P9-CQU-582

1979 Writer's Market

1979 Writer's Market

Edited by
Bruce Joel Hillman

Assisted by
Judith Ann Beraha

Writer's Digest Books
Cincinnati, Ohio

Published by Writer's Digest Books, 9933 Alliance Rd., Cincinnati, Ohio 45242.

Library of Congress Catalog Number 31-20772
International Standard Serial Number 0084-2729
International Standard Book Number 0-911654-54-2

Printed and bound in the United States of America

Preface

Writing is hard work. *Good* writing is exhausting. In his prime, Ernest Hemingway's work day of five or six hours left him completely sapped, and often produced no more than 500 words. Yet, thousands of people commit themselves to this painstaking task of constructing something where nothing was, from that most fragile, yet most durable of building materials—the written word.

Why do they do it?

Because they have to, and not because they must pay the rent or the butcher. Freelancing has changed over the centuries from its original meaning—roaming knight errants whose lances were for hire to any king or cause—but it still retains its romantic heritage. The modern freelancer has traded the sword for the mightier pen.

Freelancing isn't a profession like being a doctor, a technician or a lawyer; it isn't a job like working on the docks or an assembly line. You can be a doctor or a line woker and still freelance, but it takes dedication.

"The art of writing is the art of applying the seat of the pants to the seat of the chair," goes one popular quotation. This book provides some of the glue necessary to keep you there long enough to sell what you write. Its function is to lead you to editors who want to read your work—and will pay for the privilege of publishing it.

Use your *Writer's Market*. Enjoy it. Profit by it.

That's what it's for.

—Bruce Joel Hillman

Contents

On Writers and Writing **1**

How to Use Your Writer's Market **1**

Editors Need You **5**

But Where Do You Plug in the Typewriter? Tales of the Traveling Freelancer **8**

Submitting Your Work **14**

- The Query Letter 14
- The Complete Manuscript 16
- Packaging Helps Sell 19
- Sinning Against Editors: It Happens 20

Copyright: Questions & Answers **22**

Rights and the Writer: What Should I Sell? **28**

Taxes and the Writer: What Should I Pay? **30**

The Writer as Photographer **35**

Others Ways to Sell Your Writing **43**

The Markets **47**

Audiovisual **47**

Book Publishers **64**

Subsidy Book Publishers 182

Company Publications **183**

Consumer Publications **194**

Alternative 195
Animal 203
Art 210
Association, Club, and Fraternal 214
Astrology and Psychic 220
Automotive and Motorcycle 224
Aviation 235
Black 238
Business and Finance 240
CB Radio 246
Child Care and Parental Guidance 247
City 249
College, University, and Alumni 257
Comic Book Publications 258
Confession 258
Consumer Service and Business Opportunity 262
Detective and Crime 264
Education 266
Food and Drink 268
General Interest 269
Health 279
History 283
Hobby and Craft 289
Home and Garden 302
Humor 308
In-Flight 308
Jewish 312
Juvenile 315
Literary and "Little" 326
Men's 366
Military 375
Miscellaneous 381
Music 391
Mystery 400
Nature, Conservation, and Ecology 400
Newspapers and Weekly Magazine Sections 405
Op-Ed Pages 416
Photography 417
Poetry 419
Politics and World Affairs 428
Puzzle 433
Regional 434
Religious 460

Retirement 487
Science 489
Science Fiction, Speculative Fiction, and Fantasy 495
Social Science 496
Sport and Outdoor 498
Archery and Bowhunting 499
Basketball 500
Bicycling 500
Boating 500
Bowling and Billiards 505
Football 506
Gambling 506
General Sports Interest 507
Golf 509
Guns 511
Horse Racing 513
Hunting and Fishing 514
Martial Arts 523
Miscellaneous 523
Mountaineering 529
Skiing and Snow Sports 529
Soccer 533
Swimming and Diving 533
Tennis 535
Teen and Young Adult 535
Theater, Movie, TV, and Entertainment 548
Travel, Camping, and Trailer 556
Union 564
Women's 565

Gag **575**

Greeting Card Publishers **581**

Play Producers **588**

Play Publishers **597**

Potpourri **601**

Syndicates **603**

Trade, Technical, and Professional Journals **615**

Accounting 616
Advertising and Marketing 616
Agricultural Equipment and Supplies 618
Architecture 618
Auto and Truck 619
Aviation and Space 627
Baking 628
Beverages and Bottling 629
Book and Book Store Trade 630
Brick, Glass, and Ceramics 631

Building Interiors 633
Business Management 634
Church Administration and Ministry 636
Clothing and Knit Goods 639
Coin-Operated Machines 641
Confectionery and Snack Foods 642
Construction and Contracting 642
Dairy Products 646
Data Processing 646
Dental 647
Department Store, Variety, and Dry Goods 649
Drugs, Health Care, and Medical Products 650
Education 651
Electricity 660
Electronics and Communication 661
Engineering and Technology 666
Farm 668
- Crops and Soil Management 669
- Dairy Farming 671
- General Interest Farming and Rural Life 672
- Livestock 678
- Miscellaneous 682
- Poultry 682

Finance 683
Fishing 685
Florists, Nurserymen, and Landscaping 685
Food Products, Processing, and Service 687
Fur 688
Gas 688
Government and Public Service 689
Groceries 693
Grooming Products and Services 695
Hardware 695
Home Furnishings and Appliances 697
Hospitals, Nursing, and Nursing Homes 700
Hotels, Motels, Clubs, Resorts, Restaurants 702
Industrial Management 704
Insurance 707
Jewelry 708
Journalism 710
Laundry and Dry Cleaning 715
Law 716
Leather Goods 717
Library Science 718
Lumber and Woodworking 720
Machinery and Metal Trade 722
Maintenance and Safety 725
Management and Supervision 727
Marine Industries and Water Navigation 730
Medical 731
Milling, Feed, and Grain 736
Mining and Minerals 737

Miscellaneous 737
Music 744
Oceanography 746
Office Equipment and Supplies 747
Optical 748
Packing, Canning, and Packaging 748
Paint 749
Paper 750
Petroleum 751
Pets 753
Photography 755
Plastics 757
Plumbing, Heating, Air Conditioning, and Refrigeration . 757
Power and Power Plants 759
Printing 760
Public Relations 761
Railroad 762
Real Estate 762
Recreation Park and Campground Management 763
Secretarial 765
Selling and Merchandising 765
Show People and Amusements 770
Sport Trade 771
Stone and Quarry Products 776
Textile 777
Toy, Novelty, and Hobby 778
Trailers, Mobile Homes 779
Transportation 780
Travel 781
Veterinary 782
Water Supply and Sewage Disposal 784

Opportunities & Services 787

Author's Agents/Literary Services **787**

Contests and Awards **805**

Government Information Sources **825**

Picture Sources **836**

Writers' Clubs **867**

Writers' Colonies **876**

Writers' Conferences **878**

Writers' Organizations **885**

Glossary 893

Index 898

On Writers and Writing

How to Use Your Writer's Market

Writer's Market is divided into three basic sections: text/feature articles that offer insights, information and tips on issues of interest to freelance writers; The Markets, featuring thousands of buyers needing freelance material; and Opportunities and Services for Writers, a guide for the writer to additional information and research sources, photograph suppliers, writers' clubs and professional organizations offering companionship and camaraderie, agents, and more. Used carefully and correctly, *Writer's Market* can be the source of all information necessary to successfully sell your work.

Good use of *Writer's Market* begins with the text/feature articles. Here the basics of professional writing are discussed—from how and why Hank Nuwer makes his living as a freelance writer on the road, to editor Art Spikol postulating the virtues of freelance writing, and why it is needed in today's publishing world. In the face of a revised and complex new copyright law, attorney Tad Crawford gives answers to 19 of the most confusing questions asked by writers. Also, tips on making your editorial package more attractive are discussed, how to prepare a manuscript or query letter for an editor, your rights as a writer, taxes, and other major concerns facing both the pro and the novice.

The Markets section contains listings for more than 3,500 periodicals, organizations, syndicates, firms, theaters and even individuals who are willing to review freelance material for possible use. Listings are designed to relate a buyer's policies, practices and editorial needs to the writer in an efficient manner. Consider what there is to be learned from this sample listing:

AMERICAN HUMANE MAGAZINE, Coyle Publications, 2 Park Central, Suite 740, 1515 Arapahoe St., Denver CO 80202. (303)534-8843. Editor-in-Chief: William N.

Vaile. Associate Editor: Alan D. Miller. 80-90% freelance written. For "persons interested in the care and protection of animals, children, and adults. Readers are professionals in veterinary medicine, animal welfare and control, social service, education, law and medicine, as well as the pet-owning public. Monthly magazine; 48 pages. Estab. 1913. Circ. 15,000. Pays on publication. Buys all rights, but may reassign following publication. Phone queries OK. Submit seasonal/holiday material at least 4 months in advance of issue date. Photocopied and previously published submissions OK. SASE. Reports in 8 weeks. Sample copy 50¢; free writer's guidelines.

— editor's names
— percent of freelance material used
— publication's emphasis and readership makeup
— frequency of circulation
— rights purchased
— submission requirements
— reporting time
— sample copy availability

Nonfiction: How-to (concentrate on animal care and/or animal shelter operation); general interest (concentrate on animals, animal protection, and child or adult protection and welfare); humor; historical (relating to humane movement—animals or child protection); inspirational (relating to humane concerns); interview (prominent or acknowledged authority in animal/child/adult protection); personal experience (relating to *very* unusual experiences); photo feature (concentrate on newsworthy events relating to animals); and profile (prominent or acknowledged authority). No overly sentimental, mushy animal stories; no editorializing. Buys 180 mss/year. Query or submit complete ms. Length: 500-2,000 words. Pays $25 minimum.

— types of nonfiction needed
— word length
— payment

Photos: Pays $15 minimum for 8x10 b&w glossy prints. Captions preferred. Buys all rights, but may reassign following publication. Model release preferred.

— photo requirements

Columns/Departments: Update (breaking news on animal protection and welfare legislation, same for children); Point/Counterpoint (issue forum with photos related to humane aims and movement); and Profiles. Submit complete ms. Length: open. Pays $10 minimum. Open to suggestions for new columns/departments.

— column/department needs

Fiction: "We will consider nearly all types of fiction relating to animals." Adventure; fantasy; historical; humorous; mystery; suspense; mainstream; and western. No overly sentimental material or flagrant editorialization. Buys 12 mss/year. Submit complete ms. Length: 500-1,500 words. Pays $25.

— fiction requirements

Fillers: Clippings and short humor. "All must relate to humane movement." Length: open. Pays $10 minimum.

— filler requirements

Take nothing for granted when studying *Writer's Market* listings. All statements contained in them have been provided and verified by the buyer/editor (or a member of his staff) prior to our going to press, so the policies and requirements are reported precisely as the buyer/editor wanted them stated. Consider every fact, hint, tip and detail before submitting your material. If a listing states that a publication or firm wants queries only, *don't* expect to beat the crowd by sending your complete manuscript—no matter *how* extraordinary it is in your estimation. Violation of the rules as stated in a listing rarely brings more than a rejection slip—and not even that if the editor says "Enclose SASE" and you haven't.

There are almost 180 different categories of markets in the trade journals and consumer publications sections alone—so it is obvious that there is a market for almost *any* kind of writing. Don't limit your attempts to one category. Just because a magazine may be classified by its *general* slant doesn't mean it isn't interested in a broad range of material. For example, if your specialty is in sport and outdoor writing, don't try to sell just to the publications in that category. Keep in mind that editorial slants overlap, and that many general interest, travel, regional, and even Sunday magazine supplements may be glad to review your article.

If you are interested in the requirements for a particular magazine, check the index. If you *don't* have a certain magazine or area of publishing in mind that you would like to write for, glance through the table of contents. Once you find a section in which you are interested in writing for, read that section through like a book. You may find just the magazine you want, or perhaps even an idea may be spawned from the editor's words in the listings.

OK, you're now ready to use this book. But before you rush off to the keys, here are a few more pointers to help you take best advantage of *Writer's Market*.

• *Writer's Market* editors research, review and update all listings annually. However, editors come and go, addresses change and editorial needs may vary between when this book was published and when you buy it. (Drop us a note if you have any new information concerning a listing.) If you know of a freelance market not included in *Writer's Market,* write us including the name and address of the market. We'll solicit it for the next edition.

• Occasionally problems may crop up in your dealings with an editor or publisher. *Writer's Market* editors will look into complaints that deal with the following: (1) nonpayment of a promised sum for accepted material, or getting less payment than promised. Promised payment must have been made in writing; send us a photocopy of the agreement; and (2) no response from an editor/publisher on solicited material (again, send us photocopies of any correspondence). Enclose SASE with your letter to us. Letters concerning complaints other than those mentioned above will *not* be acknowledged unless the complaint is of a serious nature. However, such letters will be filed and later reviewed when we publish subsequent editions of this book.

• Listings for new markets in need of freelance material, changes in editorial needs, new editors' names and changes of address can be found throughout the year in the monthly magazine for freelancers, *Writer's Digest*.

• A publication might not be listed in *Writer's Market* for one of the following reasons: 1) It doesn't solicit freelance material; 2) It has suspended publication; 3) It doesn't pay for material (excepting those listings in the Journalism, Literary and Little, Alternative, Poetry and Education categories, which we've included because publication in any of them might be of value to the writer); 4) Complaints have been received about it and it has failed to answer

We use the US Postal Service's two-letter codes for state names in each of the listings, and a few abbreviations that you should know. Tape this to your wall or typewriter for a handy reference guide. Other terms you may be unfamiliar with can be found in the glossary.

B&W	Black-and-White
Estab.	Established
Circ.	Circulation
Ms(s)	Manuscript(s)
SASE	Self-addressed stamped envelope

STATE CODES

AK	Alaska
AL	Alabama
AR	Arkansas
AZ	Arizona
CA	California
CO	Colorado
CT	Connecticut
DC	District of Columbia
DE	Delaware
FL	Florida
GA	Georgia
HI	Hawaii
IA	Iowa
ID	Idaho
IL	Illinois
IN	Indiana
KS	Kansas
KY	Kentucky
LA	Louisiana
MA	Massachusetts
MD	Maryland
ME	Maine
MI	Michigan
MN	Minnesota
MO	Missouri
MS	Mississippi
MT	Montana
NC	North Carolina
ND	North Dakota
NE	Nebraska
NH	New Hampshire
NJ	New Jersey
NM	New Mexico
NV	Nevada
NY	New York
OH	Ohio
OK	Oklahoma
OR	Oregon
PA	Pennsylvania
PR	Puerto Rico
RI	Rhode Island
SC	South Carolina
SD	South Dakota
TN	Tennessee
TX	Texas
UT	Utah
VA	Virginia
VI	Virgin Islands
VT	Vermont
WA	Washington
WI	Wisconsin
WV	West Virginia
WY	Wyoming

Writer's Market inquiries satisfactorily; 5) It fails to OK or update its listing annually; 6) It requests not to be listed.

If you're just getting started in freelancing, write to us and request the free reprint, "Getting Started in Writing," by Allan Eckert. It covers preferred manuscript submission methods, some facts on book contracts and a sample of how to prepare your manuscript. Plus a list of the most commonly asked questions by freelancers. Send SASE to Mechanics Editor, *Writer's Market*, 9933 Alliance Rd., Cincinnati 45242.

Writer's Market is a professional tool for the freelance writer, just as a shop manual is a tool for the mechanic, or a scalpel for a surgeon. As such, it has to be used correctly and in conjunction with other tools-of-the-trade for best results. *Writer's Market* cannot replace the studying of issues of a publication or a book publisher's catalog, or writer's guidelines sheets provided by the publications/firms themselves.

Editors Need You

By Art Spikol

I'm an editor. I'm also a human being; in fact, I'm a human being first. So I tend to buy what I like, what I need and what I can afford. I won't buy from you just because you're an 80-year-old who thinks I'll want to do something nice for the elderly; I won't buy from you simply because you're a black, or a woman, or somebody else who's been discriminated against. I buy from you because you have what I want, no matter who you are.

Like you, I've met a lot of people who sell things for a living—many of them, naturally, because I buy what they sell. The best of them are the ones who really care about selling me on the quality and the appropriateness of what they're pushing; the least effective are the ones who use canned pitches and platitudes that are, at best, unbelievable. Nevertheless, I recently purchased a tape recorder from a salesman whose approach I didn't particularly like, a guy who sounded like he was reading a script, because he had the tape recorder I wanted at the price I wanted to pay.

A lot of writers feel that their chances of selling material to an editor are relatively small. I don't know of another business where the suppliers exhibit less self-confidence. But it's understandable: most freelancers work in a vacuum; their self-images are often formed exclusively from a limited amount of feedback from people they rarely see—*until* they become successful, anyway.

That's why I'm writing this: to give you a variation on the theme. Stated simply, you can count on your fingers the magazines in this country that can get along without freelance help. *We,* in other words, *need you.*

The fact of life at most magazines is that fulltime staff people are expensive. Not just in terms of salary, but paid vacations, bonuses, hospitalization and other fringe benefits, social security and so on. Freelancers don't get any of this, unless they pay for it on their own.

It may be hard for you to conceive of this as some kind of advantage. But it means that a magazine can pick up an article cheaper from you than from a staffer, and that *is* a big advantage—to the magazine. Say a staff writer earns $20,000 a year. If he or she spends a month on an article, the piece costs almost $1,700 in salary alone, not to mention all the other intangibles. If you spend a month writing an article for the majority of magazines in this country, you'll get a lot less . . . but chances are you can turn out more than one a month.

So when a magazine finds freelancers who are both dependable and write well, those writers are going to be worth their weight in gold. In fact, those are the freelancers who often end up as contributing editors—"regular" freelancers who earn a place on the masthead and some extra money through occasional raises—after which they're *still* much less expensive than staffers.

That's one good reason why you're in demand. But is that it? Is it just a matter of price?

Not by a long shot. There's versatility, too. Magazines have to use their staffers wisely, so they'll usually want them to do the "heavier" stories or the special kinds of articles at which they're best. What's left are all the peripheral articles that are done primarily by freelance talent. That's where you come in.

Art Spikol is executive editor of Philadelphia *magazine, and is a regular columnist and contributor for* Writer's Digest.

Say a magazine wants to run occasional articles on aspects of the medical field; after all, people like to read about diseases, breakthroughs, cures; and there's a strong public service aspect in publishing such articles. It doesn't pay for most general-interest magazines to hire fulltime specialists in medical subjects, so the only alternative is a freelance specialist in articles of that kind. Naturally, the same thing applies to a wide range of similarly-specialized subject matter—from business to ballet, science to self-help, as well as to review and criticism columns dealing with films, theater, books, dining and so on. And if you can do articles like these for general-interest magazines, you can often also do them for publications that deal *specifically* with your subject.

Some freelancers make the mistake of starting out trying to sell the heavyweight stuff—the in-depth profiles, the investigative pieces—because that's the kind of material that's most visible in magazines. That's the toughest way to break in. When you study magazines, look around the fringes of the staff-written articles and see what kind of material is normally purchased from freelancers. Don't try to beat the staffers at their own game when you're just trying to get your foot in the door; if you're good enough, that will come later.

Keep looking at yourself from the magazine's standpoint. For instance, freelancers give magazines a flexibility they can't get from their own staffs; that is, a battery of experts who can be called upon on a moment's notice. It's great to be one of those experts, so try to establish for yourself a reputation for quality and dependability. That way, when a staff article falls through, or when a special project comes up, you'll be one of the people the magazine will think of.

Part of that flexibility is, naturally, in the area of ideas. Most of the freelance assignments in this country go to people who come up with their own ideas for articles, *not* to people who are called by the magazines to do a specific assignment. Staff writers often develop similar styles and similar points of view, the natural consequence of working in one place for a long period of time. So magazines often look to the freelance sector for fresh ideas. I remember one freelance writer who obtained a copy of the latest crime report—something that was available to every writer (or non-writer, for that matter) in the state—and managed to extract an idea from it that took it out of the context of normally-dull statistics. We called it, "The Ten Safest Suburbs—and the Ten Most Dangerous." And we ran it as our cover story.

Freelancers keep magazines from getting stale in other ways, and new talent is one of them. There isn't an editor in the world whose pulse doesn't beat a little faster when he reads a truly different piece of writing by somebody who's never submitted anything before.

That could be you—but you gotta believe. You have to want to write, not just want to be a writer. You have to enjoy writing—and interviewing and researching, too, although not each of them equally. You have to believe in writing as your personal way to self-fulfillment; the idea of a byline has to excite you; the prospect of having thousands or even millions of people reading your words and being affected by them has to give you a sense of both accomplishment and responsibility. That alone should be enough. But there's always the chance of hitting the big time, of expanding an article into a book or even a movie.

Granted, that doesn't happen often. Freelance writing is a tough way to earn a living; that's why people do it in their spare time until they've established a market for their work. In other words, *don't* quit your job tomorrow.

But plenty of nice things can happen in the meanwhile. You can establish a reputation—fame, if you think of it that way. Lots of writers travel the speaker's circuit, getting paid to appear in front of groups to discuss the subjects about which they've written. Local TV appearances are not uncommon. And you can do most of your work at home. Once you've had a few things published, you'll probably start to meet people you'd *never* expected to meet—if only because you'll be writing about them or obtaining information from them.

Considering the potential of freelance writing to change your life, naturally you'd like to sell. And there are plenty of magazines who'd like to buy. It sounds like a symbiotic relationship, and it is. Most magazines *are* always looking for new talent. You have to remember that the big names that appear in magazines today weren't there, for the most part, ten years ago. And chances are that a whole new group of magazine writers will be on the scene one, two and three years from now. Maybe *you'll* be one of them. The public is fickle; the mere fact that you may not have broken in *yet* is meaningless.

* * * *

There are things about the magazine field that make it a haven for newcomers. First of all, nobody knows how old you are—after all, most of the freelance writing business is conducted through the mail. So if a magazine receives a query from you, it has no way of knowing whether you're 17 or 77. Don't tell them; let the story sell on its own merits. Further, nobody's going to force you to retire when you're 65—you can write as long as you can write. Also: race, religion, sex, national origin—they don't mean a thing. Also: money. You can write in your spare time; whatever you earn is gravy.

All you have to be able to do is write, and whereas if you wanted to be a doctor, you'd go to medical school, and if you wanted to be a lawyer, you'd go to law school, that doesn't hold in this field.

If you want to be a writer, you simply have to write.

And, of course, sell yourself.

Don't be afraid to break the rules. If you think you have something worth calling an editor about, call. If you write a query letter, don't follow a formula—you're supposed to be creative, and if you can't write a good, convincing letter, who can? If you think you have a terrific story idea, don't give up just because one editor won't assign it. Believe in it. Freelance writers put too much faith in the wisdom of editors despite the fact that editors, too, make mistakes. I remember two article ideas I turned down; luckily, each writer decided to go ahead anyway and write them for me on spec. Both stories were purchased, published, and went on to win national journalism awards.

You have in your hands now a publication that's the best of its kind anywhere. It's literally page after page of listings of resources—from magazines to book publishers—that buy from freelancers. Thousands of markets. This book is a gold mine, take my word for it; you'll probably come up with plenty of ideas just thumbing through its pages.

And that, you'll find, is the easy part.

But Where Do You Plug in the Typewriter? Tales of the Traveling Freelancer

By Hank Nuwer

"The great writers arrived by achieving the impossible. They did such blazing, glorious work as to burn to ashes those that opposed them. They arrived by course of miracle, by winning a thousand-to-one wager against them. They arrived because they were Carlyle's battle-scarred giants who will not be kept down."

—Jack London

Writers are creatures gifted with the ability to see, the desire to learn, and the will to endure until the special talent of each is recognized. For 15 of my 31 years, I have earned a freelance income. Until last year, however, I supplemented my often meager earnings any way I could. I worked as a steel mill employee in Buffalo, a university English instructor in Nevada and New Mexico, a summer camp director in the California Sierras, and as an associate editor of a men's magazine named *Chic*.

This last job paid $20,000 a year, and gave me the chance to edit the work of established writers such as Norman Mailer and Clifford Irving. I dated lovely *Chic* models and taught seminars in writing at UCLA and USC. My home was in Los Angeles' fashionable Topanga Canyon, my car a jaunty blue Fiat sportscar, and my record collection second to none.

But there was another detail I should mention. I was also miserable.

The reason was simply that to work for *Chic*, I had to be imprisoned from 9 to 5:30 each day in a 38th floor office in Century City. After nearly two years, I felt as though I were shackled to my desk like Van Gogh's prisoner while I edited manuscripts that I would much rather have written.

I worked on my own writing every third night or so. At two month intervals my byline appeared in *Gentlemen's Quarterly, Qui* and other magazines, but this only increased my restlessness. I burned to find out what sort of work I could turn out if left to my own devices. Finally, in December of 1977, something snapped and I handed in my notice.

At last I was free. Free to write, to travel, to meet exciting people, and to fashion my life exactly the way I wanted. I was also free to starve and to bemoan my loss of security should I fail.

Tightening Up the Belt

There was no way I could continue to live the sweet life I had been enjoying. First to go was the Fiat. In its place I purchased a green-and-white '58 Buick for $200, dropped $1100 to restore it, and wound up with a chrome laden classic which I wouldn't have traded for all the buggies in Detroit.

Out next went my three restaurant meals each day which had expanded my waistline to 36 inches. Vegetables and fruit replaced steak and potatoes. I began working out daily at a local "Y" and sweated off 18 pounds in less than a month.

Where there's a story, there's a writer to pick it up. Hank Nuwer, ex-senior associate editor of Chic *magazine, is presently picking up stories from somewhere between Los Angeles and Portland, Maine.*

Now there was no stopping me. The monthly haircut was stretched to two. I tried going on the wagon but ended up allowing myself two daily drinks. I went from drinking 15 cups of coffee daily to none. No more sugar, desserts, soda pop and sickly, starchy foodstuffs for me.

I felt better than I had in a decade. All my friends noticed the change, too. My pale skin bronzed, my gut retreated, and my energy capacity expanded.

It was time for the next logical move. In one week I sold or gave away all my possessions, and moved out of my apartment on to the road where I have remained ever since. All I own is stashed in the Buick: my portfolio of articles, a typewriter and supplies, a small stove, three suits, miscellaneous clothing, several books, a 35mm camera, a tool box, tent, sleeping bag, basketball, baseball glove, and a bottle of Amaretto.

Not that I live cheaply by any means. I still go to restaurants—but only take out magazine editors and exciting women. More often than not I pop for the tab. I want to leave the impression that I am a professional, that I am doing well, and that I am looking for work, not my next meal. The clothes I wear are expensive and carefully laundered. The plaid shirts are made by Pendleton, the dress shirts by Pierre Cardin. My letterhead stationery is engraved on expensive stock, and I keep my automobile gleaming. Because I frequently write entertainment pieces, I spend a fortune on movie and concert tickets. There are also motels and campgrounds to be paid.

''Hammerin' '' Hank Nuwer on location: a writer's odyssey of 10,000 miles, three countries, and $9,400 in assignments. ''Tomorrow, I may be in town to work on a piece that could have been yours if you hustled.''—Photo by Kim Nelson.

Roughly, I need $1200 a month to live. So, Jack Kerouac I ain't. His dreams and needs are not mine. He rode the rails; I'd rather pay trainfare and party in a Pullman. Yet I have sold blood for quick cash when I was broke and couldn't spare more than an hour from my typewriter.

What is my goal, anyway?

To become the best writer I am capable of becoming. I am not in competition with anyone. Reading the prose of good writers inspires me, never discourages me. I read a minimum of one hundred pages of fiction each day and examine over 30 magazines and newspapers each week to spot trends which lead to future article ideas. Although magazines are my meal ticket, my book agent is currently peddling a half-dozen ideas of mine around New York. The big money is in books for mass publication, and I hope to crash this market soon.

True, times are flush now. But it wasn't alway this way. In fact, until I hit paydirt as an editor at *Chic* and established contacts elsewhere, I collected hundreds of rejections and a handful of acceptances in 13 years. Yet from the time I was 16, when I sold two sports articles to the Buffalo Evening News, I never doubted I would eventually make a living as a writer.

My break came in the spring of 1976. I left behind a failed marriage in Nevada and came to LA in a battered '59 Chevy van, determined to obtain a position, any position, with a national magazine. With me were my four-year-old son Christian and a floppy old Afghan hound named Fagin. They were the only ones in the world who believed in me, and even Fagin looked doubtful at times. I knew damn well how the odds stacked up against me, but I was going to remain in Tinseltown until I succeeded.

We three camped out illegally on the beaches of Malibu for nine weeks. The police often came to evict us, but Chris charmed them every time. "Don't tell the guys on the next shift," they would say and drive away. During that time, I spent but $200, sold three newspaper articles for $65, and had a ball every day romping in the surf with my companions.

I had nothing going for me but belief in myself. But at last that combination evidently proved enough. I answered an ad which sought editors for a men's magazine named *Chic*. I was interviewed by editor John Lombardi— a past editor at *Esquire, Oui* and *New Times*—who hired me as a combination coffee gopher, bodyguard, messenger and writer for $20 a day. In one week I finished my first national magazine feature, an expose on police weapons called "Arms and the Man," and was named assistant editor of *Chic* at a decent salary. During the next year I wrote a half dozen features, several short pieces, and researched all other stories to be printed. At last I had the clips to send other editors to assure them I could write. My title at *Chic* by now was senior associate editor and my portfolio included tearsheets from *Oui, Gentlemen's Quarterly, Playgirl Advisor, New West, Mother Jones* and *Westways*.

I was convinced that I could write independently and earn my keep without a weekly paycheck to rely upon. It was not going to be easy but anything was better than the day-in, day-out pressure of putting out a monthly magazine.

Writer on the Road

The decision proved to be the right one for me. In just 30 days I managed to acquire the following contracts and hit the road for good to write them:

—*Human Behavior* ($500). A study of fraternity pledges who die during hazing. A trip to Reno, Nevada to research the recent death of an initiate who had been forced to drink 190-proof Everclear was necessary.

—*Oui* ($2100). A package of four articles of varying lengths including two Openers, a feature on America's Ten Meanest Towns, and a look at eco-raiders—conservationists who have declared war on polluters.

—*Chic* ($5000). A package involving three Close Up profiles, a media column on sport specialty magazines, a look at beer baron Joe Coors, a piece on American millionaires in strange cities, and two articles to be named later. The Coors piece required a visit to Denver, and *Chic* gave me $300 in expense money to get there.

—*Gentlemen's Quarterly* ($300). A service feature on how to purchase men's stationery.

—*Dynamic Years* ($2750). Four features for this truly underrated publication put out by the American Association of Retired Persons. One article was an interview with Tampa Bay football coach John McKay; another was a look at the problems of fathers over 50; the third was an interview with a Texas deep sea diver who searches for historical treasures; the fourth was a look at pro softball in America.

—*Ampersand* ($150). A cover story interview with comedian Martin Mull for this newspaper-format entertainment magazine aimed at a college audience.

—*Writer's Market* ($250). A feature on my life as a freelance writer.

Obviously I am faring better now than during all those years I thought the reason they called me a "*free*lancer" was because I never got paid. I don't know if I have any special secrets to reveal, but I can say with certainty what works for me.

1) The only way I can consistently turn out articles is to stick rigorously to a routine. I write or research seven days a week, from two to 20 hours a day, depending on how near a deadline looms. My favorite time to create is during the predawn hours when no one else is awake. I get six hours sleep a night and take a one hour nap before going out on the town at night.

2) I rarely send a query or a manuscript without attaching a carefully written cover letter which usually contains a personal greeting of some sort. A few editors are close acquaintances or friends of friends which makes the task easier. But when writing an editor I do not know, I introduce myself in as few words as possible and ask what themes he plans to use in forthcoming issues. This way, if my current submissions are rejected, I at least stand a good chance of learning what the editor is looking for which increases my chances of hitting the next time. Also, I have increased my chances of receiving a personal note back instead of a cold rejection slip which lets me know why my material missed the mark.

3) I never end a day of writing by pumping myself dry of all I have to say. I stop writing when I am tired, but have yet to reach that point where the words fail to come. I make a few shorthand notes as to what I want to say next, and then continue writing from that point the next day. This way, I rarely ever suffer writer's block.

4) It is difficult to produce good writing if you do not feel good about yourself. Not that my looks are going to send Robert Redford cowering behind his mirror. For one thing, my receding hairline is racing my bald spot to see which ends up in the middle of my head first. On the other hand, I now firmly believe in the importance of keeping my body hard and firm. Consequently, I work out two hours nearly every day and take vitamin supplements to keep killing stress at bay.

I also believe that something must go into a writer's head before it can come out. Therefore, I try to experience as many pleasures as possible, and I take in the sights hungrily as I drive each day to the location of my next assignment.

5) I'll do anything to grab an editor's attention. Last year, for example, I wrote a feature for *Oui* on the subject of spontaneous human combustion, a pseudo-scientific look at folks who suddenly flare up into human patty melts. When I sent the piece in, I couldn't resist lighting a match to the edges of the manuscript so that it looked as if it had been rescued from a bonfire. Forty hours later, a call came through saying the magazine had bought the article. What's more, the magazine page was illustrated to look as if it were burning up in the reader's hands.

The Best Job of All

Now that I have freelanced for some time, I often reflect on my chosen profession and what it means to me. Without a doubt it is the best job I have ever had, and I would be hardpressed to name another profession which comes even close. I have learned more from researching articles for publication that from all the education I supposedly got while taking bachelor and masters degrees in English.

What are the advantages of being a freelance writer? Well, for one thing, I've had the opportunity to meet fascinating people. I've interviewed authors and celebrities and have always come away invigorated from the opportunity to plug into the amazing store of energy which the successful invariably possess. But these aren't the only people with things to say and exciting experiences to talk about. Mechanics, waitresses, hoboes—the people on the street—have touched my life as I passed and made it richer.

Freelancing also has given me confidence in other areas of my life. Out on the road alone I find myself attacking life with the same gusto that I accord my writing. When a pretty girl passes on the street, I tell her she is attractive and ask her out on the spot. It does no good to think of clever things to say once she passes out of my life. Instead, I march up to her as I would an editor when I have a dynamite idea to sell. It is time to be direct and to the point with all the false and real courage that I can muster. If she likes my pitch, I've made a sale. If she doesn't..., well, we all get rejection slips now and then. But just as with freelance writing, when you give it all your heart, it is amazing to see how often your inquiries are met with interest.

But perhaps the best thing about writing is seeing your byline in print. I believe that the act of writing is its own reward and flatly disagree with Samuel Johnson's contention that only a blockhead ever wrote for any reason but money.

A writer has no reason to be ashamed of appearing in small magazines that pay in contributor's copies. You may not have heard of the magazines I have hit. Magazines with colorful titles like *Anvil, Brushfire,* the *South Dakota Review, The Aquarium* and *Rocks and Minerals*. I proudly carry some of these pieces in my portfolio.

For one thing, some incredibly good writing is found in little magazines that don't have a formula or a capricious publisher to dictate what is printed. For another, seeing your stuff in print is the best way to learn how to write. There is no better motivation to improve writing than to see a mistake in cold print. An awkward construction or inflated metaphor can make you feel suddenly like you've swallowed barium. But errors are all right, too. It's all part of the learning process and you can make corrections later in the collected edition of your works.

After all, writers have the opportunity to keep on growing long after their peers have stopped. Writers are an inquisitive bunch who ask questions and demand answers. Always there are new topics to be investigated, fresh concepts to be grasped, virgin ground to be covered. No matter how long a writer has been working, there's always something else to learn.

A freelance writer's life may be wrought with peril. He may face bankruptcy, starvation and law suits. But never must he endure the ennui that folks in all other professions must inevitably suffer.

Finally, for me, there's the chance to see unfamiliar things and cover stories which I could only read about when tied down by a full-time job. Tomorrow, perhaps, I may be in your town to work on a piece that could have been yours if you hustled.

You've been reading long enough. Now sit down and write!

Submitting Your Work

People take to writing for varying reasons: for love, for money; possibly for love *of* money. But no matter the personal reasons behind the act—people write *to be read.*

Getting read is the trick. There are right ways down the path to publication, and there are wrong ways. In the following four articles are given some standards, tips and hints that may help get you started on the road to being *read.*

The Query Letter

By Art Spikol

When I was first asked to write this article, part of the assignment was to include two samples: a good query letter, and a poor query letter. So I started poring through the files.

I did find "good" and "poor" query letters, of course, but not without realizing that some of the ones that I would've called poor might've been considered appropriate at some other magazines. And some of the ones I'd have called good would've been inappropriate elsewhere.

So that's the first thing to understand: there's no absolute model or formula for writing a query letter to a publication.

As an editor, I guess I've seen just about every kind of query letter imaginable. I've had queries from dentists and housewives, shoplifters and hookers, weightlifters and judo experts, government workers and student radicals, collectors, hobbyists, prisoners, and just about every other category of human being. A scant few of them have written letters that were irresistable, letters that I couldn't put down. But most have written letters that could best be described as typical.

The "typical" query starts out something like, "Do you think your readers would be interested in . . .?" or "Did you know that . . .?" When I get one of these, the first thing I wonder is, well, if that's the way you start your letter, will I want you to write an article for me? It is, to put it mildly, rather predictable.

A query letter has to grab me—just as an article would have to do. If you can't excite me about an article in a letter, you can't sell me at all—and "me" is virtually every editor out there. Forget that I have hundreds of thousands of readers, forget that I'm a name high up on a masthead, forget that I'm also supposed to conduct myself like a businessperson. Just write me an exciting letter. *Me*, not my readers. Let me hear the kind of enthusiasm you feel for the article. And write your letter to the human being in me, not the editor in me and not the businessperson in me. I'm like anybody else when it comes to reading a good story.

In fact, that has sometimes made me behave not according to form. For instance, as the executive editor of a city magazine, I should buy only articles of significant local interest. But I've purchased, on occasion, articles with very slight, almost non-existent local angles—because they were so well written that I knew my readers would enjoy them as much as I did.

Sure, I could give you the rules, but then there's always somebody who can break them effectively—and it turns out that those letters are often the ones which I read the most thoroughly. Some time ago I wrote an article about a

Ten Ways to Turn Editors Off

What you say:	What they think:
1. "Have you done a story yet about . . . ."	You should know this before you query. There are ways to find out.
2. "I am writing to give you the opportunity to publish . . ."	How did we get so lucky?
3. "Would you be interested in the truly hilarious (or tragic) story of . . . ."	I don't know if we can survive it.
4. "This is the kind of story you should be doing . . ."	Don't hold your breath.
5. "Just tell me which approach you'd like me to take . . . ."	Just tell us which approach is appropriate.
6. "The author can . . . ."	What're you, an agent?
7. "There would obviously be two sides to the story . . . ."	If it's obvious, isn't it a bit patronizing to tell us about it?
8. "I know I can write this better than so-and-so did for you some time back . . . ."	We'll bet your mother told you so.
9. "If you're not interested, please let me know, since I'm sure I can sell this elsewhere . . . ."	Go to it.
10. "I'll be willing to take a little less than your regular fee to get this published . . . ."	Yes, but we're not willing to pay less, assuming it's worth publishing.

number of things that bug editors, things any writer would be better off not doing. Not long after it appeared, a writer wrote to me, "I know I'm not supposed to do this . . . ." and then broke every rule I'd given, with excellent reasons for doing so. It was a letter that I literally couldn't stop reading.

So what do I—and most editors—want in a query letter? As far as I'm concerned, it might not be a bad idea to tack the following up over your typewriter: **I AM AN EDITOR!**

I want an opening sentence that is going to get me to the next sentence and the next, until I've read the whole letter—without trying.

I want to care about your article and the people in it. And I want to feel that I, as a reader, have a definite stake in its outcome.

I want you to tell me enough to get me involved—but not so much that you'll answer all my questions. By the time I'm finished reading your letter, I should be willing to pay to learn more. And then I will.

I want to know just what I'm getting: what kind of article, what kinds of information it will include, what will be your point of view. And don't tell me you intend to be objective; that's not your function and you can't do it anyway.

I want you to tell me why you should get the assignment. Why you? If you have some professional expertise in the subject, mention it. If you've been an interested observer of it for a long time, mention it.

I don't want to have to guess about your abilities, and just because you can write a decent letter doesn't mean that you'll get an assignment. If I don't know who you are, you'd better send samples or clips. If you don't have any, the chances of your getting an assignment other than "on spec" are small—but you can improve those chances by writing an excellent letter.

I don't want to see anything that isn't right for my market. And I don't want to see any "last resort" types of submissions.

I admire stick-to-it-iveness, but I don't want to get a query a week from anybody. There are people who send out 52 queries a year and figure to play the percentages, but all you'll get is a reputation for your lack of discretion.

In addition: I am not impressed by bad grammar, incorrect punctuation, misspellings, etc. I am not impressed by college degrees, friends of mine that you claim to know, sweeping generalizations, or language that makes you sound like you're out to dazzle me. I do not care what you think of the magazine for which I work, and particularly I don't care to know how you think I could improve it. I probably do not want to meet you now; if I ever do, it will be because I respect you as a writer or need you as a supplier.

That's it, and by this time you should be fairly well turned off. What kind of editor is this, you ask; he sounds about as friendly as a rattlesnake.

Actually, I *am* friendly. But I'm honest, too, and there's no way to say these things without just saying them. Because if you make one mistake it could cost you an assignment. Sure, you may get a very nice letter. After all, we don't want to be unkind. But neither do we have time to change the world; we don't have time to tell you everything you did wrong. A nice letter doesn't pay the rent; knowing this kind of stuff just might.

That's why I'm coming on strong now: so you won't make the mistakes. If you're going to be a professional, don't behave like an amateur. Write the editor a letter that's every bit as good, and every bit as representative of your style, as your article will be. Take it from me, we're receptive. We're waiting, always, for the blockbuster. Maybe yours.

The Complete Manuscript

By Bruce Joel Hillman

Whether you are typing an article as the result of a go-ahead from an editor on a query, or because a publication's *Writer's Market* listing says that complete manuscripts are acceptable, the *appearance* of your manuscript is second in importance only to its content. The appearance of your submission is an editor's first impression of you as a writer—and this impression could mean the difference between a sale and a rejection slip.

As a general axiom, editors consider sloppy, pencil-pocked, typo-riddled manuscripts an indication of sloppy, error-marred, ill-conceived writing. It isn't hard for an editor to separate the hacks from the pros on the basis of a manuscript's appearance. A writer who *cares* about his work and who cares about the appearance of it is a *professional*.

The first step toward professional submissions is the choice of your writing instrument. Invariably, this must be a typewriter, although whether electric or manual isn't of great importance. Handwritten submissions are tantamount to editorial suicide. In most editorial offices they are not even read before being stuffed back into the SASE (or wastebasket if no SASE has been provided).

Choosing a good machine means getting a typewriter with all keys functioning properly, that types evenly, and that doesn't shred or leave stray ink spots on the paper. As far as type styles go, *pica* and *elite* rate about the same with editors, although pica is slightly larger, thereby easier on the editor's eyes. *Stay away* from typewriters with fancy typefaces such as script, all capital letters, etc. These typefaces don't add to the attractiveness of your work—and are usually hard for the editor to read.

Once you have chosen a good typewriter—maintain it. Change the ribbon regularly and keep the keys clean. A story typed with dirty keys and a poor ribbon may be the badge of the writer's poverty, but *not* of his professionalism.

Before beginning to write, it's worth a check to see that all your "gear" is close at hand. This can eliminate frustrating interruptions later because you find you lack the proper supplies or tools. Have correction tape or fluid (the Liquid Paper Corp. of Dallas, Texas puts out a good product called Liquid Paper), pencils and scratch pad for trying out words and phrases, a dictionary, thesaurus and other reference works, and *plenty of paper*.

Paper comes in different weights, rag/wood contents, sizes and colors. For the writer's purposes there are only three solid rules: paper must be *white,* it must be size *8½x11,* and it should be of a *good bond,* preferably between sixteen and twenty-pound bond. Never use onion skin paper, colored sheets, or (because of the way it smears while being edited on) erasable bond. Erasable bond paper, though great looking and easy for the writer to use, must usually be photocopied before it can be used for editing purposes. For use as second sheets or carbon copies (always a nice practice!) a much cheaper grade of paper may be used.

Ok—your tools of the trade are readily accessible, a ream of paper beckons, and you are finally ready to create. Keep in mind as you write (or at least as you are preparing your final revision) the following standards for professional preparation and submission.

On the first page of your manuscript type your name, address, and telephone number (and any desired pseudonym) in the upper left-hand corner. In the upper right-hand corner place the estimated word count. To estimate wordage in an article of under 25 pages, count the number of words on the first three pages, divide by three, and multiply the result by the total number of pages in the article. For manuscripts over 25 pages, use the same process, but take the average from the first five pages.

Some writers wish to limit the rights (see "Rights and the Writer: What Should I Sell?") they offer to publications because of possible reprint sales. Since a large number of publications will reassign rights following publication, unless you have a specific reason for doing so, it is best to leave mention of rights off the manuscript. However, if you *do* desire to control which rights you relinquish (which may also have the effect of limiting your sales), type which rights you are offering to sell directly below the estimated word count (for example, "*first serial rights* only"). Almost all markets in *Writer's Market* state in their listing which rights they buy on accepted material. Should you desire to relinquish only certain rights, it would be wise to check individual listings for this information before submitting.

On the same page, center the title of the article or story (in capital letters) and directly below it, type your byline as you prefer it published. Then two or three lines farther down, begin typing your story.

Each consecutive page must be identified with your name and a key word from the title in the upper left-hand corner, and the page number in the upper right. Maintain a uniform number of lines on each page by making a light pencil mark at the page's lower margin to let you know when you have reached the bottom.

For pica type, your margins should be 1¼" at the top and on the left; 1" on the right; and 1" on the bottom. For elite type, use a uniform margin of 1½" on all four sides. Indent paragraphs five spaces. Always double space your copy, and type only on one side of the paper. Double space between paragraphs—do not triple space.

Letters, telegrams, newspaper clippings, etc., when used within the body of the text, should also be double spaced; however, they must be given an extra indentation of five or more spaces to make them stand out.

Book manuscripts are typed exactly the way submissions to magazines would be, with the exception that the opening page of each chapter is begun about one-third down the page. Number the pages of a book consecutively, not by chapters.

Cover letters sent with manuscript submissions to magazines or book publishers should be brief and to-the-point. Editors are not interested in the state of your health, or your life story unless such information is absolutely germane to your story. Included in a cover letter would be your qualifications to write your particular article, or any major credits. If you are submitting your manuscript in reponse to a green light given by an editor on a query, mention that in your letter or send along a photocopy of the editor's OK.

Manuscripts of five pages or less can be submitted to magazines folded in thirds (paperclipped, not stapled) in a regular business envelope, with a SASE (self-addressed, stamped envelope) enclosed for return. For articles or stories more than five pages, submit in a large (9x12) envelope with stiff cardboard backing (again, with SASE). Book manuscripts can be mailed in a box that typing paper comes in. Submit the pages loose, without stapling or binding in any way. Be sure to paperclip a mailing label addressed to yourself and enough postage for the manuscript's return to the first page of the manuscript, along with any special mailing instructions such as fourth class manuscript rate, first class, etc. Your manuscript will then usually be returned via the same box you submitted it in. To avoid confusion and the possibility of your manuscript being misplaced, mark the box "Save for return—label and postage enclosed."

Submissions to magazines and publishing houses can be made either by first class mail or by the special fourth class manuscript rate. While the fourth class rate is considerably less expensive, it is also a great deal slower, and the post office is not required to return it should it prove undeliverable.

American postage is not honored in Canada, and very often Canadian editors will not return material unless accompanied by either Canadian postage (available through the Canadian postal service) or International Reply Coupons (available at all post offices).

Organization is the mark of the professional, and good record keeping is good organization. It's embarrassing to forget just where you have submitted a manuscript, and could result in the loss of time, sales, or even your work. One reliable method of record keeping is to type the name and address of the publication to which you are submitting on the back of your carbon copy, recording the date the manuscript was mailed. If the article is returned rejected, note the date it was returned and send it off to another market. It is always wise to have three or four markets in mind for any one article, so that in the event of a rejection (and after possible reworking, rewriting, or reslanting), there is another market waiting. It is also a good practice to keep on file any correspondence with editors, or other material that may prove beneficial at some later time, such as research notes.

Remember, improperly prepared, even the best of writing may be rejected. Well prepared, you may find yourself pleasing editors—and pleased editors bring pleasing returns.

Packaging Helps Sell

By Walt Sandberg

(Editor's Note: The following article is not meant to be "the" definitive way to package your work for submission to an editor or publisher. Its main purpose is to point out that a neat package may help influence the buyer.)

Writers wishing to sell consistently might take a tip from the consumer products marketing people. These experts generally spend more time and money

Packaging — a place for everything and everything in its place. A well-organized package gives an editor a good feeling about a writer even before he reads the material. — Photo by Walt Sandberg.

developing the package than the product it contains. They know that consumers won't select poorly packaged products from crammed supermarket shelves.

The writer's market is competitive, too. And I wasn't having much success until I learned to package my product.

Walt Sandberg, a freelance sport and outdoor writer, hails from Wisconsin. His "packages" have sold to Field & Stream, Sports Afield, *and* Outdoor Life.

Now, I sell almost everything I write, usually on the first try. In the past three years, I've sold over 150 "packages" to more than a dozen national and regional publications.

My product may not be better than that of other writers, but they don't take the time to package . . . so I cash checks while they collect rejection slips.

Consider the plight of one busy editor:

First thing in the morning, the mailperson dumps a load of manuscripts on the editor's already cluttered desk. Dejectedly the editor selects one from the pile. He knows it has come from a moonlighting newspaper columnist because several yards of yellow newsprint uncoil across the desk. The copy is replete with strikeovers, x-outs, and scrawled corrections.

"What does he think I am," he fumes, "a copy editor?"

The next submission contains color slides, loose in the envelope. As he opens it some slides spill over the desk, two splash into his coffee cup, others scatter over the floor, and three fall into the wastebasket.

It's only 9:36 a.m., much to early to sneak out to lunch, so the editor returns to the pile. "One good story," he mutters. "That's all I need."

As he picks up the next envelope, his foul mood begins to evaporate. There's something about this one that makes him feel better. Sure! The addresses are typed and the envelope neatly labeled. One label cautions: *Do Not Bend.* Another proclaims: *First Class Mail.* Obviously this writer thinks highly enough of his product to take pains when submitting it.

Gingerly, he peeks into the envelope. No uncoiling newsprint, no shotgunning slides, just a single black folder. The cover is labeled: "Packaging Helps Sell, by Walt Sandberg."

"Intriguing thought," he says, opening the folder.

In the right pocket is a neatly typed script of 500 words, precisely the length needed to fill that open slot. And in the left pocket are two clear black and white glossy photos with good contrast, which appear germane to the title.

He reads the text. Not the best, but not bad either. And the quality of the photos should be enough to offset any slight defects in the writing.

Packaging helps sell. It just helped sell article No. 208 for Walt Sandberg . . . on its first trip out.

Sinning Against Editors: It Happens

By John P. Hayes

What do freelancers do that editors wish they wouldn't do? I've asked that question of more than 100 magazine editors.

Their answers could fill a book I'd call *The Sins of a Freelance Writer*. To a general audience, that title sounds like another lurid confession story, full of sex and thrills. But to an editor, *The Sins of a Freelance Writer* is all too familiar. Editors see hundreds of freelanced sins every week and they know such sins are more technical than sexual, more killing than thrilling.

So, what *do* freelancers do that editors wish they wouldn't? Here are the best of the answers:

John P. Hayes is an assistant professor of journalism at Temple University. He has freelanced to numerous national publications.

• They telephone. Don't make a practice of calling editors to inquire about your manuscript or to complain about some problem. But *do* include your telephone number in the event the editor wants to call you. Sounds unfair, but that's what editors prefer. Write if you have to; call only as a last resort.

• They don't query. Query! Unless you read otherwise, most editors say that queries save them time. And they'll save you time, too.

• They send 15 ideas in one query letter. Some editors say it's okay to send two or three ideas in one letter, but most editors prefer to see a separate query for every idea.

• They send their only copy of a manuscript. Unless you absolutely trust the postal service and have equally as much faith in an editor not misplacing your article or story, you'd better keep copies of your work.

• They send their notes. What's an editor to do with your notes? He only wants your query or manuscript. Keep your notes unless the editor *asks* to see them.

• They send dozens of samples of published and unpublished work. It's okay, say most editors, to send one or two samples of your best *published* work, but never your unpublished manuscripts.

• They forget a SASE. In these times of rising prices, few magazines will return manuscripts without a SASE. Your work may only end up in the wastebasket.

• They send batches of photos and slides and negatives. Most editors want transparencies or slides, but few prefer prints unless they work primarily in black-and-white. Some want contact sheets. It's best to let the editor know what you have and then wait for him to tell you what to send. Many editors list their preferences in *Writer's Market*.

• They wrap their manuscripts in cellophane and pretty pink bows. It's true. I saw it myself in more than one office. Once, the bow was blue. No matter, a large envelope, please, will do nicely.

• They don't read the magazine. *Thou shalt read the magazine*. One of the quickest ways to sell an article is to read the magazine to better find out what the editor(s) buys. Also it helps to address your material to the current editor. *Good Housekeeping* still gets poetry submissions addressed to an editor who hasn't been there for 10 years!

So now you know.

Copyright: Questions & Answers

By Tad Crawford

1. *What is a copyright and what does it mean to me as an author?* Your copyright is the source of the financial rewards you reap from your writing. Our nation's founding fathers provided in the constitution that "the Congress shall have the power . . . To promote the Progress of Science and useful Arts, by securing for limited Times to Authors and Inventors the exclusive Right to their respective Writings and Discoveries . . ." In the most recent revision of our federal copyright law, which took effect on January 1, 1978, Congress provided that the author of a work shall automatically have his or her copyright the moment that work is fixed in tangible form. This means that as you write each word, it is protected by copyright. Your rights as a copyright owner include the power to do or authorize any of the following: (1) to make copies of your work; (2) to prepare derivative works (such as a film made from a novel); (3) to distribute copies to the public (except that someone who has purchased lawfully made copies has a right to resell them); (4) to perform the work publicly; and (5) to display the work publicly. If anyone makes use of your work in violation of your exclusive rights, they are infringing your copyright. In sum, copyright provides you with two very important rights: (1) the right to authorize use of your work in return for suitable payments, and (2) the right to refuse to permit use of your work if the payments are inadequate, or you simply don't feel a certain person or company can do justice to what you've created.

2. *How long does copyright protection last?* This protection lasts for your life plus fifty years. If you created a work jointly with another author, it lasts until 50 years after the survivor's death. If you created the work anonymously, using a pseudonym, or as a work for hire, the copyright lasts for 100 years from the date of creation or 75 years from the date of publication, whichever term is shorter. If an author who has created a work anonymously or using a pseudonym chooses to reveal his or her identity to the Copyright Office, the term then runs for the normal period of the author's life plus fifty years. For works created prior to January 1, 1978, but never published, the copyright term is the author's life plus 50 years. For works that were published with copyright notice prior to January 1, 1978, the term will be 75 years if the copyright was renewed after 28 years as required by the old law. If a work published with the copyright notice prior to January 1, 1978 has not been renewed and has not gone into the public domain, you must file Form RE at the appropriate time for renewal.

3. *How can I transfer my copyright to someone else? Is it necessary to transfer the whole copyright, or can I transfer parts of it?* A transfer of your copyright or any exclusive right comprised in your copyright must be done in writing and signed by you or your authorized agent. For example, you or your agent must sign a written note or memorandum to transfer all rights in your copyright to a publisher. But if you want to transfer exclusive publishing rights to one company and exclusive film rights to another company, each of these transfers would also have to be in writing because they are exclusive. Exclusive rights can be sub-

---

Tad Crawford, an attorney, is the author of The Writer's Legal Guide *and* Legal Guide for the Visual Artist *(Hawthorn Books). He teaches art law courses at the School of Visual Arts in New York City and lectures frequently on legal matters pertaining to writers and artists.*

divided further. The exclusive right to publish could be subdivided by giving one publisher the right to book publication and another publisher the right to magazine publication, and so on. First North American serial rights are exclusive rights because you are giving a magazine the right to be first to publish in a geographic area. Nonexclusive rights, however, do not have to be transferred in writing. An example of nonexclusive rights would be the sale to two magazines of one-time simultaneous rights for the same geographic area. This could be agreed upon verbally, although it would be wise to have a written contract anyway. The important point here is that if you have not signed anything, you have definitely not transferred an exclusive right.

4. *If I submit an article to a copyrighted publication and it accepts it by buying all rights but states that it will reassign rights following publication, how do I go about getting those rights back?* Request a reassignment of the rights immediately after publication. They will then sign a tranfer of the copyright back to you which allows them no further use of your article. You should record this transfer with the Copyright Office within one month of receiving it, especially if you feel the article might be saleable again. Recordation gives notice to the public of your rights in the work. For this notice to be effective, the work must have been registered and the transfer must identify the work clearly. The original or a certified copy of the transfer must be accompanied by a $10 fee for recordation.

5. *If I submit an article to a copyrighted publication and it accepts it by buying first North American serial rights, can I do anything else I want with my article once it is published? Do I need to notify the first publication of further such actions?* Once the article has been published you are free to place it elsewhere. You do not have any legal obligation to inform the first publication of further actions, although as a matter of courtesy you might consider giving that publication a credit line in subsequent uses of the article.

6. *For purposes of copyright, is there any difference between dealing with a book publisher and dealing with a magazine publisher?* A book publisher will invariably have a written contract for you to sign. Often, however, magazines will not bother with any written formalities. The new law, therefore, provides a presumption as to what rights you are selling when you deal with the publisher of a collective work, which is a work composed of separate contributions. Examples of collective works are magazines, anthologies, and encyclopedias. You are the copyright owner of your contribution. If you don't make a specific transfer of rights to the publisher of the collective work, that publisher is presumed to acquire only the following nonexclusive rights: (1) to use your contribution in that particular collective work; (2) to use your contribution in later collective works in the same series; and (3) to use it in revisions of that collective work. For example, a magazine purchasing your story could run it again in a later issue of that same magazine (if you don't want this to happen, you should have a contract with the magazine stating you are only transferring one-time rights or first North American serial rights). It would have no power, however, to authorize a different magazine to use the story, even if the same company owned both magazines. Or the publisher of an anthology could use your contribution in a revision of that particular anthology, but not in a different anthology. Since nonexclusive rights require no special formalities to be transferred, you should object promptly to a publisher's letter, memorandum, or masthead notice seeking additional nonexclusive rights in your contribution, and you should refuse to sign checks with endorsements purporting to transfer such additional rights. For example, if you want to sell one-time rights, you should object to a masthead

notice or check endorsement stating that nonexclusive reprint rights are also being purchased.

7. *I have sold my work to a publication that promised to revert all rights after publication, but it now has gone out of business. Do I have to try and find some representative of the publication, or are there any special legal steps that I should take?* If a publication has agreed to revert all rights to you after publication, you should immediately follow through by demanding that assignment back to you once the issue with your contribution has appeared. If the publication goes out of business after paying you but before publication of the issue containing your contribution, you will have to find a representative of the company with whom to negotiate. Normally an agreement can be worked out to have the rights assigned back to you, perhaps in return for your promise to pay back some percentage of what you may receive from making a sale elsewhere in the future. If you can't find a representative to deal with, you should consider retaining an attorney to help you. If you feel you can't afford an attorney, one of the volunteer lawyers for the arts organizations listed at the end of this article might be able to assist you.

8. *If I submit an article to a copyrighted publication and it accepts it by buying all rights, does this mean that my work now belongs entirely (and for whatever purposes) to that publication? Can I rewrite the piece–using a new lead, a few new quotes, and a new ending–and sell it again?* If you transfer all rights, the magazine owns the copyright and is free to make whatever uses it may wish of your article. If you simply make a few cosmetic changes and use the same piece again, you will be infringing the rights that you have transferred to someone else. If you have an idea about a related topic and write a different article, you are naturally free to sell the new article wherever you wish. Even if you transfer all rights in an article, however, you do have a right to terminate that transfer during a period of five years beginning thirty-five years after the date of publication or forty years after execution of the transfer, whichever period ends earlier.

9. *OK. I now have my article ready to send off to an editor or publisher. In terms of copyright protection, what can happen to the piece from the time I send it to the time it is published?* Since copyright protection is in effect from the time of creation, you are protected by law and any infringements of your rights can result in a penalty for the offender. However, even though you are protected, there are loopholes to know about and further steps to take if the writer wants his rights to his piece forever guaranteed. For instance, if you are sending the manuscript to more than one place at a time—say, to three or four magazines which will accept simultaneous submissions—type at the top of the manuscript the words, "All rights reserved. Not previously published." The reason for this is that there is some question whether multiple submissions might constitute "publication," thereby placing your work in the public domain. If the publication in which your piece will appear is copyrighted, the copyright notice for the publication—usually appearing either on the masthead page or near the table of contents—gives you further copyright protection. The magazine editor or publisher will then formally register the magazine's copyright with the Copyright Office. However, registration of the copyright for a magazine does not register individually contributed pieces appearing in that magazine. It is up to the writer to register his individual piece in his own name if he decides it necessary to do so. So how do you decide whether or not to register your piece? The value of registration only arises if your work is ever infringed upon. Registration does the following things: (1) If you register before or within five years of first publication, there is a presumption in your favor that your copyright is valid and

everything you stated in the certificate of registration is true; (2) You must register prior to bringing suit against an infringer; (3) Registration cuts off certain defenses that an unknowing infringer might assert to avoid penalties; and (4) Registration prior to the beginning of infringement—or within three months of publication—makes you eligible to receive attorney's fees and statutory damages (which are an amount awarded in the court's discretion between $250 and $10,000 for each work infringed). The test for deciding whether or not to register is the writer's determination of the value of his work. If he fears possible infringement or sees further use of the work at a later date, the registration should be a must. The cost for registration is $10. To register his work, the writer needs to mail the completed Form TX, $10, and one complete copy of an unpublished work or two copies of the best edition of a published work to the Copyright Office. For unpublished work, you can send in a collection under a single title, such as "Writings by Alice Writer, 1979," and copyright as much of your unpublished work as you wish for one $10 fee. For published contributions to periodicals, such as magazines and newspapers, you can make a group registration of all contributions published within a 12 month period as long as copyright notice appeared in your name on each of the contributions. Thus it is a good idea for the regular contributor to ask for such notice (*note*: keep in mind that such a request may need to depend on your rapport with the editor). Group registration of published contributions is made by using Form GR/CP in conjunction with Form TX. You must deposit one copy of each magazine or section of a newspaper in which your contributions appeared. For more information on how to register your work, consult the Copyright Office.

10. *If I submit an article to a publication that is NOT copyrighted and they accept and publish it, what happens to my copyright?* You should have copyright notice in your name on your contribution at the time of publication. If copyright notice is omitted from a published work, however, your copyright will remain valid if (1) the copyright notice was only omitted from a relatively small number of copies; (2) the copyright notice was omitted from a substantial number of copies, but you register your work within five years of publication and make a reasonable effort to place the notice on the copies that don't have it; or (3) you required in writing, as a condition of allowing publication of your work, that copyright notice appear on it, but the copyright notice was omitted anyway. If your copyright notice is omitted and you do not come within one of these three saving provisions, your copyright will enter the public domain. This means that your work can be freely copied by anyone without the need to request your permission or pay you.

11. *What if I am approached–through no actions of my own–by X Magazine to do an article on assignment for an upcoming issue. Is this considered a "work-for-hire" arrangement, meaning that whatever I do my work is owned solely by the magazine?* Work for hire is the most dangerous pitfall facing the author. A work for hire is considered to be created by the employer or commissioning party, not by the author. The author has no right to get back a copyright created under a work for hire arrangement. However, a work for hire can only come into being in certain limited circumstances. If you are an employee, work prepared within the scope of your employment will be work for hire (unless you and your employer agree by contract it will not be work for hire). If, for example, you work for a magazine as an editor and also write articles on your own time for the magazine as a freelancer, your articles would not be work for hire. Freelancers can find themselves doing work for hire, but only if *all* the following conditions

are met: (1) the work is specially ordered or commissioned by the publisher; (2) the author and publisher agree in writing that the work will be considered work for hire (apparently those exact words have to be used, but as a precaution watch out for other language that sounds like it's trying to create a work for hire relationship); (3) the publisher and author both sign the contract; and (4) the work falls into one of the following categories:

- contribution to a collective work
- part of a motion picture or other audiovisual work
- a translation
- a compilation
- an instructional text
- a test or answer material for a test
- an atlas
- a supplementary work, which is a work prepared for the purpose of introducing, concluding, illustrating, explaining, revising, commenting upon, or assisting in the use of a work by another author. Examples of supplementary works would be forewords, afterwords, charts, tables, editorial notes, bibliographies, appendixes, and indexes.

If the work does not fall into one of these categories, or you do not sign anything in writing, you as a freelancer can be certain that you are not doing a work for hire.

12. *Are ideas copyrightable? What if I send a query letter to an editor with 10 ideas for articles, all returned "rejected," yet I note in the next issue two articles are on the same subjects as my ideas. Can I legally do anything?* An idea is not copyrightable, but the creative expression of an idea is protected by copyright. The reason for this is that copyright protection for ideas would effectively take ideas out of circulation, constantly narrowing what other authors could write about. The use of an idea in a written work, however, creates an expression of the idea that can be protected. For example, the idea to write a biography of a famous man cannot be protected by copyright, but the biography you in fact write does have copyright protection. If you wish to be paid for giving an idea to someone, your best approach would be to try and obtain a contract in which the publisher agrees to pay you if the idea is used. In practice, of course, this is not easy to do.

13. *What constitutes an infringement of copyright? What can I do if I note an infringement of my copyright? What type of proof do I need that I was the originator of the material and that word-for-word it's all mine?* The test for infringement of copyright is whether an ordinary observor, looking at your work and the work you claim is an infringement, would say that one work was copied from the other. If you believe a copyright of yours has been infringed, you should contact an attorney. The best proof that you were the originator of the material is for you to have registered it with the Copyright Office.

14. *In what situations can I make a "fair use" of someone else's work without infringing on their copyright?* Whether your use is a fair use or an infringement depends on the circumstances of each case. Frequently, you can make a fair use of someone else's copyrighted work without their permission for purposes such as criticism, comment, news reporting, teaching (including multiple copies for classroom use), scholarship or research. To determine whether or not a use is a fair use, the factors to be considered include: (1) the nature of the use, including whether it's commercial or nonprofit and educational; (2) the nature of the copyrighted work; (3) how much of the copyrighted work is used; and (4) what effect the use will have on the potential market for or value of the copyrighted

work. If you are in a borderline situation, the wisest step is to request permission to use the work.

15. *I have more questions about copyright. How can I get answers to more specific questions? Will the Copyright Office cut through all the legal mumbo-jumbo and give me down-to-earth answers or do I need to see an attorney? Is there any other literature available that will answer my questions?* The Copyright Office will not give legal advice or opinions, but they will provide you free of charge with their Copyright Information Kit (Register of Copyrights, Library of Congress, Washington, D.C. 20559). This contains a copy of the copyright law, the regulations, the application forms, and circulars describing numerous aspects of copyright and the operation of the Copyright Office. If you feel you need to consult an attorney but you can't afford to do so, you should consider contacting one of the volunteer lawyers for the arts groups that exist across the country. You can find out the location of the group nearest you by contacting one of the following established organizations.

Bay Area Lawyers for the Arts
25 Taylor Street
San Francisco, California 94102
(415) 775-7200

Lawyers for the Creative Arts
111 North Wabash Avenue
Chicago, Illinois 60602
(312) 263-6989

Volunteer Lawyers for the Arts
36 West 44th Street
New York, New York 10036
(212) 575-1150

A comprehensive handbook for authors that covers all of their legal concerns, including copyright, is *The Writer's Legal Guide* by Tad Crawford (Hawthorn Books). Also, *Law and the Writer* by Kirk Polking and Leonard S. Meranus (Writer's Digest Books).

Rights and the Writer: What Should I Sell?

By William Brohaugh

Selling a piece of writing is cause enough for rejoicing, but the celebration *truly* begins when that article or short story is sold again.

Unless you own the rights to that piece of writing, however, you can't resell it. If you have sold all rights to an article, for instance, it can be reprinted *without* your permission and without further reimbursement. That's why taking careful stock of what rights you sell is important.

Here are the types of rights editors/publishers most often seek:

All Rights. The writer sells all rights to a piece of writing, meaning the buyer can use the article however and as many times as he pleases, without further reimbursement offered to the writer. Selling all rights is selling, in other words, ownership of the piece. The writer cannot use the piece again in its present form.

As expected, few writers want to sell everything they own on what they write—unless, of course, the price is right. And that's why—because the price usually isn't "that right"—the writer should try to avoid selling all rights. Consider that the article you sell once can be sold again and again, but without any rights to do so, potential income is totally lost.

Many of the publications listed in *Writer's Market* indicate that they buy all rights but will reassign those rights following publication. However, the author must usually request such reassignment after the publication (see question #4 in copyright article).

First Serial Rights. The writer sells the right to use a piece of writing for the first time in a periodical—anywhere ("serial" refers to the periodical nature of publications, and does not imply "serialization"). The writer cannot allow any other periodical to use the article until the purchaser of first rights has used it. Once the buyer of first rights has used the material, you can then resell it. Selling first rights is selling the right to use a piece of writing first in anything publishable.

First North American Serial Rights. The writer sells the right to use a piece of writing for the first time in any periodical located in North America.

Reprint Rights. The writer sells the right to reprint an already published work. If you've already sold first rights on an article to a publication and it has since been used, you are selling reprint rights to other buyers of the work. Using terms like Second Reprint Rights indicates to the buyer that he is the second user of the work and that no third buyers of the work can use it before he does.

Simultaneous Rights. The writer sells the right to use a piece of writing simultaneously to more than one buyer. If you have a general feature story that is suitable for Sunday newspaper supplements, for example, you might sell simultaneous rights to a number of supplements with non-overlapping circulations. Religious magazines are another type of publication that often purchases simultaneous rights. By selling these rights, you have clarified that others are using the story. Never sell simultaneous rights unless all parties involved know you're doing so.

One-Time Rights. The writer sells the right to use a piece of writing one time. This term is most often used in regard to photographic material or other artwork, but can be applied to writing, as well.

William Brohaugh is currently editor of Songwriter's Market *and is coeditor of* Photographer's Market—*both published by* Writer's Digest Books.

Before submitting material to a market, check its listing in this book to see what rights are purchased. Some buyers are adamant about what rights they'll accept; others will negotiate. In any case, the rights purchased should be specifically stated in writing sometime during the course of the sale, either in a letter or in some sort of written agreement. *Note:* If no rights are transferred in writing, and the material is sold to a periodical, the writer is authorizing unlimited use of the piece in that magazine, or subsequent issues of it. Thus, you can't collect reprint fees if the rights weren't spelled out in advance (see question #6 in "Copyright: Questions & Answers").

Give as much attention to the rights that you *haven't* sold as you do to the rights that you have sold. Be aware of what rights you retain, with an eye out for additional sales. If you have sold all North American rights to an article, for instance, you are still perfectly free to sell the article in Europe.

Whatever rights you sell or don't sell, the most important aspect in these dealings still lies in communication. Clarify what is being sold, for how long, and with what stipulations before any actual sale. Communication, coupled with these guidelines and some common sense, will preclude any harangues with editors over rights.

Taxes and the Writer: What Should I Pay?

By Patricia Ann Fox

Some of us would lose in a raffle if there were only one other ticket. That was my luck. Then I met this guy, see, in the numbers racket (an accountant), and since I was in the letters racket (a writer) we found that we could deduct most of my writing expenses at income tax time.

If I can master enough tax know-how to save money with my writing, so can you. Try it.

You must get your Internal Revenue Service return completed and into the mail by April 15. Don't wait until April 14 to worry about it. Keep records all year. When you tally up, you're liable to find the red figures massacring the black ones. But this is no time for an ego trip. Let the figures honestly tell the story, and take solace in the deductions.

The deductions can't be determined, however, without the figures. Here are two basic sources of the numbers you'll need:

Receipts. For each pack of paper, typewriter ribbon, book, magazine or magazine subscription you buy in carrying out your profession as a writer, get a receipt.

Records. Pay bills by check and buy a ledger. (It's deductible.) No matter how tedious it may be at first, enter each expense accurately, systematically, and religiously. If you keep records hit and miss, the IRS will hit you hard and you'll miss a considerable saving on taxes.

What's Deductible

All writing supplies, including paper, carbons, pens, ribbons, envelopes, copying costs, and postage.

Repairs and maintenance of writing equipment, including typewriter, tape recorder and camera.

Courses and conferences attended to enhance you as a professional writer. It's important to realize, though, that you can't deduct courses you take to *become* a writer. The IRS rule is that courses must be "refresher" or professionally improving in nature to count. Besides deducting the costs of these, also deduct mileage (at 17 cents a mile)—or actual car expenses, whichever profits you most; cost of tickets for public transportation; cost of hotel/motel rooms; and costs of meals.

Courses taken as research on subjects you're writing about. To establish that a course is for research, it would help if you had documentation from the potential publisher of your writings—such as a favorable response to a query. Even if the magazine should not publish what you've written, the response will show the research was done in good faith.

Dues paid for membership in writer's organizations.

Home office expenses. There's been an important change in this category. Many of us have been using a portion of a dining or living room to write in and

---

Patricia Ann Fox has been a copywriter and continuity director for radio stations in New Jersey and Pennsylvania. She has written for The Revue *(Quebec) and* The Family Digest. *Special thanks to Tony Bombardiere of the IRS Public Affairs Office, who reviewed and authenticated the article.*

deducting a percentage for expenses. This is no longer allowed. To take a home office deduction, you must have a portion of your dwelling set aside solely for writing on a *regular basis*. This same rule applies to a separate structure on your property.

For example, you may not use a portion of your garage for writing and a portion for parking your car. If your goes in, your home office expense is out.

If you are using a room solely for writing, you will be able to deduct a portion for your rent and utilities.

Example: If you rent a five-room apartment for $200 a month and use one room exclusively for writing, you are entitled to deduct one-fifth of the rent, which comes to $40 a month, or $480 a year. Add to this one-fifth of your heating bill and one-fifth of your electric bill and watch the deductions mount up. Keep a list, too, of long-distance phone bills arising from your writing.

Note: There is a limit to home office expenses. You may not exceed in deductible expenses the amount of your gross income. If you made $1,000 last year, you can't deduct any more than that in home office expenses—no matter how much they came to. Just $1,000 in this case.

In taking home office expenses, you must use the designated room as your principal place of business.

If you own your home and use one room for writing, you can deduct the allocated expenses of operating that room. Among these allowable expenses are interest on mortgage, real estate taxes, repairs or additions to the home, cost of utilities, home insurance premiums, and depreciation on the room.

Example: If you own a seven-room house, one room used for writing, one-seventh of the total cost of the house can be depreciated, as well as one-seventh of the above mentioned expenses. Again, this must be your principal place of business, used solely for writing, and not exceed your amount of gross income.

Deductions for an addition to your home will require you to do a little more figuring than if you simply calculate for the cost of the unadded-to home.

Example: Let's say you have a 10-room home which cost $50,000 and which has a life-expectancy of 50 years. One of these rooms is solely for your writing. Your yearly deduction would be $100. (One-tenth of the house cost = $5,000. Fifty years into this = $100.)

Now, if you put a $5,000 addition on your $50,000 home, the basis for calculation goes up to $55,000—and your yearly allowable deduction increases to $110. If the addition cost $5,000 but has only a life expectancy of 25 years (shoddy materials, maybe) the total yearly deduction just for the addition would be $200. Your one-tenth share would be $20. You could deduct, then, $100 (depreciation on the original structure), plus $20 (depreciation on addition), or $120.

The only problem is finding a house so conducive to round-figure calculations.

Mileage. Take 17 cents a mile for the first 15,000 miles you travel on writing-related missions and 10 cents a mile for miles traveled over 15,000.

Or you may take the actual cost of operating your car—gas, oil, tires, maintenance and depreciation. (See below for figuring depreciation.) If you use your car 100 percent for writing, the total cost of operating it is deductible. If you use it only half time for writing, then half the expenses are deductible.

Compare mileage deduction to cost deduction, and use the one that gives you the bigger break.

What May Be Depreciated

You can count depreciation on your typewriter, desk, chair, lamps, tape recorder, files, camera equipment or anything else related to your writing which cost a considerable amount of money and which has a useful life of more than one year. The easiest, most common method of depreciation for the writer is the straight line method.

In straight line, you take the depreciable basis (original cost of the asset minus the "salvage value"), divide by the number of useful years, and come up with the yearly depreciation deduction. The salvage value is what you could normally sell the item for after its estimated life of usefulness to you is over.

Example: Electric typewriter, purchased January, 1976 for $350. Estimated life, five years. Salvage value at end of five years, $50. Depreciation allowable for the year ending 1976 equals $60. That's what you get when you divide the cost ($350), less salvage value ($50), by the estimated number of useful years (5).

Assets purchased later in the year must be calculated only for the months you had them.

Example: Electric typewriter purchased in May, 1976 for $350. Estimated life, five years. Depreciation allowable for the year is $40. Since the asset was yours for only eight months, you calculate depreciation by dividing 12 (months) into the yearly deduction of $60. This gives you $5 a month. This $5 multiplied by eight months gives you $40 in depreciation.

If salvage value is less than 10 percent of your depreciable basis, you can disregard it for computation. However, you can't depreciate below salvage value.

In addition to deductions and depreciation, you can make some extra gains on purchases made for your "business." For any business equipment purchased during the current tax year, the IRS allows an additional deduction. This deduction, the "investment tax credit" (ITC), is allowed for furniture, equipment, and other depreciable assets, except real estate. It is also substracted from your total tax liability.

The maximum ITC, 10 percent, occurs when the asset's useful life is seven years or more. If the useful life is only three to five years, take one-third of that 10 percent. Example: A desk with a useful life of three to five years is bought for $100. First take 10 percent ($10), then one-third ($3.33) for the total deduction.

If the asset's useful life is five to seven years, the investment tax credit is calculated on two-thirds of the 10 percent. Thus, your $100 desk, now expected to live longer, has an ITC of $6.66.

Of course, once the predicted useful life of an item goes to or beyond seven years, the maximum 10 percent of the total cost may be deducted, and the ITC for your desk would be $10.

You get the investment tax credit on eligible items no matter what time during the year they were purchased.

Finally, if after deductions you earn $400 or more, you are required to pay a Social Security tax of .079 of the earnings. And you must fill out and submit a Schedule SE (for "self-employment").

Tax Forms You Should Know

Many of us will be filling out a Form 1040 joint return with spouse. As writers, we would also be filling out a Schedule C—Profit (or Loss) from Business or Profession, a Schedule SE (see above) for Social Security, a Form 3468—Computation

Show Depreciation!

Wear and tear on equipment costs you money each year. To allow you credit for this inexact expense, the Internal Revenue Service has a depreciation formula you can follow. Generally, any item that is helpful to you as a writer is depreciable if it (1) represents a sizable expenditure, and (2) has an estimated useful life of more than one year.
For example:

Typewriter

Tape recorder

Office furniture and equipment

Camera

Photocopier

See the main article for ways of figuring depreciation.

Take It Off!

Most of the things you buy to enhance your writing profession are deductible. There are qualifications, however, and for these see the main article. Here are the most common items for which you should get and keep receipts.

Books, magazines, subscriptions

Conferences

Courses (refresher and research)

Dues for writers' organizations

Home office expenses

Mailing supplies

Mileage, or cost of car operation

Photo developing and printing

Postage

Repair and maintenance of writing-related equipment

Writing and copying supplies

of Investment Credit, and often Schedules A and B (for itemized deductions, and dividends and interest income).

You will have to read these forms carefully—but a careful reading will show how to provide the information asked for and the advantages for doing so.

When you keep accurate records throughout the year and when you get receipts and pay by check, then preparing for your April 15 deadline won't be so bad.

In the event you are faced with an audit, there are other collectibles that will lend support.

Rejection slips. Keep them.

When the subject of rejection slips comes up at writers' conferences, the instructors generally frown and tell you to throw them away. Be done with them, they advise.

Not me. I advise you to pile the slips in a folder, carton, or spare room—somewhere you won't have to look at them, but where they are accessible should you be the featured guest at a tax audit. What better way to establish you're a working writer than to hit the IRS agent (not physically) with an avalanche of rejection slips or communiques from the publishers.

Encouraging letters? Hold onto them, too, for heaven's sake. And have your *ledger, receipts,* and *canceled checks* ready. Audits, like toothaches, sometimes happen to the best of us.

Because of the 1976 rules on home office expenses, numerous accountants tell me that taking those expenses will invariably mean a tax audit. So I cannot stress too often that you must have a room just for writing and be able to prove that it is your principal place of business.

One final note: The examples used here are for guides only. Different requirements are made of people in different circumstances. For any long-term writing projects, such as novels or histories, which take more than a year to complete, consult Revenue Ruling 73-395.

After all this, doesn't writing seem easy?

The Writer as Photographer

By Ted Schwarz

For the average freelance writer, the difference between selling a magazine article and selling an *illustrated* magazine article is likely to be a minimum of $50. In many cases the photographs will bring you as much money as the text—or more. And for a few articles, such as how-to-do-it features, an unillustrated manuscript is likely to be rejected regardless of the quality of the writing.

If you are not currently a photography enthusiast or if your equipment is a battered old Brownie, my comments may sound somewhat intimidating. You have refined your writing skills to the point where you feel competitive with other freelancers. If you now have to learn to take pictures as well, you may feel you will reduce, rather than increase your sales.

Fortunately, your fears are groundless. Admittedly, a rank amateur isn't going to read this article and go forth taking pictures the old *Life* magazine would have purchased. However, you can learn enough to begin illustrating articles which will be saleable to literally thousands of magazines. More important, you can do it with almost any camera you now own, including that battered Brownie.

As an example of what can happen by illustrating your work, I once sold an article to *Nation's Cities* magazine for $150 with the promise that I would send illustrations. When the photographs reached the editor, he selected enough so that my check for the prints equalled what I had received for the text.

In another case, an article idea for *Stern* magazine (Germany) was rejected until I told the editor pictures could be provided. The text plus photographs package *was* desired and I received a check instead of a "no sale".

Getting Started: Equipment and Film

Your first step toward selling pictures with your words is getting to know the limitations of your equipment. Some cameras have interchangeable lenses, motor drives, several viewfinders, built-in light meters, make your morning coffee and draw your bathwater. They can take pictures through microscopes or provide close-ups of objects hundreds of yards away. Other, less expensive cameras are prefocused at a point approximately five feet from the lens. Everything from that distance to infinity will be sharp but you can't get closer and you can't change the lenses. Between these two extremes are numerous cameras with varying technical abilities.

The most practical way to start selling pictures with your articles is to illustrate *only* those articles you can handle with the camera you now own. For example, you should not attempt close-up, detailed studies of a button collection with a fixed focus camera. If you did an article about such a collection, you should send it not illustrated or work with a photographer who has more sophisticated equipment. However, your camera would be fine for taking pictures of a person wearing a custom-made dress utilizing those same buttons since you would be able to stand several feet from your model.

Photographer/writer Ted Schwarz is author of How to Make Money With Your Camera, How to Start a Photography Business, *and a new book* Tell Me Who I Am Before I Die. *His writing and photography have appeared in* Saturday Review, Cosmopolitan, Seventeen, *and numerous other publications.*

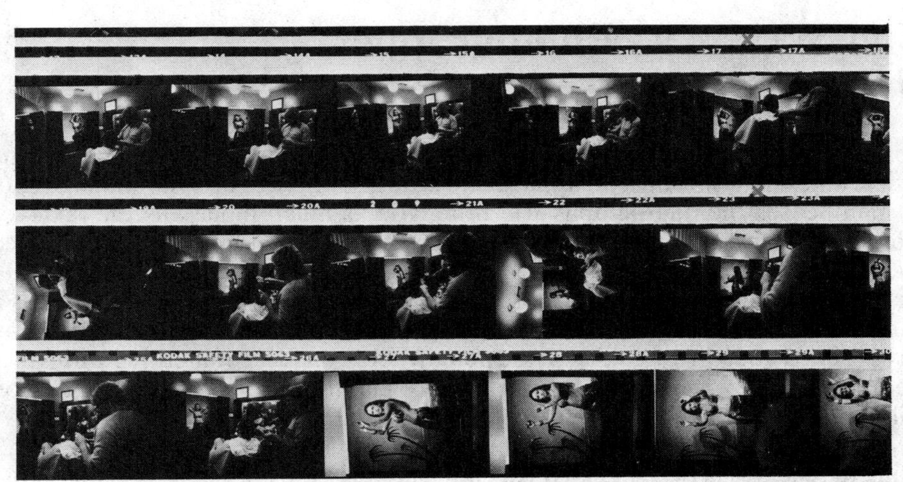

An excellent and inexpensive way to allow an editor a great deal of choice in choosing photographs is to submit a *contact sheet*. Because of the varience in quality of the images on the sheet, include two or three prints with your submission to show the editor that your photos will reproduce well when enlarged. —Photo by Ted Schwarz.

The only type of camera which cannot be easily used to sell your pictures is the Instamatic type using 110 film. Editors prefer 8x10 prints when you send black-and-white pictures, and due to the small size of 110 film negatives, 8x10s cannot easily be well made. All the other film sizes you might use—35mm, 120 roll film, etc.—can readily be made into 8x10 prints.

If you do not own a camera and are interested in buying one, the best purchase would be a 35mm single lens reflex. It should have a built-in light meter and interchangeable lens capabilities. Good equipment is available in the $200-300 line. Start with the basic camera and lens, learning how to use it and exploring its picture taking potential. Then, when you know your camera's limits and have decided what types of photographs you will need beyond the camera's present capability, buy the lens(es) and/or accessories needed. By spreading your expenses over time, the purchase can be financed by your increased sales.

The type of film you use will be determined in large measure by the publications for which you write. Most magazines want black-and-white prints. The best all-around black-and-white films are Kodak's Plus-X, when plenty of light is available, and Kodak's Tri-X, when the opposite is true.

Magazines generally prefer color slides to color prints. Slides are made from positive color film which is identifiable by the "chrome" ending in the film name. Koda*chrome*, Ekta*chrome* and Agra*chrome* are among the best known slide films, with Kodachrome providing the greatest detail and longest processed film storage life without the color deteriorating.

If you use color negative film, films with names ending with the word "color," most labs will give you prints at the time of processing. Films of this type include Koda*color*, Veri*color* and Fuji*color*, among others. Some are meant for extremely low light. All of them can be made into slides for an additional charge beyond the processing and printing price. It is usually cheapest to buy the slide film when freelancing. If you ever need color prints, they can be made from the slides.

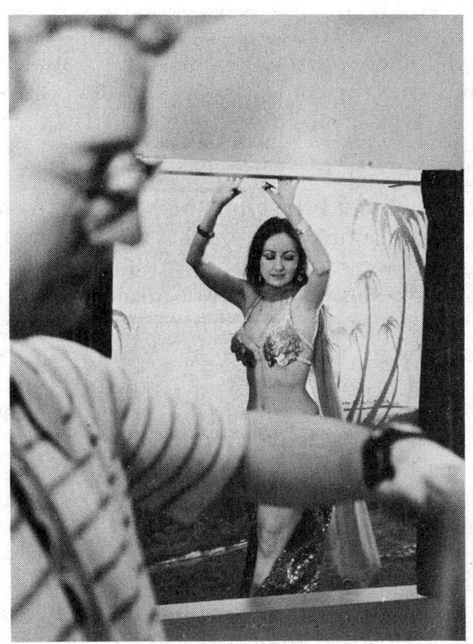

To assure that the photos you submit to a publication will fit the editor's space needs, provide both horizontal and vertical images. A series of stories on a hairstyling club which utilizes belly dancers for entertainment required extensive illustration. These two overviews, horizontal and vertical, give the reader instant information as to what is happening. — Photos by Ted Schwarz.

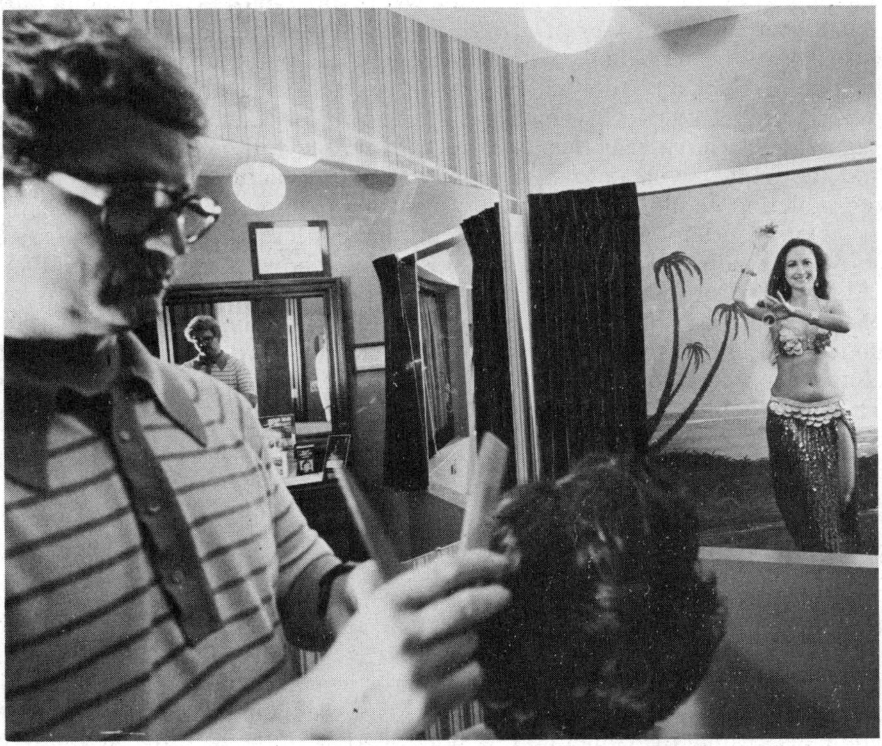

Taking the "Interesting" Photo

What makes an interesting photograph? There are many books on this subject but, basically, the answer is two-fold when it comes to writers illustrating their works. The photographs must be enjoyable to look at and/or informative.

If you write about an author, a straight head and shoulders portrait might prove adequate as an illustration, but it will not bring you much respect from the publication. An *interesting* photo of the same person might be a wide angle picture taken from a corner of his or her writing area. The author is shown surrounded by a desk, overflowing book shelves, papers scattered on the floor, a wastebasket surrounded by wads of paper and perhaps a cat perched lazily on the typewriter. It is a picture which shows the author's environment and provides insight into where and how the author works. Or you might take the author outside and photograph him or her walking with a dog through the dewy pasture land surrounding the farm the author owns.

Suppose you are writing about an athlete who won an award for track. A picture of just the athlete's head or a photo of the athlete accepting a trophy will not be very interesting or saleable. But an action portrait of the athlete leaping a hurdle or breaking the tape at the finish line will be of interest to everyone, including the editor.

Keep in mind the potential reproduction size for the publication as well. For example, suppose you are writing about a community theater. The article will appear in your local city magazine where most illustrations are run fairly small—perhaps a quarter of a page at the most. One possible photograph would be of the entire stage with the actors spread out, performing a dramatic high point. Such a picture will be extremely interesting when run as a double page spread. However, when the magazine editor reduces it to the quarter page you can more realistically expect, everyone will be squeezed together and the impact will be lost. A more interesting picture for the small size reproduction would be a close-up of just two or three actors interacting.

Don't clutter your picture with items that don't relate to what you want to show the reader. Suppose you are illustrating a how-to article on building a radio. The photos will show step-by-step construction. Try to take a close-up of the unfinished radio and the procedure being described in the text without unneeded parts or tools intruding. To do this, you might lay a piece of white cloth on a table and remove all the parts you will be using for future steps. Then place only those parts involved with that step on the cloth and take a close-up. A photo showing not only the essential parts of the illustration but also screw drivers, soldering iron, and transistors used for the whole project will be confusing—and rejected.

Use a lot of film when photographing. Take a picture standing up. Then stoop down and photograph the same image from the lower angle. Get above

Taking the Pictures

You'll need to supply both *horizontal* and *vertical* photographs for the most flexible illustration use. With most cameras, especially 35mm equipment, this just means turning the camera on its side for some of the pictures. If you have a square format camera, such as an Instamatic (126 film type) or 120 roll film the subject, behind the subject and at every other angle you can imagine. A dull situation need not be dull if you use imagination. I once had to photograph a woman watering a house plant. The image which sold was taken low, looking up through the foliage at the watering can and the woman holding it. A potentially dull photograph was made visually interesting. However, had I contented myself with just one or two pictures, I never would have discovered the angle which insured my sale.

Always take plenty of film on assignments and, if you are using 35mm equipment, buy 36 exposure rolls. Most of us have a tendency to limit our picture taking to the number of frames on a roll. The larger the roll, the more we are likely to experiment, and that experimentation can lead to your discovery of the unusual angle which sells.

Be alert to additional picture possibilities. I photographed a 90 year old blind woman who sews to illustrate an article. When photographing her at work on the ancient sewing machine she used, I noticed that her wrinkled, leathery hands were interesting by themselves. I took an extra few frames of just the hands. The images did not directly relate to the story other than the fact that they were the subject's hands. However, the editor found them interesting enough to pay to use one.

If the magazine to which you are submitting an illustrated article uses color, be very selective about what you photograph. Remember that color reproduction is expensive. Unless color is essential to an understanding of the subject, adds a definite beauty with strong eye appeal, or provides details which would not be visible in black-and-white, it should be avoided.

Before taking any photograph, ask yourself these questions:

Will this picture give the reader essential information?

Will this picture be enjoyable to look at?

If I didn't include this picture, would the article suffer in any way?

Can I show this image in a more unusual way?

Does color play an essential part in this picture?

Would this color picture be as effective if black-and-white film was used?

Have I avoided such dull approaches as showing someone staring into the camera with a dazed smile, a group of people holding a trophy, certificate or whatever, and similar trite images?

If I were the reader, why would I want to take the trouble to study this photograph?

I have found that the greatest self-education about taking interesting photographs comes from studying published work. Look at back isues of the various photography annuals which are collections of photographs accompanied by brief technical information, usually at the back of the publication. See which photographs you like, decide why they appeal and then think about how you can adapt the photographer's technique to your own work to make your pictures more appealing. Learning by such examples is an effective way to advance your skills as an article illustrator.

equipment, then plan your images so there is room to *crop* (removal of a portion of the picture) both horizontally and vertically when the prints are made. By supplying both horizontal and vertical prints, you are increasing the chances of having the pictures used. Remember that when an editor buys an illustrated article, he or she will seldom pay extra for the photographs if they can't be used due to images which fail to match space requirements.

Every set of illustrations you send a publication must include two types of photographs. Of greatest importance is a single photograph which provides an over-view of the story. For example, *Stern* asked me to photograph a barber who opened a hairstyling club where belly dancers entertain. One of my photographs included the barber cutting the customer's hair while the customer watched the belly dancer perform. All three people appeared, and that photo (one horizontal and one vertical) summed up the accompanying article I wrote.

The remainder of the photographs you send can isolate different parts of what you are trying to illustrate. In the case of the barber, there were photographs of the barber and his customer alone as well as close-ups of the dancer.

With how-to-do-it articles, one photograph might show the finished project or perhaps all the different parts used for the project. Then the rest of the images would isolate the different steps of the project.

Be certain your photographs are interesting. An article on an artist should not be illustrated by a photo of his or her receiving an award for the work. Rather it might show the artist painting or doing sculpture or whatever else won the prize.

Use of flash requires precaution. If you have a subject near a wall and aim the flash so the light strikes head on, the beam parallel with the lens, you will get a heavy shadow that is not pleasing. Either move the subject to eliminate the shadow or, if your equipment is somewhat sophisticated, direct the flash towards the ceiling so the light bounces down without leaving a shadow.

Many magazines no longer print color due to reproduction cost. When they do use color, it must be important to the image. For example, in the case of the artist at work, one photograph might include a portrait of the artist concentrating intensely. A second photograph might be taken from behind or to one side of the artist, including a painting as the main composition element. The close-up of the face, while interesting, probably will not be considered for color reproduction because the color adds nothing of value. However, the photo showing the painting will be used in color when possible because the color adds a dimension which aids the reader's understanding of the artist's work. Be certain you always check back issues of a magazine to which you are submitting your work to see whether or not it uses color. If it doesn't, provide only black-and-white photos.

Photo Processing

When you are working with black-and-white film, it is best to utilize the services of a custom lab to process the film and make your prints. Normal processing laboratories serving the general public are completely automated. Everything is printed according to pre-planned standards which may or may not be right for your negatives. Special cropping and removal of dust specks and other blemishes are not offered.

Special processing, the highest quality printing, and all manner of cropping and retouching services are offered by most custom labs. A standard lab will usually send you small prints (e.g. 3½x5) from your negatives. These are expensive, running from 20-40 cents apiece for each print.

With a custom lab, you can get a black-and-white contact sheet. The cost is seldom more than $3, much less than the $8-10 you'd have to pay to get up to 36 enlargements in the 3½x5 range. After the contact sheet is studied, the photographer can then order only those prints needed for sending with the article. These will usually be 8x10, so getting the 3½x5 size only gives you a lot of prints to clutter your files.

Often editors will ask to see the contact sheets made for the assignment. The editors would rather have the opportunity to pick the prints they want than to leave it to the writer. However, since contact sheets cannot allow for each negative to get its best possible exposure, the writer should send along several enlargements to show the true picture quality.

Submitting Your Photos

Almost every camera store sells envelopes, mailers, for mailing prints. They are slightly larger than the size print they are meant to hold and contain two pieces of corrugated cardboard. To submit your prints, insert them between the two pieces of cardboard and secure with a rubber band. Include inside the mailer envelope your cover letter and/or manuscript; a second equal-size envelope to serve as your SASE; and the photos within the cardboard. On each piece of cardboard write SAVE CARDBOARD FOR PRINT RETURN. I have known editors to throw away the cardboard and return the prints in the unprotected envelope. The prints were ruined.

Color slides can be sent in a number of ways. Many photographers mail them in the cardboard or plastic boxes supplied by the processing labs. Unfortunately, this method can result in plastic splinters puncturing the slides or the boxes being crushed. Even worse, the loose slides are frequently lost or improperly handled by the editor.

My approach is to use a heavy plastic sheet with 20 pockets, each of which holds a 2x2 (35mm size) transparency. The sheets are punched to fit three-ring notebooks for easy storage. They are available from camera stores and some coin shops, as many holders for coins are 2x2 size. The sheets fit nicely in a photo mailer and can be held up to the light for easy viewing without the risk of loss or fingerprint damage.

I try to save postage by sending photographs with an article only when it is necessary. If an article is effective without illustrations, I will let it stand on its own even though I have pictures in my files. However, the covering letter accompanying the article always states, "Illustrations are available on speculation if desired." The editor invariably does *not* ask to see the illustrations, under such circumstances, until he or she is sold on the article.

Other times, the photographs are an integral part of the article. A how-to-do-it piece, for example, can not stand alone without pictures. Under such circumstances, the photographs *must* be enclosed with the article.

Almost every camera shop or coin store sells plastic holders that can easily be used for submitting photographs to publications. They make it convenient for the editor to choose the photo he wants, and decreases the chances of damage to valuable transparencies.—Photo by William Brohaugh.

Photographs need never be enclosed with a query letter unless the illustrations are needed to make the sale in the first place. For example, suppose you have a series of pictures of a dog and cat at play which will be accompanied by a long caption rather than an actual article. Just mentioning that you have "adorable" photos you would like to send will not be good enough to get a favorable response. You will have to either send the entire set of photos or one dramatic example on speculation with your initial query in order to make the sale. However, this circumstance is rare and usually you will *not* send illustrations when making the initial query.

Send all photographs to the same editor who handles the manuscripts unless specifically told to send them elsewhere. Photo editors and art editors occasionally buy photographs on their own, especially for cover use. However, article illustrations are not purchased until the article itself has been approved. Since this is handled by the editor (managing editor, features editor or similar individual), he or she should also be sent the appropriate illustrations.

There is always the chance that the Postal Service will lose or damage some of your slides and/or prints. It is tempting to insure your package but it may not be to your benefit. When paying for damaged photos, legal precedents have been set which tend to work against you. The value is placed at the "fair market price" which, in the case of material sent on speculation, is really the cost of the materials, not the potential income if a sale is made. The only exception is a slide or print you have sold over and over again for regular fees of $10, $50, $100 or whatever. The total amount of money earned over the months or years of sales is found, then the potential future sales life is determined. Finally money is paid based on those past earnings and future life expectancy. However, you will probably not fall into this category and can only receive token payment for loss.

Generally, if you mail everything first class, it *will* arrive at its destination. I have never lost anything this way. However, if a slide is of great personal value, you can get a 4x5 internegative (smaller internegatives offered by labs are of lesser quality) for from $5-8. If the slide is lost, a print can be made from the internegative. Because of the cost, making an internegative must be reserved for very special slides only.

All prints, contact sheets, and slides you mail should have your name, address and telephone number *lightly* stamped on the back. Put the print face down on a smooth, hard surface and use a standard rubber stamp to print your identification. Such custom-made stamps are available through most office supply stores and some print shops. You can get a print face small enough so three lines fit in the white margin of a 35mm mount.

For More Information

The most concise information about selling and where to sell your photographs, as well as information about custom labs, can be found in the annual *Photographer's Market* (a Writer's Digest Book). You might also check such books as *How to Make Money With Your Camera* by Ted Schwarz (H.P. Books), *Photography: What's the Law?* by Robert Cavallo and Stuart Kahn (Crown Pub.) and Eastman Kodak's *Practical Encyclopedia of Photography* published by Amphoto.

Other Ways to Sell Your Writing

By Kirk Polking

Once a freelancer's skill with words becomes known, he, or she, is usually approached by two kinds of clients: 1) social service agencies, fund-raising organizations and church groups in the community which want the writer to "donate" his services for a worthy cause; and 2) national and local businesses which are prepared to pay. How the writer handles client number one depends on who the client is and the freelancer's personal situation as to finances, time and energy.

For example, some freelance writers just trying to get established in a community will take on a fund-raising job with minimal pay just to get exposure to other clients who are prospective paying customers. Other writers take the attitude that they have a professional marketable skill and the best way to operate from the very start is to charge for their services.

Writers approached by the second type of client are usually hired for a one-time writing assignment and are often asked to quote a fee for the job. How do you decide what to charge?

You can try contacting other writers or friends in a related business who have used freelancers, to get some idea of what's been paid for similar jobs in the past. Otherwise you have to set your fee based on two considerations: (1) how much you think your time is worth for as long as you think it will take to do the job; and (2) how much you think the client is willing, or can afford to pay for the job.

But why wait for businesses to seek *you* out? There are hundreds of freelance writing opportunities. The list which follows is only a springboard for you to start investigating your own possibilities. And keep in mind that the rates paid by advertising agencies, businesses, retail stores and other firms which are consistent users of freelance writers vary from city to city, so the rates reported to us here by freelancers can only serve as a rough guideline.

Advertising copy writing: Ad agencies need part-time help in rush seasons; but you may also wish to contact smaller merchants who can't afford an agency. Fees freelancers charge in this area range from $10-25/hour or a "package" price which might be just $25 for a press release or small ad on up to several hundred dollars for a more complex assignment.

Book publishing: Jobs for freelancers here include:

Book manuscript/copy editing: $3-5/hour and up. Occasionally 75¢/page.

Paperback cover copy: $40-75.

Proofreading paperback book page proofs: 30-40¢/page.

Preparing a book manuscript reader's report: $10 for a half-page summary of the book; half-page recommendation.

Manuscript rewriting: $1,000 and up; $350/day and up.

Kirk Polking has been both a full-time freelance writer and editor of Writer's Digest *magazine. Presently, she is director of the* Writer's Digest School.

Writing as-told-to books: author gets full advance and 50% royalties; subject gets 50% royalties.

Writing a biography for a sponsor: $500 up to $3,000 plus expenses.

Translation work: $25-50/thousand words minimum.

Business-related jobs: On the local level, this can range from copywriting ads for small retailers, to writing annual reports and anniversary booklets for local manufacturers. On the national level, major corporations hire top writers and pay top rates. Some freelance rates for both regional and national jobs here include:

Announcement folders writing: $25-350.

Annual report writing: $10-30/hour for brief report with some economic information and explanation of figures; $40-50/hour and up for a report that must meet SEC requirements, legal language, etc.

Booklets, writing and editing: $500-$1,000.

Business films: 10% of production cost of films up to $30,000. $150/day; $20/hour where percent of cost not applicable.

Catalogs or brochures for business: $60-75/printed page; more if there are many tables or charts which must be reworked for readability and consistency.

Commercial reports, for business, insurance companies, credit agencies, market research firms: $1.85-5/report.

Company newsletters, "house organs": $100-400, 2-4 pages.

Consultation fees: $75-100/hour.

Conventions, public relations for: $500-5,000.

Editing text copy for business brochures, publications: $20-35/hour.

Ghostwriting business speeches, major markets: $2,750.

House organs, writing and editing: $200-600, 2-4 pages; editing, some writing, 16-32 pages, $500-1,000/issue.

Industrial and business brochures, consultation, research and writing: $3,500.

Industrial films: $500-1,200, 10-minute reel; 5-12% of the production cost of films that run $750-1,000/release minute.

Industrial promotions: $7.50-40/hour.

Industrial slide films: 14% of gross production cost.

Industrial writing: $25-30/hour including conference interview and writing time. Long distance travel time and expenses billed separately.

Miscellaneous business writing: $25-50/hour.

New product releases, writing $300-500 plus expenses.

Newspaper ads for small businesses: $25 for small 1-column ad; $3.50/hour and up.

Retail business newsletters: $200 for 4 pages, writing, picture taking, layout and printing supervision.

Sales letter, business or industrial: $150 for one or two pages.

Shopping mall promotion: 15% of promotion budget for the mall.

Technical typing: 50¢-$1/page.

Technical typing masters for reproduction: $3/hour for rough setup then $2-4/page or $5-6/hour.

Technical translation: $2.75-3.95/150 words.

Technical writing: $10-15/hour.

Travel folder: $100.

Education-related jobs: If you're a teacher *and* a writer you have two skills to sell and the variety of buyers for them is shown here.

Audio cassette scripts: $120 for 20 minutes.

Educational film strips: $1,200.

Educational films, writing: $200 for one reeler (11 minutes of film); $1,000-1,500 for 30 minutes.

Educational grant proposals, writing: $50-125/day plus expenses.

Programmed instruction materials, writing: $1,000-3,000/hour of programmed training provided. Consulting/editorial fees: $25/hour; $200/day, plus expenses, minimum.

School public relations: $3.50-10/hour.

Slide presentation for an education institution: $1,000.

Teaching creative writing, part-time: $15-30/hour of instruction.

Teaching high school journalism, part-time: percent of regular teacher's salary.

Teaching home-bound students: $5/hour.

Magazine and newspaper work:

Editing a group of religious publications: $200-500/month.

Local criticism, art, music, drama: free tickets plus $2-5.

Magazine stringing, rates recommended by American Society of Journalists and Authors, Inc.: 20¢-$1/word, based on circulation. Daily rate: $200 plus expenses. Weekly rate: $750 plus expenses.

Newspaper column: 80¢/column inch to $20/column.

Newspaper stringing: 50¢-2.50/column inch; up to $4-5 in some national publications.

Regional magazine correspondent: $5-15/hour, plus expenses.

Reviews, art, drama, music, for national magazines: $25-50; $20-50/column for newspapers; $100-200 in Sunday supplements.

Trade journal articles, ghostwritten for someone else's byline: $250-400.

Photo/film jobs: Those writers who are also photographers or want to work with another freelancer, can seek out extra checks like these:

Audiovisual scripts: $1,000-$1,500 advance against 5-10% royalties for 5-10 script/visual units.

Photo-brochures: $700-15,000.

Slide film, single image photo: $75.

TV filmed news and features: $15/film clip.

TV news film still photo: $3-6.

TV news story: $16-25.

Publicity and Public Relations:

Library public relations: $5-25/hour.

Public relations: $200-400/day plus expenses.

Publicity writing: $30/hour; $100/day.

Retainer for fund-raising writing for a foundation: $500/month.

Retainer for publicity and PR work for an adoption agency: $200/month.

Retainer for writing for businesses, campaign funds: usually a flat fee but the equivalent of $5-20/hour.

Other ideas:

Associations, writing for, on miscellaneous projects: $10-25/hour or on a project basis.

Comedy writing, for night club entertainers: Gags only, $5-7. Routines, $100-300/minute. Some new comics try to get 5-minute routines for $100-150; but top comics may pay $1,500 for a 5-minute bit from a top writer with credits.

Family histories, writing: $200-500.

Fiction rewriting: $150 for 10-page short story to $10,000 for complete novel rewrite, under special circumstances.

Gallup Poll interviewing: $2.50/hour.

Genealogical research, local: $3-5/hour.

Ghostwriting a novel rewrite: $1,000 ($10/hour for 100 hrs. work).

Government, local, public information officer: $10/hour, to $50-100/day.

History, local, lectures: $25-100.

Photocomposition on electric typewriter: $6/hour, 5¢/line on short jobs.

Political campaign writing: $200-250/week; $35/page piecework jobs; $10/hour and up.

Ghostwriting political speeches: $10-20/hour.

Record album cover copy: $100-200.

Speeches by writers who become specialists in certain fields; $50-500 plus expenses.

Sports information director, college: $700-2,000/month.

Syndicated newspaper column, self-promoted: $2 each for weeklies; $5-25/week for dailies, based on circulation.

If there are substantial differences in the rates paid in your area for any of these jobs—or you'd like to tell us about other job categories with which you have personal experience, please drop a line with the facts to Kirk Polking, Jobs for Writers, care of *Writer's Market,* 9933 Alliance Road, Cincinnati 45242. Your comments will help other freelancers through future editions of this directory.

The Markets

Audiovisual Markets

Because producers of "software"—the trade term for nonprint materials like records, filmstrips, tape cassettes, etc., as opposed to "hardware," which refers to the machines on which they are viewed or played frequently have highly individualized editorial requirements, freelance writers are encouraged to seek firm assignments from audiovisual producers before writing or submitting finished scripts. A good query letter should outline the writer's credentials (as an educator, specialist in some subject, or professional scriptwriter), include a sample of his writing, and give details of his proposed script or series of scripts.

Many of the companies currently active in the audiovisual field are working with staff writers and do not actively seek freelance contributions. Those who are interested in staff positions will find a more complete list of audiovisual producers in the *Audiovisual Market Place* (published by R.R. Bowker).

Software producers pay on a flat fee or royalty basis, depending on the company and the quality of the writer's material. The sponsored film production company, operating on a contract basis to produce audiovisuals for the government, business or private organizations, offers a flat fee payment, which varies according to the nature of the project and the writer's credentials. If a company produces and markets its own audiovisual products (usually to the elementary and secondary school and college markets), payment is most often according to a royalty contract with the writer, but a flat fee is sometimes paid. The flat fees vary widely, but royalty agreements usually approximate the ones offered for school texts. Based on the net money the publisher receives on sales, this is 3% to 5% for elementary and secondary school materials and 8% to 12% for college textbooks. A few producers offer an even higher percentage, some going as high as 18.75% for college materials.

A/V CONCEPTS CORPORATION, 263 Union Blvd., West Islip NY 11795. (516)587-6315. Director of R&D: Dorothy M. Bogart. Estab. 1968. Produces material for el-hi language arts students, both those on grade and in remedial situations. Query. SASE. Reports on outlines in 1 week; on final scripts in 2½ months. Buys all rights. Catalog for SASE.
Needs: "Authors must receive a set of our specifications before submitting material. Manuscripts must be written using our lists of vocabulary words, and must meet readability formula requirements provided by us. Length of manuscripts and subjects will vary according to grade level for which material is prepared. Basically, we want articles and stories that will motivate people to read. Authors must be highly creative and highly disciplined." Pays $75.

ABINGDON PRESS, (Audio-Graphics Line), 201 8th Ave., S., Nashville TN 37202. For religious professionals, groups and lay persons. Buys all rights. Will send a catalog and editorial guidelines to writer on request. Looking for "people with established reputations whose names help sell the product." Query first. "Study the market. Don't submit vague plans."
Religion: Multimedia kits and prerecorded tapes and cassettes. "Study materials for religious education, educational programs for religious professionals and how-to and self-help programs for religious groups. Most of these programs produced as sets of 1, 2, or 4 audio-cassettes in a box or album accompanied by a printed guide." Offers 7½ to 10% on retail price.

ADMASTER, INC., 425 Park Ave., S., New York NY 10016. Executive Producer: Aileen Corbett. Estab. 1948. Produces material for industry (sales and training). Query with samples. SASE. Reports in 3 weeks. Buys all rights.
Needs: Education; religion; business; technical; medical; and general. Produces charts; silent and sound filmstrips; motion pictures; multi-media kits; overhead transparencies; tapes and cassettes; slides; and teaching machine programs. "No writers outside metropolitan New York (Connecticut and New Jersey). Writers must be available for meetings." Pays $500-1,000.

AERO PRODUCTS RESEARCH, INC., 11201 Hindry Ave., Los Angeles CA 90045. (213)641-7242. Contact: J. Parr. Aviation/aeroscience/aerospace education material for pilot training and schools (private and public schools from K through college). Copyrighted. SASE.
Education: "Developing and editing both technical and nontechnical material. Charts, silent filmstrips, models, multimedia kits, overhead transparencies, phonograph records, prerecorded tapes and cassettes, slides and study prints. Royalty arrangements are handled on an individual project basis. Writers should have flight instructor and ground school instructor experience."

ALLEGRO FILM PRODUCTIONS, INC., 201 W. 52nd St., New York NY 10019. President: Mr. J. Forman. Produces for the general and school markets. Buys 3-20 scripts/year. Submit resume. Buys all rights.
Needs: Science films for education, films for industry and government, and documentaries. Produces 16mm and 35mm motion pictures. Pays $1,000-1,500.

ANCO/BOSTON, INC., 80 Boylston St., Boston MA 02116. (617)482-9270. Director, Instructional Systems: R. Hoyt. Estab. 1959. Produces for the industrial and business communities. Submit resume. SASE. Reports in 1 week. Buys all rights.
Needs: "Often technical or business-oriented material on specific subjects for specific customized needs." Produces charts; sound filmstrips; multimedia kits; overhead transparencies; tapes and cassettes; and slides. Pays by outright purchase price of $400-800.

KEN ANDERSON FILMS, Box 618, Winona Lake IN 46590. (219)267-5774. President: Ken Anderson. Produces material for church-related libraries with evangelical bias; films for all ages, with particular interest in children and teenagers. Prefers true stories; rarely purchases fiction, but will consider for the younger ages. No objections to previously published material. Buys motion picture rights. Free catalog. "We cannot guarantee consideration for material unless a brief one-page story synopsis is included. Other than that, writers may send rough material, a collection of anecdotes, published material, a book or whatever form the material may be in as long as it's good film material. We like to maintain a very warm attitude toward writers and will try to give careful consideration either to queries or to full-blown material. We only produce 4-6 films/year, so our quantity needs are limited." Produces sound filmstrips; motion pictures and tapes and cassettes.
Needs: Religious material only. "We are constantly looking for good material which is positively Christian and relates realistically to today's lifestyles." Pays "as low as $100 for basic story idea which the author could then market elsewhere. But general payment runs more between

$250-1,000, depending upon story quality and adaptability for audiovisual production."

ANIMATION ARTS ASSOCIATES, INC., 2225 Spring Garden St., Philadelphia PA 19130. (215)563-2520. Contact: Harry E. Ziegler, Jr. Copyrighted. For "government, industry, engineers, doctors, scientists, dentists, general public, military." Send "resume of credits for motion picture and filmstrip productions. The writer should have scriptwriting credits for training, sales promotion, public relations." Enclose SASE.
Business: Produces 3½-minute, 8mm and 16mm film loops; 16mm and 35mm motion pictures (ranging from 5 to 40 minutes), 2x2 or 4x5 slides and teaching machine programs for training, sales, industrial and public relations. Fee arrangements dependent on client's budget.

HAL MARC ARDEN AND COMPANY, Executive Offices: 240 Central Park South, New York NY 10019. President: Hal Marc Arden. Copyrighted. "Writer must have experience in writing for motion pictures. Scripts are not solicited, but we welcome resumes." Query. SASE.
General: "Specialize in sponsored production only: documentary, educational, public service." Produces silent and sound filmstrips, 16mm motion pictures, multimedia kits, phonograph records, prerecorded tapes and cassettes, and slides. "No royalties. Fee negotiated."

AUGUST FILMS, INC., 321 W. 44th St., New York NY 10036. Produces sound filmstrips; Super 8, 16mm and 35mm motion pictures; prerecorded tapes and cassettes; 35mm slides, and video tapes. Copyrighted. Prospective writer should have had previous experience and expertise in the desired format or style. Enclose SASE.
General: Producing all kinds of audiovisual materials — from medical, educational, industrial, to feature films. Pays $75 to $100 per minute (up to 10 minutes) for educational and industrial films. Pays flat fee for longer feature films; amount depending on budget.

BACHNER PRODUCTIONS, INC., 501 Madison Ave., New York NY 10022. (212)688-2755. Produces 16mm film loops; 16mm and 35mm motion pictures, and video tape programs. Not copyrighted. Does not accept unsolicited material. Prospective writer usually must have experience in subject related to proposed film. Also needs knowledge of videotape or film requirements. Sometimes will use good writer without specialized experience and then supply all necessary research. Enclose SASE.
General: Produces training and sales films and documentaries. Subject matter and style depend upon client requirements. "Sometimes clients supply outlines and research from which our writers work. Usually pay Writer's Guild scale, depending on usage and what is supplied by us. Price varies with assignments."

BARR FILMS, 3490 E. Foothill Blvd., Pasadena CA 91107. "For all age levels; grades K through college level as well as in the public library market to the same age span and adult audience. We also have interest in materials aimed at business and industry training programs." Copyrights completed films. Catalog $1. Query. "We will assign projects to qualified writers. We would require previous experience in film writing and would want to see samples of films previously written and completed for sale in the market." SASE.
General: "We produce and distribute 16mm films in all curriculum and subject areas. We prefer a semi-dramatic form of script with a moral or informational point. The length of our films is 10 to 20 minutes. We will also consider pure informational subjects with voice over narration. Fees are entirely negotiable, but we normally pay approximately in the area of $500 per script. We will accept film treatments and/or completed visual and dialogue scripts. Please inquire prior to sending your materials to us."

BOARD OF JEWISH EDUCATION OF NEW YORK, 426 W. 58th St., New York NY 10019. (212)245-8200. Associate in curriculum materials development: Yaakov Reshef. Produces material for Jewish schools, youth groups, temples, and synagogues; for audience from kindergarten to old age. Buys 12-15 scripts/year. Submit outline/synopsis or resumé. SASE. Reports in 2-3 months. Buys first rights or all rights. Free catalog.
Needs: General, educational, and informational. "Generally length up to 20-25 minutes maximum; most material geared to 10-12 years old and up. Jewish background needed." Produces sound filmstrips, 16mm motion pictures, tapes and cassettes, and slides. Pays 10-15% royalty or $300 outright purchase price.

BOBBS-MERRILL EDUCATIONAL PUBLISHING, 4300 W. 62nd St., Indianapolis IN 46268. (317)291-3100. Contact: John Obst, Assistant Editorial Director. Query. Enclose SASE.
Education: Seeking scripts for "industrial arts, vocational/technical, business education, and

career education subjects at the junior and senior high school, technical school and junior college levels.'' Payment by royalty arrangement or fee.

ROBERT J. BRADY CO., Routes 197 & 450, Bowie MD 20715. Director, Product Development: C.R. McCarthy. Produces material for professionals and paraprofessionals in medical, allied health, nursing, emergency medicine, fire service, vocational and business fields. Buys all rights. Free catalog. ''We are always anxious to develop new writers who can blend both book skills and audiovisual skills. Since most of our writing needs would be commissioned, all submissions should be in the form of resumes, sample materials, and client and title lists.'' Query. Produces sound filmstrips; motion pictures; overhead transparencies; audio tapes and cassettes; slides (size 35mm); and books and manuals.
Needs: Educational (35mm sound/slide programs, 35mm sound filmstrips—instructional); subject areas: business (training, skills, general); medicine (allied health, nursing, emergency medicine); and fire service training. Pays $400-1,200/script.

BUSINESS PROGRAMS, INC., 985 Main St., Stamford CT 06902. (203)348-8459. President: J.F. Kilmartin. Estab. 1960. Produces material for corporations and marketing companies. Query with samples or submit resume. SASE. Reports in 1 month. Buys all rights. Free catalog.
Needs: ''All of our work is performed for basic marketing organizations and is specifically involved with preparation of New Product Introductions and National Sales Meetings.'' Produces charts; 16 and 8mm film loops; sound filmstrips; 16mm motion pictures; live shows and multi-media presentations; overhead transparencies; tapes and cassettes; and slides. Pays in outright purchase of $500-1,500.

CENTER FOR MEDIA DEVELOPMENT, INC., Box 51, Great Neck NY 11022. (212)229-0695. President/Editorial Director: S. Seltzer. Estab. 1967. Produces for the el-hi and college market. Buys material from 10-15 writers/year. Query with samples or submit resumé. SASE. Reports in 3 weeks. Buys all rights. Catalog for SASE.
Needs: El-hi and college material in various subject areas: language arts, social studies, science, math, etc. Produces charts, sound filmstrips, 16mm motion pictures, multimedia kits, tapes and cassettes and study prints. 5-10% royalty or outright purchase price.

THE CHAMBA ORGANIZATION, Box U, Brooklyn NY 11202. President: St. Clair Bourne. For ''the new hip, activist-oriented audience; the general audience (PG), and in the educational film market, we aim at high school and adult audiences, especially the so-called 'minority' audiences. Assignments are given solely based upon our reaction to submitted material. The material is the credential.'' Query first. Enclose SASE.
General: ''I concentrate primarily on feature film projects. However, I am always interested in a unique feature-length documentary film project. We prefer submission of film treatments first. Then, if the idea interests us, we then negotiate the writing of the script.'' Payment is negotiable, according to Writer's Guild standards.

CINEMAKERS, INC., 200 W. 57th St., New York NY 10019. President: Ed Schultz. Estab. 1965. ''We produce corporate sponsored audiovisuals for use in education, communication and persuasion with all kinds of audiences.'' Submit resume and sample of professionally produced film, filmstrip, or slide show. SASE. Reports in 4 weeks. Buys all rights.
Needs: ''We want to build a list of New York City freelancers who know how to write movies, video tapes, slide shows, filmstrips, teacher's guides, activity sheets, multimedia kits for use in education, training, public relations, employee relations, sales promotions, and fund raising, on topics varying from 'sewing patterns' to 'cancer in children' to 'behavorial approaches to environments.' We like easy-going, non-didactic scripts that encourage audiences to think and discover for themselves.'' Produces Super-8mm film loops; silent and sound filmstrips; 8, 16, and 35mm motion pictures; videotapes; multimedia kits; phonograph records; tapes and cassettes; and slides. Pays $25-2,000.

CK COMMUNICATIONS, 551 5th Ave., New York NY 10017. Executive Vice President: Rory Kaplan. Estab. 1971. Produces material for corporate and consumer audiences. Submit resume. Reports in 4 weeks on solicited material. Buys all rights.
Needs: Dialogue writers with TV or film background for 10-30 minute dramatic vignettes on given subjects (may be technical); and narrative/explanatory writers for given topics in the areas of business, technical, medical or general. Produces sound filmstrips; 16mm motion pictures; overhead transparencies; tapes and cassettes; slides; videocassettes and brochures. Pays by outright purchase.

COMPRENETICS, INC., 340 N. Camden Dr., Beverly Hills CA 90210. President: Ira Englander. Estab. 1967. "Target audience varies. In the health care field it goes from entry level health workers with minimal academic background to continuing education programs for physicians and health professions. In manpower training, from entry level to top supervisors; in the cultural area, all levels." Buys approximately 10-20 scripts/year. Query with samples or submit resumé. SASE. Reports in 1 month. Buys all rights.
Needs: "Films are generally 10-20 minutes in length and tend to have a dramatic framework. They are often programmed with response frames included. Subject topics include all educational areas with emphasis on health and medical films, manpower and management training and multi-cultural education. Our staff normally does subject matter research and content review which is provided for the writer who is then required to provide us with an outline or film treatment for review. Due to the extensive review procedures, writers are frequently required to modify through three or four drafts before final approval." Produces sound filmstrips; 16mm motion pictures; and tapes and cassettes. Pays $1,000-2,500.

CONCORDIA PUBLISHING HOUSE, PRODUCT DEVELOPMENT DIVISION, 3558 S. Jefferson Ave., St. Louis MO 63118. (314)664-7000. For preschool through adult; institutional and home use. Material is copyrighted. Will send a catalog to writer on request. Writer must have demonstrated skills in writing producible material for the audio and visual fields. Competence in the content area is necessary. Initial query is preferred in view of existing production commitments and necessity to maintain a satisfactory product mix. Enclose SASE.
Education and Religion: Silent and sound filmstrips, 16mm motion pictures, multimedia kits, overhead transparencies, phonograph records, prerecorded tapes and cassettes, 35mm slides and study prints. Content areas relate to the requirements of religious and moral guidance instruction. Emphasis may be curricular, quasi-curricular or enriching. Writing fees are negotiated in consideration of such factors as type of production, configuration, complexity of assignment, research required, field tests and production deadlines.

DAVID C. COOK PUBLISHING CO., 850 N. Grove Ave., Elgin IL 60120. Editor: Anne Blischke. Estab. 1876. Produces material for preschool, K-3. Buys 3 scripts/year. Query with samples or submit outline. SASE. Reports in 2 weeks. Buys all rights. Free catalog.
Needs: Education (various topics with pictures and stories for children; manual for teachers). Pays $35-60/print.

CREATIVE VISUALS, Division of Gamco Industries, Inc., Box 1911, Big Spring TX 79720. (915)267-6327. Director, New Product Development: Judith Rickey. Free catalog and author's guidelines. "We want you, as a potential author, to submit the following information. First, provide a list of your educational degrees and majors. Explain your teaching experience, including subjects taught, grades taught, and the number of years you have taught. Please describe any writing experience, and, if possible, include a sample of your published educational material currently on the market. We ask for this information because we have found that our best authors are usually experienced classroom teachers who are writing in their subject area. Once we have information about your background, we will ask you for the subject and titles of your proposed series." Produces sound filmstrips; overhead transparencies; tapes and cassettes; and study prints.
Needs: Education (grades K-12, all subjects areas). Payment by royalty; usually 7-10% of net sales.

DEFENSE PRODUCTS CO., Audiovisual Division, 645 Azalea Dr., Rockville MD 20850. (301)279-0808. Manager: Harry A. Carragher. Estab. 1958. Produces material for industrial and public relations clients and the general public. Buys 4 scripts/year. Submit outline/synopsis, complete ms, or resume. Submissions will not be returned. Reports in 2 weeks. Buys first rights. Free catalog.
Needs: Sample treatments in business, technical and general material. Produces sound filmstrips; 16mm motion pictures; multimedia kits; and slides. 5% royalty; $100 minimum outright purchase price.

MARK DRUCK PRODUCTIONS, 300 E. 40th St., New York NY 10016. Produces audiovisuals for "mostly industrial audiences or women's groups." Produces 16mm motion pictures, multimedia kits and video tape industrials. Subjects: retail items, drugs, travel, industrial products, etc. Material is sometimes copyrighted. "The whole production belongs to the client." No unsolicited scripts; only resumes, lists of credits, etc. The freelance writer must have some

expertise in the subject, and in writing A/V scripts. Enclose SASE.
General: Pays minimum of $500 per reel. No maximum. Writer will be expected to produce outline, treatment, and shooting script.

DYNACOM COMMUNICATIONS INTERNATIONAL, Box 702, Snowdon Station, Montreal, Quebec, Canada H3X 3X8. (514)342-5200. Director: David P. Leonard. Estab. 1969. Produces for industrial and business management training and development and exhibits (entertainment, PR, motivation). Buys 12 10-20 minute scripts/year. Submit resume. SAE and international reply coupons. Reports in 2-4 weeks. Buys all rights. Brochure/presentation $4.
Needs: Business (sales and marketing presentations); industry (technical and nontechnical training programs in motivation, management, etc.); education (learning modules for elementary and high school and college); and general (exhibit audiovisuals for museums, conferences, meetings). Produces charts; dioramas; super-8 and 16mm motion pictures; color television videocassettes; multimedia kits; overhead transparencies; phonograph records; tapes and cassettes; slides; and teaching machine programs. Pays in outright purchase based on length and complexity of project, research required.

EDUCATIONAL COMMUNICATIONS, INC., Box 56, Wayne PA 19087. (215)688-2002. President: Dr. Philip Minter. Estab. 1969. Produces material for trainees in all types of industry. Buys approximately 25 scripts/year. Query with samples or submit resume. SASE. Reports in 2 weeks. Buys all rights. Free catalog.
Needs: Scripts on engineering and biomedical topics. Produces sound filmstrips; 16mm motion pictures; tapes and cassettes; and slides. Pays $1,000-2,500.

EDUCATIONAL DIMENSIONS GROUP, Box 126, Stamford CT 06904. Managing Editor: Vincent J. Amato. Produces material for K-12 levels. Catalog $1. Query. Produces sound filmstrips; multimedia kits and slides (size 2¼x2¼).
Needs: 40-80 frames geared to proper grade level; all educational disciplines. Pays $100 minimum for consultation. Script writing fees vary.

EDUCATIONAL FILMSTRIPS, 1401 19th St., Huntsville TX 77340. (713)295-5767. Vice President: George H. Russell. Estab. 1953. Produces material for schools, junior high to university level. Submit complete script "with original slides in Kodak Carousel tray or original camera ready art." SASE. Reports "as soon as possible." Buys all rights. Free catalog.
Needs: Educational and technical. Produces silent and sound filmstrips. 10% royalty or outright purchase price of $100-500.

EDUCATIONAL IMAGES, Box 367, Lyons Falls NY 13368. (315)348-8211. Executive Director: Dr. Charles R. Belinky. Produces material for schools, K-college and graduate school, public libraries, parks, nature centers, etc. Buys all AV rights. Free catalog. "We are looking for complete AV programs. This requires high quality, factual text and pictures." Query. Produces silent and sound filmstrips; multimedia kits; and slides.
Needs: Science and education. Slide sets and filmstrips. Pays $150 minimum or percentage royalties.

EDUCATIONAL RESEARCH, INC., 1768 Willow Point, Shreveport LA 71119. (318)635-2111. President: Dr. James W. Stockard Jr. Estab. 1970. Produces material for schools (grades K-12) and adult education programs. "Most scripts are prepared internally; however, we have about 8 outside authors on royalty now." Query with samples. SASE. Reports in 2-4 weeks. Buys all rights. Catalog for SASE.
Needs: "Educational programs that can be produced in a lesson card/cassette tape format. The printed portion may be workbook or lesson cards. Reading aids, math aids, and special education aids are especially interesting. We market to schools through an extensive dealer network." Produces cassette tapes with accompanying visuals (lesson cards/workbooks). Pays in royalties or by outright purchase price "according to the amount of work needed at this end. Determined by agreement with author."

EMC CORPORATION, 180 E. Sixth St., St. Paul MN 55101. Book Editor: Connie McMillan. Editor-in-Chief: Northrop Dawson Jr. Produces material for children, teen-agers—primary grades through high school. Buys world rights. Catalog for SASE. "Writer, via submitted sample, must show capability to write appropriately for the medium." Query. Produces filmstrips (sound); multimedia kits and tapes and cassettes.
Needs: "No standard requirements, due to nature of educational materials publishing—subject

area, grade level, instructional objectives, etc.'' Payment varies.
For '79: ''Math materials, consumer education, special education (as related to language arts and math especially), low vocabularly but high interest fiction and nonfiction for problem readers at secondary grade levels.''

FAMILY FILMS/COUNTERPOINT FILMS, 14622 Lanark St., Panorama City CA 91402. Contact: Paul R. Kidd, Director of Product Development. For all age levels from preschool through adult. Copyrighted. Will send a catalog to writer on request. Query first. ''Majority projects are assigned and developed to our specifications. Writers may submit their credentials and experience. Some experience in writing film and filmstrip scripts is desired. A teaching credential or teaching experience valuable for our school materials. Active involvement in a mainstream church desirable for our religious projects.''
Education and Religion: ''Sound filmstrips, 16mm motion pictures and prerecorded tapes and cassettes for schools, universities, public libraries, and for interdenominational religious market. Motion pictures vary from 10 minutes to 30 to 40 minutes. Filmstrips about 50 to 60 frames with running time of 7 to 10 minutes. Emphasis on the human situation and person-to-person relationships. No royalty arrangements. Outright payment depends on project and available budget. As an example, usual filmstrip project requires 4 scripts, for which we pay $150 to $250 each. Motion picture scripts through final draft, $1,200-1,500.''

FRANCISCAN COMMUNICATIONS CENTER, 1229 S. Santee St., Los Angeles CA 90015. Associate Producer: Corinne Hart. Estab. 1946. Produces material for the educational and religious market. Buys approximately 6-15 scripts/year. Query with samples, or submit outline/synopsis or completed script. SASE. Reports in 1 month. Buys all rights. Free catalog.
Needs: 10-15 minute (maximum) dramatic scripts, with good story and well developed characters. ''Themes in value areas: personal worth, faith, problem areas for youth, caring and concern, and social responsibility. Avoid sterotyped characters representing a point of view or single dimension. Be upbeat without being simplistic; insight without didacaticism. The majority of our films are oriented toward a junior high and high school audience. However, we are always on the look out for the really good story that appeals to a wide range of people.'' Produces sound filmstrips; and 16mm motion pictures. Pays $100 maximum for story ideas; $500 for completed script.

GENERAL EDUCATIONAL MEDIA, INC., 350 Northern Blvd., Great Neck NY 11021. (516)829-5333. President: David Engler. Estab. 1973. Produces for schools, colleges, business and industry, and general adult audiences. Buys 30-40 scripts/year from 5-6 writers. Query with samples. SASE. Reports in 3 weeks. Buys all rights.
Needs: Typical length, 12-15 minute scripts; subjects, style and format variable. Produces sound filmstrips; multimedia kits; tapes and cassettes; slides; and teaching machine programs. Pays $200-500.

GIRL SCOUTS OF THE U.S.A., 830 Third Ave., New York NY 10022. For girls and adults involved in the Girl Scout movement; the general public. Will send catalog to writer on request. Query first. All projects are generated within the organization, which is not seeking proposals, treatments, or manuscripts. Credentials for writer would depend on project. Enclose SASE.
General: All audiovisuals deal with some aspect of Girl Scout movement: program, training, administration, public relations, etc. Sound filmstrips, 16mm and 8mm motion pictures, multimedia kits, overhead transparencies, phonograph records, prerecorded tapes and cassettes, 35mm slides, and flip charts. ''We work on fee basis only; the amount negotiable in terms of the assignment.''

GOLDSHOLL ASSOC., 420 Frontage Rd., Northfield IL 60093. (312)446-8300. President: M. Goldsholl. Buys all rights. Free catalog. Query. Produces sound filmstrips; motion pictures (16/35mm); multimedia kits; tapes and cassettes, and slides (size 35mm).
Needs: PR films for industry. Pays 5-10% of budgets. Also interested in short stories to be made into screenplays, filmscripts (original). ''Describe before sending.''

HANDEL FILM CORP., 8730 Sunset Blvd., West Hollywood CA 90069. Contact: Production Department. For variety of audiences, depending on film. Material becomes property of Handel Film Corp. if acquired. Submit only upon request. Do not send in unsolicited material. Query first. Enclose SASE.
Education and Documentary: 16mm motion pictures, approximately half-hour films for science, history and other areas. Payment is negotiable.

HAYES SCHOOL PUBLISHING CO., INC., 321 Pennwood Ave., Wilkinsburg PA 15221. (412)371-2373. 2nd Vice President: Clair N. Hayes III. Produces material for school teachers, principals, elementary and junior high school students. Buys all rights. Catalog for SASE. Query. Produces charts; workbooks, teachers handbooks, posters, bulletin board material, and liquid duplicating books.
Needs: Education material only ("will consider all types of material suitable for use in elementary schools and Sunday school classes."). Pays $25 and up.

HESTER & ASSOCIATES, INC., 11422 Hines Blvd., Dallas TX 75229. (214)241-4859. President: Stew Hester. Produces material for school population—kindergarten through post graduate. Buys "exclusive or non-exclusive" rights. Free catalog. "Would prefer an outline of the idea; then we can respond if there is a relevance to our needs." Query. Produces film loops (S 8mm); sound filmstrips; multimedia kits; tapes and cassettes; slides (size 35mm); and work books (with and without tapes).
Needs: Education ("Our major efforts at present are sales to school...usually workbooks and activity books in math, art and science.") Pays royalties, 5-15%.

IDEAL SCHOOL SUPPLY CO., A Division of Westinghouse Learning Corp., 11000 S. Lavergne Ave., Oak Lawn IL 60453. (312)425-0800. Editor: Carol Thompson. Estab. 1898. Produces material for primary, elementary, and high school students. "80% of our product line comes from outside sources, most of them practicing classroom teachers. The audiovisual materials have come from qualified educators or writers experienced in educational materials." Query with samples, submit synopsis/outline, or send resume. SASE. Reports in 3 months. Buys all rights. Free catalog.
Needs: "Style, format, and length vary, according to grade level and subject matter of program. We are saturated in the career area, but would be interested in reviewing programs in language arts, reading, math for all grade levels K-12, and science for elementary levels." Produces charts; models; books; printed material; multimedia kits; tapes and cassettes; and study prints. Pays in royalties; "individual should contact company for information."

IMARC CORP., Box H, Newtown Square PA 19073. (215)356-2000. President: Bob Barry. Estab. 1977. Produces material for management, sales people; customers; and trainees. "In the past 8 months we have worked with 7 writers and produced 16 audiovisual projects." Submit resume. SASE. Reports in 1 week. Buys all rights, or material is not copyrighted.
Needs: "We are very broad-based—from speech writing to full-length industrial films, brochures, technical writing, presentation formats, training and learning manuals and audiovisual projects, etc. We cover all fields, i.e., chemical, services, telephone, insurance, banks, manufacturers, etc." Produces charts; dioramas; film loops; silent and sound filmstrips; models; 16 and 35mm motion pictures; phonograph records; tapes and cassettes; and slides. Pays $300-4,000/project.

IMPERIAL INTERNATIONAL LEARNING CORP., Box 548, Kankakee IL 60901. Contact: Spencer Bernard, Director of Product Development. Produces material for schools, K-high school. Free catalog. Query. Buys considerable freelance material, but generally on assignment basis only. "Writers seeking assignments should query first. Letter should include a summary of background and professional writing experience." Reports in 6 weeks. Produces sound filmstrips (35mm); tape-centered instructional packages; paperback books; and multimedia kits.
Needs: Education; and audiovisual software appropriate for elementary school students. Pays flat fee within 90 days after acceptance of ms or reprinted contract.

INSGROUP, INC., 16052 Beach Blvd., Huntington Beach CA 92647. For industrial, military (both enlisted men and officers), public schools (K through graduate level), police, nursing, and public administrators. Material is copyrighted. Criteria for writers are determined on a project by project basis. Query first, with resumes and be prepared to submit copies of previous efforts. Enclose SASE.
General: Charts, silent and sound filmstrips, multimedia kits, overhead transparencies, prerecorded tapes and cassettes, 35mm slides, study prints, teaching machine programs, and videotapes. Insgroup develops objective-based validated audiovisual instructional programs both for commercial customers and for publication by Insgroup. These programs cover the entire range of subject areas, styles, formats, etc. Most writing is on a fee basis. Royalties, when given, are 5% to 8%.

INSTRUCTIONAL DYNAMICS INCORPORATED, 450 E. Ohio St., Chicago IL 60611. For early learning through college level. Material is copyrighted. "Writer should have valid background and experience that parallels the specific assignment. Would like to have vita as first contact. We keep on file and activate as needs arise. We use a substantial group of outside talent to supplement our in-house staff." SASE.
Education: Silent filmstrips, sound filmstrips, multimedia kits, overhead transparencies, phonograph records, prerecorded tapes and cassettes, 2x2 slides, study prints and hard copy. "Requirements for these vary depending upon assignments from our clients. Payment depends on contractual arrangements with our client and also varies depending on medium or multimedia involved."

INSTRUCTOR CURRICULUM MATERIALS, 7 Bank St., Dansville NY 14437. (716)335-2221. Editorial Director: Margie H. Richmond. "U.S. and Canadian school supervisors, principals, and teachers purchase items in our line for instructional purposes." Buys all rights. Will send a catalog to a writer on request. Writer should have "experience in preparing materials for elementary students, including suitable teaching guides to accompany them, and demonstrate knowledge of the appropriate subject areas, or demonstrable ability for accurate and efficient research and documentation. Please query." Enclose SASE for response to queries.
Education: "Elementary curriculum enrichment, all subject areas. Display material, copy, and illustration should match interest and reading skills of children in grades for which material is intended. Production is limited to printed matter: posters, charts, duplicating masters, resource handbooks, teaching guides." Length: 6,000 to 12,000 words. "Standard contract, but fees vary considerably, depending on type of project."

INTERGROUP PRODUCTIONS, INC., 300 E. 59th St., New York NY 10022. (212)832-8169. Executive Producer: Rudolf Gartzman. Estab. 1971. Produces material for industry; theatrical release, feature films; TV specials and documentaries; and dramatic nonfiction and fiction. Buys 12-15 scripts/year. Query with samples. SASE. Reports in 4-6 weeks. Buys all rights.
Needs: Industrial films and slide/sound productions; general sales, technical, promotional; and sales training material. Produces 16 and 35mm motion pictures and slides. Pays $1,000-1,800 for 15 minute script with 1 draft and 3 rewrites; "individual company standard contract for industrial material; Writers' Guild standards for film."

JANUARY PRODUCTIONS, 13-00 Plaza Rd., Fair Lawn NJ 07410. (201)797-2575. Editor: Tom Crawford. Esab. 1973. Produces elementary school curriculum material. Buys 10-20 scripts/year. Query. SASE. Reports in 1 week. Buys all rights. Free catalog.
Needs: Primarily interested in the language arts, social studies, and basic science. Length: 20-40 frames, with captions of 2-3 lines for each frame. Pays $200-300.

KEN-DEL PRODUCTIONS, INC., 111 Valley Rd., Richardson Park, Wilmington DE 19804. (302)655-7488. Contact: Ed Kennedy. For "elementary, junior high, high school, and college level, as well as interested organizations and companies." Will assign projects to qualified writers. Query first. Enclose SASE for response to queries.
General: Wants material for "topics of the present (technology, cities, traffic, transit, pollution, ecology, health, water, race, genetics, consumerism, fashions, communications, education, population control, waste, future sources of food, undeveloped sources of living, food, health, etc.); topics of the future; how-to series (everything for the housewife, farmer, banker, mechanic, on music, art, sports, reading, science, love, repair, sleep—on any subject)." Produces sound filmstrips; 8mm, 16mm, and 35mm motion pictures; 16mm film loops; phonograph records; prerecorded tapes and cassettes; slides.

LANSFORD PUBLISHING CO., Box 8711, San Jose CA 95155. (408)287-3105. Editor: Mary Chatton. Estab. 1968. Produces material for college, adult, industrial and business audiences. Buys 10-30 scripts/year. Query. SASE. Reports in 1 month. Buys all rights. Free catalog.
Needs: "Our chief sales area is in the fields of management, communication, psychology, and social problems. Produces multimedia kits; overhead transparencies (10-20 visuals plus booklet); tapes and cassettes (6 1-hour tapes per set); and slides (20 or more slides). Pays royalty.

WILLIAM V. LEVINE ASSOCIATES, INC., 18 E. 48th St., New York NY 10017. (212)751-1880. President: William V. Levine. Estab. 1967. Presentations for business and industry. Buys 18 scripts/year. Submit resume. SASE. Reports in 2 weeks. Buys all rights.

Needs: Business-related scripts for specific clients for use at sales meetings or for desk-top presentations. Also uses theme-setting scripts with inherent messages of business interest. Produces charts; silent and sound filmstrips; motion pictures; multimedia kits; tapes and cassettes and slides. Pays $250-1,500.

LYCEUM PRODUCTIONS, INC., P.O. Box 1018, Laguna Beach CA 92652. Contact: Patty Lincke. For grade levels from elementary school through college. Copyrighted. Rights purchased are subject to negotiation. Query first. No assignments are made. Enclose SASE.
Education: Produces sound filmstrips. "Most of our filmstrips provide curriculum support and enrichment in subject areas including natural science, ecology, science, social studies, language arts, art, history and citizenship. Many titles are interdisciplinary. Some titles span wide age groups while others may be more limited in scope. Whatever the concept of the filmstrip, it should stimulate the student to explore the subject more fully. Please submit an idea or an outline before sending a manuscript or transparencies. Completed material will only be considered if it has been requested upon the basis of a previous query. Our contracts provide for royalties based on sales with an advance upon acceptance. The possibilities for the unknown freelancer are difficult."

MAGNETIX CORPORATION, 770 W. Bay St., Winter Garden FL 32787. (305)656-4494. President: John Lory. Produces material for the general public. Buys all rights. "Personal contact must be made due to wide variety of very specific scripts we require. Must have ability to dramatize our subjects using sound effects, etc." Produces tapes and cassettes.
Needs: General (20-30 minute audio program with sound effects written to be sold to general public as a souvenir with some educational value.) Pays $300 and up.

ED MARZOLA & ASSOCIATES, 8831 Sunset Blvd., Suite 408, Hollywood CA 90069. (213)652-7481. Vice President/Creative Director: William Case. Estab. 1970. Produces material for educational and industrial audiences. Query with samples or submit resume. SASE. Reports in 10 days. Buys all rights.
Needs: "We now produce shows for the grammar school levels; also feature-length motion pictures for theatrical release." Produces sound filmstrips; 16 and 35mm motion pictures; and videotaped presentations. Pays by outright purchase; "we negotiate each case individually. Payment is in accordance with Writer's Guild standards."

MEDICAL MULTIMEDIA CORP., 211 E 43rd St., New York NY 10017. (212)986-0180. Administrative Assistant: Susan Flynn. Estab. 1973. Produces for the medical and paramedical professions. Buys 10-12 scripts/year. Submit resume; "scripts are purchased on assignment." Buys all rights.
Needs: "Style and format vary; however, all writing is for the medical health sciences profession." Produces charts; sound filmstrips; 16mm motion pictures; multimedia kits; tapes and cassettes; slides and teaching machine programs. Pays $200-2,000.

ARTHUR MERIWETHER, INC. Box 457, Downers Grove IL 60515. For elementary and high school students. Material is copyrighted. Will send catalog to writer for 75¢. "Prior professional experience is required. Query first. Background as an educator is often helpful." Enclose SASE.
Education: "We prefer items applying to language arts, English, sociology and drama studies to be used as a supplement to regular curriculum materials." Filmstrips (silent and sound), motion pictures, multimedia kits, and prerecorded tapes and cassettes. Games for learning also considered. Pays 5% to 10% royalty.
Religion: "Will consider filmstrip scripts that deal with subjects of contemporary religious importance for elementary and high school religious education groups. Liberal approach preferred. Professional quality only. Scripts purchased outright, or royalty arrangement."
Business: Business-oriented mss or scripts on marketing and staff training.

TOM MORRIS, INC., 621 Devon Ave., Park Ridge IL 60068. (312)825-7182. President: Tom Morris. Buys 6-8 scripts/year. Query with samples or submit resumé. SASE. Reports in 2 weeks. Buys all rights.
Needs: Industrial; religious; teaching; and training. Produces charts; silent and sound filmstrips; 16mm motion pictures; multimedia kits; tapes and cassettes; and slides. "Every job is custom, no set payment."

MOTIVATION MEDIA, INC., 110 River Rd., Des Plaines IL 60016. (312)297-4740. Executive

Producer: Frank Stedronsky. Estab. 1969. Produces material for salespeople, customers, corporate/industrial employees and distributors. Query with samples. SASE. Reports in 3-4 weeks. Buys all rights.
Needs: Material for all audiovisual media—particularly marketing oriented (sales training, sales promotional, sales motivational). Produces 8mm and 16mm film loops; sound filmstrips; 16mm motion pictures; multimedia kits; tapes and cassettes and slides. Pays $150-5,000.

MRC FILMS, Division of McLaughlin Research Corp., 71 W. 23rd St., New York NY 10010. Executive Producer: Larry Mollot. "Audience varies with subject matter, which is wide and diverse." Writer "should have an ability to visualize concepts and to express ideas clearly in words. Experience in motion picture or filmstrip script writing is desirable. Write us, giving some idea of background. Submit samples of writing. Wait for reply. We will always reply, one way or another. We are looking for new talent. No unsolicited material accepted. Work upon assignment only." Query first. Enclose SASE for response to queries.
General: "Industrial, documentary, educational, and television films. Also, public relations, teaching, and motivational filmstrips. Some subjects are highly technical in the fields of aerospace and electronics. Others are on personal relationships, selling techniques, ecology, etc. A writer with an imaginative visual sense is important." Produces silent and sound filmstrips, 16mm motion pictures, prerecorded tapes, cassettes. "Fee depends on nature and length of job. Typical fees: $500 to $1,000 for script for 10-minute film; $1,000 to $1,400 for script for 20-minute film; $1,200 to $2,000 for script for 30-minute film. For narration writing only, the range is $200 to $500 for a 10-minute film; $400 to $800 for a 20-minute film; $500 to $1,000 for a 30-minute film. For script writing services by the day, fee is $60 to $100 per day."

MULTI-MEDIA PRODUCTIONS, INC., Box 5097, Stanford CA 94305. Assistant Program Director: Mark Vining. Estab. 1967. Produces material for elementary (grades 4-6) and secondary (grades 9-12) school students. Buys 24 scripts/year. Query or submit synopsis/outline. SASE. Reports in 3 weeks. Buys all rights. Free catalog.
Needs: "Material suitable for general high school and elementary school social studies curriculums; history, biography, sociology, psychology, anthropology, archaeology, and economics. Style should be straightforward, lively and objective." Approximate specifications: 50 frames, 10 minutes/program part; 2 sentences and one visual per frame; 1 or 2 part programs. Writer supplies script, slides for filmstrip, and teachers manual (as per our format). Royalties are paid quarterly, based on 12½% of return on each program sold.

HENRY NASON PRODUCTIONS, INC., 250 W. 57th St., New York NY 10019. President: Henry Nason. Estab. 1972. Produces audiovisual media presentations for a varying audience of customers, employees, community groups, etc. Query with samples or contact for personal interview. SASE. Reports in 1 month. Buys all rights.
Needs: "Usually 10-15 minute scripts on corporate subjects, such as sales, marketing, employee benefits, products, systems, etc. Usually freestanding audiovisual modules. The style should be clear and relaxed, well researched and organized. Writers must live in the New York City area." Produces filmstrips; multimedia material; tapes and cassettes; and slides. Pays "an average of 10% of the production budget."

NEBRASKA ETV COUNCIL FOR HIGHER EDUCATION, Box 83111, Lincoln NE 68501. (402)472-3611. Senior Producer—ITV: Darrell Wheaton. Produces material for educational/instructional television programs for college students for use in college classrooms. Free catalog. "Only persons experienced in preparing material for college level instructional film need inquire. Copies of previous materials must be available for consideration. We need full scripts in production format including all dialogue and production suggestions, typed in a split column form, preferably." Query. Produces motion pictures (16mm); tapes and cassettes; and video tapes.
Needs: "Requirements are specifically tailored to the particular lesson under development; the organization prepares material in most areas of study." Pays $50-2,000.

NYSTROM, 3333 Elston Ave., Chicago IL 60618. For kindergarten through 12. Material is copyrighted. Will send catalog to writer on request. Required credentials depend on topics and subject matter and approach desired. Query first. Enclose SASE.
Education: Charts, sound filmstrips, models, multimedia kits, overhead transparencies, and realia. Social studies, earth and life sciences, career education, reading, language arts and mathematics. Payment varies with circumstances.

OUR SUNDAY VISITOR, INC., Audiovisual Department, Noll Plaza, Huntington IN 46750. Audiovisual Manager: Richard D. Hawthorne. For students (K to 12), adult religious education groups, and teacher training. Copyrighted. Will send catalog to writer on request. Query first. "We are looking for well-developed, detailed proposals. Complete program also considered. Programs should display up-to-date audiovisual technique and cohesiveness." SASE.
Education and Religion: "Broadly speaking, material should deal with religious education, including liturgy and daily Christian living, as well as structured catechesis. Must not conflict with sound Catholic doctrine. Should reflect modern trends in education. Word lengths may vary." Produces charts, sound filmstrips, overhead transparencies, phonograph records, prerecorded tapes and cassettes and 2x2 slides. "Work for hire and royalty arrangements possible."

OUTDOOR PICTURES, Box 277, Anacortes WA 98221. (206)293-3200. Contact: Ernest S. Booth. "We would like to find qualified persons to design filmstrips, take the original photos or prepare the artwork, write the scripts and submit to us the entire package ready to produce. We make the internegative master then return the originals to you. We copyright all such materials, but allow you the right to sell any of the originals to others on a one-time basis."
Needs: "We are interested in all subjects that schools will buy. You should look at audiovisual catalogs and examine existing filmstrips, and work closely with one or more teachers in the grade level where your material would be used. We pay 10% royalty on the retail price of the production. Before you begin, write us for a set of guidelines and a free catalog of our filmstrips."

PACE FILMS, INC., 411 E. 53rd St., New York NY 10022. Contact: Mr. R. Vanderbes. For "TV and theatrical audience in the U.S. and worldwide." Buys all rights. Writing assignments are handled through agencies, but independent queries or submissions are considered. Enclose SASE for response.
General: "Feature motion pictures for TV and theaters." Pays "Writers Guild of America minimums and up."

PARAMOUNT COMMUNICATIONS, A Subsidiary of Paramount Pictures Corp., 5451 Marathon St., Hollywood CA 90038. For general audiences. Material is copyrighted. Will send catalog to writer on request. Query first. SASE.
Education: 16mm motion pictures and filmstrips. "Because we are distributors as well as producers of educational films and filmstrips, much of our activity concerns post production work on films and filmstrips acquired and the marketing of these. For media which we produce, scripts are usually written on assignment by staff or educational script writers known to us; educational films have special requirements to meet school curriculum requirements. Therefore, the opportunity for freelance writers here is limited. However, if a writer has information on an unusual subject which could be of interest to schools, or a fresh approach to something which could fit into the less structured areas such as language arts or interpersonal relationships, it wouldn't hurt to query us. Also we consider the kind of films suitable for business and in some instances we sell to college, adult, church, health and vocational groups.

THE PERFECTION FORM CO., 8350 Hickman Rd., Des Moines IA 50322. Editor-in-Chief: Wayne F. DeMouth. Produces sound filmstrips, cassette programs and learning packages for use in secondary language arts and social studies education. Reports in 30 days. Write for catalog.
Filmstrips: Prefers length of 10-18 minutes, with 100 to 135 frames. Interpretive biographies and studies of historical epochs. Usually pays $500 for script (depending on amount of time needed for editorial revision).
How To Break In: "Writers should study our products carefully before trying to submit their material."

PHOTOCOM PRODUCTIONS, Box 3135, Pismo Beach CA 93449. Creative Services Director: Brenda L. Pattison. Estab. 1970. Produces material for schools, junior high to university level. Query with samples or submit synopsis/outline. SASE. Reports in 2-3 weeks. Buys all rights. Free guidelines.
Needs: "We're most interested in how-to-do-its in vocational areas that can be used in high school shop classes or adult education classes. Material that we've been buying is 60-70 frames long." Produces sound filmstrips; multimedia kits; cassettes; and slides. Pays 10-15% royalty or $200 minimum/script.

PLAYETTE CORPORATION, 301 E. Shore Rd., Great Neck NY 11023. Contact: Sidney A. Evans. For "all school levels, teachers, and libraries." Writer must have "a complete and thorough knowledge of the subject with practical applied usage. Material must have been classroom tested before submission." Query first. SASE. No phone calls.
Education and Foreign Languages: Requirements "depend on subject selected." Charts, silent filmstrips, sound filmstrips, multimedia kits, overhead transparencies, phonograph records, prerecorded tapes and cassettes, slides, study prints, and foreign language training aids and games. "Payment for each subject on a separate basis."

PRODUCERS GROUP LTD., One IBM Plaza, Suite 2519, Chicago IL 60611. (312)467-1830. For general audiences. Material is copyrighted. "Make yourself known to us. We do, on some occasions, go outside for help. There is very little point in submitting scripts unless we have a specific project in hand. First, we get the assignment; then we go into creative work. We're probably not the best market for freelance submissions. Unsolicited mss are wasteful, inappropriate. We're too specialized. When and if writer has proven record, we match project to writer's skills, expertise. Originate most of our own creative material here. We prefer any writer to have at least a B.A., or equivalent experience. Must have a record in a-v writing, and hopefully, production. We require clean shooting script, with all visuals completely designated." Query first. Enclose SASE.
Education: Film loops and sound filmstrips, 8mm and 16mm motion pictures, and multimedia kits. Business-oriented multimedia shows, educational motion pictures, and talk demonstrations. Editorial requirements vary according to assignments. Usually aim toward higher levels of educational background for business communications; aim toward specific age groups for educational films, as required. Usual lengths are 20 minutes. Again, varied according to end use. Standard fee is 10% of gross production budget. No royalty arrangements under this schedule. Straight buyout.

PROFESSIONAL RESEARCH, INC., 660 S. Bonnie Brae St., Los Angeles CA 90057. Vice-President: Richard J. Sternberg, M.D. Produces material for medical/surgical/dental/health care institutional patients, doctors, nurses, allied health professionals. "Looking for writers with experience in development of educational media for health care markets. Only require a few writers each year who must have familiarity with biological and medical/dental sciences, as well as have experience in AV writing." Query. Produces motion pictures (16mm); multimedia kits; and video tapes.
Needs: Medicine (patient education films: live action and animation, lay language, 20 minutes or less; continuing education: content and format adapted to meet subject and audience needs). Pays $350 minimum (first draft) — $1,500 (completed script maximum).

PUBLISHERS INVESTORS, INC., 134 E. 38th St., New York NY 10016. Business Manager: Carol Herrod. Buys 20% of material from freelance writers. Query with samples. SASE. Reports in 1 month. Buys all rights.
Needs: Produces multimedia kits, tapes, and cassettes. Pays $50 minimum.

Q-ED PRODUCTIONS, INC., Box 4029, Thousand Oaks CA 91359. For grade levels kindergarten through 12. Material is copyrighted. Buys all rights. Free catalog. "We are interested in reviewing completed filmstrip packages (4 to 6 filmstrips in a set) for distribution on royalty basis, or outright buy. Knowledge of the field and experience as a writer of filmstrips and films for education required. Also, demonstrated ability in research required. We look for the new approach. Unique ways of imparting information so that children will want to learn more and on their own. Definitely not interested in didactic, mundane approaches to learning." Query first. Send queries to Henry Spitzer, Vice President/Production. SASE.
Education: Grade levels K-12. Interested in core curriculum materials. Historically strong in values. Materials should be inquiry oriented, open-ended, strong objectives (cognitive, affective, psycho-motor). Royalties open on original materials. Fees range from $450 for a 10-minute film or filmstrip.

REGENTS PUBLISHING COMPANY, INC., Two Park Ave., New York NY 10016. Contact: Julio I. Andujar, President. For foreign language students, in school and at home. Copyrighted. Will send catalog to writer on request. Query with description of material, table of contents and sample portions. Enclose SASE for reply. No unsolicited mss. "It would be helpful if writer has done previous audiovisual work, has taught or is currently teaching."
Education: English as a second language. Spanish, French, German. Supplementary materials, cultural aspects of wide appeal in foreign language classes. Vocabulary within the range of

foreign language students. Sound filmstrips, multimedia kits, phonograph records, prerecorded tapes and cassettes. Pays 6% of list price.

RHYTHMS PRODUCTIONS, Whitney Bldg., Box 34485, Los Angeles CA 90034. Contact: R.S. White. "Our audience is generally educational, with projects ranging from early childhood through adult markets." Copyrighted. Query first. "We need to know a writer's background and credits and to see samples of his work." Enclose SASE for response to queries.
Education: Books, sound filmstrips, 16mm motion pictures, multimedia kits, phonograph records, prerecorded tapes and cassettes, and study prints. "Our firm specializes in creative productions, so though content is basic to the productions, a creative and imaginative approach is necessary." Usually pays $250 for filmstrip scripts.

RIDDLE VIDEO AND FILM PRODUCTIONS, INC., 507 Fifth Ave., New York NY 10017. (212)697-5895. President/Executive Producer: William Riddle. For "general public, young and old alike. Also for theater distribution." Material may be copyrighted or not copyrighted. Write for copy of guidelines for writers. Writer "must be experienced and well-qualified in the subject in order to handle work assignments satisfactorily. We must see a sample of his or her work." Query first. Enclose SASE for response to queries. Reports in 2 months.
General: "Story boards and scripts are needed." Produces 8mm, 16mm and 35mm film loops; silent filmstrips; sound filmstrips; kinescopes; models; 8mm, 16mm, and 35mm motion pictures; multimedia kits; prerecorded tapes and cassettes; slides; study prints; videotape productions. Pays "standard going rates, with bonus on super work performed."

RMI MEDIA PRODUCATIONS, INC., 701 Westport Rd., Kansas City MO 64111. (816)561-2284. President: David L. Little. Estab. 1964. Produces material for schools (grades K-12), colleges, and adults (business and industry). Query with samples or submit resume. SASE. Reports in 3 weeks. Buys all rights. Free catalog.
Needs: Vocational, technical and general training. Produces sound filmstrips and slides. Pays "negotiable" outright purchase price.

SAVE THE CHILDREN, 48 Wilton Rd., Westport CT 06880. (203)226-7272. Producer: Andrew Mollo. Generally buys all rights, "but it depends on project. We use work only written for specific assignments." Produces motion pictures (16mm); tapes and cassettes; slides (size 2x2); and posters and displays.
Needs: General (radio and TV); and education (high school, college and adult). Pays $250-500 minimum/assignment.

SEVOTE GROUP, 484 Waterloo Court, Oshawa, Ontario, Canada L1H 3X1. (416)576-0250. General Manager: Bob Stone. Produces material for educational (K-8) and secondary schools. Buys all rights. Catalog for SASE. "We are looking for new projects. Send very brief outline of concept first." Query. Produces silent and sound filmstrips; motion pictures (16mm); multimedia kits; phonograph records; tapes and cassettes; and video tapes.
Needs: Education ("we specialize in the vocal and instrument instruction field.") Pays $500 minimum.

SOUTH CAROLINA EDUCATIONAL TELEVISION NETWORK, Drawer L, Columbia SC 29250. (803)758-7261. Assistant Director for Professional Organizations/Program Development: Ms. Mickey Rogers. Estab. 1960. Produces material for the general public; training and career development for business and industry; college courses; and on-going adult education in fields of medicine, dentistry and technical education. Query or submit resume. SASE. Reports in 2 weeks. Buys all rights.
Needs: "The Department of Educational Services works in all media. Since, as a state agency, we work with other state agencies of varying needs, style, format, length, etc. are determined for each individual project." Produces kinescopes; 16mm motion pictures; multimedia kits; overhead transparencies; tapes and cassettes; slides; videotape and live in-studio television productions; also related printed materials for training programs. Payment "depends on funding governed by South Carolina state law guidelines."

SPENCER PRODUCTIONS, INC., 507 5th Ave., New York NY 10017. (212)697-5895. Contact: Bruce Spencer. For high school students, college students, and adults. Occasionally uses freelance writers with considerable talent. Query first. Enclose SASE.
Satire: 16mm motion pictures, prerecorded tapes and cassettes. Satirical material only. Pay is negotiable.

SPOKEN LANGUAGE SERVICES, INC., Box 783, Ithaca NY 14850. (607)257-0500. President: J.M. Cowan. Estab. 1972. Produces material for "any and all foreign language beginners in 30+ languages." Produces 6 new books/year. Submit resume. SASE. Reports in 2 weeks. Buys all rights. Free catalog.
Needs: Produces tapes and cassettes. Pays in outright purchase price "depending on time put in."

SPOTTSWOOD STUDIOS, 2524 Old Shell Rd., Box 7061, Mobile AL 36607. (205)478-9387. Co-owner: M.W. Spottswood. Estab. 1952. "We normally work for sponsors (not always) who seek public attention." Query with samples. SASE. Reports in 2 weeks. Buys all rights.
Needs: Business; religious; and general. Produces 16mm film loops; sound filmstrips; and slides. Pays in outright purchase price.

BILL STOKES ASSOCIATES, 5642 Dyer St., Dallas TX 75206. Contact: Bill Stokes. Audience varies with projects undertaken; everyone from children to board chairmen. Rights purchased from author as payment for work performed. Writer must have experience in script writing, ability to visualize, good research habits, with recent reel or portfolio. Jobs are let on closed contract basis only. Query first. Enclose SASE.
General: Super 8mm, 16mm and 35mm film loops, sound filmstrips, 16mm and 35mm motion pictures, multimedia kits, phonograph records, prerecorded tapes and cassettes, and 35mm slides. All materials and requirements contingent upon clients' needs. "We produce sales meetings, industrial films, educational films, animated films, slide shows, filmstrips, multimedia programs, etc., covering a wide range of subjects and applications. Writer must be sufficiently acquainted with av and motion picture production formats to write within specific budget requirements." No royalties are paid. Contract basis only.

SUMMERHILL MEDIA, LIMITED, Box 156, Station Q, Toronto, Ontario, Canada M4T 2M1. President: Ian A. Stuart. Estab. 1969. Produces material for the general public and schools. Buys 20 scripts/year. Submit outline/synopsis. Reports in 2 weeks. Buys all rights.
Needs: "All subjects are of interest in the educational area with special emphasis on crime prevention and health." Produces 16mm motion pictures. Pays 5% royalty or $250-2,500 outright purchase price.

SWIMMING WORLD, 8622 Bellanca Ave., Los Angeles CA 90045. (213)641-2727. Produces 8mm film loops, 8mm motion pictures, 35mm slides. "Our audience includes swimmers, age 10 through 25, their parents, coaches and administrators involved in the sport; high school through college level." Copyrighted. Will send copy of guidelines for writers. Query first. Enclose SASE.
Sports: Competitive swimming, diving and water polo. "Must be able to shoot good instructional films and action slides." Pays $150 for 20-minute 8mm color instructional films, plus royalty; but payment depends on project.

TALCO PRODUCTIONS, 279 E. 44 St., New York NY 10017. (212)697-4015. President: Alan Lawrence. Produces material for TV and film programming for some schools, foundations, industrial organizations, and associations. Buys all rights. "We maintain a file of writers and call on those with experience in the general category. We do not select unsolicited ms. We prefer to receive a writer's resume listing credits. If his experience merits, we will be in touch when a project seems right." Produces sound filmstrips; motion pictures; videotapes; phonograph records; tapes and cassettes; and slides.
Needs: General (client oriented productions to meet specific needs); education (peripheral market); business (public relations, documentaries, industrial); foreign language (we sometimes dub shows completed for clients for a specific market). Payment runs $500 and up; usually Writers Guild minimums apply.

TELSTAR PRODUCTIONS INC., 366 N. Prior Ave., St. Paul MN 55104. Program Consultant: Dr. Victor Kerns. Produces video material for adult, college level audience, in industry and continuing education. Buys video recording rights. Query. Produces instructional video tapes, non-broadcasting.
Needs: Education (curricular materials for small group or independent study); business (training and development material); and medicine (para-medical topics). Pays $100 plus royalties.

BOB THOMAS PRODUCTIONS, 23 Broad St., Bloomfield NJ 07003. (201)429-9000. President:

Robert G. Thomas. Buys all rights. "Send material with introductory letter explaining ideas. Submit outline or rough draft for motion picture or business matter. If possible, we will contact the writer for further discussion." Enclose SASE.

Business, Education, and General: "We produce 3 types of material for 3 types of audiences: 8mm film loops in sports and pre-teen areas (educational); 8mm and 16mm motion pictures for business (educational, distributed by agencies); 35mm motion pictures for entertainment for a general audience (theater type). General subject matter may be of any style, any length. For the future, 35mm theatrical shorts for distribution." Payment "depends on agreements between both parties. On 8mm and 16mm matter, one fee arrangement. On 35mm shorts, percentage or fee."

TROLL ASSOCIATES, 320 Rt 17, Mahwah NJ 07430. (201)529-4000. Contact: M. Schecter. Estab. 1968. Produces material for elementary and high school students. Buys approximately 200 scripts/year. Query or submit outline/synopsis. SASE. Reports in 2-3 weeks. Buys all rights. Free catalog.

Needs: Film loops; silent and sound filmstrips; multimedia kits; tapes and cassettes; and books. Pays in royalties or outright purchase.

VIDEO FILMS INC., 2211 E. Jefferson Ave., Detroit MI 48207. (313)393-0800. President: Clifford Hanna. For "adult, industrial audience." Query first, with resume of credentials. Enclose SASE.

Industry: Produces filmstrips, 8mm and 16mm motion pictures, prerecorded tapes and cassettes, and slides. Payment "negotiable."

VISUAL EDUCATION CORP., Box 2321, Princeton NJ 08540. Vice-President: Willian J. West. Estab. 1969. Produces material for elementary and high schools. Submit resumé and samples. Submissions will not be returned; "we like to keep a file of freelancers on whom we can call." Reports in 1 month. Buys all rights.

Needs: "Most of our audiovisual work is in filmstrips of about 80 frames (10 minutes). Topics range from language arts to social studies and home economics. Most use a combination of live-action photography and artwork." Produces sound filmstrips, motion pictures; teacher's guides and student activity material; multimedia kits; and tapes and cassettes. Pays $250 minimum.

VOCATIONAL EDUCATION PRODUCTIONS, California Polytechnic State University, San Luis Obispo CA 93407. (805)546-2623. Production Supervisor: Rick Smith. 3,000 color photos of "many aspects of the agricultural industry. Covers animal science, crops, machinery, horticulture, insects, weeds, poultry science, irrigation, etc. Most show people doing a task related to that branch of agriculture." Offers one-time editorial rights. Fees: $35-100 for one-time editorial use.

Needs: Produces sound filmstrips; multimedia kits; tapes and cassettes, and slides (size 35mm). "We usually furnish script development pages for the typing of final drafts, just to make it easier to work with the script. Total length of our filmstrips is about 10 minutes, or 50-70 frames. Avoid talking down to viewer. Technical accuracy is an absolute must." Pays $200/script for a series of 3-6; $400-600 for a single script.

JERRY WARNER & ASSOCIATES, 8455 Fountain Ave., #309, Los Angeles CA 90069. For business, government, schools, and television audiences. Copyright depending on client situation. "We buy full rights to writers' works for sponsored films. Writer must be a professional screenwriter or within the discipline of the special area of subject matter. Do not submit single copy material. Have material registered for datemark, or Writers Guild protection. We accept no responsibility of unsolicited mss." Will answer inquiries within the boundaries of production interest. SASE.

Business and General: Sound filmstrips, motion pictures, multimedia kits, and prerecorded tapes and cassettes. Sponsored business and government films; training, public information, public relations, sales promotion, educational, report films. Royalties are paid on proprietary films that writers take equity in rather than full fee, participations. "We read concepts for educational and documentary films and properties for feature films, but do not solicit scripts as a general rule. Fees vary and depend upon individual client or agency. We frequently pay from $75-100 per day for research periods and from $650-2,000 per reel of script. The wide variance is indicative of how each project has different scope and must be approached on the basis of talent requirement."

WILMAC RECORDS, TAPES AND FILMSTRIPS, 301 East Shore Rd., Great Neck NY 11023. Production Supervisor: Leah D. Evans. Estab. 1950. Produces foreign language-related products. Buys 10 projects/year. Submit resume. SASE. Reports in 4 weeks. Buys all rights.
Needs: Foreign Language. Produces charts; silent and sound filmstrips; multimedia kits; overhead transparencies; phonograph records; tapes and cassettes; relia; slides; and study prints. Pays no royalties; "negotiation only per project."

Book Publishers

Despite the greater impact from electronic media, literacy scandals ("Why Johnny Can't Read"), and a fear by some authorities that reading is a dying art, book publishing is a flourishing, ever expanding industry. The industry employs more than 50,000 people, and operates on a yearly budget of almost $4 billion. Each year, *millions* of dollars are invested in new and established authors. For example, a contract between Little, Brown and Company and former Secretary of State Henry Kissinger called for a reputed $2 million for the former stateman's memoirs; and *Publisher's Weekly* reports that a record $1,900,000 was paid to Harper & Row by Avon for the paperback rights to Colleen McCullough's *The Thorn Birds*.

According to *Publisher's Weekly*, 27,413 new titles were published in 1977, as opposed to 26,983 in 1976. The 84 publishing firms added to *Writer's Market* this year alone report that they expect to publish a combined total of over 2,100 titles in the next year—and need writers to produce them. So there *is* opportunity for the writer in today's book market—provided he has something to say, says it well in writing, and carefully attends to the business end of being a craftsman with a typewriter.

What is Being Published?

One important question to ask while your book is only a germ of an idea is this: *What* is being published? As in the past several years, nonfiction is by far the industry leader, accounting for over 92 percent of all book publishing in 1977. But what nonfiction is making its way from the second assistant copyreader's slush pile to the composing room? The most dramatic increase in publishing activity in 1977 was in the field of juvenile books, with a 14 percent increase over 1976, and representing a ten percent share of the total 1977 book publishing activity.

Religious titles, though down slightly from the previous year, continue to be strongly represented in publishers' catalogs. "We see especially the religious market as doing nothing but increasing," says editor-in-chief David Polek of Liguori Publications. "It seems that more and more people are searching for solid, practical, down-to-earth help and guidance." Professional and business titles also saw a hefty increase this past year. "Professional books are solid and steady, not as subject to feast/famine sales as are trade and text books," according to Allen Jossey-Bass of Jossey-Bass Publishers, Inc.

Fiction, poetry and drama publishing all lost ground in 1976, with fiction accounting for only eight percent of total publishing. Poetry and drama fared even worse, with 20 percent fewer titles published in 1977 than 1976, and now representing only three percent of publishing activity. Much of the current fiction publishing is in the "escape" genre—women's romances, gothic novels, mysteries and science fiction leading the pack. If you prefer writing science fiction, cash in quickly. "The science fiction market seems to have grown immensely, particularly in the mass market field. I can't see this boom lasting more than a few years," says editor R. Reginald of The Borgo Press. "Readers seem to be moving towards strongly-plotted adventures and romances filled with heroes and heroines they can look up to. Escape is what most people seem to want."

Submitting Your Work

The listings for book publishers in *Writer's Market* are designed to help you find the right publisher for your book. Each listing is subdivided by **boldface** headings as to the kinds of manuscripts it is soliciting (fiction, nonfiction, etc.), with information on desired specific genres contained in each heading (i.e., how-to, biography, gothic fiction, etc.). If you have one type of book in hand or in mind, thumb through the entire section to see how often it comes up. This will give you an idea of the size of the market for your work. Does it surface in the large companies that publish hundreds of titles a year, or solely in the smaller, more specialized houses?

Each listing contains the essentials for choosing the right publisher: a contact name and address (and often individual department editors' names), royalty and advance information, submission requirements, how many titles were published in 1977, 1978, and usually an estimation of how many are slated to be published in 1979, plus detailed information on just *what* that publisher wants to see. Careful study of these listings will get your manuscript off to a good start.

Many publishers of both fiction and nonfiction prefer to be queried or to be sent an outline/synopsis and a few sample chapters. If you use the latter method, type a succinct one- or two-page synopsis of your book, attach it to the first two chapters and one other chapter that is particularly well-written, add an outline of the whole work, and send the package off. *Only* in cases where a publisher's listing states that he's willing to consider complete manuscripts should you send one. Due to rising costs and sometimes small staffs, many publishing houses now return unsolicited manuscripts unopened—and unread.

What you have to say belongs in your book. A cover letter should note only that you're working on (or have finished) a book, part of it is enclosed, and would the editor care to see more? If the editor is impressed he'll ask to see the rest; if he isn't, your manuscript will be returned via the enclosed post paid return envelope you have provided.

Study the listings carefully for what each firm wants, and how the firm wants it. Don't send a query on the effects of sunburn on Alaskan polar bears to a publisher who only does material on South Pacific porpoises. That's like personally asking the editor to reject your story.

Also, study the book catalogs of the publishing houses most likely to be interested in your work. The catalog is an invaluable source of information about what types of books the publisher is interested in, what he's done lately (and so isn't anxious to do again soon) and what he needs. Checking book catalogs before you go to market may seem basic, but the anguished cries of editors wading through inappropriate manuscripts ring loudly on Publishers' Row. You can easily avoid these mistakes by studying catalogs in any major bookstore or library, or by writing directly to the publisher. Each listing states the conditions under which a publisher will send you his current catalog (either free, for SASE, or for some small charge).

Getting Paid

Publishers will sometimes offer a writer an *advance* against royalties. An advance is a sum of money paid at acceptance of the manuscript, and before the work's completion, that is later charged against the author's profit. Advances can vary greatly, depending on who you are, who your publisher is, what you've written, and how well the book is projected to sell. They can range from $100 allowances for typing fees to hundreds of thousands of dollars for major multiple book contracts. A few publishers may pay a flat fee for the manuscript, avoiding royalties.

Usually, hardbound trade books (those which are sold in bookstores) have a minimum royalty arrangement of 10% on the first 5,000-10,000 copies sold, 12½% on the next several thousand, and 15% thereafter. The percentage is based on the retail price of the book. For paperback originals (a fast-growing market), the usual royalty is 4% on the first 150,000 copies and 6% thereafter.

Other rights to be aware of are movie, TV, and book club selection rights. Generally, the first novelist receives 50% of what the publisher contracts for paperback and book club sales, and 90% on movie and television commissions.

Working With an Agent

You've written a book and now want to join the ranks of Hemingways and Steinbecks and other writers who have that common denominator—*published books*. One way to sell your book is to acquire an agent. Another way is to try selling it yourself. It's difficult to interest an agent in an unknown writer, and possibly the wisest choice is to try marketing it on your own.

Agents don't knock over first-time authors in a rush to represent them. A first book (particularly a novel) is rarely a commercial success, and an established agent will take on a new writer only when he believes in the future sales potential of his client. Some agents are willing to represent you for a fee, which ensures the agent some compensation should the book prove unmarketable.

Don't get discouraged, though frustration is probably the most common trait among unsuccessful writers. It's a tough business—and remember, as beautiful as your art is, selling that art is pure business.

Subsidy Publishing

If your book has made all the rounds it (and you) can take, but you still consider it worth publishing, you may want to turn to a subsidy publisher. A subsidy publisher will publish your book only if you pay him. He expects to profit from the venture regardless of how well the book sells. Many a subsidy publisher lacks the resources for promoting and selling your book that a standard publisher has, and your chances for turning a profit are slim.

Be cautious of the subsidy book contract. Make sure it provides all the essentials, like the number of copies to be printed (and bound), the type of paper to be used, binding, marketing, and hidden costs. Generally, subsidy publishing is a costly venture.

**Asterisk preceding a listing indicates that individual subsidy publishing (where author pays part or all of publishing costs) is also available. Those firms that specialize in total subsidy publishing are listed at the end of the book publishers' section.*

A.R.C. PUBLICATIONS, Box 3044, Vancouver, British Columbia, Canada V6B 3X5. Editorial Director: John Grayson. Publishes hardcover originals. Publishes 4 titles/ year. 10-15% royalty; no advance. Photocopied submissions OK. Reports in 3 months. SASE. Free book catalog.
Nonfiction: Contemporary fine arts, particularly contemporary music and music education. Query.

ABBEY PRESS, St. Meinrad IN 47577. (812)357-6677. Editor: John T. Bettin. Publishes original and reprint paperbacks. Royalty schedule and advances variable. Send query with outline and sample chapter. Reports in 3 weeks. SASE.
Nonfiction: "Primarily books aimed at married and family life enrichment." Recently published *Family Nights: Summer/Vacation*, by T. Reilly/M. Reilly; and *The Promise of Love*, by J. Grossman.

ABC-CLIO INC., 2040 A.P.S., Santa Barbara CA 93103. (805)963-4221. Editorial Director: Lloyd W. Garrison. Senior Editor: Shelly Lowenkopf. Publishes hardcover originals (95%) and paperback reprints (5%). Published 10 titles in 1977, 12 in 1978; will do 15 in 1979. 10-12% royalty; no advance. Photocopied submissions OK. Reports in 6-8 weeks. SASE. Free book catalog.

Nonfiction: Guides, reference books, bibliographies in the field of history and political science (specifically in ethnic studies, war/peace issues, comparative and international politics, library science—acquisition guides, collection guides for the reference librarian, or for the el-hi market). Mss on comparative politics should be forwarded directly to the series editor, Professor Peter H. Merkl; bibliographies on war/peace issues may be forwarded to Professor Richard D. Burns. Query or submit outline/synopsis and sample chapters. Recently published *The Asian in North America,* by S. Lyman; *Articles on Women Writers,* by N.L. Schwartz; and *The Korean Diaspora,* by Hyung-chan Kim.

ABINGDON PRESS, 201 Eighth Ave. S., Nashville TN 37202. (615)749-6403. Editorial Director: Ronald P. Patterson. Managing Editor: Robert Hill Jr. College Editor: Pierce S. Ellis, Jr.; Editor of Religious Books: Paul M. Pettit; Editor of General Interest Books: Richard Loller. Juvenile Editor: Ernestine Calhoun; Editor of Research Projects: Jean Hager. Payment in royalties. Published 90 titles last year. Write for guide to preparation of mss. Query first. Reports in 1 month. SASE.
Nonfiction, Juveniles, and Textbooks: Publishes religious, children's and general interest books, college texts. Length: 32-200 pages.

ACADEMIC PRESS, INC., 111 Fifth Ave., New York NY 10003. (212)741-6836. Editorial Vice-President: E. V. Cohen. Royalty varies. Published 400 titles last year. Free book catalog. Submit outline, preface and sample chapter. Reports in 1 month. SASE.
Science: Specializes in scientific, technical and medical works. Textbooks and reference works in natural, behavioral-social sciences at college and research levels.

ACADEMY PRESS LIMITED, 360 N. Michigan Ave., Chicago IL 60601. (312)782-9826. Editorial Director: Anita Miller. Senior Editors: Jill Sellers, Bruce Miller. Publishes hardcover and paperback originals (35%) and reprints (65%). Publishes 20 titles/year. 7-10% royalty; no advance. Photocopied submissions OK. Reports in 4 weeks. SASE. Free book catalog.
Nonfiction: "We are primarily interested in feminist books: children's and adult; educational, historical, etc." No how-to, cookbooks, self-help, etc. Query or submit outline/synopsis and sample chapters. Recently published *The Gender Trap: A Closer Look at Sex Roles,* by Adams/Laurikietis; *My Childbirth Coloring Book,* by Baze/Scott (sex education); and *Suburban Portraits,* by Shaderowfsky (photo book).
Fiction: "We will publish *good* fiction. We would consider mysteries and science fiction. Also good novels, but not experimental or avant-garde in an extreme sense." No "romantic" fiction, or religious or sexist material. Query or submit outline/synopsis and sample chapters. Recently published *Land of Green Ginger,* by W. Holtby.

ACE BOOKS, Editorial Department, 360 Park Ave., S., New York NY 10010. Publishes paperback originals and reprints. "Terms vary; usually on royalty basis." Published more than 200 titles last year. Query first, with detailed outline. "Do not send completed ms." Reports in 4 to 8 weeks. SASE.
Nonfiction and Fiction: Self-help, and how-to books. Does not want to see poetry or short stories. For fiction, will consider romantic suspense, westerns, science fiction, women's fiction, occult, and historical romances. Length: 75,000 to 140,000 words. Recently published *A State of Blood,* by H. Kyemba (documentary); *The Illustrated Elvis,* by W.A. Harbinson; and *Alien Meetings,* by B. Steiger.

ADDISON-WESLEY PUBLISHING CO., INC., General Books Division, Reading MA 01867. Publishes hardcover and paperback originals. Published 29 titles in 1977, 27 in 1978. Royalty varies; advance is negotiable. Simultaneous and photocopied submissions OK. Reports in 4-6 weeks. SASE. Free book catalog.
Nonfiction: Adult Trade Program: "Trade paperback and hardcover originals only. Publishes 10-15 titles/year. Subjects considered: current topics in education, psychology, women, public affairs, politics, economics, science, and the arts. Do not send transactional analysis, books of regional interest, cookbooks or humor books. Children's Book Department: Hardcover originals only, grades K-12. Subjects considered: the arts, sciences; the environment, biography and picture books. Submit outline/synopsis and sample chapters; complete ms for children's books. Recently published *Shyness: What It Is, What to do About It,* by P.G. Zimbardo (self-help); and *Take Care of Yourself,* by D. Vickery/J. Fries (medical self-care).
Fiction: Children's books: science fiction, mystery, adventure, picture books, folk tales and

poetry. No adult fiction. Submit complete ms. Recently published *Meet Guguze*, by S. Vangheli (Russian folk tale); and *Sara and the Door*, by V.A. Jensen (picture book).

ADDISONIAN PRESS AND YOUNG SCOTT BOOKS, Juvenile Division of Addison-Wesley Publishing Co., Inc., Reading MA 01867. Publishes hardcover originals. Contracts "vary." Advance is negotiable. Published 2 titles last year. Free book catalog. Send complete ms for fiction and nonfiction. Reports in 3-5 weeks. SASE.
Juveniles: Publishes books for 4-16 year olds.

AERO PUBLISHERS, INC., 329 W. Aviation Rd., Fallbrook CA 92028. (714)728-8456. Editorial Director: Ernest J. Gentle. Publishes hardcover and paperback originals. Published 12 titles in 1977, 15 in 1978; will do 20 in 1979. "Our book publishing has increased 25-40% each year for the last 5 years." 10% royalty; no advance. Simultaneous and photocopied submissions OK. Reports in 1-3 months. SASE. Free book catalog.
Nonfiction: "Manuscripts submitted must be restricted to the fields of aviation and space—and should be of a technical or nontechnical nature. Mss should be 50,000-100,000 words in length and well illustrated." No personal biographies. Submit outline/synopsis and sample chapters. Recently published *Fighter Aces of Luftwaffe*, by Toliver/Constable; *US Navel Fighters*, by L. Jones; and *Cleared To Land*, by F. Burnham.

ALASKA NORTHWEST PUBLISHING CO., Box 4-EEE, Anchorage AK 99509. Editor: Robert A. Henning. Publishes hardcover and paperback originals. "Contracts vary, depending upon how much editing is necessary. Everybody gets 10% of gross, which averages around 8% because direct mail retail sales are high. Pros may get a flat fee in addition, to increase the percentage. Advances may be paid when ms is completed." Free book catalog. "Rejections are made promptly, unless we have 3 or 4 possibilities in the same general field and it's a matter of which one gets the decision. That could take 3 months." Send queries and unsolicited mss to the Book Editor. Enclose return postage.
General Nonfiction: "Alaska, Northern B.C., Yukon, and Northwest territories are subject areas. Emphasis on life in the last frontier, history, outdoor subjects such as hunting and fishing. Writer must be familiar with the North first-hand, from more knowledge than can be gained as a tourist. We listen to any ideas. For example, we recently did a book of woodprints." Art, nature, history, sports, hobbies, recreation, pets, and travel. Length: open. Recently published *Alaska Blues: A Fisherman's Journel*, by J. Upton; *Wood Stoves–How to Make and Use Them*, by O. Wik Chow-to); and *Facts About Alaska*, by the editors of Alaska Magazine.

***ALBA HOUSE**, 2187 Victory Blvd., Staten Island, New York NY 10314. (212)761-0047. Editor-in-Chief: Anthony L. Chenevey. Hardcover and paperback originals (90%) and reprints (10%). Specializes in religious books. 10% royalty. Subsidy publishes 5% of books. Subsidy publishing is offered "if the author is able to promote the sale of a thousand copies of a book which we would not venture on our own." Published 15 titles in 1977, 20 in 1978. Query. State availability of photos/illustrations. Simultaneous and photocopied submissions OK. Reports in 2-4 weeks. SASE. Free book catalog.
Nonfiction: Publishes philosophy; psychology; religious; sociology; textbooks and Biblical books. Recently published *Thirsting for the Lord*, by C. Stuhlmueller; *Elements of Philosophy*, by W. A. Wallace; and *Proclaimed from the Rooftops*, by M. Mahning.

ALLEN PUBLISHING CO., 5711 Graves Ave., Encino CA 91316. Published 3 titles in 1978; will do 10-20 in 1979. 10% royalty; no advance. Simultaneous and photocopied submissions OK. Reports in 4-6 weeks. SASE.
Nonfiction: "Self-help and how-to material, 2,000-15,000 words, aimed at opportunity seekers, wealth-builders, or people seeking self-fulfillment. Material must be original and authoritative, not rehashed from other sources. Authentic, anecdotal case histories helpful. Most of what we market is sold via mail order in report form (8½x11 pages, offset printed and stapled) with some longer soft cover bound booklets planned." No home fix-it, hobby hints, gardening, or cooking material. Submit complete ms.

ALLYN AND BACON, INC. 470 Atlantic Ave., Boston MA 02210. Editors: William Roberts (college texts). P. Parsons (Elhi texts), John Gilman (professional books). Publishes hardcover and paperback originals. "Our contracts are competitive within the standard industry framework of royalties." Rarely offers an advance. Published 200 titles last year. Letter should accompany ms with author information, ms prospectus, etc. Query first or submit complete ms. Reports in 1 to 3 months. SASE.

Nonfiction and Textbooks: "We are primarily a textbook, technical and professional book publisher. Authoritative works of quality. No fiction or poetry." Will consider business, medicine, music, reference, scientific, self-help and how-to, sociology, sports and hobbies, technical mss and other course related texts.

ALMAR PRESS, 4105 Marietta Dr., Binghamton NY 13903. Editor-in-Chief: A.N. Weiner. Managing Editor: M.F. Weiner. Publishes hardcover and paperback originals and reprints. Published 2 titles in 1977, 6 in 1978; will do 9 in 1979. 10-12½-15% royalty; no advance. Simultaneous (if so indicated) and photocopied submissions OK. Reports in 4 weeks. SASE. Book catalog for SASE.
Nonfiction: "Publishes business, technical, and consumer booklets and reports. These main subjects include general business, financial, travel, career, technology, personal help, hobbies, general medical, general legal, and how-to. *Almar Reports* are business and technology subjects published for management use and prepared in 8½x11 format. Other publications are printed and bound in soft covers as required. Reprint publications represent a new aspect of our business—we have not published any of these as yet." Query with outline/synopsis and sample chapters. Recently published *How to Buy and Maintain Tires for Top Mileage and Maximum Safety,* by A.N. Weiner; and *How to Reduce Business Losses From Employee Theft and Customer Fraud* (Almar Report).

AMERICAN ASTRONAUTICAL SOCIETY, Box 28130, San Diego CA 92128. (714)746-4005. Editorial Director: H. Jacobs. Publishes hardcover originals. Published 10 titles in 1977, 8 in 1978; will do 10 in 1979. 10% royalty; no advance. Simultaneous and photocopied submissions OK. Reports in 4 weeks. SASE. Free book catalog.
Nonfiction: Proceedings or monographs in the field of astronautics, including applications of aerospace technology to Earth's problems. Submit outline/synopsis and sample chapters. Recently published *Space Shuttle Missions of the 80's,* edited by W.J. Burshall, et al; and *The Eagle has Returned,* edited by E.A. Steinhoff (technical).

AMERICAN CATHOLIC PRESS, 1223 Rossell Ave., Oak Park IL 60302. (312) 331-4111. Editorial Director: Father Michael Gilligan. Publishes hardcover originals (90%) and hardcover and paperback reprints (10%). Published 2 titles in 1977, 3 in 1978. "Most of our sales are direct mail, although we do work through retail outlets." Pays in outright purchase, $25-100; no advance. Simultaneous and photocopied submissions OK. Reports in 2 months. SASE. Free book catalog.
Nonfiction: "We publish books on the Roman Catholic Liturgy, for the most part books on religious music and educational books and pamphlets. We also publish religious songs for church use, including Psalms as well as choral and instrumental arrangements. We are very interested in new music, meant for use in church services. Books or even pamphlets on the Roman Catholic Mass are especially welcome. We have no interest in secular topics at all, and are not interested in religious poetry of any kind." Query. Recently published *The Role of Music in the New Roman Liturgy,* by W. Herring (educational); *Noise in our Solemn Assemblies,* by R. Keifer (educational); and *Song Leader's Handbook,* by W. Callahan (music).

AMERICAN CLASSICAL COLLEGE PRESS, P.O. Box 4526. Albuquerque NM 87196. Editor-in-Chief: Leslie Dean. Pays a flat sum plus royalties of 10-15%. Published 27 titles last year. Prefers queries. SASE.
Nonfiction: Publishes history, biography, scientific phenomena, politics, psychology and philosophy books. Also economics, Wall Street and the stock market. Mss should be short, to the point, informative, and practical. Length: 20,000 to 40,000 words. Publishes The Science of Man Research Books series.

AMERICAN MEDIA, 790 Hampshire Road, Suite H, Westlake Village CA 91361. (213)889-1231. Editor-in-Chief: G. Edward Griffin. Senior Editor: B. Corday Fain. Publishes hardcover and paperback originals and reprints. Offers 5% royalties on paperback and 10% on hardback. Advance is negotiable. Free book catalog. Will consider photocopied submissions. Query first for nonfiction. Reports in 1 month. Enclose return postage.
General: Specializes in scholarly, documentary books in the following fields: nutrition (favoring organic); creation (favoring the catastrophic, creationist viewpoint as opposed to uniformitarian evolutionist point of view); and ideology (favoring the individualistic conservative point of view as opposed to the collectivistic big government point of view). Point of view is generally controversial and not the orthodox. "Style and structure are open but all points of view must be carefully researched and documented." Publishes biography, book trade, cookbooks,

economics, history, medicine and psychiatry, multimedia material, politics, reference, scientific, self-help and how-to, and sociology.
Recent Titles: *Laetrile Case Histories: The Richardson Cancer Clinic Experience,* by J. Richardson M.D./P. Griffin, R.N. (health and medicine) and *Explosion from the Left; Political Terrorism in America,* by L. McDonald.

AMERICAN UNIVERSAL ARTFORMS CORP., Box 2242, Austin TX 78768. Editor-in-Chief: R.H. Dromgoole. Hardcover and paperback originals. 10% (of net invoice) royalty. Possibility of advance "depends on many factors." Published 4 titles in 1977, 5 in 1978. Send sample print if photos and/or artwork are to accompany ms. Simultaneous submissions OK (if so advised); photocopied submissions OK. Reports in 2-4 weeks. SASE. Book catalog for SASE.
Nonfiction: Publishes textbooks (bilingual educational material, K-12; Spanish/English); books on hobbies, how-to, humor, politics and poetry; juveniles. Submit complete ms.

AMERICANA PUBLICATIONS CO., 212 W. State Highway 38, Moorestown NJ 08057. (609)234-1200. Editor-in-Chief: Patricia F. Yula. Publishes softcover originals and reprints. Will negotiate contract and advance. Submit complete ms for nonfiction. Prefer photocopied submissions. Reports in 2 months for ms; 2 weeks for query. Enclose return postage.
Juveniles and Teaching Aids: Wants juvenile literature for children, ages 5 to 11. Nonfiction. Science and technology preferred. Should be oriented toward learning experience. Illustrations desirable. Interested in "short, exciting copy; unusual subjects or unusual approach to everyday topics." Mss should be geared to children to enhance learning, but not childish. Outlook must be open to the world, unprejudiced and curious in "how's and why's." Structure must allow for ample illustration. Also needs writers and medical illustrators for medical training programs.

AMPHOTO, American Photographic Book Publishing Co., Inc., 750 Zeckendorf Blvd., Garden City NY 11530. (516)248-2233. Editorial Director: Herb Taylor. Publishes hardcover and paperback originals. Published 30 titles in 1977, 40 in 1978; will do 50 in 1979. 10% royalty or $3,000-5,000 outright purchase; advance averages $1,500. Simultaneous and photocopied submissions OK. Reports in 2 months. SASE. Free book catalog.
Nonfiction: "Books on photography only—all phases; technical and how-to aspects. We publish very few picture-only books." Submit outline/synopsis and sample chapters. Recently published *People in Focus,* by C. Gatewood (portraiture); *Color Printing Manual,* by B. Nadler; and *Homegrown holography,* by G. Dowbenko.

ANDERSON PUBLISHING CO., 602 Main St., Suite 501, Cincinnati OH 45201. (513)421-4393. Editorial Director: Jean Martin. Publishes hardcover and paperback originals (98%) and reprints (2%). Published 14 titles in 1977. 12-15% royalty; "advance in selected cases." Simultaneous and photocopied submissions OK. Reports in 6 weeks. SASE. Free book catalog.
Nonfiction: Criminal justice, law, and law-related books and texts and social studies. Query or submit outline/synopsis and sample chapters. Recently published *The Invisible Justice System: Discretion and the Law,* by B.M. Atkins/M.R. Pogrebin; *Constitutional Law for Police,* by J.C. Klotter/J.R. Kanovitz; and *Consumer Protection: Text and Materials,* by D.P. Rothschild/ D.W. Carroll.

AND/OR PRESS, Box 2246, Berkeley CA 94702. Managing Editor: Peter Beren. Paperback originals (90%); hardcover and paperback reprints (10%). Specializes in "works on counterculture with youth market interest. We function as an alternative information resource." 5-10% royalty; advance of 10% of first print run. Published 15 titles in 1977 and 1978. Reports in 2 weeks to 3 months. SASE. Book catalog 25¢.
Nonfiction: Publishes how-to, philosophy, psychology, religious, self-help, sociology, technical, travel, human potential, psycho-pharmacology books. Also alternative lifestyles. Query or submit outline/synopsis and sample chapters. Recently published *Cosmic Trigger,* by R.A. Wilson; *Daily Planet Almanac,* by T. Reim; and *Psychedelic Encyclopedia,* by Stafford.
Special Needs: Planning a series on health, sex and old age.

ANGLICAN BOOK CENTRE, 600 Jarvis St., Toronto, Ontario, Canada M4Y 2J6. (416)924-9192. Editorial Director: Robert Maclennan. Publishes hardcover and paperback originals (90%) and reprints (10%). Published 8 titles in 1977, 10 in 1978; will do 12 in 1979. 7½% royalty; no advance. Simultaneous and photocopied submissions OK. Reports in 6 weeks. SASE.
Nonfiction: Religion—theology, self-help, Bible study, and popular theology; also social action books. Query. Recently published *It's Your Life,* by Tucker (self-help); *Growing in Christ,* by

Stuchbery (theology); and *Wake Up, My People,* by Bolton (popular theology).

ANTONSON PUBLISHING CO., (formerly Nunaga Publishing Co., Ltd.) 12165 97th Ave., Surrey, B.C., Canada V3V 2C8. (604)584-9922. Editor-in-Chief: Richard Antonson. Hardcover and paperback originals. 8-10% royalty; no advance. Published 4 titles in 1976 and 1977; will do 5 in 1978. State availability of photos and/or illustrations to accompany ms. Simultaneous and photocopied submissions OK. Reports in 2-4 weeks. SASE. Free book catalog.
Nonfiction: Publishes Canadiana; biography (Canadian emphasis); how-to (guide books); politics (Canadian perspective); history; nature and wildlife; recreation and conservation, history, reference, how-to, sociology, sports, hobbies, recreation, and travel. "We are developing a strong line of outdoor-oriented books both in the story form and in the guidebook area. Titles vary in length from 40,000 words to 60,000 words. In addition, we are planning more titles on regional and national history."

THE AQUARIAN PUBLISHING CO. (LONDON) LTD., Denington Estate, Wellingborough, Northamptonshire NN8 2RQ England. Editor-in-Chief: J.R. Hardaker. Hardcover and paperback originals. 8-10% royalty. Photocopied submissions OK. SAE and International Reply Coupons. Reports in 2-4 weeks. Free book catalog.
Nonfiction: Publishes books on astrology, magic, witchcraft, palmistry and other occult subjects. Length: 15,000-60,000 words.

THE AQUILA PUBLISHING CO., LTD., Box 1, Portree, Isle of Skye, Scotland IV51 9BT. Editor-in-Chief: J.C.R. Green. Publishes hardcover and paperback originals (99%); paperback reprints and pamphlets (1%). 10% royalty. If ms is to be illustrated, state availability of prints and send photocopies. Simultaneous submissions OK (if informed); photocopied submissions OK. Reporting time varies with workload. Query. SAE and International Reply Coupons. Free book catalog.
Nonfiction: Publishes books on art, biographies, business; cookbooks, cooking and foods; erotica, hobbies, how-to, humor, music, nature, philosophy, photography, poetry, recreation and self-help. Also publishes translations from any language and work with a Scottish/Celtic bias. Query. Recently published *Cantata Underocioh,* E. Milne (poetry); and *The Lamplighter,* by A. Buttigigg.
Fiction: Erotica, experimental, fantasy, humorous, mystery, suspense and science fiction. Work with a Scottish/Celtic bias. Recently published *In Search of Jasper McDoom,* by S. Wade.
Special Needs: "New series of pamphlet/paperbacks of critical essays on American writers and writing; the ecology, humor, etc."

ARCHER EDITIONS PRESS, Box 562, Danbury CT 06810. Editorial Director: Wanda Hicks. Publishes hardcover and paperback originals (60%) and paperback reprints (40%). Published 2 titles in 1977, 3 in 1978; will do 3 in 1979. 15% royalty; occasionally offers $250-750 advance. Simultaneous and photocopied submissions OK. Reports in 2-3 months. SASE. Free book catalog.
Nonfiction: "We are interested in books that could go to the academic and public library market in the fields of history, literature and art. We would especially like biographies in this field." Query. Recently published *Miracle of the Wilderness,* by O. Faulk/B. Jones (history); *Noa Noa,* by P. Gauguin (art/biography reprint); and *Thomas Francis Meagher,* by W.F. Lyons (Civil War reprint).

ARCHITECTURAL BOOK PUBLISHING CO., INC., 10 E. 40th St., New York NY 10016. (212)689-5400. Editor: Walter Frese. Royalty is percentage of retail price. Prefers queries, outlines and sample chapters. Reports in 2 weeks. Enclose return postage.
Architecture and Industrial Arts: Publishes architecture, decoration, and reference books on city planning and industrial arts. Also interested in history, biography, and science of architecture and decoration.

ARCO PUBLISHING CO., INC., 219 Park Ave., S., New York NY 10003. Editor-in-Chief: David Goodnough. Education Editor: Edward Turner. Medical Editor: Don Simmons. Hardcover and paperback originals (30%) and reprints (70%). 10-12½-15% royalty. Advance averages $1,000. Published 140 titles in 1977, 150 in 1978. Simultaneous and legible photocopied submissions OK. Reports in 4-6 weeks. SASE (must be large enough to contain material in case of return). Book catalog for 8½x11 SASE.
Nonfiction (in order of preference): Publishes hobbies (crafts and collecting); pets (practical and

specific); self-help (medical, mental, career guidance, economic); career guidance; medicine and psychiatry (technical and authoritative); study guides and school aides; travel (informative—not "My Trip to . . ."); sports (but not the usual stories about baseball, football, etc.); cookbooks, cooking and foods (specialized cookbooks and nutrition); how-to; medical textbooks, military history; reference. Query first or submit outline/synopsis and sample chapters.

ARKHAM HOUSE PUBLISHERS, INC., Sauk City WI 53583. Editor: James Turner. Publishes hardcover originals and reprints. 10% royalty; advance averages $1,000. Free book catalog. Reports in 4-6 weeks. Enclose return postage.
Fiction: "Arkham House is a fantasy imprint, specializing in supernatural horror and weird literature. Mss should be well-written, preferably on original fantastic themes, with particular attention to atmosphere and style." Query. Recently published *Literary Swordsmen and Sorcerers,* by L. Sprague de Camp (history of heroic fantasy); and *The Princess of All Lands,* by R. Kirk (weird tales).

***ARLINGTON HOUSE PUBLISHERS,** 165 Huguenot St., New Rochelle NY 10801. Editorial Director: Neil McCaffrey. Senior Editors: Richard Band, Karl Pflock and Kathleen Williams. Publishes hardcover originals (90%) and reprints (10%). Published 27 titles in 1977, 28 in 1978; will do 31 in 1979. Subsidy published 5-10% of titles. "If we feel the book is valuable but will not pay its way commercially we will entertain an offer for subsidy publishing. This happens rarely with us, because we believe that most books can make their way commercially if they are worth publishing." 10-12½-15% royalty; advance averages $1,500-2,500. Simultaneous and photocopied submissions OK. Reports in 2 months. SASE. Free book catalog.
Nonfiction: "We publish in three broad areas. We specialize in conservative books in any of several areas: politics, religion, history, economics, social issues—anything that is likely to interest the political or religious conservative. We publish in the nostalgia entertainment area: mainly books on old movies, jazz of the pre-modern period, popular music of the pre-rock era, and early TV. We publish in the area of financial self-help, and we tend to specialize in books that offer offbeat views of the market, e.g., books on gold and silver investing." Query or submit outline/synopsis and sample chapters. Recently published *The Truth About the Panama Canal,* by D. Kitchel; *The Power of the Positive Woman,* by P. Schlafly; and *Universal Pictures,* by M. G. Fitzgerald.

ARTISTS & WRITERS PUBLICATIONS, Box 3692, San Rafael CA 94901. (415)456-1213. Editor-in-Chief: Owen S. Haddock. Paperback originals. Specializes in how-to cookbooks. 5% minimum royalty; no advance. "We prefer all submissions to be in outline/synopsis form, not requiring return, plus a brief resume of the author." State availability of photos/illustrations. Prefers photocopied submissions. Reports in 2-4 months. SASE.
Nonfiction: Publishes business; cookbooks, cooking and foods; hobbies; how-to; law; scientific; and self-help books. "Will examine closely any book outlines which could be used as premium-promotion books for private companies." Recently published *Ghirardelli Original Chocolate Cookbook,* by P. Larsen, and *The New T-Fal French Cookbook,* by M. Pendergast.

***ASHLEY BOOKS, INC.,** 223 Main St., Port Washington NY 11050. (516)883-2221. Editorial Director: Simeon Paget. Senior Editor: Albert Young. Publishes hardcover originals. Published 35 titles in 1977, 30-35 in 1978; will do 35-40 in 1979. Subsidy publishes 2% of books based on "no definite criteria. It depends on the subject matter." May offer writers a cooperative publishing contract. 10-12½-15% royalty; advance "depends on the property and the agent." Simultaneous and photocopied submissions OK. Reports in 6 weeks. SASE. Book catalog for SASE.
Nonfiction: "We seek books like *The Surgical Beauty Racket,* by Dr. Kendall Moore and Sally Thompson which discusses the pitfalls of cosmetic surgery and the danger to the consumer; *How To Recover From A Stroke and Make a Successful Comeback,* by Clarence Longenecker, a former stroke victim who wrote a Baedeker of how to get well; and *Soul Talk: How To Rejuvenate Your Life Style* by James Jacobson, which inspires one to live fully while alive. Natural food and gourmet cookbooks are always welcome. We don't do any craft books. We habitually seek consumer material on medical topics plus explicit medical undercover vehicles and medical self-help books." Submit complete ms.
Fiction: "We seek mainstream fiction that fulfills a responsibility to the quality of life; ideas that are not repressed but breathe integrity and uphold the dignity of what human life should be about. We want books that penetrate the consciousness of the reader and awaken some sentiment be it anger, passion, excitement, sadness, or happiness; books that clamor to be talked about and remain in the mind of the reader long after they have been put aside. Books that

pertain to the changing values of life today and have appeal for a large audience. Books for people who would rather read than watch TV whether they are reading for recreation, relaxation, or just because the topic turns them on. Give them warmth or give them hate, give them fear or give them love, but write about something that will make them feel honest emotion." No juvenile or pornographic material. Recently published *Among the Carnivores,* by D. Curzon (gay mainstream fiction); *The Hospital Plot,* by C. Pugh; and *The Nuclear Catastrophe,* by B. Pohnka/B.C. Griffin.

ASI PUBLISHERS, INC., 127 Madison Ave., New York NY 10016. Editor-in-Chief: Henry Weingarten. Publishes hardcover and paperback originals and reprints. Offers 7½-10% royalty; advance varies. Published 6 titles in 1977. Book catalog for SASE. Will consider photocopied submissions. Query first. Submit outline and sample chapters. Mss should be typed, double-spaced. Enclose return postage. Reports in 1 to 3 months.
Nonfiction: "We specialize in guides to balancing inner space, e.g., acupuncture, astrology, yoga, etc. Our editors are themselves specialists in the areas published. We will accept technical material with limited sales potential." Medical editor: Barbara Somerfield. Astrology editor: H. Weingarten. Recently published *Synastry,* by R. Davison (astrology); *Complete Method of Prediction,* by R. DeLuce (astrology); and *The Day with Yoga,* by E. Haith.

***ASSOCIATED BOOKSELLERS,** 147 McKinley Ave., Bridgeport CT 06606. (212)366-5494. Editor-in-Chief: Alex M. Yudkin. Hardcover and paperback originals. 10% royalty; advance averages $500. Subsidy publishes 25% of books. Subsidy publishing is offered "if the marketing potential is limited." Published 8 titles in 1977, 9 in 1978. Query. Simultaneous and photocopied submissions OK. Reports in 2-4 weeks. SASE. Book catalog for SASE.
Nonfiction: Publishes how-to; hobbies; recreation; self-help; and sports books.
Recent Titles: *Key to Judo*; *Ketsugo*; and *Kashi-No-Bo.*

ASSOCIATED PUBLISHERS' GUIDANCE PUBLICATIONS CENTER, 1015 Howard Ave., San Mateo CA 94401. Editor: Ivan Kapetanovic. Publishes paperback originals. "Offer standard minimum book contract, but there could be special cases, different from this arrangement. We might give more to an author who can provide competent artwork, less if he uses our resources for basic material. We have not made a practice of giving advances." Published 3 titles last year. Will consider photocopied submissions. Submit outline and sample chapters, or submit complete ms. Reports in 30 days. Enclose return postage.
Education: "In addition to bibliographies, which we develop and publish ourselves, we are interested in most kinds of guidance materials. We distribute these from many sources; but would consider publication of books and pamphlets suitable for high school students, but only in the field of guidance, including occupational information, college entrance and orientation, and personal and social problems. We are less concerned with a single title than a group of related titles or a series of publications which may be developed over a period of time. We would like a series of career materials which can be produced and sold inexpensively for junior and senior high school students, with or without tape and/or filmstrip materials correlated with them. We would like materials relating to the *Dictionary of Occupational Titles* for student use; a first class student study guide or a series for different levels to and including college freshmen; a series of social dramas for junior and senior high school use; a series of pamphlets on occupations. Individually and/or in groups. Although we sell to counselors, most of our own materials are aimed at seventh- to twelfth-grade students and those constitute our main market. The vocabulary level usually should be that of average students in the seventh to tenth grades. We prefer not to publish large volumes; stay away from textbooks for school subjects where there are already many books; do not reach markets below or above high school except for additional sales beyond our primary market; do not sell to bookstores, though some buy from us; do not sell to school and public libraries. We are planning a series of occupational pamphlets, a filing system on American colleges. Someone knowledgeable in labor statistics, employment problems, etc., could do the first one; someone familiar with materials on college entrance could do the latter. Interested in publishing about the energy problem and economic conditions in terms of occupations and their impact on the growth or decline of industries over a long range of time. Definitely not interested in poetry, fiction, and pseudo-scientific material. Books published in following categories only: Economics, Self-help and How-to, Sociology, and Guidance. No strict length requirements."

ASSOCIATION PRESS, 291 Broadway, New York NY 10007. (212)374-2127. Editor-in-Chief: Robert W. Hill. Managing Editor: Robert Roy Wright. Hardcover and paperback originals. 10% royalty; advance "varies with nature of project." Published 25 titles in 1977; 30 in 1978. Query,

submit outline/synopsis and sample chapters, or complete ms. State availability of photos/illustrations. Photocopied submissions OK. Reports in 1-2 months. SASE. Free book catalog.
Nonfiction: Publishes general nonfiction, religion, youth leadership, youth problems, recreation, sports, national and international affairs, physical fitness, marriage and sex, crafts and hobbies, social work and human relations. "Word length is a function of the subject matter and market of each book;" ranges from 40,000 words up.

ATHENEUM PUBLISHERS, 122 E. 42nd St., New York NY 10017. Editor-in-Chief: Herman Gollob. Published 28 titles last year. For unsolicited mss prefer query, outline, or sample chapter. Submit complete ms for juveniles. All freelance submissions with the exception of juveniles, should be addressed to "The Editors." Reports in 4 weeks. Enclose return postage.
General Fiction and Nonfiction: Publishes adult fiction, history, biography, science (for the layman), philosophy, the arts and general nonfiction. Length: over 40,000 words.
Juveniles: Juvenile nonfiction books for ages 3 to 18. Length: open. Picture books for ages 3 to 8. "No special needs; we publish whatever comes in that interests us. No bad animal fantasy." Department Editor: Jean Karl. Margaret K. McElderry Books: Fiction and nonfiction preschool through 18. Interested in anything of quality. Editor: Margaret K. McElderry.

ATHLETIC PRESS, Box 2314-D, Pasadena CA 91108. (213)283-3446. Editor-in-Chief: Donald Duke. Paperback originals. Specializes in sports conditioning books. 10% royalty; no advance. Published 4 titles in 1977. Query or submit complete ms. "Illustrations will be requested when we believe ms is publishable." Simultaneous and photocopied submissions OK. Reports in 2-4 weeks. SASE. Free book catalog.
Nonfiction: Publishes sports books. Recently published *Triple Jump Encyclopedia,* by Bullard/Knuth; and *The Young Wrestler,* by T. Clayton.

ATLANTIC MONTHLY PRESS, 8 Arlington St., Boston MA 02116. (617)536-9500. Director: Peter Davison; Associate Director: Upton Birnie Brady; Editor-in-Chief, Children's Books: Emilie McLeod. "Advance and royalties depend on the nature of the book, the stature of the author, and the subject matter." Published 41 titles in 1976, 36 in 1977. Query letters welcomed. Mss preferred, but outlines and chapters are acceptable. Send outline and sample chapters for juvenile nonfiction; send complete ms for juvenile picture books. Enclose return postage.
General Fiction, Nonfiction and Juveniles: Publishes, in association with Little, Brown and Company, fiction, general nonfiction, juveniles, biography, autobiography, science, philosophy, the arts, belles lettres, history, world affairs and poetry. Length: 70,000 to 200,000 words. For juvenile picture books for children 4 to 8, looks for "literary quality and originality." Recently published *Eskimos, Chicanos, Indians,* by R. Coles; *Bel Ria,* by S. Burnford, and *Dear Me,* by P. Ustinov (autobiography).

AUGSBURG PUBLISHING HOUSE, 426 S. Fifth St., Minneapolis MN 55415. (612)332-4561. Director, Book Department: Roland Seboldt. Payment in royalties. Published 40 titles in 1977. Prefers queries, outlines and sample chapters. Reports in 1 month. Enclose return postage.
Fiction, Nonfiction, Juveniles, Poetry, and Religion: Publishes primarily religious books. Also nonfiction and fiction, juveniles, and some poetry. Specializes in Christmas literature; publishes "Christmas," an American Annual of Christmas Literature and Art. Length: "varied." Juveniles are usually short.

***AUTO BOOK PRESS,** 1511 Grand Ave., San Marcos CA 92069. (714)744-2567. Editorial Director: William Carroll. Publishes hardcover and paperback originals. Publishes 3 titles/year. Subsidy publishes 25% of books based on "author's exposure in the field." 15% royalty; offers variable advance. Simultaneous and photocopied submissions OK. Reports in 2 weeks. SASE. Free book catalog.
Nonfiction: Automotive material only: technical or definitive how-to. Query. Recently published *Brief History of San Marcos,* by Carroll (area history); *Honda Civic Guide,* by Carroll; and *How To Sell,* by Woodward (sales hints).

AUTUMN PRESS, INC., 7 Littell Rd., Brookline MA 02146. (617)738-5680. President/Editor-in-Chief: M. Nahum Stiskin. Managing Editor: Shirley Corvo. Publishes hardcover and paperback originals and paperback reprints. Published 5 titles in 1977, 8 in 1978. Distributed by Randon House, Inc. Standard royalty; sometimes offers a small advance. Simultaneous and photocopied submissions OK. Reports in 3 months. SASE. Free book catalog.
Nonfiction: "We are interested in books on holistic health, natural food cookbooks, alternative lifestyles, psychology and growth, philosophy and religion, Eastern and Western thought,

ecology, and environmental concerns. We're also looking for a quality line of 'New Age' children's books." No poetry. Submit outline/synopsis and sample chapters. Recently published *The Temple in Man,* by R.A. Schwaller de Lubicz; *The Looking Glass God,* by M. Nahum Stiskin; and *The Book of Kudzu,* by W. Shurtleff/A. Aoyagi.
Fiction: "We may be interested in fiction that reflects the above themes, as well as children's books that reflect these same themes."

***AVI PUBLISHING CO.,** 250 Post Rd., E., Box 831, Westport CT 06880. (203)266-0738. Editor-in-Chief: Norman W. Desrosier, Ph.D. Hardcover and paperback originals. Specializes in publication of books in the fields of food science and technology, food service, nutrition, health, agriculture and engineering. 10% royalty on the first 1,000 copies sold; $200 average advance (paid only on typing bills). Subsidy publishes 2% of titles (by professional organizations) based on "quality of work; subject matter within the areas of food, nutrition and health, endorsed by appropriate professional organizations in the area of our specialty." Published 45 titles in 1977, 52 in 1978; will do 60 in 1979. Reports in 2-4 weeks. SASE. Free book catalog.
Nonfiction: Publishes books on foods, agricultural economics, medicine, scientific, technical, textbooks; nutrition, agriculture and health books. Query or submit outline/synopsis and sample chapters.
Recent Titles: *Food for Thought,* by T.P. Labuza (nutrition); *Commericial Chicken Production Manual,* by M.O. North (agriculture); *The Meat Handbook,* by A. Levie (food technology).

AVIATION BOOK COMPANY, 555 West Glenoaks Blvd., Box 4187, Glendale CA 91202. (213)240-1771. Editor: Walter P. Winner. Publishes hardcover and paperback originals and reprints. No advance. Free book catalog. Query with outline. Reports in 2 months. Enclose return postage.
Nonfiction: Aviation books, primarily of a technical nature and pertaining to pilot training. Young adult level and up. Also aeronautical history. Recently published *Airmen's Information Manual,* by Winner (pilot training); and *Federal Aviation Regulations* (training/reference).

AVON BOOKS, 959 8th Ave., New York NY 10019. (212)262-6252. Editor-in-Chief: Walter Meade. Managing Editor: Judith Riven. Paperback originals (20%) and reprints (80%). 6-8% royalty; advance averages $2,500 "but can go much higher." Publishes about 260 titles a year. State availability of photos and/or illustrations. Simultaneous and photocopied submissions OK. Reports in 2-4 weeks. SASE. Free book catalog.
Nonfiction: Publishes biography; cookbooks, cooking and foods; how-to; juveniles; medicine and psychiatry; music; nature; pets; poetry; religious; scientific; self-help; and sociology books. Query or submit outline/synopsis and sample chapters. Recently published *People's Pharmacy,* by J. Graedon; and *Saturday Night Live,* by the cast.
Fiction: Publishes adventure (90-125,000 words); fantasy; historical (100-200,000 words); humorous (85,000 words); mainstream; religious; romance; science fiction; and suspense books. Submit complete ms. Recently published *Shanna,* by K. Woodiwiss; *Oliver's Story,* by E. Segal; and *Voyage,* by S. Hayden.

***BADGER CREEK PRESS,** Box 728, Galt CA 95632. Editor-in-Chief: James Singer. Managing Editor: Peggy Flynn. Paperback originals. Specializes in how-to (including cookbooks) pamphlets, up to 32 pages and technical health/medicine texts. Flat rate of up to $100 for pamphlets; 15% for technicals. Very small percentage of subsidy publishing. "Each subsidy is usually not paid by the author, but by his/her sponsor (university, foundation, etc.)." Photocopied submissions OK. Reports in 1-2 weeks. SASE.
Nonfiction: Publishes (in order of preference) how-to; cookbooks, cooking and foods; self-help; books on small farms; reference, medicine and psychiatry; and technical books. Query. "We do not read unsolicited mss. We send style sheet with go-ahead."
Recent Title: *Rug Tufting–How to Make Your Own Rugs,* by S. Lambert (how-to).

***BAKER BOOK HOUSE CO.,** Box 6287, Grand Rapids MI 49506. Editor-in-Chief: Dan Van't Kerkhoff. Hardcover and paperback originals (40%); paperback reprints (60%). Specializes in conservative Protestant (religious) nonfiction. 5% royalty on mass market paperbacks; 7½% on trade paperbacks; 10% on hardcover; no advance. Subsidy publishes 5% of titles; prefers religious field. Publishes 150 books a year. All mss follow the MLA Style Sheet and the Chicago *Manual of Style*. State availability of photos and/or illustrations. Simultaneous and photocopied submissions OK. Reports in 1-2 months. SASE. Free book catalog for SASE.
Nonfiction: Publishes books on humor, religion, self-help. Submit outline/synopsis and sample chapters. Recently published *Fallacies of Evolution,* by A.J. Hoover (science/religion); *Un-*

common Prayers, by D.R. Seagren; and *Ten Years To Live,* by H. Schut.
Special Needs: Booklets of puzzles and activities for children and program activities for church groups (youth, adult, and children).

BALE BOOKS, Box 2727, New Orleans LA 70176. Editor-in-Chief: Don Bale, Jr. Publishes hardcover and paperback originals and reprints. Offers standard 10-12½-15% royalty contract; "no advances." Sometimes purchases mss outright for $500. Published 12 titles last year. "Most books are sold through publicity and ads in the coin newspapers." Book catalog for SASE. Will consider photocopied submissions. "Send ms by registered or certified mail. Be sure copy of ms is retained." Reports usually within several months. SASE.
Nonfiction and Fiction: "Our specialty is coin and stock market investment books; especially coin investment books and coin price guides. We are open to any new ideas in the area of numismatics. The writer should write for a teenage through adult level. Lead the reader by the hand like a teacher, building chapter by chapter. Our books sometimes have a light, humorous treatment, but not necessarily."

BALLANTINE BOOKS, division of Random house, 201 E. 50th St., New York NY 10022. Publishes trade and mass market paperback originals and reprints. Royalty contract varies. Published 350 titles last year; about 1/4 were originals. Query first. Enclose return postage.
General: General fiction and nonfiction, science fiction and fantasy.

***BANNER BOOKS INTERNATIONAL, INC.,** 13415 Ventura Blvd., Sherman Oaks CA 91423. (213)784-9788. Executive Vice President: Ms. Terry Sherf. Editor-in-Chief: Margaret Tropp, Ph.D. Hardcover and paperback originals (90%) and reprints (10%). Specializes in "academic and scholarly books for the world college and university markets." 40% royalty; no advance. "We are co-op publishers, we co-invest with authors in books we accept for publication on a subsidy basis. We are not a vanity press nor are we a 'typical' subsidy publisher. Our co-investment in a book requires that we first substantiate its sales potential and then market it aggressively, to justify our investment." Published 100 titles in 1977; 125 in 1978; will do 137 in 1979. State availability of photos or line art. Simultaneous and photocopied submissions OK. Reports in 1-2 months. SASE. Free author's prospectus.
Nonfiction: Publishes Americana; art; biography; business; economics; education; history; law; medicine and psychiatry; military science; music; philosophy; political science; psychology; reference; religious; scientific; sociology; technical; textbooks; language textbooks; and literature translation books. Submit complete ms. Recently published *Survival in Academia,* by Dr. W.R. Dukelow (education); *So You Think You're Happy,* by Dr. A.R. Gerson (psychology); and *The Dynamics of Development,* by Dr. M.F. Jussawalla (economics).

BANTAM BOOKS, INC., 666 5th Ave., New York NY 10019. (212)765-6500. Editorial Director: Marc Jaffe. Associate Editorial Director: Allan Barnard. Executive Editor: Grace Bechtold. Publishes hardcover and paperback reprints (75%) and paperback originals (25%). Publishes approximately 375 titles/year. Royalty and advance vary. Reports in 4 weeks. SASE. Free book catalog.
Nonfiction: "We no longer accept unsolicited manuscripts. Material will be returned unread unless sent at our request. Please query as appropriate: Grace Bechtold, Executive Editor (religious and health books); Toni Burbank, Executive Editor, School & College Books (nonfiction); Jean Highland, Senior Editor (political science); and Linda Price, Senior Editor (cookbooks). Recently published *All Creatures Great and Small,* by J. Herriott; *Life After Life,* by R. Moddy, Jr., M.D.; and *Haywire,* by B. Hayward.
Fiction: "We no longer accept unsolicited manuscripts, and material will be returned unread. Please query as appropriate: Linda Price, Senior Editor (romances, historicals, general women's fiction); Sydney Weinberg, Editor (science fiction and fantasy); and Roger Cooper, Senior Editor (young adult fiction). Recently published *The Chancellor Manuscript,* by R. Ludlum; *Aspen,* by B. Hirschfeld; and *Even Cowgirls Get the Blues,* by T. Robbins.

***BANYAN BOOKS, INC.,** Box 431160, Miami FL 33143. (305)665-6011. Director: Ellen Edelen. Hardcover and paperback originals (90%) and reprints (10%). Specializes in publishing regional and natural history books. 10% royalty; no advance. Subsidy publishes 10% of books; "worthwhile books that fill a gap in the market, but whose sales potential is limited." Send prints if illustrations are to be used with ms. Photocopied submissions OK. Reports in 1 month. SASE. Free book catalog.
Nonfiction: Publishes regional history and books on nature and horticulture. Submission of outline/synopsis, sample chapters preferred, but will accept queries. Recently published *Voices*

from the Countryside, by G. Miles (documentary); *The Forgotten Frontier,* by A. Parks (history); and *They All Call It Tropical,* by Brookfield/Griswold.

BARLENMIR HOUSE PUBLISHERS, 413 City Island Ave., New York NY 10064. Editor-in-Chief: Barry L. Mirenburg. Managing Editor: Leonard Steffan. Hardcover and paperback originals. 10-12½-15% royalty; varying advance. Submit outline/synopsis and sample chapters. State availability of photos and/or illustrations to accompany ms. Simultaneous (if informed) and photocopied submissions OK. Reports in 2-4 weeks; "sometimes sooner." SASE.
Nonfiction: Publishes Americana, art, biography, business; cookbooks, cooking and foods; economics, erotica, history, hobbies, how-to, humor, law; medicine and psychiatry; multimedia material, music, nature, philosophy, photography, poetry, politics, psychology, recreation, reference, scientific, self-help, sociology, sports, technical textbooks, and travel books. "No adherence to specific schools of writing, age, or ethnic group. Acceptance based solely on original and quality work."
Recent Titles: *UFO, The Eye and The Camera,* by A. Vance (nonfiction); and *The Painterly Poets,* by F. Moramarco (nonfiction).

A.S. BARNES AND CO., INC., Cranbury NJ 08512. (609)655-0190. Editor: Dena Rogin. Publishes hardcover and paperback originals and reprints; occasionally publishes translations and anthologies. Contract negotiable: "each contract considered on its own merits." Advance varies, depending on author's previous works and nature of book. Published 90 titles last year. Will send a catalog to a writer on request. Query first. Reports as soon as possible. Enclose return postage.
General Nonfiction: "General nonfiction with special emphasis on cinema, antiques, sports, and crafts." Recently published *Dollmaking for Everyone,* by H. Young; *Films of George Pal,* by G. Hickman; and *The Complete Book of Dogs,* by M.E. Ensminger.

BARRE PUBLISHERS, Valley Rd., Barre MA 01005. Publisher: Jane West. Publishes hardcover and paperback originals. Offers standard minimum book contract. "We offer small advances." Published 10 titles last year. Free book catalog. Photocopied submissions OK. Submit outline and sample chapters or complete ms. Reports in 4 weeks. SASE.
General Nonfiction: "We specialize in fine craftsmanship and design. History, Americana, art, photography, travel, cooking and foods, nature, recreation and pets. No length requirements; no restrictions for style, outlook, or structure. Our emphasis on quality of manufacture sets our books apart from the average publications. Particularly interested in folk art and crafts." Recently published *Molas: Folk Art of the Cuna Indians;* and *Make Use of Your Garden Plants.*

BEACON PRESS, 25 Beacon St., Boston MA 02108. (617)742-2110. Editorial Director: MaryAnn Lash. Publishes hardcover originals (50%) and paperback reprints (50%). Published 31 titles in 1977, 30 in 1978; will do 30 in 1979. 7½% royalty on paperback; 10% on hardbound; advance averages $3,000. Simultaneous and photocopied submissions OK. Reports in 6-8 weeks. SASE. Free book catalog.
Nonfiction: General nonfiction; religion; world affairs; social studies; history; psychology; art; literature; and philosophy. Query. Recently published *Non-Sexist Childraising,* by C. Carmichael (social studies); *Pursuit of Dignity: New Living Alternatives for the Elderly,* by B.K. Smith (social studies); *Behind the Sex of God: Toward a New Consciousness–Transcending Matriarchy and Patriarchy,* by C. Ochs (philosophy).

R.O. BEATTY & ASSOCIATES/BEATTY BOOKS, Box 763, Boise ID 83701. (208)343-4949. Publisher: David C. Beatty. Editor: Melissa L. Dodworth. Hardcover and paperback originals. Specializes in photographic documentary books. Royalty and advance negotiable. Published 2 titles in 1977. Query. State availability of photos/illustrations. Simultaneous submissions OK. Reports in 1-2 months. SASE. Free book catalog.
Nonfiction: Publishes Americana; biography; history; juveniles; nature; photography; and travel books.
Fiction: Publishes fantasy and historical books. No romantic fiction.
Recent Titles: *Nevada: Land of Discovery,* by D. Beatty (Western Americana photographic documentary); *Sun Valley: A Biography,* by D. Oppenheimer and J. Poore (photographic documentary).

BEAU LAC PUBLISHERS, Box 248, Chuluota FL 32766. Publishes hardcover and paperback originals. Query first. Enclose S.A.S.E.

Nonfiction: "Military subjects. Specialist in the social side of service life." Recently published *The Officer's Family Social Guide,* by M.P. Gross; and *Military Weddings and The Military Ball,* by M.P. Gross.

BEEKMAN PUBLISHERS, INC., 38 Hicks St., Brooklyn Heights NY 11201. (212)624-4514. Editor-in-Chief: Stuart A. Ober. Publishes hardcover originals and reprints. Published 29 titles in 1977, 33 in 1978. 10% royalty; no advance. Simultaneous and photocopied submissions OK. Reports in 1-2 months. SASE. Book catalog for SASE.
Nonfiction: Americana; cookbooks, cooking and foods; economics; history; philosophy; politics and textbooks. Submit outline/synopsis or complete ms.
Fiction: Adventure; experimental; historical; humorous; mainstream; mystery; romance; science fiction; suspense; and western. Submit outline/synopsis or complete ms.

BELIER PRESS, Box C, Gracie Station, New York NY 10028. Editor-in-Chief: J.B. Rund. Hardcover and paperback originals and reprints. 5-7½-10% royalty; advance depends on work. Send contact sheet or prints to illustrate ms. Photocopied submissions OK. Reports "as soon as possible." SASE. Free book catalog.
Nonfiction: Publishes comics, satire, erotica, and art books. "Strictly adult". Query first. Recently published *Carload O' Comics,* by R. Crumb; *The Adventures of Sweet Gwendoline,* by J. Willie.

BELL SPRINGS PUBLISHING COMPANY, Box 322, Laytonville CA 95454. Editorial Director: Bernard Bear. Senior Editor: Bernard Kamoroff. Publishes hardcover and paperback (primarily) originals. Published 1 title in 1977, 2-3 in 1978; will do 2-3 in 1979. 8-10% royalty; no advance. Simultaneous and photocopied submissions OK. Reports in 2 weeks. SASE. Free book catalog.
Nonfiction: "We are particularly interested in how-to and self-help books on subjects of current popular interest that have not been covered before. We prefer authors who have solid, first-hand experience in the subject they write about, and who have a talent for translating complicated and detailed information into everyday, clear language." Query. Recently published *Small Time Operator,* by B. Kamoroff, CPA; and *Co-Op's,* by Blasky/Sternberg.

BENCH PRESS, Box 24635, Oakland CA 94623. Editorial Director: Pamela Yellen. Publishes hardcover and paperback originals. Published 1 title in 1977, 3 in 1978; will do 5 in 1979. Payment method "varies, sometimes by percent of profit." Advance varies. Simultaneous and photocopied submissions OK. Reports in 4-6 weeks. SASE. Book catalog for SASE.
Nonfiction: Psychology, parapsychology, philosophy, and history. "Will consider books in other areas also." Query or submit outline/synopsis and sample chapters. Recently published *Dream Reality: The Conscious Creation of Dream and Paranormal Experience,* by J.J. Donahoe (parapsychology/psychology); and *Millbrook: The True Story of the Early Years of the Psychedelic Revolution,* by A. Kleps (history/philosophy).
Fiction: "Will consider submissions."

CHARLES A. BENNETT CO., INC., 809 W. Detweiller Dr., Peoria IL 61614. (309)691-4454. Editor-in-Chief: Michael Kenny. Hardcover and paperback originals. Specializes in textbooks and related materials. 10% royalty for textbooks, "less for supplements;" no advance. Published 25 titles in 1977, 25 in 1978. Query "with a sample chapter that represents much of the book; not a general introduction if the ms is mostly specific 'how-to' instructions." Send prints if photos/illustrations are to accompany the book. Photocopied submissions OK. Reports in 2-4 weeks. SASE. Free book catalog.
Nonfiction: Publishes art (history or appreciation; possibly some how-to intended for students in junior high or above); foods (textbooks); how-to (textbooks on woodworking, metalworking, etc.); photography (textbook, high school or college level); and textbooks (home economics, industrial education, art). Recently published *Person to Person,* by C. Sasse; *Industrial Electricity,* by R. Miller; and *Today's Teen,* by J. Kelly/E. Landers.

BERKLEY PUBLISHING CORP., 200 Madison Ave., New York NY 10016. Editor-in-Chief: Page Cuddy. Managing Editor: Robin Rosenthal. Hardcover and paperback originals (50%) and paperback reprints (50%). 6% royalty to 150M copies; 8% thereafter; usually offers advance. Publishes about 165 titles a year. Submit through agent only. State availability of photos/illustrations. Simultaneous and photocopied submissions OK. Reports in 1-2 months. SASE.
Nonfiction: Publishes biography; hobbies; how-to; pets; psychology (popular); and self-help books. "We publish very little nonfiction; the categories above are the ones we are most likely to publish."

Fiction: Publishes fantasy; historical; mainstream; mystery; romance; science fiction; suspense; and western books.
Recent Titles: *Children of Dune,* by F. Herbert (science fiction); *Once an Eagle,* A. Myrer (fiction); and *The Tomorrow File,* by L. Sanders (fiction).

BETHANY FELLOWSHIP, INC., 6820 Auto Club Rd., Minneapolis MN 55438. (612)944-2121. Editor-in-Chief: Alec Brooks. Managing Editor: David Thompson. Hardcover and paperback originals (75%); paperback reprints (25%)). 10% royalty on hardcover and original trade paperback; 6% on original mass market book. No advance. Published 40 in 1977; 45 in 1978. Simultaneous and photocopied submissions OK. Reports in 1-2 months. Free book catalog.
Nonfiction: Publishes biography (evangelical Christian), nature, religious (evangelical charismatic) and self-help books. Query. Recently published *Through Sorrow to Joy,* by Salisbury; *Especially for Husbands,* by Campean; and *Of Whom the World is Not Worthy,* by Chapien.
Fiction: "We are interested in anything that is Christian and evangelical." Query.

BETHANY PRESS, Book Division of Christian Board of Education, P.O. Box 179, St. Louis MO 63166. (314)371-6900. Editor-in-Chief: Sherman R. Hanson. Publishes hardcover and paperback originals. Standard 17% royalty contract. Query. Reports in 30 days. Enclose return postage.
Nonfiction: Books dealing with Christian experience, church life, devotions, and programming, Christian education, Bible reading and interpretation. Writer should offer clear prose, readable by lay persons, speaking to their concerns as Christians and churchmen or churchwomen. Recently published *Experiment in Liberty,* by R.E. Osborn; and *Reading the Bible With Understanding,* by J. Trefzger.

BETTER HOMES AND GARDENS BOOKS, 1716 Locust St., Des Moines IA 50336. Editor: Gerold Knox. Publishes hardcover originals and reprints. "Ordinarily we pay an outright fee for work (amount depending on the scope of the assignment). If the book is the work of one author, we sometimes offer royalties in addition to the fee." Free book catalog. Prefers outlines and sample chapters. Will accept complete ms. Will consider photocopied submissions. Reports in 6 weeks. Enclose return postage.
Home Service: "We publish nonfiction in many family and home service categories, including gardening, decorating and remodeling, sewing and crafts, money management, entertaining, handyman's topics, cooking and nutrition, and other subjects of home service value. Emphasis is on how-to and on stimulating people to action. We require concise, factual writing. Audience is primarily husbands and wives with home and family as their main center of interest. Style should be informative and lively with a straightforward approach. Stress the positive. Emphasis is entirely on reader service. We approach the general audience with a confident air, instilling in them a desire and the motivation to accomplish things. Food book areas that we have already dealt with in detail are currently overworked by writers submitting to us. We rely heavily on a staff of 9 home economist editors for food books. We are interested in non-food books that can serve mail order and book club requirements (to sell at least for $8.95 and up) as well as trade. Rarely is our first printing of a book less than 100,000 copies. Then, new titles must compete with our other titles. 96-, 208- and 400-page books are lengths of 3 most popular lines. Each is heavily interspersed with illustrations ranging from 2-page spreads to 1-column, 5-inch pix." Publisher recommends careful study of specific BH&G book titles before submitting material.

***BINFORD & MORT, PUBLISHERS**, 2536 S.E. 11th Ave., Portland OR 97202. (503)238-9666. Editor-in-Chief: L.K. Phillips. President: Thomas Binford. Hardcover and paperback originals (75%) and reprints (25%). 10% royalty; advance (to established authors) varies. Occasionally does some subsidy publishing, "when ms merits it, but it does not fit into our type of publishing." Publishes about 24 titles annually. Reports in 2-4 months. SASE. Free book catalog.
Nonfiction: Publishes books about the Pacific Northwest, mainly in the historical field. Also Americana, art, biography; cookbooks, cooking and foods; history, nature, photography, recreation, reference, sports, and travel. Query. Recently published *High Desert of Central Oregon,* by R.R. Hatton; and *Tom McCall: Maverick,* by T. McCall/S. Neal.
Fiction: Publishes historical and western books. Must be strongly laced with historical background.

CLIVE BINGLEY, LTD., 16 Pembridge Rd., London W11, England. Editorial Director: Clive Bingley. Senior Editor: Clive Martin. Publishes hardcover and paperback originals (90%) and reprints (10%). Published 17 titles in 1977, 20 in 1978; will do 22 in 1979. 10% royalty; no

advance. Simultaneous and photocopied submissions OK. Reports in 4 weeks. SASE. Free book catalog.
Nonfiction: Publishes bibliographies, reference books and books on library science. Submit outline/synopsis and sample chapters. Recently published *Literature & Bibliometrics,* by Ritchie/Nicholas (literature assessment); *Archaeology: A Reference Handbook,* by A. Day (reference); and *The Subject Approach to Information,* by A.C. Foskett (student textbook).

JOHN F. BLAIR, PUBLISHER, 1406 Plaza Dr., Winston-Salem NC 27103. (919)768-1374. Editor-in-Chief: John F. Blair. Publishes hardcover originals; occasionally paperbacks and reprints. Royalty to be negotiated. Published 8 titles last year. Free book catalog. Submit complete ms. "Authors are urged to inquire if they have not received an answer within 6 weeks." SASE.
General Fiction, Nonfiction, and Juveniles: In juveniles, preference given to books for ages 10 through 14 and up; in history and biography, preference given to books having some bearing on the southeastern United States. Very little poetry. No length limits for juveniles. Other mss may be 140 pages or more. Recently published *Woodsmoke* (fiction); *Children of the Sea* (fiction); *Carnivorous Plants of the United States and Canada* (nonfiction); and *Contemporary Poetry of North Carolina* (poetry).

THE BOBBS-MERRILL EDUCATIONAL PUBLISHING CO., 4300 W. 62nd St., Indianapolis IN 46268. (317)291-3100. Editorial Director: Thomas D. Wittenberg. Published 53 titles last year. "Queries are acceptable, but do not send complete manuscripts." SASE.
Nonfiction: "We are interested in the following disciplines: business education, humanities, vocational and technical books."

THE BOBBS-MERRILL CO., INC., 4 W. 58th St., New York NY 10019. Editor-in-Chief: Daniel Moses. Publishes hardcover originals. Offers standard 10-12½-15% royalty contract. Advances vary, depending on author's reputation and nature of book. Published about 90 titles last year. Query first. No unsolicitied mss. Reports in 4 to 6 weeks. Enclose return postage.
General Fiction and Nonfiction: Publishes American and foreign novels, suspense, science fiction, film, politics, history, current events, biography/autobiography, and children's books. No poetry.

THE BOND WHEELRIGHT COMPANY, Box 296, Freeport ME 04032. (207)865-6045. Editor: Mary Louise Morris. Offers 10% royalty contract. No advance. Published 10 titles in 1977. Query. SASE.
Nonfiction: "We are interested in nonfiction only—books that have a regional interest or specialized subject matter (if the writer is an authority), or how-to-do-it books."

BOOKCRAFT, INC., 1848 W. 2300 South, Salt Lake City UT 84119. Editor: H. George Bickerstaff. Publishes hardcover originals and reprints. Offers standard 10-12½-15% royalty contract. "We rarely make an advance on a new author." Published 20 titles last year. Will send a catalog to a writer on request. Query first. Will consider photocopied submissions. "Include contents page with ms." Reports in about 2 months. Enclose return postage.
Nonfiction: "We publish for members of The Church of Jesus Christ of Latter-Day Saints (Mormons). Our books are directly related to the faith and practices of that church. We will be glad to review such mss, but mss having merely a general religious appeal are not acceptable. Ideal book lengths range from about 64 pages to 200 or so, depending on subject, presentation, and age level. We look for a fresh approach—rehashes of well-known concepts or doctrines not acceptable. Mss should be anecdotal unless truly scholarly or on a specialized subject. Outlook must be positive. We do not publish anti-Mormon works. We almost never publish fiction or poetry. Recently published *The Art of Raising Parents,* by G. Durrant (youth); *Love is the Gift,* by A.G. Affleck (motivational); and *You and Your World,* by P.H. Dunn.
Teen and Young Adult: "We are particularly desirous of publishing short books for Mormon youth, about ages 14 to 19. Must reflect LDS principles without being 'preachy;' must be motivational. 18,000-25,000 words is about the length, though we would accept good longer mss. This is a tough area to write in, and the mortality rate for such mss is high." Recently published *Charlie's Monument,* by B.M. Yorgason (allegory).

BOOKS FOR BUSINESSMEN INC., 1100 17th St., NW., Washington DC 20036. (202)466-2372. Hardcover and paperback originals (80%) and reprints. Specializes in books on business and international trade. "Usually royalties start at 10%; sometimes 5% for anthologies, but this is not a fixed rule." No advance. Send contact sheets for selection of illustrations. Simultaneous

and photocopied submissions OK. Reports in 1-2 months. Book catalog for SASE.
Nonfiction: Publishes books on business, self-help, law, reference, economics, multimedia material and technical subjects. "We can use business material from a 5,000-word pamphlet to a 100,000-word book." Submit complete ms.
Recent Titles: *Tax Havens: What They Are and How They Work,* by Starchild (business); *How the IRS Selects Individual Tax Returns for Audit,* by Starchild (business); *Islamic Law in the Modern World,* by Yemani (law).

BOOKWORM PUBLISHING CO., P.O. Box 655, Ontario CA 91761. Editor-in-Chief: Maisic Meier. Publishes paperback originals and reprints. "We publish limited library hardback editions." Offers royalty of 5% of net publisher revenues. "Author receives 1/3 of all auxillary revenues, e.g., translations, serial, TV rights, etc. We hold all copyrights ourselves in most cases." Advances paid only to previously established authors. Average advance is $500. "We rely on aggressive nontrade promotion to special outlets in addition to regular trade distribution channels, e.g., nurseries for garden books, worm farms for books on vermiculture. Books lending themselves to this additional thrust have an extra edge in our consideration." Query first. First time authors should submit complete ms. Established authors should submit outline and sample chapters. Will consider simultaneous and photocopied submissions. Typed, double-spaced ms essential. "If photos or drawings, send some samples of artist's or photographer's work." Enclose return postage if submitting complete ms on initial contact. Include phone number. Reports usually within 10 days.
Nonfiction: Any subject area related to natural or social ecology. Primary interests are agriculture, horticulture (gardening), waste management, self-sufficiency and organic living. Prefers practical "how-to-do-it" treatment. Mss may range from 7,500 to 30,000 words. "We seek mss from authors having authentic qualifications as 'authorities' in their subject areas, but qualification may be by experience as well as academic training." Interested in "needed" books either covering subjects relatively rare in existing literature or taking an unusual approach to conventional subject matter. Marketability of book is prime consideration. "We dislike issuing books which must compete in too crowded a field." See *The Elements of Style.* "We demand clear, concise, and effective use of English, appropriate to subject and intended audience. Technical terms, if used, should be defined in text on initial appearance and/or in accompanying glossary. We publish for the average person, and wish even our books for specialists to be understandable to the neophyte. We're more interested in creating books of lasting value to readers than in following current trends or fads." Abstract philosophy, poetry, fiction are "just not in our fields." Recently published *House Plants for Fun and Profit,* by D. Fell; *Begonias for Beginners,* by E. Haring; and *Living Off the Country for Fun and Profit,* by J. Parker.
Textbooks: Publishes social science texts for the elementary-high school market, emphasizing traditional values.
Business and Professional: Publishes business and "organization management."

BOREALIS PRESS, LTD., 9 Ashburn Dr., Ottawa, Ontario, Canada K2E 6N4. Editorial Director: Frank Tierney. Senior Editor: Glenn Clever. Publishes hardcover and paperback originals. Published 16 titles in 1977, 18 in 1978; will do 20 in 1979. 10% royalty; no advance. Photocopied submissions OK. Reports in 8 weeks. SASE. Book catalog for $1.
Nonfiction: "Only material Canadian in content." Query. Recently published *Seventy Years of Service: A History of the Royal Canadian Army Medical Corps,* by Col. G.W.L. Nicholson.
Fiction: "Only material Canadian in content." Query. Recently published *Song and Silence,* by D. Madott.

THE BORGO PRESS, Box 2845, San Bernardino CA 92406. (714)884-5813. Editor-in-Chief: R. Reginald. Publishes paperback originals. "About 60% of our line consists of The Milford Series: Popular Writers of Today, critical studies on modern popular writers, particularly science fiction writers." Royalty: "4% of gross, with a 6% escalator; 6-8% for second books, if the first has sold well." No advance. "At least a third of our sales are to the library market." Reports in 1-2 months. SASE. Free book catalog.
Nonfiction: Publishes literary critiques. Submit outline/synopsis and sample chapters. "We appreciate people who've looked at our books before submitting proposals; all of the books in our author series, for example, are based around a certain format that we prefer using." Recently published *Kurt Vonnegut: The Gospel from Outer Space,* by C. Mayo (literary critique).
Fiction: Fantasy and science fiction. "We only publish fiction by established authors (those with previous book credits)." Query first. Recently published *Hasan,* by P. Anthony; and *A Usual Lunacy,* by D.G. Compton.

THOMAS BOUREGY AND CO., INC., 22 E. 60th St., New York NY 10022. Editor: Ms. Debra Manette. Offers advance on publication date. Published 60 titles in 1977. Query first with description. Reports in 1 month. SASE.
Fiction: For teenagers and young adults. Publishes romances, nurse and career stories, westerns and gothic novels. Sensationalist elements should be avoided. Length: 55,000-60,000 words. Also publishes Airmont Classics Series. Recently published *Listen to Your Heart*, by D.J. Snow (romance); *Edge of Fear*, by J. Morton; and *My High Love Calling*, by E. Cary.

R.R. BOWKER CO., 1180 Avenue of the Americas, New York NY 10036. (212)764-5100. Manager, Book Editorial Department: Desmond F. Reaney; Acquisitions Editor: Judith S. Garodnick. Directories Editor: Olga S. Weber. Royalty basis by contract arrangement. Query first. Reports in 2 to 4 weeks. Enclose return postage.
Book Trade and Reference: Publishes books for the book trade and library field, reference books, and bibliographies. Recently published *Great Treasury of Western Thought*, by M. Adler/C. Van Doren (literature); and *Candid Critique of Book Publishing*, by B. Curtis (essays).

BOWLING GREEN UNIVERSITY POPULAR PRESS, Popular Culture Center, Bowling Green State University, Bowling Green OH 43403. Editor: Ray B. Browne. Publishes hardcover and paperback originals. Offers 10% royalties; no advance. Published 10 titles last year. Free book catalog. SASE.
Nonfiction: "Popular culture books generally. We print for the academic community interested in popular culture and popular media." Interested in nonfiction mss on "science fiction, folklore, black culture." Will consider any book-length mss. Submit complete ms. Recently published *Outlaw Aesthetics*, by F.E.H. Schroeder; *Arts in a Democratic Society*, by D. Mann and *Voices for the Future*, by T. Clareson.

BOWMAR/NOBLE PUBLISHING, INC., 4563 Colorado Blvd., Los Angeles CA 90039. (213)247-8995. Editor-in-Chief: Mel Cebulash. Managing Editor: Dolly Hassinbiller. Hardcover and paperback originals (80%) and reprints (20%). Specializes in El-hi educational books. Royalties or flat fees are negotiable; "there is no average advance amount, and we don't always give advances." Published 48 titles in 1977, 42 in 1978. "We sell directly to the schools: we have very few titles in bookstores." Submit complete ms. Photocopied submissions OK. Reports in 1-3 months. SASE. Book catalog for SASE.
Nonfiction: Publishes biography; business; history; juveniles; and sports books.
Fiction: Publishes adventure; mystery; science fiction, "and anything else that might be of interest to kids 8-16." Especially interested in easy reading books.

BRADBURY PRESS, INC., 2 Overhill Rd., Scarsdale NY 10583. (914)472-5100. Editor-in-Chief: Richard Jackson. Publishes hardcover originals. Published 16 titles in 1977, 18 in 1978; will do 20 in 1979. "We're distributed by E.P. Dutton." 10% royalty or 5% to author, 5% to artist; advance averages $1,000. Photocopied submissions OK. Reports in 3 months. SASE. Book catalog for 28¢.
Fiction: Contemporary fiction: adventure, science fiction, and humor. Also "stories about real kids; special interest in realistic dialogue." No fantasy or religious material. Recently published *Starring Sally J. Freedman as Herself*, by J. Blume; *Tattercoats*, by F. Steel; and *The Slave Dancer*, by P. Fox.

***BRANDEN PRESS, INC.**, 221 Columbus Ave., Boston MA 02661 (617)267-7471. Editor-in-Chief: Alice May Stark. Publishes hardcover and paperback originals (70%) and reprints (30%). 10% royalty up to 5,000 copies; 15% thereafter. "We offer an advance only on important books and cannot give an average amount. We publish some books for which the authors furnish a subsidy, or have grants." Publishes about 50 titles annually. Photos and/or illustrations are generally discussed with the author after ms is received. Photocopied submissions OK. Reports in 2-4 weeks. SASE. Free book catalog.
Nonfiction: "We publish books of all sorts and kinds and are willing to consider any ms, but are not interested in fiction." Query first.
Recent Titles: *Fundamentals of Applied Industrial Management*, by J. Glasser (educational); *Alaska–Not for a Woman*, by M. Carey (autobiographical); *House Plants That Really Grow*, by E.S. Parcher (handbook).

CHARLES T. BRANFORD CO., Box 41, 28 Union St., Newton Centre MA 02159. (617)244-6009. Editor-in-Chief: Ms. I. F. Jacobs. Hardcover and paperback originals (80%) and reprints

(20%). 10% royalty; no advance. Publishes about 10 titles annually. Photocopied submissions OK. Reports in 2 weeks. SASE. Free book catalog.
Nonfiction: Hobbies, how-to, recreation, self-help. Query first.

GEORGE BRAZILLER, INC., 1 Park Ave., New York NY 10016. Offers standard 10-12½-15% royalty contract. Advance varies, depending on author's reputation and nature of book. No unsolicited mss. Reports in 6 weeks. Enclose return postage.
General Fiction and Nonfiction: Publishes fiction and nonfiction; literature, art, philosophy, history, science.

BRASCH & BRASCH, PUBLISHERS, 220A W. 'B' St., Ontario CA 91762. (714)984-4114. Editorial Director: Walter M. Brasch, Ph.D. Publishes hardcover and paperback originals. Published 1 title in 1977, 5 in 1978; will do 10-15 in 1979. "We have full and complete marketing plans developed for every book; the nature of the book determines the means of primary marketing. But, we are aggressive in promotion of works, and will use every trick we can to get sales. It is only when we get creative in our marketing that everyone benefits." 10-12½-15% royalty. Simultaneous and photocopied submissions OK. Reports in 2 weeks on queries, 4 weeks on sample chapters, 2 months on complete mss. SASE. Book catalog for SASE.
Nonfiction: "We are especially interested in books written by journalists on topics involving society and the role of the person in society. In this aspect, we are open to many kinds of manuscripts. The writings of Lafcadio Hearn, Mark Twain, Tom Wolfe, Jimmy Breslin, John Hershey, and others who view the American scene are guidelines on topics. The ms should reflect careful research, and should be exceptionally well-written. Within this scope, there is a wide latitude of topics. No cookbooks, how-to books, crafts, sports, religious or travel material." Query or submit outline/synopsis and sample chapters. Recently published *The Buffalo Pope,* by S. Longstreet (historical); and *If Duck Droppings Fall on Your Head,* by F.P. Yariv (humor/satire).
Fiction: "We will publish at least one science fiction title per year, and at least two novels. The SciFi book *must* reflect society through a thorough comprehension of the human process of interaction. We are *not* interested in science fiction fantasy, but in SciFi as a means to understanding the present, and the human condition. Our novels must have well-developed plots that also reflect deep studies of the human condition, as seen through individuals in the novel. We are not interested in novels that 'go nowhere' or are merely stream-of-consciousness attempts to explain what probably can't be explained anyway. We would also like to see fiction that deals with Jewish themes. Our fiction must have a certain 'power' within it; a power to influence and make readers think." No westerns, mysteries, gothics, or romances. Recently published *Then, Now, and Forever,* by J. Rapisardi (autobiography); and *Time Span,* by B. Diamond (science fiction).

BREVET PRESS, INC., 519 W. 10th St., Box 1404, Sioux Falls SD 57101. Editor-in-Chief: Donald R. Mackintosh. Managing Editor: Peter E. Reid. Hardcover and paperback originals (67%) and reprints (33%). Specializes in business management, history, recipes, place names, historical marker series, fiction. 5% royalty; advance averages $1,000. Query; "after query detailed instructions will follow if we are interested." Send copies if photos/illustrations are to accompany ms. Simultaneous and photocopied submissions OK. Reports in 1-2 months. SASE. Free book catalog.
Nonfiction: Publishes Americana (L.S. Plucker, editor); business (D. P. Mackintosh, editor); cookbooks, cooking and foods (Peter Reid, editor); history (B. Mackintosh, editor); and technical books (Peter Reid, editor). Recently published *Illinois Historical Markers and Sites* (nonfiction historical series); and *Challenge,* by R. Karolevitz (history).
Fiction: Publishes historical books (T.E. Kakonis, editor). Recently published *The Thresher,* by H. Krause (historical fiction).

BRICK HOUSE PUBLISHING CO., Church Hill, Harrisville NH 03450. (603) 827-3406. Editorial Director: Jack D. Howell. Publishes hardcover and paperback originals. Published 2 titles in 1977, 3 in 1978; will do 5 in 1979. 7-10% royalty; "negotiable" advance. Photocopied submissions OK. Reports in 4 weeks. SASE. Free book catalog.
Nonfiction: Trade paperbacks generally in the $6-10 range. Alternative sources of energy material; "and would like to diversify into other how-to and alternative lifestyle books. We will consider any quality nonfiction trade material." Recently published *The Solar Home Book,* by B. Anderson/M. Riordan; and *Solar Heated Buildings of North America: 120 Outstanding Examples,* by W. Shurcliff.

***BRIGHAM YOUNG UNIVERSITY PRESS**, University Press Bldg., Provo UT 84602. Director: Ernest L. Olson. Managing Editor: John Drayton. Publishes hardcover and paperback originals (85%) and reprints (15%). Published 22 titles in 1977, 26 in 1978; will do 28 in 1979. "We subsidy publish 15% of our books. If a book has scholarly merit but little potential for repaying the cost of publication, we encourage the author to seek a subsidy from an institution or foundation." Royalties are based on estimated market potential, ranging 0-15%; no advance. Reports in 3-6 weeks. SASE. Free book catalog.
Nonfiction: Scholarly nonfiction, textbooks, and high-level popularizations. "We are interested in high-quality work from any discipline, but we focus mainly on Western regional studies, elementary education, outdoor recreation, and the social sciences, especially anthropological studies dealing with the American Indian. No length preferences. Query. Recently published *Indeh ("The Dead"): Reminiscences of an Apache,* by E. Ball; *Walk on the North Side,* by W. Primrose (music); and *An American Crusade: The Life of Charles Waddell Chesnutt,* by F. Keller (history).
Fiction and Poetry: "We publish an average of 1 book of poetry or short stories annually. We have not published a novel. We do not publish children's or juvenile literature."

BROADMAN PRESS, 127 Ninth Ave., N., Nashville TN 37234. Editor-in-Chief: Thomas L. Clark. Publishes hardcover and paperback originals (85%) and reprints (15%). Specializes in religious publishing (conservative, evangelical, Protestant viewpoint). 10% royalty for original adult hardcover; 5% for original paperbacks; no advance. Published 96 titles in 1977, and 1978; will do 100 in 1979. State availability of photos and/or illustrations to accompany ms. Reports in 1-2 months. SASE.
Nonfiction: Publishes adult religious books (William J. Fallis, editor) and children's religious books (Grace Allred, editor). Query. Recently published *A Migrant with Hope,* by E. Newby (inspirational autobiography); *The Magic of J.B.,* by C. Mays (juvenile fiction); and *I Want My Church to Grow,* by C.B. Hogue (church leadership).
Fiction: Very limited interest in religious fiction (J.S. Johnson, editor).

BROMBACHER BOOKS, 691 S. 31st St., Richmond CA 94804. (415)232-5380. Editor-in-Chief: John C. Tullis. Paperback originals (95%); paperback reprints (5%). Specializes in gardening (how-to) books. Royalty of 4% of retail price. "We also contract by the assignment for a flat, one-time, payment." State availability of photos and/or illustrations to accompany ms, or send contact sheet. Reports in 2-4 weeks. SASE. Free book catalog.
Nonfiction: Publishes books on business, (jobs/employment); cookbooks, cooking and foods; how-to (gardening, building, cooking); reference. Submit outline/synopsis and sample chapters. Recently published *Ferns For Your Home,* by Cayford; and *Cacti and Other Succulents,* by Meadow.

WILLIAM C. BROWN CO., PUBLISHERS, 2460 Kerper Blvd., Dubuque IA 52001. Publisher: Richard C. Crews. Royalties vary. Query first. Enclose return postage.
Textbooks: College textbooks.

BUCKNELL UNIVERSITY PRESS, Lewisburg PA 17837. (717)524-3674. Director: Mills F. Edgerton Jr. Associate Director: Cynthia Fell. Publishes hardcover originals. Publishes 15 titles/year. 10% royalty; no advance. Photocopied submissions OK. Reports in 3 months, "sooner if rejected." SASE. Free book catalog.
Nonfiction: Scholarly books, especially in the humanities and social sciences. No highly technical scientific or mathematical manuscripts, textbooks, general readership books, fiction, or poetry. "We publish only scholarly books written by and for the academic professional." Query; "we prefer to begin with a letter of inquiry, but once we have expressed an interest in a particular proposal, we require a complete and finished manuscript." Recently published *Cosmic Satire in the Contemporary Novel,* by J. Tilton; *The Later Philosophy of Schelling,* by R. Brown; and *H.G. Wells & Modern Science Fiction,* by D. Suvin/R. Philmus.

BUSINESS WEEK, McGraw-Hill Publications, Inc., 1221 Avenue of the Americas, 40th floor, New York NY 10020. Editorial Director: Lincoln Platt. Senior Editor: Steve M. Cohen. Publishes hardcover and paperback originals (90%) and reprints (10%). Published 4 titles in 1978; will do 6 in 1979. "Financial arrangements are made individually." Simultaneous and photocopied submissions OK. Reports in 3 weeks. SASE. Book catalog from McGraw-Hill, Inc.
Nonfiction: "*Business Week* is interested in manuscripts which appeal to the business man and woman. Mss should contribute to knowledge in a professional way. An emphasis on 'personal'

business as well as strictly financial and business books. Submit outline/synopsis and sample chapters. Recently published *Executive Health: How to Live Without Stress*, by P. Goldberg (informative look at health and well being, zeroing in on the role corporations can play to advance the health of their executives).

***C.S.S. PUBLISHING CO.**, 628 S. Main St., Lima OH 45804. (419) 227-1818. Editor-in-Chief: Wesley T. Runk. Managing Editor: Jon L. Joyce. Paperback originals. Specializes in religious books. 4-10% royalty; no advance. Subsidy publishers ½ of 1% of books. Subsidy publishing is offered "to all whose mss we reject, but we do not offer marketing for any ms outside our categories." Published 60 titles in 1977, 60 in 1978; will do 50 in 1979. Markets by direct mail and bookstores. Submit complete ms. Simultaneous submissions OK. Reports in 2-4 months. SASE. Free book catalog.

Nonfiction: "We publish titles geared to helping members of the clergy and lay leaders of all denominations in the work of their parishes. Our titles are practical helps to these leaders: worship resourses, sermon books, dramas for church use, stewardship and evangelism materials, youth programming materials, Bible study guides, children's sermon stories, pastoral care resources, and multimedia sermons and stories. Generally, the more creative and contemporary the ms is, the more likely we are to offer a contract. Length may vary from a 12-page drama to a 150-page book of sermons. Clarity and creativity should be the first consideration." Recently published *Holy Ballyhoo,* by O. Arnold (church public relations); *Wings of the Spirit,* by J. Weekley (worship); and *When Jesus Exaggerated,* by H. Sheets (sermons).

CAMARO PUBLISHING COMPANY, P.O. Box 90430, Los Angeles CA 90009. (213)837-7500. Editor-in-Chief: Garth W. Bishop. Publishes hardcover and paperback originals. "Every contract is different. Many books are bought outright." Published 5 titles last year. Query. SASE.

Nonfiction: Books on travel, food, wine and health. Recently published *Total Mind Power: How to use the Other 90% of Your Mind,* by D.L. Wilson, M.D.

CAMBRIDGE UNIVERSITY PRESS, 32 E. 57th St., New York NY 10022. Editor-in-Chief: Walter Lippincott. Publishes hardcover and paperback originals. Offers 10% list worldwide royalty contract; 6% on paperbacks. No advance. Published 350 titles in 1976 in the U.S. and England. Query first. Reports in 2 weeks to 6 months. Enclose return postage.

Nonfiction and Textbooks: Sociology, economics, psychology, upper-level textbooks, academic trade, scholarly monographs, biography, history, music. Looking for academic excellence in all work submitted. Department Editors: Ken Werner (science), Steven Fraser (economics, economic history, American history, social and political theory).

CANADIAN MUSEUMS ASSOCIATION, 331 Cooper St., Suite 400, Ottawa, Ontario, Canada K2P 0G5. (613)233-5653. Editorial Director: Barbara Riley. Senior Editor: Gary Sirois. Publishes hardcover and paperback originals. Published 9 titles in 1977, 3-4 in 1978. 10% royalty; no advance. Simultaneous submissions OK. Reports in 2-3 months. SASE. Free book catalog.

Nonfiction: Must be related to the museum and art gallery field, primarily Canadian. Museology, museography, care of collections, security, environmental control, museum architecture, exhibition care and design, cataloguing and registration, conservation methods, glossaries of terminology, staff training, extension and educational services, and technical skills. "Serious material only. Primarily concerned with the Canadian scene, with a view to the international market." Submit outline/synopsis and sample chapters. Consult Chicago *Manual of Style.* Recently published *Handbook for the Travelling Exhibitionist,* by V. Dickenson/B. Tyler; *Fellows Lecture,* by E. Turner; and *Cataloguing Military Uniforms,* by D. Ross/R. Chartrand.

CAPRA PRESS, 631 State St., Santa Barbara CA 93101. Editor-in-Chief: Noel Young. Publishes hardcover and paperback originals. Specializes in documentary lifestyle and short fiction books. 8% royalty; advance averages $1,000. Published 15 titles in 1978. State availability of photos and/or illustrations to accomany ms. Simultaneous submissions OK "if we are told where else it has been sent." Reports in 2-4 weeks. SASE. Book catalog for SASE.

Nonfiction: Publishes western contemporary nonfiction (30,000 words); biography (30,000 words); how-to; and nature books. Submit outline/synopsis and sample chapters. Recently published *Guns, Gold and Caravans,* by R. Easton (biography); *Sweat,* by M. Aalund (health/history); and *The Toilet Papers,* by S. VanderRyn.

Fiction: Publishes fantasy (like Peter Beagle); and occasional short stories. Query.

Special Needs: Noel Young Books (selected shorter works voicing the interests and concerns of America). Length not to exceed 25,000 words.

CAREER INSTITUTE, Division of Singer Communications, 1500 Cardinal Dr., Little Falls NJ 07424. (201)256-4512. Editor: Don Bolander. Publishes hardcover and paperback originals. Publishes 30-50 titles/year. Pays in royalties, or more often, in outright purchase, "which varies with size and complexity of project." No advance. Simultaneous and photocopied submissions OK. SASE. Reports in 2-4 weeks. Free book catalog.
Nonfiction: "Primarily self-study education materials or programs, or how-to-do-it books (i.e., photography, locksmithing, dress design, interior decorating, and similar subjects). Also reading programs for children and adults." Query or submit complete ms. Recently published *The Dr. Bruno Furst Memory Course*; *Automotive Locksmithing Handbook*; and *The Encyclopedia of Photography*.

CAREER PUBLISHING, INC., Box 5486, Orange CA 92667. (714)997-0130. Senior Editor: S. Michele McFadden. Publishes paperback originals. Published 14 titles in 1977, 19 in 1978; will do 24 in 1979. 10% royalty; no advance. Simultaneous (if so informed with names of others to whom submissions have been sent) and photocopied submissions OK. Reports in 1-2 months. SASE. Book catalog for 25¢.
Nonfiction: "Textbooks should provide core upon which class curriculum can be based: textbook, workbook or kit with 'hands-on' activities and exercises, and teacher's guide. Should incorporate modern and effective teaching techniques. Should lead to a job objective. We also publish support materials for existing courses, and are open to unique, marketable ideas with schools in mind. Reading level should be controlled appropriately—usually 8th-9th grade equivalent for vocational school and community college level courses. Any sign of sexism or racism will disqualify the work. No career awareness masquerading as career training." Submit outline/synopsis and sample chapters or complete ms. Recently published *Medical Office Management*, by G.E. Bonito (allied health textbook); *Medical Sound-Alikes*, by L. Rowe; and *Growing Pains*, by A. Frigone (juvenile self-help).

CARMA PRESS, Box 12633, St. Paul MN 55112. Editorial Director: Florence Nelson. Publishes paperback originals. Published 2 titles in 1977. Pays in outright purchase, $50-100; no advance. Photocopied submissions OK. Reports in 1-3 weeks. SASE.
Nonfiction: "We are looking for material in one area only: help for the non-professional teacher of adults. Our recent publication *Yes You Can Teach!* deals with teaching in general. Now we'd like to get more specific. We'd like to see various subject areas (eg. how to teach crafts, astrology, real estate, writing, etc.). Another possibility is how-to teach demonstration, lecture and discussion-type subjects. The key word is *how-to*. We need to see techniques, problem situations, how to construct and use teaching materials, etc. No theory—just plain, practical how-to. Our manuals contain 20-60 pages." Query; include 1 page for writing style and short outline. Recently published *Yes You Can Teach!*, by F. Nelson.

CATHOLIC TRUTH SOCIETY, 38/40 Eccleston Square, London, England SW1V 1PD. (01)834-4392. Editorial Director: David Murphy. Publishes hardcover and paperback originals (70%) and reprints (30%). Published 38 titles in 1977, 40 in 1978; will do 40 in 1979. Pays in outright purchase of $50-400; no advance. Simultaneous and photocopied submissions OK. Reports in 4 weeks. SASE. Free book catalog.
Nonfiction: 1) Books dealing with how to solve problems in personal relationships, parenthood, teen-age, widow-hood, sickness and death, especially drawing on Christian and Catholic tradition for inspiration; 2) simple accounts of points of interest in Catholic faith, for non-Catholic readership; and 3) books of prayer and devotion. Query, submit outline/synopsis and sample chapters, or submit complete ms. Recently published *Nuclear Energy–A Christian Concern*, by S. Triolo (phamphlet to draw attention to moral and ecological danger); *The Charismatic Prayer Meeting*, by A.D. Parry, O.S.B. (an account of features of this new movement); and *Margaret Clitheron*, by P. Casaman, S.J. (illustrated biography of a 16th century R.C. martyr).

CATHOLIC UNIVERSITY OF AMERICA PRESS, 620 Michigan Ave., N.E., Washington DC 20064. (202)635-5052. Manager: Miss Marian E. Goode. 10% royalty. Query first with sample chapter plus outline of entire work, along with curriculum vita, including a list of previous publications. Reports in 60 days. Enclose return postage.
Nonfiction: Publishes history, biography, languages and literature, philosophy, religion, church-state relations, social studies. Length: 100,000 to 500,000 words. Recently published *Walter George Smith*, by T.A. Bryson; *Christian Sacrifice*, by R.J. Daly; and *Events, Reference and Logical Form*, by R.M. Martin.

***CAVEMAN PUBLICATIONS LTD.**, Box 1458, Dunedin, New Zealand. Editor-in-Chief: Trevor Reeves. Hardcover and paperback originals (80%) and reprints (20%). 10% royalty; advance depends on circumstances. Subsidy publishes 50% of books "from government grants only, *not* from authors". Publishes 5 titles a year. Photocopied submissions OK. Reports in 1-2 months. Enclose International Reply Coupons. Free book catalog.
Nonfiction: Publishes books on the environment, conservation, energy systems; technical, nature, poetry, self-help, erotica, how-to; cookbooks, cooking and foods; economics, hobbies, medicine and psychiatry; politics, music, science, humor, photography, art. Query first.
Fiction: Publishes experimental, fantasy, erotica, humorous, confession and science fiction. Query first.
Recent Titles: *Body Needs,* by S. Monson (cookbook), *Hospital Shock,* by A. Clark (medicine).

THE CAXTON PRINTERS, LTD., P.O. Box 700, Caldwell ID 83605. Publisher: Gordon Gipson. Pays royalties of 10%; advance is negotiable. Published 7 titles last year. Catalog available on request. Query before submitting ms. Publisher does not pass on excerpts or synopses, only complete mss. Reports in 6 to 8 weeks. Enclose return postage.
Americana and Politics: Publishes adult books of nonfiction, Western Americana or occasionally of conservative political nature. No fiction, scientific mss. Length: 40,000 words and up. Recently published *Bugles, Banners and War Bonnets,* by E.L. Reedstrom; and *Sawtooth Tales,* by D. d'Easumo.

CELESTIAL ARTS, 231 Adrian Rd., Millbrae CA 94030. (415)692-4500. Editor-in-Chief: David Morris. Paperbook originals and reprints. Minimum standard royalty payment schedule; no advance. Published 41 titles in 1977, 40 in 1978. Send sample prints and/or state availability of photos and/or artwork to illustrate ms. Simultaneous and photocopied submissions OK. Reports in 1-2 months. SASE. Free book catalog.
Nonfiction: Publishes Americana, art, biography; cookbooks, cooking and foods; erotica, history, hobbies, how-to, humor, medicine and psychiatry; psychology, self-help and sociology books. Query first or submit outline/synopsis, addressed to Gail Hynes. Recently published *To the Edges of the Universe,* by D.P. DeNevi; and *The Fern Book,* by M. Crittenden.
Fiction: Publishes erotica, fantasy and science fiction. Query first or submit outline/synopsis, addressed to Gail Hynes. Recently published *Jacob Atabet: A Speculative Fiction,* by M. Murphy.

***CENTURY HOUSE, INC.**, Watkins Glen NY 14891. Editor: John C. Freeman. Standard royalty contract. Preservation Press, related to Century House, does some subsidy publishing. "Preservation Press will report on such publication costs and related distribution problems if such requests accompany mss." SASE.
Americana and Hobbies: Publishes Americana and books on American decorative arts: history, historical biography, American arts, books on antiques and other collector subjects; hobby handbooks. Pictorial preferred. No fiction
Recent Titles: *Creative Doll Making,* by D. Gottilly; *Matchcovers: A Guide to Collecting,* by E. Rancier (hobbies) and *Wish You Were Here: Centennial Guide to Postcard Collecting,* by Dr. L. Freeman (hobbies).

CHARTER HOUSE PUBLISHERS, INC., 2121 Belcourt Ave., Nashville TN 37212. (615)297-4615. Editorial Director: Denise Jones. Senior Editor: Carolyn Aylor. Publishes hardcover and paperback reprints (50%). Published 10 titles in 1977, 28 in 1978; will do 50 in 1979. 10-15% royalty; advance averages $500-1,500. Simultaneous and photocopied submissions OK. Reports in 3 months. SASE. Free book catalog.
Nonfiction: "Style and treatment would vary with topics, but basically, popular, easy-reading, direct style—always keeping the reader in mind." Publishes how-to; cookbooks; self-help and travel. No religious material. Query or submit outline/synopsis and sample chapters. Recently published *Winning,* by Morelli/Roth (self-help); *Death by Prescription,* by Siler (lay medicine); and *California Quake,* by Meyer (popular geology).
Fiction: Adventure; science fiction; mysteries; and juvenile material. Query. Recently published *Fifty,* by Kern; and *60 Hours of Darkness,* by Sederberg.

CHATEAU PUBLISHING INC., Box 20432, Herndon Station, Orlando FL 32814. (305)898-1641. Editor-in-Chief: Marcia Roen. Managing Editor: Julie Currie. Hardcover originals. 10-12½-15% royalty; no advance. Published 3 titles in 1977. State availability of photos and/or illustrations to accompany ms. Photocopied submissions OK. Reports in 2-4 weeks. SASE. Book catalog for SASE.

Nonfiction: Publishes hobbies, how-to, multimedia material, pets, poetry, politics, recreation, self help, and sports books. *No* cookbooks. Query, or submit outline/synopsis and sample chapters. Recently published *Europe–The Two-Wheeled Adventure,* by P. Philcox/B. Boe; and *Hizzoner the Mayor,* by C.T. Langford.

THE CHATHAM PRESS, a subsidiary of Devin-Adair, 143 Sound Beach Ave., Old Greenwich CT 06310. Editor: Devan A. Garrity. Publishes hardcover and paperback originals, reprints, and anthologies. "Standard book contract does not always apply if the book is heavily illustrated. Average advance is low." Published 5 titles last year. Will send a catalog to a writer on request. Send query with outline and sample chapter. Reports in 2 weeks. SASE.
General Nonfiction, The arts, and history and biography: Publishes mostly "regional history and natural history, involving almost all regions of the US, all illustrated, with emphasis on conservation and outdoor recreation, photographic works, and the arts." Recently published *Skiing Colorado, The Soft-Hackled Fly, Green Fun, Seasons of the Salt Marsh, An Age of Flowers.*

CHILDRENS PRESS, 1224 W. Van Buren St., Chicago IL 60607. (312)666-4200. Managing Editor: Joan Downing. Offers outright purchase or small advance against royalty. Published 65 titles in 1977. Reports in 3-6 weeks. SASE.
Juveniles: Publishes fiction and nonfiction for supplementary use in elementary and secondary schools; easy picture books for early childhood and beginning readers; high interest, easy reading material. Specific categories include careers, social studies, fine art, plays, and special education. Length: 50-10,000 words. For picture books, needs are very broad. They should be geared from pre-school to grade 3. Length: 50-1,000 words. Send outline with sample chapters or complete ms for picture books. Do not send finished artwork with ms. Recently published *Golden Knights, Performers in Uniform,* by Mohn; *Where is Michael,* by Hallinan; and *My Name is Jimmy Carter,* by Behrens.

CHILTON BOOK CO., 201 King of Prussia Rd., Radnor PA 19089. (215)687-8200. Editorial Director: Alan F. Turner. Managing Editor, Automotive: John Weise. Hardcover and paperback originals. Standard royalty; negotiable advance. Published 70 titles in 1978. Simultaneous and photocopied submissions OK. Reports in 2-8 weeks. SASE. Free book catalog.
Nonfiction: Publishes books on arts and crafts (35,000 words minimum: Lydia Driscoll, senior editor). Business; cookbooks, cooking and foods; hobbies, how-to, recreation, reference, self-help, sports, technical, textbooks, current events (50,000 words minimum length; Alan F. Turner, editorial director). Query or submit outline/synopsis and sample chapters. Recently published *Menopause: A Positive Approach,* by R. Reitz (health); *The New Executive Woman,* by M.G. Williams (business); and *Tennis Equipment,* by S. Fiott (sports).

CHOSEN BOOKS, Lincoln VA 22078. (703)338-4131. Executive Director: Leonard E. LeSourd. Managing Editor: Richard Schneider. Hardcover and paperback originals. 10-12½-15% royalty; advance averages $1,000. Simultaneous submissions OK. SASE. Free book catalog for SASE.
Religion: Seeks out significant developments in the Christian world to present in dramatic book form. Wants quality books that are highly interesting as well as spiritually enriching. Length: 40,000-60,000 words. Prefers complete ms but will consider outline and sample chapters. Recently published *My Glimpse of Eternity,* by Maly; *My War with Worry,* by Thomas; and *Miracle on Death Row,* by Bradford.

CHRISTIAN HERALD BOOKS, 40 Overlook Dr., Chappaqua NY 10514. (914)769-9000. Editor-in-Chief: Gary A. Sledge. Hardcover originals. Emphasizes Christian themes. 10% royalty; advance negotiable. State availability of photos and/or illustrations to accompany ms. Simultaneous and photocopied submissions OK. Reports in 1-2 months. SASE. Book catalog for SASE.
Nonfiction: Publishes religious books. Must have Christian evangelical slant or theme. Query or submit outline/synopsis and sample chapters. Recently published *This Too Shall Pass,* by L. Lance with G. Sledge; *Hagas,* by L. Henderson; and *Reaching For God,* by E. Mitson.

CHRONICLE BOOKS, 870 Market St., San Francisco CA 94102. A division of the Chronicle Publishing Co., publisher of *The San Francisco Chronicle.* Editor: R.C. Schuettge. Publishes hardcover and paperback originals, reprints, and anthologies. Offers standard royalty contract; advance varies. Published 15 titles in 1977. Send query with outline and sample chapter. "We prefer outline and sample chapter to complete ms." Reports in 1 month. Enclose return postage.
General Nonfiction: Current titles are in the fields of animals, architecture, conservation, food,

history, the outdoors, sports, and travel. Length: 60,000 to 100,000 words. Recently published *Good Life in Hard Times,* by Flamm (San Francisco history); *Historic Country Inns,* by Crain; and *Cannibal Soup,* by Thompson (lifestyle).

CITADEL PRESS, 120 Enterprise Ave., Secaucus NJ 07094. (212)736-0007. Editorial Director: Allan J. Wilson. Publishes hardcover and paperback originals (40%) and paperback reprints (60%). Published 43 titles in 1977, 50 in 1978. 10% royalty on hardcover, 5-7% on paperback; advance averages $1,000. Simultaneous and photocopied submissions OK. Reports in 2 months. SASE.
Nonfiction: Biography; film; psychology; humor; and history. Query. Recently published *Moe Howard and the Three Stooges,* by M. Howard (filmography); *The Great American Amusement Parks,* by G. Kyriazi (Americana); and *Documentary History of the Negro People in the U.S.,* by H. Aptheker (history).

***ARTHUR H. CLARK CO.**, Box 230, Glendale CA 91209. Editorial Director: Robert A. Clark. Publishes hardcover originals. Published 8 titles in 1977, 6 in 1978; will do 8 in 1979. "We market by catalog and direct mail." Subsidy publishes 24% of books based on "marketability of book's content." 10% royalty; no advance. Photocopied submissions OK. Reports in 2 months. SASE. Free book catalog.
Nonfiction: "We are publishers of documentary source material in western American history. Mss should be scholarly and well-written. Secondary historical accounts of historical events are acceptable, if documented and treated in an objective manner. Masters theses and Doctoral dissertations are welcome as first drafts for consideration. No semi-novelistic treatments of history." Query or submit outline/synopsis and sample chapters. Recently published *Recollections of the Flathead Mission,* by G. Mengarini (1840 missionary memoir); and *Man-Made Disaster,* by C.F. Outland.

CLARKE, IRWIN & CO., LTD., 791 St. Clair Ave., W., Toronto, Ontario, Canada M6C 1B8. Hardcover and paperback originals (95%) and reprints (5%). Specializes in Canadian subjects. Royalty schedule varies; minimum of 10%. Publishes about 20 titles a year. Submit outline/synopsis and sample chapters or complete ms. Must be typed double-spaced. "Don't send only copy." Send samples of prints for illustration. Photocopied submissions OK. Reports in 1-2 months. SASE.
Nonfiction: Publishes juveniles and books on Canadiana, art, biography, history, how-to, music, nature, poetry, politics, recreation, self-help, sports, textbooks, travel. Recently published *No Safe Place,* by W. Troyer; *Ken Danby,* by P. Duval (art); and *The Comedians,* by P. Morley (biography).
Fiction: Publishes adventure, historical, humorous, and mainstream books. Recently published *The Wars,* by T. Findley; *Shrewsbury,* by J. Brown; and *Holiday in the Woods,* by F. Bird.

CLIFF'S NOTES, INC., Box 80728, Lincoln NE 68501. (402)477-6971. Editor: Harry Kaste. Publishes paperback originals. Outright purchase, with full payment upon acceptance of ms. Free book catalog. Query. Contributors must be experienced teachers with appropriate special interests; usually have Ph.D. degree. Reports in 4 weeks. Enclose return postage.
Nonfiction: Currently expanding a line of paperback texts in the field of speech and hearing handicaps. Also occasional trade or textbooks of special merit.

COBBLESMITH, Box 191, RFD 1, Freeport ME 04032. Editor-in-Chief: Gene H. Boyington. Hardcover and paperback originals (90%); hardcover and paperback reprints (10%). Royalty of 8½% of list price. No advance. Simultaneous and photocopied submissions OK. SASE. Reports in 2-4 months. Free book catalog.
Nonfiction: Americana and art topics (especially New England and antiques); law (popular, self-help); cookbooks, cooking and foods; gardening, psychology (applied—not theory); how-to (home and homestead crafts); philosophy (educational and new developments); sociology (applied—not theory); material on alternative life styles; nature, travel (offbeat guide books); self-help. Query. "Unsolicited mss are often treated as though only a little better than unsolicited third class mail."
Recent Titles: *Wood Cook's Cookbook,* by S.D. Haskell (cooking); *Practical Hooked Rugs* by S.H. Rex (how-to, crafts); *Do Your Own Divorce in North Carolina* by M.H. McGee (self-help/law).

COLES PUBLISHING CO., LTD., 90 Ronson Dr., Rexdale, Ontario, Canada M9W 1C1. (416)249-9121. Vice President/Editorial Director: Jeffrey Cole. Publishes hardcover and paper-

back originals (10%) and reprints (90%). Published 200 titles in 1977, 300 in 1978; will do 350 in 1979. "We are a subsidiary company of 'Coles, The Book People,' a chain of 150 bookstores throughout North America." Pays an outright purchase, $500 to $2500; advance averages $500. Simultaneous and photocopied submissions OK. Reports in 2-3 weeks. SASE. Free book catalog.
Nonfiction: "We publish in the following areas: language, science, math, pet care, gardening, cookbooks, medicine and health, occult, business, reference, technical and do-it-yourself, crafts and hobbies, antiques, games, and sports." No philosophy, psychology, sociology, religion, history or biography. Submit outline/synopsis and sample chapters. Recently published *Guide to Canadian Business Law*, by T. Rocchi; *The Ed Allen Exercise Book*, by E. Allen; and *Landlord/Tenant Law in Ontario*, by P. Brace.

COLGATE UNIVERSITY PRESS, Hamilton NY 13346. Editor-in-Chief: R. L. Blackmore. Publishes hardcover originals, reprints, and an annual journal about the Powys family of writers and their circle. No other subjects at this time. Offers standard royalty contract: "rarely an advance." Published 4 titles last year. Free book catalog. Will consider photocopied submissions. Query first. Reports in 1 month. Enclose return postage.
Biography: "Books by or about the Powyses: John Cowper Powys, T. F. Powys, Llewelyn Powys. Our audience is general and scholarly." Length: open.

COLLECTOR BOOKS, Box 3009, Paducah KY 42001. Editor-in-Chief: Steve Quertermous. Hardcover and paperback originals. 5% royalty of retail; no advance. Published 25-30 titles in 1977. Send prints or transparencies if illustrations are to accompany ms. SASE. Reports in 2-4 weeks. Free book catalog.
Nonfiction: "We only publish books on antiques and collectibles. We require our authors to be very knowledgeable in their respective fields and have access to a large representative sampling of the particular subject concerned." Query. Recently published *Collector's Encyclopedia of Depression Glass,* by G. Florence; and *Madame Alexander Collector Dolls,* by P. Smith.

COLLIER MACMILLAN CANADA, LTD., 1125 B Leslie St., Don Mills, Ont., Canada. Published both originals and reprints in hardcover and paperback. Advance varies, depending on author's reputation and nature of book. Published 35 titles last year. Reports in 6 weeks. Enclsoe S.A.E. and International Reply Coupons.
General Nonfiction: "Topical subjects of special interest to Canadians." Query.
Textbooks: Mathematics, language arts, and reading: mainly texts conforming to Canadian curricular requirements. Also resource books, either paperback or pamphlet for senior elementary and high schools. Length: open.

COLORADO ASSOCIATED UNIVERSITY PRESS, University of Colorado, 1424 Fifteenth St., Boulder CO 80309. (303)492-7191. Editor: Margaret C. Shipley. Publishes hardcover and paperback originals. Offers standard 10-12½-15% royalty contract; "no advances." Free book catalog. Will consider photocopied submissions "if not sent simultaneously to another publisher." Query first. Reports in 3 months. Enclose return postage.
Nonfiction: "Scholarly and regional." Length: 250 to 500 ms pages. Recently published *Solar Output,* by White (scholarly); *Ford White House,* by Casserly; and *Yellowstone Story,* by Haines (regional).

***COLUMBIA PUBLISHING CO., INC.**, Frenchtown NJ 08825. (201)996-2769. Editorial Director: Bernard Rabb. Publishes hardcover originals. Published 2 titles in 1977, 6 in 1978; will do 10 in 1979. Subsidy publishes 15% of books. "If the title is a good one, in our editorial opinion, we will subsidy publish the work using our own imprint and will place it into national distribution. It will be subsidy published if, in our view, it is not expected to earn a profit. We also produce some subsidy-published titles not bearing our imprint and not placed into our distribution channels. These books are produced for a fee and are shipped, in full, to the author for distribution as the author sees fit." 10-12½-15% royalty. Simultaneous and photocopied submissions OK. Reports in 3-4 months. SASE.
Nonfiction: "We emphasize the practical. We have no interest in 'fad' books." Solid cookbooks; business; classical music; recreation; biography (well-known persons only); popular psychology; "muck-raking" books that are carefully researched and meticulously documented; and health-medicine books for a general audience. No juvenile material. Submit outline/synopsis and sample chapters. "Sample chapters should be interior chapters, as opposed to an introduction, preface, forward, or bibliography. Send minimum of 2 chapters plus itemized outline. If the book is to be illustrated, 5 samples are required." Recently published *The*

Backyard Wilderness, by V. Abraitys (nature, ecology); *Back to Nature in Canoes: A Guide to American Waters,* by R. Esslen (recreation, guidebook); and *Twenty Years of Community Medicine,* by L. Wescott, et al (medical care).
Fiction: "Serious, quality fiction." No genre fiction or poetry. Submit complete ms. Recently published *Golcz,* by W. Herrick.

COLUMBIA UNIVERSITY PRESS, 562 W. 113th St., New York NY 10025. (212)678-6777. Editor-in-Chief: John D. Moore. Publishes hardcover and paperback originals. Royalty contract to be negotiated. Published 110 titles in 1977. Query. SASE.
Nonfiction: "General interest nonfiction of scholarly value."
Scholarly: Books in the fields of literature, philosophy, fine arts, Oriental studies, history, social sciences, science, law. Recently published *The Creation of Tomorrow: Fifty Years of Magazine Science Fiction,* by P. Carter; and *Christopher Isherwood: Myth and Anti-myth,* by P. Piazza.

COMMONERS' PUBLISHING, 296 Clarence St., Ottawa, Ontario, Canada K1N 5R3. (613)233-1225. Editorial Director: Glenn Cheriton. Senior Editor: Robert Craig. Publishes hardcover and paperback originals. Published 6 titles in 1977, 8 in 1978; will do 10 in 1979. "We are strongly dependent on local market and library sales." 10% royalty; no advance. Simultaneous and photocopied submissions OK. Reports in 4 months. SASE. Book catalog for SASE.
Nonfiction: Self-help; alternative lifestyles; and crafts books. Submit complete ms. Recently published *Ottawa Valley Peoples' Yellow Pages,* by Nichiels, Brecks, et al (guidebook); and *Apple II,* by Cheriton (historical).
Fiction: Canadian short stories, plays and fiction; also full-length novels with Canadian themes, locations, and authors; and Canadian poetry. Submit complete ms. Recently published *Stations,* by P. White (poetry); *Hard Road,* by G. Forbes (humor); and *The Buffalo Trails,* by E.L. Frame (novel).

COMPUTER SCIENCE PRESS, INC., 9125 Fall River Lane, Potomac MD 20854. (301)299-2040. Editorial Director: Arthur D. Friedman. Publishes hardcover originals. Published 5 titles in 1977, 6 in 1978; will do 6 in 1979. Pays in royalties; no advance. Simultaneous and photocopied submissions OK. Reports in 3 weeks. SASE. Free book catalog.
Nonfiction: "Technical books in all aspects of computer science and computer engineering. Both text and reference books. Will also consider public appeal 'trade' books in computer science." Query or submit complete ms. "We prefer 3 copies of manuscripts." Recently published *Algorithms: Design and Analysis,* by Horowitz/Sahni (college text); and *Computer Aided Design of Digital Systems, Volume III,* by W. van Cleemput (reference bibliography).

CONCORDIA PUBLISHING HOUSE, 3558 S. Jefferson Ave., St. Louis MO 63118. Pays royalty on retail price; outright purchase in some cases. Free book catalog. Submit outline and sample chapter for nonfiction; complete ms for fiction. Reports in 3 months. Enclose return postage.
Religion, Juveniles, and Fiction: Publishes Protestant, general religious, theological books and periodicals; music works, juvenile picture and beginner books and adult fiction. "As a religious publisher, we look for mss that deal with Bible stories, Bible history, Christian missions; and mss that deal with ways that readers can apply Christian beliefs and principles to daily living. Any ms that deals specifically with theology and/or doctrine should conform to the tenets of the Lutheran Church-Missouri Synod. We suggest that, if authors have any doubt about their submissions in light of what kind of mss we want, they first correspond with us." Recently published *Theology of Concord,* by Preus; and *The Wanderers,* by Rimland.

CONDOR PUBLISHING CO., INC., 521 5th Ave., New York NY 10017. Editorial Director: Pat Connolly. Senior Editor: Carol Inouye. Publishes paperback originals and reprints. Published 14 titles in 1977, 48 in 1978; will do 52 in 1979. 6% royalty to 150,000 copies; 8% thereafter; advance averages $1,500. Simultaneous (if so notified) and photocopied submissions OK. Reports in 6-8 weeks. SASE. Book catalog for SASE.
Nonfiction: Psychology; how-to; health and nutrition; business; inspirational; self-help; and general nonfiction. No text material or poetry. Query. Recently published *The Washington Connection,* by R. Moore (investigative reporting); *A Survival Kit for a Happier Marriage,* by S. Collins Jr., M.D. (psychology); and *The Happy Heart Cookbook,* by F. Faigel, R.N. (cookbook).
Fiction: Romance novels; science fiction; mysteries; gothics; and fantasy. "Plus top-notch novels on any subject." Query. Recently published *Rotunda,* by R.S. Siegrist (suspense); *The Corruptors,* by G.G. Griffin (mystery); and *The Death Disciple,* by R. Moore (mystery).

DAVID C. COOK PUBLISHING CO., 850 N. Grove, Elgin IL 60120. (312)741-2400. Editorial Director: Lawrence P. Davis. Managing Editor: Dean Merrill. Publishes hardcover and paperback originals (90%) and paperback reprints (10%). Specializes in religious books. 6% royalty on paperbacks, 10% on hardcovers; advance "varies considerably." Query. State availability of photos and/or illustrations. Reports in 4-6 weeks. SASE. Free book catalog.
Nonfiction: Publishes juvenile, reference, religious and self-help books. All ms must pertain to religious themes. Recently published *Good News is for Sharing,* by Dr. L. Ford; *The Man Who Keeps Going to Jail,* by D. and J. Erwin (religious biography); and *The Devil's Coach,* by J. Brock/J. Gilmartin.
Fiction: "We want fiction, especially for ages 8-14, but it should have a religious theme." Recently published *Ararat,* by E. Groseclose; and *McTaggert's Promise,* by B. Palmer.

CORDOVAN CORPORATION, 5314 Bingle Rd., Houston TX 77018. (713)688-8811. Editor-in-Chief: Bob Gray. Published hardcover and paperback originals and reprints under the Cordovan Press, Horseman Books, and Fisherman Books imprints. Offers standard minimum book contract of 10-12½-15%. Published 10 titles in 1977. Marketed heavily by direct mail and through various consumer and trade periodicals. Will consider photocopied submissions. Query first or submit outline and sample chapters. Reports in 1 month. Enclose return postage.
Nonfiction: Cordovan Press, a trade book division, seeks books on Texas history for the history buff interested in Texana. Horseman Books are practical, how-to books on horse training, grooming, feeding, showing, riding, etc., either by experts in the field or as told to a writer by an expert. Fisherman Books are how-to, where-to, when-to books on fishing in Texas and/or the Southwest. Author must be noted expert on fishing, or be retelling what a noted expert told him. "The emphasis is on plain language in all of these lines. Short sentences. Make the verbs sing the song. Pungent quotes. Don't try to snow the readers; they are too sharp and already know most of the score in all areas. Use humor when it isn't forced." Length: 150 ms pages. Recently published *Rick Clunn's Championship Bass Fishing Techniques,* by R. Clunn; *Eyes of Texas Travel Guide,* by R. Miller; and *The Cowgirls,* by J.G. Roach (Americana).

CORNELL MARITIME PRESS, INC., Box 109, Cambridge MD 21613. Publisher: Robert F. Cornell. Hardcover and quality paperbacks, both originals and reprints. Payment is on regular trade publishers' royalty basis: 10% for first 5,000 copies, 12½% for second 5,000 copies, 15% on all additional. Revised editions revert to original royalty schedule. Subsidy publishing is done only in conjunction with universities. Published 10 titles last year. Free book catalog. Send queries first, accompanied by writing samples and outlines of book ideas. Reports in 2 to 4 weeks. Enclose return postage.
Marine: Nonfiction relating to marine subjects, highly technical; manuals; how-to books on any maritime subject. Recently published *Tanker Operations: A Handbook for the Ship's Officer;* and *The Deep Sea Diver: Yesterday, Today and Tomorrow.*

R.D. CORTINA CO., INC., 136 W. 52nd St., New York NY 10019. General Editor: MacDonald Brown. Pays on a fee or a royalty basis. Published 27 titles last year. Do not send unsolicited mss; send outline and sample chapter. Reports in 2 months or less.
Textbooks: Publishes language teaching textbooks for self-study and school; also publishes language teaching phonograph records and tapes. Materials of special ESL interest. Word length varies.

COURIER OF MAINE BOOKS, 1 Park Dr., Rockland ME 04841. (207)549-4401. Director: William E. Dennen. Hardcover and paperback originals (80%) paperback reprints (20%). Specializes in books about Maine only. 10% royalty; "low" advance. Published 8 titles in 1977 and 1978. Marketing is limited to people and institutions interested in Maine. Submit outline/synopsis and sample chapters. State availability of illustrations and photos. Simultaneous ("if we know about it") and photocopied submissions OK. Reports in 2-4 weeks. SASE. Free book catalog.
Nonfiction: Publishes art; biography; cookbooks, cooking and foods; economics; history; hobbies; how-to; humor; juveniles; nature; poetry; politics; recreation; reference; sociology; and travel books. All mss must pertain to Maine. Recently published *All-Maine All-Poultry,* edited by Shibles and Rogers (cookbook); *Tombstones and Paving Blocks,* by Grindle (history); and *Nature I Loved,* by Geagan.
Fiction: Adventure; historical; humorous; mainstream; and mystery books.

COWARD, McCANN & GEOGHEGAN, 200 Madison Ave., New York NY 10016. (212)576-

8900. President: John J. Geoghegan. Editor-in-Chief, adult division: Patricia B. Soliman. Editorial Director, juvenile division: Ferdinand Monjo. 5% to 10% royalties on juvenile material; for juvenile nonfiction, advance is $500 to $3,000. Unsolicited mss will be returned unread. Query the editor, who will advise whether to submit ms. Enclose return postage.
General Fiction and Nonfiction: Publishes novels, including mysteries (no westerns or salacious love stories); outstanding nonfiction of all kinds; religious, history, biography (particularly on American figures). Also interested in humor. All should have general appeal. Length: 60,000 words and up.
Juveniles: "We will look at anything. Our needs vary considerably. Want picture books for ages 4 to 12. Want nonfiction for ages 4 and up."

CRAFTSMAN BOOK COMPANY OF AMERICA, 542 Stevens Ave., Solana Beach CA 92075. (714)755-0161. Editor-in-Chief: Gary Moselle. Publishes paperback originals. Royalty of 12½ to 15% of gross revenues, regardless of quantity sold. Published 8 titles last year. "About 75% of our sales are directly to the consumer and since royalties are based on gross revenues, the actual revenue realized is maximized." Will send free catalog to writer on request. Will consider photocopied submissions. Submit outline and sample chapters. Reports in 2 weeks. Enclose return postage.
Technical: "We publish technical books and are aggressively looking for queries and outlines on manuscripts related to construction, carpentry, masonry, plumbing, civil engineering, building estimating, chemical engineering and petroleum technology. Our books are written as practical reference for professionals in their respective fields and each book should be written to answer practical questions and solve typical problems. Emphasis is on charts, graphs, illustrations, displays and tables of information. We are producing a series on how to become a construction contractor, construction estimator, etc. We can use practical, descriptive information. We don't want to see reprints of magazine articles and isolated essays which do not have the breadth or scope to warrant consideration for publication." Recently published *Building and Remodeling for Energy Savings,* by Higson; *Planning and Building the Minimum Energy Dwelling,* by Williams; and *Structures Cost Manual,* by Smith.

CRAIN BOOKS, 740 Rush St., Chicago IL 60611. Editor-in-Chief: Melvin J. Brisk. Hardcover and paperback originals. 10% royalty, "although this varies, depending on the book, its potential and the market". Makes an advance only under exceptional circumstances. Send contact sheet if photos/illustrations are to accompany ms. Simultaneous and photocopied submissions OK, "but will rarely receive priority status as compared to the exclusive submission". Reports in 2-4 months. SASE. Free book catalog.
Nonfiction: Publishes business books for the advertising and marketing professional and student, including the academic market. "We're interested in mss that have a definite communications theme, and we usually work on assignment unless the author is a professional or academician. No rehashes. We want innovative ideas that will appeal to business types looking for improvement." Recently published *100 Best Sales Promotions of 1976/77,* by W. Robinson (promotion); and *John Caples: Adman,* by G. White (advertising research).

CRANE, RUSSAK & COMPANY, INC., 347 Madison Ave., New York NY 10017. Editor-in-Chief: Ben Russak. Publishes scientific journals and scientific and scholarly books. On monographs, offers no royalty for first 1,500 copies sold, 7% on the second 2,000 copies, and 10% on all copies sold after the first 2,000. No advances. "We promote our books by direct mail to the exact market for which each book is intended." Submit outline and sample chapters. Reports in 1 month. SASE.
Technical and Reference: "We publish scientific and scholarly works at the graduate and reference level: postgraduate textbooks and reference books for scholars and research workers. Our publications also appeal to members of professional societies. We'd like to see manuscripts on large-scale systems analysis in relation to solution of large-scale social problems. But do not send any popular material or matter which is intended for sale to the general public." Length: 60,000 to 120,000 words.

CREATIVE BOOK CO., Box 214998, Sacramento CA 95821. (916)489-4390. Editor-in-Chief: Sol H. Marshall. Paperback originals. Payment by flat fee ($50-$200). Pays half on approval of outline; balance on delivery of ms. Published 20 titles in 1977; 20 in 1978; will do 12-20 in 1979. "Our catalogs and advertising go only to community organizations and educational fields. We do not use subjects in the field of commerce and industry." Send photocopies of glossy prints to accompany ms. Simultaneous and photocopied submissions OK. Reports in 2-4 weeks. SASE. Free book catalog.

Nonfiction: Publishes recreation, self-help, and textbooks. "We emphasize self-improvement for professionals in education and community organizations; public relations, administration and fund-raising for educational agencies and community organizations; adult education and gerontology. Our audience includes sophisticated lay leaders and professionals. We do not need books on 'how to run a club meeting'." Query or submit complete ms. Recently published *How to Be Your Own Publisher and Get Your Book into Print,* by P. Thompson (how-to); and *Publicize It With Pictures!,* by K. Waters.

CRESCENDO PUBLISHING CO., 200 Park Ave., S., New York NY 10003. Publishes both originals and reprints in hardcover and paperback. Offers standard 10-12½-15% royalty contract. "Advances are rare; sometimes made when we seek out an author." Published 20 titles last year. Free book catalog. Will look at queries or completed mss. SASE. Address submissions to Gerald Krimm. Reports in 4 weeks.
Music: Trade and Texts in music. Length: open.

***CRESCENT PUBLICATIONS, INC.**, 5410 Wilshire Blvd., #400, Los Angeles CA 90036. Editor-in-Chief: Joseph Lawrence. Publishes hardcover and paperback originals. Offers royalty contract "on the basis of the ms published." Does 75% subsidy publishing. Free book catalog. Will consider simultaneous submissions. Submit complete ms for fiction and nonfiction. Mss must be typed, double-spaced, on one side of paper only. Reports in 2 weeks. Enclose return postage.
Fiction, Nonfiction, Juveniles and Poetry: Publishes general trade books which are sold to book publishers and book distributors. Length: open. Also interested in Americana; politics; self-help and how-to; sports, hobbies, recreation and pets. "All subjects." Recently published *I Wonder Why,* by E.G. Klemm (poetry); *Robota,* by L. Clay (science fiction); and *How to Find a Loving Husband,* by M.S. Cagan, Ph.D. (how-to).

CRESTLINE PUBLISHING, INC., Box 48, Glen Ellyn IL 60137. (312)495-9294. Editorial Director: George H. Dammann. Publishes hardcover originals. Published 2 titles in 1977, 3 in 1978; will do 4 in 1979. Royalty varies; from $1/book sold; no advance. Simultaneous and photocopied submissions OK. Reports in 1-2 months. SASE. Free book catalog.
Nonfiction: "Our books are highly specialized and relate only to automotive history. All books are highly pictorial, arranged in either chronological or alphabetical order, and range from 320-416 pages. We are now working in 3 distinct series: automobile history by make, truck history by make, and agricultural history by type of equipment. We work hand-in-hand with the author from the start of a book through its completion, so therefore, a writer should contact us before he even begins his project. Since our books are so highly specialized in both subject matter and format, a prospective author should first check his local library for Crestline books, and study these books before contacting us. Most inquiries we get are from writers who have no idea of the type of books we publish, and consequently could not do a book in our format even if we were interested. In addition to having to have a vast knowledge of the subject upon which he wishes to write, the author also must have 2,000-5,000 illustrations to back up his work—these must either be in his possession or he must know exactly where these illustrations are and have total free access to copy them." Query. Recently published *Great American Woodies & Wagons,* by D.J. Narus; *Encyclopedia of American Cars, 1930-1942,* by J. Moloney; and *American Fire Engines Since 1900,* by W. McCall.

CRESTWOOD HOUSE, INC., Box 3427, Mankato MN 56001. (507)388-1616. Editorial Director: Karyne Jacobsen. Publishes hardcover originals. Published 17 titles in 1977, 25 in 1978; will do 35-40 in 1979. "All fees are negotiated based upon subject matter, length of publication, and additional work furnished." Occasionally offers advance. Simultaneous and photocopied submissions OK. Reports in 2-3 weeks. SASE. Free book catalog.
Nonfiction: "Crestwood House publishes only high interest, low vocabulary books for children with a reading level of grades 2-5. Our books are always published in related series of books (probably 5-10 titles per series). We do current up-to-date topics on sports, recreation, and other topics of high interest to children and young adults. Books are generally between 32-48 pages, and always include a generous number of photographs." Submit complete ms. Recently published *Bicycle Touring,* by P.B. Mohn; *Dorothy Hamill Skate to Victory,* by D. Schmitz (sports biography); and *Rodeo,* by J. Thorne.
Fiction: Same basic requirements as nonfiction. Science fiction; adventure; and sports. No material on "bears, ducks, frogs, etc." Submit complete ms. Recently published *10-5 Alaska Skip,* by B. Cunningham (CB adventure story).

THOMAS Y. CROWELL, Division of Harper & Row Publishers, 10 E. 53rd St., New York NY 10022. Send trade submissions to Acquisitions Editor; reference book submissions to Patrick Barrett; Children's book submissions to Patrick Allen. Offers standard royalty contract. Published 230 titles last year. Query first. Reports in 1-2 months. SASE.
Nonfiction, Juveniles, and Textbooks: "Trade and reference books, children's books, and college and secondary school reference books. Interested in general books of an informational nature."

CROWN PUBLISHERS, 1 Park Ave., New York NY 10016. (212)532-9200. Editor-in-Chief: Herbert Michelman. Contracts offered on basis of stature of writer, outline, subject and sample material. For juveniles, offers "10% against catalog retail price on books for older children; for picture books, 5% of the catalog retail price to the author and 5% to the artist. However, royalty scales may vary. Advance varies, depending on author's reputation and nature of book." Published 250 titles last year. Will send catalog on request. Prefers queries. Send complete ms for juvenile picture books. Address mss to department editor. Reports in 2 to 6 weeks. Enclose return postage.
General Fiction and Nonfiction: General fiction and nonfiction; pictorial histories, popular biography, science, books on decorative arts and antiques, crafts; some on music, drama and painting. Administrative Editor: Philip Winsor; Executive fiction Editor: Larry Freundlich; Arts and Crafts: Brandt Aymar; Collector's Books: Kay Pinney; Science: Paul Nadan; General nonfiction: Gig Moglen. Recently published *The Kitchen Book,* by T. Cowan (house decoration); and *The Authentic Wild West: The Outlaws,* by J.D. Horan.
Juveniles: For juvenile nonfiction for all ages, wants "contemporary issues of a social and political nature. Length depends on the book." Picture books for preschoolers to children 7 years old "should be approached in terms of telling a good story. Length depends on the book." Children's Books Editor: Norma Jean Sawicki.

CSA PRESS, Lake Rabun Rd., Lakemont GA 30552. (404)782-3931. Editorial Director: Roy Eugene Davis. Publishes hardcover and paperback originals. Publishes approximately 10 titles/year. 15% royalty based on wholesale sales; no advance. Simultaneous and photocopied submissions OK. Reports in 2 weeks. SASE. Book catalog for SASE.
Nonfiction: "We specialize in positive thinking titles, New Thought, Yoga, and all self-improvement titles." Query or submit outline/synopsis and sample chapters. Recently published *An Easy Guide to Meditation,* by R.E. Davis; *Finding the Christ,* by D. Curtis; and *Picture Yourself a Winner,* by Dr. R.E. Nichols.

CUSTOMBOOK, INCORPORATED, The Custom Bldg., South Hackensack NJ 07606. A new opportunity for writer-reporters has been developed by Custombook, Inc., nationwide producers of color editions for churches. "These limited editions are produced in conjunction with special occasions such as anniversaries, construction, renovations or for general education. As a result of major technical breakthroughs, such limited color editions are now practical for the first time. The books feature full-color photographs and the story of each church, its history, stained glass, symbolism, services, and organizations. Writers are being sought in most regions of the country to work. Recommendations are being sought from talented writers as to which churches would be the best subject for their initial Custombook. Older churches with major anniversaries (10th, 25th, 50th, 100th), new construction, or renovations (church, religious school, or convent), would be good subjects. The company will then contact the churches recommended by writers. $50 will be paid to any individual whose recommendation of a church eventually results in a Custombook. The organization will at the same time evaluate previous written efforts of this individual. If their editorial staff engages the writer to prepare the ms for the book, and the writer completes the ms himself, he will be paid $200 for his initial effort. Additional assignments may then follow from our own sources or from additional recommendations by the writer." Further details on the program are available from Mrs. Joan Curtis, Editor, at the above address.

***CYRCO PRESS, INC., PUBLISHERS**, 342 Madison Ave., New York NY 10017. (212)682-8410. Editorial Director: Benjamin Rosenzweig. Senior Editor: George Schwab. Publishes hardcover originals. Published 7 titles in 1977, 15 in 1978; will do 15 in 1979. "Our books are distributed to the trade by the Bobbs-Merrill Co., and distributed in the U.K. and Europe by Eurospan Ltd." Subsidy publishes 1-2% of books. "We do not accept subsidies from authors. Any subsidy which we have accepted has been from either a university or a nonprofit organization in the form of a co-publishing venture." 10% royalty; no advance. Simultaneous and photocopied submissions OK. Reports in 3-4 weeks. SASE. Free book catalog.

Nonfiction: Politics; history; and biography. Query. Submit introduction, table of contents, and 1-2 sample chapters. Follow Chicago *Manual of Style.* Recently published *The Politics of Defeat: America's Decline in the Middle East,* by J. Churba (political analysis); *Detente in Historical Perspective,* by G. Schwab (politics); and *The European Left,* by B. Brown (politics).

DARTNELL CORPORATION, 4660 North Ravenswood Ave., Chicago IL 60640. (312)561-4000. Editorial Director: John Steinbrink. Publishes manuals, reports, hardcovers. Royalties: sliding scale. Published 6 titles last year. Send outline and sample chapter. Reports in 4 weeks. SASE.
Business: Interested in new material on business skills and techniques in management, supervision, administration, advertising sales, etc. Recently published *Executive Compensation,* by J. Steinbrink (general business); *How to Participate Profitably in Trade Shows,* by R. Konikow (sales); and *How to Conduct Better Meetings,* by Kirkpatrick (business).

DAUGHTERS PUBLISHING CO., INC., 22 Charles St., New York NY 10014. Paperback originals (80%) and reprints (20%). 10% royalty; negotiable advance. Published 4 titles in 1976, 6 in 1977; 6 in 1978. Submit queries to Parke Bowman. Simultaneous and photocopied submissions OK. Reports in 2-4 months. SASE. Free book catalog.
Fiction: Publishes radical feminist novels. "We only do novels which reflect the current state of the women's movement." Recently published *Angel Dance,* by M.F. Beal; *I Must Not Rock,* by L. Marie; and *Applesauce,* by J. Arnold.

DAVID & CHARLES (PUBLISHERS), LTD., Brunel House, Forde Rd., Newton Abbot, Devon, England. Publishes hardcover and paperback originals. Published 160 titles in 1977, 140 in 1978; will do 140 in 1979. 10% royalty; advance "varies." Simultaneous and photocopied submissions OK. Reports in 2-3 weeks. SASE. Free book catalog.
Nonfiction: "General wide-interest 'trade' nonfiction, including lavishly illustrated and produced books; how-to books, country, outdoor, sports, natural history, hobbies, topics, history, business, travel and the arts. Treatment must vary according to the subject, market, etc., so early consultation is urged." Query or submit outline/synopsis and sample chapters. Recently published *Shell Book of Rural Britian,* by K. Mossman (country); *Lover's Companion,* by E.J. Howard (anthology); and *House Plants in Colour,* by R. Herwig (practical).

DAVIS PUBLICATIONS, INC., 50 Portland St., Worcester MA 01608. Published 10 titles last year. Write for copy of guidelines for authors. Submit complete ms. Enclose return postage.
Art and Reference: Publishes art and craft books. "Keep in mind the reader for whom the book is written. For example, if a book is written for the teacher, avoid shifting from addressing the teacher to addressing the student. Include illustrations with text. All illustrations should be collated separately from the text, but keyed to the text. Photos should be good quality original prints. Well-selected illustrations can explain, amplify, and enhance the text. It is desirable for the author's selection of illustrations to include some extras. These may be marked 'optional.' The author should not attempt to lay out specific pages. Poorly selected illustrations or too many competing illustrations in a short space can mar a book. For instance, if you are planning a 125- to 150-page book and you have over 300 photos (more than 2 photos per page, average), you probably have too many." Recently published *The Art of Sketching,* by Porter (how-to); *Painting with Oils,* by Sheaks (how-to); and *Drawing Handbook,* by Purser (text).

DAW BOOKS, INC., 1301 Avenue of the Americas, New York NY 10019. Editor: Donald A. Wollheim. Publishes paperback originals and reprints. Standard paperback book contract with advances starting at $2,000. Published 64 titles in 1977. Books are distributed nationally and internationally by The New American Library. Submit complete ms. Will not consider photocopied submissions. Reports in 4 to 8 weeks. Enclose return postage with ms.
Fiction: "Science fiction only, 5 titles a month. About 70% are original works. Mainly novels with occasional collections of the short stories of one author (name authors only). Space flight, future adventure, scientific discovery, unusual concepts, and all the vast range of s-f conceptions will be found in our works. We prefer good narrative presentation without stress on innovations, avant-garde stunts, etc." Length: 55,000 to 95,000 words.

THE JOHN DAY COMPANY, INC., (see Thomas Y. Crowell).

GERRY & HELEN DE LA REE, Scientifantasy Specialists, 7 Cedarwood Lane, Saddle River NJ 07458. (201)327-6621. Editor-in-Chief: Gerry de la Ree. Publishes paperback and hardcover originals. Offers to buy mss outright, since editions are limited. Advance varies. "We do our

own retailing through our own mailing list and also sell to wholesalers or other dealers in the fantasy field." Query first for nonfiction and fantasy artwork. Reports in 1 week under normal circumstances. Enclose return postage.
Nonfiction: "We publish books mainly in the nonfiction vein dealing with fantasy, weird, and science fiction. Over the past three years we have done such volumes on writers like the late H.P. Lovecraft, Clark Ashton Smith and Robert E. Howard; art volumes on such fantasy artists as Virgil Finlay, Hannes Bok and Stephen E. Fabian. Our most recent trend has been more toward art books and folios than articles, but we are flexible. Most of our publications have been limited editions—1,500 or less, with a certain number hardbound and the balance in paper covers. We buy first print rights and would copyright book under author's name if he so desires, and he has all future reprint rights." Not interested in new fiction or poetry. Prefer material of interest to collector in the fantasy field—articles dealing with leading authors of the recent past. Also interested in any unpublished material by these leading authors. Writers should know the fantasy field and its authors and artists. "This is a rather specialized field and we are always willing to discuss in advance any articles a writer is planning. We do not deal with agents." Recently published *Fantastic Nudes: Combined Series,* by S.E. Fabian; *Edd Cartier: The Known and the Unknown,* edited by D. Cartier; and *Fantasy by Fabian,* edited by G. de la Ree.

DELL PUBLISHING CO., INC. (including Delacorte Press), 245 E. 47th St., New York NY 10017. Book Division. Publishes hardcover and paperback originals and reprints. Standard royalty schedule. Published 416 titles last year. Query first always. "Mss that arrive without a preceding query answered in the affirmative by a member of our staff will have to be returned unread. On fiction queries, we would like to know what sort of book the author has written or proposes to write—whether straight novel, romance-suspense, mystery, historical, or Gothic. A paragraph further describing the story would also be helpful." Send complete ms for juveniles. SASE.
General Fiction and Nonfiction: Publishes adult fiction; general nonfiction including philosophy, biography, history, religion, science, the arts.
Juveniles: Delacorte Press children's books: poetry, history, sports and science for ages 12 and over; history, social science and fiction for intermediate level; picture books for the very young. Length: 30,000 to 50,000 words for ages 12 to 16. Juvenile Editor: Ronald Buehl.

***DELTA DESIGN GROUP**, 518 Central Ave., Box 112, Greenville MS 38701. (601)335-6148. Editor-in-Chief: Noel Workman. Hardcover and paperback originals. 10-12½-15% royalty; no advance. 25% of books are subsidy published. Send contact sheet to accompany ms. Simultaneous submissions OK, "but tell us what is really going on". Photocopied submissions OK. Reports in 2-4 weeks. SASE.
Nonfiction: Publishes Americana, cookbooks, cooking and foods; history, multimedia material, travel, and regional architectural subject (lower Mississippi Valley) books. "Our market is the lower Mississippi Valley (Louisiana, Mississippi, Arkansas, Tennessee, Missouri) and we edit for this audience." No autobiographies. Recently published *Son of a Seacook Cookbook,* by K. Tolliver; *75 Years in Leland,* by N. Workman (history); *A Mississippi Architectural Handbook,* by W. Lack (architecture).

T.S. DENISON & CO., INC., 5100 W. 82nd St., Minneapolis MN 55437. Editor-in-Chief: W.E. Rosenfelt. Hardcover and paperback originals. Specializes in educational publishing, textbooks, supplemental textbooks, and teacher aid materials. Royalty varies, "usually $80-100 per 1,000 copies sold; 10% on occasion; no advance. Published 30 titles in 1977, 20 in 1978; will do 20 in 1979. Send prints if photos are to accompany ms. Photocopied submissions OK. Reports in 2-4 weeks. SASE. Book catalog for SASE.
Nonfiction: Publishes textbooks and teaching aid books. Query. Recently published *How To Make Bulletin Board Designs,* by Barnes (teaching aid); and *Getting To Know You Through Art,* by Kenny (art activity book).

***DENLINGER'S PUBLISHERS, LTD.**, Box 76, Fairfax VA 22030. (703)631-1501. Editorial Director: W.W. Denlinger. Senior Editor: R.A. Rathman. Publishes hardcover and paperback originals (90%) and reprints (10%). Published 16 titles in 1977, 20 in 1978; will do 30 in 1979. "Will consider highly specialized books with limited market on a partial or fully subsidized basis. We have been successful in returning to the author his investment. Our plan is not the usual plan of subsidy publishing. Only books of worthwhile material which we would add to our list would be considered." 10% royalty or negotiable outright purchase; no advance. Simultaneous and photocopied submissions OK. Reports in 6 weeks. SASE. Free book catalog.
Nonfiction: Southern historical material. "Will consider other kinds."

THE DEVIN-ADAIR CO., INC., 143 Sound Beach Ave., Old Greenwich CT 06870. (203)637-4531. Editor-in-Chief: Devin A. Garrity. Managing Editor: Florence Norton. Hardcover and paperback originals (90%) and reprints (10%). Royalty on sliding scale, 7-12½%; advance averages $100-3,500. Publishes 12 titles annually. Send prints to illustrate ms. Simultaneous submissions OK. SASE. Free book catalog.
Nonfiction: Publishes Americana, art, biography, business, how-to, politics, cookbooks; history; medicine, nature, economics, hobbies, scientific, sports and travel books. Query or submit outline/synopsis and sample chapters. Recently published *Life's Second Half,* by J. Ellison (popular psychology); and *St. Lucia Diary,* by H. Eggliston (travel).

THE DIAL PRESS, 1 Dag Hammarskjold Plaza, New York NY 10017. (212)832-7300. Editor-in-Chief: Juris Jursevics. Executive Editor: Joyce Johnson. Publishes hardcover and paperback originals. Published 60 titles in 1977 and 1978; will do 70 in 1979. 10-12½-15% royalty. Simultaneous and photocopied submissions OK. Reports in 4 weeks. SASE. Free book catalog.
Nonfiction: "All general trade nonfiction is of interest." Submit outline/synopsis and sample chapters. Recently published *Dulles,* by L. Mosley (biography); *Tennis Begins at 40,* by P. Gonzalez (how-to); and *The Show & Tell Machine,* by R. Goldsen (sociological).
Fiction: All general adult categories. Submit outline/synopsis and sample chapters. Recently published *The Chancellor Manuscript,* by R. Ludlum (intrigue/thriller); and *Child of the Morning,* by P. Gedge (historical).

THE DIETZ PRESS, INC., 109 E. Cary St., Richmond VA 23219. Editor: August Dietz, III. Requires preliminary letter stating the subject and briefly outlining the material. SASE.
Nonfiction: Publishes biography, books of an historical nature, and Virginiana cookbooks. Length: 40,000 to 50,000 words. No poetry.

DILLON PRESS, INC., 500 S. 3rd St., Minneapolis MN 55415. (612)336-2691. Editorial Director: Uva Dillon. Senior Editor: Linda Kusserow. Publishes hardcover and paperback originals. Published 10 titles in 1977, 12-14 in 1978; will do 15-20 in 1979. 10% royalty; no advance. Simultaneous and photocopied submissions OK. Reports in 6 weeks. SASE. Book catalog for SASE.
Nonfiction: Ethnic heritage, cooking, adventure, and outdoor material for adult line; American Indian biographies, social studies, history, minority groups, social problems and environment, biographies of outstanding American women, how-to, folk art and craft books for juvenile line. Submit complete ms. Recently published *Tomo-chi-chi,* by S. Harrell (American Indian biography); *Contributions of Women: Politics and Government,* by L. Greenebaum; and *Fair Winds & Far Places,* by Z. Mann.
Fiction: Juvenile novels: adventure and American Indian material. Submit complete ms. Recently published *The Cherokee Tale-Teller Tales,* by M. Cunningham; *Ride the Red-Eyed Wind,* by J. Pearson; and *The Sea Wedding,* by S. Maas.

DIMENSION BOOKS, INC., Box 811, Denville NJ 07834. (201)627-4334. Regular royalty schedule; advance is negotiable. Book catalog for SASE. Query. Address mss to Thomas P. Coffey. Reports in 1 week on requested mss. SASE.
General Nonfiction: Publishes general nonfiction including religion, principally Roman Catholic. Also psychology and music. Length: 40,000 words and over. Recently published *Looking For Jesus,* by A. van Kaam; *Called By Name,* by P. van Breemen; and *Jesus, Set Me Free!,* by G. Maloney.

DODD, MEAD & CO., 79 Madison Ave., New York NY 10016. (212)685-6464. Executive Editor: Allen T. Klots. Royalty basis: 10% to 15%. Advances vary, depending on the sales potential of the book. A contract for nonfiction books is offered on the basis of a query, a suggested outline and a sample chapter. Write for permission before sending mss. Published 150 titles last year. Adult fiction, history, philosophy, the arts, and religion should be addressed to Editorial Department. Reports in 1 month. SASE.
General Fiction and Nonfiction: Publishes book-length mss. 70,000 to 100,000 words. Fiction and nonfiction of high quality, mysteries and romantic novels of suspense, biography, popular science, travel, yachting, music, and other arts. Very rarely buys photographs or poetry.
Juveniles: Length: 1,500 to 75,000 words. Children's Books Editor: Mrs. Joe Ann Daly.

THE DONNING COMPANY/PUBLISHERS, INC., 253 W. Bute St., Norfolk VA 23510. Editorial Director: Donna Reiss Friedman. Publishes hardcover and paperback originals. Published 19 titles in 1977, 20-25 in 1978. 10-12½-15% royalty on hardcover titles; 8-10-12% royalty on

paperback; advance "negotiable." Simultaneous (if so informed) and photocopied submissions OK. Reports in 12 weeks. SASE. Book catalog for SASE.
Nonfiction: Wants material for 3 series: 1) Portraits of American Cities Series (pictorial histories of American cities with 300 illustrations, primarily photographs, with fully descriptive captions and historical overview text of approximately 10,000 words. "The intent is to capture the character of a community in transition, from earliest known settlers to the present. Author need not be a professional historian, but must have close ties to the community and cooperation of local historians and private and public photo archives); 2) Regional Specialty Books (specialty, regional cookbooks, popular history and art collections); and 3) Unilaw Library imprint (Editor: Robert Friedman. Religious, inspirational, metaphysical subjects and themes). Query or submit complete ms. Recently published *Alexandria (VA): A Pictorial History,* by K.G. Harvey/R. Stansfield; *Virginia Supernatural Tales,* by H. Tucker; and *Frank Kelly Freas: Art of Science Fiction,* by F. Kelly Freas.
Fiction: Starblaze Editions imprint. Editors: Kelly and Polly Freas.

DOUBLEDAY & CO., INC., 245 Park Ave., New York NY 10017. (212)553-4561. Managing Editor: Pyke Johnson, Jr. Publishes hardcover and paperback originals; publishes paperback reprints under Anchor, Dolphin and Image imprints. Offers standard 10-12½-15% royalty contract. Advance varies. Reports in 1 month. Published 584 titles in 1977. Special submission requirements outlined below. Query first with outline and sample chapters for both fiction and nonfiction. "Your letter of inquiry should be addressed to the Editorial Department, Doubleday & Co. Inc., 245 Park Avenue, New York City 10017. The letter may be as short as one page, but no longer than six pages (double-spaced). The first sentence should tell us whether your book is a novel, a biography, a mystery, or whatever. The first paragraph should give us an idea of what your book is about. This description should be clear and straightforward. If your book is a novel, please give us an engaging summary of the plot and background, and a quick sketch of the major characters. If you have already been published, give us details at the end of your letter. You should also tell us of any credentials or experience that particularly qualify you to write your book. For a nonfiction book, it will be helpful to you to consult the *Subject Guide to Books in Print* (available in most libraries) so that you are aware of other books on the same or similar subjects as your own, and can tell us how your book differs from them. Finally, letters of inquiry should be inviting and typed with a good ribbon. If we ask to see your ms, it should be submitted double-spaced on white paper. You should retain a carbon copy, since we cannot assume responsibility for loss or damage to mss. Sufficient postage, in the form of loose stamps, should accompany your submission to insure the return of your ms in the event it is not accepted for publication."
Nonfiction and Fiction: "Doubleday has a policy concerning the handling of manuscripts. We return unopened and unread all complete manuscripts, accompanied by a form telling how we would like submissions made. However, in 2 areas, we will accept complete manuscripts: Mysteries and science fiction. These mss should be addressed to the appropriate editor (for example, Science Fiction Editor) and not just to Doubleday. We have a moratorium on poetry publishing and are not accepting mss."

DOUBLEDAY CANADA, LTD., 105 Bond St., Toronto, Ontario, Canada M5B 1Y3. (416)366-7891. Editorial Director: Betty Jane Corson. Publishes hardcover originals. Published 10 titles in 1977, 15 in 1978; will do 20 in 1979. Pays in royalties; advance "varies." Simultaneous and photocopied submissions OK. Reports in 2 months. SASE. Free book catalog.
Nonfiction: General interest. "We do not specialize, but the major part of our list consists of biography, popular history, and subjects of contemporary interest. Our main concern is to publish books of particular interest to the Canadian market, although our books are published in the US as well. We will consider any nonfiction proposal. We are especially anxious to consider books of Canadian interest." Query, submit outline/synopsis and sample chapters, or submit complete ms. Recently published *Bartlett: The Great Canadian Explorer,* by H. Horwood (biography/history); *Years of Sorrow, Years of Shame,* by B. Broadfoot (oral history); and *A Winter's Tale: The Wreck of the Florizel,* by C. Brown.
Fiction: "No particular preferences as to style or genre. We publish both 'literary' and 'commercial' books. Once again, we are most interested in fiction with a Canadian angle (author, setting, subject). Of course, we hope they have North American potential as well." Query or submit complete ms. Recently published *Sidehill Gouger,* by S. Dennison; *The Common Touch,* by T.A. Keenleyside; and *Snowman,* by T. York.

DOUGLAS, DAVID & CHARLES LTD., 1875 Welch St., North Vancouver, B.C., Canada V7P 1B7. (604)980-7922. Editor: Jim Douglas. Publishes hardcover originals and reprints. Offers

"normal" royalty contract. Average advance is $300 to $750. Publishes in association with David & Charles in U.K., whose yearly output is about 350 books. Published 15 titles in 1977. Style manual also available on request. Will consider photocopied submissions. No simultaneous submissions. Submit outline and sample chapters. Reports in 6 to 8 weeks. Enclose S.A.E. and International Reply coupons.
Nonfiction: Publishes practical books on all subjects. Nautical, military, gardening, cooking, photography, wildlife, education, Americana, Canadiana, art, business, economics, history, humor, law, library, medicine, music, politics, reference, travel. "Must be authoritative and at the same time readable." Mss should "address themselves to readers in the United Kingdom and Canada as well as the U.S., whenever possible. A book club is operated from the headquarters of our affiliate company in Britain, and our titles stand a good chance of adoption by the club." Length: 50,000 to 100,000 words. Recently published *Natural Resources of British Columbia and the Yukon,* by Dr. M. Barker (geography reference); and *Canadian Railways in Pictures,* by R. Legget.

DOUGLAS & McINTYRE, 1875 Welch St., N. Vancouver B.C., Canada. (604)986-4311. Editor-in-Chief: J.J. Douglas. Managing Editor: Marilyn Sacks. Publishes hardcover and paperback originals (90%) and reprints (10%). 10% royalty; $500 average advance. State availabilty of photos and/or illustrations. Photocopied submissions OK. Reports in 1-2 months. SASE. Free book catalog.
Nonfiction: Publishes reference books and books on Canadian history, nature, hobbies, recreation and sports, how-to, hobbies; cookbooks, cooking and foods; pets, self-help, music and art books. Recently published *A Cree Life: The Art of Allen Sapp,* by Bradshaw/Warner; *Vancouver's First Century,* by the editors of the *Urban Reader;* and *The Enterprising Mr. Moody, The Bumptious Capt Stamp,* by J. Morton.

DOW JONES-IRWIN, 1818 Ridge Rd., Homewood IL 60430. (312)798-6000. Publishes originals only. Royalty schedule 10% of net. Advance negotiable. Published 25 titles last year. Send completed mss to the attention of Editorial Director. SASE.
Nonfiction: Business and industrial subjects.

DRAKE PUBLISHERS, INC., 801 2nd Ave., New York NY 10017. (212)986-5100. Publisher: Ted Gottfried. Editor-in-Chief: Donald J. Davidson. Publishes hardcover and paperback originals (75%) and reprints (25%). Published 80 titles in 1977 and 1978; will do 100 in 1979. 10% royalty; advance averages $1,000. Simultaneous and photocopied submissions OK. Reports in 4-6 weeks. SASE. Book catalog for SASE.
Nonfiction: Americana; biography; business; foods; economics; history; hobbies; how-to; humor; law; medicine; nature; pets; photography; psychology; recreation; reference; self-help; sports; technical; and woodworking. No inspirational or religious books. Query or submit outline/synopsis and sample chapters. Recently published *How To Build Shaker Furniture,* by T. Moser (woodworking); *Cary Grant,* by L. Guthrie (biography); and *Dancers on Dancing,* by C. Lyle (stage and screen).

DRAMA BOOK SPECIALISTS (PUBLISHERS), 150 West 52nd St., New York NY 10019. (212)582-1475. Publishes hardcover and paperback originals. Royalties usually 10%. Advance varies. Published 19 titles in 1977. Send query only to Ralph Pine. Do not send complete mss. Reports in 4 to 8 weeks. Enclose SASE.
Drama: "Theatrical history, texts, film, and books dealing with the performing arts."

DUQUESNE UNIVERSITY PRESS, Pittsburgh PA 15219. (412)434-6610. Royalty schedule is 10%. No advance. Query first. Reports in 8 weeks. Enclose return postage.
Nonfiction: Scholarly books on philosophy and philology and psychology. Length: open. Recently published *Man and Technology,* by E.G. Ballard (philosophical); *Kierkegaard's Psychology,* by K. Nordentoft (psychological); and *Schizophrenia,* by A. De Waelhens (philosophical/psychological).

E.P. DUTTON, 201 Park Ave. S., New York NY 10003. Juvenile Department: Ann Durell. Dutton Paperback: Cyril Nelson. Sunrise: Adult Department, Henry Robbins. Windmill Books: Robert Kraus. Pays by advances and royalties. Query. Send letter with outline before submitting mss or sample material. "Policy is not to return materials unless postage is included."
General Fiction and Nonfiction: Publishes novels of permanent literary value, mystery, nonfiction, religious, travel, fine arts, biography, memoirs, belles-lettres, history, science, psychology, translations, quality paperbacks, juvenile books. Recently published *Origins,* by R.

Leakey/Roger Lewin; *True Confessions,* by J.G. Dunne; and *Trail of the Fox,* by D. Irving.

LES EDITIONS DE L'ETOILE, 325-327 Mont-Royal Est., Montreal H2T 1P8, PQ, Canada. Offers 10% royalty contract. No advance. Enclose S.A.E. and International Reply Coupons for return of submissions.
General Fiction and Nonfiction: General publisher of all types of books in French language only.

EDITS PUBLISHERS, Box 7234, San Diego CA 92107. (714)488-1666. Editorial Director: Robert R. Knapp. Publishes hardcover and paperback originals. Published 5 titles in 1977, 6 in 1978; will do 10 in 1979. Royalty "varies"; no advance. Photocopied submissions OK. Reports in 1-2 months. SASE. Book catalog for SASE.
Nonfiction: "Edits publishes scientific and text books in social sciences, particularly counseling and guidance, psychology, statistics and education." Query. Recently published *Actualizing Therapy,* by E. Shostrom (therapy text); *Naked Therapist,* by S. Kopp; and *Handbook in Research and Evaluation,* by S. Isaac.

EMC CORPORATION, 180 E. 6th St., St. Paul MN 55101. Editorial Director: Northrop Dawson Jr. Senior Editor: Constance Van Brunt McMillan. Publishes hardcover and paperback originals (90%) and reprints (10%). Publishes 40 titles/year. "We publish for the school (educational) market only, in limited runs as compared to trade publishers. Writers should not have expectations of huge quantity sales." Contract and advance "open to negotiation." Photocopied submissions OK. Reports in 4 weeks. Free book catalog.
Nonfiction: "Topics of interest to juvenile readers: sports; the media; popular entertainers; outdoor life and activity (wild animals, outdoor sports such as cross-country skiing, ballooning, etc.); "the unexplained" (supernatural, esp, etc.); unusual occupations; and biographies of achievers surmounting great odds. No how-to, religious, or travel material." Query; "send one or more samples of previously published work." Recently published *Arthur Ashe: Alone in the Crowd,* by L. Jacobs (sports biography); *Animals Around Us,* by J. Becker (wildlife/science enrichment); and *Hispanic Heroes of the U.S.A.,* by W. Wheelock (biography).
Fiction: Juvenile fiction: mystery; "the unexplained"; young detectives; stories focussing on non-stereotyped, active, aggressive girls; adventure stories involving young people; sports fiction involving juvenile athletes, both male and female; outdoor and wildlife adventure involving juveniles; realistic stories of juveniles overcoming handicaps; science fiction geared to juveniles; and stories involving animals. No religious material. Query, "send one or more samples of previously published work. After we have indicated interest in initial query, submit outline and sample chapters." Recently published *Time of Danger, Time of Courage,* by G. Gray; *No Such Things . . . ?,* by B. Hunting (series of supernatural stories); and *Sea Wolf Mysteries,* by R. Wise (outdoor mystery).

EMERSON BOOKS, INC., Reynolds Ln., Buchanan NY 10511. (914)739-3506. Managing Editor: Barry Feiden. Hardcover originals (80%) and reprints (20%). Publishes about 5 titles annually. Photocopied submissions OK. Reports in 3 months. SASE.
Nonfiction: Hobbies, how-to, recreation, self-help. Query first. Recently published *Collecting and Identifying Old Clocks,* by Harris (antiques); and *Principles of Collage,* French (crafts).

ENERGY EDUCATION PUBLISHERS, 1432 Wealthy St., SE, Grand Rapids MI 49506. Editor-in-Chief: Tom Lee. Publishes hardcover and paperback originals. Published 2 titles in 1977, 4-6 in 1978; will do 4-6 in 1979. 10% royalty. Simultaneous and photocopied submissions OK. Reports in 1-2 weeks. SASE. Book catalog for SASE.
Nonfiction: Trade, reference, and textbooks in the areas of energy, energy utilization, energy conservation and related subject areas: economics; scientific; and technical. Query. "Complete manuscripts will not be read unless submitted at the request of our editorial department." Recently published *Energy: A Critical Decision for the United States Economy,* by S. Dix; and *Energy: The Rude Awakening,* by R. Bailey.

ENGENDRA PRESS LTD., Box 235, Westmount Station, Montreal, Quebec Canada H3Z 2T2. (514)953-1476. Editor-in-Chief: Ronald Rosenthall. Publishes hardcover originals. Specializes in literature in translation. "At the present time, a royalty (and if necessary, an advance) is paid to the copyright holder or the translator, *not both.* In addition, each future book will have to be assisted by a grant, preferably from the translator/writer's university." Publishes about 4 titles annually. State availability of photos and/or illustrations to accompany ms. Reports in 1-2 weeks. SASE. Free book catalog.
Translations: "Engendra Press specializes in the publication of translations of quality writing

from the languages—though not necessarily the lands—of Continental Europe. Most of the ideas for books originate within the house, but whatever the case, we are most interested either in important authors who will be getting their first 'hearing' in English, or in those already known to English readers but in whose work in translation serious omissions exist." These books are not especially different in subject or theme from the serious side of commercial publishing or from certain of the products of some university presses. "We do, however, stress an imaginative approach to a subject's oeuvre." Query first. No unsolicited mss. "Owing to the nature of the material, only ideas will be entertained."
Recent Titles: *3 Catalan Dramatists,* edited by G. Wellwarth; *The Legacy of Jura Soyfer,* by J. Soyfer.

ENTELEK, Ward-Whidden House/The Hill, Portsmouth NH 03801. Editor-in-Chief: Albert E. Hickey. Publishes paperback originals. Offers royalty contract of 5% trade; 10% textbook. No advance. Published 8 titles last year. Will send free catalog to writer on request. Will consider photocopied and simultaneous submissions. Submit outline and sample chapters or submit complete ms. Reports in 1 week. Enclose return postage.
Nonfiction and Business: Publishes computer, calculator, math, business and how-to books. "We seek books that have not been undertaken by other publishers." Would like to see material for career guides. Length: 3,000 words minimum. Recently published *Genetic With the Computer.*

ENTERPRISE PUBLISHING CO., INC., 1300 Market St., Wilmington DE 19702. (302)575-0440. Publisher: T.N. Peterson. Editor: B.H. Kirby. Publishes hardcover and paperback originals. Published 3 titles in 1977, 6 in 1978; will do 6 in 1979. 5% royalty; advance averages $1,000. Photocopied submissions OK. Reports in 2 months. SASE. Free book catalog.
Nonfiction: General audience, self-help books relating to small business, and self-improvement. "Also material on ways the public can do something for themselves that would normally be a paid service performed by someone else. Use an entreprenuerial slant and non-academic language, geared toward do-it-yourselfers. Material must have vast market appeal." Query; all unsolicited mss are returned unopened. Recently published *How To Form Your Own Corporation,* by T. Nicholas; and *Writing Part Time–For Fun and Money,* by J.C. McLarn.

***PAUL S. ERIKSSON**, Battell Bldg., Middlebury VT 05753. (802)388-7303. Publishes hardcover and trade paperbacks. Pays standard royalty. Does 5% to 10% subsidy annually. Published 8 titles last year. Query first with outline and sample chapters. Reports within 1 month. Enclose return postage.
Fiction and Nonfiction: Trade nonfiction and fiction. Also nature and bird lore. Recently published *Three Alexander Calders,* by M.C. Hayes (biography); and *A Very Simple Garden Book: Vegetables,* by R. Ensh.

EVANS AND COMPANY, INC., 216 E. 49 St., New York NY 10017. Editor-in-Chief: Herbert M. Katz. Publishes hardcover originals. Royalty schedule to be negotiated. Publishes 30 titles/year. Will consider photocopied submissions. "No mss should be sent unsolicited. A letter of inquiry is essential." Reports in 6-8 weeks. SASE.
General Fiction and Nonfiction: "We publish a general trade list of adult fiction and nonfiction, cookbooks and semi-reference works. The emphasis is on selectivity since we publish only 30 titles a year. Our fiction list represents an attempt to combine quality with commercial potential. Our most successful nonfiction titles have been related to the behavioral sciences. No limitation on subject. A writer should clearly indicate what his book is all about, frequently the task the writer performs least well. His credentials, although important, mean less than his ability to convince this company that he understands his subject and that he has the ability to communicate a message worth hearing." Recently published *Women Who Write* and *The Marriage Premise.*

FAIRCHILD BOOKS & VISUALS, Book Division, 7 East 12th St., New York NY 10003. Manager: Ed Gold. Publishes hardcover and paperback originals. Offers standard minimum book contract. No advance. Pays 10% of net sales distributed twice annually. Published 12 titles last year. Will consider photocopied submissions. Will send free catalog to writer on request. Query first, giving subject matter and brief outline. Enclose return postage.
Business and Textbooks: Publishes business books and textbooks relating to fashion, electronics, marketing, retailing, career education, advertising, home economics, and management. Length: open. Recently published *Men's Outerwear Design,* by Kawashima; and *Fashion Advertising and Promotion,* by Winters/Goodman.

FAR EASTERN RESEARCH AND PUBLICATIONS CENTER, P.O. Box 31151, Washington DC 20031. Publishes hardcover and paperback originals and reprints. "Royalty is based on the standard rate or outright purchase. Pays up to $2,000 advance against standard royalties." Submit a synopsis or table of contents with sample chapter, along with biographical sketches, to editor-in-chief. Reports in 2 months. Enclose return postage with ms—"enough postage to cover registered mail for return of submissions."
Nonfiction: Subject emphasis: reference materials on the Far East, especially on the Chinese, Japanese, and Korean people. All lengths.

FARNSWORTH PUBLISHING CO., INC., 78 Randall Ave., Rockville Centre NY 11570. (516)536-8400. President: Lee Rosler. Publishes hardcover originals. "Standard royalty applies, but 5% is payable on mail order sales." Published 15 titles last year. Free book catalog. Reports in 3-6 weeks. SASE.
General Nonfiction, Business and Professional: "Our books generally fall into 2 categories: 1. Books which appeal to executives, lawyers, accountants, and life underwriters. Subject matter may vary from selling techniques, estate planning, taxation, money management, etc. 2. Books which appeal to the general populace which are marketable by direct mail and mail order, in addition to bookstore sales." Recently published *A Treasury of Business Opportunities,* by D.D. Seltz; *What Every Woman Should Know about Finances,* by F.A. Lumb; and *How To Make A Solid Profit in the Apartment Business,* by J. Schwartz.

FARRAR, STRAUS AND GIROUX, INC., (including Hill and Wang), 19 Union Square West, New York NY 10003. Published 150 titles last year. Prefers queries. Enclose S.A.S.E.
General Fiction, Nonfiction and Juveniles: Publishes general fiction, nonfiction and juveniles. Publishes Noonday paperbacks, scholarly reprints under Octagon Books imprint and Hill and Wang books.

FAST & McMILLAN PUBLISHERS, INC., 6000 Kingstree Dr., Charlotte NC 28210. Editorial Director: Sally Hill McMillan. Publishes hardcover and paperback originals. Published 2 titles in 1977, 4 in 1978; will do 6 in 1979. 10% royalty. Reports in 2-4 weeks. SASE. Book catalog for SASE.
Nonfiction: "We are strictly interested in the outdoors. Regional guidebooks are our specialty—hiking, fishing, skiing, etc., but anything on the outdoors will be considered." Submit outline/synopsis and sample chapters. "A list of competitive books should be submitted, along with specific reasons why this manuscript should be published. Also, any maps and art should be supplied by the author." Recently published *Canoeing the Jersey Pine Barrens,* by R. Parnes (guidebook); *Hiking Cape Cod,* by Mitchell/Griswold (guidebook); and *Rocky Mountain National Park Trails,* by Dannen (guidebook).

FAWCETT PUBLICATIONS, INC./GOLD MEDAL BOOKS, 1515 Broadway, New York NY 10036. Publishes paperback originals only. Advances and royalties are flexible and competitive. Address query first to the editors before submitting ms. Reports in 3 to 8 weeks. Enclose return postage.
Nonfiction and Fiction: Seeks books of broad, mass-market appeal.

F. W. FAXON COMPANY, INC., 15 Southwest Park, Westwood MA 02090. (617)329-3350. Publisher: Albert H. Davis, Jr. Editor-in-Chief: Beverly Heinle. Publishes hardcover originals. Published 7 titles in 1977, 10 in 1978; will do 10 in 1979. Offers 10% of sales net price for each book sold, payable at the end of each fiscal year. No advance. Books are marketed through advertising, mail campaigns, book reviews, and library conventions. Will send catalog to writer on request. Mss must be original copy, double-spaced, and must be accompanied by a copy. They should contain reference material useful to library users throughout the world. Query. Reports in 2 months. SASE.
Reference: "We publish library reference books. These are primarily indexes but we would also consider bibliographies and other material useful to library users. We would be interested in publishing indexes on topics of current interest which have not been indexed previously." Recently published *Index to America–18th Century,* by N.O. Ireland; and *Dear Faculty: A Discovery Guidebook to the High School Library,* by J.A. Nordling.

FREDERICK FELL PUBLISHERS, INC., 386 Park Ave., S., New York NY 10016. (212)685-9017. Editor-in-Chief: Charles Nurnberg. Hardcover and paperback originals (85%) and reprints (15%). 10% royalty. Published 29 titles in 1977, 30 in 1978. Query. Send sample prints or

contact sheet if photos/illustrations are to accompany ms. Simultaneous and photocopied submissions OK. Reports in 3-5 weeks. SASE. Free book catalog.
Nonfiction: Publishes Americana; business; hobbies; how-to; law; medicine and psychiatry; pets; photography; psychology; recreation; reference; self-help; and sports books. Recently published *Complete Guide To Eye Care, Eyeglasses, & Contact Lenses,* by Drs. Zinn/Soloman (medical self-help); and *Ken Rosewall on Tennis,* by K. Rosewall (sports).
Special Needs: Pet Lovers Library; Home Medical Library.

THE FEMINIST PRESS, Box 334, Old Westbury NY 11568. (516)997-7660. Publishes paperback, and occasionally hardcover originals and reprints of lost feminist works. Published 2 titles in 1977, 7 in 1978; will do 10 in 1979. 10% royalty; no advance. Simultaneous and photocopied submissions OK. Reports in 2 months. SASE. Free book catalog.
Nonfiction: Elizabeth Phillips, editor. "Women in history, literature, science, and arts will be considered. The subject matter may be from the past or the present. We publish biographies, anthologies, reprints of lost artists, bibliographies, and nonsexist educational materials." No material without a feminist viewpoint. Query or submit outline/synopsis and sample chapters. Recently published *The Mamie Papers,* by Rosen and Davidson (autobiographical letters); *Portraits of Chinese Women in Revolution,* by A. Smedley (historical reprint); *Kathe Kollwitz,* by M. Kearns (biography).
Fiction: Jeanne Bracken and Sharon Wigutoff, Children's Books editors. "We do not publish contemporary fiction in the adult department. Fiction in the children's department includes nonsexist picture books and stories for the middle reader." Query, submit outline/synopsis and sample chapters, or complete ms. Recently published *My Mother the Mailcarrier,* by I. Maury; and *ABC Workbook,* by J. Mangi.

FFORBEZ ENTERPRISES, LTD., Box 35340, Station E, Vancouver B.C., Canada V6M 4G6. (604)872-7325. Editor-in-Chief: P.W. Zebroff. Managing Editor: Tim Udd. Paperback originals. Specializes in how-to and health-oriented books. 10% royalty; no advance. Published 12 titles in 1977 and 1978. Markets books through health and book stores. Send at least 1 copy of illustration and 1 print. Simultaneous submissions OK if exclusive to Canada. Photocopied submissions OK. Reports in 2-4 weeks. SASE. Free book catalog.
Nonfiction: Publishes cookbooks, cooking and foods; how-to, multimedia material, nature, recreation, self-help, sports and health books. Submit outline/synopsis, sample chapters and table of contents. Recently published *Farewell Fatigue,* by N. Rogers (health); *Celebrity Cooks' Cookbook,* by B. Gerussi; and *Kid, Kids, Kids, and Vancouver Island,* by D. Wood/B. Campbell.

FIDDLEHEAD POETRY BOOKS, Department of English, University of British Columbia, Box 4400, Fredericton, New Brunswick, Canada E3B 5A3. Editor-in-Chief: Fred Cogswell. Paperback originals. Specializes in publishing books of poetry. Royalty of 10% of first run; no advance. "We have a fairly large list of standing orders from libraries." State availability of photos and/or illustrations to accompany ms. Simultaneous submissions OK. Reports in 1-2 months. SASE. Free book catalog, if available.
Poetry: "Canadian authors have a better chance of acceptance as our whole publicity and distribution mechanism is geared that way." Submit complete ms. Recently published *White Wings Black Dead,* by M. Bullock (poetry); and *Twenty-Five,* by G. McWhiter (poetry).

***FIDES/CLARETIAN**, Box F, Notre Dame IN 46556. Editor: James F. Burns. Publishes originals and reprints. Pays 8-10% royalty; no advance. Publishes about 1 subsidy book a year. Free book catalog. Send outline and sample chapter. Reports in 6 weeks. Enclose return postage.
Religion: Publishes religious books (Christian and ecumenical) and general nonfiction with theological, spiritual, pastoral implications. The new look in religion and religious education, and the attitude of freedom and personal responsibility. Length: religious, 20,000 words and up; general nonfiction, 20,000 words and up. Recently published *A New Look at the Sacraments,* by W.J. Bausch (pastoral theology); *A Call to Action,* by F. Manning; and *How to Pray Always without Always Praying,* by S. Fittipaldi (spirituality).

***THE FILTER PRESS,** Box 5, Palmer Lake CO 80133. (303)481-2523. Editorial Director: Gilbert L. Campbell. Senior Editor: Lollie W. Campbell. Publishes hardcover and paperback originals (50%) and reprints (50%). Publishes 8 titles/year. Subsidy publishes less than 10% of titles/year. "These are usually family histories in short runs, although subjects have ranged from preaching, ranching, history debunking, to a study of UFO's. If we feel we can market a book profitably for us and the author, and it is a good book and the author feels he needs it published, we will consider it.'' 10% royalty; no advance. Simultaneous and photocopied submissions OK. Reports in 2-3 weeks. SASE. Book catalog for SASE.

Nonfiction: ''Cookbooks must apppeal to westerners, campers, and tourists. We have one on game cookery, one on pancakes, one on camp cooking, one on southwestern Indian recipes. In prep is one on Mexican cooking for the Anglo bride (our daughter is one!). Also western legends, and other western Americana, as we are quite regional. We must stay at or near our 64-page limit, as most booklets are sold softbound, saddle stitched. We have done some verse, but prefer light verse of western interest. Our morgue of antique wood engravings is used extensively, so books with a Victorian feel fit in best. Western Americana on our list includes Indians, explorations, lawmen, and bandits. We have Butch Cassidy, Pat Garrett, and will add Jim Reavis, The Bogus Baron of Arizona, one of America's more successful swindlers. Family histories and very local history have not done well for us. Writers must remember we are small, publish few books, and they must be things that a tourist will buy to take home, although we are in many eastern bookstores. Query. Recently published *Saga of Butch Cassidy and the Wild Bunch,* by E.M. Kirby (history); *Foxgrapes,* by J.S. Isom (Cherokee verse); and *Many Moons Ago,* by I.D. Ferrin (legends).

Fiction: ''Practically all our fiction has been reprinted from 19th century authors, a distinguished group who never ask for an up-to-date royalty statement! Our poetry is evenly divided between old and new. I suppose if something very short and imaginative should come along on the 19th century west, we might do it, but . . . .'' Query.

FITZHENRY & WHITESIDE, LIMITED, 150 Lesmill Rd., Don Mills, Ontario, Canada. Editor-in-Chief: Robert Read. Publishes hardcover and paperback originals and reprints. Chiefly educational materials. Royalty contract varies; advance negotiable. Published 40 titles last year. Submit outline and sample chapters. Will consider photocopied submissions. Reports on material accepted for publication in 1 to 2 months. Returns rejected material in 2 to 3 months. Enclose return postage.

General Nonfiction, Drama and Poetry: ''Especially interested in topics of interest to Canadians.'' Biography; business; history; medicine and psychiatry; nature; politics. Canadian plays and poetry are also of interest. Length: open. Recently published *The Mind of Norman Bethune,* by R. Stewart; *Gabriel Dumont,* by G. Woodcock; and *Women in Canadian Law,* by L. Dranoff.

Textbooks: Elementary and secondary school textbooks, audiovisual materials in social studies and reading and science.

FLEET PRESS CORPORATION, 160 Fifth Ave., New York NY 10010. (212)243-6100. Editor: Susan Nueckel. Publishes hardcover and paperback originals and reprints. Royalty schedule ''varies.'' Advance ''varies.'' Published 18 titles last year. Will send a catalog to a writer on request. Send query and outline. Reports in six weeks. Enclose return postage with ms. Will not evaluate unsolicited mss.

General Nonfiction: ''History, biography, arts, religion, general nonfiction, sports.'' Length: 45,000 words.

Juveniles: Nonfiction only. Stress on social studies and minority subjects; for ages 8 to 15. Length: 25,000 words.

FODOR'S MODERN GUIDES, 750 3rd Ave., New York NY 10017. (212)949-1500. Editorial Director: Robert C. Fisher. Senior Editor: Leslie Brown. Publishes hardcover and paperback originals. Published 46 titles in 1977, 53 in 1978. Pays $50 minimum outright purchase; 10-20% advance. Simultaneous and photocopied submissions OK. Reports in 1-3 months. SASE. Book catalog for SASE.

Nonfiction: ''We publish only travel guidebooks in these two general formats: guides to individual countries, cities, areas or continents (e.g. Europe, New England, Paris, Germany); and guides for special interest travel (e.g. cruises, railways, Old West, etc.). No material unrelated to travel. Query, submit outline/synopsis and sample chapters, or complete ms. Recently published *Egypt,* by K. Showker; *Railways of the World;* and *Europe '78.*

FOLLETT PUBLISHING CO., 1010 W. Washington Blvd., Chicago IL 60607. Children's Book Department at 420 Lexington Ave., Suite 2603, New York NY 10017. Department Editorial Director: Ellen Rudin. Publishes hardcover originals and paperback reprints of Follett books. Negotiable royalty and advance. Photocopied submissions OK. Reports in 4-6 weeks. SASE. Book catalog for SASE (use Chicago address).

Nonfiction: ''We are interested in quality nonfiction of all kinds with strong, direct appeal to

children from preschool to teens. Subjects and themes not often covered in books for children are especially welcome." Query, submit outline/synopsis and sample chapters, or submit complete ms. Recently published *The Days When the Animals Talked,* by Faulkner (black slave tales and folk tales); *The Left-Hander's World,* by Silverstein/Silverstein (social science); and *Tales of the Elders,* by Bales (immigration history and photo journalism).
Fiction: "We are interested in quality fiction of all kinds, without regard to genre, if well-written and well characterized. We publish picture books for the youngest children, beginning readers, storybooks, and novels for both middle grades and teenagers." Submit complete ms. Recently published *Shadows,* by Hall; *Edward Troy and the Witch Cat,* by Sargent (junior novel); and *Fantastic Toys,* by Beisner (picture book).

FORTRESS PRESS, 2900 Queen Lane, Philadelphia PA 19129. (215)848-6800. Senior Editor: Theodore McConnel. Hardcover and paperback originals. Specializes in general religion for laity and clergy; academic texts and monographs in theology (all areas). 7% royalty on paperbacks; 10% on hardcover; modest advance. Published 65 titles in 1977, 70 in 1978. Mss must follow *Chicago Manual of Style* (17th edition). Photocopied submissions OK. Reports in 90 days. SASE. Free book catalog.
Nonfiction: Publishes philosophy, religious and self-help books. Query. Does not want religious poetry or fiction. Recently published *Karl Barth,* by E. Busch (biography); *Paul and Palestinian Judaism,* by E.P. Sanders; and *Tradition and Theology in the Old Testament,* edited by D. Knight (essays).

FOUR CORNERS PRESS, 232 Washington St., Hanover MA 02339. Editor-in-Chief: Carl W. Lindsay. Publishes paperback originals. "We buy all material outright. No byline. Payment will vary from a minimum of $25 for simple reports to well over $500 for acceptable book-length material." Published 25 titles, reports and booklets last year. Published material is sold by mail order to the public, or sold to a business and sent to their customers or prospects as if it were published by them. "Do NOT ask for samples, etc. They have no bearing on what we expect from a new submission." Query first. Reports in 2 weeks. SASE.
Nonfiction: Americana, business, humor, politics, reference, self-help and how-to, technical. "We are always on the lookout for material which can be sold by mail or syndicated." Publishes reports, short books. Most material published in report form, 8½x11 pages, offset printed, stapled rather than bound. Longer material published as saddle-stitched or softcover booklet. "Material must be useful, well researched and, hopefully, unique. This is not a market for off-the-cuff writing. Usually the writer must have some specialized knowledge or be able to do good research." Audience is specialized, but material should also be of interest to a cross-section of professional, business and personal people. Mss must be practical and useful. No preconceived notions. "Household hints are a drug on the market for us. We use no poetry but keep getting it."

FRANCISCAN HERALD PRESS, 1434 West 51st St., Chicago IL 60609. Editor: Paul J. Bernard. "Royalty schedule—10% and up with volume. Advance depends on nature and length of ms." Published 24 titles last year. Use University of Chicago *Manual of Style.* Send query and outline. Reports in 30 days. SASE.
Religion: "A Catholic publishing house with a wide range of interests in theology, sociology, culture, art and literature, reflecting, interpreting, directing the socio-religious and cultural aspects of our times." Synthesis Series of booklets (10,000 words maximum) in the filed of religion and psychology. Church history, biography and specialized publications on history, purpose and personages of the Franciscan Order. Lengths run from 5,000 to 60,000 words.

THE FREE PRESS, a Division of the Macmillan Publishing Co., Inc., 866 Third Ave., New York NY 10022. President: Edward W. Barry. Editor-in-Chief: Charles E. Smith. Royalty schedule varies. Published 80 titles in 1977. Send sample chapter, outline, and query letter before submitting mss. Reports in 3 weeks. SASE.
Nonfiction and Textbooks: Publishes college texts and adult educational nonfiction in the social sciences and humanities.

GAMBLER'S BOOK CLUB, Box4115, Las Vegas NV 89106. (702)382-7555. Editorial Director: John Luckman. Publishes hardcover and paperback originals (67%) and reprints (33%). Published 24 titles in 1977 and 1978; will do 30 in 1979. 10% royalty; advance averages $300. Photocopied submissions OK. Reports in 1 month. SASE. Book catalog for SASE.
Nonfiction: 20,000 word mss pertaining to gambling; or pertaining to games on which people wager money. Submit complete ms. Recently published *Professional Blackjack,* by S. Wong;

Poker Poker, by P. Dangel; and *Average Purse Tables,* by H. Mahl.

GARDEN WAY PUBLISHING, Charlotte VT 05445. (802)425-2171. Editor: Roger Griffith. Publishes hardcover and paperback originals. Offers a flat fee arrangement varying with book's scope, or royalty, which usually pays author 6% of book's retail price. Advances are negotiable, but usually range from $1,500 to $2,000. "We stress continued promotion of titles and sales over many years. None of our titles has yet gone out of print." Emphasizes direct mail sales, plus sales to bookstores through salesmen. Will send free catalog and editorial guidelines sheet to writer; enclose SASE. Will consider photocopied submissions. Query first for nonfiction. Enclose return postage.
Nonfiction: Books on gardening, cooking, animal husbandry, homesteading and energy conservation. Emphasis should be on how-to. Length requirements are flexible. "The writer should remember the reader will buy his book to learn to do something, so that all information to accomplish this must be given. We are publishing specifically for the person who is concerned about natural resources and a deteriorating life style and wants to do something about it." Would like to see energy books with emphasis on what the individual can do. Recently published *Woodstone Cookery,* by J. Cooper; and *Harnessing Water Power for Home Energy,* by D. McGuigan.

***GENEALOGICAL PUBLISHING CO., INC.,** 111 Water St., Baltimore MD 21202. (301)837-8271. Editor-in-Chief: Michael H. Tepper, Ph.D. Publishes hardcover originals and reprints. Offers straight 10% royalty. Does about 10% subsidy publishing. Published 79 titles last year. Will consider photocopied submissions. Prefers query first, but will look at outline and sample chapter or complete ms. Reports "immediately." Enclose SAE and return postage.
Reference, Textbooks and History: "Our requirements are unusual, so we usually treat each author and his subject in a way particularly appropriate to his special skills and subject matter. Guidelines are flexible and generous, though it is expected that an author will consult with us in depth. Most, though not all, of our original publications are offset from camera-ready typescript. Since most genealogical reference works are compilations of vital records and similar data, tabular formats are common. We hope to receive more ms material in the area of census indexes, specifically indexes to statewide decennial censuses. We also anticipate mss documenting the Revolutionary War service of large numbers of early Americans. We would like to have an on-going Revolutionary War genealogy project." Family history compendia, basic methodology in genealogy, and advanced local history (for example, county histories, particularly those containing genealogy); heraldry: dictionaries and glossaries of the art and science, armorials of families entitled to bear coat armor, manuals and craftbooks describing heraldic painting, etc. Recently published *Index to the 1820 Census of Virginia,* by J. Felldin; *Heraldic Design,* by H. Child; and *Researcher's Guide to American Genealogy,* by V. Greenwood (textbook).

GENERAL PUBLISHING CO., LTD., 30 Lesmill Rd., Don Mills, Ontario, Canada M3B 2T6. Publishes hardcover originals (70%) and hardcover and paperback reprints (30%). Publishes 75 titles/year. Royalty "depends on nature of book." Advance offered. Simultaneous and photocopied submissions OK. SASE. Reports in 5 weeks. Free book catalog.
Nonfiction: "Popular self-help and how-to-do-it books on topics relating to the consumer, Canadian politics, business, psychology and sociology." Submit outline/synopsis and sample chapters; consult Chicago *Manual of Style*. Recently published *Canadian Consumers Survival Book,* by P. Edmonston/E. Roseman; and *Teach Your Child to Read in 60 Days,* by S. Ledson.
Fiction: International interest in adventure, mystery and romance fiction. Submit outline/synopsis and sample chapters. Recently published *Bearwalk,* by L. Sallott/T. Peltier (suspense); *Divine Case of Murder,* by C. Dennis (humor); and *Indigo Nights,* by O. O'Neill (romance).

THE C.R. GIBSON CO., Knight St., Norwalk CT 06856. (203)847-4543. Editorial Director: Dee Barwick. Editors: Patricia Dreier, Stephanie Oda. Publishes hardcover and paperback originals. Publishes 20 titles/year. "Outright purchase is the usual practice, occasional royalty agreement is made; advance varies according to contractual agreement." Simultaneous and photocopied submissions OK. Reports in 2 months. SASE.
Nonfiction: "We publish gift books and inspirational pamphlets; no trade." Query or submit outline/synopsis. Recently published *Mothers Are Marvelous,* edited by B.S. Hazen (anthology about mothers); *I Love You Because . . . .,* by D. Walley; and *To Be A Friend,* edited by B.S. Hazen.

GINN AND COMPANY, 191 Spring St., Lexington MA 02173. Editor-in-Chief: Richard Morgan. Royalty schedule: from 10% of net on a secondary book to 4% on elementary materials. Published 450 titles last year. Sample chapters, complete or partially complete mss will be considered. Reports in 2 to 6 weeks. Enclose return postage.
Textbooks: Publishers of textbooks and instructional materials for elementary and secondary schools.

GLENMARK PUBLISHING CO., 5041 Byrne Rd., Oregon WI 53575. Editorial Director: Glenn Schaeffer. Senior Editor: Mike Pearlman. Publishes paperback originals. Published 2 titles in 1977, 6 in 1978; will do 10 in 1979. 5% royalty; no advance. SASE.
Nonfiction: "We deal in mail order books that have mass appeal. Our specialty is books on making money or success including such topics as real estate, stock market, starting a business, easy way to riches and so on. However we will seriously consider books that strike a nerve in the public such as on astrology, ESP, mysticism and so on. The bigger, the more exciting the idea, the better we like it." Query. Recently published *The Best Things In Life Are Free,* by G. Shay (how to get just about anything free); and *Foolproof Theory for Making a Fortune in the Stock Market,* G. Shay.

GOLDEN WEST BOOKS, Box 8136, San Marino CA 91108. (213)283-3446. Editor-in-Chief: Donald Duke. Managing Editor: Jeff Dunning. Hardcover and paperback originals. 10% royalty contract; no advance. Publishes about 7 titles annually. Simultaneous and photocopied submissions OK. Reports in 2-4 weeks. SASE. Free book catalog.
Nonfiction: Publishes western Americana and transportation Americana. Query first or submit complete ms. "Illustrations and photographs will be examined if we like ms." Recently published *Grand Central . . . World's Greatest Railway Terminal,* by W. Middleton; and *Mount Lowe Railway,* by C. Seims.

GRAPHIC ARTS CENTER PUBLISHING CO., 2000 NW Wilson St., Portland OR 97209. (503)224-7777. Executive Vice-President: Charles H. Belding. Publishes hardcover originals. Published 7 titles in 1977, 6 in 1978; will do 8 in 1979. Pays outright purchase averaging $3,000 (less for paperbacks); no advance. Simultaneous and photocopied submissions OK. Reports in 3 weeks. SASE. Free book catalog.
Nonfiction: "All titles are pictorials with text. Text usually runs separately from the pictorial treatment. State and regional book series are published under the imprint name (D.B.A.) Belding. Several theme series of pictorial books have also been begun and length and style are more flexible." Query. Recently published *New York,* by L. Atwill; *California II,* by D. Pike; and *Georgia,* by C. Wharton.

GRAY'S PUBLISHING LTD., Box 2160, Sidney, BC, Canada V8L 3S6. (604)656-4454. Editor: Maralyn Horsdal. Publishes hardcover and paperback originals. Offers standard royalty contract. Published 7 titles in 1978. Free book catalog. Query first with outline. Reports in 6 to 10 weeks. Enclose SAE and International Reply Coupons.
Nonfiction: Wants "nonfiction, Canadiana," especially Pacific Northwest. Biography, natural history, history. Indian culture. Nautical. Length: 60,000 to 120,000 words. Recently published *The Man for a New Country,* by D.R. Williams (biography); *Fifty Dollar Bride,* by J. Carpenter; and *Pére Murray and the Hounds,* by J. Gorman (biography).
Fiction: "We are beginning to accept fiction with a Pacific Northwest interest."

GREAT OUTDOORS PUBLISHING CO., 4747 28th St. N., St. Petersburg FL 33714. (813)522-3453. Editor-in-Chief: Charles Allyn. Publishes paperback originals. Offers royalty of 5% of retail price. No advance. Published 8 titles last year. Will send free catalog to writer on request. Will consider photocopied submissions and simultaneous submissions. Query first for nonfiction. Reports in 1 month. Enclose return postage.
Nonfiction: Books of regional interest. Fishing, gardening, shelling in Florida. Also publishes some cookbooks of southern emphasis. Should be straightforward, how-to style with consideration for the hobbyist or sportsman who needs the basic facts without flowery phrasing. "No other publisher is geared to the tourist market in Florida. Our books are low-cost and especially suited to their market." Would like to see more shell books with illustrations. Doesn't want to see personal narratives. Department editors: Joyce Allyn. Cooking, nature, recreation: Charles Allyn, self-help and how-to. Length: cooking 9,000 to 17,000 words; nature, 52,000 to 90,000 words; self-help, how-to, sports, hobbies, recreation and pets, 9,000 to 17,000 words.
Recent Titles: *Pelican,* by R. Ovingle (birds); and *Pine Cone Crafts,* by J. McKay (crafts).

GREEN HILL PUBLISHERS, INC., 236 Forest Park Place, Ottawa IL 61350. Editorial Direc-

tor: Jameson Campaigne Jr. Senior Editor: Richard S. Wheeler. Publishes originals (85%) and reprints (15%). Published 15 titles in 1977, 25 in 1978; will do 30 in 1979. 6-15% royalty; outright purchase averages $2,500. Advance averages $2,000. Simultaneous and photocopied submissions OK. Reports in 2 months. SASE. Book catalog for SASE.
Nonfiction: Racquet sports; pet books; and biographies (of major subjects). No autobiographies or "nostrum-peddling." Query; all unsolicited mss are returned unopened. Recently published *Watch the Ball, Bend Your Knees, That'll Be $20 Please,* by E. Collins (tennis instruction); *My Cat's First Five Years,* by Turley/Metcalf/Conrad (pet care); and *Cooper Rollow's Bears 1977 Football Book,* by C. Rollow (sports).
Fiction: Previously published, high quality fiction for mass paperback reprints; historical fiction (only well-researched, serious work); and westerns. No political fiction or romance material. Query; all unsolicited mss are returned unopened. "We prefer detailed precis with query." Recently published *Anatomy of a Murder,* by R. Traver (suspense reprint); and *Red Spring,* by J. Burke (historical).

GREEN TIGER PRESS, 7458 La Jolla Blvd., La Jolla CA 92037. Editorial Director: Harold Darling. Publishes hardcover and paperback originals (60%) and reprints (40%). Published 2 titles in 1977, 14 in 1978. Pays in royalties or outright purchase price; "variable" advance. Simultaneous and photocopied submissions OK. Reports in 2 weeks. SASE. Book catalog for 50¢.
Nonfiction: "We specialize in nonfiction works of children's illustrations, especially from an historical or cultural point of view." Submit complete ms. Recently published *Kay Nielsen,* by W. Poltarnees.
Fiction: Fantasy—especially for children. Submit complete ms. Recently published *Cabbage Moth and the Shamrock,* by E. Marback.

GREEN TREE PUBLISHING CO., LTD., 95 Grinity St., Toronto, Ontario, Canada M5A 3C7. (416)869-3321. Editor-in-Chief: W.H.P. Parr. Hardcover and paperback originals. 10% royalty; advance "depends on how badly we want the book. We've paid up to $3,500 and in many cases just a lunch." Published 12 titles in 1977; will publish 12-15 in 1978 and 1979. Simultaneous submissions OK "if we're given a date by which we must respond and given the book if we offer the best deal." Reports in 1-2 months. SASE. Free book catalog.
Nonfiction: Publishes business; economics; history; hobbies; how-to; humor; juveniles (adventure); politics; psychology (self-help type); reference; self-help; sociology; and textbooks (math). "We are a Canadian firm and publish for our market. In the craft and self-help line, there is no border. We are big on trains and welcome just about anything. No more poetry please." Query.
Special needs: "We are developing an inexpensive line of hobby/craft books. Technically simple and cheap to carry out."

***WARREN H. GREEN, INC.**, 8356 Olive Blvd., St. Louis MO 63132. Editor: Warren H. Green. Hardcover originals. Offers "10% to 20% sliding scale of royalties based on quantity distributed. All books are short run, highly specialized, with no advance." About 5% of books are subsidy published. Published 48 titles last year. "37% of total marketing is overseas." Will send a catalog to a writer on request. Will consider photocopied submissions. Submit outline and sample chapters. "Publisher requires 300- to 500-word statement of scope, plan, and purpose of book, together with curriculum vitae of author." Reports in 60 to 90 days.
Medical and Scientific: "Specialty monographs for practicing physicians and medical researchers. Books of 160 pages upward. Illustrated as required by subject. Medical books are non-textbook type, usually specialties within specialties, and no general books for a given specialty. For example, separate books on each facet of radiology, and not one complete book on radiology. Authors must be authorities in their chosen fields and accepted as such by their peers. Books should be designed for all doctors in English-speaking world engaged in full- or part-time activity discussed in book. We would like to increase publications in the fields of radiology, anesthesiology, pathology, psychiatry, surgery and orthopedic surgery, obstetrics and gynecology, and speech and hearing. Recently published *Nursing Care for Myocardial Infarction,* by M. Rubin (nursing); and *Ultrasonography,* by Brown (radiology).
Education: "Reference books for elementary and secondary school teachers. Authors must be authorities in their fields. No textbooks."

THE STEPHEN GREENE PRESS, Box 1000, Brattleboro VT 05301. (802)257-7757. Editorial Director: Castle Freeman. Publishes hardcover and paperback originals (99%); hardcover and paperback reprints (1%). Royalty varies from 8-10-12½% of net to 10-12½-15% of list; no

advance. "Ask for our list of submission requirements with your query. Refer to Chicago *Manual of Style; Elements of Style; Words into Type.*" Send contact sheet or prints to illustrate ms. Photocopied submissions OK. Reports in 1-2 months. SASE. Book catalog for SASE.
Nonfiction: Publishes Americana, biography; cookbooks, cooking and foods; history, how-to (self-reliance); nature and environment; recreation, self-help, sports (outdoor and horse); popular technology; regional (New England); and Belles-lettres. Recently published *Appalachian Odyssey,* by Sherman/Older (nature/recreation); and *Cross-Country Skiing Today,* by Caldwell (outdoor sports).

GREENLEAF CLASSICS, INC., Box 20194, San Diego CA 92120. Editorial Director: Douglas Saito. Managing Editor: James Koelmel. Paperback originals. Specializes in adult erotic fiction. Pays outright purchase price on acceptance. Publishes 360 titles/year. Submit complete ms. Reports in 2-4 weeks. SASE. Writer's guidelines for SASE.
Fiction: Publishes erotic novels. "All stories must have a sexual theme. They must be mainstream novels dealing with the serious problems of everyday people. All plots are structured so that characters must get involved in erotic situations. Write from the female viewpoint." Preferred length: 40,000 words.

GREENWICH PRESS, 335 Bleecker St., New York NY 10014. Editor: Anton Hardt. Publishes hardcover originals and reprints. Query first. Enclose return postage.
Nonfiction: "Books only on the subject of antiques and possibly allied fields."

GREGG DIVISION, McGraw-Hill Book Co., 1221 Ave. of the Americas, New York NY 10020. Vice President and General Manager: Charles B. Harrington. Publishes hardcover originals. "Contracts negotiable; no advances." Query first. "We accept very few unsolicited mss." Reports in 1 to 2 months. Enclose return postage with query.
Textbooks: "Textbooks and related instructional materials for the career education market." Publishes books on typewriting, office education, shorthand, accounting and data processing, distributing and marketing, agriculture, trade and industrial education, and health and consumer education. Recently published *Working in Plant Science,* by Bishop (career education); *Gregg Shorthand, Series 90,* by Leslie/Zoubek (business education); and *Electronic Circuits for Technicians,* by Temes (technical education).

GROSSETT AND DUNLAP, INC., (including Tempo Teenage Paperbacks and Universal Library), 51 Madison Ave., New York NY 10010. (212)689-9200. Editor-in-Chief: Robert Markel. Publishes hardcover and paperback originals and reprints, as well as a "very few" translations, and anthologies "on occasion." Royalty and advance terms generally vary. Published "close to 400" titles last year. Will send a catalog to a writer on request. Send query letter, outline, or sample chapter only; do not send complete ms. "We do not accept unsolicited manuscripts." Reports in 3 to 5 weeks. SASE.
General Fiction: "Very seldom—usually only via literary agent."
General Nonfiction and Reference: "No limits—anything and everything that would interest the 'average' American reader: sports, health, ecology, etc." Interested in history, science, religion, biography, the arts, and literature. Favors writers with strong experience and good credits.
Juveniles and Teen: Editor-in-Chief, Children's Picture Books: Doris Duenewald.

***GROSSMONT PRESS, INC.**, 7071 Convoy Court, San Diego CA 92111. Editorial Director: Joyce Schelling. Senior Editor: Ellen Squires. Publishes hardcover and paperback originals. Published 21 titles in 1977, 36 in 1978; will do 51 in 1979. 10% royalty; no advance. Subsidy publishes 75% of titles. Photocopied submissions OK. Reports in 4 weeks. SASE.
Fiction, Business, Nonfiction, Juveniles, Photography, Poetry and Textbooks: "All subjects considered." Fiction and nonfiction length requirements: 15,000 to 20,000 words. Children's books: 1,000 word minimum, "if amply illustrated." Poetry: 30 or 40 poems. "Our poetry list is expanding rapidly because of excellent sales this past year through gift shops. We are anxious to learn about trade and college textbooks, particularly in the business field. Also, we're looking for anthologies on all topics for use as supplementary readers for college level courses." Also interested in Americana; biography; book trade; economics; history; humor; law; library; medicine and psychiatry; nature; philosophy; politics; reference; religion; scientific; self-help and how-to; sociology; sports, hobbies, recreation and pets; travel. Submit outline/synopsis and sample chapters. Recently published *Somewhere the Sun is Shining,* by B./J. Calhoun (biographical); *The Weather Surfer,* by V. Morris/J. Nelson; and *The Wind Blows Death,* by D. Pierce (western novel).

GROUPWORK TODAY, INC., Box 258, South Plainfield NJ 07080. Editor-in-Chief: Harry E. Moore, Jr. Publishes hardcover and paperback originals. Offers $100 advance against royalties on receipt of contract; 10% of gross receipts from sale of book. "If a book is of special value, we will pay 10% of gross earnings on first 1,000 copies and 15% thereafter." Average advance is $100. Books are marketed by direct mail to Groupwork Agency executives and professionals (YMCA, YWCA, Scouts, Salvation Army, colleges, directors of organized camps, and libraries.) Will send catalog to a writer for $1. "Also will answer specific questions from an author considering us as a publisher." Will not consider simultaneous submissions. Submit outline and sample chapters for nonfiction. Reports in 6 to 8 weeks. Enclose return postage.
Nonfiction: "We are publishers of books and materials for professionals and volunteers who work with people in groups. Some of our materials are also suited to the needs of professionals who work with individuals. Groupwork agency management, finance, program development and personnel development are among the subjects of interest to us. Writers must be thoroughly familiar with 'people work' and have fresh insights to offer. New writers are most welcome here. Lengths are open but usually run 30,000 to 50,000 words." Readers are mainly social agency administrators and professional staff members. Groupwork materials are also read by volunteers serving in the social agencies. Mss are judged by experienced professionals in social agencies. The company is advised on policy direction by a council of advisors from national agencies and colleges across the nation. "We are planning what we are tentatively calling our 'Seminar' series to deal with the most important problems with which social work agencies must deal today. We would like to see a good work on 'Management by Objective' as applied to groupwork agency operations."

GUIDANCE CENTRE, Faculty of Education, University of Toronto, 1000 Yonge St., Toronto, Ontario, Canada M4W 2K8. (416)978-3210. Editorial Director: S.J. Totton. Senior Editor: Hazel Ross. Publishes hardcover and paperback originals. Published 19 titles in 1977, 20 in 1978. Pays in royalties. Reports in 1 month. Submissions returned "only if Canadian postage is sent." Free book catalog.
Nonfiction: "The Guidance Centre is interested in publications related to career planning and guidance and in measurement and evaluation. Also general education. No manuscripts which have confined their references and illustrations to United States material." Submit complete ms. Consult Chicago *Manual of Style*. Recently published *Saturday's Stepchildren,* by S. Shack; and *Population and Canada,* by M. Barrett/C. Taylor.

GUITAR PLAYER BOOKS, Box 615, Saratoga CA 95030. (408)446-1105. Editor-in-Chief: Jerry R. Martin. Publishes paperback originals (95%) and reprints (5%). 10% royalty; advance averages $500. Simultaneous submissions OK, "but we must be fully informed of identities of all other recipients." Reports in 2-4 weeks. SASE. Free book catalog.
Nonfiction: General interest and instructional books for guitarists of all ages. "We do not want books on chords or fingerpicking or books for fans; no general method books." Query and submit first chapter and outline. "Very clear, straightforward style; minimum personal opinion of author. Music and tablature in pencil only. Permisssions for music print rights are responsibility of author. We will consider mss of 15,000-30,000 words; double-spaced on bond paper; author should have intimate knowledge of music, including direct contact with artists, instruments, and technology. Materials should be clearly introduced and fully developed in the text. Ms should convey a sense of authority and support this sense with fresh authenticated information; write for the 18-35-year-old male market of guitar lovers of all styles. We prefer co-authorship with famed and accomplished guitar artists." Recently published *Home Recording for Musicians,* by C. Anderton; *Rock Guitarists, Volume II,* by the editors of *Guitar Player Magazine*.
Special Needs: A new imprint tentatively titled Keyboard Books will be slanted toward keyboard players.

***GULF PUBLISHING CO.**, Box 2608, Houston TX 77001. (713)529-4301. Editor-in-Chief: C.A. Umbach, Jr. Senior Editor: B.J. Lowe. Hardcover originals. 10% royalty; advance averages $300-2,000. Published 22 titles in 1977, 40 in 1978; will do 45 in 1979. Subsidy publishes 1-2 titles a year. Simultaneous and photocopied submissions OK. Reports in 1-2 months. SASE. Free book catalog.
Nonfiction: Publishes business; reference; regional trade; regional gardening; scientific and self-help books.

H.P. BOOKS, Box 5367, Tucson AZ 85703. Editor-in-Chief: Carl Shipman. Hardcover and paperback originals. Specializes in how-to books in several fields, all photo-illustrated. Pays

12½% of net; advance negotiable. Publishes approximately 12 titles/year. Query. State number and type of illustrations available. Simultaneous and photocopied submissions OK. Reports in 2-4 weeks. SASE. Free book catalog.
Nonfiction: Publishes cookbooks, cooking and foods; hobbies; how-to; leisure activities; photography; recreation; self-help; and technical books. All books 160 pages minimum, "word count varies with format." Recently published *Wok Cookery,* by C. Dyer; *SLR Handbook,* by C. Shipman; and *Handtool Handbook,* by R.J. Dechistobita.

HAMMOND, INC., 515 Valley St., Mapplewood NJ 07040. (201)763-6000. Editorial Director: Frank Brady. Hardcover and paperback originals. "Books are negotiated from flat fee for outright purchase to advances against standard royalties, depending on subject." Published 25 titles in 1977, 30 in 1978. Submit outline/synopsis and sample chapters. State availability of photos/illustrations. Simultanous submissions OK. Reports in 2-4 weeks. SASE. Book catalog for SASE.
Nonfiction: Publishes Americana, art, biography, business; cookbooks, cooking and foods; history, hobbies, how-to, humor, music, nature, photography, psychology, recreation, reference, religious, sports and travel books.
Fiction: "Perhaps mystery fiction with a strong travel or geographical plot. Author must really know the area about which he writes and work that into an intriguing plot.
Recent Titles: *Eyewitness to Disaster,* by D. Perkes (general nonfiction); *Discover Brunch,* by R. MacPherson (cookbook); and *Living Longer,* by A. and D. Geller.

HANCOCK HOUSE PUBLISHERS LTD., 3215 Island View Rd., Saanichton, B.C., Canada V05 1MO. Editor-in-Chief: David Hancock. Managing Editor: Robert Sward. Hardcover and paperback originals (97%) and reprints (3%). 10% royalty: $100 minimum advance. Published 30 titles in 1977, 35 in 1978. State availability of photos and/or illustrations to accompany ms. Reports in 1-2 months. SASE. Free book catalog.
Nonfiction: Publishes (in order of preference): nature, history, biography, reference, Americana (Canadian); cookbooks, cooking and foods; hobbies, how-to, juveniles, photography, recreation, self-help, sports, and travel books. Query. Recently published *British Columbia: Our Land,* by P. St. Pierre; and *Our UFO Visitors,* by J. Magor.

HANOVER STUDIOS, INC., Box 6013, Boston MA 02209. (617)241-8858. Editorial Director: Susan McCann. Publishes hardcover and paperback originals. Published 2 titles in 1977, 6 in 1978. 5-10-15% royalty; advance averages $1,000. Simultaneous and photocopied submissions OK. Reports in 2-4 weeks. SASE. Free book catalog.
Nonfiction: Americana (heavily illustrated historical works with general appeal); cookbooks, cooking and foods (specialties such as deer hunter's or scuba diver's cookbooks); history; recreation (where-to-go, what-to-do, who-to-see); and well illustrated sports histories. "Word length is flexible. We will rely on a lot of artwork to carry a contracted ms. A sample illustration should accompany ms, although we will supply the artist, if necessary." Submit outline/synopsis and sample chapters. Recently published *Underwater New England,* by G. Comeau/A. Bailey (scuba diver's guide); and *America's Cup,* by D. Alvord (illustrated history).

HARBINGER PUBLICATIONS, Box 891, San Francisco CA 94101. Editor-in-Chief: Patrick Fanning. Publishes paperback originals. Offers standard minimum book contract of 10-12½-15%. Published 1 title last year. "At present, our marketing and distribution is mainly by mail, so new book projects for the next year will have to be tailored to a specific market that can be reached by direct mail." Will consider photocopied submissions. Query. Conform to *Chicago Manual of Style*. Reports in 4 weeks for rejected material; 8 weeks for a manuscript accepted for publication. Enclose return postage.
Fiction: "Would like to see quality experimental fiction or traditional novels with strong personal style."
Business and Professional: "No taboos, but dislike seeing commonplace approaches to tired subjects; avoid padding a thin ms out to 'book-length.' We'd rather see the shorter version. Looking for originality and excellence." Would like to see mss in the areas of practical business handbooks, sociology, popular psychology, and alternative life styles.

HARCOURT BRACE JOVANOVICH, 757 3rd Ave., New York NY 10017. Director of General Books Department: William Jovanovich. Publishes hardcover and paperback originals and reprints. SASE.
Adult Trade Hardcovers: "We regret that all unsolicited mss for hardcover trade publication must be returned unread. Only mss submitted by agents or recommended to us by advisors or

actively solicited by us will be considered. However, we will consider queries or brief proposals."

Adult Trade Paperbacks: Editor-in-Chief: Sam Mitnick. Publishes original and reprint trade paperbacks under the Harvest imprint, including illustrated material, reprints of literary works, and novelty art, crafts, and photography.

Mass Market Paperbacks: Editor-in-Chief: Sondra Ordover. Publishes both adult and juvenile works. Mass market originals and reprints are published under the Jove/HBJ imprint. Jove/HBJ Books include category fiction plus general fiction and nonfiction. Unsolicited submissions of category fiction should be limited to the areas of romance, sagas and mysteries. Submissions in other areas may be considered for paperback original only, or a combination of hardcover/paperback publication. Refer queries and mss for adult paperbacks to Fred Graver, young adult or juvenile to Barbara Lucas.

Juveniles: Editor-in-Chief: Barbara Lucas. Fiction and nonfiction mss for beginning readers through the younger teenager. Early reading mss of special interest, especially nonfiction. Middle-grade and young adult fiction of exceptional quality only. Length: 5,000-60,000 words.

HARIAN PUBLICATIONS, 1 Vernon Ave., Floral Park NY 11001. Editor: Arthur Briskin. Advances paid on royalties. Published 8 titles last year. Will send copy of current catalog on request. Query first. Reports in 1 week. Enclose SASE.

Nonfiction: Books on travel, retirement, investments, and health. Length: 50,000 words minimum for completed mss.

HARLEQUIN BOOKS, LTD., 220 Duncan Mill Rd., Don Mills, Ontario, Canada M3B 3J5. (416)495-5860. Publishing Director: Fred Kerner. Managing Editor: George A. Glay. Publishes paperback originals (5%) and reprints (95%). Published 180 titles in 1977, 248 in 1978; will do 200+ in 1979. Photocopied submissions OK. Reports in 6-8 weeks. SASE.

Fiction: "We publish romantic fiction with no overt sex or violence. It is imperative that potential authors study a sizeable number of Harlequin titles to determine what constitutes an acceptable manuscript. Guidelines are available upon request." Submit outline/synopsis and first 40-50 pages of ms.

HARPER & ROW, PUBLISHERS, INC., (including Torchbooks, Colophon, and Perennial Library, and Barnes & Noble), 10 E. 53rd St., New York NY 10022. Publishes hardcover and paperback originals and reprints. Royalty schedule subject to negotiation, but generally 10% to 5,000; 12½% to 10,000; 15% thereafter. Published 1,700 titles last year. Query letters, sample chapters and outlines preferred. For fiction, prefers completed ms. Address General Trade Department for fiction and nonfiction. Address Junior Books Department for Juveniles. Reports in 4 to 6 weeks. Enclose return postage.

General Fiction and Nonfiction: Publishes books between 40,000 and 200,000 words in the following departments: college, elementary and high school, mail order, medical, nature and outdoor, religious, social and economic, and trade. Trade books can cover any subject of general interest, fiction or nonfiction, rather than specialized or scholarly works. Adult Trade Editor: Erwin Gilkes.

Juveniles: Charlotte Zolotow, Patricia Allen.

Textbooks: Publishes elementary and high school textbooks. Address Harrison Bell, School Department, 10 E. 53rd St., New York NY 10022. College textbooks. Address Alvin Abbott, Publisher, College Dept. Harper & Row, 10 E. 53rd St., New York NY 10022. Junior college textbooks. Address Jack Jennings, Publisher, Canfield Press, 1700 Montgomery St., San Francisco CA 94111.

HART PUBLISHING CO., INC., 15 W. 4th St., New York NY 10012. (212)260-2430. Hardcover and paperback originals. Royalty of 5% of list price for paperbacks; 10% for hardcovers. Advance averages $1,000. Published 50 titles in 1977, 60 in 1978 Reports in 1-2 weeks. SASE. Free book catalog.

Nonfiction: Publishes books on cooking and foods and cookbooks; hobbies, how-to, psychology, recreation, reference, self-help and sociology. Query first, or submit outline/synopsis and sample chapters, or complete ms.

Special Needs: "We are beginning a series of activity books for young children. We are looking for crossword puzzles, poems, short bedtime stories, games, things to make and do, puzzles and concept activities. All of these must be extremely easy to do and understand. Art may or may not be included. We pay anywhere from $5-10 per piece, depending on length and merit, more if art is included. Payment is made immediately upon acceptance. All material must be accompanied by SASE. Replies will be made within 2 weeks."

HARVARD UNIVERSITY PRESS, 79 Garden St., Cambridge MA 02138. (617)495-2600. Director: Arthur J. Rosenthal. Editor-in-Chief: Maud Wilcox. Publishes hardcover and paperback originals and reprints. Published 90 titles in 1977. Free book catalog.
Fiction: "The Harvard Program in the Short Novel is our sole source of fiction book needs. Manuscripts of any previously unpublished short novel in the English language may be submitted at any time, the length to be between 25,000-60,000 words. Send completed mss to general editor William Goodman at Harvard University Press.

HARVEST HOUSE LTD., PUBLISHERS, 4795 St. Catherine St. W., Montreal, Quebec, Canada H3G 1B4. (514)932-0666/4724. Senior Editor: Maynard Gertler. Publishes hardcover and paperback originals and translations. Published 12 titles in 1977, 15 in 1978; will do 12-15 in 1979. 8-12% royalty; advance "varies widely." Photocopied submissions OK. Reports in 3-6 weeks. SASE. Free book catalog.
Nonfiction: Social studies, science, history, philosophy, biography, education, public affairs, and general nonfiction. "Simple, untechnical language devoid of terminological snares is an advantage. We are interested in manuscripts of Canadian and general world appeal." Query or submit outline/synopsis and sample chapters. Length: 35,000 words maximum. Recently published *Social Realism in the French-Canadian Novel,* by Ben-Zion Shek (literary criticism); *Anne Savage: The Story of a Canadian Painter,* by A. MacDougall (biography); and *Greater Than Kings: Ukrainian Pioneer Settlement in Canada,* by Z. Keywan/M. Coles (history).
Fiction: Canadian science fiction and general novels. Query or submit outline/synopsis and sample chapters. Recently published *Bitter Bread,* by A. Laberge (translation novel).

HARVEY HOUSE PUBLISHERS, 20 Waterside Plaza, New York NY 10010. Editorial Director: L.F. Reeves. Managing Editor: Larry Bograd. Publishes hardcover originals. Published 14 titles in 1977, 30 in 1978; will do 30 in 1979. 5% minimum royalty; advance "depends on ms." Simultaneous (if so informed) and photocopied submissions OK. Reports in 3 weeks. SASE. Book catalog for SASE.
Nonfiction: Juvenile leisure-time activity books. "We have successful books on skateboards, minicycles, hang gliding, etc. Our biography series "Star People" covers athletes: we have books on Dorothy Hamill, Tracy Austin, Janet Guthrie, Reggie Jackson, and celebrities such as Linda Ronstadt. Also occasional science books." No religious, self-help, strictly adult, textbooks, or travel books. Query. Recently published *Soccer*, by J. Scagnetti (sports how-to); *A.J. Foyt*, by R. Olney; and *Hang Gliding*, by N. Robison.
Fiction: "We publish only a couple of novels a year. Recently have opted toward realistic fictions about contemporary problems—i.e., foster children, American Indians, etc. We are considering a line of mysteries built around leisure-time activities such as skateboarding, etc. We are always looking for good picture books." No science fiction, romances, fantasy, talking animal stories or rehashed fairy tales. Query. Recently published *Yes My Darling Daughter*, by E. Swetnam; *Malcolm Yucca Seed*, by L. Gessner; and *The Sand Lot*, by M.B. Christian.

HASTINGS HOUSE PUBLISHERS, INC., 10 E. 40th St., New York NY 10016. (212)689-5400. Editor-in-Chief: Walter Frese. Hardcover and paperback originals (80%) and reprints (20%). 10% minimum royalty. Reports in 1-2 weeks. SASE. Free book catalog.
Nonfiction: Publishes Americana, biography; cookbooks, cooking and foods; history, humor, juveniles, photography, recreation, sports and travel books. Query or submit outline/synopsis and sample chapters. Recently published *Food Processor Magic,* by Hemingway/DeLima (cooking); *Seeds of Anger,* by S.B. Smith (history); and *Cape Cod in Color,* by Lazarus/Vuilleumier (travel).

HAYDEN BOOK CO., INC., 50 Essex St., Rochelle Park NJ 07662. (201)843-0550. Editorial Director: William Cook. Publishes hardcover and paperback originals. Published 50 titles in 1977, 60 in 1978; will do 60 in 1979. 10% royalty; offers "minimal" advance. Simultaneous (if so identified) and photocopied submissions OK. Reports in 6 weeks. SASE. Free book catalog.
Technical: Publishes technician-level and engineering texts and references in many subject areas (emphasis on electronics and computer science); text and references for hotel, restaurant and institution management and other personnel (emphasis on management, food service).
Textbooks: Texts and references for senior high schools, technical institutes and community colleges in English (literature and composition) computer sciences, mathematics, and other subject areas.

HEALTH PROFESSION PUBLISHING, McGraw-Hill Book Co., 1221 Avenue of the

Americas, New York NY 10020. Editor-in-Chief: Joseph J. Brehm. Pays on royalty basis. SASE.
Textbooks: Publishes textbooks, major reference books and audiovisual materials in the fields of medicine, dentistry, nursing, and allied health.

D.C. HEATH & CO., 125 Spring St., Lexington MA 02173. (617)862-6650. Editor-in-Chief: Joseph Hodges. Economics and Math Editor: Robert Macek. History & Political Science Editor: Ann Knight. Education & Sociology Editor: Geoffery Hughes. Science Editor: Stanley Galek. Biology & Psychology Editor: Harry Herckner. Modern Langauges Editor: Mario Hurtado. Technical Editor: Michael McCarroll. English Editor: Holt Johnson. General Manager, College Division: John T. Harney. Publishes hardcover and paperback originals. Offers standard royalty rates for textbooks. Free book catalog. Query. Reports in 2 weeks. "Finished mss accepted are published within 1 year." SASE.
Textbooks: "Texts at the college level in sociology, psychology, history, political science, chemistry, math, physical science, economics, education, modern language, and English." Length varies.

HEIDELBERG PUBLISHERS, INC., 1003 Brown Bldg., Austin TX 78701. (512)451-3872. Editor-in-Chief: Vijay Parekh. Publishes hardcover originals. Offers standard minimum book contract. Advance varies. Published 4 titles last year. Will consider photocopied submissions. Query first or submit complete ms. SASE.
General Fiction and Nonfiction: "We are a general interest publisher and willing to see works of fiction (no short stories), nonfiction, biography, journalism, food and health, sociology, book trade, history, philosophy, photography, and travel."

HENDRICKS HOUSE, INC., 488 Greenwich St., New York NY 10013. (212)966-1765. Editorial Office: Putney VT 05346. Editor: Walter Hendricks. Publishes hardcover originals and hardcover and paperback reprints. Published 5 titles last year. Free book catalog. Photocopied submissions OK. Submit complete ms. Reports in 1 month. SASE.
Nonfiction: "Mainly educational." Publishes Americana, biography, history, philosophy, reference, and textbooks.

HERALD HOUSE, Drawer HH, 3225 S. Noland Rd., Independence MO 64055. (816)252-5010. Editor-in-Chief: Paul A. Wellington. Publishes hardcover originals. Standard royalty contract. Usual advance is $500, but this varies, depending on author's reputation and nature of book. Published 20 titles in 1978. Query first. Reports in 2 months. Enclose return postage.
Religion: Publishes religious books for adults and children. Fiction, poetry, doctrinal texts, history, etc. All books must be relevant to the Reorganized Church of Jesus Christ of Latter-Day Saints. Length: 30,000 to 60,000 words.

***HERALD PRESS**, 616 Walnut Ave., Scottdale PA 15683. (412)887-8500. (A division of Mennonite Publishing House.) Book Editor: Paul M. Schrock. Publishes hardcover and mass market paperback originals and reprints. Royalty schedule of 10% of retail price of book. Half royalty on bulk sales sold at more than 50% discount, such as to jobbers and book clubs. Escalator clause to 12% and 15%. Occasional advance of $500; usually, not more. Subsidy publishes 10% of books. "Only books sponsored by an official board or committee of the Mennonite Church to meet discriminating needs when a book is not otherwise economically feasible." Published 30 titles last year. Two or 3 titles a year are subsidized by church organizations. No personal subsidies. Will send catalog to writer for 50¢. No simultaneous submissions. Will consider photocopied submissions. Query first with brief outline and sample chapter. Reports within 1 month. Enclose return postage.
General Nonfiction and Fiction: "We publish books of specific interest to Mennonites, as well as books of general Christian interest in such areas as inspiration, Bible study, self-help, church history, adult fiction, devotionals, peace studies, current issues, personal experience stories showing how the Christian faith provides genuine help in facing life, missions and evangelism, family life, and Christian ethics. Our goal is to publish books which are sound in theology, honest in presentation, clear in thought, stimulating in content, and conducive to the spiritual and intellectual growth of the reader. Length varies from several thousand words (pamphlets, children's storybooks) to hundreds of thousands of words *(Mennonite Encyclopedia)*. We can handle whatever length seems appropriate for the subject matter." Recently published *Marriage in Today's World,* by C.Amstutz, MD; *Mari's Mountain,* by D. Hamilton; and *African Fables,* by E. Keidel.
Juveniles: For ages 9 and up. Length: 25,000 to 30,000 words.

***HERITAGE BOOKS, INC.**, 36 Mace Rd., Hampton NH 03842. (603)926-7332. Editorial Director: Peter E. Randall. Senior Editor: Laird C. Towle, Ph.D. Publishes hardcover and paperback originals (20%) and reprints (80%). Published 5 titles in 1977, 12 in 1978; will do 20 in 1979. Subsidy publishes 20% of titles. "Quality of the book is of prime importance; next is its relevance to our field of interest. Our subsidy jobs would be better described as 'co-publication,' and are done in collaboration with individuals, groups or organizations. We normally expect to participate extensively in the marketing of the book." 10% royalty; no advance. Simultaneous and photocopied submissions OK. Reports in 1 month. SASE. Free book catalog.
Nonfiction: "We particularly desire nonfiction titles dealing with history and genealogy including how-to and reference works, as well as conventional histories and genealogies. The titles should be either of national interest or restricted to New England. Other subject matter will be considered provided that it is of either national or New England interest. We prefer writers to 1) query, 2) submit an outline/synopsis, or 3) submit a complete ms, in that order, depending on the stage the writer has reached in the preparation of his work." Recently published *The Colonial Era History of Dover, N.H.*, by Scales; and *Dover, N.H. Vital Records*, by the Dover Historical Society.

***HERITAGE HOUSE PUBLISHERS, INC.**, Box 52298, Jacksonville FL 32203. (904)725-5053. Editor-in-Chief: Leslie E. Ellis. Hardcover and paperback originals. 10% royalty contract; no advance. Subsidy publishes 10% of books. "Generally, if we cannot offer the author a royalty contract because his work does not fit our direct needs, we will give him the option of using our Venture subsidy program. His work must be concise and well done." Published 3 titles in 1977 and 1978. State availability of photos to illustrate ms. SASE. Reports in 6-8 weeks.
Nonfiction: Americana, art, biography, business; cookbooks, cooking and foods; economics, history, hobbies, how-to, humor, juveniles, law; medicine and psychiatry; music, nature, pets, philosophy, poetry, politics, psychology, recreation, reference, religious, scientific, self-help, sociology, sports, technical, textbooks and travel topics. Query. Recently published *Mr. Easy Teaches Phonics*, by K. Bagaley; and *Lose Weight Without Dieting*, by Ellis.
For '79: "Our primary interest at the present time is in the development of a series of medically oriented books for the lay person. We are always interested in offering royalty contracts for good patient-oriented mss."

HERMAN PUBLISHING, 45 Newbury St., Boston MA 02116. Editor: M.J. Philips. Publishes hardcover and paperback originals and reprints. "Standard 10% royalty (7% on paperbacks) up to break-even point; higher beyond." Advance varies, depending on author's reputation and nature of book. Will send copy of current catalog on request. Send query, outline and sample chapter to C.A. Herman. Reports in 2 months. SASE.
General Nonfiction, Business, and Technical: Business, technical and general nonfiction; reference, science, hi-fi, music, antiques, gardening, cooking, the arts, health, self-improvement, psychology, travel, regional, religion, history, biography, ships, audio, acoustics, electronics, radio, TV, architecture, communications arts, engineering and technology, food service and home economics, health care and management, manufacturing and marketing. "It might be worth noting that we also perform a unique service. We will market to the book trade (and elsewhere possibly), books which may have been privately published by the author or by a small publisher. Naturally, we must first see a sample copy and be satisfied that we can market it." Writing must be factual and authoritative. No length limits.

LAWRENCE HILL & CO., 24 Burr Farms Rd., Westport CT 06880. (203)226-9392. Editor-in-Chief: Lawrence Hill. Managing Editor: Mercer Field. Hardcover and paperback originals. Specializes in publishing Black Studies and Third-World affairs books. Standard royalty; advance averages $500 and up. Query or submit outline/synopsis and sample chapters. State availability of photos and/or illustrations unless for children's book. For children's book send samples. Photocopied submissions OK. Reports in 2-4 weeks. SASE. Book catalog for SASE.
Nonfiction: Publishes Americana; art; biography; cookbooks; economics; history; humor; juveniles; law; psychiatry; music; nature; pets; philosophy; poetry; politics; psychology; reference (no dictionaries or encyclopedia—trade book slant); religious (trade book slant); scientific; self-help; sociology; sports; and travel books.
Fiction: Publishes adventure; experimental; historical; humorous; mainstream; mystery; religious; romance; science fiction; suspense; and western books.
Recent Titles: *The Jazz Book*, by J. Berendt (music); *The Kidnapped Saint*, by B. Traven (short stories); *The Land's Lord*, by T.O. Echewa (African fiction).

HIS PUBLISHING HOUSE, Box 245, Goodlettsville TN 37072. Editorial Director: Norma L. Boyd. Publishes hardcover and paperback originals. Published 2 titles in 1977, 4 in 1978; will do 10 in 1979. 25% net royalty; no advance. Books sold through Christian bookstores. Simultaneous and photocopied submissions OK. Reports in 2 weeks. SASE. Book catalog for SASE "when available."
Nonfiction: Religious material: meditation, study, poetry, prayers, biography, and autobiography. Submit complete ms. Recently published *From His Hand,* by D. Cusic (poetry); *The Gospel According to Common Sense,* by J. Cring (Bible study); and *LaBreeska,* by LaBreeska/Hemphill (autobiography).

HOLIDAY HOUSE, 18 E. 53rd St., New York NY 10022. (212)688-0085. Editorial Director: Margery Cuyley. Publishes hardcover originals. Published 23 titles in 1977, 25 in 1978. Pays in royalties; offers variable advance. Photocopied submissions OK. Reports in 2 months. SASE. Free book catalog.
Nonfiction and Fiction: General fiction and nonfiction for young readers—pre-school through high school. Submit outline/synopsis and sample chapters or complete ms.

HOLLOWAY HOUSE PUBLISHING CO., 8060 Melrose Ave., Los Angeles CA 90046. (213)653-8060. Editor-in-Chief: Charles D. Anderson. "Our payments are on a par with those of larger paperback book publishers, and our distribution is good. We rely heavily on promotion and advertising. A manuscript will be reviewed the same day as received. If it is unacceptable, it will be returned that day. If it is accepted for consideration, please allow 3 months for a decision."
Nonfiction and Fiction: Holloway House is in the market for adult, high-quality novels and (more rarely) nonfiction works on subjects of enduring interest. Our major concern is with the Black Experience—writings on realistic black themes. We prefer hard-hitting contemporary stories with easily identifiable characters and locations in realistic situations. Dialogue must be street-wise and strong, people and places thoroughly described, and violence graphically depicted. A strain of sex is acceptable but not essential. A manuscript without these elements is not acceptable." Query or submit outline/synopsis and sample chapters.

A.J. HOLMAN CO., A Division of J.B. Lippincott, East Washington Square, Philadelphia PA 19105. (215)574-4304. Editorial Director: Jerry L. Hooper. Publishes hardcover and paperback originals (60%) and paperback reprints (40%). Published 10 titles in 1978. 10% royalty; negotiable advance. Simultaneous and photocopied submissions OK. Reports in 4-6 weeks. SASE. Book catalog for SASE.
Nonfiction: Conservative Christian books addressed to popular readership. Devotional, how-to-do-it approach. Also Bible study aids. Submit outline/synopsis and sample chapters. Recently published *But For Our Grief,* by J. Taylor; *Death of a Guru,* by R. Maharaj; and *The Family Album,* by Demoss.

HOLT, RINEHART & WINSTON OF CANADA, LTD., 55 Horner Ave., Toronto, Ontario Canada M8Z 4X6. (416)255-4491. Editorial Director: James Mainprize. Senior Editor: Frank Barrett. Publishes hardcover and paperback originals. Published 28 titles in 1977, 40 in 1978; will do 30 in 1979. Royalty varies according to type of book; pays $200-500 for anthologies. No advance. Simultaneous and photocopied submissions OK. Reports in 1-3 months. SASE. Free book catalog.
Nonfiction: Education texts. Query. Recently published *Canadian Public Finance (Second Edition);* by J.C. Strick (college economics text); *Le Français Partout 6,* by Wright/Hathorn (secondary text); and *Ready or Not,* by J. Booth (elementary language arts text).
Fiction: "Interested in fiction with realistic Canadian background." No science fiction or romances. Query.

HOPKINSON & BLAKE, 185 Madison Ave., New York NY 10016. Editor-in-Chief: Len Karlin. Publishes clothbound and paperback originals. Offers standard 10-12½% royalty contract; average advance $1,000. Published 5 titles last year. Query. Reports in 2 weeks. SASE.
Nonfiction: Mainly for college market. "We plan to continue to publish books on motion pictures. Also going into social sciences. Cookbooks, and self-help books will also be considered."

HORIZON PRESS, 156 Fifth Ave., New York NY 10010. Royalty schedule standard scale from 10% to 15%. Published 22 titles in 1977. Free book catalog. Prefers complete ms. Reports in 6 weeks. SASE.

Nonfiction: History, literature, science, biography, the arts, general. Length: 40,000 words and up. Recently published *The Encyclopedia of Jazz in the Seventies,* by L. Feather; *Understanding Human Nature,* by J.K. Feibleman; and *Witnessing: The Seventies,* by S. Bernard.

HOUGHTON MIFFLIN CO., 2 Park St., Boston MA 02107. (617)725-5000. Editor-in-Chief: Austin G. Olney. Managing Editor: David B. Harris. Hardcover and paperback originals (90%) and paperback reprints (10%). Royalty of 7½% for paperbacks; 10-15% on sliding scale for standard fiction and nonfiction; advance varies widely. Published 154 titles in 1977, 150 in 1978. State availability of photos to accompany ms and show half a dozen sample prints. Simultaneous submissions (if informed) and photocopied submissions OK. Reports in 2-4 weeks. SASE. Book catalog for SASE.
Nonfiction: Publishes (in order of preference): nature, history, biography, juveniles, politics, poetry, hobbies, Americana, how-to; and cookbooks, cooking and foods. Query. Recently published *Air,* by D. Schorr (politics).
Fiction: Publishes (in order of preference): mainstream, suspense, mystery, and historical books. Submit outline/synopsis and sample chapters. Recently published *The Immigrants,* by H. Fast; and *The Silmarillion,* by J.R.R. Tolkien.

HOUSE OF ANANSI PRESS LIMITED, 35 Britain St., Toronto, Ont., Canada M5A 1R7. (416)363-5444. Editorial Director: James Polk. Managing Editor: Ann Wall. Hardcover and paperback originals (99%) and paperback (of out-of-print important Canadiana) reprints (1%). Royalty "varies, depending on whether we publish the book first in hardcover or paperback or both; not less than 8%;" advance averages $500, "but we also participate in the author subsidy plan of the Ontario Arts Council, and through them can offer up to $3,000." Query, submit outline/synopsis and sample chapters or complete ms. "We're flexible, but prefer for nonfiction to have a pretty good idea of what we're going to get. Don't send photos or illustrations with first submission. Tell us about them and if we're interested in the writing, we'll talk about those later." Photocopied submissions OK. Reports in 1-2 months. SASE. Free book catalog.
Nonfiction: Publishes Canadian authors only. Publishes biography; history; law; medicine and psychiatry; music; philosophy; poetry; politics; psychology; and sociology books. "We have no length requirement. A book should be as long as it has to be to cover its topic adequately, and no longer. The slant should be toward the general reader with some university education. We like well-researched but not heavy or over-footnoted books." Recently published *Six Journeys: A Canadian Pattern,* by C. Taylor (biographies); and *George Grant in Process: Essays and Conversations,* edited by L. Schmidt.
Fiction: Publishes experimental books. Recently published *The Rosedale Hoax,* by R. Wyatt and *The Garden of Delights,* by P. Carrier.

HOUSE OF COLLECTIBLES, INC., 771 Kirkman Rd., Suite 100, Orlando FL 32811. Publishes hardcover and paperback originals. Royalty is based on the stature of the author, the subject and the ms. Average advance is $1,000. Published 15 titles last year. Complete distribution and marketing range in all fields with heavy coverage on the collectible markets. Will send catalog to writer on request. Submit outline and sample chapters. Will consider photocopied submissions. Mss must be typed, double spaced with sample illustrations, when necessary. Reports within 2 months. Enclose return postage.
Nonfiction: "On the subject of collectibles (antiques, numismatics, philatelics) and how-to-do books. We prefer an author who knows his or her subject thoroughly. Style and general format are left entirely to the author. Any special treatment or emphasis is a matter of decision for the author."

HOWELL-NORTH BOOKS, 1050 Parket St., Berkeley CA 94710. (415)845-4096. President: Flora D. North. Vice President: Morgan North. Publishes hardcover and paperback originals (95%) and hardcover reprints (5%). Published 2 titles in 1977, 7 in 1978. 10% royalty; no advance. Simultaneous submissions OK. Reports in 6 weeks. SASE. Free book catalog.
Nonfiction: "We would like to see manuscripts in the transportation field—railroads and marine preferred. In the Western Americana field we would like to see books on mining, but ones with general appeal rather than those too restricted in area or subject." Query. Recently published *A History of the Lehigh Valley Railroad,* by R.A. Archer; *The Iron Horse at War,* by J. Valle; and *Eminent Women of the West,* by E. Richey.

CARL HUNGNESS PUBLISHING, Box 24308, Speedway IN 46224. (317)244-4792. Editorial Director: Carl Hungness. Senior Editor: Jerry Miller. Publishes hardcover and paperback originals. Published 4 titles in 1977, 5 in 1978; will do 7 in 1979. Pays in "negotiable" outright

purchase; advance averages $500. Reports in 3 weeks. SASE. Free book catalog.
Nonfiction: Stories relating to professional automobile racing. No sports car racing or drag racing material. Query. Recently published *Indianapolis 500 Yearbook,* by C. Hungness and others (historical); and *The Mighty Midgets,* by J.C. Fox (historical).

HURTIG PUBLISHERS, 10560-105 St., Edmonton, Alta, Canada T5H 2W7. (403)426-2359. Editor-in-Chief: Sylvia Vance. Hardcover and paperback originals (80%) and reprints (20%). 10% royalty on first 7,000 copies; 12½% on next 1,000; 15% thereafter. Advance averages $500-1,000. State availability of photos and/or illustrations to accompany ms. Photocopied submissions OK. Reports in 1-2 months. SASE. Free book catalog.
Nonfiction: Publishes biographies of well-known Canadians; cookbooks, cooking and foods; Canadian history; humor; nature; topical Canadian politics; reference (Canadian); and material about native Canadians. No reminiscences. Query or submit outline/synopsis and sample chapters; or submit complete ms. Recently published *All of Baba's Children,* by M. Kostash (sociological/historical); *Andy Russell's Adventures with Wild Animals,* by A. Russell (adventure); and *Canada Cancelled Because of Lack of Interest,* by E. Nicol/P. Whalley (political satire).

***HWONG PUBLISHING CO.**, 10353 Los Alamitos Blvd., Los Alamitos CA 90720. Editor-in-Chief: Hilmi Ibrahim. Managing Editor: Peter Staple. Publishes hardcover and paperback originals. Specializes in social science and the humanities. 10% royalty; no advance. Subsidy publishes 33% of books. Send prints of photos and/or illustrations to accompany ms. Simultaneous and photocopied submissions OK. Reports in 2-4 weeks. SASE. Free book catalog.
Nonfiction: Publishes biography, business, history, humor, politics, psychology, recreation, religious, sociology, sports, and textbooks. Submit outline and sample chapters. Recently published *Self-Hypnosis,* by G. Van Warrebey; *Introduction to Sociology;* by R. O'Brien (textbook) and *Financial Accounting,* by H. Snavely et al (textbook).
Fiction: Publishes adventure, historical, humorous, mainstream, and suspense. Submit outline and sample chapters. Recently published *Kale,* by G. Campbell (adventure); and *The Zodiac Killer,* by C. Smith.

***IDEAL WORLD PUBLISHING COMPANY**, Box 1237-EG, Melbourne FL 32935. New Idea Publishing Co. is a division of the Ideal World Publishing Company. Editor: Harold Pallatz. Publishes hardcover and paperback originals and reprints. Offers "10% on hardcover, 5% on softcover; specific contracts can go higher or lower, depending upon material. No advance is ever given." About 25% of books are subsidy published. "If the book looks like it might sell, but we are not certain of exact demand, then, instead of outright rejection, we will try subsidy. Costs vary between $1,000 and $2,000 depending upon number of pages, copies, text, etc." Published 4 titles last year. Will consider photocopied submissions. Query first. Reports in 2 to 4 weeks. "No material will be returned unless SASE is attached."
Health: "Natural approaches to good health through nutrition, herbs, vegetarianism, vitamins, unusual medical approaches for specific ailments, particularly from authorities in the field. Any style is acceptable, but it must hold the reader's attention and make for fairly smooth nonintensive (no brain taxation) requirements. Ideas should be in a simple, easygoing pace."

INDEPENDENCE PRESS, Drawer HH, 3225 S. Noland Rd., Independence MO 64055. (816)252-5010. Editorial Director: Margaret Baldwin. Publishes hardcover and paperback originals (50%) and paperback reprints (50%). Publishes 7 titles/year. 10-12½-15% royalty; advance averages $200. Simultaneous and photocopied submissions OK. Reports in 2 months. SASE. Book catalog for 50¢.
Nonfiction: "Very interested in books with strictly local themes and settings. Kansas City history, Independence history, Missouri history, Kansas City sports or sports personalities; local outlaws such as Jesse and Frank James, Quantrill, the Youngers; books on political figures such as Tom Pendergast, etc. All material should be well-researched, preferably by experts in the field. Material should be geared to the general reading public." Submit outline/synopsis and sample chapters along with a brief biographical sketch of author. Recently published *Independence, Missouri,* by B. Foerster, Ph.D.; and *Images of Greatness,* by D. Melton.
Fiction: "Fiction for young people including books of local themes either historical or current." Science fiction; adventure; mystery; historic romance for young people (no sex, clean language, little violence); westerns, and sports. "We like action stories with girls for central characters." Query or submit outline/synopsis and sample chapters. Recently published *Duster,* by F. Poderus; and *Fire Mate,* by O. Cossi.

INDIANA UNIVERSITY PRESS, 10th & Morton Sts., Bloomington IN 47401. (812)337-4203.

Director: John Gallman. Publishes hardcover and paperback originals (75%) and paperback reprints (25%). Published 60 titles in 1977, 72 in 1978; will do 75 in 1979. 10% royalty; occasional advance. Photocopied submissions OK. Reports in 3 weeks on rejections, 2 months on acceptances. SASE. Free book catalog.
Nonfiction: Scholarly books on humanities, history, philosophy, translations, semiotics, public policy, film, music, linguistics, social sciences, regional materials and serious nonfiction for the general reader. Query or submit outline/synopsis and sample chapters. "Queries should include as much descriptive material as is necessary to convey scope and market appeal to us." Recently published *A Theory of Semiotics,* by U. Eco; *Shakespeare on Film,* by J. Jorgens (film/literature criticism); and *How Animals Communicate,* edited by T. Sebeok.
Fiction: "Only translations of fiction are published." Query or submit outline/synopsis and sample chapters.

***INFORMATION PRESS SERVICE**, 5118 Rolling Hills Court, Tampa FL 33617. (813)988-6561. Editorial Director: Phil Philcox. Senior Editor: Beverly H. Boe. Publishes hardcover and paperback originals. Published 7 titles in 1977, 10 in 1978; will do 25 in 1979. Subsidy publishes 15% of titles. "We make our living off regular book sales, not subsidy publishing, so we make a decision based solely on what we think the author's book can do on the market. We're equipped to assist any author in getting his/her book published at the lowest cost possible, although we're not vanity publishers. We print, not subsidize, and turn everything over to the author with a minimum amount of expense and trouble." Market consultation available. 10-12½-15% royalty or outright purchase ranging $250-1,000; no advance. Simultaneous and photocopied submissions OK. SASE.
Nonfiction: "We're interested in nonfiction only with subjects of mass appeal. We're not interested in anything 'folksy' (cooking, needlepoint), but are very interested in how-to books on how to get rich, how to live to be 200 years old, how to be happy, how to save money traveling, and subjects currently on the top-ten nonfiction bestseller list. No religion. Write in a loose, across-the-table style as if you were talking to the reader over a cup of coffee. We want to inform our readers but not put them to sleep while doing so. This year we published *Europe, The Two-Wheeled Adventure,* a motorcyclist's guide to touring Europe and *The Freelance Artist's Handbook,* how to earn $15,000-20,000 a year at the drawing board. Keep filler material (no facts but padding) to a minimum and eliminate it entirely if possible. Submit outline/synopsis and sample chapters.

***INSTITUTE FOR THE STUDY OF HUMAN ISSUES**, (ISHI Publications), 3401 Market St., Suite 252, Philadelphia PA 19104. (215)387-9002. Director of Publications: Betty C. Jutkowitz. Managing Editor: Douglas C. Gordon. Publishes hardcover and paperback originals (85%) and hardcover reprints (15%). Published 10 titles in 1977, 20 in 1978; will do 26 in 1979. Subsidy publishes 10% of books. "Some of our books are partly subsidized by grants from other institutions, but we never ask money from an author. When financial support for a particular book (or series of books) is necessary, we seek funding from appropriate institutions." 10-12½% royalty; no advance. Photocopied submissions OK. Reports in 3 months. SASE. Free book catalog.
Nonfiction: Books on political science, history, anthropology, folklore, sociology, narcotics, and macro-economics, suitable for scholars in these fields. Submit outline/synopsis and sample chapters. Recently published *Essays in Understanding Latin America,* by K.H. Silvert (political science); *Transaction and Meaning,* edited by B. Kapferer (social anthropology); and *Red Years/Black Years: A Political History of Spanish Anarchism, 1911-1937,* by R.W. Kern (history).

***INTERMEDIA PRESS**, Box 3294, Vancouver, B.C., Canada V6B 3X9. (604)681-3592. Editors-in-Chief: Henry Rappaport, Edwin Varney. Hardcover and paperback originals. 7½-10% royalty; occasionally offers advance. Published 10 titles in 1977, 12 in 1978. Query, or submit outline/synopsis and sample chapters or complete ms. State availability of photos and/or illustrations. Photocopied ("if we can print from the original") submissions OK. Reports in 2-4 months. SASE. Book catalog $1.
Nonfiction: Dona Sturmanis, Managing Editor. Publishes art (avant-garde, personal); cookbooks, cooking and foods; erotica (in a literary context); humor (absurdist); juveniles; multimedia material; poetry; recreation; sports; textbooks; and travel books. Recently published *Hot Springs of British Columbia and the Yukon,* by J. McDonald (guidebook); and *New West Coast,* edited by F. Candelaria (poetry anthology).
Fiction: Dona Sturmanis, Managing Editor. Publishes erotica; experimental; fantasy; historical (with a Canadian content); humorous; mainstream; and science fiction books. Recently pub-

lished *The Immigrant,* by G. Szohner; *Stories for Late Night Drinkers,* by M. Tremblay; and *16 Ways to Skin a Cat,* by G. Seanto.
Special Needs: "We are especially interested in juvenile and trade books. Anthologies of poetry and fiction also."

INTERNATIONAL MARINE PUBLISHING COMPANY, 21 Elm St., Camden ME 04843. Editors: Peter Spectre and Kathleen Brandes. Publishes hardcover and paperback originals and reprints. "Standard royalties, with advances." Free book catalog. "Material in all stages welcome. Query invited, but not necessary." Reports in 4 weeks. Enclose return postage.
Marine Nonfiction: "Marine nonfiction only—but a wide range of subjects within that category: fishing, boatbuilding, yachting, sea ecology and conservation, maritime history, cruising, true sea adventure, etc.—anything to do with boats, lakes, rivers, seas, and the people who do things on them, commercially or for pleasure. No word length requirements. Pictorial books with short texts are as welcome as 60,000-word mss." Recently published *Go South Inside,* by C. Lane (cruising guide); and *The Proper Yacht,* by A. Beiser (boat design).

INTERNATIONAL SELF-COUNSEL PRESS, LTD., 306 W. 25th St., North Vancouver, B.C., Canada V7N 2G1. (604)986-3366. Editorial Director: Jack James. Senior Editor: Heather Fayers. Publishes paperback originals. Published 30 titles in 1977, 35-40 in 1978; will do 35-40 in 1979. 10% royalty; no advance. Simultaneous and photocopied submissions OK. Reports in 2 weeks. SASE. Free book catalog.
Nonfiction: "Books only on law and business for the layperson (how-to)." Submit outline/synopsis and sample chapters. Follow Chicago *Manual of Style.* Recently published *You and the Police,* by R. Stoll; *Divorce Guide for Oregon,* by K. Lamar; and *Our Accountant's Guide for Small Business,* by C.G. Cornish.

INTERNATIONAL WEALTH SUCCESS, Box 186, Merrick NY 11566. (516)766-5850. Editor: Tyler G. Hicks. Offers royalty schedule of 10% of list price. Usual advance is $1,000, but this varies, depending on author's reputation and nature of book. Will consider photocopied submissions. Query first. Reports in 4 weeks. Enclose return postage.
Self-Help and How-to: "Techniques, methods, sources for building wealth. Highly personal, how-to-do-it with plenty of case histories. Books are aimed at the wealth builder and are highly sympathetic to his problems." Financing, business success, venture capital, etc. Length 60,000 to 70,000 words.

***THE INTERSTATE PRINTERS AND PUBLISHERS, INC.**, 19-27 N. Jackson St., Danville IL 61832. (217)446-0500. Editor-in-Chief: R. L. Guin. Managing Editor: Ronald McDaniel. Hardcover and paperback originals. Usual royalty is 10% of wholesale price; no advance. Occasionally subsidy publishes books depending on the market and financial evaluation. Publishes about 60 titles annually. Markets books by mail to all elementary, junior/middle and high schools in the U.S. Reports in 1-2 months. SASE. Free book catalog.
Nonfiction: Publishes textbooks; agriculture; special education; trade and industrial; home economics; athletics; career education; outdoor education; school law; marriage counseling; and learning disabilities books. Query or submit outline/synopsis and sample chapters. Recently published *Modern Agricultural Mechanics,* by T.J. Wakeman; and *Animal Science,* by M.E. Ensminger.

INTERVARSITY PRESS, Box F. Downers Grove IL 60515. (312)964-5700. Editorial Director: James W. Sire. Publishes hardcover and paperback originals. Published 38 titles in 1977, 42 in 1978; will do 45 in 1979. 10% royalty; advance averages $500. Photocopied submissions OK. Reports in 16 weeks. SASE. Free book catalog.
Nonfiction: "InterVarsity Press publishes books geared to the presentation of biblical Christianity in its various relations to personal life, art, literature, sociology, psychology, philosphy, history and so forth. Though we are primarily publishers of trade books, we are cognizant of the textbook market at the college, university and seminary level within the general religious field. The audience for which the books are published is composed primarily of university students and graduates; stylistic treatment varies from topic to topic and from fairly simplified popularizations for college freshmen to extremely scholarly works primarily designed to be read by scholars." Query or submit outline/synopsis and sample chapters. Recently published *Fire in the Fireplace: Contemporary Charismatic Renewal,* by C. Hummel (theology); *Rich Christians in an Age of Hunger,* by R. Sider (practical theology); and *Developing a Christian Mind,* by N. Barcus (humanities).

***IOWA STATE UNIVERSITY PRESS**, S. State Ave., Ames IA 50010. (515)294-5280. Director:

Merritt Bailey. Managing Editor: Rowena Malone. Hardcover and paperback originals. 10-12½-15% royalty; no advance. Subsidy publishes 10-50% of their titles, based on sales potential of book and contribution to scholarship. Published 42 titles in 1977, 40 in 1978. Send contrasty b&w glossy prints to illustrate ms. Simultaneous submissions OK, if advised; photocopied submissions OK if accompanied by an explanation. Reports in 2-4 months. SASE. Free book catalog.
Nonfiction: Publishes biography, history, recreation, reference, scientific technical, textbooks and Iowana books. Submit outline/synopsis and sample chapters; must be double-spaced throughout. Recently published *Physics of Stereo/Quad Sound,* by J.G. Traylor (audio reference); *Those Radio Commentators,* by I.E. Fang (biography); and *Family Afoot,* by E. Young (travel).

JOHNS HOPKINS UNIVERSITY PRESS, Baltimore MD 21218. Editor-in-Chief: Michael A. Aronson. Publishes mostly clothbound originals and paperback reprints; some paperback originals. Payment varies; contract negotiated with author. Prompt report, usually 8 weeks. Published 84 titles last year. Prefers query letter first. Enclose SASE.
Nonfiction: Publishes scholarly books and journals, biomedical sciences, history, literary theory and criticism, wildlife biology and management, psychology, political science, regional material, and economics. Length: 50,000 words minimum. Recently published *The Johns Hopkins Atlas of Human Functional Anatomy,* by Schlossberg/Zuidema; and *Wild Mammals of New England,* by A. Godin.

JONATHAN DAVID PUBLISHERS, 68-22 Eliot Ave., Middle Village NY 11379. (212)456-8611. Editorial Director: Alfred J. Kolatch. Publishes hardcover and paperback originals. Published 23 titles in 1977, 24 in 1978; will do 24 in 1979. 10-12½-15% royalty; advance averages $1,500. Photocopied submissions OK. Reports in 4 weeks. SASE. Book catalog for SASE.
Nonfiction: Adult nonfiction books for a general audience. "Subjects of interest include contemporary affairs, gardening, how-to, popular medicine, movies, nature, politics, sports, crafts, and hobbies. No religious, scholarly, or esoteric material." Recently published *The Gardener's Hint Book*, by C. Wilson; *The Lilt of the Irish*, by Spalding (humor/folklore); and *The Biography of a Tree*, by Jackson (nature).

***JOSSEY-BASS, INC., PUBLISHERS**, 433 California St., San Francisco CA 94101. (415)433-1740. Editorial Director: Allen Jossey-Bass. Senior Editors: JB Hefferlin, Higher Education; William E. Henry, Social and Behavioral Science. Publishes hardcover originals. Published 50 titles in 1977, 75 in 1978; will do 75 in 1979. 10-15% royalty; no advance. Simultaneous (if so informed) and photocopied submissions OK. Reports in 4 weeks. SASE. Free book catalog.
Nonfiction: Professional, scholarly books for senior administrators, faculty, researchers, graduate students, and professionals in private practice. Research-based books developed for practical application. "We do not want undergraduate texts or collections of previously published materials." Submit outline/synopsis and sample chapters. Recently published *Problem-Solving Therapy*, by J. Haley (social and behavioral science); *The Open University*, by W. Perry (higher education series); and *Handbook of Institutional Advancement*, edited by A.W. Rowland.

JOVE/HBJ PUBLICATIONS, 757 3rd Ave., New York NY 10017. Editorial Director: Sondra Ordover. Managing Editor: Fred Graver. Publishes paperback originals (50%) and reprints (50%). Published 180 titles in 1977, 148 in 1978; will do 148 in 1979. 8-10% royalty or outright purchase price of $3,000-5,000; advance "varies." Simultaneous and photocopied submissions OK. Reports in 1-2 months. SASE. Book catalog for SASE.
Nonfiction: Publishes biography; cookbooks; cooking and foods; history; hobbies; how-to; humor; juveniles; nature; pets; politics; psychology; reference; religious; self-help; and sociology books. Submit through agent only. Recently published *Male Trouble,* by Cant (self-help); and *You Can Fight for Your Life,* by LeShan (cancer).
Fiction: Publishes adventure; historical; humorous; mainstream; mystery; romance; science fiction and suspense books. Submit through agent only. Recently published *The Lawless,* by J. Jakes (saga); *The Vallette Heritage,* by L. Bronte (saga); and *Raven,* by S. Carrol (historical romance).

JUDSON PRESS, Valley Forge PA 19481. (215)768-2116. Managing Editor: Harold L. Twiss. Publishes hardcover and paperback originals. Generally 10% royalty on first 7,500 copies; 12½% on next 7,500; 15% above 15,000. "Payment of an advance depends on author's reputation and nature of book." Published 36 titles in 1976 and 1977. Free book catalog. Prefers a query

letter accompanied by outline and sample chapter. Reports in 3 months. Enclose return postage.
Religion: Adult religious nonfiction of 30,000 to 200,000 words. Recently published *Church Treasurer's Handbook,* by L.O. Ellis; *Those Meddling Women,* by J. Bailey; and *Confronting Death,* by W. Griffith.

WILLIAM KAUFMANN, INC., 1 First St., Los Altos CA 94022. Editor-in-Chief: William Kaufmann. Hardcover and paperback originals (90%) and reprints (10%). "Generally offers standard minimum book contract of 10-12½-15% but special requirements of book may call for lower royalties;" no advance. Published 8 titles in 1976, 12 in 1977; will do 10 in 1978. State availability of photos and/or illustrations to accompany ms. Simultaneous and photocopied submissions OK. Reports in 1-2 months. SASE. Free book catalog.
Nonfiction: "We specialize in not being specialized; look primarily for originality and quality." Publishes Americana; art; biography; business; economics; history; how-to; humor; medicine and psychiatry; nature; psychology; recreation; scientific; sports; and textbooks. Does not want to see cookbooks, novels, poetry, inspirational/religious and erotica. Query. Recently published *What's So Funny About Science?,* by S. Harris; and *Draw!,* by Belliston/Hanks.

KEATS PUBLISHING, INC., 36 Grove St., P.O. Box 876, New Canaan CT 06840. Editor: Ms. An Keats. Publishes hardcover and paperback originals and reprints. Offers standard 10-12½-15% royalty contract. Advance varies. Free book catalog. Query first with outline and sample chapter. Reports in 2 months. Enclose return postage.
Nonfiction: "Natural health, special interest; industry-subsidy. Also, mss with promotion and premium potential. In natural health, anything having to do with the current interest in ecology, natural health cookbooks, diet books, organic gardening, etc." Length: open.
Religion: "Largely in the conservative Protestant field."

J.J. KELLER & ASSOCIATES, INC., 145 W. Wisconsin Ave., Neenah WI 54956. (414)722-2848. President: John J. Keller. Publishes paperback originals. Payment by arrangement. Published 5 titles in 1977. Query. SASE.
Technical and Reference: "Working guides, handbooks and pamphlets covering the regulatory requirements for the motor carrier industry at both the federal and individual state levels. Technical and consumer publications pertaining to the International System of Units (Metric system of measurement)." Contact must be made in advance to determine applicability of subject matter and method of presentation. Recently published *National Backhaul Guide* (source directory); *Hazardous Materials Shipments* (reference); and *Multi-Day Logging* (reference).

KENT STATE UNIVERSITY PRESS, Kent State University, Kent OH 44242. (216)672-7913. Director: Paul H. Rohmann. Publishes hardcover originals. Standard minimum book contract; rarely gives an advance. Published 12 titles in 1977 and 1978. Free book catalog. "Please always write a letter of inquiry before submitting mss. We can publish only a limited number of titles each year and can frequently tell in advance whether or not we would be interested in a particular ms. This practice saves both our time and that of the author, not to mention postage costs." Reports in 10 weeks. Enclose return postage.
Nonfiction: Especially interested in "scholarly works in history of high quality, particularly any titles of regional interest for Ohio. Also will consider scholarly biographies, social sciences, scientific research, the arts, and general nonfiction." Recently published *The Cistercians: Ideals and Reality,* by L.J. Lekai; *The Swastika Outside Germany,* by D.M. McKale; and *The Mapping of Ohio,* by T.H. Smith.

KIRKLEY PRESS, INC., P.O. Box 200, Timonium MD 21093. Editor: Walter Kirkley. Publishes paperback 16-page booklets. "We buy mss outright and pay upon acceptance. Payment (total) varies between $200 and $300, depending on subject and strength with which written. Sample of our material sent on request." Send complete ms. "Try to answer in 2 weeks." Enclose return postage.
Business: "We publish small booklets which are sold to businesses for distribution to the employee. They attempt to stimulate or motivate the employee to improve work habits. Basically they are pep talks for the employee. We need writers who are so close to the problems of present-day employee attitudes that they can take one of those problems and write about it in a warm, human, understanding, personal style and language that will appeal to the employee and which the employer will find to his advantage to distribute to the employees." Length: 2,400 to 2,600 words.

B. KLEIN PUBLICATIONS, Box 8503, Coral Springs FL 33065. (305)752-1708. Editor-in-Chief: Bernard Klein. Hardcover and paperback originals. Specializes in directories, annuals, who's who type of books; bibliography, business opportunity, reference books. 10% royalty, "but we're negotiable". Advance "depends on many factors". Markets books by direct mail and mail order. Simultaneous and photocopied submissions OK. Reports in 1-2 weeks. SASE. Free book catalog for SASE.
Nonfiction: Publishes books on business, hobbies, how-to, reference, self-help, directories, bibliographies. Query or submit outline/synopsis and sample chapters or complete ms.
Current Titles: *Reference Encyclopedia of the American Indian*; *Your Business, Your Son and You,* by J. McQuaig (nonfiction).

KNICKERBOCKER BOOKS, INC., 38 Hicks St., Brooklyn Heights NY 11201. (212)624-4514. Editor-in-Chief: Stuart A. Ober. Publishes hardcover originals and reprints. Published 10 titles in 1977, 20 in 1978. 10% royalty; no advance. Simultaneous and photocopied submissions OK. Reports in 1-2 months. SASE. Free book catalog.
Nonfiction: Americana; cookbooks, cooking and foods; music; politics; and sports. Submit synopsis/outline and complete ms.
Fiction: Adventure; confession; erotica; experimental; fantasy; historical; humorous; mainstream; mystery; romance; science fiction; suspense; and western. Submit outline/synopsis and complete ms.

ALFRED A. KNOPF, INC., 201 E. 50th St., New York NY 10028. (212)751-2600. Senior Editor: Ashbel Green. Children's Book Editor: Ms. Pat Ross. Publishes hardcover and paperback originals (90%) and paperback reprints (10%). Publishes 150 titles/year. Royalties and advance "vary." Simultaneous (if so informed) and photocopied submissions OK. Reports in 2-4 weeks. Book catalog for SASE.
Nonfiction: Book-length nonfiction, including books of scholarly merit on special subjects. Preferred length: 40,000 to 150,000 words. "A good nonfiction writer should be able to follow the latest scholarship in any field of human knowledge, and fill in the abstractions of scholarship for the benefit of the general reader by means of good, concrete, sensory reporting." Query. Recently published *Perjury: The Hiss-Chambers Case,* by A. Weinstein (public affairs); *The Weaving, Spinning, and Dyeing Book,* by R. Brown (crafts); and *Biohazard,* by M. Rogers (science).
Fiction: Publishes book-length fiction of literary merit by known or unknown writers. Length: 30,000 to 150,000 words. Submit complete ms. Recently published *Listening to Billie,* by A. Adams; *The Honourable Schoolboy,* by J. Le Carré; and *Song on Solomon,* by T. Morrison.

JOHN KNOX PRESS, 341 Ponce de Leon Ave., NE, Atlanta GA 30308. (404)873-1531. Director: Richard A. Ray. Publishes hardcover and paperback originals (90%) and paperback reprints (10%). 7½% royalty on paperbacks; 10% on hardcover; no advance. Published 25 titles in 1977, 28 in 1978. Photocopied submissions OK. Reporting time varies according to proposal. SASE. Free book catalog.
Nonfiction: Publishes religious, inspirational, inter-personal; and recreation topic books. Recently published *Go Out in Joy,* by N. Herman; and *UFO's, God's Chariots,* by T. Peters.

KODANSHA INTERNATIONAL, LTD., 2-12-21 Otowa, Bunkyo-Ku, Tokyo 112, Japan. Hardcover originals and a limited number of paperback originals. 3-8% royalty, either against sales or printing; determined case by case. Advance varies. Markets trade books through Harper & Row; by direct mail to Asian studies specialists. State availability of prints or transparencies to illustrate ms. Photocopied submissions OK. SAE and International Reply Coupons. Reports in 2-4 months. Free book catalog but request must be sent to the firm at 10 E. 53 St., New York NY 10022.
Nonfiction: "Books about Japan and the Far East of interest to American general readers or specialists. Books on arts and crafts of highest quality." Oriental arts, crafts of the world; especially ceramics. Books on Oriental cooking; on economics related to Japan and Asia; how-to on arts and crafts and Oriental martial arts. Philosophy, photography, politics, psychology, reference and sociology. Query. "Since we are highly specialized, we are probably a poor market for American writers, but we would welcome innovative approaches to arts and crafts subjects."
Recent Titles: *Michael Cardew,* by K. Clark (crafts; ceramics); *Dialogue in Art: Japan and the West,* by C. F. Yamada (fine art).

LANTERN PRESS, INC., 354 Hussey Rd., Mount Vernon NY 10552. (914)668-9736. Payment is on royalty basis, or outright purchase, if preferred. Usual advance is $250 on signing, $250 on

publication. Published 2 titles last year. No mss should be sent unless authorized. Query first. Reports in 3 to 4 weeks. SASE.
Nonfiction: Publishes adult nonfiction, mail-order books. Length: 2,000 to 30,000 words.
Juveniles: Juveniles for all ages. Juvenile Editor: J.R. Furman.

LAW-ARTS PUBLISHERS, 453 Greenwich St., New York NY 10013. Editorial Director: Joseph Taubman. Publishes hardcover and paperback originals (90%) and paperback reprints (10%). Published 5 titles in 1977, 7-10 in 1978; will do 10 in 1979. 10% royalty; no advance. Simultaneous and photocopied submissions OK. Reports in 1 month. SASE. Free book catalog.
Nonfiction: Legal related, in-depth textbooks; books on creative work, audiovisual techniques, management, publicity, etc. No photography books. Submit outline/synopsis and sample chapters. Recently published *Performing Arts Management and Law,* by J. Taubman; and *Professional Sports and the Law,* by L. Sobel.

SEYMOUR LAWRENCE, INC., 90 Beacon St., Boston MA 02108. Publisher: Seymour Lawrence. Editor: Merloyd Lawrence. Publishes hardcover and paperback originals. Seymour Lawrence books are published in association with the Delacorte Press. Royalty schedule: 10% to 5,000 copies; 12½% to 10,000; 15% thereafter on adult hardcover books; 10% on children's books. Published 14 titles in 1977. Send outline and sample chapters. SASE.
Nonfiction, Fiction, Juveniles: Child care and development books for the general reader; no textbooks. Adult fiction. Juvenile fiction and picture books. Recent titles include *Slapstick* (Vonnegut), *Child Health Encyclopedia* (Boston Children's Hospital) and *Doctor and Child* (Brazelton.)
Special Needs: Radcliffe Series of biographies of women.

LAWYERS AND JUDGES PUBLISHING CO., 817 E. Broadway, Box 42050, Tucson AZ 85733. Editor: Alice Evans. Publishes paperback originals. "We negotiate each title separately." No advance. Published 5 titles last year. Will consider photocopied submissions. Query first. Reports in 10 days. SASE.
Business and Law: Question and answer booklets about the law for laymen. Case organizers for lawyers and their secretaries. How-to books for lawyers and accountants. Question and answer format desired. "Lawyers purchase question and answer booklets to give to their clients at no charge, in order to reduce office time needed to educate the client. How-to books stress practical aspects of complying with the hundreds of different federal government forms. We're planning more Practical Guides, and taxes and government regulations are good themes also."

LEBHAR-FRIEDMAN, 425 Park Ave., New York NY 10022. (212)371-9400. Executive Editor: Barbara Miller. Senior Editor: Linda Marks. Publishes hardcover and paperback originals. 10% (of net) royalty. Advance depends on type of book. Published 7 titles in 1977, 15 in 1978; will do 15 in 1979. Mss must follow Chicago *Manual of Style.* Simultaneous and photocopied submissions OK. Reports in 4-8 weeks. SASE. Free book catalog.
Nonfiction: Business and professional books with emphasis on all aspects of retailing, plus management and marketing. Query or submit outline/synopsis and sample chapters. Recently published *Food Service Management and Control,* by C. Villano; *Store Planning and Design,* by A. Novak; and *Retail Personnel Management,* by R. Glaser.

HAL LEONARD PUBLISHING CORPORATION, 8112 W. Bluemound Rd., Milwaukee WI 53213. (414)774-3630. Editorial Director: Richard Peck. Publishes hardcover and paperback originals. Published 5 titles in 1978; will do 10-15 in 1979. Pays standard industry royalty; advance offered "for an especially attractive book." Simultaneous (if so notified) and photocopied submissions OK. Reports in 4 weeks. SASE. Book catalog for SASE.
Nonfiction: "The book publishing division of our company has just been established [in 1978] to serve the evangelican Christian market. Thus, all titles published will be religious. We would be willing to consider any nonfiction work (Bible study aids, reference, commentary, as well as scriptural perspectives on topics of current interest), but the majority of our books during the first 2 years will undoubtedly be either 'how-to' (based upon the Biblical 'how-to's' for a Christian life) or well written perspectives on issues confronting contemporary Christians. All books must reflect the fundamental or evangelical view of the Bible and its absolute authority in the believer's life. If the writer has any questions as to the implications of this prerequisite, he or she should query first, without sample chapters and certainly without sending the manuscript. All work must show understanding of the total Scriptural revelation, or in plain words, good, sound Bible knowledge. Works based upon unscriptural positions or incomplete understanding will be returned." Query or submit complete ms.

Fiction: "Would not rule out fiction, but most publishing will be in the nonfiction area. Fundamental/evangelical view of life must prevail. Would be particularly interested in fiction for young readers (8-16 years-old) if well written and reinforcing reader's Christian commitment. All fiction must be more than just 'recreational reading', in the sense that it should say something about the Christian's life in the 20th Century through the fictional lives portrayed." Query or submit outline/synopsis and sample chapters or complete ms.

LES FEMMES PUBLISHING, 231 Adrian Rd., Millbrae CA 94030. Publisher: Ruth Kramer. Editor: Joycelyn Moulton. Publishes paperback originals. Offers standard royalty payment schedule. Nationwide distribution, plus distribution to most English-speaking countries. Free book catalog. Will consider photocopied submissions. Query first and submit outline and sample chapters. Must be typed, double spaced. Reports in 6 weeks. Enclose return postage.
Nonfiction and Fiction: Publishes "all subjects of interest to contemporary women, especially those conveying educational or self-help benefits." Will be needing material for the Everywoman's Guide Series. Must be concise, packed with information, presenting guides on subjects of interest to women. Would also like to see material about women in sports, menopause, biographies of famous women. Does not want to see anti-male material. Submit mss about the arts, sociology, sports, hobbies, and special interest material, such as health and history. "Some highly original fiction is possible, such as science fiction, satire, etc."

LESTER AND ORPEN LIMITED, PUBLISHERS, 42 Charles St. E., 8th floor, Toronto, Ontario M4Y 1T4, Canada. (416)961-1812. Editor-in-Chief: Malcolm Lester. Publishes hardcover and paperback originals. Offers standard minimum book contract of 10-12½-15%. Published 12 titles in 1977. Free book catalog. Will consider photocopied submissions. Query first with outline and one sample chapter showing style and treatment. Submit complete ms only if writer has been published before. Reports in 6 weeks. Enclose S.A.E. and International Reply Coupons.
General Fiction and Nonfiction: "Our basic philosophy of publishing only carefully selected books is stronger than ever; each and every title reflects a uniqueness in concept, careful and imaginative editing and design, and powerful and creative promotion. Our philosophy is that the book should be as long or as short as the subject warrants." Publishes adult trade fiction, biography, sociology, economics and philosophy. Recently published *The Ion Effect,* by F. Soyka/A. Edmonds (health); *Five Lives of Ben Hecht,* by D. Fetherling (biographical); and *Stokowski,* by P. Robinson (biography).

LIBERTY FUND, INC., 7440 N. Shadeland, Indianapolis IN 46250. (317)842-0880. Director of Publications: David Franke. Publishes hardcover and paperback originals (25%) and reprints (75%). Published 9 titles in 1977, 12 in 1978; will do 15 in 1979. Pays in royalties or outright purchase; usually no advance. Simultaneous and photocopied submissions OK. Reports in 4 weeks. SASE. Free book catalog.
Nonfiction: "Liberty Fund is a foundation established to encourage study of the ideal of a society of free and responsible individuals. Under the Liberty Press imprint we publish academic-level books on political, economic and social philosophy, written from a perspective that values individual liberty. No works written on a popular level; no political activism and no fiction." Query. "Very few of our titles are published as a result of unsolicited submissions. Authors, therefore, should take care *not* to submit a ms initially, but just a letter and outline." Recently published *Adam Smith: The Man and His Works,* by E.G. West (biography); *Essays On Individuality,* edited by F. Morley (collection); and *The Roots of Capitalism,* by J. Chamberlain (history).

***LIBRA PUBLISHERS, INC.**, 391 Willets Rd., Box 165, Roslyn Hts NY 11577. (516)484-4950. Hardcover and paperback originals. Specializes in the behavioral sciences. 10-15% royalty; no advance. Subsidy publishes a very small percentage of books (those which have obvious marketing problems or are too specialized). Simultaneous and photocopied submissions OK. Reports in 1-2 weeks. SASE. Free book catalog.
and Fiction: Mss in all subject areas will be given consideration, but main interest is in the behavioral sciences. Submit outline/synopsis and sample chapters. Recently published *Emotional Aspects of Heart Disease,* by H. Giest, Ph.D. ; *The Counseling Process: A Cognitive Behavioral Approach,* by J. Lembo, Ph.D.

LIBRARIES UNLIMITED, INC., Box 263, Littleton CO 80160. (303)770-1220. Editor-in-Chief: Bohdan S. Wynar. Publishes hardcover and paperback originals (95%) and hardcover reprints (5%). Specializes in library science and reference books. 10% royalty; advance averages $500. Published 30 titles in 1977, 35 in 1978. Marketed by direct mail to 20,000 libraries in this country

and abroad. Query or submit outline/synopsis and sample chapters. All prospective authors are required to fill out an author questionnaire. Make inquiry if photos/illustrations are to accompany ms. Reports in 2-4 months. SASE. Free book catalog.
Nonfiction: Publishes reference; textbooks, and library science books. Recently published *Library Management,* by R.D. Stueart and J. T. Eastlick (textbook); and *The Islamic Near East and North Africa: An Annotated Guide to Books in English for Non-Specialists,* by D. W. Littlefield (reference).

LIGUORI PUBLICATIONS, 1 Liguori Dr., Liguori MO 63057. (314)464-2500. Editor-in-Chief: Christopher Farrell. Managing Editor: David Polek. Paperback originals. Specializes in religion-oriented materials. 8% royalty; no advance. Query or submit outline/snyopsis and sample chapters. State availability of photos and/or illustrations. Photocopied submissions OK. Reports in 2-4 months. SASE. Free book catalog.
Nonfiction: Publishes (in order of preference) religious; self-help; juvenile (with religious tone or approach); and how-to (self-help, not mechanical) books. Recently published *Mary and Your Everyday Life,* by B. Haring; and *Six Levels of a Happy Marriage,* by M. Laz.

***LION BOOKS**, 111 E. 39th St., New York NY 10016. Editorial Director: Harriet Ross. Publishes originals (80%) and reprints (20%). Published 18 titles in 1977, 20 in 1978. Subsidy publishes 5% of titles. Subsidy publishing is offered "if we feel we can move it in our market." 7-12% royalty, or pays $500-7,500 outright purchase price; advance varies. Photocopied submissions OK. Reports in 2 weeks. SASE.
Nonfiction: Beginner cat and dog books (with photos); biography (in all areas, especially political); African and Arabian tales; black historical nonfiction; womens' movement; sports (how-to on gymnastics, swimming, riding); sex and the young man; and cookbooks with story line. Query or submit complete ms. Recently published *Vince Lombardi,* by Klein; *Sports Injuries of Young Athletes,* by Schavi; and *Black Heroes,* by Lindquist.

J.B. LIPPINCOTT CO., (General Division), E. Washington Square, Philadelphia PA 19105. General Adult Book Editor: Edward L. Burlingame. Publishes hardcover and paperback originals and reprints. Standard royalty schedule. Published 161 titles last year. Free book catalog. Reports in 3 to 4 weeks. Query. SASE.
General: Publishes general nonfiction; also history, biography, nature, sports, the arts, adult fiction. Submit outline/synopsis and sample chapters.

J.B. LIPPINCOTT CO., (Juvenile Division), 521 5th Ave., New York NY 10017. Editor-in-Chief, Books for Young Readers: Dorothy Briley. Publishes trade books for kindergarten through high school. Selected titles published simultaneously in paper and hardcover. Standard royalty schedule. Free book catalog. Reports in 8-10 weeks. Enclose return postage with ms.
Juveniles: Fiction and nonfiction. Current titles include *Trial Valley* (Cleavers); *The Golem* (McDermott).

LITTLE, BROWN AND COMPANY, INC., 34 Beacon St., Boston MA 02106. Editorial Director: Robert Emmett Ginna, Jr. Publishes hardcover and paperback originals and paperback reprints. Publishes 105 titles/year. "Royalty and advance agreements vary from book to book and are discussed with the author at the time an offer is made." Simultaneous (if so notified) and photocopied submissions OK. Reports in 6-8 weeks for queries/proposals. SASE. Free book catalog.
Nonfiction: "Some how-to books, select and distinctive cookbooks, biographies, history, science and sports." Query or submit outline/synopsis and sample chapters. Recently published *Male Sexuality: A Guide to Sexual Fulfillment,* by B. Zilbergeld, Ph.D.; *The People Shapers,* by V. Packard; and *The Cop Who Would Be King,* by Daughen/Binzen.
Fiction: Contemporary popular fiction as well as fiction of literary distinction; some mysteries, suspense novels and adventure novels. "We are not particularly active in the fields of science fiction or gothic romances. Our poetry list is extremely limited; those collections of poems that we do publish are usually the work of poets who have gained recognition through publication in literary reviews and various periodicals." Query or submit outline/synopsis and sample chapters. Recently published *I Heard My Sister Speak My Name,* by T. Savage; *Daniel Martin,* by J. Fowles; and *Coma,* by R. Cook.

LOGOS INTERNATIONAL, 201 Church St., Plainfield NJ 07060. (201)754-0745. Editorial Director: Viola Malachuk. Publishes hardcover and paperback originals (95%) and paperback reprints (5%). Published 44 titles in 1977, 60 in 1978; will do 65 in 1979. 10% royalty; advance

offered "on a limited basis." Reports in 2 months. SASE. Book catalog for postage.
Nonfiction: "Logos books are primarily written to propagate and inform the charismatic movement within the Christian church. They are typically evangelical in flavor; many are by Roman Catholic authors as well; some are Messianic Jews. Frequently the books are the stories, the testimonies, of leaders in the charismatic movement; how they came to receive the Baptism of the Holy Spirit and experience the gifts of the Holy Spirit, like speaking in tongues, miracles, prophecy, etc. The first Logos book was a warning against spiritualism, seances, and the occult. The first bestseller was *Run, Baby, Run,* the story of a converted teenage gang leader, Nicky Cruz. The author must be a serious Christian who regards the Bible as authoritative; any attempt to approach this material apart from personal involvement will likely be judged unsuccessful. Especially interested in popular treatments of biblical prophecy, serious trends in discipleship, teaching for children, and biography testimony." Length: 25,000-500,000 words. Submit outline/synopsis and sample chapters. Recently published *Child of Satan, Child of God,* by S. Atkins/B. Slosser (biography); *Let My People Grow,* by M. Harper (teaching on church structure); and *Eldridge Cleaver: Reborn,* by J. Oliver (biography).

LOLLIPOP POWER, INC., Box 1171, Chapel Hill NC 27514. (919)929-4857. Collective editorship. Paperback originals; experimenting on some hardcover titles. "We currently pay $100 per book, split between author and illustrator. Hope to increase payment or begin royalties eventually. Payment is made when work is completed, regardless of when book is actually published." No advance. Photocopied submissions OK. Reports in 1-2 months. SASE. Free book catalog and information sheet for authors and illustrators.
Juveniles: Non-sexist, non-racist books for children; fiction and nonfiction. "Because commercial publishers are beginning to incorporate some of our goals into their books, we are now attempting to meet specific needs that continue to exist. We are seeking mss which include: 1) Strong female protagonists, especially Black, Spanish-American or Native American girls or women. 2) Females who are struggling to change values and behavior. 3) Friendship and solidarity among girls and women. 4) Non-heterosexist values; e.g., children and lesbian mothers, early childhood sex education materials not limited to heterosexual relationships. 5) Non-traditional family situations; e.g., single mothers, extended families, several women living with children. And we are now especially interested in biographies for children." Submit complete ms for both fiction and nonfiction. Recently published *The Clever Princess,* by A. Tompert; and *Jesse's Dream Skirt,* by B. Mack (juvenile picture book).

***LONE STAR PUBLISHERS, INC.**, Box 9774, Austin TX 78766. (512)255-2333. Editorial Director: A.J. Lerager. Publishes hardcover and paperback originals. Published 6 titles in 1978; will do 5 in 1979. Subsidy publishes approximately 1 title/year based on "the subject matter, the author's reputation, the potential market, the capital investment, etc." 12½-15% royalty; no advance. Simultaneous and photocopied submissions OK. Reports in 3 weeks. SASE. Free book catalog.
Nonfiction: College textbooks; how-to; cookbooks; self-help and sports. No poetry. Query. Recently published *The Texas Press Women's Cookbook,* by D. Hunt/K. Pill/B. Field (cookbook); *Poverty, Manpower, & Social Security,* by P. Brinker/J. Klos (college text); and *Multidimensional Marketing,* by T. Anderson, et al (college text).

LONGMAN CANADA LTD., 55 Barber Greene Rd., Don Mills, Ont., M3C 2A1 Canada. (416)444-7331. Query on general nonfiction and science; completed mss preferred in all other categories. SASE.
Fiction: Publishes adult fiction. Fiction mss should run 80,000 words or more.
Nonfiction: History (Canadian preferred), biography (lives of Canadians preferred), popular science, general nonfiction.
Textbooks: Textbooks on all levels.

LOTHROP,LEE & SHEPARD CO., 105 Madison Ave., New York NY 10016. (212)889-3050. Editor-in-Chief: Edna Barth. Hardcover originals. Royalty and advance vary according to type of book. Published 39 titles in 1977, 54 in 1978. State availability of photos and/or illustrations to accompany ms. Photocopied submissions OK, but originals preferred. Reports in 4-6 weeks. SASE. Free book catalog.
Juveniles: Publishes biography; cooking, cookbooks and foods; history; hobbies; music; poetry; self-help; and sports books. Submit outline/synopsis and sample chapters for nonfiction. Juvenile fiction includes adventure, fantasy, historical, humorous, mystery, science fiction, suspense and contemporary novels. Submit complete ms. for fiction. Recently published *Warton and Morton,* by R.E. Erickson (fantasy) and *Harvey the Beer Can King,* by J. Gibson.

Special Needs: "A series we are trying to build is the Fun-To-Read series."

ROBERT B. LUCE, INC., 2000 N St., N.W., Washington D.C. 20036. (202)296-2690. Offers standard 10-12½-15% royalty contract. Free book catalog. Address mss to assistant editor. Submit outline and sample chapter. Reports in 4 weeks. Enclose return postage.
Nonfiction and Fiction: "Books must be authoritative, informative, and written in plain language for the popular audience. Mss should be 60,000 words minimum. General nonfiction: current affairs, how-to-do-it, self-help, controversial subjects. History and biography. Public affairs and social problems. Popular science. Publishes limited fictional works."
Recent Titles: *The Zeal of the Convert,* by B. Wilkinson (biography); *A Plague on Both Your Houses,* by R. Whitaker (history); and *Developing Your Latent Powers,* by F. Gould (psychology).

McCLELLAND AND STEWART LTD., 25 Hollinger Rd., Toronto, Ontario, Canada M4B 3G2. Editor-in-Chief: Anna Porter. Publishes hardcover and paperback originals. Offers sliding scale of royalty on copies sold. Advance varies. Free book catalog. Submit outline and sample chapters for nonfiction. Submit complete ms for fiction. Reports in 6 weeks, average. Enclose S.A.E. and International Reply Coupons.
Nonfiction, Poetry and Fiction: Publishes "Canadian fiction and poetry. Nonfiction in the humanities and social sciences, with emphasis on Canadian concerns. Coffee-table books on art, architecture, sculpture and Canadian history." Will also consider general adult trade fiction, biography, history, nature, photography, politics, sociology, textbooks.

McCORMICK-MATHERS PUBLISHING CO., 450 W. 33rd St., New York NY 10001. Executive Vice-President: Anthony J. Quaglia. Publishes paperback originals. Contract negotiated by flat fee. Published 119 titles last year. Will send catalog to writer on request. Will consider photocopied submissions. Submit outline and sample chapters. Reports as soon as possible. Enclose return postage.
Textbooks and Fiction: El-hi textbooks and action fiction within the el-hi age level from short stories to novellas; rural, suburban, city and inner city subject matter; school situations, inter-peer relationships, inter-family situations. Prefers third-person narrative without flashbacks. Value based in outlook, with strong emphasis on ethical good over ethical evil. "Our books are geared primarily to students with reading difficulties who have not profited from traditional reading instructions. We rewrite submitted material."

McGRAW-HILL BOOK CO., 1221 Ave. of the Americas, New York NY 10020. Hardcover and paperback originals, reprints, translations and anthologies. 10-12½-15% royalty. Submit outline and sample chapter; unsolicited mss rarely accepted. Reports in 3 weeks. SASE.
General Trade Division: "McGraw-Hill Trade Division is no longer assessing unsolicited ms. Rising costs have made it uneconomic for us to employ skilled editors to read all mss without consideration of the company's area of interest or the chances of achieving success on publication. All mss not sought by McGraw-Hill will be returned unopened to the sender via 4th Class Mss Rate, regardless of the postal rate selected by the sender."
Professional and Reference: Publishes books for engineers, scientists, and business people who need information on the professional level. Some of these books also find use in college and technical institute courses. This Division also publishes multi-volume encyclopedias (which are usually staff-prepared using work from outside contributors who are specialists in their fields) and one-volume encyclopedias prepared by experts in a given field. The professional books are usually written by graduate engineers or scientists or business people (such as accountants, lawyers, stockbrokers, etc.) Authors of the professional books are expected to be highly qualified in their field. Such qualifications are the result of education and experience in the field; these qualifications are prerequisite for authorship. The multi-volume encyclopedias rarely accept contributions from freelancers because the above education and experience qualifications are also necessary. Single-volume encyclopedias are usually prepared by subject specialists; again freelancers are seldom used unless they have the necessary experience and educational background. Technical and Scientific Book Editor: Tyler G. Hicks; Multi/volume Encyclopedia Editor: Daniel N. Lapedes; Single-volume Encyclopedia Editor: Robert A. Rosenbaum; Business Editor: William H. Mogan; Architecture Editor: Jeremy Robinson; Handbook Editor: Harold B. Crawford.
College Textbooks: The College Division publishes textbooks. The writer must know the college curriculum and course structure. Also publishes scientific texts and reference books in business, economics, engineering, social sciences, physical sciences, mathematics, medicine and nursing. Material should be scientifically and factually accurate. Most, but not all, books should

be designed for existing courses offered in various disciplines of study. Books should have superior presentations and be more up-to-date than existing textbooks. Department Publishers: Patrick Clifford, Professional and Continuing Education; J.L. Farnsworth, Arts and Sciences.
High School and Vocational Textbooks: The Gregg Division publishes instructional materials in two main areas, business and office education (accounting, data processing, business communication, business law, business mathematics and machines, management and supervision, secretarial and clerical, records management, shorthand, typing) and career and vocational education (career development, marketing and distribution, public and personal services, applied arts and sciences, technical and industrial education, consumer education, health occupations, and agribusiness). Materials must be accurate, with clearly stated objectives, and should reflect a structuring of technical and interpersonal skills which mesh with both career clustering and course content. A. J. Lemaster, Editor-in-Chief, Shorthand. E. E. Byers, Editor-in-Chief, Business Management, and Office Education; D. Cripps, Editor-in-Chief, Accounting, Computing, and Data Processing; P. Voiles, Editor-in-Chief, Typing, Communications, and Record Management; W. A. Sabin, Publisher, Business and Office Education; D. E. Hepler, Editor-in-Chief, Trade and Technical Education; C. O'Keefe, Editor-in-Chief, Career Education
David McKay Company, Inc., 750 Third Ave., New York NY 10017. Manager, General Book Division: Alan Tucker. Offers standard royalty contract. Query first or submit outline and sample chapter. Reports in about 3 weeks. Enclose return postage.
Nonfiction and Juveniles: How-to books on the outdoors, boating and yachting, games, horses, gardening, and hobbies. "Absolutely no fiction." Nonfiction for young adults. Young Adult Editor: Alexandra Whitney.

MACMILLAN OF CANADA, 70 Bond St., Toronto, Ontario, Canada M5B 1X3. Editorial Director: Douglas M. Gibson. Senior Editor: Jan Walter. Publishes hardcover originals and paperback reprints. Published 30 titles in 1977, 34 in 1978. 10% royalty. Simultaneous and photocopied submissions OK. Reports in 6 weeks. SASE. Book catalog for SASE.
Nonfiction: "We publish Canadian books of all kinds. Biography; history; art; current affairs; juveniles; and poetry. Particularly looking for good topical nonfiction." Textbook/Educational Editor: Gladys Neale; Scientific/College Editor: Virgil Duff. Query. Recently published *By Person Unknown,* by G. Jonas/B. Amiel (crime); *Remembering the Farm,* by A. Anderson (oral history); and *Garbage Delight,* by D. Lee (juvenile).
Fiction: Query. Recently published *Sandbars,* by O. McFee; *The Invention of the World,* by J. Hodgins; and *Birds of Prey,* by J.R. Saul.

MACMILLAN PUBLISHING COMPANY, INC., 866 Third Ave., New York NY 10022. Publishes hardcover and paperback originals and reprints. Will consider photocopied submissions. Send query letter before sending ms. Address all mss except juveniles to Trade Editorial Department; children's books to Children's Book Department. Enclose return postage.
Fiction and Nonfiction: Publishes adult fiction and nonfiction. Length: at least 75,000 words.
Juveniles: Children's books.

MACRAE SMITH COMPANY, 225 S. 15th St., Philadelphia PA 19102. Pays 10% of list price. Published 12 titles last year. Will send a catalog on request. Send outline and sample chapters or complete ms and letter reviewing relevant background and experience of author. Address mss to Ruth Allan Miner. Reports in 4 to 6 weeks. Enclose return postage.
General: "Adult trade books, fiction and nonfiction. Current issues and topical concerns, adventure, mysteries and gothics, history and science, biography."
Juveniles: For nonfiction books, interested in "biographies, history of world cultures, impact of the sciences on human affairs, cultural anthropology, scientific and medical discoveries, ecology, current social concerns and theory, peace research, international cooperation and world order, controversial issues, sports. Future-oriented subjects. For all ages, but prefer 8 to 12 and junior and senior high school." Also buys adventure stories, mysteries, history and science, biography, and girls' fiction. Length: 40,000 to 60,000 words.

MAINE ELVES PRESS, INC., Box 249, Rockport ME 04856. Editor-in-Chief: Julie A. Bragdon. Hardcover and paperback originals. 10-12½-15% royalty. Advance varies, depending on projected sales, generally between $500-1,000. "We do our own marketing. We go directly to the markets ourselves, sometimes through advertising in magazines; more likely to bookstores and specialty stores." State availability of photos to illustrate ms. Reports in 1-2 months. SASE.
Nonfiction: Publishes how-to, biography, sociology and books on politics. Query. Address it to proper department (How-to Department, Biography Department, etc.).
Special Needs: "We're looking for books that appeal to young people especially. Humor is

important in the books we publish."
Recent Titles: *30 Easy Pieces of Furniture* (Made by Elves That You Can Make, Too), by M. P. Boshnack and E. M. Schoon (how-to); *Another 30 Pieces* (a sequel), by M. P. Boshnack.

MAJOR BOOKS, 21335 Roscoe Blvd., Canoga Park CA 91304. (213)999-4100. Editor-in-Chief: Harold Straubing. Managing Editor: John Mitchell. Paperback originals (75%) and reprints (25%). 4-6% royalty, breaking at 150M sales mark; average advance of $750-1,000, depending on subject matter of book and literary quality. Published 100 titles in 1977, and 1978. Submit outline/synopsis and sample chapters or complete ms. Send contact sheets or photos with submissions. Reports in 1-2 months. SASE. Book catalog for SASE.
Nonfiction: John Mitchell, senior editor. Publishes biography; cookbooks, cooking and foods; erotica; how-to; humor; law; pets; politics; self-help; and sports books. No avant-garde material. Recently published *There's A Puddle in My Parlor,* by F. Klusman (pet care); *Vince Lombardi: His Life and Times,* by R. Wells (biography); and *The New Truth About Pot,* by B. Lewin.
Fiction: Publishes adventure, erotica, historical, mystery, romance, science fiction, suspense, and western books. Recently published *The Fire and the Rose,* by V. Bloom (romance); and *Buzzard Bait,* by J. Sherman (western).

MANOR BOOKS, INC., 432 Park Ave., S., New York NY 10016. (212)686-9100. Editor-in-Chief: Bob Abel. Managing Editor: Sam Irving. Publishes paperback originals and reprints. Publishes 200+ titles/year. 6% royalty to 150,000 copies; 8% thereafter. Simultaneous (if the topic is important enough to merit multiple submissions) and photocopied submissions OK. Reports in 1 month. SASE. Writer's guidelines for SASE.
Nonfiction: "In general our nonfiction runs to important topics or personalities rather than category books. We do very little in the way of cookbooks, or travel, crafts, etc. We have done recent biographies of Bing Crosby, Prime Minister Begin and President Sudat. We of course like to sign up books on future-breaking news events or significant phenomenoa or fashion or trend, et al. On the other side of the coin, we want books that will be around for years and continue to sell as back list." Query. Recently published *Glitter and Blood,* by Robin Moore; *The Life Story of Menachem Begin,* by R.P. Greenfield/I.A. Greenfield; and *Anwar Sudat: A Man of Peace,* by G. Carpozi Jr.
Fiction: "We are soft on mysteries unless there's a unique angle. We are very interested in fantasy and science fiction and there seems to be a steady demand for war books as well. We continue to do gothics, westerns, and may be in the market for strong men's adventure. The big women's historical romance-adventure market seems to be fading because of a glut of titles, but we will publish some of them in 1978 and see how the market holds up for them. We are always in the market for sexy novels—not porn thank you—and we are trying to develop a line of sex comedies—bright, funny racy plots—and a line of historical fantasies—people going back in time and the like. We also want to try some series characters who are women in interesting occupations, but we don't have a handle on that as yet." Submit outline/synopsis and sample chapters or complete ms. Recently published *Finders Keepers,* by G. Gibbs/N. Clark; *Bernadette Black,* by C. Gabriel; and *Asylum and Circus,* by M.D. Barrett.

***MANYLAND BOOKS, INC.**, 84-39 90th St., Woodhaven NY 11421. Editor-in-Chief: Stepas Zobarskas. Publishes hardcover and paperback originals. Offers 5-10-12½-15% royalty contract; average advance, $250 to $500. About 25% of books are subsidy published. Published 5 titles last year. Photocopied submissions OK. Submit complete ms. Reports in 6 or 8 weeks. Enclose return postage with ms.
Fiction, Nonfiction, Poetry, and Juveniles: "Manyland is concerned primarily with the literature of the lesser known countries. It has already published a score of novels, collections of short stories, folk tales, juvenile books, works of poetry, essays, and historical studies. Most of the publications have more than local interest. Their content and value transcend natural boundaries. They have universal appeal. We are interested in both new and established writers. We will consider any subject as long as it is well-written. No length requirements. We are especially interested in memoirs, biographies, anthologies." Recently published *Sudiev-Goodbye!,* by E. Bates (story of an immigrant family).

MASON/CHARTER PUBLISHERS, INC., 641 Lexington Ave., New York NY 10022. Editor-in-Chief: Margaret B. Parkinson. Publishes hardcover and paperback originals and hardcover imprints. Offers standard minimum book contract of 10-12½-15%. No photocopies or simultaneous submissions. Query first. Reports in 2 months. Enclose return postage.

General Trade: Fiction; mainstream, gothic, romance, suspense. Biography, business, history, self-help and how-to, sociology, sports, technical (data processing only), textbooks.
Recent Titles: *Hamilton I & II,* by R. Hendrickson (nonfiction); *Tempestous Petticoat,* by M.A. Gibbs (fiction); and *Search for the Gold of King Tut,* by A. Brackman (nonfiction).

MASTER'S PRESS, INC., 20 Mills St., Kalamazoo MI 49001. Editorial Director: Earl O. Roe. Publishes paperback originals. Publishes 15 titles/year. 10% royalty; no advance. Simultaneous and photocopied submissions OK. Reports in 3 months. SASE. Free book catalog.
Nonfiction: Devotionals, Bible studies, practical Christian living, contemporary issues viewed from an evangelical perspective, self-help and how-to books. No poetry. Query or submit outline/synopsis and sample chapters. Recently published *Becoming a Child of God,* by Dr. S.F. Olford (basic Christian teaching); *Acceptance,* by L. Pote (Christian life); and *The Stress Mess, by R. Susek.*

***MEDCO BOOKS**, 1640 S. La Cienega Blvd., Los Angeles CA 90035. Editor-in-Chief: Gil Porter. Hardcover and paperback originals. Specializes "primarily in sex, health, wealth topics, popular medicine such as dealing with diabetes, weight, arthritis, etc." Pays $500-1,500 for outright purchase; advance averages 1/3-½ on contract, balance on acceptance. Subsidy publishes 1% of books. Subsidy publishing offered "if writer has a viable means of selling his book himself, such as personality with media access, etc. We charge our cost plus about 20% for each step of production as a working average." Query. Send prints if photos are to accompany ms. Simultaneous submissions OK. Reports in 1-2 weeks. SASE.
Nonfiction: Publishes erotica; how-to; medicine and psychiatry; and self-help books.

MEDICAL EXAMINATION PUBLISHING COMPANY, INC., 969 Stewart Ave., Garden City NY 11530. Royalty schedule is negotiable. Will send catalog on request. Send outlines to editor. Reports in 1 month. Enclose return postage.
Medical: Medical texts and medical review books; monographs and training material for the medical and paramedical professions.

***MEMPHIS STATE UNIVERSITY PRESS**, Memphis State University, Memphis TN 38152. (901)454-2752. Editor-in-Chief: James D. Simmons. Publishes hardcover and paperback originals and reprints. Offers 10% "unless an exceptional book. Each contract is subject to negotiation. We prefer not to offer an advance." Does about 10% subsidy publishing. "We don't ask a subsidy from the author and do not make subsidy contracts with authors. We do make an effort to obtain outside (other than University) money to assist books which have an identifiable source of public support; associations, commissions, museums and galleries, and the like." Free book catalog and writer's guidelines. Will consider photocopied submissions. Query first. Reports in 3 to 6 months. Enclose SASE.
General Nonfiction: Americana Editor: James D. Simmons; History Editor: Nancy Hurley. "We publish scholarly nonfiction, books in the humanities, social sciences, and regional material. Interested in nonfiction material within the Mississippi River valley. Tennessee history, contemporary philosophy, modern literature criticism, and regional folklore." Recently published *Hostile Butterflies and Other Paintings,* by C. Cloar (art); *Vision of the Voyage,* by R.C. Combs (literary criticism); and *Morality and the Good Life,* by R. Sullivan (philosphy).

ARTHUR MERIWETHER, INC., Box 457, 921 Curtiss St., Downers Grove IL 60515. Editor-in-Chief: Arthur L. Zapel, Jr. Publishes paperback originals. Royalty contract of 10%. Advance by individual negotiation. Marketed by direct mail. Book catalog 25¢. Editorial guidelines also available. Query first. "Do not send ms until after query response from us." Reports in 1 month. Enclose return postage.
Education: Mss for educational use in schools and churches. Mss for business and staff training on subjects related to business communications and advertising. Religious, self-help, how-to, sociology, and humor books are also published.
Drama: Plays on the same subjects as above.

CHARLES E. MERRILL PUBLISHING CO., a Bell & Howell Co., 1300 Alum Creek Dr., Columbus OH 43216. Publishes hardcover and paperback originals. Payment is on acceptance or on a royalty basis. "Our textbooks generally offer 6% at elementary school level; 8% at secondary school level; 10% to 15% at college level. Published 215 titles in 1977. Send brief outline and sample chapter. Reports in 4-12 weeks. SASE.
Textbooks: Education Division publishes texts, workbooks, instructional tapes, overhead pro-

jection transparencies and programmed materials for elementary and high schools in all subject areas, primarily language arts and literature, mathematics, science and social studies (no juvenile stories or novels). The College Division publishes texts and instructional tapes in all college areas, specializing in education, business and economics, math, technology, science, and speech. Editor-in-Chief, Educational Division: Buzz Ellis; Director, College Division: John Buterbaugh.

MERTON HOUSE PUBLISHING CO., 8 S. Michigan Ave., Chicago IL 60603. (312)236-2686. Editorial Director: Laurence Stevens. Publishes hardcover and paperback originals. Published 2 titles in 1977, 2 in 1978; will do 7 in 1979. "Royalties depend upon the type of book. For a travel book which requires updating and revision we pay 5-6-7½% depending on number sold, and 10% for hardcover. Specialized books for travel agents are 5-6-7½%, depending on copies sold, or we will negotiate outright purchase. Otherwise our royalties are standard." Simultaneous and photocopied submissions OK. Reports in 2 weeks-3 months. SASE. Catalog for SASE.
Nonfiction: "We are looking for manuscripts in several travel-related areas and this obviously requires that the writer know the travel, aviation, hotel and foodservice industries and the feminine travel market. Our first area of specialization is the feminine travel market, books with a slant towards the solo or single woman traveler. This series is directed towards the woman who wants, or has, to travel by herself yet at the same time wants to know where to meet men and find togetherness overseas. Such books need a woman's touch and it goes without saying that the author must know her stuff on hotels, and tours and be able to offer travel tips to women travelers. We are currently looking for books on the Caribbean, the Orient, South America, and several other locations. We will listen to almost *any* suggestion on manuscripts for our feminine travel series. Our second area of specialization is books for travel agents—books to help the travel agent run his business. If a writer is good and knows his stuff we will assign manuscripts, but he must know something about travel from the business perspective. Our third area is business books, and vocational guidance books, as well as 'different' books in the travel-related field. If a writer is imaginative and has a good idea, we welcome a query and promise a fast response. What we *don't* want are ordinary run-of-the-mill travel guides—there are too many already. We use the Chicago *Manual of Style,* and prefer a query or an outline plus 1 sample chapter so that we can judge writing ability." Recently published *Travel and the Single Woman,* by Van Campen; *Your Career in Travel & Tourism,* by Stevens; and *Guide to Buying, Selling & Starting a Travel Agency,* by Stevens.

JULIAN MESSNER (Simon & Schuster Division of Gulf & Western Corp.), 1230 Avenue of the Americas, New York NY 10020. Senior editor for elementary grades: Ms. Lee M. Hoffman. Senior editor for junior and senior high school: Iris Rosoff. Hardcover originals. Royalty varies. Advance averages $1,500. State availability of photos and/or illustrations to accompany ms. Simultaneous submissions OK from established authors who may propose two or more book ideas they would like to work on. Reports in 1-2 months. SASE. Free book catalog.
Juveniles: Nonfiction books for young people. Submit outline/synopsis and sample chapters. Recently published *The Evil that Men Do,* by A.P. Rubin; *The Hungry World,* by E. Israel; and *Is There a Loch Ness Monster?,* by G.S. Snyder.

***MIMIR PUBLISHERS, INC.**, Box 5011, Madison WI 53705. Editor-in-Chief: Henry H. Bakken. Hardcover and paperback originals. Specializes in books in the social sciences at college level. 15% royalty, "but nearly all titles are determined on a special contract." No advance. Subsidy publishes 50% of books. Subsidy publishing is offered "if the author wishes to proceed on our 50/50 type contract and share in the proceeds. Under this contract the author gets all the proceeds until he recovers his venture capital." Query or submit complete ms. Simultaneous ("if indicated") and photocopied submissions OK. Reports in 2-4 months. SASE. Free book catalog.
Nonfiction: Publishes Americana; biography (limited); business; economics; history; law; philosophy; politics; sociology; and textbooks. Recently published *Water Pollution, Causes and Cures,* by S.D. Morton; and *Wisconsin Income Tax Guide for Individuals,* by J.B. Bower.

***MODERN BOOKS AND CRAFTS, INC.**, Box 38, Greens Farms CT 06436. Editor-in-Chief: Robert Paul. Publishes paperback originals and hardcover reprints. 10% royalty; no advance. Subsidy publishes a minimal percentage of books. "We do this only if author is unknown in the field." Photocopied submissions OK. Reports in 1-2 weeks. SASE.
Nonfiction: Publishes erotica, hobbies, and psychology books. Also books on antiques.
Recent Titles: *Collector's Handbook to Marks on Porcelain and Pottery,* edited by E. Paul and A. Petersen; *Dictionary of American Painters, Sculptors and Engravers,* by M. Fielding.

MODERN CURRICULUM PRESS, INC., 13900 Prospect Rd., Cleveland OH 44136. (216)238-2222. Editorial Director: Thomas H. Hatch. Publishes hardcover and paperback originals. Published 35 titles in 1978; will do 40 in 1979. 5% royalty; no advance. Simultaneous and photocopied submissions OK. Reports in 2-4 weeks. SASE. Free book catalog.
Nonfiction: "We publish multi-ethnic, non-sexist instructional material used to teach reading, language arts, and social studies skills. We have a special need for writers who can create high-interest, controlled-vocabulary material suitable for students in grades K-6. The ability to write clear, concise Teacher's Guides and lesson plans is desirable." Submit outline/synopsis and sample chapters.
Fiction: Same requirements as nonfiction.

MONARCH PUBLISHING CO., INC., 222 Mamaroneck Ave., White Plains NY 10605. Chief Editor/Production Supervisor: Kathy L. Nelson. Publishes hardcover originals. Offers $200 royalty contract, with 2-part payment. Published 45 titles last year. Guidelines furnished on assignment. SASE.
History and Religion: Limited color editions for church, town, city and county histories. "Generally in conjunction with a major anniversary or dedication." Recently published *Our Heritage: A History of East Providence, R.I.* and *The History of St. Joseph's Church, Le Mars, Iowa.* "We are looking for freelance writers to draw up manuscripts from researched material provided by Monarch."

MONITOR BOOK COMPANY, INC., 195 S. Beverly Dr., Beverly Hills CA 90212. (213)271-5558. Editor-in-Chief: Alan F. Pater. Hardcover originals. 10% minimum royalty; also outright purchase, depending on circumstances. No advance. Send prints if photos and/or illustrations are to accompany ms. Reports in 2-4 months. SASE. Book catalog for SASE.
Nonfiction: Publishes Americana, biographies (only of well-known personalities); law and reference books.Recently published *What They Said in 1977: The Yearbook of Spoken Opinion* (current quotations).

MONTANA COUNCIL FOR INDIAN EDUCATION, 1810 3rd Ave., N., Billings MT 59101. Senior Editor: Hap Gilliland. Managing Editor: Tony Moore. Publishes paperback originals. Published 6 titles in 1977, 5-10 in 1978; will do 5-10 in 1979. Pays 1½¢/word; no advance. Simultaneous and photocopied submissions OK. Reports in 1-2 months. "All mss must be evaluated by an Indian Editorial Committee before we can publish. We immediately acknowledge the receipt of a ms, but the committee meets randomly, every month or two." SASE. Free book catalog.
Nonfiction: "We will consider material on any Indian-related subject (e.g., Indian foods, plants, herbs used medicinally and for cooking, how-to-do-it, etc.). We also encourage accurately written biographies and histories. We stress that the books are paperback, of 32-50 pages in length. That usually means that we need from 16-25 pages of text per book (double-spaced, typed) because our books are heavily illustrated. Mss can be submitted in book or story length. Most of our books are compilations of two or more stories." Submit complete ms. Recently published *Indian Canoeing,* by P. Pulling (how-to); *Chief Joseph's Own Story,* by Chief Joseph; and *A History of the Cheyenne People,* by T. Weist (history).
Fiction: Specialized fiction aimed mainly at young readers who read below the level of their class. Must be fast moving to hold interest. "We prefer Indian authors because Indian students can more easily relate to stories written by Indians, but we will consider anything that does accurately portray the Indian way of life, culture, values, etc. We will also consider adult level material. Again, we stress cultural accuracy. No stereotyped cowboy-Indian type stories. We encourage legends, folk tales and fiction stories." Submit complete ms. Recently published *In the Beginning,* by E. Clark; *The Heritage,* by Armstrong/Lee/Hildreth; and *Cheyenne Short Stories,* compiled by W. Leman.

MONTHLY REVIEW PRESS, 62 West 14th St., New York NY 10011. Director: Jules Geller. Royalty schedule. Published 40 titles last year. Current catalog available on request. Send query letter, table of contents and two sample chapters; SASE. Reports in 1 to 3 months.
Economics, History, and Politics: Publishes books on history, economics, political science, world events. Books should reflect or be compatible with the socialist point of view on world problems.

MOODY PRESS, 820 North LaSalle St., Chicago IL 60610. (312)329-4337. Editor: Leslie H. Stobbe. Publishes hardcover and paperback originals. Royalty schedule is usually 10% of the

retail. No advance. Send query with outline and sample chapters. Reports within 3 months. Enclose return postage.
Religion: Publishes books that are definitely Christian in content. Christian education, Christian living, inspirational, theology, missions and missionaries, pastors' helps. Conservative theological position. Clothbound between 45,000 and 60,000 words. Recently published *Crying Wind,* by Crying Wind (autobiography); and *Archaeology in Bible Lands,* by H. Vos.
Fiction: Adult. Length: 40,000-90,000 words. Recently published *Snare of the Fowler,* by T. Taylor and *Three Shapes of Love,* by M. Wells.
Juveniles: Fiction. Length: 25,000 to 40,000 words.

***MOREHOUSE-BARLOW CO., INC.**, 78 Danbury Rd., Wilton CT 06897. Editor-in-Chief: Margaret L. Sheriff. Publishes paperback originals (75%) and reprints (25%). Published 25 titles in 1977, 22 in 1978. Subsidy publishes "at most, one book per year. Author must come highly recommended. We do not encourage subsidy publishing." 10% royalty; advance varies. Simultaneous and photocopied submissions OK. SASE. Reports in 2 months. Free book catalog.
Nonfiction: Religious books, education, arts & crafts, books on prayer, healing, spirituality; how-to books on church related subjects, worship aids; books on all aspects of the Christian life. No biographies or autobiographies of an inspirational nature. Submit outline/synopsis and sample chapters. Recently published *Eyes to See God,* by A. Elliott (arts & crafts); *Creative Drama in Religious Education,* by I. Burger; and *God's Work of Liberation,* by R. Bennett.

MORGAN & MORGAN, INC., 145 Palisade St., Dobbs Ferry NY 10522. Editor-in-Chief: Douglas O. Morgan. Publishes hardcover and paperback originals and reprints. Offers 10% of net sales. No advance. Published 15 titles last year. Free book catalog. Submit outline and sample chapters. Reports "immediately." SASE.
Photography: Books on all phases of photography. "We want to see an outline on what the book is about; various chapter headings; and how this material will be covered in various chapters. Would like one chapter in its entirety so that we could better grasp the method of approach in writing and also would like to have writer's reasons why he feels this book would have a good sale potential. We feel that our books go into greater detail on the particular subject and reasons why the book is relevant to the person looking for help in that field. We're looking for mss dealing with the how-to side of photography aimed at the amateur market and the more serious amateur photographer." Length depends on book.

WILLIAM MORROW AND CO., 105 Madison Ave., New York NY 10016. Editor: Hillel Black. Payment is on standard royalty basis. Published 175 titles last year. Query on all books. No unsolicited mss. Address to specific department. Reports in 4 weeks. Enclose return postage.
General: Publishes fiction, nonfiction, history, biography, arts, religion, poetry, how-to books, and cookbooks, all high-quality. Length: 50,000 to 100,000 words. Recently published *The Book of Lists,* by Wallace/Wallace/Wallechinsky; *Bloodline,* by S. Sheldon (mystery/romance); and *Rachel the Rabbi's Wife,* by S. Tannenbaum.
Juveniles: Juvenile Editor: Connie C. Epstein.

MOTORBOOKS INTERNATIONAL, INC., Box 2, Osceola WI 54020. (715)294-3345. Editor-in-Chief: William F. Kosfeld. Hardcover and paperback originals. Specializes in automotive literature. Escalating royalty begins at "10% retail on each copy; 10% gross where books sold at unusually large discount such as foreign rights sales. Advance depends on reputation of author and the work being considered." Published 4 titles in 1977, 5 in 1978. Also markets books through mail order subsidiary. State availability of photos and/or illustrations and include a few photocopied samples. Photocopied submissions OK. Reports in 1-2 months. SASE. Free book catalog.
Nonfiction: Publishes automotive literature written for serious car enthusiasts (histories, biographies, photographic works). Prefers not to see anything on extremely "narrow" topics that would be more suitable for magazine articles. Recently published *The Art and Science of Grand Prix Driving,* by N. Lauda; *Shelby's Wildlife: The Cobras and Mustangs,* by W.A. Wyss; and *Hudson: The Post War Years,* by R.M. Langworth.

MOTT MEDIA, Box 236, 305 Caroline, Milford MI 48042. Editor: Diane Zimmerman. Hardcover and paperback originals (90%) and paperback reprints (10%). Specializes in religious books, including trade and textbooks. 7% base royalty with sliding scale for mass sales; usually offers advance, "varies with experience." Query for fiction and nonfiction or submit outline/synopsis and sample chapters for nonfiction, complete ms for fiction. "Request advance information form with query, return completed form with ms or synopsis." Photocopied

submissions OK. Reports in 2-4 months. SASE. Free book catalog.
Nonfiction: Publishes Americana (religious slant); biography (for juveniles on famous Christians, adventure-filled; for adults on Christian people, scholarly, new slant for marketing); how-to (for pastors, Christian laymen); juvenile (biographies, 30,000-40,000 words); politics (conservative, Christian approach); religious (conservative Christian); self-help (religious); and textbooks (all levels from a Christian perspective, all subject fields). No preschool materials or early elementary stories.
Fiction: Publishes adventure; fantasy; historical; and religious. Main emphasis of all mss must be religious. Recently published *The Separation Illustration,* by J.W. Whitehead (current issues); *Justice Through Restitution,* by R.F. Campbell; and *Please Rise,* by M. Hilliard.

***MOUNTAIN PRESS PUBLISHING CO.**, 279 W. Front, Missoula MT 59801. Publisher: David P. Flaccus. Hardcover and paperback originals (90%) and reprints (10%). Royalty of 12% of net amount received; no advance. Subsidy publishes less than 5% of books. "Top quality work in very limited market only." Published 9 titles in 1977, 10 in 1978. State availability of photos and/or illustrations to accompany ms. Simultaneous submissions OK. Reports in 2-4 weeks. SASE. Free book catalog.
Nonfiction: Publishes history (regional Northwest); hobbies, how-to (angling, hunting); medicine and psychiatry (coronary care and critical care); nature (geology, habitat and conservation); outdoor recreation (backpacking, fishing, etc.); technical (wood design and technology); and textbooks. Recently published *Roadside Geology of Oregon,* by Alt/Hyndman.

MULTIMEDIA PUBLISHING CORP. (affiliates: Steinerbooks, Rudolf Steiner Publications, Biograf Books), 72 5th Ave., New York 10011. Editor: Paul M. Allen. Publishes paperback originals and reprints. 5% to 7% royalty; advance averages $1000. Free book catalog. Query first with outline and sample chapters for nonfiction. Will consider photocopied submissions. Reports on ms accepted for publication in 60 days. Returns rejected material in 3 weeks. SASE.
Nonfiction: "Spiritual sciences, occult, philosophical, metaphysical, E.S.P. These are for our Steiner books division only. Scholarly and serious nonfiction. How-to-do or make books using our patented format of Biograf Books. Examples: origami, breadbaking, calendar. We prefer not to see any more Tarot or religious books." Department Editor, Multimedia Materials and Self-Help: Beatrice Garber; Department Editor, Philosophy and Spiritual Sciences: Gene Gollogly.

MUSEUM OF NEW MEXICO PRESS, Box 2087, Santa Fe NM 87503. (505)827-2352. Editor-in-Chief: Richard L. Polese. Hardcover and paperback originals (90%) and reprints (10%). Royalty of 10% of list after first 1,000 copies; no advance. Prints preferred for illustrations; transparencies best for color. Sources of photos or illustrations should be indicated for each. Simultaneous and photocopied submissions OK. Submit complete mss, addressed to Richard L. Polese, Editor. Mss should be typed double-spaced, follow Chicago *Manual of Style* and *Words Into Type,* and be accompanied by information about the author's credentials and professional position. Reports in 1-2 months. SASE. Free book catalog.
Nonfiction: "We publish both popular and scholarly books in anthropology, history, fine and folk arts; geography, natural history, the Americas and the Southwest; regional cookbooks; some children's and foreign language books." Art, biography (regional and Southwest); hobbies, how-to, music, nature, photography, reference, scientific, technical and travel. Recently published *Navajo Weaving Handbook,* by editors of *El Palacio; New Mexico's "Little Texas,"* by R. Polese/J.M. Burroughs (history/geography); and *Pueblo Weaving and Textile Arts,* by N. Fox.
Fiction: Historical, humorous (regional) and other regional (New Mexico/Southwest) fiction. Recently published *Riders to Cibola,* by N. Zollinger.

THE NAIAD PRESS, INC., 20 Rue Jacob Acres, Bates City MO 64011. (816)633-4136. Editorial Director: Barbara Grier. Publishes paperback originals. Published 2 titles in 1977 and 1978; will do 4 in 1979. 50% royalty; no advance. Reports in 6 weeks. SASE. Book catalog for SASE.
Fiction: "We publish Lesbian fiction, preferably Lesbian/Feminist fiction. We are not impressed with the 'oh woe' school and prefer realistic (i.e., happy) novels." Query. Recently published *Love Image,* by V. Taylor; *A Woman Appeared to Me,* by R. Vivien; and *Berrigan,* by G. Lox.

THE NATIONAL GALLERY OF CANADA, Publications Division, Ottawa, Ontario, Canada K1A 0M8. (613)995-6526. Head: Peter L. Smith. Senior Editors: Jean-Claude Champenois, Julia Findlay. Publishes hardcover and paperback originals. Published 30 titles in 1977, 32 in

1978; will do 40 in 1979. Pays in outright purchase of $1,500-2,500; advance averages $700. Photocopied submissions OK. Reports in 3 months. SASE. Free book catalog.
Nonfiction: "In general, we are exclusively interested in mss on art, particularly Canadian art, and must, by the way, publish them in English and French. Exhibition catalogs are commissioned, but we are open to mss for the various series, monographic and otherwise, that we publish. All mss should be directed to our Editorial Coordinator, who doubles as an editor. Since we publish translations into French, authors have access to French Canada and the rest of Francophonie. Also, because we are a national institution, authors have the attention of European as well as American markets." Query. Recently published *Canadian Painting in the Thirties,* by C. Hill (exhibition catalog); *Donald Judd,* by B. Smith; and *European Drawings from Canadian Collections: 1500-1900,* by M.Z. Taylor (exhibition catalog).

NATIONAL TEXTBOOK COMPANY, 8259 Niles Center Rd., Skokie IL 60076. Editorial Director: Leonard I. Fiddle. Mss purchased on either royalty or buy out basis. Published 80 titles last year. Free book catalog and writer's guidelines. Send sample chapter. Reports in 6 to 8 weeks. Enclose return postage.
Textbooks: Major emphasis being given to language arts area, especially secondary level material. Emphasis is on true orientation materials which give an accurate description of a field, its requirements and opportunities, all of which should be written for a 9th-10th grade reading level. Donna A. Drews, Language Arts Editor. Also interested in elementary education material: supplementary, enrichment, and professional materials in reading, writing, and social studies. Faith Wolfe, Elementary Education Editor.

NATUREGRAPH PUBLISHERS, INC., Box 1075, Happy Camp CA 96039. (916)493-5353. Editor-in-Chief: Sevrin Housen. Original paperbacks. "We offer 10% of wholesale; 12½% after 10,000 copies are sold. State what photographs are available in query; send with ms upon request." Photocopied submissions OK. Reports in 1-2 months. SASE. Free book catalog.
Nonfiction: Publishes (in order of preference): nature (plants, mammals, birds, reptiles, amphibians, natural history for American Wildlife Series); history (Indian lore, ethnographic studies on native Americans); how-to (on science-related matters); land and gardening books; seashore life; cookbooks, cooking and foods (modern nutritional knowledge for the layman); hobbies (nature or science-related); religious (Baha'i); geologic studies and recreation books. Query. Follow *Chicago Manual of Style.* "All material must be scientifically well-grounded. Author must not only be professional, but in good command of his/her English. Many of our authors are college professors. Some of our books are used by teachers, particularly for natural science courses and anthropology (special studies)." Recently published *Owls by Day and Night,* by H. Tyler/D. Phillips (natural history); *Propagate Your Own Plants,* by W. James; and *Wildlife Woodcraft;* by L.B. Phillips (nature/crafts).

NAZARENE PUBLISHING HOUSE, Box 527, Kansas City MO 64141. Trade name: Beacon Hill Press of Kansas City. Editor: J. Fred Parker. Publishes hardcover and paperback originals and reprints. Offers "standard contract (sometimes flat rate purchase). Advance on royalty is paid on first 1,000 copies at publication date. Pays 10% on first 5,000 copies and 12% on subsequent copies at the end of each calendar year." Published 55 titles last year. Query. Follow *Chicago Manual of Style.* Address all mss to Book Editor. Reports in 2 to 5 months. "Book Committee meets quarterly to select, from the mss which they have been reading in the interim, those which will be published." Query first. Enclose SASE.
General Fiction and Juvenile Fiction: "Must have religious content germane to plot not artificially tacked on. At the same time not preachy or moralistic." Publishes 1 adult fiction and 1 juvenile a year. "Currently a moratorium on adult fiction."
Nonfiction: "Basically religious, (inspirational, devotional, Bible study, beliefs) but of wide scope from college textbook level to juvenile. Doctrinally must conform to the evangelical, Wesleyan tradition. Conservative view of Bible. Personal religious experience. We want the accent on victorious life, definitely upbeat. Social action themes must have spiritual base and motivation. Popular style books should be under 128 pages." Interested in business and professional books on church administration, Sunday school, etc. Textbooks are "almost exclusively done on assignment. Send query first." Length: 10,000 to 30,000 words. Recently published *God, Man, and Salvation,* by W.T. Purkiser/R. Taylor/W. Taylor (biblical theology); *Get Ready to Grow,* by P.R. Orjale (church growth); and *How to Live with Less Tension,* by P.E. Spray.

NC PRESS, 24 Ryerson Ave., Toronto, Ontario, Canada M5T 2P3. (416)368-1165. Editorial Director: Caroline Walker. Publishes hardcover and paperback originals and reprints. Pub-

lished 10 titles in 1977, 8-10 in 1978. 15% royalty; "advance is negotiable." Simultaneous and photocopied submissions OK. Reports in 2 months. SASE. Free book catalog.
Nonfiction: "We generally publish books of social/political relevance either on contemporary topics of concern (current events, ecology, etc.), or historical studies. We publish primarily Canadiana, but will consider other works if they are of good quality and general interest. Occasionally we do books on particular subjects (i.e., this year a photographic history of steamboats in Canada). Not too interested in religious or sports books, though will always accept submitted outline/synopsis and sample chapters before definitely saying no." Submit outline/synopsis and sample chapters. Recently published *Yours in the Struggle,* by B. Beeching/P. Clarke (biography); *Shadd: Life and Times of Mary Shadd Cary,* by J. Beardon/L. Butler (biography); and *And the Rivers of Our Blood,* by J. McLeod (ecology).
Fiction: "We have just published our first novel. Interested primarily in classical fiction—not mysteries or science fiction. Very interested in children's books—especially those with good illustrations." Submit outline/synopsis and sample chapters. Recently published *Fallout,* by P. Such.

NELLEN PUBLISHING CO., INC., 386 Park Ave., S., New York NY 10016. (212)679-0937. Editorial Director: Nancy W. Dunn. Senior Editor: M.F. Valentine. Publishes hardcover and paperback originals. Published 5 titles in 1977, 10 in 1978; will do 12-15 in 1979. 10-12½-15% royalty; no advance. Photocopied submissions OK. Reports in 2-4 weeks. SASE. Free book catalog.
Nonfiction: "We are seeking titles that have a wide interest in both the trade and scholarly markets. Our emphasis is on the trade. If a book is addressed to the scholarly or technical market we ask our authors to rewrite with the larger market in mind. Our subject areas are wide: politics, economics, health, education, diet, crime, self-help, nutrition, business, management, public administration, sociology, etc. We are interested in books on names, such as our Smith Book; names of interest: Jones, Johnson, Jackson, etc." Submit outline/synopsis and sample chapters. "With a clear synopsis of the book we appreciate knowing something about the author. We prefer authors with published works to their credit. If not books, at least magazine or journal articles." Recently published *The Book of Smith,* by E.C. Smith (fact book); *Living with Epilespsy,* by M. Sullivan (how-to); and *TM and Crime Prevention,* by R. Lanphear.
Fiction: Our interest is in "romans a clef" only. Submit outline/synopsis and sample chapters.

THOMAS NELSON, INC., 30 E. 42nd St., New York NY 10017. (212)697-5573. Editor-in-Chief: Gloria Mosesson. Hardcover and paperback originals. 7½% royalty; advance offered. State availability of photos and/or illustrations. Photocopied submissions OK. Reports in 2-4 months. SASE. Book catalog for SASE.
Nonfiction: Publishes Americana; art; biography; business; cookbooks, cooking and foods; history; hobbies; how-to; humor; juveniles; nature; politics; psychology; recreation; reference; religious; scientific; self-help; and sports books. Query or submit outline/synopsis and sample chapters. Recently published *Terrorism,* by R. Ceston; and *It's No Sin to Be Rich: A Defense of Capitalism,* by W. Davis.
Fiction: Publishes adventure; experimental; fantasy; historical; humorous; mainstream; mystery; religious; science fiction; suspense; and western books. Submit complete ms. Recently published *A Snake Among the Sunflowers,* by J. Kingard.

NELSON-HALL, INC., 325 West Jackson Blvd., Chicago IL 60606. (312)922-0856. Publisher: V. Peter Ferrara. Editor: Elbert P. Epler. Standard royalty schedule. Rarely offers an advance. Free book catalog. Will consider photocopied and simultaneous submissions. Send query accompanied by outline and return postage. "Soundness of subject matter and its treatment more important than just 'good writing.'" Reports in about 3 weeks. Enclose return postage.
Social Sciences, Psychology, History, Biography, Health, and Applied Psychology: Publishes serious works in the behavioral sciences. Also more popular books on practical, applied psychology written by qualified writers; business subjects, employment and personnel, general self-improvement, techniques relating to memory efficiency, retirement, investment, hobbies, etc. Length: 60,000 to 100,000 words.Recently published *Brand Name Guide to Sugar,* by I.L. Shannon, M.D. (health); *How to Burglar-Proof Your Home,* by R.L. Robinson; and *The Typewriter Guerrillas,* by J.C. Behrens (journalism).
Special Needs: "Series of individual books on establishing and operating various kinds of independent businesses. Must be authoritative and specific. Full size 256-page texts.

NEW AMERICAN LIBRARY, 1301 Ave. of the Americas, New York NY 10021. (212)956-3800. Editorial Director: Elaine Geiger Koster. Executive Editors: Angela Rinaldi, Bill Contradi.

Publishes paperback originals and reprints. Publishes 300 titles/year. Royalty is "variable;" offers "substantial" advance. Simultaneous and photocopied submissions OK. Reports in 2-3 months. SASE. Free book catalog.
Nonfiction: "We will consider all nonfiction sent—educational, mystic, self-help, inspirational, topical, etc. Submit outline/synopsis and sample chapters.
Fiction: "We will consider all fiction. We publish romance sagas, gothics, romances, science fiction, contemporary, suspense, thrillers, family sagas, etc." Submit outline/synopsis and sample chapters.

NEWCASTLE PUBLISHING CO., INC., 13419 Saticoy, North Hollywood CA 91605. (213)873-3191. Editor-in-Chief: Alfred Saunders. Paperback originals (20%); and reprints (80%). 5% royalty; no advance. Publishes 8 titles/year. Send prints or copies of items to illustrate ms. Simultaneous and photocopied submissions OK. Reports in 2-4 months. SASE. Free book catalog.
Nonfiction: Publishes cookbooks, cooking and foods; how-to; juveniles; multimedia material; pets; psychology; reference; self-help; sports (horse racing); travel; books on the occult, mythology and gambling. Submit outline/synopsis and sample chapters or complete ms. Alfred Saunders and Daryl Jacoby, editors.
Fiction: Fantasy, mystery and science fiction and mythology. Submit outline/synopsis and sample chapters. Doug Menville, editor.

NEW LEAF PRESS, INC., Box 1045, Harrison AR 72061. Editor-in-Chief: Cliff Dudley. Hardcover and paperback originals (99%); paperback reprints (1%). Specializes in charismatic books. 10% royalty on first 10,000 copies, paid once a year; no advance. Send photos and illustrations to accompany ms. Simultaneous and photocopied submissions OK. SASE. Reports in 30-60 days. Free book catalog.
Nonfiction: Biography; self-help. Charismatic books; life stories; how-to live the Christian life. 100-400 pages. Submit complete ms. B. Springer, editor.
Recent Titles: *The C. M. Ward Story,* by D. Wead (biography); *Christian Catechism,* by E. B. Gentile (curriculum for non-Christians).

NEW READERS PRESS, Publishing division of Laubach Literacy International, Box 131, Syracuse NY 13210. Editorial Director: Caroline Blakely. Assistant Editorial Director: Kay Koschnick. Publishes paperback originals. Published 18 titles in 1977, 20 in 1978. "Most of our sales are to public education systems, including adult basic education programs, with some sales to volunteer literacy programs, private human-services agencies, prisons, and libraries with outreach programs for poor readers." Pays in royalties or outright purchase. "Rate varies according to type of publication and length of ms." Advance is "different in each case, but does not exceed projected royalty for first year." Photocopied submissions OK. Reports in 6 weeks-2 months. SASE. Free book catalog.
Nonfiction: "Our audience is adults and older teenagers with limited reading skills (6th grade level and below). We publish coping skills materials that are of immediate practical value to our readers in such areas as consumer education, career education, health, family life, parenting skills, self-awareness, life-span development (adolescence through old age), legal rights, community resources, and adapting to U.S. culture (for functionally illiterate English-as-a-second-language students). We are particularly interested in mss written at the 3rd-4th grade level or below. Mss must be not only easy to read but adult in tone and concepts and sensitive to the needs and circumstances of low-income adults. We also publish basic education materials in reading and writing, math, and English-as-a-second-language for double illiterates. Our *basic* programs are usually commissioned by us, but we would consider submissions of materials in areas like reading comprehension, composition, and practical math or materials for specialized audiences of non-readers, such as the learning disabled or speakers of non-standard dialects. We would prefer proposals for a cluster of related titles; we would be interested in isolated titles only if they could fit in existing clusters. We are not interested in biography, poetry, or anything at all written for children. Recently published *Learning Games for Infants and Toddlers,* by Dr. J.R. Lally/Dr. I.J. Gordon (handbook); *Settlers in America,* by B.W. Lowrie/W. Stein (text); and *It's on the Map,* by P.K. Waelder (workbook).
Fiction: "We're looking for original, realistic fiction written for adults, but written at a 3rd-grade reading level. We want well-developed believable characters in realistic situations. We want mss of approximately 10,000 words that can be published as short novels. We are not interested in genres like adventure, mystery, science fiction, gothic romances or any other kinds of formula fiction that develop plot at the expense of characterization. We do not want simplified versions of already published works." Query.

NEW REVIEW BOOKS, Box 31, Station E, Toronto, Ontario, Canada M6H 4E1. (416)536-5083. Editorial Director: Dr. Oleh S. Pidhainy. Senior Editor: Dr. Alexander S. Pidhainy. Publishes hardcover and paperback originals. Published 8 titles in 1977, will do 10 in 1978. 10% royalty to 5,000 copies, 15% thereafter; no advance. Photocopied submissions OK. Reports in 3 months. SASE. Free book catalog.
Nonfiction: Academic works in bibliography, archeology, history, international relations, politics and etc., in regard to Eastern Europe/Soviet Union. No propaganda or improperly researched works. Consult Chicago *Manual of Style*. Submit outline/synopsis and sample chapters.

NEW VIEWPOINTS, division of Franklin Watts, 730 5th Ave., New York NY 10019. Executive Editor: Will Davison. Publishes hardcover and paperback originals. Specializes in college textbooks. Standard royalty, "depending on the author's reputation, subject matter and work involved." Published 8 titles in 1977. Query. Follow MLA *Style Sheet, Words into Type,* or Chicago *Manual of Style*. Simultaneous ("if so advised") and photocopied submissions OK. Reports "immediately on queries; about 2 months on mss." Free book catalog.
Nonfiction: Publishes textbooks on history, political science and sociology. Length: 300 book pages (100,000 words). Publishes textbooks for colleges, junior and community colleges, continuing education, and upper levels of high school. Recently published *Youth and Change in American Politics,* by L.M. Seagull (political sociology text); *Sexual Deviancy in Social Context,* edited by C.M. Bryant; and *St. Louis,* edited by S. Troen/G. Holt (documentary history).

NEWBURY HOUSE PUBLISHERS, INC., 54 Warehouse Lane, Rowley MA 01969. Editor-in-Chief: R. H. Ingram. Publishes hardcover and paperback originals (75%) and reprints (25%). 5-10% royalty. Advance against royalties up to $500 in special cases. Published 17 titles in 1977, 20 in 1978; will do 25-30 in 1979. State availability of photos and/or illustrations to accompany ms. Photocopied and simultaneous submissions OK. Reports in 1-2 months. SASE. Free book catalog.
Nonfiction: "Any topic of motivating interest to the following readers: students (adult and near adult) of English as a second/foreign language." Query.
Fiction: "These materials are intended for students of English as a second language; wanted are materials created especially for the purpose, or simplified and abridged versions of already published materials. Avoid topics which may give offense to persons overseas and topics which are dated or provincial."

NICHOLS PUBLISHING CO., Box 96, New York NY 10024. Editorial Director: W.G. Nichols. Publishes hardcover originals. Published 10 titles in 1977, 20 in 1978; will do 25 in 1979. Simultaneous and photocopied submissions OK. Reports in 6 weeks. SASE. Book catalog for SASE.
Nonfiction: Professional/academic materials in architecture, business, education, library science, international affairs, marine reference, and energy topics. Query. Recently published *Resource Management at the International Level,* by O. Young; *International Dictionary of Education,* by G.T. Page et al; and *Marinas: A Working Guide to Their Development and Design,* by D. Adie.

NORTH RIVER PRESS, INC., Box 241, Croton-on-Hudson NY 10520. Publishes hardcover and paperback originals and hardcover reprints. Offers 10% of cash received on all copies sold and paid for. No advance. Published 3 titles last year. Will consider photocopied submissions. Submit outline and sample page or two. Reports in 3 weeks. Enclose S.A.E. and return postage.
Reference and History: Regional history, literature and lore. Special interest in Hudson Valley material. Reference material, especially psychiatric and psychoanalytic. No special approach. Also interested in politics.

NORTHLAND PRESS, Box N, Flagstaff AZ 86002. (602)774-5251. Hardcover and paperback originals (95%) and reprints (5%). Advance varies. Published 12 titles in 1977, 12 in 1978; will do 12-15 in 1979. Transparencies and contact sheet required for photos and/or illustrations to accompany ms. Simultaneous and photocopied submissions OK. Reports in 2-4 weeks. SASE. Free book catalog.
Nonfiction: Publishes western Americana and related regional topics. Query.

NORTHWOODS PRESS, INC., Rt. 1, Meadows of Dan VA 24120. (703)953-2388. Editor-in-

Chief: Robert W. Olmsted. Publishes hardcover and paperback originals and reprints. 10-12½-15% royalty; "we are just beginning to offer an advance for local histories or biographies 'set' at $300." Published 12 titles in 1977, 14 in 1978. Simultaneous submissions OK. SASE. Book catalog for SASE.
Nonfiction: Americana; biography; cookbooks, cooking and foods; erotica; local history; hobbies; how-to; juvenile; nature; poetry; politics; recreation; self-help; sports; textbooks; and travel. Submit complete ms. Recently published *Trails Through the Northwoods: A History of the Bigfork Trail,* by Nauratil (local history); *Grandpa and the Red Haired Black Giants,* by Menkin (juvenile); and *Shadows on Casseopia,* by Olmsted (fantasy/poetry).
Fiction: Adventure; erotica; fantasy; historical; mainstream; and western. Submit complete ms.

W. W. NORTON CO., INC., 500 Fifth Ave., New York NY 10036. (212)354-5500. Managing Editor: Sterling Lawrence. 10-12½-15% royalty; advance varies. Publishes about 200 new titles annually. Photocopied and simultaneous submissions OK. Submit outline/synopsis and sample chapters for nonfiction. Submit complete ms for fiction. Reports in 4 weeks. SASE.
Nonfiction, Fiction and Poetry: "General, adult fiction and nonfiction of all kinds on nearly all subjects and of the highest quality possible within the limits of each particular book." Last year there were 52 book club rights sales; 35 mass paperback reprint sales; "Innumerable serializations, second serial, syndication, translations, etc."

NOYES DATA CORPORATION (including Noyes Press and Noyes Art Books), Noyes Bldg., Park Ridge NJ 07656. Publishes hardcover originals. Pays 10% royalty. Advance varies, depending on author's reputation and nature of book. Free book catalog. Query Editorial Department first. Reports in 1 to 2 weeks. Enclose return postage.
Nonfiction: "Art, classical studies, archaeology, history,mental health, and other nonfiction. Material directed to the intelligent adult and the academic market."
Technical: Publishes practical industrial processing science; technical, economic books pertaining to chemistry, chemical engineering, food and biology, primarily those of interest to the business executive; books relating to international finance. Length: 50,000 to 250,000 words.

OCCUPATIONAL AWARENESS, Box 948, Los Alamitos CA 90720. Editor-in-Chief: Edith Ericksen. Publishes educational originals. Offers standard minimum book contract; advance varies. Photocopied submissions OK. Submit outline and sample chapters for books and textbooks. Reports in 1 month. SASE.
Nonfiction: Materials should relate to students, careers, personnel, teachers, counselors and administrators. "We are an educational publishing company, relating occupations to curriculum."

OCEANA PUBLICATIONS, INC., Dobbs Ferry NY 10522. (914)693-1394. President: Philip F. Cohen. Managing Editor: William W. Cowan. Legal Editor: Edwin S. Newman. Docket Series Editor: Julius Marke. Editor, Reprint Bulletin: Sam P. Williams. Pays a flat fee of $500 for a legal almanac ms; $250 on receipt of acceptable ms; $250 at date of publication. No advance. Published approximately 50 titles last year. Send outline and sample chapter. Reports in 60 days. SASE.
Nonfiction: "We publish 5 to 10 legal almanacs a year. Most of them deal with legal aspects of everyday living. The author should have legal training. The prospective author will find sample almanacs in most local libraries."

ODDO PUBLISHING, INC., P.O. Box 68, Beauregard Blvd., Fayetteville GA 30214. (404)461-7627. Managing Editor: Genevieve Oddo. Publishes hardcover and paperback originals. Scripts are usually purchased outright. "We judge all scripts independently." Royalty considered for special scripts only. Will send free catalog to writer on request. Send complete ms, typed clearly. Reports in 3 to 4 months. Return postage and envelope must be enclosed with mss.
Juveniles and Textbooks: Publishes language arts, workbooks in math, writing (English), photophonics, science (space and oceanography), and social studies for schools, libraries, and trade. Interested in children's supplementary readers in the areas of language arts, math, science, social studies, etc. Texts run from 1,500 to 5,000 words. Presently searching for mss carrying the positive mental attitude theme—how to improve oneself, without preaching. Ecology, space, oceanography, and pollution are subjects of interest. Books on patriotism. Ms must be easy to read, general, and not set to outdated themes. It must lend itself to full color illustration. No stories of grandmother long ago. No love angle, permissive language, or immoral words or statements. Recently published *Little Indians' ABC,* by F.H. Lucero; *Uncle Sam and the Flag,* by L. Mountain; and *Cotton Carta,* by G. Worsham.

ODYSSEY PRESS, A Division of Bobbs-Merrill Educational Publishing, 4300 West 62nd St., Indianapolis IN 46268. (317)291-3100. Editorial Director: Thomas D. Wittenberg. Publishes college texts. Published 10 titles last year. "No unsolicited mss at this time, but queries are acceptable."

OHIO STATE UNIVERSITY PRESS, 2070 Neil Ave., Columbus OH 43210. (614)422-6930. Director: Weldon A. Kefauver. Payment on royalty basis. Published 20 titles last year. Query letter preferred with outline and sample chapters. Reports within 2 months. Ms held longer with author's permission. Enclose return postage.
Nonfiction: Publishes history, biography, science, philosophy, the arts, political science, law, literature, economics, education, sociology, anthropology, geography, and general scholarly nonfiction. No length limitations. Recently published *The Politics of Business in California,* by M.G. Blackford (American history); *The Railroad and the City,* by C.W. Condit; and *Electing Black Mayors,* by W.E. Nelson/P.J. Meranto.

***OHIO UNIVERSITY PRESS**, Scott Quad, Ohio University, Athens OH 45701. (614)594-5505. Director: Patricia Fitch. Managing Editor: Holly Panich. Publishes hardcover and paperback originals (97%) and reprints (3%). Published 26 titles in 1977, 30 in 1978; will do 35 in 1979. Subsidy publishes 6% of titles, based on projected market. Pays in royalties starting at 1,500 copies. No advance. Photocopied submissions OK. Reports in 2-4 months. SASE. Free book catalog.
Nonfiction: "General scholarly nonfiction with particular emphasis on 19th century literary criticism. Also history, social sciences, philosophy, and regional works. We do not publish in the hard sciences." Query or submit complete ms. Recently published *Hitler's War and the Germans,* by M. Steinert; *Dimity Convictions: The American Woman in The Nineteenth Century,* by B. Welter; and *Nietzsche's Gift,* by H. Alderman.

THE OLD ARMY PRESS, 1513 Welch, Ft. Collins CO 80521. (303)484-5535. Editor-in-Chief: Michael J. Koury. Hardcover and paperback originals (90%) and reprints (10%). Specializes in Western Americana. 10% royalty; no advance. State availability of photos and/or illustrations to accompany ms. Simultaneous and photocopied submissions OK. SASE. Free book catalog.
Nonfiction: Publishes Americana (60,000 words or less); history (60,000 words or less). Query. Recently published *Washington's Eyes,* by B. Loescher; *Legend Into History,* by C. Kuhlman (western Americana); and *Dust to Dust,* by J. Gaddy.

101 PRODUCTIONS, 834 Mission St., San Francisco CA 94103. (415)495-6040. Editor-in-Chief: Jacqueline Killeen. Publishes paperback originals. Offers standard minimum book contract. Published 12 titles in 1977. Free book catalog. Will consider photocopied submissions. Query. No unsolicited mss will be read. SASE.
General Nonfiction: All nonfiction, mostly how-to; cookbooks, the home, gardening, outdoors, travel, sports, hobbies, recreation and crafts. Heavy emphasis on graphics and illustrations. Most books are 192 pages.
Recent Titles: *Greenhousing for Purple Thumbs,* by D. Fenten; and *One-Pot Meals,* by M. Gin.

OPEN COURT-LIBRARY PRESS INCORPORATED, Box 599, LaSalle IL 61301. Publisher: M. Blouke Carus. General Manager: Howard R. Webber. Editor: Thomas G. Anderson. Royalty contracts negotiable for each book. Query first. Reports in 6 to 8 weeks. Enclose return postage.
Nonfiction: Philosophy, mathematics, comparative religion, history, political science, economics, and related scholarly topics. "This is a publishing house run as an intellectual and cultural enterprise and not as an assembly line industry. Nonetheless, all the books we publish are intended to be at least adequately viable in the market."
Recent Titles: *Hazards of Learning,* by G. R. Urban (education); *The Occult Establishment,* by S. Webb (religion/history); and *Three Questions About Morality,* by W. Frankena (philosophy).

OPTIMUM PUBLISHING CO. LIMITED, 245 rue St-Jacques, Montreal, PQ, Canada H2Y 1M6. (514)282-2491. Editor-in-Chief: Michael S. Baxendale. Hardcover and paperback originals and reprints. 10% royalty. Publishes approximately 25 titles a year. Marketed internationally, mail order and direct mail. Publishes in both official Canadian languages (English and French). Query or submit outline/synopsis and sample chapters. Photocopied submissions OK. Reports in 2-4 weeks. SASE.
Nonfiction: Cookbooks, cooking and foods; history; how-to; medicine and psychiatry; nature;

photography; self-help; sports; and travel books.
Recent Titles: *How To Live With Your Heart,* by A. Vineberg, M.D. (health); *The Artic,* by F. Bruemmer (nature);and *Stew and Casserole Cookbook,* by Margo Oliver (cookbook).

ORBIS BOOKS, Maryknoll NY 10545. (914)941-7590. Editor: Philip Scharper. Publishes paperback originals. 10-12½-15% royalty; advance averages $1,000. Query with outline, sample chapters, and prospectus. Reports in 4 to 6 weeks. Enclose return postage.
Nonfiction: "Religious developments in Asia, Africa, and Latin America. Christian missions. Justice and peace. Christianity and world religions." Recently published *The Liberation of Theology,* by J.L. Segundo (theology); *In Search of the Beyond,* by C. Carretto (inspiration); and *The Gospel of Peace and Justice,* by J. Gremillion.

OREGON STATE UNIVERSITY PRESS, 101 Waldo Hall, Corvallis OR 97331. (503)754-3166. Hardcover and paperback originals. "Very seldom pay royalties." No advance. Submit contact sheet of photos and/or illustrations to accompany ms. Reports in 2-4 months. SASE. Free book catalog for SASE.
Nonfiction: Publishes Americana; biography; economics; history; nature; philosophy; energy and recreation; reference; scientific (biological sciences only); technical (energy); and American literary criticism books. Emphasis on Pacific or Northwestern topics. Submit outline/synopsis and sample chapters. Recently published *The Marine Plant Biomass of the Pacific Northwest Coast,* edited by R. Krauss (biological science); and *The Fiction of Bernard Malamud,* edited by Astro/Benson.

OUR SUNDAY VISITOR, INC., Noll Plaza, Huntington IL 46750. (219)356-8400. Book Editorial Director: Anne Geoghegan. Original hardcovers and paperbacks (80%); hardcover and paperback reprints (20%). 10% royalty of price received; advance averages $250. Published 60 titles in 1977, 50 in 1978. Send prints of photos with ms. Reports in 2 weeks on queries; 1-2 months on mss. SASE. Free book catalog.
Nonfiction: Publishes books of religious connection and value. Biography, history, how-to, philosophy, psychology, reference, religious, textbooks, and travel. Submit outline/synopsis and sample chapters. Recently published *Depression,* by J. Dominian (psychology); *Alcohol: Its Use, Abuse & Therapy,* by G. Schomp (self-help); and *Journal of an Itinerant Artist,* by D. Bacigalupa (autobiographical essays).

OXMOOR HOUSE (a division of The Progressive Farmer Co.), P.O. Box 2262, Birmingham AL 35202. Director: Bon Logan. Managing Editor: Ann Harvey. Publishes hardcover and paperback originals. Payment on royalty basis or fee. Published 11 titles last year. Send outline and sample chapter. Reports in 1 month. SASE.
General Nonfiction: "Publishes books of general interest to Southern readers—cookbooks, garden books; books on crafts, sewing, photography, art, outdoors, antiques and how-to topics. Recently published *Jericho: A Southern Album; Tracing Your Ancestry,* and *Southern Antiques and Folk Art.*

P. A. R. INCORPORATED, Abbott Park Place, Providence RI 02903. (401)331-0130. Publisher: Richard P. Thiel. President: Barry M. Smith. Hardcover and paperback originals; reprints of their own texts. Specializes in textbooks for business schools, junior or community colleges, and adult continuing education programs. 10% royalty. Advance of $500-1,000. Markets through fall and winter workshops throughout the country with special seminars that are periodically held by authors and sales staff. State availability of photos or illustrations to furnish at a later date. Simultaneous submissions OK. Reports in 2-4 months. SASE. Free book catalog.
Nonfiction: R. P. Thiel, Department Editor. Business, economics, law, politics, psychology, sociology, technical, textbooks.
Recent Titles: *Developing Leadership,* by B. L. Fischman (management); *Study Guide for Personal Selling: Choice Against Chance,* by E. M. Mazze (salesmanship).

PACIFIC BOOKS, PUBLISHERS, Box 558, Palo Alto CA 94302. (415)323-5529. Editor: Henry Ponleithner. Royalty schedule varies with book. No advance. Published 6 titles last year. Will send catalog on request. Send complete ms. Reports promptly. SASE.
Nonfiction: General interest, professional, technical and scholarly nonfiction trade books. Specialties include western Americana and Hawaiiana. Recently published *Chinatown's Angry Angel: The Story of Donaldina Cameron,* by Martin (biography); and *For Health's Sake: A Critical Analysis of Medical Care in the United States,* by Carter (history).
Textbooks and Reference: Text and reference books; high school and college.

PADRE PRODUCTIONS, Box 1275, San Luis Obispo CA 93406. Editor-in-Chief: Lachlan P. MacDonald. Hardcover and paperback originals (90%) and reprints (10%). 6% minimum royalty; advance ranges from $200-1,000. Published 5 titles in 1977, 5 in 1978; will do 8 in 1979. State availability of photos and/or illustrations or include contact sheet or stat. Simultaneous submissions OK. Reports in 2-4 weeks. SASE. Book catalog for SASE.
Nonfiction: Publishes Americana (antiques), art, collectibles; cookbooks; history (local California); hobbies; how-to; nature (with illustrations); photography; poetry (about collectibles); psychology; recreation; reference; self-help; and travel books. Query first or submit outline and sample chapters. "Ample packaging; type all material; don't send slides unless asked." Recently published *An Uncommon Guide to San Luis Obispo County California,* by Lee, et. al. (travel guide); *Want Ads: I Want to be a Woman,* by R. Hamilton (autobiography/journal); and *Where the Highway Ends,* by G. Hamilton (local history).
Fiction: Publishes (in order of preference): adventure, fantasy, experimental, mainstream, and suspense books. "Also full-length narratives for the 10-14 year group, especially adventure with either strong contemporary situations or exceptional fantasy. Submit complete ms.

PAGURIAN PRESS LTD., Suite 1106, 335 Bay St., Toronto, Ontario, Canada M5H 2R3. Editor-in-Chief: Christopher Ondaatje. Publishes paperback and hardcover originals and reprints. Offers negotiable royalty contract. Advance negotiable. Published 30 titles in 1977. Free book catalog. Will consider photocopied submissions. Submit 2-page outline; synopsis or chapter headings and contents. Reports "immediately." Enclose SAE and International Reply Coupons.
Nonfiction: Publishes general interest trade books. Would like to see outdoor topics, sports, instruction. Will consider Americana, biography, cookbooks and cooking, economics, erotic, history, reference, self-help and how-to, sports, travel. Length: 40,000 to 70,000 words. Recently published *The Last of the Artic,* by W. Kurelek; *The Agatha Christie Mystery,* by D. Murdoch (biography); and *Wilderness Living,* by B. Berglund (outdoor).

PALADIN PRESS, Box 1307 Boulder CO 80306. (303)443-7250. Editor/Publisher: Peder C. Lund. Senior Editor: Timothy J. Leifield. Publishes hardcover and paperback originals (40%) and paperback reprints (60%). Published 11 titles in 1977, 14 in 1978. 10-12½-15% royalty. Simultaneous and photocopied submissions OK. Reports in 1 month. SASE. Free book catalog.
Nonfiction: "Paladin Press primarily publishes original manuscripts on military science, weaponry, self-defense, survival, police science, guerrilla warfare, and Kieldcraft. Survival and how-to manuscripts, as well as pictorial histories, are given priority. Manuals on building weapons, when technically accurate and cleanly presented, are encouraged. If applicable, send sample photographs and line drawings with outline and sample chapters." Query or submit outline/synopsis and sample chapters. Recently published *Save Your License; A Driver's Survival Guide,* by G. Mason; *Limited War Sniping,* by P.R. Senich; and *Home Workshop Guns for Defense and Resistance,* by B. Holmes.

PANTHEON BOOKS, Division of Random House, Inc., 201 E. 50th St., New York NY 10022. Managing Editor: Kathleen Macomber. Published over 60 titles last year. Unable to read mss submitted without previous inquiry. Address queries to Wendy Wolf, Adult Editorial Department. Enclose return postage.
Fiction: Publishes fewer than 5 novels each year, primarily mysteries. Recently published *Walking Dead,* by P. Dickinson; and *Three Kingdoms,* by Lo Kuan-Chung.
Nonfiction: Books mostly by academic authors. Emphasis on Asia, international politics, radical social theory, history, medicine, and law.
Juveniles: Publishes some juveniles. Address queries specificially to Juvenile Editorial Department.

PAPERJACKS LTD., 30 Les Mill Rd., Don Mills, Ontario, Canada M3B 2T6. (416)445-3333. Associate Publisher: Susan Stoddart. Paperback originals (50%) and reprints (50%). Specializes in mass market paperbacks. 6% royalty; advance averages $1,000. Published 60 titles in 1977, and 1978. Submit outline and sample chapters. "We like to have a covering letter which describes the nature and purpose of the work and states the number of words in the ms." Send contact sheet or prints if photos are to accompany the ms. Simultaneous ("if we are informed and give our prior permission") and photocopied submissions OK. Reports in 1-2 months. SASE. Free book catalog.
Nonfiction: Publishes Canadiana; biography; business; economics; erotica; history; hobbies; how-to; humor; medicine and psychiatry; nature; pets; politics; psychology (broad appeal);

recreation; self-help; sociology (broad appeal); sports; and travel books. "The only requirement is that the work have strong mass-market appeal." Recently published *Margaret Trudeau,* by A. Johnson (biography); and *Rape of a Normal Mind,* by C. Cobb/B. Avery.
Fiction: Publishes adventure; erotica; fantasy; historical; humorous; mainstream; mystery; romance; and suspense. Recently published *A Divine Case of Murder,* by C. Dennis.

PARENTS MAGAZINE PRESS, 52 Vanderbilt Ave., New York NY 10017. (212)661-9080. Editorial Director: Selma G. Lanes. Senior Editor: Barbara Francis. Publishes hardcover and paperback originals (90%) and reprints (10%). Published 22 titles in 1977, 26 in 1978; will do 26-30 in 1979. 5% royalty for author, 5% for illustrator; advance averages $750-1,000 for author, $1,500-2,000 for illustrator. Reports in 4-6 weeks. SASE. Book catalog for SASE.
Nonfiction: "We have a series called 'Finding Out Books' for children of about 8-11. Most of the books in the series are in the fields of science and social studies and are loosely geared to the curriculum needs of grades 3-5. But we would not exclude the idea of nonfiction books in other subject areas, for the same age group. The texts generally run about 5,000-6,000 words, and are illustrated with drawings and occasionally with photographs, depending on the best way to treat the text visually." Query. Recently published *Those Mysterious UFO's,* by D.C. Knight; *American Freedom and the Bill of Rights,* by W. Wise; and *Apples: A Bushel of Fun and Facts,* by B. Kohn.
Fiction: "We are primarily a picture-book publisher (32-48 page books) for children 4-9. We favor lively stories over poetry collections or fantasies. Many of the picture-books we publish are also used by our own Read-Aloud Book Club. Recently we have branched out into the I-Can-Read book category. And we are contemplating starting a line of books for a slightly older reader (8-11); these books would probably be 64-96 pages in length and carry some illustration—the story however would be the more important element." Submit complete ms. Recently published *Merry Merry Fibruary,* by D. Orgel; *Grandpa had a Windmill, Grandma had a Churn,* by L. Jackson; and *The Substitute,* by A. Lawler.

PARKER PUBLISHING CO., West Nyack NY 10994. Publishes hardcover originals and paperback reprints. Offers 10% royalty; 5% mail order and book clubs. Published 80 titles last year. Will send catalog on request. Reports in 3 to 5 weeks.
Nonfiction: Publishes practical, self-help, how-to books. Subject areas include popular health, mystic and occult, inspiration, secretarial, selling, personal and business self-improvement, money opportunities. Length: 65,000 words. Recently published *Miracle Healing Foods,* by Adams; and *Speakers on the Spot,* by Bernhard.

PAULIST PRESS, 1865 Broadway, New York NY 10023. (212)265-4028. Publishes hardcover and paperback originals and reprints. Standard trade contract with basic royalty open to negotiation. Advance depends on length of ms. Published 70 titles last year. Send outline and sample chapter first to Editorial Department. Reports in 4 weeks. Enclose return postage.
Religion: Catholic and Protestant religious works, both popular and scholarly. Length: 30,000 words and up. "Photo books and multimedia materials, large amounts of contemporary religious education materials." Material tends to avant-garde; no homespun philosophy or pious rehashes.

PAY DAY PRESS, 8208 E. Vista Dr., Scottsdale AZ 85253. (602)994-1724. Editorial Director: David L. Markstein. Publishes paperback originals. Published 3 titles in 1977, 4-5 in 1978. 10% royalty on mail order books, 10-12½-15% on trade books; no advance. Simultaneous and photocopied submissions OK. Reports in 2 months. SASE.
Nonfiction: "Anything that can make the reader's life easier, richer, or assist him to avoid pain. Anything a wide audience will take to, which will aid that audience and make it richer or happier." Query or submit outline/synopsis and sample chapters. Recently published *Guide to Much Bigger Investment Income; Secrets of a Successful Race Handicapper.*

PEACE & PIECES FOUNDATION, P.O. Box 99394, San Francisco CA 94109. President: M. Custodio. Publishes limited edition paperback originals and chapbooks. Does not offer a royalty contract. Makes outright purchase for a small sum (minimum of $100 honorarium), plus 100 to 200 copies of the book. Publishes 6 to 10 titles a year. Reports in 3 weeks. SASE.
Nonfiction and Poetry: "This tax-deductible, nonprofit foundation is concentrating largely on anthologies, California writers, and chapbooks by Bay Area writers and poets, although we will look at mss outside these confines. Serious writers only; no amateurs." Query. Recently published *The Empire of Howard Hughes,* by T.S.J. Lawson; *In Pursuit of Images,* by E.C. Ramirez; and *Sweet Tomorrow,* by R. Laursen.

Fiction: "Interested in science fiction, fantasy and humor, and solid folk tales by professional writers. No religious or gothic material please." Submit complete ms. Recently published *The 69 Days of Easter,* by T.S. Lawson; and *Antares,* by Emanuel Ro.

PEACE PRESS, INC., 3828 Willat Ave., Culver City CA 90230. Publisher: Richard Profumo. Publishes paperback originals. Specializes in how-to, ecology, appropriate technology and self-help books. 5% royalty; no advance. Published 7 titles in 1977, 8 in 1978; will do 9 in 1979. Submit outline/synopsis and sample chapters or complete ms. State availability of photos and/or illustrations. Simultaneous and photocopied submissions OK. Reports in 2-3 months. SASE.
Nonfiction: Publishes how-to; self-help; religious; cookbooks; ecology; history; and future history. Recently published *Exo-Psychology* and *Neuropolitics,* by T. Leary (future history); and *Solar Cookery,* by B. and D. Halacy.

PEGASUS, (A Division of The Bobbs-Merrill Co., Inc.), 4300 West 62nd Street, Indianapolis IN 46268. (317)291-3100. Editorial Director: Thomas D. Wittenberg. Publishes college texts. Published 10 titles last year. Business, education, humanities, and liberal arts. "We are not interested in unsolicited mss at this time but queries are acceptable."

***PELICAN PUBLISHING CO., INC.**, 630 Burmaster St., Gretna LA 70053. (504)368-1175. Editor-in-Chief: James Calhoun. Managing Editor: Cynthia Leonard. Hardcover and paperback originals (90%) and reprints (10%). 10% royalty; advance averages $500-1,000. Subsidy publishes 5% of books. Subsidy publishing offered "only if we determine a book is not economically feasible, but subject is of great importance." Submit outline/synopsis and sample chapters. Use Chicago *Manual of Style*. Send prints if photos/illustrations are to accompany ms. Reports in 2-4 months. SASE. Free book catalog.
Nonfiction: Publishes Americana; art; biography; business; cookbooks, cooking and foods; history; hobbies; how-to; humor; juveniles; politics; religious (inspirational); self-help; textbooks; motivational and travel books.
Special Needs: "*Maverick Guide to Hawaii* (Bone) is the first in a series of foreign travel guides. The Pelican Guide Series on domestic themes has long been a staple." Recently published *Maverick Guide to Hawaii,* by Bone; *Confessions of a Happy Christian,* by Ziglar; and *New Orleans Architecture, Vol. II,* by Cleristovich.

THE PENNSYLVANIA STATE UNIVERSITY PRESS, 215 Wagner Bldg., University Park PA 16802. (814)865-1327. Editor-in-Chief: Jack Pickering. Hardcover and paperback originals. Specializes in books of scholarly value, and/or regional interest. 10% royalty; no advance. Maintains own distribution company in England which serves the British Empire, Europe, etc. Submit outline/synopsis and sample chapters or complete ms. Send prints if photos/illustrations are to accompany ms. Simultaneous and photocopied submissions OK. Reports in 2-4 months. SASE. Free book catalog.
Nonfiction: Publishes art; biography; business; economics; history; hobbies; medicine and psychiatry; multimedia material; music; nature; philosophy; politics; psychology; recreation; reference; religious; scientific; sociology; technical; textbooks; women's studies; black studies; and agriculture books.
Special Needs: Keystone Books (a paperback series concentrating on topics of special interest to those living in the mid-Atlantic states.) Recently published *Aubrey Beardsley: Imp of the Perverse,* by S. Weintraub (critical biography); and *Gymnastic Safety Manual,* by G. Wettstone.

PENNYWORTH PRESS, Box 7192, Calgary, Alberta, Canada. Editorial Director: David Foy. Publishes hardcover and paperback originals (90%) and reprints (10%). Published 3 titles in 1977, 5 in 1978. 20% royalty, after costs; "minimal" advance. Simultaneous and photocopied submissions OK. Reports in 4-8 weeks. SAE and International Reply coupons; "Our present policy is to discard unread (and unacknowledged) all manuscripts not accompanied by proper return postage. American stamps are not used in Canada, despite the advice often given by US Postal employees." Book catalog for $1.
Poetry: "Poetry only. We would especially like to see manuscripts from Canadians. Submit complete ms. Recently published *The Tightrope Walker,* by R. Ratner; *While Walking,* by R. Hoeft; and *In Transit,* by E. McNamara.

THE PEQUOT PRESS, INC., Old Chester Rd., Chester CT 06412. (203)526-9571. Editorial Director: Robert W. Wilkerson. Publishes hardcover and paperback originals (95%) and paperback reprints (5%). Published 21 titles in 1977, 15 in 1978. 10% royalty; advance offered, "but

usually just for specific expenses." Simultaneous and photocopied submissions OK. Reports in 2 weeks. SASE. Free book catalog.
Nonfiction: Publishes history, biography, special interest, and "how-to" books. Special field is New England guide books, genealogies, short walks series, New England town histories, New England historical sidelights, railways, maritime, New England arts and crafts, including antiques and architecture. Interested in Connecticut history and the arts. "For book trade and elementary and high school markets." Length: open. Recently published *Only in New England,* by J.C. Hill; *Short Walks Maine Coast,* by H. & H. Sadlier; and *25 Bird Walks in Connecticut,* by N. Proctor.

PEREGRINE SMITH, INC., 1877 E. Gentile St., Layton UT 84041. (801)376-9800. Editorial Director: Richard A. Firmage. Publishes hardcover and paperback originals (50%) and reprints (50%). Published 6 titles in 1977, 7 in 1978; will do 10 in 1979. 10-12½-15% royalty; no advance. Photocopied submissions OK. Reports in 2 weeks-3 months. SASE. Book catalog for 26¢.
Nonfiction: "Western American history, American architecture, art history, arts & crafts (including how-to) and fine arts. We consider biographical, historical, descriptive and analytical studies in all of the above. Much emphasis is also placed on pictorial content. Many of our books are used as university texts." Query or submit outline/synopsis and sample chapters. Consult Chicago *Manual of Style*. Recently published *Greene & Greene: Architecture as a Fine Art,* by R. Makinson; *Bernard Maybeck: Artisan, Architect, Artist,* by K. Cardwell; and *The American Presidency in Political Cartoons,* by Blaisdell/Selz.
Fiction: "We have mainly published reprints or anthologies of American writers; but are very interested in expanding in the areas of serious fiction: novels, short stories, drama, and poetry. This will include reprints of important work as well as new material." Query or submit outline/synopsis and sample chapters. Recently published *Wild Animals I Have Known,* by E. Thompson Seton (short stories); *The Valley of the Moon,* by J. London; and *Okies,* by G. Haslem.

***PERIVALE PRESS**, 13830 Erwin St., Van Nuys CA 91401. (213)785-4671. Editorial Director: Lawrence P. Spingarn. Publishes paperback originals (90%) and reprints (10%). Published 3 titles in 1977 and 1978. Subsidy publishes "one out of six books published in any period. If a book has permanent value but a slow rate of return, we publish on a subsidy written into the contract as 'returnable through long-term sales income'." 10% royalty; no advance. Simultaneous and photocopied submissions OK. Reports in 3 months. SASE. Book catalog for SASE.
Nonfiction: Humor, criticism, and folklore. "Books on unusual subjects from a highly original viewpoint." Query. Recently published *Not-So-Simple Neil Simon,* E. McGovern (dramatic criticism); *Contemporary French Women Poets,* by C. Hermey (poetry in translation); and *Jewish Mother Goose,* by H. Squires (ethnic humor).
Fiction: "While we cannot publish novels, we welcome short story collections with a theme that would interest young contemporary readers, college-educated (18-35 years old), but these must be published on a returnable subsidy or grant from a foundation." Query. Recently published *The Blue Door & Other Stories,* by L. Spingarn.

S.G. PHILLIPS, INC., 305 West 86th St., New York NY 10024. (212)787-4405. Editor: Sidney Phillips. Publishes hardcover originals. "Graduated royalty schedule varies where artists or collaborators share in preparation." Published 5 titles last year. Will send a catalog to a writer on request. "Query first; no unsolicited mss." Reports in 30-60 days. SASE.
General and Juveniles: "Fiction and nonfiction for children and young adults. Particular interests—contemporary fiction, mysteries, adventure, science fiction; nonfiction: biography, politics, urban problems, international affairs, anthropology, archaeology, geography. Length depends on age group."

THE PICKWICK PRESS, 5001 Baum Blvd., Pittsburgh PA 15213. Editorial Director: Dikran Y. Hadidian. Publishes paperback originals and reprints. Published 6 titles in 1977, 7 in 1978; will do 7 in 1979. 8-10% royalty; no advance. Photocopied submissions OK. Reports in 2 months. SASE. Free book catalog.
Nonfiction: Religious and scholarly mss in Biblical archaeology, Biblical studies, church history and theology. Also reprints of outstanding out-of-print titles and original texts and translations. No popular religious material. Query. Consult *MLA Style Sheet* or Turabian's *A Manual for Writers*. Recently published *Crux Imperatorum Philosophies,* by R.G. Heath; *Manipulated Man,* by C. Rokut; and *The Emergence of Contemporary Judaism,* by P. Sigal.

PICTORIAL PRESS, 1535 Francisco St., San Francisco CA 94123. (415)362-6979 Editor-in-

Chief: T.S. Connelly. Publishes paperback originals. Royalty contract and advance are negotiable. Published 4 titles last year. Will consider photocopied and simultaneous submissions. Query first and include research outline. Reports in 45 days. Enclose return postage.
Nonfiction and Art: Publishes children's art; books about cable television; broadcast radiation; radiation and electromagnetic subjects.

PILOT BOOKS, 347 Fifth Ave., New York NY 10016. (212)685-0736. Publishes paperback originals. Offers standard royalty contract. Usual advance is $250, but this varies, depending on author's reputation and nature of book. Published 20 titles in 1977, 24 in 1978. Send outline. Reports in 4 weeks. Enclose return postage.
General Nonfiction, Reference, and Business: "Publishes financial, business, travel, career, and personal guides, training manuals. Directories and books on moneymaking opportunities." Wants "clear, concise treatment of subject matter." Length: 8,000 to 20,000 words. Recently published *Curtis Casewit's Guide to Tennis Resorts,* by C. Casewit; and *Quips and Quotes about Fashion,* by E. Lambert.

PINNACLE BOOKS, 1 Century Plaza, Century City CA 90067. Editor: Andrew Ettinger. Publishes paperback originals and reprints. "Contracts and terms are standard and competitive." Published 160 titles in 1977. Will send brochure and requirements memo to a writer if SASE is enclosed. "Will no longer accept unsolicited mss. Most books are assigned to known writers or developed through established agents. However, an intelligent, literate, and descriptive letter of query will often be given serious consideration." SASE.
General: "Books range from general nonfiction to commercial trade fiction in most popular categories. Pinnacle's list is aimed for wide popular appeal, with fast-moving, highly compelling escape reading, adventure, espionage, historical intrigue and romance, science fiction, western, popular sociological issues, topical nonfiction."

PLATT & MUNK PUBLISHERS, division of Grosset & Dunlap, 51 Madison Ave., New York NY 10010. (212)689-9200. Editor-in-Chief: Kate Klimo. Hardcover originals. Pays flat fee; "if royalty, nothing above 2%; advance averages $500." Submit complete ms. Send prints, photocopies or slides if photos/illustrations are to accompany ms. Photocopied submissions OK. Reports in 2-4 weeks. SASE. Book catalog for SASE.
Nonfiction and Fiction: Publishes juvenile picture books only.

PLAYBOY PRESS, Division of Playboy Enterprises, Inc., 919 Michigan Ave., Chicago IL 60611. New York office: 747 Third Ave., New York NY 10017. (212)688-3030. Editorial Director (hardcover): Robert Gleason; Editorial Director (softcover): Mary Ann Stuart. Publishes hardcover and paperback originals and reprints. Royalty contract to be negotiated. Published 60 titles last year. Query first. SASE.
General: Fiction and nonfiction slanted to the adult male who reads *Playboy* magazine.

PLENUM PUBLISHING CORP., 227 W. 17th St., New York NY 10011. Imprints: Da Capo Press, Consultants Bureau, IFI/Plenum Data Corporation, Plenum Press, Plenum Medical Book Company, Plenum Rosetta. Publishes hardcover and paperback reprints. Offers standard minimum contract of 7½-10%. Published 450 titles last year. Query B. Friedland. SASE.
Nonfiction: Books on science, medicine, social and behavioral sciences, history, biography, art, music, photography, film, and general trade. Recently published *Portraits in Life and Death,* by P. Hujar; and *The Complete Operas of Verdi,* by C. Osborne.

POCKET BOOKS, 1230 Ave. of the Americas, New York NY 10020. Paperback originals and reprints. Published 300 titles last year. Reports in one month. Submit through agent only. Enclose return postage.
General: History, biography, philosophy, inspirational, general nonfiction and adult fiction (mysteries, science fiction, gothics, westerns). Reference books, joke books, puzzles.

POET GALLERY PRESS, 224 W. 29th St., New York NY 10001. Editor: E.J. Pavlos. Publishes paperback originals. Offers standard 10-12½-15% royalty contract. Published 4 titles last year. Submit complete ms only. Enclose return postage with ms.
General: "We are a small specialty house, and we place our emphasis on publishing the works of young Americans currently living in Europe. We are interested in creative writing rather than commercial writing. We publish for writers who live overseas, who write and live, who produce writings from the self. Our books might turn out to be commercial, but that is a secondary consideration. We expect to emphasize poetry; however, our list will be concerned with all

aspects of literature: the novel, plays, and cinema, as well as criticism. We urge that authors recognize our imposed restrictions; we can not, and do not wish at this time to compete with major publishing companies." Recently published *Sarah,* by Gamela; and *Iris Elegy,* by Hakim.

POLARIS PRESS, 16540 Camellia Terrace, Los Gatos CA 95030. (408)356-7795. Editor-in-Chief: Edward W. Ludwig. Paperback originals. Specializes in el-hi books with appeal to general juvenile public. 10% royalty; advance averages $100-300. Send contact sheets or prints if photos and/or illustrations are to accompany ms. Simultaneous and photocopied submissions OK. Reports in 1-2 weeks. SASE. Free book catalog.
Fiction: Publishes some fantasy and science fiction "Please, *no* mss which require extensive (and expensive) use of color in inner pages." Query. Recently published *A Mexican American Coloring Book,* by Rascon; and *The California Story: A Coloring Book,* by Bernal.

POPULAR LIBRARY/CBS, 600 Third Ave., New York NY 10016. Editor-in-Chief: Patrick O'Connor. Publishes originals and reprints. Royalty contract to be negotiated. Published 252 titles last year. Query first. Enclose return postage.
General: Publishes adult general fiction and nonfiction. Recently published *Don Bolles: An Investigation into His Murder,* by M. Tallberg (investigative journalism); *Delta Flame,* by M. Ross (gothic); and *Optimism One,* by F.M. Esfandiary.

G. HOWARD POTEET, INC., Box 217, Cedar Grove NJ 07009. Publishes paperback originals. Published 5 titles in 1978. 10% royalty; no advance. Simultaneous submissions OK. Reports in 1-2 weeks. SASE. Book catalog for SASE.
Nonfiction: How-to books in the areas of business, hobbies, multimedia material; photography; technical material; and textbooks. Query or submit outline/synopsis and sample chapters. Recently published *Between the Lines in the Mail Order Game,* by Matt Dol.

CLARKSON N. POTTER, INC., 1 Park Ave., New York NY 10016. (212)532-9200. Vice President/Publisher: Jane West. Senior Editor: Carol Southern. Publishes hardcover and paperback originals. 10% royalty on hardcover; 5% on paperback, varying escalations; advance depends on type of book and reputation or experience of author. Samples of prints may be included with outline. Photocopied submissions OK. Reports in 2-4 weeks. SASE. Free book catalog.
Nonfiction: Publishes Americana; art; biography; cookbooks, cooking and foods; history; how-to; humor; nature; photography; politics; scientific; self-help; and annotated literature books. "Mss must be cleanly typed on 8½x11 bond; double-spaced. Chicago *Manual of Style* is preferred." Query first or submit outline/synopsis and sample chapters. Recently published *Oysterville,* by W. Espy (biography/Americana); *Remarkable Names of Real People,* by J. Train (humor); and *Molas,* by A. Parker/A. Neal (art).

***A.R. PRAGARE CO., INC.**, 3695G N. 126th St., Brookfield WI 53005. (414)781-1430. Publisher: Robert W. Pradt. Hardcover and paperback originals (70%) and reprints (30%). Specializes in firearms, hunting, and other topics of interest in this area. 7-10% royalty; no advance. Subsidy publishes a varying percentage of books through Pine Mountain Press, a division of the corporation. "Author must be previously published with good sales record and have some knowledge of publishing (marketing) and the financing to start a publishing venture." Markets books by mail order through gun and hunting magazines. Submit outline/synopsis and sample chapters. "No onion skin paper." Send prints to illustrate ms. Reports in 1-2 months. SASE.
Nonfiction: Publishes Americana, business; cookbooks, cooking and foods; economics, history, humor, recreation, sports (limited to our area); technical (in field of guns); biographies and children's books. Recently published *Book of the Garand,* by Hatcher; and *What is Love and Where to Find It,* by Liebman.
Fiction: Publishes adventure, humorous and western fiction books.
Special Needs: Guns, hunting, related adventure and historical books for Leather Stocking division; general need for all materials in Business and Economics division.

***PRECEDENT PUBLISHING, INC.**, 520 N. Michigan Ave., Chicago IL 60611. (312)828-0420. Editorial Director: Louis A. Knafla. Senior Editor: Henry Cohen. Publishes hardcover and paperback originals. Published 2 titles in 1977, 3-4 in 1978; will do 4-5 in 1979. Subsidy publishes 10% of titles. 10% royalty; advance averages $400. Simultaneous and photocopied submissions OK. Reports in 2 weeks-1 month. SASE. Free book catalog.
Nonfiction: Scholarly books: history and historical methodology, Afro-American life,

philosophy, and science. Query, including outline of chapters, synopsis of book, maximum number of words projected, and tentative date of first draft. Recently published *Envelopes of Sound,* by Grele (oral history); *Revolutionary Guerrilla Warfare,* by Sarkesian (multidisciplinary); and *Perception, Theory, Commitment,* by Brown (philosophy/science).
Fiction: Literature depicting American life and its people, including blacks and ethnic groups; poetry; and anthologies. Submit outline/synopsis and sample chapters. Recently published *The Big Gate,* by Stuckey (poetry).

PRENTICE-HALL, INC., Englewood Cliffs NJ 07632. Editor-in-Chief, Trade Division: John Grayson Kirk. Publishes hardcover and paperback originals and reprints. Free book catalog. Submit outlines and sample chapters for nonfiction; submit complete ms for fiction. Will consider photocopied submissions. "Always keep 1 or more copies on hand in case original submission is lost in the mail." Reports in 4 to 6 weeks on trade books; reports in 2 to 4 weeks on juveniles. SASE.
General: "All types of fiction and trade nonfiction, save poetry, drama, and westerns. Average acceptable length: 80,000 words. The writer should submit his work professionally and be prepared to participate to the extent required in the book's promotion." Publishes adult trade mainstream fiction, Americana, art, biography, business, history, humor, medicine and psychiatry, music, nature, philosophy, politics, reference, religion, science, self-help and how-to, sports, hobbies and recreation.
Juveniles: "Contemporary fiction for ages 8 and up; high interest, low reading level fiction and nonfiction, project books up to age 15. Style, outlook, and structure requirements vary with each ms. They are as much an integral part of the book as the subject matter itself. In general, writers should make their material as interesting, alive, and simple as possible. We are interested in very simple concept books for preschoolers (*not* alphabet books) about 500 to 1,000 words; books for ages 9 to 14 on one aspect of American history covering a wide time and geographical span. If a book is really good, it can usually survive the fact that the subject has been worked over. Because children's books are so expensive to produce and therefore expensive to buy, the trade market is limited. Libraries are the primary market. At this point, they seem to be showing a decided preference for books in which the child can participate—instructive books, involving books." Length: 15,000 words for teenage books; 5,000 to 10,000 for fiction and nonfiction, ages 7 to 12; Editor-in-Chief, Juvenile Books: Ellen E.M. Roberts.

PRENTICE-HALL OF CANADA, LTD., 1870 Birchmont Rd., Scarborough, Ontario, Canada M1P 2J7. (416)293-3621. Editor-in-Chief: G.B. Halpin. Trade Editor: G.M. Laszloffy. Publishes hardcover and paperback originals (90%) and reprints (10%). Published 30 titles in 1977, 40 in 1978; will do 50 in 1979. 10-12½-15% royalty; advance "is determined by publication." Simultaneous and photocopied submissions OK. Reports in 4-6 weeks. SASE. Free book catalog.
Nonfiction: Publishes art, biography, history, hobbies, how-to, humor, nature, photography, politics, recreation, references, self-help, sports, and technical. Submit outline and '3-4 representative samle chapters along with brief author biography including previous publishing experience, if any." Recently published *The Art of Glen Loates,* by Loates/Duval (art); *Complete Guide to Total Fitness,* by Percival/Taylor (how-to/reference); and *The OK Way to Slim: Weight Control Through Transactional Analysis,* by Laverty (self-help).

***THE PRESERVATION PRESS**, National Trust for Historic Preservation, 740-748 Jackson Pl., N.W., Washington DC 20006. Vice-President and Editor: Mrs. Terry B. Morton. Publishes paperback reprints and originals, and hardcover originals. Offers Author's Guild and other standard publishing contracts. "Past work has generally been on honorarium or fee basis. Contracts based on flat fees often provide for partial payment upon submission of outline." About 95% of ideas coming from outside the company are published only on a subsidy basis. Also has a cooperative publication program for member organizations. Published 5 titles in 1977. Titles sold and distributed primarily by direct mail. Will send free catalog to writer on request. Will consider simultaneous and photocopied submissions. Query first. Follow Chicago *Manual of Style*. Reports as soon as possible. Enclose return postage.
Nonfiction: Publishes books about historic preservation (saving and reusing the "built" environment such as buildings, structures, sites and objects of architectural and historical importance and character). No general local history. Length: 2,000 to 20,000 words. Also publishes case studies, cookbooks; preservation law; reference and textbooks. Recently published *Built to Last: A Handbook on Recycling Old Buildings,* by G. Bunnell; and *Fabrics for Historic Buildings, What Style Is It?,* by HABS Staff.

PRESS PACIFICA, Box 47, Kailua HI 96734. Publisher: Jane Wilkins Pultz. Senior Editor:

Penny Pagliaro. Publishes hardcover and paperback originals (50%) and reprints (50%). Published 3 titles in 1977, 5 in 1978; will do 8 in 1979. 10% royalty "with escalations"; advance averages $100. Simultaneous and photocopied ("if on good white paper and very readable") submissions OK. Reports in 4 weeks-3 months. SASE. Book catalog for 50¢.
Nonfiction: History (especially women and Hawaii); Hawaiiana; women (history, biography, anthologies, feminist theory); self-help; and how-to. "We are open to new authors who have expertise in their field." No technical or supernatural material. Submit outline/synopsis and sample chapters. Recently published *Loom and Spindle,* by H.H. Robinson (women's history/autobiography); *I Like Poems and Poems Like Me,* edited by P. Pagliaro; and *Job Searching in Hawaii,* by A. Lim.
Fiction: "Good solid fiction, well crafted. We have a hard hitting novel on the brutalization of juveniles in the deliquency detention system titled *Butterflies . . . If You Throw It,* by R.C. Winslow. We're not interested in mysteries, fantasy, religious material and science fiction generally speaking, unless of unusual quality." Submit complete ms, "query if you think subject matter would limit audience."

PRICE/STERN/SLOAN INC., PUBLISHERS, 410 N. La Cienega Blvd., Los Angeles CA 90048. (213)657-6100. Editorial Director: John Dickinson Arams. Publishes hardcover and paperback originals. Published 44 titles in 1977, 51 in 1978. 6% royalty and up or $300 minimum outright purchase; "sometimes" offers advance. Simultaneous and photocopied submissions OK. Reports in 3 weeks. SASE.
Nonfiction: Humor; self-help; and satire (limited). Submit outline/synopsis and sample chapters. Recently published *Instant Photo/Instant Art,* by D. Sicilia (how-to); *Winner's Workbook,* by J. Alexander (self-improvement); and *Murphy's Law,* by A. Bloch (collection of humor).

PRINCE PUBLISHERS, 349 E. Northfield Rd., Livingston NJ 07039. Editor-in-Chief: Dick Atkins. Publishes hardcover and paperback originals. Offers standard royalty contract of 10-12½-15%. Published 3 titles last year. Submit outline and sample chapters for nonfiction and fiction. Address "Fiction Editor" or "Nonfiction Editor." Reports in 2 months. SASE.
Fiction and Nonfiction: "Prince is very selective and publishes a limited number of books each year. We're looking for mss of quality that have potential mass appeal. Also publishes mainstream adult trade fiction, and recreation.

***PRINCETON BOOK CO., PUBLISHERS**, 20 Nassau St., Princeton NJ 08540. (609)924-2244. Editorial Director: Charles Woodford. Publishes hardcover and paperback originals (70%) and reprints (30%). Published 4 titles in 1977, 5 in 1978; will do 6 in 1979. Subsidy publishes 10% of titles, based on "the marketability of the book and the expense of producing it." 10% royalty; no advance. Simultaneous and photocopied submissions OK. Reports in 6 weeks. SASE. Free book catalog.
Nonfiction: Professional books and college textbooks on education, physical education, dance, psychology, sociology, physical therapy, and recreation. No "books that have a strictly trade market." Submit outline/synopsis and sample chapters. Recently published *Making it Till Friday: A Guide to Successful Classroom Management,* by Long/Frye (college textbook); *Motor Development: Issues and Applications,* by Ridenour (professional book); and *The Dance Technique of Doris Humphrey and Its Creative Potential,* by Stodelle (text).

PROFESSIONAL EDUCATORS PUBLICATIONS, INC., Box 80728, Lincoln NE 68501. Editor-in-Chief: Harry Kaste. Publishes paperback originals. Offers outright purchase of ms for negotiated fee. Free book catalog. Will consider photocopied submissions; ribbon copy for publication. Mss for publication must be typed on good quality bond stock with generous margins. Everything must be double-spaced, including any extracts, notes, references or bibliographies. Query first. Reports in 1 month. Enclose return postage.
Textbooks: "Short texts treating special topics related to the field of professional education for use by students and faculty in schools of education and by practicing teachers." Presentation should be lucid, with a minimum of professional jargon and scholarly apparatus. Length: 35,000-75,000 words. Recently published *Lifelong Learning* (Hiemstra) and *Moral Development and Education* (Forisha/Forisha).

PRUETT PUBLISHING COMPANY, 3235 Prairie Ave., Boulder CO 80301. Managing Editor: Gerald Keenan. Royalty contract is "dependent on the price we receive from sales." No advance. "Most books that we publish are aimed at special interest groups. As a small publisher, we feel most comfortable in dealing with a segment of the market that is very clearly identifiable, and one we know we can reach with our resources." Will send free catalog to writer

on request. Mss must conform to the Chicago *Manual of Style*. No simultaneous submissions. Legible photocopies acceptable. Query first. Reports in 2-4 weeks. SASE.
General Adult Nonfiction and Textbooks: Pictorial railroad histories; outdoor activities related to the Intermountain West; some Western Americana. Textbooks with a regional (Intermountain) aspect for pre-school through college level. Also, Special Education, with emphasis on student-oriented workbooks. Does not want to see anything with the personal reminiscence angle or biographical studies of little-known personalities. "Like most small publishers, we try to emphasize quality from start to finish, because for the most part, our titles are going to a specialized market that is very quality conscious. We also feel that one of our strong points is the personal involvement ('touch') so often absent in a much larger organization." Recently published *The Queen City: A History of Denver,* by L. Dorsett (urban history); and *The Circus Moves by Rail,* by Parkinson/Fox.

PSG PUBLISHING COMPANY, INC., 545 Great Rd., Littleton MA 01460. (617)486-8971. Editor-in-Chief: Frank Paparello. Managing Editor: Margery Berube. Hardcover and paperback originals. Specializes in publishing technical medical and scientific books for the professional and graduate student market. 10% royalty; no advance. Send prints of photos to accompany ms. Simultaneous submissions OK. Reports in 2-4 weeks. SASE. Free book catalog.
Nonfiction: Margery S. Berube, Department Editor. Publishes scientific books and ones on medicine and psychiatry. Query or submit complete ms. Recently published *AMA Drug Evaluations,* by American Medical Association; *Clinical Psychopharmacology,* by J. Bernstein (drug reference); and *Malnutrition and Intellectual Development,* by J.D. Lloyd-Still.

PULSE-FINGER PRESS, Box 16697, Philadelphia PA 19139. Editor-in-Chief: Orion Roche. Publishes hardcover and paperback originals. Offers standard minimum book contract; less for poetry. Advance varies, depending on quality. "Not less than $100 for poetry; or $500 for fiction." Published 6 titles last year. Query. No unsolicited mss. Reports in 1 month. SASE.
Fiction and Poetry: "We're interested in subjects of general concern with a focus on fiction and poetry. All types considered; tend to the contemporary-cum-avant-garde. No length requirements. Our only stipulation is quality, as we see it." Recently published *Bronchitis Caper,* by DeAria; and *The Circular Seesaw,* by Finkel.

THE PURDUE UNIVERSITY PRESS, South Campus Courts—D. West Lafayette IN 47907. (317)749-6083. Director: William J. Whalen. Managing Editor: Verna Emery. Publishes hardcover and paperback originals. Specializes in scholarly books from all areas of academic endeavor. 10% royalty on gross; no advance. Published 7-8 titles in 1978. Photocopied submissions OK "if author will verify that it does not mean simultaneous submission elsewhere." Reports in 2-4 months. SASE. Free book catalog.
Nonfiction: Publishes Americana, art (but no color plates), biography, communication, history, law, music, nature, philosophy, photography, poetry, political science, psychology, reference, religious, scientific, sociology, technical, and literary criticism. "Works of scholarship only." Recently published *Phenomenology and Literature,* by R.R. Magliola; and *Meaning and Appreciation,* by M.A. Weinstein.
Fiction: Experimental. "As a university press, we are interested only in works of academic merit which display creative research and scholarship."

G.P. PUTNAM'S SONS, 200 Madison Ave., New York NY 10016. (212)576-8900. Editor-in-Chief: Phyllis Grann. Juvenile Editor-in-Chief: Charles Mercer. Publishes hardcover and paperback originals. "Payment is on standard royalty basis." Published 276 titles in 1977. Free book catalog. "Well-known authors may submit outline and sample chapter." Unsolicited mss not accepted. Reports on queries in 1 week. Enclose SASE.
Nonfiction, Fiction and Juveniles: Nonfiction in history, biography, exploration, etc. Publishes juvenile fiction and nonfiction. "Adult mss must be a bare minimum of 60,000 words; juveniles vary in length, of course, depending upon whether they are young adult or picture book texts."

***QUEENSTON HOUSE PUBLISHING, LTD.**, 102 Queenston St., Winnipeg, Manitoba, Canada R3N OW5. (204)489-6862. Editorial Director: Joan Parr. Senior Editor: Steven Benstead. Publishes hardcover and paperback originals. Published 4 titles in 1977, 12 in 1978; will do 20 in 1979. Subsidy publishes 10% of titles; "if the author, or a sponsor offers to subsidize, then we are open to negotiation." 10% royalty; no advance. Photocopied submissions OK. Reports in 3-6 months. SASE. Book catalog for SASE.
Nonfiction: Autobiography; biography; history; and political issues. Query. Recently published *Ed Schreyer: A Social Democrat in Power,* edited by P. Beaulieu; *Political Warriors,* by L.

Stinson (history); and *Paper Tomahawks,* by J. Burke (expose).
Fiction: Adventure; mystery; fantasy; and science fiction (to a smaller degree). "We are not interested in fiction of a strictly sensational nature, i.e., sex, disaster, etc. A lot depends on the quality of writing, so we will look at query letters on about any subject." Query. Recently published *Corner Stone,* by B. Kaplan; *A Small Informal Dance,* by H. Levi; and *Wanna Fight, Kid?,* by C. Duncan.

QUICK FOX, (formerly *Links Books*), 33 W. 60th St., New York NY 10023. Editor-in-Chief: Jim Charlton. Managing Editor: Jeanette Mall. Publishes paperback originals. Published 40 titles in 1977 and 1978; will do 50 in 1979. 7% royalty; advance varies. Simultaneous and photocopied submissions OK. Reports in 1 month. SASE. Free book catalog.
Nonfiction: "We publish general interest books in a special way—contemporary culture and society; practical and instructional books; and photography and art books." Query or submit outline/synopsis and sample chapters. Recently published *Good Lives,* by Wise/Weiss (home design); *Art Deco Internationale,* by Brown/Weinstein (design); and *Paul Simon* (photo/song collection).

RAINTREE PUBLISHERS LTD., 205 W. Highland, Milwaukee WI 53203. Editor-in-Chief: Russ Bennett. Publishes hardcover and paperback originals. Specializes in juvenile information series for general reader or for supplementary reading and language arts programs. May offer royalty or outright purchase; advance varies; "usually 50% of the contract fee." Query or submit outline/synopsis and sample chapters. State availability of photos/illustrations. Photocopied submissions OK. Reports in 2-4 weeks. SASE. Free book catalog.
Nonfiction: Publishes biography (juvenile, 1,500 words max); general nonfiction; sports; and reference. Recently published *Close Encounters: A Factual Report on UFO's,* by S.J. Larsen.
Fiction: Publishes juvenile books in all categories.

RAND McNALLY, P.O. Box 7600, Chicago IL 60680. Trade Division and Education Division at this address. Variable royalty and advance schedule. Trade books payment on royalty basis or outright; mass market juveniles outright. Reports in 6 to 8 weeks. Enclose return postage.
General Nonfiction: Adult manuscripts should be sent to Stephen P. Sutton, Editor, Adult Books, Trade Division, but query first on the subjects of Americana, travel, natural history, personal adventure, self-help. Contracts are sometimes offered on the basis of outline and sample chapter.
Trade Juveniles: Dorothy Haas, Editor. Picture books ages 3-8; fiction and nonfiction ages 8-12; special interest books (no fiction) for young adults. Send picture book manuscripts for review. Query on longer manuscripts.
Mass Market Juveniles: Roselyn Bergman, Editor. Picture book scripts, six years and under; Jr. Elf Books, Elf Books, activity formats. Realistic stories, fantasy, early learning material; not to exceed 600 words and must present varied illustration possibilities.
Textbooks: Education Division publishes books, equipment, other printed materials, and maps for elementary, high schools and colleges in restricted fields. Query Executive Editor, Education Division.

RANDOM HOUSE, INC., 201 East 50th St., New York NY 10022. Also publishes Vintage Books. Publishes hardcover and paperback originals and reprints. Payment as per standard minimum book contracts. Query first. SASE.
Fiction and Nonfiction: Publishes fiction and nonfiction of the highest standards.
Poetry: Some poetry volumes.
Juveniles: Publishes a broad range of fiction and nonfiction for young readers, including Beginner Books, Step-up Books, Gateway Books, Landmark Books. Particularly interested in high-quality fiction for children.

RD COMMUNICATIONS, Box 683, Ridgefield CT 06877. Editor-in-Chief: Richard Dunn. Publishes paperback originals. Straight book contract of 15%. Advance averages $500 payable in installments from time of contract to publication. Marketed by direct mail and mail order advertising. Will send catalog to writer if professional in one of their fields of specialty. Reports in 2-4 weeks. SASE.
Business, Educational, and Technical: Technology, business, professional skills, education. Author should have working background in field in which he writes. Content must have immediate practical value to professionals in the field. Emphasis is on practical application rather than general discussion or theory. Recently published *Ready for Reading,* by M. Larberg.

RED DUST, INC., 218 East 81st St., New York NY 10028. Editor: Joanna Gunderson. Publishes hardcover and paperback originals and translations. Specializes in quality work by new writers. Books printed either simultaneously in hard and paper covers or in hardcover alone, in editions of 1,000 copies. 10-12½-15% royalty; the author generally receives $300 on the signing of the contract, as an advance. Current catalog available on request. Enclose 13¢ stamp with request. Will consider photocopied submissions. "Authors should not submit photos or artwork with mss." Query with sample chapter. Reports in 2 months. SASE.
Fiction: Novels and short stories.
Nonfiction and Poetry: Scholarly, art, art history, film and poetry.

REGAL BOOKS, Division of Gospel Light Publications, 110 W. Broadway, Glendale CA 91204. (213)247-2330. Editorial Director: Olan Hendrix. Senior Editor: Fritz Ridenour. Publishes hardcover and paperback originals. Published 60 titles in 1977 and 1978; will do 80 in 1979. 6% royalty on paperback titles, 10% for curriculum books. Advance averages $1,000. Simultaneous and photocopied submissions OK. Reports in 4 weeks. SASE. Free book catalog.
Nonfiction: Missions (gift books); Bible studies (Old and New Testament); Christian Living; counseling (self-help, the future); contemporary concerns (biographies); evangelism (church growth); marriage and family; youth; children's books; handcrafts; communication resources; teaching enrichment resources; Bible commentary for Laymen Series; and material for the International Center for Learning. Query or submit outline/synopsis and sample chapters. Recently published *Lords of the Earth,* by D. Richardson (adventurous missionary story); *Measure of a Woman,* G. Getz; and *In His Strength,* by G. Wilkerson (personal experience).

THE REGENTS PRESS OF KANSAS, (formerly The University Press of Kansas), 366 Watson Library, Lawrence KS 66045. (913)864-4154. Managing Editor: John Langley. Hardcover and paperback originals. "No royalty until manufacturing costs are recovered." No advance. Published 10 titles in 1977, 16 in 1978. Markets books by direct mail, chiefly to libraries and scholars. "State availability of illustrations if they add significantly to the ms." Photocopied submissions OK. Reports in 4-6 months. SASE. Free book catalog.
Nonfiction: Publishes biography, history, literary criticism, politics, regional subjects, and scholarly nonfiction books. "No dissertations." Query first. Recently published *The Korean War: A 25-Year Perspective* edited by Francis H. Heller (history); *The Crystal Cage: Adventures of the Imagination in the Fiction of Henry James* by Daniel J. Schneider (literary criticism); and *Philosophical Scepticism and Ordinary Language Analysis* by Garrett L. Vander Veer (philosophy).

REGENTS PUBLISHING COMPANY, INC., Two Park Ave., New York NY 10016. Pays 10% to 15% royalty based on net sales. Usual advance is $500, but this varies, depending on author's reputation and nature of book. Published 50 titles last year. Prefers queries, outlines, sample chapters. Reports in 3 to 4 weeks. Enclose return postage.
Textbooks: Publishes foreign language texts, multimedia packages, English books for the foreign-born.

***RESOURCE PUBLICATIONS**, Box 444, Saratoga CA 95070. Editorial Director: William Burns. Publishes paperback originals. Published 2 titles in 1977, 4 in 1978; will do 4 in 1979. Has subsidy published 1 title; "if the author can present and defend a personal distribution effort, and the work is in our field, we will consider it." 8% royalty; no advance. Photocopied submissions (with written assurance that work is not being submitted simultaneously) OK. Reports in 2 months. SASE.
Nonfiction: "We look for creative source books for the religious education, worship, and religious art fields. How-to books, especially for contemporary religious art forms are of particular interest (dance, mime, drama, choral reading, singing, music, musicianship, banner-making, statuary, or any visual art form). No heavy theoretical, philosophical, or theological tomes. Nothing utterly unrelated or unrelatable to the religious market as described above." Query or submit outline/synopsis and sample chapters. Recently published *The Music Locator,* by Cunningham (index of published religious music).
Fiction: "Light works providing examples of good expression through the religious art forms. Any collected short works in the areas of drama, dance, song, stories, anecdotes, or good visual art. Long poems or illustrated light novels which entertain while teaching a life value which could be useful in religious education, or to the religious market at large." Query or submit outline/synopsis and sample chapters. Recently published *Pilgrim's Road,* by M. Wood (collected songs); *Picture the Dawning,* by P.F. Page (songs); and *We Believe,* by G. Collopy (assorted notepapers).

RESTON PUBLISHING COMPANY (Prentice-Hall subsidiary), 11480 Sunset Hills Rd., Reston VA 22090. President: Matthew I. Fox. Publishes hardcover originals. Offers standard minimum book contract of 10-12½-15%. Advance varies. "We are a wholly-owned subsidiary of Prentice-Hall, which has the most extensive marketing system in publishing." Published 85 titles last year. Will send free catalog to writer on request. Will consider photocopied submissions. Submit outline and sample chapters. Reports immediately. Enclose return postage.
Textbooks: "Primarily for the junior college and vocational/technical school market. Professionally oriented books for in-service practitioners and professionals. All material should be written to appeal to these markets in style and subject. We are able to attract the best experts in all phases of academic and professional life to write our books. But we are always seeking new material in all areas of publishing; any area that is represented by courses at any post-secondary level."

FLEMING H. REVELL COMPANY, Central Ave., Old Tappan NJ 07675. Editor-in-Chief: Dr. Frank S. Mead. Payment usually on royalty basis. Published 70 titles last year. Reports in a month to six weeks. SASE.
Religion: Publishers of inspirational and religious books. Also books related to Sunday School and church work. Occasional biography and more general books that might appeal to the religious market. Length: usually 40,000 to 60,000 words.

REYMONT ASSOCIATES, 29 Reymont Ave., Rye NY 10580. Editor-in-Chief: D.J. Scherer. Managing Editor: Felicia Scherer. Paperback originals. 10-12½-15½% royalty; no advance. Submit outline/synopsis and sample chapters. State availability of photos/illustrations. Simultaneous and photocopied submissions OK. Reports in 2-4 weeks. SASE. Book catalog for SASE.
Nonfiction: Publishes business; how-to; self-help; and unique directories. "Aim for 12-15,000 words."Recently published *'Til Business Do Us Part,* by Dr. E. Jerry Walker.

THE WARD RITCHIE PRESS, 474 S. Arroyo Parkway, Pasadena CA 91105. (213)793-1163. Managing Editor: William Chleboun. Offers standard 10-12½-15% royalty contract. Advance varies. Published 25 titles in 1977. Free book catalog. Query first and submit outline and 2 chapters. SASE.
Nonfiction and Fiction: Broad general interest. "Americana (quality literature pertaining to any period and place in American history); cookbooks (distinctive cookbooks only); biography, how-to (on any subject); and photo essay." Recently published *Redd Foxx Encyclopedia of Black Humor,* by R. Foxx.

RICHARDS ROSEN PRESS, 29 E. 21st St., New York NY 10010. Editor: Ruth C. Rosen. Publishes hardcover originals. "Each project has a different royalty setup." Published 41 titles last year. Wants queries with outline and sample chapter. Reports within 3 weeks. SASE.
Nonfiction: "Our books are geared to the young adult audience whom we reach via school and public libraries. Most of the books we publish are related to guidance-career and personal adjustment." Also publishes material on the theatre, science, women, as well as journalism for schools. Interested in supplementary material for enrichment of school curriculum. Preferred length: 40,000 words.

ROUTLEDGE & KEGAN PAUL, LTD., 9 Park St., Boston MA 02108. Publishes hardcover and paperback originals and reprints. Offers standard 10-12½-15% royalty contract "on clothbound editions, if the books are not part of a series"; usual advance is $250 to $2,500. Published over 200 titles last year. Query first with outline and sample chapters. Submit complete ms "only after going through outline and sample chapters step." Returns rejected material in 1 to 2 months. Reports on ms accepted for publication in 1 to 6 months. Enclose check for return postage.
Nonfiction: "Academic, reference, and scholarly levels: English and European literary criticism, drama and theater, social sciences, philosophy and logic, psychology, parapsychology, oriental religions, mysticism, history, political science, education. Our books generally form a reputable series under the general editorship of distinguished academics in their fields. The approach should be similar to the styles adopted by Cambridge University Press, Harvard University Press, and others." Interested in material for the International Library of Sociology. Length: 30,000 to 250,000 words.

RUTGERS UNIVERSITY PRESS, 30 College Ave., New Brunswick NJ 08901. Published 16 titles last year in the following categories: history, literary criticism, ornithology. Free book catalog. Prefers queries. Final decision depends on time required to secure competent professional reading reports. Enclose return postage.
Nonfiction: Scholarly books on history, literary criticism, anthropology, political science, biography, and criminal justice. Occasional titles in music, business and economics. Regional nonfiction must deal with mid-Atlantic region with emphasis on New Jersey. Length: 60,000 words and up. Recently published *Moby-Dick and Calvinism: A World Dismantled,* by Herbert; and *War and the Liberal Conscience,* by Howard.

WILLIAM H. SADLIER, INC., 11 Park Pl., New York NY 10007. Vice President, Editor-in-Chief: William J. Richardson, Ph.D. Offers 6% royalty contract for elementary textbooks; 8% for high school textbooks. Submit outline and sample chapters to Editorial Department. Reports "as soon as possible." Enclose S.A.E. and return postage.
Textbooks: Elementary and secondary textbooks. Whole or significant part of school market should be identified, competition studied, proposal developed and submitted with representative sample. Interested in language arts and social studies, economics, history, politics, religion, sociology.

ST. ANTHONY MESSENGER PRESS, 1615 Republic St., Cincinnati OH 45210. Editor-in-Chief: Rev. Jeremy Harrington, O.F.M. Publishes paperback originals. Offers 6% to 8% royalty contract. Usual advance is $500. Books are sold in bulk to groups (study clubs, high school or college classes). Will send free catalog to writer on request. Will consider photocopied submissions if they are not simultaneous submissions to other publishers. Query first or submit outline and sample chapters. Enclose return postage.
Religion: "We try to reach the Catholic market with topics near the heart of the ordinary Catholic's belief. We want to offer insight and inspiration and thus give people support in living a Christian life in a pluralistic society. We are not interested in an academic or abstract approach. Our emphasis is on the popular approach with examples, specifics, color, anecdotes." Length: 25,000 to 40,000 words. Recently published *Parent/Child/God,* by G. Schomp; and *His Way: An Everyday Plan for Following Jesus,* by D. Knight.

ST. MARTIN'S PRESS, 175 Fifth Ave., New York NY 10010. Published 350 titles last year. Query. Reports promptly. SASE.
General: Publishes general fiction and nonfiction; major interest in adult nonfiction, history, self-help, political science, popular science, biography, scholarly, technical reference, etc. "No children's books." Recently published titles include *All Things Bright and Beautiful* (Herriot).
Textbooks: College textbooks.

HOWARD W. SAMS & CO., INC., 4300 W. 62nd St., Indianapolis IN 46268. Manager, Book Division: C.P. Oliphant. Payment depends on quantity, quality, salability. Offers both royalty arrangements or outright purchase. Prefers queries, outlines, and sample chapters. Usually reports within 30 days. Enclose return postage.
Technical, Scientific, and How-To: "Publishes technical and scientific books for the electronics industry; Audel books for the homeowner, craftsman, and handyman; and books for the amateur radio field."

PORTER SARGENT PUBLISHERS, INC., 11 Beacon St., Boston MA 02108. (617)523-1670. Publishes hardcover and paperback originals, reprints, translations, and anthologies. "Each contract is dealt with on an individual basis with the author." Published 4 titles in 1978. Free book catalog. Send query with brief description of table of contents, sample chapter and information regarding author's background. Enclose return postage.
General Nonfiction, Reference, Philosophy, and Textbooks: "Handbook Series and Special Education Series offer standard, definitive reference works in private education and writings and texts in special education. The Extending Horizons Series is an outspoken, unconventional series which presents topics of importance in contemporary affairs, viewpoints rarely offered to the reading public, methods and modes of social change, and the framework of alternative structures for the expansion of human awareness and well-being." This series is particularly, although not exclusively, directed to the college adoption market." Contact Christopher Leonisio for Special Education Books; Kathryn Sargent for EHB Books.

SCHENKMAN PUBLISHING CO., INC., 3 Mt. Auburn Pl., Cambridge MA 02138. (617)492-4952. Editor-in-Chief: Alfred S. Schenkman. Managing Editor: Katherine Schlivek. Hardcover

and paperback originals. Specializes in textbooks. Royalty varies, but averages 10%. "In some cases, no royalties are paid on first 2,000 copies sold." No advance. State availability of photos and/or illustrations. Simultaneous and photocopied submissions OK. Reports in 1-2 months. SASE. Free book catalog.
Nonfiction: Publishes economics, history, psychology, sociology, and textbooks. Query.
Recent Titles: *Socialization in Drug Abuse,* by R. Coombs (sociology); and *All Their Own: People and the Places They Build,* by J. Wampler (Americana).

SCHIRMER BOOKS, Macmillan Publishing Co., Inc., 866 Third Ave., New York NY 10022. Editor-in-Chief: Ken Stuart. Hardcover and paperback originals (90%); paperback reprints (10%). Specializes in music books for college textbook, trade, professional and reference and music store markets. Pays in royalities; small advance. Submit photos and/or illustrations if central to the book, not if decorative or tangential. Photocopied and simultaneous submissions OK. Reports in 1-2 months. SASE. Book catalog for SASE.
Nonfiction: Publishes how-to, music, self-help, and textbooks. Submit outline/synopsis and sample chapters. Recently published *Beethoven,* by M. Solomon (biography); *Fats Waller,* by M. Waller/T. Calabrese; and *Sound Pleasure: A Prelude to Active Listening,* by D. Ivey.

SCHOLAR'S CHOICE, LTD., 50 Ballantyne Ave., Stratford, Ontario, Canada N5A 6T9. Editorial Director: Don Smith. Published 12 titles in 1977, 14 in 1978; will do 15 in 1979. Pays in combination royalty (3-5%) and fee. Simultaneous submissions OK. Reports in 2 months. SASE. Free book catalog.
Nonfiction: Curriculum-oriented programs in workbook, duplicating book, activity card, and poster formats relating to the following curriculum areas: language arts, mathematics, consumer studies, science, outdoor education, and Canadian studies, primarily at the elementary grade levels. Programs should be teacher-prepared and classroom tested before submission. No essays." Submit outline/synopsis and sample chapters. Recently published *My People Anishinabe,* by William and Sharon Blundell (student activity kit); and *Quoi Faire,* by C. Evans (teacher resource kit).

***"SCHOLASTICUS" PUBLISHING**, Box 2727, Springfield VA 22152. Editorial Director: E.J. Keats. Senior Editor: Dr. Leo Hecht. Publishes paperback originals. Published 20 titles in 1978; will do 30 in 1979. "In the case of a worthy book which contributes to the body of knowledge and which, we feel, would have a very weak market, we would ask the author to see to it that his university order a sufficient number of copies to cover part (not all) of the publication costs." 10% royalty; no advance. Photocopied submissions OK. Reports in 6 weeks. SASE.
Nonfiction: "Very frequently professors are required to teach innovative, specialized courses for which there is no text available. Sometimes a professor is forced to write his own text for his courses which may then be adopted by other professors at other institutions teaching similar courses. This is the market to which we wish to cater. We specifically wish to publish paperback originals for which there is a demonstrable, albeit limited, demand as university textbooks, augmentative texts, or reference handbooks. We are looking for quality rather than widespread marketability, although obviously, there must be some established need for a given book within academe." Submit outline/synopsis and sample chapters. Recently published *The USSR Today: Facts and Interpretations,* by Dr. Leo Hecht.

SCHOLIUM INTERNATIONAL, INC., 130-30 31st Ave., Flushing NY 11354. Editor-in-Chief: Arthur L. Candido. Publishes hardcover and paperback originals. Standard minimum book contract of 12½%. Published 3 titles last year. Free book catalog. Will consider photocopied submissions. Query. Reports in 2 weeks. SASE.
Science and Technology: Subjects covered are cryogenics, electronics, aviation, medicine, physics, etc. "We also publish books in other areas whenever it is felt the manuscript has good sales and reception potential. Contact us prior to sending ms, outlining subject, number of pages, and other pertinent information which would enable us to make a decision as to whether we would want to review the ms."

CHARLES SCRIBNER'S SONS, 597 Fifth Ave., New York NY 10017. Director of Publishing: Jacek K. Galazka. Publishes hardcover originals and hardcover and paperback reprints. "Our contract terms, royalties and advances vary, depending on the nature of the project." Published 300 titles last year. Query first for nonfiction (juvenile and adult), and adult fiction; complete ms preferred for juvenile fiction, "but will consider partial ms and outline." Prefers photocopied submissions. Reports in 1 to 2 months on ms accepted for publication. Returns rejected adult material in 4 to 6 weeks; returns rejected juveniles in 3 to 4 weeks. Enclose return postage.

General: Publishes adult fiction and nonfiction, practical books, garden books, reference sets, cookbooks, history, and science. Adult Trade Editors: Elinor Parker, Doe Coover, Susanne Kirk, Laurie Graham, and Charles Scribner III.
Juveniles: "We publish books for children of all ages—pre-kindergarten up through high school age. We publish picture books, fiction, and nonfiction in all subjects. We have no special requirements in regard to special treatment or emphasis and length requirements. We're interested in books on any topical subject or theme, assuming we feel the material is exciting enough." Children's Book Editor: Lee Anna Deadrick.

THE SEABURY PRESS, 815 2nd Ave., New York NY 10017. Editors: William H. Gentz, Crossroad Books (religious); Justus G. Lawler, Continuum Books (adult general); and James C. Giblin, Clarion Books (juvenile). 10% royalty; advance "depends on the author's reputation and the nature of the project." Published 100 titles in 1977, 85 in 1978; will do 85-100 in 1979. Query for fiction and nonfiction; submit complete ms for children's picture books and short novels. State availability of photos/illustrations. Photocopied submissions OK. Reports in 1-2 months. SASE. Free book catalog.
Nonfiction: Publishes Americana (adult general, juvenile); biography (adult and juvenile); cookbooks, cooking and foods; history (juvenile); humor (adult, juvenile); juveniles; medicine and psychiatry (adult general); nature (juvenile); philosophy (religious); politics; psychology; reference (adult general); religious; self-help; and sociology (adult general) books. Recently published *The Sex Atlas,* by E.J. Haeberle (illustrated educational guide); *An Elephant's Ballet,* by R.G. Kemper (biography); and *Sand Tiger Shark,* by C. Corrich (juvenile).
Fiction: Publishes adventure (juvenile); fantasy (juvenile); historical (juvenile); humorous (juvenile); science fiction (juvenile, adult general); and suspense (juvenile) books. Recently published *Keep Stompin' Till the Music Stops,* by S. Presner (juvenile).

'76 PRESS, Box 2686, Seal Beach CA 90740. (213)596-3491. Editor-in-Chief: Wallis W. Wood. Hardcover and paperback originals. 5% royalty; advance averages $2,500. Published 4 titles in 1977, 6 in 1978; will do 8-18 in 1979. State availability of photos and/or illustrations. Simultaneous and photocopied submissions OK. SASE. Free book catalog.
Nonfiction: "Economics, politics, and international relations, written from conservative, anti-big government perspective. Information on author's credentials on subject matter is very important." Submit outline/synopsis and sample chapters. Recently published *The War on Gold,* by A.C. Sutton; *Confrontation,* by M. Spring; and *The Rockefeller File,* by G. Allen.

SHEED ANDREWS AND McMEEL, INC., 6700 Squibb Rd., Mission KS 66202. Editor-in-Chief: James F. Andrews. Managing Editor: Donna Martin. Standard royalty; negotiable advance. Publishes 50 titles annually. Photocopied submissions OK. Reports in 1-2 months SASE. Book catalog for SASE.
General Nonfiction: Political history and commentary, general interest, popular philosophical, theological, cartoon collections, how-to books in home interests, photography, textbooks. Cookbooks, cooking and foods; economics, humor, politics, psychology, religious, and self-help books.
Fiction: "We are venturing into high-level fiction. Genre is not important; quality is." Recently published *Desert Notes,* by B.H. Lopez (short stories).
Recent Titles: *The Formula Book* by N. Stark (how-to); *The Yankee and Cowboy War,* by C. Oglesby (political); *The Church and the Homosexual,* by Fr. J.J. McNeill.

SHOAL CREEK PUBLISHERS, INC., Box 9737, Austin TX 78766. (512)451-7545. Senior Editor: Judy Timberg. Publishes hardcover originals (90%) and reprints (10%). Published 7 titles in 1977, 8 in 1978. 10% royalty; no advance. Simultaneous and photocopied submissions OK. Reports "as soon as practical." SASE. Free book catalog.
Nonfiction: Historical; biographical; and children's books. Submit outline/synopsis and sample chapters. Recently published *Jose Vives Atsara: His Life and His Art,* by N. West (biography); and *Waggoner Carr: Not Guilty,* by W. Carr/J. Keever.

THE SHOE STRING PRESS, INC., (Archon Books, Linnet Books), 995 Sherman Ave., Hamden CT 06514. (203)248-6307. President: Mrs. Frances T. Rutter. 10% royalty of net; no advance. Query first and include table of contents and sample chapters. Reports in 4 to 6 weeks. Enclose return postage.
Nonfiction: Publishes scholarly books: history, biography, literary criticism, reference, philosophy, bibliographies, information science, library science, education, and general adult nonfiction. Preferred length is 40,000-130,000 words, though there is no set limit. Recently

published *The Golden Age of Black Nationalism 1850-1925,* by W. Jeremiah (black studies).

GEORGE SHUMWAY PUBLISHER, R.D. 7, Box 388B, York PA 17402. (717)755-1196. Editorial Director: George Shumway. Publishes hardcover and paperback originals. Publishes 3 titles/year. Pays in royalties or outright purchase price; "We use various means depending on the situation. Most of our books are of marginal economics, so royalties are small." No advance. Simultaneous and photocopied submission OK. Reports in 2 weeks. SASE. Free book catalog.
Nonfiction: "We publish in the field of antique art and Americana, with particular emphasis on the art of the American longrifle. This is a small, very specialized field, but we get into culturally-related topics such as early American costume. The frontier arts are our bag. We are interested in manuscripts dealing with early American costume of the 18th and early 19th centuries (before the Victorian period)." Query. Recently published *Arms Makers of Maryland,* by D.D. Hartzler (Americana/art); *Rural Pennsylvania Clothing,* by E. Gehret (Americana); and *Pennsylvania Longrifles of Note,* by G. Shumway (art).

SIGNPOST PUBLICATIONS, 16812 36th Ave. West, Lynnwood WA 98036. Editor-in-Chief: Cliff Cameron. Publishes hardcover and paperback originals. Offers standard minimum book contract of 10%. Advance varies. Free book catalog. Query. Reports in 3 weeks. SASE.
Nonfiction: "Books on outdoor subjects. Limited to self-propelled wilderness activity. Also books of general interest to Northwesterners. History, natural science, related to the Pacific Northwest. Books should have strong environmental material for a general audience, where applicable. Recently published *Understanding Avalanches,* by Seiler; and *Mostly In Fun,* by Thomas.

SILVER BURDETT, Subsidiary of Scott, Foresman Co., 250 James St., Morristown NJ 07960. Publishes hardcover and paperback originals. "Textbook rates only, El-Hi range." Published approximately 180 titles last year. Query first to Barbara Howell, Editor-in-Chief, Silver Burdett Division. Enclose S.A.S.E.
Education: Produces educational materials for preschoolers, elementary and high school students, and professional publications for teachers. Among materials produced: textbooks, teachers' materials, other print and non-print classroom materials including educational games, manipulatives, and audiovisual aids (silent and sound 16mm films and filmstrips, records, multimedia kits, overhead transparencies, tapes, etc.). Assigns projects to qualified writers on occasion. Writer must have understanding of school market and school learning materials.

SILVERMINE PUBLISHERS INCORPORATED, Comstock Hill, Silvermine, Norwalk CT 06850. President: Marilyn Z. Atkin. Free book catalog. Query. SASE.
Nonfiction: Publishes general nonfiction, biography, and books dealing with fine arts and architecture. "We are not interested in name authors, but insist on good writing. Our books are designed to last (that is, they are not 1-season phenomena). Thus, a typical book over a period of 3 to 5 years may earn $3,000 to $6,000 royalties. It is our opinion that books that are solid text, unillustrated, are not salable any longer unless they are news or topical (which we are not interested in), fiction by established writers (which we are not interested in), or books on special subjects."

SIMON AND SCHUSTER, Trade Books Division of Simon & Schuster, Inc., 1230 6th Ave., New York NY 10020. "If we accept a book for publication, business arrangements are worked out with the author or his agent and a contract is drawn up. The specific terms vary according to the type of book and other considerations. Royalty rates are more or less standard among publishers. Special arrangements are made for anthologies, translations and projects involving editorial research services." Published over 200 titles in 1977. Free book catalog. "All unsolicited mss will be returned unread. Only mss submitted by agents or recommended to us by friends or actively solicited by us will be considered. Our requirements are as follows: All mss submitted for consideration should be marked to the attention of the editorial department. Mystery novels should be so labeled in order that they may be sent to the proper editors without delay. It usually takes at least three weeks for the author to be notified of a decision—often longer. Sufficient postage for return by first-class registered mail, or instructions for return by express collect, in case of rejection, should be included. Mss must be typewritten, double-spaced, on one side of the sheet only. We suggest margins of about one inch all around and the standard 8½-by-11-inch typewriter paper." Prefers complete mss.
General: "Simon and Schuster publishes books of adult fiction, history, biography, science, philosophy, the arts and religion, running 50,000 words or more. Our program does not,

however, include school textbooks, extremely technical or highly specialized works, or, as a general rule, plays. Exceptions have been made, of course, for extraordinary mss of great distinction or significance." Recently published *The Path Between the Seas,* by D. McCullough (history/current affairs); *The Second Ring of Power,* by C. Castaneda (anthropology); and *Dreams Die First,* by H. Robbins.

CHARLES B. SLACK, INC., 6900 Grove Rd., Thorofare NJ 08086. (212)285-9777. Editor-in-Chief: Kenton T. Finch. Managing Editors: Kaye Coraluzzo, Ken Senerth, Pamela Wright, and Peg Carnine. Hardcover and paperback originals (90%) and reprints (10%). Specializes in medical and health education texts. 10% (of net proceeds) royalty; advances are discouraged. Published 8 titles in 1977, 9 in 1978; will do 10 in 1979. State availability of photos and/or illustrations to accompany ms. Simultaneous submissions OK. Reports in 1-2 months. SASE. Free book pamphlet for SASE.
Nonfiction: Publishes medicine and psychiatry; psychology, scientific, and textbooks. Query, or submit outline/synopsis and sample chapters, or submit complete ms. All queries, outlines and mss should be sent to the attention of Kenton T. Finch. Recently published *Nursing Care for Parents at Risk,* by R.T. Mercer; and *Humor and the Health Profession,* by U.M. Robinson.

SLEEPY HOLLOW RESTORATIONS, INC., 150 White Plains Rd., Tarrytown NY 10591. (914)631-8200. Editor-in-Chief: Saverio Procario. Managing Editor: Bruce D. MacPhail. Hardcover and paperback originals (85%); hardcover reprints (15%). 5-10% (on net) royalty; no advance. Published 3 titles in 1977, 5 in 1978 State availability of photos and/or illustrations to accompany ms. Simultaneous and photocopied submissions OK. Reports in 1-2 months. SASE. Free book catalog.
Nonfiction: Publishes Americana, art (American decorative arts); biography; cookbooks, cooking and foods (regional, historic); history (especially American; New York state and colonial through modern times); technical (17th-19th century technology); travel (regional and New York state); American literature and literary criticism, especially 19th century. Query first, addressing it to the Managing Editor. Recently published *Life Along the Hudson,* by A. Keller (regional history); *Van Cortlandt Family Papers,* edited by J. Judd (American history); *A Century of Commentary on the Works of Washington Irving,* edited by A. Myers (American literary criticism).

THE SMITH, 5 Beekman St., New York NY 10038. Publishes hardcover and paperback originals. The Smith is now owned by The Generalist Association, Inc., a non-profit organization, which gives to writers awards averaging $500 for book projects. Free book catalog. Send query first for nonfiction; sample chapter preferred for fiction. Reports within six weeks. SASE.
Nonfiction and Fiction: "Original fiction — no specific schools or categories; for nonfiction, the more controversial, the better." Editor of Adult Fiction: Harry Smith. Nonfiction Editor: Sidney Bernard.

***SOCCER ASSOCIATES**, Box 634, New Rochelle NY 10802. Editor: Jeff Miller. Published 95 titles last year. Send finished book to Milton Miller. SASE.
Sports, Hobbies, and Recreation: Publishes sports, recreation, leisure time, and hobby books under Sport Shelf and Leisure Time Books imprints. Most titles are British and Australian although they do have a special service for authors who publish their own books and desire national and international distribution, promotion, and publicity.

SOUNDVIEW BOOKS, 100 Heights Rd., Darien CT 06820. (203)655-4918. Editorial Director: Harold Longman. Publishes hardcover and paperback originals. 10% royalty; advance averages $5,000. Simultaneous and photocopied submissions OK. Reports in 4 weeks. SASE.
Nonfiction: "Books on self-help and self-improvement, or perhaps more accurately, self-development. Books can be inspirational in nature, or they can deal with current concerns which are of general interest. The books can be practical. For example, a book on how to avoid heart attacks. If anything this specific were chosen, it would have to be well-researched, clearly and simply written. It would also help if it were interesting and, since many of these areas have already been ploughed, the book would have to contain something new that has not appeared before. If the book were more toward the inspirational, it should be sympathetically written, and provocative rather than preachy. We are new. While books are currently in the works, we have as yet published none of them. This does not mean that we are publishers of last resort, and should be the recipients of everything that everybody else has turned down. Although we can't promise stellar advances, we'll probably give the author a better break than most because we understand advertising and promotion, as most publishers do not—and we will push any book

we publish. But we're fussy. We happen to like good writing."

SOUTHERN METHODIST UNIVERSITY PRESS, Dallas TX 75275. (214)692-2263. Director: Allen Maxwell; Associate Director and Editor: Margaret L. Hartley. Payment is on royalty basis: 10% of list up to 2,500 copies; 12½% for 2,500 to 5,000 copies; 15% thereafter; no advance. Free book catalog. Appreciates query letters, outlines and sample chapters. Reports tend to be slow for promising mss requiring outside reading by authorities. Enclose return postage.
Nonfiction: Regional and scholarly nonfiction. History, Americana, economics, banking, literature, and anthropology. Length: open. Recently published *Dallas Yesterday,* by S. Ackeson (regional history); *New Perspectives for Bank Directors,* edited by R.B. Johnson; and *The Well-Tempered Lyre: Songs and Verse of the Temperance Movement,* by G.W. Ewing.

SOUTHERN PUBLISHING ASSOCIATION, Box 59, Nashville TN 37202. (615)889-8000. Editor-in-Chief: Richard W. Coffen. Hardcover and paperback originals. Specializes in religiously oriented books. 5-10% royalty; advance averages $100. Published 25 titles in 1977, 30 in 1978; will do 35 in 1979. State availability of photos and/or illustrations to accompany ms. Simultaneous and photocopied submissions OK. SASE. Reports in 2-4 months. Free book catalog.
Nonfiction: Juveniles (religiously oriented only; 20,000-60,000 words; average of 138 pages). Nature (average of 128 pages). Religious (20,000-60,000 words; average of 128 pages). Query or submit outline/synopsis and sample chapters. Recently published *Demon of Podeng,* by O. Bohner (religious/missions); *God's Hand in My Life*; and *Love is the Motive,* by C. Amen.

STACKPOLE BOOKS, Box 1831, Harrisburg PA 17105. (717)234-5091. Editorial Director: Neil McAleer. Hardcover and paperback originals (90%) and reprints (10%). Specializes in outdoor activity, craft, early Americana, the future, space and space colonization. 15% royalty of net receipts. Advance averages $1,000. Published 30 titles in 1977, 35 in 1978. Query and include author's credentials. Send prints if photos/illustrations are to accompany ms. Simultaneous ("no more than to 2 other publishers") and photocopied submissions OK. Reports in 4 weeks. SASE. Free book catalog.
Nonfiction: Publishes Americana; hobbies; how-to; nature; psychology; recreation; self-help; travel; future; space activities; and energy books.

STANDARD PUBLISHING, 8121 Hamilton Ave., Cincinnati OH 45231. (513)931-4050. Managing Editor: Carol Ferntheil. Hardcover and paperback originals (85%) and reprints (15%). Specializes in religious books. 10% maximum royalty. Advance averages $200-1,500. Published 35 titles in 1977, 40 in 1978; will do 40 in 1979. Query or submit outline/synopsis and sample chapters. State availability of photos/illustrations. Reports in 1-2 months. SASE.
Nonfiction: Publishes how-to; history; juveniles; reference; Christian education; and religious books. All ms must pertain to religion. Recently published *The Jesus Years,* by T.D. Thurman; *Grow, Christian, Grow,* by K. Staton; and *Selecting a Translation of the Bible,* by L. Foster.
Fiction: Publishes religious books. Recently published *Soaring,* by R. Elwood.

STATE HISTORICAL SOCIETY OF WISCONSIN PRESS, 816 State St., Madison WI 53706. (608)262-9604. Editorial Director: Paul H. Hass. Senior Editor: William C. Marten. Publishes hardcover and paperback originals (75%) and hardcover reprints (25%). Published 3 titles in 1977, 2 in 1978; will do 2 in 1979. Subsidy publishes 66⅔% of titles based on "an educated guess on the availability of a subsidy from some source and the strength of the market for the title." 10% royalty; no advance. Photocopied submissions OK. Reports in 8 weeks. SASE. Free book catalog.
Nonfiction: "Research and interpretation in history of the American Middle West—broadly construed as the Mississippi Valley. Must be thoroughly documented but on topics of sufficient interest to attract the layman as well as the scholar. 150,000-200,000 words of text, exclusive of footnotes and other back matter. No extremely narrowly focused monographs on non-Wisconsin subjects." Recently published *The Old Northwest in the American Revolution: An Anthology,* by D.C. Skaggs; *At Home: Domestic Life in the Post-Centennial Era, 1876-1920,* by G. Talbot; and *The History of Wisconsin, Volume 2: The Civil War Era,* by R.N. Current.

STEIN AND DAY, Scarborough House, Briarcliff Manor NY 10510. Offers standard royalty contract. Published 100 titles last year. No unsolicited mss. Nonfiction, send outline or summary and sample chapter; fiction, send first chapter only. SASE.
General: Publishes general adult fiction and nonfiction books; no juveniles or college. All types

of nonfiction except technical. Quality fiction. Length: 75,000 words. Recently published *Jerry Brown,* by R. Pack; *The Dancer,* by L. Cooley; and *Wynner,* by M. Torme.

STONE WALL PRESS, INC., 5 Byron St., Boston MA 02108. Senior Editor: Henry Wheelwright. Publishes hardcover and paperback originals. Published 4 titles in 1977, 3 in 1978; will do 3 in 1979. 7% royalty on paperback books, 10% on hardcover; no advance. Simultaneous and photocopied submissions OK. Reports in 2 weeks. SASE. Free book catalog.
Nonfiction: Regional (Northeastern USA) and National Outdoors books on specific subjects. Complete treatment is generally required—how-to, where-to, anecdotes, humor, ecology, etc. Photos/drawings to be included with the text. Query. Recently published *Movin' On: Equipment and Techniques for Winter Hikers,* by H. Roberts; *Wild Preserves: Illustrated Recipes for over 100 Natural Jams and Jellies,* by J. Freitus; and *The Northeastern Outdoors: A Field and Travel Guide,* by S. Berman.

STRAVON PUBLISHERS INC., 595 Madison Ave., New York NY 10022. Editor-in-Chief: Robert M. Segal. Hardcover and paperback originals. Specializes in how-to, popular reference books and children's science books. 10% royalty; advance of $1,500-3,000. "Our main publishing interest consists of packaging popular reference books for other publishers. Subjects include medical, general how-to, encyclopedias. Thus, we are always on the lookout for writers on special subjects on a fee or word basis (6-10¢/word)." Publishes 70 titles/year. Simultaneous and photocopied submissions OK. Reports in 1-2 weeks. SASE. Free book catalog.
Nonfiction: Publishes art, business,; cookbooks, cooking and foods; history, hobbies, how-to, humor, juveniles, medicine and psychiatry; nature, politics, psychology, reference, religion, scientific, self-help and sociology books. Query. Recently published *Dinosaur World,* by E. Colbert (science and history); *Cartooning Fundamentals,* by A. Ross (how-to); *Quick Reference Encyclopedia.*

STRAWBERRY HILL PRESS, 616 44th Ave., San Francisco CA 94121. Editoral Director: Jean-Louis Brindamour, Ph.D. Senior Editors: Jean Lesher and Catherine A. Pearsall. Publishes paperback originals. Publishes 12 titles/year. "We are a small house, proud of what we do, and intending to stay relatively small (that does not mean that we will do a less-than-professional job in marketing our books, however). The author-publisher relationship is vital, from the moment the contract is signed until there are no more books to sell, and we operate on that premise. We do no hardcovers, and, for the moment at least, our format is limited strictly to 6x9 quality paperbacks, priced between $3.95-7.95. We never print fewer than 5,000 copies in a first printing, with reprintings also never falling below that same figure. Our books are distributed to the trade by Stackpole Books. 10-20% royalty; no advance. Photocopied submissions OK. Reports in 2-3 weeks. SASE. Book catalog for SASE.
Nonfiction: Self-help; inspiration (*not* religion); cookbooks; health and nutrition; aging; diet; popular philosophy; metaphysics; alternative life styles; third world; minority histories; oral history; and popular medicine. No religion, sports, craft books, photography or fine art material. Submit outline/synopsis and sample chapters. Recently published *Cooking With Josephine,* by J. Araldo; *Fundamentally Speaking,* by H.S. Meyers Jr.; and *A Pleasure of Flowers,* by V.S. Roberts.

STRUCTURES PUBLISHING CO., P.O. Box 423, Farmington MI 48024. Editor-in-Chief: Shirley M. Horowitz. Publishes hardcover and paperback originals. Offers standard 10-12½-15% royalty contract. Advance varies, depending on author's reputation and nature of book. Published 10 titles last year. Will send a catalog to a writer on request. Submit outline and sample chapters. Will consider photocopied submissions. Reports in 4 to 6 weeks. Enclose return postage.
Technical and How-To: Books related to building. Wants to expand Successful Series which includes books published both for professionals and homeowners in paperback and hardcover. Will consider structure, construction, building and decorating-related topics. "Mss commissioned, usually. Book layout and design expertise of interest."

***SUN PUBLISHING CO.**, Box 4383, Albuquerque NM 87106. (505)255-6550. Editor-in-Chief: Skip Whitson. Publishes hardcover and paperback originals (40%) and reprints (60%). 8% royalty. No advance. Will subsidy publish "if we think the book is good enough and if we have the money to do it, we'll publish it on our own; otherwise, the author will have to put up the money." Query or submit outline/synopsis and table of contents. Send photocopies if photos/illustrations are to accompany ms. Simultaneous and photocopied submissions OK. Reports in 2-4 months. SASE. Book list for SASE.

Nonfiction: Publishes Americana; art; biography; cookbooks, cooking and foods; history; how-to; politics; scientific; self-help; metaphysical; oriental; and new age books. "40-200 page length ms are preferred." Recently published *Science and Art of Hot Air Ballooning,* by Dichtl/Jackson (science/sports); and *Meditation for Healing,* by J.F. Stone (metaphysical).
Fiction: Publishes science fiction books.
Special Needs: "The 'Sun Historical Series' is looking for short, illustrated mss on various U.S. cities and regions."

SUNSTONE PRESS, P.O. Box 2321, Santa Fe NM 87501. (505)988-4418. Editor-in-Chief: James C. Smith, Jr. Publishes paperback originals; "sometimes hardcover originals." Published 6 titles in 1977. Free book catalog. Query. Reports in 1 month. Enclose return postage.
Nonfiction: How-to series craft books. Books on the history of the Southwest; poetry. Length: open. Recently published *Woody Plants of the Southeast,* by S. Lamb; *Tamotzu in Haiku,* by H. Kimbro; and *Diehos: Sayings from the Spanish,* by C. Aranda (proverbs).

SWEDENBORG FOUNDATION, 139 East 23rd St., New York NY 10010. Chairman, Editorial and Publications Committee: C. S. Priestnal. Publishes hardcover and paperback originals and reprints (limited to Swedenborgiana). Royalties negotiable. Published 5 titles last year. Catalog available on request. Will consider photocopied submissions. Query first. Reports in 1 month. Enclose return postage with query.
Nonfiction: The life and works of Emanuel Swedenborg. Studies of Swedenborg's scientific activities as precursors of modern developments. Studies of Swedenborg's contributions to the mainstream of religious thought. Recently published *Swedenborg, Life and Teaching,* by G. Trobridge (biography); and *Heaven and Hell,* by E. Swedenborg.

***SYMMES SYSTEMS,** Box 8101, Atlanta GA 30306. Editor-in-Chief: E.C. Symmes. Publishes hardcover and paperback originals. Offers royalty contract of 10% of money received. "Contracts are usually written for the individual title and may have different terms." No advance. Does 40% subsidy publishing. Will consider photocopied and simultaneous submissions. Acknowledges receipt in 10 days; evaluation within 1 month. Query. SASE.
Nonfiction and Nature: "Our books have mostly been in the art of bonsai (miniature trees). We are publishing quality information for laypersons (hobbyists). Most of the titles introduce information that is totally new for the hobbyist." Clear and concise writing style. Text must be topical, showing state-of-the-art and suggestions on how to stay on top. All books so far have been illustrated with photos and/or drawings. Would like to see more material on bonsai, photography, collecting photographica, ferns for neophytes (along with quality photos), and other horticultural subjects. Length: open.

SYRACUSE UNIVERSITY PRESS, 1011 E. Water St., Syracuse NY 13210. (315)423-2596. Director and Editor: Arpena Mesrobian. The royalty schedule varies, but generally a royalty is paid on every title. Free book catalog. Query with outline or sample chapters. If the ms is not rejected outright, a decision may be expected in 2-4 months. SASE.
Nonfiction: Publishes nonfiction, scholarly books, including biography, regional (especially on New York State and Iroquois), literary criticism, history, politics, and educational books. "Major areas are special education, learning disabilities, rehabilitation, especially practical books directed to teachers and parents." Approximate minimum length: 50,000 words. Recently published *Our Four Boys: Foster Parenting Retarded Teenagers,* by M.V. Dickerson.
Special Needs: "Contemporary issues in the Middle East, scholarly. Especially looking for material on Iroquois, anything from scholarly to general trade."

TAB BOOKS, Sylvester Court, East Norwalk CT 06855. (203)866-5450. Editorial Director: Dorothy M. Greenberg. Senior Editors: Aircraft Series, Joe Christy; Sports Car Series, Dic Van Feen. Publishes hardcover and paperback originals and reprints. Published 8 titles in 1977, 24 in 1978; will do 24 in 1979. 10% royalty; advance averages $700. Photocopied submissions OK. Reports in 3-4 weeks. SASE. Free book catalog.
Nonfiction: Modern Sports Car Series: marque cars, sports, how-to collecting and restoration of antique, classic, milestone and special interest cars. Also vans, trucks and leisure vehicles; Modern Aircraft Series: all subjects on single and twin-engine planes of interest to private pilots; individual planes, sports, do-it-yourself, restoration, passing flight tests, etc. Submit outline/synopsis and sample chapters. Recently published *The New Mercedes Benz Guide,* by J. Oldham; and *Precision Aerobatics,* by H.D. Ettinger.

TAFNEWS PRESS, Box 296, Los Altos CA 94022. (415)948-8188. Editorial Director: Tom

Jordan. Publishes hardcover and paperback originals. Published 6 titles in 1977, 5 in 1978; will do 6 in 1979. 10% royalty; no advance. Simltaneous and photocopied submissions OK. Reports in 4 weeks. SASE. Free book catalog.
Nonfiction: Specializes in books on track and field athletics. All aspects of track and field are considered, including technique and training, biographies, motivation and psychology, history, sports injuries, etc. Submit outline/synopsis and sample chapters. Recently published *Pre!,* by T. Jordan; *Masters Age Records,* edited by P. Mundle; and *Of People and Things,* by B. Nelson.

TAFT CORPORATION, 1000 Vermont Ave., N.W., Washington DC 20005. (800)424-9477/(202)347-0788. Editor-in-Chief: Jean Brodsky. Paperback originals. Specializes in books directed toward nonprofit industry. 9% royalty on first 3,000 copies, 11% on next 2,000, 14% over 5,000; advance of $250-500. State availability of photos and/or illustrations to accompany ms "and whether right to use has already been obtained". Simultaneous and photocopied submissions OK. Reports in 1-2 months. SASE. Free book catalog.
Nonfiction: Publishes how-to and technical books. "All dealing with fund-raising and other elements of the nonprofit industry. Query or submit outline/synopsis and sample chapters. Recently published *Taft Corporate Foundation Directory,* by J. Brodsky; *Nonprofits' Handbook on Lobbying,* by J. Grupehoff/J. Murphy; and *Foundation Reporter,* by J. Brodsky.

TALON BOOKS, LTD., 201/1019 E. Cordova, Vancouver, British Columbia, Canada V6A 1M8. (604)255-5915. Editorial Director: David Robinson. Publishes paperback originals (80%) and reprints (20%). Published 16 titles in 1977, 15-20 in 1978; will do 15-20 in 1979. 10% royalty; advance averages $200-500. Simultaneous and photocopied submissions OK. Reports in 3-6 months. SASE. Free book catalog.
Nonfiction: "We publish only occasional nonfiction titles." Query. Recently published *Some Useful Wild Plants,* by Dan and Nancy Jason (guide); and *The Evelyn Roth Recycling Book,* by R. Roth (fabric recycling).
Fiction: Serious literary fiction—novels and short stories. Interested in Canadian authors first. We are interested in authors with a body of work, having previous publication experience and critical reputations." Query. Recently published *Ballad of a Stonepicker,* by G. Ryga; *Theme for Diverse Instruments,* by J. Rule; and *A Short Sad Book,* by G. Bowering.

TAMARACK PRESS, Box 5650, Madison WI 53705. (608)238-5564. Editorial Director: Jill Weber Dean. Publishes hardcover and paperback originals (75%) and reprints (25%). Published 4 titles in 1977, 5 in 1978; will do 5 in 1979. 15% royalty on net cash receipts, "if the author supplies all materials needed for book." Advance averages $500. Photocopied submissions OK. Reports in 1 week on queries, 2 months on outline/synopsis and sample chapters. SASE. Free book catalog.
Nonfiction: "We are seeking adult nonfiction books that deal in a positive way with the world of nature and the state of Wisconsin. Within the Wisconsin category, we are willing to review a broad range of subjects and approaches, but we do not want religious, academic, or technical titles. No book should deal with an area smaller than the entire state, though titles dealing with Wisconsin and neighboring states are welcome. We reach a general audience, but one that's well educated and environmentally minded. Within the 'world of nature' category, we want titles of broad national appeal, focusing on nature and the environment." Query. Recently published *Easy Going: Madison and Dane County,* by S. Rath (travel guide); *Barns of Wisconsin,* by J. Apps ("all you ever wanted to know about . . ."); and *A Sand County Almanac Illustrated,* by A. Leopold.

TANDEM PRESS PUBLISHERS, Box 237, Tannersville PA 18372. (717)629-2250. Editor-in-Chief: Judith Keith. Hardcover originals. 10-12½-15% royalty. Sometimes offers an advance. "This is handled with each author individually." Photocopied submissions OK. SASE. Reports in 2-4 weeks. Book catalog for SASE.
Nonfiction: Cookbooks, cooking and foods; how-to, multimedia material, nature, pets, psychology, recreation, self-help and sports books. Query. Recently published *I Haven't a Thing to Wear,* by J. Keith (how-to on clothes and accessories).
Fiction: Adventure, confession, fantasy, historical, mainstream, mystery, religious, romance and suspense. Submit outline/synopsis and sample chapters to Judith Keith.

TANGENT BOOKS, 114 7th Ave., N.W., Calgary, Alta., Canada T2M OA2. Editor-in-Chief: David Foy. Hardcover and paperback originals and reprints. Offers "minimum advance against larger than normal royalties after costs have been met. We are the nonfiction imprint of the *Pennyworth Press*. Expect to contract for at least 4, perhaps 12 titles this year." Query. State

availability of photos/illustrations. Photocopied submissions OK. Ms returned "only if sufficient Canadian postage or International Reply Coupons enclosed."
Nonfiction: Publishes art (especially how-to and crafts); business (oriented toward small business, especially how-to); how-to (wide open); juveniles; medicine and psychiatry (popularizations, must be authoritative); nature (current issues); photography (technical how-to aspects; no photo books); psychology (popular); reference (wide open); scientific (popular); self-help; sociology (popular); technical (popular, e.g., electronics); travel (student oriented); Third World and women's movement books.
Special Needs: "We're looking for imaginative nonfiction projects, and particularly encourage mss from Canadians on Canadian subjects."

TAPE 'N TEXT, Williamsville Publishing Co., Inc., Box 237, Williamsville NY 14221. Editor-in-Chief: William R. Parks. Publishes printed text closely coordinated with narration on cassette tape. Offers royalty contract of 10% minimum. Published 12 titles last year. Marketing currently through direct mail to schools, libraries, and through distributors. Photocopied submissions OK. Query. Reports in 6 weeks. SASE.
Education and Training: "The kind of material we want from prospective authors is either a narration on tape with printed text which is very closely coordinated, *or* taped lectures or talks. Although we are now in English, computer science, and mathematics, we have plans of going into home and hobby computer, both software and instruction, and, perhaps, other fields such as science, and art. We must have inquiries first before writers send in their material. We also request that writers consider that their educational background and experience are important factors. Authors should examine our existing Tape 'n Text titles so that they can follow this format for their development of material. It is important that the writer establish what his target audience is, i.e., level: elementary school, junior high school, high school, junior college, university, or the general trade market." Current titles include *Basic English Language Usage*, by Dr. G.H. Poteet; and *Programming in Basic*, by W.R. Parks.

J.P. TARCHER, INC., 9110 Sunset Blvd., Los Angeles CA 90069. (213)273-3274. Editor-in-Chief: Victoria Pasternack. Hardcover and paperback originals. 10-12½-15% royalty; advance averages $5-7,500. Published 12 titles in 1977, 15 in 1978. State availability of photos and/or illustrations to accompany ms. Simultaneous and photocopied submissions OK. Reports in 2-4 weeks. SASE. Free book catalog.
Nonfiction: Publishes popular psychology, self-help, sociology, medicine; cookbooks, cooking and foods; and hobbies books. Submit outline/synopsis and sample chapters. Recently published *The New Diary*, by T. Rainer; *Mother Care*, by L.D. Quadri/K. Breckinridge; and *Betrayal of Innocence*, by S. Forward/C. Buck.

***TEACHERS COLLEGE PRESS**, 1234 Amsterdam Ave., New York NY 10027. (212)678-3929. Senior Editor: Mary L. Allison. Publishes hardcover and paperback originals (90%) and reprints (10%). Published 22 titles in 1977, 25 in 1978; will do 30 in 1979. Royalty varies; "very rarely" offers advance. Reports in 3-6 months. SASE. Free book catalog.
Nonfiction: "This university press concentrates on books in the field of education in the broadest sense from early childhood to higher education: good classroom practices, teacher training, special education, innovative trends and issues, administration and supervision, film, continuing and adult education, all areas of the curriculum, comparative education, guidance and counselling and the politics, economics, philosophy, sociology and history of education. The Press also issues classroom materials for students at all levels, with a strong emphasis on reading and writing." Submit outline/synopsis and sample chapters. Recently published *Strategies for Teaching Children with Severe Language and Behavior Disorders*, by B. Van Witsen (special education).

TEN SPEED PRESS, Box 7123, Berkeley CA 94707. Editor: P. Wood. Publishes hardcover and paperback originals and reprints. Offers royalty of 10% of list price; 12½% after 100,000 copies are sold. Published 8 titles last year. Will send catalog to writer on request. Submit outline and sample chapters for nonfiction. Reports in 1 month. Enclose return postage.
Nonfiction: Americana, book trade, cookbooks, cooking and foods, history, humor, law, nature, self-help, how-to, sports, hobbies, recreation and pets, and travel. Publishes mostly trade paperbacks. Subjects range from bicycle books to Wm. Blake's illustrations. No set requirements. Some recipe books, career development books. Recently published *Who's Hiring Who?*, by Lathrop; *Mousewood Cookbook*, by Katzen; and *The Other Awkward Age*, by Page.

TEXAS WESTERN PRESS, The University of Texas at El Paso, El Paso TX 79968. (915)747-5688. Director: E.H. Antone. Publishes hardcover and paperback originals. "We are a university press, not a commercial house; therefore, payment is in books and prestige more than money. Most of our books are sold to libraries, not to the general reading public." Published 10 titles last year. Will send a catalog to a writer on request. Query first. Will consider photocopied submissions. "Follow MLA Style Sheet." Reports in 1 to 3 months. Enclose return postage.
Nonfiction: "Scholarly books. Historic accounts of the Southwest (west Texas, southern New Mexico, and northern Mexico). Some literary works, occasional scientific titles. Our Southwestern Studies use mss of 20,000 words. Our hardback books range from 30,000 words up. The writer should use good exposition in his work. Most of our work requires documentation. We favor a scholarly, but not overly pedantic, style. We specialize in superior book design." Recently published *The Paradox of Poncho Villa,* by H. Braddy; and *Down Went McGinty: El Paso in the Wonderful Nineties,* by C. Bryson.

A. THOMAS & CO., LTD., Denington Estate, Wellingborough, Northamptonshire NN8 2RQ England. Editor-in-Chief: J.R. Hardaker. Hardcover and paperback originals and reprints. Specializes in inspirational, practical psychology and self-improvement material. 8-10% royalty. Photocopied submissions OK. SAE and International Reply Coupons. Reports in 2-4 weeks. Free book catalog.
Nonfiction: Publishes books on how-to methods, psychology and self-help. Submit outline/synopsis and sample chapters.

THORSONS PUBLISHERS, LTD, Denington Estate, Wellington, Northamptonshire NN8 2RQ England. Editor-in-Chief: J.R. Hardaker. Hardcover and paperback originals and reprints. Specializes in health books, psychology, self-improvement, hypnotism, self-sufficiency; alternative medicine and business success books. 5-10% royalty. Photocopied submissions OK. SAE and International Reply Coupons. Reports in 2-4 weeks. Free book catalog.
Nonfiction: Business; cookbooks, cooking and foods; philosophy, psychology, self-help themes. Submit outline/synopsis and sample chapters.

THREE CONTINENTS PRESS, 1346 Connecticut Ave., N.W., Washington DC 20036. Editor-in-Chief: Donald E. Herdeck. Hardcover and paperback originals (90%) and reprints (10%). 10% royalty; advance "only on delivery of complete ms which is found acceptable; usually $150." Query. Prefers photocopied submissions. State availability of photos/illustrations. Simultaneous submissions OK. Reports in 1-2 months. SASE. Free book catalog.
Nonfiction and Fiction: Specializes in African and Caribbean literature and criticism, third world literature and history. Scholarly, well-prepared mss; creative writing. Fiction, poetry, criticism, history and translations of creative writing. "We search for books which will make clear the complexity and value of African literature and culture, including bilingual texts (African language/English translations) of previously unpublished authors from less well-known areas of Africa. We are always interested in genuine contributions to understanding African and Caribbean culture." Length: 50,000 words. Recently published *Fire: Six Writers from Angola, Mozambique, and Cape Verde,* by D. Bwumess; and *Bozambo's Revenge,* by B. Jumines.

TIDEWATER PUBLISHERS, Box 109, Cambridge MD 21613. Editor: Mary Jane Cornell. An imprint of Cornell Maritime Press, Inc. Publishes hardcover and paperback originals and reprints. Offers standard 10-12½-15% royalty contract. Free book catalog. Query first with outline and sample chapters. Will not consider photocopied submissions. Reports in 2 to 3 weeks. SASE.
Nonfiction: "General nonfiction on Maryland and the Delmarva Peninsula." Recently published *Pioneer Decoy Carvers,* by The Berkeys.

TIME-LIFE BOOKS INC., 777 Duke St., Alexandria VA 22314. (703)960-5000. Managing Editor: Jerry Korn. Publishes hardcover originals. "We have no minimum or maximum fee because our needs vary tremendously. Advance, as such, is not offered. Author is paid as he completes part of contracted work." Books are almost entirely staff-generated and staff produced, and distribution is primarily through mail order sale. Query first to the Director of Planning. SASE.
Nonfiction: "General interest books. Most books tend to be heavily illustrated (by staff), with text written by assigned authors. We very rarely accept mss or book ideas submitted from outside our staff." Length: open. Recently published *The Mexican War* (Old West Series); and *Amsterdam* (Great Cities Series).

TIMES BOOKS, (formerly *Quadrangle/The New York Times Book Co.*), 3 Park Ave., New York NY 10016. Editor-in-Chief: Roger Jellinek. Executive Editor: John J. Simon. Senior Editor: Marcia Magill. Publishes hardcover and paperback originals (75%) and reprints (25%). Published 79 titles in 1977, 80 in 1978; will do 80 in 1979. Standard royalty; advance offered "if circumstances so indicate." Simultaneous and photocopied submissions OK. Reports in 2 weeks. SASE. Free book catalog.
Nonfiction: Americana; art; biography; business; cookbooks; economics; history; how-to; humor; law; medicine and psychiatry; nature; photography; politics; psychology; recreation; reference; scientific; self-help; sociology; sports; and travel. Submit synopsis and sample chapters. Recently published *The Ends of Power,* by H.R. Haldeman (Watergate "insider"); *Beyond the Male Myth,* by A. Pietropinto/J. Simenaur (survey and analysis of what women want to know about male sexuality); and *The Secrets of Atlantis,* by O. Muck (solving the mystery of Atlantis).
Fiction: Adventure; fantasy; historical; mainstream; mystery; romance; science fiction; and suspense. Submit outline/synopsis and sample chapters. Recently published *Compromising Positions,* by S. Isaacs (suspense/suburban novel); *Vital Statistics,* by T. Chastain (sophisticated mystery); and *Mixed Blessings,* by M. Cockrell (old-fashioned romance).

TIMES MIRROR MAGAZINES, INC., BOOK DIVISION, (Subsidiary of Times Mirror Company), 380 Madison Ave., New York NY 10017. Publishing books in the Popular Science and Outdoor Life fields. Editor: John W. Sill. Royalties and advance according to size and type of book. Wants outlines, sample chapters, author information. Enclose return postage.
How-To and Self-Help: Publishes books in Popular Science field: energy saving, home renovation, repair and improvement, workshop, hand and power tools, automobile how-to. In the Outdoor Life field: hunting, especially big game and deer; fishing, camping, firearms. Small books to 35,000 words; large books to 150,000 words. Recently published *Home Energy How-to,* by A.J. Hand; *Complete Book of Woodworking,* by R. Capotosto; and *Basic Car Maintenance and Repairs,* by P. Weissler.
Special Needs: "Home and shop how-to books, step-by-step with photos, captions, and text."

THE TOUCHSTONE PRESS, Box 81, Beaverton OR 97005. (503)648-8081. Editor-in-Chief: Thomas K. Worcester. Paperback originals. Specializes in field guide books. Royalty of 10% of retail price; seldom offers an advance. Published 3 titles in 1977, will do 4-6 in 1979. Photocopied submissions OK. Reports in 1-2 months. SASE. Free book catalog.
Nonfiction: Publishes cookbooks, cooking and foods; history, hobbies, how-to, recreation, sports, and travel books. "Must be within the range of our outdoor styles." Query first. Recently published *Indian Heaven Back Country,* by M. Hansen (trail guide/history); *I Know You're Hurt, but There's Nothing to Bandage,* by D.D. Fisher, MD. (self-help); and *Central Oregon Hiking Tours,* by D. Love/R. Love.

TRANSACTION BOOKS, Rutgers University, New Brunswick NJ 08903. (201)932-2280. Book Division Director: Kevin McLaughlin. Publishes hardcover and paperback originals (65%) and reprints (35%). Specializes in scholarly social science books. Royalty "depends almost entirely on individual contract, we've gone anywhere from 2-15%." No advance. Published 55 titles in 1977, 60 in 1978. Query or submit outline/synopsis and sample chapters. "Send introduction or first chapter and conclusion or last chapter. Use Chicago *Manual of Style.*" State availability of photos/illustrations and send 1 photocopied example. Photocopied submissions OK "if they are perfectly clear." Reports in 2-4 months. SASE. Free book catalog.
Nonfiction: Publishes Americana; art; biography; economics; history; law; medicine and psychiatry; music; philosophy; photography; politics; psychology; reference; scientific; sociology; technical; and textbooks. "All must be scholarly social science or related." Recently published *Yankee Family,* by J.R. McGovern (social history); *Basic Human Needs,* by J. McHale/M.C. McHale (Third World public policy); and *Who Really Rules? New Haven and Community Power Reexamined,* by G.W. Domhoff.

TRANS-ANGLO BOOKS, P.O. Box 38, Corona del Mar CA 92625. Editorial Director: Spencer Crump. Royalty of 5% to 10%. Published 4 titles last year. Catalog on request. Query required; do not send mss until requested. Reports in three weeks to one month. Enclose return postage.
Nonfiction: Publishes Americana, Western Americana, biography, and railroad books. Also planning to enter the college text field. "We are not interested in family histories or local history that lacks national appeal." Most books are 8½x11 hardcover with many photos supplementing a good text of 5,000 to 15,000 words. Recently published *The Real Death Valley Story,* (biography); *Matches, Flumes and Rails* (railroadiana); *California's Spanish Missions* (Western Americana).

TREASURE CHEST PUBLICATIONS, Box 5250, Tucson AZ 85703. (602)623-9558. Contact: Sterling Mahan or Ellen L. Jensen. Publishes paperback originals. Published 4-10 titles in 1978. 5% minimum royalty; advance "depends on the situation." Simultaneous and photocopied submissions OK. Reports in 6 weeks. SASE. Free book catalog.
Nonfiction: "We specialize in books concerning the lifestyle, culture, history and arts of the Southwest, and especially would like to see related works. We are particularly interested in manuscripts by and/or about Native Americans, and works about Native American artists. Also art, history, biography, and photography with a Southwestern theme. Recently published *Indian Jewelry Making,* by O. Branson; and *Wild Brothers of the Indians,* by A. Wesche.

TREND HOUSE, Box 2350, Tampa FL 33601. (813)247-5411. Editor-in-Chief: Harris Mullen. Managing Editor: Al Petow. Hardcover and paperback originals (90%) and reprints (10%). Specializes in books on Florida and the South — all categories. 10% royalty; no advance. Books are marketed through *Florida Trend* and *The South* magazines. Query. State availability of photos and/or illustrations. Photocopied submissions OK. Reports in 2-4 weeks. SASE. Free book catalog.
Nonfiction: Publishes business; economics; history; law; politics; reference; textbooks; and travel books. "All books pertain to Florida and Southern U.S."
Recent Titles: *300 Most Abused Drugs,* by E. Bludworth (police handbook); *The Power Structure,* by L. Butcher (Florida business); *All About Wills for Florida Residents,* by R. Richards (legal information).

***TRIUMPH PUBLISHING CO.**, Box 292, Altadena CA 91001. (213)797-0075. Editor-in-Chief: William Dankenbring. Hardcover and paperback originals. 5% royalty; no advance. Subsidy publishes 10% of books; "depends on the ms". Published 3 titles in 1977 and 1978. State availability of photos and/or artwork to accompany ms. Simultaneous and photocopied submissions OK. Reports in 1-2 months. SASE. Free book catalog.
Nonfiction: Americana (inspirational); business (how-to); history (Biblical); nature (creation); psychology and scientific books (for laymen); religious and self-help. Recently published *Golden Prince,* by Ramsay (juvenile); *Ascent to Greatness,* by McNair (Americana); *Last Days,* by Dankenbring (religious).

TROUBADOR PRESS, 385 Fremont St., San Francisco CA 94105. (415)397-3716. Publisher: Malcolm K. Whyte. Production Manager: June Blackburn. Publishes hardcover and paperback originals. Published 10 titles in 1977, 10-15 in 1978. 2-10% royalty; advance averages $400-1,000. Simultaneous and photocopied submissions OK. Reports in 1 month. SASE. Book catalog for SASE.
Nonfiction: "Troubador Press publishes project, activity, entertainment, art, game, nature, craft, and cookbooks. All titles feature original art and exceptional graphics. Primarily nonfiction. Current series include creative cut-outs; in-depth, readable cookbooks; 3-D mazes and other puzzle books; color and story books; and other art and entertainment books. Interested in expanding on themes of 60 current titles. We like books which have the potential to develop into series." Query or submit outline/synopsis and sample chapters. Recently published *How To Draw Monsters,* by L. Evans; *Original Diet, Raw Vegetarian Guide and Recipe Book,* by K. Cross Whyte; and *Cats & Kittens,* by R. Warner.

TROY STATE UNIVERSITY PRESS, Troy State University, Troy AL 36081. (205)566-3000. Editor: Martin Kruskopf. Hardcover and paperback originals (80%) and reprints (20%). Royalty of 10% of published price on first 2,000 copies sold; advance averages $250. State availability of photos and/or artwork to accompany ms. Photocopied submissions OK. Reports in 2-4 months. SASE. Free sample copy.
Nonfiction: Publishes books on Alabama and regional subjects, Americana, economics, history, law, philosophy, politics, psychology, religion, sociology, science; and biographies.
Recent Titles: *The Way of Love,* by J.B. Glubb (religious); *Every Day Is Easter in Alabama,* by R.H. Couch (history); *Devils' Wine,* by S. Scalf (poetry).

TURNSTONE BOOKS, 37 Upper Addison Gardens, London W14 8AJ England. (01)602-6885. Editor-in-Chief: Alick Bartholomew. Managing Editor: Robin Campbell. Hardcover and paperback originals (90%) and reprints (10%). 7½% royalty on paperbacks; 10-15% on hardcovers. Advance of 400 pounds. Has subsidy published only one title. "We would really have chosen to publish it anyway, but the investment was too great." Published 9 titles in 1977, 9 in

1978; will do 12 in 1979. Photocopied submissions OK. SASE. Reports in 1-2 months. Free book catalog.
Nonfiction: Pre-history and ancient wisdom; alternative medicine; practical philosophy, Jungian psychology, alternative technology, mysticism and self-sufficiency topics. Query first or submit outline/synopsis and sample chapters. Recently published *Living Better on Less,* by P. Rivers (alternative lifestyles); *Journal of Insight Meditation,* by F. Lenes; and *The Childbirth Book,* by C. Beels.

CHARLES E. TUTTLE CO., INC., Publishers & Booksellers, Drawer F, 26-30 S. Main St., Rutland VT 05701. Publishes originals and reprints. Pays $250 against 10% royalty. Advance varies. Published 30 titles in 1977. Book catalog 25¢. Send complete mss or queries accompanied by outlines or sample chapters to Charles E. Tuttle Co., Inc., Suido 1--Chome, 2-6, Bunkyo-Ku, Tokyo, Japan, where the editorial and printing offices are located. Reports in 4-6 weeks. SASE.
Nonfiction: Specializes in publishing books about Oriental art and culture as well as history, literature, cookery, sport and children's books which relate to Asia, Hawaiian Islands, Australia and the Pacific areas. Also interested in Americana, especially antique collecting, architecture, genealogy and Canadiana. Not interested in travel, sociological or topical works even when in subject field. No interest in poetry and fiction except that of Oriental theme. Normal book length only.

TWAYNE PUBLISHERS, A division of G. K. Hall & Co., 70 Lincoln St., Boston MA 02111. (617)423-3990. Editor: Alice D. Phalen. Payment is on royalty basis. Query first. Reports in three weeks. Enclose return postage.
Nonfiction: Publishes scholarly books in series. Literary criticism and biography.
Special Needs: "We will publish the first 3 titles in Twayne's Theatrical Arts Series. These are consise critical studies of 176-200 pages on film directors, actors, producers, and entertainers, written with scholarly authority, but directed at a literate general audience."
Recent Titles: *Kurt Vonnegut, Jr.,* by S. Schatt (literary criticism and biography); and *The German-Americans,* by L.J. Rippley (history of immigration).

TYNDALE HOUSE PUBLISHERS, INC., 336 Gundersen Dr., Wheaton IL 60187. (312)668-8300. Managing Editor: Virginia Muir. Acquisitions Editor: Wendell Hawley. Publishes hardcover and trade paperback originals (90%) and hardcover and mass paperback reprints (10%). Published 50 titles in 1977, 60 in 1978; will do 65 in 1979. 10% royalty; negotiable advance. Simultaneous submissions OK; prefers photocopied submissions. Reports in 6 weeks. SASE. Free book catalog.
Nonfiction: Religious books only: personal experience; family living; marriage; Bible studies and commentaries; books for children; Christian living; devotional; inspirational; church and social issues; Bible prophecy; missions; theology and doctrine; counseling and Christian psychology; Christian apologetics; and church history. Submit table of contents, chapter summary, preface, 1st 2 chapters and 1 later chapter. Recently published *I Want to Be a Christian,* by J.I. Packer (theology and doctrine); and *Walking Among the Unseen,* by H. Hurnard (devotional).
Fiction: Bible and contemporary novels, children's books, religious and allegory. Submit outline/synopsis and sample chapters. Recently published *The Mantle,* by W. Stephens; and *Ivan and the Star of David,* by M. Grant.

UNITED SYNAGOGUE BOOK SERVICE, 155 Fifth Ave., New York NY 10010. (212)533-7800. Hardcover and paperback originals. 10% royalty; no advance. Free book catalog. Send query, outline, sample chapter first. Address juveniles and history to Dr. Morton Siegel; biography, philosophy and adult religion to Rabbi Marvin Wiener. "Address general inquiries to George L. Levine, Director." Reports in 1-8 weeks. SASE.
Religion: Publishes religious books only: textbooks, readers, Hebrew Language books, history, picture books. No length requirements.
Recent Title: *The Jewish Experience, Book I,* by F. Hyman (history).

UNITY PRESS, 113 New St., Santa Cruz CA 95060. (408)427-2020. Publisher: Craig Caughlan. Publishes paperback originals. Published 2 titles in 1977, 8 in 1978; will do 12 in 1979. Standard royalty; advance "depends—generally small." Simultaneous and photocopied submissions OK. Reports in 6 weeks. SASE. Free book catalog.
Nonfiction: "Our editorial direction could be defined as follows: books that bring an individual to a better understanding of self and environs. Prefer books that are on the leading edge of the

social sciences and human behavior. With each submission, author should state in 50 words or less the purpose of his book, and what makes it better than others that are available on similar subjects." Query or submit synopsis/outlines and sample chapters.
Fiction: "Our editorial direction includes fiction as well. Would like to see books on futurism." No poetry, mysteries, or romances. Query or submit outline/synopsis and sample chapters.

UNIVELT INC., Box 28130, San Diego CA 92128. (714)746-4005. Editorial Director: H. Jacobs. Publishes hardcover originals. Published 10 titles in 1977, 12 in 1978; will do 10 in 1979. 10% royalty; no advance. Simultaneous and photocopied submissions OK. Reports in 4 weeks. SASE. Free book catalog.
Nonfiction: Publishes in the field of aerospace, especially astronautics, and technical communications, but including application of aerospace technology to Earth's problems. Submit outline/synopsis and sample chapters. Recently published *Satellite Communications in the Next Decade,* by L. Jaffe; and *200 Years of Flight in America,* by E.M. Emme.

UNIVERSAL MAGAZINE, Box 1537, Palm Desert CA 92260. Editorial Director: Rev. Paul von John. Publishes paperback originals. "Our books are marketed through direct mail, and manuscripts submitted should be suitable for this type of marketing." Publishes 2 titles/year. Payment "to be arranged with author." Reports in 2-3 weeks. SASE.
Nonfiction: "We are open to see what is most interesting to us. At this time we have no plans for any one subject." Submit outline/synopsis and sample chapters to "Book Division."

***UNIVERSE BOOKS**, 381 Park Ave. S., New York NY 10016. (212)689-0276. Editor-in-Chief: Louis Barron. Hardcover and paperback originals (90%) and reprints (10%). 10% royalty on cloth, 6% on paper. Advance ranges from $500-5,000. Subsidy publishes 5% of books. Subsidy publishing is determined by "size of potential market, cost of production, and significance of material. We won't do a subsidy book unless it contributes significantly to knowledge." Published 40 titles in 1977, 50 in 1978. Query or submit outline/synopsis and sample chapters. "Please don't use corrasable bond paper." State availability of photos and/or illustrations. Simultaneous and photocopied submissions OK. Reports in 1-2 weeks. SASE. Free book catalog.
Nonfiction: Publishes art, biography; cookbooks, cooking and foods; erotica, history, how-to, music, nature, philosophy, politics, reference, sociology, alternative lifestyles and survival books. Recently published *The Dark Angel: Aspects of Victorian Sexuality,* by F. Harrison; *Gardener's Magic and Folklore,* by M. Baker; and *Plantcraft: A Guide to the Everyday Use of Plants,* by R. Mabey.

UNIVERSITY ASSOCIATES, INC., 7596 Eads Ave., La Jolla CA 92037. (714)454-8821. President: J. Wm. Pfeiffer. Vice-President and Editor-in-Chief: John E. Jones. Paperback originals (65%); reprints (35%). Specializes in practical materials for human relations trainers, consultants, etc. 10-15% royalty; no advance. Markets books by direct mail. Send prints or completed art or rough sketches to accompany ms. Simultaneous submissions OK. Reports in 2-4 months. SASE. Free book catalog.
Nonfiction: Marion Fusco, Department Editor. Publishes (in order of preference) human relations training and group-oriented material; management education and community relations and personal growth; business, psychology, sociology, and textbooks. Nothing on male/female relations or materials for grammar school or high school classroom teachers. Address query to Marion Fusco, Managing Editor. Use *American Psychological Association Style Manual.* Recently published *The 1978 Annual Handbook for Group Facilitators,* by J.W. Pfeiffer/J.E. Jones; *The Consulting Process in Action,* by R. Lippitt/G. Lippitt; and *Sociotechnical Systems: A Sourcebook,* edited by W. Pasmore/J.J. Sherwood.

UNIVERSITY OF ALABAMA PRESS, Drawer 2877, University AL 35486. Editor-in-Chief: P. Squibb. Publishes hardcover originals. "Maximum royalty is 12½%; no advances made." Published 35 titles last year. Will send a catalog to a writer on request. Will consider photocopied submissions. Submit outlines and sample chapters. Enclose return postage.
Nonfiction: Categories include biography, business, economics, history, music, philosophy, politics, religion, and sociology. Considers upon merit almost any subject of scholarly interest, but specializes in linguistics and philology, political science and public administration, literary criticism and biography, philosophy, and history. Also interested in biology, ecology, medicine, and agriculture.

UNIVERSITY OF ARIZONA PRESS, Box 3398, Tucson AZ 85722. (602)884-1446. Director:

Marshall Townsend. Publishes hardcover and paperback originals and reprints. "Contracts are individually negotiated, but as a 'scholarly publishing house' operating primarily on informational works, does not pay any advances. Also, royalty starting point may be after sale of first 1,000 copies, by virtue of the nature of the publishing program." Marketing methods "are based on 'what is considered best for the book,' giving individual treatment to the marketing of each book, rather than a generalized formula." Will send catalog to writer on request. Write for copy of editorial guidelines sheets. Will consider photocopied submissions if ms is not undergoing consideration at another publishing house. "Must have this assurance." Query first and submit outline and sample chapters. Reports on material within 90 days. SASE.
Nonfiction: "Significant works of a regional nature about Arizona, the Southwest and Mexico; and books of merit in subject matter fields strongly identified with the universities in Arizona; i.e., anthropology, arid lands studies, Asian studies, Southwest Indians, Mexico, etc. Each ms should expect to provide its own answer to the question, "Why should this come out of Arizona?" The answer would be that either the work was something that ought to be made a matter of record as a service to Arizona and the Southwest, or that it was presenting valuable information in a subject matter field with which the Arizona institutions hold strong identification. The Press strongly endorses 'the target reader' concept under which it encourages each author to write for only *one* reader, then leave it up to the publisher to reach the thousands—as contrasted with the author's trying to write for the thousands and not 'hitting home' with anyone. The Press believes this approach helps the author come to a consistent level of subject matter presentation. The press also insists upon complete departure of 'time-dating' words such as 'now,' 'recently,' and insists that the author consider how the presentation will read three years hence." Americana, art, biography, business, history, nature, scientific, technical. Length: "what the topic warrants and demands." Not interested in "personal diary types of Western Americana, mainly directed only toward family interest, rather than broad general interest." Recently published *Mexican Folk Tales,* by A.J. Campos; and *Ethnic Medicine in the Southwest,* edited by E.H. Spicec.

UNIVERSITY OF CALIFORNIA PRESS, Berkeley CA 94720; Los Angeles CA 90024. Director: James H. Clark. Los Angeles address is 60 Powell Library, Los Angeles CA 90024. Editor: Robert Y. Zachary. New York Office, Room 513, 50 E. 42 St., New York NY 10017. London Office IBEG, Ltd., 2-4 Brook St., London W1Y 1AA, England. Publishes hardcover and paperback originals and reprints. On books likely to more than return their costs, a standard royalty contract beginning at 10% is paid; on paperbacks it is less. Published 175 titles last year. Queries are always advisable, accompanied by outlines or sample material. Address to either Berkeley or Los Angeles address. Reports vary, depending on the subject. Enclose return postage.
Nonfiction: "It should be clear that most of our publications are hardcover nonfiction written by scholars." Publishes scholarly books including art, literary studies, social sciences, natural sciences and some high-level popularizations. No length preferences.
Fiction and Poetry: Publishes fiction and poetry only in translation. Usually in bilingual editions.

UNIVERSITY OF ILLINOIS PRESS, Urbana IL 61801. Hardcover and paperback originals (95%); paperback reprints (5%). "Royalty varies greatly; from zero on small edition scholarly books to sliding scale beginning at 15% of net income." Very rarely offers advance. State availability of photos and/or illustrations to accompany ms. Simultaneous (in some cases) and photocopied submissions OK. SASE. Reports in 1-2 months. Free book catalog.
Nonfiction: "Particular emphasis on American studies in history, literature, music, and other areas of specialization including anthropology, communications, urban and regional planning, and Western Americana." Query or submit complete ms. Recently published *Neighbors: An Oral History of Contemporary Cuba,* by O. Lewis, et al (anthropology).
Fiction: "We publish 4 collections of short stories each year in the Illinois Short Fiction series. Should be the kind of stories published in literary journals and quality magazines. Queries to Richard Wentworth." Recently published *One More River,* by L. Goldberg (short stories).

UNIVERSITY OF IOWA PRESS, Graphic Services Bldg., Iowa City IA 52242. (319)353-3181. Editor-in-Chief: Art Pflughaupt. Hardcover and paperback originals. 10% royalty. Subsidy publishes 5% of books. Subsidy publishing is offered "if a scholarly institution will advance a subsidy to support publication of a worthwhile book. We market mostly by direct mailing of fliers to groups with special interests in our titles." Query or submit outline/synopsis and sample chapters. Chicago *Manual of Style.* State availability of photos/illustrations. Photocopied submissions OK. Reports in 2-4 months. SASE. Free book catalog.
Nonfiction: Publishes art; economics; history; music; philosophy; reference; and scientific

books. "We do not publish children's books. We do not publish any poetry or short fiction except the Iowa Translation Series and the Iowa School of Letters Award for short fiction." Recently published *Contemporary Yugoslav Poetry,* edited by V. Mihailovich; and *The Information Process: World News Reporting to the 20th Century,* by R. Desmond.

***UNIVERSITY OF MASSACHUSETTS PRESS**, Box 429, Amherst MA 01002. (413)545-2217. Editorial Director: Leone Stein. Senior Editor: Richard Martin. Publishes hardcover and paperback originals (95%) and reprints (5%). Published 25 titles in 1977, 20 in 1978; will do 24 in 1979. "Royalties depend on character of book; if offered, generally at 10% of list price. Advance, if offered, averages $250." Subsidy publishes 10% of books; "Press Committee specifies subsidy requirement on basis on estimated edition loss." No author subsidies accepted. Simultaneous (if advised) and photocopied submissions OK. Reports in 1-2 months. SASE. Free book catalog.
Nonfiction: Publishes Americana; art; biography; history; philosophy; nature; poetry; politics; psychology; reference; scientific; and sociology. Submit outline/synopsis and sample chapters. Recently published *Ruth V. Hemenway, M.D.: A Memoir of Revolutionary China, 1924-1941,* by R.V. Hemenway, edited by F.W. Drake (history/biography); *The Culture of Inequality,* by M. Lewis (sociology); and *Crisis on the Left: Cold War Politics and American Liberals, 1947-1954,* by M.S. McAuliffe (political science/government).

UNIVERSITY OF MISSOURI PRESS, 107 Swallow Hall, Columbia MO 65201. (314)882-7641. Director: Edward D. King. Senior Editor: Susan E. Kelpe. Publishes hardcover and paperback originals. Published 20 titles in 1977, 25 in 1978. 10% royalty; no advance. Photocopied submissions OK. Reports in 3 months. SASE. Free book catalog.
Nonfiction: "Scholarly publisher interested in history, literary criticism, political science, social science, music, art, art history, and original poetry." Also regional books about Missouri and the midwest. "We do not publish very much in mathematics or hard sciences." Query or submit outline/synopsis and sample chapters. Consult Chicago *Manual of Style*. Recently published *The Arts & Architecture of German Settlements in Missouri,* by C. van Raverswaay (regional art history); *The 20th Century American West,* by G.M. Gressley (essays/history); and *Lionel Trilling,* by R. Boyers (literary criticism).
Fiction: "Will not be reading fiction manuscripts again until Jan. 1979. We publish original short fiction in Breakthrough Series, not to exceed 35,000 words. May be short story collection or novella. Also publish poetry and drama in the same series. No limitations on subject matter." Query. Recently published *Lambing Out,* by M. Clearman; *4.4.4,* by L. Gonzales/G. Lyons/R. Rath; and *Frog Gig,* by S. Morgan.

UNIVERSITY OF NEBRASKA PRESS, 901 N. 17th St., Lincoln NE 68588. Editor-in-Chief: Virginia Faulkner. Hardcover and paperback originals (60%); hardcover and paperback reprints (40%). Specializes in scholarly nonfiction (particularly literary); some regional books; reprints of western Americana; natural history. Royalty is usually graduated from 10% for original books. No advance. Published 55 titles in 1977 and 1978. SASE. Reports in 1-2 weeks on rejections; 2-4 months on acceptances. Free book catalog.
Nonfiction: Publishes Americana, biography, history, medicine and psychiatry; nature, photography, psychology, sports, literature, agriculture and American Indian themes. Query. Recently published *Anatomies of Egotism: A Reading of the Last Novels of H.G. Wells* by R. Bloom (literature); *Oglala Religion* by W.K. Powers (American Indian); *North American Game Birds of Upland and Shoreline* by P.S. Johnsgard (nature).

THE UNIVERSITY OF NORTH CAROLINA PRESS, Box 2288, Chapel Hill NC 27514. (919)933-2105. Editor-in-Chief: Malcolm Call. Publishes hardcover and paperback originals. Specializes in scholarly books and regional trade books. Royalty schedule "varies greatly. Depends on nature of ms and its marketability; zero to 15% of retail price." No advance. Published 35 titles in 1977 and 1978. "As a university press, we do not have the resources for mass marketing books." Send prints to illustrate ms only if they are a major part of the book. Photocopied submissions OK. Reports in 2-5 months on accepted mss, sooner if rejected. SASE. Free book catalog.
Nonfiction: "Our major fields are American and European history." Also scholarly books on Americana, classics, biography, economics; medicine and psychiatry; philosophy, psychology and sociology. History books on art, law, music and religious themes. Books on nature, particularly on the Southeast; literary studies. Submit outline/synopsis and sample chapters. Must follow Chicago *Manual of Style*. Recently published *Character of John Adams,* by P. Shaw (biography); *The Fledgling Province (Colonial Georgia),* by H. Davis (history); and *Fact*

and Fiction: New Journalism and Nonfiction Novel, by J. Hollowell (literary studies).

UNIVERSITY OF NOTRE DAME PRESS, Notre Dame IN 46556. Editor: Ann Rice. Publishes hardcover and paperback originals and paperback reprints. Offers standard 10-12½-15% royalty contract; no advance. Published 33 titles in 1977. Free book catalog. Will consider photocopied submissions. Query first. Reports in 2 to 3 months. SASE.
Nonfiction: "Scholarly books, serious nonfiction of general interest; book-length only. Especially in the areas of philosophy, theology, history, sociology, English literature (Middle English period, and modern literature criticism in the area of relation of literature and theology), government, international relations. and Mexican-American studies. Recently published *Anamnesis,* by E. Voegelin; *Four Hassidic Masters,* by E. Wiesel; and *Varieties of Interpretation,* by J. Mazzeo.

***UNIVERSITY OF OKLAHOMA PRESS**, 1005 Asp Ave., Norman OK 73019. (405)325-5111. Editor-in-Chief: Luther Wilson. Hardcover and paperback originals (85%); and reprints (15%). Royalty ranges from zero to 15% "depending on market viability of project". No advance. Subsidy publishes 5% of books. "If a book has scholarly merit, but is destined to lose money, we seek a subsidy." Submit sample photos or 8x10 glossy prints. Simultaneous and photocopied submissions OK. Reports in 2-4 months. SASE. Book catalog for SASE.
Nonfiction: Publishes Americana and art (western and Indian); biographies of major western and Indian figures; history, hobbies, how-to, music, nature, politics, reference, sociology, technical, textbooks, archaeology (Mesoamerican); classics, and anthropology books. Query. Recently published *Maya Ruins of Mexico in Color,* by Ferguson/Royce; *Propertius,* by Richardson (scholarly); and *The Indian Tipi,* by Laubin/Laubin.

***UNIVERSITY OF PENNSYLVANIA PRESS**, 3933 Walnut St., Philadelphia PA 19104. (215)243-6261. Director: Robert Erwin. Hardcover and paperback originals (90%) and reprints (10%). Royalty of 10% of list price on first 5,000 copies sold; 12½% on next 5,000 copies sold; 15% thereafter; no advance. Subsidy publishes 10% of books. Subsidy publishing is determined by: a) evaluation obtained by the press from outside specialists b) work approved by Press Editorial Committee c) subsidy approved by funding organization. Published 20 books in 1977 and 1978. State availability of photos and/or illustrations to accompany ms, with copies of illustrations. Photocopied submissions OK. Reports in 1-3 months. SASE. Free book catalog.
Nonfiction: Publishes Americana, biography, business (especially management); economics, history, law, medicine and psychiatry; philosophy, politics, psychology, reference, scientific, sociological, technical, folklore and folk life books. "Serious books that serve the scholar and the professional." Follow the Chicago *Manual of Style*. Query with outline and sample chapter addressed to the director. Recently published *Recycling the Past: Popular Uses of American History,* edited by L. Zenderland (history); and *Interorganizational Relations,* edited by W. Evan (sociology/management).

UNIVERSITY OF PITTSBURGH PRESS, 127 N. Bellefield Ave., Pittsburgh PA 15260. (412)624-4110. Director: Frederick A. Hetzel. Senior Editor: Louise Craft. Publishes hardcover and paperback originals. Published 25 titles in 1977, 30 in 1978; will do 30 in 1979. 12% royalty on hardcover, 8% on paperback; no advance. Photocopied submissions OK. Reports in 1-4 months. SASE. Free book catalog.
Nonfiction: Scholarly nonfiction. No textbooks or general nonfiction of an unscholarly nature. Submit outline/synopsis and sample chapters. Recently published *Fragile Families, Troubled Children: The Aftermath of Infant Trauma,* by E. Elmer; *The Overthrow of Allende & the Politics of Chile, 1964-1976,* by P.E. Sigmund; and *Ruins & Empire: The Evolution of a Theme in Augustan & Romantic Literature,* by L. Gold.

***UNIVERSITY OF THE TREES PRESS**, Box 644, Boulder Creek CA 95006. (408)338-3855. Editorial Director: Dr. D. Rozman. Senior Editor: Ann Ray, Ph.D. Publishes hardcover and paperback originals (85%) and reprints (15%). Published 10 titles in 1977, 15 in 1978; will do 20 in 1979. Will consider subsidy publishing: "have done none so far, but we are open to works of great originality. Originality of work must be high even if the market for the work may be only a few key people. If we can't make a profit on it, we would still publish it as a subsidy." 10% royalty; no advance. Simultaneous and photocopied submissions OK. Reports in 4 weeks. SASE. Book catalog for 25¢.
Nonfiction: "All our books relate to consciousness research or scientific approach to spiritual objects. We are interested in original research into dowsing, esp, brain development, evolution of forms, breath control, yoga, mental phenomena or meditation techniques. Also research into

light and energies; original spiritual guides or manuals, and education for children by new classroom techniques." Recently published *Nuclear Evolution: Discovery of the Rainbow Body,* by C. Hills, *Energy, Matter and Form,* by Bearne/Smith/Allen; and *Journey into Light,* by A. Ray.

UNIVERSITY OF UTAH PRESS, University of Utah, University Services Building, Salt Lake City UT 84112. (801)581-6771. Director: Norma B. Mikkelsen. Publishes hardcover and paperback originals, reprints, and translations. 10% royalty on first 2,000 copies sold; 12½% on 2,001 to 4,000 copies sold; 15% thereafter. No advance. Published 10 titles last year. Free book catalog. Query first with outline and sample chapter. Reports in 6-8 months. SASE.
Nonfiction: Scholarly books on history, philosophy, religion, anthropology, the arts, poetry, and general nonfiction. Length: author should specify page length in query. Recently published *The Zunis of Cibola,* by C.G. Crampton; *Country to City,* by E. Norbeck; and *The English Spenserians,* by W.B. Hunter Jr.

***UNIVERSITY OF WISCONSIN PRESS**, P.O. Box 1379, Madison WI 53701. (608)262-4928. Director: Thompson Webb. Editor: Irving E. Rockwood. Publishes hardcover and paperback originals, reprints, and translations. Offers standard royalty contract. No advance. Published 25 titles in 1976 and 1977. Send complete ms. Follow Modern Language Association Style Sheet. Reports in 3 months. Enclose return postage with ms.
Nonfiction: Publishes general nonfiction based on scholarly research. Recently published *A History of the Crusades,* edited by K. Setton; *Climates of Hunger: Mankind and the World's Changing Weather,* by R.A. Bryson/T.J. Murray; and *The People and the King,* by J.L. Phelan.

UNIVERSITY PRESS OF AMERICA, 4710 Auth Place, SE, Washington D.C. 20023. (301)899-9600. Editorial Director: James E. Lyons. Publishes hardcover and paperback originals (95%) and reprints (5%). Publishes 300 titles/year. 10% royalty; no advance. Simultaneous and photocopied submissions OK. Reports in 4 weeks. SASE. Free book catalog.
Nonfiction: Scholarly monographs, college, and graduate level textbooks in history, political science, African studies, Black studies, philosophy, religion, sociology, and education. No juvenile or El-Hi material. Submit complete ms. Send for University Press of America's author's guide. Recently published *African Society, Culture, and Politics,* edited by C. Mojekwu; *The Weimar in Crisis: Cuno's Germany,* by A. Cornebise; and *Thirteen Thinkers: An Introduction to Philosophy,* by G. Kreyche.

UNIVERSITY PRESS OF KENTUCKY, 102 Lafferty Hall, Lexington KY 40506. (606)258-2951. Editor-in-Chief: William Jerome Crouch. Managing Editor: Evalin F. Douglas. Hardcover originals (95%); paperback reprints (5%). 10% royalty after first 1,000 copies; no advance. State availability of photos and/or artwork to accompany ms. "Author is ultimately responsible for submitting all artwork in camera-ready form." Reports in 2-4 months. SASE. Free book catalog.
Nonfiction: Publishes (in order of preference): history, sociology, literary criticism and history; politics, business, law, philosophy; medicine and psychiatry; nature, psychology, and scientific books. "All mss must receive an endorsement (secured by the press) from a scholar in the appropriate area of learning and must be approved by an editorial board before final acceptance." Query or submit outline/synopsis with sample chapters. Recently published *Atlas of Kentucky,* by P.P. Karan/C. Mather (reference); *The Missile Defense Controversy,* by E. Yanarella (political science); and *The Poetic Vision of Robert Penn Warren,* by V. Strandberg.

***UNIVERSITY PRESS OF VIRGINIA**, Box 3608, University Station, Charlottesville VA 22903. (804)924-3468. Editor-in-Chief: Walker Cowen. Hardcover and paperback originals (95%) and reprints (5%). Royalty depends on the market for the book; sometimes none is made. "We subsidy publish 40% of our books, based on cost vs. probable market." Photocopied submissions OK. Returns rejected material within a week. Reports on acceptances in 1-2 months. SASE. Free book catalog.
Nonfiction: Publishes Americana, business, history, law; medicine and psychiatry; politics, reference, scientific, bibliography, and decorative arts books. "Write a letter to the director, describing content of ms, plus length. Also specify if maps, tables, illustrations, etc., are included. Please, no educational or sociological or psychological mss." Recently published *The Immigrant in Industrial America*, by R.L. Ehrlich; and *The New Humanism*, by J.D. Hoeveler Jr.

URIZEN BOOKS, INC., 66 W. Broadway, New York NY 10007. Editor-in-Chief: Michael

Roloff. Publishes paperback and hardcover originals. Offers standard minimum book contract of 10-12½-15%. Average advance is $3,000. Book catalog $1. Will consider photocopied submissions. Query first for nonfiction. Reports in 6 weeks. Enclose return postage.
Fiction, Nonfiction, Drama, Poetry: Sociology, philosophy, history of industrialization, history of economics, communication theory, "first class fiction." High caliber writing necessary.
Recent Titles: *Beautiful Days,* by F. Innerhofer (fiction); *Jesus, Son of Man,* by R. Augstein (nonfiction); and *The Soviet Union Against Dr. Mikhail Stern,* by A. Stern (nonfiction).

VALUE COMMUNICATIONS, INC., 11175 Flintcote Ave., San Diego CA 92121. (714)452-8676. Editor-in-Chief: Cynthia B. Tillinghast. Specializes in juvenile books focusing on development of personal values. Pays flat fee; variable. Advance varies. Published 7 titles in 1977, 12 in 1978. Send available prints to illustrate ms. Simultaneous and photocopied submissions OK. Reports in 2-4 weeks. SASE. Free book catalog.
Nonfiction: Publishes juveniles and biographies. Recently published *The Value of Fairness, the Story of Nellie Bly,* by A.D. Johnson (juvenile biography); and *The Value of Saving,* by S. Spenser.
Fiction: Publishes fantasy and themes that emphasize the development of personal values. Recently published *A Visit to the Forest,* by B.B. Simons.

VANGUARD PRESS, INC., 424 Madison Ave., New York NY 10017. Editor-in-Chief: Mrs. Bernice S. Woll. Publishes hardcover originals and reprints. Offers standard minimum book contract of 10-12½-15%. Published 20 titles last year. Query first with outline and sample chapters. Will not consider photocopied submissions. Reports in 4 months. SASE.
General Fiction, General Nonfiction: "We publish both fiction and nonfiction of all types. We stipulate that writers query before sending complete ms. We publish books for all audiences. Overly scholastic, or religious works are rarely published; although some exceptions are made. We seek polished, organized, typed (double-spaced) materials. We are a small, independently run house with a reputation for publishing literate, well-written books. Our size allows us to give more attention to a limited number of authors than is possible in the larger houses. We do not, however, provide free advice or rewrite poorly written material. We rely on the author to come up with a new slant or approach on the subject he is dealing with."

***VESTA PUBLICATIONS**, Box 1641, Cornwall, Ontario, Canada K6H 5V6. (613)932-2135. Editor-in-Chief: Stephen Gill. Paperback originals. 10% minimum royalty. Subsidy publishes 10% of books. "We ask a writer to subsidize a part of the cost of printing; normally, it is 50%. We do so when we find that the book does not have a wide market, as in the case of university themes and the author's first collection of poems. The writer gets 50 free copies and 10% royalty on paperback editions." No advance. Published 15 titles in 1977, 20 in 1978. State availabiliy of photos and/or illustrations to accompany ms. Simultaneous submissions OK if so informed. Photocopied submissions OK. Reports in 1-4 weeks. SASE. Free book catalog.
Nonfiction: Publishes Americana, art, biography, cookbooks, cooking and foods; history, philosophy, poetry, politics, reference, religious. Query or submit complete ms. "Query letters and mss should be accompanied by synopsis of the book and biographical notes." Recently published *English Grammar for Beginners,* by S. Gill; *Purring is My Business,* by W.A. Crawford; and *Chalk Dust in My Blood,* by D. Morgan.

VICTOR BOOKS, Box 1825, Wheaton IL 60187. (312)668-6000. Editorial Director: James R. Adair. Editor: Wightman Weese. Paperback originals. 7½-10% royalty; occasionally offers an advance. Prefers outline/synopsis and sample chapters, but queries are acceptable. Reports in 1-2 months. SASE. Free book catalog.
Nonfiction: Only religious themes. "To click with us, writers must have real substance and know the evangelical market well. Actually, most of our books are by ministers, Bible teachers, and seminar speakers. We are looking for freelancers who can furnish ideas and find experts to team up with to put together good books." Recently published *God Can Make It Happen,* by R. Johnston; and *How to Really Love Your Child,* by R. Campbell.

THE VIKING PRESS, INC., PUBLISHERS, 625 Madison Ave., New York NY 10022. Royalties paid on all books. Published over 200 titles last year. Juvenile mss should be addressed to Viking Junior Books. Adult mss should be addressed to The Viking Press. Studio mss should be addressed to Viking Studio Books. Reports in 4 to 6 weeks. Enclose return postage with ms.
General: Publishes adult and Studio books (art, photography, etc.). Also publishes Viking Portable Library and Viking Critical Library.
Juveniles: Publishes juvenile books.

VISAGE PRESS, INC., 3409 Wisconsin Ave., N.W., Washington DC 20016. (202)686-5302. Editor-in-Chief: Emilio C. Viano. Managing Editor: Sherry Icenhower. Hardcover and paperback originals. "At this time, interested in particular in how-to books and books about skiing, travel guides to skiing locations in U.S. and abroad. Also looking for a good ms on spouse abuse." 10% royalty on first 5,000 hardcover; 12% next 5,000; 14% thereafter. Paperback royalty depends on the run. "Average advance is $1,000, generally given upon receipt of acceptable ms; rarely given on basis of outline alone. For scholarly works, please follow the style of the American Sociological Review (see their Notice to Contributors), or send for style sheet." Send contact sheets (if available) or prints to illustrate ms. Pictures must always be captioned and accompanied by proper releases. Photocopied submissions OK. Reports in 1-2 months. SASE. Book catalog for SASE.
Nonfiction: Publishes biography, business; cookbooks, cooking and foods (regional cuisine and Mid-Atlantic and southern states); hobbies, medicine and psychiatry (particularly about emergencies, crisis, rape, child abuse, other victimizations, prevention of victimization); pets (a consumer guide to pet books; "gourmet" foods for pets); politics (books about behind the scenes at United Nations sought); psychology (particularly in the area of the rapist, sex offender and victims repeatedly victimized); recreation (soccer, in particular); religious (books about the coming millenium sought); sports (skiing and soccer, in particular); travel books. Query first or submit outline/synopsis and sample chapters.
Special Needs: "A series on skiing of the travel book variety, telling people where to go, what to expect in terms of facilities, schools, lifts, accommodations, etc. Also books on soccer."

VISTA AND CO., Publication Division, 9056 Santa Monica Blvd., Los Angeles CA 90069. Editor-in-Chief: Cornelius C. Welch, M.D. Hardcover and paperback originals. Specializes in general interest, religious, psychological, occult, social sciences and fiction. 10% royalty. If ms is to be illustrated, send prints. Simultaneous and photocopied submissions OK. Submit outline and sample chapters. SASE. Reports in 1-2 months. Book catalog for SASE.
Nonfiction: Publishes psychology, religious, occult, philosophy, medicine and psychiatry, self-help, nature and books on sociology.
Fiction: Occult, religious, romance, experimental, suspense and mainstream.

VULCAN BOOKS, Division of Trinity-One, Inc., Box 25616, Seattle WA 98125. Publisher: Michael H. Gaven. Publishes hardcover and paperback originals and reprints. Offers standard minimum book contract. "Advances offered only in special cases." Published 10 titles in 1978. "Our books are marketed by all major occult distributors and we sell them to practically every store in America dealing with our subject matter." Submit outline and sample chapters for nonfiction; complete ms for fiction. Reports in 4-8 weeks. SASE.
Nonfiction: "Textbooks and books for the student of astrology; no specific religious denominations whatever, but religious books that will appeal to all people of all the world. Books that cover the wave of consciousness: radionics, color, music vibration, all topics revealing the ultimate unity of ALL. Top priority for positive-oriented books on these subjects. We will reject any material that is called 'entertainment astrology', that is, perpetuating the belief that astrology is fortune-telling. We are searching for academic astrological treatises on material such as astro-cartography, weather forcasting, minor aspects, etc." Recently published *Joy of Healing, To the Devil with Satan,* and *The Hero in the Horoscope*.

WALKER AND CO., 720 5th Ave., New York NY 10019. Editor-in-Chief: Richard Winslow. Managing Editor: Andrea Curley. Hardcover and paperback originals (90%) and reprints (10%). 10-12½-15% royalty or outright purchase; advance averages $1,000-2,500 "but could be higher or lower." Publishes 80 titles annually. Query or submit outline/synopsis and sample chapters. Submit samples of photos/illustrations to accompany ms. Photocopied submissions OK. SASE. Free book catalog.
Nonfiction: Publishes Americana; art; biography; business; cookbooks, cooking and foods; histories; hobbies; how-to; juveniles; medicine and psychiatry; multimedia material; music; nature; pets; psychology; recreation; reference; religious; self-help; sports; travel; and gardening books. Recently published *The New York Philharmonic Guide to the Symphony,* by E. Downs (music nonfiction); *The Santa Claus Book,* by Jones (nonfiction); and *Collapsing Universe,* by Isaac Asimov (nonfiction).
Fiction: Mystery; science fiction; suspense; gothics; and regency books.

FREDERICK WARNE & CO., INC., 101 Fifth Ave., New York NY 10003. Editor, Books for Young People: Margaret Klee Lichtenberg. Publishes juvenile hardcover originals. Offers 10%

royalty contract. Minimum advance is $500. Will consider photocopied submissions. No simultaneous submissions. Submit outline and sample chapters for nonfiction. Submit complete ms for fiction. Reports in 10 weeks. "Ms will not be considered unless accompanied by a correct-size S.A.S.E."
Juveniles: Hardcover trade books for children and young adults. Picture books (age 4 to 7), fiction and nonfiction for the middle reader (age 7 to 12) and young adults (ages 11 and up). Mss must combine a high-interest level with fine writing. Prefers to see fewer picture books and more submissions for 8 to 12-year-olds. Recently published *After Olympic Glory: The Live of Ten Outstanding Medalists,* by L. Bortstein (sports biography); and *Ghost of Summer,* by E. Bunting.

WATSON-GUPTILL PUBLICATIONS, 1515 Broadway, New York NY 10036. Publishes originals. 10-12½-15% royalty; usual advance is $1,000, but average varies, depending on author's reputation and nature of book. Published 47 titles last year. Address queries (followed by outlines and sample chapters) to Donald Holden, Editorial Director. Reports on queries within 10 days. Enclose return postage.
Art: Publishes art instruction books. Interested only in books of a how-to-do-it nature in any field of painting, crafts, design, etc. Also interested in biographies of painters, art history books, aesthetic appreciation. Length: open.

FRANKLIN WATTS, INC., 730 Fifth Avenue, New York, NY 10019. Vice-President, Editorial Director: Jeanne Vestal. Royalty schedule varies according to the type of book. Usual advance for a series title is $1,000. Single title varies according to reputation of author and type of book. Published 130 titles last year. Current catalog available on request. Query before submitting a nonfiction title. Prefers complete manuscript on fiction. Reports in approximately six weeks. Enclose return postage.
Juveniles: Publishes quality juveniles from pre-school through senior high. Especially interested in humorous novels and science fiction for children ages 9-12. Also looking for high interest/low reading level fiction, nonfiction, and contemporary teenage fiction. No historical fiction, please. Would suggest that writers check catalog before submitting nonfiction ideas. Recent titles include: *Mob, Inc.; Metric Puzzles* and *Vampires.*

WAYNE STATE UNIVERSITY PRESS, 5959 Woodward Ave., Detroit MI 48202. (313)577-4601. Editor-in-Chief: B.M. Goldman. Managing Editor: B. Woodward. Publishes hardcover and paperback originals. "Standard royalty schedule;" no advance. Published 25 titles in 1977, 30 in 1978. Reports in 1-6 months. SASE. Free book catalog.
Nonfiction: Publishes Americana, biography, economics, history, law; medicine and psychiatry; music, philosophy, politics, psychology, religious, and sociology books. Query first or submit outline/synopsis and sample chapters. "Do not send photos unless requested, or send photocopies." Recently published *Theodore Dreiser: A Selection of Uncollected Prose,* by D. Pizer (literature); and *Latin via Ovid: a First Course,* by Goldman/Nyenhuis.

WEBSTER DIVISION, McGraw-Hill Book Co., 1221 Ave. of the Americas, New York NY 10020. General Manager: Lawrence A. Walsh. Royalties vary. "Our royalty schedules are those of the industry, and advances are not commonly given." Photocopied submissions OK. Reports in 2-4 weeks. SASE.
Textbooks: Publishes school books, films, equipment and systems for elementary and secondary schools. Juveniles, social studies, science, language arts, foreign languages, the arts, mathematics. "Material is generally part of a series, system, or program done in connection with other writers, teachers, testing experts, et al. Material must be matched to the psychological age level, with reading achievement and other educational prerequisites in mind. Interested in a Basic Reading program, a Career Education program, a Guidance program, a Health program, and a Special Education program for the elementary schools."

WESTERN ISLANDS, 395 Concord Ave., Belmont MA 02178. Editor: John W. Robbins. Publishes hardcover and paperback originals (75%) and reprints (25%). Published 5 titles in 1977, 3 in 1978. 10% royalty on hardcover, 5% on paperback; no advance. Simultaneous and photocopied submissions OK. Reports in 2 months. SASE. Book catalog for SASE.
Nonfiction: "We are interested in conservative books on current events: economics, politics, contemporary history, etc. We are not interested in biographies, autobiographies (unless by a famous conservative), fiction, poetry, etc. Anti-communist books, if not overly autobiographical, are welcome." Query or submit complete ms. Recently published *To Covet Honor,* by H. Alexander; *F.D.N.Y.,* by G. Johnson; and *The Siecus Circle,* by C. Chambers.

WESTERN PRODUCER PRAIRIE BOOKS, Box 2500, Saskatoon, Saskatchewan, Canada S7K 2C4. Editor-in-Chief: Rob Sanders. Publishes hardcover and paperback originals (95%); and reprints (5%). Specializes in nonfiction historical works set in Western Canada by Western Canadian authors. 10% (of list price) royalty. Published 10 titles in 1977, 12 in 1978. Submit contact sheets, prints if illustrations are to accompany ms. Simultaneous submissions OK. Reports in 2-4 months. SASE. Free book catalog.
Nonfiction: Publishes history, nature, photography, biography, reference, economics, politics, cookbooks, cooking and foods books. Submit outline, synopsis and sample chapters. Recently published *Uphill All the Way,* by E. Jaques (autobiography); *Our West,* by B. Phillips; and *Cornerstone Colony,* by G. Macleven.

WESTERN PUBLISHING CO., INC., 1220 Mound Ave., Racine WI 53404. Publishes hardcover and paperback juvenile books only; originals and reprints. Mss purchased outright. Published approximately 95 titles last year. Complete ms may be sent for picture books; query with outline and sample chapter on all mss over 1,000 words. Address mss and query letters for picture books to Miss Betty Ren Wright; query letters for novels to William Larson. Mss should be typed, double-spaced, with SASE enclosed. Reports in 2-6 weeks.
Juveniles: Picture book lines include Whitman Tell-a-Tale books, Big Golden books, Little Golden books, Golden Play and Learn books, Golden Shape books, and Golden Touch and Feel books. Material should be concerned with familiar childhood experiences, early learning concepts, favorite subjects (animals, cars and trucks, play activities). Urban, suburban and rural settings welcome. Unless specifically indicated, books are planned to be read to children, but vocabulary should be simple enough for easy understanding and for young readers to handle themselves if they wish. "We are especially interested in stories about animals, humorous stories, and stories that emphasize concepts important to preschool-primary learning. We have board books and cloth books for children two and under; most of our picture books are intended for ages 3 to 6. While we are definitely interested in stories that combine fun and learning, we see too many mss that are forced or uninteresting because the writer has tried too hard to make them 'educational.' Also, we see many stories that are about children without being for children. We would encourage writers to consider always whether the story is genuinely meaningful to children. We are also interested in seeing stories about little girls that enlarge upon the position of women in our society. It is easy to turn out a 'message' story, and we do not want to do that, but we would like to publish stories in which girls play a wide variety of roles." Length for picture books: 200 to 800 words. Also publishes a limited number of novel-length hardcover books and story anthologies for ages 8-14. Length: 35,000 to 60,000 words. Should deal with subjects of genuine interest to pre-teens and early teens—mystery, adventure, science fiction and sports.

WESTERNLORE BOOKS, P.O. Box 41073, 5117 Eagle Rock Blvd., Los Angeles CA 90041. Editor: Paul D. Bailey. Pays standard royalties except in special cases. Query. Unsolicited mss returned. Reports in 60 days. Enclose return postage with query.
Americana: Publishes Western Americana of the scholarly and basically researched type. "Volumes fitting our Great West & Indian Series, American Survey Series, Ghost Town Series, or Desert Series." Republication of rare and out-of-print books. Scholarly studies of the great West. Length: 25,000 to 65,000 words.
Recent Titles: *Retracing the Butterfield Trail,* by G.A. Ahmerst (history); and *Mining Camps and Ghost Towns Along the Colorado,* by F. Lowe (history).

THE WESTMINSTER PRESS, 902 Witherspoon Bldg., Philadelphia PA 19107. (215)893-4423. Juvenile Editor: Barbara S. Bates. Publishes hardcover originals. Published 17 titles in 1977, 18 in 1978; will do 18 in 1979. Royalty and advance "vary with author's experience and credentials, and the amount of illustration needed." Photocopied submissions OK. Reports in 3 months. SASE. Book catalog for SASE.
Nonfiction: Juvenile only, for readers 8-14. Career; consumer education; ecology and nature; science and math resource; social studies resource; recreation and how-to; and sports and hobbies. Query or submit outline/synopsis and sample chapters. Recently published *A Horse In Your Backyard?,* by V.P. Clemens (pet/how-to); *Ms.–Architect,* by D.X. Fenten (career); and *Who Do You Think You Are?,* by S. Hilton (hobby/social studies resource).
Fiction: Juvenile only, for ages 8-14. Adventure; humor; mystery; family; science fiction; and suspense. No picture books or stories in verse. Submit outline/synopsis and sample chapters. Recently published *Never Mind Murder,* by F. Wosmek (mystery); *I Gotta Be Free,* by R. Hallman (suspense); and *What Are You Up To, William Thomas?*, by S. Newton (humor).

***WESTVIEW PRESS**, 5500 Central Ave., Boulder CO 80301. (303)444-3541. Publisher: F.A. Praeger. Executive Editor: Lynne Rienner. Hardcover and paperback originals (90%) and reprints (10%). Specializes in scholarly monographs or conference reports. Zero to 10% royalty, depending on marketing. Subsidy publishes a limited number of books. "Only in the case of top flight, scholarly materials for a limited market and which need to be priced low, or where the mss have unusual difficulties such as Chinese or Sanskrit characters. The usual quality standards of a top-flight university press apply and subsidies must be furnished by institutions and not individuals." Published 250 titles in 1977, 350 in 1978. Markets books by direct mail. State availability of photos and/or illustrations to accompany ms. Reports in 2-4 months. SASE. Free book catalog.
Nonfiction: Publishes art, business, economics, history, law, politics, psychology, reference, scientific, sociology, and textbooks. Query and submit sample chapters (Chicago *Manual of Style*). "We do not read unsolicited mss."

WHITAKER HOUSE, Pittsburgh and Colfax Sts., Springdale PA 15144. (412)274-4444. Editor: Victoria L. Mlinar. Paperback originals (80%) and reprints (20%). "We publish only Christian books, especially dealing with charismatic Christianity. Royalty of a straight percentage (6%) of the cover price of the book. Advance is made only under certain circumstances. Publishes about 12 titles annually. "We market books in Christian book stores and in rack-jobbing locations such as supermarkets and drug stores." Looking for teaching/testimonies; typed, double-spaced, about 200 pages in length. Send prints to illustrate ms. Simultaneous and photocopied submissions OK. Reports in about 2-4 weeks. SASE. Free book catalog.
Nonfiction: Publishes biography or autobiography (testimony of spirit-filled Christians; 60,000 words); how-to (how to move on in your Christian walk; 60,000 words); religious ("don't want heavy theology"; 60,000 words). "Testimonies of drug addicts or ex-convicts are somewhat overworked. Please note that we call our books 'teaching testimonies' because they give the author's life experiences as well as solid Christian teaching." Recently published *What You Say Is What You Get,* by D. Gossett (how-to); *Yesterday at the Seventh Hour,* by J. Hale (autobiography); *Freedom to Choose,* by E.J. Gruen (how-to).

WHITMORE PUBLISHING COMPANY, 35 Cricket Terrace, Ardmore PA 19003. Contact: Linda S. Peacock. Offers "standard royalty contract, profit-sharing contract, or outright purchase." Published 10 titles last year. Reports in 2 to 3 weeks. Send queries and sample chapters or poems. SASE.
General Nonfiction and Poetry: Publishing interest focused on books that will provide the reader with insight and techniques to manage his or her life more effectively. Interests include education, nutrition, community life, philosophy, self-improvement, family study and planning, career planning; explanations of significant science and technology not broadly understood. Recently published *In the Ashes: The Story of Lebanon,* by Gabriel; and *The Pink Elephant and Other Essays: Reflections of a Rational Man,* by Semisch.

THE WHITSTON PUBLISHING CO., Box 958, Troy NY 12181. (518)283-4363. Editorial Director: Stephen Goode. Publishes hardcover originals. Published 20 titles in 1977, 25 in 1978; will do 30 in 1979. 10-12½-15% royalty; no advance. Simultaneous and photocopied submissions OK. Reports in 8-10 weeks. SASE. Free book catalog.
Nonfiction: "We publish scholarly and critical books in the arts, humanities, and social sciences. We also publish reference books, bibliographies, indexes and checklists. We do not want author bibliographies in general unless they are unusual and unusually scholarly. We are, however, much interested in catalogs and inventories of library collections of individuals, such as the Robert Graves collection at Southern Illinois, etc." Query or submit complete ms. Recently published *Two Faces of Ionesco, A Collection of 15 Essays by and about Ionesco,* edited by R. Lamont/M. Friedman.

WILDERNESS PRESS, 2440 Bancroft Way, Berkeley CA 94704. (415)843-8080. Editorial Director: Thomas Winnett. Publishes paperback originals. Published 8 titles in 1977, 9 in 1978. 8-10% royalty; advance averages $200. Simultaneous and photocopied submissions OK. Reports in 2 weeks. SASE. Book catalog for SASE.
Nonfiction: "We publish books about the outdoors. So far, most of our books are trail guides for hikers and backpackers, but we will be publishing how-to books about the outdoors and personal adventures. The manuscript must be accurate. The author must research an area thoroughly in person. If he is writing a trail guide, he must walk all the trails in the area his book is about. The outlook must be strongly conservationist. The style must be appropriate for a

highly literate audience." Query, submit outline/synopsis and sample chapters, or complete ms. Recently published *Pacific Crest Trails,* by Schaffer et al (trail guide); *Huckleberry Country,* by Thompson/Thompson (wild food plant guide); and *Waxing for Cross-Country Skiing,* by Brady/Skjemstad (how-to manual).

JOHN WILEY & SONS, INC., 605 3rd Ave., New York NY 10016. (212)867-9800. Hardcover and paperback originals. 15% (of net receipts) royalty. Follow MLA Style Sheet. Simultaneous and photocopied submissions OK. Reports in 6 months. SASE. Free book catalog.
Nonfiction: Publishes college textbooks and professional reference titles in engineering, social science, business life sciences, politics, medicine and psychology. Query first or submit outline/synopsis and sample chapters. Recently published *Zero Base Budgeting,* by Pyhrr; and *Medical Botany,* by Lewis/Lewis.

WILLAMETTE MANAGEMENT ASSOCIATES, INC., 220 S.W. Alder St., Suite 203, Portland OR 97204. (503)224-6004. Query Editor: J. Michael Reid. Publishes paperback and hardcover originals. Offers royalty contract of 10 to 15% of net. Advance varies. "We will consider photocopy, but would like to know the track record of a copied ms. (Turned down texts no problem — if they fit our needs)." Query with outline and sample chapters or completed ms. Reports in 1 month. Enclose return postage.
Business: Interested in business investment books. "They should be technical and of current interest (timing) as well as of good long-range material. We might consider business-related titles."

WILSHIRE BOOK CO., 12015 Sherman Rd., N. Hollywood CA 91605. (213)875-1711. Editorial Director: Melvin Powers. Publishes paperback originals (50%) and reprints (50%). Publishes 50 titles/year. 5-6-7% royalty; "advance varies with nature of the book." Simultaneous and photocopied submissions OK. Reports in 2 weeks. SASE. Book catalog for SASE.
Nonfiction: Business; study and reference; calligraphy; cookery and herbs; gambling and poker; health; hobbies; horse racing; humor; hypnotism; Judaica; books for women; marriage, sex and parenthood; metaphysics and occult; self-help and inspirational; sports; tennis; pets; and horse instruction. "Main interest is in self-help, psychological, and inspirational books. We are also especially interested in books dealing with how to run a successful small business or mail order business." Query. Recently published *Calligraphy,* by K. Jaffares (art); *Exuberance,* by P. Kurtz, Ph.D.; and *Manual of Horsemanship,* by H. Black.

WINCHESTER PRESS, 205 E. 42 St., New York NY 10017. (212)661-7210. Managing Editor: Jock Bartlett. Hardcover originals. 10-12½-15% royalty; $1,500 average advance. Published 28 titles in 1977, 30 in 1978. "Submit sample photos and some idea of total number projected for final book." Simultaneous and photocopied submissions OK. Reports in 3 months. SASE. Free book catalog.
Nonfiction: Main interest is in outdoor sports, crafts and related subjects. Publishes cookbooks, cooking and foods (if related to their field); how-to (sports and sporting equipment); pets (hunting dogs and horses); recreation (outdoor), sports (hunting, fishing, etc.); and technical (firearms). Submit outline/synopsis and sample chapters. Recently published *American Shotgun Design and Performance,* by L.R. Wallack; and *Wildlife Watcher's Handbook,* by F.T. Hanenkrat.

WINTERGREEN PUBLISHING CO., 40 Shallmar Blvd., Toronto, Ontario, Canada M6C 2J9. Editor-in-Chief: Ted Kosoy. Hardcover and paperback originals. Specializes in travel guides. 7½% royalty on paperbacks; 10% on hardcover; $1,500-2,000 average advance. Published 3 titles in 1977 and 1978; will do 5 in 1979. Markets books through bookstores. State availability of photos and/or illustrations. Simultaneous and photocopied submissions OK. Reports in 1-2 months. SASE. Free book catalog for SASE.
Nonfiction: Publishes books on recreation and travel. Submit outline/synopsis and sample chapters.
Recent Titles: *Kosoy's Travel Guide to Canada,* by Kosoy; *A Budget Guide to Florida;* and *A Guide to the Orient and the Pacific.*

***ALAN WOFSY FINE ARTS**, 150 Green St., San Francisco CA 94111. Publishes hardcover and paperback originals (75%); hardcover reprints (25%). Specializes in art reference books, specifically catalogs of graphic artists; bibliographies related to fine presses and the art of the book; original, illustrated books. Payment usually made on a flat fee basis, which begins at $200. Subsidy publishes 15% of books "where a very high quality of reproduction is necessary for a

very limited market, and we feel the book should be published''. No advance. Publishes 6 titles annually. SASE. Reports in 2-4 weeks. Free book catalog.
Nonfiction: Publishes reference books on art and photography. Query.

WOLF HOUSE BOOKS, Box 209-K, Cedar Springs MI 49319. (616)696-2772. Editorial Director: Richard Weiderman. Publishes hardcover and paperback originals (50%) and reprints (50%). Published 3 titles in 1978; will do 5 in 1979. 10% royalty; no advance. Simultaneous and photocopied submissions OK. Reports in 4 weeks. SASE. Book catalog for SASE.
Nonfiction: Literary criticism and biography and other studies (e.g. bibliography, etc.) on Jack London. Query. Recently published *Alien Worlds of Jack London,* by D.L. Walker; *White Logic: Jack London's Short Stories,* by J.I. McClintock; and *Jack London at Yale,* by A. Irvine.

WOODBRIDGE PRESS PUBLISHING CO., P.O. Box 6189, Santa Barbara CA 93111. Editor-in-Chief: Howard B. Weeks. Publishes hardcover and paperback originals. Standard royalty contract. Rarely gives an advance. Published 8 titles in 1977. Will consider photocopied submissions. Query first. Returns rejected material as soon as possible. Reports on material accepted for publication in 3 months. Enclose return postage with query.
General Nonfiction: "How-to books on personal health and well-being. Should offer the reader valuable new information or insights on anything from recreation to diet to mental health that will enable him to achieve greater personal fulfillment, with emphasis on that goal. Should minimize broad philosophy and maximize specific, useful information." Length: Books range from 96 to 300 pages. Also publishes cookbooks and gardening books. Recent titles include *The Oats, Peas, Beans and Barley Cookbook* (Cottrell), *More Food From Your Garden* (Mittleider) and *Butterflies in My Stomach* (Taylor).

THE WRITER, INC., 8 Arlington St., Boston MA 02116. Editor: A.S. Burack. Publishes hardcover originals. Standard royalty schedule. Advance varies. Published 5 titles last year. Catalog on request. Query first. Reports within three weeks. Enclose return postage.
Nonfiction: Books on writing for writers. Length: open.

WRITER'S DIGEST BOOKS, 9933 Alliance Rd., Cincinnati OH 45242. (513)984-0717. Publishes hardcover originals. Trade publisher for books about writing, art, crafts, songwriting, and photography. Usual royalty contract: 10% of net; advance averages $1,500. Published 6 titles in 1978 (not counting market books); will publish 10-12 titles in 1979. Books sold in bookstores and by direct mail. Query with complete chapter outline. Simultaneous (if so advised) and photocopied submissions OK. Reports in 1 month. SASE or enclose return postage. Book catalog for SASE.
Nonfiction: Wants lively, up-to-date how-to treatments on all writing genre, for pros and beginners as well. Also books about photography with emphasis on marketing, not technique. Authors should be established, and be able to write from experience — while not merely holding forth. Style should be well researched, instructive, yet conversational and anecdotal. Recently published *The Craft of Interviewing,* by J. Brady; *Magazine Writing Today,* by J. Kelly; *Law and the Writer,* edited by K. Polking/L. Meranus; and 5 hardcover annuals: *Writer's Market, Artist's Market, Craftworker's Market, Songwriter's Market,* and *Photographer's Market.*

YALE UNIVERSITY PRESS, 92A Yale Station, New Haven CT 06520. Editor-in-Chief: Edward Tripp. Executive Editor: Jane Isay. Publishes hardcover and paperback originals (96%) and reprints (4%). Published 85 titles in 1977, 90 in 1978; will do 90 in 1979. 5-10% royalty; no advance. Photocopied submissions OK. Reports in 2-3 months. SASE. Book catalog for SASE.
Nonfiction: Works of original scholarship in the humanities, social sciences and hard sciences. No fiction, cookbooks or popular nonfiction. Query or submit outline/synopsis and sample chapters. Recently published *Caught in the Web of Words,* by K.M.E. Murray; *Democracy in Plural Societies,* by A. Lijphart (political science); and *The Rise of American Philosophy,* by Kublick.
Poetry: "The only contemporary poetry we publish is the Yale Series of Younger Poets. Competition for this series is open only during the month of February; manuscripts received at other times of the year will be returned unopened. There is a $5 submission fee, which must accompany the manuscript submitted. A competitor is allowed to submit 1 manuscript in a year, from 48-64 pages long, with no more than 1 poem per page. A title page, table of contents, and page of biographical information (including a listing of previous publications) should be included. The competition is open to any American writer under 40 at the time of submission who has not published a volume of poetry." Submit complete ms "as per rules."

ZONDERVAN PUBLISHING HOUSE, 1415 Lake Drive S.E., Grand Rapids MI 49506. (616)698-6900. Managing Editor: J.E. Ruark. Textbook Editor: Paul Hillman. Publishes hardcover and paperback originals and reprints. Offers standard minimum book contract of 10%. Advances paid only on assigned projects. Published 70 titles last year. Will consider photocopied submissions. Query first with outline and sample chapters. Reports in 7 to 9 weeks. SASE.
Religious Nonfiction: For all ages. Material should be aimed at the evangelical Christian reader. Christian adult trade books, Bible study, biography, marriage and family, self-help and how-to, sports, and textbooks. Conservative and biblical. Also textbooks aimed for the Bible college or seminary market. Apologetics, applied Christianity, biblical language books, biblical studies, Christian education, communications, contemporary church, historical studies, missions, pastoral theology, psychology and counseling. Length: 12,000 to 100,000 words.

Subsidy Book Publishers

The following listings are for book publishing companies who are totally subsidy publishers, meaning they do no standard trade publishing, and will publish a work only if the author is willing to underwrite the entire amount of the venture. This can be costly, and may run into thousands of dollars, usually returning less than 25% of the initial investment.

Read any literature or contracts carefully and thoroughly, being sure that all conditions of the venture (binding, editing, promotion, number of copies to be printed, etc.) are spelled out specifically.

For more information on subsidy publishing, write to us asking for the reprint "Does It Pay to Pay to Have It Published?" Address to *Payin' For It Editor,* 9933 Alliance Rd., Cincinnati OH 45242. Enclose SASE.

Dorrance and Company, 35 Cricket Terrace, Ardmore PA 19003.

Exposition Press, 900 S. Oyster Bay Rd., Hicksville NY 11801.

Helios Publishing Co., Inc., 150 W. 28th St., New York NY 10001.

Mojave Books, 7040 Darby Ave., Reseda CA 91335.

Vantage Press, 516 W. 34th St., New York NY 10001.

Company Publications

The company publications field began in the United States in 1840 with the *Lowell Offering*, a modest house organ which printed news of the women employed by the Lowell Cotton Mills of Massachusetts. From this beginning was spawned one of the largest publishing ventures in the country today, totaling nearly 20,000 publications. Conservative estimations place the figure for the monies invested in this field at a *billion* dollars per year. In a field of this size and magnitude, freelance opportunities abound.

Company publications are those magazines, newspapers, newsletters and tabloids that are sponsored by a particular company to keep employees, customers and interested parties informed of the activities of that company. Basically, there are six kinds of company publications: *employee magazines* published to keep employees abreast of company policy and the goings-on of their co-workers; *customer magazines* edited to remind customers of the desirability of owning or using that company's products or services; *stockholder or corporate magazines* put out for the shareholder keeping him informed of financial or policy matters; *sales magazines* telling the company's field representatives how to better push their wares; *dealer magazines* published to maintain open channels of communication between manufacturer and independent dealers; and *technical service magazines* sponsored by companies to whom technical data is important in the use and application of products. A single company may publish any or all of these types, enlarging their need for well-written information regarding their products, employees and services.

What interests the editors of these publications? The trick to successful (meaning selling) writing in the field is the word *company*. These magazines are published for the sole purpose of performing a useful service to the sponsor, be that service in an *internal* publication (which is a controlled circulation magazine distributed only among the employees of a company) or an *external* publication (published for the public relations benefits to the company and circulated among the customers and users of that company's products or services). These publications vary in emphasis, some giving more space to company product-related information, and others highlighting the interesting activities or unique doings of company personnel. Manuscripts lacking a strong company tie-in, or derogatory material about the company or its goods are worthless to company publication editors.

Ideas for writing for company publications are as numerous as the number of companies that publish magazines. Stay alert for new businesses or unique applications of company's products in your own home town. Quite often, an out-of-the-ordinary use of a company's product is the way to a sure sale. Due to the limited nature of the publication, and the fact that editors have run stories on the use of their company's goods in all the conventional ways, an article about some merchant in your town who uses products in an offbeat manner will catch the editor's eye.

Photos are a must for most company publications. When doing your photo planning, be sure to ensure that your photos contain concrete references to the company's product. Show off the product in a manner which compliments its qualities. Remember, the story is about the *product* and its use, not the store owner or manager who uses it.

Company publications aren't the "puffy" magazines they were years ago. Editors are looking for articles that do more than praise the merits of their companies. They want well-developed, lively pieces that will make the reader more aware of aspects of the firm other than his own job. Writing for these publications can be profitable (paying fairly competitive rates in comparison with other publishing fields) and rewarding. The freelancer who can turn in polished copy to these busy editors may find himself more often than not on the company's payroll.

ACF HORIZONS, ACF Industries, Corporate Communications, 620 N 2nd St., St. Charles MO 63301. (314)723-9600. Editor: William W. Wallace. For "employees and the public." Quarterly. Circ. 18,000. Buys "non-exclusive" rights. Pays on publication. Free sample copy. Query first. Reports in 1 month. SASE.
Nonfiction, Photos, and Fillers: "Articles related to the products and operations of the divisions of ACF Industries: railroad equipment, automotive fuel systems, valves and fittings. Material must have ACF tie-in." Length: "the shorter the better." Pays $5 minimum. Buys 8x10 single-weight b&w glossies.

AMERICAN GENERAL JOURNAL, American General Life Insurance Co., Box 1931, Houston TX 77001. Editor-in-Chief: Richard H. Cutrer. 50% freelance written. Emphasizes life and health insurance for a "very articulate, conservative, family oriented audience, age 30-50, interested in hunting, fishing, golf, and people." Monthly magazine; 32 pages. Estab. 1964. Circ. 2,500. Pays on publication. Buys all rights. Submit seasonal/holiday material 3 months in advance of issue date. SASE. Reports in 4 weeks. Free sample copy and writer's guidelines; mention *Writer's Market* in request.
Nonfiction: "Mostly sales-oriented material." Exposé (impact of life and health insurance on US and world economy); How-to (sell life insurance, avoid call reluctance, how to deal with rejection, find prospects, use spare time wisely); general interest (any well-written, interesting article—especially behavior related—on life and health insurance); historical (how and why life and health insurance got started, when, what course it has taken or will take); and profile (we will assign a feature story on one of our agents in a specific region). No material on products or *great* salesmen. Buys 12 mss/year. Query with clips of previously published work and a 100-word biography. Length: 1,000-3,000 words. Pays 5¢/word.
Photos: State availability of photos. Pays $10-20 for 8x10 b&w glossy photos with borders.

ASHLAND NOW, Ashland Oil, Inc., Box 391, Ashland KY 41101. (606)329-3070. Publications Manager: Don Mayne. 30% freelance written. Emphasizes petroleum, chemical, construction, exploration and coal for an audience of employees, shareholders, opinion makers, and community leaders. Quarterly magazine; 24 pages. Estab. May 1977. Circ. 100,000. Pays on acceptance. Buys all rights. Phone queries OK. Submit seasonal/holiday material 2 months in advance of issue date. Previously published submissions OK. Reports in 2 weeks.
Nonfiction: How-to; general interest; historical; personal opinion; and technical. Buys 8 mss/year. Query. Length: 500-1,500 words. Pays $250-1,200.

BAROID NEWS BULLETIN, Box 1675, Houston TX 77001. Editor-in-Chief: Marvin L. Brown. Editorial Assistant: Virginia Myers. 50% freelance written. Emphasizes the petroleum industry for a substantial cross section of ages, education and interests although most readers are employed by the energy industries. Quarterly magazine; 36 pages. Estab. 1948. Circ. 20,000. Pays on acceptance. Buys first North American serial rights. Submit seasonal/holiday material 1 year in advance of issue date. SASE. Reports in 3 weeks. Free sample copy and writer's guidelines.
Nonfiction: General interest and historical. Buys 12 mss/year. Submit complete ms. Length: 1,000-3,000 words. Pays 8-10¢/word.
Photos: "Photos may be used in the publication, or as reference for illustration art." Submit b&w prints. Offers no additional payment for photos accepted with ms. Captions preferred. Buys first North American serial rights.

BARTER COMMUNIQUE, Full Circle Marketing Corp., Box 2527, Sarasota FL 33578. (813)349-2242. Editor-in-Chief: Robert J. Murely. Emphasizes bartering for radio and TV station owners, cable TV, newspaper and magazine publishers and select travel and advertising agency presidents. Semiannual tabloid; 32-40 pages. Estab. 1975. Circ. 30,000. Pays on publication. Rights purchased vary with author and material. Phone queries OK. Simultaneous, photocopied and previously published submissions OK. SASE. Reports in 4 weeks. Free sample copy and writer's guidelines.
Nonfiction: Articles on "barter" (trading products, good, and services), primarily travel and advertising. Length: 1,000 words. "Would like to see travel mss on southeast U.S. and the Bahamas, and unique articles on media of all kinds. Include photos where applicable." Pays $30-50.

THE BEAVER, 77 Main St., Winnipeg, MB, Canada. Editor: Helen Burgess. Publication of Hudson's Bay Company for "mature students and adults". Estab. 1920. Quarterly. Circ. 40,000. Buys all rights. Buys about 30 mss/year. Pays on acceptance. Free sample copy. Submit seasonal material at least 6 months in advance. Reports in 2 weeks. "Content is quite specialized; suggest query first."
Nonfiction and Photos: "Well-illustrated, authentic articles on life in the Arctic and areas of early Hudson's Bay Company activities; historical and present-day fur trade, nature subjects, Indians, and Eskimos. Accurate information must be presented in a readable way. No more articles on Arctic canoe trips." Buys informational articles, personal experience pieces, profiles, and historical articles. Length: 1,000-4,000 words. Pays minimum 7¢ a word. Photos purchased with mss; captions required. Pays minimum $7 for 8x10 b&w glossies. Pays minimum $10 for 35mm or 4¼x4¼ color slides.

THE BLOUNT BANNER, Blount Brothers Corp., 4520 Executive Park Dr., Box 949, Montgomery AL 36111. (205)272-8000. Editor-in-Chief: Victor R. McLean. Associate Editor: Phoebe Bylsma. Emphasizes construction and engineering for a business and professional audience. Bimonthly magazine; 24-28 pages. Estab. 1958. Circ. 5,000. Pays on publication. Buys all rights. Phone queries OK. Photocopied submissions OK. Reports in 3 weeks. Free sample copy; mention *Writer's Market* in request.
Nonfiction: Articles on company projects and photo features on project sites and company projects. Query. Length: 1,500-2,500 words. Pays $50-250.
Photos: "All features in our publication require photographic coverage." State availability of photos. Pays $5-50 for 5x7 b&w glossy prints; $25-125 for 35mm color transparencies. Captions required. Buys all rights. Model release required.
How To Break In: "We look forward to expanding our magazine in the future—possibly going to a larger format and requiring articles of more depth and complexity than we now feature. We may have more need in the future of freelance material."

BUSINESS ON WHEELS, Box 13208, Phoenix AZ 85002. (602)264-1579. Editor: Frederick H. Kling. "External house organ of Goodyear Tire and Rubber Company for distribution to owners and operators of truck fleets, both common carrier trucking systems and trucks used in connection with businesses of various types." Quarterly. Not copyrighted. Pays on acceptance. "Stories on assignment only. We like to choose our own subjects for case history stories." Query first. Enclose SASE.
Nonfiction and Photos: "Freelance writers and photographers (especially writer-photographer teams or individuals) are invited to send in their qualifications for assignment of articles on truck-fleet operators in their territory. Pays from $250-300, plus expenses, for complete editorial-photographic coverage, additional for color, if used."

THE CARAVANNER, 600 S. Commonwealth Ave., Los Angeles CA 90005. Contact: Editor. For persons in the 30-60 year age class; retired or semi-retired who have expressed a definite interest in the Airstream make of travel trailer. Publication of Airstream, a Division of Beatrice Foods Co., Chicago IL. Newspaper; 8 pages. Estab. 1954. Circ. 450,000. Not copyrighted. Pays on acceptance. Free sample copy. No simultaneous submissions. Returns rejected material in 2 to 3 weeks. Reports on material in 3 to 4 weeks "unless I'm on vacation." Query first. SASE.
Nonfiction: "Interesting uses of the Airstream make of travel trailers. Material must be entirely factual and not exaggerated, but upbeat. Writer must know what we usually print in our pages. We're really looking for truth; sharp analysis. The recreational vehicle, of which a travel trailer is one kind, has really encouraged or engendered a new life style in modern America —I'd like to see that examined." Personal experience, interview, profile, nostalgia, travel, and spot news. Length: 250 to 2,500 words. Usually pays $50 to $150.
Photos: Purchased with accompanying ms with no additional payment. Photos generally required with ms. Pays $5 minimum if photos are exceptional, and without accompanying ms. 8x10 b&w. Captions required.

CATERPILLAR WORLD, Caterpillar Tractor Co., 100 NE Adams AB1D, Peoria IL 61629. (309)675-4724. Editor-in-Chief: Tod Watts. 25-40% freelance written. Emphasizes "anything of interest about Caterpillar people, plants, or products. The magazine is distributed to 100,000 Caterpillar people and friends worldwide. It's printed in French, English, and Portuguese. Reader's ages, interests and education vary all over the map." Quarterly magazine; 32 pages. Estab. 1963. Circ. 100,000. Pays on acceptance. Buys one-time rights in 3 languages. Phone queries OK. "We rarely use seasonal or holiday material. All material has at least a 3 month lag time." Simultaneous and previously published submissions OK. Reports in 4 weeks. Free sample copy and writer's guidelines.

Nonfiction: "Everything must have a Caterpillar tie. It doesn't have to be strong, but it has to be there." How-to (buy one piece of equipment and become a millionaire, etc.); general interest (anything that may be of interest to Cat people worldwide); humor (it's hard to find something humorous yet interesting to an international audience; we'd like to see it, however); interview (with any appropriate person: contractor, operator, legislator, etc.); new product (large projects using Cat equipment; must have human interest); personal experience (would be interesting to hear from an equipment operator/writer); photo feature (on anything of interest to Cat people; should feature people as well as product); and profile (of Cat equipment users, etc.). "We don't want anything that has not been read and approved by the subjects of the article. Their written approval is a must." Buys 10 mss/year. Query. Length: "Whatever the story is worth." Pays $200 minimum.

Photos: "The only articles we accept without photos are those obviously illustrated by artwork." State availability of photos. Pays $25 minimum for b&w photos; $50 minimum for color. Submit contact sheets or negatives. Captions required; "at least who is in the pix and what they're doing." Buys one-time rights in 3 languages. Model release required.

How To Break In: "Best way to get story ideas is to stop in at local Cat dealers and ask about big sales, events, etc."

CHANNELS MAGAZINE, Northwestern Bell Telephone Co., 100 S. 19th St., Omaha NE 68102. Editor: G.T. Metcalf. For top level executives in Iowa, Minnesota, Nebraska, North and South Dakota. Quarterly magazine. Estab. 1966. Circ. 47,000. Pays on acceptance. Buys all rights, but may reassign following publication. SASE. Reports in 1 month.

Nonfiction: Wants mss designed to keep executives up to date on new developments and techniques in business communications such as WATS, data transmission, time-shared computers, industrial television. Also uses occasional general interest features on sports, hobbies, personalities, events and points of interest in the five states covered. "Writing must be good and it must be tight." Length: 500-1,500 words. Query. Pays $150 minimum.

CIBA-GEIGY JOURNAL, 4002 Basel, Switzerland. Editor: Stanley Hubbard. For "employees of Ciba-Geigy, together with 'opinion leaders,' customers, educational institutions, etc., in most English-speaking countries." Estab. 1971. Circ. 27,000. Rights purchased vary with author and material; may buy all rights, but will reassign rights to author after publication. Buys 4 to 6 mss a year. Pays on publication. Will send a sample copy to a writer on request. Will consider photocopied submissions. Submit seasonal material 5 months in advance. Reports in 4 weeks. Query first.

Nonfiction and Photos: "Popularized scientific and technical presentations, international cooperation subjects, regional and historical contributions related to group activities, human interest with product or operational tie-in. The approach should be literate; no writing down. The internationalism of our company is the basic determining factor — we are interpreting from continent to continent rather than talking to a homogeneous, neatly defined readership." Buys company related informational articles, think pieces, photo features, and technical articles. Length: 500 to 3,000 words. Pays minimum of $100. Photos purchased with mss; captions required. Pays $10.

THE COMPASS, Mobil Sales and Supply Corp., 150 E. 42nd St., New York NY 10017. Editor-in-Chief: R. Gordon MacKenzie. 80% freelance written. Emphasizes marine or maritime activities for the major international shipowners and ship operators. Quarterly magazine; 40 pages. Estab: 1920. Circ. 25,000. Pays on acceptance. Buys one-time rights. Submit seasonal/holiday material 1 year in advance of issue date. Simultaneous, photocopied and previously published submissions OK. SASE. Reports in 2 weeks. Free sample copy.

Nonfiction: Marine material only. General interest; humor; historical; nostalgia; new product; personal experience; and technical. No travelogues. Buys 20 mss/year. Query or submit complete ms. Length: 2,000-4,000 words. Pays $125-250.

Photos: Purchased with accompanying ms. Submit 5x7 or larger b&w prints or 35mm color transparencies. No additional payment for photos accepted with ms. Captions preferred. Buys one-time rights. Model release required.

Fiction: Marine or sea stories. Adventure; experimental; historical; humorous; mystery; science fiction; and suspense. No travel tales. Buys 20 mss/year. Query or submit complete ms. Length: 2,000-4,000 words. Pays $150-250.

CORVETTE NEWS, 2-129 General Motors Bldg., Detroit MI 48202. For Corvette owners worldwide. Bimonthly. Circ. 265,000. Buys all rights. Pays on acceptance. Free sample copy and editorial guidelines. Query first. SASE.
Nonfiction and Photos: "Articles must be of interest to this audience. Subjects considered include: (1) Technical articles dealing with engines, paint, body work, suspension, parts searches, etc. (2) Competition, 'Vettes vs. 'Vettes, or 'Vettes vs. others. (3) Profiles of Corvette owners/drivers. (4) General interest articles, such as the unusual history of a particular early model Corvette, and perhaps its restoration; one owner's do-it-yourself engine repair procedures, maintenance procedures; Corvettes in unusual service; hobbies involving Corvettes; sports involving Corvettes. (5) Road hunts. (6) Special Corvette events such as races, drags, rallies, concourse, gymkhanas, slaloms. (7) Corvette club activities." Length: 800 to 2,400 words. Pays $50 to $500, including photos illustrating article. Color transparencies or b&w negatives required. Pays additional fee of $35 for cover shot which is selected from photos furnished with article used in that issue.

CREDITHRIFTALK, CREDITHRIFT Financial, Box 59, Evansville IN 47701. (812)464-6638. Editor-in-Chief: Gregory E. Thomas. Emphasizes consumer finance. All readers are employees of CREDITHRIFT Financial or one of its financial or insurance subsidiaries, age range 18-65, with most in the 25-45 bracket. Most are high school grads with one year of college, interested in company advancement. Monthly magazine; 12-16 pages. Estab. December 1937. Circ. 3,000. Pays on acceptance. Not copyrighted. Phone queries OK. Submit seasonal/holiday material 3 months in advance of issue date. Simultaneous, photocopied and previously published submissions OK. Reports in 2 weeks. Free sample copy.
Nonfiction: Interview (must be with company employee; subject need not be limited to consumer finance and could center on employee's personal experience, hobby, volunteer work, etc.); personal opinion; photo feature (employee engaged in a unique activity); profile (employee); and finance industry trends. Query., Length: 800-3,000 words. Pays $35 minimum.
Photos: State availability of photos. Pays $5 minimum for b&w photos; submit contact sheet. Captions preferred. Buys one-time rights. Model release required "in some cases where a non-employee is included in the photo."

EUA SPECTRUM, EUA Service Corp., Box 212, Lincoln RI 02865. (401)333-1400. Editor: Jerry Campbell. Monthly. Circ: 2,500. Pays on publication. Not copyrighted. Submit seasonal or holiday material 2 months in advance. SASE. Reports in 4-6 weeks.
Nonfiction: How-to articles, humor, think pieces, new product coverage; photo and travel and safety articles. Length: open. Pays $10-50.
Photos: No additional payment for b&w glossies purchased with mss.

THE ENTHUSIAST, 3700 W. Juneau, Milwaukee WI 53208. (414)342-4680. Editor: Bob Klein. 50% freelance written. Published by Harley-Davidson Motor Co., Inc. for "motorcycle riders of all ages, education, and professions." Estab. 1916. Circ. 150,000. Quarterly magazine. Not copyrighted. Pays on publication. Will send a sample copy to a writer on request. Write for copy of guidelines for writers. Will consider photocopied submissions. Submit seasonal material 2 months in advance. Reports in 4 weeks. Query or submit complete ms. Enclose SASE.
Nonfiction and Photos: "Stories on motorcycling—humor, technical, racing, touring, adventures, competitive events. All articles should feature Harley-Davidson products and not mention competitive products. We do not want stories concerning sex, violence, or anything harmful to the image of motorcycling. We use travel stories featuring Harley-Davidson motorcycles, which must be illustrated with good quality photos of the motorcycle and travelers with scenic background taken on the trip. Also needed are stories of off-road usage, e.g., scrambles, racing, motocross, trail riding, or any other unusual usage." Informational articles, how-to's, personal experience articles, interviews, profiles, inspirational pieces, humor, historical articles, photo features, travel articles, and technical articles. Length: 3,000 words. Pays 5¢ "per published word, or as previously agreed upon." Photos purchased with mss and without mss; captions optional. Uses "quality b&w or color 4x5 prints or larger." Pays $7.50 to $15.
Fiction: "Good short stories with the image of clean motorcycling fun. No black leather jacket emphasis." Buys adventure and humorous stories. Length: 3,000 words maximum. Pays 5¢ "per published word, or as previously agreed upon."
Fillers: Short humor. Length: open. Pays $15.

FAMILY MAGAZINE, General Mills, 9200 Wayzata Blvd., Minneapolis MN 55440. Editorial Director: Syl Jones. Emphasizes plant and subsidiary company activities for employees of the corporation at every level from the president to workers in the plant. Quarterly magazine; 24 pages. Estab. 1977. Circ. 40,000. Pays on acceptance. Buys all rights. Submit seasonal/holiday

material 6 months in advance of issue date. Photocopied and previously published submissions OK. SASE. Reports in 6 weeks. Free sample copy.
Nonfiction: General interest; humor; historical; new product; and technical (for Progress Thru Research). Query. Length: 2,500 words maximum. Pays $50-250.
Photos: State availability of photos. Pays $10-50 for 8x10 b&w glossies. Captions required. Buys all rights. Model release required.

THE FLYING A, Aeroquip Corp., 300 S. East Ave., Jackson MI 49203. (517)787-8121. Editor-in-Chief: Wayne D. Thomas. 20% freelance written. Emphasizes Aeroquip customers and products. Quarterly magazine; 24 pages. Estab. 1949. Circ. 32,000. Pays on acceptance. Buys all rights. Phone queries OK. Simultaneous submissions OK. SASE. Reports in 1 month. Free sample copy; mention *Writer's Market* in request.
Nonfiction: General interest (feature stories with emphsis on free enterprise, business-related articles); interview (by assignment only); and photo feature (by assignment only). Buys 1 ms/issue. Query. Length: 1-4 printed pages. Pays $100 minimum.
Photos: "Photos are generally by specific assignment only."
Fillers: Business; economy; and educational. Pays $25.

HOBART WELDWORLD, Hobart Brothers Co., Troy OH 45273. (513)339-6509. Editor: Daniel Lea. For "men and women with engineering degrees or technical education who are practicing a technical profession related to welding fabrication or who have moved into manufacturing management posts." Estab. 1941. Quarterly. Circ. 50,000. Usually buys first rights only. Buys "a few" mss a year. Pays on publication. Will send a sample copy to a writer on request. Will consider photocopied submissions. Reports in 1 month. Query first or submit complete ms. Enclose SASE.
Nonfiction and Photos: "Technical articles on arc welding applications. The writer should submit items only about exotic or unusual applications, give full technical information, and describe the benefits of equipment or process for the application as compared with other welding methods. Give figures, if possible. Unless a specific product benefit is involved, we worry about the application and let the product references come as they may. We're interested in coverage of big construction projects, in which welding plays a major part." Length: 300 to 1,000 words. Pays $50 minimum. Mss must be accompanied by photos illustrating the application. Buys color negatives or transparencies, only. Pays $20 minimum each.
How To Break In: "We are trying to upgrade our photos as to artistic quality, impact, and information value, and will be impressed by submissions which help do this."

INDUSTRIAL PROGRESS, Box 13208, Phoenix AZ 85002. (602)264-1579. Editor: Frederick H. Kling. External house organ of Goodyear Tire and Rubber Company, for "executives, management, and professional men (designers, engineers, etc.) in all types of industry." Bimonthly. Not copyrighted. Pays on acceptance. SASE.
Nonfiction and Photos: Male-interest features: hobbies, sports, novelty, mechanical, do-it-yourself, personalities, adventure, etc. Must be strongly photographic. Some color features used. Pays from $25-50 for a single photo caption item to $150 for full-length features (up to 1,000 words) with 4 or 5 b&w photos; up to $250 for full-length color features.

INLAND, The Magazine of the Middle West, Inland Steel Co., 30 W. Monroe St., Chicago IL 60603. (312)346-0300. Managing Editor: Sheldon A. Mix. 25% freelance written. Emphasizes steel products, services and company personnel. Quarterly magazine; 24 pages. Estab. 1953. Circ. 12,000. Pays on acceptance. Buys one-time rights. Submit seasonal/holiday material at least a year in advance. Simultaneous submissions OK. SASE. Reports in 6-8 weeks. Free sample copy.
Nonfiction: Articles, essays, humorous commentaries, pictorial essays. "We like well-done individuality. Half of each issue deals with staff-written steel subjects; half with widely ranging nonsteel matter. Articles and essays related somehow to Midwest (basically Illinois, Wisconsin, Minnesota, Michigan, Missouri, Iowa, Indiana, Ohio) in such subject areas as history, folklore, sports, humor, the seasons, current scene generally; nostalgia and reminiscence if appeal is broad enough. But subject less important than treatment. Encourage individuality, thoughtful writing, fresh ideas, and approaches. Please don't send slight, rehashed historical pieces or any articles of purely local interest." Personal experience, profile, inspirational, humor, historical, think articles, nostalgia, personal opinion, photo articles. Length: 1,200 to 5,000 words, but this may vary. Pays $200 minimum.
Photos: Purchased with or without mss. Captions required. "Payment for pictorial essay same as for text feature."

JD JOURNAL, Deere & Co., John Deere Rd., Moline IL 61265. (309)752-4105. Editor-in-Chief: John J. Gerstner. 35% freelance written. For employees, retirees, and selected outside persons. Quarterly magazine; 28 pages. Estab. 1972. Circ. 100,000. Pays on acceptance. Not copyrighted. Simultaneous and photocopied submissions OK. Reports in 2 weeks. Free sample copy and writer's guidelines.
Nonfiction: Humor; interview; new product; nostalgia; personal experience; personal opinion; photo feature; profile; and travel. "All articles must be strongly related to John Deere and its employees. Within this limit, the mix of stories can be broad, ranging from what employees do after hours to features on new products." Buys 12 mss/year. Send clips of previously published work. Length: 40-150 lines, 75 characters wide. Pays $50-600.
Photos: Wayne Burkart, art director. Submit contact sheet or negatives. Pays $10-75 for b&w photos and 35mm color transparencies. Captions preferred. Buys all rights, but may reassign following publication.

LLOYD'S LISTENING POST, Box 5867, Rockford IL 61125. (815)399-6970. Editor: David M. Mathieu. For persons age 50 and over. Publication of Lloyd Hearing Aid Corp. Tabloid; 8-12 pages. Estab. 1972. Quarterly. Circ. 200,000. Not copyrighted. Buys about 25 mss per year. Pays on acceptance. Free sample copy. Will consider photocopied and simultaneous submissions. Reports in 2 weeks. Submit only complete ms. Enclose SASE.
Nonfiction and Photos: Uses "self-help; inspirational; stories on active and happy people; solutions to senior citizens' problems; nostalgia; travel; profile; how-to and informational. Keep material positive — and short. We use short features and wide variety of subjects in each issue." Would like to see mss on social security problems; travel (places and costs); "handyman" ideas around the home; relationships between old and young; profiles of active senior citizens. Length: 500 to 1,500 words. Pays 3¢ to 5¢ a word. Photos used with accompanying ms with no additional payment. Captions required.

MARATHON WORLD, Marathon Oil Company, 539 S. Main St., Findlay OH 45840. (419)422-2121. Editor-in-Chief: Robert Ostermann. 20% freelance written. Emphasizes petroleum/energy; for shareholders, educators, legislators, government officials, libraries, community leaders, students and employees. Quarterly magazine; 28 pages. Estab. 1964. Circ. 72,000. Pays on acceptance. Buys first North American serial rights. Photocopied submissions OK. SASE. Reports in 3 weeks. Free sample copy and writer's guidelines.
Nonfiction: Informational; interview and photo feature. Buys 2-3 mss/issue. Query. Length: 800-2,500 words. Pays $300-1,000.
Photos: Photos purchased with accompanying ms or on assignment. Pay negotiable for b&w and color photos. Total purchase price for a ms includes payment for photos.
How To Break In: "Because of the special nature of the *World* as a corporate external publication and the special limits imposed on content, suggest best approach is through initial query."

ONAN NEWS BRIEF/ONAN NEWS, 1400 73rd Ave., N.E., Minneapolis MN 55432. (612)574-5000. Editor: Meredith Houge. For "Onan employees, distributors, dealers, and customers." Monthly (*Onan News Brief*); bimonthly (*Onan News*). Circ. 8,000. Not copyrighted. Buys about 12 mss a year. Pays on acceptance. Free sample copy. Will not consider photocopied submissions. Reports in 30 days. Query first. SASE.
Nonfiction and Photos: "Application stories on Onan products and feature stories on Onan employees, distributors, and dealers. The story should be readable, informative, and interesting. It should be able to stand alone, and the mention of Onan products should not necessarily be important to the story line. We do not want material on recreational vehicles —our marketing emphasis has shifted." Length: "about 1,000 words, but we will look at anything on the subject, no matter how short. And if it takes 5,000 well-chosen words to put a message across, we'll consider that, too. Remuneration depends on so many things other than the number of words: difficulty in obtaining the material, accompanying photographs (we prefer contact sheets and require negatives —b&w with captions only), quality of article, timeliness, and degree of importance of theme to our audience. Our normal pay for a four-page typed article accompanied by 8 to 12 b&w negatives is $150. This includes expenses, unless an additional allowance is authorized in advance by the editor."

PGW NEWS, Philadelphia Gas Co., 1800 N. 9th St., Philadelphia PA 19122. (215)796-1260. Editor-in-Chief: Witliam B. Hall, III. Emphasizes gas utility; for employees, retirees, their families, suppliers, other utility editors in U.S. and abroad. Monthly magazine; 24 pages. Estab.

1928. Circ. 5,000. Pays on acceptance. Buys one-time rights. Submit seasonal/holiday material 3-4 months in advance. SASE. Reports in 1-2 months. Free sample copy.
Nonfiction: How-to (being a better employee); informational; inspirational (from a job approach). Send complete ms. Length: 1,000-2,000 words. Pays $25 minimum.

THE RED DEVIL, Wm. Underwood Co., 1 Red Devil Ln., Westwood MA 02090. Editor-in-Chief: Vincent G. Moloney. 25% freelance written. Emphasizes food products and history of food. Published 3 time/year magazine; 16 pages. Estab. 1968. Circ. 3,700. Pays on acceptance. Buys one-time rights. Submit seasonal/holiday material 3 months in advance of issue date. Photocopied and previously published submissions OK. SASE. Reports in 3 weeks.
Nonfiction: General interest; historical; humor; new product; and technical. "All articles must be related to food." Buys 2 mss/issue. Query. Length: 725-2,000 words. Pays $50-150.
Photos: State availability of photos with query. Pays $5-10 for b&w contact sheets. Captions preferred. Buys one-time rights. Model release required.

ROSEBURG WOODSMAN, 1220 S. W. Morrison St., Portland OR 97205. (503)227-3693. Publication of Roseburg Lumber Company. Editor: Rodger Dwight. 25% freelance written. For wholesale and retail lumber dealers and other buyers of forest products, such as furniture manufacturers and paper products companies. Monthly magazine; 8 pages. Publishes a special Christmas issue. Estab. 1955. Circ. 10,000. Buys all rights, but will reassign rights to author after publication. Buys approximately 20 mss/year. Pays on publication. Free sample copy and writer's guidelines. Will not consider photocopied or simultaneous submissions. Submit seasonal material 3 months in advance. Reports in 1 week. Query or submit complete mss.
Nonfiction and Photos: Features on the "residential, commercial and industrial applications of Roseburg's wood products, such as lumber, plywood, prefinished wall paneling, and flakeboard —vinyl-laminated and printed." Informational, how-to, interview, profile, new products, technical and merchandising techniques articles. Length: 500 to 1,000 words. Pays 10¢ per word. Pays $10 per b&w glossies purchased with mss, 8x10. Pays $25 to $50 per color transparency or print.

RURALITE, Box 557, Forest Grove OR 97116. (503)357-2105. Editor: Ken Dollinger. For primarily rural families, served by consumer-owned electric utilities in Washington, Oregon, Idaho, Nevada and Alaska. Estab. 1954. Monthly. Circ. 160,000. Buys first North American rights only. Pays on acceptance. Submit seasonal material at least three months in advance. Query. SASE.
Nonfiction and Photos: Primarily human-interest stories about rural or small town folk, preferably living in areas (Northwest states and Alaska) served by Rural Electric Cooperatives; emphasis on self-reliance, overcoming of obstacles, cooperative effort, unusual or interesting avocations, hobbies or histories, public spirit or service, humor, inspirational. Will also consider how-to, advice for rural folk, little-known and interesting Northwest history, people, or events. Good art or pix required (B/W negatives with proofsheets). Length 500-3,000 words. Pays $5-$70, depending upon length, quality, appropriateness and interest, number and quality of pix.

SAVER, First Federal Savings and Loan Association of Chicago. Box 4444, Chicago IL 60680. Editor-in-Chief: Marilyn Hopkins. Managing Editor: Chester Myszkowski. 40% freelance written. Emphasizes saving, mortgage, and lending news of the savings and loan industry for Chicago area families with middle and upper-middle incomes. Quarterly magazine; 20 pages. Estab. 1955. Circ. 220,000. Pays on publication "or acceptance if story is done a year in advance." Buys one-time rights. Submit seasonal/holiday material 1 year in advance of issue date. Simultaneous and photocopied submissions OK. Reports in 8 weeks. Free sample copy.
Nonfiction: "Articles of general interest to families in the Chicago area: travel, arts/crafts, things to do, etc." Historical (Chicago, Illinois or closeby features); interview (with well-known figure in the world of budgeting/personal finance); and travel (Chicago, Illinois, or nearby). Buys 2 mss/issue. Query including clips of previously published work. Length: 1,000-3,000 words. Pays $250 minimum.

SEVENTY SIX MAGAZINE, Box 7600, Los Angeles CA 90051. Editor: Karen Saunders. For employees, politicians, retirees and community leaders. Publication of Union Oil Company. Estab. 1920. Bimonthly. Circ. 32,000. Not copyrighted. Buys 2 or 3 mss/year. Pays on acceptance. Free sample copy and writer's guidelines. Reports "as soon as possible." SASE.
Nonfiction and Photos: "Articles about the petroleum industry, Union Oil Co., or Union Oil's employees or retirees. No articles about service stations or dealers. The history of oil or the

unusual uses of petroleum are good subjects for freelancers." No straight news. People-oriented. Does not want to see travel features. Buys informational, profile, humor, historical mss. Pays 10¢ a word minimum. Photos purchased with ms with extra payment. 8x10 b&w; 35mm color transparencies. Captions required.

SMALL WORLD, Volkswagen of America, 818 Sylvan Ave., Englewood Cliffs NJ 07632. Editor: Burton Unger. For "Volkswagen owners in the United States." Magazine; 24 pages. Circ. 300,000. 5 times/year. Buys all rights. Buys about 20 mss/year. Pays on acceptance. Free writer's guidelines. Reports in 6 weeks. "If you have a long feature possibility in mind, please query first. Though queries should be no longer than 2 pages, they ought to include a working title, a short, general summary of the article, and an outline of the specific points to be covered. Where possible, please include a sample of the photography available. We strongly advise writers to read at least 2 past issues before working on a story." SASE.
Nonfiction and Photos: "Interesting stories on people using Volkswagens; useful owner modifications of the vehicle; travel pieces with the emphasis on people, not places; Volkswagenmania stories, personality pieces, inspirational and true adventure articles. VW arts and crafts, etc. The style should be light. All stories must have a VW tie-in. Our approach is subtle, however, and we try to avoid obvious product puffery, since *Small World* is not an advertising medium. We prefer a first-person, people-oriented handling. Length: 1,500 words maximum; shorter pieces, some as short as 450 words, often receive closer attention." Pays $100 per printed page for photographs and text; otherwise, a portion of that amount, depending on the space allotted. Most stories go 2 pages; some run 3 or 4. Photos purchased with ms; captions required. "We prefer color transparencies, particularly 35mm slides. All photos should carry the photographer's name and address. If the photographer is not the author, both names should appear on the first page of the text. Where possible, we would like a selection of at least 40 transparencies. It is recommended that at least one show the principal character or author; another, all or a recognizable portion of a VW in the locale of the story. Quality photography can often sell a story that might be otherwise rejected. Every picture should be identified or explained." Model releases required. Pays $250 maximum for cover photo.
Fillers: "Short, humorous anecdotes about Volkswagens." Pays $15.

SPERRY NEW HOLLAND PUBLIC RELATIONS NEWSFEATURES, New Holland PA 17557. (717)354-1274. Contact: Don Collins, Press Relations Supervisor. For farm families. Special Thanksgiving, Christmas and July 4 issues. Estab. 1895. Buys all rights. Buys about 40 mss/year. Pays on acceptance. Write for editorial guidelines. Will consider photocopied submissions. No simultaneous submissions. Submit seasonal material 4 months in advance. Reports on mss accepted for publication in 2 weeks. Returns rejected material "immediately." Query first. Enclose SASE.
Nonfiction and Photos: "We send releases on how-to; getting the most out of; new twists in old practices; good management practices; work and time saving tips; safety tips — as these topics apply to farming and ranching. Most subjects will be owners of Sperry New Holland agricultural machinery. Give us an outline of a story of interest to a farmer magazine editor. Tell us about the operation and the farmer and equipment involved. Always looking for good freelancers we can contact with our own leads and get coverage." This publication contains newsfeature articles for farm publications and newspapers. Circulation is to various farm publications. "We discuss rates before assignment is made. We usually pay expenses involved in gathering articles. Payment for unsolicited materials, which are accepted, depends on quality and value to us. We're fair, but want only good materials that don't require a lot of rework." Buys informational mss on new farming practices, profiles of good farmers who use Sperry New Holland equipment, spot news, successful business operations of farms and Sperry New Holland dealers, and new product applications. Photos purchased with ms with extra payment, without ms, or on assignment. Captions required. Uses "good cover shots in which our equipment appears" and agricultural photos. Payment: "no set figure for photos. If they are good we'll pay a fair price." Size: 8x10 for b&w; any size color transparencies.

SUN MAGAZINE, Sun Co., 1608 Walnut St., Philadelphia PA 19103. For "local, state, and national government officials; community leaders; news and financial communicators; educators, shareholders, customers, and employees of Sun Company." Estab. 1923. Published three times/year. Circ. 140,000. Not copyrighted. Buys 1 or 2 articles/year. "Most are staff written." Pays on acceptance. Free sample copy. Reports in 3-6 weeks. Query.
Nonfiction: "Articles only. Subject matter should be related to Sun Company, oil industry, or national energy situation. Articles should be directed toward a general audience. Style: magazine feature. Approach: nontechnical. Travel themes are currently being overworked."

Buys informational articles, interviews, profiles, historical articles, think pieces, coverage of successful business operations. Length: 1,000-3,000 words. Pays $300-$800.
Photos: Purchased on assignment; captions optional. "We do not buy photos on spec." Pays $100-$400/day for photographic assignments.

THINK, 7-11 S. Broadway, White Plains NY 10601. (914)696-4755. Editor: C.B. Hansen. For company employees with interests in science, business, technology and other topics. Publication of IBM. Estab. 1935. Every 2 months. Circ. 170,000. Rights purchased vary with author and material. Usually buys first serial rights. Buys about 20 mss/year. Pays on acceptance. Free sample copy. Will consider photocopied submissions. No simultaneous submissions. Reports in 6 to 8 weeks. SASE.
Nonfiction and Photos: Art Director: Ben Carucci. Wants mss on science, technology, business, data processing and other business-related topics. Would like to see any topical themes in business such as privacy, international corporations and consumerism. Buys informational, interview, profile, "think" pieces. "Most stories done on assignment." Length: 500 to 2,000 words. Payment "varies with writer's experience. Generally adhere to going market rate." Photos purchased with accompanying ms with extra payment or on assignment. Captions required. B&w only. Payment "depends on quality and experience."

TIME BREAK, GeoSpace Corp., Box 36374, Houston TX 77036. (713)666-1611. Editor: Lee C. Dominey. 2-5% freelance written. "The purpose of *Time Break* is to inform 'friends and customers' about all products and applications plus trends and items of interest in the geophysical field. It includes technical and semi-technical articles." Semiannual magazine; 20 pages. Estab. 1962. Circ. 4,000. Pays on acceptance. Buys all rights, but may reassign following publication. Submit seasonal/holiday material 3 months in advance of issue date. Simultaneous and previously published submissions OK. SASE. Reports in 4 weeks. Free sample copy; mention *Writer's Market* in request.
Nonfiction: "All articles need to be related to seismic explorations." General interest (to people engaged in seismic exploration); historical; interview; and nostalgia. Query. Length: 500-5,000 words. Pays $50-250.
Photos: "Hopefully, *all* articles in the magazine have photos." State availability of photos with query. Pays $10-50 for b&w photos. Captions preferred. Buys all rights, but may reassign following publication. Model release required.

UNIROYAL WORLD, Oxford Management and Research Center, Middlebury CT 06749. (203)573-2218. Editor: Renee Follett. Published by Uniroyal, Inc. for "wage and salary employees, all ages and educations; they are plant, office, and management employees." Estab. 1964. 12 times a year. Circ. 65,000. Copyrighted. Pays on acceptance. Free sample copy. Photocopied submissions OK. Reports in 3 weeks. SASE.
Nonfiction and Photos: "This publication deals primarily with Uniroyal — its people, places and products. We publish general information dealing with specific aspects of Uniroyal and the rubber industry. Articles must relate to Uniroyal employees." Length: 600 to 1,200 words. Pays $10-200. 8x10 b&w glossies purchased with mss; captions required. Pays $10-50/photo.

VICKERS VOICE, Box 2240, Wichita KS 67201. (316)267-0311. Editor: Derald Linn. For employees of Vickers Petroleum Corp. Quarterly magazine; 24 pages. Estab. 1956. Quarterly. Circ. 2,000. Not copyrighted. Pays on publication. Free sample copy. Query first or submit complete ms. SASE.
Nonfiction and Photos: Articles about activities of the company, its parent company, and its subsidiaries. Articles showing, by example, how a service station owner or manager can make more money from an existing outlet; travel articles. Length: 500 to 1,000 words. Pays $100-150. Photos purchased with or without mss or on assignment. Captions required. Pays $10 for 8x10 b&w glossies.

WDS FORUM, Writer's Digest School, 9933 Alliance Rd., Cincinnati OH 45242. (513)984-0717. Editor: Kirk Polking. Emphasizes writing techniques and marketing for students of seven courses in fiction and nonfiction writing offered by Writer's Digest School. Bimonthly magazine; 16 pages. Estab. 1971. Pays on acceptance. Buys all rights, but may reassign following publication. Phone queries OK. Submit seasonal/holiday material 3 months in advance of issue date. Simultaneous, photocopied and previously published submissions OK. SASE. Reports in 3 weeks. Free sample copy.
Nonfiction: How-to (write or market short stories, articles, novels for young people, etc.); and interviews (with well-known authors of short stories, novels, and books). Buys 10 mss/year.

Query. Length: 500-1,500 words. Pays $10-30.
Photos: Pays $2-5 for 8x10 b&w prints. Captions required. Buys all rights, but may reassign following publication.

Consumer Publications

Consumer publications are the "meat and potatoes" of the freelance diet. These magazines purchase hundreds of thousands of manuscripts annually for a few dollars to over $4,000. Many have small staffs, and so rely heavily on freelancers for material.

For almost every interest, there is a magazine; for every magazine, an editor who is constantly looking for new ideas. This section contains over 50 categories packed with magazines and editors who are looking for ideas from *you*.

New magazines are often good jumping-in points for talented freelancers on the rise because they haven't as yet established good freelance contacts to feed their word mills. By signing on early with the kinds of submissions the editor wants to see, a writer can grow and prosper with these magazines as they increase in size and stature.

Traditionally, religious publications have been good springboards for new writers. Although payment is generally low, these publications offer the exposure that an unestablished writer needs, and more important, they offer a vehicle in which to practice and *perfect* the craft of writing. Opportunities are plentiful. "I think there is more room now [in the Christian field] for good writers than ever before," says Charles Brewster, managing editor of *New World Outlook*. This edition lists over 100 religious publications that need freelance material.

Regional publications are increasing in number by leaps and bounds. A quick check through the 100-plus regional markets (excluding Sunday magazine supplements and op-ed pages) shows that more than 4,500 manuscripts will be bought from freelancers this year in nonfiction *alone*.

What do regional magazines do? According to Monty Joynes, editor of *Metro, The Magazine of Southeastern Virginia,* "city magazines must surprise and entertain, as well as inform and challenge their readership."

What's being bought by editors in the consumer field? Everything—so long as it's good. The consumer field is immense, and encompasses interests from every point of the compass. Would you like to write about sports? *Writer's Market* lists 21 subcategories under the general heading Sport and Outdoor. Want to put puzzles together for fun and profit? There's a section for that, too.

Generally, people watch TV to get their fiction, and turn to magazines for their facts. For this reason, in magazines, nonfiction is more salable than fiction. But if you're a fiction afficionado, don't despair; the Literary and Little section is packed with publications that will consider your story. They may not pay as well as some of the larger markets (which *do* use a limited amount of fiction) but chances of being accepted there are much greater than if you submit your fiction to the few larger markets (such as men's and women's publications, or the general interest section).

Few people earn their bread by writing poetry. But because many people enjoy writing poetry for its own sake, the Poetry and Literary & Little categories include publications that *don't* pay for material. Often these magazines are small (some have circulations under 1,000), but they do offer exposure.

Magazine editors want their submissions in one of two ways: by query, or by submitting the completed manuscript. Before sending *anything* to a publication, check its listing to see how the editor wants material sent to him. If he says to query, write a knowledgeable, cleanly typed, one-page letter outlining your article idea. If the editor is interested, he'll get back to you, often with ideas for slanting your story to his publication. If the listing states that he'll consider complete manuscripts (as is usually the case for fiction and poetry), be sure to package your article *neatly*. Always include the proper return postage in *any* correspondence with an editor.

When waiting to hear from a publication on the outcome of a query or article, it's a good idea to allow a few more weeks than what the listing states as a reporting time. Editors *are* busy—constantly. However, once you've allowed an editor the allotted time (and a bit more), drop a gentle reminder in the mail, asking for a progress report on your submission.

The most important tenent of the freelance business is this: *Know Thy Market*. The best way to do this is to read recent issues of the publication at which you're aiming. Usually a magazine will send a sample copy (free or at some cost) to a writer; to be sure, check its listing. Before writing for an issue, check your library or local newsstand to see if you can obtain a copy there.

For the latest marketing tips and information—including news of new markets—read *Writer's Digest*. One *WD* column, The Markets, is like a monthly edition of *Writer's Market*. The magazine also includes other marketing columns and features.

Alternative Publications

Publications in this section offer writers a forum for expressing anti-establishment or minority ideas and views that wouldn't necessarily be published in the commercial or "establishment" press. Included are a number of "free press" publications that do not pay except in contributor's copies. Writers should be aware that some of these publications remain at one address for a limited time or prove unbusinesslike in their reporting on, or returning of, submissions. However, the writer will also find a number of well-established, well-paying markets in this list.

THE ADVOCATE, Liberation Publications, Inc., 1 Peninsula Place, Bldg. 1730, Suite 225, San Mateo CA 94402. Editor-in-Chief: Robert I. McQueen. For gay men and women, age 21-40; middle-class, college educated, urban. Biweekly tabloid; 80 pages. Estab. 1968. Circ. 65,000. Pays on publication. Rights purchased vary with author and material. SASE. Reports in 1 month.
Nonfiction: "Basically, the emphasis is on the dignity and joy of the gay lifestyle." News articles, interviews, lifestyle features. "Major interest in interviews or sketches of gay people whose names can be used, but who are not in The Movement." Informational, how-to, personal experience, profile, humor, historical, photo feature, spot news, new product. Query. Length: open.
Photos: "Payment for b&w photos purchased without ms or on assignment depends on size of the reproduction."

THE ARTS OBJECTIVELY, Podium II, Box 15716, Philadelphia PA 19103. Editor-in-Chief: Frederic C. Kaplan. Quarterly magazine; 35-50 pages. Estab. 1975. Circ. 1,000. Pays on publication. Buys all rights, but may reassign following publication; simultaneous rights or second serial (reprint) rights. Query about holiday/seasonal material 4 months in advance. Simultaneous and photocopied submissions OK. Previously published work OK. SASE. Reports in 6-8 weeks. Sample copy $1. Writer's guidelines for SASE.
Nonfiction: Exposes (of governmental interference into the arts of communications); informational (advice to professionals on arts of communications); interviews (with individuals involved in the arts or who have made an impact in this area). Buys 10-15/issue. Pays 1-1½¢/word.
Photos: "We are seeking photo essays of about 12 pictures." On assignment only; query. Pays $2-5.
Fiction: "Good, fast-paced stories reflecting objectivist values." Adventure, fantasy, historical, humorous, mainstream, mystery, science fiction, suspense. Buys 1-2/issue. Submit complete ms. Length: 1,500-5,000 words. Pays 1-1½¢/word.
Fillers: Clippings, newsbreaks. Buys 8-10/issue. Send fillers in. Length: 50-100 words. Pays 1-1½¢/word.

BERKELEY BARB, International News Keyus, Inc., Box 1247, Berkeley, CA 94701. (415)849-1040. Editor-in-Chief: Ray Riegert. Alternative weekly newspaper. Audience ranges from college age to upper 40s, well educated, interested in leftist politics, avant-garde art, sex, drugs and the counter-culture. Estab. 1965. Circ. 20,000. Pays on publication. Buys all right, but may reassign following publication. Phone queries OK. Submit seasonal/holiday material 6 weeks in advance. Simultaneous and photocopied submissions OK. SASE. Reports in 6 weeks.

Free sample copy and writer's guideline.
Nonfiction: Expose (mainly political, but must be hard-hitting, well substantiated, investigative journalism); historical (San Francisco Bay area historical sketches only); how-to (make a freelance living, grow your own dope, make it outside the establishment); interview (with leftist, political leaders, avant-garde artists and other counter-culture figures; write in prose narrative, not Q & A form); nostalgia (Bay area only); photo feature; and profile (of individuals, groups or movements which are leftist, avant-garde or part of the counter-culture). Buys 10 mss/issue. Send complete ms. Length: 500-2,000 words. Pays 3-5¢/word.
Photos: Ken Esiner, Photo Editor. Photos purchased with or without accompanying ms. Captions required. Pays $10-70 for b&w and color photos. Send prints and contact sheet.
Columns/Departments: Warren Sharpe, Columns/Departments Editor. Alternatives (lifestyles, energy, scams); Off-The-Wall (uncommon people, events, enterprises); Reviews (unsung heroes/heroines, innovators, writers). Buys 10 mss/year. Query. Length: 300-800 words. Pays 3¢/word.
Fillers: Jokes, gags, anecdotes and newsbreaks. Buys 6 fillers/issue. Length: 100-300 words. Pays 3¢/word.

BERKELEY MONTHLY, 2275 Shattuck Ave., Berkeley CA 94704. (415)848-7900. Publishers/Editors: Tom and Karen Klaber. Associate Editor: Mark Osaki. 60% freelance written. "Stresses variety, from practical subjects to the esoteric." Monthly tabloid; 72 pages. Estab. November 1970. Circ. 65,000. Pays on publication. Buys all rights, but may reassign following publication. Phone queries OK. Submit seasonal/holiday material 2-3 months in advance of issue dtae, "depending on subject matter and/or topical importance." Simultaneous and photocopied submissions OK. SASE. Reports in 1-2 weeks. Sample copy and writer's guidelines for SASE; mention *Writer's Market* in request.
Nonfiction: General interest (human interest articles which provoke a sense of wonder); how-to (arts, science); humor (wry, ironic—top notch only); interview (figures in arts, music, literature, science, philosophy, zen, and alternative health); personal experience (paramount interest only); photo feature (willing to consider ideas); technical (science or new technology made interesting and accesible); and travel (multileveled articles, no travelogues or senic jaunts). No politics, topical news, conventional religious tracts, sports, or personal opinion material. Buys 4-6 mss/issue. Query or submit complete ms. Length: 1,000-2,500 words. Pays $1.50/column inch minimum.
Photos: "Manuscripts with accompanying illustrations—if the article needs them—naturally stand a better chance of acceptance. Usually we provide some kind of art work for each article." Pays $5 minimum for 5x7 glossy or semi-glossy prints. Submit contact sheets. Captions required. Buys one-time rights.
Columns/Departments: Environmental Column (nature, ecology, science; nothing preachy—science made accesible to general public, sense of wonder instilled); and Photographic Journal (articles on aesthetic and philosophical aspects of the craft). Query or submit complete ms. Length: 1,000-2,500 words. Pays $1/column inch minimum.
Fiction: Erotica; humorous; and mainstream. No romance, religious, suspense, etc. Buys 1-2 mss/issue. Length: 2,000 words maximum. Pays $25 minimum.
Poetry: Avant-garde; free verse; and traditional. No "religious, political or first attempts." Buys 1-2/issue. Limit submissions to batches of 5. Length: 60 lines maximum. Pays $15 minimum.

BLACK MARIA, 815 W. Wrightwood, Chicago IL 60614. (312)929-4883. Collective editorship. Mostly for women interested in redefining women's position in society and in the family. Magazine; 64 pages. Estab. 1971. Published 3 to 4 times/year. Circ. 1,000. Rights acquired vary with author and material. May acquire all rights, with the possibility of reassigning rights to author after publication, or second serial (reprint) rights. Uses about 40 mss/year. Pays in contributor's copies and a subscription. Sample copy $1.50. Will consider photocopied submissions, but would prefer the original. Will consider simultaneous submissions. Reports in 1 month. Query first or submit complete ms. SASE.
Nonfiction and Photos: "Articles must be written by women. Subjects include those pertinent to women's liberation (e.g., redefining history to include women); life style changes through role reversals in family. Articles which are pro woman and define her as active, intelligent; a complete human being. We prefer a more subtle approach than political rhetoric. We do not want immediate, newsy articles about specific events. We prefer more general, non-transitory themes for articles." B&w photos (2x3 or 8x10) used with mss.
Fiction and Poetry: "Writer should use understatement in stories; gutsy and to the point." Experimental, mainstream, science fiction, fantasy, humorous and historical fiction. Tradi-

tional forms of poetry, free verse, light verse and avant-garde forms. Submit at least 3 poems, no more than 10. Length: 4 to 75 lines.

THE BOSTON PHOENIX, 100 Massachusetts Ave., Boston MA 02115. (617)536-5390. Editor: William Miller. 40% freelance written. For 18-35 age group, educated middle class and post-counterculture. Weekly alternative newspaper. Circ. 115,000. Buys all rights. Pays on publication. Sample copy $1. Photocopied submissions OK. Reports in 4 to 6 weeks. Query. SASE.
Nonfiction: "No set theme. Anything well written; people interest. Unsentimental; not corny or folksy; high-quality writing and observation. No humor." Pays $50 to $100.

COMMUNITY, 343 S. Dearborn St., Room 317, Chicago IL 60604. (312)939-3347. Editor: Albert Schorsch. For teachers, religious students and movement types (high school age up) interested in social change through nonviolent action. Quarterly magazine; 32 pages. Estab. 1937. Circ. 1,000. Acquires all rights, but will reassign rights to author after publication. Uses about 40 mss/year. Pays in contributor's copies. Sample copy $1. Will consider clear photocopied submissions. Occasionally considers simultaneous submissions. Reports on material accepted for publication in 6 to 8 weeks. Returns rejected material as soon as possible. Query first. SASE.
Nonfiction and Photos: "All types of material concerning movements of liberation and how to achieve such through nonviolence. Our approach is from the viewpoint of the Catholic left. We like to publish material extracted from personal experience whether theoretical or practical. All facets of the women's struggle; men's liberation. No term paper types. We also use book reviews and photo essays." Length: 2,400 words. 8x10 glossy or matte photos are used with mss.
Poetry: Johnny Baranski, poetry editor. Nothing trite. Traditional forms. Blank verse, free verse, avant-garde forms and haiku. Length: 3 to 30 lines.

COSMOPOLITAN CONTACT, Pantheon Press, Box 1566, Fontana CA 92335. Editor-in-Chief: Romulus Rexner. Managing Editor: Nina Norvid. Assistant Editor: Irene Anders. "It is the publication's object to have as universal appeal as possible—students, graduates and others interested in international affairs, cooperation, contacts, travel, friendships, trade, exchanges, self-improvement and widening of mental horizons through multicultural interaction. This publication has worldwide distribution and participation, including the Communist countries." Irregularly published 3 or 4 times a year. Magazine; 32 pages. Estab. 1962. Circ. 1,500. Pays on publication in copies. Simultaneous, photocopied and previously published submissions OK. SASE. Reports in 6 weeks. Sample copy $1.
Nonfiction: Expose (should concentrate on government, education, etc.); how-to; informational; inspiration; personal experience; personal opinion and travel. Submit complete ms. Maximum 500 words. "Material designed to promote across all frontiers bonds of spiritual unity, intellectual understanding and sincere friendship among people by means of correspondence, meetings, publishing activities, tapes, records, exchange of hospitality, books, periodicals in various languages, hobbies and other contacts."
Poetry: Haiku and traditional. Length: Maximum 40 lines.
Rejects: "We are not interested in any contribution containing vulgar language, extreme, intolerant, pro-Soviet or anti-American opinions."

EARTH'S DAUGHTERS, Box 41, Station H, Buffalo NY 14214. Collective editorship. 75-90% freelance written. For women and men interested in literature and feminism. Estab. 1971. Publication schedule varies from 2 to 4 times a year. Circ. 1,000. Acquires first North American serial rights. Pays in contributor's copies. Sample copy $1. Will consider clear photocopied submissions and clear carbons. Reports in 10 weeks. Submit complete ms. SASE.
Nonfiction and Photos: "Our subject is the experience and creative expression of women. We require a high level of technical skill and artistic intensity; although we work from a left-feminist political position, we are concerned with creative expression rather than propaganda. On rare occasions we publish feminist work by men. We rarely use nonfiction, but might be interested in reviews of work by women for an occasional review issue. Length: 1,000 words maximum. We are generally interested in photos more as free-standing artistic works than as illustrations." Pays in copies only.
Fiction: Feminist fiction of any and all modes. Length: 2,500 words maximum.
Poetry: All modern, contemporary, avant-garde forms. Length: 6 pages maximum.

EAST WEST JOURNAL, 233 Harvard St., Brookline MA 02146. (617)738-1760. Editor: Sherman Goldman. Emphasizes alternative living for "people of all ages seeking to live

harmoniously in a world of change." Monthly magazine; 80-104 pages. Estab. 1971. Circ. 40,000. Pays on publication. Buys one-time rights. Phone queries OK. Submit seasonal/holiday material 4 months in advance. Simultaneous, photocopied and previously published submissions OK. SASE. Reports in 4 weeks. Free sample copy.
Nonfiction: Vera Backstrom, editorial assistant. Expose (medicine, agribusiness), how-to (self-healing, martial arts, crafts, alternative energy), informational (American Indians, social and political alternatives, natural foods, macrobiotics), historical (mythology, nutrition and diet, cultural rise and fall, sacred wisdom), interview (innovative thinkers), photo feature (traditional cultures). Buys 60 mss/year. Query. Length: 500-5,000 words. Pays 3-9¢/word.
Photos: Purchased on assignment. Query. Pays $15 for b&w prints; $125-175 for color transparencies (cover only).
Columns/Departments: Books, Music, Cooking (natural foods), Healing (wholestic therapies, martial arts), Compass (current news items). Buys 48 mss a year. Submit complete ms. Length: 500-1,000 words. Pays $5-50. Open to suggestions for new columns and departments.

THE EMISSARY, Eden Valley Press, Box 328, Loveland CO 80537. Editor-in-Chief: Robert Moore. Managing Editor: Theodore Black. Emphasizes general reading, "dedicated to the practical art of living." Monthly magazine; 48 pages. Estab. 1975. Circ. 2,000. Acquires one-time rights. Pays in contributor's copies. Seasonal/holiday material must be submitted 3 months in advance. Photocopied and previously published submissions OK. SASE. Reports in 1 week. Free sample copy and writer's guidelines.
Nonfiction: Historical (how modern experience is connected to a historical event/person); humor; inspirational (not religious or moralistic); interview (with well-known personalities or leader in such fields as solar energy development, ecology, education, etc.); personal experience and photo feature. Uses 12 mss/year. Length: 2,500 words maximum.
Photos: B&w and color. Send contact sheet.
Columns, Departments: Historical connection, awareness forum, life sketches, TV, movie and book reviews. Buys 12 mss/year. Length: 1,500 words maximum.
Fiction: Adventure. fantasy; humorous and science fiction. Uses 6 mss/year.
Poetry: Most types. Uses 12 poems/year. Limit submissions to batches of 6.
Fillers: Clippings, puzzles and short humor. "Would use more of this type material if contributors knew magazine and sent fillers that fit our format and general tone."

FARMSTEAD MAGAZINE, Box 111, Freedom ME 04941. (207)382-6200. Eidtor-in-Chief: George Frangoulis. 95% freelance written. Emphasizes gardening, small farming, homesteading and self-sufficiency. Bimonthly magazine; 96 pages. Estab. 1974. Circ. 50,000. Pays on publication. Buys first serial and reprint rights. Phone queries OK. Submit seasonal/holiday material 3 months in advance of issue date. SASE. Reports in 3 months. Free sample copy and writer's guidelines.
Nonfiction: General interest (relating to rural living, gardening and farm life); how-to (gardening, farming, construction, conservation, wildlife livestock, crafts, and rural living); interview (with interesting and/or inspirational people involved with agriculture, farm life, or self-sufficiency); new product (reviews of new books); nostalgia (of rural living; farmlife self-sufficiency); and occasionally travel (agriculture in other lands). Buys 20 mss/year. Submit complete ms. Length: 5,000 words maximum. Pays $10-100.
Photos: State availability of photos with ms. Pays $5 for each 5x7 b&w print used. Buys all rights.

FOCUS: A JOURNAL FOR LESBIANS, Daughters of Bilitis, 1151 Massachusetts Ave., Cambridge MA 02138. A literary journal for lesbians of all ages and interests. Monthly magazine; 20 pages. Estab. 1970. Circ. 350. Pays in contributor's copies. Obtains all rights. Submit seasonal/holiday material 3 months in advance of issue date. Simultaneous and photocopied submissions OK. SASE. Reports in 3 months. Sample copy 75¢.
Nonfiction: Historical; humor; informational; interview; personal experience; personal opinion; profile and book reviews (includes monthly D.O.B. calendar). Send complete ms. Length: 2,500 maximum words.
Fiction: Relating to magazine theme. Confession; erotica; fantasy; historical; humorous; romance and science fiction. Send complete ms. Length: 2,500 words maximum.
Poetry: Avant-garde; free verse; haiku; light verse and traditional. Length: 2,500 words maximum.
Fillers: Clippings, jokes, gags, anecdotes, newsbreaks, short humor, graphics, cartoons and drawings. Send fillers. Length: 200 words maximum.

FREE FOR ALL, Box 962, Madison WI 53701. (608)255-2798. Editor-in-Chief: Michael Kaufman. Managing Editor: Tom Phillips. 50% freelance written. For the student community—university students; people with high political committments; affluent (liberal) readers; and crafts people/artists. Biweekly tabloid; 12 pages. Estab. March 1973. Circ. 10,000. Pays on acceptance. Phone queries OK. Simultaneous, photocopied and previously published submissions OK. SASE. Reports in 1 month. Sample copy 50¢; 25¢ for writer's guidelines.
Nonfiction: Exposé; general interest (children and health); historical (labor, racism, sexism, with Wisconsin angle); how-to (plumbing, carpentry, etc.); interview (political, cultural interviews); and photo feature. Submit complete ms. Length: 500-1,500 words. Pays $10.
Photos: State availability of photos with ms. Offers no additional payment for b&w contact sheets or prints.
Columns/Departments: Culture (reviews, news releases, socio-political angles); education; minorities and national/international. Open to suggestions for new columns/departments.

GAY SUNSHINE, A Journal of Gay Liberation, P.O. Box 40397, San Francisco CA 94140. (415)824-3184. Editor: Winston Leyland. 25% freelance written. For gay people of all ages throughout North America and abroad. "We especially appeal to people interested in the radical, political and literary aspects of the gay liberation movement." Quarterly newspaper; 28-36 pages. Estab. 1970. Circ. 10,000. Rights purchased vary with author and material; negotiable. Payment in contributor's copies, or negotiable. Sample copy $1. Photocopied submissions OK. Reports in 2 to 4 weeks. Submit complete nonfiction mss; query first for short fiction and graphics. SASE.
Nonfiction and Photos: Interviews, personal articles, political articles, literary essays. Particularly interested in in-depth interviews with gay people from different backgrounds. "Material should relate to gay people and the gay consciousness. Author should write to us first regarding style, structure, etc." Length: maximum of 10 to 15 double-spaced, typed pages. B&w photos are purchased on assignment. Captions required.
Fiction: Experimental and erotica. Must relate to theme. Length: maximum of 10 to 15 double-spaced, typed pages.
Poetry: Blank verse, free verse, avant-garde forms.

GNOSTICA MAGAZINE, Box 43383, St. Paul MN 55164. (612)291-1970. Editor: K. Schuster. 50% freelance written. For people interested in astrology, parapsychology, divination techniques, psychic phenomena, magic, witchcraft and alternative religions, tantra and Eastern philosophy, the tarot and the occult. Bimonthly magazine; 88-112 pages. Estab. 1971. Circ. 10,000. Pays within a month of publication. Usually buys first serial rights. Photocopied and simultaneous submissions OK. SASE. Reports in 2 months. Free sample copy.
Nonfiction: All articles deal with astrology, parapsychology and the occult. Prefers articles with a how-to or instructional theme. Length: 2,500-10,000 words. Will consider serializing some book-length mss. Pays 2¢/word, except by arrangement. Reviews of occult books. Length: 200-1,000 words. Pays 2¢/word.
Photos: Purchased with mss, or on assignment.
Columns/Departments: Material on astrology, parapsychology and the occult. Length: 500-2,000 words. Pays $10-50/column. Submit several columns at one time.

GRASS ROOTS FORUM, P.O. Box 472, San Gabriel, CA 91778. Editor: Henry Wilton. For "ages 14 to 70; from thinking, intelligent craftsmen, to Ph.D.'s, M.D.'s, etc." Estab. 1967. Monthly. Circ. 5,000. Rights acquired are open. Uses 40 mss/year. Payment in contributor's copies. Sample copy for 25¢. Submit only complete ms. Will consider photocopied submissions. Reports in 2 weeks. SASE.
Nonfiction, Photos, Poetry and Fillers: Publishes material on "political, economic, social subjects; all aspects of our culture; current events. In prose or verse; from liberal perspective. Emphasis on truth, reality, justice as it would serve the underdog. We do not want erotica, trivia, falsehoods, etc. We are seeking cogent, astute observations regarding national issues, political events; activities of dissenting groups and minorities." Buys informational, interview, humor, expose articles; book and music reviews. B&w photos must be of general interest and authentic. Photos used with or without ms and on assignment. Accepts traditional, avant-garde, blank, and free verse. Buys jokes and short humor. Payment in contributor's copies.

HARROWSMITH MAGAZINE, Camden House Publishing, Ltd., Camden East, Ontario, Canada K0K 1J0. (613)378-6661. Editor-in-Chief: James M. Lawrence. Managing Editor: Barry Estabrook. 90% freelance written. "For those interested in organic gardening, rural living, alternative energy, and alternative life styles." Bimonthly magazine; 106 pages. Estab. 1976.

Circ. 80,000. Pays on acceptance. Buys first North American serial rights. Submit seasonal/holiday material 6 months in advance of issue date. SASE. Reports in 3 weeks. Sample copy $1; free writer's guidelines.

Nonfiction: Expose; how-to; general interest; humor; interview; nostalgia; photo feature; and profile. "We are always in need of quality gardening articles geared to northern conditions. No articles whose style feigns 'folksiness.'" Buys 15 mss/issue. Query. Length: 500-4,000 words. Pays $75-300.

Photos: State availability of photos with query. Pays $25 for 8x10 glossy b&w prints; $50 for 35mm or larger color transparencies. Captions required. Buys all rights, but may reassign following publication.

How To Break In: "We have standards of excellence as high as any publication in the country. However we are by no means a closed market. Most of our material comes from unknown writers. We welcome and give thorough consideration to all freelance submissions."

HIGH TIMES, Trans-High Corporation, Box 386, Cooper Station, New York NY 10003. (212)481-0120. Managing Editor: Shelley Levitt. For persons under 35 interested in lifestyle changes, cultural trends, personal freedom, sex and drugs. Monthly magazine; 116 pages. Estab. 1974. Circ. 450,000. Buys first and second serial (reprint) rights. Submit seasonal/holiday material 6 months in advance. Pays on publication. SASE. Reports in 6-8 weeks. Sample copy $1.75.

Nonfiction: Expose; historical; humor; informational; interview; new product; photo feature; profile and travel. Buys 4 mss/issue. Send complete ms. Length: 3,000-4,000 words. Pays $250-750. Wants material on drugs and consciousness expansion; other subjects of interest to a young, hip audience. "Brevity and clarity appreciated." Also, new drugs, dope-dealing, business news, glamor drugs. Nothing on "my drug bust."

Photos: Annie Toglia, Photo Editor. Photos purchased with or without accompanying ms or on assignment. Pays $25-150 for b&w photos; $50-250 for color photos. Query. No additional payment for photos accepted with accompanying ms. Model release required.

INTEGRITY: GAY EPISCOPAL FORUM, 701 Orange St., #6, Fort Valley GA 31030. (912)825-7287. Editor: Louie Crew, Ph.D. For "gay Episcopalians and friends. About one-fourth of our readers are clergy, many of them gay themselves, and others of them trying thereby to become more informed of our basically gay point of view. We also have many non-Christian gays seeking to be informed of our Christian witness. We have now developed chapters in over 35 cities, meeting regularly for eucharist and other programs." Newsletter; 10 pages. Estab. 1974. 10 times a year. Circ. 1,000. Rights acquired vary with author and material. Usually acquires all rights, but may reassign rights to author after publication. Uses 15 to 20 mss/year. Pays in contributor's copies. Will send sample copy to writer for $1. Will consider photocopied submissions. Will consider simultaneous submissions only if other distribution is explained. Reports in 2 weeks. Query first or submit complete ms. Enclose SASE.

Nonfiction: "Personal experience items, particularly with a Christian (but not sentimental) focus, and particularly with the poignancy to be forceful about the truth of the gay experience. We like materials that discuss gay sexuality in the broader context of human sexuality." Length 25 to 2,000 words.

Poetry and Fillers: Traditional forms of poetry, blank verse, free verse, avant-garde forms, haiku. Length 2 to 25 lines. Newsbreaks, clippings, jokes, gags, anecdotes, short humor used as fillers. Length: 1 to 10 lines.

JIM'S JOURNAL, Box 3563, Bloomington IL 61701. Editor: James E. Kurtz. 50% freelance written. For young adult to middle-age readers. All professions. Interested in controversial themes. Estab. 1962. Monthly. Circ. 5,000. Not copyrighted. Payment in contributor's copies. Will not consider photocopied submissions. Reports on material accepted for publication in 4 weeks. Returns rejected material in 3 to 5 weeks. Query first or submit complete ms. SASE.

Nonfiction and Photos: Controversial, underground material, sociology, philosophy, current events, religion, men's liberation, sex. "We honestly invite stimulating material. We want well-written material and we favor the new writer. Be bold, speak out with confidence; no punches pulled. All subjects are carefully read." Informational, personal experience, inspirational, think pieces, personal opinion, expose. Length: 2,500 words maximum. 5x7 or 8x10 b&w photos used with accompanying mss. Captions required.

Fiction: Experimental, mainstream, adventure, erotica, humor, confession, condensed novels. Length: 3,000 words maximum.

THE LESBIAN TIDE, 8706 Cadillac, Los Angeles CA 90034. (213)839-7254. Collective editorship. Managing Editor: Jeanne Cordova. For feminist lesbians of any age, educational level, interests, or political viewpoints. Bimonthly magazine; 40 pages. Estab. 1971. Circ. 6,700. Not copyrighted. Uses about 50 mss/year. Sample copy $1. Will consider photocopied and simultaneous submissions. Reports in 60 days. Submit complete ms. SASE.

Nonfiction and Photos: News regarding lesbian organizations, conferences, social alternatives, "zaps," etc.; civil rights, historical/political analyses; book, film, and music reviews; interviews, profiles, instructional pieces. "Writers must be women writing for a readership of feminist lesbians of any political orientation. We will not consider material written by men." Will consider articles on lesbian child custody cases, job and credit discrimination against women, armed services discharge battles, abuse of women in prison, and general oppression of lesbians and other feminists by the legal power structure. Length: 250 to 1,500 words. Pays $10. B&w photos (any size) used with or without mss or on assignment.

Fiction and Fillers: Stories of interest to lesbians and other feminists; all types, except religious fiction. Length: 250 to 1,500 words. Short humor (100 to 200 words), jokes, gags, anecdotes, clippings, newsbreaks used as fillers.

THE MOTHER EARTH NEWS, Box 70, Hendersonville NC 28739. (704)692-4256. Editor-in-Chief: John Shuttleworth. Submissions Editor: Sonia Nordenson. Emphasizes "back-to-the-land self-sufficiency for the growing number of individuals who seek a more rational self-directed way of life." Bimonthly magazine; 180 pages. Estab. 1970. Circ. 550,000. Pays on acceptance. Buys all rights, but will reassign following publication. Submit seasonal/holiday material 3-4 months in advance. Simultaneous, photocopied and previously published submissions OK. SASE. Reports in 2-3 months. Free sample copy and writer's guidelines.

Nonfiction: How-to (*Mother* is always looking for good, well documented home business pieces and reports on alternative energy systems as well as low cost ($100 and up) housing stories and seasonal cooking and gardening articles) and profile (250-400-word thumbnail biographies of "doers" are always welcome). Buys 150-200 mss/year. Query. Length: 300-3,000 words. Pays $40-500.

Photos: Purchased with accompanying ms. Captions and credits required. Send prints or transparencies. Uses 8x10 b&w glossies; any size color transparencies. Include type of film, speed and lighting used. Total purchase price for ms includes payment for photos.

Columns/Departments: "Contributions to Mother's Down-Home Country Lore; and Successful Swaps are rewarded by a one-year subscription; Bootstrap Business pays a two-year subscription; Profiles and Newsworthies." Length: 100-500 words. Pays $25-50. Open to suggestions for new columns/departments.

Fillers: Short how-to's on any subject normally covered by the magazine. Query. Length: 150-300 words. Pays $7.50-25.

How To Break In: "Probably the best way is to send a tightly written, short (1,000 words), illustrated (with color slides) piece on a slightly offbeat facet of gardening, cooking or country living. It's important that the writer get all the pertinent facts together, organize them logically, and present them in a fun to read fashion. It's also important that the ms be accompanied by top-notch photos, which is why, as a matter of policy, we reimburse authors for the cost of hiring professional photographers."

NATURAL LIFE MAGAZINE, Natural Dynamics, Inc., Box 640, Jarvis, Ontario, Canada. Editor-in-Chief: Wendy Priesnitz. 75% freelance written. Emphasizes "back-to-the-land and ecology matters for a readership (both rural and urban) interested in natural foods, alternate energy, do-it-yourself-projects, and self-sufficiency. Bimonthly magazine; 64 pages. Estab. November 1976. Circ. 25,000. Pays on publication. Buys all rights, but may reassign following publication. Submit seasonal/holiday material 2-3 months in advance. Photocopied and previously published submissions OK. SASE. Reports in 3 weeks. Free sample copy and writer's guidelines; mention *Writer's Market* in request.

Nonfiction: How-to (on becoming self-sufficient, i.e., organic gardening, homestead carpentry, useful crafts, etc.); interview (ecology-oriented, nutritionists, alternate energy people); personal experience (with homesteading, self-sufficient lifestyle); and technical (solar and wind energy). Buys 30 mss/year. Query with clips of previously published work. Length: 2,000 words maximum. Pays $10-100.

Photos: State availability of photos with query. "Our readers want to see how everything is done, or built, etc." Offers no additional payment for photos accepted with ms. Uses b&w prints only. Captions preferred. Buys all rights, but may reassign following publication.

Columns/Departments: Book Reviews. Buys 6-7 mss/year. Query. Length: 600 words maximum. Pays $10-25.

NORTH COUNTRY ANVIL, Anvil Press, Box 37, Millville MN 55957. Editor-in-Chief: Jack Miller. Emphasizes alternatives, lifestyles, back-to-the-soil movements, and social justice. For a "midwestern audience interested in subject matter, distributed among all ages, but 25-40 age group most predominant." Bimonthly magazine; 40-44 pages. Estab. 1972. Circ. 2,200. Pays in copies. Acquires all rights, but may reassign following publication. Submit seasonal or holiday material 6-9 months in advance. Simultaneous and photocopied submissions OK. SASE. Reports in 12 weeks. Sample copy $1.
Nonfiction: Expose (mistreament and triumphs of minorities), historical (populist and land reform movements); how-to (gardening, alternative sources of energy, small scale farming), humor and informational (lifestyles). Uses 20 mss/issue. Length: 3,000 words maximum.
Poetry: Mara and Ray Smith, Poetry Editors. Uses all kinds. Uses 20 poems/issue. Pays in copies.
How To Break In: "Start by being well-informed on the subject matter, then present it in clear, concise fashion. We want our writers to touch all the bases without dying on them. We're always on the lookout for people-oriented articles, particularly when the people involved are accomplishing something worthwhile in spite of the 'establishment,' and not because of it."

PRAIRIE SUN, 1303 NE Adams St., Peoria IL 61603. (309)673-6624. Editor-in-Chief: Bill Knight. 10-20% freelance written. For music listeners who are also interested in films, books, and general entertainment. Weekly tabloid; 16 pages. Estab. 1972. Circ. 27,000. Pays on publication. Buys all rights, but may reassign following publication. Phone queries OK. Simultaneous, photocopied and previously published submissions OK. SASE. Reports in 3 weeks. Sample copy 50¢.
Nonfiction: Exposé (government and corporate interests); how-to (back to nature; gardening; living with less; alternative energy systems); interview (especially cultural and entertainment personalities); and profile (music personalities). Buys 20 mss/year. Query. Length: 400-1,000 words. Pays $15-40.

SAN FRANCISCO BAY GUARDIAN, 2700 19th St., San Francisco CA 94110. (415)824-7660. Editor: Bruce Brugmann. 25% freelance written. For "a young liberal to radical, well-educated audience." Estab. 1966. Weekly. Circ. 25,000. Buys all rights, but will reassign them to author after publication. Buys 200 mss a year. Payment on publication. Will consider photocopied submissions. Query first for nonfiction with sample of published pieces. SASE.
Nonfiction and Photos: Department Editors: Louis Dunn (photos) and Michael E. Miller (articles). Publishes "investigative reporting, features, analysis and interpretation, how-to and consumer reviews, and stories must have a Bay Area angle." Freelance material should have a "public interest advocacy journalism approach (on the side of the little guy who gets pushed around by large institutions). More interested in hard investigative pieces. Fewer stories about isolated suffering welfare mothers and other mistreated individuals; should be put in context (with facts) of groups and classes. We would like to see articles on how to survive in the city—in San Francisco." Reviews of 800 to 1,500 words pay $25 minimum; short articles of 1,500 to 2,500 words pay $35 minimum; long articles of over 2,500 words pay $50 minimum. Photos purchased with or without mss. B&w full negative prints, on 8x10 paper. Pays $15 per published photo, $40 minimum photo essay.
How To Break In: "Working with our summer volunteer projects in investigative reporting, in which we teach the techniques and send new reporters out to do investigations in the Bay Area. Submit applications in mid-Spring each year."

THE SECOND WAVE, Box 344, Cambridge A., Cambridge MA 02139. (617)491-1071. Editors: Women's Editorial Collective. For women concerned with issues of feminism. Quarterly magazine; 52 pages. Estab. 1971. Circ. 5,000. Acquires first serial rights. Uses about 20 mss a year. Pays in contributor's copies. Sample copy $1.50. Photocopied and simultaneous submissions OK. Reports in 1 to 3 months. Query first or submit complete ms. Enclose SASE.
Nonfiction and Photos: All material must be related to the theme of women's liberation. "She (the writer) should write only on issues involving women's struggle for liberation, or women's relationships with other women. We do not want work glorifying men, marriage, traditional women's roles, etc. Would like to see articles on feminism outside the big cities and in other countries; new issues being dealt with by women, etc." Informational, personal experience, interview, historical and think articles. Length: varies. B&w photos are used with or without accompanying mss. Captions optional.
Fiction and Poetry: Must relate to feminist themes. Experimental, mainstream, science fiction, fantasy. Free verse.

SIPAPU, Route 1, Box 216, Winters CA 95694. Editor: Noel Peattie. For "libraries, editors and collectors interested in Third World studies, the counterculture and the underground press." Estab. 1970. Semi-annually. Circ. 500. Buys all rights, but will reassign rights to author after publication (on request). Pays on publication. Sample copy $2. Will consider photocopied submissions. Reports on material in 3 weeks. Query first. SASE.
Nonfiction: "Primarily book reviews, interviews, descriptions of special libraries and counterculture magazines and underground papers. We are an underground 'paper' about underground 'papers.' We are interested in personalities publishing dissent, counterculture and Third World material. Informal, clear and cool. We are not interested in blazing manifestos, but rather a concise, honest description of some phase of dissent publishing, or some library collecting in this field, that the writer knows about from the inside." Personal experience, interview, successful library operations. Pays 4¢/word.

THE UNSPEAKABLE VISIONS OF THE INDIVIDUAL, Tuvoti, Inc., Box 439, California PA 15419. Editors-in-Chief: Arthur Winfield Knight, Kit Knight. For "an adult audience, generally college-educated (or substantial self-education) with an interest in Beat (generation) writing." Annual magazine/book; 176 pages. Estab. 1971. Circ. 2,000. Payment (if made) on publication. Acquires first North American serial rights. Reports in 2 months. Sample copy $2.
Nonfiction: Interviews (with Beat writers), personal experience, photo feature. Uses 20 mss/year. Query or submit complete ms. Length: 300-15,000 words. Pays 2 copies, "sometimes a small cash payment, i.e., $10."
Photos: Used with or without ms or on assignment. Captions required. Send prints. Pays 2 copies to $10 for 8x10 b&w glossies.
Fiction: Uses 10 mss/year. Submit complete ms. Length: Pays 2 copies to $10.
Poetry: Avant-garde, Free verse, traditional. Uses 15/year. Limit submissions to batches of 10. Length: 100 lines maximum. Pays 2 copies to $10.

VILLAGE VOICE, 80 University Plaza, New York NY 10003. Editor: Marianne Partridge. Emphasizes arts and politics. Weekly tabloid; 125 pages. Estab. 1956. Circ. 148,000. Pays on acceptance. Buys all rights. SASE. Reports in 3 weeks.
Nonfiction: Expose, how-to, informational, historical, humor, interview, nostalgia, personal opinion, profile, personal experience, photo feature. Query. Length: 2,000 words maximum. Pays $150 minimum for features.

WOMEN: A JOURNAL OF LIBERATION, 3028 Greenmount Ave., Baltimore MD 21218. (301)235-5245. Collective editorship. For women and men; high school education; specifically feminists. Quarterly magazine; 64 pages. Estab. 1969. Circ. 20,000. Payment in contributor's copies. Acquires all rights. Phone queries OK. Simultaneous and photocopied submissions OK. SASE. Reports in 4-5 months. Sample copy $1.25.
Nonfiction: "All articles should be related to upcoming themes and reflect nonsexist and, hopefully, a socialist/feminist approach." Uses 60 mss/year. Submit complete ms. Length: 1,000-3,000 words.
Photos: Photos used with or without mss or on assignment; 5x7 (or larger) b&w.
Columns/Departments: Uses reviews of feminist press books about women. Letters from readers are used in Our Sisters Speak column. Uses 6/year. Length: 1,000-2,000 words.
Fiction: Adventure, confession, erotica, experimental, fantasy, historical, humorous, mainstream, mystery, suspense and science fiction. Uses 6/year. Length: 4,000-5,000 words.
Poetry: Avant-garde and traditional forms; free verse, blank verse, haiku and light verse. Submit complete ms. Length: open.

WOMEN'S RIGHTS LAW REPORTER, 180 University Ave., Newark NJ 07102. (201)648-5320. Legal journal emphasizing law and feminism for lawyers, students and feminists. Quarterly magazine; 64 pages. Estab. 1971. Circ. 1,500. No payment. Acquires all rights. Submit seasonal/holiday material 3-4 months in advance. SASE. Reports in 2 months. Sample copy $3.50.
Nonfiction: Historical and legal articles. Query or submit complete ms. Length: 20-100 pages plus footnotes.

Animal Publications

These publications deal with pets, racing and show horses, and other pleasure animals. Magazines about animals bred and raised for food are classified in Farm Publications.

AMERICAN HUMANE MAGAZINE, Coyle Publications, 2 Park Central, Suite 740,1515 Arapahoe St., Denver CO 80202. (303)534-8843. Editor-in-Chief: William N. Vaile. Associate Editor: Alan D. Miller. 80-90% freelance written. For "persons interested in the care and protection of animals, children, and adults. Readers are professionals in veterinary medicine, animal welfare and control, social service, education, law and medicine, as well as the pet-owning public." Monthly magazine; 48 pages. Estab. 1913. Circ. 15,000. Pays on publication. Buys all rights, but may reassign following publication. Phone queries OK. Submit seasonal/holiday material at least 4 months in advance of issue date. Photocopied and previously published submissions OK. SASE. Reports in 8 weeks. Sample copy 50¢; free writer's guidelines.
Nonfiction: How-to (concentrate on animal care and/or animal shelter operation); general interest (concentrate on animals, animal protection, and child or adult protection and welfare); humor; historical (relating to humane movement—animals or child protection); inspirational (relating to humane concerns); interview (prominent or acknowledged authority in animal/child/adult protection); personal experience (relating to *very* unusual experiences); photo feature (concentrate on newsworthy events relating to animals); and profile (prominent or acknowledged authority). No overly sentimental, mushy animal stories; no editorializing. Buys 180 mss/year. Query or submit complete ms. Length: 500-2,000 words. Pays $25 minimum.
Photos: Pays $15 minimum for 8x10 b&w glossy prints. Captions preferred. Buys all rights, but may reassign following publication. Model release preferred.
Columns/Departments: Update (breaking news on animal protection and welfare legislation, same for children); Point/Counterpoint (issue forum with photos related to humane aims and movement); and Profiles. Submit complete ms. Length: open. Pays $10 minimum. Open to suggestions for new columns/departments.
Fiction: "We will consider nearly all types of fiction relating to animals." Adventure; fantasy; historical; humorous; mystery; suspense; mainstream; and western. No overly sentimental material or flagrant editorialization. Buys 12 mss/year. Submit complete ms. Length: 500-1,500 words. Pays $25.
Fillers: Clippings and short humor. "All must relate to humane movement." Length: open. Pays $10 minimum.

ANIMAL KINGDOM, New York Zoological Park, Bronx NY 10460. (212)220-5121. Editor: Eugene J. Walter, Jr. For individuals interested in wildlife, zoos, aquariums, and members of zoological societies. Bimonthly. Buys first North American serial rights. Pays on acceptance. Reports in 1 month. SASE.
Nonfiction and Photos: Wildlife articles dealing with animal natural history, conservation, behavior. No pets, domestic animals, or botany. Articles should be scientifically well-grounded but written for a general audience, not scientific journal readers. No poetry, cartoons, or fillers. Length: 1,500 to 3,000 words. Pays $100-$450. Payment for photos purchased with mss is negotiable.
How To Break In: "It helps to be a working scientist dealing directly with animals in the wild. Or a scientist working in a zoo such as the staff members here at the New York Zoological Society. Most of the authors who send us unsolicited mss are non-scientists who are doing their research in libraries. They're simply working from scientific literature and writing it up for popular consumption. There are a fair number of others who are backyard naturalists, so to speak, and while their observations may be personal, they are not well grounded scientifically. It has nothing to do with whether or not they are good or bad writers. In fact, some of our authors are not specially good writers but they are able to provide us with fresh, original material and new insights into animal behavior and biology. That sort of thing is impossible from someone who is working from books. Hence, I cannot be too encouraging to anyone who lacks field experience."

ANIMAL LOVERS MAGAZINE, Box 918, New Providence NJ 07974. (201)665-0812. Editor-in-Chief: Anita Coffelt. 50% freelance written. Emphasizes animals, pets for readership of animal lovers, pet owners, veterinarians, school/public libraries and 2-3 universities. Quarterly magazine; 24 pages. Estab. 1969. Circ. 3,500+. Pays on acceptance. Buys all rights, but may reassign rights to author following publication. Seasonal/holiday material must be submitted 3 months in advance. Photocopied submissions OK. SASE. Reports in 6 weeks. Sample copy 75¢; writer's guidelines for SASE.
Nonfiction: How-to; humor (between pet and owner; two pets, etc.); informational, personal experience; personal opinion (on euthanasia, veterinarian fees, cruelty, hunting, etc.) and

profile (animal lovers who have gone to extraordinary lengths to help animals). Buys 60 mss/year. Submit complete ms. Length: 300-600 words. Pays 1¢ per published word; $3-6 per article.
Photos: Purchased with or without accompanying ms. Captions required. Send b&w or color prints. Pays maximum $2 for b&w or color.
Fiction: Humorous. Buys 5 mss/year. Length: 300-600 words. Pays 1¢ per word; $3-6/ms. Send complete ms.
Fillers: Short Humor (brief incidents involving animals). Buys 5-10/year. Length: 75-200 words. Pays 1¢ per word; $1-2, maximum.
Rejects: "Poetry, cartoons, puzzles, articles or stories which depict cats stalking their prey; gory details about dying animals; stories which contain profanity or sexual overtones. We particularly do not want inconsequential accounts of pets. Manuscripts that are 1,000 words+. No poetry or foreign markets."

ANIMALS, MSPCA, 350 S. Huntington Ave., Boston MA 02130. Editor-in-Chief: Deborah Salem. 50% freelance written. For members of the MSPCA. Bimonthly magazine; 40 pages. Estab. 1868. Circ. 20,000. Pays on publication. Buys all rights, but may reassign to author following publication. Photocopied and previously published submissions OK. Reports in 2 weeks. Sample copy $1.25 with 8½x11 SASE; writers's guidelines for SASE.
Nonfiction and Photos: Uses practical articles on animal care and articles on humane/animal protection issues. Non-sentimental approach. Length: 300 to 3,000 words. Pays 2¢ per word. Photos purchased with accompanying ms with extra payment, without accompanying ms or on assignment. Captions required. Payment: $5 for b&w; $7.50 for color. Size: 5x7 minimum for b&w; color transparencies. Pays $5 to $10.

APPALOOSA NEWS, Box 8403, Moscow ID 83843. (208)882-5578. Emphasizes appaloosa horses for appaloosa owners, breeders and people interested in horses. Monthly magazine; 186 pages. Estab. 1950. Circ. 29,000. Buys all rights, but may reassign rights to author following publication. Phone queries OK. Seasonal/holiday material should be submitted 90 days in advance. SASE. Reports in 2 weeks. Free sample copy.
Nonfiction: How-to (horse-related articles); historical (history of appaloosa); humor (cartoons); informational; interview (horse-related persons—trainer, owner, racer, etc.); personal opinion (we have a forum); photo feature; profile (must be authentic) and technical. Submit complete ms. Pays $35-125, however most are gratis by owners.
Photos: Purchased with accompanying manuscript for article, without accompanying manuscript for cover. Captions are required. Send prints or transparencies. 8x10 or 5x7 b&w glossies or color transparencies for cover. No additional payment for photos accepted with accompanying ms, total purchase price for ms includes payment for photos.
Columns, Departments: For regional reports for appaloosa horse club, horse shows or sales. Send complete ms. No payment.

THE CANADIAN HORSE, 48 Belfield Rd., Rexdale, Ontario, Canada M9W 1G1. (416)249-7278. Editor: P.G. Jones. For thoroughbred horsemen. Monthly magazine. Estab. 1961. Circ. 4,500. Buys all rights. Pays on publication. Query first. Enclose SASE.
Nonfiction: Material on thoroughbred racing; racing results. Length: 2 pages. Pays $20 per page.

CAT FANCY, Fancy Publications, Inc., Box 4030, San Clemente CA 92672. (714)498-1600. Editor: Mike Criss. 90% freelance written. For men and women of all ages interested in all phases of cat ownership. Bimonthly magazine; 40 pages. Estab. 1967. Circ. 55,000. Pays on publication. Buys all rights, but may reassign following publication. Submit seasonal/holiday material 4 months in advance. Previously published submissions OK. SASE. Reports in 3 months. Sample copy $1.25; free writer's guidelines.
Nonfiction: Historical; how-to; humor; informational; personal experience; photo feature and technical. Buys 5 mss/issue. Send complete ms. Length: 500-3,500 words. Pays 3¢/word.
Photos: Photos purchased with or without accompanying ms. Pays $7.50 minimum for 8x10 b&w glossies; $50-100 for 35mm or 2¼x2¼ color photos. Send prints and transparencies. Model release required.
Fiction: Adventure; fantasy; historical and humorous. Buys 1 ms/issue. Send complete ms. Length: 500-5,000 words. Pays 3¢/word.
Poetry: Avant-garde, free verse, haiku, light verse and traditional. Buys 4 poems/issue. Length: 5-50 lines. Pays $10.
Fillers: Short humor. Buys 10 fillers/year. Length: 100-500 words. Pays 3¢/word.

CATS MAGAZINE, Box 4106, Pittsburgh PA 15202. Editor: Jean Amelia Laux. For men and women of all ages; cat enthusiasts, vets, geneticists. Monthly magazine. Estab. 1945. Circ. 50,000. Buys first North American serial rights. Buys 50 mss/year. Pays on publication. Free sample copy. Submit seasonal Christmas material 4 to 6 months in advance. Reports within 6 weeks. SASE.

Nonfiction and Photos: "Cat health, cat breed articles, articles on the cat in art, literature, history, human culture, cats in the news. Cat pets of popular personalities. In general how cats and cat people are contributing to our society. We're more serious, more scientific, but we do like an occasional light or humorous article portraying cats and humans, however, as they really are. Would like to see something on psychological benefits of cat ownership; how do cat-owning families differ from others? Also movie and book reviews." Length: 800 to 2,500 words. Pays $15 to $75. Photos purchased with or without accompanying ms. Captions optional. Pays $15 minimum for 4x5 or larger b&w photos; $100 minimum for color. Prefers 2¼x2¼ minimum, but can use 35mm (transparencies only). "We use color for cover only. Prefer cats as part of scenes rather than stiff portraits."

Fiction and Poetry: Science fiction, fantasy and humorous fiction; cat themes only. Length: 800 to 2,500 words. Pays $15 to $100. Poetry in traditional forms, blank or free verse, avant-garde forms and some light verse; cat themes only. Length: 4 to 64 lines. Pays 30¢/line.

DOG FANCY, Fancy Publications, Inc., Box 4030, San Clemente CA 92672. (714)498-1600. Editor: Mike Criss. For men and women of all ages interested in all phases of dog ownership. Bimonthly magazine; 40 pages. Estab. 1969. Circ. 40,000. Pays on publication. Buys all rights, but may reassign following publication. Submit seasonal/holiday material 4 months in advance. Previously published submissions OK. Sample copy $1.25; free writer's guidelines. SASE.

Nonfiction: Historical; how-to; humor; informational; interview; personal experience; photo feature; profile and technical. Buys 5 mss/issue. Length: 500-3,500 words. Pays 3¢/word.

Photos: Photos purchased with or without accompanying ms. Pays $7.50 minimum for 8x10 b&w glossies; $50-100 for 35mm or 2¼x2¼ color photos. Send prints and transparencies. Model release required.

Fiction: Adventure; fantasy; historical and humorous. Buys 5 mss/year. Send complete ms. Length: 500-5,000 words. Pays 3¢/word.

Fillers: "Need short punchy photo fillers and timely news items. Also need short pieces with a definite point of view to be used as editorials." Buys 10 fillers/year. Length: 100-500 words. Pays 3¢/word.

THE EQUESTRIAN IMAGE, Image Publications and Promotions, R.R. 5, Fenwick, Ontario, Canada L0S 1C0. (416)892-2222. Editor-in-Chief: Pat Mellen. Emphasizes equine world; from novice to professional, all breeds from pony to draft, all facets from breeding to clipping. Monthly magazine; 56 pages. Estab. 1973. Circ. 6,500. Pays on publication. Buys one-time rights. Submit seasonal/holiday material 1 month in advance. Simultaneous, photocopied and previously published submissions OK. SAE and International Reply Coupons. Reports in 6 weeks. Free sample copy.

Nonfiction: "All topics open to writers." Buys 6-12 mss/year. Send complete ms. Pays 40¢/column inch.

Photos: Photos purchased with accompanying ms or on assignment. Captions required. Pays $2 minimum for b&w and color photos. Send prints.

Fiction: Historical and humorous. Buys 6-12 mss/year. Send complete ms. Pays 40¢/column inch.

Fillers: Jokes, gags, anecdotes, puzzles and short humor. Buys 6-12 mss/year. Pays $3.

FAMILY PET, Box 22964, Tampa FL 33622. Editor-in-Chief: M. Linda Sabella. 25% freelance written. Emphasizes pets and pet owners in Florida. "Our readers are all ages; many show pets, most have more than one pet, and most are in Florida." Quarterly magazine; 16-24 pages. Estab. 1971. Circ. 3,000. Pays on publication. Buys one-time rights. Previously published submissions OK. SASE. Reports in 3-4 weeks. Free sample copy and writer's guidelines.

Nonfiction: Historical (especially breed histories); how-to (training and grooming hints); humor (or living with pets); informational; personal experience; photo feature and travel (with pets). Buys 1-2 mss/issue. Send complete ms. Length: 500-1,200. Pays $5-20.

Photos: Photos purchased with or without accompanying ms. Captions required. Pays $3-5 for 5x7 b&w glossies. Send prints. Total purchase price for ms includes payment for photos.

Columns/Departments: New Books (reviews of recent issues in pet field). Send complete ms. Length: 200-400 words. Pays $3-5. Open to suggestions for new columns/departments.

Poetry: Light verse, prefers rhyme. Buys 1/issue. Length: 25 lines maximum. Pays $3-5.

Fillers: Jokes, gags, anecdotes, puzzles and short humor. Buys 4-5 fillers/year. Length: 100-400 words. Pays $2-5.

HORSE AND HORSEMAN, Box HH, Capistrano Beach CA 92624. Editor: Mark Thiffault. 75% freelance written. For owners of pleasure horses; predominantly female with main interest in show/pleasure riding. Monthly magazine; 74 pages. Estab. 1973. Circ. 96,000. Buys all rights, but will reassign rights to author after publication. Buys 40 to 50 mss/year. Pays on acceptance. Free sample copy and writer's guidelines. Submit special material (horse and tack care; veterinary medicine pieces in winter and spring issues) 3 months in advance. Reports within 1 month. Query first or submit complete ms. SASE.
Nonfiction and Photos: Training tips, do-it-yourself pieces, grooming and feeding, stable management, tack maintenance, sports, personalities, rodeo and general features of horse-related nature. Emphasis must be on informing, rather than merely entertaining. Aimed primarily at the beginner, but with information for experienced horsemen. Subject matter must have thorough, in-depth appraisal. Interested in more English (hunter/jumper) riding/training copy, plus pieces on driving horses and special horse areas like Tennessee Walkers and other gaited breeds. More factual breed histories. Uses informational, how-to, personal experience, interview, profile, humor, historical, nostalgia, successful business operations, technical articles. Length: 2,000 words minimum. Pays $75 to $200. B&w photos (4x5 and larger) purchased with or without mss. Pays $4 to $10 when purchased without ms. Uses original color transparencies (35mm and larger). Will not consider duplicates. Pays $100 for cover use. Payment for inside editorial color is negotiated.

HORSE ILLUSTRATED, Box A, Lake Elsinore CA 92330. (714)674-1404. Editor-in-Chief: Richard Gibson. 80% freelance written. Bimonthly magazine; 68 pages. Estab. August 1977. Circ. 102,000. Pays on publication. Buys second serial (reprint) rights and first North American serial rights. Submit seasonal material 3 months in advance of issue date. Previously published submissions OK. SASE. Reports in 8 weeks. Sample copy 50¢; free writer's guidelines; mention *Writer's Market* in request.
Nonfiction: Exposé (BLM and wild horses); general interest (anything as long as it concerns the horse); historical (how horses were treated and their accomplishments); how-to (better ways to feed and groom horses and success in show ring or on event course); inspirational (success stories); interview (usually with show judges and trainers—tips on improving); new product (consumer information); nostalgia (movie cowboys and old cowboys in general); photo feature (as long as there is considerable caption material); profile (riders, judges, horses); technical (explaining things to readers); and travel (good places for trail riding). Buys 120 mss/year. Query. Length: 1,000-1,500 words. Pays 5-10¢/word.
Photos: State availability of photos with query. Offers no additional payment for 5x7 or 8x10 b&w glossy prints. Captions preferred. Buys all rights, but may reassign following publication.
Columns/Departments: I Learned About Horses From. Buys 4 mss/issue. Query. Length: 100-500 words. Pays $25-75. Open to suggestions for new columns/departments.
Fiction: "Would be interested if we receive well-written, interesting material." Length: 1,000-2,500 words. Submit complete ms. Pays 5-10¢/word.
Fillers: Cartoons. Pays $12.50 for each cartoon used.

HORSE LOVER'S NATIONAL MAGAZINE, Uniplan Publishing Corp., Box 640, San Martin CA 95046. (408)683-2683. Editor-in-Chief: Robert J. Lydon. Emphasizes horses and horse owners. Monthly magazine; 64 pages. Estab. 1936. Circ. 120,000. Pays on publication. Buys first North American serial rights. Phone queries OK. Submit seasonal/holiday material 6 months in advance. Photocopied and previously published submissions OK. SASE. Reports in 6 weeks. Sample copy $1.25; free writer's guidelines.
Nonfiction: Nanette Meek, associate editor. Historical, how-to; informational; interview (well known and respected horse people only); personal experience; photo feature; profile and medical (related to horses). Buys 15 mss/year. Query. Length: 1,000-2,500 words. Pays 5-10¢/word.
Photos: Photos purchased with or without accompanying ms or on assignment. Captions required. Pays $10-25 for 35mm color transparencies; no payment for 5x7 b&w glossies submitted with ms. Model release required.
Fiction: Adventure; historical; humorous; mainstream; mystery; suspense and western. Buys 1 ms/issue. Send complete ms. Length: 1,000-2,000 words. Pays $25-75. Buys some column space (800-1,200 words at 5¢/word) and poetry (for the Junior Section; no payment involved).
Fillers: Jokes, gags, anecdotes, newsbreaks and short humor. Buys 6 fillers/issue. Length: 25-200 words. Pays $5-10.

HORSE, OF COURSE, Derbyshire Publishing Co., Temple NH 03084. (603)654-6126. Editor-in-Chief: R.A. Greene. 80% freelance written. For novice, backyard horsemen. Monthly magazine; 84 pages. Estab. 1972. Circ. 120,000. Pays on publication. Buys all rights. Submit seasonal/holiday material 6 months in advance. SASE. Reports in 3 weeks. Sample copy $1.25; free writer's guidelines.
Nonfiction: How-to (about all aspects of horsemanship, horse care, and horse owning), historical (on breeds, famous horse-related people, etc., would be particularly saleable if they include some tips on riding and horse care), interview (with trainers, riders giving their methods), photo feature ('how-to' photo features). Buys 35-50 mss/year. Submit complete ms. Length: 800-3,500 words. Pays $10-200.
Photos: Purchased with accompanying ms. Captions required. Submit prints. Pays minimum $3 for 4x5 or larger b&w glossies; pays $10-50 for 35mm or 8x10 glossy color prints (for cover). Model release required.

HORSE PLAY, 443 N. Frederick Ave., Gaithersburg MD 20760. (301)840-1866. Editor-in-Chief: Susanne Saver. Managing Editor: Cordelia Doucet. 50% freelance written. Emphasizes horses and horse sports for a readership interested in horses, especially people who show, event and hunt. Monthly magazine; 48 pages. Estab. 1975. Circ. 10,000. Pays on publication. Buys first North American serial rights. Phone queries OK. Submit seasonal/holiday material 3 months in advance. SASE. Reports in 6 weeks. Sample copy $1.50; free writer's guidelines.
Nonfiction: Expose; how-to (various aspects of horsemanship, course designing, stable management, putting on horse shows, etc.); historical; humor; interview; nostalgia; personal experience; personal opinion; photo feature; profile; technical; and travel. Buys 40 mss/year. Length: 1,000-3,000 words. Pays $35-75.
Photos: Margaret Thomas, Photo Editor. Purchased on assignment. Captions required. Query or send contact sheet, prints, or transparencies. Pays $5 for 8x10 b&w glossies; $50 maximum for color transparencies.
Columns/Departments: Book Reviews, Roundup, and News Releases. Pays $10.

HORSEMAN, The Magazine of Western Riding, 5314 Bingle Rd., Houston TX 77092. (713)688-8811. Editor: Allen Bird. 80% freelance written. For people who own and ride horses for pleasure and competition. Majority own western stock horses and compete in western type horse shows as a hobby or business. Monthly. "We have 6 special emphasis issues per year, but they're not standard. Subjects may vary from year to year." Estab. 1954. Circ. 175,000. Rights purchased vary with author and material. Buys all rights, first North American serial rights, or second serial (reprint) rights. Buys approximately 110 mss per year. Payment on publication. Free sample copy and writer's guidelines. Will not consider photocopied submissions. Submit seasonal material 4 months in advance. Reports in 3 weeks. Query first. SASE.
Nonfiction, Photos, and Poetry: "How-to articles on horsemanship, training, grooming, exhibiting, nutrition, horsekeeping, mare care and reproduction, horse health, humor and history dealing with horses. We really like articles from professional trainers, or about their methods, written by freelancers. The approach should always be to provide information which will educate and inform readers as to how they can ride, train, keep and enjoy their horses more. Compared to other horse publications, we try to be more professional in our writing and really have meaningful articles in the magazine." Length: 1,000 to 2,500 words. Pays 7-10¢/word. Photos purchased with accompanying ms. Captions required. Also purchased on assignment. Pays $6 minimum for b&w 8x10 and negs; 35mm or 120 negs. $25 for inside color. Prefers transparencies. Pays $100 for covers; all rights. Buys some traditional forms of poetry. Pays $10 for all rights.

HORSEMEN'S JOURNAL, 6000 Executive Bldg., Suite 317, Rockville MD 20852. Publisher: Anthony Chamblin. For an audience composed entirely of thoroughbred running-horse owners, trainers, breeders, officials and fans. Monthly magazine; 72 pages. Special issues: May (Kentucky Derby issue); December, July and August (material relating to racehorse breeding and bloodlines); September (material relating to training). Estab. 1949. Circ. 38,000. Rights purchased vary with author and material. Buys all rights, first North American serial rights, and second serial (reprint) rights. Buys "less than 6 unsolicited mss a year; over 50 mss on assignment basis." Pays on publication. Sample copy $1. Will not consider photocopied or simultaneous submissions. Submit seasonal material first of month preceding cover date. Reports "as soon as possible." Query first. SASE.
Nonfiction and Photos: "Any material which our readership can relate to on a professional level. This includes personality pieces, interviews, how-to articles, veterinary stories and generally

material relating to happenings and economics within the racehorse industry." Length: 1,000 to 3,000 words. Pays $45 minimum. 8x10 b&w glossies are purchased with accompanying ms. Captions optional. Pays $10 each.
How To Break In: "Because of our monthly deadline and competition from dailies and weeklies, 'current events' pieces are of little use. Material should be incisive, should quote the people involved in their words and should have national import and interest."

HORSEMEN'S YANKEE PEDLAR NEWSPAPER, Wilbraham MA 01095. (413)589-9088. Editor-in-Chief: Beverly Foisy. "All-breed monthly for horse enthusiasts of all ages and incomes, from one horse owners to large commercial stables." Monthly magazine; 116 pages. Estab. 1962. Circ. 12,500. Pays on publication. Buys one-time rights. Submit seasonal/holiday material 2-3 months in advance of issue date. SASE. Reports in 4 weeks. Sample copy $1.
Nonfiction: How-to; humor; educational; interview; and nostalgia about horses and the people involved with them. Buys 50-60 mss/year. Submit complete ms or outline. Length: 1,500-2,500 words. Pays $50-100, including photos.
Photos: Purchased with ms. Captions required. Buys 1 cover photo/month. Submit b&w prints. Pays $10.
Columns/Departments: Area news column. Buys 85-95/year. Length: 1,200-1,400 words. Pays 70¢/column inch. Query.

HUNTING DOG MAGAZINE, 9714 Montgomery Rd., Cincinnati OH 45242. (513)891-0060. Editor-in-Chief: George R. Quigley. Emphasizes sporting dogs. Monthly magazine; 56 pages. Estab. 1965. Circ. 31,000. Pays on publication. Buys all rights but may reassign following publication. Phone queries OK. Submit seasonal/holiday material 5-6 months in advance. Photocopied submissions OK. Reports in 3-4 weeks. Free sample copy and writer's guidelines.
Nonfiction: How-to (training dogs, hunting with dogs, building dog-related equipment), informational, interview (with well-known outdoor and dog-related persons), personal opinion (by the experts), profile, new product, photo feature, technical (guns, dog-related items). Buys 175-200 mss/year. Query or submit complete ms. Length: 1,500-2,200 words. Pays 3¢/word minimum.
Photos: Purchased with or without accompanying ms. Captions required. Send contact sheet, prints or transparencies. Pays $5 minimum for 8x10 b&w glossy prints; $50 for 35mm or 2¼x2¼ vertical transparencies (for cover).
Fillers: "Short (200-700 words) pieces about hunting dogs or new uses for equipment." Buys 100 mss/year. Submit complete ms. Pays "3¢/word.

PRACTICAL HORSEMEN, The Pennsylvania Horse, Inc., 225 S. Church St., West Chester PA 19380. Editor-in Chief: Pamela Goold. For knowledgeable horsemen interested in breeding, raising and training thoroughbred and thoroughbred-type horses for show, eventing, dressage, race or hunt and field. Monthly magazine; 56-64 pages. Estab. 1973. Circ. 18,000. Pays on publication. Buys all rights. Simultaneous and photocopied submissions OK, but will not use any submission unless withdrawn from other publishers. SASE. Reports in 2 months. Free sample copy and writer's guidelines.
Nonfiction: How-to-do-it interviews with top professional horsemen in the hunter/jumper field; veterinary and stable management articles; and photo features and step-by-step ideas for barn building, grooming, trimming, and feeding and management tips. Buys 3-4/issue. Query with sample of writing or complete ms. Length: open. Pays $100.
Photos: Purchased on assignment. Captions required. Query. Pays $5 minimum for b&w glossies (5x7 minimum size); $40 maximum for 35mm or 2¼x2¼ color transparencies for covers.

THE QUARTER HORSE JOURNAL, Box 9105, Amarillo TX 79105. (806)376-4811. Editor-in-Chief: Audie Rackley. Official publication of the American Quarter Horse Association. Monthly magazine; 600 pages. Estab. 1948. Circ. 70,000. Pays on acceptance. Buys all rights, but on occasion will buy first rights. Phone queries OK. Submit seasonal/holiday material 2 months in advance. SASE. Reports in 2 weeks. Free sample copy and writer's guidelines.
Nonfiction: Historical (those that retain our western heritage); how-to (fitting, grooming, showing, clipping, or anything that relates to owning, showing, or breeding); informational (educational clinics, current news); interview (feature-type stories; must be on established people who have made a contribution to the business); new product; personal opinion; and technical (medical updates, new surgery procedures, etc.). Buys 15 mss/year. Length: 800-2,500 words. Pays $40-100.
Photos: Purchased with accompanying ms. Captions required. Send prints or transparencies. Uses 5x7 or 8x10 b&w glossies; 2¼x2¼ or 3x5 color transparencies. Offers no additional

payment for photos accepted with accompanying ms.

THE QUARTER HORSE OF THE PACIFIC COAST, Pacific Coast Quarter Horse Assn., Box 254822, Gate 12 Cal Expo, Sacramento CA 95825. Editor-in-Chief: Jill L. Scopinich. 90% freelance written. Emphasizes quarter horses for owners, breeders and trainers on the west coast. Monthly magazine; 150 pages. Estab. 1945. Circ. 8,200. Pays on publication. Buys all rights and first North American serial rights. Simultaneous submissions OK. SASE. Reports in 4 weeks. Sample copy $1.
Nonfiction: How-to; informational; interview; personal experience; photo feature and profile. Buys 2 mss/issue. Send complete ms. Length: 500-3,000 words. Pays $50-150.
Photos: Photos purchased with or without accompanying ms. Captions required. Pays $3-5 for 8x10 b&w glossies. Model release required.
Columns/Departments: Of Course, A Horse; Racing Room and The Stable Pharmacy. Buys 3 mss/issue. Send complete ms. Length: 500-2,000 words. Pays $50-100.
Fiction: Humorous and western. Buys 6 mss/year. Send complete ms. Length: 500-3,000 words. Pays $50-150.

TODAY'S ANIMAL HEALTH, Animal Health Foundation, 1905 Sunnycrest Dr., Fullerton CA 92635. Editor-in-Chief: Richard Glassberg, D.V.M. Managing Editor: Jane Wright. 100% freelance written. Emphasizes animal health, nutrition and care for people who own animals. Bimonthly magazine; 32-40 pages. Estab. 1970. Circ. 35,000. Pays on publication. Buys all rights. Submit seasonal/holiday material 6 months in advance of issue date. Simultaneous, photocopied and previously published submissions OK. SASE. Reports in 2 months. Sample copy $1; writer's guidelines for SASE; mention *Writer's Market* in request, to Mr. Harry Maiden, 8338 Rosemead, Pico Rivera CA 90660.
Nonfiction: Exposé; how-to; general interest; interview; photo feature; profile; and technical. Buys 6/issue. Submit complete ms. Length 250-2,000 words. Pays $5-25.
Photos: D.M. Diem, photo editor. Submit photo material with accompanying ms. Pays $5-25 for 8x10 b&w glossy prints and $5-25 for 5x7 color prints. Caption preferred. Buys all rights, but may reassign following publication.

TROPICAL FISH HOBBYIST, 211 W. Sylvania Ave., Neptune City NJ 17753. Editor: Marshall Ostrow. 75% freelance written. For tropical fish keepers; mostly male, mostly young. Monthly magazine; 100 pages. Estab. 1952. Circ. 40,000. Rights purchased vary with author and material. Usually buys all rights, but buys only serial rights in some cases. Buys 50 mss a year. Pays on acceptance. Sample copy $1. Will not consider photocopied or simultaneous submissions. Reports within 1 week. Query first or submit complete ms. SASE.
Nonfiction and Photos: "Don't submit material unless you're an experienced keeper of tropical fishes and know what you're talking about. Offer specific advice about caring for and breeding tropicals and related topics. Study the publication before submitting." Informal style preferred. Can use personality profiles of successful aquarium hobbyists, but query first on these. Pays from 1½¢ to 3¢ a word. Pays $5 for b&w glossy photos purchased with or without accompanying mss. No size limitation. Captions optional. Pays $10 for color; 35mm transparency, or larger.

THE WESTERN HORSEMAN, Box 7980, Colorado Springs CO 80933. Editor: Chan Bergen. Emphasizes western horsemanship. Monthly magazine. Estab. 1936. Circ. 195,000. Pays on acceptance. Buys one-time rights. Submit seasonal/holiday material 3 months in advance. SASE. Reports in 2-3 weeks. Sample copy $1.
Nonfiction: How-to (horse training, care of horses, tips, etc.); and informational (on rodeos, ranch life, historical articles of the west emphasizing horses). Buys 15-20/issue. Submit complete ms. Pays $35-85; "sometimes higher by special arrangement."
Photos: Purchased with accompanying ms. Captions required. Uses 5x7 or 8x10 b&w glossies. Total purchase for ms includes payment for photos.

Art Publications

THE AMERICAN ART JOURNAL, Kennedy Galleries, Inc., and Israel Sack, Inc., 40 W. 57th St., 5th Floor, New York NY 10019. (212)541-9600. Editor-in-Chief: Jane Van N. Turano. Scholarly magazine of American art history of the 17th, 18th, 19th and 20th centuries, including painting, sculpture, architecture, decorative arts, etc., for people with a serious interest in American art, and who are already knowledgeable about the subject. Readers are scholars, curators, collectors, students of American art, or persons who have a strong interest in

Americana. Quarterly magazine; 112 pages. Estab. 1969. Circ. 2,000. Pays on acceptance. Buys all rights, but may reassign following publication. Photocopied submissions OK. SASE. Reports in 2 months. Sample copy $6.
Nonfiction: "All articles are historical in the sense that they are all about some phase or aspect of American art history." Buys 25-30 mss/year. Submit complete ms "with good cover letter." Length: 2,500-8,000 words. Pays $250-300.
Photos: Purchased with accompanying ms. Captions required. Uses b&w only. Offers no additional payment for photos accepted with accompanying ms.
How To Break In: "Actually, our range of interest is quite broad. Any topic within our time frame is acceptable if it is well-researched, well-written, and illustrated. Whenever possible, all mss must be accompanied by b&w photographs which have been integrated into the text by the use of numbers."
Rejects: No how-to articles or reviews of exhibitions. No book reviews or opinion pieces. No human interest approaches to artists' lives.

AMERICAN ART REVIEW, Box 460, Laguna Beach CA 92651. (714)499-4507. Victoria Kogan. For libraries, museums, professional art historians, artists, collectors; persons interested in American art history heritage. Bimonthly magazine; 144 pages. Estab. 1973. Circ. 10,000. Rights purchased vary with author and material. May buy all rights, but will reassign rights to author after publication; or simultaneous rights. Buys 35-40 mss/year. Pays on publication. Sample copy $3.75; free writer's guidelines. Photocopied and simultaneous submissions OK. Submit special issue material 6 months in advance. Reports in 2 weeks. Query. SASE.
Nonfiction and Photos: Articles must be well-researched and documented, but can be interpretive. Should be highly readable and directed toward art historians/collectors, and concern American art history from the Colonial period to 1950. Would like to see material on American art as an investment; articles about collectors and collections; interpretations of American art history; collecting possibilities. Quality of artists or collectors must be high. Length: 1,500 to 2,000 words. Pays $25 to $150. Also uses reviews of exhibitions and art books. Pays $35 to $100. No additional payment for 8x10 b&w glossies or 4x5, 5x7 or 8x10 color transparencies used with mss. Captions required.

ART NEWS, 750 Third Ave., New York NY 10017. Editor: Milton Esterow. For persons interested in art. Monthly. Circ. 50,000. Query first. Enclose SASE.
Nonfiction: "I'm buying in-depth profiles of people in the art world—artists, curators, dealers. And investigative pieces, including some on antiques. The format is very flexible to cover personalities, trends, a single painting." Wants "humanized" art coverage. Length: 800 words; "some major pieces as long as 8,000 words." Pays $75 to $300.

ARTS MAGAZINE, 23 E. 26th St., New York NY 10010. (212)685-8500. Editor: Richard Martin. A journal of contemporary art, art criticism, and art history, particularly for artists, scholars, museum officials, art teachers and students, and collectors. Estab. 1926. Monthly, except July and August. Circ. 28,500. Buys all rights. Pays on publication. Query first. SASE.
Nonfiction and Photos: Art criticism, art analysis, and art history. Topical reference to museum or gallery exhibition preferred. Length: 1,500 to 2,500 words. Pays $100, with opportunity for negotiation. B&w glossies or color transparencies customarily supplied by related museums or galleries.

ARTS MANAGEMENT, 408 West 57th St., New York NY 10019. (212)245-3850. Editor: A.H. Reiss. 5% freelance written. For cultural institutions. Published five times/year. Circ. 6,000. Buys all rights. Pays on publication. Mostly staff written. Query. Reports in several weeks. SASE. Pays on publication. Mostly staff written. Query. Reports in several weeks. SASE.
Nonfiction: Short articles, 400 to 900 words, tightly written, expository, explaining how art administrators solved problems in publicity, fund raising, and general administration; actual case histories emphasizing the how-to. Also short articles on the economics and sociology of the arts and important trends in the nonprofit cultural field. Must be fact-filled, well-organized and without rhetoric. Payment is 2¢ to 4¢ per word. No photographs or pictures.

THE CULTURAL POST, National Endowment for the Arts, 2401 E St., NW., Washington DC 20506. Editor: George Clack. The official newspaper of the Arts Endowment, a federal agency that gives grants to nonprofit cultural institutions and individual artists. Bimonthly magazine. Buys all rights, but may reassign following publication. Reports in 1 month. SASE.
Nonfiction: "Interested in carefully researched articles on the financial or administrative side of Arts Endowment grantees, examinations of important trends or problems in various art fields,

and reports on arts activities at the state and community level.'' Buys 20 mss/year. Query. Length: 1,000-3,000 words. Pays $300-500, including photos.

DESIGN MAGAZINE, Box 1463, Indianapolis IN 46206. Editor/Publisher: Mary Alice Simpson. ''For teachers, art specialists, and administrators, who work with children in education.'' Bimonthly magazine. Estab. 1898. Pays on publication. Buys all rights. SASE. Reports in 8-10 weeks. Sample copy $1.
Nonfiction: ''We will use articles which will help to promote the following program objectives in schools: enhance instruction in basic studies with interdisciplinary arts-related activities; provide innovative staff development programs based on existing district curriculum; develop and maintain on-going arts programs which integrate community resources with district curriculum; assist in development of aural, oral, visual and non-verbal communication skills; provide experiences in a variety of arts forms in order to assist in the development of realistic self-concepts through creative processes; and strengthen and expand existing arts programs.'' Submit complete ms. Length: 1,000-1,500 words. Pays 3¢/word.

GLASS, 7830 S.W. 40th Ave., Portland OR 97219. For artists working in blown glass, stained glass, conceptual glass; collectors, museum curators, gallery and shop owners, art critics, high school and college students in the arts; general public. Monthly magazine; 68-80 pages. Estab. 1973. Circ. 7,000. Pays on publication. Buys all rights, but may reassign following publication. Simultaneous, photocopied and previously published submissions OK. SASE. Reports in 4 weeks. Sample copy $1, for postage.
Nonfiction: ''We want articles of a general nature treating the arts and crafts in the U.S. and abroad; psychology of art; urban artist. We'll gladly look at anything dealing with the arts and crafts, especially contemporary glass in the U.S. We confine our main interest to contemporary glass arts, and to subjects touching thereon, viz., the energy crisis. Art-oriented themes, reviews of shows including glass arts. Successful business operations (glass blowing or stained glass only). New product (glass oriented only). Pays $25-350.
Photos: No additional payment made for 8x10 b&w glossies used with mss. Captions required.

METROPOLITAN MUSEUM OF ART BULLETIN, Metropolitan Museum of Art, Fifth Ave. and 82nd St., New York NY 10028. Editor: Joan K. Holt. Quarterly. Query first. ''Writers contributing must write entirely on speculation. Most of our writers are scholars or have some reputation in the field, and we commission most of our freelance material.'' SASE.
Nonfiction: Each issue usually covers a single theme. Writers must be acknowledged experts in their fields. ''Our museum experts scrutinize everything very carefully.'' Length: 750 words; 1,500 to 2,000 words. Pays $75 for short pieces, $150 for longer articles.

NEWORLD: THE MULTI-CULTURAL MAGAZINE OF THE ARTS, Inner City Cultural Center, 1308 S. New Hampshire Blvd., Los Angeles CA 90006. (213)387-1161. Editor-in-Chief: Fred Beauford. Managing Editor: Paul De Ceglie. 75% freelance written. Bimonthly magazine; 60 pages. Estab. September 1974. Circ. 15,000. Pays on publication. Buys all rights, but may reassign following publication. Phone queries OK. Submit seasonal/holiday material 4 months in advance of issue date. Photocopied submissions OK. SASE. Reports in 1 week. Sample copy $1.25.
Nonfiction: ''Only articles related to dance, theatre, photography, visual arts, music and poetry.'' How-to; general interest; historical; interview; personal opinion; photo feature; and profile. Buys 3 mss/issue. Submit complete ms. Length: open. Pays $50-75.
Photos: State availability of photos with ms. Submit contact sheets. Pays $5-10/b&w photo. Captions and model release required. Buys one-time rights.
Poetry: Avant-garde; free verse; light verse; and traditional. Buys 7/issue. Limit submissions to batches of 3. Length: 42 lines maximum. No payment.

NEW YORK ARTS JOURNAL, Manhattan Arts Review, Inc., 560 Riverside Dr., New York NY 10027. (212)663-2245. Editors-in-Chief: Richard Burgin and Holland Cotter. Emphasizes the arts: visual arts, fiction, poetry, music, etc. Bimonthly tabloid; 44 pages. Estab. 1976. Circ. 15,000. Buys one-time rights. Phone queries OK. Simultaneous, photocopied and previously published submissions OK. SASE. Reports in 4 weeks. Sample copy $1.
Nonfiction: Historical, informational, interview, photo feature and profile. Buys 3-6 mss/issue. Send complete ms. Pays $3/page.
Photos: Purchased with or without accompany ms. Pays $10 for b&w photos. Send prints. ''We publish full-page portfolios of photos which stand on their own, not necessarily as illustration.''
Columns/Departments: Richard Kuczkowski, Book Review Editor, 15 Forest Glen Rd., Valley

Cottage NY 10989. Book Review, Music Review and Art Review. Send complete ms. Pays $3/page.
Fiction: Adventure, confession, erotica, experimental, fantasy, historical, humor, mystery, romance, science fiction. Buys 2 mss/issue. Send complete ms. Pays $3/page.
Poetry: David Lehman, Poetry Editor. Avant-garde, free verse and traditional. Buys 6-8 poems/issue. Pays $15/poem.

THE ORIGINAL ART REPORT, Box 1641, Chicago IL 60690. (312)588-6897. Editor and Publisher: Frank Salantrie. Emphasizes "visual art conditions for visual artists, art museum presidents and trustees, collectors of fine art, art educators, and interested citizens." Monthly newsletter; 6-8 pages. Estab. 1967. Circ. 1,000. Pays on publication. Buys all rights. Phone queries OK. SASE. Reports in 2 weeks. Sample copy $1.
Nonfiction: Expose (art galleries, government agencies ripping off artists, or ignoring them), historical (perspective pieces relating to now), humor (whenever possible), informational (material that is unavailable in other art publications), inspirational (acts and ideas of courage), interview (with artists, other experts; serious material), personal opinion, technical (brief items to recall traditional methods of producing art), travel (places in the world where artists are welcome and honored) philosophical, economic, aesthetic, and artistic. Query or submit complete ms. Length: 1,000 words maximum. Pays 1¢/word.
Columns/Departments: WOW (Worth One Wow), Worth Repeating, and Worth Repeating Again. "Basically, these are reprint items with introduction to give context and source, including complete name and address of publication. Looking for insightful, succinct commentary." Submit complete ms. Length: 500 words. Pays ½¢/word. Open to suggestions for new columns/departments.

SOUTHWEST ART, Art Magazine Publishers, Box 13037, Houston TX 77019. (713)529-3533. Editor-in-Chief: Vicki Baucum. Emphasizes art: painting and sculpture. Monthly magazine; 112 pages. Estab. 1971. Circ. 17,500. Pays on 10th of month following publication. Buys all rights, but may reassign following publication. Photocopied submissions OK. SASE. Reports in 6 weeks. Sample copy $3.
Nonfiction: Informational, interview, personal opinion, and profile. "We publish articles about artists and art trends. We primarily concentrate on artists living west of the Mississippi and on art trends occurring within the same geographical region. The articles should be informative, but not biographical. They should be in-depth pieces about the artist's opinions as to why he does what he does, and how this has developed." Buys 72 mss/year. Query; also submit 10 8x10 b&w glossies, 4 8x10 color prints and a short biography of the artist. Length: 2,000 words minimum. Pays $00-150.

TODAY'S ART, 6 E. 43rd St., New York NY 10017. Editor: George A. Magnan. For "artists (professional and amateur), art teachers, and museums." Monthly. Circulation: 86,000. Buys first rights. Pays on publication. Query first. Enclose SASE.
Nonfiction and Photos: "Only items referring to art and how-to articles in all fields of art with b&w and some color illustrations. Articles should be easy to follow. Most articles we receive are not sufficiently detailed and a lot have to be rewritten to make them more informative." Length: 400 to 850 words. Pays $25 to $50.
How To Break In: "Every now and then, someone comes up with a good idea, even if no idea can be completely new, of course. But there are many technical and esthetic possibilities in art. Indeed, there's no limit to them. If a writer, young or old, is sure he has something like that, and knows how to present it in an easily comprehensible manner, we are glad to consider the article. But we don't want philosophizing about art, and we do not wish to promote unknown artists."

WESTART, Box 1396, Auburn CA 95603. (916)885-3242 or 0960. Editor-in-Chief: Jean L. Couzens. Emphasizes art for practicing artists and artist/craftsmen; students of art and art patrons. Semimonthly tabloid; 20 pages. Estab. 1962. Circ. 7,500. Pays on publication. Buys all rights, but may reassign following publication. Phone queries OK. Submit seasonal/holiday material 2 months in advance. Photocopied submissions OK. Sample copy 50¢; free writer's guidelines.
Nonfiction: Informational; photo feature; and profile. Buys 6-8 mss/year. Query or submit complete ms. Length:7-800 words. Pays 30¢/column inch.
Photos: Purchased with or without accompanying ms. Send b&w prints. Pays 30¢/column inch.

Association, Club, and Fraternal

The following publications exist to publicize—to members, friends, and institutions—the ideals, objectives, projects, and activities of the sponsoring club or organization. Club-financed magazines that carry material not directly related to the group's activities (for example, *Manage* magazine in the Management and Supervision Trade Journals) are classified by their subject matter in the Consumer and Trade Journals sections of this book.

THE AMERICAN LEGION MAGAZINE, 1608 K St., N.W., Washington DC 20006. (202)393-4811. 75% freelance written. Monthly. Circ. 2.6 million. Reports on most submissions promptly; borderline decisions take time. Buys first North American serial rights. Pays on acceptance. Include phone number with ms. SASE.
Nonfiction: Most articles written on order. Some over transom. Writers may query for subject interest. Subjects include national and international affairs, American history, reader self-interest, great military campaigns and battles, major aspects of American life, vignettes of servicemen, veterans and their families, etc. Length: maximum of 20 double-spaced typewritten pages. Pay varies widely with length and worth of work. Research assignments for some skilled reporters. Proven pros only.
Photos: Chiefly on assignment. Some over-transom stories or photos click.
Poetry and Humor: Limited market for short, light verse, and short, humorous anecdotes, epigrams, jokes, etc. No serious verse. Taboos: old material; bad taste; amateurish work. Short humorous verse: $3.50 per line, minimum $10. Epigrams: $10. Anecdotes: $20.

AUTOMOTIVE BOOSTER OF CALIFORNIA, Box 765, LaCanada CA 91011. (213)790-6554. Editor: Don McAnally. 3% freelance written. For members of Automotive Booster clubs, automotive warehouse distributors and automotive parts jobbers in California. Estab. 1967. Monthly. Circ. 4,000. Not copyrighted. Pays on publication. Submit complete ms. SASE.
Nonfiction and Photos: Will look at short articles and pictures about successes of automotive parts outlets in California. Also can use personnel assignments for automotive parts people in California. Pays $1 per column inch (about 2¢ a word); $5 for b&w photos used with mss.

CALIFORNIA HIGHWAY PATROLMAN, California Association of Highway Patrolmen. 2030 V St., Sacramento CA 95818. (916)452-6751. Editor: Richard York. Monthly magazine; 100 pages. Estab. 1937. Circ. 16,000. Pays on publication. Buys all rights, but may reassign following publication. SASE. Reports in 1 month. Free sample copy.
Nonfiction: Publishes articles on transportation safety and driver education. "Topics can include autos, boats, bicycles, motorcycles, snowmobiles, recreational vehicles and pedestrian safety. We are also in the market for travel pieces and articles on early California. We are *not* a technical journal for teachers and traffic safety experts, but rather a general interest publication geared toward the layman. Please note that we are not a law enforcement magazine." Submit complete ms. Pays 2½¢/word.
Photos: "Illustrated articles always receive preference." Pays $2.50/b&w.

EASY LIVING MAGAZINE, The Webb Company, 1999 Shepard Rd., St. Paul MN 55116. (612)647-7304. Executive Editor: Don Picard. Editor: Adele Renee Malott. 75% freelance written. "The publication's editorial goal is to inform and entertain the readers, with emphasis on the former." Emphasizes international travel, profiles, lifestyles, family activities, and consumer and food articles; for an audience between 35 and 65; fairly high income. Distributed by Savers Travel Club, Ltd. Quarterly magazine; 36 pages. Estab. 1974. Circ. 300,000. Pays on acceptance. Buys all rights, but will reassign following publication. Submit seasonal/holiday material 6 months-1 year in advance. Photocopied submissions OK. SASE. Reports on queries in 3 weeks; on mss in 6 weeks. Free sample copy and writer's guidelines.
Nonfiction: Informational (about popular activities, new trends), profile (of known or unknown), and travel (international, Europe, Caribbean, Mexico, Far East, and Hawaii only). Query. Length: 1,000-2,500 words. Pays $150-400.
Photos: Photos purchased with or without accompanying ms (but only to illustrate ms already purchased). Captions required. Pays $35 for 8x10 b&w glossies; $75 minimum for 35mm color photos; $250 for color cover photos. Total purchase price for a ms includes payment for photos. Model release "preferred, but in some circumstances may be dispensed with."

THE ELKS MAGAZINE, 1425 W. Diversey, Chicago IL 60614. Managing Editor: Jeffrey Ball.

80% freelance written. Emphasizes general interest with family appeal. Monthly magazine; 56 pages. Estab. 1922. Circ. 1,600,000. Pays on acceptance. Buys first North American serial rights. Submit seasonal/holiday material 4-6 months in advance. Previously published submissions OK. SASE. Reports in 4-6 weeks. Free sample copy and writer's guidelines.
Nonfiction: Expose; historical (no textbook stuff); informational; and new product (like smoke detectors, etc.). Buys 3-4 mss/issue. Query. Length: 2,000-3,500. Pays $250-350.
Photos: Purchased with or without accompanying manuscript (for cover). Captions required. Query with photos or send transparencies. Uses 8x10 or 5x7 b&w glossies and 35mm or 2x2 color transparencies (for cover). Pays $250 minimum for color (cover). Total purchase price for ms includes payment for photos.
Fiction: Adventure, fantasy, historical, humorous, mainstream, mystery, science fiction, suspense and western. Buys 6 mss/year. Submit complete ms. Length: 1,500-2,500 words. Pays $150 minimum.
How To Break In: "In the past, TEM has used very little fiction. A freelancer desiring to break in would do best to think in terms of nonfiction. Since we continue to offer sample copies and guidelines for the asking there is no excuse for being unfamiliar with TEM. A submission, following a go ahead would do best to include several b&w prints, if the piece lends itself to illustration, and a short cover letter. It's not wise to try to sneak through by implying the submission is in answer to a go ahead (i.e., Here's the piece you asked to see). If we didn't ask to see it, we'll know. Short humor (1,500-2,000) has been a best bet in fiction. While TEM has not been a big fiction market, we hope to include more. Family appeal is the watchword. No query is necessary for fiction."

THE FLYFISHER, 390 Bella Vista, San Francisco CA 94127. (415)586-8332. Editor: Michael Fong. "*The Flyfisher* is the official publication of the Federation of Flyfishermen, a non-profit organization of member clubs and individuals in the US, Canada, United Kingdom, France, New Zealand, Chile and other nations. It serves an audience of sophisticated anglers." Quarterly magazine; 40 pages. Estab. 1968. Circ. 7,000. Pays on acceptance for solicited material. Buys first North American serial rights. Submit seasonal/holiday material 90 days in advance of issue date. SASE. Reports in 4 weeks. Sample copy $1.50, available from 519 Main St., El Segundo CA 90245; writer's guidelines for SASE.
Nonfiction: How-to (fly fishing techniques, flytying, tackle, etc.); general interest (any type including where to go, conservation); historical (places, people, events that have significance to fly fishing); inspirational (looking for articles dealing with Federation clubs on conservation projects); interview (articles of famous fly fishermen, fly tiers, teachers, etc.); nostalgia (articles of reminiscences on flies, fishing personalities, equipment and places); photo feature (preferably a combination of 35mm slides about places and seasons); technical (about techniques of fly fishing in salt and fresh waters). "Our readers are pretty sophisticated fly fishermen and articles too basic or not innovative do not appeal to us." Buys 7-8 mss/issue. Query. Length: 1,500-3,500 words. Pays $50-175.
Photos: Pays $15-25 for 8x10 b&w glossy prints; $40-100 for 35mm or larger color transparencies. Captions required. Buys one-time rights. Prefers a selection of transparencies and glossies when illustrating with a manuscript, which are purchased as a package.
Fiction: Adventure; confession; fantasy; historical; humorous; and suspense. Buys 2 mss/issue. Query. Length: 1,500-2,500 words. Pays $50-125.

FUTURE, Box 7, Tulsa OK 74102. (918)584-2481. Editor-in-Chief: Stephen Coury. 15% freelance written. For members of the US Jaycees; all males between 18-36, upper income for their age bracket, and community-involvement oriented. Bimonthly magazine: 32 pages. Estab. 1938. Circ. 350,000. Pays on publication. Buys all rights. Submit seasonal/holiday material 3 months in advance of issue date. Reports in 2 weeks. Free sample copy and writer's guidelines; mention *Writer's Market* in request.
Nonfiction: General interest (directed at males between 18-36; trends); how-to (fund-raising, citizen action in government; directed at non-professionals); photo feature (citizen involvement in community); and profile (a young successful man on the move). Query. Length: 500-1,200 words. Payment is year's subscription.

KANSAS MOTORIST, 4020 W. 6th, Topeka KS 66606. Editor: Ronald M. Welch. 30% freelance written. For Kansas members of the American Automobile Association. Bimonthly magazine; 16 pages. Estab. 1952. Circ. 50,000. Buys second serial (reprint) rights. Pays on acceptance. Free sample copy. Will consider photocopied and simultaneous submissions. Reports in 3 weeks. Query or submit complete ms. Enclose SASE
Nonfiction and Photos: Informative and entertaining articles of interest to the Kansas motoring

public. Primarily interested in features with regional travel, especially Kansas. Length: 1,500 words maximum. Pays 2¢ a word. High quality 8x10 or 5x7 b&w glossies purchased with mss. Captions required. Pays $2.50 to $10. The higher rate of payment is for cover shots of Kansas subjects.

THE KEY MAGAZINE, 144 W. 12th Ave., Denver CO 80204. (303)222-7734. Publication of the Inter-Community Action Association. Editor: Lou Thomas. For the general public interested in news analysis as well as news reporting. Published 6 times a year. Circ. 12,000. Buys all rights. Buys about 50 mss a year. Payment on publication. Will send sample copy to writer for 75¢. Mss must be double-spaced, with 55-character line. Reports in 3 to 4 weeks. Enclose SASE.
Nonfiction and Photos: "News summary materials of events or activities happening (or that have happened) that have national relevance though of local origin. Analysis must be included. Reports on government, culture(s), crime, law, economy, etc. All materials must provide more than one point of view. Seek freelance book, movie, and concert reviews." Buys interviews, profiles, spot news, historical and essay pieces, and photo features. Length: 2,000 to 4,000 words. Pays 1¢ to 3 ¢ a word. B&w glossies and color transparencies purchased with mss. Pays $5 to $20.
Fillers: Newsbreaks, letters to the editor. Analysis preferably included. Length: 500 to 1,500 words. Pays $5 minimum.
How To Break In: "New writers can best 'break into' our publication by providing fresh approaches to subjects not normally covered by the established news periodicals. Prefer the perspectives of cultural and ethnic groups not represented in the larger publications. Material is selected depending on how well the viewpoint (extremist or conformist) is clearly stated and the position taken is defended."

THE KIWANIS MAGAZINE, 101 E. Erie St., Chicago IL 60611. Executive Editor: David B. Williams. 90% of feature articles are freelance written. For business and professional men. Published 10 times/year. Buys first North American serial rights. Pays on acceptance. Free sample copy. Query. Reports on submission in 4 weeks. SASE.
Nonfiction and Photos: Articles about social and civic betterment, business, education, religion, domestic affairs, etc. Emphasis on objectivity, intelligent analysis and thorough research of contemporary problems. Concise writing, absence of cliches, and impartial presentation of controversy required. Length: 1,500 words to 3,000 words. Pays $300 to $600. "No fiction, personal essays, fillers, or verse of any kind. A light or humorous approach welcomed where subject is appropriate and all other requirements are observed. Detailed queries can save work and submission time. We often accept photos submitted with mss, but we do not pay extra for them; they are considered part of the price of the ms. Our rate for a ms with good photos is higher than for one without."

LEADER, The Order of United Commercial Travelers of America, 632 North Park St., Columbus OH 43215. (614)228-3276. Editor-in-Chief: James R. Eggert. 5% freelance written. Emphasizes fraternalism for its officers and active membership. Published 8 times per year; magazine; 32 pages. Estab. 1976. Circ. 25,000. Pays on publication. Buys all rights, but may reassign following publication. Submit seasonal/holiday material 3 months in advance of issue date. SASE. Reports in 1 week. Free sample copy and writer's guidelines; mention *Writer's Market* in request.
Nonfiction: General interest; how-to; humor; interview; and profile. Buys 1 ms/issue. Submit complete ms. Length: 500-3,000 words. Pays 1½¢/word.
Photos: State availability of photos with ms. Pays $5 for 5x7 b&w glossy prints. Captions preferred. Buys all rights. Model release required.
Fiction: Humorous. Buys 2 mss/year. Submit complete ms. Length: 500-1,500 words. Pays 1½¢/word.

THE LION, 300 22nd St., Oak Brook IL 60570. (312)986-1700. Editor-in-Chief: Roy Schaetzel. Senior Editor: Robert Kleinfelder. Emphasizes service club organization for Lions club members and their families. Monthly magazine; 48 pages. Estab. 1918. Circ. 670,000. Pays on acceptance. Buys all rights. Phone queries OK. Submit seasonal/holiday material 4 months in advance. Photocopied submissions OK. SASE. Reports in 2 weeks. Free sample copy and writer's guideline.
Nonfiction: Humor; informational (stories of interest to civic-minded men); and photo feature (must be of a Lions club service project). Buys 4 mss/issue. Query. Length: 500-2,200. Pays $50-400.
Photos: Purchased with or without accompanying ms or on assignment. Captions required.

Query first for photos. B&w glossies at least 5x7. Total purchase price for ms includes payment for photos.

THE LOOKOUT, Seaman's Church Institute, 15 State St., New York NY 10004. (212)269-2710. Editor: Carlyle Windley. 30% freelance written. "Basic purpose is to engender and sustain interest in the work of the Institute and to encourage monetary gifts in support of its philanthropic work among seamen." Monthly, except combined February-March and July-August issues. Magazine; 20 pages. Estab. 1909. Buys first North American serial rights. Payment on publication. Free sample copy. Query first. Reports in 1 month. Enclose SASE.
Nonfiction: Emphasis is on the merchant marine; not Navy, pleasure yachting, power boats, commercial or pleasure fishing, passenger vessels. Buys freelance marine-oriented articles on the old and new, oddities, adventure, factual accounts, unexplained phenomena. Length: 200 to 1,000 words. Pays $40 maximum, depending on quality, length, etc.
Photos: Buys vertical format b&w (no color) cover photo on sea-related subjects. Pays $20; lesser amounts for miscellaneous photos used elsewhere in the magazine.
Poetry: Buys small amount of short verse; seafaring-related but not about the sea per se and the cliches about spume, spray, sparkle, etc. Pays $5.

MR. LONGEARS MAGAZINE, The Noteworthy Company, 100 Church St., Amsterdam, NY 12010. (518)842-2660. Editor-in-Chief: Thomas B. Constantino. Official publication of the American Donkey and Mule Society. "For people that own donkeys or are interested in equines and history and role of animals." Quarterly magazine; 48 pages. Estab. 1971. Circ. 1,500. Pays on acceptance. Buys all rights, but may reassign following publication. Submit seasonal/holiday material 3 months in advance. Simultaneous, photocopied, and previously published submissions OK. SASE. Reports in 1 month. Free sample copy.
Nonfiction: Informational, historical, humor, personal experience, photo feature, and travel. Buys 2 mss/issue. Query. Pays $25.
Photos: Photos purchased with or without accompanying ms or on assignment. Send prints. Total purchase price for ms includes payment for photos.

NATIONAL 4-H NEWS, 150 N. Wacker Dr., Chicago IL 60606. (312)782-5021, Ext. 44. Editor: Bonnie B. Sarkett. For "young to middle-aged adults and older teens (mostly women) who lead 4-H clubs; most with high school, many with college education, whose primary reason for reading us is their interest in working with kids in informal youth education projects, ranging from aerospace to swimming, and almost anything in between." Monthly. Circ. 90,000. Buys first serial or one-time rights. Buys about 10 mss/year. Pays on acceptance. Free sample copy and writer's guidelines. Query first. "We are very specialized, and unless a writer has been published in our magazine before, he more than likely doesn't have a clue to what we can use. When query comes about a specific topic, we often can suggest angles that make it usable." Submit seasonal material 6 months to 1 year in advance. Reports in 3 weeks. SASE.
Nonfiction: "Education and child psychology from authorities, written in light, easy-to-read fashion with specific suggestions how layman can apply them in volunteer work with youth; how-to-do-it pieces about genuinely new and interesting crafts of any kind. This is our primary need now but articles must be fresh in style and ideas, and tell how to make something worthwhile . . . almost anything that tells about kids having fun and learning outside the classroom, including how they became interested, most effective programs, etc., always with enough detail and examples, so reader can repeat project or program with his or her group, merely by reading article. Speak directly to our reader (you) without preaching. Tell him in a conversational text how he might work better with kids to help them have fun and learn at the same time. Use lots of genuine examples (although names and dates not important) to illustrate points. Use contractions when applicable. Write in a concise, interesting way—our readers have other jobs and not a lot of time to spend with us. Will not print stories on 'How this 4-H club made good' or about state or county fair winners. Reasons for rejection of freelance submissions include: failure of the writer to query first; failure of the writer to study back issues; and mss submitted on subjects we've just covered in depth." Length: 1,700 to 3,400 words. Payment up to $100, depending on quality and accompanying photos or illustrations.
Photos: "Photos must be genuinely candid, of excellent technical quality and preferably shot 'available light' or in that style; must show young people or adults and young people having fun learning something. How-to photos or drawings must supplement instructional texts. Photos do not necessarily have to include people. Photos are usually purchased with accompanying ms, with no additional payment. Captions required. If we use an excellent single photo, we generally pay $25 and up."

PERSPECTIVE, Pioneer Girls, Inc., Box 788, Wheaton IL 60187. (312)293-1600. Editor: Julie Smith. 40% freelance written. "All subscribers are volunteer leaders of clubs, anywhere from 1-12 grade. Clubs are sponsored by evangelical, conservative churches throughout North America." Quarterly magazine; 32 pages. Estab. 1964. Circ. 20,000. Pays on acceptance. Buys first North American serial rights. Submit seasonal/holiday material 9 months in advance. Simultaneous submissions OK. SASE. Reports in 3 weeks. Sample copy $1; writer's guidelines for SASE.
Nonfiction: Julie Smith, Articles Editor. How-to (projects for girls' clubs, crafts, cooking service), informational (relationships, human development, mission education, outdoor activities), inspirational (Bible studies, women leading girls), interview (Christian education leaders), personal experience (women working with girls). Buys 4-12 mss/year. Query. Length: 200-1,500 words. Pays $5-40.
Columns/Departments: Julie Smith, Column/Department Editor. Storehouse (craft, game, activity, outdoor activity suggestions — all related to girls' club projects for any age between grades 1-12). Buys 8-10 mss/year. Submit complete ms. Length: 150-250 words. Pays $5.
Fiction: Julie Smith, Fiction Editor. Humorous (women leading girls' clubs), religious (Christian education — message inherent, not tacked on). Buys 1-2 mss/year. Query. Length: 1,000-2,000 words. Pays $20-40.
How To Break In: "Submit articles directly related to club work, practical in nature, i.e., ideas for leader training in communication, Bible knowledge, teaching skills. They must have practical application. We want substance—not ephemeral ideas."

PLANNING, 1313 E. 60th St., Chicago IL 60637. (312)947-2108. Editor: Sylvia Lewis. Publication of the American Society of Planning Officials. For urban planners, public officials, and citizens active in community groups. Magazine; 40 pages. Estab. 1972. Published 11 times/year. Circ. 15,000. Buys first serial rights. Buys about 50 mss/year. Pays on publication. Free sample copy and writer's guidelines. Photocopied submissions OK. Reports in 1 month. Query first. SASE.
Nonfiction and Photos: Articles of high quality on architecture, environment, energy, housing, health care, planning, historic preservation, land use, transportation, urban renewal, neighborhood conservation and zoning. "Articles should be written in magazine feature style. Topics should be current and stress issues, not personalities, though quotes should be used. We are national and international in perspective and are interested in stories from all parts of the country and the world." Length: 100 to 1,200 words for news; 1,200 to 3,000 for features; 300 to 800 words for book reviews. Pays $25 for book reviews; $50 for news articles, and $125 for features. B&w (8x11) glossies purchased on assignment. Pays $15 minimum.

PORTS O' CALL, Box 530, Santa Rosa CA 95402. (707)542-0898. Editor: William A. Breniman. Newsbook of the Society of Wireless Pioneers. Society members are mostly early-day wireless "brass-pounders" who sent code signals from ships or manned shore stations handling wireless or radio traffic. Twice yearly. Not copyrighted. Payment on acceptance. Query suggested. Editorial deadlines are May 15 and October 15. Reports on submissions at once. SASE.
Nonfiction: Articles about early-day wireless as used in ship-shore and high power operation. Early-day ships, records, etc. "Writers should remember that our members have gone to sea for years and would be critical of material that is not authentic. We are not interested in any aspect of ham radio. We are interested in authentic articles dealing with ships (since about 1910)." Oddities about the sea and weather as it affects shipping. Length: 500 to 2,000 words. Pays 1¢ per word.
Photos: Department Editor: Dexter S. Bartlett. Purchased with mss. Unusual shots of sea or ships. Wireless pioneers. Prefers b&w, "4x5 would be the most preferable size but it really doesn't make too much difference as long as the photos are sharp and the subject interests us." Fine if veloxed, but not necessary. Payment ranges from $2.50 to $10 "according to our appraisal of our interest." Ship photos of various nations, including postcard size, if clear, 25¢ to $1 each.
Poetry: Ships, marine slant (not military), shipping, weather, wireless. No restrictions. Pays $1 or $2.50 each.

THE ROTARIAN, 1600 Ridge Ave., Evanston IL 60201. (312)328-0100. Editor: Willmon L. White. 50% freelance written. For Rotarian business and professional men and their families; for schools, libraries, hospitals, etc. Monthly. Circ. 452,000. Usually buys all rights. Payment on acceptance. Free sample copy and editorial fact sheet. Query preferred. Reports in 2 to 4 weeks. Enclose SASE.
Nonfiction: "The field for freelance articles is in the general interest category. These run the

gamut from inspirational guidelines for daily living to such weighty concerns as world hunger, peace, and preservation of environment. Articles should appeal to an international audience and should in some way help Rotarians help other people. An article may increase a reader's understanding of world affairs, thereby making him a better world citizen. It may educate him in civic matters, thus helping him improve his town. It may help him to become a better employer, or a better human being. We are pushovers for articles on unusual Rotary club projects or really unusual Rotarians. We carry debates and symposiums, but we are careful to show more than one point of view. We present arguments for effective politics and business ethics, but avoid expose and muckraking. Controversy is welcome if it gets our readers to think but does not offend ethnic or religious groups. In short, the rationale of the organization is one of hope and encouragement and belief in the power of individuals talking and working together.'' Length: 2,000 words maximum. Payment varies.

Photos: Purchased with mss or with captions only. Prefers 2¼ square or larger color transparencies, but also uses 35mm. B&w singles and photo essays. Vertical shots preferred to horizontal. Scenes of international interest. Color cover.

Poetry and Fillers: ''Currently overstocked on serious poetry, but will look at short, light verse.'' Pays $2 a line. Pays $10 for brief poems. ''We occasionally buy short humor pieces.''

THE SPIRIT, Newsletter of Lindbergh Association. Editor: Bob Hammack. ''Writers should write Bob Hammack, Mountain View, AR 72560. Do not write *The Spirit* or *Charles A. Lindbergh Association* on outside envelope. For several reasons, this will only cause confusion at the local post office. The situation may change at a later date.'' For collectors of Charles A. Lindbergh memorabilia, conservationists, and aviators (many ''pioneer''); admirers of Lindbergh with high school to post-graduate backgrounds; ages from 15 to 75. Bimonthly magazine; 24 pages. Estab. 1975. Circ. 1,000. Buys all rights, but may reassign rights to author after publication. Buys all material from freelancers. ''Writers are eligible for Reader Survey Awards for, 'Best Collector Interest Article,' and/or, 'Best Historical Article.' '' Pays on acceptance. Sample copy $1. Will consider photocopied and simultaneous submissions. Reports on material accepted for publication in 1 month. Returns rejected material within 2 weeks. Submit complete mss. SASE.

Nonfiction and Photos: This publication is the first to concern itself with Lindbergh memorabilia, history, research, etc., and seeks anything connected with the ''Lone Eagle.'' ''We are especially interested in material dealing with his contributions to archaeology, and his scientific and medical research. If submitting collector material, give sources of supply; if historical, give addresses of museums, displays, individual authors, etc.'' Anniversaries of ''first flights,'' genealogical material and new memorials or tributes are desired. Also, personal experience, nostalgia, personal opinion, spot and photo news, and book reviews are needed. Length: 250 to 1,000 words. Pays $3 to $10 per ms. When photos are purchased with ms, they should be the same as the nonfiction article, but photos *are* purchased without accompanying ms with captions required. Pays approximately $5. No color shots. Numismatic, philatelic, and bibliographic items are needed for regular columns; pays $5 per contribution. Length: 500 words.

Poetry: ''Would like to see good narrative work regarding the 1927 Trans-Atlantic Flight.'' Will consider some traditional poetic forms, and blank and free verse. Payment varies.

Fillers: Will use newsbreaks and clippings. Length: 50 to 100 words. Pays $1 per item.

How To Break In: ''Do something on Lindbergh's 'advisory role' in either commercial or military aviation. All submitted information must show detailed research.''

STEERING WHEEL, P.O. Box 1669, Austin TX 78767. (512)478-2541. Editor: Barbara Law. Published by the Texas Motor Transportation Association for transportation management, high school libraries, state agencies, doctors, legislators, mayors, county judges, newspapers. Monthly magazine; 28 pages. Estab. 1936. Circ. 7,200. Buys about 10 mss/year. Pays on publication. Free editorial guidelines. Submit seasonal holiday material 3 months in advance. Will consider photocopied and simultaneous submissions. Query first. Reports immediately. SASE.

Nonfiction and Photos: ''Material related to motor transportation in Texas, and other subjects as they relate; highway safety, energy, etc.'' Buys interviews, profiles, historical, spot news, and coverage of successful business operations. Length: 1,000 to 2,500 words. Pays $15-75. Photos purchased with ms. Captions required.

THE TOASTMASTER, 2200 N. Grand Ave., Box 10400, Santa Ana CA 92711. (714)542-6793. Editor-in-Chief: Michael J. Snapp. Emphasizes communication and leadership techniques; self-improvement. For members of Toastmasters International, Inc. Monthly magazine; 32 pages. Estab. 1932. Circ. 60,000. Pays on acceptance. Buys all rights, but may reassign

following publication. Photocopied submissions and previously published work OK. SASE. Reports in 2 weeks. Free sample copy and writer's guidelines.
Nonfiction: How-to (improve speaking, listening, thinking skills; on leadership or management techniques, meeting planning, etc., with realistic examples), humor (on leadership communications or management techniques), interviews (with communications or management experts that members can directly apply to their self-improvement efforts; should contain "how to" information). Buys 15-20 mss/year. Query. Length: 1,500-3,000 words. Pays $25-150.
Photos: Purchased with or without ms. Query. Pays $10-50 for 5x7 or 8x10 b&w glossies; $35-75 for color transparencies. No additional payment for those used with ms.
How To Break In: "By studying our magazine and sending us (after a query) material that is related. Since we get a number of articles from our members on 'how to build a speech', freelancers should concentrate on more specific subjects such as body language, time management, etc. We're a non-profit organization, so if they're looking to get rich on one article, they can probably forget it. But we do provide a good place for the inexperienced freelancer to get published."

V.F.W. MAGAZINE, Broadway at 34th St., Kansas City MO 64111. (816)561-3420. Editor: James K. Anderson. 30-50% freelance written. For members of the Veterans of Foreign Wars, men who served overseas, and their families. They range in age from the 20's to veterans of World War I and Spanish-American War veterans. Interests range from sports to national politics. Monthly magazine; 48 pages. Estab. 1913. Circ. 1,900,000. Buys all rights. Buys 40 mss/year. Pays on acceptance. Sample copy 50¢; free writer's guidelines. Seasonal material should be submitted 3 months in advance. Query. SASE. Reports in 1 week.
Nonfiction and Photos: "Nonfiction articles on sports, personalities, and historical pieces. Special emphais within a subject, special outlook related to veterans. The Veterans of Foreign Wars organization is geared to the man who has served overseas, a distinction that other veterans organizations do not make." Buys informational, how-to, personal experience, interview, profile, historical, think articles, and travel articles. Length: 1,000 to 1,500 words. Pays 5¢ to 10¢ per word. B&w and color photos purchased with accompanying ms. Captions required. Pays $5 each.

Astrology and Psychic Publications

The following publications regard astrology, psychic phenomena, ESP experiences, and related subjects as sciences or as objects of serious scientific research. Semireligious, occult, mysticism, and supernatural publications are classified in the Alternative category.

AMERICAN ASTROLOGY, 2505 N. Alvernon Way, Tucson AZ 85712. (602)327-3476. Editor: Joanne S. Clancy. 50% freelance written. For all ages, all walks of life. Monthly magazine; 116 pages. Estab. 1933. Circ. 265,000. Buys all rights. Buys 50-75 mss/year. Pays on publication. Free writer's guidelines. Reports in 4 weeks. Submit complete ms. SASE.
Nonfiction: Astrological material, often combined with astronomy. More interested in presenting results of research material and data based on time of birth, instead of special Sun sign readings. Source of birth data must be included. Length: 3,500 words. "Payment is made according to the astrological knowledge and expertise of the writer."

ASTROLOGY GUIDE, Sterling's Magazines, Inc., 355 Lexington Ave., New York NY 10017. (212)391-1400, Ext. 21. Editor: Marsha Kaplan. For a special interest audience involved in astrology, parapsychology and the occult on all levels, from the merely curious to the serious student and practitioner. Bimonthly magazine; 96 (6½x9½) pages. Estab. 1937. Circ. 55,000. Buys all rights. Buys 30 mss/year. Pays on acceptance. Will not consider photocopied or simultaneous submissions. Submit seasonal (Christmas, vacation-time, etc.) and special (major astrological events) material 5-6 months in advance. Reports in 8-12 weeks minimum. Query first or submit complete ms. Enclose SASE.
Nonfiction: "Mostly astrological articles: Sun-sign, mundane, speculative or research. Slightly more technical for advanced readers, but prefer intelligent popular approach. Emphasis is on use of astrology and the related psychic and occult arts for self betterment in the reader's life. Very interested in buying articles on timely themes in these fields. We are more interested in featuring new ideas and new writers than in repeating what has been done in the past. We are attempting to develop a more personal, intimate approach." Would also like to see astrological "portraits" or interviews with current celebrities. Does not want to see articles based only on

the writer's knowledge of Sun signs. "They are superficial and boring. Even Sun-sign articles on the traditional themes (health, money, love) should refer (at least in preparation) to other aspects of the birth chart, and should be written by a practicing astrologer, or serious student. Length: 2,000 to 3,000 words, but will accept shorter articles. Also uses book reviews and will consider new ideas for new departments. Pays 3¢ a word minimum.
Fillers: Short humor and material on astrological experiences and insights are used as fillers. Length: 750 words maximum. Pays 3¢ per word.

ASTROLOGY '78, 124 Madison Ave., New York NY 10016. (212)679-5676. Editor-in-Chief: H. Weingarten. 40% freelance written. Quarterly magazine; 64 pages. Estab. 1968. Circ. 2,000. Pays on publication. Buys all rights, but may reassign following publication. Submit seasonal/holiday material 4-5 months in advance of issue date. Photocopied and previously published submissions OK. SASE. Reports in 2 months. Sample copy $2.
Nonfiction: How-to; interview; and technical. No sun sign articles. Buys 2 mss/issue. Query. Pays $2/page.

ASTROLOGY—YOUR DAILY HOROSCOPE, 1515 Broadway, New York NY 10036. Monthly. Buys all rights. Pays on acceptance. SASE.
Nonfiction: Articles on astrology, either popularized or moderately technical. Anxious to attract new writers and can promise a steady market plus a great deal of help from the editor. Knowledge of astrology is necessary. Length: 1,500 to 3,500 words. Pays 2¢/word, or by arrangement.

BEYOND REALITY MAGAZINE, 303 W. 42nd St., New York NY 10036. (212)265-1676. Editor: Harry Belil. 75% freelance written. Primarily for university students interested in astronomy, archaeology, astrology, the occult (the whole range); UFO's, ESP, spiritualism, parapsychology, exploring the unknown. Bimonthly magazine; 64 pages. Estab. 1971. Circ. 50,000. Buys all rights. Buys 30 to 35 mss/year. Payment on publication. Sample copy $1; writer's guidelines for SASE. Will consider photocopied submissions. Will not consider simultaneous submissions. Query first or submit complete ms. SASE.
Nonfiction and Photos: Interested in articles covering the range of their readers' interests, as well as any new discoveries in parapsychology. How-to, interview, inspirational, historical, think pieces, spot news. Length: 1,000 to 2,000 words. Pays 3¢ per word maximum, or whatever the editor feels such a feature warrants. No additional payment for b&w photos used with mss.
Fillers: "We pay $1 for clippings used."
How To Break In: "Show me some pieces you've written and if I like your style, I'll provide you with the subjects to write on. Also looking for current ideas from the campuses, so student writers should give us a try." Lack of research documentation, or re-hashing old material will bring a rejection here.

BREAKTHROUGH! Institute of Psychic Science, Inc., 2015 S. Broadway, Little Rock AR 72206. (501)372-4278. Editor-in-Chief: Korra L. Deaver. 90% freelance written. Emphasizes personal psychic development. Bimonthly magazine; 20 pages. Estab. 1971. Circ. 1,000. Pays in copies on publication. Buys all rights, but may reassign following publication. Phone queries OK. Simultaneous, photocopied and previously published submissions OK. SASE. Reports in 2 months. Sample copy for 14¢ postage; writer's guidelines.
Nonfiction: How-to (explaining how one acquires an understanding of, and personal use of, such psychic gifts as clairvoyance, precognition, astral projection, etc.); informational, personal experience, inspirational and think articles. Length: 5,000 words maximum.
Poetry: Any form; upbeat and inspirational. Buys 1/issue. Length: 4-41 lines. Pays in copies.

FATE, Clark Publishing Co., 500 Hyacinth Place, Highland Park IL 60035. Editor: Mary Margaret Fuller. 70% freelance written. Monthly. Buys all rights; occasionally North American serial rights only. Pays on publication. Query. Reports on submissions in 4-8 weeks. SASE.
Nonfiction and Fillers: Personal psychic experiences, 300 to 500 words. Pays $10. New frontiers of science, and ancient civilizations, 2,000 to 3,000 words; also parapsychology, occultism, witchcraft, magic, spiritual healing miracles, flying saucers, etc. Must include complete authenticating details. Prefers interesting accounts of single events rather than roundups. "We very frequently accept manuscripts from new writers; the majority are individuals' first-person accounts of their own psychic experience. We do need to have all details, where, when, why, who and what, included for complete documentation." Pays minimum of 3¢ per word. Fillers should be fully authenticated. Length: 100 to 300 words.
Photos: Buys good glossy photos with mss or with captions only. Pays $5 to $10.

THE HEFLEY REPORT, U.S. Research, Inc., Box 7242, Burbank CA 91510. (213)841-2733. Editor-in-Chief: Carl D. Hefley. Emphasizes psychic phenomena for a mass readership interested in the occult, psychic happenings, science, UFO's and witchcraft. Bimonthly tabloid; 36-64 pages. Estab. 1977. Pays on publication. Buys all rights, but may reassign following publication. Submit seasonal/holiday material 2 months in advance of issue date. Photocopied and previously published submisssions OK. SASE. Free sample copy and writer's guidelines.
Nonfiction: Expose; historical; how-to (develop psychic skills/abilities);informational; interview; personal experience (100-200 words); personal opinion (brief); photo feature; profile (brief); and technical (electronic equipment related to ESP/psychic). Buys 100-200 mss/year. Query. Length: 50-1,200 words. Pays $10-500.
Photos: State availability of photos with query. Pays $5-25 for 3¼x3¼ minimum glossy b&w prints. Captions required. Model release required.
Columns/Departments: Secret Psychic's Confidential Report; Health and Science; and Dream Bank. Buys 1/issue. Query. Length: 200-500 words. Pays $25-75. Open to suggestions for new columns/departments.
Fillers: Clippings and newsbreaks. Buys 3-5/issue. Length: 25-100 words. Pays $1-25.

HOROSCOPE, 1 Dag Hammarskjold Plaza, 245 E. 47th St., New York NY 10017. Editor: Julia A. Wagner. Monthly magazine; 124 pages. Estab. 1939. Circ. 300,000. Buys all rights. Buys 300 mss/year. Pays on acceptance. Free sample copy and writer's guidelines. All submissions must be accompanied by a carbon copy. Submit project forecast material at least 6 months in advance. Reports in 2 months. Query first or submit complete ms. SASE.
Nonfiction: Articles on astrology only. "Love, family, money, employment, and health are our most popular subjects. Must appeal to general readers with some knowledge of astrology. Articles dealing with prevailing conditions are always considered. We will not accept any articles relating to witchcraft." Informational, how-to, profile, inspirational. Length: 3,000 to 3,500 words. Pays 6¢/word.
Fillers: On astrology only. Length: 50-150 words. Submissions must consist of a minimum of 10 fillers. Pays 6¢/word.

HOROSCOPE GUIDE, 350 Madison Ave., Cresskill NJ 07626. (201)568-0500. Editor: Jim Hendryx. For persons interested in astrology as it touches their daily lives; all ages. Estab. 1967. Monthly. Circ. 60,000. Buys all rights, but may reassign rights to author after publication "for non-competitive use. That is, for book publication, but never for magazine resale." Buys about 40 mss per year. Pays on acceptance. Sample copy for $1. Will consider photocopied submissions. No simultaneous submissions. Submit seasonal material 5 months in advance. Submit complete ms. SASE.
Nonfiction, Poetry and Fillers: No textbook-type material. Wants anything of good interest to the average astrology buff, preferably not so technical as to require more than basic knowledge of birth sign by reader. Mss should be light, readable, entertaining and sometimes humorous. Not as detailed and technical as other astrology magazines, "with the astro-writer doing the interpreting without long-winded reference to his methods at every juncture. We are less reverent of astrological red tape." Does not want to see a teacher's type of approach to the subject. Wants mss about man-woman relationships, preferably in entertaining and humorous fashion. Length: 900 to 4,000 words. Pays 1½¢ to 2¢ per word. Buys traditional forms of poetry. Length: 4 to 16 lines. Pays $2 to $8. Also buys newsbreaks on astrology. Wants historical newsbreaks and quotes from notable persons favorable to astrology. Length: 25 to 500 words. Pays $2 to $7.50.
How To Break In: "Best way to break in with us is with some lively Sun-sign type piece involving some area of man-woman relationships — love, sex, marriage, divorce, differing views on money, religion, child-raising, in-laws, vacations, politics, life styles, or whatever.

MOON SIGN BOOK, Box 43383, St. Paul MN 55164. (612)291-1970. Editor: Carl Weschcke. For "persons from all walks of life with interests in gardening, natural living and astrology." Estab. 1906. Annual. Circ. 100,000. Rights purchased vary with author and material. Pays on publication. Query. Reports in 8 weeks. SASE.
Nonfiction and Photos: "Astrology (with emphasis on the moon) is the primary subject, but we can use material in natural medicine, healing, and living in intelligent cooperation with nature. We are a yearly publication dealing with farming, gardening, yearly forecasts for all types of activities, with informative articles on astrology. We try to be educational as well as practical." Length: 3,000 to 10,000 words. Pays 2¢ to 5¢ a word. Photos on assignment.
How To Break In: "The *Moon Sign Book* is a farming and gardening almanac emphasizing

astronomical effects on planting, growing, harvesting and using crops to maximum advantage. Since 80% of the book is taken up with tables, we have room for only a few outside articles. Those articles should have something to do with either astrology or gardening (we are also interested in herbs, herbal remedies). Since most freelancers are not astrologers I would suggest that they concentrate on the many aspects of organic gardening or possibly how-to-do features that relate in some way to farming and gardening. Short articles on the occult phenomena (enhancing growth psychically), are also good possibilities for the beginning writer. We are continually looking for astrologers capable of writing 'Sun Sign' predictions for *Moon Sign Book*. Also astrological predictions for weather, stock and commodity markets, news and political developments, etc. We generally stick with one, but we find that quality depends on a variety, and would like to find a few more writers to back us up."

NEW REALITIES, 680 Beach St., Suite 408, San Francisco CA 94109. (415)776-2600. Editor: James Bolen. 20% freelance written. For general public interested in holistic approach to living and being—body, mind, and spirit—and straightforward, entertaining material on parapsychology, consciousness research, and the frontiers of human potential and the mind. Bimonthly. Buys all rights. Pays on acceptance. Reports in 4 to 6 weeks. Query first. SASE.
Nonfiction and Photos: "Documented articles on ESP research and the psychic, holistic dimensions of man. Balanced reporting, no editorializing. No personal experiences as such. Accept profiles of leaders in the field. Must have documented evidence about holistic leaders, healers, researchers. Short bibliography for further reading." Length: 3,000 to 4,000 words. Pays $100 to $150.

THE PSYCHIC EYE, Heflin Printing Company, 521 Mulberry St., Toledo OH 43604. Editor-in-Chief: Charlie R. Brown. Managing Editor: Gary N. Gamble. Emphasizes parapsychology for readership age 18 and up. Quarterly magazine; 26-30 pages. Estab. 1972. Circ. 5,000. Pays on publication. Buys all rights, but may reassign rights to author following publication. Submit seasonal/holiday material 3 months in advance. Simultaneous and previously published submissions OK. SASE. Reports in 6 weeks. Sample copy $1.
Nonfiction: Personal experience (in psychic/occult fields, clairvoyance, etc., healing, psychic development). Buys 12 mss/year. Submit complete ms.
Photos: Purchased with accompanying manuscript. Captions required. Submit b&w prints.
Columns, Departments: Buys 1-2 mss/issue. Submit complete ms. Length: 250-500 words. Pays 1¢-2 per word; may also pay in contributor's copies. Open to suggestions for new columns/departments; address to C.R. Brown.
Fillers: Newsbreaks (in psychic field).

QUEST, North American UFO Organization, Box 2485, Cedar Rapids IA 52406. Editor-in-Chief: Kevin D. Randle. Emphasizes unusual phenomena. Bimonthly magazine; 45-60 pages. Estab. 1975. Circ. 100,000. Pays on acceptance. Buys all rights, but may reassign following publication. Phone queries OK. Simultaneous and photocopied submissions OK. SASE. Reports in 2 weeks. Free sample copy.
Nonfiction: "Exposes should show how good UFO cases have been 'edited' so the public gets only one side, either pro or con. We are interested in articles showing how information in the field differs from the public belief. All facts must be verified. Interviews, personal opinion, photo features." Length: 3,000-12,000 words. Pays $150-500.

SADIC MAGAZINE, Box 2026, N. Hollywood CA 91602. (213)762-6995. Editor-in-Chief: S.E. Adlai. Managing Editor: T.L. Adlai. 35% freelance written. Monthly magazine; 41 pages. Estab. 1976. Circ. 35,000. Pays on acceptance. Buys all rights. Simultaneous submissions OK. SASE. Reports in 3 months. Sample copy $2.
Nonfiction: "We only publish articles and research materials relating to astrology, ESP, and related subjects." General interest; historical; inspirational; interview; profile; and technical. Buys 3 mss/year. Query. Length: 200-600 words. Pays 10-25¢/word.

YOUR PERSONAL ASTROLOGY, Sterling's Magazines, Inc., 355 Lexington Ave., New York NY 10017. (212)391-1400, Ext. 33. Editor: Marsha Kaplan. For a special interest audience involved in astrology, parapsychology and the occult on all levels, from the merely curious to the serious student and practitioner. Quarterly magazine; 96 pages. Estab. 1940. Circ. 60,000. Buys 35 mss/year. Payment on acceptance. Will not consider photocopied or simultaneous submissions. Submit seasonal (Christmas, vacation-time, etc.) and special (major astrological events) material 5-6 months in advance. Reports in 8-12 weeks minimum. Query first or submit complete ms. Enclose SASE.
Nonfiction: "Mostly astrological articles: Sun-sign, mundane, speculative or research. Slightly

more technical for advanced readers, but prefer intelligent popular approach. Emphasis is on use of astrology and the related psychic and occult arts for self betterment in the reader's life. Very interested in buying articles on timely themes in these fields. We are more interested in featuring new ideas and new writers than in repeating what has been done in the past. We are attempting to develop a more personal, intimate approach." Would also like to see astrological "portraits" or interviews with current celebrities. Does not want to see articles based only on the writer's knowledge of Sun signs. "They are superficial and boring. Even Sun-sign articles on the traditional themes (health, money, love) should refer (at least in preparation) to other aspects of the birth chart, and should be written by a practicing astrologer or a serious student." Length: 2,000 to 3,500 words, but will accept shorter articles. Also uses book reviews and will consider new ideas for new departments. Pays 3¢ a word minimum.
Fillers: Short humor and material on astrological experiences and insights are used as fillers. Length: 750 words maximum. Pays 3¢ per word.

Automotive and Motorcycle

Publications listed in this section are concerned with the maintenance, operation, performance, racing, and judging of automobiles and motorcycles. Publications that treat vehicles as a means of transportation or shelter instead of as a hobby or sport are classified in the Travel, Camping, and Trailer category. Journals for teamsters, service station operators, and auto dealers will be found in the Auto and Truck classification of the Trade Journals section.

AMERICAN MOTORCYCLE (formerly *AMA News*), American Motorcyclist Association, Box 141, Westerville OH 43081. (614)891-2425. Editor: Bill Amick. For "enthusiastic motorcyclists, investing considerable time and money in the sport." Monthly magazine; 56-64 pages. Estab. 1947. Circ. 116,000. Pays on publication. Rights purchased vary with author and material. Phone queries OK. Submit seasonal/holiday material 3 months in advance. SASE. Reports in 4 weeks. Free sample copy.
Nonfiction: How-to (different and/or unusual ways to use a motorcycle or have fun on one), historical (the heritage of motorcycling, particularly as it relates to the AMA), interviews (with interesting personalities in the world of motorcycling), photo feature (quality work on any aspect of motorcycling), technical (well-researched articles on safe riding techniques). Buys 10-20 mss/year. Query. Length: 500 words minimum. Pays $2/published column inch.
Photos: Bob Pluckebaum, Photo Editor. Purchased with or without accompanying ms, or on assignment. Captions required. Query. Pays $15 minimum per photo published.

AUTOMOBILE QUARTERLY, 221 Nassau St., Princeton NJ 08540. (609)924-7555. Editor-in-Chief: Beverly Rae Kimes. Senior Editor: Stan Grayson. Emphasizes automobiles and automobile history. Quarterly hardbound magazine; 112 pages. Estab. 1962. Circ. 40,000. Pays on acceptance. Buys all rights. SASE. Reports in 2 weeks. Sample copy $7.95.
Nonfiction: Articles relating to the automobile and automobile history. Historical, humor, interview and nostalgia. Buys 5 mss/issue. Query. Length: 2,000-10,000 words. Pays $200-400.
Photos: Purchased on assignment. Captions required. Query. Uses 8x10 b&w glossies and 4x5 color transparencies. "Payment varies with assignment and is negotiated prior to assignment."

AUTOWEEK, Real Resources Group, Inc., Box A, Reno NV 89506. Editor: Bob Irvin. Managing Editor: Cory Farley. Emphasizes automobile racing and the auto industry, domestic and international. Weekly tabloid; 40 pages. Estab. 1965. Circ. 95,000. Pays on publication. Buys all rights, or simultaneous rights, or by agreement with author. Previously published submissions OK. SASE. Reports in 2-4 weeks. Free sample copy.
Nonfiction: Informational (group-based vs. assembly line system; does Volvo/Kalmar plant really work?, etc.); historical (the first Indy race, first successful Ferrari, first European assembly line, etc.); nostalgia ("we'd have room for 2-3/month if we had them on tap"). Technical articles on radical design changes. News reports on auto racing. "Any literate auto racing enthusiast can offer articles to *Autoweek*. If the beginner is at a local race and he sees no *AW* reporter around, he might try covering the event himself. If he's going to a big race, he should query first since we undoubtedly already have it covered. A number of stringers got started just that way. Industry stories may range from General Motors to consumerists. In either case, remember we're not the auto section in a family paper." Length: 2,000 words maximum. Query. Pays $3/column inch.

Photos: Purchased with or without mss, or on assignment. "Photo rates by arrangement."
Fillers: Clippings ("rewrite clips and enclose"); newsbreaks. Buys 3/issue. Send fillers in. Length: 50-500 words. Pays $3/column inch.

THE AUTOMOTIVE PAGE, The Simser Group, Box 572A, Weston, Ontario, Canada M9N 3N3. Editor: Ed King. "An automotive feature for hard-core racers to housewives." Published weekly in 42 regional editions, appearing as a supplement in newspapers thorughout the US and Canada. Estab. 1972. Pays on acceptance. Buys first North American serial rights. Photocopied submissions OK. SASE. Reports in 3 weeks. Free sample copy and writer's guidelines.
Nonfiction: "Articles and features on anything dealing with coverage of racing events, automotive legislation, interviews, and biographies. Road tests, technical and how-to pieces must be exclusive." Expose; humor; informational; interview (racing people only); new product; photo feature (racing); profile (racers only); and technical (auto or motorcycle). Buys 150 mss/year. Submit complete ms. Length: 200-2,500 words. Pays $50-300.
Photos: Pays $5-20 for 5x7 glossy b&w prints; $5-25 for 5x7 or 8x10 glossy color prints. Captions optional. Model release required.
Fillers: Newsbreaks, any length.
How To Break In: "Quality material opens the door, and consistant journalism keeps it open. The easiest way to get in is through coverage of racing events in your area. We usually assign a permanent area to local writers rather than go ourselves. But the little races are important because we publish in regions, not only nationally. National events are usually handled by us, unless you are closer. Why not drop us a line; we're open to suggestions."

BIG BIKE, Hi-Torque Publications, 16200 Ventura Blvd., Encino CA 91436. (213)981-2317. Senior Editor: Chet Carman. Emphasizes street and touring motorcycles for a "reasonably well-educated, semi-affluent, mobile readership interested in all aspects of steet/road motorcycling, travel and camping. Probably more liberal than the 'you meet the nicest people on a . . .' set, though slightly more conservative than the 'Easyrider' gang." Monthly magazine; 68 pages. Estab. 1968.Circ. under 1,000,000. Pays on publication. Buys all rights, but may reassign following publication. Phone queries OK. Submit seasonal/holiday material 4 months in advance of issue date. Simultaneous, photocopied and previously published submissions OK. SASE. Free sample copy.
Nonfiction: Expose (we love the expose—get down and get the story, show a little brass); historical (the more unusual, the better); how-to; humor (we'd love to see some *real* humor for a change); informational (make it good); interview (query first); nostalgia (groovy); personal experience (only if it's: dirty, funny, or free); photo feature (query); profile; and travel (query, we get swamped with 'me and the wife' stories). Buys 6-12 mss/year. Query or submit complete ms. Length: "whatever it takes to tell the story—no more, no less." Pays approximately $40/page.
Photos: Purchased with or without accompanying ms. Captions "strongly suggested." Uses 8x10 b&w prints or 35mm or larger color transparencies. Payment negotiable. Model release required.
Columns/Departments: Notes (bits of news, scandel and gossip relating to bike, biking, or bike people); and On the Track (news items relating to the world of competition). Query or submit complete ms. Length: 10-500 words. Pays $5-50.
Fiction: Adventure; erotica; fantasy (be sure to know what you are doing); experimental; humorous; science fiction; and western (if you write a western about motorcycling, the least we can do is read it). Buys 2-4 mss/year. Query or submit complete ms. Length: 4-12 typewritten pages. Pays approximately $40/page.
Poetry: Avant-garde; free verse; haiku; light verse; traditional; Dada; and Limricks. Limit submissions to batches of 3. Pays $1.50 maximum.
Fillers: Humorous clippings, jokes, gags, anecdotes; newsbreaks; short humor; and brainteasers. Pays $36.20 maximum.

BIKER, Cycle News, Inc., 2201 Cherry Ave., Long Beach CA 90801. (213)595-4753. Editor-in-Chief: Charles Clayton. Emphasizes road motorcycle recreation, transportation and touring. For outdoorsmen (18-50); average education. Semimonthly tabloid; 24 pages. Estab. 1975. Circ. 6,000. Pays 15th of month following publication. Buys one-time rights and rights to reprint in any other CN publication. Submit seasonal/holiday material 3 weeks in advance. Photocopied submissions OK. SASE. Reports in 6 weeks. Sample copy 60¢.
Nonfiction: Expose (government, industry); how-to (nuts and bolts, plus pix and diagrams); informational; interviews (with remarkable bikers of all ilk, except racers and off-road riders); travel (specific travel and touring experiences); photo features (custom bikes, parties — no

races); technical (any type, but road only); political action by bikers, oddball news bits, trivia. Buys 5-15 mss/issue. Submit complete ms. Length: 2,500 words maximum. Pays 50¢-$1/column inch.
Photos: Clear, sharp 5x7 or 8x10 b&w glossies purchased with or without mss. Captions required. Pays $2-5.
Columns/Departments: Runs Around the Nation. Road rides, meets, organized road recreation reports. "This is dated material and should not be more than 1 week old." Submit complete ms. Length: 100-500 words. Pays 50 cents/column inch.
How To Break In: "First, be interested in what modern day bikers are into. Become a correspondent by covering local motorcycle road runs, rallies, etc. Use sense of humor, even on serious subjects."
Rejects: Anything about death or dismemberment.

BMW JOURNAL, A. Christ Zeitschriftenverlag GmbH, Pettenkoferstrasse 22, 8000 Munich 2, W. Germany. (089)53.59.11. USA editorial office: 2540 Bonito Way, Laguna Beach CA 92651. Editor: Ron Wakefield. Editor-in-Chief: Udo Wust. An automobile customer magazine for owners and enthusiasts of BMW automobiles; upper income audience; generally, people with active life styles and an eye for the unusual. Bimonthly magazine; 52 pages. Estab. 1962. Circ. 50,000. Pays on publication. Buys all rights, but may reassign following publication. Phone queries OK. SASE. Reports in 4 weeks.
Nonfiction: Historical (having to do with places or with history of automobiles if related to BMW); informational; nostalgia, photo features; profiles (of interesting BMW owners); travel (by automobile, BMW in photos). Buys 3-5/issue. Query. Length: 500-1,500 words. Pays $75-150 per printed page.
Photos: Used with or without ms, or on assignment. Captions required. Query. No additional payment for 5x7 b&w glossies or 35mm minimum (larger preferred) color transparencies. Model release required. Need not relate to publication's subject matter; can encompass a broad range of life style themes.
Fiction: Adventure, experimental, historical, mystery, science fiction, suspense. Buys 1/issue. Query. Length: 500-1,500 words. Pays $75-150 per printed page.
How To Break In: "Author must know the magazine, available at local BMW dealers. Articles must be submitted with excellent photos, captioned."

CAR AND DRIVER, One Park Ave., New York NY 10016. (212)725-3767. Editor: David E. Davis, Jr. For auto enthusiasts; college educated, professional, median 26 to 28 years of age. Monthly magazine; 100 pages. Estab. 1957. Circ. 730,000. Rights purchased vary with author and material. Buys all rights, but may reassign rights to author after publication, or first North American serial rights. Buys 10-12 unsolicited mss/year. Pays on acceptance. No photocopied or simultaneous submissions. Submit seasonal material 4 months in advance. Query and include samples of previous work. Reports in 2 months. SASE.
Nonfiction and Photos: Nonanecdotal articles about the more sophisticated treatment of autos and motor racing. Exciting, interesting cars. Automotive road tests, informational articles on cars and equipment; some satire and humor. Personalities, past and present in the automotive industry and automotive sports. Treat readers as intellectual equals. Emphasis on people as well as hardware. Informational, how-to, humor, historical, think articles, and nostalgia. Length: 750 to 2,000 words. Pays $200 to $1,000. B&w photos purchased with accompanying mss with no additional payment. Also buys book reviews for book review department, and mini-features for FYI department. Length: about 500 words. Pays $50.
How To Break In: "It is best to start off with an interesting query and to stay away from nuts-and-bolts stuff since that will be handled in-house or by an acknowledged expert. Probably the very best way for a new writer to break in with us is with a personal, reasonably hip approach which shows a real intimacy with what we are trying to do. A while back, for instance, we ran a freelance piece on automobiles in Russia, which was the product of an interesting query. We are not like other automotive magazines inasmuch as we try to publish material which could just as well appear in the general magazines. We're not interested in unusual cars. To us the Ford Mustang is infinitely more important than a 1932 Ruxton wicker-seat five-passenger touring car. Good writing and unique angles are the key."

CAR CRAFT, Petersen Publishing Co., 8490 Sunset Blvd., Los Angeles CA 90069. (213)657-5100, ext. 345. Editor: Rick Voegelin. For men and women, 18 to 34, automotive oriented. Monthly magazine; 124 pages. Estab. 1953. Circ. 300,000. Buys all rights. Buys 12 mss/year. Pays on acceptance. Query. SASE.
Nonfiction and Photos: Photo Department Editor: Charlie Hayward. Drag racing articles,

technical car features, how-to articles, and general car features. Interview, profile, and photo features. Length: open. Pays $100 to $125 per page. Photos are purchased with or without accompanying ms. Captions optional. 8x10 b&w glossy; 35mm or 2¼ color transparencies. Pays $12.50 for b&w photos; $100 minimum (one page) color.

CARS MAGAZINE, Popular Publications, Inc., 150 E. 58th St., New York NY 10022. (212)935-7160. Editor: Steve Collison. Emphasizes automotive high performance: factory musclecars, hot street machines, drag race cars, and racing. For enthusiasts from early teens through thirties, some older; assume fair technical knowledge of cars. Monthly magazine; 82 pages. Estab. 1957. Circ. 80,000. Pays on publication. Buys one-time or all rights. Phone queries OK. SASE. Reports in 3 months. Sample copy $1.25.
Nonfiction: How-to (budget hop-ups, speed tricks, suspension modification, customizing, repair, body work, or race car building); informational and new product offerings; high-performance or automotive humor; interviews and profiles (of prominent people in drag racing or automotive field); historical and nostalgia (looking back on hot rods, muscle cars of the 50's and 60's); technical (drivetrain and suspension subjects); and some drag race coverage. Buys 12 mss/issue. Submit complete ms. Length: 500-3,000 words. Pays $100-500.
Photos: Pays $25/b&w photo (if separate from article package), 8x10 glossies preferred; $50/ color photos (35mm or larger transparencies). Model release required.

THE CLASSIC CAR, Box 3013, Orange CA 92665. Editor: William S. Snyder. For the classic car enthusiast, highly specialized in his interest. Uses writing with a "good nonfiction prose style. More interested in clear, factual writing than a lot of 'flash.'" The publication has a "finer focus than general automotive magazines. The reader is extremely knowledgeable to begin with. Accuracy is of utmost importance." Quarterly. Circ. 5,000. Buys first rights. Buys 4 to 8 mss a year from freelancers. Pays on publication. Query first. Reports in a week to 10 days. SASE.
Nonfiction and Photos: Wants "historical articles on various makes and models of classic cars (high quality cars of 1925-1942 vintage), photo articles on classics, restoration how-to articles, interviews, and profiles." Length: 500 to 5,000 words. Pays $25 to $100. 8x10 b&w glossy photos, 4x5 color transparencies. Preferred with captions only. Pays $1 to $5 for b&w; $5 to $25 for color.

CUSTOM VANS MAGAZINE, Twentieth Century Publications, Box 2547, 8943 Fullbright Ave., Chatsworth CA 91311. (213)998-7411. Editor: Dennis Adler. Emphasizes custom vans. Monthly magazine; 76 pages. Estab. 1976. Circ. 120,000. Pays on publication. Buys first North American serial rights. Phone queries OK. SASE. Reports in 4 weeks. Free sample copy.
Nonfiction: How-to and van features. Buys 10 mss/issue. Query. Length: 350-1,500 words. Pays $50-60/published page.
Photos: Purchased with accompanying ms. Captions required. Send b&w prints (8x10 for feature vans; 5x7 for how-to's) or color transparencies (35mm and 2¼x2¼). Offers no additional payment for photos accepted with mss. Model release required.
How To Break In: "Offer us some original ideas and approaches, especially with how-to stories that can save the customizer money. We're always looking for outstanding custom vans to feature, with good quality color transparencies and b&w prints."

CYCLE NEWS, WEST, 2201 Cherry Ave., Box 498, Long Beach CA 90801. (213)427-7433. Editor-in-Chief: John D. Ulrich. Publisher: Sharon Clayton. Emphasizes motorcycle recreation for motorcycle racers and recreationists west of Mississippi River. Weekly tabloid; 48 pages. Estab. 1963. Circ. 60,000. Payment on 15th of month for work published in issues cover dated previous month. Buys all rights, but may reassign rights to author following publication. SASE. Reports in 4 weeks. Free writer's guidelines.
Nonfiction: Expose; how-to; historical; humor; informational; interview (racers); personal experience (racing, non-racing with a point); personal opinion (land use, emission control, etc.); photo feature; profile (personality profiles); technical; and travel (off-road trips, "bikepacking"). Buys 1,000 mss/year. Submit complete ms. Pays $1/column inch.
Photos: Purchased with or without accompanying manuscript. Captions required. Submit contact sheet, prints, negatives or transparencies. Pays $5 minimum for 5x7 or 8x10 glossies; $10 minimum for 35mm slides or 2¼ color transparencies. Model release required. No additional payment for photos accepted with accompanying ms.

CYCLE TIMES, Multi-Media Publications, 222 W. Adams St., Suite 318, Chicago IL 60606. (312)236-5550. Managing Editor: Mark Schmidlin. For "midwestern motorcyclists, early teens and up, race oriented." Published 18 times/year. Tabloid; 24 pages (winter); 40 (summer).

Estab. 1975. Circ. 50,000. Pays on publication. Submit seasonal/holiday material 3 months in advance. SASE. Reports in 2-3 weeks. Free sample copy and writer's guidelines.
Nonfiction: How-to (motorcycle maintenance, performance modifications, repairs); informational (race coverage, event reports); interview (with midwesterners); personal (no first m/c rides, no crash/death stories); and technical. Buys 10-25 mss/issue. Submit complete ms. Length: 500-2,000 words. Pays $1/column inch.
Photos: Purchased with accompanying ms. Captions required. B&w only. Submit 5x7 (minimum size) glossy or matte. Pays $2.50/photo.Needs transparencies for cover; submit selection.
How To Break In: "Start covering the races in our 11-state circulation area. Include usable photos and a sufficient re-cap of the day's events. All of us started this way. Once we know who you are, you'll get all the work you can handle."
Rejects: "I'm very open to new submissions, but slander pieces, poetry, or too short treatments get automatic rejects."
For '79: "We're looking for a lot more contributors who like to (or have to) go to motorcycle races. If you're a literary genius, so much the better, but that's secondary to your ability to provide consistent, on-time, race coverage."

CYCLE WORLD, 1499 Monrovia Ave., Newport Beach CA 92663. Editor: Allan Girdler. For active motorcyclists, "young, affluent, educated, very perceptive." Subject matter includes "road tests (staff-written), features on special bikes, customs, racers, racing events; technical and how-to features involving mechanical modifications." Monthly. Circ. 300,000. Buys all rights, but will reassign rights to author after publication. Buys 200 to 300 mss/year from freelancers. Payment on publication. Sample copy 75¢; free writer's guidelines. Submit seasonal material 2½ months in advance. Reports in 4 to 6 weeks. Query. SASE.
Nonfiction: Buys informative, well-researched travel stories; technical, theory, and how-to articles; interviews, profiles, humor, spot news, historical pieces, think pieces, new product articles and satire. Taboos include articles about "wives learning to ride; 'my first motorcycle.'" Length: 800 to 5,000 words. Pays $75 to $100 per published page. Columns include Competition, which contains short, local racing stories with photos. Column length: 300 to 400 words. Pays $75 to $100 per published page.
Photos: Purchased with or without ms, or on assignment. Captions optional. Pays $50 for 1 page; $25 to $35 for ½ page. 8x10 b&w glossies, 35mm color transparencies.
Fiction: Humorous stories. Does not want to see racing fiction or "rhapsodic poetry." Length: 1,500 to 3,000 words. Pays $75 minimum per published page.

DIESEL MOTORIST, Box 335, Fort Lee NJ 07024. 10% freelance written. For "largely a professional readership—engineers, auto industry executives, diesel automobile owners, R/V and light truck owners, with an interest in diesel travel, economics, technical trends, etc." Quarterly magazine; 32 pages. Estab. 1977. Circ. 13,000. Pays on publication. Buys all rights, but may reassign following publication. Submit seasonal/holiday material 4-6 months in advance of issue date. Photocopied submissions OK. SASE. Reports in 6 weeks.
Nonfiction: Exposé (regulatory agencies of governments, EPA, etc.); how-to (diesel auto information); general interest (energy, economics); historical (related to automobile industry, etc.); new product (automotive and inventions); photo feature (new autos, events, etc.); profile (on assignment only); technical (automotive, particularly diesel, also petroleum, energy); and travel (vehicle). Buys 1-2 mss/issue. Query with outline of new work and clips of previously published work. Length: 600-1,500 words. Pays $25-100.
Photos: Pays $5-25 for 5x7 glossy prints. State availability of photos with query.
Fiction: Will consider queries for adventure and historical fiction. Pays $25-100.

DIRT BIKE MAGAZINE, P.O. Box 317, Encino CA 91436. Editor: Bruce Woods. For dirt bike riders. Magazine; 100 (8x10) pages. Estab. 1971. Monthly. Circ. 175,000. Buys all rights. Buys about 24 mss a year. Will consider photocopied submissions. No simultaneous submissions. Submit special material 3 months in advance. Query first. SASE.
Nonfiction and Photos: Competition reports outside of southern California of national interest. Light, humorous style, but accurate facts. Informational, how-to, expose, spot news, technical. Length: 1,000 to 8,000 words. Pays 3¢ to 5¢ a word. Hole Shot column uses opinions of general interest. Length: 1,200 to 1,500 words. Payment is the same as for articles. Photos are used in special Crash & Burn issues. Also purchased with or without ms, or on assignment. Pays $5 to $7 for 8x10 b&w glossies. Pays $25 to $50 for 35mm (or larger) transparencies.

DUNE BUGGIES & HOT VWS, Wright Publishing Co., Inc., Box 2260, Costa Mesa CA 92626.

Editor: Tom Chambers. Monthly magazine; 100 pages. Estab. 1967. Circ. 50,000. Pays on publication. Buys one-time rights. Submit seasonal or holiday material 3 months in advance. SASE. Free sample copy.
Nonfiction: Technical how-to and informational articles. Buys 6-8 per issue. Submit complete ms. Length: 500-2,000 words. Pays $50 per published page.
Photos: Purchased with ms. Captions required. Send contact sheet. Pays $10 maximum for 8x10 b&w glossies; $10 minimum for color negs or slides.
Rejects: First person articles.

EASYRIDERS MAGAZINE, Entertainment for Adult Bikers, Box 52, Malibu CA 90265. (213)880-4240. Editor: Lou Kimzey. For "adult men—men who own, or desire to own, expensive custom motorcycles. The individualist—a rugged guy who enjoys riding a chopper and all the good times derived from it." Monthly. Circ. 285,000. Buys all rights. Buys 12 to 20 mss a year. Payment on acceptance. Will send a sample copy to a writer for 25¢. Reports in 2 to 3 weeks. Enclose SASE for return of submissions.
Nonfiction, Fiction, and Fillers: Department Editor: Louis Bosque. "Masculine, candid material of interest to men. Must be bike-oriented, but can be anything of interest to a rugged man. It is suggested that everyone read a copy before submitting—it's not *Boy's Life*. Light, easy, conversational writing style wanted, like guys would speak to each other without women being around. Gut level, friendly, man-to-man. Should be bike-oriented or of interest to a guy who rides a bike. *Easyriders* is entirely different from all other motorcycle magazines in that it stresses the good times surrounding the owning of a motorcycle—it's aimed at the rider and is nontechnical, while the others are nuts and bolts. Not interested in technical motorcycle articles. We carry no articles that preach to the reader, or attempt to tell them what they should or shouldn't do." Buys personal experience, interviews, humor, expose (motorcycle-oriented) articles. Length: 1,000 to 3,000 words. Payment is usually 10¢/word, depending on length and use in magazine. "It's the subject matter and how well it's done—not length, that determines amount paid." Risque joke fillers, short humor. Length: open. Payment: open.
Photos: Department Editor: Pete Chiodo. B&w glossies, 35mm color, 2¼x2¼ color transparencies purchased with mss. "We are only interested in *exclusive* photos of exclusive bikes that have never been published in, or photographed by, a national motorcycle or chopper publication. Bikes should be approved by editorial board before going to expense of shooting. Submit sample photos—Polaroids will do. Send enough samples for editorial board to get good idea of the bike's quality, originality, workmanship, interesting features, coloring." Payment is $50 to $150 for cover, $75-$150 for centerspread, $20 for b&w and $35 for color for "In the Wind," $25 up for arty, unusual shots, and $100 to $225 for a complete feature.
Fiction: "Gut level language okay. Any sex scenes, not to be too graphic in detail. Dope may be implied, but not graphically detailed. Must be bike-oriented, but doesn't have to dwell on that fact. Only interested in hard-hitting, rugged fiction." Length: 2,000-5,000 words. Payment is usually 10¢/word, depending on quality, length and use in magazine.
How To Break In: "There is no mystery about breaking into our publication, as long as the material is aimed at our specific audience. We suggest that the writer read the requirements indicated above and seriously study a current copy of the magazine before submitting material."

FOUR WHEELER MAGAZINE, Box 547, 8943 Fullbright, Chatsworth CA 91311. (213)998-7411. Editor/Publisher: Bill Sanders. Editorial Assistant: Dale Ellen Weintraub. Emphasizes four-wheel-drive vehicles. Monthly magazine; 108 pages. Estab. 1956. Circ. 120,000. Pays on publication. Buys all rights. Phone queries OK. Submit seasonal/holiday material at least 4 months in advance. SASE. Reports in 6-12 months. Free sample copy and writer's guidelines.
Nonfiction: Historical (4 wheeling in ghost towns), how-to, interview (4WD industry), new product, profile (prominent 4WD enthusiast), technical and travel. Query or send complete ms. Length: 5-6 pages. Pays $50-250.
Fillers: Newsbreaks, cartoons and 4WD outings for "campfire". Submit fillers. Pays $15 minimum for cartoons.

HOT ROD, 8490 Sunset Blvd., Los Angeles CA 90069. (213)657-5100. Editor: Lee Kelley. For readers 10 to 60 years old with automotive high performance and racing interest, truck and van interest, drag racing and street machines. Monthly magazine; 120 pages. Estab. 1948. Circ. 800,000. Buys all rights. Buys 30 mss per year. Pays on publication. Free sample copy and editorial guidelines. Will not consider photocopied or simultaneous submissions. Submit seasonal material 3 to 4 months in advance. Reports on accepted and rejected material "as soon as possible." SASE.
Nonfiction and Photos: Wants how-to, interview, profile, photo, new product and technical

pieces. Length: 2 to 12 ms pages. Pays $100 to $125 per printed page. Photos purchased with accompanying ms with no additional payment, with extra payment, without accompanying ms and on assignment. Captions required. Pays $15 for b&w prints and $25 minimum for color.
How To Break In: "Freelance approach should be tailored for specific type and subject matter writer is dealing with. If it is of a basic automotive technical nature, then story slant and info should be aimed at the backyard enthusiasts. If the story is dealing with a specific personality, then it must include a major portion of human interest type of material. What we do is attempt to entertain while educating and offer exceptional dollar value."

KEEPIN' TRACK, Box 5445, Reno NV 89513. Editor-in-Chief: Frank Kodl. Managing Editor: Fredi Kodl. 80-90% freelance written. Emphasizes Corvettes. Monthly magazine; 48-64 pages. Estab. 1976. Circ. 35,000. Pays on publication. Buys all rights. Submit seasonal/holiday material 2-3 months in advance. Previously published submissions OK. SASE. Reports in 3 weeks. Free sample copy and writer's guidelines.
Nonfiction: Expose (telling of Corvette problems with parts, etc.); historical (any and all aspects of Corvette developments); how-to (restorations, engine work, suspension, race, swapmeets); humor; informational; interview (query); nostalgia; personal experience; personal opinion; photo feature; profile (query); technical; and travel. Buys 3-5 mss/issue. Submit complete ms. Pays $25-100.
Photos: Purchased with accompanying ms. Send contact sheet or transparencies. Offers no additional payment for photos accepted with ms.

MOTOCROSS ACTION MAGAZINE, 16200 Ventura Blvd., Encino CA 91436. (213)981-2317. Editor: Dick Miller. For "primarily young and male, average age 12 to 30, though an increasing number of females is noticed. Education varies considerably. They are interested in off-road racing motorcycles, as either professional or hobby." Monthly magazine; 72 pages. Estab. 1973. Circ. 85,000. Buys all rights but may reassign them to author after publication. Buys 20 to 25 mss/year. Pays on publication. Sample copy $1; free writer's guidelines. Will consider photocopied but no simultaneous submissions. Reports in 1 to 6 months. Query. SASE.
Nonfiction and Photos: Wants "articles on important national and international motocross events, interviews with top professionals, technical pieces, and in-depth investigative reporting. Short stories and/or poetry will be greeted with a heartfelt yawn. It's best to obtain a copy of the magazine and read recent stories. Stories should be brief and to the point, though flair is appreciated. Top photography is a must." No blatant hero worship. For the coming year, Miller also wants to see articles on "the evolution of motocross from a backyard to a big time, multi-million dollar sport and business." Takes informational, how-to, profile, humor and photo pieces. Length: 500 to 2,000 words. Pays $25 to $200. Photos purchased with accompanying ms with extra payment and on assignment. Captions optional. Pays $8 to $10 for b&w, 8x10 glossies. $25 to $50 for 35mm or 2¼ color slides.

MOTOR TREND, 8490 Sunset Blvd., Los Angeles CA 90069. (213)657-5100. Managing Editor: Cliff Creager. For automotive enthusiasts, backyard mechanics and general interest consumers. Monthly. Circ. 750,000. Buys all rights, except by negotiation. "Fact-filled query suggested for all freelancers." Reports in 30 days. SASE.
Nonfiction: Automotive and related subjects that have national appeal. Emphasis on money-saving ideas for the motorist, high-performance and economy modifications, news tips on new products, pickups, RVs, long-term automotive projects. Packed with facts. Pays $100 per printed page in magazine, or as negotiated.
Photos: Buys photos, particularly of prototype cars in Detroit area. Other automotive matter. 8x10 b&w glossies or transparencies. Pays $25 minimum.
Fillers: Automotive newsbreaks. Any length. Payment open.

MOTORCYCLIST MAGAZINE, Petersen Publishing, 8490 Sunset Blvd., Los Angeles CA 90069. Editor-in-Chief: Dale Boller. Emphasizes motorcycles for motorcycle enthusiasts. Monthly magazine; 100 pages. Estab. 1912. Circ. 150,000. Pays on publication. Buys all rights. Submit seasonal/holiday material 90 days in advance. SASE. Reports in 1 month. Free writer's guidelines.
Nonfiction: How-to, humor, informational, interview, new product, photo feature, profile and technical. Buys 12 mss/year. Query. Length: 500-2,000 words. Pays $100/published page.

NORTHEAST VAN, 70 Edwin Ave., Waterbury CT 06078. (203)755-0158. Editor: John Florian. Estab. 1975. Readers are people interested in vanning in the Northeast. Ages vary, though most are in early to late twenties, in the process of customizing a van, or a member of a van club.

Tabloid newspaper; 32-plus pages. Seasonal features considered. Monthly. Not copyrighted. Expects to buy 3 or 4 mss/issue. Pays on publication. Free sample copy and writer's guidelines. Submit seasonal material 3 months in advance. Reports on accepted and rejected material in 2 weeks. Query. SASE.
Nonfiction and Photos: "We publish 'how-to' articles about customizing vans, features about what others in the Northeast have done to their vans, and other features of interest to readers, like truck-ins, club news, maintenance/safety advice. We are open to all ideas. Material should be snappy and easy-reading, yet without a load of cliches." Wants informational, how-to, personal experience, humor, and travel articles. Length: 800-2,000 words. Pays $20 to $60; up to $80 maximum with b&w photos. "Good photos are very important to complement any article, though manuscripts will be considered without them." For photos alone, pay is $10 for each b&w 8x10.

1001 TRUCK AND VAN IDEAS MAGAZINE, Argus Publishers Corp., 12301 Wilshire Blvd., Los Angeles CA 90025. (213)820-3601. Editor-in-Chief: Phillip E. Carpenter. 40% freelance written. Emphasizes use of trucks, RVs, vans and mini-trucks for drivers who use, modify, customize and 'go fun truckin' with these vehicles. Monthly magazine; 96 pages. Estab. 1975. Circ. 200,000. Pays either on acceptance or publication. Phone queries OK. Submit seasonal/holiday material 3 months in advance. SASE. Reports in 2 weeks. Free writer's guidelines.
Nonfiction: How-to (on building interiors for custom vans and pickups, engine swaps, suspension work, etc.); informational; interview, new product, photo feature (for *Van Idea Notebook* and *Tricks For Trucks*); technical (step-by-step) and travel (tie in with type of vehicle). "No copy without photos, and no 'look, world, here's my very own custom van I built and captured on my polaroid for you' articles." Buys 6-7 mss/issue. Query. Length: 1,500 maximum. Pays $50-75/page.
Photos: Steve Reyes, Photo Editor. Photos purchased with or without accompanying ms or on assignment. Captions required. Pays $10-25 for 5x7 minimum b&w glossies; $25-75 for 2¼x2¼ or 35mm color transparencies. Total purchase price for ms includes payment for photos. Model release required.

PICKUP, VAN & 4WD MAGAZINE, CBS Consumer Publishing, 1499 Monrovia Ave., Newport Beach CA 92663. (714)646-4451. Editor: Don E. Brown. Managing Editor: Jon Thompson. For off-road vehicle enthusiasts. Monthly magazine; 104 pages. Estab. 1972. Circ. 200,000. Pays on publication. Buys all rights. Submit seasonal/holiday material 3-4 months in advance. Photocopied submissions OK. SASE. Reports 1-2 months. Free writer's guidelines.
Nonfiction: How-to (modifications to light duty trucks, such as extra seats, tool storage, etc.), historical, nostalgia (old restored trucks and 4-wheel drives), technical and travel (4-wheel drive travel only, must show vehicle being used). Buys 4-5 mss/issue. Submit complete ms. Length: 1,000-3,000 words. Pays $75/published page.
Photos: Purchased with accompanying manuscript or on assignment. Captions required. Query for photos. Pays $12.50-75 for 8x10 b&w glossies; $25-75 for 35mm or 2¼ color transparencies. Total purchase price for ms includes payment for photos. Model release required.

RACING CARS, Carl Hungness & Associates, Box 1341, Marion IN 46952. Editor-in-Chief: Jerry Miller. For automobile racing fans; 30-50; blue collar. Quarterly magazine; 64 pages. Estab. 1977. Circ. 5,000. Pays on publication. Buys first North American serial rights. Submit seasonal/holiday material two months in advance. SASE. Reports in 3 weeks.
Nonfiction: Historical (on racing in general, race cars, speedways, etc.); humor (anything to do with racing); informational (on racing personalities, profiles or specific enterprises); interviews (major racing personality; hard-hitting; not restricted to questions on racing subjects); nostalgia (old races, drivers, mechanics, cars, etc.); profiles (any racing personalities of national interest). "Remember, we cover only oval racing in America and personalities, cars, tracks associated with it. No road racing, please." Buys 24 mss/year. Query. Length: 2,000-5,000. Pays $50-100.
Photos: Purchased with or without mss or on assignment. Captions required. Send contact sheet, prints or transparencies. Pays $5-15 for 5x7 or 8x10 b&w glossies; $25 minimum for color transparencies, any size.

RIDER, 23945 Craftsman Rd., Calabasas CA 91302. Editor: Bill Estes. For owners and prospective buyers of motorcycles to be used for touring, sport riding, and commuting. Bimonthly magazine: 100 to 120 pages. Estab. 1974. Buys all rights. Pays on acceptance. Sample copy $1; free writer's guidelines. Submit seasonal material 3 months in advance. Photocopied submissions OK. Query. Reports in 1 month. SASE.
Nonfiction and Photos: Articles directly related to motorcycle touring, commuting and sport

riding including travel, human interest, safety, novelty, do-it-yourself and technical. "Articles which portray the unique thrill of motorcycling." Should be written in clean, contemporary style aimed at a sharp, knowledgeable reader. Buys informational, how-to, personal experience, profile, historical, nostalgia, personal opinion, travel and technical. Length is flexible. Pays $100-200. Photos purchased with ms with no additional payment. Captions required. "Quality photographs are critical. Graphics are emphasized in *Rider,* and we must have photos with good visual impact."

ROAD & DRIVER, Box 326, Northport NY 11768. Editor: Mel Shapiro. For car owners who are interested in getting more for their driving dollars. Magazine; 84 (8½x11) pages. Estab. 1974. Every 2 months. Circ. 250,000. Buys all rights. Buys 60 mss per year. Payment on publication. Will send sample copy to writer for 50¢. Will consider photocopied submissions. No simultaneous submissions. Submit seasonal/holiday material 4 to 5 months in advance. Reports on material accepted for publication in 3 weeks. Returns rejected material in 4 weeks. Query first. Enclose SASE.
Nonfiction and Photos: Articles on anything to do with auto economy. Safety and better driving tips. New products. Maintenance. Informational, how-to, personal experience, interview, profile, humor, travel, spot news. Length: 500 to 3,000 words. Pays $50 to $60. No additional payment is made for photos submitted with mss.
Fillers: Newsbreaks, clippings, short humor on themes pertinent to economical driving. Length: 50 to 200 words. Pays $5 to $25.

ROAD & TRACK, 1499 Monrovia Avenue, Newport Beach CA 92663. Editor: Tony Hogg. For knowledgeable car enthusiasts. Monthly magazine. Buys all rights, but may be reassigned to author after publication. Query first. Reports in 6 weeks. SASE.
Nonfiction: "The editor welcomes freelance material, but if the writer is not thoroughly familiar with the kind of material used in the magazine, he is wasting both his time and the magazine's time. *Road & Track* material is highly specialized and that old car story in the files has no chance of being accepted. More serious, comprehensive and in-depth treatment of particular areas of automotive interest." Payment is minimum 12¢ per word but often reaches 20¢ per word.

ROAD KING MAGAZINE, 233 E. Erie, Chicago IL 60611. (312)664-2959. Editor-in-Chief: William A. Coop. Managing Editor: Darlene Zonca. 20% freelance written. Emphasizes truck driving. Quarterly magazine; 48 pages. Estab. 1963. Circ. 200,122. Pays on acceptance. Buys one-time rights. Submit seasonal/holiday material 3 months in advance of issue date. Simultaneous and photocopied submissions OK. SASE. Reports in 3 months. Free sample copy; mention *Writer's Market* in request.
Nonfiction: General interest; humor; and photo feature. No articles on violence or sex. Buys 8 mss/year. Submit complete ms. Length: 500-2,500 words. Pays $50-100.
Photos: Submit photos with accompanying ms. No additional payment for b&w contact sheets or 2¼x2¼ color transparencies. Captions preferred. Buys one-time rights.
Fiction: Adventure; historical; humorous; mystery; suspense; and western. Especially about truckers. No stories on sex and violence. Buys 4 mss/year. Submit complete ms. Length: 2,500 words maximum. Pays $100.
Poetry: Light verse and traditional. No avant-garde poetry. Buys 2 poems/year. Submit 1 poem/batch. Length: 250 words. Pays $50-100.
Fillers: Jokes, gags, anecdotes, and short humor. Buys 20-25/year. Length: 50-500 words. Pays $5-50.

ROAD RIDER, Box 678, South Laguna CA 92677. Editor-in-Chief: Roger Hull. Managing Editor: R.L. Carpenter. Emphasizes touring on motorcycles for family style and fellow enthusiasts. Monthly magazine; 96 pages. Estab. 1969. Circ. 35,000. Pays on acceptance. Buys all rights, but may reassign rights to author following publication. Submit seasonal/holiday material 4 months in advance. "We schedule seasonal material 1 year in advance". SASE. Reports in 4 weeks. Free sample copy and writer's guidelines.
Nonfiction: How-to (researched method for improving facet of motorcycling/touring); informational (verified references when applicable); humor; nostalgia ("yesterday cycling", accompanied by photos); personal experience; photo feature; travel (biggest market) and technical (by assignment, must have prior outline). Buys 50 mss/year. Query. Length: maximum 2,000 words. Pays $75 minimum.
Photos: Purchased with accompanying manuscript. Captions required. B&w 5x7 glossies; 35mm or 2¼x2¼ color transparencies. Pays $50 maximum for covers. Total purchase price for ms includes payment for photos.

How To Break In: "We are an enthusiast publication—as such, it is virtually impossible to sell here unless the writer is also an enthusiast and actively involved in the sport. A good, well-written, brief item dealing with a motorcycle trip, accompanied by top quality b&w photos receives prime time editorial attention. We are always on the lookout for good material from eastern seaboard or Midwest. Best way to hit this market is to request sample and study same prior to submitting. Most of our contributors are Road Rider People. If you are unsure as to what "Road Rider People" refers, you will propably not be able to sell to this magazine."
Rejects: We continue to be overstocked on following: beginner articles (all ages, sexes, etc.), Journal-format travel articles (not welcome), travel articles from southwestern U.S.

ROAD TEST, Quinn Publishing Company, 1440 W. Walnut St., Compton CA 90220. (213)537-0857. Editor-in-Chief: Jon F. Thompson. Managing Editor: Dick Falk. Emphasizes automobiles for college-educated, professional readership. Monthly magazine; 72 pages. Estab. 1964. Circ. 80,000. Pays on publication. Buys first North American serial rights. Submit seasonal/holiday material 3 months in advance. SASE. Reports in 3 weeks. Free sample copy.
Nonfiction: How-to (make cars more reliable, responsive, economical, etc.); humor; informational; interview (racing or industry); nostalgia (old car stuff) and profile. Buys 3-4 mss/issue. Query. Length: 1,500-3,000 words. Pays $250-500.
Photos: Purchased with accompanying manuscript. Captions required. Query for photos. B&w 35mm/2¼ proof sheets and negatives; 35mm kodachrome color. Model release required.

SOUTHERN RV, Intra-South Publications, 6637 Superior Ave., Sarasota FL 33581. (813)921-5687. Editor-in-Chief: Joe Zambone. 50% freelance written. Emphasizes recreational vehicles and the outdoors for "generally middle-class, middle-aged folks who use recreational vehicles as a way of escaping the daily ratrace. Education is varied, but usually not high-brow at all." Monthly tabloid; 48 pages. Estab. June 1976. Circ. 30,000. Pays 10 days after publication. Buys all rights, but may reassign following publication. Submit seasonal/holiday material 2 months in advance of issue date. Simltaneous (but not to another publication in the southeast), photocopied and previously published submissions OK. SASE. Reports in 2 weeks. Free sample copy; mention *Writer's Market* in request.
Nonfiction: General interest (anything related in some way to the great southeastern outdoors scene, fishing, camping, but not hunting); how-to (get the most out of a camping trip, how to cook camp meals, how to do something 'outdoorsy' and do it easily); historical (short articles on historical areas of the south are welcome); humor (any tidbit of humor related to camping out or using an RV); personal experience (camping experiences not based on specific locales); photo feature (on the southeast—any area); technical (semi-technical how-to-fix-it articles would fit well occasionally); and travel (any travel experience relating to the southeast and RV's). "No advancing of favorite causes needed. No soap box oratory or bigoted material. In fact, if it doesn't relate to the southeastern USA, or travel with an RV, we probably don't need it." Buys 4 mss/issue. Submit complete ms. Length: 800-2,000 words. Pays $10-20.
Photos: "We like graphically exciting layouts. They lend credence to the stories we publish." State availability of photos with query. Offers no additional payment for photos accepted with ms, "they just make for a better article and better chances of being published." Uses 3x5 glossy b&w prints. Captions required. Buys all rights, but may reassign following publication.
Fiction: "We would consider humorous fiction as long as it is tied into the outdoors scene in some way. No soap box tirades about anything—we like to keep the paper light and interesting for all our readers. They can read other publications for controversial stuff." Query. Length: 800-1,500 words. Pays $10-20.

STOCK CAR RACING MAGAZINE, 205 S. Whiting St., Alexandria VA 22304. Editor: Dick Berggren. 75% freelance written. For stock car racing fans and competitors. Monthly magazine; 84 pages. Estab. 1966. Circ. 80,000. Pays on publication. Buys all rights, but may reassign following publication. SASE. Reports in 2-6 weeks.
Nonfiction: "Uses primarily nonfiction on stock car drivers, cars, and races. We are looking for Canadian and California people. We are interested in the story behind the story in stock car and sprint car racing. Technical articles are also sought." Query. Buys 75 mss/year. Length: 100-6,000 words. Pays $10-125.
Photos: State availability of photos with query. Pays $15 for 8x10 b&w photos; $50-150 for 35mm or larger color transparencies. Captions required.

STREET CHOPPER, 2145 W. La Palma, Anaheim CA 92801. (714)635-9040. Editor: Bob Clark. For custom and high-performance motorcycle enthusiasts. Monthly magazine; 84 pages. Estab. 1969. Circ. 100,000. Buys all rights. Buys 25-35 mss/year. Pays on acceptance. Will not consider

photocopied or simultaneous submissions. Reports within 3 months. Query first. SASE.
Nonfiction and Photos: Technical-oriented stories dealing with all aspects of motorcycles. "We deal strictly with custom and high-performance motorcycles. No off-road or dirt bikes." Material must be written in laymen's terminology. Greatest interest is in technical stories and how-to articles on motorcycles. Length: open. Pays maximum of $50/published page. Columns using freelance material include "Checkered Flag" and "Cafe Corner." Length: 2 to 5 double-spaced, typed pages. Pays $40 per published page. Pays $40 to $75 for b&w photos purchased with mss; $50 for color; 2¼ only.
Fillers: Newsbreaks. Length: 1 to 3 typed, double-spaced pages.

STREET RODDER MAGAZINE, TRM Publications, Inc., 2145 W. La Palma, Anaheim CA 92801. Editor: Patrick Ganahl. For the automotive enthusiast with an interest in street-driven, modified old cars. Monthly magazine; 76 pages. Estab. 1972. Circ. 105,000. Buys all rights, but will reassign rights to author after publication. Buys 25-35 mss/year. Pays on acceptance. Sample copy $1.50; free writer's guidelines. No photocopied or simultaneous submissions. Reports in 1 month. Query or submit complete ms. SASE.
Nonfiction and Photos: "We need coverage of events and cars that we can't get to. Street rod events (rod runs); how-to technical articles; features on individual street rods. We don't need features on local (Southern California) street rods, events or shops. We stress a straightforward style; accurate and complete details; easy to understand (though not 'simple') technical material. Need good, clear, complete and well-photographed technical and how-to articles on pertinent street rod modifications or conversions. We very seldom accept a story without photos." Length: 250 to 1500 words. Pays $25 to $150. Average payment for 2- to 3-page 5x7, 8x10 b&w feature: $75-150.

SUPER CHEVY MAGAZINE, Argus Publishers Corporation, 12301 Wilshire Blvd., Los Angeles CA 90025. (213)820-3601. Editor: Jay Amestoy. For automotive enthusiasts interested in optimum performance, efficiency, mileage and handling; for street, drag strip, and race track. Bimonthly magazine; 84 pages. Estab. 1973. Circ. 100,000. Buys first North American serial rights. Buys 90 mss a year. Pays on publication. Free sample copy. Will not consider photocopied and simultaneous submissions except to other Argus magazines. Reports in 2 months in most cases. Query first or submit complete ms. SASE.
Nonfiction and Photos: All articles should be slanted to high-performance-minded individuals. Car features, technical articles dealing with the automobile. New car introductions, new product features, and a few race reports. All cars or pickups must be 100% Chevrolet. Informational, how-to, interview, profiles. Length: open. Pays $40 per printed page. No additional payment is made for b&w photos (8x10 prints) purchased with mss. Pays $10 to $20 for those purchased separately. Pays $50 to $150 for 2¼x2¼ color transparencies.

SUPER STOCK AND DRAG ILLUSTRATED, Lopez Publications, 205 S. Whiting St., Suite 502, Alexandria VA 22304. Editor: Jim Kelly. For "mostly blue-collar males between 12-35 years old; high performance, drag racing oriented." Monthly magazine; 80 pages. Estab. 1964. Circ. 140,000. Pays on publication. Buys all rights, but may reassign following publication. Simultaneous and photocopied submissions OK. SASE. Reports in 2-6 weeks. Sample copy $1.50.
Nonfiction: Interview (with prominent drag racers); nostalgia (of famous drag racing events); profile (on local or national drag racers); photo features (on drag racing cars or racing events); and technical. Buys 120 mss/year. Query or submit complete ms. Length: 500-5,000 words. Pays $50-250.
Photos: Purchased with accompanying ms. Captions required. Submit prints or transparencies. Pays $10 for 8x10 b&w glossies; $50-150 for 35mm color transparencies.
Fiction: Adventure, humorous. Must be drag racing oriented. Submit complete ms. Length: 500-5,000 words. Pays $50-250.

TRAVELIN' 4x4's, AND OFF ROAD VEHICLES, E-Go Enterprises, Inc., 13510 Ventura Blvd., Sherman Oaks CA 91423. (213)990-2510. Editor: Jim Matthews. 50% freelance written. Emphasizes off-road vehicles and related activities. Monthly magazine; 72 pages. Estab. 1976. Circ. 135,000. Pays on publication. Buys all rights, but may reassign following publication. Phone queries OK. Submit seasonal/holiday material 4 months in advance. SASE. Reports in 2 weeks. Free sample copy and writer's guidelines.
Nonfiction: Expose (on government bills and such related to off roaders); how-to; informational; technical and travel (off-road areas). Buys 5-7 mss/issue. Query of send complete ms. Length: 1,500-3,000 words. Pays $20-35/published page.

Photos: Photos purchased with accompanying ms. Captions required. Uses 8x10 b&w photos and 35mm or 2¼x2¼ color transparencies. Send prints and transparencies. Total purchase price for ms includes payment for photos.
Columns/Departments: Dirt Freak (off-road motorcycle column); and Willie's Work Bench (budget mechanical tips). Buys 3-4/issue. Query or send complete ms. Length: 400-1,000 words. Pays $25-50.
Fillers: Clippings, jokes, gags, anecdotes and short humor. All off-road related. Buys 2/issue. Query or send fillers in. Length: 50-200 words. Pays $5-10.

VAN WORLD MAGAZINE, Hi-Torque Publications Inc., 16200 Ventura Blvd., Encino CA 91436. Editor-in-Chief: Chris Hosford. Managing Editor: Tiff Ford. 20-25% freelance written. Emphasizes custom vans for enthusiasts. Monthly magazine; 76 pages. Estab. 1973. Circ. 85,000. Pays on publication. Buys all rights. Submit seasonal/holiday material 4 months in advance. Photocopied submissions OK. SASE. Reports in 3 weeks. Sample copy $1.50; free writer's guidelines.
Nonfiction: CB (non-technical articles enabling vanners to get the most from their CBs); feature vans: (photo features with brief description); how-to (interior/exterior customizing and engine/mechanical with emphasise on economy); and photo feature (b&w, color with short article on custom vans). Buys 30-50 mss/year. Query. Length: 200-1,000 words. Pays $40 maximum/page.
Photos: Purchased with or without accompanying manuscript or on assignment. Captions required. Submit contact sheet or transparencies. Pays $5-10 for 8x10 b&w glossies; $10-25 for 35mm or 2¼ color transparencies. Total purchase price for ms includes payment for photos. Model release required.

Aviation Publications

Publications in this section aim at professional and private pilots, and at aviation enthusiasts in general. Magazines intended for passengers of commercial airlines are grouped in a separate In-Flight category. Technical aviation and space journals, and those for airport operators, aircraft dealers, or other aviation businessmen are listed under Aviation and Space in the Trade Journals.

AIR LINE PILOT, 1625 Massachussetts Ave., N.W., Washington DC 20036. (202)797-4176. Editor-in-Chief: C.V. Glines. Production Editor: Anne Kelleher. 25% freelance written. Emphasizes commercial aviation. Monthly magazine; 56 pages. Estab. 1933. Circ. 42,000. Pays on acceptance. Buys all rights, but may reassign following publication. Submit seasonal material 4 months in advance. SASE. Reports in 4 weeks. Free sample copy and writer's guidelines.
Nonfiction: Historical (aviation/personal or equipment, aviation firsts); informational (aviation safety, related equipment or aircraft aids); interview (aviation personality); nostalgia (aviation history); photo feature; profile (airline pilots; must be ALPA members); and technical. Buys 25 mss/year. Query. Length: 1,000-2,500 words. Pays $100-300.
Photos: Purchased with or without accompanying ms. Captions required. Query. Pays $10-25 for 8½x10 b&w glossies; $20-250 for 35mm or 2¼x2¼ color transparencies.
How To Break In: "Unless a writer is experienced in aviation, he is more likely to score with a pilot profile or aviation historical piece."

THE AOPA PILOT, 7315 Wisconsin Ave., Washington DC 20014. (301)654-0500. Editor: Robert I. Stanfield. 50% freelance written. For plane owners, pilots, and the complete spectrum of the general aviation industry. Official magazine of the Aircraft Owners and Pilots Association. Monthly. Circ. 205,000. Pays on acceptance. Reports promptly. SASE.
Nonfiction: Factual articles up to 2,500 words that will inform, educate and entertain flying enthusiasts ranging from the student to the seasoned professional pilot. These pieces should be generously illustrated with good quality photos, diagrams or sketches. Quality and accuracy essential. Topics covered include maintenance, how-to features, pilot reports on new or unusual aircraft or aeronautical equipment, places to fly (travel), governmental policies (local, state or federal) relating to general aviation. Additional features on weather in relation to flying, legal aspects of aviation, flight education, pilot fitness, aviation history and aero clubs are used periodically. Short features of 100 to 300 words written around a single photograph, and strong photo features are always in demand. Payment is up to $400.
Photos: Pays $15-25 for each photo or sketch used. Exceptionally good cover color transparencies also purchased.

AVIATION (formerly *Great Lakes Aircraft Bulletin*, *North Atlantic Aircraft Bulletin*, and *Southern Aviation Times*), Data Publications, Box 186, Brookfield CT 06804. (203)789-5802. Editor: David Shugarts. Published in 3 regional editions: Great Lakes, North Atlantic, and Southern. For further details, see listing for *Flight Line Times*.

AVIATION QUARTERLY, Box 606, Plano TX 75074. Publisher: Brad Bierman. Editor: David Hadeler. 100% freelance written. For the serious aviation enthusiast, interested in the history of aviation. Quarterly. Hard-bound volume with four-color illustrations. Estab. 1974. Circ. 9,500. Buys all rights. Buys about 20-25 mss/year. Pays on acceptance. Query. SASE.
Nonfiction and Photos: "We accept only the highest quality articles and photos. Photos with captions must be included or available. Subject matter should be a specific topic within the history of aviation. Writer must have acknowledged experience in his particular field, and must treat his subject in a unique way. Technical articles must also be readable. Nontechnical mss are preferred. Preferred length: 4,000-8,000 words. Payment varies, depending on subject matter and quality and acceptability of text and photos." Pays $150 to $400 per article.

AVIATION TRAVEL, Box 7070, Arlington VA 22207. For owners of business and private aircraft; interested in fishing, hunting, boating, photography, golf, sightseeing, beaches, resorts, outdoor and other sports. Offers a substantial market for writers slanting their material to aviation buffs. Bimonthly magazine. Estab. 1972. Circ. 30,000. Buys all rights. Buys about 20-30 mss/year. Pays on publication. Sample copy $1. Will consider photocopied submissions. Submit seasonal material 3 to 4 months in advance. Query first or submit complete ms. Reports in 2 months. SASE.
Nonfiction and Photos: "Short travel articles—where to go, what to see and do. We may feature a general area or special activity, event, or resort which must be accessible by private or business plane. The U.S.A., Canada, Mexico and the Bahamas are preferred. Airport and flight info are helpful, but not required. The style should be light and nontechnical. Stories must be short, informational, and specific enough to be helpful to the traveler. Destinations must be emphasized, rather than flight. Dates, admission, what to take, etc., increase the value of a story. We're the only travel-oriented aviation magazine, featuring places and events accessible by general aviation. We're interested in fly-in wilderness, fishing, hunting, golfing and camping stories at specific locations. Each issue features items of particular interest during the period immediately following." Buys informational articles, how-to's, personal experience articles, humor, historical articles, photo features, travel pieces, and technical articles. Length: 200 to 1,200 words. Pay "varies: about 5¢ per word, depending on subject and quality." Photos purchased with mss or without mss; captions required. Pay "$5 and up, depending on photo, for b&w glossies 5x7 and larger." Pays $5 and up, "depending on photo and use for transparencies only."

EXXON AIR WORLD, Exxon International Co., Div. of Exxon Corp., 115 Spring Valley Rd., Ossining NY 10562. Editor: Warren H. Goodman. 40% freelance written. For worldwide audience of technical and semitechnical aviation readers. Quarterly. Pays on publication. Query. Reports "quickly." SASE.
Nonfiction and Photos: Uses articles on aviation in action, worldwide; especially the offbeat aviation operation; technical articles. Style should be "unsensational, good 'international' English, informative accurate." Length 300 to 2,000 words. Must be accompanied with good photos. Pays about 10¢ a word. Photos must be of good quality, interesting subject, striking composition, and adequately captioned. Pays $10 minimum for photos.

FLIGHT LINE TIMES, Data Publications, Box 186, Brookfield CT 06804. (203)792-5802. Editor: David A. Shugarts. Emphasizes national issues and broad interest features from within the aviation community of pilots, student pilots, airplane owners, controllers, aviation specialists, etc. Weekly tabloid; 16 pages. Estab. 1974. Pays on publication. Buys all rights. Phone queries OK. Submit seasonal/holiday material 1½ months in advance. Photocopied submissions OK. SASE. Reports in 4 weeks. Free sample copy and writer's guidelines.
Nonfiction: Exposes (on government and industry as their decisions affect the lives of aviation people); how-to (e.g., how to fly in certain tricky conditions, such as wind shear); informational; interviews (with outstanding, important and unusual people in aviation); travel (about the features—resorts, museums, vacation spots, etc.—of places to fly.) "Our outlook is not as formal as most publications. We would rather have the material in hand to look at than to answer queries and talk about writing. We have been stung too many times by people who like to promise, but don't come across with the story. On the other hand, we provide special help and

advice for non-writers, when they show they have a commitment to fair, quick and accurate aviation reporting." Buys 10 mss/issue. Length: 800 words maximum. Pays $1/column inch (maximum $10) for news stories; $20 for features at least 15 column inches long.
Photos: Mark Lacagnina, Photo Editor. Purchased with or without mss. Captions required. Pays $2.50-5 for b&w or color prints.
Columns/Departments: Restaurant reviews. Buys 1/issue. Send complete ms. Length: 400-800 words. Pays $20. Open to suggestions for new columns/departments.

FLYING, Ziff-Davis Publishing Co., 1 Park Ave., New York NY 10016. (212)725-3500. Editor-in-Chief: Richard L. Collins. Managing Editor: Susan Crandell. 5% freelance written. For private or commercial pilots involved with, or interested in, the use of general-aviation aircraft (not airline or military) for business and pleasure. Monthly magazine; 128 pages. Estab. 1927. Circ. 450,000. Pay on acceptance. Buys all rights and first North American serial rights. Phone queries OK. Submit seasonal/holiday material 4 months in advance of issue date. SASE. Reports in 3 weeks.
Nonfiction: How-to (piloting and other aviation techniques, including a monthly series of personal experiences, "I Learned About Flying From That"); personal experience ("I Learned About Flying From That" department); and technical (aviation-related). No articles on "My Trip" travel accounts, or historical features. Buys about 12 mss/year. Submit complete ms. Length: 750-3,500 words. Pays $50-1,000.

GENERAL AVIATION NEWS, Box 1094, Snyder TX 79549. (915)573-6318. Editor-in-Chief: M. Gene Dow. 20% freelance written. Biweekly tabloid; 40 pages. Estab. 1949. Circ. 30,000. Pays on publication. Buys all rights. Phone queries OK. Submit seasonal/holiday material 1 month in advance of issue date. Photocopied submissions OK. SASE. Reports in 4 weeks. Sample copy 50¢; writer's guidelines for return postage.
Nonfiction: General interest (aviation subjects that would be of interest to nation wide audience, not regional); historical (on general aviation history, not including "War Birds"); how-to (fly better or move safely on how to use any type aviation equipment); inspirational (successful aviation businesses, pilots, and airport operations); interview (well known pilots); new product (new aviation projects); nostalgia (pioneer pilot and aircraft); personal experience (flying experiences); photo feature (unique aviation subjects); profile (aviation businessman); and technical (aviation, equipment or pilot techniques). No articles on commercial or military airlines. Buys 50 mss/year. Submit complete ms. Length: 2,000 words. Pays $25/1,000 words.
Photos: Send photo material with accompanying ms. Pays $3-5 for 4x5 b&w or color prints. Captions required. Buys all rights.

PLANE & PILOT MAGAZINE, Werner & Werner Corp., 606 Wilshire, Suite 100, Santa Monica CA 90401. (213)451-1423. Editor-in-Chief: Bill Cox. Managing Editor: Larry Collier. 60% freelance written. Emphasizes all aspects of general aviation. Monthly magazine; 80 pages. Estab. 1965. Circ. 75,000. Pays on publication. Buys all rights. Phone queries OK. Submit seasonal/holiday material 6 months in advance. SASE. Reports in 3 months. Sample copy $1.25.
Nonfiction: How-to articles (emergency procedures); informational (proficiency); humor (strongly encouraged); personal experience (regular features on "Flight I'll Never Forget"). Buys 150 mss/year. Query. Length: 1,000-2,200 words. Pays $50-250.
Photos: Purchased with mss; no additional payment. Only uses 8x10 b&w. Prefers 2¼x2¼ slides or larger, but will consider 35mm. Query.

PRIVATE PILOT, Macro/Comm Corp., 2377 S. El Camino Real, San Clemente CA 92672. (714)498-1600. Editor: Dennis Shattuck. 60% freelance written. For owner/pilots of private aircraft, for student pilots and others aspiring to attain additional ratings and experience. Estab. 1955. Circ. 100,000. Buys first North American serial rights. Buys about 60 mss/year. Pays on publication. Sample copy $2; writer's guidelines for SASE. Will consider photocopied submissions if guaranteed original. Will not consider simultaneous submissions. Reports in 30 days. Query first. SASE.
Nonfiction and Photos: Material on techniques of flying, developments in aviation, product and specific airplane test reports, travel by aircraft, development and use of airports. All must be related to general aviation field. "Freelancer must know the subject about which he is writing; use good grammar; know the publication for which he's writing; remember that we try to relate to the middle segment of the business/pleasure flying public. We see too many 'first flight' type of articles. Our market is more sophisticated than that. Most writers do not do enough research on their subject. Would like to see more material on business-related flying, more on people involved in flying." Length: 1,000 to 4,000 words. Pays $25 to $200. Material is also used in the

following columns: Business Flying, Homebuilt/Experimental Aircraft, Pilot's Logbook. Length: 1,000 words. Pays $25 to $100. 8x10 b&w glossies purchased with mss or on assignment. Pays $15. Color transparencies of any size are used for the cover. Pays $100.

WINGS MAGAZINE, (formerly *Canadian Wings*), Corvus Publishing Group Ltd., 203-2003 McKnight Blvd., Calgary, Alberta, Canada T2E 6L2. (403)277-2337 or 277-0078. Editor-in-Chief: Wayne D. Ralph. 20% freelance written. Emphasizes aviation-private, commercial & military. The audience would range from age 15-70 and are predominently people employed in aviation or with a hobbyist's interest in the field. Monthly magazine; 52 pages. Estab. 1958. Circ. 8,500. Pays on publication. Buys all rights, but may reassign following publication; one-time rights for photo material. Phone queries OK. Submit seasonal/holiday material 2 months in advance. Simultaneous, photocopied and previously published submissions OK. SASE. Reports in 1 month. Sample copy $1.
Nonfiction: Historical (mainly Canadian history); how-to (technical); humor (cartoonists' drawings); informational (technical aviation); interview (Canadian personalities in aviation circles); new product, nostalgia (historical vein); personal experience; photo feature; profile (Canadian individuals); technical; travel (flying related); aircraft handling tests and technical evaluation on new products. Buys 25 mss/year. Query. Length: 500-2,000 words. Pays $50-200.
Photos: Purchased with or without accompanying ms. Captions required. Query for photos. Pays $5-20 for 5x7 b&w glossies; $25-50 for 35mm color transparencies. No additional payment for photos accepted with accompanying ms. Total purchase price for a ms includes payment for photos.
Fillers: Clippings and newsbreaks.

Black Publications

Black general interest publications are listed in this category. Additional markets for black-oriented material are in the following sections: Business and Finance Publications, Confession Publications, Juvenile Publications, Literary and Little Publications, Poetry Publications, Politics and World Affairs Publications, Sport and Outdoor Publications, Teen and Young Adult Publications; Theater, Movie, TV and Entertainment Publications; Play Publishers, Book Publishers, Greeting Card Publishers, and Syndicates.

BLACK FORUM MAGAZINE, Box 1090, Bronx NY 10451. Editor-in-Chief: Revish Windham. Managing Editor: Julia Coaxum. 50% freelance written. For unpublished black writers interested in literary subjects. Semiannual magazine; 48 pages. Estab. 1975. Circ. 2,000. Pays on publication. Buys first North American serial rights. Photocopied submissions OK. SASE. Reports in 1-2 months. Sample copy $1.25; free writer's guidelines.
Nonfiction: Informational; interview (with black writers, artists, etc.); and profile. Buys 2 mss/issue. Submit complete ms. Length: 750-1,000 words. Pays $15 minimum.
Photos: Reginald Ward, Photo Editor. Purchased on assignment. Query for photos.
Columns, Departments: Movie, book, theater and dance reviews. Submit complete ms. Open to suggestions for new columns/departments; address to Revish Windham.
Fiction: Fred Richardson, Fiction Editor. Adventure, experimental, historical, humorous and suspense. Buys 2 mss/issue. Submit complete ms. Length: 500-750 words. Pays $15 maximum.
Poetry: Horace Mungin, Poetry Editor. Avant-garde, free verse, light verse and traditional. Limit submissions to batches of 5. Length: maximum 20 lines. Pays in copies of magazine.
Fillers: Puzzles (subject should deal with black history). Send fillers.
How To Break In: "All material will be personally read by the editor of each department. Comments and notations will accompany all returned material. We ask that freelancers read and note our comments and continue to send in material."

CORE, 200 W. 135 St., New York NY 10030. (212)368-8104. Editor: Victor Hall. Publication of the Congress of Racial Equality. Estab. 1970. Bimonthly. Circ. 30,000. Rights acquired vary with author and material. Uses about 60 freelance articles/year. "Most of our articles are donated." Free sample copy. Will consider photocopied submissions. Submit seasonal/holiday material at least 2 months in advance. Query. Reports in 6 months. SASE.
Nonfiction and Photos: "Articles about or related to the black movement, black people's oppression, projected or attempted solutions. Also profiles of Black Movement people. Interviews. Health, food, books, sports. Also interested in travel, fashion, movies or African affairs.

The writer's style and emphasis is up to him. We like variety. Of course, it helps if his outlook is black nationalist, but it's not mandatory. We try to make black nationalism (a little understood concept) digestible for the common man as well as the intellectual. Most articles are donated." Length: 500-5,000 words. Pays $25 for b&w photos on assignment. Captions optional.
Fiction: Should relate to magazine's theme. Length: 500-5,000 words. "Most are donated."
Poetry and Fillers: Free verse and avant-garde forms. Should relate. Length: open. Short humor and anecdotes. Length: 500-1,500 words. "Most are donated."

THE CRISIS, 1790 Broadway, New York NY 10019. (212)245-2100. Editor: Warren Marr, II. 80% freelance written. Official publication of the NAACP. "Our audience includes government officials, schools and libraries, representative of the leadership group in the black community across the nation, and persons involved in the broad area of human relations." Established in 1910 by W. E. B. Du Bois. Monthly (June/July, August/September issues are combined). Circ. 114,000. Acquires all rights. "In most situations, upon request, we will grant permission to reprint provided proper credit is included." Uses 50 freelance mss a year. "Our payment to writers at this time is in contributor's copies only." Submit complete ms. Reports on material within a month. SASE.
Nonfiction: "Articles dealing with civil rights and general welfare of Negroes and other minorities." Informational, interview, profile, historical, think pieces, exposes. Length: 3,000 words maximum.
Fiction: Short stories with a constructive racial theme.
Poetry: Traditional forms, blank verse and free verse. Should relate to magazine's theme. Length: 40 lines maximum.
How To Break In: "What we don't get and would appreciate is material dealing with Blacks in the arts and sciences. And that means all the arts —performing, graphic, etc. We haven't had any material on Blacks in the classical music area, for instance. When dealing with other minorities, stick to material that is applicable across the board —to minorities in general. For example, how does the struggle of a Puerto Rican writer relate to the struggle of all third world writers?"

EBONY MAGAZINE, 820 S. Michigan Ave., Chicago IL 60605. Editor: John H. Johnson. Address mss to Charles L. Sanders, Managing Editor. For black readers of the U.S., Africa, and the Caribbean. Monthly. Circ. 1,300,000. Buys all rights. Buys about 20 mss/year from freelancers. Pays on publication. Submit seasonal material 2 months in advance. Query first. Usually reports in less than 30 days, but this varies. SASE.
Nonfiction: Achievement and human interest stories about, or of concern to, black readers. Photo essays, interviews, think pieces, profiles, humor, inspirational and historical pieces are bought. Length: 2,500 words minimum. Pays $150 and up.
Photos: Purchased with mss, and with captions only. Buys 8x10 glossies, color transparencies, 35mm color. Submit negatives and contacts when possible. Photo stories. Pays $150 and up.

ESSENCE, 1500 Broadway, New York NY 10036. (212)730-4260. Editor-in-Chief: Marcia Ann Gillespie. Managing Editor: Navine Alexander. 70% freelance written. Emphasizes Black Women. Monthly magazine; 150 pages. Estab. May 1970. Circ. 600,000. Pays 30 days after publication. Buys all rights, but may reassign following publication. Submit seasonal/holiday material 6 months in advance of issue date. SASE. Reports in 6-8 weeks. Sample copy $1; free writer's guidelines.
Nonfiction: Exposé; general interest; historical; how-to; humor; interview; personal experience; personal opinion; profile; and travel. Buys 200 mss/year. Query. Length: 1,500-6,000 words. Pays $200-850.
Photos: Ray Hooper, art director. State availability of photos with query. Pays $50-300 for b&w contact sheets; $100-600 for color transparencies. Captions and model release required.
Columns/Departments: Daryl Alexander. Entertainment; Health; Travel and Work. Query. Length: 1,500-2,000 words. Pays $100 minimum.
Fiction: Adventure; experimental; fantasy; humorous; romance; condensed and serialized novels. Buys 33 mss/year. Submit complete ms. Length: 1,500 words. Pays $200.
Poetry: Alexis deVeaux, poetry editor. Avant-garde; free verse; light verse and traditional. Buys 29/year. Pays $35.

JET, 820 S. Michigan Ave., Chicago IL 60605. Executive Editor: Robert E. Johnson. For black readers interested in current news and trends. Weekly. Circ. 700,000. Study magazine before submitting. Enclose SASE. for return of submissions.
Nonfiction and Photos: Articles on topics of current, timely interest to black readers. News items

and features: religion, education, African affairs, civil rights, politics, entertainment. Buys informational articles, interviews, profiles, spot news, photo pieces, and personal experience articles. Length: varies. Payment to be negotiated.

MISS BLACK AMERICA MAGAZINE, 24 W. Chelten Ave., Phildelphia PA 19144. Executive Editor: Norman Hayes. Service magazine for Black women between the ages of 18 and 34. Quarterly magazine; 48 pages. Estab. 1969. Circ. 125,000. Pays on publication. Buys all rights. SASE. Reports in 1 month. Sample copy and writer's guidelines $1.
Nonfiction: Profiles of young Black women who have made significant achievements in the arts, entertainment, business or professions; how-to articles on fashions, beauty, careers, human relationships, money management, or any area of interest to young women. Submit complete ms. Length: 1,500-2,500 words. Pays $25.
Photos: Purchased with accompanying ms only. Pays $15/8x10 b&w print. Model release required.

SEPIA, 1220 Harding St., Ft. Worth TX 76102. Editor: A.S. "Doc" Young. For "black readers of all age groups and interests." Monthly. Circ. 160,000. Buys all rights. Buys about 75 mss a year from freelancers. Pays on acceptance. Will send a sample copy to a writer for $1. Will consider photocopied submissions. Submit seasonal material 3 months in advance. Reports in 1 week. Query first. Enclose SASE.
Nonfiction and Photos: "We are in the market for well-written, provocative, factual articles on the role of black Americans in all phases of American life. We look for a good writing style, no different from any popularly written publication. We are constantly in need of articles with current news value, but strictly projected for future publication. In this respect, we specifically look for queries on events that will be in the news when our magazine reaches its readers. Articles may be on interesting personalities, entertainers, sports figures, human interest or controversial topics. We will consider any subject if it has good reader appeal for a black audience. It cannot be overemphasized that contributors should study recent issues for general content and style." Buys interviews, profiles, historical articles, exposes, coverage of successful business operations, photo essays. Length: 3,000 words. Pays $200-$250. Photos are required with mss. B&w glossies, color transparencies.

Business and Finance Publications

National and regional publications of general interest to businessmen are listed here. Those in the National grouping cover national business trends, and include some material on the general theory and practice of business and financial management. Those in the Regional grouping report on the business climate of specific regions.

Magazines that use material on national business trends and the general theory and practice of business and financial management, but which have a technical, professional slant, are classified in the Trade Journals section, under the Business Management, Finance, Industrial Management, or Management and Supervision categories.

National

BARRON'S NATIONAL BUSINESS AND FINANCIAL WEEKLY, 22 Cortlandt St., New York NY 10007. (212)285-5245. Editor: Robert M. Bleiberg. For business and investment people. Weekly. Free sample copy. Buys all rights. Pays on publication. SASE.
Nonfiction: Articles about various industries with investment point of view; shorter articles on particular companies, their past performance and future prospects as related to industry trends for "News and Views" column. "Must be suitable for our specialized readership." Length: 2,000 words or more. Pays $200 to $500 for articles; $100 and up for "News and Views" material. Articles considered on speculation only.
How To Break In: "News and Views might be a good way, but the key thing to remember here is these pieces must be fully researched and thoroughly documented."

BLACK ENTERPRISE, 295 Madison Ave., New York NY 10017. Managing Editor: Phil W. Petrie. For black executives, professionals, and independent businessmen. Monthly. Estab. 1970. Circ. 215,000. Rights purchased vary with author and material. Buys 20 to 30 mss per year. Pays on acceptance. Will send free sample copy to writer on request. Will consider photocopied submissions. Will not consider simultaneous submissions. Reports in 6 to 8 weeks. Query first. Enclose SASE.

Nonfiction: Informational articles addressed to business and business-related interests of audience. Stress is on black perspective and economic framework. Unique, exclusive focus on black economic interests. Informational, how-to, personal experience, interview, profile, think articles, and successful business operations. Length: 1,500 words minimum. Pays up to $500 maximum.

BUSINESS WEEK, 1221 Avenue of the Americas, New York NY 10020. Does not solicit freelance material.

COMMERCIAL WEST MAGAZINE, Financial Communications, Inc., 5100 Edina Industrial Blvd., Edina MN 55435. (612)835-5853. Editor: David L. Jones. 10% freelance written. For banking and corporate executives. Weekly magazine; 40 pages. Estab. 1901. Circ. 4,700. Pays on acceptance. Buys all rights. Phone queries OK. Submit seasonal/holiday material 6 weeks in advance of issue date. Simultaneous and previously published submissions OK. SASE. Reports in 2 weeks. Sample copy $1; free writer's guidelines.
Nonfiction: Exposé; general interest; historical; inspirational; interview; personal opinion; photo feature; profile; technical; financial legislation and corporation profiles. Buys 12 mss/year. Query. Pays $100-250.
Photos: State availability of photos with query. Pays $25 for 5x7 b&w prints.

COMMODITY JOURNAL, American Assoc. of Commodity Traders, 10 Park St., Concord NH 03001. Editor-in-Chief: Arthur N. Economou. 30% freelance written. Emphasizes commodities, agriculture and energy for a highly educated and informed audience with specific interests in mind. Bimonthly magazine; 45 pages. Estab. 1965. Circ. 5,000. Pays on acceptance. Buys all rights. Phone queries OK. Simultaneous and photocopied submissions OK. SASE. Reports in 2 months.
Nonfiction: Robert F. Boucher, associate editor. Informational (of technical nature) and technical (commodities, agriculture and alternative energy). Query. Length: 2,500 words maximum. Pays 5-10¢/word.

DOLLARS & SENSE, National Taxpayers Union, 325 Pennsylvania Ave., S.E., Washington DC 20003. Editor-in-Chief: Chuck Crawford. 5-10% freelance written. Emphasizes taxes and government spending for a diverse readership. Monthly newsletter; 8-12 pages. Estab. 1970. Circ. 30,000. Pays on publication. Buys all rights. Submit seasonal/holiday material 1 month in advance. Previously published submissions OK. SASE. Free sample copy and writer's guidelines.
Nonfiction: Exposé (dealing with wasteful government spending, excessive regulation of the economy), and personal opinion. Buys 10 mss/year. Query. Length: 600-2,000 words. Pays $15-100. "We look for original material on subjects overlooked by the national press and other political magazines. Probably the best approach is to take a little-known area of government mismanagement and examine it closely. The articles we like most are those that examine a federal program that is not only poorly managed and wasteful, but also self-defeating, hurting the very people it is designed to help. We are also interested in the long term harm done by different kinds of taxation. Articles on IRS harassment and abuses are always needed and welcome. We have no use for financial or investment advice or broad philosophical pieces."

DUN'S REVIEW, Dun & Bradstreet Publications Corp., 666 5th Ave., New York NY 10019. (212)489-2200. Editor: Clem Morgello. Emphasizes business, management and finances for a readership "concentrated among senior executives of those companies that have a net worth of $1 million or more." Monthly magazine; 90-140 pages. Estab. 1893. Circ. 250,000. Pays on acceptance. Buys all rights. Submit seasonal/holiday material 3 months in advance. Photocopied submissions OK. Reports in 1 month. Sample copy $1.50.
Nonfiction: Exposé (business and government), historical (business; i.e., law or case history), how-to (hobby that would appeal to readership), humor (business), informational (business and government), interview (assigned only), personal opinion (submitted to The Forum, opinion from high ranked sources), and profile (companies, turnarounds, etc). Buys 12 mss/year. Query. Length: 1,500-3,000 words. Pays $200 minimum.
Photos: Gene Landino, Art Director. Purchased with accompanying ms. Query. Pays $75 for b&w photos; $150 for color.
Columns/Departments: Footnote (historical or important issues impacting business world), Spotlight, Forum, and The Economy (by invitation only). Buys one mss/issue. Query. Length: 1,000-1,500 words. Pays $200.

FINANCE, The Magazine of Money & Business, 8 W. 40th St., New York NY 10018. (212)221-7900. Editor: Bradbury K. Thurlow. Associate Editor: Charles B. Thurlow. 50% freelance written. For senior executives and decision makers in the business and financial communities. Monthly magazine; 48 pages. Estab. 1941. Circ. 45,000. Pays on publication. Buys all rights. Phone queries OK. Submit seasonal/holiday material 6 weeks in advance of issue date. Simultaneous and photocopied submissions OK. SASE. Reports in 3 months. Free sample copy and writer's guidelines.
Nonfiction: Interviews and profiles with high ranking business and financial executives. "No nuts-and-bolts or lower/middle management-related how-to articles." Query. Length: 1,000-5,000 words. Pays $100-500.
Photos: State availability of photos with query. Pays $10 for 5x7 glossy b&w prints; $10 for color transparencies. Captions preferred. Buys all rights, but may reassign following publication.
Columns/Departments: Buys 3 mss/year. Query. Length: 1,000-2,000 words. Pays $100. Open to suggestions for new columns/departments.

FORBES, 60 Fifth Ave., New York NY 10011. "We do not buy freelance material." But, on occasion, when a writer of some standing (or whose work is at least known to them) is going abroad or into an area where they don't have regular staff or bureau coverage, they have given assignments or sometimes helped on travel expenses.

FORTUNE, 1271 Ave. of the Americas, New York NY 10020. Staff-written, but they do buy a few freelance articles (by Irwin Ross, for example) and pay extremely well for them.

FREE ENTERPRISE, 800 2nd Ave., New York NY 10017. (212)697-3200. Publisher: Patrick H.W. Garrard. Emphasizes business opportunities and money making. Bimonthly magazine. Estab. 1971. Circ. 350,000. Pays on publication. Buys all rights. Free sample copy and writer's guidelines.
Nonfiction: "We are about business opportunities and money making—but we stay away from the ordinary, the dull, and corporate doings. We want stories about new fads and trends, told either in the second person or, as an inspirational profile, in the third person; both though, must contain in the text or in sidebars enough information (names, address, sources of information) for readers to go forth and prosper. We also want articles about individuals fighting big business (Washington, unions, City Hall, or big media) and exposés where the victim is the little guy." Query. Buys 150 mss/year. Length: 2,500 words maximum. Pays 10¢/words minimum.

INVESTMENTS/OPPORTUNITIES AROUND THE WORLD (formerly *Franchising Investments & Business Opportunities*), Box 610097, North Miami FL 33161. Editor: Edward J. Foley. For people interested in investment and business opportunities. Estab. 1966. Monthly. Circ. over 50,000. Buys all rights, but will reassign rights to author after publication. Buys about 10 mss/year. Pays on publication. Free sample copy. Will consider photocopied submissions. No simultaneous submissions. Reports on material accepted for publication in 30 days. Does not return unsolicited material which is rejected. Query first. SASE.
Nonfiction and Photos: Business and financial articles. New ideas for money-making opportunities. Articles should tie in with current market conditions and should be preceded with an outline and query. Avoid emphasis on "old" times. Informational, spot news, successful business operations, new product. Length: 1,000 to 3,000 words. Pays 2¢/word. $5 for b&w glossies purchased with mss. Captions required.

KENTUCKY BUSINESS LEDGER, Box 3508, Louisville KY 40201. (502)635-5212. Editor-in-Chief: Jim St. Clair. Managing Editor: Dot Ridings. 60% freelance written. Emphasizes Kentucky business and finance. Monthly tabloid; 32 pages. Estab. January 1976. Circ. 11,000. Pays on publication. Buys all rights, but may reassign following publication. Phone queries OK. Submit seasonal/holiday material 1 month in advance of issue date. Simultaneous, photocopied and previously published submissions OK. SASE. Reports in 2 weeks. Sample copy 75¢; free writer's guidelines.
Nonfiction: How-to (tips for businesses on exporting, dealing with government, cutting costs, increasing profits); interview (government officials on issues important to Kentucky businessmen); new product (new uses for coal); profile (of Kentucky businessmen); and articles on the meanings of government laws and regulations to Kentucky businesses. Buys 15-20 mss/issue. Query. Length: 1,250 words maximum. Pays $1/inch.
Photos: State availability of photos with query. Pays $5-25 for 8x10 b&w glossy prints; $10-35 for color transparencies.

MBA MAGAZINE, 730 3rd Ave., New York NY 10017. (212)557-9240. Editor-in-Chief: Marlene Deverell-Van Meter. Emphasizes business management. Monthly magazine; 80 pages. Estab. 1966. Circ. 200,000. Pays on the tenth of the month of publication. Buys all rights. Submit seasonal/holiday material 4 months in advance. Simultaneous and photocopied submissions OK. SASE. Reports in 3 months. Sample copy $1.25.
Nonfiction: Exposé (business and government regulations); how-to (business management and career planning); interview (business and government executives); profile; new product (for management market, e.g., calculators, computers); photo feature (business or economic); and technical (management science). Buys 5 mss/issue. Submit outline. Length: 500-2,000 words. Pays 10¢/word.
Photos: John Jay, Photo Editor. Purchased on assignment. Captions required. Query. Pays $25-50 per b&w photo; $75-100 for color. Model release required. Will make appointments to see portfolios.

MONEY, Time-Life Building, Rockefeller Center, New York NY 10020. Managing Editor: William Simon Rukeyser. "For the middle to upper middle income, sophisticated, well-educated reader. We picture our readers as neither insiders or idiots." Established in 1972. No freelance material.

MONEY STRATEGIES, Alexander Hamilton Institute, 605 Third Ave., New York NY 10016. Editor: Joseph R. Tigue. For high income individuals. Biweekly newsletter. Estab. 1909. Buys all rights. Pays on acceptance. Free sample copy. Query first. Enclose SASE.
Nonfiction: Ways to save and invest money; investment alternatives, real estate, precious metals, art, antiques. Pithy, newsletter style of writing. No puffery. Solid copy with concrete examples. Length: 500 words average. Pays 15¢ per word.

Regional

ALASKA CONSTRUCTION & OIL MAGAZINE, 109 W. Mercer St., Seattle WA 98119. Executive Editor: Roscoe E. Laing. Associate Editor: Christine Laing. For management level personnel in construction/oil/timber/mining. Monthly magazine; 100 pages. Estab. 1959. Circ. 9,500. Pays on publication. Buys first North American serial rights. Submit seasonal/holiday material 3-4 months in advance. Previously published work OK. SASE. Reports in 2 weeks. Sample copy $1. Free writer's guidelines.
Nonfiction: "Only informational articles on the fields we cover." Buys 10-15/year. Query. Length: 500-2,000 words. Pays $1.50/column inch.
Photos: Purchased with mss. Pays $10-25/5x7 or 8x10 b&w glossies; $25-50/color positives of any size.

AUSTIN MAGAZINE, Austin Chamber of Commerce, P.O. Box 1967, Austin TX 78767. Editor: Hal Susskind. A business and community magazine dedicated to telling the story of Austin and its people to Chamber of Commerce members and the community. Magazine published monthly by the Chamber; 48-64 pages. Estab. 1960. Circ. 6,500. Not copyrighted. Sample copy for $1. Will consider original mss only. Reports in 1 month. SASE.
Nonfiction and Photos: Articles should deal with interesting businesses or organizations around town with emphasis on the Austin community and Chamber of Commerce members. Articles are also accepted on Austin's entertainment scene. Length: 1,000 to 2,000 words. Pays 2½¢/word. B&w photos are purchased with mss.

B.C. BUSINESS MAGAZINE, 101-1256 W. Pender St., Vancouver, British Columbia, Canada V6E 2S8. (604)685-2376. Editor-in-Chief: J. R. Martin. Managing Editor: Kent MacKay. 20% freelance written. Emphasizes British Columbian business. Monthly magazine; 80 pages. Estab. May 1973. Circ. 20,000. Pays on publication. Buys all rights. Phone queries OK. Simultaneous and photocopied submissions OK. Reports in 2 weeks. Sample copy $1.50.
Nonfiction: Interview (B.C. business people); profile (B.C. business people); and general business (in B.C.). No items unrelated to business in British Columbia and no how-to business articles. Buys 6 mss/issue. Query. Length: 500-2,500 words. Pays $50-500.
Photos: No additional payment for 5x7 or 8x11 b&w prints. Captions required.

CALIFORNIA BUSINESS, 1060 Crenshaw Blvd., Los Angeles CA 90019. (213)937-1714. Editor: Art Garcia. For management executives, investors, bankers, other financial executives. Biweekly tabloid newspaper; 32 to 40 pages. Estab. 1965. Circ. 35,000. Buys all rights, but will reassign rights to author after publication. Buys 30 to 40 mss a year. Payment within 1 to 3 weeks after publication. Free sample copy. No photocopied or simultaneous submissions. Reports in 1 to 4 weeks. Query. SASE.

Nonfiction: Department editor: Mike Harris. Specializes in regionalized business coverage of the West. Uses business and financial news and feature stories; management, marketing,investment trend stories. Nearly all have a California or west coast angle. Virtually all stories are keyed to western readers. Informational, how-to, interview, profile, expose, personal opinion and coverage of successful business operations. Length: 250 to 2,000 words. Pays $25 to $250. Photos purchased with mss; no additional payment.

CANADIAN BUSINESS, CB Media, Ltd., 59 Front St., E., Toronto, Ontario, Canada. (416)364-4266. Editor-in-Chief: Alexander Ross. Managing Editor: John Dizard. 80% freelance written. Emphasizes general business. Monthly magazine; 120 pages. Estab. 1919. Circ. 55,000. Pays on acceptance. Buys first North American serial rights. Submit seasonal/holiday material 3 months in advance of issue date. Photocopied submissions OK. SASE. Reports in 1 month. Sample copy $2.
Nonfiction: How-to. Buys 6 mss/issue. Query. Length: 500-5,000 words. Pays $150-1,000.

CANADIAN BUSINESS MAGAZINE, 1080 Beaver Hall Hill, Montreal, H2Z 1T2, Quebec, Canada. Editor: Robin Schiele. For senior and middle management men in business and industry in late 40s or early 50s, usually educated to at least bachelor degree level. We also have significant readership among business students and university and government people. Monthly magazine. Established in 1927. Circulation: 50,000. Buys first Canadian serial rights. Buys second serial (reprint) rights, on occasion. Buys 60 to 80 mss per year. Payment on acceptance. Will send free sample copy to writer on request. Will consider photocopied submissions. Simultaneous submissions, "if so indicated." Reports within 8 weeks. Query first. Enclose SASE.
Nonfiction and Photos: Subjects pertaining directly to Canadian business, including the economic performance of the nation, a region, an industry, or a company; finance; corporate management; investments; trade relations; personnel; government action, particularly planned or newly passed legislation; how-to stories helpful to the reader in his capacity as businessman. Non-academic style, written with a complete familiarity with the Canadian scene (and how it differs from the American). Length: 1,000 to 2,500 words. Pays $100 minimum. Photos purchased with accompanying ms with no additional payment. Captions optional.

CARIBBEAN BUSINESS NEWS, 1255 Yonge St., Toronto, Ontario, Canada M4T 1W6. (416)925-1086. Managing Editor: Colin Rickards. 3% freelance written. Emphasizes business and financial news affecting the entire Caribbean area for upper and middles echelon business/managment people worldwide. Monthly tabloid; 16-20 pages. Estab. October 1969. Circ. 32,000. Pays on publication. Buys all rights, but may reassign following publication. Phone queries OK. Photocopied and previously published submissions OK. SASE. Reports in 2 weeks. Free sample copy and writer's guidelines; mention *Writer's Market* in request.
Nonfiction: General interest, interview and business/financial articles on Caribbean topics. No travel material. Buys 8 mss/year. Query. Length: 500-1,000 words. Pays $50-250.
Photos: Pays $25 minimum for 5x7 or 8x10 b&w prints. Captions required. Buys all rights, but may reassign following publication.

COMMERCE MAGAZINE, 130 S. Michigan Ave., Chicago IL 60603. (312)786-0111. Editor: Gordon A. Moon II. For top businessmen and industrial leaders in greater Chicago area. Also sent to chairmen of and presidents of Fortune 1,000 firms throughout United States. Monthly magazine; varies from 100 to 400 pages, (8¼x11¼). Established in 1904. Circulation: 12,000. Buys all rights, but will reassign rights to author after publication. Buys 30 to 40 mss per year. Pays on acceptance. Will send sample copy to writer for $1. Query first. Enclose SASE.
Nonfiction: Business articles and pieces of general interest to top business executives. "We select our freelancers and assign topics. Many of our writers are from local newspapers. Considerable freelance material is used but almost exclusively on assignment from Chicago area specialists within a particular business sector." Pays 4¢ to 8¢ a word.

FINANCIAL POST, Maclean-Hunter, Ltd., 481 University Ave., Toronto, Ontario, Canada M5W 1A7. Editor: Neville J. Nankivell. Executive Editor: Dalton S. Robertson. New Editor: A.C. Dunbar. 10% freelance written. Emphasizes Canadian business, investment/finance and public affairs. Weekly newspaper; 36-48 pages. Estab. 1907. Circ. 165,000. Pays on publication. Buys one-time rights. Reports in 2-3 weeks. Sample copy 75¢.
Nonfiction: Useful news and information for executives, managers and investers in Canada. Buys 3 mss/issue. Query. Length: 700-800 words. Pays 10-15¢/word.
Photos: State availability of photos with query. Pays $15-50 for 8x10 b&w glossy prints.

Captions required. Buys one-time rights.

HOUSTON BUSINESS JOURNAL, Cordovan Corp., 5314 Bingle Rd., Houston TX 77092. (713)688-8811. Editor-in-Chief: Mike Weingart. 10% freelance written. Emphasizes Houston business. Weekly tabloid; 40 pages. Estab. 1971. Circ. 15,000. Pays on publication. Purchases all rights. Phone queries OK ("but prefer mail"). Submit seasonal/holiday material 2 months in advance. SASE. Reports in 1 month. Free sample copy.
Nonfiction: Expose (business, if documented), How-to (finance, business, management, lifestyle), informational (money-making), interview (local business topics), nostalgia (possible, if business), profile (local business execs), personal experience and photo feature. Buys 100+ mss/year. Query or submit complete ms. Length: 500-2,000. Pays $2.50/column inch.
Photos: Purchased with or without accompanying ms or on assignment. Captions required. B&w only. Submit prints; 4x5 minimum, 11x14 maximum glossy. Pays $7.50-25.
Columns, Departments: Profile, Restaurants. Buys 100 mss/year. Query. Pays $2. Open to suggestions for new columns and departments.

NEAR EAST BUSINESS, 386 Park Ave., S., New York NY 10016. Editor: John Townsend. U.S. Editor: Martha Downing. Bimonthly magazine; 60-80 pages. For business and government leaders (English speaking) in the Arab Middle East, Iran and Turkey. Estab. 1976. Circ. 17,000. Buys first serial rights. Buys 6-8 mss/year. Pays on publication. Free sample copy. Will consider photocopied submissions. Reports in 1 month. Enclose SASE.
Nonfiction: Stories and news items relating to business, industry, markets, management in the Middle East, Iran and Turkey. Length: 1,000-2,000 words. Pays average of $175.

THE NEW ENGLANDER, Dublin NH 03444. (603)563-8111. Editor-in-Chief: Timothy Clark. Emphasizes business and public affairs in New England. For "executives and public officials in 6 New England states, age 25-65, college educated, upper income." Monthly magazine; 80 pages. Estab. 1953. Circ. 17,400. Pays on acceptance or publication. Purchases all rights, but may reassign following publication. Submit seasonal/holiday material 8-10 weeks in advance. SASE. Reports in 2 weeks. Free sample copy (if in New England).
Nonfiction: Expose (government regulation, business); How-to (business, management); informational (regional needs); interview (key business and public leaders); personal opinion; profile; personal experience; and photo feature (any related to New England business or regional interest). Buys 7 mss/issue. Query. Length: 500-2,000. Pays $300.
Photos: Bruce Hammond, photo editor. Purchased with accompanying ms or on assignment. Captions required. Submit 5x7 or 8x10 glossy for b&w, 2¼x2¼ or 4x5 for color. Query or send contact sheet. Pays $25-150 per photo for both color or b&w. Photos must relate to publication's subject matter.

NORTHWEST INVESTMENT REVIEW, 220 S.W. Alder St., Portland OR 97212. (503)224-6004. Editor-in-Chief: Shannon P. Pratt. For investors and corporate leaders who pay $135 a year to read about the 270 plus northwestern publicly held corporations covered by this publication. Newsletter; 6-20 pages. Estab. 1971. Semimonthly. Not copyrighted. Pays on publication. Will send sample packet of newsletters to writer for $2.50. No photocopied or simultaneous submissions. Reports in 2 to 4 weeks. Query first to J. Michael Reid. SASE.
Nonfiction: "We need top regional articles, appealing to investors." Corporate profiles, personnel changes, industry surveys. "If well researched in our field, we will consider freelance work; ideally, from business page writers, individuals with finance/security backgrounds." Length: 500 to 2,500 words. "With query first, we would quote what the piece would be worth to us. Many are done for a fee. No set minimum."

THE SOUTH MAGAZINE, Trend Publications, Inc., Box 2350, Tampa FL 33601. Editor-in-Chief: Roy B. Bain. Emphasizes the Southern business community and climate. Monthly magazine; 64-96 pages. Estab. January 1974. Circ. 50,000. Pays on acceptance. Buys first North American serial rights. SASE. Reports in 6 weeks. Sample copy $1; free writer's guidelines.
Nonfiction: No articles on how-to. Buys 8 mss/issue. Query. Length: 300-1,800 words. Pays $45-300.
Photos: State availability of photos with query. No additional payment for 5x7 b&w glossy prints or 35mm color transparencies. Captions required. Buys one-time rights. Model release preferred.

TIDEWATER VIRGINIAN, Box 327, Norfolk VA 23501. Editor: Marilyn Goldman. 90% freelance written. For members of Norfolk, Portsmouth, Chesapeake and Virginia Beach

chambers of commerce. Magazine; 78 pages. Monthly. Circ. 10,000. Copyrighted. Buys about 60 mss a year. Pays on publication. Sample copy for $1. Will consider photocopied and simultaneous submissions. Reports in 2 to 3 weeks. Query first or submit complete ms. SASE.
Nonfiction: Articles dealing with business and industry in Virginia, primarily surrounding area of southeastern Virginia (Tidewater area). Profiles, successful business operations, new product, merchandising techniques, book reviews. Length: 500 to 2,500 words. Pays $25-125.

CB Radio

CANADIAN TRANSCEIVER, Walgram Publishing Ltd., 75 The Donway West, Suite 1009, Don Mills, Ontario, Canada M3C 2E9. (416)496-1203. Editor-in-Chief: J.R. Graham. Managing Editor: Robert Arculli. 80% freelance written. Emphasizes CB, Ham, and commercial 2-way radio. Monthly magazine; 64 pages. Estab. 1975. Circ. 22,000. Pays on publication. Buys all rights. Phone queries OK. Submit seasonal/holiday material 3 months in advance of issue date. Photocopied submissions OK. SASE. Reports in 6-8 weeks. Free sample copy; mention *Writer's Market* in request.
Nonfiction: How-to (building electronic items, installing 2-way radios and antennas, etc.); and technical (electronics and specifically 2-way radio). Buys 60 mss/year. Query. Length: 500-1,500 words. Pays 6-10¢/word.
Photos: State availability of photos with query. Pays $5 for 3x4 b&w glossy prints; $25-50 for 2¼x2¼ color transparencies. Captions required. Buys all rights, but may reassign following publication. Model release required.

CB MAGAZINE, 531 N. Ann Arbor, Oklahoma City OK 73127. Editor-in-Chief: Leo G. Sands (212)986-6596, New York City. Managing Editor: Edward K. Minderman (405)947-6113 Oklahoma City. 50% freelance written. For operators of citizens band 2-way radiotelephones for personal and business communications. Estab. 1961. Monthly. Circ. 300,000. Full rights purchased worldwide. May buy all rights but will sometimes reassign rights to author after publication. Buys 4 or more mss/issue. Payment on publication. Free sample copy. Will not consider simultaneous submissions. Reports on material in 30 days. Query first. SASE.
Nonfiction and Photos: Case histories of use of citizens band radio in saving lives, etc. Semitechnical articles about equipment installation and repair. Interested in true life stories where CB radio was used to render public service. Interested in unusual social events concerning CB radio operator clubs. Uses informational, how-to, personal experiences articles; expose and technical. Length: 500 to 1,500 words. Payment varies. B&w photos purchased with accompanying mss; no additional payment.
How To Break In: "Report on a significant incident such as the use of CB radio in a search and rescue operation or at the scene of an accident or disaster. We cannot use material about social and fund raising activities of CB radio users."

CB TIMES, Charlton Publications, Inc., The Charlton Bldg., Derby CT 06418. (203)735-3381. Editor-in-Chief: John E. Bartimole. 80% freelance written. For anyone involved in CBing. Bimonthly magazine; 64 pages. Estab. 1976. Circ. 150,000. Pays on publication. Buys all rights. Phone queries OK. Submit seasonal/holiday material 4 months in advance. SASE. Reports in 2 weeks. Sample copy 50¢.
Nonfiction: "We want any type of article which would interest CBers. In other words, nothing to do with CBs is out of bounds. In fact, some of our most popular articles have been extremely offbeat. We pride selves on being the only CB magazine which devotes itself primarily to the 'human' side of CB. So, we're interested in humor, expose, information—just about anyting—as long as it has a shred of CB in it." Buys 8-10 mss/issue. Query or submit complete ms. Length: 1,000-11,000 words. Pays $25 minimum.
Photos: B&w (8½x11 glossies) and color (2¼x2¼ or 35mm) purchased with or without mss. Captions required. "If someone's thinking about submitting a color transparency for a cover, he might be better off querying, but we'll look at unsolicited cover shots, too." Pays $5 minimum for b&w; $25 minimum for color.
Fiction: "We pioneered the field in CB fiction—and we're always looking for fiction pieces dealing with CB and its people. We'll look at any type of fiction dealing with CB." Buys 1 ms/issue. Query or submit complete ms. Length: 1,000 words minimum. Pays $50 minimum.
Fillers: Clippings, jokes, gags, anecdotes, newsbreaks, short humor. "This is a new area for us. We're giving it a try, experimentally." Send complete ms. Length: 500 words maximum. Pays $5 minimum.
How To Break In: "Just write the best you can on any subject dealing with CB. We'll look at everything. We feel every manuscript deserves an equal shot. Everyone started out as an

'unknown' writer once—we're always looking for fresh new talent. We are currently in need of freelance material, and we sincerely hope that need never diminishes. Freelancers will be a constant source of new ideas for us. We ask freelancers to remember one thing, and this keys our whole editorial philosophy: We emphasize the 'human' side of CB. CBers are people who are interested in other people, in communicating. That's what keys our contents, good buddies!"
Rejects: Super-technical articles and unprofessional looking mss. "Neatness does count!"

Child Care and Parental Guidance Publications

The following publications are concerned with child care and parental guidance. Other categories that include markets that buy items about child care for special columns and features are: Confession, Religious, and Women's in Consumer Publications; Education Journals in Trade Journals.

AMERICAN BABY MAGAZINE, 575 Lexington Ave., New York NY 10022. (212)752-0775. Editor-in-Chief: Judith Nolte. 50% freelance written. Emphasizes how-to and medical information for expectant and new parents. Monthly magazine; 60 pages. Estab. 1938. Circ. 1,000,000. Pays on publication. Buys one-time rights. Phone queries OK. Submit seasonal/holiday material 4-5 months in advance of issue date. Simultaneous, photocopied and previously published submissions OK. SASE. Reports in 3-4 weeks. Free sample copy and writer's guidelines; mention *Writer's Market* in request.
Nonfiction: How-to (on pregnancy and child-related subjects); interview (with medical authority on some subject of interest to expectant and new parents); new product; personal experience; personal opinion; and profile (well-known figure in child care). No breast-feeding or natural childbirth experiences. Buys 5 mss/issue. Submit complete ms. Length: 500-2,000 words. Pays $50-250.
Photos: Editor: Jeanne Dzienciol. State availability of photos with query or ms. Pays $50-200 for 8x10 b&w glossy prints; and $100-300 for 35mm color transparencies. Buys one-time rights, but may reassign after publication. Model release required.
Fillers: Newsbreaks. Buys 5 mss/year. Length: 25-200 words. Pays $25-75.

BABY CARE, 52 Vanderbilt Ave., New York NY 10017. Editor: Evelyn A. Podsiadlo. Assistant Editor: Doris Youdelman. For "mothers of babies from birth through the first year." Quarterly. Circ. 500,000. Buys one-time rights. Pays on acceptance. Free sample copy and writer's guidelines. Submit seasonal material 5 to 6 months in advance. Reports in 1 to 4 weeks. SASE.
Nonfiction: Feature articles "include basic infant care (bathing, feeding, common illness, safety); emotional and physical development; how-to's; effect of new baby on family relations; seasonal topics (travel, summer or winter care). Shorter features with a humorous, narrative or reflective approach. Articles can be first-person accounts by mothers and fathers, but prefer medical subject to be written by M.D.'s and R.N.'s or writer who can work well with doctors." Worthy material is used to aid mothers of the very young child. Buys informational, how-to, personal experience, inspirational, humor, nostalgia and travel. Length: 1,000 to 1,800 words. Pays $50 to $125; and slightly higher to professionals such as M.D.'s. Regular columns that seek freelance material are: "Family Corner" —shorter anecdotes about life with the new baby. Pays $10. "Focus on You" —500-word mss focusing on a mother's feelings, personal interests or family relationships in regard to the baby. Pays $25.
Poetry: Uses poetry occasionally; all forms. Length: 4 to 24 lines. Pays $5 to $10. Should relate to subject matter.

BABY TALK, 66 E. 34th St., New York NY 10016. Editor: Patricia Irons. 50% freelance written. For new and expectant mothers interested in articles on child development and baby care. Monthly. Estab. 1934. Circ. over 750,000. Buys first North American serial rights. Pays on acceptance. Submit complete ms. SASE.
Nonfiction and Photos: "Articles on all phases of baby care. Also true, unpublished accounts of pregnancy, life with baby or young children. Write simple, true experience articles, not too lengthy. Informational, how-to, personal experience, inspirational, humor, think pieces, personal opinion, photo, travel (with babies), and new product articles. Pays $20-50. B&w and color photos are sometimes purchased with or without ms. Payment varies.

EXCEPTIONAL PARENT, Room 708, Statler Office Bldg., 20 Providence St., Boston MA

02116. (617)482-0480. Editors: Dr. Stanley D. Klein, Dr. Maxwell J. Schleifer. Associate Editor: Dr. Lewis B. Klebanoff. Managing Editor: John Griffin. Magazine provides practical guidance for parents and professionals concerned with the care of children with disabilities (physical disabilities, emotional problems, mental retardation, learning disabilities, perceptual disabilities, deafness, blindness, chronic illness, etc.). Estab. 1971. Bimonthly. Circ. 15,000. Buys all rights. Buys about 20 mss/year. Pays on publication. Sample copy for $2.50; writer's guidelines for SASE. Send query with outline. Reports in 6 months. Enclose SASE.
Nonfiction and Photos: "The general intent of the magazine is to provide practical guidance for the parents and professionals concerned with the care of children with disabilities. We print articles covering every conceivable subject within this area, including legal issues, tax information, recreation programs, parent groups, etc. This is a consumer publication within a very specialized market. That we provide practical guidance cannot be stressed too strongly. Articles should be jargon-free. Articles within special areas are checked by an advisory board in the medical and allied professions. There is no other magazine of this type." Buys how-to's, personal experience articles. Length: 200 words maximum. Pays 5¢/word. Photos accompanied by signed releases are of interest.

EXPECTING, 52 Vanderbilt Ave., New York NY 10017. Editor: Evelyn A. Podsiadlo. Assistant Editor: Doris Youdelman. Issued quarterly for expectant mothers. Circ. 1,000,000. Buys all rights or one-time rights. Pays on acceptance. Reports in 2-4 weeks. Free writer's guidelines. SASE.
Nonfiction: Prenatal development, layette and nursery planning, budgeting, health, fashion, husband-wife relationships, naming the baby, minor discomforts, childbirth, expectant fathers, working while pregnant, etc. Length: 800 to 1,600 words. Pays $50 to $125 for feature articles, somewhat more for specialists.
Fillers: Short humor and interesting or unusual happenings during pregnancy or at the hospital; maximum 100 words, $10 on publication; submissions to "Happenings" are not returned.
Poetry: Occasionally buys subject-related poetry; all forms. Length: 4-24 lines. Pays $5-10.

FAMILY, 37 Hanna Ave., Box 8, Station C, Toronto, Canada M6J 3M8. Editor-in-Chief: Mrs. Myroslava Baker. Emphasizes issues of interest to young urban women with children. Quarterly magazine; 80 pages. Estab. 1975. Circ. 700,000. Pays on publication. Buys first Canadian serial rights. Submit seasonal/holiday material 4 months in advance. Simultaneous, photocopied and previously published submissions OK. Free sample copy and writer's guidelines.
Nonfiction: Larry Osborn, Nonfiction Editor. How-to (home improvements, redecorating, gardening, landscaping); humor (directly relating to theme); informational (investigative and social nature pertaining to young Canadian family). Buys 12 mss/year. Query. Length: 450-3,150 words. Pays 5-10¢/word.
Fiction: Larry Osborn, Fiction Editor. Humor and mainstream. Buys 3 mss/year. Query. Length: 2,000-5,000 words. Pays 10¢/word.

HOME LIFE, Sunday School Board, 127 Ninth Ave., N., Nashville TN 37234. (615)251-2271. Editor-in-Chief: George W. Knight. Emphasizes Christian family life. For married adults of all ages, but especially newlyweds and middle-aged marrieds. Monthly magazine; 64 pages. Estab. 1947. Circ. 850,000. Pays on acceptance. Buys all rights. Phone queries OK, but written queries preferred. Submit seasonal/holiday material 9-10 months in advance. SASE. Reports in 6 weeks. Free sample copy and writer's guidelines.
Nonfiction: How-to (good articles on child care and marriage); informational (about some current family-related issue of national significance such as "Television and the Christian Family" or "Whatever Happened to Good Nutrition?"); personal experience (informed articles by people who have solved family problems in healthy, constructive ways). Buys 10 mss/month. Submit complete ms. Length: 1,200-2,400 words. Pays $35-70.
Fiction: "Our fiction should be family related and should show a strong moral about how families face and solve problems constructively." Buys 12/year. Submit complete ms. Length: 1,600-2,400 words. Pays $40-70.
How To Break In: "Study the magazine to see our unique slant on Christian family life. We prefer a life-centered case study approach, rather than theoretical essays on family life."

MOTHERS' MANUAL MAGAZINE, 176 Cleveland Dr., Croton-on-Hudson NY 10520. (914)271-8926. Editor-in-Chief: Beth Waterfall. Emphasizes parenting. Bimonthly magazine; 52 pages. Estab. 1964. Circ. 900,000. Pays on publication. Buys all rights. Submit seasonal/holiday material 5-6 months in advance. SASE. Reports in 6 weeks. Sample copy 75¢.
Nonfiction: How-to, humor, informational, inspirational, interview, personal experience and

personal opinion. Submit complete ms. Length: 500-2,500 words. Pays 2-5¢/published word; $10-500/article.
Poetry: Lorraine Morris, Poetry Editor. Free Verse, light verse and traditional. Buys 72/year. Pays 50¢/line; $3-30.

PARENTS' MAGAZINE, 52 Vanderbilt Ave., New York NY 10017. Editor: Genevieve Millet Landau. Special issues: March (Nutrition); September (Education); November (Health). Monthly. Circ. 1,500,000. Usually buys all rights; sometimes buys North American serial rights only. Pays on acceptance. Free sample copy. Reports on submissions in 3 weeks. Query first; enclose outline and sample opening. SASE.
Nonfiction: "We are interested in well-documented articles on the problems and success of preschool, school-age, and adolescent children—and their parents; good, practical guides to the routines of baby care; articles which offer professional insights into family and marriage relationships; reports of new trends and significant research findings in education and in mental and physical health; articles encouraging informed citizen action on matters of social concern. We prefer a warm, colloquial style of writing, one which avoids the extremes of either slanginess or technical jargon. Anecdotes and examples should be used to illustrate points which can then be summed up by straight exposition." Length: up to 2,500 words. Payment varies, starting from a base of $350.
Fillers: Anecdotes for "Family Clinic," illustrative of parental problem solving with children and teenagers. Pays $10.

YOUR BABY (service section of *Modern Romances* magazine), *Modern Romances*, Macfadden Women's Group, 205 E. 42nd St., New York NY 10017. Buys all rights. Pays on publication. Reports in 1 month. SASE.
Nonfiction: Uses warmly written, genuinely helpful articles of interest to mothers of children from birth to three years of age, dealing authoritatively with pregnancy problems, child health, child care and training. Editors recommend you study this market before trying to write for it. Length: up to 1,000 words. Pays up to $100. Submissions should be addressed to Jean Sharbel, Editor, *Modern Romances*.

City

ALIVE AND WELL IN ST. CATHARINES, 125 Ontario St., St. Catharines, Ontario, Canada L2G 7B8. (416)688-9460. Editor: Bev Delaney. 60% freelance written. Distributed to a controlled circulation of householders and businesses in St. Catharines and Niagara-on-the-Lake (no apartments). Monthly magazine; 56 pages. Estab. July 1976. Circ. 30,000. Pays on publication. Buys all rights but may reassign following publication. Phone queries OK. Submit seasonal/holiday material 3 months in advance of issue date. Photocopied and previously published submissions OK. SASE. Reports in 2 weeks. Free sample copy and writer's guidelines; mention *Writer's Market* in request.
Nonfiction: "All articles must focus on people or events in the St. Catharines area." Exposé (government, education, crime); how-to (sports); general interest; historical; interview; nostalgia; and profile. No personal experiences or opinions. Buys 3 mss/issue. Query. Length: 1,500-2,500 words. Pays $35 minimum.
Photos: Photos purchased with accompanying ms. Pays $5 minimum for 5x7 b&w glossy prints (snapshots acceptable); pays $5 minimum for 5x7 color satin-finish prints. Captions preferred. Buys all rights, but may reassign following publication.
Columns/Departments: Business (new businesses, executive changes, new products, etc.). Buys 3 columns/issue. Query with clips of previously published work. Length: 500-1,500 words. Pays $10 minimum. Open to suggestions for new columns/departments.
Fillers: Anecdotes and newsbreaks. Must have local angle. Buys 1/issue. Length: 125-375 words. Pays $5 minimum.

AVENUE M, 875 N. Michigan Ave., Chicago IL 60611. (312)787-9415. Editor: Art Desmond. 85% freelance written. Emphasizes news and features around the Magnificent Mile in Chicago for all ages. Monthly magazine; 36-48 pages. Estab. 1975. Circ. 15,000. Pays on publication. Buys all rights, but may reassign to author following publication. Phone queries OK. Photocopied and previously published submissions OK. SASE. Reports in 3 weeks. Sample copy $1; free writer's guidelines.
Nonfiction: Historical, humor, informational, inspirational, interview, nostalgia, personal experience, personal opinion, photo feature, profile and travel. Buys 80 mss/year. Query. Length: 500-750 words. Pays $25-50.

Photos: Purchased with accompanying ms. Captions required. Pays $5-10 for 8x10 b&w glossies. Offers no additional payment for photos accepted with accompanying ms. Total purchase price for ms includes payment for photos.

BOSTON MAGAZINE, Municipal Publications, 1050 Park Square Bldg., Boston MA 02116. (617)357-4000. Editor-in-Chief: George M. Gendron. For young, upscale readers; vast majority are professionals, college-educated and affluent. Monthly magazine; 160 pages. Estab. 1910 as a Chamber of Commerce publication, becoming an independent publication in 1971. Pays on acceptance. Buys all rights, but may reassign following publication. Submit seasonal/holiday material 3 months in advance. Simultaneous and photocopied submissions OK. SASE. Reports in 2 weeks.
Nonfiction: Exposé (subject matter varies); profiles (of Bostonians; sometimes, New Englanders); travel (usually only in New England or eastern Canada); personal experience. Buys about 40 mss/year. Query. Length: 1,000-10,000 words. Pays $100-500.
Photos: Ronn Campisi, Design Director, B&w and color purchased on assignment only. Query. Specifications vary. Pays $25-150 for b&w; payment for color (which is used on cover) averages $275.
Fillers: Nancy Pomerene, Department Editor. Newsbreaks. Short items of interest about Boston personalities, institutions or phenomena. Buys about 5 per issue. Send fillers in. Length: 100-500 words. Pays $5-25.
How To Break In: "If we are unfamiliar with a writer's work, we want to see clips that are representative of his/her style and range of interest and expertise. Remember, we consider ourselves in the entertainment business, so the emphasis here is on compelling, entertaining writing. The one thing that this or any other magazine can never afford to do is bore the reader."

BFLO, (formerly *Buffalo Fan*), Box 294, Buffalo NY 14240. (716)885-1500. Editor: Richard Hirsch. 80% freelance written. The city magazine of Buffalo and Western New York. Magazine; 64 pages. Estab. 1974. Buys all rights. Pays on acceptance. Photocopied submissions OK. SASE. Reports in 1 week. Sample copy $1.
Nonfiction: "Features on subjects of interest to those who live in Buffalo or western New York state." Informational; personal experience; profiles; humor; historical; "think" pieces; and nostalgia. Buys 40 mss/year. Query. Length: 1,000-2,000 words. Pays up to $125.
Photos: B&w and color photos purchased with or without accompanying ms, or on assignment. Pay varies, but pays $10 minimum for b&w; $25 for color.

CHARLESTON MAGAZINE, Box 549, 7½ State St., Charleston SC 29402. (803)577-0110. Editor: R. William Robinson: 90% freelance written. Monthly magazine; 32-56 pages. Estab. August 1975. Circ. 7,500. Pays on publication. Buys all rights. Phone queries OK. Submit seasonal/holiday material 5 months in advance of issue date. Photocopied and previously published submissions OK. SASE. Reports in 5 weeks. Sample copy $1.
Nonfiction: Exposé (government, inefficiency, etc., as relates to Charleston metro area); historical (Charleston metro area or Low County); interview; personal experience (area citizens only); photo feature (old houses, resorts in area, etc.); and travel (short excursions from metro area). No "editorial, personal opinion, crusading, glorifying, sentimental, or impressionistic material." Buys 80 mss/year. Query. Length: 800-2,400 words. Pays $40-125.
Photos: State availability of photos with query. Pays $5-10 for 5x7 matte prints; $15-25 for 3x3 color transparencies. Buys all rights, but may reassign following publication.
Columns/Departments: Low County Kitchen (regional dishes); Gardeners Corner (regional gardening). Query. Length: 500-800 words. Pays $35-50.
Fiction: "Quality original fiction. No formula fiction, please." Buys 1 ms/issue. Submit complete ms. Length: 1,800-2,600 words. Pays $40-60.
Poetry: Avant-garde and contemporary. "No sentimental, nostalgic mood pieces. New wine in old bottles is OK, but no more Civil War poems, please." Buys 1-3/issue. Limit submissions to batches of 3. Length: 4-30 lines. Pays $10.

CHICAGO MAGAZINE, 500 N. Michigan Ave., Chicago IL 60611. Editor-in-Chief: Allen H. Kelson. Editor: John Fink. 80% freelance written. For an audience which is "95% from Chicago area; 90% college-trained; upper income; overriding interests in the arts, dining, good life in the city. Most are in 30 to 50 age bracket and well-read and articulate. Generally liberal inclination." Monthly. Circ. 160,000. Buys first rights. Buys about 50 mss/year. Pays on acceptance. Free sample copy and writer's guidelines. Submit seasonal material 3 months in advance. Reports in 2 weeks. Query first. SASE.
Nonfiction and Photos: "On themes relating to the quality of life in Chicago . . . past, present,

future." Writers should have "a general awareness that the readers will be concerned, influential native Chicagoans reading what the writer has to say about their city. We generally publish material too comprehensive for daily newspapers or of too specialized interest for them." Buys personal experience and think pieces, interviews, profiles, humor, spot news, historical articles, travel, and exposés. Length: 1,000 to 6,000 words. Pays $100 to $500. Photos purchased with mss. B&w glossies, color transparencies, 35mm color, color prints.
Fiction: Mainstream, fantasy, and humerous fiction. Preferably with Chicago orientation. No word length limits, but "no novels, please." Pays $250 to $500.

CHICAGO READER, Box 11101, Chicago IL 60611. (312)828-0350. Editor: Robert A. Roth. "The *Reader* is distributed free in Chicago's lakefront neighborhoods. Generally speaking, these are Chicago's best educated, most affluent neighborhoods—and they have an unusually high concentration of young adults." Weekly tabloid; 80-100 pages. Estab. 1971. Circ. 91,000. Pays "by 15th of month following publication." Buys all rights. Phone queries OK. Photocopied submissions OK. SASE. Reports in 12 months.
Nonfiction: "We want magazine features on Chicago topics. Will also consider reviews." Buys 500 mss/year. Submit complete ms. Length: "whatever's appropriate to the story." Pays $25-300.
Photos: By assignment only.
Columns/Departments: By assignment only.

CINCINNATI MAGAZINE, Greater Cincinnati Chamber of Commerce, 120 W. 5th St., Cincinnati OH 45202. (513)721-3300. Editor-in-Chief: J.P. O'Conner. Emphasizes Cincinnati living. Monthly magazine; 88-120 pages. Estab. 1967. Circ. 18,000. Pays on acceptance. Buys all rights, but may reassign following publication. Submit seasonal/holiday material 2 months in advance. Simultaneous, photocopied and previously published submissions OK. SASE. Reports in 3 weeks.
Nonfiction: How-to; informational; interview; photo feature; profile and travel. Buys 3-4 mss/issue. Query. Length: 2,000-4,000 words. Pays $200-400.
Photos: Laurie Peterson, Photo Editor. Photos purchased on assignment only. Model release required.
Columns/Departments: Travel; How-To; Sports and Consumer Tips. Buys 6 mss/issue. Query. Length: 750-1,500 words. Pays $75-150.

CLEVELAND MAGAZINE, 1621 Euclid Ave., Cleveland OH 44115. Editor-in-Chief: Michael D. Roberts. 10-15% freelance written. Emphasizes local news and information. Monthly magazine; 190 pages. Estab. April 1972. Circ. 55,000. Pays on publication. Buys all rights. Phone queries OK. Submit seasonal/holiday material 2 months in advance of issue date. Photocopied submissions OK. SASE. Reports in 2 months. Sample copy $1.50; free writer's guidelines.
Nonfiction: Exposé (local government, business, politics, banking, etc.); general interest; historical (local or statewide); interview; photo feature; and profile. Buys 15-20 mss/year. Query. Length: 5,000 words maximum. Pays $50-700.

D MAGAZINE, Dallas Southwest Media Corp., 2902 Carlisle, Dallas TX 75204. Editor-in-Chief: Wick Allison. Managing Editor: Charles Matthews. 40% freelance written. For readers in the Dallas/Ft. Worth area; primarily the middle to upper income group. Monthly magazine; 198 pages. Estab. 1974. Circ. 55,000. Pays on publication. Buys all rights. Submit seasonal/holiday material 2 months in advance. Photocopied submissions OK. SASE. Reports in 1 month. Sample copy $2.
Nonfiction: Informational; new product; profile; travel and business. Buys 2-3 mss/issue. Query. Length: 750-4,000 words. Pays $50-400.
Photos: Photos purchased with accompanying ms or on assignment. Pays $25-150 for 8x10 b&w glossies; $50-150 for color transparencies. Model release required.
Columns/Departments: Keeping Up (arts, entertainment, books, movies, and concert reviews); Up Front (business and gossip); Dining (reviews); and Windfalls (special products and services). "All pieces must relate to Dallas and the Fort Worth area." Open to suggestions for new columns/departments.

DENVER MAGAZINE, 1763 Williams, Denver CO 80218. (303)399-5931. Publisher: Herbert Neu. Executive Editor: Mike Burke. Managing Editor: Don Russell. For an urban, sophisticated, well-educated audience interested in all aspects of contemprary living. Monthly magazine; 96 pages. Estab. 1971. Circ. 30,000. Pays on acceptance. Buys all rights, but may

reassign following publication. Submit seasonal/holiday material 4 months in advance of issue date. Photocopied submissions OK. SASE. Reports in 2-8 weeks.
Nonfiction: Exposé (anything that is a genuine scoop); informational (anything that will enhance life, happiness, and well-being of Denver and Colorado residents—where to go, what to do, etc.); interviews and profiles (famous Coloradians). Buys 100 mss/year. Query. Length: 800-1,500 words. "Payment varies depending on story quality, length, and author. Base rates range from $50 for short articles to $300 and up for major features."
Photos: B&w and color transparencies used with mss or by assignment. Payment negotiable. Query.
Fillers: Light, entertaining short pieces considered for newsletter. Both humorous and informative. "No *Reader's Digest*-type fillers.

HOUSTON, Houston Chamber of Commerce, 1100 Milam Bldg., 25th Floor, Houston TX 77002. Editor: Richard Stanley. 5% freelance written. Emphasizes the Houston business community. Monthly magazine; 64-90 pages. Estab. 1929. Circ. 15,000. Pays on acceptance or publication. Buys all rights. Phone queries OK. Photocopied submissions OK. SASE. Reporting time varies.
Nonfiction: How-to (managing a company, starting a business, motivating employees, etc.); informational (on economy, business, etc.); interview; and new product. Buys 3-4 mss/year. Query. Length: 30-120 inches. Pays $30-300. "Experienced business writers for assignment stories on such topics as oil, aviation, housing, banking, etc."

JACKSONVILLE MAGAZINE, P.O. Drawer 329, Jacksonville FL 32201. (904)353-6161. For civic-minded, concerned community types; business, community oriented interest, Jacksonville subjects. Estab. 1963. Bimonthly. Circ. 7,000. Buys all rights, Buys 20 to 25 mss/year. Pays on publication. Query. Submit seasonal material 3 to 6 months in advance. Reports in 3 weeks. SASE.
Nonfiction and Photos: Buys historical, photo, business articles. Length: usually 1,500 to 3,000 words. Pays $50 to $150. "We accept b&w glossies, good contrast; color transparencies." Pays $15 minimum for b&w; color terms to be arranged.

KANSAS CITY MAGAZINE, Box 2298, Shawnee Mission KS 66201. (913)384-0770. Editor-in-Chief: Floyd E. Sageser. Managing Editor: Paul Hohl. 85% freelance written. Emphasizes Kansas City lifestyle and business. Monthly magazine; 68 pages. Estab. January 1976. Circ. 16,000. Pays on publication. Buys all rights, but may reassign following publication. Phone queries OK. Submit seasonal/holiday material 3 months in advance of issue date. SASE. Simultaneous, photocopied and previously published submissions OK. Reports in 3 weeks. Sample copy $1.25.
Nonfiction: All material must relate to Kansas City areas, activities, or personalities. Exposé; historical; interview; nostalgia; photo feature; and profile. Buys 4 mss/issue. Query. Length: 800-2,500 words. Pays 5¢/word.
Photos: Submit photo material with accompanying query. Pays $5-10 for 5x7 or 8x10 b&w glossy prints and $25-50 for color transparencies. Captions required. Buys all rights, but may reassign following publication.
Columns/Departments: Art; Books; indoor gardening; movies and travel. Buys 5/issue. Query. Length: 400-1,500 words. Pays 5¢/word. Open to suggestions for new columns/departments.

LOS ANGELES MAGAZINE, 1888 Century Park East, Los Angeles CA 90067. Editor: Geoff Miller. Monthly. Buys first North American serial rights. Query first. SASE.
Nonfiction: Uses articles on how best to live (i.e., the quality of life) in the changing, growing, diverse Los Angeles urban-suburban area; ideas, people, and occasionally places. Writer must have an understanding of contemporary living and doing in Southern California; material must appeal to an upper-income, better-educated group of people. Fields of interest include urban problems, pleasures, personalities and cultural opportunities, leisure and trends, candid interviews of topical interest; the arts. Solid research and reportage required. No essays. Length: 1,000-3,000 words. Also uses some topical satire and humor. Pays 10¢/word minimum.
Photos: Most photos assigned to local photographers. Ocassionally buys photographs with mss. B&w should be 8x10. Pays $25-50 for single article photos.

MADISON SELECT, 5522 University Ave., Madison WI 53705. Editor: James Selk. For business, civic and social leaders of Madison. Magazine; 40-56 pages. Estab. 1958. Monthly.

Circ. 13,000. Buys all rights, but may reassign rights to author after publication. Buys 10 to 15 mss a year. Pays on publication. Sample copy $1. Reports on material accepted for publication 10 days after publication. Returns rejected material immediately. Query first. Enclose SASE.
Nonfiction and Photos: "Subjects of interest to the business, civic and social leaders in the Madison metropolitan area. We regularly review one aspect each of the business, arts, sports, society, fashion and travel scene. We like humor as well as serious material, as long as it relates to Madison or Madisonians." Length: 350 to 1,250. Pays $10 to $100. No additional payment for b&w photos used with mss. Pays $5 to $10 for b&w, $25 for color, when purchased without mss. Captions required.

MIAMI MAGAZINE, 3361 S.W. Third Ave., Miami FL 33145. (305)856-5011. Executive Editor: Cliff Yudell. For affluent, involved citizens of South Florida; generally well educated. Monthly magazine. Estab. 1975. Circ. 25,000. Rights purchased vary with author and material. Usually buys first publication rights. Buys about 200 mss/year. Pays on publication. Sample copy $1.50. Reports in 60 days. Query first or submit complete ms. SASE.
Nonfiction: Investigative pieces on the area; thorough, general features; exciting, in-depth writing. Informational, how-to, personal experience, interview, profile, humor, and expose. Strong local angle. Length: 3,000 words maximum. Pays $85-250. Departments: Film, business, books, art, travel. Length: 1,500 words maximum. Payment ranges from $50-75.

MPLS. MAGAZINE, 512 Nicollet Mall, Suite 615, Minneapolis MN 55402. (612)339-7571. Editor-in-Chief: Brian Anderson. 90% freelance written. For "professional people of middle-upper income levels, college educated, interested in the arts, dining, and the good life of Minnesota." Monthly magazine; 100 pages. Estab. 1971. Circ. 25,000. Pays on publication. Buys all rights, but may reassign following publication. Submit seasonal/holiday material 4 months in advance of issue date. Photocopied submissions OK. SASE. Reports in 3 weeks.
Nonfiction: Expose; how-to; informational; historical; humor; interview; profile; and photo feature. "We can use any of these as long as they are Minneapolis-St. Paul related." Query. Length: 300-3,000 words. Pays $20-300.
Photos: Ann Sundet, photo editor. Purchased on assignment. Query. Pays $25-100 for b&w; $25-175 for color.

MONTREAL CALENDAR MAGAZINE, 300 Place d' Youville, Montreal, Quebec, Canada H2Y 2B6. (514)844-3931. Editor: Wendy Penfield. For an audience in the top 25% income bracket in Montreal. Monthly magazine; 80 pages. Estab. 1971. Circ. 100,000. Buys all rights, but may reassign rights to author after publication. Buys about 15 mss/year. Pays on acceptance. Free sample copy. Will consider photocopied and simultaneous submissions. Submit seasonal material 1 month in advance. Reports in 2 weeks. Query first or submit complete ms. Enclose SAE and International Reply Coupons.
Nonfiction: Informational, how-to, personal experience, interview, humor, think pieces, and expose. Articles on money and events for children. Theater, stage, movies, restaurant dining, shopping bag, clubs. "Be brief, to the point, and include all essential information; addresses, phones, prices, etc. — in essence, *digest*. And remember that we speak only of subjects of interest to people who live in Montreal. Will pay from $100-400, depending on length, and from there, it depends on professionalism."

NASHVILLE! PlusMedia, Inc., 1 Vantage Way, Suite 238, Nashville TN 37228. (615)259-4600. Editor-in-Chief: C. Turney Stevens, Jr. For "upper middle class families who live in Nashville/Davidson County; business people, professionals in management positions; intelligent, educated, well-read." Monthly magazine; 120 pages. Estab. 1973. Circ. 20,500. Pays on publication. Phone queries OK. Submit seasonal/holiday material 4-5 months in advance. Simultaneous and photocopied submissions OK. SASE. Reports in 6-8 weeks. Sample copy $1.50; free writer's guidelines.
Nonfiction: Wayne Gurley, Managing Editor. Expose (politics, government); how-to (hobbies, gardening, recreational activities); historical (local only); interview; nostalgia; profile; travel; and business. Buys 80 mss/year. Query. Length: 2,000-4,000 words. Pays $100-250.
Photos: Don Milstead, Art Director. Purchased with or without accompanying ms or on assignment. Captions required. Query. Pays $5.50-15 for 5x7 or 8x10 b&w prints; $12.50-25 for 35mm or 2¼x2¼ color transparencies. Model release required.
Columns/Departments: Politics, Consumer's Notebook, People, Science, Medicine, After Hours (entertainment, recreation). Buys 36 mss/year. Query. Length: 1,500-2,500 words. Pays $75-125. Open to suggestions for new columns or departments.

NEW HAVEN INFO MAGAZINE, 53 Orange St., New Haven CT 06510. (203)562-5413. Editor: Sol D. Chain. For those interested in art, music, theater, recreational activities, etc. Monthly magazine; 40 (6x9) pages. Estab. 1952. Circ. 5,000. Not copyrighted. Buys 20 mss per year. Payment on publication. Sample copy 50¢. Will consider photocopied and simultaneous submissions. Reports on material accepted for publication in 30 days. Returns rejected material in 2 weeks. Query first. SASE.
Nonfiction: "Most of our material is on assignment. We publish articles dealing with New Haven area events and people." Personal experience, interview, profile, historical, nostalgia. Length: 350 to 700 words. Pays $10 per page (about 350 words).

NEW ORLEANS MAGAZINE, Flambeaux Publishing Co., 6666 Morrison Rd., New Orleans LA 70114. (504)246-2700. Editor: Bonnie Crone. 80% freelance written. Monthly magazine; 100 pages. Estab. October 1966. Circ. 50,000. Pays on publication. Buys all rights, but may reassign following publication. Submit seasonal/holiday material 2 months in advance of issue date. Previously published submissions OK. SASE. Reports in 2 weeks.
Nonfiction: General interest; interview; and profile. Buys 6 mss/issue. Query or submit complete ms. Length: 1,200-3,000 words. Pays $100-500.
Photos: George Bacon, art director. State availability of photos with query or ms. Offers no additional payment for b&w photos accepted with accompanying ms. Captions required. Buys one-time rights. Model release required.

NEW YORK AFFAIRS/URBAN AMERICA, 342 Madison Ave., Suite 1100, New York NY 10017. (212)953-1713. Editor-in-Chief: Dick Netzer. Emphasizes urban problems. "Readers tend to be academics, public officials, corporation presidents and intellectual types." Quarterly magazine; 128 pages. Estab. 1973. Circ. 5,000. Pays on publication. Buys all rights, but may reassign following publication. Phone queries OK. Photocopied submissions OK. SASE. Reports in 4 weeks. Sample copy $3; free writer's guidelines.
Nonfiction: Michael Winkleman, Articles Editor. Expose; interview (figures who are key to urban policymaking); and personal opinion. Buys 8 mss/year. Query. Length: 3,000-7,500 words. Pays $50-200. "We also have a section for short articles (250-3,000 words) called 'Side Streets' in which we run just about anything that is good about cities—humor especially. Most of our authors are academics whom we don't pay. For those whom we can't afford to pay, which includes most articles and Side Streets, we pay in copies of the magazine."
Columns/Departments: Book reviews. "We don't pay reviewers. They just get to keep the book." Uses 30 pages/year. Query.
How To Break In: "We are looking for hard-hitting, well-written articles on general urban problems. We especially like articles that take the unconventional approach—that transit fares should be raised, or that the cost of welfare should *not* be picked up by the Federal Government."

PHILADELPHIA MAGAZINE, 1500 Walnut St., Philadelphia PA 19102. Editor: Alan Halpern. 35-50% freelance written. For sophisticated middle- and upper-income people in the Greater Philadelphia/South Jersey area. Magazine. Estab. 1908. Monthly. Circ. 130,000. Buys all rights. Buys over 100 mss/year. Pays on publication, or within 2 months. Free writer's guidelines for SASE. Reports in 4 weeks. Queries and mss should be sent to Polly Hurst, Administrative Editor. SASE.
Nonfiction and Photos: "Articles should have a Philadelphia focus, but should avoid Philadelphia stereotypes — we've seen them all. Life styles, city survival, profiles of interesting people, business stories, music, the arts, sports, local politics, stressing the topical or unusual. No puff pieces. We're in the 'new journalism' tradition — exposes, fast-moving, first-person accounts — and we're a steady award winner, so quality and professionalism count. We offer lots of latitude for style, but before you make like Norman Mailer, make sure you have something to say." Length: 1,000 to 7,000 words. Pays $75 to $500. Photos occasionally purchased with mss at additional payment of $35 to $150.

PITTSBURGH MAGAZINE, Metropolitan Pittsburgh Public Broadcasting Inc., 4802 5th Ave., Pittsburgh PA 15213. (412)622-1300. Editor-in-Chief: Herb Stein. "The magazine is purchased on newsstands and by subscription and is given to those who contribute $17 or more a year to public TV in western Pennsylvania." Monthly magazine; 80 pages. Estab. 1970. Circ. 60,000. Pays on publication. Buys all rights, but may reassign following publication. Phone queries OK. Submit seasonal/holiday material 2 months in advance. SASE. Reports in 6 weeks. Sample copy $1.50; free writer's guidelines.
Nonfiction: Expose, historical, how-to, humor, informational, inspirational, interview, nostal-

gia, personal experience, personal opinion, profile and travel. Buys 6 mss/issue. Query or send complete ms. Length: 2,500 words. Pays $50-250.
Photos: Purchased with accompanying ms or on assignment. Captions required. Uses b&w and color. Query for photos. Model release required.
Columns/Departments: Travel; Humor; Nostalgia. "All must relate to Pittsburgh or Western Pennsylvania."

RICHMOND MAGAZINE, 5 E. Franklin, Richmond VA 23219. Editor-in-Chief: Mike Edelhart. 90% freelance written. For anyone interested in Virginia affairs. Monthly magazine; 112 pages. Estab. November 1977. Circ. 16,000. Pays on publication. Buys first North American serial rights. Phone queries OK. Submit seasonal/holiday material 3 months in advance of issue date. SASE. Reports in 5 weeks. Sample copy $1.25.
Nonfiction: Exposé (only by experienced professionals); general interest (not very many people pieces); how-to; historical (monthly local heritage column); humor (if it's really funny); interview (few); personal opinion (only by recognized local figures); and profile (only extremely unique people). "No reviews or first person stories." Buys 40 mss/year. Query. Length: 1,500-3,500 words. Pays $100-300.
Fillers: Newsbreaks and short humor. Buys 2-3 fillers/issue. Length: 50-500 words. Pays $10-25.

SAN DIEGO MAGAZINE, Box 81809, San Diego CA 92138. (714)222-0325. Editor-in-Chief: Edwin F. Self. 65% freelance written. Emphasizes San Diego. Monthly magazine; 250 pages. Estab. 1948. Circ. 35,000. Pays on publication. Buys all rights, but may reassign following publication. Submit seasonal/holiday material 3 months in advance of issue date. Simultaneous and photocopied submissions OK. SASE. Reports in 2 months. Sample copy $3.
Nonfiction: Exposé (serious, documented); general interest (to San Diego region); historical (San Diego region); interview (with notable San Diegans); nostalgia; photo essay; profile; service guides; and travel. Buys 7 mss/issue. Query, or submit complete ms with clips. Length: 3,000 words. Pays $300 maximum.
Photos: State availability of photos with query. Pays $7.50-45 for b&w contact sheets or 8x10 glossy prints; $25-100 for color transparencies. Captions required. Buys all rights. Model release required.

SEATTLE BUSINESS MAGAZINE, Seattle Chamber of Commerce, 215 Columbia St., Seattle WA 98104. (206)447-7266. Editor-in-Chief: Ed Sullivan. Emphasizes regional socio-economic affairs. For business and government leaders, civic leaders, regional businessmen, educators, opinion makers, and the general public. Bimonthly magazine; 56 pages. Estab. 1900. Circ. 5,500. Pays on publication. Buys all rights, but may reassign following publication. Submit seasonal/holiday material 2 months in advance. Previously published submissions OK. SASE. Reports in 2 weeks. Free sample copy.
Nonfiction: Informational (socio-economic affairs) and technical. Buys 1-2 mss/issue. Query. Length: 500-2,500 words. Pays $50-300.
Photos: Purchased with accompanying ms or on assignment. Captions required. Pays $50-100 for b&w photos. Total purchase price for ms includes payment for photos. Model release required.
How To Break In: "The freelancer must be able to write—and have a basic awareness of and sympathy for—the interests and problems of the business community as these relate to the community at large."

SPOKANE MAGAZINE, Box 520, Spokane WA 99210. (509)838-2012. Co-publisher/Editor: Judith Laddon. Editor-in-Chief: Lawrence Shook. 90% freelance written. "*Spokane Magazine* is designed as an editorial vehicle for exploring the color, vitality and quality of life in Spokane and the Northwest." Monthly magazine; 40 pages. Estab. May 1977. Circ. 5,000. Pays on publication. Buys one-time rights. Submit seasonal/holiday material 4 months in advance of issue date. Photocopied submissions OK. SASE. Reports in 8 weeks. Sample copy $1.25; free writer's guidelines.
Nonfiction: "Regular coverage includes politics, the environment, business, the economy, energy, education, agriculture, the arts, medicine, law, architecture, followup or unique angles on news stories with a distinct Northwest identity, the gamut of sports and recreation, profiles or interesting people whose lifestyles reflect the Northwest way of life, travel throughout the West, and fact pieces on subjects of interest to Northwesterners. Humor is always welcome." Buys 3 mss/issue. Query. Length: 500-3,000 words. Pays $50/1,000 words.
Photos: State availability of photos with query. Pays $10 for 8x10 b&w glossy prints; $35-50 for 2¼x2¼ color transparencies. Captions preferred. Buys one-time rights.

TULSA MAGAZINE, Box 1620, Tulsa OK 74101. (918)582-6576. Editor: Larry Silvey. Audience is primarily medium to upper income level Tulsans. Monthly. Circulation: 6,000. Not copyrighted. Pays on publication. Sample copy for 25¢. Deadlines are at least 6 weeks prior to publication date, which is normally on the first Thursday of each month. Reports immediately. Query first. SASE.
Nonfiction and Photos: Articles must revolve around people or how subject affects people and must have a Tulsa area slant. Style desired is informal and lively. 1,000 to 4,000 words. Payment is negotiable, $50 to $75, depending on length, research. Photos usually taken by staff or on assignment. May be purchased with mss.

TUCSON MAGAZINE, Desert Silhouette, 2500 N. Pantano Rd., Suite 106, Tucson AZ 85715. (602)886-1253. Editor-in-Chief: Dennis Nix. 60% freelance written. Monthly magazine; 64 pages. Estab. 1975. Circ. 18,000. Pays on publication. Buys one-time rights. Phone queries OK. Submit seasonal/holiday material 2 months in advance of issue date. Simultaneous, photocopied and previously published submissions OK. SASE. Reports in 2 months. Sample copy $1.
Nonfiction: All articles must have Tucson-related interest. Expose (affecting Tucson's quality of life); how-to; general interest; humor; historical; new product; and nostalgia. Buys 40 mss/year. Query with clips of previously published work. Length: 600-3,600 words. Pays $50-500.

VANCOUVER MAGAZINE, 1008 Hornby St., Vancouver, B.C., Canada V6Z 1V7. (604)685-5374. Editor: M.F. Parry. 90% freelance written. For an upper income, urban audience in Vancouver. Monthly magazine; 80-120 pages. Estab. 1967. Circ. 85,100. Rights purchased vary with author and material. Buys first serial rights or second serial (reprint) rights. Buys about 120 mss/year. Pays on acceptance. Free sample copy. Will consider photocopied and simultaneous submissions. Reports in 4 weeks. Query first or submit complete ms. Enclose SAE and International Reply Coupons.
Nonfiction and Photos: City-oriented features, consumer self-help; arts and political columns; sports, life style, entertainment. Some personality profiles on assignment. Also, informational, how-to, personal experience, interview, historical and travel articles, as well as think pieces. Article length: 600 to 4,000 words. Pays 7¢ to 10¢ a word. Column material length: 1,000 words. Pays minimum of $85. B&w glossies (5x7 minimum) and Kodachromes purchased with mss. Pays $25-100.

THE WASHINGTONIAN MAGAZINE, 1828 L St., N.W., Washington DC 20036. Editor: John A. Limpert. For active, affluent, well-educated audience. Monthly magazine; 250 pages. Estab. 1965. Circ. 95,000. Buys first rights. Buys 75 mss/year. Pays on publication. Simultaneous and photocopied submissions OK. Reports in 4-6 weeks. Query or submit complete ms. SASE.
Nonfiction and Photos: "*The Washingtonian* is written for Washingtonians. The subject matter is anything we feel might interest people interested in the mind and manners of the city. The style, as Wolcott Gibbs said, should be the author's—if he is an author, and if he has a style. The only thing we ask is thoughtfulness and that no subject be treated too reverently. Audience is literate. We assume considerable sophistication about the city, and a sense of humor." Buys how-to's, personal experience, interviews, profiles, humor, coverage of successful business operations, think pieces, and exposes. Length: 1,000 to 7,000 words; average feature, 3,000 words. Pays 10¢ a word. Photos rarely purchased with mss.
Fiction and Poetry: Department Editors: Dick Victory (fiction); Howard Means (poetry); Both must be Washington-oriented. No limitations on length. Pays 10¢ a word for fiction. Payment for poetry is negotiable.

WICHITA, Wichita Area Chamber of Commerce, 350 W. Douglas, Wichita KS 67202. (318)265-7771. Managing Editor: Gene Dickinson. Coordinating Editor: Marge Setter. Emphasizes business and community assets. Bimonthly magazine; 36 pages. Estab. 1967. Circ. 8,000. Pays 50% on acceptance, balance on publication. Buys all rights, but may reassign following publication. Submit seasonal/holiday material 2 months in advance. Simultaneous, photocopied, and previously published submissions OK. SASE. Reports in 3 weeks. Free sample copy.
Nonfiction: Informational (articles on new management techniques); interviews (with nationally known business leaders); and articles related to Wichita, past and present. Buys 2-3 mss/year. Query. Length: 300-800 words. Pays $50-175.
Photos: Purchased on assignment only. Captions required. Query. No additional payment for 5x7 b&w glossies. Model release required.
How To Break In: "Determine a topic or person that will be of specific interest to Wichita

business persons, or send a list of possible topics and/or individuals that the writer has access to for interviews."

College, University, and Alumni

The following publications are intended for students, graduates, and friends of the institution. Publications for college students in general are found in the Teen and Young Adult category.

ALCALDE, Box 7278, Austin TX 78712. (512)476-6271. Editor-in-Chief: Sarah Jane English. 50% freelance written. Bimonthly magazine; 58 pages. Estab. 1913. Circ. 32,000. Pays on acceptance. Buys all rights. Submit seasonal/holiday material 5 months in advance of issue date. SASE. Reports in 2 weeks. Free sample copy and writer's guidelines; mention *Writer's Market* in request.

Nonfiction: General interest; historical (University of Texas, research, and faculty profile); humor (humorous University of Texas incidents or profiles which include background data); interview (University of Texas subjects); nostalgia (University of Texas traditions); profile (faculty or alumni); and technical (University of Texas research on a subject or product). "We do not want subjects lacking taste or quality or not connected with the University of Texas." Buys 30 mss/year. Query. Length: 1,000-1,800 words. Pays 4¢/word.

CLIFTON MAGAZINE, University of Cincinnati, 204 Tangeman University Center, Cincinnati OH 45221. (513)474-6379. Editor: Deborah Kopka. For the entire university community (students, faculty, administration and employees), and residents of the Clifton area. Estab. 1972. Circ. 1,200. Pays on publication. Buys all rights, but may reassign following publication. Submit seasonal/holiday material 3 months in advance of issue date. Photocopied submissions OK. SASE. Reports in 4-6 weeks. Free writer's guidelines.

Nonfiction: Exposé (government, education, environmental, consumer, lifestyle, industry); historical (but only if of Clifton community or old Cincinnati); how-to (survival type, but no recipes); humor (especially satire); informational (especially dealing with the bureaucracy); minority affairs; interview; profile; and photo feature. Buys 5 mss/issue. Query. Length: 1,000-6,000 words. Pays $10-20.

Photos: 5x7 or 8x10 b&w glossies used with ms; no additional payment.

Fiction: Experimental (thematic); fantasy (no science fiction); humorous; traditional; erotica (if responsible and in good taste). Buys 1-2 mss/issue. Length: 1,000-6,000 words. Pays in contributor's copies.

DePAUW UNIVERSITY ALUMNUS MAGAZINE, Greencastle IN 46135. (317)653-9721, ext. 480. Editor-in-Chief: Patrick Aikman. Managing Editor: Greg Rice. 25% freelance written. Emphasizes alumni activities and institutional developments. Quarterly magazine; 40 pages. Estab. 1926. Circ. 23,500. Pays on publication. Buys all rights. Submit seasonal/holiday material 3 months in advance of issue date. SASE. Reports in 3 weeks. Sample copy $1.

Nonfiction: General interest; historical; humor; inspirational; interview; nostalgia; personal experience; personal opinion; photo feature; and profile. Buys 2 mss/issue. Submit clips of previously published work. Length: 1,000-4,000 words. Pays $50-150.

Photos: State availability of photos with query. Pays $5-25 for b&w 8x10 or contact sheets; $2-25 for 35mm color transparencies. Captions required. Buys all rights.

MISSISSIPPI STATE UNIVERSITY ALUMNUS, Mississippi State Univ. Alumni Assoc., Editorial Office, Box 4930, Mississippi State MS 39762. (601)325-6343. Editor-in-Chief: Bob V. Moulder. Emphasizes articles about Mississippi State graduates and former students. For well-educated and affluent audience. Quarterly magazine; 32 pages. Estab. 1921. Circ. 13,875. Pays on publication. Buys one-time rights. Phone queries OK. Submit seasonal/holiday material 3 months in advance. Simultaneous, photocopied and previously published submissions OK. SASE. Reports in 1 month. Free sample copy.

Nonfiction: Historical, humor (with strong MSU flavor; nothing risque), informational, inspirational, interview (with MSU grads), nostalgia (early days at MSU), personal experience, profile and travel (by MSU grads, but must be of wide interest). Buys 2-3 mss/year ("but welcome more submissions.") Send complete ms. Length: 500-2,500 words. Pays $10-25 (including photos, if used).

Photos: Photos purchased with accompanying ms. Captions required. No additional payment for photos accepted with accompanying ms. Uses 8x10 b&w photos.

Columns/Departments: Statesmen "A section of the Alumnus that features briefs about alumni

achievements and professional or business advancement. We do not use engagements, marriages or births. There is no payment for Statemen briefs.")
How To Break In: "We welcome articles about MSU grads in interesting occupations and have used stories on off-shore drillers, miners, horse trainers, etc. We also want profiles on prominent MSU alumni and have carried pieces on Senator John C. Stennis, comedian Jerry Clower and baseball manager, Alex Grammas."

Comic Book Publications

GOLD KEY COMICS, 850 Third Ave., New York NY 10022. Editor: Wallace I. Green. For children, ages 6 to 15. "Most titles are issued every 2 months or monthly." Circ. 100,000 to 200,000. Buys all rights. Pays on acceptance. SASE.
Comics: "Our main product is comic books; 40 titles. We publish our own animated and adventure titles as well as licensed animated and adventure properties; e.g., Bugs Bunny, Heckle and Jeckle. I would prefer that potential authors *do not write us just to inquire* as to whether or not we are interested and what kind of material to submit. I suggest the following procedure: Buy copies of our various comics, particularly those you think you can write. If you don't know which ones suit you, you can determine that after reading them. Become familiar with the characters and the kinds of stories we use in particular titles. Write a number of story synopses (keep them brief, please) aimed for particular publications. At the same time, let us know whether you have had any experience writing comics so we'll know how much instruction to give you about the form to follow when writing a script. This last applies only if we like the synopses. We prefer to deal personally with authors, rather than through the mails. But I'd rather anyone who is interested send in his first synopses. We can meet personally later if it seems worthwhile. Our manuscript rate is $10 per page (mss are written page for page with the printed comic). Since we have several writers who produce stories on a more or less regular basis, I do not want to sound overly encouraging. But ours is not a closed shop. There's always room for someone with original and imaginative ideas who can turn them into sound, workable scripts."

Confession Publications

The confession market has come a long way since the old hide-under-the-mattress days, upgrading itself to "family counselor" status. Although a very lucrative market for writers (especially personal experience stories), editors still invent titles that often make even a veteran confession writer blush. Such titles are usually come-ons.

Another concern among freelancers is the cheaper looking appearance of even the best confession magazines. Those magazines that used to be slick are apparently caught in the paper crunch, using part pulp and part coated stock. What's ahead if the paper shortage continues? Will a cheapened appearance cost the reader and writer the respect the markets have gained in recent years? This is unlikely since readers are becoming used to this stock in other publications, as well.

Marketing Tip: Confession magazines may use psychic phenomena and supernatural stories, even though some use them very rarely. These stories should not be in the realm of fantasy; they must be plausible. Male-narrator or humorous stories might be another type they'll consider. Suspense crime yarns are always well received if the confessional tone is preserved. Courtroom stories and mental health problems are usually sure sales. It might be wise to query the confession editor first about these out-of-the ordinary stories.

BRONZE THRILLS, 1220 Harding St., Ft. Worth TX 76102. Editor: Mrs. Edna K. Turner. Monthly magazine; 96 pages. Estab. 1957. Circ. 80,000. Buys all rights. Buys 60 mss/year. Pays on acceptance. Free sample copy and writer's guidelines. Reports in 90 days. Submit complete ms. SASE.
Fiction: All material must relate to blacks. Romance or confession; black-oriented. Particularly interested in occult themes or those concerned with UFO's or mental illness. Does not want to see anything dealing with pregnancy, venereal disease, virginal girls getting pregnant after "first mistake" or old woman/young man love affairs unless the story has an unusual angle. Length: 4,000 to 6,000 words. Pays $30.

Photos: B&w and color photos are purchased on assignment. 8x10 b&w glossies. 2¼x2¼ or 4x5 color transparencies. Pays $35 for b&w; $50 for color.

INTIMATE ROMANCES, Rolat Publishing Corp., 667 Madison Ave., New York NY 10021. Editorial Director: Cara Sherman. Requirements same as *Intimate Secrets*.

INTIMATE SECRETS, Rolat Publishing Corp., 667 Madison Ave., New York NY 10021. Editorial Director: Cara Sherman. For women between the ages 16-30. Magazine. Circ. 170,000. Pays on acceptance. Buys all rights. Submissions addressed to *Intimate Secrets* are also considered for publication for *Intimate Romances*, and *True Secrets*. Reports in 4-6 weeks. Free writer's guidelines.
Nonfiction: "Though we do not purchase much nonfiction, if the subject is of interest, relevance, and handled appropriately for our readership, we'll consider it." Length: 3,000-5,000 words. Pays $125-150.
Fiction: "We look primarily for tender love stories, touching baby stories, and stories dealing with identifiable marital problems, particularly sexual. We are interested in realistic teen stories, and on occasion, male-narrated stories, and tales with supernatural overtones. Stories should be written in the first-person. They should deal with a romantic or emotional problem that is identifiable and realistically portrays how the narrator copes with her conflict and resolves it. We reject stories based on hackneyed themes and outdated attitudes. In our contemporary society, stories condemming premarital sexual experience, abortion, and those that preach chastity, etc., are unsuitable for our needs." Length: 1,500-6,000 words. Pays $75-150.
How To Break In: Avoid the "sin-suffer-repent" syndrome. Tailor your needs to suit a young, rural audience who, though unsophisticated, no longer live by Puritanical values."

INTIMATE STORY, 2 Park Ave., New York NY 10016. Editor: Janet Wandel. 95% freelance written. For women; 14- to 70-years-old; small minority men; blue-collar. Monthly magazine; 74 pages. Estab. 1948. Circ. 170,000. Buys all rights. Buys about 100 mss/year. Pays on acceptance. Rarely sends sample copies. No photocopied or simultaneous submissions. Submit seasonal material 6 months in advance. Reports in 2 months. SASE.
Fiction: "Sex oriented and human interest stories; all types of fictional confession stories. Always first person; always enough dialogue. Our stories are within the realm of the believable." Does not want to see anything with the theme of hopelessness. No depressing situations. All titles are house-generated. Length: 2,000 to 7,000 words. Pays 3¢ per word; $165 maximum.

LOPEZ ROMANCE GROUP: REAL ROMANCES, REAL STORY, 21 W. 26th St., New York NY 10010. (212)689-3933. Editor: Ardis Sandel. For housewives, teenagers, and working women. Monthly magazines; 72 pages. Buys all rights. Buys about 350 mss/year. Pays on publication. Sample copy 75¢. No photocopied or simultaneous submissions. Reports in 6 to 8 weeks. Submit seasonal or holiday material 6 months in advance. Submissions addressed to individual publications in this listing will be considered by all of the publications. SASE.
Nonfiction and Fiction: "First person confession stories and service articles on sex, decorating, arts and crafts, fashions, homemaking, beauty, cooking, children, etc. Stories must be well-plotted, have realistic situations, motivation and characterization." Writer should read several issues for style and approach. Strong emphasis on realism. No racial stories. "Sexy passages and dialogue are okay if integral part of the story." Mss should feature a different twist or angle to make the story usable. Lengths from short-shorts to 7,500 words maximum. Pays $150 maximum, depending on length.

MODERN ROMANCES, Macfadden Women's Group, Inc., 205 E. 42nd St., New York NY 10017. (212)983-5644. Editor: Jean Sharbel. 100% freelance written. For 18-35 year-old blue collar, family-oriented women. Monthly magazine; 80 pages. Estab. 1929. Circ. 200,000. Pays on publication. Buys all rights. Submit seasonal/holiday material 4 months in advance of issue date. SASE. Reports in 4-8 weeks.
Nonfiction: General interest; how-to (homemaking subjects); humor; inspirational; and personal experience. Submit comlete ms. Length: 200-1,500 words. Pay "depends on merit."
Fiction: "Confession stories with reader identification and a strong emontional tone. No third person material" Buys 10 mss/issue. Submit complete ms. Length: 1,500-7,000 words. Pays 5¢/word.
Poetry: "Light, romantic poetry, to 24 lines." Buys 36/year. Pay "depends on merit."

PERSONAL ROMANCES, Ideal Publishing Corp., 2 Park Ave., New York NY 10016. Editor:

Debbie Weisman. Monthly. Buys all rights. Pays on acceptance. Reports on submissions in 6-8 weeks. SASE.
Fiction: First-person stories told in strong up-to-date terms by young marrieds, singles, and teens revealing their emotional, sexual, and family conflicts and their search to resolve personal problems. Blue-collar, white collar group identification. Length: 2,000 to 6,000 words. Top pay is up to $160, based on 3¢ a word.

REAL CONFESSIONS, MODERN LOVE CONFESSIONS, Sterling Library Inc., 261 Fifth Ave., New York NY 10016. Editor: Susan Silverman. 50% freelance written. For female readers from teenage on up. Monthly. Circ. 300,000. Buys all rights. Pays on publication. Will not consider photocopied or simultaneous submissions. Submit seasonal material 5 months in advance. Reports within 1 month. Submit only complete ms. SASE.
Fiction: "Current sexual themes; quantity of description, although it should not be too explicit." Payment: "In the area of 3¢/word."

REAL ROMANCES, 21 W. 26th St., New York NY 10010. See Lopez Romance Group.

REAL STORY, 21 W. 26th St., New York 10010. See Lopez Romance Group.

REVEALING SECRETS, E-Go Enterprises, Inc., 13510 Ventura Blvd., Sherman Oaks CA 91423. (213)990-2510. Editor: Charles E. Fritch. "Slanted toward women of all ages." Bimonthly magazine; 68 pages. Estab: 1976. Circ: 175,000. Pays on publication. Buys one-time rights. Phone queries OK. Submit seasonal/holiday material 4 months in advance. SASE. Reports in 6 weeks. Sample copy $1; writer's guidelines for SASE.
Nonfiction: Francine Dupar, Articles Editor. How-to (be a better wife, mother, woman, human being; beauty hints, hobbies, etc.). Buys 4 mss/issue. Length: 1,000-2,500 words. Pays 1½¢/word.
Fiction: Confession stories. "Stories must be first person female, with a likable protagonist, someone the reader can cry with and root for. The problem must be a realistic one. Stories should be emotionally charged and written in an easy to read conversational tone. Endings need not be happy, but the protagonist must have learned something from her unhappy experience." Buys 7 mss/issue. Submit complete ms. Length: 1,500-7,000 words. Pays 1½¢/word.

SECRETS, Macfadden Women's Group, 205 E. 42nd St., New York NY 10017. (212)983-5644. Editor: Jean Press Silberg. For blue-collar family women, ages 18 to 35. Monthly magazine; 80 pages. Estab. 1936. Buys all rights. Buys about 150 mss/year. Pays on publication. No photocopied or simultaneous submissions. Submit seasonal material 4 to 5 months in advance. Submit only complete ms. Reports in 4 weeks. SASE..
Nonfiction, Fiction and Poetry: Wants confession stories; self-help or inspirational fillers. Stories should have realistic plotting with strong emotional tone. Length: 300 to 1,000 words for nonfiction; 1,500 to 7,500 words for confession mss. Pays 3¢ a word for confession mss. Greatest need: 2,000-5,000 words. Also buys light, romantic verse. Length: 24 lines maximum.

TRUE CONFESSIONS, Macfadden Women's Group, 205 E. 42 St., New York NY 10017. Editor: Barbara J. Brett. For blue-collar women, teens through maturity. Monthly magazine. Estab. 1922. Circ. 350,000. Buys all rights. Pays on publication. No photocopied or simultaneous submissions. Submit seasonal material at least 5 or 6 months in advance. Reports in 8-12 weeks. Submit complete ms. SASE.
Fiction, Nonfiction, and Fillers: Realistic life stories within the confession frame. Humor, romance, and suspense fiction. All must be of interest to women in their new and ever-changing role in today's world. Some stories may have a seasonal tone. Careful study of a current issue is suggested. Length: 2,000-7,000 words; 5,000 word stories preferred; also book-lengths of 10,000-12,000 words. Pays 5¢/word. Also, articles, regular features, and short fillers.
Poetry: Romantic poetry, free verse and traditional, of interest to women. Limit submissions to batches of 4. Pays $10.

TRUE EXPERIENCE, Macfadden Women's Group, 205 E. 42 St., New York NY 10017. Editor: Lydia E. Paglio. For young marrieds, blue-collar, high school education. Interests: children, home, arts, crafts, family and self-fulfillment. Monthly magazine; 80 pages. Estab. 1925. Circ. 225,000. Buys all rights. Buys about 150 mss/year. Pays on publication. "Study the magazine for style and editorial content." No photocopied or simultaneous submissions. Submit seasonal material for holiday issues 5 months in advance. Reports in 3 months. Submit complete ms. SASE.

Fiction and Nonfiction: Stories on life situations, i.e., death, love, sickness. Romance and confession, first-person narratives with strong identification for readers. Articles on health, self-help, child care. "Remember that we are more contemporary. We deal more with women's self-awareness, and consciousness of their roles in the seventies." Length: 250 to 1,000 words for nonfiction; 1,000 to 7,500 words for fiction. Pays 3¢ a word.
Poetry: Only traditional forms. Length: 4 to 20 lines. Payment varies.

TRUE LIFE SECRETS, Charlton Publications, Charlton Building, Derby CT 06418. (203)735-3381. Editor-in-Chief: John E. Bartimole. 90% freelance written. Bimonthly magazine; 64 pages. Estab. 1960. Circ. 150,000. Pays on publication. Buys all rights, but may reassign following publication. Phone queries OK. Submit seasonal/holiday material 6 months in advance of issue date. Photocopied submissions OK. SASE. Reports in 4-8 weeks. Sample copy and writer's guidelines for SASE; mention *Writer's Market* in request.
Nonfiction: How-to (sex-aids, guide to sex, and anything of interest to women). Buys 1 ms/issue. Query or submit complete ms. Length: 1,000-2,500 words. Pays $25.
Fiction: Confession. "We welcome manuscripts on a racier theme than most confession magazines. We welcome the new writer and anticipate our needs to remain high for the next several issues." Buys 6-7 mss/issue. Submit complete ms. Length: 3,000-10,000 words. Pays $75 minimum.

TRUE LOVE, Macfadden Women's Group, 205 E. 42 St., New York NY 10017. Editor: Erma E. Benedict. For young, blue-collar women. Monthly magazine; 80 pages. Estab. 1924. Circ. 225,000. Buys all rights. Buys about 150 mss a year. Pays on publication. No photocopied or simultaneous submissions. Submit seasonal material (Christmas, Easter, Thanksgiving Day, Mother's Day, Father's Day, Valentine's Day) at least 6 months in advance. Reports in 3 months. Submit complete ms. Enclose SASE.
Fiction: Confessions, true love stories; problems and solutions. Graphic sex is to be avoided. Stories dealing with reality, current problems, everyday events, with emphasis on emotional impact. Length: 1,500 to 8,000 words. Pays 3¢ a word.
Nonfiction: Informational and how-to articles. Length: 250 to 800 words. Pays 5¢ a word minimum.

TRUE ROMANCE, Macfadden Women's Group, 205 E. 42nd St., New York NY 10017. (212)983-5644. Editor: Jean Sharbel. "Our readership ranges from teenagers to senior citizens. The vast majority of them, however, are young, high school educated, blue-collar wives, the mothers of young children. They have high moral values, are family and love oriented." Monthly magazine; 80 pages. Estab. 1923. Circ. 225,000. Pays on publication. Buys all rights. Submit seasonal/holiday material at least 4 months in advance. SASE. Reports in 4-8 weeks.
Nonfiction: How-to; informational; and personal experience (inspirational—300-500 words). Submit complete ms. Length: 300-1,000 words. Pays 3¢/word, special rates for short features and articles.
Fiction: Confession. Buys 10 stories/issue. Submit complete ms. Length: 2,000-7,500. Pays 3¢/word; slightly higher flat rate for short-shorts.
Poetry: Free verse and traditional. Buys 20/year. Length: 4-20 lines. Pays minimum $10.
How To Break In: "The freelance writer is needed and welcomed. A timely, well-written story that is centered around sympathetic characters, that reaches a strong climax and that sees the central problem through to a satisfying resolution is all that is needed to 'break into' *True Romance*."

TRUE SECRETS, Rolat Publishing Corp., 667 Madison Ave., New York NY 10021. Editorial Director: Cara Sherman. Requirements same as *Intimate Secrets*.

TRUE STORY, Macfadden Women's Group, 205 E. 42 St., New York NY 10017. Editor: Helen Vincent. 80% freelance written. For young married, blue-collar women, 20 to 35; high school education; increasingly broad interests; home-oriented, but increasingly looking beyond the home for personal fufillment. Monthly magazine; 104 pages. Estab.1919. Circ.1,700,000. Buys all rights. Buys about 125 full-length mss/year. Pays on publication. No photocopied or simultaneous submissions. Submit seasonal material 4 months in advance. Make notation on envelope that it is seasonal material. Query first for nonfiction. Submit only complete mss for fiction. Reports in 2 to 3 months. Enclose SASE..
Nonfiction, Photos, Fiction, and Fillers: "First-person stories covering all aspects of women's interest: love, marriage, family life, careers, social problems, etc. Nonfiction would further explore same areas. The best direction a new writer can be given is to carefully study several

issues of the magazine; then submit a fresh, exciting, well-written story. We have no taboos. It's the handling that makes the difference between a reject and an accept." How-to, personal experience, inspirational. Length: 1,000 to 2,500 words. Pays 5¢ to 10¢ or more per word. Also seeks material for Women are Wonderful column. Length: 1,500 words maximum. Pays 5¢ per word. Pays a flat rate for column or departments, announced in the magazine. Query Art Director, Gus Gazzola, about all possible photo submissions. Fiction; romance and confession. Length: 1,500 to 8,000 words. Pays 5¢ a word; $100 minimum. Regular departments, New Faces and Children's Corner, bring $5 each item.

Consumer Service and Business Opportunity Publications

Magazines in this classification are edited for individuals who don't necessarily have a lot of money, but who want maximum return on what they do have—either in goods purchased or in earnings from investment in a small business of their own. Publications for business executives are listed under Business and Finance. Those on how to run specific businesses are classified in Trade, Technical, and Professional Journals.

BUYWAYS, 1000 Sunset Ridge Rd., Northbrook IL 60062. (312)777-7000. For members of NACT, Inc.; National Association of Consumers and Travelers, United Farmers Association and United Builders Association. Association members are middle income, high school graduates. They joined their association to save money on a variety of products (for example, new cars, motels, group travel, car rental, appliances, etc.). Quarterly magazine; 16-24 pages. Estab. 1972. Circ. 60,000. Buys first North American serial rights. Buys 12 to 16 mss a year. Payment on acceptance. Will consider photocopied and simultaneous submissions. Query first. Reports in 6 weeks. SASE.
Nonfiction and Photos: "Consumer-oriented articles on how to save, how to buy wisely (money and management); travel articles (domestic and foreign). Emphasis on wise buying for home and travel. Looking for well-researched articles. Informational, how-to, personal experience, interview, profile, humor, historical, photo, travel, successful business operations, and new product articles. Length: 500 to 2,500 words. Pays 10¢ to 20¢/word. Color transparencies purchased with or without ms, or on assignment. Captions optional. Payment depends on size and use.

CANADIAN CONSUMER, Consumers' Association of Canada, 200 1st Ave., Ottawa, Ontarion, Canada K1S 2G6. (613)233-9383. Editor: Michael Segal. 40% freelance written. Emphasizes consumer information for a "very broad readership." Bimonthly magazine; 48-56 pages. Estab. 1963. Circ. 145,000. Pays on acceptance. Buys all rights. Phone queries OK. Submit seasonal/holiday material 3 months in advance of issue date. Simultaneous and photocopied submissions OK. SASE. Reports in 1 month. Free sample copy.
Nonfiction: "Anything of general interest to consumers." Expose; how-to; general interest; interview; and new product. Buys 18 mss/year. Submit complete ms. Length: 700-2,700 words. Pays $25-50.
Photos: State availability of photos with ms. Pays $10-25 for 8½x11 b&w glossy prints; $10-25 for 35mm color transparencies. Captions preferred. Buys all rights, but may reassign following publication.
Columns/Departments: Book Reviews. Buys 6/year. Submit complete ms. Length: 700-1,500 words. Pays $25.
Fillers: Newsbreaks. Buys 6/year. Length: 50-200 words. Pays $5-10.

COMMON CENTS, 432 Park Ave., S., Suite 1205, New York NY 10016. (212)889-1527. Editor-in-Chief: Roy A. Lord. Managing Editor: Chet Meyer. 70% freelance written. Emphasizes family money management. Monthly tabloid; 24 pages. Estab. March 1977. Circ. 2 million. Pays on publication. Buys all rights, but may reassign following publication. Phone queries OK. Submit seasonal/holiday material 3 months in advance of issue date. Prefer previously unpublished submissions. SASE. Reports in 3-6 weeks. Sample copy 35¢ in stamps on large SASE; writer's guidelines for SASE; mention *Writer's Market* in request.
Nonfiction: General interest (travel tips, shopping, 'buymanship,' the home, energy conservation, food, car care, retirement, health, community issues and involvement, and finances); how-to (hobbies, do-it-yourself); interview (must be vital and lively as well as informative); new product (mention no brand names, must be generic in nature); photo feature (with text, usually outdoor subjects like sports or camping); technical (in a how-to or fix-it area, with photos); and

travel (short pieces). Buys 10 mss/issue. Query or submit complete ms. Length: 200-1,800 words. Pays 8¢/edited word.
Columns/Departments: Travel Tips, Shopping, Hobbies, Energy, Food, Getting On (retirement); AdolesCents; The Home, Car Care, Health, and Finances (not investment). Query or submit complete ms. Length: "varies each issue." Pays 8¢/edited word.

CONSUMER REPORTS, 256 Washington St., Mt. Vernon NY 10550. Editor: Irwin Landau. Staff-written.

CONSUMERS DIGEST, 4001 W. Devon, Chicago IL 60646. Editor: Arthur Darack. 35% freelance written. For high school and college educated do-it-yourselfers. Bimonthly magazine; 32 pages. Estab. 1958. Circ. 650,000. Buys all rights. Buys 15-20 mss/year. Pays on acceptance. Sample copy for 50¢. Query. Enclose SASE.
Nonfiction: Material on investments, self-help, products and services, health and food, best buys, analysis of cars, appliances, etc. Also how-to's on car, appliance and house repair. Approach is systematic with mass appeal. Not interested in exposes, but will consider material on successful business operations and merchandising techniques and for legal and medical columns. Article length: 1,000 words minimum. Column length: 3,000 words. Pays 5¢ a word.

CONSUMERS' RESEARCH MAGAZINE, Washington NJ 07882. Editor: F.J. Schlink. 5% freelance written. Monthly. Copyrighted. Limited amount of freelance material used. Query first. SASE.
Nonfiction and Photos: Articles of practical interest to ultimate consumers concerned with tests and expert judgment of goods and services which they buy. Must be accurate and careful statements, well-supported by chemical, engineering, scientific, medical, or other expert or professional knowledge of subject. Pays approximately 2¢ per word. Buys b&w glossies with mss only. Pays $5 minimum. "Photos are accepted only if they are clearly relevant to the article being published."

ECONOMIC FACTS, The National Research Bureau, Inc., 424 N. 3rd St., Burlington IA 52601. Editor-in-Chief: Barbara Pollard. Managing Editor: Ronald Walker. 95% freelance written. For industrial workers of all ages. Published 3 times/year. Magazine; 16 pages. Estab. 1970. Circ. 30,000. Pays on publication. Buys all rights, but may reassign following publication. Submit seasonal/holiday material 3-4 months in advance of issue date. Previously published submissions OK. SASE. Reports in 1 week. Free sample copy and writer's guidelines; mention *Writer's Market* in request.
Nonfiction: Barbara Boeding, articles editor. General interest (private enterprise, government data, graphs, taxes, and health care). Buys 2-3 mss/issue. Query with outline of article. Length: 400-600 words. Pays $20 minimum.

FDA CONSUMER, 5600 Fishers Lane, Rockville MD 20857. (301)443-3220. Editor: Ellis Rottman. 10% freelance written. For "all consumers of products regulated by the Food and Drug Administration." A Federal Government publication. Monthly magazine, 40 pages. Estab. 1967. December/January and July/August issues combined. Circ. 20,000. Not copyrighted. "All purchases automatically become part of public domain." Buys 4 to 5 freelance mss a year, by contract only. Payment on publication. Query first. "We cannot be responsible for any work by writer not agreed upon by prior contract." SASE.
Nonfiction and Photos: "Articles of an educational nature concerning purchase and use of FDA regulated products and specific FDA programs and actions to protect the consumer's health and pocketbook. Authoritative and official agency viewpoints emanating from agency policy and actions in administrating the Food, Drug and Cosmetic Act and a number of other statutes. All articles subject to clearance by the appropriate FDA experts as well as the editor. The magazine speaks for the Federal Government only. Articles based on facts and FDA policy only. We cannot consider any unsolicited material. All articles based on prior arrangement by contract. The nature and subject matter and clearances required are so exacting that it is difficult to get an article produced by a writer working outside the Washington DC metropolitan area." Length: average, 2,000 words. Pays $500. B&w photos are purchased on assignment only.

HOME BUDGET & CONSUMER, DTM Publications, Box 207, Brookline NH 03033. Editor-in-Chief: Joseph F. Harrity. 80% freelance written. Emphasizes conservation of family expenses for a readership consisting of low-middle and middle income family members, mostly housewives, with an interest in gaining the most value for funds spent in household operations. Biweekly magazine; 12 pages. Estab. 1977. Pays on publication. Buys all rights. Submit

seasonal/holiday material 4 months in advance of issue date. Simultaneous and photocopied submissions OK. SASE. Reports in 3-4 weeks. Free sample copy and writer's guidelines.
Nonfiction: "Writers should make articles meaningful and concise. All submissions should be as short as possible without losing purpose. No brand name is to be used unless it is essential to the article." How-to (conserving the family budget, gaining top value for expenditures made for the home); and new product (those that can eliminate the workload in the home without adding great expense). Buys 5-7 mss/issue. Submit complete ms. Length: 300-700 words. Pays 3-7¢/word.

INCOME OPPORTUNITIES, 380 Lexington Ave., New York NY 10017. Editor: Joseph V. Daffron. Managing Editor: Frances Freilich. 98% freelance written. For all who are seeking business opportunities, full- or part-time. Monthly magazine. Estab. 1956. Buys all rights. Buys 100 mss/year. Will not consider photocopied or simultaneous submissions. Two special directory issues contain articles on selling techniques, mail order, import/export, franchising and business ideas. Reports in 1 to 2 weeks. Query. SASE.
Nonfiction and Photos: Regularly covered are such subjects as mail order, direct selling, franchising, party plans, selling techniques and the marketing of handcrafted or homecrafted products. Wanted are ideas for the aspiring entrepreneur; examples of successful business methods that might be duplicated. No material that is purely inspirational. "Payment rates vary according to length and quality of the submission from a minimum of $50 for a short of a maximum of 800 words, to $200 for a major article of 2,000 to 3,000 words. Illustrations are considered part of the manuscript purchase."
How To Break In: "Study recent issues of the magazine. Best bets for newcomers: Interview-based report on a successful small business venture."

INTERNATIONAL ENTREPRENEURS' MAGAZINE, 631 Wilshire Blvd., Suite 200, Santa Monica CA 90401. Editor-in-Chief: Chase Revel. Managing Editor: John Hiatt. 10% freelance written. For a readership looking for highly profitable opportunities in small businesses, as owners, investors or franchisees. Monthly magazine; 52 pages. Estab. 1972. Circ. 40,000. Pays on acceptance. Buys all rights. Submit seasonal/holiday material 2 months in advance of issue date. Photocopied submissions OK. SASE. Reports in 4 weeks. Sample copy $1; free writer's guidelines.
Nonfiction: How-to (in-depth start-up details on 'hot' business opportunities like skateboard parks or computer stores). Buys 12 mss/year. Query with clips of previously published work. Length: 3,500-4,000 words. Pays $300-700 for features; $100 for featurettes.
Photos: "We need good b&w glossies to illustrate articles." Offers no additional payment for photos accepted with ms. Uses 8x10 b&w glossy prints or standard transparencies. Captions preferred. Buys one-time rights. Model release required.
Columns/Departments: New Products; New Ideas; Promo Gimmicks; and Frauds. Query. Length: 200-500 words. Pays $25-50.

MONEYTREE NEWSLETTER, Task Bldg., Kerrville TX 78028. Editor: Marshall Sideman. Pays on acceptance. Send #10 SASE and $1 for sample copy.
Fillers: "Items dealing with money. How to invest it, make it grow rapidly, how to get big savings—these have the best chance of acceptance. Our readers want to get rich, or if wealthy already, stay rich." Also uses capsule articles on health, self-help, vocational training, practical science, money-making opportunities, etc. Also capsulized write-ups about free publications, product samples, items of value, etc. All submissions must be documented by author. Length: 10 to 60 words. Pays $5.

SUBURBAN SHOPPER, Box 208, East Millstone NJ 08873. (201)873-2156. Editor-in-Chief: Kevin K. Kopec. 100% freelance written. For convenience shoppers, working women who are interested in savings and unusual gagets/home items. Quarterly tabloid; 24 pages. Estab. February 1978. Pays on publication. Buys one-time rights. Phone queries OK. Submit seasonal/holiday material 1 month in advance of issue date. Simultaneous, photocopied, and previously published submissions OK. SASE. Reports in 3 weeks. Sample copy $1.25; free writer's guidelines; mention *Writer's Market* in request.
Nonfiction: General interest (any aspect of mail order shopping-buying tips, etc.); and new product (mail order product reviews). Buys 5 mss/issue. Submit complete ms. Length: 500-1,000 words. Pays $5-10.

Detective and Crime Publications

Publications listed in this section provide markets for nonfiction accounts of true crimes. Markets for criminal fiction (mysteries) are listed in Mystery Publications.

DETECTIVE CASES, Detective Files Group, 1440 St. Catherine St., W., Montreal, Quebec, Canada H3G 1S2. Editor-in-Chief: Dominick A. Merle. Art Director: Art Ball. Bimonthly magazine; 72 pages. See *Detective Files*.

DETECTIVE DRAGNET, Detective Files Group, 1440 St. Catherine St., W., Montreal, Quebec, Canada H3G 1S2. Editor-in-Chief: Dominick A. Merle. Art Director: Art Ball. Bimonthly magazine; 72 pages. See *Detective Files*.

DETECTIVE FILES, Detective Files Group, 1440 St. Catherine St., W., Montreal, Quebec, Canada H3G 1S2. Editor-in-Chief: Dominick A. Merle. Art Director: Art Ball. Bimonthly magazine; 72 pages. Pays on acceptance. Buys all rights. Submit seasonal/holiday material 4 months in advance. Photocopied submissions OK. SASE. Reports in 4 weeks. Free sample copy and writer's guidelines.
Nonfiction: True crime stories. "Do a thorough job; don't double-sell (sell an article to more than one market), and deliver and you can have a steady market. Neatness, clarity and pace will help you make the sale." Query. Length: 3,500-6,000 words. Pays $175-300.
Photos: Purchased with accompanying ms; no additional payment. B&w only. Model release required.

FRONT PAGE DETECTIVE, INSIDE DETECTIVE, Official Detective Group, R.G.H. Publishing Corp. 235 Park Ave., S., New York NY 10003. Editor-in-Chief: Albert P. Govoni. Editor: Diana Lurvey.
Nonfiction: The focus of these two publications will be quite similar to the others in the Official Detective Group, but will concentrate less on pre-trial stories. For further details, see *Official Detective*.

HEADQUARTERS DETECTIVE, Detective Files Group, 1440 St. Catherine St., W., Montreal, Quebec, Canada H3G 1S2. Editor-in-Chief: Dominick A. Merle. Art Director: Art Ball. Bimonthly magazine; 72 pages. See *Detective Files*.

MASTER DETECTIVE, Official Detective Group, R.G.H. Publishing Corp., 235 Park Ave., S., New York NY 10003. Editor-in-Chief: Albert P. Govoni. Managing Editor: Walter Jackson. Monthly. Estab. 1929. Circ. 350,000; Buys 9-10 mss/issue. See *Official Detective*.

OFFICIAL DETECTIVE, Official Detective Group, R.G.H. Publishing Corp., 235 Park Ave., S., New York NY 10003. Editor-in-Chief: Albert P. Govoni. Manager Editor: Walter Jackson. "For detective story or police buffs whose tastes run to *true*, rather than fictional crime/mysteries." Monthly magazine; 80 pages. Estab. 1930. Circ. 500,000. Pays on acceptance. Buys all rights. Phone queries OK. Buys 11-12 mss/issue. SASE. Reports in 2 weeks.
Nonfiction: "Only *fact* detective stories. We are actively trying to develop new writers, and we'll work closely with those who show promise and can take the discipline required by our material. It's not difficult to write, but it demands meticulous attention to facts, truth, clarity, detail. Queries are essential with us, but I'd say the quickest rejection goes to the writer who sends in a story on a case that should never have been written for us because it lacks the most important ingredient, namely solid, superlative detective work. We also dislike pieces with multiple defendants, unless all have been convicted." Buys 150 mss/year. Query. Length: 4,500-6,500 words. Pays $200-400.
Photos: Purchased with accompanying mss. Captions required. Send prints for inside use; transparencies for covers. Pays $12.50 minimum for b&w glossies, 4x5 minimum. Pays $200 minimum for 2¼x2¼ or 35mm. Model release required for color used on cover.

TRUE DETECTIVE, Official Detective Group, R.G.H. Publishing Corp., 235 Park Ave., S., New York NY 10003. Editor-in-Chief: Albert P. Govoni. Managing Editor: Walter Jackson. Monthly. Estab. 1924. Circ. 500,000. Buys 11-12 mss/issue. See *Official Detective*.

STARTLING DETECTIVE, Detective Files Group, 1440 St. Catherine, W., Montreal, Quebec, Canada H3G 1S2. Editor-in-Chief: Dominick A. Merle. Art Director: Art Ball. Bimonthly magazine; 72 pages. See *Detective Files*..

TRUE POLICE CASES, Detective Files Group, 1440 St. Catherine St., W., Montreal, Quebec,

Canada H3G 1S2. Editor-in-Chief: Dominick A. Merle. Art Director: Art Ball. Bimonthly magazine; 72 pages. See *Detective Files*.

Education Publications

Magazines in these listings approach the subject of education with the interests of parents and the general public in mind. Journals for professional educators and teachers are included under Education in the Trade Journals section. Because of their value to educators and parents, nonpaying markets are included in this section.

AMERICAN EDUCATION, U.S. Office of Education, 400 Maryland Ave. SW, Washington DC 20202. (202)245-8907. Editor: William A. Horn. Managing Editor: Gertrue Mitchell. Presents successful education programs with some federal involvement for readership of education professionals and others with special interest in the field. Monthly magazine; 36-42 pages. Estab. 1965. Circ. 40,000. Pays on acceptance. Buys all rights. Submit seasonal/holiday material 4 months in advance. Photocopied submissions OK. SASE. Reports in 2-3 weeks. Free sample copy and writer's guidelines.
Nonfiction: Informational (successful projects or programs with federal involvement). Buys 30 mss/year. Query. Length: average 2,500 words. Pays $350 and up, depending on quality.
Photos: Alice Jackson, Photo Editor. Purchased with accompanying manuscript. Submit b&w glossy photos and contact sheet. Pays $15 minimum.

AMERICAN TEACHER, 11 Dupont Circle, N.W., Washington DC 20036. Editor: Gail Miller. For "members of the American Federation of Teachers, AFL-CIO, and other classroom teachers." Monthly except July and August. Buys first North American serial rights; will buy simultaneous rights. Pays on publication. Free sample copy. Prefers query first. Reports in 4 months. SASE.
Nonfiction and Photos: "We want material directly concerned with our primary interests: educational innovation, academic freedom, the teacher union movement, better schools and educational methods, legislation concerning teachers, etc. Pays $25 to $70. Photos purchased with and without mss; captions required. "Stock photos of classroom scenes." Subjects must be in range of subject interest. No specific size. Pays $15.

CANADIAN CHILDREN'S MAGAZINE, 4150 Bracken Ave., Victoria B.C. Canada, V8X 3N8. (604)479-6906. Editor-in-Chief: Evelyn Samuel. "This magazine is geared toward children 6-12 years old in Canada or interested in Canadian materials." Quarterly magazine; 48 pages. Estab. 1976. Circ. 25,000. Pays in copies. Acquires one-time rights. Phone queries OK. Submit seasonal/holiday material 6 months in advance. Photocopied submissions OK. SASE. Reports in 1 month. Sample copy $1.25; free writer's guidelines.
Nonfiction: How-to (always with a Canadian slant—ethnic, Indian, or regional), historical (Canadian material only), and informational (current Canadian contributions, inventions, etc). Uses 25 mss/issue. Query. Length: 500-1,500 words. Pays in copies.
Fiction: Uses 2 mss/year. Query. Length: 500-1,500 words. Pays in copies.

CAREER WORLD, Curriculum Innovations, Inc., 501 Lake Forest Ave., Highwood IL 60040. (312)432-2700. Editor: Bonnie Bekker. 80% freelance written. Emphasizes career education for junior and senior high school students at approximately 9th grade reading level. Teacher's edition aimed at guidance and career education personnel. Monthly (September-May) magazine; 32 pages. Estab. 1972. Circ. 130,000. Pays on publication. Buys all rights. Submit seasonal/holiday material 4 months in advance. SASE. Reports in 2 weeks.
Nonfiction: How-to, informational, interview, profile, photo feature. Buys 9 mss/year. Query. Length: 750-3,000 words. Pays 4¢/word minimum.
Columns, Departments: Lifestyle (worker profile), Opening Door (profile of minority or handicapped worker), New Careers, Teachers' Edition (activities and news for teachers). Buys 9/year. Query. Length: 500-1,500 words. Pays 4¢/word and up. Open to suggestions for new columns or departments.

CHANGE MAGAZINE, Educational Change, Inc., NBW Tower, New Rochelle, NY 10801. Editor-in-Chief: George W. Bonham. Emphasizes higher learning/higher education. "*Change* is an opinion magazine broadly concerned with academic matters, social issues, and subject matter of intellectual interest." Monthly magazine; 69 pages. Estab. 1969. Circ. 26,000. Pays on acceptance. Buys all rights. Simultaneous and photocopied submissions OK. SASE. Reports in

6 weeks. Sample copy $1.
Nonfiction: Joyce Hermel, Articles Editor. Informational; interview; personal opinion; and profile. Buys 150 mss/year. Length: 1,200-10,000 words. Pays $100-300.
Columns, Departments: Cullen Murphy, Column, Department Editor. Book Reviews (topnotch reviews of books on education, social issues, intellectual interests), Community Colleges (first-rate reports on community colleges and their programs and problems), Media (broad-based pieces on all forms of media, educational and others). Buys 2/issue. Query. Length: 1,600-2,000 words. Pays $100-150. Open to suggestions for new columns and departments.

CURRENT CONSUMER, Curriculum Innovations, Inc., 501 Lake Forest Ave., Highwood IL 60040. (312)432-2700. Editor: Jan Farrington. 25% freelance written. Emphasizes consumer education. For junior and senior high school students at approximately 9th grade reading level. Teacher's edition aimed at home economics, business, economics and consumer education teachers. Monthly during the school year (Sept-May). Magazine; 32 pages. Estab. 1976. Circ. 65,000. Pays on publication. Buys all rights. Submit seasonal/holiday material 4 months in advance. Simultaneous, photocopied or previously published submissions OK. SASE. Reports in 2 weeks.
Nonfiction: "Our editorial philosophy is to educate young people toward becoming effective and aware consumers. We do not take an advovacy stance or endorse singular viewpoints. Material submitted for our consideration must correspond to this philosophy." How-to (on ways to becoming a more effective and confident consumer); informational (on anything a junior or senior high school student should know as a future consumer); interview; profile (of a consumer who has a valuable story to tell or lesson to teach); new product (that offers unique alternatives or advantages to the consumer); personal experience, and photo feature. Buys 9/year. Query. Length: 750-3,000 words. Pays 4¢/word and up.
Photos: Purchased with or without accompanying ms or on assignment. Query. Pays $10 minimum for 8x10 b&w glossies; $25 minimum for 35mm or larger transparencies. Model release required.
Columns, Departments: Marketplace (guide to buying goods and services—no product listing or rating), Money Management, Consumer Law, Teacher's Edition (activities for teachers). Buys 10-15/year. Query. Length: 750-1,000 words. Pays $75 for short features. Open to suggestions for new columns or departments.
Fillers: Clippings, puzzles (consumer related), short humor. Buys 20/year. Pays $5-15.

DAY CARE AND EARLY EDUCATION, 72 5th Ave., New York NY 10011. Contact: Editor. 40% freelance written. For day care professionals—teachers, aides, administrators, and parents. Quarterly magazine; 64 pages. Estab. 1973. Circ. 20,000. Pays on publication. Buys all rights, or "will make arrangements with authors." Submit seasonal/holiday material 6 months in advance of issue date. Photocopied submissions OK. SASE. Reports in 2 months. Free sample copy and writer's guidelines.
Nonfiction: How-to (activity ideas, staff training, administrative ideas); interview (on research or innovations in day care or educational programs); photo feature; and travel (child care in other countries). No "highly technical, jargon-filled research." Buys 5 mss/issue. Query. Length: 1,000-3,000 words. Pays $35-150.
Photos: State availabilty of photos with query. No additional payment for 8x10 glossy b&w photos accepted with ms. Captions preferred. Buys all rights.
Fiction: "We discourage fiction submissions unless *unusual*. Must be for young children. Very little published. We prefer that there be non-stereotyped situations and characters, teaching a useful lesson." Buys 2 mss/year. Submit complete ms. Length: 1,000-2,000 words. Pays $35-75.

THE EDUCATIONAL ABC OF INDUSTRY, 2212-11th St., Niagara Falls NY 14305. Editor-in-Chief: Terence J. Hughes. Managing Editor: Terry Whelpton. 20% freelance written. For students aged 12-16 and teachers of grades 7-10. Annual magazine; 30 pages. Estab. 1957. Circ. 2,800,000. Pays on publication. Buys first North American serial rights. Submit seasonal/holiday material 5 months in advance of issue date. Photocopied submissions OK. SASE. Reports in 10 weeks. Free sample copy; mention *Writer's Market* in request.
Nonfiction: Dennis G. Adair and Janet Rosenstock, editors. "All of our articles are educational in nature and must be aimed at students 12-16. Articles must be informative, concise, documented and interesting at the same time. We require a pre-statement on the article and teaching questions, project bibliography, and class discussion questions. All articles should lead to resources. We are interested in articles from educators that can be understood. No Jargon." How-to; historical; interview (sometimes); personal experience (from students only); photo feature; profile; and travel. Buys 2 mss/issue. Length: 3,000-5,000 words. Query. Pays $300-400.

Columns/Departments: Careers; Sports; Communications; Social Science; Science; and Coming Across. Query. Length: 1,000-3,000 words. Pays $250-300. Open to suggestions for new columns/departments.

READ MAGAZINE, 245 Long Hill Rd., Middletown CT 06457. (203)347-7251. Editor: Edwin A. Hoey. 10% freelance written. For high school students. Biweekly magazine; 32 pages. Estab. 1951. Circ. 796,305. Rights purchased vary with author and material. May buy second serial (reprint) rights or all rights. Buys about 20 mss a year. Pays on acceptance. Free sample copy and writer's guidelines. Will consider photocopied submissions. No simultaneous submissions. Reports in 3 to 4 weeks. Submit complete ms. SASE.
Drama and Fiction: First emphasis is on plays; second on fiction with suspense, adventure, or teenage identification themes. "No preachy material. Plays should have 12 to 15 parts and not require complicated stage directions, for they'll be used mainly for reading aloud in class. Remember that we try to be educational as well as entertaining." No kid detective stories or plays. No obscenity. Pays $50 minimum.

SCHOOL AND FAMILY DIGEST, Rt. 2, Box 156, Landenberg PA 19350. Editor-in-Chief: Lloyd W. Kline. 50% freelance written. For parents concerned about the education of their own children, kindergarten through college. Magazine published 4 times/school year; 16 pages. Estab. 1978. Pays on publication. Buys all rights, but may reassign following publication. Submit seasonal/holiday material 6 months in advance of issue date. Previously published submissions OK. SASE. Reports in 2 weeks. Free sample copy and writer's guidelines; mention *Writer's Market* in request.
Nonfiction: How-to (educate your child; interact constructively with schools; influence school programs as they affect your child); interview (outstanding parents/educators on school-home relationships); new product (for home use in educational ways); photo feature; profile (good home-school programs); and travel (as family education). Buys 20 mss/year. Submit complete ms. Length: 200-2,000 words. Pays $10-200.
Photos: State availability of photos with ms. Pays $5-25 for 5x7 b&w glossy prints. Buys all rights, but may reassign following publication. Model release required.
Fillers: Clippings, anecdotes, and newsbreaks. Buys 40/year. Length: 50-300 words. Pays $2-10.

Food and Drink Publications

Magazines classified here aim at individuals who are interested in and appreciate fine wines and fine foods. Journals aimed at food processors, manufacturers, and retailers will be found in the Trade Journals.

BON APPETIT, Knapp Communications, 5900 Wilshire Blvd., Los Angeles CA 90036. Editor-in-Chief: Paige Rense. Managing Editor: Pat Brown. 90% freelance written. Emphasizes food, cooking and wine "for affluent young, active men and women, interested in the good things of life." Monthly magazine; 120 pages. Circ. 1 million. Pays on acceptance. Rights purchased vary. Submit seasonal/holiday material 6 months in advance of issue date. Photocopied and previously published submissions OK. SASE. Reports in 6 weeks.
Nonfiction: Arline Inge, articles editor. How-to cook, and food articles with recipes. No historical food pieces. Query. Length: 2,000 words. Pay varies.

GOURMET, 777 Third Ave., New York NY 10017. Managing Editor: Miss Gail Zweigenthal. For moneyed, educated, traveled, food-wise men and women. Monthly. Purchases copyright, but grants book reprint rights with credit. Pays on acceptance. Suggests a study of several issues to understand type of material required. Reports within 2 months. Query first. "We prefer published writers, so if you haven't written for us before, you should enclose some samples of previous work." SASE.
Nonfiction: Uses articles on subjects related to food and wine—travel, adventure, reminiscence, fishing and hunting experiences. Prefers personal experiences to researched material. Recipes included as necessary. Not interested in nutrition, dieting, penny-saving, or bizarre foods, or in interviews with chefs or food experts, or in reports of food contests, festivals, or wine tastings. Buys recipes only as part of an article with interesting material to introduce them and make them appealing. "Gourmet Holidays" written by staff contributors only. The same is true for material including specific hotel or restaurant recommendations. Sophisticated, light, nontechnical. Length: 2,500 to 3,000 words. Current needs include American regional pieces (no restaurants). Pays $650 minimum.

Poetry and Verse: Light, sophisticated with food or drink slant. Pays $50 minimum.
How To Break In: "Personal reminiscences are the easiest way to break in, since we always use staff writers when recommending hotels or restaurants. Our biggest problem with freelancers is that they are not familiar with our style or that they fail to treat their material with enough sophistication or depth. We don't want pieces which sound like press releases or which simply describe what's there. We like to really cover a subject and literary value is important. We'd very much like to see more regional American material. It seems to be much easier to get people traipsing around Europe."

WINE WORLD MAGAZINE, 15101 Keswick St., Van Nuys CA 91405. (213)785-6050. Editor-Publisher: Dee Sindt. For the wine loving public (adults of all ages) who wish to learn more about wine. Bimonthly magazine; 48 pages. Estab. 1971. Buys first North American serial rights. Buys about 72 mss/year. Payment on publication. Free sample copy and writer's guidelines. Will not consider photocopied submissions. Will consider simultaneous submissions, "if spelled out." Reports in 30 days. Query first. SASE.
Nonfiction: "Wine-oriented material written with an in-depth knowledge of the subject, designed to meet the needs of the novice and connoisseur alike. Wine technology advancements, wine history, profiles of vintners the world over. Educational articles only. No first-person accounts. Must be objective, informative reporting on economic trends, new technological developments in vinification, vine hybridizing, and vineyard care. New wineries and new marketing trends. We restrict our editorial content to wine, and wine-oriented material. No restaurant or food articles accepted. No more basic wine information. No articles from instant wine experts. Authors must be qualified in this highly technical field." Length: 750 to 2,000 words. Pays $50 to $100.

WOMEN'S CIRCLE HOME COOKING, Box 338, Chester MA 01011. Editor: Barbara Hall Pedersen. For women (and some men) of all ages who really enjoy cooking. "Our readers collect and exchange recipes. They are neither food faddists nor gourmets, but practical women and men trying to serve attractive and nutritious meals. Many work full-time, and most are on limited budgets." Magazine; 72 (5x7¼) pages. Monthly. Circ. 225,000. Buys all rights, but will reassign rights to author after publication. Buys about 50 mss a year. Pays on publication. Will send sample copy to writer for SASE. Holiday food articles are always welcome, especially if accompanied by photos, and should be submitted 6 months in advance. Submit complete ms. Reports in 2 to 8 weeks. Enclose SASE.
Nonfiction and Photos: "We like a little humor with our food, for the sake of the digestion. Keep articles light. Stress economy and efficiency. Remember that at least half our readers must cook after working a full-time job. Draw on personal experience to write an informative article on some aspect of cooking. We're a reader participation magazine. We don't go in for fad diets, or strange combinations of food which claim to cure anything." Informational, how-to, inspirational, historical, expose, nostalgia, photo, and travel also considered. Length: 50 to 1,000 words. Pays 2¢ to 5¢ per word. Columns and regular features by arrangement. Photos purchased with ms or on assignment. Captions optional. 4x5 b&w, sharp, glossy. 2¼ color, but prefers 4x5. Pays $5 for b&w, $20 or more for color, by arrangement.
Fiction, Poetry, and Fillers: Humorous fiction, related to cooking and foods. Length: 1,200 words maximum. Pays 2¢ to 5¢ per word. Light verse related to cooking and foods. Length: 30 lines maximum. No payment. Short humorous fillers, 100 words maximum. Pays 2¢ to 5¢ per word.

General Interest Publications

Publications classified here are edited for national, general audiences and carry articles on any subject of interest to a broad spectrum of people. Other markets for general interest material will be found in the Black, In-Flight, Men's, Newspapers and Weekly Magazine Sections, Regional, City magazine, and Women's classifications in the Consumer section.

ACCENT, 1720 Washington Blvd., Box 2315, Ogden UT 84404. (801)394-9446. Editor: Helen S. Crane. 75% freelance written. For "a wide segment, from the young couple to the retired one." Estab. 1968. Monthly. Circ. 600,000. Rights purchased vary with author and material. Buys about 100 mss/year. Pays on acceptance. Free sample copy. Submit seasonal/holiday material 11 months in advance. Query. SASE.

Nonfiction and Photos: "We consider interest-capturing, short features from freelancers. Since our emphasis is on pictures, and our copy space limited, we require concise, informative, yet lively writing that covers a lot in a few words. We want pieces of lasting general interest suitable for the family. We do not need rambling experience pieces, or ecology features; nor do we want holiday material. We use a few travel vignettes about exciting yet well-known spots and pieces showing glimpses of life and unusual activities. Writing should be in a fresh, sparkling style." Pays about 10¢/word. Photos purchased with mss; captions required. "For the most part, we prefer views without people, unless actively engaged in interesting ways. Subjects must be eyecatching and colors sharp." For 8x10 b&w glossies, pays $20. For color transparencies ("some 35mm, prefer larger"), pays $25 minimum ("more for larger views or covers").

THE ATLANTIC MONTHLY, 8 Arlington St., Boston MA 02116. (617)536-9500. Editor-in-Chief: Robert Manning. For a professional, academic audience. Monthly. Circ. 325,000. Buys first North American serial rights. Pays on acceptance. Sample copy for $1. Reports in 2 weeks to several months. SASE.
Nonfiction: "We prefer not to formulate specifications about the desired content of *The Atlantic* and suggest that would-be contributors examine back issues to form their own judgment of what is suitable." Length: 2,000 to 5,000 words. Rates vary from $100 per magazine page base rate. Author should include summary of his qualifications for treating subject.
Fiction: Short stories by unestablished writers, published as Atlantic "Firsts" are a steady feature. Two prizes of $750 and $250 are awarded to the best of these when a sufficient number of stories are published. Candidates should so label their submissions and list their previous publications, if any, as authors whose stories have appeared in magazines of national circulation are not considered eligible. Will also consider stories by established writers in lengths ranging from 2,700 to 7,500 words. Payment depends on length, but also on quality and author.
Poetry: Uses three to five poems an issue. These must be of high literary distinction in both light and serious poetry. Interested in young poets. Base rate for poetry is $2/line.

BLACKWOOD'S MAGAZINE, William Blackwood & Sons, Ltd., 32 Thistle St., Edinburgh, Scotland EH2 IHA. (031)225-3411. Editor-in-Chief: David Fletcher. 80% freelance written. Monthly magazine; 96 pages. Estab. 1817. Circ. 8,500. Pays on publication. Buys first British serial rights. Phone queries OK. Submit seasonal/holiday material 3 months in advance. SAE and International Reply Coupons. Reports in 1 week. Sample copy $1.50; free writer's guidelines.
Nonfiction: Historical; nostalgia; personal experience; personal opinion; and travel. "Would-be contributors should first study the magazine." Buys 50 mss/year. Submit complete ms. Length: 2,500-9,000 words. Pays 5-8 pounds/1,000 words.
Fiction: Adventure, historical; humorous; mainstream; mystery; and religious. Buys 50 mss/year. Submit complete ms. Length: 2,500-9,000 words. Pays 5-8 pounds/1,000 words.
Poetry: Traditional forms, free verse and light verse. Buys 12/year. Length: 14-69 lines. Pays 8 pounds/poem.
How To Break In: "*Blackwood's* is one of the world's oldest monthlies and we are always keen to see work by U.S. and Canadian writers. But writers must, first of all, have studied the magazine and remember that material must not have appeared in print before submission to us."

CAPPER'S WEEKLY, Stauffer Communications, Inc., 616 Jefferson St., Topeka KS 66607. (913)295-1108. Editor: Dorothy Harvey. Emphasizes home and family. Biweekly tabloid; 24-36 pages. Estab. 1879. Circ. 425,000. Pays for poetry and cartoons on acceptance; articles on publication. Buys first North American serial rights. Submit seasonal/holiday material 2 months in advance. SASE. Reports in 2-3 weeks, 6-8 months for serialized novels. Sample copy 35¢.
Nonfiction: Historical (local museums, etc.), inspirational, nostalgia, travel (local slants) and people stories (accomplishments, collections, etc.). Buys 2-3 mss/issue. Submit complete ms. Length: 700 words maximum. Pays $1/inch.
Photos: Purchased with accompanying ms. Submit prints. Pays $5 for 8x10 b&w glossy prints. Total purchase price for ms includes payment for photos.
Columns/Departments: Heart of the Home (homemakers' letters, hints), Hometown Heartbeat (descriptive). Submit complete ms. Length: 500 words maximum. Pays $2-10.
Fiction: Novel length mystery and romance mss. Buys 2-3 mss/year. Query. Pays $200.
Poetry: Free verse, haiku, light verse, traditional. Buys 7-8/issue. Limit submissions to batches of 5-6. Length: 4-16 lines. Pays $3-5.

CARTE BLANCHE, 3460 Wilshire Blvd., Los Angeles CA 90010. (213)480-3328. Editor: Margaret M. Volpe. 75% freelance written. For affluent professional people and their families;

highly educated, well-read, well-traveled; have much leisure time; interested in fine food and drink. Bimonthly magazine; 72-84 pages. Estab. 1964. Circ. 700,000. Pays on acceptance. Buys one-time reproduction rights. Submit seasonal/holiday material 5-6 months in advance. Photocopied submissions OK. SASE. Reports in 4 weeks. Sample copy and writer's guidelines for SASE.
Nonfiction: "We publish articles relating to our travel, dining and entertaining format. Photos are very important. Food stories should have expository text, recipes and photos. Some articles on crafts, hobbies, sports, art, or personality profiles (no film stars). We occasionally give assignments." Buys 12-20 mss/year. Query or submit complete ms. Length: 2,000-3,000 words. Pays $300-400.
Photos: Purchased with or without accompanying ms. Captions preferred. Send list of stock photos. Uses any size b&w prints or color transparencies from 35mm and larger.

CHANGING TIMES, The Kiplinger Service for Families, 1729 H St., N.W., Washington DC 20006. Editor: Sidney Sulkin. For general, adult audience interested in personal finance, family money management and personal advancement. Estab. 1947. Monthly. Circ. 1,500,000. Buys all rights. Pays on acceptance. Reports in 30 days. SASE.
Items: "Original topical quips and epigrams for our monthly humor feature, 'Notes on These Changing Times.' Almost all other material is staff-written." Pays $10.

COMMENTARY, 165 East 56th St., New York NY 10022. Editor: Norman Podhoretz. Monthly magazine, 96 pages. Estab. 1945. Circ. 60,000. Buys all rights. "All of our material is done freelance, though much of it is commissioned." Payment on publication. Query first, or submit complete ms. Reports in 4 weeks. SASE.
Nonfiction and Fiction: Nonfiction Editor: Brenda Brown. Fiction Editor: Marion Magid. Thoughtful essays on political, social, theological, and cultural themes; general, as well as with special Jewish content. Informational, historical, and think articles. Length: 3,000 to 7,000 words. Pays approximately $30 a page. Uses some mainstream fiction. Length: flexible.

EASY TIMES MAGAZINE, Fantasma Productions of Florida, Inc., 1675 Palm Beach Lakes Blvd., Suite 902, Forum III, West Palm Beach FL 33401. (305)686-6387. Editor: M.M. McClung. 30% freelance written. Emphasizes general interest features for a young adult readership interested in music, sports, health, travel and clothes. Monthly magazine; 40 pages. Estab. April 1974. Circ. 62,500. Pays on publication. Buys simultaneous and second serial (reprint) rights. Phone queries OK. Submit seasonal/holiday material 2 months in advance of issue date. Simultaneous, photocopied and previously published submissions OK. SASE. Reports in 6 weeks. Free sample copy and writer's guidelines.
Nonfiction: How-to (look better, feel better, make money, entertain, build something cheaply, or attain credit); general interest (all phases of music, sports, health, food, fashion, etc.); humor (we are interested in starting a humor column); interview or profile (with any big-name starts in the entertainment field using a question and answer or bio format); photo feature (on concerts, the outdoors, name stars, sports); and travel (focus on Florida, Key West, Bahamas, low cost travel ideas). Buys 36 mss/year. Query or submit complete ms. Length: 400-1,000 words. Pays $25-40.
Photos: "Each feature is illustrated in some way. Sending photos along makes our job easier." Submit photo material with accompanying ms. Pays $5-10 for 5x7 b&w prints. Captions preferred. Buys all rights, but may reassign following publication.
Columns/Departments: "We do not accept freelance for our standard columns, but we are interested in starting a humor column open to freelancers." Query or submit complete ms. Length: 500-850 words. Pays $25-30. Open to suggestions for new columns/departments.
How To Break In: "Keep the writing concise and light, with a strong identification for the young adult. Four letter words are cool, but don't over-do. Keep an 'up' attitude and entertain as well as inform. Articles that contain personal experiences as well as informative reading are great. Don't have to overdose with factual writing, but give the readers enough meat to chew on."

FORD TIMES, Ford Motor Company, Room 332, 3000 Schaefer Rd., Dearborn MI 48121. Managing Editor: Richard L. Routh. 85% freelance written. "Family magazine designed to attract all ages." Monthly. Circulation: 1,700,000. Buys first serial rights. Buys about 150 mss/year. Pays on acceptance. Free sample copy and writer's guidelines. Query first. Submit seasonal material 6 months in advance. Reports in 2 to 4 weeks. SASE.
Nonfiction and Photos: "Almost anything relating to American life, both past and present, that is in good taste and leans toward the cheerful and optimistic. Topics include motor travel, sports, fashion, where and what to eat along the road, vacation ideas, reminiscences, big cities and

small towns, the arts, Americana, and the outdoors. We strive to be colorful, lively and engaging. We are particularly attracted to material that presents humor, anecdote, first-person discourse, intelligent observation and, in all cases, superior writing. We are committed to originality and try as much as possible to avoid subjects that have appeared in other publications and in our own. However, a fresh point of view and/or exceptional literary ability with respect to an old subject will be welcomed." Length: 1,500 words maximum. Pays $250 and up for full-length articles. "We prefer to have a suitable ms in hand before considering photos or illustration. Speculative submission of good quality color transparencies and b&w photos is welcomed. We want bright, lively photos showing people. Writers may send snapshots, postcards, brochures, etc., if they wish."

GOOD READING, Henry F. Henrichs Publications, Litchfield IL 62056. (217)324-2322. Editor: Mrs. Monta Crane. 60% freelance written. "A magazine with the human touch." Monthly. Not copyrighted. Estab. 1964. Circ. 75,000. Buys 50-75 mss/year. Pays on acceptance. Sample copy 50¢; free writer's guidelines. Submit seasonal/holiday material 4 months in advance. Reports in 1 to 2 months. SASE.
Nonfiction and Photos: Articles on "current or factual subjects, and articles based on incidents related to business, personal experiences that reveal the elements of success in human relationships. All material must be clean and wholesome and acceptable to all ages. Material should be uplifting, and non-controversial." Length: 500-1,000 words. Pays $20-60. B&w glossies purchased with mss occasionally.

GREEN'S MAGAZINE, Box 313, Detroit MI 48231. Editor: David Green. 100% freelance written. For a general audience; the more sentient, literate levels. Quarterly magazine; 100 pages. Estab. 1972. Circ. 1,000. Buys first North American serial rights. Buys 48 mss a year. Payment on publication. Sample copy for $1.50. Will not consider photocopied or simultaneous submissions. Reports in 6 weeks. Submit complete ms. SASE.
Fiction: Mainstream, suspense, humorous, must have a realistic range in conflict areas. Slice of life situations enriched with deep characterization and more than superficial conflict. Avoid housewife, student, businessmen problems that remain "so what" in solution. Open on themes as long as writers recognize the family nature of the magazine. Length: 1,000 to 3,000 words. Pays $15 to $25.
Poetry: Haiku, blank verse, free verse. Length: about 36 to 40 lines. Pays $2 to $3.

GRIT, 208 W. Third St., Williamsport PA 17701. (717)326-1771. Editor: Terry L. Ziegler. For "residents of all ages in small-town and rural America who are interested in people and generally take a positive view of life." Tabloid newspaper; 44 pages. Estab. 1882. Weekly. Circ. 1,300,000. Buys first serial rights and second serial (reprint) rights. Buys 800 to 1,000 mss/year. Pays on acceptance for freelance material; on publication for reader participation feature material. Free sample copy and writer's guidelines. No photocopied or simultaneous submissions. Reports in 2 to 4 weeks. Query first or submit complete ms. SASE.
Nonfiction and Photos: Feature Editor: Kenneth D. Loss. Wants mss demonstrating the power of free enterprise as a desirable and vital aspect of life in the U.S., with emphasis on specific examples. Mss should show "value of honesty, thrift, hard work and generosity as keys to better living." Also wants patriotic stories which have an immediate tie-in with a patriotic holiday. Avoid sermonizing, but mss should be interesting and accurate so that readers may be inspired. Also mss about men, women and teenagers involved in unusual occupations, hobbies or significant personal adventures. "*Grit* seeks to present the positive aspect of things. When others point out the impending darkness, *Grit* emphasizes the beautiful sunset or approaching rest before another day." Does not want to see mss promoting alcoholic beverages, immoral behavior, narcotics, unpatriotic acts. Wants good Easter, Christmas and holiday material. Mss should show some person or group involved in an unusual and/or uplifting way. "We lean heavily toward human interest, whatever the subject. Writing should be simple and down-to-earth." Length: 300 to 800 words. Pays 5¢ a word for first or exclusive rights; 2¢ a word for second or reprint rights. Photos purchased with or without ms. Captions required. Size: prefers 8x10 for b&w, but will consider 5x7; color transparencies or slides only. Pays $10 for b&w photos accompanying ms; for accompanying color transparencies, $35 each.
Fiction and Poetry: Department Editor: Mrs. Fran Noll. Buys only reprint material for fiction. Western, romance. Pays 2¢ per word. Buys traditional forms of poetry and light verse. Length: 32 lines maximum. Pays $4 for 4 lines and under, plus 25¢ per line for each additional line.

HARPER'S MAGAZINE, 2 Park Ave., Room 1809, New York NY 10016. (212)481-5220. Editor: Lewis H. Lapham. 90% freelance written. For well-educated, socially concerned,

widely read men and women and college students who are active in community and political affairs. Monthly. Circ. 325,000. Rights purchased vary with author and material. Buys approximately 12 non-agented, non-commissioned, non-book-excerpted mss a year. Pays on acceptance. Sample copy $1.25. Will look only at material submitted through agents or which is the result of a query. Reports in 2 to 3 weeks. SASE.
Nonfiction: "For writers working with agents or who will query first only, our requirements are: Public affairs, literary, international and local reporting, humor." Also buys exposes, think pieces, and profiles. Length: 1,500 to 6,000 words. Pays $200 to $1,500.
Photos: Department Editor: Sheila Berger. Occasionally purchased with mss. Others by assignment. Pays $35 to $400.
Fiction: On contemporary life and its problems. Also buys humorous stories. Length: 1,000 to 5,000 words. Pays $300 to $500.
Poetry: 60 lines and under. Pays $2 per line.

MACLEAN'S, 481 University Ave., Toronto, Ont., Canada M5W 1A7. (416)595-1811. Editor: Peter C. Newman. For general interest audience. Biweekly. Newsmagazine; 90 pages. Circ. 750,000. Buys first North American serial rights. Pays on acceptance. Will send free sample copy to writer on request. Will consider photocopied submissions; no simultaneous submissions. "Query with 200- or 300-word outline before sending any material." Reports in 2 weeks. Enclose S.A.E. and International Reply Coupons.
Nonfiction: "We have the conventional newsmagazine departments (science, medicine, law, art, music, etc.) with slightly more featurish treatment than other newsmagazines. We usually have 3 middle-of-the-book features on politics, entertainment, etc. We buy short features, but book reviews and columns are done by staffers or retainer freelancers. Freelancers should write for a free copy of the magazine and study the approach." Length ranges from 400 to 3,500 words. Pays $300 to $1,000.

MIDNIGHT/GLOBE, 200 Railroad Ave., Greenwich CT 06830. Editor: Selig Adler. "For everyone in the family over 18. *Midnight/Globe* readers are the same people you meet on the street, and in supermarket lines, the average hard-working American who finds easily digestible tabloid news the best way for his information." Weekly national tabloid newspaper. Estab. 1954. Circ. 2,000,000. Buys more than 1,000 mss/year. Pays on acceptance. "Writers should advise us of specializations on any submission so that we may contact them if special issue or feature is planned." Submit special material 2 months in advance. Reports within 1 week. SASE.
Nonfiction, Photos, and Fillers: Photo Department Editor: Alistair Duncan. "Sex and violence are taboo. We want upbeat human interest material, of interest to a national audience. Stories where fate plays a major role are always good. Always interested in features on well-known personalities, offbeat people, places, events and activities. Current issue is best guide. Stories are best that don't grow stale quickly. No padding. Grab the reader in the first line or paragraph. Tell the story, make the point and get out with a nice, snappy ending. Don't dazzle us with your footwork. Just tell the story. And we are always happy to bring a new freelancer or stringer into our fold. No cliques here. If you've got talent, and the right material—you're in. Remember—we are serving a family audience. All material must be in good taste. If it's been written up in a major newspaper or magazine, we already know about it." Buys informational, how-to, personal experience, interview, profile, inspirational, humor, historical, expose, nostalgia, photo, spot news, and new product articles. Length: 1,000 words maximum; average 500 to 800 words. Pays $50 to $300. Photos are purchased with or without ms, and on assignment. Captions are required. Pays $25 minimum for 8x10 b&w glossies. "Competitive payment on exclusives." Buys puzzles, quizzes, and short humor.
How To Break In: "*Midnight/Globe* is constantly looking for human interest subject material from throughout the United States and much of the best comes from America's smaller cities and villages, not necessarily from the larger urban areas. Therefore, we are likely to be more responsive to an article from a new writer than many other publications. This, of course, is equally true of photographs. A major mistake of new writers is that they have failed to determine the type and style of our content and in the ever-changing tabloid field, this is a most important consideration. It is also wise to keep in mind that what is of interest to you or to the people in your area may not be of equal interest to a national readership. Determine the limits of interest first. And, importantly, the material you send us must be such that it won't be 'stale' by the time it reaches the readers."

MODERN PEOPLE, Aladdin Dist., 11058 W. Addison St., Franklin Park IL 60131. Editor-in-Chief: Ray Bachar. Emphasizes celebrities, consumer affairs and offbeat stories for white lower

and middle class, blue collar, non-college educated people with religious, patriotic, conservative background. Weekly tabloid; 32 pages. Estab. 1969. Circ. 200,000. Pays on acceptance. Buys all rights. Submit seasonal/holiday material 6-8 weeks in advance. Photocopied submissions OK. SASE. Reports in 2 weeks. Free sample copy and writer's guidelines.
Nonfiction: Bernard Whalen, Nonfiction Editor. Expose (consumer ripoffs); how-to (get rich, save money, be healthy, etc.); interviews (celebrities); photo feature (offbeat subjects). Buys 10 mss/issue. Query. Length: 150-500 words. Pays $10-150.
Photos: Bernard Whalen, Photos Editor. Photos purchased with accompanying ms. Pays $5-15 for 8½x11 b&w glossies; $25-200 for 8x5.5 pica color slides or transparencies. Total purchase price for ms includes payment for photos. Model release required.
Columns/Departments: Bernard Whalen, Columns/Departments Editor. Psychic Prediction; TV Soap Operas, Celebrity Gossip and Dieting. Buys 2 mss/issue. Query. Length: 15-300 words. Pays $25-50. Open to suggestions for new columns/departments.

NATIONAL ENQUIRER, Lantana FL 33464. Editor: Iain Calder. Correspondence to "Freelance Editor." Weekly tabloid. Circ. 6,000,000. Pays on publication. Buys first North American serial rights. Query. "Story idea must be accepted first. No longer accepting unsolicited mss and all spec material will be returned unread." SASE.
Nonfiction and Photos: Wants story ideas on any subject appealing to a mass audience. Requires fresh slant on topical news stories, waste of taxpayers' money by government, the entire field of the occult, how-to articles, rags to riches success stories, medical firsts, scientific breakthroughs, human drama, adventure, personality profiles. "The best way to understanding our requirements is to study the paper." Pays $325-500 for most completed features, plus separate lead fees; more with photos. "Payments in excess of $1000 are not unusual; will pay more for really top, circulation-boosting blockbusters." Uses single or series b&w photos that must be attention-grabbing. Wide range; anything from animal photos to great action photos. "We'll bid against any other magazine for once-in-lifetime pictures."

NATIONAL GEOGRAPHIC MAGAZINE, 17th and M Streets, N.W., Washington DC 20036. Senior Assistant Editor: James Cerruti. Editor: Gilbert M. Grosvenor. For members of the National Geographic Society. Monthly. Circ. 9,325,000. Buys first publication rights with warranty to use the material in National Geographic Society copyrighted publications. Buys 40-50 mss/year. Pays on acceptance. Sample copy $1.25. Returns rejected material and acknowledges acceptance of material in 2 to 4 weeks. Query first. Writers should study several recent issues of *National Geographic* and send for leaflets "Writing for National Geographic" and "National Geographic Photo Requirements." SASE.
Nonfiction and Photos: "First-person narratives, making it easy for the reader to share the author's experience and observations. Writing should include plenty of human-interest incident, authentic direct quotation, and a bit of humor where appropriate. Accuracy is fundamental. Contemporary problems such as those of pollution and ecology are treated on a factual basis. The magazine is especially seeking short American place pieces with a strong regional 'people' flavor. The use of many clear, sharp color photographs in all articles makes lengthy word descriptions unnecessary. Potential writers need not be concerned about submitting photos. These are handled by professional photographers. Historical background, in most cases, should be kept to the minimum needed for understanding the present." Length: 8,000 words maximum for major articles. Shorts of 2,000 to 4,000 words "are always needed." Pays from $1,500 to $4,000 (and, in some cases, more) for acceptable articles; from $250 per page for color transparencies. A paragraph on an article idea should be submitted to James Cerruti, Senior Assistant Editor. If appealing, he will ask for a one- or two-page outline for further consideration. Photographers are advised to submit a generous selection of photographs with brief, descriptive captions to Mary G. Smith, Assistant Editor.
How To Break In: "Send 4 or 5 one-paragraph ideas. If any are promising, author will be asked for a one- to two-page outline. Read the latest issues to see what we want."

NATIONAL INFORMER, Aladdin Distributing Corp., 11058 W. Addison St., Franklin Park IL 60131. Editor-in-Chief: Jack Steele. Managing Editor: Norton Newcomb. "Our audience is a sophisticated group of adults in the 25-75 age group that enjoys sex-oriented material." Weekly tabloid; 32 pages. Estab. 1964. Circ. 500,000. Pays on acceptance. Buys all rights. Phone queries OK. Submit seasonal/holiday material 2 months in advance. Simultaneous and previously published submissions OK. SASE. Reports in 2 weeks. Sample copy $1; free writer's guidelines.
Nonfiction: "Adult expose (this is our forte!), humor, and sex-oriented material and subject matter." Buys 500 mss/year. Query. Length: 800-1,200 words. Pays $25-75.

Photos: Pays $5-25 for 8x10 b&w photos. Query. Model release required.

NATIONAL INSIDER, 2713 N. Pulaski Rd., Chicago IL 60639. Editor: Robert J. Sorren. For a general audience. Weekly newspaper; 20 pages. Estab. 1962. Rights purchased vary with author and material. Usually buys all rights but will sometimes reassign rights to author after publication. Buys 500 to 600 mss a year. Payment on acceptance. Will send free sample copy to writer on request. Write for copy of guidelines for writers. Will not consider photocopied or simultaneous submissions. Reports in 2 weeks. Query first. Enclose SASE.
Nonfiction and Photos: "We are looking for a variety of human interest stories. These generally should be upbeat human interest stories about persons who have overcome handicaps, or beat City Hall, or made millions from a small investment, etc. We're also interested in articles on wasteful government practices, unexplained phenomena, murder mysteries. (The emphasis here must be on the mystery surrounding the crime and good detective work. No gore photos or stories with the emphasis on sex crimes. No fictionalized accounts.) In the past we have published articles relating to sex and sex scandals. We are no longer interested in such material." B&w photos (8x10) purchased with or without mss, or on assignment. Captions required. Payment varies.

NEW TIMES, 1 Park Ave., New York NY 10016. (212)889-6900. Editor: Jonathan Z. Larsen. Executive Editor: Jane Amsterdam. 70% freelance written. General interest news magazine; average reader age 31. Biweekly magazine; 76 pages. Estab. 1973. Circ. 350,000. Pays on acceptance. Buys second serial and first North American serial rights. Submit seasonal/holiday material 3 months in advance of issue date. SASE. Reports in 3-4 weeks.
Nonfiction: Exposé (any area); general interest; humor (hopefully with a political edge); interview (rarely); new product (possible); nostalgia (rarely); photo feature (seldom) and profile (very interested). Buys 4 mss/issue. Query. Length: 2,500-5,000 words. pays $500-750.
Photos: State availability of photos with query. Buys one-time rights. Model release required.
Column/Departments: "We publish any number of 1,000 word one-sheet columns on a variety of news topics." Buys 3-4 mss/issue. Query. Length: 850-1,500 words. Pays $250/page; $300/1½ page.

THE NEW YORKER, 25 W. 43rd St., New York NY 10036. Editor: William Shawn. Weekly. Reports in two weeks. Pays on acceptance. SASE.
Nonfiction, Fiction, and Fillers: Single factual pieces run from 3,000 to 10,000 words. Long fact pieces are usually staff-written. So is "Talk of the Town," although ideas for this department are bought. Pays good rates. Uses fiction, both serious and light, from 1,000 to 6,000 words. About 90 percent of the fillers come from contributors with or without taglines (extra pay if the tagline is used).

PEOPLE ON PARADE, Meridian Publishing Co., 1720 Washington Blvd., Box 2315, Ogden UT 84404. (801)394-9446. Senior Editor: Dick Harris. For employees, stockholders, customers and clients of 2,000 business and industrial firms. Monthly magazine; 28 pages. Estab. 1976. Circ. 450,000. Pays on acceptance. Buys one-time rights. Submit seasonal/holiday material 9 months in advance. SASE. Reports in 3-4 weeks. Sample copy 35¢; free writer's guidelines.
Nonfiction: Valerie Sagers, articles editor. "*POP* focuses on people—active, interesting, exciting, busy people; personality profiles on people succeeding, achieving, doing things." Humorous, informational, inspirational. "We want material from all regions of the country and about all types of people. Big name writers are fine, but we know there is a lot of talent among the little knowns, and we encourage them to submit their ideas. We read everything that comes in, but writers will save their time and ours by writing a good, tantalizing query." Buys 10 mss/issue. Length: 400-1,000 words. Pays 10¢/word.
Photos: Purchased with or without mss or on assignment. Captions required. Pays $20/8x10 b&w glossy; $25 for 35mm, 2¼x2¼ or 4x5 color used inside; up to $400 for cover color. Model release required.
Fillers: "We welcome fillers and shorts with a humorous touch, featuring interesting, successful, busy people." Buys 1-2/issue. Send fillers in. Length: 200-300 words. Pays 10¢/word.
How To Break In: "*POP* has a strong family-community orientation. Without being maudlin or pious, we cherish the work ethic, personal courage and dedication to the American dream. So we look for material that reflects positively on the man/woman who succeeds through diligence, resourcefulness, and imagination, or finds fulfillment through service to community or country. He/she may be a captain of industry, a salvage yard operator, country school teacher, medical technician, or bus driver. Tell us about people whose lives and accomplishments inspire and encourage others. We like humor and nostalgia. We want tight writing, with lively quotes and

anecdotes. Pictures should be fresh, sharp, unposed, showing action, involvement."

PEOPLE WEEKLY, Time Inc., Time & Life Bldg., Rockefeller Center, New York NY 10020. Editor: Richard B. Stolley. For a general audience. Estab. 1974. Weekly. Circ. 2,000,000. Rights purchased vary with author and material. Usually buys first North American serial rights with right to syndicate, splitting net proceeds with author 50/50. Payment on acceptance. Query first. SASE.
Nonfiction and Photos: "Nearly all material is staff produced, but we do consider specific story suggestions (not manuscripts) from freelancers. Every story must have a strong personality focus. Payment varies from $100 for Lookouts to $1,000 for Bios. Photo payment is $200/page for b&w, minimum $75. Prefer minimum size of 8x10 from original negatives."

PERSONALITIES IN REVIEW, 6125 E. Indian School Rd., Scottsdale AZ 85251. (602)946-8010. Editor-in-Chief: Justin Case. 70-80% freelance written. For a general audience; "but central thrust is the emphasis on interesting stories about facinating people." Monthly magazine; 24 pages. Estab. March 1978. Pays on acceptance. Buys all rights, but may reassign following publication. Phone queries OK. Submit seasonal/holiday material 4-5 months in advance of issue date. Simultaneous, photocopied and previously published submissions OK. SASE. Reports in 6 weeks. Free sample copy and writer's guidelines; mention *Writer's Market* in request.
Nonfiction: "We are especially interested in writers who may have on hand material about someone who has made a success in an unusual business or overcome a physical handicap or other adversity, and survived beautifully. We have a strong proclivity for the Horatio Algier flavor. This publication is upbeat, reflecting some of the best qualities of our capitalistic system . . . the fulfillment of the American Dream." No environmental, political, religious, technical, controversial, or erotic material. "These stories will be seen in various company publications, published for our clients all over the US." Buys 100 mss/year. Submit complete ms. Length: 500-3,000 words. Pays 10¢/word.
Photos: Submit photos with ms. Pays $10-25 for 5x7 or 8x10 b&w glossy photos; $40-100 for 35mm or larger color transparencies.

QUEST/78, 1133 Avenue of the Americas, New York NY 10036. Editor-in-Chief: Robert Shnayerson. Managing Editor: Molly McKaughan. Emphasizes "the pursuit of human excellence for an educated, intelligent audience, interested in the positive side of things; in human potential, in sciences, the arts, good writing, design and photography. We have no connection with the feminist magazine, *Quest*." Bimonthly magazine; 112 pages. Estab. 1977. Circ. 350,000. Pays on acceptance. Buys all rights. Submit seasonal/holiday material 4 months in advance. Photocopied submissions OK. Free writer's guidelines.
Nonfiction: Margaret Staets, articles editor. Humor (short pieces deflating or satirizing world views or "good" things), interviews (with fascinating individuals in government, the arts, business, science), personal experience (adventures, unusual experiences), profiles (of risk taking people, great craftsmen, adventurers), reviews (books, products, thoughts, places, etc.), and technical (new inventions, applications of science). Query. Length: 500-5,000 words. Pays $600-2,500.
Columns/Departments: Book Reviews (William Plummer, editor); Potentials (Tony Jones, editor). Also reviews of all other cultural, political, art, or commercial events. Buys 100 mss/year. Length: 500-2,000 words. Pays $100-1,000.
Fiction: Bill Plummer, fiction editor. Adventure, fantasy, humorous, mainstream, science fiction. Buys 6 mss/year. Query. Length: 500-6,000 words. Pays$600-2,000.
Poetry: Luke Matthiessen, poetry editor. Buys 6-12 poems/year. Query. Limit submissions to batches of 5. Length: 5-50 lines. Pays $5/line.

READER'S DIGEST, Pleasantville NY 10570. Monthly. Buys all rights to original mss. "Items intended for a particular feature should be directed to the editor in charge of that feature, although the contribution may later be referred to another section of the magazine as seeming more suitable. Manuscripts cannot be acknowledged, and will be returned —usually within eight or ten weeks —only when return postage accompanies them."
Nonfiction: "*Reader's Digest* is interested in receiving First Person and Premonition articles. An article for the First Person series must be a previously unpublished narrative of an unusual personal experience. It may be dramatic, inspirational or humorous, but it must have a quality of narrative and interest comparable to stories published in this series. An article for the Premonition series must be a previously unpublished narrative of an unusual psychic experience, verifiable through witnesses or appropriate documentation. Contributions for either series must

be typewritten, double-spaced, no longer than 2,500 words, and accompanied by SASE. Pays $3,000 on acceptance. Address: Premonition or First Person Editor. Base rate for *general* articles is $2,400 for first sale."

Fillers: "Life in These United States contributions must be true, unpublished stories from one's own experience, revelatory of adult human nature, and providing appealing or humorous sidelights on the American scene. Maximum length: 300 words. Address Life in U.S. Editor. Payment rate on publication: $300. True and unpublished stories are also solicited for Humor in Uniform, Campus Comedy and All in a Day's Work. Maximum length: 300 words. Payment rate on publication: $300. Address Humor in Uniform, Campus Comedy or All in a Day's Work Editor. Toward More Picturesque Speech: The first contributor of each item used in this department is paid $35. Contributions should be dated, and the sources must be given. Address: Picturesque Speech Editor. For items used in Laughter, the Best Medicine, Personal Glimpses, Quotable Quotes, and elsewhere in the magazine, payment is made at the following rates: to the *first* contributor of each item from a published source, $35. For original material, $15 per *Digest* two-column line, with a minimum payment of $35. Address: Excerpts Editor."

READERS NUTSHELL, Box 9820, Fort Worth TX 76107. Editor: Elinor Musick Hubbard. 75% freelance written. Emphasizes safety and insurance. Bimonthly magazine; 16 pages. Pays on acceptance. Buys first North American serial rights. Submit seasonal/holiday material 8 months in advance of issue date. Simultaneous and previously published submissions OK. SASE. Reports in 1 month.

Nonfiction: General interest; how-to; and humor. No articles on drinking and sex. Buys 3 mss/issue. Submit complete ms. Length: 500-1,000 words. Pays 5¢/accepted word.

Photos: State availability of photos with ms or submit with accompanying ms. Pays $5 for 5x7 b&w glossy prints. Model release required.

THE SAMPLE CASE, Box 159019, 632 N. Park St., Columbus OH 43215. (614)228-3276. Editor: James R. Eggert. For members of the United Commercial Travelers of America, located throughout the U.S. and Canada; 18 years of age and older, with a wide range of interests, educations, and occupations. Estab. 1891. Quarterly. Rights purchased vary with author and material. Buys all rights, but will reassign rights to author after publication; buys first North American serial rights; first serial rights; second serial (reprint) rights; simultaneous rights. Buys 5-10 mss/year. Payment on publication. Free sample copy and writer's guidelines. Will consider photocopied submissions. Submit seasonal material 6 months in advance. Reports in 4 months. SASE.

Nonfiction and Photos: "Especially interested in general interest nonfiction. We pay special attention to articles about mental retardation, youth, safety, and cancer." Informational, personal experience, interview, some humor. Length: 500 to 2,000 words. Pays 1½¢ per word. Additional payment for good quality color and b&w glossies purchased with mss. Captions required.

THE SATURDAY EVENING POST, The Curtis Publishing Co., 1100 Waterway Blvd., Indianapolis, IN 46202. (317)634-1100. Editor-in-Chief: Cory Ser Vaas M.D. Managing Editor: Starkey Flythe, Jr. For general readership. Magazine, published 9 times a year; 144 pages. Estab. 1728. Circ. 460,000. Pays on publication. Buys all rights. Phone queries OK. Simultaneous and photocopied submissions OK. SASE. Reports in 1 month. Sample copy $1; free writer's guidelines for SASE.

Nonfiction: Ms. Betty White, Nonfiction Editor. Historical (especially nostalgia and Americana); how-to (health, general living); humor; informational (people; celebrities and ordinary but interesting personalities); inspirational (for religious columns); interview; nostalgia; personal experience (especially travel, yachting, etc.); personal opinion; photo feature; profile (especially government figures); travel and small magazine "pick-ups." Buys 5 mss/issue. Query. Length: 1,500-3,000 words. Pays $100-1,000.

Photos: Janet Kioski, photo editor. Photos purchased with or without accompanying ms. Pays $25 minimum for b&w photos; $50 minimum for color photos. Total purchase price for ms includes payment for photos. Model release required.

Columns/Departments: Editorials ($100 each); Food ($150-450); Medical Mailbox ($50-250); Religion Column ($100-250) and Travel ($150-450).

Fiction: Sam Walton, fiction editor. Adventure; fantasy; humorous; mainstream; mystery; romance; science fiction; suspense; western and condensed novels. Buys 5 mss/issue. Query. Length: 1,500-3,000 words. Pays $150-750.

Poetry: John D. Craton, poetry editor. Free verse, light verse and traditional. Buys 1 poem/issue. Pays $15-150.

Fillers: Ms. Louise Fortson, fillers editor. Jokes, gags, anecdotes, cartoons, postscripts and short humor. Buys 1 filler/issue. Length: 500-1,000 words. Pays $10-100.
How To Break In: "Interested in topics relating to science, government, the arts, personalities with inspirational careers and humor. We read unsolicited material."

SATURDAY NIGHT, New Leaf Publications, Ltd., 69 Front St., E., Toronto, Ontario, Canada M5E 1R3. (416)362-5907. Editor: Robert Fulford. Managing Editor: Bernadette Sulgit. 70% freelance written. Emphasizes "politics, business/economics, lifestyles and literary topics for readers ranging in age between 18-49, heavier on the young side; well-educated, with a high percentage in managerial/professional occupations." Published 10 times/year. Magazine; 88 pages. Estab. 1887. Circ. 100,000. Pays on acceptance. Buys first North American serial rights in French and English. Phone queries OK., Submit seasonal/holiday material 4 months in advance of issue date. Photocopied submissions OK. SASE. Reports in 4 weeks. Sample copy $1.25.
Nonfiction: General interest (Canadian government, business, the arts, lifestyles); interview (in-depth profiles of interest to Canadians); and profile. Buys 4 mss/issue. Query. Length: 1,500-3,500 words. Pays $400-1,000.
Fiction: "High quality writing by new or established writers. No restrictions on theme but should appeal to a fairly sophisticated audience who do not read literary journals. Buys 10 mss/year. Submit complete ms. Length: 2,500-4,000 words. Pays $1,000 maximum.

SATURDAY REVIEW, 1290 Ave. of the Americas, New York NY 10019. Editor: Carl Tucker. Managing Editor: Peter Young. "A review of ideas, the arts, and the human condition for above average educated audience. Biweekly magazine; 64 pages. Estab. 1924. Circ. 550,000. Usually pays on publication. Buys first North American serial rights. Photocopied submissions OK. SASE. Reports in 3-4 weeks. Free writer's guidelines.
Nonfiction: Expose (government, education, science); informational (analytical pieces on national or international affairs, sciences, education, and the arts); interview; and profile. Buys 100 mss/year. Query. Length: 2,500 words maximum. Pays $200/page.

SIGNATURE—The Diners' Club Magazine, 260 Madison Ave., New York NY 10016. Managing Editor: Ernest Baxter. For Diners' Club members—"businessmen, urban, affluent, traveled, and young." Monthly. Circ. 800,000. Buys first rights. Buys approximately 75 mss/year. Pays on acceptance. Write for copy of guidelines for writers. Submit seasonal material, including seasonal sports subjects, at least 3 months in advance. Returns rejected material in 2 weeks. Query. SASE.
Nonfiction: "Articles aimed at the immediate areas of interest of our readers—in travel, social issues, personalities, sports, entertainment, food and drink, business, humor. *Signature* runs 5 to 8 nonfiction articles an issue, all by freelancers." Subjects covered in past issues of *Signature* include profiles of Norman Lear and Pete Rose. Articles on secretarial crisis, Wall Street reform, British TV invasion, natural foods dispute and small town U.S.A. restoration. Travel pieces require a *raison d'etre,* a well-defined approach and angle. Eschew destination or traditional travel piece. Feature articles run 2,500 words maximum. Also buy shorter 1,500-word pieces which are a slice of some travel experience and usually written in very personal style. These pay $450 and up. It's important that writer be familiar with our magazine."
Photos: "Picture stories or support are usually assigned to photographers we have worked with in the past. We rarely ask a writer to handle the photography also. But if he has photos of his subject, we will consider them for use." Pays $50 minimum per photo; $200/page.

THE STAR, 730 3rd Ave., New York NY 10017. (212)557-9200. Editor: Ian Rae. Managing Editor: Mike Nevard. 25-40% freelance written. "For every family; all the family—kids, teenagers, young parents and grandparents." Weekly tabloid; 48 pages. Estab. February 1974. Circ. 3,000,000. Pays on publication. Buys all rights, but may reassign following publication, second serial (reprint) rights, and first North American serial rights. Submit seasonal/holiday material 2-3 months in advance of issue date. SASE. Free sample copy and writer's guidelines.
Nonfiction: Peter Faris, chief of staff. Exposé (government waste, consumer, education, anything affecting family) general interest (human interest, consumerism, informational, family and women's interest); how-to (psychological, practical on all subjects affecting readers); inspirational (off-beat personal experience, religious, and psychic); interview (celebrity or human interest); new product (but not from commercial interests); personal experience (adventure, human drama, etc.); photo feature; profile (celebrity or national figure); travel (how to cheaply); health; medical; and diet. Buys 50 mss/issue. Query or submit complete ms. Length: 500-2,000 words. Pays $50-1,000.

Photos: State availability of photos with query or ms. Pays $25-100 for 8x10 b&w glossy prints, contact sheets or negatives; $125-1,000 for 35mm color transparencies. Captions required. Buys one-time, all rights, and all rights, but may reassign following publication.
Fillers: Statistical-informational. Length: 50-400 words. Pays $15-40.

SUNSHINE MAGAZINE, Henry F. Henrichs Publications, Litchfield IL 62056. (217)324-3425. Editor: Mrs. Monta Crane. 40% freelance written. For general audience of all ages. Monthly magazine. Estab. 1924. Circ. 225,000. Not copyrighted. Buys 75 to 100 mss per year. Payment on acceptance. Sample copy 50¢; free writer's guidelines. Submit seasonal material 6 months in advance. Reports in 1-3 months. SASE.
Nonfiction: "We accept some short articles, but they must be especially interesting or inspirational. *Sunshine Magazine* is not a religious publication, and purely religious material is rarely used. We desire carefully written features about persons or events that have real human interest—that give a 'lift'." Length: 250 to 1,200 words. Pays $20-100.
Fiction: "Stories must be wholesome, well-written, with clearly defined plots. There should be a purpose for each story, but any moral or lesson should be well-concealed in the plot development. Avoid trite plots that do not hold the reader's interest. A surprising climax is most desirable. Material should be uplifting, and non-controversial." Length: 400 to 1,300 words. Pays $10-40.

SWINGERS WORLD, 8060 Melrose Ave., Los Angeles CA 90046. Editors: Norman Scott, Michael Carey. 90% freelance written. For "swingers and would-be swingers." Estab. 1972. Subject matter must be "swinger oriented." Bimonthly. Buys first North American serial rights. Buys 50 mss/year. Pays on publication. Sample copy $2.75; free writer's guidelines. Reports in 3-4 weeks. Query. SASE.
Nonfiction: "Articles must be pro-swinger. Slick. We like new information on sex-oriented subjects, with an occasional allied subject acceptable. Even if it is humorous in treatment (which we do like), your research must be thorough." Length: 1,500-3,000 words. Pays $65-150.

TOWN AND COUNTRY, 717 Fifth Ave., New York NY 10022. Managing Editor: Jean Barkhorn. For upper-income Americans. Monthly. Not a large market for freelancers. Always query first. Enclose SASE.
Nonfiction: Department Editors: Richard Kagan and Frank Zachary. "We're always trying to find ideas that can be developed into good articles that will make appealing cover lines." Wants provocative and controversial pieces. Length: 1,500 to 2,000 words. Pays $300. Also buys shorter pieces for which pay varies.

WOODMEN OF THE WORLD MAGAZINE, 1700 Farnam St., Omaha NE 68102. (402)342-1890, Ext. 302. Editor: Leland A. Larson. 20% freelance written. Published by Woodmen of the World Life Insurance Society for "people of all ages in all walks of life. We have both adult and children readers from all types of American families." Estab. 1891. Monthly. Circ. 460,000. Not copyrighted. Buys 25 mss a year. Pays on acceptance. Will send a sample copy to a writer on request. Will consider photocopied and simultaneous submissions. Submit complete ms. Submit seasonal material 3 months in advance. Reports in 5 weeks. SASE.
Nonfiction: "General interest articles which appeal to the American family—travel, history, art, new products, how-to-do-it, sports, hobbies, food, home decorating, family expenses, etc. Because we are a fraternal benefit society operating under a lodge system, we often carry stories on how a number of people can enjoy social or recreational activities as a group. No special approach required. We want more 'consumer type' articles, humor, historical articles, think pieces, nostalgia, photo articles." Length: 10 to 1,800 words. Pays $10 minimum, 2½¢ a word depending on word count.
Photos: Purchased with or without mss; captions optional "but suggested." Uses 8x10 glossies, 4x5 tranparencies ("and possibly down to 35mm"). Payment "depends on use." For b&w photos, pays $25 for cover, $10 for inside. Color prices vary according to use and quality. Minimum of $25 for inside use; up to $100 for covers.
Fiction: Humorous and historical short stories. Length: 600 to 2,000 words. Pays "$10 or 2½¢ a word, depending on count."

Health Publications

Nearly every publication is a potential market for an appropriate health article, particularly the General Interest publications.

ACCENT ON LIVING, P.O. Box 700, Bloomington IL 61701. (309)378-4213. Editor: Raymond C. Cheever. For physically disabled persons and rehabilitation professionals. Quarterly magazine, 112 pages. Estab. 1956. Circ. 18,000. Buys all rights. Buys 20-40 mss/year. Payment on publication. Sample copy $1; free writer's guidelines. Will consider photocopied submissions. Will not consider simultaneous submissions. Reports in 2 weeks. SASE.

Nonfiction: Articles about seriously disabled people who have overcome great obstacles and are pursuing regular vocational goals. Home business ideas with facts and figures on how someone confined to their home can run a business and make an average income. Especially interested in new technical aids, assistive devices, devised by an individual or available commercially, such as: bathroom and toilet aids and appliances, clothes and aids for dressing and undressing, aids for eating and drinking, as would be helpful to individuals with limited physical mobility. Intelligent discussion articles concerning the public image of and acceptance or non-acceptance of the physically disabled in normal living situations. Articles reporting on lawsuits, demonstrations or protests by handicapped individuals or consumer groups to gain equal rights and opportunities. Length: 200 to 750 words. Pays $5-100.

Photos: B&w photos purchased with accompanying ms. Captions required. Pays $5 to $25.

ARISE, American Research Foundation in Special Education, 55 W. Park Ave., New Haven CT 06511. Editor: Eric Sandahl. For "all persons concerned with the welfare and advancement of the mentally and physically handicapped." Monthly magazine; 32 pages. Estab. September 1977. Pays on acceptance. Buys all rights, but may reassign following publication. Submit seasonal/holiday material 3 months in advance of issue date. Previously published submissions OK "depending on the medium in which previously published." SASE. Reports in 2 weeks. Free sample copy and writer's guidelines.

Nonfiction: Informational; inspirational (if not too 'shmaltzy'); interview; personal experience; photo feature; and profile. Buys 6-8 articles/issue. Submit complete ms. Length: 1,000 words minimum. Pays 5¢/word for up to 1,000 words; payment thereafter negotiable.

Photos: Submit photo material with accompanying ms. Pays $10-25 for 5x7 or 8x10 b&w glossy prints. Model release required.

How To Break In: "Send us a straightforward, crisp, simply written manuscript dealing with a mentally or physically handicapped person or group. Manuscripts which show concrete gains made in behalf of a handicapped person or group, or which pinpoint obstacles to such gains, will have priority."

BESTWAYS MAGAZINE, 466 Foothill Blvd., La Canada CA 91011. Editor/Publisher: Barbara Farr Bassett. 30% freelance written. Emphasizes health and nutrition. Monthly magazine; 100 pages. Estab. 1973. Circ. 125,000. Pays on publication. Buys all rights, but may reassign following publication. Submit seasonal/holiday material 6 months in advance of issue date. SASE. Reports in 6 weeks. Sample copy and writer's guidelines for SASE; mention *Writer's Market* in request.

Nonfiction: General interest (nutrition, preventive medicine, vitamins and minerals); how-to (natural cosmetics, diet and exercise); personal experience; profile (natural life style); and technical (vitamins, minerals, and nutrition). "No direct or implied endorsements of refined flours, grains or sugar, tobacco, alcohol, caffeine, drugs or patent medicines." Buys 6 mss/issue. Query. Length: 2,500 words. Pays $50.

Photos: State availability of photos with query. Pays $5 for 4x5 b&w glossy prints; $15 for 2x2 color transparencies. Captions preferred. Buys all rights, but may reassign following publications. Model release required.

Column/Departments: Well, Naturally! Buys 6 mss/year. Query. Length: 1,500 words. Pays $25.

BODY FORUM MAGAZINE, Cosvetic Laboratories, Box 80883, Atlanta GA 30305. Editor: Louis Rinald. Emphasizes "health and beauty from standpoint of nutrition for an audience mid 20's to 60's with 50% below 38. Education level high school to post grad. Average income $16,000." Monthly magazine; 42 pages. Estab. 1976. Circ. 2.2 million. Pays on acceptance. Buys all rights. Phone queries OK "from authors whose written inquiries we follow up." Submit seasonal/holiday material 3 months in advance. Photocopied and previously published submissions OK. SASE. Reports in 4 weeks. Free sample copy.

Nonfiction: Expose, how-to, informational, interview and technical. "We are trying to interpret what is happening in governmental and university research projects for the general public. We focus on anti-aging nutrition, exercise physiology, relaxation techniques and congressional legislation affecting nutrition. The aim is for each article to show the reader how this new piece of information can be used to give him a better, more healthy life style. We are particularly interested in new developments from reputable scientists. These would discuss how some new piece of research can be applied by the average person to better his life. An example would be a report by a university researcher showing that 200 mg of vitamin E per day could cut heart attacks in half." Buys 12 mss/issue. "Prefer ms, but will work with query." Length: 1,000-1,800 words. Pays $100-225; "specialist articles at negotiated rates."

THE CRITICAL LIST MAGAZINE, 32 Sullivan St., Toronto, Ontario, Canada M5T 1B9. (416)923-0716. Editor-in-Chief: Jerry Green, M.D. 80% freelance written. Readership is male and female, ages 30-35, interested in health issues and natural lifestyle. Quarterly magazine; 32 pages. Estab. 1975. Circ. 17,000. Pays on publication. Buys all rights. Phone queries OK. Submit seasonal/holiday material 2 months in advance of issue date. SASE. Reports in 12 weeks. Sample copy and writer's guidelines $2; mention *Writer's Market* in request.
Nonfiction: Exposé (documented articles exposing failings of medical profession and alternative methods of health care practice); and interview (interviews with prominent members of alternative health care movement). No personal experience, technical and personal opinions. Buys 24 mss/year. Query. Length: 1,000-3,000 words. Pays 3-20¢/word.
Photos: State availability of photos with query. Pays $5-10 for b&w contact sheet(s); and $10-15 for color contact sheet(s). Buys all rights.
Columns/Departments: Books; health news analysis; and newsbriefs. Buys 2 mss/issue. Query. Length: 300-1,000 words. Pays 3-20¢/word. Open to suggestions for new columns/departments.
Fiction: Humorous (short jokes, and cartoons). Buys 8 mss/year. Query. Pays 3-20¢/word.
Poetry: Avant-garde; free verse; haiku; light verse; traditional; and anything pertaining to health care issues. Buys 9/year. Limit submissions to batches of 10. Length: 5-25 lines. Pays 10¢/word.
Fillers: Clippings; jokes; gags; anecdotes; newsbreaks; puzzles; short humor; and "any other as long as copy is relevant." Buys 8 mss/year. Length: 5-20 lines. Pays 10¢/word.

FAMILY HEALTH, 149 Fifth Ave., New York NY 10010. Editor: Dahna Heyn. For health-minded young men and women. Magazine; 66 pages. Special issues: April and November (food and nutrition); October (baby and child care). Estab. 1969. Monthly. Circ. 1,000,000. Rights purchased vary with author and material. May buy all rights but may reassign rights to author after publication; first North American serial rights. Buys most of their articles from freelance writers. Pays within 6 weeks of acceptance. Will send sample copy to writer for $1. No photocopied or simultaneous submissions. Submit special issue material 3 months in advance. Reports in 6 weeks. Query first for most nonfiction. Submit complete ms for first-person articles. SASE.
Nonfiction: Articles on all aspects of health, both mental and physical; safety, new advances in medicine. Fresh, new approaches essential. No "all about" articles (for example, "All About Mental Health"). Informational, how-to, personal experience, interview, profile, think articles, expose; book reviews. Length: 500 to 3,000 words. Pays $350 to $750.

FOUNDATION, Baptist Hospitals Foundation, Inc., 3201 4th Ave., S., Birmingham AL 35222. (205)322-7501. Editor: Jim Reed. 10% freelance written. Emphasizes self-care and health care for general consumers. Quarterly magazine; 32 pages. Estab. 1974. Circ. 20,000. Pays on acceptance. Buys all rights. Simultaneous, photocopied and previously published submissions OK. SASE. Reports in 3 months. Free sample copy.
Nonfiction: General interest (health); how-to; and photo feature. Buys 1 mss/issue. Query. Length: open. Pays $150.

HEALTH, American Osteopathic Association. 212 E. Ohio St., Chicago IL 60611. (312)944-2713. Editor-in-Chief: George W. Northup, D.O. Executive Editor: Barbara E. Peterson. 50% freelance written. For patients in osteopathic hospitals and doctor's offices. Bimonthly magazine; 32 pages. Estab. 1956. Circ. 127,000. Pays on acceptance. Buys first North American serial rights. Submit seasonal/holiday material 3 months in advance of issue date. SASE. Reports in 6 weeks. Free sample copy and writer's guidelines.
Nonfiction: General interest (health-related); interview; and personal opinion. Buys 3 mss/issue. Submit complete ms. Length: 1,200-1,500 words. Pays 6¢/word.
Photos: Submit photo material with accompanying ms. Pays $10 for 5x7 b&w glossy prints and more for color transparencies. Captions required. Buys all rights. Model release required.
Column/Departments: To Your Good Health (hygiene, nutrition, and physical fitness); and Viewpoint (national health issues). Submit complete ms. Length: 800-1,200 words. Pays 6¢/word. Open to suggestions for new columns/departments.
Fillers: Jokes, gags, puzzles, anecdotes and cartoons. Pays $15.

HEALTHWAYS MAGAZINE, 2200 Grand Ave., Des Moines IA 50312. Editor: Maryann Smith. 75% freelance written. Emphasizes chiropractice medicine and health. Bimonthly magazine; 50 pages. Estab. 1946. Circ. 100,000. Pays on acceptance. Buys one-time rights. Submit seasonal/holiday material 6 months in advance of issue date. Simultaneous submissions OK. SASE. Reports in 3 weeks. Free sample copy and writer's guidelines.
Nonfiction: General interest; humor; photo feature; travel and articles on chiropractice, nutrition and exercise. Buys 30 mss/year. Query or submit complete ms. length: 400-1,200 words. Pays $10-75.
Photos: State availability of photos with query or ms. Pays $2.50-25 for 8x10 b&w glossy prints and $15-50 for 35mm color transparencies. Captions required. Buys one-time rights. Model release is required.
Poetry: Light verse. "No long maudlin stuff." Buys 8 mss/issue. Length: 4-10 lines. Pays $1-5.

LIFE AND HEALTH, 6856 Eastern Ave., N.W., Washington DC 20012. Editor: Leo van Dolson. Estab. 1884. Monthly. Circ. 100,000. Buys all rights. Buys 100-150 mss/year. Pays on acceptance. Sample copy 50¢; free writer's guidelines. Complimentary copies automatically to authors published. No query. Submit seasonal health articles 6 months in advance. Reports on material within two months. SASE.
Nonfiction, Photos, Poetry, and Fillers: General subject matter consists of "short, concise articles that simply and clearly present a concept in the field of health. Emphasis on prevention; faddism avoided." Approach should be a "simple, interesting style for laymen. Readability important. Medical jargon avoided. Material should be reliable and include latest findings. We are perhaps more conservative than other magazines in our field. Not seeking sensationalism." Buys informational, interview, some humor. "Greatest single problem is returning articles for proper and thorough documentation. References to other lay journals not acceptable." Regular columns that seek freelance material are Youth Corner and Man and His Spirit. Length: up to 1,500 words. Pays $50 to $150. Purchases photos with mss. 5x7 or larger b&w glossies. Pays $7.50. Color photos usually by staff. Pays $75. Buys some health-related poetry, minimum of $10.

LISTEN MAGAZINE, 6830 Laurel St., N.W., Washington DC 20012. (202)723-0800. Editor: Francis A. Soper. 75% freelance written. Slanted primarily for teens. *Listen* is used in many high school curriculum classes, in addition to use by professionals; medical personnel, counselors, law enforcement officers, educators, youth workers, etc. Monthly magazine, 28 pages. Estab. 1948. Circ. 200,000. Buys all rights. Buys 100 to 200 mss per year. Payment on acceptance. Free sample copy and writer's guidelines. Will not consider photocopied submissions or simultaneous submissions. Reports within 4 weeks. Query first. SASE.
Nonfiction: Specializes in preventive angle, presenting positive alternatives to various drug dependencies. Especially interested in youth-slanted articles or personality interviews encouraging nonalcoholic and nondrug ways of life. Teenage point of view is good. Popularized medical, legal, and educational articles. "We don't want typical alcoholic story/skid-row bum, AA stories." Length: 500 to 1,500 words. Pays 2-5¢/word.
Photos: Purchased with accompanying ms. Captions required. Pays $5-15 per b&w (5x7, but 8x10 preferred). Color done on assignment.
Poetry and Fillers: Blank verse and free verse only. Some inspirational poetry; short poems preferred. Word square/general puzzles are also considered. Pays $5 for poetry. Payment for fillers varies according to length and quality. Pays $15 for puzzles.
How To Break In: "Personal stories are good, especially if they have a unique angle. Other authoritative articles need a fresh approach."

MUSCLE MAGAZINE INTERNATIONAL, Unit 1, 270 Rutherford Rd., S., Brampton, Ontario, Canada. L6W 3K7. Editor: Robert Kennedy. 80% freelance written. For 20- to 30-year-old men interested in physical fitness and overall body improvement. Quarterly magazine; 116 pages. Estab. 1974.Circ. 110,000. Buys all rights. Buys 80 mss/year. Pays on acceptance. Sample copy $1. No photocopied or simultaneous submissions. Reports in 1 week. Submit complete ms. SAE and International Reply Coupons.
Nonfiction and Photos: Articles on ideal physical proportions and importance of protein in the diet. Should be helpful and instructional and appeal to young men who want to live life in a vigorous and healthy style. "We do not go in for huge, vein-choked muscles and do not want to see any articles on attaining huge muscle size. We would like to see articles for the physical culturist or an article on fitness testing." Informational, how-to, personal experience, interview, profile, inspirational, humor, historical, expose, nostalgia, personal opinion, photo, spot news, new product, merchandising technique articles. Length: 1,200 to 1,600 words. Pays 6¢

per word. Columns purchasing material include Nutrition Talk (eating ideas for top results) and Shaping Up (improving fitness and stamina). Length: 1,300 words. Pays 6¢ per word. B&w and color photos are purchased with or without ms. Pays $8 for 8x10 glossy exercise photos; $16 for 8x10 b&w posing shots. Pays $100 for color; 2¼x2¼ or larger.
Fillers: Newsbreaks, clippings, puzzles, jokes, short humor. Length: open. Pays $5, minimum.
How To Break In: "Best way to break in is to seek out the muscle-building 'stars' and do in-depth interviews with biography in mind. Picture support essential."

NUTRITION HEALTH REVIEW, Box 221, Haverford PA 19041. Editor-in-Chief: Frank Ray Rifkin. 70% freelance written. Emphasizes nutrition, vegetarianism and health for all ages. Quarterly tabloid; 30 pages. Estab. 1976. Circ. 110,000. Pays on publication. Buys all rights, but may reassign following publication. Submit seasonal/holiday material 90 days in advance. Photocopied and previously published submissions OK. SASE. Reports in 5 weeks. Sample copy 75¢.
Nonfiction: William Renaurd, Nonfiction Editor. Expose, historical, how-to, humor, informational, interview, new product, personal experience, photo feature, technical and travel. All must be related to nutrition and health. Buys 15-20 mss/issue. Send complete ms. Length: 400 words maximum. Pays $10 minimum.
Photos: Purchased without accompanying ms. Pays $15 minimum for b&w photos. Send prints. Total purchase price for ms includes payment for photos. Model release required.
Columns/Departments: Vegetarianism, Health Hints and Medical Research. Buys 15-20 mss/issue. Send complete ms. Length: 400 words maximum. Pays $10 minimum. Open to suggestions for new columns/departments.

WEIGHT WATCHERS MAGAZINE, 149 FIfth Ave., New York NY 10011. (212)475-5400. Editor: Bernadette Carr. For middle class females, mostly married, with children. Monthly magazine, 64 pages. Estab. 1968. Circ. 780,000. Buys all rights. Buys 3-5 mss per month. Payment on acceptance. Sample copy for 75¢. Will not consider photocopied or simultaneous submissions. Submit seasonal material 5 months in advance. Reports within 4 weeks. SASE.
Nonfiction: "Subject matter should be related to weight control, although we are not interested in diet pieces. We are interested in developing medical and psychological pieces related to weight, or humor, or weight control articles with a male slant. We are not interested in women's articles per se, or in fiction, or in fashion or beauty pieces. We don't want recipes, either." Informational, how-to, humor, think articles. Particularly open to new material on both children and money, but stay away from narrow, personal experience pieces like "How to Have a Garage Sale." Length: 3,000 maximum. Pay varies, usually $300-600.

WELL-BEING MAGAZINE, 833 W. Fir, San Diego CA 92101. (714)234-2211. Editor: Barbara Salat. Reports on "do-it-yourself" healing techniques for readers interested in change for the better, for the individual and the planet. Monthly magazine; 64 pages. Estab. 1975. Circ. 30,000. Pays on publication. Phone queries OK. Submit seasonal/holiday material 1 month in advance. Photocopied and previously published submissions OK. Reports in 1-2 months. Sample copy $1; free writer's guidelines.
Nonfiction: Reports on various life styles and healing techniques, alternative and traditional. Subjects include diet, massage, herbs, exercise, positive thought, life styles, gardening, recycling, alternatvie energy, wild foods, wholistic medicine, home birth, etc. How-to (use solar energy, recycling methods, garden naturally, conserve, improve health); informational (effects of common foods, drugs, additives, flavorings, colorings); inspirational (achieving inner peace; outer harmony through relationship; work, prayer, positive thought, service, sharing); interviews (with folks who live natural, positive, healthy, active lives; healers, doctors, midwives, inventors, musicians, "new age" business people); new products (natural—can be made at home); nostalgia (living on the land, homesteading); personal experience (self-healing, home birth, new herbal uses); profiles (natural life style personalities); photo features (related to individual and/or planetary healing) and technical (how to build single, inexpensive solar devices, composters, etc., for the home). Buys 2-3/issue. Length: 500-5,000 words. Pays $5-200.
Photos: Purchased with or without mss, or on assignment. Query. Pays $10/page (published). Send 8x10 b&w glossies. Color slides by arrangement.

History Publications

THE ALASKA JOURNAL, Alaska Northwest Publishing Co., Box 4-EEE, Anchorage AK 99509. (907)243-1723. Editor-in-Chief: William S. Hanable. 90% freelance written. Quarterly

magazine; 96 pages. Estab. 1971. Circ. 10,000. Pays on publication. Buys first North American serial rights. SASE. Reports in 4 weeks. Sample copy $1.
Nonfiction: Historical (Alaska, Northern Canada, Arctic), and articles on Northern art and artists, present and past. Buys 30-36 mss/year. Query. Length: 1,000-6,000 words. Pays 2-4¢/word.
Photos: Purchased with accompanying ms. Captions required. Pays $2-5 for 5x7 or 8x10 b&w photos; $5-10 for 35mm color transparencies.

AMERICAN HERITAGE, 10 Rockefeller Plaza, New York NY 10020. Editor: Alvin M. Josephy, Jr. Estab. 1954. Bimonthly. Circ. 170,000. Buys all rights. Buys about 20 uncommissioned mss a year. Pays on acceptance. Before submitting, "check our five- and ten-year indexes to see whether we have already treated the subject." Submit seasonal material 8 months in advance. Returns rejected material in 1 month. Acknowledges acceptance of material in 1 month, or sooner. Query first. SASE.
Nonfiction: Wants "historical articles intended for intelligent lay readers rather than professional historians." Emphasis is on authenticity, accuracy, and verve. Style should stress "readability and accuracy." Length: 4,000 to 5,000 words. Pays $350 minimum.
Fillers: "We occasionally buy shorts and fillers that deal with American history."
How To Break In: "Our needs are such that the criteria for a young, promising writer are unfortunately no different than those for an old hand. Nevertheless, we have over the years published quite a few 'firsts' from young writers whose historical knowledge, research methods, and writing skills meet our standards from the start. Everything depends on the quality of the material. We don't really care whether the author is twenty and unknown, or eighty and famous."

AMERICAN HISTORICAL REVIEW, Ballantine Hall, Indiana University, Bloomington IN 47401. Editor: Otto Pflanze. Associate Editor: Paul Lucas. For professional historians, educators, others interested in history. Estab. 1895. Five times a year. Circ. 23,000. Acquires all rights. Uses about 20 mss/year. No payment. Will consider photocopied submissions. No simultaneous submissions. Reports in 2 to 3 months. Submit 2 copies of complete ms. SASE.
Nonfiction: Scholarly articles of historical nature to appeal to a general audience (not specialized). Reviews of history books.

AMERICAN HISTORY ILLUSTRATED, CIVIL WAR TIMES ILLUSTRATED, Box 1831, Harrisburg PA 17105. (717)234-5091. Editor: William C. Davis. Aimed at general public with an interest in sound, well-researched history. Monthly except March and September. Buys all rights. Pays on acceptance. Sample copy $1.25; free writer's guidelines. Suggestions to freelancers: "Do not bind ms or put it in a folder or such. Simply paperclip it. We prefer a ribbon copy, not a carbon or xerox. No multiple submissions, please. It is best to consult several back issues before submitting any material, in order to see what we have already covered and to get an idea of our editorial preferences. Please include informal annotations and a reading list of materials used in preparing the article." Reports within two weeks. Query first. SASE.
Nonfiction: U.S. history, pre-historic to the 1960's, biography, military, social, cultural, political, etc. Also the U.S. in relation to the rest of the world, as in World Wars I and II, diplomacy. The Civil War, military, biography, technological, social, diplomatic, political, etc. Style should be readable and entertaining, but not glib or casual. Slant generally up to the author. Taboos: shallow research, extensive quotation. 2,500 to 5,000 words. Pays $50 to $350.
Photos: Buys only occasionally with mss; 8x10 glossies preferred. Does welcome suggestions for illustrations. Address to Frederic Ray, Art Director.

THE AMERICAN WEST, 20380 Town Center Ln., Suite 160, Cupertino CA 95014. Senior Editor: Pamela Herr. Editor: Ed Holm. Published by the Buffalo Bill Historical Society, Cody WY. Emphasizes Western American history. Sponsored by the Western History Association. Bimonthly magazine; 64 pages. Estab. 1964. Circ. 25,000. Pays within 30 days of acceptance. Buys all rights. Submit seasonal/holiday material 6 months in advance. Photocopied submissions OK. SASE. Reports in 6 weeks. Free sample copy and writer's guidelines.
Nonfiction: Historical (carefully researched, accurate, lively articles having some direct relationship to western American history) and photo feature (essays relating to some specific historical theme). Buys 5 mss/issue. Length: 2,000-5,000 words. Pays $100-250.
Photos: Purchased with or without accompanying ms. Captions required. Query. Pays $25 for 8x10 b&w photos; $50 for 4x5 color transparencies.
How To Break In: "We publish a relatively small number of articles, emphasizing careful research (preferably based on primary resources) and historical accuracy. The articles should

be written with a general audience in mind and should be lively in tone. Most accepted mss fall into the following subject areas: biography (noteworthy men and women figuring in the western American heritage); historical narrative; personal experience (accounts by senior citizens having some relation to the western heritage); and 'living history' (articles on museums, historical reenactments, or other events). Geographic area is limited to anything west of the Mississippi River."

ART AND ARCHAEOLOGY NEWSLETTER, 243 East 39 St., New York NY 10016. Editor: Otto F. Reiss. 5% freelance written. For people interested in archaeology; educated laymen, educators, some professional archaeologists. Quarterly newsletter, 20 pages. Estab. 1965. Circ. 1,800. Buys all rights, but will reassign rights to author after publication; buys second serial (reprint) rights. Buys 1 or 2 mss per year. Payment on publication. Will send sample copy to writer for $1.50 in 13¢ stamps. Will consider photocopied or simultaneous submissions. Reports in 2 weeks. Query first. SASE.
Nonfiction: "Ancient history, archaeology, new discoveries, new conclusions, new theories. Our approach is similar to the way *Time Magazine* would treat archaeology or ancient history in its science section. A lighter tone, less rigidly academic. Don't avoid mystery, glamor, eroticism. Primarily interested in Old World antiquity. Would like intriguing articles on Aztecs, Mayas, Incas, but not travel articles a la *Holiday*. Definitely not interested in Indian arrowheads, Indian pots, kivas, etc." Length: 400 to 2,500 words. Pays $20.
Photos: Purchased with accompanying ms with no additional payment. Purchased also without ms for $5 minimum for b&w. Information (data) required for all b&w photos. No color. Will write own captions.
How To Break In: "Spend five years reading books about archaeology and ancient history so that you become something of an expert on the subject. Be prepared to give precise sources, with page and paragraph, for factual statements. Some freelance writers, pretending to submit nonfiction, invent their material. Don't know what is on their mind, perhaps the ambition to be a pocket-size Clifford Irving. Altogether, dealing with freelance people in this field is more trouble than it is worth. But hope blooms eternal. Perhaps there's another enthusiast who sneaked his way into an Alexander's Tomb."

CANADA WEST, Box 3399, Langley, British Columbia, Canada V3A 4R7. (604)534-8222. Editor-in-Chief: T.W. Paterson. 75% freelance written. Emphasizes pioneer history, primarily of Alberta, British Columbia and the Yukon. Quarterly magazine; 40 pages. Estab. 1969. Circ. 5,000. Pays on publication. Buys First North American serial rights. Phone queries OK. Previously published submissions OK. SASE. Reports in 2 months. Free sample copy and writer's guidelines.
Nonfiction: How-to (related to gold panning and dredging); historical (pioneers, shipwrecks, massacres, battles, exploration, logging, Indians, and railroad). Buys 28 mss/year. Submit complete ms. Length: 2,000-3,500. Pays 2¢/word.
Photos: All mss must include photos or other artwork. Submit photos with ms. Pays $5 maximum for 5x7 or larger b&w glossy prints. Captions preferred. "Photographs are kept for future reference with the right to re-use. However, we do not forbid other uses, generally, as these are historical prints from archives."
Columns/Departments: Open to suggestions for new columns/departments.

CANADIAN FRONTIER, P.O. Box 157, New Westminster, British Columbia, Canada V3L 4Y4. Editors: Brian Antonson, Gordon Stewart. For people of all ages interested in Canadian history. Annual magazine; 124 pages. Estab. 1972. Circ. 5,000. Copyrighted. Buys 24 mss/year. Pays on publication. Sample copy $3.50; free writer's guidelines. Photocopied and simultaneous submissions OK. Query first or submit complete ms, including a brief author's biography and bibliography. SAE and International Reply Coupons. Annual submissions deadline: March 1.
Nonfiction and Photos: Authoritative, accurate accounts of people, incidents, etc., in Canada's pre-1900 history. Completely factual material, with complete bibliographies, where possible. Length: 1,500-3,000 words. Pays $50 minimum, and $2/photo used. Captions required.

CHICAGO HISTORY, Chicago Historical Society, Clark St. at North Ave., Chicago IL 60614. (312)642-4600. Editor-in-Chief: Fannia Weingartner. 30% freelance written. Emphasizes history for history scholars, buffs and academics. Quarterly magazine; 64 pages. Estab. 1970. Circ. 6,500. Pays on acceptance. Buys all rights (but may reassign following publication), second serial (reprint) rights and one-time rights. Ribbon copy preferred. SASE. Reports in 2 weeks. Sample copy $1; free writer's guidelines.
Nonfiction: Historical (of Chicago and the Old Northwest). "Articles should be well researched,

analytical, informative, and directed at a popular audience, but one with a special interest in history." Buys 6 mss/issue. Query. Length: 4,500 words maximum. Pays $75-250.

EL PALACIO, QUARTERLY JOURNAL OF THE MUSEUM OF NEW MEXICO, Museum of New Mexico Press, Box 2087, Santa Fe NM 87503. (505)827-2352. Editor-in-Chief: Richard L. Polese. Emphasizes anthropology, history, folk and fine arts, natural history and geography. Quarterly magazine; 48 pages. Estab. 1913. Circ. 2,500. Pays on publication. Buys all rights, but may reassign following publication. Phone queries OK. Submit seasonal/holiday material 9 months-1 year in advance. Photocopied submissions OK. SASE. Reports in 2-6 weeks. Sample copy $2; free writer's guidelines.
Nonfiction: Historical (on Southwest; technical approach OK); how-to (folk art and craft, emphasis on the authentic); informational (more in the fields of geography and natural history); photo feature; technical; and travel (especially if related to the history of the Southwest). Buys 1 ms/issue. Send complete ms. Length: 1,750-5,000 words. Pays $15 minimum.
Photos: Photos purchased with or without accompanying ms or on assignment. Captions required. Pays "on contract" for 5x7 (or larger) b&w photos and 5x7 or 8½x11 prints or 35mm color transparencies. Send prints. Total purchase price for ms includes payment for photos.
Columns/Departments: Museum Notes, Photo Essay, Books (reviews of interest to *El Palacio* readers). The following pertains to Books: Query or send complete ms. Length: 250-1,000 words. Pays in copies. Open to suggestions for new columns/departments.
How To Break In: "*El Palacio* magazine offers a unique opportunity for writers with technical ability to have their work reach publication and be seen by influential professionals as well as avidly interested lay readers. The magazine is highly regarded in its field, despite the fact that we still infrequently pay for articles, except on contract."

FRONTIER TIMES, Western Publications, Inc., Box 3338, Austin TX 78764. Bimonthly. See *True West*.

HISTORIC PRESERVATION, National Trust for Historic Preservation, 740-748 Jackson Place, N.W., Washington DC 20006. Vice President and Editor: Mrs. Terry B. Morton. Organizational publication emphasizing historic preservation. For members of the National Trust for Historic Preservation and others interested in or involved with historic preservation efforts. Quarterly magazine; 48 pages. Estab. 1949. Circ. 110,000. Pays on publication. Rights purchased vary; may buy all, second serial (reprint), or one-time rights. Photocopied and previously published submissions OK. SASE. Reports in 2-4 weeks. Free sample copy and writer's guidelines.
Nonfiction: "Little freelance work used, but willing to review queries on subjects directly related to historic preservation, including efforts to save buildings, structures, neighborhoods of historical, architectural and cultural significance. No local history; must relate to sites, objects, buildings and neighborhoods specifically. Most material prepared on a commission basis. Writer must be very familiar with our subject matter, which deals with a specialized field, in order to present a unique publication idea." Length: 1,000-2,500 words. Pays $250 maximum.
Photos: Additional payment not usually made for photos purchased with mss. Query or send contact sheet. Pays $10-50 for 8x10 b&w glossies purchased without mss or on assignment; $50 maximum for color.

JOURNAL OF AMERICAN HISTORY, Ballantine Hall, Indiana University, Bloomington IN 47401. (812)337-3034. Interim Editor: Robert Gunderson. For professional historians of all ages. Quarterly journal, 350 pages. Estab. 1907. Circ. 12,500. Buys all rights. Pays on acceptance. Reports in 10 to 12 weeks. Submit 2 copies of complete ms. SASE.
Nonfiction: Material dealing with American history; analytical for the audience of professional historians. Length: 900 to 1,500 words. Pays $5/ page.

JOURNAL OF GENEALOGY, Anderson Publishing Co., Inc., Box 31097, Omaha NE 68131. (402)554-1800. Editor-in-Chief: Robert D. Anderson. Emphasizes genealogy and history. Monthly magazine; 48 pages. Estab. 1976. Circ. 10,000. Pays on publication. Buys all rights, but may reassign following publication. Submit seasonal/holiday material 4 months in advance. Previously published submissions OK. SASE. Reports in 4 weeks. Sample copy $1; writer's guidelines for SASE.
Nonfiction: Historical (on places or obscure pioneers, place names, etc), how-to (new or different ways to trace ancestors, new ways to keep notes, or new ways to diagram a pedigree chart), interview (of well-known persons involved in genealogy), new product (about innovations in capturing, storing, indexing, and retrieving data—such as computors and microfiche

relating to historical or genealogical data), personal experience (must have profound impact on genealogical research), personal opinion (must be in-depth and scholarly dealing with genealogy and/or history), profile, travel (genealogists like to combine a vacation with genealogical research), and scholarly (we need thought provoking articles on the science of genealogy and how it relates to other sciences). Buys 20 mss/year. Query. Length: 750-4,500 words; "longer considered, but need natural breaks for serialization." Pays 2¢/word.
Photos: Purchased with or without accompanying ms or on assignment. Captions required. Query. Pays $5-25 for 8x10 b&w photos. Model release required.
Columns/Departments: Society Station (this column is devoted to helping genealogical and historical societies in their day-to-day activities, i.e., "How to Write a News Release" or "Should We File for Non-Profit Status?"). Query. Length: 750-2,000 words. Pays 2¢/word. Open to suggestions for new columns/departments.
How To Break In: "We want articles that will help the most people find the most genealogy. Always ask yourself, as we do, 'is it meaningful?' We need good articles on researching in foreign countries."

NORTH CAROLINA HISTORICAL REVIEW, Historical Publications Section, Archives and History, 109 E. Jones St., Raleigh NC 27611. (919)733-7442. Editor: Memory F. Mitchell. Emphasizes scholarly historical subjects for students and others interested in history. Quarterly magazine; 100 pages. Estab. 1924. Circ. 2,200. Buys all rights, but may reassign following publication. Phone queries OK. SASE. Reports in 3 months. Free writer's guidelines.
Nonfiction: Articles relating to North Carolina history in particular, southern history in general. Topics about which relatively little is known or are new interpretations of familiar subjects. All articles must be based on primary sources and footnoted. Length: 15-25 typed pages. Pays $10/article.

NORTH SOUTH TRADER, 8020 New Hampshire Ave., Langley Park MD 20783. (301)434-2100. Editor: Wm. S. Mussenden. For Civil War buffs, historians, collectors, relic hunters, libraries and museums. Magazine; 52 to 68 (8½x11) pages. Estab. 1973. Every 2 months. Circ. 5,000. Rights purchased vary with author and material. Usually buys all rights. Buys 70 mss a year. Pays on publication. Sample copy and writer's guidelines $1. Will consider photocopied and simultaneous submissions. Reports within 2 weeks. Query first or submit complete ms. Enclose SASE.
Nonfiction and Photos: General subject matter deals with battlefield preservation, relic restoration, military artifacts of the Civil War (weapons, accoutrements, uniforms, etc.); historical information on battles, camp sites and famous people of the War Between the States. Prefers a factual or documentary approach to subject matter. Emphasis is on current findings and research related to the places, people, and artifacts of the conflict. Not interested in treasure magazine type articles. Length: 500 to 3,000 words. Pays 2¢ a word.
Columns/Departments: Columns and departments include Relic Restoration, Lost Heritage and Interview. Length: 1,000 to 1,500 words. Pays 2¢ a word. B&w photos are purchased with or without ms. Captions required. Pays $2.

OLD WEST, Western Publications, Inc., Box 3338, Austin TX 78764. (512)444-3674. Editor: Pat Wagner. See *True West*.

PERSIMMON HILL, 1700 N.E. 63rd St., Oklahoma City OK 73111. Editor: Dean Krakel. Senior Editor: Sara Dobberteen. For a Western art, Western history, ranching, and rodeo oriented audience; historians, artists, ranchers, art galleries, schools, libraries. Publication of the National Cowboy Hall of Fame and Western Heritage Center. Estab. 1970. Quarterly. Circ. 25,000. Buys all rights. Buys 12-14 mss/year. Pays on publication. Sample copy $3. Reporting time on mss accepted for publication varies. Returns rejected material immediately. Query. SASE.
Nonfiction and Photos: Historical and contemporary articles on famous Western figures connected with pioneering the American West; Western art; rodeo; cowboys; etc., or biographies of such people; stories of Western flora and animal life; environmental subjects. Only thoroughly researched and historically authentic material is considered. May have a humorous approach to subject. Not interested in articles that re-appraise, or in any way put the West and its personalities in an unfavorable light. Length: 2,000 to 3,000 words. Pays a minimum of $150. B&w glossies or color transparencies purchased with or without ms, or on assignment. Pays according to quality and importance for b&w and color. Suggested captions appreciated.

TRUE WEST, Western Publications, Inc., Box 3338, Austin TX 78764. (512)444-3674. Editor:

Pat Wagner. Bimonthly magazine. Estab. 1953. Circ. 155,000. Pays on acceptance. Buys first North American serial rights. "Magazine is distributed nationally, but if not on the newsstands in a particular location will send sample copy for 75¢." SASE.
Nonfiction and Photos: "Factual accounts regarding people, places and events of the frontier West (1850-1910). Sources are required. If based on family papers, records, memoirs, etc., reminiscences must be accurate as to dates and events. We strive for stories with an element of action, suspense, heroics, and humor, but those about the better known outlaws, Indians, lawmen, and explorers will probably overlap material we have already run. At present we are receiving too much material from the 1920's, '30's, and '40's. We regret that many first-hand accounts have to be retuned because the happenings are too recent for us. We also receive considerable material which is good local history, but would have limited appeal for a national readership." Length: 750-4,000 words. pays 2¢/word minimum, plus allowances for photos. "We usually buy mss and photos as a package."

VIKINGSHIP, Leif Ericson Society, Box 301, Chicago IL 60690. (312)761-1888. Editor: W.R. Anderson. 40% freelance written. Emphasizes medieval American history for a readership interested in pre-Columbian American exploration by Norse Vikings. Quarterly newsletter; 10 pages. Estab. 1965. Circ. 1,200. Pays on acceptance. Buys first North American serial rights. Photocopied submissions OK. SASE. Reports in 1 week. Sample copy $1.
Nonfiction: Historical articles on Norse Viking exploration in America from the 10th-14th centuries. "We have no interest in run-of-the-mill rehashes of well-known evidence. Our readers are very sophisticated in the subject." Buys 5-10 mss/year. Submit complete ms. Length: 300-1,000 words. Pays $10 minimum.

VIRGINIA CAVALCADE, Virginia State Library, Richmond VA 23219. Primarily for Virginians and others with an interest in Virginia history. Quarterly magazine; 48 pages. Estab. 1951. Circ. 17,000. Buys all rights. Buys 15-20 mss/year. Pays on acceptance. Sample copy $1; free writer's guidelines. Rarely considers simultaneous submissions. Submit seasonal material 15 to 18 months in advance. Reports in 4 weeks to 1 year. Query first. SASE.
Nonfiction and Photos: "We welcome readable and factually accurate articles that are relevant to some phase of Virginia history. Art, architecture, literature, education, business, technology, and transportation are all acceptable subjects, as well as political and military affairs. Articles must be based on thorough, scholarly research. We require footnotes but do not publish them. Authors should avoid contemporary political and social topics on which people hold strong and conflicting opinions. Any period from the age of exploration to the mid-twentieth century, and any geographical section or area of the state may be represented. Must deal with subjects that will appeal to a broad readership, rather than to a very restricted group or locality. Fresh and little known themes are preferred; manuscripts on more familiar subjects must treat them in a new light or rest on new documentary evidence. Articles must be suitable for illustration, although it is not necessary that the author provide the pictures. If the author does have pertinent illustrations or knows their location, the editor appreciates information concerning them." Uses 8x10 b&w glossies; color transparencies should be at least 4x5. Length: approximately 3,500 words. Pays $100.

VIRGINIA MAGAZINE OF HISTORY AND BIOGRAPHY, Virginia Historical Society, P.O. Box 7311, Richmond VA 23221. Editor: William M.E. Rachal. 95% freelance written. Quarterly for serious students of Virginia history. Usually buys all rights. Pays on publication. Reports in one month. Enclose SASE for return of submissions.
Nonfiction: Carefully researched and documented articles on Virginia history, and well-edited source material relating to Virginia. Must be dignified, lucid, scholarly. Length: 1,500 to 15,000 words. Appropriate illustrations are used. Pays $2 per printed page.

THE WESTERN PRODUCER, Box 2500, Saskatoon, Saskatchewan, Canada. (306)665-3500. Publisher: R.H.D. Phillips. Editor: R.H.D. Phillips. 6% freelance written. Emphasizes Western Canadian agriculture for farm families, children to grandparents. Weekly newspaper; 56 pages. Estab. 1923. Circ. 145,000. Pays on acceptance. Buys first North American serial rights. Submit seasonal/holiday material 2 months in advance of issue date. Previously published submissions OK. SASE. Reports in 2 weeks. Free writer's guidelines.
Nonfiction: How-to; general interest; historical (Western Canada); inspirational; nostalgia; personal experience; photo feature; and profile. Buys 1,200 mss/year. Submit complete ms. Pays $5-300.
Photos: Submit photos with ms. Pays $5-25 for 5x7 b&w prints. Captions and model release required. Buys one-time rights.

Fiction: Adventure; historical; humorous; mainstream; mystery; religious; romance; suspense; and Western Canadian subjects. Buys 20 mss/year. Length: 1,500 words maximum. Pays $25-100.
Poetry: Traditional. Buys 51/year. Pays $5-15.

Hobby and Craft Publications

Publications in this section are for collectors, do-it-yourselfers, and craft hobbyists. Publications for electronics and radio hobbyists will be found in the Science classification.

ACQUIRE: THE MAGAZINE OF CONTEMPORARY COLLECTIBLES, 170 5th Ave., New York NY 10010. Editor: R. C. Rowe. For collectors, mostly 30 to 65 in age, many rural and suburban, affluent and reasonably well educated. Published 5 times a year. Estab. 1973. Circ. 50,000. Rights purchased vary with author and material. Buys all rights, but will reassign rights to author after publication; first North American serial rights; first serial rights; second serial (reprint) rights; simultaneous rights. Buys 15 to 30 mss a year. "First assignments are always done on a speculative basis." Payment on acceptance. Will send sample copy to writer for $1. Will consider photocopied submissions and simultaneous submissions. Query first, with an outline. Reports within 1 month. Enclose SASE.
Nonfiction: "Short features about collecting, written in tight, newsy style. We specialize in contemporary (postwar) collectibles. Particularly interested in items affected by scarcity." Informational, how-to, interview, profile, expose, nostalgia. Length: 500 to 2,500 words. Pays $50 to $150. Columns cover stamps, cars, porcelains, glass, western art, and graphics. Length: 750 words. Pays $75.
Photos: Department Editor: S. Linden. B&w and color photos purchased with accompanying ms with no additional payment. Also purchased without ms and on assignment. Captions are required. Wants clear, distinct, full frame image that says something. Pays $10 to $50.

AIRFIX MAGAZINE, PSL Publications Limited, Bar Hill, Cambridge CB3 8EL England. (0954)80010. Editor-in-Chief: Bruce Quarrie. 90% freelance written. Emphasizes plastic modeling. Monthly magazine; 68 pages. Estab. 1960. Circ. 37,000. Pays on publication. Buys all rights. Phone queries OK. Photocopied submissions OK. SASE. Reports in 2 months. Free sample copy and writer's guidelines.
Nonfiction: How-to (on plastic model construction and conversion); historical (military, aviation, naval); photo features and technical (military, aeronautical, naval). Buys 120 mss/year. Query. Length: 500-3,000 words. Pays $10-100.
Photos: Purchased with or without mss or on assignment. Pays $1-10 for half plate b&w glossies; $10-25 for 35mm, 2¼x2¼ or 4x5 color.
How To Break In: "By covering air shows, military rallies, etc., outside the United Kingdom and submitting illustrated write-ups."

AMERICAN COLLECTOR, Crain Communications, Inc. 740 Rush St., Chicago IL 60611. Editor: Merle Kingman. Managing Editor: John Maloney. 80% freelance written. Emphasizes collecting for antique buffs , collectors of all kinds, dealers, and investors. Monthly tabloid; 48 pages. Estab. 1970. Circ. 100,000. Pays on publication. Buys all rights, but may reassign following publication. Submit seasonal/holiday material 3 months in advance of issue date. SASE. Reports in 1 month. Sample copy $1; free writer's guidelines.
Nonfiction: Exposé (fake collectibles and fake antiques); how-to (evaluate, protect an item, tips on finding or buying, and prices); historical (related to a collectible or type of collectible); interview; nostalgia; personal experience (related to collecting); and photo feature (related to collecting). Buys 100 mss/year. Submit complete ms. Length: 500-1,200 words. Pays 3¢/inch.
Photos: Submit photo material with accompanying ms. Pays $5 for 8x10 b&w glossy prints and $10-20 for 2x2 color transparencies. Captions required. Buys all rights, but may reassign following publication.

AMERICAN GRAPHICS, Box 363W, Salisbury CT 06068. Editor: Tryntje Van Ness Seymour. 75% freelance written. Emphasizes fine art prints for members of mail order book club. Quarterly bulletin; 24 pages. Estab. 1978. Pays on acceptance. Buys first or second serial (reprint) rights. Simultaneous, photocopied, and previously published submissions OK. SASE. Reports in 4 weeks. Free sample copy.
Nonfiction: How-to articles on printmaking, care of prints, framing, etc; and interviews and

profiles of printmakers, print collectors, museum print curators and master printers. No art criticism articles. Buys 8-12 mss/year. Query or submit complete ms. Length: 1,000-2,500 words. Pays $50-150.
Photos: "Illustrated articles are preferred in all cases." Pays $5-25 for 5x7 or 8x10 b&w glossy prints. Captions required. Buys one-time rights.

AMERICANA, 10 Rockefeller Plaza, New York NY 10020. Editor: Michael Durham. For "a very well-educated, mature audience, interested in American history, especially such things as architecture, design, crafts, travel, etc." Estab. 1973. Bimonthly. Circ. 250,000. Buys all rights. Payment on acceptance. Query first. SASE.
Nonfiction: "Materials of the broadest range of American creation from gardens to cut glass; from collecting Revere silver to automobile hood ornaments. We are interested in anything Americans have created. Our special approach is that, although we are interested in the creative American past, we are a contemporary magazine. The ideal reaction to any story is that the reader will want to and be able to do something about it now; to go to that place, prepare that meal, collect that object, now." Length: 1,500 to 2,500 words. Pays $200 to $300.

THE ANTIQUARIAN, 13 Cheshire St., Huntington Station NY 11746. (516)271-8990. Editor-in-Chief: Marguerite Cantine. Managing Editor: Elizabeth Kilpatrick. Emphasizes antiques, and 19th century or earlier art. Monthly (except January) magazine; 40 pages. Estab. 1974. Circ. 10,000. Pays on publication. Buys all rights, but may reassign following publication. Submit seasonal/holiday material 3 months in advance of issue date. Photocopied and previously published (if not published in antiques publication) submissions OK. SASE. Reports in 6 weeks. Sample copy for SASE; mention *Writer's Market* in request.
Nonfiction: How-to (refinish furniture, repair glass, restore old houses, paintings, rebind books, resilver glass, etc.); general interest (relations of buyers and dealers at antique shows/sales, auction reports); historical (data, personal and otherwise, on famous people in the arts and antiques field); interview; photo feature (auctions, must have caption on item including price it sold for); profile (want articles around movie stars and actors who collect antiques, query); and travel (historical sites of interest in New York, New Jersey, Pennsylvania and Deleware). Wants no material on art deco, collectibles, anything made after 1900, cutesy things to 'remake' from antiques, or flea markets and crafts shows. Buys 6 mss/year. Submit complete ms. Length: 200-2,000 words. Pays ½¢/word.
Photos: Pays $.50-1 for 3½x5 glossy b&w prints. Captions required. Buys all rights, but may reassign following publication. Model release required.
Fillers: Newsbreaks. Length: 100-200 words. Pays ½¢/word.
How To Break In: "Don't write an article unless you *love* this field. Antiques belong to a neurotic group. Collecting is a sickness as expensive as gambling, and twice as hard to break, because we are all content in our insanity. Don't write like a textbook. Write as though your were carrying on a nice conversation with your mother. No pretentions. No superiority. Simple, warm, one-to-one, natural, day-to-day, neighbor-over-coffee writing."

THE ANTIQUE TRADER WEEKLY, Box 1050, Dubuque IA 52001. (319)588-2073. Editor: Kyle D. Husfloen. 75% freelance written. For collectors and dealers in antiques and collectibles. Weekly newspaper; 90-120 pages. Estab. 1957. Circ. 80,000 to 90,000. Buys all rights, but will reassign rights to author after publication. Buys about 200 mss/year. Payment at end of month following publication. Free sample copy and writer's guidelines. Will consider photocopied and simultaneous submissions. Submit seasonal material (holidays) 3 to 4 months in advance. Prompt reports. Query first or submit complete ms. SASE.
Nonfiction and Photos: "We invite authoritative and well-researched articles on all types of antiques and collectors' items. Submissions should include a liberal number of good b&w photos. We also welcome feature cover stories which are accompanied by a good, clear color transparency which illustrates the feature. The feature should also have several b&w photos to illustrate the inside text. A color transparency of 4x5 is desirable for use as cover photo, but a smaller transparency is sometimes acceptable." Pays $5 to $35 for feature articles; $35 to $100 for feature cover stories. "We do not pay for brief information on new shops opening or other material printed as service to the antiques hobby."

ANTIQUES JOURNAL, Babka Publishing Co., Box 1046. Dubuque IA 52001. Emphasizes antiques and collecting for "experienced and incipient antiques collectors and dealers from age 20-80 interested in learning the background of both the older antiques and the more recent collectible objects." Monthly magazine; 68 pages. Estab. 1946. Circ. 36,000. Pays on acceptance. Buys first North American serial rights. Submit seasonal/holiday material 10 months in

advance. SASE. Reports in 2 weeks. Sample copy $1.25.
Nonfiction: Historical; informational; interview (only occasionally); and nostalgia (if related to collectible objects of the 1920s-50s). Buys 100 mss/year. Query. Length: 300-2,000 words. Pays $35-105.
Photos: Photos purchased with accompanying ms. Captions required. Uses 4x5 or 8x10 b&w glossies; pays $35-40 for 35mm-4x5 color transparencies (for cover). Total purchase price for ms includes payment for photos (excluding color transparencies for cover). Model release required.

THE BOOK-MART, 3110 1st Ave., N., St. Petersburg FL 33713. Editor/Publisher: David G. MacLean. 60% freelance written. Emphasizes book collecting and the used-book trade. Monthly tabloid; 8 pages. Estab. March 1977. Circ. 1,500. Pays on publication. Buys one-time rights. Submit seasonal/holiday material 6 weeks in advance of issue date. Simultaneous, photocopied and previously published submissions OK. SASE. Reports in 4-6 weeks. Sample copy for 13¢ in postage; mention *Writer's Market* in request.
Nonfiction: "Especially need articles of interest to book dealers and collectors containing bibliographical and pricing data." Exposé (literary forgeries); general interest (articles about regional authors, expecially those highly collected); historical (about books, authors, publishers, printers, booksellers); how-to (book conservation and restoration techniques, no amateur binding); interview (if in field of interest); nostalgia (articles about paper collectibles, especially those with pricing information); personal experience; and travel (literary landmarks). "No rambling accounts with no specific focus or articles about an unknown poet who has published his/her first book." Buys 2 mss/issue. Query. Length: 1,000-2,500 words. Pays 30¢/column inch.
Photos: State availability of photos with query. Pays $5 minimum for 5x7 or larger b&w glossy or matte finish prints. Buys one-time rights.
Columns/Departments: Auction Report and Books in Review. Query "unless of a timely nature." Pays 30¢/column inch.

CANADA CRAFTS, G.P. Page Publications, 380 Wellington St., Toronto, Ontario, Canada M5V 1E3. Editor-in-Chief: G.P. Dempsey. 20-40% freelance written. "Readers are typically in their mid 20's to 30's and are trained craftspeople with at least some university training." Bimonthly magazine; 48-52 pages. Circ. 12,000. Pays on publication. Buys one-time rights. Simultaneous and previously published submissions OK. SASE. Reports in 2 months. Sample copy $2.
Nonfiction: Historical (development of a craft technique, style; especially if there is a Canadian angle); how-to; interview; photo feature (on a particular artist's work and his technique); profile; and technical. Query. Pays 5¢/printed word.
Photos: "Often the articles we use require photos to explain what the article discusses. Our magazine relies on photos for its look." Pays $10 for b&w photos. Submit contact sheet. Buys one-time rights.

COIN WORLD, Box 150, Sidney OH 45367. Editor: Margo Russell. For "coin collectors, mostly specialists in U.S. or world coins, or related numismatic items such as medals, tokens, and paper money." Weekly. Circ. 96,000. Buys first rights. Buys 100 mss/year. Pays on publication. Returns rejected material in 2 weeks. Acknowledges acceptance of material in 4 weeks. Query first. SASE.
Nonfiction and Photos: "Articles on U.S. and world coins or related subjects, especially those based on original research or personal experience." Buys personal experience and historical pieces. Length: 250 to 4,000 words. Pays 2¢ per published word with additional allowance for art. Photos purchased with mss. B&w glossies.

COLLECTIBLES AND ANTIQUES MONTHLY, 1944 NE 151st St., North Miami FL 33162. (305)944-0719. Editor-in-Chief: Arthur Brickman. Managing Editor: Nettie Brickman. Emphasizes all collectibles and antiques including rare books. Monthly magazine; 52 pages. Estab. 1977. Circ. 5,000. Pays on publication. Buys all rights, but may reassign following publication. Phone queries OK. Submit seasonal/holiday material 3 months in advance of issue date. Simultaneous and photocopied submissions OK. SASE. Reports in 2 weeks. Free sample copy and writer's guidelines.
Nonfiction: Sal Perrine, articles editor. Informational; historical; interview; nostalgia; personal opinion; photo feature and technical. Buys 100-120 mss/year. Query or submit complete ms. Length: 300-1,500 words. Pays 4¢/word.
Photos: Lee Gottlieb, photo editor. Pays $3 for b&w photos. Captions required.
Fillers: Clippings, newsbreaks and short humor. Pays $2.

COLLECTORS NEWS, P.O. Box 156, 606 8th St., Grundy Center IA 50638. (319)824-5456. Editor: Mary E. Croker. For dealers in, and collectors of, antiques. Monthly tabloid newspaper; 64-72 pages. Estab. 1960. Circ. 30,000. Buys 60 mss/year. Pays on publication. Free sample copy. No photocopied or simultaneous submissions. Submit seasonal material (holidays) 2 months in advance. Reports in 30 days. Query first or submit complete ms. SASE.
Nonfiction and Photos: Only factual articles pertaining to some phase of collecting or interesting collections. Informational, profile, nostalgia. Length: 1,200 words minimum; 1,600 words average. Pays 50¢ per column inch. No additional payment for b&w photos used with mss. Captions required.

CRAFT HORIZONS, 44 West 53rd St., New York NY 10019. Editor-in-Chief: Rose Slivka. Bimonthly. Circ. 40,000. Published by American Crafts Council for professional craftspeople, artists, teachers, architects, designers, decorators, collectors, connoisseurs and the consumer public. Copyrighted. Pays on publication. Free sample copy. Reports as soon as possible. Query first. SASE.
Nonfiction and Photos: Articles and accompanying photos on the subject of creative work in ceramics, weaving, stitchery, jewelry, metalwork, woodwork, etc. Discussions of the technology, the materials and the ideas of artists throughout the world working in the above media. Length: 1,000 words. Pays $75 to $100 per article. Accompanying photos should be 8x10 b&w glossies. Pays $7.50 per b&w glossy.

CREATIVE CRAFTS, Carsten's Publications, Inc., Box 700, Newton NJ 07860. Editor-in-Chief: Sybil C. Harp. 80-90% freelance written. Emphasizes crafts for the serious adult hobbyist. Bimonthly (with a Christmas annual) magazine; 76 pages. Estab. 1967. Circ. 75,000. Pays on publication. Buys all rights. Submit seasonal/holiday material 7 months in advance. SASE. Reports in 4 weeks. Sample copy $1; free writer's guidelines.
Nonfiction: How-to (step-by-step of specific projects or general techniques; instructions must be clearly written and accompanied by b&w procedural photos and/or drawings). Buys 50-60 mss/year. Query. Length: 1,200 words average. Pays $50/magazine page. No human interest articles.
Photos: Purchased with accompanying ms. "We give $35 maximum allowance for photo expenses."
Columns/Departments: Going Places (articles dealing with annual fairs, craft "villages" or museums of special interest to craft enthusiasts). Buys 1 mss/issue. Query. Length: 1,200 words average. Pays $50/magazine page without advertising; $25/page mixed. Open to suggestions for new columns/departments.
Special Needs: "In the market for articles on dollhouse miniatures for a special 'miniature' section of each issue. Must be written by serious miniaturists who understand the hobby and do miniature crafts themselves."

DECORATING & CRAFT IDEAS MADE EASY, 1303 Foch, Ft. Worth TX 76107. (817)338-4401. Editor: Fredrica Daugherty. For people whose main interests are crafts and decorating. Magazine; 80 pages. Estab. 1970. Monthly except January and July. Circ. 650,000. Buys all rights, but may reassign rights to author after publication. Buys 10 mss a year. Pays on publication. Free sample copy. Submit seasonal (Christmas) material 6 months in advance. Reports as soon as possible. Query first, with snapshot of project. SASE.
Nonfiction and Photos: Material on craft projects, craft-related travel, sewing projects, needlework projects. Simple, straightforward approach; clear, concise, complete instructions. In crafts, the emphasis must be on what makes the project unique. "We explain a craft project, show it close-up, in a decorative manner and completely explain how a reader can reproduce the project. We do a '100 Ideas' type article for Christmas, so we're on the lookout for small Christmas projects." Length: 600 to 1,000 words, not including instructions. Rate of payment is variable and is negotiated with each writer. Payment for photos depends on article.
How To Break In: "Query first with an explanation of the project and clear snapshots of the completed object. Projects offering *original* patterns for unique, well-made items are of highest interest and appeal."

DELTIOLOGY, 3709 Gradyville Rd., Newtown Square PA 19073. (215)353-1689. Editor: James L. Lowe. For collectors of antique picture postcards from around the world. Bimonthly magazine; 16 pages. Estab. 1960. Circ. 2,600. Rights purchased vary with author and material. Usually buys first U.S. rights. Buys 6 to 10 mss/year. Pays on publication. Sample copy 50¢. Will consider photocopied and simultaneous submissions. Reports in 2 months. Query first or

submit complete ms. SASE.
Nonfiction and Photos: Informative articles pertaining to antique picture postcards, primarily those issued prior to 1915, dealing with specific publishers and artists. Length: 500-2,000 words. Pays $10/article minimum. No additional payment for b&w photos used with mss.

EARLY AMERICAN LIFE, Early American Society, P.O. Box 1831, Harrisburg PA 17105. Editor: Robert G. Miner. Executive Editor: Frances Carnahan. 70% freelance written. For "people who are interested in capturing the warmth and beauty of the 1600 to 1850 period and using it in their homes and lives today. They are interested in arts, crafts, travel, restoration, collecting." Bimonthly magazine; 100 pages. Estab. 1970. Circ. 300,000. Buys all rights. Buys 50 mss/year. Payment on acceptance. Free sample copy and writer' guidelines. Will consider photocopied submissions. Will not consider simultaneous submissions. Reports in 1 month. Query first or submit complete ms. SASE.
Nonfiction and Photos: "Social history (the story of the people, not epic heroes and battles); crafts such as woodworking and needlepoint; travel to historic sites; country inns; antiques and reproductions; refinishing and restoration; architecture and decorating. We try to entertain as we inform, but always attempt to give the reader something he can do. While we're always on the lookout for good pieces on any of our subjects, the 'travel to historic sites' theme is most frequently submitted. Would like to see more how-to-do-it (well-illustrated) on how real people did something great to their homes." Length: 750 to 3,000 words. Pays $50-400. Pays $10 for 5x7 (and up) b&w photos used with mss; minimum of $25 for color. Prefers 2¼ and up, but can work from 35mm.
How To Break In: "Get a feeling for 'today's early Americans', the folks who are visiting flea markets, auctions, junkyards, the antiques shops. They are our readers and they hunger for ideas on how to bring the warmth and beauty of early America into their lives. Then, conceive a new approach to satisfying their related interests in arts, crafts, travel to historic sites, and the story of the people of the 1600 to 1850 period. Write to entertain and inform at the same time, and be prepared to help us with illustrations, or sources for them."

GEMS AND MINERALS, Box 687, Mentone CA 92359. (714)794-1173. Editor: Jack R. Cox. Monthly for the amateur gem cutter, jewelry maker, mineral collector, and rockhounds. Buys first North American serial rights. Buys 15 to 20 mss/year. Payment on publication. Free sample copy and writer's guidelines. Query first. Reports within a month. SASE.
Nonfiction and Photos: Material must have how-to slant. No personality stories. Field trips to mineral or gem collecting localities used; must be accurate and give details so they can be found. Instructions on how to cut gems; designs and creations of jewelry. Four to eight typed pages plus illustrations preferred, but do not limit if subject is important. Frequently good articles are serialized if too long for one issue. Pays 50¢ per inch for text and pix as published.
How To Break In: "Because we are a specialty magazine, it is difficult for a writer to prepare a suitable story for us unless he is familiar with the subject matter: jewelry making, gem cutting, mineral collecting and display, and fossil collecting. Our readers want accurate instructions on how to do it and where they can collect gemstones and minerals in the field. The majority of our articles are purchased from freelance writers, but most of them are hobbyists (rockhounds) or have technical knowledge on one of the subjects. Infrequently, a freelancer with no knowledge of the subject interviews an expert (gem cutter, jewelry maker, etc.) and gets what this expert tells him down on paper for a good how-to article. However, the problem here is that if the expert neglects to mention all the steps in his process, the writer does not realize it. Then, there is a delay while we check it out. My best advice to a freelance writer is to send for a sample copy of our magazine and author's specification sheet which will tell him what we need. We are interested in helping new writers and try to answer them personally, giving any pointers that we think will be of value to them. Let us emphasize that our readers want how-to and where-to stories. They are not at all interested in personality sketches about one of their fellow hobbyists."

HOBBY ARTIST NEWS, R. #2, Fort Atkinson IA 52144. Editor: Ray Gillem. 10% freelance written. For artists, hobbyists and authors. Bimonthly magazine; 8 to 12 pages. Estab. 1970. Circ. 500. Not copyrighted. Pays on publication. Sample copy 75¢; free writer's guidelines. Reports on material accepted for publication in 2 to 3 weeks. Submit complete ms. SASE.
Nonfiction: How-to and moneymaking idea type of articles on art, artists, handicrafts, song writing. Should be informative, educational, entertaining, first-person material on actual experiences. How-to articles on greeting cards and "new ways for an artist to make a buck." Length: 300 to 500 words. Pays ½¢ a word.

HOBBY COMPUTER HANDBOOK, Davis Publications, Inc., 380 Lexington Ave., New York NY 10017. (212)949-9190. Editor-in-Chief: Julian S. Martin. Managing Editor: Alan Rose. 100% freelance written. Emphasizes home hobby computers and theory. Annual magazine; 112 pages. Estab. 1978. Pays on acceptance. Buys all rights. Previously published submissions OK. SASE. Reports in 4-6 weeks. Free writer's guidelines; mention *Writer's Market* in request.
Nonfiction: "The nature of the magazine's title limits the manuscript contributions to the subject matter. Aim at the hobbyist who is a beginner, or working with his first computer. Stick to theory articles, how to ideas that are universal to hobby computers and simple project ideas. If you know nothing about hobby computers, have not worked with a hobby computer, don't write to us! You can't fake it in this field." Buys 350 mss/year. Query. Length: 1,000-3,500 words. Pays $150-250.
Photos: State availability of photos with query. Offers no additional payment for b&w negatives with proof sheet. Buys all rights. "In most cases, we give permission for author and/or photographer to use material in other publications after publication date. Authorization given in-writing only.
Fillers: Jokes, gags, anecdotes. Buys 3/issue. Pays $20-30.

JOEL SATER'S ANTIQUES & AUCTION NEWS, 225 W. Market St., Marietta PA 17547. (717)426-1956. Managing Editor: Joel Sater. Editor: Denise Murphy. For dealers and buyers of antiques, nostalgics, and collectibles; and those who follow antique shows and shops. Biweekly tabloid; 24 pages. Estab. 1967. Circ. 80,000. Pays on publication. Buys all rights. Phone queries OK. Submit seasonal/holiday material 6 weeks to 3 months in advance. Simultaneous (if so notified), photocopied and previously published submissions OK. SASE. Reports in 6 weeks. Free sample copy (must identify *Writer's Market*).
Nonfiction: Historical (related to American artifacts or material culture); how-to (restoring and preserving antiques and collectibles); informational (research on antiques or collectibles; "news about activities in our field"); interview; nostalgia; personal experience; photo feature; profile; and travel. Buys 100-150 mss/year. Query or submit complete ms. Length: 500-2,500 words. Pays $5-25.
Photos: Purchased with or without accompanying ms. Captions required. Send prints. Pays $2-10 for b&w photos. Total purchase price for ms includes payment for photos.

LAPIDARY JOURNAL, P.O. Box 80937, San Diego CA 92138. Editor: Pansy D. Kraus. For "all ages interested in the lapidary hobby." Estab. 1947. Monthly. Circ. 66,250. Rights purchased vary with author and material. Buys all rights, or first serial rights. Payment on publication. Free sample copy and writer's guidelines. Will consider photocopied submissions. Query first. SASE.
Nonfiction and Photos: Publishes "articles pertaining to gem cutting, gem collecting and jewelry making for the hobbyist." Buys informational, how-to, personal experience, historical, travel, and technical articles. Pays 1¢ a word. Buys good contrast b&w photos. Contact editor for color. Payment varies according to size.

LOST TREASURE, Box 328, Conroe TX 77301. Editor: John H. Latham. 95% freelance written. For treasure hunting hobbyists, bottle and relic collectors, amateur prospectors and miners. Monthly magazine; 72 pages. Estab. 1969. Circ. 100,000. Buys all rights, but will reassign rights to author after publication. Buys 180 mss a year. Payment on acceptance. Free sample copy and writer's guidelines. Will consider photocopied submissions. Will not consider simultaneous submissions. Reports in 3 to 4 weeks. Submit complete ms. SASE.
Nonfiction and Photos: Articles about lost mines and buried and sunken treasures. Avoid writing about the more famous treasures and lost mines. Length: 100 to 3,000 words. Pays 2¢ per word. Pays $5 for b&w glossies purchased with mss. Captions required. Pays $75 for color transparencies used on cover; 2¼x2¼ minimum size. "Treasure Nuggets" section uses short articles on publication's theme. Length: 100 to 250 words. Pays $12.50.

McCALL'S NEEDLEWORK & CRAFTS MAGAZINE, 230 Park Ave., New York NY 10017. Managing Editor: Margaret Gilman. Quarterly. All rights bought for original needlework and handcraft designs. SASE.
Nonfiction: Accepts the made-up items accompanied by the directions, diagrams, and charts for making them. Preliminary photos may be submitted. Variety of payment depends on items sent in. The range of payment could be from a few dollars to a few hundred dollars.

MAGICIAN'S WEEK, Box P, Hewitt NJ 07421. Editor-in-Chief: Robert G. Bott. For all professional and amateur magicians, and people interested in magic and magic history. Weekly newspaper; 16-24 pages. Estab. January 1978. Pays on publication. Buys simultaneous, second serial (reprint), and one-time rights. Simultaneous, photocopied and previously published submissions OK. SASE. Reports in 1 month.

Nonfiction: How-to (magic tricks, build magic equipment, and work to an audience); historical (history of magic, equipment, and magicians); humor (of interest to magicians or humor that magicians can use in act); interview (with magicians or those in magic business); new product (new magic); nostalgia (the "I remember famous magician's performance" type of articles); photo feature (art illustrations); profile (of magicians or manufactures of magic equipment); technical (magic tricks); and travel (where to see magic). Buys 4 mss/issue. Submit complete ms. Length: 500-full page. Pays 2¢/word.

Photos: State availability of photos with ms. Pays $5-10 for 5x7 b&w glossy prints. Captions required. Model release preferred.

Columns/Departments: Close Up Magic (how-to); Illusions (how-to); Slight of Hand (how-to); Stage Magic (how-to). "We would like to devote a page or half page to the young magician, i.e. simple tricks, puzzles, etc. for children 10-16 years of age." Submit complete ms. Length: 500-1,000 words. pays 2¢/word.

Fillers: Clippings; jokes, gags, anecdotes; newsbreaks; puzzles; and short humor. Submit fillers. Pays 2¢/word.

MAINE ANTIQUE DIGEST, Box 358, Waldoboro ME 04572. (207)832-7534. Editor: Samuel Pennington. For collectors and dealers in early Americana, antique furniture (country and formal), marine, redware, folk art, "Shaker things." Tabloid newspaper; 113 pages. Estab. 1973. Monthly. Circ. 13,000. Buys first North American serial rights. May buy second serial (reprint) rights for use in their annual. Buys about 60 mss/year. Pays on acceptance. Free sample copy. No photocopied or simultaneous submissions. Reports in 1 week. Query first or submit complete ms. SASE.

Nonfiction and Photos: Auction and show articles (mostly assigned); on antiques from 1700 to 1875. "We want writers who are very knowledgeable about antiques; writers who can write with feeling and 'tell it like it is' about the antiques business and collecting. We would be particularly interested in articles (chapters or selections) by authors of forthcoming antique books." Length: 1,000 words minimum. Pays $50-75. No additional payment for b&w photos used with mss. Captions required.

MAKE IT WITH LEATHER, Box 1386, Fort Worth TX 76101. (817)335-8500. Editor: Earl F. Warren. Buys all rights. Bimonthly. Estab. 1956. Circ. 60,000. Buys 60 mss/year. Pays on publication. Free sample copy and writer's guidelines. Reports in 6 to 8 weeks. SASE.

Nonfiction and Photos: "How-to-do-it leathercraft stories illustrated with cutting patterns, carving patterns. First-person approach even though article may be ghosted. Story can be for professional or novice. Strong on details; logical progression in steps; easy to follow how-to-do-it." Length: 2,000 words maximum. Payment starts at $25 to $50 plus $5 to $10 per illustration. "Most articles judged on merit and may range to '$200 plus' per ms. Depends on project and work involved by author." 5x7, or larger, b&w photos of reproduction quality purchased with mss. Captions required. Pays $5 minimum. Color of professional quality is used. Ektachrome slides or sheet film stock. Negs needed with all print film stock. Pays $8.50 minimum. All photos are used to illustrate project on step-by-step basis, and also finished item. "We can do photos in our studio if product sample is sent. No charge, but no payment for photos to writer. Letting us 'do it our way' does help on some marginal story ideas and mss since we can add such things as artist's sketches or drawings to improve the presentation."

Fillers: "Tips and Hints." Short practical hints for doing leathercraft or protecting tools, new ways of doing things, etc. Length: 100 words maximum. Pays $5 minimum.

How To Break In: "There are plenty of leathercraftsmen around who don't feel qualified to write up a project or who don't have the time to do it. Put their ideas and projects down on paper for them and share the payment. We need plenty of small, quick, easy-to-do ideas; things that we can do in one page are in short supply."

MILITARY COLLECTORS NEWS, P.O. Box 7582, Tulsa OK 74105. Editor: Jack Britton. For amateur and advanced collectors of all types of military items. Estab. 1967. Monthly. Circ. 3,200. Buys or acquires all rights. Buys or uses about 12 mss a year. Payment in contributor's copies or cash. "Since we receive many articles from our readers for which no payment other than contributor's copies is made, writers should let us know whether or not payment is expected." Sample copy 50¢. Reports in 1 week. Submit complete ms. SASE.

Nonfiction and Photos: Articles on the identification of military items (insignia, medals, uniforms, flags, weapons, aircraft, armor), anything that is of a military nature. Covers all periods

(Vietnam, Korea, WW I, WW II, Civil War; all earlier periods). Also, military history. Informational, humor, historical, nostalgia. Length: 100 to 2,000 words. Pays 1¢ per word, or 2 to 20 copies of the magazine. "We need photos of WW II, men in uniform, foreign weapons, tanks, etc. (WW I, or earlier)." Captions optional. Pays 50¢ to $1, or 2 to 4 copies of the magazine.
Fillers: Clippings, jokes. Length: half page or less. Pays 50¢ to $1, or 2 to 4 copies of the magazine.

MODEL RAILROADER, 1027 N. 7th St., Milwaukee WI 53233. Editor: Russell G. Larson. For hobbyists interested in scale model railroading. Monthly. Buys exclusive rights. Study publication before submitting material. Reports on submissions within 4 weeks. Query first. SASE.
Nonfiction: Wants construction articles on specific model railroad projects (structures, cars, locomotives, scenery, benchwork, etc.). Also photo stories showing model railroads. First-hand knowledge of subject almost always necessary for acceptable slant. Pays base rate of $36 per page.
Photos: Buys photos with detailed descriptive captions only. Pays $7.50 and up, depending on size and location. Color: double b&w rate. Full color cover: $112.

99 IC PROJECTS, Davis Publications, Inc., 380 Lexington Ave., New York NY 10017. (212)949-9190. Editor-in-Chief: Julian S. Martin. Managing Editor: Alan Rose. 100% freelance written. Emphasizes home hobby projects and theory. Annual magazine; 112 pages. Estab. January 1979. Pays on acceptance. Buys all rights. Previously published submissions OK. SASE. Submit seasonal/holiday material 1 month in advance of issue date. Reports in 4-6 weeks.
Nonfiction: "We are looking for brief, simple IC construction ideas that authors have assembled and operated. Refer to *101 Electronic Projects* for style and size." Buys100 mss/issue. Query. Length: 1,00-150 words. Pays $25-50/project.
Photos: State availability of photos with query. Offers no additional payment for b&w negatives with proof sheet. Buys all rights. "In most cases, we give permission for author and/or photographer to use material in other publications after publication date. Authorization given in writing only."
Fillers: Jokes, gags, anecdotes. Buys 3/issue. Pays $20-30.

OHIO ANTIQUE REVIEW, Box 538, Worthington OH 43085. (614)885-9757. Editor-in-Chief: James Lowder. Managing Editor: James Loeffler. 60-70% freelance written. For an antique-oriented readership, "generally well educated, interested in folk art and other early American items." Monthly tabloid; 60-68 pages. Estab. September 1975. Circ. 6,000. Pays on publication. Buys all rights, but may reassign following publication. Phone queries OK. Submit seasonal/holiday material 2 months in advance of issue date. Photocopied submissions OK. SASE. Reports in 2 weeks. Free sample copy and writer's guidelines; mention *Writer's Market* in request.
Nonfiction: "The articles we desire concern history and production of furniture, pottery, china, and other antiques of the period prior to the 1880's. In some cases, contemporary folk art items are acceptable. We are also interested in reporting on antique shows and auctions with statements on conditions and prices. We do not want articles on contemporary collectibles." Buys 5-8 mss/issue. Query with clips of previously published work. Length: 200-2,000 words. Pays $25-60.
Photos: State availability of photos with query. Payment included in ms price. Uses 3x5 or 5x7 glossy b&w prints. Captions required.

THE OLD BOTTLE MAGAZINE, Box 243, Bend OR 97701. (503)382-6978. Editor: Shirley Asher. For collectors of old bottles, insulators, relics. Monthly. Circ. 11,000. Buys all rights. Buys 35 mss a year. Pays on acceptance. Will send a sample copy to a writer on request. No query required. Reports in 1 month. Enclose SASE for return of submissions.
Nonfiction, Photos, and Fillers: "We are soliciting factual accounts on specific old bottles, canning jars, insulators and relics." Stories of a general nature on these subjects not wanted. "Interviews of collectors are usually not suitable when written by non-collectors. A knowledge of the subject is imperative. Would highly recommend potential contributors study an issue before making submissions. Articles that tie certain old bottles to a historical background are desired." Length: 250 to 2,500 words. Pays $20 per published page. B&w glossies and clippings purchased separately. Pays $5.

OLD CARS NEWSPAPER, Krause Publications, 700 E. State St., Iola WI 54945. (715)445-2214. Editor: Terry Boyce. 40% freelance written. "Our readers collect, drive, and restore everything

from 1899 locomobiles to '76 Cadillac convertibiles. They cover all age and income groups." Weekly tabloid; 80 pages. Estab. October 1971. Circ. 95,000. Pays on publication. Buys all rights, but may reassign following publication. Phone queries OK. Photocopied submissions OK. SASE. Reports in 2 months. Sample copy 50¢; mention *Writer's Market* in request.
Nonfiction: Historical (sites related to auto history, interesting oldsters from the automobile past, etc.); how-to (good restoration articles); interview (with important national level personages in the car hobby); new product (for regular column); nostalgia (auto-related, and only occasionally); and photo feature (by knowing hobby reporters, definite query). No "local man restores Model T Ford, Local club sponsors parking lot show, or local couple takes trip in Model A" type stories. Buys 4 mss/issue. Query. Pays 3¢/word.
Photos: State availability of photos with query. Pays $5 for 5x7 b&w glossy prints. Captions required. Buys all rights, but may reassign following publication.
Columns/Departments: Book reviews (new releases for hobbyists). Buys 1 ms/issue. Query. Pays 3¢/word. Open to suggestions for new columns/departments.
Fillers: Newsbreaks. Buys 20/year. Pays 3¢/word.

PERSONAL COMPUTING, 1050 Commonwealth Ave., Boston MA 02215. (617)232-5470. Editor-in-Chief: Harold G. Buchbinder. Assistant Editor: Ellen Stein. 95% freelance written. Emphasizes personal and small business computing. Monthly magazine; 132 pages. Estab. 1977. Circ. 40,000. Pays on publication. Buys all rights. Phone queries OK. Submit seasonal/holiday material 2-3 months in advance of issue date. Photocopied submissions OK. SASE. Sample copy $2; free writer's guidelines; mention *Writer's Market* in request.
Nonfiction: Exposé (comparison pieces, product reviews, manufactures evaluations); general interest (editorials, evaluations); historical (original pieces concerning computer history); how-to (program, use, debug, buy, sell, insure, sell services with/for computers); humor (fiction relating to computers and personal stories concerning computers); interview (with prominent figures in the field); new product (review, but not promo piece, must be objective; especially good, new product or comparison pieces); nostalgia (only if by someone of note or in the form of fiction); personal experience (someone who has bought, built, or worked with a specific system and has learned something readers can benefit from); personal opinion (editorials, or opinion of someone in field); photo feature (only if accompanied by article); profile (of prominent person in field); and technical (program writing, debugging, testing, especially good, applications for business, education, or home use). No articles on product hype, personal experiences that don't pass anything on to the reader, games that have been published in similar form already, and puzzles. Buys 20 mss/issue. Query or submit complete ms. Length: 1,000 words minimum. Pays $25/printed page minimum.
Photos: State availability of photos with query or ms. Offers no additional payment for b&w or color pictures. Captions preferred. Buys all rights.
Columns/Departments: Editorials (on any topic in the field); Future Computing (a detailed look at one or more aspects of what's going on in the field and what's projected); PC Interview (relating to prominent figures in the field); Random Access (unusual applications, going on, or stories about computers); and What's Coming Up (product reviews, comments on, criticism of, and comparison). Query or submit complete ms. Length: 1,000 words. Pays $25/printed page; Random Access pieces are paid anywhere from $5-25. Re-written press releases are not acceptable.
Fiction: "Fiction should relate to computers—minis, micros, or maxis . . . science fiction relating to computers also acceptable." Buys 1 ms/issue. Submit complete ms. Length: 750 words minimum. Pays $25/printed page.

POPULAR HANDICRAFT HOBBIES, Tower Press, Inc., Box 428, Seabrook NH 03874. Editor-in-Chief: Karen P. Sherrer. "Our readers are primarily women interested in crafts and hobbies. Many are looking for projects suitable for sale at church bazaars and fund-raising events. They also like crafts that are easy and inexpensive to do." Bimonthly magazine; 72 pages. Estab. 1966. Circ. 140,000. Pays on acceptance. Buys all rights, but may reassign following publication. Submit seasonal/holiday material 8-10 months in advance. SASE. Reports in 6-8 weeks. Free sample copy and writer's guidelines.
Nonfiction: How-to (illustrated with color slides and b&w photos; craft projects to make); informational (about new craft projects or techniques); historical (material about collecting as a hobby); humor (craft-related); profile (people who have an interesting hobby or do an unusual craft); new product; and photo feature. Buys 15 mss/issue. Query. Length: 200-1,500 words. Pays 2¢/word.
Photos: Purchased with accompanying ms. Submit prints or transparencies. Pays $5 minimum

for 4x5 or larger b&w glossy prints; $20 minimum for 35mm, 2¼x2¼ or 4x5 color transparencies. Model release required.

QUILTER'S NEWSLETTER MAGAZINE, Box 394, Wheatridge CO 80033. Editor: Bonnie Leman. Estab. 1968. Monthly. Circ. 80,000. Buys first or second North American serial rights. Buys about 15 mss a year. Pays on acceptance. Free sample copy. Will consider photocopied submissions. No simultaneous submissions. Reports in 2 to 3 weeks. Submit complete ms. SASE.
Nonfiction, Photos and Fillers: "We are interested in articles, fillers and photos on the subject of quilts and quiltmakers *only*. We are not interested in anything relating to 'Grandma's Scrap Quilts', but could use material about contemporary quilting." Pays 1½¢ a word minimum. Additional payment for photos depends on quality.

RADIO-ELECTRONICS, 200 Park Ave., S., New York NY 10003. (212)777-6400. Editor: Larry Steckler. Managing Editor: Arthur Kleiman. 85% freelance written. For electronics professionals and hobbyists. Monthly magazine; 120 pages. Estab. 1929. Circ. 188,000. Pays on acceptance. Buys all rights, second serial (reprint rights), first North American serial rights, and all rights, but may reassign following publication. Phone queries OK. Submit seasonal/holiday material 6-8 months in advance of issue date. Previously published submissions OK. SASE. Reports in 2-4 weeks. Free sample copy and writer's guidelines; mention *Writer's Market* in request.
Nonfiction: General interest; how-to; new product; photo feature; profile; and technical. Buys 10 mss/issue. Query or submit complete ms. Length: 1,000-1,500 words. Pays $50-500.
Photos: State availability of photos with query. Offers no additional payment for 4x5 or larger b&w prints or 35mm color transparencies. Captions preferred. Buys one-time, all rights, and all rights, but may reassign following publication. Model release required.
Columns/departments: Computer Corner and Hobby Corner. Buys 1,000 words/issue. Submit complete ms. Pays $50-200. Open to suggestions for new columns/departments.
Fillers: Short technical fillers. Buys 5/issue. Length 50-100 words. Pays $15-35.

RAILROAD MODEL CRAFTSMAN, P.O. Box 700, Newton NJ 07860. (201)383-3355. Managing Editor: Tony Koester. 75% freelance written. For "adult model railroad hobbyists, above average, including mature youngsters. All gauges, scales, plus collecting, railfanning." Estab. 1933. Monthly. Circ. 97,000. Buys all rights. Buys 50 to 100 mss/year. Payment on publication. Sample copy $1. Submit seasonal material six months in advance. SASE.
Nonfiction and Photos: "How-to model railroad features written by persons who did the work. They have to be good. Glossy photos a must. Drawings where required must be to scale, accurately and completely rendered. Some railroad prototype features if of interest to modelers and with modelers' slant. All of our features and articles are written by active model railroaders familiar with the magazine and its requirements. 'Outsiders' don't have the technical know-how to write for us. Non-model railroad writers invariably write up some local hobbyist as 'Joe Doaks has a railroad empire in his basement made all by himself,' treating him as some kind of nut. We do not want the cartoon of little men tying the little girl to model railroad track. We do want topnotch how-to model railroading articles." Purchases photos with and without mss. Captions required. Buys sharp 8x10 glossies and 35mm transparencies. Minimum payment: $1 per column inch of copy ($30 per page); $5 for photos ($1 per diagonal inch of published b&w photos, $3 for color transparencies); $75 for covers (must tie in with feature material in that issue).
How To Break In: "Frankly, there is virtually no chance of making a sale to us unless the author is a very experienced hobbyist in our field. I doubt that a non-model railroad hobbyist has authored a single line of copy for us in the past 40 years, so it's 'hobbyist first, author second' as far as we're concerned. Our material is for the serious hobbyist, not the general public trying to better understand our hobby, as a rule."

RAPIDFIRE REVIEW, Box 779, Glendora CA 91740. Editor-in-Chief: Ted Mauritzen. Emphasizes automatic weaponry collecting. Bimonthly magazine; 34 pages. Estab. 1977. Circ. 5,000. Pays on publication. Buys all rights, but may reassign following publication. Submit seasonal/holiday material 6 months in advance. Photocopied submissions OK. SASE. Reports in 4 weeks. Sample copy $2. Free writer's guidelines.
Nonfiction: Historical (information on all types of automatic and semiautomatic firearms. Museum collections with photos); how-to (shooting and servicing automatic firearms and ammunitions); informational; interview (with important collectors and ATF officials); new product; nostalgia, personal experience (military combat experience especially); personal opinion (range reports, etc.); photo feature (on special historical guns); technical (ballistics, etc.);

and travel (museums around the world with gun collections). Buys 4-6 mss/issue. Query. Length: 1,000-3,500 words. Pays $50-175.
Photos: Photos purchased with or without accompanying ms. Captions required. Pays $3-5 for 8x10 b&w glossies; $2-25 for 35mm, 2¼x2¼ or 4x5 color photos. Query. Send contact sheet. Total purchase price for ms includes payment for photos.
Fillers: Clippings and newsbreaks. Buys 10-15 fillers/issue. Length: 200-500 words. Pays $2-15.
How To Break In: "Have factual material that is timely. Come up with new ideas for articles that would be of interest to the automatic weapons buff. No dry writing or warmed over stories from other publications. This is a trial balloon. We are on a tight budget and are starting slowly. If all goes well, *Rapidfire Review* should be a fertile market for the novice who has an interest in guns and military ordnance. Those who stick with us will reap the rewards as we grow."

RELICS, Western Publications, Inc., Box 3338, Austin TX 78764. (512)444-3674. Editor: Pat Wagner. 90% freelance written. Bimonthly to collectors of Americana. Buys North American serial rights and occasionally reprint rights based on where the article originally appeared. Sample copy 35¢. Pays on acceptance. Query appreciated. Reports in 4 to 6 weeks. SASE.
Nonfiction and Photos: "General subject matter includes collectibles of any kind except those of museum quality. We are not as much devoted to the coverage of true antiques as to the myriad assortment of nostalgic items. Also pieces pertaining to personal collections if specific information is given, such as current value, how to judge, where to find, how to preserve. Articles must contain useful hints for the collector. 2,500 words is tops." Pays 2¢/word minimum. No mss considered unless accompanied by photos (b&w preferably) or drawings of item. Photos and drawings are returned after publication.

ROCK & GEM, 16001 Ventura Blvd., Encino CA 91436. (213)788-7080. Senior Editor: W.R.C. Shedenhelm. 95% freelance written. For amateur lapidaries and rockhounds. Monthly magazine; 100 pages. Estab. 1971. Circ. 75,000. Rights purchased vary with author and material. May buy first North American serial rights or first serial rights. Pays on publication. Sample copy $1. No photocopied or simultaneous submissions. Reports on material accepted for publication in 1 month. Returns rejected material immediately. Query first or submit complete ms. SASE.
Nonfiction and Photos: Knowledgeable articles on rockhounding and lapidary work; step-by-step how-to articles on lapidary and jewelry making. Length: open. Pays $40-50/published page. No additional payment for 8x10 b&w glossies used with mss. Color for cover (4x5 transpariencies) is by assignment only.

ROCKHOUND, P.O. Box 328, Conroe TX 77301. Editor: John H. Latham. For gem and mineral hobbyists. Bimonthly magazine; 52 pages. Estab. 1971. Circ. 20,000. Buys all rights, but will reassign rights to author after publication. Buys 75 to 100 mss/year. Pays on acceptance. Free sample copy and writer's guidelines. Will consider photocopied submissions. Will not consider simultaneous submissions. Reports in 3 to 4 weeks. Submit complete ms. SASE.
Nonfiction and Photos: Articles on where and how to find gems and minerals. "We cover only where and how to collect gems and minerals; not the whole lapidary field." Length: 250 to 3,000 words. Pays 2¢ per word. B&w glossies of any size purchased with mss. Captions required. Pays $5. Pays $5 to $35 for color transparencies used on cover.
How To Break In: "Write about collecting sites anywhere in the U.S., except the western states. We receive a glut of mss from the West. We particularly welcome new writers who write about the East, North, South, or Midwest. A bit of research on collecting sites (for gems and minerals) in these parts of the country will really sell us."

SCOTT'S MONTHLY STAMP JOURNAL, 3 E. 57th St., New York NY 10022. (212)371-5700. Editor: Paula Pines. For stamp collectors, from the pre-teenage beginner to the sophisticated philatelist. Monthly magazine; 64 pages. Estab. 1922. Circ. 24,000. Rights purchased vary with author and material. Usually buys all rights. Buys 12-24 mss/year. Pays on publication. Free sample copy. Will consider photocopied and simultaneous submissions. Submit seasonal or holiday material 3 months in advance. Reports in 4 weeks. Query first. SASE.
Nonfiction and Photos: "Stories about *stamps only*. Human interest and historical perspective very important. Must be lively, well-researched articles. Emphasize philatelic detail and human interest at the same time. Stamps capture the time and place of events. An interesting article might be one of a period in a country's stamp history such as 'Sweden, 1800 to 1900' or whatever historical events define as a period. We recently published a story about stamp collecting in the U.S.S.R." Length: 500 to 4,000 words. Pays $50 to $250. No additional payment is made for b&w photos used with mss.

How To Break In: "*Scott's Monthly Stamp Journal* is undergoing a complete change. Although all material deals with stamps, new writers are invited to seek assignments. It is not necessary to be a stamp collector or a published professional. You must (1) be a good writer, and (2) be willing to do careful research on strong material. Because our emphasis is on lively, interesting articles about stamps, including historical perspectives and human interest slants, we are open to writers who can produce the same. Of course, if you are an experienced philatelist, so much the better. We do *not* want to see finished manuscripts. What we *do* want is this: A query letter with paragraph summaries of suggested articles, followed by a phone call. Because our magazine does require philatelic detail, phone contact throughout the assignment is necessary. Long distance — please call collect."

THE SPINNING WHEEL, Everybodys Press, Inc., Hanover PA 17331. (717)632-3535. Editor: A. Christian Revi. For antique collectors and dealers. 10 times a year. Pays on publication. Buys exclusive rights unless author wishes some reservations. SASE.
Nonfiction: Authentic, well-researched material on antiques in any and all collecting areas; home decorating ideas with antiques. Prefers combined scholar-student-amateur appeal. No first-person or family history. Prefers draft or outline first. Requires bibliography with each ms. Quality illustrations. Length: 500 to 1,500 words. Pays minimum $1 per published inch, including pictures.
Photos: Photos and professional line drawings accepted. Photos should be top quality b&w, no smaller than 5x7. If of individual items shown in groups, each should be separated for mechanical expediency. Avoid fancy groupings.

STITCH 'N SEW, Tower Press, Box 338, Chester MA 01011. Editor: Barbara Hall Pedersen. For women of all ages who like to sew. Magazine published every 2 months; 64 pages, (8x11). Estab. 1968. Circ. 200,000. Buys all rights. Buys 50 mss a year. Payment on publication. Will send free sample copy to writer on request, if large S.A.S.E. is enclosed. Write for copy of guidelines for writers. Submit holiday crafts, especially Christmas, 6 months in advance. Query first or submit complete ms. Reports in 2 to 8 weeks. Enclose SASE.
Nonfiction, Photos, and Fillers: "Articles on various facets of needlework; knitting, crocheting, garment construction, embroidery, tatting, gift and toy making, decorative items for the home. Our emphasis is on old-fashioned practicality. Our projects appeal to the woman on a tight budget. We like 'scratch' projects which utilize readily available materials which do not cost much. How-to articles must include either a sharp photograph, or drawing or actual sample." Length: 1,500 words maximum. Pays $5 to $50. B&w and color photos purchased with accompanying ms. jcaptions required. Pays $35 for 4x5 color transparency used on cover.

TODAY'S FILM MAKER, 250 Fulton Ave., Hempstead NY 11550. Editor: Arnold F. Kroekman. 60% freelance written. For amateur movie makers and hobbyists. Quarterly magazine; 50 pages. Estab. 1971. Circ. 40,000. Rights purchased vary with author and material. May buy all rights, but will reassign rights to author after publication; first North American serial rights or first serial rights. Buys 25 to 30 mss/year. Pays on publication. Free sample copy and writer's guidelines. Will consider photocopied submissions. No simultaneous submissions. Reports in 1 week. Query first. SASE.
Nonfiction and Photos: How-to articles; Super 8 film techniques. All material should tell the amateur how to better use his equipment to achieve professional results. Informational, personal experience, interviews, think pieces, personal opinion, reviews. Captions required for photos used with mss. Pays minimum of $35 per published page; $5 for accompanying photos.

TREASURE, Jess Publishing, 16146 Covello St., Van Nuys CA 91406. (213)988-6910. Editor-in-Chief: David Weeks. Managing Editor: Richard Fales. Emphasizes treasure hunting and metal detecting. Monthly magazine; 74 pages. Estab. 1969. Circ. 100,000. Pays on publication. Buys all rights, but may reassign following publication. Phone queries OK. Submit seasonal/holiday material 4 months in advance. Previously published submissions OK. SASE. Reports in 1 month. Free writer's guidelines.
Nonfiction: Jim Williams, Articles Editor. How-to (coinshooting and treasure hunting tips); informational and historical (location of lost treasures with emphasis on lesser known); interviews (with treasure hunters); profiles (successful treasure hunters and metal detector hobbyists); personal experience (treasure hunting); technical (advice on use of metal detectors and metal detector designs). Buys 6-8 mss/issue. Send complete ms. Length: 300-3,000 words. Pays $15-150. "Our rate of payment varies considerably depending upon the proficiency of the author, the quality of the photographs, the importance of the subject matter, and the amount of useful information given."

Photos: No additional payment for 5x7 or 8x10 b&w glossies used with mss. Pays $50 minimum for color transparencies (120 or 2¼x2¼). Color for cover only. Model release required.

TRI-STATE TRADER, 27 N. Jefferson St., Knightstown IN 46148. (317)345-5134. Managing Editor: Kevin Tanzillo. Editor: Elsie Kilmer. 75% freelance written. For persons interested in antiques, history, restorations, etc. Weekly newspaper; 40 pages. Estab. 1968. Circ. 29,000. Not copyrighted. Pays on 10th of month following publication. Free sample copy and writer's guidelines. Submit seasonal (Christmas, Easter, Halloween) material 4 months in advance. Query first. SASE.
Nonfiction and Photos: Prefers material that deals with antiques, collectibles, or places of historical interest; restored homes, etc. Chiefly in the North Central and border states. Interested in material on less commonly found antiques, but not museum type pieces; including origin, date of manufacture, unique features; pattern names of glassware; ceramics with dates and origin (including foreign ceramics); trademarks. Much of the material received is too general in content and omits dates, styles, names of firms, etc. Also uses auction reports and nostalgic material related to antiques and collectibles. Length: 1,200 words maximum. Pays $5 to $25. Pays $3 to $5 for b&w photos purchased with or without ms. $2 for Polaroids.
Fillers: In areas of this newspaper's interests; specific information on subjects of antique and historical interests; used as fillers. Length: 500 words maximum. Pays 25¢ per published inch.

WOMEN'S CIRCLE, Box 428, Seabrook NH 03874. Editor: Marjorie Pearl. For women of all ages. Monthly magazine; 72 pages. Buys all rights. Buys 150 mss/year. Pays on acceptance. Sample copy 75¢. Submit seasonal material 7 months in advance. Reports in 1 to 3 months. Query first or submit complete ms. SASE.
Nonfiction: How-to articles on hobbies, handicrafts, etc. Also food, recipes, needlework, dolls, home, family and children. Informational approach. Needs Christmas crafts for Christmas annual. Length: open. Pays 3¢ per word.

THE WORKBASKET, 4251 Pennsylvania, Kansas City MO 64111. Editor: Mary Ida Sullivan. Issued monthly. Buys first rights. Pays on acceptance. Query. Reports in six weeks. SASE.
Nonfiction and Photos: Uses articles, 400 to 500 words, which explain how a person or a family has benefited, financially or otherwise, by sewing, needlecraft, etc. Interested in step-by-step directions for making project. Also has a how-to short-stuff section which uses material on hobbies, ideas for pin-money and the like. These are limited to 250 words or under and bring a flat sum of $5. Pays 4¢ a word for articles, plus $5 to $7 for accompanying art. 5x7 or 8x10 pix with mss.

WORKBENCH, 4251 Pennsylvania Ave., Kansas City MO 64111. (816)531-5730. Editor: Jay W. Hedden. 65% freelance written. For woodworkers. Estab. 1946. Circ. 500,000. Pays on publication. Buys all rights, but returns all but first magazine rights on request, after publication. Reports in 10-14 days. Query. SASE.
Nonfiction and Photos: "In the last couple of years, we have increased our emphasis on home improvement and home maintenance, and now are getting into alternate energy projects. Ours is a nuts-and-bolts approach, rather than telling how someone has done it. Because most of our readers own their own homes, we stress 'retrofitting' of energy-saving devices, rather than saying they should rush out and buy or build a solar home. Energy conservation is another subject we cover thoroughly; insulation, weatherstripping, making your own storm windows. We still are very strong in woodworking, cabinetmaking and furniture construction. Projects range from simple toys to complicated reproductions of furniture now in museums. We pay a minimum of $150/published page. Shop tips bring $20 maximum with drawing and/or photo. If we pay less than the rate, it's because we have to supply photos, information, drawings or details the contributor has overlooked. Contributors should look over the published story to see what they should include next time. Our editors are skilled woodworkers, do-it-yourselfers and photographers. We have a complete woodworking shop at the office and we use it often to check out construction details of projects submitted to us."

WORKING CRAFTSMAN, Box 42, 1290 Shermer Rd., Northbrook IL 60062. Editor: Marilyn Heise. For serious craftsmen (both professional and part-time), teachers, shopowners who sell handcrafted items, suppliers; others seriously interested in crafts. Quarterly magazine; 40 pages. Estab. 1971. Circ. 10,000. Buys first rights. Buys about 8 mss/year. Pays on publication. Sample copy $2.25. Reports on material accepted for publication by return mail. Returns rejected material in 3 months. Query first. SASE.
Nonfiction and Photos: Emphasis is on how to market crafts. Also, ideas for teaching for art

departments or home studio teachers; new products; trends in the crafts field; new books, careers in crafts, ideas for operating successful shops or galleries. Does not want to see anything on crafts as a hobby, or how-to pieces on individual crafts. Uses articles based on personal experience, and those dealing with successful business operations and merchandising techniques. Interviews, profiles, inspirational, humorous and historical articles. Length: 50 to 1,500 words. Pays $5 to $35, except for humorous and historical material. Payment for these is $5 to $20 or $25. Pays $5 to $50 for photo articles of 25 to 1,500 words. $5-$20 for reviews of craft shows; 50 to 600 words; 5x7 or 8x10 b&w or color photos of craftsmen seriously involved in crafts; teachers, schools. These are purchased with mss or on assignment. Pays $5 minimum. Captions required.

Home and Garden Publications

APARTMENT LIFE, 1716 Locust, Des Moines IA 50336. Editor: David Jordan. For apartment residents. Monthly magazine; 108 pages. Estab. 1968. Circ. 850,000. Buys all rights. Buys 60 to 100 mss a year. Payment on acceptance. Will not consider photocopied or simultaneous submissions. Submit seasonal material 5 to 6 months in advance. Reports in 2 months. Query first. Enclose SASE.
Nonfiction and Photos: "Service material specifically for people who live in cities and apartments. Thorough, factual, informative articles always slanted toward the apartment situation." Informational, how-to, travel. Length: 300 to 1,000 words. Pays $250 to $400. B&w photos and color are purchased only on assignment.

BETTER HOMES AND GARDENS, 1716 Locust St., Des Moines IA 50336. (515)284-9011. Editor: James A. Autry. For "middle-and-up income, homeowning and community-concerned families." Monthly. Circ. 8,000,000. Buys all rights. Pays on acceptance. Query preferred. Submit seasonal material 1 year in advance. Mss should be directed to the department where the story line is strongest. SASE.
Nonfiction: "Freelance material is used in areas of travel, health, cars, money management, and home entertainment. Reading the magazine will give the writer the best idea of our style. We do not deal with political subjects or areas not connected with the home, community and family." Pays top rates based on estimated length of published article; $100 to $2,000. Length: 500 to 2,000 words.
Photos: Shot under the direction of the editors. Purchased with mss.
How To Break In: "Follow and study the magazine, to see what we do and how we do it. There are no secrets, after all; it's all there on the printed page. Having studied several issues, the writer should come up with one or several ideas that interest him, and, hopefully, us. We consider freelance contributions in the areas of health, education, cars, money matters, home entertainment, and travel. The next step is to write a good query letter. It needn't be more than a page in length (for each idea), and should include a good stab at a title, a specific angle, and a couple of paragraphs devoted to the main points of the article. This method is not guaranteed to produce a sale, of course; there is no magic formula. But it's still the best way I know to have an idea considered."

THE CANADIAN LOG HOUSE, Box 1205, Prince George, B.C., Canada V2L 4V3. Editor-in-Chief: B. Allan Mackie. 40% freelance written. "For a middle and upper income audience; well educated, otherwise all ages and sexes. Everyone needs a home, but these are the people who have the energy, the drive, the intelligence to want to create a superior home with their own hands." Annual magazine; 70 pages. Estab. 1974. Circ. 20,000. Pays on acceptance. Buys one-time rights. Annual deadline is October 1. Reports in 1 week.
Nonfiction: Historical (on excellent log construction methods), how-to (do any part/portion of a good solid timber house), informational, humor, inspirational, interview (with a practicing, professional builder, or a factual one on an individual who built a good house), new product (if relevant), personal experience (house building), photo feature (on good log buildings of a permanent residential nature; absolutely no cabins or rotting hulks), and technical (preservatives, tools). Query. Length: 3,000 words maximum. Pays $50 minimum.
Photos: Mary Mackie, Photo Editor. Purchased with accompanying ms. Captions required. Send contact sheet. Pays $3 minimum for 5x7 b&w glossy photos (negatives appreciated); $10 minimum for 2¼x2¼ transparencies.

FAMILY FOOD GARDEN, Box 1014, Grass Valley CA 95945. (916)273-3354. Editor: George S. Wells. For gardeners. Magapaper (magazine in newspaper format) published 10 times/year; 24 pages. Estab. 1973. Circ. 250,000. Buys all rights, but will reassign rights to author upon request.

Buys about 50 mss a year. Pays on publication. Free sample copy and writer's guidelines. Will not consider photocopied or simultaneous submissions. Submit seasonal material 3 months in advance. Reports in 3 weeks. Query first. SASE.
Nonfiction and Photos: "Our approach is 'practical' food growing, We prefer gardening advice based on personal experience, or sometimes third-person accounts. Not interested in inspirational approach, but in practical, usable advice on all aspects of growing fruit, vegetables and meat. We do not cover flower gardening except very incidentally. We are interested in articles in which the economics of home raising of food are spelled out; exact costs, food budget savings, etc. We do not want recipes, except as inclusions in articles about particular foods. Inspirational gardening articles or very long articles do not have much chance." Length: 300 to 1,200 words. Pays $25-50 for illustrated articles. No additional payment for b&w used with mss. Snapshot size acceptable for b&w; any size color transparencies, but b&w is more often used.

FLOWER AND GARDEN MAGAZINE, 4251 Pennsylvania, Kansas City MO 64111. Editor-in-Chief: Rachel Snyder. 20-50% freelance written. For home gardeners. Monthly. Picture magazine. Circ. 600,000. Buys first rights. Pays on acceptance. Free writer's guidelines. Query first. Reports in 6 weeks. SASE.
Nonfiction: Interested in illustrated articles on how-to-do certain types of gardening, descriptive articles about individual plants. Flower arranging, landscape design, house plants, patio gardening are other aspects covered. "The approach we stress is practical (how-to-do-it, what-to-do-it-with). We try to stress plain talk, clarity, economy of words. We are published in 3 editions: Northern, Southern, Western. Some editorial matter is purchased just for single edition use. Most, however, is used in all editions, so it should be tailored for a national audience. Material for a specific edition should be slanted to that audience only." Length: 1,000 to 1,200 words. Pays 5¢/word or more, depending on quality and kind of material.
Photos: Buys photos submitted with mss or with captions only. Pays up to $12.50 for 5x7 or 8x10 b&w's, depending on quality, suitability. Also buys color transparencies, 35mm and larger. Pays $20 to $125 for these, depending on size and use.
How To Break In: "Prospective author needs good grounding in gardening practice and literature. Then offer well-researched and well-written material appropriate to the experience level of our audience. Illustrations help sell the story."

GARDEN MAGAZINE, The Garden Society, A Division of the New York Botanical Garden, Bronx Park, Bronx NY 10458. Editor: Ingrid Eisenstadter. 30% freelance written. Emphasizes horticulture, environment, and botany for a diverse readership, largely college graduates and professionals united by a common interest in plants and the environment. Bimonthly magazine; 44 pages. Estab. March 1977. Circ. 20,000. Buys all rights, but may reassign following publication. Submit seasonal/holiday material 4 months in advance of issue date. Photocopied and previously published submissions OK. SASE. Reports in 2 months. Sample copy $2.
Nonfiction: Ann Botshon, associate editor. "All articles must be of high quality, meticulously researched and botanically accurate." Exposé (environmental subjects); how-to (horticultural techniques, must be unusual and verifiable); general interest (plants of interest, botanical information); humor (pertaining to botany and horticulture); photo feature (pertaining to plants and the environment); and travel (great gardens of the world). Buys 1-2 mss/issue. Query with clips of previously published work. Length: 500-2,500 words. Pays $50-300.
Photos: Carol Dethloff, designer. Pays $35-50 for 5x7 glossy b&w prints; $40-150 for 4x5 or 35mm color transparencies. Captions preferred. Buys one-time rights.

HOME, THE CANADIAN FAMILY MAGAZINE, Home Info Distributing, Ltd., 59 G Howden Rd., Scarborough, Ontario, Canada M1R 3C7. (416)759-0215. Managing Editor: Marian den Boer. 50% freelance written. Emphasizes homes, gardens, cooking and crafts for Canadian homeowners. Bimonthly magazine; 64 pages. Estab. 1976. Circ. 40,000. Pays on publication. Buys all rights. Phone queries OK. Submit seasonal/holiday material 4 months in advance of issue date. SASE. Reports in 2 months. Free sample copy and writer's guidelines; mention *Writer's Market* in request.
Nonfiction: How-to (do-it-yourself projects for the home, crafts, decorating, cooking); new product (of use to the homeowner available in Canada, must be new); and technical (energy saving techniques, wood, wind, solar energy, written specifically for a Canadian readership). Buys 4-5 mss/issue. Query with clips of previously published work. Length: 1,500-3,000 words. Pays $25-150.
Photos: State availability of photos with query. Offers no additional payment for photos accepted with ms. Captions preferred. Buys all rights, but may reassign following publication.

HOMEOWNERS HOW TO HANDBOOK, The Make-It, Fix-It, Grow-It Magazine, 380 Madison Ave., New York NY 10017. Editor: Jim Liston.90% freelance written. A Popular Science publication of Times Mirror Magazines. Estab. 1974. Quarterly. Circ. 300,000. Buys all rights. Pays on acceptance. Sample copy $1.50; address request to: Milton J. Norcross, Homeowners How To Handbook Subscription Department, 380 Madison Ave., New York NY 10017. No photocopied or simultaneous submissions. Submit seasonal material 7 months in advance. Reports in 3 weeks. SASE.
Nonfiction and Photos: Wants how-to information based on facts and experience — not theory. "Design ideas should be original and uncomplicated. They should be directed at young homeowners working with simple tools, and, if possible, the kind of project that can be completed on a weekend. All articles should contain a list of necessary materials and tools. Photos are as important as words. B&w preferred. 4x5's are OK, but 8x10's are better." Length: 1,800 words maximum. Pays $150 per published page maximum. No additional payment for b&w photos used with mss.
Fillers: Problem Solvers, a regular filler feature, pays $25 per captioned photo that contains a work-saving hint or solves a problem.

HORTICULTURE, 300 Massachusetts Ave., Boston MA 02115. Editor: Esther Mackintosh. Published by the Massachusetts Horticulture Society. Monthly. "We buy only first and exclusive rights to mss; one time use rights for photos." Pays after publication. Query first. Reports in 6 weeks. SASE.
Nonfiction and Photos: Uses authentic articles from 500 to 1,000 words on plants and gardens, indoors and out, based on actual experience. Study publication. Pays 2¢ to 3¢ per word, more for special features. Photos: color must be accurate tones, transparencies only, preferably not Ektachromes "and accurately identified."

HOUSE AND GARDEN, The Conde Nast Building, 350 Madison Ave., New York NY 10017. Editor-in-Chief: Mary Jane Pool. For homeowners and renters in middle and upper income brackets. Monthly. Circ. 1,136,444. Buys all rights. Pays on acceptance. Will not send sample copy. "Study magazine before querying." Reports immediately. Query first and include sample of previous writing. SASE.
Nonfiction and Photos: Subjects of interest to "families concerned with their homes. Nothing for young marrieds specifically." Anything to do with the house or garden and affiliated subjects such as music, art, books, cooking, etc. Length: about 1,500 words. Payment varies. Jerome H. Denner, Assistant Managing Editor, is department editor. Photos purchased with mss only.
How To Break In: "This is a very tough market to break into. We very seldom use unsolicited material, but if anything is going to have a chance of making it here, it should be on a news breaking item. It must be something which has not already been covered in the other major magazines. It must have a new slant. Read the magazine closely for style and avoid things we've already done. We get too many freelancers sending us material on subjects for which the crest of wave has already passed. There's no guarantee that providing a short item (say, for Gardener's Notes, which is mostly staff-written) will be an easier way in, but if you understand our needs and provide something that's really good, there's always a chance. It's best to send a query and a sample of previous writing."

HOUSE BEAUTIFUL, The Hearst Corporation, 717 5th Ave., New York NY 10022. Editor-in-Chief: Doris Shaw. Executive Editor: Norma Skurka. Emphasizes design, architecture and building. Monthly magazine; 200 pages. Estab. 1896. Circ. 850,000. Pays on acceptance. Submit seasonal/holiday material 4 months in advance of issue date. SASE. Reports in 5 weeks.
Nonfiction: Carol Cooper Garey, copy editor. Historical (landmark buildings and restorations); how-to (kitchen, bath remodelling service oriented); humor; interview; new product; profile and travel. "No articles on religion." Buys 10 mss/year. Submit complete ms. Length: 300-1,500 words. Pays $150-400.
Photos: State availability of photos with ms. Offers no additional payment for photos.

HOUSE PLANTS AND PORCH GARDENS, Scrambling Press, Inc.,1 Aldwyn Center, Villanova PA 19085. (215)527-5100. Editor-in-Chief: Peter Tobey. Emphasizes house plants and porch or terrace gardens. Monthly magazine; 96 pages. Estab. 1976. Circ. 250,000. Pays on publication. Buys all rights. Phone queries OK. Submit seasonal/holiday material 5-6 months in advance. Photocopied submissions OK. SASE. Reports in 3 weeks. Sample copy $1.50; free writer's guidelines.
Nonfiction: Ava Seave, Managing Editor. How-to (building plant-oriented projects, i.e., making terrariums, work areas, containers, etc.); informational (care and culture of specific plant

families or individual plants); profile (on renowned horticulturists who have done interesting or unusual things in the plant world, generally in interview format). Buys 2-3 mss/issue. Send sample of writing along with resume, outline of proposed article, with a 1-2 page introduction, and a list of areas of expertise. Length: 1,200-6,000 words. Pays $100/1,000 words, pre-editing.
Photos: Purchased with or without mss, or on assignment. Captions required. Send b&w prints or color transparencies. Pays $10-25 for 8x10 b&w glossies; $25-50 for color used inside.
Columns, Departments: Artificial Light Gardening (all aspects); Basics (of indoor gardening); Potpourri (short, interesting bits about all aspects of gardening); Weird but Lovable (house or greenhouse plants that are odd in color, size, shape); Greenhouse (all aspects of greenhouse gardening); All columns are geared to amateur gardeners. Buys 20% of column material per year. Length: 1,200-3,500 words. Send sample of writing, with resume, outline of proposed article, with a 1-2 page introduction. Pays $100/1,000 words, pre-editing. Open to suggestions for new columns and departments.
Fillers: Clippings; gardening tips; jokes, gags, anecdotes. All plant-oriented. Send fillers in. Buys 2-3/issue. Length: 25-200 words. Pays 10¢/word, pre-editing.

HOUSEHOLD GARDENING AND HOUSE PLANTS, Box 874, Oak Bluffs MA 02557. Editor: Louise Aldrich Bugbee. 99% freelance written. For growers of home gardens and house plants. Magazine; 72 pages. Estab. 1975. Buys all rights. Pays on publication. Writer's guidelines for SASE. Will consider photocopied submissions. Submit seasonal material 8 months in advance. Reports in 2 months. Submit complete ms. SASE.
Nonfiction, Photos and Fillers: How-to articles on gardens and house plants, unusual flowers and vegetables. Either serious or light material. Should be slanted to appeal to ordinary readers, interested in gardens and plants. "Our aim is garden talk among friends and neighbors." Length: About 500 words for articles; 25 to 100 words for fillers. Pays $5-15.

HOUSTON HOME AND GARDEN, Bayland Publishing, Inc., Box 25386, Houston TX 77005. Editor-in-Chief: Karleen Koen. Emphasizes shelter. Monthly magazine; 200 pages. Estab. 1974. Circ. 60,000. Pays on publication. Buys all rights, but may reassign following publication. Submit seasonal/holiday material 4-6 months in advance. Photocopied and previously published submissions OK. SASE. Reports in 2 months. Sample copy $1.50; free writer's guidelines.
Nonfiction: How-to (home maintenance and repairs); informational (city, tax information) and new product (short description). Buys 40 mss/year. Query. Length: 1,000-2,000 words. Pays $2.50/published inch.
Photos: Photos purchased with accompanying ms. Captions required. Pays $15-20 for 8x10 b&w glossies. Model release required.
Fillers: Informative, how-to pieces. Buys 2 fillers/issue. Length: 500-1,000 words. Pays $25-50.

ORGANIC GARDENING AND FARMING, Rodale Press Publications, 33 E. Minor St., Emmaus PA 18049. (215)967-5171. Managing Editor: Jeff Cox. For a readership "ranging the full scope of public now aware and interested in growing plants, vegetables and fruits, as well as concerned about environmental problems." Monthly magazine; 160 to 240 pages. Estab. 1942. Circ. 1,300,000. Buys all rights and the right to reuse in other Rodale Press Publications with agreed additional payment. Buys 400 to 500 mss/year. Payment on publication (actually, on preparation for publication). Free sample copy and writer's guidelines. Reports in 4 to 6 weeks. Query first or submit complete ms. SASE.
Nonfiction, Photos and Fillers: "Factual and informative articles or fillers especially on backyard gardening, family farming, plus stressing organic methods. Interested in all crops, soil topics, livestock, indoor gardening, greenhouses; natural foods preparation, storage, etc.; biological pest control; variety breeding, nutrition, recycling, energy conservation; community and club gardening. Strong on specific details, step-by-step how-to, adequate research. Good slant and interesting presentation always help. We do not want to see generalized garden success stories. And some build-it-yourself topics are often repeated. We would like to see material on development, techniques, different approaches to organic methods in producing fruit crops, grains, new and old vegetables; effective composting, soil building, waste recycling, food preparation. Emphasis is on interesting, practical information, presented effectively and accurately." Length: 1,200 to 2,500 words for features. Pays $100-350. B&w and color purchased with mss or on assignment. Enlarged b&w glossy print and/or negative preferred. Pays $15-25. 2¼x2¼ (or larger) color transparencies. Fillers on above topics are also used. Length: 150 to 500 words. Pays $35 to $50.

PERFECT HOME MAGAZINE, 427 6th Ave., S.E., Cedar Rapids IA 52401. Editor: Donna Nicholas Hahn. For "homeowners or others interested in building or improving their homes."

Estab. 1929. Monthly. Buys all rights. Pays on acceptance. Study magazine carefully before submitting. No seasonal material used. Submit editorial material at least 6 months in advance. Reports "at once." Free sample copy. Query first. SASE.

Nonfiction: "Ours is a nationally syndicated monthly magazine sponsored in local communities by qualified home builders, real estate companies, home financing institutions, and lumber and building supply dealers. We are primarily a photo magazine that creates a desire for an attractive, comfortable home. We need homebuilding, decorating, and remodeling features, decorating idea photographs, complete home coverage, and plans on homes." No do-it-yourself features. Length: 1 to 3 meaty paragraphs. No set price. "Each month we feature one nationally known guest editor on the theme 'What Home Means to Me.' Check with us before contacting a celebrity since we have had so many of them." Length: 500 to 1,000 words. Pays $50, including copy, photos, signature, and signed release from individual.

Photos: Purchases photos with articles on home building, decorating and remodeling; also purchases photos of interest to homeowners with captions only. Buys either b&w or color; color 3¼x4¼ up. "We return color; keep b&w unless return is requested as soon as issue has been printed. May hold photos 1 year." Photos must be well-styled and of highest professional quality. No models in pictures. Interested in series (for example, several pictures of gates, bay windows, window treatment, fireplaces, etc.). Pays $25 minimum.

PLANTS ALIVE, 5509 1st Ave., S., Seattle WA 98108. Publisher: Theodore R. Marston. Managing Editor: John McClements. 88% freelance written. Emphasizes houseplants, greenhouses some outdoor gardening. For an audience extremely interested in gardening (indoors and outdoors). Monthly magazine; 100 pages. Estab. 1972. Circ. 140,000. Pays on publication. Buys all rights, but may reassign following publication. Submit seasonal/holiday material at least 3 months in advance. Photocopied submissions OK. SASE. Reports in 4 weeks-12 months. Free sample copy and writer's guidelines.

Nonfiction: Chris Miller, Assistant Editor. How-to (related to growing plants, building plant equipment, greenhouses); informational (to help readers with all aspects of gardening); histories (of popular flowers, usually combined with useful information); interviews (with leading growers or horticulturists, especially if article includes useful information for readers); travel (pieces on unique and unusual gardens around the world); new product (will it help our readers or is it a dud?) and newsworthy, first person accounts on gardening; capillary watering, plant photography and personality articles (how this person built a greenhouse or an indoor atrium, etc.). Buys 220 mss/year. Query or submit complete ms. Length: 300-2,000 words. Pays 4¢/word.

Photos: Norm Comp, Art Director. Purchased with mss. Pays $10 for 8x10 b&w glossies; $35 for color transparencies (35mm minimum). Model release required.

Columns/Departments: How-to (ideas on building plant stands, light units, greenhouses, planters). Plant Propagation (how to increase plants in general or a specific kind of plant, or by one particular method). Buys 24 mss/year. Query or send complete ms. Pays 4¢/word plus $10 for each drawing or b&w photo used.

How To Break In: "Freelancer should be specific, know subject and be accurate. Article shouldn't be too technical, though. Organize thoughts and present in logical manner. Ideas should be somewhat newsworthy; not something that has appeared in other publications. Leads should be snappy. Copy should be clear with no extra baggage."

POOLIFE, Olin Corp., 120 Long Ridge Rd., Stamford CT 06904. (203)356-3251. Editor: Russell Pendergast. Managing Editor: Eileen Sharkey. For "a broad based family audience of men, women, and children with the bulk of readers consisting of young adults (18-35) and adults (35-54). Their common bond is ownership of a home swimming pool and a lifestyle that is heavily oriented toward the home, home entertaining, family leisure activities (cooking, gardening, etc.) and backyard sports and games." Semiannual magazine; 40 pages. Estab. 1970. Circ. 700,000. Pays on acceptance. Buys all rights. Submit seasonal/holiday material 8 months in advance of issue date. Photocopied and previously published submissions OK. SASE. Reports in 4 weeks. Free sample copy.

Nonfiction: Humor (poolside anecdotes); how-to (improve life in and around the pool—landscaping, building, poolside structures, energy saving, decorating, cooking and entertaining); informational (health, safety, swimming); interview (related to poolside living); and photo feature (related to pools). Buys 10-16 mss/year. Query. Length: 550-2,000 words. Pays $200 minimum.

Photos: Offers no additional payment for photos accepted with accompanying ms. Uses all types of color transparencies and 8x10 b&w prints. Captions and model release required.

POOL 'N PATIO, 3923 W. 6th St., Los Angeles CA 90020. Editor: Fay Coupe. Issued once

yearly, in April, to residential owners of swimming pools. Buys all rights. Pays on publication. Reports on submissions at once. SASE.
Nonfiction and Photos: Articles on how to make pool maintenance easier; technical articles on equipment, unusual use of pools, or unusual pools; human interest or glamour stories on pool owners. Pays 5¢/word. Length: 500 to 1,500 words. Photos purchased with mss. Pays $5 minimum.

REAL ESTATE, P.O. Box 1689, Cedar Rapids IA 52406. (319)366-1597. Editor: C.K. Parks. 65% freelance written. "A publication sponsored by real estate brokers for distribution to homebuyers, clients, and community leaders." Bimonthly magazine; 16 pages. Special Christmas issue. Estab. 1972. Circ. 80,000. Buys all rights. Buys about 24 mss/year. Pays on acceptance. Free sample copy. Photocopied submissions OK. No simultaneous submissions. Submit seasonal material 4 months in advance. Reports in 30 days. Enclose SASE.
Nonfiction and Photos: "The work of freelance writers fits particularly well into this type of publication because we are looking for nontechnical material of interest to the general public." Wants mss about how-to projects that can be done around the home, decorating in the home, and investing in real estate. Length: 700 to 1,200 words. Pays $100 to $150. Photos purchased with accompanying ms with extra payment. No color. Pays $10 for first photo; $5 per additional photo. Size: 5x7.

SELECT HOME DESIGNS, 382 W. Broadway, Vancouver, British Columbia, Canada V5Y 1R2. (604)879-4144. Editor-in-Chief: Ralph Westbrook. Managing Editor: Brian Thorn. 50% freelance written. Emphasizes building, renovation, and interior design of single family homes. Quarterly magazine. Estab. 1948. Circ. 110,000. Pays on publication. Buys all rights, but may reassign following publication. Phone queries OK. Submit seasonal/holiday material 60 days in advance of issue date. Simultaneous, photocopied and previously published submissions OK. SASE. Reports in 2 weeks. Free sample copy and writer's guidelines; mention *Writer's Market* in request.
Nonfiction: General interest (explaining new products or innovations in methods relating to home and cottage); how-to (pertaining to home or cottaging); new product (energy sources, interior design products, lighting, etc.); photo feature (furniture, interiors, housing in general); and technical (new products or techniques relative to home or cottage). Buys 4-5 mss/issue. Query. Length: 250-2,000 words. Pays 3-10¢/word.
Photos: Geoffrey Noble, artistic director. "We are a 4-color consumer magazine. We prefer color photography for maximum effect." Pays $2 minimum for 8x10 glossy b&w prints; $5 minimum for 35mm color transparencies. Captions preferred. Buys all rights, but may reassign following publication. Model release required.
Columns/Departments: "We have no established columns or departments, but are open to their establishment on a continuing basis." Query. Length: 250-1,000 words. Pays 3-10¢/word.

WOMAN TALK MAGAZINE, Box 356, Blackwood NJ 08012. Editor: Elizabeth Ettore.For women of all ages with interests in all areas of homemaking. Bimonthly; 36 pages. Estab. 1973. Circ. 1,200. Not copyrighted. Buys 30 mss/year. Pays on publication. Sample copy $.60. Will consider photocopied submissions. Will not consider simultaneous submissions. Submit seasonal material 3 to 4 months in advance. Reports in 2 months. Query first or submit complete ms. SASE.
Nonfiction and Photos: Articles on goal achievement, interesting women, homemakers, gardening, animals, spare-time earning. "We emphasize a person-to-person relationship between our book and the reader and try gently to broaden the horizons of our readers. Our size makes it absolutely necessary that articles be concise. Style is open, but we do prefer a light approach. This does not preclude thoughtful subject matter, but nothing on the sensational side." Informational, how-to, interview, profile, humor, historical. Length: no minimum; 1,000 words maximum. Prefers 400 to 600 words. Pays ½¢ a word. Columns and departments include: Garden Corner, Pet Page, and recipes for Quik-E Page. Items on needlework of all kinds are always needed. Pays ½¢ a word.

YOUR HOME, P.O. Box 2315, Ogden UT 84403. (801)394-9446. Editor: Helen S. Crane. 30% freelance written. For young marrieds of middle income and better than average education who own their homes and are interested in improving them. Monthly magazine; 16 pages. Estab. 1945. Circ. 650,000. Buys all rights, but may reassign rights to author after publication. Buys about 20 mss/year. Pays on acceptance. Free sample copy. Query first, with copies of published material. SASE.
Nonfiction and Photos: "Articles on decorating the home, small vignettes on lifestyles past or

present. Our emphasis is on articles that can be illustrated effectively. We want short, but pertinent, pieces that give the reader new ideas. Articles must be general in scope and timeless in appeal; short, yet meaty. We don't want to see amateur photos of one's own do-it-yourself project, nor do we want heavy, pedantic tomes on nutrition or any household tips." Length: 400-700 words. Pays $40-70. Pays $15-20 for b&w glossies purchased with mss. Can use 35mm color transparencies, but prefers larger. "Must be sparkling." Pays $25 minimum.

Humor Publications

Publications in this category specialize in humor. Other publications that use humor can be found in nearly every category in this book. Some of these have special needs for major humor pieces; some use humor as fillers; many others are simply interested in material that meets their ordinary fiction or nonfiction requirements but has a humorous slant.

MAD MAGAZINE, 485 Madison Ave., New York NY 10022. Editor: Al Feldstein. Buys all rights.
Nonfiction: "You know you're *almost* a *Mad* writer when: You include a self-addressed, stamped envelope with each submission. You realize we are a visual magazine and we don't print prose, text or first/second/third person narratives. You don't send us stuff like the above saying, 'I'm sure one of your great artists can do wonders with this.' You first submit a 'premise' for an article, and show us how you're going to treat it with three or four examples, describing the visuals (sketches not necessary). You don't send in 'timely' material, knowing it takes about 6 months between typewriter and on-the-stands. You don't send poems, song parodies, fold-ins, movie and/or TV show satires, Lighter Sides or other standard features. You understand that individual criticism of art or script is impossible due to the enormous amount of submissions we receive. You don't ask for assignments or staff jobs since *Mad* is strictly a freelance operation. You concentrate on new ideas and concepts other than things we've done (and over-done), like 'You Know You're a . . . When . . . '."

ORBEN'S CURRENT COMEDY, ORBEN'S COMEDY FILLERS, 1200 N. Nash St. Arlington VA 22209. (703)522-3666. Editor: Robert Orben. For "speakers, toastmasters, businessmen, public relations people, communications professionals." Biweekly; monthly. Buys all rights. Pays at the end of the month for material used in issues published that month. "Material should be typed and submitted on standard size paper. Please leave 3 spaces between each item. Unused material will be returned to the writer within a few days if SASE is enclosed. We do not send rejection slips. Please do not send us any material that has been sent to other publications. If SASE is not enclosed, all material will be destroyed after being considered except for items purchased."
Fillers: "We are looking for funny, performable one-liners, short jokes, and stories that are related to happenings in the news, fads, trends, and topical subjects. The accent is on comedy, not wit. Ask yourself, 'Will this line get a laugh if performed in public?' Material should be written in a conversational style and, if the joke permits it, the inclusion of dialogue is a plus. We are particularly interested in material that can be used by speakers and toastmasters: lines for beginning a speech, ending a speech, acknowledging an introduction, specific occasions, anything that would be of use to a person making a speech. We can use lines to be used at sales meetings, presentations, conventions, seminars, and conferences. Short, sharp comment on business trends, fads, and events is also desirable. Please do not send us material that's primarily written to be read rather than spoken. We have little use for definitions, epigrams, puns, etc. The submissions must be original. If material is sent to us that we find to be copied or rewritten from some other source, we will no longer consider material from the contributor." Pays $3.

In-Flight Publications

This list consists of publications read by commercial airline passengers. They use freelance material of general interest such as travel articles, etc., as well as general interest material on aviation.

AIR CALIFORNIA MAGAZINE, The Publishing Co., Box 707, South Laguna CA 92677. (714)494-9393. Editor-in-Chief: Michael McFadden. Emphasizes all aspects of California for airline passengers on the world's 2nd largest intra-state airline. Monthly magazine; 84 pages.

Estab. 1967. Circ. 225,000. Pays on publication. Buys one-time rights. Phone queries OK. Submit seasonal/holiday material 3 months in advance. Simultaneous, photocopied and previously published submissions OK. SASE. Reports in 2 months. Sample copy $1.
Nonfiction: Sheldon Kilbane, Nonfiction Editor. Historical; humor; informational (travel); inspirational (if not sentimental); interview (California personalities); nostalgia; photo feature; profile and travel (California or international). Buys 35 mss/year. Query. Length: 1,500-5,000 words. Pays $50-150.
Photos: Photos purchased with accompanying ms or on assignment. Captions required. Pays $10-25 for 8x10 b&w photos; $25-50 for 35mm color photos. No additional payment for photos accepted with accompanying ms. Model release required.

ALOFT, Wickstrom Publishers, Inc., 2701 South Bayshore Dr., Suite 501, Miami FL 33133. (305)858-3546. Editor: Karl Wickstrom. 90% freelance written. For National Airlines passengers. Travel-oriented. Offbeat places, things to see and do along NAL route or connecting areas. Designed for light upbeat entertainment. Bimonthly. Rights to be negotiated. Pays on publication. Sample copy 25¢. Will consider photocopied submissions. Reports in 4-6 weeks. Query. Address query to Ms. Pat Pinkerton, Executive Editor. SASE.
Nonfiction and Photos: Articles on unusual or little-known places rather than national monuments, historical sites, and the usual commercial attractions. New emphasis on leisure activity of interest to the affluent male. Each issue contains at least one piece by or about a known personality. NAL city restaurant dining (with recipes), book reviews and fashion, are handled by staff or contributing editors. No controversial or expose articles. Length: 800 to 1,500 words. Pays $150 and up for articles. Color transparencies are purchased with mss or captions on travel, sports, adventure. Must be top quality with imaginative approach. Payment negotiated. Photo Editor: Theodore R. Baker.

CALIFORNIA, East/West Network, Inc., 5900 Wilshire Blvd., Suite 300, Los Angeles CA 90036. (213)937-5810. Editor: John Johns. Managing Editor: Pam Gates. 90% freelance written. Monthly magazine; 160 pages. Pays within 60 days after acceptance. Buys all rights, but may reassign following publication. Submit seasonal/holiday material 4 months in advance of issue date. Simultaneous and photocopied submissions OK. SASE. Sample copy $1.
Nonfiction: Prefers California slant. General interest; humor; interview (top-level government, entertainment, sports figures); new product (trends, survey field); profile; and business (with California orientation). Buys 10 mss/issue. Query. Length: 500-2,000 words. Pays $100-400.
Photos: Jim Cornfield, photo editor. State availability of photos with query. Pays $50-100 for b&w contact sheets or negatives; pays $75-175 for 35mm or 2¼x2¼ color transparencies. Captions required. Buys one-time rights. Model release required.
Columns/Departments: Business Trends. Buys 1 ms/issue. Query. Length: 700-1,500 words. Pays $100-300.
Fiction: Adventure; experimental; humorous; mystery and science fiction. No esoteric or historic fiction. Buys 3 mss/year. Submit complete ms. Length: 500-1,500 words. Pays $100-200.
Fillers: Short humor. Buys 4/year. length: 500-700 words. Pays $100.

THE CALIFORNIA MAGAZINE, East/West Network, 5900 Wilshire Blvd., Suite 300, Los Angeles CA 90036. See *East/West Network*.

CLIPPER, East/West Network, 488 Madison Avenue, New York NY 10022. Editorial Director: Fred R. Smith. See *East/West Network*.

EAST/WEST NETWORK, INC., 5900 Wilshire Blvd., Suite 300, Los Angeles CA 90036. (213)937-5810. Editorial Director: Fred R. Smith. Publishes *The California Magazine, Clipper, Flightime, Mainliner, ReView, Sky, Sundancer, Companion* and *Reflections*. In-flight magazines for Allegheny Airlines, Continental Airlines, Delta Airlines, Eastern Airlines, Hughes Airwest, Ozark Airlines, Pacific Southwest Airlines, Pan Am and United Airlines. In-room magazines for Holiday Inn and Ramada Inn. Monthly magazines. Estab. 1968. Circ. (combined) 18 million. Pays within 60 days of acceptance. Buys all *East/West Network* rights. SASE. Reports in 1 month. All inquiries except for *The California Magazine* and *Sundancer* should be sent to Fred R. Smith, 488 Madison Ave., New York NY 10022.
Nonfiction: "On business, topical subjects, sports, personalities, trends, and destinations." Length: 1,000-2,000 words. Pays $75-1,000.

FLAIR MAGAZINE, 6500 Midnight Pass Rd., Penthouse Suite 504, Sarasota FL 33581. (813)921-5513. Editor: Robert J. Murley. For the passengers of Florida Air Lines, Air South and

Shawnee Airlines. Tabloid; 24 pages. Established in 1975. Monthly. Circulation: 20,000. Acquires all rights. Buys about 36 mss a year. Pays on publication. Will send sample copy to writer on request. Write for copy of guidelines for writers. Will consider photocopied submissions. No simultaneous submissions. Reports in 30 days. Query first or submit complete ms. Enclose SASE.
Nonfiction and Photos: Upbeat articles on travel and vacation. Items of regional interest (the Southeast and the Bahamas), business-oriented articles. Short, personal experience articles on travel and leisure activities. Length: 1,000 words. Pays 2¢ to 3¢ a word; $50 maximum. No additional payment for b&w photos used with mss. Captions required.

FLIGHTIME, East/West Network, 488 Madison Ave., New York NY 10022. Editorial Director: Fred R. Smith. See *East/West Network.*

FLYING COLORS, Halsey Publishing Co., 15383 N.W. 7th Ave., Miami FL 33021. Editor-in-Chief: Seymour Gerber. 80% freelance written. In-flight magazine of Braniff International Airlines. Monthly magazine; 56 pages. Estab. 1972. Circ. 1,000,000. Pays on publication. Buys all rights, but may reassign following publication. Previously published submissions OK. SASE. Reports in 3 months. Sample copy $2; writer's guidelines for SASE.
Nonfiction: Humor; informational, interview (question and answer); and travel (Braniff International destination cities). Buys 24 mss/year. Query. Length: 1,500-2,000 words. Pays $175-250.
Photos: Purchased with accompanying ms. Captions required. Send transparencies. Uses 35mm, 2¼x2¼ or 4x5 color transparencies. Total price for ms includes payment for photos. Model release required.

INTERLUDE, Box 6680, Vancouver, British Columbia, Canada V6B 4L4 (604)732-1371. Editor/Publisher: W.J.B. Mayrs. Assistant Editor: Elspeth Woodske. 75% freelance written. Emphasizes local material on Pacific Western Airlines destinations. Bimonthly magazine; 40 pages. Estab. 1976. Circ. 50,000. Pays on publication. Buys first North American serial rights. Phone queries OK. Submit seasonal/holiday material 6 months in advance of issue date. Photocopied submissions OK. SASE. Free sample copy and writer's guidelines.
Nonfiction: General interest (western Canada); how-to (travel); humor; interview (western or travel personalities); photo feature; and travel (P.W.A. destinations). No "heavy subject" articles. Buys 30 mss/year. Query or submit complete ms. Length: 500-1,500 words. Pays $25-100.
Photos: "No articles are used without some visual material; accompanying photos make this easier." Submit photo material with accompanying query or mss. Pays $10 for 5x7 b&w glossy prints and $10-100 for 35mm color transparencies. Captions and model release required. Buys one-time rights.
Fillers: Off Spottin's (funny photos in British Columbia, Alberta, or the Northwest Territory); That: trivia or unusual bits of information. Length: 50-150 words. Pays $10-35.

LATITUDE/20, 1649 Kapiolani Blvd., #28, Honolulu HI 96814. Editor: Jeri Bostwick. For Hawaiian Air passengers; affluent tourists and local people traveling inter-island. Monthly magazine; 34-48 pages. Estab. 1974. Circ. 2,500,000. Not copyrighted. Buys about 30 mss/year. Pays on publication. Sample copy for $1. Will consider photocopied submissions. No simultaneous submissions. Reports in 2 months. Query first. SASE.
Nonfiction and Photos: Primarily interested in Hawaiiana. Practical information and historical facts. Self-improvement articles. Travel-related humor. Ethnic stories are always welcome (Japanese, Chinese, Korean, Filipino, Hawaiian, Samoan, Portuguese). No word pictures of swaying palms and scarlet sunsets. Length: 1,000 to 1,500 words. Pays $50. No additional payment for photos used with mss. Pays $50 for cover photos; model release required.

MAINLINER, East/West Network, 488 Madison Ave., New York NY 10022. Editorial Director: Fred R. Smith. See *East/West Network.*

METRO, Box 60033, Houston TX 77205. (713)443-6256. Managing Editor: Art Young. "An in-flight publication for commuter airlines covering East Texas and the Gulfcoast." Pays on publication. Buys first rights. Phone queries OK. Submit seasonal/holiday material 3 months in advance of issue date. SASE.
Nonfiction: Informational; historical; humor; interview; nostalgia; profile; travel; photo feature and technical articles (if directed toward laymen). Articles should be aimed at the traveling salesman whose first interest is to learn about the area to which he is traveling. Also needs general interest material. Query. Length: 500-1,500 words. Pays 3-5¢/word.

Photos: Purchased with or without mss, or on assignment. Query. Captions required. Pays $5-25 for 8x10 b&w glossy prints. Fee for color transparencies or negatives is negotiable.

NORTHWEST PASSAGES, The Webb Co., 1999 Shepard Rd., St. Paul MN 55116. Editor-in-Chief: Jean Marie Hamilton. Managing Editor: Jim Carney. 80% freelance written. For Northwest Orient Airlines passengers. Monthly magazine. Pays on acceptance. Buys all rights, but may reassign following publication. Buys 61 mss/year. Reports in 2-4 weeks. Query with samples of published work. No complete mss accepted. SASE. Sample copy $1; free writer's guidelines.
Nonfiction: Controversial ("rather than pure expose, but we want to explore both sides of any controversy"); how-to (on business, health, etc.,—no crafts); informational (sports, business trends, modern living, current issues); historical (with current peg); interviews and profiles (on interesting people who are saying things of significance); personal opinion (only from writers with the proper credentials); travel (no broadbrush, what-to-see, where-to-stay pieces) and business management. Length: 1,500-2,200 words. Pays $75-500.
Photos: Purchased with mss and on assignment. Query. Pays $25-75/b&w; $50-100/color; $200/cover shots. For photos purchased with mss, "the package price is negotiated ahead of time." Model release required.

REVIEW, East/West Network, 488 Madison Ave., New York NY 10022. Editorial Director: Fred R. Smith. See *East/West Network*.

ROYALE, Box 60033, Houston TX 77205. (713)443-6256. Managing Editor: Art Young. An in-flight publication for commuter airlines in Louisiana. For further details, see the *Metro* listing.

SKY, East/West Network, 488 Madison Ave., New York NY 10022. Editorial Director: Fred R. Smith. See *East/West Network*.

SOUTHWEST AIRLINES MAGAZINE, Summit Publishing Co., 11824 Radium, San Antonio TX 78216. (512)349-1281. Editor-in-Chief: Al Mogavero. Managing Editor: Dani Presswood. 50% freelance written. "Readership consists primarily of passengers of Southwest Airlines, which serves the major cities of Texas." Monthly magazine; 80 pages. Estab. 1971. Pays on acceptance. Buys first North American serial rights. Submit seasonal/holiday material at least 3 months in advance of issue date. Photocopied and previously published submissions OK. SASE. Reports in 2-4 weeks. Sample copy $1.50.
Nonfiction: "Most articles have a Texas orientation; however, there are some of a general nature with no local connection, for example, "The Psychology of Color." General interest ("these make up the majority of our stories. We're looking for interesting and unusual articles that will hold the reader's attention as he/she flies the airline. Recent example are "Houston's Boy in the Plastic Bubble" and "The Newton Boys: Uvalde's Favorite Bank Robbers."); how-to (e.g., "How to Diet When You're Traveling", "How to Cope with Stress"); interview (question & answer format; subject must be well-known in his/her field); photo feature; profile (subject must be a Texan who has succeeded in his field or line of work); and articles of particular interest to business executives. No personal opinion or experience articles. Buys 50 mss/year. Query or submit complete ms. Length: 1,500-3,000 words. Pays $60-125.
Photos: Franco Cernero, photo editor. State availability of photos with query or ms. Offers no additional payment for photos accepted with accompanying ms. Uses 5x7 or 8x10 b&w glossy prints. Buys one-time rights. Model release required.

SUNDANCER, East/West Network, 5900 Wilshire Blvd., Suite 300, Los Angeles CA 90036. See *East/West Network*.

TIME ZONES, 15383 N. W. 7th Ave., Miami FL 33169. Semiannual. See *Flying Colors*.

TWA AMBASSADOR (for Trans World Airlines), The Webb Co., 1999 Shepard Rd., St. Paul MN 55116. Editor-in-Chief: James Morgan. 90% freelance written. "For TWA passengers, top management executives, professional men and women, world travelers; affluent, interested and responsive." Monthly magazine. Estab. 1968. Circ. 321,000. Pays on acceptance. Buys first and second rights. Submit seasonal/holiday material 6 months in advance. SASE. Reports in 2-4 weeks. Sample copy $1; free writer's guidelines.
Nonfiction: Controversial (rather than the pure expose; we insist on exploring all sides in any topic), historical (with current peg), how-to (in business subjects, health; no crafts or hobbies),

humor (on current topics), informational (sports, business, modern living, current issues, etc.), interview (with interesting people who are saying something of significance), personal opinion (from writers with the proper credentials), profile (people who're topical, timely; covered in-depth. Not just what they do, but why they do it), travel (no "where-to-go, what-to-see" pieces) and business management. Buys 72 mss/year. Query. Length: 800-2,000 words. Pays $100-600.

Photos: Purchased with accompanying ms. Query. Pays $25-75 for b&w photos; $50-150 for 35mm and larger color transparencies ($250 for cover). "We often buy photos with mss; the package price is negotiated ahead of time." Model release required.

Columns/Departments: Health, Travel, Sports, Food and Drink, Technology, Management, Education, Art, etc. "We buy short (800-900 words) pieces and run them as columns, under the appropriate heading." Pays $150 maximum. Open to suggestions for new columns/departments.

VOYAGER, Trent Press, Ltd., 63 Shrewsbury Ln., Shooters Hill, London, England SE18 3JJ. Editor: Dennis Winston. 80% freelance written. 20% of material from American/Canadian writers. Emphasizes travel for "a reasonably sophisticated audience, middle to upper income and intelligence, both sexes, all ages." Quarterly magazine; 32 pages. Estab. 1973. Circ. 15,000. Pays on publication. Buys one-time rights. Submit seasonal/holiday material 6 months in advance. Photocopied and previously published submissions OK ("if not previously published in U.K."). SASE. Reports in 1 month.

Nonfiction: Humor (real-life travel experiences), informational (articles concerning business and/or holidays in areas with which magazine is concerned), and travel (relevant to area served by magazine). "*Voyager* is the free in-flight magazine for passengers of British Midland Airways, which has several domestic routes within the U.K., and international routes to France, West Germany, Belgium, Holland, and the Republic of Ireland. A new route to Denmark is expected soon. Our need is for well-informed, entertaining articles about business, tourism, and facets of life in those countries and in others for which those countries are gateways." Buys 6 mss/issue. Submit complete ms. Length: 1,000-2,000 words maximum. Pays 25-45 pounds.

Photos: Purchased with accompanying ms. Captions required. Submit prints or transparencies. Pays 3-12 pounds for 8x6 b&w glossies; 7-20 pounds for color transparencies. Total purchase price for ms includes payment for photos.

How To Break In: "Articles must be informative, specific (e.g., name hotels and restaurants, give prices), not outdated, entertaining. First person material is welcomed."

WESTERN'S WORLD, 141 El Camino, Beverly Hills CA 90212. (213)273-1990. Editor: Frank M. Hiteshew. Assistant Editor/Art Director: Tom Medsger. Published by Western Airlines for the airline traveler. Established in 1970. 6 times a year. Circulation: 250,000. Buys all rights. Buys 20 to 25 mss a year. Pays on publication. Will consider photocopied submissions. Submit seasonal material 12 months in advance of issue date. Reports in 1 to 3 months. Query first. Enclose SASE.

Nonfiction: "Articles should relate to travel, dining, or entertainment in the area served by Western Airlines: Hawaii, Minneapolis/St. Paul, Alaska to Mexico, Miami and between. General interest (non-travel) articles are welcome too, as a change of pace. Compared to other airline magazines, *Western's World* strives for a more editorial approach. It's not as promotional-looking; all articles are bylined articles. Some top names in the field." Buys photo features and travel articles. Length: 1,000 to 2,000 words. Pays 10¢ a word.

Photos: Department Editor: Tom Medsger. Purchased with or without mss or on assignment; captions required. Uses 8x10 b&w glossies, but "rarely." Pays $25. Uses 35mm, 4x5, and larger color transparencies. Pays $25 to $125; "more for cover, subject to negotiation."

Fiction: Short stories, fantasy, and humor. "Rarely printed because we've seen so few good ones. Should relate to the geographic areas served by Western Airlines. No personality profiles." Length: 1,000-2,000 words. Pays 10¢/word.

Jewish Publications

The publications which follow use material on topics of general interest slanted toward a Jewish readership. Publications using Jewish-oriented religious material are categorized in Religious Publications.

AMERICAN JEWISH TIMES-OUTLOOK, Box 10674, Charlotte NC 28234. (704)372-3296. Editor: Ronald D. Unger. For Jewish middle and upper class; religious; primarily own their own

businesses or corporations; most of the women are club oriented. Monthly magazine; 24 pages. Special issues for Rosh Hashanah, Hanukkah, Purim and Passover. Circ. 5,000. Not copyrighted. Buys 12 to 15 mss a year. Pays on publication. Free sample copy and writer's guidelines. Will consider photocopied and simultaneous submissions. Submit special holiday material at least 2 months in advance; usually earlier. Length of time in which reports are given on material accepted for publication depends on material. Returns rejected material in 7 to 10 days. Query first. SASE.
Nonfiction and Photos: Articles primarily dealing with Jewish topics of interest: economic news, Israel, Soviet Jewry, holy days, Jewish personalities, art, music, sports, etc. Book reviews and short features. Articles usually take an analytical, rather than reportive, style. A more condensed style is preferred. Length: maximum of 3 typed, double-spaced pages. Pays $10 per article. No additional payment for b&w photos used with mss.
Fiction, Poetry and Fillers: Fantasy, humorous, religious, and historical fiction. If timely, may be linked to Holy Days. Pays $25. Traditional and avant-garde forms of poetry, blank verse, free verse, haiku. Must relate to publications's theme. Pays $10 minimum. Groups of jokes, gags, anecdotes; and short humor used as fillers. Pays $10 minimum.

THE AMERICAN ZIONIST, Zionist Organization of America, 4 E. 34th St., New York NY 10016. Editor-in-Chief: Elias Cooper. 15% freelance written. Political journal pertaining to Israel, Middle East, and Jewish affairs. Monthly magazine; 40 pages. Estab. 1910. Circ. 44,000. Pays "some time after publication." Buys all rights, but may reassign following publication. Photocopied submissions OK. SASE.
Nonfiction: Expose, historical, humor, informational, inspirational, interview, nostalgia, profile, and travel. Buys 64 mss/year. Length: 2,000-3,000 words. Pays $50-100.
Poetry: "Mainly used as filler material." Buys 4 poems/year. Pays $15.

CANADIAN ZIONIST, 1310 Greene Ave., Montreal, Quebec, Canada H3Z 2B2. Editor-in-Chief: Dr. Leon Kronitz. Associate Editor: Rabbi Sender Shizgal. Assistant Editor: Irene Welik. 40% freelance written. Emphasizes Zionism. Published 7-8 times/year. 40-48 pages. Estab. 1934. Circ. 34,000. Pays on publication. Submit seasonal/holiday material 2 months in advance of issue date. Photocopied submissions OK. Reports in 3 weeks. Free sample copy.
Nonfiction: General interest (Jewish or Zionist current events); historical (Jewish or Zionist history); interview (with prominent figures in Israeli politics, art or science); profile (on Israeli political figures); and technical (Zionism, Jewish interest, Middle East politics). No stories on personal experiences or travel to Israel. Buys 10 mss/year. Query with clips of previously published work. Length: 1,500-2,500. Pays $125 maximum.
Photos: State availability of photos with query. No additional payment for b&w prints.

JEWISH CURRENT EVENTS, 430 Keller Avenue, Elmont NY 11003. Editor: S. Deutsch. 25-30% freelance written. For Jewish children and adults; distributed in Jewish schools. Biweekly. Pays on publication. No sample copies available. No query required. Reports in 1 week. SASE.
Nonfiction: All current event items of Jewish content or interest; news; featurettes; short travel items (non-Israel) relating to Jewish interests or descriptions of Jewish communities or personalities; life in Jewish communities abroad; "prefer items written in news-style format." Length must be short. Pays anywhere from $10 to $300, depending on content, illustrations, length and relevance.
Photos: Purchased with mss, if available, but not required. All items of Jewish content or interest. B&w snapshots only. Payment varies.

THE JEWISH DIGEST, 1363 Fairfield Ave., Bridgeport CT 06605. Editor: Bernard Postal. For "urban, well-educated families, interested in topics of Jewish interest." Estab. 1955. Monthly. Circ. 15,000. Occasionally buys first North American serial rights. Pays on acceptance. Sample copy for $1. Submit seasonal material (Jewish holidays) six months in advance. Will consider photocopied submissions. Reports in 2 weeks. SASE.
Nonfiction: Subject matter should be of "Jewish interest. Jewish communities around the world, and personality profiles. Contemporary topics about and relating to Jews in the U.S. and abroad. We would like to see personal experiences, biographic sketches, impressions of the Jewish community here and abroad." Length: 2,000 words. Pays 1¢ to 2¢ a word with $30 maximum.

JEWISH TELEGRAPH, Telegraph House, Bury Old Rd., Manchester M2S 8HH, England. Editor: Frank Harris. Weekly. Estab. 1950. Circ. 11,500, Copyrighted. Pays on publication.

SAE and International Reply Coupons. Free sample copy.
Nonfiction: Exclusive news and humorous and historical articles of Jewish interest. Pays 3 pounds minimum.

MIDSTREAM, 515 Park Ave., New York NY 10022. Editor: Joel Carmichael. Monthly. Circ. 14,000. Buys first rights. Pays on publication. Reports in 2 weeks. SASE.
Nonfiction and Fiction: "Articles offering a critical interpretation of the past, searching examination of the present, and affording a medium for independent opinion and creative cultural expression. Articles on the political and social scene in Israel, on Jews in Russia and the U.S.; generally it helps to have a Zionist orientation. If you're going abroad, we would like to see what you might have to report on a Jewish community abroad." Buys historical and think pieces and fiction, primarily of Jewish and related content. Pays 7¢ minimum per word.
How To Break In: "A book review would be the best way to start. Send us a sample review or a clip, let us know your area of interest, suggest books you would like to review."

MOMENT MAGAZINE, 55 Chapel St., Newton MA 02160. (617)964-2512. Editor-in-Chief: Leonard Fein. Emphasizes Jewish affairs. Monthly magazine; 80 pages. Estab. 1975. Circ. 25,000. Pays on publication. Buys all rights. Phone queries OK. Submit seasonal/holiday material 6 months in advance. Reports in 4 weeks. Sample copy $2.
Nonfiction: Expose, how-to, informational, historical, humor, nostalgia, profile, personal experience. Top literary quality only. Buys 100 mss/year. Query or submit complete ms. Length: 1,000-5,000 words. Pays $50-400.
Fiction: Anne Fishman, Fiction Editor. "We use only the highest quality fiction. If you wouldn't send it to the *New Yorker,* don't send it to us. Stories must have high Jewish content." Buys 8 mss/year. Submit complete ms. Length: 1,000-5,000 words. Pays $100-400.
How To Break In: "We rarely publish beginners. Best way to break in is to have published in other quality magazines."
Rejects: "We don't want anything sentimental or cliched. We receive far too many mss on the Holocaust. No room for memoirs or family stories."

THE NATIONAL JEWISH MONTHLY, 1640 Rhode Island, N.W., Washington DC 20036. (202)857-6645. Editor: Charles Fenyvesi. Published by B'nai B'rith. Monthly magazine. Buys North American serial rights. Pays on publication. SASE.
Nonfiction: Articles of interest to the Jewish community: economic, demographic, political, social, biographical. Length: 4,000 words maximum. Pays 10¢/word maximum.

RECONSTRUCTIONIST, 432 Park Ave., S., New York NY 10016. (212)889-9080. Editor: Dr. Ira Eisenstein. A general Jewish religious and cultural magazine. Monthly. Estab. 1935. Circ. 6,000. Buys all rights. Buys 10 mss/year. Payment on publication. Free sample copy. Query first. SASE.
Nonfiction: Publishes literary criticism, reports from Israel and other lands where Jews live, and material of educational or communal interest. Also uses interviews and features dealing with leading Jewish personalities. Preferred length is 3,000 words and payment is from $15 to $25.
Fiction and Poetry: Uses a small amount of poetry and fiction as fillers.

SOUTHERN JEWISH WEEKLY, Box 3297, Jacksonville FL 32206. (904)355-3459. Editor: Isadore Moscovitz. 10% freelance written. For a Jewish audience. Estab. 1924. General subject matter is human interest and short stories. Weekly. Circ. 28,500. Not copyrighted. Buys 15 mss/year. Payment on acceptance. Will send a free sample copy to a writer on request. Will send editorial guidelines sheet on request. Submit seasonal material one month in advance. Reports in 10 days. Enclose SASE.
Nonfiction and Photos: Approach should be specifically of "Southern Jewish interest." Length: 250 to 500 words. Pays $10 to $25. Buys b&w photos with mss.

WORLD OVER, 426 W. 58th St., New York NY 10019. Editor: Stephen Schaffzin. 50% freelance written. Buys first serial rights only. Pays on acceptance. Reports within three to four weeks. Query first. SASE.
Nonfiction, Photos, and Fiction: Uses material of Jewish interest, past or present for ages 8-13 and up. Articles up to 1,700 words. Fiction should be Jewish in content. Length: 600-800 words. Pays 6¢/word minimum. B&w glossies purchased with mss.

Juvenile Publications

This section of *Writer's Market* includes publications for children ages 2 to 12. Magazines for young people 12 to 25 appear in the Teen and Young Adult category.

Most of the following publications are produced by religious groups, and wherever possible, the specific denomination is given. For the writer with a story or article slanted to a specific age group, the sub-index which follows is a quick reference to markets for his story in that age group.

Those editors who are willing to receive simultaneous submissions are indicated. (This is the technique of mailing the same story at the same time to a number of low-paying religious markets of nonoverlapping circulation. In each case, the writer, when making a simultaneous submission, should so advise the editor.) The few mass circulation, nondenominational publications included in this section which have good pay rates are not interested in simultaneous submissions and should not be approached with this technique. Magazines which pay good rates expect, and deserve, the exclusive use of material.

Writers will also note in some of the listings that editors will buy "second rights" to stories. This refers to a story which has been previously published in a magazine and to which the writer has already sold "first rights." Payment is usually less for the re-use of a story than for first-time publication.

Juvenile Publications Classified by Age

Two-to Five-Year Olds: Children's Playmate, Children's Service Programs, The Friend, Happy Times, Highlights for Children, Humpty Dumpty's Magazine, Jack and Jill, The Kindergartner, Nursery Days, Our Little Friend, Ranger Rick's Nature Magazine, Story Friends.

Six-to Eight-Year-Olds: Child Life, Children's Playmate, Children's Service Programs, Cricket, Crusader, The Friend, Highlights for Children, Humpty Dumpty's Magazine, It's Our World, Jack and Jill, Jet Cadet, Let's Find Out, Primary Treasure, R-A-D-A-R, Ranger Rick's Nature Magazine, Story Friends, Video-Presse, The Vine, Weekly Bible Reader, Wonder Time, Wow, Young Crusader, Young Judaean.

Nine-to Twelve-Year-Olds: The Beehive, Child Life, Children's Service Programs, Cricket, Crusader, Crusader Magazine, Discoveries, Discovery, Ebony, Jr., The Friend, Highlights for Children, It's Our World, Jack and Jill, On the Line, Primary Treasure, R-A-D-A-R, Rainbow, Ranger Rick's Nature Magazine, Sprint Magazine, Story Friends, Trails, Video-Presse, The Vine, Wee Wisdom, Young Crusader, Young Judaean, Young Musicians.

THE BEEHIVE, 201 8th Ave., S., Nashville TN 37203. Editor: Martha Wagner. Published monthly in weekly format for children in grades five and six in United Methodist Church schools. Free sample copy. Buys all rights. Pays on acceptance. Submit double-spaced copy, 65-character line count. Reports on submissions within three months. SASE.

Nonfiction and Photos: Most articles requested by editor from writers. Subject matter relates to or correlates with church school curriculum and interests of children in grades 4, 5 and 6. Should not be overly moralistic or didactic. May provide information to enrich cultural understanding in religion and in relationships with other people. Also well-written biography, not composed from encyclopedias. Length: 200 to 800 words. Pays 3¢ a word. Photos purchased with mss. B&w glossies; color transparencies. Pays $1 to $25.

Fiction and Poetry: Modern day life, problems. Unusual historical stories; church history. No slang, references to drinking, or smoking. Might-have-happened Biblical stories. "Many stories are too long, too unrealistic, or goody-goody." Length: about 700 words. Poetry to 20 lines. Pays 50¢ per line.

CHILD LIFE Mystery and Science Fiction Magazine, Saturday Evening Post Co., Youth Publications, 1100 Waterway Blvd., Box 567B, Indianapolis IN 46206. Editor: Peg Rogers. For children to age 14. Monthly (except bimonthly issues in June/July, August/September) magazine; 48 pages. Estab. 1921. Pays on publication. Buys all rights. Submit seasonal/holiday

material 8 months in advance. Photocopied submissions OK. SASE. Reports in 8-10 weeks. Sample copy 50¢; free writer's guidelines.
Nonfiction: How-to (crafts for children up to 14, using easy to find items or articles around the home); informational (science, mysteries of nature, space-related subjects); historical (mysterious happenings); humor (always needed and appreciated); interview (famous TV personalities connected with space and mystery). Buys 1-2 mss/issue. Submit complete ms. Length: 500-1,000 words. Pays 3¢/word.
Photos: Purchased with accompanying ms. Captions required. Submit prints or transparencies. Pays $2.50 for b&w glossy prints; $5 for color transparencies. Model release required.
Fiction: Adventure; fantasy; humorous; mystery; suspense; and science fiction. All fiction must appeal to children to age 14. Buys 3-6 mss/issue. Submit complete ms. Length: 1,200-4,000 words. Pays 3¢/word.
How To Break In: "We encourage new authors. The most important factors are interest levels and length of ms. Good mystery and science fiction stories are accepted. Authors must remember that our readers are up to 14 years old, and endeavor to keep their words and sentence lengths to that level."

CHILDREN'S PLAYMATE, 1100 Waterway Blvd., Box 567B, Indianapolis IN 46206. (317)634-1100, Ext. 296. Editor: Beth Wood Thomas. For children, ages 3 to 8. 10 times a year. Buys all rights. Pays on publication. Sample copy for 50¢; free writer's guidelines. No query. "We do not consider resumes and outlines. Reading the whole ms is the only way to give fair consideration. The editors cannot criticize, offer suggestions, or review unsolicited material that is not accepted." Submit seasonal material 8 months in advance. Simultaneous submissions not accepted. Reports in 8 to 10 weeks. Sometimes may hold mss for up to 1 year; with author's permission. "Material will not be returned unless accompanied by a self-addressed envelope and sufficient postage."
Fiction: Short stories, not over 600 words for beginning readers. No inanimate, talking objects. Humorous stories, unusual plots. Vocabulary suitable for ages 3 to 8. Pays about 3¢ per word.
Nonfiction: Beginning science, not more than 600 words. Monthly "All About...." feature, 300 to 500 words, may be an interesting presentation on animals, people, events, objects, or places. Pays about 3¢ per word.
Fillers: Puzzles, dot-to-dots, color-ins, mazes, tricks, games, guessing games, and brain teasers. "Attention to special holidays and events is sometimes helpful." Payment varies.

CHILDREN'S SERVICE PROGRAMS, Concordia Publishing House, 3558 S. Jefferson Ave., St. Louis MO 63118. (314)664-7000. Issued annually by The Lutheran Church—Missouri Synod, for children, aged three through eighth grade. Buys all rights. Receipt of children's worship scripts will be acknowledged immediately, but acceptance or rejection may require up to a year. All mss must be typed, double-spaced on 8½x11 paper. SASE. Write for details.
Nonfiction and Drama: "Two Christmas worship service programs for congregational use published yearly. Every script must include usual elements embodied in a worship service. Children lead the worship with adults participating in singing some of the hymns. Youth and adult choir selections optional. Every script must emphasize the Biblical message of the Gospel through which God shares His love and which calls for a joyful response from His people. Services requiring elaborate staging or costumes not accepted." Pays $125 but buys few mss.

CRICKET, Box 100, LaSalle IL 61301. Editor: Marianne Carus. For children ages 6 to 12. Monthly magazine; 96 pages. Estab. 1973. Rights purchased vary with author and material. May buy all rights, first serial rights, or second serial (reprint) rights. Buys about 100 mss per year. Pays on publication. Sample copy $1.50; free writer's guidelines. Special material should be submitted 9 to 12 months in advance. "We work 1 year in advance of publication." Reports on material accepted for publication in 6 to 8 weeks. Returns rejected material in 6 to 8 weeks. Submit complete ms. SASE.
Nonfiction: "We are interested in high-quality material written for children, not down to children." Biography, science, history, foreign culture, informational, humor, travel. Pays up to 25¢ per word.
Fiction: Realistic and historic fiction; fantasy, myth, legend, folk tale. Does not want to see life-cycle, natural history, or retold folk tales that appear in standard story collections and anthologies. Length: 200 to 2,000 words. Pays up to 25¢ per word.
Poetry: Traditional forms, light verse, limericks, nonsense rhymes. Length: 100 lines maximum. Pays up to $3 per line.
Fillers: Short humor, puzzles, songs, crafts, recipes. Length: 200 words maximum. Pays up to 25¢ per word.

CRUSADER, 1548 Poplar Ave., Memphis TN 38104. (901)272-2461. Editor: Phil Burgess. For boys ages 6 through 11, who are part of a boys' program in Southern Baptist Churches called Royal Ambassadors. Estab. 1970. Monthly. Circ. 100,000. Rights purchased vary with author and material. May buy first North American serial rights, first serial rights, second serial (reprint) rights, simultaneous rights. Buys 25-50 mss/year. Pays on acceptance. Free sample copy and writer's guidelines. Will consider photocopied submissions. Submit seasonal material 8 to 10 months in advance. Reports within 3 months. SASE.
Nonfiction and Photos: "Articles of general interest to the age group. Articles should often aid the child's interest in the world around him and increase his appreciation for cultures other than his own." Informational, how-to (simple), humor, historical (limited), photo, and travel articles. Nature articles almost always require photos. Query. Length: maximum 750 words, but prefers 500. Pays minimum $5, no maximum. Photos are purchased with or without manuscripts. Captions optional. Prefers 5x7 b&w or larger glossy. Pays $5 and up per photo. "Nonfiction photo stories involving boys as well as self-explanatory photos without copy involving boys."
Fiction and Fillers: 12 to 15 short stories are purchased each year. Mainstream, mystery, adventure, humorous, and religious fiction (no sermonizing!). Length: no minimum, maximum 900 words. Pays 2½¢ a word. Prefers simple puzzles involving drawing.

CRUSADER MAGAZINE, Box 7244, Grand Rapids MI 49510. Editor: David Koetse. For boys, age 9 to 14. Magazine; 24 pages, in cartoon format. Estab. 1962. Published seven times/year. Circ. 12,000 Rights purchased vary with author and material. Buys 15 to 20 mss a year. Pays on acceptance. Free sample copy and writer's guidelines. Will consider photocopied and simultaneous submissions. Submit seasonal material (Christmas, Easter) at least 4 months in advance. Reports on material accepted for publication in 30 days. Returns rejected material in 30 to 60 days. Query first or submit complete ms. SASE.
Nonfiction and Photos: Articles about young boys' interests: sports, outdoor activities, bike riding, science, crafts, etc., and problems. Emphasis is on a Christian perspective, but no simplistic moralisms. Material appropriate to Christmas and Easter. Informational, how-to, personal experience, interview, profile, inspirational, humor. Length: 500 to 1,500 words. Pays 2¢ to 5¢ a word. Pays $4 to $25 for b&w photos purchased with mss.
Fiction and Fillers: "Fiction is used sparingly, but fast-moving stories that appeal to a boy's sense of adventure or sense of humor are always welcome. Avoid 'preachiness'. Avoid simplistic answers to complicated problems. Avoid long dialog and little action." Length: 500 to 1,200 words. Pays 2¢ to 5¢ a word. Uses short humor and any type of puzzles as fillers.

DASH, Box 150, Wheaton IL 60187. Editor: Paul Heidebrecht. 50% freelance written. For boys 8 to 11 years of age. Most subscribers are in a Christian Service Brigade program. Monthly magazine; 32 pages. Established in 1972. Circulation: 32,000. Rights purchased vary with author and material. Usually buys all rights, but will sometimes reassign rights to author after publication. Buys 5 mss a year. Payment on publication. Submit seasonal material 4 months in advance. Reports on material accepted for publication as soon as possible. Returns rejected material in 4 weeks. Query first. Enclose S.A.S.E.
Nonfiction and Photos: "Our emphasis is on boys and how their belief in Jesus Christ works in their everyday life." Uses short articles about boys of this age; problems they encounter. Material on crafts and games. Interview, profile. Length: 1,000 to 1,500 words. Pays $30 to $60. Pays $7.50 for 8x10 b&w photos purchased with ms. Captions required.
Fiction: Religious. Length: 1,000 to 1,500 words. Pays $20 to $60.

DISCOVERIES, 6401 The Paseo, Kansas City MO 64131. Editor: Ruth Henck McCreery. 100% freelance written. For boys and girls 9 to 12. Weekly. Buys first and some second rights. No query required. "No comments can be made on rejected material."SASE.
Nonfiction: Articles on nature, travel, history, crafts, science, Christian faith, biography of Christian leaders, Bible manners and customs, home craft ideas. Should be informal, spicy, and aimed at fourth and fifth grade vocabulary. Sharp photos and artwork help sell features. Length: 400 to 800 words. Pays 2¢ a word.
Photos: Sometimes buys pix submitted with mss. Buys them with captions only if subject has appeal. Send quality photos, 5x7 or larger.
Fiction: Stories with Christian emphasis on high ideals, wholesome social relationships and activities, right choices, Sabbath observance, church loyalty, goodwill, and missions. Informal style. Length: 1,000 to 1,250 words. "Or serials of 2 to 4 parts, average 1,250 words per installment." Pays 2¢ a word.
Poetry: Nature and Christian thoughts or prayers, 4 to 16 lines. Pays $1 for each 4 lines.

DISCOVERY, Free Methodist Publishing House, 999 College Ave., Winona Lake IN 46590. (219)267-7161. Editor-in-Chief: Vera Bethel. 100% freelance written. For "57% girls, 43% boys, age 9-11; 48% city, 23% small towns." Weekly magazine; 8 pages. Estab. 1929. Circ. 15,000. Pays on acceptance. Rights purchased vary; may buy simultaneous, second serial or first North American serial rights. Submit seasonal/holiday material 3 months in advance. Simultaneous and previously published submissions OK. Reports in 4 weeks. Free sample copy and writer's guidelines.
Nonfiction: How-to (craft articles, how to train pets, party ideas, how to make gifts); informational (nature articles with pix); historical (short biographies except Lincoln and Washington); and personal experience (my favorite vacation, my pet, my hobby, etc.). Buys 150 mss/year. Submit complete ms. Length: 300-1,000 words. Pays 2¢/word.
Photos: Purchased with accompanying ms. Captions required. Submit prints. Pays $5-10 for 8x10 b&w glossy prints. $2 for snapshots.
Fiction: Adventure; humorous; mystery; and religious. Buys 100 mss/year. Submit complete ms. Length: 1,200-2,000 words. Pays 2¢/word.
Poetry: Free verse; haiku; light verse; traditional; devotional; and nature. Buys 100/year. Limit submissions to batches of 5-6. Length: 4-16 lines. Pays 25¢/line.
How To Break In: "Send interview articles with children about their pets, their hobbies, a recent or special vacation—all with pix if possible. Kids like to read about other kids."

EBONY JR!, Johnson Publishing Co., 820 S. Michigan Ave., Chicago IL 60605. (312)786-7722. Managing Editor: Mary C. Lewis. For all children, but geared toward black children, ages 6-12. Monthly magazine (except bimonthly issues in June/July and August/September); 48 pages. Estab. 1973. Circ. 75,000. Pays on acceptance. Buys all rights, but may reassign following publication, or second serial (reprint) rights or first North American serial rights. Submit seasonal/holiday material 4 months in advance. Previously published work OK. SASE. Reports in 3 weeks to 3 months. Sample copy 75¢. Free writer's guidelines.
Nonfiction: How-to (make things, gifts and crafts; cooking articles); informational (science experiments or articles explaining how things are made or where things come from); historical (events or people in black history); inspirational (career articles showing children they can become whatever they want); interviews; personal experience (taken from child's point of view); profiles (of black Americans who have done great things—especially need articles on those who have not been recognized). Buys 3/issue. Query or submit complete ms. Length: 500-1,500 words. Pays $75-400.
Photos: Purchased with or without mss. Must be clear photos; no instamatic prints. Pays $10-15/b&w; $25 maximum/color. Send prints and transparencies. Model release required.
Columns/Departments: Ebony Jr! News uses news of outstanding black children, reviews of books, movies, TV shows, of interest to children. Pays $25-100.
Fiction: Must be believable and include experiences black children can relate to. Adventure, fantasy, historical (stories on black musicians, singers, actors, astronomers, scientists, inventors, writers, politicians, leaders; any historical figures who can give black children positive images). Buys 2/issue. Query or submit complete ms. Length: 300-1,500 words. Pays $75-200.
Poetry: Free verse, haiku, light verse, traditional forms of poetry. Buys 2/issue. Send poems in. No specific limit on number of submissions, but usually purchase no more than two at a time. Length: 5-50 lines; longer for stories in poetry form. Pays $15-100.
Fillers: Jokes, gags, anecdotes, newsbreaks and current events written at a child's level. Brain teasers, word games, crossword puzzles, guessing games, dot-to-dot games; games that are fun, yet educational. Pays $15-85.

THE FRIEND, 50 East North Temple, Salt Lake City UT 84150. (801)531-2210. Managing Editor: Lucile C. Reading. 75% freelance written. Appeals to children from age 4 to 12. Publication of the Church of Jesus Christ of Latter-day Saints. Issue feature different countries of the world, its culture, and children. Special issues: Christmas and Easter. Estab. 1970. Monthly. Circ. 190,000. Pays on acceptance. Free sample copy and guidelines for writers. Submit only complete ms. Submit seasonal material 6 months in advance. SASE.
Nonfiction: Subjects of current interest, science, nature, pets, sports, foreign countries, and things to make and do. Length: 1,000 words maximum. Pays 3¢ a word and up.
Fiction: Seasonal and holiday stories; stories about other countries and children in them. Wholesome and optimistic; high motive, plot, and action. Also simple, but suspense-filled mysteries. Character-building stories preferred. Length: 1,200 words maximum. Stories for younger children should not exceed 700 words. Pays 3¢ a word and up.
Poetry: Serious or humorous; holiday poetry. Any form. Good poetry, with child appeal. Pays 25¢ a line and up.

How To Break In: "Do you remember how it feels to be a child? Can you write stories that appeal to children ages four to twelve in today's world? We're interested in stories with an international flavor and those that focus on present day problems."

HIGHLIGHTS FOR CHILDREN, 803 Church St., Honesdale PA 18431. Editors: Walter B. Barbe and Caroline C. Myers. For children 2 to 12. 11 times/year. Circ. approximately 1,000,000. Buys all rights. Pays on acceptance. Write for copy of guidelines for writers. No query. Submit complete ms only. Reports in 2 months. Enclose S.A.S.E.
Nonfiction: Most factual features, including history and science, are written on assignment by persons with rich background and mastery in their respective fields. But contributions always welcomed from new writers, especially science teachers, engineers, scientists, historians, etc., who can interpret to children useful, interesting, and authentic facts, but not of the bizarre or "Ripley" type; also writers who have lived abroad and can interpret well the ways of life, especially of children in other countries, and who don't leave the impression that our ways are always the best. Sports material, biographies, articles about sports of interest to children. Direct, simple style, interesting content, without word embellishment; not rewritten from encyclopedias. State background and qualifications for writing factual articles submitted. Include references or sources of information with first submission. Length: 1,000 words maximum. Pays minimum $50. Also buys original party plans for children 7 to 12, clearly described in 600 to 800 words, including pencil drawings or sample of items to be illustrated. Also, novel but tested ideas in arts and crafts, with clear directions, easily illustrated, preferably with made-up models. Projects must require only salvage material or inexpensive, easy-to-obtain material. Especially desirable if easy enough for early primary grades and appropriate to special seasons and days. Also, fingerplays with lots of action, easy for very young children to grasp and parents to dramatize, step-by-step, with hands and fingers. Avoid wordiness. Pays minimum $30 for party plans; $10 for arts and crafts ideas; $25 for fingerplays.
Fiction: Unusual, wholesome stories appealing to both girls and boys. Vivid, full of action and word-pictures, easy to illustrate. Seeks stories that the child 8 to 12 will eagerly read, and the child 2 to 6 will like to hear when read to him. "We print no stories just to be read aloud; they must serve a two-fold purpose. We encourage authors not to hold themselves to controlled word lists. Especially need humorous stories, but also need winter stories; urban stories; horse stories; and especially some mystery stories void of violence; and stories introducing characters from different ethnic groups; holiday stories void of Santa Claus and the Easter Bunny. Avoid suggestion of material reward for upward striving. Moral teaching should be subtle. The main character should preferably overcome difficulties and frustrations through his own efforts. The story should leave a good moral and emotional residue. War, crime, and violence are taboo. Some fanciful stories wanted." Length: 400 to 1,000 words. Pays minimum 5¢ a word.
How To Break In: "We are pleased that many authors of children's literature report that their first published work was in the pages of *Highlights*. It is not our policy to consider fiction on the strength of the reputation of the author. We judge each submission on its own merits. With factual material, however, we do prefer either authorities in their fields or people with first-hand experience. In this manner we can avoid the encyclopedic-type article which merely restates information readily available elsewhere. A beginning writer should first become familiar with the type of material which *Highlights* publishes. We are most eager for the easy-type story for very young readers, but realize that this is probably the most difficult kind of writing. The talking animal kind of story is greatly overworked. A beginning writer should be encouraged to develop first an idea for a story which must involve only a small number of characters and likely a single-incident plot. The story must contain a problem or a dilemma which is clearly understood and presented early. It is then clearly resolved at the end of the story. Description should be held to a minimum. Dialogue is a requirement for it is a means by which children can identify with the characters in the story."

HUMPTY DUMPTY'S MAGAZINE, Parents' Magazine Enterprises, Inc., 52 Vanderbilt Ave., New York NY 10017. Editor: Stephanie Calmenson. For children, 3 to 7 years of age. Magazine published monthly except June and August. Estab. 1952. Circ. 1,000,000. Rights purchased vary with author and material. Usually buys all rights. Buys 25 or more freelance story mss a year. Payment on acceptance. Write for copy of guidelines for writers enclosing self-addressed, stamped envelope. No sample copies. Will consider photocopied submissions. Will not consider simultaneous submissions. Submit seasonal material 6 to 8 months in advance. Reports in 2 to 6 weeks. Submit complete ms. SASE.
Fiction: "Like stories with real-life children, not all suburban types; more urban material. One thing that's always anathema to me is the animated inanimate object. Yet I just bought an

excellent piece in that genre. I also dislike cliche pieces about sugar girls with dolls at tea parties. We use old-fashioned stories and folk tales — but real children must be up-to-date. We're cautious about adaptations because we don't want to give our readers something they have seen before." Length: 900 to 1,000 words maximum. Pays $50 minimum.
Poetry: Rhyme or free verse. Length: 4 to 16 lines. Pays $10.

IT'S OUR WORLD, 800 Allegheny Ave., Pittsburgh PA 15233. Editor: Thomas F. Haas. For boys and girls in Catholic elementary schools in the United States, ages 6 to 13. Quarterly. Two-color, four-page newsletter. Established in 1974 by the Holy Childhood Association. Circ. 3.1 million. Buys simultaneous rights. Payment on acceptance. Will send free sample copy to writer on request. Write for copy of guidelines for writers. Will consider photocopied and simultaneous submissions. Submit seasonal material 4 months in advance. Reports on material within a month. Submit complete ms. SASE.
Nonfiction: "Ours is a publication of mission news for children, dealing with children in other countries, especially those in the developing countries (Third World or mission countries). Stories about children in other countries should show an appreciation for that country's culture, and not give the impression that our culture is better." Interested in current events reports, stories about life in other countries, stories about the legends, culture or customs of various countries (with documentation). Uses informational, how-to, personal experience, interview, profile, inspirational, humor, adventure, biographical, historical, travel and think articles. Length: 600 to 800 words. Pays minimum of $25.
Fiction: Experimental, mainstream, mystery, suspense, adventure, science fiction, fantasy, humorous, religious and historical fiction. Length: 600 to 800 words. Pays minimum of $25.
Poetry: Traditional forms, light verse and poems written by children. Length: open. Pays $15 to $25.

JACK AND JILL, 1100 Waterway Blvd., Box 567B, Indianapolis IN 46206. (317)634-1100. Editor: William Wagner. For children 5 to 12. 10 times a year. Buys all rights. Pays on publication. Sample copy to writer for 50¢; free writer's guidelines. Submit seasonal material 8 months in advance. Reports in approximately 8 weeks. May hold material seriously being considerated for up to 6 months or 1 year. "Material will not be returned unless accompanied by self-addressed envelope with sufficient postage."
Nonfiction and Photos: "*Jack and Jill*'s primary purpose is to encourage children to read for pleasure. The editors are actively interested in material that will inform and instruct the young reader and challenge his intelligence, but it must first of all be enjoyable reading. Submissions should appeal to both boys and girls." Current needs are for "short factual articles concerned with nature, science, and other aspects of the child's world. Longer, more detailed features: 'My Father (or My Mother) Is a ...'; first-person stories of life in other countries; some historical and biographical articles." Where appropriate, articles should be accompanied by good 35mm color transparencies, when possible. Pays approximately 3¢ a word. Pays $2.50 for each b&w photo. Pays $5 each for color photo.
Fiction: "May include, but is not limited to, realistic stories, fantasy, adventure—set in the past, present, or future. All stories need plot structure, action, and incident. Humor is highly desirable." Length: 500 to 1,200 words, short stories; 1,200 words per installment, serials of 2 or 3 parts. Pays approximately 3¢ a word.
Fillers and Drama: "Short plays, puzzles (including varied kinds of word and crossword puzzles), riddles, jokes, songs, poems, games, science projects, and creative construction projects. Instructions for activities should be clearly and simply written and accompanied by models or diagram sketches. We are also in need of projects for our feature, For Carpenters Only. Projects should be of the type our young readers can construct with little or no help. Be sure to include all necessary information—materials needed, diagrams, etc. Whenever possible, all materials used in projects should be scrap materials that can be readily found around the workshop and home." Payment varies for fillers. Pays approximately 3¢ per word for drama.
How To Break In: "We have been accused of using the same authors over and over again, not keeping an open mind when it comes to giving new authors a chance. To some extent, perhaps we do lean a little heavier toward veteran authors. But there is a good reason for this. Authors who have been published in *Jack and Jill* over and over again have shown us that they can write the kind of material we are looking for. They obtain *current* issues of the magazine and *study* them to find out our present needs, and they write in a style that is compatible with our current editorial policies. That is the reason we use them over and over; not because they have a special 'in.' We would reject a story by the world's best known author if it didn't fit our needs. After all, our young readers are more interested in reading a good story than they are in reading a good by-line. We are constantly looking for new writers that have told a good story with an interesting

slant—a story that is not full of outdated and time-worn expressions. If an author's material meets these requirements, then he stands as good a chance of getting published as anyone."

THE KINDERGARTNER, The United Methodist Publishing House, 201 Eighth Ave. S., Nashville TN 37202. Editor: Arba O. Herr. 98% freelance written. For children of kindergarten age. Monthly in weekly parts. Magazine; 4 pages per week. Estab. 1964. Circ. 190,000. Pays on acceptance. Buys all rights. Submit seasonal/holiday material 1½ years in advance. SASE. Reports in 4 weeks. Free sample copy and writer's guidelines for SASE.
Nonfiction: How-to (inexpensive craft ideas, simple science discoveries that kindergartners can experiment with, gift ideas, games); informational (about nature, animals, or community services such as doctors, plumbers, etc.); inspirational (prayers and Biblical stories); personal experience (any that would be of interest to a kindergarten age child); and photo feature. Buys 60 mss/year. Query. Length: 250-300 words. Pays 2-3¢/word.
Photos: Purchased with or without accompanying ms. Query. Pays $10-15 for 8x10 glossy b&w photos; $35-40 for 2x2 color transparencies. Model release required.
Fiction: Adventure; experimental ("in the area of Bible stories there often is not sufficient dialogue or background to make a story. Therefore, we add experiences typical of the historical period—but not really authentic as to the Biblical account. Also, since the child learns by experience, we often use stories about children whose experiences are typical but at the same time fictitious"); humorous; and religious. Buys 60 mss/year. Query. Length: 200-300 words. Pays 2-3¢/word.
Poetry: Free verse, traditional. Buys 60/year. Query. Length: 8-12 lines. Pays $.50-1/line.

MY DEVOTIONS, Concordia Publishing House, 3558 S. Jefferson Ave., St. Louis MO 63118. For young Christians, 8 through 13 years of age. Buys little freelance material. Write for guidelines, enclosing 13¢ postage. Material is rejected here because of poor writing, lack of logic, and lack of Lutheran theology. Pays $7.50 per printed devotion.

NURSERY DAYS, The United Methodist Publishing House, 201 8th Ave., S., Nashville TN 37202. Editor-in-Chief: Dr. Ewart Watts. Children's Editor: Leo Kisrow. 100% freelance written. A story paper for children 2-4 years of age, distributed through Sunday school classes of the United Methodist Church and Christian Church. Weekly magazine; 4 pages. Circ. 125,000. Pays on acceptance. Buys all rights. Submit seasonal/holiday material 12 months in advance. SASE. Reports in 1-2 months. Free sample copy and writer's guidelines.
Nonfiction: Doris Willis, Nursery Editor. Informational (Biblical, nature, seasonal); inspirational (Biblical, church, family, prayers, etc.); and personal experience (familiar to children 2-4 years old). Buys 1 ms/issue. Length: 250 words maximum. Pays 4¢/word.
Photos: Dave Dawson, Photo Editor. Purchased without accompanying ms. Send prints or transparencies. Pays $15-30 for 8x10 b&w glossies; $25-125 for 35mm color transparencies. Model release required.
Fiction: Religious (Jesus, God, prayer, church, Bible). Buys 1 ms/issue. Submit complete ms. Length: 250 words. Pays 4¢/word.
Poetry: Doris Willis, Nursery Editor. Free verse and light verse. Buys 3-4/issue. Length: 4-12 lines. Pays 75¢/line.

ON THE LINE, Menonite Publishing House, 616 Walnut Ave., Scottdale PA 15683. (412)887-8500. Editor: Helen Alderfer. For 10-14-year-olds. Weekly magazine; 8 pages. Estab. 1970. Circ. 17,650. Pays on acceptance. Buys one-time rights. Submit seasonal/holiday material 6 months in advance. Simultaneous, photocopied and previously published submissions OK. SASE. Reports in 2 weeks.
Nonfiction: How-to (things to make with easy-to-get materials); and informational (500-word articles on wonders of nature, people who have made outstanding contributions). Buys 25-40 mss/issue. Length: 500-1,200 words. Pays $10-24.
Photos: Photos purchased with or without accompanying ms. Pays $5-25 for 8x10 b&w photos. Total purchase price for a ms includes payment for photos.
Columns/Departments: Fiction; adventure; humorous and religious. Buys 25 mss/year. Send complete ms. Length: 800-1,200 words. Pays $15-24.
Poetry: Light verse and religious. Length: 3-12 lines. Pays $5-15.

OUR LITTLE FRIEND, PRIMARY TREASURE, Pacific Press Publishing Association, 1350 Villa St., Mountain View CA 94042. (415)961-2323, Ext. 335. Editor: Louis Schutter. Published weekly for youngsters of the Seventh-Day Adventist church. *Our Little Friend* is for children ages 2 to 6; *Primary Treasure*, 7 to 9. Rights purchased vary with author and material. Buys first serial rights (international); second serial (reprint) rights (international). "The payment we

make is for one magazine right. In most cases, it is for the first one. But we make payment for second, third rights also." Query on serial-length stories. Will accept simultaneous submissions. "We do not purchase material during June, July, and August." SASE.
Nonfiction and Fiction: All stories must be based on fact, written in story form. True to life, character-building stories; written from viewpoint of child and giving emphasis to lessons of life needed for Christian living. True to life is emphasized here more than plot. Nature or science articles, but no fantasy; science must be very simple. All material should be educational or informative and stress moral attitude and religious principle. Honesty, truthfulness, courtesy, health and temperance, along with stories of heroism, adventure, nature and safety are included in the overall planning of the editorial program. *Our Little Friend* uses stories from 700 to 1,000 words. *Primary Treasure*, 600 to 1,200 words. Fictionalized Bible stories are not used. Pays 1¢ per word.
Photos, Poetry, and Fillers: 8x10 glossies for cover. "Photo payment: sliding scale according to quality." Juvenile poetry; up to 12 lines. Puzzles.

PIZZAZZ, Marvel Comics Group, 575 Madison Ave., New York NY 10022. Editor: Bobby Miller. Monthly magazine; 48 pages. Estab. October 1977. Circ. 300,000. Pays on acceptance. Buys first North American and foreign serial rights. Submit seasonal/holiday material 4 months in advance of issue date. Photocopied and previously published (if published in book form) submissions OK. SASE. Reports in 1 month. Free sample copy and writer's guidelines; mention *Writer's Market* in request.
Nonfiction: "Only material of interest to our audience (10-14 year-old children) is requested. Writing style must be colorful, sophisticated, and personal, *not* school-booky." How-to; humor; and interview. Query with clips of previously published work or submit complete ms. Length: 600-1,000 words. Pays $150 minimum.
Photos: State availability of photos with query. Pays $50-100 for color transparencies.
Fiction: "Style is as important as subject matter in these very short stories." Humor, fantasy and science fiction. Submit complete ms. Length: 600-1,000 words. Pays $150-250.

PRIMARY TREASURE, Pacific Press Publishing Association, 1350 Villa St., Mountain View CA 94042. See *Our Little Friend*.

R-A-D-A-R (formerly *Jet Cadet*), 8121 Hamilton Ave., Cincinnati OH 45231. (513)931-4050. Editor: Dana Eynon. 75% freelance written. For children 8 to 11 years old in Christian Sunday schools. Weekly. Rights purchased vary with author and material. Buys first serial rights or second serial (reprint) rights. Occasionally overstocked. Pays on acceptance. Will send a sample copy to a writer on request. Submit seasonal material 12 months in advance. Reports in 4 to 6 weeks. SASE.
Nonfiction: Articles on hobbies and handicrafts, nature (preferably illustrated), famous people, seasonal subjects, etc., written from a Christian viewpoint. Length: 500 to 1,000 words. Pays up to 1½¢ a word.
Fiction: Short stories of heroism, adventure, travel, mystery, animals, biography. True or possible plots stressing clean, wholesome, Christian character-building ideas, but not preachy. Make prayer, church attendance, Christian living a natural part of the story. "We correlate our fiction and other features with a definite Bible lesson." Length: 900 to 1,200 words; 2,000 words complete length for 2-part stories. Pays up to 1½¢ per word.
Fillers: Bible puzzles and quizzes. Pays up to 1½¢ a word.
How To Break In: "We give the same consideration to a new writer as we do to regular contributors. We just checked our files, and this past year purchased mss from 35 new writers. We look for (1) Christian character-building stories, filled with action and conversation, based on true-to-life situations; (2) articles on a wide range of subjects, filled with accurate facts, and written from a Christian viewpoint. Writers may send for list of themes coming up, and submit stories that correlate with the lesson stressed in a particular issue."
Rejects: Talking animal stories, science fiction, Halloween stories, first-person stories from an adult's viewpoint, non-Biblical puzzles, and articles about saints of the opposite, or historical figures with an absence or religious implication.

RAINBOW, American Baptist Board of Educational Ministries, Valley Forge PA 19481. Editor: Gracie McCay. 95% freelance written. Emphasizes religion for children in Baptist churches; ages 8-11. Monthly magazine; 32 pages. Estab. 1974. Circ. 10,000. Pays on acceptance. Buys first North American serial rights. Submit seasonal/holiday material 8 months in advance. Simultaneous and previously published submissions OK. SASE. Reports in 6 months. Free sample copy and writer's guidelines.

Nonfiction: Historical; how-to (projects of interest to children, including recipes); humor; informational; inspirational; and photo feature. Buys 10-12 mss/year. Length: 800-1,000 words. Pays 3¢/word.
Photos: Purchased without accompanying ms. Send contact sheet or prints. Pays $7.50-15 for 8x10 b&w glossies. Model release required.
Fiction: Adventure; historical; humorous; religious; science fiction; and suspense. Buys 200 mss/year. Submit complete ms. Length: 800-1,500 words. Pays 3¢/word.
Poetry: Free verse; haiku; light verse and traditional. Buys 25-30/year. Limit submissions to batches of 5. Pays 25¢/line.
Fillers: Puzzles appropriate for children—wide variety. Buys 30/year. Pays $8/puzzle.
Note: Will cease publication in February 1979.

RANGER RICK'S NATURE MAGAZINE, National Wildlife Federation, 1412 Sixteenth St., N.W., Washington DC 20036. (202)797-6800. Editorial Director: Trudy D. Farrand. For "children from ages 4 to 12, with the greatest concentration in the 7-10 age bracket." Monthly. Buys all rights. Pays on acceptance. Anything written with a specific month in mind should be in our hands at least 8 months before that issue date." Query first. SASE.
Nonfiction and Photos: "Articles may be written on any phase of nature, conservation, environmental problems, or natural science. Do not try to humanize wildlife in features. We limit the attributing of human qualities to animals in our regular feature, 'Ranger Rick and His Friends.' The publisher, National Wildlife Federation, discourages wildlife pets because of the possible hazards involved to small children. Therefore, pets of this kind should not be mentioned in your copy." Length: 900 words maximum. Pays from $10 to $250 depending on length. "If photographs are included with your copy, they are paid for separately, depending on how they are used. However, it is not necessary that illustrations accompany material."

SPRINT MAGAZINE, Scholastic Magazines, Inc., 50 W. 44th St., New York NY 10036. Editor: Vicky Chapman. 20-40% freelance written. Magazine (14 times/school year); 16 pages. Pays on acceptance. Usually buys all rights. SASE. Reports as soon as possible.
Nonfiction and Fiction: Michael Bonner. Assistant Editor. Accepts some feature articles on sports, career education, other topics of interest to pre-teens. "Main need is for very short fiction, plays (450-900 words), short stories (200-450 words), unique and creative items teaching reading skills (word games, etc.) Fiction subjects include action, adventure, mystery, science fiction, sports, humor, family, friend, and school situations. Stories often work best when they (1) are heavy on dialogue; (2) concentrate on developing insight into at least one character, and/or (3) have a 'twist' ending. No overt moralizing. No talking animals." Pays $80 minimum.

STORY FRIENDS, Mennonite Publishing House, 616 Walnut Ave., Scottdale PA 15683. (412)887-8500. Editor: Marjorie Waybill. For children 4-9 years of age. Published monthly in weekly parts. Not copyrighted. Pays on acceptance. Submit seasonal/holiday material 6 months in advance of issue date. SASE. Free sample copy.
Nonfiction and Fiction: "The over-arching purpose of this publication is to portray Jesus as a friend and helper—a friend who cares about each happy and sad experience in the child's life. Persons who know Jesus have values which affect every area of their lives. Stories of everyday experiences at home, at church, in school, or at play can provide models of these values. Of special importance are relationships, patterns of forgiveness, respect, honesty, trust, and caring. Prefer short stories that are exciting but plausible, offer a wide variety of settings, acquaint children with a wide range of friend, and mirror the joys, fears, temptations and successes of the readers. Length: 300-800 words. Pays 2½-3¢/word.
Poetry: Traditional and free verse. Length: 3-12 lines. Pays $5.

TOUCH, P.O. Box 7244, Grand Rapids MI 49510. Editor: Joanne Ilbrink. Assistant Editor: Jennifer Seel. 50-60% freelance written. For girls, usually members of Calvinette clubs, ages 8-15. Monthly magazine; 24 pages. Estab. 1970. Circ. 14,000. Pays on acceptance. Buys simultaneous, second serial and first North American serial rights. Submit seasonal/holiday material 3-5 months in advance. Simultaneous, photocopied or previously published submissions OK. SASE. Reports in 3 weeks. Free sample copy and writer's guidelines.
Nonfiction: How-to (crafts girls can make easily and inexpensively), informational (write for issue themes), humor (needs much more), inspirational (seasonal and holiday), interview, travel, personal experience (avoid the testimony approach), and photo feature (query first). "Because our magazine is published around a monthly theme, requesting the letter we send out twice a year to our established freelancers would be most helpful. We do not want easy solutions or quick character changes from bad to good. No pietistic characters. Constant mention of God is not necessary, if the moral tone of the story is positive. We do not want stories that always

have a good ending.'' Buys 20 mss a year. Submit complete ms. Length: 100-1,000 words. Pays 2¢/word, depending on the amount of editing.
Photos: Purchased with or without ms. Submit 3x5 clear glossy prints. B&w only. Pays $5-25.
Fiction: Adventure (that girls could experience in their home towns or places they might realistically visit), fantasy (fables welcome), humorous, mystery (believable only), romance (stories that deal with awakening awareness of boys are appreciated), suspense (can be serialized), and religious (nothing preachy). Buys 20 mss/year. Submit complete ms. Length: 300-1,500 words. Pays 2¢/word.
Poetry: Free verse, haiku, light verse, traditional. Buys 10/year. Length: 50 lines maximum. Pays $5 minimum.
Fillers: Jokes, gags, anecdotes, puzzles, short humor and cartoons. Buys 6/issue. Pays $2.50-7.

TRAILS, Pioneer Girls, Inc., Box 788, Wheaton IL 60187. Editor-in-Chief: Dr. Sara Robertson. Managing Editor: Frances Price. Emphasizes Christian education for girls, 7-12, most of whom are enrolled in the Pioneer Girls club program. It is kept general in content so it will appeal to a wider audience. Bimonthly magazine; 32 pages. Estab. 1962. Circ. 23,000. Pays on acceptance. Buys first, second, or simultaneous rights. Submit seasonal/holiday material 6 months in advance. Simultaneous and previously published submissions OK. SASE. Reports in 4 weeks. Sample copy $1; free writer's guidelines.
Nonfiction: How-to (crafts and puzzles); humor; informational; inspirational; and interview. Query or submit complete ms. Length: 800-1,500 words. Pays $20-30.
Fiction: Adventure; fantasy; historical; humorous; mainstream; mystery; and religious. Buys 6 mss/issue. Query or submit complete ms. Length: 800-1,500 words. Pays $25-40.
Fillers: Jokes, gags, anecdotes, and short humor. Buys 4/issue. Pays $5-15.

VIDEO-PRESSE, 3965 est, boul. Henri-Bourassa, Montreal H1H 1L1, Que., Canada. Editor: Pierre Guimar. For ''French Canadian boys and girls of 8 to 15.'' Monthly. Circulation: 45,000. Buys all rights. Buys 20 to 30 mss a year. Pays on publication. Will send a sample copy to a writer on request. Reports in 2 weeks. Enclose SASE.
Nonfiction: ''Material with a French Canadian background. The articles have to be written in French, and must appeal to children aged 8 to 15.'' Buys how-to's, personal experience articles, interviews, profiles, humor, historical articles, photo features, travel pieces. Length: 1,500 to 3,000 words. Pays 3¢ a word.
Photos: B&w glossies, color transparencies; with captions only. Pays $7.50.
Fillers: Puzzles, jokes, short humor.

THE VINE, 201 Eighth Ave., S., Nashville TN 37202. (615)749-6369. Editor: Betty M. Buerki. Publication of The United Methodist Church. For children in grades 3 and 4. Monthly in weekly parts. Buys all rights. Pays on acceptance. Free sample copy. Deadlines are 18 months prior to publication date. Reports in 1 month. SASE.
Nonfiction and Photos: Desires articles about science, nature, animals, customs in other countries, and other subjects of interest to readers. Length: approximately 500 words. Pays 3¢ a word. Photos usually purchased with manuscripts only. Uses photo features. Prefers 8x10 glossies. Also uses transparencies.
Fiction: Historical stories should be true to their setting. Stories which make a point about values should not sound moralistic. Also accepts stories written just for fun. Length: 500 to 800 words. Writers must know children. Fictionalized Bible stories must be based upon careful research. Pays 3¢ a word.
Poetry: Accepts light verse or religious verse. Pays 50¢ to $1 per line.
Fillers: Puzzles, quizzes, and matching games. Pays 3¢ minimum per word. Pays more for clever arrangements. Puzzles, such as crossword, mazes, etc.; pays $4.50 to $12.50.

WEE WIDSOM, Unity Village MO 64065. Editor: Colleen Zuck. 10 issues per year. A Christian magazine for boys and girls aged 13 and under dedicated to the truths: that each person is a child of God and that as a child of God each person has an inner source of wisdom, power, love, and health from their Father that can be applied in a practical manner to every-day life. Free sample copy, editorial policy on request. Buys first North American serial rights only. Pays on acceptance. SASE.
Nonfiction: Entertaining nature articles or projects, activities to encourage appreciation of all life. Pays 3¢/word minimum.
Fiction: Character-building stories that encourage a positive self-image. Although entertaining enough to hold the interest of the older child, they should be readable by the third grader. Characters should be appealing but realistic; plots should be plausible, and all stories should be

told in a forthright manner but *without preaching*. Life itself combines fun and humor with its more serious lessons, and our most interesting and helpful stories do the same thing. Language should be universal, avoiding the Sunday school image. Length: 500 to 800 words. Pay 3¢ per word minimum.
Poetry: Very limited. Pays 50¢ per line. Prefers short, seasonal or humorous poems. Also buys rhymed prose for "read alouds" and pays $15 up.
Fillers: Pays $3 up for puzzles and games.

WEEKLY BIBLE READER, Standard Publishing, 8121 Hamilton Ave., Cincinnati OH 45231. Editor: Barbara Cuttrell. For children 6 and 7 years of age. Quarterly in weekly parts; 4 pages. Established in 1965. Circulation: 95,459. Buys first serial rights. Payment on acceptance. Will send free sample copy to writer on request. Write for copy of guidelines for writers. Will not consider photocopied or simultaneous submissions. Submit seasonal material 18 months in advance. Reports on material accepted for publication in about 1 month. Returns rejected material in about 2 weeks. Query first or submit complete ms. Enclose SASE.
Nonfiction, Photos, and Poetry, and Fillers: Religious-oriented material. Stories with morals, short fiction (150 to 250 words in length) fun poems, puzzles and other interesting items. Emphasis is on material that can be read by children themselves. "No fanciful material, superstitions or luck, things that talk, fairies, Easter rabbits, or Santa Claus. We'd like to see material on things children can do to help others; to be pleasing to God, etc." Do not send Bible stories or Buzzy Bee items, as these are staff-written from preplanned outlines. Length for fiction and nonfiction: 300 words maximum. Pays $1 to $10. B&w photos purchased with or without mss. Pays $10. Light verse. Length: 12 lines maximum. Very simple puzzles for this age group. Pays 50¢ to $10.

WONDER TIME, 6401 The Paseo, Kansas City MO 64131. (816)333-7000. Editor: Evelyn Beals. Published weekly by Church of the Nazarene for children ages 6 to 8. Free sample copy. Buys first rights. Pays on acceptance. SASE.
Fiction and Poetry: Buys stories portraying Christian attitude, without being preachy. Uses stories for special days, stories teaching honesty, truthfulness, helpfulness or other important spiritual truths, and avoiding symbolism. God should be spoken of as our Father who loves and cares for us; Jesus, as our Lord and Savior. Length: 400-650 words. Pays 2¢ a word on acceptance. Uses verse which has seasonal or Christian emphasis. Length: 8 to 12 lines. Pays 25¢/line minimum.

WOW, American Baptist Board of Educational Ministries, Valley Forge PA 19481. Editor: Gracie McCay. 95% freelance written. Emphasizes religion for children in Baptist churches, ages 6-7. Weekly magazine; 4 pages. Estab. 1974. Circ. 10,000. Pays on acceptance. Buys simultaneous, first North American and one-time rights. Submit seasonal/holiday material 8 months in advance. Simultaneous and previously published submissions OK. SASE. Reports in 6 months. Free sample copy and writer's guidelines.
Photos: Purchased without accompanying ms. Send contact sheet or prints. Pays $7.50-15 for 8x10 b&w glossies. Model release required.
Fiction: Adventure; fantasy; historical; humorous; religious; science fiction and suspense. Buys 100 mss/year. Length: 200-400 words. Pays 3¢/word.
Poetry: Free verse; haiku; light verse; and traditional. Buys 25-30/year. Limit submissions to batches of 5. Pays 25¢/line.
Fillers: Jokes, gags, anecdotes and puzzles. Buys 25-30/year. Pays $5-8.

THE YOUNG CRUSADER, 1730 Chicago Ave., Evanston IL 60201. (312)864-1396. Managing Editor: Michael Vitucci. For children ages 6 to 12. Monthly. Not copyrighted. Pays on publication. Free sample copy. Submit seasonal material 6 months in advance. SASE.
Nonfiction and Fiction: Uses articles on total abstinence, character building, love of animals, Christian principles, world friendship. Also science stories. Length: 650 to 800 words. Pays ½¢ per word.

YOUNG JUDAEAN, 817 Broadway, New York NY 10003. (212)260-4700. Editor: Barbara Gingold. For Jewish children aged 8 to 13, and members of Young Judaea. Publication of Hadassah Zionist Youth Commission. All material must be on some Jewish theme. Special issues for Jewish/Israeli holidays, or particular Jewish themes which vary from year to year; for example, Hassidim, Holocaust, etc. Estab. 1916. Monthly (November through June). Circ. 8,000. Rights purchased vary with author and material. Buys all rights, but will reassign rights to author after publication; buys first North American serial rights; buys first serial rights. Buys 10 to 20 mss a year. Payment in contributor's copies or small token payment. Sample copy and annual list of themes for 25¢. Prefers complete ms only. Will consider photocopied and simultaneous submissions. Submit seasonal material 4 months in advance. Reports in 3 months. SASE.

Nonfiction and Photos: "Articles about Jewish-American life, Jewish historical and international interest. Israel and Zionist-oriented material. Try to awaken kids' Jewish consciousness by creative approach to Jewish history and religion, ethics and culture, politics and current events. Style can be didactic, but not patronizing." Informational (300 to 1,000 words), how-to (300 to 500 words), personal experience, interview, humor, historical, think articles, photo, travel, and reviews (books, theater, and movies). Length: 500 to 1,200 words. Pays $5-25. "Token payments only, due to miniscule budget."

Photos: Photos purchased with accompanying mss. Captions required. 5x7 maximum. B&w prefered. Payment included with fee for article. Illustrations also accepted.

Fiction: Experimental, mainstream, mystery, suspense, adventure, science fiction, fantasy, humorous, religious, and historical fiction. Length: 500 to 1,000 words. Pays $5 to $25. Must be of specific Jewish interest.

Poetry and Fillers: Traditional forms, blank verse, free verse, avant-garde forms, and light verse. Poetry themes must relate to subject matter of magazine. Length: 25-100 lines. Pays $5-15. Newsbreaks, jokes, and short humor purchased for $5.

How To Break In: "Think of an aspect of Jewish history/religion/culture which can be handled in a fresh, imaginative way, fictionally or factually. Don't preach; inform and entertain."

YOUNG MUSICIANS, 127 Ninth Ave., N., Nashville TN 37234. Editor: Jimmy R. Key. 5-10% freelance written. For boys and girls age 9 to 11, and their leaders in children's choirs in Southern Baptist churches (and some other churches). Monthly magazine; 52 pages. Estab. 1963. Buys all rights. Buys 5 or 6 mss a year. Payment on acceptance. Free sample copy. Will not consider photocopied or simultaneous submissions. Query first. SASE.

Nonfiction: "All material is slanted for use with and by children in church choirs. Music study materials related to study units in *The Music Leader*. Ours is a curriculum magazine written almost entirely on assignment." Informational, how-to, historical. Length: 300 to 900 words. Pays approximately 3¢ per word.

Fiction: Child-centered stories related to church music and music in the home. Length: 600 to 900 words. Pays approximately 2½¢ per word.

Literary and Little Publications

Many of the publications in this category do not pay except in contributor's copies. Nonpaying markets are included because they offer the writer a vehicle for expression that often can't be found in the commercial press. Many talented American writers found first publication in magazines like these. Writers are reminded that many "littles" remain at one address for a limited time; others are notoriously unbusinesslike in their reporting on, or returning of submissions. University-affiliated reviews are conscientious about manuscripts but some of these are also slow in replying to queries or returning submissions.

Magazines that specialize in publishing poetry or poetry criticism are found in the Poetry category. Many "little" publications that offer contributors a forum for expression of minority opinions are classified in the listings for Alternative Publications.

AMERICAN MERCURY, Box 1306, Torrance CA 90505. Managing Editor: La Vonne Furr. Quarterly. Write for copy of guidelines for writers. "All mss must be typed, double-spaced, clean, ready for printer, left margin at least 1½ inches. Break up articles with periodic italicized paragraphs and/or subheads. Authors should submit biographical material to aid editor in preparing a suitable introduction." SASE.

Nonfiction: *Mercury*'s editorial policy is nonpartisan but generally conservative. "It will stress the positive and hopeful aspects of life and Western tradition through reliable and well-written exposes. Articles on fads, dances, narcotics, crime, entertainers are generally unwanted." Wants Americana, nature briefs, humorous comment on everyday life, politics, science, health; particular emphasis on heroic and patriotic themes; satire. "Precede book reviews with a very brief title, then describe book: Title of book in caps, by (name of author), number of pages, publisher, date of publication." Length: 1,000 words maximum for book reviews; 900 to 2,000 words for articles. Payment ranges from one-year complimentary subscription to $50 for unsolicited articles.

AMERICAN NOTES AND QUERIES, Erasmus Press, 225 Culpepper, Lexington KY 40502. (606)266-1058. Editor: John Cutler. Ten times a year. No payment. SASE.
Nonfiction: Historical, artistic, literary, bibliographical, linguistic and folklore matters, scholarly book reviews and reviews of foreign reference books; items of unusual antiquarian interest.

AMERICAN QUARTERLY, Van Pelt Library, University of Pennsylvania, 3420 Walnut St., Philadelphia PA 19104. (215)243-6252. Editor: Dr. Bruce Kuklick. For college professors, teachers, museum directors, researchers, students, college and high school libraries. Readers professionally interested in American studies. Acquires all rights. Does not pay. Reports in 2-4 months. SASE and 2 copies of article.
Nonfiction and Photos: Scholarly, interdisciplinary articles on American studies, about 20 pages. August issue contains bibliographic essays, dissertation listings, American Studies programs. Occasionally uses photos.

THE AMERICAN SCHOLAR, 1811 Q St., N.W., Washington DC 20009. (202)265-3808. Editor: Joseph Epstein. For college educated, mid-20's and older, rather intellectual in orientation and interests. Quarterly magazine, 144 pages. Estab. 1932. Circ. 40,000. Buys all rights, but will reassign rights to author after publication. Buys 20 to 30 mss a year. Pays on publication. Sample copy $2; free writer's guidelines. Will consider photocopied submissions. Will not consider simultaneous submissions. Reports within 3 weeks. Query first, with samples, if possible. SASE.
Nonfiction and Poetry: "The aim of the *Scholar* is to fill the gap between the learned journals and the good magazines for a popular audience. We are interested not so much in the definitive analysis as in the lucid and creative exploration of what is going on in the fields of science, art, religion, politics, and national and foreign affairs. Advances in science particularly interest us." Informational, interview, profile, historical, think articles, and book reviews. Length: 3,500 to 4,000 words. Pays $250 per article and $50 for reviews. Pays $35 to $75 for poetry on any theme. Approximately 5 poems published per issue. "We would like to see poetry that develops an image or a thought or event, without the use of a single cliche or contrived archaism. The most hackneyed subject matter is self-conscious love; the most tired verse is iambic pentameter with rhyming endings. The usual length of our poems is 10-12 lines. From 1-4 poems may be submitted at one time; *no more* for a careful reading. We urge prospective contributors to familiarize themselves with the type of poetry we have published by looking at the magazine."

ANTHELION, Box 614, Corte Madera CA 94925. Editor: Wm. Whitney. 30-40% freelance written. For "a university level readership." Bimonthly. Purchases all rights with return of reprint rights upon request. Pays on publication. Reports in 4 to 6 weeks. Authors should include a brief resume and cover letter with submissions. SASE.
Nonfiction and Fiction: "Devoted in alternate months to the fields of literature, social and cultural comment, and philosophy. January and July issues are devoted to literary articles and stories. Interviews, reviews and like articles are used to augment our basic copy. We stress that all copy must be verifiable and logical. We seek the new writer with new insights into our modern world. Our pay for articles varies from contributor's copies up to 5¢ a word." Length: 2,500 words maximum.

THE ANTIGONISH REVIEW, St. Francis Xavier University, Antigonish, Nova Scotia, Canada B2G 1C0. Editor: R.J. MacSween. For "those with literary interests." Quarterly magazine; 100 pages. Circ. 500. Pays in copies only. Not copyrighted. Photocopied submissions OK. SASE. Reports in 6 weeks. Free sample copy.
Nonfiction: Literary articles of general interest. Submit complete ms.
Fiction: Fantasy; experimental; and mainstream. No erotica. Submit complete ms.
Poetry: Avant-garde and traditional. Uses 30/issue.

ANTIOCH REVIEW, Box 148, Yellow Springs OH 45387. Editor: Robert S. Fogarty. For general, literary and academic audience. Quarterly. Buys all rights. Pays on publication. Reports in 4 to 6 weeks. SASE.
Nonfiction: Contemporaneous articles in the humanities and social sciences, politics, economics, literature and all areas of broad intellectual concern. Somewhat scholarly, but never pedantic in style, eschewing all professional jargon. Lively, distinctive prose insisted upon.

Length: 2,000 to 8,000 words. Pays $8 per published page.
Fiction: No limitations on style or content. Pays $8 per published page.
Poetry: No light or inspirational verse. Contributors should be familiar with the magazine before submitting. Rarely uses traditional, or rhymed verse.

APALACHEE QUARTERLY, Box 20106, Tallahassee FL 32304. Collective Editorship. For an artistic/critical audience; 20 to 60 years of age. Quarterly magazine; 44 to 60 pages. Estab. 1972. Circ. 400. Acquires all rights. Uses about 80 mss a year. Payment in contributor's copies. Sample copy for $1. No simultaneous submissions. Reports in 1 to 10 weeks. Submit complete ms. SASE.
Nonfiction and Photos: Emphasis is on creative writing, rather than criticism. Uses interviews and reviews of fiction and poetry. Length: 300 to 3,000 words. B&w photos purchased without ms. Captions optional.
Fiction and Poetry: Short stories, experimental or mainstream. Length: 300 to 6,000 words. Traditional forms of poetry, blank verse, free verse, avant-garde forms. Length: 3 to 100 lines.

ARION, University Professors, Boston University, Rm. 607, 745 Commonwealth Ave., Boston MA 02215. (617)353-4025. Editors-in-Chief: William Arrowsmith and D. S. Carne-Ross. "Journal of humanities and classics for persons interested in literature of the classical periods of Greece and Rome." Estab. 1962. Quarterly journal, 128 pages. Circ. 1,000. No payment. Acquires all rights, but will reassign rights to author after publication. Sample copy for $3. Query first or submit complete ms. Will consider photocopied submissions. Reports in 3 months. SASE.
Nonfiction: Uses articles on literature, Greece and Rome. The articles printed are in the form of literary essays. "We deal with the classics as literature, rather than philology." Length: 10 to 40 pages.

ARIZONA QUARTERLY, University of Arizona, Tucson AZ 85721. Editor: Albert F. Gegenheimer. 80% freelance written. For a university-type audience. Quarterly. "We acquire all rights, but freely give authors permission to reprint. We require editors of anthologies, etc., to obtain permission of authors as well as of ourselves." Payment is in copies and a one-year subscription to the magazine. There are annual awards for the best poem of the year, the best article of the year, the best story of the year and the best book review of the year. Reports in 3 to 4 weeks except during summer. SASE.
Nonfiction: "Always interested in articles dealing with the Southwest, but open to articles on any topic of general interest."
Fiction: "Quality" fiction. Southwestern interest preferred, but not essential. Length: normally not over 3,000 words.
Poetry: Uses 4 or 5 poems per issue on any serious subject. Prefers short poems; up to 30 lines can be used most readily. The author must have something to say and be equipped to say it.

THE ARK RIVER REVIEW, c/o A. Sobin, English Department, Wichita State University, Wichita KS 67208. Editors-in-Chief: Jonathan Katz, A.G. Sobin. 100% freelance written. For "the well-educated, college age and above; poets, writers, and the readers of contemporary poetry and fiction." Published 3-4 times a year. Magazine; 52 pages. Estab. 1971. Circ. 1,000. Pays on publication. Buys all rights, but will reassign to author following publication. Photocopied submissions OK. Reports in 1-3 weeks. Sample copy $1.
Fiction: "Conventional fiction stands little chance. We are interested only in highly innovative and sophisticated material. Type and subject matter is far less important to us than the way in which the story is written. We are looking for freshness in approach, style and language. We suggest strongly that you read back issues before submitting." Buys 3 mss/issue. Send complete ms. No length limit (no novels). Pays $40/story and contributor's copies.
Poetry: "Poetry should be substantial, intelligent and serious (this doesn't mean it can't be funny). Any form is OK, though we almost never print rhyming poems." Buys 30/issue. Limit submissions to batches of 5. No length limits. Pays $10/poem.
How To Break In: "Your work should demonstrate to us that you know what has gone on in literature in the last 50 years, and that you're working toward something better."

ART AND LITERARY DIGEST, Summer address: Madoc-Tweed Art Centre, Tweed, Ontario, Canada. Winter address: 1109 N. Betty Lane, Clearwater FL 33515. Editor: Roy Cadwell. "Our readers are the public and former students of the Art and Writing Centre. As an educational publication we welcome new writers who have something to say and want to see their name in print and get paid for it." Quarterly. Estab. 1969. Circ. 1,000. Not copyrighted. Payment on publication. Will send sample copy for $1. Photocopied mss are accepted, but not returned. Unless notified, you may submit elsewhere after 30 days. Original mss must be accompanied by return envelope and unattached postage. SASE.

Nonfiction and Fiction: How-to articles, inspirational, humorous, travel and personality improvement. "Good writing is essential with integrity and knowledge. Ask yourself, 'What have I to say?' Slant toward students and alumni. Our readers want to be informed and, hopefully, learn how to live better." Personal experience articles and "I was there" type of travel articles are appreciated. Length: 500 words. Pays $5. "We need digests of articles on art, music, poetry and literary subjects." Pays 1¢ per word.

Fillers: Ideas and short humor. Length: 500 words or less. Pays 1¢ per word.

Poetry: All types. Free verse, light verse, blank verse, traditional and avant-garde. Length: usually 12 lines, but no limit. Payment in contributor's copies.

ASPECT, 66 Rogers Ave., Somerville MA 02144. Collective Editorship. 90% freelance written. Primarily for people interested in new and experimental, as well as traditional and widely accepted writing. Many readers are themselves involved in the field of writing. Quarterly magazine; 80-100 pages. Estab. 1969. Circ. 800. Pays in copies. Acquires first North American serial and one-time anthology rights. Photocopied submissions OK. SASE. Reports in 1-3 months. Sample copy $1.50.

Nonfiction: Informational; historical (social, political or literary subjects); humor; interview (with emerging, exciting poets and writers or people involved in alternative literary publishing); personal experience; personal opinion (social, political or literary subjects); photo feature (social, political, literary, historical focus). Buys 6-8 mss/year. Query. Length: 5,000 words maximum. Pays in copies.

Columns/Departments: News & Reviews (short news pieces about the field of alternative literary publishing; magazine and small press manuscript needs; Reviews of little magazines and small press books). Uses 15/issue. Submit complete ms. Length: 400 words for news; 300-1,000 for reviews.

Fiction: Adventure; experimental; historical; humorous; mainstream; and science fiction.

Poetry: Avant-garde; free verse; traditional. Uses 30/issue. Limit submissions to batches of 3-6.

How To Break In: "Subject area is broad, but tends to focus most on literature, and secondly, politics, broadly defined. We are a mature (in growth stage) independent literary magazine that still publishes, almost entirely, work by unknowns. Know what you're doing, and try to do it very well."

ASPEN ANTHOLOGY, The Aspen Leaves Literary Foundation, Box 3185, Aspen CO 81611. (303)925-8750. Editor-in-Chief: Kurt N. Brown. For poets, novelists, teachers, and literate readers. Biannual magazine; 130 pages. Estab. 1973. Circ. 1,000. Pays in contributor's copies. Acquires all rights, but may reassign following publication. Phone queries OK. SASE. Reports in 4 weeks. Sample copy $2.75.

Fiction: J.D. Muller, John Sabella, Hancel McCord, Fiction Editors. Experimental. Uses 2 mss/issue. Submit complete ms. No length requirement. Pays in 2 copies.

Poetry: Jim Lindsey, Virginia Slachman, Rosemary Thompson, Poetry Editors. Any style. Uses 50/issue. No length limit. Pays in two copies.

AT RISE: MAGAZINE, 9838 Jersey Ave., Santa Fe Springs CA 90670. Editor-in-Chief: Stella Hardy. Managing Editor: Howard D. Hunter. 75-85% freelance written. "For all ages interested in excellent original one-act plays. Cater most specifically to high school, college, and community theater." Quarterly magazine; 90 pages. Estab. January 1977. Circ. 200. Pays on publication. Buys publication and amateur performance rights. Photocopied submissions OK. SASE. Reports in 6-10 weeks. Sample copy $1; free writer's guidelines.

Fiction: "One-act plays only. We are interested in anything well-written, but do not appreciate foul language with no reason for it." Buys 16 plays/year. Submit complete ms. Length: 15-45 minutes. Pays $25, "plus standard royalty contract for amateur performances."

BACHY, Papa Bach Bookstore, 11317 Santa Monica Blvd., Los Angeles CA 90025. Estab. 1972. Circ. 800. Published 3 times/year. Buys first North American serial rights only. Will send sample copy to writer for $3. Submit complete ms. Will consider photocopied submissions. Reports within 8 weeks. SASE.

Fiction, Poetry: Serious poetry and fiction of highest quality, avant-garde or traditional forms; any length: "*Bachy* is dedicated to the discovery and continued publication of serious new writers and poets."

BACK ROADS, Box 543, Cotati CA 94928. Editor/Publisher: Stella Monday. 50% freelance written. Emphasizes literature and art for a general adult audience. Annual magazine; 120 pages. Estab. 1971. Circ. 2,500. Pays on publiation, in copies. Buys all rights, but may reassign following publication. Simultaneous, photocopied and previously published submissions OK. SASE. Reports in 2 months. Sample copy $1.50; mention *Writer's Market* in request.
Nonfiction: "Material must be revelant to annual theme; query." Expose; how-tos; general interest; humor; historical; interview; nostalgia; personal opinion; photo feature; profile; and reviews. Query. Length: 3,000 words maximum. Pays copies - $20.
Photos: Pays copies - $10 for 8½x11 b&w prints. Query for theme.
Fiction: Must be revelant to annual theme. Experimental; fantasy; humorous; mainstream; and science fiction. Query. Length: 3,000 words. Pays in copies.
Poetry: Avant-garde; free verse; haiku; light verse; traditional; experimental; concrete forms; and sound poems. Uses 25/issue. Limit submissions to batches of 3. Length: 60 lines maximum. Pays copies - $5. Query for theme.
Fillers: Clippings, jokes, gags, anecdotes, puzzles and short humor. Length: 50 words maximum. Pays in copies. Query for theme.

BALL STATE UNIVERSITY FORUM, Ball State University, Muncie IN 47306. (317)285-7255. Editors: Merrill Rippy and Frances Mayhew Rippy. 90% freelance written. For "educated readers interested in nontechnical studies of humanities, fine arts, sciences, social sciences, history, and education." Quarterly. Estab. 1959. Acquires all rights, "but author may always reprint at his own request without charge, so long as *Forum* is notified and international copyright held by *Forum* is acknowledged." Pays in 5 contributor's copies. Will send a sample copy to a writer on request. Contributors should accompany their entries with a 2-sentence description of their academic background or position, their other publications, and their special competence to write on their subject. Contributors submitting multiple copies cut 1 month from reading time: poems, 7 copies; short stories, 7 copies; plays, 7 copies; articles, 2 copies. Special issues planned on American literature, British literature, education. Reports in 2 weeks to 4 months. SASE.
Nonfiction, Fiction, Drama, and Poetry: Articles that are reasonably original, polished, and of general interest. Length: 50 to 3,000 words. Short stories, 1-act plays. Length: 50 to 2,000 words. Uses 5 to 30 poems per issue. Length: 5 to 200 lines.

BLACK AMERICAN LITERATURE FORUM, Indiana State University, Parsons Hall 237, Terre Haute IN 47809. (812)232-6311, ext. 2664. Editor-in-Chief: Joe Weixlmann. 90% freelance written. Emphasizes black American literature. Quarterly magazine; 40 pages. Estab. 1967. Circ. 850. Pays in copies. Acquires simultaneous rights. Phone queries OK. Submit seasonal/holiday material at least 3 months in advance. Simultaneous and photocopied submissions OK. SASE. Reports in 3 months. Free sample copy and writer's guidelines.
Nonfiction: "We publish scholarly criticism and bibliographies of black American writers, also pedagogical articles and curricular evaluations. We also use poetry by black writers and original graphic work by black artists."
Photos: Sketches and photos used without accompanying ms. Pays $15/graphic work.

BLACK SCHOLAR, Box 908, Sausalito CA 94965. Editor: Robert Allen. Mainly for black professionals, educators, and students. Monthly journal of black studies and research, 64 pages. Estab. 1969. Circ. 20,000. Acquires all rights. Uses about 60 mss per year. Payment in contributor's copies. Free sample copy and writer's guidelines. Will consider photocopied submissions. Will consider simultaneous submissions, "but must be so informed." Reports within 2 months. Query first about upcoming topics. SASE.
Nonfiction: "We seek essays discussing issues affecting the black community (education, health, economics, psychology, culture, literature, etc.). Essays should be reasoned and well-documented. Each issue is organized around a specific topic: Black education, health, prisons, family, etc., with a variety of viewpoints." Informational, interview, profile, historical, think articles, and book and film reviews. Length: 1,500 to 7,000 words.

THE BLACK WARRIOR REVIEW, The University of Alabama, Box 2936, University AL 35486. (205)348-7839. Editor-in-Chief: Rodney Simard. Emphasizes fiction and poetry. Semiannual magazine; 80 pages. Estab. 1974. Circ. 1,000. Pays in copies. Acquires all rights, but may reassign following publication. Phone queries OK. Submit seasonal material for fall/July 1; for spring/January 1. SASE. Reports in 2 months. Sample copy $2.00.
Nonfiction: Interview and criticism of contemporary literature. Buys 4 mss/year. Query.
Fiction: Ross White, fiction editor. Experimental and mainstream. "Acceptance depends on

quality, not subject matter, genre or treatment." Buys 1-3 mss/issue. Submit complete ms.
Poetry: Clark Powell, poetry editor. Avant-garde, free verse and traditional. Buys 20/issue.

BLACKBERRY, Box 4757, Albuquerque NM 81796. Editor: Jeanne Shannon. 95% freelance written. For readers interested in literature, especially poetry. Estab. 1975. Quarterly. Circ. 100. Acquires first North American serial rights. Uses about 90 mss a year. No payment, but contributors may buy copies of issues containing their work at reduced rate. Sample copy $2. Photocopied and simultaneous submissions OK. Reports in 2 weeks. SASE.
Nonfiction and Poetry: "We use a few reviews, primarily of poetry books and magazines. How-to articles; i.e., lessons in poetry and fiction writing. Personal experiences of writers in learning their craft. Interviews with writers and poets." Length: 800 words maximum. Traditional and avant-garde forms of poetry; blank verse, free verse and haiku. Length: 30 lines maximum.

BOOK ARTS, The Center For Book Arts, 15 Bleeker St., New York NY 10012. (212)260-6860. Editor-in-Chief: Patricia Nedds. Managing Editor: Joanne Deveraux-Caputi. Emphasizes bookbinding and exploring the arts of the book. "Occasional" magazine; 60 pages. Estab. 1974. Circ. 5,000. Pays in copies. Acquires all rights, but may reassign following publication. Submit seasonal/holiday material 3 months in advance. Simultaneous, photocopied, and previously published submissions OK. Reports in 2 months. Sample copy $3.
Nonfiction: Expose (on banning books in schools, other censorship, etc.); historical (bookburnings, looking at the history of watermarks and any other book experience); interview (with book artists) and technical (e.g. "William Blake's Method of Printing"). Query. Pays in copies.

BOOK FORUM, Hudson River Press, 38 E. 76th St., New York NY 10021. (212)861-8328. Editor-in-Chief: Marshall Hayes. Managing Editor: Marilyn Wood. Emphasizes contemporary literature, the arts, and foreign affairs for "intellectually sophisticated and knowledgeable professionals—university-level academics, writers, people in government, and the professions." Quarterly magazine; 192 pages. Estab. 1974. Circ. 5,200. Pays on publication. Buys all rights, but may reassign following publication. Phone queries OK. Photocopied submissions OK. SASE. Reports in 2 weeks. Sample copy $3.
Nonfiction: "We seek highly literate essays that would appeal to the same readership as, say, the London *Times Literary Supplement* or *Encounter*. Our readers are interested in professionally written, highly literate and informative essays, profiles and reviews in literature, the arts, behavior, and foreign and public affairs. We cannot use material designed for a mass readership, nor for the counter-culture. Think of us as an Eastern establishment, somewhat snobbish literary and public affairs journal and you will have it right." General interest; interview (with select contemporary writers); personal opinion (some personal essays which exhibit an exceptional level of literary skill and originality of viewpoint); profiles, and essays about contemporary writers. Buys 20 mss/year. Query. Length: 1,400-3,000 words. Pays $25-75.

BOSTON UNIVERSITY JOURNAL, Room 333, West Tower Three, 704 Commonwealth Ave., Boston MA 02215. (617)353-2699. Editor: Paul Kurt Ackermann. For libraries and universities.Magazine; 72 pages. Estab. 1966. Three times a year. Circ. 3,000. Buys all rights, but may reassign rights to author after publication. Buys 30 mss a year. "Read the magazine and query first before submitting mss." Reports in 1 month. SASE.
Nonfiction, Photos, Fiction, and Poetry: "Literary criticism, poetry (all forms), scholarly, well-written and lively articles on a variety of subjects (must be written clearly, without jargon), a few short stories." No limitations on length. "We also take reviews and b&w photos." Pays $10 per printed page; $25 minimum.

BOX 749, Box 749, Old Chelsea Station, New York NY 10011. (212)989-0519. Editor: David Ferguson. 75% freelance written. For "people of diverse background, education, income and age—an audience not necessarily above or underground. Such an audience is consistent with our belief that literature (plus art and music) is accessible to and even desired by a larger and more varied portion of society than has generally been acknowledged." Biannual magazine; 68-100 pages. Estab. 1972. Circ. 2,500. Acquires all rights, but will reassign rights to author after publication. Uses about 100 mss a year. Payment in contributor's copies. Will send sample copy to writer for $2. Will consider photocopied submissions. Will not consider simultaneous submissions. Reports in 1 to 4 months. Submit complete ms. SASE.
Fiction, Drama, Music and Poetry: "We publish poetry and fiction of every length and any theme; satire, belles-lettres, plays, music and any artwork reproducible by photo-offset. We will consider (and have serialized) long fiction. We will consider full-length plays. We have no

particular stylistic or ideological bias."

BULLETIN OF BIBLIOGRAPHY & MAGAZINE NOTES, F. W. Faxon Company, Inc., Publishing Division, 15 Southwest Park, Westwood MA 02090. Editor: Sandra J. Conrad. 100% freelance written. For college and university professors, undergraduate and graduate students, reference and serials librarians and the general public. Quarterly scholarly journal; 56 pages. Estab. 1897. Circ. 1,500. Copyrighted. Pays in contributor's copies. Uses about 30 mss a year. Reports within 12 weeks. SASE.
Bibliographies: "We publish bibliographies (primary and/or secondary, annotated or unannotated) on a wide range of topics within the humanities and social sciences. Articles are indexed or abstracted in 9 indexes and abstracting journals every year."
How To Break In: "We publish many bibliographies by researchers in specialized fields who find themselves hampered by incomplete or inaccurate bibliographies on particular subjects. Librarians, high school and college teachers, and graduate students often compile checklists for their own use which would be of value to scholars or the general public."

THE CALIFORNIA QUARTERLY, 100 Sproul, University of California, Davis CA 95616. Editor: Elliot Gilbert. 95% freelance written. "Addressed to an audience of educated, literary and general readers, interested in good writing on a variety of subjects, but emphasis is on poetry and fiction." Quarterly. Usually buys first North American serial rights. Reports in 4 to 6 weeks but the editorial office is closed from July 1 to September 30. SASE.
Fiction and Nonfiction: Department Editor: Diane Johnson. "Short fiction of quality with emphasis on stylistic distinction; contemporary themes, any subject." Experimental, mainstream. Length: 8,000 words. Original, critical articles, interviews and book reviews. Length: 8,000 words maximum. Pays $2 per published page.
Poetry: Department Editor: Sandra M. Gilbert. "Original, all types; any subject appropriate for genuine poetic expression; any length suitable to subject." Pays $3 per published page.

CANADIAN FICTION MAGAZINE, Box 46422, Station G, Vancouver B.C., Canada V6R 4G7. Editor-in-Chief: Geoffrey Hancock. 95% freelance written. Emphasizes Canadian fiction, short stories and novel excerpts. Quarterly magazine; 128 pages. Estab. 1971. Circ. 1,800. Pays on publication. Buys first North American serial rights. SASE (Canadian stamps). Reports in 4-6 weeks. Sample copy $2.50 (in Canadian funds); free writer's guidelines.
Nonfiction: Interview (must have a definite purpose, both as biography and as a critical tool focusing on problems and techniques) and book reviews (Canadian fiction only). Buys 35 mss/year. Query. Length: 1,000-3,000 words. Pays $3/printed page plus one-year subscription.
Photos: Purchased on assignment. Send prints. Pays $5 for 5x7 b&w glossies; $20 for cover. Model release required.
Fiction: "No restrictions on subject matter or theme. We are open to experimental and speculative fiction as well as traditional forms. Style content and form are the author's prerogative. We also publish self-contained sections of novel-in-progress and French-Canadian fiction in translation. Please note that *CFM* is an anthology devoted exclusively to Canadian fiction. We publish only the works of writers and artists residing in Canada and Canadians living abroad."

THE CANADIAN FORUM, 3 Church St., Suite 401, Toronto, Ont., Canada M5E 1M2. Editor-in-Chief: Denis Smith. Managing Editor: Susan Glorer. Emphasizes Canadian arts, letters, affairs for a highly educated readership interested in and committed to Canadian affairs. Monthly magazine; 60 pages. Estab. 1920. Circ. 20,000. Pays on publication. Buys one-time rights. SASE. Reports in 1-2 months. Sample copy $1.25
Nonfiction: Canadian political and literary commentary. Must be intellectual. Preferred subjects are research, politics, sociology and art. Length: 2,000-3,000 words.
Poetry: Avant-garde; free verse; haiku; light verse; and traditional.
How To Break In: "We accept very little material from the U.S. and are not a 'commercial' market for writers. However, we have published poetry and occasional articles about politics, economics, social analysis, etc., written by Americans."

CANADIAN LITERATURE, University of British Columbia, Vancouver V6T 1W5, B.C., Canada. Editor: W.H. New. Quarterly. Circ. 2,500. No fiction, fillers or photos. Not copyrighted. Pays on publication. Study publication. Query advisable. Enclose SAE and International Reply Coupons.
Nonfiction: Articles of high quality on Canadian books and writers only. Articles should be scholarly and readable. Length: 2,000 to 5,500 words. Pays $40 to $120 depending on length.

CAROLINA QUARTERLY, Greenlaw Hall, O66-A, University of North Carolina, Chapel Hill NC 27514. Editor: Katherine Kearns. 3 issues per year. Reprint rights revert to author on request. Pays on publication. Will send sample copy to a writer for $1.50. Reports in 6 to 8 weeks. Submissions should be marked Fiction or Poetry on envelope. SASE.
Fiction: "Quality. A place for both the new writer and the professional. Mainly interested in new writers who demonstrate both control of material and sophistication of language. We publish a significant number of unsolicited mss." Pays $3 a printed page. A contest in fiction and poetry for new writers, with cash prizes and publication, is held annually with a deadline of February 1. Only major restriction is that entrant not have published a book-length ms in the field of entry.
Poetry: "Quality; poems must have original subjects or points of view and demonstrate maturity in technique and in use of language. Popular or conventional verse not wanted." Pays $5 per poem.
How To Break In; "Writer, first of all, needs experience in writing even if unpublished. We publish only those pieces that show evidence of craft. Second, writer would benefit from perusal of recent copy of magazine to appreciate the type of thing we publish. After that, it's a matter of quality and editorial taste."

CHELSEA, P.O. Box 5880, Grand Central Station, New York NY 10017. Editor: Sonia Raiziss. Acquires first North American serial rights, but returns rights to author on request. Payment in copies. SASE.
Nonfiction, Fiction, and Poetry: "Poetry of high quality; short fiction; occasional nonfiction articles, interviews, and special issues. Accent on style. Also interested in fresh, contemporary translations."
How To Break In: "Best thing to do: Read several issues of the magazine to get the tone/content, themes, penchants, and range of contributions."

CHICAGO REVIEW University of Chicago, Faculty Exchange Box C, Chicago IL 60637. (312)753-3571. Editors: Cheryl Glickfield, M. Marks. Readership interested in contemporary literatures and criticisms. Quarterly magazine; 140 pages. Estab. 1946. Circ. 3,000. Pays in copies. Acquires all rights, but may reassign following publication. Photocopied submissions OK. SASE. Reports in 2 months. Sample copy $2.85; free writer's guidelines.
Nonfiction: David L. Smith, nonfiction editor. Informational and interview. "We consider essays on and reviews of contemporary writing and the arts." Submit complete ms. Length: 500-5,000 words.
Graphics: Buzz Spector, graphics editor. Accepted without accompanying ms. Submit b&w prints or transparencies.
Fiction: Thomas Mair, fiction editor. Experimental and mainstream. "We welcome the work of younger, less established writers." Uses 3-12/issue. Submit complete ms.
Poetry: Catherine Mouly, Mara Anne Tapp, poetry editors. Avant-garde; free verse; translations, and traditional. Uses 12/year. Limit submissions to batches of 3-5.

CHICAGO SUN-TIMES SHOW/BOOK WEEK, Chicago Sun-Times, 401 N. Wabash Ave., Chicago IL 60611. (312)321-2659. Editor: Jean Adelsman. Emphasizes entertainment, arts and books. Weekly newspaper; 10 pages. Circ. 750,000. Pays on publication. Buys all rights. Submit seasonal/holiday material at least 2 months in advance. Photocopied and previously published work OK. SASE. Reports in 2 weeks.
Nonfiction: "Articles and essays dealing with all the serious and lively arts—movies, theater (pro, semipro, amateur, foreign), filmmakers, painting, sculpture, music (all fields, from classical to rock—we have regular columnist in these fields). Our Book Week columns have from 5 to 10 reviews, mostly assigned. Material has to be very good because we have our own regular staffers who write almost every week. Writing must be tight. No warmed-over stuff of fan magazine type. No high schoolish literary themes." Query. Length: 500-800 words. Pays $50-100.

CIMARRON REVIEW, Oklahoma State University, Stillwater OK 74074. Editor-in-Chief: Clinton Keeler. Managing Editor: Jeanne Adams Wray. 100% freelance written. For educated readers, college and university oriented. Quarterly magazine, small and humanistic, 72 pages, (6x9). Estab. 1967. Circ. 1,500. Acquires all rights. Payment in contributor's copies. Will send free sample copy to writer on request. Reports within 5 months. Submit only complete ms. SASE.
Nonfiction and Fiction: "Stories, articles, often grouped in specific issues around a theme; such as women, aging, the dignity of work, etc. We are particularly interested in articles that show man triumphant in a polluted, technological world. Contemporary. Grace, lucidity in style;

optimistic or positive in outlook. We prefer to do theme issues. No adolescent, adjustment problems in fiction."

COLLAGE, Box 965, Los Gatos CA 95030. (408)264-5504. Editor: Timothy Seidler. Literary Arts Editor: Cheryl Kidder. Monthly tabloid; 20 pages. Estab. May 1977. Circ. 100,000. Phone queries OK. Submit seasonal/holiday material 3 months in advance. Simultaneous and photocopied submissions OK. SASE. Reports in 3-5 weeks. Free sample copy.
Nonfiction: Informational; interview (we try to have 1/month with a 'name' person or an 'unknown' doing something interesting); personal opinion; photo feature; and profile. Uses 24 mss/year. Query or submit complete ms. Length: 1,000-3,500 words. Pays 2¢/word.
Photos: Uses 5x7 b&w prints. Pays $5 minimum.
Columns/Departments: Movie Reviews; Book Reviews; and Record reviews. Uses 72 mss/year. Submit complete ms. Length: 400-750 words. Pays 2¢/word. Open to suggestions for new columns/departments.
Fiction: Adventure; fantasy; humorous; mainstream; mystery; science fiction; and suspense. Uses 12 mss/year. Submit complete ms. Length: 1,200-3,500 words. Pays 2¢/word.
Poetry: Free verse; and avant-garde. Uses 72/year. Submit up to 20 poems. Pays 2/word.

THE COLORADO QUARTERLY, Hellems 134C, University of Colorado, Boulder CO 80309. Editor: Walter G. Simon. Quarterly magazine. Estab. 1952. Circ. 700. Buys all rights, "but liberal on returning rights." Reports in 3-4 weeks. SASE. Publishes Award Issue each spring; devoted to one author or artist. Carries $1,000 award. Must be able to fill 1 issue. Deadline: December 31. Also publishes bonus issues sponsored by private businesses or individuals. "These contain materials felt worthy of publication but not in keeping with the format of regular *Quarterly* issues. Payment determined by staff—up to $500. 4-5 issues scheduled this year." Sample copy $2.50; mention *Writer's Market* in request.
Nonfiction: Articles written by experts on any subject for the general educated reader in nontechnical, nonacademic style. Length: 4,000-6,000 words. Pays $50.
Fiction: Interested in all styles. Length: 4,000-6,000 words. Pays $20.
Poetry: Interested in all styles. Pays $20.

CONFRONTATION, Long Island University, 1 University Plaza, Brooklyn NY 11201. (212)834-6170. Editor-in-Chief: Martin Tucker. 90% freelance written. Emphasizes creative writing for a literate, educated, college graduate audience. Semiannual magazine; 190 pages. Estab. 1968. Circ. 2,000. Pays on publication. Buys all rights, but may reassign following publication. Phone queries OK. Simultaneous and photocopied submissions OK. SASE. Reports in 2 months. Sample copy $1.
Nonfiction: "Articles are, basically, commissioned essays on a specific subject." Memoirs wanted. Buys 6 mss/year. Query. Length: 1,000-3,000 words. Pays $10-50.
Fiction: Ken Bernard, Fiction Editor. Fantasy, experimental, humorous, mainstream. Buys 20 mss/year. Submit complete ms. Length: "completely open." Pays $20-75.
Poetry: W. Palmer, Poetry Editor. Avant-garde, free verse, haiku, light verse, traditional. Buys 40/year. Limit submissions to batches of 10. No length requirement. Pays $10-40.

CONNECTICUT FIRESIDE AND REVIEW OF BOOKS, Box 5293, Hamden CT 06518. (203)248-1023. Editor-in-Chief: Albert E. Callan. Emphasizes writing and literary subjects for an intelligent, well-educated readership interested in writing. Quarterly magazine; 96 pages. Estab. 1972. Circ. 1,500. Pays in copies on publication. Acquires first North American serial rights. Phone queries OK. Simultaneous, photocopied and previously published submissions OK. Reports in 2 weeks. Sample copy $1.25.
Nonfiction: Historical (have had an article about a Connecticut person, usually literary, in each issue so far); and humor. Uses 4 mss/year. Submit complete ms. Length: 1,000-2,500 words.
Photos: "We would use good art photos if offered, otherwise we take our own. We are interested in anything of artistic nature."
Columns/Departments: L.R. Langley, Reviews Editor. "We have about 20 pages of tradebook reviews/issue. Also 5 pages of small press books and poetry chapbooks." Length: 500 words minimum.
Fiction: Confession; experimental; fantasy; historical; humorous; mystery; and suspense. Uses 16-20/issue. Submit complete ms. Length: 1,500-5,000 words.
Poetry: Avant-garde; free verse; haiku; light verse; and traditional. Uses 160/year. Length: 30 lines or less.
How To Break In: "We need articles about Connecticut literary people, or literary people associated with Connecticut in some way, or with New England. Such articles should have a

fresh viewpoint, or new information to offer. We also need good serious fiction, nothing commercial."

CONTEMPORARY LITERATURE, Dept. of English, Helen C. White Hall, University of Wisconsin, Madison WI 53706. Editor: L.S. Dembo. Quarterly. "All details should conform to those recommended by the *MLA Style Sheet*." Does not encourage contributions from freelance writers without academic credentials. SASE.
Nonfiction: A scholarly journal which examines various aspects of contemporary literature, from generalizations on current trends and themes, to studies of a writer, his technique, and/or his work, to other specialized treatments or studies in modern literature.

CONTEMPORARY REVIEW, 61 Carey St., London, W.C. 2, England. Editor: Rosalind Wade. Monthly magazine. Estab: 1866. SAE and International Reply Coupons. Reports within a week or so.
Nonfiction, Fiction, and Poetry: "We are completely 'independent' although 'liberal' in origin. We can provide a platform for a very wide range of ideas. Our circulation is greater in the U.S.A. than in England. Freshness of approach and some new and authoritative information is essential. Only material written with authority can be considered." Buys interviews, profiles, and personal experience articles on "the arts, history, home and international politics, domestic subjects, theology, etc." Occasionally buys "short stories and poems of the highest literary merit." Length: 1,500 to 3,000 words for articles; 4,000 words maximum for fiction. Pays 3 pounds per 1,000 words.

CREAM CITY REVIEW Department of English, Box 413, University of Wisconsin-Milwaukee, Milwaukee WI 53201. Co-editors: Sheri Gibbs, Debra Vest. 100% freelance written. Emphasizes poetry, fiction, criticism, reviews, graphics, and interviews. "We have existed very locally for 3 years, and are just coming under the direction of the English Department, and will soon be distributed over a 5 state area of the midwest. Libraries, universities, high schools, etc., subscribe." Published 3 times/year. Magazine; 65 pages. Estab. 1973. Circ. 500 at present. Pays in copies. Obtains all rights, but may reassign following publication. Submit seasonal/holiday material 1 month in advance of issue date. Simultaneous, photocopied, and previously published submissions OK. SASE. Reports in 2-4 weeks. Sample copy $1.50; free writer's guidelines; mention *Writer's Market* in request.
Nonfiction: General interest (of or pertaining to established writers or writing); historical; humor; interview (of literary or creative interest); personal opinion (as in book reviews, reviews of readings, etc.); and profile (of writers past and present). "Religious, patriotic, sentimental things are not for us—our readership is always excited by the newness of what we try to print." Submit complete ms. Length: 3,000 words maximum.
Fiction: Adventure; experimental (as long as there is a discernable beginning, middle, and end); fantasy; historical; humorous; mainstream; suspense;condensed novels; and serialized novels. Uses 3-5 mss/issue. Submit complete ms. Length: 15 pages maximum.
Poetry: All types. Uses 60-90/year. Limit submissions to batches of 4.

CREATIVE PITTSBURGH, 841 Broadway, East McKeesport PA 15035. (412)824-7746. Editor-in-Chief: Daniel B. Edwards. Managing Editor: G. Ulrich Musinsky. For a readership 18 years old and up, ranging from the general public to the academia. Semiannual magazine; 52-72 pages. Estab. 1976. Circ. 1,500. Pays in copies on publication. Buys all rights, but may reassign following publication. Previously published submissions OK. SASE. Reports on queries in 2 weeks; complete mss in 6 months. Sample copy $2.75; writer's guidelines for SASE.
Nonfiction, Fiction, and Poetry: "*Creative Pittsburgh* is a journal designed to publish contemporary literature that major literary magazines pass by. The contention of our staff is that major American literary magazines, in an effort to keep up with the times, are overlooking the type of short stories, essays and poetry that coincide with the traditions of the media. We do not limit our publication to new fads in literature or specified styles. Our criteria is very open, requiring material of high quality. We believe it takes more than words, trends, or styles to be literary. *Creative Pittsburgh* is a magazine that is read, not only looked at." Submit complete ms. Length: 500-6,000 words. Payment in contributor's copies.

CRITICISM, Wayne State University, Dept. of English, Detroit MI 48202. Editor: Alva Gay. For college and university audience of humanities scholars and teachers. Quarterly. No payment. Reports in 3 months. Enclose SASE.
Nonfiction: Articles on literature, music, visual arts; no particular critical "school." Style should be clear and to the point. Length: 15 to 20 typewritten pages.

CRITIQUE: STUDIES IN MODERN FICTION, Department of English, Georgia Institute of Technology, Atlanta GA 30332. Editor: James Dean Young. For college and university teachers and students. Estab. 1956. Triannual. Circ. 1,500. Acquires all rights. Pays in contributor's copies. Submit complete original ms. Writers should follow the *MLA Style Sheet*. Reports in 4 to 6 months. Enclose SASE.
Nonfiction: "Critical essays on writers of contemporary fiction. We prefer essays on writers from any country who are alive and without great reputations. We only rarely publish essays on well-known, established writers such as Conrad, James, Joyce, and Faulkner." Uses informational articles and interviews. Length: 4,000 to 8,000 words.

DARK HORSE, 47 Stearns, Cambridge MA 02138. (617)492-0040. Editor: Jane Barnes. Estab. 1974. Quarterly. Circ. 3,000. Copyrighted. Uses about 120 mss a year. Pays in contributor's copies. Sample copy $1.25. No photocopied or simultaneous submissions. Reports in 1 to 12 weeks. SASE.
Nonfiction and Photos: "We welcome intelligent reviews of poetry and fiction books. We welcome work of prisoners, the gay community, minorities, translations, Blacks, Puerto Ricans, Indians, etc. News about literary events in New England; small press publishing. Techniques of printing, running a small press, distribution, literary cooperatives, setting type, etc." Length: 600-1,200 words. B&w and color photos used with mss.
Fiction and Poetry: Experimental, and mainstream. No science fiction; serialized novels. Length: 4,000 words maximum. Traditional and avant-garde forms of poetry. Blank verse, free verse. "Open to all non-cliched poetry. Fold poems together. Identify each page with name and address."

DE KALB LITERARY ARTS JOURNAL, 555 N. Indian Creek Dr., Clarkston GA 30021. (404)292-1520. Editor: William S. Newman. 90% freelance written. For those interested in poetry, fiction and/or art. Quarterly. Magazine; 100 pages. Estab. 1966. Circ. 5,000. Acquires first serial rights. Pays in contributor's copies. Sample copy for $1.50 (cost plus postage). "Look for announcements of special issues." Seeking material for National Poets Issue. Submit complete ms. Reports in 2-3 months. SASE.
Nonfiction, Fiction, Photos, and Poetry: Subject matter is unrestricted. "We consider all types of nonfiction and fiction. Our decisions are based on quality of material. Traditional, blank verse, free verse, light verse, and avant-garde forms of poetry." B&w photos are used with mss; 8x10 glossies preferred.

THE DENVER QUARTERLY, University of Denver, Denver CO 80208. (303)753-2869. Editor-in-Chief: Leland Chambers. Assistant Editor: Rhondala Shafner. For an intellectual/university readership. Quarterly magazine; 125-160 pages. Estab. 1965. Circ. 800. Pays on publication. Buys first North American serial rights. Phone queries OK. Photocopied (if explained as not simultaneous) submissions OK. SASE. Reports in 4 weeks. Sample copy $2. "Each issue focuses on a topic of contemporary concern. Beginning with Fall 1978: Mexican letters since 1968, Australian Literature, American Translators, and the 70's novel. Submissions need not conincide with these topics."
Nonfiction: Historical; humor; personal opinion and profile. Buys 10-12 mss/year. Send complete ms. Pays $5/printed page.
Fiction: Adventure; fantasy; experimental; historical; humorous; mainstream and science fiction. Buys 8-10 mss/year. Send complete ms. Pays $5/printed page.
Poetry: Avant-garde, free verse and traditional. Buys 30 poems/year. Send poems. Pays $10/printed page.
How To Break In: "We decide on the basis of quality only. Prior publication is irrelevant. Promising material, even though rejected, will receive some personal comment from the editor; some material can be revised to meet our standards, through such criticism. Rejection via a printed form only means the editor sees nothing worth encouraging.

DESCANT, Texas Christian University Press, Department of English, TCU, Fort Worth TX 76129. (817)926-2461. Editor-in-Chief: Betsy Feagan Colquitt. Quarterly magazine; 48 pages. Estab. 1956. Circ. 650. Pays in contributor's copies on publication. Acquires all rights, but will reassign following publication. Phone queries OK. Simultaneous and photocopied submissions OK. SASE. Reports in 6 weeks. Sample copy $1; free writer's guidelines.
Nonfiction: Informational (articles used are literary criticism, with examination of modern literature as principal concern of the essay). Uses 4 mss/year. Submit complete ms. Length: 3,000-5,000 words.

Fiction: Fantasy, confession, experimental, historical. Uses 10-12 mss/year. Submit complete ms. Length: 2,000-6,000 words.
Poetry: Avant-garde, free verse, traditional. Uses 40/year. Limit submissions to batches of 6. Length: 10-40 lines.

THE DRAMA REVIEW, New York University, 51 W. 4th St., Rm. 300, New York NY 10012. (212)598-2597. Editor-in-Chief: Michael Kirby. 75% freelance written. Emphasizes avant-garde performance art for professors, students and the general theater and dance-going public as well as professional practitioners in the performing arts. Quarterly magazine; 144 pages. Estab. 1955. Circ. 10,000. Pays on publication. Reassigns rights following publication. Phone queries OK. Submit seasonal/holiday material 4 months in advance. Photocopied and previously published (if published in another language) submissions OK. SASE. Reports in 3 months. Sample copy $3.50. Free writer's guidelines.
Nonfiction: Terry Helbing, Managing Editor. Historical (the historical avant-garde in any performance art, translations of previously unpublished plays, etc.) and informational (documentation of a particular performance). Buys 10-20 mss/issue. Query. Pays 1¢/word for translations; 2¢/word for other material.
Photos: Terry Helbing, Managing Editor. Photos purchased with or without accompanying ms or on assignment. Captions required. Pays $10 for b&w photos. No additional payment for photos accepted with accompanying ms.
Rejects: "No criticism in the sense of value judgments—we are not interested in the author's opinions. We are only interested in documentation theory and analysis."

EL VIENTO, 348 7th Street, Huntington WV 25701. Editor: William Lloyd Griffin. Estab. 1967. Semiannual. "All rights revert to the authors." Pays in contributor's copies. Will consider photocopied submissions. Reports in 6 weeks. SASE. Free sample copy.
Fiction, Nonfiction, Poetry, and Drama: "We use fiction, nonfiction, poetry, and one-act plays. No taboos except low quality material." Length: 500 to 3,000 words for fiction and nonfiction.

EPOCH, A Magazine of Contemporary Literature, 245 Goldwin Smith Hall, Cornell University, Ithaca NY 14853. 3 times yearly. Acquires first serial publication rights. Payment in copies. Reports in 2 months or more. SASE.
Fiction: "Quality. Would like to see more stories which combine a fresh, honest transcription of human experience with power or meaningfulness, but are not adverse to experimental forms." Length: 1,500 to 5,000 words.
Poetry: Approximately 30 to 40 pages each issue devoted to poetry.

EVENT, Douglas College, Box 2503, New Westminster, B.C., Canada V3L 5B2. For "those interested in literature and writing." Biannual magazine; 135-150 pages. Estab. 1970. Circ. 800. Uses 65-75 mss/year. Small payment and contributor's copies. Photocopied and simultaneous submissions OK. Reports in 4 months. Submit complete ms. Enclose SAE and International Reply Coupons.
Nonfiction, Fiction, Poetry and Drama: "High-quality work." Reviews, essays, the novella, the short story, poetry, and drama.

THE FAULT, 33513 6th St., Union City CA 94587. (415)487-1383. Editor: Rustie Cook. Emphasizes innovative literature for the small press collector, libraries, anyone interested in experimental and contemporary works of art. Semiannual magazine; 125 pages. Estab. 1971. Circ. 500. Payment 1 year after publication "if grant is awarded." Buys 1-time and reprint rights. Phone queries OK. Submit seasonal/holiday material 2 months in advance. Photocopied and previously published submissions OK. SASE. Reports in 4 weeks. Sample copy $1.50. Free writer's guidelines.
Photos: Purchased without accompanying manuscript. Send prints. Pays $5-10 for 5x7 b&w; $5-10 for color. No additional payment for photos accepted with accompanying ms.
Fiction: Science fiction, dada, visual, erotica, experimental, fantasy and mainstream. Buys 10 mss/year. Send complete ms. Length: 100-5,000 words. Pays $5-10.
Poetry: Avant-garde and free verse. Buys 40 poems/year. Limit submissions to batches of 10. Length: 2-100. Pays $5-10.
Fillers: Collages. Buys 10/year. Length: 1-100 words. Pays $5-10.
How To Break In: "No need for formula fiction filled with cliches and unimaginative writing. Poetry with end rhymes filled with abstractions and archaic ideas. Any work that lacks style, invention, originality."

FICTION, City College, English Department, 138th St. and Convent Ave., New York NY 10031. (212)690-8170. Editor: Mark Mirsky. Published by a cooperative of writers. For individual subscribers of all ages; college libraries, bookstores, and college bookstores. Published 3 times a year. Book; 15-250 pages. Estab. 1972. Circ. 5,000. Acquires all rights, but will reassign rights to author after publication. Payment in contributor's copies only. Will send free sample copy to writer on request. Submit complete ms. Reports as soon as possible, but time "depends on the backlog of material." SASE.
Fiction and Photos: "We publish only fiction. There really is no minimum or maximum length, because we edit many pieces. No payment for writers." Photos purchased without accompanying ms. Photo Editor: Inger Grytting.

FICTION INTERNATIONAL, Department of English, St. Lawrence University, Canton NY 13617. Editor: Joe David Bellamy. For "readers interested in the best writing by talented writers working in new forms or working in old forms in especially fruitful new ways; readers interested in contemporary literary developments and possibilities. Not considering manuscripts at present because of our decision to publish our forthcoming issue as a collection of stories by one author. We will not be reading again for an open-anthology issue until Summer, 1979."

FIRELANDS ARTS REVIEW, Firelands Campus, Huron OH 44839. Editor: Joel D. Rudinger. For general educated audience. Annual magazine, 80 pages. Estab. 1972. Circulation: 1,000. Acquires first serial rights. Uses 50 mss a year. Pays in copies. Will send sample copy to writer for $2.30. Submit only complete ms. Accepts mss from October to March of each year. Reports within 8 weeks. SASE.
Fiction: "Any style and approach and subject matter as long as the quality is professional and mature. Length: 3,000 words maximum. Will also accept short prose sketches and characterizations sensitive to the human condition. We need stories that display humor or clever ironic twist."
Photos: 5x7 or 8x10 b&w's. Any non-cliched subject or style. Unusual perspective, high contrast, experimental materials are of interest as well as fresh approaches to traditional photography.
Poetry: Poems must be original and mature in use of language. Any subject, any theme, any style, any length. High quality and awareness of the art of writing poetry essential.

FOLKLORE FORUM, 504 North Fess, Bloomington IN 47401. For folklorists, graduate students in the humanities and social sciences. Quarterly magazine; 80 pages, Estab. 1968. Circ. 350. Not copyrighted. Payment in contributor's copies. Will send sample copy to writer for $2. Will consider photocopied and simultaneous submissions. Query first or submit complete ms. Reports within 2 months. SASE.
Nonfiction: Articles, bibliographies; translations; book, record, and ethnographic film reviews on topics in folklore. "We encourage short comments and queries. Our objective is to serve as a medium of communication among folklorists. We have a special interest in popular culture and folklore."

FORMS, The Review of Anthropos Theophoros, Box 3379. San Francisco CA 94044. (415)768-6963. Editor-in-Chief: Emily McCormick. 90% freelance written. For adults interested in ideas, especially as related to all forms of art. Quarterly magazine; 36 pages. Estab. 1976. Circ. 200. Pays on publication. Buys one-time rights. Phone queries OK. Submit seasonal/holiday material 2 months in advance of issue date. Simultaneous and photocopied submissions OK. SASE. Reports in 1 month. Sample copy 50¢; mention *Writer's Market* in request.
Nonfiction: Exposé; general interest; humor; historical; interview; personal opinion; profile; travel; "and music, art, and book reviews of more than topical interest." Buys 5 mss/issue. Submit complete ms. Length: 500-5,000 words. Pays $50 maximum.
Fiction: Adventure; experimental; fantasy; humorous; and mainstream. Buys 4 mss/issue. Submit complete ms. Length: 500-5,000 words. Pays $50 maximum.
Poetry: Avant-garde, free verse, haiku, light verse; and traditional. Buys 4/issue. Limit submissions to batches of 10. Length 4-200 words. Pays $25 maximum.

FORUM, University of Houston, Cullen Blvd., Houston TX 77004. (713)749-4710. Editor: William Lee Pryor. Primarily for a sophisticated audience; most of the contributors are university professors. Quarterly. Acquires all rights, but will reassign rights to author after publication. Pays in contributor's copies. "A query letter is a welcome courtesy, although we do not specifically request one." SASE.
Nonfiction: "We feature articles dealing with the humanities and the fine arts. For articles, we

stress the scholarly approach and originality. We recommend use of the *MLA Style Sheet*. An informal style is not objectionable, but research, if any, should be accurate, thorough, and carefully documented. Our format differs from those publications of a similiar orientation in that we attempt to combine scholarship with an appealing, aesthetic setting. We are very much interested in good articles on literature, music, dance, architecture, sculpture, etc., not only for our regular issues, but also for special numbers which focus on a particular theme."
Fiction: "We are open on story themes, and we stress originality and quality. Up to now we have not found it possible to publish condensed or serialized novels."
Poetry: "We can use a limited number of poems, and we stress originality and quality."

FOUR QUARTERS, LeSalle College, Olney Ave. at 20th St., Philadelphia PA 19141. Editor: John C. Kleis. For college educated audience with literary interest. Quarterly. Circ. 700. Buys all rights; grants permission to reprint on request. Buys 10 to 12 short stories, 30 to 40 poems, 4 articles a year. Pays on publication. Sample copy for 50¢. Reports in 6-8 weeks. "Do not submit during July and August." SASE.
Nonfiction: "Lively critical articles on particular authors or specific works. Think pieces on history, politics, the arts. Prefer footnotes incorporated. Style must be literate, lively, free of jargon and pedantry." Length: 1,500 to 5,000 words. Payment is up to $25.
Fiction: "Technical mastery gets our attention and respect immediately. We admire writers who use the language with precision, economy, and imagination. But fine writing for its own sake is unsatisfying unless it can lead the reader to some insight into the complexity of the human condition without falling into heavy-handed didacticism." Length: 2,000 to 5,000 words. Pays up to $25.
Poetry: "Quality poetry from 8 to 32 lines. Some shorter ones used as fillers without payment." Payment is up to $5.

GALLIMAUFRY PRESS, Box 32364, Calvert St. Station, Washington DC 20007. Editor-in-Chief: Mary MacArthur. Emphasizes literature. Semiannual magazine; 150 pages. Estab. 1973. Circ. 1,500. Pays on publication in copies. Acquires all rights, but may reassign to author following publication. Simultaneous submissions (if notified) OK. SASE. Reports in 3 months. Sample copy $3.50.
Fiction: Contemporary—both traditional and experimental. Uses 50 mss/year. Send complete ms.

GRAFFITI, English Department, Box 418, Lenoir Rhyne College, Hickory NC 28601. Editor: Kermit Turner. For writers, college students, faculty and all persons interested in literature. Semiannual magazine; 44 pages. Estab. 1972. Circ. 250. Acquires first serial rights. All rights return to author after publication. Uses 6 to 8 short story mss a year; about 80 poems. Payment in contributor's copies. Sample copy $1. Will not consider photocopied or simultaneous submissions. Reports on material accepted for publication in 4 months. Returns rejected material in 6 weeks. Submit complete ms. SASE.
Fiction: Short stories; experimental, mainstream. Length: 2,000 to 5,000 words.
Poetry: Traditional forms; free verse. Will consider any length.

THE GREAT LAKES REVIEW, Central Michigan University, Mt. Pleasant MI 48858. Editors: Ronald Primeau, Martha Brown. Mostly for scholars and academics who are interested in Midwest studies. Semi-annual magazine, 100 pages. Estab. 1974. Circ. 1,000. "We require no rights outside of copyright." Payment in contributor's copies. Write for editorial guidelines for writers. Query first or submit complete ms. Will consider photocopied and simultaneous submissions. Reports in 6 months. SASE.
Nonfiction and Poetry: Scholarly articles, bibliographies, interviews, poetry features, personal narratives.

GREAT RIVER REVIEW, 211 W. 7th St., Winona MN 55987. (507)454-1212. Editors: Emilio DeGrazia, David Robinson and Sandra Bennett. Published 3 times/year. Magazine; 120 pages. Estab. November 1977. Pays on publication. Submit seasonal material 3-4 months in advance of issue dates. Photocopied submissions OK. SASE. Reports in 6 weeks. Sample copy $2.75.
Nonfiction: Articles on midwestern authors. Submit complete ms. Pays $20-50.
Fiction: Experimental and mainstream. "We are not interested in most mass-circulation type fiction. We give priority to midwestern, especially Minnesota writers." Buys 6 mss/issue. Submit complete ms. Length: 2,000-10,000 words. Pays $20-50.
Poetry: Avant-garde; free verse; and traditional. No newspaper poetry. Buys 30 poems/issue.

Limit submissions to batches of 10-15. Pays modest rates for poetry.

GRUB STREET, Grub Street Press, Box 91, Bellmore NY 11710. (212)733-3922. Editor: Alan Ball. 95% freelance written. For anyone interested in modern literature. Semiannual magazine; 48 pages. Estab. 1969. Circ. 1,000. Pays on publication. All rights revert to author. Phone queries OK. Simultaneous, photocopied, and previously published submissions OK. SASE. Reports in 3-6 weeks. Sample copy 50¢; writer's guidelines for SASE.
Fiction: "We are a magazine of modern culture, which publishes mainly, but is not restricted to, verse, fiction, and graphics. We do seek mss of high quality from professional as well as relatively unknown writers. We are a literary magazine, hoping to appeal to a diverse audience. At the same time we seek readable material of significant interest, we encourage experimentation. No taboos, no restrictions on subject matter or length, except that we try to publish a diverse collection, so shorter works have a certain advantage." Buys 1-2 mss/issue. Send first 2 pages only if ms is over 2,000 words. Length: 5,000 maximum. Pays in copies.
Poetry: Avant-garde, free verse and traditional. Buys 20 poems/issue. Pays in copies. 1 featured poet per issue is paid a cash award.
Rejects: No racist or sexist material.

HANGING LOOSE, 231 Wyckoff St., Brooklyn NY 11217. Editors: Dick Lourie, Emmett Jarrett, Ron Schreiber, Robert Hershon. Quarterly. Acquires first serial rights. Payment in copies. Will send sample copy to writer for $1.50. Reports in 2 to 3 months. SASE.
Poetry and Fiction: Fresh, energetic poems of any length. Excellent quality. Experimental fiction. "Space for fiction very limited."

HARVEST, Box 78, Farmington CT 06032. Contact: Robert T. Casey. "A forum for literary work by members of the Connecticut Writers League. Membership in the league is $10/year, and is open to all, regardless of state." Magazine; 75 pages. Estab. 1974. Annually (October). Acquires first North American serial rights. No payment. Sample copy $1.95. Will consider photocopied and simultaneous submissions. Writer's guidelines available. SASE.
Nonfiction, Fiction and Poetry: Essays, short fiction, parts of novels, poetry. Satire and other types of humor would also be welcome. Length for fiction: 2,000 words. No limit on length for poetry.

HEIRS MAGAZINE, 657 Mission St., Room 205, San Francisco CA 94105. Editor: Alfred Durand Garcia. For educators, artists, students, professionals, poets, libraries and public institutions; specifically people interested in art and literature viewed from a multi-culture perspective. Quarterly magazine; 80 pages. Estab. 1968. Circ. 2,000. Rights acquired vary with author and material. May acquire first North American serial rights, first serial rights, or all rights. Token monetary payment and/or copies. Sample copy $3; free writer's guidelines. Will consider photocopied submissions. No simultaneous submissions. Reports in 6 to 8 weeks. Submit complete ms. SASE.
Nonfiction and Photos: Art criticism, feature articles on art and artists. Must be written from a humanistic perspective. Book reviews. Reviews of Third World literature and women's literature. B&w photos used with or without mss. "Because of our unique format, we suggest that writers see a sample copy first since we publish major articles in English, Spanish and Chinese." Length: 1,500 words.
Fiction and Poetry: Experimental fiction. Length: 1,500 words. Blank verse, free verse and avant-garde forms of poetry.

THE HUDSON REVIEW, 65 E. 55th St., New York NY 10022. Managing Editor: Marianne Clay. Quarterly. Pays on publication. Reports in 6 to 8 weeks. SASE for return of submissions.
Nonfiction, Fiction, and Poetry: Uses "quality fiction up to 10,000 words, articles up to 8,000 words; translations, reviews and poetry." Pays 2½¢ a word for prose, and 50¢ a line for poetry.

THE HUMANIST, 923 Kensington Ave., Buffalo NY 14215. (716)837-0306. Editor: Paul Kurtz. 90% freelance written. For college graduates; humanists with a wide range of interests. Published every 2 months; 48 to 64 pages. Estab. 1941. Circ. 28,500. Copyrighted. Pays on publication. Will send free sample copy to writer on request. Will consider photocopied submissions. Query first. Reports "immediately." SASE.
Nonfiction: "General informative articles of an intellectual nature. A thorough treatment of the subject material covered. We're considered to be quite innovative in the types of articles

published. Particularly interested in articles on frontier issues, especially on changing ethical and value issues." Informational, think articles, and book, movie, and TV reviews. Length: 1,000 to 5,000 words. Pays $50 to $150.

IN A NUTSHELL, Hibiscus Press, Box 22248, Sacramento CA 95822. (916)428-2766. Editor-in-Chief: Margaret Wensrich. 99% freelance written. Emphasizes poetry and fiction. Quarterly magazine; 40 pages. Estab. 1975. Circ. 5,000. Pays on publication. Buys one-time rights. Submit seasonal/holiday material 6 months in advance. Photocopied submissions OK. SASE. Reports in 4 weeks. Sample copy $2; writer's guidelines for SASE.
Fiction: Adventure, fantasy, confession, experimental, historical, humorous, mystery, romance, suspense, mainstream, science fiction, western. Buys 12 mss/year. Submit complete ms. Length: 1,500-3,500 words. Pays ½¢/word.
Poetry: Joyce Odam, Poetry Editor. Free verse, haiku, light verse, traditional. "We put no restrictions on poetry." Buys 60-80/year. Limit submissions to batches of 4-6. No length limit. Pays $2 minimum. "We have an annual poetry and short story contest. We give cash and other awards. Winners are published *In A Nutshell.* Send SASE for contest rules and entry form."

INLET, Virginia Wesleyan College, Norfolk VA 23502. Editor: Joseph Harkey. Poetry and fiction for liberally educated readership of all ages. Annual magazine; 30 pages. Estab. 1971. Circ. 700. Pays in copies. Acquires all rights, but will reassign rights to author following publication. Photocopied submissions OK. Submissions accepted September 1-March 15. SASE. Reports in 2 months. Sample copy for 35¢ in postage.
Fiction: Any type that is handled successfully. Especially interested in engaging, well-written short shorts of 600-1,500 words, but will consider mss up to 3,000 words long. Uses 1-4 mss/year.
Poetry: "Anything that is not mauldlin will be considered. The only requirement is good writing." Preferred lengths: 2-30 lines, 40-80 lines, or 100-160 lines. "The longer the poem, the better it has to be." Uses 20-40 poems/year. Limit submissions to batches of 5.

INTER-AMERICAN REVIEW OF BIBLIOGRAPHY, Organization of American States, Washington DC 20006. Editor: Elena Castedo-Ellerman. Quarterly magazine; 120-150 pages. Estab. 1951. Circ. 3,000. Pays in subscription to magazine. Sample copy $1.50; free writer's guidelines.
Nonfiction: Scholarly material only in literature and philosophy. Uses 16 mss/year. Query.
Columns/Departments: Book reviews on serious literature and humanistic studies dealing with the American continent, especially Latin America and the Caribbean. Also News and Notes about cultural news dealing with same. Submit complete ms. Length: 20-30 pages for articles; 2 pages for book reviews; 1 paragraph for news. Pays in copy of book to be reviewed.

THE INTERCOLLEGIATE REVIEW, Intercollegiate Studies Institute, 14 S. Bryn Mawr Ave., Bryn Mawr PA 19010. (215)525-7501. Editor-in-Chief: Robert A. Schadler. Emphasizes intellectual conservatism on cultural, economic, political, literary and philosophical issues. Quarterly magazine; 64 pages. Estab. 1975. Circ. 30,000. Pays on publication. Buys all rights. Phone queries OK. SASE. Reports in 6 months. Free sample copy.
Nonfiction: Historical; informational and personal. Buys 4 mss/issue. Query. Length: 1,000-5,000 words. Pays $50-150.

INTERMEDIA, Century Club Educational Arts Project, 10508 W. Pico Blvd., Los Angeles CA 90026. Editor-in-Chief: Harley W. Lond. Emphasizes art and literature for college educated writers and artists interested in new literature. Triquarterly magazine; 48 pages. Estab. 1974. Circ. 2,000. Pays on publication. Acquires all rights, but may reassign following publication. Simultaneous, photocopied, and previously published submissions OK. SASE. Reports in 1 month. Sample copy $1.
Nonfiction: Informational articles on art groups, media groups, dance, theater, etc. Interviews, personal opinion articles, profiles, photo features on the same themes. "We're wide open on articles on art and media, particularly those covering avant-garde art of all disciplines; video, film, theater, dance, etc." Buys 9-15 mss/year. Query. Length: 5,000 words. Pays in contributor's copies.
Photos: B&w only. Used with or without mss. Query. Pays in contributor's copies.
Fiction and Poetry: "Both should be highly experimental." Buys 1-2 mss/issue. Query. Pays in contributor's copies.

INTERSTATE, Box 7068, University Station, Austin TX 78712. Editors: Loris Essary and Mark Loeffler. For "anyone interested in creative arts." Quarterly magazine; 54 pages. Estab. 1974. Circ. 500. Acquires all rights, but will reassign rights to author after publication. Payment in contributor's copies. Sample copy $2. Photocopied submissions OK. Reports in 1-3 weeks. "Occasionally longer." No query necessary. SASE.
Nonfiction and Photos: "We actively seek nonfiction in the form of 'creative essays.' Such work is best defined by reference to John Cage, Norman O. Brown and Merleau-Ponty. We accept mss and then fit them to the issues for the year. Frequently, we have holdover." Increasingly emphasis on theatre and performance pieces. Photos used with and without mss. Size: open. "Must be b&w glossies."
Fiction and Poetry: All forms and subjects open. Length: open. "Piece should be creative in either terms of style or theme. We are interested in seeing all forms of creative material, particularly experimental. We are not interested in ill-thought-through political diatribes."

THE IOWA REVIEW, 308 EPB, The University of Iowa, Iowa City IA 52242. (319)353-6048. Editor: David Hamilton. Fiction Editor: Frederick Bush. Poetry Editor: Stanley Plumly. Quarterly magazine; 96-128 pages. Estab. 1970. Buys first rights, but may reassign following publication. Photocopied submissions OK. SASE. Reports in 1 week-3 months.
Nonfiction, Fiction and Poetry: "We publish essays, stories and poems. We are more interested in essays than in academic criticism and are willing to consider writing that do not fall neatly into one of those categories." Buys 100 mss/year. Query or submit complete ms. Pays $1/line for verse; $5/page for prose.

JOHNSONIAN NEWS LETTER, 610 Philosophy Hall, Columbia University, New York NY 10027. Co-editors: James L. Clifford and John H. Middendorf. For scholars, book collectors and all those interested in 18th century English literature. 4 times a year. No payment. Reports immediately. SASE.
Nonfiction: Interested in news items, queries, short comments, etc., having to do with 18th century English literature. Must be written in simple style. Length: maximum 500 words.

THE JOURNAL OF MEXICAN AMERICAN HISTORY, Box 13861-UCSB, Santa Barbara CA 93107. (805)968-5915. Editor-in-Chief: Joseph Peter Navarro. Emphasizes history for specialists in Mexican American history, including professors, graduate and undergraduate students. Annual magazine; 150-200 pages. Estab. 1970. Circ. 1,500. No payment. Acquires simultaneous rights. Phone queries OK. Submit seasonal/holiday material 6-12 months in advance. Photocopied submissions OK. SASE. Reports in 2 weeks. Sample copy $17.50.
Nonfiction: Historical (Mexican American history from 1848 to present); interview; personal experience (documented carefully); personal opinion; photo feature (if historical and pertinent). Send complete ms. Length: 1,500-4,500 words. Prize of $100 for best article. Captions required for b&w photos used.

JOURNAL OF MODERN LITERATURE, Temple University, 1241 Humanities Bldg., Philadelphia PA 19122. (215)787-8505. Editor-in-Chief: Maurice Beebe. Managing Editor: Kathleen Quinn. Emphasizes scholarly literature for academics interested in literature of the past 100 years. Quarterly magazine; 160-200 pages. Estab. 1970. Circ. 2,000. Buys all rights, but may reassign rights to author following publication. Phone queries OK. Photocopied submissions OK. SASE. Reports in 8 weeks. Free sample copy.
Nonfiction: Historical (20th century literature); informational (20th century literature); and photo feature on art and literature. Buys 30 mss/year. Query or send complete ms. Pays $50-100.
Photos: Purchased only with accompanying nonfiction manuscript. Total purchase price for ms includes payment for photos.

JOURNAL OF THE NORTH AMERICAN WOLF SOCIETY, Box 118, Eatonville WA 98328. Editor: Sandra L. Gray. For audience with interest in "conservation issues and a strong concern for the preservation and promotion of the wolf and its habitat, and other wild canids of North America." Estab. 1975. Quarterly. Circ. 350. Rights acquired vary with author and material. Acquires all rights, but may reassign rights to author after publication; first North American serial rights; or simultaneous rights. Payment in contributor's copies. Will send sample copy to writer for $1. Write for editorial guidelines sheet. Will consider simultaneous and photocopied submissions. Reports in 4 to 6 weeks. Query not necessary. SASE.

Nonfiction: "Subject matter must be relevant to wolves, or other wild canids such as coyotes, their prey, their habitat, or activities of individuals or groups on their behalf. Our approach is factual and objective. We try to provide space for as many positions as possible in this complex and emotional subject, as long as these positions have their bases in fact and are rationally presented. We generally like to see sources and references though they may not be published with the article." Length: 600 to 1,800 words. For personal opinion, 300 to 600 words. For reviews, 150 to 300 words. Regular columns: "Thinking It Over" and "Views and Reviews."
Photos and Fillers: "No specific requirements yet for photos, will negotiate on individual basis." Uses newsbreaks and clippings.

JOURNAL OF POPULAR CULTURE, University Hall, Bowling Green State University, Bowling Green OH 43402. (419)372-2610. Editor: Ray B. Browne. 100% freelance written. For students and adults, interested in popular culture, TV, films, popular literature, sports, music, etc. Quarterly magazine, 256 pages, (6x9). Estab. 1967. Circ. 3,000. Acquires all rights, but will reassign rights to author after publication. Payment in copies. Sample copy $4. Will consider photocopied submissions. Reports within 3 to 6 months. SASE.
Nonfiction and Photos: "Critical essays on media, books, poetry, advertising, etc." Informational, interview, historical, think pieces, nostalgia, reviews of books, movies, television. Length: 5,000 words maximum. Payment in contributor's copies (25 reprints). Uses b&w glossies.

JOURNALISM MONOGRAPHS, School of Journalism, University of Kentucky, Lexington KY 40506. (606)258-2671. Editor: Bruce H. Westley. For all journalism educators in the U.S., Canada and the world. Magazine; 30 to 85 (6x9) pages. Estab. 1966. Published serially, 1 ms per issue; 4 to 6 issues per year. Circ. 1,600. "Author grants all rights." Uses 4 to 6 mss a year. No payment. Sample copy $2.50; free guidelines for writers. Will consider photocopied submissions. No simultaneous submissions. Reports on material accepted for publication in 1 to 6 months. Query first or submit complete ms. SASE.
Nonfiction: "Scholarly articles (any methodology) in the field of journalism and mass communications. We do not encourage freelancers without scholarly discipline."

KANSAS QUARTERLY, Dept. of English, Kansas State University, Manhattan KS 66502. (913)532-6716. Editors: Harold W. Schneider and Ben Nyberg. For "adults, mostly academics, and people interested in creative writing, literary criticism, midwestern history, and art." Estab. in 1968. Quarterly. Circ. 1,100. Acquires all rights, but will reassign them to author after publication. Pays in contributor's copies. Sample copy $2.50. Query first for nonfiction. "Follow *MLA Style Sheet* and write for a sophisticated audience." Reports in about 2 to 4 months. Enclose SASE for return of submissions or reply to queries.
Nonfiction, Photos, Fiction, and Poetry: Accepts poetry, short stories; art, history and literary criticism on special topics. "We emphasize the history, culture, and life style of the Mid-Plains region. We do not want children's literature, 'slick' material, or special interest material not in keeping with our special numbers." Accepts historical articles on "special topics only." Photos should have captions; 4x6 b&w preferred. Accepts experimental and mainstream fiction. Length: 250 to 10,000 words. Accepts traditional and avant-garde forms of poetry, blank verse, and free verse. Poetry themes open.

KARAMU, English Department, Eastern Illinois University, Charleston IL 61920. (217)345-5013. Co-Editors: Carol Elder, Ray Schmudde. For literate, university-educated audience. Estab. 1967. Annually. Circ. 300. Acquires first North American serial rights. Uses 25 mss/year. Payment in 2 contributor's copies. Sample copy $1.50. Submit complete ms. Reports on material in 5 months. SASE.
Nonfiction: Articles on contemporary literature. Length: open.
Fiction: Experimental, mainstream. Length: 2,000 to 8,000 words.
Poetry: Traditional forms, free verse, avant-garde. Dept. Editor: Carol Elder.

KENTUCKY FOLKLORE RECORD, Box U-169, College Heights Station, Western Kentucky University, Bowling Green KY 42101. (502)745-3111. Editor: Charles S. Guthrie. 80% freelance written. For libraries and individuals having a professional or personal interest in folklore as a learned discipline. Estab. 1955. Quarterly. Circ. 400. Uses 20 mss/year. Payment in contributor's copies. Sample copy 30¢ postage. Will not consider photocopied submissions. Follow *MLA Style Sheet*. Usually reports on material in 4 weeks. Query first or submit complete ms. SASE.
Nonfiction and Photos: "Our main emphasis is on Kentucky material. Articles dealing primarily

with folklife, folk speech, folktales, folksong (songs collected from oral tradition) of Kentucky. Some material pertaining to other areas is used also. Book reviews dealing with recent publications that treat some aspect of folklore. Study an issue of the journal." Also interested in Child ballads, folk children's games, nursery rhymes, black folklore, folklore in literature. Not interested in seeing anything pertaining to "Nashville" music. Length: 200 to 2,000 words. B&w photos with good contrast, 8x10 preferred, used with mss. Must relate to the journal's theme.

THE LAKE SUPERIOR REVIEW, Box 724, Ironwood MI 49938. (906)667-3781. Editors: Faye Korpi, Cynthia Willoughby, and Lee Merrill. Emphasizes contemporary poetry and short stories for readership interested in good contemporary literature. Published 2 times a year; 52-60 pages. Estab. 1970. Circ. 500. Pays on publication in copies. Buys first North American serial rights. Phone queries OK. Reports in 2 weeks-6 months. Sample copy $2.
Photos: Dail Willoughby, Photo Editor. Purchased without accompanying manuscript. Maximum size b&w without reduction 5x8. "Can be an expression or piece of art in itself."
Fiction: Adventure; erotica; experimental; fantasy; historical; humorous; mainstream; mystery and science fiction. Uses 12 mss/year. Length: 4,000 words maximum.
Poetry: Avant-garde; free verse; haiku; light verse and traditional. Uses 90 poems/year. Limit submissions to batches of 6-8.

L'ESPRIT CREATEUR, Box 222, Lawrence KS 66044. (913)864-3164. Editor: John D. Erickson. Bilingual journal for persons interested in French literature (educators, critics). Quarterly, 95 to 100 pages, (8¾x6). Estab. 1961. Circ. 1,250. Acquires all rights, but will reassign rights to author after publication. Uses about 30 mss a year. Payment in 5 contributor's copies. Will send sample copy to writer for $2.25. Prefers the *MLA Style Sheet* style. "All issues are devoted to special subjects, though we print book reviews and review articles of critical works that do not correspond to the issue subject. Please note subjects of coming issues, listed in each issue. Submit July 1 for spring issue, Oct. 1 for summer issue, Feb. 1 for fall issue, and April 1 for winter issue." Reports within 3 to 6 months. Query first or submit complete ms. Enclose SASE.
Nonfiction: "Criticism of French literature centered on a particular theme each issue; interviews with French writers or critics that appear irregularly; book reviews of critical works on French literature. Critical studies of whatever methodological persuasion that observe the primacy of the text. We notice a bit too much emphasis on extra-literary matters and a failure to note the special issues scheduled. Interested in new critical practices in France. We prefer articles that are direct, honest, avoid pedantry, respect the integrity of the literary work and have something intelligent to say." Length: 12 to 15 double-spaced typed pages, or 3,500 to 4,000 words.

LETTERS, Mainespring Press, Box 82, Stonington ME 04681. (207)367-2484. Editor-in-Chief: Helen Nash. For general literary audience. Quarterly magazine; 4-10 pages. Estab. 1972. Circ. 6,500. Pays on acceptance. Buys all rights. Submit seasonal/holiday material 5 months in advance. Simultaneous and photocopied submissions OK. SASE. Reports in 1 month. Sample copy for SASE.
Nonfiction: "Any subject within moral standards and with quality writing style." Query. Length: 100-500 words. Pays 5¢/word.
Fiction: No porno or confession and no religious or western. Buys 5 mss/year. Query. Pays 5¢/word.
Poetry: G.F. Bush, Poetry Editor. Avant-garde, free verse, haiku, light verse, traditional, blank verse, humorous and narrative. Buys 15/year. Length: 30-42 lines. Pays $1/line maximum.

LITERARY REVIEW, Fairleigh Dickinson University, 285 Madison Ave., Madison NJ 07940. (201)377-4050. Editors: Martin Green, Harry Keyishian. For international literary audience, largely libraries, academic readers and other poets and writers. Quarterly magazine; 100 pages. Estab. 1956. Circ. 1,000. Pays in copies. Acquires first North American serial rights. Photocopied submissions OK. Reports in 2-3 months. Sample copy $3.50.
Nonfiction: Literary criticism on contemporary American and world literature; themes, authors and movements aimed at non-specialist audience. Uses 2-3 mss/issue.
Fiction: Experimental or traditional. "We seek literary stories, not slick types." Uses 3-4/issue.
Poetry: Avant-garde, free verse and traditional. Uses 5-10/issue.

LITERARY SKETCHES, P.O. Box 711, Williamsburg VA 23185. (804)229-2901. Editor: Mary Lewis Chapman. For readers with literary interests; all ages. Monthly magazine; 16 pages. Estab. 1961. Circ. 500. Not copyrighted. Buys about 24 mss a year. Pays on publication. Will

send free sample copy to writer on request, if a stamped, self-addressed envelope is enclosed. Will consider photocopied and simultaneous submissions. Reports in 1 month. Submit complete ms. SASE.
Nonfiction: "We use only interviews of well-known writers and biographical material on past writers. Very informal style; concise. Centennial or bicentennial pieces relating to a writer's birth, death, or famous works are usually interesting. Look up births of literary figures and start from there." Length: 1,000 words maximum. Pays ½¢ per word.

THE LONDON COLLECTOR, 2807 Sycamore Ave., Muncie IN 47302. (317)289-3934. Editor-in-Chief: Dennis E. Hensley. Managing Editor: Richard Weiderman. 80% freelance written. For students, book collectors, readers, fans, and professors who are interested in the career and life of Jack London. Magazine published 3 times/year; 32 pages. Estab. 1968. Circ. 322. Pays in bylines and copies. Buys first North American serial rights. SASE. Reports in 2 weeks. Sample copy $2.
Nonfiction: Book reviews (any and all reviews of books and monographs written about Jack London); general interest (literary analysis of London's writings); historical (London family history); humor (articles on London's use of humor in his articles, novels and short stories). Buys 12 mss/year. Submit complete ms with clips of previously published work. Length: 250-1,400 words. Pays 4 copies.
Photos: State availability of photos with ms. Offers no additional payment for 5x7 b&w glossy prints. Captions preferred. Buys one-time rights. Model release required.
Fillers: Clippings; and newsbreaks. Buys 7/year. Length: 50-175 words.

LONG ISLAND REVIEW, 360 W. 21st St., New York NY 10011. Editors: Stephen Sossaman and Edward Faranda. For those interested in contemporary literature and criticism. Biased only toward the well-crafted and intelligent. Semiannual magazine. Estab. 1973. Circ. 500. Acquires first or second (reprint) serial rights; all rights are returned to author. Payment in contributor's copies. Will consider photocopied submissions. "We're open to new writers, but send a cover letter telling us who you are. We advise writer to see a sample issue first." Will send sample copy to writers for $1. Uses 50 mss/year. Reports in 4 to 5 weeks. Enclose SASE.
Nonfiction: Literary criticism and articles on literature as craft or as art; psychology of the creative process; sociology of literary forms; any length. Book reviews to about 800 words. Seeks articles for occasional special issues which are announced in the magazine.
Fiction: Experimental or traditional. Length: 3,500 words maximum.
Poetry: Any form, style, or length, but content or message cannot make up for deficiencies in language. Poetry as social criticism, and poetry by Vietnam veterans.

MARK TWAIN JOURNAL, Kirkwood MO 63122. Editor: Cyril Clemens. For those interested in American and English literature. Semiannual magazine. Estab: 1936. Not copyrighted. SASE. Sample copy $1. Pays in contributor's copies. Reports in 2 weeks. "Queries welcome."
Nonfiction: Critical and biographical articles dealing with Mark Twain and other American, English, and foreign authors.

THE MARKHAM REVIEW, Horrmann Library, Wagner College, Staten Island NY 10301. (212)390-3000. Editor: Joseph W. Slade. For academics; specialists in American culture. Newsletter; 20 pages. Estab. 1968. Quarterly. Circ. 1,000. Rights purchased vary with author and material. Usually buys all rights, but may reassign rights to author after publication. Buys 15 to 20 mss/year. Pays in contributor's copies. Will send free sample copy to writer on request. No photocopied or simultaneous submissions. Reports in 4 weeks. Query first or submit complete ms. Enclose SASE.
Nonfiction: Inter-disciplinary treatments of any aspect of American culture between 1965 and 1940. Scholarly approach following *MLA* style. Does not want articles on Henry James or Ernest Hemingway or other major writers. Would consider material on the history of science and technology. Length: 6,000 words maximum.

THE MASSACHUSETTS REVIEW, Memorial Hall, University of Massachusetts, Amherst MA 01003. Editors: Lee R. Edwards, Mary T. Heath, John Hicks, and Robert Tucker. Quarterly. Buys first North American serial rights. Pays on publication. Reports promptly. SASE.
Nonfiction: Articles on literary criticism, women, public affairs, art, philosophy, music, dance. Average length: 6,500 words. Pays $50.
Fiction: Short stories or chapters from novels when suitable for independent publication. Pays $50.

MICHIGAN QUARTERLY REVIEW, 3032 Rackham Bldg., University of Michigan, Ann Arbor MI 48109. Editor: Laurence Goldstein. Quarterly. Circ. 2,000. Pays on acceptance. Buys all rights. Reports in 4 weeks September-May; in Summer, 8 weeks. SASE. Sample copy $1.50.
Nonfiction: "*MQR* is open to general articles directed at an intellectual audience. Essays ought to have a personal voice and engage a significant subject. Scholarship must be present as a foundation but we are not interested in specialized essays full of facts and figures. We prefer ruminative essays, written in a fresh style, which reach interesting conclusions. Length: 2,000-5,000 words. Pays $80-150, sometimes more.
Fiction and Poetry: No restrictions on subject matter or language. "We publish about 12 stories a year and are very selective." Pays $5-8/published page.

THE MIDWEST QUARTERLY, Kansas State College of Pittsburg, Pittsburg KS 66762. (316)231-7000. Editor: V. J. Emmett, Jr. 95% freelance written. Published "for an educated adult audience interested in contemporary thought in a variety of scholarly disciplines." Magazine; 100 pages. July issue is all literary analysis. Estab. 1959. Quarterly. Circ. 1,000. Acquires all rights, but may reassign rights to author after publication. Uses 24 articles; 48 poems/year. Payment in contributor's copies. Will send free sample copy to writer on request. Will consider photocopied submissions. No simultaneous submissions. Submit seasonal material 6 to 9 months in advance. Reports in 3 months for prose; 6 months for verse. SASE.
Nonfiction and Poetry: "Literary analysis, history, social sciences, art, musicology, natural science in nontechnical language. Write standard literary English without jargon or pedantry. No footnotes, minimum parenthetical documentation and a short bibliography. We do not use fiction. Would like to see more history and social science." Length: 3,500 to 5,000 words. Publishes traditional forms of poetry, blank verse, free verse, avant-garde forms and haiku. Subject: open. Length: 4 to 200 lines. Poetry Editor: Michael Heffernan.

MISSISSIPPI REVIEW, Center for Writers, University of Southern Mississippi, Southern Station, Box 5144, Hattiesburg MS 39401. (601)266-7180. Editor: Frederick Barthelme. For general literary audiences, including students, libraries and writers. Published 3 times/year; 120 pages. Estab. 1972. Buys all rights, but may reassign following publication. Pays in copies. SASE. Reports in 8-10 weeks. No submissions in June or July. Sample copy $2.50.
Fiction: All types considered.
Poetry: All types considered.

MISSISSIPPI VALLEY REVIEW, Department of English, Western Illinois University, Macomb IL 61455. Editor: Forrest Robinson. For persons active in creating, teaching, or reading poetry and fiction. Magazine; 64 pages. Estab. 1971. Published twice a year. Circ. 400. "Permission to reprint must be gained from individual authors." Accepts 80 to 100 mss/year. Payment in 2 contributor's copies, plus a copy of the next 2 issues. Will send sample copy to writer for $1.50 plus postage. Will consider "only excellent" photocopied submissions. Will consider simultaneous submissions only if the author "notifies us immediately upon receipt of an acceptance elsewhere. We try to return mss within 3 months. We do not mind writers asking for progress reports if we are a bit late. Allow for no ms reading during summer." Submit complete ms. SASE.
Fiction and Poetry: Publishes stories and poems. Not interested in long poems. Tries to provide a range and variety of style and subject matter. "*Writer's Market* guidelines for ms submission suggested. We take pride in trying to help those who are breaking in. We publish no articles. We usually solicit our reviews." Fiction Editor: Loren Logsdon. Long poems are discouraged. Length: 2 printed pages, maximum. Poetry Editor: John Mann.

MODERN FICTION STUDIES, Dept. of English, Purdue University, W. Lafayette IN 47907. (317)493-1684. Editors: William T. Stafford and Margaret Church. For students and academic critics and teachers of modern fiction in all modern languages. Quarterly magazine, 140 to 160 pages, (6x9½). Estab. 1955. Circ. 4,000. Acquires all rights, but with written stipulated agreement with author permitting him or her to republish anywhere, any time as long as *MFS* is cited, and splitting 50/50 with him reprints by others of his agreed-to-be-reprinted material. No payment. Reports in 2 to 4 months. "Every other issue is a special issue. See current copy for future topics. Submit material any time before announced deadline for special issue." SASE.
Nonfiction: Interested in critical or scholarly articles on American, British, and Continental fiction since 1880. Length: notes, 500 to 2,500 words; articles, 3,000 to 7,000 words.

MOONS AND LION TAILES, Permanent Press, Box 8434, Lake St. Station, Minneapolis MN 55408. (612)377-4384. Managing Editor: H. Schjotz-Christensen. Emphasizes contemporary

literature for professional people, teachers, high school and college students. Quarterly magazine; 100 pages. Estab. 1973. Circ. 1,500. Pays on publication. Buys all rights. Submit seasonal/holiday material 2-3 months in advance. SASE. Reports in 2 months. Sample $1.75. Free writer's guidelines.
Nonfiction: Informational (reviews of current poetry publications) and profile (each issue publishes an article or essay on the work on a contemporary poet). Buys 8-10 mss/issue. Query. Length: 800-1,600 words. Pays $15-50.
Photos: Photos purchased on assignment. Pays $10 maximum for b&w photos. No additional payment for photos accepted with accompanying ms.
Columns/Departments: Poets on Poetry. Buys 1-2 mss/issue. Query. Length: 800-1,000 words. Pays $15-50. Open to suggestions for new columns/departments.
Fiction: Experimental. Buys 1-2 mss/issue. Send complete ms. Length: 2,000-5,000 words. Pays in copies for fiction. Buys some translations (pays $15/page).
Poetry: Avant-garde, free verse, haiku; "poetry in free forms preferred." Buys 35-40 poems/issue. Limit submissions to batches of 10. Pays in copies. Buys some translations (pays $15/page).

MOUNTAIN REVIEW, Box 660, Whitesburg KY 41858. (606)633-4811. Editor: Betty Edwards. For Appalachians of all ages and backgrounds and others interested in life in the mountains. Quarterly magazine; 48 pages. Estab. 1974. Circ. 2,000. Acquires all rights, but may reassign rights to author after publication. Uses about 50 mss/year. No payment. Will send sample copy to writer for $1.50. Will consider photocopied submissions. No simultaneous submissions. Submit seasonal material (spring, summer, fall, winter) 4 months in advance. Reports in 3-6 months. SASE.
Nonfiction and Photos: "We publish articles, preferably by mountain people, about some aspect of life in the mountains; life — not repetitions of old stereotypes. The material we choose deals with Appalachia, but in a fresh (often surprising) way." Personal experience, interview, historical, think pieces, expose, nostalgia, personal opinion articles and reviews of books about the mountains. Query or submit complete ms. Length: open. B&w glossies used with or without mss.
Fiction and Poetry: Open to all writing by Appalachian writers, including, but not limited to, themes that deal with some aspect of mountain life. Traditional and avant-garde forms of poetry, blank verse, free verse, haiku.

MOUNTAIN SUMMER, Glen Antrim, Sewanee TN 37375. (615)598-5795. Editor: Don Keck DuPree. For literary, college and university audience. Estab. 1972. Published annually. Circ. 1,000. Acquires all rights, but may reassign rights to author after publication. Uses 12 to 16 mss/year. Pays in contributor's copies. Sample copy $2. Will consider photocopied and simultaneous submissions. Reports in 2 to 4 weeks. SASE.
Poetry and Nonfiction: "We publish material which shows an interest in traditional English forms." Likes "good sound material." Poetry and essays. Preferred submission time: March 15 to July 15. Length for poetry: 4 to 48 lines.

MOVING OUT, Wayne State University, 4866 3rd, Detroit MI 48202. Editors: Margaret Kaminsk and Gloria Dyc. Feminist literary and arts journal for college and career women and others interested in women's studies and writing. Magazine; 2 times a year; 50 pages. Estab. 1971. Circ. 800. Pays in contributor's copies. Acquires all rights, but may reassign following publication. Phone queries OK. Simultaneous and photocopied submissions OK. SASE. Reports in 3-6 months. Sample copy $1.25. Writer's guidelines for 15¢ stamp.
Nonfiction: Literary criticism (not too academic in style); reviews of women's books; magazines, records or film reviews of interest to women. Historical (papers on famous women writers, artists, etc.). Interviews and personal experience (diary excerpts). Photo features (portfolios of fine art photography or artwork, graphics, paintings, etc.); uses 1/issue. Query or submit complete ms. Length: about 20 pages.
Fiction: Must be related to women's experience. Also uses novel excerpts. Query or submit complete ms. Length: 20 pages.
Poetry: Free verse, haiku, prose poems, feminist poetry.

MUNDUS ARTIUM, A Journal of International Literature and the Arts, University of Texas at Dallas, Box 688, Richardson TX 75080. Editor: Rainer Schulte. 30-50% freelance written. For all levels except the scholarly, footnote-starved type. Semiannual magazine; 160 pages. Estab. 1967. Circ. 2,000. Buys all rights, but will reassign rights to author after publication. Buys about 50 mss/year. Pays on publication. Sample copy $3. Will consider photocopied submissions. No

simultaneous submissions. Reports in 30 days. Submit complete ms. SASE.
Nonfiction and Photos: "In articles, we look for people who are able to talk about our non-traditional, conceptual kind of orientation from a broad, esthetic point of view. We like interdisciplinary emphasis. We don't want scholarly articles, kitsch, or social-political material, or descriptive, representational work." Length: open. Pays $15 to $100. Only avant-garde photography is acceptable.
Fiction: Experimental and fantasy. Must be non-traditional and conceptual. Length: open. Pays minimum of $5 per page.
Poetry: Avant-garde forms. Prefers to publish young, outstanding poets from the international and American scene who, as yet, are unrecognized. Pays minimum of $5 per page.
How To Break In: "Since we have a bilingual format, translations of contemporary international poets is a good way. Otherwise, creative work which goes beyond description and regional, national restrictions."

NATCHEZ TRACE LITERARY REVIEW, The Bluff Press, Box 6945, Jackson MS 39212. Editor-in-Chief: Rosalie Daniels. Emphasizes poetry and fiction. For an educated, literary audience. Semiannual magazine; 16-20 pages. Estab. 1976. Circ. 200. Pays on acceptance. Acquires all rights. Submit seasonal/holiday material 3 months in advance. SASE. Reports in 2 months. Sample copy $2; writer's guidelines $2.
Fiction: Experimental. Buys 3 mss/issue. Send complete ms. Length: 3,000-3,500 words. Pays in copies.
Poetry: Avant-garde, free verse, haiku and traditional. Buys 14 poems/issue. Limit submissions to batches of 2. Pays in copies.

NEBULA, 970 Copeland St., North Bay, Ontario, Canada P1B 3E4. (705)472-5127. Editor-in-Chief: Ken Stange. Managing Editor: Ursula Stange. Emphasizes literature for an intellectually sophisticated readership. Semiannual magazine; 88 pages. Estab. 1974. Circ. 750. Pays on publication in copies and grants. Buys first North American serial rights. Phone queries OK. SAE and International Reply Coupons. Reports in 5 weeks. Sample copy and writer's guidelines $1.00.
Nonfiction: Interview (with literary figures); and personal opinion (critical essays). Submit complete ms.
Fiction: Erotica; experimental; fantasy; mainstream and science fiction. Submit complete ms.
Poetry: Quality poetry of all kinds.
How To Break In: We do thematic issues, the themes announced in preceeding issues, so a would-be contributor is advised to send for a recent sample. Seeing the type of material we publish generally and learning what specific themes we will be exploring in future issues is the best guide to any writer considering our publication.
Rejects: "We are very tired of receiving submissions from the states where the postage affixed to the return envelope is American. Canada is a separate country and has its own postal system. Canadian postage or International Reply Coupons should accompany submissions."

NEW BOSTON REVIEW, 77 Sacramento St., Somerville MA 02143. Editors: Gail Pool, J.M. Alonso, Lorna Condon. For people interested in the arts. Bimonthly magazine; 28-32 pages. Estab. 1975. Circ. 12,000. Acquires all rights, unless author requests otherwise. Pays in copies. Photocopied and simultaneous submissions OK. SASE. Reports in 4-6 weeks. Sample copy $1.
Nonfiction, Fiction and Poetry: Critical essays and reviews in all the arts: literature, painting, music, film, theatre, photography, dance. Length: 1,000-3,000 words. Accepts 20 mss/year. Fiction length: 2,000-4,000 words.

THE NEW ENGLAND QUARTERLY, Hubbard Hall, Brunswick ME 04011. (207)725-8731, Ext. 289. Managing Editor: Herbert Brown. For historians and scholars. Estab. 1928. Quarterly. Acquires all rights. Does not pay. Usually reports in 4 weeks. SASE.
Nonfiction: Wants scholarly articles on New England life and letters. Length: "essays should be limited to 25 pages, including documentation."

THE NEW INFINITY REVIEW, Box 412, South Point OH 45680. (614)377-4182. Editor: James R. Pack. Manuscript Editor: Ron MO HIN. For the lovers of new writing with "pizzazz and verve." Quarterly magazine; 56 pages. Estab. 1969. Circ. 500. Acquires North American serial rights. Pays in copies or gift subscriptions. Free sample copy and writer's guidelines. Photocopied submissions OK "if readable." All submissions should be accompanied by a brief autobiography, stressing the individual and his/her unique personality, and including current activities and publication credits. Reports in 4 weeks. SASE.

Nonfiction and Photos: "Essays and articles on literature, drama and art that chronicle new perspectives, the mysteries and fantastic. Subjects can range from the psychic to the sociological." Length: 3,000 words maximum. Accompanying photos or illustrations are welcome.
Fiction: "We publish stories that are mentally exciting. Mystery, science fiction and fantasy find an eager eye." Length: 4,000 words maximum.
Poetry: "Send as large a sample as possible (4-20). We try to feature one poet every issue, using 4-8 or more poems. Free verse; experimental; avant-garde; and all poetry approaching the visual are encouraged. What we seek most is clear voice and lots of energy. No length limit."
How To Break In: "We especially need good short fiction, 3-6 pages, that deals with the new and the strange."

NEW ORLEANS REVIEW, Loyola University, New Orleans LA 70118. (504)865-2294. Editor-in-Chief: Dawson Gaillard. Managing Editor: Susan Lindsay. For "anyone interested in literature and culture." Published 3 times/year. Magazine; 96 pages. Estab. 1968. Circ. 1,000. Pays on publication. Buys all rights, but may reassign following publication. Photocopied submissions OK. SASE. Reports in 2 months. Sample copy $1.50; free writer's guidelines.
Nonfiction: Interviews with writers, photographers, film directors, producers and artists. "We are also interested in articles dealing with science and the humanities. These must be directed to an educated *lay* audience. We are not interested in academic articles." Buys 6 mss/year. Query. Length: 2,000-5,000 words. Pays $25-50.
Fiction: Quality fiction. Buys 9 mss/year. No length restrictions. Submit complete ms. Pays $50 minimum.
Poetry: Shael Herman, poetry editor. "All types, as long as it is *good*." Buys 75 poems/year. Pays $10.

THE NEW YORK TIMES BOOK REVIEW, 229 West 43rd St., New York NY 10036. Editor: Harvey Shapiro. Weekly.
Nonfiction: "Occasional book reviews and essays. Almost all reviewing is done on an assignment basis."

NEWSART, 5 Beekman St., New York NY 10038. Editor: Harry Smith. Newspaper. Estab. 1974. Published 2 times a year, as a supplement to *The Smith*. Circulation: 5,000. Buys first rights. Buys 50 to 100 mss/year. Pays on acceptance. Sample copy $1. Will consider photocopied and simultaneous submissions. Reports in 4 weeks. Query first for nonfiction. Submit complete ms for fiction and poetry. SASE.
Nonfiction, Fiction and Poetry: Essays, book reviews, humor, interviews. Pays $15 minimum for nonfiction. Fiction "should be reasonably short for newspaper format — newsy element helpful." Pays $15 minimum for fiction. Poetry should be short, though occasional longer poems are used. Pays $5 for poetry.
Photos: Purchased with accompanying ms with extra payment and purchased without accompanying ms. B&w only. "8x10 best but not exclusively used." Pay: open.

NIMROD, University of Tulsa, 600 South College, Tulsa OK 74104. (918)939-6351. Editor: Francine Ringold. For readers and writers interested in good literature and art. Semiannual magazine; 96 (6x9) pages. Estab. 1955. Circ. 1,000. Acquires all rights but will return rights to author on request. Payment in contributor's copies and $5/page when funds are available. Will consider photocopied submissions, but they must be very clear. No simultaneous submissions. Reports in 3 to 6 months. Query first or submit complete ms. SASE.
Nonfiction: Interviews and essays. Length: open.
Fiction and Poetry: Experimental and mainstream fiction. Traditional forms of poetry; blank verse, free verse and avant-garde forms. "We are interested in quality and vigor. We often do special issues. Writers should watch for announced themes and/or query."

NIT & WIT LITERARY ARTS MAGAZINE, 1908 W. Oakdale, Chicago IL 60657. (312)248-1183. Publisher: Kathy Cummings. Editor: Lenny Dominquez. 100% freelance written. Monthly magazine; 32 pages. Estab. July 1977. Circ.5,000. Pays in copies. Rights reassigned following publication. Phone queries OK. Submit seasonal/holiday material 2 months in advance of issue date. Simultaneous, photocopied and previously published submissions OK. SASE. Reports in 4 weeks. Sample copy for 25¢ postage; mention *Writer's Market* in request.
Nonfiction: "Anything well-written will be considered." Exposé (social commentary and critiques); how-to; general interest; humor; historical; inspirational; interview; nostalgia; personal experience; personal opinion; photo feature; profile and travel. Uses 36 mss/year. Submit complete ms. Length: 2,000 words maximum.

Photos: Submit photos with accompanying ms. Uses 5x7 or 5x3 b&w glossy prints. Captions preferred; model release required.
Fiction: Adventure; confession; erotica (light erotica is OK); experimental; fantasy; historical; humorous; mainstream; mystery; religious; romance; science fiction; and suspense. "Will not use material in bad taste." Uses 12 mss/year. Length: 2,000 words maximum. Submit complete ms.
Poetry: Avant-garde; free verse; haiku; light verse; traditional; and senryu. Uses 150/year.

NITTY-GRITTY, Goldermood Rainbow Publisher, 331 W. Bonneville, Pasco WA 99301. (509)547-5525. Editor-in-Chief: W.R. Wilkins. Each issue has a "tool-theme" subject. Triannual magazine; 100 pages. Estab. 1975. Circ. 3,000. Pays on acceptance. Buys all rights, but may reassign following publication. Submit seasonal/holiday material 2 months in advance. Photocopied submissions OK. SASE. Reports in 2 months. Sample copy $4; free writer's guidelines.
Nonfiction: Humor; interview; personal experience; personal opinion and profile. Buys 60-70 mss/issue. Send complete ms. Length: 100-3,000 words. Pays $2-15.
Fiction: Adventure; experimental, fantasy, historical; humorous; mainstream; mystery; romance; science fiction and suspense. Send complete ms. Length: 1,000-10,000 words. Pays $15 minimum.
Poetry: Free verse. Buys 50 poems/issue. Limit submissions to batches of 4. Length: 100 lines maximum. Pays $2.
Fillers: Clippings, jokes, gags, anecdotes and short humor. Buys 20 fillers/issue. Length: 50-1,000 words. Pays $2-15.

NORTH AMERICAN MENTOR MAGAZINE, 1745 Madison St., Fennimore WI 53809. (608)822-6237. Editors: John Westburg, Mildred Westburg. 95% freelance written. For "largely mature readers, above average in education, most being fairly well-to-do; many being retired persons over 60; college personnel and professional writers or aspirants to being professional." Quarterly. Acquires all rights, but may reassign rights to author after publication. Payment in contributor's copies. Sample copy $1. Photocopied and simultaneous submissions OK. Reports in 1 week to 6 months. SASE.
Nonfiction: "Desire writing to be in reasonably good taste; traditional is preferable to the vulgar, but emphasis should be on creativity or scholarship. I know of no other of the small magazine genre that is like this one. We make no claim to being avant-garde, but have been accused of being a rear guard periodical, for we try to follow the general traditions of western civilization (whatever that might be). Would be interested in readable articles on anthropology, archaeology, American Indians, black or white Africa. Do not want vulgarity or overworked sensationalism. No stuff on riots, protests, drugs, obscenity, or treason. We do not want to discourage a writer's experimental efforts. Let the writer send what he thinks best in his best style. Study a current issue first, though." Length: "maximum about 5,000 words."
Photos: "Please make inquiry about photographs in advance. We like to use them if they can be reproduced on multilith offset masters."
Fiction: "Short stories should have a plot, action, significance, and depth of thought, elevating rather than depressing; would be glad to get something on the order of Dickens, Thackeray or Dostoyevsky rather than Malamud, Vidal or Bellow. Sustained wit without sarcasm would be welcome; propaganda pieces unwelcome." Length: 1,000 to 4,000 words.
Poetry: Accepts traditional, blank and free verse, avant-garde forms and light verse. "Poetry from many cultures." Length: 50 lines maximum.

THE NORTH AMERICAN REVIEW, University of Northern Iowa, Cedar Falls IA 50613. (319)273-2681. Editor: Robley Wilson, Jr. Quarterly. Circ. 3,000. Buys all rights for nonfiction and North American serial rights for fiction and poetry. Pays on publication. Sample copy $1. Familiarity with magazine helpful. Reports in 8 to 10 weeks. Query first for nonfiction. SASE.
Nonfiction: No restrictions, but most nonfiction is commissioned by magazine. Rate of payment arranged.
Fiction: No restrictions; highest quality only. Length: open. Pays minimum $10 per page.
3Poetry: Department Editor: Peter Cooley. No restrictions; highest quality only. Length: open. Pays 50¢ per line minimum.

NORTHWEST REVIEW, 369 P.L.C., University of Oregon, Eugene OR 97403. (503)686-3957. Editor-in-Chief: Michael Strelow. 85% freelance written. For literate readership whether university or non-university. "We have one issue per year with Northwest emphasis, the other two are of general interest to those who follow American/world poetry and fiction." Published 3

times/year; 130 pages. Estab. 1958. Circ. 20,000. Pays on publication in copies. Buys all rights, but may reassign rights to author following publication. Phone queries OK. Submit seasonal/holiday material 6 months in advance. Photocopied submissions OK. SASE. Reports in 6-8 weeks. Sample copy $1.50. Free writer's guidelines.
Photos: Purchased without accompanying manuscript. Send prints. Total price for ms includes payment for photos.
Fiction: Deb Casey, Fiction Editor. All types. Uses 5 mss/issue. Send complete ms.
Poetry: Jay Williams, Poetry Editor. Uses 30-35 poems/issue. Limit submissions to batches of 10-15.

NORTHWOODS JOURNAL, A Magazine for Writers, R.D. #1, Meadows of Dan VA 24120. (703)952-2388. Editor-in-Chief: Robert W. Olmsted. 95% freelance written. Readers are all writers. Monthly (except summer and January) magazine; 35-52 pages. Estab. 1972. Circ. 1,000. Pays on acceptance. Buys all rights. Submit seasonal or holiday material 4-6 months in advance. SASE. Reports in 4 weeks. Sample copy 50¢.
Nonfiction: Expose (about writing con games); historical; how-to; humor; informational; nostalgia; personal opinion; profile; technical (as pertains to small press publishing only). Buys 1-2 mss/issue. Submit complete ms. Length: 400-2,400 words. Pays $5-40.
Photos: Purchased with accompanying ms. Captions required. Query. Pays $5-25 for 8x10 b&w photos. Total purchase price for ms includes payment for photos. Model release required.
Columns/Departments: Paul Hodges, Review Editor. Reviews (small press and self-published books only). Submit complete ms. Length: 100-1,000 words. Pays $1-4. Open to suggestions for new columns/departments.
Fiction: "Anything that is superb." Buys 8-16 mss/year. Submit complete ms. Length: 500-5,000 words. Pays $5-25.
Poetry: Avant-garde; free verse; haiku; and traditional. Buys 80/year. Pays 50¢-$3.

THE NOTEBOOK & OTHER REVIEWS, The Notebook Press, Box 180, Birmingham MI 48012. Editor-in-Chief: Michael O'Neill. 65% freelance written. Emphasizes the arts, literature and humanities (and "intelligent writing"). Magazine, published 10 times/year; 32 pages. Estab. 1975. Circ. 300. Pays on acceptance. Buys all rights. Submit seasonal/holiday material 6 months in advance. Photocopied submissions OK. SASE. Reports in 2-4 weeks. Sample copy 75¢.
Nonfiction: Humor; interview and personal opinion. Buys 1-2 mss/issue. Query. Length: 400-4,000 words. Pays $10-50.
Photos: Photos purchased without accompanying ms. Pays $5-10 for 5½x8½ b&w glossies. Send contact sheet. Model release required.
Columns/Departments: Reviews (new books); Reports (a look at various publications) and Hindsight (reviews of previous issue by readers). Buys 3 mss/issue. Query. Length: 250-1500 words. Pays $5-25. Open to suggestions for new columns/departments.
Fiction: Rottinger McTaggert, Fiction Editor. Experimental, humorous; mainstream; mystery and suspense. Buys 1 ms/issue. Send complete ms. Length: 750-4,000 words. Pays $5-100.
Poetry: Avant-garde, free verse, light verse and traditional. Buys 5/issue. Pays $1-25.
Fillers: Clippings, jokes, gags, anecdotes, newsbreaks, and short humor. Buys 5/year. Length: 25-250 words. Pays $1-5.

THE OHIO JOURNAL, A Magazine of Literature and the Visual Arts, Department of English, Ohio State University, 164 W. 17th Ave., Columbus OH 43210. Editor: William Allen. Magazine; 3 times a year. Estab. 1972. Circ. 1,250. Pays in contributor's copies. Acquires all rights, but will reassign rights following publication. Photocopied and simultaneous submissions OK. SASE. Reports in 6 weeks.
Nonfiction and Photos: Material of interest to an audience knowledgeable of literature and the arts, but not of an academic nature. Interviews and photo essays welcome. No color reproductions.
Fiction and Poetry: Gordon Grigsby, Poetry Editor. No restrictions as to category or type. Maximum length for fiction: 10,000 words.

THE OHIO REVIEW, Ellis Hall, Ohio University, Athens OH 45701. (614)594-5889. Editor: Wayne Dodd. "A balanced, informed engagement of contemporary American letters, special emphasis on poetics." Published 3 times yearly. Estab. 1959. Circ. 1,000. Rights acquired vary with author and material. Acquires all rights or first North American serial rights. Will send sample copy to writer for $2. Submit complete ms. Unsolicited material will be read only September-June. Reports in 6 to 8 weeks. SASE.
Nonfiction, Fiction, and Poetry: Buys essays of general intellectual and special literary appeal.

Not interested in narrowly focused scholarly articles. Seeks writing that is marked by clarity, liveliness, and perspective. Interested in the best fiction and poetry. Pays minimum $5 a page, plus copies.

OHIOANA QUARTERLY, Ohioana Library Association, 65 S. Front St., 1105 Ohio Departments Bldg., Columbus OH 43215. (614)466-3831. Editor: James Barry. Quarterly magazine; 60 pages. Estab. 1943. Circ. 1,800. No payment. Phone queries OK. Reports in 2 weeks.
Nonfiction: "Limited to articles about Ohio authors, musicians, or other artists, and current book reviews; or articles by published Ohio authors." Query. Length: 500-3,000 words.

OMEGA, 145 E. Main St., Cambridge NY 12816. Editor: J. Geoffrey Jones. For "people interested in literature and art in a permanent way; collectors of literary rarities." Magazine; 30 pages. Estab. 1975. Published irregularly. Circ. 1,000. Acquires first serial rights. Uses 40 mss a year. Payment in contributor's copies. Sample copy $2. Reports in 4 weeks. Query first for nonfiction. Submit complete ms for fiction and poetry. SASE.
Nonfiction, Fiction and Poetry: "*Omega* is the voice of the Graycroft Press, founded in memory of Elbert Hubbard's Roycroft Press. We are concerned with printing as a permanent art form and enjoy combining high quality literature with high quality format. All the type is set by hand and the sheets hand-pulled from an 1890 press. *Omega* wishes to explore the work of well-known creators in areas not as often noticed (see Vol. 1, No. 1, 'Ray Bradbury As Poet'). We also wish to bring light to gifted unknowns, and forgotten writers of importance. We publish articles, short stories and serious poetry, which must be clear and without contrived obscurity."

OPINION, Box 3563, Bloomington IL 61701. Editor: Dr. James E. Kurtz. 80% freelance written. For readers from 18 and older; people who have an appetite for invigorating, inspiring, thought-provoking articles. Numerous teachers, clergymen, and professional people. Monthly magazine, 16 (8½x11) pages. Estab. 1957. Circ. 3,700. Not copyrighted. Uses about 38 mss a year. Pays in contributor's copies. Will send sample copy to writer for 30¢. Will consider photocopied submissions and simultaneous submissions. Submit complete ms. Reports in 3 to 5 weeks. SASE.
Nonfiction: "We publish articles dealing with social problems, philosophical themes, theological studies. Our articles are on current subjects but inspirational as well. Controversy but not just for the sake of being 'different'. Our writers believe in what they write. Be yourself. Take a deep subject and make it simple—don't write down to people but lift people up to a higher level of understanding. *Opinion* is down to earth. We carry some in-depth essays but for the most part we present to our readers, articles that hit the nail on the head. We are informal but we adhere to the old principles of good writing. Articles on marriage problems are a bit heavy and we prefer to see more material on philosophy and theology. Common sense philosophy. Particularly we want articles on religious adventure; new trends, new happenings." Informational, personal experience, profile, inspirational, historical, think articles, expose, nostalgia, personal opinion, spot news, and new product. Length: 1,500 words maximum.
Photos: Uses 5x7 or 8x10 b&w glossies. Captions optional.
Poetry: Traditional forms, free verse and light verse.

OUT THERE MAGAZINE, 552 25th Ave., San Francisco CA 94121. Editor: Stephen M. H. Braitman. For a literary audience with science fiction interests. Quarterly; 25 (8½x11) pages. Estab. 1967. Circ. 1,000. Acquires first North American serial rights. Uses 4 mss a year. Payment in contributor's copies. Will send sample copy to writer for 75¢. Will consider photocopied and simultaneous submissions. Reports in 1 month. Submit complete ms. Enclose SASE.
Nonfiction: Informational, interview, humor, historical, nostalgia, personal opinion and book and film reviews. Length: 1,500 words.
Fiction: Science fiction and fantasy; anything above the average of "tameness." Must be quality writing; literature, not pulp. Uses experimental, mainstream, mystery, suspense, adventure, erotica, science fiction, fantasy and humorous fiction. Length: 500 to 2,000 words maximum.
Poetry and Fillers: Sci-fi poetry, blank verse, free verse, avant-garde forms; light verse. Length: open. Jokes and relevant short humor used as fillers.

PAINTBRUSH, Department of English, Northeastern University, Boston MA 02115. Editor: B. M. Bennani. For professional and "up-and-coming" writers, college and university groups; teachers. Magazine; 65 (5½x8½) pages. Estab. 1974. Semiannually. Circ. 500. Buys all rights, but may reassign rights to author after publication. Buys about 50 mss a year. Pays on publication. Will send sample copy to writer for $2. No photocopied or simultaneous submis-

sions. Reports in 2 to 4 weeks. Query first for interviews. SASE.
Nonfiction and Photos: Criticism, nonscholarly articles, translations from any language. Interviews with known writers and poets. Length: 2,000 to 3,000 words. Book reviews of small press publications are always welcome. Length: 300 words maximum. "No soul-searching, back-scratching junk. No book reviews that begin with 'This is a terrific book'. No politically inspired propaganda. Only the best goes." Would like to see work on "popularizing poetry without barbarizing it." Pays $5 per published page. B&w glossies (minimum 3x5) are used only with interviews.
Poetry: "All schools are welcome but, please, no four-letter rhymes or jingles." Traditional forms of poetry, blank verse, free verse, prose poems. Short lyrics preferred; 30 lines maximum. Pays $5 per poem per page.

PANACHE, Box 77, Sunderland MA 01375. Editors: Candice Ward, David Lenson. "A small press publication specializing in experimental and other fiction and poetry. For a small but sophisticated audience, by and large educated." Semiannual magazine; 64 pages. Estab. 1965. Circ. 800. Pays on acceptance. Buys all rights, but may reassign following publication. Photocopied submissions OK. SASE. Reports in 6 weeks. Sample copy $1.
Fiction: Experimental; adventure; erotica (of literary quality); fantasy; historical (if imaginative); humorous; mainstream. Buys 10 mss/year. Submit complete ms. Length: 1-50 pages. Pays $25-100. "Fiction reading period is August-October."
Poetry: Avant-garde, free verse. Buys 40/year. Limit submissions to batches of 7. No length requirements. Pays $5-40. Submit February-April.
How To Break In: "*Panache* is an eclectic publication belonging to no school or movement, or, better yet, to all schools and movements. We rely on freelance material as a matter of principle, in order to bring to a discriminating audience that which is new and exciting at the grass roots level of American literature. In addition, we are also interested in poetry translations, line drawings, and word-pictures."

PARABOLA, 150 5th Ave., New York NY 10011. (212)924-0004. Executive Editor: Lorraine Kisly. Managing Editor: Susan Bergholz. "Audience shares an interest in exploring the wisdom and truth transmitted through myth and the great religious traditions." Quarterly magazine; 136 pages. Estab. 1974. Circ. 14,000. Buys all rights, but will reassign following publication, or reprint rights. Pays on publication. Photocopied submissions OK. SASE. Reports in 3-5 weeks. Free writer's guidelines.
Nonfiction: "We handle work from a wide range of perspectives—from comparative religion and anthropology to psychology and literary criticism. We seek to use these disciplines in the quest for meaning. Don't be scholarly, don't footnote, don't be dry. We want fresh approaches to timeless subjects. Length: 5,000 words maximum. Buys 30 mss/year. Query. Pays $25-150.
Photos: Purchased with or without accompanying ms.No color. Pays $25.
Fiction: Prefers retellings of traditional stories, legends, myths. Length: 3,000 words maximum. Pays "negotiable rates."

THE PARIS REVIEW, 45-39 171 Place, Flushing NY 11358. Editor: George A. Plimpton. Quarterly. Buys all rights. Pays on publication. Address submissions to proper department. SASE.
Fiction: Study publication. No length limit. Pays up to $150. Fiction should be sent to Flushing office. Makes award of $500 in annual fiction contest.
Poetry: Study publication. Pays $10 to 25 lines; $15 to 50 lines; $25 to 100 lines; $50 thereafter. Poetry mss must be submitted to Michael Benedikt at 541 E. 72nd St., New York NY 10021.

THE PENNY DREADFUL, c/o The Department of English, Bowling Green State University, Bowling Green OH 43403. Editors: Robert W. Johnson, Jr. and Michael McCall. Tabloid format. Estab. 1972. Published irregularly. Circ. 500. "All rights returned to author after publication." Pays in contributor's copies. Will send a sample copy to a writer for 50¢. Reports in 2 weeks. Enclose SASE for return of submissions.
Nonfiction, Fiction, Drama and Poetry: The editors encourage submission of poems, fiction, one-act plays, book reviews, interviews, and critical essays. No particular themes. Length: 500 to 3,500 words for fiction and nonfiction; 2 to 120 lines for poetry.

PERFORMING ARTS REVIEW, The Journal of Management and Law of the Arts, 453 Greenwich St., New York NY 10013. Editor: Joseph Taubman. 90% freelance written. Estab. 1970. For lawyers, theater managers, academic libraries in law and arts. Quarterly. Circ. 2,200. Acquires primary or secondary U.S. or Canadian rights. Payment in contributor's copies (10 to

each author). Free sample copy. Will consider photocopied submissions. Reports in 2 months. Query first. SASE.
Nonfiction: "Articles on theater, law-management, and creativity in the arts. Academic outlook; professional tone. Writer should be experienced in the field of entertainment law or the theater (pro or amateur)." Length: 1,000 to 7,000 words.

THE PERSONALIST, School of Philosophy, University of Southern California CA 90007. Editor: John Hospers. Quarterly. No honorarium. Follow the *MLA Style Sheet*. Put footnotes at end of article. Reports in approximately 4 months. Enclose SASE for return of submissions.
Nonfiction: Uses critical articles pertaining only to the field of philosophy.

PERSPECTIVES, English Department, West Virginia University, Morgantown WV 26506. (304)293-5525. Editor: Arthur C. Buck. A column of literature, philosophy, and education. Associated with the Charleston *Gazette-Mail State Magazine*. Circ. 110,000. Appears on a space-available basis. Not copyrighted. Space for freelance material is strictly limited. Pays after publication. No sample copies available. Reports in 1 month. SASE.
Nonfiction: Short, informal personal essays on literature, philosophy, higher education, and linguistics. Interesting, informal style desired. Preference is given to informational or interpretive essays or essays of personal opinion. Pays on the average of 2¼¢ per word. Length: 500 to 900 words preferred. Longer articles are rarely used. Satire is sometimes used.
Poetry: Length: 30 lines maximum. Any style. No payment. Limit submissions to batches of 3.
Rejects: Seasonal material, formal research or scholarly articles, previously published work, poorly prepared mss, simultaneous submissions, photocopied submissions.

PIERIAN SPRING, Brandon University Press, Brandon University, Brandon, Manitoba, Canada R7A 6A9. Editor: Dr. Robert W. Brockway. 90% freelance written. For a readership of all ages, predominantly university level, aimed at readers interested in the products of fledgling writers. Published autumn and spring. Magazine; 70-100 pages. Estab. 1969. Circ. 200. Pays in copies. Buys all rights. Submit seasonal/holiday material 3 months in advance. Photocopied and previously published submissions OK. SASE. Reports in 4 weeks. Sample copy and writer's guidelines $1.
Nonfiction: Linda West, Articles Editor. Historical; humor; interview; nostalgia; personal experience; personal opinion; photo feature (if brief); profile; inner self-expression. "In general, imaginative, subjective, experimental, observations, vignettes, and memoirs. We are less interested in political or religious writing, not at all in polemics of any kind or crank articles." Uses 4-6 mss/issue. Submit complete ms. Length: 2,000 words maximum.
Photos: Curt Shoultz, Art Editor. "We can publish pen and ink drawings, possibly photography, whatever can be done on university offset press." Captions required. Send b&w prints. "In general, we would be interested in art photos, photography as an art medium."
Fiction: Darlene Perkin, Barbara Farough, Fiction Editors. "Any type of short fiction (up to 2,000 words) or short prose, vignettes, memoirs, etc." Submit complete ms.
Poetry: Frances Spafford, Barbara Farough, Poetry Editors. Avant-garde; free verse; haiku; light verse; traditional. Uses 70/issue. Limit submissions to batches of 5.
How To Break In: "Our publication was founded to provide another outlet for the beginning writer, although we very much welcome poems and brief articles from established writers as well. We publish in order of priority poetry, short short stories, subjective prose such as personal experiences or observations, and fillers."

PIG IRON MAGAZINE, Box 237, Youngstown OH 44501. (216)744-2258. Editor-in-Chief: Jim Villani. 70% freelance written. Emphasizes literature/art for general audience. Semiannual magazine; 104 pages. Estab. 1975. Circ. 1,000. Pays on publication. Buys one-time rights. Submit seasonal/holiday material 6 months in advance of issue date. Photocopied and previously published submissions OK. SASE. Reports in 4 months. Sample copy $2; free writer's guidelines.
Nonfiction: Exposé; general interest; humor; interview; photo feature; and technical. Buys 6 mss/year. Query. Length: 1,000-20,000 words. Pays $1/page.
Photos: Submit photo material with accompanying query. Pays $1 minimum for 5x7 b&w glossy prints. Buys one-time rights.
Fiction: Rose Sayre, fiction editor. Fantasy; experimental; humorous; science fiction; suspense; and condensed novels. No traditional stories. Buys 10/year. Submit complete ms. Length: 1,000-20,000 words. Pays $1/page.
Poetry: Terry Murcko, poetry editor. Avant-garde, experimental, and free verse. Buys 60/year. Submit in batches of 10 or less. Length: 1 line minimum. Pays $1/page.

PLOUGHSHARES, Box 529, Dept. M., Cambridge MA 02139. Editor: DeWitt Henry. For "readers of serious contemporary literature; students, educators, adult public." Quarterly magazine; 188 pages. Estab. 1971. Circ. 3,000. Rights purchased vary with author and material. Usually buys all rights, but may reassign rights to author after publication; or may buy first North American serial rights. Buys 50 to 100 mss per year. Pays on publication. Sample copy $2.95. Photocopied submissions OK. No simultaneous submissions. Reports in 3 months. SASE.
Nonfiction, Poetry and Fiction: "Highest quality poetry, fiction, criticism." Interview and literary essays. Length: 5,000 words maximum. Pays $50. Reviews (assigned). Length: 500 words maximum. Pays $15. Fiction. Experimental and mainstream. Length: 300 to 6,000 words. Pays $5 to $50. Poetry. Buys traditional forms, blank verse, free verse, avant-garde forms. Length: open. Pays $10/poem.

POTPOURRI-AN ANTHOLOGY., Box 6183-WM, Wyomissing PA 19610. Editor-in-Chief: Elizabeth M. Downing. Managing Editor: Lenny Fields. 100% freelance written. "Devoted to the advancement of authors; read primarily by other writers, editors, and publishers." Bimonthly book; 100 pages. Estab. 1975. Buys one-time rights. Submit seasonal/holiday material 6 months in advance of issue date. Photocopied and previously published (if so stated) submissions OK. SASE. Reports in 2-4 months. Sample copy $6.50; free writer's guidelines; mention *Writer's Market* in request.
Nonfiction: "Interested in all types of articles except photo features and pornographic material." Buys 50 mss/year. Query. Length: 6,500 words maximum. Pays $10-300.
Fiction: Interested in all forms of short stories. Will consider condensed and serialized novels. No pornographic material. Buys 50 mss/year. Query. Length: 6,500 words maximum. Pays $10-300.
Poetry: Avant-garde; free verse; haiku; light verse; and traditional. Buys 300/year. Query. Length: 32 lines maximum, "preferrably, but may consider longer poems." Pays $5-200.

PRAIRIE SCHOONER, Andrews Hall, University of Nebraska, Lincoln NE 68588. Editor: Bernice Slote. Quarterly. Usually acquires all rights, unless author specifies first serial rights only. Small payment, depending on grants, plus copies of the magazine, offprints, and prizes. Reports usually in 1 month. SASE.
Nonfiction: Uses 2 or 3 articles per issue. Subjects of general interest. Seldom prints extremely academic articles. Length: 5,000 words maximum.
Fiction: Uses several stories per issue.
Poetry: Uses 20 to 30 poems in each issue of the magazine. These may be on any subject, in any style. Occasional long poems are used, but the preference is for the shorter length. High quality necessary.

PRISM INTERNATIONAL, Department of Creative Writing, University of British Columbia, Vancouver, B.C., Canada V6T 1W5. Editor-in-Chief: Dona Sturmanis. Emphasizes contemporary literature, including translations. For university and public libraries, and private subscribers. Semiannual magazine; 200 pages. Estab. 1959. Circ. 1,000. Pays on publication. Buys first North American serial rights. Photocopied submissions OK. SAE and International Reply Coupons. Reports in 10 weeks. Sample copy $2.75.
Fiction: Experimental and traditional. Buys 12 mss/issue. Send complete ms. Length: 5,000 words maximum. Pays $5/printed page.
Poetry: Avant-garde and traditional Buys 60 poems/issue. Limit submissions to batches of 6. Pays $5/printed page.

PULP, c/o Sage, 720 Greenwich St., New York NY 10014. Editor: Howard Sage. For writers and any persons interested in quality fiction, poetry, art. Quarterly tabloid; 16 pages. Estab. 1975. Circ. 2,000. Acquires all rights, but will reassign rights to author after publication. Payment in contributor's copies. Sample copy 50¢. Will consider photocopied submissions. No simultaneous submissions. Reports in 1 month. Submit complete ms. SASE.
Fiction and Poetry: "Fiction topics of human relations (especially intercultural relations)." Experimental fiction and serialized novels. Length: open. "Poems on all topics as long as subject is well handled and control is deft." Traditional and avant-garde forms; free verse. Length: open.

PULP: FICTION & POETRY, Box 243, Narragansett RI 02882. Editor: Robert E. Moore. Poetry Editor: Pat Leitch. For a general, educated readership. Quarterly magazine. Estab.

1975. Circ. 600. Acquires first North American serial rights. Pays in contributor's copies. Photocopied submissions OK. SASE. Reports in 6-10 weeks.
Fiction: Mainstream; humorous; historical; mystery; suspense; adventure; fantasy; science fiction and "shades between." Also considers serialized novels and continuing sagas. Length: 10,000 words maximum. Uses 6 mss/issue. Submit complete ms.
Poetry: All forms. Limit submissions to batches of 5. Uses 6-16/issue.

THE REMINGTON REVIEW, 505 Westfield Ave., Elizabeth NJ 07208. Editors: Joseph A. Barbato and Dean Maskevich. Published 2 times/year. All rights revert to author upon publication. Reports as soon as possible. Pays in contributor's copies. SASE.
Fiction, Poetry, and Photos: Department Editors: Joseph A. Barbato (fiction); Dean Maskevich (poetry). "A magazine of new writing and graphics; short stories, poems, parts of novels, and art which, we hope, have a spark of life. We will look at quality fiction and poetry of any school, by new as well as established writers. However, we tend to shy away from work that indicates the contributor has just learned how toes freeze when it gets too cold outside. But if you and your work are alive, by all means let us see something. We want to do what we can to bring promising talent and an appreciative audience together." Fiction length: 1,500 to 10,000 words. Poetry length should not exceed 100 lines. Drawings and photos suitable for b&w, offset reproduction.

RENASCENCE, Essays on Values in Literature, Marquette University, Milwaukee WI 53233. Editor: Dr. John D. McCabe. For college teachers of English, French and theology. Quarterly magazine, 56 pages. Estab. 1949. Circ. 675. Acquires all rights. Payment in contributor's copies. Submit only complete ms for literary essays. Reports in 4 to 6 weeks. SASE.
Nonfiction: Scholarly and critical articles on literary works of the nineteenth century and, especially, of the twentieth century. Primarily devoted to the study of values in literature. Often invites papers on special topics through announcements in its issues. Length: 2,500 to 5,000 words.

REVISTA/REVIEW INTERAMERICANA, G.P.O. Box 3255, San Juan, Puerto Rico 00936. (809)767-4240. Editor: John Zebrowski. For "mostly college graduates and people with higher degrees." Publication of the Inter American University of Puerto Rico. Estab. 1971. Quarterly. Circ. 2,000. Acquires all rights, "but will pay 50% of money received if reprinted or quoted." Uses about 75 mss/year. Payment in reprints (25) mailed to author. Free sample copy. Query first or submit complete ms. Will consider photocopied submissions. No simultaneous submissions. Submit seasonal material at least 3 months in advance. Reports in 3 months. SASE.
Nonfiction: "Articles on the level of educated laymen; bilingual. Also book reviews. Multidisciplinary with preference to Puerto Rican and Caribbean and Latin American themes from multidisciplinary approach." Length: maximum 10,000 words.
Photos: B&w glossies, 4x5 minimum. Captions required. No color.
Fiction and Poetry: "Bilingual; Spanish or English." Experimental, fantasy, humorous and historical fiction. Blank verse, free verse; experimental, traditional and avant-garde forms of poetry.

ROMANCE PHILOLOGY, University of California, Berkeley CA 94720. Editor: Yakov Malkiel, Department of Linguistics. For college and university professors, including graduate students. Quarterly magazine, 120 pages. Estab. 1947. Circ. 1,200. Copyrighted. No payment. Write for copy of editorial guidelines for writers. Query first. Reports within 6 weeks. SASE.
Nonfiction: "Scholarly articles, notes, review articles, book reviews, brief reviews, editorial comments, and technical essays. Examine very carefully some of the recent issues." General linguistics, theory of literature, historical grammar; dialectology, textual criticism applied to older Romance materials.

RUSSIAN LITERATURE TRIQUARTERLY, 2901 Heatherway, Ann Arbor MI 48104. (313)971-2367. Editors: Carl R. and Ellendea Proffer. For "readers of material related to Russian literature and art." Estab. 1971. 3 times a year. Circ. 1,000. Acquires all rights. Uses about 50 mss/year. Except for photographs, payment is made in contributor's copies. Will send sample copy for $5. Query first or submit complete ms. Will consider photocopied and simultaneous submissions. Reports on material in 1 to 2 months. SASE.
Nonfiction and Photos: Translations of Russian criticism, bibliographies, parodies, texts and documents from English literature. Critical articles. All in English. Interviews and reviews of Russia-related books. Payment by arrangement for b&w glossies or negatives. "Only requirement is relation of some kind to Russian art, literature."

THE RUSSIAN REVIEW, Hoover Institution, Stanford CA 94305. (415)497-2067. Editor: Terence Emmons. Quarterly journal; 128 pages. Estab. 1941. Circ. 1,850. Free sample copy. Will consider photocopied submissions. No simultaneous submissions. Reports in 4 to 6 weeks. Query first. SASE.
Nonfiction: A forum for work on Russia past and present. Uses material of high quality in the fields of Russian history, politics and society, literature and the arts. Scholarly reviews. Length: 2,500 to 7,500 words.

ST. CROIX REVIEW, Religion Society Inc., Box 244, Stillwater MN 55082. Editor-in-Chief: Angus MacDonald. For an audience from college presidents to students. Bimonthly magazine; 48 pages. Estab. 1968. Circ. 2,000. Pays in copies. Buys all rights. Submit seasonal/holiday material 2 months in advance. Simultaneous, photocopied and previously published submissions OK. SASE. Reports in 2 weeks. Free sample copy.
Nonfiction: "Articles must be germane to today's problems." Scholarly, but not pedantic articles on religion and/or society for intelligent and concerned American and foreign audience. Must analyze and evaluate current problems in terms of West European intellectual heritage. Editorial viewpoint is classical liberalism. Length: 5,000 words maximum.

SALT LICK PRESS, Box 1064, Quincy IL 62301. Editor-in-Chief: James Haining. Emphasizes literature. Published irregularly; magazine; 68 pages. Estab. 1969. Circ. 1,500. Pays by arrangement. Photocopied and previously published submissions OK. SASE. Reports in 2 weeks. Sample copy $2.
Nonfiction: Informational and personal opinion. Send complete ms.
Photos: Photos purchased with accompanying ms. Send contact sheet. Total purchase price for ms includes payment for photos.
Fiction: Experimental. Send complete ms.
Poetry: Open to all types. Limit submissions to batches of 4.
Fillers: Query.

SAMISDAT, Box 231, Richford VT 05476. Editor-in-Chief: Merritt Clifton. 85% freelance written. Emphasizes literature, art and aesthetics for a primarily college-educated audience "alienated from commercial and academic tastes, yet not aligned with the conventional underground either. Highly demanding, most are themselves well published writers with a lifelong commitment to alternative and rebel literature." Monthly magazine; 60-80 pages. Estab. 1973. Circ. 500. Pays in copies on publication. SASE. Reports in 1 month. Sample packet $2.
Nonfiction: Robin Clifton, Nonfiction Editor. Expose (of commercial publishing practices; corruption in both big and little publishing circles; name names and be accurate); historical (background on little magazine and small pressmanship; contemporary small press criticism within historical context); interview; personal opinion; and profile. Buys 6 mss/year. Send complete ms, "but be familiar with the publication." Length: 1,000-5,000 words.
Fiction: June Kemp, Fiction Editor. Experimental; fantasy; humorous; mainstream; and science fiction. "We do not use mere 'genre' material; give us stories that make us think and rouse our emotions as well as our intellects. No mock Henry James or James Joyce." Uses 50 mss/year. Send complete ms. Length: 500-3,000 words.
Poetry: Avant-garde and free verse. "Read and understand our critical manifesto, *The Pillory Poetics*. We are open to imagism and surrealism, but only so long as the devices make a point and statement beyond themselves." Uses 200 poems/year.

SAN FRANCISCO REVIEW OF BOOKS, 2140 Vallejo St., #10, San Francisco CA 94123. Editor: Ron Nowicki. For a college-educated audience interested in books and publishing. Monthly magazine; 28 pages. Estab. 1975. Circ. 15,000. Acquires all rights, but will reassign rights to author after publication. Uses about 180 mss/year. Payment in contributor's copies and subscription. Sample copy $1. No photocopied or simultaneous submissions. Reports on material accepted for publication in 4-6 weeks. Query first for nonfiction; submit complete ms for book reviews. SASE.
Nonfiction: Book reviews; articles about authors, books, and their themes. "No glib, slick writing. Primarily serious; humor occasionally acceptable. No restrictions on language provided it is germane to the book or article." Interviews, profiles, historical and think articles. Length: 1,000 words maximum for reviews; 2,000 words maximum for articles.

SAN JOSE STUDIES, San Jose State University, San Jose CA 95192. (408)277-3460. Editor: Arlene N. Okerlund. For the educated, literate reader. Academic journal; 112 pages. Estab.

1975. Three times a year; February, May and November. Circ. 500. Acquires first serial rights. Uses about 40 mss/year. Pays in contributor's copies. Sample copy $3.50. No photocopied or simultaneous submissions. Reports in 2 to 3 months. Submit complete ms. SASE.
Nonfiction and Photos: In-depth, erudite discussions of topics in the arts, humanities, sciences, and social sciences. Review essays of authors. Informational, interview, profile, humor. Photo essays can be free-wheeling. "We need more science articles and more in-depth review essays of significant, but little known, contemporary writers." Recently published articles include previously unpublished letters of William James; "Deriddling Tillie Olsen's Writings," "Of Mice and Marshes" and "The Political Odyssey of George D. Herron". Length: 5,000 words maximum. Payment consists of 2 copies of the journal.
Fiction and Poetry: Experimental, mainstream, fantasy, humorous, mystery and science fiction. Length: 5,000 words maximum. Traditional and avant-garde forms of poetry; blank verse and free verse. Themes and length are open.

SCHOLIA SATYRICA, Department of English, University of South Florida, Tampa FL 33620. (813)974-2421. Editor: R. D. Wyly. For professors of English in American universities and scholars having an interest in satire. Quarterly magazine; 40-48 pages. Estab. 1975. Acquires first North American serial rights or second serial (reprint) rights. Uses about 40 mss/year. Pays in contributor's copies. Sample copy $1. Will consider photocopied submissions. No simultaneous submissions. Reports in 1 month. Submit complete ms. SASE.
Nonfiction: Serious, critical articles on the nature of satire itself, and original satire that mocks the scholarly community, its 4 horsemen, and its sacred cows. Length: 5,000 words maximum; shorter length preferred.
Fiction, Poetry and Fillers: Humorous fiction and erotica. Length: 5,000 words maximum, but prefers shorter material. Satiric blank verse and free verse. Satiric fillers.

SECOND COMING, Box 31249, San Francisco CA 94131. Editor-in-Chief: A.D. Winans. Semiannual magazine; 80-120 pages. Estab. 1972. Circ. 1,000. Pays in copies. Acquires one-time rights. Previously published submissions OK, if accompanied by release. SASE. Reports in 1-4 weeks. Sample copy $2.
Fiction: Experimental (avant-garde), humorous. Uses 2-4 mss/year. Submit complete ms. Length: 1,000-2,000 words. Pays in copies.
Poetry: Avant-garde, free verse, traditional, surrealism. Uses 160-200/year. Limit submissions to batches of 6. No length requirement. Pays in copies.
Photos: Pays $5 plus copies for b&w photos.

SEQUOIA, Storke Publications Bldg., Stanford University, Stanford CA 94305. Editor: Ted Gioia. 80% freelance written. "At present *Sequoia* serves the Stanford College community, but is planning to expand to a more widespread audience." Quarterly magazine; 100 pages. Estab. 1956. Circ. 1,200. Pays in copies. Not copyrighted. Submit seasonal/holiday material 3 months in advance of issue date. Photocopied submissions OK. SASE. Reports in 4-6 weeks. Sample copy $1.
Nonfiction: Interviews with writers. Uses 1-2 mss/issue. Submit complete ms. Length: 30 pages maximum.
Fiction: Rica Leiderman, fiction editor. "The only criteria is quality." Uses 2 mss/issue. Submit complete ms. Length: 30 pages maximum.
Poetry: Avant-garde; free verse; haiku; light verse; and traditional. Nothing "trite and conventional." Uses 20/issue. Length: 20 pages maximum.

SEWANEE REVIEW, University of the South, Sewanee TN 37375. (615)598-5931. Editor: George Core. For audience of "variable ages and locations, mostly college-educated and with interest in literature." Quarterly. Circ. 3,900. Buys all rights. Pays on publication. Sample copy $2.75. Returns in 2-4 weeks. SASE.
Nonfiction and Fiction: Short fiction (but not drama), essays of critical nature on literary subjects (especially modern British and American literature), essay-reviews and reviews (books and reviewers selected by the editors). Payment varies: averages $10 per printed page.
Poetry: Selections of 4 to 6 poems preferred. In general, light verse and translations are not acceptable. Maximum payment is 60¢ per line.

THE SHAKESPEARE NEWSLETTER, University of Illinois at Chicago Circle, English Department, Chicago IL 60680. (312)996-3289. Editor: Louis Marder. 20% freelance written. For professors of English, students, and Shakespeare enthusiasts. Published 6 times per academic year. Estab. 1951. Circ. 2,790. Not copyrighted. Payment in contributor's copies. Sample copy

$1. Will consider photocopied submissions. Will not consider simultaneous submissions. Query first or submit complete ms. "Send the conclusions and I will tell you if I want the facts." SASE.
Nonfiction: Solid, original articles. Wants new facts on Shakespeare. Scholarly, yet popular. Articles must show thorough knowledge of the literature on the subject. Length: 1,500 words maximum.
Poetry and Fillers: Occasional poems. No abstract poetry. Shakespeare only; anything that works. Length: 20 lines maximum. Newsbreaks, clippings, jokes, and short humor. Length: 75 words or so.

SHAW REVIEW, S-234 Burrowes Bldg., University Park PA 16802. (814)865-4242. Editor: Stanley Weintraub. For scholars and writers and educators interested in Bernard Shaw and his work, his milieu, etc. Published every 4 months. Estab. 1954. Circ. 800. Copyrighted. Pays in contributor's copies. Will consider photocopied submissions. Submit complete ms. Reports in 6 weeks. SASE.
Nonfiction: "Articles must pertain to G.B. Shaw, his writing life and environment." Uses informational and historical articles and interviews. Length: open.

SIGNS: Journal of Women in Culture & Society, Barnard College, 307 Barnard Hall, New York NY 10027. Editor: Catharine R. Stimpson. For academic and professional women; women and men interested in the study of women. Journal; 196 (6x9) pages. Estab. 1975. Quarterly. Circ. 7,000. Acquires all rights. Payment in copies and offprints. Write for copy of guidelines for writers. Will consider photocopied submissions. No simultaneous submissions. Reports on material accepted for publication in 4 to 6 months. Returns rejected material in 2-3 months. SASE.
Nonfiction: "Scholarly essays exploring women, their roles and culture, their relations with society, etc. We are especially looking for articles with larger theoretical implications." Length: 20 to 45 typed, double-spaced pages.

THE SMALL POND MAGAZINE OF LITERATURE, 10 Overland Dr., Stratford CT 06497. (203)378-9259. Editor: Napoleon St. Cyr. For "high school students, mostly poets, the rest college and college grad students who read us in college libraries, or in general the literati." Published 3 times a year. 40 pages. Estab. 1964. Circ. 300. Acquires all rights. Uses about 100 mss/year. Payment in contributor's copies. Sample copy $1.25. Will consider photocopied submissions. Will not consider simultaneous submissions. Query first or submit complete ms. Reports within 1 month. SASE.
Nonfiction, Photos, and Poetry: "About 2/3 poetry, the rest is open to any and all subjects, essays, articles, and stories. We've had an uncanny knack for discovering talent which has gone on and risen rapidly in the literary field. We don't want anything on the high school and college drug scene, or fiction based on 'Love Story'. Particularly interested in authoritative inside exposes (not rabid yellow journalism) of some aspect of business, government, international affairs, or even the world of literature and performing arts." Nonfiction length: 2,500 words maximum. Experimental, mainstream, fantasy, historical, and humorous fiction. Length: 200 to 2,500 words. Traditional and avant-garde forms of poetry, blank, free and light verse. Length: 100 lines maximum.

SMALL PRESS REVIEW, Box 1056, Paradise CA 95969. Editor: Len Fulton. Associate Editor: Ellen Ferber. Managing Editor: K. Patrick Conner. For "people interested in small presses and magazines, current trends and data; many libraries." Monthly. Circ. 3,000. Accepts 50-200 mss/year. Free sample copy. "Query if you're unsure." Reports in 1 to 2 months. SASE.
Nonfiction and Photos: "News, short reviews, photos, short articles on small magazines and presses. Get the facts and know your mind well enough to build your opinion into the article." Uses how-to's, personal experience articles, interviews, profiles, spot news, historical articles, think pieces, photo pieces, and coverage of merchandising techniques. Length: 100 to 200 words. Uses b&w glossy photos.

THE SMITH, 5 Beekman St., New York NY 10038. Editor: Harry Smith. 75% freelance written. For writers, professors, librarians, others who are interested in literature as art and revolutionary thought. 2 book-size issues, plus supplements. Book format magazine. Estab. 1964. Circ. 2,500. Buys first North American serial rights and second serial (reprint) rights. Buys 200 mss/year. Payment on acceptance. Sample copy $1. Query first for nonfiction. Submit complete ms for fiction and poetry. Reports in 6-8 weeks. SASE.
Nonfiction: Department Editor: Sidney Bernard. Speculative essays. No taboos. Length: 2,500 words or less. Payment is "modest," by arrangement.

Fiction and Poetry: Department Editor (fiction): Raphael Taliaferro. Long stories and novellas as well as short-shorts and vignettes of under 2,000 words. Modest payment by arrangement. Has published poems as long as 52 pages. Pays $5 per short poem.
How to Break In: "The only thing I can say about the trend in this office in the use of over-the-transom mss is that the best chance lies in poetry and fiction. We don't tend to encourage new people to do reviews for a couple of reasons—they usually tend to be too formalistic and conventional (in the style of *Saturday Review, The Yale Review,* or *The New York Review*), and besides we have a number of people in the office and outside who have been doing them. Newcomers might want to try their hands at topical essays, perhaps with a polemical stroke, on the aesthetics of literature. But query first. I should point out that we prefer the unknown to the known. It's partly the sense of discovery and also because we're not that crazy about many of the knowns."

SOUTH ATLANTIC QUARTERLY, Box 6697, College Station, Durham NC 27708. Editor: Oliver W. Ferguson. For the academic profession. Quarterly. No payment. Proceeds of sale of rights to reprint divided with author. Reports in 6 weeks. SASE.
Nonfiction: Articles on current affairs, literature, history and historiography, art, education, essays on most anything, economics, etc. — a general magazine. No taboos. Length: 4,500 words maximum.

SOUTH CAROLINA REVIEW, English Dept., Clemson University, Clemson SC 29631. (803)656-3229. Editors-in-Chief: R. Calhoun, R. Hill. Managing Editor: F. Day. Publishes in April and November. Magazine; 72 pages. Estab. 1965. Circ. 500. Pays in copies. Acquires all rights, but may reassign following publication. Phone queries OK. Submit seasonal/holiday material 3 months in advance. Simultaneous and photocopied submissions OK. SASE. Reports in 2 months. Free sample copy.
Nonfiction: Literary criticism, literary history and history of ideas. Submit complete ms. Pays in copies.
Fiction: "We have no set types; if it's fiction, we'll look at it." Submit complete ms.
Poetry: "If it's poetry, we'll look at it."

SOUTH DAKOTA REVIEW, Box 11, University Exchange, Vermillion SD 57069. (605)677-5229. Editor: John R. Milton. For a university audience and the college educated, although reaches others as well. Quarterly. Acquires North American serial rights and reprint rights. Pays in contributor's copies. Reports within 4 weeks. SASE.
Nonfiction: Prefers, but does not insist upon, Western American literature and history; especially critical studies of western writers. Open to anything on literature, history, culture, travel, the arts, but selection depends on patterns and interests of individual numbers within each volume. Contents should be reasonably scholarly, but style should be informal and readable. All well-written mss will be considered. Length: 6,000 words maximum, but at times has used longer.
Fiction: Contemporary Western setting preferred (Great Plains, Rockies, Southwest), but receptive to almost anything that is disciplined and original. Quality is more important than subject or setting. No excessive emotions. Rarely uses hunting, fishing, or adolescent narrator or subject studies. Open to paramyth, Jungian treatments, serious themes. Length: 6,000 words maximum, but has used longer at times.
Poetry: Prefers poetry which is disciplined and controlled, though open to any form (tends to prefer traditional free verse). Any length considered, but prefers 10 to 30 lines.

THE SOUTHERN REVIEW, Drawer D, University Station, Baton Rouge LA 70893. (504)388-5108. Editors: Donald E. Stanford and Lewis P. Simpson. For academic, professional, literary, intellectual audience. Quarterly. Circ. 3,000. Buys first rights. Pays on publication. Will send sample copy to writer for $1.50. No queries. Reports in 2 to 3 months. SASE.
Nonfiction: Essays; careful attention to craftsmanship and technique and to seriousness of subject matter. "Willing to publish experimental writing if it has a valid artistic purpose. Avoid extremism and sensationalism. Essays exhibit thoughtful and sometimes severe awareness of the necessity of literary standards in our time." Emphasis on contemporary literature, especially Southern culture and history. Minimum number of footnotes. Length: 4,000 to 10,000 words. Pays 3¢ per word minimum.
Fiction and Poetry: Short stories of lasting literary merit, with emphasis on style and technique. Length: 4,000 to 8,000 words. Pays minimum of 3¢ per word. Pays $20 per page for poetry.

SOUTHWEST REVIEW, Southern Methodist University, Dallas TX 75275. (214)692-2263.

Editor: Margaret L. Hartley. For adults, college graduates, literary interests, some interest in the Southwest, but subscribers are from all over America and some foreign countries. Quarterly magazine; 120 pages. Estab. 1915. Circ. 1,000. Buys all rights, but will reassign rights to author after publication. Buys 65 mss/year. Payment on publication. Sample copy $1. Query first for nonfiction. Submit only complete ms for fiction and poetry. Reports within 3 months. SASE.
Nonfiction and Photos: "Articles, literary criticism, social and political problems, history (especially Southwestern), folklore (especially Southwestern), the arts, etc. Articles should be appropriate for a literary quarterly; no feature stories. Critical articles should consider a writer's whole body of work, not just one book. History should use new primary sources or a new perspective, not syntheses of old material. We're regional but not provincial." Interviews with writers, historical articles, and book reviews of scholarly nonfiction. Length: 1,500 to 5,000 words. Pays ½¢ a word. Regular columns are Regional Sketchbook (southwestern) and Points of View (excellent personal essays). Uses b&w photos only occasionally for cover.
Fiction: No limitations on subject matter for fiction. No experiences of adolescents—that's overworked. Experimental (not too far out), and mainstream fiction. Length: 1,500 to 5,000 words. Pays ½¢ per word. The John H. McGinnis Memorial Award is made in alternate years for fiction and nonfiction pieces published in *SR*.
Poetry: No limitations on subject matter. "We don't care for most religious and nature poetry." Free verse, avant-garde forms (not too far out), and open to all serious forms of poetry. Length: prefers 18 lines or shorter. Pays $5 per poem.

SOU'WESTER, Department of English, Southern Illinois University, Edwardsville IL 62025. Editor: Lloyd Kropp. For "poets, fiction writers, teachers, and anyone else connected with or interested in the small press scene." Magazine; 92 pages. Estab. 1960. Three times a year. Circ. 500. Acquires all rights, but will return rights to author after 12 months, upon request. Uses about 70 mss/year. Payment in contributor's copies. Several prizes are offered yearly for fiction and poetry. Sample copy $1.50. Will consider photocopied submissions. Reluctantly considers simultaneous submissions. Reports in 4 to 6 weeks except in the summer. "We do not read mss during June, July and August." Submit complete ms. SASE.
Fiction and Poetry: "We publish mostly fiction and poetry. We do not have any particular editorial bias, but we do insist on meaningful, imaginative development and technical proficiency. No doggerel; no old-fashioned magazine fiction aimed at old-fashioned housewives." Experimental, mainstream, fantasy, historical and science fiction. Length: 10,000 words maximum. Traditional and avant-garde forms of poetry; blank verse, free verse, haiku. Length: 80 lines maximum.

SUNSTONE REVIEW, Box 2321, Sante Fe NM 87501. Publisher: James Clois Smith, Jr. Editor: Sandra Edelman. Estab. 1974. Quarterly. Circ. 500. Acquires all rights, but will give permission to reprint. Payment in contributor's copies. Sample copy $1.50. Reports in 6 weeks. SASE.
Nonfiction, Fiction, Poetry, and Photos: "Interested in new writers as well as those well known. Material selected on merit only. Accepts poetry (any form, any length), short fiction, b&w photos, drawings, criticism and short articles."

THE TEXAS ARTS JOURNAL, Box 7458, Dallas TX 75209. Editor: Cameron Northouse. Emphasizes art, literature, history and biography. Annual magazine; 250 pages. Estab. 1977. Circ. 4,000. Pays on publication. Photocopied submissions OK. SASE. Reports in 3 weeks. Sample copy $2.95.
Nonfiction: Donna M. Northouse, Articles Editor. Historical; informational; interview; personal experience; personal opinion; photo feature; profile and travel. Buys 5 mss/issue. Send complete ms. Pays $8/page.
Photos: Photos purchased with or without accompanying ms or on assignment. Pays $10 minimum for 5x7 b&w glossies. Model release required.
Fiction: Experimental, mainstream, science fiction and serialized novels. Buys 6 mss/year. Send complete ms. Length: open. Pays $8/page.
Poetry: J.W. Brown, Poetry Editor. Avant-garde, free verse and traditional. Buys 20 poems/year. Pays 40¢/line.

13TH MOON, Box 3, Inwood Station, New York, NY 10034. Editor-in-Chief: Ellen Marie Bissert. Emphasizes quality work by women for a well-read, collegiate audience of professors and graduates. Semiannual magazine; 96-112 pages. Estab. 1973. Pays in copies. Acquires all rights, but will reassign following publication. SASE. Reports in 2 months. Sample copy $1.75.
Nonfiction: Literary criticism and aesthetics. Query.
Photos: Photos used without accompanying ms. Uses b&w photos. Send prints.

Fiction: Experimental. "Send complete ms, but study magazine first."
Poetry: Avant-garde and free verse.

THOUGHT, The Quarterly of Fordham University, Fordham University Press, Box L, Fordham University, The Bronx NY 10458. Editor: G. Richard Dimler, S.J.. Acquires all rights. Payment in copies. Reports within a month. SASE.
Nonfiction and Poetry: A review of culture and idea, *Thought* discusses questions of permanent value and contemporary interest in every field of learning and culture in a scholarly but not excessively technical way. Articles vary from 5,000 to 10,000 words. Publishes a page or 2 of poetry in each issue.

TOWN AND COUNTRY JOURNAL, 101½ Mill St., Coudersport PA 16915. Editor: Geraldine R. Miller. For natives and newcomers of this area. Special double winter issue, January/February. Estab. 1972. Monthly. Circ. 2,000. Not copyrighted. Pays in contributor's copies. Will send free sample copy to writer on request. Will consider photocopied submissions. Submit special issue material 3 months in advance. Reports on material accepted for publication in 1 month. Returns rejected material in 2 weeks. Query first or submit complete ms. Enclose SASE.
Nonfiction and Photos: Articles on the history of the area, local government, nature, real estate, antiques, gardening, subdivision, zoning. May have inspirational or mild ecology theme. Snowmobile and other winter sport material is used for the winter issue; material on fairs is used for the August issue. Other interests include informational, how-to, interviews, profile, nostalgia, merchandising techniques, successful business operations, book reviews. Length: 1,500 to 5,000 words. 8x10 b&w glossy photos purchased with mss. Captions required.
Poetry: Free verse, light verse. Length: 4 to 20 lines.

TRI-QUARTERLY, Fiction Editor, 1735 Benson Ave., Northwestern University, Evanston IL 60201. (312)492-3490. Editor: Elliott Anderson. 3 times yearly. For an intellectual and literary audience. "Our format is extremely eclectic. The tone and intentions of each issue may vary." Buys first serial rights. Reports on unsolicited mss within 4-6 weeks; solicited mss immediately. Pays on publication. Study publication before submitting mss; enclose SASE.
Fiction and Photos: No length limits. "We are not committed to the short story as the only publishable form of fiction. Frequently excerpts from longer works tell us more about an author and his work." Payment at $10 per page, if possible. Occasionally uses photos.

UNICORN, A Miscellaneous Journal, 345 Harvard St., #3B, Cambridge MA 02138. Editor: Karen S. Rockow. 75% freelance written. Estab. 1967. Mainly for college and graduate school students and faculty. "Well-educated and sophisticated. Not jaded." Published irregularly. Circ. 700. Acquires all rights, but will reassign rights to author after publication. Uses 15 to 25 freelance mss a year. Pays an honorarium only for nonfiction. Submit complete ms. Generally reports in 3 to 4 weeks, longer over summer, and for poetry and short stories. Sample copy $1. Will consider photocopied submissions. SASE.
Nonfiction and Photos: "*Unicorn* is a community of writers and readers brought together to share their favorite books and topics. Primarily, we publish essays. These range from personal essays to graceful, scholarly papers directed at a general audience. Areas of greatest interest are folklore, popular culture (especially fantasy literature, detective fiction, children's books) and medieval studies, but we will consider mss on any subject. Scholarly and semischolarly papers may include footnotes (use *MLA* form). The supporting scholarship must be rigorous, but avoid 'intellectualese'. Also have a very offbeat foods column, The Galumphing Gourmet, and publish many reviews, long and short. We are looking for crisp, honest prose and stand committed against pretentiousness. We pay $5 honorarium for each article and essay accepted." B&w glossies, any size. Payment in cost of film plus extra roll and offprints. Optimum length: 2,500 to 5,000 words; 7,500 words maximum, but will break longer articles and consider series.
Fiction: Department Editor: Stuart Silverman. Satire, short stories. Fantasy, detective fiction. Experimental, mainstream, science fiction, humorous fiction. "We publish 1 short story per issue, plus perhaps, a parody or humorous piece." Length: 2,500 words maximum. Payment in copies plus offprints.
Poetry: Department Editor: Stuart Silverman. "We are heavily overstocked with poetry at present time. This does not preclude any current acceptances, but does make us more selective. Please limit number of submissions at any one time to 3 poems, unless they are very short. Publication of poetry may be delayed several issues." Traditional forms, blank verse, free verse, avant-garde forms, light verse and "concrete" poetry. Length: 1 line to 1 single-spaced page. Payment in copies plus offprints.

UNIVERSITY OF TORONTO QUARTERLY, University of Toronto Press, Toronto, Ontario M5S 1A6. Editor-in-Chief: W.J. Keith. Emphasizes literature and the humanities for the university community. Quarterly magazine; 96 pages. Estab. 1931. Pays on publication. Buys all rights. Photocopied submissions OK. SASE. Sample copy $3.50.
Nonfiction: Scholarly articles on the humanities; literary criticism and intellectual discussion. Buys 15 mss/year. Pays $50 maximum.

UNIVERSITY OF WINDSOR REVIEW, Windsor, Ontario, Canada. N9B 3P4 (519)253-4232. Editor: Eugene McNamara. For "the literate layman, the old common reader." Estab. 1965. Biannual. Circ. 300 plus. Acquires first North American serial rights. Accepts 50 mss/year. Sample copy $1.75 plus postage. Follow *MLA Style Sheet*. Reports in 4 to 6 weeks. Enclose SAE and International Reply Coupon .
Nonfiction and Photos: "We publish articles on literature, history, social science, etc. I think we reflect competently the Canadian intellectual scene, and are equally receptive to contributions from outside the country; I think we are good and are trying to get better. We are receiving too many poems, too many short stories. Everybody in the world is writing them. Too many articles on literature itself. Not enough in the other areas: history, etc." Seeks informational articles. Length: about 6,000 words. Pays $25. For photos, please inquire to Evelyn McLean.
Fiction: Department Editor: Alistair MacLeod. Publishes mainstream prose with open attitude toward themes. Length: 2,000-6,000 words. Pays $25.
Poetry: Department Editor: John Ditsky. Accepts traditional forms, blank verse, free verse, and avant-garde forms. No epics. Pays $10.

UNMUZZLED OX, Box 840, Canal St. Station, New York NY 10013. (212)431-8829. Editor-in-Chief: Michael Andre. Emphasizes art and poetry. Quarterly magazine; 140 pages. Estab. 1971. Circ. 4,000. Pays on publication. Buys all rights, but may reassign following publication. Photocopied submissions OK. SASE. Reports in 1 month. Sample copy $3.
Nonfiction: Interviews (artists, writers and politicians). Buys 1 ms/issue. Query. Pays $1-50.
Photos: Photos purchased on assignment only. Pays $1-25 for photos. Model release required.
Fiction: Ellen Kahow, Fiction Editor. Experimental. Buys 1 ms/issue. Mostly solicited. Pays $1-50.
Poetry: Avant-garde. Pays $1-25.

VAGABOND, Box 879, Ellensburg WA 98926. Editor: John Bennett. For "libraries, poets, writers, sensitive and free spirits, minority groups, people of all ages, varied education and with an interest in life ..." Estab. 1966. Quarterly. Circ. 700. Acquires all rights, but will reassign them to author after publication. Uses about 80 mss/year. Pays in contributor's copies. Sample copy $1.50. Query first for nonfiction. Reports in 3 to 4 weeks. SASE.
Nonfiction: "I would prefer not to see work that was written with a market in mind. I would like to see material that deals with life and death and all their accoutrements ... joy, laughter, love and hate." Accepts interviews, reviews and personal opinion articles. Length: not more than 5,000 words.
Fiction and Poetry: Publishes genuine experimental, suspense, adventure, erotica, fantasy, humorous fiction. Length: 5,000 words maximum. Traditional and avant-garde forms of poetry; blank verse, free verse and haiku.

VALLEY VIEWS MAGAZINE, Box 39096, Solon OH 44139. (216)248-4048. Editor: Patricia R. Yunkes. Managing Editor: Nelson P. Bard. Quarterly magazine; 44 pages. Estab. 1964. Circ. 5,000. Pays in copies on publication. "Author retains all rights except for those we need to print the story." Submit seasonal/holiday material 6 months in advance. SASE. Reports in 2 months.
Nonfiction: Historical; humor; nostalgia; personal experience; photo feature; and travel. Uses 8 mss/year. Submit complete ms. Length: 3,000 words maximum.
Photos: Purchased with accompanying ms. Send prints. Uses b&w prints (at least 3 inch square) and 5x7 or 8x10 color glossy prints. Model release required.
Fiction: Adventure; historical; humorous; mystery; science fiction; suspense and western. Uses 110 mss/year. Submit complete ms. Length: 3,000 words maximum.
Poetry: Free verse; light verse; traditional; and humorous. Uses 15/issue. Limit submissions to batches of 10.

THE VILLAGER, 135 Midland Ave., Bronxville NY 10708. (914)337-3252. Editor: Amy Murphy. Publication of the Bronxville Women's Club. For club members and families; professional people and advertisers. Estab. 1929. Monthly, October through June. Circ. 750. Acquires all rights. Uses 40 mss/year. Pays in copies only. Will send sample copy to writer for 50¢. Submit

seasonal material (Thanksgiving, Christmas, Easter) 2 months in advance. Submit only complete ms. Reports within 2 weeks. SASE.
Nonfiction, Fiction, and Poetry: Short articles about interesting homes, travel, historic, pertinent subjects, sports, etc. Informational, personal experience, inspirational, humor, historical, nostalgia, travel. Mainstream, mystery, suspense, adventure, humorous, romance, and historical fiction. Length: 900 to 2,500 words. Traditional forms of poetry, blank verse, free verse, avant-garde forms, light verse. Length: 20 lines.

VILTIS (Hope), Box 1226, Denver CO 80201. (303)534-2025. Editor: V.F. Beliajus. For teenagers and adults interested in folk dance, folk customs and folklore; all professions and levels of education. Bimonthly magazine; 40 pages. Estab. 1942. Circ. 2,500. Acquires all rights, but will reassign rights to author after publication on request. No payment. Free sample copy. Query first. SASE.
Nonfiction: Uses articles on folklore, legends, customs and nationality backgrounds. Folkish (not too erudite) but informative. Can be any length. Everything must be based on custom, interview, profile, humor, expose reportage. Length: 500 to 3,500 words. Dept. Editor: Robert Friedman.

THE VIRGINIA QUARTERLY REVIEW, 1 West Range, Charlottesville VA 22903. (804)924-3124. Editor: Staige Blackford. Quarterly. Pays on publication. Reports on submissions in 2 weeks. SASE.
Nonfiction: Articles on current problems, economic, historical; literary essays. Length: 3,000-6,000 words. Pays $10/345-word page.
Fiction: Good short stories, conventional or experimental. Length: 2,000-7,000 words. Pays $10/350-word page. Prizes offered for best short stories and poems published in a calendar year, beginning in 1978.
Poetry: Generally publishes 10 pages of poetry in each issue. No length or subject restrictions. Pays $1/line.

WALT WHITMAN REVIEW, Business Office: Wayne State University Press, Detroit MI 48202. (313)626-6404. Editorial Office: Journalism Program, Communication Arts Department, Oakland University, Rochester MI 48063. Editors: William White and Charles E. Feinberg. For specialists in American literature. Quarterly. Payment in contributor's copies. Wayne State University Press and author share all rights. Reports within a few days. SASE.
Nonfiction: All articles and book reviews, notes and queries should deal with Walt Whitman and his writings. Length: 500 to 6,000 words.

WASCANA REVIEW, University of Regina, Saskatchewan, Canada. Editor-in-Chief: W. Howard. Emphasizes literature and the arts for readers interested in serious poetry, fiction and scholarship. Semiannual magazine; 90 pages. Estab. 1966. Circ. 300. Pays on publication. Buys all rights. Photocopied submissions OK. SAE and International Reply Coupons. Reports in 6-8 weeks.
Nonfiction: Literary criticism and scholarship in the field of English, American, Canadian, French or German literature and drama; reviews of current books (2,000-6,000 words). Buys 1-4 mss/issue. Send complete ms. Pays $3-4/page.
Fiction: Quality fiction with an honest, meaningful grasp of human experience. Any form. Buys 5-10 mss/issue. Send complete ms. Length: 2,000-6,000 words. Pays $3/page.
Poetry: Avant-garde, free verse, haiku, light verse and traditional. Buys 10-15 poems/issue. Length: 2-100 lines. Pays $10/page.

WAVES, Room 128, Founders College, York University, 4700 Keele St., Downsview, Ontario, Canada L4J 1P2. Editor: Bernice Lever. For university and high school English teachers and readers of literary magazines. Magazine published 3 times a year; 80 (5x8) pages. Estab. 1972. Circ. 1,000. Acquires first North American serial rights. Payment in contributor's copies. Sample copy $1. Will consider photocopied submissions. Will not consider simultaneous submissions. Reports in 6 weeks. Submit complete ms. Enclose SAE and International Reply Coupons.
Nonfiction and Photos: "Intelligent, thorough, unique, humanitarian material. Good quality; yet wide variety of genres and styles. Avoid pornography and carelessness. No 'copies' of Jonathan Livingston Seagull." Uses interviews, essays, literary think pieces and book reviews. Length: 250 to 7,000 words. B&w photos and graphics are used.
Fiction: Experimental, mainstream, fantasy, humorous and science fiction. Length: 500 to 5,000 words.

Poetry and Drama: Formal and free verse. Playlets. Length: 2,000 words maximum.

WAYSIDE QUARTERLY, P.O. Box 475, Cottonwood AZ 86326. Editors: Joan Atwater and Mary Radcliffe. 35% freelance written. Quarterly magazine; 100 pages. Estab. 1972. Circ. 500. Not copyrighted. Uses 10 or more articles a year; 30-50 poems. Pays in contributor's copies. Sample copy for 30¢ postage. Will consider photocopied and simultaneous submissions. Reports on material accepted for publication in 2 weeks. Submit complete ms. SASE.
Nonfiction: "Articles should reflect some interest in self-understanding, personal growth. Material should reflect some serious thought on the part of the writer, contribute some real experience of the writer that can be shared with others." Informational, personal experience, inspirational, nutritional information, nutritional recipes. Length: flexible, but averages 1,200 to 1,500 words. Pays $1/page and copies.
Poetry: Same themes as for nonfiction; also nature or descriptive poems. Traditional forms, blank verse, free verse, light verse, haiku.

WEBSTER REVIEW, Webster College, Webster Groves MO 63119. (314)432-2657. Editor: Nancy Schapiro. For "academics, students, all persons interested in contemporary international literature." Magazine; 64 pages. Estab. 1974. Quarterly. Circ. 400. Not copyrighted. Uses about 200 mss per year. Pays in copies. Free sample copy. Will consider photocopied and simultaneous submissions. Reports on mss accepted for publication in 1 month. Returns rejected material in 3 weeks. SASE.
Fiction and Poetry: "Stories, poems, excerpts from novels, essays and English translations of foreign contemporary literature. Subject matter is not important, but quality is. Our emphasis is on international as well as American contemporary quality writing." No restrictions on length.

WEST END MAGAZINE, Box 354, Jerome Ave. Station, Bronx NY 10468. Editor-in-Chief: Gail Darrow Kaliss. Emphasizes poetry, short fiction and politics for readers interested in poetry and in the movement for social change in America. "We hope to appeal to working people." Quarterly magazine; 48 pages. Estab. 1971. Acquires all rights, but may reassign following publication. Pays in copies. Simultaneous and photocopied submissions OK. SASE. Reports in 1-3 months.
Nonfiction and Fiction: Stories about people's lives: realistic with a social message. Proletarian writings. We don't really want protest literature. We want material telling us how it feels to work in America." Personal experience. Also uses fiction.Length: 1,500-2,000 words.
Poetry: Free verse and avant-garde. Length: 1-200 lines.

WESTERN HUMANITIES REVIEW, University of Utah, Salt Lake City UT 84112. (801)581-7438. Editor-in-Chief: Jack Garlington. For educated, university-centered, sophisticated readers. Quarterly magazine; 96 pages. Estab. 1947. Circ. 1,000. Pays on acceptance. Buys all rights, but may reassign following publication. Phone queries OK. Simultaneous and photocopied submissions OK. SASE. Reports in 4 weeks.
Nonfiction: Historical; informational; interview; personal experience; personal opinion; profile and travel. "We need articles related to issues in the humanities." Buys 2-5 mss/issue. Send complete ms. Pays $25-150.
Fiction: Adventure; experimental; fantasy; historical; and humorous. Buys 2 mss/issue. Send complete ms. Pays $25-150.
Poetry: Avant-garde; free verse; haiku; light verse and traditional. Buys 5-10 poems/issue. Pays $25-50.

WHISKEY ISLAND QUARTERLY (formerly *Dark Tower Magazine*), University Center, Cleveland State University, Cleveland OH 44115. (215)687-2056. Editor: Arvydas Valiukas. For those interested in literature, poetry, etc. Published 3 times/year. Estab. 1977. Circ. 700. Acquires first serial rights. Uses 6 mss/year. Pays on publication in copies. Sample copy $1.50. Simultaneous and photocopied submissions OK. Submit no more than 6 poems at one time. Reports within 2 months. SASE.
Nonfiction, Photos, Fiction, Drama and Poetry: "We have no thematic restrictions and no structural or stylistic restrictions. Poetry, short stories, literary criticism, and plays. But no pornography or political treatises, and nothing occult." Length: 3,000 words maximum. Captions optional. Experimental, erotica, fantasy, humorous, and prose poems, poetic fiction considered. Length: 3,000 words maximum. Traditional forms of poetry, blank verse, free verse, light verse, or avant-garde forms. Concrete poetry. Length: 2 to 250 lines.

WIND/LITERARY JOURNAL, R.F.D. 1, Box 809K, Pikeville KY 41501. (606)631-1129.

Editor: Quentin R. Howard. For literary people. Magazine; 96 pages. Estab. 1971. Quarterly. Circ. 500. Copyrighted. Uses about 500 mss a year. Payment in contributor's copies. Sample copy $1.25. No photocopied or simultaneous submissions. Reports on material accepted for publication in 5 to 15 days. Returns rejected material in 5 days. Submit complete ms. SASE.
Nonfiction, Fiction, Drama and Poetry: Short essays and book reviews (preferably from small presses) are used, as well as short stories and 1-act plays. Blank verse, traditional and avant-garde forms of poetry, free verse, haiku.

WISCONSIN REVIEW, Box 145, Dempsey Hall, University of Wisconsin-Oshkosh, Oshkosh WI 54901. Editors: Lynn Abraham, Miekal And, Patty Plowman, Perry Peterson. Quarterly magazine; 40 pages. Estab. 1966. Circ. 1,500. Acquires first rights. Pays in contributor's copies. Sample copy $1.25. Reports in 2-3 months. Submit complete ms. SASE.
Poetry, Prose and Art: "Looking for fresh poetry, prose and art. Experimental, concrete, avant-garde, and surrealist forms welcome. Keep poetry mss to 3-4 pages; prose up to 4,000 words (exceptions made). Need imaginative b&w art and photos. We're tired of reading the same old thing."

WOMEN ARTISTS NEWS, Midmarch Associates, Box 3304 Grand Central Station, New York NY 10025. Editor-in-Chief: Cynthia Navaretta. For "artists, museum and gallery personnel, students, teachers, crafts personnel, art critics, writers." Monthly magazine; 12 pages. Estab. 1975. Circ. 5,000. "Payment is modest and is based on a recent grant from the New York State Council of the Arts to pay authors. When grant runs out, we may be forced to revert to 'no payment'." Buys all rights, but may reassign following publication. Submit seasonal/holiday material 1-2 months in advance. SASE. Reports in 1 month. Free sample copy.
Nonfiction: Judy Seigel, Articles Editor. Expose; how-to; informational; historical; interview; personal opinion; profile; personal experience; photo feature; and technical. Uses 4-6 mss/issue. Query or submit complete ms. Length: 500-1,000 words. Pays $5-10 when grants are available.
Photos: Used with or without accompanying ms. Captions required. Query or submit contact sheet or prints. Pays $5 for 5x7 b&w prints when money is available.

WORLD LITERATURE TODAY, 630 Parrington Oval, Room 110, University of Oklahoma, Norman OK 73019. Editor: Ivar Ivask. University of Oklahoma holds all rights to materials published unless otherwise noted. SASE.
Nonfiction: Articles (maximum length 3,000 words) concerned with contemporary literature; book reviews of 200 to 300 words on new, important, original works of a literary nature in any language. All contributions in English. Payment only in offprints (25) of a major article, plus 3 complimentary copies.

THE YALE REVIEW, 1902A Yale Station, New Haven CT 06520. Editor: J.E. Palmer. Managing Editor: Mary Price. Buys all rights. Pays on publication. SASE.
Nonfiction and Fiction: Authoritative discussions of politics, literature, and the arts. Pays $75 to $100 per article. Buys quality fiction. Length: 3,000 to 5,000 words. Pays $75 to $100 per story.

ZVEZDA, University of California, Box 9024, Berkeley CA 94709. Editor-in-Chief: Mark Osaki. Managing Editor: Steven Mikulan. 99% freelance written. Semiannual magazine; 40-50 pages. Estab. 1976. Circ. 500. Pays in copies on publication. Buys all rights, but may reassign following publication. Photocopied submissions OK. SASE. Reports in 1-3 months. Sample copy 50¢.
Nonfiction: Interview (poets, writers, artists, on topics of craft, style and their projects and work); and personal opinion (in form of literary or art reviews). Query. Length: 500-3,000 words.
Fiction: Sabrina Sam, fiction editor. Erotica; fantasy; experimental; and serialized novels. "Please keep fiction short (1-6 pages)." Query.
Poetry: Avant-garde; free verse; haiku; light verse; and traditional. "Unless your work is of the caliber of Milton, Donne, Eliot, etc., do not submit religious poetry." Length: 5 pages maximum.

Men's Publications

ADAM, Publishers Service Inc., 8060 Melrose Ave., Los Angeles CA 90046. 90% freelance written. For the adult male. General subject: "Human sexuality in contemporary society." Monthly. Circ. 500,000. Buys first North American serial rights. Occasionally overstocked.

Pays on publication. Writer's guidelines for SASE. Reports in 3-6 weeks, but occasionally may take longer. Query. SASE.

Nonfiction: "On articles, please query first. We like hard sex articles, but research must be thorough." Length: 2,500 words. Pays $100 to $200.

Photos: All submissions must contain model release including parent's signature if under 21; fact sheet giving information about the model, place or activity being photographed, including all information of help in writing a photo story, and SASE. Photo payment varies, depending upon amount of space used by photo set.

AFFAIR, Sunway Periodicals, Inc., 21335 Roscoe Blvd., Canoga Park CA 91401. Editor: Herb Hills. For uninhibited young men from about 21 to 35, with above average interest in erotic entertainment and improving their sex lives. Magazine; 84 pages. Established in 1975. Every 2 months. Circulation: 65,000. Buys first North American rights. Buys about 75 mss a year. Pays on acceptance. No photocopied or simultaneous submissions. Reports in 3 to 4 weeks. Query first or submit complete ms. Enclose SASE.

Nonfiction and Fiction: "We're looking for things that are warm and enjoyable, not so super-slick that they're over the heads of most of our readers. Articles and fiction pieces with sexual and erotic themes. Areas covered are self-help, do-it-yourself or how-to articles; new trends, humor, entertainment (of the reader), all with a strong man-woman orientation. Articles should be helpful to the male reader and give him insights and appraoches to better relations with women. Writers with interesting personal experiences should have an edge in this approach. Fiction must have strong, action plots with erotic orientation and activity." Length (for both fiction and nonfiction): 2,500 to 3,000 words. Pays $75 minimum.

How To Break In: "Submit an article or a piece of fiction for our consideration, and then suggest several other ideas that could be developed (with our approval) into other submissions.

ARGOSY, 150 E. 58 St., New York NY 10022. Editor: Lou Sahadi. For the "adult male, with at least high school education, interested in outdoors, nature, adventure, exploration, camping, hunting, fishing, travel, history, automobiles, sports." Monthly. Circ. 150,000. Rights bought "depend on individual arrangements." Buys 100 mss/year. Payment upon publication; sometimes later. Reports in 1 month. Query first. Enclose SASE.

Nonfiction: Articles of personal adventure—humor, offbeat and exotic travel, treasure hunts, unusual outdoor stories—everything of interest to the active, intelligent male except overly sexy material. Must be documented and authentic. "We like to feel that the author was actually on the scene. We don't need anything on the movies or for our regular columns." Length: 2,500 to 3,000 words. Pays $250 to $500.

How To Break In: "To break into the pages of *Argosy* for the first time, a new writer would first have to submit a story idea that we like. It could be just 2 or 3 paragraphs. And he would also have to include the possibility of good photos. If he's a photographer himself, this would be to his credit. Then, if his story idea is accepted, we would ask him to do the piece on speculation, obviously because we have no idea of how well he can write since, as a beginner, he will have no samples of published stories. In *Argosy* there is no such thing as a small sale; we run only full-length features, no shorts."

BEAVER, Reese Publishing Co., Inc., 235 Park Ave., S., New York NY 10003. Editor: Jayson Rollands. 90% freelance written. For men, age 18 to 34; high school education; interested in sex, cars, scandal in government, etc. Magazine; 80 pages. Published 8 times/year. Estab. 1976. Circ. 200,000. Buys first North American serial rights. Buys about 24 mss a year. Pays on acceptance. Will consider photocopied submissions. Reports in 1 month. Query first for nonfiction. Submit complete ms for fiction. SASE.

Nonfiction and Photos: "Articles of interest to our male readers." Informational, personal experience, humor, historical, expose. Length: 5,000 words. Pays $300-500. Spot news (humorous items). Pays $25 maximum. Sets of nudes are purchased without mss. Pays $500 for 35mm transparencies.

Fiction: "Short, erotic fiction. The approach should be fresh, explicit and very erotic. It should be a real turn on. We don't want to see anything like the typical fiction run in other men's books." Experimental, adventure, erotica, science fiction. Length: 5,000 words. Pays $300-500.

CASINO (formerly *Nymphet)*, Sunway Periodicals, 21335 Roscoe Blvd., Canoga Park CA 91401. Editor-in-Chief: Jay Randolph. Managing Editor: Rose Knight. Emphasizes adult male topics, especially as they relate to young women. For the active, sexually motivated male; 21-40. Bimonthly magazine; 100 pages. Estab. 1972. Pays 30-60 days after acceptance. Buys

first rights. Submit seasonal/holiday material 6 months in advance of issue date. Reports in 4 weeks. Free editorial guidelines.
Photos: Kevin Rawls, department editor. Purchased on assignment. Query preferred. Pays $10. Model release required.
Fiction: Adventure; erotica; fantasy; confession; experimental; humorous; mystery; suspense; and mainstream. Buys 25 mss/year. Query or submit complete ms. Length: 2,000-3,500 words. Pays $100, "but may pay less for shorter material."

CAVALIER, Suite 209, 316 Aragon Ave., Coral Gables FL 33134. Editor: Douglas Allen. For "young males, 18 to 29, 80% college graduates, affluent, intelligent, interested in current events, ecology, sports, adventure, travel, clothing, good fiction." Monthly. Circ. 250,000. Buys first and second rights. Buys 35 to 40 mss a year. Pays on publication or before. See past issues for general approach to take. Submit seasonal material at least 3 months in advance. Reports in 3 weeks. Query first except on fiction. SASE.
Nonfiction and Photos: Personal experience, interviews, humor, historical, think pieces, expose, new product. "Frank—open to dealing with controversial issues." Does not want material on Women's Lib, water sports, hunting, homosexuality, or travel, "unless it's something spectacular or special." Length: 2,800 to 3,500 words. Payment to $300. Photos purchased with mss or with captions. No cheesecake.
Fiction: Department Editor: Nye Willden. Mystery, science fiction, humorous, adventure, contemporary problems. Length: 3,000 to 4,000 words. Payment to $300, "higher for special."
How To Break In: "Our greatest interest is in originality—new ideas, new approaches; no tired, overdone stories—both feature and fiction. We do not deal in sensationalism but in high-quality pieces. Keep in mind the intelligent 18- to 29-year-old male reader."

CHIC MAGAZINE, Larry Flynt Publications, 2029 Century Park East, Suite 3800, Los Angeles CA 90067. Editorial Director: Ben Pesta. For affluent men, 20-35 years old, college educated and interested in current affairs, luxuries, entertainment, sports, and fashion. Monthly magazine; 115 pages. Estab. 1976. Circ. 450,000. Pays 30 days after acceptance. Buys all rights, but may reassign following publication. Submit seasonal/holiday material 5-6 months in advance. SASE. Reports in 3-4 weeks. Writer's guidelines for SASE.
Nonfiction: Expose (national interest only); how-to (male-oriented consumer interest); historical (sexual slant only); humor (parody, satire); informational (entertainment, fashion, food, drink, etc.); interview (personalities in news and entertainment); celebrity profiles; travel (rarely used, but will consider). Buys 90 mss/year. Query. Length: 750-3,200 words. Pays $500-1,200.
Photos: Bob Elia, Photo Editor. Purchased with or without mss, or on assignment. Query or send transparencies. Pays $35-100/8x11 b&w glossies; $50-150/transparency. Model release required.
Columns/Departments: David Harrison, editor-in-chief. Chic Thrills (front of the book shorts; study the publication first). Pays $50-75/250-450 words. Media (trends in TV, journalism, radio, etc.). Pays $250/1,200 words. Close Up (profiles of celebrities and future celebrities; one Q/A interview/month) pays $100-150/300-700 words. Buys 150/year. Query. Open to suggestions for new columns/departments.
Fiction: "No porn. Only *Chic* characters in *Chic* situations." Buys 14/year. Send complete ms. Length: 2,000-3,000 words. Pays $500-750.
How To Break In: "Break in with short pieces for the front-of-the-book section (Chic Thrills). Study the magazine. Don't send us your worst stuff if you want to receive serious consideration now or in the future."

CLUB, Box 5220, FDR Station, New York NY 10022. Editor: David Jones. 100% freelance written. Monthly magazine; 100 pages. Estab. 1975. Circ. 1,000,000. Pays on publication. Buys North American and U.K. rights. SASE. Reports in 4 weeks.
Nonfiction: "While the emphasis remains on sex for the 25-35 year-old male, the magazine currently publishes straight fiction, investigative reports and topical features of national interest." Buys 2 mss/issue. Submit complete ms. Length: 2,000-3,000 words. Pays $600 minimum.

DAPPER, Sunway Periodicals, Inc., 21335 Roscoe Blvd., Canoga Park CA 91401. Publisher: Kent Roland. Managing Editor: Dan Jackson. 100% freelance written. Emphasizes adult male topics. For the active, sexually motivated male; 21-40. Bimonthly magazine; 100 pages. Estab. 1972. Pays 30-60 days after acceptance. Buys first rights. Submit seasonal/holiday material 3 months in advance. Reports in 2-3 weeks. Free writer's guidelines.

Nonfiction: Expose; how-to; informational; humor. Buys about 65 mss/year. Query or submit complete ms. Length: 2,500-3,500 words. Pays $100.
Photos: B&w and color purchased on assignment. Query or send prints and/or transparencies. Pays $10 maximum for b&w; payment for color varies. Model release usually required.
Fiction: Adventure; erotica; fantasy; confession; experimental; humorous; mystery; suspense; and mainstream. Buys 25 mss/year. Query or send complete ms. Length: 2,500-3,500 words. Pays $100.

DUDE, GENT, NUGGET, Suite 209, 316 Aragon Ave., Coral Gables FL 33134. (305)443-2378. Editor: Bruce Arthur. 80% freelance written. "For men 21 to ?; adventure and sex are their interests." Male-oriented subject matter. Every 2 months. Buys first North American serial rights. Buys about 100 mss a year. Pays on publication. Submit complete ms. Reports on material in 6 to 8 weeks. SASE.
Nonfiction and Photos: "Articles which are male oriented; primarily concerning sex or adventure." Informational, how-to, personal experience, interview, humor, historical, personal opinion and travel. Length: 1,500-4,000 words. Pays $100-200. Photos purchased with mss.
Fiction: Adventure, erotica, science fiction, humorous. Length: 1,500 to 3,500 words. Pays $100-200.

ELITE MAGAZINE, 606 Avenue Rd., Suite 404, Toronto, Ontario, Canada M4U 2K9. Editor-in-Chief: David Wells. Managing Editor: Christine Curl. 60% freelance written. Emphasizes male entertainment. Monthly magazine; 100 pages. Estab. 1975. Circ. 500,000. Pays on publication. Buys all rights and First North American serial rights. Submit seasonal/holiday material 4 months in advance of issue date. Simultaneous and photocopied submissions OK. SASE. Reports in 4 weeks. Sample copy $1; free writer's guidelines.
Nonfiction: Exposé ; general interest (anything topical); humor (satire); interview (topical personalities); photo feature; and travel. Buys 3mss/issue. Submit complete ms. Length: 2,000-4,000 words. Pays $100-400.
Fiction: Adventure; erotica; fantasy; and humorous. Buys 12 mss/year. Submit complete ms. Length: 2,500-3,500 words. Pays $150-400.
Photos: Gerry L'orange, Photo Editor. Purchased with or without accompanying ms. Send contact sheet or transparencies. Pays $20-100 for standard size b&w photos; $40-400 for 35mm or 2¼x2¼ transparencies. Offers no additional payment for photos accepted with ms. Model release required.
Columns/Departments: Reviews of film, books and pop music. Submit complete ms. Length: 500-1,000 words. Pays $50-100. Open to suggestions for new column/departments.
Fiction: Adventure; erotica; fantasy; humorous; and science fiction. Buys 12 mss/year. Length: 1,500-3,000 words. Pays $150-400.
Fillers: Clippings; jokes, gags, anecdotes; and newsbreaks. Pays $20-50.

ESCAPADE MAGAZINE, Escapade Corp., 210 E. 35th St., New York NY 10016. Editor-in-Chief: Christopher Watson. 75% freelance written. Emphasizes sophisticated sex. Readers are 18-40, high school educated, interested in sexual entertainment. Monthly magazine; 100 pages. Estab. 1955. Circ. 150,000. Pays 2-3 weeks after scheduling for specific issue. Buys first North American serial rights. Submit seasonal/holiday material 6 months in advance. SASE. Reports in 2-3 weeks.
Nonfiction: "Material in keeping with contemporary 'sophisticate' magazine standards; must be frank in sexual detail without being tasteless (racist, etc.). Expose (of sexual nature); interviews (with sex personalities); photo features (nudes). Buys about 6 mss/issue. Send complete ms. Length: 2,500-3,500 words. Pays $75-125.
Photos: B&w and color purchased with or without mss. Send contact sheet or transparencies. Pays $10 minimum for b&w contacts; $15-20 for 2¼x2¼ or 35mm color. Model release required. All photos must relate to theme of magazine.
Columns, Departments: Offbeat sex news, sex puzzles (crossword), pieces with reader involvement (sexual). Buys 1-2/issue. Length: 1,000-1,500 words. Pays $35-50. Open for suggestions from freelancers for new columns or departments.
Fiction: Adventure, erotica, fantasy, confession, experimental (sexual). Buys 3 mss/issue. Send complete ms. Length: 2,500-4,000 words. Pays $100-150.

ESQUIRE, 488 Madison Ave., New York NY 10022. Editor: Clay Felker. Biweekly. Usually buys all rights. Payment on acceptance. Reports in 3 weeks. "We depend chiefly on solicited contributions and material from literary agencies. Unable to accept responsibility for unsolicited material." Query first. SASE.

Nonfiction: Articles vary in length, but usually average 3,000 words and rarely run longer than 4,000 words. Articles should be slanted for sophisticated, intelligent readers; however, not highbrow in the restrictive sense. Wide range of subject matter. Rates run roughly between $350 and $1,250, depending on length, quality, etc. Expenses are sometimes allowed, depending on the assignment.
Photos: Art Director, Milton Glaser. Accepts both contacts and 11x14 b&w matte prints. Uses 35mm and larger Ektachrome and Kodachrome color transparencies. Buys all rights. Payment depends on how photo is used, but rates are roughly $25 for single b&w; $100-200 for b&w full page; $150 to $350 for full color page. Guarantee on acceptance. Prefers to be queried. Gives assignments and pays some expenses.
Fiction: Rust Hills, Fiction Editor. "Literary excellence is our only criterion, but we accept only solicited contributions and material from literary agents." Length: about 1,000 to 6,000 words. Payment: $350 to $1,500.

FLING, 1485 Bayshore Blvd., San Francisco CA 94124. Editor/Publisher: Arv Miller. For male readership, 25- to 35-years old, college-educated and "hip in the sense that he knows what rings true and what sounds phony." Magazine. Estab. 1957. Bimonthly. Buys first rights (additional payment if reprinted in Fling Festival annual); first or second rights for photos, with additional payment for reprint use. Pays on acceptance. Query for nonfiction. SASE. Sample copy for 70¢ in postage; free writer's guidelines.
Nonfiction: "We want contemporary subjects that have a special interest to men. Areas such as crime, film reviews, sport figures, personality profiles, new sexual activities, foreign travel, pornography, health-diets, making money and sexual news items are currently needed. Style of text should reflect a modern-day, sophisticated approach to prose. No long-winded, scholarly sentences or paragraphs. We want the writer's personal feelings to come through." Quotes and anecdotes important to mss. Also buys humor-fillers, personalities and investigative reporting. Length: 2,500 to 4,500 words. Pays $125 to $350 on acceptance.
Fiction: Wants "up-beat, happy-goofy pieces that contain elements of sharp, contemporary dialogue and spaced-out sexual expisodes." Fiction should be slightly fantasized without being too far-fetched.

GALLERY, Montcalm Publishing Corp., 99 Park Ave., New York NY 10016. (212)986-9600. Editorial Director: Eric Protter. For men; 18-34. Monthly magazine; 132 pages. Estab. 1972. Circ. 800,000. Pays in-part before publication. Rights purchased vary. May buy first North American serial rights or all rights. Submit seasonal/holiday material 4-6 months in advance. Photocopied submissions OK. SASE. Reports in 4-8 weeks.
Nonfiction: F. Joseph Spieler, Executive Editor. Investigative articles, informational, humor, interview, profile, new product, photo features and expose. Buys about 80 mss/year. Send complete ms. Length: 2,500-6,500 words. Pays $300-750. Special arrangements for higher fees.
Photos: Payment varies for color sets of nude female photography. Model release required.
Columns/Departments: On movies, music, books. Query. Length: 800-1,500 words. Pays $150-200. Open to suggestions for new columns/departments.
Fiction: Adventure, erotica, fantasy, humorous, suspense. Buys 12 mss a year. Length: 2,500-6,000 words. Pays $300-500.

GENESIS MAGAZINE, 770 Lexington Ave., New York NY 10021. Editor: Joseph Kelleher. Monthly magazine; 110 pages. Estab. 1973. Circ. 600,000. Query. Reports in 2-3 weeks. SASE.
Nonfiction, Photos and Fiction: "Newsmaking articles, interviews with celebrities—political and entertainment, and erotic photo essays of beautiful women. Remember that we are, male-entertainment oriented. We want top quality first and foremost. Nothing downbeat, depressing or nostalgic."

GENTLEMEN'S QUARTERLY, Esquire, Inc., 488 Madison Ave., New York NY 10022. Editor-in-Chief: Jack Haber. Managing Editor: Roger C. Sharpe. Emphasizes fashion and service features for men in their late 20's, early 30's, with a large amount of discretionary income. Published 10 times/year. Pays between acceptance and publication. Submit seasonal/holiday material 4-6 months in advance. Photocopied submissions OK. SASE. Reports in 3 weeks.
Nonfiction: "Content is mostly geared toward self-help and service areas. Subject should cover physical fitness, psychological matters (different types of therapy, etc), health, money and investment, business matters—all geared to our audience and filling our format." Buys 6-10 mss/issue. Query with outline of story content. Length: 1,500-2,500 words. Pays $300-450.
Columns/Departments: Aileen Stein, Associate Editor. Shaping Up (physical fitness); Money (investments); Selling Yourself; Business Wise; and Living (catchall for various stories that fit

magazine format). Buys 5-8/issue. Query. Length: 1,500-2,500 words. Pays $300-400. Open to suggestions or new columns/departments.

HUSTLER MAGAZINE, 2029 Century Park East, floor 38, Los Angeles CA 90067. (213)556-9200. Editorial Director: Bruce David. Monthly magazine; 140 pages. Estab. 1974. Circ. 3 million. Rights purchased vary with author and material. Usually buys all rights, but may reassign rights to author after publication, or first world serial rights. Buys about 72 mss per year. Pays on acceptance. Write for editorial guidelines. Will consider photocopied submissions (although original is preferred). Reports in 6-8 weeks. Query first for nonfiction. Query first or submit complete ms for other material. SASE.
Nonfiction, Photos and Fiction: Department Editors: Zbigniew Kindela, articles; Francis DeLia, photos. Will consider expose, profiles, interviews. Should be hard-hitting, probing, behind-the-scenes material. ''We do not want fluff pieces or P.R. releases. Avoid overly complex sentence structure. Writing should nonetheless be sophisticated and contemporary, devoid of any pretensions, aggressive and down-to-earth, exhibiting no-nonsense attitude. We deal in a realistic world where people sweat and pick their noses. We mirror the reality of the 70's.'' The publication is ''sexually explicit but no pornography. No interviews or profiles on porno actors or actresses.'' Wants expose material, particularly exposes/in political/celebrity/business world. Length: 4,000 to 5,000 words. Pays $500 to $1,500. Material also needed for regular columns, ''Kinky Korner'' and ''Sex Practices.'' Length: 2,000 words for ''Korner''; 1,500 to 2,000 words for ''Practices.'' Pays $100 for 'Korner''; $350 for ''Practices.'' Photos used with mss with no additional payment. Size: 35mm Kodachrome. Buys ''total exclusive rights.'' Pays $300 per page for color. ''Check a recent copy to see our style. Slides should be sent in plastic pages. Soft-focus and diffusion are not acceptable.'' Considers all good fiction. Length: 4,000 to 5,000 words. Pays $500 to $1,000.

KNIGHT, Publishers Service Inc., 8060 Melrose Ave., Los Angeles CA 90046. 90% freelance written. For male adults. Monthly. Buys all rights, but author may ask for and receive all rights other than first North American serial rights after publication. Pays on publication. Query first on articles. SASE.
Nonfiction: ''Broad variety of subjects of interest to male adults. Sophisticated, sexual slant preferred. Profiles of contemporary personalities; reports on new life styles; latest trends in erotic films, art, theater; photojournalism, coverage of current social movements. Interested in articles in the subjective 'new journalism' style, as well as carefully researched reportage, but all must be erotically oriented. No interest in true adventure pieces or how-to-do-it material.'' Length: 2,500 to 4,000 words. Pays $50-250, based on quality and editorial needs.
Photos: All photo submissions must contain the following: 1) An acceptable release (containing the model's name and signature) for all models used. If the model is under 21 years old (18 if married), the signature of a parent or guardian is required. A sample model release is available on request. 2) A stamped, self-addressed envelope. 3) A fact sheet giving information about the model. 4) Place or activity being photographed. Include all information that may be of help in writing an interesting text for photo story. Sample fact sheet available on request. Uses b&w photo stories for personality profiles; photo stories covering events, places, or unusual activities, plus special material, such as erotic art, nude theater, etc. Photos bring $15 each when used to illustrate a story. Purchased separately at time issue goes to press. If submitting an entire layout, an effort should be made to capture a model in the midst of various activities; clothed and unclothed shots should be intermingled; interesting settings and backgrounds are essential. ''Keep in mind that the model will become a personality if used in the magazine and emphasis should be as much on who she is as what her body looks like. Natural, real girls with whom men can easily identify are most desirable.''

MACHO, Relim Publishing Co., Inc., 1485 Bayshore Blvd., San Francisco CA 94124. Managing Editor: David Harrison. For ''liberated men — young, hip, somewhat sophisticated guys.'' Magazine. Published every other month. Enclose SASE.
Nonfiction: ''If it's not offbeat, upbeat, or a bit on the kinky side — it's not right for Macho.'' Expects top-notch writing. Uses ''investigative reporting, celebrity profiles, sexposes, New Journalism, photojournalism and controversial articles on contemporary topics. Articles submitted to *Macho* should reflect the male chauvinistic attitude.'' Length: 2,000 to 5,000 words. Pays $100 to $350.
Fiction: Publishes ''one solid fictional story per issue, along with one or two humor pieces. Fiction must be offbeat, kinky, fast-paced and contemporary in theme, subject matter and dialogue. Characters must be sharply drawn figures from the modern American landscape. First person stories which are obviously thinly-veiled vignettes from the writer's life are immediately

rejected.'' Rarely accepts any mss written in the first person. Also wants ''hilarious spoofs of modern fads and foibles, biting satire that is funny as well as pungent, offbeat tales of humorous sexual episodes.'' Length: 2,000 to 4,000 words. Pays $100 to $200.

MAN TO MAN, MR., SIR, 21 W. 26th St., New York NY 10010. (212)889-0878. Editor: Adam Blake. Monthly. Buys all rights, but usually returns specific rights to author on request. Usually pays on publication. Enclose SASE.
Nonfiction and Photos: Sharply angled articles that reflect contemporary trends in such subjects as travel, music, sex, new art forms, unusual entertainment, and other activities of interest to men. Length: 2,000 to 5,000 words. Pays $100 and up. Typical payment for article with 1 or 2 good b&w photos, $150.
Fiction: ''Strong, imaginative stories in modern mood that include man-woman relationships; no one stereotype is demanded. Taboos are against hackneyed plotting and dull writing rather than particular themes or points of view. No rewriting is done in this market, so the original must be mature and professional in execution, as well as fresh in concept.'' Length: 1,500-5,000 words. Pays $100 minimum.

ONE MAN'S OPINION, Box 3563, Bloomington IL 61701. For young to middle-age men; semi-professional. Monthly magazine; 32 pages. Estab. 1972. Circ. 5,000. Pays on publication. Buys all rights, but may reassign following publication. Simultaneous submissions OK. SASE. Reports in 6 weeks. Writer's guidelines 25¢.
Nonfiction: Expose (all types); personal opinion (provocative); personal experience; photo feature (men's type). Buys 48 mss/year. Submit complete ms. Length: 250-1,500 words. Pays $100-500.
Photos: Purchased with or without mss. Query first. Pays $5-25 for 5x7 or 8x10 b&w glossies. Model release required.
Fiction: Erotica, confession, romance, mainstream. Buys 25 stories a year. Query or submit complete ms. Length: 500-1,500 words. Pays 4¢/word.
How To Break In: ''We are looking for strong fiction/nonfiction. No punches pulled. Heavy on man/woman relationships, sex, forceful and fast-moving stories—good dialogue.''
Rejects: ''Clever'' or ''cute'' approaches. Wants the ''meat and potatoes'', not the overly intellectual stuff.

OUI MAGAZINE, 8560 Sunset Blvd., Los Angeles CA 90069. (213)652-7870. Executive Editor: Richard Cramer. For young, well-educated, urban-oriented men. Monthly. Estab. 1972. Circ. over 1 million. Buys all rights. Buys over 200 mss/year. Pays on acceptance. Seasonal material for year-end holidays must be submitted 6 months in advance. Reports within 4 weeks. Query first. Submit only complete ms for fiction. SASE.
Nonfiction and Photos: ''Articles dealing with subjects of national and international interest (including travel) as well as pop culture (including entertainment), sex, sports, service, human behavior. Humor and satire are especially welcome. All material should be characterized by irreverence, wit, humor.'' Informational, interview, profile, humor, nostalgia, photo, travel, and spot news. Length: 4,000 words maximum. Pays $750 to $1,200 for full-length article. Spot news is used for regular column, Openers. Photos (both b&w and color) are purchased without accompanying ms or on assignment. Pays $200 to $400.
Fiction: Contemporary, experimental, mainstream, mystery, suspense, erotica, fantasy, and humorous fiction. Length: 1,500 to 2,500 words. Pays $750 up.

PENTHOUSE, 909 Third Ave., New York NY 10022. Editorial Director: James Goode. For male (18 to 34) audience; upper income bracket, college educated. Estab. 1965. Monthly. Circ. 5,350,000. Buys all rights. Buys 70-80 mss a year. Payment on acceptance. Will consider photocopied submissions. Reports in 2-4 weeks. Query first. SASE.
Nonfiction: Department Editor: Peter Bloch. Articles on general themes, but not sport or family orientated; money, sex, humor, politics, health, crime, etc. Male viewpoint only. Length: 3,500 to 5,000 words. General rates: $1,000 and up.
Fiction: Department Editor: Paul Breshick. Quality fiction. Experimental, mainstream; mystery, suspense and adventure with erotic flavor; erotica, and science fiction. Length: 3,500 to 5,000 words. Pays $750 and up.
Photos: Purchased without mss and on assignment. Pays $200 minimum for b&w; $350 for color. Spec sheet available from Art Director Joe Brooks.

PLAYBOY, 919 N. Michigan, Chicago IL 60611. Editor-Publisher: Hugh M. Hefner; Editorial Director: Arthur Kretchmer; Managing Editor: Sheldon Wax. Monthly. Reports in 2 weeks.

Buys first rights and others. SASE.

Nonfiction: Department Editor: Laurence Gonzales. "Articles should be carefully researched and written with wit and insight; a lucid style is important. Little true adventure or how-to material. Check magazine for subject matter. Pieces on outstanding contemporary men, sports, politics, sociology, business and finance, games, all areas of interest to the urban male." A query is advisable here. Length is about 4,000 to 6,000 words. On acceptance, pays $2,000 minimum. If a commissioned article does not meet standards, will pay a turn-down price of $400. The Playboy interviews run between 8,000 and 15,000 words. After getting an assignment, the freelancer outlines the questions, conducts and edits the interview, and writes the introduction. Pays $2,500 on acceptance. Also, selected shorts pays $750 for 1,000-word essays on contemporary topics; query first. For interviews and selected shorts, contact G. Barry Golson, Executive Editor.

Photos: Gary Cole, Photography Editor, suggests that all photographers interested in contributing make a thorough study of the photography currently appearing in the magazine. Generally all photography is done on assignment. While much of this is assigned to *Playboy*'s staff photographers, approximately 50% of the photography is done by freelancers and *Playboy* is in constant search of creative new talent. Qualified freelancers are encouraged to submit samples of their work and ideas. All assignments made on an all rights basis with payments scaled from $600 per color page; $300 per b&w page; cover, $1,000. Playmate photography for entire project: $6,000. Assignments and submissions handled by Associate Editor: Janice Moses, Chicago; Hollis Wayne, New York; Marilyn Grabowski, Los Angeles. Assignments made on a minimum guarantee basis. Film, processing, and other expenses necessitated by assignment honored.

Fiction: Department Editor: Vickie Haider. Both light and serious fiction. Entertainment pieces are clever, smoothly written stories. Serious fiction must come up to the best contemporary standards in substance, idea, and style. Both, however, should be designed to appeal to the educated, well-informed male reader. General types include comedy, mystery, fantasy, horror, science fiction, adventure, social-realism, "problem," and psychological stories. *Playboy* has serialized novels by Ian Fleming, Vladimir Nabokov, Graham Greene, Michael Crichton, and Irwin Shaw. Other fiction contributors include Saul Bellow, John Cheever, Bernard Malamud, and Kurt Vonnegut. Fiction lengths are from 3,000 to 6,000 words; short-shorts of 1,000 to 1,500 words are used. Pays $2,000; $1,000 short-short. Rates rise for additional acceptances. Rate for Ribald Classics is $400. Unsolicited mss must be accompanied by stamped, self-addressed envelope.

Fillers: Party Jokes are always welcome. Pays $50 each on acceptance. Also interesting items for Playboy After Hours, front section (best check it carefully before submission). The After Hours, front section, pays anywhere from $50 for humorous or unusual news items (submissions not returned) to $350 for original reportage. Subject matter should be new trends, fads, personalities, cultural developments. Has movie, book, record reviewers but solicits queries for short (1,000 words or less) pieces on art, places, people, trips, adventures, experiences, erotica, television—in short, open-ended. *Playboy*'s Pipeline pay $500 for 900 word how-to's. Ideas for Playboy Potpourri pay $75 on publication. Query first.

PLAYERS MAGAZINE, Players International Publications, 8060 Melrose Ave., Los Angeles CA 90046. (213)653-8060. Editor-in-Chief: Michael St. John. Managing Editor: Monica Fisher. For the black male. Monthly magazine; 94 pages. Estab. 1973. Circ. 400,000. Pays on publication. Buys all rights. Phone queries OK. Submit seasonal/holiday material 4-6 months in advance. Photocopied submissions OK. SASE. Reports in 3 months. Free writer's guidelines.

Nonfiction: "*Players* is *Playboy* in basic black." Expose; historical; humor; inspirational; sports, travel; reviews of movies, books and records; profile and interview (on assignment). Length: 1,000-5,000 words. Pays 6¢/word. Photos purchased on assignment (pays $25 minimum for b&w; $500 and expenses for 100 shots). Model release required.

Fiction: Adventure; erotica; fantasy; historical (black); humorous; science fiction and experimental. Length: 1,000-4,000 words. Pays 10¢/word.

RAMPAGE, 11058 West Addison St., Franklin Park IL 60131. Editor: Jack Tyger. For sophisticated, cosmopolitan adults. Weekly. Circulation: 300,000. Buys all rights. Buys 600 mss a year. Pays on acceptance. Will send a sample copy to a writer for $1. Query first or submit complete ms. SASE.

Nonfiction and Photos: "Our audience consists of sophisticated, cosmopolitan adult readers who enjoy reading witty, humorous and satirical sex-oriented articles. Our readers also prefer reading shocking expose features. We're always in the market for features on current trends in sex. These features should have a strong humorous or satirical slant. Humorous first-person confession stories are also in order. Writer should know how to put humor, wit and satire to good use in his features. Features must be entertaining. Rather than treating readers as groups of buyers, we try to reach each and every reader on an individual basis." Length: 600 to 1,200 words. Payment is up to 2¢ a word. B&w glossy photos purchased with mss. Payment is $5 to $100.

SAGA, Gambi Publications, Inc., 333 Johnson Ave., Brooklyn NY 11206. (212)456-8600. Editor-in-Chief: David J. Elrich. General interest men's magazine. "We offer an alternative to the many 'skin' magazine across the country in that we give an exciting, contemporary look at America today without the porn. A man's magazine that can be read by the entire family." Monthly magazine; 80 pages. Estab. 1950. Circ. 300,000. Pays on acceptance. Buys all rights, but may reassign following publication. Phone queries OK. Submit seasonal/holiday material 3 months in advance. SASE. Reports in 3-4 weeks. Sample copy $1.
Nonfiction: Expose (government); how-to (save money); humor (topical); interview; new product; profile and travel. Buys 12 mss/issue. Query. Length: 1,500-3,500 words. Pays $250-600.
Photos: Photos purchased with accompanying ms or on assignment. Captions required. Pays $35 minimum for b&w photos; $75 minimum for 35mm color photos. Query for photos. Model release required.

SCREW, Box 432, Old Chelsea Station, New York NY 10011. Managing Editor: Larry Wichman. For a predominantly male, college-educated audience; 21 through mid-40's. Tabloid newspaper; 48 pages. Estab. 1968. Weekly. Circ. 125,000. Buys all rights. Buys 150 to 200 mss a year. Pays on publication. Free sample copy and writer's guidelines. Reports in 2 to 4 weeks. Submit complete ms for first-person, true confessions. Query first on all other material. SASE.
Nonfiction and Photos: "Sexually related news, humor, how-to articles, and first-person, true confessions. Frank and explicit treatment of all areas of sex; outrageous and irreverent attitudes combined with hard information, news and consumer reports. Our style is unique. Writers should check several recent issues." Length: 1,000-3,000 words. Pays $100-200. Will also consider material for "Letter From...", a consumer-oriented wrapup of commercial sex scene in cities around the country; and "My Scene," a sexual true confession. Length: 1,000 to 1,200 words. Pays about $40. B&w glossies (8x10 or 11x14) purchased with or without mss or on assignment. Pays $10 to $50.

SWANK, 888 7th Ave., New York NY 10019. Editor-in-Chief: Herman Petras. Managing Editor: Halsey Munson. For urban men, ages 18-40. Monthly magazine; 108 pages. Circ. 350,000. Pays 60 days following acceptance. Buys first North American serial rights and second serial (reprint) rights (for books). Submit seasonal/holiday material 4 months in advance. SASE. Reports in 4 weeks. Sample copy $2.
Nonfiction: Expose (on government, big business, and organized crime); how-to (get a raise, find a divorce lawyer, seduce women); humor; interview (must be established names); photo feature (usually nude sets); profile; and travel (with a strong men's slant). Buys 5-6 mss/issue. Length: 3,000 words maximum (except for *very* strong investigative pieces). Pays $200 minimum.
Photos: Norman Oberlander, Art Director. Purchased without accompanying ms. Send transparencies. Pays $400/set for 2x2 color transparencies. Model release required. "There should be some notation here that the photos we're looking for are female nudes, not your kids, your puppy, your vacation, etc."
Fiction: Adventure; erotica; humorous; mystery; science fiction; suspense; western. Buys 1 mss/issue. Length: 3,000 words. Pays $200 minimum.
How To Break In: "The best way is to read several issues which will give you an idea of what we do. Local events and celebrities that are singular enough to be of national interest are usually good query material. With your query, enclose tearsheets of pieces you've written that are fairly close in style to what you'd like to do for us. Don't just list your credits. We have to know if you can write."

WEEKDAY, Enterprise Publications, 20 N. Wacker Dr., Suite 3417, Chicago IL 60606. For the average employee in business and industry. Estab. 1953. Circ. 30,000. Buys all rights. Pays on acceptance. SASE.
Nonfiction and Photos: Uses articles slanted toward the average man, with the purpose of increasing his understanding of the business world and helping him be more successful in it. Also uses articles on "How to Get Along with Other People." and informative articles on meeting everyday problems — consumer buying, legal problems, community affairs, real estate, education, human relations, etc. Length: approximately 1,000 words or less. Pays $20-40 for these. Uses b&w human interest photos.

Military Publications

Technical and semitechnical publications for military commanders, personnel, and planners, as well as those for military families and civilians interested in Armed Forces activities are listed here. All of these publications require submissions emphasizing military subjects or aspects of military life.

AIR UNIVERSITY REVIEW, United States Air Force, Air University, Bldg. 1211, Maxwell Air Force Base AL 36112. (205)293-2773. Editor: Glenn E. Wasson, Col., USAF. 95% freelance written. Professional military journal for military supervisory staff and command personnel and top level civilians. Circ. 20,000. Not copyrighted, Buys no mss, but gives cash awards on publication. Reports in 6 weeks. Query first.
Nonfiction and Photos: "Serves as an open forum for exploratory discussion. Purpose is to present innovative thinking and stimulate dialogue concerning Air Force doctrine, strategy, tactics, and related national defense matters. Footnotes as needed. Prefer the author to be the expert. Reviews of defense related books. Expository style. B&w glossy photos or charts to supplement articles are desired. Length: 1,500 to 3,500 words. Cash awards up to $150 unless written by U.S. Federal personnel on duty time.

ARMED FORCES JOURNAL, 1414 22nd St., N.W., Washington DC 20037. Editor: Benjamin F. Schemmer. For "senior career officers of the U.S. military, defense industry, Congressmen and government officials interested in defense matters, international military and defense industry." Estab. 1863. Monthly. Circ. 20,000. Buys all rights. Buys 25-45 mss/year. Pays on publication. Sample copy $2.75. Photocopied submissions OK. Reports in 2-4 weeks. Submit complete ms. SASE.
Nonfiction: Publishes "national and international defense issues: weapons programs, research, personnel programs, international relations (with emphasis on defense aspect). Also profiles on retired military personnel. We do not want broad overviews of a general subject; more interested in detailed analysis of a specific program or international defense issue. Our readers are decision makers in defense matters—hence, subject should not be treated too simplistically. Be provocative. We are not afraid to take issue with our own constituency when an independent voice needs to be heard." Buys informational, profile, think articles. Length: 1,000 to 3,000 words. Pays $50-100/page.

ARMY MAGAZINE, 1529 18th St., NW. Washington DC 20036. (202)483-1800. Editor-in-Chief: L. James Binder. Managing Editor: M.D. Walker. 80% freelance written. Emphasizes military interests. Monthly magazine; 72 pages. Estab. 1898. Circ. 110,000. Pays on publication. Buys all rights. Submit sesonal/holiday material 3 months in advance of issue date. Photocopied submissions OK. SASE. Free sample copy and writer's guidelines.
Nonfiction: Historical (military and original); humor (military feature length articles and anecdotes); interview; new product; nostalgia; personal experience; photo feature; profile; and technical. No rehashed history. Buys 10 mss/issue. Submit complete ms. Length: 4,000 words. Pays 7-10¢/word.
Photos: Michael Dunbar, photo editor. Submit photo material with accompanying ms. Pays $15-50 for 8x10 b&w glossy prints; $25-150 for 8x10 color glossy prints or 2¼-2¼ color transparencies, but will accept 35mm. Captions preferred. Buys all rights.
Columns/Departments: Eric C. Ludvigsen, department editor. Military news; books, comment (New Yorker-type 'talk of the town' items). Buys 8/issue. Submit complete ms. Length: 1,000 words. Pays $30-100. Open to suggestions for new columns/departments.

ARMY RESERVE MAGAZINE, DAAR-PA, The Pentagon, Washington DC 20310. (202)697-2470. Editor: Bernard F. Halloran. For civilians who find the military a hobby. Bimonthly magazine; 32 pages. Estab. 1954. Circ. 720,000. Not copyrighted. Payment in contributor's copies. Various prizes are awarded from time to time. Free sample copy and writer's guidelines. Reports on accepted or rejected material in 6 weeks. Answers queries in 1 week. Query first. SASE.
Nonfiction: "We use news and personality features, consumer information, articles on happenings in world military affairs, weapons, foreign armies, off-duty activities, and happenings in the Army, Army Reserve and ROTC units. And good, amusing military history. Since *Reserve* is designed for a primarily non-military audience, buzz words are not used; humor is. We assume

the reader knows nothing about the subject and develop it carefully attempting to find a universal level of interest. Articles are short, to the point, filled with information and often written tongue in cheek." Length: 1,200 to 2,500 words.
Fillers: Newsbreaks, anecdotes; short humor. Length: 150 to 500 words.

BATTLE FLAG 1832 Highland Dr., Carrollton TX 75006. Editor-in-Chief: Larry Herndon. Managing Editor: Donald J. Maris. Emphasizes military history for an audience 18-45 years-old, with interests in history, war games, the military, social events, etc. Monthly tabloid; 32 pages. Estab. 1977. Circ. 3,000. Pays on acceptance. Buys all rights, but may reassign following publication, or second serial (reprints) rights. Simultaneous, photocopied and previously published submissions OK. SASE. Reports in 2-3 weeks. Sample copy $1; free writer's guidelines.
Nonfiction: "We're interested in buying well-done articles on any subject that's considered 'military history.' I realize that's a wide area, but that's our interest. Our special wants are well researched features on ancient warfare (Carthage, Roman Empire, the Vikings, Egypt, etc.) and World War II. I'd love to see biographical articles on Field Marshall Rommel, Hannibal, any of the ancient Aztec kings, Alexander the Great, etc. The possibilities are almost endless. I also want articles on little-known battles or wars—such as the ancient Persian wars, the French and Indian Wars, the campaigns in Africa during WW I., etc. And ... articles on the weapons of war: aircraft, cannons, ships, swords, even uniforms. As I said, the list is endless as to what we're looking for." Submit complete ms. Length: 3,000-20,000 words. Pays $20-150.
Photos: "Obviously, articles with photos will earn more." Submit 5x7 b&w prints.
Columns/Departments: New Books (reviews of new history and military books. Uses 20 mss/year. Submit complete ms. Length: 200-500 words. Pays $3-5. Open to suggestions for new columns/departments.

AT EASE, Division of Home Missions, Assemblies of God, 1445 Boonville Ave., Springfield MO 65802. Editor: T.E. Gannon. Managing Editor: Mark Ellis. For military personnel. Bimonthly magazine; 4 pages. Circ. 10,000. Buys all rights. "We are quite limited in what we would accept from freelance writers. Everything has to be slanted to Assemblies of God readers." Pays on publication. Free sample copy and writer's guidelines. "If we can't use a submission and we think another department can, we usually let them see it before replying. Otherwise, as soon as we reject it, we return it." Query first. SASE.
Nonfiction and Photos: Materials that will interest military men and women. Must have some religious value. Length: 500 to 800 words. Pays minimum of 2¢ a word. Payment for b&w and color photos subject to author's stated fee and size of picture.

INFANTRY, Box 2005, Fort Benning GA 31905. (404)545-2350. Editor: LTC Thomas J. Barham. Published primarily for combat arms officers and noncommissioned officers. Bimonthly magazine; 64 pages. Estab. 1921. Circ. 25,000. Not copyrighted. Pays on publication. Payment cannot be made to US employees. Free sample copy and writer's guidelines. SASE. Reports in 30 days.
Nonfiction and Photos: "Interested in current information on US military organization, weapons, equipment, tactics, and techniques; foreign armies and their equipment; lessons learned from combat experience, both past and present; solutions to problems encountered in the Active Army and the Reserve components. Departments include Letters, Features and Forum, Training Notes, Book Reviews. Length of articles: 1,500-3,500 words. Length for Book Reviews: 500-1,000 words. Query. Accepts 75 mss/year.

LADYCOM, Downey Communications, Inc., 1800 M St. NW, Suite 650 S., Washington DC 20036. Editor-in-Chief: Anne Taubeneck. 75% freelance written. For wives of military men who live in the U.S. or overseas. Published eight times a year. Magazine; 64 pages. Estab. 1969. Circ. 400,000. Pays on publication. Buys first North American serial rights. Submit seasonal/holiday material 4 months in advance. Previously published submissions OK. SASE. Reports in 2-3 weeks. Free sample copy and writer's guidelines.
Nonfiction: All articles must have special interest for military wives. How-to (crafts, food), humor, interview, personal experience, personal opinion, profile and travel. Buys 10-12 mss/issue. Query. Length: 1,200-3,000 words. Pays $75-400/article.
Photos: Purchased with accompanying ms and on assignment. Captions required. Query for photos. 5x7 or 8x10 b&w glossies; 35mm or larger color transparencies. Total purchase price for a ms includes payment for photos. Model release required.
Columns, Departments: It Seems to Me—"personal experience" pieces by military wives. Pros & Cons—opinion pieces on a controversial topic of interest to military wives. Buys 2-3/issue. Query. Length: 1,200-1,800 words. Pays $75-175. Open to suggestions for new columns/

departments; address to Anne Taubeneck.
Fiction: Mystery, romance and suspense. Buys 6-8 mss/year. Query. Length: 1,800-2,500 words. Pays $100-250.
How To Break In: "Our ideal contributor is a military wife who can write. However, I'm always impressed by a writer who has analyzed the market and can suggest some possible new angles for us."

LEATHERNECK, Box 1775, Quantico VA 22134. (703)640-3171. Editor: Ronald D. Lyons. Managing Editor: Tom Bartlett. 10% freelance written. Emphasizes all phases of Marine Corps activities. Monthly magazine; 64 pages. Estab. 1917. Circ. 50,000. Pays on acceptance. Buys all rights. Phone queries OK. Submit seasonal/holiday material 3 months in advance of issue date. SASE. Reports in 2 weeks. Free sample copy and writer's guidelines; mention *Writer's Market* in request.
Nonfiction: "All material submitted to *Leatherneck* must pertain to the U.S. Marine Corps and its members." General interest; how-to; humor; historical; interview; nostalgia; personal experience; profile; and travel. No articles on politics, subjects not pertaining to the Marine Corps, and subjects that are not in good taste. Buys 12 mss/year. Query. Length: 1,500-3,000 words. Pays $100 minimum.
Photos: "We like to receive a complete package when we consider a mss for publication." State availability of photos with query. No additional payment for 4x5 or 8x10 b&w glossy prints. Captions required. Buys all rights. Model release required.
Fiction: Adventure; historical; and humorous. All material must pertain to the U.S. Marine Corps and its members. Buys 3 mss/year. Query. Length: 1,000-3,000 words. Pays $100 minimum.
Poetry: Free verse; light verse; and traditional. No poetry that does not pertain to the U.S. Marine Corps. Buys 40 mss/year. Length: 12 lines. Pays $10-20.

MARINE CORPS GAZETTE, Marine Corps Association, Box 1775, MCB, Quantico VA 22134. Editor: Col. Bevan G. Cass, U.S.M.C. (Ret.). May issue is aviation oriented. November issue is historically oriented. Monthly. Circ. 25,000. Buys all rights. Buys 140 to 160 mss a year. Pays on publication. Free sample copy and writer's guidelines. Submit seasonal or special material at least 2 months in advance. Query first. Reports in 30 to 60 days. SASE.
Nonfiction: Uses articles up to 5,000 words pertaining to the military profession. Keep copy military, not political. Wants practical articles on military subjects, especially amphibious warfare, close air support and helicopter-borne assault. Also uses any practical article on artillery, communications, leadership, etc. Particularly wanted are articles on relationship of military to civilian government, in-depth coverage of problem areas of the world, Russian and Chinese military strategy and tactics. Also historical articles about Marines are always needed for the November issue, the anniversary of the Marine Corps. Otherwise, historical articles not wanted unless they have a strong application to present day military problems. All offerings are passed on by an editorial board as well as by the editor. Does not want "Sunday supplement" or "gee whiz" material. Pays 3¢ to 6¢ per word.
Photos: Purchased with mss. Pays $5 each. 4x5 glossies preferred.

THE MILITARY ENGINEER, Suite 905, 740 15th St., N.W., Washington DC 20005. (202)638-4010. Editor: Brig. Gen. William C. Hall, USA, Ret. Managing Editor: John J. Kern. 98% freelance written. Bimonthly magazine. Estab. 1919. Circ. 22,000. Pays on publication. Buys all rights. Phone queries OK. SASE. Reports in 1 month. Sample copy and writer's guidelines $3.
Nonfiction: Well-written and illustrated semi-technical articles by experts and practitioners of civil and military engineering, constructors, and architect/engineers on these subjects and on subjects of military biography and history. "Subject matter should represent a contribution to the fund of knowledge, concern a new project or method, be on R&D in these fields; investigate planning and management techniques or problems in these fields, or be of militarily strategic nature." Buys 80-100 mss/year. Length: 2,000-4,000 words. Query.
Photos: Mss must be accompanied by 6-8 well-captioned photos, maps or illustrations; b&w, generally. Pays $20/page.

MILITARY JOURNAL, 218 Beech St., Bennington VT 05201. (802)447-0313. Executive Editor: Ray Merriam. 80% freelance written. Emphasizes military history from 1900 to present time. Bimonthly magazine; 48 pages. Estab. 1977. Circ. 2,000. Pays on publication. Buys all rights. Phone queries OK. Submit seasonal/holiday material 6 months in advance of issue date. Photocopied and previously published submissions OK. SASE. Reports in 4 weeks. Sample copy $1; free writer's guidelines; mention *Writer's Market* in request.

Nonficition: Exposé (military subjects-past and present); humor (military-oriented); historical (military history—battles, personalities, weapons, equipment, uniforms, insignia, unit histories, personal accounts, etc.); interview (with military personalities); nostalgia ("What it was like"-type accounts-in military, home front, etc.); personal experience (military subjects, home front, etc.); photo feature (anything military); and technical (military weapons, equipment, tactics, etc.). "No fiction or how-to-do-it, hobby pieces." Buys 15 mss/issue. Query. Pays 50¢/column inch.
Photos: State availability of photos with query. Pays $2 for any size b&w prints. Captions required. Buys one-time rights.
Columns/Departments: Book Reviews (military history books); Medal of Honor (accounts of winners of award); Military Briefs (unusual, littleknown facts and oddities); and Signs of the Times (military signs, illustrations and description). Query. Length: 200-500 words. Pays 50¢/column inch.
Fillers: Clippings, jokes, gags, anecdotes, newsbreaks, and short humor. Buys 12 fillers/issue. Length: 250-1,000 words.

MILITARY LIVING, Box 4010, Arlington VA 22204. (703)521-7703. Editor: Ann Crawford. For military personnel and their families. Monthly. Circ. 30,000. Buys first serial rights. "Very few freelance features used last year; mostly staff-written." Pays on publication. Sample copy for 50¢ in coin or stamp. "Slow to report due to small staff and workload." Submit complete ms. SASE.
Nonfiction and Photos: "Articles on military life in greater Washington DC area. We would especially like recreational features in the Washington DC area. We specialize in passing along morale boosting information about the military installations in the area, with emphasis on the military family—travel pieces about surrounding area, recreation information, etc. We do not want to see depressing pieces, pieces without the military family in mind, personal petty complaints or general information pieces. Prefer 700 words or less, but will consider more for an exceptional feature. We also prefer a finished article rather than a query." Payment is 1¢ to 1½¢ a word. Photos purchased with mss. 8x10 b&w glossies. Payment is $5 for original photos by author.

MILITARY LIVING AND CONSUMER GUIDE'S R&R REPORT, P.O. Box 4010, Arlington VA 22204. Publisher: Ann Crawford. For "military consumers worldwide who are subscribers to the Military Living R&R Report." Newsletter. Bimonthly. "Please state when sending submission that it is for the *R&R Report Newsletter* so as not to confuse it with our monthly magazine which has different requirements." Buys first rights, but will consider other rights. Pays on publication. Sample copy 50¢. SASE.
Nonfiction: "We use information on little-known military facilities and privileges, discounts around the world and travel information. Items must be short and concise. Stringers wanted around the world. Payment is on an honorarium basis—1¢ to 1½¢ a word."

MILITARY REVIEW, US Army Command and General Staff College, Fort Leavenworth KS 66027. (913)684-5642. Editor-in-Chief: Col. Edward Bradford. Managing Editor: Maj. Albert Bundons. Emphasizes the military for senior military officers, students and scholars. Monthly magazine; 96 pages. Estab. 1922. Circ. 21,000. Pays on publication. Buys one-time rights. Phone queries OK. Photocopied submissions OK. SASE. Reports in 4 weeks. Free sample copy and writer's guidelines.
Nonfiction: Historical, humor, informational, new product, personal opinion and technical. Buys 5-7 mss/issue. Query. Length: 2,000-4,000 words. Pays $10-50.
Photos: Purchased on assignment. Captions required. Send b&w/color prints. Offers no additional payment for photos accepted with accompanying ms. Model release required.

NATIONAL DEFENSE, 819 Union Firs Bldg., Washington DC 20005. (202)347-7250. Editor: D. Ballou. For members of industry and U.S. Armed Forces. Publication of the American Defense Preparedness Association. Bimonthly magazine; 80 pages. Estab. 1920. Circ. 30,000. Buys all rights, Buys 6 to 12 mss a year. Pays on publication. Sample copy $2; free writer's guidelines. Will consider photocopied submissions. No simultaneous submissions. Reports on material accepted for publication in 2 to 3 weeks. Returns rejected material in 4 weeks. Query first or submit complete ms. Enclose S.A.S.E.
Nonfiction: Military-related articles: weapons, systems, management, production. "We emphasize industrial preparedness for defense and prefer a news style, with emphasis on the 'why'." Length: 1,500 to 2,500 words. Pays $25 per published page. Book reviews are sometimes used, but query is required first and no payment is made.

NATIONAL GUARDSMAN, 1 Massachusetts Ave., N.W., Washington DC 20001. (202)789-0031. Editor: Bruce Jacobs. 98% freelance written. For officers and enlisted men of the Army and Air National Guard. Monthly except August. Circ. 62,000. Rights negotiable. Buys 10-12 mss/year. Pays on publication. Query first. SASE.

Nonfiction and Photos: Military policy, strategy, training, equipment, logistics, personnel policies: tactics, combat lessons learned as they pertain to the Army and Air Force (including Army National Guard and Air National Guard). No history. Material must be strictly accurate from a technical standpoint. Writer must have military knowledge. "It helps if he knows enough about Guard or other reserve forces to orient his piece toward the Guardsman's frame of reference. Style should be easy to read, serious but not pedantic." Does not want exposes. Length: 2,000 to 3,000 words. Payment is 3¢ a word and up, depending on originality, amount of research involved, etc. B&w glossy photos occasionally purchased with mss. Payment is $5 to $10.

Fillers: True military anecdotes (but not timeworn jokes). Length: 50 to 200 words. Payment is $10.

OFF DUTY, 250 E. 63rd St. New York NY 10021. Editor: Jim Shaw. For members of the U.S. military and dependents living overseas and the mainland West Coast, with much interest in travel and hobbies. Monthly magazine; 56-60 pages. Estab. 1971. Circ. 275,000. Pays on publication in most cases, but sometimes pays on acceptance. Buys one-time rights. Submit seasonal or holiday material 4 months in advance. Simultaneous and photocopied submissions OK. Previously published work OK. SASE. Reports in 6 weeks. Free sample copy and writer's guidelines.

Nonfiction: How-to articles on getting started in hobbies, getting around in exotic countries, household hints for women, latest travel information, shopping bargains, etc. Travel articles (how to get there, what to see and do, tariffs, hidden costs, anecdotes, etc.) New product (chiefly cars, hobby and recreational equipment). Personal experience (only to enlighten readers on pitfalls or discoveries in travel stories). Buys 8-100/year. Query or submit complete ms. Length: 300-2,500 words. Pays 7-10¢/word.

Photos: Purchased with mss. Captions required. Pays $10-20/5x7 b&w glossies; $15-100/35mm (and up) transparencies. Query or send contact sheet or transparencies.

OFF DUTY EUROPE, Eschersheimer Landstrasse 69, 6-D Frankfurt/Main, West Germany. Editor-in-Chief: Patricia Graves. (Submissions may be sent through New York. Address to Graves, Off Duty, 250 E. 63rd St., New York NY 10021). For "U.S. servicemen and their families, mostly between 18-30 years old. Interested in travel, sports, audio and sports equipment, cars, hobbies." Monthly magazine; 104 pages. Estab. 1969. Circ. 100,000. Pays on acceptance. Buys second serial or one-time rights. Submit seasonal or holiday material 2-3 months in advance. Photocopied and previously published (if not in conflicting distribution) submissions OK. SASE. Free sample copy and writer's guidelines.

Nonfiction: "We like articles on travel, hobbies, recreation, entertaining, motoring, family activities, the home, and budget saving ideas. Emphasis is on things to do. In travel articles we like anecdotes, lots of description, color and dialogue. Our readers are not looking to relax in unspoiled scenery. They want to know what to do." Buys 8-10 mss/issue. Query. Length: 850-2,500 words. Pays 10-12¢/word.

Photos: Clothild Lucey, Photo Editor. Purchased with accompanying ms. Captions required. Send contact sheet. Pays $20 for b&w photos; $40-100 for color transparencies. More for covers. Model release required. Photos often decisive in acceptance of article.

Rejects: "No fiction, poetry, war stories, GI humor, personality feature, cartoons, medicine, diets, occult or mysticism."

OVERSEAS LIFE, Postfach 29, 6382 Friedrichsdorf 2, West Germany. Editor-in-Chief: Bruce Thorstad. General entertainment magazine serving American and Canadian military personnel stationed throughout Europe. Specifically directed to 18-30 year old males. Monthly magazine; 64 pages. Estab. 1973. Circ. 82,000. Pays on publication. Buys all rights, but will reassign following publication. Submit seasonal/holiday material 3 months in advance of issue date. Simultaneous, photocopied and previously published submissions OK. SAE and International Reply Coupons (not US postage). Sample copy for 1 International Reply Coupon.

Nonfiction: "We are a commercial giveaway magazine looking for flashy, sexy, young-male-interest writing and photography. In the past we've bought how-to (travel by bike, van, foot, motorcycle; how to photograph girls, rock stars, traveling subjects); and do-it-yourself-sports (skiing, kayaking, sailing, soccer, tennis). Also need music features—rock, soul, C&W, espe-

cially on musicians soon coming to Europe. We're looking for a new kind of travel article: the "in scenes" of Europe written up especially for our young GI's. Should include nightlife, discos, bars, informal eating out, good music scenes rather than fancy restaruants, cathedrals, or museums. Above all, tell our servicemen where the *girls* are. Buys 40 mss/year. Length: 800-1,500 words. Pays 6.5¢/word; "but our rates are computed in Deutschmarks and will vary with exchange rate."
Photos: Purchased with accompanying ms. Captions required. Send b&w or color transparencies.
Rejects: "We get far too many mss written by would-be 19th century aristocrats for other would-be 19th century aristocrats. Our military readers are not taking the Grand Tour, they are on a tour of duty and travel when they can. Seeing the best of Europe cheaply takes information and ingenuity."

PARAMETERS: JOURNAL OF THE U.S. ARMY WAR COLLEGE, U.S. Army War College, Carlisle Barracks PA 17013. (717)245-4943. Editor: Colonel Paul R. Hilty, Jr., U.S. Army. 49% freelance written. For military audience (large percentage of graduate level degrees) interested in national and international security affairs, defense activities and management; also a growing audience among civilian academicians. Quarterly. Circ. 6,500. Not copyrighted. Unless copyrighted, articles may be reprinted. Please credit the author and *Parameters, Journal of the U.S. Army War College*. Payment on publication. Reports in 2 months.
Nonfiction and Photos: The purpose of *Parameters* is to provide a forum for the expression of mature, professional thought on national and international security affairs, military history, military strategy, military leadership and management, the art and science of land warfare, and other topics of significant and current interest to the U.S. Army and the Department of Defense. Further, it is designed to serve as a vehicle for continuing the education, and thus the professional development, of War College graduates and other military officers and civilians concerned with military affairs. Military implications should be stressed whenever possible. Length: 5,000-7,000 words. B&w glossies purchased with mss. Pays $25 minimum; $100 maximum (to include half-tones, artwork, charts, graphs, maps, etc.).

PERIODICAL, Council on Abandoned Military Posts, 4970 N. Camino Antonio, Tucson AZ 85718. Editor-in-Chief: Dan L. Thrapp. 100% freelance written. Emphasizes old and abandoned forts, posts and military installations; military subjects for a professional, knowledgeable readership interested in one-time defense sites or other military installations. Quarterly magazine; 40-64 pages. Estab. 1967. Circ. 1,500. Pays on publication. Buys one-time rights. Simultaneous, photocopied and previously published (if published a long time ago) submissions OK. SASE. Reports in 3 weeks. Sample copy 50¢.
Nonfiction: Historical; personal experience; photo feature; technical (relating to posts, their construction/operation and military matters) and travel. Buys 4-6 mss/issue. Query or send complete ms. Length: 300-4,000 words. Pays minimum $2/page.
Photos: Purchased with or without accompanying ms. Captions required. Query. Glossy, single weight, b&w up to 8x10. Offers no additional payment for photos accepted with accompanying ms.

THE RETIRED OFFICER MAGAZINE, 1625 Eye St., N.W., Suite 503, Washington DC 20006. (202)331-1111. Editor: Colonel Minter L. Wilson, Jr., USA-Ret. For "officers of the 7 uniformed services and their families." Estab. 1945. Monthly. Circ. 265,000. Rights purchased vary with author and material. May buy all rights or first serial rights. Pays on publication. Free sample copy. Will consider photocopied submissions "if clean and fresh." Submit seasonal material (holiday stories in which the Armed Services are depicted) at least 3 months in advance. Reports on material accepted for publication within 6 weeks. Returns rejected material in 4 weeks. Submit complete ms. SASE.
Nonfiction and Photos: History, humor, cultural, second-career opportunities and current affairs. "Currently topical subjects with particular contextual slant to the military; historical events of military significance; features pertinent to a retired military officer's milieu (second career, caveats in the business world; wives' adjusting, leisure, fascinating hobbies). True military experiences (short) are also useful, and we tend to use articles less technical than a single-service publication might publish." Length: 1,000 to 2,500 words. Pays $25 to $250. 8x10 b&w photos (normal halftone). Pays $5. Color photos must be suitable for color separation. Pays $25 if reproduced in color; otherwise, same as b&w. Department Editor: Sharon F. Golden.

RUSI JOURNAL, Royal United Services Institute for Defense Studies, Whitehall SW1A 2ET,

England. Editor: Rear Admiral E.F. Gueritz. Deputy Editor: Jenny Shaw. Emphasizes defense and military history. Quarterly magazine; 100 pages. Estab. 1857. Circ. 7,000. Pays on publication. Buys all rights, but may reassign following publication. Photocopied submissions OK. SAE and International Reply Coupons. Sample copy, $5.
Nonfiction: Informational articles on British and U.S. defense; historical military articles with particular reference to current defense problems; weapon technology; international relations and civil/military relations. Buys 10/issue. Query. Length: 2,500-6,000 words. Pays 8 pounds/ printed page.
Photos: No additional payment is made for photos, but they should accompany articles whenever possible.

SEA POWER, 818 Eighteenth St., N.W., Washington DC 20006. Editor: James D. Hessman. Issued monthly by the Navy League of the U.S. for naval personnel and civilians interested in naval maritime and defense matters. Buys all rights. Pays on publication. Will send free sample copy to a writer on request. Reports in 1 to 6 months. Query first. Enclose S.A.S.E.
Nonfiction and Photos: Factual articles on sea power in general, and the U.S. Navy, the U.S. Marine Corps, U.S. Coast Guard, U.S. merchant marine and naval services and other navies of the world in particular. Should illustrate and expound the importance of the seas and sea power to the U.S. and its allies. Wants timely, clear, nontechnical, lively writing. Length: 500 to 2,000 words. Does not want to see historical articles, commentaries, critiques, abstract theories, poetry or editorials. Pays $50 to $200, depending upon length and research involved. Purchases 8x10 glossy photos with mss.

U.S. NAVAL INSTITUTE PROCEEDINGS, Annapolis MD 21402. (301)268-6110. Editor: Clayton R. Barrow, Jr. Managing Editor: Paul Stillwell. Emphasizes sea services (Navy, Marine Corps, Coast Guard) for sea services officers and enlisted personnel, other military services in the US and abroad and civilians interested in naval/maritime affairs. Monthly magazine; 120 pages. Estab. 1873. Circ. 65,000. Pays on acceptance. Buys all rights. Phone queries OK, but all material must be submitted on speculation. Submit seasonal/anniversary material 6 months in advance. Photocopied submissions OK. SASE. Reports in 2 weeks (queries); 3 months (manuscripts). Free sample copy.
Nonfiction: Historical (based on primary sources, unpublished and/or first-hand experience); humor; informational; nostalgia; personal experience; personal opinion; photo feature; technical; professional notes; and book reviews. Query. Length: 4,000 words maximum. Pays $200-400.
Photos: Purchased with or without accompanying ms or on assignment. Captions required. Query. Pays $15 maximum for b&w 8x10 glossies. "We pay $2 for each photo submitted with articles by people other than the photographer."
Columns/Departments: Fred Rainbow, Column/Department Editor. Comment and Discussion (comments 500-700 words on new subjects or ones previously covered in magazine); Professional Notes; Nobody Asked Me, But... (700-1,000 words, strong opinion on naval/maritime topic); and Book Reviews. Buys 35 Book Reviews; 35 Professional Notes; 100 Comment and Discussion and 10 NAMB/year. Pays $25-50.
Fillers: Patricia Perry, Fillers Editor. Jokes, gags, anecdotes. Buys 25 fillers/year. Length: maximum 200 words. Pays $25 flat rate.
How To Break In: "The Comment and Discussion section is our bread and butter. It is a glorified letters to the editor section and exemplifies the concept of the *Proceedings* as a forum. We particularly welcome comments on material published in previous issues of the magazine. This offers the writer of the comment an opportunity to expand the discussion of a particular topic and to bring his own viewpoint into it. This feature does not pay particularly well, but it is an excellent opportunity to get one's work into print."

Miscellaneous Publications

A BETTER LIFE FOR YOU, 424 N. 3rd St., Burlington IA 52601. Editor-in-Chief: B. Pollard. Managing Editor: R. Walker. 95% freelance written. For industrial workers of all ages. Quarterly magazine: 32 pages. Estab. 1956. Circ. 45,000. Pays on publication. Buys all rights, but may reassign following publication. Previously published submissions OK. SASE. Reports in 1 week. Free sample copy and writer's guidelines; mention *Writer's Market* in request.
Nonfiction: General interest (steps to better health, on the job attitudes); how-to (perform better on the job, how-to do home repair jobs, and how-to keep up maintenance on a car). Buys 5-6 mss/issue. Query or send outline. Length: 400-1,000 words. Pays $20.

ALTERNATIVE SOURCES OF ENERGY MAGAZINE, Route 2, Box 90A, Milaca MN 56353. (612)983-6892. Editor-in-Chief: Donald Marier. Emphasizes alternative energy sources and appropriate technology for a predominately male, age 36, college educated audience, conscious of environmental and energy limitations. Bimonthly magazine; 64 pages. Estab. 1972. Circ. 5,000. Pays on acceptance. Buys all rights, but may reassign following publication. Phone queries OK. Simultaneous, photocopied, and previously published submissions OK, "if specified at time of submission." SASE. Reports in 2 weeks. Sample copy $1.
Nonfiction: Expose (government, industry), historical (solar, wind, water, etc.), how-to (plans, kits, etc.), humor, informational (new sources of data, products, etc.), interview (any active person), and technical (plans, kits, designs). Buys 90 mss/year. Submit complete ms. Length: 500-6,000 words. Pays "generally $20-30/page."
Photos: Susan Pauls, Photo Editor. Photos purchased with or without accompanying ms or on assignment. Captions required. Send contact sheet or prints. Pays $5-25 for 8x10 b&w glossy photos. Total purchase price for ms includes payment for photos. Model release required. "We prefer to purchase pix with mss rather than alone."
Fillers: Susan Pauls, Fillers Editor. Clippings, jokes, gags, anecdotes, newsbreaks. Length: 25-100 words. Pays $5 minimum.
How To Break In: "We need well-researched articles emphasizing alternative or appropriate sources of energy; solar, water, wind, biofuels, etc."

AMERICAN DANE MAGAZINE, Danish Brotherhood in America, Box 31748, Omaha NE 68131. (402)341-5049. Administrative Editor: Howard Christenson. Emphasizes Danish heritage and traditions. Monthly magazine; 20-28 pages. Estab. 1920. Circ. 11,000. Pays on publication. Buys all rights, but will reassign to author following publication. Submit seasonal/holiday material 4 months in advance (particularly Christmas). Photocopied or previously published submissions OK. SASE. Reports in 1 month. Sample copy 50¢. Free writer's guidelines.
Nonfiction: Historical; humor (satirical, dry wit notoriously Scandinavian); informational (Danish items, Denmark or Danish-American involvements); inspirational (honest interrelationships); interview; nostalgia; personal experience; photo feature and travel. Buys 35-40 mss/year. Query. Length: maximum 1,500 words. Pays $25.
Photos: Purchased on assignment. Query. Pays $10-25 for b&w. Total purchase price for a ms includes payment for photos. Model release required.
Columns, Departments: Grandmother's Kitchen (unusual, unique, or traditional Danish or Scandinavian recipes); Book, film, play reviews (relating to Denmark or the Danes, Danish authors, playwrights, etc.). Buys 20/year. Query. Length: maximum 500 words. Pays $10-25.
Fiction: Adventure; historical; humorous; mystery; romance; and suspense. Must have Danish or Scandinavian appeal. Buys 12 mss/year. Query. Length: 500-2,000 words. Pays $25.
Poetry: Avant-garde, free verse, haiku, light verse and traditional. Buys 6-8 poems/year. Query. Limit submissions to batches of 5. Length: maximum 40 lines. Pays $25-75.
Fillers: Clippings, jokes, gags, anecdotes, puzzles (crossword, anagrams etc.) and short humor. Buys 10-12 fillers/year. Query. Length: 50-300 words.

ANDY WARHOL'S INTERVIEW MAGAZINE, 860 Broadway West, New York NY 10003. (212)533-4700. Editor: Bob Colacello. For those interested in fashion, movies, art and music. Estab. 1970. Monthly. Circ. 82,000. All rights purchased but will negotiate on individual basis. Buys 25 mss a year. Payment on publication. Will send sample copy for $1. Query first. Enclose SASE.
Nonfiction and Photos: Features exclusive interviews with interesting people in fashion, art, movies, television, music, books, and whatever is happening now. Length: 10,000 words maximum. Pays $25. Prefer 8x10 or larger b&w photos.
How To Break In: "We are interested in interviews with entertainment figures as well as with *entertaining* figures. Usually with famous people with whom I want an interview, I'll assign it to someone I know. So the best way to break in is either with a well-known person to whom you happen to have some kind of access or, more likely, a lesser known *entertaining* person who you can get to yourself. If we like what you do—and I don't know how to describe it; basically what you need is a good interviewing personality rather than writing skill—then I will certainly want to use you in the future and will arrange access for you when it comes to interviewing the more famous types."

ARARAT, The Armenian General Benevolent Union, 628 2nd Ave., New York NY 10016. Editor-in-Chief: Leo Hamalian. Emphasizes Armenian life and culture for Americans of Armenian descent; Armenian immigrants. "Many are well-educated; some are Old World." Quarterly magazine; 48 pages. Estab. 1960. Circ. 2,000. Pays on publication. Buys first North

American serial rights. Submit seasonal/holiday material at least 3 months in advance. Photocopied, and previously published submissions OK. SASE. Reports in 6 weeks. Sample copy $1.50.
Nonfiction: Historical (history of Armenian people, of leaders, etc.); interviews (with prominent or interesting Armenians in any field, but articles are preferred); profile (on subjects relating to Armenian life and culture); personal experience (revealing aspects of typical Armenian life); travel (in Soviet Armenia). Buys 3 mss/issue. Query. Length: 1,000-6,000 words. Pays $25-100.
Columns/Departments: Reviews of books by Armenians or relating to Armenians. Buys 6 per issue. Query. Pays $20. Open to suggestions for new columns/departments.
Fiction: Any stories dealing with Armenian life in America or in the old country. Religious stories relating to the Armenian Church. Buys 2 mss/year. Query. Length: 2,000-5,000 words. Pays $35-75.
Poetry: Any verse that is Armenian in theme. Buys 6 per issue. Pays $10.
How To Break In: "Read the magazine, and write about the kind of subjects we are obviously interested in, i.e., Kirlian photography, Aram Avakian's films, etc. Remember that we have become almost totally ethnic magazine in subject matter, but we want articles that present the Armenian to the rest of the world in an interesting way."

C.S.P. WORLD NEWS, Editions Stencil, Box 2608, Station D, Ottawa, Ontario, Canada K1P 5W7. Editor-in-Chief: Guy F. Claude Hamel. Emphasizes book reviews. Monthly newsletter; 20 pages. Estab. 1965. Circ. 200,000. Buys all rights. Photocopied submissions OK. SASE. Reports in 2 months. Sample copy $1.
Nonfiction: Publishes exposes about law enforcement and courts. Buys 12/year. Send complete ms. Length: 2,600-5,000 words. Pays $1-2 per typewritten, double-spaced page. Submit complete ms.
Columns, Departments: Writer's Workshop material. Buys 12 items/year. Send complete ms. Length: 20-50 words. Pays $1-2.
Poetry: Publishes avant-garde forms. Buys 12/year. Submit complete ms; no more than 2 at a time. Length: 6-12 lines. Pays $1.
Fillers: Jokes, gags, anecdotes. Pays $1-2.

CANADIAN GEOGRAPHICAL JOURNAL, 488 Wilbrod St., Ontario, Canada, K1N 6M8. (613)236-7493. Editor-in-Chief: David Maclellan. Managing Editor: Enid Byford. Assistant Editor: Frank B. Edwards. 100% freelance written. Readership is adult, with some university education, and has a high interest in learning more about Canada (especially its geography). Bimonthly magazine; 84 pages. Estab. 1930. Circ. 50,000. Pays on publication. Buys first North American serial rights. Phone queries OK. Submit seasonal/holiday material 6 months in advance of issue date. Photocopied submissions OK. SASE. Reports in 6 weeks. Sample copy $2.50; free writer's guidelines.
Nonfiction: General interest (relating to Canadian geography); photo feature (must be of superb quality if it is to be used with minimal or no text); and technical or scientific (must be written for laymen and deal with a subject related to Canadian geography). "We do not want poorly researched, non-factual stories on topics which are not about Canada". Buys 60 mss/year. Query or submit complete ms. Length: 1,500-3,000 words. Pays 5½¢/word, but good photos will raise payment substantially ($150-200/article).
Photos: State availability of photos with query or send photo material with accompanying ms. "If an author can get photo material from other sources (corporations and government agencies) with reproduction permission, we will pay standard photo rates." Pays $6-15 for 8x10 b&w glossy prints and $10-35 for 35mm color transparencies. Detailed caption information required. Buys one-time rights.

CA$H NEWSLETTER, 2232 Arrowhead Ave., Brooksville FL 33512. Editor-in-Chief: G. Douglas Hafely, Jr. Managing Editor: K.R. Baker. Emphasizes "making, saving, and investing money." Monthly newsletter; 8 pages. Estab. 1976. Pays on acceptance. Buys all rights. Submit seasonal/holiday material 2 months in advance. Simultaneous and photocopied submissions OK. SASE. Reports in 2 weeks. Sample copy 50¢.
Nonfiction: Expose (rags to riches, how the little guy got started and made it big; need full details on how); humor (pertaining to making and saving money); how-to (make, save, keep, use, and invest money; how to get services, information and goods free); informational (ways for anyone to succeed); inspirational (hope for the small man); interview (with successful people who started small), new product (hot items for resale, new items of interest to mass audience, how to buy and save), personal experience (if from small to successful); technical (on interesting new ways to invest; market projections and contacts); and travel (any inexpensive and/or unusual

vacations). Buys 2-10 mss/issue. Submit complete ms. Length: 100-1,000 words. Pays $2-10.
Photos: Purchased with or without accompanying ms. Captions required. Send prints. Pays $2-5 for 4x5 b&w glossies. No additional payment for photos accepted with accompanying ms.
Fillers: Clippings, newsbreaks. Buys 1-10/issue. Length: 5-50 words. Pays 50¢-$2.

THE CIVIL LIBERTIES REVIEW, ACLU Foundation, 22 E. 40th St., New York NY 10016. (212)689-8142. Editor-in-Chief: Alan F. Westin. Executive Editor: Albert Robbins. 5-10% freelance written. Emphasizes civil liberties/civil rights for a well-educated readership, committed to the protection of constitutional rights. Bimonthly magazine; 80-96 pages. Estab. 1973. Circ. 11,000. Pays on publication. Buys all rights, but may reassign following publication. SASE. Reports in 6 weeks. Sample copy $3; mention *Writer's Market* in request.
Nonfiction: "We accept little freelance work because of the nature of our publication. In general, our articles are written by leading academics, lawyers, activists and journalists, and they encompass both theoretical essays and narrative nonfiction about current trends and events in American civil liberties. However, now and then, a thoughtful, well written piece submitted by a freelancer arrives in our office. In general, these deal with a specific problem area, and may take the form of an essay or a narrative of some civil liberties case, following it through from beginning to end, and, necessarily, drawing appropriate conclusions. We like brightly written prose here which sparkes with wit while delving into complex issues." Expose; general interest; and historical. Buys 6 mss/year. Query. Length: 1,000-3,000 words. Pays $50-300.
Photos: State availability of photos with query. Pays $10-25 for b&w glossy prints. Buys all rights, but may reassign following publication.

C-ME MAGAZINE, P.O. Box 48487, Los Angeles CA 90048. (213)382-6341 and (213)382-9857. Editor: Freeda C. Jordan. Monthly magazine; 50 pages. For general audience. Estab. 1975. Circ. 10,000. Buys all rights. Pays on acceptance. Sample copy 75¢. Will consider simultaneous submissions. Submit seasonal material 6 months in advance. Reports in 4 weeks. Query first. Enclose SASE.
Nonfiction, Photos, Fiction, Poetry and Fillers: Wants mss dealing with music, the arts and entertainment fields; inspiration, "you can do it." Writers should "study and become familiar with format." Length: 3,000 words maximum for fiction and nonfiction. Pays $125 maximum for fiction and nonfiction. 8x10 b&w photos used with accompanying ms with no additional payment. Captions required. Poetry. Length: 50 words maximum. Pays $5 to $10. Buys various types of fillers. Length varies. Payment varies.

COFFEE BREAK, Box 103, Burley WA 98322. Editor-in-Chief: Dolores Nicolai. 80% freelance written. "Our objective is to provide the reader with brief reading material to brighten their coffee breaks, lunch hours, commuting time, and other hum-drum lulls." Biannual magazine; 112 pages. Estab. June 1977. Circ. 6,000. Pays on publication. Buys one-time rights. Submit seasonal/holiday material 4-6 months in advance of issue date. Photocopied and previously published submissions OK. SASE. Reports in 6-8 weeks. Sample copy $1; free writer's guidelines; mention *Writer's Market* in request.
Nonfiction: Historical (northwest only); how-to (home, house, garden, juvenile or sports); humor (keeping in mind we are a family magazine all humor is welcome; especially need the male point of view); nostalgia (on occasion); personal experience (if it relates to the over all feel of the magazine, always humor); photo feature (northwest preferred); profile (query first); and adventure (juvenile). "We will not consider politics, religion, erotica or pornography." Buys 30 mss/issue. Submit complete ms. Length: 1,500 words. Pays $5-25.
Photos: State availability of photos with ms. Offers no additional payment for 5x7 b&w glossy prints. Captions preferred. Buys one-time rights. Model release required.
Fiction: Adventure (masculine and juvenile appeal); experimental (open to new ideas); fantasy (juvenile or adult); historical (northwest themes preferred); humorous (adult and juvenile); mainstream; mystery; romance; science fiction; suspense; and western. Buys 10 mss/issue. Submit complete ms. Length: 1,500 words. Pays $5-25.
Poetry: Free verse; haiku; light verse; and traditional. Buys 6/issue. Pays $5-10.
Fillers: Jokes, gags, anecdotes; puzzles (juvenile); and short humor. Pays $5.

CREATIVE LIVING, 488 Madison Ave., New York NY 10022. (212)752-4530. Editor: Robert H. Spencer. Published by Northwestern Mutual Life. Estab. 1972. Quarterly. Circ. 200,000. Rights purchased vary with author and material. Usually buys all rights but may reassign rights to author after publication. Buys 40 to 50 mss a year. Occasionally overstocked. Payment on publication. Free sample copy and writer's guidelines. Prefers items not written in first person. Will not consider photocopied submissions. Submit seasonal sports material 6 months in

advance. Reports on material in 2 to 3 months. Query first, with writing sample. SASE.
Nonfiction: "We publish *Creative Living* because we think it helps turn people on to themselves. We think it totally conceivable that people who read articles about others living their lives to the hilt might be motivated to think of themselves in a brighter, more creative light. Writers should bone up a bit on what makes the creative process tick. Get behind the facts. Many people lead creative lives. Importantly, we want to know their philosophical basis for living. Stress individuality and use specific examples. Give advice to the reader for gaining greater self-fulfillment. We try to avoid sex and partisan politics." Length: 600 to 2,500 words with greater need for short manuscripts. Pays $50 to $300, sometimes more for complex assignments.

CREDIT UNION LIFE, Division of Modern Communications, Inc., 409 S. Barstow Commons, Eau Claire WI 54701. (715)832-4934. Editor-in-Chief: Stephen A. Franzmeier. Quarterly magazine; 64 pages. Estab. 1977. Circ. 40,000. Pays on acceptance. Buys one-time rights. Phone queries OK. Submit seasonal/holiday material 2 months in advance. Photocopied submissions OK. SASE. Reports in 1 week. Free writer's guidelines.
Nonfiction: Informational (fresh subject matter, offbeat angle, upper Midwest locale); interview (remarkable philosophies of life, spectacular achievement by an unsung and unusual personality); personal experience (escapist in nature); photo feature (people at work, body language, facial expressions, gestures are important); profile (unique but unknown personalities, men or women great in their own domain); pieces on non-ordinary life styles and leisure-time activities. Buys 2/issue. Send complete ms. Length: 750-1,500 words. Pays $200-250.
Photos: Purchased without mss. Captions required. Send contact sheet. Pays $30-50/5x7 or 8x10 b&w glossy; $45-65/35mm or 4x5 or 2¼x2¼ color transparency.
Columns/Departments: Ms. Lucille Schaff, Department Editor. Strange and Unexplained column buys 750 words/issue. Send complete ms. Length: 500-750. Pays $100-175. Open to suggestions for new columns/departments.
How To Break In: "Send a people-centered article that deals with people who live in Wisconsin, but not Milwaukee residents. Column ideas are in particular demand. We need columns about leisure-time activities that appeal to a large proportion of the population."

THE DEAF CANADIAN MAGAZINE, Box 1291, Edmonton, Alta., Canada T5J 2M8. Editor-in-Chief: David Burnett. For "general consumers who are deaf, parents of deaf children/adults, professionals on deafness, teachers, ministers, and government officials." Bimonthly magazine; 24 pages. Estab. 1972. Circ. 125,000. Pays on publication. "Although the publication is copyrighted, we do not purchase any rights which are reserved to the individual contributor." Submit seasonal/holiday material 2 months in advance. Simultaneous, photocopied and previously published submissions OK. SASE. Reports in 4 months. Sample copy $1; free writer's guidelines.
Nonfiction: Expose (education), how-to (skills, jobs, etc.), historical, humor, informational (deafness difficulties), inspirational, interview, new product, personal experience, personal opinion, photo feature (with captions), profile, technical and travel. "Mss must relate to deafness or the deaf world." Buys 1-10 mss/issue. Submit complete ms. Length: 3,000 words maximum. Pays $20-75. "Articles should be illustrated with at least 4 good b&w photos."
Photos: Purchased with accompanying ms or on assignment. Captions required (not less than 25 words). Query. Pays $5 for 5x7 b&w glossy or matte finish photos; $20 for color transparencies used as cover. Total purchase price for ms includes payment for photos.
Columns/Departments: Here and There, Sports and Recreation, Foreign, Cultural Events and Books. Submit complete ms. Length: 1 page maximum. Pays $25-100. Open to suggestions for new columns/departments.
Fiction: Adventure, experimental, historical, humorous, mystery, mainstream, religious, romance, science fiction, suspense, condensed novels, and serialized novels. Buys 1-10 mss/issue. Length: 3,000 words maximum. Pays $25-100.
Fillers: Clippings, jokes, gags, anecdotes, newsbreaks, puzzles, and short humor. Must be related to deafness or the deaf world. Buys 1-20 mss/issue. Submit complete ms. Length: ½ page maximum. Pays $5-30.

DIRECTORS & BOARDS, The Journal of Corporate Action, Information for Industry Inc., 1621 Brookside Rd., McLean VA 22101. (703)534-7771. Editor-in-Chief: Stanley Foster Reed. Emphasizes corporate decisionmaking at board level. Quarterly magazine; 64 pages. Estab. 1976. Circ. 3,000. Pays 21 days after publication. Buys all rights. Photocopied submissions OK. SASE. Reports in 4-6 weeks. Free sample copy and writer's guidelines.
Nonfiction: Sue Duncan, senior editor. "*D&B* article topics usually fall into one of three categories: (a) specific, detailed ideas (generally from seasoned directors) for improving board

function, structure, or performance; (b) analyses of legal, social, or industrial developments in the U.S. or abroad, examined from the perspective of evolving board responsibilities; (c) board considerations of subjects that come before directors for review and/or approval—for example, long-range strategic planning, executive succession and compensation, corporate performance appraisals, compliance audits, shareholder relations, annual reports, disclosure standards, corporate social responsibilities, etc." Buys 20 mss/year. Length: 5,000-15,000 words. Pays $100-$1,000, depending on length of article, amount of research involved, and stature of author.

EL EXCENTRICO MAGAZINE, Garcia Enterprises, 274 Terraine St., San Jose CA 95110. (408)294-4040. Editor/Publisher: Bert Garcia. "Our audience is almost exclusively Mexican-American, family-orientated, non-radical, lower to middle income, conscious of Chicano strife. We distribute in Santa Clara County CA." Biweekly magazine; 40 pages. Estab. 1949. Circ. 20,000. Pays on publication. Buys simultaneous, second serial and one-time rights. Submit seasonal/holiday material 2 months in advance. Simultaneous, photocopied and previously published submissions OK. SASE. Free sample copy and writer's guidelines.
Nonfiction: Historical (of interest to Mexican-Americans), humor, informational (on any Chicano-related issue), inspirational (written by a Hispanic), interview (any prominent Latino, local or national), foods (Mexican recipes), personal experience (personal struggle as a Chicano), photo feature (Mexican politicians or related news events), profile, sports, and travel (Mexico, Spain, Latin America). Buys 50-75 mss/year. Submit complete ms. Length: 50-1,000 words. Pays $5-60.
Photos: Purchased with accompanying ms. Captions required. Query. Pays $5-15 for 4x5 or 8x10 b&w photos. Model release required.
Columns/Departments: Profiles of prominent Chicanos, Foods (Mexican recipes), Movies, and interviews with successful Chicanos, business or political. Buys 50-100 mss/year. Submit complete ms. Length: 250-750 words. Pays $5-50. Open to suggestions for new columns/ departments.
Poetry: "Poems must be relating to issues concerning Mexican-Americans." Buys 5 poems/ year. Pays $5-20.
How To Break In: "In the past we have dealt with local people and issues. We are now expanding our coverage to include state and national concerns. Additionally, we are interested in regular departments such as Foods, Music, News Brief; this is an excellent opportunity for interested writers because we are very much in need of their services."

FAR WEST, Box 2260 Costa Mesa CA 92626. (714)979-2560. Editor-in-Chief: Scott R. McMillan. 100% freelance written. Emphasizes western fiction set before 1920. Monthly magazine; 126 pages. Estab. February 1977. Circ. 150,000. Pays on publication by contract. Buys all rights, but may reassign following publication. Phone queries OK. Submit seasonal/holiday material 6 months in advance of issue date. Previously published submissions OK. SASE. Reports in 8-12 weeks. Sample copy $1.25; writer's guidelines for SASE.
Fiction: Western (tightly written, action packed westerns set in the period 1830-1920). No animal stories, range romances, avant garde writing styles, sex-in-the-sage brush, and poetry or fictionalized accounts of true incidents or real people. Buys 80 mss/year. Submit complete ms. Length: 2,000-35,000 words. Pays $150 minimum.

FIREHOUSE MAGAZINE, 33 E. 53rd, New York NY 10022. (212)935-4550. Editor-in-Chief: Dennis Smith. 75% freelance written. For volunteer firefighters, as well as paid firefighters and their families. Monthly magazine; 72 pages. Estab. 1976. Circ. 100,000. Pays on publication. Buys all rights, but may reassign following publication. Submit seasonal or holiday material 4 months in advance. Photocopied submissions OK. SASE. Reports in 6 weeks. Sample copy $1.50. Free writer's guidelines.
Nonfiction: How-to (firefighting); informational (family activities); historical (great fires); profiles (achieving firefighters); new product; personal experience (firefighting); photo features (recent fires); technical (fire science and medicine); and stories on recent large and unusual fires or disasters involving firefighters. Buys 120 mss/year. Query. Length: 1,000-2,000 words. Pays 10¢/word.
Photos: Purchased with or without ms, or on assignment. Captions required. Query. Pays $10-25 for 8x10 glossies or color transparencies.

JOURNAL OF GRAPHOANALYSIS, 325 W. Jackson Blvd., Chicago IL 60606. Editor: V. Peter Ferrara. For audience interested in self-improvement. Monthly. Buys all rights. Pays on acceptance. Reports on submissions in 1 month. Enclose S.A.S.E.
Nonfiction: Self-improvement material helpful for ambitious, alert, mature people. Applied

psychology and personality studies, techniques of effective living, etc.; all written from intellectual approach by qualified writers in psychology, counseling and teaching, preferably with degrees. Length: 2,000 words. Pays about 5¢ a word.

MASTHEAD, Box 1009, Marblehead MA 01945. (617)581-0198. Editor-in-Chief: Walter A. Day, Jr. "A journal for teaching history with old newspapers" for teachers, genealogists, collectors and people interested in printing, journalism and general history. Tabloid; 9 times/year; 20 pages. Estab. 1977. Circ. 6,000. Pays on publication. Not copyrighted. Phone queries OK. Simultaneous, photocopied, and previously published submissions OK. SASE. Reports in 2 weeks. Sample copy $1.
Nonfiction: Informational; historical; humor (in historical vein); interviews (with people in history field); nostalgia, profile; travel; personal experience. Length: 500-5,000 words. Query. Pays 1¢/word.
Photos: Used with mss with no additional payment for 5x7 glossies. Model release required.
Columns/Departments: Open Forum (letters on developments in printing, journalism and collecting history); The Hidden Side to History (articles tracing the original, firsthand account in a newspaper of an historical event tempered with a current perspective). Length: 100-750 words. Pays 1¢/word. Open to suggestions for new columns/departments.

THE NEW HARBINGER: A Journal of the Cooperative Movement, NASCO, Box 1301, Ann Arbor MI 48106. (313)663-0889. Editor-in-Chief: Margaret Lamb. Managing Editor: Jonathan Klein. Emphasizes consumer cooperatives. Readership is mostly consumer co-op members and leaders, and others interested in social change. Quarterly magazine; 64 pages. Estab. 1971. Circ. 2,000. Pays on publication. Buys all rights, but may reassign following publication. Phone queries OK. Simultaneous, photocopied, and previously published submissions OK. SASE. Sample copy $1; free writer's guidelines.
Nonfiction: Interview, personal opinion; personal experience; technical; investigative reporting; and theory analysis. "We want articles on all types of consumer cooperatives, their activities and initiatives." Buys 5 mss/year. Query. Length: 1,000-4,000 words. Pays $10-50.

THE NEW YORK ANTIQUE ALMANAC, The New York Eye Publishing Co., Inc., Box 335, Lawrence NY 11559. (516)371-3300. Editor-in-Chief: Carol Nadel. Emphasizes antiques, art, investments, nostalgia for an audience above average in income and intelligence. Monthly tabloid; 24 pages. Estab. 1975. Circ. 18,000. Pays on publication. Buys all rights, but may reassign following publication. Phone queries OK. Submit seasonal/holiday material "whenever available." Previously published submissions OK. SASE. Reports in 4 weeks. Free sample copy.
Nonfiction: Expose (fradulent practices), historical (museums, exhibitions, folklore, background of events), how-to (clean, restore, travel, shop, invest), humor (jokes, cartoons, satire), informational, inspirational (essays), interviews (authors, shopkeepers, show managers, appraisers), nostalgia ("The Good Old Days" remembered various ways), personal experience (anything dealing with antiques, art, investments, nostalgia), personal opinion, photo feature (antique shows, art shows, fairs, crafts markets, restorations), profile, technical (repairing, purchasing, restoring), travel (shopping guides and tips) and investment, economics, and financial reviews. Buys 9 mss/issue. Query or submit complete ms. Length: 3,000 words maximum. Pays $15-35. "Expenses for accompanying photos will be reimbursed."
Photos: "Occasionally, we have photo essays (auctions, shows, street fairs, human interest) and pay $3/photo with caption."
Fillers: Jokes, gags, anecdotes. "Limited only by author's imagination." Buys 45 mss/year. Pays $5-15.

THE NEWS CIRCLE, Box 74637, Los Angeles CA 90004. (213)469-7004. Editor: Joe Haiek. For Arab Americans. Monthly newspaper; 16 pages. Estab. 1972. Circ. 5,000. Not copyrighted. Buys 18 to 35 mss/year. Payment on publication. Free sample copy. Will consider photocopied and simultaneous submissions. Reports in 1 week. Query first with title of proposed article. SASE.
Nonfiction, Photos and Fillers: Wants mss about Middle East issues; mainly business, and economic conditions. Would like to see mss on Mideast business conferences and expos. Length: 400 words maximum. Pays 5¢ to 10¢. Photos purchased with accompanying ms with extra payment and purchased on assignment. Captions required. Pays $5 to $10. Also buys newsbreaks, clippings on Mideast business. Pays 10¢ to 15¢ a word.

NUESTRO: THE MAGAZINE FOR LATINOS, 1140 Avenue of the Americas, New York NY

10036. Editor-in-Chief: Charles R. Rivera. Managing Editors: José Ferrer III, Philip Herrera. 85% freelance written. Monthly magazine; 64 pages. Estab. April 1977. Circ. 150,000. Pays on publication. Buys all rights, but may reassign following publication. Phone queries OK. Photocopied submissions OK. SASE. Reports in 6 weeks. Free sample copy and writer's guidelines; mention *Writer's Market* in request.
Nonfiction: General interest material relating to Latinos living in US. Query or submit complete ms. Length: 750-3,000 words. Pays $50-500.
Photos: Donna Nicholson, photo editor. State availability of photos with query or ms. Pays $50-100 for 8x10 b&w semi-glossy prints; $75-150 for 35mm color transparencies. Buys first North American serial rights. Model release "preferred, but it depends on the situation."
Columns/Departments: Yesterday (articles on events of recent or distant past); Travel; Fashions; Food; Beauty Tips; and Reviews (books, movies, and arts). "All material must relate directly to Latinos." Query or submit complete ms. Length: 500-2,000 words. Pays $35-100/printed page. Open to suggestions for new columns/departments.
Fiction: "Submissions must be in English, of high quality and have a Latino slant." No erotica. Query or submit complete ms. Length: 2,000-3,000 words. Pays $100/printed page.

PILLOW TALK, 208 E. 43rd St., New York NY 10017. Editorial Director: Jesse James Leaf. 100% freelance written. "For people interested in all areas of human relationships—meetings, dating, arguing, making up, sex (in all aspects). We're a light, fun, but helpful and reliable publication—a counselor, a friend, a shoulder to lean on, and an entertainment." Monthly magazine; 96 pages. Estab. July 1976. Pays on publication. Buys all rights, but may reassign following publication. Simultaneous and photocopied submissions OK. SASE. Reports in 1 week. Sample copy $1; free writer's guidelines for SASE; mention *Writer's Market* in request.
Nonfiction: How-to (romantic and sexual techniques, meeting new people, handling relationships, overcoming emotional hurdles); humor (sexual, romantic); interview (maybe in rare cases); personal experience (sexual/romantic scenarios if they illustrate a specific topic); and technical (lightly done on sexual topics). "No out-and-out pornography." Buys 11 mss/issue. Query. Length: 1,000-3,000 words. Pays $80-300.
Photos: State availability of photos with query. Pays $25-50 for b&w; $250 for color covers. Buys all rights, but may reassign following publication. Model release required.
Columns/Departments: Different Strokes. Buys 1 ms/issue. Query or submit clips of previously published work. Length: 1,250 words. Pays $100. Open to suggestions for new columns/departments.
Fiction: "All must have sensual/sexual under current or feel." Adventure; confession; erotica; fantasy; historical; humorous; mainstream; mystery; romance; science fiction; suspense; and western. "No straight pornography or anything without sensual/sexual attraction." Buys 1 ms/issue. Query. Length: 6,000-7,750 words. Pays $300.
Fillers: Clippings and newsbreaks (funny, unusual relating to the broad area of sex). Buys 6 clippings/issue. Pays $5.

PRACTICAL KNOWLEDGE, 325 W. Jackson Blvd., Chicago IL 60606. Editor: Lee Arnold. Bimonthly. A self-advancement magazine for active and involved men and women. Buys all rights, "but we are happy to cooperate with our authors." Pays on acceptance. Reports in 2 to 3 weeks. SASE.
Nonfiction and Photos: Uses success stories of famous people, past or present; applied psychology; articles on mental hygiene and personality by qualified writers with proper degrees to make subject matter authoritative. Also human interest stories with an optimistic tone. Up to 5,000 words. Photographs and drawings are used when helpful. Pays a base rate of 5¢ a word; $10 each for illustrations.

READERS REVIEW, The National Research Bureau, Inc., 424 N. 3rd St., Burlington IA 52601. Editor-in-Chief: B. Pollard. Managing Editor: R. Walker. 95% freelance written. "For industrial workers of all ages." Bimonthly magazine; 32 pages. Estab. 1956. Circ. 45,000. Pays on publication. Buys all rights, but may reassign following publication. Previously published submissions OK. SASE. Reports in 1 week. Free sample copy and writer's guidelines; mention *Writer's Market* in request.
Nonfiction: R. Wilson, editor. General interest (steps to better health, attitudes on the job); how-to (perform better on the job, do home repairs, car maintenance); and travel. Buys 4-5 mss/issue. Query with outline. Length: 400-1,000 words. Pays $20.

REVIEW, Center for Inter-American Relations, 680 Park Ave., New York NY 10021. (212)249-8950. Editor-in-Chief: Ronald Christ. Emphasizes "views, reviews, interviews, news

on Latin-American literature and arts." Published spring, fall, and winter. Magazine; 95 pages. Estab. 1968. Circ. 2,000. Pays on publication. Buys all rights, but may reassign following publication. Phone queries OK. Previously published submissions OK (if originally published in Spanish). Reports in 2 months. Free sample copy.
Nonfiction: Interview, personal opinion, personal experience, literary essays on Latin American authors, art, film. Buys 30 mss/year. Length: 8-14 pages. Pays $35-75.
Fiction: "All types—but has to be by Latin Americans." Buys 3/issue. Query. No length requirement. Pays $6.50/1,000 words.
Poetry: Uses all types. Buys 3/issue. Limit submissions to batches of 3.

ROSICRUCIAN DIGEST, Rosicrucian Order, AMORC, Rosicrucian Park, San Jose CA 95191. (408)287-9171, ext. 213. Editor-in-Chief: Robin M. Thompson. 50-60% freelance written. Emphasizes mysticism, science, the arts. For "men and women of all ages, many well-educated, and into alternative answers to life's questions." Monthly magazine; 40 pages. Estab. 1916. Circ. 70,000. Pays on acceptance. Buys first rights and rights to reprint. Phone queries OK. Submit seasonal or holiday material 5 months in advance. Photocopied and previously published submissions OK. SASE. Reports on submissions in 4 weeks. Free sample copy and writer's guidelines.
Nonfiction: How-to (deal with life's problems and opportunities in a positive and constructive manner); informational (new ideas and developments in science, the arts, philosophy, and thinking), historical (biographies, historical sketches, human interest), inspirational (no religion articles—we are looking for articles with a constructive, uplifting outlook; philosophical approach to problem solving), interview (occasionally, but we would definitely have to work with author on this), philosophy, psychology. Buys 40-50 mss a year. Query. Length: 1,000-1,700 words. Pays 4¢/word for first rights.
Photos: Purchased with accompanying ms. Send prints. Pays $3 per 8x10 b&w glossy.
Fillers: Short inspirational or uplifting (not religious) anecdotes or experiences. Buys 6 a year. Query. Length: 25-250 words. Pays 2¢/word.
How To Break In: "Be specific about what you want to write about—the subject you want to explore—and be willing to work with editor. Articles should appeal to worldwide circulation.
Rejects: Religious, political, or articles promoting a particular group or system of thought.

SAVING ENERGY, Box 75837 Sanford Station, Los Angeles CA 90075. (213)874-1453. Editor/Publisher: Larry Liebman. 20% freelance written. Emphasizes energy conservation, ideas and case histories aimed at business, industry and commerce. Monthly newsletter; 8 pages. Estab. February 1977. Pays on acceptance. Buys all rights. Phone queries OK. SASE. Reports in 2 weeks. Free writer's guidelines.
Nonfiction: "I need good, tightly written case histories on how industry and commerce are saving energy, listing problems and solutions. The item should present an original energy saving idea. Include full name and address of business so readers can contact for follow-up." How-to (conserving energy, what the problem was, how it was resolved, cost, how fast the payback was, etc.); and technical (case histories). Buys 5 mss/issue. Submit complete ms. Length: 200-800 words. Pays $10-25.

SCANDINAVIAN REVIEW, American-Scandinavian Foundation, 127 E. 73rd St., New York NY 10021. (212)879-9779. Editor-in-Chief: Nadia Christensen. "The majority of our readership is over 30, well educated, and in the middle income bracket. Most similar to readers of *Smithsonian* and *Saturday Review*. Have interest in Scandinavia by birth or education." Quarterly magazine; 112 pages. Estab. 1913. Circ. 7,000. Pays on publication. Buys all rights. Submit seasonal/holiday material 9 months in advance. Previously published material (if published abroad) OK. SASE. Reports in 1 month. Sample copy $3. Free writer's guidelines.
Nonfiction: Historical, informational, interview, photo feature and travel. "Modern life and culture in Scandinanvia." Buys 35 mss/year. Send complete ms. Length: maximum 2,500 words. Pays $50-100.
Photos: Purchased with accompanying ms. Captions required. Submit prints or transparencies. Prefers sharp, high contrast b&w enlargements. Total purchase price for ms includes payment for photos.
Fiction: Adventure, fantasy, historical. Prefers work translated from the Scandinavian. Buys 8 mss/year. Send complete ms. Length: 2,000 words maximum. Pays $50-100.
Poetry: Translations of contemporary Scandinavian poetry and original poems with a Scandinavian theme. Buys 5-15 poems/year. Pays $10.

SELECTED READING, The National Research Bureau, Inc., 424 N. 3rd St., Burlington IA

52601. Editor-in-Chief: Barbara Pollard. Managing Editor: Ronald Walker. 95% freelance written. For industrial workers of all ages. Bimonthly magazine; 16 pages. Estab. 1956. Circ. 35,000. Pays on publication. Buys all rights, but may reassign following publication. Submit seasonal/holiday material 2 months in advance of issue date. Previously published submissions OK. SASE. Reports in 1 week. Free sample copy and writer's guidelines; mention *Writer's Market* in request.
Nonfiction: Barbara Boeding, articles editor. General interest (economics, health, safety, working relationships); how-to; and travel. Buys 2-3 mss/issue. Query with outline. Length: 400-600 words. Pays $20 minimum.

SMITHSONIAN MAGAZINE, 900 Jefferson Drive, Washington DC 20560. Editor: Edward K. Thompson. For "associate members of the Smithsonian Institution; 85% with college education." Monthly. Circ. 1,500,000. "Our material is automatically copyrighted. In the case of selling off second rights, *Smithsonian* keeps half, gives the rest to writer. Payment for each article to be negotiated depending on our needs and the article's length and excellence." Pays "first half on assignment or tentative acceptance, remainder on scheduling." Submit seasonal material 3 months in advance. Reports "as soon as possible." Query first. SASE.
Nonfiction: "Our mandate from the Smithsonian Institution says we are to be interested in the same things which now interest or should interest the Institution: folk and fine arts, history, natural sciences, hard sciences, etc." Length and payment "to be negotiated."
Photos: Purchased with or without ms and on assignment. Captions required. Pays "$300 a color page, $250 b&w."

STEREO, ABC Leisure Magazines, Inc., The Publishing House, State Rd., Great Barrington MA 01230. (413)528-1300. Editor-in-Chief: John W.P. Mooney. 10% freelance written. Emphasizes high quality home audio equipment. Quarterly magazine; 96 pages. Estab. 1960. Circ. 50,000. Pays on acceptance. Buys all rights. Phone queries OK. Submit seasonal/holiday material 6 months in advance. Photocopied submissions OK. SASE. Reports in 2 weeks. Free writer's guidelines.
Nonfiction: How-to (technically expert articles dealing with audio equipment), humor, interview (with personalities in audio field) and technical (workings of audio equipment). Buys 1-2 mss/year. Query. Length: 2,000-5,000 words. Pays 8¢-10/word.
How To Break In: "We are interested in the small minority of freelancers who are genuine audio experts with the training and experience that qualifies them to write with real authority. *Stereo* is almost entirely staff-written. At the moment, we buy very few manuscripts. However, we would buy more if material meeting our very high technical standards were available. Because every issue is themed to a specific aspect of audio, and all articles are written on assignment, it is *imperative* that freelancers query us before writing."
Rejects: "We are not interested in record buffs with 'golden ears'."

SUCCESS UNLIMITED, 6355 Broadway, Chicago IL 60660. Contact: Editor. "Average reader is 25-40, married with 2 children; working in professional, sales or management capacity; college educated (85%), with a strong motivation to go into business for himself. Financially, he's doing fine—but wants to do even better." Monthly magazine; 95-128 pages. Estab. 1954. Circ. 180,000. Pays on acceptance. Rights purchased vary with author and material. Free sample copy and writer's guidelines. SASE.
Nonfiction: "Our publication continues to stress the importance of a positive mental attitude (PMA) in all areas of endeavor." Uses material on self-motivation and the psychology of success; profiles of business leaders and successful (not necessarily wealthy) persons of all types—especially individuals who have overcome adversity to achieve success. How-to articles on entrepreneurship, management techniques, health, moneymaking ideas and investments. Length: 500-2,500 words. Pays 10¢/word. Query.

VEGETARIAN TIMES, Box A3104, Chicago IL 60690. Editor: Paul Obis, Jr. For "non meat eaters and people interested in organic food. Well educated, sincere, ecologically minded. Interests in do-it-yourself food preservation, preparation, cooking, growing, and with a compassion for animals other than homo sapiens." Monthly magazine; 60 pages. Estab. 1973. Circ. 10,000. Rights purchased vary with author and material. Will reassign all rights to author after publication, or will buy first serial or simultaneous rights. Buys 50 mss/year. Pays on acceptance. Sample copy $1. Will consider photocopied and simultaneous submissions. Submit seasonal material 2 to 3 months in advance. Reports in 8 weeks. Query first. Enclose SASE.
Nonfiction and Photos: Features concise articles related to "vegetarianism (cooking, humanism, pacifism), environment, self-sufficiency, animal welfare and liberation, articles about vegeta-

rian nutrition — all material should be well-documented and researched. It would probably be best to see a sample copy — remember that despite our name, we are beholden to our readers and we do not want the health food stores to sell more vitamins. We are not in the business of selling health foods. We are strongly pro consumer and this means making your own Granola. We are not interested in personal pet stories or wonder cure all foods.'' Informational, how-to, personal experience, interview, profile, historical, expose, personal opinion, successful health food business operations, and restaurant reviews. Length: 500 to 3,000 words. Pays 1¢ per word minimum. Will also use 500- to 1,000-word items for regular columns. Pays $10 apiece. Pays $5 total for photos purchased with accompanying ms. No color; b&w ferrotype preferred.

WEIRD TRIPS, Krupp Comic Works, Inc., Box 7, Princeton WI 54968. (414)295-3972. Editor-in-Chief: Denis Kitchen. Emphasizes the bizarre and exotic for young and ''hip'' audience. Annual magazine; 48 pages. Estab. 1971. Circ. 25,000. Pays on acceptance. Buys all rights, but may reassign following publication. Phone queries OK. Simultaneous, photocopied, and previously published submissions OK. SASE. Reports in 2 weeks. Sample copy $1.50, postpaid.
Nonfiction: Expose (government, institutions, Army); historical and humor (relating to hip and drug culture); profile (subculture figures); travel (to exotic places—Nepal, etc.); new product (if unusual); personal experience (UFO's, drugs, bizarre sex); photo feature (of bizarre nature). Buys 6-8/issue. Query or submit complete ms. Pays $25-400.
Photos: Michael Jacobi, Department Editor. Purchased with or without mss. Captions required. Send b&w prints. Query for color. Pays $10-30 for 8x10 b&w glossies. Model release required.
How To Break In: ''By offering items usually too bizarre or offbeat to be accepted in most other publications, but writing must be of good quality as well.''

WESTERN & EASTERN TREASURES, People's Publishing, Inc., 1440 W. Walnut St., Box 7030, Compton CA 90224. (213)537-0896. Managing Editor: Ray Krupa. Emphasizes treasure hunting for all ages, entire range in education, coast-to-coast readership. Monthly magazine; 68 pages. Estab. 1966. Circ. 70,000. Pays on publication. Buys all rights, but may reassign rights to author following publication. SASE. Reports in 2-3 weeks. Free sample copy and writer's guidelines.
Nonfiction: How-to (use of equipment, how to look for rocks, gems, prospect for gold, where to look for treasures, rocks, etc., ''first person'' experiences). Buys 150 mss/year. Submit complete ms. Length: maximum 1,500 words. Pays maximum 2¢ per word.
Photos: Purchased with accompanying ms. Captions required. Submit prints or transparencies. Pays $5 maximum for 3x5 and up b&w glossies; $10 maximum for 35mm and up color transparencies. Model release required.
Columns/Departments: Treasures in the Headlines, Look What They Found, Off Road/This & That and Around the Campfire. Buys 50/year. Send complete ms. Length: 800-1,500 words. Pays maximum 2¢ per word. Open to suggestions from freelancers for new columns or departments; address Ray Krupa.

WHAT MAKES PEOPLE SUCCESSFUL, The National Research Bureau, Inc., 424 N. 3rd St., Burlington IA 52601. Editor-in-Chief: Barbara Pollard. Managing Editor: Ronald Walker. 95% freelance written. For ''industrial workers of all ages.'' Published 3 times/year. Magazine; 16 pages. Estab. 1951. Circ. 30,000. Pays on publication. Buys all rights, but may reassign following publication. Submit seasonal/holiday material 3-4 months in advance of issue date. Previously published submissions OK. SASE. Reports in 1 week. Free sample copy and writer's guidelines; mention *Writer's Market* in request.
Nonfiction: How-to (be successful); general interest (personality, employee morale, guides to successful living, biographies of successful persons, etc.); personal experience; personal opinion; and travel. Buys 2-3 mss/issue. Query with outline. Length: 400-600 words. Pays $20.

THE WITTENBURG DOOR, 861 Sixth Ave., Suite 411, San Diego CA 92101. (714)234-6454. Editor: Denny Rydberg. For men and women, usually connected with the church. Bimonthly magazine; 36 pages. Estab. 1968. Circ. 9,100. Buys all rights, but may reassign rights to author after publication. Buys about 12 mss/year. Payment on publication. Free sample copy. Reports in 2 weeks. Query first or submit complete ms. SASE.
Nonfiction: Articles on church renewal, the Christian life, book reviews, satire and humor. Length: 2,500 word maximum. Pays $15 to $40.

Music Publications

ACCENT Magazine, 1418 Lake St., Evanston IL 60204. (312)328-6000. Editor: Elizabeth F. von Bergen. 80% freelance written. ''Our readers are serious junior and senior high school musi-

cians. The magazine focuses on styles of music ranging from classical to jazz." Published bimonthly during the school year. Magazine; 32 pages. Estab. January 1976. Pays on publication. Buys all rights, but may reassign following publication. Phone queries OK. Submit seasonal/holiday material at least 3 months in advance of issue date. Photocopied submissions OK. SASE. Reports in 8 weeks. Free sample copy and writer's guidelines; mention *Writer's Market* in request.
Nonfiction: General interest (areas of music relating to young musicians, including interviews with artists); historical (some areas of musc history, not straight biography of Bach, Mozart, etc.); how-to (improve playing technique, take care of instruments, enjoy music more); humor (anything relating to the experience of a high school musician); interview (performers, composers, teac ers); photo feature (featuring a musical event or process, such as building an instrument); and technical (Checking Out Colleges column features one music school/issue). "No condescending articles for grade-school level students. Emphasis is on instrumental and piano students. Articles shouldn't be written like a textbook—they should be lively and practical." Buys 40 mss/year. Query or submit complete ms. Pays $20/magazine page.
Photos: "Good photos can be helpful, although they're not essential. Payment is calculated into overall payment for article." Submit color transparencies. Captions preferred. Buys all rights, but may reassign following publication.
Columns/Departments: Checking Out Colleges (features 1 college or music school/issue); Good Vibrations (a potpourri column of newsbriefs, musical jokes and puzzles, new product descriptions, and book and record reviews); and Musical Brain Teaser (a full-page music note puzzle). Query for College reviews, submit complete ms for others. Length: 1,000-2,500 words. Pays $5 minimum; "College profiles and Musical Brain Teasers are paid at same rate as articles."

AUDIO MAGAZINE, 401 N. Broad St., Philadelphia PA 19108. Editor: Gene Pitts. For persons interested in high fidelity components, electronics and music. Monthly magazine; 120 pages. Estab. 1947. Circ. 130,000. Buys all rights. Buys about 15 mss/year. Pays on publication. Free sample copy. Will consider photocopied submissions. No simultaneous submissions. Reports in 3 to 6 weeks. Query recommended, but not required. SASE.
Nonfiction and Photos: Articles on hi-fi equipment, design technique, hi-fi history; explanations for buffs and of widely known commercial uses. Pays $35 per published page minimum. No additional payment made for photos used with mss.

AUDIOSCENE CANADA, MacLean-Hunter, Ltd., 481 University Ave., Toronto, Ontario, Canada M5W 1A7. (416)595-1811. Editor-in-Chief: Ian G. Masters. 50% freelance written. Emphasizes high fidelity and music. Monthly magazine; 60 pages. Estab. 1964. Circ. 25,000. Pays on publication. Buys all rights, but may reassign following publication. Submit seasonal/holiday material 2 months in advance. SASE. Reports in 4 weeks. Free sample copy; mention *Writer's Market* in request.
Nonfiction: How-to (must have first-hand technical knowledge); interview; and technical. Buys 6-8 mss/year. Query. Length: 1,500-2,500 words. Pays 10¢/word.
Photos: Wants photos for personality pieces and appropriate artwork for technical material. Pays $15 minimum for 4x5 or 8x10 b&w glossy prints. Captions preferred. Buys all rights. Model release required.

BLUEGRASS UNLIMITED, Box 111, Broad Run VA 22014. (703)361-8992. Editor-in-Chief: Peter V. Kuykendall. Managing Editor: Marion C. Kuykendall. 50% freelance written. Emphasizes old-time traditional country music for musicians and devotees of bluegrass, ages from teens through the elderly. Monthly magazine; 48 pages. Estab. 1966. Circ. 14,000. Pays on publication. Buys all rights, but may reassign to author following publication. Phone queries OK. Submit seasonal/holiday material 2-3 months in advance. Photocopied and previously published submissions OK. SASE. Reports in 1 month. Free sample copy and writer's guidelines.
Nonfiction: Historical, how-to, humor, informational, interview, nostalgia, personal experience, personal opinion, photo feature, profile and technical. Buys 20-40 mss/year. Query. Length: 500-5,000 words. Pays 3½-4¢/word.
Photos: Purchased with or without accompanying ms. Query for photos. Pays $15-20/page for 5x7 or 8x10 b&w glossies, 35mm or 2¼ color transparencies; $40 for covers.
Columns, Departments: Record and book reviews. Buys 5-10/year. Query. Length: 100-500 words. Pays 3½-4¢/word.
Fiction: Adventure and humorous. Buys 5-7 mss/year. Length: 500-2,500 words. Pays 3½-4¢/word.

CONCERT LIFE, Box 1152, Mechanicsburg PA 17055. (717)766-2901. Editor: Cheri. 10% freelance written. Emphasizes gospel music. Bimonthly magazine; 48 pages. Estab. 1974. Buys all rights, but may reassign following publication. Submit seasonal/holiday material 2-4 months in advance. Simultaneous submissions OK. SASE. Reports in 6 months. Sample copy 30¢ (stamps only).
Nonfiction: Informational; inspirational; interview; nostalgia (in gospel field); and personal experience. Buys 5 mss/issue. Query. Length: 600-1,000 words. Pays $5 minimum.
Fiction: Religious. Query. Length: 600-1,000 words. Pays $5 minimum.

CONTEMPORARY KEYBOARD MAGAZINE, The GPI Corp., Box 615, Saratoga CA 95070. (408)446-3220. Editor: Tom Darter. For those who play piano, organ, synthesizer, accordion, harpsichord, or any other keyboard instrument. All styles of music; all levels of ability. Monthly magazine; 68 pages. Estab. 1975. Circ. 54,000. Pays on acceptance. Buys all rights. Phone queries OK. SASE. Reports in 1 week. Free sample copy and writer's guidelines.
Nonfiction: "We publish articles on a wide variety of topics pertaining to keyboard players and their instruments. In addition to interviews with keyboard artists in all styles of music, we are interested in historical and analytical pieces, how-to articles dealing either with music or with equipment, profiles or well-known instrument makers and their products. In general, anything that amateur and professional keyboardists would find interesting and/or useful." Buys 6-7 mss/issue. Query. Length: 8-20 double-spaced pages. Pays $50-125.
Photos: Purchased with or without accompanying ms. Captions required. Pays $25-40 for 5x7 or 8x10 b&w glossies; $100 for 35mm transparencies (for cover).

CORNHUSKER COUNTRY, Box 42, Louisville NE 68037. Editor: Robert Everhart. 50% freelance written. Emphasizes traditional country music. Monthly magazine; 36 pages. Estab. 1976. Circ. 2,000. Pays on acceptance. Buys one-time rights. Submit seasonal/holiday material 3 months in advance of issue date. Simultaneous, photocopied and previously published submissions OK. SASE. Reports in 4 weeks. Free sample copy.
Nonfiction: Historical (relating to country music); how-to (play, write, or perform country music); inspirational (on country gospel); interview (with country performers, both traditional and contemporary); nostalgia (pioneer living); personal experience (country music); and travel (in connection with country music contests or festivals). Buys 6 mss/year. Query. Length: 200-2,000 words. Pays $20-50.
Photos: State availability of photos with query. Payment is included in ms price. Uses 5x7 b&w prints. Captions and model release required. Buys one-time rights.
Poetry: Free verse and traditional. Buys 1/issue. Length: 3-15 lines. Limit submissions to batches of 3. Pays in copies.

COUNTRY MUSIC MAGAZINE, KBO Publishers, 475 Park Ave., S., New York NY 10016. Editor-in-Chief: Michael Bane. 80% freelance written. Monthly magazine; 64 pages. Estab. September 1972. Circ. 211,000. Pays on publication. Buys all rights, but may reassign following publication. Submit seasonal/holiday material at least 4 months in advance of issue date. Photocopied and previously published (book excerpts) OK. SASE. Reports in 3-4 weeks. Free sample copy and writer's guidelines.
Nonfiction: General interest (about country music or subjects of interest to a country music audience); humor (some, but must be taken article by article); historical (about music, items of interest to our audience); interview (country artist, craftsman, etc.); photo feature; profile; and travel. Buys 6-10 mss/issue. Query with clips of previously published work. Length: 1,500-3,500 words. Pays $250-400.
Photos: Cheh Nam Low, photo editor. State availability of photos with query. Pays $25/b&w photos; $50/35mm color transparencies. Captions required. Buys all rights, but may reassign following publication.
Columns/Departments: Record reviews. Buys 5-10/issue. Query. Length: 100-250 words. Pays $25.

COUNTRYSTYLE, 11058 W. Addison, Franklin Park IL 60131. (312)455-7178. Editor: Vince Sorren. Emphasizes country music and country life style. Bimonthly tabloid; 48 pages. Estab. 1976. Circ. 425,000. Pays on acceptance. Buys all rights, but may reassign following publication. Phone queries OK. Submit seasonal/holiday material 3 months in advance. Photocopied submissions and previously published work OK. SASE. Reports in 2 weeks. Sample copy $1. Free writer's guidelines.
Nonfiction: Harry Morrow, Department Editor. Expose, informational, interview, nostalgia,

profile, photo feature. Buys 100 mss/year. Query. Length: 500-2,000 words. Pays minimum of $10 per ms page.

Photos: Purchased with or without ms, or on assignment. Send contact sheet, prints or transparencies. Pays $15-100 for 8x10 b&w glossies; $35-250 for color. Prefers 2¼x2¼, but color negatives OK.

Columns, Departments: Country Music. Record Review. Send complete ms. Length: 100-500 words. Pays 5-10¢/word.

Fiction: Western. Buys 10/year. Query. Pays minimum of $10/ms page.

Fillers: Newsbreaks. Buys 40/year. Length: 100-300 words. Pays $5-15.

How To Break In: "With a timely (in the sense that the artist has a hot song on the charts) feature with good color art. But, no microphones, please."

CREEM, 187 S. Woodward Ave., Suite 211, Birmingham MI 48011. (313)642-8833. Editor: Susan Whitall. Estab. 1969. Buys all rights. Pays on publication. Query first. Reports within 2 weeks. Enclose SASE.

Nonfiction and Photos: Freelance photos and articles, mostly music oriented. "We bill ourselves as America's Only Rock 'n' Roll Magazine." Pays $125 minimum, more for the right story. Pays $35 minimum for reviews.

FORECAST!, 8615 Ramsey Ave., Silver Spring MD 20910. Editor-in-Chief: Richard W. Mostow. 10% freelance written. Emphasizes FM radio, Fine Arts, Performing Arts. Monthly magazine; 112 pages. Estab. 1963. Circ. 23,000. Pays on publication. Buys all rights. Submit seasonal/holiday material 45 days in advance. SASE. Reports in 2-4 weeks.

Nonfiction: Faith P. Moeckel, Articles Editor. Expose, historical, how-to, humor, informational, interview, new product, nostalgia, personal experience, personal opinion, photo feature, profile and technical. "Fine Arts, Performing Arts, Music—concentrating on events occurring locally in the Washington/Baltimore area to preview outstanding performances and/or performers of the month and to enhance enjoyment of performing and fine arts in general." Buys 2-3 mss/issue. Query. Length: 1,000-2,000. Pays $25-75.

FUGUE, Watts & Johnson Publications, Ltd., York Square, 49 Avenue Rd., Toronto, Ontario, Canada. (416)364-2486. Editor and Publisher: Diane Watts. 90% freelance written. Emphasizes classical music. Published 10 times/year. Magazine; 48-56 pages. Estab. September 1976. Circ. 25,000. Pays 30 days after acceptance. Buys all rights, but may reassign following publication. Phone queries OK. Submit seasonal/holiday material 3½ months in advance of issue date. SASE. Reports in 2 weeks. Free sample copy; mention *Writer's Market* in request.

Nonfiction: How-to (record buying, how to build a record collection, National Price Survey, etc.); general interest (features on performers, composers, new works); humor (examples: concert etiquette, the influence of the cat in music, etc.); historical (features on performers, composers, eg., Tchaikovsky's Traumatic Life, The Mystique of Mahler, etc.); interview (performers, composers, conductors, impresarios); personal experience (of famous performers, composers); personal opinion (record and book reviews usually staff assigned); photo feature (orchestras and artists on tour, eg., Canadian Brass goes to China); travel (visiting famous birthplaces) and technical (critical evaluations of musical works). Buys 5-6 mss/issue. Query. Pays $50-150.

Photos: David Campbell, photo editor. State availability of photos with query. Pays $10-50 for 8x10 b&w glossy prints or color transparencies. "Obviously assignments are negotiated at different rates than stock photos." Captions preferred. Buys one-time rights. Model release required.

How To Break In: "*Fugue* is somewhat untypical of 'arts' magazines in that we are commercially oriented. The audience for classical music is large, and we do not want to discourage newsstand sales by appearing intimidating, scholarly, dusty, and 'hard-going." Articles even on solid subjects should be written in an accessible way. We are attempting to apply commercial magazine principles to an arts magazines."

THE FUGUE, SJR Communications, Inc., 2951 S. Bayshore Dr., Miami FL 33133. (305)443-5251. Executive Editor: Lawrence Litt. 50% freelance written. Emphasizes classical music, jazz, ballet and opera for a middle and upper income readership, well educated with an interest in higher forms of culture. Monthly magazine; 68 pages. Estab. 1970. Circ. 40,000. Pays on publication. Buys all rights, but may reassign following publication. Phone queries OK. Submit seasonal/holiday material 3 months in advance of issue date. Simultaneous and previously published submissions OK. SASE. Reports in 3 weeks. Sample copy $1; free writer's guidelines.

Nonfiction: "*The Fugue* is glad to consider manuscripts from anybody at any time on most musical subjects. Feel free to submit any items or articles you think might be good reading for people who love fine music. We are interested in light, informative articles that hold the reader's attention. If you use a technical musical term you must define it the first time its used in the piece. We have a record reviewer, but we're always interested in the possibility of guest reviews. Our point of view is that fine arts music is for everyone, not the culturally sophisticated audience. Keep in mind that we are aware of new recordings and are especially interested in tie-in article topics such as crossovers, young new stars, and people who support and promote fine arts music of all types. If we don't accept an article that doesn't mean we won't assign an article to a writer if he or she writes well. Mathematical or technical discourses are not welcome unless they are presented in a breezy, readable style that will hold the interest of the reader of average intelligence." General interest (on music and the Arts; Travel for music); historical (music history, especially American); and interview (composers, conductors, musicians, artists, producers and important people in the field). No academic or scholastic treatises on music or the arts. "We are a general consumer magazine, and our readers want to enjoy reading about their favorite forms of entertainment." Buys 60 mss/year. Query with clips of previously published work. Length:800-2,000 words. Pays $40-150.
Columns/Departments: Record reviews and puzzles and quizes with a musical point of view. Query with clips of previously published work. Length: 500-750 words. Pays $15-50. Open to suggestions for new columns/departments.
Fillers: Clippings, newsbreaks, puzzles, and short humor. Buys 3-5/issue. Length: 500-1,000 words. Pays $15-50.

GIG, 415 Lexington Ave., New York NY 10017. Editor: Jean-Charles Costa. "We rarely buy freelance material. We're just swamped with material."

GUITAR PLAYER MAGAZINE, Box 615, Saratoga CA 95070. (408)446-1105. Editor: Don Menn. For persons "interested in guitars and guitarists." 12 times a year. Circ. 127,800. Buys all rights. Buys 60-80 mss/year. Pays on acceptance. Will send a sample copy to a writer on request. Returns rejected material in 1 week. Acknowledges acceptance in 1 week. Query first. Enclose SASE.
Nonfiction and Photos: Publishes "wide variety of articles pertaining to guitars and guitarists: interviews, guitar craftsmen profiles, how-to features—anything amateur and professional guitarists would find fascinating and/or helpful. On interviews with 'name' performers, be as technical as possible regarding strings, guitars, techniques, etc. We're not a pop culture magazine, but a music magazine." Also buys features on such subjects as a "guitar museum, the role of the guitar in elementary education, personal reminiscences of past greats, technical gadgets and how to work them, analysis of flamenco, etc." Length: open. Pays $50 to $200. Photos purchased with mss. B&w glossies. Pays $25 to $35. Buys 35mm color slides. Pays $150 (for cover only). Buys all rights.

HI-FI STEREO BUYERS' GUIDE, 380 Lexington Ave., New York NY 10017. Editor-in-Chief: Julian S. Martin. Editor: Christine Begole. Bimonthly magazine whose function is to assist the prospective buyer of high fidelity components in their purchase. Writers are advised to obtain a copy of the magazine and examine it carefully for content. "If you think you can write for us, we suggest you submit to us a precis of the story you would like to write, and await our comments. We pay on impulse before publication." SASE.
Nonfiction: "We run a short jazz column and a comprehensive record-review column on classical music. Also, we have a continuing series on opera which takes about 2 pages in the magazine. We don't plan to increase this coverage, nor do we plan to take on additional freelancers to assist us in this area. We are interested in discovering new authors who are familiar with the buying habits of the audiophile and know the current audio marketplace. Average payment is about $200."

HIGH FIDELITY, The Publishing House, State Road, Great Barrington MA 01230. Editorial Director: Robert Clark. For well-educated, young, affluent readers, interested in home recording and playback systems (all disc and tape formats) and music. Special issues: August, tape; June, speakers; September, new recordings and new equipment; December, year's best recordings. Monthly magazine. Estab. 1951. Circ. 365,000. Buys all rights. Buys 36-42 mss/year. Payment on acceptance. Will consider photocopied submissions, "if they are legible." Submit seasonal material 5 months in advance. Reports in 1 month. Query first or submit complete ms. Enclose SASE.
Nonfiction: "Material for feature articles is divided between consumer and semipro audio

equipment and music makers. Equipment articles should be backed up with as much technical sophistication as possible and appropriate and readily understandable to the lay reader. Music articles should be slanted toward the classical or popular musician's recording career or recordings of his works or aimed at increasing the reader's understanding of music. Articles are sophisticated, detailed, and thoroughly backgrounded." Regular columns include: interviews with noted music and recording personalities about their work. Behind the Scenes, reports of in-progress recording sessions here and abroad. Length: 1,000 to 3,000 words. Pays $200-500.
Photos: Purchased with accompanying manuscripts. Captions required, 8x10 b&w glossy payment included in ms payment. Color rarely used; inquire first.

HIGH FIDELITY/MUSICAL AMERICA, 130 E. 59th St., New York NY 10022. Editor: Shirley Fleming. Monthly. Estab. 1888. Circ. 25,000. Buys all rights. Pays on publication. SASE.
Nonfiction and Photos: Articles, musical and audio, are generally prepared by acknowledged writers and authorities in the field, but does use freelance material. Length: 3,000 words maximum. Pays $25 minimum. New b&w photos of musical personalities, events, etc.

INTERNATIONAL MUSICIAN, 1500 Broadway, New York NY 10036. (212)869-1330. Editor: J. Martin Emerson. For professional musicians. Monthly. Copyrighted. Pays on acceptance. Free sample copy. Reporting time varies. Query first. SASE.
Nonfiction: Articles on prominent instrumental musicians (classical, jazz, rock, or country). Pay negotiable.

KEYBOARD WORLD, Box 4399, Downey CA 90241. (213)923-0331. Editor-in-Chief: Bill Worrall. Emphasizes organ, piano and synthesizer music. Monthly magazine; 48-52 pages. Estab. 1972. Circ. 18,000 U.S. and Canada; 10,000 Australia. Pays on acceptance. Buys all rights, but may reassign following publication. Phone queries OK. Submit seasonal/holiday material at least 4 months in advance. Simultaneous and photocopied submissions OK. Previously published work OK, if author owns rights. SASE. Reports in 4 weeks. Sample copy $1; mention *Writer's Market* in request.
Nonfiction: Jean Garland, Articles Editor. How-to (playing technique, forming clubs, fixing, building instruments, theory of music, information for teachers); informational (profiles of teachers, news of concerts, conventions); historical (keyboard instrument history, history of composers, songs—but related to the present, restoring old instruments); inspirational (human interest on handicapped, etc., musicians who are nevertheless outstanding); interview (with organ/piano and all keyboard teachers and musicians, and others related to this field); nostalgia (old theatre organs, older songs, musicians of the past); personal opinion (letters to the editor welcomed); profile (of teachers and musicians); new product (reviews of books and records); personal experience (human interest about relationships with teachers, musicians, students overcoming difficulties); photo feature (good, clear pix of concerts, etc., especially candid shots, rather than posed); technical (advice on fixing/tuning instruments and on teaching/practice/learning methods). Query. Length: 500-4,000 words. Pays ½-1¢/word.
Photos: David Rivas, Art Director. Purchased with or without mss or on assignment. Captions optional, "but must have names and situation info". Send prints. Pays $2 minimum for b&w and color; $25 for cover use. Model release required.
Fillers: Clippings, jokes, anecdotes, newsbreaks, short humor related to keyboard music. Send fillers in. Pays $1 minimum.
How To Break In: "Read *Keyboard World*. Most of our material is contributed free. Therefore, we want something we can't readily get from the experts who write for us. Well-researched and slanted material, especially on pianos and synthesizers, and for children."

THE LAMB, 5518 Chaucer, Houston TX 77005. (713)526-7793. Editor-in-Chief: Michael Point. Emphasizes music for a readership interested in the current shape and future course of contemporary music. Primary readership lies in the 20-30-year-old bracket with some college affiliation (past or present) and a serious interest in music. Monthly tabloid; 28 pages. Estab. 1976. Circ. 30,000. Pays on publication. Buys all rights, but may reassign rights to author following publication. Phone queries OK. Photocopied (if clean and clear) submissions OK. SASE. Reports in 4 weeks. Sample copy 50¢.
Nonfiction: Historical, informational, interview, nostalgia, personal opinion, photo feature and profile. "All articles must deal with music, musicians or the music world." Buys 50 mss/year. Query. Length varies. Pays minimum $10.
Photos: Geary Davis, Photo Editor. Purchased with or without accompanying ms or on assignment. Captions required. Pays minimum $5 for 8x10 b&w glossies. Send contact sheet or prints. Total purchase price for ms includes payment for photos.

Fiction: Adventure, confession, erotica, experimental, fantasy, historical, humorous and science fiction. Buys 10 mss/year. Query. Pays minimum $10.
Poetry: Nancy McKinney, Poetry Editor. Avant-garde, free verse, haiku, light verse and traditional. Buys 50 poems/year. Send poems. Pays minimum $5.
How To Break In: "*The Lamb* is not a teen or pop music oriented publication. It deals with "progressive music" of all styles (jazz, rock, classical, etc.) and requires writers able to communicate to an audience of musically informed and interested readers. *The Lamb* is open to all forms of alternative expression dealing with music and invites writers, photographers, etc., to use their creativity when submitting material. Remember that this is a music magazine and, as such, concentrates almost exclusively on the permutations of the music world. Album reviews and performance reviews are customary starting points for new writers."

MELODY MAKER, IPC Specialist & Professional Press Ltd., 24/34 Meymott St., London SE1 9LU, England. Editor-in-Chief: Ray Coleman. Emphasizes popular music. Weekly magazine; 64 pages. Estab. 1926. Circ. 147,000. Pays on publication. Buys all rights. Submit seasonal/holiday material 2-3 weeks in advance. SAE and International Reply Coupons.
Nonfiction: Concert reviews; folk, rock, pop, jazz, country artists. Interviews with personalities. Length: 400-1,000 words. Pays $17-100.

MODERN DRUMMER, 47 Harrison St., Nutley NJ 07110. (201)667-2211. Editor-in-Chief: Ronald Spagnardi. 70% freelance written. For "student, semi-pro, and professional drummers at all ages and levels of playing ability, with varied specialized interests within the field." Quarterly magazine; 40 pages. Estab. 1975. Circ. 10,000. Pays on publication. Buys all rights. Phone queries OK. Photocopied and previously published submissions OK. SASE. Reports in 8 weeks. Sample copy $1.75; free writer's guidelines.
Nonfiction: How-to; informational; interview; personal opinion; new product; personal experience; and technical. "All submissions must appeal to the specialized interests of drummers." Buys 5-10 mss/issue. Query or submit complete ms. Length: 500-2,000 words. Pays 5-10¢/word.
Photos: Purchased with accompanying ms. Considers 8x10 b&w and color glossies. Submit prints or negatives. Total ms purchase price includes payment for photos. Model release required.
Columns, Departments: Jazz Drummers Workshop, Rock Perspectives, Rudimental Symposium, Complete Percussionist, Teachers Forum, Drum Soloist, Record, Book and Live Action Review, Shop Talk. "Technical knowledge of area required for all columns." Buys 5-8 mss/issue. Query or submit complete ms. Length: 500-1,500 words. Pays 5-10¢/word. Open to suggestions for new columns and departments.
Fillers: Jokes, gags, anecdotes. Buys 3 fillers an issue. No length requirement. Pays $2-5.

MUSIC CITY NEWS, 1302 Division St., Nashville TN 37203. (615)244-5187. Managing Editor: Lee Rector. Emphasizes country music. Monthly tabloid; 40 pages. Estab. 1963. Circ. 80,000. Buys all rights. Phone queries OK. Submit seasonal or holiday material 2 months in advance. Photocopied submissions OK. SASE. Reports in 8-10 weeks. Free sample copy.
Nonfiction: "We prefer interview type articles with country music personalities, not question/answer but narrative/quote interviews leaning toward the personality telling his own story. Prefer new slants to biographical." Buys 4-5 mss per issue. Query. Length: 500-1,250 words. Pays $1.05/column inch.
Photos: Purchased on assignment. Query. Pays $10 maximum for 8x10 b&w glossies.

MUSIC JOURNAL, 149 Hampton Rd., Southampton NY 11968. Editor: Hannah Hanani. 70% freelance written. Emphasizes serious music for college and conservatory faculty and students, professional and amateur musicians, and music lovers. Published 10 times/year, magazine. Pays on publication. Submit seasonal/holiday material 4 months in advance of date. Simultaneous and photocopied submissions OK. SASE. Reports in 6 weeks. Sample copy $1.50.
Nonfiction: General interest (composers, performers, music festivals, instruments, new trends, recordings, music business, and audio); interview (important figures in the music world); profile (important figures in the music world); technical (new compositions, and new techniques in audio music); and travel (as related to classical music or jazz). Buys 35 mss/year. Query with 3 clips of previously published work. Length: 1,000-3,000 words. Pays $75-200.
Photos: State availability of photos with query. No additional payment for b&w prints. Buys one-time rights.

OPERA CANADA, 366 Adelaide St., E., Suite 533, Toronto, Ontario Canada M5A 1N4. (416)363-0395. Editor: Ruby Mercer. For readers who are interested in serious music; specifi-

cally, opera. Quarterly magazine; 52 pages. Estab. 1960. Circ. 5,000. Not copyrighted. Buys about 10 mss/year. Pays on publication. Sample copy $2. Will consider photocopied and simultaneous submissions. Reports on material accepted for publication within 1 year. Returns rejected material in 1 month. Query first or submit complete ms. Enclose SAE and International Reply Coupons.
Nonfiction and Photos: "Because we are Canada's opera magazine, we like to keep 75% of our content Canadian, i.e., by Canadians or about Canadian personalities/events. We prefer informative and/or humorous articles about any aspect of music theatre, with an emphasis on opera. The relationship of the actual subject matter to opera can be direct or barely discernible. We accept record reviews (*only* operatic recordings); book reviews (books covering any aspect of music theatre) and interviews with major operatic personalities. Please, no reviews of performances. We have staff reviewers." Length (for all articles except reviews of books and records): 350 to 5,000 words. Pays $25-50. Length for reviews: 50 to 100 words. Pays $10. No additional payment for photos used with mss. Captions required.

PAID MY DUES: JOURNAL OF WOMEN AND MUSIC, Box 6517, Chicago IL 60680. Editor: Althea Majajna. For everyone interested in feminist and women's music; all aspects from technical to "herstorical," as well as coverage of the contemporary scene. Magazine; 48 pages. Estab. 1974. Circ. 1,200. Rights purchased vary with author and material. Buys all rights, but may reassign rights to author after publication; first serial rights or simultaneous rights. Buys about 15 mss per year. Pays on publication. Free writer's guidelines. Will consider photocopied submissions. May consider simultaneous submissions. Reports in 6 weeks. Query first. SASE.
Nonfiction and Photos: "We focus exclusively on women and use articles about women (alive or dead) who are prominent in music (or should be prominent in music); interviews with musicians who are women; songs, reviews of records, concerts. Emphasis is on the work itself (concert, musician, etc.), as well as the approach of the woman to her music. No articles on 'how bad things are for women in music'." Informational, how-to, personal experience, profile, humor, historical, think pieces, personal opinion and travel articles. All must relate to women in music. Length: 300 words minimum. Pays $5-10/ms. B&w photos purchased with or without mss. 2x2, minimum size. Prefers 5x7 or larger. Pays $2.

PICKIN' MAGAZINE, North American Publishing Co., 401 N. Broad St., Philadelphia PA 19108. (215)574-9600. Editor-in-Chief: Don Kissil. Managing Editor: Marilyn Kochman. 60-70% freelance written. For people who play, but who also listen and collect records of old time bluegrass, country, folk, jazz and all of the specialty type musics with a special emphasis on stringed instruments. Monthly magazine; 74-96 pages. Estab. February 1974. Circ. 100,000. Pays on publication. Buys all rights, but may reassign following publication. Phone queries OK. Submit seasonal/holiday material 6-8 months in advance of issue date. Photocopied and previously published submissions OK. SASE. Reports in 4-6 weeks. Free sample copy and writer's guidelines; mention *Writer's Market* in request.
Nonfiction: "All related to our kind of music or instruments." General interest; historical; how-to; humor; interview; new product (unusual, not commercial); nostalgia; personal experience (music tablature for Pickers, lifestyles and fashions for "down home folk"); personal opinion; photo feature; profile; technical (instrument making); and travel (festivals). No articles of promo pieces on bands or artists. Buys 100 mss/year. Query with clips of previously published work. Length: 500-5,000 words. Pays 4-10¢/word.
Photos: State availability of photos with query. Pays $5-50 for b&w contact sheets or prints; $10-200 (cover only) for 35mm color transparencies or contact prints. Captions required. Buys all rights, but may reassign following publication. Model release required.
Columns/Departments: Across the Pond (overseas music); Crafts Corner (instrument repair tips); Music Book Reviews (stringed); Music Tablature; Record Reviews; Workbench (on building instruments); and Song Book Reviews. Query. Length: 300-12,000 words. Pays $15-50. Open to suggestions for new columns/departments.
Poetry: "Related to our music only." Avant-garde, free verse, haiku, light verse, and traditional. Buys 4/year. Submit in batches of 2. Pays $10-20.
Fillers: Jokes, gags, anecdotes, puzzles, short humor and cartoons. Buys 10/year. Pays $5-25.

RIFFS, Box 1324, Arlington TX 76010. (817)261-3584. Editor: Les Ross. 65% freelance written. Emphasizes Texas jazz and blues for afficiondos of all ages. Monthly magazine; 20 pages. Estab. December 1977. Circ. 5,000. Pays on publication. Buys one-time rights. Phone queries OK. Submit seasonal/holiday material 3 months in advance of issue date. Simultaneous, photocopied and previously published submissions OK. SASE. Reports in 4 weeks. Sample copy $1; writer's guidelines for SASE.

Nonfiction: General interest (on Texas jazz and blues musicians); historical (to reveal jazz or blues impact or significance to culture); interiew (with Texas jazz and blues personalities, uses 10 angled nationally/year); personal experience (concert reviews of Texas concerts); personal opinion (record reviews, 300-400 words); profile (on anyone significant to the national or Texas jazz or blues scene). Buys 12 mss/year. Query or submit complete ms. Length: 300-1,500 words. Pays $5-50.

ROLLING STONE, 745 5th Ave., New York NY 10022. Editor: Jann S. Wenner. "Seldom accept freelance material. All our work is assigned or done by our staff."

THE $ENSIBLE SOUND, 403 Darwin Dr., Snyder NY 14226. Editor/Publisher: John A. Horan. 50% freelance written. "All readers are high fidelity enthusiasts, and many have a high fidelity industry-related job." Quarterly magazine; 48 pages. Estab. 1976. Circ. 3,650. Pays on acceptance. Buys all rights. Simultaneous, photocopied and previously published submissions OK. SASE. Reports in 2 weeks. Sample copy $1; mention *Writer's Market* in request.
Nonfiction: Exposé; how-to; general interest; humor; historical; interview (people in hi-fi business, manufacturers or retail); new product (all type of new audio equipment); nostalgia (articles and opinion on older equipment); personal experience (with various types of audio equipment); photo feature (on installation, or how-to tips); profile (of hi-fi equipment) and technical (pertaining to audio). "Subjective evaluations of Hi-Fi equipment make up 70% of our publication. Will accept 10/issue." Buys 2 mss/issue. Submit outline. Pays $25 maximum.
Columns/Departments: Bits & Pieces (short items of interest to hi-fi hobbyists); Ramblings (do-it-yourself tips on bettering existing systems); Record Reviews (of records which would be of interest to audiophiles). Query. Length: 25-400 words. Pays $5 maximum.
Fillers: Clippings, jokes, gags, anecdotes, and newsbreaks. Buys 2/issues. Length: 25-400 words. Pays $10 maximum.

SONO, 625 President Kennedy Ave., Montreal, Quebec, Canada H3A 1K5. (514)845-5141. Editor: Paul Saint-Pierre. For amateurs and fanatics of music and of musical instruments. Although this publication is in French, English mss are considered. Annual magazine; 100 pages. Estab. 1973. Circ. 15,000. Buys all rights, but will reassign rights to author after publication. Pays on acceptance. Reports in 1 week. Query first or submit complete ms. Enclose SAE and International Reply Coupons.
Nonfiction: Interviews with singers, technical articles on quadraphony; on new equipment, trends; reviews of new records, audiolab, etc. Informational, how-to, profile, technical. Length: 600 to 1,200 words. Pays $100 minimum.

SOUNDS, 332 E. Camelback, Phoenix AZ 85012. (602)265-4830. Senior Editor: William Niblick. Editor: Bob Henchen. 50% freelance written. Emphasizes music, audio, performing and visual arts entertainment for audiophiles, music listeners and anyone interested in what is "happening" in music, dance, theater, film, audio both nationally and locally (Arizona). Monthly tabloid; 24 pages. Estab. 1973. Circ. 25,000. Pays on publication. Buys all rights, but may reassign rights to author following publication. Phone queries OK. Simultaneous, photocopied and previously published submissions OK. SASE. Reports in 3 weeks. Sample copy and writer's guidelines for 9x12 SASE and 35¢ postage.
Nonfiction: Expose (music); interview; new product (audio or music); essays; record and performance reviews. Buys 12-25 mss/year. Query or send complete ms. Length: 50-400 words for record reviews; 400-1,500 words for articles. Pays 1-5¢/word.
Photos: Purchased with or without accompanying ms. Query or send contact sheet. Pays maximum $5 for b&w any finish at least 4x5. Total purchase price for ms includes payment for photos.

TRIAD MAGAZINE, 401 W. Fullerton Pkwy., Chicago IL 60614. (312)871-1900. Managing Editor: Bill Paige. 100% freelance written. Emphasizes rock music, films, books, theatre and dance and other cultural aspects of Chicago. "Late teens to 30ish orientation." Monthly tabloid; 40 pages. Estab. 1971. Circ. 40,000. Pays on publication. Buys all rights, but may reassign following publication. Phone queries OK. Simultaneous and photocopied submissions OK. SASE. Reports in 1 month. Sample copy $1; writer's guidelines for SASE.
Nonfiction: Humor (if it concerns the rock & roll music life); interview (with music personalities; narrative preferable, but question and answer format acceptable); profile (of mainstream music

artist or group); and concert and record reviews. Also articles concerning the arts in Chicago. Buys 4 mss/issue. Query or submit complete ms. Length: 800-3,000 words; shorter for reviews. Pays $20-80.

Photos: State availability of photos with query or ms. Pays $10-20 for 5x7 b&w prints.

Mystery Publications

ALFRED HITCHCOCK'S MYSTERY MAGAZINE, Davis Publications Inc., 380 Lexington Ave., New York NY 10017. Editor: Eleanor Sullivan. Associate Editor: Sally Smith. Emphasizes mystery fiction. Monthly magazine; 130 pages. Estab. 1956. Circ. 145,000. Pays on acceptance. Buys all rights. Submit seasonal/holiday material 7 months in advance. Simultaneous and photocopied submissions OK. SASE. Reports in 6 weeks. Free writer's guidelines.

Fiction: Original and well-written mystery, suspense and crime fiction. No reprints or true crimes. "A 'now' feeling is preferred for every story, both as to plot urgency and today's world. Plausibility counts heavily even in supernatural stories." Length: 1,000-10,000 words. Rates are basically the same as those paid by *Ellery Queen's Mystery Magazine*.

How To Break In: "Think Hitchcock. It's the master's brand of suspense that we want. Avoid gore, profanity and explicit sex."

ELLERY QUEEN'S MYSTERY MAGAZINE, Davis Publications, Inc., 380 Lexington Ave., New York NY 10017. Editor-in-Chief: Ellery Queen. Managing Editor: Eleanor Sullivan. Monthly magazine; 160 pages. Estab. 1941. Circ. 340,000. Pays on acceptance. Buys first North American serial rights. Submit seasonal/holiday material 7 months in advance. Simultaneous, photocopied and previously published submissions OK. SASE. Reports in 6 weeks. Free writer's guidelines.

Fiction: "We publish every type of mystery: the suspense story, the psychological study, the deductive puzzle—the gamut of crime and detection from the realistic (including the policeman's lot and stories of police procedure) to the more imaginative (including 'locked rooms' and impossible crimes). We need private-eye stories, but do not want sex, sadism, or sensationalism-for-the-sake-of-sensationalism" Buys 13 mss/issue. Length: 6,000 words maximum. Pays 3-8¢/word.

How To Break In: "We have a department of First Stories to encourage writers whose fiction has never before been in print. We publish an average of 24 first stories a year."

MIKE SHAYNE MYSTERY MAGAZINE, Renown Publications, Inc., Box 69150, Los Angeles CA 90069. Editor-in-Chief: Cylvia Kleinman. 100% freelance written. Monthly magazine; 128 pages. Estab. 1956. Pays on acceptance. Buys magazine serial rights only. Submit seasonal/holiday material 4 months in advance. Photocopied submissions OK. SASE. Reports in 2 weeks.

Fiction: Strong, fast-moving mystery stories. Buys 8 mss/issue. Length: 1,000-6,000 words. Pays 1¢/word minimum.

How To Break In: "Study the type of material we use. Know pace of story, type of mystery we buy. Best to send very short material to start, as the new author doesn't handle novelette lengths convincingly."

Nature, Conservation, and Ecology Publications

The magazines classified here are "pure" nature, conservation, and ecology publications—that is, they exist to further the study and preservations of nature and do not publish recreational or travel articles except as they relate to conservation or nature. Other markets for this kind of material will be found in the Regional; Sport and Outdoor; and Travel, Camping, and Trailer categories, although the magazines listed there require that nature or conservation articles be slanted to their specialized subject matter and audience.

AUDUBON, 950 Third Avenue, New York NY 10022. "Not soliciting freelance material; practically all articles done on assignment only. We have a backlog of articles from known writers and contributors. Our issues are planned well in advance of publication and follow a theme."

ENVIRONMENT, 4000 Albemarle St. NW., Washington DC 20016. Managing Editor: Barbara Ferkiss. For citizens, scientists, teachers, high school and college students interested in envi-

ronment or effects of technology and science in public affairs. Magazine; 48 pages. Estab. 1958. Ten times a year. Circ. 20,000. Buys all rights. Pays on acceptance to professional writers. Sample copy $3. Will consider photocopied submissions. No simultaneous submissions. Reports in 6-8 weeks. Query first or submit complete ms. SASE.
Nonfiction and Photos: Scientific and environmental material; effects of technology on society. Pays $100-150, depending on material. 8x10 b&w photos purchased with or without mss. Pays $3 on acceptance, $7 on publication. Photographer must submit an invoice.
Poetry: Environmental and satiric poems. Pays $10.

ENVIRONMENTAL ACTION, 1346 Connecticut Ave., Washington DC 20036. Editor: Deborah Baldwin. 20% freelance written. Emphasizes citizen action and legislative/governmental activity affecting the environment for a well-educated, sophisticated, politically oriented readership. Semimonthly magazine; 16 pages. Estab. April 1970. Circ. 19,000. Pays on publication. Buys all rights, but may reassign following publication. Simultaneous (if so identified), photocopied and previously published submissions OK. SASE. Reports in 6 weeks. Free sample copy.
Nonfiction: "All articles must be written for a sophisticated, politically oriented audience, well informed on environmental issues." Expose; general interest; and profile. Buys 10 mss/year. Query. Length: 1,000-2,500 words. Pays $25-225.
Photos: State availability of photos with query. Pays $5-25 for 8x10 b&w glossy prints. Buys all rights, but may reassign following publication.

THE EXPLORER, Cleveland Museum of Natural History, Wade Oval, University Circle, Cleveland OH 44106. (216)231-4600. Editor: Bill Baughman. 50% freelance written. For readers with a strong interest in natural history and science. Estab. 1938. Quarterly. Circ. 25,000. Audience are members of 15 museums and many independent subscribers. Buys one-time rights. Payment in contributor's copies. Submit seasonal material 6 months in advance. Reports in 3-4 weeks. SASE.
Nonfiction and Photos: "We are especially concerned with interpreting the natural history and science of North America, but mostly U.S. We endeavor to give a voice to the natural scientists and naturalists functioning within these geographical boundaries and feel an obligation to make our readers aware of the crucial issues at stake in the world regarding conservation and environmental problems. Now assigning most articles, but will consider articles by scientists, naturalists and experts in nature, ecology, and environmental areas. Writing should have a lively style and be understandable to scientists of all ages. Exploring nature can be exciting. Your writing should reflect and encourage the exploring mind." Length: 1,000 to 4,000 words. B&w (8x10) photos. Some color transparencies and color prints are used. 35mm Kodachrome color, 2¼x2¼, and 4x5 transparencies are acceptable for inside editorial and cover illustrations. All photos, particularly close-ups of birds and animals, must be needle-sharp. Also interested in b&w photo essays (12 photos maximum) on natural history topics.

FRONTIERS, A Magazine of Natural History, Academy of Natural Sciences, 19th and the Parkway, Philadelphia PA 19103. Editor: Mrs. Vi Dodge. Published 4 times per year. Circ. 6,000. Rights purchased vary with author and material. May buy first North American serial rights or all rights, but may reassign rights to author after publication. Pays on publication. Sample copy $1. Reports in 4 to 6 weeks. SASE.
Nonfiction and Photos: Articles on natural science and ecology, written for high school and adult laymen, but scientifically accurate. Length: 500 to 3,000 words. Pays $50 to $100. Articles with b&w photos usually given preference. Accuracy, originality, and neatness all weigh heavily. 8x10 b&w photos purchased with mss.
Fillers: Natural science puzzles and short humor. Length: 10 to 50 words. Pays $15 to $25.

INTERNATIONAL WILDLIFE, 225 E. Michigan, Milwaukee WI 53202. Editor: John Strohm. 80% freelance written. For persons interested in natural history, outdoor adventure and the environment. Bimonthly. Buys all rights to text; usually one-time rights to photos and art. Payment on acceptance. Query first. "Now assigning most articles but will consider detailed proposals for quality feature material of interest to broad audience." Reports in 2 weeks. SASE.
Nonfiction and Photos: Focus on world wildlife, environmental problems and man's relationship to the natural world as reflected in such issues as population control, pollution, resource utilization, food production, etc. Especially interested in articles on animal behavior and other natural history, little-known places, first-person experiences, timely issues. "Payment varies according to value and use of feature articles, but usually begins at $750. Purchase top-quality

color and b&w photos; prefer 'packages' of related photos and text, but single shots of exceptional interest and sequences also considered. Prefer Kodachrome transparencies for color, 8x10 prints for b&w."

JOURNAL OF FRESHWATER, Freshwater Biological Research Foundation, 2500 Shadywood Rd., Box 90, Navarre MN 55392. (612)471-7467. Editor: Richard A. Hughes. 50% freelance written. Emphasizes freshwater/environmental issues. Quarterly magazine; 32 pages. Estab. January 1977. Pays on acceptance. Buys all rights, but may reassign following publication. Phone queries OK. Submit seasonal/holiday material 6 months in advance of issue date. SASE. Reports in 4-6 weeks. Sample copy $3; free writer's guidelines.
Nonfiction: "We will consider virtually any material dealing with freshwater environment as long as it is well-written, interesting, etc. We're always looking for new slants and ideas." How-to; general interest; humor; interview; nostalgia; personal opinion; photo feature; profile; and technical. "No 'bumper-sticker' philosophies, please; and no dry encyclopedia-type articles or obviously slanted, unresearched material." Buys 15-20 mss/year. Submit complete ms. Length. "However long it takes—and not a word more." Pays $100-300 (more with photos or art).
Photos: Submit photos with accompanying ms. Payment for photos is included in purchase price of article. Uses 5x7 minimum b&w glossy photos or 35mm, 2¼x2¼ or larger color transparencies. Captions preferred. Buys all rights, but may reassign following publication. Model release required.
Fiction: "We have never purchased any fiction, since we have not received good fiction material. But we're always open to something new." Experimental and humorous. Pays $50-300.
Poetry: Avant-garde; free verse; haiku; light verse; and traditional. Buys 4-6/issue. Limit submissions to batches of 5-10. Pays $20-50.

THE LIVING WILDERNESS, 1901 Pennsylvania Ave. NW., Washington DC 20006. (212)293-2732. Editor: James G. Deane. For members of the Wilderness Society, libraries and educational institutions. Estab. 1975. Circ. 70,000. Quarterly. "There may be a considerable wait for return of unsolicited materials." Pays on publication. SASE. Sample copy $1.50; free writer's guidelines.
Nonfiction, Poetry and Photos: Articles on wilderness preservationa and appreciation and on wildlife conservation. Special interest in threats to North American wild areas. Occasional articles on other environmental issues and natural history; occasional nature-oriented essays and high-caliber wilderness oriented poetry. Some book reviews are assigned. Mss should be of professional quality. Payment depends on character of material. Editors consider only highest quality photographs relevant to the foregoing subjects, usually to illustrate specific articles. Pays $25 minimum for b&w; $75 minimum for color, except when bought in article photo package.

LOUISIANA CONSERVATIONIST, 400 Royal St., Room 110, New Orleans LA 70130. Editor: Bob Dennie. For the outdoorsman and his family. Publication of Louisiana Wildlife and Fisheries Commission. Estab. 1931. Bimonthly. Circ. 190,000. Not copyrighted. Payment in contributor's copies. Free sample copy. Will not consider photocopied submissions. Returns rejected material in 2 weeks. Reports on mss accepted for publication in 6 to 8 weeks. Query first. "We will look at outlines with query letters." SASE.
Nonfiction and Photos: "We use feature-length articles, including how-to's if they are informative and concisely written, of the outdoor variety. We also consider 'offbeat' pieces if they are written to interest a general outdoor audience. Studying the style of the staff writers and published authors in the magazine is the best advice interested writers could get. To be avoided are wordiness, cute tricks, writing with adjectives, and the outmoded 'me and Joe' articles. It is important that a writer be active in the outdoor writing field in order to submit to our magazine." Length: 800 to 2,000 words. Mss should be illustrated with color slides (originals only); 35mm or 2¼x2¼.

NATIONAL PARKS & CONSERVATION MAGAZINE, 1701 18th St., N.W., Washington DC 20009. (202)265-2717. Editor: Eugenia Horstman Connally. For a mature, high-education audience interested in out-of-doors and environmental matters. Monthly magazine; 32 pages. Estab. 1919. Circ. 45,000. Buys North American serial rights. Almost all material used is purchased from freelance writers. Payment on acceptance. Sample copy $2; free writer's guidelines. Submit seasonal material 4 months in advance. Reports on material accepted for publication in 4-6 weeks. Returns rejected material promptly. Query first. SASE.

Nonfiction and Photos: Articles about national parks and monuments, stressing threats confronting them or their particularly significant floral, faunal, geological, or historical features; endangered species of plants or animals and suggestions to save them; protection of natural resources; environmental problems and programs to solve them. Length: 1,500 to 2,000 words. Pays $75-200 for acceptable illustrated articles. No additional payment for b&w and color used with mss, unless selected for cover. Pays $15-50 for 8x10 b&w glossies purchased without mss; $25 to $75 for 4x5 color transparencies (some slides) purchased without mss. Captions required. "Photos generally not purchased unless a relevant article is on file. Send list of subjects and a few samples for files."
How To Break In: "Excellent market for new writers. 'Adventures in the national parks' articles are welcome, particularly those on backcountry hiking, mountain climbing, river running, spelunking. Emphasize conservation and protection of natural resources."

NATIONAL WILDLIFE, 225 E. Michigan Ave., Milwaukee WI 53202. Editor-in-Chief: John Strohm. Emphasizes wildlife. Bimonthly magazine; 56 pages. Estab. 1962. Circ. 800,000. Pays on acceptance. Buys all rights. Submit seasonal/holiday material 6 months in advance. Previously published submissions OK. SASE. Reports in 2 weeks. Free writer's guidelines.
Nonfiction: Mark Wexler, Nonfiction Editor. How-to; humor; informational; interview; personal experience; photo feature and profile. Buys 5 mss/issue. Query. Length: 2,000-3,000 words. Pays $500-1,000.
Photos: Karen Altpeter, Photo Editor. Photos purchased with or without accompanying ms or on assignment. Pays $35-100 for 8x10 b&w glossies; $75-150 for 35mm color kodachromes.

NATURAL HISTORY, 79th and Central Park West, New York NY 10024. Editor: Alan Ternes. For "well-educated, ecologically aware audience. Includes many professional people, scientists, scholars." Monthly. Circ. 450,000. "Copyright on text of articles is held by The American Museum of Natural History." Buys 20 mss a year. Pays on publication. Sample copy $1.25. Submit seasonal material 6 months in advance. Query first or submit complete ms. SASE.
Nonfiction: Uses all types of scientific articles except chemistry and physics—emphasis is on the biological sciences and anthropology. Prefers professional scientists as authors. "We always want to see new research findings in almost all the branches of the natural sciences —anthropology, archaeology, zoology, ornithology. We find that it is particularly difficult to get something new in herpetology (amphibians and reptiles) or entomology (insects) and we would like to see material in those fields. We lean heavily toward writers who are scientists or professional science writers. High standards of writing and research. Favor an ecological slant in most of our pieces, but do not generally lobby for causes, environmental or other. Writer should have a deep knowledge of his subject. Then submit original ideas either in query or by ms. Should be able to supply high-quality illustrations." Length: 2,000 to 4,000 words. Pays $300-750, plus additional payment for photos used.
Photos: Uses some 8x10 b&w glossy photographs; pays up to $100 per page. Much color is used; pays $150 for inside and up to $250 for cover. Photos are purchased for one-time use.
How To Break In: "Learn about something in depth before you bother writing about it."

THE NATURALISTS' DIRECTORY AND ALMANAC (INTERNATIONAL), Box 505, Kinderhook NY 12106. (518)758-7219. Editor-in-Chief: Ross H. Arnett, Jr. Emphasizes outdoor natural history recreation. Annual magazine; 250 pages. Estab. 1877. Circ. 5,000. Pays on publication. Buys all rights. Phone queries OK. Submit seasonal or holiday material any time. Photocopied submissions and previously published work OK. SASE. Reports in 2 months. Sample copy $4.50. Free writer's guidelines.
Nonfiction: Informational (sources must be documented) and historical articles. "Some suggested subjects are: nature sayings; records such as tallest trees, smallest living organisms; value of minerals; where and what to collect; poisonous plants and animals; state trees, state birds, state fish, state mammals, state insects, etc." Buys 40 mss a year. Pays $10 minimum.
Photos: Purchased with or without mss, or on assignment. Captions required. Send b&w prints and color transparencies. Pays $5-50 for b&w glossies (at least 5x7); $10-50 for 35mm, 2¼x2¼ or 2¼x3¼ color transparencies. No prints.
How To Break In: "Material must be technically accurate. Most freelance material is too elementary or is written in newspaper style, and is not acceptable."
Rejects: Humorous or sensational material; hunting and fishing themes.

PACIFIC DISCOVERY, California Academy of Sciences, Golden Gate Park, San Francisco CA 94118. (415)221-5100. Editor: Bruce Finson. 100% freelance written. A journal of nature and culture around the world, read by scientists, naturalists, teachers, students, and others having a

keen interest in knowing the natural world more thoroughly. Estab. 1928. Published every 2 months by the California Academy of Science. Circ. 12,000. Buys first North American serial rights of articles, one-time use of photos. Usually reports within 3 months; publishes accepted articles in 2 to 4 months. Pays on publication. Send query first, with 100-word summary of projected article for review before preparing finished ms. SASE.
Nonfiction and Photos: "Subjects of articles include behavior and natural history of animals and plants, ecology, anthropology, geology, paleontology, biogeography, taxonomy, and related topics in the natural sciences. Occasional articles are published on the history of natural science, exploration, astronomy, and archaeology. Types of articles include discussions of individual species or groups of plants and animals that are related to or involved with one another, narratives of scientific expeditions together with detailed discussions of field work and results, reports of biological and geological discoveries and of short-lived phenomena, and explanations of specialized topics in natural science. Authors need not be scientists; however, all articles must be based, at least in part, on firsthand fieldwork." Length: 1,000 to 3,000 words. Pays $50 to $150. B&W photos or color slides must accompany all mss or they will not be reviewed. Send 15 to 30 with each ms. Photos should have both scientific and aesthetic interest, be captioned in a few sentences on a separate caption list keyed to the photos and numbered in story sequence. Some photo stories are used. Pays $10 per photo. All slides, negatives, and prints are returned soon after publication.

SAERCH, Social Science and Environmental Research, Box 614, Corte Madera CA 94925. Editor: William Whitney. For professionals in the environmental and sociological fields. Bimonthly magazine; 52 pages. Estab. 1975. Circ. 5,000. Rights purchased vary with author and material. Buys all rights, but may reassign rights to author after publication, or first serial rights, or simultaneous rights. Buys about 20 mss a year. Pays on acceptance. Sample copy $1. No photocopied submissions. Will consider simultaneous submissions. Reports in 8 to 10 weeks. Query first or submit complete ms. SASE.
Nonfiction, Photos and Fillers: "Our material centers on the subjects of environmental science, impacts on sociological areas, etc. All material should be up-to-date and informative. Our readers are aware of their fields and the need to stay abreast of new developments. The writer's approach and outlook should be problem oriented with stress on solutions to the multi-faceted sciences of today. Nothing trite or generalized. We would like to see more coverage of current debates in the fields of environmental and sociological science. Our recent coverage has included activities of the Sierra Club, as well as specific topics such as shell oil retrieval." Informational, interview, profile, historical, think pieces, expose and technical articles. Length: 2,000 to 3,500 words. Pays 3¢ to 10¢ a word. Spot news. Length: 500 to 750 words. Pays 3¢ to 10¢ a word. Pays $5 to $20 for 8x10 b&w glossies used with mss. Pays $10 to $50 for color transparencies used with mss. 35mm minimum. Newsbreaks of 500 to 750 words used as fillers. Same rate of payment as for other material.

SIERRA, THE SIERRA CLUB, 530 Bush Street, San Francisco CA 94108. Editor-in-Chief: Frances Gendlin. Managing Editor: David Gancher. 30% freelance written. Emphasizes conservation & environmental politics for young adults on up who are well educated, activist, outdoor-oriented, and politically well informed with a dedication to conservation. Published 10 times/year. Magazine; 48 pages. Estab. 1892. Circ. 180,000. Pays on publication. Buys one-time rights. Submit seasonal/holiday material 3 months in advance. Simultaneous and photocopied submissions OK. SASE. Reports in 3 weeks. Free sample copy and writer's guidelines.
Nonfiction: Expose (well-documented on environmental issues of national importance such as energy, forestry, fisheries, etc.); general interest (well-researched pieces on areas of particular environmental concern); historical (relevant to environmental concerns); how-to (sophisticated how-to's on camping, climbing, outdoor photography, etc.); interview (with very prominent figures in the field); personal experience (by or about children and wilderness); photo feature (photo essays on threatened areas); and technical (on energy sources, wildlife management land-use, solid waste management, etc.). No "My trip to . . ."; or why we must save wildlife/nature articles; poetry or general superficial essays on environmentalism and local enviromental issues. Buys 2-3 mss/issue. Query with clips of previously published work. Length: 800-3,000 words. Pays $100.
Photos: Catherine Gasparini, production editor. State availability of photos with query letter. Pays $50 maximum for b&w contact sheets; $50-100 for color transparencies. Buys one-time rights.
Columns/Departments: Book Reviews. Buys 5 mss/year. Length: 800-2,000 words. Query. Open to suggestions for new columns/departments. Submit to Carey Charlesworth, editorial assistant.

SNOWY EGRET, 205 S. Ninth St., Williamsburg KY 40769. (606)549-0850. Editor: Humphrey A. Olsen. For "persons of at least high school age interested in literary, artistic, philosophical, and historical natural history." Semiannual. Circ. less than 500. Buys first North American serial rights. Buys 40-50 mss/year. Pays on publication. Sample copy $1. Usually reports in 2 months. SASE.

Nonfiction: Subject matter limited to material related to natural history, especially literary, artistic, philosophical, and historical aspects. Criticism, book reviews, essays, biographies. Pays $2 per printed page.

Fiction: "We are interested in considering stories or self-contained portions of novels. All fiction must be natural history or man and nature. The scope is broad enough to include such stories as Hemingway's 'Big Two-Hearted River' and Warren's 'Blackberry Winter.'" Length: maximum 10,000 words. Payment is $2 a printed page. Send mss and books for review to Dr. William T. Hamilton, Dept. of English, Otterbein College, Westerville OH 43081. "It is preferable to query first."

Poetry: No length limits. Pays $4 per printed page, minimum of $2. Send poems and poetry books for review to Dr. Hamilton, Literary Editor, and to West Coast Editor, Gary Elder, 22 Ardith Ln., Alamo CA 94507.

Newspapers and Weekly Magazine Sections

This section includes daily newspapers as well as Saturday and Sunday magazine sections of daily newspapers. They are listed geographically by state headings although some cover wider areas (such as *Michiana* which serves both Michigan and Indiana).

Most of these markets require submissions to be about persons, places, and things in their specific circulation areas. However, some large city and national newspapers that welcome general interest material from nonlocal writers are also included in this list. Newspapers with specialized subject matter or audiences, like *The Wall Street Journal* are classified with magazines dealing with the same subject matter or audience.

A few editors report that some correspondents in their area are attracted to small feature items but let big news stories from their communities slip through their fingers. Freelancers, on the other hand, report that some busy newspaper editors return their submissions without even a rejection slip—or in a few cases, fail to return it at all, even when it's accompanied by a stamped, self-addressed envelope. (Since newspaper editors receive many submissions from public relations firms and other individuals who do not expect return of their material, they sometimes automatically toss material they're not interested in publishing. That means a retyping job for the freelancer. It also means you should be wary of sending photographs which are your only copies.)

Arizona

ARIZONA MAGAZINE, Box 1950, Phoenix AZ 85001. (602)271-8291. Editor: Bud DeWald. For "everyone who reads a Sunday newspaper." Weekly; 60 pages. Estab. 1953. Circ. 400,000. Copyrighted. Buys 250 mss/year. Payment on scheduling. Free sample copy and guidelines for writers. Will consider photocopied submissions. Will consider simultaneous submissions if exclusive regionally. Reports on material accepted for publication in 2 weeks. Returns rejected material in 1 week. Query first or submit complete ms. Enclose SASE.

Nonfiction and Photos: "General subjects that have an Arizona connection. Should have a bemused, I-don't-believe-it approach. Nothing is that serious. Should have an abundance of quotes and anecdotes. Historical and travel subjects are being overworked. We don't need someone's therapy." Length: 1,000 to 3,000 words. Pays $50-225. B&w and color photos purchased with or without mss or on assignment. Pays $10 to $25 for 8x10 b&w glossies; $15 to $70 for color (35mm or 8x10).

How To Break In: "Find a good personal subject and write about him so the reader will feel he is with the subject. Describe the subject in anecdotes and let him describe himself by his quotes."

California

CALIFORNIA TODAY, 750 Ridder Park Dr., San Jose CA 95190. (408)289-5563. Editor: John Parky. For a general audience. Weekly newspaper. Circ. 250,000. Not copyrighted. Buys 100

mss a year. Payment on acceptance. Free sample copy. Will consider photocopied and simultaneous submissions, if the simultaneous submission is out of their area. Submit seasonal material (skiing, wine, outdoor living) 3 months in advance. Reports in 4 weeks. Query first. SASE.
Nonfiction and Photos: A general newspaper requiring that all subjects be related to California and interests in that area. Will consider subjects outside California if subject is of broad or national appeal. Length: 500 to 3,500 words. Pays $25-350. Payment varies for b&w and color photos purchased with or without mss. Captions required.

THE SACRAMENTO BEE, Box 15779, Sacramento CA 95813. For a general readership; higher than average education; higher than average interest in politics, government; outdoor-activity oriented. Newspaper; 48 pages. Estab. 1857. Daily. Circ. 190,000 daily; 220,000 Sunday. Not copyrighted. Buys about 200 mss/year. Pays on publication. Will consider simultaneous submissions if they are not duplicated in Northern California. Reports in 2 weeks. Query or submit complete ms to Features Editor. SASE.
Nonfiction and Photos: Human interest features, news background. Prefers narrative feature style. Does not want to see sophomoric humor. Will consider interviews, profiles, nostalgic and historical articles; expose; personal experience. Length: 100 to 1,500 words. Pays $20 to $100. B&w glossies and color (negatives) purchased with or without mss. Pays $15 to $75 for b&w; $25 to $100 for color. Captions required.

SACRAMENTO WEEKENDER, *Sacramento Union,* 301 Capitol Mall, Sacramento CA 95812. Editor: Jackie Peterson. Weekly. Not copyrighted. Buys about 30 mss a year. "We cannot be responsible for return of unsolicited material." Query first. SASE.
Nonfiction and Photos: "We are becoming more and more local in our approach to all subjects, such as leisure activities, outings, travel, the arts, music, entertainment, hobbies, how-to crafts, area personalities." Length: 1,200 words maximum. Pays $25 minimum; $35 to $50 with b&w photos; $45-90, depending on number used, with color photos.

Colorado

CONTEMPORARY MAGAZINE, Sunday supplement to *The Denver Post*, 650 15th St., Denver CO 80201. Editor: Joan White. For "young adults to senior citizens (both sexes), aware of today's world." Newspaper format. Buys first rights. Pays on publication. Free sample copy. No query required. "We are being very selective and use a very limited amount of freelance material." Submit seasonal material 3 months in advance. Reporting time varies. SASE.
Nonfiction: "Mostly a family and women's interest magazine." Articles of 500 to 1,500 words. Payment is $50 to $75.

EMPIRE MAGAZINE, *The Denver Post*, P.O. Box 1709, Denver CO 80201. (303)297-1687. Editor: Carl Skiff. Weekly. Estab. 1950. Buys about 250 mss a year. Buys first rights. Payment on acceptance for nonfiction; on publication for photos. Query first. SASE.
Nonfiction and Photos: "A rotogravure magazine covering the general scene in our circulation area. We are looking for material of national magazine quality in interest and writing style, but with a strong, regional peg. Our region focuses on Colorado, Wyoming, Utah, New Mexico, western Kansas and Nebraska. We need solidly researched articles about exciting things, personalities and situations. We also need light humor and reminiscences." Length: 2,500 words maximum. Pays about 5¢ per word. "Photographs can help sell a story." B&w photos are purchased with ms or as singles or series or as picture stories (500 words). Five to 8 photos are used with picture stories. Query first about these. Pays $50 for color transparencies used for cover; $100 for double spread; $25 for singles (color) used inside; $10 for b&w.

District of Columbia

PRESERVATION NEWS, National Trust for Historic Preservation, 740-748 Jackson Place, N.W., Washington DC 20006. Vice President and Editor: Mrs. Terry B. Morton. Organizational publication for members of the National Trust for Historic Preservation. Emphasizes historic preservation. Monthly newspaper; 12-16 pages. Estab. 1961. Circ. 135,000. Pays on publication. Rights purchased vary; may buy all, second serial (reprint) or one-time rights. Photocopied submissions and previously published work OK. SASE. Reports in 4-6 weeks. Free sample copy and editorial guidelines.
Nonfiction: Carleton Knight, Associate Editor. "Most of our material is prepared in-house, but

willing to review queries on subjects directly related to historic preservation, including efforts to save and re-use buildings, structures, and to restore neighborhoods of historical, architectural and cultural significance. Writer must be very familiar with our subject matter, which deals with a specialized field, in order to present a unique publication idea." Length: 750 words maximum. Buys about 12 mss a year. Pays 10¢/word.
Photos: Additional payment not usually made for photos used with mss. Pays $10-25 for 8x10 b&w photos purchased without mss or on assignment. Query or send contact sheet. No conversions from slides.

Florida

THE FLORIDIAN, Box 1211, St. Petersburg FL 33731. Editor: Judy Sedgeman. For middle income readers with contemporary outlook. Weekly magazine; 24-40 pages. Estab. 1967. Circ. 200,000. Pays on acceptance. Buys first North American serial, second serial and simultaneous rights; exclusive rights within Florida. Simultaneous and photocopied submissions OK. SASE. Free writer's guidelines.
Nonfiction: Incisive articles should focus on Florida. Subject areas include government and politics, consumer issues, business and finance, health, leisure and recreation, food, fashion, interior design, architecture, and profiles of high-interest personalities. "Presentation should be crisp, original, innovative. No once-over-lightly features. Articles must be validated by substantial research and a high degree of professionalism is expected. Style is as important as substance. Buys 200 mss/year. Length: 1,000-3,000 words. Pays $75-500.

THE TAMPA TRIBUNE, Box 191, Tampa FL 33601. Features Editor: Leland. Hawes. For a general circulation, newspaper audience. Newspaper; 80 to 160 pages. Estab. 1894. Daily. Circ. 175,000 to 210,000. Not copyrighted, but special stories are copyrighted. Buys limited number of mss (primarily from area freelancers). Pays 2-4 weeks after publication. Will consider photocopied submissions. Simultaneous submissions considered (but not if made to nearby publications). Reports on material accepted for publication within a month. Returns rejected material within 2 weeks. Query first or submit complete ms. SASE.
Nonfiction and Photos: Articles on travel, history, news events, sports, fashion, profiles, trends, etc. Must have central Florida emphasis or tie-in. Open to any literate style. Informational, how-to, personal experience, interview, humor, think pieces, spot news. Length: 150-3,000 words. Pays $25-200. Pays $5 to $25 for b&w glossies purchased with or without ms. Pays $15 to $50 for color transparencies purchased with or without ms.

Idaho

COUNCIL RECORD, Box 67, Council ID 83612. Editor-in-Chief: Anson J. Longtin. 5% freelance written. Emphasizes news old and new, historical items, jokes, household hints, etc. Weekly newspaper; 14 pages. Estab. 1977. Circ. 4,500. Pays on acceptance. Buys all rights, but may reassign following publication. Submit seasonal/holiday material 2 months in advance of issue date. SASE. Reports in 4 weeks. Sample copy 10¢; mention *Writer's Market* in request.
Nonfiction: "Old natural health remedies, edible greens and recipes". How-to; historical; humor; inspirational; new product; nostalgia; personal experience; photo feature; and household hints to save money on items. Submit complete ms. Length: 400-1,500 words.
Photos: State availability of photos with ms. Buys b&w prints. Captions and model release required. Buys all rights, but may reassign following publication.
Columns/Departments: From Soup To Nuts; Horse Talk; I Remember; and Pastor's Corner. Submit complete ms. Length: 400-1,500 words. Open to suggestions for new columns/departments.
Fiction: Adventure; experimental; fantasy; historical; humorous; mainstream and western. "No articles on sex, pornographic or cheap language." Submit complete ms. Length: 400-1,500 words.
Fillers: Clippings; jokes, gags, anecdotes; newsbreaks and short humor.

Illinois

CHICAGO TRIBUNE MAGAZINE, 435 N. Michigan Ave., Chicago IL 60611. Editor: Robert Goldsborough. "The magazine is largely staff-written, but we do use a limited number of freelance articles. Query first, however." Pays $200 and up. Length: 1,500 to 3,000 words.

Indiana

INDIANAPOLIS STAR MAGAZINE, 307 N. Pennsylvania St., Indianapolis IN 46206. Editor-in-Chief: Fred D. Cavinder. 10-15% freelance written. Emphasizes subjects of interest in Indiana. Weekly magazine section of newspaper; 40 pages. Estab. 1947. Circ. 380,000. Pays on publication. Buys one-time rights. Phone queries OK. Submit seasonal/holiday material 2 months in advance. Simultaneous and photocopied submissions OK. SASE. Reports in 2 weeks. Free sample copy.
Nonfiction: Informational; historical and interview (Indiana only); profiles (Hoosiers or ex-Hoosiers only); and technical (health/medical developments). "Too many freelancers send us too general material. We are not interested in household hints, consumer tips, oddities, celebrities, etc. We want stories which would be of specific interest to Indiana readers. That is, if the story doesn't include some relationship to Indiana, the subject must be of significant universal interest. An example would be a health breakthrough, major social development, or a new national trend. But our overwhelming topic is Indiana, her people or her former residents." Buys 50/year. Query. Length: 5,000 words maximum. Pays $25-75.
Photos: Purchased with mss. Query or send prints or transparencies. Pays $5-7.50 for 5x7 or larger b&w glossies or mattes; $7.50-10 for 35mm (or larger) color transparencies.

MICHIANA, *The South Bend Tribune,* Colfax at Lafayette, South Bend IN 46626, (219)233-6161. Editor: Bill Sonneborn. 70% freelance written. For "average daily newspaper readers; perhaps a little above average since we have more than a dozen colleges and universities in our area." Weekly; 24 pages. Estab. 1873. Circ. 125,000. Rights purchased vary with author and material. May buy first North American serial rights or simultaneous rights providing material offered will be used outside of Indiana and Michigan. Buys about 200 mss a year. Payment on publication. Will consider photocopied submissions if clearly legible. Submit special material for spring and fall travel sections at least 1 month in advance. Reports in 10 days. Submit complete ms. SASE.
Nonfiction and Photos: "Items of general and unusual interest, written in good, clear, simple sentences with logical approach to subject. We like material oriented to the Midwest, especially Indiana, Michigan, Ohio and Illinois; also some religious material if unusual." Humor, think pieces, travel, photo articles with brief texts. "We avoid all freelance material that supports movements of a political nature. We do not like first-person stories, but use them on occasion. We can use some offbeat stuff if it isn't too far out." Length: 800 to 3,000 words. Payment is $50 to $60 minimum, with increases as deemed suitable. All mss must be accompanied by illustrations or b&w photos or 35mm or larger color transparencies.

Iowa

DES MOINES SUNDAY REGISTER PICTURE MAGAZINE, *Des Moines Register*, 715 Locust St., Des Moines IA 50309. Editor: Charles J. Nettles. 5-10% freelance written. For mass newspaper audience, metropolitan and rural. Estab. 1950. Weekly. Circ. 440,000. Buys first rights. Buys 12-15 mss a year. Payment on publication. Submit seasonal material 8 weeks in advance. SASE.
Nonfiction and Photos: "Articles heavily concentrated on Iowa, mostly picture stories; interest material. Anything interesting in Iowa, or interesting elsewhere with some kind of tie to Iowans." Length: 1,500 words maximum. Material must lend itself to strong photographic presentation. If the idea is good, a photographer will be assigned, if writer does not have professional quality photos. Pays $100-200. Photos purchased with or without mss. Captions required. Prefers 8x10 b&w glossies. Pays $15 minimum. 35mm or larger transparencies. Pays $50 minimum for cover; $25 for inside use.

Kentucky

THE COURIER-JOURNAL MAGAZINE, 525 West Broadway, Louisville KY 40207. Publisher: Barry Bingham Jr. Editor: James Pope. 25% freelance written, mostly from regular professional sources. For general readership in Kentucky and Indiana. Monthly magazine; 52 pages. Estab. 1942. Circ. 350,000. Pays on publication. Buys one-time rights. Submit seasonal/holiday material 2 months in advance of issue date. Simultaneous, photocopied and previously published submissions OK. SASE. Reports in 4 weeks.
Nonfiction: General interest; how-to; humor; photo feature; and profile. Buys 100 mss/year. Query or submit complete ms. Length: 1,500-3,000 words. Pays $100-300.
Photos: State availability of photos with query or submit with accompany mss. Pays $15-25 for 10x12 b&w glossy prints and $20-40 for color transparencies. Captions required. Buys one-time rights.

THE VOICE-JEFFERSONIAN, Chenoweth Sq., St. Matthews KY 40207. (502)895-5436. Editor: Bruce B. VanDusen. For middle and upper income suburban audience. Family readership, but no taboos. Weekly. "No copyright unless the story is super-special and exclusive to us." SASE.
Nonfiction and Photos: News and Features departments. 300 to 1,500 words on local (East Jefferson County) subjects. "Manuscripts must have a local angle. Writers persistently ignore this fundamental standard." 5x7 b&w glossies. Pays 25¢ to $1 per inch; $5 to $15 for photos.

Louisiana

SUNDAY ADVOCATE MAGAZINE, Box 588, Baton Rouge LA 70821. (504)383-1111, Ext. 319. Editor: Charles H. Lindsay. Buys no rights. Pays on publication. SASE.
Nonfiction and Photos: Well-illustrated, short articles; must have local, area or Louisiana angle, in that order of preference. Photos purchased with mss. Rates vary.

Massachusetts

THE CHRISTIAN SCIENCE MONITOR, 1 Norway St., Boston MA 02115. (617)262-2300, Ext. 2321. Editor: John Hughes. International newspaper issued daily except Saturdays, Sundays and holidays in North America; weekly international edition. Special issues: travel, winter vacation and international travel, summer vacation, autumn vacation, cruise section, and others. February and September: fashion. Estab. 1908. Circ. 188,000. Buys all rights. Buys about 3,700 mss a year. Payment on acceptance or publication, "depending on department." Submit seasonal material 2 months in advance. Reports within 4 weeks. Submit only complete ms. Enclose SASE.
Nonfiction: Features Editor: Alan Bunce. In-depth news analysis, features, and essays. Style should be bright but not cute, concise but thoroughly researched. Try to humanize news or feature writing so the reader identifies with it. Avoid sensationalism, crime and disaster. Accent constructive, solution-oriented treatment of subjects. Can use news-in-the-making stories not found elsewhere if subject has sufficient impact on current history (600 to 1,500 words). Feature pages use colorful human interest material not exceeding 800 words, and humorous anecdotes. Home Forum page buys essays of 400 to 800 words; education, arts, real estate, travel, women, fashion, furnishings, consumer, environment, and science-technology pages will consider articles not usually more than 800 words appropriate to respective subjects." Pays from $20 to $100. Some areas covered in travel pages include: Swiss, N.E., British, Canadian, Hawaiian, and Caribbean.
Photos: Department Editor: Gordon Converse. Purchased with or without mss. Captions required. Pays $10 to $50 depending upon size and where used in paper.
Poetry: Home Forum Editor: Henrietta Buckmaster. Home Forum uses poetry. Wide variety of subjects and treatment; traditional forms, blank and free verse, but the poetry must be of high quality and proficiency. Short poems preferred. Pays $20-40.

NEW ENGLAND MAGAZINE, *Boston Globe*, Boston MA 02107. Editor-in-Chief: Anthony C. Spinazzola. 40% freelance written. Weekly magazine; 44 pages. Estab. 1936. Circ. 606,353. Pays on publication. Buys one-time rights. Submit seasonal/holiday material 3 months in advance. Reports in 2 weeks.
Nonfiction: Karen Dobkin, Articles Editor. Expose (variety of issues including political, economic, and scientific); informational; humor (limited use, but occasionally published in short columns of 1,000 words); interview; personal opinion (1,000 words); and profile. Buys 100-150 mss/year. Query. Length: 1,000-3,000 words. Pays $150-400.
Photos: Purchased with accompanying ms or on assignment. Captions required. Send contact sheet. Pays $25-75 for b&w photos; $50-225 for color. Total purchase price for ms includes payment for photos.
Columns/Departments: Karen Dobkin, Column/Department Editor. In Personal Terms (humor, personal experiences, opinion). "This column is a magazine op-ed page, which allows the opportunity to air views, joys, angers, and experiences through quality writing." Buys 52 mss/year. Submit complete ms. Length: 1,000-1,200 words. Pays $175.

NORTH SHORE MAGAZINE, Essex County Newspapers, Inc., Whittemore St., Gloucester MA 01930. Editor: Tom Meade. 80% freelance written. Emphasizes regional features on Massachusetts' North Shore. Weekly tabloid; 32 pages. Estab. 1964. Circ. 38,700. Pays on publication. Buys all rights, but may reassign following publication. Submit seasonal/holiday

material 2 months in advance of issue date SASE. Reports in 3 weeks.
Nonfiction: How-to (fishing, hunting, outdoor family sports, etc.); general interest; historical (as long as the article is relevant to today); photo feature; and profile. All material must pertain to Massachusetts' North Shore. Buys 4 mss/issue. Query with clips of previously published work. Pays $30-70.
Photos: State availability of photos with query. Pays $5-25 for b&w photos; $15-50 for 35mm color transparencies. Captions required. Buys all rights, but may reassign following pbulciation. Model release required.
Poetry: John Ronan, poetry editor. "Poems must reflect the New England experience." Free verse; haiku; light verse; and traditional. Buys 1/issue. Limit submissions to batches of 5. Pays $10.

SUNDAY MORNING MAGAZINE, Worcester Sunday Telegram, 20 Franklin St., Worcester MA 01613. (617)755-4321. Sunday News Editor: Charles F. Mansbach. 25% freelance written. Sunday supplement serving a broad cross-section of Central Massachusetts residents; 16 pages. Estab. 1933. Circ. 110,000. Pays on acceptance. Buys first North American serial rights. Phone queries OK. Submit seasonal/holiday material 2 months in advance. SASE. Free sample copy.
Nonfiction: Expose (related to circulation area); informational (should have broad application); personal experience (something unusual); photo feature and profile. Buys 2 mss/issue. Query. Length: 600-2,400 words. Pays $50-100. "All pieces must have a local angle."
Photos: Photos purchased with or without accompanying ms or on assignment. Captions required. Pays $5 for 5x7 b&w glossies.
Columns/Departments: City Life ("a brief slice-of-life piece that says something about life in our city; heavy on dialogue and description.") Query. Length: 600-1,200 words. Pays $32-50. Open to suggestions for new columns/departments.

Maryland

PERSPECTIVE, The Baltimore Sun, 501 N. Calvert St., Baltimore MD 21203. Editor: Richard O'Mara. 50% freelance written. Emphasizes current affairs, national and international politics, social issues, etc. Weekly newspaper section; 3 pages. Estab. 1968. Circ. 300,000. Pays on publication. Buys all rights, but may reassign following publication. Phone queries OK. SASE. Reports in 3-4 weeks. Free sample copy.
Nonfiction: "We are looking for tightly-written articles on current issues, politics, national and international affairs. We run articles similar to those of the New York Times, and occasionally an offbeat piece, but never any fiction. We will look at humour pieces, but they must be well executed to make it." Buys 4 mss/issue. Query. Length: 1,000-5,000 words. Pays $125.

Michigan

DETROIT MAGAZINE, *The Detroit Free Press,* 321 Lafayette Blvd., Detroit MI 48231. (313)222-6490. Editor: Rogers Worthington. For a general newspaper readership; urban and suburban; relatively high educational level. Weekly magazine. Estab. 1965. Circ. 714,000. Pays within 6 weeks of publication. Buys first rights. Reports in 3-4 weeks. SASE. Sample copy for SASE.
Nonfiction: "Seeking quality magazine journalism or subjects of interest to Detroit and Michigan readers: lifestyles and better living, trends, behavior, health and body, business and political intrigue, crime and cops, money, success and failure, sports, fascinating people, arts and entertainment. *Detroit Magazine* is bright and cosmopolitan in tone. Most desired writing style is literate, but casual, and reporting must be impeachable. We also use guides or service pieces." Buys 65-75 mss/year. Query or submit complete ms. Length: 3,000 words maximum. Pays $125-250.
Photos: Purchased with or without accompanying ms. Pays $25 for b&w glossies or color transparencies used inside; $100 for color used as cover. (Covers are usually free-standing, non-story related.)

FENTON INDEPENDENT, 112 E. Ellen St., Fenton MI 48430. (313)629-2203. Editor: Robert G. Silbar. Weekly. Newspaper, not a magazine supplement. Buys all rights. Query first. SASE.
Nonfiction and Photos: News stories, features, photos of local interest. Wants local material on local people, not generalized articles. Appreciates opinion articles on local topics. All material must have local flavor. Pays 25¢ per column inch.

New York

FAMILY WEEKLY, 641 Lexington Ave., New York NY 10022. Executive Editor: Scott DeCarmo. Managing Editor: Tim Mulligan. 60% freelance written. No longer accepting unsolicited mss, but will consider queries. SASE.
Fillers: Will consider short jokes and humor items. Pays $10.

LI MAGAZINE, *Newsday,* 550 Stewart Ave., Garden City NY 11530. (516)222-5126. Managing Editor: Stanley Green. For well-educated, affluent suburban readers. Established in 1972. Weekly. Circulation: 450,000. Buys all rights. Pays on publication. Query. SASE.
Nonfiction and Photos: Art Director: Cliff Gardiner. "Stories must be about Long Island people, places or events." Length: 600 to 2,500 words. Pays $100 to $600. B&w contacts and 35mm transparencies purchased on assignment. Pays up to $100 per page for b&w; $200 per page for color, including cover.

NATIONAL EXAMINER, Box 711, Rouses Point NY 12979. (514)866-7744. Editor-in-Chief: John Elder. For a contemporary, upbeat audience. Weekly color tabloid. Pays on publication. Buys first North American serial rights. Phone queries OK. SASE.
Nonfiction: Informational; how-to; personal experience; interview; profile; inspirational; humor; historical; expose; nostalgia; photo feature; spot news; and new product. Especially interested in pieces on ghosts, psychics and astrology. Query.
Photos: Purchased with or without accompanying ms. "Celebrities, off-beat shots, humorous and spot news photos always in demand." Send prints or transparencies.

NEW YORK NEWS MAGAZINE, *New York Daily News*, 220 E. 42 St., New York NY 10017. Editor: Richard C. Lemon. For general audience. Weekly. Circulation: over 3 million. Buys first serial rights. Buys about 40 mss a year. Payment on acceptance. Will send free sample copy to a writer on request. Submit seasonal material 2 months in advance. Will consider photocopied submissions. Reports in 4 weeks. Query first. "If you have published before, it is best to include a sample clip." Enclose SASE.
Nonfiction and Photos: "Interested in all sorts of articles: most interested in human interest stories, articles about people (famous or unknown) and service pieces; least interested in essays and discussion pieces. Continuing need for New York City area subjects. Freelancer should use his own approach to material. Entertainment pieces seem to be over-abundant. We use a number, but they are mostly staff written." Buys informational, personal experience, interview, profile, humor, nostalgia, and photo articles. Length: 600 to 3,000 words. Pays $50 to $750. Photos purchased with or without mss. Captions are required. Specifications for b&w glossies or jumbo contacts: 8x10. Pays $25 for single, $150 for complete picture story. Color specifications: 2½, 4x5 or 35mm transparency. Pays from $35 for single, $200 for set.
How To Break In: "For new writers, the key thing to remember is to start with a suggestion that grabs us and keep your material within screaming distance of New York City."

THE NEW YORK TIMES, 229 W. 43 St., New York NY 10036. Enclose SASE for reply to queries or return of mss.
Nonfiction and Photos: *The New York Times Magazine* appears in *The New York Times* on Sunday, and is edited by Edward Klein. "We are looking for fresh, lively and provocative writing on national and international news developments, science, education, family life, social trends and problems, arts and entertainment, personalities, sports, the changing American scene. Freelance contributions are invited. Articles must be timely. They must be based on specific news items, forthcoming events, significant anniversaries, or they must reflect trends. Our full-length articles run from 2,500-5,000 words, and for these we pay $850 on acceptance. ($1,000 after two prior acceptances). Our shorter pieces run from 1,500-2,500 words, and for these, we pay $500 on acceptance. We pay a basic minimum of $50 for photos." *Travel and Resorts* section buys "literate, sophisticated, factual articles, evoking the experience of travel with quotes, anecdotes and even-handed reportage. Authors must be personally familiar with subjects about which they write, free to praise or criticize; under no circumstances will we publish articles growing out of trips in any way subsidized by airlines, hotels or other organizations with direct or indirect interest in the subjects. All submissions are to be considered on speculation; payment upon publication is approximately 10¢ a word; maximum $250 per article; additional $50 for each photo used." *Travel and Resorts* Editor: Robert Crandall. *Arts and*

Leisure section of *The New York Times* appears on Sunday. Wants "to encourage imaginativeness in terms of form and approach —stressing ideas, issues, trends, investigations, symbolic reporting and stories delving deeply into the creative achievements and processes of artists and entertainers —and seeks to break away from old-fashioned gushy, fan magazine stuff." Length: 750-2,000 words. Pays $100-$250 depending on length. Pays $50 for photos. *Arts and Leisure* Editor: William H. Honan.
How To Break In: "The Op Ed page is always looking for new material and publishes many people who have never been published before. We want material of universal relevance which people can talk about in a personal way. When writing for the Op Ed page there is no formula but the writing itself should have some polish. Don't make the mistake of pontificating on the news. We're not looking for more political columnists. Op Ed length runs about 700 words, and pays about $150."

NEWSDAY, 550 Stewart Ave., Garden City NY 11566. Travel Editor: Steve Schatt. For general readership of Sunday Travel Section. Newspaper. Estab. 1947. Weekly. Circ. 515,000. Buys all rights for the New York area only. Buys 100 mss a year. Pays on publication. Will consider photocopied submissions. Simultaneous submissions considered if others are being made outside of New York area. Reports in 4 weeks. Submit complete ms. SASE.
Nonfiction and Photos: Travel articles with strong focus and theme for the Sunday Travel Section. Emphasis on accuracy, honesty, service, quality writing to convey mood and flavor. Destination pieces must involve visit or experience that typical traveler can easily duplicate. Skip diaries, "My First Trip Abroad" pieces or compendiums of activities; downplay first person. Length: 600 to 1,750 words, but use more 800-1,000—word pieces. Pays $60-175. Also, regional "weekender" pieces of 700-800 words plus service box, but query subject first.

PARADE, The Sunday Newspaper Magazine, 733 Third Ave., New York NY 10017. (212)953-7557. Weekly. Circ. over 21 million. Buys first North American serial rights. Pays on acceptance. Query first. SASE.
Nonfiction: "Interested in features that will inform, educate or entertain a mass circulation domestic audience. Exclusive, news-related articles and photos are required. Subjects may include: well-known personalities, sports, religion, education, community activities, family relations, science and medicine. Articles should be current, factual, authoritative." Length: about 1,500 words. Pays up to $2,500.
Photos: "Photos should have visual impact and be well composed with action-stopping qualities. For the most part, color is used on cover. Transparencies of any size are accepted. Either b&w 8x10 enlargements or contact sheets may be submitted. Accurate caption material must accompany all photos."

Ohio

THE BLADE TOLEDO MAGAZINE, 541 Superior St., Toledo OH 43660. (419)259-6132. Editor: Tom Gearhart. General readership. Weekly magazine; 32 pages. Estab. 1948. Circ. 210,000. Pays on publication. Buys one-time rights. Phone queries OK. Submit seasonal/holiday material 6 months in advance. Simultaneous, photocopied and previously published submissions OK. SASE.
Nonfiction: Historical (about Ohio); humor; informational; interview; personal experience and photo feature. Buys 1 ms/issue. Query. Length: 600-2,000 words. Pays $35-100.
Photos: Photos purchased with accompanying ms. Captions required. Pays $7.50-15 for 8x10 b&w glossies; $10-45 for 35mm, 2¼x2¼ or 8x10 color glossies. Total purchase price for ms includes payment for photos. Model release required.

COLUMBUS DISPATCH SUNDAY MAGAZINE, 34 South Third St., Columbus OH 43216. (614)461-5250. Editor: Hal Schellkoph. 50% freelance written. Buys one-time rights. Payment after publication. Enclose SASE.
Nonfiction and Photos: "We accept offerings from beginning writers, but they must be professionally written, and a good picture helps." Strong Ohio angle is essential in all material. Buys singles, photo series, and illustrated articles. Length: 1,000 to 1,500 words. Pays minimum of 3¢ per word. B&w photos only. Pays $5 per photos. "Pay is flexible, depending on how good the piece is, how much effort has apparently been put into it, etc."

DAYTON LEISURE, *Dayton Daily News*, Fourth and Ludlow Sts., Dayton OH 45401. (513)225-2240. Editor: Jack M. Osler. Sunday supplement. Circ. 225,000. Pays on publication.

Usually reports within 1 week. Enclose SASE.
Nonfiction and Photos: Magazine focuses on leisure time activities particularly in Ohio—that are interesting and unusual. Emphasis is on photos supplemented by stories. Up to 1,000 words. Photos should be glossy. "*The Daily News* will evaluate articles on their own merits. Likewise with photos. Average payment per article: $30." Payments vary depending on quality of writing.

THE ENQUIRER MAGAZINE, 617 Vine St., Cincinnati OH 45201. (513)721-2700. Editor: Graydon DeCamp. Art Director: Ron Huff. Weekly newspaper supplement; 52 pages. Circ. 290,000. Pays on publication. Free writer's guidelines. Photocopied and simultaneous submissions OK. Submit "dated" material at least 2 months in advance. SASE.
Nonfiction: Local articles, current subjects, issues, trends, personalities, topical material, "think" pieces. Will use some local nostalgia/history. "Will not accept manuscripts about any organization or event written by anyone connected with that organization or event, except in unusual first-person cases." Buys 100 mss/year. Query. Length: 1,500-3,000 words. Pays $50-200.
Photos: Will buy photos with ms; must be of professional quality. Pays $10-50 for 8x10 b&w prints.

Oregon

NORTHWEST MAGAZINE, *The Sunday Oregonian*, 1320 S.W. Broadway, Portland OR 97201. Editor: Joseph R. Bianco. For a family type of audience with somewhat higher education level in Oregon than average. Weekly Sunday supplement magazine; 28 to 40 pages. Estab. 1965. Circ. about 400,000. Buys all rights, but will reassign rights to author after publication. Buys 600 to 650 mss a year. Pays in the closest period to the 15th of the month following publication. Will not consider photocopied submissions. Will consider simultaneous submissions. Reports on material accepted for publication in 10 days. Returns rejected material in 2 weeks. Query first or submit complete ms. Enclose SASE.
Nonfiction and Photos: "Articles of interest to the Northwest. Topical and (sometimes) controversial. Periodically, issue is devoted to a theme. For example, the theme of 'Outdoors' is how-to. How to do the hockey stop in skiing, how to find a remote hiking ridge, etc. Keep Northwest articles short, topical, and of interest to the Northwest. Ecology, environment, and social mores are always subjects of interest. Also, personality profiles of people of interest." Length: 800 to 1,500 words. Pays $40. 8x10 b&w glossies are purchased with mss or on assignment. Captions required. Pays $15.

Pennsylvania

THE PITTSBURGH PRESS, 34 Blvd. of Allies, Pittsburgh PA 15230. (412)263-1100. Features Editor: William Allan. For general newspaper readers. Estab. 1920. Publishes 3 weekly magazines. Circ. 700,000. Not copyrighted. Buys 25 to 50 mss a year. Pays on publication. Reports in 2 weeks. Submit complete ms. Enclose SASE.
Nonfiction and Photos: Picture-oriented material for the Roto Magazine; family type stories for Family Magazine. Must be local subjects with good general interest. Informational, how-to, personal experience, profile, inspirational, humor, historical, nostalgia. Pays $25 per published page. Some additional payment for b&w photos used with mss.
How To Break In: "Submit good copy."

TODAY MAGAZINE, Philadelphia Inquirer, 400 N. Broad St., Philadelphia PA 19101. Editor-in-Chief: David Boldt. Managing Editor: John Lubell. Sunday magazine section for city and suburban readers. Weekly; 42 pages. Circ. 850,000. Pays on publication. Buys first North American serial rights. Submit seasonal/holiday material 3 months in advance of issue date. Photocopied submissions OK. SASE. Reports in 2 months. Free sample copy.
Nonfiction: "Most of our material is written by freelance writers. Articles run from 300-7,000 words. Occasionally we run first-person articles but they are the exception to our general rule of reporting on and analysis of local issues and personalities. Query. Pays $125-500.

Rhode Island

RHODE ISLANDER, *The Providence Journal*, Providence RI 02902. (401)277-7263. Editor: Douglas Riggs. Sunday magazine section. Circ. 210,000. Buys first rights. Pays on publication.

Free sample copy. Reports in 2 weeks. Query first or submit complete ms. SASE.
Nonfiction and Photos: "Always looking for new writers with real talent. Prefer articles with 'new journalism' flavor (anecdotal, subjective, highly descriptive, thought-provoking, etc.). Strongly oriented toward Rhode Island and southern New England." Pays $50 to $200. Photos purchased with mss. Their weekly "Speaking Out" feature uses expressions of opinions on any topic. Length: 750 words maximum. Pays $50.
How To Break In: "A phone call or personal visit is better than a query letter. If you have some specific story ideas, you are always welcome. Read the magazine first; sample copies sent on request. Personal contact with writer may mean difference between rejection slip and letter suggesting revisions. But if your stuff is really good, we'll buy it if it comes in by pony express. We're always looking for new talent, especially in southern New England."
Rejects: "Light" essays on homey topics, historical narrations unrelieved by anecdotes, commentary on national events, single photographs.

Texas

MIDLAND REPORTER-TELEGRAM, Box 1650, Midland TX 79701. Managing Editor: Tom Rutland. City Editor: Tom Nickell. Primarily for oilmen, ranchers, office workers; all ages, varied interests. Daily newspaper. Estab. 1890. Circ. 23,000. Pays on publication. Buys one-time rights. Query. Phone queries OK. Submit seasonal/holiday material 1 month in advance. Reports in 2-3 weeks. Sample copy 50¢.
Nonfiction: Informational, historical, interviews, profiles, travel articles; photo features. Should be related to the oil business or be of interest to West Texas readers. Query. Length: 200 words minimum. Pays $5-10.
Photos: Purchased with or without mss or on assignment. Captions required. Query. Pays $3-10 for 8x10 b&w glossies. Model release required.
Columns/Departments: Material for Oil/Energy, Travel and Outdoors columns. Query. Length: 200 words minimum. Pays $3-10. Address suggestions for new columns and departments to Tom Rutland.

Washington

PANORAMA MAGAZINE, *The Everett Herald,* Box 930, Everett WA 98206. (206)259-5151. Editor: Jeanne Metzger. Weekly magazine section; 20 pages. Estab. 1973. Circ. 56,000. Pays on publication. Buys one-time rights. Phone queries OK. Submit seasonal/holiday material 6 weeks in advance. Simultaneous, photocopied and previously published submissions OK. SASE. Reports in 1 month.
Nonfiction: Historical (Pacific Northwest history); humor; interview and profile; nostalgia; personal experience; photo feature and some travel. Query or send complete ms. Pays $15-60.
Photos: Photos purchased with or without accompanying ms. Pays $30 for good color photos to go with 'people' covers. No payment for b&w photos accompanying ms.

SEATTLE TIMES MAGAZINE, Seattle Times Co., Box 70, Seattle WA 98111. (206)464-2283. Editor: Larry Anderson. 40% freelance written. For people 20-80, above average in education and income. Weekly newspaper supplement; 16 pages. Circ. 250,000. Pays on publication. Buys first rights. Submit seasonal/holiday material 2 months in advance. Photocopied and previously published submissions OK. SASE. Reports in 1 week. Free sample copy and writer's guidelines.
Nonfiction: Humor; informational; inspirational; interview; personal experience and profile. Buys 3 mss/issue. Query or send complete ms. Length: 200-1,500 words. Pays $40-60/page.
Photos: Photos purchased with accompanying ms. Captions required. Pays $10-20 for b&w glossies. Query or send prints.

SEATTLE TIMES PICTORIAL, P.O. Box 70, Seattle WA 98111. Editor: Tom Stockley. For a general audience, above average in education. Sunday newspaper supplement. Circ. 325,000. Buys first rights. Pays on publication. Reports in 1 week. SASE.
Nonfiction and Photos: Looking for pictorial essays on regional (Washington, British Columbia) material. Uses b&w photos inside with possible tie-in color (4x5 transparencies) cover. B&w, submit negatives with contact sheets. Text length: 500 to 1,000 words. Pays $30 to $50 for text. Pays $125 for color cover; $30/page for b&w. Unused negatives and transparencies returned after publication.

SUNDAY MAGAZINE, *Tacoma News Tribune*, 1950 S. State St., Tacoma WA 98411. (206)597-8671. Editor: Dick Kunkle. 15% freelance written. Sunday supplement. Circ. 100,000. Pays on publication. Query first. Reports immediately. SASE.
Nonfiction and Photos: Articles and photos about Pacific Northwest, particularly the Puget Sound area. Historical, biographical, recreational stories. Length: 1,000 words maximum. Pays $50/printed tabloid page, whether pictures, text or both. Also occasionally buys a color cover transparency for $60. Northwest subjects only.

TOTEM TIDINGS MAGAZINE, *The Daily Olympian*, Box 407, Olympia WA 98507. Editor: Dennis Anstine. For newspaper readers. Sunday tabloid; 16 pages. Estab. 1974. Weekly. Circ. 27,000. Not copyrighted. Buys about 50 mss a year. Pays on publication. Free sample copy to writer on request if postage is included. Write for copy of guidelines for writers. No photocopied or simultaneous submissions. Reports in 30 days. Query first. SASE.
Nonfiction and Photos: Washington state-oriented articles, preferably from southwestern part of state. Must be bright and fast-paced material. People, places or things —but no first-person articles. Historical, water-oriented and topical pieces dealing with the immediate area. Informational, how-to, interview, profile, humor, historical, nostalgia, travel (but only in the northwest). Length: 1,440 words maximum. Pays $35. Buys color transparencies or b&w (8x10) prints with mss. Pays $5 for both b&w and color.

West Virginia

PANORAMA, *The Morgantown Dominion-Post*, Greer Bldg., Morgantown WV 26505. Sunday supplement issued weekly. Editor: Sarah Stevenson. Rights purchased are negotiable. Pays on publication. Reports in 2 weeks. Query first. Enclose SASE.
Nonfiction: "While we have considerable material from our regular sources, we are interested in 1,500- to 2,000-word nonfiction about West Virginia places, people, customs and events and about the Appalachian area immediately surrounding the state. We are always looking for the regional tie-in, no matter how slim." Pays $7.50 to $25.

STATE MAGAZINE, *Sunday Gazette-Mail*, 1001 Virginia St., E, Charleston WV 25330. Editor: Harold C. Gadd. 50% freelance written. For family newspaper readers. Weekly newspaper magazine. Estab. 1952. Circ. 110,000. Not copyrighted. Buys 150 to 200 mss a year. Pays on publication. Sample copy for 25¢. Will consider photocopied submissions. Simultaneous submissions are considered, if not made to other West Virginia newspapers. Submit special issue material by May 1. Reports in 30 to 90 days. Query first. SASE.
Nonfiction and Photos: Emphasis is on West Virginia material; articles and photo essays. "Simple, lucid, tight writing with a logical organization. Writer must want to catch and hold readers' attention in a busy, busy world. We do not want to see material that has obviously been rejected by other publications. We're easy to sell, but not that easy." Length: 500 to 1,500 words. Pays $10 to $50. Annually publishes a special issue on West Virginia: Vacationland, in which articles on enjoyable West Virginia vacation locales are used. Length: 500 to 1,000 words. Pays $10 to $50. B&w photos with good contrast, good composition, and sharp focus purchased with or without ms. Pays $5. Ultra-sharp, bright, 35mm (or up to 4x5) color transparencies purchased with or without ms. Pays $20.
How To Break In: "Always query first. Beginning West Virginia writers have best chance. Our freelance policy is designed to encourage them to write about their home state."

Wisconsin

INSIGHT MAGAZINE, *Milwaukee Journal*, 333 W. State, Milwaukee WI 53201. (414)224-2341. Editor: Mike Moore. Emphasizes general interest reading for a cross-section of Milwaukee. Weekly magazine; 48 pages. Estab. 1969. Circ. 530,000. Pays on acceptance. Buys one-time rights. Phone queries OK. Submit seasonal/holiday material at least 2 months in advance. Simultaneous, photocopied and previously published submissions OK. SASE. Reports in 1-2 weeks. Free sample copy.
Nonfiction: Humor; interview; nostalgia; personal experience; personal opinion; and profile. Buys 50 mss/year. Query. Length: 1,000-3,000 words. Pays $50-250.
How To Break In: "We are not a good market for out-of-state writers. We may buy reprints from time to time from established writers."

MIDWEST ROTO, Rural Gravure Service, Inc., 6501 Mineral Point Rd., Madison WI 53719. Editor-in-Chief: Jerry C. Curren. Managing Editor: Bonnie Currie. Emphasizes "hometown midwest America. A newspaper supplement which carries human interest articles about the midwest and midwest people. Circulates in 150 newspapers." Monthly magazine; 16 pages. Estab. 1936. Circ. 651,000. Pays on publication. Buys simultaneous rights. Submit seasonal/holiday material 6 months in advance. Simultaneous and previously published submissions OK. SASE. Reports in 1 week.

Nonfiction: Historical; humor; interview; nostalgia; photo feature; and profile. Mss must relate to midwest people and places. Buys 4-6/issue. Submit complete ms. Length: 1,000-3,000 words. Pays $50-300.

Photos: Purchased with accompanying ms. Captions required. Send prints. Pays $15-150 for 8x10 b&w glossies. Total purchase price for ms includes payment for photos. Model release required.

Canada

THE CANADIAN MAGAZINE, The Simpson Tower, 401 Bay St., Toronto M5H 2Y8, Ontario, Canada. (416)363-7151. Editor: Patrick Scott. Buys North American serial rights. Pays on acceptance. "We only consider mss written with a very strong Canadian slant." Query first. Enclose SAE and International Reply Coupons.

Nonfiction: Department Editor: Arthur Rowson, Managing Editor. Looking for articles of interest to Canadians from coast to coast, on Canadian subjects, written in a lively and informative manner with plenty of human interest. Effective use of anecdotes quite frequently provides this human interest; therefore, use an anecdotal approach to the subject. Articles submitted may cover a wide range of topics—human affairs, religion, science, politics, personalities, humor and sport, hobbies, cookery and fashion. Looking for good literary quality. Strongly recommend an outline letter, of 200 to 300 words, staking out the extent and burden of the article. Length: 1,100 to 3,000 words. Pays $300 to $900.

THE ISLANDER MAGAZINE, *The Daily Colonist*, Victoria B.C., Canada. (604)383-4111. Editor: Alec Merriman. For "just about everyone who lives on Vancouver Island". Weekly; 16 pages. Estab. 1858. Circ. 50,000. Not copyrighted. Buys 400 to 500 mss a year. Pays on publication. Free sample copy. Will not consider simultaneous submissions. Reporting time varies "from a week or two to a year, if it is an article we hope to use." Submit complete ms. SASE.

Nonfiction and Photos: "*The Islander* is very personally Pacific Northwest, mainly Vancouver Island, and takes a folksy, homespun, almost chatty outlook. We aim at our local market and don't try to compete with the syndicated magazine sections with articles of wide-ranging general interest. We use feature articles about people, places and things, with a Pacific Northwest slant, plus a heavy interest in Northwest history. All material must have the Pacific Northwest angle." Length: 500 to 2,000 words. Pays about $25/magazine page. Prefers 5x7 or 8x10 b&w glossies, but sometimes uses snapshots. Pays $3 for photos used with ms; $7.50 for cover use (always a local scene). Captions required.

How To Break In: "*The Islander* leans heavily toward the local slant which is an advantage for Pacific Northwest writers. But, a person from this area who is doing something unique or making a success of living elsewhere always makes an acceptable feature. Travel literature is distributed freely by the yard, so a local and different slant must be sought."

WEEKEND MAGAZINE, The Montreal Standard Limited/Limitee, 390 Bay St., Suite 504, Toronto, Ontario Canada M5H 2Y2. Editor: John Macfarlane. Weekly section of 23 newspapers. Circ. 1,700,000. Buys first North American rights. Buys 100 mss/year. Pays on acceptance. "All mss and photos sent in are done so on a speculative basis only and should be addressed to the Editor or Art Director respectively." Query before submitting material. Enclose SAE and International Reply Coupons with mss and queries.

Nonfiction and Photos: "Articles should be about some person, event or activity of interest to Canadians. We don't use travel articles or fillers." Length: 1,500 to 2,500 words. Pays $400-800. If photos or transparencies are sent in and used in addition to the ms, payment is adjusted accordingly. "Our photographic requirements are for all sizes of color from 35mm up; we prefer color transparencies and b&w prints." Pays from $75-250.

Op-Ed Pages

Within the last few years, a new forum for opinion and observation (and freelance opportunity) has emerged—the Op-Ed Page. The Op-Ed page is that page in a newspaper *opposite* the editorial page which solicits commentary on any subject concerning its readers.

Here are the requirements for two of the largest and best known newspapers who solicit material for their Op-Ed pages. Be sure to check with your own local newspaper to see if it contains an Op-Ed page, or if it solicits freelance material for use on its editorial page.

NEW YORK TIMES, 229 W. 43rd St., New York NY 10036. Op-Ed Page Editor: Charlotte Curtis. Daily. Copyrighted, if requested. Submit complete ms. SASE. "No limit to topics, just something of interest to the public. However, it should be an opinion or commentary. No news reports. We are always looking for new and exciting writers to add to the page." Length: 700 words maximum. Pays $150 maximum.

NEWSDAY, 550 Stewart Ave., Garden City NY 11550. Editorial Page Editor: William C. Sexton. Daily. Copyrighted. SASE. Seeks "opinion on current events, trends, issues—whether national or local government or lifestyle. Must be timely, pertinent, articulate and opinionated. Strong preference for authors within the circulation area, and it's best to consult before you start writing." Length: 600-2,000 words. Pays $50-500.

Photography Publications

CAMERA 35, Popular Publications, 150 E. 58th St., New York NY 10022. (212)935-7160. Editor: Willard Clark. "A very special magazine within a vertical field, directed at thinking photographers." Semiannual magazine. Estab. 1957. Circ. 115,000. Buys first North American serial rights. Pays on publication. Query first. Reports in 1 to 3 months. SASE.
Photos: "Photography published in form of portfolios and essays. No taboos for either words or pictures, as long as they fit our needs. To determine needs, study at least 3 recent issues. Good literate writing mandatory." Payment rates negotiable prior to acceptance.

PETERSEN'S PHOTOGRAPHIC MAGAZINE, Petersen Publishing Co., 8490 Sunset Blvd., Los Angeles CA 90069. (213)657-5100. Publisher: Paul R. Farber. Editor: Karen Geller. Emphasizes photography. Monthly magazine; 112 pages. Estab. 1972. Circ. 230,000. Pays on publication. Buys one-time rights. Submit seasonal/holiday material 5 months in advance. Photocopied submissions OK. SASE. Reports in 2 months. Sample copy $2.
Nonfiction: Merrill Roseman, Nonfiction Editor. How-to. Buys 3 mss/issue. Send story outline. Pays $60/printed page.
Photos: David B. Brooks, Photo Editor. Photos purchased with or without accompanying ms. Pays $25-35 for b&w and color photos. Model release required.

PHOTO INSIGHT, Suite 2, 91-24 168th St., Jamaica NY 11432. Editor-in-Chief: Conrad Lovelo, Jr. 95% freelance written. Emphasizes photography. For amateur and professional photographers interested in photography contests. Bimonthly newsletter; 8 pages. Estab. 1975. Circ. 1,000. Pays on publication. Buys one-time rights. Submit seasonal or holiday material 3 months in advance. Simultaneous and previously published submissions OK. SASE. Reports in 1 month. Sample copy $1.
Nonfiction: How-to (tips on winning contests), humor, inspirational and new products (related to photography). Buys 2 mss/issue. Length: 800-1,000 words. Pays $30.
Photos: Photos purchased with accompanying ms. Captions required. Pays $35 for 8x10 or 4x5 b&w glossies. Total purchase price for ms includes payment for photos. Model release required.
Columns/Departments: Gallery Insight (photo show reviews) and In The News (new products or seminars). Buys 1 ms/issue. Query. Length: 100-300 words. Pays $10. Open to suggestions for new columns/departments.
Poetry: Edwardo Braithwaite, Poetry Editor. Traditional. Length: 4-12 lines. Pays $5.
Fillers: Jokes, gags and anecdotes. Pays $5.

PHOTOMETHODS, Ziff-Davis Publishing Co., 1 Park Ave., New York NY 10016. (212)725-3942. Editor-in-Chief: Fred Schmidt. Managing Editor: Richard Cooper. 90% freelance written. Emphasizes photography (still, motion, video) as a tool for "all adult ages; most are college or technical school graduates, many readers are in science, engineering or education." Monthly magazine; 80 pages. Estab. 1970. Circ. 50,000. Pays on publication. Buys one-time rights. Phone queries OK. SASE. Reports in 4 weeks. Free sample copy and writer's guidelines; mention *Writer's Market* in request.
Nonfiction: How-to (application stories to help readers in his/her work); interview; personal

experience (that will benefit the reader in his/her work); photo feature (rare, but will consider); profile; and technical (always interested in 'popularizing' highly technical applications). No material dealing with amateur photography or snapshooters. Buys 60-70mss/year. Query. Length: 1,500-3,000 words. Pays $75-300.
Photos: Mary Sealfon, art director. State availability of photos with query. Offers no additional payment for photos accepted with ms. Uses 5x7 and up matte dried or glossy b&w prints and 35mm and up color transparencies. Captions required. Buys one-time rights. Model release required.
Columns/Departments: How I Solved The Problem. Submit complete ms. Length: 1,000-1,500 words. Pays $75 minimum.

POPULAR PHOTOGRAPHY, 1 Park Ave., New York NY 10016. Editor: Kenneth Poli. "Mostly for advanced hobby photographers; about 90% are men." Also publishes 6 annuals or one-shots. Monthly. Circ. 800,000. "Rights purchased vary with author and material, but usually buys one-time if story is author's idea, not ours." Buys 35 to 50 mss/year, "mostly from technical types already known to us." Pays on acceptance. Submit material 4 months in advance. Reports in 3 to 4 weeks. Query first. SASE.
Nonfiction: This magazine is mainly interested in instructional articles on photography that will help photographers improve their work. This includes all aspects of photography, from theory to camera use and darkroom procedures. Utter familiarity with the subject is a prerequisite to acceptance here. It is best to submit article ideas in outline form since features are set up to fit the magazine's visual policies. "Style should be very readable but with plenty of factual data when a technique story is involved. We're not quite as 'hardware' oriented as some magazines. We use many equipment stories, but we give more space to cultural and aesthetic aspects of the hobby than our competition does." Buys how-to's, interviews, profiles, historical articles, new product coverage, photo essays. Length: 500 to 2,000 words. Pays $120 per b&w display page; $200 for color page.
Photos: Interested in seeing b&w prints of any type finish that are 8x10 or larger. Also uses any size color transparency. Buys one-time rights except when assigned, then all-time. No additional payment is made. Gives few assignments.
Fillers: Uses featurettes that run from 1 to 2 columns to 1-pagers and "Photo Tips," which are short how-to-do-its, illustrated by a single picture. Featurette length should be from 500 to 1,000 words; for the "Photo Tips," less than 100 words or whatever is necessary to give all pertinent information. Pays $25 to $75 for featurettes, depending on use; $25 for illustrated "Photo Tips."

STUDENT FORUM, 2519 De La Vina #5, Santa Barbara CA 93105. (805)682-5530. Editor-in-Chief: Glen Serbin. Managing Editor: V. Montmorency. 75% freelance written. Emphasizes student photographic work. Bimonthly magazine; 65 pages. Estab. November 1978. Pays on publication. Buys all rights. Simultaneous and previously published submissions OK. SASE. Reports in 3 weeks.
Nonfiction: Exposé; general interest and historical. "Articles must deal with some aspect of photography or student photography." Interviews (how one got started, views on the different schools); profile (of schools); and photo feature. "No technical articles." Submit complete ms. Length: 500-3,000 words. Pays $40.
Photos: State availability of photos with ms. Pays $35 for 5x7 or 8x10 b&w matt prints. Buys one-time rights. Model release is required.
Columns/Departments: Book Review; Historical Analysis; Interview; and School Profile. Buys 6 mss/issue. Submit complete ms. Length: 500-3,000 words. Pays $35. Open to suggestions for new columns/departments.
Fillers: Cartoons or anything else that may be of interest to student photographers. Pays $10.

UNDERWATER PHOTOGRAPHER, Drawer 608, Dana Point CA 92629. Editor/Publisher: F.M. Roberts. 25% freelance written. Bimonthly magazine; 32 pages. Estab. 1973. Circ. 2,000. Pays on publication. Buys one-time rights. Submit seasonal/holiday material 6 months in advance. Simultaneous and photocopied submissions OK. SASE. Reports in 3-4 months. Sample copy $1.
Nonfiction: General interest; how-to (building equipment); interview (with well-known underwater photographers); photo feature; technical (on photography); and travel. Buys 3-4 mss/year. Query. Length: 1,000-2,000 words. Pays 1¢/word.
Photos: State availability of photos with query. Pays $5 for 5x7 or 8x10 glossy b&w prints; $5-25 for 35mm or 2¼x2¼ color transparencies. Captions required. Buys one-time rights. Model release required.

Poetry Publications

This category includes publications that exist to discuss and publish poetry. A few newspapers and other special media using poetry are also included. Many publications in the Literary and Little category are also interested in poetry submissions. Various other poetry markets are listed in other categories throughout the Consumer section.

Many of the markets that follow pay in contributor's copies, prizes or some form of remuneration other than money. We have included such markets because there are limited commercial outlets for poetry and these at least offer the poet some visibility.

Poetry manuscripts should have the poet's name and address typed in the upper left-hand corner. Total number of lines in the poem should appear in the upper right-hand corner. Center the title of the poem 8 to 10 lines from the top of the page. The poem should be typed, double-spaced. The poet's name should again appear at the end of the poem. In the case where the poet submits more than one poem to the editor, each poem should always be typed on a separate sheet of paper. Always enclose SASE with poetry submissions.

ADVENTURES IN POETRY MAGAZINE, 3915 SW Military Dr., San Antonio TX 78211. (512)923-8407. Editor-in-Chief: Dr. Stella Woodall. Bimonthly magazine; 60 pages. Estab. 1968. Circ. 500. Submit seasonal/holiday material 3 months in advance. Previously published submissions OK. SASE. Reports in 8 weeks. Sample copy $2.
Poetry: Free verse; haiku; light verse; traditional and sonnet. Uses 60 poems/issue. "We have prizes for each issue, contest prizes of $25, $15 and $10 and annual prizes for those registering for Patriotic Poetry Seminar, up to $500 in prizes."

AMERICAN POETRY LEAGUE MAGAZINE, 3925 SW Military Dr., San Antonio TX 78211. (512)923-8407. Editor-in-Chief: Dr. Stella Woodall. Quarterly magazine. See *Adventures in Poetry Magazine*.

ASFA POETRY QUARTERLY, Alabama School of Fine Arts, 820 N. 18th St., Birmingham AL 35203. Editor: Charles Ghigna. For high school and college audience. Poetry quarterly. Estab. 1975. Circ. 1,000. Pays in contributor's copies. Submit complete poem and brief biography. SASE.
Poetry: Wants poetry that is "fresh, concise; strong use of imagery." No sentimental lyrics.

BARDIC ECHOES, 1036 Emerald Ave., N.E., Grand Rapids MI 49503. (616)454-9120. Editor: Clarence L. Weaver. Quarterly. Copyrighted. Payment in contributor's copies. Will send sample copy to writer for 50¢. Reports in 1 to 3 months. Limit submissions to no more than 5 poems. Occasionally overstocked. SASE.
Poetry: Poetry may be on any subject, but in good taste. Varied style. Length: 40 lines maximum including title, byline, and stanzaic spaces (one full page).

BELOIT POETRY JOURNAL, Box 2, Beloit WI 53511. Editors: David Stocking, Marion Stocking. "Our readers are people of all ages and occupations who are interested in the growing tip of poetry." Quarterly magazine; 40 pages. Estab. 1950. Circ. 1,100. Pays in copies on publication. Acquires all rights, but may reassign following publication. Photocopied submissions OK. SASE. Reports in 4 months; "actually most rejections are within a week; four months would be the maximum for a poem under serious consideration." Sample copy $1; free writer's guidelines.
Poetry: Avant-garde; free verse; and traditional. Uses 60/year. Limit submissions to batches of 6. "We publish the best contemporary poetry submitted, without bias as to length, form, school, or subject. We are particularly interested in discovering new poets, with strong imagination and intense, accurate language."

BIRTHSTONE MAGAZINE, Box 27394, San Francisco CA 94127. (415)334-4681. Editor-in-Chief: Daniel Brady. Emphasizes poetry, graphics, and photography. Quarterly magazine; 16 pages. Estab. 1975. Circ. 500. Pays in copies. Acquires all rights but may reassign following publication. Photocopied and previously published submissions OK.
Photos: B&w glossies, maximum size 7x10. No additional payment for photos accepted with accompanying ms. "We use pen and ink graphics.
Poetry: Avant-garde, free verse, haiku, light verse, traditional, and "anything that we agree is

good." Buys 20-25 poems/issue. Limit submissions to batches of 5. Length: 1-48 lines, but "will consider longer if very good." Pays in copies.

BITTERROOT, International Poetry Magazine, Blythebourne Station, P.O. Box 51, Brooklyn NY 11219. Editor: Menke Katz. Quarterly. Copyrighted. Payment in 1 contributor's copy. SASE.
Poetry: "We need good poetry of all kinds. If we think a poem is very good, we will publish a two-page poem; mostly however, we prefer shorter poems, not longer than one page. We always discourage stereotyped forms which imitate fixed patterns and leave no individual mark. We inspire all poets who seek their own selves in original forms of many moods, in harmony with their poems which may be realistic or fantastic, close to earth and cabalistic." We have an annual contest with awards amounting to $325. December 31 of each year is the deadline for the Kaitz award and the William Kushner award.

BLUE UNICORN, 22 Avon Rd., Kensington CA 94707. Editors: Ruth G. Iodice, B. Jo Kinnick, Harold Witt. "We appeal especially to the discriminating lover of poetry, whatever his/her taste runs to." Published 3 times/year. Magazine; 40-50 pages. Estab. 1977. Circ. 500. Pays in copies on publication. Buys one-time rights. Photocopied submissions OK. SASE. Reports in 3-4 months. Sample copy $2.50.
Poetry: "The main criterion is excellence. We like poems which communicate in a memorable way whatever is deeply felt by the poet—ones which delight with a lasting image, a unique twist of thought, and a haunting music. We don't want the hackneyed, the trite, or the banal." Uses 150 poems/year. Limit submissions to batches of 3-4. Prefers shorter verse; "rarely use poetry over 1 page in length." Pays 1 copy.

BONSAI, A QUARTERLY OF HAIKU, Bonsai Press, Box 580, Prescott AZ 86302. Editor-in-Chief: Jan Streif. Emphasizes haiku poetry and related prose. Quarterly magazine; 36 pages. Estab. 1975. Circ. 350. No payment. Buys first rights. SASE. Reports in 1 week-2 months. Sample copy $1.25.
Nonfiction: "We are looking for penetrating essays dealing with the haiku of the 1970's, some reviews and other contemporary work in the haiku/senryu field. Length: short or long; no limit."
Poetry: "All schools of haiku are welcome, but the standard is high. We look for haiku that captures a moment, not just talks about it."

THE CAPE ROCK, Southeast Missouri State University Press, English Department, Cape Girardeau MO 63701. (314)334-8211, Ext. 278. Editor: R.A. Burns. For libraries and persons interested in poetry. Estab. 1964. Semiannual. Circ. 500. Acquires all rights, but may reassign rights to author after publication. Uses about 100 mss per year. Pays in contributor's copies. Sample copy $1; writer's guidelines for SASE. Will consider photocopied submissions. No simultaneous submissions. Reports in 1 to 4 months. SASE.
Poetry: "Publish poetry — any style, subject. Avoid obscene or profane diction, sentimentality, didacticism. We have summer and winter issues and try to place poetry in the appropriate issue, but do not offer strictly seasonal issues." Photos acquired with accompanying ms with no additional payment; also used without accompanying ms. B&w only. Pays 2 copies. Length: 70 lines maximum. Pays 2 copies.

CEDAR ROCK, 1121 Madeline, New Braunfels TX 78130. (512)625-6002. Editor-in-Chief: David C. Yates. For "persons with an active interest in poetry." Quarterly tabloid; 24 pages. Estab. 1975. Circ. 400. Pays on acceptance. Buys all rights but may reassign following publication. Phone queries OK. Photocopied submissions OK. SASE. Reports in 3 weeks. Sample copy $1.25; free writer's guidelines.
Poetry: Avant-garde; free verse; haiku; light verse; and traditional. "No deliberately obscure poems." Buys 200 poems/year. Limit submissions to 6 at one time. Length: 3-75 lines. Pays $2-100.
Fiction: Buys 2/issue. Pays $2-100. Submit to R.S. Gwynn, Dept. of English, Lamar University, Beaumont TX 77710.

CHOOMIA Collections of Contemporary Poetry, Yarrow Press, Box 40322, Tuson AZ 85717. Editor-in-Chief: Jay Barwell. Managing Editor: Ann Guido. Semiannual magazine; 60 pages. Estab. 1975. Circ. 400. Pays in copies on publication. Acquires all rights, but may reassign following publication. Photocopied submissions OK. SASE. Reports in 3 months. Sample copy $1.

Poetry: "We have an extremely high standard and are not interested in seeing poetry that is written "out of fun and enjoyment" rather than commitment." Any form. No length restrictions.

CHRISTIAN POETRY JOURNAL, Arkadelphia AR 71923. Editor: Gilbert Morris. "The purpose of *Christian Poetry Journal* is to furnish a platform for poets who can embody conservative religious truth in quality poetry." Published 3 times/year. Magazine; 35 pages. Estab. 1976. Pays in copies. Obtains all rights, but may reassign following publication. Photocopied submissions OK. SASE. Reports in 6 weeks. Sample copy 50¢.
Poetry: "We will accept any form, formal or free verse, and we are not interested in re-written hymns. Fresh imagery is an absolute necessity." Uses 75 poems/year. Limit submissions to batches of 8.

CIRCUS MAXIMUS, Garretson Graphics, Box 3251, York PA 17402. Editor: Pete Garretson, Jr. For an intellectual readership of all ages. Quarterly magazine; 40 pages. Estab. 1975. Circ. 400-500. Pays on acceptance. Buys one-time rights. Photocopied and previously published submissions OK. SASE. Reports in 2 weeks. Sample copy $2; free writer's guidelines.
Poetry: Free verse, haiku and traditional. Buys 40-50 poems/issue. Limit submissions to batches of 5. Pays $2/poem.
How To Break In: "We prefer imaginative language poems which use concrete imagery to create a 'scene' with a beginning, a middle and an end. The message or experience should suddenly come alive for the reader so that he/she can leave the poem with a fresh emotional/intellectual perception that was not present in the mind's eye before reading the poem."

CONNECTIONS MAGAZINE, Bell Hollow Rd., Putnam Valley NY 10579. Editor-in-Chief: Toni Ortner-Zimmerman. Annual magazine; 70 pages. Estab. 1971. Circ. 600. Pays in copies. SASE. Reports in 2 weeks. Sample copy $2.
Poetry: Avant-garde, free verse and traditional. Limit submissions to batches of 5. Length: 50 lines maximum.

CREATIVE REVIEW, 1718 S. Garrison, Carthage MO 64836. Editor: Glen Coffield. For hobbyists, educated, retired, handicapped, educators. Quarterly mimeographed magazine; 14 to 18 pages. Estab. 1961. Not copyrighted. Uses 250 poems a year. Payment in contributor's copies. Sample copy 50¢. Reports within 3 months. Submit complete ms; "one poem to a page (8½x11)." SASE.
Poetry: "Poems on creativity, good description, local history, examples of good writing, pictures of life, positive approach, good taste, simple and clear. Good grammar and punctuation, logical structure, understandable to the average reader; interesting beginnings, strong endings, objective imagery, not too abstract. We're perhaps more selective and demanding; more traditional in a knowledgeable sense. We don't want anything risque, no negativism or tearing down, no difficult typographical experiments, no excess verbosity and repetition, no intellectual snobbery or trite sophistication. No personal frustrations. Not especially interested in the topical, except positive suggestions on current problems." Length: 32 lines maximum. "Quality demands are greater the longer the poem."

DRAGONFLY: A QUARTERLY OF HAIKU, 4102 NE 130th Pl., Portland OR 97230. Editor-in-Chief: Lorraine Ellis Harr. For all ages. Quarterly magazine; 68 pages. Estab. 1965. Circ. 500. Pays in copies. Some awards. Reassigns rights on request. SASE. Reports in 1 month. Sample copy $1.25; free writer's guidelines.
Nonfiction: 300-word articles on haiku or related matter. "Must be concise and have something to say." Uses 2-3 mss/issue.
Poetry: Uses some senryu poetry and oriental forms, but mostly haiku. Uses 150 poems/issue. Limit submissions to batches of 5.

EN PASSANT POETRY QUARTERLY, 1906 Brant Rd., Wilmington DE 19810. Editor: James A. Costello. For an audience interested in poetry. Magazine; 44 pages. Estab. 1975. Quarterly. Circ. 500. Acquires all rights, but will reassign rights to author after publication. Uses about 25 to 30 mss per issue. Payment in contributor's copies. Sample copy $1.50. Reports in 3 weeks. Submit complete ms. SASE.
Poetry: Poetry of insight and clear imagery. Poetry in translation.

ENCORE, A Quarterly of Verse and Poetic Arts, 1121 Major Ave., N.W., Albuquerque NM 87107. (505)344-5615. Editor: Alice Briley. For "anyone interested in poetry from young people

in high school to many retired people. Good poetry on any theme." Estab. 1966. Quarterly. Circ. 600. Acquires all rights but will reassign rights to author after publication. Uses 300 mss a year. Payment in contributor's copies. Sample copy 30¢. Will consider photocopied submissions "provided the author is free to assign rights to *Encore*. Will require assurance if poem is accepted." Submit seasonal material 6 to 9 months in advance. Reports on material within a month. Submit complete poetry ms. Query first, for short reviews. SASE.
Nonfiction, Poetry and Photos: "Particularly like poetry which illustrates the magazine's theme that poetry is a performing art. Fresh approach greatly desired. Poetry by students as well as established poets." Traditional forms, blank verse, free verse, avant-garde and light verse. Limit submissions to batches of 4. Some articles on related subjects. Profiles of poets, poetry reviews, technical verse writing. Length: open, but "very long articles rarely used." Prefer no larger than 5x8 b&w glossy photos with good contrast. Pays in contributor's copies. Also has poetry contests. "My poetry contests have grown considerably. Continuous contests have November 1 and May 1 deadlines. In addition, there are often very good special contests."

THE FREE LANCE, A Magazine of Poetry & Prose, 6005 Grand Ave., Cleveland OH 44104. Editors: Russell Atkins, Casper L. Jordan. For college students, teachers and persons who practice the creative arts. Estab. 1950. Published irregularly. Circ. 600. Copyrighted. Pays in contributor's copies. No sample copies. Will not consider photocopied or simultaneous submissions. Reports in 6 months. Query first for book reviews. SASE.
Nonfiction, Fiction and Poetry: "Largely avant-garde, emphasis on literary techniques and ideas, should be experimental. Book reviews. We are more creative than 'topical,' consequently there are not many themes we would single out." Fiction. Length: 3,000 words maximum. Poetry; mainstream, contemporary and avant-garde forms. "Not in the market for poetry or verse that rhymes, or verse that has a message on social problems, or work that is rigidly traditional in form, etc." Length: open.

GRAVIDA, Box 76, Hartsdale NY 10530. Editor: Lynne Savitt. Quarterly magazine; 44-60 pages. Estab. 1973. Circ. 1,000. Pays in copies on publication. Acquires all rights, but may reassign following publication. Submit seasonal/holiday material 6 months in advance. Photocopied submissions OK. SASE. Reports in 2 weeks. Sample copy $1; free writer's guidelines.
Poetry: Avant-garde; free verse; haiku; light verse; traditional. Uses 120/year. Limit submissions to batches of 5. Pays in 2 copies and a $25 prize for best poem in each issue.

HAPPINESS HOLDING TANK, 1790 Grand River Ave., Okemos MI 48864. Editors: Albert and Barbara Drake. For "poets of various ages, interests; other editors; students." Triannual magazine; 45 pages, (8½x11). Estab. 1970. Circ. 300 to 500. All rights revert to author automatically. Payment in contributor's copies. Sample copy $1. Reports in 1 to 3 weeks. Not reading during summer months. Submit complete ms. SASE.
Nonfiction and Poetry: Publishes "poems of various kinds, somewhat eclectic—looking for 'excellence.' Essays and articles on modern poetry. Emphasis on younger but unestablished poets: their work to date. Emphasis on information of various kinds—to make magazine useful. Interested in printing methods of all kinds." Buys informational, how-to, and poetry book reviews. Uses all forms of poetry except light verse. Now doing chapbooks and poetry posters.
Rejects: "What we see repeatedly, and do not want, is a kind of poem which can best be described as a 'beginner's poem.' It's usually entitled 'Reflections' or 'Dust' or 'Spring' and has to do with death, love, etc. These are abstractions and the poet treats them in an abstract way. This kind of poem has to be written, but shouldn't be published."

THE HARTFORD COURANT, THIS SINGING WORLD, 285 Broad St., Hartford CT 06115. Poetry Editor: Malcolm L. Johnson. For a general audience. Weekly poetry column in newspaper. Estab. 1764. Circ. 180,000. Not copyrighted. Uses about 200 poems a year. Payment in tearsheets. "We are not set up to send free copies." Will consider photocopied submissions and simultaneous submissions. "Christmas poetry is wanted for the weekend before Christmas. Seasonal poetry is usually not used out of season." Submit seasonal poetry 1 month in advance. Reports usually within 2 weeks, unless it is being considered for publication; may take up to 3 months. Submit complete ms. SASE.
Poetry: "Any sort of poetry is eligible, but the general readership means that graphically erotic or violent poetry cannot be used. In general, we strive for the same sort of poetry that might be published in a literary magazine. The only guideline would be that the poetry must necessarily be rather short. 50 lines is about the maximum. Seasonal and poet's soul poetry always seem overworked, but creative approaches to these subjects are still welcome. It would be pleasant to receive more light or satirical verse, but these seem difficult genres for many poets." Length: 2 to 50 lines.

HIRAM POETRY REVIEW, P.O. Box 162, Hiram OH 44234. (216)569-3211. Editor: David Fratus. Published 2 times a year; magazine, 40 to 60 pages, (6x9). "Since our chief subscribers are libraries in major cities or libraries of colleges and universities, our audience is highly literate and comprises persons who are actively interested in poetry of high quality." Estab. 1967. Circ. 500. Copyrighted. Acquires all rights, but will reassign rights to author upon written request. Uses approximately 75 poems a year. Payment in 2 contributor's copies plus one year's subscription. Free sample copy. Reports in 8 weeks. Submit only complete ms. SASE.
Poetry: "All forms of poetry used. No special emphasis required. Length: open, but we have printed few very long poems." Limit submissions to 4-6 to a batch.

HUERFANO, Daran, Inc., 5730 N. Via Elena, Tucson AZ 85718. Editor-in-Chief: Randell Shutt. Semiannual magazine; 40 pages. Estab. 1972. Circ. 250. Pays in copies. Acquires all rights, but may reassign following publication. Photocopied submissions OK. SASE. Reports in 1 month. Sample copy $1. Free writer's guidelines.
Poetry: Vicki Thompson, Poetry Editor. Free verse, light verse and traditional. Uses 50-60 poems/year. Length: 4-50 lines. "Daran Award of $50 to one of our published poets annually."

IDEALS, 11315 Watertown Plank Rd., Milwaukee WI 53201. Editorial Director: James Kruse. Managing Editor: Ralph Luedtke. Payment for poems or articles made at time of publication ($10 and a copy of the issue). Buys one-time rights. Free sample copy. Reports in 2 weeks. SASE.
Nonfiction, Poetry and Photos: "*Ideals* are books containing clean, wholesome, old-fashioned American ideals, homey philosophy and general inspirational, patriotic, religious, seasonal, family, childhood or nostalgic material. Poems and articles submitted will be carefully reviewed, and such material that we believe will lend itself to use in *Ideals* will be retained in our permanent review files. Such material is carefully reviewed during the preparation of each new book. We cannot definitely guarantee that we will feature the poems or articles which we retain, but we shall make a sincere effort to do so. We assume the privilege of editing retained material where necessary. If, for any reason, you do not want us to enter your material into our review files, kindly advise us when submitting it so that we can promptly return it to you. Please do not send us your original poems or articles. Send only copies. We cannot return your submitted material after it has been entered into our review files. B&w photos should be sharp, clear 8x10 glossies. We pay $20 minimum when purchased for immediate use. We prefer 4x5 or 8x10 color transparencies, for which pay is $75 minimum. 35mm transparencies are accepted, provided they are mounted on a sheet of acetate in groups of at least 20 so they may be easily reviewed."

KOSMOS, 130 Eureka, San Francisco CA 94114. (415)863-4861. Editor: Kosrof Chantikian. Biannual magazine; 64 pages. Estab. 1975. Circ. 750. Pays in copies on publication. Acquires all rights, but may reassign following publication. Previously published submissions OK. SASE. Reports in 7-9 weeks. Sample copy $2.50.
Poetry: No restrictions.

LIGHT: A POETRY REVIEW, Box 1105M, Stuyvesant PO, New York NY 10009. Editor-in-Chief: Roberta C. Gould. Annual magazine; 64 pages. Estab. 1973. Circ. 800. Pays in copies. Acquires first North American serial rights. Submit seasonal/holiday material 3 months in advance. SASE. Reports in 3 months. Sample copy $1.25. Uses graphics and some 7½x5 b&w photos.
Poetry: Avant-garde, free verse, haiku and traditional. Uses 40 poems/issue. Limit submissions to batches of 4. Length: 5-40 words.

THE LITTLE MAGAZINE, Box 207, Cathedral Station, New York NY 10025. Managing Editor: Felicity Thoet. Quarterly magazine; 64 pages. Circ. 1,000. Pays in copies. Acquires all rights, but may reassign following publication. Photocopied submissions OK. SASE. Reports in 2-6 weeks. Sample copy $1.50; free writer's guidelines.
Fiction: Uses all types. Uses 12 mss/year.
Poetry: Avant-garde; free verse; light verse; traditional. Uses 75/year. Limit submissions to batches of 10.

THE LITTLE REVIEW, English Department, Marshall University, Huntington WV 25701. Editor: John McKernan. Biannual. Circ. 1,000. Acquires first rights. No payment. Sample copy $1.25. Reports in 2 months or more. Enclose SASE.

Nonfiction and Poetry: "Poetry, translations, critical reviews of contemporary poets, parodies, and satire. We are mainly a poetry magazine."

THE LYRIC, 307 Dunton Dr., SW, Blacksburg VA 24060. Editor-in-Chief: Leslie Mellichamp. Quarterly magazine; 26 pages. Estab. 1921. Circ. 1,000. Pays in prizes only $25-100. Acquires first North American serial rights. Submit seasonal/holiday material 3-6 months in advance. Photocopied submissions OK. SASE. Reports in 2 weeks.
Poetry: Light verse and traditional. Uses 40 poems/issue. Limit submissions to batches of 5. Length: 36 lines maximum.

THE MODULARIST REVIEW, Wooden Needle Press, 65-45 Yellowstone Blvd., #3-D, Forest Hills NY 11375. Editor: R.C. Morse. Annual magazine. Estab. 1972. Circ. 1,000. Pays in contributor's copies. Acquires all rights but may reassign following publication. SASE. Reports in 3 months.
Fiction, Photos, Poetry: "All literary, visual and plastic arts. Work submitted must be Modularist: Based on the concept that time is not the fourth dimension, but is composed of four dimensional elements, the simultaneous, contiguous, recursive and disparate (which correspond to length, width and depth, the dimensional elements of space) and thereby conceived from a seven-dimensional space/time perspective." Length: Short fiction mss preferred, but will consider long poems.

NEW COLLAGE MAGAZINE, 5700 N. Trail, Sarasota FL 33580. (813)355-7671, Ext. 203. Editor: A. McA. Miller. For poetry readers. Magazine; 24 pages minimum. Estab. 1971. Triquarterly. Circ. 2,000. Acquires all rights, but usually reassigns rights to author after publication. Uses 80 poems per year. Token payment or 3 contributor's copies. Sample copy $1, together with editorial guidelines sheet. Will consider photocopied submissions. No simultaneous submissions. Reports in 3 weeks. SASE.
Poetry: "We want poetry as a fresh act of language. No tick-tock effusions about everyday sentiments, please. First, read a sample copy. Then, and only then, send us poems. We especially want strong poems, more in Yeats' vein than in W. C. Williams, but we are open to any poem that sustains clear imagery and expressive voice." Length: 150 lines maximum.

NEW EARTH REVIEW, Box 83, Murfreesboro NC 27855. (919)398-3341. Editor: Robert G. Mulder. For "wide audience of readers." Most readers are women poets, although many men subscribe. Magazine; 20 to 30 pages. Estab. 1975. Quarterly. Circ. 1,500. Acquires all rights, but may reassign rights to author after publication. Uses 500 poems per year. Pays in contributor's copies for most poetry. Sample copy $1; free writer's guidelines. Will consider photocopied submissions. No simultaneous submissions. Reports in 2 weeks. SASE.
Poetry: "We only publish poems of our selection trying to get a good representation of poets across the U.S." Sometimes publishes essays pertinent to poetry. Uses traditional forms, blank verse, free verse, light verse, avant-garde forms, haiku, experimental forms and prose poetry. Length: 4 to 16 lines. Pays $5 per poem "in some cases for poem-of-the-issue. Other payment in contributor's copies."

NEW WORLDS UNLIMITED, Box 556-WM, Saddle Brook NJ 07662. Editor-in-Chief: Sal St. John Buttaci. Managing Editor: Susan Linda Gerstle. For "professional and aspiring poets of all ages from here and abroad. We've published high school students, college students, graduates, and people from all walks of life who write good poetry." Annual hardcover anthology; 130 pages. Estab. 1974. Circ. 500-700. No payment. Obtains all rights, but may reassign following publication. Photocopied submissions OK. SASE. Reports in 6 months. Writer's guidelines for SASE.
Poetry: "We want previously unpublished poems rich in imagery, poems that show intelligent treatment of universal themes and reveal the poet's understanding, even limited, of the poetry craft." Avant-garde; free verse; haiku; light verse; and traditional. Uses 400/issue. Limit submissions to batches of 5. Length; 2-14 lines

NORTHERN LIGHT, University of Manitoba Printers, 605 Fletcher Argue Bldg., University of Manitoba, Winnipeg, Manitoba R3J 2E4. (204)474-8145. Editor-in-Chief: George Amabile. Audience is poets, libraries, professors, teachers, English students and lighthouse keepers. Semiannual magazine; 64 pages. Estab. 1968. Circ. 1,000. Pays on either acceptance or publication. Buys all rights, but may reassign following publication. Phone queries OK. Simultaneous submissions OK. SASE and International Reply Coupons. Reports in 4 weeks. Sample copy $1.50. Free writer's guidelines.

Nonfiction: Reviews of recent poetry publications and interviews with poets. Buys 2 mss/issue. Send complete ms. Length: 1,000-1,800 words. Pays $5/page.
Photos: Pamela McLeod, Photo Editor. Photos purchased without accompanying ms. Pays $5/page for 8x10 b&w photos.
Poetry: Avant-garde, free verse, haiku, light verse and traditional. Buys 30 poems/issue. Pays $5/page.
How To Break In: "We prefer to publish Canadians, so Americans have to be good."

OUTPOSTS, 72 Burwood Rd., Walton-on-Thames, Surrey KT12 4AL. Editor-in-Chief: Howard Sergeant. Quarterly magazine; 40 pages. Estab. 1944. Circ. 1,500. Pays on publication. Buys first serial rights. Photocopied submissions OK. SAE and International Reply Coupons. Reports in 2 weeks. Sample copy $2.
Nonfiction: Articles on poetry or critical studies of poetry. Buys 4/year. Length: 1,000-2,500 words. Pays about 2 pounds/page.
Poetry: Any type of poetry, but not of epic length. Buys 25-50/issue. Limit submissions to 6. Length: 80 lines maximum. Pays about 2 pounds/page.

POEM, P.O. Box 1247, West Station, Huntsville AL 35807. Editor: Robert L. Welker. For adults; well-educated, interested in good poetry. Published 3 times a year; magazine, 65 pages. Estab. 1967. Circ. 500. Acquires all rights, but will reassign rights to author after publication. Uses 200 poems a year. Payment in contributor's copies. Reports within 2 months. Submit complete ms only. SASE.
Poetry: "We use nothing but superior quality poetry. Good taste (no pornography for its own sake) and technical proficiency. We give special attention to young and less well-known poets. Do not like poems about poems, poets, and other works of art." Traditional forms, blank verse, free verse, and avant-garde forms. Length and theme: open.

THE POET, 2314 W. 6th St., Mishawaka IN 46544. (219)255-8606. Editor: Doris Nemeth. For professional people, freelance writers, students, etc. Anthology; 200 pages. Estab. 1963. Twice a year. Circ. 25,000. Acquires first North American serial rights. Uses about 1,000 mss a year. No payment. Sample copy $4.50. Will consider photocopied and simultaneous submissions. Reports in 4 to 6 weeks. Submit complete ms. SASE.
Poetry and Photos: "All forms of poetry. No set rules. We read all manuscripts. We prefer not to see religious material." Length: 16 lines maximum. Uses 8x10 (or smaller) b&w glossies.

POETRY, The Modern Poetry Association, 1228 N. Dearborn Pkwy., Chicago IL 60610. Editor-in-Chief: John F. Nims. Monthly magazine; 64 pages. Estab. 1912. Circ. 7,000. Pays on publication. Buys all rights, but may reassign following publication. Submit seasonal/holiday material 9 months in advance. SASE. Reports in 4-6 weeks. Sample copy $2; writer's guidelines for SASE.
Poetry: "We consistently publish the best poetry being written in English. All forms may be acceptable." Buys 500/year. Limit submissions to batches of 6-8. Pays $1/line.

POETRY NEWSLETTER, Department of English, Temple University, Philadelphia PA 19122. (215)787-1778. Editor: Richard O'Connell. For readers of serious poetry. Quarterly newsletter; 20-40 pages. Estab. 1971. Circ. 500 to 1,000. Not copyrighted. Payment in contributor's copies. Will send sample copy to writer for $1. Will consider photocopied submissions. No simultaneous submissions. Reports in 1 to 3 months. Submit complete ms. SASE.
Poetry: "Poetry of high literary quality. No biases. Commercial verse will not be considered. The news is the poetry."

POETRY NORTHWEST MAGAZINE, *The Oregonian,* 1320 SW Broadway, Portland OR 97201. Editor: Penny Avila. Poetry column in Sunday magazine of newspaper. Pays on 10th of month following publication. Buys first newspaper rights which revert to poet after publication. SASE. Reports in 2-3 weeks.
Poetry: "We publish 3 poems/week from many schools and disciplines old and new. Rarely use religious poems. Seek fresh metaphor and imagery in issue and ethic oriented poems. Welcome the new and experimental, but in good taste." Length: 21 lines maximum. Pays $5.

POETRY VENTURE, Valkyrie Press, Inc., 8245 26th Ave., N., St. Petersburg FL 33710. Editor and Publisher: Marjorie Schuck. For poets, writers, scholars. Semiannual magazine; 64 to 72 pages. Estab. 1968. Circ. 1,000 to 2,000. Acquires all rights, but will reassign rights to author after publication. Payment in contributor's copies and subscription. Sample copy $1.25. Will

consider photocopied submissions. Will not consider simultaneous submissions. Reports on material within 6 months. Query first on poetry essays. SASE.
Nonfiction and Poetry: Poetry essays on poetry and/or related topics (the literary scene, contemporary poetry, etc.). Brief articles on individual poets. Commentaries, anthology reviews, poetical analyses. Often features foreign poetry published in both the original and the English translation. Length: 100 to 1,500 words. Traditional forms of poetry, blank verse, free verse, innovative poetry. Length: 112 lines maximum.

POETRY VIEW, 1125 Valley Rd., Menasha WI 54952. Editor: Dorothy Dalton. Published weekly as half-page in *View,* magazine section of the *Post-Crescent*. Estab. 1970. Circ. 50,000. Not copyrighted. Buys 250 poems per year. Payment on 10th of month following publication. Prefers original submissions; not photocopies. Will not consider simultaneous submissions. Submit seasonal material 2 to 3 months in advance. Reports in 2 to 3 months. SASE.
Poetry: Well-written poetry, showing a fresh use of language. No religious poetry or poetry that is overly sentimental. Uses some traditional forms, free verse, and light verse. Length: serious poetry, to 24 lines; light verse, 4 to 8 lines. Pays $3 per poem.

POETRY WINDSOR POESIE, Box 7186 Sandwich Station, Windsor, Ontario, Canada N9C 3Z1. Editor-in-Chief: Alexandre L. Amprimoz. Managing Editor: Robert Billings. 100% freelance written. Emphasizes Canadian poetry and writing. Published 3 times/year. Magazine; 60-65 pages. Estab. 1975. Circ. 300. Pays in copies on publication. Buys first North American serial rights. Photocopied submissions OK. SASE. Reports in 2 months. Sample copy $2.50.
Nonfiction: Interviews with Canadian writers (in French or English) and articles on Canadian writing. Uses 5 mss/year. Submit complete ms. Length: 1,000-3,000 words. Pays in copies.
Fiction: Short stories in French or English. Uses 5-6 mss/year. Submit complete ms. Length: 1,000-3,000 words. Pays in copies.
Poetry: Avant-garde; free verse; and haiku. "No theraputic, closet, or imitative poetry." Uses 120-180/year. Limit submissions to batches of 15-20. Pays in copies.

SEVEN, 115 South Hudson, Oklahoma City OK 73102. Editor: James Neill Northe. Published 4 times a year on an irregular basis. Estab. 1954. Circ. 1,000. Buys all rights. Payment on acceptance. Will send sample copy to writer for $1.25. Will not consider photocopied submissions. Will consider simultaneous submissions. Reports on material accepted for publication in 10 days. Returns rejected material immediately. Submit complete ms. SASE.
Poetry: "We strive to present only the most sheerly lyrical, poignant and original material possible. Seven poems and 1 reprint are used in each issue. We prefer the classical sonnet over the variations, accenting adherence to the form. Free verse is acceptable, but not as chopped prose. Good ballads are always acceptable. We like titles, punctuation and capitalization where needed. We like well-written and finely expressed spiritual poems, but they must be spiritual (not religious). We prefer the universal approach, rather than the personal. We want lines that communicate; not rambling, disjointed, chopped prose in or out of rhyme, lacking the rhythm and power of free verse." No restrictions as to form or subject. Length: open. Pays $4 per poem.

SEVEN STARS POETRY, Realities Library, Box 33512, San Diego CA 92103. Editor-in-Chief: Richard A. Soos, Jr. Emphasizes poetry/modern literature. Monthly magazine; 40 pages. Estab. 1975. Circ. 800-1,000. Pays on acceptance. Buys all rights, but may reassign following publication. Photocopied and previously published submissions OK. SASE. Reports in 3 weeks. Sample copy $1.50; writer's guidelines for SASE.
Poetry: Avant-garde, free verse, haiku, dada/surreal. Buys 50-60 poems/issue. Limit submissions to batches of 5. Pays 50¢-$1.
Nonfiction: Interviews with any modern poet, or fictional interview with a historic poet. Query. No length requirement. Pays $1/printed page.
Columns, Departments: Reviews on poetry books and TV poetry. Buys 10 mss/issue. Query. No length requirements. Pays 1¢/word. Open to suggestions for new columns, departments.
Fiction: Adventure, erotica, fantasy, experimental, humorous, suspense, science fiction, serialized novels. Buys "1 or less" an issue. Query. No length requirements. Pays $1/printed page.

SPARROW POVERTY PAMPHLETS, (formerly *Sparrow*), Sparrow Press, 103 Waldron St., West Lafayette, IN 47906. Editor-in-Chief: Felix Stefanile. Semiannual magazine; 32 pages. Estab. 1954. Circ. 800. Pays on publication. Buys first North American serial rights. "We retain anthology rights." Previously published submissions OK. SASE. Reports in 6 weeks. Sample copy $1.50.

Poetry: "No form bias. Mature, serious work in the modern manner. Poetry must be human and relevant." Buys 20-30 poems/issue. Pays $15 plus royalties.

SPRING RAIN PRESS, P.O. Box 15319, Seattle WA 98115. Editor: Karen Sollid. Yearly anthology. 50 to 60 (8½x5) pages. Estab. 1971. Circ. 500. Acquires all rights, but will reassign rights to author after publication. Payment in contributor's copies. Will send sample copy to writer for $3. Write for copy of guidelines for writers, but SASE must be enclosed. Will consider photocopied submissions. Will not consider simultaneous submissions. Reports in June each year. Submit representative sample ms. SASE.
Poetry: Traditional forms, blank verse, free verse, avant-garde forms, lyric poetry. "We avoid sentimental poetry." Length: open.

STAR WEST, P.O. Box 731, Sausalito CA 94965. Editor: Leon Spiro. Semiannual newspaper, with mini-supplements. Estab. 1963. Circ. 1,000. Not copyrighted. Payment in contributor's copies. Will send sample copy to writer for $1. Reports in 2 to 4 weeks. SASE.
Poetry: Traditional, contemporary, avant-garde, light verse, surrealism. "Poetry that's dynamic, from Black English to haiku." Length: 16 lines maximum.

STONE COUNTRY, 20 Lorraine Rd., Madison NJ 07940. (201)377-3727. Editor: Judith Neeld. For mature and young adults who have a participating interest in all forms of poetry. Magazine, published 3 times a year; 40 pages. Circ. 400. Acquires first North American serial rights. Accepts 100 to 150 poems a year. Payment in contributor's copies. Sample copy $1.50. Reports in 1 month, "more or less". Query first or submit complete ms. SASE.
Poetry and Graphics: Art Editor: Pat McCormick. "We publish poetry, poetry criticism, and graphics. No thematic or stylistic limitations, but we are unable to publish long narrative poems in full. Overworked approaches include adolescent love, explicit sex, or use of Anglo-Saxonisms. (Have no objections to these poems, just not in quantity, usually badly done.) All themes must be handled maturely and with a search for language, not just the first word that comes to mind or the obvious shocker." Traditional forms, blank verse, free verse, avant-garde forms. Length: 40 lines maximum. Limit submissions to 5 poems at a time.

UT REVIEW, University of Tampa, Tampa FL 33606. Editor-in-Chief: Duane Locke. Quarterly magazine; 32 pages. Estab. 1972. Circ. 500. Pays in copies on publication. Buys all rights, but may reassign following publication. Photocopied and previously published submissions OK. SASE. Reports in 1 week. Sample copy $2.50.
Poetry: Avant-garde. Buys 32-128 poems/issue. "Each issue is devoted to the work of one poet. Write poetry similar to that of Alan Britt, Silvia Schiebli, Nico Suarez, or Paul Roth."

VOICES INTERNATIONAL, South and West Inc., 6804 Cloverdale Dr., Little Rock AR 72209. Editor-in-Chief: Clovita Rice. Quarterly magazine; 32 pages. Pays in copies on publication. Acquires all rights. Submit seasonal/holiday material 1 year in advance. SASE. Reports in 3 weeks. Sample copy $1.50.
Poetry: Free verse. Uses 50-60 poems/issue. Limit submissions to batches of 5. Length: 3-40 lines. Will consider longer ones if good.
How To Break In: "We accept poetry with a new approach, haunting word pictures and significant ideas. Language should be used like watercolors to achieve depth, to highlight one focal point, to be pleasing to the viewer, and to be transparent, leaving space for the reader to project his own view."

WEST COAST POETRY REVIEW, 1335 Dartmouth Dr., Reno NV 89503. Editor-in-Chief: William L. Fox. Emphasizes conventional and experimental literature. *WCPR* if often used in college writing courses. Semiannual magazine; 80 pages. Estab. 1970. Circ. 750. Pays in copies on publication. Acquires first North American serial rights. SASE. Reports in 1 week. Sample copy $2.
Nonfiction: Criticism of contemporary poetry only. Query. Uses some fiction.
Poetry: Avant-garde and free verse. Uses 50 poems/issue. Limit submissions to batches of 10.

WESTERN POETRY QUARTERLY, 3253-Q San Amadeo, Laguna Hills CA 92653. Editor: Joseph Rosenzweig. For a well-educated audience with a wide range of interests. Quarterly; 32 to 40 (5½x8½) pages. Estab. 1974. Circ. 200. Acquires first North American serial rights. Uses 120 to 160 mss a year. Payment in 1 contributor's copy. Will send sample copy for $1.25. Reports in 10 days. Submit complete ms. SASE.
Poetry: "We accept all types of quality poetry; traditional, contemporary, free form and

humorous verse and are not limited as to theme. Contributors are asked to submit at least 3 poems for consideration." Length: 8 to 24 lines, but exceptions are made on very high quality poems. Best of issue cash awards are also made.

THE WINDLESS ORCHARD, English Department, Indiana-Purdue University, Ft. Wayne IN 46805. Editor: Dr. Robert Novak. For poets and photographers. Estab. 1970. Quarterly. Circ. 300. Acquires all rights, but will reassign rights to author after publication. Payment in contributor's copies. Reports in 3 to 14 weeks. Submit complete ms. SASE.
Poetry and Photos: Avant-garde forms of poetry, free verse and haiku. Use of photos restricted to b&w.

THE WORMWOOD REVIEW, P.O. Box 8840, Stockton CA 95204. Editor: Marvin Malone. Quarterly. Circ. 700. Acquires all rights, but will reassign rights to author on request. Pays in copies or cash equivalent. Pays on publication. Will send sample copy to writer for $1.50. Reports in 2 to 8 weeks. SASE.
Poetry: Modern poetry and prose poems that communicate the temper and depth of the human scene. All styles and schools from ultra avant-garde to classical; no taboos. Especially interested in prose poems or fables. 3 to 500 lines.
How To Break In: "Be original. Be yourself. Have something to say. Say it as economically and effectively as possible. Don't be afraid of wit and intelligence."

XANADU, c/o Beverly Lawn, RD 3, Huntington NY 11743. Editors: Beverly Lawn, Coco Gordon. For a college-educated audience, interested in reading the best new poetry being written. Magazine; 60 (5½x8½) pages. Estab. 1974. Biannually. Circ. 1,000. Acquires all rights, but will reassign rights to author after publication if proper credit line is given. Uses about 90 poems a year. Payment in 3 contributor's copies. Will send sample copy to writer for $1.50. No photocopied or simultaneous submissions. Reports in 2 months. Query first for nonfiction. Submit complete poetry mss. SASE.
Poetry, Nonfiction, Graphics, and Photos: "We publish only poems and materials related to poetry; intelligent criticism, interviews with up-and-coming poets we respect; possible reviews of new books. Our main criteria for poetry are excellence of craft and clarity and force of vision. Only the highest quality contemporary poetry. We like to see at least 5 poems by a contributor at one time. Strongly realized poems rooted in human experience have an edge. We would prefer not to see sloppy, poorly crafted work. Any theme is acceptable, if it is approached with integrity, although we are not a good market for pornographic material pretending to be erotic, or for tedious avant-garde experiments, or for trite or sentimental verse. Poems incorporating recent scientific knowledge, poems confronting important political, moral, and ethical issues, and poems reaching into the realm where the ordinary and the dramatic or visionary are one would be most welcome." B&w photos and line drawings appropriate to size of publication are used without mss.

Politics and World Affairs Publications

Other categories in *Writer's Market* include publications that will also consider articles about politics and world affairs. Some of these categories are Business and Finance, Regional, City magazines, General Interest, and Newspapers and Weekly Magazine Sections.

AFRICA REPORT, 833 United Nations Plaza, New York NY 10017. (212)949-5731. Editor: Anthony J. Hughes. 60% freelance written. For U.S. citizens, residents with a special interest in African affairs for professional, business, academic or personal reasons. Not tourist-related. Estab. 1956. Every 2 months. Circ. 10,500. Rights purchased vary with author and material. Usually buys all rights. Buys about 70 mss per year. Pays on publication. Will send sample copy to writer for $2.25. Write for editorial guidelines sheet. SASE.
Nonfiction and Photos: Interested in mss on "African political, economic and cultural affairs, especially in relation to U.S. foreign policy and business objectives. Style should be journalistic but not academic or light. Articles should not be polemical or long on rhetoric but may be committed to a strong viewpoint. I do not want tourism articles." Would like to see in-depth topical analyses of lesser known African countries, based on residence or several months stay in the country." Pays $150 for nonfiction. Photos purchased with or without accompanying mss with extra payment. B&w only. Pays $25. Submit 12x8 "half-plate."

AMERICAN OPINION MAGAZINE, Belmont MA 02178. Managing Editor: Scott Stanley, Jr. "A conservative, anti-communist journal of political affairs." Monthly except August. Circ. 50,000. Buys all rights. Pays on publication. Sample copy $1.50. SASE.
Nonfiction: Articles on matters of political affairs of a conservative, anti-communist nature. "We favor highly researched, definitive studies of social, economic, political and international problems which are written with verve and originality of style." Length should not exceed 4,000 words nor be less than 3,000. Pays $25 per published page.

AMERICAS, Organization of American States, Washington DC 20006. Managing Editor: Flora L. Phelps. 10% freelance written. Official organ of Organization of American States. Audience is persons interested in inter-American relations. Editions published in English, Spanish, Portuguese. Monthly. Circ. 100,000. Buys first publication and reprint rights. Pays on publication. Free sample copy. Articles received only on speculation. Include cover letter with writer's background. Reports within two months. Not necessary to enclose SASE.
Nonfiction: Articles of general hemisphere interest on history, art, literature, music, development, travel, etc. Taboos are religious and political themes or articles with non-international slant. Photos required. Length, about 3,000 words. Pays about $75.

THE ASIA MAIL, Potomac-Asia Communications, Inc., Box 1044, Alexandria VA 22313. (703)548-2881. Editor and Publisher: Edward Neilan. Associate Editor: Donna Gays. Emphasizes "American perspectives on Asia and the Pacific" for business executives, opinion leaders, diplomats, scholars, and other Americans who travel, do business or have demonstrated an interest in Asia and Asian affairs. Monthly tabloid; 28 pages. Estab. 1976. Circ. 30,000. Pays on publication. Buys first North American serial rights. SASE. Reports in 4 weeks. Free sample copy and writer's guidelines.
Nonfiction: "The *Asia Mail* will purchase about 4-5 mss from freelance writers each month. The Asia-related articles must show a U.S. interest in an Asian country or Asian interests within the U.S. The publication is comprehensive in business and scholarly aspects and includes articles of information, nostalgia, personal interest, historic interest, as well as reviews of books, art and theatre." Query. Length: 1,500 words maximum for features; 800 words maximum for reviews. Pays $50-150, "higher by special assignment."

CALIFORNIA JOURNAL, California Center for Research and Education in Government. 1617 10th St., Sacramento CA 95814. (916)444-2840. Editor-in-Chief: Ed Salzman. Associate Editor: Alice Nauman. Emphasizes California politics and government. Monthly magazine; 40 pages. Estab. 1970. Circ. 16,500. Pays on publication. Buys all rights. Phone queries OK. SASE. Reports immediately. Free sample copy.
Nonfiction: Profiles and state and local government and political analysis. No outright advocacy pieces. Buys 75 mss/year. Query. Length: 900-6,000 words. Pays $50/printed page.

CONSERVATIVE DIGEST, 7777 Leesburg Pike, Suite 416, Falls Church VA 22043. (703)893-1411. Editor-in-Chief: Brien Benson. 10% freelance written. Monthly magazine; 56 pages. Estab. 1974. Circ. 100,000. Pays on publication. Buys second serial and one-time rights. Submit seasonal/holiday material 3 months in advance of issue date. SASE. Simultaneous, photocopied and previously published submissions OK. Reports in 3 weeks. Sample copy $1.50; free writer's guidelines.
Nonfiction: Exposé (government); how-to (political ideas); and interview. Buys 1ms/issue. Submit complete ms. Length: 750-1,200 words. Pays 10¢/word.
Fillers: Susan Fourt, fillers editor. Clippings, jokes, gags, anecdotes, newsbreaks; puzzles (political crossword) and short humor. Buys 20 mss/issue. Pays $15-25.

CURRENT HISTORY, 4225 Main St., Philadelphia PA 19127. Editor: Carol L. Thompson. Monthly. Pays on publication. Reports in one to two weeks. Query preferred. "All articles contracted for in advance." SASE.
Nonfiction: Uses articles on current events, chiefly world area studies, stressing their historical, economic, and political background, 3,500 to 4,000 words in length. Academician contributions almost exclusively. Pays an average of $100.

EUROPEAN COMMUNITY, 2100 M St., N.W., Washington DC 20037. Editor: Walter Nicklin. For anyone with a professional or personal interest in Western Europe and European—U.S. relations. Monthly magazine; 50 pages. Estab. 1954. Circ. 40,000. Copyrighted. Buys about 50 mss/year. Pays on acceptance. Free sample copy. Will consider photocopied and simultaneous submissions. Submit seasonal material 3 months in advance. Reports in 2-4 weeks. Query first or submit complete ms. Include resume of author's background and qualifications with query or ms. SASE.

Nonfiction and Photos: Interested in current affairs (with emphasis on economics and politics), the Common Market and Europe's relations with the rest of the world. Publishes occasional cultural pieces, with European angle. High quality writing a must. "Please, no more M.A. theses on European integration. Looking for European angle in topics current in the U.S." Length: 250 to 2,000 words. Average payment is $250. Photos purchased with or without accompanying mss. Also purchased on assignment. Captions optional. Buys b&w and color. Average payment is $25 to $35 per b&w print, any size; $100 for inside use of color transparencies; $200 to $300 for color used on cover.

FOREIGN AFFAIRS, 58 E. 68th St., New York NY 10021. (212)734-0400. Editor: William P. Bundy. For academics, businessmen (national and international), government, educational and cultural readers especially interested in international affairs of a political nature. Estab. 1922. Quarterly. Circ. 75,000. Buys all rights. Buys 45 mss a year. Payment on publication. Will send sample copy to writer for $3.50, post paid. Will consider photocopied submissions. Reports in 2 to 4 weeks. Submit complete ms. SASE.

Nonfiction: "Articles dealing with international affairs; political, educational, cultural, philosophical and social sciences. Develop an original idea in depth, with a broad basis on topical subjects. Serious, in-depth, developmental articles with international appeal." Length: 2,500 to 6,000 words. Pays $300.

THE FREEMAN, 30 S. Broadway, Irvington-on-Hudson NY 10533. (914)591-7230. Editor: Paul L. Poirot. 60% freelance written. For "fairly advanced students of liberty and the layman." Monthly. Buys all rights, including reprint rights. Buys about 44 mss a year. Pays on publication. SASE.

Nonfiction: "We want nonfiction clearly analyzing and explaining various aspects of the free market, private enterprise, limited government philosophy, especially as pertains to conditions in the United States. Though a necessary part of the literature of freedom is the exposure of collectivistic cliches and fallacies, our aim is to emphasize and explain the positive case for individual responsibility and choice in a free economy. Especially important, we believe, is the methodology of freedom; self-improvement, offered to others who are interested. We try to avoid name-calling and personality clashes, and find satire of little use as an educational device. Ours is a scholarly analysis of the principles underlying a free market economy." Length: not over 3,500 words. Payment is 5¢ a word.

THE NATION, 333 Sixth Ave., New York NY 10014. Editor: Victor Navasky. Weekly. Query first. SASE.

Nonfiction and Poetry: "We welcome all articles dealing with the social scene, particularly if they examine it with a new point of view or expose conditions the rest of the media overlooks. Poetry is also accepted." Length and payment to be negotiated.

How To Break In: "We are absolutely committed to the idea of getting more material from the boondocks. For instance, a fellow in Denver just sent us a piece we're printing on the firings that are going on at the newspaper there. Right now we're getting stuff at the ratio of about 10 to one from the New York area and I would like to reverse that ratio. If you live somewhere where you think nothing is going on, look again! If you do a piece for us from someplace where we don't have anyone, you could develop into a stringer."

NATIONAL DEVELOPMENT, Intercontinental Publications, Inc., 15 Franklin St., Westport CT 06880. (203)226-7463. Editor-in-Chief: Martin Greenburgh. Emphasizes 3rd world infrastructure. For government officials in 3rd world—economists, planners, engineers, ministers. Monthly magazine; 120 pages. Estab. 1960. Circ. 23,000. Pays on acceptance. Buys all rights, but may reassign following publication. Phone queries OK. Previously published submissions OK. SASE. Reports in 4 weeks. Free sample copy and writer's guidelines.

Nonfiction: How-to (tourism, case studies, government management, planning, telecommunications), informational (agriculture, economics, public works, construction management), interview, photo feature, technical. Buys 6-10 mss/issue. Query. Length: 1,800-3,000 words. Pays $150-250.

Photos: B&w and color. Captions required. Query. Total price for ms includes payment for photos.

Columns, Departments: Managing Maintenance (public works maintenance from managerial viewpoint), Financial Technology (finances as they might affect 3rd world governments). Buys

4 mss/issue. Query. Length: 750-1,500 words. Pays $75-150. Open to suggestions for new columns/departments.

NATIONAL JOURNAL, 1730 M St., N.W., Washington DC 20036. (202)857-1400. Editor: Richard Frank. "Very limited need for freelance material because full-time staff produces virtually all of our material."

NATIONAL REVIEW, 150 E. 35th St., New York NY 10016. (212)679-7330. Editor: Wm. F. Buckley, Jr. Issued fortnightly. Buys all rights. Pays on publication. Will send sample copy. Reports in a month. SASE.
Nonfiction: Kevin Lynd, articles editor. Uses articles, 1,000 to 3,500 words, on current events and the arts, which would appeal to a politically conservative audience. Pays about 7½¢/word. Inquiries about book reviews, movie, play, TV reviews, or other cultural happenings, or travel should be addressed to Chilton Williamson, Jr., 150 E. 35th St., New York NY 10016.
Poetry: Uses only short, satirical poems of a political nature. Should not run over 30 lines.

NEW GUARD, Young Americans for Freedom, Woodland Rd., Sterling VA 22170. (703)450-5162. Editor-in-Chief: David Boaz. Emphasizes libertarian or conservative political ideas for readership of mostly young people with a large number of college students. Age range 14-39. Virtually all are politically conservative or libertarian with interests in politics, economics, philosophy, current affairs. Mostly students or college graduates. Monthly magazine; 32 pages. Estab. 1961. Circ. 12,000. Pays on publication. Buys all rights. Phone queries OK. Seasonal/holiday material should be submitted 2-3 months in advance. SASE. Reports in 1 month. Free sample copy.
Nonfiction: Expose (government waste, failure, mismanagement, problems with education or media); historical (illustrating political or economic points); humor (satire on current events); interview (politicians, academics, people with conservative viewpoint or something to say to conservatives); personal opinion and profile. Buys 40 mss/year. Submit complete ms. Length: 3,500 words maximum. Pays $10-60/article.
Photos: Purchased with accompanying manuscript.
Fiction: Humorous (satire or current events). Buys 5 mss/year. Submit complete ms. Length: 1,800 words maximum. Pays $10-40.

THE NEW REPUBLIC—A Weekly Journal of Opinion, 1220 Nineteenth St., N.W., Washington DC 20036. Managing Editor: Michael Kinsley. 50% freelance written. Estab. 1914. Circ. 90,000. Buys all rights. Pays on publication. SASE.
Nonfiction: This liberal, intellectual publication uses 1,000- to 1,500-word comments on public affairs and arts. Pays 8¢ per published word.

NEWSWEEK, 444 Madison Ave., New York NY 10022. Staff-written. Unsolicited mss accepted for "My Turn," a column of personal opinion. Length: 1,100 words maximum.

PRACTICAL POLITICS, Box 2495, Springfield IL 62705. (217)522-5328. Editor: Terry Lutes. 80% freelance written. Emphasizes campaign politics for elected officials and their aides, party officials, political consultants, writers, and election officials. Bimonthly magazine; 40 pages. Estab. 1977. Circ. 8,000. Pays on acceptance. Buys first North American serial rights. Phone queries OK. Submit seasonal/holiday material 3 months in advance of issue date. Simultaneous, photocopied and previously published submissions OK. SASE. Reports in 1 month. Sample copy $1; free writer's guidelines.
Nonfiction: How-to (campaigns, media preparation, research); historical (past campaigns); interview (elected officials, candidates, consultants, writers); new product (campaign techniques); personal experience (campaign); personal opinion (electoral change); and photo feature (campaign activity). No partisan or idealigical opinion. Buys 40mss/year. Query. Length: 500-2,000 words. Pays $15-60.
Photos: Pays $5-50 for b&w photos. Buys one-time rights.
Columns/Departments: Donna Vaught, department editor. Book Reviews (on campaign books). Buys 12/year. Query. Length: 500-1,500 words. Pays $15-45. Open to suggestions for new columns/departments.
Fillers: Clippings. Length: 10-60 words. Pays $5-10.

PRESENT TENSE: THE MAGAZINE OF WORLD JEWISH AFFAIRS, 165 E. 56th St., New York NY 10022. (212)751-4000. Editor: Murray Polner. For college-educated, Jewish-oriented audience interested in Jewish life throughout the world. Quarterly magazine; 80 pages. Estab.

1973. Circ. 25,000. Buys all rights, but will reassign rights to author after publication. Buys 60 mss a year. Payment on acceptance. Sample copy $2.50. Will not consider photocopied or simultaneous submissions. Reports in 6 to 8 weeks. Query first. SASE.
Nonfiction: Quality reportage of contemporary events (a la *Harper's, Atlantic, New Yorker*, etc.) and well-written memoirs. Personal experience, profiles, essay reviews and photo essays. Length for essay reviews: 800 words maximum. Length for other material: 3,000 words maximum. Pays $100 to $250.

THE PROGRESSIVE, 408 W. Gorham St., Madison WI 53703. (608)257-4626. Editor: Erwin Knoll. Issued monthly. Buys all rights. Pays on publication. Reports in two weeks. Query first. SASE.
Nonfiction: Primarily interested in articles which interpret, from a progressive point of view, domestic and world affairs. Occasional lighter features. Up to 3,000 words. Pays $50-$200 per ms.

REASON MAGAZINE, Box 40105, Santa Barbara CA 93103. (805)962-1079. Editor: Robert Poole, Jr. 50% freelance written. For a readership interested in individual liberty, economic freedom, private enterprise alternatives to government services, protection against inflation and depressions. Monthly; 52 pages. Estab. 1968. Circ. 20,000. Rights purchased vary with author and material. May buy all rights; but will sometimes reassign rights to author after publication; first North American serial rights or first serial rights. Buys 40 mss a year. Payment on publication. Sample copy $1; free guidelines for writers. "Manuscripts must be typed, double- or triple-spaced on one side of the page only. The first page (or a cover sheet) should contain an aggregate word count, the author's name and mailing address, and a brief (100- to 200-word) abstract. A short biographical sketch of the author should also be included." Will consider photocopied submissions. Reports in 3 months. Query first. SASE.
Nonfiction and Photos: "*Reason* is a libertarian publication, dealing with social, economic and political problems, and supporting both individual liberty and economic freedom. Articles dealing with the following subject areas are desired: analyses of current issues and problems from a libertarian viewpoint (e.g., education, pollution, victimless crimes, regulatory agencies, foreign policy, etc.). Discussions of social change, i.e., strategy and tactics for moving toward a free society. Discussions of the institutions of a free society and how they would deal with important problems. Articles on self-preservation in today's environment (economic, political, cultural). Lessons from the past, both revisionist history and biographical sketches of noteworthy individuals. Case studies of unique examples of the current application of libertarian/free-market principles." Length: 1,500-5,000 words. Book reviews are needed. No additional payment is made for b&w photos. Captions required.

THIS MAGAZINE, Red Maple Publishing Co., Ltd., 3 Church St., Suite 401, Toronto, Ontario, Canada M5E 1M2. (416)364-2431. Managing Editor: Lorraine Filyer. 60% freelance written. Emphasizes Canadian education, culture and politics for a well-educated readership of teachers, professors, students, radicals, union leaders and community workers. Bimonthly magazine; 36 pages. Estab. 1966. Circ. 6,000. Pays on publication. Buys all rights, but may reassign following publication. Submit seasonal/holiday material 3 months in advance of issue date. Photocopied and previously published submissions OK. SASE. Reports in 1 month. Free sample copy; mention *Writer's Market* in request.
Nonfiction: Humour (add a bit of it to everything); historical (analysis of political events, labour events, etc.); interview (with people making important contributions to the Canadian experience); personal opinion (on any field: labour, education, culture); photo feature (include 300-500 words); and in-depth analysis on matters relating to the Canadian experience, i.e., Canada and the Third World, Canada's economy, etc. Buys 4 mss/issue. Submit complete ms. Length: 2,000-3,500 words. Pays $10-25.
Photos: Submit photos with accompanying ms. Pays $15 for b&w glossy prints. captions preferred. Buys one-time rights.
Fiction: Adventure; experimental; fantasy; humorous; mystery; science fiction; and suspense. Buys 1 ms/issue. Submit complete ms. Length: 2,000-3,500 words. Pays $15-25.

TIME, Rockefeller Center, New York NY 10020. Staff-written.

US NEWS & WORLD REPORT, 2300 N. St., NW, Washington DC 20037. "We are presently not considering unsolicited freelance submissions."

WASHINGTON MONTHLY, 1028 Connecticut Ave., N.W., Washington DC 20036. Editor:

Charles Peters. For "well-educated people interested in politics and government; well-read." Monthly. Circ. 30,000. Rights purchased depend on author and material. Buys all rights or first rights. Buys about 40 mss a year. Pays on publication. Sample copy $1.75. Sometimes does special topical issues. Query or submit complete ms. Tries to report in 2-4 weeks. SASE.
Nonfiction and Photos: Responsible investigative or evaluative reporting about the U.S. government, business, society, the press, and politics. Length: "average 2,000 to 6,000 words." Pays 5¢ to 10¢ a word. Buys b&w glossies.

WASHINGTON WOMEN'S REPRESENTATIVE, 854 National Press Bldg., Washington DC 20045. (202)347-3553. Editor: Brynda Pappas. 25% freelance written. Emphasizes "legislative, judicial and political actions by and affecting women at federal, state, and local levels for professionals whose profession is women, and women activists of all ages and occupations." Semimonthly newsletter; 12 pages. Estab. January 1976. Circ. 1,400. Pays on publication. Buys all rights, but may reassign following publication. Phone queries OK. Submit seasonal/holiday material 2 weeks in advance of issue date. Simultaneous and photocopied submissions OK. SASE. Reports in 2 weeks. Free sample copy and writer's guidelines; mention *Writer's Market* in request.
Nonfiction: Exposé (we are looking for the inside story on any governmental or political action affecting women; just the facts, no opinion); general interest (innovative government or political action; stories on the group or individual who has adopted new strategies to bring about change); interview (occasionally, if interpretive); and profile (interpretive). "We do not want personal opinion pieces. Our emphasis is on current news of national interest." Buys 4 mss/issue. Query. Length: 50-750 words. Pays $10.
Columns/Departments: "We currently run a freelance health column and are considering the development of other regular features written by freelancers. Writers must be experts in the fields they write about. We are open to ideas for regular features."

WORLD POLITICS, Corwin Hall, Princeton NJ 08540. Editors: Klaus Knorr, Cyril E. Black, Gerald Garvey, Walter F. Murphy, Leon Gordenker. Issued quarterly to academic readers in social sciences. Pays on publication. Buys all rights. Reports in one to six months. SASE.
Nonfiction: Uses articles based on original scholarly research on international aspects of the social sciences. Mss should be double-spaced throughout (including footnotes), and have wide margins. Footnotes should be placed at the end of article. Length: 3,000 to 5,000 words. Pays $50 per article.

WORLDVIEW, 170 E. 64th St., New York NY 10021. Phone: (212)838-4120. Managing Editor: Susan Woolfson. For "the informed and concerned reader who insists that discussion of public issues must take place within an ethical framework." Monthly. Buys all rights. Pays on publication. Study the magazine and query first. SASE.
Nonfiction: Articles on public issues, religion, international affairs, world politics, and moral imperatives. "The editors believe that any analysis of our present cultural and political problems which ignores the moral dimension is at best incomplete—at worst, misleading. *Worldview* focuses on international affairs, puts the discussion in an ethical framework, and relates ethical judgment to specifically religious traditions." Article length: 2,500 to 5,000 words; "Excursus", 300-1,000 words; Book reviews: 1,000 words. Payment depends on length and use of material.
How To Break In: "Short pieces for the 'Excursus' section must be as well written and have the same degree of ethical orientation as the longer ones, but it is one way to break in. Book reviews are also a possibility. If a writer sends some samples of previous work and a list of the types of literature he is interested in, we might try him out with an assignment."

Puzzle Publications

This category includes only those publications devoted entirely to puzzles. The writer will find many additional markets for crosswords, brain teasers, acrostics, etc., by reading the Filler listings throughout the Consumer, Trade, Technical, and Professional sections of this book. Especially rich in puzzle markets are the Religious, Juvenile, Teen and Young Adult, and General Interest classifications in the Consumer section.

OFFICIAL CROSSWORDS, DELL CROSSWORDS, POCKET CROSSWORDS, DELL WORD SEARCH PUZZLES, DELL PENCIL PUZZLES AND WORD GAMES, DELL CROSSWORD ANNUALS, DELL CROSSWORD PUZZLES, PAPERBACK BOOK SERIES, DELL PUZZLE

PUBLICATIONS, 245 East 47 St., New York NY 10017. Editor: Kathleen Rafferty. For "all ages from '8 to 80'—people whose interests are puzzles, both crosswords and variety features." Buys all rights. SASE.
Puzzles: "We publish puzzles of all kinds, but the market here is limited to those who are able to construct quality pieces which can compete with the real professionals. See our magazines. They are the best guide for our needs. We publish quality puzzles, which are well-conceived and well edited, with appeal to solvers of all ages and in about every walk of life. We are the world's leading publishers of puzzle publications and are distributed in many countries around the world in addition to the continental U.S. However, no foreign language puzzles, please! Our market for crosswords and anacrostics is very small, since long-time contributors supply most of the needs in those areas. However, we are always willing to see material of unusual quality, or with a new or original approach. Since most of our publications feature variety puzzles in addition to the usual features, we are especially interested in seeing quizzes, picture features, and new and unusual puzzle features of all kinds. Please do not send us remakes of features we are now using. We are interested only in new ideas. Kriss Krosses are an active market here. However, constructors who wish to enter this field must query us first before submitting any material whatever. Prices vary with the feature, but ours are comparable with the highest in the general puzzle field."

ORIGINAL CROSSWORD, EASY-TIMED, CROSSWORD'S WORD HUNT, 575 Madison Ave., New York NY 10022. (212)838-7900. Editorial Director: Arthur Goodman. Bimonthly. Buys all rights. Pays on acceptance. Refer to current issue available on newsstand as guide to type of material wanted. Submissions must be accompanied by self-addressed, stamped envelope for return.
Puzzles: Original adult crossword puzzles; sizes 15x15 and 13x13; medium and not hard. Same requirements for diagramless, but 15x15 irregular patterns only. Pays $7 to $20.

Regional Publications

General interest publications slanted toward residents of and visitors to a particular region are listed below. Since they publish little material that doesn't relate to the area they cover, they represent a limited market for writers who live outside their area. Many buy manuscripts on conservation and the natural wonders of their area; additional markets for such material will be found under the City, Nature, Conservation, and Ecology, and Sport and Outdoor headings.

Publications that report on the business climate of a region are grouped in the regional division of the Business and Finance category. Newspapers and weekly magazine sections, which also buy material of general interest to area residents, are classified separately under that category heading.

ADIRONDACK LIFE, Box 137, Keene NY 12942. Editor-in-Chief: Bernard R. Carman. Emphasizes the Adirondack region of New York State for a readership aged 30-60, upper-educated, whose interests include outdoor activities, history, and natural history directly related to the Adirondacks. Bimonthly magazine; 64 pages. Estab. 1970. Circ. 42,000. Pays on publication. Buys all rights, but may reassign following publication. Submit seasonal/holiday material 4 months in advance. Previously published book excerpts OK. SASE. Reports in 4 weeks. Free sample copy and writer's guidelines.
Nonfiction: Historical (Adirondack relevance only); how-to (should relate to activities and lifestyles of the region, e.g., how to make your own maple syrup); informational (natural history of the region); interview (Adirondack personalities); personal experience; photo feature (Adirondack relevance required); profile; and travel (Adirondacks only). Buys 6-8 mss/issue. Query. Length: 1,500-3,500 words. Pays $75-200.
Photos: Purchased with or without mss or on assignment. Captions required (Adirondacks locale must be identified). Submit contact sheet or transparencies. Pays $10 for 8x10 glossy, semi-glossy or matte photos; $25-50 for 35mm or larger color transparencies.
How To Break In: "Start with a good query that tells us what the article offers—its narrative line and, most importantly, its relevance to the Adirondacks. We tolerate all sorts of aberrations at least once. The exception: failure to determine what the magazine is all about. At the risk of being tiresome, let me repeat again: it's all about the Adirondacks, broadly concieved—and not about anything else."

ALASKA MAGAZINE, Box 4-EEE, Anchorage AK 99509. (Writers living outside of Alaska should submit to the magazine's Lower 48 office: 130 2nd Ave., S., Edmonds WA 98020.) Managing Editor: Marty Loken. 80% freelance written. Monthly magazine. Pays on publication. Buys first North American serial rights. SASE.
Nonfiction and Photos: "*Alaska Magazine's* subtitle is 'The Magazine of Life on the Last Frontier,' and, as implied, our interests are broad. We're heavy on sharp color photographs of Alaska and northwestern Canada, buying about 1,000 transparencies each year, and rely heavily on freelance writers. Feature subjects include backpacking, resource management, sport fishing, wildlife encounters, kayaking and canoeing, trapping, cross-country skiing, snowshoeing, hunting, travel in Alaska, commercial fisheries, Native affairs, mining, arts and crafts, mountaineering, bush-country life, profiles of Alaskans, history, town profiles, and wilderness photo essays. Manuscripts may run up to about 4,000 words, but we prefer shorter photo-illustrated pieces in the 1,000-2,000 word range. Rates for illustrated material range from $50-400, depending on length."
Photos: "Photos should ideally be Kodachrome or Ektachrome color slides—no duplicates, please—with attention given to sharpness. Rates are $100 for covers, $75 for 2-page spreads, $50 for full-page; and $25 for half-page.
Columns/Departments: "Regular monthly features include full-page color photos, letters, book reviews, personality profiles, bush-living tips, and short factual stories on Alaskan creatures."

ARIZONA HIGHWAYS, 2039 W. Lewis Ave., Phoenix AZ 85009. (602)258-6641. Editor: Tom. C. Cooper. "We are drastically overstocked on copy and photos."

ARCTIC IN COLOUR, Northern News Service, Box 2728 Yellowknife, Northwest Territories, Canada XOE 1HO. (403)873-2117. Editor-in-Chief: Brad Henderson. 85% freelance written. Emphasizes polar regions. Quarterly magazine; 48 pages. Estab. 1967. Circ. 40,000. Pays on acceptance or publication. Buys one-time rights. Phone queries OK. Submit seasonal/holiday material 3 months in advance of issue date. Simultaneous, photocopied and previously published submissions OK. Reports in 2 weeks. Free sample copy and writer's guidelines; mention *Writer's Market* in request.
Nonfiction: All material must have a Northern content and interest. General interest; historical; interview; personal experience; photo feature; profile; and travel. Buys 4 mss/issue. Submit complete ms. Length: 800-5,000 words. Pays $50-200.
Photos: Submit photo material with accompanying ms. Pays $10-200 for b&w negatives; $15-300 for 35mm color transparencies. Captions required. Buys one-time rights.

THE ATLANTIC ADVOCATE, University Press of New Brunswick Ltd., Gleaner Bldg., Fredericton, NB., Canada E3B 5A2. (506)455-6671. Editor-in-Chief: H.P. Wood. Emphasizes The Atlantic Provinces for junior high school to octogenarian. Monthly magazine; 72 pages. Estab. 1950. Circ. 22,000. Pays on publication. Buys first North American serial rights. Phone queries OK. Submit seasonal/holiday material 3 months in advance. SASE. Reports in 2 weeks. Sample copy 50¢.
Nonfiction: Historical, humor, informational, interview, nostalgia, personal experience and profile. Buys 150-200 mss/year. Send complete ms. Length: 500-2,000 words. Pays 5¢/word.
Photos: Purchased with accompanying ms. Submit transparencies. Pays $5-10 for b&w; $25 for color (covers only). Model release required. "Our cover shots are scenes taken in the Atlantic Provinces. We try to be seasonal."
Fiction: Adventure, historical and humorous. Buys 15-30 mss/year. Send complete ms. Length: 1,500-2,000 words. Pays 5¢/word.
Poetry: Free verse and traditional. Buys 12-20 poems/year. Limit submissions to batches of 6. Length: 15-50 lines. Pays $10-50.
How To Break In: "We encourage new writers and read every manuscript that is relevant to the Atlantic area. We write letters, even if brief, and have no rejection cards or slips. We're friendly people with a sincere love for writers, artists and photographers, but don't abuse our good nature."

BC OUTDOORS, Box 900, Postal Station A, Surrey, B.C., Canada. (604)574-5211. Editor: Art Downs. Monthly magazine; 68 pages. Estab. 1945. Circ. 30,000. Buys first North American serial rights. Buys 70-80 mss/year. Pays on acceptance. Free sample copy. Submit seasonal material 4 months in advance. Reports in 2 to 4 weeks. Query first or submit complete ms. Enclose SAE and International Reply Coupons.
Nonfiction and Photos: Anything of a factual nature about B.C./Yukon, including conservation,

history, travel, fishing, camping and wildlife. Must be of general interest. Length: 1,500 to 3,000 words. Pays $100-250. 8x10 or 6x9 b&w photos purchased with or without accompanying ms. Pays $10. 35mm color used for covers. Pays $50-75.

BAJA CALIFORNIA BULLETIN, J L Publications, Apdo. Postal 127, La Paz, Baja California Sur, Mexico. Co-editors: Luisa Porter, Jerry Klink. Emphasizes tourism in Baja California. Bimonthly magazine; 32 pages. Estab. 1972. Circ. 10,000. Pays on acceptance. Buys all rights, but may reassign following publication. Submit seasonal/holiday material 4 months in advance of issue date. Previously published submissions OK. SASE. Reports in 4 weeks. Free sample copy.
Nonfiction: Historical (Pre-Columbian Baja California and Mexican Indian lore, mission stories, revolutionary highlights); how-to (and where-to on camping, scuba-diving, shopping for bargains); humor (anything humorous about travel in Mexico, but nothing about poverty); informational (towns visited, off-beat areas); interview (with famous person who travels in Baja California, relating to his experiences on the peninsula); nostalgia (Mexico or Baja in earlier times, personal experience only); and photo feature (sports, bullfights, off-road racing, boat racing); and animal and plant life of Baja. Buys 12 mss/year. Submit complete ms. Length: 500-1500 words. Pays $15-35.
Photos: Purchased with accompanying ms, no additional payment. Submit 5x7 or larger b&w prints. Captions optional.
Fiction: Historical (if related to Baja California). Submit complete ms. Length: 1,500 words maximum. Pays $10-30.
Fillers: Joke, gags, anecdotes and short humor. Buys 2-3/year. Length: 100-300 words. Pays $4-10.

BEND OF THE RIVER MAGAZINE, Box 239, Perrysburg OH 43551. (419)874-1691. Editors: Christine Raizk Alexander and Lee Raizk. For readers interested in history, antiques, etc. Monthly magazine; 24 pages. Estab. 1972. Circ. 2,000. Rights purchased vary with author and material. Usually buys all rights, but will reassign rights to author after publication. Buys 50 to 60 mss a year. Payment on publication. Sample copy for 10¢. Will not consider photocopied or simultaneous submissions. Submit seasonal material 2 months in advance; deadline for holiday issue is October 15. Reports in 2 months. Submit complete ms. SASE.
Nonfiction and Photos: "We deal heavily in Ohio history. We are looking for articles about modern day pioneers, doing the unusual. Another prime target is the uplifting feature, spiritual and/or religious sketch or interview. Don't bother sending anything negative; other than that, we can appreciate each writer's style. We'd like to see interviews with historical (Ohio) authorities; travel sketches of little known but interesting places in Ohio; grass roots farmers; charismatic people. Nostalgic pieces will be considered. Our main interest is to give our readers happy thoughts. We strive for material that says 'yes' to life, past and present." Length: open. Pays minimum of $5. Purchases b&w photos with accompanying mss. Pays minimum of $1. Captions required.
How To Break In: "Send us any unusual piece that is either cleverly humorous, divinely inspired or thought provoking. We like articles about historical topics treated in down-to-earth conversational tones. And *any* Toledo area history will be put on top of the heap!"

BLUENOSE MAGAZINE, Box 580, Port Maitland, Nova Scotia, Canada BOW 2VO. (902)649-2789. Editor-in-Chief: Bill Crowell. Managing Editor: Frances Crowell. 75% freelance written. Quarterly magazine; 50 pages. Estab. 1976. Circ. 3,000. Pays on acceptance. Buys first North American serial rights. Submit seasonal/holiday material 6 months in advance of issue date. SASE. Reports in 3 months. Sample copy $1; free writer's guidelines.
Nonfiction: How-to (environmental, gardening, energy alternatives); historical (regional); interview (Bluenose character); new product (regional,crafty); and nostalgia (regional). Buys 48 mss/year. Query or submit complete ms. Length: 500-1,500 words. Pays 1¢/word.
Photos: "No payment for non-copyrighted work except by arrangement." Pays $2.50-5 for any size b&w prints. Captions preferred. Buys one-time rights.
Fiction: Historical; humorous; and nostalgia. Buys 4 mss/year. Submit complete ms. Length: 1,500 words maximum. Pays 1¢/word.
Poetry: Free verse; haiku; light verse; and traditional. Buys 16/year. Length: 5-10 lines. Pays $3-7.

BOULDER DAILY CAMERA FOCUS MAGAZINE, Box 591, Boulder CO 80306. (303)442-1202. Editor-in-Chief: W. Michael Barry. 50% freelance written. Emphasizes subjects of particular interest to Boulder County residents. Weekly tabloid.; 40 pages. Estab. 1964. Circ.

28,000. Pays on first of month following publication. Buys one-time rights. Phone queries OK. Submit seasonal/holiday material 6-8 weeks in advance. Photocopied submissions OK. SASE. Reports in 2 weeks.

Nonfiction: Expose (anything relevant to Boulder County that needs exposing); informational (emphasis on good writing, warmth and impact); historical (pertaining to Boulder County or Colorado in general); interview and profile (stress local angle); photo feature (featuring Boulder County or areas in Colorado and Rocky Mountain West where Boulder County residents are apt to go). Buys 35 mss/year. Query. Length: 700-3,300 words. Pays 30-50¢ a column inch.

Photos: Purchased with or without mss, or on assignment. Captions required. Query. Pays $3-6 for 8x10 b&w glossies; $4-8 for 35mm or 2¼x2¼ (or larger) color transparencies.

BROWARD LIFE, Brenda Publishing Co., 3081 E. Commercial Blvd., Fort Lauderdale FL 33308. (305)491-6350. Editor-in-Chief: Joanne Myers. 50% freelance written. Emphasizes leisure activities in Broward County. Monthly magazine; 72 pages. Estab. 1974. Circ. 20,000. Pays on publication. Rights purchased vary with author and material; buys all rights, but may reassign following publication, or first North American serial rights. Phone queries OK. Submit seasonal/holiday material 1 month in advance. Simultaneous, xeroxed and previously published submissions OK. SASE. Reports in 6 weeks. Sample copy for $1.

Nonfiction: Expose (must pertain to persons or events in Broward County), how-to (must appeal to high-income lifestyles), humor (especially *New Yorker* type), interview (Broward County oriented), profile (Broward County resident), travel, new product, photo feature. Buys 2 mss/issue. Submit complete ms. Length: 1,000-2,000 words. Pays $25-100. "We will consider students' work for credits only. Writers previously published in other magazines will be given preference."

Photos: Michael O'Bryon, Photo Editor. Purchased with or without accompanying ms or on assignment. Captions required. Pays $5-50 for b&w or 35mm color transparencies. Query or send contact sheet. Model release required.

Columns, Departments: Movies, Books, Theatre, Cooking, Business (taxes, new laws), quizzes. Buys 6 mss/issue. Submit complete ms. Length: 500-1,500 words. Pays $25-75.

Poetry: Avant-garde, free verse, haiku, light verse, humorous. Buys 4/issue. Limit submissions to 6 at one time. Length: 50 line maximum. Pays $5-25.

Fillers: Jokes, gags, anecdotes, crossword puzzles, short humor. Buys 3/issue. Length: 100 words maximum. Pays $5-25.

BUFFALO SPREE MAGAZINE, P.O. Box 38, Buffalo NY 14226. (716)839-3405. Editor: Richard G. Shotell. For "a highly literate readership." Estab. 1967. Quarterly. Circ. 18,000. Buys first serial rights. Buys 30 to 35 mss a year. SASE.

Nonfiction and Fiction: Department Editor: Gary Goss. "Intellectually stimulating prose exploring contemporary social, philosophical, and artistic concerns. We are not a political magazine. Matters of interest to western New York make up a significant part of what we print." Length: 3,000 words maximum. Pays about $75 for a lead article. "We print fiction, but it must be brilliant." Length: 3,000 words maximum. Pays $75.

Poetry: Department Editor: Janet Goldenberg. "Serious, modern poetry of nature and of man's relationship with nature interests us, provided it is of the highest quality." Pays $15 minimum.

CANADIAN FRONTIER ANNUAL, Antonson Publishing Ltd., Box 157, New Westminster, B.C., Canada V3L 4Y4. (604)584-9922. Editor-in-Chief: Gordon Stewart. Emphasizes Canadian history (pre-1900). For "anybody at all who is interested in Canadian history." Annual magazine; 124 pages. Estab. 1972. Circ. 5,000. Pays on publication. Buys first North American serial rights. "All material should be submitted by April of publication year." Simultaneous, photocopied and previously published submissions OK. Reports in 1 month. Sample copy $3.50; free writer's guidelines.

Nonfiction: Historical (Canadian history, pre-dating 1900. Only true, accurate and factual material will be accepted). Buys 24 ms/issue. Length: 2,000-3,000 words. Pays $50 minimum.

Photos: Purchased with accompanying ms. Captions required. Send prints. Pays $2 for any size b&w photos.

CANADIAN GOLDEN WEST MAGAZINE, 1012-16 Ave. NW., Calgary, Alberta, Canada T2M 0K5. (403)282-9181. Editor: Pat Donaldson. For residents and visitors to Western Canada. Magazine; 40 to 48 pages. Estab. 1965. Quarterly. Circ. 9,750. Buys first North American serial rights. Buys about 50 mss per year. Pays on acceptance. Will send free sample copy to writer on request. Submit seasonal material 3 months in advance. Reports in 4 weeks. SASE.

Nonfiction and Photos: Uses Canadian writers only. "Emphasis on the history, fine arts, people,

places and opinions of Western Canada; well-illustrated with b&w photos. No Wild West cowboy and Indian stuff!" Prefers informal, relaxed writing in third person, but first-person narratives considered if the writer was personally involved in an event of major importance. "Golden Notes" features true anecdotes and original humor. Pays $5 to $15 for 100 to 600 words. Indian stories accepted only if they are written by Indians. Would like to see personality profiles on public figures. "The magazine, being quarterly, likes to run material that corresponds to the seasons — historical slant appreciated." Length: 1,000-3,000 words. Pays 3-5¢/word. "Regular contributors are paid more, as are writers who have done original historical research." Photos purchased with mss with no additional payment. Captions optional, but some explanation preferred.
Fiction and Fillers: Buys fiction with Western Canadian slant. Will consider mystery, suspense, adventure, Western, science fiction and historical. Buys 1 ms/issue. Pays 1¢ to 5¢ per word. "Average article is paid 3¢/word." Will consider fillers with Canadian slant. Buys crossword and word puzzles, jokes, gags, anecdotes, and short humor. Pays $5 to $15.

CASCADES EAST, 1230 NE 3rd St., Bend OR 97701. (503)382-0127. Editor: George W. Linn. 20% freelance written. For "all ages as long as they are interested in outdoor recreation in Central Oregon: fishing, hunting, sight-seeing, hiking, bicycling, mountain climbing, backpacking, rockhounding, skiing, snowmobiling, etc." Quarterly magazine; 48 pages. Estab. May 1976. Circ. 10,000. Pays on publication. Buys all rights, but may reassign following publication. Submit seasonal/holiday material 6 months in advance of issue date. SASE. Reports in 4 weeks. Sample copy $1.
Nonfiction: General interest (first person experiences in outdoor Central Oregon—with photos, can be dramatic, humorous, or factual); historical (for feature, "Little Known Tales from Oregon History," with photos); and personal experience (needed on outdoor subjects—dramatic, humorous or factual). "No articles that are too general, sight-seeing articles that come from a travel folder, or outdoor articles without the first person approach." Buys 1-2 mss/issue. Query. Length: 1,000-3,000 words. Pays 3-4¢/word.
Photos: "Old photos will greatly enhance chances of selling a historical feature. First person articles need black and white photos, also." Pays $5-10 for b&w; $15-50 for color transparencies. Captions preferred. Buys one-time rights.

CHESAPEAKE BAY MAGAZINE, 130 Severn Ave., Annapolis MD 21403. (301)263-2662. Editor: Betty D. Rigoli. 45% freelance written. "*Chesapeake Bay Magazine* is a regional publication for those who enjoy reading about the Bay and its tributaries. Our readers are yachtsmen, boating families, fishermen, ecologists—anyone who is part of Chesapeake Bay life." Monthly magazine; 56 pages. Estab. 1971. Circ. 10,000. Pays on either acceptance or publication, depending on "type of article, timeliness and need." Buys all rights or first North American serial rights. Submit seasonal/holiday material 3 months in advance of issue date. Simultaneous (if not overlapping circultions) and photocopied submissions OK. SASE. Reports in 1 month. Sample copy $1; writer's guidelines for SASE.; mention *Writer's Market* in request.
Nonfiction: "All material must be about the Chesapeake Bay area—land or water." How-to (fishing, hunting, and sports pertinent to Chesapeake Bay); general interest; humor (welcomed, but don't send any 'dumb boater' stories where common safety is ignored); historical; interviews (with interesting people who have contributed in some way to Chesapeake Bay life: authors, historians, sailors, oystermen, etc.); nostalgia (accurate, informative and well-paced. No maudlin ramblings about 'the good old days'); personal experience (drawn from experiences in boating situations, adventures, events in our geographical area); photo feature (with accompanying ms); profile (on natives of Chesapeake Bay); technical (relating to boating, hunting, fishing); and Chesapeake Bay Folklore. "We do not want material written by those unfamiliar with the Bay area, or general sea stories. No personal opinions on environmental issues." Buys 3 mss/issue. Query or submit complete ms. Length: 1,000-3,000 words. Pays $35-75.
Photos: Joe Wadsworth, art director. Submit photo material with ms. Uses 8x10 b&w glossy prints; pays $25-50 for 35mm, 2¼x2¼ or 4x5 color transparencies used for cover photos. Captions preferred. Rights "negotiable." Model release required.
Fiction: "All fiction must deal with the Chesapeake Bay, and be written by persons familiar with some facet of Bay life." Adventure; fantasy; historical; humorous; mystery; and suspense. "No general type stories with Chesapeake Bay superimposed in an attempt to make a sale." Buys 8 mss/year. Query or submit complete ms. Length: 1,250-3,000 words. Pays $35-75.
Poetry: Laura Oliver, poetry editor. Free verse; haiku; and traditional. "We want well crafted, serious poetry. Do not send in short, 'inspired' sea-sick poetry or 'sea-widow' poems." Buys 6/year. Limit submissions to batches of 4. Length: 5-30 lines. Pays $5-15.
How To Break In: "At present, we are the only regional publication entirely about the

Chesapeake Bay. Our readers are true 'Bay' lovers, and look for stories written by others who obviously share this love. We are particularly interested in material from the lower bay (Virginia) area and the upper Bay (Maryland-Delaware) area."

COAST, Box 2448, Myrtle Beach SC 29577. Managing Editor: Helen Sisson. For tourists to the Grand Strand. Magazine; 180 (5½x8½) pages. Estab. 1955. Weekly. Circ. 17,500. Buys all rights. Buys 5 or 6 mss a year. Pays on acceptance. Free sample copy. Will consider photocopied and simultaneous submissions. Reports on material accepted for publication in 60 to 90 days. Returns rejected material in 2 weeks. Query first. SASE.
Nonfiction and Photos: "Timely features dealing with coastal activities and events, and an occasional historical article related to the area. Submit an idea before a manuscript. It should be directly related to this coastal area. No vague, general articles." Emphasis is on informational and historical articles. Length: 800 to 1,000 words. Pays $25 to $30. B&w photos purchased with mss. Prefers 5x7. Pays $5 to $10 for b&w. Buys some color for editorial purposes. Must relate to area. Pays $15 to $25.

COASTLINE MAGAZINE, P.O. Box 914, Culver City CA 90230. (213)839-7847. Editor/Publisher: Robert M. Benn. For zone 9 audience in major urban complexes; age 24-48. Quarterly magazine; 64 pages. Estab. 1973. Rights purchased vary with author and material. May buy all rights, with the possibility of reassigning rights to author after publication, first North American serial rights, first serial rights, or second serial (reprint) rights. Pays on publication. Sample copy $2; free writer's guidelines. Photocopied submissions OK. No simultaneous submissions. Reports on mss accepted for publication in 3 to 7 weeks. Returns rejected mss in 4 to 6 weeks. Query first. SASE.
Nonfiction: Department Editor: Stephen Lawrence Berger. Will consider mss about regional lifestyles, investigative articles (municipal to international); socially significant trends in the arts (reviews, columns, events); and expanded print/electronic media-related mss. Establishment, avant-garde approach. Writer should study sample copy and contributor guidelines before submitting. Favors regional artists and writers. "We favor in-depth over gimmick and consider all, not merely a portion of our region." Interested in non-specific promotion of travel, restaurants and specific city cultural events. Length: 400 to 6,000 words. Pays $10 to $600. Length preferred for regular columns: 200 to 300 words. Pays minimum of $45.
Photos: Contact: Art Director. Purchased with ms with extra payment, without ms, or on assignment. Captions required. B&w only. Pays $5 to $25. Size: 8x10 b&w glossies or very clear 35mm transparencies.
Fiction and Poetry: Poetry Editor: Charles Price. Uses "significant fiction (especially novel excerpts); and major poetry tied in with West Coast slant." Buys experimental, mainstream, erotica, science fiction, humorous, historical, condensed novels and serialized novels. Length: 500 to 4,000 words. Pays $25 minimum. Buys blank verse, free verse, traditional forms, and avant-garde forms of poetry. Length: 4 to 50 lines (2 columns wide). Pays $5 to $50.

THE COLORADO EXPRESS, Box 18214, Capitol Hill Station, Denver CO 80218. Editor-in-Chief: Karl Kocivar. 80% freelance written. Emphasizes "the outdoors, travel, food, consumer information, crafts, essential living and natural sciences for educated, well-informed people of all ages who *read* rather than skim." Semianual magazine; 96 pages. Estab. 1972. Pays on publication. Buys all rights. Submit seasonal/holiday material 6 months in advance of issue date. Simultaneous, photocopied, and previously published submissions OK. SASE. Reports in 5-8 weeks. Sample copy $3.50.
Nonfiction: "*The Express* covers a wide range of interest areas. Features might fall under the headings of how-to, personal experience, nostalgia and travel all at once. They are complete to the extent that a reader must rarely feel the need to go elsewhere for more information. But should he feel that need, he can find 'elsewhere' in *the Express*. Each feature is a complete reference and each volume is designed to be kept, read and used. So timely pieces about something that happened last week are not what we're looking for. Nor are straight technical pieces. What we search for is readable, literate, but not literary, writing about almost anything educated, active people who participate in life might enjoy involving themselves with through reading. Our readers are looking for useful information that often isn't readily available through other sources. Features have included glaciers, lightning and winter camping for example; and consumer pieces on banking services and charge cards and how they work. How-to pieces should not be limited to a dozen candlemaking recipes; they should include historical and anecdotal information as well. Travel pieces shouldn't be limited to the ten best hotels in your favorite city." Buys 5 mss/issue. Submit complete ms. Length: 2,500-7,000 words. Pays $50-400.

Photos: Send photo material with accompanying ms. Pays $10-50 for 8x10 b&w glossy prints. Captions required. Buys all rights, but may reassign following publication.

COLORADO MAGAZINE, Titsch Publication, Inc., 1139 Delaware Plaza, Suite 200, Denver CO 80204. (303)573-1433. Editor-in-Chief: Paul S. Maxwell. Managing Editor: Rich Marschner. Emphasizes the scenic/lifestyle Rocky Mountain West, (Colorado, Wyoming, Utah, Montana, Idaho, New Mexico, Nevada and Arizona only). Bimonthly magazine; 100 pages. Estab. 1965. Circ. 175,000. Pays on acceptance. Buys all rights (one-time rights for photos). Submit seasonal/holiday material 3-6 months in advance. Simultaneous, photocopied and previously published submissions OK. SASE. Reports in 4 weeks. Free sample copy and writer's guidelines.
Nonfiction: Historical (old West); how-to (Rocky Mt. flavor); informational (useful 'where-to' lifestyle); personal experience (adventure, sports, recreation); photo feature; and profile (''Faces''—people who are fascinating and from the Western states). Buys 5-8 mss/issue. Query or send complete ms. Length: 1,500-2,500 words. Pays 12¢/word.
Photos: Ann Tait, Photo Editor. Photos purchased with or without accompanying ms or on assignment. Captions required. Uses b&w and 35mm color photos. Total purchase price for a ms includes payment for photos. Model release required. ''Attractive views of Western mountains, lakes, streams, ranches, ghost towns, sunsets, flowers, animals, outdoor sports.''

COMMONWEALTH, Virginia State Chamber of Commerce, 611 E. Franklin St., Richmond VA 23219. (804)643-7491. Editor-in-Chief: James S. Wamsley. Emphasizes Virginia. Monthly magazine; 48 pages. Estab. 1934. Circ. 11,000. Pays on publication. Buys all rights, but may reassign following publication. Submit seasonal/holiday material 4 months in advance. Photocopied submissions OK. SASE. Reports in 6 weeks. Sample copy 75¢.
Nonfiction: Informational; historical; humor; interview; nostalgia; profile; travel; and photo feature. Buys 25-30 mss/year. Query or submit complete ms. Length: 1,200-3,000 words. Pays $75-150.
Photos: Purchased with or without accompanying ms or on assignment. Captions required. Query. Pays $5-10 for 8x10 b&w glossy prints; $50 maximum for 35mm color transparencies.
How To Break In: ''Very difficult for a non-Virginian, or one not familiar with the magazine. We always need good ideas but find most outside freelancers want to provide subjects which are cliches to our readers.''

THE COUNTY MAGAZINE, Box 4233, Mt. Penn PA 19606. Editor: Darlene M. Roth. Executive Editor: B.R. Roth. 50% freelance written. Emphasizes ''all aspects of culture, people, history and trends in the tri-county area of Berks, Lancaster and Lebanon, counties. Monthly magazine; 64 pages. Estab. September 1975. Circ. 10,000. Pays on publication. Buys all rights, but may reassign following publication. Submit sesonal/holiday material 2-3 months in advance of issue date. Photocopied submissions OK. SASE. Reports in 6-8 weeks. Sample copy $1; free writer's guidelines; mention *Writer's Market* in request.
Nonfiction: All articles must be localized to the region of Berks-Lancaster-Lebanon-York counties in southeastern Pennsylvania.'' Exposé; general interest; humor; historical; interview (we use several of these per issue); nostalgia; photo feature; profile; technical and travel (within a day's journey of the area—no tourist traps). No crafts articles. Buys 4-5 mss/issue. Query or submit complete ms. Length: 600-2,000 words. Pays $35-75.
Photos: State availability of photos with query or ms. Pays $30 minimum/double-page spread for 5x7 b&w photos; $40 minimum/double-page spread for 35mm color transparencies. Captions required. Buys all rights, but may reassign following publication. Model release required.
Poetry: Kathy McCoy, poetry editor. Very little poetry used. Free verse; and traditional. No rhymed poetry. Buys 8/year. Limit submissions to batches of 3. Pays $10-20.

CUE MAGAZINE, 545 Madison Ave., New York NY 10022. (212)371-6900. Editor-in-Chief: Jeremiah E. Flynn. Emphasizes leisure and entertainment for sophisticated New Yorkers knowledgeable in all areas of the arts. Biweekly magazine; 144 pages. Estab. 1935. Circ. 300,000. Pays on publication. Buys all rights, but may reassign to author following publication or buys first North American serial rights. Phone queries OK. Submit seasonal/holiday material 2 months in advance. SASE. Reports in 2 weeks. Free sample copy.
Nonfiction: Informational, interview and travel. Buys 3 mss/issue. Query. Length: 500-2,500. Pays $100 minimum.
Photos: Judy Greer, Photo Editor. Purchased with accompanying ms. Query for photos. Offers no additional payment for 8x10 b&w/color photos accepted with accompanying ms. Model release required.

DELAWARE TODAY MAGAZINE, 2401 Pennsylvania Ave., Wilmington DE 19806. (302)655-1571. Editor-in-Chief: Leondard A. Quinn. 95% freelance written. Monthly magazine; 68 pages. Estab. 1962. Circ. 8,000. Pays on publication. Buys all rights, but may reassign following publication. Submit seasonal/holiday material 3 months in advance. Photocopied submissions OK. SASE. Reports in 4-6 weeks.
Nonfiction: Expose, historical, informational, inspirational, interview, new product, nostalgia, personal experience, profile, arts/crafts, hobbies and fashion. "The material must always relate to Delaware; it must have substance and holding power. Contemporary articles on social or political issues will be considered as well as consumer, ecological and economic pieces that are bright in style and locally oriented, especially in-depth, well-researched work." Buys 65 mss/year. Query or send complete ms. Length: 500-6,000 words. Pays $15-200.
Photos: Purchased with accompanying manuscript. Captions required. Pays $5-50 for b&w; $5-50 for color. Query for photos. Total purchase price for ms includes payment for photos. Model release required.

DELTA SCENE, Box B-3, Delta State University, Cleveland MS 38733. (601)846-1976. Editor-in-Chief: Dr. Curt Lamar. Managing Editor: Ms. Cary Thomas Cefalu. For an art-oriented or history-minded audience wanting more information (other than current events) on the Delta region. Quarterly magazine; 32 pages. Estab. 1973. Circ. 700. Pays on publication. Buys one-time rights. Submit seasonal/holiday material at least 4 months in advance. Simultaneous, photocopied, and previously published submissions OK. SASE. Reports in 4 weeks. Sample copy 50¢.
Nonfiction: "Only local writers should apply." Historical and informational articles; interviews, profiles and travel articles; technical articles (particularly in reference to agriculture). "We have a list of articles available free to anyone requesting a copy." Buys 2-3 mss/issue. Query. Length: 1,000-2,000 words. Pays $5-20.
Photos: Purchased with or without ms, or on assignment. Pays $5-15 for 5x7 b&w glossies or any size color transparency.
Fiction: Humorous and mainstream. Buys 1/issue. Submit complete ms. Length: 1,000-2,000 words. Pays $10-20.
Poetry: Traditional forms, free verse and haiku. Buys 1/issue. Submit unlimited number. Pays $5-10.

DOWN EAST MAGAZINE, Camden ME 04843. (207)236-4354. Editor-in-Chief: Davis Thomas. Focuses on Maine people, places, events and heritage. Monthly magazine; 116 pages. Estab. 1954. Circ. 70,000. Pays on acceptance for text, on publication for photos. Buys first North American serial rights. Phone queries OK. Submit seasonal/holiday material 6 months in advance of issue date. SASE. Reports in 2-3 weeks. Sample copy $1.25; free writer's guidelines.
Nonfiction: Submit to Manuscript Editor. "All material must be directly related to Maine: profiles, biographies, nature, gardening, nautical, travel, recreation, historical, humorous, nostalgic pieces, and photo essays and stories" Length: 600-2,500 words. Pays up to $250, depending on subject and quality.
Photos: Purchased on assignment or with accompanying ms. Captions required. Pays page rate of $50. Accepts 8x10 b&w, 35mm, 2¼x2¼ or 4x5 color transparencies and large color prints. Also purchases single color scenics for calendars. Model release required.
Columns/Departments: Short travel (600-1,500 word tightly written travelogues focusing on points of scenic, historic, or local interest); I Remember (short personal accounts of some incident in Maine, less than 1,000 words); and It Happened Down East (1- or 2- paragraph Maine anecdotes, pays $10). Pay depends on subject and quality.

THE DRUMMER, 250 W. Girard Ave., Philadelphia PA 19123. Editor: Jon Crane. Tabloid newspaper; 24 pages. Estab. 1967. Weekly. Circ. 60,000. Rights purchased vary with author and material. Usually buys all rights, but will reassign rights to author after publication. Buys about 50 mss a year. Pays on publication. Free sample copy. Will consider photocopied submissions. No simultaneous submissions. Reports as soon as possible. Query first. SASE.
Nonfiction and Photos: "Articles that, we hope, will either edify or entertain, with a decided emphasis on Philadelphia. This emphasis is most important. We like clarity and brevity and would prefer not to see think pieces." Interview, profile, humor, expose. Length: 750 to 1,000 words. Pays $5 to $50. 8x10 b&w glossies purchased with or without ms. Pays $5 to $10.

ENCHANTMENT MAGAZINE, 614 Don Gaspar Ave., Santa Fe NM 87501. (505)982-4671. Editor: John Whitcomb. 10% freelance written. For diversified audience. Estab. 1950. Monthly.

Circ. 71,000. Rights purchased vary with author and material. May buy all rights, with the possibility of returning rights to author after publication, or second serial reprint rights, or simultaneous rights. Buys 12 to 15 mss per year. Pays on publication. Free sample copy. Will consider photocopied and simultaneous submissions. Reports as soon as possible. SASE.
Nonfiction, Fiction and Photos: Buys historical features about rural New Mexico. Also occasional short stories on wide range of subjects. Length: 600-1,200 words. Pays $15 maximum. Photos purchased with accompanying ms with extra payment. Captions required. Pays $5. B&w only.

ENTERTAINER MAGAZINE, 940 Main St., W., Hamilton, Ontario, Canada L8P 3Y2. (416)528-0253. Editor: Chuck Wilson. Associate Editor: Joan Smith. 30% freelance written. Emphasizes leisure activities and entertainment for a controlled circulation of middle income readers in southern Ontario. Monthly tabloid; 44 pages. Estab: October 1973. Circ: 100,000. Pays 1 month after publication. Buys all rights, but may reassign following publication. Phone queries OK. Submit seasonal/holiday material 2 months in advance of issue date. SASE. Reports in 2 months. Free sample copy; mention *Writer's Market* in request.
Nonfiction: How-to (occasional crafts pieces); humor (related to leisure time); interview (with celebrities scheduled to appear in this area—South Ontario); nostalgia (about things, people and places relating to this area); personal opinion (about a performance, restaurant, travel experience); photo feature (fashion with a local interest); profile (of personalities in sports or entertainment or local notables); and travel (with information on prices, quality of accommodations, food, transportation, etc.). Query with clips of previously published work. Length: 800-1,200 words. Pays $25-50.
Photos: Pays $10/published b&w photo. Buys all rights, but may reassign following publication.

FAIRFIELD COUNTY MAGAZINE, County Communications, Inc., Playhouse Square, Box 269, Westport, CT 06880. (203)227-3706. Editor-in-Chief: Elizabeth Hill O'Neil. Emphasizes regional material of interest to high-salaried, well-educated readers. Monthly magazine; 72-96 pages. Estab. 1959. Circ. 26,500. Pays on publication. Buys all rights, but may reassign rights following publication. Phone queries OK. Submit seasonal/holiday material 3-4 months in advance. Photocopied submissions OK. SASE. Reports in 3 weeks. Sample copy $1.
Nonfiction: How-to, informational, historical, interview, profile, travel. Buys 5 mss/issue. Query. Length: 750-2,000 words. Pays $50-200.
Photos: Photos purchased with accompanying ms or on assignment. Pays $15-30 for 5x7 b&w glossies. Color photos for cover only. Total purchase price for ms includes payment for photos.
Columns/Departments: Travel, Nature, Sports, Music, Books, At Home, Executive Profile, and Lifestyle. Buys 3-4 mss/issue. Query. Length: 750-1,000 words. Pays $75-150. Open to suggestions for new columns/departments.
How To Break In: "Make your presence known, via resume or phone call. Tell of any specialty or experience. Write on-target articles."

FLORIDA KEYS MAGAZINE, Island Communications, Inc., 851 43rd St. Gulf, Marathon FL 33050. (305)743-3721. Editor/Publisher: Bill Beach. 70% freelance written. "Our audience is primarily affluent, early retirees, hard working, above average executives and tourist oriented folks." Quarterly magazine; 60 pages. Estab. 1977. Circ. 7,500. Pays on publication. Buys all rights, but may reassign following publication. Phone queries OK. Submit seasonal/holiday material 1 month in advance of issue date. Simultaneous and previously published (if not in conflicting area) submissions OK. SASE. Reports in 2 weeks. Sample copy 50¢.
Nonfiction: Features and articles on the Keys or similar sub-tropic living. Articles should deal with 'how-to' in this or similar areas with regard to efficient use of water and ecological topics unless specifically geared to Keys life and people. "While our articles are primarily pointed toward the Florida Keys they are not restricted to that content. For example, a how-to article on energy saving in southern California would certainly apply to us. A slice of life, especially with some humor, would do good. The watchword is *quality*. We have people for correcting breeches of the language but we do not want to see a manuscript which needs to be revised as to content." Buys 3-5 mss/issue. Query with clips of previously published work. "We maintain an open mind as to the length of an article. Keep in mind that the publisher is an old newspaper man. Use as many words as needed to tell the story, but don't use one damn word more than it takes." Pays 3-5¢/word.
Photos: "Photos must be of top quality for reproduction, and applicable to subject of article." State availability of photos with query. Pays $10-75 for b&w photos; $50-100 for 2¼x2¼ color transparencies. Captions preferred. Buys all rights, but may reassign following publication.
Fiction: Adventure; fantasy; historical; humorous (especially); suspense; and serialized novels.

Submit complete ms. Length: 1,000-3,000 words. Pays 6¢/word.
Fillers: Short humor. Pays $10.

FOCUS/MIDWEST, 928a N. McKnight, St. Louis MO 63132. (314)991-1698. Editor: Charles L. Klotzer. For an educated audience in Illinois, Missouri and the Midwest. Bimonthly magazine; 28 to 42 pages. Estab. 1962. Circ. 7,500. Buys all rights. Pays on publication. Reports in 4-6 weeks. SASE.
Nonfiction: Controversial articles; main emphasis on Illinois and Missouri. Facts, interpretation, analyses presenting political, social, cultural and literary issues on the local, regional and national scene of direct interest to the reader in or observer of the Midwest. Informational, interview, profile, think pieces. Length: open. Pays minimum of $25.
Poetry: Blank verse and free verse. Length: open. Pays minimum of $10.

GLIMPSES OF MICRONESIA AND THE WESTERN PACIFIC, Box 3191, Agana, Guam 96910. Editor-in-Chief: Robert Kiener. 90% freelance written. "A regional publication for Micronesia lovers, travel buffs and readers interested in the United States' last frontier. Our audience covers all age levels and is best described as well-educated and fascinated by our part of the world." Quarterly magazine; 80 pages. Estab. 1974. Circ. 15,000. Pays on publication. Buys one-time rights. Submit seasonal/holiday material 8 months in advance. Previously published work OK. SASE. Reports in 2 weeks. Sample copy $2; free writer's guidelines.
Nonfiction: Expose (well-documented of Micronesian cover-ups; mismanagement of funds, etc. CIA bugging is recent example); historical (anything related to Micronesia and the Western Pacific that is lively and factual); interviews; personal experience (first person adventure as in our recently published piece about 1,000-mile open-ocean outrigger canoe trip across Micronesia). Photo features (very photo-oriented magazine—query us on Island or Pacific themes); profiles (of outstanding Micronesian or Western Pacific individuals—e.g., looking for Lee Marvin's relationship with Micronesia); travel (use one/issue about areas reachable from Micronesia). Buys 30 mss/year. Query. Length: 5,000 words maximum. Pays 5¢/word.
Photos: Purchased with or without accompanying ms. Pays minimum of $15 for 8x10 b&w prints or 4x5 color transparencies or 35mm slides. Pay $200-300 for photo essays; $75 for covers. Captions required. Model release required.
Fiction: Adventure (believable; related to Micronesia); historical (as long as it's related to our part of the world). Buys 2 mss/year. "Most fiction is rejected because of poor quality." Submit complete ms. Length: 4,000 words maximum. Pays 10¢/word.
Poetry: "Use very little, but willing to look at Pacific-related themes to be used with photos." Only traditional forms. Pays $10 minimum.
How To Break In: "Writers living in or having first-hand experience with Micronesia and the Western Pacific are scarce. (That's because we *truly* are the United States' last frontier). Therefore, we'll work with a writer on making his manuscript suitable for publishing in *Glimpses*. If a writer has a good idea and is willing to work, we have the time to spare."

GULFSHORE LIFE, Gulfshore Publishing Co., Inc., 1039 Fifth Ave., N., Naples FL 33940. (813)649-9125. Editor: Lanny Sherwin. For an upper income audience of varied business and academic backgrounds. Published monthly, November through April. Magazine; 56 pages. Estab. 1970. Circ. 15,000. Buys all rights, with permission in writing to reproduce. Buys 6 mss a year. Payment on publication. Will consider photocopied or simultaneous submissions. Submit seasonal material 3 months in advance. Reports in 2 months. Query first. SASE.
Nonfiction: "Basically personal journalism of people, sports, homes, boats; pinpointing all features to seasonal residents, year-round residents and visitors. Travel, fishing, environmental articles are also used, but must be tied into personalities. Emphasis on "at home" life styles. Yachting, personality profiles; some historical material. Everything must be localized in line with our personal journalism concept." Length: 500 to 1,000 words. Pays $15 to $50.
How To Break In: "Only to be on location: Naples, Marco Island, Ft. Myers, Ft. Myers Beach, Sanibel-Captiva, Whiskey Creek, Punta Gorda Isles, Port Charlotte."

HIGH COUNTRY, The Idaho Mountain Record, Box 494, Council ID 83612. (208)253-4551. Editor-in-Chief: Leo Peurasaari. Managing Editor: D.E. Jones. Monthly tabloid: 32 pages. Estab. 1977. Circ. 8,000. Pays on acceptance. Buys all rights, but may reassign following publication. Phone queries OK. Submit seasonal/holiday material 3 months in advance of issue date. Simultaneous, photocopied and previously published submissions OK. SASE. Reports in 4-6 weeks. Sample copy 50¢; free writer's guidelines.
Nonfiction: Historical (we are interested in historical articles pertaining to the old west with a new slant); how-to (interested in rural lost arts, 'back-to-Mother Earth-type' skills); humor

(humorous articles are welcome especially relating to Idaho or the Northwest); interviews (with local Idaho or outstanding western figures); new product (concerning offbeat or unusual inventions); nostalgia (welcome, especially with an original or offbeat slant); and photo feature (articles accompanied by photos have the best change of acceptance). "We like articles about the eccentricities of people." Buys 150 mss/year. Submit complete ms. Length: 400-1,500 words. Pays 3-5¢/word.
Photos: Pays $2-8 for 4x5 glossy b&w prints. Captions and model release required.
Fiction: Historical; humorous (if short); and western. Buys 6 mss/year. Submit complete ms. Length: 400-1,000 words. Pays 3-5¢/word.
Poetry: Light verse; traditional; and western. Buys 12/year. Limit submissions to batches of 3. Length: 25-100 lines. Pays $2-5.
Fillers: Clippings, jokes, gags, anecdotes, newsbreaks, puzzles, short humor or unusual facts. Buys 60/year. Length: 25-200 words. Pays $2-5.

HUDSON VALLEY MAGAZINE, Suburban Publishing Inc., Box 265, Main St., Pleasant Valley NY 12569. (914)635-8822. Editor: Joan Loven. 95% freelance written. Emphasizes regional entertainment and leisure. Monthly magazine; 48 pages. Estab. 1972. Circ. 26,000. Pays 8-12 weeks after publication. Buys all or first North American serial rights. Submit seasonal/holiday material 2-3 months in advance. Simultaneous and photocopied submissions OK. SASE. Reports in 4-6 weeks. Sample copy $1; free writer's guidelines.
Nonfiction: All types of articles if regionally oriented to Hudson Valley. Buys 1-4 mss/issue. Query with tentative short outline and sample tentative introduction. Send samples of previous work. Length: 1,200-3,000 words. Pays 3¢/word.
Photos: Purchased on assignment. Uses b&w; payment depends on assignment. Query for photos. Offers no additional payment for photos accepted with accompanying ms. Model release required.
Fillers: Jokes, cartoons. Buys 1-2 fillers/issue. Send fillers. Pays about $5/cartoon.

ILLINOIS ISSUES, Sangamon State University, 226 CC, Springfield IL 62708. Acting Publisher: J. Michael Lennon. Managing Editor: Caroline Gherardini. Emphasizes Illinois government and issues for state and local government officials and staff plus citizens and businessmen concerned with Illinois and its government (local government also). Monthly magazine; 36 pages. Estab. 1975. Circ. 6,000. Pays on publication. Buys all rights. SASE. Reports in 4 weeks. Sample copy $1.75; free writer's guidelines.
Nonfiction: How-to (use state services and processes as a citizen); informational (explaining state/local government agency in Illinois, detailing new process initiated by state legislation, city or county ordinance); interview (Illinois government or political leaders) and technical (relating to government policy, services with issues stressed, i.e., energy). Buys 7 mss/issue. Query. Length: 800-2,500 words (best chance: 1,200 words). Pays 4¢-10¢/word.
How To Break In: "Local issues tied to state government in Illinois have a good chance, but writer must research to know state laws, pending legislation and past attempts that relate to the issue."

INDIANAPOLIS MAGAZINE, 320 N. Meridian St., Indianapolis IN 46204. (317)635-4747. Editor: Craig J. Beardsley. Publication of the Indianapolis Chamber of Commerce for members and others interested in Indianapolis. Established in 1964. Monthly. Buys first rights. Buys about 50 mss a year. Pays on publication. Will consider photocopied submissions. Seasonal material should be sent 6 months in advance. Reports on material within 10 days. Query first, "but if story is already completed, mail it on in." Enclose SASE.
Nonfiction and Photos: In-depth features of and about Indianapolis. Also interested in people who once lived in Indianapolis. Controversial articles welcomed, but must have Indianapolis-oriented slant to them. Anything that deals with informational, how-to, personal experience, interview, profile, humor, historical, think pieces, exposes, nostalgia, personal opinion, travel, successful business operations, new product, merchandising techniques. Length: 500 to 5,000 words. Pays $100 and as high as $200 for an exceptional article. Editor will make arrangements for photography after ms has been accepted. Uses both b&w and color photos. Pays between $50 and $100.
Fiction and Fillers: Uses very little fiction, unless it's Indianapolis oriented. Short (500 to 1,500 words) humor pieces welcome. Pays $50 to $100.

INLAND SHORES, 11050 W. Bluemound Rd., Milwaukee WI 53226. (414)774-8555. Editor-in-Chief: Van B. Hooper. Managing Editor: P. R. Dawley. 80% freelance written. Emphasizes travel and tourism in the Great Lakes states region and Ontario. Quarterly magazine; 56 pages.

Estab: December 1977. Pays on publication. Buys one-time rights. Phone queries OK. Submit seasonal/holiday material 4-6 months in advance. Simultaneous (if so identified), photocopied, and previously published (note where previously published) submissions OK. SASE. Reports in 6-8 weeks. Sample copy $2.50; free writer's guidelines.
Nonfiction: General interest; historical; interview (if appropriate); nostalgia; photo feature (beautiful 4-color); profile; and travel. Wants no material not relevant to travel/tourism. Buys 50 mss/year. Submit complete ms. Length: 1,000-5,000 words. Pays 5¢/word.
Photos: Submit photos with accompanying ms. Pays $10-20 for 8½-11 b&w glossy prints; $25-35 for 35mm, 2¼x2¼, or 4x5 color transparencies; $75-100 for cover photos. Captions required. Buys one-time rights. Model release required.

THE IRON WORKER, Lynchburg Foundry, A Mead Company, Drawer 411, Lynchburg VA 24505. (804)847-1724. Editor-in-Chief: Patrick M. Early. 50% freelance written. Emphasizes Virginia-related history for customers and schools. Quarterly magazine; 28 pages. Estab: 1919. Circ: 9,500. Pays on acceptance. Buys all rights, but may reassign following publication. Simultaneous and photocopied submissions OK. SASE. Reports in 6 weeks. Free sample copy and writer's guidelines.
Nonfiction: Historical (Virginia-related). "No dull, badly researched articles without a strong tie to Virginia." Buys 6 mss/year. Query. Length: 3,000-5,000 words. Pays $200-600.

JAPANOPHILE, Box 223, Okemos MI 48864. Editor: Earl R. Snodgrass. 65% freelance written. For people who have visited Japan or are interested in Japan; all ages. Magazine; 50 (7x10) pages. Estab. 1974. Quarterly. Circ. 800. Rights purchased vary with author and material. Buys all rights, but will reassign rights to author after publication; buys first North American serial rights; second serial (reprint) rights. Buys 50 mss a year. Pays on acceptance. Sample copy $1.75; free writer's guidelines. Will consider photocopied and simultaneous submissions. Submit seasonal material (each issue is built around a season) 4 months in advance. Reports in 2 months. Query preferred, but not required. SASE.
Nonfiction and Photos: Department Editors: Robert Cavera (nonfiction); Robert Copland (photos). "Articles that have to do with Japan or Japanese culture. We welcome material about Americans and other non-Japanese who practice a Japanese art in their own country. Hawaii, Los Angeles, and other locations have activity in the Japanese arts as well as Tokyo. Stories must be informed and accurate. We would like more on how Japan retains its culture and tradition while becoming a modern nation." Buys informational, personal experience, interview, profile, inspirational, humor, historical, think articles, nostalgia, personal opinion, photo, travel, book and film reviews, successful business operations. Length: 1,200 words maximum. Pays $5 to $20. Regular columns and features are San Francisco Scene, Tokyo Scene and Profiles of Artists. Length 1,000 words. Pays $20 maximum. Photos purchased with or without accompanying ms. Captions required. Pays $5 for b&w.
Fiction, Poetry, and Fillers: Department Editors: Earl Snodgrass (fiction and fillers); Carol Schumacher (poetry). Experimental, mainstream, mystery, adventure, science fiction, humorous, romance, and historical. Themes should relate to Japan. Length: 1,000 to 5,000 words. Pays $20. "We particularly need profiles of people practicing Japanese art forms, and well-written short stories with a setting in Japan." Traditional forms of poetry; avant-garde forms, and light verse. Should relate to Japan and to a season. Length: 3 to 50 lines. Pays $1 and up. Newsbreaks, puzzles, clippings, short humor. Length: 200 words maximum. Pays $1 to $5.

KANSAS!, Kansas Department of Economic Development, 503 Kansas Ave., 6th Floor, Topeka KS 66603. (913)296-3810. Editor: Ronald M. Welch. 60% freelance written. Emphasizes Kansas "faces and places for all ages, occupations and interests." Quarterly magazine; 32 pages. Estab: 1965. Circ: 25,000. Pays on acceptance. Buys all rights, but may reassign following publication. Phone queries OK. Submit seasonal/holiday material 3 months in advance of issue date. Simultaneous, photocopied and previously published submissions OK. SASE. Reports in 2 months. Free sample copy and writer's guidelines.
a3Nonfiction: "Material must be Kansas oriented and well-written." General interest; humor; historical; interview; nostalgia; photo feature; profile; and travel. No exposés. Buys 4 mss/issue. Query. Length: 1,000-2,000 words. Pays $100-150.
Photos: "We are a full-color photo/manuscript publication." State availability of photos with query. Pays $10-25 ("generally included in mss rate") for 35mm color transparencies. Captions required. Buys all rights, but may reassign following publication.

LAS VEGAS REVIEW-JOURNAL, Donrey Media Group, Inc., Box 70, Las Vegas NV 89101. (702)385-4241. Editor-in-Chief: Don Digilio. Emphasizes stories about Nevada, either a timely or interesting feature or a historical piece. "We accept freelance work only for our Sunday Nevada magazine." Daily newspaper; 64 pages. Circ. 72,000. Pays on publication. Buys all rights, but may reassign following publication. Phone queries OK. Submit seasonal/holiday material 1 month in advance. Photocopied submissions OK. SASE. Reports in 1 month. Free sample copy.

Nonfiction: A.D. Hopkins, nonfiction editor. Historical (on Nevada only); how-to; informational; interview; photo feature (on Nevada only). Send complete ms. Length: 800 words. Pays $30 minimum.

Photos: Rene Germanier, Photo Editor. Photos purchased with accompanying ms. Captions required. Pays $10 minimum for 8x10 b&w glossies; $10 minimum for color photos. Send prints and transparencies.

MAINE LIFE, RFD 1, Liberty ME 04949. (207)589-4351. Editor: Dave Olson. For middle age and over, urban or rural, 70% Maine; balance in other states to persons who have either an interest or love for the state of Maine. Monthly magazine; 64 pages. Estab. 1946. Circ. 26,000. Rights purchased vary with author and material. May buy all rights, but will reassign rights to author after publication or second serial (reprint) rights. Buys 110 mss a year. Payment on publication. Will send sample copy to writer for 30¢ in stamps. Will consider photocopied submissions and simultaneous submissions. Submit seasonal material 2 months in advance. Reports in 1 week. Query first. Enclose SASE.

Nonfiction and Photos: "Largely historical (Maine), non-controversial 'good-news' type of publication. Slogan is "For Those Who Love Maine.' Down-to earth material; more general interest, historical type." Interview, profile, humor, historical, nostalgia, personal opinion. Length: 500 to 2,000 words. Pays $10 to $35. B&w photos purchased with accompanying ms. Captions required. Pays $2 to $3.

THE MAIN SPORTSMAN, Box 365, Augusta ME 04330. Editor: Harry Vanderweide. 80-90% freelance written. Monthly tabloid; 32 pages. Estab: 1972. Circ: 17,000. Pays "shortly after publication." SASE. Reports in 2-4 weeks.

Nonfiction: "We publish only articles about Maine outdoor activities. Any well written, researched, knowledgable article about that subject area is likely to be accepted by us." Expose; how-to; general interest; interview; nostalgia; personal experience; personal opinion; profile; and technical. Buys 20-25 mss/issue. Submit complete ms. Length: 200-3,000 words. Pays $20-70.

Photos: "We can have illustrations drawn, but prefer 1-3 b&w photos." Submit photos with accompanying ms. Pays $5-20 for any size b&w print.

METRO, THE MAGAZINE OF SOUTHEAST VIRGINIA, Suite 304, Holiday Inn Scope, Norfolk VA 23510. (804)622-4122. Editor-in-Chief: St. Leger "Monty" Joynes. 75% freelance written. For urban adults with a concern for a lifestyle that provides cultural and social enrichment. Monthly magazine; 100 pages. Estab. 1970. Circ. 20,000. Pays on publication. Buys all rights, but may reassign following publication. Phone queries OK. Submit seasonal/holiday material 3 months in advance. Simultaneous, photocopied and previously published submissions OK. SASE. Reports in 2 weeks. Sample copy $1. Free writer's guidelines.

Nonfiction: Expose (regional controversies), historical (regional events, personalities), how-to (purchasing consumer goods), interview (regional), photo feature (society), and travel (major cities, sun and ski spots). Buys 4 mss/issue. Query. Length: 2,000-5,000 words. Pays $100-150.

Photo: Coco Smith, Photo Editor. Photos purchased with accompanying ms or on assignment. Captions required. Pays $25-100 for 8x10 b&w glossies. $50-150 for 35mm, 2¼x2¼ or 4x5 color transparencies. No additional payment for photos accepted with accompanying ms. Model release required.

Columns/Departments: Coco Smith, Columns/Departments Editor. Fashion (trends, male and female), Gourmet (restaurant reviews), Business (regional commentary), Books (by Southern authors), Arts (reviews, personalities), and Newsmakers. Buys 6 mss/issue. Query. Length: 1,000-1,750 words. Pays $75-100. Open to suggestions for new columns/departments.

MONDAY MAGAZINE, Box 1390, Victoria, British Columbia, Canada V8W 3C4. (604)382-6188. Editor: Derry McDonell. 30% freelance written. Emphasizes public affairs, art, and entertainment for a professional, white collar readership, interested in entertainment, dining out, social and family issues and urban affairs. Weekly magazine; 36 pages. Estab. July 1975. Circ. 21,000. Pays on publication. Phone queries OK. Submit seasonal/holiday material 1 month in advance of issue date. Previously published submissions OK. SASE. Reports in 3 weeks. Sample copy 50¢.

Nonfiction: Exposé (government, especially local/municipal); general interest (public affairs

features on current issues); humor (700-1,000 words maximum if fictional); interview (question and answer format preferred); personal experience; and profile (biographical). Buys 2-3 mss/issue. Submit complete ms. Length: 1,000-3,500 words. Pays $50-150.
Photos: Submit photos with accompanying ms. Pays $10 for b&w photos. Captions preferred. Model release required.
Columns/Departments: Book; Records and Pop music concert reviews. Buys 3/issue. Submit complete ms. Length: 500-1,500 words. Pays $25-50; "if review copies are kept, the pay rate is decreased accordingly." Open to suggestions for new columns/departments.

MISSOURI LIFE, 1209 Elmerine Ave., Jefferson City MO 65101. (314)635-4011. Editor: W.R. Nunn. 95% freelance written. For readers whose ages range from the upper twenties to retirees; education varies from high school to Ph.D's. Occupations range from farmers to professionals, such as doctors, lawyers, engineers, etc. Bimonthly magazine; 56 (9x12) pages. Estab. 1973. Circ. 33,000. Buys all rights, but will reassign rights to author after publication. Buys 20 mss a year. Payment on publication. Sample copy $2.50. Will consider photocopied and simultaneous submissions. Submit seasonal material 3 months in advance. Reports on material in 3 weeks. Query first or submit complete ms. SASE.
Nonfiction and Photos: "Almost any kind of material if it's about Missouri or Missourians. History, travel, recreation, human interest, personality profiles, business, scenic, folklore. The emphasis is on the approach and quality. Because it is a bimonthly, *Missouri Life* must look for the different angle, the human interest, the long-lasting information and appeal, the timelessness of quality and beauty. Prospective contributors would best be guided by recent issues of *Missouri Life*." Does not want to see "the stereotyped Ozark hillbilly piece, the travelogue with no feel of the country, the 'social message'." Seasonal material should have a different approach, with a seasonal flavor. Back issues are the best reference. Length: 1,200 to 2,500 words. 8x10 b&w glossy prints and color transparencies purchased with mss. Pays $50 for ms with b&w; $75 for mss with color transparencies; more if exceptional.

MONTANA MAGAZINE, Box 5630, Helena MT 59601. (406)443-2842. Editor: Rick Graetz. For residents of Montana and out of state residents with an interest in Montana. Estab. 1970. Bimomthly. Pays on publication. Sample copy $1.25; free writer's guidelines. Will consider photocopied and simultaneous submissions. Reports in 8 weeks. Query first. SASE.
Nonfiction and Photos: Articles on life in Montana; history, recreation. "How-to, where and when type articles." Limited usage of material on Glacier and Yellowstone National Park. Prefers articles on less publicized areas. Informational, profile, think pieces, nostalgia, travel, history. Length varies. Pays $20-35 for short articles with b&w photos; $35-125 for longer articles and accompanying b&w photos. Photo size: 5x7 or 8x10. "We can make b&w photos from color transparencies at a cost of $5 each. This amount would be deducted from the fee for the article."

NEVADA MAGAZINE, Carson City NV 89710. (702)885-5416. Editor-in-Chief: Caroline J. Hadley. Managing Editor: David Moore. 50% freelance written. Quarterly magazine; 64 pages. Estab. 1936. Circ. 55,000. Pays on publication. Buys first North American serial rights. Phone queries OK. Submit seasonal/holiday material 4 months in advance of issue date. SASE. Reports in 2 months. Sample copy $1; free writer's guidelines.
Nonfiction: Nevada topics only. Historical; nostalgia; photo feature; profile; recreational; and travel. Buys 10 mss/issue. Submit complete ms. Length: 500-2,500 words. Pays $75-300.
Photos: Send photo material with accompanying ms. Pays $10-50 for 8x10 glossy prints; $15-100 for color transparencies. Captions required. Buys one-time rights.

THE NEVADAN, Box 70, Las Vegas NV 89101. (702)385-4241. Editor-in-Chief: A.D. Hopkins. 15% freelance written. For Las Vegas and surrounding small town residents of all ages (those who take our Sunday paper. Affluent, outdoor-oriented.) Weekly tabloid; 12 pages. Estab. 1968. Circ. 76,000. Pays on publication. Buys one-time rights. Phone queries OK. Submit seasonal/holiday material 2 months in advance of issue date. Photocopied and previously published submissions OK. SASE. Reports in 3 weeks. Free sample copy and writer's guidelines; mention *Writer's Market* in request.
Nonfiction: General interest (contemporary off-beat features on Nevada's outdoors, mining towns and back country); historical (more of these than anything else, always linked to Nevada, southern Utah, N. Arizona, and Death Valley); how-to (on nostalgic arts, i.e. recent article on how to play mumbly-peg); nostalgia (about small-town life in Nevada mining camps); personal experience (any with strong pioneer Nevada angle, pioneer can be 1948 in some parts of Nevada); and travel (interesting new Nevada destinations). "No articles on history that is based

on doubtful sources; any current showbusiness material; any commercial plugs." Buys 52 mss/year. Query. Length: 1,000-3,000 words. Pays $40.
Photos: State availability of photos with query. Pays $5 for 5x7 or 8x10 b&w glossy prints; $15 for 105mm color transparencies. Captions required. Buys one-time rights.

NEW ALASKAN, Rt. 1, Box 677, Ketchikan AK 99901. Publisher: R.W. Pickrell. 75% freelance written. For residents of southeast Alaska. Tabloid magazine; 28 pages. Estab. 1964. Monthly. Circ. 15,000. Rights purchased vary with author and material. May buy all rights, but will reassign rights to author after publication; or second serial (reprint) rights. Buys about 40 mss a year. Pays on publication. Sample copy 50¢. Will consider photocopied submissions. Submit complete ms. SASE.
Nonfiction and Photos: Feature material about southeast Alaska. Emphasis is on full photo or art coverage of subject. Informational, how-to, personal experience, interview, profile, inspirational, humor, historical, nostalgia, personal opinion, travel, successful business operations, new product. Length: minimum of 1,000 words. Pays 1½¢ a word. B&w photos purchased with or without mss. Minimum size: 5x7. Pays $5 per glossy used. Pays $2.50 per negative (120 size preferred). Negatives are returned. Captions required.
Fiction: Historical fiction related to Alaska. Length: open. Pays 1½¢ per word.

NEW ENGLAND GALAXY, Old Sturbridge Village, Sturbridge MA 01565. Editor: Catherine Fennelly. 99% freelance written. For all ages, people interested in New England history and museums. Quarterly magazine; 60 pages. Estab. 1959. Circ. 11,500. Rights purchased vary with author and material. Buys all rights, but will occasionally reassign rights to author after publication; buys first North American serial rights. Buys 26 mss a year. Payment on publication. Free sample copy. Will consider photocopied submissions. Reports within 6 weeks. Query first for nonfiction. SASE.
Nonfiction and Photos: "Articles on any aspect of New England history, but not on a specific historic house open to the public. We're aimed at the general public, but emphasize the historical knowledge, original research and accuracy. We like to see the author's bibliography, which, however, will not be published." Biography, social customs, etc. Profile, historical, occasionally nostalgia articles. Length: 2,000 to 3,500 words. Pays $75 to $150. B&w photos purchased with or without ms. 8x10 photos of New England subjects. Pays $10.
Poetry and Fillers: Traditional forms, blank verse, and free verse. New England themes. Length: 6 to 30 lines. Pays $50. Pays $10 for quotes from New England historical sources.

THE NEW ENGLAND GUIDE, Stephen W. Winship & Co., Box 1108-12 Green St., Concord NH 03301. (603)224-4231. Editor-in-Chief: Stephen W. Winship. Detailed travelers'/vacationers' guide to New England. Annual magazine; 166 pages. Estab. 1958. Circ. 133,000. Pays on publication. Buys one-time rights. Deadline for queries is October 1. Reports in 2-3 weeks. Sample copy $1.50. Free writer's guidelines.
Nonfiction: Historical (New England subjects only, off-beat material preferred. "We didn't run a piece on Paul Revere's ride, but we did on the man who hung the lanterns"); humor (as an essay); informational (personal experience while traveling in New England, or a piece on a New England institution, such as antiquing, auctions, country fairs); nostalgia (this is tricky going); and profile (of little known but unusual people). Buys 6 mss/issue. Query. Length: 400-700 words. Pays $40-75.
Fillers: Anecdotes "one paragraph long, short and sharp history info is preferred. These tend to have a bit of wry humor to them, and that is preferred." Buys 10 mss/year. Length: 20-110 words. Pays $10.
How To Break In: "There is such a vast reservoir of history, legend and folklore on New England that we want the more off-beat variety. We don't pan individuals, groups, or hotels. Writing is to a large extent expository and sources are needed."

NEW HAMPSHIRE PROFILES, 2 Steam Mill Court, Concord NH 03301. (603)224-5193. Editor: Sharon L. Smith. 70% freelance written. For young to middle aged, college educated, high income readership interested in learning how to make the most of living in New Hampshire. Monthly magazine; 72 pages. Estab. December 1951. Circ. 20,000. Pays on publication. Buys First North American serial rights. Submit seasonal/holiday material 4 months in advance of issue date. Simultaneous and photocopied submissions OK. SASE. Reports in 4 weeks. Sample copy $1; free writer's guidelines; mention *Writer's Market* in request.
Nonfiction: "In each case, must relate to New Hampshire living". Historical; how-to; humor; photo feature (scenic color or telling a story); profile (of a newsmaker in New Hampshire); and travel (within New Hampshire; what to see and where to go and stay). "No poetry or fiction. No

stories on New Hampshire craftspersons and artists." Buys 5 mss/issue. Query. Length: 1,200-2,000 words. Pays $60-225.
Photos: State availability of photos with query. Pays $5-15 for 5x7 or 8x10 b&w glossy prints and $25-50 for 2¼x2¼ color transparencies. Captions required. Buys one-time rights. Model release required.
Columns/Departments: The Last Word (personal opinion on subjects previously covered in *Profiles*). Buys 1 ms/issue. Submit complete ms. Length: 850 words. Pays $60-150. Open to suggestions for new columns/departments.

NEW JERSEY MONTHLY, 1101-I State Rd., Princeton NJ 08540. Editor: Michael Aron. Managing Editor: Nancy Doherty. 70% freelance written. Emphasizes New Jersey interests. Monthly magazine; 108 pages. Estab. November 1976. Circ. 100,000. Pays on acceptance. Buys all rights. Submit seasonal/holiday material 4 months in advance of issue date. SASE. Reports in 6 weeks.
Nonfiction: Exposé (government or any institution in New Jersey); general interest (people doing unusual things, in-depth look at situations which define a community); how-to (service pieces must cover entire state; should concentrate on living the "better" life at reasonable cost); interview (people who are living and doing something in New Jersey—something that affects our readers, as opposed to someone who is from New Jersey and hasn't lived here in years); and personal experience (only if it sheds light on something going on in the state). "We're interested in high-quality magazine writing and original thinking." Buys 4-6 mss/issue. Query. Length: 1,500-6,000 words. Pays $250-1,500.
Columns/Departments: Departments run shorter than articles and include sports, media, politics, money and others. "Also have an arts section—800-1,200 word pieces on a subject concerning movies, music, art, dance, and theatre—no reviews, just pieces that deal with the ongoing arts scene in New Jersey." Buys 3 mss/issue. Query. Length: 1,000-2,000 words. Pays $50-300.

NEW MEXICO MAGAZINE, Bataan Memorial Bldg., Santa Fe NM 87503. (505)827-2642. Editor-in-Chief: Sheila Tryk. Associate Editor: Richard Sandoval. 75% freelance written. Emphasizes the Southwest, especially New Mexico, for a college-educated readership above average income, interested in the Southwest. Monthly magazine; 48 pages. Estab. 1923. Circ. 80,000. Pays on acceptance for mss; on publication for photos. Buys first North American serial or one-time rights for photos/compilation. Submit seasonal/holiday material 8 months in advance. SASE. Reports in 10 days-4 weeks. Sample copy $1.
Nonfiction: "New Mexico subjects of interest to travelers. Historical, cultural, humorous, nostalgic, and informational articles." Buys 5-7 mss/issue. Query. Length: 500-2,000 words. Pays $25-300.
Photos: Purchased with accompanying ms or on assignment. Captions required. Query, or send contact sheet or transparencies. Pays $15-30 for 8x10 b&w glossies; $25-35 for 35mm; prefers Kodachrome; (photos in plastic pocketed viewing sheets). Model release required.
How To Break In: "Send a superb short (1,000 words) manuscript on a little known event, aspect of history or place to see in New Mexico. Inaccurate research, faulty 'facts' will immediately ruin a writer's chances for the future. Good style, good grammar, please!"
Rejects: No generalized odes to the state or the Southwest. No Anglo, sentimentalized, paternalistic views of the Indians or of the Hispanos. No glib, gimmicky "travel brochure" writing.

NEW YORK MAGAZINE, 755 2nd Ave., New York NY 10017. (212)986-4600. Editor: James Brady. For intelligent readers in the New York area. Circ. 375,000. Buys all rights. Pays on publication. Query first. Reports in 1 month. Enclose SASE.
Nonfiction: Articles with ample reportage (not essays) about genuinely new or important aspects of the New York scene. Length: 1,000 to 3,500 words. Pays $250 to $1,000.

NORTH/NORD, 6th Floor, Les de la Chaudiére, Hull, Quebec Canada K1A OH4. Editor: Robert F.J. Shannon. For a varied audience, from libraries and educational institutions to businessmen and diplomats, Canadian and international. Special issues on various special subjects in the North. Bimonthly. Estab. 1959. Circ. 19,500. Rights purchased vary with author and material. Buys full rights to publish and permit to be republished. Buys 100 mss a year. Payment on acceptance. Free sample copy and writer's guidelines. Submit seasonal material 4 months in advance. Reports in 6 weeks. Submit only complete original mss.
Nonfiction: "Subjects must pertain to Canada's north or other northern areas of the world such as Alaska and Scandinavia. Topics can include resource development (business, mining, pipeline, construction and oil and gas industries); history (exploration, archaeology, fur trade);

conservation (wilderness, wildlife, national parks, geology); adventure and human interest stories; the arts (folklore, sculpture, print making, etc.); life in the north (housing, transportation, education, communications, health and welfare, government, entertainments); native peoples (customs, life styles, organizations etc.); features on outstanding personalities of the north as well as northern communities." Length: 750-3,000 words. Pays $50-300.
Photos: Purchased with or without mss. "We use mainly color transparency or print film; some black and white." Pays from $10-50 for single shot; $50 for "Face of the North," a photo feature profile of a northern personality. Pays $100-200 for cover photo and center spread scenic.

NORTHERN VIRGINIAN, 127 Park St., Box 334, Vienna VA 22180. (703)938-0666. "Freelance manuscripts welcomed on speculation. B&w photos as appropriate, with mss enhances publication probability." Reports in 30 days. Free sample copy and writer's guidelines.
Nonfiction: "Particularly interested in historical articles about or related to Northern Virginia."

NOVA SCOTIA HISTORICAL QUARTERLY, Box 1102, Halifax, Nova Scotia, Canada B3J 2X1. Editor-in-Chief: William H. McCurdy. 100% freelance written. "For a readership interested in the history of Nova Scotia, Canada." Quarterly magazine; 100 pages. Estab: 1971. Circ: 550. Pays on publication. Buys one-time rights. Simultaneous and photocopied submissions OK. SASE. Reports in 1 week. Free sample copy and writer's guidelines; mention *Writer's Market* in request.
Nonfiction: Historical (factual articles only). "No personal remenicences, please." Buys 20 mss/year. Submit complete ms. Length: 2,500-5,000 words. Pays $25-50.

NOW in Stark County Magazine, Box 9120, Canton OH 44711. (216)453-0305. Editor-in-Chief: William R. Moushey Jr. Managing Editor: Doborah Dommer. 30% freelance written. For residents of Stark County in Northeastern Ohio. Monthly magazine; 75 pages. Estab. January 1978. Circ. 11,300. Pays on publication. Buys all rights. Phone queries OK. Submit seasonal/holiday material 2½ months in advance of issue date. Simultaneous and previously published submissions OK. SASE. Reports in 2 weeks. Sample copy $1; free writer's guidelines; mention *Writer's Market* in request.
Nonfiction: "We will print anything that is well-writen and germane to the people of Stark County." Exposé; general interest; historical; how-to; humor; inspirational; interview; new product; nostalgia; personal experience; personal opinion; photo feature; profile; technical; and travel. "No porno articles." Buys 10 mss/issue. Query. Pays $1.30/column inch.
Photos: State availability of photos with query. Pays $1.30/inch for b&w contact sheets; negotiable for 2¼ color transparencies. Captions preferred. Buys all rights. Model release required.
Columns/Departments: Books; Film; Food; Sports; Theater; and Travel. Buys 10 mss/issue. Query. Pays $1.30/inch.
Fiction: "Will look at all types of Fiction." Buys 1 ms/issue. Submit complete ms with clips of previously published work. Pays $1.30/inch.
Poetry: Avant-garde, free verse, haiku, light verse, and traditional. Buys 10/issue. Pays $1.30/inch.
Fillers: Clippings; jokes, gags, anecdotes; newsbreaks; puzzles; and short humor. Buys 10/issue. Length: 20-100 words. Pays $1.30/inch.

OHIO MAGAZINE, Flynt Publications, 40 W. Gay St., Columbus OH 43215. (614)464-2068. Publisher: Robert Burdock. Managing Editor: J. Porter. Emphasizes news and feature material of Ohio for an educated, upper middle class readership. Monthly magazine; 96-156 pages. Estab. 1977. Circ. 125,000. Pays on publication. Buys all rights, but may reassign following publication; second serial (reprint), or one-time rights. Phone queries OK. Submit seasonal/holiday material 2 months in advance of issue date. Simultaneous, photocopied and previously published submissions OK. SASE. Reports in 8 weeks. Free writer's guidelines.
Nonfiction: Exposé (business, political, and news stories); historical (must have Ohio significance or flavor); how-to (consumer stories—how to find good firewood, best deal on a car, etc.); humor (Ohio flavor); informational (what is going on, and where); inspirational (Ohio significance); interview (Ohio person); new product (where you can find it, how much, is it any good?); nostalgia (Ohio object, person or event); personal experience (either humor or straight); personal opinion (reviews of books, movies, theatres, etc.); photo feature (must deal with Ohio, color or b&w); profile (business, sports, entertainment, limited only by imagination); technical (information must be useful to Ohioans); and travel (in Ohio, or where Ohioans can go). Buys 8-10 mss/issue. Query or submit complete ms. Length: 2,000-5,000 words. Pays $200-850.
Photos: Pays $25-50 for 8x10 glossy prints; $30-75 for 35mm and up color transparencies.

Captions and model release required.
Columns/Departments: Ohio Reporter (Ohio news generally not carried in newspapers, or more in-depth); Ohioans (people pages—must be Ohioans); Bill of Fare (Ohio restaurant reviews); and book, movie and theatre reviews. Buys 2-5/issue. Query or submit complete ms. Length: 200-2,000 words. Pays $50-300. Open to suggestions for new columns/departments.
Fillers: Clippings; jokes, gags, anecdotes; newsbreaks; crossword puzzles; and short humor. Buys 4-10/issue. Length: 50-1,000 words. Pays $50-150.

OREGON TIMES MAGAZINE, New Oregon Publishers, Inc., 1000 S.W. 3rd Ave., Portland OR 97204. (503)223-0304. Editor-in-Chief: Tom Bates. Managing Editor: David Kelly. Emphasizes Oregon for an adult, college-educated readership. Monthly magazine; 80 pages. Estab. 1971. Circ. 25,500. Pays on publication. Buys all rights, but may reassign following publication. Phone queries OK. Submit seasonal/holiday material 3 months in advance. Photocopied submissions OK. SASE. Reports in 3 weeks. Free writer's guidelines.
Nonfiction: Expose; historical; photo feature; profile; and travel. All articles must have an Oregon focus. Buys 4 mss/issue. Query. Length: 1,500-10,000 words. Pays $100-400.
Photos: Purchased with accompanying ms. Query. Pays $5-30 for 8x10 b&w glossies, uncropped, preferably full frame print; $10-40 for any size color transparencies. Model release required.
Columns/Departments: Grass Mountain Lookout (short news, interesting facts, bizarre opinion); Grapevine (gossip). Query. Pays $5-25.

OREGON VOTER DIGEST, 108 N.W. 9th, Portland OR 97209. (503)222-9794. Editor: C. R. Hillyer. For top echelon of leaders and decisionmakers in private industry and government in Oregon. Magazine; 40 pages. Frequent topical issues; apply for schedule. Estab. 1915. Monthly. Circ. 3,000. Not copyrighted. Pays on publication. Will send sample copy to writer on request. Will consider photocopied and simultaneous submissions. Submit topical issue material 1 month in advance. Reports on material accepted for publication in 1 month. Returns rejected material in 1 week. Query first or submit complete ms. Enclose SASE.
Nonfiction and Photos: News of business and industry, public affairs, legislation; statewide or affecting Oregon. Land use planning, forest industry, big government, economic trends, political items. "Looking for short political items (in state or affecting Oregon) of an expose or investigative nature. A writer's approach should be traditional, conservative stance, in support of private enterprise, against sprawling bureaucracy of government. Remember that this is not a mass consumer readership." Length: 500 words maximum. Pays 4¢ per word minimum. B&w glossies purchased with mss. Pays $7 minimum.

ORLANDO-LAND MAGAZINE, Box 2207, Orlando FL 32802. (305)644-3355. Editor-in-Chief: E.L. Prizer. Managing Editor: Carole De Pinto. Emphasizes central Florida information for a readership made up primarily of people new to Florida—those here as visitors, traveling businessmen, new residents. Monthly magazine; 112 pages. Estab. 1946. Circ. 28,000. Pays on acceptance. Buys all rights, but may reassign following publication; or first North American serial rights. Phone queries OK. Submit seasonal/holiday material 2 months in advance. Photocopied and previously published submissions OK. SASE. Reports in 6 weeks. Sample copy $1.
Nonfiction: Historical, how-to, informational. "Things involved in living in Florida."
How To Break In: "Always in need of *useful* advice-type material presented as first person experience. Central Florida subjects only."

OUTDOOR INDIANA, Room 612, State Office Building, Indianapolis IN 46204. (317)633-4332. Editor: Herbert R. Hill. 2% freelance written. For subscribers who seek information regarding programs, projects, services and facilities of the Indiana Department of Natural Resources. Published 10 times/year. Circ. 33,000. Buys first serial rights. Pays on publication. Reports on submissions in 1 to 4 weeks. Query preferred. Enclose SASE.
Nonfiction and Photos: Informative, concise, illustrative, bright articles on Indiana-related topics only. No fiction, essays or verse. Length: 1,000 to 2,000 words. Usually pays 2¢ a word. Photos of Indiana interest only; purchased with mss or with captions only. B&w photos, 8x10; color transparencies, 2¼x2¼ or larger. Pays $5 for b&w; $25 for color; $50 for color cover.

OUTDOORS IN GEORGIA, 270 Washington St., S.W., Atlanta GA 30334. (404)656-5660. Editor: Aaron Pass. Published by Georgia Department of Natural Resources for a male audience of hunters, fishermen, campers, environmentalists. Monthly magazine; 32 pages. Estab. 1966. Circ. 35,000. Copyrighted. Buys 12-15 mss a year. Pays on acceptance. Free sample copy and writer's guidelines. No photocopied or simultaneous submissions. Reports on material ac-

cepted for publication in 4 to 6 weeks. Returns rejected material 2 weeks after decision. Query first. SASE.
Nonfiction and Photos: "Material designed for reader use and relating to the outdoors (how-to and where-to in Georgia), the environment and natural/cultural history. Always need good articles on hunting, fishing, boating, hiking, etc. Must be both factual and entertaining. Informational, how-to, personal experience, interview, profile, historical articles. No "me and Joe" type articles. Length: 900-2,000 words. Pays $30-100, but payment depends on length, quality, and editorial needs. No additional payment made for b&w glossies or color transparencies used with mss, but "number and quality of photos may result in higher offer for story."

PALM BEACH LIFE, Post Office Box 1176, Palm Beach FL 33480. (305)655-5755. Managing Editor: Christopher Salisbury. "*Palm Beach Life* caters to a sophisticated, high-income readership and reflects its interests. Readers are affluent ... usually over 40, well-educated." Special issues on the arts (February), travel (March), yachting (November), and elegant living, interiors, etc. (September-October). Estab. 1906. Monthly with combined September-October issue. Circ. 12,000. Buys first North American rights. Payment on acceptance. Will consider photocopied submissions. Submit seasonal material 5 months in advance. Reports in 3 weeks. Query first. SASE. Sample copy $1.81.
Nonfiction and Photos: Subject matter involves "articles on fashion, travel, music, art and related fields; subjects that would be of interest to the sophisticated, well-informed reader. We feature color photos, 'but are crying for good b&w'. Buys informational, interview, profile, humor, historical, think, photo, and travel articles. Length: 1,000 to 2,500 words. Pays $100-300. Purchases photos with and without mss, or on assignment. Captions are required. Buys 8x10 b&w glossies at $10 each. Also buys 35mm or 2¼x2¼ transparencies and photo stories. Pay is negotiable.

PALM SPRINGS LIFE MAGAZINE, Desert Publications, Inc., 250 E. Palm Canyon Dr., Palm Springs CA 92262. (714)325-2333. Editor-in-Chief: Milton W. Jones. Managing Editor: Robert W. Vivian. 30-40% freelance written. Emphasizes "the lifestyle of the desert resort area." Monthly magazine; 220 pages. Estab. 1957. Circ. 65,000. Pays on publication. Buys all rights, but may reassign following publication. Submit seasonal/holiday material 4 months in advance of issue date. Simultaneous and previously published submissions OK. SASE. Reports in 1 month. Free sample copy and writer's guidelines; mention *Writer's Market* in request.
Nonfiction: General interest (for affluent audience); historical (Palm Springs/Southern California area); interview (with famous people); nostalgia (Palm Springs/Southern California area); profile (celebrities, movie stars, business leaders); and travel (areas which appeal to the affluent). "We're looking for material that will appeal to a highly affluent, well-traveled audience. We do not seek exposés or investigative pieces." Buys 20-25 mss/year. Query. Length: 1,000-3,500 words. Pays 6-10¢/word.
Photos: State availability of photos with query letter. Pays $5-25 for b&w photos; $25-150 for 35mm color transparencies. Captions required. Buys all rights, but may reassign following publication. Model release required.

PENINSULA LIVING, Box 300, Palo Alto CA 94302. (415)326-1200. Editor: Carolyn Snyder. For higher educated newspaper readers; median income over $20,000. Weekly tabloid newspaper; 24 pages. Estab. 1952. Circ. 65,000. Not copyrighted. Buys 10 mss/year. Pays 10th of month after publication. No photocopied or simultaneous submissions. Reports in 1 to 3 weeks. Query first. Enclose SASE.
Nonfiction and Photos: "Regional 'soft news'. Unusual hobbies, community trends, personalities, regional travel, regional history with popular 'hook', homes and gardens. No rigid structure. We seek good writing, unusual approach, impeccable accuracy. We don't want to see weak Erma Bombeck-type humor pieces, or out-of-area travel and history pieces, or themes not applicable to our audience." B&w glossies (8x10) purchased with mss. Pays $10 minimum.

PENINSULA MAGAZINE, Box 11701, Palo Alto CA 94306. (415)327-6666. Editor/Publisher: Mike Harris. "For alert, active and aware individuals who have a strong desire to know what's going on right in their own backyard." Monthly magazine; 80 pages. Estab. 1975. Circ. 12,000. Pays on publication. Buys first North American serial rights. Photocopied submissions OK. SASE. Reports in 4 weeks. Free sample copy and writer's guidelines.
Nonfiction: Expose, how-to, informational, humor, interview, new product, personal experience, photo feature, profile and travel. Buys 3 mss/issue. Query or send complete ms. Length: 1,500-3,500 words. Pays 3¢/word.
Photos: Steve Davis, Photo Editor. Purchased with or without accompanying ms or on assign-

ment. Captions required. Pays $5-10 for b&w 5x7 or 8x10. Query for photos.
Columns/Departments: Profiles buys 3 mss/issue, 350-500 words. Notable, interesting Peninsula residents, business, professional, civic, artistic. El Camino Real—hard-to-find services and items; 250 words. Interview—Q&A format; 500 words. Also potpourri-humor, vignettes, new products and services; 250 words maximum, photo and art. Query or send complete ms. Pays 3¢/word; $15 maximum. Open to suggestions from freelancers for new columns/departments; address to Mike Harris.
How To Break In: "All items must strictly and definitely have a real and believable Peninsula angle. We define the Peninsula as running bayside and coastside from the city/county line of San Francisco to and including San Jose."

PENNSYLVANIA ILLUSTRATED, Box 657, Camp Hill PA 17011. Editor-in-Chief: Albert E. Holliday. 50% freelance written. Audience is 35-50 years old, some college education, interested in self-improvement, civic and state affairs, history. Bimonthly magazine; 68 pages. Estab. 1976. Circ. 45,000. Pays on publication. Buys first North American serial rights. Submit seasonal/holiday material 6 months in advance. Simultaneous, photocopied and previously published submissions OK. SASE. Reports in 2-3 weeks. Sample copy $1.25; free writer's guidelines.
Nonfiction: Expose; how-to (any general interest subject); informational; historical; humor; interview (with prominent Pennsylvanians); nostalgia; profile; travel; new product (made in Pennsylvania); personal experience (unique); and photo feature. Buys 5-7 mss/issue. Query. Length: 500-2,000 words. Pays $50-200.
Photos: Purchased with or without accompanying ms or on assignment. Captions required. Query. Pays $5-10 for 5x7 b&w glossies or semiglossies; $25-50 for 2¼x2¼ color transparencies.

PERIODICAL OF ART IN NEBRASKA, University of Nebraska at Omaha, P-A-N, U.N.O., Annex 21, Box 688, Omaha NE 68101. (402)554-2771. Editor-in-Chief: Pat Gray. Emphasizes "literature and the arts in Nebraska." For students, writers and artists. Quarterly tabloid; 24 pages. Estab: 1974. Circ: 5,000. Payment is at the end of the publishing year. Purchases all rights. Phone queries OK. SASE. Submit seasonal/holiday material 3 months in advance. Reports in 3 months. Free sample copy.
Nonfiction: Interview; nostalgia; personal opinion; and profile on arts in Nebraska only. Buys 8 mss/year. Submit complete ms. Length: 1,000-6,000 words. Pays in surplus divided at end of year.
Fiction: Experimental; humorous; mainstream; western; and serialized novels. Buys 4 mss/year. Submit complete ms. Length: 1,000-6,000 words. Surplus divided at end of year.
Poetry: Avant-garde, free verse, haiku, traditional. Buys 60/year. Limit submissions to 5 at a time. No length requirement.

PHOENIX MAGAZINE, 4707 N. 12th St., Phoenix AZ 85014. (602)248-8900. Editor: Anita J. Welch. 75% freelance written. For professional, general audience. Monthly magazine. Estab. 1966. Circ. 60,000. Buys all rights, but will reassign rights to author after publication. Buys about 60 mss a year. Payment on publication. Sample copy $1. February issue: Real Estate; March issue: Arizona Lifestyle; August issue: Annual Phoenix Progress Report; June issue: Salute to Summer. Submit special issue material 3 months in advance. Reports in 1 month. Query first or submit complete ms. SASE.
Nonfiction and Photos: Predominantly features on some aspect of Phoenix life; urban affairs, arts, life style, etc. Subject should be locally oriented. Informational, how-to, interview, profile, historical, photo, successful local business operations. Length: 1,000 to 3,000 words. Pays $50 to $100, but payment is negotiable. Photos are purchased with ms with no additional payment, or on assignment.

ST. LOUISAN, 7110 Oakland Ave., St. Louis MO 63117. (314)781-8787. Editor: Greg Holzhauer. For "those interested in the St. Louis area, recreation issues, etc." Estab. 1969. Monthly. Circ. 20,000. Buys all rights, but will reassign rights to author after publication; buys second serial (reprint) rights. Buys 60 mss a year. Payment on publication. Will not consider photocopied submissions. Submit seasonal material 4 months in advance. Reports on material in 2 months. Query first or submit complete ms. Enclose SASE.
Nonfiction and Photos: "Articles on the city of St. Louis, metro area, arts, recreation, media, law, education, politics, timely issues, urban problems/solutions, environment, etc., generally related to St. Louis area. Looking for informative writing of high quality, consistent in style and timely in topic." Informational, how-to, personal experience, interview, profile, humor, histor-

ical, think pieces, expose, nostalgia, personal opinion, travel. Length: 1,000 to 5,000 words. Pays $100 to $200. 8x10 b&w glossies purchased on assignment. "Shooting fee plus $10 to $20 per print used. All color on individual basis."

SAN ANTONIO MAGAZINE, Greater San Antonio Chamber of Commerce, Box 1628, San Antonio TX 78296. (512)227-8181. Editor-in-Chief: Sammye Johnson. 75% freelance written. Emphasizes quality of life articles about San Antonio. Monthly magazine; 88 pages. Pays on publication. Buys all rights, but may reassign following publication. Phone queries OK. Photocopied submissions OK. SASE. Reports in 1 month. Free sample copy and writer's guidelines.
Nonfiction: "The magazine's purpose is to inform, educate and entertain readers about the quality of life in San Antonio. We're looking for articles that reflect life in San Antonio today." Expose; informational; historical; humor; nostalgia; personal opinion; profile (personality profiles of people who are interesting, colorful and quotable—must be a San Antonian or have ties to the city); travel; personal experience; and photo features. Buys 65 mss/year. Query or send complete ms. Length: 800-3,000 words. Pays $50-300.
Photos: Purchased with mss or on assignment. Captions required. Query. Pays $10-25 for 8x10 b&w glossies. Prefers to pay according to the number of photos used in an article, a bulk rate.
Columns/Departments: Personality profiles of a San Antonian who is involved in the arts, in education, in the medical field, etc., who is interesting, colorful, quotable. Buys 12/year. Query. Length: 1,000-1,500 words. Pays $100.
How To Break In: "The best way is to be a resident of San Antonio and, therefore, able to write on assignment or to query the editor personally. Again, we are looking for material which is related to the city of San Antonio and its people. We consider all possible angles and tie-ins."

THE SAN GABRIEL VALLEY MAGAZINE, Miller Books, 409 San Pasqual Dr., Alhambra CA 91801. (213)284-7607. Editor-in-Chief: Joseph Miller. For upper-middle income people who dine out often at better restaurants in Los Angeles County. Bimonthly magazine; 52 pages. Estab. 1976. Circ. 3,400. Pays on publication. Buys simultaneous, second serial (reprint) and one-time rights. Phone queries OK. Submit seasonal/holiday material 1 month in advance. Simultaneous, photocopied and previously published submissions OK. SASE. Reports in 2 weeks. Sample copy $1.
Nonfiction: Expose (political); informational (restaurants in the valley); inspirational (success stories and positive thinking); interview (successful people and how they made it); profile (political leaders in the San Gabriel Valley); and travel (places in the valley). Buys 2 mss/issue. Length: 500-10,000 words. Pays 5¢/word.
Columns/Departments: Restaurants, Education, Valley News and Valley Personality. Buys 2 mss/issue. Send complete ms. Length: 500-1,500 words. Pays 5¢/word.
Fiction: Historical (successful people) and western (articles about Los Angeles County). Buys 2 mss/issue. Send complete ms. Length: 500-10,000 words. Pays 5¢/word.
How To Break In: "Send us a good personal success story about a valley or a California personality."

SANDLAPPER—The Magazine of South Carolina, Greystone Publishers, Inc., Box 1668, Columbia SC 29202. Editor-in-Chief: Bob Rowland. 95% freelance written. "We reach an affluent, educated audience interested in the state of South Carolina, its past and present." Monthly magazine; 72 pages. Estab. 1968. Circ. 25,000. Pays on publication. Buys all rights, but may reassign following publication. Submit seasonal/holiday material 6-8 months in advance. Photocopied submissions OK. SASE. Reports in 2 weeks. Free sample copy and writer's guidelines.
Nonfiction: Harry Hope, History Editor. Historical (sound, articulate insights into South Carolina history); humor (frustrations of daily living); nostalgia; profiles (of living South Carolinians); photo feature; folk heritage; and leisure/recreation. Buys 10 mss/issue. Query. Length 1,500-3,000 words. Pays $50-350.
Photos: Purchased with accompanying ms. Captions required. Send contact sheet. Pays $6-10 for 5x7 or larger glossy finish b&w; $12-35 for 35mm or 2¼x2¼ transparencies. Maximum payment is for cover.
Columns/Departments: Dining Out (notable restaurants around the state); Folkroots (folk heritage material); Styles in Living (notable South Carolina homes); Leisure Living; and Bookshelf (book reviews relating to South Carolina or Southern experience). Buys 6 mss/issue. Query. Length: 300-500 words. Pays $50 maximum.
Fiction: Franklin Ashley, Fiction Editor. "We are interested in Southern regional fiction, with themes, characterization, 'sense of place'—all inherent in the genre. The writer should avoid melodrama, triviality, cliches, schmaltz, and anything that smacks of 'Lil Abner.'. . . ."

Buys 12 mss/year. Submit complete ms. Length: 1,500-4,000 words. Pays $150-250.
Poetry: Eugene Platt, Poetry Editor. Avant-garde, free verse, traditional. "No patriotic, religious, or inspirational verse." Buys 20/year. Length: 50 lines maximum. Pays $10-15.

SHOWCASE MAGAZINE, 103 W. Colorado Ave., Colorado Springs CO 80901. (303)633-3881. Editor-in-Chief: E. Thomas McClanahan. 90% freelance written. For "the younger reader, around 18-35, interested in light features on popular arts and leisure with a state or regional angle." Sunday supplement of the Colorado Springs Sun; 16 pages. Estab. 1948. Circ. 25,000. Pays on publication. Buys all rights, but may reassign following publication. Phone queries OK. Submit seasonal/holiday material 1 month in advance of issue date. Simultaneous, photocopied and previously published submissions OK. SASE. Reports in 4 weeks. Free sample copy; mention *Writer's Market* in request.
Nonfiction: General interest (emphasis on entertainment and leisure in the Pikes Peak region, or Colorado); humor; interview; personal experience; profile; and developments in Colorado arts. No governmental exposes. Buys 120 mss/year. Query. Length: 500-2,000 words. Pays $10-50.
Photos: State availability of photos with query. Pays $5-10 for 8x10 b&w prints or contact sheets; $8-13 for color transparencies. Captions required. Buys one-time rights. Model release required.

SOUTH CAROLINA MAGAZINE, Box 89, Columbia SC 29202. (803)796-9200. Monthly. Buys all rights. Pays on publication. Reports in about 1 week. Will send free sample copy on request. SASE.
Nonfiction and Photos: Matters of interest to South Carolinians about state history, places, people, education, art, etc. Length: 500 to 1,000 words. Pays 3¢ a word. Photos purchased with mss. Glossy prints, 8x10 or 5x7. Pays $5.

SOUTH CAROLINA WILDLIFE, Box 167, Columbia SC 29202. (803)758-6291. Editor: John Culler. Managing Editor: John Davis. For South Carolinians interested in hunting, fishing, the outdoors. Bimonthly magazine; 64 pages. Estab. 1953. Circ. 85,000. Not copyrighted. Buys 20-30 mss a year. Pays on acceptance. Free sample copy. Reports in two weeks. Submit complete ms. SASE.
Nonfiction and Photos: Articles on outdoor South Carolina with an emphasis on preserving and protecting our natural resources. Length: 1,000-3,000 words. Pays 10¢/word. Pays $35 for b&w glossies purchased with or without ms, or on assignment. Pays $75 for color.

SOUTHERN EXPOSURE, P. O. Box 230, Chapel Hill NC 27514. (919)929-2141. Editor: Bob Hall. 70% freelance written. For Southerners interested in "left-liberal" political perspective and the South; all ages; well-educated. Magazine; 100 to 230 (8x11) pages. Estab.1973. Quarterly. Circ.7,500. Buys all rights. Buys 20 mss/year. Pays on publication. Will consider photocopied and simultaneous submissions. Submit seasonal material 2 to 3 months in advance. Reports in 1 to 2 months. "Query is appreciated, but not required." SASE.
Nonfiction and Photos: "Ours is probably the only publication about the South *not* aimed at business or the upper-class people; it appeals to all segments of the population. *And,* it is used as a resource—sold as a magazine and then as a book—so it rarely becomes dated." Needed are investigative articles about the following subjects as related to the South: politics, energy, institutional power from prisons to universities, women, labor, black people, the economy. Informational interview, profile, historical, think articles, expose, personal opinion, and book reviews. Length: 6,000 words maximum. Pays $50-200. "Very rarely purchase photos, as we have a large number of photographers working for us." 8x10 b&w preferred; no color. Payment negotiable.
Fiction and Poetry: "Fiction should concern the South, i.e., black fiction, growing up Southern, etc." Length: 6,000 words maximum. Pays $50-100. All forms of poetry accepted, if they relate to the South, its problems, potential, etc. Length: open. Pays $15-200.

THE STATE, Box 2169, Raleigh NC 27602. Editor: W.B. Wright. Monthly. Buys first rights. Free sample copy. Pays on acceptance. Deadlines 1 month in advance of publication date. SASE.
Nonfiction and Photos: "General articles about places, people, events, history, general interest in North Carolina. Also reports on business, new developments within the state. Emphasis on travel in North Carolina; (devote features regularly to resorts, travel goals, dining and stopping places)." Will use humor if related to region. Length: average of 1,000 to 1,200 words. Pays $15-50. B&w photos purchased with mss. Pays average of $3-5

TAR HEEL: The Magazine of North Carolina, The New East, Inc., Wilcar Executive Center, 223 W. 10th St., Greenville NC 27834. (919)758-1288. Editor: James E. Wise. "Our magazine maintains a strict policy of being for and about North Carolina, its people, environment, culture and heritage, its nostalgia, and its character." Bimonthly magazine; 64-72 pages. Estab. 1972. Circ. 20,000. Pays on publication. Buys all rights, but may reassign following publication. Phone queries OK. Submit seasonal/holiday material 3-4 months in advance of issue date. Photocopied and previously published submissions OK. SASE. Reports in 2-3 weeks. Sample copy $1.30 plus 50¢ postage; free writer's guidelines.
Nonfiction: Historical (pertinent to North Carolina history, written in informal, anecdotal style); interview (by assignment); nostalgia (must have strong Carolina flavor and appeal; must be well-written, not maudlin); photo feature; profile; and travel (about North Carolina places, with emphasis on uniqueness, attraction, and atypical features). Buys 30-40 mss/year. Query or submit complete ms. Length: 1,200-3,000 words. Pays $30 minimum.
Fiction: Claire Pittman, fiction editor. "Generally, a recognizably Southern, preferably a North Carolina setting is needed." Adventure; historical; humorous; mystery; romance; and suspense. Buys 5-6 mss/year. Query or submit complete ms. Length: 1,800-2,200 words. Pays 2¢/word.
Poetry: Free verse; haiku; and traditional. Buys 2-3/issue. Length: 1 page maximum. Pays $10.

TEXAS MONTHLY MAGAZINE, Box 1569, Austin TX 78767. Editor: William Broyles. For Texans (in or out of state) with educated interests in politics, culture and lifestyles. Monthly magazine. Estab. 1973. Circ. 200,000. Pays on acceptance. Buys all rights, but may reassign following publication. Submit seasonal/holiday material 4 months in advance. Photocopied submissions OK. SASE. Reports in 6-8 weeks. Free writer's guidelines.
Nonfiction: Subjects must be of interest to an educated Texas readership. Informational; how-to; personal experience; interview; profile; and expose. Length: 2,500-8,000 words. Pays $500-850.
Photos: Purchased with accompanying ms. Pays $30 for b&w photos.
Columns/Departments: Travel; consumer; urban problems; and science. Length: 2,500 words maximum. Pays $300-400.

UPCOUNTRY, The Magazine of New England Living, 33 Eagle St., Pittsfield MA 01201. (413)447-7311. Managing Editor: William H. Tague. For people who are interested in the country and small town life of New England. Estab. 1973. Newsprint tabloid published 12 times a year and carried as a monthly supplement by daily newspapers in New England. Circ. 240,000. Buys all rights, but will reassign rights to author after publication. Buys 100 to 150 mss a year. Payment on acceptance. "Prefer written or telephone query in advance of sending material, although we consider everything received." SASE.
Nonfiction and Photos: "The magazine deals with life in New England as a whole, and country living, in particular; not as a fantasy, but as a reality. We look for articles on specific topics of current interest to our readership. Above all, articles must deal with New England subjects. New England writers strongly preferred. Articles concerned with moving to and living in the country; coping with country living; rural medicine, taxation, political issues affecting country life; gardening, music, art, theater, birdwatching, outdoor sports, restaurants, country inns, restorations, preservation, etc. Articles on how to come to terms with our environment; profiles of noteworthy people, interesting characters, socio-economic profiles of towns; short (1,200 words maximum) humorous pieces. How-to articles with a New England setting, on subjects relating to country or small town living." Length: 700-3,000 words. Pays $30-150. For b&w photos, payment is $10 each, or per advance arrangements. Pays $90 for color transparencies used or cover only (no inside color).
Poetry: Poetry considered, but sparingly used. Traditional forms preferred. Pays $15 minimum.

VALLEY MONTHLY MAGAZINE, 131 N. 8th St., Allentown PA 18101. (215)439-4031. Editor: Tim Whitaker. For residents of the Greater Lehigh Valley interested in everything from the arts to politics. Monthly magazine; 80 pages. Estab. 1976. Circ. 15,000. Pays on acceptance. Submit seasonal/holiday material 2 months in advance of issue date. Photocopied submissions OK. Reports in 6 weeks. Free sample copy and writer's guidelines.
Nonfiction: Exposé; how-to; historical; informational; interview; photo feature; profile; and travel. Buys 60 mss/year. Query. Length: 700-4,000 words. Pays $50-500.
Photos: State availability of photos with query. Offers no additional payment for b&w prints. Captions optional; model release required.
Columns/Departments: Dining; Film Reviews; Politics; Sports; Travel; and The Arts. Buys 36 mss/year. Query with clips. Length: 700-3,000 words. Pays $50-250.

VERMONT LIFE MAGAZINE, 61 Elm St., Montpelier VT 05602. (802)828-3241. Editor: Brian Vachon. Quarterly magazine; 64 pages. Estab. 1946. Circ. 130,000. Buys first rights. Buys about 60 mss a year. "Query is essential." SASE.
Nonfiction: Wants articles on Vermont, those which portray a typical and, if possible, unique, attractive aspect of the state or people. Style should be literate, clear and concise. Subtle humor favored. No nature close-ups and stories, Vermont dialect attempts, or an outsider's view on visiting Vermont. Word length averages 1,500 words. Payment averages 10¢ to 20¢ per word.
Photos: Buys photographs with mss and with captions only. Prefers b&w, 8x10 glossies or matte prints, except on assignment. Color submissions must be 4x5 or 35mm transparencies. Buys one-time rights, but often negotiates for re-use rights also. Rates on acceptance; b&w, $10; color, $75 inside, $200 for cover. Gives assignments but not on first trial with photographers. Query first.

WESTCHESTER ILLUSTRATED, 16 School St., Yonkers NY 10701. (914)472-2061 or 423-4722. Editor-in-Chief: Peter Porco. Emphasizes life in Westchester County, New York, for sophisticated, college-educated, 25-49 year-old suburbanites living within the New York Metropolitan area. "Interests range from participatory sports to the newest county budget, from the safety and convenience of Westchester's highways to the meaning of the latest cinema trends, from where to get the best cheesecake in the county to what their famous and not-so-famous neighbors are up to." Monthly magazine; 80 pages. Estab. 1976. Circ. 37,000. Buys all rights, but may reassign following publication. Submit seasonal/holiday material 3 months in advance of issue date. Simultaneous and photocopied submissions OK. SASE. Reports in 3-5 weeks. Sample copy $1; free writer's guidelines.
Nonfiction: "*Westchester Illustrated's* essential function is to aid survival in Westchester and make life here as pleasant and hassle-free as possible. If we can entertain readers in the process, all the better. We like 'how-to' articles, reports on new developments in county lifestyles, reports on the local effects of national or statewide trends, and profiles of local personalities, especially those currently in the news. Interviews are welcome; so is humor if it has a touch of satire. Consumer-oriented articles receive high priority—we're always looking for fresh material that people can use—material with practical value. Other favored topics are participatory sports, home care and home design, offbeat local history, local business dealings and trends, and local ecology. We do not want personal opinion, puffery or booster pieces, travel and technical writings and articles not about Westchester County. In general we want lots of personality and color—lively writing, full of anecdotes, quotes and the sounds of smells of a subject. We want to be able to visualize scenes. Stories should demonstrate genuine reporting; we're not interested in stories or essays that read as if they were reported over the telephone." Buys about 100 mss/year. Query or submit complete ms. Length: 800-4,000 words. Pays $50-250.
Photos: Purchased with or without accompanying ms, or on assignment. Detailed captions required. Pays $10-40 for minimum 5x7 b&w glossy or matte prints. Send query and contact sheet. Model release required.
Columns/Departments: Emporium (a shopper's guide and compilation of special buys and bargains in the Westchester area—$10 for 100-150 words); Locals (profiles of Westchesterites currently involved in something interesting—$25-40 for 500-1,000 words); First Cracks (series of shorts in front of book which take a look at the interesting, newsworthy, offbeat and humorous goings-on in Westchester—$10-25 for 100-500 words). Query or submit complete ms.

WESTCHESTER MAGAZINE, County Publications, 437 Ward Ave., Mamaruneck NY 10543. (914)698-8203. Editor-in-Chief: Vita Nelson. Emphasizes general interests in Westchester County and the metropolitan area. Monthly magazine; 96 pages. Estab. 1969. Circ. 30,000. Pays on publication. Buys all rights, but may reassign following publication. Submit seasonal/holiday material 3-4 months in advance. Simultaneous, photocopied, and previously published (occasionally) submissions OK. SASE. Reports in 5 weeks. Sample copy $1.25.
Nonfiction: Expose; informational (new phenomena, attitudes, new sports, hobbies, current fads); interview; profile; new product; and personal experience (only to make a point on a broader issue). Buys 5 mss/issue. Query. Length: 2,000 words minimum. Pays $75-100.

THE WESTERN RESERVE MAGAZINE, Box 243, Garrettsville OH 44231. (216)527-2030. Editor-in-Chief: Mary Folger. Managing Editor: Betty Clapp. 40% freelance written. Emphasizes historical, where-to-go, what-to-do, crafts and collectibles for Northeastern Ohioians with an interest in the region and all it has to offer an upper middle class readership. Published 8 times a year; 64 pages. Estab. 1973. Circ. 10,000. Pays on publication. Buys all rights, but may reassign following publication. Phone queries OK. Submit seasonal/holiday material 3 months in advance. Photocopied submissions OK. SASE. Reports in 1 month. Sample copy $2; free writer's guidelines.

Nonfiction: Historical (Northeastern Ohio); how-to (crafts with history); humor (if Northeastern Ohio historical slant); informational; interview (especially Northeastern Ohio historian, writer, artist, craftsman, etc.); photo feature (Western Reserve slant); profile (of famous or infamous Western Reserve person); and travel.

Photos: Purchased with accompanying ms. Uses b&w; "if sending old photo, we recommend copy—we try not to lose anything, but it can happen." Offers no additional payment for photos accepted with accompanying ms. Total purchase price for ms includes payment for photos. Model release required.

Columns/Departments: "Where to go, what to do" in Ohio and Western Pennsylvania. "New writers can break into *WRM* here and club public relations chairmen are welcome." Buys 6 (full-length "where to go, what to see" columns) per year. Send complete ms. Pays $30 for full-length article. Open to suggestions from freelancers for new columns/departments; address to Mary Folger.

How To Break In: "Our goal is to help preserve the heritage of the Western Reserve. We need *good* copy and the ability to produce it is all that's needed to break in. "Heritage" is the key here—need both history and contemporary if the contemporary preserves local heritage."

WESTWAYS, Box 2890, Terminal Annex, Los Angeles CA 90051. (213)741-4410. Editorial Chief: Frances Ring. For "fairly affluent, college-educated, mobile and active Southern California families. Average age of head of household is 42; median income of family is $15,000. Monthly. Buys first rights. Buys approximately 250 mss a year. Pays on acceptance for mss; on publication for most photos. Reports in 4 to 6 weeks. Query preferred. SASE.

Nonfiction: "Informative articles, well-researched and written in fresh, literate, honest style." This publication "covers all states west of the Rockies, including Alaska and Hawaii, western Canada and Mexico. We're willing to consider anything that interprets and illuminates the American West—past or present—for the Western American family. Employ imagination in treating subject. Avoid PR hand-out type style and format, and please know at least something about the magazine." Subjects include "travel, history, modern civic, cultural, and sociological aspects of the West; camping, fishing, natural science, humor, first-person adventure and experience, nostalgia, profiles, and occasional unusual and offbeat pieces. One article a month on foreign travel." Length: 1,000 to 3,000 words. Pays 10¢ a word and up.

Photos: Buys color and b&w photos with or without mss. Prefers 8x10 b&w glossies. Often publishes photo essays. Pays $25 minimum "for each b&w used as illustration;" $25 to $100 per transparency.

Poetry: Publishes 12 to 15 poems a year. Length: up to 24 lines; "occasionally longer." Pays $25.

WESTWORLD, Box 6680 Vancouver, British Columbia Canada V6B 4L4. (604)732-1371. Editor-in-Chief: W.J.B. Mayrs. Assistant Editor: Elspeth Woodske. 75% freelance written. Emphasis is mainly on British Columbia, but also on Alberta, Saskatchewan and Manitoba. Bimonthly magazine; 80 pages. Estab. 1975. Circ. 204,000. Pays on publication. Buys first North American serial rights. Phone queries OK. Submit seasonal/holiday material 6-12 months in advance of issue date. Photocopied submissions OK. SASE. Reports in 4-6 weeks. Free sample copy and writer's guidelines.

Nonfiction: General interest (should be British Columbia or western-Canada oriented); historical (on British Columbia); how-to (only rarely; preferably on seasonal subjects); humor; photo feature (rarely; must be western-oriented and must include copy); travel; and informational. No US subjects. Buys 40-50 mss/year. Query or submit complete ms, or submit outline and pictures. Length: 500-2,500 words. Pays $25-250.

Photos: "No articles are used without some visual material." Submit photo material with accompanying query. No additional payment for 5x7 or larger b&w glossy prints and 35mm color transparencies accepted with ms. Pays $10-100 for color cover photos. Captions required. Buys one-time rights. Model release required.

WINDOW OF VERMONT, L.L.B. Corp., Warren VT 05674. (802)496-2223. Editor-in-Chief: L.J. Aske. 75% freelance written. For "youngsters to oldsters, those who have that common desire to know and experience as much as possible about our unique state, Vermont." Monthly tabloid; 24 pages. Estab. 1969. Circ. 42,000. Pays on publication. Buys all rights but may reassign following publication. Phone queries OK. Submit seasonal/holiday material 2 months in advance. Simultaneous, photocopied and previously published submissions OK. SASE. Reports in 4 weeks. Free sample copy and writer's guidelines.

Nonfiction: Informational; historical; humor; interview; nostalgia; profile; travel; personal experience; and photo feature. "We will consider nearly any subject and approach, but the article must be definitely 'Vermont oriented'." Buys 6 mss/issue. Submit complete ms. Length: 1,000-2,000 words. Pays $15-25.
Photos: Purchased with or without accompanying ms. Pays $2-5 for b&w glossy prints. Model release required.
How To Break In: "Imagine what a tourist would like to know—about our past, our present and, in some cases, our future—our people, our towns, our farms, our way of life—and of course, our mountains and valleys, lakes and streams. Once you have this feel for what our readers want, start submitting. Chances are, we'll develop a lasting working relationship."

WINDSOR THIS MONTH MAGAZINE, Box 1029, Windsor, Ontario, Canada. (519)256-7162. Editor-in-Chief: Linda Steel. 75% freelance written. "*Windsor This Month* is mailed out in a system of controlled distribution to 20,000 households in the area. The average reader is a university graduate, middle income, and active in leisure areas." Published 9 times/year; magazine; 32-40 pages. Estab. 1974. Circ. 20,000. Pays on publication. Buys first North American serial rights. Phone queries OK. Submit seasonal/holiday material 3-4 months in advance of issue date. SASE. Reports in 1 month.
Nonfiction: General interest (Windsor oriented); how-to (generally locally oriented, but occasionally accept general interest how-to); historical (Windsor oriented); inspirational (rarely, if ever); interview (well-known area persons, or someone from the area living elsewhere); new product (occasionally, but only if available locally); personal opinion (local); photo feature (if relating to area); profile (as interview); travel (rarely); and local entertainment. Buys 10 mss/issue. Query. Length: 500-5,000 words. Pays $20-75.
Photos: State availability of photos with query. Pays $10 for first-published and $5 thereafter for b&w glossy prints and contact sheets. Captions preferred. Buys all rights.

WISCONSIN TRAILS, Box 5650, Madison WI 53705. (608)288-5564. Editor: Jill Weber Dean. For readers interested in Wisconsin, its natural beauty, history, personalities, recreation, and the arts. Magazine; 44 pages. Estab. 1960. Quarterly. Circ. 28,000. Rights purchased vary with author and material. Buys 30-40 mss/year. Pays on publication. Free sample copy and writer's guidelines. Will consider photocopied submissions. Submit seasonal material at least 1 year in advance. Reports in 1 month. Query or send outline. SASE.
Nonfiction: "Our articles focus on some aspect of Wisconsin life; an interesting site or event, a person or industry, or history and the arts. We do not use first-person essays (reminiscences are sometimes OK), ecstasies about scenery, or biographies about people who were born in Wisconsin, but made their fortunes elsewhere. No cartoons, crosswords, or fillers. Poetry exclusively on assignment." Length: 1,500 to 3,000 words. Pays $50-250, depending on length and quality.
Photos: Purchased without mss or on assignment. Captions preferred. B&w photos usually illustrate a given article. Color is mostly scenic. Pays $10 each for b&w on publication. Pays $50 for inside color; pays $100 for covers and center spreads. Transparencies; 2¼x2¼ or larger are preferred.

WORCESTER MAGAZINE, 65 Elm St., Worcester MA 01609. (617)799-0511. Editor: Dan Kaplan. 50% freelance written. Emphasizes the central Massachusetts region. Monthly tabloid; 48 pages. Estab. October 1976. Circ. 15,000. Pays on acceptance. Buys all rights. Submit seasonal/holiday material 2 months in advance of issue date. Simultaneous and photocopied submissions OK. SASE. Reports in 2 weeks. Sample copy $1; free writer's guidelines.
Nonfiction: Exposé (area government, corporate); how-to (concerning the area, homes, vacations); interview (local); personal experience; personal opinion (local); and photo feature. "We leave national and general topics to national and general publications." Buys 24 mss/year. Query with clips of previously published work. Length: 1,000-3,500 words. Pays $50-125.
Photos: State availability of photos with query. Pays $25-75 for b&w photos. Captions preferred. Buys all rights. Model release required.

YANKEE, Dublin NH 03444. (603)563-8111. Editor-in-Chief: Judson D. Hale. Managing Editor: John Pierce. Emphasizes the New England region. Monthly magazine; 176 pages. Estab. 1935. Circ. 750,000. Pays on acceptance. Buys all, first North American serial or one-time rights. Submit seasonal/holiday material at least 4 months in advance. SASE. Reports in 2 weeks-1 month. Free sample copy and writer's guidelines.
Nonfiction: Historical (New England history, especially with present-day tie-in); how-to (especially for "Forgotten Arts" series of New England arts, crafts, etc.); humor; interview (espe-

cially with New Englanders who have not received a great deal of coverage); nostalgia (personal reminiscence of New England life); photo feature (prefer color, captions essential); profile; travel (N.E. only, with specifics on places, prices, etc.); current issues; nature; antiques to look for; food. Buys 50 mss/year. Query. Length: 1,500-3,000 words. Pays $25-500.
Photos: Purchased with accompanying ms or on assignment. (Without accompanying ms for "This New England" feature only; color only). Captions required. Send prints or transparencies. Pays $15 minimum for 8x10 b&w glossies. $100/page for 2¼x2¼ or 35mm transparencies; 4x5 for cover or centerspread. Total purchase price for ms includes payment for photos.
Columns/Departments: New England Trip (with specifics on places, prices, etc.); Antiques to Look For (how to find, prices, other specifics); At Home in New England (recipes, gardening, crafts). Buys 10-12 mss/year. Query. Length: 1,000-2,500 words. Pays $150-350.
Fiction: Deborah Stone, Fiction Editor. "Emphasis is on character development." Buys 12 mss/year. Send complete ms. Length: 2,000-4,000 words. Pays $400-600.
Poetry: Jean Burden, Poetry Editor. Free verse and modern. Buys 3-4 poems/issue. Send poems. Length: 32 words maximum. Pays $25 for all rights. Annual poetry contest with awards of $150, $100, and $50 for 1st, 2nd and 3rd prizes.

YANKEE MAGAZINE'S GUIDE TO NEW ENGLAND, 581 Boylston St., Boston MA 02116. (617)266-0813. Editor: Georgia Orcutt. Emphasizes travel and leisure for a readership from New England area and from all states in the union. Biannual magazine; 160-192 pages. Estab. 1971. Circ. 110,000. Pays on acceptance. Buys first North American serial rights. Submit seasonal/holiday material 6 months in advance. Simultaneous and photocopied submissions OK. SASE. Reports in 2 weeks. Sample copy $1.50; free writer's guidelines.
Nonfiction: Informational (places to discover on a vacation, tours to take, special restaurants, related pieces); travel (New England towns/cities, specific things to see, places to stay). Buys 10-15 mss/issue. Query. Length: 500-2,500 words. Pays $50-300.
Photos: Bob Orlando, Art Director. Purchased with or without accompanying ms or on assignment. Send contact sheet or transparencies. Pays $10-75 for b&w 8x10 glossies; $25-150 for 35mm or 2¼x2¼ color transparencies.
How To Break In: "Send us a letter letting us know where you have been in New England and what ideas you think best fit our publication. Please don't send in suggestions if you have not bothered to obtain a copy of the magazine to see what we are all about! Send a query letter for your ideas, and explain why you think you are qualified to write about a given subject. Include samples."

Religious Publications

Educational and inspirational material of interest to a general audience (including students, church members, workers and leaders) within a denomination or religion is the primary interest of publications in this category. Publications intended to assist lay and professional religious workers in teaching and managing church affairs are classified in Church Administration and Ministry in the Trade Journals section. Religious magazines for children and teenagers will be found in the Juvenile, and Teen and Young Adult classifications. Jewish publications whose main concern is with matters of general Jewish interest (rather than religious interest) are listed in the Jewish Publications category.

A.M.E. REVIEW, 468 Lincoln Drive, N.W., Atlanta GA 30318. Editor-Manager: William D. Johnson. For the ministerial majority. Quarterly magazine; 68 to 70 pages. Estab. 1880. Circ. 5,000. Not copyrighted. Payment on publication. Sample copy $1.
Reports in 30 days. Query first or submit complete ms. SASE.
Nonfiction and Photos: Uses material on personal experiences and personal achievements of a religious nature; ministerial profiles, human interest articles, pulpit reviews and book reviews (religious and racial). Length: 2,500 words. Pays 10¢ a word. B&w (3x5) photos are purchased with or without accompanying mss. Pays $2.50.
Fiction: Mainstream, fantasy, humorous, religious. Length: open. Pays 8¢ a word.
Poetry: Free verse and light verse for the Poets' Corner. Length: open. Pays $5.
Fillers: Short humor with a religious slant. Pays $2 per line up to 4 lines.

AMERICA, 106 W. 56th St., New York NY 10019. (212)581-4640. Editor: Joseph A. O'Hare. Published weekly for adult, educated, largely Roman Catholic audience. Usually buys all rights.

Pays on acceptance. Reports in two or three weeks. Write for copy of guidelines for writers. SASE.

Nonfiction and Poetry: "We publish a wide variety of material on politics, economics, ecology, and so forth. We are not a parochial publication, but almost all of our pieces make some moral or religious point. We are not interested in purely informational pieces or personal narratives which are self-contained and have no larger moral interest." Articles on literature, current political and social events. Length: 1,500 to 2,000 words. Pays $50 to $75. Poetry length: 10 to 30 lines. Address to Poetry Editor.

AMERICAN REVIEW OF EASTERN ORTHODOXY, Box 447, Indian Rocks Beach FL 33535. (813)595-4415. Editor: Robert Burns, Jr. Principally for clergy, students, seminarians, prominent laity of Eastern Orthodox, Roman Catholic, Espiscopal background. Religious news magazine; 32 (6x8) pages. Estab. 1954. Published every 2 months. Circ. 3,000. Not copyrighted. Buys about 6 mss a year. Pays on acceptance. Sample copy $1. Will consider photocopied and simultaneous submissions. Reports immediately. Submit complete ms. SASE.

Nonfiction and Photos: News, short items of religious topical interest. Eastern Orthodox items principally. American view, rather than old country view. Photos and terse descriptive matter dealing with the subject are necessary. News exposes. Informational, interview, historical, and photo articles. Length: 500 to 2,500 words. Pays $10 to $25. Photos purchased with ms with no additional payment. Purchased without accompanying ms for $5 minimum. Captions required. Clear b&w glossies.

THE ANNALS OF SAINT ANNE DE BEAUPRE, Basilica of St. Anne, Quebec, Canada G0A 3C0. (418)827-4538. Editor-in-Chief: E. Lefebure. Managing Editor: Jean-Claude Nadeau. 60% freelance written. Emphasizes the Catholic faith for the general public, of average education; mostly Catholic; part of the audience is made up of people who came to The Shrine of St. Anne de Beaupre. Monthly magazine; 32 pages. Estab. 1976. Circ. 70,000. Pays on acceptance. Buys first North American serial rights. Phone queries OK. Submit seasonal/holiday material 2 months in advance. SASE. Reports in 3-4 weeks. Free sample copy and writer's guidelines.

Nonfiction: Humor (short pieces on education, family, etc.); inspirational; interview; personal experience. Buys 10 mss/issue. Query. Length: 700-1,700 words. Pays $25-35.

Photos: Purchased with or without accompanying ms. Submit prints. Pays $5-15 for b&w glossies; $25-40 for color transparencies. "We buy very few color photos." Total purchase price for ms includes payment for photos.

Columns/Departments: Query. Length: 700-1,700 words. Pays $25-35. Open to suggestions from freelancers for new columns/departments.

Fiction: Religious (Catholic faith). Buys 1 ms/issue. Query. Length: 700-1,700 words. Pays $25-35.

Poetry: Light verse. Buys 12 poems/year. Limit submissions to batches of 6. Pays $5 minimum.

Fillers: Jokes, gags, anecdotes, short humor. "We buy few fillers." Pays $5 minimum.

THE ASBURY THEOLOGICAL SEMINARY HERALD (formerly *The Herald*), SPO 11, Asbury Theological Seminary, Wilmore KY 40390. For a general Christian audience. Bimonthly magazine; 32 pages. Estab. 1888. Circ. 36,000. Copyrighted. Pays on acceptance. Simultaneous and photocopied submissions OK. SASE. Reports in 1 month. Free sample copy.

Nonfiction: G. Wayne Rogers, articles editor. "Bilbe'base material dealing with the Christian life, the work of the church, etc. Inspirational aneecdotes, personal experience, interviews, informational articles." Buys 15 mss/year. Submit complete ms. Length: open. Pays $15-35.

ASPIRE, 1819 E. 14th Ave., Denver CO 80218. Editor: Jeanne Pomranka. 50% freelance written. For teens and adults: "those who are looking for a way of life that is practical, logical, spiritual, or inspirational." Monthly; 64 pages. Estab. 1914. Circ. 2,900. Buys all rights, but may reassign to author after publication providing credit given *Aspire*. Buys 125 mss a year. Pays following publication. Sample copy 15¢. Submit seasonal material 6-7 months in advance. Reports in 2 weeks.

Nonfiction: Uses inspirational articles that help to interpret the spiritual meaning of life. Needs are specialized, since this is the organ of the Divine Science teaching. Personal experience, inspirational, think pieces. Also seeks material for God at Work, a department "written in the form of letters to the editor in which the writer describes how God has worked in his life or around him. Teen Talk includes short articles from teenagers to help other teenagers find meaning in life." Length: 100-1,000 words. Pays maximum 1¢/published word.

Fiction: "Anything illustrating spiritual law at work in life." Length: 250 to 1,000 words. Pays maximum 1¢ per published word.

Poetry: Traditional, contemporary, light verse. "We use very little poetry." Length: average 8 to 16 lines. Pays $2.

BAPTIST HERALD, 1 S. 210 Summit Ave., Oakbrook Terrace, Villa Park IL 60181. (312)495-2000. Dr. Reinhold J. Kerstan. For "any age from 15 and up, any educational background with mainly religious interests." Estab. 1923. Monthly. Circ. 10,000. Buys all rights. Payment on publication. Occasionally overstocked. Free sample copy. Submit seasonal material 3 to 4 months in advance. Enclose SASE.
Nonfiction and Fiction: "We want articles of general religious interest. Seeking articles that are precise, concise, and honest. We hold a rather conservative religious line." Buys personal experience, interviews, inspirational, and personal opinion articles. Length: 700 to 2,000 words. Payment is $5 to $10. Buys religious and historical fiction. Length: 700 to 2,000 words. Pays $5 to $10.

BAPTIST LEADER, Valley Forge PA 19481. (215)768-2158. Editor: Vincie Alessi. For ministers, teachers, and leaders in church schools. Monthly; 64 pages. Buys first rights, but may reassign rights to author after publication. Pays on acceptance. Free sample copy. Deadlines are 8 months prior to date of issue. Reports immediately. SASE.
Nonfiction: Educational topics. How-to articles for local church school teachers. Length: 1,500 to 2,000 words. Pays $25 to $40.
Photos: Church school settings; church, worship, children's and youth activities and adult activities. Purchased with mss. B&w, 8x10; human interest and seasonal themes. Pays $10-15.

BRIGADE LEADER, Box 150, Wheaton IL 60187. Editor: Don Dixon. Managing Editor: Richard Mould. 30% freelance written. For men associated with Christian Service Brigade clubs throughout U.S. and Canada. Quarterly magazine; 32 pages, (8½x11). Buys all rights; but will sometimes reassign rights to author after publication; second serial (reprint) rights. Buys 4 mss a year. Payment on acceptance. Submit seasonal material 4 months in advance. Will consider photocopied submissions. Reports in 2 months. Query first. SASE.
Nonfiction and Photos: "Articles about men and things related to them. Relationships in home, church, work. Specifically geared to men with an interest in boys. Besides men dealing with boys' physical, mental, emotional needs—also deals with spiritual needs." Informational, personal experience, inspirational. Length: 800 to 1,200 words. Pays 3¢ minimum a word. Photos purchased with or without ms. Pays $7.50 for b&w.

CALVINIST-CONTACT, 90 Niagara St., St. Catherines, Ontario, Canada L2R 4L3. (416)682-5614. Editor: Keith Knight. Christian weekly newspaper. No rights purchased. Enclose SAE and International Reply Coupons.
Nonfiction: "Any material as long as it is suitable for our publication, which has as its aim the practical application of the principles of the Bible as the only true guide in life."

CANADIAN CHURCHMAN, 600 Jarvis St., Toronto, Ont. M4Y 2J6, Canada. Editor: Jerrold F. Hames. 10-15% freelance written. For a general audience; Anglican Church of Canada; adult, with religio-socio emphasis. Monthly tabloid newspaper; 24-28 pages. Estab. 1874. Circ. 280,000. Not copyrighted. Buys 10 to 12 mss a year. Payment on publication. Will consider photocopied submissions and simultaneous submissions. Query first. SAE and International Reply Coupons.
Nonfiction: "Religion, news from churches around the world, social issues, theme editions (native rights, abortion, alcoholism, etc.). Newsy approach; bright features of interest to Canadian churchmen. Prefer rough sketch first; freelance usually on assignment only. Our publication is Anglican-slanted, progressive, heavily socially oriented in presenting topical issues." Informational, interview, spot news. Length: 750 to 1,200 words. Pays $35 to $100.

CATHOLIC LIFE, 9800 Oakland Ave., Detroit MI 48211. Editor-in-Chief: Robert C. Bayer. 75% freelance written. Emphasizes foreign missionary activities of the Catholic Church in Burma, India, Bangladesh, the Philippines, Hong Kong, Africa, etc., for middle-aged and older audience with either middle incomes or pensions. High school educated (on the average), conservative in both religion and politics. Monthly (except July or August) magazine; 32 pages. Estab. 1954. Circ. 19,200. Pays on publication. Buys all rights, but may reassign following publication. Submit seasonal/holiday material 3-4 months in advance. Simultaneous submissions OK. SASE. Reports in 2 weeks.
Nonfiction: Informational; inspirational (foreign missionary activities of the Catholic Church; experiences, personalities, etc.). Buys 30 mss/year. Query or send complete ms. Length: 1,000-1,500 words. Pays 4¢/word.

CATHOLIC NEAR EAST MAGAZINE, Catholic Near East Welfare Association, 1011 First Ave., New York NY 10022. (212)826-1480. Editor: Virginia Rohan. For a general audience with interest in the Near East, particularly its religious and cultural aspects. Quarterly magazine; 24 pages. Estab. 1974. Circ. 165,000. Buys first North American serial rights. Buys about 16 mss a year. Pays on acceptance. Free sample copy and writer's guidelines. Photocopied submissions OK if legible. Submit seasonal material (Christmas and Easter in different Near Eastern lands or rites) 6 months in advance. Reports on material accepted for publication in 3 to 4 weeks. Returns rejected material in 2 weeks. Query first or submit complete ms. SASE.

Nonfiction and Photos: "Cultural, territorial, devotional material on the Near East, its peoples and religions, (especially Eastern Rites) including profiles of noted personalities in Asia. Style should be simple, factual, concise. Articles must stem from personal acquaintance with subject matter, or through up-to-date research. No preaching or speculations." Length: 800-1,400 words. Pays 10¢/word. No additional payment for excellent quality b&w glossies used with mss. Captions required. Pays $10 to $15 for color slides or transparencies. All photos must relate to the accompanying ms.

CHICAGO STUDIES, Box 665, Mundelein IL 60060. (312)566-6401, Ext. 61. Editor: George J. Dyer. 50% freelance written. For Roman Catholic priests and religious educators. Magazine; 112 pages. Estab. 1962. Published 3 times/year. Circ. 10,000. Buys all rights. Buys 30 mss a year. Pays on acceptance. Sample copy $1. Will consider photocopied submissions. Submit complete ms. Reports within 6 weeks. SASE.

Nonfiction: Nontechnical discussion of theological, biblical, ethical topics. Articles aimed at a nontechnical presentation of the contemporary scholarship in those fields. Length: 3,000 to 5,000 words. Pays $35 to $100.

THE CHRISTIAN ATHLETE, official publication of the Fellowship of Christian Athletes, 1125 Grand, Kansas City MO 64106. (816)842-3908. Editor: Skip Stogsdill. "Aimed primarily for high school, college and professional athletes and coaches with a Christian perspective, although teenagers and adults interested in athletics/faith will find articles applicable to them." Estab. 1959. Bimonthly. Circ. 50,000. Buys first rights only. Buys 10-15 mss/year. Pays on publication. Free sample copy and writer's guidelines. Seasonal/holiday material should be submitted 3 months in advance of issue date. SASE.

Nonfiction: "We're one of the only magazines we know of bridging the worlds of sports and faith. A significant part of each issue is the personal profile on athletic figures, both the 'big names' and the benchwarmers. An article should contain an authentic spiritual emphasis depicting a real flesh and blood faith with a person's warts showing—not a pie in the sky testimony. We feature major sports like football and basketball, plus sports such as fencing and table tennis. Articles dealing positively with problem areas in athletics and the Christian application toward solution will be favorably considered. We also need down-to-earth Bible study articles. Query. Length: 200-1,200 words. Pays $15-25.

Photos: Pays $15 minimum for b&w 5x7 or 8x10 prints. "Especially want sports-related shots depicting the range of emotions that competition evokes, such as joy, drama, defeat, etc."

Poetry: Uses free and light verse with sport/faith touch and a quality of excellence about it. "Payment is at editor's descretion."

THE CHRISTIAN CENTURY, 407 S. Dearborn St., Chicago IL 60605. (312)427-5380. Editor: James M. Wall. For college-educated, ecumenically minded, progressive church people, both clergy and lay. Weekly magazine; 24-32 pages. Estab. 1884. Circ. 30,000. Pays on publication. Usually buys all rights. Query appreciated, but not essential. SASE. Reports in 3 weeks. Free sample copy.

Nonfiction: "We use articles dealing with social problems, ethical dilemmas, political issues, international affairs, and the arts, as well as with theological and ecclesiastical matters. We focus on concerns that arise at the juncture between church and society, or church and culture." Length: 2,500 words maximum. Payment varies, but averages $20/page.

CHRISTIAN HERALD, 40 Overlook Dr., Chappaqua NY 10514. (914)769-9000. Editor-in-Chief: David E. Kucharsky. Managing Editor: Jane Campbell. 80% freelance written. Emphasizes religious living in family and church. Monthly magazine; 64 pages. Estab. 1878. Circ. 270,000. Pays on acceptance. Buys all rights, but may reassign following publication. Submit seasonal/holiday material 5-6 months in advance. Photocopied submissions OK. SASE. Sample copy $1; free writer's guidelines.

Nonfiction: How-to; informational; inspirational; interview; profile; and evangelical experience. Buys 50-75 mss/year. Query or send complete ms. Length: 1,000-2,500 words. Pays $50 minimum.
Photos: Purchased with or without accompanying ms. Send transparencies. Pays $10 minimum for b&w; $25 minimum for 2¼x2¼ color transparencies.
Poetry: Light verse, traditional, religious and inspirational. Buys 30 poems/year. Length: 4-20 lines. Pays $10 minimum.

CHRISTIAN LIFE MAGAZINE, Gundersen & Schmale, Wheaton IL 60187. Editor-in-Chief: Robert Walker. Executive Editor: Janice Franzen. 75% freelance written. Religious publication. Monthly magazine; 88 pages. Circ. 80,000-150,000. Pays on publication. Buys all rights, but may reassign following publication. Submit seasonal/holiday material 8-12 months in advance of issue date. SASE. Free sample copy and writer's guidelines.
Nonfiction: Adventure articles (usually in the first person, told in narrative style); devotional (include many anecdotes, preferably from the author's own experience); general features (wide variety of subjects, with special programs of unique benefit to the community); inspirational (showing the success of persons, ideas, events and organizations); personality profiles (bright, tightly-written articles on what Christian are thinking); short stories (with good characterization and mood); news (with human interest quality dealing with trends); news feature (providing interpretative analysis of person, trend, event and ideas); and trend (should be based on solid research). Pays $175 maximum.

CHRISTIAN LIVING, Mennonite Publishing House, 616 Walnut Ave., Scottdale PA 15683. (412)887-8500. Editor: J. Lorne Peachey. For Christian families. Monthly. Buys first or second rights. Pays on acceptance. Reports in 2 weeks. Submit complete ms. SASE.
Nonfiction and Photos: Articles about Christian family life, parent-child relations, marriage, and family-community relations. Material must address itself to one specific family problem and/or concern and show how that problem/concern may be solved. If about a family activity, it should deal only with one such activity in simple, direct language. All material must relate to the adult members of a family, not the children. Length: 1,000 to 1,500 words. Pays up to $30. Additional payment for b&w photos used with mss.
Fiction and Poetry: Short stories on the same themes as above. Length: 1,000 to 2,000 words. Poems related to theme. Length: 25 lines. Pays up to $30 for fiction; minimum of $5 for poetry.

CHRISTIANITY & CRISIS, 537 W. 121st St., New York NY 10027. (212)662-5907. Editor: Wayne H. Cowan. For professional clergy and laymen; politically liberal; interested in ecology, good government, minorities and the church. Journal of 12 to 16 pages, published every 2 weeks. Estab. 1941. Circ. 19,000. Rights purchased vary with author and material. Usually buys all rights, but may reassign to author after publication. Buys 5 to 10 mss a year. Payment on publication. Free sample copy. Will consider photocopied and simultaneous submissions. Reports on material in 3 weeks. SASE.
Nonfiction: "Our articles are written in-depth, by well-qualified individuals, most of whom are established figures in their respective fields. We offer comment on contemporary, political and social events occurring in the U.S. and abroad. Articles are factual and of high quality. Anything whimsical, superficial, or politically dogmatic would not be considered." Interested in articles on bio-medical ethics, new community projects; informational articles and book reviews. Length: 500 to 5,000 words. Pays $25 to $50.
How To Break In: "It is difficult for a freelancer to break in here but not impossible. Several authors we now go to on a regular basis came to us unsolicited and we always have a need for fresh material. Book reviews are short (800 to 1,500 words) and may be a good place to start, but you should query first. Another possibility is Viewpoints which also runs short pieces. Here we depend on people with a lot of expertise in their fields to write concise comments on current problems. If you have some real area of authority, this would be a good section to try."

CHRISTIANITY TODAY, 465 Gundersen Dr., Carol Stream IL 60187. Editor-in-Chief: Kenneth Kantzee. Emphasizes religion. Semimonthly magazine; 55 pages. Estab. 1956. Circ. 150,000. Pays on acceptance. Buys all rights, but may reassign following publication. Submit seasonal/holiday material 6-8 months in advance. SASE. Reports in 4 weeks. Free sample copy and writer's guidelines.
Nonfiction: Historical and informational. Buys 4 mss/issue. Query or send complete ms. Length: 1,000-2,000 words. Pays $100 minimum.
Columns/Departments: Ministers' Workshop (practical and specific, not elementary ideas; how something *has* worked, not how it *ought* to work). Buys 12 mss/year. Send complete ms.

Length: 900-1,100 words. Pays $60 maximum.

THE CHURCH HERALD, 1324 Lake Dr., S.E., Grand Rapids MI 49506. Editor: Dr. John Stapert. For a general audience in the Reformed Church in America. Publication of the Reformed Church in America. Biweekly magazine; 32 pages. Estab. 1826. Circ. 74,000. Rights purchased vary with author and material. Buys all rights, first serial rights, or second serial (reprint) rights. Buys about 30 mss a year. Pays on acceptance. Sample copy 50¢; free writer's guidelines. Will consider photocopied and simultaneous submissions. Submit material for major Christian holidays 2 months in advance. Reports in 3 weeks. Submit complete ms only. SASE.
Nonfiction and Photos: "We expect all of our articles to be helpful and constructive, even when a point of view is vigorously presented. Articles on subjects such as Christianity and culture, government and politics, forms of worship, the media, ethics and business relations, responsible parenthood, marriage and divorce, death and dying, challenges on the campus, drug addiction, alcoholism, Christian education, human interest stories within the church, good news of God's blessings, praise, etc. Articles by or about a well-known and respected Christian doctor, attorney, businessman, teacher, judge, nurse or labor leader, showing how he faces his responsibilities, deals with his problems, and finds a Christian solution, with quotes and anecdotes to illustrate. We are also looking for material that will help us to build a somewhat younger readership, particularly readers in their teens and twenties." Length: 400 to 1,400 words. Pays 2¢ to 3¢ per word. Photos purchased with or without accompanying ms. Pays $5-15/8x10 b&w glossy.
Fiction, Poetry, and Fillers: Religious fiction. Length: 400 to 1,400 words. Pays 2¢ to 3¢ per word. Traditional forms of poetry. Length: 30 lines maximum. Pays $5 to $15. Jokes and short humor. Length: about 80 words.

CHURCH & STATE, Americans United for Separation of Church and State, 8120 Fenton St., Silver Spring MD 20910. (301)589-3707. Editor: Edd Doerr. 15% freelance written. Emphasizes religious liberty and church-state relations matters. Readership "includes the whole religious spectrum, but is predominantly Protestant and well-educated." Monthly magazine; 24 pages. Estab. 1947. Circ. 85,000. Pays on acceptance. Buys all rights, but may reassign following publication. Simultaneous, photocopied and previously published submissions OK. SASE. Reports in 4 weeks. Free sample copy and writer's guidelines.
Nonfiction: Expose; general interest; historical and interview. Buys 10 mss/year. Query. Length: 2,400 words maximum. Pays 3¢/word.
Photos: State availability of photos with query. Pays $10 for b&w prints. Captions preferred. Buys one-time rights.

THE CHURCHMAN, 1074 23rd Ave., N., St. Petersburg FL 33704. (813)894-0097. Editor: Edna Ruth Johnson. 99% freelance written. For people who think; who care about mankind. Monthly magazine. Estab. 1804. Circ. 10,000. Not copyrighted. Uses about 50 mss a year. Pays in contributor's copies. Free sample copy. Will consider photocopied submissions. No simultaneous submissions. Reports within a month. Submit complete ms. SASE.
Nonfiction: Sociological, religious and, sometimes, political material. Although founded by Episcopal leadership, this publication is interdenominational, inter-faith, humanistic, and relevant to today's troubled world. Inspirational, historical, think pieces, expose. Length: 500 to 1,000 words.

COLUMBIA, P.O. Drawer 1670, New Haven CT 06507. Editor: Elmer Von Feldt. For Catholic families; caters particularly to members of the Knights of Columbus. Monthly magazine. Estab. 1920. Circ. 1,200,000. Buys all rights. Buys 50 mss a year. Payment on acceptance. Free sample copy and writer's guidelines. Submit seasonal material 6 months in advance. Reports in 4 weeks. Query first or submit complete ms. SASE.
Nonfiction and Photos: Fact articles directed to the Catholic layman and his family and dealing with current events, social problems, Catholic apostolic activities, education, ecumenism, rearing a family, literature, science, arts, sports and leisure. Length: 1,000 to 3,000 words. Glossy photos (8x10) b&w are required for illustration. Articles without ample illustrative material are not given consideration. Payment ranges from $200 to $400, including photos. Photo stories are also wanted. Pays $15 per photo used and 10¢ per word.
Fiction and Humor: Written from a thoroughly Christian viewpoint. Length: 3,000 words maximum. Pays $300 maximum. Humor or satire should be directed to current religious, social or cultural conditions. Pays up to $100 for about 1,000 words.

COMMONWEAL, 232 Madison Ave., New York NY 10016. (212)683-2042. Editor: James

O'Gara. Edited by Roman Catholic laymen. 8% freelance written. For college-educated audience. Special book and education issues. Biweekly. Circ. 21,000. Buys 75 mss a year. Pays on acceptance. Free sample copy. Submit seasonal material 2 months in advance. Reports in 3 weeks. "A number of our articles come in over-the-transom. I suggest a newcomer either avoid particularly sensitive areas (say, politics) or let us know something about you (your credentials, tearsheets, a paragraph about yourself)." SASE.
Nonfiction: "Articles on timely subjects: political, literary, religious." Original, brightly written mss on value-oriented themes. Buys think pieces. Length: 1,000 to 2,500 words. Pays 2¢ a word.
Poetry: Department Editor: John Fanel. Contemporary and avant-garde. Length: maximum 150 lines ("long poems very rarely"). Pays $7.50 to $25.

THE COMPANION OF ST. FRANCIS AND ST. ANTHONY, Conventual Franciscan Friars, Box 535, Postal Station F, Toronto, Ontario, Canada M4Y 2L8. (416)924-6349. Editor-in-Chief: Rev. Nicholas Weiss. 75% freelance written. Emphasizes religious and human values. Monthly magazine; 32 pages. Estab. 1926. Circ. 8,000. Pays on acceptance. Buys all rights, but may reassign following publication. Phone queries OK. Submit seasonal/holiday material 2 months in advance. SASE. Reports in 3 weeks. Free writer's guidelines.
Nonfiction: Historical; how-to (medical and psychological coping); informational; inspirational; interview; nostalgia; profile; and travel. Buys 6 mss/issue. Send complete ms. Length: 1,000-1,500 words. Pays 2¢/word.
Photos: Photos purchased with accompanying ms. Captions required. Pays $5-10 for 5x7 (but all sizes accepted) b&w glossies and color photos. Send prints. Total purchase price for ms includes payment for photos.
Fiction: Adventure; humorous; mainstream and religious. Buys 1 ms/issue. Send complete ms. Length: 1,000-1,500 words. Pays 2¢/word.
How To Break In: "Mss on human interest with photos are given immediate preference."

THE CONGREGATIONALIST, 801 Bushnell, Beloit WI 53511. (608)362-4821. Editor: Dr. Louis B. Gerhardt. "This is the publication of the National Association of Congregational Christian Churches. Readers tend to be members of our churches, or generally spiritually oriented people." Monthly magazine; 24 pages (8½x11). Estab. 1840. Circ. 10,000. Rights purchased vary with author and material. Usually buys all rights. Buys 80 to 160 mss a year. Payment on publication. Will send free sample copy to writer on request. Write for copy of editorial guidelines for writers. Submit Thanksgiving, Christmas, Lent and Easter material at least 3 months in advance. Will consider photocopied and simultaneous submissions. Reports in 3 to 4 weeks. Submit only complete ms. Enclose SASE.
Nonfiction: Articles and miscellaneous features affirming the goodness of man and his spiritual nature. "We accept a wide range of religious views, and welcome views on controversial subjects not generally covered in religious magazines." Length: 300 to 2,500 words. Pays $15 to $50.
Fiction: Experimental, mainstream, religious, and historical fiction on any theme. Length: 300 to 2,500 words. Pays $15 to $50.
Poetry and Fillers: Traditional forms, blank verse, free verse, avant-garde forms, light verse, and religious poetry. Length: 2 lines minimum; no maximum. Pays $5 minimum. Pays $5 to $15 for religious puzzles.

CONTACT, United Brethren Publishing, 302 Lake St., Box 650, Huntington IN 46750. (219)356-2312. Editor-in-Chief: Stanley Peters. Managing Editor: Dennis Miller. 90% freelance written. For conservative, evangelical Christians, young and old. Weekly magazine; 8 pages. Circ. 7,000. Pays on acceptance. Buys simultaneous, second serial (reprint) and one-time rights. Submit seasonal/holiday material 6 months in advance. Simultaneous photocopied and previously published submissions OK. SASE. Reports in 4-6 weeks. Free sample copy and writer's guidelines.
Nonfiction: Historical; how-to; humor; informational; inspirational; personal experience and photo feature. Buys 2 mss/issue. Send complete ms. Length: 150-1,200 words. Pays 1¢/word maximum.
Photos: Photos purchased with or without accompanying ms. Pays $2 for 5x7 or 8x10 b&w glossies.
Fiction: Adventure, historical; humorous; and religious. Buys 30 mss/year. Send complete ms. Length: 600-1,200 words. Pays 3/4¢/word.
Fillers: Jokes, gags, anecdotes, puzzles and short humor. Buys 2 fillers/issue. Length: 25-250 words. Pays 50¢

THE COVENANT COMPANION, 5101 N. Francisco Ave., Chicago IL 60625. (312)784-3000. Editor-in-Chief: James R. Hawkinson. 25% freelance written. Emphasizes Christian life and faith. Semimonthly (monthly issues July and August) magazine; 32 pages. Circ. 28,000. Pays on publication. Buys all rights, but may reassign following publication. Submit seasonal/holiday material 3 months in advance. Simultaneous, photocopied and previously published submissions OK. SASE. Reports in 2 months. Sample copy 25¢.
Nonfiction: Humor; informational; inspirational (especially evangelical Christian); interviews (Christian leaders and personalities); and personal experience. Buys 15-20 ms/year. Length: 500-1,100 words. Pays $10-20.

DAILY MEDITATION, P.O. Box 2710, San Antonio TX 78299. Editor: Ruth S. Paterson. Issued bimonthly. Rights purchased vary with author and material. Very occasionally buys reprint material. Gives permission to writers to resubmit to others after publication. Payment on acceptance. Will send sample copy to writer on request. Reports within 60 days. Submit complete ms. SASE.
Nonfiction: Uses metaphysical teachings, inspirational articles (seasonal articles 6 months in advance), nonsectarian religious articles (emphasis on how to apply Christian principles to reader's life). Length: 750, 1,250 and 1,650 words. (Word count must be stated on ms.) Pays ½¢ to 1½¢ a word.
Poetry: Along same lines as above. Length: 16 lines maximum. Pays 14¢ per line.

DECISION MAGAZINE, 1300 Harmon Place, Minneapolis MN 55403. (612)338-0500. Editor: Roger C. Palms. Conservative evangelical monthly publication of the Billy Graham Evangelistic Association. Magazine; 16 pages. Estab. 1960. Circ. 3,000,000. Buys all rights unless otherwise arranged. Pays on publication. Reports within 2 months. SASE.
Nonfiction: Uses some freelance material; best opportunity is in testimony area (1,600 to 2,000 words). Also uses short narratives, 400 to 750 words. "Our function is to present Christ as Savior and Lord to unbelievers and present articles on deeper Christian life and human interest articles on Christian growth for Christian readers. No tangents. Center on Christ in all material."
Poetry: Uses devotional thoughts and short poetry in Quiet Heart column. Positive, Christ-centered.
Fillers: Uses fresh original quotations from known or unknown individuals, devotional thoughts. Pays $3 per item.

THE DISCIPLE, Box 179, St. Louis MO 63166. Editor: James L. Merrell. 5-10% freelance written. Published by Christian Board of Publication of the Christian Church (Disciples of Christ). For ministers and church members, both young and older adults. Semimonthly. Circ. 78,000. Buys all rights, but may reassign rights to author after publication, upon request. Payment on publication. Payment for photos made at end of month of acceptance. Sample copy 30¢; free writer's guidelines. Will consider photocopied and simultaneous submissions. Submit seasonal material at least 6 months in advance. Reports in 2 weeks to 3 months. SASE.
Nonfiction: Articles and meditations on religious themes; short pieces, some humorous. Length: 500-800 words. Pays $5-15. Also uses devotionals of 200-500 words for "A Faith for Today" page. Pays $15.
Photos: B&w glossies, 8x10. Occasional b&w glossies, any size, used to illustrate articles. Pays $10-25. Pays $25 when used for covers. No color.
Poetry: Uses 3 to 5 poems per issue. Traditional forms, blank verse, free verse and light verse. All lengths. Themes may be seasonal, historical, religious, occasionally humorous. Pays $3-5.

EMPHASIS ON FAITH & LIVING, 336 Dumfries Ave., Kitchener, Ontario, Canada N2H 2G1. Editor: Dr. Everek R. Storms. 25% freelance written. Official organ of The Missionary Church. For Church members. Magazine is published twice a month in U.S.A. but serves the Missionary Church in both the U.S. and Canada. Estab. 1969. Circ. 11,000. Not copyrighted. Buys "only a few" mss a year. Will consider photocopied and simultaneous submissions. Uses a limited amount of seasonal material, submitted 3 months in advance. Reports in 1 month. Submit only complete ms. SASE.
Nonfiction: Religious articles, presenting the truths of the Bible to appeal to today's readers. "We take the Bible literally and historically. It has no errors, myths, or contradictions. Articles we publish must have this background. No poetry, please. Especially would like articles covering the workings of the Holy Spirit in today's world." Length: approximately 500 words—"not too long". Pays $5 to $10 per ms.

ENGAGE/SOCIAL ACTION, 100 Maryland Ave., N.E., Washington DC 20002. (202)488-5632. Editor: Allan R. Brockway. 50% freelance written. For "United Methodist clergy and lay people interested in in-depth analysis of social issues, particularly the church's role or involvement in these issues." Estab. 1973. Monthly. Circ. 9,000. Rights purchased vary with author and material. May buy all rights and reassign rights to author after publication. Buys about 30 mss a year. Pays on publication. Free sample copy and writer's guidelines. Will consider photocopied submissions, but prefers original. Returns rejected material in 2 to 3 weeks. Reports on material accepted for publication in several weeks. Query first or submit complete ms. SASE.

Nonfiction and Photos: "This is the social action publication of the United Methodist Church published by the Board of Church and Society of the United Methodist Church. We publish articles relating to current social issues as well as church-related discussions. We do not publish highly technical articles or poetry. Our publication tries to relate social issues to the church—what the church can do, is doing; why the church should be involved. We only accept articles relating to social issues, e.g., war, draft, peace, race relations, welfare, police/community relations, labor, population problems. Reviews of books and music should focus on related subjects." Length: 2,000 words maximum. Pays $35 to $50. 8x10 b&w glossy photos purchased with or without mss. Captions required. Pays $15.

ETCETERA, 6401 The Paseo, Kansas City MO 64131. (816)333-7000, Ext. 277. Editor: Ernie McNaught. 50% freelance written. Published by the Church of the Nazarene for the 18-23-year-old college/university student. Monthly magazine. Circ. 18,000. Pays on acceptance. Buys first rights or second rights. Submit seasonal material 6 months in advance. SASE. Free sample copy.

Nonfiction: Articles which speak to students' needs in light of their spiritual pilgrimage. How they cope on a secular campus from a Christian life style. First-person articles have high priority since writers tend to communicate best that which they are in the process of learning themselves. Style should be evangelical...material should have "sparkle." Wesleyan in doctrine. Buys interviews, profiles, inspirational and think pieces, humor, photo essays. Length: 1,500 words maximum. Pays 2¢/word.

Photos: B&w glossies. Pays $5 to $15. Interested in photo spreads and photo essays.

THE EVANGELICAL BEACON, 1515 E. 66th St., Minneapolis MN 55423. (612)866-3343. Editor: George Keck. 30% freelance written. For Evangelical and conservative Protestant audience. Issued biweekly. Rights purchased vary with author and material. Buys first rights, second serial (reprint) rights, or all rights. Pays on publication. Free sample copy. Reports on submissions in 6-8 weeks. SASE.

Nonfiction and Photos: Devotional material, articles on the church, people and their accomplishments. "Crisp, imaginative, original writing desired — not sermons put on paper." Length: 300 to 1,500 words. Pays 2¢ per word. Prefers 8x10 photos. Pays $5 and up.

Fiction and Poetry: "Not much fiction used, but will consider if in keeping with aims and needs of magazine." Length: 100 to 1,500 words. Pays 2¢ a word. "In poetry, content is more important than form." Length: open. Pays $2.50 minimum.

EVANGELICAL FRIEND, Box 232, Newberg OR 97132. (503)538-7345. Editor: Jack Willcuts. Managing Editor: Harlow Ankeny. Readership is evangelical Christian families, mainly of the Quaker church denomination. Monthly magazine; 28 pages. Estab. 1967. Circ. 11,600. Pays on publication. Buys all rights, but may reassign following publication. Phone queries OK. Submit seasonal/holiday material 3-4 months in advance. Simultaneous, photocopied, and previously published submissions OK. SASE. Reports in 4 weeks. Free sample copy and writer's guidelines.

Nonfiction: Historical (church related); how-to (church growth methods, Christian education ideas, etc.); inspirational (Biblically based); interview; personal experience (spiritual); personal opinion (on various controversial subjects that relate to the church, etc.); photo feature (unusual people doing unusual Christian-related services). Buys 2-3 mss/year. Query. Length: 300-1,800 words. Pays $10-25.

Photos: Purchased on assignment. Send contact sheet. Pays $8-20 for b&w glossy or matte finish photos.

FAITH AND INSPIRATION, Seraphim Publishing Group, Inc., 1619-22A 3rd Ave., New York NY 10028. Publisher: Daniel E. Soyka. Executive Editor: Warner Hutchinson. 20-40% freelance written. Emphasizes religious and secular inspirational material for a family readership. Bimonthly magazine; 128 pages. Estab. January 1978. Circ. 100,000. Pays on publication. Buys all rights. Submit seasonal/holiday material 4 months in advance of issue date. Photocopied submissions OK. SASE. Reports in 30 days. Sample copy $1.25.

Nonfiction: Inspirational; interview (with evangelical religious figures); personal experience (moving articles, does not have to be religious); and profile. Buys 3-6 mss/issue. Submit complete ms. Length: 50-2,000 words. Pays $5-100.

Poems: Light verse and traditional. Buys 3 poems/issue. Limit submissions to batches of 3. Length: 5-20 lines. Pays $5-15.

Fillers: Short humor, religious and inspirational material. Buys 10/issue. Length: 25-100 words. Pays $5-15.

FAMILY LIFE TODAY MAGAZINE, 110 W. Broadway, Glendale CA 91204. (213)247-2330. Publisher: W.T. Greig, Jr. Managing Editor: Lois L. Curley. 70% freelance written. Emphasizes "helping families develop a Christian lifestyle." Monthly magazine; 32 pages. Estab. December 1974. Circ. 32,000. Pays on acceptance. Buys all rights. Submit seasonal/holiday material 9-10 months in advance of issue date. Simultaneous and previously published submissions OK. SASE. Reports in 3 months. Free sample copy and writer's guidelines; mention *Writer's Market* in request.

Nonfiction: How-to (any family-related situation. Does need narrow focus: How to help the "slow-poke" child, etc.); humor (if wholesome and family related); inspirational (especially as it deals with the practicalness of biblical principles in terms of everyday life); interview (with person who is recognized authority in area of family life); personal experience (family personal experience especially when story illustrates a Christian principle—God's help, etc.); and photo feature (family related). Buys 6 mss/issue. Query. Length: 300-1,500 words. Pays 4-5¢/word for original; 3¢/word for reprints.

Photos: State availability of photos with query. Pays $15-30 for 8x10 b&w glossy prints; $35-85 for 35mm color transparencies. Buys one-time rights. Model release preferred.

FRIAR, Butler NJ 07405. Editor: Father Rudolf Harvey. For Catholic families. Estab. 1954. 11 times a year. Not copyrighted. Pays on acceptance. SASE.

Nonfiction: Uses articles and features on current problems or events; profiles of notable individuals; trends in sociology and education. Length: 1,800 to 3,000 words. Minimum payment of $15.

FRIDAY FORUM (OF THE JEWISH EXPONENT), 226 S. 16th St., Philadelphia PA 19102. (215)893-5745. Editor: Phyllis Zimbler Miller. 95% freelance written. For the Jewish community of Greater Philadelphia. Monthly newspaper supplement. Estab. 1971. Circ. 70,000. Usually buys all rights, but will reassign rights to author after publication. Buys about 40 mss a year. Pays after publication. Free sample copy and writer's guidelines. Will consider photocopied submissions. No simultaneous submissions. Submit special material 6 months in advance. Reports on material accepted for publication in 2 months. Returns rejected material in 1 month. SASE.

Nonfiction and Photos: "We are interested only in articles on Jewish themes, whether they be historical, thought pieces, Jewish travel sites, photographic essays, or any other nonfiction piece on a Jewish theme. Topical themes are appreciated." Length: 6 to 12 double-spaced pages. Pays $35 minimum.

Poetry: Traditional forms, blank verse, free verse, avant-garde forms, light verse; must relate to a Jewish theme. Length varies. Pays $15 minimum.

GOOD NEWS, The Forum for Scriptural Christianity, Inc., 308 E. Main St., Wilmore KY 40390. (606)858-4661. Editor-in-Chief: Charles W. Keysor. For United Methodist lay people and pastors, primarily middle age and middle income; conservative and biblical religious beliefs; broad range of political, social and cultural values. Bimonthly magazine; 84 pages. Estab. 1967. Circ. 15,000. Pays on acceptance. Phone queries OK. Submit seasonal/holiday material 6 months in advance. Simultaneous, photocopied and previously published submissions OK. SASE. Reports in 2 months. Sample copy $1. Free writer's guidelines.

Nonfiction: Historical (prominent people or churches from the Methodist/Evangelical United Brethren tradition); how-to (to build faith, work in local church); humor (good taste); inspirational (related to Christian faith); personal experience (case histories of God at work in individual lives) and any contemporary issues as they relate to the Christian faith and the United Methodist Church. Buys 36 mss/year. Query. Pays $10-50.

Photos: Photos purchased with accompanying ms or on assignment. Captions required. Uses fine screen b&w glossy prints. Total purchase price for ms includes payment for photos. Payment negotiable.

Columns/Departments: Good News Book Forum. Query. Open to suggestions for new columns/departments.
Fillers: Clippings, jokes, gags, anecdotes, newsbreaks and short humor. Buys 20 fillers/year. Pays $5-10.

GOOD NEWS BROADCASTER, Box 82808, Lincoln NE 68501. (402)474-4567. Editor: Theodore H. Epp. Interdenominational magazine for adults from 16 years of age. Monthly. Circ. 190,000. Buys first rights. Buys approximately 125 mss/year. Pays on acceptance. Free sample copy and writer's guidelines. Send all mss to Thomas S. Piper, Managing Editor. Submit seasonal material at least 6 months in advance. Reports in 1 month. Query preferred, but not required. SASE.
Nonfiction and Photos: Articles which will help the reader learn and apply Christian biblical principles to his life. From the writer's or the subject's own experience. "Especially looking for true, personal experience 'salvation', church missions, 'youth' (16 years and over), 'parents', and 'how to live the Christian life' articles." Nothing dogmatic, or preachy, or sugary sweet, or without Biblical basis. Details or statistics should be authentic and verifiable. Style should be conservative but concise. Requires that Scripture references be from the New American Standard Version or the Authorized Version. Length: maximum 1,500 words. Pays 3¢/word, more in special cases. Photos sometimes purchased with mss. Pays $7-10 for b&w glossies; $25-50 for color transparencies.
How To Break In: "The basic purpose of the magazine is to accomplish one of two things—to present Christ as Saviour to the lost or to promote the spiritual growth of believers by explaining the Bible and how it is relevant to life, so don't ignore our primary purposes when writing for us. Nonfiction should be Biblical and timely; at the least Biblical in principle. Write about ways to enrich family living, give solutions to people's problems, aids to help Christians live their daily experiences while working or relaxing — on the job, at home, in church, at school, in the community, or on the home or foreign mission field. Communicate spiritual truths in a positive way and without preaching at anyone or dogmatically telling the reader what he has to do. Show a clear progression of thought throughout the article. Use illustrations of your own experiences or of someone else's when God solved a problem similar to the reader's. Be so specific that the meanings and significance will be crystal clear to all readers. We prefer third person articles as a rule."

GOSPEL CARRIER, Messenger Publishing House, Box 850, Joplin MO 64801. (417)624-7050. Editor-in-Chief: Roy M. Chappell, D.D. Managing Editor: Mrs. Marthel Wilson. Denominational Sunday school take home paper for adults, ages 20 through retirement. Quarterly publication in weekly parts; 104 pages. Circ. 3,500. Pays quarterly. Buys simultaneous, second serial and one-time rights. Submit seasonal/holiday material 1 year in advance. Simultaneous, photocopied, and previously published submissions OK. SASE. Reports in 3 months. Sample copy 50¢; free writer's guidelines.
Nonfiction: Historical (related to great events in the history of the church); informational (may explain the meaning of a Bible passage or a Christian concept); inspirational (must make a Christian point); nostalgia (religious significance); and personal experience (Christian concept). Buys 50-80 mss/year. Pays ½¢/word.
Photos: Purchased with accompanying ms. Send prints. Pays $2 for b&w glossies.
Fiction: Adventure, historical; romance; and religious. Must have Christian significance. Buys 13-20 mss/issue. Submit complete ms. Length: 800-2,000 words. Pays ½¢/word.
Fillers: Short inspirational incidents from personal experience or the lives of great Christians. Buys 52-80/year. Length: 200-500 words. Pays ½¢/word.

GOSPEL HERALD, 616 Walnut Ave., Scottdale PA 15683. (412)887-8500. Editor: Daniel Hertzler. Issued weekly (50 issues per year) for adult members of the Mennonite Church. Buys first and second rights. Pays on acceptance. SASE.
Nonfiction: "Articles discuss theological and practical Christian issues affecting Mennonite readers." Recently published articles include "Depression in the Church" and "Christ and Life's Transitions". Length: 300 to 1,500 words. Pays minimum of 1½¢ per word.

GUIDEPOSTS MAGAZINE, 747 Third Ave., New York NY 10017. Editorial Director: Arthur Gordon. 40-50% freelance written. *Guideposts* is an inspirational monthly magazine for all faiths in which men and women from all walks of life tell how they overcame obstacles, rose above failures, met sorrow, learned to master themselves, and became more effective people through the direct application of the religious principles by which they live. Buys all rights. SASE.
Nonfiction and Fillers: Articles and features should be written in simple, anecdotal style with an

emphasis on human interest. Short features up to approximately 250 words ($10 to $25) would be considered for such *Guideposts* features as "Fragile Moments," and other short items which appear at the end of major articles. Short mss of approximately 250 to 750 words ($25 to $100) would be considered for such features as "Quiet People" and general one-page stories. Full-length mss, 750 to 1,500 words ($200 to $300). All mss should be typed, double-spaced and accompanied by a stamped, self-addressed envelope. Inspirational newspaper or magazine clippings often form the basis of articles in *Guideposts,* but it is unable to pay for material of this type and will not return clippings unless the sender specifically asks and encloses postage for return. Annually awards scholarships to high school juniors and seniors in writing contest.
How To Break In: "The freelancer would have the best chance of breaking in by aiming for a 1-page or maybe 2-page article. That would be very short, say 2½ pages of typescript, but in a small magazine such things are very welcome. A sensitively written anecdote that could provide us with an additional title is extremely useful. And they are much easier to just sit down and write than to have to go through the process of preparing a query. They should be warm, well-written, intelligent, and upbeat. We like personal narratives that are true and have some universal relevance, but the religious element does not have to be hammered home with a sledge hammer." Address short items to Van Varner.

HIGH ADVENTURE, 1445 Boonville Ave., Springfield MO 65802. (417)862-2781, Ext. 264. Editor: Johnnie Barnes. For boys and men. 16 (8½x11) pages. Estab. 1971. Quarterly. Circ. 35,000. Rights purchased vary with author and material. Buys approximately 10 to 12 mss a year. Pays on acceptance. Free sample copy and writer's guidelines. Query first or submit complete ms. SASE.
Nonfiction, Fiction, Photos, and Fillers: Camping articles, nature stories, fiction adventure stories, and jokes. Nature study and campcraft articles about 500 to 600 words. Buys how-to, personal experience, inspirational, humor, and historical articles. Pays $10 per page. Photos purchased on assignment. Adventure and Western fiction wanted. Length: 1,200 words. Puzzles, jokes and short humor used as fillers.

INSIGHT, The Young Calvinist Federation, Box 7244, Grand Rapids MI 49510. (616)241-5616. Editor-in-Chief: Rev. James C. Lont. Assistant Editor: Denise Goff. For young people, 15-19, Christian backgrounds and well exposed to the Christian faith. Monthly (except June and August) magazine; 32 pages. Estab. 1921. Circ. 22,000. Pays on publication. Buys simultaneous, second serial (reprint) and first North American serial rights. Phone queries OK. Submit seasonal/holiday material 6 months in advance. Simultaneous, photocopied and previously published submissions OK. SASE. Reports in 4 weeks. Sample copy and writer's guidelines for 9x12 SASE.
Photos: Photos purchased without accompanying ms or on assignment. Pays $10-25 for 8x10 b&w glossies; $50-100 for 35mm or larger color transparencies. Total purchase price for ms includes payment for photos.
Fiction: Humorous; mainstream and religious. "I'm looking for short stories that are not preachy but that lead our readers to a better understanding of how their Christian beliefs apply to their daily living. They must do more than entertain—they must make the reader think or see something in a new light." Buys 1 ms/issue. Send complete ms. Length: 1,000-3,000 words. Pays $35-100.
Poetry: Free verse; light verse and traditional. Buys 5 poems/year. Length: 4-25 lines. Pays $10-25.
Fillers: Jokes, gags, anecdotes, puzzles and short humor. Buys 4 fillers/year. Length: 50-300 words. Pays $10-35.

INSIGHT, Review and Herald Publishing Association, 6856 Eastern Ave., Washington DC 20012. Editor-in-Chief: Donald John. "Our audience is 16-25 years old, including high school, college, graduate students, and young marrieds. We are directed primarily to Seventh-day Adventist young adults." Weekly magazine; 24 pages. Estab. 1970. Circ. 50,000. Pays on acceptance. Buys first North American serial rights. Submit seasonal/holiday material 3 months in advance. Photocopied and previously published submissions OK. SASE. Reports in 6 weeks. Sample copy and writer's guidelines for postal costs.
Nonfiction: How-to (we like practical Christian help for problems in school, dating, marriage, relating to God and man); historical (use mostly unique features about early Adventist pioneers or events); inspirational (we need factual-based stories); interview (with people who have an influence on the lives of young Christians); personal opinion (need intelligent essays that present God's character in new and enlightening ways, also discussion of problems of living in today's world); personal experience (conversion and witnessing stories handled in a fresh way); and

photo feature. Buys 3 mss/issue. Query or submit complete ms. Length: 300-1,800 words. Pays 2-4¢/word.
Photos: Byron Steele, Photo Editor. Purchased without accompanying ms. Pays $50-125 for 8x10 b&w glossies. Query. Model release required.
Columns/Departments: Critique (review of books that have a religious or moral message). Buys 12 mss/year. Query. Length: 300-800 words. Pays 2-4¢/word. Open to suggestions for new columns or departments.
Fiction: Religious (well-written parables and allegories in harmony with our Bible doctrine). Buys 10 mss/year. Query or submit complete ms. Length: 300-1,000 words. Pays 2-4¢/word.
Poetry: Free verse, haiku, light verse, traditional, inspirational. Buys 20/year. Limit submissions to batches of 5. Length: 10-12 lines. Pays $2-10.

INTERLIT, David C. Cook Foundation, Cook Square, Elgin IL 60120. (312)741-2400, ext. 142. Editor-in-Chief: Gladys J. Peterson. 90% freelance written. Emphasizes Christian communications and journalism for missionaries, broadcasters, publishers, etc. Quarterly newsletters; 20 pages. Estab. 1964. Circ. 9,000. Pays on acceptance. Buys all rights, but may reassign following publication. Photocopied submissions OK. SASE. Reports in 2 weeks. Free sample copy.
Nonfiction: Informational; interview and photo feature. Buys 7 mss/issue. Length: 500-3,000 words. Pays 2-4¢/word.
Photos: Purchased with accompanying ms or on assignment. Captions required. Query or send prints. Uses b&w. Offers no additional payment for photos accepted with ms.

LIBERTY, A Magazine of Religious Freedom, 6840 Eastern Ave., N.W., Washington DC 20012. (202)723-0800, ext. 745. Editor: Roland R. Hegstad. For "responsible citizens interested in community affairs and religious freedom." Bimonthly. Circ. 500,000. Buys first rights. Buys approximately 40 mss a year. Pays on acceptance. Free sample copy and writer's guidelines. Will consider photocopied submissions. Submit seasonal material 6 to 8 months in advance. Reports in 1-3 weeks. Query not essential, but helpful. SASE.
Nonfiction: "Articles of national and international interest in field of religious liberty, church—state relations. Current events affecting above areas (Sunday law problems, parochial aid problems, religious discrimination by state, etc.). Current events are most important; base articles on current events rather than essay form." Buys how-to's, personal experience and think pieces, interviews, profiles. Length: maximum 2,500 words. Pays up to $150.
Photos: "To accompany or illustrate articles." Purchased with mss; with captions only. B&w glossies, color transparencies. Pays $15 to $35. Cover photos to $150.

LIGHT AND LIFE, Free Methodist Publishing House, 999 College Ave., Winona Lake IN 46590. Editor: G. Roger Schoenhals. 30% freelance written. Emphasizes religion for a cross section of adults. Published 20 times yearly. Magazine; 16 pages. Estab. 1867. Circ. 60,000. Pays on publication. Buys all rights, but may reassign following publication. Submit seasonal/holiday material 6 months in advance. Previously published submissions OK. SASE. Reports in 6 weeks. Sample copy 50¢; writer's guidelines for SASE.
Nonfiction: Each issue uses a lead article (warm, positive first-person account of God's help in a time of crisis; 1,500 words); a Christian living article (a fresh, lively, upbeat piece about practical Christian living; 750 words); a Christian growth article (an in-depth, lay-level article on a theme relevant to the maturing Christian; 1,500 words); a discipleship article (a practical how-to piece on some facet of Christian discipleship; 750 words); news feature (a person-centered report of a "good news" event showing God at work at the local, conference, or denominational level of the Free Methodist Church; 500 words, 2 photographs); and a back page article (contents must be brief and attractive; poem, parable, or 400-word article, profound and unforgettable). Buys 90 mss/year. Submit complete ms. Pays 2¢/word.
Photos: Purchased without accompanying ms. Send prints. Pays $7.50-20.00 for b&w photos. Offers no additional payment for photos accepted with accompanying ms.

LIGUORIAN, Liguori MO 63057. Editor: Rev. Norman Muckerman. 50% freelance written. For families with Catholic religious convictions. Monthly. Circ. 465,000. Copyrighted. Buys 60 mss a year. Pays on acceptance. Submit seasonal material 4 months in advance. Returns rejected material in 6 to 8 weeks. SASE.
Nonfiction and Photos: "Pastoral, practical, and personal approach to the problems and challenges of people today. No travelogue approach or unresearched ventures into controversial areas." Length: 400 to 2,000 words. Pays 5-7¢/word. Photos purchased with mss; b&w glossies.

THE LITTLE FLOWER MAGAZINE, 4600 W. Davis, Dallas TX 75211. Acting Editor: Br. R.

Adam Forno, O.C.D. For Catholic readership. Bimonthly magazine; 32 pages. Estab. 1921. Circ. 30,000. Pays on publication. Simultaneous, photocopied and previously published submissions OK. SASE. Free sample copy and writer's guidelines.
Nonfiction: Simple, factual discussions of Christian living, prayer, social action, the thinking of important religious writers. "It is important that factual or doctrinal articles be about a very, very specific topic. We cannot use articles about religion in general. For example, we can always use articles on St. Therese of Lisieux; a good article could be written by referring to a good biography such as Ida Goerres' *The Hidden Face,* and concentrating on some specific topic, such as Therese's relations to nineteenth century attitudes toward women; her approach to meditation; her relationship to her superior. Since few of our readers are familiar with current religious literature, it is relatively easy to draw material from good works on specific passages in the Bible, on prayer, on current social questions, on the liturgy, etc." Avoid sentimentality and overly personal presentation. Length: 1,250-1,700 words.

LIVING MESSAGE, Box 820, Petrolia, Ontario, NON IRO, Canada. Editor: Rita Baker. For "active, concerned Christians, mainly Canadian Anglican." Publication of the Anglican Church of Canada. Estab. 1889. Monthly except July and August. Circ. 14,000. Not copyrighted. Payment on publication. Free sample copy. Will consider photocopied submissions. Submit seasonal material 5 months in advance. Reports on material in 4 weeks. Submit complete ms. Enclose SAE and International Reply Coupons.
Fiction, Nonfiction and Photos: "Short stories and articles which give readers an insight into other lives, promote understanding and stimulate action in areas such as community life, concerns of elderly, handicapped, youth, work with children, Christian education, poverty, the 'Third World', etc. No sentimentality or moralizing. Readers relate to a warm, personal approach; uncluttered writing. 'Reports' or involved explanatory articles are not wanted. The lead-in must capture the reader's imagination. A feeling of love and optimism is important." Length: up to 2,000 words. Pays $10-25. 8x10 b&w prints (with article). Pays $5. Fiction length: 1,000 to 1,500 words. Pays $15-20.

LOGOS JOURNAL, Logos International Fellowship, Inc., 201 Church St., Plainfield NJ 07060. (201)754-0745. Senior Editor: Howard Earl. Managing Editor: Carey Moore. For a readership interested in charismatic renewal. Bimonthly magazine; 80 pages. Estab. 1971. Circ. 56,000. Pays on publication; on acceptance if assigned. Buys all rights, but may reassign following publication, or first North American serial rights. Submit seasonal/holiday material 3 months in advance of issue date. Photocopied submissions OK. SASE. Reports in 3 weeks. Sample copy $1; free writer's guidelines.
Nonfiction: "Uses a testimony of healing each issue. Interested in well-researched stories having to do with the current awakening, and/or which give historical perspective. Also, how-to articles for family difficulties such as divorce, depression, etc. Articles must have Christ as center. Humor desired; personal opinion." Query. Buys 20-25 mss/year. Length: 800-2,000 words. Pays $75-200.
Photos: Purchased with accompanying ms. Pays $15-25 for 2¼x2¼ color transparencies or 5x7 b&w glossies.
Columns/Departments: "Desire first-hand reports of charismatic-oriented events/people plus news of spiritual significance." Also opinion column (informed person addressing subject significant to a sizable element in the church). Buys 1/issue. Query. Length: 800-1,000 words.

THE LOOKOUT, 8121 Hamilton Ave., Cincinnati OH 45231. (513)931-4050. Editor: Mark A. Taylor. 50% freelance written. For the adult and young adult of the Sunday morning Bible school. Weekly. Pays on acceptance. Simultaneous submissions OK. SASE. Reports in 6 weeks. Sample copy and writer's guidelines 50¢.
Nonfiction: "Seeks stories about real people or Sunday-school classes; items that shed Biblical light on matters of contemporary controversy; and items that motivate, that lead the reader to ask, 'Why shouldn't I try that?' or 'Why couldn't our Sunday-school class accomplish this?' Should tell how real people are involved for Christ. In choosing topics, *The Lookout* considers timeliness, the church and national calendar, and the ability of the material to fit the above guidelines. Tell us about ideas that are working in your Sunday school and in the lives of its members. Remember to aim at laymen." Submit complete ms. Length: 1,200-1,800 words. Pays $25-35.
Fiction: "A short story is printed in most issues; it is usually between 1,200-1,800 words long, and should be as true to life as possible while remaining inspirational and helpful. Use familiar settings and situations."
Fillers: Inspirational or humorous shorts. "About 400-800 words is a good length for these.

Relate an incident that illustrates a point without preaching. Pays 1-3¢/word.
Photos: B&w prints, 4x6 or larger. Pays $5-15. Pays $50-125 for color transparencies for covers.

THE LUTHERAN, 2900 Queen Lane, Philadelphia PA 19129. (215)848-6800. Editor: A. P. Stauderman. General interest magazine of the Lutheran Church in America. Twice monthly, except single issues in July and August. Buys first rights. Pays on acceptance. Free sample copy and writer's guidelines. SASE.
Nonfiction: Popularly written material about human concerns with reference to the Christian faith. "We are especially interested in articles in 4 main fields: Christian ideology; personal religious life, social responsibilities; Church at work; human interest stories about people in whom considerable numbers of other people are likely to be interested." Write "primarily to convey information rather than opinions. Every article should be based on a reasonable amount of research or should exploit some source of information not readily available. Most readers are grateful for simplicity of style. Sentences should be straightforward, with a minimum of dependent clauses and prepositional phrases." Length: 500 to 2,000 words. Pays $75 to $200.
Photos: Buys pix submitted with mss. Good 8x10 glossy prints. Pays $10 to $20. Also color for cover use. Pays up to $100.

LUTHERAN FORUM, 155 E. 22nd St., New York NY 10010. (212)254-4640. Editor: Glenn C. Stone. 85% freelance written. For church leadership, clerical and lay. Magazine; 40 (8½x11¼) pages. Estab. 1967. Quarterly. Circ. 5,500. Rights purchased vary with author and material. Buys all rights, but will sometimes reassign rights to author after publication; first North American serial rights; first serial rights; second serial (reprint) rights; simultaneous rights. Buys 12-15 mss a year. Pays on publication. Sample copy 75¢. Will consider photocopied and simultaneous submissions. Returns rejected material at once. Reports on ms accepted for publication in 4 to 6 weeks. Query first or submit complete ms. SASE.
Nonfiction: Articles about important issues and developments in the church's institutional life and in its cultural/social setting. Payment varies; $10 minimum. Length: 1,000 to 3,000 words. Informational, how-to, personal experience, interview, profile, think articles, expose, personal opinion. Length: 500 to 3,000 words. Pays $15 to $50.
Photos: Purchased with mss or with captions only. Prefers 8x10 prints. Uses more vertical than horizontal format. Pays $7.50 minimum.
How To Break In: "Send something for our On The Way to the Forum feature. Material for this is usually humorous or offbeat in a gentle way and should have some relation to the life of the Church at some level. Ideal length is 700 to 1,000 words. Payments range from $10 to $20."

THE LUTHERAN JOURNAL, 7317 Cahill Rd., Edina MN 55435. Editor: The Rev. Armin U. Deye. Conservative journal for Lutheran church members, middle age and older. Quarterly magazine; 32 pages, (8½x11). Estab. 1937. Circ. 105,000. Not copyrighted. Buys 12-15 mss a year. Payment on publication. Free sample copy. Submit Christmas, Easter, other holiday material 4 months in advance. Will consider photocopied and simultaneous submissions. Reports in 8 weeks. Submit complete ms. SASE.
Nonfiction and Photos: Inspirational, religious, human interest, and historical articles. Interesting or unusual church projects. Informational, how-to, personal experience, interview, humor, think articles. Length: 1,500 words maximum; occasionally 2,000 words. Pays 1¢ to 1½¢ a word. B&w and color photos purchased with accompanying ms. Captions required. Payment varies.
Fiction and Poetry: Experimental, mainstream, religious, and historical fiction. Must be suitable for church distribution. Length: 2,000 words maximum. Pays 1¢ to 1½¢ a word. Traditional poetry, blank verse, free verse, related to subject matter of magazine.

THE LUTHERAN STANDARD, 426 S. 5th St., Minneapolis MN 55415. (612)332-4561. Editor: Dr. George H. Muedeking. 50% freelance written. For families in congregations of the American Lutheran Church. Estab. 1842. Semimonthly. Circ. 535,000. Buys first rights or multiple rights. Buys 30-50 mss/year. Pays on acceptance. Free sample copy. Reports in 3 weeks. SASE.
Nonfiction and Photos: Uses human interest, inspirational articles, especially about members of the American Lutheran Church who are practicing their faith in noteworthy ways, or congregations with unusual programs. "Should be written in language clearly understandable to persons with a mid-high school reading ability." Also publishes articles that discuss current social issues and problems (crime, family life, divorce, etc.) in terms of Christian involvement and solutions. Length: 650 to 1,250 words, with pictures. Pays 4¢ and up per word. Photos used with mss.
Fiction: "We are particularly interested in getting substantive fiction with a positive Christian theme." Tie-in with season of year, such as Christmas, often preferred. Length: limit 1,200 words. Pays 4¢ per word.

Poetry: Uses very little poetry. The shorter the better; 20 lines. Pays $10 per poem.

LUTHERAN WOMEN, 2900 Queen Lane, Philadelphia PA 19129. Editor: Terry Schutz. 10% freelance written. 11 times yearly. Circ. 45,000. Official magazine for Lutheran Church Women. Acknowledges receipt of manuscript and decides acceptance within two months. Prefers to see mss 6 months ahead of issue, at beginning of planning stage. Can consider up to 3 months before issue. (December issue is nearly completed by September 1). Buys first rights. Pays on publication. SASE.
Nonfiction: Anything of interest to mothers, young or old, professional or other working women, relating to the contemporary expression of Christian faith in daily life, community action, international concerns. Family publication standards. No recipes or housekeeping hints. Length: 1,500 to 2,000 words. Some shorter pieces accepted. Pays up to $50 for full-length ms and photos.
Photos: Purchased with or without mss. Women; family situations; religious art objects; overseas situations related to church. Should be clear, sharp, b&w. No additional payment for those used with mss. Pays $5 for those purchased without mss.
Fiction: Should show deepening of insight; story expressing new understanding in faith; story of human courage, self-giving, building up of community. Not to exceed 2,000 words. Pays $30 to $40.
Poetry: "Biggest taboo for us is sentimentality. We are limited to family magazine type contributions regarding range of vocabulary, but we don't want almanac-type poetry." No limit on number of lines. Pays $10 minimum per poem.

MARIAN HELPERS BULLETIN, Eden Hill, Stockbridge MA 01262. (413)298-3691. Editor: Bro. Robert M. Doyle, M.I.C. 90% freelance written. For average Catholics of varying ages with moderate religious views and general education. Quarterly. Estab. 1947. Circ. 625,000. Not copyrighted. Buys 18 to 24 mss a year. Payment on acceptance. Free sample copy. Reports in 4 to 8 weeks. Submit seasonal material 6 months in advance. SASE.
Nonfiction and Photos: "Subject matter is of general interest on devotional, spiritual, moral and social topics. Use a positive, practical, and optimistic approach, without being sophisticated. We would like to see articles on the Blessed Virgin Mary." Buys informational and inspirational articles. Length: 300 to 900 words. Pays $25-35. Photos are purchased with or without mss; captions optional. Pays $5 to $10 for b&w glossies.

MARRIAGE & FAMILY LIVING, St. Meinrad IN 47577. (812)357-6677. Editor: Ila M. Stabile. 75% freelance written. Monthly magazine. Circ. 48,000. Pays on acceptance. Buys first North American serial rights. SASE. Reports in 3-4 weeks. Sample copy 25¢.
Nonfiction: Uses 3 different types of articles: 1) Articles aimed at enriching the husband-wife and parent-child relationship by expanding religious and psychological insights or sensitivity. (Note: Ecumenically Judeo-Christian but in conformity with Roman Catholicism.) Length: 1,000-2,000 words. 2) Informative articles aimed at helping the couple cope, in practical ways, with the problems of modern living. Length: 2,000 words maximum. 3) Personal essays relating amusing and/or heartwarming incidents that point up the human side of marriage and family life. Length: 1,500 words maximum. Pays 5¢/word.
Photos: Bob Weaver, Department Editor. B&w glossies (8x11) and color transparencies purchased with mss. Pays $125 for 4-color cover photo; $50 for b&w cover photo; $35 for 2-page spread in contents, $30 for 1 page in contents; $10 minimum. Photos of couples especially desirable. Model releases required.

MARYKNOLL MAGAZINE, Maryknoll NY 10545. Editor: Darryl Hunt. 15% freelance written. Foreign missionary society magazine. Monthly. Pays on acceptance. Free sample copy. Query before sending any material. Reports within several weeks. SASE.
Nonfiction: Articles and pictures concerning foreign missions. Articles developing themes such as world hunger, environmental needs, economic and political concerns. Length: 800 to 1,500 words. Send an outline before submitting material. Pays $50 to $150.
Photos: "We are a picture/text magazine. All articles must either be accompanied by top quality photos, or be easily illustrated with photos." Pays $15 to $25 for b&w; $25 to $50 for color. Payment is dependent on quality and relevance.

THE MENNONITE, 600 Shaftesbury Blvd., Winnipeg, Canada R3P OM4. (204)888-6781. Editor: Bernie Wiebe. 25% freelance written. For a "general readership—age span—15 to 90 years; education—from grade school to Ph.D's; interests—themes dealing with the Christian response to such issues as the family, ethics, war and peace, life style, renewal, etc." Estab.

1881. Weekly except in July and August. Circ. 16,000. Rights purchased vary with author and material. May buy first and second serial rights. Buys 100 to 125 mss a year. Payment on publication. Free sample copy. Submit seasonal material 3 months in advance. Reports in 2 months. Enclose SAE and International Reply Coupons.
Nonfiction, Photos, Fiction, and Poetry: General subject matter is "articles on Bible study, social and political issues faced by Christians, creative responses to the challenges of 20th century life; some poetry on a variety of subjects; a small amount of fiction. *The Mennonite* is a publication of an historic peace church which pays special attention to ways and means of attempting to resolve conflict at various levels of life—family, community, national and international." Buys personal experience, inspirational, think, and personal opinion articles. Length: 500 to 1,500 words. Pays 1½¢ to 2½¢ a word. Purchases photos without mss and captions are optional. Pays $5 to $10 for 5x7 or 8x10 b&w glossies. Buys religious fiction. Length: 800 to 1,500 words. Pays 1½¢ to 2½¢ a word. Buys religious poems in traditional, blank, or free verse. Length: 2 to 40 lines. Pays 35¢ a line.

MENNONITE BRETHREN HERALD, 159 Henderson Hwy., Winnipeg, Manitoba, R2L 1L4, Canada. Editor: Harold Jantz. Family publication. Biweekly. Circ. 9,600. Pays on publication. No copyrighted. Sample copy 40¢. Reports within the month. Enclose SAE and International Reply Coupons.
Nonfiction and Photos: Articles with a Christian family orientation; youth directed, Christian faith and life, current issues. 1,500 words. Pays $10 to $30 for accepted ms. Photos purchased with mss; pays $3.

MESSAGE, Southern Publishing Association of Seventh-Day Adventists, Box 59, Nashville TN 37202. Editor: Louis Reynolds. 90% freelance written. International religious journal for people of African heritage. Monthly July-October; bimonthly November-June. Pays on acceptance or publication. Buys all rights. SASE. Free sample copy and writer's guidelines.
Nonfiction: Need articles on current events; social problems such as divorce, drugs, diet, family, marriage, abortion, etc. Subjects should be examined in the light of the Holy Scriptures. New approach to doctrinal subjects such as law vs. grace, the Godhead, the birth, death, and resurrection of Christ, Second coming, millennium, the Sabbath, immortality, etc. Short, inspirational themes and unusual human interest stories welcome, but must be creative, original, warm—not the usual run-of-the-mill types. When possible, all articles should be geared to Black audience. All references should be fully documented. Length: 500-1500 words. Pays $25 for minor articles; $35 for major.
Poetry: Market is small. Buys about ten poems/year. Short poetry up to 12 lines. Free verse welcome. Not a lot of nature poems needed. Should tell of divine truths of the Christian experience—struggle and victory and praise. Pays $10 maximum.

THE MESSENGER OF THE SACRED HEART, 833 Broadview Ave., Toronto, Ont., Canada M4K 2P9. Editor: Rev. F. J. Power, S.J. 10% freelance written. For "adult Catholics in Canada and the U.S. who are members of the Apostleship of Prayer." Monthly. Circ. 22,000. Buys first rights. Buys about 12 mss a year. Pays on acceptance. Free sample copy. Submit seasonal material 3 months in advance. Reports in 1 month. Enclose SAE and International Reply Coupons.
Nonfiction: Department Editor: Mary Pujolas. "Articles on the Apostleship of Prayer and on all aspects of Christian living;" current events and social problems that have a bearing on Catholic life, family life, Catholic relations with non-Catholics, personal problems, the liturgy, prayer, devotion to the Sacred Heart. Material should be written in a popular, nonpious style. Length: 1,800 to 2,000 words. Pays 2¢ a word.
Fiction: Department Editor: Mary Pujolas. Wants fiction which reflects the lives, problems, preoccupations of reading audience. "Short stories that make their point through plot and characters." Length: 1,800 to 2,000 words. Pays 2¢ a word.

THE MIRACULOUS MEDAL, 475 E. Chelten Ave., Philadelphia PA 19144. Editorial Director: Rev. Robert P. Cawley, C.M. Quarterly. Buys first North American serial rights. Buys articles only on special assignment. Pays on acceptance. Free sample copy. SASE.
Fiction: Should not be pious or sermon-like. Wants good general fiction—not necessarily religious, but if religion is basic to the story, the writer should be sure of his facts. Only restriction is that subject matter and treatment must not conflict with Catholic teaching and practice. Can use seasonal material. Christmas stories. Length: 2,000 words maximum. Pays 2¢ and up per word. Occasionally uses short-shorts from 750 to 1,250 words.

Poetry: Maximum of 20 lines, preferably about the Virgin Mary or at least with religious slant. Pays 50¢ a line and up.

MODERN LITURGY, Box 444, Saratoga CA 95070. Editor: William Burns. For artists and musicians, creative individuals who plan group worship services; teachers of religion. Magazine: 32 pages. Estab. 1973. Eight times a year. Circ. 12,000. Buys all rights, but may reassign rights to author after publication. Buys about 10 mss a year. Pays on publication. Sample copy $2; free writer's guidelines. No photocopied or simultaneous submissions. Reports in 6 weeks. Query first. SASE.
Nonfiction and Fiction: Articles (historical and theological and practical), example services, liturgical art forms (music, poetry, stories, dances, dramatizations, etc.). Practical, creative ideas and art forms for use in worship and/or religious education classrooms. Length: 750 to 2,000 words. Pays $5 to $30.

NEW CATHOLIC WORLD, Paulist Press, 1865 Broadway, New York, NY 10023. (212)265-8181. Managing Editor: Robert Heyer. 10% freelance written. Bimonthly magazine; 52 pages. Estab. 1865. Circ. 12,700. Pays on publication. Buys all rights, but may reassign following publication. Submit seasonal/holiday material 6 months in advance. SASE. Reports in 4 weeks. Free sample copy.
Nonfiction: Inspirational and informational; personal experience and personal opinion. Query. Length: 2,000 words.
Photos: Photos purchased without accompanying ms. Pays $7-15 for b&w photos.

NEW COVENANT MAGAZINE, Charismatic Renewal Services, Inc., Box 617, Ann Arbor MI 48107. (313)761-8505. Editor-in-Chief: Bert Ghezzi. Managing Editor: Randy Cirner. Emphasizes the charismatic renewal of Christian churches. Ecumenical, with a higher percentage of Roman Catholic readers. Monthly magazine; 36 pages. Estab. 1971. Circ. 72,000. Pays on publication. Buys all rights. Photocopied submissions OK. SASE. Reports in 6-8 weeks. Free sample copy.
Nonfiction: Historical; informational (coverage of recent and upcoming events in the charismatic renewal); inspirational; interview and personal experience (life testimonials relating to the charismatic experience). Buys 2-3 mss/year. Query. Length: 1,000-3,000 words. Pays 2½-3½¢/word.
Photos: Photos purchased with or without accompanying ms or on assignment. Pays $10-35 for 8x10 b&w glossies. Send contact sheet and prints. No additional payment for photos accepted with accompanying ms. Model release required.

THE NEW ERA, 50 E. North Temple, Salt Lake City UT 84150. (801)531-2951. Editor: Brian K. Kelly. 40-60% freelance written. For young people of The Church of Jesus Christ of Latter-Day Saints (Mormon); their church leaders and teachers. Monthly magazine; 51 pages. Estab. 1971. Circ. 160,000. Buys all rights, but will reassign rights to author after publication. Buys 100 mss a year. Payment on acceptance. Will send sample copy to writer for 35¢. Will consider simultaneous submissions. Submit seasonal material 6 months to a year in advance. Reports in 30 days. Query preferred. SASE.
Nonfiction and Photos: "Material that shows how The Church of Jesus Christ of Latter-Day Saints is relevant in the lives of young people today. Must capture the excitement of being a young Latter-Day Saint. Special interest in the experiences of young Latter-Day Saints in other countries. No general library research or formula pieces without the *New Era* slant and feel." Uses informational, how-to, personal experience, interview, profile, inspirational, humor, historical, think pieces, travel, spot news. Length: 150 to 3,000 words. Pays 2¢ to 5¢ a word. Also seeks material for the FYI column (For Your Information) which uses news of young Latter-Day Saints around the world. Uses b&w photos and color transparencies with mss. Payment depends on use in magazine, but begins at $10.
Fiction: Experimental, adventure, science fiction and humorous. Must relate to their young Mormon audience. Pays minimum 3¢ a word.
Poetry: Traditional forms, blank verse, free verse, avant-garde forms, light verse and all other forms. Must relate to their editorial viewpoint. Pays minimum 25¢ a line.

NEW WORLD OUTLOOK, 475 Riverside Dr., Room 1328, New York NY 10027. (212)678-6031. Editor: Arthur J. Moore, Jr. For United Methodist lay people; not clergy generally. Monthly magazine; 50 pages (9x11¼). Estab. 1911. Circ. 40,000. Buys all rights, but will reassign to author after publication; buys first North American serial rights. Buys 15 to 20 mss a year. Payment on publication. Free sample copy and writer's guidelines. Query first or submit complete ms. SASE.

Nonfiction: "Articles about the involvement of the Church around the world, including the U.S., in outreach and social concerns and Christian witness, not solely of 1 denomination. Write with good magazine style. Facts, actualities important. Quotes. Relate what Christians are doing to meet problems. Specifics. We have too much on New York and other large urban areas. We need more good journalistic efforts from smaller places in U.S. Articles by freelancers in out-of-the-way places in the U.S. are especially welcome." Length: 1,000 to 2,000 words. Usually pays $50 to $150.

NORTH AMERICAN VOICE OF FATIMA, Fatima Shrine, Youngstown NY 14174. Editor: Steven M. Grancini, C.R.S.P. 75% freelance written. For Roman Catholic readership. Circ. 19,000. Not copyrighted. Pays on acceptance. Free sample copy. Reports in 4 weeks. SASE.
Nonfiction, Photos, and Fiction: Inspirational, personal experience, historical and think articles. Religious and historical fiction. Length: 700 words. B&w photos purchased with mss. All material must have a religious slant. Pays 1¢ a word.

THE OTHER SIDE, Box 12236, Philadelphia PA 19144. Co-editors: John Alexander, Alfred Krass, Mark Olson. A magazine of Christian discipleship, radical in tone and outlook, with a definite point of view but open to other opinions. Monthly. Estab. 1965. Circ. 7,000. Pays on publication. Buys first serial, second serial and simultaneous rights. SASE. Reports in 1-2 weeks. Sample copy $1.
Nonfiction: "Articles are not encouraged unless they are highly creative descriptions of personal experiences relative to Christian discipleship amidst current issues of society or interviews or profiles which don't just 'grind an axe' but communicate personality." Length: 250-2,500 words. Pays $10-25.
Photos: "Shots depicting 'the other side' of affluence or the juxtaposition of affluence and poverty are needed." Photo essays on social issues will be considered. Pays $10-25 for b&w photos.
Fiction: "Short pieces of creative writing on hard social issues. A Christian perspective should be clear." Length: 300-2,800 words. Pays $10-30.

OUR FAMILY, Oblate Fathers of St. Mary's Province, Box 249, Battleford, Saskatchewan, Canada S0M 0E0. (306)937-2131. Editor-in-Chief: A.J. Reb Materi, O.M.I. For average family men and women of high school and early college education. Monthly magazine; 32 pages. Estab. 1949. Circ. 12,800. Pays on acceptance. Buys all rights but may reassign following publication, simultaneous, second serial (reprint), first North American serial, and one-time rights. Phone queries OK. Submit seasonal/holiday material 4 months in advance. Simultaneous, photocopied and previously published submissions OK. SASE. Reports in 2-4 weeks. Sample copy 50¢; free writer's guidelines.
Nonfiction: Humor (relating to family life or husband/wife relations); inspirational (anything that depicts people responding to adverse conditions with courage, hope and love); personal experience (with religious dimensions); and photo feature (particularly in search of photo essays on human/religious themes and on persons whose lives are an inspiration to others).
Photos: Photos purchased with or without accompanying ms. Pays $20-25 for 5x7 or larger b&w glossies and color photos (which are converted into b&w). Total purchase price for ms includes payment for photos.
Fiction: Humorous and religious. "Anything true to human nature. No moralizing or sentimentality." Buys 1 ms/issue. Send complete ms. Length: 750-3,000 words. Pays 3¢/word minimum for original material.
Poetry: Avant-garde; free verse; haiku; light verse and traditional. Buys 4-10 poems/issue. Length: 3-30 lines. Pays $2-10.
Fillers: Jokes, gags, anecdotes and short humor. Buys 2-10 fillers/issue.

OUR SUNDAY VISITOR MAGAZINE, Noll Plaza, Huntington IN 46750. (219)356-8400. Executive Editor: Robert Lockwood. For general Catholic audience. Weekly. Circ. 400,000. Buys all rights. Buys about 200 mss a year. Pays on acceptance. Will send a sample copy to a writer on request. Submit seasonal material 2 months in advance. Reports in 1 week. Query first. Enclose SASE.
Nonfiction: Uses articles on Catholic related subjects. Should explain Catholic religious beliefs in articles of human interest; articles applying Catholic principles to current problems, Catholic profiles, etc. Payment varies depending on reputation of author, quality of work and amount of research required. Length: 1,000 to 1,200 words. Minimum payment for major features is $100 and a minimum payment for shorter features is $50 to $75.
Photos: Purchased with mss; with captions only. B&w glossies, color transparencies, 35mm

color. Pays $125 for cover photo story, $75 for b&w story; $25 per color photo. $10 per b&w photo.

PENTECOSTAL EVANGEL, The General Council of the Assemblies of God, 1445 Boonville, Springfield, MO 65802. (417)862-2781. Editor-in-Chief: Robert C. Cunningham. Managing Editor: Richard G. Champion. 33% freelance written. Emphasizes news of the Assemblies of God for members of the Assemblies and other Pentecostal and charismatic Christians. Weekly magazine; 32 pages. Estab. 1913. Circ. 266,000. Pays on publication. Buys all rights, but may reassign following publication, simultaneous, second serial (reprint) and one-time rights. Submit seasonal/holiday material 6 months in advance. Simultaneous, photocopied and previously published submissions OK. SASE. Reports in 3 months. Free sample copy and writer's guidelines.
Nonfiction: Informational (articles on home life which convey Christian teachings); inspirational; and personal experience. Buys 8 mss/issue. Send complete ms. Length: 500-2,000 words. Pays up to 2¢/word.
Photos: Photos purchased without accompanying ms. Pays $7.50-15 for 8x10 b&w glossies; $10-35 for 35mm or larger color transparencies. Total purchase price for ms includes payment for photos.
Poetry: Religious and inspirational. Buys 1 poem/issue. Limit submissions to batches of 6. Pays 15¢-30¢/line.

PENTECOSTAL TESTIMONY, 10 Overlea Blvd., Toronto Ont. M4H 1A5 Canada. Editor: Joy E. Hansell. Monthly. For Church members plus general readership. Estab. 1920. Circ. 18,000. Not copyrighted. Payment on publication. Free sample copy. Submit seasonal material at least 3 months in advance. Query first. Enclose SAE and International Reply Coupons.
Nonfiction: Must be written from Canadian viewpoint. Subjects preferred are contemporary public issues, events on the church calendar (Reformation month, Christmas, Pentecost, etc.) written from conservative theological viewpoint. Pays 1¢ per word for originals. Preferred lengths are 800 to 1,200 words.
Photos: Occasionally buys photographs with mss if they are vital to the article. Also buys b&w photos if they are related to some phase of the main topic of the particular issue. Should be 8x10 b&w prints. Payment is $6 to $10 for cover photos.
Fiction: Might use youth-slanted fiction. Same theological slant, same lengths, same payment as nonfiction.

THE PRESBYTERIAN JOURNAL, Box 3108, Asheville NC 28802. Editor-in-Chief: Rev. G. Aiken Taylor. Managing Editor: Rev. J.A. McAlpine. 10% freelance written. For "ministers and laymen of several denominations, mostly Presbyterian, concentrated in the Southeast but including all 50 states and about 20 foreign countries; educational attainments higher than average, conservative religious outlook." Weekly magazine; 20 pages. Estab. 1942. Circ. 22,000. Pays on publication. Submit seasonal/holiday material at least 2 months in advance of issue date. Simultaneous, photocopied and previously published submissions OK. SASE. Reports in 4 weeks. Free sample copy.
Nonfiction: How-to (study the Bible, increase Sunday school attendance, etc.); general interest; humor (light, nothing off color); historical; inspirational; personal experience; and personal opinion. Buys 50 mss/year. Submit complete ms. Length: 2,500 words maximum. Pays $20.

PRESBYTERIAN RECORD, 50 Wynford Dr., Don Mills, Ontario, Canada M3C 1J7. (416)429-0110. Editor: Rev. James Dickey. 40-50% freelance written. For a church-oriented, family audience. Monthly magazine. Estab. 1876. Circ. 89,500. Buys 10 mss/year. Pays on publication. Free sample copy. Submit seasonal material 3 months in advance. Reports on manuscripts accepted for publication in 2 weeks. Returns rejected material in 4 weeks. Query first. SAE and Canadian stamps.
Nonfiction and Photos: Material on religious themes. Check a copy of the magazine for style. Also, personal experience, interview, and inspirational material. Length: 800 to 1,600 words. Pays $20 to $50. Pays $5 to $12 for b&w glossy photos. Captions required. Uses positive color transparencies for the cover. Pays $30.

PURPOSE, 616 Walnut Ave., Scottdale PA 15683. Editor: David E. Hostetler. 85% freelance written. For adults, young and old, general audience with interests as varied as there are persons. "My particular readership is interested in seeing Christianity work in tough situations and come out on top." Monthly magazine. Estab. 1968. Circ. 21,500. Buys first serial rights; second serial (reprint) rights; simultaneous rights. Buys 200 mss a year. Payment on acceptance.

Free sample copy and writer's guidelines. Submit seasonal material 5 months in advance. Will consider photocopied and simultaneous submissions. Reports within 6 weeks. Submit only complete ms. SASE.

Nonfiction and Photos: Inspirational articles from a Christian perspective. "I want material that goes to the core of human problems—morality on all levels, or lack of it in business, politics, religion, sex, and any other area—and shows how Christian answers resolve some of these problems. I don't want glib, sweety-sweet, or civil religion pieces. I want critical stuff with an upbeat. *Purpose* is a story paper and as such wants truth to be conveyed either through quality fiction or through articles that use the best fiction techniques to make them come alive. Our magazine has an accent on Christian discipleship. Basically, this means we think our readers take Christianity seriously and we do not accept a compartmentalized expression of faith. Christianity is to be applied to all of life and we expect our material to show this. We're getting too much self-centered material. By that, I mean many writers see religion as a way of getting their needs met with very little concern for how the other fellow may be affected by their selfishness. I would like to see articles on how people are intelligently and effectively working at some of the great human problems such as overpopulation, food shortages, international understanding, etc., motivated by their faith." Length: 200 to 1,200 words. Pays 1¢ to 3¢ per word. Photos purchased with ms. Captions optional. Pays $5 to $35 for b&w, depending on quality. Normal range is $7.50 to $15. Must be sharp enough for reproduction; prefers prints in all cases. Can use color for halftones at the same rate of payment.

Fiction, Poetry, and Fillers: Humorous, religious, and historical fiction relating to the theme of magazine. "Should not be moralistic." Traditional poetry, blank verse, free verse, and light verse. Length: 3 to 12 lines. Pays 25¢ to 50¢ per line. Jokes, short humor, and items up to 400 words. Pays 1¢ minimum per word.

How To Break In: "We are a good market for new writers who combine Christian perceptions with craftsmanship. We are looking for articles which show Christianity slugging it out where people hurt but we want the stories told and presented professionally. Good photographs help place material with us."

QUEEN, Montfort Missionaries, 40 S. Saxon Ave., Bay Shore NY 11706. (516)665-0726. Editor-in-Chief: James McMillan, S.M.M. Managing Editor: Roger Charest, S.M.M. Emphasizes doctrine and devotion to Mary. Bimonthly magazine; 40 pages. Estab. 1950. Circ. 10,000. Pays on acceptance. Buys all rights, but may reassign following publication. Phone queries OK. Submit seasonal/holiday material 3 months in advance. SASE. Reports in 1 month.

Nonfiction: Expose (doctrinal); historical; informational; inspirational and interview. Buys 5 mss/issue. Send complete ms. Length: 1,500-2,000 words. Pays $20-40.

Fiction: Religious. Buys 1 ms/issue. Send complete ms. Length: 1,500-2,000 words. Pays $30-40.

Poetry: Free verse and traditional forms. Marian poetry only. Buys 2/issue. Limit submissions to batches of 2. Pays in free subscription for 2 years.

REVIEW FOR RELIGIOUS, 612 Humboldt Building, 539 N. Grand Blvd., St. Louis MO 63103. (314)535-3048. Editor: Daniel F. X. Meenan, S.J. 100% freelance written. Bimonthly. For Roman Catholic religious men and women. Pays on publication. Reports in about 4 weeks. SASE.

Nonfiction: Articles on ascetical, liturgical and canonical matters. Length: 2,000 to 10,000 words. Pays $6 a page.

ST. ANTHONY MESSENGER, 1615 Republic St., Cincinnati OH 45210. Editor-in-Chief: Jeremy Harrington. For a national readership of Catholic families, most of them have children in grade school, high school or college. Monthly magazine; 59 pages. Estab. 1893. Circ. 280,000. Pays on acceptance. Buys first North American serial rights. Submit seasonal/holiday material 4 months in advance. SASE. Free sample copy and writer's guidelines.

Nonfiction: How-to (on psychological and spiritual growth; family problems); humor; informational; inspirational; interview; personal experience (if pertinent to our purpose); personal opinion (limited use; writer must have special qualifications for topic); profile. Buys 12 mss/year. Length: 1,500-3,500 words. Pays 7¢/word.

Fiction: Mainstream and religious. Buys 12 mss/year. Query. Length: 2,000-3,500 words. Pays 7¢/word.

How To Break In: "The freelancer should ask why his/her proposed article would be appropriate for us, rather than for *Redbook* or *Saturday Review*. We treat human problems of all kinds, but from a religious perspective."

ST. JOSEPH'S MESSENGER & ADVOCATE OF THE BLIND, Sisters of St. Joseph of Peace,

St. Joseph's Home, Box 288, Jersey City NJ 07303. Editor-in-Chief: Sister Ursula Maphet. 50% freelance written. Quarterly magazine; 30 pages. Estab. 1900. Circ. 71,000. Pays on acceptance. Buys all rights, but may reassign following publication. Submit seasonal/holiday material 3 months in advance (no Christmas issue). Simultaneous and previously published submissions OK. Reports in 3 weeks. Free sample copy and writer's guidelines.

Nonfiction: Humor; inspirational; nostalgia; personal opinion; and personal experience. Buys 24 mss/year. Submit complete ms. Length: 300-1,500 words. Pays $3-15.

Fiction: "Fiction is our most needed area." Romance; suspense; mainstream; and religious. Buys 30 mss/year. Submit complete ms. Length: 600-1,600 words. Pays $6-25.

Poetry: Light verse, traditional. Buys 25/year. Limit submissions to batches of 10. Length: 50-300 words. Pays $5-20.

Fillers: Jokes, gags, anecdotes. Buys 30/year. Length: 25-150 words. Pays $5-10.

SANDAL PRINTS, 1820 Mt. Elliott, Detroit MI 48207. Editor: William La Forte. For people who are interested in the work of the Capuchins. Estab. 1952. Circ. 8,000. Not copyrighted. Payment on acceptance. Free sample copy. Reports on material accepted for publication in 1 week. Returns rejected material immediately. Query first. SASE.

Nonfiction and Photos: Material on the contemporary apostolates and life style of Capuchins (especially in the Midwest). "We do not use any general religious material; no topical subjects or themes accepted." Length: 2,500 words. Pays $25 to $50. Pays $5 per b&w photo.

How To Break In: "Write about actually living Capuchins and their work. Query before writing the first word."

SCOPE, 426 S. Fifth St., Minneapolis MN 55415. (612)332-4561, Ext. 397. Editor: Dr. Lily M. Gyldenvand. 30% freelance written. For women of the American Lutheran Church. Monthly. Circ. 325,000. Buys first rights. Buys 200 to 300 mss a year. Occasionally overstocked. Pays on acceptance. Free sample copy. Submit seasonal material 4 to 5 months in advance. Reports in 2 to 3 weeks. SASE.

Nonfiction and Photos: "The magazine's primary purpose is to be an educational tool in that it transmits the monthly Bible study material which individual women use in preparation for their group meetings. It contains articles for inspiration and growth, as well as information about the mission and concerns of the church, and material that is geared to seasonal emphasis. We are interested in articles that relate to monthly Bible study subject. We also want articles that tell how faith has affected, or can influence, the lives of women or their families. But we do not want preachy articles. We are interested in any subject that touches the home. The possibilities are limitless for good, sharp, stimulating and creative articles." Length: 700 to 1,000 words. Pays $10 to $50. Buys 3x5 or 8x10 b&w photos with mss or with captions only. Pays $7 to $10.

Poetry and Fillers: "We can use interesting, brief, pithy, significant, or clever filler items, but we use very little poetry and are very selective." Pays $5 to $15.

How To Break In: "Examine a copy of *Scope* and submit a well-written manuscript that fits the obvious slant and audience."

SEEK, Standard Publishing, 8121 Hamilton Ave., Cincinnati OH 45231. (513)931-4050, Ext. 164. Editor: J. David Lang. 60% freelance written. For young and middle-aged adults who attend church and Bible classes. Sunday School paper; 8 pages. Estab. 1970. Quarterly, in weekly issues. Circ. 60,000. Rights purchased vary with author and material. Prefers first serial rights. Buys 100 to 150 mss a year. Pays on acceptance. Free sample copy and writer's guidelines. No photocopied submissions. Submit seasonal (Christmas, Easter, New Year's) material 9 to 12 months in advance. Reports in 30 to 60 days. Query first or submit complete ms. SASE.

Nonfiction and Photos: "We look for articles that are warm, inspirational, devotional, of personal or human interest; that deal with controversial matters, timely issues of religious, ethical, or moral nature, or first-person testimonies, true-to-life happenings, vignettes, emotional situations or problems; communication problems, and examples of answered prayer. Article must deliver its point in a convincing manner, but not be patronizing or preachy. Must appeal to either men or women. Must be alive, vibrant, sparkling, and have a title that demands the article to be read. We will purchase a few articles that deal with faith or trials of blacks or other racial groups. Always need stories of families, marriages, problems on campus, and life testimonies." Length: 400 to 1,200 words. Pays 1½¢ to 2¢ a word. B&w photos purchased with or without mss. Pays $7.50 minimum for good 8x10 glossies.

Fiction: Religious fiction and religiously slanted historical and humorous fiction. Length: 400 to 1,200 words. Pays 1½¢ to 2¢ a word.

THE SIGN, Union City NJ 07087. (201)867-6400. Editor: Rev. Arthur McNally, C.P. 60% freelance written. Magazine; 56 pages. 10 issues per year. Buys all rights. Free sample copy. Reports in 3 weeks. SASE.
Nonfiction and Photos: Prime emphasis on religious material: prayer, sacraments, Christian family life, religious education, liturgy, social action — especially "personal testimony" genre. Length: 3500 words maximum. Pays $75 to $300. Uses photos and artwork submitted with articles.
Fiction: Uses, at most, 1 story per month. Length: 3500 words maximum. Pays $200 to $300.

SIGNS OF THE TIMES, 1350 Villa, Mountain View CA 94042. Editor: Lawrence Maxwell. Seventh-Day Adventist. For religiously inclined persons of all ages and denominations. Monthly. Buys first rights only. Reports in 1 week to several months. SASE.
Nonfiction: Uses articles of interest to the religiously inclined of all denominations. Most material furnished by regular contributors, but freelance submissions carefully read. Sincerity, originality, brevity necessary. Lengths: 700 to 1,800 words.

SISTERS TODAY, The Liturgical Press, St. John's Abbey, Collegeville MN 56321. Editor-in-Chief: Rev. Daniel Durken, O.S.B. Associate Editor: Sister Mary Anthony Wagner, O.S.B. 90% freelance written. For religious women of the Roman Catholic Church, primarily. Monthly magazine; 65 pages. Estab. 1929. Circ. 18,000. Pays on publication. Buys all rights, but may reassign following publication. Submit seasonal/holiday material 4 months in advance. SASE. Reports in 1 month. Free sample copy.
Nonfiction: How-to (pray, live in a religious community, exercise faith, hope, charity etc.); informational; and inspirational. Also articles concerning religious renewal, community life, worship and the role of Sisters in the world today. Buys 6 mss/issue. Query. Length: 500-3,000 words. Pays $5/printed page.
Poetry: Free verse; haiku; light verse and traditional. Buys 3 poems/issue. Limit submissions to batches of 4. Pays $10.

SOCIAL JUSTICE REVIEW, 3835 Westminister Place, St. Louis MO 63108. (314)371-1653. Editor: Harvey J. Johnson. Issued monthly except for combination of July-August issues. Not copyrighted; "however special articles within the magazine may be copyrighted, or an occasional special issue has been copyrighted due to author's request." Query first. SASE.
Nonfiction: Wants scholarly articles on society's economic, religious, social, intellectual and political problems with the aim of bringing Catholic social thinking to bear upon these problems. 2,000 to 3,000 words. Pays about 1¢ a word.

SPIRITUAL LIFE, 2131 Lincoln Rd., N.E., Washington DC 20002. (202)832-6622. Editor: Rev. Christopher Latimer, O.C.D. 80% freelance written. "Largely Catholic, well-educated, serious readers. High percentage are priests and religious, but also some laymen. A few are non-Catholic or non-Christian." Quarterly. Circ. 17,000. Buys first rights. Buys about 20 mss a year. Pays on acceptance. Free sample copy and writer's guidelines. "Brief autobiographical information (present occupation, past occupations, books and articles published, etc.) should accompany article. Follow *A Manual of Style* (University of Chicago)." Reports in 2 weeks. SASE.
Nonfiction: Serious articles of contemporary spirituality. Quality articles about man's encounter with God in the present-day world. Language of articles should be college-level. Technical terminology, if used, should be clearly explained. Material should be presented in a positive manner. Sentimental articles or those dealing with specific devotional practices not accepted. "*Spiritual Life* tries to avoid the 'popular,' sentimental approach to religion and to concentrate on a more intellectual approach. We do not want first-person accounts of spiritual experiences (visions, revelations, etc.) nor sentimental treatments of religious devotions." Buys inspirational and think pieces. No fiction or poetry. Length: 3,000 to 5,000 words. Pays $50 minimum. "Four contributor's copies are sent to author on publication of article." Book reviews should be sent to Brother Edward O'Donnell, O.C.D., Carmelite Monastery, 514 Warren St., Brookline MA 02146.

SPIRITUALITY TODAY (formerly *Cross and Crown*), Aquinas Institute of Theology, 2570 Asbury, Dubuque IA 52001. (319)556-7593. Editor: Rev. Christopher Kiesling O.P. 90% freelance written. "For those interested in a more knowing and intense Christian life in the 20th century." Buys all rights, but right to re-use the material is assigned back without charge if credit line is given to *Spirituality Today*. Pays on publication. Query or submit complete ms. SASE.

Nonfiction: "Articles that seriously examine important truths pertinent to the spiritual life, or Christian life, in the context of today's world. Scriptural, biographical, doctrinal, liturgical, and ecumenical articles are acceptable." Length: 4,000 words. Pays 1¢/word.

STANDARD, 6401 The Paseo, Kansas City MO 64131. Adult story paper of the Nazarene Publishing House. Copyrighted. Weekly. Will accept second rights and simultaneous submissions. Pays on acceptance. Write for copy of guidelines for writers. Reports in about 60 days. Enclose SASE.
Fiction: "Stories should vividly portray definite Christian emphasis or character-building values, without being preachy. Setting, plot, and action should be realistic." Length: 2,000 to 3,000 words. Pays $20 per 1,000 words.

SUNDAY DIGEST, 850 N. Grove Ave., Elgin IL 60120. Editor: Darlene McRoberts. 50% freelance written. Issued weekly for Christian adults. Buys all rights. Pays on acceptance. Free sample copy and writer's guidelines. Reports on submissions in 4 weeks. SASE.
Nonfiction and Photos: Needs articles applying the Christian faith to personal and social problems, articles of family interest and on church subjects, personality profiles, practical self-help articles, personal experience articles and inspirational anecdotes. Length: 500 to 1,800 words. "Study our product and our editorial requirements. Have a clear purpose for every article or story—use anecdotes and dialog—support opinions with research." Pays 3¢ per word minimum. Photos purchased only with mss. Pays about $10 each, depending on quality. Negatives requested (b&w). Return of prints cannot be guaranteed.
Fiction: Occasionally uses fiction that is hard-hitting, fast-moving, with a real woven-in, not "tacked on," Christian message. Length: 1,000 to 1,500 words. Pays 3¢ per word minimum.
Poetry: Occasionally used if appropriate to format. Pays 5¢ per word minimum.
Fillers: Anecdotes of inspirational value, jokes and short humor; must be appropriate to format and in good taste. Length: up to 500 words. Pays 5¢ per word minimum.

SUNDAY SCHOOL LESSON ILLUSTRATOR, The Sunday School Board, 127 9th Ave., N., Nashville TN 37234. Editor: William H. Stephens. For members of Sunday School classes that use the International Sunday School Lessons and other Bible study lessons, and for adults seeking in-depth Biblical information. Quarterly. Circ. 90,000. Buys all rights. Buys 25 mss/year. Pays on acceptance. Will not consider photocopied submissions. Submit seasonal material (for Christmas and Easter) 1 year in advance. Reports in 2 weeks. Query. SASE.
Nonfiction and Photos: Journalistic articles and photo stories researched on Biblical subjects, such as archaeology and sketches of biblical personalities. Material must be written for laymen but research quality must be up-to-date and thorough. Should be written in a contemporary, journalistic style. Pays 2½¢/word. B&w and color photos purchased with ms or on assignment. Captions required. Pays $7.50 to $10.
Poetry: Traditional forms of poetry. Pays $3 to $20.

THE TEXAS METHODIST/UNITED METHODIST REPORTER, Box 1076, Dallas TX 75221. (214)748-6491. General Manager/Editor: Spurgeon M. Dunnam III. For a national readership of United Methodist pastors and laypersons. Weekly newspaper. Circ. 450,000. Pays on acceptance. Not copyrighted. SASE. Free sample copy and writer's guidelines.
Nonfiction: "We welcome short features, approximately 500 words, focused on United Methodist persons, churches, or church agencies. Write about a distinctly Christian response to human need or how a person's faith relates to a given situation." Pays 3¢/word.
Photos: Purchased with accompanying ms. "We encourage the submission of good action photos (5x7 or 8x10 b&w glossies) of the persons or situations in the article." Pays $10.
Poetry: "Poetry welcome on a religious theme; blank verse or rhyme." Length: 2-12 lines. Pays $2.
Fillers: Cross-word, word-find and other puzzles on religious or biblical themes. Pays $5.

THESE TIMES, Southern Publishing Association, Box 59, Nashville TN 37202. (615)889-8000. Editor: Kenneth J. Holland. For the general public; adult. Monthly magazine; 36 pages. Estab. 1891. Circ. 207,000. Rights purchased vary with author and material. May buy first North American serial rights, second serial (reprint) rights or simultaneous rights. Buys about 50 mss a year. Pays on acceptance. Free sample copy and writer's guidelines. Will consider photocopied and simultaneous submissions. Submit seasonal material 6 months in advance. Reports on material accepted for publication in 2 weeks. Returns rejected material in 1 week. Query first. SASE.
Nonfiction and Photos: Material on the relevance of Christianity and everyday life. Inspirational

articles. How-to; home and family problems; health. Drugs, alcohol, gambling, abortion, Bible doctrine. Marriage; divorce; country living or city living. "We like the narrative style. Find a person who has solved a problem. Then, tell how he did it." Length: 250 to 2,500 words. Pays 6¢ to 10¢ a word. B&w and color photos are purchased with or without ms, or on assignment. Pays $20 to $25 for b&w; $75 to $150 for color.

TODAY'S CHRISTIAN PARENT, 8121 Hamilton Ave., Cincinnati OH 45231. (513)931-4050. Editor: Mrs. Wilma L. Shaffer. Quarterly. Rights purchased vary with author and material. Buys first North American serial rights and first serial rights. Payment on acceptance. Free sample copy. Reports on submissions within 1 month. SASE.
Nonfiction: Devotional and inspirational articles for the family. Also articles concerning the problems and pleasures of parents of preschool children, and Christian child training. Length: 600 to 1,200 words. Also can use some handcraft and activity ideas for preschoolers. Study magazine before submitting. Pays minimum of 1½¢ per word.
How To Break In: "Write about familiar family situations in a refreshingly different way, so that help and inspiration shine through the problems and pleasures of parenthood."

"TRUTH ON FIRE!" The Bible Holiness Movement, Box 223 Sta. A, Vancouver, BC V6C 2M3. (604)683-1833. Editor-in-Chief: Wesley H. Wakefield. 20% freelance written. Emphasizes Evangelism and Bible teachings. Bimonthly magazine; 32 pages. Estab. 1949. Circ. 5,000. Pays on acceptance. Buys all rights, but may reassign following publication. Simultaneous, photocopied and previously published submissions OK. SASE. Reports in 3 weeks. Free sample copy and writer's guidelines.
Nonfiction: "Evangelical articles; articles dealing with social reforms (pacifism, civil rights, religious liberty); expose (present-day slavery, cancer, tobacco, etc.), first person testimonies of Christian experience; doctrinal articles from Wesleyan interpretation. Must observe our evangelical taboos. Nothing favoring use of tobacco, alcohol, attendance at dances or theatres; nothing pro-abortion, pro-divorce-remarriage; no hip or slang. Also, we do not accept Calvinistic religious or right-wing political material. Would like to see material on Christian pacifism, anti-semitism, present-day slavery, marijuana research, religious issues in Ireland, and religious articles." Length: 300-2,500 words. Pays $5-35.
Photos: Photos purchased with or without accompanying ms. Pays $5-15 for 5x7 b&w photos. "Subjects should conform to our mores of dress (no jewelry, no makeup, no long-haired men, no mini-skirts, etc.).
Fillers: Newsbreaks, quotes. Length: 30-100 words. Pays $1-2.50.

TWIN CIRCLE, 1901 Avenue of the Stars, #1511, Los Angeles, CA 90067. (213)553-4911. Editor-in-Chief: Mrs. Geraldine Frawley. Emphasizes the Catholic community. Weekly tabloid; 20 pages. Estab. 1968. Circ. 60,000. Buys all rights, but may reassign following publication. Phone queries OK. Submit seasonal/holiday material 8 weeks in advance. Previously published submissions OK. SASE. Reports in 6 weeks. Free sample copy and writer's guidelines.
Nonfiction: How-to (problem solving, interpersonal relationships), interview, profile. Buys 4 mss/issue. Query. Length: 600-800 words. Pays $25 minimum.
Photos: Purchased with accompanying ms or on assignment. Captions required. Pays $10-25 for 8½x10 flat or glossy b&w prints. Query. Model release required.

THE UNITED CHURCH OBSERVER, 85 St. Clair Ave. E., Toronto 7, Ont., Canada. (416)925-5931. Editor: A.C. Forrest; Associate Editor: Patricia Clarke. For families in the United Church of Canada. Monthly. Pays on publication. Sample copy 50¢. Reports in 1 month. Query first. Enclose SAE and International Reply Coupons.
Nonfiction: Wants general interest articles on all subjects of interest to church people. No homiletics. Material must have some church connection. Well-researched articles on developments in religion. Also deal in international affairs. Bright, journalistic style is necessary. Preferred lengths are 1,000 to 2,500 words. Thorough knowledge of the subject, authority and topnotch writing are looked for. Pays $50 minimum.
Photos: Buys photographs with mss and occasional picture stories. Use both b&w and color; b&w should be 8x10; color, prefers 4x5 transparencies but can work from 2¼x2¼ or 35mm. Payment varies.

UNITED EVANGELICAL ACTION, Box 28, Wheaton, IL 60187. (312)665-0500. Editor: Harold Smith. 5% freelance written. For evangelical pastors and church leaders, including denominational executives. Quarterly magazine; 32 pages. Estab. 1942. Circ. 8,500. Pays on publication. Buys all rights. Phone queries OK. SASE. Reports in 4 weeks. Free sample copy and writer's guidelines.

Nonfiction: Anita Moreland, Managing Editor. Informational (new trends in evangelical denominations or missions or on practical help to local churches and pastors). Buys 3-4 mss/year. Query. Length: 1,500-2,500 words. Pays 2-5¢/word.

UNITY MAGAZINE, Unity Village MO 64065. Editor: Thomas E. Witherspoon. Publication of Unity School of Christianity. Magazine; 66 pages. Estab. 1889. Monthly. Circ. 300,000. Buys first serial rights. Buys 200 mss a year. Pays on acceptance. Free sample copy and writer's guidelines. No photocopied or simultaneous submissions. Submit seasonal material 6 to 8 months in advance. Reports in 4 weeks. Submit complete ms. SASE.
Nonfiction and Photos: "Inspirational articles, metaphysical in nature, about individuals who are using Christian principles in their living." Personal experience and interview. Length: 3,000 words maximum. Pays minimum of 2¢ a word. 4x5 or 8x10 color transparencies purchased without mss. Pays $75-100.
Poetry: Traditional forms, blank verse, free verse. Pays 50¢/line.

UNIVERSAL MAGAZINE, Box 1537, Palm Desert CA 92260. Editor-in-Chief: Rev. Paul von Johl. 50% freelance written. Emphasizes family unity. Bimonthly magazine; 12 pages. Estab. 1975. Pays on acceptance and publication. Buys all rights. Submit seasonal/holiday material 6 months in advance of issue date. Previously published work OK. SASE. Reports in 3 weeks. Sample copy and writer's guidelines 15¢ each; mention *Writer's Market* in request.
Nonfiction: How-to (as it relates to the family); inspirational (without sounding religious); new product (for better family living in relationships to the family); and family unity and help for family togetherness. No political articles. Buys 1 ms/issue. Submit complete ms. Length: 500-1,500 words. Pays $2.50-20.
Photos: Submit photo material with accompanying ms. No additional payment for photos. Captions preferred. Buys one-time rights. Model release required.
Columns/Departments: Bookshelf (reviews for books, tape clubs, "spiritial" and other publications of general interest); For Better Human Relationship (stories should be just what the title implies). Buys 1 ms/issue. Submit complete ms. Length: 500-2,500 words. Pays $2.50-20. Open to suggestions for new columns/departments.
Fiction: Humorous. Submit complete ms. Length: 250-1,000 words. Pays $3-8.
Poetry: Any style as long as it is "clean". Submit in batches of 3. Length: 4-20 lines. Pays $1 or 15¢/line.

VANGUARD: VISION FOR THE SEVENTIES, 229 College St., Toronto, Ontario, Canada M5T 1R4. Estab. 1970. 6 times/year. Circ. 2,500. "Copyright is held jointly by author and publisher." Reports in 3 weeks. Query first. Enclose SAE and International Reply Coupons.
Nonfiction: "*Vanguard* does not pay its contributors, but we welcome articles on any range of subjects: politics, economics, education, arts, urban affairs, etc., written from a Christian perspective and contributing to the development of a radical Christian consciousness and life style. Contributions are reviewed by our editorial committee."
How To Break In: "This is an idea magazine, reaching a highly educated and culturally aware audience. Freelance writers who are not recognized experts in a field should query the editor for assignments. A summary of writer's educational and journalistic background should accompany all queries."

VERONA FATHERS MISSIONS, 2104 St. Michael St., Cincinnati OH 45204. (513)921-4400. Editor: Fr. Joseph Bragotti, FSCJ. Mainly for Catholic lay and clergy interested in foreign missions efforts of the Verona Fathers. Also grade and high school librarians; churches. Bimonthly magazine; 24 pages. Estab. 1950. Circ. 24,000. Pays on publication. Will send sample copy to writer on request. Reports on material accepted for publication in 30 days. Returns rejected material immediately. Query first. Enclose SASE.
Nonfiction and Photos: Background information and human interest articles on the developing countries of Africa and Latin America. Should be written in a popular and simple style and reflect a positive outlook on efforts in religious and social fields. Informational, personal experience, interview, inspirational, travel articles. Pays $50. B&w photos purchased on assignment. Payment to be agreed upon with the photographer/writer, but begins at $10.

VISTA, Wesleyan Publishing House, Box 2000, Marion IN 46952. Address submissions to Editor of Sunday School Magazines. Publication of the Wesleyan Church. For adults. Weekly. Circ. 63,000. Not copyrighted. "Along with mss for first use, we also accept simultaneous submissions, second rights, and reprint rights. It is the writer's obligation to secure clearance from the original publisher for any reprint rights." Pays on acceptance. Free sample copy. Editorial deadlines are 9 months in advance of publication. Reports in 6 weeks. SASE.

Nonfiction and Poetry: Devotional, biographical, and informational articles with inspirational, religious, moral, or educational values. Favorable toward emphasis on: "New Testament standard of living as applied to our day; soul-winning (evangelism); proper Sunday observance; Christian youth in action; Christian education in the home, the church and the college; good will to others; worldwide missions; clean living, high ideals, and temperance; wholesome social relationships. Disapprove of liquor, tobacco, theaters, dancing. Mss are judged on the basis of human interest, ability to hold reader's attention, vivid characterizations, thoughtful analysis of problems, vital character message, expressive English, correct punctuation, proper diction. Know where you are going and get there." Length: 500 to 1,500 words. Pays 2¢ a word for quality material. Also uses verse. Length: 4 to 16 lines. Pays 25¢ a line.

Photos: Purchased with mss. 5x7 or 8x10 b&w glossies; portraying action, seasonal emphasis or scenic value. Various reader age-groups should be considered. Pays $1 to $2.50 depending upon utility.

Fiction: Stories should have definite Christian emphasis and character-building values, without being preachy. Setting, plot and action should be realistic. Length: 1,500-2,500 words; also short-shorts and vignettes. Pays 2¢ a word for quality material.

THE WAR CRY, The Official Organ of the Salvation Army, 120-130 W. 14th St., New York NY 10011. (212)691-8780. Editor: Lt. Col. William Burrows. 5% freelance written. For "persons with evangelical Christian background; members and friends of the Salvation Army; the 'man in the street'." Weekly. Circ. 290,000. Buys first rights. Buys approximately 200 mss a year. Pays on acceptance. Free sample copy. Submit seasonal material for Christmas and Easter issues at any time. "Christmas and Easter issues are 4-color. Rate of payment for material used in these issues is considerably higher than for weekly issue material." Reports in 2 months. SASE.

Nonfiction: Inspirational and informational articles with a strong evangelical Christian slant, but not preachy. Prefers an anecdotal lead. In addition to general articles, needs articles slanted toward most of the holidays, including Mother's Day, Father's Day, Columbus Day, Washington's and Lincoln's birthdays, etc. Length: approximately 1,000 words. Pays $15 to $35.

Photos: Occasionally buys pix submitted with mss, but seldom with captions only. B&w glossies. Pays $5-20.

Fiction: Prefers complete-in-one-issue stories. Stories should run 1,500 to 2,000 words and have a strong Christian slant. May have Salvation Army background, but this is not necessary and may be detrimental if not authentic. Can have modern or Biblical setting, but must not run contrary to Scriptural account. Principal Bible characters ordinarily should not be protagonists. Pays 2¢/word.

Poetry: Religious or nature poems. Uses very little poetry "except on Christmas and Easter themes." Length: 4 to 24 lines. Pays $2.50 to $15.

Fillers: Inspirational and informative items with a strong Christian slant. 1¢ to 2¢ per word.

WORLD ENCOUNTER, 2900 Queen Lane, Philadelphia PA 19129. (215)848-6800, Ext. 373. Editor: Rev. William A. Dudde. For persons who have more than average interest in, and understanding of, overseas missions and current human social concerns in other parts of the world. Quarterly magazine; 32 pages. Estab. 1963. Circ. 8,000. Buys all rights, but will reassign rights to author after publication. Buys 10 mss a year. Payment on publication. Free sample copy. Will consider photocopied, and simultaneous submissions, if information is supplied on other markets being approached. Reports in 1 month. Query first or submit complete ms. SASE.

Nonfiction and Photos: "This is a religious and educational publication using human interest features and think pieces relating to the Christian world mission and world community. Race relations in southern Africa; human rights struggles with tyrannical regimes; social and political ferment in Latin America; resurgence of Oriental religions. Simple travelogues are not useful to us. Prospective writers should inquire as to the countries and topics of particular interest to our constituents. Material must be written in a popular style but the content must be more than superficial. It must be theologically, sociologically and anthropologically sound. We try to maintain a balance between gospel proclamation and concern for human and social development. We focus on what is happening in Lutheran groups. Our standards of content quality and writing are very high." Length: 500 to 1,800 words. Pays $25 to $150. B&w photos are purchased with or without accompanying mss or on assignment. Pays $10 to $20. Captions required.

How To Break In: "Contact Lutheran missionaries in some overseas country and work out an article treatment with them. Or simply write the editor, outlining your background and areas of international knowledge and interest, asking at what points they converge with our magazine's interests.''

WORSHIP, St. John's Abbey, Collegeville MN 56321. (612)363-3765. Editor: Rev. Aelred Tegels, O.S.B. ''For readers concerned with the problems of liturgical renewal. The readership is largely Roman Catholic with a growing percentage of readers from the other Christian churches.'' Bimonthly; 96 pages. Serves as organ of the North American Academy of Liturgy, and, as such, regularly devotes its July issue to the proceedings of the annual meeting of the Academy. Buys all rights. Pays on publication. Reports in 2 to 3 weeks. SASE.
Nonfiction: ''*Worship* magazine is engaged in an ongoing study of both the theoretic and the pastoral dimensions of liturgy. It examines the historical traditions of worship in their doctrinal context, the experience of worship in the various Christian churches, the finding of contemporary theology, psychology, communications, cultural anthropology, and sociology in so far as these have a bearing on public worship. Since the Second Vatican Council, *Worship* magazine has been fully ecumenical in its editorial board and policies as well as in its contributors and contents. Study a recent issue.'' Length: 3,000 to 5,000 words. Pays 1¢ to 2¢ a word.

Retirement Publications

DYNAMIC YEARS, 215 Long Beach Blvd., Long Beach CA 90801. Executive Editor: James Wiggins. Managing Editor: Carol Powers. ''DY is the official publication of AIM—Action for Independent Maturity. AIM members are the 45 to 65 age bracket, pre-retirees.'' Estab. 1966. Bimonthly. Circ. 190,000. Rights purchased vary with author and material. May buy all rights with the possibility of reassigning rights to author after publication; or first serial rights. Buys 100 mss a year. Payment on acceptance. Will send a free sample copy to a writer on request. Submit seasonal material 4 months in advance. Reports in 2 weeks. Query first or submit complete ms. ''Submit only 1 ms at a time.'' SASE.
Nonfiction and Photos: General subject matter is ''health for middle years, pre-retirement planning, second careers, personal adjustment, well-developed hobbies, 'people in action' with useful activities, exciting use of leisure, financial preparation for retirement. We like the 'you' approach, nonpreachy, use of lively examples. We try to slant everything toward our age group. We do not want pieces about individuals long retired. Prefer not seeing poetry, fiction, nostalgia, 'inspirational' preachments.'' Buys how-to, personal experience, profile, humor, or travel articles. Length: 1,000 to 2,000 words. Pays up to $400 per article. Photos purchased with and without mss for covers. Captions required. Pays $25 for professional quality b&w photos (5x7, 8x10). Pays $100 maximum for professional quality color photos (35mm or 2¼x2¼ transparencies).

MATURE CATHOLIC, 1100 W. Wells St., Milwaukee WI 53233. (414)271-8926. Editor-in-Chief: Carol A. Mitchell. Managing Editor; Merlin Victora. 30% freelance written. Emphasizes retirement. Bimonthly newsletter; 16 pages. Estab. 1972. Circ. 6,000. Pays on acceptance. Buys first North American serial rights. Phone queries OK. Submit seasonal/holiday material 2 months in advance of issue date. Previously published submissions OK. SASE. Reports in 2 weeks. Free sample copy.
Nonfiction: General interest; historical; how-to (hobbies, fix-it, and travel); humor; inspirational (Catholic only in religious slant); interview; nostalgia; personal experience (retired); technical; and travel. ''No articles on off-color sex. Our readers are retired Catholics.'' Buys 12 mss/year. Submit complete ms. Length: 1,000 words. Pays 1¢/word.
Fiction: Adventure; historical; humorous; and religious. ''No romance or erotica.'' Buys 4 mss/year. Submit complete ms. Length: 1,000 words. Pays 1¢/word.
Fillers: Jokes, gags, anecdotes. Buys 6/year. Pays $2.

MATURE LIVING, The Sunday School Board of the Southern Baptist Convention, 127 Ninth Ave. N., Nashville, TN 37234. (615)251-2191. Editor-in-Chief: John Warren Steen. A Christian magazine for retired or about-to-be-retired senior adults. Monthly magazine; 52 pages. Estab. 1977. Pays on acceptance. Buys all rights, but may reassign following publication. Phone queries OK. Submit seasonal/holiday material 11 months in advance. SASE. Reports in 2-6 weeks. Free sample copy and writer's guidelines.
Nonfiction: How-to (easy, inexpensive craft articles made from easily obtained materials), informational (safety, consumer fraud, labor-saving and money-saving for senior adults), inspirational (short paragraphs with subject matter appealing to elders), interviews, nostalgia, personal experience, profile and travel. Buys 4-5 mss/issue. Send complete ms. Length: 400-1,400 words; prefers articles of 875 words. Pays $12-42.

Photos: Photos purchased with accompanying ms. Pays $5-15 for any size b&w glossies. Model release required.
Fiction: Everyday living, humor and religious. Buys 1 ms/issue. Send complete ms. Length: 875-1,400 words. Pays 3¢/word.
Fillers: Short humor, religious or grandparent/grandchild episodes. Length: 125 words. Pays $5.
How To Break In: "We want warmth. Presentations don't have to be moralistic or religious, but must reflect Christian standards. Use case histories and examples. Don't write down to target audience. Speak *to* senior adults on issues that interest them. They like inspirational, good-samaritan, and nostalgic articles. We'll buy some light humor and some travel. We'll continually need medium length character studies of unusual people—especially those who have triumphed over adverse circumstances."

MATURE YEARS, 201 Eighth Ave., S., Nashville TN 37202. Editor: Daisy D. Warren. 95% freelance written. For retired persons and those facing retirement; persons seeking help on how to handle problems and privileges of retirement. Estab. 1954. Quarterly. Rights purchased vary with author and material; usually buys all rights. Buys about 50 mss a year. Payment on acceptance. Write for copy of guidelines for writers. Submit seasonal material 1 year in advance. Reports within 6 weeks. Submit complete ms. SASE.
Nonfiction, Fiction and Photos: "*Mature Years* is different from the secular press in that we like material with Christian and church orientation. Usually we prefer materials that have a happy, healthy outlook regarding aging, although advocacy (for older adults) articles are at times used. Each issue is developed on a specific theme and the majority of theme-related articles are solicited. However, many freelance materials are used. Articles dealing with all aspects of preretirement and retirement living. Short stories and leisure-time hobbies related to specific seasons. Examples of how older persons, organizations, and institutions are helping others. Writing should be of interest to older adults, with Christian emphasis, though not preachy and moralizing. No poking fun or mushy, sentimental articles. We treat retirement from the religious viewpoint. How-to, humor and travel also considered." Length for nonfiction: 1,200 to 2,000 words. 8x10 b&w glossies purchased with ms or on assignment. "We buy fiction for adults. Humor is preferred. Please, no children's stories and no stories about depressed situations of older adults." Length: 1,000 to 2,000 words. Payment varies.

MODERN MATURITY, American Association of Retired Persons, 215 Long Beach Blvd., Long Beach, CA 90801. Editor-in-Chief: Hubert C. Pryor. Managing Editor: Ian Ledgerwood. 75% freelance written. For readership over 55 years of age. Bimonthly magazine; 64 pages. Circ. 10 million. Pays on acceptance. Buys all rights. Submit seasonal/holiday material 6 months in advance. Photocopied submissions OK. SASE. Reports in 2 weeks. Free sample copy and writer's guidelines.
Nonfiction: Historical; how-to; humor; informational; inspirational; interview; new product; nostalgia; personal experience; personal opinion; photo feature; profile and travel. Query or send complete ms. Length: 1,000-1,500 words. Pays $100-500.
Photos: Photos purchased with or without accompanying ms. Pays $25 minimum for 8x12 b&w glossies and color slides or prints.
Fiction: Buys some fiction, but must be suitable for older readers. Buys 2-3 mss/year. Send complete ms. Length: 1,000-1,500 words. Pays $50 minimum.
Poetry: All types. Length: 40 lines maximum. Pays $5-50.
Fillers: Clippings, jokes, gags, anecdotes, newsbreaks, puzzles (find the word, not crossword) and short humor. Length: 200-500 words. Pays $5.

NEW ENGLAND SENIOR CITIZEN/SENIOR AMERICAN NEWS, Prime National Publishing Corp., 470 Boston Post Rd., Weston MA 02193. Editor-in-Chief: Ira Alterman. 50% freelance written. For men and women aged 65 and over who are interested in travel, finances, retirement life styles, special legislation, etc. Monthly newspaper; 24-32 pages. Estab. 1970. Circ. 32,000. Pays 2-4 weeks after publication. Buys all rights. Submit seasonal/holiday material 1 month in advance. Photocopied and previously published material OK. SASE. Reports in 3-4 weeks. Sample copy 50¢.
Nonfiction: How-to (anything dealing with retirement years); informational; historical; humor; inspirational; interview; nostalgia; profile; travel; personal experience; photo features; and articles about medicine relating to gerontology. Buys 2-6 mss/issue. Submit complete ms. Length: 750-1,500 words. Pays 25¢/column inch.
Photos: Purchased with or without ms, or on assignment. Captions required. Submit prints. Pays $5 for 5x7 or 8x10 b&w glossies. Model release required.

Columns/Departments: Humor and Elderly Viewpoints. Buys 2-3/issue. Submit complete ms. Length: 500-1,000 words. Pays 25¢/column inch. Open to suggestions for new columns and departments.
Fiction: Adventure; historical; humorous; mystery; romance; suspense; and religious. Submit complete ms. Length: 750-1,500 words. Pays 25¢/column inch.
Fillers: Jokes, gags, anecdotes; newsbreaks; and short humor. Submit complete ms. Length: 50-100 words. Pays 25¢/column inch.
How To Break In: "Remember that companionship is the theme we seek to pursue. Clean, typed, top-quality copy aimed at satisfying that need would be of great interest."

NRTA JOURNAL, 215 Long Beach Blvd., Long Beach CA 90801. (213)432-5781. Editor: Hubert Pryor. 75% freelance written. Publication of the National Retired Teachers Association. For retired teachers. Bimonthly. Buys all rights. Pays on acceptance. Free sample copy. Reports in 4 weeks. SASE.
Nonfiction and Fiction: Service pieces for the retired teacher relating to income, health, hobbies, living; Americana, nostalgia, reminiscence, personality pieces, inspirational articles, current trends. "Also in market for pieces on cultural leaders, cultural subjects and Christmas and other holiday material." Buys fiction occasionally. Length: 1,000 to 1,500 words for nonfiction; 1,500 words maximum for fiction. Pays $100 to $500.
Photos: "Special consideration for picture stories, photographic portfolios, etc." Pays $25 and up each; much more for color and covers.
Fillers: Puzzles, jokes, short humor. Pays $10 and up.

RETIREMENT LIVING, 850 3rd Ave., New York NY 10022. (212)593-2100. Editor-in-Chief: Roy Hemming. Senior Editor: Helen Alpert. "A service-oriented publication (no nostalgia) for pre-retirees (age 55 up) and retirees (age 65 and up). Readers are alert, active, forward-looking, interested in all aspects of meaningful living in the middle and later years." Monthly. Buys all rights. Buys 35 to 100 mss per year. Pays on publication. Will send a sample copy for 75¢ and 18¢ postage. Write for copy of guidelines for writers (enclose SASE). Submit seasonal and holiday material 6 months in advance. Reports in 6-8 weeks. Queries preferred, but will look at complete ms. No phone inquiries. "Manuscripts must be accompanied by SASE; otherwise not returned."
Nonfiction and Photos: "We like factual articles with a strong service value or how-to with names and sources for reader follow-up. Personal experiences, humor, income ideas, money management, unusual hobbies, self-fulfillment." Unusual travel stories, directly relevant to older people, only. Length: 500 to 1,500 words. Pays $50 to $150 an article; $20 to $25 for spot news. "We reserve all rights to edit and rewrite to our style and space requirements. Photos and color slides must be of professional quality." Pays $15 minimum.
How To Break In: "Profile a dynamic person in your community whose recent retirement activities or retirement plans are unusual and could prove meaningful or instructive to another person."

Science Publications

Publications classified here aim at laymen interested in technical and scientific developments and discoveries, applied science, and technical or scientific hobbies. Journals for professional scientists, engineers, repairmen, etc., will be found in Trade Journals.

AMERICAN INVENTOR MAGAZINE, 10310 Menhart Lane, Cupertino CA 95014. (408)253-0438. Editor: Troy C. Challenger. 80% freelance written. Emphasizes the fun and joy of invention. Bimonthly magazine; 70 pages. Estab. August/September 1977. Circ. 500. Pays on acceptance. Buys simultaneous, second serial (reprint), first North American serial or one-time rights. Phone queries OK. Submit seasonal/holiday material 2 months in advance of issue date. Simultaneous, photocopied and previously published submissions OK. SASE. Reports in 2 weeks. Sample copy for 50¢ in postage.
Nonfiction: "The human element behind the new invention is the slant we demand. Humor, passion, and drama are desired. We are a people magazine more so than a nuts and bolts magazine. Everything must be taken from the inventor's point of view, who in this society is underrated, overlooked and very often swindled. *AI* seeks to give people with a good idea the information he or she needs to succeed. Articles and stories that help us to this end, we buy." Exposé (of government and private company rip-off's of inventors or hampering progress);

general interest (about the creative process, or stories about inventors enjoying the good life); how-to (getting ideas, protecting them, marketing them, developing them); inspirational (glorifying the inventor and the creative life); interview (key figures concerning issues that affect progress and invention); nostalgia (early inventions); personal experience (inventing, or making money inventing); personal opinion (if the writer is an expert in the field of comment); photo feature (on the development of some invention, or on the innovative process); profile (of local inventors playing or working); technical (unsolved problems and needs in industry and society); and travel (inventors on tour). Buys 2-5 mss/issue. Query or submit complete ms. Length: 5,000 words maximum. Pays $5-100.

Photos: "We have a mainly visually oriented readership. Photos should be people shots showing action or personality." Pays $1-5 for 5x7 b&w glossy prints. Captions preferred. Model release required. Buys one-time rights.

Columns/Departments: Markets (companies seeking new products); In the News (inventions and inventors in the news); My Secrets (tricks of the trade); Submit complete ms. Pays $1-5.

Fiction: "Stories that have creative, inventive persons as the hero will interest us." Buys 1 ms/issue. Length: 8,000 words maximum. Pays $5-35.

Poetry: "We are skeptical, but if someone out there believes they have a poem suited for *AI*, we'll give it a fair shot." Pays $1.

Fillers: "Anything that strikes a note of 'gee whiz' and stimulates the creative juices of imagination flowing interests us." Pays $1-5.

ASTRONOMY, AstroMedia Corp., 411 E. Mason St., 6th Floor, Milwaukee WI 53202. (414)276-2689. Editor: Richard Berry. Managing Editor: Penny Oldenburger. Emphasizes the science of astronomy. Monthly magazine; 80 pages. Estab. 1973. Circ. 77,000. Pays on publication. Buys all rights. SASE. Reports in 6-8 weeks. Sample copy $2; free writer's guidelines.

Nonfiction: How-to articles (build a telescope; grind a mirror); informational (latest research; what you can observe using a specific type or size of equipment, etc.). "We do not accept articles on UFO's, astrology, or religion." Buys 40-50/year. Submit complete ms. Length: 1,500-3,000 words. Pays 3-7¢/word.

Photos: Purchased with or without mss, or on assignment. B&w and color. Send prints and transparencies. Pays $7.50-10/b&w; $10 minimum for color.

Columns/Departments: Astro News and Astronomy Reviews (books). Buys 50-100/year. Query. Length: 150-500 words. Pays $1.25-1.75/typeset line. Open to suggestions for new columns/departments.

BYTE MAGAZINE, 70 Main St., Peterborough NH 03458. (603)924-7217. Editor-in-Chief: Carl T. Helmers Jr. 100% freelance written. Emphasizes personal computers for college-educated users of computers. Monthly magazine; 225 pages. Estab. September 1975. Circ. 98,000. Pays on acceptance. Buys all rights. Photocopied submissions OK. SASE. Reports in 2 months. Sample copy $2; writer's guidelines for SASE, plus 26¢.

Nonfiction: How-to (technical information about computers); and technical. Buys 240 mss/year. Submit complete ms. Length: 20,000 words maximum. Pays $45/typeset magazine page maximum.

How To Break In: "The best way for a writer to break into our publication is by totally immersing himself in computer techniques and reading the magazine for 2-3 months since we publish almost exclusively technical information written for personal computer users."

CB YEARBOOK, 380 Lexington Ave., New York NY 10017. (212)673-1300. Editor-in-Chief: Julian S. Martin. For anyone getting started in electronics as a hobby. Annual magazine; 114 pages. Estab. 1968. Circ. 315,000. Buys all rights. Pays on acceptance. Reports in 2 to 3 weeks. Query first. SASE.

Nonfiction: "We like new and exciting ideas. No padding; straight from the hip writing. Factual, with no puff. There will be a need for good stories on Citizens' Band Radio. Use our current issue as a style manual. Ask the question, is my next writing effort suitable for the issue I hold now?" How-to, personal experience, think pieces and technical articles. Length: open. Pays $100 to $250.

ELECTRONICS HOBBYIST, 380 Lexington Ave., New York NY 10017. (212)949-9190. Editor-in-Chief: Julian S. Martin. 100% freelance written. For "guys who like to build electronic projects from simple one-transistor jobs to complex digital clocks." Magazine; 112 pages. Estab. 1964. Semi-annually. Circ. 125,000. Buys all rights. Buys about 60 mss a year. Pays on acceptance. No photocopied or simultaneous submissions. Reports in 2 to 3 weeks. Query first. SASE.

Nonfiction: Construction projects only. "Write a letter to us telling details of proposed project." Length: open. Pays $100 to $250.

ELECTRONICS TODAY INTERNATIONAL, Unit 6, 25 Overlea Blvd., Toronto, Ontario, Canada M4H 1B1. (416)423-3262. Editor: Steve Braidwood. 40% freelance written. Emphasizes audio, electronics and personal computing for a wide-ranging readership, both professionals and hobbyists. Monthly magazine; 68 pages. Estab. February 1977. Circ. 23,000. Pays on publication. Buys all rights. Phone queries OK. Submit seasonal/holiday material 4 months in advance of issue date. Photocopied submissions OK. SASE. Reports in 4 weeks. Sample copy $2; free writer's guidelines; mention *Writer's Market* in request.
Nonfiction: How-to (technical articles in electronics field); humor (if relevant to electronics); new product (if using *new* electronic techniques); and technical (on new developments, research, etc.). Buys 3-4 mss/issue. Query. Length: 600-3,500 words. pays $15-30.
Photos: "Ideally we like to publish 2 photos or diagrams per 1,000 words of copy." State availability of photo material with query. Offers no additional payment for photos accepted with acoompanying ms. Captions required. Buys all rights.
Fillers: Puzzles (mathematical). Buys 10/year. Length: 50-250 words. Pays $6-10.

ELEMENTARY ELECTRONICS, 380 Lexington Ave., New York NY 10017. (212)949-9190. Editor-in-Chief: Julian S. Martin. For electronics hobbyists, amateur radio operators, shortwave listeners, CB radio operators and computer hobbyists. Bimonthly magazine; 96 pages. Estab. 1950. Circ. 250,000. Buys all rights. Buys 350 mss a year. Payment on acceptance. Free sample copy. Will not consider photocopied or simultaneous submissions. Reports on material accepted for publication in 2 to 4 weeks. Returns rejected material as soon as rejected. Query first. SASE.
Nonfiction and Photos: Construction articles are most needed; also, theory and feature articles related to hobby electronics. How-to and technical articles. "The writer should read our book and decide whether he can be of service to us; and then send us a precis of the story he wishes to submit." Length: as required to tell the story. Pays $150 to $250. No additional payment for photos used with mss.
How To Break In: "I would make three suggestions. First, how-to pieces are always winners. The same goes for construction projects. But they must be to fulfill some need, not just for the sake of selling. Finally, installation stories are very good—something that you buy and where the installation takes some degree of know-how that can be illustrated with step-by-step photos. The author will have to take the photos as he does the job. Theory pieces are tougher—you have to really know us and sense our needs and the sorts of things our readers want to learn about. Feeling and timing are key. We are about 98% freelance and most of our material originates in queries. Please read the magazine first!"

FREY SCIENTIFIC COMPANY CATALOG, 905 Hickory Lane, Mansfield OH 44905. Published annually. Buys all rights. Buys 70-100 rhymes/year. Pays "on acceptance, between October 1 and February 1. Rhymes that arrive after the latter date are held and paid for about November 1, the start of our next publication season." SASE.
Poetry: "We use humorous quatrains and limericks in our annual school science materials catalog, which is sent to every high school and college in the U.S. Each rhyme—limerick, quatrain, or couplet—is matched as best as possible to the appropriate section of our catalog. Rhymes pertaining to physics are included in the physics section, biology in the biology section, chemistry in the chemistry section, earth science to earth science, etc." Interested in buying material from writers "who can combine, in a single rhyme, our requirements of proper rhyme construction, distinct scientific reference, and humor. Generally, we will waive any of the three requirements if the rhyme is strong in the other two." Pays $5 per rhyme.

HAM RADIO MAGAZINE, Greenville NH 03048. (603)878-1441. Editor: James R. Fisk. For amateur radio licensees and electronics experimenters. Special May issue: antenna. Estab. 1968. Monthly. Circ. 55,000. Buys all rights. Buys 10 mss/month. Pays on acceptance. Free sample copy and writer's guidelines. Submit special issue material 6 months in advance. Reports in 1 month. Query helpful, but not essential. SASE.
Nonfiction and Photos: "Technical and home construction articles pertaining to amateur radio. Stress is placed on new developments. Technical articles of interest to the radio amateur, or home construction articles pertaining to amateur radio equipment. Experience has shown that writers who are not licensed amateur radio operators cannot write successfully for this publication." Length: 500 to 5,000 words. Pays approximately $35 per magazine page. Sharp, clear glossy prints (4x5 to 8x10) purchased with accompanying mss. "Don't wish to see any fiction or operating news."

MECHANIX ILLUSTRATED, 1515 Broadway, New York NY 10036. (212)975-4111. Editor: Robert G. Beason. Recreation Editor: Bill D. Miller. Home and Shop Editor: Burt Murphy. Managing Editor: Paul M. Eckstein. Special issues include boating (spring), new cars (October). Monthly magazine; 106 pages. Buys all rights except for picture sets. Pays on acceptance. Write for copy of guidelines for writers. Reports promptly. Query first. SASE.
Nonfiction: Feature articles about science, inventions, novel boats, planes, cars, electronics, recreational vehicles, weapons, health, money management, alternative energy, unusual occupations, usually with mechanical or scientific peg, but not too technical. Length: 1,500 words. Pays $400 minimum. Also uses home workshop projects, kinks, etc., for Home and Shop section. Pays $75 to $500, and higher in exceptional circumstances. "We offer a varied market for all types of do-it-yourself material, ranging from simple tips on easier ways to do things to major construction projects. Boatbuilding, furniture construction, painting, photography, electronics, gardening, astronomy, concrete and masonry work or any type of building construction or repair are just a few of the subjects that interest." Pays minimum of $15 for a tip submitted on a postcard without an illustration. Pays $20 to $25 for an illustrated and captioned tip.
Photos: Photos should accompany mss. Pays $400 and up for transparencies of interesting mechanical or scientific subjects accepted for cover; prefers 4x5, but 2¼ square is acceptable. Inside color: $300 for 1 page, $500 for 2, $700 for 3, etc. Pays $35 for single (b&w) feature photos involving new developments, etc., in the field, Home and Shop tips illustrated with 1 photo, $25. Captions are required. B&w picture sets, up to $350. Requires model releases.
Fillers: Pays $75 for half-page fillers.
How To Break In: "If you're planning some kind of home improvement and can write, you might consider doing a piece on it for us. Good how-to articles on home improvement are always difficult to come by. Aside from that, no particular part of the book is easier to break into than another because we simply don't care whether you've been around or been published here before. We don't care who you are or whether you have any credentials — we're in the market for good journalism and if it's convincing, we buy it."

OCEANS, 240 Fort Mason, San Francisco, CA 94123. Editor-in-Chief: Keith K. Howell. 100% freelance written. For people interested in the sea. Bimonthly magazine; 72 pages. Estab. 1969. Circ. 50,000. Pays on publication. Buys one-time rights. Phone queries OK. Submit seasonal/holiday material 3 months in advance. Simultaneous and photocopied submissions OK. SASE. Reports in 8 weeks. Sample copy 50¢. Free writer's guidelines.
Nonfiction: "Want articles on the worldwide realm of salt water; marine life (biology and ecology), oceanography, maritime history, geography, undersea exploration and study, voyages, ships, coastal areas including environmental problems, seaports and shipping, islands, food-fishing and aquaculture (mariculture), peoples of the sea, including anthropological materials. Writer should be simple, direct, factual, very readable (avoid dullness and pedantry, make it lively and interesting but not cute, flip or tongue-in-cheek; avoid purple prose). Careful research, good structuring, no padding. Factual information in good, narrative style. Our mag is more serious than the common run of diving mags; less technical than *Scientific American*. We do not want articles on scuba; adventuring, travel tend to be overworked. Prefer no sport fishing, boating, surfing, other purely sport-type matter. Diving okay if serious in purpose, unusual in results or story angle. We want articles on rarely visited islands, ports, or shores which have great intrinsic interest, but not treated in purely travelogue style. Can use more on environmental concerns." Length: 1,000-5,000 words. Pays $60/page.

POPULAR ELECTRONICS, 1 Park Ave., New York NY 10016. (212)725-3566. Editor: Arthur P. Salsberg. 80% freelance written. For electronics experimenters, hi-fi buffs, computer hobbyists, CB'ers, hams. Monthly. Estab. 1954. Circ. 415,000. Buys all rights. Buys about 100 ms/year. Pays on acceptance. Write for copy of guidelines for writers. Will not consider photocopied or simultaneous submissions. Reports in 2 to 4 weeks. Query first. SASE.
Nonfiction and Photos: "State-of-the-art reports, tutorial articles, construction projects, etc. The writer must know what he's talking about and not depend on 'hand-out' literature from a few manufacturers or research laboratories. The writer must always bear in mind that the reader has some knowledge of electronics." Informational, how-to, and technical articles. Length: 500 to 3,000 words. Pays $70-125 per published page with photo illustration. B&w glossies preferred.
Fillers: Electronics circuits quizzes. Length: 500 to 1,000 words. Pays $25 to $75.

POPULAR MECHANICS, 224 W. 57th St., New York NY 10019. (212)262-4815. Editor: John

A. Linkletter. Executive Editor: Robin Nelson. Managing Editor: Arthur Maher. Home and Shop Editor: Harry Wicks. Magazine; 200 pages. Monthly. Circ. 1,671,216. Buys all rights. Pays promptly. Query first. SASE.

Nonfiction: "Our principal subjects are automotive (new cars, car maintenance) and how-to (woodworking, metalworking, home improvement and home maintenance). In addition, we use features on new technology, sports, electronics, photography and hi-fi." Exciting male interest articles with strong science, exploration and adventure emphasis. Looking for reporting on new and unusual developments. The writer should be specific about what makes it new, different, better, cheaper, etc. "We are always looking for fresh ideas in home maintenance, shop technique, and crafts, for project pieces used in the back part of the book. The front of the book uses articles in technology and general science, but writers in that area should have background in science." Lengths: 300 to 2,000 words. Pays $300-$600 and up.

Photos: Dramatic photos are most important, and they should show people and things in action. Occasionally buys picture stories with short text block and picture captions. The photos must tell the story without much explanation. Topnotch photos are a must with Craft Section articles. Can also use remodeling of homes, rooms and outdoor structures. Pays $25 minimum.

Fillers: How-to-do-it articles on craft projects and shop work well-illustrated with photos and drawings. The writer must provide the drawings, diagrams, cutaways, and/or photos that would be appropriate to the piece. Finished drawings suitable for publication are not necessary; rough but accurate pencil drawings are adequate for artist's copy. Pays $15.

POPULAR SCIENCE MONTHLY, 380 Madison Ave., New York NY 10017. Editor: Hubert P. Luckett. For the well-educated adult male, interested in science, technology, new products. Monthly magazine; 200 pages. Estab. 1872. Circ. 1,800,000. Buys all rights. Buys several hundred mss a year. Payment on acceptance. Free guidelines for writers. Will not consider photocopied or simultaneous submissions. Submit seasonal material 3 to 4 months in advance. Reports in 2 to 3 weeks. Query first. SASE.

Nonfiction and Photos: "*Popular Science Monthly* is a man's magazine devoted to exploring (and explaining) to a nontechnical but knowledgeable readership the technical world around us. We are a 'thing'-oriented publication: things that fly or travel down a turnpike, or go on or under the sea, or cut wood, or reproduce music, or build buildings, or make pictures, or mow lawns. We are especially focused on the new, the ingenious, and the useful. We are consumer oriented and are interested in any product that adds to a man's enjoyment of his home, yard, car, boat, workshop, outdoor recreation. Some of our 'articles' are only a picture and caption long. Some are a page long. Some occupy 4 or more pages. Contributors should be as alert to the possibility of selling us pictures and short features as they are to major articles. Freelancers should study the magazine to see what we want and avoid irrelevant submissions." Length: 2,000 words maximum. Pays a minimum of about $150 a published page. Prefers 8x10 b&w glossies. Pays $20.

Fillers: Uses shortcuts and tips for homeowners, home craftsmen, car owners, mechanics and machinists.

How To Break In: "Probably the easiest way to break in here is by covering a news story in science and technology that we haven't heard about yet. We need people to be acting as bird-dogs for us out there and we are willing to give the most leeway on these performances. What impresses us the most in a freelance piece—when we're thinking about uncovering a good contributor for the future—is the kind of illustrations the writer supplies. Too many of them kiss off the problem of illustrations. Nothing impresses us more than knowing that the writer can take or acquire good photos to accompany his piece. We probably buy the most freelance material in the do-it-yourself and home improvement areas."

RADIO-ELECTRONICS, 200 Park Ave. S., New York NY 10003. (212)777-6400. Editorial Director: Larry Steckler. Managing Editor: Art Kleiman. For electronics professionals and hobbyists. Monthly. Circ. 185,000. Buys all rights. Pays on acceptance. Send for "Guide to Writing." Reports on submissions in 2 weeks. Enclose SASE.

Nonfiction: Interesting technical stories on electronics, TV and radio, written from viewpoint of the TV service technician, serious experimenter, or layman with technical interests. Construction (how-to-build-it) articles used heavily. Unique projects bring top dollars. Cost of project limited only by what item will do. Emphasis on "how it works, and why." Much of material illustrated with schematic diagrams and pictures provided by author. Pays about $60 to $100 per magazine page.

Photos: Purchased with mss. Model releases required. Payment included in article price. 8x10 glossy.

How To Break In: "The simplest way to come in would be with a short article on some specific construction project. Queries aren't necessary; just send the article, 5 or 6 typewritten pages."

SCIENCE DIGEST, Hearst Magazines Division, Hearst Corp., 224 W. 57th St., New York NY 10019. (212)262-4161. Editor-in-Chief: Daniel E. Button. Emphasizes sciences and technologies for all ages with a scientific bent. Monthly magazine; 100 pages. Estab. 1937. Circ. 160,000. Pays on acceptance. Buys all rights. Submit seasonal/holiday material 3 months in advance. Simultaneous and previously published submissions OK. Reports in 1 month.
Nonfiction: Informational (authentic, timely information in all areas of science); interview (with outstanding authorities in various fields of science); photo feature (usually single photos with adequate cutlines); profile; and technical (not overly so). Buys 30 mss/year. Query. Length: 750-1,500 words. Pays $50-500.
Photos: Purchased with or without accompanying ms or on assignment. Captions required. Query. Pays $25-100 for 8x10 b&w photos; $50-300 for color. Total purchase price for ms includes payment for photos. Model release required.
Fillers: Anecdotal or nostalgic. Query. Length: 50-250 words. Pays $25-50.

SCIENCE & MECHANICS, Davis Publications, 380 Lexington Ave., New York NY 10017. Editor-in-Chief: Joseph Daffron. Managing Editor: Ronald Renzulli. Published 3 times/year. Magazine; 122 pages. Estab. 1937. Pays on acceptance. Buys all rights. Submit seasonal/holiday material 5 months in advance of issue date. SASE. Reports in 2 weeks.
Nonfiction: How-to (wood, mechanical, electronic and outdoor projects, home fix-up and repair); general interest (science, mechanics, technology, energy saving); and technical (what's new, inventions, electronics, science, technology, automotive and mechanical). Buys 6-8 mss/issue. Query. Length: 2,500-4,000 words. Pays $200 minimum.
Photos: "Technical and how-to material must be illustrated; would like to see drawings and diagrams, if applicable." State availability of photos with query. Offers no additional payment for 8x10 glossy photos accepted with ms. Captions preferred. Buys all rights. Model release required.

SCIENCE NEWS, Science Service, Inc., 1719 N. St., NW, Washington DC 20036. Editor-in-Chief: Robert Trotter. For scientists and science-oriented laymen. Weekly magazine; 16 pages. Estab. 1922. Circ. 175,000. Pays on acceptance. Buys all rights. SASE.
Nonfiction: Profile and technical news. Buys 4 mss/year. Query or send complete ms. Pays $75-200. "We are primarily staff-written for two reasons: (1) Being a weekly newsmagazine, we work very close to deadline. Communications and coordination are crucial. Everyone must note what we've previously reported on the same subject and then add what's new. (2) Quality control. We have really gotten burned in the past by freelance articles that were factually inaccurate. We are occasionally in the market for prepublication excerpts from books, especially those involving a thoughtful, humanistic approach toward science, by noted scientists of established reputation; but again this is seldom."
How To Break In: "Acceptance occurs when the writer is either 1) covering a newsworthy scientific meeting that for some reason we have no reporter at or 2) has a topical news-feature article (1,500-1,800 words) on a specific science topic that we haven't already covered. For this to work for us, the writer must be vary familiar with *Science News* (suitable for scientists and the scientifically interested lay public) and for the subjects we already cover thoroughly. These include, generally, physics, astronomy, the space sciences and medical sciences. Articles must have both news and science value."

SCIENTIFIC AMERICAN, 415 Madison Ave., New York NY 10017. Articles by professional scientists only.

73 MAGAZINE, Peterborough NH 03458. (603)924-3873. Publisher: Wayne Green. For amateur radio operators and experimenters. Monthly. Buys all rights. Pays on acceptance. Reports on submissions within a few weeks. Query first. SASE.
Nonfiction and Photos: Articles on anything of interest to radio amateurs, experimenters, and computer hobbyists — construction projects. Pays approximately $40-50 per page. Photos purchased with ms as illustrations.

TECHNOLOGY REVIEW, Alumni Association of the Massachusetts Institute of Technology, Room 10-140, Massachusetts Institute of Technology, Cambridge MA 02139. Editor-in-Chief: John I. Mattill. Managing Editor: Sara J. Neustadtl. 10% freelance written. Emphasizes technology and its implications for scientists, engineers, or managers of companies based in technology. Published 8 times/year. Magazine; 72 pages. Estab. 1899. Circ. 55,000. Pays on

publication. Buys all rights, but may reassign following publication. Phone queries OK. Submit seasonal/holiday material 6 months in advance of issue date. Simultaneous and photocopied submissions OK. SASE. Reports in 4-6 weeks. Sample copy $2.
Nonfiction: General interest; interview; photo feature and technical. Buys 3-5 mss/year. Query. Length: 1,000-10,000 words. Pays $75-300.
Columns/Departments: Book Reviews; Environment; Washington Report; and Economics. Also special reports on other appropriate subjects. Buys 1 ms/issue. Query. Length: 750-1,500 words. Pays $75-150.

Science Fiction, Speculative Fiction and Fantasy Publications

ANALOG SCIENCE FICTION & SCIENCE FACT, 350 Madison Ave., New York NY 10017. Editor: Ben Bova. 100% freelance written. For general future-minded audience. Monthly. Buys all English serial rights. Pays on acceptance. Reports within 3 to 4 weeks. Query first. SASE.
Fiction: Stories of the future told for adults interested in science and technology; central theme usually interaction of strong characters with science or technology-based problems. Length: 3,000 to 60,000 words. Serials only on consultation with Editor. Pays 3¢ to 4 ¢ a word for novelettes and novels, 5¢ a word for shorts under 7,500 words.
Nonfiction and Photos: Needs illustrated technical articles. Length: 5,000 words. Pays 5¢ a word. Buys photos with mss only. Pays $5 each.

ISAAC ASIMOV'S SCIENCE FICTION MAGAZINE, Davis Publications, Inc., Box 13116, Philadelphia PA 19101. (215)382-5415. Editor-in-Chief: George H. Scithers. 95% freelance written. Emphasizes science fiction. Bimonthly magazine; 192 pages. Estab. 1976. Circ. 100,000. Pays on acceptance. Buys first North American serial rights and foreign serial rights. Photocopied submissions OK. SASE. Reports in 2-3 weeks. Writer's guidelines for SASE.
Fiction: Science fiction only. "At first, each story must stand on its own; but as the magazine progresses, we want to see continuing use of memorable characters and backgrounds." Buys 12 mss/issue. Submit complete ms. Length: 100-12,500 words. Pays 3-5¢/word.

STARWIND, The Starwind Press, Box 3346, Columbus OH 43210. Editor: Elbert Lindsey, Jr. 70-80% freelance written. For a college-educated audience (18 to 35) interested in science fiction and fantasy. Magazine; 50 to 60 pages. Estab. 1973. Twice a year (fall and spring). Circ. 2,500. Rights purchased vary with author and material. May buy first North American serial rights or second serial (reprint) rights. Buys about 25 mss a year. Pays on publication. Sample copy $2; free writer's guidelines. Will consider photocopied submissions. No simultaneous submissions. Reports on material accepted for publication in 4 to 6 weeks. Returns rejected material in 6 to 8 weeks. Submit complete ms. Enclose SASE.
Nonfiction: "Interested in analyses of works of well-known science fiction authors and genres in sf and fantasy, or interviews with sf authors or publishers. Reviews of sf books. Also interested in articles dealing with current developments or research in space exploration or colonization, artifical intelligence, genetics, bioengineering, or other subjects. Emphasis should be on extrapolations which are of interest to readers of science fiction." Length: 4,000-20,000 words. Pays ½¢ a word.
Fiction: "Classic hardcore sf, heroic fantasy, supernatural mystery and suspense, occult horror, and some space opera and softcore sf. Interested in stories with non-stereotyped women protagonists. Our prime requisite is good storytelling that is logically constructed. We consider works of unknown writers for all types of material we publish. We prefer not to see extremely short stories with trick endings, rather than well-developed plot." Length: 2,000 to 10,000 words. Pays ½¢ a word.

TESSERACT SCIENCE FICTION, 134 Windward Drive., Schaumburg IL 60194. (312)843-1319. Editors: Keven MacAnn, Nancy K. Zinserling. 80% freelance written. Emphasizes Science fiction and fantasy. Magazine published 2 times/year; 100 pages. Estab. 1977. Circ. 1000. Pays on publication. Buys first North American serial rights. Phone queries OK. Photocopied submissions OK. SASE. Reports in 2 months. Free writer's guidelines.
Fiction: Fantasy (a limited amount will be considered only, also science fantasy); and science fiction (prefer "hard core" science fiction, but will consider all types). Buys 10 mss/year. Submit complete ms. Length 15,000 words maximum. Pays ½¢/word.

WEIRDBOOK, Box 35, Amherst Branch, Buffalo NY 14226. Editor-in-Chief: W. Paul Ganley. Emphasizes weird fantasy (swords & sorcery, supernatural horror, pure fantasy) for a readership teen-age and up. Semiannual magazine; 64 pages. Estab. 1968. Circ. 900. Pays on publication. Buys first North American serial rights and right to reprint as part of entire issue. Photocopied submissions OK. SASE. "Best time to submit is in December or May if quick response is desired." Sample copy $2; writer's guidelines for SASE.
Fiction: Adventure (with weird elements); experimental (maybe, if in fantasy or horror area). Buys 6 mss/year. Submit complete ms. Length: 20,000 words maximum. Pays ¼¢/word minimum.

WHISPERS, Box 904, Chapel Hill NC 27514. Editor: Dr. Stuart David Schiff. 100% freelance written. For intelligent adults with an interest in literate horror, terror, fantasy, and heroic fantasy. Many readers collect first edition books and the like in these fields. Magazine; 64 (5x8½) pages. Estab. 1973. An approximate quarterly schedule. Circ. 3,000. Buys first North American serial rights only. Buys 15 to 20 mss a year. Pays half of fee on acceptance; balance on publication. Will consider photocopied submissions. No simultaneous submissions. Reports in 3 months. Submit complete ms. SASE.
Fiction: Stories of fantasy, terror, horror, and heroic fantasy. Does not want to see science fiction. No rocket ships, futuristic societies, bug-eyed monsters or the like. Authors whose work is most related to their needs include H. P. Lovecraft, Lord Dunsany, Edgar Allan Poe, Algernon Blackwood, Robert Bloch, Fritz Leiber, Ray Bradbury, and Clark Ashton Smith. Length: 500 to 8,000 words. Pays 1¢ a word.

Social Science Publications

HUMAN BEHAVIOR, Manson Western Corp., 12031 Wilshire Blvd., Los Angeles CA 90025. Editor-in-Chief: Marshall Lumsden. Emphasizes human behavior for college educated audience. Monthly magazine; 80 pages. Estab. 1972. Circ. 100,000. Pays on acceptance. Buys all rights, but may reassign following publication. Photocopied and previously published submissions OK. SASE. Reports in 2 months.
Nonfiction: News, trends, reports on current research and personalities in the behavioral sciences. Buys 5 mss/issue. Query or submit complete ms. Length: 1,800-5,000 words. Pays $150-500.
Photos: Purchased on assignment. Captions required. Query or send contact sheet. Pays $25-50 for b&w photos.

IMPACT OF SCIENCE ON SOCIETY, Unesco, 7 place de Fontenoy, 75700 Paris, France. (1)577-16-10. Editor: J. G. Richardson. Emphasizes science-society interactions as well as science and technology for development. Quarterly journal; 96 pages. Estab. 1950. Published in 5 languages. Pays on acceptance. Buys all rights, but may reassign following publication. Photocopied submissions OK. SASE. Reports in 2 weeks. Free sample copy.
Nonfiction: "Would like to see manuscripts dealing with research and social goals, the sea as natural resource, pros and cons of nuclear energy, physics and chemistry of the atmosphers." Informational; interview; how-to; profiles; and think pieces. Prefers not to see mystical explanations for natural phenomena or utopian solutions to problems of world development. Length: 4,500 words, illustrated. Pays up to $250.

JOINT ENDEAVOR, Box 32, Huntsville TX 77340. Editor: Stanley P. Dickens. 75% freelance written. "*Joint Endeavor* is an inmate publication published by an inmate organization and supported by freeworld sponsors, subscribers, and advertisers." Bimonthly magazine; 56 pages. Estab. 1973. Circ. 1,500. Pays on publication. Buys all rights, but may reassign following publication. Submit seasonal/holiday material 4 months in advance of issue date. Simultaneous and photocopied submissions OK. SASE. Reports in 4 weeks. Sample copy $1.50.
Nonfiction: Exposé (must be documented and not subject to extreme criticism); humor (corrections related); historical (interested in history of foreign penal institutions as well as domestic); inspirational (will consider religious and inspirational matter related to inmates of correctional institutions); interview (prominent figures in corrections related field); nostalgia (could use descriptions of old penitentiaries and out-moded methods); personal experience (if positive and well-written); and personal opinion (for those whose opinions matter). Wants no articles which exhibit a negative attitude toward the rehabilitation of offenders, or personal experience articles which are "mushy or compromising and do not relate a realistic experience." Buys 12 mss/year. Query. Length: 2,500-5,000 words. Pays $75-150.

Photos: State availability of photos with query letter. Pays $5-10 for 8½x11 b&w glossies; $10-20 for 2¼x2¼ color transparencies.

PARAPSYCHOLOGY REVIEW, 29 W. 57th St., New York NY 10019. (212)751-5940. Editor: Betty Shapin. Emphasizes psychical research, parapsychology, research and experiment pertaining to extrasensory perception. For the scientific community, academic community, lay audience with special interest in psychical research and the paranormal. Estab. 1953. Bimonthly. Circ. 2,500. Buys all rights, but will reassign to author following publication. Buys 40-50 mss/year. Pays on acceptance. Sample copy $1. Reports in 1 to 2 weeks. Query first or submit complete ms. SASE.
Nonfiction: Articles, news items, book reviews in this general subject area. Must approach psychical research in scientific, experimental fashion. Length: 500-3,000 words. Pays $50 minimum.

PERSONAL GROWTH, Box 1254, Berkeley CA 94701. (415)548-1004. Editor: James Elliott. For psychologists and well-informed lay persons. Most of them have been to (or led) 1 or more encounter groups. Monthly magazine; 24 pages. Estab. 1964. Circ. 5,000. Buys all rights, but will reassign rights to author after publication. Buys 12 mss/year. Pays on acceptance. Sample copy to writer for 2 first class postage stamps; free writer's guidelines. Will consider photocopied, cassette, and simultaneous submissions. Reports in 3-4 weeks. Query. SASE.
Nonfiction: "Anything on personal growth; the human potential movement, psychotherapy, humanistic psychology, etc. Use simple, informal language (not abstract journalese); material should be heavily researched with plenty of examples. We're like *Psychology Today* but with emphasis on personal growth. Taboos are personal accounts of group experiences; articles about the power of positive thinking; articles on 'how religion helped me'; anything featuring the medical model (i.e., 'curing' people). Particularly interested in existensialism, phenomenology and new psychotherapies—also little-known ideas of such famous psychotherapists as Freud, Jung, and Adler—guided imagery and fantasy." Informational, how-to, interview. Length: 200 to 5,000 words. Pays $15 to $200.

PSYCHOLOGY TODAY, 1 Park Ave., New York NY 10016. (212)725-3900. For social scientists and intelligent laymen concerned with society and individual behavior. Monthly. Buys all rights. Each ms will be edited by staff and returned to author prior to publication for comments and approval. Author should retain a copy. Reports within 1 month. Address all queries to Articles Editor. SASE.
Nonfiction: Most mss written by scholars in various fields. Primary purpose is to provide the nonspecialist with accurate and readable information about society and behavior. Technical and specialized vocabularies should be avoided except in cases where familiar expressions cannot serve as adequate equivalents. Technical expressions, when necessary, should be defined carefully for the nonexpert. References to technical literature should not be cited within article, but 10 to 12 general readings should be listed at end. Suggested length: 3,000 words. Payment is $500.

THE SINGLE PARENT, Parents Without Partners, Inc., 7910 Woodmont Ave., Washington DC 20014. (310)654-8850. Editor-in-Chief: Barbara C. Chase. Emphasizes marriage, family, divorce, widowhood, and children. Distributed to members of Parents Without Partners, plus libraries, universities, psychologists, psychiatrists, etc. Magazine, published 10 times/year; 48 pages. Estab. 1965. Circ. 165,000. Pays on publication. Rights purchased vary. Phone queries OK. Submit seasonal/holiday material 3 months in advance of issue date. Simultaneous, photocopied and previously published submissions OK. SASE. Reports in 6-8 weeks. Free sample copy and writer's guidelines.
Nonfiction: Informational (parenting, career development, money management, daycare); interview (with professionals in the field, with people who have successfully survived the trauma of divorce); personal experience (adjustment to living alone, to widowhood, to divorce from both the parental and child's point of view); how-to (raise children alone, travel, take up a new career, home/auto fix-up). Buys 4-5 mss/issue. Query. Length: 1,000-6,000 words. Pays $25-50.
Photos: Purchased with accompanying ms. Query. Pays $10-50 for any size b&w glossies. Model release required.
Rejects: "No first-hand accounts of bitter legal battles with former spouses. No poetry or general interest material."

TOGETHER, 200 Park Ave., S., New York NY 10003. Editor: Sherry Armstrong. For a lay readership. Monthly magazine; 80 pages. Estab. 1933. Circ. 100,000. Pays on acceptance. Buys all rights, first serial rights or second serial (reprint) rights. SASE. Reports in 4 weeks.

Nonfiction: "We are seeking articles to bring to the public authoritative and frank information that will help them integrate their sexual natures with the rest of their lives. Themes must be solidly educational or informative and, at the same time, entertaining. Our editorial aim is to provide helpful, accurate guidance and advice. We eschew sensationalism, but any solid attempt to bring information to our public is reviewed. We regularly cover 'how to' themes with specific advice on promoting compatability, including sexual acts. We seek anatomic articles (medical) about sexuality, psychological, elderly, singles, new scientific breakthroughs, sociological/philosophical perspectives, other cultures, customs (in sex and relationship) and modern appraisals of the relationship/sex theme." Query first, with outline. Length: 2,500-3,000 words. Pays $175 minimum.

TRANSACTION/SOCIETY, Rutgers University, New Brunswick NJ 08903. (201)932-2280, ext. 83. Editor: Irving Louis Horowitz. For social scientists (policymakers with training in sociology, political issues and economics). Estab. 1963. Every 2 months. Circ. 55,000. Buys all rights, but may reassign rights to author after publication. Pays on publication. Free sample copy and writer's guidelines. Will consider photocopied submissions. No simultaneous submissions. Reports in 4 weeks. Query first. SASE.
Nonfiction and Photos: Articles Editor: Stan DeViney. Photo Editor: Jim Colman. "Articles of wide interest in areas of specific interest to the social science community. Must have an awareness of problems and issues in education, population, urbanization that are not widely reported. Articles on overpopulation, terrorism, international organizations." Payment for articles is made only if done on assignment. No payment for unsolicited articles. Pays $200 for photographic essays done on assignment.

VICTIMOLOGY: An International Journal, Box 39045, Washington DC 20016. Editor-in-Chief: Emilio C. Viano. "We are the only magazine specifically focusing on the victim, on the dynamics of victimization; for social scientists, criminal justice professionals and practitioners, social workers and volunteer and professional groups engaged in prevention of victimization and in offering assistance to victims of rape, spouse abuse, child abuse, natural disasters, etc." Quarterly magazine. Estab. 1976. Circ. 2,500. Pays on publication. Buys all rights. SASE. Reports in 6-8 weeks. Sample copy $5; free writer's guidelines.
Nonfiction: Expose; historical; how-to; informational; interview; personal experience; profile; research and technical. Buys 10 mss/issue. Query. Length: 500-5,000 words. Pays $5-50.
Photos: Purchased with accompanying ms. Captions required. Send contact sheet. Pays $15-30 for 5x7 or 8x10 b&w glossies.
Poetry: Avant-garde; free verse; light verse; and traditional. Length: 30 lines maximum. Pays $10-25.
How To Break In: "Focus on what is being researched and discovered on the victim, the victim-offender relationship, treatment of the offender, the bystander-witness, preventive measures, and what is being done in the areas of service to the victims of rape, spouse abuse, neglect and occupational and environmental hazards."

Sport and Outdoor Publications

The publications listed in this category are intended for active sportsmen, sports fans, or both. They buy material on how to practice and enjoy both team and individual sports, material on conservation of streams and forests, and articles reporting on and analyzing professional sports.

Writers will note that several of the editors mention that they do not wish to see "Me 'n Joe" stories. These are detailed accounts of one hunting/fishing trip taken by the author and a buddy—starting with the friends' awakening at dawn and ending with their return home, "tired but happy."

For the convenience of writers who specialize in one or two areas of sport and outdoor writing, the publications are subcategorized by the sport or subject matter they emphasize. Publications in related categories (for example, Hunting and Fishing; Archery and Bowhunting) often buy similar material (in this case articles on bow and arrow hunting). Consequently, writers should read through this entire Sport and Outdoor category to become familiar with the subcategories and note the ones that contain markets for their own type of writing.

Publications concerned with horse breeding, hunting dogs, or the use of other animals in sport are classified in the Animal category. Publications dealing with automobile or motorcycle racing will be found in the Automotive and Motorcycle category. Outdoor publications that exist to further the preservation of nature, placing only secondary emphasis on preserving nature as a setting for sport, are listed in the Nature, Conservation, and Ecology category. Newspapers and Magazine Sections, as well as Regional and City magazines are frequently interested in conservation or sports material with a local angle. Camping publications are classified in the Travel, Camping, and Trailer category.

Archery and Bowhunting

ARCHERY WORLD, 225 E. Michigan, Milwaukee WI 53202. Editor: Glenn Helgeland. 30-50% freelance written. For "archers—average education, hunters and target archers, experts to beginners." Subject matter is the "entire scope of archery—hunting, bowfishing, indoor target, outdoor target, field." Bimonthly. Circ. 89,000. Buys first serial rights. Buys 30 to 35 mss a year. Pays on acceptance "or as near to it as possible." Will send a free sample copy to a writer on request. Tries to report in 2 weeks. Query first. SASE.
Nonfiction: "Get a free sample and study it. Try, in ms, to entertain archer and show him how to enjoy his sport more and be better at it." Wants how-to, semitechnical, and hunting where-to and how-to articles. "Looking for more good technical stories and short how-to pieces." Also uses profiles and some humor. Length: 1,000 to 2,200 words. Payment is $50 to $150.
Photos: B&w glossies purchased with mss and with captions. "Like to see proofsheets and negs with submitted stories. We make own cropping and enlargements." Color transparencies purchased for front cover only. Will look at color prints "if that's the only photo available." Pays $5 minimum for b&w; $50 minimum for color.

BOW AND ARROW, P.O. Box HH/34249 Camino Capistrano, Capistrano Beach CA 92624. Editor: Jacqueline Farmer. 75% freelance written. For archery competitors and bowhunters. Bimonthly. Buys all rights, "but will relinquish all but first American serial rights on written request of author." Pays on acceptance. Free sample copy. Reports on submissions in 6 weeks. Author must have some knowledge of archery terms. SASE.
Nonfiction: Articles: bowhunting, major archery tournaments, techniques used by champs, how to make your own tackle, and off-trail hunting tales. Likes a touch of humor in articles. Also uses one technical article per issue. Submit complete ms. Length: 1,500 to 2,500 words. Pays $50-200.
Photos: Purchased as package with mss; 5x7 minimum or submit contacts with negatives (returned to photographer). Pays $75 to $100 for cover chromes, 35mm or larger.

BOWHUNTER MAGAZINE, P.O. Box 5377, Fort Wayne IN 46805. (219)432-5772. Editor: M. R. James. For readers of all ages, background and experience. All share 2 common passions—hunting with the bow and arrow and a love of the great outdoors. Bimonthly magazine; 80 pages. Estab. 1971. Circ. 93,000. Buys all rights, but may reassign rights to author after publication. Buys 55 mss a year. Payment on acceptance. Will send free sample copy to writer on request. Write for copy of guidelines for writers. No photocopied or simultaneous submissions. "We publish a special deer hunting annual each August. Submit seasonal material 6 to 8 months in advance." Reports within 4 to 6 weeks. Query first or submit complete ms. SASE.
Nonfiction, Photos and Fillers: "Our articles are written for, by and about bowhunters and we ask that they inform as well as entertain. Most material deals with big or small game bowhunting (how-to, where to go, etc.), but we do use some technical material and personality pieces. We do not attempt to cover all aspects of archery — only bowhunting. Anyone hoping to sell to us must have a thorough knowledge of bowhunting. Next, they must have either an interesting story to relate or a fresh approach to a common subject. We would like to see more material on what is being done to combat the anti-hunting sentiment in this country." Informational, how-to, personal experience, interview, profile, humor, historical, think articles, expose, nostalgia, personal opinion, spot news, new product, and technical articles. Length: 200 to 5,000 words. Pays $25-200. Photos purchased with accompanying ms or without ms. Captions optional. Pays $10 to $25 for 5x7 or 8x10 b&w prints; $50 minimum for 35mm or 2¼x2¼ color. Also purchases newsbreaks of 50 to 500 words for $5 to $25.
How To Break In: "The answer is simple if you know bowhunting and have some interesting, informative experiences or tips to share. Keep the reader in mind. Anticipate questions and answer them in the article. Weave information into the storyline (e.g., costs involved, services

of guide or outfitter, hunting season dates, equipment preferred and why, tips on items to bring, etc.) and, if at all possible, study back issues of the magazine. We have no set formula, really, but most articles are first-person narratives and most published material will contain the elements mentioned above."

Basketball

BASKETBALL WEEKLY, 17820 East Warren, Detroit MI 48224. (313)881-9554. Publisher: Roger Stanton. Editor: Larry Donald. 19 issues during season, September-May. Circ. 45,000. Buys all rights. Pays on publication. Sample copy for SASE. Reports in 2 weeks. Also include SASE with submissions and queries.
Nonfiction, Photos and Fillers: Current stories on teams and personalities in college and pro basketball. Length: 800 to 1,000 words. Payment is $30 to $50. 8x10 b&w glossy photos purchased with mss. Also uses newsbreaks.

HOOP, Professional Sports Publications, 600 3rd Ave., New York NY 10016. (212)697-1460. Editor: Pamela Blawie. 32-page color insert that is folded into the local magazines of each of the NBA teams. Buys all rights, but will reassign rights to author after publication, if author so requests. "For the most part, assignments are being made to newspapermen and columnists on the pro basketball beat around the country." Sample copy $1. Reports within 1 week. SASE.
Nonfiction: Features on NBA players, officials, personalities connected with league. The NBA, founded in 1946-47, is the older of the 2 established professional basketball leagues. Length: 800 to 900 words. Pays $50 per article.
How To Break In: "The best way for a freelancer to break in is to aim something for the local team section. That can be anything from articles about the players or about their wives to unusual off-court activities. The best way to handle this, is to send material directly to the P.R. person for the local team. They have to approve anything that we do on that particular team and if they like it, they forward it to me. They're always looking for new material — otherwise they have to crank it all out themselves."

Bicycling

BIKE WORLD, Box 366, Mountain View CA 94040. Editor: Bill Anderson. For bicyclists aged 5-80 interested in training, technical subjects, sophisticated touring stories at the nonbeginner level. Monthly magazine; 50 pages. Estab. 1972. Circ. 20,000. Not copyrighted. Buys 100 mss/year. Pays on publication. Free sample copy. Submit seasonal material (winter, summer and spring tours; training in winter; riding the rollers, etc.) 2 months in advance. Reports immediately. Query first or submit complete ms. Enclose SASE.
Nonfiction and Photos: Technical and touring material; physiology and race topics. "All material must be at a level beyond the beginning 'how-to'." Must be tightly written and avoid the "joys of cycling" approach. Tour stories should make the reader feel he would have a good time. Avoid chronological accounts of events that don't involve the reader. "We are more into athletics than ecology or 'romantic bikeology'." Does not want to see material on "how I bought my first 10-speed, or the Rutabaga Canners annual road race, or a peanut butter and flat tire account of a tour to Michigan's world famous glacial moraines." Would like to see material on tours that turn others on without trying to; technical articles that people can use. How to train and tour, etc. Anything of interest to cyclists who enjoy the sport. Length: open. Pays $15-20/published page; more if quality deserves it. B&w photos are purchased with or without accompanying mss or on assignment. Pays $6 for 5x7 or larger. Must have snappy contrast and be in focus. Captions required. Pays $50 for color slides used for cover. Ektachrome-X or K-II with intensity of action, mood, scenery, etc.
Fillers: News bits, technical tips. Length: 25-300 words. Pays $5 to $10.

Boating

AMERICAN BOATING ILLUSTRATED, Recreation Publications, Inc., 2019 Clement Ave., Alameda CA 94501. (415)865-7500. Managing Editor: Douglas Molitor. 75-90% freelance written. Emphasizes how-to and technical articles for an audience of boat owners who do their own work aboard; ages 20-65 with above average incomes and education. Monthly tabloid; 56 pages. Estab. January 1977. Circ. 26,000. Pays on publication. Buys all rights. Phone queries OK. Submit seasonal/holiday material 3-5 months in advance. Photocopied and previously published submissions OK. SASE. Reports in 1 month. Sample copy $1; free writer's guidelines.
Nonfiction: How-to (all manner of onboard how-to, covering cruising, fishing, electronics, sail rig and sails, onboard safety, engine repairs and installations, galley, navigation and hull and deck repairs); general interest (Update section carries general news of legislation, new safety

application, navigation rules, etc.); new product (under Gear Section, all manner of new and unusual items for onboard use: tools, adhesives, electronics, navigation, hardware, etc.); photo feature (occasionally carry photo features on one aspect of boating); how-to: (anchor stowage, rigging, galleys, etc.); and technical (how to install and do things onboard). "No first hand accounts. Nothing by novice yachtsmen." Buys 40 mss/year. Query. Length: 100-2,500 words. Pays $1.20/column inch.
Photos: "Magazine format calls for how-to articles with illustrations/photos." Pays $5 minimum for 8x10 glossies; $10 minimum for 35mm color transparencies. Captions required. Buys all rights. Model release required "if appropriate."
Columns/Departments: Handyman (short onboard how-to projects) and Ideas from Readers (a better way to do something from personal experience). Buys 12 mss/issue. Submit complete ms. Length: 100-500 words.
How To Break In: "For the boatman who's done anything aboard—building, fixing, installations, cruising, fishing—there is a wealth of personal how-to experience for *Boating Illustrated*. Write a nuts and bolts how-to piece, spelling out first a typical problem then offering a concise, step-by-step solution. The Handyman section is a great spot for short ideas."

BAY & DELTA YACHTSMAN, Recreation Publications, 2019 Clement Ave., Alameda CA 94501. (415)865-7500. Editor: Glenda Carroll. 25% freelance written. Emphasizes recreational boating for small boat owners and recreational yachtsmen in the Northern California region. Monthly tabloid newspaper; 68 pages. Estab. 1965. Circ. 17,000. Pays on publication. Buys all rights. Phone queries OK. Submit seasonal/holiday material 2 months in advance. Photocopied submissions OK. SASE. Reports in 1 month. Free writer's guidelines.
Nonfiction: Historical (nautical history of Northern California); how-to (modifications, equipment, supplies, rigging etc., aboard both power and sailboats); humor (no disaster or boating ineptitude pieces); informational (government, legislation as it relates to recreational boating); interview; new product; nostalgia; personal experience ("How I learned about boating from this" type of approach); personal opinion; photo feature (to accompany copy); profile and travel. Buys 10-15 mss/issue. Query. Length: 750-2,000 words. Pays $1/column inch.
Photos: Photos purchased with accompanying ms. Captions required. Pays $5 for b&w glossy or matte finish photos. Total purchase price for ms includes payment for photos.
Fiction: Adventure (sea stories, travel—must relate to San Francisco Bay region); fantasy; historical; humorous and mystery. Buys 5 mss/year. Query. Length: 500-1,750 words. Pays $1/columns inch.
How To Break In: "Think of our market area: the waterways of Northern California and how, why, when and where the boatman would use those waters. Think about unusual onboard application of ideas (power and sail), special cruising tips, etc. Write for a knowledgeable boating public."

BOATING, 1 Park Ave., New York NY 10016. (212)725-3972. Editor: Richard L. Rath. For powerboat enthusiasts, informed boatmen, not beginners. Publishes special Boat Show issue in January; Fall show issue in September; New York National Boat Show issue in December; Miami National Boat Show issue in February; annual maintenance issue in April. Monthly. Circ. 200,000. Buys first periodical rights. Buys 100 mss/year. Pays on acceptance. Submit seasonal material 6 to 8 months in advance. Reports in 2 months. Query first. SASE.
Nonfiction: Uses articles about cruises in powerboats with b&w or color photos, that offer more than usual interest; how-to-do-it pieces illustrated with good b&w photos or drawings; piloting articles, seamanship, etc.; new developments in boating; profiles of well-known boating people. The editor advises, "Don't talk down to the reader. Use little fantasy, emphasize the practical aspects of the subject." Length: 300-3,000 words. Payment is $25-$500, and varies according to subject and writer's skill. Regular department "Able Seaman" uses expertise on boat operation and handling; about 1,100 to 1,500 words; pays $150-300/piece.
Photos: Art Director: Shelley Heller. Buys photos submitted with mss and with captions only. 8x10 preferred, b&w. Interested in photos of happenings of interest to a national boating audience. Pays $20 to $25 each. Also buys color transparencies for both cover and interior use, 35mm slides or larger preferred. Pays $100 to $300 for one-time usage, "but not for anything that has previously appeared in a boating publication."
Fillers: Uses short items pertaining to boating that have an unusual quality of historical interest, timeliness, or instruction. Pays $50 to $100.
How To Break In: "From a time-invested standpoint, it would make sense for the beginning writer to try a short filler subject for us, rather than to go for the jackpot. Unless, of course, he has a great story or article that will sell itself. Acceptability of a piece for our magazine hinges at least as much on the quality of the writing as it does on the subject matter. One man will take a trip around the world and produce bilge water for a manuscript; another, like E. B. White, will

row across Central Park Lake and make it a great adventure in the human experience. There's no substitute for talent."

BOATING NEWS, 26 Coal Harbour Wharf, 566 Cardero St., Vancouver, British Columbia Canada V6G 2W7. Editor: Don Tyrell. 10% freelance written. Emphasizes sail and power boating. Monthly newspaper; 16 pages. Circ. 21,000. Pays on acceptance. Buys one-time rights. Phone queries OK. Submit seasonal/holiday material 2 months in advance of issue date. Simultaneous, photocopied, and previously published submissions OK. SASE. Reports in 3 weeks. Free sample copy; mention *Writer's Market* in request.
Nonfiction: How-to (useful boating tips); new product; personal experience; and photo feature. Also some news of commercial fishing activities. No long articles. Pays $25.
Photos: Pays $10 for 5x7 b&w prints. Captions required. Buys one-time rights. Model release required.
Fiction: Buys 12 mss/year. Query.

CANOE MAGAZINE, The Webb Co., 1999 Shepard Rd., St. Paul MN 55116. (612)647-7450. Editor: John Viehman. For an audience ranging from the weekend recreational canoeist to Olympic caliber flatwater, racing, marathon, poling and sailing canoe and kayak enthusiasts. Bimonthly magazine; 56 pages. Estab. 1973. Circ. 155,000. Buys all rights, but may reassign rights to author after publication. Buys about 30 mss a year. Pays on acceptance. Free sample copy and writer's guidelines. Reports in 45 days. Query or submit complete ms. SASE.
Nonfiction and Photos: "We publish a variety of canoeing and kayaking articles, but strive for a balanced mix of stories about trips and competitive events to interest all participants in the activity, recreational or competitive. Also interested in any articles dealing with conservation issues which may adversely affect the sport. Writing should be readable rather than academic; clever rather than endlessly descriptive. Diary type first-person style not desirable. A good, provocative lead is considered a prime ingredient. We want stories about trips in the contiguous 50 states that canoers/kayakers of average ability can identify with. We are interested in use of American waterways and legislation which affect that use. Also interested in articles about safety and training or expansion of the sport to the greatest number of people." Length: 2,000 words maximum. Pays $25-$150. Will consider relevant book reviews. Length: 200 to 500 words. Payment begins at $25. B&w and color purchased with accompanying ms, or on assignment. Pays $15 minimum for b&w; $25 minimum for color. Size: 35mm or larger.

CRUISING WORLD, P.O. Box 452, Newport RI 02840. (401)847-1588. Editor: Murray Davis. 75% freelance written. For all those who cruise under sail. Monthly magazine; 112 pages. Estab. 1974. Circ. 70,000. Rights purchased vary with author and material. May buy first North American serial rights or first serial rights. Pays on publication. Free guidelines for writers. Reports in about 8 weeks. Submit complete ms. SASE.
Nonfiction and Photos: "We are interested in seeing informative articles on the technical and enjoyable aspects of cruising under sail. Also subjects of general interest to seafarers." Length: 500 to 3,500 words. Pays $50 minimum. B&w prints (5x7) and color transparencies purchased with accompanying ms.

INTERNATIONAL YACHTSMAN, Hixson Industries, Inc., 4519 Admiralty Way, #206, Marina del Rey CA 90291. (213)822-9555. Editor-in-Chief: Lee Anderson. 80% freelance written. "*International Yachtsman* is designed and written as a shelf companion for other fine volumes of pictorial and literary excellence. It is edited for worldwide circulation and appeals to yachting enthusiasts, sail and motorboat owners and non-boaters with a venturesome sea spirit and an appreciation of superior waterscape photography." Quarterly magazine; 72 pages. Estab. June 1977. Circ. 10,000. Pays on acceptance. Buys one-time world rights. Phone queries OK, "but story approval is made only after submission." Simultaneous, photocopied and previously published submissions OK. Reports in 4 weeks. Sample copy "free, on approval of query;" free writer's guidelines.
Nonfiction: "Articles of interest to us must relate to one of 9 major department headings which remain constant from issue to issue. These are: On Board (pictorial tours through the interiors of the world's great yachts); Hideaways (revealing explorations into little known and intriguing resorts, harbors, and anchorages); Personality (true-life scrapbook biographies of outstanding yachtsmen and their exceptional experiences afloat); Heritage (photographically creative treatments of yachts or other watercraft of yesteryear); Artisans (reports of talented yacht craftsmen or hobbiests, including their work in painting, sculpture, model-building or design); Galley Gourmet (appetizing collections of practical recipes for the galley chef); Locale (a yachtsman's photo-guide through unusual cruising areas, highlighting their best seasons, ac-

commodations and points of interest); Fashions Afloat (the latest nautical styles captured in and about exotic waterfronts) Classic Cruises (descriptive photo-logs of rare and daring adventures on the seven seas); and Celebrity Yachtsmen (an inside look at glamorous vessels owned and operated by skippers in the public spotlight). Because *International Yachtsman* caters to a global market, all articles must be of an international nature. Any subject photographed within the continental United States will be accepted only if it commands worldwide interest as a truly unique feature in and of itself. We are not interested in technical articles, how-to features on boating equipment and techniques, and stories dealing with racing events, new products, industry news items or any other subject of a timely nature." Buys 28 mss/year. Query with clips of previously published work. Length: 1,000-3,000 words. Pays $100-500.
Photos: "We are a pictorial quarterly and selection of features is based primarily on photographic excellence. With the exception of cover shots, single photos cannot be considered for publication unless they are incorporated into a complete layout." Pays $50-150 for 35mm or larger color transparencies.

MOTORBOAT MAGAZINE, 38 Commercial Wharf, Boston MA 02110. (617)723-5800. Editor: Peter L. Smyth. For powerboat owners and devotees. Estab. 1973. Monthly. Buys all rights. Buys 50 mss per year. Payment on acceptance. Free sample copy and writer's guidelines. Photocopied submissions OK. Will not consider simultaneous submissions. Reports on material in 4 weeks. "Queries are welcome, but the editor reserves the right to withhold his final decision until the completed article has been reviewed." SASE.
Nonfiction and Photos: "We are the only magazine devoted purely to motorboating and use informative, educational articles which instruct the reader without treating him as a novice. Subject matter may cover any aspect of motorboating including profiles, technical stories, maintenance, sportfishing, cruising and seamanship. Houseboat articles with the emphasis on in-land cruising are welcome, as well as big boat cruising stories and articles dealing with mechanical subjects (engines). But, no sailing, please." Length: 2,500 words maximum. Pays $150 to $500. 8x10 b&w glossies purchased with mss. Color (35mm or larger) used on cover. Pays $300 to $400 for color used on cover.

OUTDOORS, Outdoors Bldg., Columbia MO 65201. (314)449-3119. Editor-in-Chief: Lee Cullimore. 90% freelance written. Emphasizes outdoor boating for families—fishermen, water skiers, men, women, children—boat campers. Monthly magazine; 36 pages. Estab. 1958. Pays on acceptance. Buys one-time rights. Submit seasonal/holiday material 3 months in advance. SASE. Reports in 3 weeks. Free sample copy and writer's guidelines.
Nonfiction: Historical (boating oriented); how-to (fishing, boating); informational (boat camping, hints, tips); profile (of areas, boating oriented); and travel (fishing and boating locations). Buys 8 mss/issue. Query. Length: 1,200 words maximum. Pays $25-150.
Photos: Purchased with or without (occasionally) accompanying ms. Captions required. Send contact sheet or transparencies. Uses 8x10 b&w glossies and 35mm or larger color transparencies. Total purchase for ms includes payment for photos.

POWERBOAT MAGAZINE, 15917 Strathern St., Van Nuys CA 91406. Editor: Bob Brown. 30% freelance written. For performance-conscious boating enthusiasts. January, Boat show issue; March, Jet drive issue; June, Water ski issue; October, Outboard issue; November, Stern Drive issue. Monthly. Circ. 50,000. Buys all rights or 1-time North American serial rights. Pays on publication. Free sample copy. Reports in 2 weeks. Query required. SASE.
Nonfiction and Photos: Uses articles about power boats and water skiing that offer special interest to performance-minded boaters, how-to-do-it pieces with good b&w pictures, developments in boating, profiles on well-known boating and skiing individuals, competition coverage of national and major events. Length: 1,500 to 2,000 words. Pays $100 to $150 per article. Photos purchased with mss. Prefers 8x10 b&w. 2¼x2¼ color transparency preferred for cover; top quality vertical 35mm considered. Pays $50 to $100 for 1-time use.

SAIL, 38 Commercial Wharf, Boston MA 02110. (617)227-0888. Editor: Keith Taylor. For audience that is "strictly sailors, average age 35, better than average education." Special issues: "Cruising issues, fitting-out issues, special race issues (e.g., America's Cup), boat show issues." Monthly. Buys first North American serial rights. Buys 200 mss a year. Pays on publication. Free sample copy. Submit seasonal or special material at least 3 months in advance. Returns rejected material in 4 weeks. Acknowledges acceptance of material in 1 month. SASE.
Nonfiction: Wants "articles on sailing: technical, techniques, and feature stories." Interested in how-to, personal experience, profiles, historical, new product, and photo articles. "Generally emphasize the excitement of sail and the human, personal aspect." Length: 1,000-3,000 words. Pays $100 minimum.

Photos: B&w glossies purchased with mss. Payment is from $20. Color transparencies purchased. Payment is from $35; $300 for covers.

SAILING MAGAZINE, 125 East Main St., Port Washington WI 53074. (414)284-2626. Editor: William F. Schanen III. For readers mostly between ages of 35 and 44, some professionals. About 75% of them own their own sailboat. Monthly magazine; 64 pages. Estab. 1966. Circ. 25,000. Not copyrighted. Buys 12 mss/year. Pays on publication. Write for copy of guidelines for writers. Will consider photocopied and simultaneous submissions. Reports within 1 month. Query first or submit complete ms. Enclose SASE.
Nonfiction and Photos: Micca Leffingwell Hutchins, Managing Editor. "Experiences of sailing whether curising, racing or learning. We require no special style. We're devoted exclusively to sailing and sailboat enthusiasts, and particularly interested in articles about the trend toward cruising in the sailing world." Informational, personal experience, profile, historical, travel, and book reviews. Length: open. Payment negotiable. B&w photos purchased with or without accompanying ms. Captions required. Pays $10 for each 8x10 b&w glossy used; also flat fee for series.

SEA, CBS Publications, 1499 Monrovia Ave., Newport Beach CA 92663. (714)646-4451. Editor-in-Chief: Chris Caswell. Managing Editor: Harry Monahan. 60% freelance written. Emphasizes recreational boating. Monthly magazine; 130 pages. Estab. 1884. Circ. 191,000. Pays on acceptance. Buys first North American serial rights. Submit seasonal/holiday material 6 months in advance of issue date. SASE. Reports in 5 weeks. Free sample copy and writer's guidelines.
Nonfiction: How-to (improvements to basic boat gear or procedures/techniques which will improve boat use or maintenance); interview (boating personality with a viewpoint of interest to other boat-owners); personal experience (involving use of boat, an experience profitable to other boat-owners); and travel (where-to and how-to go by boat). Buys 20 mss/issue. Query. Length: 3,000 words. Pays 10¢/word.
Photos: "Format of magazine requires illustrations for 90% of articles used; if we can't find suitable illustration material, the story is useless." State availability of photos with query or submit photo material with ms. Pays $20-25 for 8x10 b&w glossy contact sheets and negatives and $75-300 for 35mm color transparencies. Captions preferred. Buys one-time rights. Model release is required.

SPYGLASS, Spyglass Catalog Co., 2415 Mariner Square Dr., Alameda CA 94501. (415)769-8410. Managing Editor: Dick Moore. 10% freelance written. Emphasizes all aspects of sailing. "For sailors of all ages interested in the perfection of the activity, the betterment of the sailboat, the best available gear and how to apply it." Annual magazine; 480 pages. Estab. 1973. Circ. 25,000. Pays on publication. Buys first North American serial rights. Phone queries OK. Submit material 4 months prior to year's end. Previously published submissions OK. SASE. Reports in 1 month. Sample copy $1.
Nonfiction: Historical (old salts, old boats, old seaports); how-to (any build-it-yourself, repair-it-yourself, remodel-it-yourself, or rig-it-yourself hints on any facet of sailing); informational (on sailing technique, new developments in construction of the sailboat, navigation, racing or cruising); interview (or profile on noted naval architects, boatbuilders, racing or cruising personalities); personal experience (anything that is educational or has some hard lessons to be learned. No travelogues, but better ways to cruise); photo essays (emphasizing innovative apparatus utilizing stock equipment, or custom set-ups), and technical (any aspect of sails, boat construction, electronics and racing tactics). Buys 20 mss/year. Query. Length: 750-3,500 words. Pays 7½¢/word.
Photos: Photos purchased without accompanying ms. Captions required, except for full-page filler photos which should be either action or aesthetic shots. Pays $10-15 for b&w and color photos. Total purchase price for ms includes payment for photos.
How To Break In: "First, include a basic outline with the query. Too often a proposed subject melds into an overworked area of sailing. Because it's an annual, each piece must 'last' all year. We have a keen interest in the practical 'how-to' pieces. Also, we are a West Coast-based publication with a national readership and need more input from the Great Lakes, Gulf Coast and Eastern boating scene."

WOODENBOAT, Box 78, Brooklin ME 04616. Editor-in-Chief: Jonathan Wilson. Managing Editor: Jacqueline Michaud. Readership is composed mainly of owners, builders, and designers of wooden boats. Bimonthly magazine; 120 pages. Estab. 1974. Circ. 25,000. Pays on publica-

tion. Buys first North American serial rights. Photocopied and previously published submissions OK. SASE. Reports in 2 months. Sample copy $2.50; writer's guidelines for SASE.
Nonfiction: Historical (detailed evolution of boat types of famous designers or builders of wooden boats); how-to (repair, restore, build or maintain wooden boats); informational (technical detail on repairs/restoration/construction); new product (documented by facts or statistics on performance of product); personal opinion (backed up by experience and experimentation in boat building, restoring, maintaining, etc.); photo feature (with in-depth captioning and identification of boats); and technical (on adhesives and other boat-building products and materials, or on particular phases of repair or boat construction). Buys 85 mss/year. Submit complete ms. Length: 1,200-3,500 words. Pays 5¢/word.
Photos: Purchased with or without (only occasionally) accompanying ms. Captions required. Send prints, negatives or transparencies. Pays $10 for 8x10 high contrast B&w glossies; $15 minimum for color transparencies.
Columns/Departments: Newsfront (seeking news on developments and contemporary trends of wooden boat construction); and Book Reviews (on wooden boats and related subjects). Buys 1 mss/issue. Length: 300-800 words. Pays 5¢/word.
How To Break In: "Because we are bimonthly, and issues are scheduled well in advance, freelancers should bear in mind that if their material is accepted, it will inevitably be some time before publication can be arranged. We seek innovative and informative ideas in freelancers' manuscripts, and the degree to which research and careful attention has been paid in compiling an article must be apparent. We're not looking for scholarly treatises, rather detailed and thought-out material reflecting imagination and interest in the subject."

YACHTING, Yachting Publishing Corp., 50 West 44th Street, New York NY 10036. (212)391-1000. Editor: William W. Robinson. For yachtsmen interested in powerboats and sailboats. Monthly. Circ. 128,000. Buys North American serial rights only. Reports on submissions in 3 weeks. SASE.
Nonfiction and Photos: Nuts-and-bolts articles on all phases of yachting; good technical pieces on motors, electronics, and sailing gear. "We're overloaded with cruising articles —everyone seems to be going around Cape Horn in a bathtub." Length: 3,000 words maximum. Pays 10¢ per word. Article should be accompanied by 6 to 8 photos. Pays $25 each for b&w photos, "more for color when used." Will accept a story without photos, if story is outstanding.

Bowling and Billiards

BILLIARDS DIGEST, National Bowlers Journal, Inc., 875 N. Michigan Ave., Suite 3734, Chicago IL 60611. (312)266-7179. Editor-in-Chief: Larry Breckenridge. 25% freelance written. Emphasizes billiards/pool for "readers who are accomplished players and hard core fans—also a trade readership." Bimonthly magazine; 48 pages. Estab. September 1978. Circ. 5,000. Pays on publication. Buys all rights, but may reassign following publication. Phone queries OK. Submit seasonal/holiday material 2 months in advance of issue date. Simultaneous, photocopied and previously published submissions OK. SASE. Reports in 2 weeks. Sample copy $1; free writer's guidelines.
Nonfiction: General interest (tournament results, features on top players); historical (features on greats of the game); how-to (how to improve your game, your billiard room, billiards table maintenance); humor (anecdotes, any humorous feature dealing with billiards); interview (former and current stars, industry leaders); new product (any new product dealing with billiards, short 'blip' or feature); and profile (former and current stars—prefer current stars). No basic news stories. "We want features which provide in-depth material, including anecdotes, atmosphere, and facts." Buys 3 mss/issue. Query. Length: 1,000-1,500 words. Pays $40-75.
Photos: State availability of photos with query. Pays $5-25 for 8x10 b&w glossy prints; $5-25 for 35mm or 2¼x2¼ color transparencies. Captions preferred. Buys all rights.

BOWLERS JOURNAL, 875 N. Michigan, Chicago IL 60611. (312)266-7171. Editor-in-Chief: Mort Luby. Managing Editor: Jim Dressel. 30% freelance written. Emphasizes bowling. Monthly magazine: 100 pages. Estab. 1913. Circ. 18,000. Pays on publication. Buys all rights. Phone queries OK. Submit seasonal/holiday material 2 months in advance of issue date. Photocopied submissions OK. SASE. Reports in 2 weeks. Sample copy $1.
Nonfiction: General interest (stories on top pros); historical (stories of old time bowlers or bowling alleys); interview (top pros, men and women); and profile (top pros). Buys 2 mss/issue. Query. Length: 1,200-3,500 words. Pays $50-150.
Photos: State availability of photos with query. Pays $5-15 for 8x10 b&w prints; and $5-20 for 35mm or 2¼x2¼ color transparencies. Buys one-time rights.

BOWLING, 5301 S. 76 St., Greendale WI 53129. (414)421-6400. Ext. 230. Editor: David DeLorenzo. Official publication of the American Bowling Congress. Monthly. Estab. 1934. Rights purchased vary with author and material. Usually buys all rights. Pays on publication. Reports within 30 days. SASE.
Nonfiction and Photos: "This is a specialized field and the average writer attempting the subject of bowling should be well-informed. However, anyone is free to submit material for approval." Wants articles about unusual ABC leagues and tournaments, personalities, etc., featuring male bowlers. Length: 500 to 1,200 words. Pays $25 to $100 per article; $10 to $15 per photo.
How To Break In: "Submit feature material on bowlers, generally amateurs competing in local leagues, or special events involving the game of bowling. Should have connection with ABC membership."

STRIKE, The Magazine for Bowlers, Box 428, Cocoa Beach FL 32931. Executive Editor: Edith Stull. 10% freelance written. Emphasizes Florida bowling. Monthly magazine; 28 pages. Estab. 1977. Pays on publication. Buys all rights. Submit seasonal/holiday material 3 months in advance of issue date. Simultaneous, photocopied, and previously published submissions OK. SASE. Reports in 2 weeks. Free sample copy; mention *Writer's Market* in request.
Nonfiction: General interest (to Florida bowlers); historical (on bowling); interview; new product; photo feature; and profile. Query. Pays $10 minimum.
Photos: State availability of photos with query. Pays $5 for b&w contact sheets. Captions required. Buys one-time rights.

THE WOMAN BOWLER, 5301 S. 76th St., Greendale WI 53129. (414)421-9000. Editor: Mrs. Helen Latham. Emphasizes bowling for women bowlers, ages 8-90. Monthly (except for combined May/June, July/August issues) magazine; 48 pages. Estab. 1936. Circ. 135,000. Pays on acceptance. Buys all rights. Phone queries OK. Submit seasonal/holiday material 2 months in advance. Photocopied and previously published submissions OK. SASE. Reports in 1 month. Free sample copy and writer's guidelines.
Nonfiction: Historical (about bowling and of national significance); interview; profile; and spot news. Buys 25 mss/year. Query. Length: 1,000 words maximum (unless by special assignment). Pays $15-50.
Photos: Purchased with accompanying ms. Identification required. Query. Pays $5-10 for b&w glossies. Model release required.

Football

ALL SOUTH CAROLINA FOOTBALL ANNUAL, Box 3, Columbia SC 29202. (803)796-9200. Editor: Sidney L. Wise. Associate Editor: Doug Murphy. Issued annually, August 1. Buys first rights. Pays on publication. Deadline for material each year is 10 weeks preceding publication date. Query first. SASE.
Nonfiction and Photos: Material must be about South Carolina high school and college football teams, players and coaches. Pays 3¢ minimum a word. Buys photos with ms. Captions required. 5x7 or 8x10 b&w glossies; 4x5 or 35mm color transparencies. Uses color on cover only. Pays $5 minimum for b&w; $10 minimum for color.

FOOTBALL NEWS, 17820 E. Warren, Detroit MI 48224. Editor: Roger Stanton. 25% freelance written. For avid grid fans. Weekly tabloid published during football season; 24 pages. Estab. 1939. Circ. 100,000. Not copyrighted. Buys 12 to 15 mss a year. Payment on publication. Will send sample copy to writer for 25¢. Reports in 1 month. Query first. SASE.
Nonfiction: Articles on players, officials, coaches, past and present, with fresh approach. Highly informative, concise, positive approach. Interested in profiles of former punt, pass and kick players who have made the pros. Interview, profile, historical, think articles, and exposes. Length: 800-1,000 words. Pays $35-75/ms.

Gambling

GAMBLING TIMES MAGAZINE, 839 Highland Ave., Hollywood CA 90038. (213)466-5261. Editor: Len Miller. 25% freelance written. Monthly magazine; 100 pages. Estab. February 1977. Circ. 100,000. Pays on publication. Buys first North American serial rights. Submit seasonal/holiday material 3-6 months in advance of issue date. Photocopied and previously published submissions OK. SASE. Reports in 1 month. Free writer's guidelines; mention *Writer's Market* in request.

Nonfiction: Roger Dionne, features editor. How-to (relating to gambling systems, betting methods, etc.); humor; photo feature (race tracks, jai alai, casinos); and travel (gambling spas and resort areas). "Also interested in articles on gambling personalities, the history of gambling, and local gambling activities around the United States and the world." Buys 100 mss/year. Query. Length: open. Pays $50-150.
Fiction: "We only use gambling related material." Buys 12 mss/year. Submit complete ms. Pays $50-150.
Fillers: Gambling types only. Jokes, gags, anecdotes, and short humor. Buys 12/issue. Pays $5-25.

THE PLAYERS' NEWSLETTER, 1019 Beacon St., Boston MA 02146. Editor-in-Chief: S.D. Bort. For consumers and sports fans of billiards, pool, and all other sports. Monthly newsletter; 8 pages. Pays on publication. Buys simultaneous rights. Submit seasonal/holiday material 4 months in advance of issue date. Simultaneous and previously published submissions OK. SASE. Reports in 1-2 months.
Nonfiction: Exposé (all types); how-to; humor; informational; new product; and photo feature. Buys 6 mss/issue. Submit complete ms. Pays $20-750.
Photos: State availability of photos with ms. Pays $20-200 for b&w prints; $20-350 for color. Model release required.
Fiction: Erotica; fantasy; and science fiction. Buys 25 mss/year. Submit complete ms. Pays $20-750.
Fillers: Clippings; and newsbreaks. Submit fillers. Length: 15-150 words. Pays $5-50.

REFEREE, Mano Enterprises, Inc., Box 161, Franksville WI 53126. (414)632-8855. Editor-in-Chief: Barry Mano. For well-educated, mostly 26-50-year-old male sports officials. Monthly magazine; 48 pages. Estab. 1976. Circ. 32,000. Pays either on acceptance or publication. Buys all rights. Submit seasonal/holiday material 3 months in advance. Photocopied and previously published submissions OK. SASE. Reports in 4 weeks. Free sample copy.
Nonfiction: How-to; informational; humor; interview; profile; personal experience; photo feature and technical. Buys 54 mss/year. Query. Length: 1,850-3,000 words. Pays $75-150. "No general sports articles."
Photos: Tom Hammill, Photo Editor. Purchased with or without accompanying ms or on assignment. Captions required. Send contact sheet, prints, negatives or transparencies. Pays $10-20 for 8x10 b&w prints; $25-50 for 35mm or 2¼x2¼ color transparencies.
Columns/Departments: The Arena (bios) and Guest Editorial (controversial topics). Buys 24 mss/year. Query. Length: 1,200-1,800 words. Pays $50 minimum.
Fillers: Rudy Mano, Fillers Editor. Jokes, gags, anecdotes, puzzles, sport shorts. Query. Length: 50-200 words. Pays $10-15.

General Sports Interest

AAU NEWS, Amateur Athletic Union of the United States, AAU House, 3400 W. 86th St., Indianapolis IN 46268. (317)297-2900. Editor: Martin E. Weiss. Asssociate Editor: Pete Cava. Emphasizes amateur sports. Monthly magazine; 16 pages. Estab. 1925. Circ. 15,000. Pays on publication. Buys one-time rights. Phone queries OK. SASE. Reports in 2 weeks. Free sample copy.
Nonfiction: "General subject matter is profiles of top amateur athletes and athletic volunteers or leaders. Reports on AAU championships, previews of coming seasons, etc. Buys interviews, profiles, photo features, sport book reviews and spot news articles. Length: 1,000 words maximum. Pays $10-50.
Photos: Photos purchased with or without accompanying ms or on assignment. Captions required. Pays $5-25 for 8½x11 b&w glossies; $10-25 for any size color transparencies. No additional payment for photos accepted with accompanying ms. Model release required.
How To Break In: "By staying within the framework of AAU sports: Basketball, baton twirling, bobsledding, boxing, diving, gymnastics, handball, horseshoe pitching, judo, karate, luge, powerlifting, physique, swimming, synchronized swimming, taekwondo, track and field, volleyball, water polo, weightlifting, wrestling and trampoline and tumbling; also AAU Junior Olympics and all matters pertaining to Olympic development in AAU sports."

ALL OUTDOORS, 13222 Saticoy St., N. Hollywood CA 91605. (213)982-3700. Editor-in-Chief: Don Magary. "We are a family outdoors magazine." Monthly magazine; 64 pages. Estab. 1968. Circ. 50,000. Pays on publication. Buys first North American serial rights. Submit seasonal/holiday material 6 months in advance of issue date. SASE. Reports in 1 month. Sample copy

$1.25; writer's guidelines for SASE.
Nonfiction: Pat Corsa, articles editor. How-to; historical; interview; new product; nostalgia; photo feature; profile; outdoor leisure (family activities); and travel. No "Me and Joe" articles. Buys 10 mss/issue. Query. Length: 1,500-2,000 words. Pays $50-150.
Photos: Offers no additional payment for b&w photos accepted with ms. Submit 8x10 b&w glossy prints; pays $25-75 for 35mm color transparencies. Captions required. Buys all rights, but may reassign following publication.
Fillers: Short humor. Buys 2-3/issue. Pays $25.

OUTDOOR CANADA MAGAZINE, 181 Eglinton Ave. E., Suite 201, Toronto, Ontario Canada M4P 1J9. (416)487-1159. Editor-in-Chief: Sheila Kaighin. 50% freelance written. Emphasizes non-competitive outdoor recreation. Published 7 times/year; magazine; 64-80 pages. Estab. December 1972. Circ. 50,079. Pays on publication. Buys all rights, but may reassign following publication. Phone queries OK. Submit seasonal/holiday material 5-6 months in advance of issue date. Photocopied submissions OK. SASE. Reports in 4 weeks. Sample copy $1; free writer's guidelines; mention *Writer's Market* in request.
Nonfiction: Exposé (only as it pertains to the outdoors, i.e. wildlife management); and how-to (in-depth, thorough pieces on how to select equipment for various subjects, or improve techniques only as it relates to outdoor subjects covered). Buys 35-40 mss/year. Submit complete ms. Length: 1,000-3,500 words. Pays $50-150.
Photos: Submit photo material with accompanying ms. Pays $5-25 for 8x10 b&w glossy prints and $35-100 for 35mm color transparencies. Captions preferred. Buys all rights. Model release required.
Fillers: Outdoor tips. Buys 7/year. Length: 350-500 words. Pays $20.

SOUTHWEST SPORTS, Box 25024, Albuquerque NM 87125. (505)265-8478. Editor: Greg Lay. 45-65% freelance written. Emphasizes health, regional sports and recreation. Monthly magazine: 56 pages. Estab. 1978. Circ. 20,000. Pays on publication. Buys all rights, but may reassign following publication; and second serial rights. Submit seasonal/holiday material 4 months in advance of issue date. Photocopied and previously published (in different region) submissions OK. SASE. Reports in 2-4 weeks. Sample copy $1.00; free writer's guidelines; mention *Writer's Market* in request.
Nonfiction: Expose (amateurism, sports government); how-to (something unique, not trite advice column); general interest; humor; historical (talk about people, not dry facts); inspirational; interview (stars or other athletes with something to say, coaches); new product (sports equipment, recreational travel); nostalgia; personal experience; opinion (how to improve sports or recreationl facilities); photo feature; profile; and travel (southwest recreational). "We use very little material that does not fit our *regional* approach." Buys 5-10 mss/issue. Query on major projects; submit complete ms on short articles. Length: 500-5,000 words. Pays $25-200.
Photos: Submit photo material with accompanying query or ms. Pays $5-100 for 5x7 or 8x10 b&w glossy prints; $5-150 for 5x7 or 8x10 matte color prints or 2¼x2¼ transparencies. Captions and model release required. Buys all rights, but may reassign following publication.
Columns/Department: Book reviews (sports and southwest); editor's page (opinion or sidelights); equipment (evaluation of sports, travel and equipment); poetry (southwest); profiles (200 words of sports achievements); and schools (sports programs and facilities at southwest colleges). Submit complete ms. Length: 200-1,000 words. Pays $5-50. Open for suggestions for new columns/departments.
Fiction: Adventure (sports, outdoors) historical (outdoors); humorous (sports, health, and outdoors); western (possibly); and serialized novels (possibly). Submit complete ms. Length: 500-5,000 words. Pays $25-1,500.
Poetry: Avant-garde, free verse, light verse, traditional and southwest outdoors. Buys 1-4/issue. Limit submissions to batches of 3. Length: 4-64 words. Pays $5-25.

SPORTING NEWS, 1212 N. Lindbergh Blvd., St. Louis MO 63132. "We do not actively solicit freelance material."

SPORTS ILLUSTRATED, Time & Life Bldg., Rockefeller Center, New York NY 10020. Outside Text Editor: Robert Creamer. Primarily staff-written, with small but steady amount of outside material. Weekly. Reports in 2 to 3 weeks. Pays on acceptance. Buys all rights or North American serial rights. SASE.
Nonfiction: Material falls into two general categories: regional (text that runs in editorial space accompanying regional advertising pages) and long text. Runs a great deal of regional advertising and, as a result, considerable text in that section of the magazine. Regional text does not

have a geographical connotation; it can be any sort of short feature (600 to 2,000 words): historical, humor, reminiscence, personality, opinion, first-person, but it must deal with some aspect of sports, however slight. Long text (2,000 to 5,000 words) also must have sporting connection, however tenuous; should be major personality, personal reminiscence, knowing look into a significant aspect of a sporting subject, but long text should be written for broad appeal, so that readers without special knowledge will appreciate the piece. Wants quality writing. Pays $250 minimum for regional pieces, $1,000 minimum for long text. Smaller payments are made for material used in special sections or departments.
Photos: "Do not care to see photos until story is purchased."
How To Break In: "One possibility would be an item for the section, As I Saw It. These can be as short as 950 words; can be a personal experience. A happening in sports which occurred prior to the inception of the magazine in 1954 is called Yesterday."

THE SPORTS INFORMER, 3437 NE 12th Terrace, Fort Lauderdale FL 33334. (305)563-8331. Editor-in-Chief: Peter Fiocco. 90% freelance written. Emphasizes sports, nutrition, and conditioning. Biweekly tabloid; 40 pages. Estab. February 1978. Pays on publication. Buys all rights, but may reassign following publication. Phone queries OK. Submit seasonal/holiday material 2 months in advance of issue date. Simultaneous, photocopied and previously published submissions OK. SASE. Free sample copy; mention *Writer's Market* in request.
Nonfiction: Exposé; general interest; historical; how-to; humor; interview; personal opinion; profile; and technical. Buys 120 mss/year. Submit complete ms. Length: 500 words. Pays 5-8¢/word.
Photos: State availability of photos with ms. Pays $10 for b&w prints. Buys all rights, but may reassign following publication.
Fillers: Clippings, joke, gags, anecdotes and newsbreaks. Pays 5-8¢/word.

THE SPORTS JOURNAL, 206-110A Meridian Rd., NE., Calgary, Alberta, Canada T2A 2N6. (403)273-5141. Editor-in-Chief: Richard J. Mackay. 80% freelance written. Monthly tabloid; 32 pages. Estab: May 1976. Circ. 30,000. Pays on publication. Buys all rights. Phone queries OK. Submit seasonal/holiday material 1 month in advance of issue date. Simultaneous, photocopied and previously published submissions OK. SASE. Reports in 1 month. Free sample copy and writer's guidelines; mention *Writer's Market* in request.
Nonfiction: General interest; interview (sports figures); nostalgia (sports history); personal opinion (on sports-related topics); and profile. Buys 15-25 mss/issue. Submit complete ms. Length: 200-600 words. Pays $10-75.
Photos: "We do not pay extra for photos accompanying mss, but the ms stands a much better chance for publication if photos are included." Submit photos with ms. Uses b&w prints. Buys one-time rights.
Columns/Departments: "We cover all major sports; coverage can be by league, team, or invividual players." Submit complete ms. Length: 200-600 words. Pays $10-75.

SPORTSHELF NEWS, P.O. Box 634, New Rochelle NY 10802. Editor: Irma Ganz. For "all ages interested in sports." Estab. 1949. Bimonthly. Circ. 150,000. Pays on acceptance. Query first required. SASE.
Nonfiction: Subject matter is exclusively sports. Buys how-to articles. Payment varies, "averages about $50 for 1,000 words."

TEXAS OUTDOOR GUIDE, Box 55573, Houston TX 77055. (713)525-1026. Managing Editor: Stan Slaton. 100% freelance written. Emphasizes outdoor sports. Bimonthly magazine; 84 pages. Estab. 1968. Circ. 100,000. Pays on publication. Buys all rights but may reassign following publication. Phone queries OK. Submit seasonal/holiday material 3 months in advance. SASE. Reports in 3 months. Free sample copy and writer's guidelines.
Nonfiction: How-to (sporting ideas, hunting and fishing tips, etc.); interview, new product and photo feature. Buys 30 mss/year. Query. Length: 1,000-3,000 words. Pays $50-500.
Photos: Purchased with accompanying ms or on assignment. Captions required. Considers b&w or color. Query. Total purchase price for ms includes payment for photos. Model release required.

Golf

CAROLINA GOLFER, Box 3, Columbia SC 29202. (803)796-9200. Editor: Sydney L. Wise. Associate Editor: Doug Murphy. Bimonthly. Buys first rights. Payment on publication. Free sample copy. Reports in 3 to 8 weeks. SASE.

Nonfiction and Photos: Articles on golf and golfers, clubs, courses, tournaments, only in the Carolinas. Stories on the various courses should be done "in the manner that would give the reader a basic idea of what each course is like." Length: 1,200 to 1,500 words. Pays according to quality of ms; 3¢ minimum per word. Buys photos with mss. 5x7 or 8x10 b&w glossies. Color should be 4x5 or 35mm transparencies. Pays $5 minimum for b&w; $25 for color transparencies used for cover.

COUNTRY CLUB GOLFER, 2171 Campus Dr., Irvine CA 92715. (714)752-6474. Editor: Edward F. Pazdur. For private country club members and club golfers; professional, affluent, college-educated. Magazine; 60 pages. Estab. 1972. Monthly. Circ. 65,000. Buys all rights, but may reassign rights to author after publication. Buys about 6 mss a year. Pays on publication. Sample copy for $1. Will consider photocopied and simultaneous submissions. Reports in 10 days. Query first with 1-page outline. SASE.
Nonfiction and Photos: Editorial material is confined to country club activities, primarily golf. Anything reflecting country club life styles will be considered; golfing or social activities, etc. No specific style, but prefers informative articles slanted toward the more mature, affluent golfer. Informative features on fashions for country clubs, as well as on how to entertain, give parties, etc. Tips on golfing better. "But, we are not heavily golf instruction oriented since we are the *Esquire* of golf for more mature golfers." Length: open. Pays minimum of $75. No additional payment for b&w glossies or 35mm transparencies purchased with mss. Captions required.
Poetry: Traditional and avant-garde forms of poetry; must be golf-related. Length: 4 to 16 lines. Pays $5 to $10.

GOLF DIGEST, 495 Westport Ave., Norwalk CT 06856. (203)847-5811. Editor: Nick Seitz. 10% freelance written. Emphasizes golfing. Monthly magazine; 130 pages. Estab. 1950. Circ. 915,000. Pays on publication. Buys all rights. Phone queries OK. Submit seasonal/holiday material 4 months in advance. Photocopied submissions OK. SASE. Reports in 4-6 weeks. Free writer's guidelines.
Nonfiction: Expose; how-to; informational; historical; humor; inspirational; interview; nostalgia; personal opinion; profile; travel; new product; personal experience; photo feature; and technical; "all on playing and otherwise enjoying the game of golf." Buys 6 mss/issue. Query. Length: 1,000-2,500 words. Pays 20¢/edited word minimum.
Photos: Pete Libby, Photo Editor. Purchased without accompanying ms. Pays $10-150 for 5x7 or 8x10 b&w prints; $25-300 for 35mm color transparencies. Model release required.
Columns/Departments: John P. May, Column/Department Editor. Junior & Senior Golf. Buys 2-6 mss/issue. Length: 500-1,000 words. Pays 20¢/edited word. Open to suggestions for new columns/departments.
Poetry: Lois Haines, Poetry Editor. Light verse. Buys 1-2/issue. Length: 4-8 lines. Pays $10-25.
Fillers: Lois Haines, Fillers Editor. Jokes, gags, anecdotes. Buys 1-2/issue. Length: 2-6 lines. Pays $10-25.

GOLF JOURNAL, United States Golf Association, Far Hills NJ 07931. (201)234-2300. Editor: Robert Sommers. For golfers of all ages and both sexes. Official publication of the U.S. Golf Association. Magazine; 32 pages. Estab. 1948. 8 times/year. Circ. 70,000. Buys all rights. Buys about 30 mss a year. Payment on acceptance. Free sample copy. Will not consider photocopied or simultaneous submissions. Reports in 2 weeks. Query first. SASE.
Nonfiction and Photos: "As the official publication of the United States Golf Association, our magazine is strong on decisions on the rules of golf, USGA championships, history of the game, and on service articles directed to the club golfer. All facets of golf, its history, courses, and clubs. Instructions. Humor." Length: 500 to 2,000 words. Pays maximum of $300. Pays a minimum of $15 for b&w photos. Captions required.

GOLF MAGAZINE, Times Mirror Magazines, Inc., 380 Madison Ave., New York NY 10017. (212)687-3000. Editor-in-Chief: John M. Ross. 20% freelance written. Emphasizes golf for males, ages 25-65, college educated, professionals. Monthly magazine; 130 pages. Circ. 700,000. Pays on acceptance. Buys all rights. Submit seasonal/holiday material 3 months in advance. Photocopied submissions OK. SASE. Repor in 4 weeks. Sample copy $1.25.
Nonfiction: How-to (improve game, instructional tips); informational (news in golf); humor, profile (people in golf); travel (golf courses, resorts); new product (golf equipment, apparel, teaching aids); and photo feature (great moments in golf; must be special. Most photography on assignment only). Buys 4-6 mss/year. Query. Length: 1,200-2,500 words. Pays $350-500.
Photos: Purchased with accompanying ms or on assignment. Captions required. Query. Pays

$25-50 for 8½x11 glossy prints (with contact sheet and negatives); $50 minimum for 3x5 color prints. Total purchase price for ms includes payment for photos. Model release required.
Columns/Departments: Golf Reports (interesting golf events, feats, etc.). Buys 4-6 mss/year. Query. Length: 250 words maximum. Pays $35. Open to suggestions for new columns/ departments.
Fiction: Humorous, mystery. Must be golf-related. Buys 2-4 mss/year. Query. Length: 1,200-2,000 words. Pays $350-500.
Poetry: Light verse. Buys 4-6/year. Limit submissions to batches of 6. Length: 7-15 lines. Pays $20.
Fillers: Short humor. Length: 20-35 words. Pays $5-10.
How To Break In: "Best chance is to aim for a light piece which is not too long and is focused on a personality or is genuinely funny. Anything very technical that would require a consumate knowledge of golf, we would rather assign ourselves. But if you are successful with something light and not too long, we might use you for something heavier later. Probably the best way to break in would be by our Golf Reports section in which we run short items on interesting golf feats, events and so forth. If you send us something like that, about an important event in your area, it is an easy way for us to get acquainted."

GOLF SCORE, Werner Book Corp., 606 Wilshire Blvd., Santa Monica CA 90401. Editor-in-Chief: Donald Werner. Managing Editor: Steve Werner. For "golfers from their mid-teens to seniors who are avid enthusiasts. They play at least once a week and often travel to participate in the sport." Monthly, eight times/year. Magazine; 68 pages. Estab: 1976. Circ: 75,000. Pays on publication. Buys first North American serial rights. Phone queries OK. Submit seasonal/ holiday material 3 months in advance. Simultaneous submissions OK. SASE. Reports in 2 weeks.
Nonfiction: How-to; informational; historical; humor; interview; nostalgia; profile; travel; new product; photo feature and technical. Don't send "how-to articles which are not by established professionals or authorities. When this is not the case, the article should at least quote such authorities." Buys 64 mss/year. Query or submit complete ms. Length: 1,500-2,000 words. Pays $100-300.
Photos: Purchased with or without accompanying ms or on assignment. Captions required. Pays $10-25 for 8x10 b&w glossies; $50-150 for 35mm, 2¼x2¼ or 4x5 transparencies. Model release required.

Guns

THE AMERICAN SHOTGUNNER, P.O. Box 3351, Reno NV 89505. Editor: Bob Thruston. Monthly tabloid magazine; 48 pages. Estab. 1973. Circ. 123,000. Buys all rights. Buys 24-50 mss/year. Pays on publication. Free sample copy and writer's guidelines. Submit special material (hunting) 3 to 4 months in advance. Reports on material accepted for publication in 30 days. Returns rejected material immediately. Submit complete ms. SASE.
Nonfiction and Photos: All aspects of shotgunning, trap and skeet shooting and hunting, reloading; shooting clothing, shooting equipment and recreational vehicles. Emphasis is on the how-to and instructional approach. "We give the sportsman actual material that will help him to improve his game, fill his limit, or build that duck blind, etc. Hunting articles are used in all issues, year round." Length: open. Pays $75 to $250. No additional payment for photos used with mss. "We also purchase professional cover material. Send transparencies (originals)."
Fillers: Tips on hunting, shooting and outdoor themes; short humor. Pays minimum of $10.

BLACK POWDER TIMES, P.O. Box 842, Mount Vernon WA 98273. (206)424-3881. Editor: Fred Holder. 25-30% freelance written. For people interested in shooting and collecting black powder guns, primarily of the muzzle-loading variety. Tabloid newspaper; 20 pages. Estab. 1974. Monthly. Not copyrighted. Pays on publication. Sample copy 75¢. Will consider photocopied and simultaneous submissions. Reports on material accepted for publication in 2 to 4 weeks. Returns rejected material in 2 weeks. Query first. SASE.
Nonfiction: Articles on gunsmiths who make black powder guns, on shoots, on muzzle-loading gun clubs, on guns of the black powder vintage, and anything related to the sport of black powder shooting and hunting. Emphasis is on good writing and reporting. As an example of recently published material, see "Spring Rendezvous at Camus Meadows" and "Bad Luck Flintlock Hunt". Informational, how-to, personal experience, interview, profile, historical articles and book reviews. Length: 500 to 2,000 words. Pays 2¢ a word.

COLT AMERICAN HANDGUNNING ANNUAL, Aqua-Field Publications, Inc., 728 Beaver

Dam Rd., Point Pleasant NJ 08742. (201)899-4200. Editor and Publisher: Stephen Ferber. For outdoor sportsmen. Magazines; 100 pages. Estab. 1974. Annually. Circ. 150,000. Buys all rights, but may reassign rights to author after publication. Buys all of its mss from freelance writers. Pays on acceptance or on publication; varies with contributor. Will send sample copy to writer for 50¢. No photocopied or simultaneous submissions. Submit seasonal (fall) material in the spring. Reports in 2 weeks. Query first or submit complete ms. Enclose SASE.
Nonfiction and Photos: Original how-to articles on hunting, shooting, and hand-loading. No "me and Joe" stories. "Just good writing with investigative approach to journalism." Emphasis is on interesting and authoritative material with an original approach and good photos. Length: 1,500 to 2,500 words. Pays $150 to $250. Nuts & Bolts column uses how-to material or pieces on new techniques. Length: 1,000 words. Pays $100. No additional payment for b&w glossies (8x10) used with mss. Pays $10 to $15 for b&w's purchased without mss. Pays $50 for color transparencies (35mm or 4x5) purchased with mss.

GUN WEEK, Amos Press, Box 150, 911 Vandemark Rd., Sidney OH 45365. (513)492-4141. Editor-in-Chief: James C. Schneider. News Editor: Marianne R. Sailor. 60% freelance written. Emphasizes gun hobby; sports, collecting and news. Weekly newspaper; 28 pages. Estab. 1966. Circ. 50,000. Pays on publication. Buys first North American serial rights. Phone queries OK. Submit seasonal/holiday material 6 weeks in advance. Simultaneous and photocopied submissions OK. SASE. Reports in 6 weeks. Free sample copy and writer's guidelines.
Nonfiction: Historical (history of firearms or how they affected an historical event); how-to (dealing with firearms, construction, care, etc.); informational (hunting, firearms, legislative news on the west coast); interview (gun-related persons, heads of college shooting programs, etc.); new product (firearms, ammunition, cleaners, gun-related products, hunting accessories); photo feature (conservation interests); profile (hunters, gun buffs, legislators, conservationists, etc.); technical. Buys 500 mss/year. Query or send complete ms. Length: 125-3,000 words. Pays 50¢/column inch.
Photos: Purchased with or without accompanying ms. Captions required. Send contact sheet, prints and/or slides. Pays $3 minimum for 5x7 or 8x10 b&w glossies; $5 minimum for 35mm color slides. (50¢/column inch with manuscript). Total purchase price for ms includes payment for photos. Model release required.
Columns/Departments: Buys 150-300 mss/year. Query or submit complete ms. Length: 500-1,500 words. Pays $20-35. Open to suggestions from freelancers for new columns/departments; address to James C. Schneider. "Our freelance writers are writing under one designated column, 'Muzzle Loader'—Don Davis, etc. We are looking for possible columnists in firearms collecting, history, hunting and conservation."
Fillers: Clippings, jokes, gags, anecdotes, facts. Send fillers. Length: 25-100 words.

GUN WORLD, Box HH, 34249 Camino Capistrano, Capistrano Beach CA 92624. Editorial Director: Jack Lewis. 50% freelance written. For ages that "range from mid-twenties to mid-sixties; many professional types who are interested in relaxation of hunting and shooting." Estab. 1960. Monthly. Circ. 129,000. Buys all rights but will reassign them to author after publication. Buys "50 or so" mss a year. Payment on acceptance. Free sample copy. Will not consider photocopied submissions. Submit seasonal material 4 months in advance. Reports in six weeks, perhaps longer. SASE.
Nonfiction and Photos: General subject matter consists of "well-rounded articles—not by amateurs—on shooting techniques, with anecdotes; hunting stories with tips and knowledge integrated. No poems or fiction. We like broad humor in our articles, so long as it does not reflect upon firearms safety. Most arms magazines are pretty deadly and we feel shooting can be fun. Too much material aimed at pro-gun people. Most of this is staff-written and most shooters don't have to be told of their rights under the Constitution. We want articles on new development; off-track inventions, novel military uses of arms; police armament and training techniques; do-it-yourself projects in this field." Buys informational, how-to, personal experience, and nostalgia articles. Pays $250 maximum. Purchases photos with mss and caption required. Wants 5x7 b&w.

GUNS & AMMO MAGAZINE, Petersen Publishing Company, 8490 Sunset Blvd., Los Angeles CA 90069. Editor-in-Chief: Howard E. French. Managing Editor: E.G. Bell. Emphasizes the firearms field. Monthly magazine; 108 pages. Estab. 1958. Circ. 450,000. Pays on publication. Buys all rights. Submit seasonal/holiday material 4 months in advance. SASE. Reports in 1 month. Free writer's guidelines.
Nonfiction: Informational and technical. Buys 7-10 mss/issue. Send complete ms. Length: 1,200-3,000 words. Pays $125-350.

Photos: Purchased with accompanying ms. Captions required. Uses 8x10 b&w glossies. Total purchase price for ms includes payment for photos. Model release required.

GUNS MAGAZINE, 591 Camino de la Reina, San Diego CA 92108. (714)297-5352. Editor: J. Rakusan. Estab. 1955. Monthly for firearms enthusiasts. Circ. 135,000. Buys all rights. Buys 100 to 150 mss a year. Pays on publication. Will send free sample copy to a writer on request. Reports in 2 to 3 weeks. SASE.
Nonfiction and Photos: Test reports on new firearms; how-to on gunsmithing, reloading; round-up articles on firearms types. Historical pieces. Does not want to see anything about "John and I went hunting" or rewrites of a general nature or controversy for the sake of controversy, without new illumination. Length: 1,000 to 2,500 words. Pays $75 to $175. Major emphasis is on good photos. No additional payment for b&w glossies purchased with mss. Pays $50 to $100 for color; 2¼x2¼ minimum.

THE RIFLE MAGAZINE, P.O. Box 3030, Prescott AZ 86301. (602)445-7814. Editor: Neal Knox. 50% freelance written. Bimonthly. For advanced rifle enthusiasts. Pays on publication. Buys North American serial rights. Reports in 30 days. "A detailed query will help, and is preferred." SASE.
Nonfiction and Photos: Articles must be fresh and of a quality and style to enlighten rather than entertain knowledgeable gun enthusiasts. Subject matter must be technical and supported by appropriate research. "We are interested in seeing new bylines and new ideas, but if a writer doesn't have a solid knowledge of firearms and ballistics, he's wasting his time and ours to submit." Length: 1,500 to 3,000 words. Pays $75 to $200. Photos should accompany ms. Buys ms and photos as a package.

SHOOTING TIMES, News Plaza, Peoria IL 61601. Executive Editor: Alex Bartimo. "The average *Shooting Times* reader is 29 years old. He has an above average education and income. He is probably a semiskilled or skilled or professional worker who has an avid interest in firearms and the shooting sports." Special reloading issue in February; handgun issue in March. Monthly. Circ. 167,000. Buys all rights. Buys 85 to 90 mss/year. Pays on acceptance. Free sample copy and writer's guidelines. Submit seasonal or special material 4 or 5 months in advance. Reports in 4 to 5 weeks. Query first. SASE.
Nonfiction and Photos: "Presents a well-balanced content ranging from nontechnical through semitechnical to technical stories covering major shooting sports activities—handguns, rifles, shotguns, cartridge reloading, muzzle loading, gunsmithing, how-to's, and hunting, with a major emphasis on handguns. Hunting stories must be 'gunny' with the firearm(s) and ammunition dominating the story and serving as the means to an end. Articles may run from 1,000 to 2,000 words and must be accompanied by 10 to 12 b&w glossies, 8x10, including 1 or 2 'lead' pictures." Payment is $150 to $300.

Horse Racing

AMERICAN TURF MONTHLY, 505 8th Avenue, New York NY 10018. Editor: Howard Rowe. 50% freelance written. For "horse racing bettors." Buys 50 to 100 mss a year. Pays before publication. SASE.
Nonfiction: General subject matter is "articles, systems and material treating horse racing." Approach should be "how to successfully wager on racing. It is the only publication in the country devoted exclusively to the horse bettor. We have a staff capable of covering every facet aside from system articles." Length: 1,500 to 3,000 words. Pays $40 minimum.

THE BACKSTRETCH, 19363 James Couzens Highway, Detroit MI 48235. (313)342-6144. Editor: Ruth A. LeGrove. For thoroughbred horse trainers, owners, breeders, farm managers, track personnel, jockeys, grooms and racing fans which span the age range from very young to very old. Publication of United Thoroughbred Trainers of America, Inc. Quarterly magazine, approximately 100 pages. Estab. 1962. Circ. 20,000. Rights purchased vary with author and material. Pays on publication. Sample copy $1. Will not consider photocopied submissions. Will consider simultaneous submissions. Reporting time varies, but returns rejected material immediately. Submit only complete ms. SASE.
Nonfiction: "Mostly general information. No fiction. Articles deal with biographical material on trainers, owners, jockeys, horses and their careers, historical track articles, etc. Unless his material is related to thoroughbreds and thoroughbred racing, he should not submit it. Otherwise, send on speculation. Payment is made after material is used. If not suitable, it is returned immediately. We feel we have more readable material in *The Backstretch*, and we vary our

articles sufficiently to give the reader a variety of reading. Articles of a historical nature or those not depending on publication by a certain date are preferable. No special length requirements. Payment depends on material."

TURF & SPORT DIGEST, 511 Oakland Ave., Baltimore MD 21212. Editor-in-Chief: Allen Mitzel, Jr. For an audience composed of thoroughbred horseracing fans. Monthly magazine; 64 pages. Estab. 1924. Circ. 40,000. Buys all rights, but may reassign following publication. Phone queries OK. Submit seasonal/holiday material 3 months in advance. Photocopied submissions and previously published work OK. SASE. Reports in 3 weeks. Free sample copy.
Nonfiction: Historical, humor, informational and personal experience articles on racing; interviews and profiles (racing personalities). Buys 4 mss/issue. Query. Length: 300-3,000 words. Pays $60-220.
Photos: Purchased with or without mss. Send contact sheet. Pays $15-25/b&w, $100/color.

Hunting & Fishing

AMERICAN FIELD, 222 W. Adams St., Chicago IL 60606. Editor: William F. Brown. Issued weekly. Buys first publication rights. Pays on acceptance. Will send sample copy on request. Reports usually within 10 days. SASE.
Nonfiction and Photos: Always interested in factual articles on breeding, rearing, development and training of hunting dogs, how-to-do-it material written to appeal to upland bird hunters, sporting dog owners, field trialers, etc. Also wants stories and articles about hunting trips in quest of upland game birds. Length: 1,000 to 2,500 words. Pays $50 to $200. Uses photos submitted with manuscripts if they are suitable and also photos submitted with captions only. Pays $5 minimum for b&w.
Fillers: Infrequently uses some 100- to 250-word fillers. Pays $5 minimum.

THE AMERICAN HUNTER, 1600 Rhode Island Ave., N.W., Washington DC 20036. Editor: Ken Warner. Managing Editor: Earl Shelsby. 90% freelance written. For sport hunters who are members of the National Rifle Association; all ages, all political persuasions, all economic levels. Estab. 1973. Circ. over 160,000. Buys first North American serial rights "and the right to reprint our presentation." Buys 200 mss a year. Payment on acceptance. Free sample copy and writer's guidelines. Would prefer not to see photocopied submissions or simultaneous submissions. Reports in 1 to 3 weeks. Query first or submit complete ms. SASE.
Nonfiction and Photos: "Factual material on all phases of sport hunting and game animals and their habitats. Good angles and depth writing are essential. You have to *know* to write successfully here." Not interested in material on fishermen, campers or ecology buffs. Length: open. Pays $25 to $900. No additional payment made for photos used with mss. Pays $10 to $25 for b&w photos purchased without accompanying mss. Pays $20 to $100 for color.

THE AMERICAN RIFLEMAN, 1600 Rhode Island Ave., N.W., Washington DC 20036. Editor: Ken Warner. Monthly. Official journal of National Rifle Association of America. Buys first North American serial rights, including publication in this magazine, or any of the official publications of the National Rifle Association. Residuary rights will be returned after publication upon request of the author. Pays on acceptance. Free sample copy and writers' guidelines. Reports in 1-4 weeks. SASE.
Nonfiction: Factual articles on hunting, target shooting, shotgunning, conservation, firearms repairs and oddities accepted from qualified freelancers. No semifictional or "me and Joe" type of yarns, but articles should be informative and interesting. Will not consider anything that "winks" at lawbreaking, or delineates practices that are inimical to the best interests of gun ownership, shooting, or good citizenship. Articles should run from one to four magazine pages. Pays about $100-600.
Photos: Full-color transparencies for possible use on cover and inside. Photo articles that run one to two magazine pages. Pays $35 minimum for inside photo; $100 minimum for cover; payment for groups of photos is negotiable.

ANGLER, Box 12155, Oakland CA 94604. Managing Editor: Dan Blanton. 50% freelance written. Bimonthly magazine; 84 pages. Estab. 1974. Circ. 15,000. Pays on acceptance. Buys one-time rights. Submit seasonal/holiday material 4 months in advance of issue date. Photocopied submissions OK. SASE. Reports in 2 weeks. Sample copy $1.50; free writer's guidelines.
Nonfiction: How-to; humor; inspirational; and travel. Buys 24 mss/year. Query. Length: 1,500-3,000 words. Pays $100-200.

Fiction: Buys 3 mss/year. Query. Length: 1,000-2,500 words. Pays $50-100.

THE ANGLER AND HUNTER IN ONTARIO, Ontario Outdoors Publishing, Ltd., Box 1541, Peterborough, Ontario, Canada K9J 7H7. (705)743-3891. Editor-in-Chief: Jack Davis. 75% freelance written. Emphasizes outdoor activities in Ontario. Monthly magazine; 32 pages. Estab. 1975. Circ. 21,000. Pays on publication. Buys all rights, but may reassign following publication. Phone queries OK. Submit seasonal/holiday material 2 months in advance of issue date. Previously published submissions OK. SASE. Reports in 3 weeks. Sample copy for 30¢ postage; free writer's guidelines.
Nonfiction: Expose (pollution or factors affecting the environment of people in Ontario); how-to (new angles or techniques of interest to the outdoorsman); general interest (articles of interest to Ontario hunters and anglers); historical; new product; personal experience (of unusual outdoor interest). No material "that is objectionable to family readership." Buys 8-10 mss/issue. Query with clips of previously published work. Length: 1,500-2,500 words. Pays $25-100.
How To Break In: "How-to-do-its with a new angle suitable for angler, hunter, or camper. All material should have a 'where-to-go, how-to-do-it' content."

THE CAROLINA SPORTSMAN, Wing Publications, Inc., Box 9248, Charlotte NC 28299. Editor-in-Chief: Sidney Wise. Managing Editor: Mike Norris. 80% freelance written. Emphasizes outdoor activities. Bimonthly magazine; 32 pages. Estab. 1962. Circ. 4,000. Pays on publication. Buys all rights, but may reassign following publication. Phone queries OK. Submit seasonal/holiday material 3 months in advance of issue date. Simultaneous, photocopied and previously published submissions OK. SASE. Reports in 3 weeks. Sample copy for "minimal cost"; free writer's guidelines; mention *Writer's Market* in request.
Nonfiction: Exposé (relating to outdoors matters); general interest (relating to outdoors); how-to (particularly hunting, fishing and camping); humor; historical; nostalgia; new product (related to outdoors); personal experience; photo feature (related to outdoors); profile; and travel (should be written so they will be of interest to people in North and South Carolina). "We do not want to see extremely general encyclopedia entries". Buys 30 mss/year. Submit complete ms. Length: 2,000 words. Pays 3-7¢/word.
Photos: Submit photo material with accompanying ms. Pays $5-25 for 5x7 b&w glossy prints and $5-25 for any size color transparencies. Captions preferred. Buys all rights, but may reassign following publication.
Columns/Departments: "We use a Wildlife Afield column which deals with hunting and fishing with no particular slant". Buys 1 ms/issue. Submit complete ms. Length: 500-1,500 words. Pays 3-7¢/word. Open to suggestions for new columns/departments.
Fiction: Adventure (related to outdoors-fast moving dialogue); confession (related to outdoors); historical; humorous; mainstream (related to outdoors); mystery (related to outdoors "Bigfoot" type things); and suspense (related to outdoors). "No stories in which nothing of significance happens." Buys 1 ms/issue. Submit complete ms. Length: 2,500 words maximum. Pays 3-7¢/word.
Poetry: Free verse; haiku; light verse; and traditional. Would like to see poetry related to outdoors. Pays 3-7¢/word.
Fillers: Jokes, gags, anecdotes; newsbreaks and short humor. Buys 3/issue. Length: 200 words. Pays 3-7¢/word.

DAIWA FISHING ANNUAL, Aqua-Field Publications, Inc., 728 Beaver Dam Rd., Point Pleasant NJ 08742. (201)899-4200. Editor and Publisher: Stephen Ferber. For outdoor sportsmen. Magazine; 100 pages. Estab. 1974. Annually. Circ. 150,000. Buys all rights, but may reassign rights to author after publication. Buys all of its mss from freelance writers. Pays on acceptance or on publication; varies with contributor. Will send sample copy to writer for 50¢. No photocopied or simultaneous submissions. Submit seasonal material (spring) during prior winter. Reports in 2 weeks. Query first or submit complete ms. Enclose SASE.
Nonfiction and Photos: Original how-to articles on fishing. Must be good writing with an investigative approach to journalism. No "me and Joe" stories. All material must be interesting and authoritative, with an original approach and good photos. Length: 1,500 to 2,500 words. Pays $150 to $250. Nuts & Bolts column pieces on new techniques or how-to's. Length: 1,000 words. Pays $100. No additional payment for b&w glossies (8x10) used with mss. Pays $10 to $15 for b&w's purchased without mss. Pays $50 for color transparencies (35mm or 4x5) purchased with mss.

EASTERN OUTDOORS, 24 Legendary Rd., East Lyme CT 06333. (203)739-9256. Editor: John H. Brett Jr. 75% freelance written. For fishermen, hunters, and campers in the eastern state of

Pennsylvania, New York, New Jersey, Connecticut, Rhode Island, Massachusetts, New Hampshire, Vermont, and Maine. Monthly magazine; 60 pages. Estab. 1977. Circ. 110,000. Pays on publication. Buys all rights. Phone queries OK. Submit seasonal/holiday material 3 months in advance of issue date. Simultaneous and photocopied submissions OK. SASE. Reports in 4 weeks. Free sample copy; writer's guidelines for 9x12 (52¢) SASE.
Nonfiction: General interest; how-to (fishing, hunting, camping); humor; interview; new product; personal experience; personal opinion; photo feature; and travel. "How-to and where-to will receive top priority." Buys 96 mss/year. Query or submit complete ms. Length: 2,000-3,000 words. Pays $150-225.
Photos: "Photos are especially important with fishing and hunting stories." Submit photos with query or ms. Pays $15-30 for b&w contact sheets; $25-50 for 35mm color transparencies. Captions required. Buys all rights, but may reassign following publication.
Columns/Departments: Guns; Muzzle Loading; Camping; Fishing; Archery; and Boating. Buys 100 mss/year. Submit complete ms. Length: 1,000 words. Pays $50-75. Open to suggestions for new columns/departments.
Fiction: "Humorous fiction on occasion." Submit complete ms. Length: 2,000-3,000 words. Pays $150-225.
Fillers: Jokes, gags, anecdotes, newsbreaks and short humor. Buys 70/year. Length: 50-200 words. Pays $10-50.

FERBER'S FRESHWATER FISHERMAN, Aqua-Field Publications, Inc., 728 Beaver Dam Rd., Point Pleasant NJ 08742. (201)899-4200. Editor-in-Chief: Steve Ferber. Managing Editor: Stan Meseroll. 100% freelance written. Annual magazine; 96 pages. Estab. March 1978. Circ. 110,000. Pays on publication. Buys all rights. Submit seasonal/holiday material 6 months in advance of issue date. SASE. Reports in 2 weeks. Sample copy 30¢; free writer's guidelines.
Nonfiction: How-to (tactics, making fishing lures, equipment). No 'me and Joe' stories. Buys 20 mss/issue. Submit complete ms. Length: 500-750 words. Pays $50-100.
Photos: "All material is photo-feature style." Submit photos with accompanying ms. Offers no additional payment for 8x10 b&w glossy photos; pays $50-100 for any size color tranparencies. Captions required. Buys all rights.
Columns/Departments: Baitcasting; Flyfishing; Spinfishing; and Spincasting. Buys 4/issue. Submit complete ms. Length: 1,000-1,250 words. Pays $75.

FIELD AND STREAM, 383 Madison Ave., New York NY 10017. Editor: Jack Samson. 30% freelance written. Monthly. Buys all rights. Reports in 4 weeks. Query. SASE.
Nonfiction and Photos: "This is a broad-based outdoor service magazine. Editorial content ranges from very basic how-to stories that tell either in pictures or words how an outdoor technique is done or device made. Articles of penetrating depth about national conservation, game management, resource management, and recreation development problems. Hunting, fishing, camping, backpacking, nature, outdoor, photography, equipment, wild game and fish recipes, and other activities allied to the outdoors. The 'me and Joe' story is about dead, with minor exceptions. Both where-to and how-to articles should be well-illustrated." Prefers color to b&w. Submit outline first with photos. Length, 2,500 words. Payment varies depending upon the name of the author, quality of work, importance of the article. Pays 18¢ per word and up. Usually buys photos with mss. When purchased separately, pays $150 and up for color.
Fillers: Buys "how it's done" fillers of 150-500 words. Must be unusual or helpful subjects. Payment is $250.

FISH AND GAME SPORTSMAN, Box 737, Regina, Sask., Canada S4P 3A8. (306)523-8384. Editor: J. B. (Red) Wilkinson. 90% freelance written. For fishermen, hunters, campers and others interested in outdoor recreation. "Please note that our coverage area is Alberta and Saskatchewan." Quarterly magazine; 64-112 pages. Estab. 1968. Circ. 17,000. Rights purchased vary with author and material. May buy first North American serial rights or second serial (reprint) rights. Buys about 80 mss a year. Payment on publication. Sample copy $1.25; free writer's guidelines. "We try to include as much information on all subjects in each edition. Therefore, we usually publish fishing articles in our winter magazine along with a variety of winter stories. If material is dated, we would like to receive articles 4 months in advance of our publication date." Will consider photocopied submissions. Reports in 4 weeks. Submit only complete ms. Enclose SAE and International Reply Coupons.
Nonfiction and Photos: "It is necessary that all articles can identify with our coverage area of Alberta and Saskatchewan. We are interested in mss from writers who have experienced an interesting fishing, hunting, camping or other outdoor experience. We also publish how-to and other informational pieces as long as they can relate to our coverage area. Too many writers

submit material to us which quite frankly we don't believe. We call these puff stories and generally after reading the first page or two they are returned to the writers without further reading. Our editors are experienced people who have spent many hours afield fishing, hunting, camping etc., and we simply cannot accept information which borders on the ridiculous. The record fish does not jump two feet out of the water with a brilliant sunset backdrop, two-pound test line, one-hour battle, a hole in the boat, tumbling waterfalls, all in the first paragraph. We are more interested in articles which tell about the average guy living on beans, guiding his own boat, stalking his game and generally doing his own thing in our part of western Canada than a story describing a well-to-do outdoorsman traveling by motorhome, staying at an expensive lodge with guides doing everything for him except landing the fish, or shooting the big game animal. The articles that are submitted to us need to be prepared in a knowledgeable way and include more information than the actual fish catch or animal or bird kill. The story should discuss the terrain, the people involved on the trip, the water or weather conditions, the costs, the planning that went into the trip, the equipment and other data closely associated with the particular event in a factual manner. We like to see exciting writing, but leave out the gloss and nonsense. We are very short of camping articles and how-to pieces on snowmobiling, including mechanical information. We generally have sufficient fishing and hunting data but we're always looking for new writers. I would be very interested in hearing from writers who are experienced campers and snowmobilers.'' Length: 1,500 to 3,000 words. Pays $40 to $175. Photos purchased with ms with no additional payment. Also purchased without ms. Pays $7 per 5x7 to 8x10 b&w print; pays $100 for 35mm minimum transparencies.

FISHING AND HUNTING NEWS, Outdoor Empire Publishing Company, Inc., 511 Eastlake Ave. E., Box C-19000, Seattle WA 98109. (206)624-3845. Managing Editor: Vence Malernee. Emphasizes fishing and hunting. Weekly tabloid; 16 pages. Estab. 1944. Circ. 129,000. Pays on acceptance. Buys all rights, but may reassign following publication. Submit seasonal/holiday material 3 months in advance. Photocopied submissions OK. Free sample copy and writer's guidelines.
Nonfiction: How-to (fish and hunt successfully, things that make outdoor jaunts more enjoyable/productive); photo feature (successful fishing/hunting in the western U.S.); informational. Buys 70 mss/year. Query. Length: 100-1,000 words. Pays $10 minimum.
Photos: Purchased with or without accompanying ms. Captions required. Submit prints or transparencies. Pays $5 minimum for 8x10 b&w glossies; $10 minimum for 35mm or 2¼ color transparencies. Model release required.

FISHING WORLD, 51 Atlantic Ave., Floral Park NY 11001. Editor: Keith Gardner. Bimonthly. Circ. 265,000. Buys first North American serial rights only. Pays on acceptance. Free sample copy. Will consider photocopied submissions. Reports in 2 weeks. Query first. SASE.
Nonfiction and Photos: ''Feature articles range from 1,000-2,000 words with the shorter preferred. A good selection of color transparencies and b&w glossies should accompany each submission. Subject matter can range from a hot fishing site to tackle and techniques, from tips on taking individual species to a story on one lake or an entire region, either freshwater or salt. However, how-to is definitely preferred over where-to, and a strong biological/scientific slant is best of all. Where-to articles, especially if they describe foreign fishing, should be accompanied by sidebars covering how to make reservations and arrange transportation, how to get there, where to stay. Angling methods should be developed in clear detail, with accurate and useful information about tackle and boats. Depending on article length, suitability of photographs and other factors, payment is up to $250 for feature articles accompanied by suitable photography. Color transparencies selected for cover use pay an additional $150. Black-and-white or unillustrated featurettes are also considered. These can be on anything remotely connected with fishing. Length to 1,000. Payment $25-$100 depending on length and photos. Detailed queries accompanied by photos are preferred. Cover shots are purchased separately, rather than selected from those accompanying mss. The editor favors drama rather than serenity in selecting cover shots.''

FUR-FISH-GAME, 2878 E. Main, Columbus OH 43209. Editor: A. R. Harding. For outdoorsmen of all ages, interested in fishing, hunting, camping, woodcraft, trapping. Magazine; 64 pages. Estab. 1925. Monthly. Circ. 190,000.Buys 150 mss/year. Pays on acceptance. Sample copy 60¢; free writer's guidelines. No simultaneous submissions. Reports in 4 weeks. Submit complete ms. SASE.
Nonfiction and Photos: Articles on outdoor-related subjects. Articles on hunting, fishing, trapping, camping, boating, conservation. Must be down-to-earth, informative and instructive. Informational, how-to, personal experience, inspirational, historical, nostalgia, personal opin-

ion, travel, new product, technical. Length: 2,000 to 3,000 words. Pays $50 to $75. Also buys shorter articles for Gun Rack, Fishing, Dog and Trapping departments. Length: 1,000 to 2,000 words. Pays $20 to $35. No additional payment for 8x10 b&w glossies used with ms.

GRAY'S SPORTING JOURNAL, 1330 Beacon St., Brookline MA 02146. Editor/Publisher: Ed Gray. Managing Editor: Ted Williams. 95% freelance written. Emphasizes hunting, fishing and conservation for sportsmen. Published 7 times/year. Magazine; 98 pages. Estab. November 1975. Circ. 50,000. Buys First North American serial rights. Phone queries OK. Submit seasonal material 4 months in advance of issue date. SASE. Reports in 3 months. Sample copy $3; writer's guidelines for SASE.
Nonfiction: Reed Austin, Assistant Editor. Articles on hunting and fishing experiences. Humor; historical; personal experience; personal opinion and photo feature. Buys 10/issue. Submit complete ms. Length: 500-5,000 words. Pays $500-1000. "Please inquire about delayed payment schedule."
Photos: Submit photo material with accompanying ms. Pays $50-300 for any size color transparencies. Captions preferred. Buys one-time rights.
Fiction: Reed Austin, assistant editor. Adventure (mostly thoughtful and low key); and humor. Submit complete ms. Length: 500-5,000 words. Pays $500-1000.
Poetry: Free verse; light verse and traditional. Buys 1/issue. Submit in batches of 5. Pays $50-75.

ILLINOIS WILDLIFE, P.O. Box 116-13005 S. Western Ave., Blue Island IL 60406. (312)388-3995. Editor: Ace Extrom. 35% freelance written. For conservationists and sportsmen. "Tabloid newspaper utilizing newspaper format instead of magazine type articles." Monthly. Circ. 35,000. Buys one-time rights. Pays on acceptance. Will send a sample copy to a writer for 25¢. Reports in 2 weeks. SASE.
Nonfiction and Photos: Want "material aimed at conserving and restoring our natural resources." How-to, humor, photo articles. Length: "maximum 2,000 words, prefer 1,000-word articles." Pays 1½¢ per word. B&w glossies. Prefers 5x7. Pays $7.50.

MARYLAND CONSERVATIONIST, Tawes State Office Building C-2, Annapolis MD 21401. Editor: Raymond Krasnick. 95% freelance written. For "outdoorsmen, between 10 and 100 years of age." Bimonthly. Circ. 8,000. Not copyrighted. Buys 20 to 30 mss a year. Pays on publication. Free sample copy. Reports within 30 days. Query first. SASE.
Nonfiction: "Subjects dealing strictly with the outdoor life in Maryland. Nontechnical in content and in the first or third person in style." How-to, personal experience, humor, photo, travel articles. Overstocked with material on pollution and Maryland ecology. Length: 1,000 to 1,500 words. Payment is 5¢ a word.
Photos: 8x10 b&w glossies purchased with mss. Payment is $15/photo, $35/slide used with article, $10/b&w photo appearing in photo essay. Color transparencies and 35mm color purchased for covers. Payment is $50.

MICHIGAN OUT-OF-DOORS, Box 30235, Lansing MI 48909. (517)371-1041. Editor-in-Chief: Kenneth S. Lowe. 50% freelance written. Emphasizes outdoor recreation, especially hunting and fishing; conservation; environmental affairs. Monthly magazine; 116 pages. Estab. 1947. Circ. 100,000. Pays on publication. Buys first North American serial rights. Phone queries OK. Submit seasonal/holiday material 6 months in advance. Photocopied and previously published (if so indicated) submissions OK. SASE. Reports in 1 month. Sample copy 50¢; free writer's guidelines.
Nonfiction: Expose, historical, how-to, informational, interview, nostalgia, personal experience, personal opinion, photo feature and profile. "Stories *must* have a Michigan slant unless they treat a subject of universal interest to our readers." Buys 15 mss/issue. Send complete ms. Length: 300-2,100 words. Pays $5-100.
Photos: Purchased with or without accompanying ms. Pays $10 minimum for any size b&w glossies; $50 maximum for color (for cover). Offers no additional payment for photos accepted with accompanying ms.

ONTARIO OUT OF DOORS, 11 King St. W., Toronto, Ontario Canada M5H 1A3. (416)361-0434. Editor-in-Chief: Burton J. Myers. 75% freelance written. Emphasizes hunting, fishing, camping, and conservation. Monthly magazine; 72 pages. Estab. 1968. Circ. 23,000. Pays on acceptance. Buys all rights, but may reassign following publication. Phone queries OK. Submit seasonal/holiday material 3 months in advance of issue date. Photocopied submissions OK. Reports in 6 weeks. Free sample copy and writer's guidelines; mention *Writer's Market* in request.

Nonfiction: Exposé (conservation practices); how-to (improve your fishing and hunting skills); humor; photo feature (on wild life); travel (where to find good fishing and hunting); and any news on Ontario. "Avoid 'Me and Joe' articles." Buys 240 mss/year. Query. Length: 150-3,500 words. Pays $15-200.
Photos: Submit photo material with accompanying query. No additional payment for b&w contact sheets and 35mm color transparencies. "Should a photo be used on the cover an additional payment of $150-200 is made."
Fiction: Humorous (occasionally). Buys 12 mss/year. Submit complete ms. Length: 500-1,000 words. Pays $50-100.
Fillers: Outdoor tips. Buys 48 mss/year. Length: 20-50 words. Pays $10.

THE OREGON ANGLER, Box 337, Boring OR 97009. Publisher/Editor: Pete Heley. 50% freelance written. Emphasizes fishing in the Northwest and Oregon. Bimonthly magazine; 48 pages. Estab. May 1977. Circ. 3,500. Pays on acceptance. Buys first North American serial rights. Phone queries OK. Submit seasonal/holiday material at least 2 months in advance of issue date. Simultaneous, photocopied and previously published submissions OK. SASE. Reports in 3 weeks. Sample copy $1; free writer's guidelines.
Nonfiction: Expose (must concern Northwest angling and/or anglers); how-to (on fishing); humor (concerning fishing); historical (fishing); interview (1/issue on noted angler); new product (fishing product articles always considered); personal experience; personal opinion (must be backed up by research and concern Northwest angling in some way); profile (noted angler or conservationist); technical (on building fishing products); and travel (fishing spots). Buys 18-30 mss/year. Query or submit complete ms. Length: 800-3,000 words. Pays $20-100.
Columns/Departments: Buys 18 mss/year. Query with clips of previously published work. Length: 800-2,000 words. Pays $10-30.
Fiction: Humorous stories concerning fishing. Buys 1 mss/year. Submit complete ms. Length: 1,200-2,000 words. Pays $30 minimum.
Fillers: Jokes, gags, anecdotes and newsbreaks. Length: 200-1,000 words. Pays $10-30.

OUTDOOR LIFE, 380 Madison Ave., New York NY 10017. Editor: Lamar Underwood. For the active sportsman and his family, interested in fishing and hunting and closely related subjects, such as camping, boating and conservation. Buys first North American serial rights. Pays on acceptance. Query first. SASE.
Nonfiction and Photos: "What we publish is your best guide to the kinds of material we seek. Whatever the subject, you must present it in a way that is interesting and honest. In addition to regular feature material, we are also interested in combinations of photos and text for self-contained 1-, 2-, or 4-page spreads. Do you have something to offer the reader that will help him or her? Just exactly how do you think it will help? How would you present it? Material should provide nuts and bolts information so that readers can do likewise. We are interested in articles in which the author is actually a reporter interviewing and gathering information from expert sportsmen. Good geographic balance in these articles is essential. We also like spectacular personal adventure and ordeal pieces and we will even assign a staff man to help with the writing if the story really interests us." B&w photos should be professional quality 8x10 glossies. Color photos should be original positive transparencies and 35mm or larger. Comprehensive captions are required. Pays $500-1,000 for 3,000 words, depending on quality, photos and timeliness.
How To Break In: "We are the only magazine of the big three outdoor sports publications with regional sections and that's probably the best in for a writer who is new to us. Check the magazine for one of the 5 regional editors who would be responsible for material from your area and suggest an item to him. Our regional news pieces cover things from hunting and fishing news to conservation topics to new record fish to the new head of a wildlife agency. You have an advantage if you can provide us with quality photos to accompany the story. These pieces range from 300 to 1,000 words. In addition to the news section of the regionals, the Yellow Pages also include a regional feature each month. Emphasis in the regional features is *not* on species hunted or fished across the country (deer, bass), but rather on regional species (e.g. cutthroat trout in the West; garfish in the Southeast or searun white perch in the Northeast, etc.). The major function of these features is to provide specific information that will be of value to a sportsman who goes in pursuit of the subject species. 'Me and Joe' stories are out. Lively, first-person description of a trip should be considered a 'stepping stone' only for the author to branch out and tell the reader how and where he can also make such a trip in his own area. A regional feature should also give readers information on the natural history of a species: e.g., its habits, its range, its history in the region, and so on. Pay for regional features is $300 minimum for 2,500 to 3,000 words plus photographs (b&w preferred). Another opportunity for writers is the magazine's food page. These articles include a short introduction about the subject species, perhaps an

anecdote, and from three to five *tested* recipes. Articles on preparation (smoking, freezing, etc.) of fish and game will also be considered." Pays $50 for 2 to 4 double-spaced manuscript pages and photos.

THE OUTDOOR PRESS, N. 2012 Ruby St., Spokane WA 99207. (509)328-9392. Editor: Fred Peterson. 10% freelance written. For sportsmen: hunters, fishermen, RV enthusiasts. Weekly tabloid newspaper; 16 pages. Estab. 1966. Circ. 6,000. Rights purchased vary with author and material. Usually buys first North American serial rights. Buys about 63 mss a year. Pays on acceptance. Will send sample copy to writer for 25¢. Will consider photocopied and simultaneous submissions. Submit seasonal material 2 months in advance. Reports in 2 weeks. Query first or submit complete ms. SASE.
Nonfiction and Photos: How-to-do-it stories; technical in detail. Would like to see material on crabs, clams, salmon, fly fishing. Does not want anything on ecology. Length: 750 to 1,000 words. Pays $20 to $50. B&w photos (5x7 or larger) purchased with or without ms, or on assignment. Pays $10 to $20. Captions required.

OUTDOORS TODAY, 569 Melville, St. Louis MO 63130. Editor: Gary Dotson. For outdoorsmen: hunters, fishermen, campers, boaters. Weekly newspaper tabloid; 12-24 pages. Estab. 1970. Circ. 90,000. Buys all rights, but will reassign rights to author after publication. Buys over 200 mss/year. Pays on 10th of month following publication. Free sample copy. Will consider photocopied and simultaneous submissions. Submit seasonal material 30 days in advance. Reports 60 days. Submit complete ms. SASE.
Nonfiction and Photos: Outdoor-oriented material dealing with the midwestern United States. Emphasis on area news, i.e., opening of deer season in Missouri; pheasant season roundups by state, etc. Informational, how-to, personal experience, interview, profile, inspirational, humor, historical, think pieces, expose, nostalgia, personal opinion, lake features, photo and travel features. Length: 500 to 750 words. Pays $15 to $100. No additional payment for first photo used with mss. Additional payment for other photos used.

PENNSYLVANIA GAME NEWS, Box 1567, Harrisburg PA 17120. (717)787-3745. Editor-in-Chief: Bob Bell. 85% freelance written. Emphasizes hunting in Pennsylvania. Monthly magazine; 64 pages. Estab. 1929. Circ. 210,000. Pays on acceptance. Buys all rights, but may reassign following publication. Phone queries OK. Submit seasonal/holiday material 6 months in advance. Photocopied submissions OK. SASE. Reports in 1 month. Free sample copy and writer's guidelines.
Nonfiction: Historical, how-to, informational, personal experience, photo feature and technical. "Must be related to outdoors in Pennsylvania." Buys 4-8 mss/issue. Query. Length: 2,500 words maximum. Pays $250 maximum.
Photos: Purchased with accompanying ms. Pays $5-20 for 8x10 b&w glossies. Model release required.

PETERSEN'S HUNTING, Petersen Publishing Co., 8490 Sunset Blvd., Los Angeles, CA 90069. (213)657-5100. Editor-in-Chief: Ken Elliott. Emphasizes sport hunting. Monthly magazine; 84 pages. Estab. 1973. Circ. 165,000. Pays on publication. Buys all rights. Submit seasonal/holiday material 6 months in advance. SASE. Reports in 2 months. Sample copy $1.25. Free writer's guidelines.
Nonfiction: How-to (how to be a better hunter, how to make hunting-related items), personal experience (use a hunting trip as an anecdote to illustrate how-to contents). Buys 3 mss/issue. Query. Length: 1,500-2,500 words. Pays $200-300.
Photos: Photos purchased with or without accompanying ms. Captions required. Pays $15 minimum for 8x10 b&w glossies; $50-150 for 2¼x2¼ or 35mm color transparencies. Total purchase price for ms includes payment for photos. Model release required.

SALMON TROUT STEELHEADER, P.O. Box 02112, Portland OR 97202. Editor: Frank W. Amato. For sport fishermen in Oregon, Washington, and California. Bimonthly. Buys first serial rights. Pays on publication. Will send free sample copy on request. Reports in 2 weeks. Query first. Enclose SASE.
Nonfiction and Photos: Articles on fishing for trout, salmon, and steelhead. How-to's and where-to's. Length: 1,000 to 2,500 words. B&w photos purchased with mss. Pays $40-150.

SALT WATER SPORTSMAN, 10 High St., Boston MA 02110. (617)426-4074. Editor-in-Chief: Frank Woolner. Managing Editor: Rip Cunningham. 85% freelance written. Emphasizes saltwater fishing. Monthly magazine; 120 pages. Estab. 1937. Circ. 115,000. Pays on acceptance.

Buys first North American serial rights. Phone queries OK. Photocopied submissions OK. SASE. Reports in 4 weeks. Free sample copy and writer's guidelines.
Nonfiction: How-to, personal experience, technical and travel (to fishing areas). Buys 8 mss/issue. Query. Length: 2,500-3,000 words. Pays 5¢/word.
Photos: Purchased with or without accompanying ms. Captions required. Uses 5x7 or 8x10 b&w prints. Pays $200 minimum for 35mm, 2¼x2¼ or 8x10 color transparencies for cover. Offers no additional payment for photos accepted with accompanying ms.

SOUTHERN ANGLER'S GUIDE, SOUTHERN HUNTER'S GUIDE, P.O. Box 2188, Hot Springs AR 71901. Editor: Don J. Fuelsch. Covers the southern scene on hunting and fishing completely. Buys all rights. Issued annually. Query first. SASE.
Nonfiction: Hunting, fishing, boating, camping articles. Articles that have been thoroughly researched. Condensed in digest style. Complete how-to-do-it rundown on tricks and techniques used in taking various species of fresh and saltwater fish and game found in the southern states. Interested in new and talented writers with thorough knowledge of their subject. Not interested in first person or "me and Joe" pieces. Length is flexible, 750 and 1,800 words preferred, although may run as high as 3,000 words. Pays 5¢ to 30¢ a word.
Photos: Buys photographs with mss or with captions only. Fishing or hunting subjects in southern setting. No Rocky Mountain backgrounds. B&w only—5x7 or 8x10 glossies.

SPORTS AFIELD, 250 West 55 St., New York NY 10019. Editorial Director: Ted Kesting. For people of all ages whose interests are centered around the out-of-doors (hunting and fishing especially) and related subjects. Monthly magazine. Estab. 1887. Circ. 700,000. Buys first North American serial rights. Pays on acceptance. "Our magazine is seasonal and material submitted should be in accordance. Fishing in spring and summer; hunting in the fall; camping in summer and fall." Submit seasonal material 6 months in advance. Reports within 30 days. Query first or submit complete ms. SASE.
Nonfiction and Photo: "Informative how-to articles, and dramatic personal experiences with good photos on hunting, fishing, camping, boating and related subjects such as conservation and travel. Use informative approach. More how-to, more information, less 'true-life' adventure. General hunting/fishing yarns are overworked. Our readers are interested in becoming more proficient at their sport. We want brief, concise, how-to pieces and first-class writing and reporting." Buys how-to, personal experience, interview, nostalgia, and travel. Length: 500 to 2,000 words. Pays $600 or more, depending on length and quality. Photos purchased with or without ms. Pays $25 minimum for 8x10 b&w glossies. Pays $50 minimum for 2¼ or larger transparencies; 35mm acceptable.
Fillers: Mainly how-to-do-it tips on outdoor topics with photos or drawings. Length: self-contained 1 or 2 pages. Payment depends on length. Regular column, Almanac, pays $10 and up depending on length, for newsworthy, unusual or how-to nature items.

THE TEXAS FISHERMAN, Voice of the Lone Star Angler, Cordovan Corporation, 5314 Bingle, Houston TX 77092. Editor: Marvin Spivey. For freshwater and saltwater fishermen in Texas. Monthly tabloid; 40 (10¼x14) pages. Estab. 1973. Circ. 80,000. Rights purchased vary with author and material. Usually buys second serial (reprint) rights. Buys 6 to 8 mss per month. Payment on publication. Free sample copy and writer's guidelines. Will not consider photocopied submissions. Will consider simultaneous submissions. Reports in 4 weeks. Query first. SASE.
Nonfiction and Photos: General how-to, where-to, features on all phases of fishing in Texas. Strong slant on informative pieces. Strong writing. Good saltwater stories (Texas only). Length: 2,000 to 3,000 words, prefers 2,500. Pays $35-125, depending on length and quality of writing and photos. Mss must include 8 to 10 good action b&w photos or illustrations.

TURKEY CALL, Wild Turkey Bldg., Box 467, Edgefield SC 29824. (803)637-3106. Editor: Gene Smith. 30% freelance written. An educational publication for the wild turkey enthusiast. Bimonthly magazine; 24-40 pages. Estab. 1973. Circ. 15,000. Buys all rights. Buys 20 mss/year. Pays on publication. Free sample copy when supplies permit. No photocopied or simulanteous submissions. Reports in 3 weeks. Query first or submit complete ms. SASE.
Nonfiction and Photos: "Feature articles dealing with the history, management, restoration, harvesting techniques and distribution of the American wild turkey. These stories must consist of accurate information and must appeal to the dyed-in-the-wool turkey hunter, as well as management personnel and the general public. While there are exceptions, we find the management slanted article particularly well suited to us." Length: 1,200-1,500 words. Pays $30 minimum. "How-to and where-to-go articles, along with 'how the wild turkey became re-

established' articles of most any length, with specific information and practical hints for success in harvest and management of the wild turkey are what we are seeking. We use color transparencies for the cover; full of action, atmosphere or human interest. We want action photos submitted with feature articles; mainly b&w. For color, we prefer transparencies. We can use 35mm slides. We prefer 8x10 b&w glossies, but will settle for smaller prints, if they are good quality. For contacts, we must have the negatives and contact prints. We want action shots, not the typical 'dead turkey' photos. We are allergic to posed photos. Photos on how-to should make the techniques clear.'' Pays $10 minimum for b&w.

VIRGINIA WILDLIFE, Box 11104, Richmond VA 23230. (804)786-4974. Editor: Harry L. Gillam. 70% freelance written. For sportsmen and outdoor enthusiasts. Pays on acceptance. Buys first North American serial rights. Free sample copy. SASE.
Nonfiction: Uses factual outdoor stories, especially those set in Virginia. ''Currently need boating subjects, women and youth in the outdoors, wildlife and nature in urban areas. Always need gotd fishing and hunting stories—not of the 'Me and Joe' genre, however. Slant should be to enjoy the outdoors and what you can do to improve it. Material must be applicable to Virginia, sound from a scientific basis, accurate and easily readable.'' Length: prefers approximately 1,200 words. Pays 3-4¢/word.
Photos: Buys photos with mss; ''and good photos anytime.'' Prefers color transparencies, but also has limited need for 8x10 glossy b&w prints. Pays $5-7.50/b&w photo; $7-15 for color.

WASHINGTON FISHING HOLES, Snohomish Publishing Company Inc., 114 Avenue C, Snohomish WA 98290. (206)568-4121. Editors: Milt Keizer, Terry Sheely, John Thomas. 15-25% freelance written. For anglers from 8-80, whether beginner or expert, interested in the where-to and how-to of Washington fishing. Magazine published every two months; 64 pages. Estab. 1974. Circ. 3,500. Pays on publication. Buys first North American serial rights. Submit seasonal/holiday material 30-60 days in advance. SASE. Reports in 3 weeks. Free sample copy and writer's guidelines.
Nonfiction: How-to (angling only); informational (how-to). Buys 8-12 mss/year. Query. Length: 800-1,200 words. Pays $25-60.
Photos: Purchased with accompanying ms. Captions required. Send prints. Buys 5x7 b&w glossies or 35mm color transparencies with article. Offers no additional payment for photos accepted with accompanying ms. Model release required.
Fillers: How-to (only). Buys 4-6 fillers/year. Query. Length: 250-300 words. Pays $10 maximum.
For '79: ''Would like to see some pieces on striped bass, shad fishing at mouth of Columbia River and Olympic Peninsula steelheading.''

WESTERN OUTDOORS, 3939 Birch St., Newport Beach CA 92660. (714)546-4370. Editor-in-Chief: Burt Twilegar. Emphasizes hunting, fishing, camping, boating for 11 Western states only. Monthly magazine; 88 pages. Estab. 1966. Circ. 150,000. Pays on publication. Buys one-time rights. Phone queries OK. Submit seasonal/holiday material 4-6 months in advance. Photocopied submissions OK. SASE. Reports in 4-6 weeks. Sample copy 50¢; free writer's guidelines.
Nonfiction: How-to (catch more fish, bag more game, improve equipment, etc.); informational; photo feature and technical. Buys 130 mss/year. Query or send complete ms. Length: 1,000-1,500 words maximum. Pays $80-150.
Photos: Purchased with accompanying ms. Captions required. Uses 8x10 b&w glossies; prefer Kodachrome II 35mm. Send prints or transparencies. Offers no additional payment for photos accepted with accompanying ms.

WISCONSIN SPORTSMAN, Box 1307 Oshkosh WI 54901. Editor: Tom Petrie. 30% freelance written. Emphasizes Wisconsin fishing, hunting, and outdoors. Bimonthly magazine; 64-72 pages. Estab. April 1972. Circ. 45,000. Pays on publication. Buys all rights, but may reassign following publication. Submit seasonal/holiday material 5 months in advance of issue date. Previously published submissions OK. SASE. Reports in 2-3 weeks.
Nonfiction: Historical (Wisconsin state history); how-to (fishing/hunting-oriented, with photos or illustrations if applicable); photo feature (color transparencies on Wisconsin wildlife or touring); and travel (with pix). No 'why-I-hunt' or 'what the outdoors means to me' style articles. Buys 18 mss/year. Query or submit complete ms. Length: 300-2,000 words. Pays $25-250.
Photos: Submit photos with query or ms. Offers no additional payment for photos accepted with ms. Uses 8x10 glossy b&w prints and 35mm color transparencies. Captions preferred. Buys all rights, but may reassign following publication.

Martial Arts

AMERICAN JUDO, United States Judo Association, 6417 Manchester Ave., St. Louis MO 63139. Managing Editor: Jack Murray. Emphasizes Judo for a readership of judo instructors, teen-agers, and young adults. Bimonthly tabloid; 20 pages. Estab. 1960. Circ. 20,000. Pays on publication. Buys all rights, but may reassign following publication. Phone queries OK. Submit seasonal/holiday material 3 months in advance. Photocopied submissions OK. SASE. Reports in 3 weeks. Sample copy 50¢; free writer's guidelines.
Nonfiction: How-to (technical articles on technique or officiating); and photo feature (minimum of 6 photos). Buys 3 mss/year. Query. Length: 750-1,000 words. Pays $15-25.
Photos: Purchased with accompanying ms. Captions required. Uses 5x7 or larger b&w glossies. Total purchase price for ms includes payment for photos.
Columns/Departments: "Champions in Review" (a personality profile of an outstanding competitor). Buys 1/issue. Query. Length: 500-750 words. Pays $10-20. Open to suggestions for new columns/departments.

BLACK BELT, Rainbow Publications, Inc., 1845 W. Empire, Burbank CA 91504. (213)843-4444. Editor-in-Chief: Han Kim. Emphasizes martial arts for both practitioner and layman. Monthly magazine; 72 pages. Estab. 1961. Circ. 75,000. Pays on publication. Buys all rights. Submit seasonal/holiday material 6 months in advance. Simultaneous and photocopied submissions OK. SASE. Reports in 4 weeks. Free sample copy.
Nonfiction: Expose, how-to, informational, interview, new product, personal experience, profile, technical and travel. Buys 6 mss/issue. Query or send complete ms. Length: 100-1,000 words. Pays 4¢-10/word.
Photos: Purchased with or without accompanying ms. Captions required. Send transparencies. Pays $4-7 for 5x7 or 8x10 b&w or color transparencies. Total purchase price for ms includes payment for photos. Model release required.
Fiction: Historical. Buys 1 ms/issue. Query. Pays $35-100.
Fillers: Send fillers. Pays $5 minimum.

KARATE ILLUSTRATED, Rainbow Publications, Inc., 1845 W. Empire Ave., Burbank CA 91504. (213)843-4444. Editor-in-Chief: Han Kim. Emphasizes Karate and Kung Fu. Monthly magazine; 64 pages. Estab. 1969. Circ. 67,000. Pays on publication. Buys all rights. Submit seasonal/holiday material 6 months in advance. Simultaneous and photocopied submissions OK. SASE. Reports in 4-6 weeks. Free sample copy.
Nonfiction: Expose; historical; how-to; informational; interview; new product; personal experience; personal opinion; photo feature; profile; technical and travel. Buys 6 mss/issue. Query or submit complete ms. Pays $35-150.
Photos: Purchased with or without accompanying ms. Submit 5x7 or 8x10 b&w or color photos. Total purchase price for ms includes payment for photos.
Columns/Departments: Reader's Photo Contest and Calendar. Query. Pays $5-25. Open to suggestions for new columns/departments.
Fiction: Historical. Query. Pays $35-150.
Fillers: Newsbreaks. Query. Pays $5.

OFFICIAL KARATE, 351 W. 54th St., New York NY 10019. Editor: Al Weiss. For karatemen or those interested in the martial arts. Estab. 1968. Monthly. Circ. 100,000. Rights purchased vary with author and material; generally, first publication rights. Buys 60 to 70 mss a year. Pays on publication. Free sample copy. Will consider photocopied submissions. Reports in 1 month. Query first or submit complete ms. SASE.
Nonfiction and Photos: "Biographical material on leading and upcoming karateka, tournament coverage, controversial subjects on the art ('Does Karate Teach Hate?', 'Should the Government Control Karate?', etc.) We cover the 'little man' in the arts rather than devote all space to established leaders or champions; people and happenings in out-of-the-way areas along with our regular material." Informational, how-to, interview, profile, spot news. Length: 1,000 to 3,000 words. Pays $50 to $150. B&w contacts or prints. Pays $5.

Miscellaneous

APPALACHIAN TRAILWAY NEWS, Box 236, Harpers Ferry WV 25425. (304)535-6331. Editor-in-Chief: Lyn Anderson. 90% freelance written. Emphasizes hiking/backpacking on the Appalachian Trail. Bimonthly magazine; 20 pages. Estab. 1939. Circ. 11,500. Pays on publica-

tion. Buys all rights, but may reassign following publication. Previously published submissions OK. SASE. Reports in 2 weeks. Sample copy $1.25; free writer's guidelines.
Nonfiction: Exposé; general interest; historical; how-to; humor; inspirational; interview; new product; nostalgia; personal experience; personal opinion; photo feature; profile; technical; and travel. Buys 12 mss/year. Query. Length: 500-2,000 words. Pays $25-200.
Photos: State availability of photos with query. Offers no additional payment for b&w contact sheets or color transparencies. Captions required. Buys all rights, but may reassign following publication. Model release required.
Fillers: Clippings; jokes, gags, anecdotes; newsbreaks; puzzles; and short humor. Buys 5/year. Length: 30-100 words.

BACKPACKER, 65 Adams St., Bedford Hills NY 10507. Editor: Andrea Scott. Managing Editor: Greg Hoffman. 80% freelance written. Emphasizes backpacking, cross country skiing, nature photography for backpackers and wilderness enthusiasts. Bimonthly magazine; 100 pages. Estab. 1973. Circ. 120,000. Pays on acceptance. Buys all rights, but may reassign following publication. Submit seasonal/holiday material 1 year in advance. SASE. Reports in 4 weeks. Sample copy $2.50; writer's guidelines for SASE.
Nonfiction: "We especially need articles on backpacking trips in the US, with photos. Historical (mountain profiles; conservationists who have made a mark on the world); interview (wildlife photographers, leaders in conservation or land management); new product (prefer short release, not article); nostalgia (backpacking in the past, Indians, early explorers, etc.); photo feature; and profile (mountains). Buys 5 mss/issue. Query. Length: 500-3,000 words. Pays $50-500.
Photos: Purchased with or without accompanying ms or on assignment. Captions required. Query. Pays $5-100 for 8x10 b&w photos; $25-200 for 35mm and larger transparencies. Model release usually required.
Columns/Departments: Movable Feasts (recipes for backpackers); Equip & Go (making your own equipment); and Write Time (reader action on conservation issues that may effect backpackers). Buys 2/issue. Submit complete ms. Length: 25-200 words. Pays $5.
How To Break In: "We receive some 3,000 freelance submissions a year. Many of them are rejected because the author is not familiar with *Backpacker* magazine. Generalized articles just don't work here; our readers are terribly sophisticated backpackers and can spot writing by someone who does not intimately know his subject within ten seconds. Articles on trips must have an angle, as well as where you went, what you took, when you ate, etc."

BACKPACKING JOURNAL, Davis Publications, 380 Lexington Ave., New York NY 10017. Editor-in-Chief: Andrew J. Carra. Managing Editor: Lee Schreiber. 80-90% freelance written. Emphasizes hiking and backpacking. Quarterly magazine; 96 pages. Estab. 1975. Circ. 45,000. Pays on acceptance. Buys all rights, but may reassign following publication. Submit seasonal/holiday material 4-6 weeks in advance. SASE. Reports in 2 months. Sample copy $1.60.
Nonfiction: Expose (government, parks service, trail organizations); historical (biographies of conservationists, etc.); how-to; humor; informational; interview; new product; personal experience; personal opinion; profile; technical; travel; and equipment. Buys 12-15 mss/issue. Length: 500-3,000 words. Pays $50-250.
Photos: Purchased with or without accompanying ms. Query or send transparencies. Uses 8x10 b&w glossies or 35mm transparencies. Pays $200-250 for cover. Offers no additional payment for photos accepted with accompanying ms.
Columns/Departments: Opinion. Buys 2 mss/issue. Query. Length: 1,000-2,000 words. Pays $150-200.
Fillers: Jokes, gags, anecdotes, newsbreaks, and short humor. Query. Length: 100-500 words. Pays $25-50.

GAMEKEEPER AND COUNTRYSIDE, Gilbertson & Page Limited, Corry's, Roestock Lane, Colney Heath, St. Albans, Hertfordshire AL4 0QW England. Editor-in-Chief: Edward Askwith. 90% freelance written. Emphasizes field sports for gamekeepers, members of shooting syndicates, landowners, farmers, fly fishermen, and coarse fishermen. Also strong on natural history and conservation. Monthly magazine; 36 pages. Estab. 1896. Circ. 6,478. Buys first British serial rights. Simultaneous and photocopied submissions OK. Previously published work OK. SAE and International Reply Coupons. Reports in 2-3 weeks. Sample copy $1.
Nonfiction: How-to articles (field sports techniques, keepering techniques, shoot management); informational (natural history case histories and experiences); interviews. Buys 180-200 mss/year. Submit nonreturnable photocopy of ms (not the original). Length: 400-1,300 words. Pays approximately $16/1,100 words.
Photos: Purchased with or without ms. Pays $6-8 for half-plate or 8x10 b&w glossy. Model release required.

GEORGIA SPORTSMAN MAGAZINE, Box 741, Marietta GA 30061. Editor: John Spears. Emphasizes hunting and fishing and outdoor recreational opportunities in Georgia. Monthly magazine; 64 pages. Estab. 1976. Circ. 30,000. Pays on publication. Phone queries OK. Submit seasonal/holiday material 4 months in advance. Simultaneous, very legible photocopied and previously published submissions OK. Source must be identified for previously published work. SASE. Reports in 4 weeks. Sample copy $1; free writer's guidelines.
Nonfiction: Expose, how-to, informational; historical (acceptable on a very small scale) humor; interviews with fishermen or hunters known statewide; nostalgia (antique weapons such as percussion guns) and articles concerning major legislation and environmental issues affecting Georgia. Length 1,000-2,000 words. Pays 7¢/word minimum.
Photos: B&w and color purchased with or without mss or on assignment. Pays $100 for cover use.
Fillers: Newsbreaks (explanation of source must accompany them) and illustrations. "We are always in the market for illustrations depicting outdoor scenes. Send samples." Newsbreak length: 500 words average. Pays 7½¢/word minimum.

HANDBALL, United States Handball Association, 4101 Dempster St., Skokie IL 60076. (312)673-4000. Editor-in-Chief: Terry Muck. 25% freelance written. For active handball players from 15 to 70. Bimonthly magazine; 70 pages. Estab. 1951. Circ. 15,000. Pays on publication. Buys all rights, but may reassign following publication. Phone queries OK. Submit seasonal material 2 months in advance. SASE. Reports in 2 months.
Nonfiction: How-to (instructional); historical (I remember so and so); humor (funny experiences with handball); and personal opinion (handball improvement). "Our biggest demand is for instructional articles, with first person types second." Buys 1-3 mss/issue. Send complete ms. Length: 1,000-2,000 words. Pays $100-200.
Photos: Purchased without accompanying ms. Captions required. Send prints. Pays $10-50 for any size b&w glossies. Total purchase price for ms includes payment for photos. No additional payment for photos accepted without accompanying ms.

HOCKEY ILLUSTRATED, 333 Johnson Ave., Brooklyn NY 11206. Editor: Randy O'Neil. For young men and women interested in hockey. Estab. 1960. Published 6 times a year. Circ. 150,000. Buys all rights, but will reassign rights to author after publication. Buys 65 mss a year. Payment on acceptance. Will not consider photocopied submissions. Submit seasonal material 3 months in advance. Reports immediately on material accepted for publication. Returns rejected material in 1 month. Query first. SASE.
Nonfiction and Photos: Player profiles, in-depth interviews, humor; informational, historical, expose, personal opinion. Length: 2,000 words. Pays $100 to $150. Pays $10 for 8x10 glossy b&w purchased with ms, without ms or on assignment. Captions required. Color: pays $150 for cover; $50 to $75 for inside use for 35mm.
How To Break In: "An opportunity for the new writer is our news item department, Off the Ice. We use lots of little bits and pieces here for which there is no pay. But I'll be grateful and willing to work with a writer who comes in this way."

MOPED BIKING, Columbia Communications, Inc., 370 Lexington Ave., New York NY 10017. (212)532-9290. Editor: Bill Kanner. 70% freelance written. "*Moped Biking* is aimed at the active Mopedder. Readers vary in age from teens to seniors. A large part of our readership comes from high school and college students." Bimonthly magazine; 100 pages. Estab. November 1977. Circ. 100,000. Pays on publication. Buys all rights, but may reassign following publication. Phone queries OK. Submit seasonal/holiday material 4 months in advance of issue date. Simultaneous and photocopied submissions OK. SASE. Reports in 3 weeks. Free sample copy and writer's guidelines; mention *Writer's Market* in request.
Nonfiction: How-to (customize your Moped, add a CB radio, decarbonize your engine, etc.); general interest (adventure—How I took my Moped to some place, etc.); nostalgia (what Mopedding was like in the early days, or early Mopeds); technical; and travel (places to go on Mopeds; must have color photos). Buys 60 mss/year. "We will look at a work in virtually any form but handwritten. It's prudent to query first." Length: 1,500-3,500 words. Pays 10¢/word.
Photos: "*Moped Biking* is a visual magazine. All pieces must be illustrated. The how-to articles and travel pieces require photography or art." Offers no additional payment for photos accepted with ms. Captions preferred. Buys all rights, but may reassign following publication. Model release required.
Columns/Departments: Moped Maintenance (how-to pieces on care and feeding of Mopeds);

and Miscellany (captioned photos of unusual or comic interest involving Mopeds). Buys 2/issue. Query. Length: 1,000-1,500 words. Pays $100-150; $5/miscellany item (caption and photo). Open to suggestions for new columns/departments.

PADDLE WORLD, 370 Seventh Ave., New York NY 10001. Managing Editor: Marilyn Nason. 50% freelance written. For amateur platform tennis players. Magazine; 36 or more pages. Estab. 1975. Published 5 times/year. Circ. 15,000. Buys all rights. Buys 5 mss/year. Pays on publication. Sample copy $1.25. Reports in 8 to 10 weeks. Query first, briefly stating credentials. SASE.
Nonfiction: Articles on interesting installations, tournaments, "names" who play platform tennis for fun. Length: open. Pays $2 per printed page minimum.

RACING PIGEON PICTORIAL, Coo Press, Ltd., 19 Doughty St., London, England WCIN 2PT. Editor-in-Chief: Colin Osman. Emphasizes racing pigeons for "all ages and occupations; generally 'working class' backgrounds, both sexes." Monthly magazine; 32 pages. Estab. 1970. Circ. 13,000. Pays on publication. Buys all rights, but may reassign following publication. Submit seasonal/holiday material 3 months in advance. Photocopied and previously published submissions OK. Reports in 5 weeks. Sample copy $2; free writer's guidelines.
Nonfiction: Michael Shepherd, Articles Editor. How-to (methods of famous fanciers, treatment of diseases, building lofts, etc.); historical (histories of pigeon breeds); informational (practical information for pigeon fanciers); interview (with winning fanciers); and technical (where applicable to pigeons). Buys 4 mss/issue. Submit complete ms. Length: 6,000 words minimum. Pays £5/page minimum.
Photos: Rick Osman, Photo Editor. Purchased with or without accompanying ms or on assignment. Captions required. Send 8x10 b&w glossy prints or 2¼x2¼ or 35mm color transparencies.

RODEO SPORTS NEWS, 2420 W. 26th Ave., Suite 140-D, Denver CO 80211. Publisher: Ken Stemler. Editor: Bill Crawford. For avid rodeo fans and professional rodeo cowboys. Tabloids newspaper; 16-32 pages, published every other Wednesday. Annual edition published in January. Estab. 1952. Pays within 10 days of acceptance. Reports in 2 weeks. SASE. Sample copy $1.
Nonfiction: "All material published in *RSN* must relate directly to our 8,000 members and permit holders (apprentice prorodeo cowboys), and to the 580-600 PRCA-approved rodeos held annually in the US and Canada. We do not use material about amateur, high school, junior college, or so-called team rodeo. All material must be accurate and attributable; no 'informed sources' or 'highly placed officials.' No movie-type treatments with more emphasis on events outside the arena than inside; PRCA contestants are professional athletes who compete in a physically demanding sport—80-100 rodeos a year—and when not competing are usually traveling long distances enroute to a rodeo. They do not abuse their bodies and talent by the incessant drinking, womanizing, brawling, etc., depicted in most movies. Avoid overusing dialect, the countrified bit; most of our members and readers are family men who met their wives in college. Features must have a focus." Query or submit complete ms. Length: 500-2,500 words. Pays $1.35/column inch.
Photos: "Black and white—8x10 glossies only, rodeo action and human interest, including behind-the-chutes pix. Color: uses one color photo an issue. Pays $5 for b&w; $25 minimum for color."

RUNNER'S WORLD MAGAZINE, World Publications, Box 366, Mountain View CA 94040. (415)965-8777. Managing Editor: Richard Benyo. 70% freelance written. Emphasizes the sport of running, primarily long distance running; for avid runners, coaches, equipment manufacturers and salesmen, race promoters, etc. Monthly magazine; 112 pages. Estab. 1966. Circ. 210,000. Pays on publication. Buys all rights, but may reassign following publication. Submit seasonal/holiday material 3-4 months in advance. Previously published submissions OK. SASE. Reports in 2-4 weeks. Free sample copy and writer's guidelines.
Nonfiction: Expose; historical (where-are-they-now articles, primarily); how-to (improving one's own running and health); humor; informational; inspirational; interview; personal opinion (featured in column "Runner's Forum"); technical and profile. Buys 5 mss/issue. Query. Length: 1,000-5,000 words. Pays $25-350.
Photos: Photos purchased with or without accompanying ms or on assignment. Pays $15-25 for 5x7 or 8x10 b&w glossies; $50-100 for 35mm or 2¼x2¼ color transparencies. Query and send photos. Total purchase price for ms includes payment for photos.
Columns/Departments: Runner's Forum (1,000 words maximum). Buys 6 mss/issue. Pays $25 flat fee/ms.

SIGNPOST MAGAZINE, 16812 36 Ave., W., Lynnwood WA 98036. Editor-in-Chief: Louise Marshall. About hiking, backpacking, and other muscle-powered travel sports of interest to residents of the Pacific Northwest and Western Canada. Monthly published in half-tab format in newsprint. Estab. 1966. Will consider any rights offered by author. Buys 10 mss a year. Payment on publication. Free sample copy. Will consider photocopied submissions. Reports in 3 weeks. Query first or submit complete ms. SASE.
Nonfiction and Photos: "Most material is donated by subscribers or is staff written. Payment for purchased material is low, usually less than $10. Part of the reward has to be a sense of helping *The Signpost.*"

SKATEBOARD WORLD, Hi-Torque Publications, 16200 Ventura Blvd., Encino CA 91436. (213)981-2317. Editor-in-Chief: Jill Sherman. Primarily for skateboard enthusiasts. Monthly magazine; 160 pages. Estab. 1977. Circ. 250,000. Pays on publication. Buys all rights. Phone queries OK. Submit seasonal/holiday material 3 months in advance. SASE. Reports in 4 weeks.
Nonfiction: How-to (skateboard tricks); informational (skateboarding); interview (skaters out of southern California area); new product; nostalgia (riders from clay-wheel days); photo feature (especially out of California or USA locales); and profile (pro-am riders). Buys 72 mss/year. Submit complete ms. Length: 200 words. Pays $25-100.
Photos: Purchased with or without accompanying ms or on assignment. Captions required. Send contact sheet, prints, or transparencies. Pays $10-40 for any size b&w photo; $15-40 for 35mm Kodacolor transparencies. Model and photographer release required.
Columns/Departments: New Faces (any riders or personalities new to the skateboard world). Buys 36/year. Length: 200-1,000 words. Pays $25-100. Open to suggestions for new columns/departments.

SKATE WORLD NEWS, 8820 Sepulveda Blvd., suite 204, Los Angeles CA 90045. (213)641-4800. Editor-in-Chief: Mark Lawrence. Managing Editor: Jack Singer. 40% freelance written. Emphasizes skateboarding. Monthly tabloid; 60 pages. Estab. November 1977. Circ. 100,000. Pays on publication. Buys second serial (reprint) rights. Phone queries OK. Submit seasonal/holiday material 2 months in advance of issue date. Simultaneous and photocopied submissions OK. SASE. Reports in 6 weeks. Sample copy 50¢; free writer's guidelines; mention *Writer's Market* in request.
Nonfiction: Exposé (business or insurance fraud); general interest; how-to (start a club, get city council approval for a park, accomplish maneuvers); humor (must not be objectionable to any race, creed, color, or sex); inspirational (good sportsmanship); interview; new product; personal experience; personal opinion; photo feature; profile; technical; and travel. "We're looking to report what's happening *now*. We want new, fresh material. We do *not* want re-hashed items." Buys 30 mss/issue. Submit complete ms. Length: 250-2,500 words. Pays $10-35.
Photos: Submit photo material with ms. Pays $10-35 for b&w negatives; $25-100 for color transparencies. Captions required. Buys reprint rights.
Columns/Departments: Music Review (popular artists' music to skateboard to); Business & Finance (skatepark development operations); Competition (professional and amateur tournaments); and News From Around the World (skateboard-related, general interest). Submit complete ms. Length: 250-500 words. Pays $10-35. Open to suggestions for new columns/departments.
Fiction: Adventure; fantasy; and science fiction. "Must be related to skateboarding." Submit complete ms. Length: 500-2,500 words. Pays $10-35.
Poetry: Free verse; haiku; light verse; and traditional. Limit submissions to batches of 5. Length: 10-20 lines. Pays $10.
Fillers: Jokes, gags, anecdotes, newsbreaks and puzzles. Length: 100-300 words. Pays $10-25.

SOUTHERN OUTDOORS MAGAZINE, B.A.S.S. Publications, Number 1 Bell Rd., Montgomery, AL 36117. (205)277-3940. Editor: Dave Ellison. Emphasizes a broad range of Southern outdoor activities, including hunting, fishing, boating, travel, water skiing, diving, conservation, controversy, camping, canoeing, RVs, dogs, sailing, backpacking, hiking, powerboat racing, wildlife photography, various community outdoor events or projects, and, occasionally, offbeat topics such as snuff dipping, tobacco spitting, turtle racing, etc. Published 8 times/year; 80-96 pages. Estab. 1940. Circ. 200,000. Pays on acceptance. Buys all rights but may reassign rights following publication. No phone queries. Submit seasonal/holiday material 6 months in advance. SASE. Reports in 4 weeks. Writers should be thoroughly familiar with "To Know Us Is To Sell To Us," a comprehensive, free writers'/photographers' manual available from *Southern Outdoors*.

Nonfiction: Must have obvious, legimitate Sourthern outdoors slant. Subjects can vary widely. All submissions must be compatible with guidelines; seldom are first-person stories purchased. Article should inform and entertain. Buys 100+/manuscripts a year. Query. Length: up to 3,500 words with sidebars and photos. Pays $200 to $700.
Photos: Purchased with or without accompanying ms. Captions required. Pays $10 minimum for 8x10 b&w glossies or 35mm color transparencies and larger. Offers no additional payment for photos accepted with accompanying ms, unless cover is obtained, then additional payment, on publication, of $150-$300 is remitted.
Fillers: 25-1,500 words on outdoor topics, especially how-to and travel in the outdoors. Payment $20-300. Special "Southern Outsiders" short features personality sketches of interesting Southerners. Length: 350-500 words with minimum of two b&w 8x10 glossies. Payment: $125.
Fiction: Nostalgia, Humor: Length: 500-3,000 words. Payment: $75-$500.

STRENGTH & HEALTH Magazine, S&H Publishing Co., Inc., Box 1707, York PA 17405. (717)848-1541. Editor-in-Chief: Bob Hoffman. Managing Editor: John Grimek. 35% freelance written. Emphasizes Olympic weightlifting and weight training. Bimonthly magazine; 74 pages. Estab. 1932. Circ. 100,000. Pays on publication. Buys all rights, but may reassign following publication. Submit seasonal/holiday material 4-5 months in advance. SASE. Reports in 2 months. Free sample copy.
Nonfiction: Bob Karpinski, Articles Editor. How-to (physical fitness routines); interview (sports figures); and profile. Buys 15 mss/year. Submit complete ms. Length: 1,500-3,000 words. Pays $50-100.
Photos: Sallie Sload, Photo Editor. Purchased with accompanying ms. Captions required. Query. Pays $5-10 for b&w glossy or matte finish; $50-100 for 2x2 color transparencies (for cover). Model release preferred.
Columns/Departments: Robert Denis, Department Editor. Barbells on Campus (weight training program of college or university; captioned photos required, at least one photo of prominent building or feature of campus); In the Spotlight (profile of a championship caliber weightlifter, training photos as well as "behind the scenes" shots). Buys 1-2/issue. Submit complete ms. Length: 1,500-2,500 words. Pays $50-100.

TRACK & FIELD NEWS, Box 296, Los Altos CA 94022. Managing Editor: Garry Hill. For anyone interested in the sport of track and field. Magazine; 64 (8x10) pages. Estab. 1947. Irregular monthly; 9 times first half of year. Circ. 25,000. Not copyrighted. Buys 10 to 20 mss a year. Pays on publication. Will send free sample copy to writer on request. Will consider photocopied submissions and (if advised) simultaneous submissions. Reports on material accepted for publication in 10 days. Returns rejected material as soon as possible, if requested. Query first. Enclose SASE.
Nonfiction and Photos: Generally, news-oriented material (current track news), with features angled to those who are making the news and current issues. Knowledge of the sport is almost mandatory. "We are very factually oriented and have an audience that is composed of the cognoscenti. Be realistic. Tell it like it is." Informational, how-to, personal experience, interview, profile, historical, think pieces, personal opinion, technical articles. Length: 500 to 4,000 words. Pays minimum of $10 per published page. B&w (8x10) glossies purchased without ms. Pays $5-15. Captions required.

THE WORLD OF RODEO, Rodeo Construction Agency, Box 660, Billings MT 59103. Editor-in-Chief: Leslie Stanley. "We reach all of these facets of rodeo: All-girls rodeo, little britches, college, and high school rodeo, Canadian rodeo, and oldtimers rodeo. Audience age: 17-60." 24 times/year. Tabloid; 24-40 pages. Estab. 1977. Circ. 20,000. Buys all rights. Phone queries OK. Submit seasonal/holiday material 1 month in advance. Simultaneous and previously published submissions OK. SASE. Reports in 2-3 weeks. Free sample copy and writers' guidelines.
Nonfiction: Expose (personality); historical (oldtimers and famous rodeo animals); humor (pertaining to cowboys); informational (reports on current rodeo events); interview (with controversy or strong message); photo feature (emphasis on quality rodeo action and/or drama); profile (short in-depth sketch of person or persons); Buys 15/issue. Query or submit complete ms. Length: 500-1,000 words. Pays $15-100.
Photos: Purchased with or without mss. Captions required. Send prints. Pays $5/8x10 b&w glossy with good contrast; $35-50/2¼x2¼, 35mm or 8x10 matte or glossy with good color balance.

Mountaineering

CLIMBING MAGAZINE, Box E, 310 Main Street, Aspen CO 81611. (303)925-3414. Editor: Michael Kennedy. For "mountaineers of the U.S. and Canada." Published 6 times a year. Estab. 1970. Circ. 3,000. Rights purchased vary with author and material. Buys 48 mss a year. Payment on publication. Will consider photocopied submissions. Reports in 2 weeks. Query first or submit complete ms. SASE.
Nonfiction and Photos: General subject matter concerns "technical rockclimbing, mountaineering, and ski touring. Articles can be highly technical—our audience is select. Articles with general appeal also sought with a conservationist slant. We try to be a forum for all mountaineers. We would like to see articles on rock preservation, women in climbing, and attitudes toward mechanization of mountaineering." Buys informational, how-to, personal experience, interviews, profile, inspirational, humor, historical, think, personal opinion, photo, travel, mountaineering book reviews, spot news, new product and technical articles. Photos purchased with or without mss, on assignment; and captions are optional. Pays $5 per photo used; $30 for cover. Either b&w or color transparencies (35mm or 2¼x2¼) accepted. Magazine does b&w conversions from transparencies.
Fiction: Buys experimental, mainstream, adventure, humorous, historical, condensed novels, and serialized novels. Length: 1,000 to 3,000 words. Pays $5 minimum.
Poetry: Buys traditional and avant-garde forms, and free, blank, and light verse. Pays $5 minimum.

MOUNTAIN GAZETTE, 745 Walnut, Boulder CO 80205. (303)444-6213. Editor: Gaylord T. Guenin. A general magazine on mountain subjects from outdoor activities to politics and the environment. Also an emphasis on travel to remote mountain regions of the world. Monthly magazine; 36-42 pages. Estab. 1966. Circ. 17,500. Buys first North American serial rights. Pays on acceptance. Sample copy and writer's guidelines for $1. Reports in 2 weeks to several months. SASE.
Nonfiction: "We're interested in articles on almost any mountain subject, from mountaineering to politics to bluegrass music, but seek the unusual in treatment. Prefers manuscript to query letter. Length varies from 1,500 to 6,000 words, but will occasionally consider longer manuscripts." Pays $50 to $300.
Photos: Purchased with or without mss. B&w 8x10 prints only. "Our photography is more often artistic than journalistic." Pays $10-75.
Fiction: Length 500 to 8,000 words. Payment $50 to $300.
Poetry: Traditional forms, free verse, and avant-garde forms. Should relate, however metaphorically, to the mountains.

Skiing and Snow Sports

CANADIAN SKATER, Canadian Figure Skating Association, 333 River Rd., Ottawa, Ontario, Canada K1L 8B9. (416)746-5953. Editor: Linda Jade Stearns. 60% freelance written. "*Canadian Skater* appeals to skaters and skating fans of all ages—children, teenagers and adults who skate for fun; coaches, skating officials, and parents who spend on the average of $1,000-2,000 a year on young recreational skaters. Published 4 times/year during winter. Magazine; 52 pages. Estab. 1974. Circ. 12,000. Pays on publication. Buys first North American serial rights or one-time rights. Phone queries OK. Submit seasonal/holiday material 2½ months in advance. Simultaneous and photocopied submissions OK. SASE. Reports in 2-3 months. Free sample copy and writer's guidelines.
Nonfiction: "Articles dealing with Canada and the world's best amateur figure skaters, and the amateur figure skating scene in general." How-to (produce skating carnivals, raise funds, administer a skating club); general interest; humor; historical (Canadian figure skating); interview (top world and Canadian skaters, skating personalities actively involved in the amateur skating world); nostalgia; personal experience; personal opinion; photo feature; profile (special club activities); technical (figure skating skills) and competition reports or evaluations. No articles concentrating on professional rather than amateur skaters. Buys 5-8 mss/issue. Query. Length: 500-2,500 words. Pays $25-75.
Photos: "We do not have photographers on staff, and sometimes find it difficult to obtain the photos we wish." Pays $5-25 for 8x10 b&w glossy prints; $15-40 (for cover) for 2¼x2¼ color transparencies. Captions required. Buys one-time rights. Model release required.
Columns/Departments: Former Canadian Champions; You and Your Instructor; Carnival Productions; Clubs in Canada (special activities); and Book Reviews. Buys 4/issue. Query with clips of previously published work. Length: 500-1,500 words. Pays $20-50.
Fiction: "Fiction relating to figure skating, especially children's stories." Adventure; fantasy; historical; and humorous. Buys 1/issue. Query with clips of previously published work. Length:

500-2,500. Pays $20-50.
Poetry: Free verse; light verse; traditional; and children's poetry. Buys 1/issue. Pays $15-30.
Fillers: Anecdotes, newsbreaks and short humor. Buys 6/issue. Length: 75-150 words. Pays $10-15.
How To Break In: "We depend on freelancers and so are always on the lookout for new contributors, especially in the Western and Atlantic provinces. We appreciate seeing samples of previously published work when inquiries are made."

HOSPICE, 22 High St., Brattleboro VT 05301. (802)254-6077. Editor: Mike Brophy. 50% freelance written. Emphasizes Nordic Skiing. Tabloid; published 4 times/year. Estab. 1977. Circ. 5,300. Pays on acceptance. Buys all rights, but may reassign following publication. Phone queries OK. Submit seasonal/holiday material 1 month in advance of issue date. Simultaneous, photocopied, and previously published submissions OK. SASE. Reports in 1 week. Free sample copy; mention *Writer's Market* in request.
Nonfiction: Articles on Nordic Skiing. Buys 5 mss/issue. Submit complete ms. Pays $30.
Photos: State availability of photos with ms. Pays $30 for 5x7 b&w glossy prints.

NORTHWEST SKIER, 903 N.E. 45th St., Seattle WA 98105. (206)634-3620. Publisher: Ian F. Brown. Biweekly. Circ. 15,000. Not copyrighted. Pays on publication. Will send sample copy to writer for 50¢. Reports on submissions immediately. SASE.
Nonfiction: Well-written articles of interest to winter sports participants in the Pacific Northwest and Western Canada, or pieces of a general scope which would interest all of the winter sporting public. Character studies, unusual incidents, slants and perspectives. Must be authoritative, readable and convincingly thorough. Humor accepted. "Politics are open, along 'speaking out' lines. If you're contemplating a European trip or one to some other unusual recreation area, you might query to see what current needs are. When submitting article, consider pictures to supplement your text." Length: 250 words and up. Pays $10 minimum per article.
Photos: Purchased both with mss and with captions only. Wants strong graphics of winter sports scene. Doesn't want posed shots. 8x10 glossies. Pays $2 minimum per photo.
Fiction: Uses very little and use depends on quality and uniqueness. Will use humorous fiction and short-shorts. Length: 250 words and up. Pays 75¢ per column inch.

POWDER MAGAZINE, Surfer Publications, Box 1028, Dana Point CA 92629. (714)496-6424. Editor-in-Chief: Neil Stebbins. Magazine; 6 times/year; 100 pages. Estab. 1972. Circ. 100,000. Pays on publication. Buys first North American serial rights. Phone queries OK. Submit seasonal/holiday material 2-3 months in advance. Simultaneous, photocopied, and previously published submissions OK. SASE. Reports as soon as possible. Sample copy 50¢; free writers' guidelines.
Nonfiction: Expose (inside insights into personalities, organizations, their motives and actions); how-to (emphasize advanced skiing techniques); informational (preferably personality oriented or illustrated by adventures); historical (again, only if the work has personality interest to supplement facts and dates); humor (satire, hyperbole, fiction, whatever, but must be in good taste); inspirational (not religious, but philosophic or psychologically stimulating concept articles will be considered); interviews (even with unknown personalities or local characters, as well as ski celebrities); personal opinion (guest editorials are a regular feature); travel (as long as it's not dry, stuffy, bored, or typically informative); new product (short news release items will be considered if products are exceptional); photo features (high quality slides and b&w will be accepted); and technical articles (only if interesting for an expert audience), Buys 5-10/issue. Query or submit complete ms. Length: 300-3,000 words. Pays 6-10¢/word.
Photos: Purchased with or without ms or on assignment. Query or send contact sheets or negatives or transparencies. Pays $200 for b&w and 35mm slides or large format transparencies.
Fiction: "Our fiction requirements correspond to our nonfiction types, with emphasis on originality, style, competence, interest and applicability to our format and involvement with skiing." Buys 2/year. Query or submit complete ms. Length: 250-3,000 words. Pays 6-10¢/word.
Fillers: Clippings, jokes, gags, anecdotes, newsbreaks, short humor. Buys 2/year. Query or send complete ms. Length: 1,000 words maximum. Pays 6-10¢/word.

SKATING, United States Figure Skating Association, Sears Crescent, Suite 500, City Hall Plaza, Boston MA 02108. (617)723-2290. Editor-in-Chief: Gregory R. Smith. Managing Editor: Roy Winder. Monthly magazine; 64 pages. Estab. 1923. Circ. 31,000. Pays on publication. Buys all rights. Phone queries OK. Submit seasonal/holiday material 3 months in advance. Photocopied and previously published submissions OK. SASE. Reports in 1 month. Sample copy and writer's guidelines for SASE.

Nonfiction: Historical; how-to (photograph skaters, train, exercise); humor; informational; interview; new product; personal experience; personal opinion; photo feature; profile (background and interests of national caliber skaters); technical and competition reports. Buys 4 mss/issue. Query or send complete ms. Length: 500-1,000 words. Pays $50.

Photos: Valerie Bessette, Photo Editor. Photos purchased with or without accompanying ms. Pays $15 for 8x10 or 5x7 b&w glossies and color slides. Query.

Columns/Departments: European Letter (skating news from Europe); Ice Abroad (competition results and report from outside of U.S.); Book Reviews; People; Club News (what individual clubs are doing) and Music column (what's new and used for music for skating). Buys 1 ms/issue. Query or send complete ms. Length: 100-500 words. Pays $35. Open to suggestions for new columns/departments.

Fillers: Newsbreaks, puzzles (skating related) and short humor. Buys 2 fillers/issue. Query. Length: 50-250 words. Pays $25.

SKI, 380 Madison Ave., New York NY 10017. (212)687-3000. Editor: Richard Needham. 15% freelance written. 7 times/year, September through spring. Buys first-time rights in most cases. Pays on publication. Reports within 1 month. SASE.

Nonfiction: Prefers articles of general interest to skiers, travel, adventure, how-to, budget savers, unusual people, places or events that reader can identify with. Must be authoritative, knowledgeably written, in easy, informative language and have a professional flair. Cater to middle to upper income bracket readers who are college graduates, wide travelers. Length: 1,500 to 2,000 words. Pays $100 to $250.

Fiction: Fiction is seldom used, unless it is very unusual. Pays $100 to $250.

Photos: Buys photos submitted with manuscripts and with captions only. Good action shots in color for covers. Pays minimum $150. B&w photos. Pays $25 each; minimum $150 for photo stories. (Query first on these.) Color shots. Pays $50 each; $100 per page.

How To Break In: "We also publish *Guide to Cross Country Skiing* for which we need individual text and photo stories on cross-country ski touring and centers. We're looking for 1,000 to 2,000 words on a particular tour and it's an excellent way for us to get acquainted with new writers. Could lead to assignments for *Ski.* Photos are essential. Another possibility is our monthly column, Ski People, which runs 300- to 400-word items on unusual people who ski and have made some contribution to the sport. For another column, Personal Adventure, we welcome 2,000- to 2,500-word 'It Happened to Me' stories of unique (humorous, near disaster, etc.) experiences on skis. Payment is $100."

SKI COMPETITION EAST, United States Ski Association, 22 High St., Brattleboro VT 05301. (802)254-6077. Editor-in-Chief: Hank McKee. 80% freelance written. For racers, coaches, and parents thereof; single focal point is ski racing, touching all ages and educations. Interest includes aspects of competition. Seminmonthly tabloid; 8-32 pages. Circ. 9,000. Pays on publication. Buys all rights but may reassign following publication. Phone queries OK. Submit seasonal/holiday material 2 weeks in advance of issue date. Simultaneous and photocopied submissions OK. SASE. Free sample copy; mention *Writer's Market* in request.

Nonfiction: General interest (as long as it relates to skiing and ski competition); how-to (instructional pieces are of interest to racers and therefore to *Ski Competition East*); interview (with figures in the ski racing world of interest today); new product (racers are always interested in products which might improve their chances of success); and personal opinion (if from person of knowledge in the field). Query. Length: 30-1,000 words. Pays $100 minimum.

Photos: State availability of photos with query. Pays $30 for 5x11 b&w prints. Captions preferred. Buys one-time rights.

SKIERS DIRECTORY, Ski Earth Publications, Inc., 38 Commercial Wharf, Boston MA 02110. Editor-in-Chief: Neil R. Goldhirsh. Managing Editor: Tina Bently. Emphasizes skiing for travelers. For male and female traveling skiers age 20-50. Annual magazine; 296 pages. Estab. 1973. Circ. 108,000. Pays on publication. Buys all rights, but may reassign following publication. Photocopied submissions encouraged. SASE. Reports in 2 weeks. Sample copy $2.95. Free editorial guidelines.

Nonfiction: General interest articles for traveling skiers; special aspect of a resort, etc. How to do anything regarding skiing (how to take a ski vacation; how to repair your skis, etc.) Informational articles on skiing resorts, races. Personality interviews. Personal experience articles dealing with memorable skiing. Travel articles on new places to see and explore. Query or submit complete ms. Length: 1,500 words minimum. Pays $350 maximum.

Photos: No additional payment for b&w and color used with mss. Model release required.

SKIING MAGAZINE, Ziff-Davis Publishing Co., 1 Park Ave., New York NY 10016. Editor-in-Chief: Alfred H. Greenberg. Managing Editor: Robert Morrow. Published 7 times/year (September-March). Magazine; 175 pages. Estab. 1949. Circ. 450,000. Pays on acceptance. Buys all rights. Submit seasonal/holiday material 3 months in advance. Simultaneous and photocopied submissions OK. SASE. Sample copy $1.
Nonfiction: "This magazine is in the market for any material of interest to skiers. Material must appeal to and please the confirmed skier. Much of the copy is staff prepared, but many freelance features are purchased provided the writing is fast-paced, concise, and knowledgeable." Buys 10 mss/year. Submit complete ms. Length: 1,500-3,000 words. Pays 10¢/word.
Photos: Ed Sobel, Photo editor. Purchased with or without accompanying ms or on assignment. Send contact sheet or transparencies. Pays $100/full page for 8x10 b&w glossy or matte photos; $125/full page for 35mm kodachrome transparencies. Total purchase price for ms includes payment for photos. Model release required.

SNOTRACK, Market Communications, Inc., 225 E. Michigan Ave., Milwaukee WI 53202. (414)276-6600. Editor-in-Chief: Bill Vint. 20-25% freelance written. Emphasizes snowmobiling for "almost exclusively northern snowbelt residents; a pickup truck and C.B. radio group." Published 6 times yearly (October-April) magazine; 56 pages. Estab. 1971. Circ. 60,000. Pays on publication. Buys one-time rights. Phone queries OK. Submit seasonal/holiday material 60-90 days in advance. SASE. Reports in 2-3 weeks. Free sample copy and writer's guidelines.
Nonfiction: How-to (make your own accessories, repairs); informational (great places to go snowmobiling); interview (prominent snowmobile personalities and their influence in the sport); photo feature (snowmobile adventures; how-to-make-it; other activities); and technical (how a snowmobile works, how to make it work better). Buys 2-3/issue. Query. Length: 1,500-3,000 words. Pays $50-150.
Photos: Purchased with or withour accompanying ms or on assignment. Captions required. Send contact sheet and negatives. Pays $15-25 for 8x10 b&w glossies; $50-100 for 35mm or larger color transparencies.
Fillers: Clippings. Buys 10-20/year. Pays $1.

SNOW GOER, 1999 Shepard Rd., St. Paul MN 55116. (612)647-7269. Editor: Jerry Bassett. For snowmobilers. Published monthly September through January. Magazine, 60 to 104 pages. Estab. 1968. Circ. 3,000,000. Buys all rights. Pays on acceptance. Free sample copy. Submit special issue material 4 months in advance. Reports in 1 month. Query first or submit complete ms. SASE.
Nonfiction and Photos: Features on snowmobiling with strong secondary story angle, such as ice fishing, mountain climbing, snow camping, conservation, rescue. Also uses about 25% mechanical how-to stories, plus features relating to man out-of-doors in winter. "'Me and Joe' articles have to be quite unique for this audience." Length: 5,000 words maximum. Pays $100 to $400. Photos purchased with mss and with captions to illustrate feature articles. 5x7 or larger b&w; 35mm color. Payment usually included in package price for feature.

SNOWMOBILE NEWS (formerly *Chicagoland Snowmobiler*), Multie-Media Publications, Inc., 222 W. Adams St., Chicago IL 60606. (312)236-5550. Managing Editor: Paul Hertzberg. Emphasizes snowmobiling. Published 6 times yearly (Sept.-Feb.). Tabloid; 32 pages. Estab. 1972. Circ. 40,000. Pays on publication. Buys all rights, but may reassign to author following publication. Phone queries OK. Submit seasonal/holiday material 2 months in advance. Free sample copy.
Nonfiction: How-to (technical features on repairing snowmobiles), humor (winter related), travel (snowmobile travel features in the Midwest). Buys 15 mss/year. Submit complete ms. Length: 1,000-5,000 words. Pay $1/column inch.

SNOWMOBILE WEST, 521 Park Ave., Box 981, Idaho Falls ID 83401. Editor: Darryl Harris. 50% freelance written. For owners of snowmobiles; all ages. Magazine; 48 pages. Estab. 1974. Published four times during winter. Circ. 30,000. Buys first North American serial rights. Buys 10 mss/year. Pays on publication. Free sample copy and writer's guidelines. Reports in 2 months. Query first. SASE.
Nonfiction and Photos: Articles about trail riding in the Western U.S.A. Informational, how-to, personal experience, interview, profile, travel. Length: 500 to 2,000 words. Pays 3¢ a word. B&w (5x7 or 8x10) glossies and color transparencies (35mm or larger) purchased with mss. Pays $5 for b&w; $10 for color.

Soccer

AMERICAN SOCCER MAGAZINE, 211 Culver Blvd. Playa del Rey CA 90291. Editor-in-Chief: Donald R. Edgington. 25% freelance written. Bimonthly magazine; 32 pages. Estab. September 1976. Circ. 210,000. Pays on publication. Buys all rights. Simultaneous and previously published submissions OK. SASE. Reports in 2 weeks. Sample copy 50¢ and free writer's guidelines; mention *Writer's Market* in request.
Nonfiction: How-to (soccer drills, skills); humor (cartoons); interview (pro players of national stature); photo feature (action of championship calibre games-youth); and profile (pro and youth players of national stature). Buys 8 mss/year. Query. Length: 650-1,800 words. Pays $25-50.
Photos: State availability of photos with query. Offers no additional payment for 8x10 b&w glossy prints or 35mm color transparencies. Captions and model release required. Buys one-time rights.

SOCCER AMERICA, Box 23704, Oakland CA 94623. (415)549-1414. Editor-in-Chief: Lynn Berling. For a wide range of soccer enthuiasts. Weekly magazine; 32 pages. Estab. 1971. Circ. 6,000. Pays on publication. Buys all rights, but may reassign following publication. Submit seasonal/holiday material 14 days in advance. SASE. Reports in 1 month. Free sample copy and writer's guidelines.
Nonfiction: Expose (why a pro franchise isn't working right, etc.); historical; how-to; informational (news features); inspirational; interview; photo feature; profile and technical. Buys 1-2 mss/issue. Query. Length: 200-2,000 words. Pays 1¢/word.
Photos: Photos purchased with or without accompanying ms or on assignment. Captions required. Pays $5-15 for 5x7 or larger b&w glossies. Query. Total purchase price for ms includes payment for photos.
Columns/Departments: Book Reviews. Buys 25 mss/year. Send complete ms. Length: 200-1,000 words. Pays 1¢/word. Open to suggestions for new columns/departments.

SOCCER WORLD, Box 366, Mountain View CA 94042. (415)965-8777. Editor: Kevin Shafer. For U.S. soccer enthusiasts, including players, coaches, and referees. Predominantly high school players and adult coaches. Bimonthly magazine; 80 pages. Estab. 1974. Buys all rights, but will reassign rights to author after publication. Free sample copy and writer's guidelines. Will consider photocopied submissions. No simultaneous submissions. Reports on material accepted for publication within 2 months. Returns rejected material as soon as required. Query first. SASE.
Nonfiction and Photos: "Articles are primarily of the how-to variety, but usually include a personality feature with each issue. The foremost consideration is always practical value, i.e., Can a player, coach, or referee improve his performance through the information presented? We are interested in anything on soccer skills and techniques." Length: 1,000 words. Pays $10 to $25 per published page. Pays $2.50 to $15 for 5x7 (or larger) b&w glossies; snappy contrast. Pays $50 for 35mm (or larger) color transparencies for cover use. Must be high impact and vertical format.

Swimming and Diving

DIVER, Seagraphic Publications, Ltd., Boaters Village, 1601 Granville St., Vancouver, British Columbia V6Z 2B3. (604)689-8688. Editor-in-Chief: Peter Vassilopoulos. Associate Editor: Peter Golding. 45% freelance written. Emphasizes scuba diving, ocean science and technology (commercial and military diving) for a well educated, outdoor-oriented readership. Published 8 times/year. Magazine; 48 pages. Estab. March 1975. Circ. 20,000. Payment "follows publication." Buys first North American serial rights. Phone queries OK. Submit seasonal/holiday material 3 months in advance of issue date. SASE. Reports in 6 weeks.
Nonfiction: How-to (underwater activities such as photography, etc.); general interest (underwater oriented); humor; historical (shipwrecks, treasure artifacts, archaeological); interview (underwater personalities in all spheres—military, sports, scientific or commercial); personal experience (related to diving); photo feature (marine life); technical (relating to oceanography, commercial/military diving, etc.); and travel (dive resorts). No subjective product reports. Buys 25 mss/year. Submit complete ms. Length: 800-2,000 words. Pays 5¢/word.
Photos: "Features are mostly those describing dive sites, experiences, etc. Photo features are reserved more as specials, while almost all articles must be well illustrated." Submit photo material with accompanying ms. Pays $5 minimum for 5x7 or 8x10 glossy or matte finish b&w prints; $10 minimum for 35mm color transparencies. Captions required. Buys one-time rights.

Columns/Departments: Book reviews. Submit complete ms. Length: 200 words maximum. Pays $25. Open to suggestions for new columns/departments.
Fillers: Clippings, jokes, gags, anecdotes, newsbreaks and short humor. Buys 3-4/year. Length: 50-150 words. Pays $5.

SKIN DIVER, 8490 Sunset Blvd., Los Angeles CA 90069. (213)657-5100. Editor/Publisher: Paul J. Tzimoulis. Circ. 166,000. Buys only 1-time rights. Pays on publication. Acknowledges material immediately. All model releases and author's grant must be submitted with mss. Manuscripts reviewed are either returned to the author or tentatively scheduled for future issue. Time for review varies. Mss considered "accepted" when published; all material held on "tentatively scheduled" basis subject to change or rejection up to time of printing. Submit complete ms. Enclose SASE.
Nonfiction and Photos: Stories and articles directly related to skin diving activities, equipment or personalities. Features and articles equally divided into following categories: adventure, equipment, underwater photography, wrecks, treasure, spearfishing, undersea science, travel, marine life, boating, do-it-yourself, technique and archaeology. Length: 1,000 to 2,000 words, well illustrated by photos; b&w at ratio of 3:1 to color. Pays $35 per printed page. Photos purchased with mss; b&w 8x10 glossies; color 35mm, 2¼x2¼, or 4x5 transparencies; do not submit color prints or negatives. All photos must be captioned; marked with name and address. Pays $35 per published page for inside photos; with name and address. Pays $35 per published page for inside photos; $100 for cover photos.

SURFER, Box 1028, Dana Point CA 92629. (714)496-5922. Editor: Jim Kempton. For late teens and young adults. Slant is toward the contemporary, fast-moving and hard core enthusiasts in the sport of surfing. Monthly. Rights purchased vary with author and material. Payment on publication. Sample copy $1. Reports on submissions in 2 weeks. SASE.
Nonfiction: "We use anything about surfing if interesting and authoritative. Must be written from an expert's viewpoint. We're looking for good comprehensive articles on any surfing spot—especially surfing in faraway foreign lands." Length: open. Pays 5-10¢/word.
Photos: Buys photos with mss or with captions only. Likes 8x10 glossy b&w proofsheets with negatives. Also uses expert color 35mm and 2¼ slides carefully wrapped. Pays $10-40/b&w; $25-125/35mm transparency.

SWIMMING WORLD, 8622 Bellanca Ave., Los Angeles CA 90045. (213)641-2727. Editor: Robert Ingram. 2% freelance written. For "competitors (10 to 24), plus their coaches, parents, and those who are involved in the enjoyment of the sport." Estab. 1959. Monthly. Circ. 37,000. Buys all rights, but may reassign rights to author after publication. Buys 10 to 12 mss a year. Pays on publication. Reports in 1 to 2 months. Query first. SASE.
Nonfiction: Articles of interest to competitive swimmers, divers and water poloists, their parents and coaches. Can deal with diet, body conditioning, medicine, as it applies to competitive swimming. Nutrition, stroke and diving techniques, developments in pool purification. Psychology and profiles of athletes. Must be authoritative. Does not want results of competitions. Length: 1,500 words maximum. Pays $50 maximum.
Photos: Photos purchased with mss. Does not pay extra for photos with mss. 8x10 b&w only. Also photos with captions. Pays $2 to $3.

UNDERCURRENT, Box 1658, Sausalito CA 94965. (415)332-3684. Editor-in-Chief: K.L. Smith. Managing Editor: K.L. Smith. 20-50% freelance written. Emphasizes scuba diving. Monthly newsletter; 10 pages. Estab. August 1975. Circ. 11,200. Pays on publication. Buys all rights, but may reassign following publication. Submit seasonal/holiday material 2-3 months in advance of issue date. Simultaneous (if to other than diving publisher), photocopied and previously published submissions OK. SASE. Reports in 2-4 weeks. Free sample copy and writer's guidelines; mention *Writer's Market* in request.
Nonfiction: Equipment evaluation; how-to; general interest; new product; and travel. Buys 2 mss/issue. Query. Length: 2,000 words maximum. Pays $50-200.
Fillers: Buys clippings and newsbreaks. Buys 20/year. Length: 25-500 words. Pays $5-25.

THE WATER SKIER, Box 191, Winter Haven FL 33880. (813)324-4341. Editor: Thomas C. Hardman. 15% freelance written. Published 7 times/year. Circ. 18,500. Buys North American serial rights only. Buys limited amount of freelance material. Pays on acceptance. Free sample copy. Reports on submissions within 10 days. SASE.
Nonfiction and Photos: Occasionally buys exceptionally offbeat, unusual text/photo features on the sport of water skiing. Pays $25 and up per article.

Tennis

TENNIS, 495 Westport Ave., Norwalk CT 06856. Publisher: Howard R. Gill, Jr. Editor: Shepherd Campbell. For persons who play tennis and want to play it better. Monthly magazine. Estab. 1965. Circ. 425,000. Buys all rights. Pays on publication. SASE.
Nonfiction and Photos: Emphasis on instructional and reader service articles, but also seeks lively, well-researched features on personalities and other aspects of the game, as well as humor. Query. Length varies. Pays $100 minimum per article, considerably more for major features. $15 to $50 per 8x10 b&w glossy or color transparency.

TENNIS USA, Chilton Co., Chilton Way, Radnor PA 19089. (215)687-8200. Official publication of the United States Tennis Association for members and those with a serious interest in the sport. Editor: Bob Gillen. 30% freelance written. Monthly magazine. Estab. 1937. Circ. 100,000. Buys all rights. Pays on acceptance. Free sample copy. Query first. SASE.
Nonfiction and Photos: "Writer must have in-depth knowledge of the subject necessary to do an interesting, innovative piece." Features and news stories on tennis events and personalities; instructional articles on how to improve skills; testing and review articles on new equipment, court construction and other technical aspects of the sport; fashion and travel features. Pays $100 to $300.

Teen and Young Adult Publications

The publications in this category are for young people aged 12 to 26. Publications aimed at 2- to 12-year-olds are classified in the Juvenile category.

ALIVE! FOR YOUNG TEENS, P.O. Box 179, St. Louis MO 63166. (314)371-6900. Editor: Darrell Faires. 90% freelance written. A publication of the Christian Church (Disciples of Christ) for youth in junior high school. Monthly. Circ. 19,000. Not copyrighted. Payment on publication. Sample copy 25¢. Submit seasonal material 9 months in advance. "Youth are strongly encouraged to be 'co-creators' of the magazine by their contribution of articles, poems, etc." Reports usually within 4 weeks. SASE.
Nonfiction: "We seek to affirm and celebrate the aliveness of young teens, and to call them to new 'alive-ability.' We seek to stimulate the thinkings, feelings and doings of youth so that they come alive to the creative possibilities of themselves and their world. Emphasis on first-person articles, articles about outstanding youth, or youth programs, projects and activities (with photos)." Length: 1,500 words maximum. Pays 2¢ a word.
Photos: 8x10 b&w glossies preferred; mostly of youth (preferably junior high age) and youth activities. Pays $8-12.
Fiction: Should be related to real life issues of young teens. "We don't like fiction which is too moralistic or preachy; characters who do not come across as real, believable, contemporary persons." Length: 1,500 to 2,000 words. Pays 2¢ per word.
Poetry: Personal insight, affirmation and humorous verse. 16 lines maximum. Pays 25¢ per line.
Fillers: Short humor and puzzles pay 2¢ per word or $3 to $10 per item.

AMERICAN GIRL MAGAZINE, Girl Scouts USA, 830 3rd Ave., New York NY 10022. Editor-in-Chief: Cleo Mitchell Paturis. Monthly magazine; 72 pages. Estab. 1924. Circ. 650,000. Pays on acceptance. Buys all rights for one year. Submit seasonal/holiday material 4 months in advance. SASE. Reports in 2 weeks. Free sample copy and writer's guidelines.
Nonfiction: "We like articles about teens or subjects that teens would be interested in." Query. Length: 500-1,200 words. Pays $75-150.
Fiction: Mainstream; mystery; and adventure. Length: 800-1,200 words. Pays $75-150.
How To Break In: "This is a very tight market now, money is low. Any writer who's trying to make it in this tight economy should think to himself/herself whether the story might be available to me through some other channel. Writers query me all the time about material I can get through the Girl Scout's PR people free. I'm still buying several freelance pieces per issue, but you've got to provide me with something that I wouldn't have any other way of knowing about, and that wouldn't be available to me through some other source."

AMERICAN NEWSPAPER CARRIER, American Newspaper Boy Press, 915 Carolina Ave., N.W., Winston-Salem NC 27101. Editor: Charles F. Moester. 10% freelance written. Buys all rights. Pays on acceptance. Will send list of requirements on request. Reports in 10 days. SASE.

Fiction: Uses a limited amount of short fiction, 1,500 to 2,000 words. It is preferable, but not required, that the stories be written around newspaper carrier characters. Before writing this type of fiction for this market, the author should consult a newspaper circulation manager and learn something of the system under which the independent "little merchant" route carriers operate generally the country over. Stories featuring carrier contests, prize awards, etc., are not acceptable. Humor and mystery are good. Stories are bought with the understanding that *American Newspaper Carrier* has the privilege of reprinting and supplying the material to other newspaper carrier publications in the U.S., and such permission should accompany all mss submitted. Pays $15 and up for stories.

THE BLACK COLLEGIAN, 3217 Martin Luther King Jr. Blvd., New Orleans LA 70125. (504)522-2372. Editor: Kalamu Ya Salaam. 55% freelance written. For black college students and recent graduates with an interest in black cultural awareness, sports, fashion, news, personalities, history, trends, current events, and job opportunities. Published bimonthly during school year; 96-page magazine. Estab. 1970. Circ. 225,000. Rights purchased vary with author and material. Usually buys first North American serial rights. Buys 15 mss a year. Payment on publication. Will send free sample copy to writer on request. Write for copy of guidelines for writers. Will consider photocopied and simultaneous submissions. Submit special material (Career Issue in September; Travel Issue in January; History Issue in November; Jobs Issue in March; Entertainment Issue in May) 2 months in advance. Returns rejected material in 1 month. Query first. SASE.
Nonfiction and Photos: Material on careers, sports, fashion, black history, news analysis. Articles on problems and opportunities confronting black college students and recent graduates. Informational, personal experience, profile, inspirational, humor, think pieces, nostalgia, personal opinion, travel. Length: 1,000 to 3,000 words. Pays $10-150. Department and column material includes book and record reviews, how-to, interviews, historical, expose. Length: 2,000 words. Pays $20. B&w photos or color transparencies purchased with or without mss. 5x7 preferred. Pays $5 for b&w; $10 to $50 for color.

BOYS' LIFE, Boy Scouts of America, National Headquarters, North Brunswick NJ 08902. "We are shifting emphasis to staff-written material. Fiction will be drawn from present inventory." Not presently considering freelance submissions.

BREAD, 6401 The Paseo, Kansas City MO 64131. Editor: Debbie Salter. Teens' magazine with a point of view that attempts to mold as well as reflect the junior and senior high school Christian teen, sponsored by the youth organization of the Church of the Nazarene. Monthly. Pays on acceptance. Accepts simultaneous submissions. Buys second rights. Free sample copy and editorial specifications sheet. Reports on submissions in 6 weeks. SASE.
Nonfiction: Helpful articles in the area of developing the Christian life; first person, "this is how I did it" stories about Christian witness. Length: up to 1,500 words. Articles must be theologically acceptable and make the reader want to turn over the page to continue reading. Should not be morbid or contain excessive moralizing. Looking for fresh approach to basic themes. The writer should identify himself with the situation but not use the pronoun "I" to do it. Also go easy on "you" (unless the second approach is desired). The moral or application should not be too obvious. Also needs articles dealing with doctrinal subjects, written for the young reader. Pays a minimum of 2¢ per word. Works 6 months ahead of publication.
Photos: 8x10 b&w glossies of teens in action. Payment is $10 and up. Also considers photo spreads and essays. Uses 1 color transparency per month for cover.
Fiction: "Adventure, school, and church-oriented. No sermonizing." Length: 1,500 words maximum. Payment is a minimum of 2¢ a word.

CAMPUS AMBASSADOR MAGAZINE (CAM), 1445 Boonville Ave., Springfield MO 65802. Editor: Dave Gable. For students on secular campuses only. Published by Christ's Ambassadors Department, Assemblies of God. Published 6 times a year (October, November, January through April); magazine, 16 pages, (7x10). Circ. 12,000. Buys all rights, but will reassign rights to author after publication. Buys 6 mss a year. Payment on acceptance or on publication. "It varies according to type of material." Will send free sample copy to writer on request. Submit Christmas and Easter material 6 months in advance. Will consider photocopied submissions. Reports in several weeks. Enclose SASE.
Nonfiction: College-age slanted, religious nonfiction on personal evangelism, missions, Bible doctrines, Christianity and the sciences, devotional material. 400 to 1,200 words. Pays 2½-3½¢/word.
Photos: Purchased with mss. Prefers 5x7 b&w glossy. Payment varies according to quality and use.

Poetry: Must have spiritual significance and collegiate relevance. Very little used. Length: 50 lines maximum. Pays 20¢ per line.

CAMPUS LIFE MAGAZINE, Youth For Christ International, Box 419, Wheaton IL 60187. Editor-in-Chief: Philip Yancey. Editorial Assistant: Becky Petersen. 10% freelance written. For a readership of young adults, high school and college age, interested in photography, music, bicycling, cars and sports. Monthly magazine; 100 pages. Estab. 1946. Circ. 200,000. Pays on publication. Buys one-time rights. Submit seasonal/holiday material 4 months in advance of issue date. Simultaneous, photocopied and previously published submissions OK. SASE. Reports in 1 week. Sample copy $1.50; writer's guidelines for SASE.
Nonfiction: How-to; humor; personal experience; photo feature; and travel. Buys 3 mss/year. Submit complete ms. Length: 1,000-3,000 words. Pays $125-175.
Photos: Steve Lawhead, photo editor. Pays $25 for 8x10 b&w glossy prints; $50 for color transparencies; $125 for cover photos. Buys one-time rights.
Poetry: Steve Lawhead, poetry editor. Free verse. No "rhyming, sing-songy poetry." Buys 2/year. Pays $25-50.

CHRISTIAN ADVENTURER, Messenger Publishing House, Box 850, Joplin MO 64801. (417)624-7050. Editor-in-Chief: Roy M. Chappell, D.D. Managing Editor: Mrs. Marthel Wilson. A denominational Sunday school take-home paper for teens, 13-19. Quarterly; 104 pages. Circ. 3,500. Pays quarterly. Buys simultaneous, second serial (reprint) and one-time rights. Submit seasonal/holiday material 1 year in advance. Photocopied and previously published submissions OK. SASE. Reports in 4-6 weeks. Sample copy 50¢. Free writer's guidelines.
Nonfiction: Historical (related to great events in the history of the Church); informational (explaining the meaning of a Bible passage or a Christian concept); inspirational; nostalgia; and personal experience. Buys 13-20 mss/issue. Send complete ms. Length: 500-1,000 words. Pays ½¢/word.
Photos: Photos purchased with accompanying ms. Pays $2 for any size b&w glossies.
Fiction: Adventure; historical; religious and romance. Buys 13-20 mss/issue. Length: 800-2,000 words. Pays ½¢/word.
Fillers: Puzzles (must be Bible based and require no art). Buys 13-20 fillers/issue. Length: 200-500 words. Pays ½¢/word.

CHRISTIAN LIVING FOR SENIOR HIGHS, David C. Cook Publishing Co., 850 N. Grove, Elgin IL 60120. (312)741-2400. Editor: C. Lawrence Brook. "Geared toward senior high teens who attend Sunday school." Quarterly magazine; 4 pages. Estab. 1895. Pays on acceptance. Buys all rights. Phone queries OK. Submit seasonal or holiday material 12 months in advance. SASE. Reports in 3-5 weeks. Free sample copy and writer's guidelines.
Nonfiction: How-to (youth projects), historical (with religious base), humor (from Christian perspective), inspirational (non-preachy) interview (some connection to teens and Christianity), personal experience (Christian), and photo feature (Christian subject). Buys 10 mss/issue. Submit complete ms. Length: 1,200-1,800 words. Pays $60-75.
Photos: Kathleen Johns, Photo Editor. Photos purchased with or without accompanying ms or on assignment. Send contact sheet, prints or transparencies. Pays $10-35 for 8½x11 b&w photos; $50 minimum for color transparencies. Model release required.
Fiction: Adventure (with religious theme), historical (with Christian perspective), humorous, mystery, and religious. Buys 5 mss/issue. Submit complete ms. Length: 1,200-1,800 words. Pays $60-75. "No preachy experiences."

CIRCLE K MAGAZINE, 101 E. Erie St., Chicago IL 60611. Executive Editor: Mike Wujcik. "Our readership consists almost entirely of college students interested in the concept of voluntary service. They are politically and socially aware and have a wide range of interests." Published 5 times yearly. Magazine; 16 pages. Estab. 1967. Circ. 11,000. Pays on acceptance. Buys first North American serial rights. Submit seasonal/holiday material 4 months in advance. SASE. Reports in 4 weeks. Free sample copy and writer's guidelines.
Nonfiction: Informational (general interest articles on any area pertinent to concerned college students); interview (notables in the fields of sports, entertainment, politics); and travel (from a student's angle; how to budget, what to take, where to go, etc.). Buys 7-10 mss/year. Query or submit complete ms. Length: 1,500-2,500 words. Pays $50-125.
Photos: Purchased with accompanying ms. Captions required. Query. Total purchase price for ms includes payment for photos.

CO-ED, Scholastic Magazines, Inc., 50 W. 44th St., New York NY 10036. For girls and boys ages 13 to 18. Monthly. Buys all rights. Pays on acceptance. Free sample copy. Query first. SASE.
Fiction: "Stories dealing with problems of contemporary teenagers. (We prefer stories about older teenagers, 16, 17, 18 years old.) Emphasis on personal growth of one or more characters as they confront problems with friendships, dating, family, social prejudice. Suggested themes: finding identity, reconciling reality and fantasy, making appropriate life decisions. Although we do *not* want stories with a preachy, moralistic treatment, we do look for themes that can be a starting point for class discussion, since our magazine is used as a teaching tool in home economics classrooms. Try for well-rounded characters and strong, logical plots. Avoid stereotyped characters and cliched, fluffy romances. If girls with conventional 'feminine' interests are portrayed, they should nonetheless be interesting, active and realistic people. Humor, sports and adventure stories in colorful local or foreign settings." Length: 3,000 words maximum. Pays $300 maximum.

EVANGEL, Free Methodist Publishing House, 999 College Ave., Winona Lake IN 46590. (219)267-7161. Editor-in-Chief: Vera Bethel. 100% freelance written. Audience is 65% female, 35% male; married, 25-31 years old, mostly city dwellers, high school graduates, mostly non-professional. Weekly magazine; 8 pages. Estab. 1897. Circ. 35,000. Pays on acceptance. Buys simultaneous, second serial or one-time rights. Submit seasonal/holiday material 3 months in advance. Simultaneous and previously published submissions OK. SASE. Reports in 4 weeks. Free sample copy and writer's guidelines.
Nonfiction: Interview (with ordinary person who is doing something extraordinary in his community, in service to others); profile (of missionary or one from similar service profession who is contributing significantly to society); personal experience (finding a solution to a problem common to many; coping with handicapped child, for instance, or with a neighborhood problem. Story of how God-given strength or insight saved a situation). Buys 100 mss/year. Submit complete ms. Length: 300-1,000 words. Pays 2¢/word.
Photos: Purchased with accompanying ms. Captions required. Send prints. Pays $5-10 for 8x10 b&w glossy prints; $2 for snapshots.
Fiction: Religious themes dealing with contemporary issues dealt with from a Christian frame of reference. Story must "go somewhere." Buys 50 mss/year. Submit complete ms. Length: 1,200-1,800 words. Pays 2¢/word.
Poetry: Free verse, haiku, light verse, traditional, religious. Buys 50/year. Limit submissions to batches of 5-6. Length: 4-24 lines. Pays 35¢/line.
How To Break In: "Seasonal material will get a second look (won't be rejected so easily) because we get so little."

EXPLORING, Boy Scouts of America, Route 130, North Brunswick NJ 08902. Editor-in Chief: Robert Hood. Executive Editor: Annette Stec. For "ages 14 to 21. High school, some college age. Members of co-ed BSA Exploring program. Interests are education, colleges, careers, music, sports, cars, fashions, food, camping, backpacking." Published every 2 months. Buys first North American serial rights or first serial rights. Buys about 40 mss a year. Pays on acceptance. Free sample copy for large SASE. Reports in 2 weeks. Query. SASE.
Nonfiction and Photos: Interested in material slanted toward the interests of their audience. "We feature young adults involved in the BSA Exploring program. Write *for* young adults, not at them. Keep articles exciting and informational. Support opinions with quotes from experts. We prefer not to see anything on hang gliding, martial arts, or air ballooning." Personal experience, interviews, and profiles. Length: 250-750 words. Payment is $150 to $500. B&w and color photos purchased with mss or on assignment.

FACE-TO-FACE, 201 Eighth Ave. S., Nashville TN 37202. (615)749-6219. Editor: Sharilyn S. Adair. For United Methodist young people, ages 15 to 18 inclusive. Published by the Curriculum Resources Committee of the General Board of Discipleship of The United Methodist Church. Quarterly magazine; 48 pages. Estab. 1968. Circ. 30,000. Rights purchased vary with author and material. Buys first North American serial rights, or simultaneous rights. Buys about 8 mss a year. Payment on acceptance. Submit Christmas, Easter and summertime material 8 to 9 months in advance. Reports in 1 to 2 months. Query first. SASE.
Nonfiction: "Our purpose is to speak to young person's concerns about their faith, their purpose in life, their personal relationships, goals, and feelings. Articles and features (with photos) should be subjects of major interest and concern to high school young people. These include home and family life, school, extracurricular activities, vocation, etc. Satires, lampoons, related to the themes of an issue are also used." Length: 1,800 words maximum. Pays 3¢ a word minimum.

Photos: Uses 8x10 b&w glossies with high impact and good contrast. Pays $15 for one-time use of b&w. "We buy stock photos and those especially taken to illustrate articles."
Fiction: Must deal with major problems and concerns of older teens—such as finding one's own identity, dealing with family and peer-group pressures, and so forth. No straight moral fiction or stories with pat answers or easy solutions used. Story must fit themes of issue. No serials. Length: 2,500 to 3,000 words. Pays 3 ¢ per word.
Poetry: Related to the theme of an issue. Free verse, blank verse, traditional and avant-garde forms. Length: 10 to 150 lines. Pays 25¢ per line.

FREEWAY, Scripture Press, Box 513, Glen Ellyn IL 60137. Publication Editor: Anne Harrington DeWolf. For "Christian high school and college Sunday school class kids." Estab. 1943. Weekly. Circ. 80,000. Buys all rights, "but passes along reprint fees to author, when material is picked up after publication." Buys 100 mss a year. Free sample copy and writer's guidelines. Will not consider photocopied submissions. Reports on material accepted for publication in 4 to 6 weeks. Returns rejected material in 2 to 3 weeks. Query first or submit complete ms. SASE.
Nonfiction and Photos: "Mostly person-centered nonfiction with photos. Subject must have had specific encounter with Christ. Direct tie-in to faith in Christ. No simply religious or moral stories; subjects must be specifically Christ-centered. Christian message must be woven naturally into a good, true, dramatic, human interest story. Current interest is in the occult, Satanism, witchcraft and battles by Christians against grief, tragedy, danger, etc." Thought articles on Biblical themes. Length: 500 to 1,500 words. Pays $15 to $85. Pays $3-25 for 5x7 and 8x10 b&w photos.
Fiction: Same themes, lengths and rate of payment as nonfiction. Rarely publishes fiction.

GROUP, Thom Schultz Publications, Box 481, Loveland CO 80537. (303)669-3836. Editor-in-Chief: Thom Schultz. 60% freelance written. For members and leaders of high-school-age Christian youth groups; average age 16. Tabloid, published 8 times a year; 24 pages. Estab. 1974. Circ. 20,000. Pays on publication. Buys all rights, but may reassign following publication. Phone queries OK. Submit seasonal/holiday material 5 months in advance. Simultaneous, photocopied and previously published submissions OK. SASE. Reports in 3-4 weeks. Sample copy $1; free writer's guidelines for SASE.
Nonfiction: How-to (fund-raising, membership building, worship, games, discussions, activities, crowd breakers, simulation games); informational; (drama, worship, service projects); inspirational (issues facing young people today); interview and photo feature (group activities). Buys 3 mss/issue. Query. Length: 500-3,000 words. Pays $15-100.
Photos: Photos purchased with or without accompanying ms or on assignment. Captions required. Pays $15-75 for 8x10 b&w glossies and 35mm color transparencies.
Columns/Departments: Try This One (short ideas for games; crowd breakers, discussions, worships, fund raisers, service projects, etc.). Buys 6 mss/issue. Send complete ms. Length: 500 words maximum. Pays $5. Open to suggestions for new columns/departments.
For '79: Special Easter, Thanksgiving and Christmas issues.

GUIDE, 6856 Eastern Ave., Washington DC 20012. (202)723-3700. Editor: Lowell Litten. 90% freelance written. A Seventh-Day Adventist journal for junior youth and early teens. Weekly magazine; 32 pages. Estab. 1953. Circ. 60,000. Buys first serial rights. Buys about 500 mss/year. Pays on acceptance. Reports in 1 month. SASE.
Nonfiction and Poetry: Wants articles and stories of character-building and spiritual value. All stories must be true and include dialogue. Should emphasize the positive aspects of living — faithfulness, obedience to parents, perseverance, kindness, gratitude, courtesy, etc. "We do not use stories of hunting, fishing, trapping or spiritualism." Length: 1,500 to 2,500 words. Pays 2¢ to 3¢. Also buys serialized true stories. Length: 10 chapters. Buys traditional forms of poetry; also some free verse. Length: 4-16 lines. Pays 50¢-$1/line.

HI-CALL, Gospel Publishing House, 1445 Boonville Ave., Springfield MO 65802. (417)862-2791, Ext. 261. Editor-in-Chief: Dr. Charles W. Ford. Managing Editor: Kenneth D. Barney. Sunday school take-home paper for church-oriented teenagers, 12-19. Weekly magazine; 8 pages. Estab. 1954. Circ. 160,000. Pays on acceptance. Buys all rights but may reassign following publication, simultaneous or second serial (reprint) rights. Submit seasonal/holiday material 12 months in advance. SASE. Simultaneous and previously published submissions OK. SASE. Reports in 3 weeks. Free sample copy and writer's guidelines.
Nonfiction: Historical; humor; informational; inspirational and personal experience. "All pieces should stress Christian principles for everyday living." Buys 125 mss/year. Send complete ms.

Length: 500-1,000 words. Pays 1-2¢/word.
Photos: Photos purchased with or without accompanying ms or on assignment. Pays $10 for 8x10 b&w glossies; $15-35 for 35mm or 4x5 color transparencies.
Fiction: Adventure (strong Biblical emphasis, but not preachy); humorous; mystery; religious; romance; suspense and western. Buys 130 mss/year. Send complete ms. Length: 1,200-1,800 words. Pays 1-2¢/word.

HIS, 5206 Main St., Downers Grove IL 60515. (312)964-5700. Editor: Linda Doll. Issued monthly from October-June for collegiate students, faculty, administrators, and graduate students belonging to the evangelical Christian church. Buys first rights. Pays on acceptance. Reports in 3 months. SASE.
Nonfiction and Fiction: "Articles dealing with practical aspects of Christian living on campus, relating contemporary issues to biblical principles. Should show relationships between Christianity and various fields of study, Christian doctrine, or missions." Length: up to 1,500 words. Pays $25-50.
Poetry: Pays $10-15.

IN TOUCH, Wesleyan Publishing House, Box 2000, Marion IN 46952. For teens, ages 13-18. Weekly. Special issues for all religious and national holidays. Not copyrighted. Pays on acceptance. Submit holiday/seasonal material 9 months in advance. SASE. Reports in 6 weeks. Free sample copy.
Nonfiction: Features of youth involvement in religious and social activity; true life incidents and articles on Christian growth. Avoid implied approval of liquor, tobacco, theatres, and dancing. Length: 500-800 words. Pays 2¢/word.
Fiction: Stories with definite Christian emphasis and character-building values, without being preachy. Mystery stories. Setting, plot and action should be realistic. Length: 1,200 words minimum. Pays 2¢/word.
Photos: Purchased with accompanying ms, portraying action or the teenage world, or with seasonal emphasis. Pays $1-10 for 5x7 or 8x11 b&w glossies.
Poetry: Religious and/or seasonal, expressing action and imagery. Length: 4-16 lines. Pays 25¢/line.

JUNIOR BOWLER, 5301 S. 76th St., Greendale WI 53129. (414)421-4700. Official publication of American Junior Bowling Congress. Editor: Jean Yeager. 30% freelance written. For boys and girls ages 21 and under. Estab. 1946 as *Prep Pin Patter*; in 1964 as *Junior Bowler*. Monthly, November through April. Circ. 89,000. Buys all rights. Pays on publication. Reports within 10 days. Query first. SASE.
Nonfiction and Photos: Subject matter of articles must be based on tenpin bowling and activities connected with American Junior Bowling Congress only. Audience includes youngsters down to 6 years of age, but material should feature the teenage group. Length: 500 to 800 words. Accompanying photos or art preferred. Pays $30 to $100 per article. Photos should be 8x10 b&w glossies related to subject matter. Pays $5 minimum.
How To Break In: "We are primarily looking for feature stories on a specific person or activity. Stories about a specific person generally should center around the outstanding bowling achievements of that person in an AJBC sanctioned league or tournament. Articles on special leagues for high average bowlers, physically or mentally handicapped bowlers, etc. should focus on the unique quality of the league, *Junior Bowler* also carries articles on AJBC sanctioned tournaments, but these should be more than just a list of the winners and their scores. Again, the unique feature of the tournament should be emphasized."

KEYNOTER MAGAZINE, 101 E. Erie St., Chicago IL 60611. (312)943-2300. Ext. 226. Executive Editor: John A. Mars. 50% freelance written. An organizational publication of Key Club International. For a high school audience, male and female, 15 to 18, members of Key Club, a Kiwanis International sponsored youth organization; service oriented. Published 7 times a year; magazine, 16 pages. Circ. 90,000. Not copyrighted. Buys about 10 mss a year. Pays on acceptance. Free sample copy. Prompt reports on material accepted for publication. Returns rejected material in about a month. Query first. SASE.
Nonfiction and Photos: "Topical material directed to mature, service-oriented young men and women. We publish articles on current social concerns and entertaining, though not juvenile, articles. Most of our readers are intelligent and leaders in their communities and schools. Articles should be timely and informative, without talking down to the reader. We also use features on concern areas (aging, consumer protection, etc.). All material should be applicable to all geographic areas covered by our magazine. Keep in mind that our audience is Canadian as

well as American. We don't take political or religious stands, so nothing in that area, unless it is strictly informational.'' Length: 1,200 to 2,500 words. Pays $75 minimum. Additional payment is not usually made for b&w photos used with mss. Payment for those purchased on assignment varies with use and quality.

LIVE, 1445 Boonville Ave., Springfield MO 65802. (417)862-2781. Editor: Gary L. Leggett. 100% freelance written. For young people and adults in Assemblies of God Sunday Schools. Weekly. Special issues during Easter, Thanksgiving, and Christmas use articles of a devotional nature. Circ. 225,000. Not copyrighted. Buys about 100 mss a year. Payment on acceptance. Free sample copy and writer's guidelines. Submit seasonal material 12 months in advance. Reports on material within 6 weeks. SASE.
Nonfiction and Photos: ''Articles with reader appeal, emphasizing some phase of Christian living, presented in a down-to-earth manner. Biography or missionary material using fiction techniques. Historical, scientific or nature material with a spiritual lesson. Be accurate in detail and factual material. Writing for Christian publications is a ministry. The spiritual emphasis must be an integral part of your material.'' Length: 1,000 words maximum. Pays 1¢ to 2¢ a word, according to the value of the material and the amount of editorial work necessary. Color photos or slides purchased with mss, or on assignment. Pay open.
Fiction: ''Present believable characters working out their problems according to Bible principles; in other words, present Christianity in action, without being preachy. We use very few serials, but we will consider 4- to 6-part stories if each part conforms to average word length for short stories. Each part must contain a spiritual emphasis and have enough suspense to carry the reader's interest from one week to the next. Stories should be true to life, but not what we would feel is bad to set before the reader as a pattern for living. Stories should not put parents, teachers, ministers or other Christian workers in a bad light. Setting, plot and action should be realistic, with strong motivation. Characterize so that the people will live in your story. Construct your plot carefully so that each incident moves naturally and sensibly toward crisis and conclusion. An element of conflict is necessary in fiction. Short stories should be written from one viewpoint only.'' Length: 1,200 to 2,000 words. Pays 1¢ to 2¢ per word.
Poetry: Buys traditional, free, and blank verse. Length: 12 to 20 lines. Pays 20¢ per line.
Fillers: Brief, purposeful, usually containing an anecdote, and always with a strong evangelical emphasis.

LOOKING AHEAD, 850 N. Grove, Elgin IL 60120. (312)741-2400. Editor: Kristine Miller. For junior high school age students who attend Sunday School. Special Christmas, Easter and Thanksgiving issues. Estab. 1895. Weekly. Buys all rights, but may reassign rights to author after publication. Buys 50 to 75 mss per year. Pays on acceptance. Free sample copy and writer's guidelines. Rarely considers photocopied or simultaneous submissions. Submit seasonal material 1 year in advance. Reports on mss accepted for publication in 1½ to 2 months. Returns rejected mss in 3 to 4 weeks. Query first for nonfiction with statement of writer's qualifications. Submit only complete ms for fiction and poetry. SASE.
Nonfiction, Fiction and Photos: Photo Editor: William Patton. Wants ''very short stories (1,500 to 1,800 words); articles reporting on teen involvement in church/community projects; special how-to mss on earning money, dealing with difficult situations and emotional needs of the age level.'' All mss should present a Christian approach to life. ''Because it is used as part of a dated Sunday school curriculum, articles follow a weekly theme.'' Pays $60 for nonfiction. Length for fiction: 1,200 to 1,500 words. Pays $60 for fiction. Photos purchased with or without ms or on assignment. Captions optional. Pays $15 for b&w 8x10 glossies. Pays $50 for color transparencies. Color photos rarely used.

THE MODERN WOODMEN, 1701 First Ave., Rock Island IL 61201. (309)786-6481. Editor: Robert E. Frank. For members of Modern Woodmen of America, a fraternal insurance society. Bimonthly magazine; 24 pages. Estab. 1883. Circ. 325,000. Not copyrighted. Payment on acceptance. Free sample copy and writer's guidelines. Will consider photocopied and simultaneous submissions. Reports in 3 to 4 weeks. Submit only complete ms. Enclose SASE.
Nonfiction, Fiction, and Photos: ''Nonfiction may be either for children or adults. Fiction should be slanted toward children up to age 16. Our audience is broad and diverse. We want clear, educational, inspirational articles for children and young people. We don't want religious material, teen romances, teen adventure stories.'' Buys informational, how-to, historical, and technical articles. Length: 1,500 to 2,000 words. Pays $35 per ms. Mainstream, and historical fiction. Length: 1,500 to 2,500 words. Pays $35. B&w photos purchased with ms. Captions optional. Prefers vertical, b&w glossy photos for cover use. Payment varies with quality and need.

NOW, FOR TODAY'S YOUNG TEENS, Standard Publishing Co., 8121 Hamilton Ave., Cincinnati OH 45231. (513)931-4050. Editor-in-Chief: Sherry Morris. 80% freelance written. "Teens, age 12-15, from Christian backgrounds generally receive this publication in their Sunday-school classes or through subscriptions." Weekly (published quarterly) magazine; 4 pages. Estab. September 1977. Circ. 70,000. Pays on acceptance. Buys all rights, simultaneous, or second serial (reprint) rights. Submit seasonal/holiday material 9 months in advance of issue date. Simultaneous, photocopied and previously published submissions OK. SASE. Reports in 3-6 weeks. Sample copy and writer's guidelines for SASE; mention *Writer's Market* in request.
Nonfiction: How-to (religious-oriented topics, maybe activities for youth groups or Sunday classes); general interest; humor; inspirational (personal testimonies by teens); interview (religious leaders, Christian teens, atheletes, etc.); nostalgia (humorous); personal experience; and personal opinion (teen only). Wants "no articles that stand out against Christian ethics and ideals, and that promote worldliness to teens. Articles that handle sex, drugs, etc., should do so tastefully and with Christ in mind." Buys 35-40 mss/year. Submit complete ms. Length: 800-1,100 words. Pays 2¢/word.
Photos: Submit photos with ms. Pays $10-25 for 8x10 b&w glossy prints. Captions required. Buys one-time rights. Model release should be available.
Columns/Departments: Self-Expression (teen poetry only); The Bookshelf (book reviews, preferably new or recent books with Christian emphasis); and Sound Waves (record reviews on current, modern Christian records). Buys 25-30/year. Submit complete ms. Length: 250-600 words. Pays 2¢/word. Open to suggestions for new columns/departments.
Fiction: Adventure; experimental; fantasy; historical; humorous; religious; science fiction; and suspense. "All fiction should have some type of identifiable purpose, some message for the modern Christian teen—whether it is a clue to coping with the world or another way of seeing one of Christ's truths. Fiction should deal with all subjects in a forthright manner, without being preachy and without talking down to the young teens. No tasteless manuscripts with blatant sex, or that promote anything adverse to the Bible's teachings. Our audience is composed of Christians—so no idealizing gangsters, smoking, drinking, nudity, etc." Buys 100 mss/year. Submit complete ms. Length: 1,000-1,600 words. Pays 2¢/word, less for reprints.

PROBE, Baptist Brotherhood Commission, 1548 Poplar Ave., Memphis TN 38104. (901)272-2461. Editor-in-Chief: Mike Davis. 5% freelance written. For "boys age 12-17 who are members of a missions organization in Southern Baptist churches." Monthly magazine; 32 pages. Estab. 1970. Circ. 45,000. Pays on acceptance. Buys one-time rights. Phone queries OK. Submit seasonal/holiday material 6 months in advance. Simultaneous submissions OK. SASE. Reports in 1 month. Free sample copy and writer's guidelines.
Nonfiction: How-to (crafts, hobbies); informational (youth, religious especially); inspirational (personalities); personal experience (any first person by teenagers—especially religious); photo feature (sports, teen subjects). Buys 12 mss/year. Submit complete ms. Length: 500-1,500 words. Pays 2½¢/word.
Photos: Purchased with accompanying ms or on assignment. Captions required. Query. Pays $10 for 8x10 b&w glossy prints.

REFLECTION, Pioneer Girls, Inc., Box 788, Wheaton IL 60187. Editor-in-Chief: Dr. Sara Robertson. Managing Editor: Frances Price. 75% freelance written. Emphasizes Christian education with subjects related to today's girl in today's world. Bimonthly magazine; 32 pages. Estab. 1961. Circ. 12,000. Pays on acceptance. Buys first, second, and simultaneous rights. Submit seasonal/holiday material 6 months in advance. Simultaneous and previously published submissions OK. SASE. Reports in 4 weeks. Sample copy and writer's guidelines $1.
Nonfiction: How-to (crafts geared especially to teenage girls); humor; inspirational; interview; and personal experience. Buys 8 mss/issue. Length: 800-1,500 words. Pays $15-30.
Fiction: Adventure; fantasy; historical; humorous; mystery; religious; romance; and suspense. Buys 12 mss/year. Length: 900-1,500 words. Pays $20-35.
Fillers: Jokes, gags, anecdotes, puzzles, short homor. Buys 12/year. Submit complete ms. Pays $5-15.

SCHOLASTIC SCOPE, Scholastic Magazines, Inc., 50 W. 44th St., New York NY 10036. Editor: Katherine Robinson. Circ. 1,324,451. Buys all rights. Issued weekly. 4th to 6th grade reading level; 15 to 18 age level. Reports within 4 to 6 weeks. Query first. SASE.
Nonfiction and Photos: Articles with photos about teenagers who have accomplished something against great odds, overcome obstacles, performed heroically, or simply done something out of the ordinary. Prefers articles about people outside New York area. Length: 400 to 1,200 words. Pays $125 and up.

Fiction and Drama: Problems of contemporary teenagers (drugs, prejudice, runaways, failure in school, family problems, etc.); relationships between people (inter-racial, adult-teenage, employer-employee, etc.) in family, job, and school situations. Strive for directness, realism, and action, perhaps carried through dialogue rather than exposition. Try for depth of characterization in at least one character. Avoid too many coincidences and random happenings. Although action stories are wanted, it's not a market for crime fiction. Looking for material about American Indian, Chicano, Mexican-American, Puerto Rican, and Black experiences among others. Occasionally uses mysteries and science fiction. Length: 400 to 1,200 words. Uses plays up to 3,000 words. Pays $150 minimum.

SEVENTEEN, 850 Third Ave., New York NY 10022. Managing Editor: Ray Robinson. Monthly. Circ. 1,500,000. Buys all rights for nonfiction and poetry. Buys first rights on fiction. Pays on acceptance. Reports in about 2 weeks. SASE.
Nonfiction and Photos: Articles and features of general interest to young women who are concerned with the development of their own lives and the problems of the world around them; strong emphasis on topicality and helpfulness. Send brief outline and query, summing up basic idea of article. Also like to receive articles and features on speculation. Length: 2,000 to 3,000 words. Pays $100 to $500 for articles written by teenagers but more to established adult freelancers. Articles are commissioned after outlines are submitted and approved. Fees for commissioned articles generally range from $500 to $1,350. Photos usually by assignment only. Tamara Schneider, Art Director.
Fiction: Phyllis Schnieder, Fiction Editor. Top-quality stories featuring teenagers—the problems, concerns, and preoccupations of adolescence, which will have recognition and identification value for readers. Does not want "typical teenage" stories, but high literary quality. Avoid oversophisticated material; unhappy endings acceptable if emotional impact is sufficient. Humorous stories that do not condescend to or caricature young people are welcome. Best lengths are 2,500 to 3,000 words. Occasionally accepts 2- or 3-part stories such as mysteries and science fiction with adolescent protagonist and theme. Pays $50 to $300. Conducts an annual short story contest.
Poetry: By teenagers only. Pays $5 to $25. Submissions are non-returnable unless accompanied by SASE.
How To Break In: "The best way for beginning teenage writers to crack the *Seventeen* lineup is for them to contribute suggestions and short pieces to the Free-For-All column, a literary format which lends itself to just about every kind of writing: profiles, puzzles, essays, exposes, reportage, and book reviews."

SEVENTEEN "MINI-MAG," Triangle Communications, 850 3rd Ave., New York NY 10022. Executive Editor: Midge Turk Richardson. *Mini-Mag* Editor: Linda Konner. 50% freelance written. For 13-19 year-old girls. Monthly magazine; 200 pages. Estab. April 1975. Circ. 1,500,000. Pays on acceptance. Buys all rights. Submit seasonal/holiday material 3-4 months in advance of issue date. SASE. Reports in 3-4 weeks.
Nonfiction: How-to ("Here's How"—regular *Mini-Mag* feature; past articles having included fixing bikes, decorating straw hats, coping with gym class, etc.); general interest (teen problems, interfaith dating, holiday lonliness, new findings on love); humor; interview ("17-Second Interviews" with someone of interest to teens; just send background info—staff does interviews by phone); new trends ("Hot Lines"—quick news items under 300 words); career; health; and quizzes. No personal opinion, essays, fiction, poetry, or anything not related to teen-age girls. Buys 8 mss/issue. Query. Length: 650 words for lead pieces; under 300 words for "Hot Lines;" 450-550 for other articles. Pays $25-125.

THE STUDENT, 127 Ninth Ave. N., Nashville TN 37234. Editor: W. Howard Bramlette. Publication of National Student Ministries of the Southern Baptist Convention. For college students; focusing on freshman and sophomore level. Published 12 times during the school year. Circ. 25,000. Buys all rights. Will buy first rights on request. Payment on acceptance. Free sample copy. Mss should be double spaced on white paper with 70-space line, 25 lines per page. Prefers complete ms rather than query. Reports usually in 6 weeks. SASE.
Nonfiction: Contemporary questions, problems, and issues facing college students viewed from a Christian perspective. The need to develop high moral and ethical values. The struggle for integrity in self-concept and the need to cultivate interpersonal relationships directed by Christian love. Length: 1,500 to 1,800 words. Satire and parody on college life, humorous episodes; emphasize clean fun and the ability to grow and be uplifted through humor. Length: 1,500 words maximum. Pays 3¢ a word after editing with reserved right to edit accepted material.

TEEN MAGAZINE, 8490 Sunset Blvd., Hollywood CA 90069. Editor: Roxanne Camron. For teenage girls. Monthly magazine; 100 pages. Estab. 1957. Circ. 900,000. Buys all rights. Predominantly staff written. Freelance purchases are limited. Reports in 6 to 8 weeks. SASE.
Fiction: Feature Editor: Judi Marks. Stories up to 3,500 words dealing specifically with teenagers and contemporary teen issues. More fiction on emerging alternatives for young women. Experimental, suspense, humorous, and romance. Length: 2,000 to 3,000 words. Pays $100 to $150.

TEENS TODAY, Church of the Nazarene, 6401 The Paseo, Kansas City MO 64131. (816)333-7000. Managing Editor: Roy F. Lynn. 80% freelance written. For senior high teens, ages 14-18 attending Church of the Nazarene Sunday school. Weekly magazine; 16 pages. Circ. 67,000. Pays on acceptance. Buys all rights, but may reassign following publication. Submit seasonal/holiday material 10 months in advance. Simultaneous, photocopied and previously published submissions OK. SASE. Reports in 6-8 weeks. Free sample copy and writer's guidelines.
Nonfiction: How-to (mature and be a better person in Christian life); humor (cartoons); personal experience and photo feature. Buys 1 ms/issue. Send complete ms. Length: 500-1,500 words. Pays $10-30.
Photos: Photos purchased with or without accompanying ms or on assignment. Pays $10-25 for 8x10 b&w glossies; $15-50 (sometimes $100) for 8x10 color glossies or any size transparencies. Additional payment for photos accepted with accompanying ms. Model release required.
Columns/Departments: To Be Whole (helping teens be well-rounded persons, build self-worth); Direction (specific instructions gained from a passage of scripture); Last Word (the everyday life of teens—350 words maximum); and Review (review of contemporary youth reading). Buys 2 mss/issue. Send complete ms. Length: 350-1,000 words. Pays 2¢/word. Open to suggestions for new columns/departments.
Fiction: Adventure (if Christian principles are apparent); humorous; religious and romance (keep it clean). Buys 1 ms/issue. Send complete ms. Length: 1,500-2,500 words. Pays 2¢/word.
Poetry: Free verse; haiku; light verse and traditional. Buys 15 poems/year. Pays 20-25¢/line.
Fillers: Puzzles (religious). Buys 15 fillers/year. Pays $5-10.

TIGER BEAT MAGAZINE, 7060 Hollywood Blvd., #800, Hollywood CA 90028. (213)467-3111. Editor: Sharon Lee. For young teenage girls and subteens. Median age: 13. Monthly magazine; 100 pages. Estab. 1960. Circ. 700,000. Buys all rights. Buys 10 mss per year. Payment on acceptance. Free sample copy. Query first. SASE.
Nonfiction and Photos: Stories about young entertainers; their lives, what they do, their interests. Quality writing expected, but must be written with the 12 to 16 age group in mind. Length: depends on feature. Pays $50 to $100. Pays $15 for b&w photos used with mss: captions optional. $50 for color used inside; $75 for cover. 35mm slides preferred.
How To Break In: "We're mostly staff-written; a freelancer's best bet is to come up with something original and exclusive that the staff couldn't do or get."

VENTURE MAGAZINE, Box 150, Wheaton IL 60187. Managing Editor: Rick Mould. 50% freelance written. Publication of Christian Service Brigade. For young men 12 to 18 years of age. Most participate in a Christian Service Brigade program. Monthly magazine. Estab. 1959. Circ. 55,000. Rights purchased vary with author and material. Buys all rights, but will sometimes reassign rights to author after publication. Buys 2 mss a year. Payment on publication. Sample copy for $1. Submit seasonal material 6 to 7 months in advance. Reports within 6 weeks. Query first. SASE.
Nonfiction and Photos: "Family-based articles from boys' perspective; family problems, possible solutions. Assigned articles deal with specific monthly themes decided by the editorial staff. All material has an emphasis on boys in a Christian setting." Length: 400 to 1,200 words. Pays $25 to $75. No additional payment is made for 8x10 b&w photos used with mss. Pays $15 for those purchased on assignment.
Fiction: "Some religious-oriented fiction dealing with religious related experiences or purposes. No far-out plots or trite themes and settings. Length: 800 to 1,200 words. Pays $25-75.

VISIONS, Our Sunday Visitor, Noll Plaza, Huntington IN 46750. (219)356-8400. Editor: Marianna McLoughlin. For Catholic junior high school students of above average intelligence. Magazine, published 27 times during the school year; 12 pages. Estab. 1974. Circ. 46,000. Buys all rights, but may reassign following publication. Pays on publication. SASE. Free sample copy. Reports in 3 weeks.

Nonfiction and Fiction: "I will be happy to read manuscripts that will appeal to the junior high level. We avoid overly pious pieces. Fiction and nonfiction are acceptable with lengths from 500-750 words, but can be longer if the topic so warrants. Subject matter should relate to the young Catholic Christian's life directly or indirectly." Pays $35-75.

WIND, The Wesleyan Church, Box 2000, Marion IN 46952. (317)674-3301, Ext. 146. Editor: Robert E. Black. 40% freelance written. For teen readers. Monthly magazine; 8 pages. Circ. 7,000. Buys first rights or second (serial) reprint rights. Buys 15-20 mss/year. Pays on publication. Will send free sample copy to writer on request. Write for copy of guidelines for writers. Will consider photocopied and simultaneous submissions. Submit seasonal material at least 3 months in advance. Reports in 10 days to 2 weeks. Query or submit complete ms. Enclose SASE.
Nonfiction: "Our publication attempts to promote Bible study, personal piety and aggressive evangelism. We attempt to appeal not only to youth within the church, but also to unchurched youth. We publish short, inspirational articles, full-length articles and features. Themes may include spiritual life, personal problems or areas of concern; personality and character development, relationships with others; moral issues such as drugs, etc.; seasonal, historical and informative articles." Length: 1,000 words maximum. Pays 2¢ a word for first rights; 1¢ a word for second rights.
Fiction: Religious short stories. "We do not use a great amount of fiction, but will occasionally print a piece that fits a theme. Please, no 'easy way out' endings. Be realistic. Even problems that are solved can leave a scar. Sometimes a problem is never solved, but is for the purpose of teaching a lesson. Be honest." Length: 1,000 words maximum. Pays 2¢ a word for first rights; 1¢ a word for second rights.
Poetry: Related to theme. Pays 25¢ a line.

WORKING FOR BOYS, Box A, Danvers MA 01923. Editor: Brother Jerome, C.F.X. 37% freelance written. For junior high, parents, grandparents (the latter because the magazine goes back to 1884). Quarterly magazine; 28 pages. Estab. 1884. Circ. 23,875. Not copyrighted. Buys 50 mss a year. Payment on acceptance. Free sample copy. Submit special material (Christmas, Easter, sports, vacation time) 6 months in advance. Reports in 1 week. Submit only complete ms. Address all mss to the Associate Editor, Brother Alois, CFX, St. John's High School, Main St., Shrewsbury MA 01545. SASE.
Nonfiction and Photos: "Conservative, not necessarily religious, articles. Seasonal mostly (Christmas, Easter, etc.). Cheerful, successful outlook suitable for early teenagers. Maybe we are on the 'square' side, favoring the traditional regarding youth manners: generosity to others, respect for older people, patriotism, etc. Animal articles and tales are numerous, but an occasional good dog or horse story is okay. We like to cover seasonal sports." Buys informational, how-to, personal experience, historical and travel. Length: 500 to 1,000 words. Pays 3¢ a word. 6x6 b&w glossies purchased with ms for $10 each.
Fiction: Mainstream, adventure, religious, and historical fiction. Theme: open. Length: 500 to 1,000 words. Pays 3¢ a word.

YOUNG ADVENTURES, 107 N. Washington, McLeansboro IL 62859. (618)643-2018. Editor-in-Chief: T.L. Chamberlin. 80% freelance written. For 10-16 year olds interested in mystery and adventure. Monthly magazine; 96-128 pages. Estab. October 1978. Circ. 50,000. Pays on publication. Buys all rights, but may reassign following publication. Phone queries OK. Submit seasonal/holiday material 4-6 months in advance of issue date. Simultaneous, photocopied and previously published submissions OK. SASE. Reports in 2-3 weeks. Free sample copy and writer's guidelines; mention *Writer's Market* in request.
Nonfiction: General interest (the effects of world behavior on the youth of today); historical (persons with humble beginnings who have figured in the course of history); how-to (enjoy being young, illustrated arts and crafts); humor (situations that might have happened to the writer as a young person, with a humorous ending); inspirational (currently relevent situations facing youth in the family, school and social area); interview (with youth and those involved with youth); photo feature (on individuals and families who have overcome hardships spotlighting "that your not out until you quit"); and travel (travel adventure). Buys 120 mss/year. Query or submit complete ms. Length: 300-800 words. Pays 2-5¢/word.
Columns/Departments: What To Do (entertainment). "Material should include available activities for Christian youth." Query or submit complete ms. Pays 1-3¢/word.
Fiction: "All material to be written with the Christian principals in mind. Strict code of right and wrong." Adventure; experimental; humorous; mystery; religious; romance; science fiction; suspense; and western. Buys 96 mss/year. Query or submit complete ms. Length: 1,500-3,000 words. Pays 3-6¢/word.

Poetry: Traditional. Buys 2/issue. Pays $5.
Fillers: Jokes, gags, anecdotes; newsbreaks; and puzzles. Buys 150-200/year. Length: 25-150 words. Pays $3-12.

YOUNG AMBASSADOR, The Good News Broadcasting Association, Inc., Box 82808. Lincoln NE 68501. (402)474-4567. Editor-in-Chief: Melvin A. Jones. Managing Editor: Robert H. Sink. Emphasizes Christian living for church-oriented teens, 12-15. Monthly magazine; 52 pages. Estab. 1946. Circ. 90,000. Buys second serial (reprint) and first North American serial rights. Phone queries OK. Submit seasonal/holiday material 6 months in advance. Previously published submissions OK. SASE. Reports in 3 weeks. Free sample copy and writer's guidelines.
Nonfiction: Historical; how-to (church youth group activities); informational; inspirational; interview; personal experience and photo feature. Buys 2 mss/issue. Query or send complete ms. Length: 500-1,800 words. Pays 3¢/word. "Material that covers social, spiritual and emotional needs of teenagers. Interviews with teens who are demonstrating their Faith in Christ in some unusual way. Biographical articles about teens who have overcome obstacles in their lives."
Photos: Photos purchased with or without accompanying ms. Pays $5-7 for b&w photos; $25-50 for color transparencies. Query. Total purchase price for ms includes payment for photos.
Columns/Departments: Life as a Missionary Kid; Teen Scene (teen activities) and Book Reviews. Buys 2 mss/issue. Query. Length: 300-1,800 words. Pays 3¢/word.
Fiction: Adventure; historical; mystery; religious and suspense. "All submissions must relate to teenagers living the Christian life". Buys 45 mss/year. Query or send complete ms. Length: 500-1,800 words. Pays 3¢/word. "Stories of interest to early teenagers with strong, well-developed plot and a definite spiritual tone. Prefer not to see 'preachy' stories. Seasonal stories needed. Should have a realistic, contemporary setting and offer answers to the problems teens are facing."
Fillers: "Submitted by teens." Jokes and puzzles. Query. Length: 200-750 words. Pays 3¢/word.

YOUNG ATHLETE, Box 513, Edmonds WA 98020. (206)774-3589. Editor-in-Chief: Dan Zadra. Managing Editor: Bob Hinz. 75% freelance written. Emphasizes youth and amateur sports, recreation and health, ages 10-20. "Also, large peripheral readership of coaches, physical education teachers and athletic directors who work with these athletes." Bimonthly magazine; 76 pages. Estab. 1975. Circ. 200,000. Pays on publication. Buys all rights, but may reassign following publication. Submit seasonal/holiday material 3½ months in advance. Simultaneous, photocopied and previously published submissions OK. SASE. Reports in 5 weeks. Sample copy $1.25; free writer's guidelines.
Nonfiction: "Interested in any sports-related ms that enlightens, encourages, instructs, challenges or inspires young readers, without preaching or talking down. We cover every sport possible—from marbles to football—from sandlot to the Olympic Games. Want personality features. Length: 250 words for inspirational mss about boys and girls who have achieved in sports at the local level; 800-1,200 words for mss giving insights into the aspirations, philosophies and training techniques of well-known 'Olympic class' amateur athletes; 1,000-1,800 words for mss giving nostalgic glimpses into the early lives, development and eventual rise to fame of today's great professional athletes. Personality features should be liberally spiced with recent quotes from the athlete. How-to mss should be loaded with accurate details. Interested in interpretive articles on new trends in youth or amateur sports; delightful photo stories of little children in various sports; laudatory reports of new and worthwhile sports programs, leagues or organizations for youth." Buys 50 mss/year. Query. Pays $25-200.
Photos: Bob Honey, Photo Editor. Photos purchased with or without accompanying ms. Captions required. Pays $5-15 for b&w photos; $25 minimum for color photos. Query.
How To Break In: "Writing style should be lively, fast-paced, directly involving and easy to understand. Avoid hero worship, cynicism or 'winning at any cost' philosophy. Our posture: Winning is fine, but participation, personal growth, health, fun and fair play for everyone are what it's all about."

YOUNG MISS, 52 Vanderbilt Ave., New York NY 10017. Editor: Rubie Saunders. 75-80% freelance written. Monthly, except June and August, for girls 10 to 14. Buys all rights. Pays on acceptance. Editorial requirement sheet for SASE. Query on nonfiction. Reports on submissions in 3-4 weeks. All mss must be typed, double-spaced. SASE.
Nonfiction: No food, fashion or beauty articles are wanted, but practically everything else goes. Hobbies, unusual projects, self-improvement (getting along with parents, brothers, etc.);

how-to articles on all possible subjects. Length: about 1,500 words. Pays $50 minimum. Do not submit illustrations. Rough sketches may accompany a how-to article.
Fiction: "All fiction should be aimed at girls 10 to 14, with the emphasis on the late 12- to 14-year olds. Stories may be set in any locale or time—urban, western, foreign, past, contemporary, or future. Boys may be involved, even in a romantic way, as long as it is tastefully done. Mystery and adventure stories are also welcomed. Stories of today are particularly desirable. Especially interested in fiction with an urban setting dealing with the *real* problems today's young teens face. Overstocked on stories about middle income, small town girls who seem to have no problems greater than getting a date for a school dance or adjusting to a new neighborhood." Length: 2,000 to 2,300 words. Pays $50 minimum.
Fillers: Crossword puzzles and short quizzes on general information and personality subjects. Pays $10 to $25. Occasionally uses how-to fillers; currently overstocked on these.

YOUNG WORLD, The Saturday Evening Post Co., Youth Division, P.O. Box 567B, Indianapolis IN 46206. (317)634-1100. Editor: Julie Plopper. For young people 10 to 14 years old. Monthly, except June/July and August/September. Buys all rights. Pays on publication. Sample copy 50¢; free writer's guidelines. Submit seasonal material at least 8 months in advance. Minimum reporting time is 10 to 12 weeks. Mss will not be returned unless accompanied by sufficient postage and SAE.
Nonfiction and Photos: Historical, scientific, contemporary articles, and articles dealing with community involvement. "We are particularly interested in articles about young people doing things: community projects, sports, business enterprises. Also good are informational, how-to, interview, profile, and humorous articles and photo features. We are always interested in contemporary craft projects with clear directions and photos of the finished product. Articles based on interviews with sports or entertainment personalities or teenagers who have accomplished significant things are welcome." Length: 900 words maximum. Pays approximately 3¢ a word. Photos are purchased with accompanying ms. Captions required. Pays $2.50 for each b&w; $5 for color.
Fiction: Adventure, mystery, humor, suspense, westerns, science fiction, romance, and historical fiction. Length: 1,800 words maximum; slightly shorter preferred. Limited number of two-part suspense stories accepted; total word limit 3,500 words. Pays about 3¢ a word.
Poetry: Humorous poetry for young teenagers. Traditional forms, blank and free verse, and light verse. Theme is open. No length limits. No fixed rate of payment.
Puzzles: All types desired; math or word. Should be difficult enough for this age group. No fixed rate of payment.

YOUTH ALIVE!, 1445 Boonville Ave., Springfield MO 65802. Editor: Carol A. Ball. "Official youth organ of the Assemblies of God, slanted to high school teens." Monthly. Circ. 15,000. Buys some first rights, but "we are interested in multiple submissions, second rights, and other reprints." Pays on acceptance. Will send a free sample copy to a writer on request. Reports in 6 weeks. Enclose SASE.
Nonfiction, Photos, and Poetry: "Purpose is to provide news of the Pentecostal youth scene, to inspire to Christlike living, and to be used as a witnessing tool. We can use photo features, photos, interviews, biographical features, reports on outstanding Christian youth, how-to-do-it features, some fiction, some poems, humor, news, motivational articles, seasonal material (4 months prior to special day), personal experiences. Avoid cliches, unexplained theological terms, sermonizing, and 'talking down' to youth. Read *Youth Alive!* to get our style, but don't be afraid to submit something different if you think we might like it." Length of articles: 300 to 1,200 words. Payment is 1½¢ a word minimum. Teen-slanted human interest photos purchased with mss. 8x10 b&w glossies or color transparencies. Payment is $10-30. Payment for poetry is 20¢ a line.

YOUTH IN ACTION, Free Methodist Church, 901 College Ave., Winona Lake IN 46590. (219)267-7621. Executive Editor: David Markell. For junior high and high school youth. Monthly magazine; 32 pages. Estab. 1956. Circ. 2,700. Pays on publication. Buys one-time rights. Phone queries OK. Simultaneous, photocopied and previously published submissions OK. SASE. Reports in 4 weeks. Free sample copy and writers' guidelines.
Nonfiction: How-to (subjects dealing with religious themes such as prayer, Bible study, etc.); humor (any subject relevant to teens); inspirational (anything of a religious nature); interviews (with people who are in situations that would relate to our themes); personal experience (which would illustrate a spiritual truth); personal opinion and photo features (on issues and subjects that relate to our theme); profiles; (well-known people, especially teenagers who have become Christians). Buys 10-12/year. Send complete ms. Length: 500-2,000 words. Pays 2¢/word.

Photos: Purchased with or without ms or on assignment. Send 8½x11 prints. Pays $15-25/b&w; $25-50/color.
Fiction: Humorous subjects that relate to teenage interests. Religious themes "along our denominational standards". Buys 5/year. Send complete ms. Length: 500-2,000 words. Pays 2¢/word.
Poetry: Avant-garde and traditional forms; free verse, haiku, light verse. Buys 10/year. Pays $10 minimum.

Theater, Movie, TV, and Entertainment Publications

For those publications whose emphasis is on music and musicians, see the section on Music Publications. Nonpaying markets for similar material are listed in the Literary and "Little" Publications category.

ADAM FILM WORLD, 8060 Melrose Ave., Los Angeles CA 90046. (213)653-8060. Editor: Edward S. Sullivan. For fans of X- and R-rated movies. Bimonthly magazine; 96 pages. Estab. 1966. Circ. 250,000. Buys first North American serial rights. Buys about 18 mss per year. Pays on publication. Will send sample copy to writer for $1.50. No photocopied or simultaneous submissions. Reports on mss accepted for publication in 1 to 2 months. Returns rejected material in 2 weeks. Query first. SASE.
Nonfiction and Photos: "All copy is slanted for fans of X- and R- movies and can be critical of this or that picture, but not critical of the genre itself. Our main emphasis is on pictorial layouts, rather than text; layouts of stills from erotic pictures. Any article must have possibilities for illustration. We go very strong in the erotic direction, but *no* hard-core stills. We see too many fictional interviews with a fictitious porno star, and too many fantasy suggestions for erotic film plots. No think pieces wanted. We would consider articles on the continuing erotization of legitimate films from major studios, and the increasing legitimization of X- and R- films from the minors." Length: 1,000 to 3,000 words. Pays $80 to $210. Most photos are bought on assignment from regular photographers with studio contacts, but a few 8x10 b&w's are purchased from freelancers for use as illustrations. Pays minimum of $10 per photo.

AFTER DARK, 10 Columbus Circle, New York NY 10019. (212)399-2400. Editor: William Como. For an audience "20 to 55 years old." Monthly. Circ. 360,000. Buys first rights. Buys about 30 mss/year. Pays on publication. Sample copy $2. Submit seasonal material 4 months in advance. Reports in 3 to 4 weeks. Query first, including copies of previously published work. SASE.
Nonfiction and Photos: Articles on "every area of entertainment—films, TV, theater, nightclubs, books, records." Length: 2,500 to 3,000 words. Pays $75 to $150. Photos with captions only. B&w glossies, color transparencies. Pays $20 to $50.
How To Break In: "The best way to crack *After Dark* is by doing a piece on some new trend in the entertainment world. We have people in most of the important cities, but we rely on freelancers to send us material from out-of-the-way places where new things are developing. Some of our contributing editors started out that way. Query first."

AFTERNOON TV, 2 Park Ave., New York NY 10016. Monthly. For soap opera viewers. Reports at once. Enclose SASE.
Nonfiction and Photos: Interviews with afternoon TV stars. Pays $100 for eight-page story. Minimum length: 4 typewritten pages. Photos purchased with mss. Pays up to $15 per photo.
How To Break In: "We're a very tough market to break into. Everything we do is interviews with daytime TV performers which makes us a market as specialized as *Popular Mechanics*. If a writer has some credits elsewhere and has done personality pieces before, the best way to break in here would be with a story about a lesser star in one of the New York soaps. We have a West Coast editor and a regular staff of writers out there, and besides, New York has 11 soaps while there are only three in California. The interview doesn't have to be with a performer we've never interviewed before, but it should have some new angle."

AMERICAN FILM, American Film Institute, Kennedy Center, Washington DC 20566. (202)833-9300. Editor: Hollis Alpert. 80% freelance written. For film professionals, students, teachers, film enthusiasts. Monthly magazine; 80 pages. Estab. 1975. Circ. 80,000. Buys First North American serial rights. Buys 20 to 30 mss a year. Copyrighted. Payment on acceptance. Sample copy $1. Will consider photocopied submissions, but not simultaneous submissions.

Submit seasonal material 3 months in advance. Reports in 1 to 2 weeks. Query first. SASE.
Nonfiction: In-depth articles on film and television-related subjects. "Our articles require expertise and first-rate writing ability." Buys informational, profile, historical and "think" pieces. No film reviews. Length: 2,000 to 3,000 words. Pays $250 to $500.

AMERICAN SQUAREDANCE, Box 788, Sandusky OH 44870. Editors-in-Chief: Stan & Cathie Burdick. 50% freelance written. Emphasizes squaredancing. Monthly magazine; 100 pages. Estab. 1945. Circ. 11,500. Pays on publication. Buys all rights. Submit seasonal/holiday material 3-4 months in advance. SASE. Reports in 1 week. Free sample copy.
Nonfiction: How-to; informational; historical; humor; inspirational; interview; nostalgia; personal opinion; profile; travel; personal experience; photo feature; and technical. All articles must have dance theme. Buys 18 mss/year. Submit complete ms. Length: 1,000-2,500 words. Pays $10-25.
Photos: Purchased with accompanying ms. Captions required. B&w glossy prints. Pays $2-10.
Fiction: Fantasy; historical; humorous; romance; suspense; science fiction; and western. Must have dance theme. Buys 6 mss/year. Length: 1,500-2,500 words. Pays $10-30.
Poetry: Haiku, light verse, traditional. Must be on a dance theme. Buys 6 poems/year. Limit submissions to 3 at a time. Pays $5-10.
Fillers: Crossword and word puzzles with dance theme. Buys 4/year. Pays $5.

APPLAUSE: San Diego Magazine of the Arts, 545 Olive St., San Diego CA 92103. Editor: Judith Friedel. Managing Editor: Nancy Sprague. Distributed at performances of the San Diego opera, symphony and other cultural events. Monthly magazine; 52 pages. Circ. 60,000. Pays on publication. Buys all rights, but may reassign following publication. Submit seasonal/holiday material 3 months in advance. SASE. Reports in 2 weeks. Sample copy $1; writer's guidelines for SASE.
Nonfiction: "Primary editorial emphasis is on the San Diego opera, symphony and Old Globe Theatre. We look for articles that will get an 'I-didn't-know-that' reaction from our readers. We also cover other aspects of both performing and visual arts. Our pages are open to your suggestions." Length: 1,000-2,000 words. Pays $1.04/column inch.

BLACK STARS, Johnson Publishing Company, Inc., 820 S. Michigan Ave., Chicago IL 60605. (312)786-7668. Managing Editor: Ariel Perry Strong. 20% freelance written. Emphasizes entertainment. Monthly magazine; 74 pages. Estab. 1971. Circ. 350,000. Pays on publication. Buys all rights, but may reassign following publication. Seasonal/holiday material should be submitted 3 months in advance. SASE. Reports in 3 weeks. Sample copy $1-2; free writer's guidelines.
Nonfiction: Personal experience and photo feature. "Only articles on black entertainers." Buys 600 mss/year. Query. Length: 4,500 words maximum. Pays $100-200.
Photos: Purchases 8x10 b&w or transparencies. Query, submit prints or transparencies.

CANADIAN THEATRE REVIEW, 4700 Keele St., Downsview, Ontario, Canada M3J 1P3. (416)667-3768. Editor-in-Chief: Don Rubin. Business Manager: Lynn McFadgen. 80% freelance written. Emphasizes theatre for academics and professionals. Quarterly magazine; 144 pages. Estab. 1974. Circ. 5,000. Pays on publication. Buys one-time rights. SASE. Reports in 10-12 weeks. Sample copy $3.
Nonfiction: Historical (theatre in Canada); interview (internationally known theatre figures); and photo feature (theatre world-wide). Buys 40 mss/year. Length: 1,500-5,000 words. Query or submit complete ms. Pays $15/published page.
Photos: State availability of photos with query or mss.

CINEFANTASTIQUE, P.O. Box 270, Oak Park IL 60303. (312)383-5631. Editor: Frederick S. Clarke. For persons interested in horror, fantasy and science fiction films. Magazine; 48 pages. Estab. 1970. Quarterly. Circ. 8,000. Rights purchased are all magazine rights in all languages. Pays on publication. Photocopied submissions OK. No simultaneous submissions. Reports on material accepted for publication in 4 weeks. Returns rejected material "immediately." SASE.
Nonfiction: "We're interested in articles, interviews and reviews which concern horror, fantasy and science fiction films." Pays 10¢/column line. Line varies from 30-40 spaces.

DANCE MAGAZINE, 10 Columbus Circle, New York NY 10019. (212)399-2400. Editor: William Como. Monthly. For the dance profession and members of the public interested in the art of dance. Buys all rights. Pays on publication. Sample copy $2. Query. SASE.
Nonfiction: Personalities, knowledgeable comment, news. Length: 2,500 to 3,000 words. Pays $25 to $50.

Photos: Purchased with articles or with captions only. Pays $5-15.
How To Break In: "Do a piece about a local company that's not too well known but growing; or a particular school that is doing well which we may not have heard about; or a local dancer who you feel will be gaining national recognition. Query first."

DANCE SCOPE, American Dance Guild, 1619 Broadway, Room 603, New York NY 10019. Editor-in-Chief: Richard Lorber. 95% freelance written. Emphasizes dance and related performing/visual/musical arts. For performers, university teachers and students, general public audiences, other artists, arts administrators, critics, historians. Semiannual magazine; 80 pages. Estab. 1965. Circ. 5,000. Pays on publication. Buys all rights. Submit seasonal or holiday material 6 months in advance. Photocopied submissions OK. SASE. Reports in 1 month. Sample copy $2.50.
Nonfiction: Informational (contemporary developments, trends, ideas); historical (synthesis of ideas, not narrowly academic); inspirational (documentation and think pieces); interviews (with commentary, intros, etc.); personal experience (with broad relevance). Buys 12 mss per year. Query. Length: 1,500-3,000 words. Pays $25-50.
Photos: No additional payment for b&w glossies used with mss. Captions required. Query. Model release required.

DRAMATICS MAGAZINE, International Thespian Society, 3368 Central Pkwy, Cincinnati OH 45225. (513)541-7379. Editor-in-Chief: S. Ezra Goldstein. 25-30% freelance written. For theatre arts students, teachers and others interested in theatre arts education. Magazine published bimonthly in September, November, January, March and May. 48 pages. Estab. 1929. Circ. 50,000. Pays on acceptance. Buys first North American serial rights. Phone queries OK. Submit seasonal/holiday material 3 months in advance. Simultaneous, photocopied and previously published submissions OK. SASE. Reports in 3 weeks. Sample copy $1; free writer's guidelines.
Nonfiction: Historical; how-to (technical theatre); informational; interview; photo feature; profile and technical. Buys 30 mss/year. Submit complete ms. Length: 2,500 words minimum. Pays $25-100.
Photos: Purchased with accompanying ms. Uses b&w photos. Query. Total purchase price for ms includes payment for photos.
Columns/Departments: Technicalities (theatre how-to articles); Tag Line (editorials on some phase of the theatre) and Promptbook (entertainment arts news relevant to an educational magazine). Buys 15 mss/year. Send complete ms. Length: 250-1,000 words. Pays $15-40.
Fiction: Drama (one-act plays). Buys 5 mss/year. Send complete ms. Pays $40-100.

DRAMATIKA, 390 Riverside Dr., Suite 10B, New York NY 10025. Editors: John and Andrea Pyros. Magazine; 40 pages. For persons interested in the theater arts. Estab. 1968. Published 2 times/year. Circ. 500-1,000. Buys all rights. Buys 6-12 mss/year. Pays on publication. Sample copy $1. Will consider photocopied submissions. Will also consider simultaneous submissions "if advised." Reports in 1 month. SASE.
Drama and Photos: Wants "performable pieces — plays, songs, scripts, etc." Will consider plays on various and open themes. Length: 20 pages maximum. Pays about $25 per piece; $5-10 for smaller pieces. B&w photos purchased with ms with extra payment. Captions required. Pays $5. Size: 8x11.

E W TV GUIDE, Box 614, Corte Madera CA 94925. (415)397-9242. Editor-in-Chief: William Whitney. Emphasizes television programming and stars. Distributed to television audiences through local trade media. Weekly tabloid; 16-24 pages. Estab. 1971. Circ. 50,000. Pays on publication. Buys one-time rights. Submit seasonal or holiday material 3 months in advance. Simultaneous, photocopied, and previously published submissions OK. SASE. Reports in 2-4 weeks. Sample copy 25¢.
Nonfiction: Carol Williams, Nonfiction Editor. Expose, informational, humor, interview, photo feature, and profile. Buys 5-6 mss/issue. Send complete ms. Length: 500-2,000 words. Pays 2-10¢/word.
Photos: Photos purchased with or without accompanying ms or on assignment. Pays $2-5 for 5x7 b&w glossies. Total purchase price for ms includes payment for photos. Model release required.
Fillers: Clippings, jokes, gags, anecdotes, puzzles. Buys 2-5 fillers/issue. Submit complete ms. Length: 200-500 words. Pays $5-15.

FILM COMMENT, 1865 Broadway, New York NY 10023. Editor: Richard Corliss. For film students, teachers and scholars. Has select group of writers which usually fills its needs. Query. SASE.

FILM QUARTERLY, University of California Press, Berkeley CA 94720. (415)642-6333. Editor: Ernest Callenbach. 100% freelance written. Issued quarterly. Buys all rights. Pays on publication. Query first. SASE.
Nonfiction: Articles on style and structure in films, articles analyzing the work of important directors, historical articles on development of the film as art, reviews of current films and detailed analyses of classics, book reviews of film books. Length: 6,000 words maximum. Must be familiar with the past and present of the art; must be competently, although not necessarily breezily, written; must deal with important problems of the art. Payment is about 1½¢ per word; higher for material on films not in ordinary theatrical release.

FM GUIDE, 20 Hampton Rd., Box 1592, Southampton NY 11968. (516)283-2360. Editor: Bonnie P. Barton. For the hi-fi and radio enthusiast; especially interested in classical music. Publication of FM Music Program Guide Inc. Magazine; 64 pages. Estab. 1965. Monthly. Circ. 100,000. Buys all rights. Buys about 36 mss per year. Pays on publication. Will send free sample copy to writer on request. No photocopied or simultaneous submissions. Reports on mss accepted for publication in 2 months. Returns rejected material in 6 months. Enclose SASE.
Nonfiction and Photos: Publishes "radio-oriented nonfiction and hi-fidelity information, equipment stories, general interest in the musical world. Write within a musical interest framework. We cater to radio listeners with guides to programming and composers." Length: informational, 1,200 to 2,500 words; manufacturer profile, 800 to 1,200 words. Pays $25 to $100. Photos purchased with ms with no additional payment. Captions optional.

MOTION, 211 Stewart St., Ottawa, Ontario, Canada. (613)237-5360. Editor-in-Chief: P.M. Evanchuck. Managing Editor: James McLarty. 70-80% freelance written. Emphasizes Canadian film, TV, and theater. Bimonthly magazine; 40 pages. Estab. November 1972. Circ. 10,000. Pays on publication. Buys all rights, but may reassign following publication. Phone queries OK. Submit seasonal/holiday material 2 months in advance of issue date. Photocopied and previously published submissions OK. SASE. Reports in 1 month. Free sample copy.
Nonfiction: Exposé; general interest; historical; how-to; interview; new product; nostalgia; personal experience; personal opinion; photo feature; profile and technical. Buys 6-10 mss/issue. Query or submit complete ms. Length: 500-2,000 words. Pays $20-100.

MOVIE LIFE, Ideal Publishing Co., 2 Park Ave., New York NY 10016. Editor: Seli Groves. "Basically, for women, from 9 to 90, interested in peeking at the private lives of entertainment stars." Estab. 1938. Monthly. Circ. 225,000. Buys all rights. Buys about 150 mss a year. Payment on publication. Will not consider photocopied or simultaneous submissions. Reports on material in 3 to 6 weeks. Query first. Enclose SASE.
Nonfiction and Photos: Feature articles on well-known movie and television personalities. Interviews. Length: 1,500 to 2,000 words. Pays $125 to $200. 8x10 b&w photos purchased with accompanying mss for $25, or without extra payment, depending on the article and photos.
How To Break In: "Let's suppose Elvis comes to town. Check with the local paper to find out who is handling publicity for him. Then see if you can arrange an interview. Also, please get a letter from the press person acknowledging that such an interview actually took place. I'm afraid to say, we sometimes get accounts of meetings which never happened, so we do have to check. You should read our magazine and become familiar with the style. We like first-person accounts and can help out with the style if the facts are good. Our stories tend to be very personal—more visceral then intellectual. Don't be blunted by what you think I might not like. And don't overlook doing some library research for some interesting background on your subjects."

MOVIE MIRROR, MODERN SCREEN, TV PICTURE LIFE, PHOTO SCREEN, 355 Lexington Ave., New York NY 10017. Editor of *Movie Mirror:* Joan Goldstein. Editor of *TV Picture Life:* Pegi Adams. Editor of *Photo Screen:* Marsha Daly. Editor of *Modern Screen:* Connie Berman. Monthlies. Buys 10 to 12 mss a month. Pays on acceptance. Submit complete ms. Reports promptly. SASE.
Nonfiction: "The most desired sort of story is the fresh and strongly angled, dramatically told article about the private life of a leading motion picture or television star. Categories of stories popular with readers (they've changed little over the years): romantic love, weddings, married life, babies, parent/child relationships, religion, health, extra-marital affairs, divorces, dangerous moments survived, feuds. The major difference in fan mag writing then and now is the increased frankness permissible in today's articles. When many stars talk forthrightly about living together without marriage, bearing children out of wedlock, personal sexual inclinations,

etc., fan magazine editors have little choice but to go along with contemporary trends. The object, no matter the category of article, is to tell the reader something she did not already know about a favorite performer, preferably something dramatic, provocative, personal. Our readers are female (over 90% of them), youngish (under 45), and often are wives or daughters of bluecollar workers. It is our purpose to bring a bit of vicarious excitement and glamour to these readers whose own lives may not be abundantly supplied with same. Stars they want to read about now are: (TV) Dean Martin, Mary Tyler Moore, Redd Foxx, Carol Burnett, Peter Falk, William Conrad, and the leads of 'All In The Family,' 'The Waltons,' 'M*A*S*H,' and 'Maude'; (Movies) Elvis Presley, Liz Taylor, Barbara Streisand, Liza Minnelli, Paul Newman, Steve McQueen, John Wayne, Robert Redford. While most of our manuscripts are written by top magazine and newspaper writers in Hollywood and New York, we have an open-door policy. Any writer able to meet our specific editorial needs will get a 'read' here. Until we know your work, however, we would have to see completed manuscripts rather than outlines. Writers outside the two show biz meccas might keep in mind that we are particularly interested in hometown stories on contemporary celebrities. Average length for articles is 2,000 words. Pay starts at $75, going considerably higher for genuine scoops."

MOVIE STARS, Ideal Publishing Co., 2 Park Ave., New York NY 10016. Editor: Ronnie Blum. For anyone from their teens to their sixties who's interested in the lives of top TV and screen personalities. Estab. 1935. Buys all rights. Buys 100 mss/year. Pays on publication. Query. SASE.
Nonfiction and Photos: General subject matter consists of "human interest articles on movies and television personalities." Pays $150 for a 7- to 8-page article. Pays $25 per b&w photo.
How To Break In: "Submit an interview with a secondary character on a popular TV series, or a featured actor in several films, whose face has become known to the public. It is best if you query first, presenting your interview idea and including some personal information about yourself—a resume and some previously published material, for example"

PERFORMING ARTS IN CANADA, Box 517, Station F, Toronto, Ontario, Canada M4Y 1T4. (416)921-2601. Managing Editor: Linda Kelley. 50% freelance written. For professional performers and general readers with an interest in Canadian theatre, dance and music. Quarterly magazine. Circ. 40,000. Pays 2 weeks following publication. Buys first rights. Reports in 3-6 weeks. SAE, and International Reply Coupons. Sample copy 50¢.
Nonfiction: "Lively, stimulating, well researched articles on Canadian performing artists or group." Buys 25-35 mss/year. Query. Length: 1,500-2,000 words. Pays $100.

PHOTO SCREEN, Sterling's Magazines, Inc., 356 Lexington Ave., New York NY 10017. (212)391-1400. Editor: Marsha Daly. 50-60% freelance written. Emphasizes TV and movie news of star personalities. Monthly magazine; 75 pages. Estab. 1960. Circ. 300,000. Pays on publication. Buys all rights. SASE. Reports in 6 weeks.
Nonfiction: Exposes (on stars' lives); informational (on Hollywood life); interviews (with stars); photo features (on stars' personal lives). Buys 5-6 mss/month. Query. Pays $75-200.
Photos: Roger Glazer, department editor. Purchased without ms; mostly on speculation. Pays $25-35 for 8x10 b&w (glossy or matte); $50 minimum for color. Chromes only; 35mm or 2¼x2¼.

PLAYBILL MAGAZINE, 151 E. 50th, New York NY 10022. Issued monthly; free to theatergoers. Buys first and second U.S. magazine rights. SASE.
Nonfiction: The major emphasis is on current theater and theater people. On occasion, buys humor or travel pieces if offbeat. Wants sophisticated, informative prose that makes judgments and shows style. Uses unusual interviews, although most of these are staff written. Style should be worldly and literate without being pretentious or arch; runs closer to *Harper's* or *New Yorker* than to *Partisan Review*. Wants interesting information, adult analysis, written in a genuine, personal style. Humor is also welcome. Between 1,000 and 2,500 words for articles. Pays $100 to $400 each.
How To Break In: "We're difficult to break into and most of our pieces are assigned. We don't take any theater pieces relating to theater outside New York. We also have short features on boutiquing, fashions, men's wear, women's wear. The best way for a newcomer to break in is with a short humorous or satirical piece or some special piece of reporting on the Broadway theater — no more than 700 to 1,000 words. A number of people have come in that way and some of them have subsequently received assignments from us."

PRE-VUE, Box 31255, Billings MT 59107. Editor-Publisher: Virginia Hansen. "We are the cable-TV guide for southern Montana; our audience is as diverse as people who subscribe to

cable TV." Weekly magazine; 32 to 40 pages. Estab. 1969. Circ. 15,000. Not copyrighted. Payment on publication. Reports in 8 weeks. Query. SASE.
Nonfiction and Photos: "Subject matter is general, but must relate in some way to television or our reading area (southern Montana). We would like articles to have a beginning, middle and end; in other words, popular magazine style, heavy on the hooker lead. We're interested in holidays and special events in our reading area." Informational, how-to, interview, profile, humor, historical, travel, TV reviews. Feature length: 500-800 words. Pays minimum of 2¢/word. 8x10 (sometimes smaller) b&w photos purchased with mss or on assignment. Pays $3 to $6. Captions required. Department Editor: Virginia Hansen.
Poetry: Traditional forms; haiku; and light verse. Buys 20/year. Length: 2 to 8 lines. Pays $2.
Fillers: Short humor, local history and oddities. Buys 12/year. Length: 50-200 words. Pays minimum of 2¢ per word.

PROLOG, 104 N. St. Mary, Dallas TX 75204. (214)827-7734. Editor: Mike Firth. 10% freelance written. For "playwrights and teachers of playwriting." Quarterly newsletter; 8 pages. Estab. 1973. Circ. 200. Not copyrighted. Buys 8 mss per year. Pays on acceptance or publication; "may hold pending final approval." Sample copy $1. Will consider photocopied and simultaneous submissions. Reports on mss accepted for publication in "over 3 months." Returns rejected material in 1 or 2 months. SASE.
Nonfiction: Wants "articles and anecdotes about writing, sales and production of play scripts. Style should be direct to reader (as opposed to third-person observational)." Does not want to see general attacks on theater, personal problems, problems without solutions of general interest. Pays ½¢/word.

SAN FRANCISCO THEATRE MAGAZINE, 408 Columbus, San Francisco CA 94133. (415)986-6042. Editor-in-Chief: David Hett. Assistant Editor: Kasey Arnold. 25% freelance written. Emphasizes theatre and theatre-related topics. Quarterly magazine; 98 pages. Estab. August 1977. Circ. 20,000. Pays after publication. Buys all rights, but may reassign following publication. Submit seasonal/holiday material 2 months in advance of issue date. Simultaneous, photocopied and previously published submissions OK. SASE. Reports in 1 month. Sample copy $2; free writer's guidelines; mention *Writer's Market* in request.
Nonfiction: General interest (interviews and articles on theatre, theatrical personalities); interview; personal opinion (critiques, etc.); and profile (scholars, directors, personalities). Buys 3-4 mss/issue. Query. Pays 3½¢/word.
Photos: "If we have a choice between a good article with photos and one without, we will take the one with, as our magazine relies on strong visual augmentation to articles." Pays $5 minimum for 8x10 glossy b&w and color prints. Captions preferred. Buys all rights, but may reassign following publication.
Columns/Departments: Book Reviews (theatrical books); reports on technical aspects of theatre; and reports from cities other than San Francisco on major theatrical events in that area. Buys 3-4/issue. Query. Pays 3½¢/word. Open to suggestions for new columns/departments.

SCREEN AND TV ALBUM, Ideal Publishing Corp., 2 Park Ave., New York NY 10016. Editor: Ronnie Blum. Entertainment news magazine published every 2 months. Audience ranges from sub-teens to mature people in their 60's and "we try to fill the magazine with personalities appealing to these various ages." Buys all rights. Buys 4 to 6 mss a year. Pays on publication. Will send sample copy to writer for 75¢. Query first. Reports within 10 days. Enclose SASE.
Nonfiction and Photos: Stories concerning popular personalities of film, TV and recording industries must be of human interest, concerned with some personal, not professional, aspect of personality's life. "Give me your ideas on a story, plus your sources for same. Interviews (caution) will be checked through from this end with the personality before any such article is purchased. Check the new TV shows, the new films, and write about them." Interview and photo articles. Length: 1,000 to 3,500 words. "Payments arranged per article prior to transfer of material from writer to editor. I will quote price or discuss asked-for payment." Please query Ms. Sheila Steinach on any photo submission.
How To Break In: "One thing you might try to do is take a look at the second banana on a hit TV show and see what he's doing. We're interested in new personal angles —perhaps he was adopted and is willing to talk about it. We're using longer pieces now and more photos. The main thing a freelancer has to prove to me is that he is dependable, can meet deadlines, can take positive editorial criticism, and is accurate."

SHOWBILL, 105 Davenport Rd., Toronto, Ontario, Canada M5R 1H6. (416)928-0268. Editor: Margo Raport. 90% freelance written. Emphasizes film, film personalities, and concept pieces.

Bimonthly magazine; 64 pages. Estab. 1975. Circ. 400,000. Pays on publication. Buys all rights. Phone queries OK. Submit seasonal/holiday material 2 months in advance of issue date. Previously published submissions OK. SASE. Reports in 3 weeks. Free sample copy and writer's guidelines; mention *Writer's Market* in request.

Nonfiction: Articles on American, Canadian and foreign films; personalities in the industry (directors, actors, etc.); concept pieces (who's who, the New Hollywood, etc.); expose (on personalities or names in the news); how-to (getting started in the business); general interest; humor; historical; inspirational; interview (exclusive); new product; nostalgia; personal experience (from people in the industry); personal opinion (good foundation for critique); photo feature; profile and technical. Buys 10 mss/issue. Submit complete ms and clips of previously published work. Length: 400-1,200 words. Pays $50-200.

Photos: State availability of photos with query. Pays $15-50 for b&w photos; $25-60 for color. Captions preferred. Buys all rights, but may reassign following publication.

SOAP OPERA DIGEST, 420 Lexington Ave., New York NY 10017. Executive Editor: Ruth J. Gordon. 5% freelance written. Monthly magazine; 128 pages. Estab. 1975. Circ. 600,000. Pays on publication. Buys all rights. Submit seasonal/holiday material 4 months in advance of issue date. Photocopied submissions OK. SASE. Reports in 1 month.

Nonfiction: "Articles only directly about daytime personalities or soap operas." Interview (no telephone interviews); nostalgia; photo feature (must be recent); and profile. No summaries, personal opinions or analysis of shows. Buys 1-2 mss/issue. Query with clips of previously published work. Length: 1,000-2,000 words. Pays $75-100.

Photos: State availability of photos with query. Offers no additional payment for photos accepted with ms. Captions preferred. Buys all rights.

SUPER-8 FILMAKER, PMS Publishing Co., 3161 Fillmore St., San Francisco CA 94123. Editor-in-Chief: Bruce Anderson. 90% freelance written. Emphasizes filmmaking in Super-8, for amateur and professional filmmakers, students and teachers of film. Magazine (8 times a year); 66 pages. Estab. 1973. Circ. 46,000. Pays on publication. Buys all rights. Submit seasonal/holiday material 8 months in advance. SASE. Reports in 1 week. Sample copy $1.25; free writer's guidelines.

Nonfiction: How-to; informational and technical (dealing with filmmaking only). Buys 5 mss/issue. Query. Length: 2,000-3,000 words.

How To Break In: "We are a consumer publication, not a trade publication. Articles written for *Super-8 Filmaker* should contain technical information, but they should not be written in technical terminology. All technical terms and concepts should be defined simply and concisely."

TAKE ONE, Box 1778, Station B., Montreal H3B 3L3. Que., Canada. (514)843-7733. Editor: Phyllis Platt. Publisher/Editor-in-Chief: Peter Lebensold. 90% freelance written. For anyone interested in films in modern society. Not a fan magazine. Bimonthly. Circ. 25,000. Buys about 150 mss a year. Buys North American serial rights. Pays on publication. Free sample copy. Reports in 3 weeks. Query preferred. Enclose SAE and International Reply Coupons.

Nonfiction and Photos: Interviews, articles, photo stories, reviews. Anything having to do with film. Articles on directors, actors, etc. On new or classic films, on aspects of the industry, current or historical, on aesthetic developments. Anything of interest in this broad area of the communication arts. No taboos at all. Style should be lively, informed and opinionated rather than "newspaperese." Length: 700 to 5,000 words; 1,000 words maximum, reviews. Pays about 3¢ per word. Prefers photos with mss. Events, people in film and/or (occasionally) TV. 8x10 b&w glossy.

How To Break In: "Most writers who have been published in our magazine started out by sending us a review, interview or article on some subject (a film, a filmmaker) about which they cared passionately and (more often than not) had —as a result of that caring —a particular degree of expertise. Often they just happened to be in the right place at the right time (where a film was being made, where a filmmaker was making a public appearance or near where one lived)."

THEATER ACROSS AMERICA, 104 N. St. Mary, Dallas TX 75214. (214)827-7734. Editor: Mike Firth. 10% freelance written. For adults interested in theater. Most have experience with theater in school; some with professional experience. Magazine; 6-10 pages. Estab. 1975. Published 5 times per year. Circ. 500. Rights purchased vary with author and material. Usually buys first serial rights. Buys 5-200 mss per year. Pays on acceptance or publication. "May hold after advising author." Sample copy $1. Will consider photocopied and simultaneous submissions. Submit seasonal material 5 months in advance. Reports on mss accepted for publication in 4 months. Returns rejected material in 1 month. SASE.

Nonfiction, Photos and Fillers: Wants mss containing useful information about theater; experiences which have a general application for others in theater, technical, organizational, financial. Does not want material that is too academic. Would like to see mss on summer theater, Christmas or holiday shows, working with festivals. Buys informational, how-to, personal experience, humor, photo, book reviews, successful business operations, new product, merchandising techniques, technical mss. Length: 50 to 1,250 words. "Word rates will be the same for all items and will depend on number of subscribers. We will start at 1¢ a word and go up with the number of subscribers." Open to suggestions for new columns or departments. Photos purchased with mss with extra payment and purchased without mss "on occasion." Captions required. No color. Pays $5 minimum for b&w. Size: 5x7 glossy or larger. Also buys anecdotes and short humor.

TV AND MOVIE SCREEN, 355 Lexington Ave., New York NY 10017. (212)391-1400. Editorial Director: Roseann C. Hirsch. Editor: Kathy Loy. Managing Editor: George W. Anderson. 90% freelance written. For people interested in television and show business personalities. Magazine; 74 pages. Monthly. Circ. 500,000. Rights purchased vary with author and material. Usually buys all rights. Buys 65 mss a year. Pays on publication. Query first. Reports immediately. SASE.

Nonfiction and Photos: Celebrity interviews and angle stories; profile articles. Punchy, enticing and truthful. Length: 1,000 to 1,500 words. Pays $100 to $150. Photos of celebrities purchased without ms or on assignment. Pays $25 each.

TV DAWN TO DUSK, 2 Park Ave., New York NY 10016. Editor: Sherry Armstrong. 60% freelance written. For daytime television viewers. Estab. 1970. Monthly. Circ. 200,000. Buys all rights. Pays on publication. Query. SASE.

Nonfiction: "I'd like some new ideas, such as 'round-ups (i.e., 'my most embarrassing moment on a soap opera'); information on *how* the show is put together; why so many people get caught up in daytime drama, etc. I'd also like stories on interesting storylines such as the wife-beating plot on *Days of Our Lives*, or alcoholism in teen-agers on the soaps." Personality pieces with daytime TV stars of serials and quiz shows; main emphasis is on serial stars. Also interested in some women's interest material. Buys interviews, personality pieces, round-up articles, how-to's, profiles, and personal experience articles related to daytime TV only. Length: approximately 1,500 words. Pays $125 minimum.

How To Break In: "The key thing for breaking in here is to have access to one of the daytime TV personalities. Try to choose a character whose story line is evolving into a bigger and more important role. But query first; don't waste your time doing a story on a character who will be going off the show soon. For writers who don't have this kind of access, the best bet is a career retrospective of one of the major characters who has been on for years. You'll need to check a library for clippings."

TV GUIDE, Radnor PA 19088. Executive Editor: Roger Youman. Published weekly. Study publication. Query first (with outline) to Andrew Mills, Assistant Managing Editor. SASE.

Nonfiction: Wants offbeat articles about TV people and shows. This magazine is not interested in fan material. Also wants stories on the newest trends of television, but they must be written in layman's language. Length: 200 to 2,000 words.

Photos: Uses professional high-quality photos, normally shot on assignment, by photographers chosen by *TV Guide*. Prefers color. Pays $150 day rate against page rates—$250 for 2 pages or less.

TV RADIO TALK, 2 Park Ave., New York, NY 10016. Monthly. Buys first rights. 100% freelance. Reports in three weeks. Query first. SASE.

Nonfiction and Photos: "Uses interview and third person stories on TV stars, movie stars, record personalities and others who are famous. The stories should be factual. We do not print fiction. We like stories that are fresh and exclusive. There should be conflict in any story suggestion. The slant is usually for the star. The writing should fit the subject; if a love story, tender; if a scoop, exciting." Length: up to 2,000 words. Pays maximum of $125 on publication. Pays $20 up for photos; any size.

TV STAR PARADE, 2 Park Ave., New York NY 10016. (212)683-4200, Ext. 16. Editor: Jean Thomas. For "males and females of all ages interested in private lives of TV and movie stars." Monthly. Circ. 400,000. Buys all rights. Payment on publication. Submit seasonal material 2

months in advance. Reports in 2 to 3 weeks. Query first required with basic outline of proposed feature. SASE.
Nonfiction and Photos: General subject matter consists of interviews, "backstage stories," romance, etc. Approach should be a "chatty style with special attention to dialog, quotes from the stars. We like to use as many real interviews as possible. We never publish made up quotes or interviews. We do not want angles that have been dredged up time and again just to fill space. Interested in timely material." Buys informational, personal experience, interviews, profile, nostalgia, photo articles. "I would appreciate new ideas for columns." Length: 1,000-1,500 words. Pays $100-150. Photos are purchased without mss and on assignment. Captions are optional. Wants candid b&w. Pays $25 per photo on publication.

VIDEOGRAPHY, United Business Publications, 475 Park Ave., S., New York NY 10016. (212)697-8300. Editor: Peter Caranicas. 50% freelance written. For professional users of video; video hobbyists. Monthly magazine; 72 pages. Estab. April 1976. Circ. 17,000. Pays 1 month after publication. Buys all rights. Phone queries OK. SASE. Reports in 1 month. Free sample copy and writer's guidelines; mention *Writer's Market* in request.
Nonfiction: Any article about the use of video in business, education, medicine, etc. Especially interested in stories about the use of new home video devices such as Betamax, Vidstar, etc. Buys 4 mss/issue. Query with clips of previously published work. Length: 1,000-3,000 words. Pays $50.
Photos: Submit photo material with accompanying query. Offers no additional payment for 5x7 b&w glossy prints or color transparencies. Captions required. Buys all rights, but may reassign following publication.

Travel, Camping, and Trailer Publications

Publications in this category tell campers and tourists where to go, where to stay, how to get there, how to camp, or how to select a good vehicle for travel or shelter. Publications that buy how-to camping and travel material with a conservation angle are listed in the Nature, Conservation, and Ecology classification. Newspapers and Weekly Magazine Sections, as well as Regional Publications, are frequently interested in travel and camping material with a local angle. Hunting and fishing and outdoor publications that buy camping how-to's will be found in the Sport and Outdoor category. Publications dealing with automobiles or other vehicles maintained for sport or as a hobby will be found in the Automotive and Motorcycle category. Many publications in the In-Flight category are also in the market for travel articles and photos.

ABC INTERNATIONAL TRAVEL MAGAZINE, 30943 Club House Lane, Farmington Hills MI 48018. Editor/Publisher: Theresa Mitan. 25% freelance written. Emphasizes international travel for a general audience. Bimonthly magazine; 66 pages. Estab. May 1977. Circ. 40,000. Pays on publication. Buys all rights, but may reassign following publication. SASE. Reports in 1 month. Sample copy $1.
Nonfiction: International travel material. General interest; nostalgia; photo feature; profile; and travel. Buys 3 mss/issue. Submit complete ms. Length: 1,000 words. Pays 10¢/word.
Photos: Send photo material with accompanying ms. Pays $10-20 for b&w prints. Captions required. Buys all rights.

ADVENTURE TRAVEL, 444 NE Ravenna Blvd., Seattle WA 98115. (206)527-1621. Editor-in-Chief: Robert Citron. Managing Editor: Knute Berger. 75% freelance written. For 25-50 year-old active adventurers and travelers; well-educated, experienced, interested in conservation. Bimonthly magazine; 80 pages. Estab. June 1978. Circ. 75,000. Pays on publication. Buys first North American serial rights. Submit seasonal/holiday material 6 months in advance of issue date. Simultaneous, photocopied, and previously published submissions OK. SASE. Reports in 4 weeks. Free sample copy and writer's guidelines for SASE; mention *Writer's Market* in request.
Nonfiction: Exposé (articles on adventure travel industry); general interest (accounts of adventure trips open to members of the public, worldwide, including everything the reader needs to know to do it); historical (profiles of famous adventurers and adventures of the past); how-to (articles on travel tips for adventure travelers, photography, equipment use, expedition prep-

aration, etc.); conservation (stories on adventure and conservation, including environmentally-minded stories on wildlife viewing, visiting remote tribes, etc.); interview (with noted, controversial, articulate people in adventure today); new product (latest on outdoor or camera equipment, new travel books and maps); personal experience (first person accounts of adventure trip experiences); photo feature (people participating in adventurous activities); profile (of interesting adventures today); and travel (stories on adventure trips). "No articles on hunting and fishing, non-adventure travel (i.e., tours); or sexist or non-environmental material." Buys 4-5 mss/issue. Query. Length: 1,000-3,000 words. Pays $200-1,000.

Photos: Carol Baker, photo coordinator. "*Adventure Travel* uses top-quality color photography. We are always on the lookout for unique, exciting pictures of remote areas and adventure trips. We choose manuscripts frequently on the basis of the photos." Pays $50-500 for any size color transparencies; originals only. Captions and model release required. Buys one-time rights.

Columns/Departments: Gear; Reading; News; and Photography. Buys 2-3/issue. Query. Length: 800-1,500 words. Pays $150-300. Open to suggestions for new columns/departments.

THE ALBERTA MOTORIST, Kingsway Publishing (Western), Ltd., 11230-110 St., Edmonton, Alberta, Canada T5L 4J7. (403)474-8713. Editor: Stuart P. Hertzog. Managing Editor: F.W. (Bud) Hoffman. 30% freelance written. Emphasizes travel, leisure living, and automobiles for a readership consisting of 40% of all registered car-owners in Alberta. Quarterly magazine; 40 pages. Estab. 1926. Circ. 180,000. Pays on publication. Buys all rights, but may reassign following publication. Phone queries OK. Submit seasonal/holiday material 2 months in advance of issue date. Simultaneous, photocopied and previously published submissions OK. SASE. Reports in 6 weeks. Free sample copy; mention *Writer's Market* in request.

Nonfiction: How-to (automobile, camping, skiing, hiking, crafts); historical (Alberta and western Canada); interview (revelant to Canada); leisure activities; new product (revelant to transportation, automobiles, sports, etc.); photo feature (color only); technical (automobile, RV vehicles); and travel (world, Canada/US, Alberta, preferably with color photos). Buys 1-3 mss/issue. Query or submit complete ms. Length: 1,200-3,500 words. Pays 10-15¢/word.

Photos: "We are four-color magazine, essentially stressing visuals. Each article should have at least one *good* color photo suitable for reproduction. Articles will be considered unillustrated, though." Pays $3-35 for 3½x3½ or 8x10 b&w glossy prints; $5-50 for 5x8 or 8x10 color prints or 35mm transparencies. Captions preferred; "at least give explaination and location of each photo." Buys all rights, but may reassign following publication.

Columns/Departments: Automobile Connection and RV Roundup (ownership, operation, maintenance, and new developments); Transportation News (general interest news); CB Callsign (what's new in radio, how to use and maintain); Camping and Backpacking (equipment, hints, where to go); and material on all outdoor sports (skiing, hanggliding, riding, snowmobiles, etc.). Buys 2-3 columns/issue. Query. Length: 350-1,200 words. Pays 5-15¢/word.

Fiction: Adventure (for general readership stressing travel and exploration); historical (discovery, settlement of western Canada, especially Alberta); humorous (general appeal); and suspense (not bloody). Query or submit complete ms. Length: 2,000-4,000 words. Pays 10-15¢/word.

Poetry: "Would consider poetry if accompanied by *outstanding* color photos,"

How To Break In: "Best way is by personal contact. We are especially looking for freelancers in Alberta. Preference is given to Canadian residents. We need freelancers 'on tap' for regular contributions. We are a travel and leisure magazine, but can expand into general interest areas."

AWAY, 888 Worcester St., Wellesley MA 02181. (617)237-5200. Editor: Gerard J. Gagnon. For "members of the ALA Auto & Travel Club, interested in their autos and in travel. Ages range from approximately 20 to 65. They live primarily in New England." Slanted to seasons. Quarterly. Circ. 230,000. Buys first serial rights. Pays on acceptance. Free sample copy. Submit seasonal material 6 months in advance. Reports "as soon as possible." Although a query is not mandatory, it may be advisable for many articles. SASE.

Nonfiction and Photos: Articles on "travel, tourist attractions, safety, history, etc., preferably with a New England angle. Also, car care tips and related subjects." Would like a "positive feel to all pieces, but not the Chamber of Commerce approach." Buys both general seasonal travel and specific travel articles, for example, travel-related articles (photo hints, etc.); outdoor activities; for example, gravestone rubbing, snow sculpturing; historical articles linked to places to visit; humor with a point, photo essays. "Would like to see more nonseasonally oriented material. Most material now submitted seems suitable only for our summer issue. Avoid pieces on hunting and about New England's most publicized attractions, such as Old Sturbridge

Village and Mystic Seaport." Length: 800 to 1,500 words. "preferably 1,000 to 1,200." Pays approximately 10¢ per word. Photos purchased with mss; with captions only. B&w glossies. Pays $5 to $10 per b&w photo, payment on publication based upon which photos are used.

CAMPING JOURNAL, Davis Publications, 380 Lexington Ave., New York NY 10017. Editor-in-Chief: Andrew J. Carra. Managing Editor: Lee Schreiber. 75% freelance written. Emphasizes outdoor recreation. Published 8 times/year. Magazine; 64-80 pages. Estab. 1962. Circ. 285,000. Pays on acceptance. Buys all rights, but may assign following publication. Submit seasonal/holiday material 6 months in advance of issue date. Photocopied submissions OK. SASE. Reports in 6 weeks. Sample copy $1; free writer's guidelines.

Nonfiction: General interest (travel); how-to (equipment); humor (personal experience); new product; personal experience; photo feature; and travel. Buys 100 mss/year. Query. Length: 1,500-3,500 words. Pays $100-300.

Photos: Jacquelyn Brown, photo editor. State availability of photos with query. No additional payment for 8x10 b&w glossy prints and 2¼x2¼ or 35mm color transparencies. Pays $200-250 for cover photos. Captions preferred. Buys all rights, but may reassign after publication. Model release required.

Columns/Departments: Open to suggestions for new columns/departments.

CHEVRON USA, Box 6227, San Jose CA 95150. (408)296-1060. Editor: Helen Bignell. 80% freelance written. For members of the Chevron Travel Club. Quarterly. Buys first North American serial rights. Pays for articles on acceptance. Pays for photos on publication. Reports in 4 to 6 weeks. SASE. Free sample copy, writer's guidelines, and coverage map.

Nonfiction: "We need well-organized articles with sense of activity, packed with see-and-do information geared to the average family. State seasonal or specific slant early. Enthusiasm for, and knowledge of, subject should show. We want the topic's flavor. Subjects should have broad appeal. No public relations, brochure approach; no historical treatises." Length: 500 to 1,500 words. Pays 15¢ a word and up.

Photos: Subject matter same as nonfiction. No empty scenics. Majority of photos must have active people in them. Prefers 2¼ square or 4x5, top quality 35mm. Pays $150 full page for color, minimum $75. For b&w, pays $50 full page, $35 minimum.

Fillers: Anecdotal material. Must be about travel, personal experiences. Must be original. Length: about 200 to 250 words. Pays $25 each.

DESERT MAGAZINE, Box 1318, Palm Desert CA 92260. (714)346-8144. Editor: William Knyvett. 100% freelance written. Emphasizes Southwest travel and history. For recreation-minded families—middle class income, RV owners, bikers and backpackers. Monthly magazine; 48 pages. Estab. 1937. Circ. 40,000. Pays on publication. Buys first North American serial rights. Submit seasonal or holiday material 6 months in advance. SASE. Reports in 4 weeks. Free sample copy and writer's guidelines.

Nonfiction: Historical, informational, personal experience, travel. Buys 8 articles/issue. Query. Length: 500-2,500 words. Pays $20-100.

Photos: Photos purchased with or without accompanying ms. Captions required. Pays $5 for 8x10 b&w glossies; $25 for inside color photos; $35 for 4x5 color cover photos. "2¼x2¼ preferred over 35mm."

DISCOVERY MAGAZINE, Allstate Plaza, Northbrook IL 60062. Editor: Alan Rosenthal. 75% freelance written. For motor club members; mobile familes with above average income. "All issues pegged to season." Estab. 1961. Quarterly. Circ. 940,000. Buys first North American serial rights. Buys 40 mss a year. Payment on acceptance. Free sample copy and writer's guidelines. Submit seasonal material 8 to 12 months in advance. Reports in 3 weeks. Query first. SASE.

Nonfiction and Photos: "Primarily travel subjects. Also automotive and safety. First-person narrative approach for most travel articles. Short pieces on restaurants must include recipes from the establishment." Travel articles and photos often are purchased as a package. Rates depend on how the photos are used. Color transparencies (35mm or larger) are preferred. Photos should show people doing things; captions required. Send transparencies by registered mail, with plenty of cardboard protection. Buys one-time rights for photography. Color photos are returned after use. Length: 1,000 to 2,500 words. "Rates vary, depending on type of article, ranging from $200-400 for full-length features." Photos purchased with accompanying mss; captions required. Photos also purchased on assignment.

Fillers: True, humorous travel anecdotes. Length: 50 to 150 words. Pays $10.

FAMILY MOTOR COACHING, 8291 Clough Pike, Cincinnati OH 45244. (513)474-3622. Editor: Stephen Collins. Managing Editor: Pamela S. Gramke. 75% freelance written. Emphasizes travel with motor home modifications. Monthly magazine; 130 pages. Estab. February 1964. Circ. 22,000. Pays on acceptance. Buys all rights, but may reassign following publication. Phone queries OK. Submit seasonal/holiday material 3 months in advance of issue date. SASE. Reports in 2 weeks. Sample copy $2; free writer's guidelines.
Nonfiction: General interest (travel and cooking on the road); historical (various areas of country accessible by motor coach); how-to (modify motor coach with added and changing features); nostalgia; and travel. Buys 3 mss/issue. Query. Length: 1,500 words. Pays $50-200.
Photos: State availability of photos with query. No additional payment for b&w contact sheet(s) or 35mm and 2¼x2¼ color transparencies. Captions preferred. Buys first rights.

HANDBOOK AND DIRECTORY FOR CAMPERS, 1999 Shepard Rd., St. Paul MN 55116. (612)647-7290. Editor: Don Picard. 75% freelance written. For families whose members range in age from infancy to past retirement, and whose leisure interests are aimed primarily at outdoor recreation and travel with recreational vehicles providing the means to enjoyment of this new life style. Estab. 1971. Annual. Circ. 1,500,000. Buys all rights, but will reassign rights to author after publication. Buys 6 to 12 mss a year. Payment on acceptance. Free sample copy and writer's guidelines. Will consider photocopied submissions. Reports in 30 days. Query first. SASE.
Nonfiction: "General articles on outdoor living and travel including how to prepare for trip and ways to gain more enjoyment from the going, staying, and coming home portions of it. In all cases, emphasis should be on the positive, fun aspects of travel and camping, not on the problems sometimes encountered. Writing should be readable rather than academic, clever rather than endlessly descriptive, tight rather than verbose. A good lead is considered essential. First-person articles and stories about personal experiences are not acceptable. We try to emphasize that camping is not only fun in itself, but is the means to all kinds of peripheral activities not normally available to the average family. Editorial slant is consistently on the enjoyment aspects of the experience." Informational, how-to, profile, humor, historical, nostalgia, photo, and travel articles. Length: 700 to 1,500 words. Pays $75 to $275.
Photos: Purchased with accompanying mss or on assignment. Captions optional. Uses color; 35mm and larger. Pays $200 for cover; $50 each for inside use.

LEISUREGUIDE, 1515 N.W. 167th St., Miami FL 33169. Editor-in-Chief: Andrew Delaplaine. 75% freelance written. An in-room hotel guide book emphasizing information for travelers in Chicago, Louisville, Cincinnati, Philadelphia, Boston, Houston, Charleston, the Florida Gold Coast (Palm Beach to Miami), and South Carolina's Grand Strand (Myrtle Beach). Annual hard-covered magazine; 140-150 pages. Estab. 1971. Circ. 210,000. Pays on publication. Buys all rights, but may reassign following publication. Submit seasonal/holiday material 3 months in advance. Photocopied submissions and previously published work OK. SASE. Reports in 2 weeks. Sample copy $2.
Nonfiction: Informational (of interest to sophisticated transients in our cities); historical (of interest to our transient reader—usually of light, humorous vein); travel (articles concentrated on the cities in which we publish); photo feature (must be color of very high quality and concentrate on some aspect of interest to the cities served). Buys 50 mss/year. Query. Length: 1,000-3,500 words. Pays $100-500.
Photos: Purchased without mss or on assignment. Query. "A good shot can come from any locale, but be appropriate (because of its general nature) to any of our editions." Pays $10-75 for b&w; $20-125 for color.
Rejects: "We almost never accept the general 'traveler' article to be found in publications such as in-flight magazines. Our articles must relate specifically to the areas we serve and tell the readers something about these areas."

THE LUFKIN LINE, Lufkin Industries, Inc., P.O. Box 849, Lufkin TX 75901. Editor: Miss Virginia R. Allen. For men in oil and commercial and marine gear industries; readers mostly degreed engineers. Each issue devoted to different areas where division offices located; that is, West Coast, Canada, Mid-Continent, Rocky Mountain, Texas, Gulf Coast, International. Estab. 1924. Quarterly. Circ. 12,000. Not copyrighted. Buys 4 to 8 mss a year. Payment on acceptance. Free sample copy and writer's guidelines. Will not consider photocopied submissions. Submit seasonal material 3 to 4 months in advance. Reports in 1 month. Query first. SASE.
Nonfiction and Photos: "Travel articles. Subjects dealing with U.S. and Canada, and (rarely) foreign travel subjects. Product articles staff written. Length: 1,000 to 1,200 words. Pays $75 per

ms with illustrating photos. Color transparencies or prints of seasonal subjects are purchased for front cover; pays $50. Illustrations for travel articles may be color prints or transparencies (no smaller than 2¼x2¼). No b&w photos are purchased. Color photos for travel articles may be secured from state tourist or development commissions.

MIDLANTIC CAMPING TRAILS, (formerly *Metro East Outdoor News*), Delaware Valley Outdoor News, Inc., Box 162, Ambler, PA 19002. (215)628-4784. Editor-in-Chief: Charles E. Myers. 50% freelance written. Emphasis on recreation vehicle camping and travel. Monthly (except Dec. and Feb.) tabloid; 36 pages. Estab. 1973. Circ. 50,000. Pays on publication. Buys simultaneous, second serial (reprint) and regional rights. Submit seasonal/holiday material 3-4 months in advance. Simultaneous, photocopied and previously published submissions OK. SASE. Reports in 1 month. Free sample copy and writer's guidelines.
Nonfiction: Historical (when tied in with camping trip to historical attraction or area); how-to (selection, care, maintenance of RVs, accessories and camping equipment); humor; personal experience and travel (camping destinations within 200 miles of Philadelphia-D.C. metro corridor). Buys 75 mss/year. Query. Length: 1,200-2,000 words. Pays $40-75.
Photos: Photos purchased with accompanying ms. Captions required. Uses 5x7 or 8x10 b&w glossies. Total purchase price for ms includes payment for photos.
Columns/Departments: RV Handyman (RV maintenance, repair and improvement ideas) and Camp Cookery (ideas for cooking in RV galleys and over campfires. Should include recipes). Buys 10 mss/year. Query. Length: 1,000-2,000 words. Pays $40-75.
How To Break In: "Articles should focus on single attraction or activity or on closely clustered attractions within reach on the same weekend camping trip rather than on types of attractions or activities in general. We're looking for little-known or offbeat items. Emphasize positive aspects of camping: fun, economy, etc."

THE MIDWEST MOTORIST, 201 Progress Pkwy., Maryland Heights MO 63043. Editor: Martin Quigley. For the motoring public of Missouri, Southern Illinois, and eastern Kansas (Kansas City area). Publication of The Auto Club of Missouri. Bimonthly. Circ. 280,000. Not copyrighted. Payment on acceptance. Free sample copy. Reports in 2 to 6 weeks. Query first. SASE.
Nonfiction and Photos: "Features of interest to our motoring public. Articles cover important auto-oriented consumer issues as well as travel and auto interest pieces. We seek serious, well-documented consumer and ecology pieces, and are also interested in lighter material, focusing on unusual places to visit." Length: about 1,200 words. Pays $50 to $200. B&w glossy photos purchased with mss. No color.

MINNESOTA AAA MOTORIST, Minnesota State Automobile Association, 7 Travelers Trail, Burnsville MN 55337. (612)890-2500. Editor: Candy Kumerfield. 15% freelance written. Monthly magazine. Estab. 1957. Circ. 270,000. Buys first North American serial rights. Buys 15-20 mss/year. Pays on acceptance. Free sample copy and writer's guidelines. Reports in 3 weeks. Submit complete ms. SASE.
Nonfiction and Photos: "Nonfiction articles on domestic and foreign travel, motoring, car care, outdoor recreation, Minnesota people, places and events. Submissions should entertain and educate our readers. Our emphasis is on the quality, not the quantity, of work." Buys how-to's, personal experience articles, interviews, humor, historical and travel articles, photo essays. Length: 800 to 1,000 words. Pays $150 minimum. Good b&w, 8x10, glossy photos or 35mm transparencies purchased with mss.

MOBILE LIVING, Box 1418, Sarasota FL 33578. Editor: Frances Neel. Bimonthly. Buys first rights only. Pays on publication. Free sample copy. Reports on submissions within 1 month. SASE.
Nonfiction: Articles on recreational vehicle experiences and travel via recreational vehicles. In travel articles, include names of parks to stay at while seeing the sights, etc. Hobbies involving recreational vehicles and how-to-do-it articles that apply to a general audience also wanted. Length: 1,500 words maximum. Pays 1¢ per word.
Photos: With captions and illustrating articles. B&w glossies only. Returned after use. Pays $3 each.

THE MOBILE TRAVELLER IN ONTARIO, Box 1509, Peterborough, Ontario, Canada K9J 7H7. Editor-in-Chief: Steve Bronson. 5% freelance written. For users of recreational vehicles, trailers, motorhomes, campers, etc. Published 10 times/year. Magazine; 32 pages. Estab. 1975. Circ. 24,000. Pays on publication. Buys first North American serial rights. Submit seasonal/

holiday material 1 month in advance of issue date. SASE. Reports in 2 weeks. Free sample copy and writer's guidelines; mention *Writer's Market* in request.
Nonfiction: How-to (haul, repair, buy, or build recreational vehicles); general interest (of interest to campers); historical (camping); interview (with RV manufacturers and associated products); new product (in camping); and technical (on RV products). Buys 20 mss/year. Query. Length: 500-1,500 words. Pays $35-100.
Photos: No additional payment for photos accepted with accompanying ms. Uses b&w prints. Captions preferred. Buys all rights, but may reassign following publication.
Columns/Departments: The Frying Pan (outdoor cooking); and Humour (outdoor and recreational vehicle owners with pix if possible). Buys 10 mss/year. Query. Length: 250-1,000 words. Pays $25-100. Open to suggestions for new columns/departments.

MOTOR NEWS—MICHIGAN LIVING, Automobile Club of Michigan, Auto Club Dr., Dearborn, MI 48126. (313)336-1504. Editor-in-Chief: Len Barnes. 50% freelance written. Emphasizes travel and auto use. Monthly magazine; 48 pages. Estab. 1922. Circ. 800,000. Pays on acceptance. Buys first North American serial rights. Submit seasonal/holiday material 3 months in advance. SASE. Reports in 4-6 weeks. Free sample copy and writer's guidelines.
Nonfiction: Marcia Danner, Managing Editor. Travel articles on US and Canadian topics. Buys 30 mss/year. Send complete ms. Length: 800-2,000 words. Pays $75-200.
Photos: Photos purchased with accompanying ms. Captions required. Pays $25-150 for color transparencies; total purchase price for ms includes payment for b&w photos.
How To Break In: "In addition to descriptions of things to see and do, articles should contain accurate, current information on costs the traveler would encounter on his trip. Items such as lodging, meal and entertainment expenses should be included, not in the form of a balance sheet but as an integral part of the piece."

MOTORHOME LIFE, Trailer Life Publishing Co., Inc., 23945 Craftsman Rd., Calabasas CA 91302. (213)888-6000. Editor: Denis Rouse. For owners and prospective buyers of motorhomes, mini-motorhomes, campers, camping-converted vans. Estab. 1962. Published 9 times/year. Circ. 125,000. Buys all rights. Buys about 50 mss a year. Pays on publication. Sample copy for $1; free writer's guidelines. Submit seasonal material 3 months in advance. Reports in 1 month. SASE.
Nonfiction and Photos: "Articles which tell the owner of a self-propelled RV about interesting places to travel, interesting things to do. Human interest and variety articles sought as well. All material must be tailored specifically for our audience." Informational, personal experience, humor, historical, personal opinion, travel, new product, and technical articles. Length: 2,500 words maximum. Pays $75-200. Photos purchased with accompanying ms with no additional payment.

NATIONAL MOTORIST, National Automobile Club, 1 Market Plaza, #300, San Francisco CA 94105. (415)777-4000. Editor: Jim Donaldson. 75% freelance written. Emphasizes motor travel in the West. Bimonthly magazine; 32 pages. Estab. 1924. Circ. 300,000. Pays on acceptance for article, layout stage for pix. Buys first publication rights. Submit seasonal/holiday material 3 months in advance. Reports in 1 week. Free sample copy.
Nonfiction: How-to (care for car, travel by car, participate in outdoor sports and hobbies); historical (interesting history and significant historical personalities behind places and areas readers might visit); humor (occasionally buys a story treating something in motoring from a humorous angle); profile (of someone with unusual skills or engaged in some interesting and unusual art, hobby or craft); and travel (interesting places and areas to visit in the 11 western states). Buys 5-8 mss/issue. Query. Length: "around 500 words *or* around 1,100 words." Pays 10¢/word and up.
Photos: Purchased with accompanying ms. Captions optional, "but must have caption info for pix." Send prints or transparencies. Pays $20 and up for 8x10 b&w glossies; $30 and up for 2¼x2¼ or 4x5 color transparencies. Model release required.

NORTHEAST OUTDOORS, 70 Edwin Ave., Waterbury CT 06708. (203)755-0158. Editor: John Florian. 70% freelance written. Monthly. Circ. 20,000. Buys all rights. Pays on publication. Free sample copy. "Queries are not required, but are useful for our planning and to avoid possible duplication of subject matter. If you have any questions, contact the editor." Deadlines are on the 21st of the month preceding publication. Reports in 15 to 30 days. SASE.
Nonfiction and Photos: Interested in articles and photos that pertain to outdoor activities in the Northeast. Recreational vehicle tips and campgrounds are prime topics, along with first-person travel experiences in the Northeast while camping. "While the primary focus is on camping, we

carry some related articles on outdoor topics like skiing, nature, hiking, fishing, canoeing, etc. In each issue we publish a 'Favorite Trip' experience, submitted by a reader, relating to a favorite camping experience, usually in the Northeast. Payment for this is $20 and writing quality need not be professional. Another reader feature is 'My Favorite Campground'. Payment is $10. Our pay rate is flexible, but generally runs from $30 to $40 for features without photos, and up to $80 for features accompanied by 2 or more photos. Features should be from 300 to 1,000 words. Premium rates are paid on the basis of quality, not length. For photos alone we pay $10 for each 8x10 b&w print we use."

OHIO MOTORIST, Box 6150, Cleveland OH 44101. Editor: A. K. Murway, Jr. 10-15% freelance written. For AAA members in 7 northeast Ohio counties. Estab. 1909. Monthly. Circ. 245,000. Buys one-time publication rights. Buys 30 mss a year. Payment on acceptance. Free sample copy. Submit seasonal material 2 months prior to season. Reports in 2 weeks. Submit complete ms. SASE.
Nonfiction and Photos: "Travel, including foreign; automotive, highways, etc.; motoring laws and safety. No particular approach beyond brevity and newspaper journalistic treatment. Articles for travel seasons." Length: 2,000 words maximum. Pays $50-200/article including b&w photos. 8x10 b&w photos preferred. Purchased with accompanying mss. Captions required. Pays $8 to $20 for singles, although "rarely" purchases singles.
Poetry: Humorous verse. Length: 4 to 6 lines. Pays $7.50 to $12.

OUTSIDE MAGAZINE, Straight Arrow Publishers, Inc., 625 3rd St., San Francisco CA 94107. Editor-in-Chief: Jann Wenner. Managing Editor: Will Hearst. Emphasizes travel and the outdoors. Monthly magazine. Estab. 1977. Pays on publication. Rights purchased "vary." Reports in 1 month. SASE. Free sample copy and writer's guidelines.
Nonfiction: *Outside* considers only the highest quality writing. Query with clips of previously published work.

PACIFIC BOATING ALMANAC, Box Q, Ventura CA 93001. (805)644-6043. Publisher/Editor: William Berssen. For "boat owners in the Pacific Southwest." Estab. 1965. Published in 3 editions to cover the Pacific Coastal area. Circ. 36,000. Buys all rights. Buys 12 mss/year. Pays on publication. Sample copy $5.25. Submit seasonal material 3 to 6 months in advance. Reports in 4 weeks. Query. SASE.
Nonfiction and Photos: "This is a cruising guide, published annually in 3 editions, covering all of the navigable waters in the Pacific coast. Though we are almost entirely staff-produced, we would be interested in well-written articles on cruising and trailer-boating along the Pacific coast and in the navigable lakes and rivers of the western states from Baja, California to Alaska inclusive." Pays $50 minimum. Pays $10 for 8x10 b&w glossies.

TRAILER BOATS MAGAZINE, Poole Publications, Inc., 1440 W. Walnut, Compton CA 90220. (213)537-1037. Editor-in-Chief: Ralph Poole. Associate Editor: Jim Youngs. 40% freelance written. Emphasizes trailerable-size boats and related activities. Monthly magazine; 74 pages. Estab. 1971. Circ. 75,000. Pays on publication. Buys all rights, but may reassign following publication. Submit seasonal/holiday material 3 months in advance of issue date. SASE. Reports in 2-4 weeks. Free sample copy and writer's guidelines; mention *Writer's Market* in request.
Nonfiction: How-to (boat, motor and trailer maintenance, helpful and labor saving tips, finishing, etc.); general interest; humor; historical; interview; nostalgia; personal experience; photo feature; technical; and travel. Buys 6-8 mss/issue. Query. Length: 500-2,000 words. Pays $50 minimum.
Photos: Pays $7-50 for 8x10 b&w glossy prints; $15-100 for 35mm or 2¼x2¼ color transparencies. Captions preferred. Buys all rights, but may reassign following publication.
Columns/Departments: Mini-Cruise (travel type featuring a cruise to a place for a day or weekend, telling how to get there, where to stay, what to do, activities, etc.); Over the Transom (photos only, showing humorous or wierd situations in the boating world). Buys 2-4 mss/issue. Query. Length: 300-500 words. Pays $75 minimum. Open to suggestions for new columns/departments.
Fiction: Adventure; historical; humorous; and science fiction. Buys sporadicly." Query. Length: 200-1,500 words. Pays $50 minimum.

THE TRAVEL ADVISOR, #15 Park Place, Bronxville NY 10708. Editor-in-Chief: Hal E. Gieseking. 55% freelance written. Monthly newsletter; 12 pages. Estab. March 1976. Circ. 80,000. Pays on publication. Buys all rights. SASE. Reports in 4 weeks. Free sample copy and writer's guidelines.

Nonfiction: "Send us short, *very candid* items based on the writer's own travel experience—*not* written first person. A baggage rip-off in Rome; a great new restaurant in Tokyo (with prices)." Expose (candid look at the travel industry); and how-to (good, inside information on how travelers can avoid problems, save money, etc.). "No typical travel articles that extoll the setting sun." Buys 100 mss/year. Submit complete ms. Length: 20-150 words. Pays $20/item. Also buys candid destination reports. Length: 2,500 words. Query. Pays $250 maximum.

TRAVEL AND LEISURE, 1350 Avenue of the Americas, New York NY 10019. (212)586-5050. Editor-in-Chief: Pamela Fiori. 80% freelance written. Monthly. Circ. 800,000. Buys first North American serial rights. Pays on acceptance. Reports in 1 week. Query first. SASE.
Nonfiction and Photos: Uses articles on travel and vacation places, food, wine, shopping, sports. Most articles are assigned. Length: 1,000 to 2,500 words. Pays $750 to $1,500.
Photos: Makes assignments to photographers. Pays expenses.
How To Break In: "New writers might try to get something in one of our regional editions (East, West, South, and Midwest). They don't pay as much as our national articles ($200-400), but it might be a good way to start. We use a lot of these pieces and they need be no more than 800-1,200 words. They cover any number of possibilities from traveling a river in a certain state to unusual new attractions."

TRAVEL SMART, Communications House, Inc., Dobbs Ferry NY 10522. (914)693-4208. Editor: H.J. Teison. 60% freelance written. Emphasizes "budget/smart, good value travel." Monthly mewsletter; 10 pages. Estab. April 1976. Circ. 7,000. Pays on publication. Buys all rights. Phone queries OK. Photocopied submissions OK. SASE. Reports in 3-4 weeks. Free sample copy; mention *Writer's Market* in request.
Nonfiction: Expose (travel rip-off's); how-to (traveling smart); and travel. Query. Length: 200-1,000 words. Pays $10-150.

TRAVELER MAGAZINE (Wisconsin AAA) (formerly *Wisconsin AAA Motor News*), 433 W. Washington Ave., Madison WI 53703. (608)257-0711. Editor: Hugh P. (Mickey) McLinden. 30% freelance written. Aimed at an audience of domestic and foreign motorist-travelers. Monthly magazine. Pays on publication. Buys all rights. Reports immediately. SASE.
Nonfiction and Photos: Domestic and foreign travel; motoring, safety, highways, new motoring products. Length: 1,000 words maximum. Pays $50 minimum. Photos purchased with ms or with captions only. B&w and color. Pays $15 minimum.

TRAVELIN' VANS, 13510 Ventura Blvd., Sherman Oaks CA 91423. (213)990-2510. Editor: Jim Matthews. 40-50% freelance written. For van owners and their families. Magazine; 64 pages. Estab. 1976. Monthly. Circ. 80,000. Buys all rights, but may reassign rights to author after publication. Buys 25 to 35 mss per year. Pays on publication. Free sample copy and editorial guidelines. Submit seasonal material 3 months in advance. Reports in 2 weeks. Query first. SASE.
Nonfiction and Photos: Wants mss about methods of customizing, feature articles on outstanding vans, coverage of "van happenings" rallies, charity activities, special purpose vans and related subjects. Wants how-to and semi-technical mss. "Keep in mind our audience at all times. Generally thought of as a youth group, they are very solid reliable citizens who spend hours and countless dollars making their vans unique and comfortable." No travel articles unless specifically related to van events. "Never, never any emphasis on antisocial behavior." Would like to see mss on van events in many areas of the country far from Southern California. Buys informational, how-to, profile and nostalgia. Length: 1,200 to 1,600 words. Pays $35 per page in finished book. "Approximately 50% photos." Photos purchased with ms with no additional payment. Captions required. B&w primarily; color of outstanding vans.

TRAVELORE REPORT, 225 S. 15th St., Philadelphia PA 19102. Editor: Ted Barkus. For affluent travelers; businessmen, retirees, well educated; interested in specific tips, tours, and value opportunities in travel. Monthly newsletter; 4 pages. Estab. 1972. Circ. 10,000. Buys all rights, but will reassign rights to author after publication. Buys 25 to 50 mss a year. Pays on publication. Sample copy $1. Submit seasonal material 2 months in advance.
Nonfiction and Fillers: "Brief insights (25 to 200 words) with facts, prices, names of hotels and restaurants, etc., on offbeat subjects of interest to people going places. What to do, what not to do. Supply information. We will rewrite if acceptable. We're candid—we tell it like it is with no sugar coating. Avoid telling us about places in United States or abroad without specific recommendations (hotel name, how much, why, how long, etc.)." Pays $5.

VAN WORLD, 16200 Ventura Blvd., Encino CA 91436. Editor: Chris Hosford. Associate Editor: D. Tiffany Ford. For custom/recreational van owners/campers. Estab. 1973. Monthly. Circ. 80,000. Buys all rights. Payment on publication. Free sample copy. Write for copy of editorial and photo requirements. Submit seasonal material at least 4 months in advance. (Winter material needed in mid-summer.) Reports on material in 1 to 2 weeks. Query first. SASE.

Nonfiction and Photos: "No travel articles of any kind are used unless directly related to how van was used in traveling, advantages, drawbacks, etc." How-to articles related to custom-van enthusiast-type and/or repair or maintenance. Semitechnical, and technical articles related to custom vans and/or van camping. Simple, straightforward style. Any technical material must be accurate. No personal experience used as a rule, although there may be the odd exception if story merits special consideration. Length: about 2,000 words, or more. Pays $40 per printed magazine page (with 50 percent photos). Can use negatives and contact sheets; crisp focus, clean background. Captions must accompany articles. Use separate sheet(s) keyed to numbers of photos. Buys complete editorial package; copy and photos as single unit. No additional payment for photos. Color transparencies; 35mm or larger. No color prints of any type accepted.

WOODALL'S TRAILER & RV TRAVEL, 500 Hyacinth Place, Highland Park IL 60035. (312)433-4550. Editor: Kirk Landers. 50% freelance written. For recreational vehicle owners and enthusiasts whose interests include travel-camping in North America, and buying, maintaining and customizing their vehicles. Magazine; 125 pages. Estab. 1936. Monthly. Circ. 300,000. Rights purchased vary with author and material. Usually buys all rights, but may reassign rights to author after publication. Buys about 50 mss a year. Pays on acceptance. Free sample copy and writer's guidelines. No photocopied or simultaneous submissions. Submit seasonal material 4 to 6 months in advance. Reports in 4 weeks. Query first or submit complete ms. SASE.

Nonfiction and Photos: "Travel guides and narratives providing comprehensive views of great camping areas. Also, humor, profiles (especially of those who live and work on the road); recipe and menu ideas; money-saving tips; vehicle maintenance and improvement; insurance, equipment, etc. Our greatest joy is a thoroughly researched article in which facts, figures, quotes and conclusions are presented in clear, concise prose, and in a logical sequence. We avoid material that is slanted exclusively to the raw beginner. Would consider winter camping ideas; pieces on rainy day recreation for families; RV retirement; new, uncrowded, warm weather retreats for winter migrants." Length: 1,000 to 3,000 words. Pays $150 to $300; more on assignment. Seasonal photo essays are used when good color is available. B&w and color purchased with or without mss. Pays $25 minimum for b&w; $50 minimum for color. Captions required.

How To Break In: "A background in this special interest field is a must; so is a familiarity with our editorial style and format. The ripest subject areas are probably general interest material, profiles, and humor. Also, writers with a specific field of expertise — be it bird-watching, interior decorating, engineering or what have you — tend to do well with us by presenting their credentials and a few article ideas in a query. We don't always like their ideas, but if their credentials are right, we often come back to them with our own suggestions."

Union Publications

OCAW UNION NEWS, P.O. Box 2812, Denver CO 80201. (303)893-0811. Editor: Jerry Archuleta. Official publication of Oil, Chemical and Atomic Workers International Union. For union members. Monthly tabloid newspaper; 12 pages. Estab. 1944. Circ. 180,000. Not copyrighted. Payment on acceptance. Free sample copy. Reports in 30 days. Query first. SASE.

Nonfiction and Photos: Labor union materials, political subjects and consumer interest articles, slanted toward workers and consumers, with liberal political view. Interview, profile, think pieces and exposes. Most material is done on assignment. Length: 1,500 to 1,800 words. Pays $50 to $75. No additional payment is made for 8x10 b&w glossy photos used with mss. Captions required.

UTU NEWS, United Transportation Union, 14600 Detroit Ave., Cleveland, OH 44107. (216)228-9400. Editor-in-Chief: Jim Turner. For members of the union (250,000) working in the crafts of engineer, conductor, firemen and brakemen on North American railroads. Weekly newspaper; 4 pages. (Also one monthly tabloid; 8 pages). Estab. 1969. Pays on publication. Buys all rights. Phone queries OK. Reports at once.

Photos: Current news shots of railroad or bus accidents, especially when employees are killed or injured. Captions required. Pays $15 minimum for any size b&w glossies.

Women's Publications

The publications listed in this category specialize in material of interest to women. Other publications which occasionally use material slanted to women's interests can be found in the following categories: Alternative, Child Care and Parental Guidance; Confession, Education, Food and Drink; Hobby and Craft; Home and Garden; Religious, and Sport and Outdoor publications.

AAUW JOURNAL, 2401 Virginia Ave., NW., Washington DC 20037. (202)785-7700. Publication of American Association of University Women. Editor: Patricia Jenkins. For women of all ages who have at least a bachelor's degree. Published 6 times/year. Circ. 190,000. Buys first serial rights. Pays on publication. Sample copy $1. SASE.
Nonfiction and Photos: "Material used is usually related to broad themes with which AAUW is concerned, including the Equal Rights Amendment, laws and public policies affecting women, education, community issues, cultural affairs and international relations. Emphasis is on women and their efforts to improve society. Articles must be thoroughly researched, well thought through, and competently written. We pay extra for high-quality photos related to the article." Pays "generally $100 maximum."

ALASKA WOMAN MAGAZINE, TAWN, Inc., 2701 Denali, Suite 6, Anchorage AK 99503. Editor: J.A. Brown. Emphasizes "articles of interest to women of all ages who are residents of the Pacific Northwest, specifically Alaska. The majority of current readers are generally well-educated, very independent, and interested in things of past and trends of the future. They enjoy good poetry, stimulating fiction, and stories of successful women." Bimonthly magazine; 100 pages. Estab. 1977. Circ. 8,000. Pays 2 weeks after publication. Buys first rights "with by-line given to *Alaska Woman* upon reprint." Phone queries OK. Submit seasonal/holiday material 2 months in advance. Simultaneous and photocopied submissions OK. Reports in 1 month. Sample copy $1.25.
Nonfiction: Robert Yaskell, Edward Barrington, articles editors. Expose (consumer products, women and medicine, etc.); historical (women's rights movement, women in art, women in Alaska, Gold Rush era, Northwest native women); How-to (crafts and arts which would be of interest to women, gardening, outdoor activities); humor (women and the great outdoors, problems related to living in Alaska and the Northwest); informational (credit, marriage, medical problems of women, nutrition); interview (contemporary women in career and home, political female figures, etc.); new products (contraceptives and pregnancy-related); nostalgia (old-time fashions and fads, Gold Rush memories, etc.); personal experience (coping with marital and career problems, solutions, big city vs. rural, self-improvement); photo feature (must be related to Alaska); and travel (vacation spots, as Alaskans like to travel, especially in winter). Buys 60 mss/year. Query. Length: 600-4,000 words. Pays 5¢/word.
Photos: Purchased with accompanying ms or on assignment. Pays $5 for 5x7 or 8x10 b&w prints; $5 for 35mm color transparencies. Model release required.
Columns/Departments: Karen Baker, editor. News: Outside (news of interest to women that is happening outside of Alaska); News: Inside (news of interest to women that is happening inside Alaska and the Pacific North west); Memoirs: Gleanings from the the Female Past (interesting sidelights on items from the past relating to women in history). Buys 12 pages of column/department material/year. Submit complete ms. Length: 1,200 words maximum. Pays in by-line credit only.
Fiction: Robert Yaskell, Ed Barrington, editors. Adventure (must relate strongly to woman as heroine, etc.); erotica (of interest to women, not 'hard-core); fantasy (of interest to women); historical (special emphasis on Alaska/Pacific Northwest); humorous (relating to women); mystery (featuring heroine and specially for women); romance (not necessarily gothic); science fiction (women-oriented); and suspense. Buys 20 mss/year. Submit complete ms. Length: 800-4,000 words. Pays 2¢/word.
Poetry: Avant-garde; free verse; haiku; light verse; and traditional. Buys 24 poems/year. Pays $5.
How To Break In: "As a new publication, we are interested in bringing to our readers a wide variety of articles and stories dealing with women past and present with a special emphasis on our locale. We are excited about hearing from more talented freelancers outside Alaska. We have many talented people here, but want to keep abreast of the field outside."

THE AUSTRALIAN WOMEN'S WEEKLY, Australian Consolidated Press Ltd., 54 Park St., Sydney, NSW, Australia 2000. Editor-in-Chief: Ita Buttrose. For women, mainly ages 14 and older. "25% of our readership is male, they are from all walks of life." Weekly. Estab. 1933. Circ. 830,000. Pays on acceptance or publication. Buys Australian first serial rights. SASE. Sample copy $1.50.
Nonfiction and Fiction: Buys informational; how-to; personal experience; interview; profile; inspirational; humor; historical; "think" pieces; nostalgia; personal opinion; photo; travel; spot news; successful business operations; new product; film, book and theater reviews. Length: 1,000 to 3,000 words. Pays $60 minimum. "We don't have a maximum payment. Depends on article and standard of writing." Publishes all fiction: experimental, mainstream, mystery, suspense, adventure, western, science fiction, fantasy, humorous, romance, historical, condensed novels, serialized novels. Payment: negotiated.
Photos: Purchased with accompanying ms with or without additional payment. Also purchased without accompanying ms. Captions required. Payment: negotiated. Buys 6x8 glossy prints (preferably), and 2¼ or 35mm transparencies.
Fillers: Buys jokes, gags, anecdotes, short humor. Length: open. Payment: negotiated. Also open to suggestions for new columns or departments.

BEAUTY HANDBOOK, 420 Lexington Ave., New York NY 10017. (212)687-2113. Editor-in-Chief: Eileen Dougherty. Emphasizes beauty, grooming and exercise. Quarterly magazine; 84 pages. Estab. 1975. Circ. 1½ million. Pays on publication. Buys all rights. Submit seasonal/holiday material 4 months in advance. Simultaneous, photocopied, and previously published submissions OK. SASE. Reports in 2 weeks. Free sample copy.
Nonfiction: G. Shakel, Articles Editor. Uses articles on beauty, health, exercise, etc. Buys 40 mss/year. Query. Length: average 300 words. Payment negotiable.
Photos: John McAuliffe, Photo Editor. Purchased with or without accompanying ms or on assignment. Captions required. Query. Submit contact sheet, prints, negatives or transparencies. Offers no additional payment for photos used with ms. Model release required.

BRANCHING OUT, New Woman's Magazine Society, Box 4098, Edmonton, Alberta, Canada T6E 4T1. (403)433-4021. Editor-in-Chief: Sharon Batt. For Canadian women. "The majority are women with a variety of interests (art, literary, political, feminist); 25-50 years of age." Bimonthly magazine; 48 pages. Estab. 1973. Circ. 4,000. Pays on publication. Buys first North American serial rights. Photocopied submissions OK. SAE and International Reply Coupons. Sample copy $1.25; free writer's guidelines.
Nonfiction and Photos: "Unsolicited manuscripts from Canadian women only." Photo features with 4-5 photographs in a series. Buys 60-70/year. Query. Length: 500-3,500 words. Pays $5-15. B&w photos purchased with or without mss. Query. Pays $5-15.
Columns/Departments: Material for all columns and features should take a feminist point of view. Book reviews and columns on law and films. Query. Length: 300-1,500 words. Pays $5-15.
Fiction: "High quality fiction by Canadian women. Experimental and mainstream. Fiction must be good, not sentimental, tightly constructed, high quality writing." Submit complete ms. Length: 1,000-5,000 words. Same rate of payment as nonfiction.
Poetry: Avant-garde, free verse, haiku. Buys 3-4/issue. Limit submissions to batches of 8. Pays $5-15.

BRIDE'S, Condé Nast Building, 350 Madison Ave., New York NY 10017. (212)692-5032. Editor-in-Chief: Barbara D. Tober. For the first or second-time bride in her early twenties, her family and friends, the groom and his family. Magazine published 6 times/year. Estab. 1934. Circ. 300,000. Buys all rights. Buys about 30 mss/year. Pays on acceptance. Free writer's guidelines. Reports in 8 weeks. Query or submit complete ms. Address mss to Copy and Features Department.
Nonfiction: "We want warm, personal articles, optimistic in tone, with help offered in a clear, specific way. All issues should be handled within the context of marriage. How-to features on all aspects of marriage: communications, in-laws, careers, money, sex; informational articles on the realities of marriage, the changing roles of men and women, the kinds of troubles in engagement that are likely to become big issues in marriage; and first-person narratives or stories from couples or marriage authorities that illustrate marital problems and solutions to men and women both." Length: 1,800-3,000 words. Pays $200-550.
How To Break In: "Send us a well-written article that is both easy to read and offers real help for the bride as she adjusts to her new role. No features on wedding and reception planning, home furnishings, cooking, fashion, beauty, travel—these are all staff-written. For examples of the

kinds of features we want study any issue; read articles listed in table of contents under Planning for Marraiage."

CHATELAINE, 481 University Ave., Toronto, Canada M5W 1A7. Editor-in-Chief: Mildred Istona. General interest magazine for Canadian women, from age 20 up. Monthly magazine. Estab. 1928. Circ. 1 million. Pays on acceptance. Buys First North American serial rights. Submit seasonal/holiday material 4 months in advance of issue date. SASE. Free sample copy and writer's guidelines.
Nonfiction: Michele Landsburg, articles editor. How-to; general interest; interview; personal experience; profile; and travel. Length: 2,000-3,600 words. Pays $600 minimum.
Fiction: Barbara West, fiction editor. Confession; humorous; mainstream; romance; and condensed novels. No short shorts. Length: 3,000-4,000 words. Pays $400 minimum.

COMMUNITY WOMAN, 1133 W. Struck Ave., Orange CA 92667. (714)997-9660. Editor-in-Chief: Cheryl Pruett. Managing Editor: Colleen A. Huber. 75% freelance written. For women, 20-80 years-old, interested in home, children, business, personal care, and continuing education (formal and informal). "Our readers are predominately college trained graduates." Monthly tabloid; 16 pages. Estab. 1977. Circ. 15,000. Pays on publication. Not copyrighted. Phone queries OK. Submit seasonal/holiday material 2 months in advance of issue date. Photocopied and previously published submissions OK. SASE. Reports in 2 months. Free sample copy and writer's guidelines; mention *Writer's Market* in request.
Nonfiction: Exposé (consumer frauds or shabby practices, how red tape affects prices, etc.); general interest (successful individual and women's organizations, not women's liberation); historical (women who have shaped history: inventors, writers, politicians, etc.); how-to (saving, decorating, carpentry, painting, establishing a home business); humor (funny situations developed out of home life); inspirational (overcoming obstacles of women); new product (especially if it makes women's role easier). "No put-downs of men or women's liberation themed material." Buys 60-100 mss/year. Query or submit complete ms. Length: 100-1,000 words. Pays $5-15.
Photos: Pays $2.50-10 for b&w prints. Captions and model release required.

COSMOPOLITAN, 224 West 57th St., New York NY 10019. Editor: Helen Gurley Brown. Managing Editor: Guy Flatley. For career women, ages 18 to 34. Monthly. Circ. 2,500,000. Buys all rights. Pays on acceptance. Not interested in receiving unsolicited manuscripts. Most material is assigned to established, known professional writers who sell regularly to top national markets, or is commissioned through literary agents.
Nonfiction and Photos: Not interested in unsolicited manuscripts; for agents and top professional writers, requirements are as follows: "We want pieces that tell an attractive, 18- to 34-year-old, intelligent, good-citizen girl how to have a more rewarding life—'how-to' pieces, self-improvement pieces as well as articles which deal with more serious matters. We'd be interested in articles on careers, part-time jobs, diets, food, fashion, men, the entertainment world, emotions, money, medicine and psychology, and fabulous characters." Uses some first-person stories. Logical, interesting, authoritative writing is a must, as is a feminist consciousness. Length: 1,200 to 1,500 words; 3,000 to 4,000 words. Pays $200 to $500 for short pieces, $1,000 to $1,750 for longer articles. Photos purchased on assignment only.
Fiction: Department Editor: Harris Dienstfrey. Not interested in unsolicited manuscripts; for agents and top professional writers, requirements are as follows: "Good plotting and excellent writing are important. We want short stories dealing with adult subject matter which would interest a sophisticated audience, primarily female, 18 to 34. We prefer serious quality fiction or light tongue-in-cheek stories on any subject, done in good taste. We love stories dealing with contemporary man-woman relationships. Short-shorts are okay but we prefer them to have snap or 'trick' endings. The formula story, the soap opera, skimpy mood pieces or character sketches are not for us." Length: short-shorts, 1,500 to 3,000 words; short stories, 4,000 to 6,000 words; condensed novels and novel excerpts. "We also use murder or suspense stories of about 25,000 to 30,000 words dealing with the upper class stratum of American living. A foreign background is acceptable, but the chief characters should be American." Has published the work of Agatha Christie, Joyce Carol Oates, Evan Hunter, and other established writers. Pays about $1,000 and up for short stories and novel excerpts, $4,500 and up for condensed novels.

FAMILY CIRCLE MAGAZINE, 488 Madison Ave., New York NY 10022. (212)593-8000. Editor: Arthur Hettich. 60% freelance written. For women/homemakers. Published 14 times/year. Usually buys all rights. Pays on acceptance. Reports in 6 weeks. Query. "We like to see a strong query on unique or problem-solving aspects of family life, and are especially interested in

writers who have a solid background in the areas they suggest." SASE.
Nonfiction: Women's interest subjects such as family and social relationships, children, humor, physical and mental health, leisure-time activities, self-improvement, popular culture, travel. Service articles. For travel, interested mainly in local material, no foreign or extensive travel. "We look for human stories, told in terms of people. We like them to be down-to-earth and unacademic." Length: 1,000 to 2,500 words. Pays $250 to $2,500.
Fiction: Occasionally uses fiction relating to women. Buys short stories, short-shorts, vignettes. Length: 2,000 to 2,500 words. Payment negotiable. Minimum payment for full-length story is $500.

FARM WIFE NEWS, 733 N. Van Buren, Milwaukee WI 53202. (414)272-5410. Managing Editor: Judy Borowski. For farm and ranch women of all ages; nationwide. Estab. 1970. Circ. 200,000. Copyrighted. Buys over 400 mss a year. Pays on publication. Sample copy $1; free writer's guidelines. Will consider photocopied submissions. Submit seasonal material 4 to 6 months in advance. Reports in 4 to 6 weeks. Query first or submit complete ms. SASE.
Nonfiction and Photos: "We are always looking for good freelance material. Our prime consideration is that it is farm-oriented, focusing on a farm woman or a subject that would appeal especially to her." Uses a wide variety of material: articles on vacations, daily life, sewing, gardening, decorating, outstanding farm women, etc. Topic should always be approached from a rural woman's point of view. Informational, how-to, personal experience, interview, profile, inspirational, humor, think pieces, nostalgia, personal opinion, travel, successful business operations. Length: 1,000 words maximum. Departments and columns which also use material are: A Day in Our Lives, Besides Farming, Farm Woman on the Go, Country Crafts, Sewing and Needlecraft, Gardening, Decorating, I Remember When, Farm Nature Stories. Pays $20 to $100. B&w photos are purchased with or without accompanying mss. Color slides and transparencies are also used. They look for scenic color photos which show the good life on the farm. Captions required. Payment depends on use, but begins at $10 for b&w photos; at $25 for color slides or transparencies.
Fiction: Mainstream, humorous. Themes should relate to subject matter. Length: 1,000 words maximum. Pays $40 to $75.
Fillers: Word puzzles and short humor. Pays $15 to $30.

GLAMOUR, 350 Madison ave., New York NY 10017. (212)692-5500. Editor-in-Chief: Ruth Whitney. Features Editor: Wenda Wardell Morrone. For women, 18-35-years old. Circ. 6.5 million. SASE.
Nonfiction: "Editorial approach is 'how-to' with articles that are relevant in the areas of careers, health, psychology, interpersonal relationships, etc. Fashion, beauty, decorating and travel are all staff-written. Short articles (1,500-2,000 words) pay $500-750; longer mss (2,500-3,000 words) pay $850 and up.

GOOD HOUSEKEEPING, Hearst Corp., 959 Eighth Ave., New York NY 10019. Editor-in-Chief: John Mack Carter. Executive Editor: Mina Mulvey. Managing Editor: Mary Fiore. Mass women's magazine. Monthly; 200 pages. Estab. 1885. Circ. 5,000,000. Pays on acceptance. Rights very with author and material. Submit seasonal/holiday material 6-8 months in advance. SASE. Reports as soon as possible.
Nonfiction: John Block, articles editor. Expose; how-to; informational; humor; inspirational; interview; nostalgia; personal experience; photo feature; profile and travel. Buys 8-10 mss/issue. Query. Length: 1,000-5,000 words. Pays $500-5,000.
Photos: Herbert Bleiweiss, Art Director. Photos purchased with or without accompanying ms or on assignment. Captions required, (pic information only). Pays $50-250 for b&w photos; $50-350 for color photos. Query. Model release required.
Columns/Departments: Robert Liles, Features Editor. Light Housekeeping (humorous short-short prose and verse) and The Better Way (ideas and depth research, edited by Dick Teresi). Query. Pays $25-350. "Only outstanding material has a chance here."
Fiction: Naome Lewis, Fiction Editor. Romance; mainstream; suspense; condensed novels and serialized novels. Buys 3 mss/issue. Send complete ms. Length: 1,000 words (short-shorts)-10,000 words (novels); average: 4,000 words. Pays $1,000.
Poetry: Leonhard Dowty, Poetry Editor. Light verse and traditional. Buys 3 poems/issue. Pays $25 minimum.
Fillers: Robert Liles, Features Editor. Jokes, gags, anecdotes, and short humor, cartoons, and epigrams. Pays $25-100.

HADASSAH MAGAZINE, 50 W. 58th St., New York NY 10022. Editorial Director: Helen G.

Lusterman. Executive Editor: Jesse Zel Lurie. For members of Hadassah. Monthly, except combined issues (June-July and August-September). Circ. 360,000. Buys U.S. publication rights. Pays on publication. Reports in 6 weeks. SASE.
Nonfiction: Primarily concerned with Israeli, the American Jewish community and American civic affairs. Length: 1,500 to 3,000 words. Pays $200-350.
Photos: "We buy photos only to illustrate articles, with the exception of outstanding color from Israel which we use on our covers. We pay $100 and up for a suitable color photo."
Fiction: Short stories with strong plots and positive Jewish values. Length: 3,000 words maximum. Pays $300 and up.

HARLEQUIN, 220 Duncan Mill Road, Don Mills, Ontario, Canada M3B 3J5 Editor: Beth McGregor. Emphasizes romance and escape reading; for women of all ages, all walks of life. Monthly magazine; 72 pages. Estab. 1973. Circ. 225,000. Pays on acceptance. Buys second serial (reprint) and first North American serial rights. Submit seasonal/holiday material 6 months in advance. Simultaneous, photocopied and previously published submissions OK. SASE and International Reply Coupons. Reports in 4-6 weeks. Free sample copy and writer's guidelines.
Nonfiction: How-to (crafts and home-oriented items); humor (clean, light reading); inspirational; personal experience (triumph over adversity, emotional experiences—prefer photos here); profile (photos required) and travel (armchair traveler material). Buys 30 mss/year. Query. Length: 2,000-3,000 words. Pays $75-200.
Photos: Photos purchased with or without accompanying ms. Captions required. Pays $35 for b&w photos; $75 for 35mm, 2¼x2¼ and 4x5 color photos. Model release required. "Mostly purchase scenic and travel pics."

HARPER'S BAZAAR, 717 Fifth Ave., New York NY 10022. Editor-in-Chief: Anthony Mazzola. For "women, late 20's and above, middle income and above, sophisticated and aware, with at least 2 years of college. Most combine families, professions, travel, often more than one home. They are active and concerned over what's happening in the arts, their communities, the world." Monthly. Rights purchased vary with author and material. May buy first North American serial rights. No unsolicited mss. Query first. Enclose SASE.
Nonfiction and Photos: "We publish whatever is important to an intelligent, modern woman. Fashion questions plus beauty and health—how the changing world affects her family and herself; how she can affect it; how others are trying to do so; changing life pattern and so forth. Query us first."

HERS, I.P.C. Magazines Ltd., King's Reach Tower, Stamford St., London SE1 9LS, England. Editor-in-Chief: Jack McDavid. 80% freelance written. For British readers; young, married women, low income interested in self-identification through first-person real-life stories. Buys 30-40 mss/year from American/Canadian writers. Monthly magazine; 64 pages. Estab. 1965. Circ. 150,000. Pays on acceptance. Buys all rights. Submit seasonal/holiday materal 4 months in advance. SAE and International Reply Coupons. Reports in 6 weeks. Free sample copy and writer's guidelines.
Photos: Jo Gange, photo editor. Uses 35mm or 2¼x2¼ color transparencies. Model release required.
Fiction: Rosalind Davis, fiction editor. Confessions. Buys 12 mss/issue. Send complete ms. Length: 1,500-5,000 words. Pays £10-15.

IN TOUCH: THE JOURNAL OF PERSONAL POSSIBILITIES, Box 3471, Santa Barbara CA 93105. (805)967-7914. Editor: Earbara Hinrichs. For women from all walks of life who want to reinforce a winning self-image. Newsletter; 12 pages. Estab. 1974. Monthly. Circ. 1,000. Buys all rights, but may reassign rights to author after publication. Buys 50 to 100 mss per year. Pays on publication. Sample copy $1. Will consider photocopied and simultaneous submissions. Reports on mss accepted for publication "immediately." SASE.
Nonfiction: "We try to develop each issue around a theme and include book reviews and other resources that tie in with the central theme. Need short articles about women who are living their lives in creative ways. We consider ourselves feminist — with a positive attitude toward solving the problems encountered by women in both their personal and professional lives. Our top concern is always to turn women on to developing their own potential. Our aim is to inspire — no dreary stories about people who are concerned about anything less than excellence. Not interested in hearing about small thinkers." Query. Length: 500 to 750 words. Pays $5. Regular column on women's business enterprises. Length: 500 words. Pays $5. Also uses clippings, but no payment is made.

LADIES' HOME JOURNAL, 641 Lexington Ave., New York NY 10022. Editor: Lenore Hershey. Pays on acceptance. Issued monthly. "We have in the last year initiated the policy of only accepting manuscripts that are submitted to us through literary agents." SASE.
Nonfiction: "Articles that address themselves to the many issues, emotions, concerns and joys women face today — as wives, mothers, citizens, workers, and as human beings. Factual information, concrete advice, humor, and first-person 'shared experience' approaches are welcomed. Send queries to Kathleen D. Fury, Articles Editor."
Fiction: "We are sorry to announce a new policy under which we will no longer consider short stories sent through the mail. We do not have facilities that permit proper handling. Please do not send in manuscripts as we will be unable to return them."

LADY'S CIRCLE MAGAZINE, Lopez Publications, Inc., 21 West 26th St., New York NY 10010. Editor: Susan Lapinski. For homemakers. Monthly. Buys all rights. Pays on publication. Reporting time varies from 1 week to 3 months. Query first, with brief outline. SASE.
Nonfiction and Photos: Particularly likes first-person or as-told-to pieces about health and doing good. Also how homemakers and mothers make money at home. Hobbies and crafts. Also articles on baby care, home management, gardening, as well as problems of the homemaker. Also, stories of people who have overcome illnesses or handicaps. Articles must be written on specific subjects and must be thoroughly researched and based on sound authority. Length: 2,500 words. Pays $125 and up. Pays $15 for good b&w photos accompanying articles.

McCALL'S, 230 Park Ave., New York NY 10017. Editor: Robert Stein. "Study recent issues." Monthly. Circ. 6,500,000. Pays on acceptance. "All mss must be submitted on speculation and *McCall's* accepts no responsibility for unsolicited mss." Reports in 4 to 6 weeks. Query first. SASE.
Nonfiction: Department Editor: Helen Markel. No subject of wide public or personal interest is out of bounds for *McCall's* so long as it is appropriately treated. The editors are seeking meaningful stories of personal experience. They are on the lookout for new research that will provide the basis for penetrating articles on the ethical, physical, material and social problems concerning readers. They are most receptive to humor. *McCall's* buys between 200 and 300 articles a year, many in the 1,000- to 1,500-word length. Miss Lisel Eisenheimer is Editor of Nonfiction Books from which *McCall's* frequently publishes excerpts. These are on subjects of interest to women: biography, memoirs, reportage, etc. Address queries for "Right Now" column to Mary McLaughlin. Subjects can be education, medicine, social and community affairs (new ideas and trends), problems being solved in new ways, ecology, women doing interesting things, women's liberation, any timely subject. Short pieces with a news or service angle. Length: 300 to 500 words. Payment is up to $300. The magazine is not in the market for new columns. Almost all features on food, household equipment and management, fashion, beauty, building and decorating are staff-written.
Fiction: Department Editor: Helen DelMonte. "Again the editors would remind writers of the contemporary woman's taste and intelligence. Most of all, fiction can awaken a reader's sense of identity, deepen her understanding of herself and others, refresh her with a laugh at herself, etc. *McCall's* looks for stories which will have meaning for an adult reader of some literary sensitivity. *McCall's* principal interest is in short stories; but fiction of all lengths is considered." Length: about 4,000 words. Length for short-shorts: about 2,000 words. Payment begins at $1,250.
How To Break In: "Your best bet is our monthly newsletter section, Right Now. It's an eight-page section and we buy a lot of freelance material for it, much of that from beginning writers. Some people have gone on from Right Now to do feature material for us."

MADEMOISELLE, 350 Madison Ave., New York NY 10017. Editor-in-Chief: Edith Raymond Locke. 60% freelance written. Directed to college-educated women between the ages of 18 to 30. Circ. 882,000. Reports on submissions in 3 to 4 weeks. Buys first North American serial rights. Pays on acceptance. Prefers written query plus samples of work, published or unpublished. SASE.
Nonfiction: Mary Cantwell, Senior Editor, Features. Particular concentration on articles of interest to the intelligent young woman that concern the arts, education, careers, European travel, current sociological and political problems. Articles should be well-researched and of good quality. Prefers not to receive profile articles of individuals or personal reminiscences. Length: "Opinion" essay column, 1,300 words; articles, 1,500 to 6,000 words. Pays $300 for "Opinion" essay column; articles $100 minimum.
Photos: Department Editor: Susan Niles. Commissioned work assigned according to needs.

Photos of fashion, beauty, travel; career and college shots of interest to accompany articles. Payment ranges from no-charge to an agreed rate of payment per shot, job series, or page rate. Buys all rights. Pays on publication for photos.
Fiction: Department Editor: Mary Elizabeth McNichols. High-quality fiction by both name writers and unknowns. Length: 1,500-3,000 words. Pays $300 minimum. Uses short-shorts on occasion. "We are particularly interested in encouraging young talent, and with this aim in mind, we conduct a college fiction contest each year, open to men and women undergraduates. A $500 prize is awarded for each of the two winning stories which are published in our August issue. However, our encouragement of unknown talent is not limited to college students or youth. We are not interested in formula stories, and subject matter need not be confined to a specific age or theme." Annually awards 2 prizes for short stories.
Poetry: Department Editor: Mary Elizabeth McNichols. Must be of very high literary quality, under 65 lines. Pays $25 minimum. Annually awards 2 prizes for poetry.

MODERN BRIDE, 1 Park Ave., New York NY 10016. Executive Editor: Cele G. Lalli. Bimonthly. Buys all rights. Pays on acceptance. Reports in 2 weeks. SASE.
Nonfiction: Uses articles of interest to brides-to-be. "We prefer articles on etiquette, marriage, planning a home, and travel from honeymoon point of view. *Modern Bride* is divided into three sections: the first deals with wedding dresses; the second with home furnishings; the third with travel. We buy articles for all three; we edit everything, but don't rewrite without permission." Length: about 2,000 words. Payment is about $200 minimum.
Poetry: Occasionally buys poetry pertaining to love and marriage. Pays $15 to $25 for average short poem.

MS. MAGAZINE, 370 Lexington Ave., New York NY 10017. Editor-in-Chief and Publisher: Patricia Carbine. Editor: Gloria Steinem. For "women predominantly; varying ages, backgrounds, but committed to exploring new life styles and changes in their roles and society." Estab. 1972. Monthly. Circ. over 400,000. Rights purchased vary with author and material. Pays on acceptance. Will consider photocopied submissions. Submit seasonal material at least 3 months in advance. Reports in 4-6 weeks. Query first for nonfiction only, "with ideas and outline, and include samples of previous work." Address to Query Editor. Submit complete ms for fiction. Enclose SASE.
Nonfiction: "Articles, features on the arts, women's minds, women's bodies that relate to exploring new life styles for women and changes in their roles and society. We are a how-to magazine—how a woman may gain control of her life. We are hoping to change the status quo—to treat women as human beings, and not to insult their personhood with down-putting editorializing or insensitive advertising. We encourage women to live their lives as unique people, not role players. We would like more input on what women are doing politically in their communities." Buys informational articles, how-to's, personal experience articles, interviews, profiles, inspirational articles, humor, historical articles, think articles, exposes, personal opinion pieces, photo articles, new product articles, coverage of successful business operations, and art, book, and film reviews. Length varies. Pays $100 to $500. Send to Manuscript Editor.
Photos: Purchased with mss, without mss, or on assignment. Payment "depends on usage." Address to Art Department.
Fiction, Poetry and Fillers: Personal experience, fantasy, humorous, historical; condensed novels, serialized novels. Length: 3,000 words maximum. Pays up to $500. Address to Fiction Editor. Traditional forms, blank verse, free verse, avant-garde forms and light verse, relating to magazine subject matter. Address to Poetry Editor. "We accept nonfiction filler length material only for the Gazette section of the magazine; news from all over." Length: filler length to 3,000 words maximum. Pays up to $500.
How To Break In: "The Gazette section which features short news items is the easiest way to get published here. We use a lot of material from all over the country on politics, the women's movement, human interest material, women profiles. Regional material from outside New York stands the best chance, but nothing is a sure bet. We get a lot of material we can't use from people who don't understand the kind of orientation we seek. It is possible to move from the Gazette to do other work for *Ms*."

NATIONAL BUSINESS WOMAN, 2012 Massachusetts Ave. N.W., Washington DC 20036. (202)293-1100. Editor: Louise G. Wheeler. For "all mature, educated, employed women." Estab. 1919. 10 times a year. Buys all rights and second serial rights. Buys 10 or 12 mss a year. Payment on acceptance. Sample copy $1. Will consider photocopied submissions. Reports in 6 weeks. SASE.

Nonfiction: "Originality preferred. Written specifically for members of the National Federation of Business and Professional Women's Clubs, Inc. No fiction or poems." Buys informational, biographical, and articles of current interest to business and professional women. Length: 1,000 to 1,200 words. Pays $10 to $35.

NEW DAWN, North American Publishing Co., 545 Madison Ave., New York NY 10022. Editor-in-Chief: Gay Bryant. 50% freelance written. For a readership of women, 18-34 years of age, active and open-minded. "She's a first-time woman— first relationship, first apartment, first trip abroad, etc.—the young Mary Tyler Moore and *not* the New York sophisticate. She reads, works, has had a fair amount of college and has some money to spend." Bimonthly magazine; 96 pages. Estab. April 1975. Circ. 350,000. Pays on publication. Buys all rights, but may reassign following publication, or first North American serial rights. Submit seasonal/ holiday material 4 months in advance of issue date. Photocopied and previously published submissions OK. SASE. Reports in 4 weeks. Free writer's guidelines; mention *Writer's Market* in request.
Nonfiction: *New Dawn* is a general service magazine for young women and covers fashion, beauty, health, food, travel and investigative topics—"from Solar Energy to Women in the KKK. That's an ingredient that most other women's magazines don't have—some of our articles could just as easily be found in *Playboy* or *New Times*." Buys 2-4 mss/issue. Query with clips of previously published work. Length: 500-5,000 words. Pays $100-500.

PLAYGIRL MAGAZINE, 1801 Century Park East, Los Angeles CA 90067. (213)553-8006. Editor-in-Chief: Barbara Cady. For an aware, contemporary female audience of all ages, today's multi-faceted women in all occupations, who are interested in a wide range of subjects. Monthly magazine; 124 pages. Estab. 1973. Circ. 1,100,000. Rights purchased vary with author and material. May buy all rights. Buys about 100 mss/year. Pays within 30 days of acceptance. Sample copy $1.75. Will consider photocopied submissions. Will not consider simultaneous submissions. Submit seasonal material for all of the traditional holidays 5 months in advance. Reports in 1 month. Query first for nonfiction. Submit complete ms for fiction. SASE.
Nonfiction and Photos: "*Playgirl* does not believe in limiting women's horizons, as most women's magazines do. We use material on any area of concern to women, not just the traditional areas of home and children. Must be totally professional. We are most concerned with literary quality and slant. Articles must be well-researched and tightly written and must demonstrate a respect for the intelligence of our readers." Uses informational, how-to, personal experience, think pieces, nostalgia, and career articles. Length: 1,500-3,000 words. Pays $250/1,000 words. B&w and color photos are purchased on assignment only.
Fiction: "Stories may be sexually oriented, but not salacious. Female characters should be three-dimensional and portrayed realistically." Experimental, mainstream, mystery, suspense, erotica, fantasy, humorous, romance, excerpts from novels. Length: 1,000 to 5,500 words. Rates vary.

REDBOOK MAGAZINE, 230 Park Ave., New York NY 10017. Issued monthly. Rights purchased vary with author and material. Reports in 6-8 weeks. Pays on acceptance. SASE.
Nonfiction: Articles relevant to the magazine's readers, who are young women in the 18- to 34-year-old group. Also interested in submissions for "Young Mother's Story." "We are interested in stories offering practical and useful information you would like to share with others on how you, as a mother and a wife, are dealing with the changing problems of marriage and family life, such as the management of outside employment, housework, time, money, the home and children. Stories also may deal with how you, as a concerned citizen or consumer, handled a problem in your community." Please don't hesitate to send it because you think your spelling or punctuation may be a bit rusty; we don't judge these stories on the basis of technicalities and we do make minor editing changes. For each 1,000 to 2,000 words accepted for publication, we pay $500. Mss accompanied by a large, stamped, self-addressed envelope, must be signed, and mailed to: Young Mother's Story, c/o *Redbook Magazine*. Stories do not have to be typed, but we appreciate it when they are legibly written." Length: articles, 3,500 to 4,500 words; short articles, 2,000 to 2,500 words.
Fiction: Eileen Schnurr, fiction editor. Uses a great variety of types of fiction, with contemporary stories appealing especially to women in demand. Short stories of 3,500-5,000 words are always needed. Also short-shorts of 1,400-1,600 words. Payment begins at $850 for short-shorts; $1,000 for short stories.
How To Break In: "It is very difficult to break into the nonfiction section, although two columns—Young Mothers and To Be A Woman—which publish short personal experience pieces (1,000-1,500 words) do depend on freelancers. The situation for fiction is quite different.

We buy about a third of our stories from writers whose stories come in from the cold in the mail or from writers who were originally found in our unsolicited mail. We buy about 50 stories a year. This is clearly the way to break into *Redbook*. Many of the stories we're proudest of—the fresh material that gives *Redbook* fiction its distinctiveness—are from people we've discovered in the mail. So when we open those brown envelopes it is with a great deal of hope."

S.E.W. MAGAZINE, Deerfield Communications, 444 Madison Ave., New York NY 10022. (212)688-5666. Editor-in-Chief: Alison Beyea. Managing Editor: Mike Hoffman. 35% freelance written. Emphasizes home sewing, crafts, home furnishings, and women's interests. Quarterly magazine; 72 pages. Estab. October 1977. Circ. 250,000. Pays on acceptance. Buys one-time rights. Phone queries OK. Submit seasonal/holiday material 6 months in advance of issue date. Simultaneous and photocopied submissions OK. SASE. Reports in 1 month. Free sample copy.
Nonfiction: How-to (sewing hints, special projects, crafts, etc.); general interest (anything in women's field—beauty, exercise, fashion, etc.); interview (celebrity sewers or designers); new product; personal experience; and technical. "No cutesy home sewing articles. We stress fashion, practicality, ease of doing and new original ideas." Buys 4-5 mss/issue. Length: 2,000 words maximum. Pays $150-350.

SPHERE MAGAZINE, 500 N. Michigan Ave., Chicago IL 60611. Editor: Joan Leonard. Monthly. Study several issues of the publication and query first. SASE. Unsolicited mss not accepted.

VIVA, 909 Third Ave., New York NY 10022. For predominantly female audience between 18 and 27. Monthly. Pays within 30 days following publication. Usually reports in 6 weeks. Submit complete ms. SASE.
Fiction: Experimental, mainstream, suspense, adventure, humorous and science fiction. Writers must consider the nature of the magazine before submitting material. Should have strong narrative structure. Avoid mediocrity and the cliche. Length: 1,000 to 4,000 words. Pays about 25¢ per word.

VOGUE, 350 Madison Ave., New York NY 10017. Editor: Grace Mirabella. Issued monthly. For highly intelligent women. Query first. Enclose SASE.
Nonfiction: Feature Editor: Leo Lerman. Uses articles and ideas for features, 2,000 to 2,500 words. Fashion articles are staff-written. Material must be of high literary quality, contain good information. Pays $300 and up, on acceptance.

W, *Women's Wear Daily*, 7 East 12th St., New York NY 10003. Completely staff-written newspaper.

WOMAN'S DAY, 1515 Broadway, New York NY 10036. Editor: Geraldine Rhoads. 14 issues/year. Circ. over 8,000,000. Buys first and second North American serial rights. Pays on acceptance. Reports within 2 weeks on queries; longer on mss. Submit detailed queries first to Rebecca Greer, Articles Editor. SASE.
Nonfiction: Uses articles on all subjects of interest to women—marriage, family life, child rearing, education, homemaking, money management, travel, family health, and leisure activities. Also interested in fresh, dramatic narratives of women's lives and concerns. Length: 500 to 3,000 words, depending on material. Payment varies depending on length, whether it's for regional or national use, etc.
Fiction: Department Editor: Eileen Herbert Jordan. Uses little fiction; high-quality, genuine human interest romance and humor, in lengths between 1,500 and 3,000 words. Payment varies. "We pay any writer's established rate, however."
Fillers: Brief (500 words maximum), factual articles on contemporary life, community projects, unusual activities are used—condensed, sprightly, and unbylined—in "It's All in a Woman's Day" section. "Neighbors" column also pays $25 for each letter and $5 for each brief practical suggestion on homemaking or child rearing. Address to the editor of the appropriate section.

WOMEN IN BUSINESS, Box 8728, Kansas City MO 64114. (816)361-6621. Editor: Rita R. Rousseau. 25% freelance written. For working women in all fields and at all levels; largely middle-aged women in traditional "women's" fields. Monthly (combined issues in March/April, July/August, and November/December) magazine; 28 pages. Estab. 1949. Circ. 101,000. Pays on acceptance. Buys all rights, but may reassign following publication. Phone queries OK. Submit seasonal/holiday material 3 months in advance of issue date. SASE. Reports in 2 months. Free sample copy and writer's guidelines.

Nonfiction: General interest; how-to; historical; new product; technical; and travel. No articles of interviews or profiles of individuals; no food, fashion, child care or anything else that general interest women's magazines carry. Buys 9 mss/year. Query or submit complete ms. Length: 1,000-2,000 words. Pays $50-150.
Photos: State availability of photos with query or submit with accompanying ms. Pays $25-60 for 8x10 b&w glossy contact sheets; $75 cover color transparencies. Captions preferred. Buys all rights, but may reassign following publication. Model release required.
Columns/Departments: Books Briefly (short reviews); Business Communications (letters, speeches, and memos); Personal Business (financial)' The Management Woman (tips); and Your Personality (pop psychology). Buys 9/year. Query. Length: 500-1,200 words. Pays $35-50.

WOMEN STUDIES ABSTRACTS, Rush Publishing Co., Inc., Box 1, Rush NY 14543. Editor-in-Chief: Sara Stauffer Whaley. Educational publication for women (libraries, professors of women's studies, psychologists, college administrators). Quarterly magazine; 100 pages. Estab. 1972. Circ. 1,500. Pays on acceptance. Buys all rights but may reassign following publication. Phone queries OK. Simultaneous, photocopied, and previously published submissions OK. SASE. Reports in 4 weeks. Sample copy $4.50.
Nonfiction: "Bibliographical articles or bibliographies with introduction only. Must be non-sexist, non-racist material written from scholarly knowledge of our field. Must be very accurate in biographical citations." Query. Pays $50-150, "plus percentage of reprints, if made."

WOMEN'S DIGEST, 342 Madison Ave., New York NY 10017. Editor-in-Chief: Jane Alexander. Bimonthly magazine; 80 pages. Estab. 1977. Pays on publication. Buys first North American serial rights. Submit seasonal/holiday material 3 months in advance of issue date. Simultaneous and photocopied submissions OK. SASE. Reports in 2 months.
Poetry: Free verse; light verse; and traditional. Submit in batches of 5 or 6. Length: 4-13 lines. Pays $5-25.

WOMEN'S RIGHTS, 610 N. Fairbanks Court, 3rd Floor, Chicago IL 60611. (312)644-3850. Editor: Ron Fenton. Emphasizes "facts for the divorced or separated woman." Bimonthly magazine; 84 pages. Estab. 1977. Circ. 100,000. Pays 30 days after publication. Buys all rights and second serial rights. Phone queries OK. Submit seasonal/holiday material 2 months in advance of issue date. Photocopied and previously published submissions OK. SASE. Reports in 2 weeks. Free writer's guidelines.
Nonfiction: Material of interest to divorced and separated women. How-to; informational; inspirational; interview; personal experience; and profile. Buys 6-10 mss/issue. Query or submit complete ms. Length: 1,000-3,000 words. Pays $100-300.
Fiction: Humorous; romance; and serialized novels. Buys 1 mss/issue. Query or submit complete ms. Length: 1,000-3,000 words. Pays $100-300.
Poetry: Avant-garde; free verse; haiku; light verse; and traditional. Buys 1-2/issue. Limit submissions to batches of 3. Pays $100.

Gag Markets

Markets in this section include information about cartoonists who are looking for gags. Submissions to cartoonists should be made on 3x5 slips of paper. Briefly suggest the scene and add the gagline. For convenience in identifying the gag, include some identifying code number at the upper left-hand side of the gag slip. Your name and address should be typed on the reverse side of the gag slip in the upper left-hand corner.

It should be noted that payment is usually not made for cartoon gags until the cartoonist has sold the cartoon and received his payment. Most of the listings for cartoonists indicate the number of gags they will consider as a single submission. The usual average is 10 to 20. Cartoonists usually return gags in 1 to 3 weeks. Individual listings cite the variations in reporting time, but cartoonists may want to keep ideas they've converted into cartoons for many years. They try to get them circulated everywhere, and in some cases, they may even resubmit them.

Originality is essential, but switching with a fresh idea is allowable. Allowances are made for coincidence since many gag men frequently come up with similar ideas. But submissions of "many that have been done before" will "turn off" the knowledgeable cartoonist and editor.

RAE AVENA, 36 Winslow Rd., Trumbull CT 06611. Cartoonist since 1965. Likes to see all types of gags. Has sold to *National Enquirer, New York Times,* and Pyramid Publications (paperbacks). "Gagwriters should send around 12 gags. Keep descriptions short." Pays 25% commission. Returns rejected material "as soon as possible." Enclose SASE for return of submissions.

DOROTHY BOND ENTERPRISES, 2450 N. Washtenaw Ave., Chicago IL 60647. "Been in the cartooning industry since 1944, and have successfully hit all bases. Have sold panels and comic strips to top syndicates and single cartoons to publications in almost every field. When we receive your gag, it is carefully reviewed and, if we think it's salable, it is drawn up at once and sent on its quick way to a wide list of top cartoon buyers. If we reject your gag, it is returned to you within 3 days. Unsold, retained gags are returned to you within 3 months. We are happy to see all gags, with the exception of pornography, cannibal, monkey or elephant gags. Any common topic with a new, funny slant sells quickly. Also, more women should enter the gagwriting field because many top magazines welcome submissions with a woman's funny viewpoint. And cartoons *should* be funny since they are meant to amuse and entertain. Bitterness and cruelty should be left out. Be professional and type your gags on 3x5 cards with your name and address on the back, and always enclose SASE. We send you 40% of the sale check the same day we receive it. Please no clips or rubber bands, or letters with your submissions. We do your accepted submissions as expertly and as cleverly as anyone can. We want to sell them as badly as you do. Trust us, and good luck to us both."

BILL BOYNANSKY, Apt. 13/20, Ansonia Hotel, 2109 Broadway, New York NY 10022. (212)787-2520. Estab. 1936. Purchased over 300 gags last year. Submit 15-20 gags at one time. Pays "25% for regular, 35% for captionless; all others—regular payment." Reports in 3 days to 2 months. SASE.
Needs: General, male, female, sexy, girlie, family, children's, adventure, medical. "Prefer to see captionless gag ideas on all subject matter, but no beginners; only those who know their business. I prefer to deal with cartoonists by letter or phone because it saves me time. However, I will respect and consider all mail replies."

ASHLEIGH BRILLIANT, 117 W. Valerio St.. Santa Barbara CA 93101. Estab. 1967. Sells to newspapers. Has sold to the *Chicago Tribune-New York Times News Syndicate*. Reports in 2 weeks. Pays $10.

Needs: "My work is so different from that of any other cartoonist that it must be carefully studied before any gags are submitted. Any interested writer not completely familiar with my work should first send $1 for my catalog of 1,000 examples. Otherwise, their time and mine will be wasted."

JOE BUSCIGLIO, 420 W. North Bay, Tampa FL 33603. Cartoonist since 1941. Query first. State experience and if you are currently selling. General and family gags only. No sex. Pays 25% commission on sale. Currently selling to newspapers, trade journals, and house organs; also "ad" type art and some editorial panels. Will return promptly if material (gags) not adequate. Enclose SASE. No returns otherwise.

ARTEMAS COLE, Box 408, La Puente CA 91747. Estab. 1974. Buys 30-50 gags/year for use in national magazines (medical, girlie, etc.). Has sold to *National Enquirer*, *Good Housekeeping*, *Boys Life*, etc. Submit gags on 3x5 slips; 10-20/batch. Reports in 1-2 weeks. Pays 30% plus "bonus payment of 50% for every tenth sale." SASE.
Needs: "Basically any general or family gags that are funny and fresh. Humor through children especially. Will look at girlie material, adult attitudes, and humor with sex. Business and home repair gags sought. I do *not* want to see raunchy sex or children engaged in sex with adults. These items are my taboos. I do not find anything funny with child molester humor. I make this statement emphatic because I've received a lot of this type of material lately."

COMEDY UNLIMITED, Suite 625, Jack Tar Office Bldg., 1255 Post St., San Francisco CA 94109. Contact: Jim Curtis. "We are always looking for fresh, new premise ideas for unique and creative standup comedy monologues, as well as clever and original sight gags, and crazy pieces of business. We also buy original one-liners tailored especially for any of the following: comedians, public speakers, singers, magicians, or jugglers. Since we build everything from night club acts to humorous corporate speeches, it would be advisable not to submit any material until you have sent an SASE and request our current projects list to find out exactly what we're most interested in buying during any given quarter. Keep in mind we are exclusively concerned with material intended for oral presentation." If SASE is not enclosed with submission, all material will be destroyed after being considered, except items purchased. Pays $1 to $3 per line, on acceptance, and considerably more for zany, new premise ideas and sight gags. Reports in 2 weeks.

CREATIVE CARTOON SERVICE, 3109 West Schubert Ave., Chicago IL 60647. Contact: Peter Vaszilson. Cartoonist since 1965. "Creative Cartoon Service is an art brokerage service, arranging for sale of artwork between cartoonists, gagwriters and publishers. Please inquire before submitting your work to us." SASE.

THOMAS W. DAVIE, 1407 S. Tyler, Tacoma WA 98405. Cartoonist since 1960. Interested in general gags, medicals, mild girlies, sports (hunting and fishing), business and travel gags. Gags should be typed on 3x5 slips. Prefers batches of 5 to 25. Sold to *Medical Economics, Sports Afield*, King Features, *Chevron USA, Rotarian, Saturday Evening Post, Ladies' Home Journal, Playgirl* and *Boys' Life*. 25% commission. Returns rejected material within 4 weeks. SASE.

LEE DeGROOT, Box 115, Ambler PA 19002. Estab. 1956. Now interested in receiving studio greeting card ideas only. "I draw up each idea in color before submitting to greeting card publishers. Therefore, giving the editors a chance to visualize the idea as it would appear when printed...and thus increasing enormously the chances of selling the idea. Writer's percentage is 25% of selling price."

GEORGE DOLE, Box 3168, Sarasota FL 33578. Estab. 1952. Has sold to *Playboy, Parade, Penthouse*. Submit 12 gags at one time. Pays 25% commission. Reports in 1 week. SASE.
Needs: General, male, female, sexy, girlie, family, children's, sports, medical. Must be sophisticated, funny, etc., and submitted on standard index cards.

JAMES ESTES, 1103 Callahan, Amarillo TX 79106. "Primarily interested in seeing good, funny material of a general nature. Always interested in a good strip idea. Most themes are acceptable, but the usual taboos apply. Submit on 3x5 cards or paper, 10 to 20 gags per submission; clear, concise ideas set down without excessive wordiness. Wholesome, family, general material wanted. I don't do sexy, girlie cartoons at all and it's a waste of gagwriters' postage to send that type gag." Has been selling cartoons for 7 years. Currently selling to *Changing Times, Wall*

Street Journal, Saturday Review, Physician's Management, Reader's Digest, Medical Economics, Boys' Life, National Enquirer, Saturday Evening Post and *The Christian Science Monitor*, including several farm magazines, horse and western magazines. Returns rejected material as quickly as possible, usually in 2 to 3 days. Pays 25% of what cartoon sells for. SASE.

DON ERIK GJERTSEN, 338 N. Forest Ave., Rockville Centre NY 11570. Estab. 1967. Has sold to *Gallery, Genesis, Writer's Digest, Skiing*, etc. Submit gags on 3x5 file cards "typed or neatly written with gagwriter's name and address on the back;" 20/batch. Reports in 1-2 weeks. Pays 25% for gags with captions; 30% for captionless. SASE.
Needs: "Girlie" (but not gross); general; sports and outdoors; business; technology; medical; food and dining; and historical. No gross sex; "the higher paying markets don't want it, and the publications that do don't pay enough for the cartoonist, much less a gagwriter."

RANDY HALL, 1121 N. Tulane, Liberal KS 67901. (316)624-2431. Estab. 1974. Purchased 400 gags last year. Has sold to *New Woman, American Legion, VFW Magazine, Medical Times, Modern Medicine, Channels, Wallace's Farmer, Farmer/Stockman, Christian Century, Instructor, Massachusetts Teacher, King Features*. Submit 10-25 gags at one time. Pays 25% commission. Returns rejects the same day received, but "keeps gags going forever if there's a chance of selling them." SASE.
Needs: General, male, female, sexy, girlie, family, industrial, professional, children's, sports, medical, farm, religious, antique, education. "Must be original. I see far too much plagiarism. If it's not original, don't send it. Be consistent and don't send me 25th-round rejects. I like to get first looks occasionally, too."

CHARLES HENDRICK JR., Old Fort Ave., Kennebunkport ME 04046. (207)967-4412. Estab. 1942. Purchased 100 gags last year. Sells to local markets. Submit 10 gags at a time. Pays 50% of commission. Reports in 10-30 days. SASE.
Needs: General family, trade (hotel, motel, general, travel, vacationers). Safe travel ideas—any vehicle. Gags must be clean; no lewd sex.

DAV HOLLE, Box L, Naperville IL 60540. (812)533-1474. Estab. 1977. Buys 200 gags/year. "I work the generals, men's and women's publications, as well as some trade journals. My work appears in the local weekly as well." Has sold to *Ele Ela, Datamation*, and *Writer's Digest*. Submit gags on 3x5 slips, sketched or typed. "If writers draw stick figures, it gets the gag into the cartoon spirit." Reports in 5 working days. Pays 25%. SASE.
Needs: "I look for imagination at work to produce gags suited to the panel (vs. other types of humor). I enjoy seeing material for captionless panels."

DAVID R. HOWELL, 338 North E St., Porterville CA 93257. (209)781-4999. Estab. 1974. Purchased 120 gags last year. Has sold to *Writer's Digest, New Woman, Modern Medicine, Easyriders, Road King, Inside Detective, Western Horseman, American Machinist, California Dental Survey, Graphic Arts Monthly*. Submit 6-10 gags at one time. Pays 25-30% commission. Returns rejected gags same day as received. SASE.
Needs: General, female, family, trade (printing), professional, children's, medical, dental, horses. "I need gags that depend on the drawing to show idea; very original—not old, wornout type ideas. No girlies, or suggestive or offensive gags. I do a weekly panel for local paper on the printing and graphic arts trade. Have sold many cartoons to *Graphic Arts Monthly* which very much warrants my need for gags on the printing and graphic arts industry."

LARRY (KAZ) KATZMAN, 101 Central Park, W., Apt. 4B, New York NY 10023. (212)724-7862. Estab. 1949. Purchased over 100 gags last year. Has sold to *Modern Medicine, Medical Economics* and "Nifty Nellie" (syndicated feature). Submit 12-15 gags at one time. Pays 25% commission. Reports in 1 week. SASE.
Needs: "I use only medical (doctor, nurse, hospital) gags; no others." Must be submitted on numbered, separate slips.

JEFF KEATE, 1322 Ensenada Dr., Orlando FL 32807. Cartoonist since 1936. Interested in general situation and timely gags, sports gags (all sports in season) for "Time Out" sports panel. "Be funny. No puns, No oldies. No old hat situations." Has sold all of the major publications over the past 30 years. Currently doing syndicated newspaper cartoon panels for Field Newspaper Syndicate. Pays 25% commission. Bought close to 200 gags from freelancers last year. Holds unsold gags for "approximately 2 years unless gagwriter requests gag back sooner." Returns rejected material immediately. Enclose SASE for return of submissions.

STEVE KELL, 733 Waimea Dr., El Cajon CA 92021. (714)440-5749. Estab. 1966. Buys 60 gags/year for use in men's and women's publications, all general markets. Has sold to *Playgirl*, *Penthouse*, *Esquire*, etc. Submit gags in batches of 10-15. Reports in 1 week. Pays 25%. SASE.
Needs: "All fresh and surprising slants accepted."

REAMER KELLER, Box 3557, Lantana FL 33462. (305)582-2436. Estab. 1940. Buys "several hundred" gags/year for use in general markets, newspapers and trade magazines. Has sold to *Cosmopolitian*, *Medical Economics*, *National Enquirer*, etc. Submit gags in batches of 20-30. Reports in 2 weeks. Pays 25%. SASE.
Needs: "Action, short captions and captionless." General; medical; hospital; girly; "timely stuff, homey."

MILO KINN, 1413 S.W. Cambridge St., Seattle WA 98106. Cartoonist since 1942. Interested in medical gags, male slant, girlie, captionless, adventure, and family gags. Wants anything that is funny. Sells trade journals, farm, medical, office, and general cartoons. Sold to *Medical Economics, Modern Medicine, Farm Wife News, Private Practice, Wallace's Farmer,* etc. Pays 25% commission. SASE.

FRANK J. LEWIS, 2867 Gloucester Ct., Woodbridge VA 22191. (703)221-1789. Estab. 1957. Has sold to *Extra, Potomac News, Army Times* and *Navy Times*. Submit no more than 10 gags at one time. Pays 30% commission. Reports in 1 week. SASE.
Needs: "Looking for gags with political accent on anything from the Washington scene to small town politics to include social, environmental or economics. Also willing to work in conjunction with a writer on a strip idea."

LO LINKERT, 1333 Vivian Place, Port Coquitlam, B.C., Canada V3C 2T9. Cartoonist since 1957. Interested in clean, general, male, medical, family, office, outdoors gags; captionless ideas; greeting card ideas. "Make sure your stuff is funny. No spreads." Wants "action gags—not two people saying something funny." Has sold to *National Enquirer, Parade, Field and Stream,* and others. Prefers batches of 10 to 15 gags. Pays 25% commission; $25 for greeting card ideas. Returns rejected material in 1 week. Enclose SAE and International Reply Coupons for return of submissions or 13¢ U.S. postage.

ART McCOURT, 3819 Dismount, Dallas TX 75211. (214)339-6865. Estab. 1952. Purchased 300 gags last year. Has sold to *Arizona Republic, Wallace's Farmer, Independent Banker, Prairie Farmer, American Legion, Mechanix Illustrated* and King Features. Submit 10-15 gags at one time. Pays 25% commission. Reports in 1 week. SASE.
Needs: "Something unique and up-to-date." Does not want to see anything on "crowds, TV, mothers-in-law or desert islands".

MASTERS AGENCY, Box 427, Capitola CA 95010. Editorial Director: George Crenshaw. Pays $15-20 for finished cartoon roughs on banking, outdoors, religion, education, and all US holidays.

BILL MAUL, 492 Bethune Dr., Virginia Beach VA. Estab. 1970. Sells to men's and women's publications and general interest magazines. Has sold to *Better Homes & Gardens*, *Playgirl*, *TV Guide*, *Family Circle*, etc. Submit gags on 3x5 cards or paper, 10-15 in a batch. Reports in 1 week. Pays 25%; "raises to 30% after a successful collaboration period." SASE.
Needs: "Will consider all topics, but the writer should concentrate on general, family-type gags. Topics such as TV, current events and trends warrant special consideration. Sight gags are always desireable."

HAROLD B. MONEY ("Halm"), 1206 Dover Ave., Wilmington DE 19805. (302)994-0272. Estab. 1950. Buys 400 gags/year for use in men's publications. Has sold to *Nugget*, *Dude*, *Gent*, *Beaver*, and *Hustler*. Submit "brief, concise, neatly-typed gags;" 10-15/batch. Reports in 3-4 days. Pays 25% on sales to $10; 30% thereafter. SASE.
Needs: "Strictly girlie slant gags with a fresh viewpoint on what is essentially a limited human activity, and 'punchy' gaglines. No general or trade journal gags. No orgy scenes, VD gags, flashers, bride & groom, or multi-panel ideas."

RAY MORIN, 140 Hamilton Ave., Meriden CT 06450. (203)237-4500. Estab. 1959. Purchased about 10 gags last year. Has sold to *Boys' Life, Wall Street Journal,* McNaught Syndicate and

King Features. Submit 7-10 gags at one time. Pays 25% commission. Holds gags "indefinitely", trying to redraw the cartoon from a different angle. SASE.
Needs: General, family, children's, medical and business. "I do 95% of my own gags, but am willing to look."

MICHAEL J. ("SKI") PELLOWSKI, Box 726, Bound Brook NJ 08805. Estab. 1973. Buys 20-30 gags/year for use in illustrated humor publications, trade journals, special interest and hobby publications. Has sold to *Sick* magazine, *Trucking*, and *Crazy*. Submit gag slips or gags typed on a page with triple spacing. Pays $1-5 outright purchase or 10% royalty. SASE.
Needs: Banking, business, safety and general work themes. Also 1-2 page panel-to-panel material for publication in illustrated humor magazines and comic books. Sells jokes, gags, and one-liners to well known stand up comedians. Buys performable comedy material for outright fee and polishes same for sale. Will look at anything that can be performed in night clubs or on TV.

IRV PHILLIPS, 2807 East Sylvia St., Phoenix AZ 85032. Interested in general, pantomime, and word gags. Submit on 3x5 cards. Pays 25% commission; $10 minimum on syndication. Also looking for beginning gagwriters to work with beginning cartoonists from his classes at Phoenix College. Enclose SASE for return of submissions.

ANDREW PRESLAR, 133 N. 5th St., La Puente CA 91744. Estab. 1975. Buys 100 gags/year for use in general magazines and trade journals. Has sold to *Life Association News*, *Dental Survey*, and *Western Horseman*. Submit gags on 3x5 slips of paper; 10/batch. Reports in 2-3 weeks. Pays 25%. SASE.
Needs: "Sophisticated generals, general family, new woman, dental and some office gags."

DOM RINALDO, 29 Bay, 20 St., Brooklyn NY 11214. Estab. 1960. Buys 50-70 gags/year, for use in men's publications, "but would like to see trade journal gags as well." Has sold to *Cavalier*, *Oui*, *Saturday Evening Post*, *Hustler*, etc. Submit gags on 3x5 cards, numbered or coded. "Keep gag brief." Reports immediately. Pays 25%. SASE.
Needs: 'Girlie'; family; and trade. No golf gags, or making fun of religion.

LEE RUBIN, 9 Murray Ave., Port Washington NY 11050. Interested in gags concerning eyesight, eyeglasses and optometrists. Submit maximum of 25 gags at a time. Pays 40% commission. Bought about 33 gags last year. Reports in 1 month. May hold gags for 2 months. SASE.

FRANK ("DEAC") SEMATONES, 5226 Mt. Alifan Dr., San Diego CA 92111. (714)279-7178. Estab. 1950. Purchased "hundreds of gags" last year. Has sold to *National Enquirer* and male and girlie magazines. Pays 25% commission. Reports "immediately, but will keep unsold gags going forever unless return is requested." SASE.
Needs: Male, sexy, girlie. Must be new, fresh and funny.

JOSEPH SERRANO, Box 42, Gloucester MA 01930. Cartoonist since 1950. Seasonal and social comment preferred. Has sold to most major and middle markets. Pays 25% commission. SASE.

HARRY SEVERNS, 1623 Boyd, St. Joseph MO 64505. Prefers batches of 12 to 15 gags. Pays 30% commission. Has sold to *Modern Medicine, Private Practice, Dakota Farmer* and *Telebriefs*. Enclose SASE for return of submissions.
Needs: Interested in gags for telephone, medical, farm, sports, auto, business, hunting-fishing. No general or girlie gags.

E.G. SHIPLEY, 4725 Homesdale Ave., Baltimore MD 21206. Estab. 1977. Sells to trade journals and general magazines. Has sold to *Industry Mart*. Submit gags typed on 3x5 cards; 15-20 to a batch. Reports in 10 days. Pays 35%.
Needs: Needs general, computer, farming, and machine shop gags. "I am doing mostly trade journal cartoons." No medical gags.

JOHN W. SIDE, 335 Wells St., Darlington WI 53530. Cartoonist since 1940. Interested in "small town, local happening gags with a general slant." Pays 25% commission. Will send a sample cartoon to a gagwriter for $1. Does not return unsold gags. Returns rejected material "immediately." Enclose SASE for return of submissions.

SCOTT SMITH, 170 Madison Ave., Danville KY 40422. (606)236-9390. Estab. 1962. Buys 1,000 gags/year for use in men's and general interest magazines and newspapers. Has sold to *Independent Banker*, *Saturday Evening Post* and *Changing Times*. Submit gags on 3x5 cards; 10-15/batch. Reports "immediately." Pays 30%. SASE.
Needs: "General topics suitable for *National Inquirer*, *Saturday Evening Post*, etc. Would also like lawyer and court gags (mainly on lower courts). These have to be new and not switched. I will look closely at ideas for a small town lawyer-judge type strip."

JOHN STINGER, Box 202, New Hope PA 18938. Cartoonist since 1967. Interested in general, family, and general business gags. Interested in business-type gags first. Would like to see more captionless sight gags. Currently doing a syndicated panel on business, for which funny ideas are needed. Has sold to *Argosy, True, Industry Week* and other major markets. "Index cards are fine but please keep short." Pays 25% commission; "more to top writers." Bought about 50 gags last year. Can hold unsold gags for as long as a year. SASE.

TOM STRATTON, S. 4211 Lake Shore Rd., Hamburg NY 14075. Estab. 1970. Buys 100 gags/year for use in men's and women's publications and general interest magazines. Has sold to *New York Times*, *Cosmopolitian*, *Saturday Review*, *Hustler*, etc. "Submit gags on file cards in batches of 10, no more than 3 times a month. I don't want to be inundated—I can't swim." Reports in 2-3 days. Pays 25%. SASE.
Needs: General, sex, and off-the-wall humor. "An oblique way of looking at things. Nothing normal." Will also look at ideas for satires and parodies. No cliches or forced puns.

BOB THAVES, P.O. Box 67, Manhattan Beach CA 90266. Cartoonist for over 20 years. Interested in gags "dealing with anything except raw sex. Also buy gags for syndicated (daily and Sunday) panel, 'Frank & Ernest.' Prefer offbeat gags (no standard, domestic scenes) for that, although almost any general gag will do." Will look at batches containing any number of gags. Pays 25% commission. Returns rejected material in 1 to 2 weeks. May hold unsold gags indefinitely. Enclose SASE for return of submissions.

MARVIN TOWNSEND, 631 West 88th St., Kansas City MO 64114. Full-time cartoonist for over 20 years. Interested in gags with a trade journal or business slant. Such as office executives, professional engineers, plant managers, doctors, etc. "Religious and children gags also welcome. Captioned or captionless. No general gags wanted. Don't waste postage sending general gags or worn-out material." Sells to trade and business publications and church and school magazines. Prefers batches of 12 gags. Pays 25% commission. Enclose SASE for return of submissions.

BARDULF UELAND, Halstad MN 56548. Estab. 1969. Has sold to *Parade, Legion, New Woman,* King Features, McNaught Syndicate. Submit 12-15 gags at one time. Pays 25% commission. Reports in 1-3 days, but holds unsold gags indefinitely unless return is requested. SASE.
Needs: General, family, medical and farm gags. No sex.

ART WINBURG, 21 McKinley Ave., Jamestown NY 14701. Cartoonist since 1936. Will look at all types of gags; general, family, trade and professional journals, adventure, sports, medical, children's magazines. Gagwriter should "use variety, be original, and avoid old cliches." Would prefer not to see gags about "smoke signals, flying carpets, moon men, harems, or cannibals with some person in cooking pot." Has sold to *National Star, VFW Magazine, Physician's Management, American Legion, Modern Medicine, New Woman, Highlights for Children*. Pays 25% commission. Returns rejected material "usually within a week, sometimes same day as received." Will return unsold gags "on request. Always a possibility of eventually selling a cartoon." SASE.

ANDY WYATT, 10960 SW 174th Terrace, Miami FL 33157. (305)233-9418. Cartoonist since 1960. Interested in general, topical, family, and business. "I like visual gags, but any good gag is okay." Pays 25% commission. Bought "over 100" gags from gagwriters last year. Returns rejected material in "1 to 2 weeks if I definitely can't use; sometimes longer if I feel there's a possibility." May hold unsold gags "until I sell, unless a writer specifies he wants gags back at a certain time." SASE.

Greeting Card Publishers

Greeting card companies have specialized editorial needs, just as magazines and publishing houses do, so the successful greeting card writer must learn what kinds of cards each company buys. Many companies produce only a few kinds of cards; even big companies which produce all the standard kinds of cards may have staff writers to prepare some categories, so they may buy only a few kinds and ideas from freelance writers.

To submit conventional greeting card material, type or neatly print your verses on either 4x6 or 3x5 slips of paper or file cards. For humorous or studio card ideas, either use file cards or fold sheets of paper into card dummies about the size and shape of an actual card. Neatly print or type your idea on the dummy as it would appear on the finished card. Put your name and address on the back of each dummy or card, along with a code number of some type, such as 1, 2, 3, etc. The code number makes it easier for the editor to refer to your idea when writing to you, and also helps you in keeping records. Always keep a file card of each idea. On the back of each file card, keep a record of where and when the idea was submitted. Submit from 10 to 15 ideas at a time (this makes up a "batch"); be sure to include a stamped, self-addressed return envelope. Keep the file cards for each batch together until the ideas (those rejected) come back. For ideas you write that use attachments, try to get the actual attachment and put it on your dummy; if you cannot, suggest the attachment. For mechanical card ideas, you must make a workable mechanical dummy. Most companies will pay more for attachment and mechanical card ideas.

The listings below give the publishers' requirements for verse, gags, or other product ideas. Artwork requirements are also given for companies that are interested in buying a complete card from a greeting card specialist who can supply both art and idea.

Brief descriptions for the many types of greeting cards and terms used within the listings are as follows:

Contemporary card: upbeat greeting; studio card belonging to the present time; always rectangular in shape.

Conventional card: general card; formal or sentimental, usually verse or simple one-line prose.

Current needs list: see Market Letter.

Cute card: informal, gentle humor; slightly soft feminine-type card in which the text is closely tied to the illustration.

Everyday card: for occasions occurring every day of the year, such as birthdays and anniversaries.

Humorous card: card in which the sentiment is expressed humorously; text may be either verse or prose, but usually verse; illustrations usually tied closely to the text, and much of the humor is derived from the illustration itself; often illustrated with animals.

Informal card: see Cute card.

Inspirational card: slightly more poetic and religious sounding card within the conventional card line; purpose is to inspire, and is usually poetical and almost Biblical in nature.

Juvenile card: designed to be sent to children up to about age 12; text is usually written to be sent from adults.

Market letter: current needs list; list of categories and themes of ideas and kinds of cards an editor currently needs; some companies publish monthly market letters; others only when the need arises.

Mechanical: card that contains an action of some kind.
Novelty: refers to ideas that fall outside realm of greeting cards, but sent for the same occasion as greeting cards; usually boxed differently and sold at different prices from standard greeting card prices.
Other Product Lines: booklets, books, bumper stickers, buttons, calendars, figurines, games, invitations and announcements, mottoes, note papers, placemats, plaques, postcards, posters, puzzles, slogans, stationery, and wall hangings.
Pop-up: a mechanical action in which a form protrudes from the inside of the card when the card is opened.
Promotions: usually a series or group of cards (although not confined to cards) that have a common feature and are given special sales promotion.
Punch-outs: sections of a card, usually Juvenile, that are perforated so they can be easily removed.
Risque: card that jokes about sex.
Seasonal card: published for the several special days that are observed during the year; Christmas, Easter, Graduation, Halloween, etc.
Sensitivity card: beautiful, sensitive, personal greeting.
Soft line: gentle me-to-you message in greeting form.
Studio: contemporary cards using short, punchy gags in keeping with current humor vogues and trends; always rectangular in shape; often irreverent.
Topical: ideas or cards containing subjects that are currently the topic of discussion.
Visual gags: a gag in which most, if not all, the humor depends upon the drawing or series of drawings used in the card; similar to captionless cartoons.

Study the various types of cards available at your local card shops to see what's currently selling. Another excellent source for learning to write for the greeting card publishers is the complete handbook on writing and selling greeting cards—*The Greeting Card Writer's Handbook,* edited by H. Joseph Chadwick (*Writer's Digest*).

AMBERLEY GREETING CARD CO., P.O. Box 37902, Cincinnati OH 45222. (513)242-6630. Editor: Dah Crown. Buys all rights. Send for list of current needs. Submit ideas on regular 3x5 cards. "We always take a closer look if artwork (a rough sketch on a separate sheet of paper that shows how the card would appear) is submitted with the gag. It gives us a better idea of what the writer has in mind." Do not send conventional cards. Reports in 3 to 4 weeks. May hold ideas for approximately 2 weeks. Enclose S.A.S.E. for return of submissions.
Humorous, Studio and Promotions: Buys all kinds of studio and humorous everyday cards, "including odd captions such as promotion, apology, etc. Birthday studio is still the best selling caption. We never get enough. We look for belly laugh humor, not cute. All types of risque are accepted. No ideas with attachments. We prefer short and snappy ideas. The shorter gags seem to sell best. We are in special need of get well and hospital studio." Would prefer not to see Easter, Mother's Day, and Father's Day ideas. Pays $25. Occasionally buys promotion ideas. Payment negotiable, "depending entirely upon our need, the quantity, and work involved."
Other Product Lines: Promotions, plaques, mottoes, postcards, buttons, and bumper stickers. "Humor is what we look for in other product lines." Pays $25 for mottoes and bumper stickers.

AMERICAN GREETINGS CORPORATION, 10500 American Rd., Cleveland OH 44144. Buys all rights. Pays on acceptance. "Always research the card racks before submitting ideas. Like to see total card-line concepts as well as individual card ideas." Reports in 4 weeks. Enclose SASE.
Conventional: Considers holiday material, but chances are always better with everyday occasions. No limits on the type of material used, as long as it's of professional quality, and salable. Most sales made are by copy which captures some fundamental aspect of people-to-people sentiment. Verse, or prose; any length. Material should be directed to Editor, General Editorial.
Soft Touch: " 'Conversational' is the word to describe our style here. We are looking for sincere and simple (but not trite) ways to say 'Happy Birthday', 'Get better soon', 'I love you'' and 'I'm glad we're friends'. We look at any idea, any time, and are in the market for the captions mentioned above." Direct material to Soft Touch Editor.

Humorous: "Our humorous line ranges from whimsical compliments to zap-em punch lines. Besides the usual birthday, get well and friendship directions, we're in the market for family captions, especially mother, father, brother, sister, daughter and son. We don't buy *much* here, but we're always interested in new and original approaches." Send ideas to Humor Editor.
Studio: "We're looking for funny and fresh material — try for the unexpected inside line. We look at anything, any time — birthdays, get well, friendship, holiday." These ideas should be addressed to Studio Editor.
Juvenile: "Our juvenile cards range from baby's first birthday to young adult. We don't buy many freelance verses, but we are always interested in concept directions in the things-to-do or novelty areas." Juvenile concepts should be directed to the Juvenile Editor.
Other Product Lines: Calendars, books and promotional concepts.

BARKER GREETING CARD CO., Rust Craft Park, Dedham MA 02026. Humorous Director: Bill Bridgeman. Submissions should be typed or neatly printed on separate 3x5 cards or folded paper. Name, address and a code number should be on back of each idea submitted. SASE must accompany each batch. Artwork on ideas is not necessary. Reports in 1-3 weeks. Buys all rights. Pays on acceptance. Send SASE for Market Letter.
Needs: Studio card ideas for all everyday and seasonal captions; special need for card ideas involving the use of mechanicals and attachments. Some risque (sex and physical humor) ideas are also needed. Specific needs are detailed in their periodic Market Letter. Seasonal needs include Christmas, Hanukkah, Valentine's Day, St. Patrick's Day, Mother's Day, Father's Day, graduation, Halloween and Thanksgiving. Everyday captions are birthday, friendship and get well. "All verse should be as concise as possible." Promotions, mottoes, etc., may be submitted at any time.
Payment: Humorous and studio, $25.

BRILLIANT ENTERPRISES, 117 W. Valerio St., Santa Barbara CA 93101. Editor: Ashleigh Brilliant. Buys all rights. Will send a catalog and sample set for $1. Submit seasonal material any time. "Submit words and art in black on 5½x3½ horizontal, thin white paper. Regular bond okay, but no card or cardboard." Does not want to see "topical references, subjects limited to American culture, or puns." Reports "usually in 10 days." Enclose SASE.
Other Product Lines: Postcards. "All our cards are everyday cards in the sense that they are not intended only for specific seasons, holidays, or occasions." Messages should be "of a highly original nature, emphasizing subtlety, simplicity, insight, wit, profundity, beauty, and felicity of expression. Accompanying art should be in the nature of oblique commentary or decoration rather than direct illustration. Messages should be of universal appeal, capable of being appreciated by all types of people and of being easily translated into other languages. Since our line of cards is highly unconventional, it is essential that freelancers study it before submitting." Limit of 17 words per card. Pays $25 for "complete ready-to-print word and picture design."

COLORTYPE SERVICES OF LOS ANGELES, INC., 4374 E. La Palma Ave., Anaheim CA 92807. Reports in 4 to 6 weeks. SASE.
Sensitivity and Studio: Friendship and nature themes only. No everyday general cards. Body humor and risque. Brevity is important. Contemporary themes only. Payment negotiable, but conforms with established schedules.

CREATIVE PAPERS, INC., Box 448, Jaffrey NH 03452. Director: Lew Fifield. "Send photocopies that we can keep, simply because we do not have the time to write to each individual that submits work. If work is submitted to be returned, include a cover note and SASE." Reports in 4 weeks. Buys all reproduction rights to the concept of existing art, or reproduction rights for a specified product, or the original art and exclusive reproduction rights. Pays on acceptance. Free information sheet and registration form available for postcard request.
Needs: "We are looking for a fresh approach to copy ideas—clever, sophisticated. We are interested in verse and *good* poetry that expresses popular sentiments, and 1- and 2-line copy and card ideas." Especially interested in material for Christmas, Valentine's Day, get well, Easter, birthday, love, sorry, thank you, congratulations, thinking of you, best wishes and invitations. Does not want to see copy for studio cards. Seasonal/holiday material must be submitted a year in advance. "We prefer simple verse rather than long, melodramatic verses—copy that is intelligent, sensitive, and thoughtful." Open for new ideas for posters, puzzles, gift books, greeting books, postcards, games, calendars and buttons.
Payment: Soft line, sensitivity, humorous, conventional, inspirational, informal, juvenile, invitations, announcements, $10.

CUSTOM CARD OF CANADA, LTD., 1239 Adanac St., Vancouver, B.C., Canada V6A 2C8. (604)253-4444. Editor: E. Bluett. Estab. 1964. Submit ideas on 3x5 cards or small mock-ups in batches of ten. Reports in 3-6 weeks. Buys world rights. Pays on acceptance. Current needs list for SASE.
Needs: All types, both risque and non-risque. "The shorter, the better." Birthday, belated birthday, get well, anniversary, thank you, congratulations, miss you, new job, etc. Seasonal ideas needed for Christmas by March; Valentine's Day (September); graduation (December); Mother's Day and Father's Day (December).
Payment: Studio, etc., $25 minimum.

THE DRAWING BOARD, INC., 256 Regal Row, Dallas TX 75221. (214)637-0390. Editorial Director: Jimmie Fitzgerald. Estab. 1956. Purchases approximately $10,000 worth of freelance material annually. Submit ideas on 3x5 cards, typed, with name and address on each card; 20/batch. SASE. Reports in 2 weeks. Pays on acceptance. Market list for SASE.
Needs: Announcements; conventional; humorous; informal; inspirational; everyday; seasonal; invitations; juvenile; and studio cards. No 'blue' or sex humor. Pays $30-50.
Other Product Lines: Calendars. Pays $200-600.

THE EVERGREEN PRESS, P.O. Box 4971, Walnut Creek CA 94596. (415)825-7850. Editor: Malcolm Nielsen. Buys all rights. Pays on publication. Write for specifications sheet. Submit Christmas material any time. "Initial offering may be in the rough. Will not publish risque or 'cute' art." Reports in 2 weeks. Enclose SASE.
Conventional, Inspirational, and Studio: Interested in submissions from artists. Publishes everyday cards in a "very specialized series using verse from Shakespeare, for example. Our major line is Christmas. We avoid the Christmas cliches and attempt to publish offbeat type of art. For Christmas cards, we do not want Santa Claus, Christmas trees, wreaths, poodle dogs or kittens. We don't want sentimental, coy or cloying types of art. For everyday greeting cards we are interested in series of cards with a common theme. We are not interested in single designs with no relation to each other. We can use either finished art which we will separate or can use the artist's separations. Our studio lines are a complete series with a central theme for the series. We do not try to compete in the broad studio line, but only with specialized series. We do not purchase verse alone, but only complete card ideas, including verse and art." Payment for art on "royalty basis, depending on the form in which it is submitted."
Other Product Lines: Bookplates, note papers, invitations, children's books, stationery. Payment negotiated.

D. FORER AND CO., 511 E. 72 St., New York NY 10021. Editor: Barbara Schaffer. Buys all rights. Pays on acceptance. Sometimes holds material up to 3 weeks. SASE.
Informal and Humorous: Anniversary, thank you, new home, birthday, get well, engagement, and general cards. A hint of sophisticated. Cute humor. "We read all occasions all year round; Valentine, Christmas, Father's Day, Mother's Day. We prefer 3-to-4 line verse. Pays $20 for verse, $50 for humorous ideas."

FRAN MAR GREETING CARDS, LTD., Box 1057 Mt. Vernon NY 10550. (914)664-5060. President: Stan Cohen. Estab. 1958. Buys 100-300 items/year. Submit ideas in small batches (no more than 15 in a batch) on 3x5 sheets or cards. SASE. Reports in 1-2 weeks. Buys all rights. Pays on the 15th of the month following acceptance.
Needs: Soft line; invitations; and studio cards. "We are currently in need of risque, birthday, friendship, anniversary, and get well card ideas. Copy should be short and have a punch." No juvenile or seasonal material.
Other Product Lines: Promotions (pays $15-50); and plaques (pays $15). "We are currently in need of stationery and pad ideas (with or without captions, humorous or functional); novelty ideas in the paper area; and tote and accessory bag captions."

FREEDOM GREETING CARD CO., INC., 409½ Canal's End Rd., Bristol PA 19007. (215)785-4042. President: Jerome Wolk. Estab. 1969. Buys 200 ideas/year. Query. Limit submissions to batches of 12. Submit seasonal/holiday material 1 year in advance. SASE. Reports in 4-6 weeks. Buys all rights. Pays on acceptance. Needs list for SASE.
Needs: Announcements; conventional; humorous; inspirational; invitations; juvenile; sensitivity; and Spanish. Pays $1/line.

GIBSON GREETING CARDS, INC., 2100 Section Rd., Cincinnati OH 45237. Submit ideas on file cards, 10-15 at one time. SASE. Address materials to editor of appropriate line: seasonal,

everyday, studio, humorous, juvenile, cute, ancillary products. Reports in 2-3 weeks. Buys all rights. Pays on acceptance. Writer's guidelines sheet for SASE.
Needs: Humorous, studio, conventional, everyday and seasonal, cute and juvenile. "For humorous and studio, we look for short, original, punchy, funny, sendable, contemporary ideas. We can't use attachments or very tricky hand folds, but are always interested in clever use of a simple fold. We look for a different idea and/or an original way of expressing the usual sentiments. Prose, or rhymed verse. We'd like to see more good, fresh, humorous material—short, clever ideas with good illustration possibilities for an unexpected ending inside. Also, good conventional rhymed verse, both everyday and seasonal, a fresh approach, with good rhyme and meter, and contemporary wording with different rhyming words. We do not purchase inspirational material; we use Helen Steiner Rice's material for our inspirational line. However, we do purchase religious verse and prose for the major sending situations and seasons. We can't use poetry, except as it ties in with a direct message and greeting card category. Send ideas for all the usual seasons; Christmas and Valentine's Day are the largest, followed by Mother's and Father's Day, and Easter. Need various family categories and combination relatives for all of these (except, no family categories for studio). We work about 1½ years ahead of season. Need everyday cards for general and family birthdays; wedding anniversaries, sympathy and illness. We'd like to see more combinations of material; rhymed verse plus prose; quotes with prose or rhymed verse, etc. Most conventional verse runs 4 to 8 lines, but can run to 16 or even 20, for a special 'page-2'."
Payment: Humorous (needs good, short humor for relatives), $25-50; studio $50; and conventional prose, $20.

VIVIAN GREENE, INC., 15240 N.W. 60th Ave., Miami Lakes FL 33014. President: Vivian Greene. Buys all rights. SASE. Pays on acceptance.
Needs: Only humorous, whimsical comic cards.
Payment: Humorous/studio, $25-150.
Other Product Lines: Gift books, $100-300. Greeting books, $75-300.

HALLMARK CARDS., INC., Contemporary Design Department, 25th and McGee, Kansas City MO 64141. Editor, Contemporary & Humorous: Nancy Saulsbury. Estab. 1910. Submit ideas either on card mock-ups or 3x5 cards; 10-20/batch. SASE. Reports in 2-3 weeks. Buys all rights. Pays on acceptance; "must have writer's Social Security number in order to pay." Market list for SASE.
Needs: Humorous and Studio cards. Pays $55 maximum. "Will pay $40 for an idea needing major or complete change in editorial content."

INTERMART, INC., Box 432, Cambridge MA 02139. (617)963-4400. President: V.G. Badoian. Reports in 2 months. Buys all rights. Pays on acceptance.
Needs: Will consider ideas and material for all types of cards, promotions, mottoes, posters, puzzles, figurines, gift books, greeting books, plaques, postcards, games. Copy limited to 4 lines. Payment by negotiation prior to acceptance begins at $100.

KALAN, INC., 7002 Woodbine Ave., Philadelphia PA 19151. President: M. Kalan. SASE. Reports in 1 week. Copyrighted. Pays on acceptance.
Needs: Ideas for good humor studios and adult (X-rated) studios; primarily birthday. Short verse preferred.
Payment: Humorous, $10-20.
Other Product Lines: Posters (humorous, clever), $10-20.

ALFRED MAINZER, INC., 39-33 29th St., Long Island City NY 11101. (212)786-6840. Editor: Arwed Baenisch. Buys all rights. SASE.
Conventional, Inspirational, Informal, and Juvenile: All types of cards and ideas. Traditional material. All seasonals and occasionals wanted. Payment for card ideas negotiated on individual basis only.

THE MAKEPEACE COLONY, INC., Box 111, Stevens Point WI 54481. (715)344-2636. President: James L. Murat. "Contact us before submitting material." SASE. Reports in 4-12 weeks. Rights purchased vary. Pays on acceptance or on publication, depending on the product.
Needs: "We occasionally purchase soft humor, friendship and other related greeting card and poster lines, plus occasionally some poetry."
Payment: Soft line, sensitivity, humorous, conventional, inspiration; $10 minimum. Greeting books and plaques, $10 minimum.

MARK I, 1733 W. Irving Park Rd., Chicago IL 60613. Editor: Alex H. Cohen. Buys all rights. Reports within 2 weeks. Enclose SASE for return of submissions.
Sensitivity, Humorous, Studio, Invitations, and Announcements: "The verse should fit the cards; humorous for the studio cards; sensitive for the 'tenderness' line. Also interested in Christmas, (both sensitivity and studio) and Valentine's Day (sensitivity only), Mother's Day and Father's Day (studio). Verse should be short and direct, typewritten on one side of 3x5 card." Length: 3 to 4 lines. Pays $25 for studio ideas; $25 for verse; $25 for sensitivity ideas; $25 for humorous ideas, and $125 to $150 for photographs.
Other Product Lines: Wall plaques and poster verse.

MILLER DESIGNS, INC., 9 Ackerman Ave., Emerson NJ 07630. Editor: Whitney McDermot. Buys all rights. Submit seasonal ideas any time. Reports in 3 to 4 weeks. Enclose SASE.
Soft Line, Humorous, Conventional, Informal and Juvenile: Birthday, anniversary, get well, friendship, bon voyage, birth, as well as ideas for invitations and announcements. Mechanicals if possible, whimsical ideas, clever, witty, and humorous. Also buys Christmas, Easter, Valentine's Day and Mother's Day. Prefers 1 line for front of card and no more than 2 lines for the inside. Pay is open.

NORCROSS, INC., 950 Airport Rd., West Chester PA 19380. (215)436-8000. Art Services Manager: Nancy Lee Fuller. Submit ideas on 3x5 cards with writer's name on each card and SASE. Reports in 3 weeks. Buys all rights. Pays on acceptance. Current needs list available on request.
Needs: Conventional verse and prose in any category (up to 8 lines). All types of humor for all occasions (prose and verse) with or without mechanicals. Risque is OK, short of X-rated type. Especially interested in general, relative and love prose and humorous verse (relative and all-occasion). Ideas for all seasonals also sought. Seasonal schedule available on request. No juvenile or X-rated material.
Payment: Regular verse, $3/line; short prose, $12 minimum; studio/humor, $25/idea minimum.

PATTIES PRINTS, INC., Box 341601, Coral Gables FL 33134. President: Robert Shea. Query first with samples. Verses should be submitted on individual index cards, with sender's name and address on the back. Reports in 4-6 weeks. Buys all rights. Pays on publication.
Needs: "Looking for strong new ideas in whimsical areas to promote friendship, birthday and get well wishes. Verses should be short (1-2 lines), sincere, but not sentimental. Open to all areas and ideas, except religious themes." Also seeking material for anniversary, wedding, engagement, thank you, travel, baby, etc. Special interest in the juvenile line for ages 3-8, as well as seasonals for Valentine's Day and Christmas.
Payment: Soft line, conventional, informal, juveniles, invitations, announcements, $25.

QUALITY INDUSTRIES, 2293 Amber Dr., Hatfield PA 19440. (215)822-0125. Vice President: John D. Harrison Jr. Estab. 1912. Limit submissions to batches of 12. Submit seasonal/holiday 1 year in advance. SASE. Reports in 4 weeks. Buys all rights. Pays "at the end of each year".
Needs: General, poetic, religious, humorous ideas. Nothing risque. No seasonals. Pay $25/accepted idea.
Other Product Lines: Ideas and copy for bookmarks. Pays $25.

RUNNING STUDIO, INC., 1020 Park St., Paso Robles CA 93446. (805)238-2232. Editor: Judi Gorham. Submit ideas on 3x5 cards. SASE. Reports in 2 weeks. Buys all rights. Pays on acceptance.
Needs: Captions and sentiments for two quality card lines: A contemporary, studio line and a more formal, elegant line. "We're looking for humorous, catchy, and lighthearted captions for all everyday occasions to go with cute and whimsical art, all in good taste. These should be clever and can be punchy, but not sarcastic or heavy gags. No Christmas. Our second line of pretty and elegant designs need soft, meaningful and more sincere type sentiments. Sensitive, traditional expressions in everyday language for all card sending occasions plus Easter, Valentine, graduation, Mother's Day and Father's Day."

RUST CRAFT GREETING CARDS, INC., Rust Craft Park, Dedham MA 02026. (617)329-6000. Editorial and Creative Planning Director: Richard E. Myles. Submit ideas on individual coded cards (one for each sentiment). Submit around 20 at a time to save postage costs, and enclose SASE. Reports in 2-3 weeks. Buys all rights. Pays on acceptance.
Needs: "New material needed most for masculine relations and double relatives, but will

purchase material for any title if it is fresh and original, and usable to our market. We're trying to use more imagery in our line, as well as more additional copy for value at higher prices." Also needs ideas for all major seasons (Christmas, Easter, etc.). Particularly need good material for Father's Day and graduation. "Send ideas all year long. Freelancers should request our market letter to find out upcoming needs for particular seasons, however. We buy ideas for any season at any time, if they are good ones." Does not want to see humorous and studio ideas. Rejects short prose unless it is very distinctive and expresses an idea that is very original. Also rejects highly traditional verse that sounds like copy already on the greeting card racks. Verse length: No longer than 24 lines. Juvenile material: 12 lines.
Payment: Sensitivity, $10-25; conventional and inspirational, $15-40; informal, $15-30; juvenile $15-40; invitations and announcements, $10-25. Usable quotations (must be in public domain), $5-10; negotiable rates for promotional ideas and copy.
Other Product Lines: Mottoes, $15-30; posters, $15-45; calendars, $30-50. "Generally shorter material preferred. Need material which is cute and light in tone, but inspirational in message. Copy that suggests a design is also good. Can be verse or prose, and we do use some very long inspirational copy in the general style of *Desiderata*."

SANGAMON COMPANY, Route 48 West, Taylorville IL 62568. Editor: Stella Bright. Buys all rights. Reports in 2 weeks. Enclose SASE.
Everyday and Humorous: Verse for "everyday" and all seasons; also cute and humorous gags. Payment depends on quality, usually $1.50 a line for verse, and up to $20 for gags. Length: 4 to 8 lines.

STRAND ENTERPRISES, 1809½ N. Orangethorpe Pk., Anaheim CA 90630. (714)871-4744. President: S. S. Waltzman. SASE. Reports in 2 weeks. Buys all rights. Pays on acceptance.
Needs: Notecards that express one's feelings about love and friendship; philosophical and inspirational; faith; on marriage; children, human relationships; nature in short, poetic form (not too deep), prose or statement. Not over 16 lines.
Payment: Soft line, sensitivity, humorous, inspirational, $5-15.
Other Product Lines: Seeking ideas for humorous posters. Pays $15-25.

VAGABOND CREATIONS, 2560 Lance Drive, Dayton OH 45409. Editor: George F. Stanley, Jr. Buys all rights. Submit seasonal material any time; "we try to plan ahead a great deal in advance." Submit on 3x5 cards. "We don't want artwork—only ideas." Reports within same week usually. May hold ideas 3 or 4 days. Enclose SASE for return of submissions.
Soft Line and Studio: Publishes contemporary cards. Studio verse only; no slams, puns, or reference to age or aging. Emphasis should be placed on a strong surprise inside punch line instead of one that is predictable. Also prefers good use of double entendre. "Mildly risque." Purchases copy for Christmas, Valentine's and graduation. Wants "one short line on front of card and one short punch line on inside of card." Pays $10 "for beginners; up to $15 for regular contributors."
Other Product Lines: Interested in receiving copy for mottoes and humorous buttons. "On buttons we like double-entendre expressions—preferably short. We don't want the protest button or a specific person named. We pay $10 for each button idea." Mottoes should be written in the "first person" about situations at the job, about the job, confusion, modest bragging, drinking habits, etc. Pays $10 for mottoes.

VISUAL CREATIONS, 25 Hamilton Dr., Novato CA 94947. Editor: David Lieberstein. Buys all rights. Send for current needs list. Sometimes holds material for 3 to 6 weeks. Enclose SASE.
Informal, Studio, Soft Line and Promotional: Short, simple, original and clever messages for birthday, anniversary, friendship, get well, invitations. "Only ideas pertaining to everyday general occasions. No other seasons. And no photographs." 2 lines only. Buys all year. Seeking original artwork ideas for promotional card line. Pays $25 per verse. Professional only. No strained humor, rhymes, poetry or "love" verse. "For our new studio line, we want original, humorous gags, slightly risque, to go with funny animals or graphic ideas." Pays $25/verse.

Play Producers

Producers of Broadway, Off-Broadway, and Off-Off-Broadway plays are listed below. Entries are also given for resident professional companies, amateur community theaters, and theater workshops in the United States. Non-paying theater workshops are included in this list because the experience and exposure offered by these outlets can introduce talented new playwrights and give them a better chance for commercial production of their plays.

ALLEY THEATRE, 615 Texas Ave., Houston TX 77002. A resident professional theatre; large stage seating 798; arena stage seating 296. Wants good plays, with no length restriction. Not interested in musicals. Royalty arrangements vary. Send complete script. Enclose S.A.S.E. Reports in 6-12 weeks. Produces 6 to 8 plays a year.

AMERICAN STAGE FESTIVAL, Box 225, Milford NH 03055. Producing Director: T.C. Lorden. Plays performed at summer festival (professional equity company) for audience of all ages, interests, education and sophistication levels. Produces 6 plays/year. Query with synopsis. 5% standard royalty; "sometimes an additional stipend to playwright if Festival wishes to retain some continuing rights to the script." SASE. Reports in 1 month.
Needs: "The Festival can do comedies, musicals, and dramas. However, the most frequent problems come from plays not fitting into the resident acting company system (all men, all young, all black, for examples) and/or which are bolder in language and action than a general mixed audience will accept. We emphasize plays which move; long and philosophical-discussion oriented plays are generally not done. Festival plays are chosen to present scale and opportunities for scenic and costume projects far beyond the 'summer theatre' type of play." Length: 2- or 3-acts.

THE BACK ALLEY THEATRE, 617 F St., N.W., Washington DC 20001. Producing Director: Naomi Eftis. Produces quality plays including 6 premieres each year of works by new and established playwrights. Submit complete script. Royalties negotiable. SASE. Reports in 6 months.
Needs: "Any length, any type, serious, comic, experimental. Space is limited and we like to take successful productions into the parks and nearby communities, so small casts and modest set demands are a factor in choosing scripts. We do favor plays that deal with social issues and contemporary problems such as women's rights, minorities, etc. General contract involves percentage for 1-3 years on playwright's future earnings from final date of last performance of our production."

BARTER THEATRE, Main St., Abingdon VA 24210. Producer: Rex Partington. Looks for good plays, particularly comedies. Two or three acts, preferably, but will consider good quality plays of shorter length. Pays 5% royalties. Send complete script only. SASE.

BERKSHIRE THEATRE FESTIVAL, INC., East Main St., Stockbridge MA 01262. Artistic Director: Allan Albert. Estab. 1928. Produces 17-19 plays/year for summer theatre audience in Stockbridge, MA; professional productions. Submit complete ms. reports in 4-6 months. Rights purchased "depend on the level of production given." Pays in royalties for full production, in fees for reading. SASE.
Needs: "The Berkshire Theatre Festival tends to concentrate on plays that illuminate or describe the American experience, either fictive or factual."

THE BOLTON HILL DINNER THEATRE, 1111 Park Ave., Baltimore MD 21201. Manager: A.L. Dorsett. Professional dinner theatre. Public audience, middle-aged, who prefer comedy. No more than 7 characters in cast. 2-act, 3-act, comedy and revue material. Payment is negotiable. Rarely copyrights plays. Send complete script SASE. Produces about 10 plays a year.

BROWN UNIVERSITY, Program in Theatre Arts, Box 1897, Providence RI 02912. Plays will be produced for summer theater or during academic year. For students and university-related, sophisticated audience. Uses 1, 2 and 3 act plays. Pays $100. Not copyrighted. Produces 8 to 12 plays a year. Send complete script only. Reports in 2 months. Enclose SASE.

GERT BUNCHEZ AND ASSOCIATES, INC., 7730 Carondelet, St. Louis MO 63105. Contact: Gert Bunchez, President. "We feel that the time is propitious for the return of stories to radio. It is our feeling that it is not necessary to 'bring back' old programs, and that there certainly should be contemporary talent to write mystery, detective, suspense, soap operas, etc. We syndicate radio properties to clients and stations. Requirements are plays with sustaining lead characters, 5 minutes to 30 minutes in length, suitable for radio reproduction. Disclaimer letter must accompany scripts. Rates from $100 per script if acceptable for radio production and actually produced." Enclose SASE.

CENTER THEATRE GROUP/MARK TAPER FORUM, 135 N. Grand Ave., Los Angeles CA 90012. (213)972-7353. Literary Manager: David Copelin. Plays to be performed in the Mark Taper Forum, a 750-seat resident theater with a thrust stage; or in the Forum/Laboratory, a 99-seat flexible space. For "an intelligent, sensitive open-minded audience of all ages and classes who are interested in serious classic and contemporary interpretations of the real world." Produces up to 20 plays/year. Submit complete script. Pays 5% of gross receipts less ticket broker commissions for plays performed in the Mark Taper Forum; $100 for plays performed in the Forum/Laboratory. SASE. Reports in 2-4 months.
Needs: "Imaginative contemporary comedies or dramas on any topic, but if the topic has been done to death the writing had better be extraordinary, or the insight and passion unusual. Social issues with a poet's consciousness, and the inner life of man theatricalized." Length: 2- or 3-acts. "Smaller casts are easier but not always necessary. Our stage has minimal wings and flies—so heavy sets/changes are hard. But if the writing is exciting, we'll do what we can."

THE CHANGING SCENE THEATER, 1527½ Champa St., Denver CO 80202. Year-round productions in theater space. Cast may be made up of both professional and amateur actors. For public audience; age varies, but mostly youthful, and interested in taking a chance on new and/or experimental works. No limit to subject matter or story themes. Emphasis is on the innovative. "Also, we require that the playwright be present for at least one performance of his work, if not for the entire rehearsal period. We have a small stage area, but are able to convert to round, semi-round, or environmental. Prefer to do plays with limited set and props." 1-act, 2-act, and 3-act. Also interested in musicals. "We do not pay royalties, or sign contracts with playwrights. We function on a performance share basis of payment. Our theater seats 78, the first 35 seats go to the theater, the balance is divided among the participants in the production. The performance share process is based on the entire production run, and not determined by individual performances. We do not copyright our plays." Send complete script. Enclose SASE. Reporting time varies; usually several months. Produces approximately 10 to 15 new plays a year.

CHELSEA THEATER CENTER, 407 W. 43rd St., New York NY 10036. Artistic Director: Robert Kalfin. Looking for full-length plays "that stretch the bounds of the theater in form and content. No limitation as to size of cast or physical production." Pays $500 for a 6-month option for an off-Broadway production." Works 10 months in advance. No unsolicited ms. Submit synopsis. SASE.

ALFRED CHRISTIE, 405 E. 54th St., New York NY 10022. "The theatre is a summer stock theatre and many of the people in the audience are on vacation, most are over age 30." Professional cast. Two-act or three-act plays. "We would like funny situation, contemporary farces or light comedies. Scripts that are sensational in theme, that can compete with today's frank and modern films are also possible. We like a well-written play with interesting switches or avant-garde scripts that are based on reality and make sense. We would expect the author to copyright the play but if the show moves on to other theatres or Broadway or to a film, etc., we would like a small percentage of the action. We want no family situation shows, no period plays involving many period costumes. We prefer small cast, single-set shows, but if a script is good we would do a larger cast and multiple set production." Produces 6 to 10 full productions yearly. Payment varies. A percentage or a flat fee is possible. "Does the author want to come and work with the people and on the play?" Send synopsis or complete script. "We like scripts by March of each year because we must arrange publicity, hire actors, etc." Enclose SASE for return of submissions.

THE CLEVELAND PLAY HOUSE, Box 1989, Cleveland OH 44106. Robert Snook, New Scripts Department. Plays performed in professional LORT theater for the general public. Produces 10 plays/year. Submit complete script. Buys stock rights, and sometimes first class options. Payment varies. SASE. Reports in 6 months.
Needs: "No restrictions. Vulgarity and gratuitous fads are not held in much esteem." Length: 3-acts.

DAVID J. COGAN, 350 Fifth Ave., New York NY 10001. (212)563-9555. Produces 3-act plays. Chiefly interested in contemporary topical material. Looks for special qualities of character development, comedy. Pays royalties on production; percentage of box office. Gives average advance of $2,500. Charges $15 reading fee. Send complete script. Reports in 1 to 2 months. Enclose SASE.

CREEDE REPERTORY THEATRE, Box 269, Creede CO 81130. (303)658-2540. Managing Director: Stephen B. Scott. Estab. 1966. Produces 6 plays/year. "Plays are produced each summer in repertory in

the Creede Opera House; production dates are mid-June through Labor day. The Creede Repertory Theatre is a non-Equity professional theatre." Submit complete ms. Reports in 3 months. Buys performance rights only; "except for plays written under the auspices of the Creede Theatre." Pays 15-25% royalty or $15-30/performance. SASE.
Needs: "The Creede Theatre produces plays from a number of different genres, including musicals, modern comedies, absurdist plays, mysteries, period comedies and dramas, modern dramas, original and published children's plays, one-act plays. No complicated technical pieces, or plays that require large casts; also, because of the nature of the audiences that attend our plays, no plays with required nudity or excessive vulgarity can be produced." Cast size: 6 men, 5 women.

CRESSON LAKE PLAYHOUSE, Box 368, Spangler PA 15775. Artistic Director: Kenny Resinski. Estab. 1976. Produces 1 original play/year; performed in 200 seat summer barn theatre for 13 performances. Submit query and synopsis. Reports in 1 month. Pays $50/performance. SASE.
Needs: "Original works dealing with occupations, trades, or professions, or life styles, that would relate to a rural mountainous area. Minimal set, minimal number of men, maximal number of women." No Broadway comedies.

JEAN DALRYMPLE, 130 W. 56th St., New York NY 10019. Producer: Jean Dalrymple. Plays performed on Broadway, off-Broadway, Show Case or summer theatres for the general public. Produces 1 play/year. Submit through agent only. Royalty as per Dramatists Guild contract. SASE. Reports in 2 weeks-1 month.
Needs: "Comedy or suspenseful drama. 2-3 acts at most; regular play format. No pornography."

EARPLAY, Vilas Communication Hall, 821 University Ave., Madison WI 53706. Produces radio dramas for National Public Radio Stations in the United States; jointly sponsored by the Corporation for Public Broadcasting, National Endowment for the Arts, WHA Radio/University of Wisconsin Extension. Scripts are accepted throughout the year with primary interest in plays demonstrating strong character treatment and clear and compelling plot lines. All work which makes creative use of the medium will be considered. Because of broadcast schedules, the 1-hour play is best suited for production. Payment: $2,000 for 60 minutes, first rights; $1,000 for 60 minutes, previously performed. Not interested in the following: drama aimed at children, religious drama, educational/instructional material. Send SASE for writers' fact sheet to obtain complete submission details. It takes 2 to 3 months for a script to be given thorough consideration. Enclose SASE with all submissions and inquiries.

EAST CAROLINA PLAYHOUSE, East Carolina University, Greenville NC 27834. Plays will be performed at the University Theatre, for the general public. All types and lengths of plays considered. Not copyrighted. Send complete script only. Reports usually in 6 weeks-2 months. SASE.

ZELDA FICHANDLER, c/o Arena Stage, 6th and M Sts., S.W., Washington DC 20024. Wants original plays preferably (but not necessarily) submitted through agents. "Plays with relevance to the human situation—which cover a multitude of dramatic approaches—are welcome here." Pays 5 percent of gross. Reports in 6 months. Enclose SASE.

H.D. FLOWERS, II, Dept. of Speech and dramatic Arts, University of Arkansas at Pine Bluff, Pine Bluff AR 71603. Summer educational theater for college and community audience. Plays with black themes are needed. Style does not matter. Will consider 1-, 2- and 3-act plays. Pays $50 to $75 per performance. Produces 4-6 plays/year. Send complete script only. SASE.

FOLGER THEATRE GROUP, 201 E. Capitol St., Washington DC 20003. Produced in professional theatre, AEA LORT Contract, for general public. All kinds of plays. "Since we produce 2 Shakespeare productions a season, we would rather not read Shakespearean adaptations or treatments." No limitations in cast, props; stage is small but flexible. Any length play. Payment negotiable. Send complete script or submit through agent. SASE. Reports "as soon as possible, usually 8 to 10 weeks." Produces 3 new plays a year, and various Shakespearean productions.

GALWAY PRODUCTIONS, c/o New Jersey Shakespeare Festival, Madison NJ 07940. Director: Paul Barry. Looks for controversial plays on any subject. Pays standard Dramatists Guild royalty percentage. All scripts must be free and clear of subsidiary rights commitments. No musicals or one-acts. Submit synopsis or full-length play. SASE.

WILLIAM GARDNER, Academy Festival Theatre, Barat College, Lake Forest IL 60045. Plays will be performed by a professional cast during summer theater. Audience: well-educated, intelligent, 3-act plays considered. Pays 6% for new scripts. Not copyrighted. "We ask certain vested rights." Submit through agent only. SASE. Reports in 6 weeks to 6 months. Produces about 4 plays per year.

JAMES GLASS, Box 56, Cecilwood Theatre, Fishkill NY 12524. (914)896-6273. Producer: James Glass. Plays performed in professional equity summer theater. 30th year of operation. Produces 6-8 plays/year. Submit complete script to J. Glass, 240 W. 98th St., 11B, New York NY 10025. Pays flat fee or percentage. SASE. Reports in 1 month.
Needs: Intelligent comedies. Casts of 2-7; contemporary settings, single set, uncomplicated props. "No plays with filthy language or over-sexed subjects." Length: 2- or 3-acts.

HARWICH JUNIOR THEATRE, Box 168, West Harwich MA 02671. President: Marguerite Donovan. Plays performed in summer theatre with semi-professional and amateur casts for children. Produces 4 plays/year. Query with synopsis. Pays $10-15/performance. SASE. Reports in 1 year.
Needs: "We produce plays for children; adventure stories and fairy tales." Length: 2- or 3-acts; 1½ hours maximum.

CHARLES HOLLERITH, JR., 18 W. 55th St., New York NY 10019. Produces Broadway and off-Broadway plays for the general public. Pays Dramatist Guild rates. Submit through agent only. Reports in 2 weeks. Produces 1 play a year. Length: open. Copyrighted.

HONOLULU THEATRE FOR YOUTH, P.O. Box 3257, Honolulu HI 96801. Artistic Director: Wallace Chappell. Produces plays of "1 hour without intermission. Plays are produced in Honolulu in various theater buildings; also, an annual tour in theater buildings on Neighbor Islands, state of Hawaii. Casts are amateur with professional direction and production; adult actors, with children as needed. Plays are produced for school children, grades 2 through 12, individual plays directed to specific age groups; also public performances." Interested in "historical (especially American) plays, plays about Pacific countries and Pacific legends, and Asian legends and Asian history. Plays must have strong character with whom young people can identify, with stress on action rather than exposition, but not at the expense of reality (i.e., not slapstick). Plays should be reasonably simple technically and use primarily adult characters. Fairy tales (especially mod versions) are at the bottom of the priority list, as are elaborate musicals requiring large orchestras. Casts up to 15, preferably. Technical requirements should be reasonably simple, as sets have to be built at one place and trucked to the theater." Produces 5-6 plays/year. Royalty fee is based on number of performances. Query first with synopsis only. Reports in 1 to 2 months. Enclose SASE for reply to queries.

WILLIAM E. HUNT, 801 West End Ave., New York NY 10025. Interested in reading scripts for stock production, off-Broadway and even Broadway production. "Small cast, youth-oriented, meaningful, technically adventuresome; serious, funny, far-out. Must be about people first, ideas second. No political or social tracts." Pays royalties on production. Off-Broadway, 5%; on Broadway, 5%, 7½% and 10%, based on gross. Reports in "a few weeks." SASE.

IRON SPRINGS CHATEAU, c/o Mrs. Doug Jensen, 1805 Mesa Rd., Colorado Springs CO 80904. Professional cast will perform plays at a summer theater, for a general audience. "Old fashioned, western, comedy melodramas only. Song parodies and sight gags may be included." Cast limitation of 8. Drops preferred to sets or flats. Looking for 3-act plays only; 90-minute length. Rate of payment is "$125 to $300 per show." Send complete script only. SASE. Reports in 1 week. Produces 4 plays/year.

DOUG JENSEN-JENSEN ENTERPRISES, 444 Ruxton Ave., Manitou Springs CO 80829. (303)685-5104. Secretary: Sharon Rose. Estab. 1960. Produces 3 plays/year. Plays are performed at the Iron Springs Chateau Dinner Theatre for summer tourist audiences. Submit complete ms. Reports in 2 months. Buys exclusive rights. Pays $200-300. SASE.
Needs: "We produce *only* old-fashioned comedy 'mellerdramas' with western themes around 1890; approximately 1½ hours long; song parodies, sight gags, dancing, satire, puns and exaggerated gestures included. Plays are performed as a parody of old Victorian dramas. Audience participation is encouraged. There's nothing serious about our shows—they verge on being zany. Themes of mining towns and the Civil War are also welcome. Fast paced action that is relatively simple."

JON JORY, Producing Director, Actors Theatre of Louisville, 316 W. Main St., Louisville KY 40202. Actors Theatre of Louisville is a resident professional theatre operating under a L.O.R.T. contract for a 35-week season from September to June. Subscription audience of 16,000 from extremely diverse backgrounds. "Plays with a strong story line and a basically positive life view. We are not interested in situation comedies or 'absurdists' work. We are particularly interested in new musicals and small cast straight plays. No one-acts. No more than 12 to 15 actors. There are 2 theatres, one a 640-seat thrust and one seating 200. Multiple set shows are impossible here." Payment is negotiated. Submit mss to Elizabeth Mahan, Assistant to Producer. SASE. Reports in 4 months. Produces 6-8 new scripts/year, in addition to conventional subscription season.

LORETTO-HILTON REPERTORY THEATRE, 130 Edgar Rd., St. Louis MO 63119. Regional repertory theatre, professional equity company, for general public. Plays varied in themes. Interested in any play suitable for a subscription audience of over 17,000. Also seeking small-cast, single-set plays for small experimental theater. No one-acts. Royalty payments negotiable; usually between 4% and 5% of gross. Send complete script. Enclose SASE. Reports within 4 months during the winter season; closed over the summer. Produces 8 plays/year, at least 2 of them original productions.

THE MAC-HAYDN THEATRE, INC., Box 204, Chatham NY 12037. (518)392-9292 (summer). Producers: Lynne Haydn, Linda MacNish. Estab. 1969. Produces 6-15 plays/year. "This is a resort area, and our audiences include rural residents and summer residents from the metropolitan New York City and Albany areas who demand professional quality productions. Submit complete ms; we can only consider a complete script and written score, and would prefer that at least a piano tape be included of the score." Reports in 2 months. Buys exclusive rights to stage production. Pays $25-100/performance. SASE.
Needs: "We are interested in musicals which are wholesome family entertainment; these should be full-length musicals, although we might consider one-act musicals in the future. There is no limitation as to topic, so long as the object is to entertain. We will consider original material as well as adaptations, but any adaptations of copyright material must include proper clearances. We are most interested in legitimate music for trained voices, no rock or fad music. We are looking for scripts which have a story to tell, and which build to a climax; no vignettes, slice of life or character study. We prefer a fast pace and good emotional content, and the score should extend the action, not cause it to stop. We are not interested in political muck-raking or controversy unless it has high entertainment value, and we will not consider obscenity, nudity or bad writing."

MAGIC THEATRE, INC., Building 314, Fort Mason, San Francisco CA 94123. (415)441-8001. Script Reader: Suresa D. Galbraith. "Oldest experimental theatre in California, established in 1967." For public audience, generally college educated. General cross-section of the area with an interest in alternative theatre. Plays produced in the Off-Broadway manner. Cast is part equity, part non-equity. Produces 10 plays/year. Submit complete ms. SASE.
Needs: "The director of the Magic Theatre's concept leans toward the Surrealist movement in the arts. The playwright should have an approach to his writing with a specific intellectual concept in mind or specific theme of social relevance. We don't want to see scripts that would be television or 'B' movies-oriented. 1 or 2 act plays considered. We pay 5% of gross; $100 advance."

MANHATTAN THEATRE CLUB, Stephen Pascal, Associate Artistic Director, 321 E. 73 St., New York NY 10021. A three theatre, performing arts complex classified as off-off Broadway, using professional actors. "We have a large, diversified audience which includes a large number of season subscribers. We want plays about contemporary problems and people. No special requirements. No verse plays or historical dramas or large musicals. Very heavy set shows or multiple detailed sets are out. We prefer shows with casts not more than 15. No skits, but any other length is fine." Payment is negotiable. Query first with synopsis. SASE. Reports in 6 months. Produces 20 plays/year.

CHRISTIAN H. MOE, Theater Department, Southern Illinois University, Carbondale IL 62901. Plays will be performed in a university theater (either a 580-seat theater or an experimental theater which can seat 100 to 150). Cast will be non-equity. Audience is a public one drawn from a university community with disparate interests. Largest percentage is a student and faculty audience. Student age range is roughly from 16 to 25. Also a children's theatre audience ranging from pre-school to 13 years. "Submissions are restricted to children's theatre plays. We prefer dramas with small casts, not exceeding a running time of 50 minutes. A limited budget prohibits lavish set or property demands." Normally pays $15/performance. Special arrangements are made for plays that tour. Query with synopsis. SASE. Reports in 3 months. Produces 2-3 children's plays/year.

DOUG MOODY MYSTIC SOUND STUDIO'S MYSTIC MUSIC CENTRE, 6277 Selma Ave., Hollywood CA 90028. For home entertainment, all ages. Works produced on phonograph albums and cassette tapes. "We are looking for works capable of being performed within one hour, non-visual. Can be musical. Can rely on sound effects to replace visual effects. Think about the medium!" Payment depending upon royalties to artists and musical copyright royalties. Buys phonograph and audio rights. Query first with synopsis only. SASE.

OLD LOG THEATER, Box 250, Excelsior MN 55331. Producer: Don Stolz. Produces 2-act and 3-act plays for "a professional cast. Public audiences, usually adult. Interested in contemporary comedies. Small number of sets. Cast not too large." Produces about 14 plays/year. Payment by Dramatists Guild agreement. Send complete script only. SASE.

OMAHA COMMUNITY PLAYHOUSE, 6915 Cass St., Omaha NE 68132. (402)553-4890. Contact: Christopher Rutherford, Artist-in-Residence. Plays performed by an amateur cast in either studio or proscenium theater for an adult, scholastically minded, theatre-oriented audience. Produces 10 plays/year. "Works to be submitted in bound ms form and professional appearance." Does not copyright plays. SASE. Pays $35 for first performance; $25 for each performance thereafter. Some residencies available. Reporting time varies according to need and current demand.
Needs: "Any subject or theme dealt with in a competent manner; hopefully the play will also be of an entertaining nature. Prime consideration given to smaller (2-15) cast shows and preference toward simpler demands on our limited budgets for sets, costumes, musicians. Do not send musicals without *complete* score."

OPERA VARIETY THEATER, 3944 Balboa St., San Francisco CA 94121. Director: Violette M. Dale. Plays to be performed by professional and amateur casts for a public audience; all ages, generally families; upper educational level. Submit complete script. "Everyone (cast, author, technical people, publicity, etc.) receives equal percentage." SASE. Reports in 6 months.
Needs: "Prefer musicals (but must have singable, tuneful material; arranged, ready to cast). Plays or music on most any theme that conservative audiences would enjoy. Must have substantial, believable plot and good characterizations. Must be simple to produce; fairly small cast, easy setting, etc. (small backstage area limits cast, props, staging, etc.). Emphasis is on entertainment rather than social reform." Length: 1-, 2- or 3-acts. "No vulgarity in language or action; no wordy preaching."

OTRABANDA COMPANY, 900 Camp St., New Orleans LA 70130. (504)566-7729. Vice President: John Maynard Jr. Estab. 1971. Produces 2-6 plays/year. "Professional productions for touring to universities, and in residence in New Orleans. Audience is primarily adult. We also do an annual production for rural audiences along the Mississippi River; this production is suitable for all ages, and uses a great deal of comedy and popular style." Submit query letter and synopsis. Reports in 6 weeks. Buys exclusive performing rights for 15 months. Pays 5-7½% royalty. SASE.
Needs: "One style should be serious drama for adults, covering any topic of interest to the writer. Play should be 1-1½ hours in length, and suitable for highly physical theatrical techniques; i.e., open to moments of choreography with the actors. The second style is popular theatre, using elements of satire, music, vaudeville, and circus. Play must have comedy. Cast size is usually limited to 10. The company often performs and tours with small sets, preferring to stress the use of props of all sizes. Playwrights must be capable of rehearsing the play in conjunction with actors and director; changes in script will result out of collaborative work over a 2-3 month period.

OTTERBEIN COLLEGE THEATRE, Westerville OH 43081. Contact: Dr. Charles W. Dodrill. Plays will be performed by the Otterbein College Theatre cast, with a professional guest actor; also summer theatre. For a central-Ohio public. Will not use radical plays. Should be 3-act plays. Not copyrighted. Reports in 6 weeks. Produces 11 plays/year. Send synopsis or complete ms. SASE.

JOSEPH PAPP PRODUCER, New York Shakespeare Festival, 425 Lafayette St., New York NY 10003. (212)677-1750. Gail Merrifield, Director of Play Development. Interested in full-length plays and musical works. No restrictions as to style, historical period, traditional or experimental forms, etc. New works produced on 7 stages at the Public Theater. Standard option and production agreements. Reports in 6 weeks. SASE.

PETERBOROUGH PLAYERS, Box 1, Peterborough NH 03458. Artistic Director: Charles Morey. Estab. 1933. Produces 5 plays/year. Professional summer theatre (Equity). Query with synopsis or submit complete ms. "Submissions will be accepted September-February of the year. Mss should be submitted during that period to Charles Morey, Peterborough Players, 718 W. 171st St., #51, New York NY 10032. Buys single production rights only (10 performances). Pays $500 minimum. SASE.
Needs: "Interested in all types of material. Quality is the only guideline."

THE PLAY GROUP INC., 1538 Laurel Ave., Knoxville TN 37916. (615)523-7641. Writer-in-residence: David McIntosh. Estab. 1973. "We are a professional non-equity company performing in our home theater and touring nationally, particularly in the Southeast and on the alternative theater circuit." Submit complete ms; "we are particularly interested in writers who know our work, and in collaborations with writers." Reports in 2 months. Rights "vary; depending on the collaborative nature of the project." Pay ranges from $300 flat fee for one year rights, to full salary ($100/week) during development. Submissions

which have been previously produced are thrown out; new work is carefully returned."
Needs: "Full-length adult plays on any theme; one-act children's plays; women's and Southern themes; innovative musicals; and poetic drama. We tend to have small casts, need variable staging, and don't like heavy set pieces. We are not particularly interested in seeing *most* work with the three unities, and we are *not* interested in being #476 on a writer's mailing list."

THE PLAYWRIGHTS' LAB, 2010 Minnehaha, Minneapolis MN 55404. "Plays given readings and semi-professional productions. A staff of 6 playwrights-in-residence reads and critiques plays. Reports in 6 months. 1-act plays have best chance and please send SASE. A minimum royalty-stipend is available. The lab has operated for more than 5 years and in that time has produced some 60 plays by more than 30 playwrights."

POET'S REPERTORY THEATRE, 20 Academy Lane, Bellport NY 11713. Both a tour program and a resident theater program. The tour program plays for any host organization, especially libraries, churches, public schools, colleges, arts conferences, private homes. Resident theater wing plays in four permanent locations twice each year, three performances per production per location. Audiences are both public and private, and are composed of all interests, intelligences, and educational levels. Shorter plays are wanted for tour program, 5 minutes to 55 minutes. Some longer plays for the resident theater program. No restriction on subject or theme. Small casts, preferably no more than 3 for the shorter plays to be toured (although 4 or 5 might get by), and 5 for the longer plays. Avoid extremes of age (no parts for children or the elderly); the play should be able to be cast with persons who are in the age range of 18 to 50. The play should not rely for its impact upon tricky lighting or scenery. No nudity, no on-stage sexual intercourse. 1-act, 2-act, 3-act, or skits considered. "Royalty payments may range between $5 and $20 per performance for shorter plays; about $40 for longer plays. It should be stressed that we are in the context of the experimental and art theater movement and will only use material that is within that context." Send synopsis or complete script. Enclose SASE. Reports usually in 3 to 5 weeks. Produces about 12 plays a year.

REPERTORY THEATER OF AMERICA/ALPHA-OMEGA PLAYERS, Box 1296, Rockport TX 78382. Director: Drexel H. Riley. Plays performed on the college and country club circuit (professional national tour); also local churches and civic groups. For a private audience, college age and over; majority are college graduates; wide range of geographic and religious backgrounds and tastes. Produces 4 plays/year. Query with synopsis. Pays $10-20/performance; averages approximately 100 performances per play per year. SASE. Reports in 3 weeks.
Needs: "Comedies that are fast-paced and adaptable to a dinner theater setting. Adaptations of works by well-known American authors, especially short stories. Historical drama featuring famous religious figures." Length: 2-acts; total running time 1½ hours. No plays with casts larger than 4 (2 men, 2 women). Limited sound facilities, minimum props. "No guerrilla theater, obscenity, intellectualizing, or bad writing."

ST. CLEMENTS, 423 W. 46 St., New York NY 10036. Plays will be produced at St. Clement's, an off-off Broadway theater; all productions are fully professional for public performances; audiences expect off-off Broadway to be somewhat experimental or innovative. 1-act, 2-act, or 3-act plays. "Our productions are presented under the terms of the Equity Showcase Code. There are no royalties. It is a showcase for the playwrights." Send complete script or submit through agent. Enclose SASE. Reports in 3 to 6 months. Produces 4 or 5 major plays a year and 10 or 12 readings.

ST. NICHOLAS THEATER, 2851 N. Halsted St., Chicago IL 60657. Produces 10 plays/year. "Plays are done mainstage plus works in progress children's theater." Submit complete ms. Reports in 6 months. "Royalty information cannot be published." SASE.
Needs: One-act and full length plays, children's theater, and musicals. "Must be original, previously unproduced plays. Prefer small casts (6-10)."

SCORPIO RISING THEATRE FOUNDATION, 426 N. Hoover St., Los Angeles CA 90004. For an audience of selected theatre buffs. "Scorpio Rising Theatre is a repertory theatre dedicated to the works of new playwrights, and winner of Los Angeles drama critics' Circle Award. Looking for all kinds of plays, but prefer contemporary themes. We don't want any situation comedies or Broadway type musicals. Simple cast, props, stage, etc. 1-act, 2-act, 3-act, but open to all." Also interested in developmental work with playwrights-in-residence. Buys amateur performance rights. Payment to be negotiated. Produces 12 plays a year. Send script to Louise Newmark. Send complete script only. Reports in 1 to 2 months. SASE.

SCRANTON THEATRE LIBRE, INC., 512-514 Brooks Bldg., Scranton PA 18503. Executive Director: John J. White. Plays performed by semiprofessional casts for the general public. Produces 6 plays/year.

Submit synopsis or complete script. 5% royalty. SASE. Reports in 3 months.
Needs: "Only original scripts of any kind; any format."

SEATTLE REPERTORY THEATRE, Box B, Queen Anne Station, Seattle WA 98109. Plays will be produced on either main stage, or in second theatre, with professional casts in both cases. The second house performs younger, more avant-garde and special interest plays. Audience for main stage is middle class; high percentage of college graduates; ages ranging from teens to advanced middle age. Plays for second house, particularly, will involve novel forms of stage, experiments in style; particular interest in works that explore new ways to use language. In main house, more conventional plays with themes related to present time. Almost any format is acceptable providing the writing is of high quality. No limitations in cast, but prefers 3-act plays. Payment depends on the plays; a guarantee against a percentage of the gross, usually starting at 4%. "When negotiating a new script, we retain a financial interest in subsequent productions of the play for a specified period of time." Send synopsis, with a dozen or so pages of script to give feeling of style, etc. SASE. Reports in about 3 months. Produces about 12 plays/year.

LORAINE SLADE, General Manager, Virginia Museum Theatre, Boulevard and Grove Ave., Richmond VA 23221. For public, well-educated, conservative, adventurous audiences. Professional repertory theatre. Looking for biography, experimental styles. Standard format of presentation. Light comedies, musicals. 2-act and 3-act plays considered. Payment is negotiable. For a premiere, theatre requires share in future income. Produces one new script a year. Send complete script only. Reports in 3 to 5 months. Enclose SASE for return of submissions.

CHARLES STILWILL, Managing Director, Community Playhouse, Box 433, Waterloo IA 50704. (319)235-0367. Plays performed at Waterloo Community Playhouse with a volunteer cast. "We have 5,485 season tickets holders. Average attendance at main stage shows is 5,663; at studio shows 1,657. We try to fit the play to the theatre. We try to do a wide variety of plays." Looking for good plays with more roles for women than men. Our public isn't going to accept nudity, too much sex, too much strong language. We don't have enough black actors to do all black shows. We have done plays with as few as 3 characters, and as many as 54. On the main stage we usually pay between $300 and $500. In our studio we usually pay between $50 and $300." Send synopsis or complete script. SASE. Reports negatively within 3 months, but acceptance takes longer because they try to fit a wanted script into the balanced season. Produces 6 plays a year: 1 musical, 3 comedies, 2 dramas.

JOE SUTHERIN, c/o St. Bart's Playhouse, 109 E. 50th St., New York NY 10022. Plays will be produced at St. Bart's Playhouse, a 350-seat community theater. "I am also looking for material to produce in other (professional) situations." For public/commercial "sophisticated" audience. Looking for revue, comedy material, or writer who likes to do same. Does not want to see material that relies heavily on sex, four-letter words, etc., to make it viable. Payment varies. Copyright negotiable. Send synopsis or complete script. Enclose SASE. Reports in "3 months if I'm not snowed under." Produces 2 to 4 plays per year; (also 2 musicals).

TACONIC THEATRE COMPANY, Rhinebeck NY 12572. Director: Michael T. Sheehan. Plays performed at 1) staged readings; 2) summer and winter season; 3) professional workshop/studio productions; and 4) possibly full-scale production for a contemporary audience, 20-70 age range; college graduates, middle to upper income; sophisticated. Produces 8-10 plays/year. Submit complete script. No payment for staged readings series; pays $5-25 per use of skits and less than full-length plays; $25-50 for full-length. SASE. Reports in 2-4 weeks.
Needs: Small cast and simple technical requirements preferred; also children's plays. "Nothing overtly political, sexual or antagonistic. Try to avoid need for flying scenery, heavy projections, and complicated props and costumes."

THEATRE AMERICANA, Box 245, Altadena CA 91001. Attn: Playreading Committee. In operation for 43 seasons. For public general audience. Local theatre. Showcase for unknowns in all phases of theater. Awards for best director, set designer, actors, as well as best play. Looking for plays with quality and originality. Any subject matter. Selections not made on the basis of any set structure, but if new forms are used, they must work successfully from an audience viewpoint. 2-act or 3-act plays, 1½ to 2 hours playing time. Not interested in trite material; pornography for shock value unacceptable. Modern verbiage in a valid characterization not censored. Musicals should include piano arrangements. Plays with a Christmas theme or setting are welcomed. No royalties can be paid, but the 4 original plays produced each year are eligible to compete for the $300 C. Brooks Fry Award. Authors copyright own plays. Send complete script only. Reporting time is "very slow. Read year-round. Play finalists retained until April 1, when 4 are selected for next season's production." Enclose SASE for return of submissions.

THE THEATRE IN SEARCH OF PLAYWRIGHTS PROJECT, Theatre Arts-University Theatre, Virginia Polytechnic Institute and State University, Blacksburg VA 24061. "Plays produced as part of Major Production Series-Theatre Arts-University Theatre and as part of studio theatre series. Casts are students, with occasional guest performers drawn from faculty or from visiting performers." Adult audience in university community. Should be full length, previously unproduced scripts of interest to adult audiences. Fresh, attractive, controversial subject matter is desired. Uses 2- and 3-act plays. Offers royalties of $50 for first performance; $25, additional performances; negotiated rates for musical scripts. "We prefer copyrighted material." Send complete script only. Playwright's biography or resume requested. Follow standard play-duplication service procedures. Use tight binders or covers. Reports in 1 month. Produces about 15 plays a year. Enclose SASE.

THEATRE RAPPORT, 8128 Gould Ave., Hollywood CA 90040. Artistic Director: Crane Jackson. Equity company. Produces plays of 1, 2, and 3 acts. Produces gutsy, relevant plays on highly artistic level and true subjects. No unjustified homosexuality, nudity or profanity; realistic acceptable. For a sophisticated, educated, non-fad, conservative (although venturesome) audience looking for something new and different. Not avant-garde, but a strong point of view is an asset. Approach must be unique. All plays must be West Coast premieres. Pays 20% of gross. Send complete script. Response if interested. All mss read, but none are returned. Produces 6 plays a year.

THEATRE UNDER THE STARS, 1999 W. Gray, Houston TX 77019. Contact: Frank Young. Professional stock theatre in Houston. Possible New York production following Houston run. For the general public. Musical comedies only, including musical dramas and operettas. No grand opera. Product must be commercial. "Any material will be considered if well done." Will consider any length. Payment negotiated. Not all plays are copyrighted. Enclose SASE. Produces 10 plays each year.

UNIVERSITY AND FESTIVAL THEATRE, John R. Bayless, Business Manager, 137 Arts Bldg., The Pennsylvania State University, University Park PA 16802. (814)863-0381. For general audience 6-60 years of age. Produced at either the Pavilion or the Playhouse Theatres located at University Park. University Theatre is an educational program; the Festival Theatre is an equity/student theatre program offered during the summer. Any kind of play is considered. Usually does not copyright plays. For a straight play, pays between $35 and $50 per performance. Produces 6 plays/year. Send complete script only. Reports in 1 month. Enclose SASE.

UNIVERSITY OF MINNESOTA DEPARTMENT OF THEATRE, Marshall Performing Arts Center, Deluth MN 55812. (218)726-8562. Department Head: Rick Graves. Estab. 1851. Produces 15-20 plays/year. Plays are performed in the theatre of the Marshall Arts Performing Center; audience is about ½ students and ½ community adults. Submit query and synopsis. Reports in 1 month. Buys "the right to perform the script for a single engagement. Pays $25-50/performance and occasionally fees to bring the playwright on campus during rehearsals." SASE.
Needs: "The department is committed to the development of young playwrights whose works have not attracted wide commercial attention." Opera; dance; "and all types of drama and musical theatre."

YALE REPERTORY THEATRE, Literary Manager, 222 York St., New Haven CT 06520. Resident professional theatre. For University-oriented audience, but with appeal to a larger community. No limitations of age or special interests, but emphasis on an audience with serious perceptual intelligence, receptive to experiment and innovation. No limitations on subject matter or theme, but not interested in Broadway-type plays, conventional musicals, domestic dramas, etc. "We are generally limited to what the imagination can summon up on a small thrust stage with no flies and little wing space. Full-evening works preferred." Offers standard L.O.R.T. author contract. Copyright remains with author. "We retain limited residual rights and a small percentage of author's proceeds on subsequent sales of the work." Send complete script. Enclose SASE. Reports in about 4 months. Produces 7 or 8 full professional productions a year, plus a variety of student full productions, workshops, and cabaret productions.

Play Publishers

There are several markets for the playwright's work: play publishers, whose names and addresses follow; play producers, listed in the Play Producers section; television producers, and motion picture producers. Film producers, like television producers, will not look at scripts submitted directly by the writer. They must be submitted through recognized literary agents. A list of these appears in the Authors' Agents section.

Publications which do not primarily publish plays but occasionally may publish dramatic material in some form are listed in the Juvenile, Literary and "Little", and Theater, Movie, TV, and Entertainment categories in the Consumer Publications section. The playwright should also check the Book Publishers for additional play markets.

BAKER'S PLAY PUBLISHING CO., 100 Chauncy St., Boston MA 02111. Editor: John B. Welch. Plays performed by amateur groups; high school, children's theatre, churches and community theatre groups. Submit complete script. Copyrighted. Pay varies; outright purchase price to split in production fees. $75 for 1-act plays that need work. SASE. Reports in 2-3 months.
Needs: "1-acts (specifically for competition use). Quality children's theater scripts. Chancel drama for easy staging—voice plays ideal. Long plays only if they have a marketable theme. Include as much stage direction in the script as possible." Emphasis on large female cast desired.

CONTEMPORARY DRAMA SERVICE, Box 457, Downers Grove IL 60515. Editor: Arthur Zapel. Plays performed in churches and school classrooms with amateur performers for age level high school to adult; church material for young children, 8-12 years old. Publishes 25-30 plays/year. Submit synopsis or complete script. Usually buys all rights. 10% royalty up to an agreed maximum. Will negotiate for complete rights. SASE. Reports in 1 month.
Needs: "In the church field we are looking for chancel drama for presentation at various holidays: Thanksgiving, Mother's Day, Christmas, Easter, etc. School drama materials can be reader's theatre adaptations, drama rehearsal scripts, simple dialogues and short action plays. We like a free and easy style. Nothing formal. Short sentences and fast pace. Humor also welcomed where possible." Length: 1-act, skits, or short games. Casts not to exceed 9 players.

DODD, MEAD & COMPANY, 79 Madison Ave., New York NY 10016. Executive Editor: Allen T. Klots. Only interested in "playwrights after professional production, who promise to contribute to the literature of the theater." Royalty negotiated. Buys book rights only. Reports in about 4 weeks. Enclose SASE.

DAVID EASTWOOD, P.O. Box 266, Lake George NY 12845. Plays will be for professional casts in summer theater. Audience: public, tourists. Would like to see "Neil Simon-type comedies." Send synopsis. No drama. Maximum of 8 characters; 2 sets. Will consider 3-act plays; 2½ hours in length. Payment is flexible. Not copyrighted. Query first with synopsis only. Enclose SASE.

ELDRIDGE PUBLISHING CO., Drawer 209, Franklin OH 45005. (513)746-6531. Editor/General Manager: Kay Myerly. Plays performed in high schools and churches; some professional—but most are amateur productions. Publishes plays for all age groups. Publishes 20-25 plays/year. Send synopsis or complete script. Buys all rights "unless the author wishes to retain some rights." Pays $75-100 for 1-act plays; $350 for 3-acts. SASE. Reports in 60-90 days.
Needs: "We are looking for good straight comedies which will appeal to high and junior-high age groups. We do not publish anything which can be suggestive. Most of our plays are published with a hanging indentation—2 ems. All stage, scenery and costume plots must be included." Length: One-acts from 25-30 minutes; 2-acts of around 2 hours; and skits of 10-15 minutes.

SAMUEL FRENCH, INC., 25 W. 45th St., New York NY 10036. "We publish 10-15 manuscripts a year from freelancers. In addition to publishing plays, we also act as agents in the placement of plays for Broadway, Off-Broadway, regional, stock, and dinner theatre productions. Pays on royalty basis. Submit complete ms (bound). Reports in 10 weeks. SASE.
Needs: "Willing at all times to read manuscripts of plays, screenplays, and TV pilots. No verse plays, motion picture scenarios, Biblical plays, seasonal plays, huge cast plays, 'costume dramas', or children's plays on 'traditional' subjects (i.e., fairy tales)."

HEUER PUBLISHING CO., 233 Dows Building, P.O. Box 248, Cedar Rapids IA 52406. Amateur productions for schools and church groups. Audience consists of junior and senior high school students and some intermediate groups. Needs 1- and 3-act plays. Prefers comedy, farce, mystery, mystery/comedy. Uses 1-act plays suitable for contest work, (strong drama). "Suggest potential authors write for our brochure on types of plays." Taboos include sex, controversial subjects and family scenes. Prefers 1 simple setting and non-costume plays. Current need is for plays with a large number of characters, (16 to 20 characters). 1-act plays should be 30 to 35 minutes in length; 3-act, 90 to 105 minutes. Most mss purchased outright, with price depending on quality. Minimum of $500 usually. Copyrighted, however, contract stipulates amateur rights only, so author retains professional rights to TV, radio, etc. Query first with synopsis only. Enclose SASE. Reports in 1 week to 10 days. Publishes 5 to 20 plays a year.

THE INNER CITY CULTURAL CENTER, 1308 S. New Hampshire Ave., Los Angeles CA 90006. (213)387-1161. Director/Readers Theatre Program: Gene Boland. Estab. 1967. Produces 4-6 plays/year, plus Readers Theatre (semimonthly). Produced in professional West Coast theatre under Equity's 99-seat waiver. Query with synopsis. Reports in 4 weeks. "We request non-returnable manuscripts."
Needs: "Primarily those plays by or about ethnic minorities (Asians, Blacks, Hispanics, and Native Americans)."

NEW PLAYS, INC., Box 273, Rowayton CT 06853. Publisher; Patricia Whitton. Estab. 1964. Publishes 2-4 plays/year. "We are publishers of children's plays; for colleges, high schools, community theatre groups, Junior leagues, summer camps, etc." Query with synopsis. Reports in 1-2 months. Buys "exclusive rights to publish acting scripts and act as agent for productions—but the author remains the owner of the script." Pays 50% of performance royalties; "we charge our customers a royalty of $35 for the first performance and $25 for each subsequent performance. The author gets one-half of this." SASE.
Needs: "Generally, plays of approximately 45 minutes up to one and a half hours in length, for teenagers and adults to perform for children. *Not* plays for children to perform, such as assembly skits. Looking for originality in form or content. Don't want adaptations of material that has already been done a great deal, such as Rumplestiltskin, or Sleeping Beauty. Plays have to have been successfully produced by at least one organization before being published."

THE NEW PLAYWRIGHTS' THEATRE OF WASHINGTON, 1742 Church St., NW, Washington DC 20036. (202)232-1122. Scripts Editor: Bob Bowen. Estab. 1972. Produces 7 full productions plus numerous works in progress/year. "Plays are produced in semi-professional productions, for general Washington audiences." Submit complete ms, "typed to form, suitably bound." Reports in 3-4 months. "Rights purchased and financial arrangements are individually negotiated." SASE.
Needs: "All styles, traditional to experimental, straight plays to musicals and music-dramas, revues and cabaret shows, one-acts, and full-lengths. Plays must have ultimately an affirmative point-of-view. No plays that have had major, full-scale, professional productions, or that have been published." Cast: 8-12 characters. Staging: "unit settings basically."

PERFORMANCE PUBLISHING CO., 978 N. McLean Blvd., Elgin IL 60120. Editor: Virginia Butler. "We publish one, two and three-act plays and musicals suitable for stock, summer, college, high school and childrens' theatre. We're looking for comedies, mysteries, dramas, farces, etc. with modern dialogue and theme. Plays for and about high school students are usually the most remunerative and we publish 50% high school, 15% childrens' theatre and 35% for the balance of the market. The new writer is advised to obtain experience by limiting himself to one-acts until he has been published. We offer a standard royalty contract. Plays are usually copyrighted in the name of the author and we acquire all publication and stage rights. First-class professional, radio, film and TV rights remain the author's property. Approximately 40 plays/year published. Authors should retain a copy of any script mailed. Publisher is not responsible for manuscripts. No insured, certified or registered scripts accepted. SASE. Manuscript response in 3 months."

PIONEER DRAMA SERVICE, 2172 S. Colorado Blvd., Box 22555, Denver CO 80222. (303)759-4297. Publisher: Shubert Fendrich. Plays are performed by high school, junior high and adult groups, colleges and recreation programs for audiences of all ages. Publishes 15 plays/year. Submit synopsis or complete script. Buys all rights. Pays "usually 10% royalty on copy sales; 50% of production royalty and 50% of subsidiary rights with some limitations on first-time writers." SASE. Reports in 30-60 days.
Needs: "We are looking for adaptations of great works in the public domain or plays on subjects of current interest. We use the standard 1-act and 3-act format, 2-act musicals, melodrama in all lengths and plays for children's theater (plays to be done by adult actors for children). Length: 1-acts of 15-30 minutes; 2-acts of 90 minutes; 3-acts of 2 hours; and children's theater of 1 hour. "We do not want plays with predominantly male casts, or highly experimental works. Plays should be mature without being obscene or profance."

PLAYS, The Drama Magazine for Young People, 8 Arlington Street, Boston MA 02116. Associate Editor: Sylvia E. Kamerman. Publishes approximately 90 1-act plays each season. Interested in buying good plays to be performed by young people of all age groups—junior and senior high, middle grades, lower grades. In addition to comedies, farces, melodramas, skits, mysteries and dramas, can use plays for holidays and other special occasions, such as Book Week. Adaptations of classic stories and fables, historical plays, plays about other lands, puppet plays, plays for all-girl or all-boy cast, folk tales, fairy tales, creative dramatics, plays dramatizing factual information and on such concepts as good government, importance of voting, involvement and participation as citizens, and plays for conservation, ecology or human rights programs are needed. Prefers one scene; when more than one is necessary, changes should be simple. Mss should follow the general style of *Plays*. Stage directions should not be typed in capital letters or underlined. Every play ms should include: a list of characters, an indication of time, a description of setting; an "At Rise," describing what is taking place on stage as curtain rises; production notes, indicating the number of characters and the playing time, describing the costumes, properties, setting and special lighting effects, if any. Playwrights should not use incorrect grammar or dialect. Characters with physical defects, speech impediments should not be included. Desired lengths for mss are: Junior and Senior high—20 to 25 double-spaced ms pages (25 to 30 minutes playing time). Middle Grades—12 to 15 pages (15 to 20 minutes playing time). Lower Grades—6 to 10 pages (8 to 15 minutes playing time). Pays "good rates on acceptance." Reports in 3-4 weeks. SASE. "Manuscript specification sheet sent on request."

ROANOKE ISLAND HISTORICAL ASSOCIATION, Box 40, Manteo NC 27954. (919)473-2127. Assistant General Manager: Rock Kershaw. Estab. 1937. Produces 6 plays/year; "audience ranges widely from children to families to senior citizens." Query with synopsis. Reports in 2 weeks. Buys production rights. Pays $10-30/performance. SASE.
Needs: Children's fantasy; musicals; dance productions; comedies; light opera; and heavy drama. Scripts should be submitted by May 15th.

STAGE SOUTH, 829 Richland St., Columbia SC 29201. Assistant Director of Development: Tim Beall. Estab. 1973. Produces 2 plays/year. "Stage South, the state theatre of South Carolina and a program of the South Carolina Arts Commission, is a professional, regional touring operation. At present, its season consists of an educational, theatre-for-youth production in the fall—generally an original, commissioned script celebrating the history and folklore indigenous to the state; and a community tour in the spring. Stage South productions are intended to appeal to a wide range of the South Carolina population." Query or submit complete ms with vita or resume. Reports in 2 months. Rights are negotiable. Pays $300-1,000; "payment varies, depending on the reputation and experience of the playwright." SASE.
Needs: "Plays submitted to Stage South should be suitable for touring to urban and rural communities in South Carolina. We are especially interested in material that speaks to the history and cultural uniqueness of the state. Generally, all plays submitted to Stage South are read and evaluated. Scripts submitted should specify reasonable, tourable sets and should ordinarily require no more than ten actors. We are especially favorable to realistic, convincing characters that command sympathy or identification from the audience. We are open to experimental approaches, formats or structures in this regard."

THEATER WORLD PUBLISHING CO., 8707 Terrace Dr., El Cerrito CA 94530. (415)525-9341. Editor/Publisher: Frank Anderson. Plays are performed in high schools, community colleges,

and church groups, in smaller towns and rural areas. Audience is comprised of families with conservative middle-American values. Publishes 20 plays/year. Submit script, or send SASE for writer's guidelines. 10-50% royalty. Reports in 90 days.
Needs: "Broad comedy; principally, our need is for wholesome treatments of up-to-date themes with emphasis on action and broad humor. Will also consider serious material based on character conflict if strong on tension and resolution is positive." Length: mainly 3-acts; some 1-acts. Prefers casts of 12-20 for 3-acts, 6 or more for 1-acts; predominately female. No sex, sexual innuendos or offensive language, smoking or drinking on stage, or controversial subject matter regarding morals, politics, or religion. "Adaptations OK, if in public domain."

Potpourri

The following section contains listings for *oddball* markets for freelance writing—those individuals and firms who will review (and purchase) freelance writing, but whose editorial requirements are such that they don't fit into any of the regular *Writer's Market* classifications. These markets include advertising and public relations writing, one-liners for radio disc jockeys, and even a motion picture producer in need of scripts and ideas.

Because of the very specialized needs of these markets, writers in doubt of any of the firm's practices and policies should contact the listed contact name before submitting material.

COOPER RAND CORP., 127 E. 62nd St., New York NY 10021. (212)355-5505. Director: Leslie Shiffrin. Query with resume of credits. SASE. Reports in 2 weeks. Free sample brochures; mention *Writer's Market* in request.
Needs: Cooper Rand seeks local freelancers to write direct mail brochures that are inserted into statements sent to Master Charge, Visa, oil company and travel credit card holders. These brochures market products like housewares, clothes, and tools. The first brochure was produced in 1972, and are now sent to 4,000,000 people each month. All are freelance written. Pays $200 minimum/job.

HUMORETTES, Casino Loot Productions, 232 8th St., Brooklyn NY 11215. (212)768-1587. Editor: Frank Michael Cotolo. Managing Editor: Thom Savino. Comedy service supplying jokes to radio personalities. "The humor is usually quick and concise, due to the time allowed most DJ's." Pays on acceptance. Buys all rights. Submit seasonal/holiday material 1 month in advance. Photocopied submissions OK. SASE. Reports in 3 weeks. Sample copy $5; free writer's guidelines.
Needs: It Could Have Been Different (funny thoughts about topical or historical people if they had done something other than what they are famous for); Psychic Predictions (zany forecasts for the future with an emphasis on puns); People, Places, and Things (true or untrue news items with humorous comments); Your Stars Today (wacky horoscopes); and Funny Spots (zany commercials or public service announcements). "We cannot stress enough the importance of studying the format before expecting a good financial return from material submitted. This is excellent practice for any writer who wants to eventually write for the media because all humor is performed on the air by radio DJ's." Length: 160 words maximum. Pays $1/page of 5 items; 15¢/one-liner. Open to suggestions for new departments.

MANNING, SELVAGE & LEE, 666 5th Ave., New York NY 10019. Executive Vice-President: Lloyd N. Newman. Public relations firm. Query with resumé of credits.
Needs: "Our need for freelance writers varies from time to time depending on our account needs. Most frequently, we seek speech-writers knowledgeable in a specialized area, i.e., pharmaceutical economics; health care law and finance; and public issues of various types. In addition, we use specialized freelance writers for brochures, films, and audiovisual presentations. Third, we use freelance writers to research and prepare preliminary drafts for technical product publicity stories. Our interests here are in health care, chemicals, plastics, metals and metal technology, scientific instrumentation and about 20 other areas, depending on our clients." Pays $500-1,500 for speeches up to 30 minutes long; $5,000-7,000 for film treatments and shooting scripts.

O'LINERS, 366 W. Bullard Ave., Fresno CA 93704. Publisher: Dan O'Day. "*O'Liners* is a monthly humor service published primarily for disc jockeys around the world."
Needs: "I'm looking for bright, funny one-liners to be delivered on-the-air; therefore, all material should be written in a conversational style. My primary need is for clever, sharp, topical lines—the kind you expect from a Johnny Carson monologue. Merely commenting on the news won't do the job; you've got to say something about a current event that will make me laugh. Topical lines are related to politics, the economy, fashions, fads, persons in the news—whatever people are talking about at the moment. We are not interested in ethnic humor, 'fat'

jokes, mother-in-law jokes, prune jokes, etc. Neither are we interested in material that consistently reveals a racist or sexist attitude. Remember, this material is for DJ's. We're not interested in poems, limericks, toastmaster lines, short stories, etc. All submissions must be 100% original. If items are sent to us that we find to be copied, or rewritten, or from any source other than the contributor's own talent and creativity, then we will no longer consider further material from that contributor. Before submitting any material, the writer *must* send a long SASE for guidelines.'' Pays $1/line, on acceptance. Reports in 10 days. SASE.

PAMPHLET PUBLICATIONS, Box 41372A, Cincinnati OH 45241. (513)563-9502. Vice-President: Ms. Kim Brooks.
Needs: ''Our needs right now are pamphlets on controversial subjects about social issues today, and religious matters.'' The pamphlets are distributed to public and college libraries, bookstores and high schools, and other outlets. ''We're always open to suggestions that you, the author, may have. There's always room for a different view.'' Buys 300 pamphlets/year. Length: 8,000-12,000 words. Pays 10% royalty on gross profits. Sample pamphlets $1. Reports in 3-4 weeks. SASE.

SCHICK SUNN CLASSIC PICTURES, 556 E. 200 S., Salt Lake City UT 84102. Director, Product Acquisition: Richard Staley. Estab. 1969. Film production company. Reports in 4 weeks-6 months. Buys all rights.
Needs: ''As to our areas of interest, because we do strictly ''G'' rated films that must appeal to a wide cross-section audience we have certain obvious limits. A caveat: 'G' need not be pap. Many people also equate 'G' films with Walt Disney. We like to say we are the second largest producer of family films, but we do not do Disney-type films. We will consider such concepts, but our past market testing shows that our audience is made up of adults who bring their children to a film perceived to be interesting, somewhat educational, and to a degree morally uplifting. Disney-type films are aimed at children who bring their parents. We are very interested in material the major studios probably would not do. This includes projects with religious overtones (*Beyond and Back* and *In Search of Noah's Ark*) but of basically general interest level. Some of the films that have worked best for us in the past are of the 'unexplained phenomena' genre. In the past, Sunn Classic Pictures has very successfully done outdoor action adventures (*The Life and Times of Grizzly Adams*), and docu-drama 'phenomena' pictures (*The Lincoln Conspiracy*, *The Bermuda Triangle*). While we will still consider ideas in either of these genres, we very much want to continue artistic and professional growth and thus encourage story ideas from any field that will attract adults and their children, and which strictly limit sex, violence, or vulgar language. We will also consider TV series ideas. Payment is less ($250) because our staff writers must completely develop ideas from concepts. Minimum feature film payment has been raised to $1,000. We also seek to determine if a writer whose concepts we buy has files, or personal expertise that would make him or her particularly valuable to us as a consultant, researcher, or technical advisor. If this is the case, a separate contract and payment exclusive of the initial acquisition agreement may be negotiated. On the approach writers should take in submitting materials to us: First, we need a postcard inquiry specifying whether the writer intends to submit TV or feature film story concepts, so we can send the appropriate 'submissions package.' Submissions (or 'concepts') must be limited to 500 words and must be submitted on one of Schick Sunn's submissions forms. We can only accept complete screenplays from recognized agents. With just 500 words to work with a writer should imagine he or she is doing a 60-second radio commercial. Essentially, that's all the time they have to sell their story. So, the concept should move the plot along simply, contain as much visual imagery as possible and as many exciting elements as can be squeezed into the alotted space.''

Syndicates

Syndicates sell editorial copy to publishers on a commission basis, with the author receiving 40 to 60 percent of the gross proceeds. Some syndicates, however, pay the writer a salary or a minimum guarantee. Writers of top syndicated columns may earn $50,000 or more per year. The aspiring syndicate writer must first make sure his work won't be competing in an already flooded field. Second, he must select a syndicate which will properly promote his material. The larger syndicates, of course, usually have better promotional facilities. (A list of syndicates which includes all the titles of the columns and features they handle appears in the *Editor and Publisher Syndicate Directory* ($5) published at 850 Third Avenue, New York NY 10022.) It's best to query the syndicate editor first, enclosing a half-dozen sample columns or feature ideas and a self-addressed, stamped envelope. Some writers self-syndicate their own material. The writer here earns 100% of the proceeds but also bears the expense of soliciting the clients, reproducing and mailing the features, billing, etc. See the chapter "How to Syndicate Your Own Column" in the *Writer's Digest* book, *The Creative Writer*.

AMERICAN FEATURES SYNDICATE, 964 Third Ave., New York NY 10022. Editor: Robert Behren. Copyrights material. Will consider photocopied submissions. Reporting time "varies." Query. SASE.
Nonfiction: Travel and true adventure. Buys single features and article series. Does not contract for columns. Length: 1,000-5,000 words. Pays $100-$750. Usual outlets are newspapers and regional magazines, including some trade publications.

AP NEWSFEATURES, 50 Rockefeller Plaza, New York NY 10020. General Executive: Dan Perkes. SASE.
Nonfiction and Photos: Buys article series or column ideas "dealing with areas of science, social issues that can be expanded into book form. Do not usually buy single features." Length: 600 to 1,000 words. Pays minimum $25.

ARKIN MAGAZINE SYNDICATE, 761 N.E. 180th St., North Miami Beach FL 33162. Editor: Joseph Arkin. "We regularly purchase articles from several freelancers, most of whom belong to ABWA, for syndication in trade and professional magazines." Submit complete ms. SASE. Reports in 3 weeks. Buys all North American magazine and newspaper rights.
Needs: Magazine articles (nonfiction; 800-1,800 words, directly relating to business problems common to several (not just one) business firms, in different types of businesses); and photos (purchased with written material). "We are in dire need of the 'how-to' business article." Will consider article series; "will buy after we make placement, all submissions are on speculation." Pays 3-10¢/word; $5-10 for photos; "actually line drawings are preferred instead of photos."

AUTHENTICATED NEWS INTERNATIONAL, ANI, 170 Fifth Avenue, New York NY 10010. (212)243-6995. Editor: Sidney Polinsky. Syndication and Features Editor: Dan Dougherty. Supplies material to national magazines, newspapers, and house organs in the United States and important countries abroad. Buys exclusive and non-exclusive rights. Reports in 3 months. Enclose SASE.
Nonfiction and Photos: Can use photo material in the following areas: hard news, photo features, ecology and the environment, science, medical, industry, education, human interest, the arts, city planning, and pertinent photo material from abroad. 750 words maximum. Prefers 8x10 b&w glossies, color transparencies (4x5 or 2¼x2¼, 35mm color). Where necessary, model releases required. Pays 50% royalty.

AUTO NEWS SYNDICATE, Box 2085, Daytona Beach FL 32015. Editor: Don O'Reilly. Unsolicited material is acknowledged or returned within a few days, "but we cannot be responsible for loss." SASE.
Nonfiction and Photos: Syndicated articles, photos on automotive subjects and motor sports.

Newspaper articles ("Dateline: Detroit" and "Inside Auto Racing"). Magazine articles. Radio broadcasts ("Inside Auto Racing"). 50% commission. "Payment is made between acceptance and publication." No flat fees.

BUDDY BASCH FEATURE SYNDICATE, 771 West End Ave., New York NY 10025. Publisher: Buddy Basch. Buys all rights. Will consider photocopied submissions. Query first or submit complete ms. Reports in 1 week to 10 days. Enclose SASE.
Nonfiction, Humor, Photos, and Fillers: News items, nonfiction, humor, photos, fillers, puzzles, and columns and features on travel and entertainment. "Mostly staff written at present. Query first."

CANADIAN SCENE, Suite 305, 2 College St., Toronto, Ont., Canada. M5G 1K3. Editor: Miss Ruth Gordon. Query first. Submit seasonal material 3 months in advance. Reports in 1 week. Pays on acceptance. Enclose SAE and International Reply Coupons for reply to queries.
Nonfiction: "Canadian Scene is a voluntary information service. Its purpose is to provide written material to democratic, foreign language publications in Canada. The material is chosen with a view to directing readers to an understanding of Canadian political affairs, foreign relations, social customs, industrial progress, culture, history, and institutions. In a 700-word article, the writer can submit almost any subject on Canada, providing it leaves the newcomer with a better knowledge of Canada. It should be written in a simple, tightly knit, straightforward style." Length: 500 to 1,000 words. Pays 3¢ a word.

CHICAGO TRIBUNE-NEW YORK NEWS SYNDICATE, INC., 220 East 42nd St., New York NY 10017. Editor: Don Michel. Supplies material to Sunday supplements and newspapers in North America and abroad. Buys worldwide rights, where possible; must have North American rights to be interested. Submit at least 6 samples of any submission for continuing feature. Enclose SASE for return of submissions.
Columns, Puzzles: No fiction. Material must be extremely well-written and must not be a copy of something now being marketed to newspapers. Length varies, though columns should generally be 500 words or less. Pay varies, depending on market; usually 50-50 split of net after production on contractual material.

COLLEGE PRESS SERVICE, 1764 Gilpin St., Denver CO 80218. (303)388-1608. Contact: Jay Karl Stevens. Estab. 1965. "We work with about 10-15 freelancers a year." Query with clips of published work. SASE. Reports in 2-3 weeks. Material is not copyrighted. Writer's guidelines for SASE.
Needs: Magazine and newspaper features; newspaper columns; news items; fillers; and radio broadcast material. Pays $10-15.

COLUMBIA FEATURES, INC., 36 West 44 St., New York NY 10036. Editor: William H. Thomas. Buys all rights and world rights, all media. Will consider photocopied submissions. Submit complete ms. Pays on a regular monthly basis for continuing column or contract. Reports in 2 to 4 weeks. Enclose SASE for return of submissions.
Humor and Puzzles: Cartoons, comic strips, puzzles, and columns on a continuing basis. Features for special sections: family, home, women's, Sunday supplements. No single features, except series of 6 to 12 parts, about 750 to 1,000 words each article. Lengths vary according to features. Columns: 500 to 750 words. Pays 50% usually.

COMMUNITY AND SUBURBAN PRESS SERVICE, 100 E. Main St., Frankfort KY 40601. Managing Editor: Mike Bennett. Buys second serial (reprint) rights. Pays on acceptance. SASE.
Humor and Photos: Cartoons, gag panels, human interest photos. 8x10 glossy photos purchased without features. Captions required. Pays $15 per cartoon or photo.

CONTEMPORARY FEATURES SYNDICATE, INC., Box 1258, Jackson TN 38301. Editor: Lloyd Russell. Associate Editor: Kathy L. Turner. Currently has 3 columns in syndication; buys several dozen mss/year for syndication to newspapers (columns) and magazines (single features). Submit complete ms and credits. SASE. Photocopied submissions OK "if not submitted elsewhere also." Reports in 6-8 weeks, sometimes longer. Buys all rights.
Needs: News items (not looking for hard news, but rather the story behind the news); fiction (occasional short story, but no longer fiction); fillers (no rehash of the history book; entertain and inform; usually handled on consignment); and photos (purchased with or without written material or on assignment. Captions required). "We believe our product is a line of 'human

interest' features and we want to read about people and their relationships.'' Article series considered if ''there is a story too long to be easily and completely told in one article. Have something to say rather than just lots of words.'' Pays 50% commission on sales; minimum guarantee of $25 for full-length features to magazines; photos bring $5 minimum. Usually pays on acceptance.
Tips: ''Be professional. Be patient. And be realistic. Quality material is a must. Selling *any* material takes time to get the top dollar and the best treatment. No one should expect to get rich or famous overnight. It's all summed up in the abused term 'hard work'. That's what it is all about, and that's what it takes.''

CREATIVE COMMUNICATIONS, Division of Creative Enterprises, Box 377, Centreville VA 22020. Editor: Irene Brannon. Buys material for syndication to weekly newspapers. Submit complete ms. Prefers photocopied submissions. Buys all rights, first rights and second serial (reprint) rights. SASE.
Needs: Weekly columns of current interest: self-improvement, politics, health, nutrition, ecology, child development, and consumer interest. Prefers columns of 500 words or less. Pays 50% of price of item sold, on purchase of the article by a newspaper or periodical.

CRUX NEWS SERVICE, Shickshinny PA 18655. Editor: Thourot Pichel. Does not copyright material. Buys ''very few'' features a year from freelancers. Will consider photocopied submissions. SASE.
Nonfiction: ''History and political only.'' Buys single features. Does not buy article series or columns. Pays ''nominal standard.''

CURIOUS FACTS FEATURES, 1449 Glenview Dr., Lebanon OH 45036. Editor: Donald Whitacre. Buys all rights. Pays on publication. Reports in 2 weeks. Enclose SASE.
Nonfiction: Uses ''oddities'' of all types including strange animals, strange laws, people, firsts, etc. Length: 50 to 100 words. Pays $10 to $15.

DIDATO ASSOCIATES, 280 Madison Ave., New York NY 10016. Rights purchased vary with author and material. Will consider photocopied submissions. Query first or submit complete ms. Pays on acceptance, or on publication. Reports immediately. SASE.
Nonfiction: Quizzes which have a behavior science or psychology angle. Must have solid research references by behavior scientists or related professionals. Single feature examples: your clothes tell your personality; study reveals sex attitudes of teenagers; depression linked up with job blahs; terrorists are suicidal personalities, survey shows. Length: 500 to 2,000 words. Pays negotiable rates. Especially needs news-related story ideas and leads in outline form of about 100 words; also with one or more research references. Pays $10 to $50 for leads and psychology quizzes.

DORN-FREDRICKS PUBLISHING CO., 35 East 35 St., Suite 7-H, New York NY 10016. Editor: Dona Davis Grant. Buys all rights, worldwide, foreign rights. Query first. Enclose SASE.
Nonfiction, Humor, Poetry, and Fillers: Gossip columns of worldwide interest; material for feminine markets; fashion, beauty, etc. Single features include: ''Harvest Time of Life'' (column), ''Mighty Mixture'' (column), ''Famous Mothers,'' ''Your Key to Courage,'' ''How the West Was Won,'' ''Crafts'' and ''Homemaker's New Ideas.'' Interested in humor columns of approximately 800 words. Famous personalities, and beauty. Column length: 800 words. Pays 3¢ a word minimum, depending on name value.

EDITORIAL CONSULTANT SERVICE, Box 524 West Hempstead NY 11552. Editorial Director: Arthur A. Ingoglia. Estab. 1965. ''We work with 75 writers in the US and Canada.'' Syndicates material to newspapers, magazines, and radio stations. Query. SASE. Reports in 3-4 weeks. Buys all rights. Writer's guidelines for SASE.
Needs: Magazine and newspaper columns and features; news items; and radio broadcast material. Prefers material with automotive slant. Also considers trade features. Will consider article series. Author's percentage varies; usually averages 50%. Additional payment for 8x10 b&w and color photos accepted with ms. Currently syndicates *Let's Talk About Your Car* , by R. Hite; *Book Talk* , by L. Stevens; and *Car World* , by A. Ingoglia.

ENTERPRISE SCIENCE NEWS, 230 Park Ave., New York NY 10017. Editor: David Hendin. Buys all rights. Pays on acceptance. Query first. Reports in 2 to 4 weeks. Enclose SASE for reply to queries.

Nonfiction: "We only buy from professional science-medical writers." Wants feature-type newspaper stories on scientific subjects of current interest. The science should be interesting and applicable to the reader. Must be clear, concise, accurate and objective. Stories with good art receive preference. Length: 700 to 1,200 words. Pays $30 to $500, "depnding on author, length and type of story, quality of writing, whether commissioned or not, etc."
Photos: Bought with features only.

FACING SOUTH, Box 230, Chapel Hill NC 27514. (919)929-2141. Co-Editors: Jennifer Miller and Kathleen Zobel. Buys 52 columns/year for syndication to newspapers. Query or submit complete ms. SASE. Reports in 5 weeks. Buys all rights.
Needs: "650-700-word columns focusing on a southern individual, allowing that person to tell a story. Each week a different writer does a column, although we will use more than one column by the same writer—just spread them over several months." Pays $50. "Writers must send for our guidelines before attempting a column." No payment for photos; "we just need some kind of a snapshot that our artist can use to do an illustration."

FIELD NEWSPAPER SYNDICATE, 401 N. Wabash Ave., Chicago IL 60611. President/Editor: Richard Sherry. Estab. 1925. Syndicates material to newspapers. Submit "examples of work with explanatory letter." SASE. Reports in 1-2 months. Rights purchased vary. Free writer's guidelines.
Needs: Newspapers columns (should be 500-800 words in length and should appeal to a wide audience. Subject matter should not be too specialized because syndicates sell columns to newspapers all over the US and Canada). "Occasionally we use four-part series (approximately 5,000 words) covering a wide variety of subjects." Currently syndicates *Ann Landers*, by Ann Landers; *At Wit's End*, by Erma Bombeck; and *Washington Insight*, by Joseph Kraft.

GLOBAL COMMUNICATIONS, 303 Fifth Ave., Suite 1306, New York NY 10016. President: Timothy Green Beckley. "We supply material to publications in the U.S. and overseas." Rights purchased vary with author and material. Usually buys second serial (reprint) rights or simultaneous rights. Buys about 600 features a year. Will consider photocopied submissions. Send complete ms. Reports in 2 weeks. Enclose SASE.
Nonfiction, Fiction and Fillers: "Our interests are varied and include almost every area. Short fiction doesn't move very well. We go in for straight reporting and investigative pieces." Writing should be colorful, to the point, good news angle. "In addition to original material for U.S. and foreign syndication, we are always looking for previously published pieces which the writer owns foreign rights to. Our material goes to publications in about 13 foreign countries. Our standard commission is 1/3 on all sales. However, sometimes we do purchase outright. Writers should send tearsheets and a letter stating they have rights to sell outside U.S. from original publisher." Currently, best markets include celebrity interviews and profiles, true psychic/UFO pieces (must be well researched), adult fiction and nonfiction, human interest and, in general, "anything that is a bit unusual. We do *not* buy continuing columns." Sometimes will purchase material outright for $35 to $500, but 95% of material is handled on a commission basis. Mainly buys adult (sex) fiction; also adventure, Western, erotica, science fiction, religious. Length: 2,000 to 5,000 words. Buys fillers: jokes, gags, anecdotes, short humor. Pays $5 to $25. Buys all rights. No poetry. "We try to give help and advice when possible and are always looking for 'newcomers' to work with. We have about a dozen stringers who send us stories constantly. Always room for more."
Photos: Photos purchased with accompanying ms with no additional payment. Or purchased with or without ms with extra payment. Captions required. Pays $15 minimum for b&w (8x10) and $25 minimum for color slides.
Columns: "Psychic Celebrities" and "Saucers and Celebrities." Materials for these columns are purchased outright. Payment: $50. Buys all rights. No byline.

DAVE GOODWIN & ASSOCIATES, P.O. Drawer 54-6661, Surfside FL 33154. Editor: Dave Goodwin. Rights purchased vary with author and material. May buy first rights or second serial (reprint) rights. Will handle copyrighted material. Buys about 25 features a year from freelancers. Query first or submit complete ms. Reports in 3 weeks. SASE.
Nonfiction: "Money-saving information for consumers: how to save on home expenses; auto, medical, drug, insurance, boat, business items, etc." Buys article series on brief, practical, down-to-earth items for consumer use or knowledge. Rarely buys single features. Currently handling "Insurance for Consumers." Length: 300 to 5,000 words. Pays 50% on publication.

HARRIS & ASSOCIATES PUBLISHING DIVISION, 247 South 800 East, Logan UT 84321. (801)753-3587. President: Dick Harris. Rights purchased vary with author and material. May buy all rights or first rights. Does not purchase many mss per year since material must be in their special style. Pays on publication; sometimes earlier. Not necessary to query. Send sample or representative material. Reports in less than 30 days. Enclose SASE.
Nonfiction, Photos, and Humor: Material on driver safety and accident prevention. Humor for modern women (not women's lib); humor for sports page. "We like to look at anything in our special interest areas. Golf and tennis are our specialties. We'll also look at cartoons in these areas. Will buy or contract for syndication. Everything must be short, terse, with humorous approach." Action, unposed, 8x10 b&w photos are purchased without features or on assignment. Captions are required. Pays 10¢ minimum per word and $15 minimum per photo.

HER SAY, 950 Howard St., San Francisco CA 94103. (415)956-3555. Editor/Publisher: Marlene Edmunds. Editors: Shelly Buck, Ann Milner, Marcia Bauman. Estab. May 1977. Buys approximately 110 items/year for use in radio, magazines and newspapers. Query; submissions will not be returned. Reports in 3 weeks. Material is not copyrighted. Writer's guidelines for SASE.
Needs: "*Her Say* is a national women's weekly news service, going out to a number of radio news outlets and publications around the country, in Canada, and in Europe. We are looking for in-put from researchers, writers and reporters from everywhere to help us keep posted on events concerning women. We would like items which can be rewritten to 75-250 word stories for both print and radio outlets. Current status of legislation, socio-political research on, by, or for women, humorous items, new breakthroughs in medicine, scientific studies, and Third World news—these are the types of stories we would like to see." Pays $10/item.

HOLLYWOOD INSIDE SYNDICATE, Box 49957, Los Angeles CA 90049. Editor: John Austin. Purchases mss for syndication to newspapers in San Francisco, Philadelphia, Detroit, Montreal, London, and Sydney. Query or submit complete ms. SASE. Reports in 4-6 weeks. Buys first rights or second serial (reprint) rights.
Needs: News items (column items concerning entertainment (motion picture) personalities and jet setters for syndicated column; 750-800 words). Also considers series of 1,500-word articles; "suggest descriptive query first." Pay negotiable. Pays on acceptance "but this is also negotiable because of delays in world market acceptance."

INTERNATIONAL EDITORIAL SERVICES/NEWSWEEK, INC., 444 Madison Ave., New York NY 10022. Vice President: R.J. Melvin. Offers on speculation to listing of Newsweek worldwide associates first sights on second serial (reprint) rights. Offers 50 to 100 features, over 1,000 photos and graphics a year. Will consider photocopied submissions. Query first. Reports within 3 months. Enclose SASE.
Nonfiction and Photos: News items, backgrounders, personalities in the news. News-related features suitable for international syndication. Prefers approximately 1,200 words for features. Pays 50% on publication. Photos purchased with features. Pays $25-75 for b&w if purchased separately.

INTERPRESS OF LONDON AND NEW YORK, 400 Madison Ave., New York NY 10017. (212)832-2539. Editor: Jeffrey Blyth. Buys British and European rights mostly, but can handle world rights. Will consider photocopied submissions. Query first or submit complete ms. Pays on publication, or agreement of sale. Reports immediately or as soon as practicable. SASE.
Nonfiction and Photos: "Unusual stories and photos for British and European press. Picture stories, for example, on such 'Americana' as a five-year-old evangelist; the 800-pound 'con-man,' the nude-male calendar; tallest girl in the world; interviews with pop celebrities such as Yoko Ono, Bob Dylan, Sen. Kennedy, Valarie Perrine, Priscilla Presley, Bette Midler, Liza Minelli; cult subjects such as voodoo, college fads, anything amusing or offbeat. Extracts from books such as Earl Wilson's *Show Business Laid Bare*, inside-Hollywood type series ('Secrets of the Stuntmen,' 'My Life with Racquel Welch'). Real life adventure dramas ('Three Months in an Open Boat,' 'The Air Crash Cannibals of the Andes'). No length limits—short or long, but not too long. Payment varies; depending on whether material is original, or world rights. Pay top rates, up to several thousand dollars, for exclusive material. Photos purchased with or without features. Captions required. Standard size prints, suitable for radioing if necessary. Pay $50 to $100, but no limit on exclusive material."

KEISTER ADVERTISING SERVICE, Strasburg VA 22657. Editor: G. Walton Lindsay. Buys approximately 25-30 mss/year for syndication to newspapers. Query with samples/credits.

SASE. Reports in 1-2 months. Buys all rights.
Needs: "Our copy is limited to about 150 words and deals with human-interest illustrations that lead casually but persuasively into a plea for church membership and attendance. Style should compete with rest of newspaper and not be of a 'preachy' sermonette-like nature." Photos purchased without features; captions required. Pays $15-20/item. Pays on acceptance.

KING FEATURES SYNDICATE, INC., 235 E. 45th St., New York NY 10017. (212)682-5600. Executive Editor: Allan Priaulx. Estab. 1920. "We have about 55 regular text features, and add one to five new features annually." Syndicates material to newspapers. Submit "brief cover letter with samples of feature proposals." SASE. Reports in 2-3 weeks. Buys all rights.
Needs: Newspaper features and columns. Will consider article series. Pays "revenue commission percentage."

KNOWLEDGE NEWS & FEATURES SYNDICATE, Kenilworth IL 60043. (312)256-0059. Executive Editor: Dr. Whitt N. Schultz. Rights purchased vary with author and material. Usually buys all rights. Will consider photocopied submissions. Query first. Reports in 10 days. Enclose SASE.
Business Features, Photos and Nonfiction: News items; humor; fillers; business, knowledge and education articles; "success stories." Buys article series. May buy single features. Will contract for columns for syndication. Length: 1,000 minimum for features; 500 minimum for columns. Payment negotiable. Photos purchased with features and also on assignment. Captions required. Buys 8x10 glossy photos. Payment negotiable.
Tips: "Clear, crisp, concise, urgent writing—easy to read—open—spotlight success, inspiration; positive news features."

MIKE LeFAN FEATURES, 1802 S. 13th, Temple TX 76501. Editor: Mike LeFan. Estab. 1974. Buys "about 50 items annually. Much of the outside material used is submitted by readers of my features, but I'm quite willing to pay for suitable pieces from freelancers. My syndicated features appear in both magazines, and in daily and weekly newspapers." Submit complete ms; 1 item to a page. SASE. Reports in 3 weeks. Material is not copyrighted.
Needs: Fillers (practical, usable items on how people can get more for their money, up to 250 words). "An acceptable filler tells the average man or woman how to get more for their money on food, utilities, travel, clothing, auto, household needs, entertainment, or any other area of daily life, but the ideas must be practical and useful. There are no by-lines as such, but items will be credited within the text of a particular column to identify the writer." Pays $2/filler. Currently syndicates More For Your Money, and Elks Family Shopper.

MEDIA WEST, E. 302-26th, Spokane WA 99203. (509)624-7290. President: George Cole. Estab. 1974. "On the average, I will purchase 1-2 features a week for use in newspapers, newsletters and radio programs." Submit complete ms; for broadcast material submit tape. SASE. Reports in 3 weeks. Buys first North American serial rights. Writer's guidelines $1.
Needs: Newspaper features (prefer lively style); news items (200-800 words); fillers; and radio-broadcast material (prefer interviews or produced features, 1-10 minutes in length). Also interested in longer 'how-to' material, information about job markets, media, trends, life styles. "My radio 'Magazine' series can use book reviews, film reviews, interviews, and features for a general audience." Pays minimum guarantee $10; "will go higher if work so merits." Pays $7-20 for 5x7 or 8x10 b&w glossy photos. Currently syndicates Careers Today, Media report, and Survival Guide.

NATIONAL CATHOLIC NEWS SERVICE, 1312 Massachusetts Ave., N.W., Washington DC 20005. Editor: Richard W. Daw. "We are served by a number of stringers as well as freelancers. We provide a daily service and have a fairly constant market. Inquiries are welcomed, but they should be both brief and precise. Too many inquiries are coy and/or vague. Will consider photocopied submissions." Pays on publication. Reports in 4-5 weeks. Enclose SASE for reply to queries.
Nonfiction: Short news and feature items of religious or social interest, particularly items with a Catholic thrust. Buys single features and article series. Feature examples: FCC plagued by letters about non-existent petition from atheist; clown tours America as God's Good Humor Man; bishop lives in house heated 20 degrees cooler than White House. Series examples: Moral implications and religious involvement in capital punishment issue; Catholic schools and integration. Contracts for columns: "This is a highly competitive market and we are extremely selective. Our columns range from labor concerns to the liturgy." Length for single features: no minimum, maximum of 800 words. Article series: maximum of 3 parts, about 700 words each.

Columns: open in length; generally, the shorter the better. Generally pays a maximum of 5¢ a word for news and feature copy. Buys book reviews at a rate of 3¢ a word for a maximum of 500 words. Does not buy *unsolicited* reviews, but welcomes queries. "We market primarily to more than 100 Catholic weekly newspapers. We also serve foreign Catholic agencies and U.S. Catholic weekly newspapers."
Photos: Purchased with or without features. Captions required. News and feature photos of interest to Catholic periodicals. "We operate a photo service that mails to clients four times a week." Pays from $5 to $15 for each photo, depending on quality and originality.

NATIONAL FEATURES SYNDICATE, INC., 11620 Wilshire Blvd., 10th floor, Los Angeles CA 90025. Managing Editor: Fred Rosenblatt. "Subscribers are the media, especially if involved in the health industry." Submit complete ms. SASE. Reports in 2 weeks. Buys first North American serial rights. Writer's guidelines for SASE.
Needs: Newspaper features and news items concerning the health industry. Will consider single features and articles series. Pays $5-100.

NCT FEATURES, Box 11623, Chicago IL 60611. Contact: Neesa Sweet. "*NCT Features* is a feature service supplying over 120 magazines and newspapers throughout the country with feature material. Our clients include newspaper feature departments, Sunday magazine sections, travel and sports sections, sponsored publications, consumer publications and general interest magazines. SASE. Buys all rights.
Needs: "We deal in a wide variety of topics: travel pieces, adventure, consumer articles, personality profiles, how-to's, sports, column ideas, recreation features, topical stories, comic strips, science, food, history, and anything else that is different and unusual. Articles vary from 500-3,000 words, and price depends on the article and the market. We are particularly on the lookout for story-photo packages—first class words and pictures on unusual exotic and hard hitting topic areas. Photography is handled on a commission basis. Transparencies should be 35mm or larger submitted in plastic viewing files, with the photographer's name and caption information on each slide."

NEW YORK TIMES SYNDICATION SALES CORPORATION, 200 Park Avenue, New York NY 10017. (212)972-1070. Editor of Special Features: Marian Taylor. Estab. 1970. Syndicates "about one book or feature per week" in magazines, "but primarily in newspapers." Also included in foreign magazines. Query, or "if the feature is not long, like a 2,500 word one-shot, send the complete manuscript. If longer, send one part first." Phone queries OK. SASE. Prefers world rights but often buys North American second serial rights; for books, "first, second or both" rights.
Needs: "We're willing to encourage young writers." Wants magazine and newspaper features; magazine and newspaper columns; and book series. "Medical subjects are good, exclusive interviews with personalities (especially if they are those who don't normally give interviews), how-tos, biographies of stars, and education." Recently ran the Haldeman memoirs. "Don't send anything fancy, cute or tricky. The field is pretty wide open, but use facts not widely diseminated—news pegs are always good ideas. We recently received a piece about the Amish, but there was no news peg. It was a *National Geographic* kind of story and I didn't think it would sell so we didn't use it." Advances are rare. After production costs are taken, the syndication usually offers the author a 50-50 split of the profit. Total purchase price includes payment for photos. "If you don't have to include photos, don't." Currently syndicates The Dividing Line by Patrick Buchanan.

NEW YORK TODAY, INC., NEWS SERVICE, 850 7th Ave., Suite 1200, New York NY 10019. Editor: Ray Wilson. Query first. SASE.
Nonfiction: Food, restaurants, entertainment, travel and astrology material for newspapers, radio, television and magazines. Authoritative stories on wine. "We buy something that fits into our scheme of things. Criswell Predicts, Ray Wilson on Broadway, Bob Dana on Wine and Food, and Travel by Hermes, are a few examples of columns we now handle." Length: 750 words. "We have no established rate of payment. We use writers on assignment basis only if our staff cannot cover. Other material is submitted for our approval through query. Then we contact the writer."

NEWS FLASH INTERNATIONAL INC., 508 Atlanta Ave., North Massapequa NY 11758. Editor: Jackson B. Pokress. Supplies material to Observer newspapers and Champion sports publications. "Contact editor prior to submission to allow for space if article is newsworthy." Will consider photocopied submissions. Pays on publication. SASE.

Nonfiction: "We have been supplying a 'ready-for-camera' sports page (tabloid size) complete with column and current sports photos on a weekly basis to many newspapers on Long Island as well as pictures and written material to publications in England and Canada. Payment for assignments is based on the article. It may vary. Payments vary from $20 for a feature of 800 words. Our sports stories feature in-depth reporting as well as book reviews on this subject. We are always in the market for good photos, sharp and clear, action photos of boxing, football and baseball. We cover all major league ball parks during the baseball and football seasons. We are accredited to the Mets, Yanks, Jets and Giants. During the winter we cover basketball and hockey and all sports events at the Nassau Coliseum."
Photos: Purchased on assignment; captions required. Uses "good quality 8x10 b&w glossies; good choice of angles and lenses." Pays $7.50 minimum for b&w photos.

NEWSPAPER ENTERPRISE ASSOCIATION, INC., 200 Park Ave., New York NY 10017. (212)557-5870. Executive Editor: David Hendin. Estab. 1902. Syndicates material to newspapers. Query or submit complete ms. SASE. Reports in 3 weeks. Buys all rights.
Needs: Newspaper columns and features; fillers; and comics. Will consider article series. Pays $25 and up. Photos should accompany all submissions; no additional payment.

NEWS WORLD SYNDICATE, 401 5th Ave., New York NY 10016. (212)532-8300. Editor-in-Chief: Harold F. Fuller Jr. Estab. 1977. "We have purchased 9 columns this year and as the syndicate grows, we will buy more columns and feature articles;" for use in daily and weekly newspapers. Query with clips of previously published work. Submissions will not be returned; "they will be filed for future consideration. This way the writer always has a chance with us." Reports in 4-6 weeks. Buys first North American and Philippine serial rights.
Needs: Newspaper features (will consider all types, 900 words maximum); newspaper columns (all types, 900 words maximum); and fiction (1,500 words maximum; submit to Larry Moffitt). Will consider article series of 5-6 parts, 900 words/part. Pays 50% author's percentage. Currently syndicates Pop, Rock, and Soul, by Irwin Stambler (popular music); Through A Woman's Eye, by Edith Carter (viewpoints); and Spin Off, by Harold Fuller (jazz music).

NORTH AMERICAN NEWSPAPER ALLIANCE, 200 Park Ave., New York NY 10017. Executive Editor: Sidney Goldberg. Editor: Sheldon Engelmayer. Supplies material to leading U.S. and Canadian newspapers, also to South America, Europe, Asia and Africa. Rights purchased vary with author and material. May buy all rights, or first rights, or second serial (reprint) rights. Pays "on distribution to clients." Query first or submit complete ms. Reports in 2 weeks. SASE.
Nonfiction and Photos: In the market for background, interpretive and news features. Life style trends, national issues that affect individuals and neighborhoods. The news element must be strong and purchases are generally made only from experienced, working newspapermen. Wants timely news features of national interest that do not duplicate press association coverage but add to it, interpret it, etc. Wants first-class nonfiction suitable for feature development. The story must be aimed at newspapers, must be self-explanatory, factual and well condensed. It must add measurably to the public's information or understanding of the subject, or be genuinely entertaining. Broad general interest is the key to success here. Length: 300 to 800 words. Rarely buys columns. Looking for good 1-shots and good series of 2 to 7 articles. Where opinions are given, the author should advise, for publication, his qualifications to comment on specialized subjects. The news must be exclusive to be considered at all. Length: 800 words maximum. Rate varies depending on length and news value. Minimum rate $25, but will go considerably higher for promotable copy. Buys 8x10 glossy photos when needed to illustrate story, pays $5 to $10.

NUMISMATIC INFORMATION SERVICE, Rossway Rd., Rt. 4, Box 232, Pleasant Valley NY 12569. Editor: Barbara White. Estab. 1961. Buys 5 features/year. Query. SASE. Reports in 1-2 weeks. Buys all rights.
Needs: Newspaper columns (anything related to numismatics and philately, particularly the technical aspects of the avocations); news items (relative to the world of coin and stamp collecting); and fillers (on individual coins or stamps, or the various aspects of the hobbies). Pays $5/500 word article; 50¢ additional payment for b&w photos accepted with ms.

OCEANIC PRESS SERVICE, Box 4158, North Hollywood CA 91607. Editor: John Taylor. Buys from 12-15 writers annually, "using their published work" for use in magazines, newspapers or books. Query with clips of published work. SASE. Reports in 3 weeks. Buys all rights, or second serial (reprint) rights. Writer's guidelines $1.

Needs: "We like authors and cartoonists but, for our mutual benefit, they must fit into our editorial policies. The following list will give an idea of the kind of materials we want: interviews or profiles (world figures only); recipes, with color transparencies or b&w pictures; home building and home decoration features with photos; haristyle features with photos; published cartoons and cartoon books; interviews with movie and TV stars with photos; current books to be sold for translation to foreign markets: mysteries, biographies, westerns, science fiction, romance, psychological, and gothic novels; features on family relations, sex, gambling, heroism, and ecology; features on water sports, with color transparencies; and newspaper columns with illustrations. We are always happy to obtain reprint rights, especially book excerpts or serializations. Payment is outright or on a 50/50 basis. We take care of foreign language translations."

PACIFIC NEWS SERVICE, 604 Mission St., Room 1001, San Francisco CA 94105. (415)986-5690. Editors: Sandy Close, Mark Shwartz, Jon Stewart and Diane Lindquist. Associate Editors: Rasa Gustaitis, Clark Norton and Frank Mrowning. Buys approximately 300 mss/year from between 100-200 writers for syndication to newspapers ranging from major dailies to weeklies and monthlies, including the college and ethnic press and national magazines. Query or submit complete ms. SASE. Photocopied submissions OK. Reports in 2 weeks. Rights purchased vary with author and material; buys first or second serial (reprint) rights.
Needs: News items (uses news stories, features and analyses of issues and trends that are ignored or poorly covered by major media outlets; stories that look behind the news to help illuminate long-range trends in U.S. foreign policy or domestic politics. Style must be suitable for major newspaper readership: clear, concise and without undocumented opinion and rhetoric. Length about 1,000 words. Welcomes submissions from freelancers and others with specialized knowledge on subjects of importance, foreign and domestic, to U.S. readers); and photos (purchased with written material. Captions required). "We need articles examining the outlook for America's third century; top-notch reporting on the future of cities, the search for social justice." Buys occasional article series, but prefers single features. Pays $50 and up for assigned stories; $35 and up for stories submitted on speculation. Photo brings $5-10. Pays on publication.
Tips: "Write for a broad-ranged audience. *PNS* is subscribed to by 150 newspapers across the country, from *The WAshington Post* to *SF Examiner*. Document every assertion. Look for the national angle in any local story or the U.S. angle in any foreign story."

PUNGENT PRAYER, 404 E. Elm, West Frankfort IL 62896. (618)937-2898. Editor: Phil E. Pierce. Estab. 1969. Buys 52 items/year for use in secular newspapers. Query with clips of previously published work or submit complete ms. SASE. Reports in 3 weeks. "Writers may choose to copyright material or not." Writer's guidelines for SASE.
Needs: "*Pungent Prayer* is a weekly feature syndicated to a few secular newspapers. We buy colorful prayers aimed toward the interests of non-churchmen, stories of answered prayer, and once or twice only each year, an inspiring poem about prayer. Our maximum is 300 words or 37 lines (of 51 spaces each). We are not interested in general religious items nor ordinary prayers. The prayers (poetry or prose) should carry human interest—family or personal problems, social concerns, pathos, candor, joy or especially humor. The prayers of children and youth frequently qualify. We welcome special day and holiday prayers (poetry seems to fit here)." Pays $2-8.

THE REGISTER AND TRIBUNE SYNDICATE, INC , 715 Locust St., Des Moines IA 50304. President: Dennis R. Allen. Buys material for syndication in newspapers. Submit complete ms. SASE. Photocopied submissions preferred. Reports in 6 weeks. Buys all rights.
Needs: News items (nonfiction); and photos (purchased with written material). Buys article series "from 500-700 words on current topics such as the metric system, motorcycles, self-improvement programs, seasonal series for Christmas and Easter. Pays in royalties. Pays on publication.

RELIGIOUS NEWS SERVICE, 43 W. 57th St., New York NY 10019. Editor-in-Chief: Lillian R. Block. Managing Editor: Gerald Renner. Supplies material to "secular press, religious press of all denominations, radio and TV stations." Enclose SASE for return of submissions.
Nonfiction and Photos: "Good news stories on important newsworthy developments. Religious news." Will buy single features "if they have news pegs. Most of our article series are produced by our own staff." Length: 200 to 1,000 words. Pays 2¢ a word. Photos purchased with and without features and on assignment; captions required. Uses b&w glossies, preferably 8x10. Pays $5 minimum.

SAWYER PRESS, Box 46-578, Los Angeles CA 90046. Editor: E. Matlen. Buys all rights. Buys 50 cartoons/year. Will consider photocopied submissions. Submit complete cartoons only. Reports in 1 week. SASE.
Cartoons: Editorial cartoons suitable for college newspapers. Sophisticated social commentary. Royalty or outright purchase; varies with quality of material. Also looking for Barbarella/John Wiley/Stanton type of illustrating and cartoon strips, b&w and color.

THE SIMSER GROUP OF COMPANIES OF AMERICA (CANADA), LTD., Box 572A, Weston, Ontario, Canada M9N 3N3. Managing Editor: Ed King. Estab. 1972. Buys "about 600 pieces/year from nearly 200 writers;" for use in magazines, newspapers, and 'owned' publications. Submit complete ms. SASE. Reports in 3 weeks. Buys first North American serial rights.
Needs: Newspaper features (nudes, political or humorous material); magazine columns (interviews and biographies of racing figures and music stars); newspaper features (automotive or pop music oriented); fillers (pop music news items and automotive oriented cartoons and news items); and radio broadcast material (jokes and one-liners). Will consider article series. Pays 60% authors' percentage. Pays $5-250 for 5x7 or 8x10 b&w or color glossy prints accepted with ms. Currently syndicates Record Review, by Justin Tyme; Bio Feedback, and The Automotive Page.

BP SINGER FEATURES, INC., 3164 W. Tyler Ave., Anaheim CA 92801. (714)527-5650. Acting President: Eldon Maynard. Estab. 1940. Syndicates to newspapers, magazines, and book publishers. Query with clips of published work. SASE. Reports in 3 weeks. Buys all rights, or domestic and foreign reprint rights. Writer's guidelines $1.
Needs: Magazine and newspaper features with international interest; fiction slanted to women readers; and fillers (juvenile puzzles, games, and how-to's). Will consider article series if previously published. Pays 50% author's commission. Pays $25-50 for 8x10 b&w photos or 120mm or 4x5 color transparencies. Currently syndicates *Solv-A-Crime*, by A.C. Gordon (mystery series); and *Celebrities Speak*, by J. Finletter (interviews). Serializes books (Romance, Western, mysteries, war, historical romance, doctor-nurse books). Published books only.

SOCCER ASSOCIATES, Box 634, New Rochelle NY 10802. Managing Director: Irma Ganz Miller. Estab. 1947. Query. SASE. Reports in 2 weeks. Buys all rights.
Needs: Newspaper features. Payment "varies with assignment." Currently syndicates *Soccer Shots; Book Reviews; and New Products.*

SUMMIT PRESS SYNDICATE, 918 N. 4th St., Milwaukee WI 53202. Contact: Patrick or Maureen Reardon. Estab. 1976. "We will pick up a maximum of 4 standing features (columns, cartoons, etc.) a year. We intend to never get so big that we can't give our contributors' careers a great deal of special and personal attention. The usual outlet is newspapers, but we have syndicated a TV and radio show and will also deal with magazines." Query. SASE. Reports in 4 weeks.
Needs: Magazine features and columns; newspaper features and columns; new items (must be significant topic of national interest); fiction (book excerpts for Black Life package); and radio and TV broadcast material. Will consider article series; "on any subject suitable for newspapers, including lifestyle, sports, how-to, etc." Pays 50% of profits on standing columns and series. Buys b&w glossy photos with ms. Currently syndicates Black Life (modular package of features); Chalk, by Cissie Peltz (multi-media cartoon); and Chasing a Career, by Kirby Stanat (job column).

TEENAGE CORNER, INC., 37-688 Peacock Circle, Rancho Mirage CA 92270. President: David J. Lavin. Estab. 1959. Buys 122 items/year for use in newspapers. Submit complete ms. Reports in 1 week. Material is not copyrighted.
Needs: 500 word newspaper features. Pays $25.

TRANS-WORLD NEWS SERVICE, INC., Box 2801, Washington DC 20013. (202)638-5568. Managing Editor: G. Richard Ward. Estab. 1924. "We purchase or market 8,000-10,000 articles a year internationally." Query with clips of published work. SASE. Reports in 4-6 weeks. Buys all rights. Writer's guidelines for SASE.
Needs: Newspaper features (400-750 words, prefers balanced articles); newspaper columns (400-800 words; most any subject with continuity); fillers (10-60 words; any suitable subject); radio broadcast material (recorded programs for syndication or scripts 2-30 minutes in length). Buys one-shot features on science, travel, women's material or collectibles. Article series not to

exceed 6 in series, average 450-800 words on political, historical, consumer expose, etc. Pays 50% commission or $25-200. Pays $10-100 for 5x7 or larger b&w glossy photos accepted with ms. Currently syndicates *The Handicapped*, by M. Becker (health); *Miracle of Faith*, by G. Katz (religion); and *International Dateline*, by W. Halterman.

UNITED FEATURE SYNDICATE, 200 Park Ave., New York NY 10017. Managing Editor: Sidney Goldberg. Supplies material to newspapers throughout the world. Will handle copyrighted material. Buys 25 to 50 series per year, preferably 3 to 7 articles (world rights preferred). Buys first and/or second rights to book serializations. Query first with outline. Reports in 3 months. SASE.
Nonfiction, Comic Strips and Puzzles: News, features, series, columns, comic strips, puzzles. Current columnists include Jack Anderson, Marquis Childs, Henry Taylor, Virginia Payette, Barbara Gibbons. Comic strips include Peanuts, Nancy, Tarzan. Rates negotiable for one-shot purchases. Standard syndication contracts are offered for columns and comic strips.

UNITED PRESS INTERNATIONAL (UPI), 220 E. 42nd St., New York NY 10017. Editor-in-Chief: H.L. Stevenson. "We seldom, if ever, accept material outside our own ranks."

U.S. NEWS SERVICE, Suite 1006, International Bldg., 1800 K St., N.W., Washington DC 20006. Bureau Chief: Walter Fisk. Buys all rights. May handle copyrighted material. May not return rejected material. Enclose S.A.S.E. for return of submissions.
Nonfiction, Humor, Fiction, Photos, Fillers, and Poetry: Buys single features and column ideas. Length varies. Payment varies. 8x10 single weight glossies purchased with features, without features, and on assignment. Captions required.

UNIVERSAL PRESS SYNDICATE, 6700 Squibb Rd., Mission KS 66202. Editor: James F. Andrews. Buys syndication rights. Reports normally in 4 weeks. SASE.
Nonfiction: Looking for features—columns for daily and weekly newspapers. "Any material suitable for syndication in daily newspapers." Currently handling the following: Doonesbury by G.B. Trudeau, Garry Wills column, etc. Payment varies according to contract.

UNIVERSAL TRADE PRESS SYNDICATE, 85 South St., New York NY 10038. Editor: Paul Gruberg. Buys first trade paper rights only. Query first. SASE.
Nonfiction: Buys art features in all fields; fine art merchandising at the retail level; features on galleries, museums, artists. Length: 1,250 words. Pays 65%.

DOUGLAS WHITING LIMITED, 930 De Courcelle St., Montreal H4C 3C8, Que., Canada. Editor: D.P. Whiting. Supplies material to "all major dailies in Canada and many in the United States." Buys all newspaper rights. No query required. Reports in 4 to 6 weeks. Enclose SAE and International Reply Coupons.
Nonfiction: Science panels, contest promotions, puzzle features and feature columns. "The freelancer should look for ideas and content that are unique. Too much of the sample material received by us is very similar to established syndicated features. Bear in mind, too, that we are a Canadian syndicate. Most of the material received is too American." Does not buy single features. Length: 150 to 250 words, daily columns; 700 to 1,000 words, weekly columns. "Usually author's share is 40% of net after production costs are deducted. Costs do not include our sales calls and promotion material."

WILLIAMS NEWSPAPER FEATURES SYNDICATE, INC., Box 8005, Charlottesville VA 22906. (804)293-4709. Vice President/Art Director: Jean S. Lindsay. Estab. 1939. Buys 52 features/year for use in newspapers. Query. SASE. Reports in 2 weeks. Buys all rights.
Needs: Newspaper features and religious advertising copy suitable for illustration. Pays $25. Pays $25 for photos purchased with accompanying ms; "must be suitable for 4-5 column reproduction in newspapers." Currently syndicates You in the Church; The Church in You.

WILSON FEATURES, Box 369, Marysville OH 43040. President: Rick Wilson. Estab. October 1974. Buys approximately 50-100 cartoons, fillers, editorial features and informational columns for use in newspapers and magazines. Query with clips of previously published work. SASE. Reports in 2-3 weeks. Buys second serial (reprint) rights.
Needs: Newspaper features columns, and fillers. Pays 50% author's percentage. Currently syndicates Tornado, by Rick Wilson (informational cartoon strip); Editorial cartoons, by Dana Summers, and From the Kitchen Shelf, by Doris Smith (cooking column).

WOMEN'S NEWS SERVICE, 200 Park Ave., New York NY 10017. Editor: Sidney Goldberg. Buys 300 features/year for syndication for newspapers. Query or submit complete ms. SASE. Reports in 3 weeks. Buys all rights, first rights, or second serial (reprint) rights.
Needs: News items (news features, backgrounders, sidebars to events in the news of interest to women's and lifestyles pages; best length is 400-600 words); fiction (outline of plot and description of characters, with one sample chapter); fillers (news-pegged fillers preferred, 100-150 words; of interest to women's and lifestyle pages) and photos (purchased with written material; captions required). Considers "series of 3-6 articles, 700 words or so each. Series should be pegged on news event or a trend, unless service oriented." Pays minimum of $150 for series; $25 minimum for one-shots "higher depending on importance or interest;" $5-15 for fillers. Photos bring $5-15 for b&w glossies.
Tips: "Put your headline material in your lead, keep your stories short; avoid folksy essays, type accurately with plenty of space for editing. If we like your one-shots and use them frequently, we'll be open to a percentage arrangement."

WORLD-WIDE NEWS BUREAU, 309 Varick St., Jersey City NJ 07302. Editor: Arejas Vitkauskas. Enclose SASE for return of submissions.
Nonfiction: "Our multiple writeups (separate, and in our weekly columns), start in greater New York publications, then go simultaneously all over the U.S.A. and all over the world where English is printed. News from authors, or literary agents, or publishers on books planned, or ready, or published. Anything from poetry and children's books, to space technology textbooks. We cover over eighty different trade fields."

ZODIAC NEWS SERVICE, 950 Howard St., San Francisco CA 94103. (415)956-3555. Editor: Jon Newhall. Estab. 1972. "We purchase about 1,000 pieces of material from a loose network of 100+ stringers in the United States and Canada, for radio use mainly, with a few magazines, newspapers, and TV stations." Submissions returned "if specifically requested. We usually assume SASE's are for payment, not return of submissions, so please note otherwise." Buys first North American serial rights; "we want exclusive rights for 48 hours." Writer's guidelines for SASE.
Needs: "We are a reliable source of up-to-date news which is often ignored, overlooked, or misinterpreted by the major wire services. Our clients are primarily radio stations, ranging from progressive FM and college radio outlets to top-40 and all-news formats. Although we are based in San Francisco, our coverage is international, and so, we are looking for stringers world-wide. If you have story leads, ideas or news items that can be reported in a radio format (i.e., within the frustrating confines of 200 words) please telephone or mail them to our San Francisco office. We pay $10 for each story lead or item used. Most of our successful stringers receive regular payments by spotting ZNS-type items, which are often overlooked by the major wire services in daily or weekly publications."

Trade, Technical, and Professional Journals

Trade magazines make up one of the most diverse and challenging segments of the freelance market, ranging from *Convenience Store News* to *Search and Rescue Magazine*. They are numerous, and they pay moderately well. And often they don't require as much technical expertise as you might think.

For instance, Dave Kaiser is an editor at one trade magazine and a stringer for about a dozen other periodicals. But he's not afraid of diving into new trade specialties. "Heck, no," says Kaiser, the managing editor of *Swimming Pool Age/Weekly*. "As long as you have the basic reporting skills, it shouldn't be any problem at all."

That's apparently the key to successful trade freelancing: solid reporting. Although some trade magazines are probably too specialized for the general writer (and their listings usually indicate this), others are open to the freelancer who can grasp a subject quickly and write clearly and tightly.

Most trade journals appeal to one of three audiences: *retailers*, who are interested in unusual store displays, successful sales campaigns, etc.; *manufacturers*, who want stories on how one plant solved an industry problem, how certain equipment performed in production; and *professionals and industry experts*, interested in technical developments.

Whatever its audience, the trade magazine has one purpose: to help its reader do his job better. *Your* job is to find successful businesses in your area — and explain to the reader in detail what accounts for their success.

Where can you find story ideas? "If it's wet, that's where the ideas are," says David R. Getchell, editor of *National Fisherman*. "One of every two people you stop on the waterfront has probably got a first-rate story in him — and he doesn't even know it, in most cases. Almost all of the businesses and certainly all of the boats have stories. It's just the ability to sound out the story."

Kitchen Business advises: "Just go ahead and do it. Select the best-looking kitchen firm in your area, go in and tell the boss you're a writer and want to do a story for *Kitchen Business*. Interview him on a single how-to-do-it topic, shoot some pictures to illustrate the points in the interview, and take a chance. . . . It will work for anyone who has any reporting talent at all."

Take a walk through the Yellow Pages, suggests Kaiser of *Swimming Pool Weekly/Age*. "Hop on the wire and call the builder and say, 'Do you have any special sales methods?' "

But "the most valuable thing around is the daily newspaper," says Kaiser. Ben Russell, editor of *American Laundry Digest*, thinks the freelancer can find more than hamburger bargains by flipping through the ads. A creative advertisement indicates a creative plant owner, he says. "Usually it pays off to go in and talk to him."

Ginny Ade, a freelancer with a specialty in camping articles, suggests that the writer begin with the library. Read back copies and make notes on the kinds of articles the camping magazines use; then look for like articles at trade conventions and campgrounds. But Ade adds, "I get the greatest share of my ideas when I go camping."

Generally, of course, the freelancer must approach the editor — but sometimes the editor may approach *you* if you make your presence known. When Kaiser needs a writer in a certain area, he may call a local newspaper for names. So let your newspaper know you're available as a freelancer — both to that paper and to magazines.

"Don't worry about style," says *American Laundry Digest*. "What we want is good writing. We like a lead that grabs the reader's attention, logical development, copy free of cliches, and completeness (all significant details included)."

Although trade magazines want simple writing, they won't tolerate sloppy writing. *Specialty & Custom Dealer* rejects "hyperbolic accounts of business. Those that read like public relations releases. Broad generalizations concerning 'a great product' without technical data behind the information. Lack of detail concerning business operations."

But any trade magazine welcomes concise and informative writing, based on detailed interviewing. Minding the other guy's business can be good business for you.

Accounting

CGA MAGAZINE, #700-535 Thurlow St., Vancouver, British Columbia, Canada V6E 3L2. (604)681-3538. 25% freelance written. For accountants and financial managers. Magazine published 9/year; 44 pages. Circ. 25,000. Pays on acceptance. Buys one-time rights. Phone queries OK. Simultaneous and photocopied submissions OK. SASE. Reports in 2-4 weeks. Free sample copy and writer's guidelines.
Nonfiction: "Accounting and financial subjects of interest to highly qualified professional accountants as opposed to accountants in public practice. All submissions must be relevant to Canadian accounting. All material must be of top professional quality, but at the same time written simply and interestingly." How-to; humor; informational; personal experience; personal opinion; and technical. Buys 36 mss/year. Query. Length: 1,500-2,000 words. Pays $100-500.
Photos: State availability of photos with query. Offers no additional payment for 8x10 b&w glossy prints.

Advertising and Marketing

Trade journals for professional advertising executives, copywriters and marketing men are listed in this category. Those whose main interests are the advertising and marketing of specific products (such as Groceries or Office Equipment and Supplies) are classified under individual product categories.

AD TECHNIQUES, ADA Publishing Co., 19 W. 44 St., New York NY 10036. (212)986-4930. Managing Editor: Elaine Louie. 10% freelance written. For advertising executives. Monthly magazine; 50 pages. Estab: 1965. Circ: 4,500. Pays on acceptance. Not copyrighted. Reports in 1 month. Sample copy 85¢.
Nonfiction: Articles on advertising techniques. Buys 10 mss/year. Query. Pays $25-50.

ADVERTISING AGE, 740 N. Rush, Chicago IL 60611. Managing Editor: L.E. Doherty. Currently staff-produced.

ART DIRECTION, Advertising Trade Publications, Inc., 19 W. 44 St., New York NY 10036. (212)986-4930. Managing Editor: Elaine Louie. 15% freelance written. Emphasis on advertising design for art directors of ad agencies (corporate, in-plant, editorial, freelance, etc.). Monthly magazine; 100 pages. Estab: 1949. Circ: 12,000. Pays on publication. Buys one-time rights. SASE. Reports in 3 months. Sample copy $1.50.
Nonfiction: How-to articles on advertising campaigns. Pays $25 minimum.

THE COUNSELOR, 2nd & Clearview Aves., Trevose PA 19047. Editor-in-Chief: Paul Camp. Managing Editor: Carol Keough. 10% freelance written. Emphasizes advertising specialties. Monthly magazine; 200 pages. Estab. 1954. Circ. 5,000. Pays on publication. Buys first North American serial rights. Simultaneous, photocopied and previously published submissions OK. Reports in 1 month. Free writer's guidelines; mention *Writer's Market* in request.
Nonfiction: How-to (sell, write ad copy and design imprints); new product; nostalgia (old advertising items); and travel. Buys 2 mss/issue. Query or submit clips of previously published

work. Length: 1,000 words. Pays $75-100.
Fillers: Short humor. Buys 5 mss/issue. Length 25-75 words. Pays $5.

INCENTIVE MARKETING/INCORPORATING INCENTIVE TRAVEL, Bill Communications, Inc., 633 Third Ave., New York NY 10017. (212)986-4800. Editor-in-Chief: Murray Elman. For buyers of merchandise used in motivational promotions. Monthly magazine; 200 pages. Estab: 1905. Circ: 37,000. Pays on acceptance. Buys all rights, but may reassign following publication. SASE. Reports in 2 weeks. Free sample copy and writer's guidelines.
Nonfiction: Informational, case histories. Buys 60-75 mss a year. Query. Length: 1,500 words minimum. Pays $85-125.

MAC/WESTERN ADVERTISING, 6565 Sunset Blvd., Los Angeles CA 90028. Editor: Lee Kerry. For "people involved in advertising: media, agencies, and client organizations as well as affiliated businesses." Weekly. Buys all rights. Pays on acceptance. Reports in 1 month. Query. SASE.
Nonfiction and Photos: "Advertising in the West. Not particularly interested in success stories. We want articles by experts in advertising, marketing, communications." Length: 1,000-1,750 words. Pays $100. Photos purchased with mss.

MARK II, THE SALES AND MARKETING MANAGEMENT MAGAZINE, 2175 Sheppard Ave., E., Suite 110, Willowdale, Ontario, Canada MJ2 1W8. Editor/Publisher: Harold L. Taylor. For "Canadian marketing, sales management, advertising, and agency executives." Buys first rights. Pays on publication. Free sample copy. Reports "in a few days." Enclose SAE and International Reply Coupons.
Nonfiction: "Case histories, conceptual articles. Innovative; lively style. Should have a Canadian slant. Not a market for beginners." Pays $50 for 600-1000 words; $125 for 1,500-2,000 words.

THE PRESS, 302 Grote St., Buffalo NY 14207. (716)876-6410. Editor-in-Chief: Janet Tober. 90% freelance written. For advertising men/women at retail stores, newspapers, and advertising agencies. Bimonthly tabloid; 8-12 pages. Estab. January 1977. Circ. 3,000. Pays on acceptance. Buys all rights, but may reassign following publication. Phone queries OK. Simultaneous, photocopied and previously published submissions OK. SASE. Reports in 4 weeks. Sample copy with writer's guidelines 50¢.
Nonfiction: "College stories, about scholarships, college students in Europe exchange programs, unusual occupation, continuing education, travel, resorts, music, art, and vacations that would be interesting to businessmen. Short biographies on artists, politicians, businessmen, entertainers, and sport figures. Hobbies or leisure time activities such as yachting, skiing and backpacking. Literature and history (old homes in America)." Query. Length: 800-1,000 words. Pays $100-250.
Photos: State availability of photos with query. No additional payment for b&w or color prints. Buys all rights, but may reassign following publication.

SALES & MARKETING MANAGEMENT, 633 Third Ave., New York NY 10017. (212)986-4800. Editor: Robert H. Albert. For sales and marketing and other business executives responsible for the sale and marketing of their products and services. Magazine published 17 times a year. Established in 1918. Circulation: 43,168. Buys all rights. Buys the occasional outstanding article on selling and marketing; domestic and international. Payment on publication. Will send free sample copy to writer on request. Reports in 2 weeks. Query first. Enclose S.A.S.E.
Nonfiction: "Articles on the sales and marketing operations of companies, concerning the evaluation of markets for products and services; the planning, packaging, advertising, promotion, distribution and servicing of them, and the management and training of the sales force." Informational, how-to, personal experience, interview, profile, humor, think pieces, expose, spot news, successful business operations, new product, merchandising techniques, technical. Length: 500 to 1,800 words. Payment negotiable.

VISUAL MERCHANDISING, S.T. Publications, 407 Gilbert Ave., Cincinnati OH 45202. Editor: Richard Faust. Emphasizes store design and display. Monthly magazine; 72 pages. Circ: 9,500. Pays on publication. Submit seasonal or holiday material 8 months in advance. Simultaneous, photocopied and previously published submissions OK. SASE. Reports in 1 month. Sample copy $1; free writer's guidelines.
Nonfiction: Expose, how-to (display), informational (store design, construction, merchandise display), interview (display directors and shop owners), nostalgia (store architecture, display,

etc.), profile (new and remodeled stores), new product, photo feature (window display), technical (store lighting, carpet, wallcoverings, fixtures). Buys 24 mss a year. Query or submit complete ms. Length: 500-2,000 words. Pays $75-125.
Photos: Purchased with or without accompanying ms or on assignment. Pays $5 for 5x7 b&w glossies. Submit contact sheet. Seeks photos or general subjects on lighting, planning, design and merchandising.
How To Break In: "Be fashion and design conscious and reflect that in the article. Submit finished mss with photos always. Look for stories on department store display directors (profiles, methods, views on the industry, sales promotions and new store design or remodels)."

Agricultural Equipment and Supplies

CUSTOM APPLICATOR, Little Publications, 6263 Poplar Ave., Suite 540, Memphis TN 38138. Editor: Tom Griffin. For "firms that sell and custom apply agricultural chemicals." Circ. 17,000. Buys all rights. Pays on publication. "Query is best. The editor can help you develop the story line regarding our specific needs." SASE.
Nonfiction and Photos: "We are looking for articles on custom application firms telling others how to better perform jobs of chemical application, develop new customers, handle credit, etc. Lack of a good idea or usable information will bring a rejection. If the idea is good and the information is good (developed), we can always run it through a typewriter." Length: 1,000-1,200 words "with 3 or 4 b&w glossies." Pays 10¢/word.

FARM SUPPLIER, Watt Publishing Co., Sandstone Bldg., Mount Morris IL 61054. (815)734-4171. Editor-in-Chief: Ray Bates. For retail farm supply dealers and managers over the U.S. Monthly magazine; 64 pages. Estab: 1927. Circ: 20,000. Pays on acceptance. Buys all rights in competitive farm supply fields. Phone queries OK. Submit seasonal or holiday material 3 months in advance. Photocopied submissions OK. SASE. Reports in 2 weeks.
Nonfiction: How-to; informational; interview; new product; and photo feature. "Articles emphasizing product news, how new product developments have been profitably re-sold, or successfully used." Buys 20 mss/year. Query. Length: 300-1,500 words. Pays $20-100. "Longer articles must include photos, charts, etc."
Photos: Purchased with accompanying ms. Submit 5x7 or 8x10 b&w prints; 35mm or larger color transparencies. Total purchase price for a ms includes payment for photos.

Architecture

Architects and city planners whose primary concern is the design of buildings and urban environments are the target audience for the journals in this category. Those that emphasize choice of materials, structural details, and methods of constructing buildings are classified in the Construction and Contracting category.

INLAND ARCHITECT, 1800 S. Prairie, Chicago IL 60616. Editor: M. W. Newman. For architects, planners, engineers, people interested in architecture (buffs) or urban affairs. Monthly magazine; 36 (8½11) pages. Established in 1957. Not copyrighted. Buys 24 mss a year. Payment on publication. Will send sample copy to writer for $1. Will not consider photocopied submissions. Will consider simultaneous submissions. Two triple-spaced copies of each submission are required. Reports in 1 month. Query first. Enclose S.A.S.E.
Nonfiction and Photos: "Articles cover appraisal of distinguished buildings, profiles of individual architects and firms, historic buildings and preservation, related education, architectural philosophy, interior design and furnishing, building technology, architectural education, economics of the architectural field, and the business operation of an architect's office. In addition, periodic articles concern such urban matters as city planning, housing, transportation, population shifts, and ecology. The emphasis is regional (Chicago and Illinois) with occasional forays into the greater Midwest. Approach should be one of serious criticism and investigative journalism in journalistic style." Length: flexible, but is usually 1,000 to 2,500 words. Pays $50 to $100. B&w glossy photos are purchased with mss; no additional payment. Captions (and identifications) required.

PROGRESSIVE ARCHITECTURE, 600 Summer St., Stamford CT 06904. Editor: John M. Dixon. Monthly. Buys first-time rights for use in architectural press. Pays on publication. SASE.

Nonfiction and Photos: "Articles of technical professional interest devoted to architecture and community design and illustrated by photographs and architectural drawings. Also use technical articles, which are prepared by technical authorities and would be beyond the scope of the lay writer. Practically all the material is professional, and most of it is prepared by writers in the field who are approached by the magazine for material." Pays $50-$250. Buys one-time reproduction rights to b&w and color photos.

Auto and Truck

The journals below aim at automobile and truck dealers, repairmen, or fleet operators. Publications for highway planners and traffic control experts are classified in the Government and Public Service category. Journals for traffic managers and transportation experts (who route goods across the continent) will be found in Transportation.

AUTO LAUNDRY NEWS, Columbia Communications, 370 Lexington Ave., New York NY 10017. (212)532-9290. Editor-in-Chief: J.R. Peterson. For sophisticated carwash operators. Monthly magazine; 52 pages. Estab: 1925. Circ: 18,000. Pays on publication. Buys all rights. Phone queries OK. Submit seasonal/holiday material 60 days in advance. Photocopied and previously published submission OK. SASE. Reports in 4 weeks. Free sample copy.
Nonfiction: How-to; historical; humor; informational; new product; nostalgia; personal experience; technical; interviews; photo features; and profiles. Buys 40 mss/year. Query. Length: 1,500-3,000 words. Pays $75-175.

AUTOMOTIVE NEWS, 965 E. Jefferson Ave., Detroit MI 48207. Editor: Robert M. Lienert. For management people in auto making and auto dealing. Weekly. Estab. 1925. Circ. 60,000. Buys all rights. Pays on acceptance. Free sample copy. Query. SASE.
Nonfiction and Photos: News material valuable to the auto trade. "Current and complete familiarity with the field is essential, so we don't use much freelance material." Articles must be accurate with the emphasis on the how rather than the what. Ideas must be helpful to dealers, and written in a news style. Pays $3 inch of type (about 50 words). Photos are purchased with mss.

AUTOMOTIVE REBUILDER MAGAZINE, Babcox Publications, Inc. 11 S. Forge St. Akron OH 44304. (216)535-6117. Editor-in-Chief: Andrew J. Doherty. Assistant Editor: Paul R. Grant. Emphasizes the automotive and heavy duty mechanical/parts rebuilding industry and jobber machine shops. Monthly magazine: 90 pages. Estab. 1964. Circ. 17,000. Pays on publication. Buys all rights. Phone queries OK. Submit seasonal/holiday material 6 weeks in advance of issue date. Simultaneous, photocopied and previously published submissions OK. SASE. Reports in 2 weeks. Free sample copy.
Nonfiction: How-to (technical writing); humor (we particularly like humor, must be relevant to rebuilders); historical (historical automotive); inspirational (concentrate on how a rebuilder overcomes disaster or personal handicap); interview (concentrate on growth or success stories); nostalgia (only if it applies to rebuilding); personal experience (experiences with rebuilding); personal opinion (comment on legislation affecting rebuilders); photo feature (on machine shops, try to get people in photos, we want photo journalism, not photo illustration); profile (about individual rebuilder; perhaps the small rebuilder); technical (you must know what you're talking about, rebuilders don't just fall off Christmas trees) and articles on regulation at the state and local level (excise tax, zoning laws). Buys 2 mss/year. Query. Length: 500-1,500 words. Pays 4-6¢/word.
Columns/Departments: People (profile or close-up of industry figures welcome); Tech Notes (this entails technical how-to writing); new product (we generally do this ourselves); and The Forum Guest (opinions on current events relevant to rebuilders). Buys 1 ms/year. Query. Length: 200-1,500 words. Pays 4-6¢/word. Open to suggestions for columns/departments.

THE BATTERY MAN, Independent Battery Manufacturers Association, Inc., 100 Larchwood Dr., Largo FL 33540. (813)586-1409. Editor-in-Chief: Dan A. Noe. Emphasizes SLI battery manufacture, applications, new developments. For battery manufacturers and retailers (garage owners, servicemen, fleet owners, etc.). Monthly magazine; 24 pages. Estab. 1919. Circ. 7,000. Pays on acceptance. Buys all rights. Submit seasonal/holiday material 2 months in advance. Simultaneous, photocopied and previously published submissions OK. SASE. Reports in 2 weeks. Free sample copy.
Nonfiction: Technical articles. Submit complete ms. Length: 1,200-1,500 words. Pays $70-90.

BRAKE & FRONT END SERVICE, 11 S. Forge St., Akron OH 44304. (216)535-6117. Editor: Jeffrey S. Davis. 5-10% freelance written. For owners of automotive repair shops engaged in brake, wheel, suspension, chassis and frame repair, including: specialty shops; general repair shops; new car and truck dealers; gas stations; mass merchandisers and tire stores. Monthly magazine; 68 pages. Estab: 1931. Circ: 28,000. Pays on publication. Buys all rights. SASE. Reports immediately. Sample copy and editorial schedule $1.
Nonfiction and Photos: Specialty shops taking on new ideas using new merchandising techniques; growth of business, volume; reasons for growth and success. Expansions, and unusual brake shops." Query. Length: about 1,500-2,000 words. Pays 7-9¢/word. Pays $5 for b&w glossies purchased with mss.

CANADIAN AUTOMOTIVE TRADE MAGAZINE, MacLean-Hunter, Ltd., 481 University Ave., Toronto, Ontario, Canada M5W 1A7. (416)595-1811. Editor-in-Chief: Edward Belitsky. 30% freelance written. Emphasizes the automotive aftermarket and for mechanics, service station and garage operators, new car dealers and parts jobbers. Monthly magazine; 60 pages. Estab: 1919. Circ: 39,000. Pays on publication. Buys all rights, but may reassign following publication. Phone queries OK. Submit seasonal/holiday material 2 months in advance. Photocopied submissions OK. SASE. Reports in 2 months. Free sample copy and writer's guidelines.
Nonfiction: Informational; new product; technical; interviews; and profiles. "We can use business articles every month from the 4 corners of Canada. Service articles can come from anywhere." Buys 3 mss/issue. Length: 600-1,400 words. Pays $40-160.
Photos: Purchased with accompanying ms. Captions required. Send contact sheet and/or transparencies. Pays $5-20 for 4x5 b&w prints or 35mm color transparencies. Model release required.

CANADIAN DRIVER/OWNER, 481 University Ave., Toronto, Ont., Canada M5W 1A7. (416)595-1811. Editor: Simon Hally. 50% freelance written. For owner/operators of heavy-duty trucks in Canada. Bimonthly magazine; 48 pages. Estab. 1972. Circ. 17,000. Rights purchased vary with author and material. Usually buys first rights. Buys 25 to 30 mss/year. Pays on acceptance. Free sample copy. Reports in 1-2 weeks. Query or submit complete ms. SAE and International Reply Coupons.
Nonfiction and Photos: Articles on trucks, truck components, maintenance and repair, small business management, CB radio, legal aspects of trucking, country music, etc. Informal, light style. Special emphasis on the Canadian independent trucking scene since the publication is aimed exclusively at Canadian owner-operators, as opposed to company drivers, truck fleets or U.S. truckers. Material on brokers' contracts and new federal (Canadian) highway vehicle legislation would be of interest. Length: 500-1,200 words except for how-to material which usually runs 200-1,200 words. Pays 8-12¢/word. B&w photos purchased with or without mss, or on assignment. Pays according to quality. Captions required.

CANADIAN ROAD KNIGHT, 475 St. Andrews St. W., Fergus, Ontario, Canada N1M 1P2. (519)843-5900. Editor-in-Chief: Ted Stevens. Managing Editor: Sherry Clarke. 65% freelance written. Emphasizes the Canadian trucking industry. Monthly magazine: 48 pages. Estab. April 1971. Circ. 7,000. Pays on publication. Buys one-time rights. Phone queries OK. Submit seasonal/holiday material 30-45 days in advance of issue date. Simultaneous, photocopied and previously published submissions OK. Reports in 3 weeks. Free sample copy; mention *Writer's Market* in request.
Nonfiction: Interested in all subjects as long as the theme is trucking. Buys 2-3 mss/issue. Query or submit complete ms. Length: open. Pays $5-50.
Photos: Submit photos with accompanying ms. Pays $2-7 for b&w prints; $25 for color transparencies (for front cover only). Buys one-time rights.
Fiction: Adventure; experimental; historical; humorous; mainstream; mystery; and suspense. Buys 1 ms/year. Query. Length: open. Pays $5-50.
Fillers: Puzzles (crossword and anagrams). Pays $5-10.

THE CHEK-CHART SERVICE BULLETIN, Box 6227, San Jose CA 95150. Editor-in-Chief: Ken Layne. Managing Editor: Gordon Clark. 20% freelance written. Emphasizes trade news and how-to articles on automobile service for professional mechanics. Monthly newsletter; 8 pages. Estab. 1929. Circ. 20,000. Pays on acceptance. Buys all rights. Submit seasonal/holiday material 3-4 months in advance of issue date. SASE. Reports in 2 weeks. Free sample copy and writer's guidelines; mention *Writer's Market* in request.
Nonfiction: "The *Service Bulletin* is a trade newsletter, *not* a consumer magazine. How-to

articles and service trade news for professional auto mechanics, also articles on merchandising automobile service. No 'do-it-yourself' articles." Buys 1-2 mss/issue. Query. Length: 700-1,100 words. Pays $75-125.
Photos: State availability of photos with query. Offers no additional payment for photos accepted with ms. Uses 8x10 b&w glossy photos. Captions and model release required. Buys all rights.

COMMERCIAL CAR JOURNAL, Chilton Way, Radnor PA 19089. Editor: James D. Winsor. Monthly. Buys all rights. Pays on acceptance. "Query first with article outline." Enclose SASE.
Nonfiction: "Articles and photo features dealing with management, maintenance, and operating phases of truck and bus fleet operations. Material must be somewhat specialized and deal with a specific phase of the operation." Length: open. Pays $50 to $150.
Photos: "Occasionally use separate photos with captions." Pays $10-25.

CONOCO TODAY, Box 2197, Houston TX 77001. Editor: John H. Walker. Continental Oil Company. Bimonthly. Buys all rights. Pays on acceptance. Free sample copy. Query first. Reports at once. SASE.
Nonfiction: Conoco service station operation and wholesale distributor operations, news and ideas. Length: 1,000 words. Pays 7¢ a word.
Photos: Purchased with mss. B&w 8x10, pays $10.

FLEET MAINTENANCE & SPECIFYING, 7300 N. Cicero, Lincolnwood IL 60646. (312)588-7300. Editor: Tom Gelinas. For those directly responsible for specification, purchase, repair and maintenance of on-road vehicles of 10,000 GVW or more. Monthly magazine. Estab. 1974. Circ. 50,000. Buys all rights. Pays on publication. Free sample copy. Photocopied submissions OK. Reports as soon as possible. SASE.
Nonfiction and Photos: Articles on troubleshooting repair and maintenance of trucks. Articles on fleets and their maintenance programs; management technique stories. "Our publication is technically oriented. Our only interest is in generally superior work." Does not want to see product-oriented job stories, but will consider industry reports or articles on safety. Length: 2,000 to 5,000 words. Pays $25 per printed page minimum, without photos. Pays extra for 4-color transparencies. No additional payment is made for large format transparencies used with articles.

GO WEST MAGAZINE, 1240 Bayshore Highway, Burlington CA 94010. Editor-in-Chief: Bill Fitzgerald. Managing Editor: James Sterling. 15% freelance written. Emphasizes truck transport. Monthly magazine; 80 pages. Estab. 1941. Circ. 51,000. Pays on acceptance. Buys all rights. Phone queries OK. Submit seasonal/holiday material 6 months in advance of issue date. SASE. Reports in 2 weeks. Free sample copy; mention *Writer's Market* in request.
Nonfiction: Exposé; general interest; historical; how-to; humor; interview; and new product. Buys 2 mss/issue. Query. Length: 500-3,500 words. Pays $200-600.
Photos: State availability of photos with query. Pays $5-15 for b&w photos; $100 for 2¼x2¼ color transparencies. Captions required. Buys all rights.

JOBBER NEWS, Wedham Publications, Ltd., 109 Vanderhoof Ave., Toronto, Ontario, Canada M4G 2J2. (416)425-9021. Editor-in-Chief: Sam Dixon. Emphasizes auto parts merchandising and management for owners and managers of automotive wholesaling establishments, warehouse distributors, and engine rebuilding shops in Canada. Monthly magazine; 58 pages. Estab. 1932. Circ. 8,000. Pays on acceptance. Buys all rights. Phone queries OK. Submit seasonal/holiday material 2 months in advance. Simultaneous, photocopied, and previously published submissions OK. SASE. Reports in 2 weeks. Free sample copy and writer's guidelines.
Nonfiction: How-to articles. Must have authentic Canadian application. Query. Length: 2,000-3,000 words. Pays $50-125.

JOBBER/RETAILER, Bill Communications, Box 5417, Akron OH 44313. Editor: Sarah Frankson. 10% freelance written. "Readership is the independent automotive parts jobber who has entered the world of retailing to the automotive do-it-yourselfer. Editorial slant is merchandising/marketing with news secondary." Monthly tabloid; 56 pages. Estab. April 1977. Circ. 31,000. Pays on publication. Buys all rights, but may reassign following publication. Submit seasonal/holiday material 1-2 months in advance of issue date. Simultaneous, photocopied and previously published submissions OK. SASE. Free sample copy and writer's

guidelines; mention *Writer's Market* in request.
Nonfiction: How-to (merchandising do-it-yourself auto parts, store layout and design, transforming traditional jobber facilities to retail operations as well); interview (of jobber/retailers who have done an excellent job in retail merchandising or a particular item or product line); and technical (on do-it-yourself repairs). Submit complete ms. Length: 2,500 words maximum. Pays $125-175.

JOBBER TOPICS, 7300 N. Cicero Ave., Lincolnwood IL 60646. (312)588-7300. Articles Editor: Jack Creighton. For automotive parts and supplies wholesalers. Monthly. Buys all rights. Pays on acceptance. Query with outline. SASE.
Nonfiction and Photos: Most editorial material is staff written. "Articles with unusual or outstanding automotive jobber procedures, with special emphasis on sales and merchandising; any phase of distribution. Especially interested in merchandising practices and machine shop operation." Length: 2,000 words maximum. Pays 4¢ a word minimum. 5x7 or 8x10 b&w glossies purchased with mss.

MAGIC CIRCLE, c/o Aitkin-Kynett, 4 Penn Center, Philadelphia PA 19102. For the automobile mechanic in his own shop, in the service station, fleet garage, repair shop or new car dealership. Company publication of the Dana Corporation. Magazine; 20 pages. Established in 1955. Quarterly. Circulation: 80,000. Buys all rights, but will reassign rights to author after publication. Buys 2 or 3 mss a year. Pays on acceptance. A free sample copy will be sent only if a viable query is sent at the same time. Will consider photocopied submissions and may consider simultaneous submissions. Reports in 2 weeks. Query first. Enclose SASE.
Nonfiction and Photos: "Articles on anything that will make the mechanic a better, more efficient, more profitable mechanic and businessman. We need a light style, but with plenty of detail on techniques and methods." Informational, how-to, travel, successful business operations, merchandising techniques, technical articles. Length: 500 to 2,000 words. Pays $150 maximum. B&w and color photos are purchased with or without ms. Captions required. Pays $25 for b&w 8x10 glossies; $50 for 2¼x2¼ or 35mm color.

MERCHANDISER, Amoco Oil Company, P.O. Box 6110-A, Chicago IL 60680. Editor: Robert P. Satkoski. For Amoco service station dealers, jobbers. Quarterly. Circulation: 30,000. Buys all rights, but will reassign after publication. Buys 3 or 4 mss a year. Pays on publication. Query recommended. Enclose SASE.
Nonfiction and Photos: Short, to-the-point, success stories and how-to stories, that will trigger creative thinking by the reader. Storylines are most often in the merchandising, motivational, and educational areas. Length: 750 words maximum. Payment varies, with minimum of $100. Uses b&w and color photos

MODERN BULK TRANSPORTER, 4801 Montgomery Lane, Washington DC 20014. (301)654-8802. Editor: Don Sutherland. 10% freelance written. For "management of companies operating tank motor vehicles which transport liquid or dry bulk commodities." Monthly. Buys first rights only. Pays on acceptance. Will consider photocopied submissions, but "we're prejudiced against them." Enclose SASE.
Nonfiction and Photos: "Articles covering the tank truck industry; stories concerning a successful for-hire tank truck company, or stories about use of tank trucks for unusual commodities. We especially seek articles on successful operation of tank trucks by oil jobbers or other so-called 'private carriers' who transport their own products. Approach should be about specific tank truck problems solved, unusual methods of operations, spectacular growth of a company, tank truck management techniques, or other subjects of special interest. Articles should speak to management of companies operating tank trucks, *in their terms,* not to truck drivers. Simple description of routine operations not acceptable." Length: 1,000-3,000 words, "preferably accompanied by pictures." Pays minimum 5¢/word. Pays minimum $30/published page "for general articles exclusive in trucking field only (such as maintenance and mechanical subjects)." Pays minimum $25 for reporter assignments — producing fact sheet for rewrite. Pays $7 for 8x10 or 5x7 glossies purchased with exclusive features.

MODERN TIRE DEALER, Box 5417, 77 N. Miller Rd., Akron OH 44313. (216)867-4401. Editor: Stephen LaFerre. For independent tire dealers. Monthly magazine. Pays on publication. Buys all rights. Photocopied submissions OK. Query. Reports in 1 month. SASE.
Nonfiction, Photos, and Fillers: "How TBA dealers sell tires, batteries, and allied services, such as brakes, wheel alignment, shocks, mufflers. The emphasis is on merchandising. We prefer the writer to zero in on some specific area of interest; avoid shotgun approach." Length: 1,500

words. Pays $50-$100. 8x10, 4x5, 5x7 b&w glossies purchased with mss. Pays $5. Buys 300-word fillers. Pays $5 to $10.

MOTOR, 1790 Broadway, New York NY 10019. Editor: J. Robert Connor. For automobile service and repairshop operators, dealer service managers. Monthly. Buys all rights. Pays on acceptance. Query first. Reports in 1 week. Enclose SASE.
Nonfiction: Specializes in service and repair of both domestic and foreign cars for professional mechanics. Merchandising, sales promotion and management articles containing ideas that can be adapted by independent garages and service stations. Emphasis on how-to material. Wants stories on wholesalers, jobbers, and interviews with executives for 8-page section in Aftermarket Journal edition. Length: 1,200-1,500 words. Pays $100-300; sometimes higher for exceptional pieces.
Photos: Purchased with mss or with captions, of interest to readership. 8x10 glossies. Pays $25 for single b&w photo; $400 for cover color photo.

MOTOR NORTH MAGAZINE, 6215 Brooklyn Dr., Minneapolis MN 55430. (612)566-6437. Publisher: Gary Jacobson. For service stations, automotive repair garages, parts jobbers, car dealers, fleets. Magazine; 48 pages. Established in 1972. Monthly. Circulation: 12,900. Rights purchased vary with author and material. Usually buys all rights, but may reassign rights to author after publication. Buys 5 to 10 mss a year. Pays on publication. Will send sample copy to writer on request. Will consider photocopied and simultaneous submissions. Submit seasonal material 3 months in advance. Reports on material accepted for publication in 1 month. Returns rejected material at time of decision. Query first or submit complete ms. Enclose SASE.
Nonfiction and Photos: Technical, sales-oriented, and human interest material relating to the automotive parts and service industry. Articles on transportation-related subjects; fuel shortage, etc. Seasonal material pertaining to automobiles, such as winter-starting, is used. Pays $10 to $40, depending on subject matter. Tips for mechanics used in columns and departments. Length: 1 to 2 double-spaced, typewritten pages. Pays 2¢ a word. Will also accept suggestions for new columns and departments. B&w (8x10) or color (3x5 or 8x10) purchased with mss. Pays $10 for b&w; $20 for color. Captions required.

MUFFLER DIGEST, 1036 S. Glenstone, Springfield MO 65804. (417)866-3917. Editor: J. M. Ryan. For professional installers and manufacturers of exhaust systems and exhaust system components. Monthly magazine; 60-80 pages. Estab. 1976. Circ. 10,000. Pays on acceptance. Buys all rights, but may reassign following publication. Simultaneous and photocopied submissions OK. SASE. Reports in 1 week. Free sample.
Nonfiction: How-to; humor (in the muffler field); informational; interview (good interviews with shop owners); and profile (industry people). "We're not interested in 'How I Got Ripped Off at....' types of features." Buys 6-10 mss/year. Submit complete ms. Length: 1,000-1,500 words. Pays 3-5¢/word.
Photos: Purchased with accompanying ms. Captions required. Query. Pays $5 for b&w photos.
Columns/Departments: How-To column (could be a shop-talk type of article). Query. Length: 500 words. Pays 3-5¢/word.
How To Break In: "We are covering the professional exhaust system installer in the U.S., Mexico, and Canada. When we talk about professional we are talking about muffler specialty shops—Midas, Tuffy and other franchise chain operators as well as independents. We are not interested in service stations, Sears, Wards, etc. We would prefer to see more stories on successful independent installers; how they got started, what special tricks have they picked up, what is their most successful merchandising tool, etc."

NTDRA DEALER NEWS, 1343 L St., N.W., Washington DC 20005. Editor: Donald L. Thompson. 1-2% freelance written. For tire dealers and retreaders. Publication of the National Tire Dealers & Retreaders Association. Weekly magazine; 24 pages. Established in 1935. Circulation: 7,500. Occasionally copyrighted, depending on content. Buys 10 to 15 mss a year. Will send free sample copy on request. Wil consider photocopied and simultaneous submissions. Reports immediately. Query first. Enclose SASE.
Nonfiction: Articles relating to retailing and marketing, with special emphasis on the tire dealer, retreader and small businessman in general. "Industry news, business aids, new products. Dealer and consumer comments regarding this industry. Most articles received are of too general interest." Uses informational, technical, how-to, interview, think pieces and material on successful business operations and merchandising techniques. Pays $150 to $200.

O AND A MARKETING NEWS, Box 765, LaCanada CA 91011. (213)790-6554. Editor: Don

McAnally. 5% freelance written. For "service station dealers, garagemen, TBA (tires, batteries, accessories) people, oil company marketing management." Bimonthly. Circ. 15,000. Not copyrighted. Pays on publication. Reports in 1 week. SASE.
Nonfiction and Photos: "Straight news material; management, service, and merchandising applications; emphasis on news about or affecting markets and marketers within the publication's geographic area of the 7 western states. No restrictions on style or slant. We could use straight news of our industry from some western cities, notably Las Vegas, Reno, and Salt Lake City." Query. Length: maximum 1,000 words. Pays $1/column inch (about 2¢ a word). Photos purchased with or without mss; captions required. Pays $5.

OHIO TRUCK TIMES, Mezzanine Floor, Neil House Hotel, Columbus OH 43215. Editor: David F. Bartosic. Publication of the Ohio Trucking Association. Quarterly. Buys material for exclusive publication only. Pays on publication. Free sample copy. Reports in 30 days. SASE.
Nonfiction: Modern developments in truck transportation, particularly as they apply to Ohio industry and truck operators. Submit complete mss. Length: 1,500 words. Pay negotiable.
Photos: With mss or with captions only. Transportation subjects. Pay negotiable.

OPEN ROAD, 1015 Florence St., Fort Worth TX 76102. Editor: Chris Lackey. For "professional over-the-road truck drivers of America." Monthly. Buys North American serial rights. Pays on publication. Will send a sample copy to a writer on request. Query first. Reports in 2 to 4 weeks. Enclose SASE.
Nonfiction and Photos: "Pieces on truck drivers—articles about new model heavy trucks and equipment, acts of heroism, humor, unusual events, special driving articles, advice to other drivers, drivers who do good jobs in community life or civic work, etc." Recently sponsored two special events: selection of an outstanding woman trucker, "Queen of the Road," for 1978; and Truck Drivers Country Music Awards Competition, a national poll among professional truck drivers, picked outstanding artists in 10 country music categories. Length: "prefer 1,000 to 1,500 words, usually." Pays "about 6¢ a word." 5x7 or 8x10 b&w glossies purchased with mss. Pays $5 to $10, depending on quality and newsworthiness, "more for covers."

OWNER OPERATOR MAGAZINE, Chilton Co., 1 Chilton Way, Radnor PA 19089. (215)687-8200. Editor-in-Chief: Brant Clark. Managing Editor: Leon E. Witconis. 20% freelance written. For one truck owner/operators. Bimonthly magazine; 160 pages. Estab. 1970. Circ. 100,000. Pays on publication. Buys all rights, but may reassign following publication. Submit seasonal/holiday material 6 months in advance of issue date. Previously published submissions OK. SASE. Reports in 3 weeks. Sample copy $1.25.
Nonfiction: Exposé (government, unions, trucking companies, brokers, trucking associations); historical (trucking industry); how-to (perform maintenance, repairs or fix-up on heavy duty trucks); humor; interview (top trucking officials or unusual occupations in trucking); personal experience (only from truckers); photo feature (occupational, with pix); profile; and technical (truck). Buys 3-4 mss/issue. Submit complete ms and clips of previously published work. Length: 600 words maximum. Pays $50-300.
Photos: Submit photos with accompanying ms. Payment included in ms price. Uses 8x10 b&w prints. Buys all rights, but may reassign following publication. Model release required.
Columns/Departments: Chatterbox (interviews with owner/operators at truck stops with pix). Buys 6/year. Query. Length: 300-450 words. Pays $150-200.

REFRIGERATED TRANSPORTER, 1602 Harold St., Houston TX 77006. (713)523-8124. 5% freelance written. Monthly. Not copyrighted. Pays on publication. Reports in 1 month. Enclose SASE.
Nonfiction and Photos: "Articles on fleet management and maintenance of vehicles, especially the refrigerated van and the refrigerating unit; shop tips; loading or handling systems, especially for frozen or refrigerated cargo; new equipment specifications; conversions of equipment for better handling or more efficient operations. Prefer articles with illustrations obtained from fleets operating refrigerated trucks or trailers." Pays minimum $45 per page or $2 per inch.
Fillers: Buys newspaper clippings. "Do not rewrite."

SERVICE STATION AND GARAGE MANAGEMENT, 109 Vanderhoof Ave., Suite 101, Toronto, Ont. M4G 2J2, Canada. Editor: Frank Fragan. For "service station operators and garagemen in Canada only." Estab. 1956. Monthly. Circ. 24,000. Buys first Canadian serial rights. Buys 1 or 2 articles a year. Pays on acceptance. Sample copy for 50¢. Query first. Reports in 2 days. Enclose SAE and International Reply Coupons.
Nonfiction and Photos: "Articles on service station operators in Canada only; those who are

doing top merchandising job. Also on specific phases of service station doings: brakes, tune-up, lubrication, etc. Solid business facts and figures; information must have human interest angles. Interested in controversial legislation, trade problems, sales and service promotions, technical data, personnel activities and changes. No general, long-winded material. The approach must be Canadian. The writer must know the trade and must provide facts and figures useful and helpful to readers. The style should be easy, simple, and friendly—not stilted.'' Length: 1,000 words. Pays 4¢ to 5¢ a word average, ''depending on the topic and the author's status.'' Photos purchased with mss and without mss ''if different or novel''; captions required. Pays $5 for 5x7 or 8x10 b&w glossies.

SOUTHERN AUTOMOTIVE JOURNAL, 1760 Peachtree Rd., N.W., Atlanta GA 30357. (404)874-4462. Editor: William F. Vann. For service stations, auto dealers, garages, body shops, fleets, warehouse distributors, machine shops, and parts jobbers. Monthly. Buys all rights. Sample copy for $1. Query first. Enclose SASE.
Nonfiction and Photos: ''Articles of interest to the automotive aftermarket.'' Length: open. Payment varies. Photos purchased with ms.

SOUTHERN MOTOR CARGO, Box 4169, Memphis TN 38104. Editor: William H. Raiford. For ''trucking management and maintenance personnel of private, contract, and for-hire carriers in 16 southern states (Ala., Ark., Del., Fla., Ga., Ky., La., Md., Miss., N.C., Okla., S.C., Tenn., Tex., Va., and W. Va.) and the District of Columbia.'' Special issues include ''ATA Convention,'' October; ''Transportation Graduate Directory,'' December; ''Mid-America Truck Show,'' February. Monthly. Circ. 40,000. Buys first rights within circulation area. Pays on publication. Free sample copy. Reports ''usually in 3 weeks.'' SASE.
Nonfiction: ''How a southern trucker builds a better mousetrap. Factual newspaper style with punch in lead. Don't get flowery. No success stories. Pick one item, i.e. tire maintenance, billing procedure, etc., and show how such-and-such carrier has developed or modified it to better fit his organization. Bring in problems solved by the way he adapted this or that and what way he plans to better his present layout. Find a segment of the business that has been altered or modified due to economics or new information, such as 'due to information gathered by a new IBM process, it has been discovered that an XYZ transmission needs overhauling every 60,000 miles instead of every 35,000 miles, thereby resulting in savings of $$$ over the normal life of this transmission.' Or, 'by incorporating a new method of record keeping, claims on damaged freight have been expedited with a resultant savings in time and money.' Compare the old method with the new, itemize savings, and get quotes from personnel involved. Articles must be built around an outstanding phase of the operation and must be documented and approved by the firm's management prior to publication.'' Length: 1,500-3,500 words. Pays minimum 4¢ a word for ''feature material.''
Photos: Purchased with cutlines; glossy prints. Pays $5.

SPECIALTY & CUSTOM DEALER, Babcox Publishing, 11 S. Forge St., Akron OH 44304. (216)535-6117. Editor: Walt Frazier. ''Audience is primarily jobbers and retailers of specialty automotive parts and accessories. Average reader has been in business for 10 years, and is store owner or manager. Educational background varies, with most readers in the high school graduate with some college category.'' Monthly magazine; 56 pages. Estab. 1965. Circ. 20,000. Pays on publication. Buys all rights. Submit seasonal or holiday material 90 days in advance. SASE. Reports in 6 weeks. Sample copy $1.50.
Nonfiction: Publishes informational (business techniques), interview, new product, profile, and technical articles. ''No hyperbolic accounts of business or those that read like public relations releases. No broad generalizations concerning a 'great product' without technical data behind the information. Lack of detail concerning business operations.'' Buys 24 mss a year. Query. Length: 1,000-2,000 words. Pays $50-100.
How To Break In: ''For the most part, an understanding of automotive products and business practices is essential. Features on a specific retailer, his merchandising techniques and unique business methods are most often used. Such a feature might include inventory control, display methods, lines carried, handling obsolete products, etc.''

TIRE REVIEW, 11 S. Forge St., Akron OH 44304. (216)535-6117. Editor: William Whitney. For ''independent tire dealers and retreaders, company stores, tire company executives, some oil company executives.'' Monthly. Circulation: 34,000. Buys first rights. Buys 6 or 7 mss a year. Pays on publication. Will send a free sample copy to a writer on request. Query first. Reports in 1 week. Enclose SASE.
Nonfiction and Photos: ''Tire industry news, including new product news, research and market-

ing trends, legislative news, features on independent tire dealers and retreaders, news of trade shows and conventions, tire and related accessory merchandising tips. All articles should be straightforward, concise, information-packed, and not slanted toward any particular manufacturer or brand name. Must have something to do with tires or the tire industry, particularly independent dealers doing brake and front-end services." Length: "no limitations." Pays 4-5¢/word. B&w glossies purchased with and without mss. Pays "$5 a photo with story, $8.50 for photos used alone."

TODAY'S TRANSPORT INTERNATIONAL/TRANSPORTE MODERNO, International Publications, Inc., 15 Franklin St., Westport CT 06880. (203)226-7463. Editor: Martin Greenburgh. 100% freelance written. Emphasizes "fleet operations and materials handling for vehicle fleet operators and materials handling executives in 150 developing countries in Africa, Asia, Middle East, and Latin America." Bimonthly magazine; 48-72 pages. Estab. 1953. Circ. 39,000. Pays on acceptance. Buys all rights, but may reassign following publication. Phone queries OK. Previously published submissions OK. SASE. Free sample copy and writer's guidelines.
Nonfiction: How-to (run a fleet, specify equipment, etc.); informational (fleet operations, new technologies); interview (with fleet executives discussing problem solving); photo feature (fleets and materials handling); and technical (vehicle/bus/truck systems, fork lifts, material handling) articles. Buys 24-30 a year. Query. Length: 1,500-3,000 words. Pays $150-200. No articles about US or developed countries without direct relevance to the 3rd world.
Photos: Purchased with accompanying ms. Captions required. Query. Total purchase price for a ms includes payment for photos.
Columns/Departments: Materials Handling (tips and methods for materials handling personnel.) Buys 1 ms/issue. Query. Length: 750-1,500 words. Pays $75-100. Open to suggestions for new columns or departments.
How To Break In: "Articles must be written for readers in the 3rd world. Avoid U.S.-oriented approach. Our readers are administrators and executives — address them."

TOW-AGE, Box 2627, Framingham MA 01701. (617)879-0383. Editor: J. Kruza. For readers who run their own service business. Published every 6 weeks. Circ. 15,000. Buys all rights, but may reassign to author after publication. Buys about 12 mss/year. Pays on acceptance. Sample copy $1; free writer's guidelines. Photocopied and simultaneous submissions OK. Reports in 1-4 weeks. SASE.
Nonfiction and Photos: Articles on business, legal and technical information for the towing industry. "Light reading material; short, with punch." Informational, how-to, personal experience, interview, profile. Query or submit complete ms. Length: 200 to 800 words. Pays $20 to $40. Spot news and successful business operations. Length: 100 to 500 words. Pays $20. Technical articles. Length: 100 to 1,000 words. Pays $20. Regular columns sometimes use material of 200 to 400 words. Pays $20. Up to 8x10 b&w photos purchased with or without mss, or on assignment. Pays $15 for first purchase; $5 for each additional purchase.

WARD'S AUTO WORLD, 28 W. Adams, Detroit MI 48226. (313)962-4433. Editor-in-Chief: David C. Smith. Managing Editor: Erwin Maus III. 10% freelance written. For top and middle management in all phases of auto industry. Monthly magazine; 72 pages. Estab. 1965. Circ. 60,000. Pays on publication. Buys all rights. Phone queries OK. Submit seasonal/holiday material 1 month in advance of issue date. SASE. Reports in 2 weeks. Free sample copy and writer's guidelines.
Nonfiction: Exposé; general interest; historical; humor; interview; new product; nostalgia; personal experience; photo feature; and technical. No consumer-type articles. Buys 12 mss/year. Query. Length: 2,000-4,000 words. Pay $200-600.
Photos: Submit photo material with query. Pay varies for 8x10 b&w prints or color transparencies. Captions required. Buys all rights.

WAREHOUSE DISTRIBUTION, 7300 N. Cicero Ave., Lincolnwood, Chicago IL 60646. (312)588-7300. Editor: Syd Cowan. For "businessmen in the auto parts distribution field who are doing above one million dollars business per year." Published 10 times/year. Circ. 27,000. Buys all rights. Pays on publication. Most material is staff written. Reports "within a reasonable amount of time." SASE.
Nonfiction and Photos: "Business management subjects, limited to the automotive parts distribution field." Query. Length: 1,500-2,000 words. Pays 4¢-10¢ a word, "based on value to industry and the quality of the article." Photos purchased with and without mss; captions required. Wants "sharp 5x7 prints." Pays maximum $6.

WAREHOUSE DISTRIBUTOR NEWS, 11 S. Forge St., Akron OH 44304. Editor: John B. Stoner. 10% freelance written. For warehouse distributors and redistributing jobbers of automotive parts and accessories, tools and equipment and supplies (all upper management personnel). Magazine; 60 pages. Estab. 1967. Monthly. Circ. 14,000. Rights purchased vary with author and material. May buy all rights or simultaneous rights. Buys about 12 mss/year. Pays on publication. Sample copy $1. Photocopied and simultaneous submissions OK. Reports at once. SASE.
Nonfiction and Photos: Automotive aftermarket distribution management articles and those on general management, success stories, etc., of interest to the industry. Articles on manufacturers and their distributors. Must be aftermarket-oriented. Each issue centers around a theme, such as rebuilt parts issue, import issue, materials handling issue, etc. Schedule changes yearly based on developments in the industry. Does not want to see freelance material on materials handling, or product information. Would be interested in merchandising articles; those on EDP startup, and interviews with prominent industry figures. Query. Length: open. Pays 5-9¢/word. B&w (5x7) photos purchased with or without ms. Captions required.

Aviation and Space

In this category are journals for aviation businessmen and airport operators and technical aviation and space journals. Publications for professional and private pilots are classified with the Aviation magazines in the Consumer Publications section.

AIRPORT SERVICES MANAGEMENT, Lakewood Publications, 731 Hennepin Ave., S., Minneapolis MN 55403. (612)333-0471. Managing Editor: Richard A. Coffey. 20% freelance written. Emphasizes management of airports and airport business. Monthly magazine; 50 pages. Estab. June 1961. Circ. 20,000. Pays on publication. Buys all rights, but may reassign following publication. Phone queries OK. Submit seasonal/holiday material 3 months in advance of issue date. Photocopied submissions OK. SASE. Reports in 8 weeks. Free sample copy and writer's guidelines.
Nonfiction: How-to (how to manage an aviation business, service organization, work with local governments, etc.); interview (with a successful operator); and technical (how to manage a maintenance shop, snow removal operations, bird control, security operations). "No flying, no airport nostalgia, or product puff pieces. Just plain 'how-to' story lines, please." Buys 10-12 mss/year. Query. Length: 500-1,500 words. Pays $50/published page.
Photos: State availability of photos with query. Payment for photos is included in total purchase price. Uses 5x7 or 8x10 glossy b&w photos.

BUSINESS AND COMMERCIAL AVIATION, Hangar C-1, Westchester County Airport, White Plains NY 10604. Editor: John Olcott. For "corporate pilots and business aircraft operators." Monthly. Circ. 52,000. Buys all rights. Buys "very little" freelance material. Pays on acceptance. Sample copy $1. Reports "as soon as an evaluation is made." SASE.
Nonfiction and Photos: "Our readers are pilots and we have found general articles to be inadequate. Writers with a technical knowledge of aviation would be most suitable." Wants "reports on business aviation operations, pilot reports, etc." Query. Length: "no limits." Pays $100-$300. B&w photos of aircraft purchased with mss. Pays $15-$20. Pays $300 for cover color photos. Uses very little freelance photography.

GENERAL AVIATION BUSINESS, Box 1094, Snyder TX 79549. (915)573-6318. Editor: M. Gene Dow. For people in business phases of general aviation. Tabloid newspaper; 40 pages. Estab. 1973. Monthly. Circ. 16,000. Buys all rights. Pays on acceptance. Sample copy 50¢; free writer's guidelines. Photocopied submissions OK. Reports in 1 month. SASE.
Nonfiction and Photos: Informative, entertaining, technical, how-to, new products, etc., of general aviation (non-airline, non-military). Knowledgeable aviation articles. All types of articles on aviation subjects. Reviews of aviation books. Pays $25 per 1,000 words. Pays $15 for 30 column inches for regular columns or departments. Photos purchased with accompanying ms or on assignment. Captions required. Pays $3 for b&w and color.
Fillers: Aviation subjects. Newsbreaks, clippings, jokes, short humor and informative items. Pays $3.

INTERLINE REPORTER, 2 W. 46th St., New York NY 10036. (212)575-9000. Editor: Eric Friedheim. An inspirational and interesting magazine for airline employees. Buys first serial rights. Query first. SASE.

Nonfiction and Photos: Wants nontechnical articles on airline activities; stories should be slanted to the sales, reservations and counter personnel. Articles on offbeat airlines and, most of all, on airline employees —those who lead an adventurous life, have a unique hobby, or have acted above and beyond the call of duty. Personality stories showing how a job has been well done are particularly welcome. Length: up to 1,200 words. Payment is $50 to $75 for articles with photographic illustrations.

INTERNATIONAL AVIATION MECHANICS JOURNAL, 211 S. 4th St., Basin WY 82410. (307)568-2413. Editor: Will Triol. For governmentally licensed airframe and powerplant mechanics involved in maintaining general aviation airplanes. Monthly magazine; 72 pages. Estab. 1970. Circ. 12,500. Buys all rights, but may reassign rights to author after publication. Pays within 30 days of publication. Free sample copy. Photocopied submissions OK. Reports in 30 days. SASE.
Nonfiction and Photos: Technical articles on aircraft maintenance procedures and articles helping the mechanics to be more efficient and productive. All material should be written from the point of view of an aircraft mechanic, helping him solve common field problems. Buys 30-40 mss/year. Query or submit complete ms. Informational (length: 500-2,000 words. Pays $25-$100); How-to (length: 100 to 500 words. Pays $25); Photo articles (length: 50 to 100 words. Pays $20); and Technical (length: 500 to 4,000 words. Pays $25 to $150).

JET CARGO NEWS, 5314 Bingle Rd., Houston TX 77092. (713)688-8811. Editor: Britt Martin. For "traffic and distribution managers, marketing executives, sales executives, and corporate management who use or may sometime use air transportation to ship their company's products." Established in 1968. Monthly. Circulation: 20,333. Buys all rights. Buys 6 to 10 mss a year. Pays on publication. Will send a sample copy to a writer on request. Write for copy of guidelines for writers. Will not consider photocopied submissions. Submit seasonal material 2 weeks in advance of issue date. Reports within a month, if postage is included. Submit complete ms. Enclose SASE.
Nonfiction and Photos: "Air marketing success stories, cargo rate changes, new ideas on packaging and/or sales. The writer's message should be to the shipper, not to or about airlines. We feel the shipper wants to know how an airline can help him, and that he's not particularly interested in the airline's economics. Use a tight, magazine style. The writer must know marketing. We want depth, how-to material. We don't like the 'gee whiz' approach to product marketing by air. We are not particularly interested in rare items moving by air frieght. Rather, we are interested in why a shipper switches from surface to air transportation." Buys informational articles, how-to's, interviews, and coverage of successful business operations. Length: maximum 2,500 words. Pays 5¢/word; 7¢/word for air marketing success stories. 7x10 b&w glossies purchased with and without mss; captions required. Pays $7.50.

Baking

BAKING INDUSTRIES JOURNAL, Maclaren Publishers, Ltd., Box 109, Davis House, 69-77 High St., Croydon, CR9 1QH, England. (01)688-7788. Editor: Chris Whitehorn. Up to 40% freelance written. For the large scale bakery industry. Monthly magazine; 36 pages. Circ. 2,500. Copyrighted. SAE and International Reply Coupons. Sample copy $1.
Nonfiction: Features on baking and allied subjects. Length: 1,000-3,000 words. Submit complete ms. Pays $60/1,000 words.
Photos: B&w glossies used with mss. Captions required. Query.

PACIFIC BAKERS NEWS, Route 2, Belfair WA 98528. (206)275-6421. Publisher: Leo Livingston. 50% freelance written. Business newsletter for commercial bakeries in the western states. Monthly. Pays on publication. "We don't require SASE."
Fillers: Uses bakery business reports and news about bakers. Buys only brief "boiled-down news items about bakers and bakeries operating only in Alaska, Hawaii, Pacific Coast and Rocky Mountain states. Welcome clippings. Need monthly news reports and clippings about the baking industry and the donut business. "We don't use how-to and think pieces or feature articles." Length: 10 to 200 words. Pays 4¢ a word for clips and news used.
How To Break In: "Send brief news reports or clippings on spot business news about bakers and bakeries in the following western states: California, Arizona, Nevada, New Mexico, Colorado, Utah, Wyoming, Montana, Idaho, Oregon, Washington, Alaska, and Hawaii."

Beverages and Bottling

The following journals are for manufacturers, distributors, retailers of soft drinks and alcoholic beverages. Publications for bar and tavern operators and managers of restaurants are classified in the Hotels, Motels, Clubs, Resorts, and Restaurants category.

BEVERAGE WORLD, 150 Great Neck Rd., Great Neck NY 11021. Editor: Richard V. Howard. (516)829-9210. Monthly magazine; 75 pages. Estab. 1882. Monthly. Buys all rights. Pays on publication. Buys about 6 mss per year. Free sample copy. Will not consider photocopied or simultaneous submissions. Reports in 1 month. SASE.
Nonfiction and Photos: "Articles on any subject pertaining to manufacturers of carbonated and non-carbonated soft drinks, wine or beer. Emphasis should be on sales, distribution, merchandising, advertising, and promotion. Historical articles and 'how-to dissertations' are not desired; no shorts, fillers or rewritten newspaper clippings." Most mss rejected because the writers usually don't have a "thorough understanding of what they're writing about. Pieces often shallow and too generalized." Should be written in crisp, clear style. Pays $35 per printed page (about 1,200 words). "Illustrations should be supplied where possible." Pays $5 for each photo used.

MARYLAND-WASHINGTON BEVERAGE JOURNAL, 2 W. 25th St., Baltimore MD 21218. (301)235-1716. Editor: Anna A. Pumphrey. For retailers in the alcohol beverage industry in Maryland-Washington-Delaware. Monthly magazine; 210 pages. Estab. 1938. Circ. 12,300. Not copyrighted. Buys about 5 mss/year. Pays on publication. Sample copy $1. Simultaneous submissions OK. Submit seasonal material (for December holiday sales) 3 months in advance. Reports promptly. SASE.
Nonfiction and Photos: Articles of local interest regarding the beer, wine, and liquor industry. Biographical stories on local retailers, stories on bars, package goods, restaurants, etc. Emphasis on innovative trends in the industry; articles to interest and educate Maryland-Washington-Delaware retailers. Merchandising trends; advertising; informational, how-to, interview, profile, successful business operations, merchandising techniques. Query or submit complete ms. Length: 1,000-2,000 words. Pays $15-100. No additional payment for b&w photos used with mss.

MICHIGAN BEVERAGE NEWS, 24681 Northwestern Highway, Suite 408, Southfield MI 48075. Editor: Larry Stotz. For "owners of bars, taverns, package liquor stores, hotels, and clubs in Michigan." Semimonthly. Buys exclusive rights to publication in Michigan. Pays on publication. Free sample copy. Reports "immediately." SASE.
Nonfiction and Photos: "Feature stories with pictures. Unusual attractions and business-building ideas in use by Michigan liquor licensees. Profit tips, success stories, etc., slanted to the trade, not to the general public. Especially interested in working with freelancers in Grand Rapids, Flint, Kalamazoo, Marquette, Saulte Ste. Marie, and Bay City areas." Query. Length: 500-750 words. Pays $.75/column/inch. Buys photos of Michigan licensees engaged in business activities. Pays $.75/column inch.

MID-CONTINENT BOTTLER, Box 2298, Shawnee Mission, Kansas City MO 66201. (913)384-0770. Publisher: Floyd E. Sageser. 3% freelance written. For "soft drink bottlers in the 20-state midwestern area." Bimonthly. Not copyrighted. Pays on acceptance. Free sample copy. Reports "immediately." SASE.
Nonfiction and Photos: "Items of specific soft drink bottler interest with special emphasis on sales and merchandising techniques. Feature style desired." Length: 2,000 words. Pays $15-$50. Photos purchased with mss.

MODERN BREWERY AGE, Box 5550, East Norwalk CT 06856. Editorial Consultant: Howard Kelly. For "brewery executives on the technical, administrative, and marketing levels." Bimonthly. Buys North American serial rights. Pays on publication. Reports "at once." SASE.
Nonfiction and Photos: "Technical and business articles of interest to brewers." Query. Length: "no more than 6 or 7 double-spaced typewritten pages." Pays "$35 per printed page (about 3 to 3½ pages double-spaced typewritten ms)." Photos purchased with mss; captions required. Pays $7.50.

REDWOOD RANCHER, 756 Kansas St., San Francisco CA 94107. (415)824-1563. Editor: Sally Taylor. 50% freelance written. For winemakers, grape growers, and other California north coast ranchers. Magazine; 48 pages. Special issues: Vintage (September). Viticulture (February). Established in 1945. Bimonthly. Circulation: 7,000. Buys 20 to 35 mss a year. Pays on publication. Free sample copy (to writers "in our area"). Photocopied and simultaneous submissions

OK. Submit special issue material at least 2 months in advance. Reports on material accepted for publication in 2 to 4 weeks. Returns rejected material as soon as possible. Query first. Enclose S.A.S.E.
Nonfiction and Photos: "All material must be locally oriented." Technical articles on the wine industry viticulturists, and country people. "Down-to-earth, humorous, with technical savvy." Articles on pest control, carbonic maceration, pruning, chemical control, new equipment. Informational, personal opinion, how-to, interview, profile, exposes run from 100 to 3,000 words. Pays $15 to $300. Pays $10 to $150 for historical articles of 100 to 2,000 words. Pays $10 to $50 for spot news, articles on successful business operations, new products, merchandising techniques; technical. Length: 25 to 200 words. 8x10 b&w glossies and color (separations preferred) purchased with mss or on assignment. Pays $7.50 for b&w; $25 for color.

SOUTHERN BEVERAGE JOURNAL, Box 561107, Miami, FL 33156. (305)233-7230. Editor-in-Chief: Raymond G. Feldman. 25% freelance written. For owners of package stores, bars and restaurants throughout the South. Monthly magazine; 100 pages. Estab. 1947. Circ. 21,000. Pays on publication. Buys all rights. Submit seasonal/holiday material 4 months in advance of issue date. Reports in 2 months. Free sample copy and writer's guidelines.
Nonfiction: How-to articles on improving business practices, etc. Buys 12 mss/year. Submit complete ms. Pays 4¢-6/word.
Photos: State availability of photos with ms. Pays $5 for b&w or color prints. Captions preferred. Buys all rights.

WINES & VINES, 703 Market St., San Francisco CA 94103. Editor: Philip Hiaring. For everyone concerned with the wine industry including winemakers, wine merchants, suppliers, consumers, etc. Monthly magazine. Estab. 1919. Circ. 5,500. Buy first North American serial rights or simultaneous rights. Pays on acceptance. Free sample copy. Will not consider photocopied or simultaneous submissions. Submit special material (brandy, January; vineyard, February; champagne, June; marketing, September; aperitif/dessert wines, November) 3 months in advance. Reports in 2 weeks. SASE.
Nonfiction and Photos: Articles of interest to the trade. "These could be on grapegrowing in unusual areas; new winemaking techniques; wine marketing, retailing, etc." Interview, historical, spot news, merchandising techniques, technical. Does not want to see stories with a strong consumer orientation as against trade orientation. Author should know the subject matter, i.e., know proper winegrowing/winemaking terminology. Buys 4-5 ms/year. Query. Length: 1,000-2,500 words. Pays $25- $50. Pays $5-$10 for 4x5 or 8x10 b&w photos purchased with mss. Captions required.

Book and Book Store Trade

AB BOOKMAN'S WEEKLY, Box AB, Clifton NJ 07015. (201)772-0020. Editor-in-Chief: Jacob L. Chernofsky. For professional and specialist booksellers, acquisitions and academic librarians, book publishers, book collectors, bibliographers, historians, etc. Weekly magazine; 160 pages. Estab. 1948. Circ. 8,000. Pays on publication. Buys all rights. Phone queries OK. Submit seasonal or holiday material 1-2 months in advance. Simultaneous and photocopied submissions and previously published work OK. SASE. Reports in 4 weeks. Sample copy $2.
Nonfiction and Photos: How-to (for professional booksellers); historical (related to books or book trade or printing or publishing). Personal experiences, nostalgia, interviews, profiles. Query. Length: 4,000 words minimum. Pays $60 minimum. Photos used with mss.

BOOK COLLECTOR'S MARKET, Box 50, Cooper Station, New York NY 10003. Editor: Denis Carbonneau. For booksellers and book collectors. Bimonthly magazine; 40 pages. Estab. 1975. Circ. 4,800. Buys all rights. Pays on acceptance. Sample copy and writer's guidelines $2.Photocopied submissions OK. Reports almost immediately. SASE.
Nonfiction: "We publish articles about the rare, out-of-print and antiquarian book market from a business/finance point of view. Material must appeal to book collectors and rare book dealers. Emphasis is placed on determining market forces in the trade." Query. Length varies. Pays $25 minimum.

CHRISTIAN BOOKSELLER, Gundersen & Schmale Rd., Wheaton IL 60187. (312)653-4200. Editor-in-Chief: Jan Lokay. 50% freelance written. Emphasizes "any products that are found in the religious bookstore." Monthly magazine; 68 pages. Circ. 10,000. Pays on publication. Phone queries OK. Submit seasonal/holiday material 2½ months in advance of issue date. Photocopied

and previously published submissions OK. SASE. Reports in 2 weeks. Free Sample copy and writer's guidelines.
Nonfiction: "*Christian Bookseller* is a trade magazine serving religious bookstores . Needed are successful business stories—reports of Christian bookstores that are utilizing unique methods of merchandising promotions, have unique departments, etc." Query. Length: 1,500-2,000 words. Pays $60-75.
Photos: "Photos are to accompany successful business stories." State availability of photos with query. Pays $10 for any size b&w prints.

COLLEGE STORE EXECUTIVE, Box 788, Lynbrook, New York NY 11563. (516)887-1800. Editor: Sandra J. Beckerman. 25% freelance written. Emphasizes merchandising and marketing in the college store market. Publishes 10 issues/year tabloid; 40 pages. Estab. 1970. Circ. 10,000. Pays on publication. Buys all rights. Submit seasonal/holiday material 2 months in advance of issue date. Photocopied submissions OK. SASE. Reports in 3 weeks. Sample copy $1; free writer's guidelines; mention *Writer's Market* in request.
Nonfiction: Exposé (on inadequate stores; problems in college market); general interest (to managers); how-to (advertise, manage a store, store profile); inspirational (how to be successful in the college store market); interview (with bookstore managers or people in markevertising); personal experience (someone who worked for a publisher selling to bookstores); personal opinion (from those who know about the market); photo feature (on specific colleges in the country or outside); and technical (how to display products). No articles on the typical college student. Buys 40 mss/year. Query. Length: 1,000 words. Pays 5¢/word.
Photos: State availability of photos with query. Pays $5-10 for any size b&w prints or contact sheets. Captions preferred. Buys all rights.

PUBLISHERS WEEKLY, 1180 Ave. of the Americas, New York NY 10036. Editor-in-Chief: Nat Brandt. Weekly. Buys first North American rights only. Pays on publication. Reports "in several weeks." SASE.
Nonfiction and Photos: "We rarely use unsolicited mss because of the highly specialized audience and their professional interests, but we can sometimes use news items of bookstores or store promotions for books, or stories of book promotion and design." Payment negotiable; generally $50 to $75 per printed page. Photos purchased with and without mss "occasionally."

QUILL & QUIRE, 59 Front St., E., Toronto, Ont. M5E 1B3, Canada. Editor: Susan Walker. 30% freelance written. For professional librarians, writers, booksellers, publishers, educators, media people; anyone interested in Canadian books. Monthly newspaper; 48 pages. Estab. 1935. Circ. 12,000. May buy all rights or second serial (reprint) rights. Buys 120 mss/year. Pays on acceptance. Free sample copy. Reports in 1 week. Enclose SAE and International Reply Coupons.
Nonfiction and Photos: Interviews, profiles, commentary. Strong emphasis on information. Subject must be of Canadian interest. Query. Length: 1,000-2,000 words. Pays $100-350. B&w photos purchased with mss. Pays $15.

Brick, Glass, and Ceramics

AMERICAN GLASS REVIEW, Box 2147, Clifton NJ 07015. (201)779-1601. Editor-in-Chief: Donald Doctorow. Managing Editor: Susan Grisham. 20% freelance written. Monthly magazine; 32 pages. Pays on publication. Phone queries OK. Buys all rights. Submit seasonal/holiday material 3 months in advance of issue date. SASE. Reports in 2-3 weeks. Free sample copy; mention *Writer's Market* in request.
Nonfiction: Technical (problems in the glass industry and supply problems). No articles on glass blowers. Buys 2 mss/issue. Query. Length: 1,000-3,000. Pays $40-50.
Photos: State availability of photos with query. No additional payment for b&w contact sheets. Captions preferred. Buys all rights but may reassign following publication.

AUTO AND FLAT GLASS JOURNAL, 1929 Royce Ave., Beloit WI 53511. Editor: Gretchen E. Weis. For owners and employees of auto glass shops. Monthly magazine; 36 pages. Estab. 1953. Circ. over 3,500. Rights purchased vary with author and material; usually buys all rights. Buys 12 mss/year. Pays on acceptance. Will send sample copy to writer for 50c (plus SASE and 7x10 envelope). Will consider photocopied submissions only with guarantee of priority within the trade. Submit seasonal material 3 months in advance. Reports on material accepted for publication in 2 weeks. Returns rejected material in 10 days. Query first or submit complete ms. SASE.

Nonfiction and Photos: Self-help pieces and successful shop features. Emphasis is on what another shop owner/manager would gain from what a particularly successful owner/manager has to say. Would like to see something on a catchy, successful way of promoting a shop; offbeat angles within the trade. Holiday-oriented features of substance. No locally oriented stories about kind-hearted persons who made good. Length: 1,000 to 2,000 words. Pays minimum of 3¢/word. Buys 8x10 b&w photos, with or without ms. Pays $5.
Fillers: Jokes and short humor related to the trade. Length: 100 words minimum. Pays $5.

BRICK AND CLAY RECORD, 5 S. Wabash Ave., Chicago IL 60603. (312)372-6880. Managing Editor: Phil Jeffers. For "the heavy clay products industry." Monthly. Buys all rights. Pays on publication. Query first. Reports in 15 days. Enclose SASE.
Nonfiction and Photos: "News concerning personnel changes within companies; news concerning new plants for manufacture of brick, clay pipe, refractories, drain tile, face brick, glazed tile, lightweight clay aggregate products and abrasives; news of new products, expansion, new building." Pays minimum 8¢ "a published line. Photos paid for only when initially requested by editor."
Fillers: "Items should concern only news of brick, clay pipe, refractory, or clay lightweight aggregate plant operations. If news of personnel, should be only of top-level plant personnel. Not interested in items such as patio, motel, or home construction using brick; of weddings or engagements of clay products people, unless major executives; obituaries, unless of major personnel; items concerning floor or wall tile (only structural tile); of plastics, metal, concrete, bakelite, or similar products; items concerning people not directly involved in clay plant operation." Pays $3 "per published 2- or 3-line brief item." Pays minimum $3 for "full-length published news item, depending on value of item and editor's discretion. Payment is only for items published in the magazine. No items sent in can be returned."

CERAMIC INDUSTRY, 5 S. Wabash, Chicago IL 60603. Editor: J. J. Svec. For the ceramics industry; manufacturers of glass, porcelain, enamel, whitewares and electronic/industrial newer ceramics. Magazine; 50 to 60 pages. Established in 1923. Monthly. Circulation: 7,500. Buys all rights. Buys 10 to 12 mss a year (on assignment only). Pays on acceptance. Will send free sample copy to writer on request. Reports immediately. Query first. Enclose SASE.
Nonfiction and Photos: Semitechnical, informational and how-to material purchased on assignment only. Length: 500 to 1,500 words. Pays $35 per published page. No additional payment for photos used with mss. Captions required.

CERAMIC SCOPE, Box 48643, Los Angeles CA 90048. (213)939-4821. Editor-in-Chief: Mel Fiske. Managing Editor: Victoria Crenson. 25% freelance written. For "ceramic hobby business people (many emerging housewives, many retired couples) with a love for ceramics but with meager business education." Monthly magazine; 64 pages. Estab. 1964. Circ. 6,300. Pays on acceptance. Buys all rights. Phone queries OK. Submit seasonal/holiday material 3 months in advance of issue date. Simultaneous, photocopied and previously published submissions OK. SASE. Reports in 2 weeks. Free sample copy.
Nonfiction: "Articles on how business principles are applied in ceramic hobby shops, and how they work specifically, with in-depth examples. "We don't need biographical material, or how the business started in the garage or kitchen." Buys 20-25 mss/year. Query with clips of previously published work. Length: 1,000-2,500 words. Pays $100-200.
Photos: State availability of photos with query. Pays $5-10 for 5x7 glossy prints; $25-50 for 35mm color transparencies. Buys all rights.

GLASS DIGEST, 15 E. 40th St., New York NY 10016. (212)685-0785. Editor: Oscar S. Glasberg. Monthly. Buys all rights. Pays on publication "or before, if ms held too long." Will send a sample copy to a writer on request. Reports "as soon as possible." Enclose SASE for return of submissions.
Nonfiction and Photos: "Items about firms in glass distribution, personnel, plants, etc. Stories about outstanding jobs accomplished—volume of flat glass, storefronts, curtainwalls, auto glass, mirrors, windows (metal), glass doors; special uses and values; who installed it. Stories about successful glass/metal distributors, dealers, and glazing contractors—their methods, promotion work done, advertising, results." Length: 1,000 to 1,500 words. Pays 6¢/word, "occasionally more. No interest in bottles, glassware, containers, etc., but leaded and stained glass OK." B&w photos purchased with mss; "8x10 preferred." Pays $6, "occasionally more."
How To Break In: "Find a typical dealer case history about a firm operating in such a successful way that its methods can be duplicated by readers everywhere."

Building Interiors

DECOR, The Magazine of Fine Interior Accessories, 408 Olive, St. Louis MO 63102. (314)421-5445. Managing Editor: G. Cotner. For retailers of art, picture framing and decorative interior accessories. Subscribers include gallery directors/owners, custom and do-it-yourself picture framers, accessories shop owners, and managers of picture/accessories departments in department and home furnishings stores. Monthly magazine; 200 pages. Estab. 1880. Circ. 16,000. Pays on acceptance. Buys exclusive rights. Simultaneous submissions OK. SASE. Reports in 30 days. Submit seasonal/holiday material 3 months in advance of issue date. Sample copy $1; free writer's guidelines.
Nonfiction and Photos: "How-to articles (how to advertise, how to use display space, how to choose product lines, how to use credit) giving, in essence, new and better ways to show a profit. Most often in the form of single store interviews with a successful store manager. No editorializing by the freelancer, unless he has proper credentials. Our emphasis is on useful material, not merely general interest. How does this businessman keep his customers, get new ones, please the old ones, etc." Query. Length: open. Pays $65 to $125. No additional payment for 5x7 or 8x10 b&w photos used with mss.

KITCHEN BUSINESS, 1515 Broadway, New York NY 10036. Editor and Publisher: Patrick Galvin. For "kitchen cabinet and countertop plants, kitchen and bath planning specialists, and kitchen—bath departments of lumber, plumbing, and appliance businesses." Monthly. Buys all rights. Pays on acceptance. Will consider photocopied submissions. Often overstocked. Reports in 1 month. SASE.
Nonfiction and Photos: "Factual case histories with illustrative photos on effective selling or management methods; picture tours of outstanding kitchen showrooms of about 1,000 words; articles on management methods for kitchen distributorships which handle a full range of kitchen products; 'how-to' shop stories on kitchen cabinet shops or countertop fabricators, or stories on how they adapt to growth problems." Length: "600 words and 2 photos to 2,000 words and 10 photos." Pays $100 and up, on a page basis, as estimated at the time of acceptance." Photos purchased with mss.
How To Break In: "Just go ahead and do it. Select the best looking kitchen firm in your area, go in and tell the boss you're a writer and want to do a story for *Kitchen Business*, ask him to let you sit down and read an issue or two, interview him on a single how-to-do-it topic, shoot some pictures to illustrate the points in the interview, and take a chance. Include his phone number so I can check with him. If it's good, you'll get paid promptly. If it shows promise, I'll work with you. If it's lousy, you'll get it back. If it's in between, you might not hear for a while because I hate to send them back if they have any value at all. This worked for me through a dozen years of highly successful freelancing. It will work for anyone who has any reporting talent at all."

PROFESSIONAL DECORATING & COATING ACTION, Painting and Decorating Contractors of America, 7223 Lee Hwy., Falls Church VA 22046. (703)534-1201. Editor/Manager: Heskett K. Darby. Emphasizes professional decorating, painting, wallcovering and sandblasting for painting contractors and their top assistants. Monthly magazine; 48-56 pages. Estab. 1938. Circ. 12,000. Pays on acceptance. Buys all rights, but may reassign following publication. Submit seasonal or holiday material 2 months in advance. SASE. Reports in 3 weeks. Free sample copy.
Nonfiction: Publishes how-to and informational articles. Buys 17-20 mss/year. Query. Length: preferably under 1,000 words. Pays 10¢/word maximum.
Photos: Purchased with accompanying ms. Captions required. Pays $7.50-9.50 for professional quality 8½x11 or 4x5 glossy b&w prints. Model release required.

WALLS AND CEILINGS, 14006 Ventura Blvd., Sherman Oaks CA 91423. (213)789-8733. Editor-in-Chief: Robert Welch. Managing Editor: Don Haley. 10% freelance written. For contractors involved in lathing and plastering, drywall, acoustics, fireproofing, curtain walls, movable partitions and their mechanics; together with manufacturers dealers, and architects. Monthly magazine; 32 pages. Estab. February 1938. Circ. 10,000. Pays on publication. Buys first North American serial rights. Phone queries OK. Submit seasonal/holiday material 3 months in advance of issue date. SASE. Reports in 3 weeks. Sample copy $1.
Nonfiction: How-to (drywall and plaster construction and business management); and interview. Buys 5 mss/year. Query. Length: 200-1,000 words. Pays $75 maximum.
Photos: State availability of photos with query. Pays $5 for 5x7 b&w prints. Captions required. Buys one-time rights. Model release required.

Business Management

The publications listed here are aimed at owners of businesses and top level business executives. They cover business trends and general theory and practice of management. Publications that use similar material but have a less technical or professional slant are listed in Business and Finance in the Consumer Publications section. Journals dealing with banking, investment, and financial management are classified in the Finance category in this section.

Publications dealing with lower level management (including supervisors and office managers) will be found in Management and Supervision. Journals for industrial plant managers are listed under Industrial Management, and under the names of specific industries such as Machinery and Metal Trade or Plastics. Publications for office supply store operators will be found with the Office Equipment and Supplies Journals.

ADMINISTRATIVE MANAGEMENT, Geyer-McAllister Publications, 51 Madison Ave., New York NY 10010. Editor-in-Chief: Walter A. Kleinschrod. Managing Editor: Bea Scala. 33% freelance written. Emphasizes office management and equipment systems. Monthly magazine; 120 pages. Estab. 1939. Circ. 52,900. Pays on publication. Buys all rights. Photocopied submissions OK. Reports in 8 weeks. Sample copy $1.75; free writer's guidelines.
Nonfiction: Exposé (what's wrong with certain management theories or office products); general interest (business operations); and how-to (run an efficient office operation of some kind).
Photos: State availability of photos with query or submit photo material with accompany query. Possible additional payment for b&w prints or contact sheets or color contact sheets. Captions preferred. Buys one-time rights.

EXECUTIVE REVIEW, 224 S. Michigan Ave., Chicago IL 60604. (312)922-4083. Editor-in-Chief: Harold Sabes. 15% freelance written. For management of small and middle-class companies, middle management in larger companies and enterprises. Monthly magazine; 32 pages. Estab. 1955. Circ. 25,000. Pays on publication. Buys one-time and second rights. Submit seasonal/holiday material 6 months in advance of issue date. Simultaneous, photocopied, and previously published submissions OK. SASE. Reports in 4 weeks. Free sample copy and writer's guidelines; mention *Writer's Market* in request.
Nonfiction: How-to (how to do it articles that will be of interest to businessmen in the operation of their companies, and ideas that can be adapted and successfully used by others); interview; personal experience (business); profile; and travel. Buys 7 mss/issue. Submit complete ms. Length: 1,000-1,500 words. Pays $15-50.

HARVARD BUSINESS REVIEW, Soldiers Field, Boston MA 02163. (617)495-6800. Editor: Ralph F. Lewis. For top management in US industry, and in Japan and Western Europe; younger managers who aspire to top management responsibilities; policymaking executives in government, policymakers in noncommercial organizations, and professional people interested in the viewpoint of business management. Published 6 times/year. Buys all rights. Pays on publication. Reports in 2 to 6 weeks. SASE.
Nonfiction: Articles on business trends, techniques and problems. "*Harvard Business Review* seeks to inform executives about what is taking place in management, but it also wants to challenge them and stretch their thinking about the policies they make, how they make them, and how they administer them. It does this by presenting articles that provide in-depth analyses of issues and problems in management and, wherever possible, guidelines for thinking out and working toward resolutions of these issues and problems." Length: 3,000 to 6,000 words. Pays $100.

MARKETING COMMUNICATIONS, United Business Publications, Inc., 475 Park Ave., S., New York NY 10016. Editor-in-Chief: Ronnie Telzer. 70% freelance written. Emphasizes marketing and promotion. Monthly magazine; 90 pages. Estab: 1976. Circ: 25,000. Pays on publication. Buys all rights, but may reassign (with credit to *MC*) following publication. Submit seasonal or holiday material 2-3 months in advance. Photocopied submissions OK (if exclusive). Reports in 2 months. Sample copy $1.50; free writer's guidelines.
Nonfiction: "The preferred format for feature articles is the case history approach to solving marketing problems. Critical evaluations of market planning, premium and incentive programs, point-of-purchase displays, direct mail campaigns, dealer/distributor meetings, media advertising, and sales promotion tools and techniques are particularly relevant." How-to articles

(develop successful product campaigns); informational (marketing case histories); personal opinion (guest editorials by marketing executives); profiles (on a given industry, i.e., tobacco, razors, food); technical articles (technology updates on a field of interest to marketing people). Buys 3 mss/issue. Length: 750-1,250 words. Pays $75-250.
Photos: Prefers 8x10 b&w glossies with mss, or 2¼x2¼ color transparencies; other formats acceptable. Submit prints and transparencies. Captions required. No additional payment.

MAY TRENDS, 111 S. Washington St., Park Ridge IL 60068. (312)825-8806. Editor: J.J. Coffey, Jr. 100% freelance written. For chief executives of businesses, trade associations, government bureaus, Better Business Bureaus, educational institutions, newspapers. Publication of George S. May International Company. Magazine published 3 times a year; 28 to 30 pages. Established in 1967. Circulation: 10,000. Buys all rights. Buys 15 to 20 mss a year. Payment on acceptance. Will send free sample copy to writer on request. Reports on material accepted for publication in 1 week. Returns rejected material immediately. Query first or submit complete ms. Enclose SASE
Nonfiction: "We prefer articles dealing with problems of specific industries (manufacturers, wholesalers, retailers, service businesses) where contact has been made with key executives whose comments regarding their problems may be quoted." Avoid material on overworked, labor-management relations. Interested in small supermarket success stories vs. the "giants"; automobile dealers coping with existing dull markets; contractors solving cost—inventory problems. Will consider material on successful business operations and merchandising techniques. Length: 1,500 to 3,000 words. Pays $100 to $250.

SMALL BUSINESS MAGAZINE, Small Business Service Bureau, Inc., 544 Main St., Box 1441, Worcester MA 01601. (617)756-3513. Editor: Jeanne Blum Kissane. Emphasizes small businesses with 1-100 employees. "Audience is primarily self-employed or small business people with fewer than 50 employees; generally their only interest is surviving and improving their business." Bimonthly magazine; 32 pages. Estab. 1976. Circ. 18,000. Pays on acceptance. Buys all rights, but may reassign following publication. SASE. Reports in 4-6 weeks. Free sample copy.
Nonfiction: How-to (business related, bookkeeping, retail display, direct mail, advertising, etc.); informational (about using government resources, new programs, loan sources, legislation, etc.); interview (legislators and regulators with ties to small business); personal experience (short pieces on how you improved your business — i.e. "how I foiled bad check passers"); Buys 25-30 mss/year. Query. Length: 1,200-2,500 words. Pays $75-200.
Photos: Photos purchased with accompanying ms. Prefers contact sheets and negatives but will accept b&w glossy prints. Total purchase price for a ms includes payment for photos. Captions required.
Columns/Departments: Consultus (how-to, especially on technical and legal subjects). Buys 1 ms/issue. Query. Length: 900-2,000 words. Pays $75-125. Open to suggestions for new columns/departments (except ones on taxes).
How To Break In: "We are looking for people to contribute regularly and grow with us. Please try to be original and easy to read. You would have to be patient with our payment schedule and lack of space, but we do intend to grow fairly rapidly over the next few years."

SMALL BUSINESS NEWSLETTER, 7514 N. 53rd St., Milwaukee WI 53223. Editor/Publisher: Don Ristow. For small business owners and managers. Monthly newsletter; 4 pages. Estab. 1977. Circ. 500. Pays on publication. Buys one-time rights. Submit seasonal/holiday material 1 month in advance of issue date. Simultaneous, photocopied and previously published submissions OK. SASE. Reports in 1 month. Sample copy and writer's guidelines for $1.
Nonfiction: General interest; how-to (cut taxes, improve management, advertise/promote, etc.); inspirational; new product (for small business use); and technical (taxes, administration, other small business interests). Submit complete ms. Pays $10-100.
Fillers: Jokes, gags, and anecdotes (tax or business related). Pays $5.

TRAINING MANAGEMENT MOTIVATION & INCENTIVES, North American Publishing Co., 401 N. Broad St., Philadelphia PA 19180. (215)574-9600. Editor: John Denlinger. 80% freelance written. "Readership is primarily professional training directors and managers interested in seeking ways to improve their firm's training programs through case studies and new products." Published 3 times/year. Magazine; 40 pages. Estab. January 1975. Circ. 47,000. Pays on publication. Buys all rights, but may reassign following publication. Phone queries OK. Submit seasonal/holiday material 2 months in advance of issue date. Photocopied submissions OK. SASE. Reports in 3 weeks. Free sample copy and writer's guidelines; mention *Writer's Market* in request.

Nonfiction: How-to (interested in how other firms are developing successful programs); interview (with someone involved in training development); new product (first person contact or development reports); personal experience (from people involved in setting up and establishing programs); and photo feature (on any facet of training). No light humor or writers' opinions. Buys 15 mss/year. Query or submit complete ms. Length: 1,200-2,500 words. Pays $50-100.
Photos: State availability of photos with query or ms. Offers no additional payment for 5x7 b&w glossy prints. Buys one-time rights. Model release required.

Church Administration and Ministry

THE CHRISTIAN MINISTRY, 407 S. Dearborn St., Chicago IL 60605. (312)427-5380. Editorial Director: James M. Wall. 10% freelance written. For the professional clergy (primarily liberal Protestant). Bimonthly magazine; 40 pages. Estab. 1925. Circ. 12,000. Buys all rights. Buys about 50 mss/year. Pays on publication. Free sample copy. Reports in 2 weeks. SASE.
Nonfiction: "We want articles by clergy-theologians who know the clergy audience. We are interested in articles on local church problems and in helpful how-to as well as "think" pieces. Query. Length: 1,200-1,800 words. Pay varies, $10/page minimum.

CHURCH ADMINISTRATION, 127 Ninth Ave., N., Nashville TN 37234. (615)251-2060. Editor: George Clark. 75% freelance written. For Southern Baptist pastors, staff, and volunteer church leaders. Monthly. Buys all rights. Will also consider second rights. Uses limited amount of freelance material. Pays on acceptance. Free sample copy and writer's guidelines. SASE.
Nonfiction and Photos: "How-to-do-it articles dealing with church administration, including church programming, organizing, and staffing, administrative skills, church financing, church food services, church facilities, communication, pastoral ministries, and community needs." Length: 750-1,500 words. Pays 2½¢ a word. Pays $7.50 to $10 for 8x10 b&w glossies purchased with mss.
How To Break In: "A beginning writer should first be acquainted with organization and policy of Baptist churches and with the administrative needs of Southern Baptist churches. He should perhaps interview one or several SBC pastors or staff members, find out how they are handling a certain administrative problem such as 'enlisting volunteer workers' or 'sharing the administrative load with church staff or volunteer workers.' I suggest writers compile an article showing how *several* different administrators (or churches) handled the problem, perhaps giving meaningful quotes. Submit the completed manuscript, typed 54 characters to the line, for consideration."

CHURCH MANAGEMENT-THE CLERGY JOURNAL, 4119 Terrace Lane, Hopkins MN 55343. (612)933-6712. Editor: Manfred Holck, Jr. 80% freelance written. For professional clergy and church business administrators. Monthly (except June and December) magazine; 38 pages. Estab. 1924. Circ. 12,000. Pays on publication. Buys all rights, but may reassign following publication. Submit seasonal/holiday material 6 months in advance of issue date. Photocopied submissions OK. SASE. Reports in 6 weeks. Sample copy $1.25.
Nonfiction: How-to (be a more effective minister or administrator); and inspirational (seasonal sermons). No poetry or personal experiences. Buys 5 mss/issue. Submit complete ms. Length: 1,000-1,500 words. Pays $10-25.

CHURCH TRAINING, 127 Ninth Ave., N., Nashville TN 37234. (615)251-2843. Publisher: The Sunday School Board of the Southern Baptist Convention. Editor: Richard B. Sims. For all workers and leaders in the Church Training program of the Southern Baptist Convention. Established in 1926. Monthly. Circulation: 40,000. Buys all rights. Buys about 25 freelance mss a year. Pays on acceptance. Will send sample copy to writer on request. Write for copy of guidelines for writers. No photocopied or simultaneous submissions. Reports on material accepted for publication in 6 weeks. Returns rejected material immediately. Query first, with rough outline. Enclose SASE.
Nonfiction: "Articles that pertain to leadership training in the church. Success stories that pertain to Church Training. Associational articles. Informational, how-to's that pertain to Church Training." Length: 500-1,500 words. Pays 3¢/word.

THE EDGE on Christian Education, Nazarene Publishing House, 6401 The Paseo, Kansas City MO 64131. Editor: Melton Wienecke. Emphasizes Christian/religious education for Sunday School teachers, pastors Sunday School superintendents, supervisors and workers. Quarterly magazine; 48 pages. Estab. 1973. Circ. 40,000. Pays on acceptance. Buys all rights, second serial (reprint) rights, or one-time rights. Submit seasonal/holiday material 12 months in ad-

vance. Simultaneous, photocopied, and previously published submissions OK. SASE. Reports 10-12 weeks. Free sample copy and writer's guidelines.
Nonfiction: Publishes how-to, humor, informational, inspirational new product, personal experience, and technical articles; interviews, profiles of trends, photo features, and articles on philosophy of Christian education. Length: 1,000 words maximum. Buys 150 mss a year. Query first with tearsheets of published work. Pays 2¢/word.
Photos: B&w and color purchased with or without mss, or on assignment. Send prints and transparencies. Pays $6 minimum.
Fiction: Considered if it is short and deals with a problem in the field. Length: 1,000 words maximum. Pays 2¢/word.
Poetry: Publishes light verse or poetry in traditional forms. Buys 10 a year. Submit complete ms. Pays $10 minimum.

EMMANUEL, 194 E. 76th St., New York NY 10021. (212)861-1076. Editor: Rev. Paul J. Bernier, S.S.S. Monthly. For the Catholic clergy. Estab. 1895. Circ. 15,000. Rights to be arranged with author. Buys 5 or 6 mss a year. Pays on publication. Will consider photocopied submissions. No simultaneous submissions. Submit seasonal material 3 to 4 months in advance. Reports in 5 weeks. SASE.
Nonfiction: Articles of Catholic (especially priestly) spirituality; can be biographical, historical or critical. Articles on Eucharistic theology, and those which provide a solid scriptural and/or theological foundation for priestly spirituality (prayer, applied spirituality, etc.). Aims at providing today's priest and involved Catholics with an adequate theology and philosophy of ministry in today's church. Length: 1,500 to 3,000 words. Usually pays $50.

ENDURING WORD ADULT TEACHER, 6401 The Paseo, Kansas City MO 64131. (816)333-7000. Editor: John B. Nielson. 10% freelance written. For teachers of adults. Quarterly. Buys first and second rights; will accept simultaneous submissions. Pays on acceptance. Will consider photocopied submissions. Reports in 6 weeks. Enclose SASE.
Nonfiction: Department Editor: John B. Nielson. "Articles of interest to teachers of adults and articles relevant to the Enduring Word Series Sunday school lesson outline." Length: 1,300 words maximum. Pays minimum $20 per 1,000 words.
Photos: Purchased with captions only. Pays minimum $5; 4 color up to $100.
Poetry: Inspirational, seasonal, or lesson-related poetry. Length: 24 lines maximum. Pays minimum 25¢ per line.

KEY TO CHRISTIAN EDUCATION, Standard Publishing, 8121 Hamilton Ave., Cincinnati OH 45231. (513)931-4050. Editor-in-Chief: Marjorie Miller. 50% freelance written. For "church leaders of all ages; Sunday school teachers and superintendents; ministers; Christian education professors; youth workers." Quarterly magazine; 48 pages. Estab. 1962. Circ. 65,000. Pays on acceptance. Buys first North American serial rights. Phone queries OK. Submit seasonal/holiday material 15 months in advance. Photocopied and previously published submissions OK. SASE. Reports in 4 weeks. Free sample copy and writer's guidelines.
Nonfiction: How-to (programs and projects for Christian education), informational; interview; personal opinion; and personal experience. Buys 10 mss/issue. Query or submit complete ms. Length: 700-2,000 words. Pays $20-50.
Photos: Purchased with or without accompanying ms. Submit prints. Pays $5-25 for any size glossy finish b&w prints. Total price for ms includes payment for photos. Model release required.
Fillers: Purchases short ideas on "this is how we did it" articles. Buys 10 mss an issue. Submit complete ms. Length: 50-250 words. Pays $5-10.

PASTORAL LIFE, Society of St. Paul, Route 224, Canfield OH 44406. Editor: Victor L. Viberti, S.S.P. For priests and those interested in pastoral ministry. Magazine; 64 pages. Monthly. Circulation: 8,600. Buys first rights. Payment on acceptance. Will send sample copy to writer on request. "Queries appreciated before submitting mss. New contributors are expected to accompany their material with a few lines of personal data." Reports in 7 to 10 days. Enclose SASE.
Nonfiction: "Professional review, principally designed to focus attention on current problems, needs, issues and all important activities related to all phases of pastoral work and life. Avoids merely academic treatments on abstract and too controversial subjects." Length: 2,000 to 3,400 words. Pays 3¢ a word minimum.

THE SERRAN, Serra International, 22 W. Monroe St., Chicago IL 60603. (312)782-2163.

Editor: Ray Prost. 20% freelance written. Emphasizes Catholic priestly and religious vocations for a readership 90% of whom are affluent Catholic laymen and 10% clergymen (bishops, priests). Bimonthly magazine; 16-24 pages. Estab. 1944. Circ. 15,000. Pays on publication. Buys all rights; "the message of our apostolate is spread frequently by the reprinting in the publications of our affiliates and other organizations of material from the *Serran*." Submit seasonal/holiday material 3 months in advance of issue date. Simultaneous and photocopied submissions OK. SASE. Reports in 4 weeks. Sample copy 50¢.
Nonfiction: "Articles should be altruistic and in keeping with our purposes: fostering and preserving Catholic priestly and religious vocations, and assisting our members to fulfill their own Christian vocations to service." Inspirational (religious, priests, nuns, etc.); interview (occasionally on assignment); and photo feature (occasionally, if in keeping with objectives of our apostolate). Buys 6 mss/year. Query. Length: 250-1,800 words. Pays $20-100.
Photo: Pays $5-10 for glossy b&w prints; $2-5 for glossy color prints. "We prefer b&w square photos or horizontal or verticals based on multiples of a square (but not essential)." Captions preferred "for information, subject to editing." Buys all rights. Model release required.

SUCCESS, Box 15337, Denver CO 80215. Editor: Edith Quinlan. 90% freelance written. Quarterly magazine. Reports in 2-3 weeks. SASE. Free sample copy and writer's guidelines.
Nonfiction: "Articles should be from 500-2,000 words in length, and should provide ideas helpful to workers in Christian education. We are more interested in receiving articles from people who know Christian education, or workers who have accomplished something worthwhile in Sunday school and youth work, than from experienced writers who do not have such background. A combination of both, however, is ideal. Articles may be of a general nature, or be slanted to specific age groups, such as preschool, elementary, youth and adult." Pays 3¢/word.

SUNDAY SCHOOL COUNSELOR, General Council of the Assemblies of God, 1445 Boonville Ave., Springfield MO 65802. (417)862-2781, ext. 433. Editor-in-Chief: Sylvia Lee. "Our audience consists of local church school teachers and administrators. These are people who, by and large, have not been professionally trained for their positions but are rather volunteer workers. Most would have not more than a high school education." Monthly magazine; 32 pages. Estab. 1939. Circ. 45,000. Pays on acceptance. Buys all rights, but may reassign following publication; or simultaneous rights. Submit seasonal/holiday material 9 months in advance. Simultaneous and previously published submissions OK. SASE. Reports in 4-6 weeks. Free sample copy and writer's guidelines.
Nonfiction: How-to (Sunday school teaching, crafts, discipline in the Sunday school, building student-teacher relationships); inspirational (on the teaching ministry); and personal experience (as related to teaching ministry or how a Sunday school teacher handled a particular situation). Buys 70 mss/year. Submit complete ms. Length: 400-1,000 words. Pays 1-3¢/word.
Photos: Purchased with accompanying ms or on assignment. Send prints or transparencies. Pays $5-8 for 5x7 b&w photos; $10-70 for 2¼x2¼ color transparencies. Model release required.
How To Break In: "A freelancer can break into our publication by submitting a first person account of a Sunday school experience. This must be actual, and contain a new slant or insight on an old topic. We are a good freelance market providing the person has taken time to study our publication first and to see our needs and slant."

YOUR CHURCH, Religious Publishing Co., 198 Allendale Rd., King of Prussia PA 19406. Editor: Phyllis Mather Rice. Associate Editor: Norman Lock. 30% freelance written. Bimonthly magazine; 56 pages. Estab. 1955. Circ. 188,000. Pays on publication. Buys all rights. Photocopied submissions OK. SASE. Reports in 2-3 months.
Nonfiction: "Articles for pastors, informative and cogently related to some aspect of being a pastor (counseling, personal finance, administration, building, etc.)." Buys 15-20 mss/year. Length: 5-15 typewritten pages. Pays $4/page, not to exceed $75.

THE YOUTH LEADER, 1445 Boonville Ave., Springfield MO 65802. Editor: Glen Ellard. For "ministers of youth (Christian)." Evangelical Christianity and Christian activism. Special issues at Christmas and Easter. Estab. 1944. Monthly. Circ. 5,000. Buys all rights, but will reassign rights to author after publication. Buys first North American serial rights, second serial (reprint) rights and simultaneous rights. Buys 20-30 mss/year. Pays on acceptance. Free sample copy. Photocopied submissions OK. Submit seasonal material 4 months in advance. Reports in 6 weeks. SASE.
Nonfiction: "How-to" articles (e.g., "How to Evangelize Youth Through Music," "How to Study the Bible for Personal Application," "How to Use the Media for the Christian Message"); skits and role-plays; Bible raps, original choruses, Bible verses set to music, ideas for

youth services, socials, and fund raising; interviews with successful youth leaders. Avoid cliches (especially religious ones); educational philosophy; youth (or student) centered instead of adult (or teacher) centered; relational approach instead of preaching. Submit complete ms. Length: 500-2,500 words. Pays 2½¢-3½¢/word.

Clothing and Knit Goods

APPAREL INDUSTRY MAGAZINE, 6226 Vineland Ave., North Hollywood CA. (213)766-5291. Associate Editor: Ellen Robbins. For executive management in apparel companies with interests in equipment, government intervention in the garment industry; finance, management and training in industry. Monthly magazine; 70-100 pages. Estab. 1946. Circ. 16,000. Not copyrighted. Buys 40 to 50 mss/year. Pays on publication. Sample copy $1. Will consider legible photocopied submissions. No simultaneous submissions. Reports in 3 to 4 weeks. Query first. SASE.
Nonfiction and Photos: Articles dealing with equipment, training, finance; state, federal government, consumer interests, etc., related to the industry. "Use concise, precise language that is easy to read and understand. In other words, because the subjects are technical, keep the language comprehensible. No general articles on finance and management. Material must be precisely related to the apparel industry." Informational, interview, profile, successful business operations, technical articles. Length: 500 to 1,000 words. Pays 2½¢ to 3¢ a word. No additional payment for b&w photos.

BODY FASHIONS/INTIMATE APPARAL, Harcourt Brace Jovanovich Publications, 757 Third Ave., New York NY 10017. Editor-in-Chief: Ms. Deane L. Moskowitz. Emphasizes information about men's and women's hosiery and underwear; women's undergarments, lingerie, sleepwear, robes, hosiery, leisurewear. For merchandise managers and buyers of store products, manufacturers and suppliers to the trade. Monthly tabloid insert, plus 7 regional market issues called Market Maker; 24 pages minimum. Estab. 1913. Circ: 13,500. Pays on publication. Buys all rights. Phone queries OK. Submit seasonal/holiday material 2 months in advance. Previously published submissions OK. SASE. Reports in 4 weeks. Free sample copy.
Columns/Departments: New Image (discussions of renovations of Body Fashions/Intimate Apparel department); Creative Retailing (deals with successful retail promotions); Ad Ideas (descriptions of successful advertising campaigns). Buys 1 feature/issue. Query first. Length: 500-2,500 words. Pays 15¢/word. Open to suggestions for new columns and departments.
Photos: B&w (5x7) photos purchased without mss. Captions required. Send contact sheet, prints or negatives. Pays $5-25. Model release required.

KNITTING TIMES, National Knitted Outerwear Association, 51 Madison Ave., New York NY 10010. (212)683-7520. Editor: Eric Hertz. For the knitting industry, from the knitter to the cutter and sewer to the machinery manufacturer, to the fiber and yarn producer, chemical manufacturer, and various other suppliers to the industry. Weekly magazine; 58 pages. Estab. 1933. Circ: 6,100. Pays on publication. Buys all rights. Submit seasonal or holiday material 1 month in advance. SASE. Reports in 4 weeks. Free sample copy and writer's guidelines.
Nonfiction: Historical (various parts of the knitting industry; development of machines, here and abroad); how-to (cut and sew various outer garments; knit, dye and finish; needle set-outs for various knit constructions); informational (market or show reports, trends, new fabrics, machine, fiber, yarn, chemical developments); interviews (with leading figures in the industry; may be knitter, head of fiber company etc. Must say something significant such as new market development, import situation, projections and the like). New product (on anything in the industry such as machines, fibers, yarns, dyeing and finishing equipment, etc.). Photo features (on plants or plant layouts, how to cut and sew sweaters, skirts, etc.). Profiles (can be on industry leaders, or on operation of a company; specifically plant stories and photos). Technical (on machines, chemical processes, finishing, dyeing, spinning, texturing, etc.) Length: 750 words minimum. Query first. Pays $.70-1 an inch.
Photos: B&w glossies (8x10) purchased with mss. Query first. Pays $3 for glossies; $5/diagram.

MEN'S WEAR, Fairchild Publications, 7 E. 12th St., New York, NY 10003. Editor-in-Chief: Becki Levine. Emphasizes men's and boy's apparel retailers. Semimonthly magazine; 46 pages. Estab. 1896. Circ. 26,700. Pays on acceptance. Buys all rights. SASE. Reports in 3 weeks. Free sample copy.
Nonfiction: Expose (pertaining to men's wear industry companies or issues), how-to (on making men's wear retailing more profitable, sales promotions, advertising, displays). Buys 2-3 mss/

year. Query. Length: Flexible, from 1,000 words. Pays $100-200.

TACK 'N TOGS MERCHANDISING, P. O. Box 67, Minneapolis MN 55440. Address mss to The Editor. For "retailers of products for horse and rider and Western and English fashion apparel." Estab. 1970. Monthly. Circ. 16,000. Rights purchased vary with author and material; may buy all rights. Buys 5-10 mss/year. Pays on acceptance. Will send a sample copy to a writer on request. Write for copy of guidelines for writers. Query first. Enclose SASE.
Nonfiction and Photos: "Case histories, trends of industry." Buys informational articles, how-to's, interviews, profiles, coverage of successful business operations, and articles on merchandising techniques. Length: open. Pays "up to $100." B&w glossies and color transparencies purchased with mss.

TEENS & BOYS, 71 W. 35th St., New York NY 10001. Editor-in-Chief: Ellye Bloom. 20% freelance written. For retailers, manufacturers, resident buying offices in male apparel trade. Monthly magazine; 75-100 pages. Estab. 1919. Circ. 8,200. Pays on publication. Buys one-time rights. Submit seasonal/holiday material 6 months in advance of issue date. SASE. Free writer's guidelines; mention *Writer's Market* in request.
Nonfiction: "*Teens & Boys* is edited for retailers of apparel for boys and male teenage students, aged 4-18. It forecasts style trends, reports on retail merchandising, stock control, promotion, display, new products and industry news. All factual, carefully researched, pertinent articles presented in a lively style will be considered." Buys 2 mss/issue. Query. Length: 1,000-2,000 words. Pays $30-150.
Photos: State availability of photos with query. Pays $7.50-10 for contact sheets, negatives or 5x7 b&w glossy prints. Captions required. Buys one-time rights.

WESTERN OUTFITTER, 5314 Bingle Rd., Houston TX 77092. (713)688-8811. Editor: M.J. House. For "owners and managers of retail stores in all 50 states and Canada. These stores sell clothing for riders and equipment for horses, both Western and English style. Mostly Western." Monthly. Buys all rights. Pays on publication. Query first. Enclose SASE.
Nonfiction: Method stories; "in-depth treatment of subjects each merchant wrestles with daily. We want stories that first describe the problem, then give details on methods used in eliminating the problem. Be factual and specific." Subjects include merchandising, promotion, customer contact, accounting and finance, store operation, merchandise handling, and personnel. "To merit feature coverage, this merchant has to be a winner. It is the uniqueness of the winner's operation that will benefit other store owners who read this magazine." Length: 1,000 to 1,500 words for full-length feature; 500 to 600 words for featurette. Pays 3¢ per published word for shortcut featurettes; 5¢ per published word for full-length feature, and featurettes. "Send us copies of stories you have done for other trade magazines. Send us queries based on visits to Western dealers in your territory."
Photos: "Excellent photos make excellent copy much better. Plan photos that bring to life the key points in your text. Avoid shots of store fixtures without people. Submit photos in glossy finish, in 8x10 size or smaller. Sharp focus is a must." Captions required. "Cover photos: We will pay $40 for a 2¼x2¼ color transparency if used for a cover. Your 35mm shots are fine for interior b&w art." Pays $6 per photo used with ms. Also uses "single photos, or pairs of photos that show display ideas, tricks, promotional devices that are different and that bring more business." Pays $10.

WESTERN WEAR & EQUIPMENT MAGAZINE, Bell Publications, 2403 Champa St., Denver CO 80205. Editor-in-Chief: Allen Bell. Managing Editor: Susan H. Barocas. 20-25% freelance written. Emphasizes Western/English retailing operations and products for retailers, salespeople and manufacturers in the Western/English industry. Monthly magazine; 44 pages. Estab. 1959. Circ. 11,800. Pays on publication. Not copyrighted. Submit seasonal/holiday material 2 months in advance of issue date. Photocopied submissions OK. SASE. Reports in 1 month. Free sample copy and writer's guidelines; mention *Writer's Market* in request.
Nonfiction: Exposé (clothing/equipment industry, Federal Trade Commission, government as related to industry); general interest (rodeoing, country-western music or entertainment, related people features); historical (fashion); how-to (retailing management and sales, stock, inventories, and all data related specifically to the industry); humor (events, people, anecdotes related to western retailing); interview (people in industry or rodeo, knowledgeable about retailing); new product (monthly column for new products that could be sold in stores); and photo feature (Western/English apparel and equipment stores, manufacturers). Buys 2-3 mss/issue. Submit complete ms with clips of previously published work. Length: 1,000 words maximum. Pays $75 maximum.

Photos: "Magazine has photo/essay format." Pays $5 for 5x7 or 8x10 b&w prints; $5-50 for 8x20 glossy color prints (for cover). Buys one-time rights. Captions required.

Coin-Operated Machines

AMERICAN COIN-OP, 500 N. Dearborn St., Chicago IL 60610. (312)337-7700. Editor: Ben Russell. Managing Editor: Phil Sneiderman. For businessmen and businesswomen who own coin-operated laundry and drycleaning stores; operators, distributors and industry leaders. Monthly magazine; 48 pages. Estab. 1960. Circ. 22,000. Rights purchased vary with author and material but are exclusive to the field. Buys 25 mss/year. Pays two weeks prior to publication. Free sample copy. Reports decision on material as soon as possible; usually in 2 weeks. SASE.
Nonfiction and Photos: "We emphasize store operation and management and use features on industry topics: utility use and conservation, maintenance, store management, customer service, and advertising. A case study should emphasize how the store operator accomplished whatever he did — in a way that the reader can apply in his own operation. Mss should have no-nonsense, businesslike approach and be brief. Uses informational, how-to, interview, profile, think pieces, spot news, successful business operations articles. Length: 500 to 3,000 words. Pays minimum of 4¢/word. Pays minimum $5 for 8x10 b&w glossy photos purchased with mss. Must be clear and have good contrast.
Fillers: Newsbreaks, clippings. Length: open. Pays 3¢ per word; $3 minimum.
How To Break In: "Query first about subjects of current interest. Be observant of coin-operated laundries — how they are designed and equipped; how they serve customers; how (if) they advertise and promote their services. Report anything unusual. Even one-sentence query reports themselves are sometimes bought and published. Most general articles turned down because they are not aimed well enough at audience. Most case histories turned down because of lack of practical purpose (nothing new or worth reporting)."

COIN LAUNDERER & CLEANER, 525 Somerset Dr., Indianapolis IN 46260. For owners, operators, and managers of coin-operated and self-service laundry and drycleaning establishments. Monthly. Buys all rights. Enclose SASE.
Nonfiction: "Our requirements are for self-service coin laundry and drycleaning store management articles which specify the promotion, service, or technique used by the store owners; the cost of this technique; and the profit produced by it. Freelance writers must be familiar with coin laundry and drycleaning industry to prepare an article of sufficient management significance." Pays 5¢ per printed word.

COINAMATIC AGE, 60 E. 42nd St., New York NY 10017. (212)682-6330. Editor: C. F. Lee. For operators/owners of coin-operated laundries; dry cleaners. Bimonthly. Buys all rights. Pays on publication. "Queries get same-day attention." SASE.
Nonfiction and Photos: "We are currently considering articles on coin-operated laundries, and/or in combination with drycleaners. Slant should focus on the unusual, but at the same time should stress possible adaptation by other coinamat operators. Particular interest at this time centers on energy conservation methods. We are interested in promotional and advertising techniques; reasons for expansion or additional locations; attached sidelines such as carwashes and other businesses; Main Street vs. shopping center operations; successes in dealing with permanent press garment laundering and cleaning; ironing services; and, primarily, financial success, personal satisfaction, or any other motivation that the owner derives from his business. Give the story punch, details, and applicability to the reader. Include a list of specifications, detailing the number of units (washers, dryers, etc.), the different pound-loads of each machine and the make and model numbers of all of these, as well as any vending machines, changemakers, etc. Three action photos (preferably a minimum of 6) must accompany each article. At this time, we are especially interested in combined laundry/drycleaning articles. Submitted photos must include an exterior shot of the installation and interior shots showing customers. Where possible, a photo of the owner at work is also desired. If you have a far-out slant, query first." Pays 3¢ to 4¢ a word, depending on need to rewrite. Length: 1,200 to 2,000 words. No "plugola" for manufacturers' products, please. Photos purchased with mss. Pays $12 for 3 photos and $6 for each additional photo.

PLAY METER MAGAZINE, Skybird Publishing Co., Inc., Box 24170, New Orleans LA 70184. Editor-in Chief: Ralph C. Lally. Managing Editor: David Pierson. 25% freelance written. Trade publication for owners/operators of coin-operated amusement machine companies, eg., pinball machines, video games, arcade pieces, jukeboxes, etc. Monthly magazine; 70 pages. Estab.

December 1974. Circ. 5,400. Pays on publication. Buys all rights. Submit seasonal/holiday material 2 months in advance of issue date. Photocopied and previously published submissions OK. SASE. Reports in 2 months. Free sample copy and writer's guidelines.

Nonfiction: General interest (seldom used, but usually this area focuses on a successful operator, operation or manufacturer; include 'trade secrets'); how-to (get better locations for machines, how to promote tournaments, etc., how to evaluate profitability of route); interview (with industry leaders); new product (if practical for industry, not interested in vending machines); and photo feature (with some copy). "No 'puff' or 'plug' pieces about new manufacturers. Our readers want to read about how they can make more money from their machines, how they can get better tax breaks, commissions, etc. Also no stories about *playing* pinball. Our readers don't play the game per se; they buy the machines and make money from them." Buys 1 mss/issue. Submit complete ms. Length: 300-2,500 words. Pays $25-150.

Photos: "The photography should depict some action, not a 'stand 'em up-shoot 'em down' group shoot." Pays $10 minimum for 5x7 or 8x10 b&w prints; $10 for color negatives or contact sheets. Captions preferred. Buys all rights, but may reassign following publication.

VENDING TIMES, 211 E. 43rd St., New York NY 10017. Editor: Arthur E. Yohalem. For operators of vending machines. Monthly. Circulation: 13,500. Buys all rights. Pays on publication. Query first; "we will discuss the story requirements with the writer in detail." Enclose SASE.

Nonfiction and Photos: Feature articles and news stories about vending operations; practical and important aspects of the business. "We are always willing to pay for good material. Primary interest is photo fillers." Pays $10/photo.

Confectionery and Snack Foods

CANDY AND SNACK INDUSTRY, 777 Third Ave., New York, NY 10017. (212)838-7778. Editor: Myron Lench. For confectionery and snack manufacturers. Monthly. Buys all rights. Reports in 2 weeks. SASE.

Nonfiction: "Feature articles of interest to large scale candy, cookie, cracker, and other snack manufacturers that deal with activities in the fields of production, packaging (including package design), merchandising; financial news (sales figures, profits, earnings), advertising campaigns in all media, and promotional methods used to increase the sale or distribution of candy and snacks." Length: 1,000-1,250 words. Pays 5¢/word; "special rates on assignments."

Photos: "Good quality glossies with complete and accurate captions, in sizes not smaller than 5x7." Pays $5. Color covers.

Fillers: "Short news stories about the trade and anything related to candy and snacks." Pays 5¢/word; $1 for clippings.

CANDY MARKETER, 777 Third Ave., New York NY 10017. (212)838-7778. Editor: Mike Lench. For owners and executives of wholesale and retail businesses. Monthly magazine. Estab. 1967. Circ. 14,000. Buys all rights. Buys 20 mss/year. Pays on acceptance. Free sample copy. Photocopied submissions OK. Submit seasonal material at least 6 months in advance. Reports within 2 weeks. SASE.

Nonfiction, Photos, and Fillers: News and features on the candy trade. "Describe operation, interview candy buyer or merchandise manager; quote liberally. More interested in mass operations, than in unusual little shops." Informational, how-to, interview, profile, spot news, successful business operations, merchandising techniques. Annual issues on Halloween merchandising, Christmas merchandising and Easter merchandising are published in May, June and November (respectively). Length: 1,000-2,500 words. Pays 5¢/word. 5x7 or 8½x11 b&w photos and color transparencies or prints purchased with or without mss. Captions required. Pays $5 for b&w; $15 for color. Pays $1 for each clipping used.

Construction and Contracting

Journals aimed at architects and city planners will be found in the Architecture category. Those for specialists in the interior aspects of construction are listed under Building Interiors.

ABC AMERICAN ROOFER AND BUILDING IMPROVEMENT CONTRACTOR, Shelter Publications, Inc., 915 Burlington St., Downers Grove IL 60515. (312)964-6200. Editor-in-Chief:

J.C. Gudas. For roofing industry contractors. Monthly magazine; 20-32 pages. Estab. 1911. Circ. 28,800. Pays on publication. Buys all rights. Submit seasonal/holiday material 4 months in advance. SASE. Reports in 1 week. Free sample copy.
Nonfiction: Publishes how-to (apply various kinds of material on roofs, preferably unusual kinds of data), historical, humor (if original), interview, photo feature (unusual types of roofing), profile (on industry men), and technical. Buys 5 mss a year. Query. Length: 1,500 words maximum. Pays $10-50. Editorial schedule available.
Photos: 8Purchased with accompanying ms. Captions required. Pays $5-25 for any size b&w glossy prints. Query or submit prints.
How To Break In: "Mss must pertain to our industry. Be consise and brief. Spaced-out wordings are not tolerated — articles must be well condensed, yet carry all the pertinent facts."
Rejects: "No generalized industry articles; no women in industry stories unless the job is the important part of the article."

AUTOMATION IN HOUSING & SYSTEMS BUILDING NEWS, CMN Associates, Inc., Box 205, Skokie IL 60076. (312)674-8392. Editor-in-Chief: Don Carlson. Specializes in management for industrialized (manufactured) housing and volume home builders. Bimonthly magazine; 44 pages. Estab. 1964. Circ. 23,000. Pays on acceptance. Buys first North American serial rights or one-time rights. Phone queries OK. SASE. Reports in 2 weeks. Free sample copy and writer's guidelines.
Nonfiction: Case history articles on successful home building companies which may be 1) production (big volume) home builders; 2) mobile home manufacturers; 3) modular home manufacturers; 4) prefabricated home manufacturers or 5) house component manufacturers. Also uses interviews, photo features and technical articles. Buys 6-8 mss/year. Query. Length: 2,500 words maximum. Pays $250 minimum.
Photos: Purchased with accompanying ms. Captions required. Query. No additional payment for 4x5, 5x7 or 8x10 b&w glossies or 35mm or larger color transparencies.

BATIMENT, 625 President Kennedy Ave., Montreal 111, Que., Canada. (514)845-5141. Editor: Marc Castro. Published in French for "contractors, architects." Established in 1927. Monthly. Circulation: 6,000. Rights purchased vary with author and material. Buys about 25 mss a year. Pays on acceptance. Will send a sample copy to a writer on request. Write for copy of guidelines for writers. Enclose S.A.E. and International Reply Coupons.
Nonfiction: "Articles on new techniques in construction and subjects of interest to builders. Interested in residential, apartment, office, commercial, and industrial buildings—not in public works. Generally, articles written in English are rejected." Length: 500 to 1,000 words. Pays $75-100.

CALIFORNIA BUILDER & ENGINEER, 4110 Transport St., Palo Alto CA 94303. Editor: Cole N. Danehower. "For contractors, engineers, machinery distributors for the construction industry, and civic officials concerned with public works. Coverage limited to California, Hawaii, western Arizona, and western Nevada." Published semimonthly. Estab. 1894. Circ. 12,500. Pays on publication. Not copyrighted. SASE.
Nonfiction: "We are particularly interested in knowledgeable articles on non-construction issues that affect the large and small contractor in our rerion. For example, accounting for the contractor, labor issues, pending legislation, or ecology. These articles must be written with rigid accuracy, often requiring specialized knowledge. We are also interested in job stories from Hawaii on heavy public construction. We are not interested in residential construction. Field experience and in-depth knowledge of the industry are essential in writing for us. Query. Length: 1,500-2,200 words.

CONSTRUCTION EQUIPMENT OPERATION AND MAINTENANCE, P.O. Box 1689, Cedar Rapids IA 52406. (319)366-1597. Editor: C.K. Parks. 15% freelance written. For users of heavy construction equipment. Bimonthly. Buys all rights. Pays on acceptance. Query first. Reports in 1 month. SASE.
Nonfiction and Photos: "Articles on selection, use, operation, or maintenance of construction equipment; articles and features on the construction industry in general; job safety articles." Length: 1,000-2,000 words. Also buys a limited number of job stories with photos, and feature articles on individual contractors in certain areas of U.S. and Canada. Length varies. Pays $50 to $200.

CONSTRUCTION SPECIFIER, 1150 17th St., N.W., Washington DC 20036. Editor: Thomas A. Cameron. 100% freelance written. Professional society journal for architects, engineers, specification writers, contractors. Monthly. Circ. 12,000. Buys all rights. Pays on publication. Free sample copy. Deadlines are 45 days preceding publication on the 10th of each month. Reports in 4 to 7 days. SASE.

Nonfiction and Photos: "Articles on building techniques, building products and material." Query. Length: minimum 3,500 words. Pays $200-400. Photos "purchased rarely; if purchased, payment included in ms rate." 8x10 glossies.

CONSTRUCTIONEER, 1 Bond St., Chatham NJ 07928. Editor: Ken Hanan. 10% freelance written. For contractors, distributors, material producers, public works officials, consulting engineers, etc. Estab. 1945. Biweekly. Circ. 18,000. Buys all rights but will reassign rights to author after publication. Buys 10 mss/year. Pays on acceptance. Sample copy $1; free writer's guidelines. Photocopied submissions OK. Submit seasonal material 2 months in advance. Reports in 30 to 60 days. SASE.

Nonfiction and Photos: Construction job stories; new methods studies. Detailed job studies of methods and equipment used; oriented around geographical area of New York, New Jersey, Pennsylvania and Delaware. Winter snow and ice removal and control; winter construction methods. Current themes: public works, profiles, conservation. Query. Length: 1,500-1,800 words. Pays $100-$200. B&w photos purchased with or without accompanying ms or on assignment. Pays $5 to $8.

CONSTRUCTOR MAGAZINE, 1957 E St., N.W., Washington DC 20006. Editor: Elena Cunningham. Publication of the Association of General Contractors of America for "men in the age range of approximately 25 to 70 (predominantly 40's and 50's), 50% with a college education. Most own or are officers in their own corporations." Estab. 1902. Monthly. Circ. 27,500. Buys all rights, but will reassign after publication. Buys about 30 mss a year. Pays on publication. Will send a sample copy to a writer for 50¢. Query first or submit complete ms. Reports in 30 days. Enclose SASE.

Nonfiction: "Feature material dealing with labor, legal, technical, and professional material pertinent to the construction industry and corporate business. We deal only with the management aspect of the construction industry. No articles on computers and computer technology." Buys informational articles, interviews, think pieces, exposes, photo features, coverage of successful business operations, and technical articles. Length: "no minimum or maximum; subject much more important than length." Pays $50 to $300.

DIXIE CONTRACTOR, Box 280, Decatur GA 30031. (404)377-2683. Editor: Russell K. Paul. 20% freelance written. For contractors, public officials, architects, engineers, and construction equipment manufacturers and dealers. Biweekly magazine; 125 pages. Estab. 1926. Circ. 9,000. Pays on publication. Buys all rights. Phone queries OK. Submit seasonal/holiday material 2 months in advance of issue date. Photocopied submissions OK. SASE. Reports in 2 weeks. Free sample copy.

Nonfiction: How-to (articles on new construction techniques and innovations); and interview (with government officials influencing construction, or prominent contractors). Buys 7 mss/year. Query or submit complete ms. Length: 1,500-2,000 words. Pays $25 minimum.

Photo: State availability of photos with query or ms. Captions and model release required. Buys all rights.

Columns/Departments: Labor-Management relations in Construction. Buys 26 mss/year. Submit complete ms. Length: 1,000-1,500 words. Pays $25 minimum.

ENGINEERING AND CONTRACT RECORD, 1450 Don Mills Road, Don Mills, Ont., Canada M3B 2X7. (416)445-6641. Editor: Nick Hancock. For contractors in engineered construction and aggregate producers. Estab. 1889. Monthly. Circ. over 18,000. Buys first and second Canadian rights. Pays on publication. Free sample copy. Reports in 2 weeks. Enclose SAE and International Reply Coupons.

Nonfiction and Photos: "Job stories. How to build a project quicker, cheaper, better through innovations and unusual methods. Articles on construction methods, technology, equipment, maintenance and management innovations. Management articles. Stories are limited to Canadian projects only." Buys 12-15 mss/year. Query. Length: 1,000 to 1,500 words. Pays 13¢/printed word and $5/8x10 printed photo. B&w glossies purchased with mss. 8x10 preferred.

FARM BUILDING NEWS, 733 N. Van Buren, Milwaukee, WI 53202. Managing Editor: Don Peach. For farm structure builders and suppliers. 6 times a year. Buys all rights. Pays on acceptance. Will send a free sample copy on request. Query suggested. Deadlines are at least 4 weeks in advance of publication date; prefers 6 to 8 weeks. Reports immediately. Enclose SASE.

Nonfiction and Photos: Features on farm builders and spot news. Length: 600 to 1,000 words. Pays $150 to $200. Buys color and b&w photos with ms.

FENCE INDUSTRY, 6285 Barfield Rd., Atlanta GA 30328. (404)393-2920. Editor: Bill Coker. For retailers of fencing materials. Monthly magazine; 48 to 80 pages. Estab. 1958. Circ. 12,000. Buys all rights. Buys 25 to 35 mss a year. Pays on publication. Free sample copy. No photocopied or simultaneous submissions. Reports on material accepted for publication in 3 months. Returns rejected material in 2 weeks. Query first or submit complete ms. Enclose SASE.
Nonfiction and Photos: Case histories, as well as articles on fencing for highways, pools, farms, playgrounds, homes, industries. Surveys, and management and sales reports. Interview, profile, historical, successful business operations, and articles on merchandising techniques. Length: open. Pays 5¢ a word. Pays $10 for 8x10 b&w photos purchased with mss. Captions required.

JOURNAL OF COMMERCE, 2000 West 12th Ave., Vancouver, B.C., Canada. V6J 2G2. Editor: L.F. Webster. For engineers, architects, contractors, developers and construction industry specialists. Weekly. General business newspaper, tabloid 20 pages, with emphasis on construction. Estab. 1911. Circ. 9,000. Buys all rights. Payment on publication. Query first. Enclose SAE and International Reply Coupons.
Nonfiction and Photos: Specialized technical articles on construction methodology and equipment. Take the approach of writing a newspaper feature, interview, or report. "Many publications deal with construction projects, etc., but not for an audience that knows the field thoroughly; we go beyond 'daily' style of how much, how big, etc." Particularly interested in articles about Canadian products being employed in the U.S. construction field. Length: 2,000 words maximum. Pays 8¢ a word. Captioned photos are purchased with accompanying ms. Pays $5 each.

MID-WEST CONTRACTOR, Box 766, Kansas City MO 64141. (816)842-2902. Editor: Gilbert Mulley. Buys all rights. Pays on acceptance. Query first. SASE.
Nonfiction and Photos: "Limited market for articles relating to large construction contracts in the Midwest only — Iowa, Nebraska, Kansas, and Missouri. Such articles would relate to better methods of building various phases of large contracts, ranging anywhere from material distribution to labor relations. Also interested in articles on outstanding construction personalities in territory." Query. Length: open. Pays $50 minimum per article. Photos purchased with and without mss. Captions required. Pays $5 minimum per photo.

MODERN STEEL CONSTRUCTION, American Institute of Steel Construction, 1221 Avenue of the Americas, New York NY 10020. Editor: Mary Anne Stockwell. 10% freelance written. For architects, engineers, and builders. Quarterly. Not copyrighted. Pays on acceptance. Query first. SASE.
Nonfiction and Photos: "Articles with pictures and diagrams, of new steel-framed buildings and bridges. Must show new and imaginative uses of structural steel for buildings and bridges; new designs, new developments." Length: "1 and 2 pages." Pays $100 maximum. Photos purchased with mss.

WESTERN CONSTRUCTION, Box 2328, Eugene OR 97402. (503)689-2711. Editor: David C. Etheridge. For "heavy constructors and their job supervisors." Monthly. Buys all rights and simultaneous rights. Pays on acceptance. SASE.
Nonfiction and Photos: "Methods articles on street, highway, bridge, tunnel, dam construction in 13 western states. Slant is toward how it was built rather than why." Writers in this field should have a background in civil engineering, heavy machine operation, or writing experience in associated fields such as commercial building construction. Academic training not as important as field experience and firsthand knowledge of the writer's subject. Query. Length: 1,500 to 2,500 words and 6 photos. Pays minimum $40 "per printed magazine page."

WORLD CONSTRUCTION, 666 Fifth Ave., New York NY 10019. (212)489-4652. Editor: Henry Mozdzer. 10-20% freelance written. For "English-speaking engineers, contractors, and government officials in the Eastern hemisphere and Latin America." Monthly. Buys all rights. Pays on publication. Will send a sample copy to a writer on request. Query first. Reports in 1 month. Enclose SASE.
Nonfiction and Photos: "How-to articles which stress how contractors can do their jobs faster, better, or more economically. Articles are rejected when they tell only what was constructed,

but not how it was constructed and why it was constructed in that way." Length: about 1,000 to 6,000 words. Pays $75/magazine page, or 4 typed ms pages. Photos purchased with mss; b&w glossies no smaller than 4x5.

Dairy Products

DAIRY RECORD, 3460 John Hancock Center, Chicago IL 60611. (312)943-5300. Editor: Herb Saal. Monthly. For the dairy processing industry. Not copyrighted. Pays on publication. Enclose SASE.
Nonfiction: Contributions must be confined to spot news articles and current events dealing with the dairy processing industry, especially news and news commentary of fluid milk distribution and the manufacturing and processing of dairy products. "News clips are okay. Not interested in items dealing with cows, dairy farms, herd management, etc." Pays $1 for every item published.

DAIRY SCOPE, 756 Kansas St., San Francisco CA 94107. Editor-in-Chief: Sally Taylor. Managing Editor: Linda Clark. 50% freelance written. Bimonthly magazine; 16 pages. Estab. 1901. Circ. 1,500. Pays on publication. Buys one-time rights. Photocopied submissions OK. SASE. Reports in 4 weeks. Free sample copy and writer's guidelines.
Nonfiction: How-to (new or interesting techniques in dairy processing); general interest (to the western dairy processing industry); historical (western dairy industry); and technical (western dairy processing). Buys 24 mss/year. Query. Length: 100-2,000 words. Pays $2.50/column inch.
Photos: State availability of photos with query. Pays $5-25 for 8x10 b& w glossy prints, contact sheets and negatives. Captions preferred. Buys one-time rights. Model release required.
Fillers: Clippings. Pays $2.

Data Processing

CANADIAN DATASYSTEMS, 481 University Ave., Toronto, Ont., Canada M5W 1A7. (416)595-1811. Editor: Tom Kelly. For data processing managers, computer systems managers, systems analysts, computer programmers, corporate management and similar people concerned with the use of computers in business, industry, government and education. Monthly magazine; 70 pages. Estab. 1969. Circ. 15,000. Buys first Canadian rights. Pays on acceptance. Free sample copy. No photocopied or simultaneous submissions. Reports in 1 month. Enclose SAE and International Reply Coupons.
Nonfiction: Articles of technical, semi-technical and general interest within the general area of data processing. How-to features, application reports, descriptions of new techniques, surveys of equipment and services. Emphasis should be placed on the use of data processing equipment and services in Canada. Articles must be technical enough to satisfy an informed readership. Buys 20 mss/year. Query or submit complete ms. Length: 2,000 words maximum. Pays $50 per feature article minimum.

COMPUTER DECISIONS, 50 Essex St., Rochelle Park NJ 07662. Editor: Hesh Wiener. 50% freelance written. For computer professionals, computer-involved managers in industry, finance, academia, etc. Well-educated, sophisticated, highly paid. Computer trade journals; 64 pages plus supplements. Estab. 1969. Monthly. Circ. 110,000. Buys first serial rights. Buys 12-24 mss/year. Pays on publication. Free sample copy to writer "who has a good background." Will consider photocopied submissions. Reports in 4 weeks. Enclose SASE.
Nonfiction: Department Editor: Larry Lettieri. "Mainly serious articles about technology, business practice. Interviews. Informational, technical, think pieces, exposes, spot news. News pieces about computers and their use. Articles should be clear and not stylized. Assertions should be well-supported by facts. We are business-oriented, witty, more interested in the unusual story, somewhat less technical than most. We'll run a good article with a computer peg even if it's not entirely about computers. Business analysis done by people with good backgrounds. Investigative stories on computers and crime." Length: 300 to 1,000 words for news; 1,000 to 5,000 words for features. Pays 3-10¢/word.

COMPUTER DESIGN, 11 Goldsmith St., Littleton MA 01460. Editor: John A. Camuso. 35% freelance written. For digital electronic design engineers. Monthly. Buys all rights and simultaneous rights. Pays on publication. Free sample copy. Reports in 4-8 weeks. SASE.
Nonfiction: Publishes engineering articles on the design and application of digital circuits, equipment, and systems used in computing, data processing, control and communications.

Query. Pays $30 to $40/page.

COMPUTERWORLD, 797 Washington St., Newton MA 02160. Editor: E. Drake Lundell, Jr. 10% freelance written. For management-level computer users, chiefly in the business community, but also in government and education. Estab. 1967. Weekly. Circ. 87,000. Buys all rights, but may reassign rights to author after publication. Pays on publication. Free sample copy, if request is accompanied by story idea or specific query. Free writer's guidelines. Photocopied submissions OK, if exclusive for stated period. No simultaneous submissions. Submit special issue material 2 months in advance. Reports in 2 to 4 weeks. SASE.
Nonfiction and Photos: Articles on problems in using computers; educating computer people; trends in the industry; new, innovative, interesting uses of computers. "We stress impact on users and need a practical approach. What does a development mean for other computer users? Most important facts first, then in decreasing order of significance. We would be interested in material on factory automation and other areas of computer usage that will impact society in general, and not just businesses. We prefer *not* to see executive appointments or financial results. We occasionally accept innovative material that is oriented to unique seasonal or geographical issues." Buys 100 mss/year. Query. Length: 250 to 1,200 words. Pays 10¢/word. B&w (5x7) glossies purchased with ms or on assignment. Captions required. Pays $5 to $10.
Fillers: Newsbreaks, clippings. Length: 50 to 250. Pays 10¢/word.

CREATIVE COMPUTING, Box 789-M, Morristown NJ 07960. Publisher: David Ahi. Editor-in-Chief: Stephen B. Gray. Managing Editor: Burchenal Green. Emphasizes the use of computers in homes and schools for students, faculty, hobbyists, everyone interested in the effects of computers on society and the use of computers in school, at home, or at work. Bimonthly magazine; 144 pages. Estab. 1974. Circ. 50,000. Pays on acceptance. Buys all rights, but may reassign following publication. Submit seasonal/holiday material at least 4 months in advance. SASE. Reports in 4-5 weeks. Sample copy $2.
Nonfiction: How-to articles (building a computer at home; getting a computer system to work); informational (computer careers, simulations on computers, problem solving techniques, use in a particluar institution or discipline such as medicine, education, music, animation, space exploration, business or home use); historical articles (history of computers, or of a certain discipline, like computers and animation); interviews (with personalities in the hobbyist field, old-timers in the computer industry or someone doing innovative work); personal experience (first person account of using hardware or software actively sought); and technical articles on programs, games, simulations (with printout). Buys 300 mss/year. Length: 500-3,000 words. Pays $10-300.
Photos: Usually purchased with mss, with no additional payment, but sometimes pays $3-50 for b&w glossies or $3-110 for any size color.
Columns/Departments: Compendium uses interesting, short articles about crazy, silly, unfortunate, interesting uses of computers (some human interest) about use in menu planning, pole vaulting, exploring, mistakes in computer programming, etc. Length: 50-500 words. Pays $5-30. Pays in copy of book for book reviews (all books on computer use). Complete Computer Catalog accepts only press releases on new products.
Fiction: Humorous fiction, mysteries, science fiction. "Must be specifically related to computer use. Stories that are of an interesting style that show how computers can benefit society are sought. Stories must keep in mind that people program computers and should program them for people's benefit. Stories dealing with new field of computers in the home are also sought." Buys 30 mss/year. Submit complete ms. Length: 500-3,000 words. Pays $15-400.
Poetry: Avant-garde, free verse, haiku, light verse, traditional forms and computer-generated poetry. Buys about 30/year. Submit complete poem. Pays $10-100.
Fillers: Jokes, gags, anecdotes, puzzles, short humor. Buys 20/year. Send fillers in. Pays $3-25.

JOURNAL OF SYSTEMS MANAGEMENT, 24587 Bagley Road, Cleveland OH 44138. (216)243-6900. Publisher: James Andrews. 100% freelance written. For systems and procedures and management people. Monthly. Buys all serial rights. Pays on publication. Will send a free sample copy on request. Query first. Reports as soon as possible. Enclose SASE.
Nonfiction: Uses articles on case histories, projects on systems, forms control, administrative practices, computer operations. Length: 3,000 to 5,000 words. Maximum payment is $25.

Dental

CAL MAGAZINE, 3737 West 127th St., Chicago IL 60658. Editor: M.E. Yukich. For dentists,

dental assistants and dental technicians. Estab. 1935. Monthly. Circ. 50,000. Buys all rights, but will reassign to author after publication. Pays on acceptance. Will send free sample copy on request. Submit complete ms only. Reports in 6 weeks. Enclose SASE.
Nonfiction and Photos: Articles pertaining to or about dentists and dentistry; accomplishments of dentists in other fields. History, art, humor, adventure, unusual achievements, successful business operations, new products, merchandising techniques and technical. Length: 1,500 to 2,000 words. Pays $25 to $100. B&w photos only, 8x10 or 5x7 glossy, purchased with mss or captions only. Pays $25 to $50.
Fiction: "Related in some way to dentistry." Length: 1,500 to 2,000 words. Pays $25 to $100.
Poetry and Fillers: Light verse. "Related to dentistry." Puzzles, short humor. Pays $3 minimum.

CONTACTS, Box 407, North Chatham NY 12132. Editor: Joseph Strack. For laboratory owners, managers, and dental technician staffs. Estab. 1938. Bimonthly. Circ. 1,200. Pays on acceptance. Free sample copy. Reports in 1-2 weeks. SASE.
Nonfiction and Photos: Writer should know the dental laboratory field or have good contacts there to provide technical articles, how-to, and successful business operation articles. Query. Length: 1,500 words maximum. Pays 3¢ to 5¢ a word. Willing to receive suggestions for columns and departments for material of 400 to 800 words. Payment for these negotiable.

DENTAL ECONOMICS, Box 1260, Tulsa OK 74101. Editor: Pat Redmond. 60% freelance written. Emphasizes "practice management for dentists." Monthly magazine; 90 pages. Estab. 1911. Circ. 103,000. Pays on acceptance. Buys all rights, but may reassign following publication. Submit seasonal/holiday material 6 months in advance of issue date. SASE. Reports in 4 weeks. Free sample copy and writer's guidelines.
Nonfiction: Exposé (closed panels, NHI); how-to (hire personnel, bookkeeping, improve production); humor (in-office type); investments (all kinds); interview (doctors in the news, health officials); personal experience (of dentists, but only if related to business side of practice); profile (a few on doctors who made dramatic lifestyle changes); and travel (only if dentist is involved). Buys 120 mss/year. Query or submit complete ms. Length: 600-3,500 words. Pays $50-500.
Photos: State availability of photos with query or submit photos with ms. Pays $5 minimum for 8x10 glossy photos; $15 minimum for 35mm color transparencies. Captions and model release required. Buys one-time rights.
Columns/Departments: Viewpoint (issues of dentistry are aired here); and Tip of the Month (250 words on an idea that aids dental office management). Buys 2 mss/issue. Submit complete ms. Length: 600-1,500 words. Pays $50-125. Open to suggestions for new columns/departments.

DENTAL MANAGEMENT, Harcourt Brace Jovanovich, 757 3rd Ave., New York NY 10017. Editor: M.J. Goldberg. 25% freelance written. "*Dental Management* is the national business publication for dentists." Monthly magazine; 100 pages. Estab. January 1961. Circ. 100,000. Pays on acceptance. Buys all rights, but may reassign following publication. Submit seasonal/holiday material 4 months in advance of issue date. Photocopied and simultaneous submissions OK. SASE. Reports in 2 weeks. Free writer's guidelines.
Nonfiction: "The editorial aim of *Dental Management* is to help the dentist to build a bigger, more successful practice, to help him conserve and invest his money, and to help him keep posted on the economic, legal, and sociological changes that affect him." Exposé; general interest; how-to; and interview. Buys 2-4 mss/issue. Query. Length: 1,000-2,500 words. Pays 10-15¢/word.

THE JOURNAL OF ORAL IMPLANTOLOGY, 469 Washington St., Abington MA 02351. Editor: Dr. Isaih Lew. Executive Director: John P. Winiewicz. For the dental profession and related areas of medicine and technology. Magazine; 150 pages. Estab. 1970. Quarterly. Circ. 2,000. Not copyrighted. Time of payment depends on arrangements made to the convenience of the author. Will send sample copy to writer on request. Write for copy of guidelines for writers. Will consider photocopied submissions. May consider simultaneous submissions. Submit complete ms. Enclose SASE.
Nonfiction and Photos: Technical articles on all related areas of dental implantology to include materials and devices, medical research that relates to this field. Basic research, basic technology and any new research being done on new materials. Length: open. Pays $25 minimum, based on acceptability of material supplied and approval by the editorial board. No additional payment for photos used with mss.

PROOFS, The Magazine of Dental Sales, Box 1260, Tulsa OK 74101. (918)835-3161. Publisher: Joe Bessette. Monthly. Pays on acceptance. Will send free sample copy on request. Query first. Reports in a week. Enclose SASE.
Nonfiction: Uses short articles, chiefly on selling to dentists. Must have understanding of dental trade industry, and problems of marketing and selling to dentists and dental laboratories. Pays about $75.

TIC MAGAZINE, Box 407, North Chatham NY 12132. (518)766-3047. Editor: Joseph Strack. For dentists, dental assistants, and oral hygienists. Monthly. Buys first publication rights in the dental field. Pays on acceptance. Reports in 2 weeks. SASE.
Nonfiction: Uses articles (with illustrations, if possible) as follows: 1. Lead feature: Dealing with major developments in dentistry of direct, vital interest to all dentists. 2. How-to-do-it pieces: Ways and means of building dental practices, improving professional techniques, managing patients, increasing office efficiency, etc.; 3. Special articles: ways and means of improving dentist-laboratory relations for mutual advantage, of developing auxiliary dental personnel into an efficient office team, of helping the individual dentist to play a more effective role in alleviating the burden of dental needs in the nation and in his community, etc. 4. General articles: Concerning any phase of dentistry or dentistry-related subjects of high interest to the average dentist. Query. Length: 800 to 3,200 words. Pays 4¢ minimum per word.
Photos: Photo stories: four to ten pictures of interesting developments and novel ideas in dentistry. B&w only. Pays $10 minimum per photo.
How To Break In: "We can use fillers of about 300 words or so. They should be pieces of substance on just anything of interest to dentists. A psychoanalyst broke in with us recently with pieces relating to interpretations of patients' problems and attitudes in dentistry. Another writer just broke in with a profile of a dentist working with an Indian tribe."

Department Store, Variety, and Dry Goods

JUVENILE MERCHANDISING, 370 Lexington Ave., New York NY 10017. (212)532-9290. Editor-in-Chief: Joseph Feldmann. 25% freelance written. For retail store owners, buyers and manufacturers of juvenile products. Monthly magazine; 52 pages. Circ. 11,000. Pays on publication. Buys all rights, but may reassign following publication. Phone queries OK. Submit seasonal/holiday material 4 months in advance of issue date. Simultaneous, photocopied and previously published submissions OK. Reports in 2 weeks. Free sample copy and writer's guidelines; mention *Writer's Market* in request.
Nonfiction and Photos: "Stories should emphasize how sales and profits can be increased. How-to articles, merchandising stories, juvenile store coverage, etc. Solid features about a phase of juvenile operation in any of the above-mentioned retail establishments. Not interested in store histories. Mss on successful displays, methods for more efficient management; also technical articles on stock control or credit or mail promotion—how a specific juvenile store uses these, why they were undertaken, what results they brought. Factual material with pertinent quotes. Emphasis on benefits to other retail operations. Illustrated interviews with successful dealers." Length: 1,000-1,500 words. Pays $50-$75.

MILITARY MARKET, Army Times Publishing Co., 475 School St., S.W., Washington DC 20024. (202)554-7180. Editor-in-Chief: Tony Polozzolo. For store managers, headquarters personnel, Pentagon decision-makers, Congressional types, wholesalers to the military, manufacturers. Monthly magazine; 56 pages. Estab. 1954. Circ. 13,500. Pays on acceptance. Buys all rights, but may reassign following publication. Phone queries OK. Submit seasonal or holiday material 4 months in advance. SASE. Reports in 2 months. Free sample copy.
Nonfiction: Publishes how-to articles (directed toward improving management techniques or store operations); humor (funny aspects of the business); informational (implementation of policies and directions); interviews (notables in the field); technical (store operations). Buys 1 ms a year. Length: 1,000-4,000 words. Query first. Pays $75-300.

SEW BUSINESS, 666 5th Ave., New York NY 10019. Editor: Cristina Holmes. For retailers of home-sewing and needle-work merchandise. Monthly. Circ. 14,000. Not copyrighted. Pays on publication. Free sample copy. Reports in 1 month. SASE.
Nonfiction and Photos: Articles on department store or fabric shop operations, including coverage of art needlework, piece goods, patterns, sewing accessories and all other notions. Interviews with buyers—retailers on their department or shop. "Unless they are doing something

different or offbeat, something that another retailer could put to good use in his own operation, there is no sense wasting their or your time in doing an interview and story. Best to query editor first to find out if a particular article might be of interest to us.'' Buys 100 mss/year. Query. Length: 500 to 1,500 words. Pays $85 minimum. Photos purchased with mss. ''Should illustrate important details of the story.'' Sharp 8x10 b&w glossies. Pays $5.
Fillers: $2.50 for news items less than 100 words. For news item plus photo and caption, pays $7.50.

Drugs, Health Care, and Medical Products

CANADIAN PHARMACEUTICAL JOURNAL, 175 College St., Toronto, Ontario, Canada M5T 1P8. (416)979-2431. Editor: N.A. McIver. 75% freelance written. For pharmacists. Monthly magazine; 40 pages. Estab. 1868. Circ. 8,700. Pays on publication. Buys all rights, but may reassign following publication. Phone queries OK. SASE. Reports in 1 month. Free sample copy and writer's guidelines.
Nonfiction: Publishes exposes (pharmacy practice, education and legislation); how-to (pharmacy business operations); historical (pharmacy practice, legislation, education); interviews with and profiles on pharmacy figures. Buys 2-4 mss/year. Length: 1,000-3,000 words. Query first. Payment is contingent on value; usually 8¢/word.
Photos: B&w (5x7) glossies and color transparencies purchased with mss. Captions required. Payment by arrangement. Model release required.

DRUG SURVIVAL NEWS, c/o Do It Now Foundation, Box 5115, Phoenix AZ 85010. (602)257-0797. Editor: Michael Burkett. For directors and workers in drug abuse and alcoholism field; schools, counselors, nurses, state and local mental health agencies, military drug and alcohol programs, and interested people concerned with the problems of drug and alcohol abuse. Bimonthly tabloid newspaper; 16 pages. Estab. 1970. Circ. 20,000. Buys all rights, but may reassign rights to author after publication. Retains the option of publishing later as a pamphlet or part of a collection. Pays on publication. Free sample copy. Photocopied submissions OK. Simultaneous submissions are considered only when they know name of publication to which other submission was sent. Reports in 1 month. SASE.
Nonfiction and Photos: Research, news and articles about effects of various chemicals. In-depth articles about prominent programs and the people who run them. Writers should have experience with these subjects, either professionally or subjectively (as a former user, etc., but not prejudiced against the topics beforehand). Would like to see over-the-counter drug stories, but nothing on marijuana, or articles by ex-addicts or ex-alcoholics telling about their lives. Informational, interview, profile, historical, personal opinion, photo features, book reviews, spot news, successful program operations, new product and technical articles. Query. Length: 100 to 2,000 words. Pays $5 to $50. B&w photos purchased with mss or on assignment. Captions required. Pays $5 to $10.
Fillers: Drug-related newsbreaks, jokes, gags, anecdotes. Length: 100-300 words. Pays $5 to $10. Pays less for clippings.

DRUG TOPICS, 680 Kinderkamack Rd., Oradell NJ 07649. (201)262-3030. Editor: Barbara Johnson. Executive Editor: Ralph M. Thurlow. For retail drug stores and wholesalers, manufacturers, and hospital pharmacists. Monthly. Circ. over 70,000. Buys all rights. Pays on acceptance. SASE.
Nonfiction: News of local, regional, state pharmaceutical assocations, legislation affecting operation of drug stores, news of pharmacists in civic and professional activities, etc. Query first on drug store success stories which deal with displays, advertising, promotions, selling techniques. Query. Length: 1,500 words maximum. Pays $5 and up for leads, $25 and up for short articles, $50 to $200 for feature articles, ''depending on length and depth.''
Photos: May buy photos submitted with mss. May buy news photos with captions only. Pay $20.

PATIENT AID DIGEST, 2009 Morris Ave., Union NJ 07083. (201)687-8282. Editor: Laurie N. Cassak. For pharmacists, home health care managers and manufacturers of patient aid products. Estab. 1970. Bimonthly. Circ. 11,000. Buys all rights. Pays on publication. Free sample copy and writer's guidelines. Photocopied and simultaneous submissions OK. Reports in 8 weeks. SASE.
Nonfiction and Photos: ''Articles about existing home health care centers or opportunities for proprietors; human interest stories that deal with health care; helpful hints for the pharmacist. It

is essential to understand your reading audience. Articles must be informative, but not extremely technical." Buys informational, how-to, interview, photo articles. Query. Length: 1,000-1,500 words. Pays 5¢/word. Photos purchased with accompanying ms with no additional payment. Captions optional.

WHOLESALE DRUGS, 1111 E. 54th St., Indianapolis IN 46220. Editor: William F. Funkhouser. Bimonthly. Buys first rights only. Query first. SASE.
Nonfiction and Photos: Wants features on presidents and salesmen of Full Line Wholesale Drug Houses throughout the country. No set style, but subject matter should tell about both the man and his company—history, type of operation, etc. Pays $50 for text and pictures.

Education

Professional educators, teachers, coaches, and school personnel read the journals classified here. Publications for parents, or the general public interested in education-related topics are listed under Education in the Consumer Publications section.

THE AMERICAN SCHOOL BOARD JOURNAL, National School Boards Association, 1055 Thomas Jefferson St., N.W., Washington DC 20007. (202)337-7666. Editor-in-Chief: James Betchkal. Emphasizes public school administration and policymaking. For elected members of public boards of education throughout the U.S. and Canada, and high level administrators of same. Monthly magazine; 64 pages. Estab. 1891. Circ. 50,000. Pays on acceptance. Buys all rights. Phone queries OK. Submit seasonal or holiday material 4-6 months in advance. Photocopied submissions OK. SASE. Reports in 3 months. Free sample copy.
Nonfiction: Publishes how-to articles (solutions to problems of public school operation including political problems); interviews with notable figures in public education. Buys 20 mss a year. Query first. Length: 400-2,000 words. Payment varies, "but never less than $100."
Photos: B&w glossies (any size) and color purchased on assighnment. Captions required. Pays $10-50. Model release required.

AMERICAN SCHOOL & UNIVERSITY, North American Publishing Co., 401 N. Broad St., Philadelphia PA 19108. Editor-in-Chief: Rita Robison. Emphasizes "facilities and business office matters of schools, colleges, and universities (no curriculum, etc)." For "administrators such as superintendents of buildings and grounds, business officials, school superintendents, college vice-presidents of operations, etc." Monthly magazine; 70-120 pages. Estab. 1928. Circ. 41,000. Pays on publication. Buys all rights, but may reassign following publication. Reports in 3-6 weeks.
Nonfiction: Photo feature (new or renovated buildings, with architectural/engineering description), technical (energy conservation measures, solar energy applications, business practices that save money). "We prefer the 'this was the problem and this is how it was solved' approach." Buys 3-4 mss a year. Query. Length: 500-1,800 words. Pays $25/page minimum.
Photos: Used with accompanying ms for no additional payment. Submit 8x10 b&w glossies or 4x5 color transparencies.

ARTS & ACTIVITIES, 591 Camino de la Reina, San Diego CA 92108. (714)297-5352. Editor-in-Chief: Dr. Leven C. Leatherbury. 90% freelance written. Emphasizes art education. Monthly (except July and August) magazine; 72 pages. Estab. 1937. Circ. 30,000. Pays on publication. Buys all rights, but may reassign following publication. Phone queries OK. Submit seasonal/holiday material 3 months in advance of issue date. Reports in 3 weeks. Free sample copy and writer's guidelines.
Nonfiction: How-to (describing specific lessons and projects which have proved successful); and articles on art history and art education. Buys 10-13 mss/issue. Submit complete ms. Length: 500 words average. Pays $20-80.
Photos: Submit photo material with accompanying ms. No additional payment for 5x7 b&w glossy prints or color transparencies. Captions preferred. Buys all rights, but may reassign following publication.

THE ARTS IN EDUCATION, 501 N. Virginia Ave., Winter Park FL 32789. Editor-in-Chief: Joan L. Wahl. 50% freelance written. Emphasizes art, craft, music, dance and theatre for school teachers in elementary and Jr. High grades, workshop teachers, scout leaders, and professors in education course studies in elementary education. Monthly magazine: 36 pages. Estab. November 1977. Pays on publication. Buys all rights, but may reassign following publication.

Submit seasonal/holiday material 2 months in advance of issue date. Photocopied submissions OK. SASE. Reports in 2 weeks. Sample copy $1.75; writer's guidelines for SASE; mention *Writer's Market* in request.
Nonfiction: How-to (geared toward classroom teacher on visual arts and performing arts); profile (on a professional artist only). Buys 6 mss/issue. Query. Length: 500-1,000 words. Pays 2¢/word.
Photos: State availability of photos with query. Pays $1-5 for 3½x5 or 5x7 b&w prints. Captions required. Buys all rights, but may reassign after publication. Release required.
Fiction: Adventure (plays for children with "goodness and righteousness reigning over all."); fantasy (plays for children grades 3-9); humorous (plays only); mystery (plays only); and science fiction (plays only). Buys 10 mss/year. Query. Length: 8-30 min. Pays $10-15.

CATECHIST, Peter LI, Inc., 2451 E. River Rd., Dayton OH 45439. Editor: Patricia Fischer. Emphasizes religious education for professional and volunteer religious educators working in Catholic schools. Monthly (September-May) magazine; 40 pages. Estab. 1966. Circ. 82,000. Pays on publication. Buys all rights. Submit seasonal or holiday material 3 months in advance. SASE. Reports in 1 month. Sample copy 50¢; free writer's guidelines.
Nonfiction: Publishes how-to articles (methods for teaching a particular topic or concept); informational (theology and church-related subjects, insights into current trends and developments); personal experience (in the religious classroom). Length: 1,500 words maximum. Buys 45 mss a year. Query first. Pays $30-75.
Photos: B&w (8x10) glossies purchased without mss. Send contact sheet. Pays $15-25.
How To Break In: "By writing articles that would be of practical use for the teacher of religion or an article that results from personal experience and expertise in the field."

CHILDREN'S HOUSE, P.O. Box 111, Caldwell NJ 07006. Editor: Kenneth Edelson. 75% freelance written. For teachers and parents of young children. Magazine; 32 (8½x11) pages. Established in 1966. Every 2 months. Circulation: 50,000. Buys all rights. Buys 20 to 30 mss a year. Pays on publication. Sample copy for $1.25; free writer's guidelines. Will consider photocopied submissions. Reports on material accepted for publication in 3 to 6 months. Query first or submit complete ms. Enclose SASE.
Nonfiction and Photos: Department Editor: Margery Mossman. Articles on education, Montessori, learning disabilities, atypical children, innovative schools and methods; new medical, psychological experiments. "We're not afraid to tackle controversial topics such as sex education, etc., but we don't want to see personal or family histories. No 'why-Johnny-can't-read' articles." Informational, how-to, profile, think articles. Length: 1,200 to 2,000 words. Pays 2¢/word, and up "conditionally". 5x7 or 7x9 b&w glossies purchased on assignment. Pays minimum of $5.
Fillers: Newsbreaks, clippings. Length: 1 or 2 paragraphs. Pays minimum of $5/inch "conditionally".

CHRISTIAN TEACHER, Box 550, Wheaton IL 60187. (312)665-0786. Editor: Herman Van-Schuyver. For "members of the National Association of Christian Schools. They are mostly grade school teachers; also, high school teachers, principals, board members, parents." Estab. 1964. Bimonthly, except during summer. Circ. 3,500. Not copyrighted. Free sample copy. Reports "quickly." SASE.
Nonfiction and Photos: "Educational trends, reports, how-to—mostly informative or inspirational. Our publication deals with education from a Christian point of view." Query. Length for articles: 500-2,000 words. Payment: "Token payment for acceptable articles."

COMMUNITY COLLEGE FRONTIERS, Sangamon State University, Shepherd Rd., Springfield IL 62708. Editor-in-Chief: J. Richard Johnston. 80-85% freelance written. For all persons interested in two-year post-secondary educational institutions, especially faculty, administrators, trustees and students in public community colleges. Quarterly magazine; 56 pages. Estab. 1972. Circ. 5,000. Pays in contributor's copies. Acquires all rights, but will reassign following publication. Phone queries OK. All material should be given minimum of 3 months' lead time. SASE. Reports in 6-8 weeks. Free sample copy and writer's guidelines.
Nonfiction: Publishes historical articles (of community colleges); how-to (college teaching strategies to organize subject material and motivate students); humor (satire on stuffy, pompous educators); informational (analytical reports on college instructional programs); inspirational (individual students/adults; sincerity, handicapped, etc.). Query first.
Photos: Uses B&w glossies (8x10) with captions and credit line. Send contact sheet.
Columns, Departments: Say It With Words (stuffy, pretentious, academic language and style;

funny errors; play on words, etc.); Frontiers Exchange (brief information on special programs, techniques, or ideas). "We are especially interested in informal learning networks for adults, cooperatives, collective, non-profit enterprises, etc." Length: 300 words maximum. Query with sample lead paragraph.
How To Break In: "Writing fresh viewpoints (critical views are welcome) upon college education in clear, simple language. Personal experience related to important general principles make good material for us."

CURRICULUM REVIEW, Curriculum Advisory Service, 500 S. Clinton St., Chicago IL 60607. (312)939-1333. Editor-in-Chief: Irene M. Goldman. For teachers K-12, curriculum planners, librarians, graduate schools of education. 5 times yearly magazine; 80 pages. Estab. 1961. Circ. 2,000. Pays on publication. Buys all rights, but will reassign following publication. Phone queries OK. Photocopied submissions OK. Reports in 6 weeks. Free sample copy and writer's guidelines.
Nonfiction: Charlotte H. Cox, Articles Editor. Informational (on education or curriculum for K-12, current trends, methods, theory). Buys 20 essay mss a year. Query. Length: 1,000-2,000 words. Pays $30-50. Also publishes 300-400 book reviews/year on an assigned basis; classroom text materials in language arts, mathematics, science, social studies. Pays $10-50 a review depending on scope and difficulty of materials. Send educational vita. "We are especially interested in innovative articles by curriculum planners, school superintendents, deans of graduate education, or interdisciplinary specialists on new educational approaches."
For '79: "We will feature environmental studies, women's studies, career education, values education, and metrics, among other topics. Schedule available on request."

EDUCATIONAL STUDIES: A Journal in the Foundations of Education, 107 Quadrangle, Ames IA 55011. (515)294-7327. Editor-in-Chief: Dr. L. Glenn Smith. 85% freelance written. Emphasizes research, reviews and opinions in the foundations of education. Quarterly magazine; 120 pages. Estab. 1970. Circ. 1,500. Pays on publication. Buys all rights, but may reassign following publication. Phone queries OK. Photocopied submissions OK. SASE. Reports in 3 months. Free sample copy and writer's guidelines.
Nonfiction: Historical and informational articles; must relate to the Foundations of Education. Also uses pieces on experimental research. Buys 8-12 mss/year. Submit 3 copies of complete ms. Length: 1,000-3,500 words. Pays $25 maximum, but sometimes no payment is made.
Photos: No additional payment for 8x10 b&w glossies used with mss. Captions required. Send contact sheet or prints. Model release required.
Poetry: Traditional forms, free verse, haiku and light verse. Length: 4-24.

FORECAST FOR HOME ECONOMICS, 50 W. 44th St., New York NY 10036. (212)867-7700. Editor-in-Chief: Gloria S. Spitz. Managing Editor: Renee Maccarrone. 10% freelance written. Monthly (September-June) magazine; 80 pages. Estab. 1954. Circ. 78,000. Pays on publication. Buys all rights. Submit seasonal/holiday material 6-8 months in advance of issue date. SASE. Free writer's guidelines.
Nonfiction: Current consumer/home economics related issues, especially energy, careers, family relations/child development, teaching techniques, health, nutrition, metrics, mainstreaming the handicapped, appealing to both boys and girls in the classroom, money management, housing, crafts, bulletin board and game ideas. Buys 3 mss/issue. Query. Length: 1,000-3,000 words. Pays $25 minimum.
Photos: State availability of photos with query. No additional payment for b&w glossy prints. Captions required. Model release required.

HOSPITAL/HEALTH CARE TRAINING MEDIA PROFILES, Olympic Media Information, 71 W. 23 St., New York NY 10010. (212)675-4500. Publisher: Walt Carroll. 100% freelance written. For hospital education departments, nursing schools, schools of allied health, paramedical training units, colleges, community colleges, local health organizations. Serial, in loose leaf format, published every 2 months. Established in 1974. Circulation: 1,000 plus. Buys all rights. Buys about 240 mss a year. Payment on publication. Will send free sample copy to writer on request. "Send resume of your experience to introduce yourself." Will not consider photocopied or simultaneous submissions. Reports in 1 month. Query first. Enclose SASE.
Nonfiction: "Reviews of all kinds of audiovisual media. We are the only existing review publication devoted to evaluation of audiovisual aids for hospital and health training. We have a highly specialized, definite format that must be followed in all cases. Samples should be seen by all means. Our writers should first have a background in health sciences, secondly, some experience with audiovisuals; and third, follow our format precisely. Besides basic biological

sciences, we are interested in materials for nursing education, in-service education, continuing education, personnel training, patient education, patient care, medical problems. Contact us and send a resume of your experience in writing for hospital, science, health fields. We will assign audiovisual aids to qualified writers and send them these to review for us. Unsolicited mss not welcome." Pays $10/review.

ILLINOIS SCHOOLS JOURNAL, Chicago State University, 95th St. at King Drive, Chicago IL 60628. Editor: Virginia McDavid, Department of English, room E-356. Primarily for teachers and professional educators. Quarterly magazine; 64 to 80 pages. Estab. 1906. Circ. 7,000. Acquires all rights, but will reassign rights to author after publication. Pays in contributor's copies. Free sample copy and writer's guidelines. Photocopied submissions OK. No simultaneous submissions. Reports in 3 months. SASE.
Nonfiction: Educational subject matter. Concentrate on practical aspects of education. Submit complete ms. Length: 2,000 to 3,000 words.

INDUSTRIAL EDUCATION, 77 Bedford St., Stamford CT 06901. For administrators and instructors in elementary, secondary, and post-secondary education in industrial arts, vocational, industrial and technical education. Monthly, except July and August and combined May-June issue. Buys all rights. Pays on acceptance. Free writer's guidelines. Deadline for Shop Planning Annual is Dec. 29; for Back to School and Projects, July 1. Reports in 5 weeks. Enclose SASE for return of submissions.
Nonfiction and Photos: "Articles dealing with the broad aspects of industrial arts, vocational, and technical education as it is taught in our junior and senior high schools, vocational and technical high schools, and junior colleges. We're interested in analytical articles in relation to such areas as curriculum planning, teacher training, teaching methods, supervision, professional standards, industrial arts or vocational education, industrial practice, relationship of industrial education to industry at the various educational levels, current problems, trends, etc. How-to-do, how-to-teach, how-to-make articles of a very practical nature which will assist the instructor in the laboratory at every level of industrial education. Typical are the 'activities' articles in every instructional area. Also typical is the article which demonstrates to the teacher a new or improved way of doing something or of teaching something or how to utilize special teaching aids or equipment to full advantage—activities which help the teacher do a better job of introducing the industrial world of work to the student." Length: maximum 2,500 words. Pays 5¢/word. 8x10 b&w photos purchased with ms.
Fillers: Short hints on some aspect of shop management or teaching techniques. Length: 25 to 250 words.

INSTRUCTOR MAGAZINE, 7 Bank St., Dansville NY 14437. (716)335-2221. Editor-in-Chief: Leanna Landsmann. Administrative Editor: Rosemary Alexander. 30% freelance written. Emphasizes elementary education. Monthly magazine; 180 pages. Estab. 1889. Circ. 275,000. Pays on acceptance. Buys all rights, but may reassign following publication. Phone queries OK. Submit seasonal/holiday material 6 months in advance of issue date. Photocopied submissions OK. SASE. Reports in 6 weeks. Free sample copy and writer's guidelines; mention *Writer's Market* in request.
Nonfiction: How-to articles on elementary classroom practice—practical suggestions as well as project reports. Buys 10-15 mss/year. Query. Length: 750-2,500 words. Pays $10-500.

JGE: The Journal of General Education, Penn State University Press, 215 Wagner Bldg., University Park PA 16802. Editors-in-Chief: Caroline and Robert Eckhardt. 99% freelance written. Emphasizes general education, for teachers of undergraduates in colleges and universities. Quarterly magazine; 104 pages. Estab. 1946. Circ. 1,450. Acquires all rights, but may reassign following publication. SASE. Reports in 4 weeks. Free sample copy and writer's guidelines.
Nonfiction: How-to (teaching specific topics), informational (new ideas, fresh approaches, findings). Uses 30 mss a year. Query. Length: No limits. Pays in 25 offprints of the article.

JOURNAL OF ENGLISH TEACHING TECHNIQUES, University of Michigan, Flint MI 48503. (313)767-4000. Editor: Dr. F.K. Bartz. For public school English teachers, English professors in colleges and universities. Estab. 1968. Quarterly. Circ. 500. Acquires all rights. Pays in contributor's copies. Sample copy $1. Reports in 6 weeks. SASE.
Nonfiction: Articles on the teaching of English; book reviews; short features; bibliographies. exercises; and anything of interest to English teachers. All material must follow the *M.L.A. Style Sheet*. Query or submit complete ms.

JOURNAL OF READING, THE READING TEACHER, International Reading Association, 800 Barksdale Rd., Box 8139, Newark DE 19711. (302)731-1600. Editor-in-Chief: Dr. Janet R. Binkley. 90% freelance written. For teachers, reading specialists, or other school personnel; college and university faculty, independent researchers. Monthly (October-May) magazines; 132 pages *(The Reading Teacher);* 96 pages *(Journal of Reading).* Estab: 1948 *(The Reading Teacher);* 1957 *(Journal of Reading).* No payment. Phone queries OK. Photocopied submissions OK. SASE. Reports in 3 months. Sample copy $2.
Nonfiction: Publishes articles that deal with reading, teaching reading, learning to read; about children or adults. Theory, techniques, research, mental processes, history, humor; current events in reading education, etc. Articles about learners through grade 6 go to *The Reading Teacher;* articles about secondary and adult learners, go to *Journal of Reading.* Length: 100-3,000 words. Submit complete ms.
Photos: "We have no budget for photos, but are delighted to use reading-related photos (b&w) with articles and on *Journal of Reading* covers, when donated."
Columns/Departments: Tips on effective teaching techniques for Interchange *(The Reading Teacher)* and Open to Suggestion *(Journal of Reading).*
Poetry: "We don't buy poetry, but would gladly publish more than is contributed at present." Avant-garde, free verse, haiku, light verse and traditional forms acceptable.

LEARNING, The Magazine for Creative Teaching, 530 University Ave., Palo Alto CA 94301. Editor: Morton Malkofsky. 45% freelance written. Emphasizes elementary and junior high school education topics. Monthly during school year. Magazine; 150 pages. Estab. 1972. Circ. 225,000. Pays on acceptance. Buys all rights, but may reassign following publication. Submit seasonal/holiday material 6 months in advance of issue date. Photocopied submissions OK. SASE. Reports in 2 months. Free sample copy and writer's guidelines.
Nonfiction: "We publish manuscripts that describe innovative teaching strategies or probe controversial and significant social/political issues related to the professional and classroom interest of preschool to 8th grade teachers". How-to (classroom mangement, specific lessons or units or activities for children—all at the elementary and junior high level, and hints for teaching math and science); interview (with teachers who are in unusual or innovative teaching situations); new product; personal experience (from teachers in elementary and junior high school); and profile (with teachers who are in unusual or innovative teaching situations). Buys 6 mss/issue. Query. Length: 1,500-3,500 words. Pays $150-350.
Photos: State availablity of photos with query. Offers no additional payment for 8x10 b&w glossy prints or 35mm color transparencies. Captions preferred. Buys all rights, but may reassign following publication. Model release required.
Columns/Departments: Book Reviews (educational); Short Stuff (new/old news in education); and Swap Shop (how-to's $25.). Query or submit complete ms with SASE. Open to suggestions for new columns/departments.

THE LIVING LIGHT, 1312 Massachusetts Ave., N.W., Washington DC 20005. An interdisciplinary review for "professionals in the field of religious education, primarily Roman Catholics." Estab. in 1964. Quarterly. Buys all rights but will reassign rights to author after publication. Pays on publication. Sample copy $3.50. Reports in 30-60 days. SASE.
Nonfiction: Articles that "present development and trends, report on research and encourage critical thinking in the field of religious education and pastoral action. Academic approach." Buys 4 mss/year. Submit complete ms. Length: 2,000 to 5,000 words. Pays $40 to $100.

THE MANITOBA TEACHER, 191 Harcourt St., Winnipeg, Manitoba, Canada R3J 3H2. (204)888-7961. Editor: Mrs. Miep van Raalte. 25% freelance written. For teachers in the public schools of Manitoba. Published 10 times/year. Tabloid; 8-12 pages. Estab. 1919. Circ. 17,300. No payment. Phone queries OK. Submit seasonal/holiday material 3 months in advance of issue date. Photocopied and previously published submissions OK. SASE. Reports in 4 weeks. Free sample copy and writer's guidelines.
Nonfiction: How-to (teach a particular subject, introduce new programs or approaches, etc.); humor (related to education in Manitoba); interview (dealing with education); personal opinion (issues pertaining to education in Manitoba); profile (of special interest to teachers in Manitoba); personal experience (classroom experiences); and photo feature (educational event). No lengthly scholarly essays. Submit complete ms. Length: 200-1,500 words.
Photos: State availability of photos with ms. Uses any size glossy b&w or color prints.
Columns/Departments: Reaction, Readers Write, News Briefs, President's Message, and General Secretary Comments. Submit complete ms. Length: 300-800 words. Open to suggestions for new columns/departments.

MEDIA & METHODS, 401 N. Broad St., Philadelphia PA 19108. Editor: Anthony Prete. For English and social studies teachers who have an abiding interest in humanistic and media-oriented education, plus a core of librarians, media specialists, filmmakers; the cutting edge of educational innovators. Magazine; 56 to 64 (8½x11) pages. Estab. 1964. Monthly (September through May). Circ. 50,000. Rights purchased vary with author and material. Normally buys all rights. About half of each issue is freelance material. Pays on publication. Free writer's guidelines to qualified writers. Will consider photocopied submissions. No simultaneous submissions. Reports on material in 2-4 months. Submit complete ms or query first. Enclose SASE.
Nonfiction: "We are looking for the middle school, high school or college educator who has something vital and interesting to say. Subjects include practical how-to articles with broad applicability to our readers, and innovative, challenging, conceptual-type stories that deal with educational change. Our style is breezy and conversational, occasionally offbeat. We make a concentrated effort to be non-sexist; mss filled with 'he', 'him', and 'mankind' (when the gender is unspecified) will pose unnecessary barriers to acceptance. We are a trade journal with a particular subject emphasis (media-oriented English and social studies), philosophical bent (humanistic, personal), and interest area (the practical and innovative)." Length: 2,500 words maximum. Pays $15 to $100.

MOMENTUM, National Catholic Educational Association, 1 Dupont Circle, Suite 350, Washington DC 20036. (202)293-5954. Editor: Carl Balcerak. For Catholic administrators and teachers, some parents and students, in all levels of education (preschool, elementary, secondary, higher). Quarterly magazine; 56 to 64 pages. Estab. 1970. Circ. 14,500. Buys all rights. Buys 28 to 36 mss per year. Pays on publication. Free sample copy. Will consider photocopied and simultaneous submissions. Submit special issue material 3 months in advance. Query first. Reports in 2 weeks. SASE.
Nonfiction and Photos: "Articles concerned with educational philosophy, psychology, methodology, innovative programs, teacher training, etc. Catholic-oriented material. Book reviews on educational-religious topics. Innovative educational programs; financial and public relations programs, management systems applicable to nonpublic schools. No pious ruminations on pseudoreligious ideas. Also, avoid general topics, such as what's right (wrong) with Catholic education. In most cases, a straightforward, journalistic style with emphasis on practical examples, is preferred. Some scholarly writing, but little in the way of statistical. All material has Catholic orientation, with emphasis on professionalism; not sentimental or hackneyed treatment of religious topics." Length: 2,500 to 3,000 words. Pays 2¢ per word. Pays $5 for b&w glossy photos purchased with mss. Captions required.

NATIONAL ON-CAMPUS REPORT, 621 N. Sherman Ave., Suite 4, Madison WI 53704. (608)249-2455. Editor: William H. Haight. 15% freelance written. For education administrators, college student leaders, journalists, and directors of youth organizations. Estab. 1972. Monthly. Not copyrighted. Pays on publication. Sample copy and writer's guidelines for SASE. Photocopied submissions OK. Reports in 1 month. SASE.
Nonfiction and Fillers: Short, timely articles relating to events and activities of college students. "No clippings of routine college news, only unusual items of possible national interest." Also buys newsbreaks and clippings related to college students and their activities. "We particularly want items about trends in student media: newspapers, magazines, campus radio, etc." Buys 100 mss/year. Submit complete ms. Length: 25-800 words. Pays 10¢ to 12¢-word.

NJEA REVIEW, New Jersey Education Association, 180 W. State St., Trenton NJ 08608. Editor-in-Chief: George Adams. 20% freelance written. For members of the association employed in New Jersey schools; teachers, administrators, etc. Monthly (September-May) magazine; 56 pages. Estab. 1922. Circ. 105,000. Pays on acceptance. Buys all rights, but may reassign following publication. Previously published submissions OK. SASE. Reports in 1-2 months. Free sample copy and writer's guidelines.
Nonfiction: How-to (classroom ideas), informational (curriculum area), personal opinion articles (on educational issues) and interviews with "names" in education. Length: 2,500-3,000 words maximum. Buys 15-20 mss/year. Query or submit complete ms. Pays $35 minimum.
Photos: B&w (5x7 or 8x10) glossies purchased with ms. Query first. Pays $5 minimum. Model release required.
How To Break In: "Needed are well-researched articles (but no footnotes, please) on new trends in education (such as teaching and curriculum experimentation) and subject area articles. These are especially suitable if they grow directly out of experience in a New Jersey school or college.

Human interest stories about people, teaching situations, or education in general also often acceptable."

OEA COMMUNIQUE, Office Education Association, 1120 Morse Rd., Columbus OH 43229. Editor: Sandy Fekete. Emphasizes business and office trends. Quarterly (during school year). Magazine; 24 pages. Estab. September 1976. Circ. 71,000. Pays on publication. Not copyrighted. Submit seasonal/holiday material 3 months in advance of issue date. Simultaneous, photocopied and previously published submissions OK. SASE. Reports in 3 weeks. Free sample copy and writers's guidelines; mention *Writer's Market* in request.
Nonfiction: General interest; how-to; humor; interview; new product; personal experience; profile; and technical. Query. Length: 6-12 pages. Pays $50-100.

PHI DELTA KAPPAN, 8th & Union Sts., Bloomington IN 47401. Editor: Stanley Elam. For educators, especially those in leadership positions, such as administrators; mid-forties; all hold BA degrees; one-third hold doctorates. Monthly magazine; 72 pages. Estab. 1915. Circ. 118,000. Buys all rights, but will sometimes reassign rights to author after publication (this varies with the author and material). Pays on publication. Free sample copy. Reports in 1 to 2 months. SASE.
Nonfiction and Photos: Feature articles on education, emphasizing policy, trends, both sides of issues, controversial developments. Also, informational, how-to, personal experience, interview, profile, inspirational, humor, think articles, expose. "Our audience is scholarly but hard-headed." Buys 10-15 mss/year. Submit complete ms. Length: 500 to 3,000 words. Pays $25-$250 per ms. "We pay a fee only occasionally, and then it is usually to an author whom *we* seek out. We do welcome inquiries from freelancers, but it is misleading to suggest that we buy very much from them." Pays average photographer's rates for b&w photos purchased with mss, but captions are required. Will purchase photos on assignment. Sizes: 8x10 or 5x7 preferred.

THE PROGRESSIVE TEACHER, 2678 Henry St., Augusta GA 30908. Editor: M.S. Adcock. For teachers, school superintendents, school board members, and others engaged in the instruction of children and youth. Bimonthly magazine. Estab. 1899. Circ. 4,350. Copyrighted. Pays on publication. Free sample copy SASE.
Nonfiction: Material of interest and help to teachers and other professional educators on methods, units of work. Professional articles for school administrators and others engaged in guidance and instruction. Especially interested in material other educators have found helpful. Submit complete ms. Length: 1,500 to 2,000 words. Pays $1 per column.

SCHOOL ARTS MAGAZINE, 72 Printers Bldg., Worcester MA 01608. Editor: David W. Baker. For art and craft teachers and supervisors from grade school through high school. Monthly, except July and August. Will send a sample copy to a writer on request. Pays on publication. Reports in 90 days. Enclose SASE.
Nonfiction and Photos: Articles, with photos, on art and craft activities in schools. Length: 1,000 words. Payment is negotiable but begins at $25/article.

THE SCHOOL MUSICIAN, AmMark Publications, Box 245, Joliet IL 60434. (815)726-4788. Editor: George Littlefield. 85% freelance written. For school and college band directors, orchestra and choir directors, music teachers and students. Monthly (except July and August) magazine; 75 pages. Estab. 1929. Circ. 10,000. No payment; "We do not pay, but publicity from writing for us can be of use to people in the music education field." Obtains all rights, but may reassign following publication. Phone queries OK. Submit seasonal/holiday material 2½ months in advance of issue date. Photocopied submissions OK. SASE. Reports in 2 months. Free sample copy and writer's guidelines; mention *Writer's Market* in request.
Nonfiction: How-to (improve your performance as a music teacher); interview (with prominent band leader or educator); nostalgia (pertaining to music education); personal experience (in band directing); personal opinion (on facets of music education); photo feature (band or orchestra at work); profile (school music personalities); technical (care and maintenance of all instruments); and travel (band and orchestra tours). Uses 60 mss/year. Query. Length: 5-8 pages.

SCHOOL SHOP, 416 Longshore Dr., Ann Arbor MI 48107. Editor: Lawrence W. Prakken. For "industrial and technical education personnel." Special issue in April deals with varying topics for which mss are solicited. Monthly. Circ. 45,000. Buys all rights. Pays on publication. Query first: "direct or indirect connection with the field of industrial and/or technical education preferred." Submit mss to Howard Kahn, Managing Editor. Submit seasonal material 3 months

in advance. Reports in 6 weeks. SASE.
Nonfiction and Photos: Uses articles pertinent to the various teaching areas in industrial education (woodwork, electronics, drafting, machine shop, graphic arts, computer training, etc.). "Outlook should be on innovation in educational programs, processes, or projects which directly apply to the industrial-technical education area." Buys how-to's, personal experience and think pieces, interviews, humor, coverage of new products. Length: 500 to 2,000 words. Pays $15 to $40. 8x10 photos purchased with ms.

SCIENCE ACTIVITIES, Room 504, 4000 Albermarle St., N.W., Washington DC 20016. (202)362-6445. Publisher: Cornelius W. Vahle, Jr. Editor: Jane Powers Weldon. For science teachers (high school, junior high school, elementary and college). Quarterly magazine; 40-48 pages. Estab. 1969. Circ. 3,000. Pays on publication. Sample copy for $3. Reports in 90 days. SASE.
Nonfiction and Photos: "Articles on creative science projects for the classroom, including experiments, explorations, and projects in every phase of the biological, physical and behavioral sciences." Buys 50 mss/year. Length: 1,500-3,000 words. Pays $10/printed page. Photos purchased with ms; no additional payment. Captions required.

SCIENCE AND CHILDREN, National Science Teachers Association, 1742 Connecticut Ave., N.W., Washington DC 20009. (202)265-4150. Editor-in-Chief: Phyllis Marcuccio. 70% freelance written. Emphasizes elementary school science for teachers and educational personnel of all levels, kindergarten through college. Monthly (8 issues during academic year) magazine; 48 pages. Estab. 1963. Circ. 23,000. No payment except for subscription. Phone queries OK. Submit seasonal/holiday material 6-8 months in advance. Photocopied submissions OK. SASE. Reports in 2-3 months. Free sample copy and writer's guidelines.
Nonfiction: How-to (science projects and activities for elementary students); informational (relating to science or elementary science programs); inspirational (relating to children and science); personal experience (with an aspect of elementary school science); photo feature (relating to science); research on science education. Submit complete ms. Length: 1,500 words maximum.
Photos: Used with mss. Send prints. Prefers 8x10 b&w glossies. Model release required.
Columns, Departments: Research in Education. Current research, in particular, relating to science at the elementary level. Send complete ms. Length: 1,200-1,500 words.
Rejects: "Material that would not be appropriate for elementary school level. The magazine is read by teachers. It is not a children's audience. However, the teachers look for material they can use in the classroom or material that would be relevant to them."

SIGHTLINES, Educational Film Library Association, Inc., 43 W. 61st St., New York NY 10023. (212)246-4533. Editor: Nadine Covert. 80% freelance written. Emphasizes the non-theatrical film world for librarians in university and public libraries, independent filmmakers, film teachers on the high school and college level, film programmers in the community, university, religious organizations, film curators in museums. Quarterly magazine; 44 pages. Estab. 1967. Circ. 3,000. Pays on publication. Buys all rights, but may reassign following publication. Phone queries OK. SASE. Reports in 2 months. Free sample copy.
Nonfiction: Informational (on the production, distribution and programming of non-theatrical films), interview (with filmmakers who work in 16mm, video; who make documentary, avant-garde, children's, and personal films), new product, and personal opinion (for regular Freedom To View column). Buys 4 mss/issue. Query. Length: 4,000-6,000 words. Pay 2½¢/word.
Photos: Purchased with accompanying ms. Captions required. Offers no additional payment for photos accepted with accompanying ms. Model release required.
Columns/Departments: Who's Who in Filmmaking (interview or profile of filmmaker or video artist who works in the non-theatrical field). Buys 1 ms/issue. Query. Pays 2½¢/word. Open to suggestions for new columns or departments.

SPECIAL EDUCATION: FORWARD TRENDS, 12 Hollycroft Ave., London NW3 7QL., England. Editor: Margaret Peter. Quarterly. Estab: 1974. Circ: 6,500. Pays on publication. SAE and International Reply Coupons.
Nonfiction: Articles on the education of all types of handicapped children. "The aim of this journal of the National Council for Special Education is to provide articles on special education and handicapped children which will keep readers informed of practical and theoretical developments not only in education but in the many other aspects of the education and welfare of the handicapped. While we hope that articles will lead students and others to further related reading, their main function is to give readers an adequate introduction to a topic which they

may not have an opportunity to pursue further. References should therefore be selective and mainly easily accessible ones. It is important, therefore, that articles of a more technical nature (e.g., psychology, medical, research reviews) should, whenever possible, avoid unnecessary technicalities or ensure that necessary technical terms or expressions are made clear to non-specialists by the context or by the provision of brief additional explanations or examples." Length: 750 to 3,750 words. Payment by arrangement.

TEACHER, Macmillan Professional Magazines, 77 Bedford St., Stamford CT 06901. (203)357-7714. Editor-in-Chief: Joan S. Baranski. Emphasizes education at the elementary school level. Monthly magazine; 150 pages. Estab. 1883. Circ. 250,000. Pays on acceptance. Buys all rights, but may reassign following publication. Submit seasonal/holiday material 6 months in advance. Photocopied submissions OK. SASE. Reports in 3 months. Free sample copy and writer's guidelines.
Nonfiction: Jeanette Moss, articles editor. "In evaluating potential articles for *Teacher,* we try to keep one thought uppermost in mind: Can an elementary school teacher gain some practical help from this material? We're most interested in the article that says, 'Here's how I did it and it works.' We want teachers talking to teachers as peers who understand and face similar problems. We are not interested in material that is basically theoretical or in the form of a research paper or a textbook-style unit. If you want to describe a successful project or unit, put it into article form." Publishes interviews, personal experience and personal opinion articles: trends in education, newsworthy programs and techniques, short teaching tips. Length: 1,000-1,500 words. Buys 15 mss per issue. Query first.
Photos: Vincent Ceci, department editor. B&w and color used with mss. Query first. Model release required.

TODAY'S CATHOLIC TEACHER, 2451 E. River Rd., Dayton OH 45439. (513)294-5785. Editor-in-Chief: Ruth A. Matheny. 25% freelance written. For administrators, teachers, parents concerned with Catholic schools, both parochial and CCD. Monthly 8 times/year magazine; 72 pages. Estab. 1967. Circ. 65,000. Pays on publication. Buys all rights, but may reassign following publication. Phone queries OK. Submit seasonal/holiday material 3 months in advance of issue date. SASE. Sample copy 50¢; free writer's guidelines; mention *Writer's Market* in request.
Nonfiction: How-to (based on experience, particularly in Catholic situations, philosophy with practical applications); inspirational (tribute to teacher); interview (of practicing educators, educational leaders); personal experience (classroom happenings); and profile (of educational leader). Buys 40-50 mss/year. Submit complete ms. Length: 800-2,000 words. Pays $15-75.
Photos: State availability of photos with ms. Offers no additional payment for 8x10 b&w glossy prints. Captions preferred. Buys all rights, but may reassign following publication. Model release required.

TODAY'S EDUCATION, National Education Association, 1201 16th St., NW., Washington DC 20036. (202)833-5442. Editor-in-Chief: Walter A. Graves. For elementary, secondary and higher education teachers. Quarterly magazine; 96 pages. Estab. 1913. Circ. 1,800,000. Pays on acceptance. Buys all rights, but may reassign following publication. Phone queries OK. Submit seasonal/holiday material 3 months in advance of issue date. SASE. Reports in 4 weeks. Free writer's guidelines.
Nonfiction: How-to (teach); interview (teachers); and nostalgia (early schools and teachers). Buys 5 mss/year. Submit complete ms. Length: 1,600-3,200 words. Pays $200-1,000.
Photos: Submit photo material with accompanying ms. Pays $50 for 8x10 b&w glossy prints; $150 for 35mm color transparencies. Buys onetime rights. Model release required.

TRAINING FILM PROFILES, Olympic Media Information, 71 W. 23 St., New York NY 10010. (212)675-4500. Editor: Walt Carroll. For colleges, community colleges, libraries, training directors, manpower specialists, education and training services, career development centers, audiovisual specialists, administrators. Serial in looseleaf format, published every 2 months. Estab. 1967. Circ. 1,000. Buys all rights. Pays on publication. "Send resume of your experience to introduce yourself." Will not consider photocopied or simultaneous submissions. Reports in 2 months. SASE.
Nonfiction: "Reviews of instructional films, filmstrips, videotapes and cassettes, sound-slide programs and the like. We have a highly specialized, rigid format that must be followed without exception. Ask us for sample 'Profiles' to see what we mean. Besides job training areas, we are also interested in the areas of values and personal self-development, upward mobility in the world of work, social change, futuristics, management training, problem solving, and adult

education." Buys 200-240 mss/year. Query. Pays $5 to $15 per review.

Electricity

Publications classified here aim at electrical engineers, electrical contractors, and others who build, design, and maintain systems connecting and supplying homes, businesses, and industries with power. Journals dealing with generating and supplying power to users will be found in the Power and Power Plants category. Publications for appliance servicemen and dealers will be found in the Home Furnishings classification.

CEDA CURRENT, Kerrwil Publications, Ltd., 20 Holly St., Suite 201, Toronto, Ontario, Canada M4S 2E8. (416)487-3461. Editor-in-Chief: Bryan S. Rogers. 50% freelance written. For "marketing and operating personnel in electrical maintenance and construction as well as distributors." Bimonthly magazine; 20 pages. Estab. 1969. Circ. 13,000. Pays on acceptance. Buys first North American serial rights. Phone queries OK. Submit seasonal/holiday material 4 months in advance of issue date. Previously published submissions "sometimes considered." SASE. Reports in 2 weeks. Free sample copy; mention *Writer's Market* in request.
Nonfiction: Canadian content only. How-to (problem solving, wiring, electrical construction and maintenance); general interest (to the electrical industry); interview (with electrical distributors and maintenance men); new product (from manufacturers, we don't pay for news releases); and technical. Query. Length: 500-1,500 words. Pays 5-10¢/word.
Photos: State availability of photos with query. Pays $5 for b&w photos; "negotiable" payment for color transparencies. Captions required. Buys one-time rights.

ELECTRICAL APPARATUS, Barks Publications, Inc., 400 N. Michigan Ave., Chicago IL 60611. (312)321-9440. Editorial Director: Elsie Dickson. Editor-in-Chief: H.B. Barks. 10-15% freelance written. Emphasizes industrial electrical maintenance and repair. Monthly magazine; 60 pages. Estab: 1948. Circ: 15,000. Pays on acceptance. Buys all rights, but may reassign following publication. Phone queries OK. Submit seasonal/holiday material 3 months in advance. SASE. Reports in 2 weeks. Sample copy $1.50.
Nonfiction: Publishes how-to, informational, and technical articles. Buys 1-2/issue. Length: 1,000-2,000 words. Query first. Pays $50-200.
Photos: B&w glossies (5x7 or 8x10) purchased with mss or on assignment. Query first. Pays $10-25.

ELECTRICAL CONTRACTOR, 7315 Wisconsin Ave., Washington DC 20014. (301)657-3110. Editor: Larry C. Osius. 10% freelance written. For electrical contractors. Monthly. Buys first rights, reprint rights, and simultaneous rights. Will send free sample copy on request. Freelance material bought on assignment following query. Usually reports in 1 month. Enclose SASE.
Nonfiction and Photos: Installation articles showing informative application of new techniques and products. Slant is product and method contributing to better, faster, more economical construction process. Length: "1 column to 4 pages." Pays $60 per printed page, including photos and illustrative material. Photos should be sharp, reproducible glossies, 5x7 and up.

ELECTRICAL CONTRACTOR & MAINTENANCE SUPERVISOR, 481 University Ave., Toronto, Ont., M5W 1A7, Canada. Editor: Richard Willingham. For "men who either run their own businesses or are in fairly responsible management positions. They range from university graduates to those with public school education only." Estab. 1952. Monthly. Circ. 13,400. Rights purchased vary with author and material. "Depending on author's wish, payment is either on acceptance or on publication." free sample copy. Query first. Enclose SAE and International Reply Coupon.
Nonfiction and Photos: "Articles that have some relation to electrical contracting or maintenance and related business management. The writer should include as much information as possible pertaining to the electrical field. We're not interested in articles that are too general and philosophical. Don't belabor the obvious, particularly on better business management. We're interested in coverage of labor difficulties, informational articles, how-to's, profiles, coverage of successful business operations, new product pieces, and technical articles." Length: "no minimum or maximum." Pays "8¢ a published word or 6¢ a word on submitted mss, unless other arrangements are made." Photos purchased with mss or on assignment; captions optional. Pays "$7 for the first print and $2 for each subsequent print, plus photographer's expenses."

Electronics and Communications

Listed here are publications for electronics engineers, radio and TV broadcasting managers, electronic equipment operators, and builders of electronic communication systems and equipment, including stereos, television sets, and radio-TV broadcasting systems. Journals for professional announcers or communicators will be found under Journalism; those for electronic appliance retailers will be found in Home Furnishings; publications on computer design and data processing systems will be found in Data Processing. Publications for electronics enthusiasts or stereo hobbyists will be found in Hobby and Craft or in Music in the Consumer Publications section.

BROADCAST, 111A Wardour St., London W1V 3TD, U.K. (01)439-9756. Editor-in-Chief: Rod Allen. 10-20% freelance written. Emphasizes broadcasting for a totally professional audience in the TV and radio industries in the U.K. and Europe. Weekly magazine; 28 pages. Estab. 1973. Circ. 3,500. Buys first Britain serial rights. Enclose International Reply Coupons.
Nonfiction: Information articles (professional only); interviews with important industry figures; new product articles (if genuinely new and not promotional); technical articles (by broadcast professionals). Length: 3,000 words maximum. Query. Pays £20-27/1,000 words.
Fillers: Newsbreaks are published only if they're important to the trade. Length: 25-250 words. Query first. Pays £2-10.
How To Break In: "The problem is finding people who understand the needs of our European readership, who aren't particularly interested in the internal wranglings of the U.S. broadcasting industry. There aren't too many of them around, but we'd sure like to be in touch with anyone who fills the bill."

BROADCAST ENGINEERING, 9221 Quivira Rd., Overland Park KS 66212. Editor: Ron Merrell. For "owners, managers, and top technical people at AM, FM, TV stations, cable TV operators, educational and industrial TV and business communications, as well as recording studios." Estab. 1959. Monthly. Circ. 30,000. Buys all rights. Buys about 50 mss/year. Pays on acceptance; "for a series, we pay for each part on publication." Free sample copy and writer's guidelines. Will not consider photocopied submissions. Reports in 2 weeks. SASE.
Nonfiction: Wants technical features dealing with design, installation, modification, and maintenance of radio and TV broadcast equipment; interested in features of interest to communications engineers and technicians as well as broadcast management, and features on self-designed and constructed equipment for use in broadcast and communications field. "We use a technical, but not textbook, style. Our publication is mostly how-to, and it operates as a forum. We reject material that is far too general, not on target, or not backed by evidence of proof. Our 'Station-to-Station' column provides a forum for equipment improvement and build-it-yourself tips. We pay up to $30. We're especially interested in articles on recording studios and improving facilities and techniques." Query. Length: 1,500-2,000 words for features. Pays $75-200.
Photos: Photos purchased with or without mss; captions required. Pays $5-10 for b&w prints; $10-35 for 2¼x2¼ or larger color transparencies.

BROADCAST EQUIPMENT TODAY, Diversified Publications Limited, Box 423, Station J, Toronto, Ontario, Canada M4J 4Y8. (416)463-5304. Editor-in-Chief: Doug Loney. 50% freelance written. Emphasizes broadcast engineering. Bimonthly magazine; 50 pages. Estab. 1975. Circ. 3,600. Pays on publication. Buys all rights. Phone queries OK. Photocopied and previously published submissions OK. SASE. Free writer's guidelines.
Nonfiction: Technical articles on developments in broadcast engineering, especially pertaining to Canada. Query. Length: 1,000-2,000 words. Pays $50-150.
Photos: Purchased with accompanying ms. Captions required. Query for b&w or color. Total purchase price for a ms includes payment for photos.

BROADCAST MANAGEMENT/ENGINEERING, 295 Madison Ave., New York NY 10017. (212)685-5320. Editor: J. Lippke. 5% freelance written. For general managers, chief engineers, program directors of radio and TV stations. Estab. 1964. Monthly. Circ. 28,000. Buys all rights, but will reassign rights to author after publication. Buys 1 to 3 mss a year. Pays on publication. Reports in 4 weeks. Query first. Enclose SASE.
Nonfiction: Articles on cost-saving ideas; use of equipment, new programming ideas for serving the public. Tone of all material is professional to professional. "We're interested in the profile or

program sound of competitive stations in a market.'' Length: 1,200 to 3,000 words. Pays $25 to $100.

BROADCAST PROGRAMMING & PRODUCTION, Box 2449, Hollywood CA 90028. (213)467-1111. Editor-in-Chief: Gary Kleinman. 30% freelance written. Emphasizes radio and television broadcasting. Bimonthly magazine: 72 pages. Estab. 1975. Circ. 16,000. Pays on publication. Buys all rights. Phone queries OK. Photocopied submissions OK. SASE. Reports in 1 month. Sample copy $2; mention *Writer's Market* in request.
Nonfiction: How-to (articles on radio/TV programming, production, and engineering); interview (with important figures in broadcast field); profile (on the production of network or syndicated TV shows); and technical (radio & TV programming production and engineering). No articles on publicity items. Buys 12 mss/year. Query. Length: 2,000-5,000 words. Pays 3¢/word.

BROADCASTER, 77 River St., Toronto, Ont. M5A 3P2 Canada. (416)363-6111. Editor: Michael L. Pollock. For the Canadian ''communications industry — radio, television, cable, ETV, advertisers, and their agencies.'' Estab. 1942. Monthly. Circ. 10,000. Buys all rights, but may reassign rights to writer after publication. Buys 50 to 60 mss per year. Pays on publication. Will send sample copy to writer for $2. Will not consider photocopied or simultaneous submissions. Reporting time for mss accepted for publication: variable. Returns rejected material ''as soon as possible.'' Enclose SAE and International Reply Coupons.
Nonfiction: ''Publish profiles, some technical and general interest articles about the broadcasting industry almost exclusively Canadian. Style is relatively free but articles should follow, for the most part, format of magazine. Although the magazine is basically a trade publication, it has far more general appeal than magazines of this type.'' Length: 1,000 to 2,000 words. Pays $25 to $200.
Photos: ''Depending on circumstances, ways of purchase vary.'' Captions required. Pays $25 for b&w; $100 to $150 for color. Print or negative should be submitted for b&w; submit transparency for color.

CABLEVISION, Titsch Publishing, Inc., Box 4305, Denver CO 80204. (303)573-1433. Editor-in-Chief: Paul Fitzpatrick. Semimonthly magazine; 100 pages. Estab. September 1975. Circ. 5,600. Pays on publication. Buys all rights. Submit seasonal/holiday material 2 months in advance of issue date. Simultaneous, photocopied and previously published submissions OK. SASE. Reports in 1 month. Free sample copy; mention *Writer's Market* in request.
Nonfiction: Exposé (governmental, financial, educational, dealing specifically with the cable TV industry); how-to (safety methods, field procedures, use of products in cable TV industry); interview (people involved in the cable TV, film, satellite and TV industries); new product (dealing specifically with the cable TV industry); and technical. Buys 6-12 mss/year. Query or submit complete ms. Length: 750-2,000 words. Pays 5¢/word minimum.
Photos: Offers no additional payment for photos used with accompanying ms. Uses 5x7 glossy b&w prints or color transparencies. Buys all rights.

CANADIAN ELECTRONICS ENGINEERING, 481 University Ave., Toronto M5W 1A7, Ontario, Canada. (416)595-1811, Ext. 636. Editor: John Lott. For technically trained users of professional electronics products. Monthly. Buys Canadian serial rights. Pays on acceptance. Free sample copy. Reports in 2-4 weeks. Enclose SAE and International Reply Coupons.
Nonfiction: Science and technology involving professional electronic products and techniques. Must have direct relevance to work being done in Canada. Query with brief outline of article. Length: maximum about 1,500 words. Pays 8¢ to 10¢/word depending on importance of subject, amount of research, and ability of writer.
Photos: Purchased with mss. 4x5 to 8x10 b&w glossy prints; must provide useful information on story subject. Pays average professional rates for time required on any particular assignment.

COMMUNICATIONS NEWS, 124 S. 1st St., Geneva IL 60134. (312)232-1400. Editor: Bruce Howat. 5% freelance written. For managers of communications systems including telephone companies, CATV systems, broadcasting stations and private systems. Estab. 1964. Monthly. Circ. 40,000. Buys all rights. Pays on publication. Free sample copy. Photocopied submissions OK. Reports in 4 weeks. SASE.
Nonfiction: Case histories of problem-solving for communications systems. Factual reporting about new communications products, systems and techniques. Must be terse, factual, helpful. Informational news and how-to articles; think pieces. Buys 3-10 mss/year. Query or submit complete ms. Length: 1,600 words maximum. Pays 3¢/word.
Photos: Department Editor: Don Wiley. Purchased with accompanying ms with no additional

payment or without accompanying ms. Captions optional. Pays $10 for b&w glossy prints.

COMMUNICATIONS RETAILING, 325 E. 75th St., New York NY 10022. (212)794-0500. Editor-in-Chief: Richard Ekstract. Editor: Mitchell Ratliff. 5% freelance written. For "retailers and manufacturers in the consumer communications industry. More specialty stores than mass merchants. Adult audience, professional people." Monthly tabloid; 45 pages. Estab. October 1976. Circ. 32,000. Pays 6 weeks after publication. Buys all rights. Phone queries OK. Submit seasonal/holiday material 2 months in advance of issue date. Photocopied submissions OK. SASE. Reports in 2 weeks. Free sample copy.
Nonfiction: Exposé (price-cutting, transshipping of goods, etc.); how-to (any way the communications retailer can better market, sell, merchandise, display, price, obtain positive cash flow, etc.); interview; new product; profile; and technical. Buys 3 mss/issue. Query. Length: 500-1,000 words. Pays 10¢/word.

ELECTRONIC BUYERS' NEWS, 333 East Shore Rd., Manhasset NY 11030. (516)829-5880. Editor: James Moran. The purchasing publication for the electronics industry. Newspaper; 64 pages. Estab. 1972. Circ. 35,000. Pays on publication. Usually buys first rights. SASE. Reports in 2-3 months. Rejected material not returned unless requested. Free sample copy.
Nonfiction: "Each issue features a specific theme or electronic component. Articles are usually accepted from companies involved with that component. Other stories are accepted occasionally from authors knowledgeable in that field." All material is aimed directly at the purchasing profession. Length: open. Pays $100 minimum.

ELECTRONICS INDUSTRY, Lesterstar, Ltd., 375 Upper Richmond Rd., West., London SW14 7NX England. (01)878-4852. Editor-in-Chief: Mike Dance. Managing Editor: Simon Henley. For professional electronic engineers. Monthly magazine; 70 pages. Circ. 20,000. Pays on publication. Buys all United Kingdom rights. Phone queries OK. SAE and International Reply Coupons. Reports in 1 month. Sample copy $5 plus postage. Free writer's guidelines.
Nonfiction: How-to articles (make best use of electronics devices); informational (comprehensive or specialist studies on some aspect of electronics technology); technical articles. Buys 2/issue. Query. Length: 1,000-4,000 words. Pays $40/published page (about 1,300 words).
Photos: No additional payment for b&w glossies used with ms. Send prints with ms.

ELECTRONICS JOURNAL, 1001 E. Touhy Ave., Suite 112, Des Plaines IL 60018. (312)297-1000. Publisher: William C. Sands Jr. Managing Editor: Ron Stewart. 15-18% freelance written. "Readers are electronic engineers, technicians, buyers or sales personnel." Monthly newspaper; 40 pages. Estab. February 1976. Circ. 31,000. Pays on publication. Buys all rights, but may reassign following publication. Phone queries OK. Submit seasonal/holiday material 3 months in advance of issue date. Photocopied and previously published submissions OK. SASE. Reports in 4 weeks. Free sample copy.
Nonfiction: Exposé (especially dealing with buyers who are 'on the take'); general interest (any unique application of electronics); historical (dealing with the fathers of electricity or electronics, Tesla, Edison, etc.); how-to (dealing with microcomputers); humor (dealing with manufacturer's reps or industrial distributors); interview (with a CEO of an electronics firm); personal experience (limited to CEO's and award winners); photo features (for big shows, new systems, etc.); profile (CEO's or award winners); technical ("state of the art"). No opinion pieces. Buys 1-2 mss/issue. Query or submit complete ms. Length: 400-600 words. Pays $25-100.
Photos: "We are dedicated to illustrated articles especially in those which deal with important people in electronics." Offers no additional payment for photos accepted with ms. Uses 5x7 glossy b&w prints and 3x5 color prints. Captions preferred. Buys all rights, but may reassign following publication. Model releases required.
Columns/Departments: Book Reviews (of books published in last 120 days); Lest We Forget (any historical or nostalgia piece about pioneers of electronics); and Around the Great Lakes (any article of commercial use of electronics in Ohio, Illinois, Indiana, Michigan and Wisconsin). Query or submit complete ms. Length: 200 words. Pays $30-50.
Fillers: Clippings, jokes, gags, anecdotes, newsbreaks, puzzles, and short humor. "Any items which deal with electronics in industry." Buys 5-10/issue. Length: 25-100 words. Pays $5-20.
How To Break In: "We are genuinely interested in any articles about the leaders in our field, and are eager to receive articles about the history of specific components such as resistors, capacitors, transformers, power supplies, microcomputers and microprocessors. We do not pay as much as some of the large publications, but we are still growing. We do pay promptly and we do advise the writer as soon as we know if we will use the piece or not."

ELECTRONIC PACKAGING AND PRODUCTION, Kiver Publications, 222 W. Adams St., Chicago IL 60606. (312)263-4866. Editor: Donald J. Levinthal. Managing Editor: Howard W. Markstein. 40% freelance written. Emphasizes electronic equipment fabrication for engineering and production personnel, including product testing. Monthly magazine; 150 pages. Estab. 1961. Circ. 27,000. Pays on publication. Buys all rights, but may reassign following publication. Phone queries OK. Photocopied submissions OK. SASE. Reports in 3 weeks. Free sample copy and writer's guidelines.
Nonfiction: How-to (innovative packaging, production or technique); interview (newsy features about technological trends in electronics) and technical (articles pertaining to the electronic packaging, production, and testing of electronic systems, hybrids, and semiconductors). "No single-product-oriented articles of a commercial sales-pitch nature." Buys 40 mss/year. Query or submit complete ms. Length: 1,000-2,500 words. Pays $30-150.
Photos: State availability of photos with query or submit photos with ms. Offers no additional payment for 4x5 or larger b&w or color prints. Captions preferred. Buys all rights, but may reassign following publication.

ELECTRONIC TECHNICIAN/DEALER, 43 E. Ohio, Chicago IL 60611. (312)467-0670. Editor: Richard Lay. For owners, managers, technician employees of consumer electronic sales and/or service firms. Magazine; 72 pages. Estab. 1953. Monthly. Circ. 70,000. Buys all rights. Pays on acceptance. Free sample copy and writer's guidelines. Simultaneous submissions OK. No photocopied submissions. Reports immediately. SASE.
Nonfiction and Photos: Feature articles of a practical nature about consumer electronic technology and servicing techniques; business profiles and/or business management. No generalization; must have concise, practical orientation; a specific approach. No business management articles which are too general and superficial. Informational, how-to, interview, profile, technical articles and those on successful business operations. Buys 36 mss/year. Query or submit complete ms. Length: 1,200-2,500 words. Pays $100-$175. No additional payment for b&w photos purchased with mss. Captions required.

ELECTRONICS, 1221 Avenue of the Americas, New York NY 10019. Editor: Kemp Anderson. 10-15% freelance written. Biweekly. Buys all rights. Query first. Reports in 2 weeks. SASE.
Nonfiction: Uses copy about research, development, design and production of electronic devices and management of electronic manufacturing firms; articles on "descriptions of new circuit systems, components, design techniques, how specific electronic engineering problems were solved; interesting applications of electronics; step-by-step, how-to design articles; monographs, charts, tables for solution of repetitive design problems." Length: 1,000 to 3,500 words. Pays $30/printed page.

ELECTRONICS RETAILING, 645 Stewart Ave., Garden City NY 11530. Editor: Tom Ewing. For independent, department, chain and discount stores; buyers of consumer electronics (hi-fi, TV, autosound, calculators, electronic watches, and related products). Tabloid; 24 pages. Estab. 1975. Monthly. Circ. 35,000. Buys all rights, but will reassign rights to author after publication. Buys about 500 mss a year. Pays on publication. Will send free sample copy to writer on request. Write for copy of guidelines for writers. No photocopied or simultaneous submissions. SASE.
Nonfiction and Photos: "We are looking primarily for hard news stories about the retailers in our audience. We prefer a straight news style and more extensive coverage of broader product areas. Length: 100-500 words. Pays 10¢ a word. B&w photos (5x7 or larger; no Polaroids) should support accompanying ms. Pays $10.
How To Break In: "Query first. We have occasional openings for stringers in some parts of the country."

JOB LEADS, Media Service Group, 1680-CP Vine St., Hollywood CA 90028. Editor: Tim Baskerville. For job seekers in the media field and managers and personnel executives of media companies, particularly radio and TV stations. Weekly newsletter; 4 pages. Estab. 1973. Pays on acceptance. Buys all rights. Simultaneous, photocopied and previously published submissions OK. SASE. Reports in 2-6 weeks. Free sample copy.
Nonfiction: "Our weekly newsletter is staff written. However, we do buy special reports and articles for supplements and premiums. Titles recently purchased: 'Broadcaster's Guide to Resume Preparation' and 'Broadcaster's Legal Handbook of Hiring Practices.' We are open to just about any length, as the format for each project varies. Writers without expertise in a technical or narrow area are discouraged from proposing an idea in that area. For that reason,

for example, an attorney who is also a freelance writer got the assignment for the legal handbook mentioned above. We will also consider distributing self-published booklets or reports in our subject area. Send sample for review.'' How-to (get a job, prepare an audition tape, handle a job interview); and technical (technical and legal guidelines for employers and subjects of interest to broadcasting executives). Buys 6 mss/year. Query for articles over 1,500 words; submit complete ms for mss under 1,500 words. Length: 750 words minimum. Pays $50-500, depending on length and complexity.

MICROWAVES, 50 Essex St., Rochelle Park NJ 07662. (201)843-0550. Editor: Stacy V. Bearse. 50% freelance written. Emphasizes microwave electronics. ''Qualified recipients are those individuals actively engaged in microwave research, design, development, production, and application engineering, engineering management, administration or purchasing departments in organizations and facilities where application and use of devices, systems and techniques involve frequencies from VHF through visible light.'' Monthly magazine; 100 pages. Estab. March 1962. Circ. 40,217. Pays on publication. Buys all rights. Phone queries OK. Photocopied submissions OK. SASE. Reports in 4 weeks. Free sample copy and writer's guidelines; mention *Writer's Market* in request.
Nonfiction: ''Interested in material on research and development in microwave technology and economic news that affects the industry.'' How-to (microwave design); new product; personal opinion; and technical. Buys 60 mss/year. Query. Pays $25-30/published page.
Fillers: Newsbreaks. Pays $10 (minimum).

MILITARY ELECTRONICS/COUNTERMEASURES, Hamilton-Burr Publishing Co., 2065 Martin Ave., Suite 104, Santa Clara CA 95050. (408)985-2280. Editor: Richard Hartman. 40% freelance written. Emphasizes military electronics systems for military and industry engineers and program managers in electronics. Monthly magazine; 64 pages. Estab. 1975. Circ. 20,000. Pays on publication. Buys all rights. Submit seasonal/holiday material 60 days in advance of issue date. SASE. Reports in 2 months. Sample copy $5; free writer's guidelines.
Nonfiction: Exposé (very few, non-destructive, military related); new product (systems); and technical. Buys 10 mss/year. Query with outline. Length: 1,500-7,500 words. Pays 10¢/word.
Photos: State availability of photos with query. Uses 5x7 b&w glossy prints. Offers no additional payment for photos accepted with ms. Captions required. Buys all rights, but may reassign following publication.

MONITOR, SFM Media Service Corp., 6 E. 43rd St., New York NY 10017. (212)682-0760. Editor: Gary Thomas Lico. 90% freelance written. For members of the National Honorary Broadcasting Society and members of the broadcast industry. Quarterly magazine; 32 pages. Estab. 1943. Circ. 3,000. Pays on publication. Buys one-time rights. Simultaneous, photocopied and previously published submissions OK. SASE. Reports in 3 weeks. Free sample copy and writer's guidelines; mention *Writer's Market* in request.
Nonfiction: Exposé (relating to broadcasting); how-to; general interest; historical (development, growth, etc.); humor (true-life incidents, reflections, etc.); interview; new product (broadcast technology); nostalgia (within reason); personal experience; personal opinion; photo feature (relating to a certain program or treatment of an issue); profile (broadcasters); and technical (interesting articles of this nature are hard to find). Submit complete ms. Length: 200-2,000 words. Pays: $0-200.
Photos: State availability of photos with ms. Pays $10 maximum for b&w prints. Buys one-time rights. Model release required.
Columns/Departments: Book Reviews. Query. Length: 200-2,000 words. Pays $100 maximum. Open to suggestions for new columns/departments.
Fiction: Fantasy (industry-related, but of a 'what-if?' nature); and humorous (fiction treatment of factual situations). Buys 2 mss/issue. Submit complete ms. Length: 200-2,000 words. Pays $50 maximum.
Poetry: Industry related poems. Buys 1/issue. Pays $25 maximum.
Fillers: Short humor (industry related). Buys 5/issue. Length: 10-50 words. Pays $5 maximum.

PAY TELEVISION MAGAZINE, P.O. Box 2430, Hollywood CA 90028. (213)876-2219. Editor: Al Preiss. For management executives of the communications industry. Magazine; 52 pages. Estab. 1975. Every 2 months. Circ. 5,000. Rights purchased vary with author and material. Usually buys ''magazine'' rights. Pays on publication. Will send sample copy to writer for $5. Write for copy of guidelines for writers. No photocopied or simultaneous submissions. Reports in 30 days. Query first. Enclose SASE.
Nonfiction and Photos: Articles on the need for pay television. Profiles. Length: 5 double-

spaced, typed pages. Pays minimum of $150. B&w photos purchased with or without mss. Captions required. Pays minimum of $25.

RADIO-TV EDITORIAL JOURNAL, Foundation for American Communications, 20121 Ventura Blvd., Woodland Hills CA 91364. (213)999-6772. Editor-in-Chief: George Mair. For editorial writers, news directors, and general managers of radio and television stations. Monthly magazine; 32 pages. Estab. 1976. Circ. 10,600. Pays on publication. Buys all rights. Phone queries OK. Submit seasonal/holiday material 2 months in advance. Simultaneous, photocopied and previously published submissions OK. SASE. Reports in 1 month.
Nonfiction: Informational (political and social issues), personal opinion. Buys 12 mss/year. Query. Length: 1,000-2,000 words. Pays $25.

RECORDING ENGINEER/PRODUCER, Box 2449, Hollywood CA 90028. (213)467-1111. Editor: Martin Gallay. 100% freelance written. Emphasizes recording technology and concert sound for "all levels of professionals with the recording industry as well as high level amateur recording interests." Bimonthly magazine; 100-108 pages. Estab. 1970. Circ. 10,500. Pays on publication. Buys first publication rights. Photocopied submissions OK. SASE. Reports in 4 weeks. Sample copy $1.50.
Nonfiction: Interview (known engineering and producing personalities from the recording industry); new product (as related to technological advances within the recording and concert sound industry); and technical (recording and concert sound information, both technical and semi-technical). Buys 6 mss/issue. Query. Pays $100-250.

TELEPHONY MAGAZINE, 55 E. Jackson Blvd., Chicago IL 60604. Editor: Leo Anderson. 30% freelance written. For people employed by telephone operating companies. Weekly. Buys all rights. Pays on publication. SASE.
Nonfiction: Technical or management articles describing a new or better way of doing something at a telephone company. "Feature articles range from highly technical state-of-the-art presentations to down-to-earth case studies. Case-history articles should cover a new or particularly efficient way of handling a specific job at a specific telephone company." Query. Length: 1,500 words. Generally pays $30/published magazine page.

TELEVISION INTERNATIONAL MAGAZINE, P.O. Box 2430, Hollywood CA 90028. (213)876-2219. Editor: Al Preiss. For management/creative members of the TV industry. Estab. 1956. Every 2 months. Circ. 8,000 (USA); 4,000 (foreign). Rights purchased vary with author and material. Pays on publication. Will send sample copy to writer for $2. Will consider photocopied submissions. No simultaneous submissions. Reports in 30 days. Query first. Enclose SASE.
Nonfiction and Photos: Articles on all aspects of TV programming. "This is not a house organ for the industry. We invite articles critical of TV." Pays $150 to $350. Column material of 600 to 800 words. Pays $75. Will consider suggestions for new columns and departments. Pays $25 for b&w photos purchased with mss; $35 for color transparencies.

VIDEO SYSTEMS, Box 12901, Overland Park KS 66212. (913)888-4664. Editor/Publisher: George Laughead. 80% freelance written. For qualified persons engaged in various applications of closed-circuit communications who have operating responsibilities and purchasing authority for equipment and software in the video systems field. Monthly magazine; 60 pages. Estab. November 1975. Circ. 14,600. Pays on acceptance. Buys one-time rights. Submit seasonal/holiday material 2 months in advance of issue date. Photocopied submissions OK. SASE. Reports in 2 months. Free sample copy and writer's guidelines.
Nonfiction: General interest (about professional video); how-to (use professional video equipment); historical (on professional video); new product; and technical. Buys 3 mss/issue. Submit complete ms. Length: 1,000-3,000 words. Pays $125.
Photos: State availability of photos with ms. Pay varies for 8x10 b&w glossy prints; $100 maximum for 35mm color transparencies. Model release required.

Engineering and Technology

Publications for electrical engineers are classified under Electricity; journals for electronics engineers are classified with the Electronics and Communications publications.

CANADIAN CONSULTING ENGINEER, 1450 Don Mills Rd., Don Mills, Ontario, M3B 2X7,

Canada. Managing Editor: Russell B. Noble. 80% freelance written. For private engineering consultants. Buys exclusive rights preferably; occasionally exclusive to field or country. Pays on publication. Reports in 15 days. Enclose SAE and International Reply Coupons.
Nonfiction: "We serve our readers with articles on how to start, maintain, develop and expand private engineering consultancies. Emphasis is on this management aspect. We are not a how-to magazine. We don't tell our readers how to design a bridge, a high rise, a power station or a sewage plant. Paradoxically, we are interested if the bridge falls down, for engineers are vitally interested in Errors and Omissions claims (much like journalists are about libel suits). We have articles on income tax, legal problems associated with consulting engineering, public relations and interviews with political figures. When we write about subjects like pollution, we write from a conceptual point of view; i.e., how the environmental situation will affect their practices. But because our readers are also concerned citizens, we include material which might interest them from a social, or educational point of view. The word to remember is *conceptual* (new concepts or interesting variations of old ones)." Usually pays $50 to $175, but this is dependent on length and extent of research required.

DESIGN ENGINEERING, Maclean-Hunter, Ltd., 481 University Ave., Toronto, Ontario, Canada M5W 1A7. (416)595-1811. Editor-in-Chief: Royston H. Linnegar. Emphasizes O.E.M. and in-plant design engineering for professional engineers, consultants, engineering schools, draftsmen, plant engineers, product development engineers, R&D departments. Monthly magazine; 60 pages. Estab. 1955. Circ. 14,000. Pays on acceptance. Buys first North American serial rights. Phone queries OK. Previously published submissions OK. SASE. Reports in 2 weeks. Free sample copy and writer's guidelines.
Nonfiction: How-to (on use of materials, new techniques in successful design engineering, value engineering); informational (new products, trends, state-of-the-art articles on fluid power, mechanical power, electric/electronics, drawing office, automation (in-plant); ecology-oriented products, energy-conservative products, etc.). Length: 750-1,500 words. Buys up to 12 mss/ year. Query. Pays $75-200.
Photos: B&w photos (5x7 or 8x10) purchased with mss or on assignment. Pays $5 minimum. Query or send contact sheet, or send prints. Color used only on cover, by assignment. Model release required.
Columns, Departments: World Design, Ottawa Report, Careers. Query first. Length: 500 words maximum. Pays $40 minimum. Open to suggestions for new columns and departments.

DETROIT ENGINEER, 25875 Jefferson, St. Clair Shores MI 48081. Editor: Jack Grenard. For "members of the Engineering Society of Detroit. They are engineers, architects, and persons in other related fields. The median age is about 45; mostly affluent, with wide-ranging interests." Estab. 1945. Monthly. Circ. 7,000. Rights purchased vary with author and material; may buy all rights, but will reassign rights to author after publication. Buys about 20 mss/year. Pays on publication. Sample copy $1. Submit complete ms. Will not consider photocopied submissions. Submit seasonal material 3 to 4 months in advance. Returns rejected material "usually in 2 weeks." Acknowledges acceptance of material in 4 to 6 weeks. SASE.
Nonfiction: "*Detroit Engineer* publishes articles on subjects of regional, southeastern Michigan interest not covered in other publications. We are only interested in the unusual and highly specific technical or man-oriented pieces, such as an expose on the Wankel engine or a new way to harness solar energy—subjects of wide interest within the scientific community." Buys exposes and technical articles. Length: 500 to 1,000 words. Pays $50.
Photos: Buys 4x5 to 8x10 b&w glossies; "any surface." Pays $5 to $15. Buys 8x10 color prints or any size transparencies for cover use. Pays minimum $25.

ELECTRO-OPTICAL SYSTEMS DESIGN MAGAZINE, Room 900, 222 W. Adams St., Chicago IL 60606. (312)263-4866. Editor: Richard Cunningham. Monthly. Circ. 26,000. Buys all rights. Pays on publication. Will send a sample copy to a writer on request. Write for copy of guidelines for writers. Will consider cassette submissions. Query required. Editorial deadlines are on the 25th of the 2nd month preceding publication. Enclose SASE.
Nonfiction and Photos: Articles and photos on lasers, laser systems, and optical systems aimed at electro-optical scientists and engineers. "Each article should serve a reader's need by either stimulating ideas, increasing technical competence, improving design capabilities in the following areas: natural light and radiation sources, artificial light and radiation sources, light modulators, optical components, image detectors, energy detectors, information displays, image processing, information storage and processing, system and subsystem testing, materials, support equipment, and other related areas." Rejects flighty prose, material not written for type of readership, and irrelevant material. Pays $30 per page. Submit 8x10 b&w glossies with ms.

LIGHTING DESIGN & APPLICATION, 345 E. 47th St., New York NY 10017. (212)644-7922. Editor: Chuck Beardsley. 25% freelance written. For "lighting designers, architects, consulting engineers, and lighting engineers." Estab. 1971. Monthly. Circ. 13,500. Rights purchased vary with author and material. Buys about 20 mss/year. Pays on acceptance. Will not consider photocopied submissions. Query first. Enclose SASE.
Nonfiction: "Lighting application, techniques, and trends in all areas, indoors and out. Our publication is the chief source of practical illumination information. Interviews with lighting designers stand a better chance of acceptance than do 'how-to' articles on plant lighting or installation stories. Folksy accounts of home relighting are not wanted." Buys informational and think articles. Length: 500 to 2,000 words. Pays $150.

NEW ENGINEER, MBA Communications, 730 Third Ave., New York NY 10017. (800)223-6806. Editor-in-Chief: Steven S. Ross. 66% freelance written. Published 11 times a year, magazine; 60 pages. Estab. October 1971. Circ. 100,000. Pays on publication. Buys all rights, but may reassign following publication, and first North American serial rights. Phone queries OK. Submit seasonal/holiday material 3 months in advance of issue date. Photocopied submissions OK. SASE. Reports in 2 months. Free sample copy and writer's guidelines; mention *Writer's Market* in request.
Nonfiction: Exposé (government corporations); humor (slanted to engineering but not simply general humor with engineer in lead role); interview (engineers and government leaders); personal opinion (dealing with engineering subjects); profile; and travel (for "off hours" section). Buys 40 mss/year. Query. Length: 1,000-10,000 words. Pays $15-50.
Photos: State availability of photos with query. Pays $25-100 for 5x7 b&w matte prints; and $100-500 for 4x5 color transparencies. Buys one-time rights. Model release required.
Columns/Departments: Book reviews; and happenings (news items). Buys 11/year. Query. Length: 100-300 words. Pays $25.

PARKING MAGAZINE, National Parking Association, Inc., 1101 17th St., NW., Washington DC 20036. (202)296-4336. Editor-in-Chief: Norene Dann Martin. Associate Editor: David L. Ivey. 10% freelance written. "The bulk of our readers are owners/operators of commercial, off-street parking facilities in major metropolitan areas. The remainder is made up of architects, engineers, city officals, planners, retailers, contractors, and service equipment suppliers." Quarterly magazine; 60 pages. Estab. 1951. Circ. 5,500. Pays on acceptance. Buys onetime rights. Phone queries OK. Submit seasonal/holiday material 3 months in advance of issue date. Simultaneous, photocopied and previously published submissions OK. Reports in 1 week. Free sample copy and writer's guidelines; mention *Writer's Market* in request.
Nonfiction: General interest (pieces on revitalization of central business districts have a high current priority); how-to (new construction, design, equipment or operational techniques); historical (could deal with some aspect of history of parking, including piece on historic garage, etc.); new product (parking-related equipment); photo feature (range of facilities in a particular city); and travel (parking in other countries). "No general, nebulous pieces or ones not dealing with most current trends in the industry." Query. Length: 1,000-5,000 words. Pays $50-150, or negotiable.
Photos: State availability of photos with query. Pays $5-15 for 8x10 b&w glossy prints and $10-25 for 2x2 or larger color transparencies. Captions preferred. Buys onetime rights. Model release required.
Columns/Departments: Open to suggestions for new columns/departments.

Farm

Today's farmer is a businessman in bib-overalls with a six-figure investment in producing foodstuffs for the country and the world. Today's farm magazines reflect this, and the successful farm freelance writer is the person who grasps this fact and turns his attentions to the business end of farming. "We need management articles," says Dick Hanson, editor of *Successful Farming*. "We don't need nostalgic treatises or ax-grinding material. Our readers are interested in dollars and cents, profit and loss."

Do you need to be a farmer to write about farming? The general consensus is yes, and no, depending on just what you're writing about. For more technical articles, most editors feel that you should have a farm background (and not just summer visits to Aunt Rhodie's farm, either) or some technical farm education. But there are plenty of writing opportunities for the general freelancer, too. Easier stories to undertake for farm publications include straight reporting of agricultural events; meetings of national agricultural organizations; or coverage of agricultural legislation. Other ideas might be articles on rural living, rural health care or transportation in small towns.

Always a commandment in any kind of writing, but possibly even more so in the farm field, is the tenet *"Study Thy Market."* The following listings for farm publications are broken down into seven categories, each specializing in a different aspect of farm publishing: crops and soil management; dairy farming; general interest farming and rural life (both national and local); livestock; miscellaneous; and poultry.

The best bet for a freelancer without much farming background is probably the general interest, family-oriented magazines. These are sort of the *Saturday Evening* Posts of the farm set. The other six categories are more specialized, dealing in only one aspect of farm production. If you do choose to try a specialized magazine, heed this advice from Richard Krumme, managing editor of *Successful Farming:* "The writer must know what he's talking about. If he doesn't, it's terribly easy to look foolish in the trade (farming) business when you're dealing with readers who are specialists."

Where should a writer go for information about farming specialities? Go to a land-grant university; there's one in every state. According to Krumme, "there's a wealth of information there, from a variety of sources. He (the writer) could start with the information branch that each land-grant university has. They have literally thousands, probably millions, of publications about current agriculture. An assortment of these would give him the fastest and best background in a short period of time that he could get anywhere." Also try farming seminars or the county extension offices.

As you can see, there's no room for hayseeds in the farm writing field. But for the freelance writer who is willing to plow in and study, there's a good chance he'll find himself in the middle of a cash crop.

Crops and Soil Management

COTTON FARMING MAGAZINE, Little Publications, 6263 Poplar Ave., Memphis TN 38138. Editor: Tom Griffin. Buys all rights. Pays on publication. Free sample copy and outline of requirements. Reports in approximately 3 to 6 weeks. SASE.
Nonfiction and Photos: Continually looking for material on large-acreage cotton farmers (200 acres or more). Likes stories on one phase of a grower's production such as his weed control program, insect control, landforming work, or how he achieves higher than average yields. Length: 1,000 to 1,200 words with at least 3 in-the-field photos. Payment is 10¢ a word.

THE FLUE CURED TOBACCO FARMER, 559 Jones Franklin Rd., Suite 150, Raleigh NC 27606. Editor: Stephen Denny. For farmers who produce 5 or more acres of flue cured tobacco. Magazine; 40 pages. Estab. 1964. Published eight times/year. Circ. 45,500. Buys all rights, but will reassign rights to author after publication. Buys 24 mss a year. Pays on publication. Free sample copy. Reports immediately. Query first. SASE.
Nonfiction and Photos: Production and industry-related articles. Emphasis is on a knowledge of the industry and the ability to write specifically for it. All material must be in-depth and be up to date on all industry activities. Informational, how-to, personal experience, interview, profile, personal opinion, successful business operations. Length: open. Pays $2 per column inch. B&w glossies (5x7) purchased with mss. Pays $10. Captions required.

THE PEANUT FARMER, 559 Jones Franklin Rd., Suite 150, Raleigh NC 27606. Editor: Stephen Denny. For peanut farmers with 15 or more acres of peanuts. Magazine; 32 pages. Estab. 1965. Published eight times/year. Circ. 28,500. Buys all rights, but will reassign rights to author after publication. Buys about 24 mss a year. Pays on publication. Free sample copy. Reports immediately. Query first or submit complete ms. SASE.
Nonfiction and Photos: Production and industry-related articles. Must be in-depth and up to date

on all industry activities. Informational, how-to, personal experience, interview, profile, personal opinion, successful business operations. Length: open. Pays $2 a column inch. Pays $10 for 5x7 b&w glossies purchased with mss. Captions required.

POTATO GROWER OF IDAHO, Harris Publishing, Inc., Box 981, Idaho Falls ID 83401. (208)522-5187. Editor/Publisher: Darryl W. Harris. 25% freelance written. Emphasizes material slanted to the potato grower and the business of farming related to this subject — packing, shipping, processing, research, etc. Monthly magazine; 32-56 pages. Estab. 1972. Circ. 14,500. Pays on publication. Buys all rights, but may reassign following publication. Phone queries OK. Submit seasonal/holiday material 6 weeks in advance. Photocopied submissions and previously published work OK. SASE. Reports in 1 month. Free sample copy and editorial guidelines.
Nonfiction: Expose (facts, not fiction or opinion, pertaining to the subject); how-to (do the job better, cheaper, faster, etc.); informational articles; interviews (can use one of these a month, but must come from state of Idaho since this is a regional publication, though serving the nation, tells the nation "how Idaho grows potatoes"); all types of new product articles pertaining to the subject; photo features (story can be mostly photos, but must have sufficient outlines to carry technical information); technical articles (all aspects of the industry of growing, storage, processing, packing, and research of potatoes in general, but must relate to the Idaho potato industry). Buys 24 mss/year. Query. Length: 750 words minimum. Pays 3¢/word.
Photos: B&w glossies (any size) purchased with mss or on assignment; use of color limited. Captions required. Query if photos are not to be accompanied by ms. Pays $5 minimum; $25 for color used on cover. Model release required.
How To Break In: "Choose one vital, but small, aspect of the industry; research that subject, slant it to fit the readership and/or goals of the magazine. All articles on research must have valid source for foundation. Material must be general in nature about the subject or specific in nature about Idaho potato growers. Write a query letter, noting what you have in mind for an article; be specific."

RICE FARMING MAGAZINE, Little Publications, 6263 Poplar Ave., Suite 540, Memphis TN 38138. Editor: Tom Griffin. Buys all rights. Pays on publication. Will send a free sample copy and writer's guidelines. Reports in 3-6 weeks. SASE.
Nonfiction and Photos: Continually looking for material on large acreage rice farmers (200 acres or more). Stories on one phase of grower's production such as his weed control program, insect control, landforming work, or how he achieves higher than average yields. Include at least 3 in-the-field photos. Length: 1,000-1,200 words. Pays 10¢/word.

THE RICE JOURNAL, Box 714, Mclean VA 22101. Editor: Gordon Carlson. For readers interested in rice and rice farming and marketing. Magazine; 40 to 120 (8½x11) pages. Estab. 1897. Monthly. Circ. 10,000. Buys all rights, but will reassign rights to author after publication. Buys about 12 mss a year. Pays on publication. Reports in 10 days. Query first. Enclose SASE.
Nonfiction and Photos: Informational, profile, humor and travel; related to rice industry. Articles on duck hunting. Length: open. Pays minimum of $40 for articles, less for fillers. B&w photos and color transparencies purchased without mss. Pays $25 for b&w; $50 for color.

SOYBEAN DIGEST, Box 158, Hudson IA 50643. (319)988-3295. Editor/General Manager: James Bramblett. Managing Editor: Grant Mangold. 80% freelance written. Emphasizes soybean production and marketing. Monthly magazine; 40 pages. Estab. 1940. Circ. 78,000. Pays on acceptance. Buys all rights, but may reassign following publication. Phone queries OK. Submit seasonal material 2 months in advance of issue date. Photocopied submissions OK. Reports in 3 weeks. Sample copy 50¢; mention *Writer's Market* in request.
Nonfiction: How-to (soybean production and marketing); and new product (soybean productiona and marketing). Buys 100 mss/year. Query or submit complete ms. Length: 1,000-2,000 words. Pays $50-200.
Photos: State availability of photos with query. Pays $5-35 for 5x7 b&w prints and $50-100 for 35mm color transparencies. Captions preferred. Buys all rights, but may reassign following publication.

THE SUGAR BEET, The Almalgamated Sugar Co., Box 1520, Ogden UT 84402. (801)399-3431. Editor-in-Chief: A.L. Hanline. "Primarily for beet growers in Idaho, Oregon, and Utah. Also goes to research personnel, agricultural companies, local bankers, equipment dealers, etc., and other beet sugar companies." Quarterly magazine; 24 pages. Estab. 1937. Circ. 4,500. Pays on publication. Not copyrighted. Phone queries OK. Submit seasonal/holiday material 3-6 months in advance. Previously published submissions OK, "if timely and appropriate." Reports in 2

weeks. Free sample copy and writer's guidelines.
Nonfiction: How-to, informational, interview, personal experience, technical. Buys 3-4 mss/year. Query. Length: 500-2,000 words. Pays $50-100.
Photos: Purchased with accompanying ms. Captions required. No additional payment for photos accepted with ms. Send 5x7 b&w glossies. Query. Model release required.

WESTERN FRUIT GROWER, 300 Valley St., Sausalito CA 94965. (415)332-5006. Editor: Harold T. Rogers. For commercial fruit and nut growers in the Western U.S. Monthly magazine; 50 pages. Estab. 1950. Circ. 22,000. Not copyrighted. Buys 10 to 15 mss/year. Pays on publication. Free sample copy. Reports in 2 weeks. Query first. SASE.
Nonfiction and Photos: Wants mss dealing with production and marketing operations, semi-technical production research and farm experience operation. Prefers business magazine approach. Pays $50 to $100 for nonfiction mss. Length: 700 to 1,000 words. B&w photos used with mss with no extra payment. Color purchased only on assignment.

Dairy Farming

Publications for dairymen are classified here. Publications for farmers who raise animals for meat, wool, or hides are included in the Livestock category. Other magazines that buy material on dairy herds will be found in the General Interest Farming and Rural Life classification. Journals for dairy products retailers will be found under Dairy Products.

DAIRY GOAT JOURNAL, Box 1908, Scottsdale AR 85252. Editor: Kent Leach. 40% freelance written. Monthly for breeders and raisers of dairy goats. Generally buys exclusive rights. Pays on acceptance. Free sample copy. Reports in 10 days. Query. SASE.
Nonfiction and Photos: Uses articles, items, and photos that deal with dairy goats, and the people who raise them. Goat dairies and shows. How-to-do-it articles up to 1,000 words. Pays 7¢/word. Also buys 5x7 or 8x10 b&w photos for $1 to $15.

DAIRY HERD MANAGEMENT, Miller Publishing Co., Box 67, Minneapolis MN 55440. (612)374-5200. Editor: George Ashfield. 50% freelance written. Emphasizes dairy farming. Monthly magazine; 60 pages. Estab. 1963. Circ. 55,000. Pays on acceptance. Buys all rights, but may reassign following publication. Submit seasonal/holiday material 2 months in advance. Photocopied and previously published submissions OK. SASE. Reports in 3-6 weeks. Free sample copy and writer's guidelines.
Nonfiction: How-to, informational, technical. Buys 12-15 mss/year. Query. Length: 1,000-3,000 words. Pays $75-200. "Articles should concentrate on useful management information. Be specific rather than general."

THE DAIRYMAN, Box 819, Corona CA 91720. Editor: Dolores Davis Mullings. For large herd dairy farmers. Monthly. Buys reprint rights. Pays on publication. Free sample copy. Reports in 3 weeks. SASE.
Nonfiction and Photos: Uses articles on anything related to dairy farming, preferably anything new and different or substantially unique in operation, for U.S. subjects. Acceptance of foreign dairy farming stories based on potential interest of readers. Pays $2 per printed inch. Buys photos with or without mss. Pays $10 each.

DAIRYMEN'S DIGEST (Southern Region Edition), P.O. Box 809, Arlington TX 76010. Editor: Phil Porter. For commercial dairy farmers and their families, throughout the central U.S., with interests in dairy production and marketing. Magazine; 32 (8½x11) pages. Estab. 1969. Monthly. Circ. 9,000. Not copyrighted. Buys about 34 mss a year. Pays on publication. Will send free sample copy to writer on request. Reports in 3 weeks. SASE.
Nonfiction and Photos: Emphasis on dairy production and marketing. Buys articles of general interest to farm families, especially dairy-oriented. Seeks unusual accomplishments and satisfactions resulting from determination and persistence. Must be positive and credible. Needs newsbreaks, fresh ideas, profile, personal experience articles. Buys some historical, inspirational or nostalgia. Also articles of interest to farm wives. Length: 50 to 1,500 words. Pay varies from $10 to $125 per article, plus additional amount for photos, depending on quality.

SOUTHEASTERN DAIRY REVIEW, Dairy Farmers, Inc., Box 7775, Orlando FL 32804.

Editor-in-Chief: Melissa Reeves. 15% freelance written. For Dairy farmers in Florida, veterinarians, legislators, extension agents, educators, and allied tradesmen. Monthly magazine; 20 pages. Estab. 1960. Circ. 1,600. Pays on publication. Not copyrighted. Phone queries OK. Submit seasonal/holiday material 3 months in advance of issue date. Simultaneous, photocopied and previously published submissions OK. SASE. Reports in 3 months. Free sample copy and writer's guidelines; mention *Writer's Market* in request.
Nonfiction: How-to (improvement in related dairy fields); general interest; new product; and profile. Buys 5 mss/year. Submit complete ms. Pays $5-20.
Photos: Offers no additional payment for 5x7 b&w photos accepted with accompanying ms.

General Interest Farming and Rural Life

The publications listed here aim at farm families or farmers in general and contain material on sophisticated agricultural and business techniques. Magazines that specialize in the raising of crops will be found in the Crops and Soil Management classification; publications exclusively for dairymen are included under Dairy Farming; publications that deal exclusively with livestock raising are classified in the Livestock category; magazines for poultry farmers are grouped under the Poultry classification. Magazines that aim at farm suppliers are grouped under Agricultural Equipment and Supplies.

National

AGWAY COOPERATOR, Box 1333, Syracuse NY 13201. (315)477-6488. Editor: James E. Hurley. For farmers. Monthly. Pays on acceptance. Usually reports in 1 week. SASE.
Nonfiction: Should deal with topics of farm or rural interest in the northeastern U.S. Length: 1,200 words maximum. Payment is $75, usually including photos.
Photos: Payment is $10 for photos purchased singly.

AG WORLD, 20 N. Kent St., St. Paul MN 55102. (612)225-6211. Managing Editor: Rudolf Schnasse. Emphasizes economic and social aspects of agriculture. Monthly tabloid; 16 pages. Estab. 1975. Circ. 5,000. Pays on publication. Buys all rights, but may reassign following publication. Phone queries OK. Simultaneous, photocopied, and previously published submissions OK. SASE. Reports in 4 weeks. Sample copy $1.
Nonfiction: Expose, informational and personal opinion articles; interviews and profiles. Submit complete ms. Length: 750-3,000 words.

THE COUNTRY GENTLEMAN, 1100 Waterway Blvd., Indianapolis IN 46202. Editor-in-Chief: Starkey Flythe, Jr. Managing Editor: Michael New. Emphasizes country living. Quarterly magazine; 120 pages. Circ. 250,000. Pays on publication. Usually buys all rights, first rights or second serial (reprint) rights. Photocopied submissions OK. SASE. Reports in about 4 weeks. Sample copy, $1.
Nonfiction: Articles and stories on how to acquire and care for a country place. How-to's, personalities, travel, food and humor. Recent articles have dealt with greenhouses, iris propagation, English country houses, keeping a horse in the suburbs, recycling log cabins, the American rifle, Teddy Roosevelt's Bully Hilltop and fly tying. Length: 2,000 words maximum. Pays $50-200.
Photos: "We buy color photographs and illustrations having to do with rural life in America and abroad." Pays $25-75.
Fiction: Mainstream, mystery, adventure, western and humorous stories. Length: 2,000 words maximum. Pays $75-200.
Poetry: Traditional forms of poetry, blank verse, free verse, light verse and humorous or serious poetry on country or outdoor themes. Length: 5-30 lines. Pays $10-50.

COUNTRYSIDE, 312 Highway 19 E., Waterloo WI 53594. (414)478-2118. Editor: Jerome D. Belanger. Emphasizes practical small farming and organic agriculture; homesteading. Monthly magazine; 88 pages. Estab. 1917. Circ. 29,000. Pays on publication. Buys all rights, but may reassign following publication. Submit seasonal/holiday material 6 months in advance. SASE. Reports in 2 months. Free sample copy and writer's guidelines.
Nonfiction: Expose (agri-business); how-to (organic farming and gardening, practical self-sufficiency); informational (soil science, biological insect control, intermediate technology, alternative sources of energy, nutrition); interviews (farmers, researchers, agricultural consul-

tants, politicians); and personal experience (as it relates to farming on a small scale or using organic methods). Buys 70-100 mss/year. Query or submit complete ms. Length: 750-3,500 words. Pays $25 minimum.
Photos: Lea Landmann, Photo Editor. Purchased with or without accompanying ms or on assignment. Send contact sheet or transparencies. Pays $2.50-5 for b&w photos; $35 for color transparencies. Total purchase price for ms includes payment for photos.
Columns/Departments: Cow Barn (material on keeping a family cow or small dairy herd) and Pig Pen (small scale commercial swine production or for family meat supply). Also needs material on sheep, bees, poultry, rabbits and small farm machinery. Buys 10-12/year. Query or submit complete ms. Length: 750-1,500 words. Pays $25-50.

FARM JOURNAL, Washington Square, Philadelphia PA 19105. Editor: Lane Palmer. 15% freelance written. Many separate editions for different parts of the U.S. Material bought for one or more editions depending upon where it fits. Buys all rights. Payment made on acceptance and is the same regardless of editions in which the piece is used. Query before submitting material. SASE.
Nonfiction: Timeliness and seasonableness are very important. Material must be highly practical and should be helpful to as many farmers as possible. Farmers' experiences should apply to one or more of these 8 basic commodities: corn, wheat, milo, soybeans, cotton, dairy, beef, and hogs. Technical material must be accurate. Pays $25 minimum.
Photos: Much in demand either separately or with short how-to material in picture stories and as illustrations for articles. Warm human interest pix for covers—activities on modern farms. For inside use, shots of homemade and handy ideas to get work done easier and faster, farm news photos, and pictures of farm people with interesting hobbies. In b&w, 8x10 glossies are preferred; color submissions should be 2¼x2¼ for the cover, and 35mm for inside use. Pays $50 and up for b&w shot; $75 and up for color.

THE FURROW, Deere & Co., John Deere Rd., Moline IL 61265. Executive Editor: Ralph E. Reynolds. 10% freelance written. For commercial farmers and ranchers. Magazine; 8 times/year; 40 pages. Estab. 1895. Circ. 1.2 million. Buys all rights, but may reassign following publication. Phone queries OK. Submit seasonal/holiday material at least 6 months in advance. SASE. Reports in 2 weeks. Free sample copy and writer's guidelines.
Nonfiction: George R. Sollenberger, North American Editor. "We want articles describing new developments in the production and marketing of crops and livestock. These could be classified as how-to, informational and technical, but all must have a news angle. All articles should include some interviews, but we rarely use straight interviews. We publish articles describing farmers' personal experiences with new practices. We occasionally use photo features related to agriculture, as well as occasional guest editorials on the Commentary page." Buys 10-15 mss/year. Submit complete ms. Length: 300-1,000 words. Pays $100-400.
Photos: Wayne Burkart, Art Editor. Original color transparencies (no copies) or color negatives of any size used only with mss. Captions required. Send negatives or transparencies with ms. No additional payment.

THE NATIONAL FUTURE FARMER, Box 15130, Alexandria VA 22309. (703)360-3600. Editor-in-Chief: Wilson W. Carnes. For members of the Future Farmers of America who are students of vocational agriculture in high school, ranging in age from 14-21; major interest in careers in agriculture/agribusiness and other youth interest subjects. Bimonthly magazine; 52 pages. Estab. 1952. Circ. 528,656. Pays on acceptance. Buys all rights, but may reassign following publication. Submit seasonal/holiday material 3-4 months in advance. SASE. Usually reports in 2 weeks. Free sample copy and writer's guidelines.
Nonfiction: How-to for youth (outdoor type such as camping, hunting, fishing); informational (getting money for college, farming; other help for youth). Informational, personal experience and interviews are used only if FFA members or former members are involved. Buys 2-3 mss/issue. Query or send complete ms. Length: 1,200 words maximum. Pays 2½-6¢/word.
Photos: Purchased with mss (5x7 or 8x10 b&w glossies; 35mm or larger color transparencies). Pays $5-7.50 for b&w; $25-35 for inside color; $100 for cover.
How To Break In: "Find an FFA member who has done something truly outstanding which will motivate and inspire others, or provide helpful information for a career in farming, ranching or agribusiness."

REPORT ON FARMING, Free Press, 300 Carlton St., Winnipeg, Manitoba, Canada R3C 3C1. (204)269-4237. Managing Editor: Leo Quigley. For "upper income, progressive farmers." Monthly tabloid. Estab. 1880. Circ. 170,000. Pays on acceptance. Buys one-time rights. Phone

queries OK. Submit seasonal/holiday material 5 weeks in advance. Simultaneous, photocopied and previously published submissions OK. SASE. Reports in 4 weeks. Free sample copy.
Nonfiction: "Will look at ideas for agricultural news features. Most, however, will be done by assignments." Submit complete ms. Length: 1,500 words maximum. Pays $20 for news stories; $50-150 for solid features.
Photos: Purchased with accompanying ms. Captions required. Pays $5-20 for b&w prints.

SUCCESSFUL FARMING, 1716 Locust St., Des Moines IA 50336. (515)284-9204. Editor: Dick Hanson. 30% freelance written. For top farmers. Estab. 1902. 13 times/year. Circ. 750,000. Buys all rights. Pays on acceptance. Reports in 4-6 weeks. Query. SASE.
Nonfiction: Semi-technical articles on the aspects of farming with emphasis on how to apply this information to one's own farm. "Most of our material is too limited and unfamiliar for freelance writers — except for the few who specialize in agriculture, have a farm background and a modern agricultural education." Length: about 1,500 words maximum. Pays competitive rates.
Photos: Ralph Figg, Art Director, prefers 8x10 b&w glossies to contacts; color should be 2¼x2¼, 4x5 or 8x10. Buys exclusive rights and pays $20 for b&w, more for color. Assignments are given, and sometimes a guarantee, provided the editors can be sure the photography will be acceptable. Pays for meals, phone, lodging.

WORK SAVER-FARM, Webb Company, 1999 Shepard Rd., St. Paul MN 55116. Editor: Greg Northcutt. For farm families throughout the United States and Canada. Magazine published 6 times/year. Pays on acceptance. Buys all rights. SASE.
Nonfiction: "Covers whole range of business and life on the farm. Emphasis on entertaining, as well as informative. Production and marketing articles, whether crops or livestock, must be thoroughly researched, technically accurate and concisely written". Query or submit complete ms. Length: 1,000-1,500 words. Pays $200-400.
Photos: State availability of photos with query. Pays $50 minimum for b&w glossy prints or color transparencies.

Local

AGROLOGIST, Agricultural Institute of Canada, 151 Slater St., Suite 907, Ottawa, Ontario, Canada K1P 5H4. Managing Editor: W. E. Henderson. For professionals in agriculture: scientists, researchers, economists, teachers, extension workers; most are members of the Agricultural Institute of Canada. Quarterly magazine; 40 pages. Estab. 1934. Circ. 6,500. Not copyrighted. Buys 1-2 mss a year. Pays on acceptance; occasionally in contributor's copies. Free sample copy. No photocopied submissions but will consider simultaneous submissions, if so identified. Reports in 1 to 2 weeks. Query first or submit complete ms. Enclose SAE and International Reply Coupons.
Nonfiction and Photos: Articles on subjects of interest to a wide range of disciplines within agriculture, such as results and applications of new research, economic implications, international agricultural trends, overviews, transportation, education, marketing, etc. Highly technical and specialized material presented as much as possible in layman's language. Main interest is not in new facts, but in the interpretation and implication of facts and situations. "We don't publish 'as is' technical papers (such as those prepared for symposia) or scientific journal material. But we will look at it. If the information is of interest, we could suggest how it might be rewritten for our use. We are particularly interested in articles that highlight how some action of agriculture is affecting nonagriculture areas; e.g., ecology topics, food crisis, etc." Length: 500 to 2,500 words. Most articles are not paid for; those that are average $100 for 1,500 words. No additional payment for b&w photos used with mss. Pays $5 to $15 for 8x10 b&w glossies purchased without mss or on assignment.

BUCKEYE FARM NEWS, Ohio Farm Bureau Federation, Box 479, Columbus OH 43216. (614)225-8906. Editor-in-Chief: S.C. Cashman. Emphasizes agricultural policy. Monthly magazine; 53 pages. Estab. 1922. Circ. 85,000. Pays on acceptance. Buys all rights, but may reassign following publication. Phone queries OK. Submit holiday/seasonal material 3 months in advance. Simultaneous, photocopied, and previously published submissions OK. SASE. Reports in 3 weeks. Free sample copy.
Nonfiction: Exposes (on government, agriculture); humor (light pieces about farm life); informational (but no nuts-and-bolts farming); inspirational (as long as they're not too heavy); personal opinion; and interview. Buys 20 mss/year. Query. Length: 500-2,000 words. Pays $25-100.
Photos: B&w and color purchased with mss or on assignment. Captions required. Send prints and transparencies. Pays $5-10 for b&w.

Poetry: Traditional forms and light verse. Buys 12/year. Limit submissions to batches of 3. Pays $10-25.
Fillers: Buys about 6 newsbreaks/year. Length: 100-250 words. Pays $10-25.

CAROLINA COOPERATOR, 125 E. Davie, Raleigh NC 27601. (919)828-4411. Editor: Robert J. Wachs. For Carolina farmers. Monthly. Buys all rights. Not many freelance articles bought. Pays on publication. Free sample copy. Reports as soon as possible. SASE.
Nonfiction: Interested only in material related to Carolina agriculture, rural living, and farmer co-ops. Newsy features on successful or unusual farmers and their methods, with the intent to entertain or inform. Length: 1,200 words maximum. Payment is $35 to $50 per published page.

COUNTRY JOURNAL, 1600 E. Lincoln Ave., Suite 1, Decatur IL 62521. Editor-in-Chief: Arnie Weissmann. 10% freelance written. "*Country Journal* goes out to grain elevator operators and their farmer-customers. Ages and education vary greatly. All live in Illinois, Indiana, Iowa, Missouri and Ohio." Monthly magazine; 24-36 pages. Estab. 1972. Circ. 30,000. Pays on publication. Buys all rights. Phone queries OK. Submit seasonal/holiday material 3 months in advance of issue date. SASE. Reports in 4 weeks. Sample copy 75¢.
Nonfiction: "Articles must have source in, or be of interest to the states of Illinois, Indiana, Iowa, Missouri and Ohio." General interest (farm); historical; how-to; humor; inspirational (feature Country Pastor of the month); interview (agricultural personalities); new product (if writer is not connected with firm); nostalgia; personal experience; photo feature; profile (of farmers and elevators); and technical. Buys 2 mss/issue. Query or submit complete ms. Length: 200-1,500 words. Pays $25 minimum.
Photos: "About half our editorial space goes to photos. We feature photo pages prominently, and are always looking for an attractive cover photo." Pays $5 minimum per photo used; send b&w negatives and contact sheets; $10 minimum for color transparencies. Captions required. Buys all rights, but may reassign following publication.
Columns/Departments: Perspectives (opinion pieces on current topics); Farmer of the Month (photo feature); and Elevator of the Month (photo feature). Buys 2/issue. Length: 200-1,500 words. Pays $25 minimum.

COUNTRY WORLD, Box 1770, Tulsa OK 74102. (918)583-2161, Ext. 230. Editor: Herb Karner. For a rural, urban, and suburban readership. Monthly. Buys first serial rights. Pays on publication. Query. SASE.
Nonfiction and Photos: Wants farm and ranch success stories; also suburban living, homemaking, youth, 4-H, and F.F.A. Effective photo illustrations necessary. Preferred length: 700 to 800 words. Pays $7.50 a column, sometimes more for exceptional copy. Photos purchased with mss and occasionally with captions only. Prefers b&w glossies, at least 5x7.

THE DAKOTA FARMER, Box 1950, Aberdeen SD 57401. (605)225-5170. Editor: Russ Oviatt. 10% freelance written. For farmers and families in North and South Dakota. "All have agriculturally related occupations and interests." Special issues include Beef issue (August). Monthly. Circ. 80,000. Rights bought "depend on story and author. We are flexible." Buys 15-25 mss/year. Pays on publication. Free sample copy. Submit seasonal material 3 to 4 months in advance. Returns rejected material in approximately 15 days. Query. SASE.
Nonfiction: "Human interest features of Dakota farm people, history, or events. Keep in mind we write for Dakotans. Stories should be geared to that audience. Articles should be objective. We take sides on controversial issues on our editorial page only." Buys how-to's, personal experience stories, interviews, new product articles, photo essays, and successful business operation coverage. Length: 500-1,000 words. Payment based on "sliding scale."
Photos: Purchased with mss. With captions only. B&w glossies.

FARM & COUNTRY, Agricultural Publishing Co., Ltd., 10 St. Mary St., Toronto, Ontario, Canada M4Y 1P9. (416)924-6209. Editor-in-Chief: John Phillips. Managing Editor: Corinne Jefferey. 35% freelance written. Emphasizes farm news, business, and management. Semimonthly tabloid; 40 pages. Estab. 1936. Circ. 84,000. Pays on publication. Buys all rights, but may reassign following publication. Phone queries OK. Submit seasonal/holiday material 6 weeks in advance of issue date. Simultaneous photocopied and previously published submissions OK. SASE. Reports in 4 weeks. Free sample copy and writer's guidelines; send request to News Editor.
Nonfiction: Expose (government, education, corporate domination); general interest (what's new in farming); how-to (farm application); new product; photo feature; and technical. No 'folksy' material. Buys 10 mss/issue. Query with clips of previously published work. Length: 200-750 words. Pays $3-5/column inch.

Photos: "We use lots of pix." Pays $10-20 for 5x7 glossy b&w prints. Captions required. Buys one-time rights.

FARMFUTURES, 225 E. Michigan, Milwaukee WI 53202. (414)276-6600. Editor: Royal Fraedrich. For high income farmers. Monthly magazine; 32 pages. Estab. 1973. Circ. 42,500. Buys all rights. Pays on publication. Free sample copy. No photocopied or simultaneous submissions. Reports in 30 days. Query first. SASE.
Nonfiction and Photos: "Ours is the only national farm magazine devoted exclusively to marketing and the financial management side of farming. We are looking for case histories of successful use of commodity futures markets by farm operators. Major articles deal with marketing and financial strategies of high income farmers. Major commodity interests include corn, cattle, hogs, soybeans, wheat, cotton, and other grains. Market material must be current; thus, must be written within 2 to 3 weeks of publication." Interviews, profiles, personal experience and successful business operation articles pertaining to agricultural commodity markets. Length: 1,000 to 2,000 words. Pays $50 to $250. No additional payment for b&w photos used with mss.

FARMLAND NEWS, Box 7305, Kansas City MO 64116. Editor: Frank C. Whitsitt. For rural members of farmer co-ops. Tabloid newspaper; 24-32 pages. Estab. 1932. Not copyrighted. Buys 25 to 50 mss/year. Free sample copy. No photocopied or simultaneous submissions. Submit seasonal material (Christmas, Thanksgiving, Easter) 6 months in advance. Reports on material accepted for publication in 1 to 2 weeks. Returns rejected material in a few days. Query first. SASE.
Nonfiction: "We try to personalize and humanize stories of broad significance. We use features of interest to our rural audience, as well as holiday-slanted material (Christmas, Thanksgiving, Easter)." Length: open. Pays $25-125.

FLORIDA GROWER & RANCHER, 559 Jones Franklin Rd., Suite 150, Raleigh NC 27606. Editor: Stephen Denny. For citrus grove managers and production managers; vegetable growers and managers. Monthly magazine; 24 pages. Estab. 1912. Circ. 12,000. Buys all rights, but will reassign rights to author after publication. Buys about 40 mss a year. Pays on publication. Will send free sample copy to writer on request. Reports on material immediately. Query first or submit complete ms. SASE.
Nonfiction and Photos: Articles on production and industry-related topics. In-depth and up to date. Writer must know the market and write specifically for it. Informational, how-to, personal experience, interview, profile, personal opinion, successful business operations. Length: open. Pays $2 a column inch. Pays $10 for 5x7 b&w glossies used with mss. Captions required.

FLORIDAGRICULTURE, P.O. Box 730, Gainesville FL 32602. (904)378-1321, ext. 307. Editor: Andy Williams. 25% freelance written. For members of the Florida Farm Bureau Federation. Monthly magazine; 32-48 pages. Estab. 1941. Circ. 68,000. Pays on acceptance. Buys first North American serial rights. Phone queries OK. Submit seasonal/holiday material 3 months in advance. Previously published submissions OK. SASE. Reports in 4 weeks.
Nonfiction and Photos: "We cover the broad spectrum of Florida farming and use articles of general interest to Florida farmers. We can't stress the word 'Florida' enough. The outlook is always toward the Florida farmer. The Federation serves all farmers, not specialized interests. Our theme is 'The Voice of Agriculture.' Articles on the economic problems facing the farmer and how he can best meet them would be of interest. And remember, understand your subject matter thoroughly because the farmer will. We like crisp, provocative writing. Don't make it so folksy as to appear to be writing down to your reader. Please, no stories on why the farmer isn't to blame for high food prices. And, no stories on part-time farmers, or on people who have moved from the big city to get back to rural life." Length: 750-2,000 words. Pays 6¢/word. No additional payment for b&w photos used with mss. But b&w photo essays of Florida farm scenes will be considered. Payment negotiable.

MICHIGAN FARMER, 3303 W. Saginaw St., Lansing MI 48917. (517)372-4407. Editor: Richard Lehnert. 10-20% freelance written. Semimonthly. Buys first North American rights. Pays on acceptance. Reports in 1 month. Query first. SASE.
Nonfiction: Uses articles of interest and value to Michigan farmers, which discuss Michigan agriculture and the people involved in it. "These are fairly technical. Also articles for home section about Michigan farm housewives and what they are doing. Although articles are technical, lucid easy-to-understand writing is desired. Length depends on topic." Rates are 2¢ a word minimum; special stories bring higher rates.

Photos: Buys some b&w singles; also a few color transparencies, for cover use. Pays $2 to $5 each for b&w, depending on quality. Pays $60 for selected cover transparencies of identifiable Michigan farm or rural scenes.

MONTANA RURAL ELECTRIC NEWS, Montana Associated Utilities, Inc., Box 1641, Great Falls MT 59403. (404)454-1412. Managing Editor: Martin L. Erickson. Emphasizes rural life. For farmers, ranchers and rural dwellers. Monthly magazine; 32 pages. Estab. 1951. Circ. 40,000. Pays on publication. Buys one-time rights. Phone queries OK. Simultaneous photocopied, and previously published submissions OK. SASE. Reports in 3 weeks. Free sample copy.
Nonfiction: How-to, informational, historical, humor, inspirational, nostalgic and travel articles; interviews and photo features. Query. Length: 500-2,000 words. Pays $15 minimum.
Photos: Purchased with mss or on assignment. Captions required. Query. Pays $10 minimum for 8x10 (or 5x7 minimum) b&w glossies. Model release required.

NEBRASKA FARMER, Box 81208, Lincoln NE 68501. (402)489-9331. Editor-in-Chief: Robert L. Bishop. Managing Editor: Dave Howe. 5% freelance written. For "9 out of ten Nebraska farmers." Semimonthly magazine; 80 pages. Estab. 1859. Circ. 80,000. Pays on acceptance. Buys all rights, but may reassign following publication. Phone queries OK. Submit seasonal/holiday material 6 months in advance of issue date. SASE. Reports in 2 weeks.
Nonfiction: How-to and new product articles of interest to Nebraska farmers. No human interest material. Buys 10-12 mss/year. Query. Length: 500-2,500 words. Pays $25-250.
Photos: State availability of photos with query. Pays $5-15 for b&w prints; $25-50 for color transparencies. Captions and model release required. Buys one-time rights.

THE OHIO FARMER, 1350 W. 5th Ave., Columbus OH 43212. (614)486-9637. Editor: Andrew Stevens. For Ohio farmers and their families. Biweekly magazine; 50 pages. Estab. 1848. Circ. 103,000. Rights purchased vary with author and material. Usually buys all rights, but may reassign rights to author after publication. Buys 15 to 20 mss per year. Pays on publication. Sample copy $1; free writer's guidelines. Will consider photocopied submissions. No simultaneous submissions. Reports in 2 weeks. Submit complete ms. SASE.
Nonfiction and Photos: Technical and on-the-farm stories. Buys informational, how-to, personal experience. Length: 600 to 700 words. Pays $15. Photos purchased with ms with no additional payment, or without ms. Pays $5 to $25 for b&w; $35 to $100 for color. Size: 4x5 for b&w glossies; transparencies or 8x10 prints for color.

RURAL ELECTRIC MISSOURIAN, 2722 E. McCarty St., Jefferson City MO 65101. (314)635-6857. Editor: Steve Rudloff. 50% freelance written. For rural readers (farm and nonfarm). Monthly. Not copyrighted. Buys exclusive Missouri first rights. Pays on acceptance. Usually reports in 30 to 120 days. Query. SASE. Sample copy 50¢.
Nonfiction: Needs human interest material, preferably with a humorous rural flavor. Length: 500-1,500 words. Payment varies and is negotiated.
Photos: 8x10 b&w glossies occasionally purchased either with mss or with captions only. Payment varies; minimum $5 a photo.
Poetry: "Short, human interest, rural items needed." Pays $7.

WALLACES FARMER, 1912 Grand Ave., Des Moines IA 50305. (515)243-6181. Editor: Monte N. Sesker. For Iowa farmers and their families. Semimonthly. Buys Midwest States rights (Nebraska, Minnesota, Wisconsin, Illinois, Missouri, South Dakota, and Iowa). Pays on acceptance. Reports in 2 weeks. SASE.
Nonfiction and Photos: Occasional short feature articles about Iowa farming accompanied by photos. Payment varies. Length: 500 to 750 words. Pays about $50. Photos purchased with or without mss. Should be taken on Iowa farms. Pays $7 to $15 for 5x7 b&w; $50 to $100 for 4x5, 2¼x2¼ color transparencies. See recent issue covers for examples.

WYOMING RURAL ELECTRIC NEWS, 340 West B St., Casper WY 82601. (307)234-6152. Editor: Jim McAllister. For rural farmers and ranchers. Monthly magazine; 20 pages. Estab. 1954. Cir. 21,000. Not copyrighted. Buys about 12 mss per year. Pays on publication. Free sample copy. Will consider photocopied and simultaneous submissions. Submit seasonal material 2 months in advance. Reports immediately. SASE.
Nonfiction, Photos and Fiction: Wants "feature material, historical pieces about the West, things of interest to Wyoming's rural people." Buys informational, humor, historical, nostalgia and photo mss. Length for nonfiction and fiction: 1,200-1,500 words. Pays $10-25. Photos purchased

with accompanying ms with no additional payment, or purchased without ms. Captions required. Pays $25 for cover photos. B&w preferred. Buys experimental, western, humorous and historical fiction. Pays $25.

Livestock

Publications in this section are for farmers who raise cattle, sheep, or hogs for meat, wool, or hides. Publications for farmers who raise other animals are listed in the Miscellaneous category; also many magazines in the General Interest Farming and Rural Interest classification buy material on raising livestock. Magazines for dairymen are included under Dairy Farming. Publications dealing with raising horses, pets, or other pleasure animals will be found under Animal in the Consumer Publications section.

AMERICAN HEREFORD JOURNAL, 715 Hereford Dr., Kansas City MO 64105. Editor: Bob Day. Monthly. Buys first North American serial rights. Pays on publication. Reports in 30 days. Query. SASE.
Nonfiction and Photos: Breeding, feeding, and marketing of purebred and commercial Herefords, with accent on well-substantiated facts; success-type story of a Hereford cattleman and how he did it. Length: 1,000 to 1,500 words. Pays average of 2½¢ to 3¢ a word. Buys 5x7 b&w glossy photos for use with articles. Pays $3 each.

ARKANSAS CATTLE BUSINESS, 208 Wallace Bldg., Little Rock AR 72201. (501)372-3197. Editor: Mary Hinkle. For beef cattlemen. Not copyrighted. Buys 2 to 3 mss a year. Pays on acceptance. Will send a free sample copy to a writer on request. Reports in 2 weeks. Query first. Enclose SASE.
Nonfiction and Photos: Articles related to beef cattle production and allied interests, with an Arkansas slant. Could also use historical articles on Arkansas. Length: 1,000 to 2,000 words. Pays 2¢ a word maximum. Photos purchased with mss. Payment varies.

BEEF, The Webb Co., 1999 Shepard Rd., St. Paul MN 55116. (612)647-7374. Editor-in-Chief: Paul D. Andre. Managing Editor: William D. Fleming. 5% freelance written. For readers who have the same basic interest—making a living feeding cattle. Monthly magazine; 40 pages. Estab. 1964. Circ. 61,000. Pays on acceptance. Buys one-time rights. Phone queries OK. Submit seasonal material 3 months in advance. SASE. Reports in 6-8 weeks. Free sample copy and writer's guidelines.
Nonfiction: How-to and informational articles on doing a better job of feeding cattle, market building, managing, and animal health practices. Buys 8-10 mss/year. Query. Length: 500-2,000 words. Pays $25-200.
Photos: B&w glossies (8x10) and color transparencies (35mm or 2¼x2¼) purchased with or without mss. Captions required. Query or send contact sheet or transparencies. Pays $10-50 for b&w; $25-100 for color. Model release required.
How To Break In: "Be completely knowledgeable about cattle feeding. Know what makes a story. We want specifics, not a general roundup of an operation. Pick one angle and develop it fully."

BIG FARMER CATTLE, DAIRY AND HOG GUIDES, 131 Lincoln Highway, Frankfort IL 60423. (815)469-2163. Editor: Greg Northcutt. "To qualify for this controlled circulation publication, the reader must gross $20,000-plus annually." Estab. 1970. Monthly, except June, July and December. Circ. 100,000. Rights purchased vary with author and material; may buy all rights, but will reassign rights to author after publication. Pays on acceptance. Will send a sample copy to a writer on request. Will not consider photocopied submissions. Will consider cassette submissions. "We prefer articles typed at 37 characters wide and no longer than 6 typewritten pages." Submit seasonal material 3 months in advance. Reports in 1 month. Query first or submit complete ms. Enclose SASE.
Nonfiction and Photos: "Management articles must be on specific areas; not general features about an operator's operation. Articles must be to the point and acceptable for livestock producers across the country. We'd like to see articles on marketing strategies." Buys informational and how-to articles, interviews, and coverage of successful business operations. Length: 2,000 words maximum. Pays $100 minimum. Captioned photos purchased with and without mss. Pays $15 for 8x10 or 5x7 glossy prints "if not submitted with ms." Pays $25 minimum for

color transparencies "from 35mm and up."

THE CATTLEMAN MAGAZINE, Texas & Southwestern Cattle Raisers Association, 410 E. Weatherford, Ft. Worth TX 76102. (817)332-7155. Editor-in-Chief: Paul W. Horn. Emphasizes beef cattle production and feeding. "Readership consists of commercial cattlemen, purebred seedstock producers, cattle feeders, horsemen in the Southwest." Monthly magazine; 200 pages. Estab. 1914. Circ. 27,000. Pays on acceptance. Buys all rights but may reassign following publication. Submit seasonal/holiday material 3 months in advance. SASE. Reports in 3 weeks. Free sample copy and writer's guidelines.
Nonfiction: Need informative, entertaining feature articles on specific commercial ranch operations, cattle breeding and feeding, range and pasture management, profit tips. Will take a few historical western lore pieces. Must be well-documented. No first person narratives or fiction. Buys 36 articles/year. Query. Length open. Pays $25-200. No articles pertaining to areas outside of southwestern U.S.
Photos: Photos purchased with or without accompanying ms. Captions required. Pays $10-25 for 8x10 b&w glossies; $25-100 for color photos. Total purchase price for ms includes payment for photos. Model release required.

CATTLEMEN, The Beef Magazine, Public Press, 1760 Ellice Ave., Winnipeg, Manitoba R3H 0B6 Canada. (204)774-1861. Editor-in-Chief: Harold Dodds. 10% freelance written. For beef producers. Monthly magazine; 50 pages. Estab. 1938. Circ. 40,000. Pays on publication. Buys all rights. Phone queries OK. Submit seasonal/holiday material 3 months in advance. Reports in 2 weeks. Free sample copy and writer's guidelines.
Nonfiction: Industry articles, particularly those on raising and feeding beef in Canada. Also how-to-do-it and success stories with good management slant. Writer must be informed. Uses an occasional historical item. Pays up to $150 for industry and historical articles, more for special assignments.
Photos: Canadian shots only, purchased with mss and for cover. B&w and color for cover. Pays up to $10 for b&w; up to $75 for color.

FEEDLOT MANAGEMENT, Box 67, Minneapolis MN 55440. Editorial Director: George Ashfield. 50% freelance written. For agri-businessmen who feed cattle and/or sheep for slaughter. Special issues include waste management (April); and feeder cattle (September). Monthly. Circ. 20,000. Not copyrighted. Pays on acceptance. Free sample copy. Reports in 1 to 5 weeks. Query. SASE.
Nonfiction: Wants detailed, thorough material relating to cattle or lamb feeding and related subject areas—waste management, nutrition, marketing and processing, feeding, animal health. "Write for a copy of the magazine. Writers should know something about the industry in order to get the information that's important. We can accept highly technical articles, but there's no room for simple cursory articles. Feature articles on feedlots should include photos." No length restriction. Pays $30 to $200.
Photos and Fillers: 8x10 and 5x7 b&w glossies purchased with mss and with captions only. Pays 50¢ an inch for newsbreaks and clippings.

GULF COAST CATTLEMAN MAGAZINE, Box 29367, San Antonio TX 78229. (512)344-8300. Editor: Jimmy Guillot. For commercial cattlemen, purebred livestock breeders and others interested in beef cattle production in the Gulf Coast states (mainly Texas, Louisiana, Mississippi, Alabma, Oklahoma and Florida). Monthly magazine; 40-50 pages. Estab. 1935. Circ. 7,000. Pays on acceptance. Buys all rights. Phone queries OK. Submit seasonal/holiday material 2 months in advance of issue date. SASE. Reports in 2 weeks. Sample copy for 50¢ postage.
Nonfiction: Exposé (government, FDA, EPA, etc., as they affect the cattle industry); historical (regarding the beef cattle industry); how-to (making a farm or ranch work easier via a new idea, management practice, or piece of equipment); human (about ranches, people in our area); new product (about work-saving devices to be used in cattle operations); and nostalgia (about well-known persons in our area talking about past days of the cattle business). Buys 8-10 mss/year. Query or submit complete ms. Length: 500-1,200 words. Pays $35-50.
Photos: Pays $5 for 5x7 or larger b&w prints; $25 for color transparencies bought for cover. Model release required.
Fiction: Humorous; western (humorous cowboy fiction). Buys 2 mss/year. Length: 250-1,000 words. Pays $25-50.
Fillers: Cowboy or ranch related jokes. Length: 10-100 words. Pays $3-5.

IBIA NEWS, Box 1127, Ames IA 50010. Publisher: Angus Stone. 10% freelance written. Published for the Iowa Beef Improvement Association. For cow-calf producers (farmers) in the Corn Belt states. Tabloid style magazine; 24 (11½x17) pages. Estab. 1968. Monthly. Circ. 48,000. Not copyrighted. Pays on acceptance. Will send free sample copy to writer on request. Will consider photocopied and simultaneous submissions. Returns rejected material immediately. Query first or submit complete ms. Enclose SASE.
Nonfiction and Photos: "Our only interest is genetic improvement of beef cattle and updated cattle raising procedures. Success stories on beef cattle producers (not feeders) who participate in a program of performance testing. Articles on new equipment, products or procedures applicable to cow-calf operations. We prefer a conservative, typical Midwest farm approach." Interview, profile, successful business operations and technical articles. Length: 1,000 to 1,500 words. Pays $40 to $100. Photos are purchased with mss or on assignment. No additional payment is made for those purchased with mss.

THE KANSAS STOCKMAN, Kansas Livestock Association, 2044 Fillmore, Topeka KS 66604. Editor-in-Chief: Kendall Frazier. Emphasizes cattle ranching and feeding for farmers, ranchers and feeders (over 3 million cattle). Monthly magazine; 75 pages. Estab. 1916. Circ. 8,500. Buys one-time rights. Submit seasonal/holiday material 2 months in advance. Simultaneous, photocopied, and previously published submissions OK. Reports in 3 months. Sample copy 50¢.
Nonfiction: Exposes (government—added costs or inefficiencies, etc.); historical (livestock business, ranching in 19th century—*not* just cattle drives); how-to (management/scientific); humor (cattle business oriented—must be esoteric); interviews. Buys 6 mss/year. Query. Length: 750-2,000 words. Pays 3¢/word minimum.
Photos: B&w and color purchased with mss. Captions required. Send contact sheet or prints. Pays $5 minimum for b&w; $25 minimum for color.
Special Issues: Cow/calf/stocker issue (March); beef month (May); cattle feeder emphasis (July); marketing emphasis (September); convention and trade show (November).

NATIONAL WOOL GROWER, 600 Crandall Bldg., Salt Lake City UT 84101. (801)363-4484. Editor: Vern Newbold. 1% freelance written. Not copyrighted. A very limited market. Best to query first here. Reports in 4 to 5 days. Enclose SASE.
Nonfiction: Material of interest to sheepmen. Length: 2,000 words. Pays 1¢ per word for material used.

NEW MEXICO STOCKMAN, Livestock Publications, Inc., Box 7127, Albuquerque NM 87104. (505)247-8192. Editor: Carol Cohen. 5% freelance written. For ranchers, farmers, horsemen, feedlot operators of all ages. "Women and youngsters are some of our best supporters." Monthly magazine; 70 pages. Estab. 1935. Circ. 11,000. Pays on publication. Buys one-time rights. Phone queries OK. Simultaneous, photocopied, and previously published submissions OK. Reports on material accepted for publication on first of month prior to publication. Free sample copy and writer's guidelines.
Nonfiction: Historical (articles relating the rich culture and heritage of southwestern agriculture, the people and events that made it so); how-to (articles that teach people who depend on agriculture for a living how to better manage their resources); informational (articles that relate new concepts and research in agricultural management techniques); interviews (with anyone who has made a contribution to southwestern agriculture); material on ag-related new products; profiles (which relate the goals, accomplishments and achievements of the movers of southwestern agriculture); technical articles (horse pedigrees, artificial insemination, research on crops and animals that may lead to more profitable management). Buys 3-8 mss/issue. Query. Unsolicited mss are not returned. Length: 250-1,250 words. Pays 5-10¢/word.
Photos: B&w glossies (5x7 or 8x10) or color (35mm or 2¼x2¼) purchased with mss. Captions required. Query. Pays $5-10 for b&w; $25-40 for color.

THE OKLAHOMA COWMAN, 2500 Exchange Ave., Oklahoma City OK 73108. For cattle producers and feedlot owners (mostly within Oklahoma) who are members of the Oklahoma Cattlemen's Association and are deeply involved in the actual business of producing and selling beef cattle. Monthly magazine; 40 pages. Estab. 1961. Circ. 6,300. Buys all rights, but will reassign rights to author after publication. Buys 2 or 3 mss a year. Pays on publication. Will send sample copy to writer for $1. Will consider photocopied submissions. Simultaneous submissions considered if assured of first publication rights. Submit seasonal material (geared to management practices) 1 month in advance. Reports in 2 weeks. SASE.
Nonfiction and Photos: "We are exclusively interested in beef cattle and centered around field crops, horses, etc., as they relate directly to cattle production. Mostly reports of state activity in

education, extension, etc., to inform the cattleman. Also, regular feature stories on historical significance of Oklahoma's cattle background. All material dealing with management practices should be geared to season. New ideas on more intensive production practices and 'success' stories on Oklahoma cattle people, as well as adaptability of cattle people to the current economic drain on their land, labor and capital. No Wild West fictionalized articles.'' Length: 500 to 750 words. Pays $10 to $25. ''Photos may make the difference in acceptance of articles. They should be an integral part of the subject.'' No additional payment. Captions required.

POLLED HEREFORD WORLD, #1 Place, 4700 E. 63rd St., Kansas City MO 64130. (816)333-7731. Editor: Ed Bible. For ''breeders of Polled Hereford cattle—about 80% registered breeders, about 5% commercial cattle breeders; remainder are agri-businessmen in related fields.'' Estab. 1947. Monthly. Circ. 20,000. Not copyrighted. Buys ''very few mss at present.'' Pays on publication. Will send a sample copy to a writer on request. Will consider photocopied submissions. Submit seasonal material ''as early as possible; 2 months preferred.'' Reports in 1 month. Query first for reports of events and activities. Query first or submit complete ms for features. SASE.

Nonfiction: ''Features on registered or commercial Polled Hereford breeders. Some on related agricultural subjects (pastures, fences, feeds, buildings, etc.). Mostly technical in nature; some human interest. Our readers make their living with cattle, so write for an informed, mature audience.'' Buys informational articles, how-to's, personal experience articles, interviews, profiles, inspirational articles, humor, historical and think pieces, nostalgia, photo features, coverage of successful business operations, articles on merchandising techniques, and technical articles. Length: ''varies with subject and content of feature.'' Pays about 5¢ a word (''usually about 50¢ a column inch, but can vary with the value of material'').

Photos: Purchased with mss, sometimes purchased without mss, or on assignment; captions required. ''Only good quality b&w glossy prints accepted; any size. Good color prints or transparencies.'' Pays $2 for b&w photos, $2 to $25 for color. Pays $25 for color covers.

THE RECORD STOCKMAN, 4700 A Packinghouse Rd., Denver CO 80216. Editor: Fred Wortham Jr. For purebred and commercial ranchers and feeders, and others in fields related to the cattle industry. Weekly newspaper; annual magazine. Estab. 1889. Circ. 20,000. Copyrighted. Pays on publication. Will send free sample copy to writer on request. Reports in 2 weeks. Query first or submit complete ms. SASE.

Nonfiction and Photos: Wants ''interesting, informative articles on commercial ranchers, feedlot operators, etc., who are doing something innovative in their field. Writers should be familiar with livestock and the cattle industry.'' Buys informational, how-to, interview, successful business operations mss. Length: 500 to 1,000 words for newspaper; 1,500 to 4,000 words for magazine. Pays about $35 for newspaper-length mss; more for magazine articles. Photos purchased with accompanying mss. Captions required.

SIMMENTAL JOURNAL, Box 410, Cody WY 82414. (307)587-5987. Editor: John McGee. For cattle breeders. Tabloid; 16 pages. Estab. 1975. Every two weeks. Circ. 7,000. Buys first serial rights. Buys about 20 mss a year. Pays on publication. Will consider photocopied and simultaneous submissions. Reports in 1 month. Query first or submit complete ms. Enclose SASE.

Nonfiction and Photos: Articles on individual Simmental ranches or ranchers. Informational, how-to, personal experience, profile, interview, successful business operations. Length: 1,000 words maximum. Pays 80¢/column inch. Pays $15 for 8x10 b&w glossy prints purchased with or without ms; $25 for color transparencies or negatives.

SIMMENTAL SCENE, 310 9th Ave., SW., Suite 120, Calgary, Alberta, Canada T2P 1K5. Editor-in-Chief: Ron Driskill. 10-20% freelance written. Emphasizes the breeding of Simmental cattle. Monthly magazine; 52 pages. Estab. March 1973. Circ. 5,400. Pays on publication. Buys all rights, but may reassign following publication. Submit seasonal/holiday material 4 months in advance of issue date. SASE. Reports in 2 weeks. Free sample copy; mention *Writer's Market* in request.

Nonfiction: General interest (on unique aspects of beef cattle production, producers, or a farm story with a unique twist); how-to (on modern beef production methods, improvements, breeding techniques or applications of technological breakthroughs); interview (with Simmental breeders that have a significant or unique aspect to their farm or ranch); new product (having an affect or serving modern Simmental beef cattle producers); profile; and technical (on breakthroughs or advances in the breeding, maintenance or production of beef cattle). ''We cannot use anything that pertains to dairy cattle.'' Buys 5-10 mss/year. Query. Length: 500-2,000 words. Pays 2-5¢/word.

Photos: "We like photos and will always choose manuscripts with photos if it is a decision between with or without." Pays $0-50 for 5x7 glossy b&w prints; $0-100 for 2¼x2¼ color transparencies or 11x14 glossy or matte finish color prints. Captions and model release required. Buys one-time rights.

SIMMENTAL SHIELD, Box 511, Lindsborg KS 67456. Editor: Chester Peterson, Jr. Official publication of American Simmental Association. Readers are purebred cattle breeders and/or commercial cattlemen. Monthly; 130 pages. Circ. 10,000. Buys all rights. Pays on publication. Will send free sample copy to writer on request. February is AI issue; August is herd sire issue; November is brood cow issue. Submit material 3 to 4 months in advance. Reports in 1 week. Query first or submit complete ms. SASE.
Nonfiction, Photos, and Fillers: Farmer experience; management articles with emphasis on ideas used and successful management ideas based on cattleman who owns Simmental. Research: new twist to old ideas or application of new techniques to the Simmental or cattle business. Wants articles that detail to reader how to make or save money or pare labor needs. Buys informational, how-to, personal experience, interview, profile, humor, think articles. Rates vary, but equal or exceed those of comparable magazines. Photos purchased with accompanying ms with no additional payment. Interested in cover photos; accepts 35mm if sharp, well-exposed.

Miscellaneous

GLEANINGS IN BEE CULTURE, 623 West Liberty St., Medina OH 44256. Editor: Lawrence R. Goltz. For beekeepers. Monthly. Buys first North American serial rights. Pays on publication. Reports in 15 to 90 days. SASE.
Nonfiction and Photos: Interested in articles giving new ideas on managing bees. Also uses success stories about commercial beekeepers. Length: 3,000 words maximum. Pays $23 a published page. Sharp b&w photos pertaining to honeybees purchased with mss. Can be any size, prints or enlargements, but 4x5 or larger preferred. Pays $3 to $5 a picture.
How To Break In: "Do an interview story on commercial beekeepers who are cooperative enough to furnish accurate, factual information on their operations."

THE SUGAR PRODUCER, Harris Publishing, Inc., 520 Park, Box 981, Idaho Falls ID 83401. (208)522-5187. Editor/Publisher: Darryl W. Harris. 25% freelance written. Emphasizes the growing, storage, use and by-products of the sugar beet. Magazine published 7 times a year; 32 pages. Estab. 1975. Circ. 20,000. Pays on publication. Buys all rights, but may reassign following publication. Phone queries OK. Photocopied submissions and previously published work OK. SASE. Reports in 30 days. Free sample copy and writer's guidelines.
Nonfiction: "This is a trade magzine, not a farm magazine. It deals with the business of growing sugar beets, and the related industry. All articles must tell the grower how he can do his job better, or at least be of interest to him, such as historical, because he is vitally interested in the process of growing sugar beets, and the industries related to this." Expose (pertaining to the sugar industry or the beet grower); how-to (all aspects of growing, storing and marketing the sugar beet); interview, profile, personal experience; technical (material source must accompany story—research and data must be from an accepted research institution). Query or send complete ms. Length: 750-2,000 words. Pays 3¢/word.
Photos: Purchased with mss. Captions required. Pays $5 for any convenient size b&w; $25 for color print or slide used on cover. Model release required.

Poultry

The publications listed here specialize in material on poultry farming. Other publications that buy material on poultry will be found in the General Interest Farming and Rural Life classification.

CANADA POULTRYMAN, 605 Royal Avenue, New Westminster B.C. Canada V3M 1J4. Editor: Fred W. Beeson. For poultry producers and those servicing this industry. Magazine; 56 pages. Estab. 1912. Monthly. Circ. 12,000. Buys all rights. Pays on publication. Will send free sample copy to writer on request. Submit seasonal material 2 months in advance. Reports on material accepted for publication in 1 month. Returns rejected material in 1 month. Submit complete ms. Enclose S.A.E. and International reply Coupons.

Nonfiction and Photos: Canadian market facts, management material, pieces on persons in the industry. Length: 200 to 2,000 words. Pays 4¢ to 5¢ a word. Photos (up to 5x7) purchased with mss for $3. Captions required.

INDUSTRIA AVICOLA (Poultry Industry), Watt Publishing Co., Mt. Morris IL 61054. (815)734-4171. Editor: Gary Buikema. 15-20% freelance written. For "poultry producers (minimum 1,000 hens and/or 20,000 broilers annually and/or 1,000 turkeys annually) who have direct affiliation with the poultry industry in Latin America." Circ. 12,000. Buys all rights. Pays on acceptance. Free sample copy. "Prefer mss written in English." Reports in 10 days. Query. SASE.
Nonfiction and Photos: Specialized publication "for poultry businessmen of Latin America. Printed only in Spanish. Emphasis is to aid in production, processing, and marketing of poultry meat and eggs. Keep readers abreast of developments in research, breeding, disease control, housing, equipment, marketing production and business management. Analytical and trend articles concerning the poultry industry in Latin countries are given preference." Length: up to 1,000 to 1,500 words. Pays $40 to $130 depending on content and quality. Photos are purchased with mss. No size requirements.

TURKEY WORLD, Mount Morris IL 61054. Editor: Bernard Heffernan. Bimonthly. Reports on submissions in two weeks. Buys all rights. Pays on acceptance. Query first. Enclose SASE.
Nonfiction and Photos: Clear, concise, simply written, factual articles beamed at producers, processors and marketers of turkeys and turkey products. Length: 1,200 to 2,000 words. Pays $50-150.

Finance

The magazines listed below deal with banking, investment, and financial management. Magazines that use similar material but have a less technical or professional slant are listed in the Consumer Publications under Business and Finance.

BANK SYSTEMS & EQUIPMENT, 1515 Broadway, New York NY 10036. Editor: Alan Richman. For bank and savings and loan association operations executives. Monthly. Circ. 22,000. Buys all rights. Pays on publication. Query first for style sheet and specific article assignment. Mss should be triple spaced on one side of paper only with wide margin at left-hand side of the page. SASE.
Nonfiction: Third-person case history articles and interviews as well as material relating to systems, operations and automation. Charts, systems diagrams, artist's renderings of new buildings, etc., may accompany ms and must be suitable for reproduction. Prefers one color only. Length: open. Pays $75 for first published page, $45 for second page, and $40 for succeeding pages.
Photos: 5x7 or 8x10 single-weight glossies. Candids of persons interviewed, views of bank, bank's data center, etc. Captions required. "We do not pay extra for photos."

BANKING, Journal of the American Bankers Association, 350 Broadway, New York NY 10013. (212)966-7700. Editor/Publisher: Harry Waddall. Managing Editor: Joe W. Kizzia. 15-20% freelance written. Monthly magazine; 120 pages. Estab. July 1908. Circ. 41,000. Pays on publication. Buys all rights. Phone queries OK. Photocopied submissions OK. SASE. Reports in 4-6 weeks. Sample copy sent to writer "only if a manuscript is commissioned."
Nonfiction: How-to; new product; and articles dealing with banking. Buys 24-36 mss/year. Query. Average length: 2,000 words. Pays $100/magazine page, including headlines, photos and artwork.
Photos: State availability of photos with query. Uses 8x10 b&w glossy prints and 35mm color transparencies. Buys one-time rights.

BURROUGHS CLEARING HOUSE, Box 418, Detroit MI 48232. (313)972-7936. Managing Editor: Norman E. Douglas. For bank and financial officers. Monthly. Buys all publication rights. Pays on acceptance. Free sample copy. Query first on articles longer than 1,800 words. SASE.
Nonfiction: Uses reports on what banks and other financial institutions are doing; emphasize usable ideas. "We reject an article if we question its authenticity." Length: 1,000-2,000 words; also uses shorter news items. Pays 10¢/word. Additional payment of $5 for usable illustrations.
Photos: Should be 8x10 glossy b&w. Also buys pix with captions only. Pays $5.

THE CANADIAN BANKER & ICB REVIEW, The Canadian Bankers' Association, Box 282, T-D Centre, Toronto, Ontario Canada M5K 1K2. Editor: Brian O'Brien. 90% freelance written. Emphasizes banking in Canada. Bimonthly magazine; 72 pages. Estab. 1893. Circ. 45,000. Buys first North American serial rights. SASE. Reports in 1 month. Free sample copy.
Nonfiction: Informational articles on international banking and economics; interviews, nostalgic and personal opinion articles; book reviews. Query. Length: 750-2,000 words. Pays $100-250. "Freelancer should be an authority on the subject. Most contributors are bankers, economists and university professors."

COMMODITIES MAGAZINE, 219 Parkade, Cedar Falls IA 50613. (319)677-6341. Publisher: Merrill Oster. Editor: Darrell Jobman. For private, individual futures traders, brokers, exchange members, agri-businessmen; agricultural banks; anyone with an interest in commodities. Monthly magazine; 48-64 pages. Estab. 1971. Circ. 50,000. Buys all rights, but will reassign rights to author after publication. Payment on publication. Free sample copy. Photocopied submissions OK. Reports in 1 month. Query first or submit complete ms. SASE.
Nonfiction and Photos: Articles analyzing specific commodity futures trading strategies; fundamental and technical analysis of individual commodities and markets; interviews, book reviews, "success" stories; news items. Material on new legislation affecting commodities, trading, any new trading strategy (results must be able to be substantiated); personalities. Does not want to see "homespun" rules for trading and simplistic approaches to the commodities market. Treatment is always in-depth and broad. Informational, how-to, interview, profile, technical. "Articles should be written for a reader who has traded commodities for one year or more; should not talk down or hypothesize. Relatively complex material is acceptable." Buys 30-40 mss/year. Length: No maximum or minimum; 2,500 words optimum. Pays 6¢/word. Pays $15 for glossy print b&w photos. Captions required.

COMMODITY JOURNAL, The American Association of Commodity Traders, 10 Park St., Concord NH 03301. Editor-in-Chief: Arthur N. Economou. Mainly for members of the American Association of Commodity Traders, the journal serves an educational function for them, because of its design as a clearinghouse for exchanges of ideas and opinions. Bimonthly magazine. Estab. 1965. Circ. 4,000. Pays on publication. Buys all rights. Simultaneous submissions OK. SASE. Reports in 1 month.
Nonfiction: "Only feature articles dealing with commodities; preferably of a technical nature. We are interested in fresh material concerning alternatives to the commodity futures industry operant in the US today. Special emphasis should be given the spot and forward selling methods and markets. Rather than assigning specific articles, we prefer to consider the ideas of interested writers." Length: 2,500 words maximum. Pays 5-10¢/word. Query.

FINANCIAL QUARTERLY, P. O. Box 14451, North Palm Beach FL 33408. Editor: Thomas A. Swirles. For "bank and savings and loan presidents, vice-presidents, etc. We now go to major credit unions as well." Estab. 1969. Quarterly. Circ. 64,000. Rights purchased vary with author and material. Pays on publication. Will send a sample copy to a writer on request. Submit complete ms. Will consider photocopied submissions. Reports on material accepted for publication "at closing." Returns rejected material in 1 month. Enclose SASE.
Nonfiction and Photos: "Bank product information, trends in banking, etc." Buys informational articles, how-to's, interviews, and coverage of merchandising techniques. Length: 500 to 750 words. Pays $200 to $500. Photos purchased with mss.

FLORIDA BANKER, Box 6847, Orlando FL 32803. Editor: William M. Taylor. 20% freelance written. Monthly magazine; 52 pages. Estab. September 1974. Circ. 5,300. Pays on publication. Buys all rights. SASE. Reports in 8 weeks. Free sample copy and writer's guidelines; mention *Writer's Market* in request.
Nonfiction: General interest (business oriented); historical (on banking); how-to (anything in banking industry or trade); inspirational (occasionally, must deal with banking); interview; nostalgia; photo feature; profile; technical; and travel. Buys 2-3 mss/issue. Query. Length: 600-8,000 words. Pays $200-250.
Photos: State availability of photos with query. Pays $10-100 for 5x7 b&w glossy prints; $20-200 for 35mm color transparencies. Captions and model release required. Buys all rights, but may reassign following publication.
Columns/Departments: Inspiration; Interviews; and Potpourri. Query. Length: 600-2,000 words. Pays $20 minimum. Open to suggestions for new columns/departments.

THE INDEPENDENT BANKER, Box 267, Sauk Centre MN 56378. Editor-in-Chief: Al Blair.

Emphasizes banking. Monthly magazine; 32 pages. Circ. 10,000. Pays on acceptance. Buys all rights. Reports in 1-2 weeks. Free sample copy.
Nonfiction: How-to and informational articles "that will appeal to officers of independent banks in small communities." Query or send complete ms. Pays 5¢ per published word.
Photos: Pays $5 each for 8x10 or 5x7 b&w glossies.

MERGERS & ACQUISITIONS, 1621 Brookside Rd., McLean VA 22101. Editor: Stanley Foster Reed. For presidents and other high corporate personnel, financiers, buyers, stockbrokers, accountants, and related professionals. Quarterly. Buys all rights. Pays 21 days after publication. Will send a free sample copy to a writer on request. Highly recommends query with outline of intended article first. Include 50-word autobiography with mss. Enclose SASE.
Nonfiction: "Articles on merger and acquisition techniques (taxes, SEC regulations, anti-trust, etc.) or surveys and roundups emphasizing analysis and description of trends and implications thereof. Articles should contain 20 to 60 facts per 1,000 words (names, dates, places, companies, etc.). We reject articles that are badly researched. We can fix bad writing but not bad research. Accurate research is a must and footnote references should be incorporated into text. Avoid 'Company A, Company B' terminology." Length: maximum 10,000 to 15,000 words. Pays $50 to $100 per 1,000 printed words for freelance articles; $200 honorarium or 200 reprints for articles by professional business persons, such as lawyers, investment analysts.

Fishing

CANADIAN FISHERMEN AND OCEAN SCIENCE, 27 Centrale St., LaSalle, Quebec, Canada. H8R 2J1. (514)457-3250. Editor: Wayne Paterson. Not copyrighted. Pays on publication. Free sample copy. reports in 1 month. Enclose SAE and International Reply Coupons.
Nonfiction: Articles describing new developments in commercial fisheries and oceanography. Will also consider sketches and controversial articles about Canadian fisheries and oceanological developments. Style should be strictly factual and easy to read. Length: up to 1,000 words. Pays 5¢ to 8¢/word.
Photos: Buys photos with mss and with captions only. Pays $5 and up.

MAINE COMMERCIAL FISHERIES, Box 37, Stonington ME 04681. (207)367-5590. Managing Editor: Nat Barrows. 33% freelance written. Emphasizes commercial fisheries. Monthly newspaper; 24 pages. Estab. 1974. Circ. 3,200. Pays on publication. Copyrighted. SASE. Reports in 2 weeks. Sample copy $1.
Nonfiction: "Material strictly limited to coverage of commerical fishing, technical and general; occasional environment, business, etc., articles as they relate to commercial fishing." Query first. Pays $50-75.

NATIONAL FISHERMAN, Diversified Communications, 21 Elm St., Camden ME 04843. (207)236-4344. Editor-in-Chief: David R. Cetchell. News Editor: Stephen A. Saft. 65% freelance written. For amateur and professional boat builders, commercial fishermen, armchair sailors, bureaucrats and politicans. Monthly tabloid; 102 pages. Estab. 1946. Circ. 63,000. Pays in month of acceptance. Buys one-time rights. Phone queries OK. Submit seasonal/holiday material 3 months in advance of issue date. Photocopied submissions OK. SASE. Reports in 4 weeks. Free sample copy and writer's guidelines; mention *Writer's Market* in request.
Nonfiction: Exposé; how-to; general interest; humor; historical, inspirational; interview; new product; nostalgia, personal experience; personal opinion; photo feature; profile and technical. No articles about sailboat racing, cruising and sportfishing. Buys 40/issue. Submit complete ms. Length: 100-3,500 words. Pays $10 minimum and $125-250 maximum.
Photos: State availability of photos with ms. Pays $5-15 for 5x7 or 8x10 b&w prints. Buys one-time rights.
Columns/Departments: Boatyard news (photos with captions of new boats, commercial fishboats favored); fishing highlights (short articles on catches); marine book review and seafood recipes. Buys 5/issue. Submit complete ms. Length: 50-1,000 words. Pays $10 "at 2.5¢/word". Open to suggestions for new columns/departments.

Florists, Nurserymen, and Landscaping

FLORAFACTS, Florafax International, Inc., Box 45745, Tulsa OK 74145. (918)622-8415. Editor-in-Chief: Angela H. Caruso. For retail florists, wholesalers, suppliers, students of floriculture, horticulture, floral designers. Monthly magazine; 70 pages. Estab. 1961. Circ.

22,500. Pays on acceptance. Buys all rights, but may reassign following publication. Phone queries OK. Submit seasonal/holiday material 6 months in advance. Previously published submissions OK. SASE. Free sample copy and writer's guidelines.
Nonfiction: Expose (floral industry), how-to (floral designs, business, staff, and customer relations), informational, historical, humor (floral trade), interview, nostalgia, personal opinion, profile, travel, new product, personal experience, photo feature, technical. Buys 48 mss/year. Query or submit complete ms. Length: 1,000-3,000 words. Pays 3-8¢/word.
Photos: Elaine Simpson, Photo Editor. Purchased with or without accompanying ms or on assignment. Captions required. Query or submit prints, negatives, or transparencies. Pays $10-25 for 8x10 b&w glossy prints; $15-35 for 2¼x2¼ color transparencies. Model release required.
Columns, Departments: Length: 500-1,000 words. Pays $15. Open to suggestions for new columns and departments.

FLORIST, Florist's Transworld Delivery Association, 29200 Northwestern Hwy., Box 2227, Southfield MI 48037. (313)355-9300. Editor-in-Chief: William P. Golden. Managing Editor: Bill Gubbins. 5% freelance written. For retail florists, floriculture growers, wholesalers, researchers, and teachers. Monthly magazine; 96 pages. Estab. 1967. Circ. 24,000. Pays on acceptance. Buys one-time rights. Phone queries OK. Submit seasonal/holiday material 3-4 months in advance of issue date. Simultaneous, photocopied and previously published submissions OK. SASE. Reports in 1 month.
Nonfiction: How-to (more profitably run a retail flower shop, grow and maintain better quality flowers, etc.); general interest (to floriculture and retail floristry); and technical (on flower and plant growing, breeding, etc.). Buys 10-12 mss/year. Query with clips of previously published work. Length: 1,200-3,000 words. Pays 6¢/word.
Photos: "We do not like to run stories without photos." State availability of photos with query. Pays $10-25 for 5x7 b&w photos or color transparencies. Buys one-time rights.

FLOWER NEWS, 549 W. Randolph St., Chicago IL 60606. (312)236-8648. Managing Editor: Jean Onerheim. For retail, wholesale florists, floral suppliers, supply jobbers, growers. Weekly newspaper; 40 pages. Estab. 1947. Circ. 13,060. Pays on acceptance. Not copyrighted. Submit seasonal/holiday material at least 2 months in advance. Photocopied submissions and previously published work OK. SASE. Reports immediately. Free sample copy.
Nonfiction: How-to articles (increase business, set up a new shop, etc.; anything floral-related without being an individual shop story); informational (general articles of interest to industry); and technical (grower stories related to industry, but not individual grower stories). Submit complete ms. Length: 3-5 typed pages. Pays $10.
Photos: "We do not buy individual pictures. They may be enclosed with ms at regular ms rate (b&w only).

TELEFLORIST (formerly *Teleflora Spirit*), 2400 Compton Blvd., Redondo Beach CA 90278. Editor: Karen Charest. Official publication of Teleflorists, Incorporated, for retail florist subscribers to Teleflora's flowers-by-wire service. Positioned as "The Magazine of Professional Flower Shop Management." Monthly. Circ. 16,000. Buys one-time rights in floral trade magazine field. Most articles are staff-written. Pays on publication. Reports in 2 to 3 weeks. SASE.
Nonfiction and Photos: Articles dealing with buying and selling profitably, merchandising of product, management, designing, shop remodeling, display techniques, etc. Also, allied interests such as floral wholesalers, growers, tradespeople, gift markets, etc. All articles must be thoroughly researched and professionally relevant. Any florist mentioned must be a Teleflorist. Length: 1,000-3,000 words. Pays 8¢/published word. Photos purchased with mss or with captions only. 8x10 b&w glossies preferred. Captions required. Pays $7.50.

WEEDS TREES & TURF, Harvest Publishing Co., 9800 Detroit Ave., Cleveland OH 44102. Editor: Bruce Shank. For "turf managers, parks, superintendents of golf courses, airports, schools, landscape architects, landscape contractors, and sod farmers." Monthly magazine; 72 pages. Estab. 1964. Circ. 45,000. Pays on publication. Buys all rights. Submit seasonal/holiday material 4 months in advance. Photocopied submissions OK. SASE. Reports in 6 weeks. Free sample copy.
Nonfiction: Publishes how-to, informational, and technical articles. Buys 24 mss/year. Query or submit complete ms. Length: 750-2,000 words. Pays $50-150.

Food Products, Processing, and Service

In this list are journals for food wholesalers, processors, warehousers, caterers, institutional managers, and suppliers of grocery store equipment. Publications for grocery store operators are classified under Groceries. Journals for food vending machine operators will be found under Coin-Operated Machines.

FAST SERVICE, Harcourt Brace Jovanovich, Inc., 757 Third Ave., New York NY 10017. (212)754-4324. Editor: Tom Farr. Estab. 1940. Monthly. Circ. 50,800. Buys all rights. Buys 20 mss a year. Pays on acceptance. Reports on material accepted for publication in 2 weeks. Returns rejected material immediately. Query first. Enclose SASE.
Nonfiction and Photos: Articles on operations and case histories of all phases of fast service restaurant operations. Length: 1,500 to 2,000 words. Pays 10¢ a word. B&w photos (5x7 or 8x10) purchased with mss or with captions only. Pays $7 to $10. Color transparencies used for cover and for feature article illustration. Fee is negotiated for all color photography. Prefers 2¼x2¼ transparencies or larger, but will accept 35mm work if of high quality.

KITCHEN PLANNING, 757 Third Ave., New York NY 10017. Editor: Thomas Farr. Buys all rights. Pays on acceptance. Query first. Enclose SASE.
Nonfiction and Photos: How-to, in-depth articles on designing commercial and institutional kitchens—installations based on actual experience of specific operation—with quotes, facts, figures. Length: 1,000 to 1,500 words. Kitchen floor plans must accompany ms. B&w glossies purchased with ms. Pays 7¢ to 10¢ a word. Pays $5 for each photo.

MEAT MAGAZINE, 86 Long Lane, London EC1A 9ET, England. Editor-in-Chief: Marihelen Hawleins. For meat product manufacturers, wholesale and multiple butchers, self-help stores, supermarkets, freezer centers and poultry packers. Magazine; 10 times a year; 68 pages. Pays on publication. Buys all rights, but will reassign following publication. Phone queries OK. Submit seasonal/holiday material 2 months in advance. Photocopied submissions OK. SAE and International Reply Coupons. Reports in 2 weeks. Free sample copy and writer's guidelines.
Nonfiction: Exposes (any problem areas revealed in the meat industry in the U.S. or Canada); interviews (in-depth insights into "meat" men in America, especially heads of meat processing companies); profiles (of successful meat companies or people); technical articles (meat packing, processing, storing, transporting, cutting, etc.). Length: 1,500-3,500 words. Buys 4 mss/issue. Query or submit complete ms. Pays $36-100.
Photos: B&w glossies purchased with mss. Captions required. Send contact sheet. Pays $5-15.

MEAT PLANT MAGAZINE, 9701 Gravois Ave., St. Louis MO 63123. (314)638-4050. Editor: Tony Nolan. For meat processors, locker plant operators, freezer provisioners, portion control packers, meat dealers, and food service (food plan) operators. Bimonthly. Pays on acceptance. Reports in 2 weeks. Enclose SASE for return of submissions.
Nonfiction, Photos, and Fillers: Buys feature-length articles and shorter subjects pertinent to the field. Length: 1,000 words for features. Pays 1½¢ a word. Pays $3.50 for photos.

PRODUCE NEWS, 333 Slyvan Ave., Englewood Cliffs NJ 07632. Editorial Director: Jeffery King. For "commercial growers and shippers, receivers, and distributors of fresh fruits and vegetables, including chain store produce buyers and merchandisers." Estab. 1897. Weekly. Circ. 5,300. Not copyrighted. Pays on publication. Free sample copy. "Our deadline is Wednesday afternoon before Friday press day each week." SASE.
Nonfiction, Fillers and Photos: "News is our principal stock in trade, particularly trends in crop growing, distributing, and marketing. Tell the story clearly, simply, and briefly." Buys informational articles, how-to's, profiles, spot news, coverage of successful business operations, new product pieces, articles on merchandising techniques. Query. Length: "no special length." Pays 50¢ a column inch for original material, 40¢ a column inch for clippings. 8½x11 b&w glossies purchased with ms.

QUICK FROZEN FOODS, Harcourt & Brace Jovanovich, 757 3rd Ave., New York NY 10017. (212)888-3300. Editor-in-Chief: Sam Martin. Managing Editor: Richard Hodgens. 5-10% freelance written. For executives of processing plants, distributors, warehouses, transport companies, retailers and food-service operators involved in frozen foods. Monthly magazine; 100 pages. Estab. August 1938. Circ. 25,000. Pays on acceptance. Buys all rights, but may reassign following publication. Submit seasonal/holiday material 3 months in advance of issue date.

SASE. Reports in 1 week. Free sample copy; mention *Writer's Market* in request.
Nonfiction: Interview; new product; photo feature; profile; and technical. Buys 12 mss/year. Query or submit complete ms. Length: 1,500-3,000 words. Pays 3¢/word.
Photo: State availability of photos with query or ms. Pays $5 for 4x5 b&w smooth prints. Captions required. Buys all rights, but may reassign following publication.

SNACK FOOD, HBJ Publications, Inc., 1 E. 1st St., Duluth MN 55802.(218)727-8511. Editor-in-Chief: Jerry L. Hess. 10-15% freelance written. For manufacturers and distributors of snack foods. Monthly magazine; 60 pages. Estab. 1912. Circ. 10,000 Pays on acceptance. Buys all rights, but may reassign following publication. Phone queries OK. Submit seasonal/holiday material 2-3 months in advance. Photocopied submissions OK. SASE. Reports in 2-3 weeks. Free sample copy and writer's guidelines.
Nonfiction: Informational, interview, new product, nostalgia, photo feature, profile and technical articles. "We are beginning a new format which will allow us to use a greater variety of mini news-features and personality sketches. We are looking for regional correspondents who will be able to move quickly on leads furnished as well as develop articles on their own. A directory of processors in their areas will be furnished upon making working agreement." Length: 300-600 words for mini features; 1,000-1,500 words for longer features. Pays $50-300.
Photos: Purchased with accompanying ms. Captions required. Pays $10-15 for 5x7 b&w photos; $15-50 for 4x5 color transparencies. Total purchase price for a ms includes payment for photos.

Fur

U.S. FUR RANCHER, 3055 N. Brookfield Rd., Brookfield WI 53005. (414)786-7540. Publisher: Bruce W. Smith. For mink farmers. Monthly. Buys first world rights. Pays on publication. Will send free sample copy on request "by letter, not postcard. Queries imperative, including names and addresses of proposed interview subjects." Reports "immediately." Enclose SASE.
Nonfiction and Photos: "Articles and photos on mink-ranch operations, based on interviews with manager or owner. Not interested in any fur-bearing animals except mink. Opportunities for freelancers traveling to foreign nations in which mink are raised. We reject an article if we find factual errors resulting from carelessness in interviewing and research." Length: 1,000 to 2,000 words. Pays $30 to $75 per article, including four contact prints at least 2¼ square.

Gas

BUTANE-PROPANE NEWS, P.O. Box 1408, Arcadia CA 91006. (213)446-4607. Editor-Publisher: William W. Clark. 15% freelance written. For LP-gas distributor dealers with bulk storage plants, LP bottled gas dealers and manufacturers of appliances and equipment. Monthly. Buys all rights. Pays on publication. Free sample copy. Query. Reports in 1 week. Enclose SASE.
Nonfiction: Articles on advertising and promotional programs; plant design, marketing operating techniques and policies; management problems; new, unusual or large usages of LP-gas; how LP-gas marketers are coping with the energy crisis. Completeness of coverage, reporting in depth, emphasis on the why and the how are musts. "Brevity essential but particular angles should be covered pretty thoroughly." Pays $50 per magazine page. "We also publish *The Weekly Propane Newsletter,* which is a market for newsclippings on propane, butane, and other energy related matters." Will send clipping tips on request.
Photos: Purchased with mss. 8x10 desired but not required; can work from negatives. Pays $6.
Fillers: Clippings and newsbreaks pertinent to LPG industry. Clippings regarding competitive fuels (electricity, oil) with relationship that would have impact on LPG industry. Pays $5 minimum for clippings.

GAS DIGEST, Box 35819, Houston TX 77035. (713)723-7456. Editor: Ken Kridner. 50% freelance written. For operating personnel of the gas industry. Monthly magazine; 50 pages. Estab. 1975. Circ. 9,000. Rights may be retained by the author. Pays on publication. Sample copy for $2; free writer's guidelines. Will consider photocopied submissions. No simultaneous submissions. Reports in 10 days. Query first. Enclose S.A.S.E.
Nonfiction and Photos: Applications stories; new developments. All material must be operations oriented and meaningful to one working in the gas industry. How-to, interviews, technical articles. Length: 1,000 words. Pays 2.5¢ per word minimum. B&w photos purchased with mss or on assignment. Pays $5 minimum.

LP-GAS, 1 East First St., Duluth MN 55802. Editor: Zane Chastain. For liquefied petroleum gas (propane, 'bottled gas') marketers. Monthly. Buys all rights. Pays on acceptance. Query first. Enclose SASE.
Nonfiction: Uses dealer and LP-gas utilization articles, how-to features on selling, delivery, service, etc. Tersely written, illustrated by photo or line for documentation. Length: maximum 1,500 words. Pays 5 ¢ a word.
Photos: Pix with mss or captions only; not less than 2¼x2¼. Pays $5 to $7.

SOONER LPG TIMES, 2910 N. Walnut, Suite 114-A, Oklahoma City OK 73105. (405)525-9386 Editor: John E. Orr. 33% freelance written. For "dealers and suppliers of LP-gas and their employees." Monthly. Not copyrighted. Pays on publication. Reports in 3 weeks. Enclose SASE.
Nonfiction: "Articles relating to the LP-gas industry, safety, small business practices, and economics; anything of interest to small businessmen." Length: 1,000 to 2,000 words. Pays $10 to $15.

Government and Public Service

Below are journals for individuals who provide governmental services, either in the employ of local, state, or national governments or of franchised utilities. Included are journals for city managers, politicians, civil servants, firemen, policemen, public administrators, urban transit managers, utilities managers, etc.

Publications that emphasize the architectural and building side of city planning and development are classified in Architecture. Publications for lawyers are found in the Law category. Journals for teachers and administrators in the schools are found in Education. Publications for private citizens interested in politics, government, and public affairs are classified with the Politics and World Affairs magazines in the Consumer Publications section.

CAMPAIGN INSIGHT, Campaign Associates, Inc., 516 Petroleum Bldg., Wichita KS 67202. (316)265-7421. Editor-in-Chief: Hank Parkinson. Emphasizes political techniques, for readers who are interested in new politics methodology. Monthly newsletters; 16 pages. Estab. 1969. Circ. 4,300. Pays on acceptance. Buys all rights. Phone queries OK. Previously published submissions OK. SASE. Reports in 6 weeks. Free sample copy and writer's guidelines.
Nonfiction: How-to (projects other candidates used that have application in most other campaigns); informational (campaign overviews, if replete with how-to examples); interviews ("Playboy-style" interviews are used to lead off every issue and are in great demand). Length: 100-1,000 words. Buys about 75 mss/year. Query. Pays 5¢/word.
How To Break In: "We work only from queries and assigned items. A new writer should request a free copy of the newsletter, study the style and format; then query. He must have a grasp of new political technologies and be interested in modern campaigning."

THE CRIMINOLOGIST, Box No. 18, Bognor, Regis, Sussex, UK P022 7AA. For professionals and students interested in public affairs, criminology, forensic science, the law, penology, etc. Quarterly. Query. SAE and International Reply Coupons. Sample copy $3.
Nonfiction: Considers articles of very high standards, authoritatively written and factually sound, informative and sober, and not in a popular or sensational style. All material must have attached list of references or sources (title of source, author or editor, town of publication, date, and, if a periodical, page number, issue number, and volume). Articles from police officials, experts, etc., are welcomed. Length: 2,000 to 3,000 words.
Photos: Purchased with mss. Payment negotiable.

FIRE CHIEF MAGAZINE, 625 N. Michigan Ave., Chicago IL 60611. (312)642-9862. Editor: William Randleman. 25% Freelance written. For chiefs of volunteer and paid fire departments. Buys all rights. Will not consider simultaneous submissions or material offered for second rights. Pays on publication. Reports in 10 days. SASE.
Nonfiction: Wants articles on fire department administration, training, or fire-fighting operations. Will accept case histories of major fires, extinguished by either volunteer or paid departments, detailing exactly how the fire department fought the fire and the lessons learned from the experience. "Prefer feature articles to be bylined by a fire chief or other fire service

authority.'' Writing must be simple, clear, and detailed, preferably conversational in style. Pays $1-1.50 per column inch.
Photos: Used with mss or with captions only. 4x5 or larger; Polaroid or other small prints of individuals or small subjects accepted. Pays up to $35 for acceptable color photos. Pays nothing for public domain photos, up to $5 for exclusives, $1 for mug shots.

FIRE ENGINEERING, 666 Fifth Ave., New York NY 10019. Editor: James F. Casey. For commissioners, chiefs, senior officers of the paid, volunteer, industrial, and military fire departments and brigades. Buys first serial rights. Pays on publication. Reports in 3 weeks. SASE.
Nonfiction and Photos: Wants articles on fire suppression, fire prevention, and any other subject that relates to fire service. Length: 750-1,500 words. Pays minimum 3¢/word and up. Good photos with captions always in demand. Particular need for color photos for cover; small print or slide satisfactory for submission, but must always be a vertical or capable of being cropped to vertical. Transparency required if accepted. Pays $75 for color shots used on cover, $15 and up for b&w shots.

FIRE TIMES, American Fire Fighters Association, 1100 N.E. 125th St., North Miami FL 33161. (305)891-9800. Editor-in-Chief: Tom Moore. Emphasizes fire fighting services. Bimonthly magazine; 24 pages. Estab. 1975. Circ. 22,000. Pays on publication. Buys all rights, but may reassign following publication. Phone queries OK. Submit seasonal/holiday material 3 months in advance. SASE. Reports in 4 weeks. Sample copy 50¢; free writer's guidelines.
Nonfiction: How-to, informational, historical, interview, profile, new product, personal experience, photo feature, technical articles. Buys 15-20 ms/issue. Send complete ms. Length: 400-1,200 words. Pays $5-25.
Photos: Purchased with ms. Captions required. Send prints. Pays $5-25 for 8x10 b&w glossies. Except for photos of public officials, captions are required.
How To Break In: ''By remembering that this publication is aimed at the volunteer fire fighters in the small towns and that we need pictures of new buildings, equipment and activity.''

FOREIGN SERVICE JOURNAL, 2101 E St., N.W., Washington DC 20037. (202)338-4045. Editor: Shirley R. Newhall. For Foreign Service officers and others interested in foreign affairs and related subjects. Monthly. Buys first North American rights. Pays on publication. SASE.
Nonfiction: Uses articles on ''international relations, internal problems of the State Department and Foreign Service, informative material on other nations. Much of our material is contributed by those working in the fields we reach. Informed outside contributions are welcomed, however.'' Query. Length: 2,500-4,000 words. Pays 2¢-3¢/word.

GOVERNMENTAL PURCHASING, Box 8307, Trenton NJ 08650. (609)443-1072. Managing Editor: Isabelle Selikoff. 95% freelance written. For government purchasing and administrative officials. Monthly magazine: 38 pages. Estab. 1978. Circ. 5,000. Pays on publication. Buys all rights, but may reassign following publication. Phone queries OK. Submit seasonal/holiday material 4 months in advance of issue date. SASE. Reports in 4 weeks. Free sample copy and writer's guidelines; mention *Writer's Market*, in request.
Nonfiction: Exposé (ex-bid-rigging problem, graft and corruption in government purchasing); general interest; how-to (buy anything) from police walkie-talkies to heavy equipment, solar heating, cost management, etc.) interview (with purchasing officials); new product; personal experience; personal opinion (only from experienced officials or vendors selling to government); profile (purchasing officials; and technical. Buys 4 mss/issue. Query. Length: 2,400-3,600 words. Pays $100.
Photos: State availability of photos with query. Offers no additional payment for b&w contact sheets. Captions required. Buys one-time rights.
Columns/Departments: Kaleidoscope. Buys 1 ms/issue. Submit complete ms. Length: 600-800 words. Pays $50.
Fillers: Clippings; jokes, gags, anecdotes; newsbreaks; and short humor. Buys 12/year. Length: 50-100 words. Pays $5.

MODERN GOVERNMENT (SERVICIOS PUBLICOS), Box 5017, Westport CT 06880. (203)226-7463. Editor: Martin Greenburgh. For government officials, private contractors and executives of public utilities and corporations in Latin America and Spain (Spanish) and Asia, Australasia, Africa, the Middle East and the Caribbean (English). 9 times a year. Circ. 50,000. Buys international rights. Pays on acceptance. Free sample copy. Query advised. Reports in 2 weeks. SASE.

Nonfiction and Photos: All material should be of interest to government officials in developing nations. Strong "how to do it" angle on infrastructure development, public works, public transportation, public health and environmental sanitation, administrative skills, etc. Avoid strictly U.S. orientation. Publications go only overseas. Articles are bought in English and translated into Spanish. Length: 1,500 to 3,500 words. Pays $200; for article with photos: $250.

PASSENGER TRANSPORT, 1100 17th St. N.W., Washington DC 20036. Editor: Albert Engelken. Published by the American Public Transit Association for those in urban mass transportation. Pays on publication. Very little material bought. Enclose SASE.
Nonfiction: Uses short, concise articles which can be documented on urban mass transportation. Latest news only. No airline, steamship, intercity bus or railroad news. Pays 40¢ per column inch.
Photos: Sometimes buys photographs with mss and with captions only, but standards are high. 8x10's preferred. No color.

POLICE TIMES MAGAZINE, 1100 N. E. 125th St., N. Miami FL 33161. (305)891-1700. Editor: Donald Anderson. 90% freelance written. For "law enforcement officers; federal, state, county, local, and private security." Monthly. Circ. 50,000. Buys all rights. Buys 10 to 20 mss a year. Pays on publication. Sample copy for 50¢ postage. No query required. Reports "at once." Enclose SASE.
Nonfiction and Photos: Interested in articles about local police departments all over the nation. In particular, short articles about what the police department is doing, any unusual arrests made, acts of valor of officers in the performance of duties, etc. Also articles on any police subject from prisons to reserve police. "We prefer newspaper style. Short and to the point. Photos and drawings are a big help." Length: 300 to 1,200 words. Payment is $5 to $15—up to $25 in some cases based on 1¢ a word. Uses b&w Polaroid and 8x10 b&w glossies, "if of particular value." Pays $5-15 for each photo used.

PUBLIC UTILITIES FORTNIGHTLY, Suite 500, 1828 L St. N.W., Washington, DC 20036. Editor-in-Chief: Neil H. Duffy. For utility executives, regulatory commissions, lawyers, etc. Semimonthly. Pays on publication. "Study our publication." Reports in 3 weeks. SASE.
Nonfiction: Length: 2,000-3,000 words. Pays $25-200.

RESERVE LAW, P.O. Box 17807, San Antonio TX 78217. Editor: Otto Vehle. 20% freelance written. Publication of Reserve Law Officers Association of America. For sheriffs, chiefs of police, other law enforcement officials and their reserve components. Estab. 1969. Bimonthly. Circ. "over 10,000." Not copyrighted. Payment on publication. Will send free sample copy to writer on request. Submit complete ms. Will consider photocopied submissions. Enclose SASE.
Nonfiction and Photos: "Articles describing police reserve and sheriff reserve organizations and their activities should be informative and interesting. Style should be simple, straightforward, and with a touch of humor when appropriate. We need current features on outstanding contemporary lawmen, both regular officers and reserves. We are still hoping to attract freelance writers who have some law enforcement orientation as it actually is, not based upon experiences gained from watching TV. Yet, highly technical writing is not sought. Reserve Law Officers are businessmen and women who generally have incomes considerably above that of the average law officer and who find great staisfaction in donating their time to a law enforcement agency. These few hours per month they donate might possibly produce some excitement and adrenalin flow, but such occasions are rare since most police work is rather dull and monotonous. Therefore, articles submitted to us should contain some thrills, excitement, danger (much like a story submitted to a fishing magazine would place the reader in the big game fishing chair as the line spins off the reel)" Length: 500-2,000 words. "In most cases, ms should be accompanied by high contrast 8x10 b&w action photos, properly identified and captioned." Pays minimum of $10; plus $5 for first photo and $2.50 for additional photos used in same article. Also seeks material for the following columns: "Ichthus," a chaplain's column dealing with Christian law officers (100 to 500 words); "Law-Haw," humorous anecdotes about police work (40 to 60 words); "Fundamentals," basic "how-to's" of law enforcement (100 to 500 words). Payment in contributor's copies or a maximum of $50.
Fiction: "Fictionalized accounts of true police cases involving reserve officers will be accepted if they meet our needs." Length: 200 to 800 words. Pays maximum of $50.
Fillers: Jokes and short humor "of the law enforcement type." Length: 20 to 80 words. Pays maximum of $10.

ROLL CALL, 428 8th St., S.E., Washington DC 20003. (202)546-3080. Editor: Sidney Yudain. For US Congressmen, political buffs, editors and TV commentators. Weekly newspaper. Estab. 1955. Circ. 9,000. Buys first North American serial rights. Pays on acceptance. Photocopied and simultaneous submissions OK. Reports in 1 week. Query first or submit complete ms. SASE.
Nonfiction and Photos: Profiles, humor, historical, and nostalgic articles. "Political satire material must measure up to the work of the noted satirists we usually publish." Buys 10 mss/year. Length: 500 to 2,000 words. Pays $5 to $25. No additional payment for b&w photos used with articles.
Poetry and Fillers: Light verse related to subject matter. Puzzles on a Congressional or political theme and short humor on political topics are used as fillers. Pays $2 minimum.

SEARCH AND RESCUE MAGAZINE, Box 153, Montrose CA 91020. (213)248-3057. Publisher: Dennis Kelley. For volunteer and paid professionals involved in search and rescue. Estab. 1973. Quarterly. Circ. 30,000. Buys all rights, but will reassign rights to author after publication. Pays on publication. Sample copy for $2.25. Reports in 2 months. SASE.
Fiction, Nonfiction and Photos: All material must be related to search and rescue work. Particularly likes photo essays. Buys 40 mss/year. Query or submit complete ms. Pays $25 to $100. No additional payment for b&w photos used with mss. Captions required.

STATE & COUNTY ADMINISTRATOR, Box 272, Culver City CA 90230. For "top officials, managers, administrators and legislators in state government of all 50 states and 3,104 counties." Published 12 times/year. Circ. 31,000. Buys all rights. Pays on publication. Free sample copy. Submit seasonal material at least 2 months in advance of issue date. Reports in 4 to 6 weeks. Query first or submit complete ms. SASE.
Nonfiction and Photos: "A great amount of free material comes in from states, counties, and PR departments. Innovative methods that states are employing to increase the efficiency of administration, personnel management and training, revenue programs, issues facing states, new methods, procedures, and systems to reduce costs. We are management and administration oriented, as opposed to public works oriented. We are interested in environmental/pollution coverage." Length: 1,000 to 1,500 words. Pays 2¢ a word. 8x10 b&w glossies purchased with mss; captions required. Pays $2.50.

TODAY'S FIREMAN, Box 594, Kansas City MO 64141. (816)474-3495. Editor: Donald Mack. For persons involved in and interested in fire service. Quarterly magazine. Estab. 1960. Circ. 10,000. Copyrighted. Pays on acceptance or publication. Sample copy for $2. Photocopied and simultaneous submissions OK. Reports in 1 month. SASE.
Nonfiction, Photos and Fillers: Approach should be expository with research. Interested in psychological and philosophical aspects of current problems. Buys informational, interview, humor, nostalgia, new product, merchandising techniques, and technical articles (Length: 50-1,500 words. Pays $15-40); historical (length: 500-2,500 words. Pays $20-40); exposé (Length: 500 words; pays $15-40). Buys 6 mss/year. Query. Would like to see humorous articles with photos. Occasionally buys material for 2 regional editions, covering the Eastern U.S. and Western U.S. Writers may also submit suggestions for new columns or departments. Photos purchased with accompanying mss with no additional payment. Also purchased without ms. Pays $10 for b&w glossies. Captions required. Puzzles, jokes, gags, short humor. Pays $5 to $25.

VIRGINIA MUNICIPAL REVIEW, Review Publishing Co., Inc., Box 100, Richmond VA 23201. (804)643-1113. Editor-in-Chief: Ralph L. Dombrower, Sr. Emphasizes governmental subjects: federal, state, city, town and county. Monthly magazine; 32 pages. Estab. 1921. Circ. 2,500. Pays on publication. Buys all rights. Submit seasonal/holiday material 3 months in advance. Photocopied submissions OK. SASE. Free sample copy and writer's guidelines.
Nonfiction and Photos: Articles on governmental subjects. Well-researched, informative; current problems. Length: 500 words maximum. Pays 10¢/word. No additional payment made for b&w photos used with mss.

WESTERN FIRE JOURNAL, 9072 E. Artesia Blvd., Suite 7, Bellflower CA 90706. (213)866-1664. Editor-in-Chief: Dick Friend. 8% freelance written. For fire chiefs of paid, volunteer departments in metropolitan and small communities located in the 11 Western states. Also read by other fire department officers and personnel. Monthly magazine; 56 pages. Estab. 1956. Circ. 4,600. Pays on publication. Buys one-time rights. Phone queries OK. Simultaneous and photocopied submissions OK. SASE. Reports in 2 weeks. Sample copy $1; free writer's guidelines; mention *Writer's Market* in request.

Nonfiction: How-to (develop or build a new piece of fire protection equipment or facility); interview (leaders recognized in fire protection with something constructive to say); and technical (new ideas in fire protection techniques, training and prevention). Topics must concern *Western* fire service activities. No articles on a fire fighter's day. Buys 20 mss/year. Query. Pays $1.50-1.75/inch.
Photos: State availability of photos with query. Pays $4-10 for 5x7 b&w dull prints or $10-25 for 35mm color transparencies. Captions preferred. Buys one-time rights.

WORKLIFE, Dept. of Labor PH 10141, Washington DC 20213. Editor: Walter Wood. For employment training, poverty and education specialists. Monthly. Circ. 30,000. Not copyrighted. Pays on publication. Will send a free sample copy on request. Query preferred. Enclose SASE.
Nonfiction: Articles on government and private efforts to solve human resources, training, and education problems, particularly among the disadvantaged. Length: 600 to 4,000 words. "Payment for unsolicited articles used in the magazine is $100 to $200. For articles done by outside writers on assignment, payment is negotiable."

Groceries

The journals that follow are for owners and operators of retail food stores. Journals for food wholesalers, packers, warehousers, and caterers are classified with the Food Products, Processing, and Service journals. Publications for food vending machine operators are found in the Coin-Operated Machines category.

A.G. NEWS AND A.G. NEWSLETTER, 5151 Bannock St., Denver CO 80217. (303)534-1155. Editor-in-Chief: Virginia A. Valenze. 5% freelance written. Emphasizes grocery and food distribution for a readership interested in both wholesale retail operations and development. Monthly tabloid: 12 pages. Estab. 1949. Circ. 3,000. Pays on publication. Phone queries OK. Submit seasonal/holiday material 2 months in advance of issue date. Simultaneous, photocopied and previously published submissions OK. SASE. Free sample copy and writer's guidelines; mention *Writer's Market* in request.
Nonfiction: General interest (trends in the grocery industry, outlook for future of independent grocer); how-to (grocery market operations, personnel, security, management, energy conservation, and equipment use); new product (effect on market success in other parts of the country). Buys 2-3 mss/year. Query. Length: 500-2,000 words. Pays $100.
Photos: State availability of photos with query. Pays $25 for 5x7 b&w contact sheet and glossy prints. Captions required.
Columns/Departments: Energy conservation; legislation/consumer news; meat/produce/general merchandise; retail service management; and security. Buys 1-2 mss/year. Submit clips of previously published work. Length: 100-500 words. Pays $50 minimum.
Fillers: Jokes gags, anecdotes, newsbreaks and short humor. Length: 25-100 words. Pays $25 mimimum.

CHAIN STORE AGE SUPERMARKETS, 425 Park Ave., New York NY 10022. (212)371-9400. Editor: David Mahler. For chain, cooperative and voluntary executives; buyers, store supervisors, managers, food brokers, rack jobbers, associations, colleges and government agencies. Monthly magazine; 80 pages. Estab. 1925. Circ. 105,000. Buys all rights, Pays on publication. Will consider photocopied submissions. No simultaneous submissions. Reports in 2 weeks. Query first. SASE.
Nonfiction and Photos: News magazine technique of reporting and interpreting trends, developments and events of interest to chain supermarket segment of industry. This technique is combined with feature articles especially suited for chain supermarket headquarters and multi-unit stores. Articles of interest to buyers, merchandisers, trainers, supervisors, as well as management and operations. At the store level, article emphasis is on store management, meat management and produce management; display, training, and supervision. Assigns articles to freelance writers as need for coverage arises. Pays $75/printed page minimum. No additional payment for b&w photos used with mss. Captions optional.

FOODSMAN, 1001 E. Main St., Richmond VA 23219. (804)644-0731. Editor: Brian F. Daly. 10% freelance written. For food retailers, wholesalers, distributors. Monthly magazine; 22-34

pages. Estab. 1939. Circ. 7,000. Not copyrighted. Payment on publication. Will send free sample copy to writer on request. Query first. Queries handled immediately. Enclose SASE.
Nonfiction and Photos: "Consumer articles; anything of interest to food people. From attitude surveys, operational studies, general interest articles or photo layouts on store design. Emphasis is on Virginia and helpful ideas to be implemented by either food retailers, wholesalers or distributors." Informational, interviews with government officials, profiles, think pieces, training reviews, spot news, successful business operations, new product, merchandising techniques. Length: open. Pays 5¢/word.

IGA GROCERGRAM, 5725 E. River Rd., Chicago IL 60631. (312)693-4520. Editor-in-Chief: Marianne Beaudoin. Associate Editor: Pam Cheuvront. 5% freelance written. For "largely independent supermarket owners, managers, and department heads, *not* concentrated in metropolitan areas." Monthly magazine; 36 pages. Estab. 1926. Circ. 10,000. Pays on acceptance. Buys all rights. Phone queries OK. Submit seasonal/holiday material 4 months in advance of issue date. SASE. Reports in 2 months. Sample copy $1.
Nonfiction: General interest (about supermarket industry/operations); how-to; interview; and photo feature (operations, displays, unusual sales, IGA stores only). Buys 5 mss/year. Query. Length: "As long as is necessary to tell the story." Pays $50 minimum.
Photos: "We seldom publish a manuscript without photos." State availability of photos with query. Payment for photos is included in ms price. Uses 5x7 glossy b&w prints or color transparencies. Captions preferred. Buys all rights.

PENNSYLVANIA GROCER, 3701 N. Broad St., Philadelphia PA 19140. (215)228-0808. Editor: John McNelis. For grocers, their families and employees, store managers; food people in general. Monthly magazine; 16 pages. Estab. 1913. Circ. 3,500. Copyrighted. Pays on publication. Sample copy for 75¢. Reports in 30 days. SASE.
Nonfiction and Photos: Articles on food subjects in retail food outlets; mainly local, in Pennsylvania and surrounding areas. Informational, interviews, profiles, historical, successful business operations, new product, merchandising technique and technical articles. Buys 10-15 mss/year. Query or submit complete ms. Length: 500-900 words. Pays $25. Pays $25 maximum for minimum of 2 b&w photos purchased with mss.

PROGRESSIVE GROCER, 708 Third Ave., New York NY 10017. (212)490-1000. Editor: Edgar B. Walzer. For supermarket operators, managers, buyers; executives in the grocery business. Monthly magazine; 150 pages. Estab. 1922. Circ. 90,000. Rights purchased vary with author and material; may buy all rights, but will reassign rights to author after publication; first North American serial rights; first serial rights; second serial (reprint) rights or simultaneous rights. Pays on acceptance. Photocopied and simultaneous submissions OK. Submit seasonal merchandising material (spring, summer, fall, holiday) 3 months in advance. Reports in 2-3 weeks. SASE.
Nonfiction and Photos: Department Editor: Mary Ann Linsen. Articles on supermarket merchandising; success stories; consumer relations pieces; promotional campaigns; personal pieces about people in the business. How grocers manage to relate and communicate with consumers via smart programs that really work. Tight, direct, informal, colorful writing needed. Does not want to see anything about quaint little "mom and pop" stores or "run of mill" stores with nothing more than half-hearted gourmet sections. Buys 20 mss/year. Query. Length: open. Pays minimum of 5¢/word. Pays minimum of $15 for b&w glossies; $25 for color. Captions required.

SUPERMARKETING MAGAZINE, 1515 Broadway, New York NY 10036. (212)869-1300. Editor: Ralph Selitzer. 10% freelance written. For supermarket retailers; chains, independents, convenience stores, supermarket wholesalers; voluntaries, cooperatives. Monthly magazine; 60-68 pages. Estab. 1945. Circ. 80,000. Rights purchased vary with author and material. Pays on publication. Photocopied submissions OK. Immediate reports on queries. Unsolicited material is not returned. SASE.
Nonfiction and Photos: Material with a heavy retail orientation, usually based on interviews with buyers at retail and/or wholesale operations. "I don't like to see the canned management or how-to-do-it material that a writer is trying to sell to umpteen different magazines. Material must exhibit a special knowledge of our field's problems. Do not submit on speculation. Material will not be returned. Await detailed instructions in reply to your query." Buys 10-20 mss/year. Query. Length: 5 to 6 double-spaced, typewritten pages. Pays $120-170. No additional payment for b&w photos used with mss.

TELEFOOD MAGAZINE, Davies Publishing Co., 136 Shore Dr., Hinsdale IL 60521. (312)325-2930. Editor: Barbara Pattarozzi. Emphasizes only specialty and gourmet foods for retailers, gourmet shops and delicatessens, manufacturers/distributors, food brokers, media and advertisers. Monthly magazine; 50-60 pages. Estab. 1935. Circ. 15,000. Pays on publication. Buys all rights, but may reassign following publication. Phone queries OK. Submit seasonal or holiday material 2-3 months in advance. Photocopied submissions and previously published work OK. SASE. Reports in 1-3 weeks. Free sample copy and writer's guidelines.
Nonfiction: "Our needs are for articles on issue themes as determined by demands of readership; for interviews and coverage of gourmet and specialty food shops, business, manufacturers, distributors, large delicatessen operations including those within major supermarket chains or department stores. Prefer contributions from various geographical areas particularly the West and Southwest." Can be in the form of informational articles or interviews. Buys 1-2/issue. Length: 500-2,000 words. Query. "We must approve subject covered." Pays $50 minimum.
Photos: B&w glossies must accompany articles; 5x7 or 8x10. Captions required. Query and send contact sheet. Additional payment.

Grooming Products and Services

AMERICAN HAIRDRESSER/SALON OWNER, 100 Park Ave., New York NY 10017. (212)532-5588. Editor: Louise Cotter. For beauty salon owners and operators. Monthly. Buys all rights. Pays on publication. Reports "6 weeks prior to publication." SASE.
Nonfiction: "Technical material; is mainly staff-written." Pays $25 per magazine page.

HAIRSTYLIST, Allied Publications Inc., Box 23505, Fort Lauderdale FL 33307. Associate Editor: Marie Stilkind. Buys North American serial rights only. Pays on acceptance. Query not necessary. Reports in 2 to 4 weeks. SASE.
Nonfiction and Photos: Wants "articles of general interest to the professional beautician." Interested in how-to's, interviews, and profiles. Length: 500 to 1,000 words. Payment is 5¢/word. Pays $5 for b&w glossy photos of hairstyles.

PROFESSIONAL MEN'S HAIRSTYLIST, 100 Park Ave., New York NY 10017. Editor: Sandra Kosherick. For "men and women serving the men's hairstyling and barbering profession." Monthly. Circ. 65,000. Rights purchased vary with author and material. Pays on publication. Free sample copy and writer's guidelines. Submit seasonal/holiday material 2 months in advance of issue date. SASE.
Nonfiction and Photos: "Matter only relating to the hairstyling profession. Material should be technical—written from the viewpoint of professionals. Currently overworked are articles on female barbers or hairstylists and unisex salons. We're interested in articles on new trends in men's hairstyling." Buys informational articles, how-to's, interviews, coverage of successful business operations, articles on merchandising techniques, and technical articles. Buys 10-12 mss/year. Query. Length: 750 to 2,500 words. Pays $25-50. 8x10 b&w glossies purchased with mss and on assignment. Pays $25.

WOMAN BEAUTIFUL, Allied Publications, Inc., Box 23505, Fort Lauderdale FL 33307. Associate Editor: Marie Stilkind. For "students at beauty schools and people who go to beauty salons." Buys North American serial rights only. Pays on acceptance. Reports in 2 to 4 weeks. SASE.
Nonfiction and Photos: "Articles on hairstyling, beauty, and fashion." Length: 500 to 1,000 words. Pays 5¢/accepted word. Pays $5 for photos of hairstyles.

Hardware

In this classification are journals for general hardware wholesalers and retailers, locksmiths, and retailers of miscellaneous special hardware items. Journals specializing in the retailing of hardware for a certain trade, such as plumbing or automotive supplies, are classified with the other publications for that trade.

CHAIN SAW AGE, 3435 N.E. Broadway, Portland OR 97232. Editor: Norman W. Raies. For "mostly chain saw dealers (retailers); small businesses—typically small town, typical ages, interests, education." Monthly. Circ. 15,000. Not copyrighted. Buys "very few" mss a year. Pays on acceptance or publication—"varies." Free sample copy. Will consider photocopied

submissions. Query first. SASE.
Nonfiction and Photos: "Must relate to chain saw use, merchandising, adaptation, manufacture, or display." Buys informational articles, how-to's, personal experience articles, interviews, profiles, inspirational articles, personal opinion articles, photo features, coverage of successful business operations, and articles on merchandising techniques. Length: 500 to 1,000 words. Pays $20 to $50 ("2½¢ a word plus photo fees"). Photos purchased with mss, without mss, or on assignment; captions required. For b&w glossies, pay "varies."

CHAIN SAW INDUSTRY AND POWER EQUIPMENT DEALER, Louisiana Bank Bldg., Box 1703, Shreveport LA 71166. (318)222-3062. Editor: O.M. Word. For chain saw and outdoor power equipment dealers. Monthly. Buys first rights. Pays on publication. Free sample copy. Reports as quickly as possible. SASE.
Nonfiction: Articles on successful or unusual chain saw and other small outdoor power equipment dealers, explaining factors which make them so. Human interest material necessary. Articles on unusual uses or unusual users of these tools. Articles on dealers whose profits have increased through diversification of stock. Information on new markets and accessory items. Slant to help dealers do a better job of merchandising. Reader audience varies from large hardware dealers in major cities to crossroad filling station shops in rural areas. Buys 1-2 mss/issue. Query. Length: 1,000-1,500 words. Pays 3½¢/word.
Photos: Purchased with mss or with captions. B&w, sharp, action if possible; caption must include identification. Pays $5.

DOORS AND HARDWARE, 1815 N. Fort Myer Dr., Suite 412, Arlington VA 22209. (703)527-2060. Executive Editor: Richard M. Hornaday, CAE. Managing Editor: Donald L. Day. All freelance written. "Readership includes manufacturers, distributors, and special consultants in the wholesale builders hardware trade, plus architects and related engineers/designers in the industry." Monthly magazine; 48 pages. Estab. 1936. Circ. 9,000. Pays on publication. Buys all rights, but may reassign following publication. Phone queries OK. Submit seasonal/holiday material 3 months in advance of issue date. Photocopied and previously published (if in another field) submissions OK. SASE. Reports in 8 weeks. Free sample copy and writer's guidelines; mention *Writer's Market* in request.
Nonfiction: General interest; historical; how-to (management techniques); interview; new product; photo feature; profile and technical. Buys 3-5 mss/year. Query. Length: 4,000-12,000 words. Pays $25 minimum.
Photos: "We try to be highly graphically oriented, and believe illustrations, if well done and appropriate, add to the magazine as well as to the article itself." State availability of photos with query. Pays $5 for b&w photos; "negotiable" payment for color. Captions and model release required. Buys all rights, but may reassign following publication.
How To Break In: "Despite the technical nature of the industry, we welcome queries. We shall be pleased to direct writers to responsible individuals in their geographic region who can give them a good idea of the concerns and background of this type of material."

HARDWARE AGE, Chilton Co., Chilton Way, Radnor PA 19089. (215)687-8200. Editor-in-Chief: Jon Kinslow. Editor: Jay Holtzman. 5% freelance written. Emphasizes retailing, distribution, and merchandising of hardware and building materials. Monthly magazine; 180 pages. Estab. 1855. Circ. 56,000. Buys first North American serial rights. Submit seasonal/holiday material 3 months in advance of issue date. Simultaneous, photocopied and previously published submissions OK, if exclusive in the field. SASE. Reports in 1-2 months. Free sample copy and writer's guidelines; mention *Writer's Market* in request.
Nonfiction: Tim Wright, news editor. How-to (more profitably run a hardlines store or a department within a store. "We particularly want stories on local hardware stores and home improvement centers, with photos. Stories should concentrate on one particular aspect of how the retailer in question has been successful); and technical (possibly will accept stories on retail accounting or inventory management by qualified writers). Buys 2-3 mss/issue. Submit complete ms. Length: 500-2,500 words. Pays $25-125.
Photos: "We like store features with b&w or color photos. Usually use b&w for small freelance features." Send photos with ms. Pays $10 for 4x5 glossy b&w prints; $15 for color contact sheets or transparencies. Captions preferred, Buys one-time rights.
Columns/Departments: Focus on Law and Money Savers. Buys 1-2 mss/issue. Query or submit complete ms. Length: 1,000-1,250 words. Pays $35. Open to suggestions for new columns/departments.
Fillers: "Would like a *good* hard crossword puzzle related to hardware." Pays $25-50.

HARDWARE MERCHANDISING, MacLean-Hunter Co., Ltd., 481 University Ave., Toronto, Ontario, Canada M5W 1A7. (416)595-1811. Ext. 702. Editor-in-Chief: William Kennedy. 25% freelance written. For hardware retailers, followed by home center and building supply operators in Canada. Monthly magazine: 35 pages. Estab. 1889. Circ. 10,500. Pays on publication. Buys all rights. Phone queries OK. SASE. Reports in 1 month. Free sample copy and writer's guidelines; mention *Writer's Market* in request.
Nonfiction: How-to; interview; new product; photo feature (stores); and profile (retailers). Buys 12 mss/year. Query. Pays $75/magazine page.
Photos: State availability of photos with query. Pays $10 for b&w contact sheets. Captions required. Buys all rights. Model release required.

NORTHERN HARDWARE TRADE, 5901 Brooklyn Blvd., Suite 112, Minneapolis MN 55429. (612)533-0066. Editor: Edward Gonzales. 1% freelance written. For "owners, managers of hardware and discount stores and lumber yards and home centers; hardware, sporting good, wholesalers." Estab. 1890. Monthly. Circ. 16,500. Not copyrighted. Pays on publication. Submit seasonal material 3 months in advance of issue date. SASE.
Nonfiction and Photos: "Case histories on successful retail stores." Buys how-to's and articles on successful business operations. Query or submit complete ms. Pays 4¢/word. B&w photos purchased with mss. Pays $5.

OUTDOOR POWER EQUIPMENT, 3339 W. Freeway, Box 1570, Fort Worth TX 76101. Publisher: Bill Quinn. 5-7% freelance written. Estab. 1959. Monthly. Circ. 10,000. Not copyrighted. Pays on publication. SASE.
Nonfiction and Photos: Photo-story of a single outstanding feature on power equipment stores (lawnmower, snowblower, garden tractors, chain saws, tiller, snowmobiles, etc.). Feature can be a good display, interior or exterior; sales tip; service tip; unusual sign; advertising or promotion tip; store layout; demonstrations, etc. Photos must be vertical. One 8x10 glossy sufficient. Query. Length: 200-300 words. Pays $32.50-37.50.

SOUTHERN HARDWARE, W.R.C. Smith Publishing Co., 1760 Peachtree Rd., NW., Atlanta GA 30357. (404)874-4462. Editor-in-Chief: Ralph E. Kirby. 50% freelance written. For retailers of hardware and allied lines, located in the Southern states. Monthly magazine; 80 pages. Estab. 1900. Circ. 16,000. Pays on acceptance. Buys all rights. Phone queries OK. Submit seasonal/holiday material 3 months in advance of issue date. SASE. Free sample copy and writer's guidelines; mention *Writer's Market* in request.
Nonfiction: How-to (how a store can achieve greater results in selling lines or a line of merchandise). "No articles on history of business." Buys 4 mss/issue. Query. Length: 500-1,000 words. Pays $75-150.
Photos: State availability of photos with query. Offers no additional payment for 5x7 or 8x10 b&w prints. Buys all rights.

Home Furnishings and Appliances

APPLIANCE SERVICE NEWS, 5841 Montrose Ave., Chicago IL 60634. Editor: William Wingstedt. For professional service people whose main interest is the repairing of major and portable household appliances. Their jobs consists of either service shop owner, service manager, or service technician. Monthly "newspaper style" publication; 24 pages. Estab. 1950. Circ. 41,000. Buys all rights. Buys about 2 mss/issue. Pays on publication. Sample copy 50¢; free writer's guidelines. Will not consider photocopied submissions. Will consider simultaneous submissions. Reports in about 1 month. SASE.
Nonfiction and Photos: James Hodl, associate editor. "Our main interest is in technical articles about appliances and their repair. We also consider articles on the business of running a successful service agency. Material should be written in a straightforward, easy-to-understand style. It should be crisp and interesting, with a high informational content. Our main interest is in the major and portable appliance repair field. We are not interested in retail sales." Query. Length: open. Pays 5-7¢/word. Pays $10 for b&w photos used with ms. Captions required.

BEDDER NEWS, 1102 Main St., Lewiston ID 83501. (208)746-9888. Editor: Kenny Wayne. 15% freelance written. Emphasizes the waterbed industry for waterbed retailers, distributors, and manufacturers, including furniture stores and decorators. Monthly tabloid; 28 pages. Pays on publication. Buys all rights, but may reassign following publication. Phone queries OK. Submit seasonal or holiday material 3 months in advance. SASE. Reports in 4 weeks. Sample copy $1.

Nonfiction: Medical stories relating to waterbeds, interviews with people in the waterbed industry, material on old types or use of waterbeds, new product, photo feature and technical. Buys about 25 mss/year. Length: 500-1,500 words. Submit complete ms.
Photos: B&w glossies (5x7) purchased with ms or on assignment. Captions required. Send prints.
Fillers: Clippings, jokes, anecdotes related to waterbeds. Pays $1-5.

CHINA GLASS & TABLEWARE, Ebel-Doctorow Publications, Inc., Box 2147, Clifton NJ 07015. (201)779-1600. Editor-in-Chief: Susan Grisham. 30% freelance written. Monthly magazine; 40 pages. Pays on publication. Buys all rights. Phone queries OK. Submit seasonal/holiday material 3 months in advance of issue date. SASE. Reports in 2-3 weeks. Free sample copy and writer's guidelines; mention *Writer's Market* in request.
Nonfiction: Technical (on the business aspects of retailing china, glassware and flatware). No articles on how-to or gift shops. Buys 2-3 mss/issue. Query. Length: 1,000-3,000 words. Pays $40-50 per page.
Photos: State availability of photos with query. No additional payment for b&w contact sheets or color contact sheets. Captions required. Buys one-time rights.
Fillers: Clippings. Buys 2/issue. Pays $3-5.

COMPETITIVEDGE, 405 Merchandise Mart, Chicago IL 60654. (312)527-3070. Editor: Peggy Heaton. For top management of stores specializing in all home furnishings products. Monthly magazine; 80-100 pages. Estab. 1923. Circ. 15,000. Buys all rights. Buys 2-3 mss/year. Pays on publication. Free sample copy. Reports immediately. Query. SASE.
Nonfiction and Photos: Articles on managing, merchandising, operating the home furnishings store in all facets from advertising to warehousing. Concise and very factual reporting of new developments or activities within the retail store with explanation of why and how something was accomplished, and results or benefits. "We largely present 'success' stories that give ideas the reader might want to adapt to his own inidividual operation." Interested in material on special services to consumers, internal cost-cutting measures, traffic-building efforts; how the small store competes with the giants; unusual display techniques or interesting store architecture. Does not want to see straight publicity or "puff" articles about store owners or their operations, with no news value or interest to others on a national basis, or articles that are too general with no specific point. Length: 800-2,000 words. Pays 4½¢/word. 5x7 b&w glossy photos are purchased with or without mss, or on assignment. Pays $5. Captions optional.

FLOORING MAGAZINE, 757 Third Ave., New York NY 10017. Editor: Michael Korsonsky.10% freelance written. For floor covering retailers, wholesalers, floor covering specifiers, architects, etc. Monthly. Circulation: 20,000. Buys all rights. Buys 10 to 12 mss a year. Payment on acceptance. Will send free sample copy to writer on request. Query first. Reports on material in 2 to 4 weeks. Enclose S.A.S.E.
Nonfiction and Photos: "Merchandising articles, new industry developments, unusual installations of floor coverings, etc. Conversational approach; snappy, interesting leads; plenty of quotes." Informational, how-to, interview, successful business operations, merchandising techniques, technical. Length: 1,500 to 1,800 words. Pays 5¢ to 7¢ a word. 5x7 or 8x10 b&w photos. Pays $5. Color transparencies (when specified). Pays $7.50. Captions required.

FURNITURE & FURNISHINGS, 380 Wellington St., W., Toronto, Ontario, Canada M5V 1E3. Editor: Ronald H. Shuker. For an audience that includes all associated with making and selling furniture, floorcoverings and fabrics, as well as suppliers in the trade; lamps and accessories manufacturers and dealers; decorators and designers; domestic and contract readers (not consumers). Monthly magazine; 40-150 pages. Estab. 1910. Circ. 11,500. Buys first Canadian serial rights. Buys 20 mss a year. Payment on publication. Free sample copy. Will not consider photocopied submissions if they have been made to other Canadian media. Submit special material for Market Previews and Product Reports 1 month in advance. Reports on material accepted for publication in 1 month. Returns rejected material immediately. Query. SASE.
Nonfiction and Photos: "The magazine is not news-oriented. Rather, it is more feature-oriented, covering various subjects in depth. Very much a merchandising magazine for home furnishings retailers in Canada. We publish merchandising and retailer success stories; product trends; management articles; promotion/advertising programs. Styles, designs, color trends. Emphasis is on how-to—what retailers can learn from what others are doing. Writing is tight, semi-aggressive, and interesting. We'd like to see feature reports analyzing the retail situation in various cities and towns in Canada; who are the top retailers in each center and why; or personality profiles of people in this industry. We do not want U.S. or foreign-oriented articles

unless they report on trends in styles, designs, colors and materials used in furniture, floorcoverings, fabrics appearing in major trade shows in the U.S. and Europe with photos showing examples of these trends. Must be aimed at Canadian readers.'' Length: 500 to 2,000 words. Pays $100 or more, ''depending on length and use of real examples.'' Pays $10 for b&w photos purchased with mss. Captions required.

GIFTS + TABLEWARE, 1515 Broadway, New York NY 10036. (212)764-7317. Editor: Christiane Michaels. For ''merchants (department stores buyers, specialty shop owners) engaged in the resale of giftwares, china and glass, decorative accessories.'' Monthly. Circ. 36,000. Buys all rights. Pays on acceptance. Will send a sample copy to a writer on request. Query first or submit complete ms. Will consider photocopied submissions. Reports ''immediately.'' SASE.
Nonfiction: ''Retail store success stories. Describe a single merchandising gimmick. We are a magazine format—glossy stock. Descriptions of store interiors are less important than a sales performance unless display is outstanding. We're interested in articles on aggressive selling tactics. We cannot use material written for the consumer.'' Buys coverage of successful business operations and merchandising techniques. Length: 750 words maximum.
Photos: Purchased with and without mss and on assignment; captions required. ''Individuals are to be identified.''

GIFTS & DECORATIVE ACCESSORIES, 51 Madison Ave., New York NY 10010. (212)689-4411. Editor-in-Chief: Phyllis Sweed. Managing Editor: Douglas Gilbert-Neiss. 10% freelance written. Published primarily for quality gift retailers. Monthly magazine; 250 pages. Estab. 1907. Circ. 32,000. Pays on publication. Buys all rights. Submit seasonal/holiday material 6 months in advance of issue date. Photocopied submissions OK. SASE. Reports ''as soon as possible.'' Free writer's guidelines.
Nonfiction: ''Merchandising how-to stories of quality stores—how they have solved a particular merchandising problem, or successfully displayed or promoted a particularly difficult area.'' Nothing about discount stores or mass merchants, Buys 12 mss/year. Query or submit complete ms. Length: 500-1,500 words Pays $25-100.
Photos: ''Photos should illustrate merchandising points made in a story.'' Pays $5-7.50 for 5x7 glossy b&w prints; $7.50-15 for 4x5 color transparencies. Captions required. Buys all rights, but may reassign following publication.

HOME LIGHTING & ACCESSORIES, Box 2147, Clifton NJ 07015. (201)779-1600. Editor-in-Chief: Herb Ballinger. 35% freelance written. For lighting stores. Monthly magazine; 80 pages. Estab. 1923. Circ. 7,000. Pays on publication. Buys all rights, but may reassign following publication. Phone queries OK. Submit seasonal/holiday material 6 months in advance of issue date. SASE. Free sample copy.
Nonfiction: How-to (run your lighting store/department, including all retail topics); interview (with lighting retailers); personal experience (as a business person involved with lighting); personal opinion (about business approaches and marketing); profile (of a successful lighting retailer/lamp buyer); and technical (concerning lighting or lighting design). Buys 30 mss/year. Query. Pays $50/page.
Photos: State availability of photos with query. Offers no additional payment for 5x7 or 8x10 b&w glossy prints and 35mm color transparencies. Captions required. Buys all rights, but may reassign following publication.

LINENS, DOMESTICS AND BATH PRODUCTS, 370 Lexington Ave., New York NY 10017. (212)532-9290. Editor: Alyson Fendel. For department store, mass merchandiser, specialty store and bath boutiques. Published 6 times/year. Buys all rights. Pays on publication. Reports in 4-6 weeks. SASE.
Nonfiction and Photos: Merchandising articles which educate the buyer on sales and fashion trends, promotions, industry news, styles; in-depth articles with photos on retail stores/departments for bath accessories, linens and sheets, tablecloths, napkins and placemats, towels, and comforters. Especially focusing on interesting promotions and creative displays within these departments. Length: 700 to 1,500 words. Pays 10¢/word. Photos purchased with mss. For b&w glossies, pays $6.

MART MAGAZINE, Berkshire Common, Pittsfield MA 01201. (413)499-2550. Editor-in-Chief: Wallis E. Wood. Managing Editor: Ken Lilienthal. 50% freelance written. For retailers (independent dealers, buyers for department and discount stores, etc.) of major appliances, consumer electronics, and electric housewares. Semimonthly magazine; 48 pages. Estab. 1953. Circ. 45,000. Pays on acceptance. Buys all rights, but may reassign following publication.

SASE. Reports in 2 weeks. Free sample copy and writer's guidelines.
Nonfiction: "We are edited for all retailers of these products: independent appliance-TV dealers, department stores, audio specialists, discount chains, catalog showrooms, drug chains, hardware stores and buying offices. We want articles about large stores and small, well-known or unknown. The question we ask about every articles is: 'How does this help the guy in the store?' One natural story is how a dealer solved some problem. The problem could be almost anything: financial management, direct mail, radio or TV advertising, salesmanship, etc. We want stories about manufacturers as long as they are directed to retailers." Buys 15 mss/issue. Query. Length: 200-2,500 words. Pays $35-500.
Photos: "We do not run any stories that are all text." Pays $15 minimum for b&w contact sheets or negatives; $50 minimum for 2¼x2¼ color transparencies. Captions required. Buys all rights, but may reassign following publication.

RETAILER AND MARKETING NEWS, Box 57194, Dallas TX 75207. (214)528-5910. Editor: Michael J. Anderson. For "retail dealers and wholesalers in appliances, television, and furniture." Monthly. Circ. 10,000. Free sample copy. Photocopied submissions OK. Mss will not be returned unless SASE is enclosed.
Nonfiction: "How a retail dealer can make more profit" is the approach. Wants "sales promotion ideas, advertising, sales tips, business builders, and the like, localized to the southwest and particularly to north Texas." Submit complete ms. Length: 100 to 500 words. Payment is $100.

SOUTHWEST HOMEFURNISHINGS NEWS, 4313 N. Central Expressway, Dallas TX 75206. Editor: Frank Northcut. For retail home furnishing business people; home furnishings manufacturers, and others in related fields. Magazine; 50 to 100 pages. Estab. 1923. Circ. 12,000. Not copyrighted. Buys 2 mss/year. Pays on publication. Sometimes pays in copies only. Free sample copy. No photocopied or simultaneous submissions. Reports in 2 weeks. Query first. SASE.
Nonfiction: Informational articles about selling, construction of furniture, credit, business, freight, and transportation. "Must have honest, well-researched approach." Interview, nostalgia, new product, merchandising techniques, technical. Length: 750-2,000 words. Pays $50 maximum. Prior agreement must be reached before submitting.

Hospitals, Nursing, and Nursing Homes

In this section are journals for nurses; medical and nonmedical nursing home, clinical, and hospital staffs; and laboratory technicians and managers. Journals for physicians in private practice or that publish technical material on new discoveries in medicine will be found in the Medical category.

DOCTORS' NURSE BULLETIN, 9600 Colesville Rd., Silver Spring MD 20901. (301)585-1056. Editor: Bob Bickford. Quarterly. Occasionally copyrighted. Pays on publication. Reports in a few days. Enclose SASE.
Nonfiction: Uses articles of interest to the doctor's nurse. Pays from $5 to $50, depending on length and value.
Photos: Buys photographs with mss and with captions only. B&w only. Pays $3 minimum.

HOSPITAL FORUM, Association of Western Hospitals, 830 Market St., San Francisco CA 94102. (415)421-8720. Editor: Margaret Hirtz. Emphasizes hospital administration. Magazine published 7 times/year; 32-40 pages. Estab. 1959. Circ. 10,000. Buys one-time rights. Phone queries OK. SASE. Reports in 2 months. Free guidelines for writers.
Nonfiction: Publishes informational and how-to articles on hospitals. Length: 500-5,000 words. Pays $50 maximum. Query first.

HOSPITAL PROGRESS, The Catholic Hospital Association, 1438 S. Grand Blvd., St. Louis MO 63104. (314)773-0646. Editor: Robert S. Stephens. For hospital and nursing home administrators, trustees and department heads. Monthly magazine; 100 pages. Estab. 1920. Circ. 15,000. Buys all rights. Phone queries OK. SASE. Photocopied submissions OK. SASE. Reports in 3 months. Free guidelines for writers.
Nonfiction: Publishes how-to, and informational articles and interviews with government and hospital leaders. Must be in-depth (not superficial) reports of hospital administration. Buys 5 mss a year. Length: 1,000-2,000 words. Query first. Pays $1 per column inch.

HOSPITAL SUPERVISOR'S BULLETIN, Bureau of Business Practice, 24 Rope Ferry Rd.,

Waterford CT 06386. Editor: Susan Brodkin. For hospital supervisors. Semimonthly newsletter; 8 pages. Estab. 1968. Circ. 8,000. Pays on acceptance. Buys all rights. Submit seasonal/holiday material 6 months in advance. Photocopied submissions OK. SASE. Reports in 4 weeks. Free sample copy and writer's guidelines.
Nonfiction: Publishes interviews with hospital department heads. "You should ask supervisors to pinpoint current problems in supervision, tell how they are trying to solve these problems and what results they're getting — backed up by real examples from daily life." Also publishes articles on people problems and good methods of management. People problems include the areas of training, planning, evaluating, counseling, discipline, motivation, supervising the undereducated, getting along with the medical staff, etc., with emphasis on good methods of management. "We prefer 4- 6-page typewritten articles, based on interviews." Pays 10¢/word after editing.

THE JOURNAL OF NURSING CARE (formerly *Nursing Care*), 265 Post Rd., W., Westport CT 06880. (203)226-7203. Editor: Ellen Marcus. For licensed practical nurses. 12 times a year. Circ. 70,000. Buys North American serial rights. Pays on acceptance. Free sample copy. SASE.
Nonfiction: Nursing articles geared specifically to licensed practical nurses and their profession. "We prefer clinical teaching material from which our readers can learn, keep up to date on new medical developments, or refresh their skills. I would also like more articles on the nurse as a person; articles that improve her self-esteem and relationships with people (not just with patients); assertiveness, training, supervisory skills, coping with a career and a family at the same time, etc. I'd like more first-person stories from nurse-writers and more on nutrition." Query. Length: maximum 2,500 words. Pays $20/published page; 2 to 3 typewritten pages usually equal 1 published page.

JOURNAL OF PRACTICAL NURSING, 122 E. 42nd St., New York NY 10017. (212)682-3400. Editorial Director: Freda Baron Friedman. Editor: Eve Hammerschmidt. 75% freelance written. For practical vocational nurses, practical nurse educators, registered nurses, hospital and nursing home administrators, and other allied health professionals. Monthly magazine; 42-48 pages. Estab. 1950. Circ. 40,000. Pays on publication. Buys all rights, but may reassign following publication. Submit seasonal/holiday material 3 months in advance of issue date. Reports in 4-6 weeks. Free sample copy and writer's guidelines; mention *Writer's Market* in request.
Nonfiction: General interest (to LPNs); historical (relating to nursing, medicine); how-to (care for patients and their needs); humor (if relevant); inspirational (if relevant); interview (with relevant people); personal experience (of LPN in health situations); personal opinion (on issues of relevance to LPNs); photo feature (of innovative practical nursing programs); profile (of interest and news-worthy); and technical. Buys 36 mss/year. Query. Length: 700-2,100 words. Pays $10-100.
Photos: State availability of photos with query. No additional payment for photos purchased with accompanying ms. Buys b&w contact sheets or glossy prints. Captions preferred. Buys one-time rights. Model release required.
Columns/Departments: Books. Query. Length: 400-1,000 words. Open to suggestions for new columns/departments.
Fillers: Crossword puzzles and short humor. Buys 8/year. Pays $5-15.

PROFESSIONAL MEDICAL ASSISTANT, One East Wacker Dr., Chicago IL 60601. Editor: Susan S. Croy. "About 95% of our subscribers belong to the American Association of Medical Assistants. They are professional people employed by a doctor of medicine." Estab. 1957. Bimonthly. Circ. 21,000. Rights purchased vary with author and material. Pays on publication. Free sample copy. Photocopied submissions OK. Reports in 2 weeks. SASE.
Nonfiction and Photos: "Articles dealing with clinical and administrative procedures in a physician's office. Request our publication to study for the style we require." Buys informational articles, how-to's, and humor. Buys 2 mss/year. Submit complete ms. Length: 500-2,500 words. Pays $15 to $50.
Fillers: Crosswords for allied health personnel, find the word, or "word-search" puzzles. Pays $7.50.

RN, 680 Kinderkamack Rd., Oradell NJ 07649. (201)262-3030. Editor: Don L. Berg. For registered nurses, mostly hospital-based but also in physicians' offices, public health, schools, industry. Monthly magazine; 100 pages. Estab. 1937. Circ. 240,000. Buys all rights. Pays on acceptance. Free sample copy and writer's guidelines. Reports in 6-8 weeks. SASE.
Nonfiction: "If you are a nurse who writes, we would like to see your work. Editorial content:

diseases, clinical techniques, surgery, therapy, research, equipment, drugs, etc. These should be thoroughly researched and sources cited. Personal anecdotes, experiences, observations based on your relations with doctors, hospitals, patients and nursing colleagues. Our style is simple, direct, not preachy. Do include examples, case histories that relate the reader to her own nursing experience. Talk mostly about people, rather than things. Dashes of humor or insight are always welcome. Include photos where feasible.'' Buys 20-30 mss/year. Query or submit complete ms. Length: 8 to 10 double-spaced, typewritten pages. Payment varies.

Hotels, Motels, Clubs, Resorts, Restaurants

Journals which emphasize retailing for bar and beverage operators are classified in the Beverages and Bottling category. For publications slanted to food wholesalers, processors, and caterers, see Food Products, Processing, and Service.

CLUB EXECUTIVE, 1750 Old Meadow Rd., McLean VA 22101. Editor: Paul E. Reece. 20% freelance written. For military club managers. Monthly. Not copyrighted. Pays on publication. Reports in 2 weeks. SASE.
Nonfiction: Articles about food and beverages, design, equipment, promotional ideas, etc. Length: 1,500-2,000 words. Pays 4¢/word.

EXECUTIVE HOUSEKEEPER, North American Publishing Co., 401 N. Broad St., Philadelphia PA 19108. (215)574-9600. Editor: Kay Blumenthal. 80% freelance written. Emphasizes institutional (hospital, hotel, school) housekeeping management. ''Most readers have received certification in their field and/or recieved training through continuing education courses. Interested in how to manage their departments effectively.'' Monthly magazine; 56 pages. Circ. 14,000. Pays on publication. Buys all rights. Submit seasonal/holiday material 2 months in advance of issue date. SASE. Reports in 2 months. Free sample copy and writer's guidelines; mention *Writer's Market* in request.
Nonfiction: General interest (mostly management-related topics about running the Housekeeping Department, improving communication with employees and administration, training, etc.); how-to (maintenance in institutional housekeeping departments); humor (humorous treatments of experiences relating to the Executive Housekeeper's job—anecdotal); interview; personal experience; personal opinion (on topics such as contract cleaning); profile (of Executive Housekeepers); and technical (proper use of chemical supplies and equipment, infection control, carpet maintenance). Buys 3 mss/issue. Submit complete ms. Length: 1,000-2,000 words. Pays $75-125.

FOOD EXECUTIVE, 508 IBM BUILDING, Fort Wayne IN 46815. (219)484-1901. Editor: Carleton B. Evans. 15% freelance written. For restaurant, hotel, cafeteria owners and managers. Bimonthly. Not copyrighted. Pays on acceptance. Query first. Enclose SASE.
Nonfiction: Material dealing with restaurant, institutional, industrial, and catering food service (includes government and military) operation and techniques such as cost control, personnel, portion control, layout and design, decor, merchandising. Also new trends in the food service industry, general economic problems, labor situations, training programs for personnel. Must be written for professionals in the field. Length: 500 to 2,000 words. Pays 1½¢ per word.
Photos: ''Pertinent photos.'' Pays $3 to $5.

INNKEEPING WORLD, Motel Services, Inc., Box 15208, Seattle WA 98115. Editor/Publisher: C.W. Nolte. 50% freelance written. Emphasizes the lodging industry and travel. Bimonthly newsletter; 8 pages. Estab. 1975. Circ. 1,500. Pays on acceptance. Buys one-time rights. Submit seasonal/holiday material 1 month in advance of issue date. Simultaneous and previously published submissions OK. SASE. Reports in 4 weeks. Free sample copy.
Nonfiction: How-to (increase business, cut expenses, treat guests and anything that would help hotel/motel managers); technical (maintenance, repairing, upgrading of hotels/motels); and travel (statistics). Buys 2 mss/issue. Query. Length: 100-500 words. Pays 10¢/word.
Columns/Departments: Advertising/Promotion; Cutting expenses; Increasing business; Labor incentives/relations; accounting & taxes; and news, trends and ideas (for fillers). Buys 2/issue. Length: 50-500 words. Pays 10¢/word.

KANSAS RESTAURANT MAGAZINE, 359 South Hydraulic St., Wichita KS 67211. (316)267-

8383. Editor: Neal D. Whitaker. For food service operators. Special issues: Christmas, October Convention, Who's Who in Kansas Food Service, Beef Month, Dairy Month, Wheat Month. Monthly. Circ. 1,400. Not copyrighted. Pays on publication. Sample copy for 50¢. Reports "immediately." SASE.
Nonfiction and Photos: Articles on food and food service. Length: 1,000 words maximum. Pays $10. Photos purchased with ms.

LODGING AND FOOD SERVICE NEWS, 131 Clarendon St., Boston MA 02116. Managing Editor: Mrs. Susan G. Holaday. For managers and executives of hotels, motels, restaurants, fast food operations, contract feeders, country clubs, etc. Estab. 1925. Every 2 weeks. Circ. 8,000. Not copyrighted. Pays on publication. Will send sample copy to writer on request. Submit seasonal material 6 months in advance. Reports in 1 month. Query first. Enclose SASE.
Nonfiction and Photos: News relating to hotels, restaurants, etc. Travel and tourism trends. Features on unusual operations. Stories on new chains and expansions. Must have hard-breaking news orientation. Stories on food service promotions for the holidays and summer merchandising news. Length: 16 to 80 double-spaced lines. Pays $25 minimum. Pays $5 for 8x10 b&w glossies used with mss.

MANAGING THE LEISURE FACILITY, Billboard Publications, Inc., 1717 West End Ave., Nashville TN 37203. (615)329-3925. Editor: Irwin Kirby. Emphasizes operational aspects of amusement/recreation facilities for management and department heads. Bimonthly magazine; 36 pages. Estab. 1977. Circ. 17,000. Pays upon determination of payment based on typeset galleys. Buys all rights, but may reassign following publication. Phone queries OK. Simultaneous, photocopied and previously published submissions OK. SASE. Reports in 2 weeks. Free sample copy and writer's guidelines.
Nonfiction: How-to; informational; photo feature and technical. "The writing style is straightforward, based on plain language and logical grammatical construction. Unjustified contractions and breeziness are contrary to our dignified approach. The same inhibition would apply to superlatives and hyperbole." Buys 6 mss/issue. Query or submit complete ms, "but query is a time saver for original work." Length: 250-2,500 words. Pays $20-250.
Photos: State availability of photos with query. Pays $3-5 for 5x7 or 8x10 b&w glossy prints or color transparencies.

MOTEL/MOTOR INN JOURNAL, Box 769, Temple TX 76501. (817)778-5115. Editor: Walter T. Proctor. For owners and managers of motels, motor inns and resorts in the US. Monthly magazine; 42-100 pages. Estab. 1937. Circ. 29,000. Buys all rights. Buys 15 mss/year. Pays on acceptance. Free sample copy and writer's guidelines. Simultaneous submissions OK. Submit seasonal (holiday) material 2 months in advance. Reports in 10 days. Query first. Enclose SASE.
Nonfiction and Photos: Factual articles designed to help owners/managers to be more effective, and to become more profitable operators of such properties. How-to articles on profitable holiday promotions. "We stress less emphasis on big hotels; more on medium-sized to large motels and motor inns and resorts. We don't want general articles on community relations, or how to be a better manager, etc." Length: "4 to 6 pages, double-spaced." Pays $10 per double-spaced, typed page. B&w photos (5x7 or 8x10) and top-quality color transparencies purchased with mss. Pays $5 for b&w; $10 for color.

NATION'S RESTAURANT NEWS, 425 Park Ave., New York NY 10022. Editor: Charles Bernstein. "National business newspaper for food service chains and independents." Biweekly newspaper. Circ. 52,000. Pays on acceptance.
Nonfiction: "News and newsfeatures, in-depth analyses of specific new types of restaurants, mergers and acquisitions, new appointments, commodity reports, personalities. Problem: Most business press stories are mere rehashes of consumer pieces. We must have business insight. Sometimes a freelancer can provide us with enough peripheral material that we'll buy the idea, then assign it to staff writers for further digging." Length: 500 words maximum. Pays $5-$75.
Photos: B&w glossies purchased with mss and captions only. Pays $10 minimum.
How To Break In: "Send most wanted material, such as personality profiles, business-oriented restaurant news articles, but no how-to stories."

RESORT & MOTEL MAGAZINE, Page Publications, Ltd., 380 Wellington St., W., Toronto, Ontario, Canada M5V 1E3. (416)366-4608. Editor: Henry Wittenberg. For resort owners and managers; hotels, motels, etc. Bimonthly magazine; 32 pages. Estab. 1962. Circ. 10,000. Buys one-time rights. Pays on publication. Free sample copy. Reports in 6 weeks. Enclose SAE and

International Reply Coupons.
Nonfiction: Informational, technical and how-to articles. Canadian content required. Interviews; articles on travel, successful business operations, new products, and merchandising techniques. Length: open. Pays 5¢/word.

RESORT MANAGEMENT, P.O. Box 4169, Memphis TN 38104. (901)276-5424. Editor: Allen J. Fagans. 40% freelance written. For "the owners and/or managing executives of America's largest luxury vacation resorts." Monthly. Buys first rights only. Pays on publication. Sample copy for SASE. Query. "Editorial deadline is the 1st of the previous month; i.e., January material must be received by December 1." Reports in 10 days. Enclose SASE.
Nonfiction and Photos: "This is not a travel or tourist publication. It is a 'how-to-do-it' or 'how-it-was-done' business journal. Descriptive background of any sort used to illustrate the subject matter must be held to a minimum. Our material helps managers attract, house, feed and provide entertainment for guests and their friends, and bring them back again and again. Any facet of the resort operation could be of interest: guest activities, remodeling, advertising and promotion, maintenance, food, landscaping, kitchen, personnel, furnishings, etc. We do not want to see material relating to any facet of commercial hotels, motels, motor courts, fishing and hunting camps, housekeeping or other facilities serving transients. Material submitted must be accurate, to the point, and supported by facts and costs, plus pertinent examples illustrating the subject discussed." Length: 800 to 1,000 words. Pays 60¢ per inch for a 20-em column; 40¢ per inch for a 13-em column. "Photos of the resort and of its manager, and the subject(s) being discussed are a must." Pays $5/photo.
Fillers: Uses clippings related to resorts and resort area organizations only. Promotions: president, general manager, resident manager (including changes from one resort to another). Resort Obituaries: president, owner, general manager. Resort construction: changes, additions, new facilities, etc. New resorts: planned or under construction. Changes in resort ownership. Resort news: factual news concerning specific resorts, resort areas, state tourism development. Not interested in clippings about city hotels, roadside motels, motor inns or chain (franchise) operations. Clippings must be pasted on individual sheets of paper, and addressed to Clipping Editor. Your complete mailing address (typed or printed) must be included, as well as the name of the newspaper or magazine and date of issue. Do not send advertisements or pictures. Clippings will not be returned unless a self-addressed envelope and sufficient postage is enclosed. Pays $1 per clipping used.

Industrial Management

The journals that follow are for industrial plant managers, executives, distributors, and buyers; some industrial management journals are also listed under the names of specific industries, such as Machinery and Metal Trade. Publications for industrial supervisors are listed in Management and Supervision.

COMPRESSED AIR, 253 E. Washington Ave., Washington NJ 07882. Managing Editor: S.M. Parkhill. 5% freelance written. Emphasizes "the application of pneumatics for middle and upper management personnel in all industries." Monthly magazine; 48 pages. Estab. 1896. Circ. 150,000. Pays on publication. Buys all rights. Submit seasonal/holiday material 6 months in advance of issue date. SASE. Reports in 4-6 weeks. Free sample copy and writer's guidelines; mention *Writer's Market* in request.
Nonfiction: "Articles must be reviewed by experts in the field." How-to (save costs with air power); and historical (engineering). Buys 5 mss/year. Query. Pays $60/published page.
Photos: State availability of photos in query. Payment for 8x10 glossy b&w photos is included in total purchase price. Captions required. Buys all rights.

ENERGY NEWS, Energy Publications—division of Harcourt Brace Jovanovich, Box 1589, Dallas TX 75221. (214)748-4403. Managing Editor: Gregory Martin. 5% freelance written. Emphasizes natural gas production, transmission, distribution, regulation, and projects for executives or managers of energy, supply and financial, companies or the government; particularly utilities. Biweekly newsletter; 4 pages. Estab. 1970. Circ. 500. Pays on publication. Buys all rights. Phone queries OK. Simultaneous and photocopied submissions OK. SASE. Reports in 4 weeks. Free sample copy and writer's guidelines.
Nonfiction: Interviews with energy industry or government leaders keyed to recent news and technical articles on natural gas projects, trends, prices, or new technologies. "Can't use

anything not related to natural gas or utilities." Buys 1-2 mss/issue. Length: 250 words maximum. Pays 15¢/word.

ENERGY WEEK, Energy Publications—division of Harcourt Brace Jovanovich, Box 1589, Dallas TX 75221. (214)748-4403. Editor: Ernestine Adams. Assistant Editor: Gregory Martin. 5% freelance written. Emphasizes energy production, transmission, regulation, prices, etc., for executives or management of energy supply or financial companies or the government. Biweekly newsletter; 4 pages. Estab. 1973. Circ. 500. Pays on publication. Buys all rights. Phone queries OK. Simultaneous and photocopied submissions OK. SASE. Reports in 4 weeks. Free sample copy and writer's guidelines.
Nonfiction: Interview (with energy industry trend-setters, should be keyed to recent news); and technical (new energy technologies, feasibility, costs, or technical features). "No stories dealing with the surface rather than the inner core of energy developments. Our readers are aware of news related to energy; they want to know *why* and how *they* are affected." Buys 1-2 mss/issue. Submit complete ms. Length: 250 words maximum. Pays 15¢/word.

HANDLING AND SHIPPING, 614 Superior Ave. W., Cleveland OH 44113. (216)696-0300. Editor: H.G. Becker, Jr. 25-30% freelance written. For operating executives with physical distribution responsibilities in transportation, material handling, warehousing, packaging, and shipping. Monthly. Buys all rights. Pays on publication. "Query first with 50-word description of proposed article." Enclose SASE.
Nonfiction and Photos: Material on aspects of physical distribution management, with economic emphasis. Informational and successful business operations material. Writer must know the field and the publications in it. Not for amateurs and generalists. Length: 1,500 to 3,000 words. Pays minimum of $30 per published page. Additional payment is made for b&w photos used with mss, but they must be sharp, for good reproduction. No prints from copy negatives. Any size. Color used may be prints or transparencies.

INDUSTRIAL DISTRIBUTION, 205 E. 42 St., New York NY 10017. (212)573-8100. Editor: George J. Berkwitt. Monthly. Buys all rights. Will consider cassette submissions. Enclose SASE.
Nonfiction: "Articles aimed at making industrial distributor management, sales and other personnel aware of trends, developments and problems and solutions in their segment of industry. Articles accepted range widely; may cover legislation, sales training, administration, Washington, marketing techniques, case histories, profiles on industry leaders, abstracted speeches—any area that is timely and pertinent and provides readers with interesting informative data. Use either roundups or bylined pieces." Length: 900 words minimum. Pays "flat fee based on value; usually $100 per published page."

INDUSTRIAL DISTRIBUTOR NEWS, 1 West Olney Ave., Philadelphia PA 19120. Managing Editor: Stephen A. Albertini. For industrial distributors, wholesalers of industrial equipment and supplies; business managers and industrial salesmen. Estab. 1959. Monthly. Circ. 32,000. Free sample copy. Reports on material within 6 weeks. "Company policy dictates no bylined articles except when noted by publisher. Therefore, no freelance material used unless assigned through initial query first." Enclose SASE.
Nonfiction and Photos: "Factual feature material with a slant toward industrial marketing. Case studies of distributors with unusual or unusually successful marketing techniques. Avoid triteness in subject matter. Be sure to relate specifically to industrial distributors." Informational, how-to, interview. Length: 500 to 3,000 words. B&w 8x10 or 2¼x2¼ color transparencies.

INDUSTRIAL NEWS *(Southern California Industrial News, Northern California Industrial News, Southwest Industrial News, Pacific Northwest Industrial News, Southwest Electronics News)*, Box 3631, Los Angeles CA 90051. Editor: Peter Lichtgarn. For manufacturing executives and industrial suppliers, as well as technical people (engineers and chemists). Tabloid newspapers. Estab. 1948. *Southern California Industrial News* is published weekly. The balance are monthlies. Circ. over 24,000. Buys simultaneous rights. Payment on publication. Will send free sample copy to writer on request. Will consider photocopied and simultaneous submissions. Reports in 2 weeks. Query first. SASE.
Nonfiction and Photos: Hard news, industry oriented. Should pertain to the area of each publication. Should be to the point, not long-winded or overly technical. Not interested in energy crisis stories by instant experts. Does like to see the how-to approach in all industrial situations, without it being a "puff" for a particular producer. Informational, interview, profile,

expose, spot news, successful business operations, new products, merchandising techniques. Length: 50 to 100 typewritten lines. Pays $10 to $50. No additional payment for b&w photos used with mss. Captions required.

INDUSTRIAL WORLD, 386 Park Ave., S., New York NY 10016. (212)689-0120. Editor and Publisher: S. W. Kann. For plant managers abroad. Monthly. Buys first world rights. Pays on publication. Will send a sample copy to a writer on request. Query first. Formal outlines not required; paragraph of copy sufficient. Reports in 30 days. Enclose SASE.
Nonfiction and Photos: "Interested primarily in articles dealing with application of U.S. industrial machinery and know-how abroad. Clear, factual data necessary. Articles of more than passing interest to plant managers on production tools, techniques, unusual installation, new or novel solutions to production problems, etc. Should be slanted for the overseas plant manager." Length: 1,000 to 3,000 words. Pays "$75 for first printed page of article, $50 for each subsequent page." Photos purchased with mss. 5x7 or 8x10 glossies only; must be clean, professional, quality. ("If necessary, we will make prints from author's negatives which will be returned. Photos supplied, however, are usually not returned.")
How To Break In: "Concentrate on the adaptations of industrial know-how in the developing nations. Your best chance of getting an assignment will be if you are planning to travel in one of the less frequently traveled areas and have an idea for a story of this kind. We tend to rely on regular contributors in certain areas and if you plan to stay abroad, you could become a stringer."

INDUSTRY WEEK, Penton/IPC, Inc., 1111 Chester Ave., Cleveland OH 44114. (216)696-7000. Editor-in-Chief: Stanley Modic. 5-10% freelance written. Emphasizes manufacturing and related industries for top or middle management (administrating, production, engineering, finance, purchasing or marketing) throughout industry. Biweekly magazine; 100 pages. Estab. 1882. Circ. 250,000. Pays on publication. Buys all rights. Phone queries OK. Submit seasonal or holiday material 3 months in advance. Simultaneous and photocopied submissions OK. Previously published work OK. SASE. Reports in 4 weeks. Sample copy $2.
Nonfiction: How-to and informational articles (should deal with areas of interest to manager audience, e.g., developing managerial skills or managing effectively). Length: 1,000-4,000 words. Buys 15-20 a year. Query first. Pays $60/published page.No product news or clippings.
Photos: Chris Nehlen, department editor. B&w and color purchased with ms or on assignment. Query first. Pays $35 minimum. Model release required.

MODERN PLANT OPERATION AND MAINTENANCE, 209 Dunn Ave., Stamford CT 06905. (203)322-7676. Editor: Kenneth V. Jones. For plant engineers and managers. Quarterly. Circ. 55,000. Buys all rights. Pays on acceptance. "We reject all unsolicited material unseen, as we are not set up to handle it. All assignments come from us and we can use only the people who truly know the field. Send letter stating qualifications and availability." SASE. Do not send query letters.
Nonfiction and Photos: Length: 600 to 1,000 words. Pays $100 to $150.

NORTHEASTERN INDUSTRIAL WORLD, 2 Penn Plaza, Suite 1950, New York NY 10001. (212)564-0340. Managing Editor: Robert Hardt. For senior executives in northeastern manufacturing, service and industrial development. Monthly magazine; 40 pages. Estab. 1955. Circ. 150,000. Pays on publication. Buys all rights, but may reassign following publication. Phone queries OK. Submit seasonal or holiday material 2 months in advance. Previously published work OK. SASE. Reports in 2 weeks. Free sample copy and writer's guidelines.
Nonfiction: "Feature articles deal with energy, finance, legislation, economic and community development and innovations in industrial techniques and theories." Expose, historical, how-to, informational, new product and technical articles; interviews and profiles. "Best potential area for freelancers are expose and historical." Length: 1,800-2,700 words. Query. Purchases very few mss; must be material unavailable from industry sources. Pays $50-200.
Photos: B&w glossies (8x10) used with mss. Captions required. Query. No additional payment.

THE PHILADELPHIA PURCHASOR, 1518 Walnut St., Suite 610, Philadelphia PA 19102. Editor-in-Chief: Howard B. Armstrong, Jr. 35% freelance written. For buyers of industrial supplies and equipment, including the materials of manufacture, as well as the maintenance, repair and operating items; and for buyers of office equipment and supplies for banks and other industries. Monthly magazine; 65 pages. Estab. 1926. Circ. 4,000. Not copyrighted. Pays on acceptance. Free sample copy and writer's guidelines. Photocopied and simultaneous submissions OK. Reports in 1 month. SASE.

Nonfiction and Photos: "We use articles on industrial, service and institutional purchasing—*not* consumer. We also use business articles of the kind that would interest purchasing personnel. Ours is a regional magazine covering the middle Atlantic area, and if material takes this into account, it is more effective." Buys 25-35 mss/year. Query or submit complete ms. Length: 900-1,200 words. Pays minimum of $15. No additional payment for b&w photos used with mss.

PLANT MANAGEMENT & ENGINEERING, MacLean Hunter, 481 University Ave., Toronto, Ontario, Canada M5W 1A7. Editor: Tony Thompson. 20% freelance written. For Canadian plant managers and engineers. Monthly magazine; 60 pages. Estab. 1940. Circ. 18,000. Pays on publication. Buys first Canadian rights. Phone queries OK. Previously published submissions OK, if not published in Canada. SASE. Reports in 2-3 weeks. Free sample copy.
Nonfiction: How-to, technical, and some management technique articles. Must have Canadian slant. Query. Pays 10¢/word.
Photos: State availability of photos with query. Pays $25-50 for b&w prints; $50-100 for 2¼x2¼ color transparencies. Captions preferred. Buys one-time rights.

PRODUCTION ENGINEERING, Penton Plaza, Cleveland OH 44114. (216)696-7000. Editor-in-Chief: Larry Boulden. Executive Editor: John McRainey. 20% freelance written. For "men and women in production engineering—the engineers who plan, design, and improve manufacturing operations." Monthly magazine; 100 pages. Estab. 1954. Circ. 95,000. Pays on publication. Buys all rights, but may reassign following publication. Phone queries OK. Photocopied submissions OK, if exclusive. SASE. Reports in 2 weeks. Free sample copy and writer's guidelines.
Nonfiction: How-to (engineering, data for engineers); personal experience (from *very* senior production or manufacturing engineers only); and technical (technical news or how-to). "We're interested in solid, hard-hitting technical articles on the gut issues of manufacturing. Not case histories, but no-fat treatments of manufacturing concepts, innovative manufacturing methods, and state-of-the-art procedures. Our readers also enjoy articles that detail a variety of practical solutions to some specific, everyday manufacturing headache." Buys 2 mss/issue. Query. Length: 800-3,000 words. Pays $25-150.
Photos: "Sell me the manuscript, then we'll talk about photos."

PURCHASING, 221 Columbus Ave., Boston MA 02116. Editorial Director: Robert Haavind. For purchasing specialists, primarily in manufacturing industries. Semimonthly. Circ. 77,000. Buys all rights. Buys about 20 mss a year. Payment on publication. Free sample copy. Submit seasonal material 3 months in advance. Reports in 10 days. Query first. SASE.
Nonfiction: Some news items (on price shifts, purchasing problems, etc.) from stringers. Features on better purchasing methods (with real examples), on evaluating or specifying. Items must be generalized and objective. Back up topics with good data, examples, charts, etc. No product pitches. Particularly interested in contract writing, negotiating techniques. Informational, how-to, and spot news. Length: 500 to 1,500 words. Pays $50 to $150.

THE WASHINGTON PURCHASER, Box 9038, Seattle WA 98109. Associate Editor: Christine Laing. 10% freelance written. For readers who are responsible for purchasing for commercial, government and industrial firms. Monthly magazine; 52-84 pages. Estab. 1925. Circ. 2,500. Buys first North American serial rights. Pays on publication. Will send sample copy to writer on request. Write for copy of guidelines for writers. No photocopied or simultaneous submissions. Reports in 1 week to 1 month. Query first. Enclose SASE.
Nonfiction: Articles on techniques for buying, from office supplies to heavy industrial materials and general business and economic trends. "Use of freelance material is limited and writers must follow typical rules of style, remembering that readers want concise material that must benefit them in their jobs as buyers of various commodities." Informational, how-to, interview, new product, merchandising techniques, technical articles. Pays $10 to $25.

Insurance

BUSINESS INSURANCE, 740 N. Rush Street, Chicago IL 60611. Editor: Susan Alt. For "corporate risk managers, insurance brokers and agents, insurance company executives. Interested in insurance, safety, security, consumerism, employee benefits." Special issues on safety, pensions, health and life benefits, international insurance. Biweekly. Circ. 35,000. Buys all rights. Buys 75 to 100 mss a year. Pays on publication. Submit seasonal or special material 2 months in advance. Reports in 2 weeks. Query required. Enclose SASE.

Nonfiction: "We publish material on corporate insurance and employee benefit programs and related subjects. We take everything from the buyers' point of view, rather than that of the insurance company, broker, or consultant who is selling something. Items on insurance company workings do not interest us. Our special emphasis on corporate risk management and employee benefits administration requires that freelancers discuss with us their proposed articles before going ahead. Length is subject to discussion with contributor." Payment is $2.50 a column inch.

EQUIFAX, Box 4081, Atlanta GA 30302. (404)875-8321. Editor: H.A. McQuade. For "management employees of most American corporations, especially insurance companies. This includes Canada and Mexico. Pass-along readership involves sub-management and non-management people in these firms. Distributed by Equifax, Inc." Quarterly. Circ. 89,000. Copyrighted; "we allow customer publications free reprint privileges. Author free to negotiate fee independently, however." Buys 3 to 5 mss a year. Pays on acceptance. Will send a sample copy to a writer on request. Query first: "present idea in paragraph outline form. Accepted queries should result in authors' submitting double-spaced copy, typed 35 characters to the line, 25 lines to the page." Reports in 2 to 3 weeks. Enclose SASE.
Nonfiction and Photos: "Insurance-related articles —new trends, challenges, and problems facing underwriters, actuaries, claim men, executives, and agents; articles of general interest in a wide range of subjects —the quality of life, ecology, drug and alcohol-related subjects, safe driving, law enforcement, and insurance-related Americana; inspirational articles to help managers and executives do their jobs better. Write with our audience in mind. Only articles of the highest quality will be considered. Especially interested in material written by insurance underwriters, executives, college instructors, and college professors on previously unpublished or updated facets of our area of interest. More than 90% of our readers are customers of Equifax, Inc., or its various affiliates, and they expect to see articles that help them know and understand the business information business." Buys inspirational articles, think pieces about insurance industry needs for business information services, etc. Length: 1,000 to 2,000 words. Pays 1¢ to 2¢ a word, "depending on quality and importance of material, but not less than $25." B&w glossies relating to theme of article purchased with mss; 5x7 or 8x10. Pays $5 to $15.

LINES MAGAZINE, Reliance Insurance Co., 4 Penn Center, Philadelphia PA 19103. Editor: Beverly Braun. 80% freelance written. Emphasizes insurance and business for "middle-aged, college educated business people interested in business trends and opinion." Quarterly magazine; 20 pages. Estab. 1977. Circ. 9,000. Pays on acceptance. Not copyrighted. Submit seasonal/holiday material 2 months in advance of issue date. SASE. Reports in 2 weeks. Free sample copy; mention *Writer's Market* in request.
Nonfiction: Expose (anything insurance related, directly or indirectly); general interest (could be dealing with medical, natural disasters, environment, etc.); interview (with prominent business leaders who might forecast of offer opinion on insurance industry-related matters); nostalgia (insurance, old fire companies); personal experience (interesting and extremely unusual claims); technical (insurance, property/casualty or life). Buys 20 mss/year. Query. Length: 1,500 words minimum.
Fillers: Newsbreaks. Buys 5/issue. Length: 50 words.

Jewelry

AMERICAN HOROLOGIST & JEWELER, 2403 Champa St., Denver CO 80205. (303)572-1777. Managing Editor: Kathleen P. Egan. 30% freelance written. Emphasizes Watch/Clock making and jewelry. Monthly magazine; 68 pages. Estab. January 1936. Circ. 13,100. Pays on publication. Phone queries OK. Buys all rights, but may reassign following publication. Submit seasonal/holiday material 3 months in advance of issue date. Previously published submissions OK. SASE. Reports in 2-3 weeks. Free sample copy and writer's guidelines.
Nonfiction: How-to (repair articles for watch, clock, jewelry trades, and how-to merchandise, make profits); new product (pertaining to industry and of an unusual nature); photo feature (antique clocks, watches); and technical (repair of jewelry or watches). Buys 10 mss/year. Query or submit complete ms. Length: 1,000-6,000 words. Pays $10-150.
Photos: Submit photo material with accompanying query or ms. No additional payment for b&w glossy prints. Captions preferred. Buys all rights, but may reassign following publication. Model release required.
Columns/Departments: Buys 6/issue. Query. Pays $50. Open to suggestions for new columns/departments.

AMERICAN JEWELRY MANUFACTURER, 340 Howard Bldg., 155 Westminster St., Providence RI 02903. (401)274-3840. Editor: Steffan Aletti. For manufacturers of supplies and tools for the jewelry industry; their representatives, wholesalers and agencies. Estab. 1956. Monthly. Circ. 5,000. Buys all rights (with exceptions). Buys 2 to 5 mss a year. Free sample copy and writer's guidelines. Will consider photocopied submissions. Submit seasonal material 3 months in advance. Reports on material within a month. Query first. SASE.
Nonfiction and Photos: "Topical articles on manufacturing; company stories; economics (i.e., rising gold prices). Story must inform or educate the manufacturer. Occasional special issues on timely topics, i.e., gold; occasional issues on specific processes in casting and plating. We reject material that is not specifically pointed at our industry; i.e., articles geared to jewelry retailing, not the manufacturers." Informational, how-to, interview, profile, historical, expose, successful business operations, new product, merchandising techniques, technical. Length: open. Payment "usually around $25." B&w photos purchased with ms. 5x7 minimum.

THE DIAMOND REGISTRY BULLETIN, 30 W. 47th St., New York NY 10036. Editor-in-Chief: Joseph Schlussel. Managing Editor: Esther Borenstein. 15% freelance written. Monthly newsletter. Pays on publication. Buys all rights, but may reassign following publication. Submit seasonal/holiday material 1 month in advance of issue date. Simultaneous and previously published submissions OK. SASE. Reports in 3 weeks. Sample copy $5.
Nonfiction: Prevention advise (on crimes against jewelers); how-to (ways to increase sales in diamonds, improve security, etc.); and interview (of interest to diamond dealers or jewelers). Submit complete ms. Length: 50-500 words. Pays $10-150.

JEWELER'S CIRCULAR-KEYSTONE, Chilton Company, Radnor PA 19089. Editor: George Holmes. For retail jewelers. Monthly. Circ. 30,000. Buys all rights. Pays on publication. SASE.
Nonfiction: Wants "how-to-articles, case history approach, which specify how a given jeweler solved a specific problem. No general stories, no stories without a jeweler's name in it, no stories not about a specific jeweler and his business." Buys 10-12 mss/year. Length: 1,000 to 2,000 words.

MODERN JEWELER, 15 W. 10th St., Kansas City MO 64105. Managing Editor: Dorothy Boicourt. For retail jewelers and watchmakers. Monthly. Pays on acceptance. Will send sample copy only if query interests the editor. Reports in 30 days. SASE.
Nonfiction and Photos: "Articles with 3 or 4 photos about retail jewelers—specific jewelers, with names and addresses, and how they have overcome certain business problems, moved merchandise, increased store traffic, etc. Must contain idea adaptable to other jewelry operations; 'how-to' slant. Informal, story-telling slant with human interest. We are not interested in articles about how manufacturing jewelers design and make one-of-a-kind jewelry pieces. Our readers are interested in retail selling techniques, not manufacturing processes. Photos must include people (not just store shots) and should help tell the story. We reject poor photography and articles written as local newspaper features, rather than for a business publication." Pays average $70-$90 for article and photos.

THE NORTHWESTERN JEWELER, Washington and Main Sts., Albert Lea MN 56007. Publisher: John R. Hayek. Monthly. Not copyrighted. Pays on publication. SASE.
Nonfiction and Photos: Uses news stories about jewelers in the Northwest and Upper Midwest and feature news stories about the same group. Also buys retail jeweler "success" stories with the "how-to-do" angle played up, and occasionally a technical story on jewelry or watchmaking. Pictures increase publication chances. Pays 1¢ a published word. Pays $2.50 per photo.

PACIFIC GOLDSMITH, 41 Sutter St., San Francisco CA 94104. (415)986-4323. Editor: Robert B. Frier. For jewelers and watchmakers. Monthly magazine; 80-90 pages. Estab. 1903. Circ. 6,000. Not copyrighted. Pays on acceptance. Sample copy $1. No photocopied or simultaneous submissions. Submit seasonal (merchandising) material 3 to 4 months in advance. Reports in 1 week. SASE.
Nonfiction and Photos: "Our main interest is in how western jewelers can do a better selling job. We use how-to-do-it merchandising articles, showing dealers how to sell more jewelry store items to more people, at a greater profit. Seasonal merchandising articles are always welcome, if acceptable." Buys 12 mss/year. Query or submit complete ms. Length: 1,500 to 2,000 words. Pays 2¢/word. Pays $5 for b&w photos used with mss; 3x5 minimum. Captions required.

SOUTHERN JEWELER, 75 Third St., N.W., Atlanta GA 30308. (404)881-6442. Editor: Charles

Fram. For southern retail jewelers and watchmakers. Monthly. Circ. 4,400. Not copyrighted. Pays on publication. Submit seasonal material 2 months in advance. SASE.
Nonfiction: Articles relating to southern retail jewelers regarding advertising, management, and merchandising. Buys spot news about southern jewelers and coverage of successful business operations. Prefers *not* to see material concerning jewelers outside the 14 southern states. Length: open. Pays 1¢ per word. $1/clipping.
Photos: Buys b&w glossies. Pays $4.

Journalism

Because many writers are familiar with the journals of the writing profession and might want to submit to them, those that do not pay for contributions are identified in this list. Writers wishing to contribute material to these publications should write the editors for their requirements or query before submitting work.

THE CALIFORNIA PUBLISHER, 1127 11th St., Suite 1040, Sacramento CA 95814. (916)443-5991. Editor: Harvi Callaham. Does not pay.

CANADIAN AUTHOR & BOOKMAN, Canadian Authors' Association, Box 120, Niagara-on-the-Lake, Ontario, Canada L0S 1J0. (416)468-7391. Editor: Duncan S. Pollock. 75% freelance written. "For writers—all ages, all levels of experience." Quarterly magazine; 48 pages. Estab. 1921. Circ. 3,500. Pays on publication. Buys first North American serial rights. Phone queries OK. Submit seasonal/holiday material 1 year in advance of issue date. Simultaneous, photocopied and previously published submissions OK. SASE. Reports in 2 months. Free sample copy and writer's guidelines.
Nonfiction: How-to (on writing, selling; the specifics of the different genres—what they are and how to write them); informational (the writing scene—who's who and what's what); interview (on writers, mainly leading ones, but also those with a story that can help others write and sell more often); and personal opinion. Buys 40 mss/year. Query. Length: open. Pays 1¢/word and up.
Photos: "We're after an interesting looking magazine and graphics are a decided help." State availability of photos with query. Offers no additional payment for b&w photos accepted with ms. Buys one-time rights.
Poetry: "We use nothing but the best. Major poets publish with us—others need to be as good." Buys 50 poems/year. Pays $2-5.

THE CATHOLIC JOURNALIST, 119 N. Park Ave., Rockville Center NY 11570. "We are no longer buying freelance material."

COLLEGE PRESS REVIEW, Department of Journalism, Bradley University, Peoria IL 61625. (309)676-7611. Editor: John W. Windhauser. For members of the National Council of College Publications staffs, editors, and faculty advisers; staff members of student publications, journalism professors and others interested in the student communication media. Estab. 1956. Quarterly. Circ. 1,500. Acquires all rights, but may reassign rights to author after publication. No payment. Sample copy $1.50; free writer's guidelines. Photocopied submissions OK. No simultaneous submissions. Reports in 1-4 months. Query first or submit complete ms. SASE.
Nonfiction and Photos: Articles by, about, and of interest to college publication staffs, editors, and faculty advisers. Articles should focus on the editing, advising, and production of college newspapers, magazines, and yearbooks. "We like to use articles on research and opinion in the student communications media and related areas. We also like to use features on journalism techniques. The writer should write in a readable style. We will accept no manuscripts that read like term papers." Topical subjects of interest include use of new technology on campus publications; case studies of censorship problems at private schools; tips on purchasing new equipment; the adviser's role in revitalizing a dying publication. Length: 3,000 words maximum. B&w glossy photos used with ms. Captions required.

COLUMBIA JOURNALISM REVIEW, 700 Journalism Building, Columbia University, New York NY 10027. (212)280-3872. Editor: Kenneth M. Pierce. "We welcome queries concerning the media, as well as subjects covered by the media. All articles are assigned. We reject sloppy, incomplete reporting and lack of clear, carefully thought-out point of view (judgment and analysis)."

EDITOR & PUBLISHER, 575 Lexington Ave., New York NY 10022. (212)752-7050. Editor: Robert U. Brown. For newspaper publishers, editors, executives, employees and others in communications, marketing, advertising, etc. Weekly magazine; 60 pages. Estab. 1884. Circ. 26,000. Pays on publication. Sample copy 50¢. SASE.
Nonfiction: Department Editor: Jerome H. Walker, Jr. Uses newspaper business articles and news items; also newspaper personality features. Query.
Fillers: "Amusing typographical errors found in newspapers." Pays $2.

FEED/BACK, THE JOURNALISM REPORT AND REVIEW, Journalism Department, San Francisco State University, 1600 Holloway, San Francisco CA 94132. (415)469-1689. Editors: B.H. Liebes, Lynn Ludlow. Managing Editor: David M. Cole. 40-50% freelance written. For the working journalist, the journalism student, the journalism professor, and the journalistic layman. Magazine; 60 pages. Estab. 1974. Quarterly. Circ. 1,750. Not copyrighted. Pays in subscriptions and copies. Will send free sample copy to writer. Will consider photocopied and simultaneous submissions. Reports on material accepted for publication in 1 month. Returns rejected material in 2 weeks. Query first. Enclose SASE.
Nonfiction and Photos: In-depth views of journalism in Northern California. Criticism of journalistic trends throughout the country, but with a local angle. Reviews of books concerning journalism. Informational, interview, profile, humor, historical, think pieces, expose, nostalgia, spot news, successful (or unsuccessful) business operations, new product, technical; all must be related to journalism. "Articles must focus on the news media and be of interest to professional journalists—they are our audience. We like articles that examine press performance—strengths and weaknessess; we also like personality articles on offbeat or little known editors and journalists who escape national attention." Rejects articles that are not documented, or those in which the subject matter is not pertinent or those which show personal prejudice not supported by evidence. Length: 1,000 to 10,000 words. B&w glossies (8x10 or 11x14) used with or without mss. Pays in subscriptions and/or copies, tearsheets for all material.

FOLIO: The Magazine for Magazine Management, 125 Elm St., Box 697, New Canaan CT 06840. (203)972-0761. Editor: Charles I. Tannen. Managing Editor: James McNally. 5-10% freelance written. Emphasizes magazine management. Monthly magazine. Estab. June 1972. Circ. 7,300. Pays on publication. Buys all rights. Photocopied and previously published submissions OK. SASE. Reports in 3 weeks. Free sample copy.
Nonfiction: How-to (any aspect of magazine publishing); personal opinion; and technical articles. Buys 1-2 mss/issue. Query. Length: 1,500-3,000 words. Pays $100 minimum.

THE JOURNALISM EDUCATOR, Department of Journalism, University of Wyoming, Laramie WY 82071. (307)766-3122. Editor: William Roepke. For journalism professors, administrators, and a growing number of news executives in the U.S. and Canada. Published by the Association for Education in Journalism. Founded by the American Society of Journalism Administrators. Quarterly. Enclose SASE.
Nonfiction: "We do accept some unsolicited manuscripts dealing with our publication's specialized area — problems of administration and teaching in journalism education. Because we receive more articles than we can use from persons working in this field, we do not need to encourage freelance materials, however. A writer, generally, would have to be in journalism/communications teaching or in some media work to have the background to write convincingly about the subjects this publication is interested in. The writer also should become familiar with the content of recent issues of this publication." Maximum length: 2,500 words. Does not pay.

JOURNALISM QUARTERLY, School of Journalism, Ohio University, Athens OH 45701. (614)594-6710. Editor: Guido H. Stempel, III. 100% freelance written. For members of Association for Education in Journalism; also, other academicians and journalism practitioners. Estab. 1923. Quarterly. Usually acquires all rights. Circ. 4,000. Write for copy of guidelines for writers. Will consider photocopied submissions. Submit only complete ms "in triplicate." Reports in 4 to 6 months. Enclose SASE for return of submissions.
Nonfiction: Research in mass communication. Length: 4,000 words maximum. No payment.

MATRIX, Women in Communications, Inc., Box 9561, Austin TX 78766. (512)345-8922. Editor-in-Chief: Ernestine Wheelock. 95% freelance written; "mostly by WICI members and usually without pay." Quarterly magazine; 32 pages. Estab. 1915. Circ. 8,400. Pays on acceptance. Buys all rights, but may reassign following publication. Photocopied and previously published submissions OK. SASE. Reports in 2 weeks. Sample copy $1.

Nonfiction: General interest (media, freedom of information, legislation related to communications); how-to (improve graphics, take better photos, write a better story, do investigative reporting, sell ideas, start a magazine or newspaper, improve journalism education, reach decision-making jobs, etc.); personal experience (self-improvement, steps to take to reach management-level jobs); profile (people of interest because of their work in communications); and technical (advancements in print or electronic media). Buys 4-6 mss/year. Query. Length: 1,000-4,000 words. Pays $25-150.
Photos: Offers no additional payment for photos accepted with ms. State availability of photos with query. Use b&w prints. Captions required. Buys one-time rights.

MEDICAL COMMUNICATIONS, 4404 Sherwood Rd., Philadelphia PA 19131. (215)877-1137. Editor: Edith Schwager. For medical libraries, members of the American Medical Writers Association, physicians, journal and magazine editors, medical illustrators and pharmaceutical advertising people. Quarterly, 24- to 32-page digest size magazine. Estab. 1971. Circ. over 2,000. Acquires first North American serial rights. Uses 6 to 8 freelance mss/issue. Payment in contributor's copies. Sample copy for $1.25. Will not consider photocopied or simultaneous submissions. Submit seasonal or special material 2 to 3 months in advance. Reports on material accepted for publication in 6 weeks. Returns rejected material in 4 weeks. Query first. SASE.
Nonfiction and Photos: Articles relating to any aspect of medical communications including inter- and intra-personal writing. May be either philosophic or how-to with the proviso that it must tell the medical communicator something that will enrich his professional goals and achievements. "We are more of a journal than a magazine, but like to take a less formal approach in the hopes of improving an article's readability across the broad range of AMWA membership." Uses fairly serious, straightforward style. Humor accepted, but rarely. Footnotes may be required. Does not want to see anything on "how doctors can't communicate with their patients. We know this, and improving the situation is a major purpose of our organization." Length: 1,500 to 3,000 words. Charts and photos are used with mss, if needed. Payment in copies.

MILITARY MEDIA REVIEW, Defense Informational School, Bldg. 400, Fort Benjamin Harrison IN 46216. (317)542-2173. Editor-in-Chief: Connie McKean. 100% freelance written. For military and Civil Service employees of the Department of Defense and all military branch services in the fields of information/public affairs, print, broadcast, and photojournalism. Quarterly magazine; 32 pages. Estab. 1972. Circ. 15,000. Pays in copies on publication. Not copyrighted. Phone queries OK. Submit seasonal/holiday material 5 months in advance of issue date. Simultaneous, photocopied and previously published submissions OK. Reports in 4 weeks. Free sample copy and writer's guidelines; mention *Writer's Market* in request.
Nonfiction: "Military Media Review prints how-to articles in the fields of military public affairs, print, broadcast, and photojournalism. A sample topic might be 'How to Run a Military Press Center,' or 'How to Design a Post Newspaper,' etc. Occasionally, we run an interview or profile of an outstanding figure in our field. Personal opinion and experience features must be informative. They must relate information our readers will find useful in the field. Photo features and technical articles also must relate to the field." Query or submit complete ms. Length: 1,000-4,000 words.
Photos: State availability of photos with query or submit with ms. Uses 8x10 b&w glossy prints. Model release required.

MORE, A Critical Review of the Nation's Media, 40 W. 57th St., New York NY 10019. (212)757-3040. Editor: Robert Friedman. For "both men and women active in media, and readers and viewers interested in how media operates." Monthly. Circ. 20,000. Rights purchased vary with author and material. Usually buys all rights, but will reassign them to author after publication. Pays on publication. Sample copy $1.25. Reports promptly. SASE.
Nonfiction: Publishes "critical evaluations of the media—print and electronic, overground and underground. Heavy emphasis on solid reporting and good writing. Length: 500-5,000 words. Pays 12¢/word.

THE PEN WOMAN MAGAZINE, 1300 17th St., N.W., Washington DC 20036. Editor: Wilma W. Burton. For women who are professional writers, artists, composers. Publication of National League of American Pen Women. Magazine; 32-36 pages. Estab. 1920. Published 9 times/year, October through June. Circ. 6,000. Rights purchased vary with author and material. Pays on publication. Sample copy for SASE. Will "sometimes" consider photocopied submissions. No simultaneous submissions. Submit seasonal material 3 to 4 months in advance. Reports in 6 weeks. SASE.

Nonfiction: "We are overstocked from our own members. Only on occasion do we accept freelance material which must be of unusual appeal in both information and inspiration to our readers." Mss (slanted toward the professional writer, composer and artist) should be 300 to 1,500 words.
Fiction: Department Editor: Rosemary Stephens. "Usually purchase or use reprints from recognized magazines; use some original materials."
Poetry: Department Editor: Anne Marx. Uses traditional forms, blank verse, experimental forms, free verse, light verse and haiku. "We encourage shorter poems under 36 lines."

PHILATELIC JOURNALIST, Box 150, Clinton Corners NY 12514. (914)266-3150. Editor: Gustav Detjen, Jr. For "journalists, writers, columnists in the field of stamp collecting." Estab. 1971. Bimonthly. Circ. 1,000. Not copyrighted. Pays on publication. Free sample copy. Will consider photocopied submissions. Submit seasonal material 2 months in advance. Reports in 2 weeks. Query first. SASE.
Nonfiction and Photos: "Articles concerned with the problems of the philatelic journalist, how to publicize and promote stamp collecting, how to improve relations between philatelic writers and publishers and postal administrations. Philatelic journalists, many of them amateurs, are very much interested in receiving greater recognition as journalists. Any criticism should be coupled with suggestions for improvement." Buys profiles and personal opinion articles. Length: 250 to 500 words. Pays $15 to $30. Photos purchased with ms; captions required.

PNPA PRESS, 2717 N. Front St., Harrisburg PA 17110. (717)234-4067. Editor: Ruth E. Kuhn. No payment.

THE QUILL, Magazine for Journalists, 35 E. Wacker Dr., Chicago IL 60601. Editor: Charles Long. Associate Editor: Halina J. Czerniejewski. 50% freelance written. For newspaper reporters, editors and photographers; television newsmen and women; magazine journalists; freelance writers; journalism educators and students of journalism. Monthly magazine; 36 pages. Estab. 1912. Circ. 34,000. Pays on publication. Buys all rights. Submit seasonal/holiday material 2 months in advance of issue date. SASE. Reports in 3 weeks. Free sample copy and writer's guidelines; mention *Writer's Market* in request.
Nonfiction: Exposé (ethical questions related to the practice of journalism and articles dealing with First Amendment questions related to the press); general interest; and personal opinion (we have a guest opinion page entitled "Remark", of course, we welcome "letters to the editor"). Buys 25 mss/year. Query with clips of previously published work. Length: 200-2,500 words. Pays $25-250.

ST. LOUIS JOURNALISM REVIEW, 928 N. McKnight, St. Louis MO 63132. (314)991-1699. A critique of St. Louis media, print and broadcasting, by working journalists. Bimonthly. Buys all rights. SASE.
Nonfiction: "We buy material which analyzes, critically, local (St. Louis area) institutions, personalities, or trends. Payment starts at $20."

SCHOLASTIC EDITOR, 720 Washington Ave., S.E., Suite 205, University of Minnesota, Minneapolis MN 55414. Editor: Judy Schell. For high school and college journalism students, publications editors, staffs and advisers as well as mass media people. Published 6 times/year. Magazine; 32 pages. Estab. 1921. Circ. 3,000. Buys all rights, but will reassign rights to author after publication. Pays in contributor's copies. Free sample copy. Photocopied submissions OK. Reports in 2-4 weeks. SASE.
Nonfiction and Photos: "How-to articles on all phases of publication work, photography, classroom TV and the general field of communications. How to save money setting up a darkroom, make your yearbook layouts exciting with press-on lettering, etc. Style should avoid using first person. Looking for articles that have a lively, exciting approach. Especially interested in articles that suggest interesting illustration possibilities." Informational, how-to, personal experience, profile, photo feature, spot news, successful business operations, new product articles, merchandising techniques, technical; journalism and mass media topics book reviews. Uses 30 mss/year. Query or submit complete ms. Length: 5-15 typed, double-spaced pages for articles. Regular columns are Reading Between the Lines (book reviews), and People, Products, Etc., and Publicity (news releases). Length: 2 pages, double-spaced, typed. 8x10 b&w glossies wanted, but will accept smaller. Captions optional. Have occasional use for mood photos.

WASHINGTON JOURNALISM REVIEW, 3122 M St., NW Washington DC 20007. (202)338-

2495. Publisher: Roger Kranz. For "journalists, academics, trade associations, and mediaphiles." Monthly magazine; 64 pages. Estab. 1977. Circ. 10,000. Pays on publication. Buys all rights, but may reassign following publication. Phone queries OK. Simultaneous and photocopied submissions OK. SASE. Reports in 2 weeks. Sample copy $2.
Nonfiction: Exposé; historical; humor; informational;interview; nostalgia; personal experience; personal opinion; photo feature; profile and technical. Buys 10-15 mss/issue. Query. Length: 500-5,000 words. Pays 5-10¢/word.
Photos: State availability of photos with query. Pays $15-20 for 8½x11 b&w photos; $10-35 for color transparencies.

THE WRITER, 8 Arlington St., Boston MA 02116. Editor: A.S. Burack. Monthly. Pays on acceptance. Uses very little freelance material. Enclose SASE.
Nonfiction: Articles of instruction for writers. Length: about 2,000 words. Pays minimum $35.

WRITER'S DIGEST, 9933 Alliance Rd., Cincinnati OH 45242. (513)984-0717. Editor: John Brady. For writers. Estab. 1919. Circ. 140,000. Monthly magazine. Buys first magazine rights. Pays on acceptance. Photocopied submissions OK but "good quality, please." Submit seasonal/holiday material 8 months in advance of issue date. SASE. Reports in 3 weeks. Free sample copy.
Nonfiction: "Practical, instructional features on specific types of writing for the freelance market. In-depth market features on major magazine and book publishing houses; interviews with outstanding writers. Articles by working editors in special fields advising the freelancers on how to write and sell to the fields are always welcome. Discussions of specialized fields of writing, such as wire service reporting, comedy writing, script writing, new potential freelance markets, etc. Articles on how to sell and promote a book, or on new trends in publishing and how the writer can address them are needed. Regular columns cover poetry, nonfiction, fiction, and photojournalism. We also publish articles on subjects related to the business aspects of writing for publication. Our style is lively and anecdotal. We see—and reject—too many articles that *tell*, but do not *show*. Our motto here at camp: No generalizations without examples. We also prefer articles with *solid reportorial underpinning*. Our writers should treat how-to articles as they would feature assignments for a city or business magazine. They should interview other writers for their hints and stories, and dig in the library for material that will give the article perspective. The freelancer who *reports* as well as writes for us will stand a much better chance than the freelancer who merely draws from personal experience and holds forth on a topic. At the moment we're short on articles on writing techniques—writing transitions, plotting in fiction, characterization, organizing an article. We also need more material on writing books and new money making fields of endeavor for the writer. Profiles and Q&A's *must* be accompanied by candid and tight mug shots, taken against the background of the interview." Query first for in-depth features. Length: 500-3,000 words. Buys about 65 mss/year. Pays 10¢/word; more for outstanding pieces.
Photos: "Well-known writers, the writing life, for inside use with articles and cover use." Submit contact sheet first. Pays $20-50 for b&w only.
Fillers: Clippings, etc., about well-known writers. Will not be returned. Pays $2-5.
How To Break In: "We have several editorial departments that are fertile ground for a hard-working freelancer. The Writing Life uses brief, robust items that are offbeat and on-the-scene. Items are generally 100-500 words—the shorter the better. The reporting must be fresh, the writing polished. Light verse welcome, too. We pay $20-50 for articles; $10-20 for verse. We want items from writers who have a valuable hint to share in 500 words or less. We're more interested in pieces on researching and writing techniques than in pieces on how to convert old envelopes into files. We pay $25-50. Writing Life also features mini-profiles of writers—the famous, the infamous and the obscure. Must be lively and balanced; no valentines, please—and no brickbats. Pieces won't sell here without fresh and lively quotes from the subject—as well as tight and crisp shots that have a sense of place as well as of person. Package is usually a 500-word ms and one or two contrasting b&w photos. We pay $75. We're always looking for freelancers who can deliver responsible reporting and lively writing. A writer who can produce polished and balanced spots for our editorial departments stands a good chance of getting an assignment when she/he queries us later on a useful full-length feature. You might go to market for us. Is your specialty wine magazines, or Tasmanian religious journals? Let's see an article—1,500 words or less—on how to write for that market. We're interested in your material researching and *writing* techniques for a particular field. And—last and never least—*read the magazine*—give us fresh ideas, or new approaches to old problems facing the writer today. Our slant is simple: how the freelancer can turn out good work and make money. Any manuscript that does not satisfy that slant will be rejected—no matter how well-written it is. Your best bet is to sit

down with a year's backlog of *WD* and study it. What areas have we missed? What questions have we left unanswered? What new opportunities for the freelancer are we leaving untouched? Tell us that, and you'll have our full attention. Any maybe our money."

WRITER'S YEARBOOK, 9933 Alliance Rd., Cincinnati OH 45242. Editor: John Brady. For writers, writer/photographers and cartoonists. Estab. 1930. Annual. Buys first rights only. Buys about 20 mss/year. Pays on acceptance. Sample copy $2.50. "Writers should query in spring with ideas for the following year." Will consider *good-quality* photocopied submissions. SASE.
Nonfiction: "I want articles that reflect the current state of writing in America," says editor Brady. "Trends, inside information, money-saving and money-making ideas for the freelance writer. Material on writer's hardware—typewriters, cameras, recorders, etc.—and how they can be used to make writing easier or more lucrative. I'm also interested in the writer's spare time—what she/he does to retreat occasionally from the writing wars; where to refuel and replenish the writing spirit. I also want a big interview (or profile) or two, always with *good* pictures. Articles on writing techniques that are effective today are always welcome." Length: 750-4,500 words. Pays 10¢/word.
Photos: Usually purchased with manuscripts as part of package; b&w only; depending on use, pay is $20 to $50 per published photo.

WRITING, Sean Dorman Manuscript Society, 4 Union Pl., Fowey, Cornwall, U.K. PL23 1BY. Editor-in-Chief: Sean Dorman. For writers of all ages and education. Quarterly tabloid; 52 pages. Estab. 1959. Circ. 500. Pays on publication. All rights reserved to the author. Simultaneous and photocopied submissions and previously published work OK. Reports in 1 month. Sample copy $1.
Nonfiction: How-to and informational articles about writing in any form. Buys 4 mss/issue. Length: 300-350 words. Submit complete ms. Pays 2 pounds for double use in linked issues. ("The same articles appear in the spring and summer issues, and in the linked autumn and winter issues.")
Poetry: Traditional forms, free verse and light verse. Buys 4/issue. Submit poems. Pays 2 pounds for double use in a pair of linked issues.

Laundry and Dry Cleaning

Some journals in the Coin-Operated Machines category are also in the market for material on laundries and dry cleaning establishments.

AMERICAN DRYCLEANER, 500 N. Dearborn St., Chicago IL 60610. (312)337-7700. Editor: Paul T. Glaman. For professional drycleaners. Monthly. Circ. 30,000. Buys all rights. Pays on publication. Will send free sample copy on request. Reports "promptly." Enclose SASE.
Nonfiction and Photos: Articles on merchandising, diversification, sales programs, personnel management, consumer relations, cost cutting, workflow effectiveness, drycleaning methods. "Articles should help the drycleaner build his business with the most efficient utilization of time, money and effort, inform the drycleaner about current developments within and outside the industry which may affect him and his business, introduce the drycleaner to new concepts and applications which may be of use to him, teach the drycleaner the proper methods of his trade. Tight, crisp writing on significant topics imperative. Eliminate everything that has no direct relationship to the article's theme. Select details which add depth and color to the story. Direct quotes are indispensable." Pays 3¢ to 5¢ per word. Photos purchased with mss; quality 8x10 b&w glossies. Photos should help tell story. No model releases required. Pays $5.

AMERICAN LAUNDRY DIGEST, American Trade Magazines, Inc., 500 N. Dearborn St., Chicago IL 60610. (312)337-7700. Editor-in-Chief: Ben Russell. 13-26% freelance written. For a professional laundering, linen supply, uniform rental audience. Monthly magazine; 52 pages. Estab. 1936. Circ. 16,000. Pays 2 weeks prior to publication. Buys all rights. Phone queries OK. Photocopied submissions OK. SASE. Reports in 2 weeks. Free sample copy and writer's guidelines.
Nonfiction: How-to articles about how laundrymen have cut costs, increased production, improved safety, gained sales, etc. "Interviews with laundrymen about how they run a successful plant would be welcome." Query. Length: 300-3,000 words. Pays 4¢/word.
Photos: B&w glossies (8x10 preferred; 5x7 acceptable) purchased with mss. Send contact sheet. Pays $5.

INDUSTRIAL LAUNDERER, 1730 M St., N.W., Suite 613, Washington DC 20036. (202)296-6744. Editor: James W. Roberts. 15-20% freelance written. For decisionmakers in the industrial laundry industry. Publication of the Institute of Industrial Launderers, Inc. Magazine; 124 pages. Estab. 1949. Monthly. Circ. over 3,000. Buys all rights, but will reassign rights (with some exceptions) to author after publication. Buys 15 to 20 mss a year. Pays on publication. Will send free sample copy to writer on request. Write for copy of guidelines for writers. No photocopied or simultaneous submissions. Reports in 1 week. Query first. Enclose SASE.
Nonfiction and Photos: General interest pieces for the industrial laundry industry; labor news, news from Washington; book reviews on publications of interest to people in this industry. Technical advancements and "people" stories. Informational, personal experience, interview, profile, historical, successful business operations, merchandising techniques. Length: no less than 750 words. Payment negotiable. No additional payment for 8x10 b&w glossies used with ms. Pays minimum of $5 for those purchased on assignment. Captions required.

WESTERN CLEANER AND LAUNDERER, Box 722, La Canada CA 91011. (213)247-8595. Editor: Monida Urquhart. 15% freelance written. For owner/managers and key employees of drycleaning, laundry, rug cleaning, drapery, and cleaning plants. Monthly tabloid; 28 pages. Estab. 1959. Circ. 11,000. Pays on publication. Buys all rights, but may reassign following publication. Phone queries OK. Submit seasonal/holiday material 2 months in advance of issue date. SASE. Reports in 4 weeks. Free sample copy.
Nonfiction: General interest (successful operation of drycleaning or laundry business); how-to (operate a cleaning/laundry plant); new product; and profile. Buys 10-12 mss/year. Query. Length: 400-1,200 words. Pays 5¢/word.
Photos: State availability of photos with query. Pays $4 each for 4x5 b&w glossy prints for number used with story. Captions and model release required. Buys all rights, but may reassign following publication.

Law

BARRISTER, American Bar Association Press, 1155 E. 60th St., Chicago IL 60637. (312)947-4072. Managing Editor: Elizabeth H. Cameron. For young lawyers who are members of the American Bar Association, concerned about practice of law, improvement of the profession and service to the public. Quarterly magazine; 64 pages. Estab. 1974. Circ. 115,000. Pays on acceptance. Buys all rights, but may reassign following publication; or first serial rights or second serial (reprint) rights, or simultaneous rights. Photocopied submissions OK. SASE. Reports in 4-6 weeks. Free sample copy.
Nonfiction: "As a magazine of ideas and opinion, we seek material that will help readers in their inter-related roles of attorney and citizen. Major themes in legal and social affairs. Reference to legal questions in a topic may be helpful; we examine the inter-relationship between law and society. Expository or advocacy articles welcome; position should be defended clearly in good, crisp, journalistic prose." Length: 1,000-3,000 words. Query first, Pays $150-400.
Photos: Donna Tashjian, department editor. B&w (8x10) glossies and 35mm color transparencies purchased without accompanying ms. Pays $35 minimum for b&w; $50 minimum for color.

JURIS DOCTOR MAGAZINE FOR THE NEW LAWYER, 730 Third Ave., New York NY 10017. Editor: Zachary Sklar. For "young lawyers, ages 25 to 37." Published 11 times/year. Circ. 160,000. Buys first rights. Pays on publication. Free sample copy. Reports in 5 weeks. SASE.
Nonfiction: Wants articles on the legal profession, as well as travel and leisure items. Writer should show a knowledge of law, but should not be overly technical. Willing to research. "Most articles are muckraking pieces about the profession—the organized bar, law schools, new areas of legal practice. We also run book reviews." Interested in how-to, interviews, and profiles. Buys 30 mss/year. Query. Length: 1,000-3,500 words. Book reviews, 900 words. Payment is 10¢/word. $50 for reviews.
Photos: B&w glossies purchased with mss and with captions only. Payment is $25.

LAWYER'S NEWSLETTER, 1180 S. Beverly Dr., Los Angeles CA 90035. Editor: Stephan Z. Katzan. 40% freelance written. For attorneys. Bimonthly. Buys all rights. Pays on publication. Will send a sample copy to a writer on request. Reports in 2 weeks. Enclose SASE.
Nonfiction: "Our publication's main purpose is to increase the efficiency of attorneys and of law office operations. We are interested in suggestions and ideas for improvement of office operations as well as articles on legal economics." Length: 2,000 words maximum. Pays $100 per article.

LEGAL ECONOMICS, 1155 E. 60th St., Chicago IL 60637. Editor: Robert P. Wilkins. For the practicing lawyer. Quarterly magazine; 56-68 pages. Estab. 1975. Circ. 18,000. Rights purchased vary with author and material. Usually buys all rights, but may reassign rights to author after publication for special purposes. Pays on publication. Free sample copy and writer's guidelines. Returns rejected material in 90 days, if requested. Query first. SASE.
Nonfiction and Photos: "We assist the practicing lawyer in operating and managing his office in an efficient and economical manner by providing relevant articles and editorial matter written in a readable and informative style. Editorial content is intended to aid the lawyer by informing him of management methods which will allow him to provide legal services to his clients in a prompt and efficient manner at reasonable cost." Pays $50-100. Pays $10-20 for b&w photos purchased with mss; $15-25 for color.

STUDENT LAWYER, American Bar Association, 1155 E. 60th St., Chicago IL 60637. (312)947-4077. Editor: David Martin. Associate Editor: Michael VerMeulen. Monthly (during school year) magazine; 56 pages. Estab. 1952. Circ. 40,000. Pays on publication. Buys all rights, but may reassign following publication. Submit seasonal/holiday material 2 months in advance of issue date. Photocopied submissions OK. SASE. Reports in 2 weeks. Sample copy $1; free writer's guidelines.
Nonfiction: Exposé (government, law, education and business); profiles (prominent persons in law-related fields); personal opinion (on matters of current legal interest); essays (on legal-affairs); interviews and photo features. Buys 8 mss/issue. Query. Length: 3,000-6,000 words. Pays $100-300.
Photos: State availability of photos with query. Pays $35-75 for 8x10 b&w prints; $50-150 for color. Model release required.
Columns/Departments: Briefly (short stories on unusual and interesting developments in the law); Legal Aids (highlighting specific products of interest to law students and attorneys); Review (short essay on literature and the arts, popular culture, assignment only); and Status (news stories on legal education, programs, and personalities). Buys 4-8 mss/issue. Length: 50-1,500 words. Pays $25-100.
Fiction: "We buy fiction when it is very good and deals with the issues of law in the contemporary world. No mystery stories accepted." Buys ms only when interested. Pays $50-200.
How To Break In: "Student Lawyer actively seeks good, new writers. Legal training definitely not essential; writing talent is. The writer should not think we are a law review; we fall somewhere between The Nation, Newsweek and Rolling Stone. Past articles concerned gay rights, prison reform, the media, affirmative action and architecture."

TODAY'S POLICEMAN, Box 594, Kansas City MO 64141. (816)474-3495. Editor: Donald Mack. For persons employed in and interested in police services. Quarterly magazine. Estab. 1960. Circ. 10,000. Copyrighted. Pays on acceptance or publication. Sample copy $2. Photocopied and simultaneous submissions OK. Reports in 1 month. SASE.
Nonfiction, Photos and Fillers: Buys informational, interview, humor, nostalgia, new product, merchandising techniques, technical articles (length: 500 to 1,500 words. Pays $15 to $40); historical (length: 500 to 2,500 words. Pays $20 to $40); and expose (length: 500 words. Pays $15 to $40). Approach should be expository with research. Interested in psychological and philosophical aspects of current problems. Would like to see humorous articles with photos. Buys 6 mss/year. Query. Occasionally buys material for 2 regional editions, covering the eastern U.S. and western U.S. Writers may also submit suggestions for new columns or departments. Photos purchased with accompanying ms with no additional payment. Also purchased without ms. Pay: $10 for b&w glossy. Captions required. Fillers: puzzles, jokes, gags, short humor. Pays $5 to $25.

Leather Goods

LUGGAGE AND LEATHERGOODS NEWS, G.P. Page Publications, Ltd., 380 Wellington St., W., Toronto, Ontario, Canada M5V 1E3. (416)366-4608. Editor: Henry Wittenburg. 10-15% freelance written. "The majority of our readers are retailers of luggage, leathergoods, handbags, and related products. The remainder are those who supply the luggage retailers with product. 99.9% of all that I buy is of Canadian content." Published 9 times/year. Tabloid; 16 pages. Circ. 4,700. Pays on publication. Buys all rights, but may reassign following publication. Phone queries OK. Submit seasonal/holiday material 3-4 months in advance of issue date. SASE.

Reports in 3 weeks. Free sample copy; mention *Writer's Market* in request.
Nonfiction: How-to (more effectively sell luggage and leathergoods; articles must be based on the experiences of a retailer); interview (with Canadian industry leaders only); and photo features (open to b&w only). Buys up to 9 mss/year. Query. Length: 500-1,200 words Pays 5¢/word.
Photos: "There's no point in buying an article from a freelancer in another country if I have to go (or send someone) to take photos. Works of art are not necessary—just *good* b&w photos." State availability of photos with query. Pays $5 for 5x7 or 8x10 b&w prints.

Library Science

AMERICAN LIBRARIES, 50 E. Huron St., Chicago IL 60611. (312)944-6780. Editor: Arthur Plotnik. For librarians. "A highly literate audience. They are for the most part practicing professionals with high public contact and involvement interest." 11 times a year. Circ. 36,000. Buys first North American serial rights. Will consider photocopied submissions if not being considered elsewhere at time of submission. Submit seasonal material 9 months in advance. Reports within 12 weeks. SASE.
Nonfiction, Photos, and Fillers: "Material reflecting the special and current interests of the library profession. Non-librarians should browse recent journals in the field, available on request in medium-sized and large libraries everywhere. Topic and/or approach must be fresh, vital, or highly entertaining. Stereotyped stories about old maids, overdue books, fines, etc., are unacceptable. Our first concern is with the American Library Association's activities, and how they relate to the 36,000 reader/members. Tough for an outsider to write on this topic, but not to supplement it with short, offbeat library stories and features. Will look at all good b&w, natural light photos of library situations, and at color transparencies for possible cover use." Pays $5 to $150 for fillers and articles. Pays $5 to $50 for photos.
How To Break In: "With a sparkling, 300-word report on a true, offbeat library event, or with an exciting photo and caption."

CATHOLIC LIBRARY WORLD, 461 W. Lancaster Ave., Haverford PA 19041. (215)649-5251. Editor-in-Chief: John T. Corrigan, CFX. 75% freelance written. Emphasizes libriarianship for librarians and educators in academic, school, public, special, seminaries, medical and health, archives/libraries. Monthly magazine; 48 pages. Estab. 1929. Circ. 3,500. Not copyrighted. No payment. Phone queries OK. Submit seasonal or holiday material 3 months in advance. SASE. Reports in 2 weeks. Free sample copy and writer's guidelines.
Nonfiction: "We cover a broad range of library services on a thematic approach (e.g., library services to the poor) and use materials of interest to librarians and educators; research bibliographies and comments on the library profession."

EMERGENCY LIBRARIAN, 46 Gormley Ave., Toronto, Ontario, Canada M4V 1Z1. Co-Editor: Sherrill Cheda. Bimonthly magazine; 24 pages. Estab. October 1973. Circ. 1,300. Pays on publication. Not copyrighted. Photocopied submissions OK. SASE. Reports in 4-6 weeks. Free sample copy.
Nonfiction: Exposeé (of library practice); how-to (do it better in libraries); interview (with person in alternative librarianship); and profile. Also annotated bibliographies. Buys 3 mss/issue. Query. Length: 1,000-3,500 words. Pays $25.
Columns/Departments: Book Reviews (of small press or Canadian or feminist and socialist books). Query. Length: 250-500 words. Payment consists of book reviewed.

THE HORN BOOK MAGAZINE, 31 St. James Ave., Park Square Bldg. Boston MA 02116. (617)482-5198. Editor-in-Chief: Ethel L. Heins. Assistant Editor: Karen M. Klockner. 50% freelance written. For librarians, teachers, parents, authors, illustrators, and publishers. Bimonthly magazine; 100 pages. Estab. 1924. Circ. 24,500. Pays on publication. Buys all rights. Phone queries OK. Submit seasonal/holiday material 4 months in advance of issue date. Photocopied submissions OK. SASE. Free sample copy and writer's guidelines.
Nonfiction: "All related to children's books." General interest; historical; humor; inspirational; personal experience; personal opinion; profile; and travel. Query. Pays $20/page.
Poetry: Free verse, haiku, and traditional. Buys 1-6 mss/year. Pays $20.

LIBRARY JOURNAL, 1180 Avenue of the Americas, New York NY 10036. Editor: John N. Berry III. For librarians (academic, public, special, school). 115-page (8½x11) magazine pub-

lished every 2 weeks. Estab. 1876. Circ. 40,000. Buys all rights. Buys 50 to 100 mss a year (mostly from professionals in the field). Payment on publication. Submit complete ms. Enclose SASE.
Nonfiction and Photos: "*Library Journal* is a professional magazine for librarians. Freelancers are most often rejected because they submit one of the following types of article: 1) 'A wonderful, warm, concerned, loving librarian who started me on the road to good reading and success'; 'How I became rich, famous, and successful by using my public library'; 'Libraries are the most wonderful and important institutions in our society, because they have all of the knowledge of mankind — praise them.' We need material of greater sophistication, dealing with issues related to the transfer of information, access to it, or related phenomena. (Current hot ones are copyright, censorship, the decline in funding for public institutions, the local politics of libraries, trusteeship, etc.)" Professional articles on criticism, censorship, professional concerns, library activities, historical articles and spot news. Outlook should be from librarian's point of view. Length: 1,500 to 2,000 words. Pays $50 to $250. Payment for b&w glossy photos purchased without accompanying mss is $25. Must be at least 5x7. Captions required.

MEDIA: LIBRARY SERVICES JOURNAL, 127 Ninth Ave., N., Nashville TN 37234. (615)251-2752. Editor: Floyd B. Simpson. For adult leaders in church organizations and people interested in library work (especially church library work). Quarterly magazine; 50 pages. Estab. 1970. Circ. 17,500. Pays on publication. Buys all rights. Phone queries OK. Submit seasonal/holiday material 14 months in advance. Previously published submissions OK. SASE. Reports in 1 month. Free sample copy and writer's guidelines.
Nonfiction: "Primarly interested in articles that relate to the development of church libraries in providing media and services to support the total program of a church and in meeting individual needs. We publish personal experience accounts of services provided, promotional ideas, exciting things that have happened as a result of implementing an idea or service; human interest stories that are library related; media education (teaching and learning with a media mix). Articles should be practical for church library staffs and for teachers and other leaders of the church." Buys 15-20 mss/issue. Query first. Pays 3¢/word.

MICROFORM REVIEW, 520 Riverside Ave., Box 405, Saugatuck Station, Westport CT 06880. (203)226-6967. Editor-in-Chief: Allen B. Veaner. For librarians and educators at the college and university level. Bimonthly magazine; 64 pages. Estab. 1972. Circ. 1,800. Pays on publication. May buy all rights. Phone queries OK. Submit seasonal material 3 months in advance. Simultaneous, photocopied, and previously published submissions OK. SASE. Reports in 3 weeks. Free sample copy and writer's guidelines.
Nonfiction: How-to articles (technical, dealing with micrographic equipment; innovative use of microform in libraries; new product articles (in photographic field); photo features and technical articles; profiles and interviews. "We are interested in articles dealing with micropublication libraries and research using micropublications. Also problems libraries have using microforms, and solutions to those problems." Buys 1 ms per issue. Length: 1,000-3,000 words. Query first. Pays $10-50.
Photos: B&w glossies purchased with mss. Captions required. Query first. Pays $5-10.

THE PAMPHLETEER MONTHLY, 55 E. 86 St., New York NY 10028. (212)722-7272. Editor: William Frederick. 20% freelance written. A review source for paper-covered materials; from single-page leaflets to booklets and pamphlets/books up to and beyond 160 pages. For the library trade; buying guide for public school, college, university and special libraries; book review source. Magazine; 48 (6x9) pages. Estab. 1940. Monthly except July/August. Circ. 6,000. Buys all rights. Pays on assignment. Query. Send in a resume and clips of previous reviews or published writing.
Nonfiction: Book reviews on assignment only. Length: 50 words, average. Pays $1. (Usually, 50 to 100 assigned reviews at a time.)

SCHOOL LIBRARY JOURNAL, 1180 Avenue of the Americas, New York NY 10036. Editor: Lillian N. Gerhardt. For librarians in schools and public libraries. Monthly (September-May) magazine; 88 pages. Estab. 1954. Circ. 45,000. Buys all rights. Pays on publication. Reports in 3 months. SASE.
Nonfiction: Articles on library services, local censorship problems, how-to articles on programs that use books or films. Informational, personal experience, interview, expose, successful business operations. "Interested in history articles on the establishment/development of children's and young adult services in schools and public libraries." Buys 6 mss/year. Length: 2,500 to 3,000 words. Pays $100.

WILSON LIBRARY BULLETIN, 950 University Ave., Bronx NY 10452. (212)588-8400. Editor: William R. Eshelman; Associate Editor: Harriet E. Rosenfeld. For professional librarians and those interested in the book and library worlds. Monthly (September-June). Circ. 30,000. Buys North American serial rights only. Pays on publication. Sample copies may be seen on request in most libraries. "Ms must be original copy, double spaced; additional Xerox copy or carbon is appreciated. Deadlines are a minimum 2 months before publication." Reports in 8-12 weeks. SASE.
Nonfiction: Uses articles "of interest to librarians throughout the nation and around the world. Style must be lively, readable and sophisticated, with appeal to modern professionals; facts must be thoroughly researched. Subjects range from the political to the comic in the world of media and libraries, with an emphasis on the human as well as the technical aspects of any story. No condescension: no library stereotypes." Length: 3,000 to 6,000 words. Pays about $50 to $150, "depending on the substance of article and its importance to readers."
How To Break In: "With a first rate b&w photo and caption information on a library, library service, or librarian that departs completely from all stereotypes and the commonplace. Note: Libraries have changed! You'd better first discover what is now commonplace."

Lumber and Woodworking

B.C. LUMBERMAN MAGAZINE, 2000 W. 12th Ave., Vancouver, British Columbia, Canada, V65 2G2. (403)731-1171. Editor-in-Chief: Len Webster. Managing Editor: Brian Martin. 60% freelance written. Emphasizes forest industry of Canada and US Pacific Northwest. Monthly magazine; 75 pages. Estab. 1916. Circ. 8,500. Pays on acceptance. Buys all rights, but may reassign following publication. Phone queries OK. Submit seasonal/holiday material 2 months in advance of issue date. Reports in 2 weeks. Free sample copy; mention *Writer's Market* in request.
Nonfiction: How-to (technical articles on any aspect of the forest industry); general interest (anything of interest to persons in forest industies in Western Canada or US Pacific Northwest); interview (occasionally related to leading forestry personnel); and technical (forestry). Buys 8 mss/issue. Query with clips of previously published work. Length: 1,500-5,000 words. Pays 9¢/word.
Photos: State availability of photos with query. Pays $5-25 for b&w negatives and $50-80 for 8x10 glossy color prints. Captions required. Buys one-time rights.

CANADIAN FOREST INDUSTRIES, 1450 Don Mills Rd., Don Mills, Ont., M3B 2X7, Canada. Editor: Rich Letkeman. 25% freelance written. For forest companies, loggers, lumber-plywood-board manufacturers. Estab. 1882. Monthly. Circ. 12,000. Buys first North American serial rights. Pays on publication. Free sample copy. Reports in 1 month. Enclose SAE and International Reply Coupons.
Nonfiction: Uses "articles concerning industry topics, especially how-to articles that help businessmen in the forest industries. All articles should take the form of detailed reports of new methods, techniques and cost-cutting practices that are being successfully used anywhere in Canada, together with descriptions of new equipment that is improving efficiency and utilization of wood. It is very important that accurate descriptions of machinery (make, model, etc.) be always included and any details of costs, etc., in actual dollars and cents can make the difference between a below-average article and an exceptional one." Buys 20 mss/year. Query. Length: 1,200 to 2,500 words. Pays 12¢/word minimum, more with photos.
Photos: Buys photos with mss, sometimes with captions only. Should be 8x10, b&w glossies or negatives.

DIXIE LOGGER AND LUMBERMAN, 210 N. Main St., Wadley GA 30477. (912)252-5237. Publisher/Executive Editor: Jack Smith. 10% freelance written. For management personnel in the forest products industry. Monthly magazine; 44 pages. Estab. 1952. Circ. 18,000. Pays on acceptance. Buys all rights. Phone queries OK. SASE. Reports in 2 weeks. Sample copy $1.
Nonfiction: How-to (equipment maintenance); and photo feature (timber harvesting scenes). Buys "very few articles, as most freelancers don't understand our field." Query. Pays $50.
Photos: "A photo is worth a thousand words." Offers no additional payment for photos accepted with ms. Uses glossy b&w prints and 2¼x2½ color transparencies. Model release and captions required. Buys all rights.

LOGGING MANAGEMENT, Vance Publishing Corp., 300 W. Adams, Chicago IL 60606.

Editor-in-Chief: Monte Mace. Executive Editor: Duane Mason. 10-15% freelance written. "For management and operating executives involved in forest management, growing, felling, extraction, loading, shipping, and exporting of timber." Bimonthly magazine. Estab. 1977. Circ. 21,000. Pays on publication. Buys one-time rights. Submit seasonal/holiday material 3 months in advance of issue date. Simultaneous, photocopied (if exclusive in field); and previously published submissions OK. SASE. Reports in 2 weeks. Free sample copy and writer's guidelines.
Nonfiction: Exposé (government activities, upcoming regulations); how-to (increase production, efficiency, improve business operations); humor (if related to industry); interview (industry, government leaders, environmentalists); new product (a product offering truely new technology, not just a new capscrew); and photo feature (unusual or outstanding logging operations). Buys 10 mss/year. Query. Length: 500-1,500 words. Pays $75 minimum.
Photos: State availability of photos with query. Offers no additional payment for photos accepted with ms. Uses b&w prints and color transparencies. Captions required. Buys one-time rights.
Columns/Departments: Up Front (personalities, humor, behind the scenes); and Trends & News (news developments). Buys 6/year. Query. Length: 500-750 words. Pays $75.

NATIONAL HARDWOOD MAGAZINE, Box 34908, Memphis TN 38134. (901)372-8280. Editor: Floyd Keith. For "hardwood lumber mills and furniture manufacturers; their education varies, as do their interests." Estab. 1927. Monthly. Circ. 5,000. Buys all rights. Pays on acceptance. Free sample copy and writer's guidelines. Will not consider photocopied submissions or clippings. Reports in 3-4 weeks. SASE.
Nonfiction and Photos: "Furniture plant stories on those using large amounts of hardwood lumber; also, other plants that use hardwoods: casket firms, etc. We're the only publication dealing exclusively with hardwood lumber producers and users." Each plant story should include the following: Name of company and location, names of officers and plant manager, products manufactured, size of plant, number of employees, average number of hours per week the plant runs, sales force (do they have their own? Where's the sales office located? Where are the showrooms?). Complete descriptions of outstanding features or production ideas (how they work; what has been accomplished since their installation, etc.) Quantities, grades, thicknesses of lumber purchased annually; kinds of dimension used and for what purpose. Species of veneer purchased and for what purpose. Make of dry kilns, number, their capacity and moisture content of the lumber dried. Size of lumberyard and average inventory carried. History of the company and its growth; future plans. Dollar value of plant. Description of the flow of material through the plant from the back door to the front (lumberyard to the shipment of the finished product). In human interest articles, look for the following: An unusual request from a customer which the company fulfilled. The struggles the infant company went through to get established. The life of the man behind the company; how he got started in the business, etc. Has the company a unique record or reputation throughout the industry? What is it and how did it come about? 5x7 (or smaller) b&w glossies purchased with mss; captions required. Buys 12-24 mss/year. Query. Usually pays $150 for complete story and photographs.

THE NORTHERN LOGGER & TIMBER PROCESSOR, Box 69, Old Forge NY 13420. (315)369-3078. Editor: George D. Fowler. 10-20% freelance written. Monthly magazine; 48 pages. Estab. 1952. Circ. 7,300. Pays on publication. Buys all rights, but may reassign following publication. Phone queries OK. Submit seasonal/holiday material 3 months in advance of issue date. Previously published submissions OK. SASE. Reports in 4 weeks. Free sample copy; mention *Writer's Market* in request.
Nonfiction: General interest; historical; how-to; interview; new product; and technical. Buys 2-3 mss/year. Query. Length: 1,500-6,000 words. Pays $50-150.
Photos: State availability of photos with query. Pays $5-15 for 5x7 or 8x10 b&w glossy prints; $15-30 for 35mm or larger color transparencies. Captions required. Buys all rights, but may reassign following publication.

PLYWOOD AND PANEL MAGAZINE, Box 567B, Indianapolis IN 46206. (317)634-1100. Editor: Aimee Koch. For manufacturers and industrial fabricators of plywood, veneer and composite board. Monthly. Buys all rights. Pays on publication. SASE.
Nonfiction: "Factual and accurate articles concerning unusual techniques or aspects in the manufacturing or processing of veneer, plywood, particleboard, hardboard; detailing successful and/or unusual marketing techniques for wood panel products; or concerning important or unusual industrial end-uses of these materials in the production of consumer goods." Length: 1,000 words maximum. Pays maximum 5¢/word.
Photos: Of good quality and directly pertinent to editorial needs. Action photos; no catalog

shots. No in-plant photos of machinery not operating or not manned in natural fashion. Must be completely captioned; 5x7 b&w or larger preferred. Pays up to $5 per photo.

WOOD & WOOD PRODUCTS, 300 W. Adams St., Chicago IL 60606. Editor-in-Chief: Monte Mace. Managing Editor: Ellen Farnsworth. 10-15% freelance written. For owners and management of sawmills, plywood mills, particleboard mills, wood products such as laminated panels or millwork, and furniture. Monthly magazine; 84 pages. Circ. 30,000. Pays on publication. Buys all rights unless otherwise specified. Phone queries OK. Submit seasonal/holiday material 3 months in advance of issue date. Simultaneous, photocopied and previously published submissions OK. SASE. Reports in 2 weeks. Free sample copy and writer's guidelines.
Nonfiction: Exposé (Govt. upcoming regulations); how-to (increase production, efficiency, and profits); humor (if related to industry in some way); interview (industrial and government leaders); new product (one offering truly new technology, not just a new cap screw); photo feature (how-to, plant story); and technical. No articles on hobbyist wood working. Buys 15 mss/year. Query. Length: 500-1,500 words. Pays $75 minimum.
Photos: State availability of photos with query. Offers no additional payment for b&w contact sheets or prints; 35mm color transparencies. Captions required. Buys one-time rights.
Columns/Departments: Production Ideas (efficiency tips, how a company solved a problem). Buys 10/year. Query. Length: 500-750 words. Pays $75.

WOODWORKING & FURNITURE DIGEST, Hitchcock Bldg., Wheaton IL 60187. (312)665-1000. Editor: Richard D. Rea. For industrial manufacturers whose products employ wood as a basic raw material. Monthly. Buys all rights. Pays on publication. Will send free sample copy to serious freelancer on request. Query first. Reports in 10 days. Will sometimes hold ms for further evaluation up to 2 months, if it, at first, appears to have possibilities. Enclose SASE.
Nonfiction and Photos: "Articles on woodworking and furniture manufacturing with emphasis on management concepts, applications for primary raw materials (including plastics, if involved with wood), technology of remanufacturing methods and machines, and news of broad industry interest. Articles should focus on cost reduction, labor efficiency, product improvement, and profit. No handcraft, do-it-yourself or small custom shopwork. Present theme, or why reader can benefit, in first paragraph. Cover 'feeds and speeds' thoroughly to include operating data and engineering reasons why. Leave reader with something to do or think. Avoid mechanically handled case histories and plant tours which do not include management/engineering reasons." Photos, charts and diagrams which tell what cannot be told in words should be included. "We like a balance between technical information and action photos." Length: "no length limit, but stop before you run out of gas!" Pays $35 to $50 per published page. Photos purchased with mss. Good technical quality and perception of subject shown. No posed views. Prefers candid action or tight closeups. Full-color cover photo must be story-related.

Machinery and Metal Trade

ASSEMBLY ENGINEERING, Hitchcock Publishing Co., Wheaton IL 60187. Editor: Robert T. Kelly. 30% freelance written. For design and manufacturing engineers and production personnel concerned with assembly problems in manufacturing plants. Monthly. Buys first publication rights. Pays on publication. Sample copy will be sent on request. "Query first on leads or ideas. We report on ms decision as soon as review is completed and provide edited proofs for checking by author, prior to publication." SASE.
Nonfiction and Photos: Wants features on design, engineering and production practices for the assembly of manufactured products. Material should be submitted on "exclusive rights" basis and, preferably, should be written in the third person. Subject areas include selection, specification, and application of fasteners, mounting hardware, electrical connectors, wiring, hydraulic and pneumatic fittings, seals and gaskets, adhesives, joining methods (soldering, welding, brazing, etc.), and assembly equipment; specification of fits and tolerances; joint design; design and shop assembly standards; time and motion study (assembly line); quality control in assembly; layout and balancing of assembly lines; assembly tool and jig design; programming assembly line operations; working conditions, incentives, labor costs, and union relations as they relate to assembly line operators; hiring and training of assembly line personnel; supervisory practices for the assembly line. Also looking for news items on assembly-related subjects, and for unique or unusual "ideas" on assembly components, equipment, processes, practices and methods. Requires good quality photos or sketches, usually close-ups of specific details. Pays $30 minimum/published page.

AUTOMATIC MACHINING, 65 Broad St., Rochester NY 14614. (716)454-3763. Editor: Donald E. Wood. For metalworking technical management. Buys all rights. Query first. SASE.
Nonfiction: "This is not a market for the average freelancer. A personal knowledge of the trade is essential. Articles deal in depth with specific job operations on automatic screw machines, chucking machines, high production metal turning lathes and cold heading machines. Part prints, tooling layouts always required, plus written agreement of source to publish the material. Without personal background in operation of this type of equipment, freelancers are wasting time." Length: "no limit." Pays $20/printed page.

CANADIAN MACHINERY AND METALWORKING, 481 University Ave., Toronto Ont., Canada M5W 1A7. (416)595-1811. Editor: J. Davies. Monthly. Buys first Canadian rights. Pays on acceptance. Query first. Enclose SAE and International Reply Coupons.
Nonfiction: Technical and semitechnical articles dealing with metalworking operations in Canada and in the U.S., if of particular interest. Accuracy and service appeal to readers is a must. Pays minimum 7¢ a word.
Photos: Purchased with mss and with captions only. Pays $5 minimum for b&w features.

CUTTING TOOL ENGINEERING, P.O. Box 937, Wheaton IL 60187. (312)653-3210. Editor: N.D. O'Daniell. For metalworking industry executives and engineers concerned with the metal-cutting/metal-removal/abrasive engineering function in metal working. Bimonthly. Circ. 33,000. Buys all rights. Pays on publication. Will send free sample copy on request. Query required. SASE.
Nonfiction: "Intelligently written articles on specific applications of all types of metal cutting tools—mills, drills, reamers, etc. Articles must contain all information related to the operation, such as feeds and speeds, materials machined, etc. Should be tersely written, in-depth treatment. In the Annual Diamond/Superabrasive Directory, published in May/June, we cover the use of diamond/superabrasive cutting tools and diamond/superabrasive grinding wheels." Length: 1,000 to 2,500 words. Pays "$35 per published page, or about 5¢ a published word."
Photos: Purchased with mss. 8x10 b&w glossies preferred.

DETROIT INDUSTRIAL MARKET NEWS, 29501 Greenfield, Suite 214, Southfield MI 48076. Editor-in-Chief: Stan Stein. 65% freelance written. Readers are generally officers of metalworking plants in Metropolitan Detroit, Northern Ohio and other parts of Michigan. Monthly magazine; 28 pages. Estab. August 1976. Circ. 15,000. Pays on publication. Buys all rights, but may reassign following publication. Submit seasonal/holiday material 2 months in advance of issue date. Simultaneous, photocopied and previously published submissions OK. SASE. Free sample copy; mention *Writer's Market* in request.
Nonfiction: How-to (be a better businessman, heavy on financial tricks, very industry oriented, upper level management); general interest (stories could be success stories on particular corporation, small businesses or new product development); interview (wtih people idustrial-types are interested in, such as politicians invovled with industrial decisions or important tax matters); new product (would include revolutionary ideas that might affect the metalworking industry); photo feature; profile (of a corporate magnate); and technical (writing at the industries level might be effective, especially if it affects metal industry, but not heavy on automobilies). Buys 24 mss/year. Query. Length: 1,000-2,500 words. Pays $40-100.
Photos: State availability of photos with query. Pays $5-10 for 8x10 b&w glossy prints and $15-25 for color contact sheets. Captions preferred. Buys all rights, but may reassign following publication.
Columns/Departments: Buys 12 mss/year. Query. Length: 800-2,000 words. Pays $40-100. Open to suggestions for new columns/departments.

FOUNDRY MANAGEMENT AND TECHNOLOGY, Penton Plaza, Cleveland OH 44114. (216)696-7000. Editor: J. C. Miske. Monthly. Reports in 2 weeks. SASE.
Nonfiction and Photos: Uses articles describing operating practice in foundries written to interest companies producing metal castings. Length: maximum 3,000 words. Pays $35/printed page. Uses illustrative 8x10 photographs with article.

INDUSTRIAL FINISHING, Hitchcock Building, Wheaton IL 60187. (312)665-1000. Editorial Director: Richard Rea. Monthly. Circ. 44,500. Buys first rights. Buys 3-4 mss/year. Pays on acceptance. Free sample copy. Query. SASE.
Nonfiction and Photos: "Remember that we cover the oem (original equipment manufacturers, such as Ford or General Motors). We do not cover the after-market which is concerned with supplying equipment, materials, and services for repair or replacement." Wants "technical

articles on finishing operations for oem products." Style should be "direct and to the point." Photos purchased with mss. Pays $35-50/page.

INDUSTRIAL MACHINERY NEWS, 29516 Southfield Rd., C.S. #5002, Southfield MI 48037. (313)557-0100. Editor-in-Chief: Lucky D. Slate. Emphasizes metalworking for buyers, specifiers, manufacturing executives, engineers, management, plant managers, production managers, master mechanics, designers and machinery dealers. Monthly tabloid; 200 pages. Estab. 1953. Circ. 65,000. Pays on publication. Buys first North American serial rights. Phone queries OK. Submit seasonal/holiday material 3 months in advance. Simultaneous, photocopied, and previously published submissions OK. SASE. Reports in 3-5 weeks. Sample copy $1.50; free writer's guidelines.
Nonfiction and Photos: Articles on "metal removal, metal forming, assembly, finishing, inspection, application of machine tools, technology, measuring, gauging equipment, small cutting tools, tooling accessories, materials handling in metalworking plants, safety programs. We give our publication a newspaper feel — fast reading with lots of action or human interest photos." Buys how-to's. Pays $25 minimum. Length: open. Photos purchased with mss; captions required. Pays $5 minimum.
Fillers: Newsbreaks, puzzles, jokes, short humor. Pays $5 minimum.
How To Break In: "Stories on old machine tools — how they're holding up and how they're being used."

MODERN MACHINE SHOP, 600 Main St., Cincinnati OH 45202. Editor: Fred W. Vogel. Monthly. Pays 30 days following acceptance. Query first. Reports in 5 days. Enclose SASE.
Nonfiction: Uses articles dealing with all phases of metal manufacturing and machine shop work, with photos. Length: 1,500 to 2,000 words. Pays current market rate.

ORNAMENTAL METAL FABRICATOR, Suite 106, 443 E. Paces Ferry Rd., N.E., Atlanta GA 30305. Editor: Blanche Blackwell. For fabricators of ornamental metal who are interested in their businesses and families, their community and nation. Most are owners of small businesses employing an estimated average of 10 persons, usually including family members. Official publication of the National Ornamental and Miscellaneous Metals Association. Magazine published every 2 months; 24 pages. Estab. 1958. Circ. 5,500. Not copyrighted. Buys 6 mss a year. Payment on acceptance. Will send free sample copy to writer on request. Will not consider photocopied or simultaneous submissions. Submit seasonal material 2 months in advance. Reports immediately. Query first. Enclose SASE.
Nonfiction and Photos: "Our publication deals solely with fabrication of ornamental metal, a more creative and aesthetic aspect of the metals construction industry. Special emphasis on ornamental metal trade. How-to articles that will help our readers improve their businesses. Articles on use and history of ornamental metal; on better operation of the business; on technical aspects. News about the association and its individual members and about 6 regional chapters affiliated with the national association. Articles on the effects of steel shortage on ornamental metal fabricator and how a typical firm is handling the problem; the search for qualified employees; successful prepaint treatments and finishes." Prefers not to see "character study" articles. Length: 1,000 to 5,000 words. Pays 3¢ per word. B&w glossy photos purchased with accompanying mss. Pays $4. Color is not accepted.

POWER TRANSMISSION DESIGN, 614 Superior Ave., W., Cleveland OH 44113. (216)696-0300. Editor-in-Chief: Tom Hughes. Managing Editor: Leslie B. Strater. 10% freelance written. Emphasizes power transmission systems. Monthly magazine; 96 pages. Estab. 1959. Circ. 46,800. Pays on publication. Buys all rights. Simultaneous and previously published submissions OK. Reports in 3 weeks. Free sample copy and writer's guidelines.
Nonfiction: Articles on how-to design or imporve a power transmission system involving bearings, controls, motors, and drive components. Buys 5 mss/issue. Query. Pays $30/page.

PRODUCTION, Box 101, Bloomfield Hills MI 48013. (313)647-8400. Editor: Robert F. Huber. For "managers of manufacturing." Monthly. Circ. 80,000. Buys all rights. Buys "a few" mss a year. Pays on acceptance. Query first. SASE.
Nonfiction and Photos: "Trends, developments, and applications in manufacturing." Length: open. Pays $50 to $350. Photos purchased with mss; captions required.

PRODUCTS FINISHING, 600 Main St., Cincinnati OH 45202. Editor: Gerard H. Poll, Jr. Monthly. Buys all rights. Pays within 30 days after acceptance. Reports in 1 week. SASE.
Nonfiction: Uses "material devoted to the finishing of metal and plastic products. This includes

the cleaning, plating, polishing and painting of metal and plastic products of all kinds. Articles can be technical and must be practical. Technical articles should be on processes and methods. Particular attention given to articles describing novel approaches used by product finishers to control air and water pollution, and finishing techniques that reduce costs.'' Pays 8¢ minimum/word.
Photos: Wants photographs dealing with finishing methods or processes. Pays $10 minimum for each photo used.

STEEL '78, 1000 16th St., N.W., Washington DC 20036. Editor: Thomas D. Patrick. For ''opinion leaders; all ages and professions.'' Estab. 1933. Quarterly. Circ. 110,000. Buys all rights. Buys 4 to 6 mss a year. Payment on acceptance. Free sample copy. Query first. SASE.
Nonfiction and Photos: Articles on the environmental, energy, economics, international trade, new technology aspects of the steel industry. ''No product articles.'' Interviews, think pieces, technical. Length: 50 to 2,000 words. Pays $25 to $400. Photos purchased with or without accompanying ms or on assignment. Proofsheets and negatives. Color transparencies. Pays $15 to $100. Captions required. Freelance articles on assignment only.

33 METAL PRODUCING, McGraw-Hill Bldg., 1221 Avenue of the Americas, New York NY 10020. (212)997-3330. Editor: Joseph L. Mazel. For ''operating managers (from turn foreman on up), engineers, metallurgical and chemical specialists, and corporate officials in the steelmaking industry. Work areas for these readers range from blast furnace and coke ovens into and through the steel works and rolling mills. *33*'s readers also work in nonferrous industries.'' Monthly. Buys all rights. Pays on publication. Free sample copy. Query required. Reports in 3 weeks. SASE.
Nonfiction and Photos: Case histories of primary metals producing equipment in use, such as smelting, blast furnace, steelmaking, rolling. ''Broadly speaking, *33 Metal Producing* concentrates its editorial efforts in the areas of technique (what's being done and how it's being done), technology (new developments), and equipment (what's being used). Your article should include a detailed explanation (who, what, why, where, and how) and the significance (what it means to operating manager, engineer, or industry) of the techniques, technology or equipment being written about. In addition, your readers will want to know of the problems you experienced during the planning, developing, implementing, and operating phases. And, it would be especially beneficial to tell of the steps you took to solve the problems or roadblocks encountered. You should also include all cost data relating to implementation, operation, maintenance, etc., wherever possible. Benefits (cost savings; improved manpower utilization; reduced cycle time; increased quality; etc.) should be cited to gauge the effectiveness of the subject being discussed. The highlight of any article is its illustrative material. This can take the form of photographs, drawings, tables, charts, graphs, etc. Your type of illustration should support and reinforce the text material. It should not just be an added, unrelated item. Each element of illustrative material should be identified and contain a short description of exactly what is being presented. We reject material that lacks in-depth knowledge of the technology on operations involved in metal producing.'' Pays $35/published page. Minimum 5x7 b&w glossies purchased with mss.

THE WELDING DISTRIBUTOR, 614 Superior Ave., W., Cleveland OH 44113. Executive Editor: Charles Berka. For wholesale and retail distributors of welding equipment and safety supplies and their sales staffs. Bimonthly. Buys all rights. Pays on publication. SASE.
Nonfiction: Categories of editorial coverage are: management, process/product knowledge, profiles, selling and safety. Pays 2½¢ a word.

Maintenance and Safety

BUILDING SERVICES CONTRACTOR, NacNair-Donland Co., 101 W. 31st St., New York NY 10001. (212)279-4455. Editor-in-Chief: John Vollmuth. Managing Editor: Joe Thorsen. 10% freelance written. Monthly magazine; 60 pages. Estab. 1963. Circ. 6,000. Pays on publication. Buys all rights, but may reassign following publication. Phone queries OK. Submit seasonal/holiday material 2-3 months in advance of issue date. SASE. Reports in 2 weeks. Free sample copy and writer's guidelines.
Nonfiction: General interest; historical; interview; new product; personal experience; photo feature; profile; and technical. Submit complete ms. Length: 800-1,500. Pays $90-135.
Photos: Submit photo material with accompanying ms. No additional payment for b&w prints. Buys all rights, but may reassign following publication.

HEAVY DUTY EQUIPMENT MAINTENANCE, 7300 N. Cicero Ave., Lincolnwood IL 60646. (312)588-7300. Editor: Greg Sitek. 10% freelance written. Magazine; 76-110 pages. Estab. 1972. Monthly. Circ. 47,000. Rights purchased vary with author and material. Usually buys all rights, but may reassign rights to author after publication. Buys about 12 mss a year. Pays on publication. Free sample copy. No photocopied or simultaneous submissions. Reports in 4 weeks. Query first, with outline. Enclose SASE.
Nonfiction and Photos: "Our focus is on the effective management of equipment through proper selection, careful specification, correct application and efficient maintenance. We use job stories, technical articles, safety features, basics and shop notes. No product stories." Length: 2,000 to 5,000 words. Pays $25 per printed page minimum, without photos. Uses 35mm and 2¼ or larger color transparencies with mss. Pays $50 per printed page when photos are furnished by author.

MAINTENANCE SUPPLIES, 101 W. 31st St., New York NY 10001. (212)279-4455. Editor-in-Chief: John Vollmuth. Managing Editor: Ed Pasternack. 10% freelance written. For distributors of janitorial supplies. Monthly magazine; 100 pages. Estab. 1955. Circ. 11,000. Pays on publication. Buys all rights, but may reassign following publication. Phone queries OK. Submit seasonal/holiday material 2-3 months in advance of issue date. SASE. Reports in 2 weeks. Free sample copy.
Nonfiction: General interest; historical; interview; new product; personal experience; photo feature; profile; and technical. Buys 2 mss/issue. Submit complete ms. Length: 800-1,500 words. Pays $90-135.
Photos: Submit photo material with accompany ms. Offers no additional payment for b&w prints. Buys all rights, but may reassign following publication.
Columns/Departments: New Literature and New Products. Buys 1/issue. Submit complete ms. Length: 500-800 words. Pays $50. Open to suggestions for new columns/departments.

OCCUPATIONAL HAZARDS, 614 Superior Ave. W., Cleveland OH 44113. (216)696-0300. Editor: Peter J. Sheridan. "Distributed by function to middle management officials in industry who have the responsibility for accident prevention, occupational health, plant fire protection, and plant security programs. Job titles on our list include: safety directors, industrial hygienists, fire protection engineers, plant security managers, and medical directors." Monthly. Buys first rights in field. Pays on publication. Reports in 30 days. Enclose SASE.
Nonfiction: "Articles on industrial health, safety, security and fire protection. Specific facts and figures must be cited. No material on farm, home, or traffic safety. All material accepted subject to sharp editing to conform to publisher's distilled writing style. Illustrations preferred but not essential. Work is rejected when story is not targeted to professional concerns of our readers, but rather is addressed to the world at large." Length: 300 to 2,000 words. Pays 5¢/word minimum.
Photos: Accepts 4x5, 5x7 and 8x10 photos with mss. Pays $5.

PEST CONTROL MAGAZINE, 9800 Detroit Ave., Cleveland OH 44102. (216)651-5500. Editor: David Schneider. For professional pest control operators and sanitation workers. Monthly magazine; 44 pages. Estab. 1933. Circ. 14,000. Buys all rights. Buys about 6 mss/year. Pays on publication. Sample copy $1. Submit seasonal material 2 months in advance. Reports in 30 days. Query first or submit complete ms. Enclose SASE.
Nonfiction and Photos: Business tips, unique control situations, personal experience articles. Must have trade or business orientation. No general information type of articles desired. "Remember that we are oriented toward the owner-manager more than the serviceman. We might consider something on the view of an outsider to the pest control operator's job, or a report by an outsider after spending a day with a PCO on a route." Length: 4 double-spaced pages. Pays $25 minimum. Regular columns use material oriented to this profession. Length: 8 double-spaced pages. Pays 4¢ a word. No additional payment for photos used with mss. Pays $5 to $25 for 5x7 b&w glossies purchased without mss; $15 to $50 for 8x10 color or slide.

SDM: SECURITY DISTRIBUTING & MARKETING, 2639 S. La Cienega Blvd., Los Angeles CA 90034. Editor: Larry Oppen. For security products dealers, distributors, manufacturers; electrical and electronics engineering background; technically oriented. Buys 10 to 12 mss a year. Pays on publication. Free sample copy. Submit complete ms. Reports in 1 week. SASE.
Nonfiction and Photos: News items, case histories, how-to articles (how to advertise and promote, etc.). Interested in obtaining stories about dealers who installed burglar alarms that worked when needed. Can be obtained from news stories in papers and followed up with

personal interview with dealer.'' Length: 1,500-5,000 words. Pays 5¢/word. Photos purchased with accompanying ms.

Management and Supervision

This category includes trade journals for lower level business and industrial managers, including supervisors and office managers. Journals for business executives and owners are classified under Business Management. Those for industrial plant managers are listed in Industrial Management.

THE BUSINESS QUARTERLY, School of Business Administration, University of Western Ontario, London, Ontario N6A 3K7, Canada. (519)679-3222. Editor: Doreen Sanders. For persons in upper and middle management, university education, interested in continuing and updating their management education. Estab. 1933. Quarterly. Circ. 11,500. Buys all rights. Buys 35 mss/year. Pays on publication. Reports in 3 months. Query first with brief outline of article. Enclose SAE and International Reply Coupons.
Nonfiction: Articles pertaining to all aspects of management development. Must have depth. ''Think'' articles and those on successful business operations. Length: 2,000 to 5,000 words. Pays $100.

CONSTRUCTION FOREMAN'S & SUPERVISOR'S LETTER, Bureau of Business Practice, 24 Rope Ferry Rd., Waterford CT 06386. (203)442-4365. Emphasizes all aspects of construction supervision. Semimonthly newsletter; 4 pages. Estab. 1967. Buys all rights. Phone queries OK. Submit seasonal or holiday material at least 4 months in advance. SASE. Reports in 4-6 weeks. Free sample copy and writer's guidelines.
Nonfiction: Publishes solid interviews with construction managers or supervisors on how to improve a single aspect of the supervisor's job. Buys 100 a year. Length: 360-720 words. Pays 7-10¢/word.
Photos: B&w head and shoulders ''mug shots'' of person interviewed purchased with mss. Send prints. Pays $7.50.

CONSTRUCTION LETTER, Bureau of Business Practice, 24 Rope Ferry Rd., Waterford CT 06386. (203)442-4365. For front-line supervisors and foremen of construction workers. Newsletter; 4 pages. Estab. 1967. Published every 2 weeks. Circ. 8,000. Buys all rights. Buys about 100 mss per year. Pays on acceptance. Will send free sample copy and editorial guidelines sheet to writer on request. Will not consider photocopied or simultaneous submissions. Reports on mss accepted for publication in 4 to 8 weeks. Returns rejected material in 3 to 6 weeks. Query first. Enclose SASE.
Nonfiction and Photos: ''Material must deal with a single aspect of a supervisor's (foreman's) job — preferably: How to improve that aspect of his or her job.'' Length: 360 to 720 words. Pays 7¢ to 10¢ per word. Open to suggestions for new columns and departments. Query editor. Photos purchased with accompanying ms with extra payment. Pays $5. No color. Photos should be of head and shoulders of interviewee.

EMPLOYEE RELATIONS BULLETIN, Bureau of Business Practice, 24 Rope Ferry Rd., Waterford CT 06386. (203)442-4365. Supervisory Editor: Sue Ellen Thompson. Managing Editor: Wayne Muller. 50% freelance written. Emphasizes employee relations and human resources for top-level executives in the personnel field. ''This includes personnel directors, company presidents and vice presidents in charge of industrial or employee relations.'' Semimonthly magazine; 12 pages. Estab. 1960. Pays on acceptance, after editing. Buys all rights. Phone queries OK. Submit seasonal/holiday material 4-6 months in advance of issue date. SASE. Reports in 2 weeks. Free sample copy and writer's guidelines; mention *Writer's Market* in request.
Nonfiction: ''We purchase only interview-based articles with personnel or human resource executives on subjects of interest to their peers in business or industry.'' Buys 96 mss/year. Length: 1,000-1,800 words. Pays $50-150.

THE FOREMAN'S LETTER, National Foremen's Institute, 24 Rope Ferry Rd., Waterford CT 06386. (203)442-4365. Editor: Frank Berkowitz. For industrial supervisors. Semimonthly. Buys all rights. Pays on acceptance. ''Query preferred only if out-of-pocket expenses may be involved.'' Interested in regular stringers (freelance) on area exclusive basis. SASE.

Nonfiction: Interested primarily in direct in-depth interviews with industrial foremen in the U.S. and Canada, written in newspaper feature or magazine article style, with concise, uncluttered, non-repetitive prose as an essential. Subject matter would be the interviewee's techniques for managing people, bolstered by illustrations out of the interviewee's own job experiences. Slant would be toward informing readers how their most effective contemporaries function, free of editorial comment. "Our aim is to offer information which, hopefully, readers may apply to their own professional self-improvement." Pays 8¢-10½¢/word "after editing."
Photos: Buys photos submitted with mss. "Captions needed for identification only." Head and shoulders, any size b&w glossy from 2x3 up. Pays $7.50.

INSTITUTIONAL MANAGEMENT, North American Publishing Co., 401 N. Broad St., Philadelphia PA 19108. (215)574-9600. Editor: Tom Bluesteen. 60% freelance written. For "management in the health care, lodging and education fields; the publication focuses on the physical structures these people operate." Monthly news magazine; 36 pages. Estab. 1972. Circ. 70,000. Pays on publication. Buys all rights. Phone queries OK. Submit seasonal/holiday material 2-3 months in advance of issue date. Simultaneous (if not to overlapping readership) and previously published submissions OK. SASE. Reports in 2 weeks. Free sample copy and writer's guidelines; mention *Writer's Market* in request.
Nonfiction: Exposé (cost containment in hospitals, security in schools, open atrium design in hotels); how-to (save money; institutional executives will read about anything that will tell them how to save money); interview (with institutional executives); new product; personal experience (case history); photo feature; profile; and technical (new construction techniques). No articles relating to medicine or education. "While we cover hospitals and schools, we concentrate on the buildings and orgaizations these people run." Buys 4-5 mss/issue. Query. Length: 200-2,000 words. Pays $50 minimum.
Photos: "Illustration material can make an article more interesting. Sometimes, a good photo can carry a story." State availability of photos with query. Pays $10 minimum for 8x10 b&w photos; $15 minimum for color transparencies. Captions and model release required. Buys one-time rights.
Columns/Departments: People in the News (promotions, noteworthy developments of executives); and Editorial Viewpoint. Buys 6 mss/year. Query. Length: 200-1,000 words. Pays $25 minimum.

LE BUREAU, 625 President Kennedy, Montreal H3A 1K5, Que., Canada. (514)845-5141. Editor: Paul Saint-Pierre. For "office executives." Estab. 1965. Published 6 times/year. Circ. 7,500. Buys all rights, but will reassign rights to author after publication. Buys about 10 mss/year. Pays on acceptance. Free sample copy. Query first or submit complete ms. Submit seasonal material "between 1 and 2 months" in advance of issue date. Enclose SAE and International Reply Coupons for return of submissions.
Nonfiction and Photos: "Our publication is published in the French language. We use case histories on new office systems, applications of new equipment, articles on personnel problems. Material should be exclusive and above-average quality." Buys personal experience articles, interviews, think pieces, coverage of successful business operations, and new product articles. Length: 500-1,000 words. Pays $50-$75. B&w glossies purchased with mss. Pays $10 each.

MANAGE, 2210 Arbor Blvd., Dayton OH 45439. (513)294-0421. Editor-in-Chief: Douglas E. Shaw. Managing Editor: Dot Reagan. 60% freelance written. For first line and middle management and scientific/technical managers. Bimonthly magazine; 32 pages. Estab. 1925. Circ. 55,000. Pays on acceptance. Buys North American magazine rights with reprint privileges; book rights remain with the author. Phone queries OK. Submit seasonal/holiday material 3 months in advance of issue date. SASE. Reports in 1 month. Free sample copy and writer's guidelines; mention *Writer's Market* in request.
Nonfiction: "All material published by *Manage* is in some way management oriented. Most articles concern one or more of the following categories: communications; cost reduction; economics; executive abilities; health and safty; human relations; job status; labor relations; leadership; motivation and productivity; and professionalism. Articles should be specific and tell the manager how to apply the information to his job immediately. Be sure to include pertinent examples, and back up statements with facts and, where possible charts and illustrations. *Manage* does not want essays or academic reports, but interesting, well-written and practical articles for and about management." Buys 6 mss/issue. Submit complete ms. Length: 600-2,000 words. Pays 5¢/word.

MODERN BUSINESS REPORTS, Alexander Hamilton Institute, 605 3rd Ave., New York NY

10016. Editor-in-Chief: Frank Milburn. 50% freelance written. For management and business methods personnel. Monthly newsletter; 8 pages. Estab. 1974. Pays on acceptance. Buys all rights. SASE. Reports in 4 weeks. Free sample copy and writer's guidelines; mention *Writer's Market* in request.
Nonfiction: How-to; interview; new product; and technical. Buys 40 mss/year. Query. Length: 1,000-1,400 words.

PERSONNEL ADVISORY BULLETIN, Bureau of Business Practice, 24 Rope Ferry Rd., Waterford CT 06386. (203)442-4365. Editor-in-Chief: C. Starnella. Emphasizes all aspects of personnel management for personnel managers in all types and sizes of companies, both white collar and industrial. Semimonthly newsletter; 4 pages. Estab. 1973. Pays on acceptance. Buys all rights. Phone queries OK. Submit seasonal/holiday material 4 months in advance of issue date. SASE. Reports in 2 weeks. Free sample copy and writer's guidelines.
Nonfiction: Interviews with personnel managers or human resource executives on topics of current interest in the personnel field. buys 30 mss/year. Query. length: 600-1,000 words. Pays 10¢/word after editing.

SUPERVISION, 424 N. 3rd St., Burlington IA 52601. Editor-in-Chief: B. Pollard. Managing Editor: R. Walker. 65% freelance written. For firstline foremen, supervisors, and office managers. Monthly magazine; 24 pages. Estab. 1938. Circ. 8,175. Pays on publication. Buys all rights, but may reassign following publication. Phone queries OK. Previously published submissions OK. SASE. Reports in 3 weeks. Free sample copy and writer's guidelines; mention *Writer's Market* in request.
Nonfiction: How-to (cope with supervisory problems, discipline, absenteeism, safety, productivity, goal setting, etc.); personal experience (unusual success story of foreman or supervisor); and photo feature (will use manuscript plus 2-3 photos to illustrate it). Buys 7 mss/issue. Query. Length: 800-2,000 words. Pays 5¢/word.
Photos: State availability of photos with query. Pays $5 for b&w glossy prints. Buys all rights, but may reassign following publication.

TRAINING, The Magazine of Human Resources Development, 731 Hennepin Ave., Minneapolis MN 55403. (612)333-0471. Editor: Philip Jones. For persons who train people in business, industry, government and health care. Age 25 to 65. Magazine; 75 pages. Estab. 1964. Monthly. Circ. 40,000. Rights purchased vary with author and material. Usually buys all rights, but may reassign rights to author after publication; first North American serial rights; first serial rights; or all rights. Buys 30 to 50 mss per year. Payment on acceptance. Will send sample copy to writer for $1. Write for editorial guidelines sheet. Will consider photocopied submissions. No simultaneous submissions. Reports in 4 weeks. Query. SASE.
Nonfiction and Photos: Articles on management and techniques of employee training. "Material should discuss a specific training problem; why the problem existed; how it was solved, the alternative solutions, etc. Should furnish enough data for readers to make an independent judgment about the appropriateness of the solution to the problem. We want names and specific details on all techniques and processes used." Would like to see "interesting examples of successful training and management development programs; articles about why certain types of the above seem to fail; articles about trainers and training directors who have become company presidents or top execs." Most mss should be 200 to 3,000 words. Informational. Length: 200 to 2,000 words. Book reviews. Length: 50 to 1,000 words. Successful business operations. Length: 50 to 3,000 words. Pays maximum of $75 per printed page. "In general, we pay more for tightly written articles." No extra payment for photos. No payment for unsolicited material; query only. B&w only. Captions optional.

UTILITY SUPERVISION, Bureau of Business Practice, 24 Rope Ferry Rd., Waterford CT 06386. (203)442-4365. Editor: Peter W. Hawkins. Emphasizes all aspects of utility supervision. Semimonthly newsletter; 4 pages. Estab. 1966. Pays on acceptance. Buys all rights. Phone queries OK. Submit seasonal material 4 months in advance. SASE. Reports in 4-6 weeks. Free sample copy and writer's guidelines.
Nonfiction: Publishes how-to (interview on a single aspect of supervision with utility manager/supervisor concentrating on how reader/supervisor can improve in that area). Buys 100 mss/year. Query. Length: 360-720 words. Pays 6-10¢/word.
Photos: Purchased with accompanying ms. Captions required. Pays $7.50 for b&w prints of "head and shoulders 'mug shot' of person interviewed." Total purchase price for ms includes payment for photos.
How To Break In: "Write solid interview articles on a single aspect of supervision in the utility

field. Concentrate on how the reader/supervisor can improve his/her own performance in that area."

Marine Industries and Water Navigation

In this list are journals for seamen, boatbuilders, navigators, boat dealers, and others interested in water as a means of travel or shipping. Journals for commercial fishermen are classified with Fishing journals. Publications for scientists studying the ocean will be found under Oceanography.

AMERICAN SHIPPER, Box 4728, Jacksonville FL 32201. Editor: David A. Howard. For businessmen in shipping, transportation and foreign trade. Monthly magazine; 48 pages. Estab. 1958. Circ. 12,000. Not copyrighted. Buys 12 mss/year. Pays on acceptance. Reports in 1 month. SASE.
Nonfiction and Photos: "In-depth features. Analytical pieces (based on original data or research). Port finances. Other transportation (in-depth) with solid figures. News approach, basically. No 'old salt' human interest." Length: "depends on need of subject." Pays $100 to $150. Photos purchased with accompanying ms.

BOATING BUSINESS, 120-14 Barbados Blvd., Scarborough, Ontario, Canada M1J 1L2. (416)267-2878. Editor-in-Chief: Jim Punfield. 35% freelance written. Emphasizes retail marine trade. Quarterly magazine: 32 pages. Estab. September 1976. Circ. 5,400. Pays on acceptance. Not copyrighted. Phone queries OK. Submit seasonal/holiday material 3 months in advance of issue date. Photocopied submissions OK. SASE. Reports in 2 weeks. Free sample copy; mention *Writer's Market* in request.
Nonfiction: How-to (make more profit from your marine dealership, how-to sell more boats, motors, and accessories); inspirational (how one dealer overcame lack of working capital); and interview (successful operations—must be adaptable to Canadian readership). "Articles must either relate to our Canadian readership or be adaptable." Buys 3 mss/issue. Query or send complete ms. Length: 300-800 words. Pays $25-100.
Photos: Submit photo material with accompanying ms. No additional payment for 5x7 or 8x10 glossy b&w prints. Captions preferred. Buys one-time rights.

THE BOATING INDUSTRY, 850 3rd Ave., New York NY 10022. Editor: Charles A. Jones. For "boating retailers and distributors." Estab. 1929. Monthly. Circ. 26,000. Buys all rights, but will reassign rights to author after publication. Buys 10 to 15 mss a year. Pays on publication. "Best practice is to check with editor first on story ideas for go-ahead." Submit seasonal material 3 to 4 months in advance of issue date. Returns rejected material in 2 months. Acknowledges acceptance of material in 1 month. Enclose SASE.
Nonfiction and Photos: Uses "boat dealer success stories." No clippings. Pays 7¢ to 10¢ a word. B&w glossy photos purchased with mss.

MARINA MANAGEMENT/MARKETING, Box 373, Wilmette IL 60091. (312)256-4560. Editor: E.E. DuVernet. For marina owners, operators and other personnel. Monthly magazine; 64 pages. Estab. 1975. Circ. 15,000. Pays on publication. Buys all rights, but may reassign following publication, or second serial (reprint) rights. Simultaneous and photocopied submissions OK. SASE. Reports in 3 weeks. Free sample copy.
Nonfiction: Publishes material relating to the operation of marinas, boatyards and yacht clubs; including articles on dockage, maintenance, repair services, rentals, marina stores, boat dealerships; adjoining motels and recreational facilities. Informational, how-to, successful business operations, new product, merchandising techniques and technical articles; interviews and profiles. Length: 1,000-5,000 words. "Study previous issues." Pays $30-200.
Photos: B&w glossies (8x10) purchased with mss. Captions required. Pays $5-10. Color by assignment only

MARINE BUSINESS, 38 Commercial Wharf, Boston MA 02110. (617)227-0888. Editor: Paul W. Kellam. Associate Editor: Stewart Alsop II. 50% freelance written. For retailers in the recreational boating business. Monthly magazine; 144 pages. Estab. January 1978. Circ. 28,000. Pays on acceptance. Buys all rights, but may reassign following publication. Submit seasonal/holiday material 3 months in advance of issue date. SASE. Reports in 4-6 weeks. Free sample copy and writer's guidelines.

Nonfiction: "We're looking for articles with a direct benefit for marine retailers. These articles explore one unique aspect of a specific store and how the owner solved a problem that other retailers often face. No general profiles, success stories, business history, or stock articles. In-depth articles on industry problems are usually staff-written, but don't hesitate to query. Particularly interested in making contact with writers with background in and understanding of the marine business." Buys 50 mss/year. Query. Length: 1,200-3,000 words. Pays $150-500.
Columns/Departments: General Management; Financial Management; Personnel; Service; Marketing; Merchandising; Promotion; Sales Techniques; Taxes & Law; and Marinas. Buys 50 mss/year. Query. Length: 800-1,500 words. Pays $50-200.
Fillers: Ideas for simplifying day-to-day business for "Profitbuilders" or "Charting your business course" departments. Buys 25/year. Length: 25-50 words. Pays $25.

SEAWAY REVIEW, The Jorunal of the Great Lakes/St. Lawrence Seaway Transportation System, Harbor Island, Maple City Postal Station MI 49664. Senior Editor: Jacques LesStrang. Associate Editor: B.L. Hills. 10% freelance written. For "the entire Great Lakes maritime community, executives of companies that ship via the Great Lakes, traffic managers, transportation executives, federal and state government officials and manufacturers of maritime equipment." Quarterly magazine; 64 pages. Estab. 1970. Circ. 14,000. Pays on publication. Buys first North American serial rights. Submit seasonal/holiday material 2 months in advance of issue date. Photocopied submissions OK. SASE. Reports in 2 weeks. Sample copy $1.
Nonfiction: "Articles dealing with Great Lakes shipping, shipbuilding, marine technology, economics of 8 states in Seaway region (Michigan, Minnesota, Illinois, Indiana, Ohio, New York, Pennsylvania, and Wisconsin), port operation, Seaway's role in economic development, historical articles dealing with Great Lakes shipping, current events dealing with commercial shipping on Lakes, etc." Submit complete ms. Length: 1,000-2,000 words. Pay "varies with value of subject matter and knowledgeability of author, up to $250."
Photos: State availability of photos with query. Pays $10-50 for 8x10 glossy b&w prints; $10-100 for 8x10 glossy color prints. Captions required. Buys one-time rights.
Poetry: "We accept only poetry that is related to ports or shipping on the Great Lakes." Buys 2/year. Limit submissions to batches of 3. Pays $10-50.
Fillers: Clippings and spot news relating to ports and the Seaway system. Buys 3/issue. Length: 50-500 words. Pays $5-50.

SHIP & BOAT INTERNATIONAL, S-15030 Mariefred, Sweden. For naval architects, shipbuilders, owners, consultants, engineers, equipment manufacturers. Monthly. Estab. 1947. Pays on publication. Buys all rights. Submit seasonal material 2 months in advance. Enclose SAE and International Reply Coupons for reply to queries.
Nonfiction: Technical material regarding design and construction of commercial craft. Does not want to see "anything with a personal angle." Buys coverage of successful business operations and new products. Length: 500 to 1,500 words. Pays 0.25 Swedish krona per word as published.

THE WORK BOAT, Box 217, Mandeville LA 70448. (504)626-3151. Publisher/Editor: Harry L. Peace. Monthly. Buys first rights. Pays on publication. Query first. Reports in 2 week. Enclose SASE.
Nonfiction and Photos: "Articles on waterways, river terminals, barge line operations, work boat construction and design, barges, dredges, tugs. Best bet for freelancers: One-angle article showing in detail how a barge line, tug operator or dredging firm solves a problem of either mechanical or operational nature. This market is semitechnical and rather exacting. Such articles must be specific, containing firm name, location, officials of company, major equipment involved, by name, model, power, capacity and manufacturer; with b&w photos." Length: 1,000 to 5,000 words. Pays $90 minimum. 5x5 or 5x7 b&w; 4x5 color prints only. No additional payment for photos.

Medical

Publications that are aimed at private physicians or which publish technical material on new discoveries in medicine are classified here. Journals for nurses, laboratory technicians, hospital resident physicians, and other medical workers will be found with the Hospitals, Nursing, and Nursing Homes journals. Publications for druggists and drug wholesalers and retailers are grouped with the Drugs, Health Care, and Medical Products journals.

AMERICAN FAMILY PHYSICIAN, 1740 W. 92nd St., Kansas City MO 64114. (816)333-9700. Publisher: Walter H. Kemp. Monthly. Circ. 126,000. Buys all rights. Pays on publication. "Most articles are assigned." Query first. Reports in 2 weeks. Enclose SASE.
Nonfiction: Interested only in clinical articles. Length: 2,500 words. Pays $50-250.

AUDECIBEL, Journal of the National Hearing Aid Society, 20361 Middlebelt, Livonia MI 48152. (313)478-2610. Editor: Anthony DiRocco. Assistant Editor: Lila R. Johnson. For "otologists, otolaryngologists, hearing aid specialists, educators of the deaf and hard of hearing, clinical audiologists, and others interested in hearing and audiology." Estab. 1951. Quarterly. Circ. 15,600. Buys all rights. "Most articles published are from authorities in the field who publish for professional recognition, without fee." Pays on publication. Free sample copy and writer's guidelines. Query first or submit complete ms. SASE.
Nonfiction and Photos: "Purpose of the magazine is to bring to the otologist, the clinical audiologist, the hearing aid audiologist and others interested in the field authoritative articles and data concerned with current issues, research, techniques, education and new developments in the field of hearing and hearing aids. In general, *Audecibel*'s editorial policy emphasizes a professional and technical approach rather than a sales and merchandising approach. Eight types of articles are used: technical articles dealing with hearing aids themselves; technical articles dealing with fitting hearing aids; case histories of unusual fittings; technical articles dealing with sound, acoustics, etc.; psychology of hearing loss; medical and physiological aspects; professional standards and ethics, and current issues in the hearing health care fields. We are not interested in human interest stories, but only in carefully researched and documented material." Length: 200 to 2,000 words; "will consider longer articles if content is good." Pays 1¢ to 2½¢ per word. Photos purchased with mss; captions optional. Pays $3 to $5.

BEHAVIORAL MEDICINE (formerly *Practical Psychology for Physicians*), Magazines for Medicine, Inc., 475 5th Ave., New York NY 10017. (212)889-1050. Editor-in-Chief: Robert McCrie. Emphasizes behavioral sciences for physicians. Monthly magazine; 66 pages. Estab. 1972. Circ. 109,000. Pays on publication. Buys all rights, but may reassign following publication. Phone queries OK. Submit seasonal/holiday material 3 months in advance. Simultaneous and photocopied submissions OK. SASE. Reports in 2 weeks. Free writer's guidelines.
Nonfiction: "Useful information from the behaviorial sciences for primary care physicians. We need one type of article more than any other: practical, clinical-related, slightly offbeat mss that are of value to busy primary care physicians." Buys 1-3 mss/issue. Query. Length: 1,500-2,000 words. Pays $200-300.
Photos: Purchased with or without accompanying ms. Captions required. Query. Offers additional payment for photos accepted with accompanying ms up to $350 per complete article. "We like to use photo articles of physicians in practice. Would also like picture articles that tell a story of interest to physicians."
Rejects: "Articles in which author 'tells off' physicians for bad techniques or communications. Also, we never use highly personal articles from physicians about patients. Mss on depression or general psychosomatic complaints have been done to death."

CANADIAN DOCTOR, 310 Victoria Ave., Suite 201, Montreal, Quebec Canada H3Z 2M9. (514)487-2302. Editor-in-Chief: Peter N. Williamson. Assistant Editor: Linda Scovill Kramer. Monthly magazine; 20 pages. Estab. October 1935. Circ. 34,000. Pays on acceptance. Buys all rights. SASE. Reports in 3 weeks. Free sample copy and writer's guidelines; mention *Writer's Market* in request.
Nonfiction: How-to (run a physician's practice efficiently); interview (with Canadian doctor, perhaps those who have moved to U.S.); personal experience (from Canadian doctors); personal opinion (from Canadian doctor about the profession); profile (of Canadian doctor); and travel (only on assignment). Query. Length: 500-2,500 words. Pays $25-150.
Photos: State availability of photos with query. Pays $15 for b&w glossy prints. Captions required. Buys one-time rights. Model release required.

CONTEMPORARY SURGERY, Bobit Publishing, 2500 Artesia Blvd., Redondo Beach CA 90278. Editor: Barbara O'Reilly, M.P.A. Managing Editor: Peggy Plendl. 50% freelance written. Emphasizes clinical surgery for surgeons-in-practice and surgical residents. Monthly magazine; 60 pages. Estab. 1972. Circ. 40,000. Pays on publication. Buys all rights, but may reassign following publication. Photocopied and previously published (if identified) submissions OK. SASE. Reports in 3 weeks. Free writer's guidelines; mention *Writer's Market* in request.

Nonfiction: Interview; new product (if used by surgeons); profile (medical); technical; and clinical surgery-related topics. Query or submit complete ms. Length: 6,000 words maximum. Pays $50-300.
Photos: Submit photos or illustrations with query or ms. May offer additional payment for photos accepted with ms. Submit b&w or color photos, slides, or contact sheets. Model release required.

DRUG THERAPY MEDICAL JOURNAL, Biomedical Information Corp., 919 Third Ave., New York NY 10022. (212)758-6104. Editor-in-Chief: Genell Subak-Sharpe. Published in 2 editions: Office edition for practicing physicians; Hospital edition for hospital personnel. Emphasizes drug therapy for physicians in all the clinical specialties as well as internists, residents and attendants in the hospital setting throughout the U.S. Monthly magazine; 175 pages. Estab. 1970. Circ. 140,000. Pays on publication. Phone queries OK. Submit seasonal or holiday material 4 months in advance. Simultaneous and photocopied submissions OK. Previously published work acceptable as long as reprint rights are clear. SASE. Reports in 1-3 weeks. Free sample copy and editorial guidelines.
Nonfiction: How-to (diagnosis and treatment as clinical entity); informational (use of drugs, new drugs, how a drug works, etc.). Technical and new product articles. Buys 10-15 mss per issue. Query. Length: 1,000 words minimum. Pays $300.
Photos: No additional payment for b&w or color used with mss.

FACETS (formerly *MD's Wife*), American Medical Association Auxiliary, Inc., 535 N. Dearborn St., Chicago IL 60610. (312)751-6166. Editor-in-Chief: Ludel B. Sauvageot. Managing Editor: Kathleen T. Jordan. For physicians' spouses. Quarterly magazine; 32 pages. Circ. 90,000. Pays on acceptance. Buys all rights, but may reassign following publication. Submit seasonal/holiday material 4 months in advance of issue date. Simultaneous, photocopied and previously published submissions OK. SASE. Reports in 6 weeks. Free sample copy and writer's guidelines.
Nonfiction: All articles must be related to the experiences of physicians' wives. Historical; how-to; humor; informational; inspirational; interview; personal experience; personal opinion; and profile. Buys 2 mss/year. Query. Length: 1,000-2,500 words. Pays $50-500.
Photos: State availability of photos with query. Uses 8x10 glossy b&w prints and 2x2 color transparencies.

HEALTH CARE WEEK, 1515 Broadway, New York NY 10036. (212)869-1300. Editor-in-Chief: I.E. Levine. Managing Editor: Bruce Buckley. 15% freelance written. For "a cross section of administrators and professionals working in the health care field, including doctors, nurses, Blue Cross executives, government officials, and hospital administrators." Weekly newspaper; 16-32 pages. Estab. July 1977. Circ. 22,000. Pays on acceptance. Buys all rights. Submit seasonal/holiday material 1 month in advance of issue date. Photocopied and previously published submissions OK. SASE. Reports in 2 weeks. Free sample copy; mention *Writer's Market* in request.
Nonfiction: Exposé (feature or magazine-type treatment on impact of new or little known practices that endanger society, e.g., use of untried drugs, kickbacks, use of uncertified surgeons, etc.); general interest (articles dealing with major problems in health field, such as over-regulation); interview (with important figures in government or the health care field); new product (only those that represent a significant breakthrough, pix highly desirable); personal opinion (knowledgeable opinion on any aspect of health care, especially timely issues); and photo feature (on new facilities, health/delivery systems, innovative programs, etc.). "We are not interested in straight news coverage pieces." Buys 50-60 mss/year. Query. Length: 500-2,000 words. Pays 3-5¢/word.
Photos: "We are always interested in good photo features, so that if the pix are good, we might buy a manuscript that ordinarily might just miss." State availability of photos with query. Pays $5-10 for 8x10 b&w glossy photos. Captions preferred. Buys one-time rights.
Columns/Departments: "We do consider freelance material for book reviews related to health care, but the writer must establish qualifications." Buys 50/year. Query with clips of previously published work. Length: 400-900 words. Pays 3-5¢/word.

HOSPITAL PHYSICIAN MAGAZINE, 405 Lexington Ave., New York NY 10017. Editor: Peter Frishauf. For doctors. Monthly magazine; 60 pages. Circ. 80,000. Rights purchased vary with author and material. Usually buys all rights or First North American serial rights. Buys 35 mss/year. Pays on acceptance. Free sample copy. Photocopied submissions and simultaneous submissions OK. Reports in 1 month. Query first or submit complete ms. SASE.

Nonfiction: Uses medical information stories, "the patient's view" and clinical tips. Must be of interest to interns and residents in hospitals throughout the country. "We deal with the patient's view, with ethical questions in medicine, and especially with the particular problems of house-staff." Not interested in "one-shot" interviews. Length: 700-3,000 words. Pays $50.

LAB WORLD, North American Publishing Co., 401 N. Broad St., Philadelphia PA 19108. (215)574-9600. Editorial Director: A.E. Woolley. 50% freelance written. Emphasizes laboratory medicine for pathologists, lab chiefs, medical technologists, medical technicians and other staff members of laboratories. Monthly magazine; 100 pages. Estab. 1947. Circ. 62,000. Pays on acceptance. Buys first North American serial or one-time rights. Submit seasonal/holiday material 4-6 months in advance of issue date. SASE. Reports in 2 weeks. Sample copy $2.50.
Nonfiction: All articles must pertain to the laboratory field. General interest; humor; inspirational; interview; photo feature and profile. No technical papers. Buys 20-50 mss/year. Query. Length: 750-7,000 words. Pays $100-300.
Photos: State availability of photos with query. Pays $50-150 for 5x7 or 8x10 b&w semiglossy photos; $100-200 for 35mm color transparencies. Captions and model release required. Buys one-time rights.

THE LIFE LINE, California Paramedic Association, 9999 E. Imperial Highway, Downrey CA 90241. (213)923-2831. Editor-Publisher: S.W. Deeble. 50% freelance written. Emphasizes paramedic techniques and fire suppression. Monthly tabloid; 12 pages. Estab. 1973. Circ. 25,000. Pays on publication. Not copyrighted. Simultaneous, photocopied and previously published submissions OK. SASE. Sample copy and writer's guidelines $2.
Nonfiction: General interest; historical; humor; inspirational; nostalgia; personal opinion; profile; new product; personal experience; photo feature and technical. Material must be paramedic/medical-emergency related. Submit complete ms and clips of previously published work. Length: 2-2½ pages. Pays $10-150.
Photos: "I would much prefer for my reader to see as well as read the body of an article." Pays $3-15 for 3x3 b&w or color prints. Captions required.

THE MAYO ALUMNUS, Mayo Foundation, 200 SW 1st St., Rochester MN 55901. (507)284-2511. Editor: David E. Swanson. For physicians, scientists, and medical educators who trained at the Mayo Clinic. Quarterly magazine; 40 pages. Estab. 1965. Circ. 9,000. Pays on acceptance. Buys all rights. Phone queries OK. Submit seasonal/holiday material 6 months in advance of issue date. Previously published submissions OK. SASE. Reports in 2 months. Free sample copy; mention *Writer's Market* in request.
Nonfiction: "We're interested in seeing interviews with members of the Mayo Alumni Association—stories about Mayo-trained doctors/educators/scientists/researchers who are interesting people doing interesting things in medicine, surgery or hobbies of interest, etc." Query with clips of previously published submissions. Length: 1,000-3,000 words. Pays 5¢/word.
Photos: "We need art and must make arrangements if not provided with the story." Pays $5 for b&w photos. State availability of photos with query. Captions preferred. Buys all rights.

MEDICAL CENTER NEWS, 5440 Cass Ave., Suite 811, Detroit MI 48202. (313)831-3323. Editor: Merry M. Miller. 50% freelance written. For health care professionals. Weekly tabloid; 16 pages. Estab. May 1976. Circ. 15,000. Pays on publication. Buys all rights, but may reassign following publication or simultaneous rights. Phone queries OK. Submit seasonal/holiday material 1 month in advance of issue date. Simultaneous, photocopied and previously published submissions OK. SASE. Reports in 4 weeks. Free sample copy; mention *Writer's Market* in request.
Nonfiction: "*Medical Center News* is a news/feature publication for medical professionals filling the gap between the daily newspapers and medical journals offering medical news in a basically non-technical format." Historical; interview; new product; personal opinion; photo feature; and profile. "No medical items written for general public." Buys 3-4 mss/issue. Query with clips of previously published work. Length: 500-12,500 words. Pays $20-50.
Photos: State availability of photos with query. Pays $3-5 for 5x7 or 8x10 b&w glossy prints. Captions preferred. Buys all rights, but may reassign following publication.

MEDICAL ECONOMICS, 680 Kinderkamack Rd., Oradell NJ 07649. (201)262-3030. Editor-in-Chief: A.J. Vogl. Executive Editor: James A. Reynolds. Emphasizes "the business side of medical practice for office-based physicians in private practice." Bimonthly magazine; 200-300 pages. Estab. 1923. Circ. 165,000. Pays on acceptance. Buys all rights, but may reassign following publication. Submit seasonal/holiday material 2 months in advance of issue date.

Previously published submissions OK. SASE. Reports in 3 weeks. Free sample copy and writer's guidelines.
Nonfiction: "Articles tell the doctor how to manage his practice, his financial affairs, and his dealings with fellow professionals. Major subjects include medicolegal matters, health legislation, investments, fees, hospital problems, taxes, cars, and doctor-patient relations. The subject matter is nonmedical, nonclinical and nondiagnostic." Buys 24 mss/year. Query. Length: 1,000-3,000 words. Pays $500-1,200.
Fillers: Jokes, gags, and anecdotes. Buys 100-150/year. Length: 250 words maximum. Pays $30-35.

MEDICAL OPINION, 575 Madison Ave., New York NY 10022. Editor: Genell Subak-Sharpe. For physicians primarily in private practice. Monthly. Circ. 130,000. Buys all rights. Buys 30-55 mss/year. Pays on acceptance. Query first. Reports in 4 to 6 weeks. Enclose SASE.
Nonfiction: "Interested in articles written by physicians which are reflective and informative on specific aspects of modern medical practice. Clinical topics are preferred, with an emphasis on topics of practical interest to medical practitioners. We are not a news magazine. Wo do not feature products or immediate breakthroughs, but rather subjects and therapeutic areas that have been at least partially exposed to our audience. No fiction, poetry, or 'cute pieces'. All articles should offer a clearly defined opinion. Style is not technical, but follows the more lively consumer magazine style. Be careful not to oversimplify or to confuse medical terms with clear writing." Length: 1,500 to 2,500 words. Pays $150 to $350.

THE MEDICAL POST, 481 University Ave., Toronto, Ont., M5W 1A7, Canada. Editor: Derek Cassels. For the medical profession. Published every 2nd Tuesday. Will send sample copy to medical writers only. Buys first North American serial rights. Pays on publication. Enclose SAE and International Reply Coupons.
Nonfiction: Uses "newsy, factual reports of medical developments. Must be aimed at professional audience, and not written in 'popular medical' style." Length: 300 to 800 words. Pays 12¢ a word.
Photos: Uses photos with mss or captions only, of medical interest; pays $10 up.

THE NEW PHYSICIAN, 14650 Lee Rd., Chantilly VA 22021. Editor: Todd Dankmyer. 50% freelance written. For medical students, interns and residents. Monthly magazine; 72 pages. Estab. 1952. Circ. 78,000. Buys all rights. Buys 6-12 mss/year. Pays on publication. Free sample copy. No photocopied submissions. Will consider simultaneous submissions. Reports in 4 to 6 weeks. Query first. SASE.
Nonfiction and Photos: "Articles on social, political, economic issues in medicine/medical education. Our readers need more than a superficial, simplistic look into issues that affect them. We want skeptical, accurate, professional contributors to do well-researched, comprehensive reports, and offer new perspectives on health care problems." Not interested in material on "my operation," or encounters with physicians, or personal experiences as physician's patient. Occasionally publishes special topic issues, such as those on emergency care and foreign medical graduates. Informational articles, interviews, and exposes are sought. Length: 500 to 2,500 words. Pays $25 to $250. Pays $10 to $25 for b&w photos used with mss. Captions required.

PHYSICIAN'S LIFE, Arthur Retlaw & Associates, 1603 Orrington Ave., Evanston IL 60201. (312)869-6840. Editor-in-Chief: Jack Challem. Editor: Karen Stipp. 50% freelance written. For Physicians, M.D.'s and D.O.'s. Bimonthly tabloid; 40-48 pages. Estab. July 1978. Circ. 80,000. Pays on publication. Buys all rights. Phone queries OK. Submit seasonal/holiday material 4-6 months in advance of issue date. Photocopied submissions OK. SASE. Reports in 2-3 weeks. Free sample copy of writer's guidelines; mention *Writer's Market* in request.
Nonfiction: Interview (M.D.'s and D.O.'s with interesting hobbies, pastimes and interests); and profile (with extended quotes from interviewee). Buys 30 mss/year. Query with clips of previously published work. Length: 1,500 words. Pays $100-200.
Photos: State availability of photos with query. Offers no additional payment for b&w contact sheets. captions preferred. Buys all rights, but may reasign following publication. Model release required.
Fillers: Cartoons. Pays $10-20.

PHYSICIAN'S MANAGEMENT, Harcourt Brace Jovanovich Health Care Publications, 757 Third Ave., New York NY 10017. (212)754-2938. Editor: Jim Hayes. Emphasizes finances, investments, small office administration, practice management and taxes for physicians in

private practice. Monthly magazine; 90 pages. Estab. 1960. Circ. 180,000. Pays on acceptance. Buys all rights, but may reassign following publication. Submit seasonal or holiday material 5 months in advance. SASE. Reports in 2-4 weeks. Sample copy $2; free writer's guidelines.
Nonfiction: "*Physician's Management* is a socio-economic publication, not a clinical one." Publishes how-to articles (limited to medical practice management); informational (when relevant to audience); personal experience articles (if written by a physician). Length: 500-3,000 words. Buys 3-5 an issue. Query first. Pays $50-400.
How To Break In: "Talk to doctors first about their practice, financial interests, and day-to-day non-clinical problems and then query us. Use of an MD byline helps tremendously! Also, the ability to write a concise, well-structured and well-researched magazine article is essential. Most freelancers think like patients and fail with us. Those who can think like MD's are successful."

PRIVATE PRACTICE, 5100 N. Brookline, Suite 700, Oklahoma City OK 73112. Editor: Llewellyn H. Rockwell, Jr. For "medical doctors in private practice." Monthly. Buys first North American serial rights. Pays on acceptance. Query first. Enclose SASE.
Nonfiction and Photos: "Articles which indicate importance of maintaining freedom of medical practice or which detail outside interferences in the practice of medicine, including research, hospital operation, drug manufacture, etc. Straight reporting style. No cliches, no scare words, no flowery phrases to cover up poor reporting. Stories must be actual, factual, precise, correct. Copy should be lively and easy-to-read. Also publish travel, sports, leisure, historical, offbeat, and humorous articles of medical interest." Length: up to 2,500 words. Pays "usual minimum $150." Photos purchased with mss only. B&w glossies, 8x10. Payment "depends on quality, relevancy of material, etc."

SURGICAL BUSINESS, 2009 Morris Ave., Union NJ 07083. Editor: Adrian Comper. For medical/surgical dealers and dealer/salesmen. Monthly magazine; 92 pages. Estab. 1938. Circ. 7,000. Buys exclusive industry rights. Buys 5-10 mss/year. Pays on publication. Free sample copy and writer's guidelines. Will consider photocopied and simultaneous submissions. Reports in 3 months. Query first or submit complete ms. SASE.
Nonfiction and Photos: "We publish feature-length articles dealing with manufacturers within the industry, as well as domestic and international meeting coverage and general information within the industry. We do not desire promotional material about a company or product. Mss should be objective and to the point." No additional payment for b&w photos used with mss. Length: approximately 2,500 words. Pays 5¢/word.

UROLOGY TIMES, OPHTHALMOLOGY TIMES, Murray Communications, 79 Madison Ave., New York NY 10016. (212)889-6210. Editor: Zee King. Monthly magazine; 40 pages. Estab. 1973. Circ. 8,200, 10,727 respectively. Buys about 12 mss a year. Pays on publication. Will send sample copy to writer on request. Write for copy of guidelines for writers. Will consider photocopied submissions. No simultaneous submissions. Reports in 8 weeks. Query first. SASE.
Nonfiction: "Our object is to act as the bridge between the academician and the clinician. We use reports on work in urology and ophthalmology; all with a reportorial approach." Recently published articles include "Immunologic Effects of Surgery." Length: 1,000 to 5,000 words. Pays $80 to $320.

Milling, Feed, and Grain

FEED INDUSTRY REVIEW, 3055 N. Brookfield Rd., Brookfield WI 53005. (914)786-7540. Publisher: Bruce W. Smith. For manufacturers of livestock and poultry feed. Quarterly. Circ. 8,000. Buys all rights. Pays on publication. Will send a free sample copy on receipt of letter only, no postcards. Query first. Reports in one week. Enclose SASE.
Nonfiction: "Profile articles on progressive feed manufacturing operations, including data on plant layout and equipment, research, and distribution. This is a market for factual reporters, not creative writers. Market extremely limited; queries imperative prior to submitting completed articles." Length: 1,500 to 2,200 words. Pays $20 to $75.
Photos: Usually buys only with mss, occasional exceptions. Subject matter should be agribusiness, plants, or other physical facilities. B&w glossies, horizontal prints. Pays $7 to $10.

THE WHEAT SCOOP, 606 25th St. North, Box 6699, Great Falls MT 59406. Editor: Ray Fenton. 8 times a year. Not copyrighted. Query first. "Very little freelance material purch-

ased." Enclose SASE.
Nonfiction: Uses "articles on grain research, freight rates, fertilizers, domestic markets and foreign markets as they pertain to Montana. Clarity and precision necessary. Authenticity, definite Montana tie-in are musts." Length: 100 to 1,000 words. Payment negotiated.
Photos: Buys photos with mss and with captions only. Particularly needs art wheat photos, from seeding to harvesting, b&w or color; unusual or art type.

Mining and Minerals

AMERICAN GOLD NEWS, Box 457, Ione CA 95640. (209)274-2196. Editor: Cecil L. Helms. 25% freelance written. For anyone interested in gold, gold mining, gold companies, gold stocks, gold history, gold coins, the future of gold in our economy. Monthly tabloid newspaper; 20 pages. Estab. 1933. Circ. 3,500. Not copyrighted. Pays on acceptance. Free sample copy and writer's guidelines. No photocopied or simultaneous submissions. Submit seasonal material (relating to seasonal times in mining country) 2 months in advance. Reports in 2 to 4 weeks. Query first or submit complete ms. SASE.
Nonfiction and Photos: "This is not a literary publication. We want information on any subject pertaining to gold told in the most simple, direct, and interesting way. How to build gold mining equipment. History of mines (with pix). History of gold throughout U.S. Financial articles on gold philosophy in money matters. Picture stories of mines, mining towns, mining country. Would like to see more histories of mines, from any state. Length: 500 to 2,000 words. Pays $10 to $25. B&w photos purchased with or without ms. Must be sharp, if not old, historical photos. Pays $2.50 to $25. Captions required.

COAL AGE, 1221 Avenue of the Americas, New York NY 10020. Editor: Joseph F. Wilkinson. For supervisors, engineers and executives in coal mining. Monthly. Circ. 20,000. Buys all rights. Pays on publication. Query. Reports in two-three weeks. SASE.
Nonfiction: Uses some technical (operating type) articles; some how-to pieces on equipment maintenance; management articles. Pays $150 per page.

COAL WEEK, 441 National Press Bldg., Washington DC 20045. (202)624-7379. Editor: Roseann Schwaderer. For executives in coal producing, consuming and related industries, observers in the financial and academic communities, and government officials. Newsletter; 10 pages. Estab. 1975. Weekly. Buys all rights. Pays on acceptance. Will send sample copy to writer on request. Write for copy of guidelines for writers. No photocopied or simultaneous submissions. Query first. Enclose SASE.
Nonfiction: Spot news; brief news reports on developments which will affect the coal market. Length: 500 words maximum. Pays $5 to $7.50 per inch.

SILVER AND GOLD REPORT, Box 325, Newtown CT 06470. (203)427-8522. Editor: James R. Blakely. Emphasizes investments, precious metals, economics of the commodity markets, finance and gold and silver for the "well-to-do older investor; heavy New York and California concentration." Semimonthly newsletter; 8 pages. Estab. 1976. Circ. 12,000. Pays on acceptance. "We pay for research time if article is not accepted because of editorial deficiencies, providing the research is worthy." Buys all rights. Phone queries OK. Photocopied submissions OK. SASE. Reports in 2 weeks. Free sample copy and writer's guidelines.
Nonfiction: Exposé (of the cost to consumers of government regulation); how-to (ways on investing in precious metals, tax shelters); informational (numismatics); historical (runaway inflation of Germany 1920-23, gold legislation of the 1930's, etc.); interview (with experts on precious metals, international monetary affairs, international currency); new product (precious metals-related investment vehicles, such as gold IRA and Keough plans); personal experience (living through hyperinflation); and technical (use of straddles in the silver futures market). Query with clips of previously published work. Length: 500-8,000 words. Pays $400 minimum.

Miscellaneous

AMERICAN FARRIERS' JOURNAL, Drawer 151, Arcadia FL 33821. Editor-in-Chief: Henry Heymering. Emphasizes horseshoeing. Quarterly magazine: 20 pages. Estab. 1975. Circ. 1,500. Pays on publication. Buys all rights. Submit seasonal/holiday material 4-5 months in advance of issue date. SASE. Reports in 3 weeks. Free sample copy; mention *Writer's Market* in request.
Nonfiction: Historical (old companies and methods); how-to; informational; interview (with shoers or manufacturers); technical; and research findings (news coverage of contests and

competitions). Query. Length: 800-2,000 words. Pays $1/column inch.
Photos: State availability of photos with query. Pays $5-25 for b&w prints.

THE ANTIQUES DEALER, 1115 Clifton Ave., Clifton NJ 07013. Editor: Stella Hall. 90% freelance written. For antiques dealers. Monthly magazine. Estab. 1949. Circ. 10,000. Rights purchased vary with author and material. May buy all rights or first North American rights or exclusive rights in this field. Buys 40 mss a year. Payment on publication. Will send free sample copy to writer on request. Will consider photocopied submissions "if clear". Enclose SASE.
Nonfiction: "Remember that we are a trade publication and all material must be slanted to the needs and interests of antique dealers. We publish nothing of a too general ("be a good salesman") or too limited (eastern Pennsylvania chairs) nature." Only articles of national interest to dealers; may be tutorial if by authority in one specific field; otherwise of broad general interest to all dealers and news of the international antique trade. Emphasis is currently on heirlooms (50-100 years old), as well as antiques (over 100 years old). Length: no minimum; maximum 2-part article, about 7,000 words; 3,500 words if one-part. Pays $30 a page for features; $1.50 for few sentence obit. Columns cover trade news; anything from a couple of sentences to about 200 words, with photo or two. Usually pays just $1.50 if very short.
Photos: Purchased with or without accompanying mss, or on assignment. Pays $5 per b&w used inside, $10 for covers; no smaller than 5x7 (glossy). Professional quality only; no Polaroids.
Fillers: Suitable for professional dealers; any type of fillers. Length: 300 to 400 words. Pays approximately $15 for half-page.

APA MONITOR, 1200 17th St., N.W., Washington DC 20036. Editor: Pamela Moore. For psychologists, interested in behaviorial science and mental health. Monthly newspaper; 32 pages. Estab. 1970. Circ. 55,000. Buys all rights. Buys about 25 mss/year. Pays on publication. Free sample copy. Will not consider photocopied or simultaneous submissions. Query.
Nonfiction and Photos: News and features about psychology and political, social, economic developments that affect psychology; APA (American Psychological Association) affairs. "We put more emphasis on organizational and political aspects of psychology as a profession; less on interpretation of scientific findings to the public. Keep in mind that the reader is probably better informed about the substantive science and practice of psychology than the writer." Informational, interview, profile, humor, historical, think articles, expose, new product, photo. Length: 300 to 1,000 words.

ART DEALER & FRAMER, Box 1096, Alton IL 62002. (618)465-0041. Editor-in-Chief: Gretchen Schmitz. Emphasizes picture framing and art resale. Monthly magazine. Estab. 1973. Circ. 10,600. Pays on publication. Buys all rights. SASE. Reports in 3 weeks. Free sample copy and writer's guidelines; mention *Writer's Market* in request.
Nonfiction: General interest (articles on "background" material that will be of interest and aid in framing or selling art); how-to (articles on galleries and frame shops that contain ideas people can adapt to their own operations); interview (infrequent in-depth interviews with artists of note); photo feature (as would relate to how-to articles or interviews); and technical (articles on the subject of picture and frame conservation and restoration). Buys 8 mss/year. Query. Pays $35-100.
Photos: State availability of photos with query. Offers no additional payment for photos accepted with accompanying ms. Uses 5x7 b&w glossy prints. Captions required. Buys all rights.

CANADIAN FUNERAL DIRECTOR, Peter Perry Publishing, Ltd., 1658 Victoria Park Ave., Suite 5, Scarboro, Ontario, Canada M1R 1P7. (416)755-7050. Managing Editor: Peter Perry. 15% freelance written. Emphasizes funeral home operation. Monthly magazine; 60 pages. Estab. 1924. Circ. 1,700. Pays on publication. Buys one-time rights. Phone queries OK. Reports in 30-60 days. Simultaneous and photocopied submissions and previously published work OK. SASE. Reports in 3 weeks. Free sample copy.
Nonfiction: Informational, historical, humor, interview, personal opinion, profile, photo feature, technical. Buys 12 mss a year. Query. Length: 200-1,500 words. Pays $40 per 1,000 words.
Photos: Purchased with or without ms. Captions required. Query or send contact sheet. Pays $5-10 for 5x7 or 8x10 b&w glossies.

CANADIAN RENTAL SERVICE, J. Peter Watkins, Ltd., 49 Queens Dr., Weston, Ontario, Canada M9N 2H3. (416)241-4724. Editor: Naomi Watkins. Emphasizes general rental business. Bimonthly magazine; 44 pages. Estab. 1976. Circ. 2,500. Pays on publication. Buys one-time rights. Phone queries OK. Submit seasonal/holiday material 2 months in advance. Photocopied

submissions and previously published work OK. SASE. Reports in 12 weeks. Free sample copy.
Nonfiction: Profiles and technical articles. Buys 1-2 per issue. Query. Length: 1,000 words maximum. Pays $50/page minimum.
Photos: Purchased with ms or on assignment. Captions required. Query. Pays $20 minimum for 5x7 b&w glossies. Model release required.
Columns, Departments: Trade News, Association News, Appointments. Query. Length: 1 typewritten page.
Fillers: Clippings, newsbreaks. Buys 1-2 per issue. Send complete ms. Pays $10-20.
Rejects: Material relating to rental of items not rented by the field involved. Material relating to renting in the U.S.A.

C & S (Casket and Sunnyside), 274 Madison Ave., New York NY 10016. (212)685-8310. Editor: Howard Barnard. 10% freelance written. "This magazine is circulated to funeral directors of all ages, more and more who are becoming college educated." Monthly magazine; 48 pages. Estab. 1871. Circ. 12,000. Pays on publication. Buys all rights. Submit seasonal/holiday material 2 months in advance of issue date. SASE. Reports in 2 weeks.
Nonfiction: General interest (stories on mortuaries); historical (articles dealing with embalming, early funeral vehicles and ambulances, etc.); how-to (handle difficult or unusual restorative art or embalming cases); inspirational (public realtions achievements); and "short items or new products in the funeral field." Buys 20 mss/year. Query. Length: 1,500-2,500 words. Pays $75.
Photos: State availability of photos with query. Pays $5 for 5x7 or 8x10 b&w prints. Captions required. Buys all rights.
Fillers: Clippings, obituaries and items concerning various activities of funeral directors. Buys 10-15/issue. Pays $3.

COACHING: WOMEN'S ATHLETICS, Intercommunications, Inc., Box 867, Wallingford CT 06492. (203)265-0937. Editor-in-Chief: William J. Burgess. For administrators of athletic and/or physical education departments of public, private and parochial junior and senior high schools, preparatory schools, junior colleges and universities. Bimonthly (except July/August) magazine; 90 pages. Estab. 1975. Circ. 10,000. Pays on publication. Buys all rights. Phone queries OK. SASE. Reports in 2 weeks. Sample copy $2; free writer's guidelines.
Nonfiction: How-to; interview; personal experience; and profile. Buys 100 mss/year. Length: 2,500 words maximum. Pays 5¢/word.
Photos: Purchased with or without accompanying ms. Captions required. Query. Uses 4x5, 5x7, or 8x10 clear finish glossy prints; 35mm, 2¼x2¼ or 4x5 color transparencies. Pays $100-250 for cover color transparencies. Model release required.

COUNTERFORCE, Taggart Publishing Co., Box 26804, El Paso TX 79926. Editor-in-Chief: Frank W. Taggart. Managing Editor: Gavin de Becker. 50% freelance written. For "executives and security directors in business, industry and government concerned about the threat posed by terrorists around the world." Monthly magazine; 40 pages. Estab. January 1977. Circ. 2,000. Pays on acceptance. Buys all rights, but may reassign following publication. Submit seasonal/holiday material 2 months in advance of issue date. Simultaneous, photocopied and previously published submissions OK. SASE. Reports in 2 weeks. Sample copy $1.50.
Nonfiction: Expose (terrorist, subversive or underground groups and organizations); interview (experts in dealing with terrorists); new product (anti-terrorist devices); personal opinion (best ways to combat terrorism); profile (terrorist groups and organizations); and technical (anti-terrorist devices). Buys 3-5 mss/issue. Query. Length: 500-2,000 words. Pays $25 minimum.

EMERGENCY (formerly *Emergency Product News*), Box 159, Carlsbad CA 92008. Managing Editor: Linda Olander. 20% freelance written. Emphasizes emergency medical services for anyone involved in emergency services, including ambulance personnel, paramedics, emergency room personnel, law enforcement personnel and firefighters. Monthly magazine; 84 pages. Estab. 1970. Circ. 35,000. Pays on publication. Buys all rights. Submit seasonal/holiday material 4 months in advance of issue date. SASE. Reports in 2 months. Free sample copy and writer's guidelines.
Nonfiction: How-to (better execute a certain emergency procedure, guidelines for emergency medical techniques). Buys 3 mss/issue. Query. Length: 800-1,500 words. Pays $50-150.
Photos: State availability of photos with query. Pays $10 minimum for 5x7 b&w glossy prints; $10-25 for 35mm color transparencies. Captions required. Buys all rights.
Columns/Departments: News Briefs (short items of interest to emergency personnel); Legislative Updates (items pertaining to national or local legislation on emergency care); and Funds and

Grants (allocated for improvement of emergency care). Buys 10/year. Query. Length: 50-100 words. Pays $1/inch. Open to suggestions for new columns/departments.

HOUSEHOLD AND PERSONAL PRODUCTS INDUSTRY, 26 Lake St., Ramsey NJ 07446. Editor: Hamilton C. Carson. 5-10% freelance written. For "manufacturers of soaps, detergents, cosmetics and toiletries, waxes and polishes, insecticides, and aerosols." Estab. 1964. Monthly. Circ. 14,000. Not copyrighted. Buys 3 to 4 mss a year, "but would buy more if slanted to our needs." Pays on publication. Will send a sample copy to a writer on request. Will consider photocopied submissions. Submit seasonal material 2 months in advance. Query first. Enclose SASE.
Nonfiction and Photos: "Technical and semitechnical articles on manufacturing, distribution, marketing, new products, plant stories, etc., of the industries served. Some knowledge of the field is essential in writing for us." Buys informational articles, interviews, photo features, spot news, coverage of successful business operations, new product articles, coverage of merchandising techniques, and technical articles. Length: 500-2,000 words. Pays $10-150. 5x7 or 8x10 b&w glossies purchased with mss. Pays $5-10.

THE INDIAN TRADER, Box 31235, Billings MT 59107. (406)245-0507. Editor-in-Chief: Ms. Jo Smith. 70% freelance written. For traders in the Indian arts, crafts and culture. Monthly tabloid; 88 pages. Estab. 1970. Circ. 10,000. Pays on publication. Buys all rights, but may reassign following publication. Phone queries OK. Submit seasonal/holiday material 2 months in advance. Reports in 3-6 weeks. Free sample copy and writer's guidelines.
Nonfiction: Historical (must be accurately researched and of special interest to collectors of Indian artifacts, traders, or those interested in current American activities); informational (characters of historical interest, their descendants, etc.); interviews (with exceptional Indian craftsmen, collectors, shows, pow-wows, etc.); photo features (coverage of Indian affairs, reservation happenings, etc.); and travel (visits to Indian ruins, trading posts, similar material in areas of the Northwest or Northeast, or Canada). Buys 8-10 mss/issue. Pays 50¢-$1.50/column inch. "This usually works out to about 2-4¢/word, but we do pay by the column inch."
Photos: B&w (8x10) glossies preferred. Purchased with or without mss or on assignment. Captions optional, but information must be included if captionless. Query or send prints. Pays $2-15 when additional payment is made. Total purchase price sometimes includes payment for photos.
Columns/Departments: Buys 1-3 book reviews/issue. Query. Pays 50¢-$1.50/column inch.

INFO FRANCHISE NEWSLETTER, 11 Bond St., St. Catharines, Ontario, Canada L2R 4Z4. (716)754-4669, ext. 5. Editor-in-Chief: E.L. Dixon Jr. Managing Editor: Mrs. D. Hill. Monthly newsletter; 4-6 pages. Estab. May 1977. Circ. 1,500. Pays on publication. Buys all rights, but may reassign following publication. Photocopied submissions OK. SASE. Reports in 4 weeks. Sample copy $1.50.
Nonfiction: "We are particularly interested in receiving articles regarding franchise legislation, franchise litigation, franchise success stories, and new franchises. Both American and Canadian items are of interest. We do not want to receive any information which is not fully documented; or articles which could have appeared in any newspaper or magazine in North America. An author with a legal background, who could comment upon such things as arbitration and franchising, collective bargaining and franchising or class actions and franchising would be of great interest to us." Expose; how-to; informational; interview; profile; new product; personal experience and technical. Buys 5-10 mss/year. Length: 25-1,000 words. Pays $10-300.

LAWN CARE INDUSTRY, Harvest Publishing Co., 9800 Detroit Ave., Cleveland OH 44102. (216)651-5500. Editor: Bob Earley. 10% freelance written. For lawn care businessmen. Monthly tabolid; 40 pages. Estab. 1977. Circ. 8,000. Pays on acceptance. Buys all rights, but may reassign following publication. Phone queries OK. Submit seasonal/holiday material 3 months in advance of issue date. Simultaneous and photocopied submissions OK. SASE. Reports in 2 weeks. Free sample copy.
Nonfiction: General interest (articles related to small business operation); how-to (running a lawn care business); interview (with lawn care operator or industry notable); new product (helping to better business practices); and profile (of lawn care businessmen). Buys 3 mss/issue. Query. Length: 500-1,000 words. Pays $50-250.
Photos: State availability of photos with query. Pays $10-100 for 5x7 glossy b&w prints; $50-250 for 35mm color transparencies. Captions required. Buys one-time rights.

MANAGING THE LEISURE FACILITY, Billboard Publications, Inc., 1717 West End Ave.,

Nashville TN 37203. (615)329-3925. Editor: Irwin Kirby. 90% freelance written. Emphasizes mass entertainment facility operations for professional managers. Bimonthly magazine; 48 pages. Estab. 1977. Circ. 17,000. Pays on acceptance. Buys all rights, but may reassign following publication. Phone queries OK. Simultaneous and previously published submissions OK. SASE. Reports in 4-6 weeks. Free sample copy and writer's guidelines; mention *Writer's Market* in request.
Nonfiction: How-to (as applies to operational areas, concerning maintenance, security, etc. at arenas, auditoriums, fairs, theme parks and movie theaters); interview; new product; and technical. Buys 46 mss/issue. Query. Length: 200-1,800 words. Pays $1.50-3/column inch.
Photos: State availability of photos with query. Pays $3-5 for 8x10 glossy b&w prints; $10-15 for 35mm color transparencies. Captions preferred. Buys one-time rights. Model release required.
Columns/Departments: Security; Maintenance; Finance; Concessions; Personnel; Purchasing; Sound/light and Parking. Query. Length: 200-1,000 words. Pays $1.50-3/column inch.

MEETINGS & CONVENTIONS, Ziff-Davis Publishing Co., 1 Park Ave., New York NY 10016. Editor-in-Chief: Mel Hosansky. 15% freelance written. For association and corporate executives who plan sales meetings, training meetings, annual conventions, incentive travel trips, and any other kind of off-premises meeting. Monthly magazine; 150 pages. Estab. 1966. Circ. 73,500. Pays on acceptance. Buys all rights. Submit seasonal or holiday material 6 months in advance. Photocopied submissions and previously published work (if not published in a competing publication) OK. SASE. Reports in 1-2 months.
Nonfiction: "Publication is basically how-to. We tell them how to run better meetings; where to hold them, etc. Must be case history, talking about specific meeting." Query. Length: 250-2,000 words. Pays $35-300.
Photos: Purchases 8x10 b&w glossies with mss. Captions required. No additional payment. Query.

MEETINGS & EXPOSITIONS, 22 Pine St., Morristown NJ 07960. (201)538-9470. Editorial Director: William F. Kaiser. Managing Editor: Gale Dopp Curtis. 10% freelance written. Emphasizes meetings, expositions, and incentive travel for "meeting planning" executives in companies and associations. Monthly magazine; 48-64 pages. Estab. 1973. Circ. 42,000. Pays on publication. Buys all rights, but may reassign following publication. Phone queries OK. Submit seasonal/holiday material 6 months in advance of issue date. Simultaneous submissions OK. SASE. Reports in 2 weeks. Free sample copy and writer's guidelines.
Nonfiction: "*ME*'s editorial philosophy centers on in-depth coverage of the five specific major areas of most importance to meetings, expositions, and incentive travel planners: improving meetings; meeting locations; meetings associations meetings; trade shows and expositions; and incentive travel. In brief, it is *ME*'s editorial philosophy to provide, simple and directly, useful information and a most energetic support for the professional meeting planners who want to hold better meetings, more successful expositions, and more productive incentive trave promotions." Buys 10-12 mss/year. Query. Length: 1,000-3,000 words. Pays $35-100.
Photos: Offers no additional payment for 8x10 or 5x7 b&w glossy prints. Captions preferred. Buys one-time rights.

MILLIMETER MAGAZINE, 12 E. 46th St., New York NY 10017. (212)867-3636. Editor: Alice C. Wolf. 75% freelance written. For personnel in motion picture, TV, and videotape industries, ad agencies, film schools (students), and equipment rental services. Monthly magazine; 112 pages. Estab. 1974. Circ. 17,653. Pays on publication. Buys all rights. Phone queries OK. Submit seasonal/holiday material 6 months in advance of issue date. Photocopied submissions OK. SASE. Reports in 3 weeks. Free sample copy.
Nonfiction: "Production stories that deal with entertainment industries of motion pictues and television programming, including TV commercials. Stories should be somewhat technical, involving equipment used, anecdotal, problems encountered and solved, and deal with nationally known production figures. Also interviews with heads of production of current motion pictures and television personnel. Examples: directors, producers, cinematographers, scriptwriters. No personality pieces on 'stars.' " Buys 8 mss/issue. Query. Length: 2,000-4,000 words. Pays $100 minimum.

NARD JOURNAL, 1750 K St., NW., Suite 1200, Washington DC 20006. Editor: Barry Fishler. Director of Communications: Ron Grandon. "Readership is made up of independent community pharmacists who own either one pharmacy or a small chain. Because of the ownership factor, our reader is likely to be a bit older. They are college educated, professional registered pharmacists and small business entrepreneurs." Monthly magazine; 48-64 pages. Estab. 1901. Circ. 23,000. Pays on acceptance. Buys all rights, but may reassign following publication.

Submit seasonal/holiday material "at least 4 months in advance of issue date; 8-9 months for Christmas." SASE. Reports in 3-4 weeks. Free sample copy and writer's guidelines; mention *Writer's Market* in request.
Nonfiction: Expose (hard hitting, documented stories about government bureaucracy's treatment of independent pharmacies as opposed to large chains); general interest (anything that would be of interest to community pharmacists as business types or professionals); interview (with key government figures affecting pharmacy, or with prominent NARD members); personal experience (get a member pharmacist to relate his experience, peg to current issue, extract and summarize the lesson); and profile (key government figures or successful independents). Buys 3-4 mss/year. Query. Length: 1,000-2,000 words. Pays $100-200.
Photos: "Photos are welcome if they help clarify material in the article. Don't send merely to pad the package. For space reasons articles should be capable of standing alone, if convenient." State availability of photos with query. Pays $5-25 for 5x7 b&w glossy prints; $25-35 for 35mm color transparencies. Captions and model release required. Buys all rights, but may reassign following publication.

NATIONAL MALL MONITOR, Suite 500, Arbor Office Center, 1321 US 19 S., Clearwater FL 33516. (813)531-5893. Editor-in-Chief: Barbara D. Engel. 25-40% freelance written. For shopping center industry developers, mall managers, financing institutions, architects, engineers, commercial brokers, and retailers. Bimonthly magazine; 56 pages. Estab. 1970. Circ. 7,000. Pays on publication. Buys all rights. Phone queries OK. Submit seasonal/holiday material 4 months in advance of issue date. Photocopied submissions OK. SASE. Reports in 6 weeks. Sample copy $4 plus postage; free writer's guidelines.
Nonfiction: Wants concise, factual, well-written mss that will keep readers informed of the latest happenings within the industry and allied fields. "The pieces should be cleared through the proper channels for accuracy and authenticity and must be written on a free and easy style, similar to consumer magazines". Buys how-to articles (such as the best way to build, renovate or maintain a shopping center). Stories about unusual specialty or theme centers always in demand. "Always looking for articles about noted architects, engineers, designers, as long as they have something to say to the industry that it doesn't already know". No articles on pageants, auto shows, band concerts or local promotional activities. Buys 20 mss/year. Query. Length: 500-2,000 words. Pays 7½¢/word for 1st sale and 10¢/word for each subsequent sale.
Photos: State availability of photos with query. Pays $9 minimum for 5x7 b&w glossy prints and 8x10 glossy color prints or 2x2 mounted transparencies. Captions required. Buys all rights. Model release required.
Columns/Departments: Spotlights leasing, management and promotion. Query. Length: 800-1,200 words. Pays 7½¢/word for 1st sale and 10¢/word for each subsequent sale. Open to suggestions for new columns/ departments.

NON-FOODS MERCHANDISING, Charleson Publishing Co., 125 E. 40th St., New York NY 10024. Editor-in-Chief: Jerry Whitman. Managing Editor: Alice Ely. 40% freelance written. For buyers, manufacturers, and distributors of health and beauty aids and general merchandise (non-food) in the supermarket. Monthly tabloid; 65 pages. Estab. 1957. Circ. 17,000. Pays on publication. Buys all rights. Photocopied submissions OK. SASE. Reports in 4 weeks.
Nonfiction: "Reports on aspects of our business." Buys 6 mss/issue. Query. Length: 500-2,000 words. Pays $50-150.

PROBLEMS OF COMMUNISM, PGM/PM, International Communication Agency, 1776 Pennsylvania Ave., N.W., Washington DC 20547. (202)632-5119. Editor: Paul A. Smith, Jr. For scholars and decisionmakers in all countries of the world with higher education and a serious interest in foreign area studies and international relations. Estab. 1952. Circ. 25,000. Not copyrighted. Buys 60 to 70 mss/year. Pays on acceptance. Free sample copy. Will consider photocopied submissions. Reports in 3 months. Query first or submit complete ms. SASE.
Nonfiction and Photos: "*Problems of Communism* is one of a very few journals devoted to objective, dispassionate discourse on a highly unobjective, passionately debated phenomenon: communism. It is maintained as a forum in which qualified observers can contribute to a clearer understanding of the sources, nature and direction of change in the areas of its interest. It has no special emphasis or outlook and represents no partisan point of view. Standards of style are those appropriate to the field of international scholarship and journalism. We use intellectually rigorous studies of East-West relations, and/or related political, economic, social and strategic trends in the USSR, China and their associated states and movements. Length is usually 5,000 words. Essay reviews of 1,500 words cover new books offering significant information and analysis. Emphasis throughout *Problems of Communism* is on original research, reliability of

sources and perceptive insights. We do not publish political or other forms of advocacy or apologetics for particular forms of belief." Pays $400 for articles; $175 for essay reviews. Pays $35 for b&w glossies.

SANITARY MAINTENANCE, Box 694, Milwaukee WI 53201. (414)271-4105. Editor-in-Chief: Jack Pomrening. Managing Editor: Don Mulligan. 5% freelance written. For distributors of sanitary supplies. Monthly magazine; 110 pages. Estab. 1943. Circ. 11,800. Pays on publication. Buys all rights. Photocopied submissions OK. SASE. Free sample copy and writer's guidelines.
Nonfiction: How-to (run a janitorial supply business, hold seminars, etc.); interview (with men in the field); and technical. Buys 3 mss/year. Query. Length: 1,500-3,000 words. Pays $100-150.
Photos: State availability of photos with query. Offers no additional payment for 5x7 b&w glossy prints. Captions preferred. Buys all rights.

SHOPFITTING INTERNATIONAL, (incorporating *Display International),* Link House, Dingwall Ave., Croydon CR9 2TA England. Editor: Martin Staheli. Monthly newspaper for retailers with purchasing and specifying powers, property and premises managers, architects, designers, shopfitters, display managers, woodworking and metalworking equipment manufacturers, management and executive staffs in all retail trades and in most major commercial organizations which meet the public on their premises. Estab. 1955. Circ. 10,000. Pays on publication. Copyrighted. SAE and International Reply Coupons. Query or submit complete ms. Free sample copy.
Nonfiction: News items and features on the fitting-out of shops, departmental stores, restaurants, hotels (public areas only), showrooms, offices, board rooms, bars, night clubs, theaters, banks, building societies; the materials and techniques used; the design brief for interior and exterior; use of sub-contractors, cost of job. Pays 30 pounds minimum.

SMALL BUSINESS COMPUTOR, 349 Warren St., Needham MA 02192. "*SBC*'s target audience is, in general, the end-users of small business computors and computor services. The publication's prime orientation is to small business executives and professionals servicing them that desire information on the managerial aspects of computers such that the small business can be better managed and controlled." Quarterly newsletter; 16-32 pages. Estab. 1977. Pays on publication. Buys all rights. Submit material 3 months in advance. Simultaneous and photocopied submissions OK. SASE. Reports in 1-2 months. Writer's guidelines for SASE.
Nonfiction: Exposé; how-to; informational; interview; new product; personal experience; personal opinion; profile, technical,and managerial. Buys 8-16 mss/year. Query. Length: 250-1,500 words. Pays $10-300.
Photos: State availability of photos with query. Uses b&w photos.
Fillers: Clippings, jokes, gags, anecdotes, newsbreaks, and short humor. Buys 2-4/issue. Length: 250-1,500 words. Pays $10-300.

SOLAR ENERGY DIGEST, P.O. Box 17776, San Diego CA 92117. Editor: William B. Edmondson. 5-10% freelance written. For manufacturers, scientists, engineers, architects, builders, developers, technicians, energy experts, teachers, inventors, and others interested in solar energy conversion. Newsletter; 12 pages. Estab. 1973. Monthly. Circ. 15,000. Buys all rights, but may reassign rights to author after publication. Buys 60 to 75 mss per year. Payment on publication. Will send free sample copy to writer on request, if S.A.S.E. is enclosed. Will not consider photocopied or simultaneous submissions. Reports on mss accepted for publication in 2 to 3 weeks. Returns rejected material in 1 to 2 weeks. Enclose SASE.
Nonfiction and Fillers: Wants mss about new developments in any facet of solar energy conversion, including applications in agriculture, architecture, cooking, distillation, mechanical engines and pumps, photo-electricity, steam generation, flat plate and concentrating collectors, sea thermal plants, furnaces, heat and energy storage, photosynthesis, wind power, wave power, etc. "Assume that the reader knows the fundamentals of the subject and plunge right in without a long introduction. Keep it simple, but not simplistic." No generalized papers on solar energy. "We like to cover a specific new development in each story." Length: 100 to 1,000 words. Length preferred for regular columns: 1,000 words maximum. Pays 2¢ to 5¢ per word. Also buys news clippings on solar energy. Pays $2.50 maximum for accepted clips. Buys fillers; shorts on solar energy. Length: 25 to 200 words. Pays $1 to $5.
Photos: Purchased with accompanying ms with extra payment or without ms. Captions required. Pays $1 to $5 for b&w. Size: 4x5 minimum.

TOBACCO REPORTER, 757 Third Ave., New York NY 10017. Editor: John Karolefski. For tobacco growers, processors, warehousemen, exporters, importers, manufacturers and dis-

tributors of cigars, cigarettes, and tobacco products. Monthly. Buys all rights. Pays on publication. SASE.
Nonfiction and Photos: Uses original material on request only. Pays approximately 2½¢ a word. Pays $3 for photos purchased with mss.
Fillers: Wants clippings on new tobacco product brands, local tobacco distributors, smoking and health, and the following relating to tobacco and tobacco products: job promotions, obituaries, honors, equipment, etc. Pays minimum 25¢ a clipping on use only.

WEIGHING & MEASUREMENT, Key Markets Publishing Co., Box 5867, Rockford IL 61125. (815)399-6970. Editor: David M. Mathieu. For users of industrial scales and meters. Monthly tabloid; 24 pages. Estab. 1913. Circ. 25,000. Pays on acceptance. Buys all rights, but may reassign following publication. Reports in 2 weeks. Free sample copy.
Nonfiction: Interview (with presidents of companies), personal opinion (guest editorials on government involvement in business, etc.), profile (about users of weighing and measurement equipment) and technical. Buys 25 mss/year. Query on technical articles; submit complete ms for general interest material. Length: 750-2,500 words. Pays $45-125.

WIRE JOURNAL, Box H, 1570 Boston Post Rd., Guilford CT 06437. Editor: Donald K. Walker. Assistant Editor: Anita M. Oliva. Technical journal for wire and cable manufacturers and for manufacturers of products using wire and cable. Monthly magazine; 120 pages. Estab. 1964. Circ. 10,500. Pays on publication. Buys all rights. Photocopied submissions OK. SASE. Reports in 1 month. Sample copy $3.
Nonfiction: Historical (background on wire and cable manufacturers); personal experience (only if from someone in the wire industry); and technical (wiredrawing, stranding, insulating). Query. Length: 2,500 words maximum. Pays $50-200.

Music

THE CANADIAN COMPOSER, Creative Arts Co., #401, 1240 Bay St., Toronto, Ont., Canada M5R 2A7. (416)925-5138. Editor-in-Chief: Richard Flohil. For "composers of music in Canada; 10% 'serious', the rest involved in various kinds of popular music." Published 10 times/year. Magazine; 48 pages. Estab. 1966. Pays on publication. Buys one-time rights. Phone queries OK. Submit seasonal/holiday material 3 months in advance. Photocopied submissions OK. SASE. Reports in 1 week. Free sample copy.
Nonfiction: Informational, interview and profile. Buys 4 mss/issue. Query. Length: 2,500 words. Pays $90-125.
Photos: Purchased with accompanying ms or on assignment. Captions required. Query or submit contact sheet. Pays $10-20 for 8x10 b&w glossies.

THE CHURCH MUSICIAN, 127 Ninth Ave. N., Nashville TN 37234. (615)251-2953. Editor: William Anderson. 30% freelance written. Southern Baptist publication. For Southern Baptist church music leaders. Monthly. Circ. 20,000. Buys all rights. Pays on acceptance. Free sample copy. No query required. Reports in 2 months. SASE.
Nonfiction: Leadership and how-to features, success stories, articles on Protestant church music. "We reject material when the subject of an article doesn't meet our needs. And they are often poorly written, or contain too many 'glittering generalities' or lack creativity." Length: maximum 1,300 words. Pays up to 3½¢/word.
Photos: Purchased with mss; related to mss content only.
Fiction: Inspiration, guidance, motivation, morality with Protestant church music slant. Length: to 1,300 words. Pays up to 3½¢/word.
Poetry: Church music slant, inspirational. Length: 8 to 24 lines. Pays $5 to $10.
Fillers: Puzzles, short humor. Church music slant. No clippings. Pays $3 to $5.
How To Break In: "I'd advise a beginning writer to write about his or her experience with some aspect of church music; the social, musical, and spiritual benefits from singing in a choir; a success story about their instrumental group; a testimonial about how they were enlisted in a choir—especially if they were not inclined to be enlisted at first. A writer might speak to hymn singers—what turns them on and what doesn't. Some might include how music has helped them to talk about Jesus as well as sing about Him. We would prefer most of these experiences be related to the church, of course, although we include many articles by freelance writers whose affiliation is other than Baptist. We are delighted to receive their manuscripts, to be sure. A writer might relate his experience with a choir of blind or deaf members. Some people receive benefits from working with unusual children—retarded, or culturally deprived, emotionally

unstable, and so forth. Photographs are valuable here."

CLAVIER, 1418 Lake Street, Evanston IL 60204. (312)328-6000. Editor: Beverly McGahey. Magazine; 48 pages. Estab. 1962. 9 times a year. Buys all rights, but may reassign rights to author after publication. Pays on publication. Free sample copy. No simultaneous submissions. "Suggest query to avoid duplication." Reports in 4 weeks on very good or very bad mss, "quite slow on the in-betweens." SASE.
Nonfiction and Photos: Wants "articles aimed at teachers of piano and organ. Must be written from thoroughly professional point of view. Avoid, however, the thesis-style subject matter and pedantic style generally found in scholarly journals. We like fresh writing, practical approach. We can use interviews with concert pianists and organists. An interview should not be solely a personality story, but should focus on a subject of interest to musicians. Any word length. Photos may accompany ms." Pays $20/printed page. Need color photos for cover, such as angle shots of details of instruments, other imaginative photos, with keyboard music themes."

HIGH FIDELITY TRADE NEWS, 6 E. 43rd St., New York NY 10017. Editor: Ronald Marin. For "retailers, salesmen, manufacturers, and representatives involved in the high fidelity/home entertainment market." Estab. 1956. Monthly. Circ. 23,000. Buys all rights. Buys about 36 to 50 mss a year. Pays on acceptance. Will send a sample copy to a writer on request. Query first; "all work by assignment only." Enclose SASE.
Nonfiction: "Dealer profiles, specific articles on merchandising of high fidelity products, market surveys, sales trends, etc." Length: "open." Pay varies "as to type of article."
How To Break In: "We prefer to rely on our own resources for developing story ideas. Let us know about your willingness to work and submit, if possible, some samples of previous work. Even if you're a new writer, we're still likely to try you out, especially if you know the business or live in a market area where we need coverage. Articles on merchandising, product reports, and dealer profiles."

THE INSTRUMENTALIST, 1418 Lake St., Evanston IL 60204. Editor: Kenneth L. Neidig. For instrumental music educators. Estab. 1946. Monthly except in July. Circ. 21,193. Buys all rights. Buys 200 mss a year. Payment on publication. Sample copy $1. Will consider photocopied submissions. Submit seasonal material 3 months in advance. New Products (February); Summer Camps, Clinics, Workshops (March); Marching Bands (June); Back to School (September); Music Industry. (August). Reports on material accepted for publication within 4 months. Returns rejected material within 3 months. Query first. SASE.
Nonfiction and Photos: "Practical information of immediate use to instrumentalists. Not articles 'about music and musicians,' but articles by musicians who are sharing knowledge, techniques, experience. 'In-service education.' Professional help for instrumentalists in the form of instrumental clinics, how-to articles, new trends, practical philosophy. Most contributions are from professionals in the field." Interpretive photojournalism. Length: open. Pays $10 to $100, plus 3 contributor's copies. Quality b&w prints. Pays $5. Color: 35mm and up. Pays $25 if used for cover.

MUSIC EDUCATORS JOURNAL, 1902 Association Dr., Reston VA 22091. (703)860-4000. Editor: John T. Aquin. For professional music educators in elementary and secondary schools and universities. Monthly (September-May) magazine; 120 pages. Estab. 1914. Circ. 70,000. Pays on acceptance. SASE. Reports in 1-8 weeks. Free sample copy and 9-page author's guidesheet.
Nonfiction: "We publish articles on music education at all levels — not about individual schools, but about broad issues, trends, instructional techniques. Also articles on music, aside from teaching it. Particularly interested in solid, heavily researched pieces on individual aspects of American music, and interviews with important but lesser known composers, performers and educators. We do not want to see articles about 'the joys of music', or about personal experiences. We are not a homey type of publication." Length: 1,000-3,000 words. Query first. Pays $75-200 for assigned articles.

MUSIC JOURNAL, 370 Lexington Ave., New York NY 10017. Editor: Guy Freedman. For music faculties and students of universities, colleges, libraries, and professionals, music lovers, in general. 50-page magazine published 10 times a year; monthly, September through May, plus summer and winter annuals. Estab. 1943. Circ. 24,170. Rights purchased vary with author and material. Usually buys first North American serial rights. Buys 30 to 35 mss a year. Payment on publication. Will send sample copy to writer for 50¢. Will not consider photocopied or simultaneous submissions. Submit special issue material (folk, country/western, rock, jazz) 3 months

in advance. Reports on material accepted for publication in 3 weeks. Returns rejected material immediately. Query first or submit complete ms. Enclose SASE.
Nonfiction and Photos: "We embrace all musical subject areas, exploring the many mansions of the composer, conductor, performer, private teacher, student, educator, artist, manager and music lover." Does not solicit material on the opera. Uses informational articles, personal experience, humorous, historical and nostalgic articles, as well as those dealing with personal opinion, spot news, new products, technical. Length: 500 to 1,200 words. Pays $25 to $50. No additional payment is made for photos used with mss.
Poetry: Traditional forms, blank verse, free verse, avant-garde forms, light verse. Must relate to music. Length: open. Pays $5.
How To Break In: "Stories of special interest to instrumentalists are the hardest to come by and would be the best way to break in. Otherwise, the key thing to keep in mind is that we are trying to be timely."

MUSIC TRADES MAGAZINE, Box 432, Englewood NJ 07631. (201)871-1975. Editor-in-Chief: J. Majeski. Managing Editor: G. Frary. 5% freelance written. For music store owners and salesman; manufacturers of pianos, organs, band instruments, and guitars. Monthly magazine; 120 pages. Estab. 1890. Circ. 6,800. Pays on publication. Copyrighted, but rights remain with author. Simultaneous submissions OK. SASE.
Nonfiction: How-to and general interest. Query. No limit on length. Payment negotiable.

THE MUSICAL NEWSLETTER, 654 Madison Ave., Suite 1703, New York NY 10021. Editor: Patrick J. Smith. For "amateur and professional music lovers who wish to know more about music and be given more specific information." Estab. 1971. Quarterly. Circ. 600. Rights purchased vary with author and material; may buy first serial rights in English or second serial rights. Pays on acceptance. Sample copy $1. Will consider photocopied submissions. Query first for nonfiction, "giving a list of subjects of possible interest and outlines, if possible." SASE.
Nonfiction: "Articles on music and the musical scene today. The bulk of articles are on 'classical' music, but we also publish articles on jazz and pop. Articles need not pertain to music directly, such as socio-economic articles on performing entities. As the level of our publication is between the musicological quarterly and the record review magazine, what we want is readable material which contains hard-core information. We stress quality. We are always happy to examine freelance material on any aspect of music, from articles on composers' works to philosophical articles on music or reportorial articles on performing organizations. We discourage reviews of performances and interviews, which we feel are adequately covered elsewhere." Length: 3,000 words maximum. Pays 10¢/word.

OPERA NEWS, 1865 Broadway, New York NY 10023. Editor: Robert Jacobson. For all people interested in opera; opera singers, opera management people, administrative people in opera, opera publicity people, artists' agents; people in the trade and interested laymen. Magazine; 32 to 72 pages. Estab. 1933. Weekly. (Monthly in summer.) Circ. 76,000. Copyrighted. Pays on publication. Will send sample copy to writer for $1. Query first. Enclose SASE.
Nonfiction and Photos: Most articles are commissioned in advance. In summer, uses articles of various interests on opera; in the fall and winter, articles that relate to the weekly broadcasts. Emphasis is on high quality in writing and an intellectual interest in the opera-oriented public. Informational, how-to, personal experience, interview, profile, humor, historical, think pieces, personal opinion; opera reviews. Length: 300 words maximum. Pays 10¢ per word for features; 8¢ a word for reviews. Pays minimum of $25 for photos purchased on assignment. Captions required.

SOUTHWESTERN MUSICIAN, P.O. Box 9908, Houston TX 77015. Editor: J.F. Lenzo. 20% freelance written. For music teachers. Monthly (August through May). Buys all rights. Pays on acceptance. Reports in 30 days. Enclose SASE.
Nonfiction: Wants "professionally slanted articles of interest to public school music teachers." Pays $25 to $50.

Oceanography

The journals below are intended primarily for scientists who are studying the ocean. Publications for ocean fishermen will be found under Fishing. Those for persons interested in water and the ocean as a means of travel or shipping are listed with the

Marine Industries and Water Navigation journals.

SEA FRONTIERS, 3979 Rickenbacker Causeway, Virginia Key, Miami FL 33149. (305)361-5786. Editor: F.G.W. Smith. 90-95% freelance written. For "members of the International Oceanographic Foundation. For the lay person—anyone with an interest in the sea; professional people for the most part; people in executive positions and students." Estab. 1954. Bimonthly. Circ. 70,000. Buys all rights. Buys 20 to 25 mss a year. Payment on publication. Free sample copy and writer's guidelines. Will consider photocopied submissions "if very clear." Reports on material within 6 weeks. Query first. SASE.
Nonfiction and Photos: "Articles (with illustrations) covering explorations, discoveries or advances in our knowledge of the marine sciences, or describing the activities of oceanographic laboratories or expeditions to any part of the world. Emphasis should be on research and discoveries rather than personalities involved." Length: 500 to 3,000 words. Pays $20-30/page. 8x10 b&w glossy prints and 35mm (or larger) color transparencies purchased with ms. Pays $50 for color used on front and $25 for the back cover. Pays $15 for color used on inside covers.

Office Equipment and Supplies

GEYER'S DEALER TOPICS, 51 Madison Ave., New York NY 10010. (212)689-4411. Editor: Neil Loynachan. For independent office equipment and stationery dealers, and special purchasers for store departments handling stationery and office equipment. Monthly. Buys all rights. Pays on acceptance. Query first. Reports "immediately." SASE.
Nonfiction and Photos: Articles on merchandising and sales promotion; programs of stationery and office equipment dealers. Problem-solving articles relating to retailers of office supplies, social stationery items, gifts (if the retailer also handles commercial supplies), office furniture and equipment and office machines. Minimum payment, $35, but quality of article is real determinant. Length: 300 to 1,000 words. B&w glossies are purchased with accompanying ms with no additional payment.

OFFICE PRODUCTS, Hitchcock Building, Wheaton IL 60187. (312)665-1000. Editorial Director: Thomas J. Trafals. For "independent dealers who sell all types of office products—office machines, office furniture, and office supplies." Estab. 1904. Monthly. Circ. 25,000. Buys all rights, but will reassign rights to author after publication. Pays on acceptance. Article deadlines are the 1st of the third month preceding date of issue. News deadlines are the 1st of each month. Reports in 3 to 4 weeks. Query first on any long articles. SASE.
Nonfiction: "We're interested in anything that will improve an office product dealer's methods of doing business. Some emphasis on selling and promotion, but interested in all phases of dealer operations." Length: "that which tells the story, and no more or less." Pays $25 to $150 "based on quality of article."
Photos: Purchased with mss.

OFFICE WORLD NEWS, 645 Stewart Ave., Garden City NY 11530. Editor: Alec W. Shapiro. 5% freelance written. For independent office products dealers. Bimonthly; 24 to 60 tabloid pages. Estab. 1972. Circ. 16,000. Buys all rights. Payment on publication. Free sample copy. Will not consider photocopied or simultaneous submissions. Reports in 2 weeks. Query first. SASE.
Nonfiction and Photos: "All freelance material is written on assignment or following queries by our freelance 'stringers'. Our published material consists of news and news-related features. Straight news reporting, with emphasis on the effect on office product dealers. No textbook management articles will be accepted. We try to limit our content to hard news." Length: 100 to 500 words. Pays 10¢ per word. B&w photos are purchased with mss or on assignment. $10 for 5x7 (minimum) b&w.
How To Break In: "Will consider any experienced newswriter for stringer assignments, except in New York metropolitan area."

PACIFIC STATIONER, 41 Sutter St., San Francisco CA 94104. Editor: Robert B. Frier. Monthly magazine; 60 to 70 pages. Estab. 1908. Circ. 5,500. Not copyrighted. Buys about 12 mss/year. Pays on acceptance. Sample copy $1. No photocopied or simultaneous submissions. Submit seasonal (merchandising) material 3 to 4 months in advance. Reports on material accepted for publication in 1 week. Returns rejected material immediately. Query first or submit complete ms. SASE.
Nonfiction and Photos: "Our main interest is in how western retailers of stationery and office

products can do a better selling job. We use how-to-do-it merchandising articles showing dealers how to sell more stationery and office products to more people at a greater profit. Seasonal merchandising articles always welcome, if acceptable.'' Informational, how-to, personal experience, interview, successful business operations. Length: 1,000 to 1,500 words. Pays 2¢ a word. Pays $5 for b&w photos used with mss; 3x5 minimum. Captions required.

SOUTHERN STATIONER AND OFFICE OUTFITTER, 75 Third St. N.W., Atlanta GA 30308. Editor: Earl Lines, Jr. For retailers of office products in the Southeast and Southwest. Monthly. Not copyrighted. Pays on publication. Free sample copy. Query required. Reports promptly. SASE.

Nonfiction: Can use articles about retailers in the Southeast and Southwest regarding problems solved concerning store layout, inventory, personnel, etc. ''We want articles giving in-depth treatment of a single aspect of a dealer's operation rather than superficial treatment of a number of aspects.'' Must be approved by subject. Length: 1,000 to 1,400 words. Pays 2¢ to 4¢ a word.

Photos: Purchased with mss. Pays $5.

Optical

THE DISPENSING OPTICIAN, Opticians Association of America, 1250 Connecticut Ave., N.W., Washington DC 20036. Editor: James M. McCormick. 50% freelance written. For dispensing opticians. Published 11 times a year. Magazine; 36-48 pages. Estab. 1950. Circ. 5,800. Pays ''when issue is locked up.'' Buys all rights, but may reassign following publication. Photocopied submissions OK. SASE. ''Reports are slow due to clearance by editorial board (up to 60 days).'' Will send sample copy to writer ''only when we're interested in an article suggestion.''

Nonfiction: Publishes informational, how-to, interview, profile, historical, photo feature, successful business operations, merchandising techniques, and technical articles. ''All must specifically pertain to or interest the dispensing optician, and profiles and successful business operations must be of Association members.'' Query. Buys 10-20 mss/year. Length: 400-2,000 words. Pays 9-15¢/word.

Photos: Purchased with or without accompanying ms, or on assignment. Caption material required. Pays $5-50 for 5x7 or 8x10 b&w prints. Query.

N.J. JOURNAL OF OPTOMETRY, County Line Professional Bldg., W. County Line Rd., Jackson NJ 08527. (201)364-4111. Editor: Errol Rummel, O.D. For doctors of optometry practices located in New Jersey. Magazine; 35 to 40 pages. Estab. 1955. Quarterly. Circ. 1,200. Not copyrighted. Will consider photocopied submissions. No simultaneous submissions. Reports in 3 weeks. Query first. Enclose S.A.S.E.

Nonfiction and Photos: Technical articles on eye care, exam techniques, etc.; news reports on eye care, either national or local; practice management articles. Writer must remember that this is a professional, knowledgeable audience. Length: 1,000 to 2,000 words. Pays 3¢ per word minimum.

Packing, Canning, and Packaging

Journals in this category are for packaging engineers and others concerned with new methods of packing, canning, and packaging foods in general. Other publications that buy similar material will be found under the Food Processing, Products, and Services heading.

FOOD AND DRUG PACKAGING, 777 Third Ave., New York NY 10017. Editor: Ben Miyares. For packaging decisionmakers in food, drug, cosmetic firms. Estab. 1959. Biweekly. Circ. 56,000. Rights purchased vary with author and material. Pays on acceptance. ''Queries only.'' SASE.

Nonfiction and Photos: ''Looking for news stories about local and state (not federal) packaging legislation, and its impact on the marketplace. Newspaper style.'' Length: 1,000 to 2,500 words; usually 500 to 750 words. Payments vary; usually 5¢ a word. Photos purchased with mss. 5x7 glossies preferred. Pays $5.

How To Break In: ''1) Get details on local packaging legislation's impact on marketplace/sales/consumer/retailer reaction, etc. 2) Keep an eye open for *new* packages. Query when you think you've got one. New packages move into test markets every day, so if you don't see anything new this week, try again next week. Buy it; describe it briefly in a query."

MODERN PACKAGING, Morgan Grampian Publishing Corp., 205 E. 42nd St., New York NY 10017. (212)573-8109. Editor-in-Chief: Gary M. Reicsfad. For product manufacturers who package or have contract-packaged their product lines, suppliers of packaging material and equipment. Monthly magazine; 70 pages. Estab. 1927. Circ. 61,000. Pays on publication. Buys all rights. Photocopied submissions OK. SASE. Reports in 6 weeks. Free sample copy. Guidelines for writers (only on technical articles).
Nonfiction: How-to, informational and new product articles. Trend reports, engineering and technical reports. Length: open. Query first. Pays $35/printed page.
Photos: B&w and color photos purchased with mss or on assignment. Query, or send contact sheets or prints. Pays $5 minimum. Model release required.

PACKAGE PRINTING, North American Publishing Co., 401 N. Broad St., Philadelphia PA 19108. Editor-in-Chief: Walter Kubilius. Managing Editor: Hennie Marine. 20% freelance written. Emphasizes "any sort of package printing (food, peanuts, candy, etc.) for the plant superintendent or general manager of the company's package printing department." Monthly magazine; 74 pages. Estab. 1970. Circ. 8,000. Pays on acceptance. Buys all rights. Phone queries OK. Simultaneous and photocopied submissions OK. SASE. Reports in 2 weeks. Sample copy $1.
Nonfiction: "Generally a 'plant' story on the operation of the printing department of a packaging concern. The writer may not know a flexographic machine from a gravure machine or any other, but we expect him to interview the plant manager and get all the technical details. How is the package printed? What is the paper/film/foil used? How many? What kinds? Names and speed of all machines used; number of employees in production; everything relating to the manufacture and printing of any sort of package (look in any supermarket for 1,000 examples of packages." Query. Pays $50/printed page.
Photos: State availability of photos with query. Pays $10 for 5x7 or 8x10 b&w prints. Captions required. Buys all rights, but may reassign following publication.

THE PACKER, Box 1279. Kansas City KS 66117. (913)281-3073. Editor: Paul Campbell. 5% freelance written. For shippers, fruit and vegetable growers, wholesalers, brokers, retailers. Newspaper; 36 pages. Estab. 1893. Weekly. Circ. 16,500. Buys all rights, but may reassign rights to author after publication. Buys about 10 mss a year. Pays on publication. Will send free sample copy to writer on request. Write for copy of guidelines for writers. Will consider simultaneous submissions. No photocopied submissions. Reports on material accepted for publication in 2 weeks. Returns rejected material in 1 month. Query first or submit complete ms. Enclose SASE.
Nonfiction: Articles on growing techniques, merchandising, marketing, transportation, refrigeration. Emphasis is on the "what's new" approach in these areas. Length: 1,000 words. Pays $40 minimum.

PACKING AND SHIPPING, 735 Woodland Ave., Plainfield NJ 07062. Editor: C.M. Bonnell, Jr. For "packaging engineers, traffic managers, shipping managers, and others interested in physical distribution, industrial packaging and shipping." 9 times a year. Buys all rights. Pays on publication. Query first. Reports "promptly." SASE.
Nonfiction: Packing, handling and physical distribution procedure by land, water and air as related to large company operations. Pays 1¢ a word.

Paint

Additional journals that buy material on paint, wallpaper, floor covering, and decorating products stores are listed under Building Interiors.

AMERICAN PAINT & COATINGS JOURNAL, American Paint Journal Co., 2911 Washington Ave., St. Louis MO 63103. (314)534-0301. Editor: Fred Schulenberg. 10% freelance written. For the coatings industry (paint, varnish, lacquer, etc.); manufacturers of coatings, suppliers to coatings industry, educational institutions, salesmen. Weekly magazine; 78 pages. Estab. 1916. Circ. 7,300. Pays on publication. Buys all rights. Phone queries OK. Simultaneous and photocopied submissions OK. SASE. Reports in 3 weeks. Free sample copy and writer's guidelines.
Nonfiction: Informational, historical, interview, new product and technical articles and coatings industry news. Buys 2 mss/issue. Query before sending long articles; submit complete ms for

short pieces. Length: 75-1,200 words. Pays $5-100.
Photos: B&w (5x7) glossies purchased with or without mss, or on assignment. Query first. Pays $3-10.

AMERICAN PAINT AND WALLCOVERINGS DEALER, 2911 Washington Ave., St. Louis MO 63103. (314)534-0301. Editor-in-Chief: Clark Rowley. Assistant Editor: Cathy Hardin. 20% freelance written. Monthly magazine; 60 pages. Estab. 1908. Circ. 33,000. Pays on publication. Buys all rights. Phone queries OK. Submit seasonal/holiday material 2 months in advance of issue date. Reports in 2 weeks. Free sample copy and writer's guidelines.
Nonfiction: Informational articles that will be of interest to paint and wallcoverings dealers; usually articles on other successful stores. No articles about name-brand products. Buys 10 mss/year. Submit complete ms. Pays $100-125.
Photos: Submit photos with accompanying ms. Pays $10 for b&w prints; $25 for color transparencies. Captions preferred. Buys one-time rights.

AMERICAN PAINTING CONTRACTOR, American Paint Journal Co., 2911 Washington Ave., St. Louis MO 63103. (314)534-0301. Editor-in-Chief: John L. Cleveland. For painting and decorating contractors, in-plant maintenance painting department heads, architects and paint specifiers. Monthly magazine; 80 pages. Estab. 1923. Circ. 33,000. Buys all rights, but may reassign following publication. Phone queries OK. Submit seasonal/holiday material 2 months in advance. Simultaneous and photocopied submissions OK. SASE. Reports in 3 weeks. Free sample copy and writer's guidelines.
Nonfiction: Historical, how-to, humor, informational, new product, personal experience, personal opinion and technical articles; interviews, photo features and profiles. Buys 4 mss an issue. "Freelancers should be able to write well and have some understanding of the painting and decorating industry. We do not want general theme articles such as 'How to Get More Work Out of Your Employee' unless they relate to a problem within the painting and decorating industry. Query before submitting copy." Length: 1,000-2,500 words. Pays $75-100.
Photos: B&w and color purchased with mss or on assignment. Captions required. Send contact sheets, prints or transparencies. Pays $15-35.

CANADIAN PAINT AND FINISHING MAGAZINE, 481 University Ave., Toronto, Ont., Canada M5W 1A7. (416)595-1811. Editor: Andrew Douglas. Monthly. Buys first North American serial rights. Pays on acceptance for mss, on publication for photos. Query first. Reports in 1 week. Enclose SAE and International Reply Coupons.
Nonfiction and Photos: "Semitechnical and news articles on paint manufacturing, industrial finishing techniques, new developments. Also interested in electroplating. Mostly Canadian material required." Accompanied by photos. Length: 1,500 words. Pays minimum 10¢ a word.

WESTERN PAINT REVIEW, 2354 W. 3rd St., Los Angeles CA 90057. (213)389-4151. Editor: Ernest C. Ansley. For painting and decorating contractors, retail paint dealers and paint manufacturers. Estab. 1920. Monthly. Circ. 18,000. Buys first North American serial rights. Buys 25 to 30 mss/year. Pays on publication. Will consider photocopied submissions. Submit seasonal material 2 months in advance. Reports on material within 3 weeks. Query first. SASE.
Nonfiction and Photos: Articles on successful business operations, merchandising techniques. Technical articles. Length: 500 to 3,000 words. Pays 4¢ a word minimum. 4x5 minimum glossy b&w photos purchased with ms. Captions required. Pays $4.

Paper

FORET ET PAPIER, 625 President Kennedy Ave., Montreal, Quebec, Canada H3A 1K5. (514)845-5141. Editor: Paul Saint-Pierre, C. Adm. For engineers and technicians engaged in the making of paper. Quarterly magazine; 50 pages. Estab. 1975. Circ. 7,000. Rights purchased vary with author and material. Buys first North American serial rights, second serial (reprint) rights, and simultaneous rights. Buys about 12 mss per year. Pays on acceptance. Will consider photocopied submissions. Reports on mss accepted for publication in 1 week. Returns rejected material in 2 days. Enclose SASE.
Nonfiction and Photos: Uses technical articles on papermaking. Buys informational, how-to, personal experience, interview, photo, and technical articles. Length: 1,000 words maximum. Pays $25 to $150. Photos purchased with accompanying ms with extra payment or purchased on assignment. Captions required. Pays $25 for b&w. Color shots must be vertical. Pays $150 maximum for color cover shots.

PAPERBOARD PACKAGING, 777 Third Ave., New York NY 10017. (212)838-7778. Editor: Joel J. Shulman. For "managers, supervisors, and technical personnel who operate corrugated box manufacturing and folding cartons converting companies and plants." Estab. 1916. Monthly. Circ. 10,000. Buys all rights. Pays on publication. Will send a sample copy to a writer on request. Will consider photocopied submissions. Submit seasonal material 3 months in advance. Query first. Enclose SASE.
Nonfiction and Photos: "Application articles, installation stories, etc. Contact the editor first to establish the approach desired for the article. Especially interested in packaging systems using composite materials, including paper and other materials." Buys technical articles. Length: open. Pays "$50 per printed page (about 1,000 words to a page), including photos. We do not pay for commercially oriented material. We do pay for material if it is not designed to generate business for someone in our field. Will not pay photography costs, but will pay cost of photo reproductions for article."

Petroleum

THE DRILLING CONTRACTOR, International Association of Drilling Contractors, 7400 Harwin Dr., Suite 305, Houston TX 77036. Editor-in-Chief: Tony Simmons. Managing Editor: Lillian Martin. 20% freelance written. Emphasizes oilwell drilling for management of drilling contractor firms. Bimonthly magazine; 100 pages. Estab. 1942. Circ. 12,000. Pays on acceptance. Buys all rights, but may reassign following publication. Submit seasonal/holiday material 2 months in advance of issue date. Simultaneous, photocopied and previously published submissions OK. SASE. Reports in 2 weeks. Free sample copy and writer's guidelines.
Nonfiction: Historical (oilfields, drilling); how-to; and drilling articles. Buys 2 mss/issue. Query. Length: 200-2,000 words. Pays $50 minimum.

ENERGY MANAGEMENT REPORT, Box 1589, Dallas TX 75221. (214)748-4403. Editor-in-Chief: Ernestine Adams. Assistant Editors: Julie Fonner, Gregory Martin. 7-10% freelance written. Emphasizes energy for operating management of oil/gas operating companies and supply/service companies. Monthly magazine; 16 pages. Estab. October 1929. Circ. 52,000. Pays on publication. Buys all rights. SASE. Reports in 2 months. Free sample copy; mention *Writer's Market* in request.
Nonfiction: Uses energy briefs and concise analysis of energy situations. "Across-the-board interpretive reporting on current events." Publishes briefs about energy world news, international design and engineering, offshore energy business, environmental action, energy financing, and new products. Pays 10¢/word.

FUELOIL AND OIL HEAT, 200 Commerce Rd., Cedar Grove NJ 07009. (201)239-5800. Feature Editor: M. F. Hundley. For distributors of fueloil, heating and air conditioning equipment dealers. Monthly. Buys first rights. Pays on publication. Reports in 2 weeks. Enclose SASE.
Nonfiction: Management articles dealing with fueloil distribution and oilheating equipment selling. Length: up to 2,500 words. Pays $35 a printed page.

HUGHES RIGWAY, Hughes Tool Co., Box 2539, Houston TX 77001. Editor-in-Chief: Ken Whanger. For oilfield drilling personnel. Quarterly magazine; 28 pages. Estab. 1963. Circ. 14,000. Pays on acceptance. Buys first North American serial rights. Simultaneous and photocopied submissions OK. SASE. Reports in 1 month. Free sample copy and writer's guidelines.
Nonfiction and Photos: "Character-revealing historical narratives about little-known incidents, heroes, or facts, particularly those which contradict conventional concepts. Also, topical reportorial features about people in oil or drilling. Must be thoroughly documented." Length: 2,000 to 2,500 words. Pays 10¢ a word. Photos purchased with mss.
Fiction: "Top-quality fiction in oilfield settings." Length: 2,000 to 2,500 words. Pays 10¢ a word.

HYDROCARBON PROCESSING, Box 2608, Houston TX 77001. Editor: Frank L. Evans. 95% freelance written. For personnel in oil refining, gas and petrochemical processing or engineering-contractors, including engineering, operation, maintenance and management phases. Special issues: January, Maintenance; April, Natural Gas Processing; September, Refining Processes; November, Petrochemical Processes. Monthly. Buys all rights. Write for copy of guidelines for writers. SASE.
Nonfiction: Wants technical manuscripts on engineering and operations in the industry which

will be of help to personnel. Also nontechnical articles on management, safety and industrial relations that will help technical men become managers. Length: open, "but do not waste words." Pays about $25 per printed page.

How To Break In: "Articles must all pass a rigid evaluation of their reader appeal, accuracy and overall merit. Reader interest determines an article's value. We covet articles that will be of real job value to subscribers. Before writing—ask to see our Author's Handbook. You may save time and effort by writing a letter, and outline briefly what you have in mind. If your article will or won't meet our needs, we will tell you promptly."

NATIONAL PETROLEUM NEWS, 1221 Avenue of the Americas, New York NY 10020. (212)997-2361. Editor: William Olcott. For businessmen who make their living in the oil marketing industry, either as company employees or through their own business operations. Monthly magazine; 90 pages. Estab. 1909. Circ. 20,000. Rights purchased vary with author and material. Usually buys all rights. Buys 2 mss a year. Payment on acceptance if done on assignment. Payment on publication for unsolicited material. "The occasional freelance copy we use is done on assignment." Query first. SASE.

Nonfiction and Photos: Department Editor: Carolyn DeWitt. Material related directly to developments and issues in the oil marketing industry and "how-to" and "what-with" case studies. Informational; successful business operations. Length: 2,000 words maximum. Pays $60 per printed page. Payment for b&w photos "depends upon advance understanding".

OCEAN INDUSTRY, Gulf Publishing Co., Box 2608, Houston TX 77001. (713)529-4301. Editor-in-Chief: Donald M. Taylor. Associate Editor: Scott Weeden. 25% freelance written. "Our readers are generally engineers and company executives in companies with business dealings with off-shore petroleum and deepsea mining interests." Monthly magazine; 116 pages. Estab. 1966. Circ. 33,000. Pays on publication. Buys all rights. Phone queries OK. Photocopied and previously published submissions OK. SASE. Reports in 2 months. Free sample copy and writer's guidelines.

Nonfiction: New product (items on new equipment and instruments which can be used offshore); and technical (articles relating to hydrocarbon exploration and development, diving, deepsea mining, oil terminals, and oil and LNG shipping). No oceanographic, fisheries, aquaculture or mariculture material. Buys 120-140 mss/year. Query. Length: 300-1,500 words. Pays $35-50/published page.

Photos: "Technical concepts are easier to understand when illustrated." State availability of photos with query. No additional payment for 5x7 or 8x10 glossy b&w or color prints. Captions required. Buys all rights.

Columns/Departments: New Literature (brochures on company's work); New Equipment; New Instruments; New Business Ventures; Gas & Oil Wrap-up; and New Drilling Rigs. Buys 2-3 mss/issue. Query. Length: 100-500 words. Pays $2/inch.

OFFSHORE, The Petroleum Publishing Co., 1200 S. Post Oak Rd., Houston TX 77056. (713)621-9720. Editor-in-Chief: Robert Burke. Emphasizes offshore operations—oil, marine, construction, marine transportation, diving, engineering for management, engineers, operational people, geologists, technicians. Monthly (2 June issues) magazine. Estab. 1959. Circ. 19,000 Pays on publication. Buys all rights. Phone queries OK. Submit seasonal and holiday material 3 months in advance. Photocopied submissions OK. SASE. Reports in 3 weeks. Free sample copy.

Nonfiction: Publishes how-to and informational articles (specific operational articles; how to do a job better); new product articles, photo features, interviews; technical articles (good, strong details). Length: 800-2,500 words.

Photos: B&w glossies and color purchased with or without mss, or on assignment. Captions required. Query first.

OILWEEK, 918 6th Ave., S.W., #200, Calgary, Alberta, Canada T2P 0V5. Editor: Vic Humphreys. For senior management, engineers, etc., in the energy industries. Magazine; 36 to 100 pages. Estab. 1948. Weekly. Circ. 11,000. Rights purchased vary with author and material. Usually buys all rights. Pays on publication. Will send free sample copy to writer on request. Write for copy of guidelines for writers. Reports on material accepted for publication in 2 weeks. Returns rejected material in 2 weeks. Query first. Enclose SAE and International Reply Coupons.

Nonfiction: News or semitechnical articles which have a Canadian content or Canadian application, directed toward the petroleum, or in some instances, energy field. Length: 1,500 words maximum. Pays 10¢ a word minimum.

PETROLEUM INDEPENDENT, 1101 16th St., N.W., Washington DC 20036. (202)466-8240. Editor-in-Chief: Robert Gouldy. For "college-educated men and women involved in high-risk petroleum ventures. Contrary to popular opinion, they are not all Texans. They live in almost every state. These people are politically motivated. They follow energy legislation closely and involve themselves in lobbying and electoral politics." Bimonthly magazine; 64-88 pages. Estab. 1929. Circ. 13,000. Pays on acceptance. Buys all rights but may reassign following publication. Photocopied submissions OK. SASE. Reports in "5-15 minutes." Sample copy $1.
Nonfiction: "Articles need not be limited to oil and natural gas—can reflect on other energy." Expose (bureaucratic blunder), informational, historical (energy-related, accurate, with a witty twist), humor (we're still looking for a good humor piece), interview (with energy decisionmakers. Center with questions concerning independent petroleum industry. Send edited transcript plus tape), personal opinion, profile (of Independent Petroleum Association of America members), photo feature. Buys 30 mss/year. Query. Length: 750-3,000 words. Pays $40-300.
Photos: Purchased with or without accompanying ms or on assignment. Pays $15-75 for b&w and color photos. $50-200 (for cover only) for 35mm or 2¼x2¼ transparencies. Send contact sheet; prints or transparencies.
Fiction: Experimental, historical, science fiction. Buys 1 ms an issue. Submit complete ms. Length: 750-2,000 words. Pays $40-200.

PETROLEUM MARKETER, 636 First Ave., West Haven CT 06516. (203)934-5288. Editor: Henry F. Harris. For "independent oil jobbers, major oil company operations and management personnel, and petroleum equipment distributors." Bimonthly. Circ. 20,000. Buys North American serial rights. Pays on publication. Will send a sample copy to a writer on request. Query first. Reports in 1 week. Enclose SASE.
Nonfiction and Photos: "Success stories on how an oil jobber did something; interpretive marketing stories on local or regional basis. We want straightforward, honest reporting. Treat the subject matter with dignity." Length: 1,200 to 2,500 words. Pays "$35 per printed page." Photos purchased with and without mss; captions required. "Glossies for reproduction by engraving; subject matter decided after consultation." Pays $5.

PIPELINE & GAS JOURNAL, Box 1589, Dallas TX 75221. (214)748-4403. Editor-in-Chief: Dean Hale. 2% freelance written. Emphasizes energy transportation (oil, gas and coal) by pipeline. Monthly magazine; 100 pages. Estab. July 1859. Circ. 25,000. Pays on publication. Buys all rights. Phone queries OK. Photocopied submissions OK. SASE. Reports in 6-10 weeks. Free sample copy.
Nonfiction: Technical. No articles on management. Buys 5-6 mss/year. Query. Length: 800-1,500 words. Pays $25/printed page.
Photos: State availability of photos with query. No additional payment for 8x10 b&w glossy prints and 5x7 or 8x10 color glossy prints. Captions required. Buys all rights, but may reassign following publication. Model release required.

PIPELINE & UNDERGROUND UTILITIES CONSTRUCTION, Box 22267, Houston TX 77027. (713)622-0676. Editor: Oliver Klinger. Magazine; 48 pages. For underground utilities construction market; "mostly management and supervision level ... international level." Estab. 1945. Monthly. Circ. 13,500. Buys all rights, but may reassign rights to author after publication. Buys 10 to 15 mss per year. Pays on publication. Free sample copy and writer's guidelines. Submit seasonal material 3 months in advance. Reports in 1 month. SASE.
Nonfiction and Photos: Uses how-to, technical and semi-technical articles on construction of underground facilities. Does not want to see copies of newspaper articles, general success stories, articles not pertaining to the construction market. Length: 750 to 1,500 words. Pays $50 per printed page. Photos purchased with accompanying ms with no additional payment. Captions required.

THE REVIEW, 111 St. Clair Ave. W., Toronto, Ont. M5W 1K3, Canada. Editor: Kenneth Bagnell. Bimonthly. Buys all rights. Payment on acceptance. Free sample copy. Query first. Reports in 1 week. Enclose SAE and International Reply Coupons.
Nonfiction: "Subject matter is general. Articles specifically about the oil industry are generally staff-written. Material must be Canadian." Length: 2,500 words maximum. Pays $400 minimum.

Pets

Listed here are publications for professionals in the pet industry; wholesalers, manufacturers, suppliers, retailers, owners of pet specialty stores, pet groomers. Also aquarium retailers, distributors, manufacturers and those interested in the fish industry.

FROM THE KENNELS, Box 1369, Vancouver WA 98660. (206)696-2971. Editor-in-Chief: J.C. Perkins. Emphasizes material of interest to owners of purebred dogs. Semimonthly newspaper; 16-32 pages. Pays on publication. Not copyrighted. Simultaneous, photocopied, and previously published submissions OK. SASE. Reports in 2 weeks. Sample copy 50¢. Guidelines for writers for SASE.
Nonfiction: Exposes (of dog show behaviour of individuals). Must be related to the showing of purebred dogs. Query.
Photos: Purchased with accompanying ms. Captions required. Uses b&w only. Query. No additional payment for photos accepted with ms.

THE PET DEALER, Howmark Publishing Corp., 225 W. 34th St., New York NY 10001. (212)279-0800. Editor-in-Chief: William G. Reddan. Managing Editor: Marjorie Zinman. 15% freelance written. Emphasizes merchandising, marketing and management for owners and managers of pet specialty stores, departments, and dog groomers and their suppliers. Monthly magazine; 80 pages. Estab. 1950. Circ. 10,000. Pays on publication. Phone queries OK. Submit seasonal/holiday material 3 months in advance of issue date. SASE. Reports in 1 week. Free sample copy and writer's guidelines.
Nonfiction: How-to (store operations, administration, merchandising, marketing, management, promotion, and purchasing). Buys 2 mss/issue Length: 1,000-1,200 words. Pays $25-100.
Photos: Submit photo material with ms. No additional payment for 5x7 b&w glossy prints. Captions required. Buys all rights. Model release required.
How To Break In: "We're interested in store profiles outside the New York area. Photos are of key importance. Good photos and lots of them can sell an otherwise inadequate piece. The story we can always fix up, but we can't run out and take the photos. The best thing to do is send a sample of your work and some story proposals. Even if your proposals are not that strong, we still might want to use you on one of our own ideas. Articles focus on new techniques in merchandising or promotion."

PETS/SUPPLIES/MARKETING, Harcourt Brace Jovanovich Publications, 1 E. First St., Duluth MN 55802. (218)727-8511. Editor-in-Chief: Paul Setzer. For pet retailers (both small, "mom-and-pop" stores and chain franchisers); livestock and pet supply wholesalers, manufacturers of pet products. Monthly magazine; 100 pages. Estab. 1946. Circ. 14,500. Pays on acceptance. Buys all rights. Phone queries OK. Submit seasonal/holiday material 2 months in advance. Photocopied submissions OK. SASE. Reports in 4 weeks. Free sample copy and writer's guidelines.
Nonfiction: How-to (merchandise pet products, display, set up window displays, market pet product line); humor (pertaining to pets and/or their retail sale); interviews with pet store retailers); personal opinion (of pet industry members or problems facing the industry); photo features (of successful pet stores or effective merchandising techniques and in-store displays); profiles (of successful retail outlets engaged in the pet trade); technical articles (on more effective pet retailing; i.e., building a central filtration unit, constructing custom aquariums or display areas). Length: 1,000-2,500 words. Buys 5-6 per issue. Query. Pays 5-10¢/word.
Photos: Purchased with or without mss or on assignment. "We prefer 5x7 or 8x10 b&w glossies. But we will accept contact sheets and standard print sizes. For color, we prefer 35mm transparencies or 2¼x2¼." Pays $6-7.50 for b&w; $12.50-15 for color.
Columns/Departments: Barbara Trelevan, Department Editor. Short, human interest items on the pet trade for Up Front; factual news items on members of the pet industry for Industry News. Buys 3/issue. Submit complete ms. Length: 25-100 words. Pays 5-10¢/word. Suggestions for new columns or departments should be addressed to Paul Setzer.
Fillers: Terry Kreeger, Department Editor. Clippings, jokes, gags, anecdotes, newsbreaks, puzzles, short humor; anything concerned with the pet industry. Buys 3-4/issue. Send fillers in. Length: 25-100 words. Pays $10-25.
How To Break In: "Send a letter of introduction and we will send our guidelines for writers and a sample copy of the magazine. After studying each, the freelancer could visit a number of pet stores and if any seem like interesting material for *PSM*, query us. We will check them out through our wholesalers and, if recommended by them, will assign the article to the freelancer.

Once we have bought several articles from a writer, we will send the person out on specific assignments."

Photography

AMERICAN CINEMATOGRAPHER, A.S.C. Holding Corp., 1782 N. Orange Dr., Hollywood CA 90028. (213)876-5080. Editor-in-Chief: Herb A. Lightman. Specializes in coverage of 16mm and 35mm motion picture production. For an audience ranging from students to retirees; professional interest or advanced amateurs in cinematorgraphy. Monthly magazine; 116 pages. Estab. 1921. Circ. 18,500. Time of payment depends on nature of article. Buys all rights, but may reassign rights after publication. Phone queries OK. Simultaneous and photocopied submissions OK. SASE. Free sample copy.
Nonfiction: How-to articles must be unusual type of treatment, or technique used in filming a production. Interviews with cinematographers. New product pieces on 16mm and 35mm cinematographic items. "The articles we use are primarily those submitted by the photographers of motion pictures. Other material is submitted by the manufacturers of equipment important in our industry. The magazine is technical in nature and the writer must have a background in motion picture photography to be able to write for us." Buys 1 ms per issue. Query first. Length varies with interest. Pays $75-125.
Photos: B&w and color purchased with mss. No additional payment.

BUSINESS SCREEN, 165 W. 46th St., New York NY 10036. For sponsors, producers and users of business, commercial advertising and industrial motion pictures, slidefilms and related audiovisual media. Bimonthly. Buys all rights. Pays on publication. Query first. Reports in 2 weeks. Enclose SASE.
Nonfiction: "Short articles on successful application of these 'tools' in industry and commerce, but only when approved by submission of advance query to publisher's office. Technical articles on film production techniques, with or without illustrations, science film data and interesting featurettes about application or utilization of films in community, industry, etc., also welcomed." Pays up to 5¢ a word.

THE CAMERA CRAFTSMAN, 2000 W. Union Ave., Englewood CO 80110. Editor: Ann McLendon. For camera repair technicians, or people with a specialized interest in photographic equipment. Bimonthly magazine; 32-40 pages. Estab. 1955. Circ. 16,000. Rights purchased vary with author and material. Usually buys first rights. Buys about 6 mss a year. Pays on acceptance. Free sample copy. Will consider photocopied and simultaneous submissions. Reporting time varies, but tries to report in 30 days. Query first on technical articles. On others, will consider complete mss. SASE.
Nonfiction and Photos: "Technical articles on camera disassembly repair and service; articles of interest to small service businesses (on business management or other appropriate subjects). We do not want superficial or outdated business management articles, many of which are rehashes of publications issued by the Small Business Administration. We are interested in seeing current, problem-solving articles for small businesses. However, our principal interest is in technical articles on photographic equipment; also on related fields, such as optics. We are not interested in reviewing how-to articles on picture taking, or photography as such." Length: 1,000 to 5,000 words. Pays minimum of 5¢ a word. B&w glossies purchased with mss. Captions preferred. Pays minimum of $1.50.

FUNCTIONAL PHOTOGRAPHY, The Magazine of Photographic Applications in Science, Technology and Medicine, 250 Fulton Ave., Hempstead NY 11550. Editor: Michael Munzer. For scientists, engineers, doctors, etc., who must use image-production techniques to document or present their work. Magazine; 48 pages. Estab. 1966. Bimonthly. Circ. 44,000. Not copyrighted. Pays on publication. Free sample copy and writer's guidelines. No photocopied or simultaneous submissions. Reports in 1 month. Query. Describe illustrations to be supplied. SASE.
Nonfiction and Photos: "We publish reports of major conferences of interest to our readers, 'spectrum' features discussing overall photographic set-ups; specific application articles discussing any field where an image making process is involved; reports of interesting and new techniques developed in the field and portfolios in both b&w and color of work done by our readers. Use of videotape, CCTV and other audiovisual equipment is also of interest, as well as 'exotic' uses of photographic technology which might be applied to other areas." Length: 6-10 pages, typed, double-spaced. "Minimum payment is $35/display page."

INDUSTRIAL PHOTOGRAPHY, 750 3rd Ave., New York NY 10017. (212)697-8300. Editor: Barry Ancona. "For photographers working in or for business and industry, government, military, scientific, educational and other organizations." Monthly magazine. Estab. 1952. Circ. 40,000. Pays on publication. Buys first North American serial rights. SASE. Reports in 3 weeks. Free sample copy and writer's guidelines.
Nonfiction: "Our staff and contributing editors write more than 60% of the magazine; our readers almost all of the balance. It would be extremely difficult for a freelancer not familiar with both professional photography and in-plant photo department operations to submit an acceptable ms. We are more interested in applications of photography and in management of photographic operations than in 'gee whiz, new products' or personality pieces. Our readers earn their livings with cameras and want to be taken seriously." Buys 1 ms/issue. Query. Pays $75-200.
Photos: Offers no additional payment for photos used with mss. Uses glossy b&w prints and color transparencies of any size.

KELLNER'S MONEYGRAM, 1768 Rockville Dr., Baldwin NY 11510. (516)868-3177. Editor: Henry T. Kellner. 100% freelance written. For photographers, art directors, photo editors and anyone interested in selling photos. Monthly newsletter; 8 pages. Estab. January 1977. Circ. 2,000. Pays on publication. Buys one-time rights. Phone queries OK. Submit seasonal/holiday material 6 months in advance of issue date. Simultaneous and previously published submissions OK. SASE. Reports in 2-3 weeks. Sample copy $1; free writer's guidelines.
Nonfiction: Exposé (unscrupulous editors/agents, buyers who didn't pay); how-to (sell photos, preferably based on first-hand experience); humor (events that occur on assignment); inspirational (how a photographer overcame an obstacle and became successful); interview (famous photographers or editors/art directors who buy photos); nostalgia (old times in photography); personal experience (how I got an assignment, how I contact editors, how I combine writing and photography); and travel (how I made money with vacation photos). Buys 22-33 mss/year. Submit complete ms. Length: 300-350 words. Pays 2½-5¢/word.

PHOTO ARTIST USA, Sun Country Enterprises, Inc. 501 N. Virginia Ave. Winter Park FL 32789. Editor-in-Chief: J.L. Wahl. 50% freelance written. For professional photographers. Monthly magazine; 32-36 pages. Estab. October 1975. Circ. 3,152. Pays on publication. Buys all rights, but may reassign following publication. Submit seasonal/holiday material 3 months in advance of issue date. Photocopied submissions OK. SASE. Reports in 3 weeks. Sample copy $1.75.
Nonfiction: How-to (unusual framing and matting, multiple images, 3-D effects in prints); interview (well known persons in photography); personal experience (that will help other photo-artists); profile (on photo artists who are selling); and travel (unusual photo-sites). No nudes or porno. Buys 40 mss/year. Submit complete ms. Length: 500-1,000 words. Pays $10-20.
Photos: Submit photo material with accompanying ms. Uses 8x10 b&w matte finish prints or 2¼x2½ color transparencies (cover only). Captions preferred. Buys all rights, but may reassign after publication.

PHOTOMETHODS, Ziff-Davis Publishing Co., 1 Park Ave., New York NY 10016. (212)725-3942. Editor-in-Chief: Fred Schmidt. For professional, in-plant image-makers (still, film, video, graphic arts, micrographics) and functional photographers. Monthly magazine; 64 pages. Estab. 1958. Circ. 50,000. Pays on publication. Buys one-time rights. Phone queries OK. SASE. Reports in 2 months. Free sample copy and writer's guidelines.
Nonfiction: How-to and photo features (solve problems with image-making techniques—photography, etc.); informational (to help the reader in his/her use of photography, cine and video); interviews (with working pros); personal experience (in solving problems with photography, cine and video); profiles (well-known personalities in imaging); and technical (on photography, cine and video). Buys 5 mss/issue. Length: 1,500-3,000 words. Pays $75 minimum.
Photos: Mary Sealfon, Department Editor. B&w photos (8x10 matte) and color (35mm transparencies minimum or 8x10 print, matte) purchased with or without mss, or on assignment. Captions required. Query or submit contact sheet. Pays $25 for b&w; $35 for color. Model release required.

THE RANGEFINDER, 1312 Lincoln Blvd., Santa Monica CA 90406. (213)451-8506. Editor-in-Chief: Janet Marshall Victor. Associate Editor: Jan Miller. 15% freelance written. Emphasizes professional photography. Monthly magazine; 100 pages. Estab. June 1952. Circ. 43,500. Pays on publication. Buys first North American serial rights. Phone queries OK. SASE. Reports in 2

weeks. Sample copy $1.50; free writer's guidelines.
Nonfiction: How-to (solve a photographic problem; such as new techniques in lighting, new poses or setups); interview (success stories); new product (test reports of product in use); and technical (roundup style on equipment in use such as light meters, front projection, large format cameras, etc.). "No biographical articles." Buys 3 mss/issue. Query. Length: 750-2,000 words. Pays $24-36/published page.
Photos: State availability of photos with query. Offers no additional payment for 8x10 b&w glossy prints. Captions preferred. Buys one-time rights. Model release required.

STUDIO PHOTOGRAPHY, PTN Publishing Corp., 250 Fulton Ave., Hempstead NY 11550. (516)489-1300. Editor: Arnold Krockman. Associate Editor: Audrey Perel. 35-40% freelance written. Monthly magazine; 60 pages. Estab. 1964. Circ. 40,000. Pays on publication. Not copyrighted. Submit seasonal/holiday material 3 months in advance of issue date. SASE. Reports in 3 weeks. Free sample copy and writer's guidelines.
Nonfiction: Interview; personal experience; personal opinion; photo feature; and technical. No travel articles. Buys 2-3 mss/issue. Length: 1,700-3,000 words. Pays $35 minimum/published page.
Photos: State availability of photos with query. Pays $25 minimum for 5x7 b&w prints and color transparencies.
Columns/Departments: Point of View (any aspect of photography dealing with professionals only). Buys 1 ms/issue. Length: 1,700 words minimum. Pays $35 minimum.

TECHNICAL PHOTOGRAPHY, PTN Publishing Corp., 250 Fulton Ave., Hempstead NY 11550. Editor-in-Chief: Michael A. Munzer. 50% freelance written. Publication of the "on-staff (in-house) industrial, military and government still, cine, and AV professional who must produce (or know where to get) visuals of all kinds." Monthly magazine; 64 pages. Estab. 1968. Circ. 46,000. Pays on publication. Buys first North American Serial rights. SASE. Reports in 4 weeks. Free sample copy and writer's guidelines.
Nonfiction: Publishes how-to, humor, interview, photo feature, profile (detailed stories about in-house operations), and technical articles. "All mss must relate to industrial, military or government production of visuals." Buys 12-20 mss a year. Query. Length: "As long as needed to get the information across." Pays $35 minimum/display page.
Photos: Purchased with accompanying ms. Captions required. Query.

Plastics

CANADIAN PLASTICS, 1450 Don Mills Rd., Don Mills, Ont., Canada. M3B 2X7. (416)445-6641. Managing Editor: Joanne Meithner. For management people in the plastics industry. Monthly. Buys first rights. Pays on publication. Query first. Reports in 2 to 4 weeks. Enclose SAE and International Reply Coupons.
Nonfiction: Accurate technical writing. Accuracy is more important than style. "We reject some freelance material because of lack of Canadian relevance; we like to publish articles that are meaningful to the reader; something he can use for his benefit as a businessman." Pays 7¢ a word.
Photos: Buys photos submitted with ms. Pays $5.
Fillers: Buys newsbreaks. Pays $5 for news items; $15 for longer features.

PLASTICS TECHNOLOGY, 633 3rd Ave., New York NY 10017. (212)986-4800. Editor: Malcolm W. Riley. For plastic processors. Circ. 40,000. Buys all rights. Pays on publication. Will send free sample copy on request. Query preferred. Reports in 2 weeks. Enclose SASE.
Nonfiction and Photos: Articles on plastics processing. Length: "no limits." Pays $30 to $35 per published page. Photos and all artwork purchased with ms with no additional payment.

Plumbing, Heating, Air Conditioning, and Refrigeration

Publications for fuel oil dealers who also install heating equipment are classified with the Petroleum journals.

AIR CONDITIONING, HEATING AND REFRIGERATION NEWS, Box 6000. Birmingham MI 48012. (313)642-3600. Editor-in-Chief: Gordon D. Duffy. Managing Editor: John O. Sweet. 20%

freelance written. "An industry newspaper that covers both the technology and marketing of air conditioning, heating and refrigeration." Weekly tabloid: 30 pages. Estab. 1926. Circ. 31,000. Pays on publication. Buys all rights, but may reassign following publication. Phone queries OK. Submit seasonal/holiday material 1 month in advance of issue date. Simultaneous and photocopied submissions OK. Reports in 2-3 weeks. Free sample copy.
Nonficton: How-to (basic business management applied to contracting operations; sophisticated technical problems in heating, air conditioning, and refrigeration); interview (check first); new product (check first); nostalgia; profile; and technical. Buys 2-4 mss/issue. Query. Length: 1,500 words. Pays $1.25-1.70/column inch.
Photos: State availability of photos with query or ms. Pays $10-35 for 5x7 or 8x10 b&w glossy prints. Captions required. Buys all rights, but may reassign following publication.

CONTRACTOR MAGAZINE, Berkshire Common, Pittsfield MA 01201. Editor: Seth Shepard. 33% freelance written. For mechanical contractors, wholesalers, engineers. Newspaper; 70 (11x15) pages. Established in 1954. Twice a month. Circ. 43,000. Not copyrighted. Buys 50 mss/year. Pays on publication. Sample copy for $2. Photocopied submissions OK. No simultaneous submissions. Reports in 1 month. Query first or submit complete ms. Enclose SASE.
Nonfiction and Photos: Articles on materials, use, policies, and business methods of the air conditioning, heating, plumbing industry. Topics covered include: interpretive reports, how-to, informational, interview, profile, think articles, expose, spot news, successful business operations, merchandising techniques, technical. Pays $200 maximum. 5x7 b&w glossies purchased with or without ms. Pays $5. Captions required.

DOMESTIC ENGINEERING, 110 N. York Rd., Elmhurst IL 60126. Editor-in-Chief: Stephen J. Shafer. Managing Editor: Donald T. Michard. 15% freelance written. Emphasizes mechanical contracting, piping, plumbing, heating, and air conditioning. Monthly magazine; 100 pages. Estab. 1881. Circ. 40,000. Pays on publication. Buys all rights, but may reassign following publication. Simultaneous, photocopied and previously published submissions OK. SASE. Sample copy $1.50.
Nonfiction: Exposé (government, labor, and anti-trust); how-to (technical articles, short management pieces, and merchandising); interview (could be assigned); new product (all types); personal experience (possible); photo feature; profile; technical; and management material for contractors. No articles on fiction and humor. Buys 12 mss/year. Query. Pays $25 and up.
Photos: State availability of photos with query. Pays $5 for 5x7 b&w glossy contact sheets. Captions required. Buys all rights, but may reassign following publication. Model release preferred.

EXPORT, 386 Park Ave., S., New York NY 10016. Editor: M. Downing. For importers and distributors in 165 countries who handle hardware, air conditioning and refrigeration equipment and related consumer hardlines. Bimonthly magazine; 60 to 80 pages in English and Spanish editions. Estab. 1877. Circ. 38,500. Buys first serial rights. Buys about 10 mss a year. Pays on acceptance. Reports in 1 month. Query first. SASE.
Nonfiction: News stories of products and merchandising of air conditioning and refrigeration equipment, hardware and related consumer hardlines. Informational, how-to, interview, profile, successful business operations. Length: 1,000 to 3,000 words. Pays 10¢ a word, maximum.
How To Break In: "One of the best ways to break in here is with a story originating outside the U.S. or Canada. Our major interest is in new products and new developments—but they must be available and valuable to overseas buyers. We also like company profile stories. A key thing we look for in writers is some kind of expertise in our field. Departments and news stories are staff written."

HEATING/PIPING/AIR CONDITIONING, Two Illinois Center, Chicago IL 60601. (312)861-0880. Editor: Robert T. Korte. Monthly. Buys all rights. Pays on publication. Query first. Reports in 2 weeks. Enclose SASE.
Nonfiction: Uses engineering and technical articles covering design, installation, operation, maintenance, etc., of heating, piping and air conditioning systems in industrial plants and large buildings. Length: 3,000 to 4,000 words maximum. Pays $30 per printed page.

HEATING, PLUMBING, AIR CONDITIONING, 1450 Don Mills Rd., Don Mills, Ont., Canada M3B 2X7. (416)445-6641. Editor: Ronald Shuker. For mechanical contractors; plumbers; warm air heating, refrigeration, ventilation and air conditioning contractors; wholesalers; architects; consulting and mechanical engineers who are in key management or specifying positions in the plumbing, heating, air conditioning and refrigeration industries in Canada. Monthly. Circ.

13,500. Buys North American serial rights only. Pays on publication. Free sample copy. Reports in 1 to 2 months. SASE.
Nonfiction and Photos: News, technical, business management and "how-to" articles which will inform, educate and motivate readers who design, manufacture, install, service, maintain or supply fuel to all mechanical components and systems in residential, commercial, institutional and industrial installations across Canada. Length: 1,000 to 1,500 words. Pays 10¢/word. Photos purchased with mss. Prefers 5x7 or 8x10 glossies.

IOWA PLUMBING, HEATING, COOLING CONTRACTOR, 301 Insurance Exchange Bldg., Des Moines IA 50309. Editor: Denny Werning. For those in the plumbing-heating-cooling contracting industry plus state procurement authorities. Monthly. Circ.3,500. Not copyrighted. Pays on publication. Free sample copy. SASE.
Nonfiction, Photos, and Fiction: Articles on development, engineering problems and improvements in general covering new equipment, new materials, legal review, state news, national news; other topics. Photos and fiction appropriate to format. Pays 2½¢ a word; $5 each for photos.

SNIPS MAGAZINE, 407 Mannheim Rd., Bellwood IL 60104. (312)544-3870. Editor: Nick Carter. For sheet metal, warm air heating, ventilating, air conditioning, and roofing contractors. Monthly. Buys all rights. "Write for detailed list of requirements before submitting any work." Enclose SASE.
Nonfiction: Material should deal with information about contractors who do sheet metal, warm air heating, air conditioning, ventilation and roofing work; also about successful advertising campaigns conducted by these contractors and the results. Length: "prefers stories to run less than 1,000 words unless on special assignment." Pays 2¢ each for first 500 words, 1¢ each for additional words.
Photos: Pays $2 each for small snapshot pictures, $4 each for usable 8x10 pictures.

Power and Power Plants

Publications in this listing aim at company managers, engineers, and others involved in generating and supplying power for businesses, homes, and industries. Journals for electrical engineers who design, maintain, and install systems connecting users with sources of power are classified under the heading Electricity.

DIESEL & GAS TURBINE PROGRESS, Box 26308, Milwaukee WI 52336. Editor-in-Chief: Bruce W. Wadman. Managing Editor: J. Kane. Associate Editor: Mike Osenga. 5% freelance written. Monthly magazine; 88 pages. Estab. 1935. Circ. 25,000. Pays on publication. Buys all rights. Submit editorial material 6 weeks in advance of issue date. Previously published submissions OK. SASE. Reports in 4 weeks. Sample copy $1; mention *Writer's Market* in request.
Nonfiction: "The articles we would consider from freelancers would be technical descriptions of unique diesel or gas turbine engine applications. Including extensive technical descriptions of the installation, the method of operation and maintenance". Buys 20 mss/year. Query and submit clips of previously published work. Length: 1,600-2,400 words. Pays $75 page.
Photos: "All stories are illustrated and photos of the engine installation must accompany the text, or it is really of little value." State availability of photos with query. No additional payment for 8x10 b&w glossy prints and 8x10 glossy color prints (cover only). Captions preferred. Buys all rights, but may reassign following publication.

POWER ENGINEERING, 1301 S. Grove Ave., Barrington IL 60010. (312)381-1840. Editor: John Papamarcos. Monthly. Buys first North American serial rights. "Must query first." Enclose SASE.
Nonfiction and Photos: "We do not encourage freelance writers in general. We do review anything that is sent to us, but will generally accept articles only from people who are involved in the power field in some way and can write to interest engineers and management in the field." Articles on electric power field design, construction, and operation. Length: 500 to 1,500 words. Pays $80 to $200, "depending on published length." Uses 8x10 glossies with mss.

PUBLIC POWER, 2600 Virginia Ave., N.W., Washington DC 20037. (202)333-9200. Editor: Ron Ross. Estab. 1942. Bimonthly. Not copyrighted. Pays on publication. Query first. Enclose SASE.

Nonfiction: News and features on municipal and other local publicly owned electric systems. Payment negotiable.

RURAL ELECTRIFICATION, 2000 Florida Ave., N.W., Washington DC 20009. Editor: J. C. Brown, Jr. For managers and boards of directors of rural electric systems. Monthly. Buys all rights or reprint rights. Pays on acceptance. Will send sample copy on request. Query first. Reports in one month. Enclose SASE.
Nonfiction: Uses articles on the activities of rural electric systems which are unusual in themselves or of unusually great importance to other rural electric systems across the country. Length: "open." Pay "negotiable, but usually in $50 to $250 range."
Photos: Uses photos with or without mss, on the same subject matter as the articles; 8x10 glossies. Pays $5 for b&w; $10 for color.

Printing

AMERICAN INK MAKER, 101 W. 31st St., New York NY 10001. (212)279-4455. Editor-in-Chief: John Vollmuth. 2% freelance written. Monthly magazine; 70 pages. Estab. 1923. Circ. 5,700. Pays on publication. Buys all rights, but may reassign following publication. Phone queries OK. Submit seasonal/holiday material 2 months in advance of issue date. Simultaneous, photocopied and previously published submissions OK. SASE. Reports in 2 weeks. Free sample copy.
Nonfiction: General interest; historical; humor; interview; new product; personal experience; personal opinion; profile; and technical. Buys 4 mss/year. Submit complete ms. Length: 800-1,500 words. Pays $90-135.
Photos: No additional payment for photos with accompanying ms. Captions preferred. Buys all rights, but may reassign following publication.

GRAPHIC ARTS MONTHLY, Dun-Donnelley Corp., 222 S. Riverside Plaza, Chicago IL 60606. Editor-in-Chief: Burt D. Chapman. Managing Editor: Donald Curda. 10% freelance written. For "printers and persons in graphic communications, composition, plate-making, color separations, ink, press room chemicals, etc." Monthly magazine; 170 pages. Estab. 1928. Circ. 80,000. Pays on acceptance. Buys all rights, but may reassign following publication. Submit seasonal/holiday material 2-3 months in advance of issue date. SASE. Reports in 2 weeks. Free sample copy and writer's guidelines.
Nonfiction: Historical; how-to; interview; new product; photo feature; and technical. "We accept articles directly related to the printing trades. Following criteria to be followed: material should be written objectively, and should stress the savings of cost, enhancement of quality, increased productivity or maximize safety." Query with clips of previously published work. Length: 1,000-2,500 words. Pays 7-10¢/word.
Photos: State availability of photos with query. Pays $10 for 5x7 or 8x10 b&w prints. Captions preferred. Buys all rights, but may reassign following publication.

THE INLAND PRINTER/AMERICAN LITHOGRAPHER, 300 W. Adams St., Chicago IL 60606. Editor: Michael Chazin. 60-70% freelance written. For qualified personnel active in any phase of the graphic arts industry. Established in 1883. Monthly. Circ. 68,000. Buys all rights, unless otherwise specified in writing at time of purchase. Pays on publication. Free sample copy to a writer on request. Submit seasonal material 2 months in advance. "Study publication before writing." Query first. Enclose SASE.
Nonfiction: Articles on management; technical subjects with illustrations with direct bearing on graphic arts industry. Length: 1,500 to 3,000 words. Pays $50 to $200.
Photos: Purchased with mss; also news shots of graphic arts occurrences. 5x7 or 8x10 glossy. Pays $5 to $10.

NEWSPAPER PRODUCTION, North American Publishing Co., 401 N. Broad St., Philadelphia PA 19108. (215)574-9600. Editor-in-Chief: Jeffrey Markow. 50% freelance written. For the newspaper industry; production personnel through management to editor and publisher. Monthly magazine; 56 pages. Estab. 1972. Circ. 17,500. Pays on publication. Buys all rights. Phone queries OK. Photocopied submissions OK. SASE. Reports in 3 weeks. Free sample copy.
Nonfiction: Publishes historical articles (production case histories) and how-to articles (production techniques). Length: 1,500 words minimum. Query first or submit complete ms. Pays $35 minimum.

Photos: B&w and color purchased with or without mss, or on assignment. Captions required. Query first or submit contact sheet or prints. No additional payment for those used with mss. Model release required.

PLAN AND PRINT, 10116 Franklin Ave., Franklin Park IL 60131. (312)671-5356. Editor-in-Chief: James C. Vebeck. 50% freelance written. For commercial reproduction companies and in-plant reproduction, printing, drafting and design departments of business and industry. Monthly magazine; 46 pages. Estab. 1928. Circ. 23,000. Pays on publication. Buys all rights. Submit seasonal/holiday material 4-6 months in advance of issue date. SASE. Reports in 2 weeks. Free sample and writer's guidelines.
Nonfiction: How-to (how certain problems may have been solved; new methods of doing certain kinds of reproduction and/or design/drafting work); and technical (must relate to industry). Buys 50 mss/year. Query. Length: 250-5,000 words. Pays $25-300.
Photos: State availability of photos with query. Pays $5-10 for 8x10 b&w glossy prints. Captions required. Buys all rights. Model release required.
Columns/Deaprtments: Open to suggestions for new columns/departments.
Poetry: Light verse related to the industry. Buys 6/year. Length: 4-12 lines. Pays $5-10.
Fillers: Puzzles related to the industry. Buys 6/year. Pays $5-10.

SCREEN PRINTING, 407 Gilbert Ave., Cincinnati OH 45202. (513)421-2050. Editor: Jonathan E. Schiff. For the screen printing industry, including screen printers (commercial, industrial and captive shops), suppliers and manufacturers, ad agencies and allied professions. Monthly magazine; 88-96 pages. Estab. 1953. Circ. 9,000. Buys all rights, but may reassign rights to author after publication. Pays on publication. Free writer's guidelines. Will not consider photocopied submissions. Will consider simultaneous submissions. Reporting time varies. SASE.
Nonfiction and Photos: "Since the screen printing industry covers a broad range of applications and overlaps other fields in the graphic arts, it's necessary that articles be of a significant contribution, preferably to a specific area of screen printing. Subject matter is fairly open, with preference given to articles on administration or technology; trends and developments. We try to give a good sampling of technical articles, business and management articles; articles about unique operations. We also publish special features and issues on important subjects, such as material shortages, new markets and new technology breakthroughs. While most of our material is nitty-gritty, we appreciate a writer who can take an essentially dull subject and encourage the reader to read on through concise, factual, flairful and creative, expressive writing. Interviews are published after consultation with and guidance from the editor." Interested in stories on unique approaches by some shops on how to lick the problems created by the petroleum shortage (the industry relies heavily on petrol products). Length: 1,500 to 2,000 words. Pays minimum of $125 for major features; minimum of $50 for minor features; minimum of $35 for back of book articles. Pays $15 for photos used on cover; b&w or color. Published material becomes the property of the magazine.

SOUTHERN PRINTER & LITHOGRAPHER, 75 Third St., N.W., Atlanta GA 30308. Editor: Roy Conrad. For commercial printing plant management in the 14 southern states. Estab. 1924. Monthly. Circ. 3,600. Not copyrighted. Payment on publication. Reporting time on submissions varies. Query first. SASE.
Nonfiction and Photos: Feature articles on commercial printing plants in the 14 southern states and their personnel. Length: 1,000 to 1,500 words. Pays 1¢ a word. B&w photos. Pays $4.

Public Relations

PUBLICIST, Published by Public Relations Aids, Inc., 221 Park Ave. S. New York NY 10003. Editor-in-Chief: Lee Levitt. 25% freelance written. Devoted entirely to professional publicity/public relations. For "a controlled circulation of people engaged in publicity on a national or major regional scale." Bimonthly tabloid. Estab. 1976. Circ. 14,000. Pays on acceptance. Buys all rights, but may reassign to author following publication. Submit seasonal/holiday material 6 months in advance. Simultaneous photocopied and previously published material OK. SASE. Reports in 1 month. Free sample copy and writer's guidelines.
Nonfiction: How-to, informational, humor, interview, nostalgia, profile, personal experience, photo feature and technical. "The subject of every article must be publicity, or organizations or persons engaged in publicity. We cover only national projects." Buys 5 mss/issue. Query. Length: 400-1,500 words. Pays $30-250.

Photos: Purchased with or without accompanying ms or on assignment. Captions required. Uses b&w only. Query. Prefers 8x10's. Pays $20-50 per photo.
Fiction: Humorous, condensed novels, mainstream, serialized novels. "All fiction must concern publicity people in a realistic, professional situation; must exhibit sophisticated comprehension of big time PR practice." Query. Length: 500 words minimum. Pays $50-400.
Fillers: Clippings, jokes, gags, anecdotes, newsbreaks, short humor on professional public relations. Buys 2 an issue. Length: 50-400 words. Pays $2-40.
How To Break In: "We are most likely to accept case histories of national publicity projects; the article must include details of the project's cost; you must send documentation of the project. All our articles are in newspaper style: flat, abrupt leads, attributions for all important statements, no editorial comment."

Railroad

THE SIGNALMAN'S JOURNAL, 601 West Golf Rd., Mt. Prospect IL 60056. (312)439-3732. Editor: Robert W. McKnight. Monthly. Buys first rights. Query first. Reports in 3 weeks. SASE.
Nonfiction: Can use articles on new installations of railroad signal systems, but they must be technically correct and include drawings and photos. "We do not want general newspaper type writing, and will reject material that is not of technical quality." Length: 3,000 to 4,000 words. Pays $10 per printed page, and up.
Photos: Photographs dealing with railroad signaling. Pays $5.

Real Estate

APARTMENT MANAGEMENT NEWSLETTER, Mattco Equities, Inc., 48 W. 21st St., New York NY 10010. Editor: Mark Krangle. 20% freelance written. Emphasizes apartment management. Monthly newsletter; 8 pages. Estab. 1975. Circ. 5,000. Pays on publication. Buys all rights. Submit seasonal/holiday material 2 months in advance of issue date. Photocopied submissions OK. SASE. Reports in 8 weeks. Sample copy $2.25.
Nonfiction: How-to (maintenance, occupancy, cost-cutting); informational (taxes, gas, oil, trends affecting apartments) interviews (with successful managers); profiles (successful apartment complexes), new products (snow throwers, rugs, windows, etc.); and technical (for all the foregoing; can include graphs, charts). Query or submit complete ms. Length: 250-1,000 words. Pays $5-10/page.

AREA DEVELOPMENT MAGAZINE, 432 Park Ave., S., New York NY 10016. (212)532-4360. Editor-in-Chief: Albert H. Jaeggin. 50% freelance written. Emphasizes corporate facility planning and site selection. Monthly magazine; 100-130 pages. Estab. 1965. Circ. 32,000. Pays when edited. Buys all rights. Photocopied submissions Ok. Reports in 1- 3 weeks. Free sample copy and writer's guidelines.
Nonfiction: How-to (case histories of companies; experiences in site selection and all other aspects of corporate facility planning); historical (if it deals with corporate facility planning); interview (corporate executives and professional developers); personal experience (of corporate executives); personal opinion; and photo feature (pictures of new plants, offices and warehouses). Buys 1-5 mss/issue. Query. Pays $40/printed page, including illustrations.
Photos: State availability of photos with query. No additional payment for 8x10 or 5x7 b&w glossy prints or color transparencies. Captions preferred. Buys all rights, but may reassign following publication.

COMMUNITY DEVELOPMENT DIGEST, 399 National Press Bldg., Washington DC 20045. (202)638-6113. Managing Editor: Byron Fielding. Predominantly for Federal/state/local agencies interested in housing and community development. Semimonthly newsletter; 18 pages. Estab. 1965. Pays end of month following publication. Not copyrighted. Phone queries OK. Simultaneous and photocopied submissions OK. SASE. Reports in 2 weeks. Sample copy and writer's guidelines for SASE.
Fillers: Uses contributions of newspaper clippings on housing and community development; substantive actions and litigations, that would be of interest to housing and community development professionals beyond immediate area. "We reject material when the territory has already been covered; material not of interest to our needs." Particularly wants regular contributors for multistates, region, or at least a full state, especially state capitals. Normally pays $1.75 for each clipping used.

EMPIRE STATE REALTOR, New York State Association of Realtors, Executive Park Tower, Western Ave. at Fuller Rd., Albany NY 12203. Editor: W. Kresge. For professional real estate salespeople in New York. Quarterly magazine; 20 pages. Estab. 1977. Circ. 22,000. Pays on publication. Buys all rights, but may reassign following publication. Photocopied submissions OK. SASE. Reports in 6 weeks. Free sample copy.
Nonfiction: "Our readers want information which will help them sell homes. Articles should be specific to that end and may include technical information." How-to (sell a home, must have professional approach); informational (new trends in home selling, mortgage and financial trends); humor (personal experiences while selling or buying a home); and technical (financing a home, office lay-out). Buys 4 mss/year. Submit complete ms Length: 1,000 words maximum. Pays $25.

PROPERTIES MAGAZINE, 4900 Euclid Ave., Cleveland OH 44103. (216)431-7666. Editor: Gene Bluhm. Monthly. Buys all rights. Pays on publication. Query first. SASE.
Nonfiction and Photos: Wants articles of real estate and construction news value. Interested primarily in articles relating to northeastern Ohio. Length: up to 900 words. Buys photographs with mss, 5x7 preferred.

PROPERTY MANAGEMENT JOURNAL, Box 853, Temple City CA 91780. Editor: Gladys Dickholtz. For owners and managers of rental property in southern California, realtors and property management firms. Monthly tabloid newspaper. Estab. 1971. Circ. 10,000. Buys first serial rights. Buys 5 mss/issue. Pays on acceptance. Sample copy for $1. Reports in 4 weeks. Query or submit complete ms. SASE.
Nonfiction and Photos: How-to articles of vital interest to owners and property managers who control the purchasing of services and products in the rental housing industry. Topics could be on carpet care, painting, draperies, appliance sales and service, electrical and plumbing repair, decorating, swimming pool maintenance, roof repair, laundry services, fire and building safety, etc. Writers should remember that subjects should be applicable to southern California readers — no snowplows or storm window stories. Length: 3 pages, typed, double-spaced. Also uses shorter humorous articles about apartment hunting, resident managers, tenant relations, etc. Length: 1, 2 or 3 pages, typed, double-spaced. Pays $5-15. Will buy b&w photos, if applicable, at $5 each.

SHOPPING CENTER WORLD, Communication Channels, Inc., 6285 Barfield Rd., Atlanta GA 30328. (404)393-2920. Editor-in-Chief: Gail E. Brown. 30% freelance written. Emphasizes shopping center/retailing world for shopping center developers, builders, owners and managers; chain store executives, store planners, and others in the industry. Monthly magazine; 72 pages. Estab. February 1972. Circ. 22,000. Pays on acceptance. Buys all rights. Submit seasonal/holiday material 8 weeks in advance of issue date. Photocopied and previously published submissions OK. SASE. Reports in 4 weeks. Free sample copy and writer's guidelines.
Nonfiction: General interest (trends, interesting developments, etc.); how-to (concentrating on saving time and money to get something done); interview (top industry names only); and personal opinion (cut-and-dried opinions by industry people on current topics). "No articles that are consumer oriented." Query. Length: 2,000 words. Pays $50-200.
Photos: State availability of photos with query. Pays $5 for 8x10 b&w glossy prints; $10 for color negatives or transparencies. Captions preferred. Buys all rights.
Columns/Departments: People & Places (industry news). Submit complete ms. Length: 250 words. Pays $5-25.
Fillers: Clippings. Buys 30/issue. Pays $1.50 for clippings only.

Recreation Park and Campground Management

CAMPGROUND AND RV PARK MANAGEMENT, Rt. 1, Box 780, Quincy CA 95971. (916)283-0666. Editor: Bill Shepard. 8 times a year. Circ. 14,000. Buys all rights. Pays on publication. Will send a free sample copy on request. "Best to query first." Reports in 1 month. SASE.
Nonfiction and Photos: Success stories and management information articles for owners of campgrounds and recreation vehicle parks. News stories about campgrounds, campground associations, campground chains and any other subjects helpful or of interest to a campground operator. Also uses features about such subjects as a specialized bookkeeping system for campground operations, an interesting traffic circulation system, an advertising and promotion

program that has worked well for a campground, an efficient trash collection system. Successful operation of coin-operated dispensing machines, successful efforts by a campground owner in bringing in extra income through such means as stores, charge showers, swimming fees, etc. Use newspaper style reporting for news items and newspaper feature style for articles. Length: 500 to 700 words, news stories; 300 to 1,200 words, features. Pays $20 to $50. "B&w photos should accompany articles whenever practicable."
Fillers: Pays $2 to $5 for ideas which eventually appear as stories written by staff or another writer; $5 to $10 for newsbreaks of one paragraph to a page.

CAMPING INDUSTRY, 225 E. Michigan, Milwaukee WI 53202. (414)276-6600. Editor: Arlyn D. Horn. 20% freelance written. Published 8 times/year; magazine 60 pages. Estab. 1966. Circ. 16,100. Pays on acceptance. Buys all rights, but may reassign following publication, simultaneous, and one-time rights. Phone queries OK. Submit seasonal/holiday material 3 months in advance of issue date. Simultaneous submissions OK. Reports in 2-3 weeks. Free sample copy and writer's guidelines.
Nonfiction: Selling camping equipment plus dealer stories; interview; new product; photo feature; and technical. No consumer "I went camping stories". Buys 1-2 mss/issue. Query. Length: 1,000-2,500. Pays $75-150.
Photos: State availability of photos with query or submit photo material with accompanying query. Pays $10 for 8x10 b&w contact sheets, negatives or prints. Captions required. Buys one-time rights.

PARK MAINTENANCE, P.O. Box 1936, Appleton WI 54911. (414)733-2301. Editor: Erik L. Madisen, Jr. For administrators of areas with large grounds maintenance and outdoor recreation facilities. Special issues include March, Swimming Pool and Beach; July, Turf Research and Irrigation Annual; October, Buyer's Guide issue. Estab. 1948. Monthly. Circ. 17,000. Buys all rights. Buys 4 or 5 mss a year. Pays on acceptance. Will send a sample copy to a writer on request. Write for copy of guidelines for writers. Will consider photocopied submissions "if exclusive to us." Query first. "Outline material and source in letter, and include SASE.Deadlines are the first of the month preceding publication. Reports in 2 weeks.
Nonfiction: How-to, case history, technical or scientific articles dealing with maintenance of turf and facilities in parks, forestry, golf courses, campuses. These may be new or unique ideas adopted by park systems for greater use or more efficient and economical operation. Also, methods of dealing with administrative, financial, personnel and other problems; new phases of landscape architecture and building design. Buys how-to's and interviews. Length: up to 1,000 words. Pays 2¢ a word.
Photos: Purchased with mss if applicable; 8x10 or 5x7 b&w glossies. "Captions required." Pays minimum of $2 each; $5 for front cover.

TOURIST ATTRACTIONS AND PARKS, 327 Wagaraw Rd., Hawthorne NJ 07506. (201)423-2266. Editor-in-Chief: Martin Dowd. 10% freelance written. For managers, owners of amusement parks, theme parks, tourist attractions, interested in improving promotion and personnel handling in theme parks and tourist attractions. Biannually magazine; 64 pages. Estab. 1972. Circ. 6,500. Pays between publication and acceptance. Phone queries OK. Buys first North American serial rights. SASE. Reports in 2 weeks. Free sample copy and writer's guidelines.
Nonfiction: How-to; new product (must be really new and worthwhile); personal experience (only with a management technique or new type of ride, or of system that improves an amusement park or theme parks operations); technical (a device that does job better or less expensively, a description of a new technique that is successful—a ride or a way to attract visitors). "No articles on travel pieces of scenic wonder or a national or state park." Buys 2 mss/issue. Query. Length: 1,000-3,000 words. Pays 1-2¢/inch.
Photos: State availability of photos with query. Pays $10 for 8x10 b&w glossy with white borders prints. Captions preferred. Buys one-time rights.

WOODALL'S CAMPGROUND MANAGEMENT, 500 Hyacinth Place, Highland Park IL 60035. (312)433-4550. Editor/Associate Publisher: James Saul. Audience is the owners and managers of private campgrounds in the U.S., Canada and Mexico. Monthly tabloid; 24 pages. Estab. 1970. Circ. 16,000. Pays on publication. Buys all rights, but may reassign following publication. Phone queries OK. Submit seasonal/holiday material 2 months in advance. Photocopied (if statement is enclosed stating that material has not been published or accepted elsewhere) and previously published submissions OK. SASE. Reports in 4 weeks. Sample copy 25¢; free writer's guidelines.
Nonfiction: Expose (governmental practices detrimental to private campground industry);

how-to (any type that will provide practical, usable information in operation of campgrounds); informational; interview; new product; personal experience (experiences of campground owners/managers); photo feature; and technical. Buys 40-50 mss/year. Query. Length: 500-2,500 words. Pays $35-100.
Photos: Purchased with or without accompanying ms or on assignment. Captions required. Query. Pays $2.50-7.50 for 5x7 minimum b&w glossy; $20 minimum for 120mm and larger color transparencies. Offers no additional payment for photos accepted with ms "except for page 1 color transparencies; pays $20 additional whether part of editorial package or not." Model release required.
Fillers: Clippings and newsbreaks. Buys 10-12/year. Length: 50-250 words. Pays $2.50-15.
How To Break In: "We are seeking freelancers from throughout the country who can provide factual, useful articles pertinent to the private campground industry; new ideas that work, success stories, how to solve a problem. Facts and figures must be included."

Secretarial

MODERN SECRETARY, Allied Publications, Box 9820, Ft. Worth TX 76107. Editor-in-Chief: Louise Hinton. Associate Editor: Didi Scott. Bimonthly magazine; 16 pages. Pays between acceptance and publication. Buys simultaneous rights. Submit seasonal/holiday material 6 months in advance of issue date. Simultaneous, photocopied and previously published submissions OK. SASE. Reports in 2 months. Sample copy $1; writer's guideline for SASE.
Nonfiction: Office tips for secretaries and picture stories of secretaries of famous personalities. How-to; general interest; humor; historical; interview; new product; nostalgia; personal experience; profile; technical; and travel. Nothing controversial or suggestive. Submit complete ms. Length: 300-1,000 words. Pays 5¢/accepted word.
Photos: Pays $5 for 8½x11 b&w glossy prints. Captions required. Buys simultaneous rights.

TODAY'S SECRETARY, McGraw-Hill, Inc., 1221 Avenue of the Americas, New York NY 10020. (212)997-2166. Editor: Nhora Cortes-Comerer. 75% freelance written. "For a primarily female readership, between 15-21, enrolled in high school, junior college and private business school secretarial programs." Monthly (October-May) magazine; 32 pages. Estab. 1898. Circ. 60,000. Pays on publication. Buys all rights. Submit seasonal/holiday material 6 months in advance of issue date. SASE. Reports in 2-3 months. Free sample copy and writer's guidelines; mention *Writer's Market* in request.
Nonfiction: General interest (women's issues, consumer topics); historical (related to business and offices); how-to (crafts, cooking, decorating, office procedures); humor (office situations); interview (interesting secretaries); new product (office products and supplies). Buys 32 mss/year. Query with clips of previously published work. Length: 800-3,000 words. Pays $75-350.
Columns/Departments: Word Teasers (grammatical points); Consumer Wise (consumer information); and Think It Out (secretarial procedure). Buys 24 mss/year. Query. Length: 800-2,000 words. Pays $75-200.
Fillers: Adventure; fantasy; historical; humorous; mystery; suspense; science fiction; and western. No violence, sex or heavy romance. Buys 8 mss/year. Submit complete ms. Length: 800-1,000 words. Pays $75.
How To Break In: "The best way to break in would be with a short piece of fiction (800 words). Keep in mind that our audience is mostly women, age 16 to 22, in high school or business school. Also, the stories shouldn't be too heavy—we print them in shorthand as a skills exercise for our readers. Other good freelance possibilities include profiles of secretaries with unusual job responsibilities or in an unusual field, and secretarial procedure stories—tips on filing, making travel arrangements for your boss, etc."

Selling and Merchandising

In this category are journals for salesmen and merchandisers who publish general material on how to sell products successfully. Journals in nearly every other category of this Trade Journal section will also buy this kind of material if it is slanted to the specialized product or industry they deal with, such as clothing or petroleum. Publications for professional advertising and marketing men will be found under Advertising and Marketing Journals.

AGENCY SALES MAGAZINE, Box 16878, Irvine CA 92713. (714)752-5231. Editor: Dan Bayless. 60% freelance written. For independent sales representatives and the manufacturers they represent. Publication of Manufacturers' Agents National Association. Magazine; 40 pages. Estab. 1950. Monthly. Circ. 11,000. Rights purchased vary with author and material. May buy all rights, with the possibility of reassigning rights to author after publication, or simultaneous rights. Buys about 36 mss/year. Pays on publication. Free sample copy and writer's guidelines. Will consider photocopied and simultaneous submissions. Reports on mss accepted for publication in 1 to 2 months. Returns rejected material in 1 month. Query first. SASE.
Nonfiction and Photos: Articles on independent sales representatives, the suppliers and customers, and their operations. Must be about independent selling from the agent's point of view. Uses how-to, profile, interview, successful business techniques. "Articles about selling should not be too general — specifics a must." Length: 500 to 2,500 words. Ideal length is 1,500 words. Pays $50 to $100. Photos purchased with accompanying ms with extra payment. Captions required. B&w glossies only. Pays $10 to $15. Size: 3x5, 8x10.

AMERICAN FIREARMS INDUSTRY, American Press Media Association, Inc., 7001 N. Clark St., Chicago IL 60626. Specializes in the sporting arms trade. Monthly magazine; 58 pages. Estab. 1972. Circ. 19,000. Pays on publication. Buys all rights, but may reassign following publication. Submit seasonal/holiday material 60 days in advance. SASE. Reports in 2 weeks. Sample copy, $1.
Nonfiction: John Cahill, Department Editor. Publishes informational, technical and new product articles. Buys 60 mss/year. Query first. Length: 900-1,500 words. Pays $75.
Photos: B&w (8x10) glossies. Mss price includes payment for photos.

ARMY/NAVY STORE AND OUTDOOR MERCHANDISER, 225 W. 34 St., New York NY 10001. (212)279-0800. Editor: Michael Spielman. 15-20% freelance written. For the owners of army/navy surplus and outdoor goods stores. Estab. 1947. Circ. 3,000. Buys all rights. Buys 30 mss/year. Pays on publication. SASE. Reports in 1 month. Sample copy $1.
Nonfiction and Photos: Articles on the methods stores use to promote items; especially on how army/navy items have become fashion items, and the problems attendant to catering to this new customer. Sources of supply, how they promote, including windows, newspapers, etc. "If the guy wants to tell his life story, listen and take notes. Use simple words. Stick to a single subject, if possible. Find out how the man makes money and tell us. The true 'success' story is the most frequently submitted and the most dreadful; yet nothing is of more interest if it is done well. No one truly wishes to tell you how he earns money." Length: open. Pays $50 minimum. "Most articles—especially on stores—must have photos included; minimum 5x7 b&w glossies with captions."
How To Break In: "Am anxious to build our coverage of camping departments. The best material always has a unique—but not forced—slant to most routine store stories."

AUDIO TRADE MERCHANDISING (formerly *The Audio Retailer*), Maclean-Hunter Ltd., 481 University Ave., Toronto, Ontario, Canada M5W 1A7. (416)595-1811. Editor: Greg Gertz. 40-50% freelance written. For retailers of high-quality audio equipment and operators of stereo stores. Monthly; 40 pages. Estab. 1972. Circ. 6,000. Pays on publication. Buys first North American serial rights. Phone queries OK. Submit seasonal/holiday material 3 months in advance. Previously published submissions OK. SASE. Reports in 3 weeks.
Nonfiction: How-to (run a successful audio retail outlet); profiles (successful dealers); interviews (with top executives in the audio equipment manufacturing industry). Buys 2 mss/issue. Length: 500-2,000 words. Query. "Most freelance material comes to us from regular contributors. Anything else must be either very new, very exciting, or very controversial. Strong Canadian angle required." Pays 10¢/word average.
Photos: Purchased with mss B&w only. Captions required. Query. Pays $10/photos.

AUTOMOTIVE AGE, Freed-Crown Publishing, 6931 Van Nuys Blvd., Van Nuys CA 92405. (213)873-1320. Editor: Art Spinella. For a primarily male audience with income in the upper middle and upper brackets; sole owners or partners in multi-million dollar businesses. Monthly magazine; 140-150 pages. Estab. 1967. Circ. 47,000. Pays on publication. Buys all rights, but may reassign after publication. Phone queries OK. Simultaneous submissions OK, if list of other publications receiving same or similar story is furnished. SASE. Reports in 2 weeks. Free sample copy.
Nonfiction: Publishes humorous articles relating to retail sales, auto repair, or of general interest to men meeting readers' demographics; informational articles (sales techniques, dealership/

retail promotions); interviews (with men in government or industry; auto dealers); nostalgia (automotive and sales related); travel (to places where men meeting their demographics would find new and different). "Clean, sophisticated copy that talks to the audience on a professional level." Buys 10 mss per issue. Query first. Length: 300-2,000 words. Pays $5 per column inch, or $7 per hour, plus expenses.
Photos: Pays $25 per b&w photo used with articles, columns or departments.
Columns/Departments: Promo Beat (unique auto dealership promotions for new and used car sales, service or parts departments). Buys 12 items per issue. Query. Length: 700-1,000 words. Pays $5 per column inch. Open to suggestions for new columns and departments.
Fillers: Buys 15 clippings per issue. Pays $1 per clipping or tip leading to a published item.

CAMPGROUND MERCHANDISING, 327 Wagaraw Rd., Hawthorne NJ 07506. Editor: Debby Roth. For owners and managers of recreation vehicle campgrounds who sell merchandise or equipment to people who vacation in recreation vehicles. Magazine published 3 times a year; 56 (5½x8½) pages. Estab. 1972. Circ. 6,500. Buys first North American serial rights. Buys 5 mss a year. Payment on acceptance. Free sample copy to writer on request. Will not consider photocopied or simultaneous submissions. Submit seasonal material 3 months in advance. Reports in 2 weeks. Query first or submit complete ms. SASE.
Nonfiction and Photos: "We specialize in RV campgrounds that resell equipment or merchandise to RV'ers who are visiting the RV campground. We use articles about how to best operate a recreation vehicle campground. The best approach is to interview managers of recreation vehicle campgrounds about their operations. Not interested in RV campgrounds selling, bread, milk, ice cream. Main interest is in their sales of equipment or merchandise wanted only by RV'ers, and how the resale of merchandise and equipment in an RV campground made it profitable." Informational, how-to, personal experience, interview, successful business operations, merchandising techniques. Length: 800 to 1,500 words. Pays about 4¢ a word. Prefers 8x10 b&w glossies, but can use 5x7. Pays $10 for each one used with ms. No color. Captions optional.
Fillers: Clippings are purchased only if about RV parks and newsworthy. Pays 80¢ per inch used.

CHAIN STORE AGE, GENERAL MERCHANDISE EDITION, 425 Park Ave., New York NY 10022. Publisher: Paul J. Reuter. Editor: John Lightfoot. For major chain store executives, field and store management personnel in the general merchandise chain field. Estab. 1925. Monthly. Circ. 33,500. Buys all rights. Purchases of mss are limited to special needs and commitments: "12 columns in fashions (from London), 12-plus pages of government news from Washington." Pays on publication. Will send free sample copy to writer on request. Reports in 2 weeks. Submit complete ms. SASE.
Nonfiction: Retail-related news across a wide band of merchandise categories (housewares, home sewing, toys, stationery, fashionwear, etc.). News about companies, promotions, people-on-the-move. Sharp, to the point, strong on facts. Subjects that are on the tip of chain retailers' minds about their business. How chain retailers are coping with traffic fall-off by tightening productivity screws in day-to-day operations. "We have one defiinite 'no-no' —sloppy copy that is not proofread." Length: 250 to 300 words. Pays minimum of $10 per page.

CONVENIENCE STORE MERCHANDISER, Associated Business Publications, 101 Park Ave., Suite 1838, New York NY 10017. (212)689-5111. Editor-in-Chief: Bill Schnirring. For owners of convenience stories, suppliers, manufacturers of products sold in convenience stores. Monthly magazine; 68 pages. Estab. 1973. Circ. 28,000. Pays on publication. Buys all rights, but may reassign following publication. Phone queries OK. Submit seasonal/holiday material 2½ months in advance. Simultaneous submissions OK, if not competing. Photocopied submissions and previously published work OK. SASE. Reports in 2 weeks. Free sample copy and writer's guidelines.
Nonfiction: Publishes how-to articles (wholesaler, or manufacturer who does something different or better and makes money with it); interviews; new product items; personal opinion; profiles of stores or manufacturers; technical articles. "We don't care how clean the store is, how pretty it is, or how the manager used to be a clerk. As similar as many of the stores are in appearance and items stocked, we need the unique or superior." Buys 2 mss/issue. Length: "Whatever it takes to tell the story." Pays $100.
Photos: Purchased with or without mss, or on assignment. B&w, 5x7 or larger; glossy or semi-matte. "We work with b&w veloxes and need properly exposed pix." Pays $10 minimum. Color transparencies; 35mm or 2¼x2¼ slides. Pays $50 minimum for those used on cover.

CRAFT & ART MARKET, Dept. WM, P.O. Drawer 1, Greenwood MS 38930. (601)453-5822. Managing Editor: John Ashcraft.For retail store owners, wholesalers, mass merchandise buyers of art and craft material. Monthly magazine; 44 pages. Estab. 1975. Circ. 15,000. Pays on publication. Buys all rights. Submit seasonal/holiday material 5 months in advance. Simultaneous and photocopied submissions OK. SASE. Reports in 6 weeks. Free sample copy, if request is on business stationary.
Nonfiction: Connie Adams, Department Editor. Business and how-to articles, interviews and photo features. Submit complete ms. Length: 500-3,000 words. Pays $50-200.
Photos: B&w glossies (5x7) purchased with mss. Captions required. Pays $5.

GIFTWARE NEWS, 1111 E. Touhy Ave., Des Plaines IL 60018. Editor: Cholm Houghton. For retailers, gift stores, florists, stationers, department stores, jewelry and home furnishings stores. Bimonthly magazine; 80 pages. Estab. 1975. Circ. 41,000. Rights purchased vary with author and material. Buys about 24 mss/year. Pays on publication. Sample copy $1; free writer's guidelines. Submit seasonal material (related to the gift industry) 2 months in advance. Reports in 1 to 2 months. Query first or submit complete ms. SASE.
Nonfiction and Photos: Trade material. Only informative articles written in a manner applicable to daily business and general knowledge; not mere rhetorical exercises. Articles on store management, security, backgrounds (history) of giftwares, i.e., crystals, silver, (methods, procedures of manufacture); porcelain, etc. Informational, interview, profiles, material on new products and merchandising techniques. Length: 500 words minimum. Pays $40 minimum. Pays $10 minimum for b&w photos used with mss. Captions optional.

HEALTH FOODS BUSINESS, Howmark Publishing Corp., 225 W. 34th St., New York NY 10001. (212)279-0800. Editor-in-Chief: Michael Spielman. 20% freelance written. For owners and managers of health food stores. Monthly magazine; 100 pages. Estab. 1954. Circ. over 5,000. Pays on publication. Buys simultaneous rights, second serial (reprint) rights or first North American serial rights. Phone queries OK. Simultaneous and photocopied submissions OK if exclusive to their field. Previously published work OK. SASE. Reports in 1 month. Sample copy $1.
Nonfiction: Exposes (government hassling with health food industry); how-to (unique or successful retail operators); informational (how or why a product works; technical aspects must be clear to laymen); historical (natural food use); interviews (must be prominent person in industry or closely related to the health food industry); and photo features (any unusual subject related to the retailer's interests). Buys 2-3 mss/issue. Query first for interviews and photo features. Will consider complete ms in other categories. Length: 1,000 words minimum. Pays $25/published page minimum.
Photos: "Most articles must have photos included"; minimum 5x7 b&w glossies. Captions required. Send contact sheet, prints or negatives. No additional payment.

HOUSEWARES, Harcourt Brace Jovanovich Publications, Inc., 757 Third Ave., New York NY 10017. Editor: Jack BenAry. Emphasizes the retail merchandising of housewares. Published 18 times/year. Tabloid; 50 pages. Estab. 1892. Circ. 12,500. Pays on publication. Buys all rights. SASE. Reports in 3 weeks. Free sample copy.
Nonfiction: Photo features. "Articles without photos are rarely acceptable. We are picture-oriented." Buys 35 mss/year. Query. Length: 1,000-2,500 words. Pays 15¢/word maximum.
Photos: Purchased with accompanying ms. Captions required. Query. Submit 5x7 or 8x10 b&w glossy; transparencies for color. Total price for ms includes payment for photos. Model release required.

KEY NEWSLETTER, Voice Publications, Rt. 1, Box 157A, Goreville IL 62939. (618)995-2027. Editor-in-Chief: Bernard Lyons. 5% freelance written; "but would like to see more." Emphasizes direct marketing/mail order, specifically for those using classified columns of national magazines. Monthly newsletter; 4 pages. Estab. 1960. Circ. 5,000. Pays on acceptance. Buys all rights. Submit seasonal/holiday material 2 months in advance of issue date. Photocopied submissions OK. SASE. Reports in 2 weeks. Sample copy $1; mention *Writer's Market* in request.
Nonfiction: Exposé (fraud in mail order/direct marketing); historical (old classified ads); how-to (write classified ads, match markets, increase response to ads); humor (funny classifieds); inspirational (examples of successful classifieds, personal stories of successful mail order through classifieds); interview (with successful mail order/direct market persons using classifieds); new product (if of help to small business); personal experience (summary of test results); profile (successful users of classifieds, written in first person); and technical (math for

mail order/direct marketing). Buys 10 mss/year. Submit complete ms. Length: 50-1,500 words. Pays $10-75.

PHOTO MARKETING, 603 Lansing Ave., Jackson MI 49202. Managing Editor: Michael F. Buda. For camera store dealers, photofinishers, manufacturers and distributors of photographic equipment. Publication of the Photo Marketing Association, International. Monthly magazine; 62 pages. Estab. 1924. Circ. 13,000. Buys all rights. Pays on publication. Reports in 7 days. Query with outline and story line. SASE.
Nonfiction and Photos: Business features dealing with photographic retailing or photofinishing operations, highlighting unique aspects, promotional programs, special problems. Length: 300-500 typewritten lines. Pays 5-7¢/word minimum. Pays $10-15/published 5x7 glossy photo.

SALESMAN'S OPPORTUNITY MAGAZINE, 1460 John Hancock Center, 875 N. Michigan Ave., Chicago IL 60611. Managing Editor: Jack Weissman. 30% freelance written. "For anyone who is interested in making money, full or spare time, in selling or in independent business program." Monthly magazine; veried size/issue. Estab. 1923. Circ. 176,000. Pays on publication. Buys all rights. Submit seasonal/holiday material 6 months in advance of issue date. SASE. Free sample copy and writer's guidelines.
Nonfiction: "We use articles dealing with sales techniques, sales psychology or general self improvement topics." How-to; inspirational; and interview (with successful salespeople who are selling products offered by direct selling firms, especially concerning firms which recruit salespeople through *Salesman's Opportunity Magazine*). Submit complete ms. Length: 250-900 words. Pays $20-35.
Photos: State availability of photos with ms. Offers no additional payment for 8x10 b&w glossy prints. Captions required. Buys all rights. Model release required.

SELLING TODAY, Automotive Service Industry Association, 444 N. Michigan Ave., Chicago IL 60611. Director of Communications: John Corkery. 60% freelance written. Emphasizes selling to automotive service markets by wholesalers/distributors, salesmen and countermen. Bimonthly magazine; 24 pages. Estab. 1959. Circ. 10,000. Pays on acceptance. Buys all rights. Submit seasonal/holiday material 2 months in advance of issue date. Photocopied and previously published submissions OK. SASE. Reports in 2 weeks. Free sample copy; mention *Writer's Market* in request.
Nonfiction: How-to articles on selling the automotive industry. Query. Length: 750-3,000 words. Pays $30-100.

SOLUTION, One Jake Brown Road, Old Bridge NJ 08857. (201)679-4000. Editor: George S. Bahue. 20% freelance written. For persons involved in television servicing; most own their own stores. Also for trade school graduates. Publication of Blonder-Tongue Labs. Estab. 1967. Quarterly. Circ. 30,000. Buys all rights. Buys about 6 mss/year. Pays on publication. Free sample copy. Will consider photocopied and simultaneous submissions. Reports in 1 month. SASE.
Nonfiction and Photos: General interest articles on TV and signal distribution, MATV systems, and cable television systems. General knowledge of electronics is a must. Author must be able to talk the language. "Will consider short features." Buys informational, new product and technical articles. Length: 750 to 1,500 words. Pays $250 minimum. Photos purchased with accompanying mss with no additional payment.

SPECIALTY SALESMAN MAGAZINE, Communications Channels, Inc., 307 N. Michigan Ave., Chicago IL 60601. (312)726-0743. Editor-in-Chief: Yale A. Kale. Associate Editor: Susan Loeb. 75% freelance written. For independent businessmen and women who sell door-to-door, store-to-store, office-to-office and by the party plan method as well as through direct mail and telephone solicitation; selling products and services. Monthly magazine; 64 pages. Estab. 1915. Circ. 500,000. Pays on acceptance. Buys all rights. Submit seasonal/holiday material 1 month in advance of issue date. SASE. Reports in 3 months. Free sample copy and writer's guidelines.
Nonfiction: How-to (sell better; increase profits); historical (related to the history of various kinds of sales pitches, anecdotes, etc.); humor (cartoons); inspirational (success stories, "rags to riches," type of stories); personal experience; and profile (on the lines of success story). Buys 6 mss/issue. Query or submit complete ms. Length: 500-1,500 words. Pays 3¢/word.
Columns/Departments: Ideas Exchange (generated from our readers). Submit complete ms. Open to suggestions for new columns/departments.
Fillers: Jokes, gags, anecdotes, and short humor. Buys 2/issue. Length: 150-500 words. Pays 3¢/word.

WALLCOVERINGS MAGAZINE, Publishing Dynamics, Inc., 209 Dunn Ave., Stamford CT 06905. Managing Editor: Janet Verdeguer. Emphasizes retail merchandising of wallcoverings. Monthly magazine; 60 pages. Estab. 1921. Circ. 9,000. Pays on publication. Buys all rights. SASE. Reports in 2 weeks. Sample copy $1,50; free writer's guidelines.
Nonfiction: Jean Hatfield, articles editor. Informational (retail merchandising of wall coverings) and interview (with innovative retailers). Buys 2 mss/year. Submit complete ms. Length: 1,000-4,000 words. Pays $20-50/published page.
Photos: Purchased with or without accompanying ms or on assignment. Captions required. Submit 5x7 or 8x10 b&w prints. Total purchase price for ms includes payment for photos. Model release required.

Show People and Amusements

AMUSEMENT BUSINESS, Billboard Publications, Inc., 1717 West End Ave., Nashville TN 37203. (615)329-3925. Editor: Tom Powell. Managing Editor: Tim Taggart. 30% freelance written. Emphasizes the amusement and mass entertainment industry. Weekly tabloid: 24-48 pages. Estab. 1960. Circ. 15,000. Pays on publication. Buys all rights, but may reassign following publication. Phone queries OK. SASE. Submit seasonal/holiday material 2-3 weeks in advance of issue date. Reports in 1 month. Free sample copy and writer's guidelines; mention *Writer's Market* in request.
Nonfiction: How-to (case history of successful promotions); interview; new product; and technical (how "new" devices, shows or services work at parks, fairs, auditoriums and conventions). No personality pieces or interviews with stage stars. Buys 500-1,000 mss/year. Query. Length: 400-700 words. Pays $1-2.50/published inch.
Photos: State availability of photos with query. Pays $3-5 for b&w 8x10 glossy prints. Captions required. Buys all rights, but may reassign after publication. Model release required.
Columns/Departments: Auditorium arenas; fairs, fun parks; food concessions; merchandise; new products; promotion; shows (carnival and circus); shopping centers; talent; and tourist attractions. Query. Length: 25-700 words. Pays $2-2.50/published inch. Open to suggestions for new columns/departments.

THE BILLBOARD, 9000 Sunset Blvd., Los Angeles CA 90069. Editor-in-Chief and Publisher: Lee Zhito. Managing Editor: Eliot Tiegel. Special Issues Editor: Earl Paige. (All Los Angeles). Record Review Editor: Ed Harrison; Talent Editor: Jean Williams; Marketing News Editor: John Sippel; Radio/TV Editor: Doug Hall; Country Music Editor: Gerry Wood (Nashvilte); Classical: Alan Penchansky (NY). Weekly. Buys all rights. Payment on publication. SASE.
Nonfiction: "Correspondents are appointed to send in spot amusement news covering phonograph record programming by broadcasters and record merchandising by retail dealers. Concert reviews, interviews with artists; stories on discotheques. We are extremely interested in blank tape, and tape playback, and record hardware stores." Length: short. Pays 25¢ to $1 per published inch; $5 per published photo.

MOTION, Box 5490, Station A, Toronto, Ontario, Canada M5W 1N7. Editor/Publisher: P.M. Evanchuck. Managing Editor: James McLarty. 80% freelance written. Emphasizes film, TV, and theater (primarily Canadian). Bimonthly magazine; 40 pages. Estab. 1972. Circ. 10,000. Pays on publication. Buys all rights, but may reassign following publication. Phone queries OK. SASE. Reports in 4 weeks. Free sample copy and writer's guidelines.
Nonfiction: Exposé; general interest; historical; how-to; humor; interview; new product; personal experience; personal opinion; photo feature; profile and technical. Buys 8-12 mss/issue. Length: 500-2,000 words. Pays 2¢/word.

PERFORMANCE, 2929 Cullen St., Fort Worth TX 76107. (817)338-9444. Editor-in-Chief: Stephen Fuchs. "Performance publishes tour routing information, updated on a weekly basis. These itineraries, along with box office reports, street news, live performance reviews and industry features are of interest to our readers." Weekly magazine; 50 pages. Circ. 10,000. Pays in 3-4 weeks. Buys all rights. Phone queries OK. Submit seasonal/holiday material 2 months in advance of issue date. Simultaneous, photocopied and previously published submissions OK. SASE. Reports in 1 month. Sample copy and writer's guidelines $1; mention *Writer's Market* in request.
Nonfiction: "This is a trade publication, dealing basically with the ins-and-outs of booking live entertainment. We are interested in adding freelancers from major cities around the US to

provide us with "street news" and spot information on sound and lighting, clubs, ticketing, facilities, and college news relevant to live entertainment. Also publish interviews and overviews from time to time." Interviews; personal opinion and profile.
Photos: State availability of photos with ms. Pays $1-3 for 8x10 b&w matt prints; $20 for 35mm color transparencies selected for cover use. Captions preferred. Buys all rights, but may reassign following publication.

G-STRING BEAT, Atlanta Enterprises, Box 007, Gays Mills WI 54631. Editor-in-Chief: Rita Atlanta. 10% freelance written. Emphasizes burlesque and allied fields of entertainment. Quarterly magazine; 48 pages. Estab. 1973. Circ. 12,000. Pays on publication. Buys all rights. SASE. Reports in 2-3 weeks.
Nonfiction: Publishes in-depth, hard-edged profiles of performers. Buys 6-10 mss/year. Submit complete ms. Length: 1,000-2,500 words. Pays $75-150.
Photos: Query first. "We have about 5,000 pix on hand and pix must be exceptional for us to buy."
Fiction: John Bane, Department Editor. Publishes mystery, humorous and suspense fiction. "Very little fiction is accepted because freelance writers have a limited 'feel' (no pun intended) of burlesque. The tensions of the business are rarely understood by outsiders. Would say that this is one of the hardest markets to please." Buys 2-3 a year. Submit complete ms. Length: 2,500-5,000 words. Pays $100-250.

VARIETY, 154 W. 46th St., New York NY 10036. Executive Editor: Syd Silverman. Does not buy freelance material.

Sport Trade

AMERICAN BICYCLIST AND MOTORCYCLIST, 461 Eighth Ave., New York NY 10001. (212)563-3430. Editor: Stan Gottlieb. For bicycle sales and service shops. Estab. 1879. Monthly. Circ. 7,854. Buys all rights. Pays on publication. Query first. Reports within 10 days. SASE.
Nonfiction and Photos: Typical story describes (very specifically) unique traffic-builder or merchandising ideas used with success by an actual dealer. Articles may also deal exclusively with moped sales and service operation within conventional bicycle shop. Emphasis is on showing other dealers how they can follow a similar pattern and increase their business. Articles may also be based entirely on repair shop operation, depicting efficient and profitable service systems and methods. Length: 1,800 to 2,800 words. Pays 4¢ a word, plus bonus for excellent manuscript. Relevant b&w photos illustrating principal points in article purchased with ms. 5x7 minimum. No transparencies. Pays $5 per photo.

ARCHERY RETAILER, Market Communications, Inc., 225 E. Michigan, Milwaukee WI 53202. (414)276-6600. Editor-in-Chief: Glenn Helgeland. 30-40% freelance written. Emphasizes archery retailing. Published 5 times/year. Magazine; 54 pages. Estab. 1976. Circ. 9,000. Pays between acceptance and publication. Buys one-time rights. Phone queries OK, "but prefer mail queries." Submit seasonal/holiday material 4 months in advance of issue date. SASE. Reports in 3 weeks. Free sample copy and writer's guidelines.
Nonfiction: How-to (better buying, selling, displaying, advertising, etc.); interview, profile. "No stories about dinky shops selling because they love archery but have no idea of profitability." Buys 1-2 mss/issue. Query. Length: 500-2,000 words. Pays $35-125.
Photos: Purchased with or without accompanying ms. Captions required. Pays $10-25 for 8x10 b&w glossies.

BICYCLE DEALER SHOWCASE, Box 19531, Irvine CA 92713. Editor: Steve Ready. For bicycle/moped dealers and industry personnel. Monthly magazine: 70-90 pages. Estab. 1972. Circ. 9,000. Buys all rights. Buys about 12 mss/year. Pays on publication. Free sample copy and writer's guidelines. Submit seasonal material 2 months in advance of issue date. Reports in 3-4 weeks. Query or submit complete ms. SASE.
Nonfiction and Photos: Articles dealing with marketing bicycle products; financing, better management techniques, current trends, as related to bicycle equipment or selling. Material must be fairly straightforward, with a slant toward economic factors or marketing techniques. Informational, how-to, interview, profile, humor, successful business operations, merchandising techniques, technical. Length: 1,000-1,500 words. Pays $35-50. 8x10 b&w glossies purchased with mss. Pays $5 for each published b&w photo.

BICYCLE JOURNAL, 3339 W. Freeway, Fort Worth TX 76101. Publisher: Bill Quinn. Estab. 1947. Monthly. Circ. 7,500. Not copyrighted. Pays on publication. Enclose SASE for return of submissions.
Nonfiction and Photos: Wants stories only about dealers who service what they sell. Stories of a single outstanding feature of a bike store, such as a good display, interior or exterior; sales tip; service tip; unusual sign; advertising or promotion tip; store layout, etc. Photo must be vertical. One 8x10 photo is sufficient. Length: 200 to 300 words. Pays $32.50 to $37.50.

BOWLERS JOURNAL, 875 N. Michigan Ave., Chicago IL 60611. (312)266-7171. Editor-in-Chief: Mort Luby. 30-50% freelance written. For tournament bowlers and billiard players and a trade audience of proprietors, dealers, distributors. Monthly magazine; 90 pages. Estab. 1913. Circ. 17,000. Pays on publication. Buys all rights, but may reassign following publication. Phone queries OK. Submit seasonal/holiday material 1 month in advance of issue date. Simultaneous and photocopied submissions OK. SASE. Reports in 3 weeks.
Nonfiction: Uses illustrated articles about successsful bowling and billiard room proprietors who have used unusual promotions to build business, profiles of interesting industry personalities (including bowlers and billiard players). and coverage of major competitive events, both bowling and billiards. "We publish some controversial matter, seek out outspoken personalities. We reject material that is too general; that is, not written for high average bowlers and bowling proprietors who already know basics of playing the game and basics of operating a bowling alley." Length: 1,500-2,500 words. Pays $150-$175.
Photos: B&w (8x10) glossies and color (35mm or 120 or 4x5) transparencies purchased with mss. Captions required. Pays $5-10 for b&w; $15-25 for color.

THE BOWLING PROPRIETOR MAGAZINE, Box 5802, Arlington TX 76011. (214)460-2121. Editor-in-Chief: Enid Gail Barron. Assistant Editor: Deborah West. Monthly magazine; 72 pages. Estab. November 1954. Circ. 5,000. Pays on publication. Buys all rights. Phone queries OK. Submit seasonal/holiday material 2-3 months in advance of issue date. Simultaneous and photocopied submissions OK. SASE. Reports in 6 months. Sample copy and writer's guidelines for $1; mention *Writer's Market* in request.
Nonfiction: How-to (concerning a bowling center operation; interview (member proprietors); new product (for large buildings or maintenance); photo feature (personality feature, league play); technical (bowling industry); and articles on small businessmen. Buys 4 mss/year. Query. Length: 500-10,000 words. Pays $25 minimum.
Photos: State availability of photos with query. No additional payment for 5x7 or 8x10 b&w glossy contact sheets or 35mm, 120mm or 4x5 color transparencies. Color on cover only. Captions required. Buys all rights. Model release required.

GOLF BUSINESS (formerly *Golfdom),* Harvest Publishing Co./Div. of Harcourt Brace Jovanovich, 9800 Detroit Ave., Cleveland OH 44102. (216)651-5500. Editor-in-Chief: David J. Slaybaugh. Emphasizes golf and country club industry. For the management personnel at golf courses and country clubs. Monthly magazine; 60 pages. Estab. 1927. Circ. 35,000. Pays on publication. Buys all rights. Phone queries OK. Submit seasonal/holiday material 4 months in advance. SASE. Reports in two months. Free sample copy and writer's guidelines.
Nonfiction: Expose (may focus on industry problem that would uncover information new and beneficial to business); how-to (find something new that a club or course is doing that can be applied to whole industry); informational (new concepts in club management); interview (with industry or governmental individual involved in business); new product (also interested in new services which are in the news); photo feature (if it demonstrates a new technique in course or club operation, new food service or turfgrass operations). Buys 7 mss/year. Query. Length: 1,500-3,000 words. Pays $50-100.
Photos: Used with ms with no additional payment. Query or send contact sheet. B&W glossies, at least 5x7 or color transparencies.
How To Break In: "Calling first is important. If we know what the story idea is, we can guide the writer directly without further hangups due to correspondence. We can find out about the writer quicker. After contact, submission, including photos, is important as soon as possible."
Rejects: "We don't want to see articles that may have originally been speeches, digested into pieces and then, warmed over."
For '79: Budgeting and planning issue (September) — technical articles on how to prepare for a new year. Profile of today's golfer (November) — regional reports on what the golfer/customer thinks of his facility.

GOLF INDUSTRY, Industry Publishers, Inc., 915 N.E. 125th St., Suite 2-C, North Miami FL

33161. (305)893-8771. Executive Editor: Michael J. Keighley. Editor: Joan Whaley. Emphasizes the golf industry for country clubs, pro-owned golf shops, real estate developments, municipal courses, military and schools. Bimonthly magazine; 75 pages. Estab. 1975. Circ. 17,000. Pays on publication. Buys all rights. Submit seasonal/holiday material 2-3 months in advance. SASE. Reports "usually in 6-8 weeks." Free sample copy and writer's guidelines.
Nonfiction: Publishes informational articles "dealing with a specific facet of golf club or pro shop operations, i.e., design, merchandising, finances, etc." Buys 20 mss/year. Submit complete ms. Length: 2,500 words minimum. Pays 5¢/word.
How To Break In: "Since we don't make freelance assignments, a query is not particularly important. We would rather have a complete ms which conforms to our policy of general, but informative, articles about one specific facet of the business of golf merchandising, financing, retailing, etc. Well done mss, if not used immediately, are often held in our files for use in a future issue."
Rejects: "We never publish articles concentrating on one specific manufacturer, or extolling the virtues of one product over another. We seldom feature one club or retail outlet. We don't deal with the game itself, but with the business end of the game."

GOLF SHOP OPERATIONS, 495 Westport Ave., Norwalk CT 06856. (203)847-5811. Editor: Nick Roman. For golf professionals at public and private courses, resorts, driving ranges. Magazine; 36 pages. Published 6 times a year. Estab. 1963. Circ. 10,700. Copyrighted. Buys 12 mss a year. Payment on publication. Free sample copy. Will consider photocopied submissions. Will not consider simultaneous submissions. Submit seasonal material (for Christmas and other holiday sales) 3 months in advance. Reports in 4 weeks. Query first or submit complete ms. SASE.
Nonfiction and Photos: "We emphasize improving the golf professional's knowledge of his profession. Articles should describe how pros are buying, promoting, merchandising and displaying wares in their shops that might be of practical value to fellow professionals. Must be aimed only at the pro audience. We would be interested in seeing material on how certain pros are fighting the discount store competition." How-to, profile, successful business operations, merchandising techniques. Pays $50 to $100. Pays $15 for b&w photos purchased with or without mss. Captions required.

MOTORCYCLE DEALER NEWS, Box 19531, Irvine CA 92713. Editor: John Rossmann. 10% freelance written. For motorcycle dealers and key personnel of the industry. Monthly. Buys first serial rights. Payment on publication. Free sample copy and writer's guidelines. Query. Reports in 4 weeks. SASE.
Nonfiction and Photos: "Looking for articles that examine problems of dealers and offer a solution. These dealer articles are not a history of the business, but one unique aspect of the store and its attempt to hurdle an obstacle that may aid other dealers in a similar situation. This is not to be a success story, but rather a fresh look at tackling problems within the industry. Tips for dealers on selling merchandise, creating new displays and improving basic business knowledge are also needed. In-depth articles regarding liability insurance, warranty, land usage, noise pollution and advertising. Usually, in-depth articles about current problems are staff written. However, do not hesitate to query. We do not use articles of a general or unspecific nature. Concrete examples are a must. Photos help sell the article." Length: 750-2,500 words. Pays $50-100. 8x10 b&w glossy photos purchased with mss or with captions only. Modern stores, dealer awards, etc. Minimum payment for photo not accompanied by ms is $5.

POOL NEWS, Leisure Publications, 3923 W. 6th St., Los Angeles CA 90020. (213)385-3926. Editor-in-Chief: Fay Coupe. 40% freelance written. Emphasizes news of the swimming pool industry for pool builders, pool retail stores, and pool service firms. Monthly magazine; 56 pages. Estab. 1961. Circ. 10,000. Pays on publication. Buys all rights, but may reassign following publication. Phone queries OK. Photocopied submissions OK. SASE. Reports in 2 weeks. Free writer's guidelines.
Nonfiction: Interview, new product, profile, and technical. Length: 500-2,000 words. Pays 5¢/word. Pays $5 per b&w photo used.

RVR, RECREATIONAL VEHICLE RETAILER, 23945 Craftsman Rd., Calabasas CA 91302. (213)888-6000. Editorial Director; Alice Robison. 50% freelance written. For men and women of the RV industry, primarily those involved in the sale of trailers, motorhomes, pickup campers, to the public. Also, owners and operators of trailer supply stores, plus manufacturers and executives of the RV industry nationwide and in Canada. Monthly magazine; 100 pages. Estab. 1972. Circ. 28,000. Buys all rights. Buys 100 to 150 mss a year. Pays on publication. Free sample

copy and writer's guidelines. Reports on material in 3 weeks. Query first. SASE.
Nonfiction and Photos: "Stories that show trends in the industry; success stories of particular dealerships throughout the country; news stories on new products; accessories (news section); how to sell; how to increase profits, be a better businessman. Interested in broadbased, general interest material of use to all RV retailers, rather than mere trade reporting." Informational, how-to, personal experience, interview, profile, humor, think articles, successful business operations, and merchandising techniques. Length: 1,000 to 2,000 words. Pays $100-175. Shorter items for regular columns or departments run 800 words. Pays $50 to $75. Photos purchased with accompanying ms with no additional payment. Captions required.
Fillers: Dealer/industry items from over the country; newsbreaks. Length: 100 to 200 words; with photos, if possible. Payment based on length.

SELLING SPORTING GOODS, 717 N. Michigan Ave., Chicago IL 60111. (312)944-0205. Managing Editor: Thomas B. Doyle. For owners and managers of retail sporting goods stores. Estab. 1945. Monthly. Circ. 22,000. Buys all rights. Buys 12 mss/year. Pays on acceptance. Free writer's guidelines. Submit seasonal material 3 months in advance. SASE.
Nonfiction and Photos: Articles on "full-line and specialty sporting goods stores. Informational articles, how-to's; articles on retail sporting goods advertising, promotions, in-store clinics/ workshops; employee hiring and training; merchandising techniques. Articles should cover one aspect of store operation in depth." Length: 750 to 1,000 words. Pays 8-10¢/word. B&w glossy photos purchased with or without accompanying ms. 5x7 minimum. Captions required. Color transparencies acceptable. Pays $100 for cover transparency.
How To Break In: "Practice photography! Most stories, no matter how good, are useless without quality photos. They can be submitted as contact sheets with negatives to hold down writers' cost."

THE SHOOTING INDUSTRY, 291 Camino de la Reina, San Diego CA 92108. (714)297-5352. Editor: J. Rakusan. For manufacturers, dealers, sales representatives of archery and shooting equipment. 12 times a year. Buys all rights. Buys about 135 mss/year. Pays on publication. Free sample copy. Query first. Reports in 2 to 3 weeks. SASE.
Nonfiction and Photos: Articles that tell "secrets of my success" based on experience of individual gun dealers; articles of advice to help dealers sell more guns and shooting equipment. Also, articles about and of interest to manufacturers and top manufacturers' executives. Length: up to 3,000 words. Pays $50 to $150. Photos essential; b&w glossies. Purchased with ms.

SKATEBOARD INDUSTRY NEWS, 15720 Ventura Blvd., Encino CA 91436. (213)995-0257. Editor-in-Chief: Martin Mazner. Managing Editor: Phillip Missimore. For sporting goods retailers and skateboard park operators. Bimonthly magazine; 80 pages. Estab. 1977. Circ. 22,000. Pays on publication. Buys one-time rights. Phone queries OK. Submit seasonal/holiday material 2-3 months in advance of issue date. Photocopied and previously published submissions OK. SASE. Reports in 1 month. Sample copy $1.
Nonfiction: How-to (sell skateboards); interview (with successful skateboard retailer or park operator); new product (skateboard related). "This is strictly a trade magazine going to sporting goods retailers." Buys 5-7 mss/year. Query. Length: 500-2,500 words. Pays $40-150.
Photos: State availability of photos with query. Pays $20-50 for 8x10 b&w glossy prints; $35-60 for 35mm or 2¼x2¼ color transparencies. Captions and model release required.

SKI BUSINESS, 380 Madison Ave., New York NY 10017. (212)687-3000. Editor: Seth Masia. 50% freelance written. Tabloid newspaper; 28 pages. For ski retailers and instructors Estab. 1960. Monthly. Circ. 15,000. Buys about 150 mss per year. Pays on publication. Will send free sample copy to writer on request. Write for guidelines for writers. Will consider photocopied submissions. No simultaneous submissions. Submit seasonal material 3 weeks in advance. Reports on mss accepted for publication in 1 month. Returns rejected material in 1 week. Query first or submit complete ms. SASE.
Nonfiction and Photos: Will consider ski shop case studies; mss about unique and succesful merchandising ideas, and ski area equipment rental operations. "All material should be slanted toward usefulness to the ski shop operator. Always interested in interviews with successful retailers." Uses round-ups of pre-season sales and Christmas buying across the country during September to December. Would like to see reports on what retailers in major markets are doing. Length: 800 to 1,500 words. Pays $35 to $75. Photos purchased with accompanying mss. Buys b&w glossy 8x10 photos. Pays $10.

SKI INFO, 20 Hill St., Morristown NJ 07960. (201)267-9088. Editor: Jim Avalanche Smith. 40% freelance written. For the skiing public. Soft-cover book; 300 pages. Estab. 1975. Annually. Circ. 20,000. Buys all rights, but may reassign rights to author after publication. Buys 5 to 7 mss a year. Pays on publication. Sample copy for $5.95. Will consider photocopied submissions. No simultaneous submissions. Submit seasonal material 3-4 months in advance. Reports in 4 weeks. Query first or submit complete ms. SASE.
Nonfiction and Photos: Technical articles are used in this ski reference book on equipment, and other ski related topics. Helpful hints, etc. Length: 2,000 words minimum. Pays 5¢ a word. B&w photos purchased with mss, or on assignment. Pays $10 minimum.

SKIING TRADE NEWS, One Park Ave., New York NY 10016. Editor: William Grout. For ski shop owners. Annual magazine; 150 pages. Estab. 1964. Circ. about 5,000. Buys first North American serial rights. Buys 14 mss/year. Payment on acceptance. Reports in 30 days. Query first. SASE.
Nonfiction: Factual how-to or success articles about buying at the ski trade shows, merchandising ski equipment, keeping control of inventory, etc. Length: 2,000 words. Pays 10¢ a word.
How To Break In: "Find a ski shop that is a success, one that does something (merchandising, etc.) differently and makes money at it. Research the reasons for the shop's success and query."

THE SPORTING GOODS DEALER, 1212 North Lindbergh Blvd., St. Louis MO 63166. (314)997-7111. Editor: C. C. Johnson Spink. Managing Editor: Gary Goldman. For members of the sporting goods trade; retailers, manufacturers, wholesalers, representatives. Monthly magazine. Estab. 1899. Circ. 15,746. Buys second serial (reprint) rights. Buys about 15 mss a year. Payment on publication. Sample copy $1 (refunded with first mss); free writer's guidelines. Will not consider photocopied or simultaneous submissions. Reports in 2 weeks. Query first. SASE.
Nonfiction and Photos: "Articles about specific sporting goods retail stores, their promotions, display techniques, sales ideas, merchandising, timely news of key personnel; expansions, new stores, deaths—all in the sporting goods trade. Specific details on how specific successful sporting goods stores operate. What specific retail sporting goods stores are doing that is new and different. We would also be interested in features dealing with stores doing an outstanding job in retailing of baseball, fishing, golf, tennis, camping, firearms/hunting and allied lines of equipment. Query first on these." Successful business operations, merchandising techniques. Does not want to see announcements of weddings and engagements. Length: open. Pays $2 per 100 published words. Also looking for material for the following columns: Terse Tales of the Trade (store news); Selling Slants (store promotions); Open for Business (new retail sporting goods stores or sporting goods departments). All material must relate to specific sporting goods stores by name, city, and state; general information is not accepted. Pays minimum of $3.50 for sharp and clear b&w photos; size not important. These are purchased with or without mss. Captions optional, but identification requested.
Fillers: Clippings. These must relate directly to the sporting goods industry. Pays 1¢ to 2¢ per published word.

SPORTING GOODS TRADE, Page Publications, Ltd., 380 Wellington St., W., Toronto, Ontario, Canada M5V 1E3. (416)366-4608. Editor: Timothy Miller. 20-30% freelance written. For sporting goods retailers, manufacturers, wholesalers, jobbers, department and chain stores, camping equipment dealers, bicycle sales and service, etc. Bimonthly magazine; 50-100 pages. Estab. 1972. Circ. 9,000. Pays on publication. Free sample copy. Reports in 2 months. Query. Enclose SAE and International Reply Coupons.
Nonfiction: Technical and informational articles. Articles on successful business operations, new products, merchandising techniques; interviews. Length: open. Pays 4¢ a word or $25/published page.

SPORTS MERCHANDISER, W.R.C. Smith Publishing Co., 1760 Peachtree Rd., NW., Atlanta GA 30357. (404)874-4462. Editor: Eugene R. Marnell. For retailers and wholesalers of sporting goods in all categories: independent stores, chains, specialty stores, department store departments. Monthly tabloid; 100 pages. Estab. 1964. Circ. 40,000. Pays on acceptance. buys all rights. Submit seasonal/holiday material 3-4 months in advance of issue date. SASE. Reports in 1-4 months. Free sample copy and writer's guidelines; mention *Writer's Market* in request.
Nonfiction: "Articles telling how retailers are successful in selling a line of products, successful merchandising programs, and advertising program successes. No articles on business history." Uses 10-20 mss/year. Query. Length: 500-1,500 words. Pays $75-175.
Photos State availability of photos with query. Offers no additional payment for 5x7 or 8x10 b&w

prints. Captions required. Buys all rights.

SWIMMING POOL WEEKLY/AGE, Hoffman Publications, Inc., Box 11299, Fort Lauderdale FL 33339. (305)566-8401. Managing Editor: Dave Kaiser. Emphasizes pool industry. Bimonthly tabloid; 36 pages. Estab. 1928. Circ. 16,000. Pays on acceptance. Buys all rights for industry. Phone queries OK. Submit seasonal/holiday material 1 month in advance. SASE. Reports in 2 weeks. Writer's guidelines for SASE.
Nonfiction: Expose (if in industry, company frauds), how-to (stories on installation techniques done with an expert in a given field); interview (with important poeple within the industry); photo feature (pool construction or special pool use); technical (should be prepared with expert within the industry). Buys 50-80 mss/year. Query. Length: 1,000 words maximum. Pays $35-50.
Photos: Purchased with or without accompanying ms or on assignment. Captions required. Query or send contact sheet. Pays $5-20 for any size larger than 5x7 b&w photo; $15-25 for any size above 35mm color transparencies.
Columns/Departments: "Short news on personality items always welcome at about $10-15 for 25-100 words."

TENNIS INDUSTRY, Industry Publishers, Inc., 915 N.E. 125th St., Suite 2-C, North Miami, FL 33161. (305)893-8771. Editor: Michael J. Keighley. Emphasizes the tennis industry for teaching pros, pro shop managers, specialty shop managers, country club managers, coaches, athletic directors, etc. Monthly magazine; 200 pages. Estab. 1972. Circ. 19,000. Pays on publication. Buys all rights. Submit seasonal or holiday material 2-3 months in advance. Previously published submissions OK. SASE. Reports "usually in 6-8 weeks." Free sample copy and writer's guidelines.
Nonfiction: Publishes informational articles dealing "with specific facets of the tennis club or pro shop operation, i.e., design, merchandising, finances, etc." Buys 20 mss a year. Submit complete ms. Length: 2,500 words maximum. Pays 5¢/word.
How To Break In: "Since we do not make freelance assignments, a query is not particularly important. We would rather have a complete ms which conforms to our policy of general, but informative articles about one specific facet of the business of tennis merchandising, financing, retailing, etc. Well done ms, if not used immediately, are often held in our files for use in a future issue."
Rejects: "We never publish articles concentrating on one specific manufacturer, or extolling the virtues of one product over another. We seldom feature one club or retail outlet. We don't deal with the game itself, but with the business end of the game."

TENNIS TRADE MAGAZINE, 370 7th Ave., New York NY 10001. Editor-in-Chief: Robert E. Abrams. Managing Editor: Marilyn Nason. 10% freelance written. Emphasizes all racquet/paddle sports. Monthly magazine 44 pages. Estab. 1971. Circ. 26,000. Pays on publication. Buys all rights. SASE. Sample copy $1.
Nonfiction: How-to articles related to the tennis/racquet and paddle businesses.

Stone and Quarry Products

CONCRETE, Cement and Concrete Association, 52 Grosvenor Gardens, London SW1W OAQ. (01)235-6661. Editor-in-Chief: R.J. Barfoot. Emphasizes civil engineering and building and construction. Monthly magazine; 60 pages. Estab. 1969. Circ. 13,000. Pays on publication. Phone queries OK. Submit seasonal/holiday material 6 weeks in advance. Photocopied submissions OK. Free sample copy and writer's guidelines.
Nonfiction: Historical, new product, and technical articles dealing with concrete and allied industries. Buys 12 mss/year. Query or submit complete ms. Length: 1,000-3,000 words. Pays $10-30.

CONCRETE CONSTRUCTION MAGAZINE, 329 Interstate Rd., Addison IL 60101. Editor: William C. Panarese. For general and concrete contractors, architects, engineers, concrete producers, cement manufacturers, distributors and dealers in construction equipment, testing labs. Monthly magazine; 52 pages. Estab. 1956. Circ. 60,000. Buys all rights. Buys 50 mss/year. Pays on acceptance. Free sample copy and writer's guidelines. Photocopied and simultaneous submissions OK. Reports on material accepted for publication in an indefinite time. Returns rejected material in 1 to 2 months. Submit complete ms. SASE.
Nonfiction and Photos: "Our magazine has one topic to discuss: cast-in-place (site cast) concrete. Our articles deal with tools, techniques and materials which result in better handling,

better placing, and ultimately an improved final product. We are particularly firm about not using proprietary names in any of our articles. Manufacturers and products are never mentioned; only the processes or techniques that might be of help to the concrete contractor, the architect or the engineer dealing with the material. We do use 'bingo cards' which accomplish the purpose of relaying reader interest to manufacturers, but without cluttering up the articles themselves with a lot of name dropping." Does not want to see job stories or promotional material. Length: 300 to 3,500 words. Pays 7¢ per published word. Pays $10 for b&w glossy photos and color used with mss. Photos are used only as part of a completed ms.

MINE AND QUARRY, Ashire Publishing Ltd., 42 Gray's Inn Rd., London WC1X 8LR, England. Editor-in-Chief: Cyril G. Middup. For senior management at mines and quarries. Monthly magazine; 80 pages. Estab. 1924. Circ. 4,600. Buys all rights, but may reassign following publication. Phone queries OK. Submit seasonal/holiday material 2 months in advance. Simultaneous, photocopied, and previously published submissions OK. SAE and International Reply Coupons. Reports in 2 months. Free sample copy and writer's guidelines.
Nonfiction: Technical and new product articles related to the industry. Buys 20 mss/year. Submit complete ms. Length: 200-1,000 words. Pays $10-20.
Photos: B&w glossies and color transparencies purchased with or without mss. Captions required. Send contact sheet, prints, or transparencies. Pays $3-6.

ROCK PRODUCTS, 300 W. Adams St., Chicago IL 60606. (312)726-2802. Editor: Roy A. Grancher. For nonmetallic minerals mining producers. Monthly. Buys all rights. Pays on publication. Query first. Reports within 4 weeks. Enclose SASE.
Nonfiction and Photos: "Covers the construction minerals segment of the non-metallic (industrial) minerals industry. Uses articles on quarrying, mining, and processing of portland cement, lime, gypsum, sand and gravel, crushed stone, slag, and expanded clay and shale. Other non-metallic metals covered include dimension stone, asbestos, diatomite, expanded fly ash, vermiculite, perlite. Equipment and its applications are emphasized in the operating and technical coverage. Feature articles describe complete plant operations, design and planning, company profiles, marketing, and management techniques." Length: open. $35 per published page.

STONE IN AMERICA (formerly *Monumental News Review*), American Monument Association, 6902 N. High St.,Worthington OH 43085. (614)885-2713. Editor-in-Chief: William A. Kistner. Emphasizes the granite and marble memorial industry for quarriers and manufacturers of memorial stone products in the U.S. and Canada; retail memorial dealers, cemeterians and funeral directors. Monthly magazine; 48 pages. Estab. 1889. Circ. 2,375. Pays on publication. Buys all rights, but may reassign following publication. Phone queries OK. Submit seasonal/holiday material 2 months in advance of issue date. Simultaneous and photocopied submissions and previously published work OK. SASE. Reports in 2 weeks. Free sample copy and writer's guidelines, but adequate postage must accompany request.
Nonfiction: How-to (setting memorials, carving memorials, selling, managing); historical, informational, inspirational, new product, nostalgia, photo features, profiles; anything of interest to the industry. Technical articles on abrasive technology, diamond technology; tool/machine and product technology. Buys 15 mss/year. Length: 300-5,000 words. Query first or submit complete ms.
Photos: Uses b&w glossies (5x7) with or without mss. Send contact sheet or prints. Captions required. No additional payment for those used with mss. Model release required.
Columns/Departments: Buys 50- to 500-word items for Tool Chest, Films (Business/Technical), Commerative Art, Marketing—Sales techniques, Small Business Management, Stone (Granite & Marble). Buys 15/year. Query first or submit complete ms. Open to suggestions for new columns/departments.
Fiction: Adventure, experimental, historical, humorous, mystery, religious, suspense; appropriate to the industry. Length: 1,000-5,000 words.
Poetry: Published avant-garde forms, haiku, free verse and light verse; epitaphs. Buys 10/year. Limit submissions to batches of 20. Length: 5-65 lines. Pays $5-50.

Textile

AMERICA'S TEXTILE REPORTER/BULLETIN, Box 88, Greenville SC 29602. Editor: Prentice Thomas. For "officials and operating executives of manufacturing corporations and plants in the basic textile yarn and fabric industry." Monthly. Estab. 1878. Circ. 22,000. Not copyrigh-

ted. Buys "very few" mss/year. Pays on publication. Sample copy $1; free writer's guidelines "only if background is suitable." Query. "It is extremely difficult for non-textile industry freelancers to write for us." SASE.
Nonfiction: "Technical and business articles about the textile industry." Length: open. Pays $25-50/printed page.

TEXTILE WORLD, 1175 Peachtree St., N.E., Atlanta GA 30361. Editor-in-Chief: Laurence A. Christiansen. Monthly. Buys all rights. Pays on acceptance. SASE.
Nonfiction and Photos: Uses articles covering textile management methods, manufacturing and marketing techniques, new equipment, details about new and modernized mills, etc., but avoids elementary, historical, or generally well-known material. Pays $25 minimum per page. Photos purchased with accompanying ms with no additional payment, or purchased on assignment.

Toy, Novelty, and Hobby

MODEL RETAILER MAGAZINE, Clifton House, Clifton VA 22024. (703)830-1000. Editor-in-Chief: David A. Ritchey. 60-70% freelance written. "For hobby store owners—generally well-established small business persons, fairly well educated, and very busy." Monthly magazine; 120 pages. Estab. 1975. Circ. 4,500. Pays on publication. Buys "all rights in our field." Phone queries OK. Submit seasonal/holiday material 2-3 months in advance of issue date. Simultaneous, photocopied and previously published submissions OK. SASE. Reports in 3 weeks. Sample copy $1.50; free writer's guidelines.
Nonfiction: Hobby store visiting articles; interview (of hobby industry figures); nostalgia (the way things were in the hobby industry); and photo feature (if photos tie in with marketing techniques or hobby store operation, etc.). Buys 5-6 mss/issue. Query. Length: 3,000 words maximum. Pays 5¢/word minimum.
Photos: "Photos that explain the manuscript and are of good quality will help the article, particularly if it concerns business operation." Pays $5 minimum for 3x5 b&w prints. Buys all rights, but may reassign following publication.

PROFITABLE CRAFT MERCHANDISING, News Plaza, Box 1790, Peoria IL 61656. (309)682-6626. Editor: Geoffrey Wheeler. For craft retailers. Monthly magazine; 112 pages. Circ. 17,500. Buys all rights. Buys 40-50 mss/year. Pays on acceptance. Free sample copy and writer's guidelines. Will consider simultaneous submissions only if not submitted to a competitive publication. Submit seasonal material for Christmas merchandising issue, which is published in August, 6-8 months in advance. Reports in 6-8 weeks. Query. SASE.
Nonfiction and Photos: Articles on store management techniques. Craft retailer success stories. Coverage of news events such as trade shows and conventions and better consumer shows that have heavy retailer participation. Store management oriented articles. Does not want to see interviews of craft retailers. "Keep in mind that the primary purpose of *Profitable Craft Merchandising* is to tell the retailer how to make money." Informational, how-to, personal experience, spot news, new product, successful business operations, and merchandising techniques. Length: 1,000-2,500 words. Pays $45-250. 4 to 10 good quality 8x10 or 5x7 b&w glossy photos are usually used with mss. No additional payment. Captions required. Color photos are not used unless especially requested.

SOUVENIRS AND NOVELTIES, 327 Wagaraw Rd., Hawthorne NJ 07506. (201)423-2266. Editor-in-Chief: Martin Dowd. 20% freelance written. For managers and owners of souvenir shops in resorts, parks, museums, and airports. Bimonthly magazine; 88 pages. Estab. 1962. Circ. 6,000. Pays on publication. Buys first North American serial rights. Phone queries OK. Submit seasonal/holiday material 4 months in advance of issue date. Photocopied and previously published submissions OK. SASE. Reports in 2 weeks. Free sample copy and writer's guidelines.
Nonfiction: How-to (operate and improve souvenir shops) interview and profile. "No travel articles on the beauty of an area". Buys 20 mss/year. Query. Length: 1,000-2,000 words. Pays 4-6¢/word.
Photos: State availability of photos with query. Pays $10 for 5x7 or 8x10 glossy prints. Captions preferred. Buys one-time rights.
Fillers: Clippings. Pays 80¢/inch clipping.

THE STAMP WHOLESALER, P.O. Box 529, Burlington VT 05402. Editor: Lucius Jackson. 50% freelance written. For small-time independent businessmen; many are part-time and/or

retired from other work. Published 21 times a year; 68 pages. Estab. 1936. Circ. 9,500. Buys all rights. Buys 40 mss a year. Payment on acceptance. Will send free sample copy to writer on request. Will not consider photocopied or simultaneous submissions. Reports on material accepted for publication in 1 day to 1 year. Returns rejected material when decision is reached. Submit complete ms. Enclose SASE.
Nonfiction: How-to information on how to deal more profitably in postage stamps for collections. Emphasis on merchandising techniques and how to make money. Does not want to see any so-called "humor" items from nonprofessionals. Length: 1,500 to 2,000 words. Pays 3¢ per word minimum.

TOY & HOBBY WORLD, 124 E. 40th St., New York NY 10016. For everyone in the toy and hobby and craft industry from manufacturer to retailer. Magazine. Monthly. Estab. 1961. Circ. 16,500. Not copyrighted. Buys 5 mss a year. Payment on publication. Will send sample copy to writer for 50¢. Will consider photocopied submissions. Will not consider simultaneous submissions. Returns rejected material when requested. Query first. Enclose SASE.
Nonfiction and Photos: Merchandising and news. Informational, how-to, new product. Technical articles for manufacturers; features about wholesalers, retailers, chains, department stores, discount houses, etc., concerned with their toy operations. Prefers stories on toy wholesalers or retailers who have unusual success with unusual methods. Also interested in especially successful toy departments in drug stores, supermarkets, hardware stores, gas stations, etc. No interest in mere histories of run-of-the-mill operators. Use a news style. Length: 1,000 to 3,000 words. Payment commensurate with quality of material. Buys 8x10 b&w photos with mss and with captions only. Must be glossy on singleweight paper. No color. Pays $6 plus word rate. Prefers captions.

TOYS & GAMES, G.P. Page Publications, Limited, 380 Wellington St. W., Toronto, Ontario, Canada M5V 1E3. (416)366-4608. Editor-in-Chief: Henry Wittenberg. 10-25% freelance written. For toy retailers, wholesales and jobbers; owners of department stores, variety stores, hobby and handicraft stores, drug stores; arts and craft suppliers. Bimonthly magazines; 32 pages. Estab. 1972. Circ. 8,500. Pays on publication. Buys all rights, but may reassign following publication. Phone queries OK (but prefer written). SASE. Free sample copy; mention *Writer's Market* in request.
Nonfiction: How-to (more effectively sell toys and games); interview (with industry leaders in Canada only); photo features (open to suggestions for b&w only); and profile (of retailers in Canada doing a good job or retailing toys and games). "No general articles which can be used anywhere with only the names requiring a change. All articles must be written for this industry." Buys 6 mss/year. Query. Length: 500-1,200 words. Pays $25/page.
Photos: State availability of photos with query. Pays $5 for 5x7 or 8x10 b&w prints. Captions preferred. Buys all rights, but may reassign following publication.

Trailers, Mobile Homes

MOBILE HOME MERCHANDISER, 5225 Old Orchard Rd., Suite 7, Skokie IL 60076. (312)967-0430. Editor/Assistant Publisher: Jim Mack. 5% freelance written. "Primary audience is mobile home retailers—those engaged in selling manufactured housing to the consumer. We also reach housing manufacturers, suppliers to those builders, and other related industry professionals." Monthly magazine; 70 pages. Estab. November 1952. Circ. 20,037. Pays on publication. Buys one-time rights. Submit seasonal/holiday material "at least 6 months in advance of issue date, but this type of material isn't really relevant—writer would need a good slant to fit in this industry with holiday material." Photocopied and previously published submissions OK. SASE. Reports in 3 months. Sample copy $2; free writer's guidelines.
Nonfiction: How-to (sell, merchandise, display, accessorize, promote, advertise, etc.); interview (with retailers detailing how they perform some aspect of sales); photo features (retail story on how he/she does something better—photos illustrate copy explanation, which could be short); and technical (advancements in mobile housing or the products used therein). "No general success stories about mobile home retailers; stories should focus on a specific aspect of business operation." Buys 4-5 mss/year. Query. Pays $35/printed page, including photos.
Photos: "Good photos which illustrate the story are almost mandatory." State availability of photos with query. Uses 5x7 b&w and color prints with borders. Offers no payment for photos accepted with ms. "Will pay $50 for a shot I can use on the cover." Captions required. Buys one-time rights.

MOBILE-MODULAR HOUSING DEALER MAGAZINE, 6229 Northwest Highway, Chicago IL 60631. (312)774-2525. Editor: James Kennedy. 25% freelance written. For dealers, manufacturers and suppliers concerned with the industry. Monthly magazine; 130 pages. Estab. 1949. Circ. 18,110. Buys all rights, but will reassign rights to author after publication. Pays on publication. Free sample copy and writer's guidelines. Reports as soon as possible. Query. SASE.

Nonfiction and Photos: "Dealer success stories; in-depth techniques in dealership operations; service articles; financing, features; dealer/manufacturer relationships. Every article should be dealer oriented, pointed to the dealer for the benefit of the dealer. Focus on some one or two aspects of the dealer operation largely responsible for the company's success. A general overall description of the dealership is necessary for a well-rounded story, but an important aspect of the firm's operation should be developed, such as merchandising the product, unique inventory control; before and after sales service; financing procedures; salesmen programs,n ,,s accessories and parts success." Also uses warrantee features, material on manufacturers and dealer franchise agreements; consumerism and service articles. Length: 500-2,000 words. Pays $2/column inch (13 picas wide). 7x10 b&w glossy photos purchased with mss or on assignment. Pays $7. Captions required.

TRAILER/BODY BUILDERS, 1602 Harold St., Houston TX 77006. (713)523-8124. Editor: Paul Schenck. 5% freelance written. For the manufacturers and builders of truck trailers, truck bodies, truck tanks, vans, cargo containers, plus the truck equipment distributors. Monthly. Not copyrighted. Pays on publication. Free sample copy. Reports in 30 days. SASE.

Nonfiction: "Material on manufacturers of truck trailers, and truck bodies, school bus bodies, also their sales distributors. These also go under the names of semitrailer manufacturing, custom body builders, trailer sales branch, or truck equipment distributor. No travel trailers, house trailers, mobile homes, or tire companies, transmission people or other suppliers, unless it directly affects truck body or truck trailer. Need shop hints and how-to features. Many stories describe how a certain special truck body or truck trailer is built." Length: 900-1,000 words. Pays $2/inch or $50/page.

Photos: Buys photos appropriate to format. Study publication. Pays $10.

Fillers: "New products and newspaper clippings appropriate to format. Do not rewrite clippings." Pays $2/inch or better on news items.

Transportation

These journals aim at traffic managers and transportation experts (who route goods across the continent). Publications for automobile and truck dealers, repairmen, or fleet operators are classified in the Auto and Truck category. Journals for highway planners and traffic control experts are in the Government and Public Service listings.

DEFENSE TRANSPORTATION JOURNAL, 1612 K St., N.W., Washington DC 20006. Publisher and Editor: Gerald W. Collins. For "transportation executives and managers of all ages and military transportation officers. Generally educated with college degree." Estab. 1945. Bimonthly. Circ. 10,000. Rights purchased vary with author and material; may buy all rights, but may reassign rights to author after publication. Buys 5 to 10 mss a year. Pays on acceptance. Free sample copy and writer's guidelines. Submit seasonal material 2 to 3 months in advance. Reports in 2 to 3 weeks. SASE.

Nonfiction: "Articles on transportation, distribution, and traffic management in the U.S. and abroad. This publication emphasizes transportation as it relates to defense and emergency requirements." Buys informational and personal experience articles. Length: 2,500-3,000 words, with photos or sketches. Pays $100.

TRAFFIC MANAGER MAGAZINE, 206 Graphic Arts Bldg., 108 N.W. 9th, Portland OR 97209. (503)222-9794. Editor: C.R. Hillyer. For professionals in the freight transportation industry in the Pacific Northwest; shipper and carrier firms. Magazine; 32 pages. Special issue: National Transportation Week issue annually in May. Estab. 1925. Every 2 months. Circ. 3,500. Not copyrighted. Buys no more than 6 mss a year. Pays on publication. Will send sample copy to writer on request. Will consider photocopied and simultaneous submissions. Submit special issue material 2 months in advance. Reports in 2 weeks. Query first or submit complete ms. Enclose SASE.

Nonfiction and Photos: Industry news, semi-technical features about traffic management, materials handling, carrier services. Regionally oriented, personal coverage of management individuals and specific firms. Profiles of firms or executives; personal opinion articles on transportation regulation topics, or related. Length: 300 to 700 words. Pays $10 to $25. Technical articles. Length: 200 to 500 words. Pays $10 to $20. Pays $5 for each b&w glossy (5x7 or larger) used with mss. Captions required.

Travel

ASTA TRAVEL NEWS, 488 Madison Ave., New York NY 10022. Editor-in-Chief: Coleman Lollar. Managing Editor: Kathi Froio. 75% freelance written. Emphasizes travel, tourism and transportation. Monthly magazine; 120 pages. Estab. January 1931. Circ. 19,000. Pays on acceptance. Buys all rights. Submit seasonal/holiday material 3 months in advance of issue date. Simultaneous and photocopied submissions OK. Reports in 4 weeks. Free sample copy.
Nonfiction: How-to; interview; new product; profile; technical; and travel. No first person personal experience. Buys 75 mss/year. Query. Length: 500-3,000 words. Pays $50-200.
Photos: Submit photo material with accompanying query. No additional payment for b&w prints or color transparencies. Captions required.

A.S.U. TRAVEL GUIDE, 1335 Columbus Ave., San Francisco CA 94133. Editor-in-Chief: Ronald Folkenflik. Managing Editor: Pearl Furman. 100% freelance written. All readers are airline employees interested in interline travel benefits and related topics. Quarterly magazine; 288 pages. Estab. 1968. Circ. 30,000. Pays on publication. Buys all rights. Submit seasonal/holiday material 3 months in advance of issue date. Photocopied and previously published submissions OK. SASE. Free sample copy and writer's guidelines; mention *Writer's Market* in request.
Nonfiction: General interest (travel destinations); interview (with airline related personnel); personal experience (travel related); personal opinion (of destinations); profile (prominent airline industry figures); and travel (destinations with emphasis on interline discounts). Buys 4-5 mss/issue. Query with clips of previously published work. Length: 1,200-1,500 words. Pays $75-100.
Photos: State availability of photos with query. Pays $25 for 8½x11 b&w finished prints and $75 for 35mm color transparencies. Captions preferred. Buys one-time rights.

PACIFIC TRAVEL NEWS, 274 Brannan St., San Francisco CA 94107. (415)397-0070. Editor: Frederic M. Rea. 10% freelance written. For travel trade—travel agencies, transportation companies. Monthly. Buys one-time rights for travel trade publications. Pays on publication unless material is for future use; then on acceptance. Free sample copy. All material purchased on assignment following specific outline. Query about assignment. "Do not send unsolicited mss or transparencies." Reports in 1 to 3 weeks. SASE.
Nonfiction: Writer must be based in a country in coverage area of the Pacific from Hawaii west to India, south to Australia and New Zealand. "We are not interested in how-to articles, such as how to sell, decorate your windows, keep your staff happy, cut costs." Pays $250 maximum.
Photos: Purchased with mss or captions only. Related to travel attractions, activities within Pacific area. Sometimes general travel-type photos, other times specific photos related to hotels, tours, tour equipment, etc. Buys mainly b&w glossy, 5x7 or larger. Also buys about 18 color transparencies a year, 35mm top quality. Pays up to $10 for b&w; up to $50 for inside color; $75 for color used on cover.

THE STAR SERVICE, Sloane Agency Travel Reports, Box 15610, Ft. Lauderdale FL 33318. (305)472-8794. Editor: Robert D. Sloane. Editorial manual sold to travel agencies on subscription basis. Buys all rights. Buys about 2,000 reports a year. Pays on publication. Write for instruction sheet and sample report form. Initial reports sent by a new correspondent will be examined for competence and criticized as necessary upon receipt, but once established, a correspondent's submissions will not usually be acknowledged until payment is forwarded, which can often be several months, depending on immediate editorial needs. Query first. SASE.
Nonfiction: "Objective, critical evaluations of worldwide hotels and cruise ships suitable for North Americans, based on inspections. Forms can be provided to correspondents so no special writing style is required, only perceptiveness, experience, and judgment in travel. No commercial gimmick—no advertising or payment for listings in publication is accepted." With query, writer should "outline experience in travel and specific forthcoming travel plans, time available for inspections. Leading travel agents throughout the world subscribe to Star Service. No credit

or byline is given correspondents due to delicate subject matter often involving negative criticism of hotels. We would like to emphasize the importance of reports being based on current experience and the importance of reporting on a substantial volume of hotels, not just isolated stops (since staying in hotel is not a requisite) in order that work be profitable for both publisher and writer. Experience in travel writing is desirable.'' Length: ''up to 350 words, if submitted in paragraph form; varies if submitted on printed inspection form.'' Pays $5 minimum per report used. ''Guarantees of acceptance of set numbers of reports may be made on establisment of correspondent's ability and reliability, but always on prior arrangement. Higher rates of payment sometimes arranged, after correspondent's reliability is established.''

TRAVELAGE WEST, The Reuben H. Donneley Corp., 582 Market St., San Francisco CA 94104. Managing Editor: Donald C. Langley. 5% freelance written. For travel agency sales counselors in the western U.S. and Canada. Weekly magazine; 60 pages. Estab. 1969. Circ. 13,500. Pays on publication. Buys all rights. Submit seasonal/holiday material 2 months in advance. SASE. Reports in 4 weeks. Free writer's guidelines.
Nonfiction: Travel. Buys 15 mss/year. Query. Length: 1,000 words maximum. Pays $1.50/column inch. ''No promotional tones of voice or any hint of do-it-yourself travel.''

THE TRAVEL AGENT, 2 W. 46th St., New York NY 10036. Editor: Eric Friedheim. For ''travel agencies and travel industry executives.'' Estab. 1929. Semiweekly. Circ. 22,000. Not copyrighted. Pays on acceptance. Query first. Reports ''immediately.'' SASE.
Nonfiction and Photos: Uses trade features slanted to travel agents, sales and marketing people, and executives of transportation companies such as airlines, ship lines, etc. No travelogues such as those appearing in newspapers and consumer publications. Articles should show how agent and carriers can sell more travel to the public. Length: up to 2,000 words. Pays $50 to $100. Photos purchased with ms.

TRAVELAGE MIDAMERICA, Reuben H. Donnelley, A Dunn & Bradstreet Co., 2416 Prudential Plaza, Chicago IL 60601. (312)861-0432. Editor/Publisher: Martin Deutsch. Managing Editor: Linnea Smith Jessup. 5% freelance written. ''For travel agents in the 13 midAmerica states and in Ontario and Manitoba.'' Biweekly magazine; 30-50 pages. Estab. March 1975. Circ. 13,000. Pays on publication. Buys simultaneous rights. Submit seasonal/holiday material 6 months in advance of issue date. Simultaneous, photocopied and previously published submissions OK. SASE. Reports in 2 weeks. Free sample copy and writer's guidelines.
Nonfiction: ''News on destinations, hotels, operators, rates and other developments in the travel business. No general destination stories, especially ones on ''do-it-yourself'' travel. Buys 8-10 mss/year. Query. Length: 400-1,500 words. Pays $1.50/column inch.
Photos: State availability of photos with query. Pays $1.50/column inch for glossy b&w prints.

TRAVELSCENE MAGAZINE, 888 Seventh Ave., New York NY 10019. Managing Editor: Curt Schleier. For three diverse audiences: airline reservationists, travel agents, and corporate travel planners. Magazine; 60 pages. Estab. 1965. Monthly. Circ. 100,000. Buys all rights. Buys 30 to 40 mss a year. Payment on acceptance. Free sample copy. No photocopied or simultaneous submissions. Submit special issue material 5 months in advance. Reports in 2 to 6 weeks. Query first. SASE.
Nonfiction and Photos: ''*TravelScene* is the largest circulation magazine in the travel industry and runs articles on important trade issues, destinations, personalities, how-to's and other topics designed to help professional travel planners do a better job and gain a better perspective on their profession.'' Recently published articles have dealt with the politician/travel agent, women's roles in the airlines, and how tipping can run up the cost of a business meeting. B&w and color photos purchased on assignment. Pays $10-25 for photos; $100 for 2,000 word articles.
How To Break In: ''Writer should submit past samples of work, an outline of proposal(s), and include SASE and phone number. Getting a first assignment may not be too difficult, if the writer can write. We are looking for and need good writers. If stories are submitted, they must be an average of 8 to 12 pages, double spaced; 13 to 15 maximum. Please do not send queries for destination pieces unless you have a specific angle. We have never given an assignment to someone who merely writes, 'I'm going to London. Can I give you something on it?' Also, we rarely buy destination pieces since we can get those articles in exchange for the trips we offer.''

Veterinary

CANINE PRACTICE JOURNAL, FELINE PRACTICE JOURNAL, Veterinary Practice Pub-

lishing Co., Box 4506, Santa Barbara CA 93103. (805)965-1028. Editor: Dr. Anna P. Clarke. For graduate veterinarians working primarily in small animal practice, or in mixed practices (large and small) which do a substantial volume of dog and cat practice. Published every two months; magazines, 60 pages. *Feline Practice Journal* established in 1971. Circ. 6,800. *Canine Practice Journal* established in 1974. Circ. 5,230. Rights purchased vary with author and material. Buys all rights, but will reassign rights to author after publication. Buys second serial (reprint) rights. "Strictly technical medical and surgical content written so far exclusively by graduate veterinarians." Payment on publication. Will send free sample copy to writer on request, if an apparently legitimate author in this field. Write for copy of editorial guidelines for writers. Will consider photocopied submissons. Query first. Reports within 4 weeks. Enclose SASE.
Nonfiction and Photos: "Strictly technical medical and surgical articles for veterinarians, by veterinarians. One of our magazines deals exclusively with feline (cat) medicine and surgery; the other, with canine (dog) medicine and surgery. Writer would first have to be a veterinarian, or a scientist in one of the life sciences fields (for example, biology, nutrition, zoology). We send an author's guide on request. Our journals are specifically vertical magazines in a field heretofore served by horizontal magazines. That is, we publish single-species journals, the others publish multi-species journals." Length: 300 to 5,000 words. Pays $10 per published page. 4x5 to 8x10 b&w matte or glossy. 35mm or 4x5 color transparencies or negatives.

MODERN VETERINARY PRACTICE, American Veterinary Publications, Inc., Drawer KK, 300 E. Canon Perdido, Santa Barbara CA 93102. 75% freelance written. For graduate veterinarians. Monthly magazine; 90 pages. Estab. 1920. Circ. 15,400. Pays on publication. Buys all rights, but may reassign following publication. Phone queries OK. Submit seasonal/holiday material 3 months in advance. SASE. Reports in 4 weeks. Sample copy $1.50.
Nonfiction: How-to articles (clinical medicine, new surgical procedures, business management); informational (business management, education, government projects affecting practicing veterinarians, special veterinary projects); interviews (only on subjects of interest to veterinarians; query first); technical articles (clinical reports, technical advancements in veterinary medicine and surgery). Buys 25-30 mss/year. Submit complete ms, but query first on ideas for pieces other than technical or business articles. Pays $15/page.
Photos: B&w glossies (5x7 or larger) and color transparencies (5x7) ueed with mss. No additional payment.
How To Break In: "Contact practicing veterinarians or veterinary colleges. Find out what interests the clinician, and what new procedures and ideas might be useful in a veterinary practice. Better yet, collaborate with a veterinarian. Most of our authors are veterinarians or those working with veterinarians in a professional capacity. Knowledge of the interests and problems of practicing veterinarians is essential."

NORDEN NEWS, 601 W. Cornhusker Highway, Lincoln NE 68521. (402)475-4541. Editor-in-Chief: Patricia Pike. 10% freelance written. Emphasizes veterinary medicine. Quarterly magazine; 36 pages. Estab. 1919. Circ. 36,000. Pays on publication. Buys one-time rights. SASE. Reports in 2-3 weeks. Free sample copy.
Nonfiction: How-to (only if it deals with veterinary medicine or operation of a veterinary clinic); and technical (veterinary medicine, unusual case histories). No articles about veterinarians which are written for lay readers. Buys 3 mss/year. Query or submit complete ms. Length: 500-2,000 words. Pays $100-150.
Photos: State availability of photos with query or ms. Pays $7.50-15 for 8½x11 or 5x7 b&w glossy prints and $40-100 for 35mm color transparencies. Buys one-time rights. Model release required.

VETERINARY ECONOMICS MAGAZINE, 2728 Euclid Ave., Cleveland OH 44115. Editorial Director: John D. Velardo. For all practicing veterinarians in the U.S. Monthly. Buys exclusive rights in the field. Pays on publication. SASE.
Nonfiction and Photos: Uses case histories telling about good business practices on the part of veterinarians. Also, articles about financial problems, investments, insurance and similar subjects of particular interest to professional men. "We reject articles with superficial information about a subject instead of carefully researched and specifically directed articles for our field." Pays $20-30/printed page depending on worth. Pays maximum $100. Photos purchased with ms. Pays $7.50.

VETERINARY MEDICINE/SMALL ANIMAL CLINICIAN, 144 N. Nettleton Ave., Bonner Springs KS 66012. (913)422-5010. Editor-in-Chief: Dr. C.M. Cooper. Managing Editor: Ray Ottinger. 5% freelance written. For graduate veterinarians, student veterinarians, libraries,

representatives of drug companies and research personnel. Monthly magazine; 146 pages. Estab. 1905. Circ. 17,500. Pays on publication. Buys first North American serial rights. Phone queries OK. Submit seasonal/holiday material 5-6 months in advance of issue date. Previously published submissions OK. SASE. Reports in 2-3 weeks. Free writer's guidelines.
Nonfiction: Accepts only articles dealing with medical case histories, practice management, business, taxes, insurance, investments. Photo feature (new hospital, floor plan, new equipment; remodeled hospital). No "cutesy" stories about animals. Buys 3 mss/issue. Submit complete ms. Length: 1,500-5,000 words. Pays $15-75.
Photos: State availability of photos with ms. Pays $2.50 for 5x7 b&w glossy prints; $2.50 for 4x7 glossy prints or 35mm color transparencies. Captions required. Buys one-time and reprint rights. Model release required.

Water Supply and Sewage Disposal

GROUND WATER AGE, 110 N. York Rd., Elmhurst IL 60126. (312)833-6540. Editorial Director: Gene Adams. Managing Editor: Pam Smith. 20% freelance written. For water well drilling contractors and water systems specialists. Monthly magazine; 76 pages. Estab. 1965. Circ. 15,200. Pays on acceptance. Buys all rights. Phone queries OK. Submit seasonal/holiday material 4 months in advance of issue date. Photocopied and previously published submissions OK. SASE. Reports in 2 weeks. Free sample copy and writer's guidelines; mention *Writer's Market* in request.
Nonfiction: General interest; historical; how-to; humor; interview; nostalgia; personal opinion; photo feature; profile; and technical. Buys 18 mss/year. Query or submit complete ms. Length: 3,000 words. Pays 4-8¢/word.
Photos: "State availability of photos with query or submit photos with ms. Pays $5-15 for 4x5 matte b&w prints; $25-75 for 8x10 matte color prints. Captions and model release required. Buys all rights, but may reassign following publication.

SOLID WASTES MANAGEMENT, Communication Channels, Inc., 461 8th Ave., New York NY 10001. (212)239-6200. Editor-in-Chief: Alan Novak. Emphasizes refuse hauling, landfill transfer stations, and resource recovery for private haulers, municipal sanitation and consulting engineers. Monthly magazine; 100 pages. Estab. 1958. Circ. 21,000. Pays on acceptance. Buys all rights, but may reassign following publication. Phone queries OK. Submit seasonal or holiday material 3 months in advance. Photocopied submissions OK. SASE. Reports in 4 weeks. Sample copy 50¢. Free writer's guidelines.
Nonfiction and Photos: Case studies of individual solid wastes companies, landfills, transfer stations, etc. Material must include details on all quantities handled, statistics, equipment used, etc. Informational, how-to, interview, historical, think pieces and technical articles. Length: 1,500 words minimum. Pays $75-150.

WATER & SEWAGE WORKS, Scranton Publishing Co., 434 S. Wabash, Chicago IL 60605. (312)922-4950. Editorial Director: Frank Reid. Managing Editor: Francis Kelsey. Emphasizes wastewater and water pollution engineering for engineers and directors of municipal sewage treatment plants. Monthly magazine; 120 pages. Estab. 1882. Circ. 32,000. Pays on acceptance. Buys all rights. Photocopied submissions OK. SASE. Reports in 3-4 weeks. Free sample copy and writer's guidelines.
Nonfiction: General interest (pertaining to water pollution); how-to (best type for our publication, how to solve a pollution problem at a treatment plant); new product; personal experience (if it applies to the subject); photo feature; and technical. Buys 6 mss/year. Query. Length: 5,000 words maximum. "Payment negotiable prior to acceptance.
Photos: State availability of photos with query. Offers no additional payment for photos accepted with ms. Uses 5x7 or larger b&w prints; any size color transparencies. Captions required. Buys all rights, but may reassign following publication.

WATER WELL JOURNAL, 500 W. Wilson Bridge Rd., Suite 130, Worthington OH 43085. (614)436-0580. Editor-in-Chief: Jay H. Lehr. Editor: Anita Stanley. 10% freelance written. Emphasizes water well drilling/hydrology. Monthly magazine; 100 pages. Estab. 1946. Circ. 20,300. Pays on publication. Buys all rights, but may reassign following publication. Phone queries OK. Submit seasonal/holiday material 4 months in advance of issue date. Photocopied submissions OK. SASE. Reports in 10 weeks. Free sample copy and writer's guidelines; mention *Writer's Market* in request.

Nonfiction: Historical (pump, drilling rigs); interview (with drillers, geologists, politicians); new product (all related); photo feature (of related equipment or workers); profile; and technical (geology/hydrology specifics). Buys 6 mss/year. Query with clips of previously published work. Pays $50/printed page.
Photos: State availability of photos with query. Pays $10-25 for b&w photos; $15-35 for 2¼x2¼ color transparencies; $75-125 for cover photos. Captions preferred. Buys all rights, but may reassign following publication.
Columns/Departments: Industry News/Views; Industry Changes; OSHA Corner; Bureaucratic Jungle; and Coming Events. Pays $10-25.
Fillers: Clippings, jokes, gags, anecdotes and short humor. Pays $5-25.

Opportunities and Services

Authors' Agents/Literary Services

At any gathering of two or more writers who are establishing themselves in the literary community, the issue of authors' agents invariably pops into the conversation. Frequently overheard are questions like "Do I really *need* an agent? How do I get a good one? What can an agent *do* for me?"

Briefly, an authors' agent is the person responsible for any business concerning the sale of a client's written material. It's an agent's job to stay on top of the field—to know *who* needs *what,* and what is the highest price they're willing to pay for it. In short, an agent is the personal door-to-door salesman of a writer's goods.

It's best that the beginning writer market his own work. This is a good way to become familiar with the writing field, and much can be learned from personal contact between editor and writer. This open-door communication proves invaluable when an editor has an assignment that could be right for a writer with whom he has established a good rapport and working relationship.

Normally a top agent *won't* consider taking on a writer without a proven track record. After all, the agent makes his living from a 10-20 percent commission of his clients' sales, and unless a writer is producing quality work prior to signing with the agent, the investment in time and promotion isn't worth the risk. Some agencies charge prospective clients *reading fees* (ranging from around $25 for short stories and articles, to over $100 or more for novels and stage plays) to insure them some compensation should the material prove unsaleable. In such cases, the listing in *Writer's Market* for the agency states this, and generally gives the amount of the fees.

Once a writer is selling regularly to the major markets, he may want to acquire an agent, thus relieving him of the task of marketing his work, and freeing him to concentrate on his writing. Agents prefer to represent authors who are primarily doing books as commissions on book sales are greater than the fees received from magazine sales.

Be careful in signing any contract with an agent. Be sure you know what rights he's handling for your material, and check to see that there are no charges for services other than those you have contracted for (such as editing or marketing fees or charges for criticism). Some agencies legitimately charge for these services (at about the same prices as are charged for reading fees; sometimes higher for in-depth evaluation), but always take special care to be aware of "hidden" costs or extra charges.

The listings in the following category include information as to what kinds of materials the agency is willing to handle, what percentage the agent receives as his commission, and what fees for reading, evaluating, or critiquing, if any, are charged.

A&A AGENCY, Box 103, Rt. 2, Molalla OR 97038. (305)829-6982. Director: Y.D. Gerald. Obtains new clients through *Writer's Market,* authors' and editors' recommendations, and other ads. Made 4 sales in 1977, "hope to double or triple this in 1978." Will read unsolicited mss for $35 to 25,000 words; $50 for 50,000 words; $100 for 75,000 words. Will read unsolicited queries. SASE. Charges $200 marketing fee for novices, no fee for established writers. Agent receives 10% commission.
Will Handle: Magazine articles and fiction; novels; textbooks; nonfiction books; and syndicated material.
Recent Sales: "A Nice Room to Die In," by J. Martin (*Nugget*) and "Sea Urchins Provide Kidneys and Lungs," by Y. Gerald (*Medical Post*).
Criticism Services: Critique of all types of material included in the above fee.

DOMINICK ABEL LITERARY AGENCY, 498 West End Ave., New York NY 10024. (212)877-0710. Estab. 1975. Obtains new clients through recommendations, solicitation, and blind submissions. Will not read unsolicited mss, will read queries and outlines. SASE. Agent receives 10% commission on US sales; 20% on foreign.
Will Handle: Novels, nonfiction books and syndicated material.

ADAMS, RAY & ROSENBERG, 9200 Sunset Blvd., Los Angeles CA 90069. Estab. 1963. Obtains new clients through recommendation only. Will not read unsolicited mss. Agent receives 10% commission.
Will Handle: Novels (motion picture, publication and TV rights), motion pictures, stage plays (film rights), and TV scripts.

DOROTHY ALBERT, 162 W. 54th St., New York NY 10019. Estab: 1959. Obtains new clients through recommendations of editors, educational establishments, contacts in the film industry, and inquiries. Writers should send letter of introduction, description of material, and list of previous submissions, if any. Will not read unsolicited mss; will read unsolicited queries and outlines. SASE. Agent receives 10% on domestic sales; 20% on foreign.
Will Handle: Novels, nonfiction books, motion pictures (completed, no treatments), stage plays (musicals), TV scripts, juvenile and how-to. No poetry, short stories, textbooks, articles, documentaries, or scripts for established episode shows. "We are interested in novels which are well-plotted suspense; quality drama, adult fiction and human relations. The writer should have some foreknowledge of structure and endurance, whether it be motion pictures, television, or books."

AMERICAN PLAY CO., INC., 52 Vanderbilt Ave., New York NY 10017. (212)686-6333. President: Sheldon Abend. Estab. 1889. Obtains new clients through private referrals and unsolicited submissions. Will read unsolicited mss for a fee of $55-75. "We refund the readers' fee if we license the author's mss." Will read unsolicited outlines and queries. "We waive a reading fee when the writer has been published within the last 7 years." SASE. Agent receives 10% commission on U.S. sales; 20% on foreign.
Will Handle: Novels, nonfiction books, motion pictures, stage plays and TV scripts.
Criticism Services: "We have three readers critiquing the new mss, and make a master composite critique and supply a copy to the writer and the publishing and producing companies."

MARCIA AMSTERDAM, 41 W. 82nd St., New York NY 10024. (212)873-4945. Obtains new clients through client or editor referrals; ocassionally through queries. Made 3 sales in 1977, 5 in 1978. Will read unsolicited mss, queries or outlines. "We prefer queries or partials to complete manuscripts." SASE. Agent receives 10% on domestic sales.
Will Handle: Novels and nonfiction books. "The usual requirements—a good story, well told."
Recent Sales: *The Lords of Dair,* by H. Wieselberg (Putnam); *The Great American Alimony*

Escape, by D. Rogers (Fawcett); and *World on a String: The Yo-Yo Book,* by H. Zeiger (Contemporary).

CUTTY ANDERSON ASSOCIATES, INC., 521 5th Ave., New York NY 10017. Executive Senior Associate: H.M. Rothstein. Estab. 1974. Obtains new clients through personal recommendations and some advertising in professional publications. Will not read unsolicited mss; will read unsolicited queries and outlines. SASE. Made 200 sales in 1977, 250 in 1978. Agent receives 10-15% on domestic sales, 20% on foreign and media rights.
Will Handle: Magazine articles and fiction, novels, textbooks, nonfiction books, poetry, motion pictures, stage plays, TV and radio scripts, syndicated material. "We run heavily into journalistic style features and investigative materials."
Criticism Services: "We will only ctitique materials sent to us after initial query. Rates sent upon request."

ARIZONA LITERARY AGENCY, 1540 W. Campbell Ave., Phoenix AZ 85015. Representative: Jenelle Tuttle. "New clients have been obtained by word-of-mouth from past or presently satisfied clients and/or other professional people in the field. Some of our writers are already established professional writers. We are always interested in new talent." Will not read unsolicited mss; will read queries and outlines. SASE. Agent receives 10% commission.
Will Handle: Novels (material that is geared to the reading public's interest); textbooks (specialize in parapsychology, psychology and science); nonfiction books (interested in the lives of famous people, how-to's on the unusual, ancient history, philosophy, theology, paranormal experiences, and travel); motion pictures (we are presently in negotiation with 2 film companies on properties; however, we are extremely select in representing a client in this field).

AUTHOR AID ASSOCIATES, 340 E. 52nd St., New York NY 10022. (212)758-4213. Editorial Director: Arthur Orrmont. Estab. 1967. Obtains new clients through word-of-mouth, referrals, listings and advertisements. Will read unsolicited mss for fees (available upon request); will read unsolicited queries and outlines. SASE. Agent receives 10% commission on domestic sales; 20% on foreign.
Will Handle: Magazine articles and fiction, novels, nonfiction books, textbooks, poetry (collections only), motion pictures, stage plays, TV scripts and juvenile fiction and nonfiction.
Criticism Services: Will critique all materials. Fees available on request.

AUTHORS' ADVISORY SERVICE, 51 E. 42nd St., New York NY 10017. (212)687-2971. Literary Agent: Marcy Ring. Estab. 1975. Obtains new clients through recommendations, listings in *LMP* and *Writer's Market;* also some direct solicitation. Will read unsolicited mss for $100 (up to 100,000 words). "Reading fee is refundable against commission if work is sold." SASE. Agent receives 10% commission.
Will Handle: Magazine articles and fiction, novels, nonfiction books, poetry, stage plays, and juvenile fiction and nonfiction.
Criticism Services: Will critique material as above. Charges $100 for mss up to 100,000 words, combined rate offered for 2 or more mss (i.e., 2 for $150, 3 for $200). "Rule of thumb: $1/page."

THE BALKIN AGENCY, 403 W. 115th St., New York NY 10025. President: Richard Balkin. Estab. 1973. Obtains new clients through recommendations, over-the-transom inquiries, and solicitation. Will not read unsolicited mss; will read unsolicited queries, or outlines and 2 sample chapters. SASE. Agent receives 10% commission on domestic sales, 20% on foreign.
Will Handle: Magazine articles (only as a service to clients who primarily write books), textbooks (college only), nonfiction books, and professional books (on occasion).
Recent Sales: *Middle Eastern Literature,* by L. Hamalian (New American Library); *Film/Cinema/Movie,* by G. Mast (Harper & Row); and *The Programmable Pocket Calculator,* by H. Mullish (John Wiley & Sons).

THE JOSEPH A. BARANSKI LITERARY AGENCY, 427 Borden, West Seneca NY 14224. Contact: Dennis A. Baranski at the Midwest office, Box 4527, Topeka KS 66604. Estab. 1972. "Most new authors are obtained through recommendations and referrals. However we are always interested in writers with potential, regardless of their previous track record." Will read unsolicited mss subject to a reading fee of $15 for mss under 10,000 words; $35 for mss over 10,000 words. "This fee will be assessed to writers who have not met a $5000 sales requirement in the last 18 months." Will read unsolicited queries and outlines. SASE. Agent receives 10% commission on domestic sales; 20% on foreign sales.
Will Handle: Fiction and nonfiction books, stage and screen plays, magazine articles, and short fiction. "Concentrate on submitting professionally prepared material. The basics of proper

paper, clear type, and standard ms format are very important in this highly competitive field. Study your specific market with regard to the length of your ms. We deal on an international basis representing over 200 clients on 4 continents. We hope to expand our facilities to handle a maximum of 300 clients by 1980. We will begin an expanded search for new writing talent in the fall of 1978. We are especially interested in works dealing with provocative social and political issues as well as mystery fiction."

BLOOM, BECKETT, LEVY & SHORR, 449 S. Beverly Dr., Beverly Hills CA 90212. (213)553-4850. Estab. 1977; "however, the forerunner of the firm has been in existence for fifteen years." Obtains new clients by recommendations of writers, directors, producers, and studio executives. Also by reading unsolicited motion picture screenplays. Will read unsolicited mss. SASE. Made approximately 250 sales in 1977, 250 in 1978. Agent receives 10% commission.
Will Handle: "We will read only completed motion picture screenplays. This may include screenplays for feature films as well as television. We will not read outlines, treatments, or scripts for eposodic or situation comedy television."
Recent Sales: *Thaddeus, Rose and Eddy,* by W. Wittliff (CBS); *A Different Story,* by H. Olek (Avco Embassy); and *Specter,* by D. Kinghorn (Universal).

GEORGES BORCHARDT, INC., 136 E. 57th St., New York NY 10022. (212)753-5785. Estab. 1967. Obtains new clients "mainly through authors already represented by us who refer others." Potential clients "must be highly recommended by someone we know." Will not read unsolicited mss; will read unsolicited queries from established writers. Made approximately 220 U.S. book sales in 1977. Agent receives 10% commission.
Will Handle: Magazine articles and fiction, novels, and nonfiction books.
Recent Sales: *Dickens,* by E. Johnson (Viking); *How to Enjoy Ballet,* by D. McDonagh (Doubleday); and *The Public Burning,* by R. Coover (Viking).

AARON BOWMAN COMPANY, P.O. Drawer 1389, Granite City IL 62040. (618)451-1620. Chief Agent: Aaron Bowman. Estab: 1972. Obtains new clients through *Writer's Market.* Will read unsolicited mss for a fee of $50. SASE. Made 32 sales in 1977. Agent receives 10% commission. "Reading and analysis fee is returned upon sale of ms."
Will Handle: Novels, textbooks, nonfiction books, short stories, plays, and poetry books.
Criticism Services: "We critique all material not submitted to publishers, a service included in the $50 reading/analysis fee required with all mss."

BRANDT & BRANDT, 101 Park Ave., New York NY 10017. (212)683-5890. Estab: 1914. Obtains new clients through recommendations of clients and editors. Will not read unsolicited mss; will read unsolicited queries and outlines. Agent receives 10% commission.
Will Handle: Magazine articles and fiction, novels, nonfiction books, motion pictures, and stage plays.

BROOME AGENCY, INC./BROOME LITERARY SERVICE, Box 3649, Sarasota FL 33578. President: Sherwood Broome. Estab. 1957. Obtains new clients "mainly by response to our ads in *Writer's Digest,* plus our listing in *Writer's Market.*" Will read unsolicited mss. SASE. Agent receives 10% commission on domestic sales, 15% on Canadian, 20% on foreign.
Will Handle: Magazine articles and fiction, novels, and nonfiction books.
Criticism Services: Will critique short stories, articles, novels, and nonfiction books. Submissions must be in professional format. Charges $25 minimum for short stories and articles (to 5,000 words); $175 minimum for book length mss (to 37,500 words). Rates increase according to length and complexity.

JAMES BROWN ASSOCIATES, INC., 25 W. 43rd St., New York NY 10036. (212)736-3777. Estab. 1949. Potential clients "must be professional, not necessarily published." Will read unsolicited queries. SASE. Agent receives 10% commission on domestic sales, 20% on British and translation countries.
Will Handle: "We handle writers concentrating on books." For writers represented will handle all rights, foreign, performance, etc., and magazine articles and fiction.

SHIRLEY BURKE AGENCY, 370 E. 76th St., New York NY 10021. (212)861-2309. Estab. 1948. Obtains new clients through recommendations. Potential clients must have published at least one book. Will not read unsolicited mss; will read unsolicited queries. SASE. Agent receives 10% commission.
Will Handle: Magazine fiction, novels, and nonfiction books.

CHARLES R. BYRNE LITERARY AGENCY, 1133 Avenue of the Americas, 28th Floor, New York NY 10036. (212)221-3145. President: Charles R. Byrne. Estab. 1974. Obtains new clients through recommendations from publishers/editors, other agents, and from present clients. Will read unsolicited mss for a fee "depending on length of mss." Will read unsolicited queries and outlines. SASE. Made 30 sales in 1977 and 1978; will do 30 in 1979. Agent receives 10% commission on domestic sales; 20% on foreign.
Will Handle: Novels, textbooks (a limited number), nonfiction books, young adult novels and nonfiction books.
Recent Sale: *A Private Vendetta,* by R. Grant (Charles Scribner's Sons).

RUTH CANTOR, LITERARY AGENT, 156 5th Ave., New York NY 10010. Estab. 1951. Obtains new clients through recommendations by writers, publishers, editors, and teachers. Potential clients "must be of proven competence as a writer. This means either some publishing record or a recommendation from someone likely to be a competent critic of his work—a teacher of writing, another writer, etc." Will not read unsolicited mss; will read unsolicited queries and outlines. SASE. "Send a letter giving publishing history and writing experience, plus concise outline of proposed project or of ms you want to send. Do not phone." Agent receives 10% commission on domestic sales; 20% on foreign.
Will Handle: Novels, nonfiction books and childrens' books.
Recent Sales: *Perky,* by G. Bond (Western); *This Savage Land,* by B. Womack (Fawcett); and *Abigail Scott Dunaway,* by D. Morrison (Atheneum).

CHRISTOPHER CLARK ASSOCIATES, Box 3109, Tempe AZ 85281. Obtains new clients through referrals and advertising. Will read unsolicited ms for $25. "The important thing here is that the writer should first send for our information sheet (with SASE)." SASE. Agent receives 10% commission on domestic sales, 20% on foreign.
Will Handle: Novels, textbooks and nonfiction books. "Our emphasis is on selectivity. We're trying to put together a small corp of fresh new writers who in our opinion have long term marketing potential."

HY COHEN LITERARY AGENCY, LTD., 111 W. 57th St., New York NY 10019. (212)757-5237. President: Hy Cohen. Estab. 1975. Obtains new clients through recommendations. Will read unsolicited mss, queries and outlines. SASE. Agent receives 10% commission.
Will Handle: Magazine articles and fiction, novels, and nonfiction books.
Recent Sales: *The Secret Isaac,* by J. Charyn (Arbor House); *Manifest Destiny,* by E.I. Shedley (Viking Press); and *Projections,* by S. Robinett (Analog Books).

COLLIER ASSOCIATES, 280 Madison Ave., New York NY 10016. (212)685-5516. Owner: Lisa Collier. Estab. 1976. Obtains new clients through recommendations of existing clients, editors, friends, and through various listings. Will read unsolicited queries and outlines. SASE. Made 77 sales in 1977, 100 in 1978. Agent receives 10% commission on domestic sales; 15% on British; and 20% on foreign.
Will Handle: Novels and nonfiction books. "Not interested in travel, astrology, occult or porno."
Recent Sales: *The Secret Life of Henry Ford,* by F.S. Leighton (Bobbs-Merrill); *The Political Memoirs of Senator Barry Goldwater* (Harcourt); and *The Cosgrove Report* (Rawson).

BILL COOPER ASSOCIATES, INC., 16 E. 52nd St., New York NY 10022. (212)758-6491. Estab. 1963. Obtains new clients through recommendations and personal pursuit. Will read unsolicited mss. SASE. Marketing fee "subject to submitting source." Agent receives 10% commission.
Will Handle: Novels, nonfiction books, motion pictures, stage plays, and TV scripts (game shows, situation comedies; only original concepts for series, with fully developed presentation of theme, characters, and a pilot script).
Recent Sales: *Rocky Marciano,* by E. Skehan (Houghton Mifflin); and *Rebellion of the White Rose,* by R. Hanser (G.P. Putnam's Sons).

CREATIVE ENTERPRISES, Box 377, Centreville VA 22020. (703)830-3711. Director: Joyce Wright. Estab. 1975. Obtains new clients through recommendations of other writers, writer's organizations, and *Writer's Market.* Will read unsolicited queries and outlines. SASE. "Prefer that new authors send a comprehensive chapter outline, background data on himself, and the first four chapters of his ms when querying." Agent receives 10% commission.

Will Handle: Novels and nonfiction books. Will also handle magazine articles and fiction, motion pictures, and TV scripts for established clients. Specializes in fiction, how-to, self-help, and career guidance.
Criticism Services: Will critique novels, self-help books, biographies of historical or literary figures, and career guidance books. Mss must be neatly typed, double-spaced, with 1" margins at top, bottom and sides, author's name in left-hand corner, number in right-hand corner. Prefers photocopies for editorial comments. Charges $100 flat fee.
Recent Sales: *Theraputic Hypnosis,* by Dr. M.M. Miller (Human Sciences Press); *Tall Men! Tall Timber,* by C.J. Lind (Hancock House Ltd.); and *The Witch of Natchez Under-the-Hill,* by Roche (Dial).

CREATIVE WRITERS AGENCY, INC., Box 2280, Satellite Beach FL 32937. (305)773-3622. President: John C. Roach, Jr. Estab. 1971. Obtains new clients through *Writer's Market,* authors' recommendations, and advertisements. Will read unsolicited mss. SASE. Charges unpublished authors $300 marketing fee (returnable upon sale of material); no marketing fee for published authors. Made 3 sales in 1977, 6 in 1978. Agent receives 10% commission; 15% for movie rights.
Will Handle: Novels, textbooks, nonfiction books, motion pictures, stage plays and TV scripts. Specializes in material adaptable to motion pictures.
Criticism Services: Novels, textbooks, nonfiction books, motion pictures, stage plays and TV scripts. Charges $25 for mss under 25,000 words; $50 over 25,000 words; $100 over 75,000 words.
Recent Sales: *Starring John Wayne,* by G. Fernett (Neptune Books); *Dos Compadres,* by D. Bostick (Neptune Books); and *Ghost of the Java Coast,* by W. Winslow (Coral Reef Publishing, Inc.).

MARJEL DE LAUER AGENCY, 8961 Sunset Blvd., Los Angeles CA 90069. Obtains new clients through referrals from clients and producers. Made 9 sales in 1977, 20 in 1978. "Writers must be published or have motion picture or TV credits. Will not read unsolicited mss; will read queries and outlines. SASE. Agent receives 10% commission.
Will Handle: Novels (will accept unpublished authors—if outline and first 3 chapters are submitted); nonfiction (must see outline and complete mss); motion pictures; and TV scripts.
Recent Sales: "Men to Match My Mountains," by I. Stone (Universal Studios); and *Virgin Kisses,* by G. Nagy (Chelsea House Publishers).

ANITA DIAMANT: THE WRITERS WORKSHOP, INC., 51 E. 42nd St., New York NY 10017. (212)687-1122. President: Anita Diamant. Estab. 1917. Obtains new clients through recommendations by publishers or other clients. Potential clients must have made some professional sales. Will not read unsolicited mss; will read unsolicited queries. SASE. Agent receives 10% commission.
Will Handle: Magazine articles and fiction, novels, nonfiction books, motion pictures, and TV scripts.
Recent Sales: *Justice Crucified: The Story of Sacco and Vanzetti,* by R.S. Feuerlicht (McGraw-Hill); *Stop Running Scared,* by J. Baer/Dr. H. Fensterheim (Rawson Associates); and *The Secret of Blackoaks,* by A. Carter (Fawcett Gold Medal).

PATRICIA FALK FEELEY, INC., AUTHORS' REPRESENTATIVE, 52 Vanderbilt Ave., New York NY 10017. Estab. 1975. Obtains new clients through referrals by clients and editors and by inquiries. Will not read unsolicited mss; will read unsolicited queries and outlines. SASE. Made approximately 40 sales in 1977. Agent receives 10% commission on domestic sales, 15% on British; 20% on foreign.
Will Handle: Novels and nonfiction books.
Recent Sales: *A Love So Bold,* by A. Kamada (Warner Paperback); *Sandy,* by W. Berloni/A. Thomas (Simon & Schuster); and *Mao Tse Tung: On Guerilla Warfare,* by General S.B. Griffith (Doubleday).

BARTHOLD FLES LITERARY AGENCY, 507 5th Ave., New York NY 10017. Contact: Barthold Fles or Vikki Power. Estab. 1933. Obtains new clients through recommendations of clients and editors, scouting tips, and writers' conferences. Will not read unsolicited mss. Agent receives 10% commission on domestic sales; 15% on British; and 20% on foreign.
Will Handle: Novels and nonfiction books. Specializes in intermediate and teenage juveniles; no picture books.

THE FOLEY AGENCY, 34 E. 38th St., New York NY 10016. (212)686-6930. Estab. 1956. Obtains new clients through recommendations. Will read unsolicited queries. SASE. Made approximately 65 sales in 1977. Agent receives 10% commission.
Will Handle: Novels and nonfiction books.

PEGGY LOIS FRENCH AGENCY, 26051 Birkdale Rd., Sun City CA 92381. (714)679-6325. Estab. 1952. Obtains new clients through referrals and word-of-mouth. Will read unsolicited mss and queries. "Minimal reading fees for beginners; none for the established professional who has credits with a major publisher or film producer." Agent receives 10% commission.
Will Handle: "We need strong, well-plotted stories, both juvenile and adult. We are one of the few agencies who will develop a writer with talent and work him through submission, a sale, and the signing of contracts." Will handle magazine fiction of high quality, significant novels (juvenile and adult), nonfiction book, motion pictures, stage plays and TV scripts.

FULP LITERARY AGENCY, 62 Maple Rd., Amityville NY 11701. (516)842-0972. Agency Representative: M.L. Fulp. Estab. 1976. Will read unsolicited mss, queries or outlines. SASE. Charges $25 marketing fee for all material once client is accepted. Made 2 sales in 1977. Agent receives 10% commission.
Will Handle: Magazine articles and fiction, novels, and nonfiction books. "I like to receive mss from minority writers and females."

JAY GARON-BROOKE ASSOCIATES, INC., 415 Central Park West, New York NY 10025. (212)866-3654. President: Jay Garon. Obtains new clients through referrals; "however, we will read and answer query letters wherein material is briefly described." Will not read unsolicited mss; will read queries and outlines. SASE. Agent receives 10% commission.
Will Handle: Novels (general and category fiction suitable for hardcover or paperback publication); textbooks (rarely consider professional and technical material unless there is a clear application to a trade market); nonfiction books (biography, autobiography, self-help and/or improvement, popular history—but generally any nonfiction oriented toward popular appeal or interest); motion pictures (finished screenplays accompanied by treatment only); stage plays and TV scripts (accompanied by treatment).
Recent Sales: *Why Not Everything,* by B. Hirschfield (Morrow/Bantam Books); *Love's Pagen Heart,* by P. Matthews (Pinnacle Books, Inc.); and *Lord Sin,* by C. Gluyas (New American Library).

MAX GARTENBERG, LITERARY AGENT, 331 Madison Ave., New York NY 10017. (212)661-5270. Estab. 1954. Obtains new clients through referrals and solicitations. Will not read unsolicited mss; will read unsolicited queries. SASE. Agent receives 10% commission.
Will Handle: Novels and nonfiction books.
Recent Sales: *The Great Klamath County Mouse War,* by W. Ashworth (Hawthorn Books); *The Smoking Mirror,* by L. Daniels (Charles Scribner's Sons); and *Mystical Union,* by D. Robertson (G.P. Putnam's Sons).

GLORIA GEALE & ASSOCIATES, 9000 Sunset Blvd., Suite 814, Los Angeles CA 90069. (213)657-2125. Contact: Gloria Geale or Lt. Col. Ben Novom. Obtains new clients through recommendations. Made 2 sales in 1977. Will not read unsolicited mss; will read queries. SASE.
Will Handle: Novels; nonfiction books; motion pictures; and TV scripts.

LUCIANNE GOLDBERG LITERARY AGENCY, 255 W. 84th St., New York NY 10024. (212)787-2717. Contact: Patricia Roberts. Estab. 1974. Obtains new clients through referrals and/or contacts in publishing and journalism. Will read unsolicited mss for $100 up to 100,000 words, if author is previously unpublished. Fee waived if author is accepted for representation. Will read outlines and queries. SASE. Agent receives 10% commission, 20% on dramatic and foreign sales.
Will Handle: Nonfiction and fiction (magazine articles only if author is previously published).
Criticism Services: "$100 reading fee covers an in-depth report on ms, including constructive suggestions for revision and restructuring with an eye to making work a viable product."
Recent Sales: *Jimmy Carter, the Man and the Myth,* by V. Lasky (Richard Marek Publishing); *A Walk in the Moonflower Garden,* by Y. Kapralov (St. Martin's Press); and *Moonstruck,* by J. Vitek/A. Tate (William Morrow Co.).

GRAHAM AGENCY, 317 W. 45th St., New York NY 10036. Owner: Earl Graham. Estab. 1971. Obtains new clients through queries and recommendations. "Will accept any writer whose

work I feel is saleable, and occasionally will work with a writer whose initial effort may not be saleable, but whom I feel is talented, and whose work I feel merits encouraging.'' Will read unsolicited queries. Agent receives 10% commission.
Will Handle: Full-length stage plays (including musicals); fiction and nonfiction. No screenplays, teleplays or poetry.

VANCE HALLOWAY AGENCY, Box 518, Pearblossom CA 93553. (714)249-3818 or 327-9653. Agent: Vance Halloway. Estab. 1954. Free reading of unsolicited mss to 60,000 words; will read unsolicited queries and outlines. SASE. Agent's commission ''depends on transaction. All contracts are directed to agency and commissions are deducted from advances and royalty payment.'' Charges marketing fee ''only if I cannot foresee an immediate sale.''
Will Handle: Novels, nonfiction books, and stage plays. ''Book properties that are geared for possible series like our Death Merchant, Kung Fu, and Murder Master series, contracted to this agency.''
Criticism Services: Will criticize commercially slanted material. Submit precis and sample chapters. Fee depends on amount of labor required.
Recent Sales: *Hell in Om's Eden,* by Nace (Manner Books); and *The Brazos River,* by D.C. Fontana (Lenox Hill Press).

HEINLE AND HEINLE ENTERPRISES, 29 Lexington Rd., Concord MA 01742. (617)369-4858. Senior Member: Charles A.S. Heinle. Estab. 1973. Obtains new clients through word-of-mouth, *Writer's Market,* activities as resident agents at Cape Code Writer's Conference, and recommendations by clients. ''We are less concerned that a writer is unpublished, as long as we believe in the writer and the future.'' Will not read unsolicited mss; will read unsolicited queries and outlines. SASE. Made 4 sales in 1977; will make 5-9 in 1979. Agent receives 10% commission.
Will Handle: Magazine fiction, novels, textbooks, and nonfiction books. ''We are most interested in materials with a New England theme, past, present, and future, but of course, good writing is the main consideration. We handle some textbooks in the foreign language area, and some reference materials as bibliographies in selected fields.''
Recent Sales: *Vida Y Voces Del Mundo Hispanico Level 2,* by Smith, et al (Rand); *Dear Faculty: A Discovery Method Guidebook to the High-School Library,* by J. Nordling (F.W. Faxon Co.); and *Hebrew by the Audio-Visual Method,* by Enoch/Cais (Marcel Didier of Canada).

SANDRA HINTZ LITERARY AGENCY, 2879 N. Grant Blvd., Milwaukee WI 53210. Obtains new clients through ''referrals from clients and editors . . . some from queries.'' Made 6 sales in 1977, 15 in 1978. Will not read unsolicited mss; will read outlines and queries. SASE. Agent receives 10% commission.
Will Handle: Novels (adult and juvenile); nonfiction books; and religious fiction and nonfiction.
Recent Sales: *A Grief Endured,* by E. Teicher (Beta Book Co.); *A Book of Yes,* by J. Petersen O.S.F. (Argus Communications); and ''Milgitha,'' by S. Regina Koehler (*Highlights Magazine*).

HOME CRAFT UNLIMITED, 4276 Sandburg Way, Irvine CA 92715. Director: Molli Nickell. Estab. 1969. Obtains new clients through referrals from clients and *Writer's Market.* Will read unsolicited mss for approximately $50. ''Usually advise authors on how to market their own work.'' Charges $25/hour for consultation.
Will Handle: Books, articles or syndicated material relating to creative fields: how-to's, interviews with creative people, news media, money makers in crafts, career opportunities in creative fields.
Criticism Services: Will critique material as above. Fee ''depends on work—we request writers to query first with SASE—then we advise what to send, plus fee.''

RICHARD HUTTNER AGENCY, INC., 330 E. 33rd St., New York NY 10016. Obtains new clients through ''referrals, reading recommended manuscripts, literary conferences, people in the news, queries, and *Writer's Market.* We look for publish*able* authors; this does not always mean writers who have many credits. We are selective in the writers we take on, however.'' Will read unsolicited mss, queries and outlines when accompanied by SASE. Agent receives 10% commission.
Will Handle: Magazine fiction (for major magazines only, and for our book clients only); novels; TV movies; nonfiction books; motion pictures and syndicated material. ''We love manuscripts with strong interest to women readers.''
Recent Sales: *Beloved Enemy,* by A. York (Pocket); *The Suicide's Wife,* by D. Madden

(Bobbs-Merrill); and *Sleep Less, Live More,* by E. Mattlin (Lippincott).

L.H. JOSEPH AND ASSOCIATES, 8344 Melrose Ave., Suite 23, Los Angeles CA 90069. (213)651-2322. Estab. 1954. Obtains new clients through inquiries. "We are licensed artist's managers and signatories to the Writer's Guild of America, West. We require outlines of all material prior to reading full manuscripts." SASE. Agent receives 10% commission.
Will Handle: Novels, textbooks, nonfiction books (in any field). "Motion pictures, stage plays, and TV scripts considered from industry professionals only."
Criticism Services: Will critique submissions only if so requested. Charges $75. Send check with ms.

JSL ASSOCIATES, Box 23040, San Jose CA 95153. (408)225-6902. Contact: Lynn Roberts. Estab. 1975. Obtains new clients through *Writer's Market,* referral by other clients, teachers, writer's groups or Writers Guild of America listings. "We have great success with previously unpublished/unproduced authors. We ask that the work be professional quality, that the desire to work is there, and the willingness to learn." Will read unsolicited mss, queries, or outlines. "Due to rising expenses our agency has been forced to adopt a nominal reading fee policy as follows: short stories and articles, $5; book length manuscripts, $10; short juvenile, $5; long juvenile, $10; all medial manuscripts, $10." SASE. Agent receives 10% commission on domestic sales; 15% on foreign.
Will Handle: Magazine articles and fiction, novels, textbooks, nonfiction books, motion pictures, stage plays, TV and radio scripts, syndicated material, juvenile material, and artwork. "We are willing to consider and evaluate any material, except porno."
Criticism Services: "We are going to be working with a former editor/teacher in setting up a small criticism service for those who want it made available. Fees will be made available upon request. Mss must be typed double-spaced, and must specify that it is being submitted for criticism rather than general reviewing."
Recent Sales: *Killed in the Ratings,* by B. DeAndrea (Harcourt Brace Jovanovich).

VIRGINIA KIDD WITH JAMES ALLEN LITERARY AGENTS, Box 278, Milford PA 18337. (717)296-6205. Estab. 1965. Potential client "must be a published writer; should have earned at least $1,000 (from writing) during the previous year." Will not read unsolicited mss. "I cannot take on *anyone* with no track record. If someone has a special reason for wanting me to handle them, write me a letter explaining why and enclose SASE. I'm not actively looking for new authors—my lists are full." Agent receives 10% commission on domestic sales, 15% on dramatic sales, 20% on overseas sales.
Will Handle: Magazine articles and fiction, novels, textbooks, nonfiction books, motion pictures, TV and radio scripts and science fiction.

DANIEL P. KING, LITERARY AGENT, 5125 N. Cumberland Blvd., Whitefish Bay WI 53217. (414)964-2903. Estab. 1974. Obtains new clients through listings in *Writer's Market,* and referrals from clients. Will not read unsolicited mss; will read unsolicited queries. "Reading fee is charged unpublished writers." Made 50 sales in 1977. Agent receives 10% commission.
Will Handle: Magazine articles and fiction, novels, nonfiction books, and syndicated material. "While I handle general material, I specialize in crime literature (fact or fiction)."

BERTHA KLAUSNER INTERNATIONAL LITERARY AGENCY, INC., 71 Park Ave., New York NY 10016. (212)685-2642. President: Bertha Klausner. Estab. 1938. Obtains new clients through recommendation. Will read unsolicited mss; charges reading fees. Will read unsolicited queries and outlines. SASE. Agent receives 10% commission on domestic sales.
Will Handle: Novels, textbooks, nonfiction books, stage plays, and TV and motion picture scripts. "We represent world rights for all subsidiaries and are represented by our own agents throughout the world."
Criticism Services: Will critique novels and plays. Request rate card.
Recent Sales: *Memoirs of the Nijinsky Family,* by I. Nijinsky (Holt, Rinehart & Winston); and *Shakespeare,* by R. Payne (Harper & Row).

LUCY KROLL AGENCY, 390 West End Ave., New York NY 10024. (212)877-0627. Estab. 1954. Obtains new clients through recommendations. Will not read unsolicited mss; will read unsolicited queries and outlines. SASE. Agent receives 10% commission.
Will Handle: Novels, nonfiction books, motion pictures, and stage plays.

MICHAEL LARSEN/ELIZABETH POMADA LITERARY AGENTS, 1029 Jones St., San Fran-

cisco CA 94109. (415)673-0939. Estab. 1972. Obtains new clients through personal recommendations, *Literary Market Place, Writer's Market,* etc. Will read unsolicited mss for $25 (refundable immediately upon acceptance); no reading charge for published writers. Will read unsolicited queries and outlines. SASE. Agent receives 10% commission on domestic sales; 20% on foreign.
Will Handle: Novels, nonfiction books, motion pictures, and TV scripts. "We request the original copy of the ms, typed double-spaced with pica type on 8½x11 paper; unbound, preferably boxed, with writer's name, address and phone number on the title page."
Recent Sales: *Sierra Sierra,* by J. Joss (Morrow); *Raging Winds of Heaven,* by J. Shiplett (NAL); and *Baal,* by R. McCammon (Avon).

LENNIGER LITERARY AGENCY, INC., 437 5th Ave., New York NY 10016. Contact: Paul Trevoy. Obtains new clients through recommendations. Made 100 sales in 1977 and 1978. Will read invited mss only, at no charge. SASE. Agent receives 10% commission.
Will Handle: Novels and nonfiction books.
Recent Sales: *Dare to Love,* by J. Wilde (Warner Books); *Family Ties,* by D.A. Holmes (Playboy Press); and *Stallion,* by T.V. Olsen (Fawcett).

LEVY ENTERPRISES, 1570 N. Edgemont, Suite 605, Los Angeles CA 90027. President: Ms. Lee K. Levy. Obtains new clients through referrals, recommendations, "and a good query letter showing some strong writing talent. Authors must be professional, in every sense of the word, whether published or not." Will read unsolicited mss for $50. "I will read a ms for $50 and give a critique. If I decide to take it to market, I require an additional $100 to handle marketing. Should I be successful in marketing the ms, the total of $150 is charged against my agent's commission." SASE. Agent receives 10% commission on domestic sales & 20% foreign.
Will Handle: Magazine articles (only after an author has made a sale); novels (send a short outline of the book); nonfiction books; motion pictures; and juvenile fiction (very interested in handling good, well-plotted, up-beat book-length mss for children).

DONALD MacCAMPBELL INC., 12 E 41st St., New York NY 10017. (212)683-5580. "Phone queries are preferred but will answer written inquiries that are accompanied by SASE. Agency works on 10% commission basis."
Will Handle: "Now handling book-length fiction exclusively, with emphasis upon the women's markets."

CAROL MANN LITERARY AGENCY, 519 E. 87th St., New York NY 10028. (212)879-3034. Contact: Carol Mann. Obtains new clients through "satisfied clients, editors, Author's Guild, and Society of Children's Book Writers." Made 5 sales in 1977, 15-20 in 1978. Will read unsolicited mss, queries and outlines at no charge. SASE. Agent receives 10% commission.
Will Handle: Specializes in children's books and adult nonfiction. Also handles magazine, TV and film material; novels (middle reader, young adult, and adult); and nonfiction books (juvenile and adult).
Recent Sales: *The Experts' Beauty Guide for Black Women,* by L. Powlis (Doubleday); *Ezra Pound in Italy,* by G. Ivancilh (Rizzoli International); and *Crossing the Line,* by W. Hooks (Knopf).
Criticism Services: Charges $15 for mss under 5,000 words; $25 for mss under 25,000 words; and $50 thereafter.

BETTY MARKS, 51 E. 42nd St., New York NY 10017. (212)687-1122. Estab. 1970. Obtains new clients through word-of-mouth recommendations of authors, other agents, editors, and friends. Will read unsolicited mss for $100 up to 100,000 words, if author is previously unpublished. Will read unsolicited queries and outlines. SASE. Made 75 sales in 1977. Agent receives 10% commission.
Will Handle: Magazine articles and fiction, novels, nonfiction books, poetry, stage plays, TV scripts, juvenile fiction and nonfiction.
Criticism Services: Will critique material as above. Mss must be typed double-spaced, pages unbound, standard professional format. Charges $100 for mss to 100,000 words; $150 for two mss; $200 for three mss; 50¢/page for shorter material ($25 minimum).
Recent Sales: *Watch It, Dr. Adrian,* by B. Litzinger (Putnam's); *Pending Investigation,* by R. McLaughlin (Berkley); and *A Goldmine of Money Making Ideas,* by M. Brunner (Lorenz Press).

HELEN McGRATH, WRITERS' REPRESENTATIVE, 1406 Idaho Court, Concord CA 94521.

(415)686-3380. Obtains new clients through referrals and word-of-mouth. Will not read unsolicited mss; will read queries consisting of sample chapter and outlines. Agent receives 10% commission.
Will Handle: Magazine articles and fiction (only if also handling a book for a writer); novels (submit sample chapters); textbooks (submit qualifications); and nonfiction books.

SCOTT MEREDITH LITERARY AGENCY, INC., 845 3rd Ave., New York NY 10022. (212)245-5500. President: Scott Meredith. Estab. 1941. Obtains new clients "through listings such as *Writer's Market,* recommendations by clients, and direct mail advertising. Also, many promising authors are recommended to us by editors, publishers and producers." Will read unsolicited mss, queries and outlines. "We charge a single fee for all services, including readings, criticism, assistance in revision if required, and marketing. The fee is $75 for fiction or articles to 5,000 words; $100 for scripts 5,000-10,000 words; $150 for scripts above 10,000 words; $100 for book mss below 10,000 words; $150 for book mss 10,000-150,000 words; $200 for book mss 150,000-200,000 words; $300 for book mss above 250,000 words; $150 for full-length plays or screenplays; $100 for syndicate packages of 3-6 sample columns." SASE. Made 7,400 sales in 1977. Agent receives 10% on domestic sales, 20% on foreign. "If a writer has sold to a major book publisher in the past year or has begun to make major national magazine or TV sales with some regularity, we drop fees and proceed on a straight commission basis."
Will Handle: "We handle material in all fields except single poems and single cartoons, though we do handle book-collections of poetry and cartoons."
Recent Sales: *The Dragons of Eden,* by Dr. Carl Sagan (Random House); *Elegance,* by Norman Mailer (Simon & Schuster); and *Brain 2000,* by Ernest K. Gann (Doubleday).

ROBERT P. MILLS, LTD., 156 E. 52 St., New York NY 10022. President: Robert P. Mills. Estab. 1960. Obtains new clients through recommendations "of someone I know, or if the writer has a respectable publishing history." Will not read unsolicited mss; will read unsolicited queries. SASE. Agent receives 10% commission.
Will Handle: Magazine articles and fiction, novels, nonfiction books, motion pictures, and syndicated material.
Recent Sales: *The Body Language of Sex Power and Aggression,* by J. Fast (M. Evans & Co.); *Twister,* by J. Bickham (Doubleday & Co.); and *Pele's Autobiography,* by Pele, with R.L. Fish (Doubleday & Co.).

HOWARD MOOREPARK, 444 E. 82nd St., New York NY 10028. (212)737-3961. Estab. 1946. Obtains new clients through recommendations. Will read unsolicited mss. SASE. Agent receives 10% commission.
Will Handle: Magazine articles, novels, and nonfiction books.
Recent Titles: *Love's Triumphant Heart,* by V. Ashton (Fawcett); *The Gladiators,* by A. Quiller (Pinnacle) and *Way of the Mystics,* by M. Smith (Oxford UP).

MULTIMEDIA PRODUCT DEVELOPMENT, INC., 170 S. Beverly Dr., Beverly Hills CA 90212. (213)276-6246. President: Jane Jordan Browne. Estab. 1971. Obtains new clients through recommendations and word-of-mouth. "Multimedia handles only works of professional writers who make their living as authors. The rare exceptions are celebrity autobiographies and the 'new idea' nonfiction book." Will read unsolicited mss for $150; will read unsolicited queries and outlines. SASE. Made 135 sales in 1977, 200 in 1978; will make 275 in 1979. Agent receives 10% commission on domestic sales; 20% on foreign.
Will Handle: Novels, textbooks, nonfiction books, motion picture, and TV scripts.
Criticism Services: "Will critique all material. Submissions for criticism must be submitted with the fee and SASE. All material must be typed double-spaced." Charges $150 for standard-length novels or nonfiction books; $50 for juvenile books of 50 pages or less; $75 for screenplays; and $50 for teleplays of ½-1 hour. "Although Multimedia provides criticism services, the fees are meant to discourage any non-professionals from approaching the agency."
Recent Sales: *The Memory of Eva Ryker,* by D. Stanwood (Coward, McCann); *Living for Design: The Stroy of Yves St. Laurent,* by A. Madsen; and *Like The Phoenix,* by G. Thompson (Lorimer/NBC).

N.C.T., Box 11623, Chicago IL 60611. Contact: Ronald Nielsen. Estab. 1970. Will read unsolicited mss, queries or outlines. "We do not charge a reading fee. For new writers we charge a criticism fee; no fee for established writers. A writer should have been nationally published, and published at the rate of 6 magazine articles per year, or should have published at least one book." SASE. Agent receives 10-30% commission "depending on the item and market, by

negotiation."
Will Handle: Magazine articles and fiction, juvenile articles and fiction, novels, nonfiction books, textbooks, poetry, syndicated material, photo essay material and photo books. "We handle everything if the material is quality. If a writer has not had a book published, but has a good record in the magazine area, we will consider such a writer. Query first on material. Tell us something of your background and interests, as reflected in one or two projects."

NATIONAL LAUGH ENTERPRISES, Box 835, Grand Central Station, New York NY 10017. (201)229-9472. Associate Director: Gerald Lansing. Obtains new clients through "conducting college of comedy, promoting comedy workshops, personal appearances, lecture tours, advertising, etc." Will read unsolicited mss (no more than 10 pages) at no charge. SASE. Agent receives 15% commission.
Will Handle: "We deal in new, unique comedic material, but first we like to develop a relationship with writers who have an interest in continuity of development and growth." Magazine articles (200-500 words); magazine fiction (500-2,000 words); novels ("only by people with whom we are associated"); textbooks (submit premise); nonfiction books; motion pictures (submit 2-5 page outline); stage plays (submit premise); and TV scripts (submit premise). Handles comedy material only.
Recent Sales: Gag Monologs, by S. Johnson (Joan Rivers, Rodney Dangerfield).

CHARLES NEIGHBORS, INC., 240 Waverly Pl., New York NY 10014. (212)924-8296. Estab. 1966. Obtains new clients "mostly through recommendations of existing clients, but also from editors, other agents, and occasionally from *Writer's Market*." Will not read unsolicited mss; will read unsolicited queries and outlines. SASE. Agent receives 10% commission.
Will Handle: Magazine articles and fiction, novels, nonfiction books, motion pictures, and juvenile material.
Recent Sales: *The Grab,* by M. Katzenbach (William Morrow); *The Girl with the Jade Green Eyes,* by John Boyd (Viking); and *The Commuter Lines,* by S. Fischer (Hawthorn).

B.K. NELSON LITERARY AGENCY, 600 Madison Ave., New York NY 10017. (212)371-9900. Obtains new clients through inquiries and word of mouth. Made 40 sales in 1977, 45 in 1978. Will read unsolicited mss for $50/60,000 words. Will read queries. SASE. Agent receives 10% commission.
Will Handle: Novels, textbooks; and nonfiction books.
Recent Sales: *How To Survive on Two Incomes,* by D. Young (American Management Association); *Complete Guide to Public Sales,* by K. Robinson/A. Robinson (Drake); and *Layman's Guide to Adoption,* by R. Lasnik (Drake).

NICHOLAS LITERARY AGENCY, 161 Madison Ave., New York NY 10016. Owner: Georgia Nicholas. Estab. 1934. Obtains new clients through recommendations. Will not read unsolicited mss; will read unsolicited queries and outlines and published books for reprint. SASE. Charges a one-time marketing fee of $100. Agent receives 10% commission.
Will Handle: Novels, nonfiction books, motion pictures, stage plays, TV and radio scripts.

NORTHEAST LITERARY AGENCY, 69 Broadway, Concord NH 03301. (603)225-9162. Editor: Victor Levine. Estab. 1973. Obtains new clients through listings *(Literary Market Place, Writer's Market);* recommendations from editors, clients; and display advertising. Will read unsolicited mss. SASE. "There is a one-time agency charge of $45, refundable from earned commissions. Depends on writer's credits; if extensive and/or national in scope, there is no agency charge. The charge, payable with first submission, covers our reading of *all* future mss. Time-frame is deliberately open-ended. We're hopeful it will help writers develop into valued clients....good for us as well as them. We promise a sympathetic reading and fast response. In return, we ask that writers don't dump on us soiled and otherwise unmarketworthy mss." Made 75 sales in 1977, 125 in 1978. Agent receives 10% commission on domestic sales; 20% on foreign.
Will Handle: Magazine articles and fiction, novels, textbooks, nonfiction books, poetry, motion pictures, stage plays, TV and radio scripts, and juvenile fiction/nonfiction (including picture book mss). "Particularly interested in juveniles (all kinds) and all genres in popular fiction (Gothics, romances, science fiction, etc.). Be up-front with us. Tell us where you're at in terms of your writing career: what you've done in the past, what you're presently working on; the direction you wish to go. Please be specific. We prefer to see complete mss, but will read partials by arrangement."
Recent Sales: "Vadillo," by J. Budd (The Nation); "Why Can't the U.S. Be More Like Burundi," by K. McLaren (Harper's); and *Your Guide to the New Copyright Law,* by V. Levine (FN Books).

O'NEILL & KRALIK LITERARY CONSULTANTS, Box 461, Birmingham MI 48012. Manager: Michael O'Neill. Obtains new clients through *Writer's Market,* referrals, etc. Will read unsolicited mss, queries, and outlines. SASE. Charges "minimal marketing fee under certain conditions." Agent receives 10% commission.
Will Handle: Magazine articles and fiction, novels, nonfiction books, poetry, and all secondary markets connected with novels. "Our specialty is the young and coming writer. After several years of this, the big houses are beginning to look to us for new writers of significant stature. We expect this trend to continue and increase. We are most receptive to new writers and suggest that they query us."
Criticism Services: "Our criticism service is best described as educational. We will critique mss upon request, but make no warranties. Usually, we only recommend criticism for a book that is likely to be sold, but needs a few flaws corrected. In that sense, it is more for our benefit than the writer's. That is, we are primarily concerned with the ultimate sale of the book, and not the criticism fee. Sometimes it's free, sometimes it's not."

RAY PEEKNER LITERARY AGENCY, 2625 N. 36th St., Milwaukee WI 53210. Contact: Ray Puechner. Estab. 1973. Obtains new clients through referrals from clients and editors, some from queries. Will not read unsolicited mss; will read unsolicited queries. SASE. Agent receives 10% commission.
Will Handle: Novels, nonfiction books, and young adult material.
Recent Sales: *Sherlock Holmes Vs. Dracula,* by L.D. Estleman (Doubleday); *The Night the White Deer Died,* by G. Paulsen (Thomas Nelson); and *To Love As Eagles,* by V. Connolly (Playboy Press).

MARJORIE PETERS & PIERRE LONG LITERARY AGENTS, 5744 S. Harper, Chicago IL 60637. (312)752-8377. Estab. 1955. Obtains new clients through recommendations. Will not read unsolicited mss. SASE. Agent receives 10% commission on domestic sales; 20% on foreign.
Will Handle: Magazine articles and fiction, novels, textbooks, nonfiction books, poetry, and stage plays. "Our agency specializes in fiction and serious poetry. We do not handle serious (non-humorous) sociological/political exposition."
Criticism Services: Will critique novels, short stories, poetry, articles, essays, expository books, stage plays. Submissions must be typed double-spaced, with a 1-inch margin all around. Charges $100 for novels of 200 pages or less, $50 for short stories, articles or essays of 15 pages or less, $5 per page of poetry, and $35 an act for stage plays.
Recent Sales: *Haakon,* by C.F. Griffin (Thomas E. Crowell); and *"The Booster,"* by P. Parker (Alfred Hitchcock).

ARTHUR PINE ASSOCIATES, INC. 1780 Broadway, New York NY 10019. Vice President: Richard Pine. Obtains new clients through recommendations. Made 100+ sales in 1977 and 1978. "Writers must be professional, and/or have published a book." Will read unsolicited mss for a fee "depending on length of mss." Agent receives 15% commission.
Will Handle: Novels and nonfiction books (all types with mass market appeal).
Recent Sales: *Your Erroneous Zones,* by W.D. Dyer (Funk & Wagnalls); *The Artist,* by N. Garbo (W.W. Norton Co.); and *Tennis Love,* by B.J. King (Macmillan).

THE WALTER PITKIN AGENCY, 11 Oakwood Dr., Weston CT 06883. President: Walter Pitkin. Estab. 1973. Obtains new clients by referral or direct application. Will read unsolicited queries and outlines. "Writers must write an intelligent letter of inquiry and convince us of ability to write marketable material. Inquiry should include some personal background, plus a statement of what it is that the agency would be trying to place. We will solicit the ms if we like the inquiry." SASE. Agent receives 10% commission.
Will Handle: Novels and children's and adult nonfiction books. Also "almost any other material for clients who write books."

SIDNEY E. PORCELAIN AGENCY, Box J, Rocky Hill NJ 08553. (609)924-4080. Authors' Representative: Sidney Porcelain. Associate: Dan Fox. Estab. 1951. Obtains new clients through word-of-mouth and referrals. Will read unsolicited mss, queries and outlines. SASE. Agent receives 10% commission.
Will Handle: Magazine articles and fiction, novels, nonfiction books, and TV scripts.
Recent Sales: *How to Heal Yourself and Others* (C.O.P.T. Publishing); *Walks Far Woman,* by C. Stuart (Dial); and *Bride of Belvale,* by H. Rich (Dell).

PORTER, GOULD & DIERKS, 215 W. Ohio St., Chicago IL 60610. (312)644-5457. Estab. 1958. Obtains new clients "usually by internally generated book ideas that we go out and find the authorship to work on them. We also rely on screening publications to watch for promising writing talent. And, we get many referrals from long-term contacts with critics and magazine/newspaper people who recommend us." Will read unsolicited mss for $50; will read unsolicited queries and outlines. SASE. Agent receives 10% commission.
Will Handle: Magazine articles and fiction, novels, textbooks (selectively), nonfiction books, poetry (highly selective), motion pictures, TV scripts (if the writer has credits), and syndicated material. "We are interested in any marketable writing, but do not encourage cookbooks or travel books unless the writer has a national reputation."
Recent Sales: *In the Fullness of Time,* by Carlson (Regnery); *Qeequeg's Odyssey,* by Cultra (Chicago Review Press); and *Norman Mark's Chicago,* by Mark (Chicago Review Press).

PSYCHIATRIC SYNDICATION SERVICE, INC., 22 Greenview Way, Upper Montclair NJ 07043. (201)746-5075. President: Jacqueline Simenauer. Obtains new clients through professional recommendations and advertising. "I only represent psychiatrists and psychologists. Client must either be an M.D. or a Ph.D." Will read unsolicited outlines. SASE. Agent receives 10% commission.
Will Handle: "I am only interested in nonfiction—psychiatrically oriented books aimed at the trade market, written by psychiatrists or psychologists."
Recent Sales: *Beyond the Male Myth,* by Pietropinto/Simenauer (Times Books); *Every Other Man,* by Dr. M.A. Bartusis (Dutton); and *Tennis–Mind and Body,* by Dr. B. Richmond (Macmillan).

QED LITERARY AGENCY, Box 48331 Bicentennial, Los Angeles CA 90048. President: Vincent J. Ryan. Estab. 1966. Obtains new clients "on the recommendation of established authors, but also through *Writer's Market.*" Will read unsolicited mss for $35; will read unsolicited queries, outlines, and sample chapters free of charge. SASE. Agent receives 15% initial commission, descending with increasing sales volume.
Will Handle: Scholarly nonfiction only. "Mss must be book-length. Subject areas include philosophy, anthropology, theology, sociology, psychology, phenomenology, linguistics, ethnology, archaeology, natural history, ecology, history, and historical fiction. Authors should submit abstract or outline, table of contents, and possibly 1-2 chapters of ms. Do not send complete ms initially. Include information about the number of pages and tables and illustrations. Make submissions on exclusive basis. If in process of writing, may submit ms piecemeal."

RELIGIOUS WRITERS' AGENCY, 908 N. Nottawa St., Sturgis MI 49091. (616)651-6423. Director: Pastor Gregory L. Jackson. Estab. 1976. Obtains new clients through queries. "I deal with religious writing only. Previous publication and formal training in religious studies (divinity degree, etc.) help, but are not absolutely necessary." Will read unsolicited mss, queries and outlines. SASE. Charges $20 marketing fee. "My costs are charged whether the article is accepted or not." Agent receives 10% commission on book sales.
Will Handle: Magazine articles and fiction, textbooks, nonfiction books, and scholarly journal articles.
Criticism Services: Religious articles and books, popular and scholarly. Charge $2/page.
Recent Sales: "The Tale of the Bullfrogs," by G. Meyer (*Ladies Home Journal*); and "Salvation History and Clean-up Day," by G.L. Jackson (*The Lutheran*).

BARBARA RHODES LITERARY AGENCY, 140 West End Ave., New York NY 10023. (212)580-1300. Owner: Barbara Rhodes. Estab. 1968. Obtains new clients through recommendation or inquiry letters. Will not read unsolicited mss; will read unsolicited queries. SASE. Agent receives 10% commission.
Will Handle: Novels, nonfiction books, and stage plays.

RHODES LITERARY AGENCY, 436 Pau St., Suite 6, Honolulu HI 96815. (808)946-9891. Director: Fred C. Pugarelli. Estab. 1971. Obtains new clients through advertising in *Writer's Digest,* referrals, and recommendations. Will read unsolicited mss for $10 (300-1,500 words); $25 (over 1,500 words); fee for material over 5,000 words is by arrangement. Will read unsolicited queries and outlines for $5. SASE. Made 14 sales in 1977, will make 20-40 in 1979. Agent receives 10% commission on domestic sales; 15% on Canadian; 20% on foreign.
Will Handle: Magazine articles and fiction, novels, textbooks, nonfiction books, poetry, motion

pictures, stage plays, TV and radio scripts, photos, religious, and juvenile material; photos.
Criticism Services: Will critique any material. Charges $10 for up to 1,500 words; $25 for 1,500-5,000 words; $50 over 5,000 words.
Recent Sales: "Corruption in Grandpa's Beer Hall," by Robert Andrea (*Aim* magazine); "The Power of Negative Thinking," by P.W. Lovinger (*Aim* magazine); and "Where to Dine in Hawaii," by M. Lambert *(The Waikiki News)*.

RICHMOND LITERARY AGENCY, Box 57, Staten Island NY 10307. (212)984-3658. Director: Joan Gilbert. Obtains new clients through listings in directories and other special advertising. Made 11 sales in 1977. Handling charge for all mss: $10. SASE. "After 5 book submissions, a marketing fee of $2.50 is charged per submission; after 5 queries, the charge is $1.50 per submission." Agent receives 10% commission for US sales.
Will Handle: Novels (all genres); textbooks (English and film are specialties, also considers science and social studies); nonfiction books (all types from how-to to scholarly); motion pictures (submits published fiction for motion picture consideration); stage plays (suitable for Broadway production); and TV scripts (play scripts, new series).
Recent Sales: *On the Verge of Revolt: Women in Films of the 50's*, by B. French (Ungar); *Faulkner & Film*, by B.F. Kawin (Ungar); and *Mindscreen: Bergman, Godard & First-Person Film Narrative*, by B.F. Kawin (Princeton).

MINNIE ROGERS LITERARY AGENCY, Box 714, Tracy CA 95376. (209)478-5671. Obtains new clients through referrals, queries, and announcements in *National Writer's Club Newsletter*. Will make 30 sales in 1978. Will read unsolicited mss, queries and outlines. SASE. $20 marketing charge. Agent receives 10% commission.
Will Handle: Textbooks (from basic to college); and nonfiction (how-to books are particularly welcome; no biographies, autobiographies, or cookbooks).

SCOTT LITERARY AGENCY, Box 131, Trumann AR 72472. (501)483-2486. Owner-Manager: Ruth Scott. Obtains new clients "through publishers' recommendations, *Writer's Digest*, and other writers' recommendations." Made 36 sales in 1977; plans 150 in 1978. Will read unsolicited mss for $25. "We request only 1 fee ever, with the complete understanding that if we cannot handle the manuscript at all, we return the fee with the manuscript." SASE. Agent receives 10% commission.
Will Handle: Magazine articles (on issues of our times: life, health, and religious; 1,500-2,500 words); magazine fiction (all categories but pornography: 2,000-4,000 words); novels (50,000-175,000 words); textbooks; nonfiction books (we need all types, up to 150,000 words); poetry (we are handling lots of poetry; a hard market, but we have had some success); motion pictures (we handle original screenplays and also the sale of film rights from published works); TV scripts (we like the original television script, also sit-coms); radio scripts; and syndicated material (business, finance and health).
Recent Sales: *Sinnerman*, by Rev. P. McCulley (Adcott Books); "Prescription for Living," by S. McDonald (*Service* Magazine); and "The Blue Scarf," by L.W. Pyles (*Bounty* Magazine).

JAMES SELIGMANN AGENCY, 280 Madison Ave., New York NY 10016. (212)679-3383. Contact: James F. Seligmann or Nina Seidenfeld. Obtains new clients through recommendation, personal contact, or solicitation. Will not read unsolicited mss; will read unsolicited queries and outlines. SASE. Agent receives 10% commission.
Will Handle: Novels and nonfiction books.
Recent Sales: *Sexual Enslavement of Women*, by K. Barry (Prentice-Hall); *The End of Senility*, by Dr. A.S. Freese (Arbor House); and *The Day the Bomb Fell on America*, by C.W. Burleson (Prentice-Hall).

EVELYN SINGER LITERARY AGENCY, Box 163, Briarcliff Manor NY 10510. Agent: Evelyn Singer. Estab. 1951. Obtains new clients through recommendations or if writer has earned $10,000 from freelance writing. Will not read unsolicited mss. SASE. Agent receives 10% commission.
Will Handle: Novels, nonfiction books and children's books (no picture books). "I handle all trade book material and arrange subsidiary and foreign rights. Please type (double-spaced) neatly—do not send hand-written queries. Give any literary background pertinent to your material."

ELYSE SOMMER INC., Box E, 962 Allen Ln., Woodmere NY 11598. (516)295-0046. President: Elyse Sommer. Estab. 1952. Obtains new clients through recommendations of authors, editors,

and through executives and administrators of various organizations. Will read unsolicited queries and outlines. SASE. Agent receives 10% commission.
Will Handle: Nonfiction books. "My specialty at the moment is the nonfiction book, particularly in the hobby area; also health and fitness and general lifestyle improvement. This specialty derives from my own involvement as a writer of how-to books, which has caused me to limit activities to specialty areas."
Recent Sales: *Monarch Textile Collector's Guide,* (Simon & Schuster); *Collectibles* (Houghton-Mifflin); and *Basketry* (Chilton Books).

PHILIP G. SPITZER LITERARY AGENCY, 111-25 76th Ave., Forest Hills NY 11375. (212)263-7592. Estab. 1969. Obtains new clients through recommendations of editors and clients. "No previous publication necessary, but potential clients must be working on a book." Will read unsolicited queries and outlines. SASE. Agent receives 10% commission on domestic sales; 15% on British; 20% for foreign language sales.
Will Handle: Novels, nonfiction books, motion pictures. For clients also writing books, will handle magazine articles and fiction. Specializes in general nonfiction; particular interest in sports and politics. "Because I am a one-man office I can take on few new clients. I will often decline projects I think might be salable, and this should not be taken as a reflection on the author or his presentation."
Recent Sales: *Red Snow,* by O. Lange (Seaview Books); *The High Citadel: The Influence of Harvard Law School,* by J. Seligman (Houghton, Mifflin); and *A Short Life,* by T.B. Allen (Berkley/Putnam).

C.M. STEPHAN, JR., 918 State St., Lancaster PA 17603. Estab. 1971. Obtains new clients through advertising and referral. "Writing must display potential or be competitive. Prefers to work with talented newcomers." Will read unsolicited mss for fee of $10 ($1/1000 words for book length); will read unsolicited queries. SASE. Made 5 sales in 1977, 10-12 in 1978. Agent receives 10% commission.
Will Handle: Magazine articles (personality interviews only), magazine fiction, and novels. "Quality writing, self-discipline and the ability to compromise are desirable assets."
Criticism Services: "Agency charges fee to read/evaluate; no other charges are involved."

LARRY STERNIG LITERARY AGENCY, 742 Robertson St., Milwaukee WI 53213. (414)771-7677. Estab. 1953. "I am rarely able to take on new clients; too busy with the pros I now represent." Will not read unsolicited mss. Made several hundred sales in 1976. Agent receives 10% commission.
Will Handle: Magazine articles and fiction, novels and nonfiction books.

ELLEN STEVENSON & ASSOCIATES, 1266 Windsor Place, Jacksonville FL 32205. President: Ellen Kelly. Estab. 1973. "Will handle unpublished writers if they've studied the art of writing. Charges fees to beginners for reading and evaluating ms ($30-70)." Query; will not read unsolicited mss. SASE. Agent receives 10% commission.
Will handle: "Interested in only book-length novels (fact or fiction)."

GUNTHER STUHLMANN, AUTHORS' REPRESENTATIVE, Box 276, Becket MA 01223. Associate: Barbara Ward. Obtains new clients through recommendations. Will not read unsolicited ms; will read queries and outlines. SASE. Agent receives 10% commission on US and Canadian sales, 15% on British and Commonwealth sales; 20% elsewhere.
Will Handle: Magazine articles (first serial only); novels; textbooks; nonfiction books; and motion pictures (based on established properties—no original scripts).
Recent Sales: *Delta of Venus,* by A. Nin (Harcourt Brace Jovanovich); *Decision Over Schweinfurt,* by T.M. Coffey (David McKay Co.); and *Khyber–The Story of an Imperial Migraine,* by C. Miller (Macmillan).

TWIN PINES LITERARY AGENCY, 123-6 S. Highland Ave., Apt. 4, Ossining NY 10562. (914)941-1431. Executive Director: Martin Lewis. Estab. 1970. Obtains new clients through word-of-mouth. Will read unsolicited mss for $25. Will read unsolicited queries and outlines. SASE. Charges $100 marketing fee; $75 refundable if ms is not accepted. Agent receives 10% commission.
Will Handle: Magazine articles and fiction, novels, textbooks, nonfiction books, motion pictures, stage plays, and TV scripts. "Interested only in commercially oriented material."
Criticism Services: Will critique any material. Charges $50.

AUSTIN WAHL AGENCY, LTD., 332 S. Michigan Ave., Suite 1440, Chicago IL 60604. (312)922-3329. Contact: Thomas Wahl. Estab. 1935. Obtains new clients through recommendation, referrals and solicitation. Will not read unsolicited mss; will read unsolicited queries and outlines. Agent receives 10% on domestic sales; 20% on foreign. "We sometimes make special deals to attract *name* literary figures."
Will Handle: "We do not limit ourselves into categories. We manage the careers of our clients in all areas of their artistry." Magazine articles and fiction, novels (especially those with motion picture potential), textbooks, nonfiction books, technical and reference works, motion pictures ("one of our specialties"), stage plays, TV scripts and syndicated material.

JAMES A. WARREN ASSOCIATES, 6257 Hazeltine, #2, Van Nuys CA 91403. (213)997-0956. Editors: Joseph August, Alice Hilton, Barbara Thorburn. Obtains new clients through *Writer's Market, LMP,* and word-of-mouth. Made 31 sales in 1977, 40-80 in 1978; "does not include articles and other short material." Query; will not read unsolicited ms, but does like to see work from new or undiscovered talent. Charges reading fees "if not published by a recognized publisher in the last 15 years." SASE. Agent receives 15% on first sale, 10% thereafter.
Will Handle: "This agency handles only booklength fiction and nonfiction, screenplays, television scripts, playscripts, and certain magazine material. We do not handle poetry, inspirational writing, newspaper articles, syndications, short stories or short humor."
Recent Sales: *Hannah,* by F. Rivers (Jove); *Fighting Lady,* by E. Stansfield (Ward-Ritchie Press); and *The Holistic Revolution,* by L. Grant (Ward-Ritchie Press).
Criticism Services: Will critique book manuscripts ($1.25-1.50/1,000 words); children's books ($25 and up); screenplays (query); television scripts ($50 for existing series; $75 for 90-minute specials); and magazine articles (query).

W B AGENCY, INC., 145 E. 52nd St., New York NY 10022. Obtains new clients through recommendations of clients and editors. Will not read unsolicited mss; will read queries and outlines. SASE. Agent receives 10% commission.
Will Handle: Novels; nonfiction books; and motion pictures.

WIESER & WIESER, INC., 52 Vanderbilt Ave., New York NY 10017. (212)867-5454. Principals: George or Olga Wieser. Estab. 1975. Obtains new clients through referrals from publishers and clients. Writers must be published, and must be working authors. Will read unsolicited mss for a fee of $100; will read unsolicited outlines. SASE. Made $150,000 worth of sales in 1977, $200,000 in 1978. Agent receives 10% commission; 15% for movie rights.
Will Handle: Novels, nonfiction books, motion pictures, and TV scripts.
Criticism Services: General fiction and nonfiction. Mss must be typed double-spaced, and securely bound. "We will evaluate and criticize a complete ms for $100, which will be deducted from our commission if we place the work."
Recent Sales: *The Making of Roots,* by Q. Troupe (Warner); *The River at Wounded Knee,* by D.C. Jones (Scribner's); and *The One and Only Bing,* by Associated Press (Grossett).

WILLIAMS/WESLEY/WINANT, 30 Sutton Place, New York NY 10022. (212)686-0768 or 734-5400. Obtains new clients through listing in *Writer's Market, LMP,* author's recommendations, and newsletters to college and university English and film departments. Made 5 sales in 1978. Will read unsolicited mss, queries, outlines, and screen treatments at no charge. SASE. Agent receives 10% comission on domestic sales, 20% on foreign
Will Handle: Novels (adaptable to motion pictures); motion pictures (screen treatments and shooting scripts); stage plays (musical comedies, dramas); and radio scripts (open end 15, 30, and 60 minute dramas for syndication).

WRITERS HOUSE, INC., 132 W. 31st St., New York NY 10001. Literary Agents: Amy Beckower (juveniles), Albert Zuckerman (nonfiction), and Felicia Eth (fiction). Estab. 1973. Obtains new clients through referrals by publishers or other clients. Will not read unsolicited mss; will read unsolicited queries and outlines. SASE. Agent receives 10% commission.
Will Handle: Novels, nonfiction books, cartoon, photography, and art books, and juvenile fiction and nonfiction.

THE ZALONKA AGENCY, 28 Stanton Rd., Suite 6, Brookline MA 02146. (617)566-6815. Director: J.N. Porter. Estab. 1975. Obtains new clients through word-of-mouth, small ads, and suggestions from authors and editors. Writer must be previously published. Will read unsolicited mss for a fee of $25-200, depending on length. Will read unsolicited queries and outlines. SASE. Agent receives 10% commission on books, 15% on articles, and 20% on foreign sales.

Will Handle: Magazine articles, novels, textbooks, nonfiction books, scholarly works and almanacs. "I especially cater to books dealing with sociology, psychology, and contemporary social problems as well as books dealing with Judaica, Hebraica, and the Middle East. I'm looking for well-written books dealing with contemporary social issues. Never send entire ms. Always send query letter with outline and sample of five pages, along with a short biography and history of ms. I welcome new authors, especially in the nonfiction, contemporary issues genre."
Criticism Services: Nonfiction only, especially social sciences, social problems, Jewish history, the middle East, anything dealing with World War II, religion, politics, and current events. Mss must be typed, double-spaced, one-side only, and numbered. "I will not only criticize the ms, but will also do partial editing, i.e., spelling, grammar, syntext, etc." Charges $2/page.

Contests and Awards

Unless otherwise noted, the following contests and awards are conducted annually. For information on irregular and "one shot" competitions, see The Markets column in *Writer's Digest* magazine.

Some of the listed contests and awards do not accept entries or nominations direct from writers. They are included because of their national or literary importance. When a competition accepts entries from publishers only, and the writer feels his work meets its requirements, he may wish to remind his publisher to enter his work.

To obtain specific deadline information, required entry blank, or further information, write directly to the address in the individual listing. Enclose SASE.

A.I.P.-U.S. STEEL FOUNDATION SCIENCE WRITING AWARD, Press Relations Division, American Institute of Physics, 335 E. 45 St., New York NY 10017. Awards $1,500, a certificate, and a symbolic device to stimulate and recognize distinguished writing that improves public understanding of physics and astronomy. Journalists must be professional writers whose work is aimed at the general public. Write for details and official entry form.

AAAS SOCIO-PSYCHOLOGICAL PRIZE, American Association for the Advancement of Science, 1515 Massachusetts Ave., NW., Washington DC 20005. (202)467-4470. Assistant to the Executive Officer: C. Borras. Estab. 1952. Offered annually.
Purpose: "To recognize a meritorious paper that furthers understanding of the psychological-social-cultural behavoir of human beings. The prize is intended to encourage in social inquiry the development and application of the kind of methodology that has proved so fruitful in the natural sciences." Submissions must be unpublished or published within the last 18 months. Awards $1,000. Deadline for entry: July 1. Rules and entry form for SASE.

AAAS-WESTINGHOUSE SCIENCE WRITING AWARDS, American Association for the Advancement of Science, 1515 Massachusetts Ave., NW., Washington DC 20005. (202)467-4483. Administrator: Grayce A. Finger. Estab. 1947. Annual.
Purpose: To encourage and recognize outstanding writing on the sciences and their engineering and technological application in newspapers and general circulation magazines. Submissions must be previously published between October 1-September 30. Awards $1,000 plus certificate.

AAFP JOURNALISM AWARDS, American Academy of Family Physicians, 1740 W. 92nd St., Kansas City MO 64114. (816)333-9700. Contact: Charlotte Krebs. Annual. Estab. 1969. Purpose: To recognize the most significant and informative reporting and writing on family practice and health care. Only published submissions are eligible. Award: First prize, $1,000 cash and certificate; second, $750 cash and certificate; third, $250 cash and certificate. Deadline: Mid-November. Contest rules and entry form for SASE.

ACTF STUDENT PLAYWRITING AWARDS, American College Theatre Festival, John F. Kennedy Center for the Performing Arts, Washington DC 20566. (202)254-3437. The William Morris Agency awards a cash prize of $2,500 and an agency contract to the author of the best student written play produced as part of the annual American College Theatre Festival. Plays must have been produced at a college or university to be eligible.

HERBERT BAXTER ADAMS PRIZE, Committee Chairman, American Historical Association, 400 A St. S.E., Washington DC 20003. Awards $300 annually for an author's first or second book in the field of European history.

ADIRONDACK-METROLAND—HARIAN FICTION AWARD, Box 189, Clifton Park NY 12065. Publisher: Harry Barba. Sponsor: Adirondack-Spa Writers & Educators Conference and The Harian Press. Annual. Estab. 1976. Purpose: to encourage the writing and publishing of fiction strong in characterization and plot and written in a functionally suitable style; to encourage writing with a social context (without being "preachy"), quality stories that communicate a moral texture. Writing of resolution is preferred. Unpublished submissions only.

Award: first prize, $300; each of two runners-up, $100. "If no manuscript is of sufficient merit, we reserve the right to defer awards. All submitted mss will be considered for publication." Deadline: September 1. Contest rules and entry forms for SASE.

AMATEUR POETRY CONTEST, Poetry Press, Editor, Don Peek, Box 736, Pittsburg TX 75686. Prizes of $100, $50, and $25 will go to top 3 poems. Poems should be between 4 and 16 lines. Enclose SASE.

AMATEUR RADIO BITING BUG AWARD, Harter Rd., Morristown NJ 07960. (201)538-3081. Judge: Roy Collins, WA2GBC. Estab. 1976. Annual.
Purpose: For best article about amateur radio published in a US non-amateur radio publication. Articles are judged on how well they attract newcomers to amateur radio. Category I is for articles in national publication; category II is for regional or local publications. Submissions must be previously published. Award Category I: $200 and a plaque; Category II: $100 and a plaque. Deadline for entry: January 31. Rules and entry forms for SASE.

AMERICAN ACADEMY AND INSTITUTE OF ARTS AND LETTERS AWARDS, American Academy and Institute of Arts and Letters, 633 W. 155 St., New York NY 10012. Executive Director: Margaret M. Mills. Annual awards include the Richard and Hinda Rosenthal Award ($2,000 for the best novel of the year, which, though not a commercial success, is a literary achievement); the Academy Institute Awards ($3,000 awarded to 10 non-members to further their creative work).

AMERICAN DENTAL ASSOCIATION SCIENCE WRITERS AWARD, Science Writers Award Committee, 211 E. Chicago Ave., Chicago IL 60611. Awards $1,000 for best newspaper article and $1,000 for best magazine article which broadens and deepens public understanding of dental health, dental treatment, or dental research. Write for entry rules.

AMERICAN OSTEOPATHIC ASSOCIATION JOURNALISM AWARDS, 212 E. Ohio St., Chicago IL 60611. (312)944-2713. Director, PR: Robert A. Klobnak. Annual. Estab. 1956. Purpose: to recognize the growing corps of journalists who report and interpret osteopathic medicine to the scientific community and the general public. Published submissions only. Award: $1,000 for first prize; two additional prizes of $500 each. Deadline: March 1 (for works published from January 1-December 31). Contest rules and entry forms for SASE.

AMERICAN PENAL PRESS CONTEST. Individual awards in writing categories and photography. Sweepstakes awards in 3 categories. "Only prison publications and individual entries published in prison publications are eligible." Sponsored by Southern Illinois University School of Journalism, Carbondale IL 62901. Entries considered between October 1 and September 30. Established in 1964. Write for rules and entry forms.

AMERICAN PSYCHOLOGICAL FOUNDATION NATIONAL MEDIA AWARDS, Mona Marie Olean, Public Information Officer, American Psychological Association, 1200 Seventeenth St., N.W., Washington DC 20036. Awards made in five categories (television/film, radio, magazine writing, newspaper reporting, books/monographs) to recognize and encourage outstanding, accurate reporting which increases the public's knowledge and understanding of psychology. Each winner receives $1,000, a special citation, and expenses to APA's annual convention.

ANIMAL RIGHTS WRITING AWARD, Prof. Henry Mark Holzer, Chairman, Reviewing Committee, Society for Animal Rights, Inc., 421 S. State St., Clarks Summit PA 18411. Awards $300 to the author of an exceptionally meritorious published book or article in the field of animal rights.

ASCAP-DEEMS TAYLOR AWARDS, American Society of Composers, Authors And Publishers, 1 Lincoln Plaza, New York NY 10023. (212)595-3050. Director of Public Relations: Walter Wagner. Estab. 1967. Annual.
Purpose: For non-fiction books or articles about music and/or its creators: and to encourage, recognize and reward excellence in non-fiction writing about music and/or its creators. Submissions must be published during the previous year. Awards 4 $500 prizes for books, 4 $500 prizes for articles, and plaque to publishers. Deadline for entry: March 1. Submit 4 copies of book and/or articles.

ATLANTIC FIRSTS, 8 Arlington St., Boston MA 02116. (617)536-9500. Continuously. Purpose:

first major publication of fiction by an unestablished author. Submissions must be unpublished. Award: Professional fees are paid for the stories, which are published in *The Atlantic*. Prizes of $750 and $250 are awarded for the most distinguished contributions of the preceding period. Rules available for SASE.

AVIATION/SPACE WRITERS ASSOCIATION JOURNALISM AWARDS, Aviation/Space Writers Association, Cliffwood Rd., Chester NJ 07930. Awards $100 and engraved scroll for writing on aviation and space, in 9 categories: newspapers over 200,000 circulation, newspapers under 200,000 circulation, magazines (special interest); magazines (general interest); television (news documentary); radio (news documentary); books (general nonfiction); books (technical/training); still photography.

BANCROFT PRIZES, Committee, 202 Low, Columbia University, New York NY 10027. Awards 2 prizes of $4,000 for books in American history (including biography) and diplomacy.

GEORGE LOUIS BEER PRIZE, Committee Chairman, American Historical Association, 400 A St., S.E., Washington DC 20003. Awards $300 for the best first or second book by a young scholar in the field of European international history since 1895.

MIKE BERGER AWARD Committee, Columbia University, Morningside Hts., New York NY 10027. The award, given to writers whose work best reflects the style of the late Meyer Berger, carries a cash prize of $1,500.

BEST SPORT STORIES AWARDS, 1315 Westport Lane, Sarasota FL 33580. Co-Editor: Edward Ehre. Sponsor: E.P. Dutton & Co., Publisher. Annual. Estab. 1944. Purpose: for best magazine sport story, best coverage sport story and best feature sport story. Published submissions only. Award: $250 for each category. Deadline: December 15. Contest rules and entry forms for SASE.

ALBERT J. BEVERIDGE AWARD, Committee Chairman, American Historical Association, 400 A St., S.E., Washington DC 20003. Awards $1,000 for the best book published in English on American history of the U.S., Canada, and Latin America.

BITTERROOT MAGAZINE POETRY CONTEST. Write Menke Katz, Editor-in-Chief, *Bitterroot,* Blythebourne Sta., Box 51, Brooklyn NY 11219. Awards cash prizes for poems of any genre. Annual. Deadline for entry: December 31.

IRMA SIMONTON BLACK AWARD, 610 W. 112th St., New York NY 10025. Contact: Book Award Committee, Publications Division. Sponsor: Bank Street College of Education. Annual. Estab. 1972. Purpose: for excellence of text and graphics in a book for young children published during the preceding calendar year. Published submission only. Award: author and illustrator receive a scroll; winning entry carries an award seal designed by Maurice Sendak. Deadline: end of February (for works published during the preceding year).

HOWARD W. BLAKESLEE AWARDS, Chairman, Managing Committee, American Heart Association, 7320 Greenville Ave., Dallas TX 75231. Awards $500 honorarium and a citation to each winning entry, which may be a single article, broadcast, film, or book; a series; or no more than five unrelated pieces. Entries will be judged on the basis of their accuracy and significance, and on the skill and originality with which knowledge concerning the heart and circulatory system and advances in research or in the treatment, care and prevention of cardiovascular disease are translated for the public. Send for official entry blank and more details.

BOLLINGEN PRIZE IN POETRY OF THE YALE UNIVERSITY LIBRARY, Yale University Library, New Haven CT 06520. (203)436-0236. Secretary, Yale Administrative Committee: Donald Gallup. Estab. 1950. Biennial. Awards $5,000 to an American poet whose published book of poetry represents the highest achievement in the field of American poetry.

BOSTON GLOBE-HORN BOOK AWARDS, Sarah Gagne, Children's Book Editor, The Boston Globe, Boston MA 02107. Awards $200 to a book with outstanding text, and $200 to a book with outstanding illustrations. Up to 3 honor books in each category may be designated by the judges. Books may be fiction or nonfiction. No textbooks. Books must be submitted by publisher.

BOWLING WRITING COMPETITION, American Bowling Congress, Public Relations, 5301

S. 76th St., Greendale WI 53129. $1,800 in gift certificate prizes divided equally between 4 divisions — two each in Feature and Editorial. Categories separated by daily newspaper/national publication entrants and bowling publication entrants. Top prize $200 in four divisions for published bowling stories. First through fifth place in each division.

BROOKLYN ART BOOKS FOR CHILDREN CITATIONS. Awards a citation for the recognition and encouragement of the creation of books for children which are both works of art and literature. Sponsored by the Brooklyn Museum, 188 Eastern Pkwy., Brooklyn NY 11238, and the Brooklyn Public Library, Grand Army Plaza, Brooklyn NY 11238. No deadlines. Established in 1972.

EMIL BROWN FUND PREVENTIVE LAW PRIZE AWARDS, Louis M. Brown, Administrator, University of Southern California Law Center, Los Angeles CA 90007. Awards $1,000 for a praiseworthy leading article or book, and $500 for student work in the field of Preventive Law published in a law review, bar journal or other professional publication.

RAY BRUNER SCIENCE WRITING FELLOWSHIP, American Public Health Association, 1015 18th St., NW., Washington DC 20036. (202)467-5000. Contact: Doyne Bailey. Estab. 1971. Offered annually.
Purpose: "To encourage the development of young medical/health journalists. It is awarded to a reporter with less than 2 years experience covering the health beat, and less than 5 years total journalistic experience. Entrants are judged on journalistic style, timeliness, relevance, and the contribution or potential beneficial impact of the entry on the health of people." Submissions must have been published in the preceding 2 years. Awards travel and living expenses to cover the APHA Annual Meeting, an engraved plaque, and a portable typewriter. A perpetual plaque is maintained at the Toledo Blade, with winners' names inscribed. Deadline for entry: September 1. Rules for SASE.

BULTMAN AWARD, Chairman, Department of Drama, Loyola University, New Orleans LA 70118. Awards $100 for original, unpublished and professionally unproduced plays under one hour in length, written by college students and recommended by teacher of drama or creative writing. Mss must be securely bound and accompanied by SASE, or they will not be returned. Deadline: December 1, annually.

THE CANADIAN ILLUSTRATOR'S AWARD, The Amelia Frances Howard-Gibbon Medal is awarded to the illustrator of a children's book of merit written by a Canadian, published in Canada during the previous calendar year. Sponsored by the Canadian Library Association, 151 Sparks St., Ottawa, Ontario, Canada K1P 5E3. Deadline: February 1. Established in 1971.

CAROLINA QUARTERLY FICTION — POETRY CONTEST, P.O. Box 1117, Chapel Hill, NC 27514. Fiction: Awards $150 first prize, $100 second and $50 third for unpublished manuscripts up to 6,000 words. Poetry: $100 for first, $70 second and $30 third; no limit to length. Entrant may not have published a book-length ms in field of entry.

RUSSELL L. CECIL ARTHRITIS WRITING AWARDS, Arthritis Foundation, 3400 Peachtree Rd., NE., Atlanta, GA 30326. (404)266-0795. Communications Specialist: Roy Scott. Estab. 1956. Annual.
Purpose: To recognize and encourage the writing of news stories, articles and radio/TV scripts on the subject of Arthritis. Awards presented in 4 categories: newspaper, magazine, radio, and TV. Submissions must be previously published between January 1 and December 31. Awards $1,000 in each of the 4 categories. Deadline for entry January 31. Rules and entry forms for SASE.

CHILDREN'S BOOK AWARD, Child Study Children's Book Committee, 610 W. 112 St., New York NY 10025. Given to a book for children or young people which deals realistically with problems in their world. The book, published in the past calendar year, must offer an honest and courageous treatment of its theme.

CHILDREN'S SCIENCE BOOK AWARDS, 2 E. 63rd St., New York NY 10021. (212)838-0230. Public Relations Director: Ann E. Collins. Sponsor: The New York Academy of Sciences. Annual. Estab. 1971. Purpose: for the best general or 'trade' books on science for children.
Categories: Younger Category books for children under 7 years; and Older Category books for children between 7 and 14 years. Published submissions only. Award: $250 for each category.

Deadline: November 30 (for works published from December 1-November 30 each year). Contest rules and entry forms for SASE.

CHRISTOPHER AWARDS, 12 E. 48th St., New York NY 10017. Awards Co-ordinator: Peggy Flanagan. Awards bronze medallions for motion pictures (producer, director, writer), network television (producer, director, writer), and books (author, illustrator) to recognize individuals who have used their talents constructively, in the hope that they, and others, will continue to produce high quality works that reflect sound values.

COLLEGIATE POETRY CONTEST, *The Lyric*, 307 Dunton Dr., SW, Blacksburg VA 24060. Editor: Leslie Mellichamp. Annual. Purpose: for the best original and unpublished poem of 32 lines or less, written in the traditional manner, by U.S. or Canadian undergraduates. Award: 1st prize, $100; 2nd prize, $50; and a number of honorable mentions at $25 each. Also $100 to the library of the college in which the winner of the first prize is enrolled, provided that library is on the list of subscribers to *The Lyric*. Deadline: June 1. Contest rules and entry forms for SASE.

CONSERVATION NEWS AWARD. Awards a pewter plate mounted on a walnut plaque along with an honorarium (amount varies). Usually about $200. Award is given in recognition of outstanding efforts in communicating the story of natural resource conservation through the written word in newspapers or magazines. Sponsored by the Soil Conservation Society of America, 7515 N.E. Ankeny Rd., Ankeny IA 50021. Entries must be postmarked by no later than Dec. 31. Enclose SASE with correspondence.

CONTEST FOR UNPUBLISHED THIRD WORLD WRITERS, Council on Interracial Books for Children, 1841 Broadway, New York NY 10023. Contest Director: Kattie M. Cumbo. Estab. 1968. Offered annually.
Purpose: "To promote human values in children's literature. Our goal is to encourage unpublished children's book writers to produce literature that stimulates children to become anti-racist and anti-sexist individuals. Therefore, the literature is submitted for the contest must represent, in authentic fashion, some distinctive aspect of the particular Third World culture; challenge racist, sexist or ageist stereotypes by demonstrating the full humanity and potential of people of different races, ages and sexes; and demonstrate literary merit." Submissions must be previously unpublished. Awards $500 in each category (African American, Asian American, Chicano, Native American and Puerto Rican). Entry deadline: December 31. Contest rules and entry forms for SASE.

ALBERT B. COREY PRIZE IN CANADIAN-AMERICAN RELATIONS, Office of the Executive Secretary, American Historical Association, 400 A St., S.E., Washington DC 20003. The Canadian Historical Association and American Historical Association jointly award $2,000 for the best book on the history of Canadian-United States relations, or on the history of both countries.

CPCU-HARRY J. LOMAN FOUNDATION COMMUNICATIONS AWARD, Box 566, Media PA 19063. Awards $1,000 for the best written communication promoting better understanding of the economic and social functions of the property/casualty insurance business. Eligible are editorials, articles or series published in a national business or financial publication directed toward the national business community, not primarily the insurance industry.

HAROLD C. CRAIN AWARD IN PLAYWRITING, Department of Theatre Arts, San Jose State University, San Jose CA 95192. (408)277-2763. Director of Theater: Howard Burman. Estab. 1976. Offered annually.
Purpose: For original full-length plays of substance regardless of style, subject, and theme. Awards $500 and production of play. Submit entries from September 1-November 15. Entry form for SASE.

DESIGN FOR LIVING CONTEST, 14531 Stephen St., Nokesville VA 22123. (703)791-3672. Charles A. Mills, Awards Chairman. Sponsor: The March Society. Annual. Estab. 1974. Purpose: awarded to the author of a critical essay submitted in response to a social/political question formulated annually by the awards committee. Published or unpublished submissions OK. Award: 1st prize $50; 2nd prize $25. Entries will be considered for publication in the *Journal of the March Society* at the standard rate of payment. Deadline: April 15th. Contest rules and entry forms for SASE.

THE DEVINS AWARD, University of Missouri Press, Columbia MO 65201. For poetry. Write for submission details.

DISCOVERY/THE NATION 1979, The Poetry Center of the 92nd St. YM-YWHA and *The Nation* magazine, 1395 Lexington Ave., New York NY 10028. (212)427-6000. Assistant to the Director: Betsy Dunn. Estab. 1973. Offered annually.
Purpose: "This competition is designed to call critical and popular attention to promising new poets through the combined media of publication and a poetry recital." Submissions may have been published in magazines or anthologies, but not in book form. Awards $50, publication in *The Nation* and poetry recital at the Poetry Center. Entry deadline: February 10. Rules and entry form for SASE.

DOG WRITERS' ASSOCIATION OF AMERICA ANNUAL WRITING COMPETITION, Awards given for excellence in writing about dogs in newspapers, magazines, books, club publications. Separate categories for juniors. Open to all. Details from Sara Fath, Secretary, Kinney Hill Rd., Washington Depot CT 06794. (203)868-2863.

THE DUBUQUE FINE ARTS SOCIETY NATIONAL ONE-ACT PLAYWRITING CONTEST, 422 Loras Blvd., Dubuque IA 52001. Chairman: Judy Obershasen.
Purpose: For the best submitted one-act plays. Entries must be previously unproduced. Awards $100, $75, and $50. Winning plays are performed in a reader's theater format. Entry deadline: January 15. Length: 1 hour reading time. Contest rules and entry form for SASE.

JOHN H. DUNNING PRIZE IN AMERICAN HISTORY, Committee Chairman, American Historical Association, 400 A St. S.E., Washington DC 20003. Awards $300 in even-numbered years for an outstanding monograph in manuscript or in print on any subject relating to American history.

DUTTON ANIMAL BOOK AWARD, E. P. Dutton, 2 Park Ave., New York NY 10016. Offers a guaranteed minimum $15,000, as an advance against earnings, for an original book-length manuscript concerning a living creature (only Man and Plants are excluded as subjects); fiction or nonfiction. Write for details.

EDUCATION WRITERS AWARD, James G. Trulove, Director of Communications, American Association of University Professors, Suite 500, One Dupont Circle, Washington DC 20036. Awards a citation to recognize outstanding interpretive reporting of issues in higher education, through newspapers, magazines, radio, television and films. Write for entry details. SASE.

EDUCATOR'S AWARD, Miss LeOra L. Held, Executive Secretary, Delta Kappa Gamma Society International, P.O. Box 1589, Austin TX 78767. Awards $1,000 to recognize women and their contribution to education which may influence future directions in the profession. Previously published books may be in the fields of research, philosophy, or any other area of learning which is stimulating and creative. "The book submitted must have been published during the year the award is granted." Deadline for entry: February 1.

EPILEPSY FOUNDATION OF AMERICA JOURNALISM AWARD, 1828 L St., NW, Suite 406, Washington DC 20036. (202)293-2930. Editor, National Spokesman: Ann Scherer. Annual. Estab. 1972. Purpose: for articles which generate better understanding of epilepsy and those who suffer from it. Published submissions only. Award: $500 plus plaque. Deadline: 2nd week in December (for works published from December 1, 1978-November 30, 1979). Contest rules and entry forms for SASE.

ERAS REVIEW ART & POETRY CONTEST, Earth Rare Art Society, Box 481, Clarkston GA 30021. Contest Coordinator: Lori Seifert. Estab. 1975.
Purpose: Awards $25 per issue of *ERAS Review* magazine in the following categories: 1) unpublished poems not to exceed 60 lines; 2) graphics; 3) plays; and 4) children's stories (no fairytale fantasies). Entries accepted on continuing basis.

THE EXPLICATOR LITERARY FOUNDATION, INC., 3241 Archdale Rd., Richmond VA 23235. (804)272-6890. Treasurer: J.E. Whitesell. Annual. Estab. 1956. Purpose: encouragement of *explication de texte* in books. Published submissions only. Award: $200 and bronze plaque. Deadline: March 1. Contest rules and entry forms for SASE.

JOHN K. FAIRBANK PRIZE IN EAST ASIAN HISTORY, Committee Chairman, American Historical Association, 400 A St. S.E., Washington DC 20003. Awards $300 in odd-numbered years for an outstanding book on the history of China proper, Vietnam, Chinese Central Asia, Manchuria, Mongolia, Korea, or Japan, since the year 1800.

FLORIDA THEATRE CONFERENCE PLAYWRIGHT CONTEST, 2232 NW 19th Lane, Gainsville FL 32605. President: Craig Hartley. Estab. 1969. Offered annually.
Purpose: "To encourage Florida playwrights and producing organizations to produce original scripts." Submissions must be unpublished. Awards $250 cash award, plus staged reading at FTC Spring Festival. Entry deadline: January 31. Contest rules for SASE.

THE FORUM AWARD, Atomic Industrial Forum, Inc., 7101 Wisconsin Ave., Washington DC 20014. MaryEllen Warren, Administrative Assistant. Annually. Estab. 1967. Conducted to encourage factual news coverage of all aspects of peaceful nuclear applications and to honor significant contributions by the print and electronic news mediato public understanding of peaceful uses of nuclear energy. Total of $1,000 in prize money is available in each category (print media and electronic media). Nominees must be professional members of the print or electronic media. Entry must have been available to and intended for the general public.

FREEDOMS FOUNDATION AT VALLEY FORGE AWARDS, Awards Administration, Freedoms Foundation at Valley Forge, Valley Forge PA 19481. Awards honor medal and honor certificates for the most outstanding individual contribution supporting human dignity and American freedom principles in fields of journalism, television and radio. Write for further details.

FRENCH COLONIAL HISTORICAL SOCIETY BOOK AWARD, 611 Ryan Plaza Dr., suite 1139, Arlington TX 76011. (817)265-7143. Chairman: Leon B. Blair, Ph.D. Estab. 1974. Offered annually.
Purpose: "For the best book published during the current year, in English or French, on aspects of French colonial history." Awards $500. Entry deadline: December 31. "Publishers nominate and furnish 3 copies to the chairman of the book committee, who in turn submits them to the jury. Writers are welcome to correspond."

FRIENDS OF AMERICAN WRITERS JUVENILE BOOK AWARDS, Chairman for 1977-79: Mrs. John Biella, 3470 N. Lake Shore Drive, Chicago IL 60657. Awards for a book published during current year, with a Midwestern locale or written by a native or resident author of the Middle West. Up to 2 other awards to runners up and on some occasions an award to illustrator. Books submitted by publishers only.

THE GALILEO PRIZE, *Galileo* magazine, 339 Newbury St., Boston MA 02115. Contact: Editor. Offered annually.
Purpose: "We hope that, by offering a substantial amount in the form of prize money in addition to our regular rates, both new science fiction talent and those established writers who would be more likely to spend their time on longer works, will be encouraged to submit work to *Galileo* throughout the year. All works of fiction under 3,000 words received between January 1 and December 31 will be considered for both publication in *Galileo* and the annual prize, to be awarded in the spring of the following year." Submissions must be previously unpublished. Awards $300, $200 and $100.

JOHN GASSNER MEMORIAL PLAYWRITING AWARD, The New England Theatre Conference, Inc., 50 Exchange St., Waltham MA 02154. (617)893-3120. Executive Secretary: Marie L. Philips. Estab. 1967. Offered annually.
Purpose: "To encourage writing and production of new one-act plays." Submissions must be previously unpublished. Awards $200, and $100; "occasionally, one or more honorable mentions." Prize winning plays are given a script-in-hand performance by selected New England theatre groups. Entry deadline: April 15. Contest rules and entry form for SASE.

CHRISTIAN GAUSS AWARD, Phi Beta Kappa, 1811 Q St., N.W., Washington DC 20009. Awards $2,500 for a book of literary criticism or scholarship published in the United States. Books submitted by publishers only.

GAVEL AWARDS, 77 S. Wacker Dr., 6th Floor, Chicago IL 60606. (312)621-9248. Staff Director, Special Events: Dean Tyler Jenks. Sponsor: American Bar Association. Annual.

Estab. 1958. Purpose: for outstanding public service by newspaper, television, radio, magazines, motion pictures, theatrical producers, book publishers, wire services and news syndicates in increasing public understanding of the American system of law and justice. Published submissions only. Award: silver Gavel and certificate of merit. Deadline: for books, Feb. 1; all others, March 1 (for works published from January 1-December 31, 1978). Contest rules and entry forms for SASE.

GLCA NEW WRITERS AWARDS IN POETRY AND FICTION, Great Lakes Colleges Association, Wabash College, Crawfordsville IN 47933. (317)362-1400, ext. 232. Director: Donald Baker. Estab. 1968. Offered annually.
Purpose: "Competition is for first books in poetry or fiction (either novel or volume of short fiction)." Submissions must have been published the previous year. Awards "recognition, plus invited tour of up to 12 Great Lakes Colleges in Ohio, Indiana, and Michigan, with appropriate honoraria from the schools." Entry deadline: February 28. "It should be noted that only publishers may submit entries."

GOETHE HOUSE—P.E.N. TRANSLATION PRIZE, P.E.N. American Center, 156 Fifth Ave., New York NY 10010. (212)255-1577. Awards $500 for the best translation from the German language into English, published during the calendar year under review.

GOLDEN RAINTREE AWARD, 205 W. Highland Ave., Milwaukee WI 53203. (414)273-0873. Managing Editor: Jan Celba. Sponsor: Raintree Publishers Limited. Annual. Estab. 1976. Purpose: for mss that reflect outstanding achievement in juvenile literature. Unpublished submissions only. Award: $100 cash and Golden Raintree Seal, in addition to negotiated publication fee for ms. Deadline: December 31.

GREAT AMERICAN PLAY CONTEST, Actors Theatre of Louisville, 316 W. Main, Louisville KY 40202. (502)584-1265. Assistant to the Producer: ElizaBeth Mahan. Estab. 1977. Annual.
Purpose: "To find new scripts that are ready for professional production. Plays submitted must not have had a previous Equity production, although an Equity-waiver production is allowable. Scripts with 15 or fewer characters preferred, though others will be considered. All genres (comedy, drama, tradgedy, musicals) accepted. This year, one prize of $2,500 will be awarded to a single contest winner or split between co-winners if there are 2 scripts of equal merit. In addition, if winning plays are produced, the playwright will receive royalties for the production. Note: prize changes from year to year." Deadline for Entry: June 1. Contest rules and entry forms for SASE.

GUIDEPOSTS MAGAZINE YOUTH WRITING CONTEST, Guideposts Associates, Inc. 747 3rd Ave., New York NY 10017. Editorial Assistant: Nancy C. Galya. Estab. 1964. Annual.
Purpose: "For high school juniors or seniors or students in equivalent grades overseas. For the best first-person story telling about a true memorable or moving experience they have had." Submissions should be unpublished. Awards: 1st prize, $4,000 scholarship; 2nd prize, $3,500 scholarship; 3rd prize, $3,000 scholarship; 4th prize, $2,500 scholarship; 5th prize, $2,000 scholarship; and 6th through 10th, $1,000 scholarship. Deadline for entry: November 26. Rules and entry forms for SASE.

JOHN HANCOCK AWARDS FOR EXCELLENCE IN BUSINESS AND FINANCIAL JOURNALISM, John Hancock Mutual Life Insurance Co., T-54 John Hancock Pl. Box 111, Boston MA 02117. (617)421-2270. Special Projects Administrator: Miss Jean Canton. Estab. 1967. Annual.
Purpose: "To foster increased public knowledge of, and interest in business and finance; to recognize editorial contributions to a better understanding of personal money management; to clarify the significance of political and social developments as they relate to the nation's economy; and to stimulate discussion and thought by bringing together, in an academic environment, newsmakers, reporters, faculty and students". Categories: syndicated and news service writers; writers for national magazines of general interest; writers for financial-business newspapers and magazines; writers for newspapers with circulation above 300,000; writers of newspapers with circulation 100,000 to 300,000; and writers for newspapers with circulation under 100,000. Submissions must be previously published from January 1-December 31. Award $1,000 plus AFE medallion and expenses to presentations program. Deadline for entry January 31. Rules and entry forms for SASE.

CLARENCE H. HARING PRIZE, Committee Chairman, American Historical Association, 400

A St. S.E., Washington DC 20003. Awards $500 every five years to the Latin American who, in the opinion of the committee, has published the most outstanding book on Latin-American history during the preceding 5 years. Next awarded in 1981.

HEADLINERS AWARDS, National Headliners Club, Convention Hall, Boardwalk, Atlantic City NJ 08401. (609)348-7044. Executive Secretary: Elaine Frayne. Estab. 1934. Annual.
Purpose: "To recognize the work of small circulation newspapers, smaller circulation writers, individual radio and television stations, investigative reporters and teams, and news photography in all its phases." Deadline for entries: February 28.

HEALTH JOURNALISM AWARDS, American Chiropractic Association, 2200 Grand Ave., Des Moines IA 50312. Director of Public Affairs: Dr. R.C. Schafer. Estab. 1976. Offered annually.
Purpose: "Conducted each year to recognize journalists whose constructive thoughts suggest solutions to basic health problems, motivate consumers to take care of their health, and contribute to fair and resposible health reporting." Submissions must have been published during the calendar year preceding award. Award $200 and plaque to winners in each category. Entry deadline: March 1. Contest rules and entry forms for SASE.

ERNEST HEMINGWAY FOUNDATION AWARD, P.E.N. American Center, 156 Fifth Ave., New York NY 10010. Awards $6,000 for the best first-published book of fiction, either novel or short story collection, in the English language by an American author, published by an established publishing house. Children's books are not eligible. Deadline: December 15.

SIDNEY HILLMAN PRIZE AWARD, Sidney Hillman Foundation, Inc., 15 Union Square, New York NY 10003. Awards $750 annually for outstanding published contributions in nonfiction, fiction, radio and television dealing with themes relating to the ideals which Sidney Hillman held throughout his life. Such themes would include the protection of individual civil liberties, improved race relations, strengthened labor movement, advancement of social welfare, economic security, greater world understanding and related problems. Deadline: January 15.

HAROLD HIRSCH PERPETUAL TROPHY FOR OUTSTANDING SKI WRITING, United States Ski Association, 1726 Champa St., Suite 300, Denver CO 80202. (303)825-9183. Executive Office Manager: Evelyn Masbruch. Estab. 1963. Offered annually.
Purpose: "To promote and reward excellence in ski writing. Entries are judged on editorial effect on reading public, initiative shown by writer in gathering material, excellence in writing, technical knowledge, and variety of coverage (competitive or recreational)." Submissions must have been published between May 1-April 30. Awards the Harold S. Hirsch Trophy and certificate. Entry deadline: April 24. Contest rules and entry form for SASE.

HOUGHTON MIFFLIN LITERARY FELLOWSHIP, Houghton Mifflin Co., 2 Park St., Boston MA 02107. Awards $2,500 grant and $7,500 as an advance against royalties to help authors complete projects of outstanding literary merit. Candidates should submit at least 50 pages of the actual project (fiction or nonfiction), an informal description of its theme and intention, and a brief biography. A finished ms, as well as works in progress will be eligible for an award.

THE HUMANITAS PRIZE, Executive Director, The Human Family Institute, P.O. Box 861, Pacific Palisades CA 90272. (213)454-8769. Awards $10,000 for the thirty-minute teleplay, $15,000 for the sixty-minute teleplay, and $25,000 for the teleplay of ninety minutes or longer previously produced on national network commercial television, aired during prime time hours. To promote a greater appreciation of the dignity of the human person, to deepen the human family's understanding of themselves, of their relationship with the human community, and to their Creator, to aid individuals in their search for meaning, freedom and love; to liberate, enrich and unify the human family. Submission should be made by someone other than the writer of the produced play (for example, the program producer). Write for details and entry form.

INGAA-MISSOURI BUSINESS JOURNALISM AWARDS, William McPhatter, Director, Neff Hall, School of Journalism, Columbia MO 65201. Awards $1,000 in each of four categories to honor excellence in reporting and interpreting business, economic, trade and financial news. To encourage a greater public understanding of the American economic system through coverage of U.S. business in newspapers and magazines. Write for complete details and entry form.

INTERNATIONAL POETS AND PATRONS NARRATIVE CONTEST, 8 S. 300 Blackthorne

Ln., Naperville IL 60540. Contest Chairman: Don Cornwell. Sponsor: Poets and Patrons of Chicago, Inc. Annual. Estab. 1973. Purpose: for best narrative poem (poem must tell a story—40 lines maximum, any form, any subject). Unpublished submissions only. Award: 1st prize, $25; 2nd prize, $10. Deadline: September 1.

INTERNATIONAL READING ASSOCIATION PRINT MEDIA AWARD. Entries must focus on the field of reading and are judged on the basis of journalistic quality which includes clear and imaginative writing that lifts the material out of the routine category. In-depth studies of reading activities, accounts of outstanding reading practices, relevant reading research reportage, and/or day-to-day coverage of reading programs in the community. Sponsored by the International Reading Association. Entries or requests for additional information should be sent to Public Information Officer, International Reading Association, Box 8139, Newark DE 19711. Awards $500. Deadline: January 2. Established in 1960. Rules and entry forms available at the address above.

IOWA SCHOOL OF LETTERS AWARD FOR SHORT FICTION, English-Philosophy Bldg., University of Iowa, Iowa City IA 52242. Awards $1,000 for a book-length collection of short stories by a writer who has not yet published a volume of fiction.

JOSEPH HENRY JACKSON/JAMES D. PHELAN LITERARY AWARD, 425 California St., Suite 1602, San Francisco CA 94104. (415)982-1210. Assistant Coordinator: Susan Kelly. Sponsor: The San Francisco Foundation. Annual. Estab. 1935 (Phelan contest); 1957 (Jackson contest). "The two competitions were combined in 1957 and are now administered simultaneously. One can compete for one or both depending on eligibility." Purpose: to award the author of an unpublished, partly completed book-length work of fiction, nonfictional prose, short story or poetry (Jackson); to award the author of an unpublished, incomplete work of fiction, non-fictional prose, short story, poetry or drama (Phelan). Award: Both $2,000. Deadline: January 15. Contest rules and entry forms can be obtained by calling the above number.

JACKSONVILLE UNIVERSITY PLAYWRITING CONTEST, Davis Sikes, Director, College of Fine Arts, Jacksonville University, Jacksonville FL 32211. (904)744-3950. Awards prizes up to $2,000 and premiere production of previously unproduced plays (original 1-act and full-length). Deadline: January 1. Write for contest rules. Enclose SASE.

JEWISH BOOK COUNCIL AWARD FOR A BOOK OF JEWISH THOUGHT, National Jewish Welfare Board, 15 E. 26th St., New York NY 10010. Awards $500 and a citation to the author of a published book dealing with some aspect of Jewish thought, past or present, which combines knowledge, clarity of thought, and literary merit.

JEWISH BOOK COUNCIL AWARD FOR A BOOK ON THE NAZI HOLOCAUST, National Jewish Welfare Board, 15 E. 26 St., New York NY 10010. Awards $500 and a citation to the author of a published nonfiction book dealing with some aspects of the Nazi holocaust period. Books published in English, Yiddish, and Hebrew are acceptable.

JEWISH BOOK COUNCIL AWARD FOR BOOKS OF POETRY, National Jewish Welfare Board, 15 E. 26 St., New York NY 10010. Awards $500 and a citation to the author of a book of poetry of Jewish interest. Books published in English, Yiddish, and Hebrew are acceptable.

JEWISH BOOK COUNCIL JUVENILE AWARD, National Jewish Welfare Board, 15 E. 26 St., New York NY 10010. Awards $500 and a citation to the author of a published Jewish juvenile book.

JEWISH BOOK COUNCIL WILLIAM AND JANICE EPSTEIN FICTION AWARD, National Jewish Welfare Board, 15 E. 26 St., New York NY 10010. Awards $500 and a citation to the author of a published book of fiction of Jewish interest, either a novel or a collection of short stories, which combines high literary merit with an affirmative expression of Jewish values.

ANSON JONES AWARD. $250 cash and engraved plaque in each of eight categories. For excellence in communicating health information to the public through Texas newspapers, magazines, radio and television. Sponsored by the Texas Medical Association, 1801 North Lamar Blvd., Austin TX 78701. (512)477-6704. Entries are considered between January 1 and December 31. Estab. 1956. Rules and entry forms available from the Communication Department at TMA (address above). Deadline: January 15th of following year.

FRANK KELLEY MEMORIAL AWARD, American Association of Petroleum Landmen, Box 1984, Fort Worth TX 76101. Awards $250 and a plaque in appreciation for excellence in reporting oil and gas industry information to the general public. Previously published newspaper articles only.

THE JANET HEIDINGER KAFKA PRIZE, English Department/Writers Workshop, University of Rochester, Rochester NY 14627. (716)275-2340. Dean, University College: Robert G. Koch. Estab. 1975. Offered annually.
Purpose: "The prize shall be awarded to a woman citizen of the US who has written the best book-length published work of prose fiction, whether novel, short stories, or experimental writing. Works primarily written for children and vanity house publications will not be considered." Submissions from publishers must have been published within the previous 12 months; collections of short stories must have been assembled for the first time, or at least 1/3 must be previously unpublished. Entry deadline: October 31. Contest rules and entry form for SASE.

THE ROBERT F. KENNEDY JOURNALISM AWARDS, Ruth Darmstadter, 1035 30th St., N.W., Washington DC 20007. (202)338-7444. The awards ($1,000 first prize in each category, possible additional grand prize of $2,000, honorable mentions and citations) honor journalists, broadcasters, and photographers whose work (published or broadcast during 1978) has illuminated the problmes of the disadvantaged in the United States. Write in November for complete details and entry form for the current annual competition.

LUCILLE LOY KUCK OHIOANA AWARD. 3 prizes of $250, $150 and $50 for literary excellence. Sponsored by the Martha Kinney Cooper Ohioana Library Association, 1105 Ohio Departments Bldg., Columbus OH 43215. Deadline: February 1. Rules and entry forms may be obtained from the Martha Kinney Cooper Library Association.

HAROLD MORTON LANDON TRANSLATION AWARD, The Academy of American Poets, 1078 Madison Ave., New York NY 10028. Awards $1,000 biennially to an American poet for a published translation of poetry from any language into English. Translation may be a book-length poem, collection of poems, or a verse drama translated into verse. Send published books (no manuscripts) to the Academy.

NORMAN LEAR AWARD FOR ACHIEVEMENT IN COMEDY PLAYWRITING, Executive Producer, American College Theatre Festival, John F. Kennedy Center for the Performing Arts, Washington DC 20566. (202)254-3437. Awards $2,500 and a professional assignment to write a complete teleplay for one of the series produced by Norman Lear, a trip to Los Angeles with all expenses paid to participate in story conferences and membership in the Writers Guild of America with the Writers Guild Foundation paying the usual initiation fee of $200, for the best student comedy play produced for the annual American College Theatre Festival.

LEVI'S/I.R.W.A. RODEO PRESS CONTEST, Levi Strauss & Co., in cooperation with the International Rodeo Writers Association, 2 Embarcadero Center, San Francisco CA 94106. (415)544-7217. Director, Corporate Communications: Bud Johns. Estab. 1970. Annual.
Purpose: To recognize each year the best writing and photography published on the subject of rodeo. Awards given in 3 categories: Rodeo News Story, Rodeo Feature Story and Rodeo Photography. Submissions must have been published during the previous year. Awards in each category: $100 1st prize, $50 2nd prize and $25 3rd prize; plus a pair of Levi's and a specially designed certificate. Deadline for entry: March. Rules and entry form for SASE.

JERRY LEWIS/MDA WRITING AWARDS, Horst S. Petzall, Director, Department of Public Health Education, Muscular Dystrophy Association, 810 Seventh Ave., New York NY 10019. Awards $1,000, $500, and $250, along with award plaques, to those writers whose work fosters better understanding of muscular dystrophy and related neuromuscular diseases, and contributes to public support of the effort to conquer these afflictions. Previously published articles, feature stories, editorials or poetry, as well as commentaries, documentaries, dramas, or public-service announcements aired on radio or television, are eligible.

ELIAS LIEBERMAN STUDENT POETRY AWARD. For details, send SASE to Elias Lieberman Student Poetry Award, Executive Secretary, Poetry Society of America, 15 Gramercy Park, New York NY 10003. Awards $100 for the "best unpublished poem by a high school or preparatory school student of the USA." Deadline: December 31.

LITERATURE MEDAL CONTEST, Commonwealth Club of California, 681 Market St., San Francisco CA 94105. (415)362-4903. Executive Director: Michael J. Brassington. Estab. 1931. Offered annually.
Purpose: Awards made for books in the following categories: fiction, nonfiction, juvenile, poetry, first novel, or Californiana (history, society, culture, etc.). Submissions must have been published during the year in which the book is submitted. Awards a gold or silver medal. Entry deadline: January 31. Rules and entry form for SASE.

DAVID D. LLOYD PRIZE, Chairman of the Committee, Professor Thomas C. Blaisdell, Jr., Department of Political Science, 210 Barrows Hall, University of California, Berkeley CA 94720. Awards $1,000 biennially for the best published book on the period of the presidency of Harry S. Truman. Books must deal primarily and substantially with some aspect of the political, economic, and social development of the U.S., principally between April 12, 1945 and January 20, 1953, or of the public career of Harry S. Truman. Publication period: January 1-December 31.

THE GERALD LOEB AWARDS, UCLA Graduate School of Management, Los Angeles CA 90024. (213)825-7982. Assistant Dean: Gerald F. Corrigan. Annual. Estab. 1957. Purpose: for distinguished business and financial journalism.
Categories: Single article in a newspaper with daily circulation above 350,000; single article in a newspaper with daily circulation less than 350,000; single article in a national magazine; and syndicated column or editorial. Published submissions only. Award: $1,000 for each category. Deadline: February 15 (for works published from January 1-December 31). Contest rules and entry forms for SASE.

MAN IN HIS ENVIRONMENT BOOK AWARD, E. P. Dutton, 2 Park Ave., New York NY 10016. Offers a guaranteed minimum $10,000 as an advance against earnings for an original single work of adult nonfiction on an ecological theme, dealing with the past, present or future of man in his environment, natural or man-made. Write for details.

HOWARD R. MARRARO PRIZE IN ITALIAN HISTORY, Office of the Executive Secretary, American Historical Association, 400 A St. S.E., Washington DC 20003. Awards $500 for a book or article which treats Italian history in any epoch of Italian cultural history, or of Italian-American relations. Write for submission details.

JOHN MASEFIELD MEMORIAL AWARD, Poetry Society of America, 15 Gramercy Park S., New York NY 10003. Awards $500 for an unpublished narrative poem written in English, not exceeding 200 lines, in memory of the late Poet Laureate of England. Write for submission details enclosing SASE. Deadline: December 15.

MELCHER BOOK AWARD, Unitarian Universalist Association, 25 Beacon St., Boston MA 02108. Department Director: Doris Pullen. Estab. 1964. Annual.
Purpose: Given annually to a work published in America during the previous calendar year judged to be the most significant contribution to religious liberalism. Submissions must be previously published. Awards $1,000 plus bronze medallion. Publisher submits candidate books to judges.

MODERN LANGUAGE ASSOCIATION PRIZES, Office of Research Programs, 62 Fifth Ave., New York NY 10011. Awards the annual James Russell Lowell Prize, $1,000, for an outstanding literary or linguistic study, a critical edition of an important work, or a critical biography written by a member of the Association or published in book form. The committee also awards an annual prize for an outstanding article in the *PMLA,* the William Riley Parker Prize.

JAMES MOONEY AWARD, The University of Tennessee Press/The Southern Anthropological Society, Department of Geography and Anthropology, Louisiana State University, Baton Rouge LA 70803. Contact: Miles Richardson.
Purpose: "For the book-length manuscript that best describes and interprets the people or culture of a New World population, which may be prehistoric, historic, or contemporary. The purpose of this award is to encourage distinguished writing in anthropology and any student of the cultures and societies of the New World is eligible." Submissions must be previously unpublished. Awards $1,000. Entry deadline: December 31. Contest rules and entry form for SASE.

FRANK LUTHER MOTT-KAPPA TAU ALPHA RESEARCH AWARD IN JOURNALISM, School of Journalism, University of Missouri, Columbia MO 65201. (314)882-4852. Chief, Central Office: William H. Taft. Estab. 1944. Annual.
Purpose: "To recognize outstanding research in journalism. Generally, textbooks are not considered. Books that reflect on journalism considered as well as those that depend heavily on journalism sources, such as presidential biographies, etc." Submissions must be previously published and copyrighted for year awarded, i.e. in 1979 will consider 1978 books. Awards $250 "plus beautiful hand-lettered scroll. Certificates to top five or so. At times, extra scrolls." Deadline for entry: February. "We have no special forms. We require 5 copies of each book entered. We have 5 judges, top professors across the nation".

NABW AWARDS FOR DISTINGUISHED JOURNALISM, National Association of Bank Women, Inc., 111 E. Wacker Dr., Chicago IL 60601. (312)644-6610. Contact: Public Relations Department. Estab. 1974. Offered annually.
Purpose: "To recognize and honor journalists for their interpretive articles about executive women in banking and women's contributions to, and place in, the banking industry." Submissions must have been published within one year preceding the contest closing date. Awards $300 and certificate of recognition in 2 categories: 1) US newspapers or periodicals; and 2) bank-sponsored publications. Entries must be published by June 1; received by June 10. Contest rules and entry forms for SASE.

NAEBM DIRECTORS AWARD, National Association of Engine and Boat Manufacturers, Box 5555, Grand Central Station, New York NY 10017. (212)697-1100. Public Relations Manager: Sandy Mills. Estab. 1970. Annual.
Purpose: To recognize an individual within the communications profession who has made outstanding contributions to boating and allied water sports. Submissions must be previously published. Awards $1,000 and certificate and trip to New York in January for presentation during New York National Boat Show. Deadline for entry: October 15. Rules and entry forms for SASE.

NARRATIVE POETRY, World Order of Narrative Poets, Box 412, Orinda CA 94563. President: Mr. Lynne L. Prout. Estab. 1975. Offered annually.
Purpose: "To encourage the writing and appreciation of narrative poetry forms, most of which are eliminated in the usual contests due to the longer line length often required by narratives. Most contests and publications cannot deal with lengthy poems, so this competition gives an opportunity that is badly needed to narrative poets." Submissions must be previously unpublished. Awards $55 in cash, divided in not less than 3 prizes/year. Entry deadline: September 1. Contest rules for SASE.

NATIONAL BOOK AWARDS, sponsored by the Association of American Publishers, 1 Park Ave., New York NY 10016. Awards $1,000 in each of seven categories for literature written or translated by American citizens and published in the U.S. to honor outstanding creative writing. Categories include biography and autobiography, children's literature, contemporary thought, fiction, history, poetry and translation. Deadline: September 15.

THE NATIONAL FOUNDATION FOR HIGHWAY SAFETY AWARDS, Box 3043, Westville Station, New Haven CT 06515. Annual. Estab. 1962. Purpose: to emphasize driving safety. Published submissions only. Award: U.S. Savings Bond and plaques offered to editors, reporters, cartoonists, television and radio directors. Deadline: January 31 (for works published during the year). Contest rules and entry forms for SASE.

NATIONAL HISTORICAL SOCIETY BOOK PRIZE IN AMERICAN HISTORY, Board of Judges, Box 1831, Harrisburg PA 17105. Awards $1,000 for a first book published by an author, to encourage promising historians, young and old, in producing the sound but readable history that is so necessary for portraying our past to the general public.

NATIONAL MEDIA AWARDS, American Psychological Foundation, 1200 17th St., NW., Washington DC 20036. (202)833-7600. Public Information Officer: Mona Marie Olean. Estab. 1956. Offered annually.
Purpose: "The purpose of the awards is to recognize and encourage outstanding, accurate reporting which increases the public's knowledge and understanding of psychology." Awards are made in 5 categories: 1) TV/Film; 2) Radio; 3) Newspaper reporting; 4) Magazine writing;

and 5) Books/monographs. Awards $1,000 and an invitation to attend the annual Convention of the American Psychological Association, expenses paid. Submissions must have been published in the previous calendar year. Entry deadline: May 5. Contest rules and entry form for SASE.

NATIONAL PRESS CLUB AWARD FOR EXCELLENCE IN CONSUMER REPORTING, Stan Cohen, Chairman, Consumer Awards, National Press Bldg., Washington DC 20045. Provides the Consumer Reporting Award, and Certificates of Recognition in 11 categories. For members of the working press. Deadline for entries: May 15.

NATIONAL SOCIETY OF PROFESSIONAL ENGINEERS JOURNALISM AWARDS, 2029 K St., N.W., Washington DC 20006. (202)331-7020. PR Director: Jack Cox. Annual. Estab. 1966. Purpose: for contributing to public knowledge and understanding of the role of engineering and technology in contemporary life. Published submissions only. Award: Three awards of $500, $300 and $200. Deadline: January 15 (for works published during the previous year). Contest rules and entry forms for SASE.

ALLAN NEVINS PRIZE, Professor Kenneth T. Jackson, Secretary-Treasurer, Society of American Historians, 610 Fayerweather Hall, Columbia University, New York NY 10027. Awards $1,000 and publication of winning manuscript for the best written doctoral dissertation in the field of American history, dealing historically with American arts, literature, and science, as well as biographical studies of Americans in any walk of life.

NEWCOMEN AWARDS IN BUSINESS HISTORY, c/o *Business History Review*, Harvard University, 215 Baker Library, Soldiers Field, Boston MA 02163. (617)495-6364. Editor: Albro Martin. Offered annually.
Purpose: "To the author of the article judged to be the best published in the *Business History Review* during the preceding year." Awards $250. Special award (in addition to the main award) of $100 to the article judged to be the best published in the Review during the year by a non-Ph.D., or a recent (not more than 5 years) Ph.D., and who has not published in book form. "There is no deadline for the prize; any article accepted for publication in the *Business History Review* becomes eligible for the award in the year the publication occurs." Contest rules for SASE; "but they are regularly advertised in the issues of the *Review*."

NEW YORK STATE HISTORICAL ASSOCIATION MANUSCRIPT AWARD, Lake Rd., Cooperstown NY 13326. (607)547-2508. Editorial Associate: Dr. Wendell Tripp. Estab. 1973. Offered annually.
Purpose: "The award is presented to the best unpublished, book-length monograph dealing with the history of New York State. Manuscripts may deal with any aspect of New York history including biographies, literature and the arts, provided that the methodology is historical." Submissions must be previously unpublished. Awards $1,000 and assistance in publication. Entry deadline: February 1. Contest rules and entry form for SASE.

CATHERINE L. O'BRIEN AWARD, c/o Ruder & Finn, Inc., 110 E. 59th St., New York NY 10022. (212)593-6321. Vice President: Jill Totenberg. Sponsor: Stanley Home Products, Inc. Annual. Estab. 1960. Purpose: for achievement in women's interest newspaper reporting. Published submissions only. Award: First prize; $500 and $1,000 journalism scholarship to student of choice; second prize: $300 and $750 journalism scholarship; third prize: $200 and $500 journalism scholarship. Annual deadline: January 31 (for works published from January-December of calendar year). Contest rules and entry forms available on request.

OPEN CIRCLE THEATRE PLAYWRIGHTS AWARD, Goucher College, Towson MD 21204. Director: Barry Knower. Estab. 1976. Offered annually.
Purpose: "To find challenging plays with good roles for women. At least 50% of major roles must be for women." Submissions must be unpublished and unproduced. Awards $200, and production by Open Circle Theatre. Entry deadline: December 31. Contest rules for SASE.

EARL D. OSBORN AWARD, Robert Francis Kane Associates, Inc., Public Relations, 12 E. 41st St., New York NY 10017. Sponsor: EDO Corporation. Annual. Estab. 1970. Purpose: for best writing in any medium (press, magazine, radio or TV) on general aviation. Published submissions only. Award: $500 and trophy. Deadline: February (for works published during the previous calendar year). Contest rules and entry forms for SASE.

P.E.N. TRANSLATION PRIZE, Chairman, Translation Committee, P.E.N. American Center, 156 Fifth Ave., New York NY 10010. Awards $1,000 for the best booklength translation into English from any language published in the United States. Technical, scientific, or reference works are not eligible. Sponsored by the Book-of-the-Month Club. Deadline: December 31.

FRANCIS PARKMAN PRIZE, Professor Kenneth T. Jackson, Secretary, Society of American Historians, 610 Fayerweather Hall, Columbia University, New York NY 10027. Awards $500 and a bronze medal to recognize the author who best epitomizes the Society's purpose—the writing of history with literary distinction as well as sound scholarship. Books must deal with the colonial or national history of the United States. Books submitted by publishers only.

THE DREW PEARSON PRIZE FOR EXCELLENCE IN INVESTIGATIVE REPORTING, The Drew Pearson Foundation, 1156 15 St. N.W., Washington DC 20005. Awards $5,000 for significant investigative reporting by newspaper reporters, authors of books and magazine articles and journalists involved in radio and television.

PENNEY-MISSOURI MAGAZINE AWARDS, School of Journalism, University of Missouri, Columbia MO 65201. Awards Director: Ruth D'Arcy. Annual. Estab. 1966. Purpose: for excellence in magazine coverage that enhances lifestyle in today's society.
Categories: Contemporary living; consumerism; health; personal lifestyle; expanding opportunities, and excellence in smaller magazines. Published submissions only. Award: $1,000 in each category. Deadline: May 1 (for works published from January 1-December 31). Write for centest rules and entry forms.

PFIZER AWARD, c/o Isis Editorial Office, MHT 5214, Smithsonian Institution, Washington DC 20560. (202)381-5691. After January 1, University of Pennsylvania, 215 S. 34th St., Philadelphia PA 19104. (215)263-5575. Sponsor: History of Science Society, Inc. Annual. Estab. 1958. Purpose: to recognize and reward the best published work related to the history of science in the preceding year, written by an American or Canadian author. Published submissions only. Award: $1,000 and a medal. Deadline: May 1 (for work published during the previous year).

PLAYWRITING FOR CHILDREN'S THEATRE, 5416 W. 101st Terrace, Overland Park KS 66207. Contact: Mrs. John B. Keller. Sponsor: Community Children's Theatre of Kansas City. Annual. Estab. 1951. Purpose: to encourage the writing of outstanding original scripts which are suitable for production by adults for grade school children. Unpublished submissions only. Award: $500. Deadline: First week of January. Contest rules and entry forms for SASE.

EDGAR ALLAN POE AWARDS, Mystery Writers of America, Inc., 105 E. 19 St., New York NY 10003. Awards Edgar Allan Poe statuettes in each of nine categories: best mystery novel published in America, best first mystery novel by an American author, best fact crime book, best juvenile mystery, best paperback mystery, best mystery short story, best mystery motion picture, and best television mystery.

THE POETRY CENTER DISCOVERY-THE NATION CONTEST, The Poetry Center of the 92nd St. YM-YWHA, 1395 Lexington Ave., New York NY 10028. Awards $50 to each of 4 winners, invites each winner to read at The Poetry Center in a special program and publishes one poem by each winner in *The Nation*. Open to poets whose works have not yet been published in book form. Write for details. SASE. Deadline for entry: February 23.

POETS CLUB OF CHICAGO NATIONAL SHAKESPEAREAN SONNET CONTEST. 3 prizes of $50, $25 and $10. Sponsored by the Poets Club of Chicago. Mail three copies of only one Shakespearean sonnet, typed on 8½x11 paper, to Anne Nolan, c/o Nolan Boiler Co., 8531 S. Vincennes, Chicago IL 60620. Deadline: September 1. Sonnet must be unpublished and must not have won a cash award in this contest previously. No author identification is to appear on the copies. Enclose a separate envelope with the poet's identification on a card inside it. No poems will be returned. SASE must accompany all inquiries.

PRIZE IN PHOTOGRAPHIC HISTORY, Prize Committee, Photographic Historical Society of New York, Box 1839, Radio City Station, New York NY 10019. Awards $100 to an individual who has written, edited, or produced an original work dealing with the history of photography. Books, magazine articles and monographs are eligible.

PULITZER PRIZES, Secretary, Advisory Board on the Pulitzer Prizes, 702 Journalism, Columbia University, New York NY 10027. Awards $1,000 in categories of journalism, letters, and music for distinguished work by United States newspapers, and for distinguished achievement in literature.

PUTNAM AWARDS, G. P. Putnam's Sons, 200 Madison Ave., New York NY 10016. Awards $7,500 advance against royalties for outstanding fiction and nonfiction book manuscripts. Nominations are made by the editors of G.P. Putnam's Sons from mss already under contract to the house.

ERNIE PYLE MEMORIAL AWARD, Scripps-Howard Foundation, 200 Park Ave., New York NY 10017. Awards $1,000 to the winner and medallion plaque to the paper, plus $500 second prize and hand-lettered citation to the paper, for newspaper writing which exemplifies the style, warmth, and craftsmanship of Ernie Pyle.

REAL ESTATE JOURNALISM ACHIEVEMENT COMPETITION, National Association of Realtors, 430 N. Michigan Ave., Chicago IL 60611. Assistant Media Director: Sue Davidson. Estab. 1965. Offered annually.
Purpose: "To encourage excellence in real estate reporting and writing, and to recognize winners for their accomplishments in the field." Submissions must have been published in the year previous to contest closing date. Awards "plaques and cash awards." Entry deadline: September 1. Contest rules and entry form for SASE.

REDBOOK'S YOUNG WRITER'S CONTEST III, Box F-3, 230 Park Ave., New York NY 10017.
Purpose: The contest is open to men and women 18-28 years of age at the time of entry, and who have not previously published or had accepted fiction in a magazine with a circulation over 25,000. Awards $500, and *Redbook* will buy publication rights for an additional $1,000 for 1st prize; $300 for second prize; and $100 for 3rd prize. Entry deadline: December 1978. "For a period of 6 months after the deadline, The Redbook Publishing Co. reserves the right to purchase for publication any story entered in the competition that is deemed publishable." Contest rules will appear in the October, November, and December issues of *Redbook*.

REGINA MEDAL, Catholic Library Association, 461 W. Lancaster Ave., Haverford PA 19041. Awards a silver medal for continued distinguished contribution in literature for children.

RELIGIOUS ARTS GUILD ONE-ACT PLAY COMPETITION, 25 Beacon, Boston MA 02108. (617)742-2100. Chief Judge: Dr. Richard Warye. Biannual. Estab. 1950. Unpublished submissions only. Award: $200. Deadline: January 15. Contest rules and entry forms for SASE.

DOROTHY ROSENBERG ANNUAL POETRY AWARD, 25 Beacon, Boston MA 02108. Chief Judge: Virginia Thayer. Sponsor: Religious Arts Guild. Annual. Estab. 1970. Unpublished submissions only. Award: $50. Deadline: March 31. Contest rules for SASE.

ST. LAWRENCE AWARD FOR FICTION, *Fiction International*, Department of English, St. Lawrence University, Canton NY 13617. Awards $1,000 to the author of an outstanding first collection of short fiction published by an American publisher during the current year. Editors, writers, agents, readers, and publishers are invited to suggest or submit eligible books. Publisher must submit final nominations. Deadline: January 31.

HENRY SCHUMAN PRIZE, c/o Isis Editorial Office, MHT 5214, Smithsonian Institution, Washington DC 20560. (202)381-5691. After January 1, University of Pennsylvania, 215 S. 34th St., Philadelphia PA 19104. Sponsor: History of Science Society, Inc. Annual. Estab. 1955. Purpose: for original prize essay on the history of science and its cultural influences, open to graduate and undergraduate students in any American or Canadian college. Unpublished submissions only. Papers submitted must be 5,000 words in length, exclusive of footnotes, and thoroughly documented. Award: $500. Deadline: July 1.

ROBERT LIVINGSTON SCHUYLER PRIZE, Committee Chairman, American Historical Association, 400 A St. S.E., Washington DC 20003. Awards $500 every five years for recognition of the best work in the field of Modern British, British Imperial, and British Commonwealth history written by an American citizen.

SCIENCE IN SOCIETY JOURNALISM AWARDS, Administrative Secretary, National Association of Science Writers, Box H, Sea Cliff NY 11579. Two awards of $1,000 and engraved medallions to recognize investigative and interpretive reporting about physical sciences and the life sciences and their impact for good and bad. Write for complete details and entry blank.

SCIENCE-WRITING AWARD IN PHYSICS AND ASTRONOMY, Director, Public Relations Division, American Institute of Physics, 335 E. 45 St., New York NY 10017. A single prize of $1,500, a certificate and stainless steel Moebius strip is awarded annually to an author whose work has improved public understanding of physics and astronomy. Entries must be the work of physicists, astronomers or members of AIP member and affiliated societies. Co-sponsored by the United States Steel Foundation.

SERGEL DRAMA PRIZE, The Charles H. Sergel Drama Prize, The University of Chicago Theatre, 5706 S. University Ave., Chicago IL 60637. Awards $1,500 biennially for best original play. Write for details and entry blank. Contest deadline is July 1 of the contest year. Entry blanks are available by February of the contest year.

ANNE SEXTON POETRY PRIZE, Florida International University, Miami FL 33199. (305)552-2874. Contact: Jim Hall. Estab. 1976. Offered annually.
Purpose: For the best single poem by a woman. Submissions must be unpublished. Awards $250. Entry Deadline: October 1. Rules and entry form for SASE.

THE SMOLAR AWARD, Council of Jewish Federations and Welfare Funds, Inc., 575 Lexington Ave., New York NY 10022. Director of Communications: Frank Straum. Awards a plaque to recognize outstanding journalists in North America whose work appears in English language newspapers substantially involved in the coverage of Jewish communal affairs and issues in the United States and Canada. Write for details and required entry form.

SOCIETY OF COLONIAL WARS AWARD, Awards Committee, 122 E. 58 St., New York NY 10022. Awards bronze medallion and citation to recognize contributions of outstanding excellence in the field of literature, drama, music or art relative to colonial Americana (1607-1775).

SPECIAL OLYMPICS AWARDS. For radio and television broadcasters, newspaper and magazine reporters and feature writers, news photographers, athletes, coaches and sports organizations who during the previous calendar year have made the most distinguished contributions to local, national, or international Special Olympics program. The award is presented at an annual luncheon and consists of a specially designed award. Sponsored by Special Olympics, Inc., and The Joseph P. Kennedy, Jr. Foundation. For information write: Special Olympics Awards, Joseph P. Kennedy, Jr. Foundation, 1701 K St., N.W., Suite 205, Washington DC 20006. Established in 1973.

SPUR AWARDS, Western Writers of America, Inc., Nellie S. Yost, Secretary, 1505 West D St., North Platte NE 69101. Awards the Spur Award Trophy for the best western nonfiction book, western novel, western juvenile nonfiction book, western juvenile fiction book, western television script, motion picture script, and western short material. Write for current details and submission rules.

STANLEY DRAMA AWARD, Wagner College, Staten Island NY 10301. Awards $800 for an original full-length play or musical which has not been professionally produced or received tradebook publication. Must be recommended by a theatre professional (e.g., director, actor, agent, playwright, producer, etc.). Consideration will also be given to a series of two or three thematically connected 1-act plays. Write for application. Deadline for entry: June 1.

THOMAS L. STOKES AWARD, The Washington Journalism Center, 2401 Virginia Ave. N.W., Washington DC 20037. Awards $1,000 and a citation for the best analysis, reporting or comment appearing in a daily newspaper on the general subject of development, use and conservation of energy and other natural resources in the public interest, and protection of the environment.

WALKER STONE AWARDS, The Scripps-Howard Foundation, 200 Park Ave., New York NY 10017. President: Matt Meyer.
Purpose: "To honor outstanding achievement in the field of editorial writing. The yardstick for judging will be for general excellence, which may include quality of writing, forcefulness, and importance to the public interest." Submissions must have been published in the calendar year previous to the contest closing date. Entry deadline: February 10.

JESSE STUART CONTEST, *Seven*, 115 South Hudson, Oklahoma City OK 73102. Awards $25, $15, $10, and $5 for the best unpublished poems in the Jesse Stuart tradition; any form or free verse; any length. Write for submission details. Enclose SASE.

THEATRE ARTS CORPORATION NATIONAL PLAYWRITING CONTEST, Contest Coordinator, Box 2677, Sante Fe NM 87501. (505)982-0252. Awards $500 for original and unproduced plays in each of several categories such as plays in mime and plays for children. The contest is supported by a grant from the National Endowment for the Arts in Washington DC. Contest rules and entry form for SASE.

THE PAUL TOBENKIN MEMORIAL AWARD, Graduate School of Journalism, Columbia University, New York NY 10027. Awards $250 and a certificate for outstanding achievement in the field of newspaper writing in the fight against racial and religious hatred, intolerance, discrimination and every form of bigotry.

TRA ECLIPSE AWARDS. Award consists of an "Eclipse Trophy and $500 'added money.' " Given for outstanding newspaper writing on thoroughbred racing and outstanding magazine writing on thoroughbred racing. Sponsor: Thoroughbred Racing Associations. Contact: TRA, 3000 Marcus Ave., Lake Success NY 11040. Deadline for entry: October 31, annually. Starting date for entry: November 1, annually. Estab. 1971. No entry blank necessary. Submit copy of published article showing date of publication.

TRANSLATION CENTER AWARD, 307-A Math Bldg., Columbia University, New York NY 10027. (212)280-2305. Executive Director: Ms. Dallas Galvin. Estab. 1972. Offered annually.
Purpose: "To assist in the completion of a book of literature (a novel, stories, poems) in translation. The book must be a work in progress and the application must be accompanied by a letter of intent from an interested publisher." Submissions must be unpublished. Awards $500. Entry deadline: February 15. Contest rules and entry form for SASE.

TRANSLATION CENTER FELLOWSHIP, Translation Center, 307-A Math Bldg., Columbia University, New York NY 10027. (212)280-2305. Executive Director: Ms. Dallas Galvin. Estab. 1972. Offered annually.
Purpose: "To encourage literary translators to explore lesser known languages without economic hindrance for 1 year." Submissions may be published or unpublished. Awards $10,000. Entry deadline: January 15. Contest rules and entry form for SASE.

UNICO NATIONAL LITERARY AWARD CONTEST. Sponsored by UNICO National, Italian-American service organization. Write for details to Anthony J. Forneli, 5915 W. Irving Park Rd., Chicago IL 60634. Awards a total of $3,000 to winners. To be eligible, author must be of Italian lineage and between the ages of 18 to 35.

UNITED STATES INDUSTRIAL COUNCIL EDUCATIONAL FOUNDATION EDITORIAL AWARDS COMPETITION, Box 2686. Nashville TN 37219. Awards $100-$300 for editorials, published in a daily or weekly newspaper, which best interpret the spirit and goals of the free enterprise system in the United States and which describe and analyze the achievements of this system.

VESTA AWARDS CONTEST, American Meat Institute, P.O. Box 3556, Washington DC 20007. Awards an engraved cast bronze statuette of Vesta, mythological goddess of hearth and home, for excellence in the presentation of news about food by daily newspaper food editors and writers. The annual contest is open to any editor or writer regularly employed by a daily newspaper and who is responsible for production of pages or columns dealing with food.

VETERANS' VOICES AWARDS, Hospitalized Veterans' Writing Project, Inc., 5920 Nall, Room 117, Mission KS 66202. The Hospitalized Veterans' Writing Project, which publishes *Veterans' Voices* offers cash prizes for original unpublished articles, stories, poems, light verse, and patriotic essays by hospitalized veterans of the U.S. Armed Forces, plus poetry prizes, $5.00; prose, $10.00; special awards are Joseph Posik Award, $50.00 each edition; Gladys Feld Helzberg Poetry Award, $25.00 each edition; two Charlotte Dilling Awards given in June each year for essays on "Why a Two-Party System" or "Why the Veterans Should Vote" — $125.00 first prize — $75.00 second. Also Beginners' Awards, $5.00 extra for regular prose or poetry. Manuscripts received all year long. "All material must be submitted through a VA facility." Sample copy of *Veterans' Voices,* $1.

LUDWIG VON MISES MEMORIAL ESSAY CONTEST, Intercollegiate Studies Institute, Inc., 14 S. Bryn Mawr Ave., Bryn Mawr PA 19010. $1,000 first prize, $500 second prize, $100 each to five runners-up. Open to high school and college students. Annual contest. Write for contest entry form. Deadline: July 1.

WAGNER MEMORIAL POETRY AWARD. For details, send SASE to Wagner Memorial Award, c/o Secretary, Poetry Society of America, 15 Gramercy Park, New York NY 10003. Awards $250 for the best poem worthy of the tradition of the art, any style or length. Deadline: December 31.

EDWARD LEWIS WALLANT BOOK AWARD, Dr. Lothar Kahn, Central Connecticut College, New Britain CT 06150. Awards $125 and citation for a creative work of fiction published during the current year which has significance for the American Jew.

WATUMULL PRIZE IN THE HISTORY OF INDIA, Committee Chairman, American Historical Association, 400 A St. S.E., Washington DC 20003. Awards $1,000 biennially for the best book originally published in the United States on any phase of the history of India.

BERTHA WEISZ MEMORIAL AWARD, 16000 Terrace Rd., #208, Cleveland OH 44112. Editor: Julius Weiss. Sponsor: Weiss Philatelic-Numismatic Features. Even numbered years. Estab. 1973. Purpose: for best stamp column and coin column in a newspaper with over 50,000 circulation. Contest judged on originality, research and news of subject. Published submissions only, (and from writers, not from readers). Award: $50 Bond and plaque for both categories. Deadline: December 31 (for works published from January 1-December 1). Contest rules for SASE.

WESTERN WRITERS OF AMERICA GOLDEN SPUR AWARD, Nellie Yost, 1505 West D., North Platte NE 69101. Annual. Estab. 1952.
Categories: Best western novel; best western historical novel; best western nonfiction book; best western juvenile; best western TV show; best western film script; best western short subject (fiction or nonfiction). Published submissions only. Award: Golden Spur Award given at annual convention banquet. Deadline: December 31 (for works published in that year). Contest rules and entry form for SASE.

THE WALT WHITMAN AWARD, Sponsor, The Academy of American Poets, Inc., 1078 Madison Ave., New York NY 10028. Annual. Estab. 1974. Purpose: for a book-length (50-100 pp.) manuscript of poetry by an American citizen who has not previously published a book of poems. (The winning poet may have published a chapbook or a small edition of a book of poems, and may have published poems in magazines.) Award: $1,000 cash and publication of winning ms by a major publisher. Deadline: manuscripts received between September 15 and November 15. Send SASE in late summer for contest rules and required entry form.

THOMAS J. WILSON PRIZE, Harvard University Press, 79 Garden St., Cambridge MA 02138. Awards $500 to the author of a first book by a beginning author accepted by Harvard University Press during the calendar year and judged outstanding in content, style, and mode of presentation.

LAURENCE L. WINSHIP BOOK AWARD, The Boston Globe, Boston MA 02107. (617)929-2644. The $1,000 book award is open to books of fiction or science written by American authors and submitted by U.S. publishing companies. Books must contain a New England angle either in theme, atmosphere or origin of the author.

LeROY WOLFE COMMUNICATIONS AWARDS, Cystic Fibrosis Foundation, 3379 Peachtree Rd. N.E., Atlanta GA 30326. (404)262-1100. Contact: Public Relations Department. Annual. Estab. 1975. Awards $1,000 in each of two categories: print and broadcast. To recognize outstanding writing of published news and feature stories on cystic fibrosis and other children's lung-damaging diseases. Write for details and entry blank.

AUDREY WOOD AWARD IN PLAYWRITING, Department of Performing Arts, The American University, Massachusetts and Nebraska Aves., Washington DC 20016. (202)686-2315. Director, Theatre Program: Kenneth Baker. Estab. 1970. Annual.

Purpose: To encourage "young" unproduced and unpublished writers with a place and opportunity to have their works given a public showing. Awards $500 and production, or at least a staged reading of play. Deadline for entry: May 15. Rules and entry forms for SASE.

WORLD OF POETRY CONTEST. Sponsored by *World of Poetry,* a monthly newsletter for poets. Write for details to *World of Poetry,* Box 27507, San Francisco CA 94127. Awards a $1,500 first place prize; $500 second place; plus 49 other cash or merchandise awards. Poems of all styles and any subject matter are eligible.

CAPTAIN DONALD T. WRIGHT AWARD, Southern Illinois University, Edwardsville IL 62025. Contact: Edmund C. Hasse. Sponsor: Southern Illinois University Foundation. Annual. Estab. 1971. Purpose: for distinguished journalism in maritime transportation.
Categories: Newspaper and magazine articles; books; photos and photo essays; tapes; and videotapes and films. Published submissions only. Award: bronze plaque featuring modern and historic forms of river transportation. Deadline: August 1 (for works published within the last two years). Contest rules for SASE.

WRITER'S DIGEST CREATIVE WRITING CONTEST. Write *Writer's Digest*, 9933 Alliance Rd., Cincinnati OH 45242. (513)984-0717. Awards 300 prizes worth over $5,000 (in cash value) for the best article, short story, and poetry entries. Deadline: midnight, June 30.
Nonfiction, Fiction, and Poetry: All entries must be original, unpublished, and not previously submitted to a *Writer's Digest* contest. Length: short story, 2,000 words maximum; article, 2,500 words maximum; poetry, 16 lines maximum. Entries must be typewritten, double-spaced, on 8½x11 paper with the author's name and address in the upper left corner. An entry form must accompany each entry. Each contestant is entitled to submit one entry in each category. All entries may be submitted elsewhere after they are sent to *Writer's Digest*. No acknowledgment will be made of receipt of mss. Mss will not be returned and enclosure of SASE will disqualify the entry. Announcement of this contest is made yearly in the January through July issues of *Writer's Digest*. The grand prize winner and the top 10 entries in each category will be announced in the October issue. *Writer's Digest* retains one-time rights to the 1st, 2nd, and 3rd place entries in each category.

WRITERS GUILD OF AMERICA WEST AWARDS, Allen Rivkin, Public Relations, Writers Guild of America West, 8955 Beverly Blvd., Los Angeles CA 90048. Awards plaques in screen, television, and radio categories for best written scripts, to members only.

YOUTH MAGAZINE'S CREATIVE ARTS AWARDS, Rm. 1203, 1505 Race St., Philadelphia PA 19102. Awards $25 each to all entries selected for publication in the Creative Arts issue of *Youth*. Categories are creative writing, artwork, photography and sculpture. Entrants must be between ages of 13-19. Deadline: May 15. Contest rules for SASE.

Government Information Sources

Information and statistics on just about any subject are provided by the administrative, judicial, and legislative offices of the United States government. Often a writer can locate a fact that has eluded his library research by writing a letter to the proper government agency and asking them to supply it or suggest where it might be available. The government offices in the following listings have indicated a willingness to assist writers with research in their areas of expertise. For a more comprehensive directory of government offices, see *A Directory of Information Resources in the United States* in the Federal Government (available from the U.S. Government Printing Office, N. Capitol and H St., NW., Washington DC 20401).

Most of the agencies listed here issue booklets about their operations. Copies of these are available (often at no cost) by request, from the individual agencies. The research done by these government offices is usually published in booklet or book form by the U.S. Government Printing Office. Details on getting copies of this material are given in the entry for that office.

ACTION, 806 Connecticut Ave., N.W., Washington DC 20525. Contact: Director of Public Affairs.
Purpose: Federal agency established to administer volunteer programs in the United States and overseas. Programs include Peace Corps, VISTA, Foster Grandparent Program, Retired Senior Volunteer program, and Senior Companion program.
Services: Provides writers with photos of *ACTION* program volunteers on their assignments. Writers may also obtain copies of news releases, bibliography of Peace Corps materials, bios and photos of senior personnel, and assistance in obtaining additional information sources within the agency.

ADMINISTRATIVE CONFERENCE OF THE UNITED STATES, 2120 L St. N.W., Suite 500, Washington DC 20037. Contact: Office of Chairman. Purposes are to identify the causes of inefficiency, delay and unfairness in administrative proceedings affecting private rights and to recommend improvements to the President, the agencies, the Congress and Courts. *Volumes I, II and III* of the *Recommendations and Reports of the Administrative Conference of the U.S.*, published in July 1971, June 1973, and June 1975 respectively, contain the official texts of the recommendations adopted by the Assembly, and may be obtained from Superintendent of Documents, U.S. Government Printing Office, Washington DC.

AGRICULTURAL MARKETING SERVICE, U.S. Department of Agriculture, Washington DC 20250. Contact: Director, Information Division. Responsible for market news, standardization and grading of cotton and tobacco, marketing agreements and orders, packer and stockyard regulations, and specified regulatory programs. Provides various marketing services for nearly all agricultural commodities. Provides publications, photos, a catalog of available publications, and other assistance to writers.

AGRICULTURE, DEPARTMENT OF, Independence Ave. between 12th and 14th Sts. S.W., Washington DC 20250. (202)447-5247. Contact: Director of Governmental and Public Affairs. Directed by law to acquire and diffuse useful information on agricultural subjects in the most general and comprehensive sense. Performs functions relating to research, education, conservation, marketing, regulatory work, nutrition, food programs, and rural development.

AIR FORCE, DEPARTMENT OF THE, Established writers seeking information for use in articles concerning any aspect of the U.S. Air Force should contact its Magazine and Book Branch by writing: SAF/OIPM, The Pentagon, Room 4C914, Washington, DC 20330, or calling (202)697-4065/695-7793. This branch also provides a referral service to those authors engaged in historical research on the Air Force. The Air Force also has field offices in New York City, 663

Fifth Ave., (212)753-5609; Chicago, 219 South Dearborn Ave., Room 246-D, (312)353-8300, and Los Angeles, 11000 Wilshire Blvd., Room 10114, (213)824-7517.

AMERICAN BATTLE MONUMENTS COMMISSION, 4C014 Forrestal Bldg., 1000 Independence Ave., S.W., Washington DC 20314. Contact: Col. William E. Ryan, Jr., Director of Operations.
Purpose: "The principal functions are to commemorate the services of the American Forces where they have served since April 6, 1917; to design, construct, operate, and maintain permanent American military burial grounds."
Services: "By writing to the commission, writers may obtain reference information concerning the cemeteries, photographs, individual cemetery booklets, and a general information pamphlet which briefly lists and describes the cemeteries under our care. The commission publishes an information newsletter and periodically updates it as required. A copy of the newsletter may be obtained by writing to the commission."

AMERICAN FOREST INSTITUTE, 1619 Massachusetts Ave., N.W., Washington DC 20036. Contact: Public Information Department. Information and statistics for writers relating to America's forest resources.

AMERICAN NATIONAL RED CROSS, 17th & E Sts., NW., Washington DC., 20006. (202)737-8300. Chief, News, Magazine and Photo Section: Robert Walhay.
Purpose: "Humanitarian agency, dealing primarily in disaster relief, blood collection, processing, distribution and research, first aid, water safety and nursing, and services to the armed forces, veterans and their families."
Services: Provides writers with bibliographies, reference services, reference information, photos, etc. Publishes the bimonthly *The Good Neighbor*.

ARMY, DEPARTMENT OF THE, The Pentagon, Washington DC 20310. Contact: Office, Chief of Public Affairs.

BUREAU OF MINES, U.S. Department of the Interior, 2401 E St., N.W., Washington DC 20241. (202)634-1001. Contact: R.O. Swenarton, Chief, Office of Mineral Information.
Purpose: "(1) Research on better ways of recovering, processing, using and recycling minerals, and (2) Gathering and publication of statistical and other data on the mineral industries." Programs include mine productivity research (except coal); mine health and safety research; research on mining and the environment; research on metallurgy and nonmetallics, including recycling; industry developments, trends and forecasts for major mineral commodities, excluding fuels.
Services: Provides photos (mostly of the Bureau's own research activities) obtainable from Division of Production and Distribution, Bureau of Mines, 4800 Forbes Ave., Pittsburgh PA 15213. "Minerals and Materials—A Monthly Survey" can be obtained from the Editor, Bureau of Mines, 2401 E St., N.W., Washington, D.C. 20241. "The Bureau of Mines is a good source of information on two main subjects: Its own research programs, and non-fuel mineral industry developments and trends. Most of the Bureau's publications cover these two areas; it has very few that treat current industry practice on a relatively non-technical level (for example, we do not issue publications on "How Coal is Mined" for a high school audience). The Bureau has a staff of experts on all major mineral commodities, excluding fuels, and these specialists frequently assist authors in research projects."

CENSUS, BUREAU OF THE, U.S. Department of Commerce, Washington DC 20233. Contact: Public Information Officer. Conducts and reports results of censuses and surveys of U.S. population, housing, agriculture, business, manufacturing, mineral industries, construction, foreign trade and governments. Statistical information is available for each state, county, city, metropolitan area, and for portions of cities and metropolitan areas in the U.S. 17 brochures in the *Factfinder for the Nation* series are available providing information on each of the 12 subject areas of the Census Bureau plus other topics such as census geography and minority statistics. The entire set is available for $3.25 from the Subscriber Services Section (Publications), Washington DC 20233.

CENTER FOR DISEASE CONTROL, 1600 Clifton Rd., N.E., Atlanta GA 30333. Contact: Donald A. Berreth, Director, Office of Information.
Purpose: "*CDC* is one of six agencies of the U.S. Public Health Service. It is responsible for surveillance and control of communicable and vector-borne diseases, occupational safety and

health, family planning, birth defects, lead-based paint poisoning, urban rat control, and health education. Programs include epidemic and/disease outbreaks, foreign travel (health recommendations and requirements), international activities, training of foreign health workers, etc."
Services: "*CDC* provides reference and background materials and photographs on communicable diseases and other subjects. Publishes the *Morbidity and Mortality Weekly Report* and *Surveillance Reports*. Mailing lists are maintained and anyone may request these publications."

CIVIL SERVICE COMMISSION, 1900 E St. N.W., Washington DC 20415. Contact: Office of Public Affairs. Administers the civil service merit system and is responsible for competitive examinations for entry into Federal civil service. Library at central office of Commission in Washington DC is outstanding location for research in personnel management. Material does not circulate.

COPYRIGHT OFFICE, Library of Congress, Washington DC 20559. Contact: Office of Information and Publications. Registers claims to copyright and provides copyright searches, free circulars on copyright subjects, and other related services.

DEFENSE CIVIL PREPAREDNESS AGENCY, Information Services, Defense Civil Preparedness Agency, The Pentagon, Washington DC 20301. Contact: Vincent A. Otto, Assistant Director, Information Services. Purpose is to prepare the nation to cope with the effects of nuclear attack and to help state and local governments plan and prepare to cope with these effects. An extensive file of disaster photos and movies regarding disasters and emergency preparedness available. Information for the general public is available from state or local civil preparedness agencies, and also directly from above address.

DEFENSE, DEPARTMENT OF, Room 2E773, Acquisitions Branch, A-V Division, The Pentagon, Washington DC 20301. Contact: Magazines and Books, Office of the Assistant Secretary of Defense for Public Affairs. Assists magazine and book editors and writers in gathering information about the Department of Defense and its components.

DEFENSE LOGISTICS AGENCY, Cameron Sta., Alexandria VA 22314. Contact: Chester C. Spurgeon, Special Assistant for Public Affairs. Responsible for supply support to the Military Services, administration of defense contracts and various other logistics services. Will provide writers with information on Defense Logistics Agency areas of activity. *Introduction to the Defense Logistics Agency* available upon request.

ECONOMIC ANALYSIS, BUREAU OF, U.S. Department of Commerce, Washington DC 20230. Contact: Public Information Officer. Provides basic economic measures of the national economy (such as gross national product), current analysis of economic situation and business outlook, and general economic research on the functioning of the economy.

ENERGY, DEPARTMENT OF, Washington DC 20461. Contact: Office of Public Affairs.

ENVIRONMENTAL PROTECTION AGENCY, Washington DC 20460. Contact: Public Information Center (PM215). Available literature includes popular booklets and leaflets on water and air pollution, solid waste management, radiation and pesticides control, as well as noise abatement and control. 16mm color films on pollution control and photos of pollution problems available by contacting Communications Division of Office of Public Affairs at above address.

FARM CREDIT ADMINISTRATION, 490 L'Enfant Plaza S.W., Washington DC 20578. (202)755-2170. Contact: Public Affairs Division. Responsible for the supervision and coordination of activities of the farm credit system, which consists of federal land banks and federal land bank associations, federal intermediate credit banks and production credit associations, and banks for cooperatives. Writers should confine areas of questions to agricultural finance and farm credit.

FEDERAL COMMUNICATIONS COMMISSION, 1919 M St., N.W., Washington DC 20554. Contact: Samuel M. Sharkey Jr., Public Information Officer.
Purpose: Regulation of all forms of telecommunications, broadcasting, cable, common carrier (telephone, telegraph, satellite), CB, safety or special radio.
Services: All material, except for certain special information (trade secrets, etc.) is available for public inspection. Does not do research for writers. Detailed material is available in FCC public reference rooms in Washington D.C.

FEDERAL JUDICIAL CENTER, Dolley Madison House, 1520 H St. N.W., Washington DC 20005. Contact: Mrs. Sue Welsh, Information Service. Purpose is to further the development and adoption of improved judicial administration in the courts of the United States. Information Service collection consists of books, articles, and periodicals in the field. Reference services and a few bibliographies are available. *The Third Branch*, free monthly newsletter of the federal courts, is also available. Information Service open to the public for research purposes and written requests, within the realm of jurisdiction, will be answered, with first priority to federal judicial personnel.

FEDERAL LAW ENFORCEMENT TRAINING CENTER, Glynco GA 31520. (912)267-2447. Public Information Officer: William M. Allen Jr.
Purpose: "The Federal Law Enforcement Training Center is a bureau of the Department of the Treasury which serves as an inter-agency training center for Federal police officers and investigators. The Center provides basic training for new officers and investigators from more than 30 Federal Law enforcement organizations. In addition, the Center provides administrative and logistical support for the organizations to conduct advanced and specialized training required to meet their individual needs."
Services: Photos, brochures and other descriptive printed material is available to writers. Material may be obtained by contacting the Center Public Information Office. "The Center Public Information Office will be happy to provide all available assistance to writers."

FEDERAL MEDIATION AND CONCILIATION SERVICE, 2100 K St., N.W., Washington DC 20427. Contact: John Rogers, Assistant Director of Information. Purpose is settlement and prevention of labor-management disputes. Collective bargaining is the general subject of programs. Brochures and annual reports are available.

FEDERAL POWER COMMISSION, 825 N. Capitol St. N.E., Washington DC 20426. Contact: William L. Webb, Director of Public Information. Regulation of interstate aspects of natural gas and electric power industries, and licensing of non-Federal hydroelectric power projects. FPC will provide, free of charge, lists of publications and special reports, and general information on regulatory activities. Media representatives may also receive, upon request, a complimentary copy of non-subscription items on the publications list.

FEDERAL TRADE COMMISSION, Sixth St. and Pennsylvania Ave. N.W., Washington DC 20580. (202)523-3600. Contact: Public Reference Branch. The Commission is a law enforcement agency whose mission is to protect the public (consumers and businessmen) against abuses caused by unfair competition and unfair and deceptive business practices; to guide and counsel businessmen, consumers, and federal, state, and local officials, promoting understanding among them and encouraging voluntary compliance with trade laws. Will assist a researcher with reprints, copies of speeches, or other documents pertinent to his subject. Most helpful when a writer's questions are specific rather than general. Publications available include *News Summary*, a weekly roundup of news stories emanating from the Commission.

FISH AND WILDLIFE SERVICE, Room 3240, Interior Bldg., Washington DC 20240. Contact: Office of Public Affairs.

FOOD AND DRUG ADMINISTRATION, 5600 Fishers Lane, Rockville MD 20857. Contact: Wayne Pines, Chief, Press Relations.
Purpose: "To protect consumers in the areas of food (except meat and poultry); medicines, cosmetics, medical devices, biologicals, and electronic equipment emitting radiation."
Services: Press releases available; writers can get on mailing list by writing to the above address. Brochures available on many subjects. Publishes *FDA Consumer* magazine, available by subscription through the Government Printing Office.

FOREST SERVICE, USDA, Box 2417, Washington DC 20013. (202)447-4211. Press Officer: Diane O'Connor.
Purpose: "Forest Service is dedicated to the principles of multiple-use management of the nation's forest resources for sustained yields of water, forage, wildlife, wood and recreation. Through management of the national forests and national grasslands, cooperation with states and private forest owners and forestry research, it strives, as directed by Congress, to provide increasingly greater service to a growing nation."
Services: Provides writers with reference services, reference information, photos, news releases, etc.

GENERAL SERVICES ADMINISTRATION, 19th and F Sts. N.W., Washington DC 20405. Contact: Public Information Officer, (202)566-1231. The General Services Administration (GSA) establishes policy and provides for an economical and efficient system for the management of federal property and records, including construction and operation of buildings, procurement and distribution of supplies, utilization and disposal of property, transportation, traffic and communications management, stockpiling of strategic materials and management of government-wide Automated Data Processing resources program. Writers interested in obtaining government contracts should contact any one of GSA's 13 Business Service Centers across the country for information.

INTERIOR, DEPARTMENT OF THE, Interior Bldg., Washington DC 20240. Contact: Director of Public Affairs. The nation's principal conservation agency, with responsibilities for energy, water, fish, wildlife, mineral, land, park, and recreational resources, and Indian and territorial affairs. Requests for information should be directed to the office most concerned with specific subjects of interest. See listings for individual bureaus and agencies to locate the best source for information.

INTERSTATE COMMERCE COMMISSION, 12th and Constitution Ave., Washington DC 20423. (202)275-7301. Contact: Public Information Office. Has regulatory responsibility for interstate surface transportation by railroads, trucks, buses, barges, coastal shipping, oil pipe lines, express companies, freight forwarders, and transportation brokers. Jurisdiction includes rates, mergers, operating rights, and issuance of securities. Free list of publications available.

JUSTICE, DEPARTMENT OF, Office of Public Information, 10th St. & Constitution Ave., NW, Room 5114, Washington DC 20530. (202)739-2007. Director, Public Information: Marvin D. Wall. Deputy Director, Public Information: Robert J. Havel.
Purpose: "As the largest law firm in the Nation, the Department of Justice serves as counsel for its citizens. It represents them in enforcing the law in the public interest. Through its thousands of lawyers, investigators, and agents, the Department plays the key role in protection against criminals and subversion, in ensuring healthy competition of business against criminals and subversion, in ensuring healthy competition of business in our free enterprise system, in safeguarding the consumer, and in enforcing drug, immigration, and naturalization laws. The Department also plays a significant role in protecting citizens through its efforts for effective law enforcement, crime prevention, crime detention, and prosecution and rehabilitation of offenders."

LABOR, UNITED STATES DEPARTMENT OF, 3rd and Constitution Ave. N.W., Washington DC 20210. Contact: Office of Information, Publications and Reports.

LAND MANAGEMENT, BUREAU OF, U.S. Department of the Interior. Washington DC 20240. Office of Public Affairs provides information and photos on the management of 473 million acres of National Resource Lands (Public Domain) mostly in 10 western states and Alaska; on forest, range, water, wildlife, and recreation resources; on resource uses including camping, hunting, fishing, hiking, rock-hunting, off-road vehicle use; and on primitive, historic, natural and scenic areas.

LIBRARY OF CONGRESS, Washington DC 20540. Serves as a research arm of Congress and as the national library of the U.S. Maintains reading rooms open to scholars for research on the premises. Provides bibliographic and reference information by mail only in cases where individuals have exhausted library resources of their own region. Such reference information should be sought from the General Reference and Bibliography Division. Free list of Library of Congress publications can be obtained from the Central Services Division. Photoduplicates of materials in the collections (not subject to copyrights or other restrictions) are available at set fees from the Photoduplication Service.

MANAGEMENT AND BUDGET, OFFICE OF, Old Executive Office Bldg., Washington DC 20503. Contact: Information Office.

NATIONAL ACADEMY OF SCIENCES, NATIONAL ACADEMY OF ENGINEERING, NATIONAL RESEARCH COUNCIL, INSTITUTE OF MEDICINE, 2101 Constitution Ave. N.W., Washington DC 20418. Contact: Office of Information. A private organization which acts as an official, but independent adviser to the Federal government in matters of science and technology. For writers on assignment, the Academies often can be helpful by identifying authorities in various scientific disciplines and sometimes by providing state-of-the-art reports on broad scientific and environmental subjects prepared by their committees.

NATIONAL AERONAUTICS AND SPACE ADMINISTRATION, Washington DC 20546. Contact: Public Information Office. Principal functions are to conduct research for the solution of problems of flight within and outside the earth's atmosphere and develop, construct, test, and operate aeronautical and space vehicles; conduct activities required for the exploration of space with manned and unmanned vehicles; arrange for most effective utilization of scientific and engineering resources of the United States with other nations engaged in aeronautical and space activities for peaceful purposes; provide for widest practicable and appropriate dissemination of information concerning NASA's activities and their results.

NATIONAL ARCHIVES AND RECORDS SERVICE, Pennsylvania Ave. at 8th St. N.W., Washington DC 20408. Contact: Public Information Officer. The National Archives is the repository for permanently valuable, official records of the U.S. Government. All treaties, laws, proclamations, executive orders, and bills are retained. It is also authorized to accept some private papers which deal with goverment transactions. Administering all presidential libraries from Herbert Hoover to Lyndon Johnson and 15 Federal Records centers across the nation, the National Archives was created to serve the government, scholars, writers, and students. Among its holdings are sound recordings, motion pictures, still pictures, and some artifacts.

NATIONAL CREDIT UNION ADMINISTRATION, 2025 M St., NW, Washington DC 20456. Administrator: Lawrence Connell.
Purpose: "NCUA is a Federal regulatory agency responsible for chartering, supervising, examining and insuring some 13,000 Federal credit unions and for providing federal share insurance to qualifying State credit unions requesting it. Reference services are not available, although a specific request may be honored if the information is at hand. NCUA publications available, upon request, include: *Annual Report of the Administration, Your Insured Funds, NCUA Research Report, Administrator's Letter,* and *NCUA Quarterly.*"

NATIONAL FIRE PREVENTION AND CONTROL ADMINISTRATION, U.S. Department of Commerce, Washington DC 20230. Contact: Peg Maloy, Director of Information Services.
Purpose: "To reduce human and property losses from fire, in the United States, by half, within a generation. Programs include fire prevention and control through the National Academy for Fire Prevention and Control; The National Fire Safety and research Office; the National Fire Data Center; and the Public Education Office."
Services: Publishes a monthly newsletter, *Fireword,* bulletins, news releases, public education materials, brochures, reports (such as *Arson; America's Malignant Crime*), annual reports, annual conference proceedings, etc.

NATIONAL MARINE FISHERIES SERVICE, National Oceanic and Atmospheric Administration, Department of Commerce, Washington DC 20235. Contact: Public Affairs Office. Biological and technical research, market promotion programs, statistical facts on commercial fisheries, marine game fish, and economic studies are the responsibilities of this Service.

NATIONAL PARK SERVICE, Room 3043, Interior Bldg., Washington DC 20240. (202)343-7394. Contact: Office of Communications, Tom Wilson, Director. Provides information on more than 290 areas of National Park System which the Service administers. Information available includes park acreage and attendance statistics; data on camping, swimming, boating, mountain climbing, hiking, fishing, winter activities, wildlife research and management, history, archaeology, nature walks, and scenic features. Photos of many areas and activities are available. To obtain publications, contact Division of Public Inquiries, Room 1013, Interior Bldg.; to obtain photos, contact Photo Library, Room 8060, Interior Bldg.

NATIONAL RAILROAD PASSENGER CORPORATION (AMTRAK), 400 N. Capital St., Washington DC., 20001. (202)484-7220. Director of Public Information: Brian Duff.
Purpose: "We are a nationwide intercity rail passenger service. We serve over 500 communities on a 26,000 mile network."
Services: "Press releases, background material, photographs, 35mm slides, ridership and other statistical information may be obtained by writing to Amtrak Public Affairs. The company publishes an annual report in February, a five year plan in October, a monthly ridership/one-

time performance report, and press releases and background material as needed. Writers who regularly cover transportation or travel may request to be added to the mailing list for the above publications.

NATIONAL TECHNICAL INFORMATION SERVICE, 5285 Port Royal Rd., Springfield VA 22161. (703)557-4600.
Purpose: "NTIS is an information service organization. It promotes the general welfare by channeling information about technological innovations and other specialized information to business, industry, government, and the public. Its products and services are intended to increase the efficiency and effectiveness of the US research and development enterprise, to support US foreign policy goals by assisting the social and economic development of other nations, and to increase the availability of foreign technical information in the US. NTIS undertakes and develops products and programs having the potential for self-support and which are appropriate for government, instead of private enterprise. NTIS information covers science, technology, social sciences, administration, urban planning, health, law, business, and dozens of other categories. NTIS services include: help in location of useful reports through published searches and on-line computer search service; lease of the NTIS Bibliographic data file (on magnetic tape); and current summaries of new research reports in 26 abstract newsletters—each devoted to a different subject (usually published weekly); Selected Research in Microfiche SRIM, automatically sends subscribers full texts of new research reports in their selected field of interest."

NATIONAL TRANSPORTATION SAFETY BOARD, 800 Independence Ave., S.W., Washington DC 20591. Responsibility of this agency is the investigation and cause determination of transportation accidents and the initiation of corrective measures. Work is about 80% in the field of aviation; balance is in selected cases involving highways, railroad, pipeline, and marine accidents. Provides writers with accident reports, special studies involving transportation safety. Case history details of all cases available for review are in the Public Inquiry Section of the Safety Board in Washington DC.

NATIONAL WEATHER SERVICE, National Oceanic and Atmospheric Administration, Department of Commerce, 8060 13th St., Silver Spring MD 20910. Contact: Public Affairs Officer. Reports the weather of the U.S. and its possessions, provides weather forecasts to the general public, and issues warnings against tornadoes, hurricanes, floods, and other weather hazards. Develops and furnishes specialized information which supports the needs of agricultural, aeronautical, maritime, space, and military operations. Some 300 Weather Service offices in cities across the land maintain close contact with the general public to ensure prompt and useful dissemination of weather information. Agency publications may be purchased from Superintendent of Documents, U.S. Government Printing Office, Washington DC 20402.

NUCLEAR REGULATORY COMMISSION, Washington DC 20555. Contact: Office of Public Affairs.

OCCUPATIONAL SAFETY AND HEALTH REVIEW COMMISSION, 1825 K St. N.W., Washington DC 20006. (202)634-7943. Contact: Linda Dodd, Director of Information. An independent agency of the executive branch of the government. Functions as a court by adjudicating contested cases under the Occupational Safety and Health Act of 1970. Operates under the mandates of the Freedom of Information Act. Its files are open to anyone who wishes to inspect them. Publishes press releases, *Rules of Procedure,* and a layman's "Guide to the Procedures of OSHR." Information available on written request.

OUTDOOR RECREATION, BUREAU OF, Department of the Interior, Washington DC 20240. Contact: Office of Communications. Serves as Federal coordinator of public and private outdoor recreation programs and activities; as administrator of the Land and Water Conservation Fund; as conveyor of Federal surplus properties to state and local governments for public recreation use. Provides information on national and statewide outdoor recreation planning; assistance available from other government and private sources; the L&WCF's Federal recreation land acquisition and state grant programs; Congressionally authorized resource studies for potential Federal recreation areas including national trails, wild and scenic rivers, lakeshores and seashores, Federal off-road vehicle regulations; Federal recreation area fee system; and sources of technical assistance, literature and research on outdoor recreation.

PATENT AND TRADEMARK OFFICE, U.S. Department of Commerce, Washington DC

20231. Contact: Public Information Officer. Administers the patent and trademark laws, examines applications, and grants patents when applicants are entitled to them under the law. Publishes and disseminates patent information, maintains search files of U.S. and foreign patents and a Patent Search Room for public use, and supplies copies of patents and official records to the public. Performs similar functions relating to trademarks.

RECLAMATION, BUREAU OF, U.S. Department of the Interior, Public Affairs Service Center, Denver Federal Center, Denver CO 80225. Contact: Editor.
Purpose: "Operating in the 17 western states, the Bureau of Reclamation is responsible for water resource development. The agency conserves and supplies irrigation water, avails such water for hydroelectric power, recreation, municipal and industrial use, fish and wildlife enhancement, flood control, and other related uses of water."
Services: "Writers may obtain information services by writing the Public Affairs Service Center. Requests for photographs should be addressed to Bureau Photography Coordinator. Publishes pamphlets about various projects which might be useful to writers. These may be obtained by writing to the Bureau of Reclamation, Code 900.

SECRET SERVICE, 1800 G St. N.W., Washington DC 20223. Contact: Office of Public Affairs.

SECURITIES AND EXCHANGE COMMISSION, 500 N. Capitol St., Washington DC 20549. Contact: Office of Public Information.
Purpose: "To administer the securities laws, which have two basic objectives: (1) to provide investors with financial material and other information on securities and (2) to prohibit fraud in the sale of securities."
Services: Bibliographies of Commissioners are available. Write for Publications List.

SENATE, Senate Office Bldg., Washington DC 20510.

SMITHSONIAN INSTITUTION, 1000 Jefferson Dr., SW., Washington DC 20560. (202)381-6218. Contact: Office of Public Affairs.
Purpose: "The Smithsonian is an independent trust establishment which conducts scientific and scholarly research and administers the national collections in numerous museums with exhibits representative of the arts, American history and technology, natural history, and aeronautics and space explorations."
Services: B&w prints and color transparencies representing the Smithsonian's collections are available from Photograpic services, Smithsonian Institution, Washington DC 20560. The Office of Public Affairs publishes a detailed booklet entitled "Increase and Diffusion" on Smithsonian history and general bureau activities as well as a general information leaflet on what visitors can see in each museum. *Smithsonian Institution Research Reports* is an 8-page newsletter issued quarterly with articles on scientific research conducted by Smithsonian staff and is available from the Office of Public Affairs.

SOCIAL SECURITY ADMINISTRATION, 6401 Security Blvd., Baltimore MD 21235. (301)592-1200. Contact: Michael Naver, Press Officer. Administers the Federal retirement, survivors, and disability insurance programs and health insurance for the aged and certain severely disabled people (Medicare) and a program of supplemental security income for aged, blind, and disabled people. Publications on all social security programs are available free of charge from any social security office, or from the Office of Information, above address. Writers may also obtain statistical and historical information, news releases, photos, biographies of top SSA officials, and other information materials. Cannot provide information about any individual social security record or beneficiary. Under the law, all social security records are confidential.

SOIL CONSERVATION SERVICE, U.S. Department of Agriculture, Box 2890, Washington DC 20013. (202)447-4543. Contact: Hubert Kelley, Director, Information Division. Purpose is to help landowners and operators to use their land and water in the best possible manner. Assists local groups with flood, drought, excessive sedimentation, or other water problems. Main concerns are soil, water, plant, and wildlife conservation; flood prevention; better use of water by individuals and communities; improvement of rural communities through better use of natural resources, and preservation of prime farmland. In addition to material of interest to the agricultural and outdoor media, also has work in urban and educational fields that offer article possibilities. "We provide writers with background materials on all phases of our work; arrange interviews; provide b&w and color photographs. For information, write above address. We publish a variety of general and technical publications on practically all aspects of our programs and on soil and water conservation. Single copies are available without charge from Publications Unit, Information Division, Soil Conservation Service.

SOUTHEASTERN POWER ADMINISTRATION, U.S. Department of Energy, Samuel Elbert Bldg., Elberton GA 30635. (404)283-3261. Contact: Miss Mary George Bond, Chief, Division of Administrative Management. Responsible for transmission and disposition of electrical energy generated at reservoir projects under the control of the Corps of Engineers in the southeastern U.S., and for water resources development. Will answer inquiries from writers regarding the bureau.

STANDARDS, NATIONAL BUREAU OF, U.S. Department of Commerce, Washington DC 20234. (301)921-3181. Contact: Chief, Office of Information Activities. The nation's central measurement laboratory, charged with maintaining and refining the standards and technology on which our measurement system is based. Covers the entire spectrum of the physical and engineering sciences. Provides the technical base for federal programs in environmental management, consumer protection, health, and other areas. Bureau publications are available through the U.S. Government Printing Office.

SUPREME COURT, No. 1 First St. N.E., Washington DC 20543. (202)252-3211. Contact: Barrett McGurn, Director of Public Information.

TENNESSEE VALLEY AUTHORITY, 400 Commerce Ave., E12A4 C-K, Knoxville TN 37902. Contact: Louis J. Van Mol Jr., Director of Information.
Purpose: "Regional resource development, including economic development, resource conservation and environmental protection, electric power production, waterway development, flood control, agriculture, recreation, fish and wildlife, forestry."
Services: Information available on TVA activities in all these fields. Occasional press tours are conducted for regional and national media representatives. Also, interviews and visits to TVA projects can be arranged for interested writers. Publishes *Tennessee Valley Perspective,* a quarterly employee magazine, and *Annual Report,* an various information bulletins on specific programs.

TERRITORIAL AFFAIRS, OFFICE OF, C St. between 18th and 19th N.W., Washington DC 20240. Contact: Director of Territorial Affairs.

TRANSPORTATION, U.S. DEPARTMENT OF, 400 7th St. S.W., Washington DC 20590. Contact: Office of Public Affairs, S-80. "We can supply limited photos and reference material, but we can usually put the writer in touch with the right people in the Department."

TREASURY DEPARTMENT, Room 2313, 15th St. and Pennsylvania Ave. N.W., Washington DC 20220. Contact: Public Information Office.

UNITED STATES CIVIL SERVICE COMMISSION, 1900 E St., N.W., Washington DC 20415. Contact: Director, Office of Public Affairs.
Purpose: "To administer a merit system of Federal employment. Programs include recruiting and examining, personnel investigations, equal employment opportunity, employee development and training, incentive awards, personnel management, employee benefits, intergovernmental personnel programs."
Services: Address inquiries to the Director, Office of Public Affairs. *OPA* will either respond directly, or direct inquiry to appropriate bureau or office within the commission. Publishes *The Civil Service Journal,* a quarterly for Federal and other managers; *The First Line,* a bimonthly newsletter for Federal supervisors; *The Federal News Clip Sheet,* a monthly news clip sheet for editors of Federal employees' newsletters, among others. "There are so many possible topics and approaches, it would be best to deal separately with each idea. Write or call the Office of Public Affairs, talk it over informally with an information specialist, get comments, suggestions, sources, etc., applicable to that idea."

US COMMISSION ON CIVIL RIGHTS, 1121 Vermont Ave., NW., Washington DC 20425. (202)254-6697. Director of Public Affairs: Joan Larson Kelly.
Purpose: "The Commission is an independent, bipartisan, fact-finding agency established by Congress. It appraises laws and policies concerned with the civil rights of minorities and women and makes recommendations to the President and Congress."

Services: "We can provide writers with copies of press releases on studies we have done on civil rights. Studies are available at no charge by writing the Publications Division of the Commission."

U.S. GEOLOGICAL SURVEY (Department of the Interior), National Center, Reston VA 22092. (703)860-7444. Contact: Frank H. Forrester, Information Officer.
Purpose: "Major Federal earth science research agency. Through field and lab studies and investigations, obtains fundamental data and makes assessments of the nation's mineral, energy, and water resources. Programs include resource estimates, mapping, studies of surface and ground water, supervision of leases on Federal lands, studies of geologic hazards (earthquakes, volcanoes, landslides, subsidence and glaciers)."
Services: "Our Information Office provides news media services: press releases, backgrounders, news photos, arranges interviews, etc." Publishes no periodicals or newsletters; however a variety of nontechnical leaflets are available, and writers may request press release mailings. "We would be pleased to receive inquiries from any writer on general earth science subjects, including natural resources and environmental monitoring."

U.S. GOVERNMENT PRINTING OFFICE, North Capitol and H Sts., N.W., Washington DC 20401. Contact: David H. Brown, Special Assistant to the Public Printer.
Purpose: Printing and binding services for the Congress, Judicial and Executive branches of the Federal Government; distribution of 25,000 titles of Federal documents to the public. Programs include printing production and innovations; mail order sales program.
Services: "Reference materials or information, etc., can be provided on an individual request basis. Writers may obtain Federal reference publications on a broad range of subjects—available through mail order or in 24 bookstores throughout the country."

UNITED STATES INTERNATIONAL TRADE COMMISSION, 701 E. St., NW., Washington DC 20436. (202)532-0161. Assistant Secretary, Public Information Officer: Hal Sundstrom.
Purpose: "An independent, important fact-finding federal agency, the United States International Trade Commission is empowered by statute to conduct on matters relating to international trade either on its own initiative, or at the request of the President, the Committee on Finance of the US Senate or the Committee on Ways and Means of the US House of Representatives."
Services: "Writers researching specific trade investigations, past or present, may use the resources of the Office of the Secretary, including examination of pertinent documents but excluding confidential material. The agency publishes an annual report, a monthly newsletter, and periodic publications containing the views of the Commissioners and information developed in its investigations. Copies may be obtained from the Office of the Secretary."

U.S. SAVINGS BONDS DIVISION, Department of the Treasury, Washington DC 20226. (202)634-5377. Contact: Carolyn Johnston, Director, Public Affairs Office.
Purpose: "To promote the sale and retention of U.S. Savings Bonds, to help the United States government finance its debts in the least inflationary way possible and to encourage savings."
Services: "Services offered to the extent money and time will allow. For specific, local information on the bond program, writers may contact the state savings bonds director." Publishes informational leaflets, quick reference guides. "The Office of Public Affairs, Savings Bonds, will be happy to work with writers who have specific informational requests."

VETERANS ADMINISTRATION, 810 Vermont Ave. N.W., Washington DC 20420. Contact: Information Service 063. Administers laws authorizing benefits principally for former members and certain dependents of former members of the Armed Forces. Major VA programs include medical care and research, education and training, compensation, pension, loan guaranty, certain death benefits, rehabilitation, and insurance. Information is available at 58 VA regional offices and 172 hospitals. Specialized pamphlets describing individualized VA benefits are available free from VA.

WOMEN'S BUREAU, Employment Standards Administration, U.S. Department of Labor, 200 Constitution Ave., N.W., Washington DC 20210. (202)523-6654. Contact: Information Officer.
Purpose: "To formulate standards and policies which shall promote welfare of wage-earning women, improve their working conditions, increase their efficiency, and advance their opportunities for profitable employment." Programs include sex discrimination in training and employment, nontraditional jobs for women, special needs of low-income women, minorities, youth, women offenders.

Services: ''Supplies its own statistical and other studies, bibliographies and a limited number of photos of women in work situations. Single copies of all materials are available upon request.''

Picture Sources

Libraries, museums, public relations agencies, and other organizations offer free use of photos or charge only a modest fee. In addition, stock photo companies and agencies representing groups of photographers have photographs filed by subject on almost every conceivable topic. Fees for the one-time use of such photographs may vary from $25 for a b&w photograph to several hundred dollars for the one-time reproduction of a color transparency.

Another source for photography (stock or "to order") is the membership of ASMP —The Society of Photographers in Communications. Some members are included below, and a complete list appears in the ASMP Membership Directory, which gives the name, address, and specialties of over 700 professional photographers. It is available from ASMP, 60 East 42nd St., New York NY 10017.

Writers seeking further details from any of the sources below should be sure to enclose an SASE with their inquiry.

Several of the photo agencies say they charge "ASMP rates." These are minimum fees set by ASMP as a basis for negotiation, and actual charges may be higher, depending on use. For a practical, complete guide to ASMP rates and policies, *Business Practices and Photography Guide* is available from ASMP for $5.

ASMP also sets minimum fees for member photographers working on a day rate. These are outlined in the Membership Directory.

Remember that the following listings are for agencies and institutions whose main concern is the *supplying* of photographs to writers and others. For a major directory of markets for your photography see *Photographer's Market* available from *Writer's* Digest Books.

ALASKA PICTORIAL SERVICE, Box 6144, Anchorage AK 99502. (907)344-1370. Contact: Steve McCutcheon. 60,000 b&w, 70,000 color. "All subjects pertaining to Alaska from geomorphology to politics, from scenery to ethnical. We do not ship to individuals: only to recognized business firms, publishing houses, AV productions, governmental bodies, etc." B&w and color. Reproduction rights offered depend upon type of rights the publisher wishes or the advertising agency requires. Fees: minimum $50 b&w; minimum $150 color. "We do not charge a service or search fee unless the project has been cancelled, then only minimum ($15-50) depending upon the time the search required and the cost of transportation. We will accept certain types of assignments."

J.C. ALLEN AND SON, Box 2061, West Lafayette IN 47906. (317)463-9614. Managers: John O. Allen or Chester Allen. 50,000 b&w and 12,000 color photos. "Our file of black and white agricultural illustrations was started by J.C. Allen in 1912. Most of our photos have been produced in the Corn Belt States, but we have made illustrations in travel from coast to coast. We add many new illustrations of farm crops and farm animals to our collection each year." Offers editorial, advertising and reproduction rights. Charges $25-75 for b&w one-time editorial or advertising use; $50-250 for color.

ALPHA PHOTOS ASSOCIATES, 251 Park Ave. S., New York NY 10010. Manager: Ann Schrieber. One million photos in "almost every conceivable category." Offers "any rights client is willing to purchase. Pictures can even be bought for outright purchase if desired." Fees depend on use.

ALPINE PHOTOGRAPHY, Box 731, Ephraim UT 84627. (801)283-4526. Contact: Lee Miller. 5,000 photos on file on purchase basis for all rights.
Subjects: Nature, scenics, scientific, snow crystals, winter recreation, farming, ranching, livestock, outdoor life, avalanches and snowslides. B&w (8x10) and 35mm color transparencies.

Reproduction fee: $5-500. Prints made to order/$1-35.

ALUMINUM COMPANY OF AMERICA, Alcoa Building, Pittsburgh PA 15219. Contact: A.T. Post, Manager, Financial Communication. Many thousands of photos in "color and b&w on practically everything concerning aluminum—mining, refining, smelting, fabricating, products, uses, etc." Offers worldwide rights. No fees.

THE AMERICAN MUSEUM OF NATURAL HISTORY, Photography Department, Central Park West at 79th St., New York NY 10024. The Photography Department has a library of about 16,000 color transparencies and over 500,000 b&w negatives available for reproduction. Collection includes anthropology, archaeology, primitive art, botany, geology, mineralogy, paleontology, zoology, and some astronomy. Fees and other information will be supplied on request.

AMERICAN PETROLEUM INSTITUTE, 2101 L St., N.W., Washington DC 20037. Contact: Earl A. Ross, Manager, Print Media. Photos pertaining to petroleum. B&w glossies. For non-commercial, non-advertising use only. Credit line required.

AMERICAN STOCK PHOTOS, 6842 Sunset Blvd., Hollywood CA 90028. (213)469-3908. Contact: Al Greene or Yvonne Binder. Nearly 2 million photos. "All subjects: contemporary and historical. Mostly b&w; some color transparencies 4x5 or larger." Offers any rights desired. Only restrictions are limited to previous sales; i.e., 1 year calendar exclusive. Fees: "based on public exposure. $25 minimum."

AMERICAN TRUCKING ASSOCIATIONS, INC., 1616 P St., N.W., Washington DC 20036. (202)797-5236. Contact: News Service Department, Media and Public Relations Division. B&w photographs of different types of trucks (twin trailers, auto carrier, livestock, etc.) and trucks in various situations (traffic, urban, night, etc.). Limited number of color prints available for non-commercial use only. No fees but credit line and return of pictures required. (Pictures not available for advertising purposes.)

ANIMALS ANIMALS, 203 W. 81st St., New York NY 10024. (212)580-9595. Contact: Nancy Henderson. "Hundreds of thousands of pictures of animals from all over the world in their natural habitat in color and in b&w. Mammals, reptiles, amphibians, fish, birds, invertibrates, horses, dogs, cats, etc. One-time use, world rights, foreign language. Service fee of $35 if no sale is made—applicable only on lengthy requests. All uses, if unusual, are negotiable. We follow the ASMP guidelines."

BARBARA ANTON, INC., 10 Engle St., Englewood NJ 07631. (201)871-3989. President: Barbara Anton. Photos of gemstones in jewelry, jewelry by award winning designers and designer Anton wearing her jewelry. Material is in the public domain.

APPEL COLOR PHOTOGRAPHY, Twin Lakes WI 52181. (414)877-2303. Contact: Thomas E. Appel. "Nations' largest producer and seller of outdoor color photography, stocking the nation's largest independent collection of color photographs. Will sell any rights. Coverage is national, plus some foreign, with 4-season representation. Stock nearly everything. Examples: outdoor sports (all facets), participant and spectator sports, wildlife, children and family activities, young adults, girls, historicals and points of interest, national parks and monuments, lighthouses, grist mills, bridges, famous houses, churches (including America's oldest), landscapes, farms, gardens, flowers, waterfalls, sunsets, mountains, rivers and lakes, harbors, snow, tourism, industry, food, still lifes, collectibles, fireworks, boating, and over a score of 12-picture theme sets." Return required. Fees vary upon use and nature of publication.

ARIZONA PHOTOGRAPHIC ASSOCIATES' INC., 2350 W. Holly, Phoenix AZ 85009. (602)258-6551. Contact: Dorothy McLaughlin. Over 250,000 photos available for purchase. Reproduction rights, advertising rights, first rights, second rights, editorial rights and all rights available. A collection from A-Z (animals-zoo) at ASMP code of minimum rates.

ART REFERENCE BUREAU INC., Box 137, Ancram NY 12502. Contact: Janet L. Snow. Have "access to over a million subjects in Europe: painting, sculpture, graphics, architecture, archaeology, artifacts principally from European locations. B&w glossy photos may be purchased. Color transparencies supplied on 3-month loan only. We clear reproduction rights for material supplied. Fees vary with the sources who supply material to us."

ARTISTRY INTERNATIONAL, Box 800, San Anselmo CA 94960. (415)457-1482. Contact: Dave Bartruff. 100,000 photos available on sale basis only. Reproduction rights, advertising rights, editorial rights, first rights, all rights. Subjects: World wide subjects for editorial use; color transparencies. Standard ASMP rates. Charges $35 service fee.

ASSOCIATED PICTURE SERVICE, Northside Station, Box 52881, Atlanta GA 30355. (404)948-2671. Manager: Buford C. Burch. 25,000 photos on sale basis only. Reproduction rights, advertising rights, second rights, first rights, all rights. Subjects: Nature, historical points, city/suburbs, and scenics of most major countries of the world. Charges $25-175 for one-time editorial or advertising use; $25 selection fee.

ASSOCIATION OF AMERICAN RAILROADS NEWS SERVICE, American Railroads Building, 1920 L St., N.W., Washington DC 20036. Contact: J. Ronald Shumate. B&w glossies on railroad subjects. No fees. Credit line required.

AUSTRIAN PRESS AND INFORMATION SERVICE, 31 E. 69th St., New York NY 10021. General information and b&w photos of Austria. No fees but credit line and return of pictures required.

AUTHENTICATED NEWS INTERNATIONAL, 170 Fifth Ave., New York NY 10010. (212)243-6995. Managing Editor: Sidney Polinsky. Approximately 1½ million photos, b&w and color. Photo agency for all types of domestic and foreign news photos, stock photos on all subjects, including politics, pollution, geo-thermal and solar energy, etc. 50% commission on all photos sold; b&w and color. Credit line and return of photos required.

AUTOMOBILE PHOTO ARCHIVES, 206 W. 94th St., New York NY 10025. Contact: George A. Moffitt. 2,000 photos on file; loan basis only. Reproduction rights, advertising rights, editorial rights and all rights available. Subjects: Automotive; old, classic, postwar cars shown with personalities (movie stars, etc.). Both standard cars and custom American and European. Fees: $10 service charge. Holding fee of $1/photo after 21 days. B&w additional $35 for editorial; $50 for advertising use.

ROYCE BAIR, PHOTOGRAPHER, 1481 S. Main St., Salt Lake City UT 84115. (801)467-0322 or 561-0054. 5,000 photos available for purchase of reproduction rights only; very little material is sold outright. Subjects: Western states (primarily Utah and Idaho): agriculture, industries, outdoor recreation, scenics. "I follow ASMP guidelines and business practices. I also accept assignment photography." Fees: Prints, $4/print, plus reproduction fee. Holding fee: $1/photo after 14 days.

THE BANCROFT LIBRARY, University of California, Berkeley CA 94720. Contact: Curator of Pictorial Collections. Portraits, photographs, original paintings and drawings, prints and other materials illustrating the history of California, western North America, Mexico. Researchers must consult card indexes and book catalogs to the collection. The Library cannot make selections. Photographic reference copies are available for purchase; negatives and transparencies on a loan basis only. "Commercial users of our pictorial resources are asked to make a donation comparable to the per-unit prices charged by commercial picture agencies for similar materials." Credit line required: "Courtesy, The Bancroft Library." Rights vary with material.

BILLY E. BARNES, 313 Severin St., Chapel Hill NC 27514. (919)942-6350. 65,000 photos (b&w and color) available for one-time use only. Subjects: civil rights activities, poverty problems, education, people shots, rural scenes, industrial, youth in vocational education, scenics. "Shots on file are stock from 20 years of assignments for national magazines, company publications, audiovisual firms, etc." Will send 7-page descriptive index of stock files to prospective buyers; also available for special assignment. Fees: $35/b&w; $75/color transparency. Decreasing rate for multiple frame purchases. Special assignment $175/day in North Carolina; $225 outside of state.

BUDDY BASCH FEATURE SYNDICATE, 771 West End Ave., New York NY 10025. (212)666-2300. Publisher: Buddy Basch. 5,000 b&w photos; 2,000 color. Photos of show business people from the 30's to present (mostly b&w); travel photos of cities, states, countries, sights, etc. (color and b&w); also many other smaller areas—airplanes, etc. "Will search out and supply photos to order." Offers one-time and reproduction rights. Charge "depends on circulation, use, etc., and varies widely."

BBM ASSOCIATES, Box 24, Berkeley CA 94710. (415)653-8896. Contact; Clinton Bond. 300,000 "b&w and color pictures ranging over all subject areas; emphasis on the San Francisco Bay area with a bit of everything from the rest of the world. Specialties: ecology, ethnic, children, nature, political, and radical photography." 1-time North American usage. Subsequent fees for additional reproduction. Fees: "Standard ASMP with consideration for certain budget problems."

RICHARD BELLAK — PHOTOGRAPHER, 127 Remsen St., Brooklyn NY 11201. (212)858-2417. About 10,000 photos on a wide variety of people-oriented subjects including migrant workers, Appalachia, children, elderly people, blacks in rural Alabama, youth scenes, third world people. B&w and color. Usually offers one-time, non-exclusive reproduction rights. Minimum fee for b&w is usually $50; $100 minimum for color. Unused photos may not be held longer than 10 days. All photos must be returned undamaged.

THE BETTMAN ARCHIVE, INC., 136 E. 57th St., New York NY 10022. (212)758-0362. Picture Researcher: Carol Fabian. 6,000,000 b&w and 200,000 color photos of all topics. Offers all rights. Charges $35-50 for one-time editorial or advertising use; $35 and up selection charge on larger orders.

BIOMEDICAL PHOTO LIBRARY, Camera M.D. Studios, Inc., 122 E. 76th St., New York NY 10021. (212)628-4331. Contact: Library Division. 100,000 biomedical color transparencies and b&w negatives. The biomedical photos illustrate about 30 specialty areas of medicine, such as dermatology, allergy and rheumatology, dentistry, veterinary medicine, botany, entomology and other biological sciences. Also, photos of about 60 sites of normal human anatomy are availabe of adults and children, males and females plus matching skeletal views and, where possible, matching normal x-rays. The 132-page catalog, illustrated in color and b&w, costs $5.75 plus postage.

BLACK STAR, 450 Park Ave. S., New York NY 10016. (212)679-3288. President: Howard Chapnick; Executive Vice-President: Benjamin J. Chapnick. Represents 120 photographers for assignment work. Color and b&w photos of all subjects. Two million photos in collection. One-time use or negotiations for other extended rights. $75 minimum per b&w, $150 minimum per color. Assignment rates quoted on request.

BLACKSTONE-SHELBURNE NEW YORK, INC., 3 W. 30 St., New York NY 10001. (212)736-9100. President: Ira Fontaine. 180,000 sets of negatives. Photos (portraits) of personalities, businessmen, dignitaries.

DR. BLOCK COLOR PRODUCTIONS, 1309 N. Genesee Ave., Hollywood CA 90046. Contact: Mrs. Fred Block. 3,300 color slides, 2x2. "Large collection in the art field. We have sold reproduction rights to publishers for prints in book publications." Credit line requested. Fee: "about $60 for single slide for reproduction." Requests return of originals. Request sheet available of detailed list of photos and prices.

HARRY BONNER, Freelance Outdoor Photographer and Writer, 5369 Vergara St., San Diego CA 92117. (714)571-0048. 25,000 b&w photos; 10,000 color of West Coast outdoor subjects: salt and fresh water game fish, most species; seascapes; sunsets; seabirds; boats; fishing, all phases; rivers; scenics; Mexico; whales and other marine animals; sharks and rays; few animals. Extensive fishing coverage and related subjects in Mexico, California, Oregon, Washington, and some Hawaii. Rights vary with material and use. Reproduction fee: $50 minimum.

THE BOSTONIAN SOCIETY, Old State House, 206 Washington St., Boston MA 02109. (617)523-7033. Librarian: Mary Leen. 10,000 b&w photos of people, places (i.e., buildings, streets, etc.), events relative to Boston, mostly of the 19th century, but some 20th century material. Offers one-time and reproduction rights. Charges $5-50 for one-time editorial or advertising use; $5-15 print fee.

PHIL BRODATZ, 100 Edgewater Dr., Coral Gables FL 33133. (305)858-2666. 20,000 b&w and 10,000 color photos. Subjects: nature, trees, scenics of USA and Caribbean Islands, clouds, water; textures of many kinds. Offers one-time editorial and advertising and reproduction rights. "Fees depend on use, from $25 up."

BROOKLYN PUBLIC LIBRARY, Grand Army Plaza, Brooklyn NY 11238. (212)636-3178. Contact: Elizabeth L. White or Marie Spina, Librarians. The History Division's Brooklyn Collection contains about 5,000 b&w photos of Brooklyn buildings and neighborhoods. Also has photograph file of the Brooklyn Daily Eagle, covering photographs used from c. 1905 to 1955; it contains thousands of prints of national as well as local news subjects. Some of these are wire service photos and many have been retouched. The photographs cannot be borrowed, but appointments can be made (with at least a week's notice) for the user to bring his own equipment to photograph prints. Permission to use the wire service photos must be obtained from that service. There is no other charge or rental fee for use of these photos, but a credit line to the Brooklyn Public Library: Brooklyn Collection is required.

BUFFALO AND ERIE COUNTY HISTORICAL SOCIETY, 25 Nottingham Court, Buffalo NY 14216. (716)873-9644. Contact: Curator of Iconography. "Our emphasis is historical and regional; nineteenth and twentieth century materials of the Niagara Frontier. Reproduction fee depends on project. Publications are generally $20/item/edition." Credit line required.

GUY BURGESS, PHOTOGRAPHER, 202 Old Broadmoor Road, Colorado Springs CO 80906. (303)633-1295. Contact: Guy Burgess. 1,800 5x7 color transparencies of garden scenes, plant portraits. 1-time use. Fees: $100 to $250. Return required.

CALIFORNIA STATE LIBRARY, Library and Courts Bldg., Box 2037, Sacramento CA 95809. Contact: Kenneth I. Pettitt, California Section Head Librarian. California historical pictures, portraits of Californians (mostly early residents) in b&w only. "Photocopies of specific pictures may be ordered by mail. Selection should be done at the library by the researcher. Names of private researchers, who work on a fee basis, are available. Fees for photocopies vary according to type and size of print. Credit line required."

CAMERA CLIX, INC., 404 Park Ave. S., New York NY 10016. (212)684-3526. Manager: Alix Colow. Photos of children, florals, animals, historic points, sports, major American cities, scenics, art reproductions, and human interest. "Our emphasis is the calendar and greeting card type of photograph." Large format color transparencies. Rights offered are negotiable. Fees depend on usage and area of distribution. Return of prints, and credit line, are required.

CAMERA HAWAII, INC., 206 Koula Street, Honolulu HI 96813. (808)536-2302. Contact: Photo Librarian. Estimated over 50,000 color and 20,000 b&w pictures of Hawaii; cross section of all islands, scenics, travel, aerial and general. Also selection of photos from New Zealand, Sydney, Bali, Manila, Taiwan, Hong Kong, Korea, Tokyo and parts of Japan, Guam; minor file of other areas such as Tahiti, West Coast; Washington, New York, Boston area; Quebec, Niagara Falls; spring flowers in Washington DC, New York scenes and a small selection of London, Germany, Austria, and Switzerland scenes. Usually offers one-time rights, but subject to negotiation according to needs. Fees dependent upon usage and rights required. Minimums generally in line with ASMP standards.

CAMERA M D STUDIOS INC., Library Division, 122 E. 76 St., New York NY 10021. (212)628-4331. Manager: Carroll H. Weiss. Over 100,000 photos of the health and biological sciences. Offers all rights. Credit line, tearsheets and return of prints required. ASMP rates.

CAMERIQUE STOCK PHOTOS, Box 175, Blue Bell PA 19422. (215)272-7649. Contact: Orville Johnson. B&w photos and color transparencies on a variety of subject matter. Selection can be sent on ten-day approval. One-time reproduction fee varies with importance of use, media, circulation, etc. Fee quoted on receipt of this information. Return of pictures required in 10 days, unless extended.

WOODFIN CAMP AND ASSOCIATES, 50 Rockefeller Plaza, New York NY 10020. Contact: Midge Keator or Woodfin Camp. Over 100,000 photos representing general geographic coverage of most countries in the world, with particular emphasis on India, Africa, Russia, Western Europe, South America, Southeast Asia, and the U.S. B&w and color. Fees depend on usage, beginning at $50 per b&w; $150 for color. Usually offers one-time, non-exclusive North American rights. Since most photos were produced from reportage assignments, there are no model releases for the subjects. Requests must be as specific as possible regarding the type of photo needed and its intended use, and rights required.

CANADIAN CONSULATE GENERAL, 1251 Avenue of the Americas, New York NY 10020. (Territory comprises Connecticut, New Jersey, and New York State only.) Contact: Photo Librarian. 8x10 b&w glossies of Canadian scenes and the people of Canada are available, gratis, on a loan basis from the Canadian Consulate General at the above address. Credit line required. Return of pictures requested.

CANADIAN PACIFIC, Windsor Sta., Montreal, P.Q., Canada H3C 3E4. (514)861-6811. Contact: F.E. Stelfox. "We can provide b&w and color photos of all kinds in various sizes from 4x5 to wall murals. Wide selection of historical subjects in b&w of the steam-loco era—ships, rail, logging, oil drilling, hotels, air, containerization. Senic views of Canada, cities, and numerous other subjects." Fees and credit line required.

CANADIAN PRESS, 36 King St. E., Toronto, Ontario, Canada M5C 2L9. (416)364-0321. 600,000 photos of current and historic Canadian personalities and life; mostly b&w. Canadian agents for Wide World Photos, Inc. Offers one-time rights. Charges $25-40 for b&w, depending on publication's circulation.

WILLIAM CARTER, PHOTOGRAPHER AND WRITER, 535 Everett Ave., Palo Alto CA 94301. (415)326-1382 or 328-3561. Contact: William Carter. About 30,000 photos on a variety of worldwide subjects, particularly U.S. Middle West, western ghost towns, children, show horses, Middle East, special subjects. Fees negotiable.

WALTER CHANDOHA, RFD, Annandale NJ 08801. (201)782-3666. 100,000 color and b&w pictures of "cats, dogs, horses and other animals. Nature subjects, weather situations, trees and leaves, flowers (wild, domestic, tropical); growing vegetables and fruits; sunsets, clouds, sky and scenics; water, conservation." Offers non-exclusive, limited exclusive, exclusive rights and outright purchase. Fees: Minimum $50 for b&w, minimum $150 for color and up to $3,500, depending on use. "We do not deal with authors direct; we prefer to work with their publishers."

CHICAGO HISTORICAL SOCIETY, Clark St. at North Ave., Chicago IL 60614. (312)642-4600. Contact: Larry A. Viskochil. 450,000 photos on file on Chicago history. "Collection is in the public domain. We exercise proprietary rights and sell or rent photographic copies of items in the collection." Print fee: $10 (b&w); $40 (color transparency). "In certain instances, i.e., advertising, $75." Photocopies: 15¢ plus 50¢ service charge. "Unless copies are available in our "ready" file, photo orders take 4-8 weeks for completion."

CINCINNATI HISTORICAL SOCIETY, Eden Park, Cincinnati OH 45202. Contact: Edward Malloy, Picture Librarian. Over 350,000 photos and slides of Cincinnati and Cincinnati-related material; general pictures on subjects such as World War I, urban decay, Ohio River transportation. B&w and color slides. One-time use, with fee for commercial use.

JOE CLARK, H.B.S.S. PHOTOGRAPHY, 8775 W. 9 Mile Rd., Oak Park MI 48237. (313)399-4480. 15,000 color and b&w photos on file for sale or loan. Rights vary with material and author. Subjects: city and farm subjects, Michigan, Tennessee, Ohio, Kentucky, Detroit, down South, people, pets, children, landscapes. Fees vary with material and use.

COAST GUARD NEWS & PHOTO CENTER, Third Coast Guard District, New York NY 10004. (212)264-4996. Contact: Photographic Officer. Photos available on loan. Reproduction rights available. Collection is in the public domain. Subjects: U.S. Coast Guard, search and rescue, marine safety, aids to navigation, recreational boating, oil pollution abatement, lighthouses, etc. Generally no charge to qualified sources for publication. Modest charges for personal collections, etc. Credit line required. Fees: Prints made to order, $1.25/b&w; $3-50/color. Photocopies, $3.15/b&w; $6-25/color.

BRUCE COLEMAN INCORPORATED, 15 E. 36 St., New York NY 10016. (212)683-5227. Contact: Norman Owen Tomalin. 300,000 photos available for sale or leasing. Reproduction rights, advertising rights, editorial rights, first rights, all rights. Subjects: Everything but spot news or all aspects of South America. Fees: $30 minimum service charge. $1/week minimum holding fee. ASMP reproduction fees.

COLLEGE NEWSPHOTO ALLIANCE, 342 Madison Ave., New York NY 10017. (212)697-1136. Manager: Ted Feder. 100,000 b&w photos and color transparencies of college life including political activity, people, current economic and social trends, urban and rural subjects, ecology. Offers one-time to world rights. Fees depend on the reproduction rights and size of reproduction on the page; average $50 for b&w, $125 for color.

COMPSCO PUBLISHING CO., 18 Blackrock Terrace, Ringwood NJ 07456. (201)962-4114 or (212)757-6454. Photographer: Ernst A. Jahn. 10,000 b&w and 40,000 color photos. "Subjects: Latin America, all countries Mexico, Central and South America. Cuba, Puerto Rico, Curacao, Canada, Germany, Holland, Switzerland, Greece with Aegean Islands and Rhodes, Finland, Russia, Austria, all Islands of the Windward chain from Grenada to Antigua, West Indies, Tierra del Fuego, Easter Island, Tahiti, French Polynesia Islands, Robinson Crusoe Island of Juan Fernandez, Galapagos Islands, San Blas Islands of Panama, Tunesia, South Africa. Jordan, Lebanon, Syria, Alaska, Poland. A very large file is kept on all South American countries, French Polynesian Islands, Galapagos Islands, Central America and Mexico, South Africa and Tunesia. USA: General scenery coverage of most states of the Union, including many State and National Parks. A limited selection of cities and people. All in 35mm Kodachromes, no black-white pictures. Special Studies: Flying Squirrel and regular squirrel. Many animal pictures, local and tropical animals." Offers all rights. Charges $125 minimum for one-time editorial color use, more for advertising use; $35 minimum b&w. Free catalog.

CONSOLIDATED EDISON COMPANY OF NEW YORK, INC., 4 Irving Place, New York NY 10003. Contact: William O. Farley, Director, Public Information. Single copies of prints available on electric, gas, steam generation and distribution facilities. No fees.

CONTACT PRESS IMAGES, INC., 135 Central Park West, New York NY 10023. Contact: Robert Pledge. (212)799-9570. Photos available on a loan basis for all rights. Subjects: Photojournalistic editorial photography (color and b&w) on major personalities, situations, trends, events, coutries of the world; political, economics, sociological and cultural points of view. Service charge: $25. Holding fee: $50. Minimum reproduction fee: $50. Prints made to order: $15.

CULVER PICTURES, INC., 660 First Ave., New York NY 10016. (212)684-5054. Contact: R. B. Jackson. "Widely known in historical field, with over 9 million b&w photos, old prints, engravings, posters, paintings, movie stills covering every imaginable subject, including the Seidman collection. We like to work with writers but cannot send material until acceptance of article or story by magazine or publisher is final. We have found that we cannot tie up pictures on speculative ventures." One-time reproduction fee varies; $35-100 (for cover use). Credit line and return of pictures required.

DANDELET INTERLINKS, 126 Redwood Rd., San Anselmo CA 94960. (415)456-1260. Contact: Lucile Dandelet. "We connect writers, editors and other communicators with illustration problems to photographers who are problem solvers: we rep Jon Brenneis, Philip Hyde, Fred Lyon, Dr. E.S. Ross, Ree Whitford and Franklin Wing and a periphery network beyond San Francisco Bay Area—credit lines that spell quality and professionalism. Worldwide assignments and stock, primarily color. Travel, industry, nature & entomology, book jackets, food & wine. Search fee of $35 charged, deductible from order; overlong-holding fees. Once we know your needs, fees for our solutions depend on use and rights in contract."

ALFRED DE BAT PHOTOGRAPHY, 4629 N. Dover Street, Chicago IL 60640. (312)271-9553. 50,000 pictures of "foreign travel, U.S. travel, Chicago area scenes and activities. Mainly color —some b&w." Offers world, North American, first, one-time, and stock rights. Charges standard ASMP rates.

LEO DE WYS INC., 60 E. 42nd St., New York NY 10017. (212)986-3190. Contact: Diana Ross. "We represent over 400 photographers from around the world, each with their own specialty; freelancers and staffers from companies and magazines." 500,000 (plus) photos included in collection. Scenics, education, science, religion, natural science, agriculture, music, dance, sculpture, celebrities, sports, government, foreign countries, industry, medicine, human interest photos. B&w and color photos available. Charge for making a selection is $25 outside New York state. Holding fee: $1 per photo per day, after 3 weeks. No service charge for 1 to 4 subjects. $25 for 5 or more subjects. Outright purchase price: "high." Reproduction fee: $35 minimum for b&w; $100 minimum for color. Selection on approval or in person. Prints must be returned. Credit line and tearsheets required.

DR. E. R. DEGGINGER, APSA, P.O. Box 186, Convent NJ 07961. Contact: E. R. Degginger. About 80,000 color transparencies on wide range of subject matter including pictorial and nature photography: scenics, travel, industry, science, abstracts, sports, all facets of the natural world. 35mm color. Rights to be negotiated. Charges $125 for one-time usage; covers are higher.

DELAWARE STATE TRAVEL SERVICE (formerly *Bureau of Travel Development*), 630 State College Rd., Dover DE 19901. Contact: Donald Mathewson, Tourism Coordinator. Approximately 2,000 photos. "Historic buildings and sites. Indoor-outdoor photos of museums. Camping, boating, fishing, and beach scenes. Auto, flat and harness racing. State park nature scenes. Historic churches, monuments, etc." B&w and color. Rights offered unlimited, except credit line required in some cases. No fees charged. "Released on a loan only basis. Must be returned after use."

DESIGN PHOTOGRAPHERS INTERNATIONAL, INC., 521 Madison Avenue, New York NY 10022. (212)752-3930. Contact: Alfred W. Forsyth. "Over 1½ million pictures. Comprehensive contemporary collection of worldwide subjects in color and b&w." Offers one-time reproduction rights "unless other specific terms are agreed upon and additional fee is paid for said additional rights." Fees vary "depending on media and specific use."

A. DEVANEY, INC., 415 Lexington Ave., New York NY 10017. (212)682-1017. Contact: George Marzocchi. Types of photos available: scenics, seasonal, U.S. and foreign cities, industrials, farming, human interest, religious, etc. B&w and color transparencies; no color prints. Holding fee after 10 days. 1-time reproduction fee depends on use. Credit line required for editorial use only. Return of pictures required except for those used.

DIVISION OF MICHIGAN HISTORY, Department of State, 3423 N. Logan St., Lansing MI 48918. Contact: David J. Olson, State Archivist. Files of original and reproduction prints and negatives accumulated over a period of time and depicting all phases of the Michigan scene. Approximately 100,000 photo items in the collection. The cost of an individual print varies according to the size and finish of the print desired. In those cases where the Division of Michigan History does not have a negative, an additional charge is made for a copy negative, which remains in the collections of the Division of Michigan History. In advance of placing any order, there is a charge of $1 as a service fee, payable to the State of Michigan. Checks and money orders are to be made payable to the State of Michigan. The service fee paid is solely for the cost of handling the order, and does not include the right to further reproduction or publication. If the Commission grants the right to production, the credit line "From the collections of the Michigan History Division" is requested; and, when used in publication, 2 copies of the article, publication or book are requested for inclusion in the Division's research library.

IRVING DOLIN PHOTOGRAPHY, 124 Ludlow St., New York NY 10002. (212)473-4006. Contact: Irving Dolin. Several thousand pictures. "All types of auto racing, in b&w and color. Racing drivers. Files date from 1948. Most are 35mm." Prefers to sell one-time rights; depends upon fee paid. Minimum b&w fee is $35 for one-time editorial use.

DONDERO PHOTOGRAPHY, Box 1006, Reno NV 89504. (702)786-6623. Contact: Mike Ritter. "Thousands of color and b&w pictures of all western activity in the four seasons; celebrities, mainly entertainment; gambling; legalized prostitution —mood —unidentifiable subjects." Offers one-time rights on stock pictures; exclusive rights when shooting on assignment. Fees: "one-time publication rights for area publications and small newspapers, $10 for b&w, $25 for color; standard space rates for national publications."

DRAKE WELL MUSEUM, R.D. 3, Titusville PA 16354. (814)827-2797. Contact: Jane Elder. 6,000 photographs of the 19th and 20th century petroleum industry. Reproduction rights or advertising rights. Collection is in the public domain. Available for purchase. Charges $10/hour for making selection. Print fee: $2-5. Prints made to order: $5. Photocopies: $5. Copy negative: $5.

EASTFOTO AGENCY, 25 W. 43 St., New York NY 10036. (212)279-8846. Manager: Leah Siegel. 900,000 color and b&w photos on all aspects of life in E. Europe, China, Vietnam, etc. Industrial, political, historical, entertainment, news photos. Offers one-time rights, North American, world in English, world rights in translation. Fees vary according to usage. Minimum of $50 for 1-time use of b&w photos; $125 for color.

EDITORIAL PHOTOCOLOR ARCHIVES, 342 Madison Ave., New York NY 10017. (212)697-1136. B&w photos; color transparencies: 35mm, 2¼x2¼ formats. Subjects include foreign countries and cultures, ecology, children, works of art, family life, human activities, nature. Fees vary depending on use. Generally the b&w fee is $50 and color is $125.

EKM COMMUNICATIONS, 7874 Tanglerod Lane, La Mesa CA 92041. (714)463-9513. Over 100,000 photos available for purchase. Rarely loans photos. Rights vary with material and use. All subject categories: People, animals, medical research, foreign countries, nature, Indians, sports, etc. "We also have photographers around the world who will accept assignments." Reproduction: $60 minimum. Prints made to order: $3.50/8x10, $5/11x14.

ENTHEOS/NORTHWEST, Bainbridge Island WA 98110. (206)842-3641. Contact: Steven C. Wilson. 100,000 photos in collection, "all 35mm color and 16mm color movie footage. Western U.S. and Canada, Alaska, the Arctic; nature, animals, plants, man." Rights to be negotiated with each purchase; varies from exclusive to one-time educational book rights. Fees: $100 minimum per photo for one-time book rights.

ANTHONY F. ESPOSITO, JR., 65 Lynmoor Place, Hamden CT 06517. (203)288-0588. Director: A.F. Esposito. 5,000 b&w photos; 15,000 color. Subjects: farm subjects; animal husbandry; worldwide scenics and people; children/teenagers; medical/hospital; carnivals; sports; plants and animals (scientific categories); and rural and urban America. Offers one-time, editorial, advertising, reproduction, and all rights (rarely). Charges $15-1,500 for one-time editorial or advertising use; $10 for 8x10 prints. "Query us giving as much information as possible concerning your needs. We will send you a selection on approval. Writer's obligation is to return unused slides via registered mail within 10 days. There is a charge for slides held longer than 10 days. Writers must include information on how slide will be used when querying, in order than we may provide the proper quote. We have a sliding scale based on the use made of the slide."

EUROPEAN ART COLOR, Peter Adelberg, Inc., 120 W. 70th St., New York NY 10023. (212)877-9654. Contact: Peter Adelberg. About 6,000 photos. "Archives of original color transparencies photographed on-the-spot from the original art object in museums, cathedrals, palaces, etc. Prehistoric to contemporary art; all media. Transparencies instantly available from New York office." Charges selection and holding fees. One-time reproduction fee varies from $85 and up for b&w to $150 and up for color. Credit line and return of pictures required.

FIELD MUSEUM OF NATURAL HISTORY, Roosevelt Rd. at Lake Shore Dr., Chicago IL 60605. No catalogue of photos available so it is necessary in ordering photos either to inspect the Museum albums or to write, giving precise specifications of what's wanted. Prices and requirements for permission to reproduce available on request. Write to Division of Photography.

FLORIDA CYPRESS GARDENS, INC., Box 1, Cypress Gardens FL 33880. (813)324-2111. Director of Publicity and Promotion: Pete Johnson. Photos of flowers, plants, scenics, boating, water skiing, fishing, camping, pretty girls. One-time reproduction fees; $300 without credit line or no charge with credit line. Return of pictures required. Cypress Gardens also has a staff of photographers that can take pictures in above categories. Prices available on request.

FLORIDA NEWS BUREAU, 410-C Collins Bldg., Tallahassee FL 32304. (904)488-2494. Contact: Tim Olsson. Photographs on all areas and phases of Florida; b&w available to freelancers, b&w and color transparencies to publications. "To receive the greatest value for the tax money that supports our operation, we apply the following guidelines in filling photographic requests: 1) requests direct from publications get first priority; 2) requests from freelancers who have established a record of cooperation with us (tearsheets, credit lines and other acknowledgments) receive second priority; and 3) requests from unknown freelancers are handled on a 'time available' basis. A freelancer who has not worked with us previously should allow plenty of time on photo requests." No fees but credit line and return of transparencies required.

FORD FOUNDATION PHOTO LIBRARY, 320 E. 43 St., New York NY 10017. (212)573-4815. Over 10,000 in contact sheets. Primarily b&w. All related to projects supported by the Foundation: agricultural research, family planning, reproductive biology, public and higher education, community development. Use restricted to bona fide publications; photos must be for use in context of project. No fees; only print costs.

HARRISON FORMAN WORLD PHOTOS, 555 Fifth Ave., New York NY 10017. (212)697-4165. Contact: Harrison Forman. "Over 700,000 Kodachromes on countries throughout the world. Our files are cross-filed by subjects such as: religions of the world, art and architecture, housing, flora, fauna, dances, children, education, agriculture, handicrafts, native rituals, imports and exports, transportation, natural resources, mountains, rivers, jungles, deserts, glaciers, ancient civilization, historical monuments. Special recent coverage on China with over 7,000 Kodachromes. China inventory includes color pix of light and heavy industries, art and architecture, consumer products, education, acupuncture, children, communes, transportation, irrigation products, cities, towns, villages and many more. Thousands of b&w pix of Asia dating from early 1930's. Rates vary, depending on editorial use, publication, reproduction rights offered. Our rates are in conformance with standards of ASMP. Credit line, tearsheets and return of photographs required. We are founder/members of PACA (Picture Agency Council of America)."

FOTOS INTERNATIONAL, 130 West 42nd Street, New York NY 10036. (212)695-0353. Contact: Baer M. Frimer. B&w and color transparencies "covering the entertainment field in all its phases—motion pictures (international); television, radio, stage." 1-time reproduction rights.

FOUR BY FIVE, INC., 485 Madison Ave., New York NY 10022. (212)697-8282. Manager: Joanna Ferrone. Quality stock photos of people, scenics, travel, and sports. Full-color catalogs available on subscription. Free sample. Charges $150-300 for one-time editorial or advertising use.

FRANKLIN PHOTO AGENCY, 39 Woodcrest Ave., Hudson NH 03051. (603)889-1289. Photographs available of flowers, gardens, trees, plants, wildflowers, etc.; foreign countries; interiors and exteriors of homes, scenics (all seasons), antique cars, insects and small animals, dogs (all breeds), fish pictures, horses (all breeds), fishing and hunting scenes, some sports. Mostly 4x5 color. One-time reproduction and rental fees vary according to use and quantities printed, etc. Not less than $50 minimum. Credit line requested and return of pictures required.

FREE LIBRARY OF PHILADELPHIA, Print and Picture Department, Logan Square, Philadelphia PA 19103. Contact: Robert F. Looney. Photographs available on a wide range of subjects. Original prints: historical and fine arts. Also clippings, plates, news photos. Specialties: portrait collection (300,000 items), Philadelphia history (9,000 items), Napoleonica (3,400 items), fine prints (1,000 items). "Unfortunately we cannot send out samples of literature or groups of pictures from which selections may be made." Photocopies: $3.50 each. Credit line required for original material only.

FREELANCE PHOTOGRAPHERS GUILD, 251 Park Ave. S., New York NY 10010. Contact: Ann Schneider. Photos of all countries, U.S.A., and major cities, human interest, subjects from accidents to zoot suits. 5,000,000 b&w, color photos. Reproduction fee depends on usage; $40-1,200 for b&w, $125-2,500 for color.

FREEPORT MINERALS COMPANY, 200 Park Ave.,New York NY 10017. (212)578-9200. Contact: E.C.K. Read, PR Director. Color and b&w mining and shipping photos of sulphur (including world's only offshore sulphur mine), kaolin, Indonesian copper, potash, phosphates, oil and gas, Australian nickel-cobalt operations. Usually no restrictions on rights offered. No fees charged.

LAWRENCE FRIED PHOTOGRAPHY LTD., 330 East 49th St., Studio 1A, New York NY 10017. (212)371-3636. Contact: Lawrence Fried. "500,000 subjects, ranging from travel throughout the world, international and domestic political figures, society, theatre (stage and film), sports, editorial and commercial illustration, military, medical, personalities in b&w and color." Rights offered flexible, "depending on negotiation in each individual case." Fees: minimum b&w, $135; minimum color, $135.

EWING GALLOWAY, 342 Madison Ave., New York NY 10017. Photo agency offering all types, both b&w and color. Prices are based on how and where a photo will be used.

GAMMA-LIAISON PHOTO AGENCY, 150 E. 58th St., New York NY 10022. (212)355-7310. Contact: Michael DeWan. One million b&w and color photos available for purchase or loan. Reproduction rights, advertising rights, first rights, second rights, editorial rights, all rights. Subjects: political, social, economic, religious, cultural events, newsmakers, politicians; celebrities of stage, screen and society. Human interest features, children, animals, nature, sports, fashion. Fees: $35 for making selection; $2/color photo/day holding fee, after standard holding time. Reproduction fee varies with photo and photographer, but generally $75 minimum/b&w; $125 minimum/color.

GEMINI SMITH INC., 5858 Desert View Dr., La Jolla CA 92037. (714)454-4321. Director: Bradley Smith. 7,000 b&w photos; 5,000 color. Important paintings and sculptures of the world (all periods from prehistoric to modern); folkways and scenics of the world; arts, crafts and historical sites of the US; personalities of the 30's and 40's; animal and circus photos. Offers all rights. Charges ASMP rates for one-time editorial use; and $20 service charge (deductible from purchase). Free catalog.

GENERAL PRESS FEATURES, 130 W. 57 St., New York NY 10019. (212)265-6842. Manager: Gabriel D. Hackett. Still photo archives, written and illustrated features. Photos of all subjects; lists available. Over 100,000 photos: historic and documentary, social changes (U.S. and Europe), music, fine arts, artists, Americana; pictorials (U.S. and France, Switzerland). Towns, landscapes, politicians, statesmen, celebrities. Both color and b&w. Rights offered open to negotiation. Fees are ASMP minimum code rates. Discount on larger orders.

A. JOHN GERACI, 279 E. Northfield Rd., Livingston NJ 07039. (201)992-0202. 100,000 photos available for reproduction rights, advertising rights, first rights, second rights, or editorial rights. On loan basis only. Subjects: Medical, dermatology, sports, fencing, tennis, travel, people. Fees: $20 for making selections; $20/service charge. $10 print fee. Holding fee: (over 10 days) $10/day. Copy negative, $25.

GLOBE PHOTOS, 404 Park Ave. S., New York NY 10016. (212)689-1340. Contact: Elliot Stern. 10,000,000 photos of all subjects. B&w and color. Offers first rights, all rights, second rights; depends on the price. $35 minimum for b&w, $125 minimum for color. Credit line, tearsheets and return of prints required.

GLOBE PRESS INTERNATIONAL, Box 2046, York PA 17405. (717)845-2805. Editor: William D. Reis. "We do not maintain a picture file as all of our work is done on assignment. In general we provide both copy and photos, however on occasion we have accepted photo assignments. We have photographers in all states and most foreign countries." Offers all rights. Charges $500 service charge, plus expenses.

GOVERNMENT OF SASKATCHEWAN, Photographic/Art Division, Room 3, Legislative Building, Regina, Saskatchewan, Canada. Contact: Ray W. Christensen. A large variety of photographs of all aspects of life in Saskatchewan available as prints in black and white and color, available to publishers only; supplies photos directly to publications, but not to freelance writers. Credit line required.

PETER GOWLAND, 609 Hightree Road, Santa Monica CA 90402. (213)454-7867. Contact: Peter Gowland. Over 3,000 photos catalogued and over 100,000 photos in total collection. "Beautiful women —heads, full-lengths, bathing suits, some nudes —in both b&w and color." Non-exclusive rights offered. Fees: b&w, $50/picture for circulation under 100,000, $75/picture for circulation over 100,000; color, $100-500 depending on use.

THE GRANGER COLLECTION, 1841 Broadway, New York NY 10023. (212)586-0971. Contact: William Glover, Director. A general historical picture archives encompassing the people, places, things, and events of the past in b&w prints and color transparencies. Holding fee varies and 1-time reproduction fee depends on use, but minimum fee is $35. Credit line and return of pictures required.

GREATER PROVIDENCE CHAMBER OF COMMERCE, 10 Dorrance St., Providence RI 02903. Contact: Lisbeth V.H. Pettengill, Vice President, Communications. Photos of Providence in b&w; limited 35mm color slides. Credit line and return of photos required.

HAROLD V. GREEN, 570 St. John's Blvd., Pointe Claire, Quebec, Canada. (514)697-4110. Contact: H. Green. Approximately 35,000 photos. "Wide spectrum of natural history and general biology photos, and some botanical, zoological, and crystal photomicrographs. Also places, people, landscapes, sea scapes, old farms, etc. Mainly 35mm color." One-time reproduction rights usually; other rights by agreement. Fees: $50 to $150, color; $25 to $75, b&w.

AL GREENE MURALS & EXHIBITS, 1333 S. Hope St., Los Angeles CA 90015. "100,000 scenics and points of interest around the world. Mostly color on scenics and farming, otherwise b&w." Offers normal one-time reproduction rights, exclusive rights available at additional charge. Fees: $25 minimum.

ARTHUR GRIFFIN, 22 Euclid Ave., Winchester MA 01890. (617)729-2690. Contact: Arthur Griffin. 50,000 color photos of New England and other states; Orient, the Scandinavian countries, Canada and South America; mostly scenics. All islands of the West Indies. Majority are 4x5 transparencies. Offer all rights. ASMP rates.

AL GROTELL, Underwater Photography, 170 Park Row, New York NY 10038. (212)349-3165. "Over 5,000 color transparencies available for reproduction in all media. Subjects: natural history, including underwater scenes, divers, fish corals, sponges, sunken ships, most invertabrates, marine ecology from the Caribbean and the Bahamas. Fees vary with usage."

JUDSON B. HALL, PHOTOGRAPHER, R.F.D. 3, Putney VT 05346. (802)387-6670. "Approximately 10,000 b&w pictures of Marlboro Music Festival—Rudolf Serkin, Alexander Schneider, Pablo Casals and others. Feature material on sugaring, lumbering, education, animals, seasons, Vermontiana, Sweden in 1963, Kiruna, Vasteras, Stockholm; color photos of Europe, Marlboro, Vermont scenes." Rights negotiable according to ASMP. Fees: b&w stock $35 minimum; color editorial, $100 minimum.

HARPER HORTICULTURAL SLIDE LIBRARY, 219 Robanna Shores, Seaford VA 23696. (804)898-6453. Contact: Pamela Harper. 12,000 35mm color slides of gardens, trees, shrubs, vines, perennials, alpines, wildflowers, bulbs, and houseplants. Offers all rights. Fees: $25 minimum for one-time editorial or advertising use; $10 selection fee if no photos are used. Duplicate slides $2. Catalog for $1.

HAWAII VISITORS BUREAU, 2270 Kalakaua Ave., Honolulu HI 96815. (808)923-1811. Contact: Photo Librarian. Photographs in b&w, 35mm, and 2¼x2¼ color available on evidence of firm assignment. B&w usually no charge, depends on quantity; color on loan. Credit line and return of color required.

HEDRICH-BLESSING, LTD., 11 W. Illinois St., Chicago IL 60610. (312)321-1151. Contact: Gary Knaus. 750,000 photographs in b&w and color of residential interiors and exteriors, commercial and industrial buildings, interiors and exteriors; scenics of mountains, lakes, woods, mostly without people. City views and historic architecture, especially in Chicago. 1-time reproduction fees for editorial use: color, $100 minimum; b&w, $40 minimum. $25/hour research fee required (deductible). Credit line frequently required. Return of pictures required for color.

HEILPERN PHOTOGRAPHERS INC., Box 12266, 151 Homestead Ave., Hartford CT 06112. Contact: George R. Garen. Approximately 35,000 aerial photographs, mostly b&w, "of every type of subject, from close-ups of modern buildings and highway intersections to over-all views of cities." One-time reproduction rights. $40 for 7x7 contact print, $10.50 additional for two 8x10 or 1 11x14 enlargements of entire negative or any portion.

KEN HEYMAN, 64 E. 55th St., New York NY 10022. (212)421-4512. Contact: Natalie Smith or Ken Heyman. "Over 15,000 b&w and color photos of family types—50 countries around the world; general emphasis on people. Also USA in categories; agricultural, art, cities, education, food, medicine, people, research, travel, work, women, and youth." Generally offers one-time, non-exclusive North American (or world) rights. Fees: b&w, $50 minimum; color, $125. Quantity discounts available.

THE HISTORIC NEW ORLEANS COLLECTION, 333 Royal St., New Orleans LA 70130. (504)523-7146. Contact: Research Department. Over 25,000 pictorial items available on loan basis to sister institutions with necessary insurance and professional staff. Reproduction rights available. Manuscripts Division contains family papers and other original manuscripts and supporting materials (broadsides, sheet music, newspapers); extensive library of rare books, pamphlets, and major Louisiana studies. Pictorial Division consists of engravings, lithographs, photographs, paintings, maps, original framings and artifacts. These materials cover almost every facet of New Orleans history, including architecture, culture, people, and river life, from the 17th to 20th century (largely 19th century). Reproduction fee: $30/item. Prints made to order: $6/8x10 b&w print. Color $15. Slides also available at $3.

HISTORICAL PICTURES SERVICE INC., 17 N. State St., Room 1700, Chicago IL 60602. (312)346-0599. Contact: Jeane Williams. Over 2 million engravings, drawings, photos, paintings, cartoons, caricatures, and maps, covering all important persons, places, things and events. Pictures sent on 60-day approval. 1-time, North American, world rights, or multiple use. 1-time reproduction fee: $35 average, but varies with use. Credit line and return of pictures required.

ILLINOIS STATE HISTORICAL LIBRARY, Old State Capitol, Springfield IL 62706. (217)782-4836. Contact: Janice Petterchak, Curator of Prints and Photographs. 100,000 photos on file. Rights vary with author and material. Subjects: Illinois history, (people, places and events), Abraham Lincoln, the Civil War. Fees: Prints made to order, $5-7.50/8x10 b&w glossies. Photocopies, 20¢.

THE IMAGE BANK, The Penthouse, 88 Vanderbilt Ave., New York NY 10017. (212)371-3636. Sales Managers: Advertising Lenore Herson, Editorial Marty Abrams. 1,000,000 color photos; "all subjects." Offers all rights. Fees: "ASMP minimum as applies" for one-time editorial or advertising use; $40 service charge; $75 print fee. Free catalog. "We have licensed offices in Chicago, Washington DC, San Francisco, Montreal, Toronto, Rio, Sao Paolo, Paris, Hamburg, and Tokyo to expedite the servicing of our clients on an international basis."

IMAGE FINDERS PHOTO AGENCY, INC., 134 Abbott St., Vancouver, British Columbia, Canada V6B 2K4. (604)688-3818. Manager: Dairobi Paul. 300,000 color photos. Art, architecture, historic sites, North American Indians and their culture; commerce and industry (office buildings, shops, restaurants, hotels, construction, communications, crafts, manufacturing, and people at work); sciences, transportation, foreign countries, people, parks, recreation, sports, cityscapes, cultural events, zoos, aquariums, housing and alternative energy; institutional (military, education, government, law enforcement, medical services, religion, and fire fighting); landscapes, seascapes, plants, animals, agriculture, logging, fishing, and mining. Offers one-time, editorial, advertising, reproduction and all rights. Charges $50-900 for one-time editorial or advertising use; $15 service charge. Prints made to order: $5-15. Copy negatives $5-10.

IMAGE PHOTOS, Main St., Stockbridge MA 01262. (413)298-5500. Director: Clemmens Kalischer. 500,000 b&w and color photos of abstractions, arts, architecture, children, crafts, education, ethnic groups, Western Europe, farming, human activities, India, music, Nature, New England, personalities, religion, social documentary, and theater. Offers one-time editorial and reproduction rights. Charges $50-1,500 for one-time editorial or advertising use; research charge for some requests.

IMAGES ATLANTA, 1425 Dutch Valley Place, NE, Atlanta GA 30324. (404)876-5014. Contact: Jim Ayres. 5,000 b&w photos; 2,500 color. Subjects: nature, scenics, food, architectural, people, fashion, glamour, New Orleans jazz, Great Smoky Mountains, old railroad and logging photos. Offers one-time editorial and advertising or reproduction rights. Fees: $100-1,000 for one-time editorial or advertising use; $50 selection charge, $25 service charge if no selection is used. $10 print fee. Catalog for $5.

INTERCAM, 383 E. 17th St., Brooklyn NY 11226. (212)469-9472. Owner/Photographer: Carl Frank. 10,000 b&w and 10,000 color photos. "Specializing in Latin America with subject material for textbooks, encyclopedia or advertising use." Offers "any rights purchaser requires." Fees: $45-125 for one-time editorial or advertising use.

INTERNATIONAL MUSEUM OF PHOTOGRAPHY, George Eastman House, 900 East Ave., Rochester NY 14607. Contact: Martha Jenks, Archives; Michael Kamins, Print Service. Collection spans the history of photography — 1839 to present day. Original prints do not leave the museum, except for approved traveling exhibitions. Reproduction prints must be returned, and a credit line is required. Work is listed by photographer, not subject. "Rates determined by circulation." Fee: $15 to $200, 1-time reproduction.

INTERNATIONAL REPORTS AGENCY (formerly *Reports Internationale Agency*), Box 4574, Denver CO 80204. Manager: R. Johnson. 20,000 color photos. "Strong 35mm Kodachrome inventory of the Rocky Mountain States, Canada and the Southwest, Florida, New England,

Seattle, Central America, Mexico and France. Scenics, peoples, flowers, nature, the sciences, and mountain sports a specialty." Offers one-time, editorial, advertising, and reproduction rights. Charges $25 and up for one-time editorial or advertising use.

INTERPRESS OF LONDON AND NEW YORK, 400 Madison Ave., New York NY 10017. (212)832-2839. Manager: Jeffrey Blyth. Photos of personalities; specializing in photojournalism. Topical or unusual picture stories.

ITALIAN HISTORICAL ARCHIVES (formerly *Sisto Archives*), Box 255, Berwyn IL 60402. President: John A. Sisto. 1 million photos. Subjects: old cars, old advertisements, theatre, movies, circus, women's fashions, Italian historical prints, engravings from 12th to 20th centuries, sports, medicine, religious prints, old documents, authors, World Wars I & II, Mussolini, Italian kings, queens, cities, cathedrals, musicians, artists, Popes, autographs, architecture, airplanes, dirigibles, air balloons, World War II posters, and art nouveau of Italy. Offers one-time and reproduction rights. Fees: $50-150 for one-time advertising or editorial use; $25 selection fee. Catalog for SASE.

LOU JACOBS, JR., 13058 Bloomfield St., Studio City CA 91604. Contact: Lou Jacobs, Jr. About 25,000 b&w negatives and 5,000 color slides. "All manner of subjects from animals to industry, human interest to motion picture personalities, action, children, scenic material from national parks and various states." Offers first rights on previously unpublished material; one-time reproduction rights on the remainder, except for exclusive rights by agreement. Fees: b&w minimum $50 each up to five, and $40 each for five or more; color is $150 each for one to five and $125 each for more than five.

ERNST A. JAHN, 18 Blackrock Terrace, Ringwood NJ 07456. (201)962-4114. 40,000 photos available on purchase or loan basis for reproduction rights, advertising rights, second rights, editorial rights, first rights or all rights. Subjects: Alaska, Central and South America, Europe, South Africa, Caribbean Islands, and U.S.A. coverage ranging from general scenery, cities, new buildings, ships, railways, cattle, festivals, general human interest and special studies on the flying squirrel; local and tropical animals. Reproduction fee: $125/color; $25/b&w. Holding fee: $10 after 21 days.

JUDGE STUDIO, 610 Wood St., Pittsburgh PA 15222. "500 to 1,000 old city views of Pittsburgh and air views; industrial, coal towns, bridges; all b&w prints." Offers one-time reproduction rights. $50 fee charged for 1-time.

YORAM KAHANA PHOTOGRAPHY, 1909 N. Curson Place, Hollywood CA 90046. (213)876-8208 or 876-5430. Contact: Yoram Kahana or Peggy Halper. "200,000 photos, mostly 35mm transparencies in two areas: personalities (screen, TV, rock, jazz, pop, at home sessions, portraits and in performance; and travel (emphasis on people, crafts, folkways, families; strongest in Central America, Mexico, Far East, Israel, Kenya, and US West Coast)." Sells reproduction rights only; follows ASMP guidelines for terms, rights, and fees.

CURT W. KALDOR, 603 Grandview Dr., South San Francisco CA 94080. (415)583-8704. Several thousand photos of scenic views and city-suburbs; street scenes, aircraft, people, architectural, railroads, shipping and boating, redwoods and timbering, and others. Offers all types of rights up through complete purchase. Charges a flat fee for purchase of reproduction rights. That fee is based on type of usage.

KANSAS STATE HISTORICAL SOCIETY, 10th and Jackson Sts., Topeka KS 66612. (913)296-3165. Contact: Nancy Sherbert. 80,000 photos of Indians, the American West, railroads, military, Kansas and Kansans. Reproduction rights, advertising rights, first rights, second rights. Collection is in the public domain. B&w glossy or matte finish fee: $1 (4x5); $1.50 (5x7); $2.75 (8x10); $5 (11x14); $8.50 (16x20). Minimum order $1. Color transparencies will be made in special cases where such work is feasible for $7. Mounting charge: 75¢/sq. ft. Copy fee of $1.50 if a new negative is required. Credit line required.

KENTUCKY DEPARTMENT OF PUBLIC INFORMATION, Advertising and Travel Promotion, Capitol Annex, Frankfort KY 40601. (502)564-4930. Contact: Ken Cooper, Director. B&w and color photos of scenic, historic; parks, recreation, events. No fees, but credit line and return of pictures required. General information and editorial material available on most areas.

KEYSTONE PRESS AGENCY, INC., 170 Fifth Ave., New York NY 10010. (212)924-4123.

Contact: Walter Schrenck-Szill, Managing Editor. Singles and feature sets of news, political, scientific, business, human interest, animals, inventions, education, recreation, underwater, scenics, explorers, personalities, odds, pop and hippies, art, pretty girls, medical, sports, and many more. B&w and color. Pictures must be returned within two weeks; longer period for free holding must be negotiated. One-time reproduction fee for b&w, $50 minimum. Credit line and return of pictures required.

JOAN KRAMER AND ASSOCIATES, 5 N. Clover, Great Neck NY 11021. (212)246-7600 or (212)224-1758. Contact: Joan Kramer. Over 100,000 photos including abstracts, boats, travel shots from U.S.A. and other countries, children, ethnic groups, fisheye shots, nature, people shots, scenics, teenagers, winter scenes and zoos. B&w (8x10) and color (35mm). Rights negotiable. Fees are based on budget available and photo use.

JAMES W. LA TOURRETTE, PHOTOGRAPHER, 1416 SW 15 Terrace, Ft. Lauderdale FL 33312. About 4,000 b&w and color pictures. "2¼ and 35mm underwater color transparencies of the waters in the Florida Keys and Bahama Islands. Some 4x5 color scenics. Motor sports events; boat races, sports car races; scenics, eastern U.S., West Coast, Everglades wildlife and plants." Also scenics of Germany, Austria, Japan and Hong Kong. Offers one-time rights. Fees: b&w 8x10 prints, $25; color transparencies, $75-250. "Color to be returned after use."

HAROLD M. LAMBERT STUDIOS, INC., Box 27310, Philadelphia PA 19150. (215)224-1400. Contact: R. W. Lambert. Complete photo service has over 1,000,000 b&w photos on hand to cover all subjects from babies to skydiving, plus 200,000 color transparencies covering same subjects. Rental fee varies according to use. "Average rates: $25 minimum editorial use with credit line; $40 minimum (b&w); $140 (color); minimum promotional rate."

LAS VEGAS NEWS BUREAU, Convention Center, Las Vegas NV 89109. (702)735-3611. Contact: Don Payne, Manager. B&w, color, both stills and 16mm, available from files or shot on assignment for accredited writers with bona fide assignments. Return of color required.

LATIN AMERICA PHOTOS, 3308 Legation St., NW, Washington DC 20015. (202)686-1609. Contact: Luz Mangurian. 50,000 color and b&w photos of "a wide variety of subjects from most Latin American countries including agriculture, archaeology, education, energy, folk arts, food, Indians, industry, mining, music, scenics, sports, rural and urban life, and social conditions." Offers one-time rights. Charges ASMP rates. Free stock list. "All specific queries will be answered, but will not loan pictures for articles being submitted on speculation. Prefer to deal with editors after article has been accepted. Exception: book projects. All request must be specific to receive attention."

FRED LEWIS AGENCY (formerly Frederic Lewis, Inc.), 390 Ocean Pkwy, Brooklyn NY 11218. (212)282-9219. Owner: Fred Lewis. 1,000 b&w and 5,000 color photos of "nature, people, and places inside the United States." Offers all rights. Fees: $75-200 for one-time editorial or advertising use, no selection fee, $5-10 print fee. Free catalog.

LICK OBSERVATORY, University of California, Santa Cruz CA 95064. Contact: Administrative Office. Users of astronomical photographs should make their selections from the standard list in the current catalogue of Astronomical Photographs available as slides or prints from negatives obtained at Lick Observatory, since it is not possible to supply views of other objects or special sizes. B&w, 2x2, 8x10, and 14x17. Catalogues are free upon written request. Information concerning color materials is contained in the calalogue. Purchasers are reminded that permission for use of Lick Observatory photographs for reproduction or commercial purposes must be obtained in writing in advance from the Director of the Observatory. Fee: 60¢-$6 for b&w.

LIGHTFOOT COLLECTION, Box A-F, Greenport NY 11944. (516)477-2589. Contact: Frederick S. Lightfoot. 30,000 b&w photos of "Americana—strong coverage 19th century, representation of 20th century to 1920. City, town, village and country scenes, architecture, transportation, industrial, culture, famous people, wars, agriculture, mining. Also 19th century foreign file, primarily cities and harbors." Offers all rights. Charges $15 and up for one-time editorial or advertising use; $5 print fee.

LINCOLN FARM, 140 Heatherdell Rd., Ardsley NY 10502. (914)693-4222. Contact: Harold Loren. 5,000 photos of children (7-16) in summer camp activities. Available for purchase or loan at cost of handling and postage. Reproduction rights, editorial rights, all rights.

LINCOLN PICTURE STUDIO, 225 Lookout Dr., Dayton OH 45419. Contact: Lloyd Ostendorf. Photographs in b&w, Civil War era, 1850-1870; photographs of American scenes, people, places; special collection of photographs of Abraham Lincoln, his family, friends and notables of his day. Selecting photographs for an author or publisher is often done with only a small fee for cost of prints and mailing. The reproduction fee ($50 each) is payable when user holds them for reproduction and publication. Credit line and return of photos required.

LONG ISLAND HISTORICAL SOCIETY, 128 Pierrepont St., Brooklyn NY 11201. (212)624-0890. Librarian: Anne Gordon. 6,000 b&w photos of Brooklyn, Queens, and Long Island—streets, houses, factories, landscapes, transportation and marine topics; dating from c. 1870 to present. Offers reproduction rights. Fees: $10 for one-time editorial or advertising use; $2 service charge; $12.50 print fee. "All negatives retained by the society. Credit line required."

LOUISIANA STATE LIBRARY, Box 131, Baton Rouge LA 70821. (504)389-6120. Contact: Mrs. Harriet Callahan. This is a collection pertaining to the state of Louisiana and persons prominent in Louisiana history. Most of the photographs are b&w. It does contain color pictures during the past 5 years. This is a non-circulating, historical collection. Credit line and return of pictures required.

THOMAS LOWES, PHOTOGRAPHER, 491 Delaware Ave., Buffalo NY 14202. (716)883-2650. Contact: Liz Mohring. Over 50,000 photos — yachting and boating, tall ships, Americana (people, landscapes, historic objects and landmarks), hot air ballooning, rodeos, ghost towns, Indian crafts and missions. Farming (people and equipment), Canadian provinces. Color transparencies (35mm). Fees depend on publication.

BURTON McNEELY PHOTOGRAPHY, P.O. Box 338, Land o' Lakes Fl 33539. (813)996-3025. Contact: Burton McNeely. "About 10,000 color only: recreation, travel, romance, girls, underwater, and leisure time activities." Offers any and all rights. "Fees are based on the use of the photos, such as circulation of magazine or type of book. Minimum one-time rate for any published use is $125."

MAGNUM, 15 W. 46th St., New York NY 10036. Joan Liftin, Director of library; Lee Jones, Editor. Over 1,000,000 photos. Photojournalistic reportage, documentary photography, feature and travel coverage; mainly from the thirties. B&w and color. Standard American Society of Magazine Photographers fees.

THE MAYTAG COMPANY, 403 W. Fourth St., N., Newton IA 50208. Contact: Ronald L. Froehlich, Manager, Public Information. Photos of home laundry settings; kitchens; anything in area of laundry appliances, laundering, kitchen appliances, use of dishwashers, disposers; laundering procedures. Also available are industrial shots, in-factory assembly line photos. Both b&w and color (laundry and kitchen settings), transparencies, slides. Credit line and return of color transparencies required.

MEMORY SHOP, 109 E. 12th St., New York NY 10003. (212)473-2404. 5,000,000 b&w and 1,000,000 color photos on "all various subjects, but mostly catering to the seven arts: specializing in movies, theatre, television, etc. Also categories on almost any subject from animals to zoos; sports, politicians, scenics, westerns, horror, science fiction, and classic films." Offers one-time rights. Fees: charges $15-25 for one-time editorial or advertising use; $10-25 service charge; $15-25 print fee.

LOUIS MERCIER, 342 Madison Ave., New York NY 10017. Stock photographs; color scenics USA and worldwide; personalities, fashion, food, industry, and the arts. Fees: $35 minimum for b&w; $100 for color depending on use.

MERCURY ARCHIVES, 1574 Crossroads of the World, Hollywood CA 90028. Over a million photos. "Woodcuts and engravings on all subjects; pre-1900. We operate as a stock photo rental service." Full rights offered. Fees: vary per picture on a 1-time and 1-use basis. Research/service fee charged when pictures not used for reproduction.

THE METROPOLITAN MUSEUM OF ART, Fifth Ave., at 82nd St., New York NY 10028. Contact: Photograph and Slide Library. History of art from ancient times to the present. B&w

photos: 4x5 and 8x10 for sale; color transparencies: mostly 8x10, rental, for purposes of publication only. New publication: *Color Transparencies for Rental,* $3 plus tax. These cover only paintings and other objects in the Museum's collections. Research must be done by user. Copy photo price schedule available. Fee: $5-10/8x10 photo. Credit line required. Return required on color transparencies only; photographs made to special order are sold outright with one-time reproduction rights included.

MIAMI SEAQUARIUM, 4400 Rickenbacker Causeway, Miami FL 33149. Contact: Zoe Todd. Photos in b&w and color of the Seaquarium and a variety of sea creatures. The Miami Seaquarium makes photographs available to all writers and editors free of charge, providing either the Seaquarium is given a credit line ("Photo Courtesy Miami Seaquarium"), or the Seaquarium is mentioned in the caption. Tearsheets required. Return required for color only. Nonpayment situation subject to change.

MINISTRY OF INDUSTRY AND TOURISM, Hearst Block, Parliament Bldgs., Toronto, Ontario, Canada. Contact: Bruce Reed. "About 40,000 color transparencies and b&w photos of outdoors and travel, fishing, hunting, boating, camping. To be used for travel articles only. Would appreciate a credit line." No fee.

MINNESOTA HISTORICAL SOCIETY, Audio-Visual Library, 690 Cedar, St. Paul MN 55101. (612)296-2489. Contact: Bonnie Wilson. 150,000 photos available for purchase. Reproduction rights offered for some photos. Minnesota persons, places and activities. Emphasis on Indians, agriculture, mining, lumbering, recreation, transportation and family life. Reproduction service fee: $5. Print fee: $2.50. Photocopies: 10¢. Copy negative: $2. Credit line required.

MISSISSIPPI DEPARTMENT OF ARCHIVES & HISTORY, Box 571, (100 S. State St.,) Jackson MS 39205. (601)354-6218. Contact: Jo Ann Bomar. Subjects: Civil War prints from *Harper's Weekly* and Frank Leslie's *Weekly* (some hand-colored); prominent Mississippians, historic spots and other Mississippi scenes, historic buildings and antebellum mansions, the Mississippi River and steamboats. Fees: $3.50 for positive photostat; $3/8x10 glossy. Credit line required.

MISSOURI HISTORICAL SOCIETY, Jefferson Memorial Bldg., Lindell & Debaliviere, St. Louis MO 63112. (314)361-1424. Contact: Ms. Gail R. Guidry. 100,000 photos on Missouri and western life, the World's Fair, early St. Louis, early aviation; the Lindbergh Collection and Steamboat Collection. Reproduction rights available. Reproduction fee $15/photo. Print fee: $10/8x10 b&w; $40/4x5 color transparency. "Always write if out of state and request prints. No telephone orders processed. Collection seen upon appointment."

GEORGE A. MOFFITT, COLLECTION, 306 W. 94th St., New York NY 10025. Contact: George A. Moffitt. Photos of pre-war American and Continental standard and custom cars of the movies (with stars that owned them); cars shown with public figures of the past; custom body builders' renderings; antique cars of early American production; racing car scenes, b&w and color; also post-war photos of American and Continental production. 1-time reproduction fee for editorial use: $30, b&w; $100, color.

MONTANA DEPARTMENT OF HIGHWAYS, Montana Travel Promotion Unit, Helena MT 59601. Contact: Josephine Brooker, Director. Scenic, historic, recreational, official (state seal, flag, etc.) photos in 8x10 glossy b&w and 35mm. 2¼ square, 4x5 color transparencies. Writer receives a memo invoice with shipment of color photos. If photos are returned within reasonable time, in same condition, invoice is canceled. Credit line required. Return of pictures required for color only. Editorial material also available.

MONTGOMERY PICTURES, Box 722, Las Vegas NM 87701. (505)425-3146. Contact: Mrs. C.M. Montgomery. "6,000 4x5 color transparencies and 10,000 35mm color transparencies of animals, birds, reptiles, flora, scenics, state and national parks, ghost towns, historic, Indian and petroglyphs." 1-time reproduction rights in one country preferred; all other rights by negotiation. Fees: "ASMP rates, where applicable. Otherwise, the publisher's current rates; but not less than $25 per transparency."

MUNSEY NEWS SERVICE, 41 Union Square W., New York NY 10003. (212)989-7151. Editor: Al LaPresto. 5,000 b&w photos; 2,000 color. "Photos of spot news events, World Fairs from 1939 to the present, general scenes from New York City, Montreal and most other locations in the US and Canada. We will work on assignment basis anywhere in the world." Offers all rights. Charges $5-250 for one-time editorial or advertising use. Free catalog.

THE MUSEUM OF MODERN ART, Film Stills Archive, 11 W. 53rd St., New York NY 10019. (212)956-4209. Contact: Mrs. Mary Corliss. Approximately 3,000,000 b&w stills on foreign and American productions, film personalities, and directors. Duplicates of original stills are sold at a cost of $6/still. Credit line required.

MUSEUM OF NEW MEXICO, Box 2087, Santa Fe NM 87503. (505)827-2559. Contact: Photo Archives. 80,000 photos available: archaeology, anthropology, railroads, Southwestern Americana, Southwestern Indians. Some 19th-Century foreign holdings including Oceania, Japan, Middle East. Copy prints $2 and up. Reproduction/publication fees and credit lines required. Catalogs and photographer indexes available.

MUSEUM OF SCIENCE, Science Park, Boston MA 02114. Contact: Bradford Washburn. Contact prints of Alaskan and Alpine mountains and glaciers. All b&w. Copy prints, $5 and up. One-time reproduction fees: $25 each for use on ½-page or less; $50 each for use on 1 page; $75 each for use as a double-page spread. Credit line required.

MUSEUM OF THE AMERICAN INDIAN, Broadway at 155th St., New York NY 10032. Contact: Carmelo Guadagno. The Photographic Archives of the Museum include negatives, b&w prints, and color transparencies from Indian cultures throughout the Western hemisphere. The various categories present a selection of everyday customs, ceremonial paraphernalia, costumes and accessories, dwellings and physical types from a majority of areas. B&w photos, 35mm and 4x5 color transparencies. 2,200 Kodachrome slides; list available for $1. Send stamp. 1-time editorial reproduction fee is $20 for b&w and $40 for color. Credit line required. Folder of information available; send stamp.

MUSEUM OF THE CITY OF NEW YORK, Fifth Ave. at 103rd St., New York NY 10029. (212)534-1672. Contact: Esther Brumberg. 22,000 photos on file for sale only. All rights. Subjects: New York City; all aspects of life and history; street scenes, furniture, toys, costumes, theatre, fires, police, social history, etc. Reproduction fee: $10. Prints made to order: $5 from existing negatives; $10 if new photography is required. Color transparencies available on rental basis. Photocopies: 25¢ each.

THE MUSICAL MUSEUM, S. Main St., Deansboro NY 13328. (315)841-8774. Contact: Arthur H. Sanders. Unlimited number of photos on file for all rights on purchase or loan basis. "We no longer have a staff photographer, and we cannot handle copying work, and help along this line is not in the budget. We do encourage photos and writers and even recordings, but prefer to be mentioned as photo source. Ours is a museum of odd material, some of it very colorful."

HANS NAMUTH, c/o Photoresearchers, Inc., 60 E. 56th St., New York NY 10022. "About 5,000 b&w and color photos: portraits of American artists, scenes of Guatemala, Egypt, etc." Offers reproduction rights. Fees: $75-150.

NATIONAL ARCHIVES AND RECORDS SERVICE, 8th and Pennsylvania Ave., N.W., Washington DC 20408. (202)523-3054. Contact: William H. Leary. Five million photos available for purchase. "Most are in the public domain and may be freely reproduced." Subject: "Pictorial records (primarily b&w) from some 140 Federal agencies illustrating all aspects of American history from the colonial period to the recent past, and many aspects of life in other parts of the world. Included are several large collections such as the Mathew Brady Civil War photographs, the picture file of the Paris branch of the N.Y. Times (1923-1950), and the Heinrich Hoffmann files illustrating activities of the Nazi party in Germany (1923-45)."

NATIONAL CATHOLIC NEWS SERVICE, 1312 Massachusetts Ave., N.W., Washington DC 20005. Contact: Robert A. Strawn. 20,000 photos on purchase basis only. Rights vary with material and usage. Subjects: Catholic-related news and feature and historical material. Fees vary with usage.

NATIONAL COAL ASSOCIATION, 1130 17th St. N.W., Washington DC 20036. (202)628-4322. Contact: Herbert Foster. 2,000 photos, "mostly b&w shots of bituminous coal production, transportation and use, and reclamation of mined land. Some color transparencies of coal production, many showing land reclamation. Most are modern—no historical pix." Allows free editorial use. No fees. "Credit line to NCA."

NATIONAL FILM BOARD PHOTOTHEQUE, Tunney's Pasture, Ottawa, Ontario K1A 0M9 Canada. (613)593-5826. Contact: L. Krueger, Photo Librarian. About 300,000 b&w photos and color transparencies "illustrating the social, economic and cultural aspects of Canada." Photos purchased for 1-time use only. Pictures can be purchased for editorial and commercial use. Fees vary according to the purpose for which the photos are required.

NATIONAL GALLERY OF ART, Washington DC 20565. (202)737-4215. Contact: Ira Bartfield, Photographic Services. Photographs available of major portion of objects in the Gallery's collections, from medieval to present times, including paintings, drawings, etchings, engravings, sculpture and renderings of American folk-art objects. B&w glossy prints, 8x10. Charge: $2 prepaid. Color transparencies available of many objects; rental fee to cover 3-month loan of transparencies. For details of charges, please write for further information. Permission to reproduce objects will be granted for scholarly publications after receiving written request. Permission is not granted for advertising purposes.

NATIONAL LIBRARY OF MEDICINE, 8600 Rockville Pike, Bethesda MD 20014. Contact: Chief, History of Medicine Division. Photographs available on the history of medicine (portraits, institutions, scenes), not related to current personalities, events, or medical science. B&w and color. Copy prints: 8x10, $3 and up. Credit line required. Prices vary according to service provided, and are subject to change without notice. No pictures sent out on approval.

NATIONAL PHOTOGRAPHY COLLECTION, Public Archives of Canada, 395 Wellington St., Ottawa, Canada K1A ON3. (613)992-3884. Contact: Reference Officers. 4,500,000 photos, "all Canadian subjects: documenting the political, economic, industrial, military, social and cultural life of Canada from 1850 to the present. B&w negatives and prints; color transparencies. On unrestricted or non-copyright material, reproduction rights are normally granted upon request after examination of a statement of purpose, or legitimate use in publication, film or television production, exhibition or research." Fees: b&w 8x10 print, $3.

NEBRASKA STATE HISTORICAL SOCIETY, 1500 R St., Lincoln NE 68508. Contact: Marvin F. Kivett, Director. Photographs available of historical subjects pertaining to Nebraska and trans-Missouri west; agriculture; steamboats; Indians. B&w 8x10 glossy prints $2.50. Credit line required.

NEIKRUG GALLERIES, INC., 224 E. 68th St., New York NY 10021. (212)288-7741. Owner/Director: Majorie Neikrug. Collection of antique photos, equipment, daguerrotypes. Offers reproduction rights. Also historical and current books for the researcher.

NEVILLE PUBLIC MUSEUM, 129 S. Jefferson, Green Bay WI 54301. Contact: James L. Quinn, Director. Historical photographs available pertinent to northeastern Wisconsin, especially Green Bay area in b&w and some contemporary color. Photos available at cost only for educational purposes. Museum credit line required.

THE NEW JERSEY HISTORICAL SOCIETY, 230 Broadway, Newark NJ 07104. Contact: Howard W. Wiseman, Curator. Photos available of historical New Jersey houses, buildings, streets, etc., filed by the name of the town (must know the name of town; not filed by subject matter). Charge for making selection: $1.25. 1-time reproduction fee $10 each. Print fee: about $15, depending on job. Copy negative: $5. Credit line required.

THE NEW YORK BOTANICAL GARDEN LIBRARY, Bronx Park, New York NY 10458. Contact: Charles R. Long, Administrative Librarian or Helen Schlanger, Photo Librarian. "Collection being reorganized. Limited access." B&w photos (original and copy), glass negatives, film negatives, clippings, postcards, old prints, original drawings and paintings. Subjects: botany, horticulture; portraits of botanists and horticulturists; pictures from seed catalogues. One-time reproduction fee $35 per print for original b&w photos, $100 for original 35mm color. Credit line required.

NEW YORK CONVENTION AND VISITORS BUREAU, 90 E. 42nd St., New York NY 10017. (212)687-1300. Contact: John P. MacBean. B&w glossies, and color, of New York City's sightseeing attractions and services. No factories, industrial sites, etc. Only city sights; no N.Y. State photos. Please give us specific requests (such as "Statue of Liberty") rather than "a selection of photos." Photos may be used in any legitimate news or feature sense to illustrate copy on the city. No fees, but credit line requested.

THE NEW-YORK HISTORICAL SOCIETY, 170 Central Park W., New York NY 10024. (212)873-3400. Contact: Print Room. About 300,000 photos. Subjects: American history, with emphasis on New York City and New York State; portraits. Seventeenth century to early 20th century. B&w original and copy photos, daguerrotypes, Stereograms, fine-art prints, original cartoons, architectural drawings, business ephemera, glass negatives, posters, postcards, illustrated maps and broadsides. Some material available for editorial reproduction. No loans. Charges print fees and reproduction rights fees.

NEW ZEALAND EMBASSY, 19 Observatory Circle N.W., Washington DC 20008. Contact: Information Officer. A limited number of photos of a general nature about New Zealand. No fees, but credit line and return of pictures requested.

NEWARK MUSEUM, 49 Washington St., Newark NJ 07101. Contact: W.T. Bartle. Photos available on American art (18th, 19th and 20th centuries; painting and sculpture); Oriental art (especially Tibet, Japan, and India); decorative arts (furniture, jewelry, costumes). 8x10 b&w photos. Fee: $2.50 for copy prints; $10, one-time reproduction fee. 4x5 transparencies. $65 sale or $35 for 3-month rental, including reproduction fee. Credit line required.

NEWSWEEK BOOKS, 444 Madison Ave., New York NY 10022. Collection of about 8,000 photos on art of all kinds, architecture, American and world history. B&w and color. Offers reproduction rights for 1-time, non-exclusive use. Charges $35 to $50 for b&w; up to $150 for color.

NICHOLSON PHOTOGRAPHY, 1503 Brooks Ave., Raleigh NC 27607. (919)787-6076. Contact: Nick Nicholson. 20,000 photos available for sale. Reproduction rights, advertising rights, first rights, second rights, editorial rights, all rights. Subjects: scenics, travel, leisure activity, cities, general interest. "All fees negoiated and based on rights requested plus usage. No standard rate. All material in 35mm color transparency form; b&w prints available as conversions from color slides."

NORTH CAROLINA DIVISION OF ARCHIVES AND HISTORY, 109 E. Jones St., Raleigh NC 27611. (919)733-3952. Contact: Archives Branch. 300,000 photos on file. Most are in the public domain. Subjects: "Most of the photographs in our custody pertain to North Carolina history and culture. Holdings include extensive number of pictures depicting buildings and places in North Carolina that have been nominated for or placed on the National Register of Historic Places." None are available for sale or loan, but prints can be made to order $2-8/b&w; cost, plus 15%/color. "Orders should be placed at least 2 weeks in advance. Detailed research cannot be done by mail or by telephone."

NORTH CAROLINA MUSEUM OF ART, Raleigh NC 27611. (919)733-7568. Contact: Head, Collections Research and Publications Branch. 8x10 b&w glossies; 2x2 color slides; 4x5 color transparencies on permanent collections. Fees: $1.50 for glossies; 75¢ for original slides; 50¢ for duplicate slides; $15 for 3 month rental fee for transparencies. Permission to publish is required.

NOTMAN PHOTOGRAPHIC ARCHIVES, McCord Museum, 690 Sherbrooke St., W., Montreal, Quebec, Canada. (514)392-4781. Contact: Stanley Triggs. 600,000 photos. "Portraits, landscapes, city views, street scenes, lumbering, railroad construction, trains, Indians, fishing, etc. Covers Canada coast to coast. Mostly 19th century, some 20th." Offers 1-time non-exclusive publication rights. Fees: $25 for most publications. "Photographs on loan only —to be returned after use."

NYT PICTURES, 229 W. 43rd St., New York NY 10036. (212)556-1243. Contact: Raphael Paganelli. This is the photo syndicate of the *New York Times* with almost 3 million photos available. Reproduction rights, advertising rights, editorial rights, all rights. Subjects: Personalities, politics, news and special events. Fee: $12.50/photo print. Reproduction fee: $40 minimum, depending on use of photos. "Photo research in archives by non-staff members not permitted. Photo research service in archives available at cost of $25/hour or fraction thereof."

OREGON HISTORICAL SOCIETY, 1230 S.W. Park Ave., Portland OR 97205. Contact: Janice Worden, Photographs Librarian. Several hundreds of thousands —300,000 catalogued photos.

"All subjects in geographical range: Pacific Northwest (Oregon, Washington, Idaho, British Columbia), Alaska, North Pacific. Most b&w prints and negatives; also color transparencies and negatives, engravings, lantern slides (color and b&w), etc. Virtually all material is available for publication; credit line required." Fees vary according to use.

ORGANIZATION OF AMERICAN STATES, Photographic Records, Graphic Services Unit, 19th St., and Constitution Ave., N.W., Washington DC 20006. (202)381-8700. Contact: C.L. Headen. 35,000 b&w photos available at reprint cost ($2/copy). Reproduction rights, advertising rights, editorial rights, and all rights offered. Collection is in the public domain. Subjects: Agriculture, antiquities, art, cities and towns, education, historical, industry, minerals, native activities, natural history, political, portraits, public welfare recreation, topography, transportation, Latin America, Barbados, Jamaica, Trinidad, and Tobago. Fee: $2/print. Credit line required. Return of pictures *not* required.

OUTDOOR PIX & COPY, 5639 N. 34th Ave., Phoenix AZ 85017. (602)973-9557. Contact: James Tallon. About 70,000 photos included in this collection. Photos of scenics, education, natural science, agriculture, sports, travel, wildlife, foreign countries (Mexico and Canada), human interest. "Strong on nature, hunting, fishing, camping, recreation. More than 500 selected shots of elk; 2,000 shots of cowboys on cattle drive; thousands of bird shots; lots of plant close-ups including cactus blossoms; national parks and monuments (Western); lots of sealife including fighting elephant seals. "95 percent of the people who write me for pictures find something they are looking for." 35mm color only. Rights vary with material and its use. Selection on approval. Slides must be returned unless all rights are purchased. Credit line and tearsheets appreciated. Outright purchase price: negotiable. Reproduction fee: $50 minimum. "Selections are mailed to prospective buyers within 48 hours, usually the same day requests come in. List of categories available on request."

PACIFIC AERIAL SURVEYS, 444 Pendleton, Oakland CA 94614. Contact: Jack E. Logan. 200,000 aerial photographs of western U.S. only. B&w, color. Outright purchase price: b&w 8x10, $50; color transparency, $100. 1-time reproduction fee: b&w, $30; color, $75. Credit line and return of pictures required.

PAN AMERICAN AIRWAYS, Pan Am Bldg., New York NY 10017. Attn: Photo Library. Contact: Ruth Keary, Manager, Film. Photos of Pan Am equipment (airplanes, etc.) and destination photos. B&w and color. Photos supplied for use within travel context. Charges reproduction fee (lab costs) to supply duplicates, whether b&w or color. Fee varies depending upon what is required.

PEABODY MUSEUM OF SALEM, East India Square, Salem MA 01970. (617)745-1876. Contact: Curators of the various departments. 1 million photographs available for sale. Principally maritime history and ethnology of non-European peoples; natural history. B&w and color. Reproduction, advertising and editorial rights. Credit line required. Send for free price list and descriptive brochure. Selection charge depends on research needed; reproduction fee negotiable; print fee $4 and up; photocopies 25¢/page.

PENGUIN PHOTO, 663 Fifth Ave., New York NY 10022. (212)758-7328. Contact: Mrs. Ena Fielden. Over 50,000 photos in b&w and color. Accent is on the field of entertainment: film, stage, music, dance, radio, and TV. "Photos are for strictly editorial use only." Prevalent current fees. "Photos are on loan from collection."

ROBERT PERRON, 104 E. 40th St., New York NY 10016. (212)661-8796. Photos of nature, aerials of coastal scenes, architecture, interiors, energy saving houses. About 10,000 in collection. Offers 1-time rights. Fees: $50 for b&w, $150 for color, editorial.

PHELPS & THOMPSON, INC., 1375 Peachtree St., NE, Suite 172, Atlanta GA 30309. (404)881-1925. President: Sarah Catherine Phelps. 5,000 b&w and 10,000 color photos of all subjects. "We supply editorial, advertising, corporate, and educational markets." Offers all rights. Fees: ASMP rates for one-time editorial or advertising use: $25 selection fee. Catalog for SASE.

PHILADELPHIA MUSEUM OF ART, Rights and Reproduction Department, Box 7646, Philadelphia PA 19101. 250,000 photos and color transparencies. "Paintings, prints, furniture, silver, sculpture, ceramics, arms and armor, coffers, jades, glass, metal objects, ivory objects, textiles, tapestries, costumes, period rooms; photos of works of art in our museum.'' 8x10 b&w and 5x7 and 4x5 color transparencies. Fees: $5 for 8x10 b&w; $30 rental fee for color transparencies. Reproduction fees are based on usage.

ALLAN A. PHILIBA, 3408 Bertha Dr., Baldwin NY 11510. (212)371-5220 or (516)623-7841. 25,000 photos on file. Travel specialists in color photography. Subjects: the Far East, Europe, South America, U.S.A., North Africa and the Caribbean. Fees vary with use and material.

PHOTO ARCHIVES-MUSEUM OF NEW MEXICO, Box 2087, Santa Fe NM 87503. (505)827-2087. Photographic Archivist: Arthur L. Olives. 90,000 b&w photos; 500 color. Subjects: New Mexicana; Western Americana; Indians; mining; railroads; agriculture; Latin America; and North, Central and South American archaeology. Offers one-time and reproduction rights. Send for free schedule.

PHOTO RESEARCHERS, INC., 60 E. 56th St., New York NY 10022. (212)758-3420. Contact: Sam Dasher, Natural History & National Audubon Society Collection or Marcia Mammano, General Library. Includes The National Audubon Society Collection and Rapho Division. More than 1,500,000 award-winning color transparencies and b&w prints. Special editing services. Nature, wildlife, ''beautiful people;'' all subjects and locations. ''Noted photographers available for assignments.''

PHOTO TRENDS, 1472 Broadway, New York NY 10036. Contact: R. Eugene Keesee. ''About 500,000 b&w and color (mostly 35mm) photos. Subjects: children, education, news photos from England, South Africa, and Spain; Hollywood candids from circa 1960 to date, scientific subjects such as photomicrographs, people in places around the world, scenics around the world, wonders and disasters occurring on planet Earth.'' For editorial, offers ''usually North American rights only. World rights available for 95% of the materials.'' Fees: ASMP rates.

PHOTO WORLD, 251 Park Ave. S., New York NY 10010. (212)777-4210. Manager: Selma Brackman. Photos of personalities, history, World War II, and all other subjects; some specialties. 3,000,000 photos in collection. Rights offered negotiable. Fees depend on reproduction rights.

PHOTOGRAPHY BY HARVEY CAPLIN, Box 10393, Alameda NM 87184. (505)898-2020. Contact: Harvey Caplin. 35,000 b&w and 15,000 color photos of ''all southwestern subjects including cattle, ranching, sheep, Indians, national parks and monuments, scenery, sports and recreation. Also available for assignment anywhere in the southwest.'' Offers all rights. Fees: $50 minimum for one-time b&w editorial or advertising use; $100 minimum for color. Free catalog.

PHOTOGRAPHY COLLECTION, Special Collections Division, University of Washington Libraries, Seattle WA 98195. (206)543-0742. Contact: Curator of Photography. Collection of 200,000 images devoted to history of photography in Pacific Northwest and Alaska from 1860-1920. Most early photographers of the two regions are represented, including Eric A. Hegg (Gold Rush), Wilhelm Hester (Maritime), and George T. Emmons (Anthropology). Special topical assemblies maintained for localities, industries and occupations of Washington Territory and State, for Seattle history, for Indian peoples and totem culture, for ships, whaling and for regional architects and architecture. No printed catalog available; will provide xeroxes of selected views (at 10¢ each) upon receipt of specific statements of needs. Fees by arrangement. Picture credits required for publication and television uses.

PHOTOGRAPHY FOR INDUSTRY, 850 7th Ave., New York NY 10019. (212)757-9255. Contact: Charles Rotkin. 100,000 b&w photos and 25,000 color. Subjects: US, Asia, Europe. People at home, work and play; most basic industries from raw materials to finished products; transportation: land, water, rail, and air; pollution; communications; aviation; lumbering; agriculture & food production; distribution; and housing. Offers one-time editorial and advertising or reproduction rights. Fees: ASMP recommended minimums for editorial use. Free catalog.

PHOTOPHILE, 2311 Kettner Blvd., San Diego CA 92101. (714)234-4431. Director: Linda L. Rill. 90,000 color photos of California, Mexico, Europe, worldwide travel and sports. Offers one-time editorial, advertising or reproduction rights. Fees: $100 minimum for one-time editorial or advertising use; $15 selection fee (if photos unused). Free catalog.

PHOTOVILLAGE, 117 Waverly Place, #5E, New York NY 10011. (212)260-6051 or 541-7600. Contact: Geoffrey R. Gove. Collection of over 50,000 photos, geographic coverage, as well as Americana, sports, special effects, cover graphics, personalities. B&w and color. Offers non-exclusive reproduction rights. Minimum fee of $50 for b&w; $150 minimum for color. Will shoot to order for $150 minimum purchase.

PHOTRI, Box 971, Alexandria VA 22313. (703)836-4439. Director: Col. Jack Novak, USAF Ret. 100,000 b&w photos; 200,000 color. Geographic, scientific/technical, people, space, agriculture, airplanes, ships, tanks, animals, natural history, actors, art, creative photos, holidays, and museums. Offers one-time, editorial, advertising, reproduction, and all rights. Charges $50-125 for one-time editorial or advertising use; "occasionally" charges service fee. Catalog for SASE.

PICTORIAL PARADE, INC., 130 W. 42 St., New York NY 10036. (212)695-0353. Contact: Baer M. Frimer. Photos of all subjects.

PICTUREMAKERS, INC., 1 Paul Dr., Succasunna NJ 07876. (201)584-3000. President: Bill Stahl. Photos of all subjects.

KENNETH C. POERTNER, PHOTOGRAPHER, 613 Hillview Dr., Boise ID 83702. (208)336-0499. Approximately 5,000 photos total, b&w and color. Western birds and mammals, western scenes, Idaho's land and people, western national parks and monuments. Offers one-time, editorial, and advertising rights. "Fees depend on usage and rights purchased. Credit line requested, return of color originals required. Will accept individual assignments on request."

ENOCH PRATT FREE LIBRARY, 400 Cathedral St., Baltimore MD 21201. Contact: Maryland Department. B&w 8x10 glossies of Maryland and Baltimore: persons, scenes, buildings, monuments. "Copy prints at nominal fees." Credit line required.

PUBLIC ARCHIVES OF CANADA, 395 Wellington St., Ottawa, Ontario, Canada K1A 0N3. (613)995-1300. Chief, Picture Division: George Delisle. 25,000 b&w and 800 color photos of Canadiana: historical views, events, portraits, posters, cartoons, costumes, heraldry and medals. Material is in the public domain. Minimum print fee: $2.75.

QUEENS BOROUGH PUBLIC LIBRARY, Long Island Division, 89-11 Merrick Blvd., Jamaica NY 11432. (212) 739-1900. Contact: Davis Erhardt. 20,000 b&w original photos, glass negatives, clippings, postcards, old prints. Subjects: Long Island history, all phases. "Many are historical in nature, dating back to the 1890-1920 period." Print and reproduction fees charged. Credit line required.

RAISNER PHOTOS, Box 298, Nazareth PA 18064. (215)759-5416. Contact: Richard Raisner. 1,000 b&w photos; 6,000 color. Glamour (abstract figurework, nudes, semi-nudes, bikini, ethnic women); women (headshots, at work, at recreation, personalities); and couples (sensitive, mood). Offers one-time, editorial, advertising and reproduction rights. Charges $10 minimum for b&w one-time editorial or advertising use; $25 minimum for color. Charges $2/day for extended holding period over 2 weeks. Credit line requested; return of photos required.

REFLEX PHOTO, INC., 186 5th Ave., New York NY 10010. (212)243-4432. Manager: Lawrence Woods. 100,000 b&w and 100,000 color photos of foreign countries, animals, armed forces, cities/communities, children, conservation/environment, demonstrations, politics, personalities, parks/monuments, police/firemen, picture stories, photojournalism, recreation, sports, special events, personality journalism, United Nations and peace movements. Offers all rights. "All fees are negotiable."

RELIGIOUS NEWS SERVICE, 43 W. 57th St., New York NY 10019. Contact: Jim Hansen, Photo Editor. Over 200,000 items on file. "Religious and secular topics. Largest collection of religious personalities in world. Also fine selection of scenics, human interest, artwork, seasonals, social issues, history, cartoons, etc. RNS can be called on for almost all photo needs, not just religious topics." B&w only. Offers 1-time rights. Fees variable.

REMINGTON ART MUSEUM, 303 Washington St., Ogdensburg NY 13669. (315)393-2425. Contact: Mildred B. Dillenbeck, Director. Photos of Frederic Remington paintings, watercolors, drawings, and bronzes. B&w prints and color transparencies available. The largest and most complete collection of works by Remington. Charges rental and 1-time reproduction fee. "$6 photographer's fee for b&w; $35 photographer's fee for color." Credit line and return of pictures required.

RHODE ISLAND DEPARTMENT OF ECONOMIC DEVELOPMENT, Tourist Promotion Division, One Weybosset Hill, Providence RI 02903. Contact: Leonard J. Panaggio, Assistant Director. 2,500 to 5,000 photos. Subjects deal primarily with those used in the promotion of industry tourism and the state of Rhode Island. Industrial and general picture file includes 8x10 b&w photos, 35mm color transparencies. Color transparencies must be returned. Any pictures or color transparencies can be used for editorial purposes. Any and all of material is available.

RICHARDS COMMERCIAL PHOTO SERVICE, 734 Pacific Ave., Tacoma WA 98402. (206)627-9111. Contact: Ed Richards. "Thousands of b&w and color photos of children, people, animals, farms, forests, all types of industry." Rights offered: "any required." Fees: $25 minimum.

H. ARMSTRONG ROBERTS, 4203 Locust St., Philadelphia PA 19104. (215)386-6300. 420 Lexington Ave., Room 2914, New York NY 10017. (212)682-6626. Tina Veiga, Manager. 203 N. Wabash Ave., Room 818, Chicago IL 60601. (312)726-0880. Howard Cox, Manager. Over one-half million stock photographs of all subjects in color and b&w. Also historical file. Catalog and/or 10-day fee approval submissions available. Research and holding fees may be required. Reproduction fees vary according to nature and extent of media.

LEONARD RUE III ENTERPRISES, Rt. 3, Box 31, Blairstown NJ 07825. (201)362-6616. 45,000 b&w and 50,000 color photos. "We specialize in wildlife, nature, natural history, outdoor subjects, travel, primitive people of the world. Feature North America and Africa. We have one of the largest files on wildlife in the country." Offers all rights. "All photo rates are according to usage and rights purchased."

PHOTOGRAPHY, Box 8101, Atlanta GA 30306. Manager: Ed Symmes. Photos of all subjects. "Mostly color transparencies of nature, tropical fish, horticulture, bonsai, scenics." About 5,000 photos in collection. Offers "from 1-time only to world rights." Fees depend on usage and rights purchased.

SAN FRANCISCO MARITIME MUSEUM, Foot of Polk St., San Francisco CA 94109. Contact: Isabel Bullen. Photos of West Coast shipping, deep-water sail, steamships, etc. Mostly b&w, some color (contemporary ships). Print fee: $4 (8x10 glossy). Textbooks repro fee is $7.50. Credit line required.

SANFORD PHOTO ASSOCIATES, 219 Turnpike Road, Manchester NH 03104. Contact: Mrs. Gene Tobias Sanford, Stockfile Manager. Over 100,000 photos in collection. "Color (primarily 4x5 transparencies), 35mm, 2¼, some 8x10 transparencies; color negatives — mostly New England scenics and varied all-occasion type photographs. B&w 8x10 scenics and miscellaneous subjects. Our files in both b&w and color cover a wide range of subjects: flowers, children, animals, houses, industry, pollution, soft focus, some other areas in U.S. and many foreign countries. Fees for one-time reproduction rights depend on how the photograph will be used, and on quantity of photos purchased." Minimum fee for single purchases: $35 for b&w; $125 for color.

SCALA FINE ARTS PUBLISHERS, INC., 28 W. 44th St., New York NY 10036. Manager: Ted Feder. Photos of art objects. "Chronologically, the range is from the caveman to the present; geographically, we cover all Europe, the Near East, and India with a specialty collection from Japan and a small selection of Mayan and Incan objects." Photos available of "paintings, sculpture, architecture, tapestry, pottery, manuscript illumination, and a wide variety of other art styles." Has archive of scientific subjects; "the main topics covered include botany, zoology, geography, geology, biology, medicine, marine life (with special emphasis on underwater), and a wide range of photographs of farming, industry, living conditions, etc., around the world. We represent the famous Alinari collection in the United States. These b&w photographs for rental include objects of art from Greece, Italy, Germany, France, and numerous other countries." B&w photos; color transparencies, 35mm to 8x10. Fee: "varies according to the usage. We will submit photos on approval."

SEKAI BUNKA PHOTO, 501 Fifth Ave., Room 2102, New York NY 10017. (212)490-2180. Manager: Jane Hatta. Over 100,000 color and b&w photos of Japan and the Far East for usage in New York branch, including modern scenes, historical art treasures, temples/shrines, architecture, costume, manners, etc. Expanding to similar coverage, especially of people and their life styles in the United States and Europe (including calendar pin-ups) for sale in Japan through Tokyo office. B&w are quality 5x7 or larger glossy and color are usually 2¼x3¼, 4x5 or larger. Usually offers 1-time rights, non-exclusive usage, although other rights are negotiable. Discounts from basic prices for quantity use in same work. Basic price minimums (generally $65 for b&w and $125 for color) vary depending upon usage, quantity; other factors depending upon final fee negotiations. Available for special assignments in Japan and Far East.

THE SHAKER MUSEUM, Shaker Museum Rd., Old Chatham NY 12136. Contact: Peter Laskovski, Director. Photographs of Shaker buildings and members; museum galleries; some furniture and other artifacts; B&w only. Charge for making selection $1. Print fees: for first requested copy if not in files, $12, including one 8x10 print; second prints, or if from negative in files, $6. Negative of any requested copy stays in files. Billed by photographer. Credit line required.

ANN ZANE SHANKS, 201 B East 82nd St., New York NY 10028. "About 5,000 items. Stock picture file, color and b&w of people—from the very young to the very old. Celebrities, scenes, hospitals, travel, and interracial activities." Offers first or second rights. Fees: $50 minimum, b&w; $150 minimum, color. Credit line requested.

RAY SHAW, Studio 5B, 255 W. 90th St., New York NY 10024. (212)873-0808. Worldwide editorial photo feature and annual report specialist. Animals, ballet, children, inspirational, American Indians, Mennonites, foreign countries: Algeria, Canada, Denmark, Egypt, England, France, Germany, India, Iran, Israel, Jordan, Lebanon, Luxembourg, Mexico, Morocco, Switzerland, Syria, Tunisia, Yugoslavia, etc.

SHOSTAL ASSOCIATES, INC., 60 E. 42nd St., New York NY 10017. (212)687-0696. Contact: David Forbert. Over 1 million photos available on rental basis. Reproduction rights, advertising rights, first rights, second rights, editorial rights, all rights. All subjects, U.S. and foreign. Fees vary with material and usage.

SICKLES PHOTO-REPORTING SERVICE, Box 98, 410 Ridgewood Rd., Maplewood NJ 07040. (201)763-6355. Contact: Gus Sickles, Jr. "Negatives on file cover a period of about the past 40 years, relating to business, industry, agriculture, etc., but we are basically an assignment service, rather than a supplier of stock photos." Offers all rights. Fee: ASMP rates "or will quote".

BP SINGER FEATURES, INC., 3164 W. Tyler Ave., Anaheim CA 92801. (714)537-5650. Photo Editor: Eldon Maynard. 5,000 b&w photos; 25,000 color. "Jacket cover art color transparencies is our major subject area. We have other topics too numerous to mention." Offers "negotiable" rights. "Fees are determined by usage and availability. $10 service fee, refundable if purchase is made."

SKYVIEWS SURVEY, INC., 50 Swalm St., Westbury NY 11590. (516)333-3600. President: William J. Fried. 125,000 b&w negatives, and 20,000 color photos. All aerial photography, cross-indexed geographically and by subject. Offers one-time editorial or advertising and reproduction rights. Fees: $50-250 for one-time editorial or advertising use; $15-20 holding fee.

DICK SMITH PHOTOGRAPHY, P. O. Box X, North Conway NH 03860. (603)356-2814. "10,000 b&w and 5,000 4x5 color transparencies. Scenics, tourist attractions, geologic and geographic features, farming, animals, lakes, mountains, snow scenes, historic sites, churches, covered bridges, flowers and gardens, aerials, Atlantic coast, skiing, fishing, camping, national parks. These are mostly of New England, but I do have some of the South and West." Offers usually 1-time rights for the specific use. Fees: minimum b&w $35, minimum color $100.

GEMINI SMITH, INC., 5858 Desert View Dr., La Jolla CA 92037. (714)454-4321. Contact: Bradley Smith. 5,000 photos on file. Reproduction rights, advertising rights, all rights available. B&w and color. Subjects: Important paintings and sculptures of the world (all periods, prehistoric to modern); arts, crafts, and historical sites of the U.S.; folkways and scenics (Japan, Spain, Mexico, Europe, United States, West Indies, India); animals in Africa; circus; personalities of the 40's and 50's. Holding fee: $20. Reproduction fee: $80/full-page b&w; $250/full page color.

SOPHIA SMITH COLLECTION, Women's History Archive, Smith College, Northampton MA 01060. Contact: Mary-Elizabeth Murdock, Ph.D., Director. About 5,000 photos emphasizing women's history and general subjects; abolition and slavery, American Indians, outstanding men and women, countries (culture, scenes), U.S. military history, social reform, suffrage, women's rights. Mainly b&w or sepia. Offers U.S. rights, 1-time use only. Print fee based on cost of reproduction of print plus intended use. *Picture Catalog* including fee schedule available for $6 postpaid.

HOWARD SOCHUREK, INC., 680 Fifth Ave., New York NY 10019. (212)582-1860. 250,000 photos on purchase basis only. Reproduction rights, advertising rights, first rights, second rights, editorial rights and all rights available. Subjects: Thermography, ultrasound, science, medical illustration, travel, journalism, U.S.S.R. Fees: Service charge, $50. Reproduction fee: $50/b&w minimum; $150/color minimum.

SOUTH DAKOTA STATE HISTORICAL SOCIETY, Memorial Bldg., Pierre SD 57501. (605)224-3615. Library Technician: Bonnie Gardner. 30,000 b&w photos. "The photograph collection is made up of early towns, forts, American natives, Black Hills, Badlands, farming, ranching, mining, recreation, sod houses, transportation, biographical, etc." Offers one-time rights. Prints made to order: $2 for 5x7, $4 for 8x10.

SOVFOTO/EASTFOTO, 25 W. 43rd St., New York NY 10036. Contact: Leah Siegel. Over 900,000 photos. Photographic coverage from the Soviet Union, China and all East European countries. B&w and color. Fees vary, depending on use. Minimum charge for b&w photos is $50 for 1-time use. Minimum fee for color is $125.

HUGH SPENCER PHOTOS, 3711 El Ricon Way, Sacramento CA 95825. (916)482-8454. Contact: George H. Spencer. 5,000 b&w, 3,500 35mm color. Plants and animals, biological sciences, birds, mammals, insects, reptiles, amphibians, marine life; ferns, wild flowers, trees, mosses, lichens, fungi, etc. Photomicrographs of plant tissues, sections, algae, protozoa. Offers non-exclusive rights on all subjects. Fees: "$25-40 for b&w; $75-125 for color, or will negotiate.

BOB AND IRA SPRING, 18819 Olympic View Dr., Edmonds WA 98020. (206)776-4685. 60,000 b&w and 20,000 color photos. Subjects: mountain climbing, Pacific Northwest, National parks of the Northwest, wilderness areas, wildlife, Alaska, world travel, Africa, Europe, Asia and North America. Offers one-time editorial and advertising rights. Fees: $35 and up for b&w; $100 and up for color. Free catalog.

TOM STACK & ASSOCIATES, 544 Pheasant Court, Grayslake IL 60030. (312)223-7800. Photo Research: Jamie Stack. 20,000 b&w and 500,000 color photos of nature and wildlife; all types of flora and fauna, children, sports, foreign countries, abstracts, landscapes, etc." Offers all rights. Fees: $125-600 for one-time editorial or advertising use; $5 selection fee. Catalog for SASE.

STATEN ISLAND HISTORICAL SOCIETY, 302 Center Street, Staten Island NY 10306. (212)351-1611. Contact: Raymond Fingado. 10,000 photos, "mostly Staten Island scenes, houses, landscapes. However, we own the famed Alice Austen Collection —excellent shots of New York City street scenes circa 1895 to 1910, waterfront scenes of old sailing ships, Quarantine Station, famous old steamships, immigrants, life of the society set on Staten Island." Primarily b&w. "Usually 1-time publication rights for each picture." Fees are "flexible, but generally average $30 per plate —sometimes, but rarely lower and sometimes higher. Negotiated according to the nature of the project."

STEAMSHIP HISTORICAL SOCIETY OF AMERICA, University of Baltimore Library, 1420 Maryland Ave., Baltimore MD 21201. (301)727-6350, ext. 455. Reference Librarian: James Foster. 15,000 b&w photos of steamships; oceans, coastal, inland, etc. "Photos arranged by vessel name, not by type of ship or geographical area of service." Offers one-time rights for commercial use. Fees: $5/hour service charge for inquiries involving lengthy research. Copy negatives $6.

STOCK, BOSTON, INC., 1739 Boylston St., Boston MA 02116. Contact: Mike Mazzaschi.

Over 100,000 photos on all subjects. Edited stock. Foreign and domestic. B&w and color. All rights available; 1-time use normally. Fees for reproduction vary by use. Credit line and return of photographs required.

SWEDISH INFORMATION SERVICE, 825 Third Ave., New York NY 10022. (212)751-5900. Information Officer: Ami Sandstedt. Photos of all Swedish subjects except tourism. About 15,000 photos; mostly b&w, some color. Free reproduction. Photos must be returned after use.

SWISS NATIONAL TOURIST OFFICE, 608 Fifth Ave., New York NY 10020. Contact: Walter Bruderer, Public Relations Director. No fees, but credit line and return of pictures required.

SYGMA, 322 W. 72nd St., New York NY 10023. (212)595-0077. Contact: E. Laffont. Sells reproduction and editorial rights to photos on file. Subjects: International news, feature stories, films, politics, social interest. Reproduction fee: $75/b&w minimum; $150/color minimum.

TAURUS PHOTOS, 118 E. 28th St., New York NY 10016. (212)683-4025. Contact: Ben Michalski. 100,000 photos available on loan basis only. Subjects: Animals, children, medical, mood, nature, background scenes, sunsets, fishing, marine life, photomicrography, people, scenics. Reproduction rights, advertising rights, first rights, second rights, editorial rights, all rights. Fees: Standard ASMP rates. No research fee.

MAX THARPE PHOTO LIBRARY, 520 N.E. 7th Ave., #3, Ft. Lauderdale FL 33301. (305)763-5449. (Summer address: Box 1508, Statesville NC 28677. (704)872-0471.) 10,000 photos and 20,000 negatives available for sale or rental. Reproduction rights, advertising, rights, second rights and editorial rights offered. Subjects: Human interest, children, teenagers, candid scenes, mountains, sea. B&w and color, aimed mainly for use in Christian publications. Fee varies with material and usage.

THEATRE COLLECTION—NEW YORK PUBLIC LIBRARY, 111 Amsterdam Ave., New York NY 10023. (212)799-2200, ext. 214. Curator: Paul Myers. "The Theatre Collection is primarily a research service, not a photographic sales agency." Photos of stage productions, films, radio and television personalities, circus, puppets and marionettes, vaudeville and night club acts, theatre buildings and portraits of personnel in all these areas of the performing arts. Offers one-time rights; some material is in the public domain. Fees: $25 for one-time editorial or advertising use; $3 selection fee.

THEPHOTOFILE, Pier 17, San Francisco CA 94111. (415)397-3040. Contact: Gerald L. French. 200,000 photos on file. Price depends on the following rights: reproduction, advertising, or editorial rights. Subjects: agriculture, animals, disasters, entertainment, flowers, food, industry, people, military, recreation, transportation, foreign countries, California, San Francisco, aviation, senics, and environmental. Fees: $35 search/service fee which is waived if purchase is made. Also available for assignments.

THIGPEN PHOTOGRAPHY, Box 9242, 1442 South Beltline, Mobile AL 36609. (205)666-2851. Contact: Roy M. Thigpen. About 3,000 stock photos; 1½ million job negatives. "Aerial views, architectural, historic, iron-lace, marine and yachting, sports, fishing, hunting; sea-life 'Jubilee' (exclusive coverage of this unusual phenomenon)." Rights offered "negotiable." Fees: "dependent on use."

BILL THOMAS, PHOTOJOURNALIST, Rt. 4, Box 387, Nashville TN 47448. (812)988-7865. 60,000 color transparencies available for purchase. Reproduction rights, advertising rights, first rights, second rights, editorial rights. Subjects: travel, outdoor recreation, wildlife, nature, all North America oriented. "We shoot only color transparencies, 35mm or 2¼, mostly latter. Maximum holding time of 3 months unless by arranged agreement." Transparency fee: $50 minimum.

LESTER TINKER PHOTOGRAPHY, 426 County Rd. 223, Durango CO 81301. Contact: Lester Tinker. "B&w and color photos of scenes of the west. Good selection of Rocky Mountain wildflower photos and various historic areas." Fees: $25 minimum for b&w; $100 minimum for color. Credit line requested. Except in cases of outright purchase, all transparencies must be returned.

TRANSWORLD FEATURE SYNDICATE, 141 E. 44 St., New York NY 10017. (212)986-1505.

Manager: Mary Taylor Schilling. Photos of children, special events, beauty heads, personalities, photojournalism.

TRANS-WORLD NEWS SERVICE, Box 2801, Washington DC 20013. (202)638-5568. Bureau Chief: G. Richard Ward. Director of Photography: Paul Malec. 18,000 photos of all subjects. B&w and color. Maintains considerable background motion picture footage on the Washington area as well as travel footage on a worldwide basis. 1-time rights only, except on custom photos. Fee varies from $5 to $100 depending on subject and usage.

TREVES WORKSHOP FEATURES, 311 Lake Evelyn Dr., West Palm Beach FL 33411. (305)683-5167. Contact: Ralph Treves. About 20,000 b&w photos. "Home improvement ideas, use of power tools, all home workshop procedures and materials (electric wiring, cabinetmaking, wall paneling, painting and wallpapering, plumbing, wide range of home repairs)." Offers 1-time use or by negotiation. Fee: $15 to $25 for stock photo, 8x10 print.

UNDERWOOD & UNDERWOOD NEWS PHOTOS INC., 25 E. 26th St., New York NY 10010. (212)686-5980. Director: Peter Falk. Several million photos of all subjects and personalities. Primarily b&w photos of historical signifiance from 1882 to World War II.

UNION PACIFIC RAILROAD, 1416 Dodge Street, Omaha NE 68179. Contact: Mr. Barry B. Combs, Director of Public Relations. 15,000 color transparencies and many b&w's on national parks and monuments, cities and regions covered by the railroad. Also photos on railroad equipment and operations, and western agriculture and industry. No fees, but credit line required.

UNIPHOTO, Box 3678, Washington DC 20007. (202)333-0500. Contact: William L. Tucker. 100,000 photos available for purchase only. Reproduction rights, advertising rights, first rights, all rights and editorial rights available. A full service photography agency with access to more than 100 photographers across the U.S. Also markets and syndicates feature stories (text and photos) to publications. Query or send samples. Rates vary with material and use. Coordinates photo assignments across the U.S.

UNITED NATIONS, UN Plaza and 42 St., New York NY 10017. Contact: Marvin Weill, Distribution Officer. More than 140,000 selected negatives on the work of the United Nations and its Specialized Agencies throughout the world. In addition to meeting coverage, illustrations primarily represent the work of the United Nations in economic and social development and human rights throughout the world. B&w and color. May not be used for advertising purposes and must be used in a United Nations context. B&w photos, if credited to the United Nations, are currently available for reproduction for a print fee of $1 each. There is a nonrefundable service fee of $6 per color transparency. In addition, there is a fee of $25 for each color photograph published. Unused transparencies must be returned, in usable condition, within 30 days.

UNITED PRESS INTERNATIONAL (Compix Division), 220 E. 42 St., New York NY 10017. Contact: Library Photo Sales Manager. Over 8 million negatives plus b&w print file of 2 million, plus a color transparency file of over 100,000. "Period covered (various collections) from Civil War to present time. Worldwide newsphotos, personalities, human interest and features. Photo Library contains the combined files of Acme Newspictures, International News photos, United Press news photos and the Rau Collection." B&w and color. Rights offered for editorial, advertising, and private use. "Fees range upward from a minimum of $35, depending on usage."

U.S. AIR FORCE CENTRAL STILL PHOTO DEPOSITORY (AAVS) (MAC), 1221 South Fern Street, Arlington VA 22202. Approximately 300,000 exposures with a corresponding visual print file for research use. "The collection consists of b&w and color still photos, negatives and transparencies depicting the history and progress of the U.S. Air Force. This coverage includes equipment, aircraft, personnel, missiles, officer portraits, unit insignia, etc." Fees: 75¢ to $6.50 for b&w; $1 to $17.50 for color.

US COAST GUARD, NEWS AND PHOTO CENTER, Bldg. 108, Room 1, Governors Island NY 10004. (212)264-8733. Center Supervisor: Dale L. Puckett. 2,000 b&w photos; 1,000 color slides. Subjects: search and rescue, marine safety patrols, aids to navigation, bridge construction, oil pollution clean up and control, lighthouses, fisheries conservation and management act patrols, icebreaking, etc. Material is in the public domain. No charge to publications, "small charge for personal collections."

US COAST GUARD HEADQUARTERS, 400 7th St., S.W., Room 8315, Washington DC 20590. Contact: Chief, Public Affairs Division. 100,000 photos of "vessels, light stations, other shore stations, rescues, Alaskan Patrols, Arctic, Antarctic, boating safety, and various others illustrating the multi-roles of the Coast Guard. Mostly 8x10 b&w glossies are available; some 35mm color transparency slides. Generally no fee when photos are to be used for publication. There is a fee of $1.25 for each 8x10 b&w glossy for mere personal use. Color is not available for personal use. If for publication, the Coast Guard credit line must be used. The number of photos selected must be kept within reason. Photos not used are requested to be returned."

US DEPARTMENT OF AGRICULTURE, Photography Division, Office of Governmental and Public Affairs, Washington DC 20250. Contact: Chief, Photography Division. 500,000 or more photos; some very technical, others general. B&w and color (mostly 35mm color) on agricultural subjects. Print fee: $3.30 per 8x10, 35¢ for duplicate 35mm color. Credit line requested. "Slide sets and filmstrips ($14.50 and up) available on Department programs."

US DEPARTMENT OF THE INTERIOR, Bureau of Reclamation, Room 7444, C St. between 18th and 19th Sts., N.W., Washington DC 20240. Contact: Commissioner, Att'n Code 910. B&w and 35mm color photos available on water-oriented recreation, municipal and industrial water supply, irrigation, agriculture, public works construction, processing of agricultural products, Western cities and scenery, hunting, fishing, camping, boating in the western U.S. "Staff is too limited to permit search for supplying requests for speculative inquiries. However, we are able to respond to requests from publications and from freelancers with assignments for articles." No fees, but credit line requested and return of color pictures required.

UNIVERSITY MUSEUM OF THE UNIVERSITY OF PENNSYLVANIA, 33rd and Spruce Sts., Philadelphia PA 19104. (215)386-7400, Ext. 213. Contact: Ms. Caroline G. Dosker. Over 100,000 photos available for purchase on loan basis. Reproduction rights offered. Subjects: anthropological, archaeological and ethnological. Fees: prints made to order: $15/first print; $7.50/each additional. Credit lines required.

UTAH STATE HISTORICAL SOCIETY, 307 W. 2nd South, Salt Lake City UT 84101. (801)533-8808. B&w historic photos on everything pertaining to Utah and Mormon history; industry, architecture, biography, Indians, drama and theater, athletics, musical bands, orchestras, etc. Photos are made to order; allow 10 days to two weeks for delivery. Photos are not sent on approval; they may not be returned once they are made. Print fees begin at $1.50; fees subject to change. Credit line required.

VAN CLEVE PHOTOGRAPHY, INC., Box 1366, Evanston IL 60204. (312)764-2440. Picture Librarian: R. McKenna Byrne. 100,000 b&w and 1,000,000 color photos. "We have anything and everything—nearly. Weak in celebrities and political figures and pre-1940 historical shots. Excellent in most else." Offers all rights. Charges $45-90 for one-time editorial or advertising rights for b&w photos; $75-200 for color. Holding fee where applicable, $25/week.

VISUALWORLD, Box 804, Oak Park IL 60303. (312)524-0405. Contact: Jim Kirk. 20,000 photos on file for use on loan basis only. Reproduction rights, advertising rights, editorial rights and first rights available. "Material is leased under agreement, the terms of which are standard among stock photograph suppliers." Fees: Reproduction, $35, b&w; $90-125, color (single editorial use). Print, $4/8x10 b&w. Photocopies, $2.50 (deductible from order).

JOHN WARHAM, Zoology Dept., University of Canterbury, Private Bag, Christchurch, New Zealand. "About 30,000 color (35mm to 5x4) and b&w photos of natural history subjects: birds, mammals, insects from Australia, New Zealand, the Subantarctic and Antarctic and U.K." Normally one-time, non-exclusive rights offered. Fees: $25 b&w, $100 plus for color.

ALEX WASINSKI STUDIOS, 16 W. 22nd St., New York NY 10010. (212)989-0455. Contact: Alex Wasinski. Collection of about 25,000 scenics, cityscapes (day and night), TV and film personalities; fashion, food, moody landscapes, boats, etc. B&w and color. 1-time reproduction rights. Fees for b&w begin at $200; at $250 for color. Maximum is usually $500 for 4x5 color slides.

ROBERT WEINSTEIN HISTORIC PHOTO COLLECTION, 1253 S. Stanley Ave., Los

Angeles CA 90019. (213)936-0558. Contact: Robert Weinstein. Photos available on maritime (sailing vessels largely) and western Americana, late 19th century. B&w. Fees subject to mutual agreement; dependent on use.

WEST VIRGINIA GOVERNOR'S OFFICE OF ECONOMIC AND COMMUNITY DEVELOPMENT, Advertising/Communications Division, State Capitol, Charleston WV 25305. Contact: Kathy Thomas. Photos on West Virginia subjects in 8x10 b&w glossy prints, color in 35mm. Also offers free information on West Virginia attractions and facilities. No fees, but credit line desired and return of color pictures required.

WESTERN HISTORY DEPARTMENT, Denver Public Library, 1357 Broadway, Denver CO 80203. (303)573-5152, Ext. 246. Contact: Mrs. Eleanor M. Gehres. B&w photos on the social, economic, political, and historical developments of the U.S. west of the Mississippi River, especially the Rocky Mountain states. Large holdings of Indians, railroads, towns, outlaws, irrigation, livestock, and forts. "The Department is continually adding to the collection, increasing the holdings by several thousand annually." Prints are not available to lend for consideration purposes. The Department is willing to make selections on the subjects needed. About 280,000 items in the collection. "Fee structure is based on the planned use of the photographs obtained from us."

WHALING MUSEUM, 18 Johnny Cake Hill, New Bedford MA 02740. Contact: Richard C. Kugler, Director. This museum adheres to the fee schedules recommended by the Association of Art Museum Directors. Permission to reproduce Whaling Museum material will only be granted publications protected by copyright. Such copyright, where it applies to Museum material, is understood to be waived in favor of the Whaling Museum. Credit line and return of pictures required.

THE WHEELWRIGHT MUSEUM, Box 5153, Santa Fe NM 87502. Contact: Director. Photos available in b&w and color. Copy prints, $1-15. Original work, $5-35. 1-time reproduction fee: $25, b&w; $75, color. Credit line required.

WHITNEY MUSEUM OF AMERICAN ART, 945 Madison Ave., New York NY 10021. Contact: Rights and Permissions. Color transparencies and b&w photographs are available for reproduction and reference purposes. Credit line and return of ektachromes required. Price schedule available by written request.

WIDE WORLD PHOTOS, INC., 50 Rockefeller Plaza, New York NY 10020. Contact: On Approval Section. About 50 million photos. "All subjects in b&w, thousands of them in color. Wide World Photos is a subsidiary of The Associated Press." Offers national, North American, and world rights. Fees start at $35.

WILDWOOD PHOTOGRAPHIC, 2110 Wood Ave., Colorado Springs CO 80907. Owner: Jeremy Agnew. 4,000 color transparencies. "Specializes in photographs of outdoor Colorado and the Rocky Mountains for editorial, promotional and advertising purposes: wildlife, nature, scenics, travel and vacation area, places of interest, railroad and historical mining. Offers one-time, editorial, advertising, reproduction, and all rights. Charges $25-150 for one-time editorial or advertising use. Catalog for SASE.

MARGARET WILLIAMSON, 175 E. 79th St., New York NY 10021. Collection of about 10,000 photos on European travel, as well as worldwide ice skaters. B&w and color. Charges fee according to use.

THE HENRY FRANCIS DU PONT WINTERTHUR MUSEUM, Wintherthur DE 19735. Contact: Ms. Karol A. Schmiegel, Associate Registrar. B&w photos and color transparencies of furniture, silver, ceramics, prints, paintings, textiles, and other decorative art objects made or used in America from 1640 to 1840. Selection of photos should be made from Winterthur publications or from photo files in Registrar's Office at the Museum. Fee: $10 for b&w print; charge includes print and 1-time use. Credit line required.

WOLFE WORLDWIDE FILMS, 1657 Sawtelle Blvd., Los Angeles CA 90025. About 11,000 35mm color slides, "basically travel, covering what the tourist sees." Offers non-exclusive worldwide rights. Fees vary, but are dependent upon quantity used, ranging from $50 for one slide down to $15 for a large quantity for reproduction.

GERALD WOLFSOHN PHOTOGRAPHY, 9554 S.W. 82nd St., Miami FL 33173. (305)274-9552. "Slide file of western landscapes, New York scenes, South Florida scenes, Key West, gulls, and other subjects. Specialized forensic photography on request." Fees: $50 for 1-time use. Credit line required.

WOLLIN STUDIOS, LTD., 433 Grand Canyon Dr., Madison WI 53719. (608)831-3686. President: William Wollin. 5,000 b&w and 3,000 color photos of Wisconsin scenics, buildings, sports activities, fishing, camping, etc.; University of Wisconsin and Capitol scenes; aerials. Offers all rights. Fees: $35 and up for one-time editorial or advertising use.

WYOMING STATE MUSEUM/PHOTO SECTION, Barrett Bldg., Cheyenne WY 82002. (307)777-7518. Photographic Technician: Paula West. 80,000 b&w photos relating to Western history in general, Wyoming history including ranching, rodeos, railroads, towns, scenics, industry, mining, people, forts and military. Offers all rights. Charges $25-100 for one-time editorial or advertising use; $4-10 print fee. Credit line required.

KATHERINE YOUNG (AGENCY), 140 E. 40th St., New York NY 10016. Contact: Katherine Young. Over 50,000 general world coverage photos (strong African coverage) plus European and Japanese news and feature service, historic landmarks, architecture, scenics, people, children and family situations, monuments, animals, flowers, churches and temples. Some historic prints of personalities as well as portraits of famous people. B&w and color. Offers U.S., North American and world rights; 1-time use with further option. Standard American Society of Magazine Photographers fees. Special arrangements negotiable.

LOU ZAUNER, Box 11316, Tahoe Paradise CA 95705. (916)544-4068. 1,500 b&w photos; 5,000 color. "Extensive collection of West Coast scenics and activities, particularly heavy on California and Nevada." Offers one-time rights. Charges $25 for one-time editorial or advertising use for b&w photos; $35 for color. $25 selection fee.

Writers' Clubs

The following clubs are local or regional, nonprofit social or professional groups. They are listed geographically by state, then alphabetically by club name within the state. Writers are requested to enclose a self-addressed stamped envelope when writing any club about membership, meeting times, or further information.

To obtain information on starting a writer's club, send 50¢ plus SASE for the booklet *How To Start/Run a Writer's Club* (Writer's Digest).

Alabama

ALABAMA STATE POETRY SOCIETY, Mrs. Virginia Farnell, President, 1427 Westmoreland Ave., Montgomery AL 36106. Estab. 1968. Meets quarterly.

CREATIVE WRITERS OF MONTGOMERY, Gary Earl Heath, Secretary, 3816 Governors Dr., #H-233, Montgomery AL 36111.

HUNTSVILLE WRITERS' CLUB, Georgette Perry, 2519 Roland Rd., S.W., Huntsville AL 35805.

Arkansas

ARKANSAS PIONEER BRANCH, NATIONAL LEAGUE OF AMERICAN PEN WOMEN, Ida Rice Rogers, 2409 W. 16th, North Little Rock AR 72114. Estab. 1921. Meets monthly.

AUTHORS, COMPOSERS AND ARTISTS' SOCIETY, Peggy Vining, Publicity Chairman, 6817 Gingerbread Lane, Little Rock AR 72204.

OZARK CREATIVE WRITERS, INC., Lida W. Pyles, President, Box 391, Eureka Springs AR 72632.

POETS' ROUNDTABLE OF ARKANSAS, Roberta E. Allen, 6604 Kenwood Rd., Little Rock AR 72207.

SPA WRITERS, 1100 2nd St., Hot Springs AR 71901. (501)321-1174. Secretary: Mildred Wilkinson. Estab. 1976. Meets bimonthly.

California

ASPIRING WRITERS'S CLUB, Box 7042, Long Beach CA 90807. Director: Gertrude Katz. Estab. 1973. Meets bimonthly.

CALIFORNIA STATE POETRY SOCIETY, Southern California Chapter, 743 Puma Canyon Lane, Glendora CA 91740. President: Nelle Fertig. Estab. 1974. Meets monthly.

CALIFORNIA WRITERS' CLUB, 2214 Derby St., Berkeley CA 94705. Secretary: Dorothy V. Benson. Estab. 1909. Meets monthly, except July and August. "Membership is open to prize-winning and published writers."

CUPERTINO WRITERS' WORKSHOP, 10117 N. Portal Ave., Cupertino CA 95014. (408)257-8494. Den Mother: Phyllis Taylor Pianka. Estab. 1972. Meets semimonthly.

DALY CITY CREATIVE WRITERS' GROUP, Margaret O. Richardson, President, 243 Lakeshire Dr., Daly City CA 94015. Estab. 1965. Meets monthly.

FALLBROOK WRITERS' WORKSHOP, 1541 Green Canyon Rd., Fallbrook CA 92028. President: Helen B. Hicks. Estab. 1977. Meets weekly.

FICTIONAIRES, 10792 Harrogate, Santa Ana CA 92705. Secretary: Armand Hanson. Estab.

1963. Meets simimonthly. Membership limited to 20 members.

FOUNTAIN VALLEY WRITERS WORKSHOP, Clara Schultz, 8815 Hummingbird Ave., Fountain Valley CA 92708. Estab. 1972. Meets monthly.

LITERARY HALL OF FAME, Box 20880, Long Beach CA 90801. (213)436-3132. President: Howard E. Hill. Estab. 1976. Meets monthly.

LONG BEACH WRITERS' CLUB, 1641 Chelsea Rd., Palos Verdes Estates CA 90274. President: Alice Dawson. Estab. 1939. Meets biweekly.

LOS ESCRIBIENTES, 107 Rancho Alipaz, 32371 Alipaz St., San Juan Capistrano CA 92675. Contact: Nora Collins. Estab. 1971. Meets semimonthly.

MOUNTAIN-VALLEY WRITERS, 18140 Hawthorne, Bloomington CA 92316. Secretary: Pat Wolff. Estab. 1969. Meets semimonthly. Membership limited to published writers.

NORTHERN CALIFORNIA CARTOON & HUMOR ASSOCIATION, Walt Miller, Secretary, 609 29th Ave., San Mateo CA 94403.

POMONA VALLEY WRITERS CLUB, Ontario City Library, 215 E. C St., Ontario CA 91761. (714)984-2758. President: Flo Swanson. Estab. 1936. Meets monthly.

PROFESSIONAL WRITERS LEAGUE OF LONG BEACH, Box 20880, Long Beach CA 90801. Director: Howard E. Hill. Estab. 1970. Meets monthly.

RIVERSIDE WRITERS' CLUB, 4278 Victoria Ave., Riverside CA 92507. President: John Byer. Estab. 1927. Meets monthly.

SAN DIEGO WRITERS WORKSHOP, Box 19366, San Diego CA 92119. President: Chet Cunningham. Estab. 1962. Meets semimonthly.

SAN FRANCISCO WRITERS WORKSHOP, Dean Lipton, Moderator, Louis Lurie Room, Main Library, McAllister and Larkin Sts., San Francisco CA 94102.

SHOWCASE WRITERS CLUB, Larry Stillman, 7842 Barton Dr., Lemon Grove CA 92045.

SOUTHWEST MANUSCRIPTERS, 560 S. Helberta Ave., Redondo Beach CA 90277. Founding Member: Reb Battles. Estab. 1949. Meets monthly.

SPELLBINDERS LITERARY GUILD, Box 10623, Santa Ana CA 92706. Estab. 1970. Meets monthly. "Prospective members must submit a sample of their work—published or unpublished—to our reading committee. Interested parties may come to one meeting as guests before submitting."

SURFWRITERS, 905 Calle Miramar, Redondo Beach CA 90277. Director: LaVada Weir. Estab. 1958. Meets monthly. Currently there is a waiting list for membership.

TIERA DEL SOL WRITERS' CLUB, 1430 E. Lexington, El Cajon CA Estab. 1970. Meets semimonthly.

WRITER'S CLUB OF PASADENA, 231 S. Hudson, Pasadena CA 91101. Secretary: Willard C. Hyatt. Estab. 1922. Meets monthly.

WRITERS' CLUB OF WHITTIER, 7716 Westman Ave., Whittier CA 90606. President: Fern Palmer. Estab. 1953. Meets weekly.

WRITERS' WORKSHOP WEST, 17909 San Gabriel Ave., Cerritos CA 90701. President: Bob McGrath. Estab. 1962. Meets semimonthly.

Colorado

BURNING MOUNTAIN WRITERS CLUB, 211 N. Valley Dr., Silt CO 81652. President: Robert Strong. Estab. 1973. Meets monthly.

ROCKY MOUNTAIN WRITERS GUILD, INC., 2969 Baseline Rd., Boulder CO 80303. President: Dr. James D. Hutchinson. Estab. 1967. Meets biweekly. Applicants must be published writers.

WE WRITE OF COLORADO, Box 942, Arvada CO 80001. Contact: Elaine Zimmerman.

WEST ROCKIES WRITERS CLUB, 2841 Teller Ave., Sp 10, Grand Junction CO 81501. (303)245-6448. Past President/Founder: Eva Carter. Estab. 1976. Meets monthly.

YWCA CO-ED WRITERS WORKSHOP, 3575 Benton St., Denver CO 80212. (303)420-2605. Chariman: Leota Troute. Estab. 1965. Meets weekly except in summer when meetings are monthly.

Connecticut

THE STRUGGLERS' CLUB, 231 Mile Creek Rd., Old Lyme CT 06371. Contact: Carolyn Gilbert.

WRITER'S EXCHANGE, 231 Mile Creek Rd., Old Lyme CT 06371. Moderator: Carolyn Gilbert. Estab. 1975. Meets monthly.

District of Columbia

WASHINGTON AREA WRITERS, 7631 Webbwood Ct., Springfield VA 22151. (703)451-9529. President: Joan B. Graham. Estab. 1973. Meets monthly.

WRITER'S LEAGUE OF WASHINGTON, 7602 Lynn Dr., Chevy Chase MD 20015. Secretary: Lola Dunn.

Florida

ANRALD (Absolutely No Relationship to Anyone Living or Dead) FICTION WRITERS, 651 NW 38th Court, Pompano Beach FL 33064. Club Director: Ginger Curry. Estab. 1976. Meets bimonthly.

WEST FLORIDA WRITERS GUILD, Box 4547, Pensacola FL 32507. President: Ferd Chappa.

Georgia

DIXIE COUNCIL OF AUTHORS AND JOURNALISTS, 4221 N. Shallowford Rd., Apt. 7, Chamblee GA 30341. Director: Harold Random. Estab. 1961. Meets bimonthly.

Idaho

CAMAS WRITER'S WORKSHOP, Fairfield ID 83327. (208)764-2536. Director: Penelope Reedy. Estab. 1975. Meets weekly.

Illinois

JUVENILE FORUM, 3403 45th St., Moline IL 61265. (309)762-8985. Host: David R. Collins. Estab. 1975. Meets monthly.

KANKAKEE AREA WRITERS GROUP, 202 Stevens Dr., Bourbonnais IL 60914. Secretary: Esther Lunsford. Estab. 1967. Meets semimonthly.

OFF CAMPUS WRITERS WORKSHOP, Winnetha Community House, Winnetha IL 60015. Chairman: Carol Spelius. Estab. 1945. Meets weekly.

QUAD CITY WRITERS CLUB, 3403 45th St., Moline IL 61265. President: David R. Collins. Estab. 1953. Meets monthly.

SHAGBARK SCRIBES, Ivan Sparling, Box 2400, Illinois Central College, East Peoria IL 61611.

SKOKIE'S CREATIVE WRITERS ASSN., Leo Friedman, 5256 Foster, Skokie IL 60077. Estab. 1974. Meets monthly.

WRITERS' STUDIO, 125½ 18th St., Rock Island IL 61201. President: Betty Mowery. Estab. 1967. Meets weekly.

Indiana

CENTRAL INDIANA WRITERS' ASSOCIATION, Cheryl B. Denk, Director, R.R. 5, Box 35B, Franklin IN 46131. Estab. 1976. Meets monthly.

FLAME'S WRITERS' CLUB, INC., Box 8264, Merrillville IN 46410. President: Kiro Obetkovski. Estab. 1976. Meets monthly.

POETS' STUDY CLUB OF TERRE HAUTE, Esther Alman, President, 826 S. Center St., Terre Haute IN 47807.

SOUTH BEND WRITERS' CLUB, 2419 Riverside Dr., South Bend IN 46616. President: Sonnie Miller. Estab. 1963. Meets biweekly.

Kansas

UNIVERSAL WRITERS GUILD, INC., Box 2274, Kansas City KS 66110. Estab. 1971. Meets monthly.

WICHITA LINE WOMEN, Jacquelyn Terral Andrews, 2350 Alameda Pl., Wichita KS 67211. Estab. 1966. Meets monthly.

Kentucky

KENTUCKY STATE POETRY SOCIETY, Rt. 3, Box 273, Clinton KY 42031.

JACKSON PURCHASE CREATIVE WRITER'S CLUB, Rt. 3, Box 273, Clinton KY 42031. (502)653-6795. Secretary: Diane Hopkins. Estab. 1974. Meets monthly.

LOUISVILLE WRITERS CLUB, Beverly Giammara, 2205 Weber Ave., Louisville KY 40205. Estab. 1952. Meets semimonthly.

Louisiana

SHREVEPORT WRITERS CLUB, Loma Chandler, 630 W. 74th St., Shreveport LA 71106. (318)687-0623. Estab. 1935. Meets monthly.

Maryland

WORDSMITHS: The Creative Writing Group of the Social Security Administration, 6724 Ransome Dr., Baltimore MD 21207. Chairman: Robert Hale. Estab. 1971. Meets biweekly. "Basically for employees of the Social Security Administration, but we do accept anyone."

Massachusetts

MANUSCRIPT CLUB OF BOSTON, 770 Boylston St., Boston MA 02199. Contact: Dr. Ruth E. Setterberg. Estab. 1911. Meets semimonthly.

PIONEER VALLEY SCRIPTORS, Maxine Englehardt, Box 1745, Springfield MA 01101. Estab. 1941. Meets monthly.

SOCIETY OF CHILDREN'S BOOK WRITERS, New England Region, 31 School, Hatfield MA 01038. Director: Jane Yolen. Estab. 1972. Meets annually.

TWELVE O'CLOCK SCHOLARS, Box 111, West Hyannisport MA 02672. Contact: Mrs. Marion Vuilleumier. Estab. 1952. Meets semimonthly.

Michigan

ANN ARBOR WRITERS WORKSHOP, 701 Indianola, Ann Arbor MI 48104.Contact: Judith Kirscht.

DETROIT WOMEN WRITERS, 16 Adams Lane, Dearborn MI 48120. Membership chairperson: Elaine Watson. Estab. 1900. Meets semimonthly.

POETRY SOCIETY OF MICHIGAN, S. Geneva Page, 256 Burr St., Battle Creek MI 49015.

SOUTH OAKLAND WRITERS, 21315 Pembroke, Detroit MI 48219. (313)532-3882. Membership Chairman: Helen Olmstead. Estab. 1968. Meets monthly.

Minnesota

A.A.U.W. WRITER'S WORKSHOP, Minneapolis Branch, American Association of University Women, 2115 Stevens Ave., Minneapolis MN 55427. Estab. 1932. Meets semimonthly.

EASTSIDE FREELANCE WRITERS OF MINNESOTA, Marlys B. Oliver, 139 Birchwood Ave., White Bear Lake MN 55110.

MESABI WRITERS CLUB, Mesabi Community College, Virginia MN 55792. Contact: Archie Hill. Estab. 1972. Meets monthly.

MINNEAPOLIS WRITER'S WORKSHOP INC., 2932 Colorado Ave., Minneapolis MN 55416.President: Mary Wilensky.

MINNESOTA AUTHORS GUILD, Box 2337 Loop Station, Minneapolis MN 55402. President: Jesse Miller. Estab. 1958. Meets semimonthly.

MINNESOTA CHRISTIAN WRITER'S GUILD, 1316 E. 42nd St., Minneapolis MN 55407. Secretary: Joyce Ellis. Estab. 1954. Meets monthly.

PEPIN PEN CLUB, Donna Rosen, Secretary, Pepin Apts. A101, Lake City MN 55041. Estab. 1975. Meets monthly.

Missouri

CARTHAGE WRITERS GUILD, 608 W. Highland, Carthage MO 64836. President: Jacqueline Potter. Estab. 1960. Meets monthly.

MISSOURI WRITERS' GUILD, 1712 W. McGee, Springfield MO 65807. President: Wayne Warner. Estab. 1915. Meets annually. "Any Missourian who has met at least one of the following requirements shall be eligible for membership: authorship or co-authorship of a published book; sale of three articles, stories or poems; sale of three briefs, stories, articles, or comparable materials to an educational publisher; sale of one serial or novelette to a periodical; sale of one play; or sale of one motion picture screenplay, radio or TV script."

NATIONAL LEAGUE OF AMERICAN PENWOMEN, ST. LOUIS BRANCH, Barbara L. Wolfe, President, 6918 Mackenzie Rd., St. Louis MO 63123. (314)481-6840. Estab. 1977. Meets monthly.

ST. LOUIS WRITERS' GUILD, 816 Lynda Court, St. Louis MO 63122. President: Joyce Flaherty. Estab. 1920. Meets monthly.

WRITER'S GROUP, Communiversity, c/o University of Missouri—Kansas City. For information contact Robert Patrick, Box 2512, Kansas City KS 66110. Meets weekly.

Nebraska

CHRISTIAN WRITERS OF OMAHA, Contact: Mary Brite, 11405 Farnam Circle, Omaha NE 68154. Estab. 1975. Meets monthly.

NEBRASKA WRITERS GUILD, Box 187, Ogallala NE 69153. Contact: Robert F. Lute.

NORTHEAST NEBRASKA WRITERS, 717 E. Norfolk Ave., Norfolk NE 68701. President: Leatta Stortvedt. Estab. 1974. Meets monthly.

OMAHA WRITERS' CLUB, 517 S. 51st St., Omaha NE 68106. President: Cathy Nelson. Estab. 1945. Meets monthly.

New Jersey

NEW JERSEY POETRY SOCIETY, INC., Box 217, Wharton NJ 07885.

WRITER'S ASSOCIATION OF NEW JERSEY, 9 David Ct., Edison NJ 08817. President: Mary Kuczkir. Estab. 1975. Meets monthly.

WRITERS' WORKSHOP, Ruth Fleishman, E-12, Rocky Brook Rd., East Windsor NJ 08420. Estab. 1971. Meets monthly.

New Mexico

ROSWELL WRITERS GUILD, 1104 Avenida Del Sumbre, Roswell NM 88201. Publicity Chairman: Lois Reader. Estab. 1972. Meets monthly. "We also have two workshops on the second Tuesday evening and the second Friday afternoon meeting."

New York

BROOKLYN CONTEST AND FILLER WRITING CLUB, Selma Glasser, 241 Dahill Rd., Brooklyn NY 11218.

NEW YORK POETRY FORUM, Dr. Dorothea Neale, Director, 3064 Albany Crescent, Apt. 54, Bronx NY 10463. Estab. 1958. Meets semimonthly.

THE NIAGARA FALLS ASSOCIATION OF PROFESSIONAL WOMEN WRITERS, 147 Chestnut, Youngstown NY 14174. President: Judy Kay. Estab. 1937. Meets monthly. "Full membership is limited to published writers who have been paid for their work. Associate members must be published even though unpaid. Membership is also limited to those in both New York and Canada who are within commuting distance."

North Carolina

CHARLOTTE WRITERS CLUB, 3114 Airlie St., Charlotte NC 28205. President: Deane Ritch Lomax. Estab. 1922. Meets monthly.

Ohio

GREATER CANTON WRITERS' GUILD, Malone College, 515 25th St., N.W., Canton OH 44709. President: Judi Bailey. Estab. 1966. Meets monthly.

LUNCH-BUNCH, Norma Sundberg, 1740 Mechanicsville Rd., Rock Creek OH 44084.

MANUSCRIPT CLUB OF AKRON, Tom Troyer, 4174 Kent Rd., Stow OH 44224. Estab. 1929. Meets monthly.

MEDINA COUNTY WRITER'S CLUB, Carol J. Wilcox, 3219 Country Club Dr., Medina OH 44256.

QUEEN CITY WRITERS, 6108 Joyce Lane, Cincinnati OH 45237. (513)351-1721. Contact: Rose A. Brook. Estab. 1976. Meets monthly.

SIGMA TAU DELTA, Beta Beta Chapter, 1167 Addison Rd., Cleveland OH 44103. Past President: Bernice Krumhansl. Estab. 1926. Meets monthly October-June. Applicants "must have had the equivalent of one year of college English composition, or special writing workshops. This might be waived for a published author."

TRI-STATE WRITERS, 3386 Robb Ave., Cincinnati OH 45211. (513)481-5409. President: Melba Eydel. Meets monthly.

VERSE WRITERS' GUILD OF OHIO, Jennifer Groce, President, 2384 Hardesty Drive S., Columbus OH 43204. Estab. 1928. Meets monthly.

WOMAN'S PRESS CLUB, Evelyn P. Johnston, 6350 Salem Rd., Cincinnati OH 45230. Estab. 1888. Meets monthly, except January, from October-June. "Membership is by invitation and requires evidence of written work already published and paid for."

WORD MERCHANTS, The Writer's League of Eastern Cincinnati, Box 312, Milford OH 45150. Contact: Michael A. Banks. Estab. 1978. Meets monthly.

Oklahoma

McALESTER WRITERS GUILD, 906 E. Miami, McAlester OK 74501. (918)423-4485. President: Frank D. McSherry. Estab. 1969. Meets biweekly.

SHAWNEE WRITERS ASSOCIATION, 1225 Sherry Lane, Shawnee OK 74801. Director: Ernestine Gravley. Estab. 1968. Meets monthly.

STILLWATER WRITERS, 513 S. Knoblock St., Stillwater OK 74074. Secretary: Florence French. Estab. 1932. Meets monthly. Membership limited to 15-18 members.

WRITERS GROUP OF CUSHING, South Kings Hwy., Cushing OK 74023. President: Mazie Cox Read. Estab. 1968. Meets monthly.

Oregon

GRANTS PASS WRITER'S WORKSHOP, 114 Espey Rd., Grants Pass OR 97526. Director: Dorothy Francis. Estab. 1970. Meets weekly.

WESTERN WORLD HAIKU SOCIETY, 4102 N.E. 130th Place, Portland OR 97230. Founder: Lorraine Ellis Harr. Estab. 1972. Meets semiannually.

Pennsylvania

HOMEWOOD POETRY FORUM, Mary Savage, Inner City Services, Homewood Branch Carnegie Library, 7101 Hamilton Ave., Pittsburgh PA 15206.

LANCASTER AREA CHRISTIAN WRITERS FELLOWSHIP, Mennonite Information Center, 2209 Millstream Rd., Lancaster PA 17603. (717)872-5183. Contact: John K. Brenneman. Meets bimonthly.

LEHIGH VALLEY WRITERS' GUILD, 1420 Gordon St., Allentown PA 18102. President: Phyllis Guth. Estab. 1938. Meets biweekly.

THE PITTSBURGH BRANCH OF BOOKFELLOWS, 3461 Harrisburg St., Pittsburg PA 15204. Contact: Ralph Watson/Carsten Ahrens.

THE SCRIBBLERS, Box 522, Hatboro PA 19040.

WILLIAMSPORT WRITERS FORUM, 2318 Dove St., Williamsport PA 17701. Contact: Cynthia Hoover. Estab. 1959. Meets monthly.

WRITERS CRAMP, 5349 Greene St., #1A, Philadelphia PA 19144. (215)848-7299. Contact: Beth Blakeman. Estab. 1977. Meets weekly.

WRITERS WORKSHOP OF DELAWARE VALLEY, c/o Our Lady of Angels College, Aston PA 19014.

RHODE ISLAND WRITERS' GUILD, 51 Homer St., Providence RI 02905.

South Carolina

FOOTHILLS WRITERS CLUB, Rt. 4, Pruitt Dr., Greensville SC 29605. Chairwoman: Elaine Trull. Estab. 1977. Meets monthly.

South Dakota

SIOUXLAND CREATIVE WRITERS' CLUB, Mrs. Larry Ells, 1905 S. Lake Ave., Sioux Falls SD 57105. Meets monthly.

Texas

ABILENE WRITERS GUILD, 502 E.N. 16th, Abilene TX 79601. President: Juanita Zachry. Estab. 1967. Meets monthly.

AMERICAN POETRY LEAGUE, 3915 S.W. Military Dr., San Antonio TX 78211. President: Dr. Stella Woodall. Estab. 1922. Meets annually.

BEAUMONT CHAPTER OF THE POETRY SOCIETY OF TEXAS, Violette Newton, 3230 Ashwood Lane, Beaumont TX 77703.

CHRISTIAN WRITERS' LEAGUE, 1604 E. Taylor, Harlingen TX 78550. Contact: Jean H. Dudley.

CREATIVE WRITING WORKSHOP, Pauline Neff, 10235 Best Dr., Dallas TX 75224.

NATIONAL LEAGUE OF AMERICAN PEN WOMEN, SAN ANTONIO BRANCH, Dr. Stella

Woodall, Organizer and Charter President, 3915 S.W. Military Dr., San Antonio TX 78211. Meets monthly.

PANHANDLE PEN WOMEN, Box 616, Pampa TX 79065. Director: Evelyn Pierce Nace. Estab. 1920. Meets bimonthly. "Active members must be published writers; associate members are seriously interested in writing, but have not yet been published. Meetings and opportunities are open to both active and associate members."

SOUTH PLAINS WRITERS ASSOCIATION, Box 10114, Lubbock TX 79408. Director: Arline Harris. Estab. 1955. Meets monthly, September-May.

STELLA WOODALL POETRY SOCIETY, Dr. Stella Woodall, President, 3915 S.W. Military Dr., San Antonio TX 78211. Meets monthly.

WRITER'S CLUB OF PASADENA, 2204 Cherry Lane, Pasadena TX 77502. Marketing and Library Chairman: June Caesar. Estab. 1966. Meets monthly.

Utah

LEAGUE OF UTAH WRITERS, Little Green Valley Chapter, Box 3, Monroe UT 84754. (801)527-3352. Director: Elinor C. Tuft. Estab. 1975. Meets monthly.

LEAGUE OF UTAH WRITERS, Price Chapter, 625 Washington Ave., Price UT 84501. President: Jeanette McAlpine. Estab. 1976. Meets monthly.

LEAGUE OF UTAH WRITERS, Utah Valley Chapter, 2858 Marrcrest West, Provo UT 84601. (801)377-5019. Secretary: Dorothy Dent. Estab. 1937. Meets monthly.

SEVIER VALLEY CHAPTER OF THE LEAGUE OF UTAH WRITERS, Marilyn A. Henrie, 68 E. 2nd St., South, Richfield UT 84701.

WASATCH WRITERS, UTAH LEAGUE OF WRITERS, 497 E. 400 North, Bountiful UT 84010. Contact: Steve Stumph.

Vermont

THE "NEW" WRITER'S CLUB, Richard J. Frazier, Fair Haven VT 05743.

Virginia

POETS TAPE EXCHANGE, Frances Brandon Neighbours, Director, 109 Twin Oak Dr., Lynchburg VA 24502.

TIDEWATER WRITER'S WORKSHOP, 742 Washington Park, Norfolk VA 23517. Membership Secretary: Jeanne Alkov. Estab. 1976. Meets biweekly.

THE WRITERS ASSOCIATION OF TIDEWATER, 76 Algonquin Rd., Hampton VA 23661. Chairman: Christine Sparks. Estab. 1976. Meets monthly.

Washington

LEAGUE OF WESTERN WRITERS, Philip Lewis Arena, Treasurer, 5603 239th Pl. S.W., Mountlake Terrace WA 98043.

POETRY LEAGUE OF AMERICA, Philip Lewis Arena, Poetry Manager, 5603 239th Pl., S.W., Mountlake Terrace WA 98043.

TACOMA WRITERS CLUB, Clydelle Smith, 3806 E. 104th St., Tacoma WA 98406. Meets monthly.

WRITERS AND ILLUSTRATORS CO-OP, 2102 Sullivan Dr., N.W., Gig Harbor WA 98335. Secretary: Wayne O. Clark. Estab. 1972. Meets monthly.

West Virginia

MORGANTOWN POETRY SOCIETY, 368 Brockway Ave., Morgantown WV 26505. President: Margaret Croston.

Wisconsin

GENEVA AREA WRITER'S CLUB, Route 3, Box 193, Delavan WI 53115. President: Clarice L. Moon. Estab. 1971. Meets monthly.

SHEBOYGAN COUNTY WRITERS CLUB, Marion Weber, 1929 N. 13 St., Sheboygan WI 53081. Estab. 1958. Meets monthly.

THE UPLAND WRITERS, Mrs. Harry Johns, 213 W. Chapel, Dodgeville WI 53533.

Wyoming

WYOMING WRITERS ASSOCITION, Fairgrounds, Sheridan WY. Secretary/Treasurer: Barbara Ketchan.

Canada

CANADIAN AUTHORS ASSOCIATION, 22 Yorkville Ave., Toronto, Ontario, Canada M3W 1L4.

Canal Zone

CROSSROADS WRITERS, A. Grimm Richardson, Secretary, Box 93, Gatun, Canal Zone.

Writers' Colonies

Some of the best writing of our time has been produced by writers working in the solitary confines of a writers' or artists' colony. The opportunity offered the writer by these institutions to remove himself from the grind of the day-to-day world allows him or her to proceed with his work in an atmosphere of comfort, privacy, and interaction with other working artists, which can greatly enhance the creative process.

The following listings are for Artists' Colonies that provide facilities for actively working writers. Included in the listings is information as to length of stay, colony capacity, date of yearly operation (some operate year around, others only during specific seasons or months), cost, and whether financial aid or grants are available, and eligibility requirements. Contact the individual colonies for additional information, enclosing SASE.

Alabama

CREEKWOOD COLONY FOR THE ARTS, For application write: Charles Ghigna, Poet-in-Residence, Box 88, Hurtsboro AL 36860. (205)667-7720. Established in 1974. For poets and authors. Cost: $50 weekly. The Colony consists of an 1840 ante-bellum mansion located on 100 acres of woodland in southeast Alabama. Open 40 weeks/year (closed December, January and February).The colony accommodates 10 residents. No application deadline. Length of each residency may vary from 1 to 3 weeks or more according to individual needs and availability. Xeroxed copies of published work along with date, volume, number and title of magazine are requested with each application.

Massachusetts

CUMMINGTON COMMUNITY OF THE ARTS, Cummington MA 01026. (403)634-2172. Director: Alan Newman. Founded 1923. Open to 30 adults and 12 children (summer); 15 adults (winter).

Purpose/Programs: "A place and atmosphere in which artists can work. A retreat in nature and community living (we share some maintenance and housekeeping tasks and eat dinner together). Artists come from various disciplines, age groups, and parts of the country. Aside from some group responsibilities, each artist is free to make his own schedule and priorities. Eligibility is based on excellence of work as judged by admissions committees. Fees: $200/month (September-June); $750 for adults, $375 for children in summer session (July-August)."Financial aid is available to some economically disadvantaged writers and artists."

FINE ARTS WORK CENTER, 24 Pearl St., Provincetown MA 02657. (617)487-9960. Contact: Program Coordinator. Founded 1968. Open to 20 members at one time.

Purpose/Programs: "To give young artists and writers who have finished their formal education time off to work and develop their talents outside an academic situation, but not isolated from their peers as well as older writers and artists. We give grants from $200-250 per month to approximately 20 writers and artists. Visual artists receive studios and some writers are given studio apartments. Lengh of stay is October 1-May 1. Open during winter only. There is a visiting program of readings and lectures by distinguished writers and artists. Write for application." Eligibility is based solely on samples of work. $10 application fee.

New Hampshire

MILDRED I. REID WRITERS' COLONY, Contact: Mildred I. Reid (at the colony), Contoocook NH 03229. (603)746-3625. Established in 1956. Cost: $80-95weekly includes private room, private conferences, class conferences, food. Fiction, nonfiction, plays, poetry. Length of stay: 1-9 weeks, starting June 26-August 28. No application deadline, but early reservations desirable. Scholarship available for woman acting as hostess half-time or full-time. No more than 12 writers per week accepted.

New Mexico

D.H. LAWRENCE SUMMER FELLOWSHIP, Apply to: Director, D.H. Lawrence Committee, English Dept., Rm. 217, Humanities Bldg., University of New Mexico, Albuquerque NM

87131. (505)277-6347. The fellowship is awarded annually and provides a creative writer with free housing (capacity 4 persons) at the D.H. Lawrence Ranch, plus a $700 stipend. Applications should include a curriculum vitae, work samples, and two or three letters of recommendation. Length of stay: up to 3 months, summers only. Apply by January 1.

HELENE WURLITZER FOUNDATION OF NEW MEXICO, Contact: Henry A. Sauerwein, Jr., Executive Director, Box 545, Taos NM 87571. (505)758-2413. Established in 1954. For all creative artists in every field. Free housing; residents supply their own food. No financial assistance available. Length of stay: 3 to 12 months. Open year-round. Room for 12 persons. No application deadline.

New York

MacDOWELL COLONY, For admissions, contact: The MacDowell Colony, 145 W. 58th St., #12C, New York NY 10019. Estab: 1907. For writers, sculptors, printmakers, photographers, filmmakers, painters and composers. Cost: $70/week; fellowships available. Length of stay: 1-3 months. Open all year. Accommodates 32 residents (summer); 22 (winter). Application deadlines: 6 months in advance, except June through August, when applications must be in by January 15.

MILLAY COLONY FOR THE ARTS, INC., Apply to Ann-Ellen Lesser, Project Director, Steepletop, Austerlitz NY 12017. (518)392-3103. Established in 1973. For writers, composers and visual artists. Room, board and studio space provided. Length of stay is variable. Open all year. Studio and living facilities for 5 residents. This is the former home of the poet Edna St. Vincent Millay. "Admissions committees of professional artists review applications, looking for talent and seriousness of purpose." Applications may be obtained by writing the Admissions Office at the colony, at above address.

YADDO, Contact: Curtis Harnack, Executive Director, Yaddo, Box 395, Saratoga Springs NY 12866. Began operation in 1926. Room and studio space at no cost, but voluntary contributions expected. Length of stay: 1 to 2 months. Open year-round, but primarily in summer, May through Labor Day. Literary merit, rather than popular appeal is criterion for admission. Applicants must submit work and 2 letters of recommendation. February 1 is annual deadline for applications. Open to persons of any age and nationality who have already published some work. Visual artists and composers also use Yaddo facilities.

Texas

DOBIE-PAISANO FELLOWSHIP, Contact: Audrey Slate, Dobie-Paisano Project, University of Texas at Austin, Main Bldg. 101, Austin TX 78712. (512)471-7213. Established in 1967. For persons born or living in Texas or those whose work is identified with the region. Free housing in the former Dobie ranch, plus a $6,000 stipend for 1 year, or 2-$3,000 awards for 6-months each. Length of stay: 12 months or 6 months. 1979-80 fellowships are for writers; 1978-79 for visual artists. Year begins August 1. Application deadline: March 15.

Virginia

VIRGINIA CENTER FOR THE CREATIVE ARTS AT SWEET BRIAR, Box VCCA, Sweet Briar VA 24595. (804)946-7236. Director: William Smart. Provides room, board, and individual studio space for 12 painters, writers, sculptors, and composers. Offers 1-3 month residencies year-round with longer and shorter periods considered in special circumstances. Fee: $70 weekly with a limited number of abatements available where need is demonstrated. Selective admission: application form, samples of work, curriculum vita, and letters of recommendation required.

Writers' Conferences

The following writers' conferences are usually held annually. Contact the conference direct for details about staff, workshops, manuscript criticism opportunities, fees, accommodations, length of conference and dates planned for the current year. Always enclose a self-addressed, stamped envelope when requesting any information.

Alabama

ALABAMA WRITERS' CONCLAVE, Carl Morton, 2221 Woodview Dr., Birmingham AL 35216.

Arkansas

ARKANSAS WRITERS' CONFERENCE, 510 East St., Benton AR 72015. Director: Anna Nash Yarbrough. Held each June for published and unpublished writers in Little Rock AR.

California

CABRILLO SUSPENSE WRITERS' CONFERENCE, Community Services, Cabrillo College, 6500 Soquel Dr., Aptos CA 95003. (408)425-6331. Director: Dr. Timothy Welch. Held each September for published and unpublished writers.

CALIFORNIA WRITERS CONFERENCE, Dorothy Benson, 2214 Derby St., Berkeley CA 94705. Held biannually in June or early July.

LA JOLLA SUMMER WRITERS' CONFERENCE, University Extension, Q-O14, University of California, San Diego, La Jolla CA 92093. Director: David Hellyer. Held each August for published and unpublished writers.

LITERARY HALL OF FAME WRITERS CONFERENCE, Box 20880, Long Beach CA 90801. (213)436-3132. President: Howard E. Hill. Estab. 1976. Held annually in June for published and unpublished writers.

LONG BEACH WRITERS CONFERENCE, Howard E. Hill, Director, Box 20880, Long Beach CA 90801.

PASADENA CITY COLLEGE ANNUAL WRITER'S FORUM, Sponsored by Pasadena City College Continuing Education Department, 1570 E. Colorado Blvd., Pasadena CA 91106. Contact: Dr. Joel Reid. Held Friday and Saturday of the last week in May for published and unpublished writers.

SEMINAR FOR FREELANCE WRITERS, Community Services, Canada College, 4200 Farm Hill Blvd., Redwood City CA 94061. Director: Gladys Cretan. Held each May for published and unpublished writers.

WRITER'S CLUB OF WHITTIER SEMINAR, 7716 Westman Ave., Whittier CA 90606. (213)699-5935. President: Fern Palmer. Annual. Held in March for published and unpublished writers.

WRITERS' CONFERENCE AT JULIAN, CALIFORNIA, 14560 Ringate Dr., Whittier CA 90604. President: Betty Lee Campbell. Held each April for published and unpublished writers.

WRITERS CONFERENCE IN CHILDREN'S LITERATURE, P.O. Box 296, Los Angeles CA 90066. Estab. 1970. Held annually in August for published and unpublished writers.

WRITERS' FORUM, Pasadena City College, Office of Extended Campus Programs, 1570 E. Colorado Blvd., Pasadena CA 91106. Held annually in May.

Colorado

UNIVERSITY OF COLORADO WRITERS CONFERENCE, Department of English, Creative

Writing Program, 101 Hellems, University of Colorado, Boulder CO 80309. Held each June for published and unpublished writers.

Connecticut

CONNECTICUT WRITERS' LEAGUE CONFERENCE, Box 78, Farmington CT 06032. Chairman: Eugene L. Belisle. Held each May for anyone interested in writing.

WESLEYAN-SUFFIELD WRITER-READER CONFERENCE, Jeanne B. Krochalis, Graduate Summer School, Wesleyan University, Middletown CT 06457.

District of Columbia

GEORGETOWN UNIVERSITY WRITERS CONFERENCE, Georgetown University School for Summer and Continuing Education, Washington DC 20057. Director: Dr. Riley Hughes. Held on campus each July (abroad, each June) for published and unpublished writers.

Florida

FLORIDA SUNCOAST WRITERS CONFERENCE, University of South Florida, St. Petersburg FL 33701. (813)974-2421. Director: Ed Hirshberg. Estab. 1972. Annual. Held in January for published and unpublished writers.

FLORIDA WRITERS' CONFERENCE, division of Continuing Education, University of Florida, 2012 W. University Ave., Gainsville FL 32603. (904)392-1701. Director: Suzan H. Schafer. Estab. 1970. Held annually in February for published and unpublished writers.

Georgia

DIXIE COUNCIL OF AUTHORS AND JOURNALISTS CREATIVE WRITING WORKSHOP, Harold R. Random, Director, 4221 N. Shallowford Rd., Apt. 7, Chamblee GA 30341.

SOUTHEASTERN WRITERS ASSOCIATION, INC., Mrs. Jos. E. Buffington, Executive Secretary, 3227-D Covington Dr., Decatur GA 30032.

Illinois

CHRISTIAN WRITERS INSTITUTE CONFERENCE AND WORKSHOP, Gundersen Drive and Schmale Rd., Wheaton IL 60187.

ILLINOIS WESLEYAN UNIVERSITY WRITERS' CONFERENCE, Illinois Wesleyan University, Bloomington IL 61701. Director: Mrs. Bettie W. Story. Held each July for published and unpublished writers.

INTERNATIONAL BLACK WRITERS CONFERENCE, INC., 4019 S. Vincennes Ave., Chicago IL 60053. Director: Alice C. Browning. Held each June for published and unpublished writers.

McKENDREE WRITERS' CONFERENCE, Ruth C. Auwarter, Conference Director, Box 89, Troy IL 62294.

MISSISSIPPI VALLEY WRITERS' CONFERENCE, 3403 45th St., Moline IL 61265. Director: David R. Collins. Held each June for published and unpublished writers.

WRITING '79, 125½ 18th St., Rock Island IL 61201. Secretary: June Moore. Held each March for published and unpublished writers.

Indiana

INDIANA UNIVERSITY WRITERS' CONFERENCE, Ballantine 464, Bloomington IN 47401. Director: Roger Mitchell. Estab. 1941. Held each June/July for published and unpublished writers.

MIDWEST WRITERS' WORKSHOP, English Department, Ball State University, Muncie IN 47306. Director: Tracy Norris. Held each August for published and unpublished writers.

OHIO RIVER WRITERS' CONFERENCE, 16½ SE 2nd St., Evansville IN 47708. (812)422-2111. Executive Director: Jane Moore. Estab. 1976. Held annually one weekend in August for published and unpublished writers.

Kentucky

CREATIVE WRITING CONFERENCE, Department of English, Eastern Kentucky University, Richmond KY 40475. Director: William Sutton. Held each June for published and unpublished writers.

WRITING WORKSHOP FOR PEOPLE OVER 57, Council on Aging, University of Kentucky, Lexington KY 40506. (606)258-2657. Assistant Director: Maude Higgs. Estab. 1966. Held annually in August for published and unpublished writers.

Maine

MAINE WRITERS WORKSHOP, G.F. Bush, Director, Box 82, Stonington ME 04681.

SEACOAST WRITERS CONFERENCE, 160 Goodwin Rd., Eliot ME 03903. Registrar: Mrs. Lillian H. Crowell. Held each October for published and unpublished writers.

STATE OF MAINE WRITERS' CONFERENCE, Box 296, Ocean Park ME 04063. Co-Chairman: Richard Burns. Estab. 1941. Held in August.

Massachusetts

CAPE COD WRITERS' CONFERENCE, Box 111, West Hyannisport MA 02622. Executive Secretary: Mrs. Pierre Vuilleumier. Held each August for published and unpublished writers.

SCBW NEW ENGLAND CHILDREN'S LITERATURE CONFERENCE, Box 27, Hatfield MA 01038. Director: Jane Stemple. Held each April for published and unpublished writers.

SCRIPTORS' CONFERENCE, Box 1745, Springfield MA 01101. Secretary: Maxine Englehardt. Held each summer for published and unpublished writers.

Michigan

CHRISTIAN SCRIBES WRITERS' CONFERENCE, Box 280, Cobles MI 49055. President: Elisabeth McFadden. Held each October or November for anyone interested in writing, but "we prefer Christian-oriented writers".

CLARION WRITERS' WORKSHOP IN SCIENCE FICTION & FANTASY, Justin Morrill College, Michigan State University, East Lansing MI 48824. Director: Dr. R. Glenn Wright. Held each July/August.

CRAFTSMANSHIP OF CREATIVE WRITING CONFERENCE, Conferences and Institutes, Oakland University, Rochester MI 48063. Assistant Director: Douglas Alden Peterson. Held each October for published and unpublished writers.

DETROIT WOMEN WRITERS, Oakland University, Division of Continuing Education, Rochester MI 48063. Director: Barbara Hoffman.

UNIVERSITY OF MICHIGAN CONFERENCE ON TEACHING TECHNICAL AND PROFESSIONAL WRITING, Humanities Department, College of Engineering, University of Michigan, Ann Arbor MI 48109.

Minnesota

UPPER MIDWEST WRITERS' CONFERENCE, Sr. Audré Marthaler. Bemidji State University, Bemidji MN 56601.

Missouri

MISSOURI PRESS WOMEN SPRING MEETING, Ann Fair Dodson, 1315 N. Broadway, Springfield MO 65802.

Nebraska

CHRISTIAN WRITERS CONFERENCE, 11405 Farnam Circle, Omaha NE 68154. Chairman: Mary Brite. Held annually in Fall.

OMAHA WRITERS' CLUB SPRING CONFERENCE, 517 S. 51st Ave., Omaha NE 68106. President: Cathy Nelson. Held each May for published and unpublished writers.

New Jersey

COMEDY AND HUMOR WORKSHOP, 74 Pullman Ave., Elberon NJ 07740. Director: George Q. Lewis. Held each June, July and August for published and unpublished writers.

NEW JERSEY WRITERS' ANNUAL CONFERENCE, 9 David Ct., Edison NJ 08817. President: Mary Kuczkir. Held each October for published and unpublished writers.

WILLIAM PATERSON COLLEGE WRITERS' CONFERENCE, Wayne NJ 07470.

New York

ADIRONDACK-METROLAND WRITERS & EDUCATORS CONFERENCE, Box 189, Clifton Park NY 12065. Director: Dr. Harry Barba. Held each July for published and unpublished writers.

CHAUTAUQUA WRITERS' WORKSHOP, Summer School Office, Box 28, Chautauqua NY 14722.

CHRISTIAN WRITERS WORKSHOP, Don Booth, 6853 Webster Rd., Orchard Park NY 14127. (716)662-5259.

CORNELL UNIVERSITY CREATIVE WRITING WORKSHOP, 105 Day Hall, Ithaca NY 14853. (607)256-4987. Assistant Dean: Charles W. Jermy, Jr. Estab. 1970. Annual. Held June-August for published and unpublished writers.

CREATIVE WRITING WORKSHOP, Niagara County Community College, 3111 Saunders Settlement Rd., Sanborn NY 14132.

INTERNATIONAL WOMEN'S WRITING CONFERENCE & RETREAT, Box 810, Gracie Station. New York NY 10028. (212)737-7536. Executive Director: Hannelore Hahn. Estab. 1976. Biannual. Held February (California) and July/August (east coast) for published and unpublished writers.

NATIONAL CRITICS INSTITUTE OF THE EUGENE O'NEILL MEMORIAL THEATER CENTER, Suite 1012, 1860 Broadway, New York NY 10023. Director: Ernest Schier. Held mid-July to mid-August each year for practicing arts writers and critics whose work is published regularly in newspapers or magazines.

NATIONAL PLAYWRIGHTS CONFERENCE OF THE EUGENE O'NEILL MEMORIAL THEATER CENTER, Suite 1012, 1860 Broadway, New York NY 10023. Artistic Director: Lloyd Richards. Held mid-July to mid-August each year for published and unpublished writers.

NEW YORK HOLIDAY WORKSHOP, 20 Plaza St., Brooklyn NY 11238. Director: Pauline Bloom. Held each October for published and unpublished writers.

NIAGARA FRONTIER CHRISTIAN WRITERS WORKSHOP, 6853 Webster Rd., Orchard Park NY 14157. (716)622-5259. Conference Director: Don Booth. Estab. 1970. Held annually in June for published and unpublished writers.

POETRY WORKSHOPS, The Poetry Center, YMHA, 1395 Lexington Ave., New York NY 10028.

ST. LAWRENCE UNIVERSITY FICTION INTERNATIONAL WRITERS' CONFERENCE, Joe David Bellamy, St. Lawrence University, Canton NY 13617.

SCIENCE FICTION WRITERS' WORKSHOP, 56 8th Ave., New York NY 10014. (212)741-0270. Administrator: Martin Last. Estab. 1976. Held annually in the spring and fall for published and unpublished writers.

TECHNICAL WRITERS' INSTITUTE, B.F. Hammet, Director, Rensselaer Polytechnic Institute, Troy NY 12181.

UNIVERSITY OF ROCHESTER WRITERS' WORKSHOP, Dean Robert Koch, Writers'

Workshop, Harkness Hall 102, University of Rochester, Rochester NY 14627. Held annually in July for published and unpublished writers.

North Carolina

MARTHA'S VINEYARD WRITERS WORKSHOP, Thomas Heffernan, Director, Box F9, 1020 Peace St., Raleigh NC 27605.

TAR HEEL WRITERS' ROUNDTABLE, Box 5393, Raleigh NC 27650. Director: Bernadette Hoyle. Held each August for published and unpublished writers.

WESTERN NORTH CAROLINA CHRISTIAN WRITERS' CONFERENCE, Box 188, Black Mountain NC 28711. Director: Yvonne Lehman. Held each August for published and unpublished writers.

Ohio

CUYAHOGA WRITERS' CONFERENCE, Cuyahoga Community College Eastern Campus, 25444 Harvard Rd., Cleveland OH 44122. Director: Mrs. Margaret Taylor. Held each April or May for published and unpublished writers.

MANUSCRIPT CLUB OF AKRON'S ANNUAL WORKSHOP, 4174 Kent Rd., Stow OH 44224. (216)688-1708. President: Tom Troyer. Estab. 1929. Annual. Held in May for unpublished writers.

MIAMI UNIVERSITY CREATIVE WRITING WORKSHOP, Upham Hall, Miami University, Oxford OH 45056. Director: Milton White. Held each May or June for published and unpublished writers.

MIDWEST WRITERS CONFERENCE, 515 25th St., N.W. Canton OH 44709. (216)454-3011 ext. 218. Director: John W. Oliver, Jr. Estab. 1969. Annual. Held in October for published and unpublished writers.

OHIO POETRY DAY, Evan Lodge, President, 1506 Prospect Rd., Hudson OH 44236.

WRITER'S WORKSHOP, Dr. Joseph LaBriola, Director, Sinclair Community College, 444 W. Third St., Dayton OH 45402.

Oklahoma

OKLAHOMA WRITERS FEDERATION ANNUAL CONFERENCE, Ernestine Gravley, 1225 Sherry Lane, Shawnee OK 74801. Held annually in May for published and unpublished writers.

UNIVERSITY OF OKLAHOMA ANNUAL SHORT COURSE ON PROFESSIONAL WRITING, Leonard Logan, Oklahoma Center for Continuing Education, University of Oklahoma, 1700 Asp Ave., Norman OK 73037.

Oregon

HAYSTACK WRITERS' WORKSHOPS, Dona Beattie, Box 1491, Portland OR 97207.

WILLAMETTE WRITERS CONFERENCE, Mrs. Philip C. Herzog, 3622 SE Lambert, Portland OR 97202.

Pennsylvania

PHILADELPHIA WRITERS CONFERENCE, Emma S. Wood, Registrar, Box 834, Philadelphia PA 19105.

ST. DAVIDS CHRISTIAN WRITERS' CONFERENCE, R. 2., Cochranville PA 19330. (215)593-5963. Registrar: Edna Mast. Estab. 1957. Held annually in June for published and unpublished writers, at Eastern College, St. Davids PA.

South Carolina

WINTHROP COLLEGE WRITERS CONFERENCE, Dean of Continuing Education, Joynes Center for Continuing Education, Winthrop College, Rock Hill SC 29733.

Texas

ABILENE WRITERS GUILD WORKSHOP, Pat Carden, 2809 Darrell Dr., Abilene TX 79606.

PANHANDLE PEN WOMEN AND WEST TEXAS STATE UNIVERSITY WRITERS' ROUND-UP, 6209 Adirondack, Amarillo TX 79106. Director: Dolores Spencer. Held each March or April for published and unpublished writers.

PATRIOTIC POETRY SEMINAR, 3915 S.W. Military Dr., San Antonio TX 78211. President-Director: Dr. Stella Woodall. Held each October for published and unpublished writers.

SOUTH TEXAS PRO-AM WRITERS RALLY, 1601 N. Main Ave., San Antonio TX 78284. (512)227-7156. Executive Director: Charles Bradbury. Estab. 1974. Annual. Held in October for published and unpublished writers.

SOUTHWEST WRITERS' CONFERENCE, Sherman L. Pease, Director, Continuing Education, University of Houston, 4800 Calhoun, Houston TX 77004.

Utah

LEAGUE OF UTAH WRITERS ROUNDUP, Box 144, Kaysville UT 84037. (801)466-6549. President: Esther Parks. Estab. 1936. Annual. Held in September for published and unpublished writers.

ROCKY MOUNTAIN WRITERS' CONVENTION, Special Courses and Conferences, 118 HRCB, Brigham Young University, Provo UT 84602. Director: Gary R. Bascom. Held each July for published and unpublished writers.

USU MAGAZINE ARTICLE WRITER'S WORKSHOP, Dick Harris, Director, Utah State University, Logan UT 84321. Held annually in June.

WESTERN WRITERS' CONFERENCE, Conference and Institute Division, UMC 01, Utah State University, Logan UT 84322.

Vermont

BREAD LOAF WRITERS' CONFERENCE, Middlebury College, Middlebury VT 05753. Directors: Robert Pack/Edward A. Martin. Held each August for published and unpublished writers.

GREEN MOUNTAINS WRITERS WORKSHOP, Johnson State College, Johnson VT 05656. Director: Roger Rath. Annual. Held each July for published and unpublished writers.

Virginia

JANUARY WRITERS' CONFERENCE, George Mason University, English Department, Fairfax VA 22030. (703)323-2220. Coordinator, Writing Program: Donald R. Galler. Estab. 1978. Held annually in January for published and unpublished writers.

VIRGINIA HIGHLANDS FESTIVAL CREATIVE WRITING DAY, Brookhill Estates, Abingdon VA 24210. Chairman: Douglas E. Arnold. Held each August for unpublished writers.

Washington

CENTRUM SUMMER SEASON OF THE ARTS, Fort Worden State Park, Port Townsend WA 98368.

FORT WORDEN POETRY SYMPOSIUM, Jim Heynen, Coordinator, Fort Worden State Park, Port Townsend WA 98368.

PACIFIC NORTHWEST WRITERS CONFERENCE, 1811 N.E. 199th St., Seattle WA 98155. (206)364-1293. Contact: Executive Secretary. Estab. 1956. Annual. Held in July for published and unpublished writers.

PORT TOWNSEND FICTION SEMINAR, Centrum, Fort Worden State Park, Port Townsend WA 98368. (206)385-3102. Program Coordinator: James Haynen. Estab. 1974. Held annually in July for published and unpublished writers.

PORT TOWNSEND POETRY SYMPOSIUM, Centrum, Fort Worden State Park, Port Townsend WA 98368. (206)385-3102. Program Coordinator: James Heynen. Estab. 1974. Held annually in July for published and unpublished writers.

Wisconsin

MIDWEST WRITERS' CONFERENCE, Dr. Wayne Wolfe, University of Wisconsin-River Falls, River Falls WI 54022.

OUTDOOR WRITERS ASSOCIATION OF AMERICA ANNUAL CONFERENCE, 4141 W. Bradley Rd., Milwaukee WI 53209. Held each June.

Canada

THE BANFF CENTRE, School of Fine Arts, P.O. Box 1020, Banff, Alberta T0L 0C0 Canada. Held annually in July for published and unpublished writers.

SUMMER WRITERS WORKSHOP AT NEW COLLEGE, UNIVERSITY OF TORONTO, 165 Spadina Ave., Suite 8, Toronto, Canada M5T 2C4. (416)364-3818. Director: Gerald Lampert. Estab. 1968. Annual. Held the first 2 weeks in August for published and unpublished writers.

Foreign

CARIBBEAN WRITERS WORKSHOP, branch of Maine Writers Workshop, Sapphire Bay Condominiums West, Star Route, St. Thomas USVI 00801 (December-April); Box 82, Stonington ME 04681 (May-November). Director: G. F. Bush. Estab. 1976. Held each April for unpublished writers.

EUROPEAN HOLIDAY WRITERS' WORKSHOP, 20 Plaza St., Brooklyn NY 11218. Director: Pauline Bloom. Held each September for published and unpublished writers.

COSTA RICA AND GUATEMALA HOLIDAY WRITERS' WORKSHOP, Pauline Bloom, 20 Plaza St., Brooklyn NY 11238.

SUMMER IN FRANCE, Hazel Kley, Paris American Academy, 9, rue des Ursullnes, 75005 Paris, France.

Writers' Organizations

National organizations for writers listed here usually require that potential members have attained a professional status. Local or regional writers' clubs are listed in the Writers' Clubs section. SASE must be enclosed with all correspondence with these organizations.

ACADEMY OF AMERICAN POETS, 1078 Madison Ave., New York NY 10028. Estab. 1934. President: Mrs. Hugh Bullock. Purpose of the Academy of American Poets is to encourage, stimulate, and foster the production of American poetry. Awards prizes, conducts poetry workshops, readings and other literary events.

AMERICAN ACADEMY AND INSTITUTE OF ARTS AND LETTERS, 633 W. 155th St., New York NY 10032. Executive Director: Margaret M. Mills. Estab. 1898.
Purpose: "To foster, assist, and sustain an interest in literature, music, and the Fine Arts. The goal is general, but the means are specific, aimed at singling out and encouraging individual artists and their work." Prospective members "must be native or naturalized citizens of the US, qualified by notable achievement in art, music or literature. In order to be eligible, the candidate's work must be essentially creative rather than interpretive. Candidates for membership can only be nominated by members. Candidates must qualify in their own department before they are submitted for vote to the whole membership."

AMERICAN AUTO RACING WRITERS AND BROADCASTERS ASSOCIATION, 922 N. Pass Ave., Burbank CA 91505. (213)842-7005. Established in 1955. Executive Director: Ms. Dusty Brandel. An organization of writers, broadcasters and photographers who cover auto racing throughout the U.S. Aims primarily to improve the relationship between the press and the promoters, sanctioning bodies, sponsors, and participants in the sport. Dues: $20 annually, full membership; $25 annually, associate membership.

AMERICAN MEDICAL WRITERS ASSOCIATION, 5272 River Rd., #209, Bethesda MD 20016. (301)986-9119. Executive Secretary: Lillian Sablack. Estab. 1945. 1,600 members.
Purpose: "To bring together all those engaged in medical communications and its allied professions, and is dedicated to the advancement and improvement of medical communication." Publishes a membership directory, freelance directory, newsletter and journal; also maintains a job market service. Fees: $35/year.

AMERICAN SOCIETY OF JOURNALISTS AND AUTHORS, INC., (formerly Society of Magazine Writers, Inc.), 123 W. 43rd St., New York NY 10036. Established in 1948. President: Ruth Winter. Initiation fee: $25. Annual dues for residents of New York and environs: $60. Annual dues for those residing 200 or more miles from New York: $45. For further information, contact Holly M. Redell. Administrative Secretary.

AMERICAN SOCIETY OF NEWSPAPER EDITORS, Box 551, 1350 Sullivan Trail, Easton PA 18042. Executive Secretary: Mr. Gene Giancarlo. Estab. 1922. Serves as a medium for the exchange of ideas. Membership is limited to directing editors (managing editors, executive editors, associate editors, editors of editorial pages, etc.) of daily newspapers in the U.S. Dues: $200 annually.

AMERICAN TRANSLATORS ASSOCIATION, P.O. Box 129, Croton-on-Hudson NY 10520. Executive Secretary: Mrs. Rosemary Malia. Established in 1959 as a national professional society to advance the standards of translation and to promote the intellectual and material interest of translators and interpreters in the United States. Welcomes to membership all those who are interested in the field as well as translators and interpreters active in any branch of knowledge.

ASMP-THE SOCIETY OF PHOTOGRAPHERS IN COMMUNICATIONS, 60 E. 42nd St., New York NY 10017. (212)661-6450. Executive Director: Arie Kopelman. Established to promote and further the interests of professional photographers in communications media such as journalism, corporate, advertising, fashion, books, etc. Acts as a clearinghouse for photographic information on markets, rates, and business practices of magazines, advertising agencies, publishers and electronic media; works for copyright law revision; offers legal advice, through counsel, to members concerning questions of rights, ethics and payment. Membership categories include Sustaining, General, Associate, and Student.

ASSOCIATED BUSINESS WRITERS OF AMERICA, Box 135, Monmouth Junction NJ 08852. Executive Director: William R. Palmer. Members are skilled in one or more facets of business writing (advertising copy, public relations, ghost writing, books, reports, business and technical magazines, etc.). "Members" are full-time writers. "Associates" hold other jobs. Does not place mss for its members. Provides directory profiling members to prospective mss buyers (at $6). Free membership lists mass-mailed to potential buyers. Dues: $50 annually ($30 for affiliate members); $10 initiation fee.

THE AUTHORS GUILD, INC., 234 W. 44th St., New York NY 10036. (212)398-0838. Executive Secretary: Peter Heggie. Estab. 1912.
Purpose: "To act and speak with the collective voice of 5,000 writers in matters of joint professional and business concern; to keep informed on market tendencies and practices, and to keep its members informed; to advise members on individual professional and business problems as far as possible. Those eleigible for membership include any author who shall have had a book published by an established American publisher within 7 years prior to his application; any author who shall have had 3 works (fiction or nonfiction) published by a magazine of general circulation within 18 months prior to application." Dues: $35/year.

AUTHORS LEAGUE OF AMERICA, INC., 234 West 44th St., New York NY 10036. Established in 1912. Administrative Assistant: Fay W. Glover. The Authors League membership is restricted to authors and dramatists who are members of the Authors Guild, Inc., and the Dramatists Guild, Inc. Matters of joint concern to authors and dramatists, such as copyright and freedom of expression, are in the province of the League; other matters, such as contract terms and subsidiary rights, are in the province of the guilds.

AVIATION/SPACE WRITERS ASSOCIATION, Cliffwood Rd., Chester NJ 07930. (201)879-5667. Executive Secretary: William F. Kaiser. Established in 1938. Founded to establish and maintain high standards of quality and veracity in gathering, writing, editing, and disseminating aeronautical information. The AWA numbers 1,200 members who work for newspapers, press services, TV, radio, or other media and specialize in writing about aviation or space. Dues: $10, initiation fee; $35, annual dues.

BOXING WRITERS ASSOCIATION, c/o Marvin Kohn, Secretary-Treasurer, N.Y. State Athletic Commission, 270 Broadway, New York NY 10007. Established in 1922.

CONSTRUCTION WRITERS ASSOCIATION, 202 Homer Building, Washington DC 20005. Estab. 1958. CWA offers its members a forum for the interchange of information, ideas and methods for improving the quality of reporting, editing and public relations in the construction field. It also provides contact between the membership and news-making officials in government, contracting firms, equipment manufacturers and distributors, consulting firms, and other construction trade and professional groups. Any person principally engaged in writing or editing material pertaining to the construction industry for any regularly published periodical of general circulation is eligible for membership. Any public information or public relations specialist who represents an organization or agency the existence of which depends in whole or in part on the construction industry is also eligible. Annual dues: $20.

DIRECT MARKETING WRITERS GUILD, INC., 15 W. 44th St., New York NY 10038. (212)867-6683. Contact: Michael Fabian. Founded 1964.
Purpose: "To provide a forum for learning the arts of the direct marketing writer's profession; a place where writers meet writers, and privately discuss problems and new achievements in the industry." Eligibility requires that 60% of prospective member's income comes from 1) direct response writing; 2) as a result of supervising writers; 3) as a result of employing direct response writers. Fees: $25/year if within 50 miles of New York City; $15 if more than 50 miles outside of New York.

DOG WRITERS' ASSOCIATION OF AMERICA, INC., 3 Blythewood Rd., Doylestown PA 18901. President: John T. Marvin. Secretary: Sara Futh, Kinney Hill Rd., Washington Depot

CT 06794. The association aims to promote and to encourage the exchange of ideas, methods and professional courtesies among its members. Membership is limited to paid dog writers, editors and/or publishers of newspapers, magazines and books dealing with dogs. Annual dues: $12.

THE FOOTBALL WRITERS ASSOCIATION OF AMERICA, Box 1022, Edmond OK 73034. Secretary-Treasurer: Volney Meece. Membership is mainly sports writers on newspapers and magazines who cover college football, plus those in allied fields, chiefly college sports information directors. Dues: $7.50 annually.

GARDEN WRITERS ASSOCIATION OF AMERICA, INC., 101 Park Ave., New York NY 10017. (212)685-5917. Executive Secretary: Margaret Herbst. Membership Chairman: Gladys Reed Robinson, 680 3rd Ave., Troy NY 12182. Estab. 1944.
Purpose: "Dedicated to improving the standards of horticultural writing, art, and photography in printed and broadcast media. GWAA publishes a helpful bulletin quarterly. Members also receive helpful information through ASS; Garden Bureau; *Garden News*; Plus material from various seed companies, nurseries and many others associated with the horticultural world." Annual dues: $12.50.

INTERNATIONAL ASSOCIATION OF BUSINESS COMMUNICATORS, 870 Market St., Suite 928, San Francisco CA 94102. Executive Director: John N. Bailey. Established in 1970. Dedicated to the advancement of its members and to the advancement of the communication profession. Members are active in the field of business and organizational communication.

MARIANIST WRITERS' GUILD, Marianist Community, University of Dayton, 300 College Park Ave., Dayton OH 45469. (513)229-3430. Executive Secretary: Louis J. Faerber, S.M., Ph.D. Established in 1947. Membership is limited to Marianists in America who have had at least 3 works published nationally since 1947.

MOTOR SPORTS PRESS ASSOCIATION (of Northern California), c/o Harriet Gittings, Box 484, Fremont CA 94537. Established in 1963 for the advancement of motor sports and motor sports journalism in Northern California, for the interchange of ideas and information; to provide a body to authenticate legitimate motor sports journalists, photographers, and radio and TV broadcasters, whether fully employed, part-time employed, or freelancing in Northern California. Annual dues: $12.

MUSIC CRITICS ASSOCIATION, INC., c/o Richard D. Freed, Executive Secretary, 6201 Tuckerman Lane, Rockville MD 20852. President: Patrick J. Smith. The purposes of the Association are to act as an educational medium for the promotion of high standards of music criticism in the press in America, to hold meetings where self-criticism and exchange of ideas will promote educational opportunities, and to increase the general interest in music in the growing culture of the Americas. Membership is open to persons who regularly cover musical events in the U.S. and Canada. Annual dues: $15.

MYSTERY WRITERS OF AMERICA, INC., 105 E. 19th St., New York NY 10003. Established in 1945. Executive Secretary: Gloria Amoury. An organization dedicated to the proposition that the detective story is the noblest sport of man. Membership includes active members who have made at least one sale in mystery, crime, or suspense writing; associate members who are either novices in the mystery writing field or nonwriters allied to the field; editors, publishers, and affiliate members who are interested in mysteries. Annual dues: $35 for U.S. members; $10 for Canadian and overseas members.

THE NATIONAL ACADEMY OF TELEVISION ARTS AND SCIENCES, 291 South La Cienega Blvd., Beverly Hills CA 90211. President: John Cannon. A nonprofit membership organization of professionals working in the television industry. Active members must have worked actively and creatively in television for at least 2 years. Dues: $15 to $30 annually, according to chapter.

NATIONAL ASSOCIATION OF EDUCATIONAL BROADCASTERS, 1346 Connecticut Ave., N.W., Washington DC 20036. Established in 1925. President: James A. Fellows. A professional society of individuals in educational telecommunications; composed of men and women who work in public broadcasting, instructional communications and allied fields. Annual dues: $35.

NATIONAL ASSOCIATION OF GAGWRITERS, 74 Pullman Ave., Elberon NJ 07740.

(201)229-9472. Contact: George Quipp Lewis. Estab: 1945.
Purpose: "To discover, develop, encourage, and showcase future funny men and women; to provide guidance; to coordinate careers in comedy; to promote a national sense of humor and happiness; to maintain a high standard of comedic creativity." Fees: $25/year.

NATIONAL ASSOCIATION OF HOME AND WORKSHOP WRITERS, 27861 Natoma Rd., Los Altos Hills CA 94022. President: R.J. DeCristoforo. Prospective members contact: Bob Brightman, 5 Sussex Rd., Great Neck NY 11020. (506)482-2074. Founded 1973.
Purpose: "An informal association of writers and editors in the field of home and workshop writing. We specialize in how-to activities. Members must have had at least 12 pages published in the previous year. Associate members are also welcome (part-time writers, non-voting) as well as folks interested in the how-to field. A bimonthly newsletter goes to all members, and membership list is used by industry to contact suitable writers for instruction booklets, tool use, and for general how-to projects." Fees: $25/year (full membership); $15/year (associate membership).

NATIONAL ASSOCIATION OF SCIENCE WRITERS, INC., Box H, Sea Cliff NY 11579. (516)671-1734. Established in 1934. Administrative Secretary: Rosemary Arctander. This organization was established to "foster the dissemination of accurate information regarding science through all media normally devoted to informing the public. In pursuit of this goal, NASW conducts a varied program to increase the flow of news from scientists, to improve the quality of its presentation, and to communicate its meaning and importance to the reading public. Anyone who is actively engaged in the dissemination of science information, and has two years or more experience in this field, is eligible to apply. There are several classes of membership. Active members must be principally engaged in reporting science through media that reach the public directly: newspapers, mass-circulation magazines, trade books, radio, television and films. Associate members report science through special media: limited-circulation publications and announcements from organizations such as universities, research laboratories, foundations and science-oriented corporations. Lifetime membership is extended to members after they have belonged to NASW for 25 years. Honorary membership is awarded by NASW to outstanding persons who have notably aided the objectives of the association." Annual dues: $35.

NATIONAL LEAGUE OF AMERICAN PEN WOMEN, INC., 1300 17th St., N.W., Washington DC 20036. Established in 1897. "Professionally qualified women engaged in creating and promoting letters, art, and music" are eligible for membership. Women interested in membership must qualify professionally and be presented for membership and endorsed by two active members in good standing in the League. The League holds branch, state, and national meetings. Dues: Initiation fee $5. Annual branch dues plus $15 national dues. For further information, write to national president at address given above.

NATIONAL PRESS CLUB, National Press Bldg., 529 14th St. N.W., Washington DC 20045. Initiation fee: $25-125. Dues: $40 to $244 annually, depending on membership status.

NATIONAL TURF WRITERS ASSOCIATION, Willco Bldg., Suite 317, 6000 Executive Blvd., Rockville MD 20852. Secretary/Treasurer: Tony Chamblin. Membership limited to newspaper or magazine writers who regularly cover thoroughbred racing, sports editors of newspapers which regularly print thoroughbred racing news and results, and sports columnists who write columns on thoroughbred racing. Dues: $10 annually.

NATIONAL WRITERS CLUB, INC., 1450 S. Havana, Suite 620, Aurora CO 80012. Established in 1937. Executive Director: Donald E. Bower. "Founded for the purpose of informing, aiding and protecting freelance writers worldwide. Associate membership is available to anyone seriously interested in writing. Qualifications for professional membership are publication of a book by a recognized book publisher; or sales of at least three stories or articles to national or regional magazines; or a television, stage, or motion picture play professionally produced." Annual dues: $22, associate membership; $25, professional membership; plus $7.50 initiation fee.

NEWSPAPER FARM EDITORS OF AMERICA (NFEA), 4200 12th St., Des Moines IA 50313. (515)243-4518. Established in 1953. Executive Secretary: Glenn Cunningham. Farm writers employed by newspapers, farm editors and farm writers for national wire services are eligible for membership. Dues: $20 annually.

NEWSPAPER FOOD EDITORS AND WRITERS ASSOCIATION, Established in 1973. President: Eleanor Ostman, St. Paul Dispatch & Pioneer Press, St. Paul MN 55101. To encourage communication among journalists devoting a substantial portion of their working time to the furthering of public's knowledge of food; to uphold and foster professional ethical standards for such persons; to increase their knowledge about food and to encourage and promote a greater understanding among fellow journalists and those who manage news dissemination organizations. Dues: $25 annually.

OUTDOOR WRITERS ASSOCIATION OF AMERICA, INC., 4141 W. Bradley Rd., Milwaukee WI 53209. (414)354-9690. Estab. 1927. Executive Director: Edwin W. Hanson. A nonprofit professional and educational organization comprised of newspaper and magazine writers, editors, photographers, broadcasters, artists, cinematographers, and lecturers engaged in the dissemination of information on outdoor sports such as hunting, boating, fishing, camping, etc., and on the conservation of natural resources. Its objectives are "providing a means of cross-communication among specialists in this field, promoting craft improvement, obtaining fair treatment from media, and increasing general public knowledge of the outdoors. Among other subjects, the membership deals extensively in current environmental issues." Requires that each member annually have published a specified quantity of paid material. Sponsorship by an active member of the OWAA is required for membership applicants. Dues: $25, initiation fee; $25, annual fee.

P.E.N., American Center, 156 Fifth Ave., New York NY 10010. (212)255-1977. Estab. 1921. Executive Secretary: Mel Mendelssohn. A world association of poets, playwrights, essayists, editors, and novelists, the purpose of P.E.N. is "to promote and maintain friendship and intellectual cooperation among men and women of letters in all countries, in the interests of literature, the exchange of ideas, freedom of expression, and good will." P.E.N. has 82 centers in Europe, Asia, Africa, Australia, and the Americas. "Membership is open to all qualified writers, translators, and editors who subscribe to the aims of International P.E.N." To qualify for membership, an applicant must have "acknowledged achievement in the literary field, which is generally interpreted as the publication by a recognized publisher of 2 books of literary merit. Membership is by invitation of the Admission Committee after nomination by a P.E.N. member."

PEN AND BRUSH CLUB, 16 E. 10th St., New York NY 10003. Estab. 1893. President: Margaret Sussman. "The Pen and Brush Club is a club of professional women, writers, painters, graphic artists, sculptors, and craftsmen, with a resident membership limited to 350 active members in these fields. Exhibits are held in the galleries of the clubhouse by painters, sculptors, graphic artists, and craftsmen."

POETRY SOCIETY OF AMERICA, 15 Gramercy Park, S., New York NY 10003. (212)254-9628. Executive Secretary: Charles A. Wagner. The oldest and largest group working for an appreciation of poetry and for wider recognition of the work of living American poets, the Society has a membership of traditionalists and experimentalists. Dues: $18 annually.

POETS & WRITERS, INC., 201 W. 54 St., New York NY 10019. (212)757-1766. Information Coordinator: Elliott Figman. Estab. 1971.
Purpose: "To serve as an information clearinghouse and service organization for the nation's literary community. The information center has a toll-free number, 800-223-0384, for anyone outside New York State who needs help finding the current address of a listed writer or has questions of a general literary nature. People in New York may call (212)-757-1766 collect." Publishes *Coda: Poets & Writers Newsletter* 5 times/year, and *Dispatch: Poets & Writers Bulletin* 8 times/year. Other publications: *A Directory of American Poets, A Directory of American Fiction Writers, The Supplement,* and *The Awards List*. "Anyone with an interest in contemporary literature may use our services, subscribe to our periodicals, or purchase our reference books and pamphlets. Writers who wish to be listed must meet publication requirements: for a poet—10 or more poems in 3 different US literary publications; for a fiction writer—1 book or 3 short fictions in 3 US periodicals. Work may be written in English, Spanish or Native American language. Some exceptions are made for performance poets who do not normally publish. No dues or listing fees at all."

RELIGION NEWSWRITERS ASSOCIATION, 1100 Broadway, Nashville TN 37202. (615)255-1221. Estab. 1949. President: W.A. Reed. First Vice President: Ms. Marjorie Hyer, 1150 15th St. N.W., Washington DC 20071. Officers and members of RNA comprise 110 reporters who cover news of religion for the secular press in the United States and Canada.

ROCKY MOUNTAIN OUTDOOR WRITERS AND PHOTOGRAPHERS, 1111 Morningside Dr., N.E., Albuquerque NM 87110. Contact: D. Harper Simms. Founded 1973.
Purpose: "RMOWP is a select regional organization of professional writers, photographers, artists, and lecturers residing in Arizona, Colorado, Idaho, Montana, New Mexico, Utah, or Wyoming. The organization was founded with the purpose of improving and expanding outdoor writing, photography, and other communication forms." Fees: $10 initiation, $10/year (active; $10 initiation fee; $5/year associate; $25 minimum for supporting members).

SCIENCE FICTION WRITERS OF AMERICA, Peter D. Pautz, Executive Secretary, 68 Countryside Apartments, Hackettstown NJ 07840. (201)852-8531. Membership is limited to established science fiction writers in the country. Purposes are to inform writers of matters of professional benefit, to serve as an intermediary in disputes of a professional nature, and to act as central clearinghouse for information on science fiction and science fiction writers. Dues: $20 annually, with a $12.50 installation fee for new members.

SOCIETY FOR TECHNICAL COMMUNICATION, 1010 Vermont Ave. N.W., Suite 421, Washington DC 20005. (202)737-0035. Estab. 1953. Executive Director: Curtis T. Youngblood. Dedicated to the advancement of the theory and practice of technical communication in all media, the STC aims primarily for the education, improvement, and advancement of its members. Dues: $20 annually.

SOCIETY OF AMERICAN SOCIAL SCRIBES, c/o The Plain Dealer, 1801 Superior Ave., Cleveland OH 44114. (216)523-4500. Secretary: Mary Strassmeyer. "The Society of American Social Scribes is a nonprofit organization dedicated to serving the interest of the reading public, to promote unbiased, objective reporting of social events and to promote journalistic freedom of movement. It endeavors to upgrade the professional integrity and skill of its members to work to increase the pleasures of the reading public, to support all legitimate efforts toward developing the education of its members, and to help its members offer greater service to their readers. Membership is limited to those regularly engaged as salaried society editors or devoting a substantial or regular part of their time to society coverage and the balance to other strictly editorial work. Society writers on daily newspapers with circulations of 200,000 or more and magazine writers and authors of books on the subject are also eligible for membership." Annual dues: $15.

SOCIETY OF AMERICAN TRAVEL WRITERS, 1120 Connecticut Ave., Suite 940, Washington DC 20036. (202)785-5567. Established in 1956. Administrative Coordinator: Ken Fischer. Dedicated to serving the interest of the traveling public, to promote international understanding and good will, and to further promote unbiased, objective reporting of information on travel topics. Active membership is limited "to those regularly engaged as salaried travel editors, writers, broadcasters, or photographers actively assigned to diversified travel coverage by a recognized medium or devoting a substantial or regular part of their time to such travel coverage to satisfy the Board of Directors; or to those who are employed as freelancers in any of the above areas with a sufficient steady volume of published work about travel to satisfy the Board. Associate membership is limited to persons regularly engaged in public relations or publicity within the travel industry to an extent that will satisfy the Board of Directors. All applicants must be sponsored by 2 active members with whom they are personally acquainted." Dues: $50 initiation fee for active members, $100 initiation fee for associate members; $50 annual dues for active members, $90 annual dues for associate members.

SOCIETY OF CHILDREN'S BOOK WRITERS, Box 296, Los Angeles CA 90066. President: Stephen Mooser. Founded 1968.
Purpose: "The Society of Children's Book Writers is the only national organization designed to offer a variety of services to people who write or share a vital interest in children's literature. The SCBW acts as a network for the exchange of knowledge between children's writers, editors, publishers, illustrators and agents." Fees $25/year.

SOCIETY OF PROFESSIONAL JOURNALISTS, SIGMA DELTA CHI, 35 E. Wacker Dr., Chicago IL 60601. Established in 1909. Executive Officer: Russell E. Hurst. Dedicated to the highest ideals in journalism. Membership extends horizontally to include persons engaged in the communication of fact and opinion by all media and vertically to include in its purposes and fellowship all ranks of journalists. Dues: $20 annually.

SOCIETY OF THE SILURIANS, INC., 45 John St., New York NY 10028. (212)233-1897. Secretary: James H. Driscoll. Estab. 1924. Primarily a fraternal organization. Membership totals 700. Men and women are eligible for full membership if their history in the New York City media dates back 25 years, for associate membership after 15 years, whether or not they are still so engaged. Dues: $10 annually.

UNITED STATES HARNESS WRITERS' ASSOCIATION, INC., P.O. Box 10, Batavia NY 14020. Estab. 1947. Executive Secretary: William F. Brown, Jr. 435 members. Involved in media coverage of harness racing and/or standardbred breeding. Dues: $25 annually.

WASHINGTON INDEPENDENT WRITERS ASSOCIATION, INC., 1010 Vermont St., N.W., Suite 710, Washington DC 20005. Executive Director: John McGrath. Established in 1975. Purposes are to further the common goals of reputable writers and to combat unfair practices which hamper work, and to help establish ethical guidelines for the conduct of the profession. Full membership is open to persons who have written and published for compensation 5,000 words or its equivalent during the previous year or who have authored a book commercially published within the preceding 5 years. Associate membership is open to persons with serious interest in the independent writing profession or other independent media professions. Offers workshops and meetings, an annual directory, a monthly newsletter, legal, contract and tax information, an assignment referral service, group hospitalization and a major medical plan. Its committees work on market information, problems of professional relations and development.

WESTERN WRITERS OF AMERICA, INC., 1505 W. "D" St., North Platte NE 69101. Contact: Nellie Yost. Writers eligible for membership in this organization are not restricted in their residence, "so long as their work, whether it be fiction, history, adult, or juvenile, book-length or short material, movie or TV scripts, has the scene laid west of the Missouri River."

WOMEN IN COMMUNICATIONS, INC., Box 9561, Austin TX 78766. (512)345-8922. Editor/PR Director: Ernestine Wheelock. Estab. 1909.
Purpose: "WICI was established to work for a free and responsible press; unite women engaged in all fields of communication; recognize distinguished achievements of women journalists; maintain high professional standards; and encourage members to greater individual effort." Publishes a monthly newsletter and a quarterly magazine, *Matrix*; prints a twice-monthly job information bulletin for WICI members; conducts a job and salary survey every 5 years; publishes occasional professional papers; and sponsors the Clarion Awards Contest. Dues: $35/year.

WRITERS GUILD OF AMERICA, Writers Guild of America, *East*, 22 W. 48th St., New York NY 10036. Writers Guild of America, *West*, 8955 Beverly Blvd., Los Angeles CA 90048. A labor organization representing all screen, television, and radio writers. Initiation fee: $400 (West), $400 (East). Dues: $12.50 per quarter (East), $10 per quarter (West), and 1% of gross earnings as a writer in WGA fields of jurisdiction.

Glossary

All Rights. See Article "Rights and the Writer: What Should I Sell?"

Alternative culture. The life styles, politics, literature, etc., of those persons with cultural values different from the current "establishment."

Associated Press Stylebook and Libel Manual. $3.95 from the Associated Press, 50 Rockefeller Plaza, New York City 10020.

Assignment. Editor asks a writer to do a specific article for which he usually names a price for the completed manuscript.

B&W. Abbreviation for black-and-white photograph.

Beat. A specific subject area regularly covered by a reporter, such as the police department or education or the environment. It can also mean a scoop on some news item.

Bimonthly. Every two months. See also *semimonthly*.

Biweekly. Every two weeks.

Blue-penciling. Editing a manuscript.

Caption. Originally a title or headline over a picture but now a description of the subject matter of a photograph, including names of people where appropriate. Also called cutline.

Chapbook. A small booklet, usually paperback, of poetry, ballads or tales.

Chicago Manual of Style. A format for the typing of manuscripts as established by the University of Chicago Press, 5801 S. Ellis, Chicago 60637. Send $13.95 to the attention of Sales Department.

Clean copy. Free of errors, cross-outs, wrinkles, smudges.

Clippings. News items of possible interest to trade magazine editors.

Column inch. All the type contained in one inch of a typeset column.

Contributors' copies. Copies of the issues of a magazine sent to an author in which his/her work appears.

Copy. Manuscript material before it is set in type.

Copy editing. Editing the manuscript for grammar, punctuation and printing style as opposed to subject content.

Copyright. A means to protect an author's work. See article "Copyright: Questions & Answers."

Correspondent. Writer away from the home office of a newspaper or magazine who regularly provides it with copy.

Cutline. See caption.

El-hi. Elementary to high school.

Epigram. A short, witty, sometimes paradoxical saying.

Erotica. Usually fiction that is sexually oriented; although it could be art on the same theme.

Fair use. A provision of the Copyright Law that says short passages from copyrighted material may be used without infringing on the owner's rights. See article "Copyright: Questions & Answers."

Feature. An article giving the reader background information on the news. Also used by magazines to indicate a lead article or distinctive department.

Filler. A short item used by an editor to "fill" out a newspaper column or a page in a magazine. It could be a timeless news item, a joke, an anecdote, some light verse or short humor, a puzzle, etc.

First North American serial rights. See article "Rights and the Writer: What Should I Sell?"

Formula story. Familiar theme treated in a predictable plot structure—such as boy meets girl, boy loses girl, boy gets girl.

Gagline. The caption for a cartoon, or the cover teaser line and the punchline on the inside of a studio greeting card.

Ghostwriter. A writer who puts into literary form, an article, speech, story or book based on another person's ideas or knowledge.

Glossy. A black-and-white photograph with a shiny surface as opposed to one with a non-shiny matte finish.

Gothic novel. One in which the central character is usually a beautiful young girl, the setting is an old mansion or castle; there is a handsome hero and a real menace, either natural or supernatural.

Honorarium. A token payment. It may be a very small amount of money, or simply a byline and copies of the publication in which your material appears.

Illustrations. May be photographs, old engravings, artwork. Usually paid for separately from the manuscript. See also "package sale."

International Postal Reply Coupons. Can be purchased at your local post office and enclosed with your letter or manuscript to a foreign publisher to cover his postage cost when replying.

Invasion of privacy. Cause for suits against some writers who have written about persons (even though truthfully) without their consent.

Kill fee. A portion of the agreed-on price for a complete article that was assigned but which was subsequently cancelled.

Libel. A false accusation; or any published statement or presentation that tends to expose another to public contempt, ridicule, etc. Defenses are truth; fair comment on the matter of public interest; and privileged communication—such as a report of legal proceedings or a client's communication to his lawyer.

Little magazines. Publications of limited circulation, usually on literary or political subject matter.

MLA Handbook. A format for the typing of manuscripts established by the Modern Language Association, 62 Fifth Ave., New York City 10011. $4.70.

Model release. A paper signed by the subject of a photograph (or his guardian, if a juvenile) giving the photographer permission to use the photograph, editorially or for advertising purposes or for some specific purpose as stated.

Ms. Abbreviation for manuscript.

Mss. Abbreviation for more than one manuscript.

Multiple submissions. Some editors of non-overlapping circulation magazines, such as religious publications, are willing to look at manuscripts which have also been submitted to other editors at the same time. See individual listings for which editors these are. No multiple submissions should be made to larger markets paying good prices for original material, unless it is a query on a highly topical article requiring an immediate response and that fact is so stated in your letter.

Newsbreak. A newsworthy event or item. For example, a clipping about the opening of a new shoe store in a town might be a newsbreak of interest to a trade journal in the shoe industry. Some editors also use the word to mean funny typographical errors.

Novelette. A short novel, or a long short story; 7,000 to 15,000 words approximately.

Offset. Type of printing in which copy and illustrations are photographed and plates made, from which printing is done; as opposed to letterpress printing directly from type metal and engravings of illustrations.

One-time rights. See article "Rights and the Writer: What Should I Sell?"

Outline. Of a book is usually a one-page summary of its contents; often in the form of chapter headings with a descriptive sentence or two under each one to show the scope of the book.

Package sale. The editor wants to buy manuscript and photos as a "package" and pay for them in one check.

Page rate. Some magazines pay for material at a fixed rate per published page, rather than so much per word.

Payment on acceptance. The editor sends you a check for your article, story or poem as soon as he reads it and decides to publish it.

Payment on publication. The editor decides to buy your material but doesn't send you a check until he publishes it.

Pen name. The use of a name other than your legal name on articles, stories, or books where you wish to remain anonymous. Simply notify your post office and bank that you are using the name so that you'll receive mail and/or checks in that name.

Photo feature. A feature in which the emphasis is on the photographs rather than any accompanying written material.

Photocopied submissions. Are acceptable to some editors instead of the author's sending his original manuscript. See also multiple submissions.

Plagiarism. Passing off as one's own, the expression of ideas, words of another.

Public domain. Material which was either never copyrighted or whose copyright term has run out.

Publication not copyrighted. Publication of an author's work in such a publication places it in the public domain, and it cannot subsequently be copyrighted. See article "Copyright: Questions & Answers."

Query. A letter of inquiry to an editor eliciting his interest in an article you want to write.

Reporting times. The number of days, weeks, etc., it takes an editor to report back to the author on his query or manuscript.

Reprint rights. See article: "Rights and the Writer: What Should I Sell?"

Round-up article. Comments from, or interviews with, a number of celebrities or experts on a single theme.

Royalties, standard hardcover book. 10% of the retail price on the first 5,000 copies sold; 12½% on the next 5,000 and 15% thereafter.

Royalties, standard mass paperback book. 4 to 8% of the retail price on the first 150,000 copies sold.

SAE. Self-addressed envelope.

SASE. Self-addressed, stamped envelope.

Second serial rights. See article "Rights and the Writer: What Should I Sell?"

Semimonthly. Twice a month.

Semiweekly. Twice a week.

Serial. Published periodically, such as a newspaper or magazine.

Short-short story. Is usually from 500 to 2,000 words.

Simultaneous submissions. Submissions of the same article, story or poem to several publications at the same time.

Slant. The approach of a story or article so as to appeal to the readers of a specific magazine. Does, for example, this magazine always like stories with an upbeat ending? Or does that one like articles aimed only at the blue-collar worker?

Slides. Usually called transparencies by editors looking for color photographs.

Speculation. The editor agrees to look at the author's manuscript but doesn't promise to buy it until he reads it.

Stringer. A writer who submits material to a magazine or newspaper from a specific geographical location.

Style. The way in which something is written—for example, short, punchy sentences or flowing, narrative description or heavy use of quotes or dialogue.

Subsidiary rights. All those rights, other than book publishing rights included in a book contract—such as paperback, book club, movie rights, etc.

Subsidy publisher. A book publisher who charges the author for the cost to typeset and print his book, the jacket, etc., as opposed to a royalty publisher which pays the author.

Syndication rights. A book publisher may sell the rights to a newspaper syndicate to print a book in installments in one or more newspapers.

Tabloids. Newspaper format publication on about half the size of the regular newspaper page, such as *National Enquirer*.

Tearsheet. Pages from a magazine or newspaper containing your printed story or article or poem.

Think piece. A magazine article that has an intellectual, philosophical, provocative approach to its subject.

Transparencies. Positive color slides; not color prints.

Uncopyrighted publication. Publication of an author's work in such a publication puts it in the public domain.

Unsolicited manuscripts. A story, article, poem or book that an editor did not specifically ask to see.

Vanity publisher. See subsidy publisher.

Vignette. A brief scene offering the reader a flash of illumination about a character as opposed to a more formal story with a beginning, middle and end.

Index

A. A.U.W. Writer's Workshop 871
A. G. News and A. G. Newsletter 693
A.I.P.-U.S. Steel Foundation Science Writing Award 805
A.M.E. Review 460
A.R.C. Publications 66
A.S.U. Travel Guide 781
A&A Agency 788
AAAS Socio-Psychological Prize 805
AAAS-Westinghouse Science Writing Awards 805
AAFP Journalism Awards 805
AAU News 507
AAUW Journal 565
AB Bookman's Weekly 630
Abbey Press 66
ABC American Roofer and Building Improvement Contractor 642
ABC International Travel Magazine 556
ABC-CLIO Inc. 66
Abel Literary Agency, Dominick 788
Abilene Writers Guild 873
Abilene Writers Guild Workshop 882
Abingdon Press 48, 67
Academic Press, Inc. 67
Academy of American Poets 885
Academy Press Limited 67
Accent 269, 391
Accent on Living 280
Ace Books 67
ACF Horizons 184
Acquire: The Magazine of Contemporary Collectibles 289
ACTF Student Playwriting Awards 805
Action 825
Ad Techniques 616
ADA Publishing Co. (see Ad Techniques 616)
Adam 366
Adam Film World 548
Adams Prize, Herbert Baxter 805
Adams, Ray & Rosenberg 788
Addisonian Press and Young Scott Books 68
Addison-Wesley Publishing Co., Inc. 67
Adirondack Life 434
Adirondack-Metroland Writers & Educators Conference 881
Adirondack-Metroland-Harian Fiction Award 805
Admaster, Inc. 48
Administrative Conference of the United States 826
Administrative Management 634

Adventure Travel 556
Adventures In Poetry Magazine 419
Advertising Age 616
Advertising Trade Publications, Inc. (see Art Direction 616)
Advocate, The 195
Aero Products Research, Inc. 48
Aero Publishers, Inc. 68
Affair 367
Africa Report 428
After Dark 548
Afternoon TV 548
AG World 672
Agency Sales Magazine 766
Agricultural Marketing Service 825
Agricultural Publishing Co. (see Farm & Country 675)
Agriculture, Department of 825
Agrologist 674
Agway Cooperator 672
Air California Magazine 308
Air Conditioning, Heating and Refrigeration News 757
Air Force, Department of the 825
Air Line Pilot 235
Air University Review 375
Airfix Magazine 289
Airport Services Management 627
Alabama State Poetry Society 867
Alabama Writers' Conclave 878
Aladdin Distributing Corp. (see Modern People 273, National Informer 274)
Alaska Construction & Oil Magazine 243
Alaska Journal, The 283
Alaska Magazine 435
Alaska Northwest Publishing Co. 68
Alaska Pictorial Service 836
Alaska Woman Magazine 565
Alba House 68
Albert, Dorothy 788
Alberta Motorist, The 557
Alcalde 257
Alfred Hitchcock's Mystery Magazine 400
Alive and Well in St. Catharines 249
Alive! For Young Teens 535
All Outdoors 507
All South Carolina Football Annual 506
Allegro Film Productions, Inc. 48
Allen and Son, J.C. 836
Allen Publishing Co. 68
Alley Theatre 588
Allied Publications Inc. (see Hairstylist 695, Woman Beautiful 695, Modern Secretary 765)
Allyn and Bacon, Inc. 68
Almar Press 69
Aloft 309
Alpha Photos Associates 836
Alpine Photography 836
Alternative Sources of Energy Magazine 382
Aluminum Company of America 837
AMA News (see American Motorcycle 224)
Amateur Poetry Contest 806
Amateur Radio Biting Bug Award 806
Amberley Greeting Card Co. 582
America 460
American Academy and Institute of Arts and Letters 885
American Academy and Institute of Arts and Letters Awards 806
American Art Journal, The 210
American Art Review 211
American Astrology 220
American Astronautical Society 69
American Auto Racing Writers and Broadcasters Association 885
American Baby Magazine 247
American Bar Association Press (see Barrister 716, Student Lawyer 717)
American Battle Monuments Commission 826
American Bicyclist and Motorcyclist 771
American Boating Illustrated 500
American Catholic Press 69
American Cinematographer 755
American Classical College Press 69
American Coin-Op 641
American Collector 289
American Dane Magazine 382
American Dental Association Science Writers Award 806
American Drycleaner 715
American Education 266
American Family Physician 732
American Farriers' Journal 737
American Features Syndicate 603
American Field 514
American Film 548
American Firearms Industry 766

American Forest Institute 826
American General Journal 184
American Girl Magazine 535
American Glass Review 631
American Gold News 737
American Graphics 289
American Greetings Corporation 582
American Hairdresser/Salon Owner 695
American Hereford Journal 678
American Heritage 284
American Historical Review 284
American History Illustrated, Civil War Times Illustrated 284
American Horologist & Jeweler 708
American Humane Magazine 204
American Hunter, The 514
American Ink Maker 760
American Inventor Magazine 489
American Jewelry Manufacturer 709
American Jewish Times-Outlook 312
American Judo 523
American Laundry Digest 715
American Legion Magazine, The 214
American Libraries 718
American Media 69
American Medical Writers Association 885
American Mercury 326
American Motorcycle 224
American Museum of Natural History, The 837
American National Red Cross 826
American Newspaper Carrier 535
American Notes and Queries 327
American Opinion Magazine 429
American Osteopathic Association Journalism Awards 806
American Paint & Coatings Journal 749
American Paint and Wallcoverings Dealer 750
American Painting Contractor 750
American Penal Press Contest 806
American Petroleum Institute 837
American Play Co., Inc. 788
American Poetry League 873
American Poetry League Magazine 419
American Psychological Foundation National Media Awards 806
American Quarterly 327
American Review of Eastern Orthodoxy 461
American Rifleman, The 514
American Scholar, The 327
American School & University 651
American School Board Journal, The 651
American Shipper 730
American Shotgunner, The 511
American Soccer Magazine 533
American Society of Journalists and Authors, Inc. 885
American Society of Newspaper Editors 885
American Squaredance 549
American Stage Festival 588
American Stock Photos 837
American Teacher 266
American Translators Association 885
American Trucking Associations, Inc. 837
American Turf Monthly 513
American Universal Artforms Corp. 70
American West, The 284
American Zionist, The 313
Americana 290
Americana Publications Co. 70
Americas 429
America's Textile Reporter/Bulletin 777
Amos Press (see Gun Week 512)
Amphoto 70
Amsterdam, Marcia 788
Amusement Business 770
Analog Science Fiction & Science Fact 495
Anco/Boston, Inc. 48
Anderson Associates, Inc., Cutty 789
Anderson Films, Ken 48
Anderson Publishing Co. 70 (see also Journal of Genealogy 286)
And/Or Press 70
Andy Warhol's Interview Magazine 382
Angler 514
Angler and Hunter in Ontario, The 515
Anglican Book Centre 70
Animal Kingdom 204
Animal Lovers Magazine 204
Animal Rights Writing Award 806
Animals 205
Animals Animals 837
Animation Arts Associates, Inc. 49
Ann Arbor Writers Workshop 870
Annals of Saint Anne de Beaupre, The 461
Anrald 869
Anthelion 327

Antigonish Review, The 327
Antioch Review 327
Antiquarian, The 290
Antique Trader Weekly, The 290
Antiques Dealer, The 738
Antiques Journal 290
Anton, Inc., Barbara 837
Antonson Publishing Co. 71
Anvil Press (see North Country Anvil 202)
AOPA Pilot, The 235
AP Newsfeatures 603
APA Monitor 738
Apalachee Quarterly 328
Apartment Life 302
Apartment Management Newsletter 762
Appalachian Trailway News 523
Appaloosa News 205
Apparel Industry Magazine 639
Appel Color Photography 837
Applause 549
Appliance Service News 697
Aqua-Field Publications, Inc. (see Ferber's Freshwater Fisherman 516)
Aquarian Publishing Co. (London) Ltd., The 71
Aquila Publishing Co., Ltd., The 71
Ararat 382
Archer Editions Press 71
Archery Retailer 771
Archery World 499
Architectural Book Publishing Co., Inc. 71
Arco Publishing Co., Inc. 71
Arctic in Color 435
Arden and Company, Hal Marc 49
Area Development Magazine 762
Argosy 367
Argus Publishers Corp. (see 1001 Truck and Van Ideas Magazine 231, Super Chevy Magazine 234)
Arion 328
Arise 280
Arizona Highways 435
Arizona Literary Agency 789
Arizona Magazine 405
Arizona Photographic Associates' Inc. 837
Arizona Quarterly 328
Ark River Review, The 328
Arkansas Cattle Business 678
Arkansas Pioneer Branch, National League of American Pen Women 867
Arkansas Writers' Conference 878
Arkham House Publishers, Inc. 72
Arkin Magazine Syndicate 603
Arlington House Publishers 72
Armed Forces Journal 375
Army, Department of the 826
Army Magazine 375
Army/Navy Store and Outdoor Merchandiser 766
Army Reserve Magazine 375
Army Times Publishing Co. (see Military Market 649)
Art and Archaeology Newsletter 285
Art and Literary Digest 328
Art Dealer & Framer 738
Art Direction 616
Art News 211
Art Reference Bureau Inc. 837
Artistry International 838
Artists & Writers Publications 72
Arts & Activities 651
Arts In Education, The 651
Arts Magazine 211
Arts Magazine Publishers (see Southwest Art 213)
Arts Management 211
Arts Objectively, The 195
Asbury Theological Seminary Herald, The 461
ASCAP-Deems Taylor Awards 806
ASFA Poetry Quarterly 419
Ashire Publishing Ltd. (see Mine and Quarry 777)
Ashland Now 184
Ashley Books, Inc. 72
ASI Publishers, Inc. 73
Asia Mail, The 429
Asimov's Science Fiction Magazine, Isaac 495
ASMP-The Society of Photographers in Communications 885
Aspect 329
Aspen Anthology 329
Aspire 461
Aspiring Writers' Club 867
Assembly Engineering 722
Associated Booksellers 73
Associated Business Writers of America 886

Associated Picture Service 838
Associated Publishers' Guidance Publications Center 73
Association of American Railroads News Service 838
Association Press 73
ASTA Travel News 781
Astrology Guide 220
Astrology '78 221
Astrology -- Your Daily Horoscope 221
Astronomy 490
At Ease 376
At Rise: Magazine 329
Atheneum Publishers 74
Athletic Press 74
Atlantic Advocate, The 435
Atlantic Firsts 806
Atlantic Monthly, The 270
Atlantic Monthly Press 74
Audecibel 732
Audio Magazine 392
Audio Retailer, The (see Audio Trade Merchandising 766)
Audio Trade Merchandising 766
Audioscene Canada 392
Audubon 400
Augsburg Publishing House 74
August Films, Inc. 49
Austin Magazine 243
Australian Consolidated Press Ltd. (see The Australian Women's Weekly 566)
Australian Women's Weekly, The 566
Austrian Press and Information Service 838
Authenticated News International 603, 838
Author Aid Associates 789
Authors' Advisory Service 789
Authors, Composers and Artists' Society 867
Authors Guild, Inc., The 886
Authors League of America, Inc. 886
Auto and Flat Glass Journal 631
Auto Book Press 74
Auto Laundry News 619
Auto News Syndicate 603
Automatic Machining 723
Automation in Housing & Systems Building News 643
Automobile Photo Archives 838
Automobile Quarterly 224
Automotive Age 766
Automotive Booster of California 214
Automotive News 619
Automotive Page, The 225
Automotive Rebuilder Magazine 619
Autoweek 224
Autumn Press, Inc. 74
A/V Concepts Corporation 48
Avena, Rae 575
Avenue M 249
AVI Publishing Co. 75
Aviation 236
Aviation Book Company 75
Aviation Quarterly 236
Aviation/Space Writers Association 886
Aviation/Space Writers Association Journalism Awards 807
Aviation Travel 236
Avon Books 75
Away 557

B.C. Business Magazine 243
B.C. Lumberman Magazine 720
Babcox Publications, Inc. (see Automotive Rebuilder Magazine 619, Specialty & Custom Dealer 625)
Babka Publishing Co. (see Antiques Journal 290)
Baby Care 247
Baby Talk 247
Bachner Productions, Inc. 49
Bachy 329
Back Alley Theatre, The 588
Back Roads 330
Backpacker 524
Backpacking Journal 524
Backstretch, The 513
Badger Creek Press 75
Bair, Photographer, Royce 838
Baja California Bulletin 436
Baker Book House Co. 75
Baker's Play Publishing Co. 597
Baking Industries Journal 628
Bale Books 76
Balkin Agency, The 789
Ball State University Forum 330
Ballantine Books 76
Bancroft Library, The 838
Bancroft Prizes 807
Banff Centre, The 884
Bank Systems & Equipment 683

Banking 683
Banner Books International, Inc. 76
Bantam Books, Inc. 76
Banyan Books, Inc. 76
Baptist Herald 462
Baptist Leader 462
Baranski Literary Agency, The Joseph A. 789
Bardic Echoes 419
Barker Greeting Card Co. 583
Barks Publications, Inc. (see Electrical Apparatus 660)
Barlenmir House Publishers 77
Barnes and Co., Inc., A.S. 77
Barnes, Billy E. 838
Baroid News Bulletin 184
Barr Films 49
Barre Publishers 77
Barrister 716
Barron's National Business and Financial Weekly 240
Barter Communique 184
Barter Theatre 588
Basch Feature Syndicate, Buddy 604, 838
Basketball Weekly 500
Batiment 643
Battery Man, The 619
Battle Flag 376
Bay & Delta Yachtsman 501
Bayland Publishing, Inc. (see Houston Home and Garden 305)
BBM Associates 839
BC Outdoors 435
Beacon Press 77
Beatty & Associates/Beatty Books, R.O. 77
Beau Lac Publishers 77
Beaumont Chapter of the Poetry Society of Texas 873
Beauty Handbook 566
Beaver 367
Beaver, The 185
Bedder News 697
Beef 678
Beehive, The 315
Beekman Publishers, Inc. 78
Beer Prize, George Louis 807
Behavioral Medicine 732
Belier Press 78
Bell Publications (see Western Wear & Equipment Magazine 640)
Bell Springs Publishing Company 78
Bellak-Photographer, Richard 839
Beloit Poetry Journal 419
Bench Press 78
Bend of the River Magazine 436
Bennett Co., Inc. Charles A. 78
Berger Award, Mike 807
Berkeley Barb 195
Berkeley Monthly 196
Berkley Publishing Corp. 78
Best Sport Stories Awards 807
Bestways Magazine 280
Bethany Fellowship, Inc. 79
Bethany Press 79
Better Homes and Gardens 302
Better Homes and Gardens Books 79
Better Life For You, A 381
Bettman Archive, Inc., The 839
Beverage World 629
Beveridge Award, Albert J. 807
Beyond Reality Magazine 221
BFLO 250
Bicycle Dealer Showcase 771
Bicycle Journal 772
Big Bike 225
Big Farmer Cattle, Dairy and Hog Guides 678
Bike World 500
Biker 225
Billboard, The 770
Billboard Publications, Inc. (see Managing The Leisure Facility 703, Amusement Business 770)
Billiards Digest 505
Binford & Mort, Publishers 79
Bingley, Ltd., Clive 79
Biomedical Photo Library 839
Birthstone Magazine 419
Bitterroot 420
Bitterroot Magazine Poetry Contest 807
Black American Literature Forum 330
Black Award, Irma Simonton 807
Black Belt 523
Black Collegian, The 536
Black Enterprise 240
Black Forum Magazine 238
Black Maria 196
Black Powder Times 511
Black Scholar 330
Black Stars 549, 839
Black Warrior Review, The 330

Blackberry 331
Blackstone-Shelburne New York, Inc. 839
Blackwood's Magazine 270
Blade Toledo Magazine, The 412
Blair, Publisher, John F. 80
Blakeslee Awards, Howard W. 807
Block Color Productions, Dr. 839
Bloom, Beckett, Levy & Shorr 790
Blount Banner, The 185
Blue Unicorn 420
Bluegrass Unlimited 392
Bluenose Magazine 436
The Bluff Press (see Natchez Trace Literary Review 348)
BMW Journal 226
Board of Jewish Education of New York 49
Boating 501
Boating Business 730
Boating Industry, The 730
Boating News 502
Bobbs-Merrill Co., Inc. 80
Bobbs-Merrill Educational Publishing Co., The 49, 80
Bobit Publishing (see Contemporary Surgery 732)
Body Fashions/Intimate Apparal 639
Body Forum Magazine 280
Bollingen Prize In Poetry of the Yale University Library 807
Bolton Hill Dinner Theatre, The 588
Bon Appetit 268
Bond Enterprises, Dorothy 575
Bond Wheelright Company, The 80
Bonner, Harry 839
Bonsai, A Quarterly of Haiku 420
Bonsai Press (see Bonsai, A Quarterly of Haiku 420)
Book Arts 331
Book Collector's Market 630
Book Forum 331
Bookcraft, Inc. 80
Book-Mart, The 291
Books for Businessmen, Inc. 80
Bookworm Publishing Co. 81
Borchardt, Inc., Georges 790
Borealis Press, Ltd. 81
Borgo Press, The 81
Boston Globe-Horn Book Awards 807
Boston Magazine 250
Boston Phoenix, The 197
Boston University Journal 331
Bostonian Society, The 839
Boulder Daily Camera Focus Magazine 436
Bouregy and Co., Inc., Thomas 82
Bow and Arrow 499
Bowhunter Magazine 499
Bowker Co., R.R. 82
Bowlers Journal 505, 772
Bowling 506
Bowling Green University Popular Press 82
Bowling Proprietor Magazine, The 772
Bowling Writing Competition 807
Bowman Company, Aaron 790
Bowmar/Noble Publishing, Inc. 82
Box 749 331
Boxing Writers Association 886
Boynansky, Bill 575
Boys' Life 536
Bradbury Press, Inc. 82
Brady Co., Robert J. 50
Brake & Front End Service 620
Branching Out 566
Branden Press, Inc. 82
Brandt & Brandt 790
Branford Co., Charles T. 82
Brasch & Brasch, Publishers 83
Braziller, Inc., George 83
Bread 536
Bread Loaf Writers' Conference 883
Breakthrough! 221
Brenda Publishing Co. (see Broward Life 437)
Brevet Press, Inc. 83
Brick and Clay Record 632
Brick House Publishing Co. 83
Bride's 566
Brigade Leader 462
Brigham Young University Press 84
Brilliant, Ashleigh 575
Brilliant Enterprises 583
Broadcast 661
Broadcast Engineering 661
Broadcast Equipment Today 661
Broadcast Management/Engineering 661
Broadcast Programming & Production 662
Broadcaster 662
Broadman Press 84
Brodatz, Phil 839

Brombacher Books 84
Bronze Thrills 258
Brooklyn Art Books For Children Citations 808
Brooklyn Contest and Filler Writing Club 872
Brooklyn Public Library 840
Broome Agency, Inc./Broome Literary Service 790
Broward Life 437
Brown Associates, Inc., James 790
Brown Co., Publishers, William C. 84
Brown Fund Preventive Law Prize Awards, Emil 808
Brown University 588
Bruner Science Writing Fellowship, Ray 808
Buckeye Farm News 674
Bucknell University Press 84
Buffalo and Erie County Historical Society 840
Buffalo Fan (see Bflo 250)
Buffalo Spree Magazine 437
Building Services Contractor 725
Bulletin of Bibliography & Magazine Notes 332
Bultman Award 808
Bunchez and Associates, Inc., Gert 588
Bureau of Mines 826
Burgess, Photographer, Guy 840
Burke Agency, Shirley 790
Burning Mountain Writers Club 868
Burroughs Clearing House 683
Busciglio, Joe 576
Business and Commercial Aviation 627
Business Insurance 707
Business on Wheels 185
Business Programs, Inc. 50
Business Quarterly, The 727
Business Screen 755
Business Week 84, 241
Butane-Propane News 688
Buyways 262
Byrne Literary Agency, Charles R. 791
Byte Magazine 490

C.S.P. World News 383
C.S.S. Publishing Co. 85
C & S (Casket and Sunnyside) 739
Cablevision 662
Cabrillo Suspense Writers' Conference 878
Cal Magazine 647
California 309
California Builder & Engineer 643
California Business 243
California Highway Patrolman 214
California Journal 429
California Magazine, The 309
California Publisher, The 710
California Quarterly, The 332
California State Library 840
California State Poetry Society 867
California Today 405
California Writers' Club 867
California Writers Conference 878
Calvinist-Contact 462
Camaro Publishing Company 85
Camas Writer's Workshop 869
Cambridge University Press 85
Camden House Publishing, Ltd. (see Harrowsmith Magazine 199)
Camera Clix, Inc. 840
Camera Craftsman, The 755
Camera Hawaii, Inc. 840
Camera M D Studios, Inc. 840
Camera 35 417
Camerique Stock Photos 840
Camp and Associates, Woodfin 840
Campaign Insight 689
Campground and RV Park Management 763
Campground Merchandising 767
Camping Industry 764
Camping Journal 558
Campus Ambassador Magazine (CAM) 536
Campus Life Magazine 537
Canada Crafts 291
Canada Poultryman 682
Canada West 285
Canadian Author & Bookman 710
Canadian Authors Association 875
Canadian Automotive Trade Magazine 620
Canadian Banker & ICB Review, The 684
Canadian Business 244
Canadian Business Magazine 244
Canadian Children's Magazine 266
Canadian Churchman 462
Canadian Composer, The 744
Canadian Consulate General 841
Canadian Consulting Engineer 666

Canadian Consumer 262
Canadian Datasystems 646
Canadian Doctor 732
Canadian Driver/Owner 620
Canadian Electronics Engineering 662
Canadian Fiction Magazine 332
Canadian Fisherman and Ocean Science 685
Canadian Forest Industries 720
Canadian Forum, The 332
Canadian Frontier 285
Canadian Frontier Annual 437
Canadian Funeral Director 738
Canadian Geographical Journal 383
Canadian Golden West Magazine 437
Canadian Horse, The 205
Canadian Illustrator's Award, The 808
Canadian Literature 332
Canadian Log House, The 302
Canadian Machinery and Metalworking 723
Canadian Magazine, The 416
Canadian Museums Association 85
Canadian Pacific 841
Canadian Paint and Finishing Magazine 750
Canadian Pharmaceutical Journal 650
Canadian Plastics 757
Canadian Press 841
Canadian Rental Service 738
Canadian Road Knight 620
Canadian Scene 604
Canadian Skater 529
Canadian Theatre Review 549
Canadian Transceiver 246
Canadian Wings (see Wings Magazine 238)
Canadian Zionist 313
Candy and Snack Industry 642
Candy Marketer 642
Canine Practical Journal, Feline Practice Journal 782
Canoe Magazine 502
Cantor, Literary Agent, Ruth 791
Cape Cod Writers' Conference 880
Cape Rock, The 420
Capper's Weekly 270
Capra Press 85
Car and Driver 226
Car Craft 226
Caravanner, The 185
Career Institute 86
Career Publishing, Inc. 86
Career World 266
Caribbean Business News 244
Caribbean Writers Workshop 884
Carma Press 86
Carolina Cooperator 675
Carolina Golfer 509
Carolina Quarterly 333
Carolina Quarterly Fiction-Poetry Contest 808
Carolina Sportsman, The 515
Cars Magazine 227
Carsten's Publications, Inc. (see Creative Crafts 292)
Carte Blanche 270
Carter, Photographer and Writer, William 841
Carthage Writers Guild 871
Cascades East 438
Cash Newsletter 383
Casino 367
Cat Fancy 205
Catechist 652
Caterpillar World 185
Catholic Journalist, The 710
Catholic Library World 718
Catholic Life 462
Catholic Near East Magazine 463
Catholic Truth Society 86
Catholic University of America Press 86
Cats Magazine 206
Cattlemen 679
Cattleman Magazine, The 679
Cavalier 368
Caveman Publications, Ltd. 87
Caxton Printers, Ltd., The 87
CB Magazine 246
CB Times 246
CB Yearbook 490
CBS Consumer Publishing (see Pickup, Van & 4WD Magazine 231)
Cecil Arthritis Writing Awards, Russell L. 808
Ceda Current 660
Cedar Rock 420
Celestial Arts 87
Census, Bureau of the 826
Center for Disease Control 826
Center for Media Development, Inc. 50

Center Theatre Group/Mark Taper Forum 589
Central Indiana Writers' Association 870
Centrum Summer Season of the Arts 883
Century House, Inc. 87
Ceramic Industry 632
Ceramic Scope 632
CGA Magazine 616
Chain Saw Age 695
Chain Saw Industry and Power Equipment Dealer 696
Chain Store Age, General Merchandise Edition 767
Chain Store Age Supermarkets 693
Chamba Organization, The 50
Chandoha, Walter 841
Change Magazine 266
Changing Scene Theater, The 589
Changing Times 271
Channels Magazine 186
Charleston Magazine 250
Charlotte Writers Club 872
Charlton Publications, Inc. (see CB Times 246, True Life Secrets 261)
Charter House Publishers, Inc. 87
Chateau Publishing, Inc. 87
Chatelaine 567
Chatham Press, The 88
Chautauqua Writers' Workshop 881
Chek-Chart Service Bulletin, The 620
Chelsea 333
Chelsea Theater Center 589
Chesapeake Bay Magazine 438
Chevron USA 558
Chic Magazine 368
Chicago Historical Society 841
Chicago History 285
Chicago Magazine 250
Chicago Reader 251
Chicago Review 333
Chicago Studies 463
Chicago Sun-Times Show/Book Week 333
Chicago Tribune Magazine 407
Chicago Tribune-New York News Syndicate, Inc. 604
Chicagoland Snowmobiler (see Snowmobile News 532)
Child Life 315
Children's Book Award 808
Children's House 652
Children's Playmate 316
Childrens Press 88
Children's Science Book Awards 808
Children's Service Programs 316
Chilton Book Co. 88
China Glass & Tableware 698
Choomia 420
Chosen Books 88
Christian Adventurer 537
Christian Athlete, The 463
Christian Bookseller 630
Christian Century, The 463
Christian Herald 463
Christian Herald Books 88
Christian Life Magazine 464
Christian Living 464
Christian Living For Senior Highs 537
Christian Ministry, The 636
Christian Poetry Journal 421
Christian Science Monitor, The 409
Christian Scribes Writers' Conference 880
Christian Teacher 652
Christian Writers Conference 880
Christian Writers Institute Conference and Workshop 879
Christian Writers' League 873
Christian Writers of Omaha 871
Christian Writers Workshop 881
Christianity & Crisis 464
Christianity Today 464
Christie, Alfred 589
Christopher Awards 809
Chronicle Books 88
Church Administration 636
Church & State 465
Church Herald, The 465
Church Management-The Clergy Journal 636
Church Musician, The 744
Church Training 636
Churchman, The 465
Ciba-Geigy Journal 186
Cimarron Review 333
Cincinnati Historial Society 841
Cincinnati Magazine 251
Cinefantastique 549
Cinemakers, Inc. 50
Circle K Magazine 537
Circus Maximus 421
Citadel Press 89
Civil Liberties Review, The 384
Civil Service Commission 827

CK Communications 50
Clarion Writers' Workshop in Science Fiction & Fantasy 880
Clark Associates, Christopher 791
Clark Co., Arthur H. 89
Clark, H.B.S.S. Photography, Joe 841
Clark Publishing Co., (see Fate 221)
Clarke, Irwin & Co., Ltd. 89
Classic Car, The 227
Clavier 745
Cleanings In Bee Culture 682
Cleveland Magazine 251
Cleveland Play House, The 589
Cliff's Notes, Inc. 89
Clifton Magazine 257
Climbing Magazine 529
Clipper 309
Club 368
Club Executive 702
C-Me Magazine 384
Coaching: Women's Athletics 739
Coal Age 737
Coal Week 737
Coast 439
Coast Guard News & Photo Center 841
Coastline Magazine 439
Cobblesmith 89
Co-Ed 538
Coffee Break 384
Cogan, David J. 589
Cohen Literary Agency, Ltd., Hy 791
Coin Launderer & Cleaner 641
Coin World 291
Coinamatic Age 641
Cole, Artemas 576
Coleman Incorporated, Bruce 841
Coles Publishing Co., Ltd. 89
Colgate University Press 90
Collage 334
Collectibles and Antiques Monthly 291
Collector Books 90
Collectors News 292
College Newsphoto Alliance 841
College Press Review 710
College Press Service 604
College Store Executive 631
Collegiate Poetry Contest 809
Collier Associates 791
Collier MacMillan Canada, Ltd. 90
Colorado Associated University Press 90
Colorado Express, The 439
Colorado Magazine 440
Colorado Quarterly, The 334
Colortype Services of Los Angeles, Inc. 583
Colt American Handgunning Annual 511
Columbia 465
Columbia Features, Inc. 604
Columbia Journalism Review 710
Columbia Publishing Co., Inc. 90
Columbia University Press 91
Columbus Dispatch Sunday Magazine 412
Comedy and Humor Workshop 881
Comedy Unlimited 576
Commentary 271
Commerce Magazine 244
Commercial Car Journal 621
Commercial West Magazine 241
Commodities Magazine 684
Commodity Journal 241, 684
Common Cents 262
Commoners' Publishing 91
Commonweal 465
Commonwealth 440
Communications News 662
Communications Retailing 663
Community 197
Community and Suburban Press Service 604
Community College Frontiers 652
Community Development Digest 762
Community Woman 567
Companion of St. Francis and St. Anthony, The 466
Compass, The 186
Competitivedge 698
Comprenetics, Inc. 51
Compressed Air 704
Compsco Publishing Co. 842
Computer Decisions 646
Computer Design 646
Computer Science Press, Inc. 91
Computerworld 647
Concert Life 393
Concordia Publishing House 91 (also see Children's Service Programs 316)
Concordia Publishing House, Product Development Division 51
Concrete 776
Concrete Construction Magazine 776
Condor Publishing Co., Inc. 91
Confrontation 334

Congregationalist, The 466
Connecticut Fireside and Review of Books 334
Connecticut Writers' League Conference 879
Connections Magazine 421
Conoco Today 621
Conservation News Award 809
Conservative Digest 429
Consolidated Edison Company of New York 842
Construction Equipment Operation and Maintenance 643
Construction Foreman's & Supervisor's Letter 727
Construction Letter 727
Construction Specifier 643
Construction Writers Association 886
Constructioneer 644
Constructor Magazine 644
Consumer Reports 263
Consumers Digest 263
Consumers' Research Magazine 263
Contact 466
Contact Press Images, Inc. 842
Contacts 648
Contemporary Drama Service 597
Contemporary Features Syndicate, Inc. 604
Contemporary Keyboard Magazine 393
Contemporary Literature 335
Contemporary Magazine 406
Contemporary Review 335
Contemporary Surgery 732
Contest For Unpublished Third World Writers 809
Contractor Magazine 758
Convenience Store Merchandiser 767
Cook Publishing Co., David C. 51, 92
Cooper Associates, Inc., Bill 791
Cooper Rand Corp. 601
Copyright Office 827
Cordovan Corporation 92
Core 238
Corey Prize in Canadian-American Relations, Albert B. 809
Cornell Maritime Press, Inc. 92
Cornell University Creative Writing Workshop 881
Cornhusker Country 393
Cortina Co., Inc., R.D. 92
Corvette News 187
Corvus Publishing Group, Ltd. (see Wings Magazine 238)
Cosmopolitan 567
Cosmopolitan Contact 197
Costa Rica and Guatemala Holiday Writers' Workshop 884
Cotton Farming Magazine 669
Council Record 407
Counselor, The 616
Counterforce 739
Country Club Golfer 510
Country Gentleman, The 672
Country Journal 675
Country Music Magazine 393
Country World 675
Countryside 672
Countrystyle 393
County Magazine, The 440
County Publications (see Westchester Magazine 457)
Courier of Maine Books 92
Courier-Journal Magazine 408
Covenant Companion, The 467
Coward, McCann & Geoghegan 92
CPCU-Harry J. Loman Foundation Communications Award 809
Craft & Art Market 768
Craft Horizons 292
Craftsman Book Company of America 93
Craftsmanship of Creative Writing Conference 880
Crain Award In Playwriting, Harold C. 809
Crain Books 93
Crane, Russak & Company, Inc. 93
Cream City Review 335
Creative Book Co. 93
Creative Cartoon Service 576
Creative Communications 605
Creative Computing 647
Creative Crafts 292
Creative Enterprises 791
Creative Living 384
Creative Papers, Inc. 583
Creative Pittsburgh 335
Creative Review 421
Creative Visuals 51
Creative Writers Agency, Inc. 792
Creative Writers of Montgomery 867
Creative Writing Conference 880

Creative Writing Workshop 873, 881
Credit Union Life 385
Credithriftalk 187
Creede Repertory Theatre 589
Creekwood Colony for the Arts 876
Creem 394
Crescendo Publishing Co. 94
Crescent Publications, Inc. 94
Cresson Lake Playhouse 590
Crestline Publishing, Inc. 94
Crestwood House, Inc. 94
Cricket 316
Criminologist, The 689
Crisis, The 239
Critical List Magazine, The 281
Criticism 335
Critique: Studies in Modern Fiction 336
Cross and Crown (see Spirituality Today 482)
Crossroads Writers 875
Crowell, Thomas Y. 95
Crown Publishers 95
Cruising World 502
Crusader 317
Crusader Magazine 317
Crux News Service 605
CSA Press 95
Cue Magazine 440
Cultural Post, The 211
Culver Pictures, Inc. 842
Cummington Community of the Arts 876
Cupertino Writers' Workshop 867
Curious Facts Features 605
Current Consumer 267
Current History 429
Curriculum Review 653
Curtis Publishing Co., The (see The Saturday Evening Post 277)
Custom Applicator 618
Custom Card of Canada, Ltd. 584
Custom Vans Magazine 227
Custombook, Incorporated 95
Cutting Tool Engineering 723
Cuyahoga Writers' Conference 882
Cycle News, West 227
Cycle Times 227
Cycle World 228
Cyrco Press, Inc., Publishers 95

D Magazine 251
Daily Meditation 467
Dairy Goat Journal 671
Dairy Herd Management 671
Dairy Record 646
Dairy Scope 646
Dairyman, The 671
Dairymen's Digest 671
Daiwa Fishing Annual 515
Dakota Farmer, The 675
Dalrymple, Jean 590
Daly City Creative Writers' Group 867
Dance Magazine 549
Dance Scope 550
Dandelet Interlinks 842
Dapper 368
Dark Horse 336
Dartnell Corporation 96
Dash 317
Data Publications (see Aviation 236, Flight Line Times 236)
Daughters Publishing Co., Inc. 96
David & Charles (Publishers), Ltd. 96
Davis Publications, Inc. 96
Davis Publications, Inc. (see Hobby Computer Handbook 294, 99 IC Projects 296, Camping Journal 558)
Daw Books, Inc. 96
Day Care and Early Education 267
Day Company, Inc., The John 96
Dayton Leisure 412
De Bat Photography, Alfred 842
De Kalb Literary Arts Journal 336
De La Ree, Gerry & Helen 96
De Lauer Agency, Marjel 792
De Wys Inc., Leo 842
Deaf Canadian Magazine, The 385
Decision Magazine 467
Decor 633
Decorating & Craft Ideas Made Easy 292
Defense Civil Preparedness Agency 827
Defense, Department of 827
Defense Logistics Agency 827
Defense Products Co. 51
Defense Transportation Journal 780
Degginger, APSA, Dr. E.R. 843
DeGroot, Lee 576
Delaware State Travel Service 843
Delaware Today Magazine 441
Dell Publishing Co., Inc. 97
Delta Design Group 97
Delta Scene 441
Deltiology 292

Denison & Co., Inc., T.S. 97
Denlinger's Publishers, Ltd. 97
Dental Economics 648
Dental Management 648
Denver Magazine 251
Denver Quarterly, The 336
DePauw University Alumnus Magazine 257
Derbyshire Publishing Co. (see Horse Of Course 208)
Des Moines Sunday Register Picture Magazine 408
Descant 336
Desert Magazine 558
Desert Publications, Inc. (see Palm Springs Life Magazine 452)
Design Engineering 667
Design For Living Contest 809
Design Magazine 212
Design Photographers International, Inc. 843
Detective Cases 265
Detective Dragnet 265
Detective Files 265
Detective Files Group (see Detective Cases, Detective Dragnet, Detective Files, Headquarters Detective, Startling Detective, True Police Cases 265)
Detroit Engineer 667
Detroit Industrial Market News 723
Detroit Magazine 410
Detroit Women Writers 870, 880
Devaney, Inc., A. 843
Devin-Adair Co., Inc., The 98
Devins Award, The 810
Dial Press, The 98
Diamant: The Writers Workshop, Inc., Anita 792
Diamond Registry Bulletin 709
Didato Associates 605
Diesel & Gas Turbine Progress 759
Diesel Motorist 228
Dietz Press, Inc., The 98
Dillon Press, Inc. 98
Dimension Books, Inc. 98
Direct Marketing Writers Guild, Inc. 886
Directors & Boards 385
Dirt Bike Magazine 228
Disciple, The 467
Discoveries 317
Discovery 318
Discovery Magazine 558
Discovery/The Nation 1979 810
Dispensing Optician, The 748
Diver 533
Division of Michigan History 843
Dixie Contractor 644
Dixie Council of Authors and Journalists 869
Dixie Council of Authors and Journalists Creative Writing Workshop 879
Dixie Logger and Lumberman 720
Dobie-Paisano Fellowship 877
Doctors' Nurse Bulletin 700
Dodd, Mead & Co. 98, 597
Dog Fancy 206
Dog Writers' Association of America Annual Writing Competition 810
Dog Writers' Association of America, Inc. 886
Dole, George 576
Dolin Photography, Irving 843
Dollars & Sense 241
Domestic Engineering 758
Dondero Photography 843
Donning Company/Publishers, Inc., The 98
Doors and Hardware 696
Dorn-Fredricks Publishing Co. 605
Dorrance and Company 182
Doubleday & Co., Inc. 99
Doubleday Canada, Ltd. 99
Douglas & McIntyre 100
Douglas, David & Charles, Ltd. 99
Dow Jones-Irwin 100
Down East Magazine 441
Dragonfly: A Quarterly of Haiku 421
Drake Publishers, Inc. 100
Drake Well Museum 843
Drama Book Specialists (Publishers) 100
Drama Review, The 337
Dramatics Magazine 550
Dramatika 550
Drawing Board, Inc., The 584
Drilling Contractor, The 751
Druck Productions, Mark 51
Drug Survival News 650
Drug Therapy Medical Journal 733
Drug Topics 650
Drummer, The 441
DTM Publications (see Home Budget & Consumer 263)

Dubuque Fine Arts Society National One-Act Playwriting Contest, The 810
Dude, Gent, Nugget 369
Dune Buggies & Hot VWs 228
Dunning Prize In American History, John H. 810
Dun's Review 241
Duquesne University Press 100
Dutton Animal Book Award 810
Dutton, E.P. 100
Dynacom Communications International 52
Dynamic Years 487

Early American Life 293
Earplay 590
Earth's Daughters 197
East Carolina Playhouse 590
East West Journal 197
Eastern Outdoors 515
Eastfoto Agency 843
Eastside Freelance Writers of Minnesota 871
East/West Network (see California 309, The California Magazine 309, Clipper 309, Flightime 310, Mainliner 310, Review 311, Sky and Sundancer 311)
East/West Network, Inc. 309
Eastwood, David 597
Easy Living Magazine 214
Easy Times Magazine 271
Easyriders Magazine 229
Ebel-Doctorow Publications, Inc. (see China Glass & Tableware 698)
Ebony Jr! 318
Ebony Magazine 239
Economic Analysis, Bureau of 827
Economic Facts 263
Eden Valley Press (see The Emissary 198)
Edge, The 636
Editions de l'Etoile, Les 101
Editor & Publisher 711
Editorial Consultant Service 605
Editorial Photocolor Archives 844
Edits Publishers 101
Education Writers Award 810
Educational ABC of Industry, The 267
Educational Communications, Inc. 52
Educational Dimensions Group 52
Educational Filmstrips 52
Educational Images 52
Educational Research, Inc. 52
Educational Studies 653
Educator's Award 810
E-Go Enterprises, Inc. (see Travelin' 4x4's, and Off Road Vehicles 234, Revealing Secrets 260)
EKM Communications 844
El Excentrico Magazine 386
El Palacio, Quarterly Journal of the Museum of New Mexico 286
El Viento 337
Eldridge Publishing Co. 597
Electrical Apparatus 660
Electrical Contractor 660
Electrical Contractor & Maintenance Supervisor 660
Electronic Buyers' News 663
Electronic Packaging and Production 664
Electronic Technician/Dealer 664
Electronics 664
Electronics Hobbyist 490
Electronics Industry 663
Electronics Journal 663
Electronics Retailing 664
Electronics Today International 491
Electro-Optical Systems Design Magazine 667
Elementary Electronics 491
Elite Magazine 369
Elks Magazine, The 214
Ellery Queen's Mystery Magazine 400
EMC Corporation 52, 101
Emergency 739
Emergency Librarian 718
Emergency Product News (see Emergency 739)
Emerson Books, Inc. 101
Emissary, The 198
Emmanuel 637
Emphasis on Faith & Living 467
Empire Magazine 406
Empire State Realtor 763
Employee Relations Bulletin 727
En Passant Poetry Quarterly 421
Enchantment Magazine 441
Encore 421
Enduring Word Adult Teacher 637
Energy, Department of 827
Energy Education Publishers 101
Energy Management Report 751
Energy News 704

Energy Publications-division of Harcourt Brace Jovanovich (see Energy News 704, Energy Week 705)
Energy Week 705
Engage/Social Action 468
Engendra Press, Ltd. 101
Engineering and Contract Record 644
Enquirer Magazine, The 413
Entelek 102
Enterprise Publishing Co., Inc. 102
Enterprise Science News 605
Entertainer Magazine 442
Entheos/Northwest 844
Enthusiast, The 187
Environment 400
Environmental Action 401
Environmental Protection Agency 827
Epilepsy Foundation of America Journalism Award 810
Epoch 337
Equestrian Image, The 206
Equifax 708
Eras Review Art & Poetry Contest 810
Erasmus Press (see American Notes and Queries 327)
Eriksson, Paul S. 102
Escapade Magazine 369
Esposito, Anthony F., Jr. 844
Esquire 369
Essence 239
Estes, James 576
Etcetera 468
EUA Spectrum 187
European Art Color 844
European Community 429
European Holiday Writers' Workshop 884
Evangel 538
Evangelical Beacon, The 468
Evangelical Friend 468
Evans and Company, Inc. 102
Event 337
Evergreen Press, The 584
Everybodys Press, Inc. (see The Spinning Wheel 300)
E W TV Guide 550
Exceptional Parent 247
Executive Housekeeper 702
Executive Review 634
Expecting 248
Explicator Literary Foundation, Inc., The 810
Explorer, The 401
Exploring 538
Export 758
Exposition Press 182
Exxon Air World 236

Face-To-Face 538
Facets 733
Facing South 606
Fairbank Prize in East Asian History, John K. 811
Fairchild Books & Visuals 102
Fairchild Publications (see Men's Wear 639)
Fairfield County Magazine 442
Faith and Inspiration 468
Fallbrook Writers' Workshop 867
Family 248
Family Circle Magazine 567
Family Films/Counterpoint Films 53
Family Food Garden 302
Family Health 281
Family Life Today Magazine 469
Family Magazine 187
Family Motor Coaching 559
Family Pet 206
Family Weekly 411
Fancy Publications, Inc. (see Dog Fancy 206)
Far Eastern Research and Publications Center 103
Far West 386
Farm & Country 675
Farm Building News 644
Farm Credit Administration 827
Farm Journal 673
Farm Supplier 618
Farm Wife News 568
Farmfutures 676
Farmland News 676
Farmstead Magazine 198
Farnsworth Publishing Co., Inc. 103
Farrar, Straus and Giroux, Inc. 103
Fast & McMillan Publishers, Inc. 103
Fast Service 687
Fate 221
Fault, The 337
Fawcett Publications, Inc./Gold Medal Books 103

Faxon Company, Inc., F. W. 103
FDA Consumer 263
Federal Communications Commission 827
Federal Judicial Center 828
Federal Law Enforcement Training Center 828
Federal Mediation and Conciliation Service 828
Federal Power Commission 828
Federal Trade Commission 828
Feed/Back, The Journalism Report and Review 711
Feed Industry Review 736
Feedlot Management 679
Feeley, Inc., Authors' Representative, Patricia Falk 792
Fell Publishers, Inc., Frederick 103
Feminist Press, The 104
Fence Industry 645
Fenton Independent 410
Ferber's Freshwater Fisherman 516
Fforbez Enterprises, Ltd. 104
Fichandler, Zelda 590
Fiction 338
Fiction International 338
Fictionaires 867
Fiddlehead Poetry Books 104
Fides/Claretian 104
Field and Stream 516
Field Museum of Natural History 844
Field Newspaper Syndicate 606
Film Comment 550
Film Quarterly 551
Filter Press, The 104
Finance 242
Financial Post 244
Financial Quarterly 684
Fine Arts Work Center 876
Fire Chief Magazine 689
Fire Engineering 690
Fire Times 690
Firehouse Magazine 386
Firelands Arts Review 338
Fish and Game Sportsman 516
Fish and Wildlife Service 828
Fishing and Hunting News 517
Fishing World 517
Fitzhenry & Whiteside, Limited 105
Flair Magazine 309
Flambeaux Publishing Co. (see New Orleans Magazine 254)
Flame's Writers' Club, Inc. 870
Fleet Maintenance & Specifying 621
Fleet Press Corporation 105
Fles Literary Agency, Barthold 792
Flight Line Times 236
Flightime 310
Fling 370
Flooring Magazine 698
Florafacts 685
Florida Banker 684
Florida Cypress Gardens, Inc. 844
Florida Grower & Rancher 676
Florida Keys Magazine 442
Florida News Bureau 844
Florida Suncoast Writers Conference 879
Florida Theatre Conference Playwright Contest 811
Florida Writers' Conference 879
Floridagriculture 676
Floridian, The 407
Florist 686
Flower and Garden Magazine 303
Flower News 686
Flowers, II, H.D. 590
Flue Cured Tobacco Farmer, The 669
Flyfisher, The 215
Flying 237
Flying A, The 188
Flying Colors 310
Flynt Publications, Larry (see Chic Magazine 368, Ohio Magazine 450)
FM Guide 551
Focus: A Journal for Lesbians 198
Focus/Midwest 443
Fodor's Modern Guides 105
Foley Agency, The 793
Folger Theatre Group 590
Folio 711
Folklore Forum 338
Follett Publishing Co. 105
Food and Drug Administration 828
Food and Drug Packaging 748
Food Executive 702
Foodsman 693
Football News 506
Football Writers Association of America, The 887
Foothills Writers Club 873
Forbes 242

Ford Foundation Photo Library 844
Ford Times 271
Forecast! 394
Forecast For Home Economics 653
Foreign Affairs 430
Foreign Service Journal 690
Foreman's Letter, The 727
Forer and Co., D. 584
Forest Service, USDA 828
Foret Et Papier 750
Forman World Photos, Harrison 845
Forms 338
Fort Worden Poetry Symposium 883
Fortress Press 106
Fortune 242
Forum 338
Forum Award, The 811
Fotos International 845
Foundation 281
Foundry Management and Technology 723
Fountain Valley Writers Workshop 868
Four By Five, Inc. 845
Four Corners Press 106
Four Quarters 339
Four Wheeler Magazine 229
Fran Mar Greeting Cards, Ltd. 584
Franciscan Communications Center 53
Franciscan Herald Press 106
Franklin Photo Agency 845
Free Enterprise 242
Free For All 199
Free Lance, The 422
Free Library of Philadelphia 845
Free Press (see Report On Farming 673)
Free Press, The 106
Freed-Crown Publishing (see Automotive Age 766)
Freedom Greeting Card Co., Inc. 584
Freedoms Foundation at Valley Forge Awards 811
Freelance Photographers Guild 845
Freeman, The 430
Freeport Minerals Company 845
Freeway 539
French Agency, Peggy Lois 793
French Colonial Historical Society Book Award 811
French, Inc., Samuel 598
Frey Scientific Company Catalog 491
Friar 469
Friday Forum (Of The Jewish Exponent) 469
Fried Photography, Ltd., Lawrence 845
Friend, The 318
Friends of American Writers Juvenile Book Awards 811
From The Kennels 754
Front Page Detective, Inside Detective 265
Frontier Times 286
Frontiers 401
Fueloil and Oil Heat 751
Fugue, The 394
Fulp Literary Agency 793
Functional Photography 755
Fur-Fish-Game 517
Furniture & Furnishings 698
Furrow, The 673
Future 215

G. P. Page Publications (see Canada Crafts 291, Luggage and Leathergoods News 717, Toys & Games 779)
Galileo Prize, The 811
Gallery 370
Gallimaufry Press 339
Galloway, Ewing 845
Galway Productions 590
Gambler's Book Club 106
Gambling Times Magazine 506
Gamekeeper and Countryside 524
Gamma-Liaison Photo Agency 845
Garden Magazine 303
Garden Way Publishing 107
Garden Writers Association of America, Inc. 887
Gardner, William 590
Garon-Brooke Associates, Inc., Jay 793
Gartenberg, Literary Agent, Max 793
Gas Digest 688
Gassner Memorial Playwriting Award, John 811
Gauss Award, Christian 811
Gavel Awards 811
Gay Sunshine 199
Geale & Associates, Gloria 793
Gemini Smith, Inc. 846
Gems and Minerals 293
Genealogical Publishing Co., Inc. 107
General Aviation Business 627
General Aviation News 237

General Educational Media, Inc. 53
General Press Features 846
General Publishing Co., Ltd. 107
General Services Administration 829
Genesis Magazine 370
Geneva Area Writer's Club 875
Gentlemen's Quarterly 370
Georgetown University Writers Conference 879
Georgia Sportsman Magazine 525
Geraci, A. John 846
Geyer-McAllister Publications (see Administrative Management 634)
Geyer's Dealer Topics 747
Gibson Co., The C.R. 107
Gibson Greeting Cards, Inc. 584
Gifts & Decorative Accessories 699
Gifts + Tableware 699
Giftware News 768
Gig 395
Ginn and Company 108
Girl Scouts of the U.S.A. 53
Glamour 568
Glass 212
Glass Digest 632
GLCA New Writers Awards in Poetry and Fiction 812
Glenmark Publishing Co. 108
Glimpses of Micronesia and the Western Pacific 443
Global Communications 606
Globe Photos 846
Globe Press International 846
Gnostica Magazine 199
Go West Magazine 621
Goethe House-P.E.N. Translation Prize 812
Gold Key Comics 258
Goldberg Literary Agency, Lucianne 793
Golden Raintree Award 812
Golden West Books 108
Goldsholl Assoc. 53
Golf Business 772
Golf Digest 510
Golf Industry 772
Golf Journal 510
Golf Magazine 510
Golf Score 511
Golf Shop Operations 773
Golfdom (see Gold Business 772)
Good Housekeeping 568
Good News 469
Good News Broadcaster 470
Good Reading 272
Goodwin & Associates, Dave 606
Gospel Carrier 470
Gospel Herald 470
Gourmet 268
Government of Saskatchewan 846
Governmental Purchasing 690
Gowland, Peter 846
Graffiti 339
Graham Agency 793
Granger Collection, The 846
Grants Pass Writer's Workshop 873
Graphic Arts Center Publishing Co. 108
Graphic Arts Monthly 760
Grass Roots Forum 199
Gravida 422
Gray's Publishing, Ltd. 108
Gray's Sporting Journal 518
Great American Play Contest 812
Great Lakes Aircraft Bulletin (see Aviation 236)
Great Lakes Review, The 339
Great Outdoors Publishing Co. 108
Great River Review 339
Greater Canton Writers' Guild 872
Greater Providence Chamber of Commerce 846
Green, Harold V. 846
Green Hill Publishers, Inc. 108
Green, Inc., Warren H. 109
Green Mountains Writers Workshop 883
Green Tiger Press 109
Green Tree Publishing Co., Ltd. 109
Greene, Inc., Vivian 585
Greene Murals & Exhibits, Al 847
Greene Press, The Stephen 109
Greenleaf Classics, Inc. 110
Green's Magazine 272
Greenwich Press 110
Gregg Division 110
Griffin, Arthur 847
Grit 272
Grossett and Dunlap, Inc. 110
Grossmont Press, Inc. 110
Grotell, Al 847
Ground Water Age 784
Group 539
Groupwork Today, Inc. 111
Grub Street 340

G-String Beat 771
Guidance Centre 111
Guide 539
Guideposts Magazine 470
Guideposts Magazine Youth Writing Contest 812
Guitar Player Books 111
Guitar Player Magazine 395
Gulf Coast Cattleman Magazine 679
Gulf Publishing Co. 111
Gulfshore Life 443
Gulfshore Publishing Co., Inc. (see Gulfshore Life 443)
Gun Week 512
Gun World 512
Guns & Ammo Magazine 512
Guns Magazine 513

H.P. Books 111
Hadassah Magazine 568
Hairstylist 695
Hall, Photographer, Judson B. 847
Hallmark Cards, Inc. 585
Halloway Agency, Vance 794
Halsey Publishing Co. (see Flying Colors 310)
Ham Radio Magazine 491
Hamilton-Burr Publishing Co. (see Military Electronics/Countermeasures 665)
Hammond, Inc. 112
Hancock Awards for Excellence in Business and Financial Journalism, John 812
Hancock House Publishers, Ltd. 112
Handball 525
Handbook and Directory For Campers 559
Handel Film Corp. 53
Handling and Shipping 705
Hanging Loose 340
Hanover Studios, Inc. 112
Happiness Holding Tank 422
Harbinger Publications 112
Harcourt Brace Jovanovich 112
Harcourt Brace Jovanovich Publications (see Body Fashions/Intimate Apparel 639, Dental Management 648, Fast Service 687, Quick Frozen Foods 687, Snack Food 688, Pets/Supplies/Marketing 754, Housewares 768)
Hardware Age 696
Hardware Merchandising 697
Harian Publications 113
Haring Prize, Clarence H. 812
Harlequin 569
Harlequin Books, Ltd. 113
Harper & Row, Publishers, Inc. 113
Harper Horticultural Slide Library 847
Harper's Bazaar 569
Harper's Magazine 272
Harris & Associates Publishing Division 607
Harris Publishing, Inc. (see Potato Grower Of Idaho 670, The Sugar Producer 682)
Harrowsmith Magazine 199
Hart Publishing Co., Inc. 113
Hartford Courant, This Singing World, The 422
Harvard Business Review 634
Harvard University Press 114
Harvest 340
Harvest House, Ltd., Publishers 114
Harvest Publishing Co. (see Weeds Trees & Turf 686, Lawn Care Industry 740)
Harvey House Publishers 114
Hastings House Publishers, Inc. 114
Hawaii Visitors Bureau 847
Hayden Book Co., Inc. 114
Hayes School Publishing Co., Inc. 54
Haystack Writers' Workshops 882
Headliners Awards 813
Headquarters Detective 265
Health 281
Health Care Week 733
Health Foods Business 768
Health Journalism Awards 813
Health Profession Publishing 114
Healthways Magazine 282
The Hearst Corporation (see House Beautiful 304, Good Housekeeping 568)
Heath & Co., D.C. 115
Heating/Piping/Air Conditioning 758
Heating, Plumbing, Air Conditioning 758
Heavy Duty Equipment Maintenance 726
Hedrich-Blessing, Ltd. 847
Hefley Report, The 222
Heidelberg Publishers, Inc. 115
Heidinger Kafka Prize, The Janet 815
Heilpern Photographers, Inc. 847
Heinle and Heinle Enterprises 794

Heirs Magazine 340
Helios Publishing Co., Inc. 182
Hemingway Foundation Award, Ernest 813
Hendricks House, Inc. 115
Henry F. Henrichs Publications (see Good Reading 272, Sunshine Magazine 279)
Her Say 607
Herald House 115
Herald Press 115
Heritage Books, Inc. 116
Heritage House Publishers, Inc. 116
Herman Publishing 116
Hers 569
Hester & Associates, Inc. 54
Heuer Publishing Co. 598
Heyman, Ken 847
Hibiscus Press (see In A Nutshell 341)
Hi-Call 539
Hi-Fi Stereo Buyers' Guide 395
High Adventure 471
High Country 443
High Fidelity 395
High Fidelity/Musical America 396
High Fidelity Trade News 745
High Times 200
Highlights For Children 319
Hill & Co., Lawrence 116
Hillman Prize Award, Sidney 813
Hintz Literary Agency, Sandra 794
Hiram Poetry Review 423
Hirsch Perpetual Trophy for Outstanding Ski Writing, Harold 813
HIS 540
His Publishing House 117
Historic New Orleans Collection, The 847
Historic Preservation 286
Historical Pictures Service, Inc. 848
Hitchcock Publishing Co. (see Assembly Engineering 722)
Hi-Torque Publications (see Big Bike 225, Van World Magazine 235)
Hobart Weldworld 188
Hobby Artist News 293
Hobby Computer Handbook 294
Hockey Illustrated 525
Hoffman Publications, Inc. (see Swimming Pool Weekly/Age 776)
Holiday House 117
Holloway House Publishing Co. 117
Hollywood Inside Syndicate 607
Holman Co., A.J. 117
Holt, Rinehart & Winston of Canada, Ltd. 117
Home Budget & Consumer 263
Home Craft Unlimited 794
Home, The Canadian Family Magazine 303
Home Life 248
Hox Lighting & Accessories 699
Homeowners How To Handbook 304
Homewood Poetry Forum 873
Hoop 500
Hopkinson & Blake 117
Horizon Press 117
Horn Book Magazine, The 718
Horoscope 222
Horoscope Guide 222
Horse and Horseman 207
Horse Illustrated 207
Horse Lover's National Magazine 207
Horse, Of Course 208
Horse Play 208
Horseman 208
Horsemen's Journal 208
Horsemen's Yankee Pedlar Newspaper 209
Horticulture 304
Hospice 530
Hospital Forum 700
Hospital/Health Care Training Media Profiles 653
Hospital Physician Magazine 733
Hospital Progress 700
Hospital Supervisor's Bulletin 700
Hot Rod 229
Houghton Mifflin Co. 118
Houghton Mifflin Literary Fellowship 813
House and Garden 304
House Beautiful 304
House of Anansi Press Limited 118
House of Collectibles, Inc. 118
House Plants and Porch Gardens 304
Household and Personal Products Industry 740
Household Gardening and House Plants 305
Housewares 768
Houston 252
Houston Business Journal 245
Houston Home and Garden 305

Howell-North Books 118
Howmark Publishing Corp. (see The Pet Dealer 754, Health Food Business 768)
Hudson Review, The 340
Hudson River Press (see Book Forum 331)
Hudson Valley Magazine 444
Huerfano 423
Hughes Rigway 751
Human Behavior 496
Humanist, The 340
Humanitas Prize, The 813
Humorettes 601
Humpty Dumpty's Magazine 319
Hungness Publishing, Carl 118
Hunting Dog Magazine 209
Huntsville Writers' Club 867
Hurtig Publishers 119
Hustler Magazine 371
Huttner Agency, Inc., Richard 794
Hwong Publishing Co. 119
Hydrocarbon Processing 751

IBIA News 680
Ideal Publishing Corp. (see Personal Romances 259, Movie Life 551, Movie Stars 552, Screen and TV Album 553)
Ideal School Supply Co. 54
Ideal World Publishing Company 119
Ideals 423
IGA Grocergram 694
Illinois Issues 444
Illinois Schools Journal 654
Illinois State Historical Library 848
Illinois Wesleyan University Writers' Conference 879
Illinois Wildlife 518
Image Bank, The 848
Image Finders Photo Agency, Inc. 848
Image Photos 848
Image Publications and Promotions (see The Equestrian Image 206)
Images Atlanta 848
Imarc Corp. 54
Impact of Science on Society 496
Imperial International Learning Corp. 54
In A Nutshell 341
In Touch 540
In Touch: The Journal Of Personal Possibilities 569
Incentive Marketing/Incorporating Incentive Travel 617
Income Opportunities 264
Independence Press 119
Independent Banker, The 684
Indian Trader, The 740
Indiana University Press 119
Indiana University Writers' Conference 879
Indianapolis Magazine 444
Indianapolis Star Magazine 408
Industria Avicola 683
Industrial Distribution 705
Industrial Distributor News 705
Industrial Education 654
Industrial Finishing 723
Industrial Launderer 716
Industrial Machinery News 724
Industrial News 705
Industrial Photography 756
Industrial Progress 188
Industrial World 706
Industry Week 706
Infantry 376
Info Franchise Newsletter 740
Information Press Service 120
INGAA-Missouri Business Journalism Awards 813
Inland 188
Inland Architect 618
Inland Printer/American Lithographer, The 760
Inland Shores 444
Inlet 341
Inner City Cultural Center, The 598
Innkeeping World 702
Insgroup, Inc. 54
Insight (Grand Rapids, MI) 471
Insight (Washington, DC) 471
Insight Magazine 415
Institute for the Study of Human Issues 120
Institutional Management 728
Instructional Dynamics Incorporated 55
Instructor Curriculum Materials 55
Instructor Magazine 654
Instrumentalist, The 745
Integrity: Gay Episcopal Forum 200
Inter-American Review of Bibliography 341

Intercam 848
Intercollegiate Review, The 341
Intercontinental Publications, Inc. (see National Development 430, Today's Transport International/Transporte Moderno 626)
Intergroup Productions, Inc. 55
Interior, Department of the 829
Interline Reporter 627
Interlit 472
Interlude 310
Intermart, Inc. 585
Intermedia 341
Intermedia Press 120
International Association of Business Communicators 887
International Aviation Mechanics Journal 628
International Black Writers Conference, Inc. 879
International Editorial Services/Newsweek, Inc. 607
International Entrepreneurs' Magazine 264
International Marine Publishing Company 121
International Museum of Photography 848
International Musician 396
International Poets and Patrons Narrative Contest 813
International Reading Association Print Media Award 814
International Reports Agency 848
International Self-Counsel Press, Ltd. 121
International Wealth Success 121
International Wildlife 401
International Women's Writing Conference & Retreat 881
International Yachtsman 502
Interpress of London and New York 849, 607
Interstate 342
Interstate Commerce Commission 829
Interstate Printers and Publishers, Inc., The 121
Intervarsity Press 121
Intimate Romances 259
Intimate Secrets 259
Intimate Story 259
Intra-South Publications (see Southern RV 233)
Investments/Opportunities Around The World 242
Iowa Plumbing, Heating, Cooling Contractor 759
Iowa Review, The 342
Iowa School of Letters Award for Short Fiction 814
Iowa State University Press 121
IPC Specialist & Professional Press, Ltd. (see Melody Maker 397)
Iron Worker, The 445
Islander Magazine, The 416
Italian Historical Archives 849
It's Our World 320

Jack and Jill 320
Jackson/James D. Phelan Literary Award, Joseph Henry 814
Jackson Purchase Creative Writer's Club 870
Jacksonville Magazine 252
Jacksonville University Playwriting Contest 814
Jacobs, Lou, Jr. 849
Jahn, Ernst A. 849
January Productions 55
January Writers' Conference 883
Japanophile 445
JD Journal 189
Jess Publishing (see Treasure 300)
Jet 239
Jet Cadet (see R-A-D-A-R 322)
Jet Cargo News 628
Jeweler's Circular-Keystone 709
Jewish Book Council Award for a Book of Jewish Thought 814
Jewish Book Council Award for Books of Poetry 814
Jewish Book Council Award for a Book on the Nazi Holocaust 814
Jewish Book Council Juvenile Award 814
Jewish Book Council William and Janice Epstein Fiction Award 814
Jewish Current Events 313
Jewish Digest, The 313
Jewish Telegraph 313
JGE: The Journal of General Education 654

Jim's Journal 200
J L Publications (see Baja California Bulletin 436)
Job Leads 664
Jobber News 621
Jobber/Retailer 621
Jobber Topics 622
Joel Sater's Antiques & Auction News 294
Johns Hopkins University Press 122
Johnson Publishing Co., Inc. (see Black Stars 549)
Johnsonian News Letter 342
Joint Endeavor 496
Jonathan David Publishers 122
Jones Award, Anson 814
Joseph and Associates, L.H. 795
Jossey-Bass, Inc., Publishers 122
Journal of American History 286
Journal of Commerce 645
Journal of English Teaching Techniques 654
Journal of Freshwater 402
Journal of Genealogy 286
Journal of Graphoanalysis 386
Journal of Mexican American History, The 342
Journal of Modern Literature 342
Journal of the North American Wolf Society 342
Journal of Nursing Care, The 701
Journal of Oral Implantology, The 648
Journal of Popular Culture 343
Journal of Practical Nursing 701
Journal of Reading, The Reading Teacher 655
Journal of Systems Management 647
Journalism Educator, The 711
Journalism Monographs 343
Journalism Quarterly 711
Jove/HBJ Publications 122
JSL Associates 795
Judge Studio 849
Judson Press 122
Junior Bowler 540
Juris Doctor Magazine For The New Lawyer 716
Justice, Department of 829
Juvenile Forum 869
Juvenile Merchandising 649

Kahana Photography, Yoram 849
Kalan, Inc. 585
Kaldor, Curt W. 849
Kankakee Area Writers Group 869
Kansas! 445
Kansas City Magazine 252
Kansas Motorist 215
Kansas Quarterly 343
Kansas Restaurant Magazine 702
Kansas State Historical Society 849
Kansas Stockman, The 680
Karamu 343
Karate Illustrated 523
Kaufmann, Inc., William 123
KBO Publishers (see Country Music Magazine 393)
Keats Publishing, Inc. 123
Keepin' Track 230
Keister Advertising Service 607
Kell, Steve 578
Keller & Associates, Inc., J.J. 123
Keller, Reamer 578
Kelley Memorial Award, Frank 815
Kellner's Moneygram 756
Ken-Del Productions, Inc. 55
Kennedy Journalism Awards, The Robert F. 815
Kent State University Press 123
Kentucky Business Ledger 242
Kentucky Department of Public Information 849
Kentucky Folklore Record 343
Kentucky State Poetry Society 870
Kerrwil Publications, Ltd. (see Ceda Current 606)
Key Magazine, The 216
Key Markets Publishing Co. (see Weighing & Measurement 744)
Key Newsletter 768
Key To Christian Education 637
Keyboard World 396
Keynoter Magazine 540
Keystone Press Agency, Inc. 849
Kidd With James Allen Literary Agents, Virginia 795
Kindergartner, The 321
King Features Syndicate, Inc. 608
King, Literary Agent, Daniel P. 795
Kingsway Publishing (Western), Ltd. (see The Alberta Motorist 557)
Kinn, Milo 578
Kirkley Press, Inc. 123
Kitchen Business 633

Kitchen Planning 687
Kiver Publications (see Electronic Packaging and Production 664)
Kiwanis Magazine, The 216
Klausner International Literary Agency, Inc., Bertha 795
Klein Publications, B. 124
Knickerbocker Books, Inc. 124
Knight 371
Knitting Times 639
Knopf, Inc., Alfred A. 124
Knowledge News & Features Syndicate 608
Knox Press, John 124
Kodansha International, Ltd. 124
Kosmos 423
Kramer and Associates, Joan 850
Krause Publications (see Old Cars Newspaper 296)
Kroll Agency, Lucy 795
Kuck Ohioana Award, Lucille Loy 815

La Jolla Summer Writers' Conference 878
La Tourrette, Photographer, James W. 850
Lab World 734
Labor, United States Department of 829
Ladies' Home Journal 570
Ladycom 376
Lady's Circle Magazine 570
Lake Superior Review, The 344
Lakewood Publications (see Airport Services Management 627)
Lamb, The 396
Lambert Studios, Inc., Harold M. 850
Lancaster Area Christian Writers Fellowship 873
Land Management, Bureau of 829
Landon Translation Award, Harold Morton 815
Lansford Publishing Co. 55
Lantern Press, Inc. 124
Lapidary Journal 294
Larsen/Elizabeth Pomada Literary Agents, Michael 795
Las Vegas News Bureau 850
Las Vegas Review-Journal 445
Latin America Photos 850
Latitude/20 310
Law-Arts Publishers 125
Lawn Care Industry 740
Lawrence, Inc., Seymour 125
Lawrence Summer Fellowship, D.H. 876
Lawyers and Judges Publishing Co. 125
Lawyer's Newsletter 716
Le Bureau 728
LeFan Features, Mike 608
Leader 216
League of Utah Writers (Monroe, UT) 874
League of Utah Writers (Price, UT) 874
League of Utah Writers (Provo, UT) 874
League of Utah Writers Roundup 883
League of Western Writers 874
Lear Award for Achievement in Comedy Playwriting, Norman 815
Learning 655
Leatherneck 377
Lebhar-Friedman 125
Legal Economics 717
Lehigh Valley Writers' Guild 873
Leisure Publications (see Pool News 773)
Leisureguide 559
Lenniger Literary Agency, Inc. 796
Leonard Publishing Corporation, Hal 125
Lesbian Tide, The 200
L'Esprit Createur 344
Les Femmes Publishing 126
Lester and Orpen Limited, Publishers 126
Letters 344
Levine Associates, Inc., William V. 55
Levi's/I.R.W.A. Rodeo Press Contest 815
Levy Enterprises 796
Lewis Agency, Fred 850
Lewis, Frank J. 578
Lewis/MDA Writing Awards, Jerry 815
Liberty 472
Liberty Fund, Inc. 126
Libra Publishers, Inc. 126
Libraries Unlimited, Inc. 126
Library Journal 718
Library of Congress 829
Lick Observatory 850
Lieberman Student Poetry Award, Elias 815
Life and Health 282
Life Line, The 734
Light and Life 472
Light: A Poetry Review 423
Lightfoot Collection 850
Lighting Design & Application 668

Liguori Publications 127
Liguorian 472
Limagazine 411
Lincoln Farm 850
Lincoln Picture Studio 851
Linens, Domestics and Bath Products 699
Lines Magazine 708
Linkert, Lo 578
Lion, The 216
Lion Books 127
Lippincott Co., J.B. (New York, NY) 127
Lippincott Co., J.B. (Philadelphia, PA) 127
Listen Magazine 282
Literary Hall of Fame 868
Literary Hall of Fame Writers Conference 878
Literary Review 344
Literary Sketches 344
Literature Medal Contest 816
Little, Brown and Company, Inc. 127
Little Flower Magazine, The 472
Little Magazine, The 423
Little Publications (see Custom Applicator 618, Cottom Farming Magazine 669, Rice Farming Magazine 670)
Little Review, The 423
The Liturgical Press (see Sisters Today 482)
Live 541
Living Light, The 655
Living Message 473
Living Wilderness, The 402
Lloyd Prize, David D. 816
Lloyd's Listening Post 189
Lodging and Food Service News 703
Loeb Awards, The Gerald 816
Logging Management 720
Logos International 127
Logos Journal 473
Lollipop Power, Inc. 128
London Collector, The 345
Lone Star Publishers, Inc. 128
Long Beach Writers' Club 868
Long Beach Writers Conference 878
Long Island Historical Society 851
Long Island Review 345
Longman Canada, Ltd. 128
Looking Ahead 541
Lookout, The 217, 473
Lopez Publications (see Super Stock and Drag Illustrated 234, Real Romances 259 and 260, Real Story 259 and 260, Lady's Circle Magazine 570)
Lopez Romance Group: Real Romances, Real Story 259
Loretto-Hilton Repertory Theatre 592
Los Angeles Magazine 252
Los Escribientes 868
Lost Treasure 294
Lothrop, Lee & Shepard Co. 128
Louisiana Conservationist 402
Louisiana State Library 851
Louisville Writers Club 870
Lowes, Photographer, Thomas 851
LP-Gas 689
Luce, Inc., Robert B. 129
Lufkin Line, The 559
Luggage and Leathergoods News 717
Lunch-Bunch 872
Lutheran, The 474
Lutheran Forum 474
Lutheran Journal, The 474
Lutheran Standard, The 474
Lutheran Women 475
Lyceum Productions, Inc. 56
Lyric, The 424

Mac/Western Advertising 617
McAlester Writers Guild 872
McCall's 570
McCall's Needlework & Crafts Magazine 294
MacCampbell Inc., Donald 796
McClelland and Stewart Ltd. 129
McCormick-Mathers Publishing Co. 129
McCourt, Art 578
MacDowell Colony 877
Macfadden Women's Group (see Your Baby 249, Modern Romances 259, Secrets 260, True Confessions 260, True Experience 260, True Love 261, True Romance 261, True Story 261)
McGrath, Writers' Representative, Helen 796
McGraw-Hill Book Co. 129
McGraw-Hill, Inc. (see Today's Secretary 765)
Mac-Haydn Theatre, Inc., The 592
Macho 371
McKendree Writers' Conference 879

MacLaren Publishers, Ltd. (see Baking Industries Journal 628)
MacLean-Hunter, Ltd. (see Financial Post 244, Audioscene Canada 392, Canadian Automotive Trade Magazine 620, Design Engineering 667, Hardware Merchandising 697, Plant Management & Engineering 707, Audio Trade Merchandising 766)
MacLean's 273
MacMillan of Canada 130
MacMillan Publishing Company, Inc. 130
McNeely Photography, Burton 851
MacRae Smith Company 130
Mad Magazine 308
Mademoiselle 570
Madison Select 252
Magic Circle 622
Magic Theatre, Inc. 592
Magician's Week 294
Magnetix Corporation 56
Magnum 851
Main Sportsman, The 446
Maine Antique Digest 295
Maine Commercial Fisheries 685
Maine Elves Press, Inc. 130
Maine Life 446
Maine Writers Workshop 880
Mainespring Press (see Letters 344)
Mainliner 310
Maintenance Supplies 726
Mainzer, Inc., Alfred 585
Major Books 131
Make It With Leather 295
Makepeace Colony, Inc., The 585
Man In His Environment Book Award 816
Man To Man, Mr., Sir 372
Manage 728
Management and Budget, Office of 829
Managing The Leisure Facility 703, 740
Manhattan Theatre Club 592
Manitoba Teacher, The 655
Mann Literary Agency, Carol 796
Manning, Selvage & Lee 601
Manor Books, Inc. 131
Manuscript Club of Akron 872
Manuscript Club of Akron's Annual Workshop 882
Manuscript Club of Boston 870
Manyland Books, Inc. 131
Marathon World 189
Marian Helpers Bulletin 475
Marianist Writers' Guild 887
Marina Management/Marketing 730
Marine Business 730
Marine Corps Gazette 377
Mark I 586
Mark Twain Journal 345
Mark II, The Sales and Marketing Management Magazine 617
Marketing Communications 634
Markham Review, The 345
Marks, Betty 796
Marraro Prize in Italian History, Howard R. 816
Marriage & Family Living 475
Mart Magazine 699
Martha's Vineyard Writers Workshop 882
Maryknoll Magazine 475
Maryland Conservationist 518
Maryland-Washington Beverage Journal 629
Marzola & Associates, Ed 56
Masefield Memorial Award, John 816
Mason/Charter Publishers, Inc. 131
Massachusetts Review, The 345
Master Detective 265
Masters Agency 578
Master's Press, Inc. 132
Masthead 387
Matrix 711
Mature Catholic 487
Mature Living 487
Mature Years 488
Maul, Bill 578
May Trends 635
Mayo Alumnus, The 734
Maytag Company, The 851
MBA Magazine 243
MD's Wife (see Facets 733)
Meat Magazine 687
Meat Plant Magazine 687
Mechanix Illustrated 492
Medco Books 132
Media & Methods 656
Media: Library Services Journal 719
Media West 608
Medical Center News 734
Medical Communications 712
Medical Economics 734

Medical Examination Publishing Company, Inc. 132
Medical Multimedia Corp. 56
Medical Opinion 735
Medical Post, The 735
Medina County Writer's Club 872
Meetings & Conventions 741
Meetings & Expositions 741
Melcher Book Award 816
Melody Maker 397
Memory Shop 851
Memphis State University Press 132
Mennonite Brethren Herald 486
Mennonite, The 475
Men's Wear 639
Merchandiser 622
Mercier, Louis 851
Mercury Archives 851
Meredith Literary Agency, Inc., Scott 797
Mergers & Acquisitions 685
Meridian Publishing Co., (see People on Parade 275)
Meriwether, Inc., Arthur 56, 132
Merrill Publishing Co., Charles E. 132
Merton House Publishing Co. 133
Mesabi Writers Club 871
Message 476
Messenger Of The Sacred Heart, The 476
Messenger Publishing House (see Gospel Carrier 470)
Messner, Julian 133
Metro 310
Metro East Outdoor News (see Midlantic Camping Trails 560)
Metro, The Magazine of Southeast Virginia 446
Metropolitan Museum of Art Bulletin 212
Metropolitan Museum of Art, The 851
Miami Magazine 253
Miami Seaquarium 852
Miami University Creative Writing Workshop 882
Michiana 408
Michigan Beverage News 629
Michigan Farmer 676
Michigan Out-Of-Doors 518
Michigan Quarterly Review 346
Microform Review 719
Microwaves 665
Mid-Continent Bottler 629
Midland Reporter-Telegram 414
Midlantic Camping Trails 560
Midnight/Globe 273
Midstream 314
Mid-West Contractor 645
Midwest Motorist, The 560
Midwest Quarterly, The 346
Midwest Roto 415
Midwest Writers Conference (Ohio) 882
Midwest Writers' Conference (Wisconsin) 884
Midwest Writers' Workshop 879
Military Collectors News 295
Military Electronics/Countermeasures 665
Military Engineer, The 377
Military Journal 377
Military Living 378
Military Living and Consumer Guide's R&R Report 378
Military Market 649
Military Media Review 712
Military Review 378
Millay Colony For The Arts, Inc. 877
Miller Designs, Inc. 586
Miller Publishing Co. (see Dairy Herd Management 671)
Millimeter Magazine 741
Mills, Ltd., Robert P. 797
Mimir Publishers, Inc. 133
Mine and Quarry 777
Ministry of Industry and Tourism 852
Minneapolis Writer's Workshop Inc. 871
Minnesota AAA Motorist 560
Minnesota Authors Guild 871
Minnesota Christian Writer's Guild 871
Minnesota Historical Society 852
Miraculous Medal, The 476
Miss Black America Magazine 240
Mississippi Department of Archives & History 852
Mississippi Review 346
Mississippi State University Alumnus 257
Mississippi Valley Review 346
Mississippi Valley Writers' Conference 879
Missouri Historical Society 852
Missouri Life 447
Missouri Press Women Spring Meeting 880
Missouri Writers' Guild 871
Mr. Longears Magazine 217

Mobile Home Merchandiser 779
Mobile Living 560
Mobile-Modular Housing Dealer Magazine 780
Mobile Traveller in Ontario, The 560
Model Railroader 296
Model Retailer Magazine 778
Modern Books and Crafts, Inc. 133
Modern Brewery Age 629
Modern Bride 571
Modern Bulk Transporter 622
Modern Business Reports 728
Modern Curriculum Press, Inc. 134
Modern Drummer 397
Modern Fiction Studies 346
Modern Government (Servicios Publicos) 690
Modern Jeweler 709
Modern Language Association Prizes 816
Modern Liturgy 477
Modern Machine Shop 724
Modern Maturity 488
Modern Packaging 749
Modern People 273
Modern Plant Operation and Maintenance 706
Modern Romances 259
Modern Secretary 765
Modern Steel Construction 645
Modern Tire Dealer 622
Modern Veterinary Practice 783
Modern Woodmen, The 541
Modularist Review, The 424
Moe, Christian H. 592
Moffitt, Collection, George A. 852
Mojave Books 182
Moment Magazine 314
Momentum 656
Monarch Publishing Co., Inc. 134
Monday Magazine 446
Money 243
Money, Harold B. 578
Money Strategies 243
Moneytree Newsletter 264
Monitor 665
Monitor Book Company, Inc. 134
Montana Council for Indian Education 134
Montana Department of Highways 852
Montana Magazine 447
Montana Rural Electric News 677
Montgomery Pictures 852
Monthly Review Press 134
Montreal Calendar Magazine 253
Monumental News Review (see Stone In America 777)
Moody Mystic Sound Studio's Mystic Music Centre, Doug 592
Moody Press 134
Moon Sign Book 222
Mooney Award, James 816
Moons and Lion Tailes 346
Moorepark, Howard 797
Moped Biking 525
More 712
Morehouse-Barlow Co., Inc. 135
Morgan & Morgan, Inc. 135
Morgan Grampian Publishing Corp. (see Modern Packaging 749)
Morgantown Poetry Society 874
Morin, Ray 578
Morris, Inc., Tom 56
Morrow and Co., William 135
Motel/Motor Inn Journal 703
Mother Earth News, The 201
Mothers' Manual Magazine 248
Motion 551, 770
Motivation Media, Inc. 56
Motocross Action Magazine 230
Motor 623
Motor News-Michigan Living 561
Motor North Magazine 623
Motor Sports Press Association 887
Motor Trend 230
Motorboat Magazine 503
Motorbooks International, Inc. 135
Motorcycle Dealer News 773
Motorcyclist Magazine 230
Motorhome Life 561
Mott Media 135
Mott-Kappa Tau Alpha Research Award in Journalism, Frank Luther 817
Mountain Gazette 529
Mountain Press Publishing Co. 136
Mountain Review 347
Mountain Summer 347
Mountain-Valley Writers 868
Movie Life 551
Movie Mirror, Modern Screen, TV Picture Life, Photo Screen 551
Movie Stars 552
Moving Out 347

Mpls. Magazine 253
MRC Films 57
MS. Magazine 571
Muffler Digest 623
Multimedia Product Development, Inc. 797
Multi-Media Productions, Inc. 57
Multi-Media Publications (see Cycle Times 227)
Multimedia Publishing Corp. 136
Mundus Artium 347
Municipal Publications (see Boston Magazine 250)
Munsey News Service 852
Muscle Magazine International 282
Museum of Modern Art, The 853
Museum of New Mexico 853
Museum of New Mexico Press 136
Museum of Science 853
Museum of the American Indian 853
Museum of the City of New York 853
Music City News 397
Music Critics Association, Inc. 887
Music Educators Journal 745
Music Journal 397
Music Journal 745
Music Trades Magazine 746
Musical Museum, The 853
Musical Newsletter, The 746
My Devotions 321
Mystery Writers of America, Inc. 887

N.C.T. 797
N.J. Journal of Optometry 748
NABW Awards for Distinguished Journalism 817
NAEBM Directors Award 817
Naiad Press, Inc., The 136
Namuth, Hans 853
Nard Journal 741
Narrative Poetry 817
Nashville! 253
Nason Productions, Inc., Henry 57
Natchez Trace Literary Review 348
Nation, The 430
Nation's Restaurant News 703
National Academy of Sciences, National Academy of Engineering, National Research Council, Institute of Medicine 829
National Academy of Television Arts and Sciences, The 887
National Aeronautics and Space Administration 830
National Archives and Records Service 830, 853
National Association of Educational Broadcasters 887
National Association of Gagwriters 887
National Association of Home and Workshop Writers 888
National Association of Science Writers, Inc. 888
National Book Awards 817
National Business Woman 571
National Catholic News Service 853, 608
National Coal Association 853
National Credit Union Administration 830
National Critics Institute of the Eugene O'Neill Memorial Theater Center 881
National Defense 378
National Development 430
National Enquirer 274
National Examiner 411
National Features Syndicate, Inc. 609
National Film Board Phototheque 854
National Fire Prevention and Control Administration 830
National Fisherman 685
National Foundation for Highway Safety Awards, The 817
National 4-H News 217
National Future Farmer, The 673
National Gallery of Art 854
National Gallery of Canada, The 136
National Geographic Magazine 274
National Guardsman 379
National Hardwood Magazine 721
National Historical Society Book Prize in American History 817
National Informer 274
National Insider 275
National Jewish Monthly, The 314
National Journal 431
National Laugh Enterprises 798
National League of American Pen Women, Inc. 888
National League of American Penwomen, St. Louis Branch 871
National League of American Pen Women, San Antonio Branch 873

National Library of Medicine 854
National Mall Monitor 742
National Marine Fisheries Service 830
National Media Awards 817
National Motorist 561
National On-Campus Report 656
National Park Service 830
National Parks & Conservation Magazine 402
National Petroleum News 752
National Photography Collection 854
National Playwrights Conference of the Eugene O'Neill Memorial Theater Center 881
National Press Club 888
National Press Club Award for Excellence in Consumer Reporting 818
National Railroad Passenger Corporation (AMTRAK) 830
National Research Bureau, Inc., The (see Economic Facts 263, Readers Review 388, Selected Reading 389)
National Review 431
National Society of Professional Engineers Journalism Awards 818
National Technical Information Service 831
National Textbook Company 137
National Transportation Safety Board 831
National Turf Writers Association 888
National Weather Service 831
National Wildlife 403
National Wool Grower 680
National Writers Club, Inc. 888
Natural History 403
Natural Life Magazine 201
Naturalists' Directory and Almanac (International), The 403
Naturegraph Publishers, Inc. 137
Nazarene Publishing House 137
NC Press 137
NCT Features 609
Near East Business 245
Nebraska ETV Council for Higher Education 57
Nebraska Farmer 677
Nebraska State Historical Society 854
Nebraska Writers Guild 871
Nebula 348
Neighbors, Inc., Charles 798
Neikrug Galleries, Inc. 854
Nellen Publishing Co., Inc. 138
Nelson, Inc., Thomas 138
Nelson Literary Agency, B.K. 798
Nelson-Hall, Inc. 138
Nevada Magazine 447
Nevadan, The 447
Neville Public Museum 854
Nevins Prize, Allan 818
New Alaskan 448
New American Library 138
New Boston Review 348
New Catholic World 477
New Collage Magazine 424
New Covenant Magazine 477
New Dawn 572
New Earth Review 424
New Engineer 668
New England Galaxy 448
New England Guide, The 448
New England Magazine 409
New England Quarterly, The 348
New England Senior Citizen/Senior American News 488
New Englander, The 245
New Era, The 477
New Guard 431
New Hampshire Profiles 448
New Harbinger, The 387
New Haven Info Magazine 254
New Infinity Review, The 348
New Jersey Historical Society, The 854
New Jersey Monthly 449
New Jersey Poetry Society, Inc. 871
New Jersey Writers' Annual Conference 881
New Leaf Press, Inc. 139
New Leaf Publications, Ltd. (see Saturday Night 278)
New Mexico Magazine 449
New Mexico Stockman 680
New Oregon Publishers, Inc. (see Oregon Times Magazine 451)
New Orleans Magazine 254
New Orleans Review 349
New Physician, The 735
New Plays, Inc. 598
New Playwrights' Theatre of Washington, The 598
New Readers Press 139
New Republic, The 431
New Review Books 140

New Times 275
New Viewpoints 140
New World Outlook 477
New Worlds Unlimited 424
"New" Writer's Club, The 874
New York Affairs/Urban America 254
New York Antique Almanac, The 387
New York Arts Journal 212
New York Botanical Garden Library, The 854
New York Convention and Visitors Bureau 854
The New York Eye Publishing Co., Inc. (see The New York Antique Almanac 387)
New York Historical Society, The 855
New York Holiday Workshop 881
New York Magazine 449
New York News Magazine 411
New York Poetry Forum 872
New York State Historical Association Manuscript Award 818
New York Times 417
New York Times, The 411
New York Times Book Review, The 349
New York Times Syndication Sales Corporation 609
New York Today, Inc., News Service 609
New Yorker, The 275
New Zealand Embassy 855
Newark Museum 855
Newbury House Publishers, Inc. 140
Newcastle Publishing Co., Inc. 139
Newcomen Awards in Business History 818
Neworld: The Multi-Cultural Magazine of the Arts 212
News Circle, The 387
News Flash International, Inc. 609
News World Syndicate 610
Newsart 349
Newsday 412, 417
Newspaper Enterprise Association, Inc. 610
Newspaper Farm Editors of America (NFEA) 888
Newspaper Food Editors and Writers Association 889
Newspaper Production 760
Newsweek 431
Newsweek Books 855
Niagara Falls Association of Professional Women Writers, The 872
Niagara Frontier Christian Writers Workshop 881
Nicholas Literary Agency 798
Nichols Publishing Co. 140
Nicholson Photography 855
Nimrod 349
99 IC Projects 296
Nit & Wit Literary Arts Magazine 349
Nitty-Gritty 350
NJEA Review 656
Non-Foods Merchandising 742
Norcross, Inc. 586
Norden News 783
North American Mentor Magazine 350
North American Newspaper Alliance 610
North American Publishing Co. (see Pickin' Magazine 398, New Dawn 572, Training Management Motivation & Incentives 635, American School & University 651, Executive Housekeeper 702, Institutional Management 728, Lab World 734, Package Printing 749, Newspaper Production 760)
North American Review, The 350
North American Voice of Fatima 478
North Atlantic Aircraft Bulletin (see Aviation 236)
North Carolina Division of Archives and History 855
North Carolina Historical Review 287
North Carolina Museum of Art 855
North Country Anvil 202
North River Press, Inc. 140
North Shore Magazine 409
North South Trader 287
Northeast Literary Agency 798
Northeast Nebraska Writers 871
Northeast Outdoors 561
Northeast Van 230
Northeastern Industrial World 706
Northern California Cartoon & Humor Association 868
Northern Hardware Trade 697
Northern Light 424
Northern Logger & Timber Processor, The 721
Northern Virginian 450
Northland Press 140
North/Nord 449

Northwest Investment Review 245
Northwest Magazine 413
Northwest Passages 311
Northwest Review 350
Northwest Skier 530
Northwestern Jeweler, The 709
Northwoods Journal 351
Northwoods Press, Inc. 140
Norton Co., Inc., W.W. 141
Notebook & Other Reviews, The 351
The Notebook Press (see The Notebook & Other Reviews 351)
Notman Photographic Archives 855
Nova Scotia Historical Quarterly 450
Now 450
Now, For Today's Young Teens 542
Noyes Data Corporation 141
NRTA Journal 489
NTDRA Dealer News 623
Nuclear Regulatory Commission 831
Nuestro: The Magazine for Latinos 387
Numismatic Information Service 610
Nursery Days 321
Nursing Care (see The Journal of Nursing Care 701)
Nutrition Health Review 283
Nymphet (see Casion 367)
Nystrom 57
NYT Pictures 855

O and A Marketing News 623
O'Brien Award, Catherine L. 818
OCAW Union News 564
Occupational Awareness 141
Occupational Hazards 726
Occupational Safety and Health Review Commission 831
Ocean Industry 752
Oceana Publications, Inc. 141
Oceanic Press Service 610
Oceans 492
Oddo Publishing, Inc. 141
Odyssey Press 142
OEA Communique 657
Off Campus Writers Workshop 869
Off Duty 379
Off Duty Europe 379
Office Products 747
Office World News 747
Official Crosswords, Dell Crosswords, Pocket Crosswords, Dell Word Search Puzzles, Dell Pencil Puzzles and Word Games, Dell Crossword Annuals, Dell Crossword Puzzles, Paperback Book Series, Dell Puzzle Publications 434
Official Detective 265
Official Detective Group (see Front Page Detective, Inside Detective, Master Detective, Official Detective 265)
Official Karate 523
Offshore 752
Ohio Antique Review 296
Ohio Farmer, The 677
Ohio Journal, The 351
Ohio Magazine 450
Ohio Motorist 562
Ohio Poetry Day 882
Ohio Review, The 351
Ohio River Writers' Conference 879
Ohio State University Press 142
Ohio Truck Times 624
Ohio University Press 142
Ohioana Quarterly 352
Oilweek 752
Oklahoma Cowman, The 680
Oklahoma Writers Federation Annual Conference 882
Old Army Press, The 142
Old Bottle Magazine, The 296
Old Cars Newspaper 296
Old Log Theater 592
Old West 287
O'Liners 601
Omaha Community Playhouse 593
Omaha Writers' Club 871
Omaha Writers' Club Spring Conference 880
Omega 352
On The Line 321
Onan News Brief/Onan News 189
One Man's Opinion 372
101 Productions 142
O'Neill & Kralik Literary Consultants 799
1001 Truck and Van Ideas Magazine 231
Ontario Out Of Doors 518
Open Circle Theatre Playwrights Award 818
Open Court-Library Press Incorporated 142
Open Road 624

Opera Canada 397
Opera News 746
Opera Variety Theater 593
Opinion 352
Optimum Publishing Co. Limited 142
Orben's Current Comedy, Orben's Comedy Fillers 308
Orbis Books 143
Oregon Angler, The 519
Oregon Historical Society 855
Oregon State University Press 143
Oregon Times Magazine 451
Oregon Voter Digest 451
Organic Gardening and Farming 305
Organization of American States 856
Original Art Report, The 213
Original Crossword, Easy-Timed, Crossword's Word Hunt 434
Orlando-Land Magazine 451
Ornamental Metal Fabricator 724
Osborn Award, Earl D. 818
Other Side, The 478
Otrabanda Company 593
Otterbein College Theatre 593
Oui Magazine 372
Our Family 478
Our Little Friend, Primary Treasure 321
Our Sunday Visitor, Inc. 58, 143
Our Sunday Visitor Magazine 478
Out There Magazine 352
Outdoor Canada Magazine 508
Outdoor Indiana 451
Outdoor Life 519
Outdoor Pictures 58
Outdoor Pix & Copy 856
Outdoor Power Equipment 697
Outdoor Press, The 520
Outdoor Recreation, Bureau of 831
Outdoor Writers Association of America Annual Conference 884
Outdoor Writers Association of America, Inc. 889
Outdoors 503
Outdoors in Georgia 451
Outdoors Today 520
Outposts 425
Outside Magazine 562
Overseas Life 379
Owner Operator Magazine 624
Oxmoor House 143
Ozark Creative Writers, Inc. 867

P.A.R. Incorporated 143
P.E.N. 889
P.E.N. Translation Prize 819
Pace Films, Inc. 58
Pacific Aerial Surveys 856
Pacific Bakers News 628
Pacific Boating Almanac 562
Pacific Books, Publishers 143
Pacific Discovery 403
Pacific Goldsmith 709
Pacific News Service 611
Pacific Northwest Writers Conference 883
Pacific Press Publishing Association (see Primary Treasure 322)
Pacific Stationer 747
Pacific Travel News 781
Package Printing 749
Packer, The 749
Packing and Shipping 749
Paddle World 526
Padre Productions 144
Page Publications, Ltd. (see Resort & Motel Magazine 703, Sporting Goods Trade 775)
Pagurian Press, Ltd. 144
Paid My Dues: Journal of Women and Music 398
Paintbrush 352
Paladin Press 144
Palm Beach Life 452
Palm Springs Life Magazine 452
Pamphlet Publications 602
Pamphleteer Monthly, The 719
Pan American Airways 856
Panache 353
Panhandle Pen Women 874
Panhandle Pen Women and West Texas State University Writers' Round-up 883
Panorama 415
Panorama Magazine 414
Pantheon Books 144
Pantheon Press (see Cosmopolitan Contact 197)
Paperboard Packaging 751
Paperjacks, Ltd. 144
Papp Producer, Joseph 593
Parabola 353
Parade 412
Parameters: Journal of the U.S. Army War College 380

Paramount Communications 58
Parapsychology Review 497
Parents' Magazine 249
Parents Magazine Press 145
Paris Review, The 353
Park Maintenance 764
Parker Publishing Co. 145
Parking Magazine 668
Parkman Prize, Francis 819
Pasadena City College Annual Writer's Forum 878
Passenger Transport 691
Pastoral Life 637
Patent and Trademark Office 831
Paterson College Writers' Conference, William 881
Patient Aid Digest 650
Patriotic Poetry Seminar 883
Patties Prints, Inc. 586
Paulist Press 145
Pay Day Press 145
Pay Television Magazine 665
Peabody Museum of Salem 856
Peace & Pieces Foundation 145
Peace Press, Inc. 146
Peagasus 146
Peanut Farmer, The 669
Pearson Prize for Excellence in Investigative Reporting, The Drew 819
Peekner Literary Agency, Ray 799
Pelican Publishing Co., Inc. 146
Pellowski, Michael J. ("Ski") 579
Pen and Brush Club 889
Pen Woman Magazine, The 712
Penguin Photo 856
Peninsula Living 452
Peninsula Magazine 452
Penney-Missouri Magazine Awards 819
Pennsylvania Game News 520
Pennsylvania Grocer 694
Pennsylvania Illustrated 453
Pennsylvania State University Press, The 146
Penny Dreadful, The 353
Pennyworth Press 146
Pentecostal Evangel 479
Pentecostal Testimony 479
Penthouse 372
People on Parade 275
People Weekly 276
Pepin Pen Club 871
Pequot Press, Inc., The 146
Peregrine Smith, Inc. 147
Perfect Home Magazine 305
Perfection Form Co., The 58
Performance 770
Performance Publishing Co. 598
Performing Arts In Canada 552
Performing Arts Review 353
Periodical 380
Periodical of Art in Nebraska 453
Perivale Press 147
Permanent Press (see Moons and Lion Tailes 346)
Perron, Robert 856
Persimmon Hill 287
Personal Computing 297
Personal Growth 497
Personal Romances 259
Personalist, The 354
Personalities in Review 276
Personnel Advisory Bulletin 729
Perspective 218, 410
Perspectives 354
Pest Control Magazine 726
Pet Dealer, The 754
Peter Perry Publishing, Ltd. (see Canadian Funeral Director 738)
Peterborough Players 593
Peters & Pierre Long Literary Agents, Marjorie 799
Petersen Publishing Company (see Car Craft 226, Motorcyclist Magazine 230, Guns & Ammo Magazine 512, Petersen's Hunting 520)
Petersen's Hunting 520
Petersen's Photographic Magazine 417
Petroleum Independent 753
Petroleum Marketer 753
Petroleum Publishing Co., The (see Offshore 752)
Pets/Supplies/Marketing 754
Pfizer Award 819
PGW News 189
Phelps & Thompson, Inc. 856
Phi Delta Kappan 657
Philadelphia Magazine 254
Philadelphia Museum of Art 856
Philadelphia Purchasor, The 706
Philadelphia Writers Conference 882
Philatelic Journalist 713
Philiba, Allan A. 857

Phillips, Inc., S.G. 147
Phillips, Irv 579
Phoenix Magazine 453
Photo Archives-Museum of New Mexico 857
Photo Artist USA 756
Photo Insight 417
Photo Marketing 769
Photo Researchers, Inc. 857
Photo Screen 552
Photo Trends 857
Photo World 857
Photocom Productions 58
Photography 859
Photography by Harvey Caplin 857
Photography Collection 857
Photography For Industry 857
Photomethods 417, 756
Photophile 857
Photovillage 858
Photri 858
Physician's Life 735
Physician's Management 735
Pickin' Magazine 398
Pickup, Van & 4WD Magazine 231
Pickwick Press, The 147
Pictorial Parade, Inc. 858
Pictorial Press 147
Picturemakers, Inc. 858
Pierian Spring 354
Pig Iron Magazine 354
Pillow Talk 388
Pilot Books 148
Pine Associates, Inc., Arthur 799
Pinnacle Books 148
Pioneer Drama Service 599
Pioneer Girls, Inc. (see Perspective 218, Trails 324)
Pioneer Valley Scriptors 870
Pipeline & Gas Journal 753
Pipeline & Underground Utilities Construction 753
Pitkin Agency, The Walter 799
Pittsburgh Branch of Bookfellows, The 873
Pittsburgh Magazine 254
Pittsburgh Press, The 413
Pizzazz 322
Plan and Print 761
Plane & Pilot Magazine 237
Planning 218
Plant Management & Engineering 707
Plants Alive 306
Plastics Technology 757
Platt & Munk Publishers 148
Play Group Inc., The 593
Play Meter Magazine 641
Playbill Magazine 552
Playboy 372
Playboy Press 148
Players Magazine 373
Players' Newsletter, The 507
Playette Corporation 59
Playgirl Magazine 572
Plays 599
Playwriting for Children's Theatre 819
Playwrights' Lab, The 594
Plenum Publishing Corp. 148
Ploughshares 355
Plywood and Panel Magazine 721
PMS Publishing Co. (see Super-8 Filmaker 554)
PNPA Press 713
Pocket Books 148
Poe Awards, Edgar Allan 819
Poem 425
Poertner, Photographer, Kenneth C. 858
Poet, The 425
Poet Gallery Press 148
Poetry 425
Poetry Center Discovery-The Nation Contest, The 819
Poetry League of America 874
Poetry Newsletter 425
Poetry Northwest Magazine 425
Poetry Society of America 889
Poetry Society of Michigan 870
Poetry Venture 425
Poetry View 426
Poetry Windsor Poesie 426
Poetry Workshops 881
Poets & Writers, Inc. 889
Poets Club of Chicago National Shakespearean Sonnet Contest 819
Poet's Repertory Theatre 594
Poets' Roundtable of Arkansas 867
Poets' Study Club of Terre Haute 870
Poets Tape Exchange 874
Polaris Press 149
Police Times Magazine 691
Polled Hereford World 681
Pomona Valley Writers Club 868

Pool 'N Patio 306
Pool News 773
Poolife 306
Popular Electronics 492
Popular Handicraft Hobbies 297
Popular Library/CBS 149
Popular Mechanics 492
Popular Photography 418
Popular Publications, Inc. (see Cars Magazine 227)
Popular Science Monthly 493
Porcelain Agency, Sidney E. 799
Port Townsend Fiction Seminar 883
Port Townsend Poetry Symposium 883
Porter, Gould & Dierks 800
Ports O' Call 218
Potato Grower of Idaho 670
Poteet, Inc., G. Howard 149
Potpourri-An Anthology 355
Potter, Inc., Clarkson N. 149
Powder Magazine 530
Power Engineering 759
Power Transmission Design 724
Powerboat Magazine 503
Practical Horsemen 209
Practical Knowledge 388
Practical Politics 431
Practical Psychology for Physicians (see Behavioral Medicine 732)
Pragare Co., Inc., A.R. 149
Prairie Schooner 355
Prairie Sun 202
Pratt Free Library, Enoch 858
Precedent Publishing, Inc. 149
Prentice-Hall, Inc. 150
Prentice-Hall of Canada, Ltd. 150
Presbyterian Journal, The 479
Presbyterian Record 479
Present Tense: The Magazine of World Jewish Affairs 431
Preservation News 406
Preservation Press, The 150
Preslar, Andrew 579
Press Pacifica 150
Press, The 617
Pre-Vue 552
Price/Stern/Sloan Inc., Publisher 151
Primary Treasure 322
Prince Publishers 151
Princeton Book Co., Publishers 151
Prism International 355
Private Pilot 237
Private Practice 736
Prize In Photographic History 819
Probe 542
Problems of Communism 742
Produce News 687
Producers Group Ltd. 59
Production 724
Production Engineering 707
Products Finishing 724
Professional Decorating & Coating Action 633
Professional Educators Publications, Inc. 151
Professional Medical Assistant 701
Professional Men's Hairstylist 695
Professional Research, Inc. 59
Professional Writers League of Long Beach 868
Profitable Craft Merchandising 778
Progressive, The 432
Progressive Architecture 618
Progressive Grocer 694
Progressive Teacher, The 657
Prolog 553
Proofs 649
Properties Magazine 763
Property Management Journal 763
Pruett Publishing Company 151
PSG Publishing Company, Inc. 152
PSL Publications Limited (see Airfix Magazine 289)
Psychiatric Syndication Service, Inc. 800
Psychology Today 497
PTN Publishing Corp. (see Studio Photography 757, Technical Photography 757)
Public Archives of Canada 858
Public Power 759
Public Utilities Fortnightly 691
Publicist 761
Publishers Investors, Inc. 59
Publishers Weekly 631
Publishing Co., The (see Air California Magazine 308)
Publishing House, The (see High Fidelity 395)
Pulitzer Prizes 819
Pulp 355
Pulp: Fiction & Poetry 355
Pulse-Finger Press 152

Pungent Prayer 611
Purchasing 707
Purdue University Press, The 152
Purpose 479
Putnam Awards 820
Putnam's Sons, G.P. 152
Pyle Memorial Award, Ernie 820

QED Literary Agency 800
Q-Ed Productions, Inc. 59
Quad City Writers Club 869
Quality Industries 586
Quarter Horse Journal, The 209
Quarter Horse of the Pacific Coast, The 210
Queen 480
Queen City Writers 872
Queens Borough Public Library 858
Queenston House Publishing, Ltd. 152
Quest/78 276
Quick Fox 153
Quick Frozen Foods 687
Quill, The 713
Quill & Quire 631
Quilter's Newsletter Magazine 298
Quinn Publishing Company (see Road Test 233)

R-A-D-A-R 322
Racing Cars 231
Racing Pigeon Pictorial 526
Radio-Electronics 298, 493
Radio-TV Editorial Journal 666
Railroad Model Craftsman 298
Rainbow 322
Raintree Publishers Ltd. 153
Raisner Photos 858
Rampage 373
Rand McNally 153
Random House, Inc. 153
Rangefinder, The 756
Ranger Rick's Nature Magazine 323
Rapidfire Review 298
RD Communications 153
Read Magazine 268
Reader's Digest 276
Readers Nutshell 277
Readers Review 388
Real Confessions, Modern Love Confessions 260
Real Estate 307
Real Estate Journalism Achievement Competition 820
Real Romances 260
Real Story 260
Reason Magazine 432
Reclamation, Bureau Of 832
Reconstructionist 314
Record Stockman, The 681
Recording Engineer/Producer 666
Red Devil, The 190
Red Dust, Inc. 154
Red Maple Publishing Co., Ltd. (see This Magazine 432)
Redbook Magazine 572
Redbook's Young Writer's Contest III 820
Redwood Rancher 629
Reese Publishing Co. (see Beaver 367)
Referee 507
Reflection 542
Reflex Photo, Inc. 858
Refrigerated Transporter 624
Regal Books 154
Regents Press of Kansas, The 154
Regents Publishing Company, Inc. 59, 154
Regina Medal 820
Register and Tribune Syndicate, Inc., The 611
Reid Writers' Colony, Mildred I. 876
Relics 299
Religion Newswriters Association 889
Religious Arts Guild One-Act Play Competition 820
Religious News Service 611, 858
Religious Publishing Co. (see Your Church 638)
Religious Writers' Agency 800
Relim Publishing Co., Inc. (see Macho 371)
Remington Art Museum 858
Remington Review, The 356
Renascence 356
Repertory Theater of America/Alpha-Omega Players 594
Report on Farming 673
Reserve Law 691
Resort Management 704
Resort & Motel Magazine 703
Resource Publications 154
Reston Publishing Company 155
Retailer and Marketing News 700
Retired Officer Magazine, The 380

Retirement Living 489
Revealing Secrets 260
Revell Company, Fleming H. 155
Review 311, 388
Review, The 753
Review & Herald Publishing Association (see Insight 471)
Review For Religious 480
Review Publishing Co. (see Virginia Municipal Review 692)
Revista/Review Interamericana 356
Reymont Associates 155
Rhode Island Department of Economic Development 859
Rhode Island Writers' Guild 873
Rhode Islander 413
Rhodes Literary Agency 800
Rhodes Literary Agency, Barbara 800
Rhythms Productions 60
Rice Farming Magazine 670
Rice Journal, The 670
Richards Commercial Photo Service 859
Richards Rosen Press 155
Richmond Literary Agency 801
Richmond Magazine 255
Riddle Video and Film Productions, Inc. 60
Rider 231
Riffs 398
Rifle Magazine, The 513
Rinaldo, Dom 579
Ritchie Press, The Ward 155
Riverside Writers' Club 868
RMI Media Productions, Inc. 60
RN 701
Road & Driver 232
Road & Track 232
Road King Magazine 232
Road Rider 232
Road Test 233
Roanoke Island Historical Association 599
Roberts, H. Armstrong 859
Rock & Gem 299
Rock Products 777
Rockhound 299
Rocky Mountain Outdoor Writers and Photographers 890
Rocky Mountain Writers' Convention 883
Rocky Mountain Writers Guild, Inc. 869
Rodale Press Publications (see Organic Gardening and Farming 305)
Rodeo Sports News 526
Rogers Literary Agency, Minnie 801
Rolat Publishing Corp (see Intimate Romances 259, Intimate Secrets 259, True Secrets 261)
Roll Call 692
Rolling Stone 399
Romance Philology 356
Roseburg Woodsman 190
Rosenberg Annual Poetry Award, Dorothy 820
Rosicrucian Digest 389
Roswell Writers Guild 872
Rotarian, The 218
Routledge & Kegan Paul, Ltd. 155
Royale 311
Rubin, Lee 579
Rue III Enterprises, Leonard 859
Runner's World Magazine 526
Running Studio, Inc. 586
Rural Electric Missourian 677
Rural Electrification 760
Ruralite 190
Rush Publishing Co. (see Women Studies Abstracts 574)
Rusi Journal 380
Russian Literature Triquarterly 356
Russian Review, The 357
Rust Craft Greeting Cards, Inc. 586
Rutgers University Press 156
RVR, Recreational Vehicle Retailer 773

S.E.W. Magazine 573
S.T. Publications (see Visual Merchandising 617)
Sacramento Bee, The 406
Sacramento Weekender 406
Sadlier, Inc., William H. 156
Saerch 404
Saga 374
Sail 503
Sailing Magazine 504
St. Anthony Messenger 480
St. Anthony Messenger Press 156
St. Clements 594
St. Croix Review 357
St. Davids Christian Writers' Conference 882
St. Joseph's Messenger & Advocate of the Blind 480
St. Lawrence Award for Fiction 820

St. Lawrence University Fiction International Writers' Conference 881
St. Louis Journalism Review 713
St. Louis Writers' Guild 871
St. Louisan 453
St. Martin's Press 156
St. Nicholas Theater 594
Sales & Marketing Management 617
Salesman's Opportunity Magazine 769
Salmon Trout Steelheader 520
Salt Lick Press 357
Salt Water Sportsman 520
Samisdat 357
Sample Case, The 277
Sams & Co., Inc., Howard W. 156
San Antonio Magazine 454
San Diego Magazine 255
San Diego Writers Workshop 868
San Francisco Bay Guardian 202
San Francisco Maritime Museum 859
San Francisco Review of Books 357
San Francisco Theatre Magazine 553
San Francisco Writers Workshop 868
San Gabriel Valley Magazine, The 454
San Jose Studies 357
Sandal Prints 481
Sandlapper 454
Sanford Photo Associates 859
Sangamon Company 587
Sanitary Maintenance 743
Sargent Publishers, Inc., Porter 156
Saturday Evening Post, The 277
Saturday Night 278
Saturday Review 278
Save The Children 60
Saver 190
Saving Energy 389
Sawyer Press 612
Scala Fine Arts Publishers, Inc. 859
Scandinavian Review 389
SCBW New England Children's Literature Conference 880
Schenkman Publishing Co., Inc. 156
Schick Sunn Classic Pictures 602
Schirmer Books 157
Scholar's Choice, Ltd. 157
Scholastic Editor 713
Scholastic Scope 542
"Scholasticus" Publishing 157
Scholia Satyrica 358
Scholium International, Inc. 157
School and Family Digest 268
School Arts Magazine 657
School Library Journal 719
School Musician, The 657
School Shop 657
Schuman Prize, Henry 820
Schuyler Prize, Robert Livingston 820
Science Activities 658
Science and Children 658
Science & Mechanics 494
Science Digest 494
Science Fiction Writers of America 890
Science Fiction Writers' Workshop 881
Science in Society Journalism Awards 820
Science News 494
Science-Writing Award in Physics and Astronomy 821
Scientific American 494
Scope 481
Scorpio Rising Theatre Foundation 594
Scott Literary Agency 801
Scott's Monthly Stamp Journal 299
Scrambling Press, Inc. (see House Plants and Porch Gardens 304)
Scranton Publishing Co. (see Water & Sewage Works 784)
Scranton Theatre Libre, Inc. 594
Screen and TV Album 553
Screen Printing 761
Screw 374
Scribblers, The 873
Scribner's Sons, Charles 157
Scriptors' Conference 880
SDM: Security Distributing & Marketing 726
Sea 504
Sea Frontiers 747
Sea Power 381
Seabury Press, The 158
Seacoast Writers Conference 880
Search and Rescue Magazine 692
Seattle Business Magazine 255
Seattle Repertory Theatre 595
Seattle Times Magazine 414
Seattle Times Pictorial 414
Seaway Review 731
Second Coming 358
Second Wave, The 202
Secret Service 832
Secrets 260
Securities and Exchange Commission 832
Seek 481
Sekai Bunka Photo 860
Select Home Designs 307
Selected Reading 389

Seligmann Agency, James 801
Selling Sporting Goods 774
Selling Today 769
Sematones, Frank ("Deac") 579
Seminar for Freelance Writers 878
Senate 832
$ensible Sound, The 399
Sepia 240
Sequoia 358
Seraphim Publishing Group, Inc. (see Faith and Inspiration 468)
Sergel Drama Prize 821
Serran, The 637
Serrano, Joseph 579
Service Station and Garage Management 624
Seven 426
Seven Stars Poetry 426
Seventeen 543
Seventeen "Mini-Mag" 543
Seventy Six Magazine 190
'76 Press 158
73 Magazine 494
Severns, Harry 579
Sevier Valley Chapter of the League of Utah Writers 874
Sevote Group 60
Sew Business 649
Sewanee Review 358
Sexton Poetry Prize, Anne 821
Shagbark Scribes 869
Shaker Museum, The 860
Shakespeare Newsletter, The 358
Shanks, Ann Zane 860
Shaw, Ray 860
Shaw Review 359
Shawnee Writers Association 872
Shayne Mystery Magazine, Mike 400
Sheboygan County Writers Club 875
Sheed Andrews and McMeel, Inc. 158
Ship & Boat International 731
Shipley, E.G. 579
Shoal Creek Publishers, Inc. 158
Shoe String Press, Inc., The 158
Shooting Industry, The 774
Shooting Times 513
Shopfitting International 743
Shopping Center World 763
Shostal Associates, Inc. 860
Showbill 553
Showcase Magazine 455
Showcase Writers Club 868
Shreveport Writers Club 870
Shumway Publisher, George 159
Sickles Photo-Reporting Service 860
Side, John W. 579
Sierra 404
Sightlines 658
Sigma Tau Delta 872
Sign, The 482
Signalman's Journal, The 762
Signature 278
Signpost Magazine 527
Signpost Publications 159
Signs 359
Signs of the Times 482
Silver and Gold Report 737
Silver Burdett 159
Silvermine Publishers Incorporated 159
Simmental Journal 681
Simmental Scene 681
Simmental Shield 682
Simon and Schuster 159
Simser Group of Companies of America (Canada), Ltd., The 612
Singer Features, Inc., BP 612, 860
Singer Literary Agency, Evelyn 801
Single Parent, The 497
Siouxland Creative Writers' Club 873
Sipapu 203
Sisters Today 482
Skate World News 527
Skateboard Industry News 774
Skateboard World 527
Skating 530
Ski 531
Ski Business 774
Ski Competition East 531
Ski Info 775
Skiers Directory 531
Skiing Magazine 532
Skiing Trade News 775
Skin Diver 534
Skokie's Creative Writers Assn. 869
Sky 311
Skybird Publishing Co. (see Play Meter Magazine 641)
Skyviews Survey, Inc. 860
Slack, Inc., Charles B. 160
Slade, Loraine 595
Sleepy Hollow Restorations, Inc. 160
Small Business Computor 743
Small Business Magazine 635
Small Business Newsletter 635

Small Pond Magazine of Literature, The 359
Small Press Review 359
Small World 191
Smith, The 160, 359
Smith Collection, Sophia 861
Smith, Inc., Gemini 860
Smith Photography, Dick 860
Smith, Scott 580
Smithsonian Institution 832
Smithsonian Magazine 390
Smolar Award, The 821
Snack Food 688
Snips Magazine 759
Snohomish Publishing Company Inc. (see Washington Fishing Holes 522)
Snotrack 532
Snow Goer 532
Snowmobile News 532
Snowmobile West 532
Snowy Egret 405
Soap Opera Digest 554
Soccer America 533
Soccer Associates 160, 612
Soccer World 533
Sochurek, Inc., Howard 861
Social Justice Review 482
Social Security Administration 832
Society for Technical Communication 890
Society of American Social Scribes 890
Society of American Travel Writers 890
Society of Children's Book Writers 870, 890
Society of Colonial Wars Award 821
Society of Professional Journalists, Sigma Delta Chi 890
Society of the Silurians, Inc. 891
Soil Conservation Service 832
Solar Energy Digest 743
Solid Wastes Management 784
Solution 769
Sommer Inc., Elyse 801
Sono 399
Sooner LPG Times 689
Sounds 399
Soundview Books 160
South Atlantic Quarterly 360
South Bend Writers' Club 870
South Carolina Educational Television Network 60
South Carolina Magazine 455
South Carolina Review 360
South Carolina Wildlife 455
South Dakota Review 360
South Dakota State Historical Society 861
South Magazine, The 245
South Oakland Writers 870
South Plains Writers Association 874
South Texas Pro-Am Writers Rally 883
Southeastern Dairy Review 671
Southeastern Power Administration 833
Southeastern Writers Association, Inc. 879
Southern Angler's Guide, Southern Hunter's Guide 521
Southern Automotive Journal 625
Southern Beverage Journal 630
Southern Exposure 455
Southern Hardware 697
Southern Jeweler 709
Southern Jewish Weekly 314
Southern Methodist University Press 161
Southern Motor Cargo 625
Southern Outdoors Magazine 527
Southern Printer & Lithographer 761
Southern Publishing Association 161
Southern Review, The 360
Southern RV 233
Southern Stationer and Office Outfitter 748
Southwest Airlines Magazine 311
Southwest Art 213
Southwest Homefurnishings News 700
Southwest Manuscripters 868
Southwest Review 360
Southwest Sports 508
Southwest Writers' Conference 883
Southwestern Musician 746
Souvenirs and Novelties 778
Sou'Wester 361
Sovfoto/Eastfoto 861
Soybean Digest 670
Spa Writers 867
Sparrow Poverty Pamphlets 426
Sparrow Press (see Sparrow Poverty Pamphlets 426)
Special Education: Forward Trends 658
Special Olympics Awards 821
Specialty & Custom Dealer 625
Specialty Salesman Magazine 769
Spellbinders Literary Guild 868
Spencer Photos, Hugh 861
Spencer Productions, Inc. 60

Sperry New Holland Public Relations Newsfeatures 191
Sphere Magazine 573
Spinning Wheel, The 300
Spirit, The 219
Spiritual Life 482
Spirituality Today 482
Spitzer Literary Agency, Philip G. 802
Spokane Magazine 255
Spoken Language Services, Inc. 61
Sporting Goods Dealer, The 775
Sporting Goods Trade 775
Sporting News 508
Sports Afield 521
Sports Illustrated 508
Sports Informer, The 509
Sports Journal, The 509
Sports Merchandiser 775
Sportshelf News 509
Spottswood Studios 61
Spring, Bob and Ira 861
Spring Rain Press 427
Sprint Magazine 323
Spur Awards 821
Spyglass 504
Stack & Associates, Tom 861
Stackpole Books 161
Stage South 599
Stamp Wholesaler, The 778
Standard 483
Standard Publishing 161
Standard Publishing (see Seek 481, Key To Christian Education 637)
Standards, National Bureau Of 833
Stanley Drama Award 821
Star, The 278
Star Service, The 781
Star West 427
Startling Detective 265
Starwind 495
State, The 455
State & County Administrator 692
State Historical Society of Wisconsin Press 161
State Magazine 415
State of Maine Writers' Conference 880
Staten Island Historical Society 861
Steamship Historical Society of America 861
Steel '78 725
Steering Wheel 219
Stein and Day 161
Stephan, Jr., C.M. 802
Stereo 390
Sterling Library Inc. (see Real Confessions, Modern Love Confessions 260)
Sterling's Magazines, Inc. (see Astrology Guide 220, Photo Screen 552)
Sternig Literary Agency, Larry 802
Stevenson & Associates, Ellen 802
Stillwater Writers 873
Stilwill, Charles 595
Stinger, John 580
Stitch 'n Sew 300
Stock, Boston, Inc. 861
Stock Car Racing Magazine 233
Stokes Associates, Bill 61
Stokes Award, Thomas L. 821
Stone Awards, Walker 821
Stone Country 427
Stone in America 777
Stone Wall Press, Inc. 162
Story Friends 323
Strand Enterprises 587
Stratton, Tom 580
Stravon Publishers Inc. 162
Strawberry Hill Press 162
Street Chopper 233
Street Rodder Magazine 234
Strength & Health 528
Strike 506
Structures Publishing Co. 162
Strugglers' Club, The 869
Stuart Contest, Jesse 822
Student, The 543
Student Forum 418
Student Lawyer 717
Studio Photography 757
Stuhlmann, Authors' Representative, Gunther 802
Suburban Publishing Inc. (see Hudson Valley Magazine 444)
Suburban Shopper 264
Success 638
Success Unlimited 390
Successful Farming 674
Sugar Beet, The 670
Sugar Producer, The 682
Summer in France 884
Summer Writers Workshop at New College, University of Toronto 884
Summerhill Media, Limited 61

Summit Press Syndicate 612
Summit Publishing Co. (see Southwest Airlines Magazine 311)
Sun Magazine 191
Sun Publishing Co. 162
Sundancer 311
Sunday Advocate Magazine 409
Sunday Digest 483
Sunday Magazine 415
Sunday Morning Magazine 410
Sunday School Counselor 638
Sunday School Lesson Illustrator 483
Sunshine Magazine 279
Sunstone Press 163
Sunstone Review 361
Sunway Periodicals, Inc. (see Affair 367, Casion 367, Dapper 368)
Super Chevy Magazine 234
Super Stock and Drag Illustrated 234
Super-8 Filmaker 554
Supermarketing Magazine 694
Supervision 729
Supreme Court 833
Surfer 534
Surfer Publications (see Powder Magazine 530)
Surfwriters 868
Surgical Business 736
Sutherin, Joe 595
Swank 374
Swedenborg Foundation 163
Swedish Information Service 862
Swimming Pool Weekly/Age 776
Swimming World 61, 534
Swingers World 279
Swiss National Tourist Office 862
Sygma 862
Symmes Systems 163
Syracuse University Press 163

Tab Books 163
Tack 'N Togs Merchandising 640
Tacoma Writers Club 874
Taconic Theatre Company 595
Tafnews Press 163
Taft Corporation 164
Taggart Publishing Co. (see Counterforce 739)
Take One 554
Talco Productions 61
Talon Books, Ltd. 164
Tamarack Press 164
Tampa Tribune, The 407
Tandem Press Publishers 164
Tangent Books 164
Tape 'n Text 165
Tar Heel 456
Tar Heel Writers' Roundtable 882
Tarcher, Inc., J.P. 165
Taurus Photos 862
Teacher 659
Teachers College Press 165
Technical Photography 757
Technical Writers' Institute 881
Technology Review 494
Teen Magazine 544
Teenage Corner, Inc. 612
Teens & Boys 640
Teens Today 544
Teleflorist 686
Telefood Magazine 695
Telephony Magazine 666
Television International Magazine 666
Telstar Productions Inc. 61
Ten Speed Press 165
Tennessee Valley Authority 833
Tennis 535
Tennis Industry 776
Tennis Trade Magazine 776
Tennis USA 535
Territorial Affairs, Office Of 833
Tesseract Science Fiction 495
Texas Arts Journal, The 361
Texas Fisherman, The 521
Texas Methodist/United Methodist Reporter, The 483
Texas Monthly Magazine 456
Texas Outdoor Guide 509
Texas Western Press 166
Textile World 778
Tharpe Photo Library, Max 862
Thaves, Bob 580
Theater Across America 554
Theater World Publishing Co. 599
Theatre Americana 595
Theatre Arts Corporation National Playwriting Contest 822
Theatre Collection-New York Public Library 862
Theatre in Search of Playwrights Project, The 596
Theatre Rapport 596

Theatre Under The Stars 596
Thephotofile 862
These Times 483
Thigpen Photography 862
Think 192
13th Moon 361
33 Metal Producing 725
This Magazine 432
Thomas & Co., Ltd., A. 166
Thomas, Photojournalist, Bill 862
Thomas Productions, Bob 61
Thorsons Publishers, Ltd. 166
Thought 362
Three Continents Press 166
Tic Magazine 649
Tidewater Publishers 166
Tidewater Virginian 245
Tidewater Writer's Workshop 874
Tiera Del Sol Writers' Club 868
Tiger Beat Magazine 544
Time 432
Time Break 192
Time Zones 311
Time-Life Books Inc. 166
Times Books 167
Times Mirror Magazines, Inc., Book Division 167
Tinker Photography, Lester 862
Tire Review 625
Titsch Publishing, Inc. (see Cablevision 662)
Toastmaster, The 219
Tobacco Reporter 743
Tobenkin Memorial Award, The Paul 822
Today Magazine 413
Today's Animal Health 210
Today's Art 213
Today's Catholic Teacher 659
Today's Christian Parent 484
Today's Education 659
Today's Film Maker 300
Today's Fireman 692
Today's Policeman 717
Today's Secretary 765
Today's Transport International/Transporte Moderno 626
Together 497
Totem Tidings Magazine 415
Touch 323
Touchstone Press, The 167
Tourist Attractions and Parks 764
Tow-Age 626
Tower Press, Inc. (see Popular Handicraft Hobbies 297, Stitch'n Sew 300)
Town and Country 279
Town and Country Journal 362
Townsend, Marvin 580
Toy & Hobby World 779
Toys & Games 779
TRA Eclipse Awards 822
Track & Field News 528
Traffic Manager Magazine 780
Trailer Boats Magazine 562
Trailer Life Publishing Co., Inc. (see Motorhome Life 561)
Trailer/Body Builders 780
Trails 324
Training 729
Training Film Profiles 659
Training Management Motivation & Incentives 635
Transaction Books 167
Transaction/Society 498
Trans-Anglo Books 167
Translation Center Award 822
Translation Center Fellowship 822
Transportation, U.S. Department Of 833
Transworld Feature Syndicate 862
Trans-World News Service 863
Trans-World News Service, Inc. 612
Travel Advisor, The 562
Travel Agent, The 782
Travel and Leisure 563
Travel Smart 563
Travelage Midamerica 782
Travelage West 782
Traveler Magazine 563
Travelin' 4x4's, And Off Road Vehicles 234
Travelin' Vans 563
Travelore Report 563
Travelscene Magazine 782
Treasure 300
Treasure Chest Publications 168
Treasury Department 833
Trend House 168
Trend Publications, Inc. (see The South Magazine 245)
Trent Press, Ltd. (see Voyager 312)
Treves Workshop Features 863
Triad Magazine 399
Tri-Quarterly 362

Tri-State Trader 301
Tri-State Writers 872
Triumph Publishing Co. 168
TRM Publications, Inc. (see Street Rodder Magazine 234)
Troll Associates 62
Tropical Fish Hobbyist 210
Troubador Press 168
Troy State University Press 168
True Confessions 260
True Detective 265
True Experience 260
True Life Secrets 261
True Love 261
True Police Cases 265
True Romance 261
True Secrets 261
True Story 261
True West 287
"Truth On Fire!" 484
Tucson Magazine 256
Tulsa Magazine 256
Turf & Sport Digest 514
Turkey Call 521
Turkey World 683
Turnstone Books 168
Tuttle Co., Inc., Charles E. 169
TV and Movie Screen 555
TV Dawn To Dusk 555
TV Guide 555
TV Radio Talk 555
TV Star Parade 555
TWA Ambassador 311
Twayne Publishers 169
Twelve O'Clock Scholars 870
Twentieth Century Publications (see Custom Vans Magazine 227)
Twin Circle 484
Twin Pines Literary Agency 802
Tyndale House Publishers, Inc. 169

Ueland, Bardulf 580
Undercurrent 534
Underwater Photographer 418
Underwood & Underwood News Photos Inc. 863
Unico National Literary Award Contest 822
Unicorn 362
Union Pacific Railroad 863
Uniphoto 863
Uniplan Publishing Corp. (see Horse Lover's National Magazine 207)
Uniroyal World 192
United Business Publications, Inc. (see Marketing Communications 634)
United Church Observer, The 484
United Evangelical Action 484
United Feature Syndicate 613
United Nations 863
United Press International 613, 863
U.S. Air Force Central Still Photo Depository 863
United States Civil Service Commission 833
US Coast Guard Headquarters 864
US Coast Guard, News and Photo Center 863
US Commission on Civil Rights 833
US Department of Agriculture 864
US Department of the Interior 864
U.S. Fur Rancher 688
U.S. Geological Survey 834
U.S. Government Printing Office 834
U.S. Naval Institute Proceedings 381
United States Harness Writers' Association, Inc. 891
United States Industrial Council Educational Foundation Editorial Awards Competition 822
United States International Trade Commission 834
US News & World Report 432
U.S. News Service 613
U.S. Savings Bonds Division 834
United Synagogue Book Service 169
Unity Magazine 485
Unity Press 169
Univelt Inc. 170
Universal Magazine 170, 485
Universal Press Syndicate 613
Universal Trade Press Syndicate 613
Universal Writers Guild, Inc. 870
Universe Books 170
University and Festival Theatre 596
University Associates, Inc. 170
University Museum of the University of Pennsylvania 864
University of Alabama Press 170
University of Arizona Press 170
University of California Press 171

University of Colorado Writers Conference 878
University of Illinois Press 171
University of Iowa Press 171
University of Massachusetts Press 172
University of Michigan Conference on Teaching Technical and Professional Writing 880
University of Minnesota Department of Theatre 596
University of Missouri Press 172
University of Nebraska Press 172
University of North Carolina Press, The 172
University of Notre Dame Press 173
University of Oklahoma Annual Short Course on Professional Writing 882
University of Oklahoma Press 173
University of Pennsylvania Press 173
University of Pittsburgh Press 173
University of Rochester Writers' Workshop 881
University of Toronto Quarterly 363
University of the Trees Press 173
University of Utah Press 174
University of Windsor Review 363
University of Wisconsin Press 174
University Press of America 174
University Press of Kentucky 174
University Press of Virginia 174
Unmuzzled Ox 363
Unspeakable Visions of the Individual, The 203
Upcountry 456
Upland Writers, The 875
Upper Midwest Writers' Conference 880
Urizen Books, Inc. 174
Urology Times, Ophthalmology Times 736
USU Magazine Article Writer's Workshop 883
UT Review 427
Utah State Historical Society 864
Utility Supervision 729
UTU News 564

V.F.W. Magazine 220
Vagabond 363
Vagabond Creations 587
Valkyrie Press, Inc. (see Poetry Venture 425)
Valley Monthly Magazine 456
Valley Views Magazine 363
Value Communications, Inc. 175
Van Cleve Photography, Inc. 864
Van World 564
Van World Magazine 235
Vance Publishing Corp. (see Logging Management 720)
Vancouver Magazine 256
Vanguard Press, Inc. 175
Vanguard: Vision For The Seventies 485
Vantage Press 182
Variety 771
Vegetarian Times 390
Vending Times 642
Venture Magazine 544
Vermont Life Magazine 457
Verona Fathers Missions 485
Verse Writers' Guild of Ohio 872
Vesta Awards Contest 822
Vesta Publications 175
Veterans Administration 834
Veterans' Voices Awards 822
Veterinary Economics Magazine 783
Veterinary Medicine/Small Animal Clinician 783
Vickers Voice 192
Victimology 498
Victor Books 175
Video Films Inc 62
Video-Presse 324
Video Systems 666
Videography 556
Viking Press, Inc., Publishers, The 175
Vikingship 288
Village Voice 203
Villager, The 363
Viltis 364
Vine, The 324
Virginia Cavalcade 288
Virginia Center for the Creative Arts at Sweet Briar 877
Virginia Highlands Festival Creative Writing Day 883
Virginia Magazine of History and Biography 288
Virginia Municipal Review 692
Virginia Quarterly Review, The 364
Virginia Wildlife 522
Visage Press, Inc. 176
Visions 544
Vista 485

Vista and Co. 176
Visual Creations 587
Visual Education Corp. 62
Visual Merchandising 617
Visualworld 864
Viva 573
Vocational Education Productions 62
Vogue 573
Voice-Jeffersonian, The 409
Voice Publications (see Key Newsletter 768)
Voices International 427
Von Mises Memorial Essay Contest, Ludwig 823
Voyager 312
Vulcan Books 176

W 573
WB Agency, Inc. 803
W.R.C. Smith Publishing Co. (see Southern Hardware 697, Sports Merchandiser 775)
Wagner Memorial Poetry Award 823
Wahl Agency, Ltd., Austin 803
Walgram Publishing Ltd., (see Canadian Transceiver 246)
Walker and Co. 176
Wallaces Farmer 677
Wallant Book Award, Edward Lewis 823
Wallcoverings Magazine 770
Walls and Ceilings 633
War Cry, The 486
Ward's Auto World 626
Warehouse Distribution 626
Warehouse Distributor News 627
Warham, John 864
Warne & Co., Inc., Frederick 176
Warner & Associates, Jerry 62
Warren Associates, James A. 803
Wasatch Writers, Utah League of Writers 874
Wascana Review 364
Washington Area Writers 869
Washington Fishing Holes 522
Washington Independent Writers Association, Inc. 891
Washington Journalism Review 713
Washington Monthly 432
Washington Purchaser, The 707
Washington Women's Representative 433
Washingtonian Magazine, The 256
Wasinski Studios, Alex 864
Water & Sewage Works 784
Water Skier, The 534
Water Well Journal 784
Watson-Guptill Publications 177
Watt Publishing Co. (see Far Supplier 618, Industria Avicola 683)
Watts & Johnson Publications, Ltd. (see Fugue 394)
Watts, Inc., Franklin 177
Watumull Prize in the History of India 823
Waves 364
Wayne State University Press 177
Wayside Quarterly 365
WDS Forum 192
We Write of Colorado 869
Webb Company, The (see Easy Living Magazine 214, Northwest Passages 311, TWA Ambassador 311, Canoe Magazine 502, Work-Saver-Farm 674, Beef 678)
Webster Division 177
Webster Review 365
Wedham Publications, Ltd. (see Jobber News 621)
Wee Widsom 324
Weeds Trees & Turf 686
Weekday 374
Weekend Magazine 416
Weekly Bible Reader 325
Weighing & Measurement 744
Weight Watchers Magazine 283
Weinstein Historic Photo Collection, Robert 864
Weird Trips 391
Weirdbook 496
Weisz Memorial Award, Bertha 823
Welding Distributor, The 725
Well-Being Magazine 283
Wesleyan Publishing House (see In Touch 540)
Wesleyan-Suffield Writer-Reader Conference 879
West Coast Poetry Review 427
West End Magazine 365
West Florida Writers Guild 869
West Rockies Writers Club 869
West Virginia Governor's Office of Economic and Community Development 865

Westart 213
Westchester Illustrated 457
Westchester Magazine 457
Western & Eastern Treasures 391
Western Cleaner and Launderer 716
Western Construction 645
Western Fire Journal 692
Western Fruit Grower 671
Western History Department 865
Western Horseman, The 210
Western Humanities Review 365
Western Islands 177
Western North Carolina Christian Writers' Conference 882
Western Outdoors 522
Western Outfitter 640
Western Paint Review 750
Western Poetry Quarterly 427
Western Producer, The 288
Western Producer Prairie Books 178
Western Publications (see Frontier Times 286, Old West 287, True West 287, Relics 299)
Western Publishing Co., Inc. 178
Western Reserve Magazine, The 457
Western Wear & Equipment Magazine 640
Western World Haiku Society 873
Western Writers' Conference 883
Western Writers of America, Inc. 891
Western Writers of America Golden Spur Award 823
Westernlore Books 178
Western's World 312
Westminster Press, The 178
Westview Press 179
Westways 458
Westworld 458
Whaling Museum 865
What Makes People Successful 391
Wheat Scoop, The 736
Wheelwright Museum, The 865
Whiskey Island Quarterly 365
Whispers 496
Whitaker House 179
Whiting Limited, Douglas 613
Whitman Award, The Walt 823
Whitman Review, Walt 364
Whitmore Publishing Company 179
Whitney Museum of American Art 865
Whitston Publishing Co., The 179
Wholesale Drugs 651
Wichita 256
Wichita Line Women 870
Wickstrom Publishers, Inc. (see Aloft 309)
Wide World Photos, Inc. 865
Wieser & Wieser, Inc. 803
Wilderness Press 179
Wildwood Photographic 865
Wiley & Sons, Inc., John 180
Willamette Management Associates, Inc. 180
Willamette Writers Conference 882
Williams Newspaper Features Syndicate, Inc. 613
Williams/Wesley/Winant 803
Williamson, Margaret 865
Williamsport Writers Forum 873
Wilmac Records, Tapes and Filmstrips 63
Wilshire Book Co. 180
Wilson Features 613
Wilson Library Bulletin 720
Wilson Prize, Thomas J. 823
Winburg, Art 580
Winchester Press 180
Wind 545
Wind/Literary Journal 365
Windless Orchard, The 428
Window of Vermont 458
Windsor This Month Magazine 459
Wine World Magazine 269
Wines & Vines 630
Wings Magazine 238
Winship Book Award, Laurence L. 823
Wintergreen Publishing Co. 180
Winterthur Museum, The Henry Francis Du Pont 865
Winthrop College Writers Conference 882
Wire Journal 744
Wisconsin Review 366
Wisconsin Sportsman 522
Wisconsin Trails 459
Wittenburg Door, The 391
Wofsy Fine Arts, Alan 180
Wolf House Books 181
Wolfe Communications Awards, LeRoy 823
Wolfe Worldwide Films 865
Wolfsohn Photography, Gerald 866
Wollin Studios, Ltd. 866

Woman Beautiful 695
Woman Bowler, The 506
Woman Talk Magazine 307
Woman's Day 573
Woman's Press Club 872
Women: A Journal of Liberation 203
Women Artists News 366
Women In Business 573
Women In Communications, Inc. 891
Women Studies Abstracts 574
Women's Bureau 834
Women's Circle 301
Women's Circle Home Cooking 269
Women's Digest 574
Women's News Service 614
Women's Rights 574
Women's Rights Law Reporter 203
Wonder Time 325
Wood & Wood Products 722
Wood Award in Playwriting, Audrey 823
Woodall Poetry Society, Stella 874
Woodall's Campground Management 764
Woodall's Trailer & RV Travel 564
Woodbridge Press Publishing Co. 181
Woodenboat 504
Woodmen of the World Magazine 279
Woodworking & Furniture Digest 722
Worcester Magazine 459
Word Merchants 872
Wordsmiths 870
Work Boat, The 731
Work Saver-Farm 674
Workbasket, The 301
Workbench 301
Working Craftsman 301
Working For Boys 545
Worklife 693
World Construction 645
World Encounter 486
World Literature Today 366
World of Poetry Contest 824
World of Rodeo, The 528
World Over 314
World Politics 433
Worldview 433
World-Wide News Bureau 614
Wormwood Review, The 428
Worship 487
Wow 325
Wright Award, Captain Donald T. 824
Wright Publishing Co., Inc. (see Dune Buggies & How VWS 228)
Writer, The 714
Writer, Inc., The 181
Writers and Illustrators Co-Op 874
Writer's Association of New Jersey 871
Writers Association of Tidewater, The 874
Writer's Club of Pasadena 868, 874
Writers' Club of Whittier 868
Writer's Club of Whittier Seminar 878
Writers Conference in Children's Literature 878
Writers' Conference at Julian, California 878
Writers Cramp 873
Writer's Digest 714
Writer's Digest Books 181
Writer's Digest Creative Writing Contest 824
Writer's Exchange 869
Writers' Forum 878
Writer's Group 871
Writers Group of Cushing 873
Writers Guild of America 891
Writers Guild of America West Awards 824
Writers House, Inc. 803
Writer's League of Washington 869
Writers' Studio 869
Writers' Workshop 872
Writer's Workshop 882
Writers Workshop of Delaware Valley 873
Writer's Yearbook 715
Writing 715
Writing '79 879
Writing Workshop for People Over 57 880
Writers' Workshop West 868
Wurlitzer Foundation of New Mexico, Helene 877
Wyatt, Andy 580
Wyoming Rural Electric News 677
Wyoming State Museum/Photo Section 866
Wyoming Writers Association 875

Xanadu 428

Yachting 505
Yaddo 877
Yale Repertory Theatre 596
Yale Review, The 366
Yale University Press 181
Yankee 459
Yankee Magazine's Guide to New England 460
Young Adventures 545
Young Ambassador 546
Young Athlete 546
Young Crusader, The 325
Young Judaean 325
Young (Agency), Katherine 866
Young Miss 546
Young Musicians 326
Young World 547
Your Baby 249
Your Church 638
Your Home 307
Youth Alive! 547
Youth In Action 547
Youth Leader, The 638
Youth Magazine's Creative Arts Awards 824
YWCA Co-Ed Writers Workshop 869

Zalonka Agency, The 803
Zauner, Lou 866
Ziff-Davis Publishing Co. (see Flying 237, Skiing Magazine 532, Meetings & Conventions 741, Photomethods 756)
Zodiac News Service 614
Zondervan Publishing House 182
Zvezda 366